NASCAR
ENCYCLOPEDIA

NASCAR
ENCYCLOPEDIA

Edited by Peter Golenbock and Greg Fielden

MOTORBOOKS
INTERNATIONAL

Published by MBI Publishing Company,
Galtier Plaza, Suite 200
380 Jackson Street
St. Paul, MN 55101-3885 USA

Original concept developed by Neil Reshen & Dawn Reshen-Doty of Benay Enterprises, Inc.

MBI Publishing Company books are also available at discounts in bulk quantity for industrial or sales-promotional use. For details write to:

Special Sales Manager at Motorbooks International Wholesalers & Distributors
Galtier Plaza, Suite 200
380 Jackson Street
St. Paul, MN 55101-3885 USA

ISBN 0-7603-1571-X

Electronic book design and composition by Stephen Ogata

Printed in the United States of America

CONTENTS

PREFACE

When Macmillan first published *The Baseball Encyclopedia* in 1969, it sparked an interest in baseball history and statistics that continues to this day. With the first edition of *The Stock Car Racing Encyclopedia*, fans of this popular sport have a comprehensive reference book of their own. In this second edition, *The NASCAR Encyclopedia*, every driver who ever competed in a race is listed—from Paul Aars to Ralph Zrimsek. The same way that baseball fans can look up the career records of their favorite players in *The Baseball Encyclopedia*, racing fans can get all the season and career totals for their favorite drivers. Other sections include career leaders, year-by-year breakdowns of the top 50 drivers, a section on car owners, and results of every NASCAR race from 1949 through the end of the 2002 season.

Arriving at the Bottom Line

The inaugural Winston Cup Series event, then named the Strictly Stock Division, was staged on a rutted, dusty track in Charlotte, North Carolina on June 19, 1949.

For over 50 years, NASCAR's unique brand of motorsports has grown from a playground for daring moonshine runners to the slick production we all enjoy today. This is the first encyclopedia to document Winston Cup racing over the years.

Definitive statistical records were seldom compiled in NASCAR's early years. A number of discrepancies have surfaced over the years—from driver records to race wins to money earnings. For instance, NASCAR awarded 10 driver victories for the eight races contested in 1949. Tim Flock and June Cleveland were given credit for winning races that were not part of the championship tour in 1949. In fact, the events Flock and Cleveland won were not even sanctioned by NASCAR.

Records for this *NASCAR Encyclopedia* have been tabulated from all events that have been part of the Winston Cup championship season—races that offer championship points. Finish positions in events such as the Winston Select All-Star race and Bud Shootout do not count; however, following NASCAR's procedure in recent years, earnings from these events are included in the total money won.

Allison's 85 Wins

Interpretation is a key word when tabulating NASCAR statistics. At times NASCAR has interpreted an event one way, then corrected it years later—without making necessary adjustments in similar or identical circumstances. Clearly, the most glaring inconsistency concerns Bobby Allison, long noted in "official" records as having 84 career Winston Cup victories. He actually won 85 races, but his victory in the August 6, 1971, race at Winston-Salem, North Carolina was never properly credited to him. Allison drove a Mustang to victory that day in an event that had both Winston Cup and Grand American cars competing. Allison was not competing for Winston Cup points, but he was competing in the Winston Cup race. NASCAR declared Allison the winner of the event, but that victory has never been reflected in his personal Winston Cup record sheet. His victory is reflected in this encyclopedia. This encyclopedia lists an official winner for each and every event that NASCAR regards as a Winston Cup point-paying event.

NASCAR did not originally credit Allison with a victory because he drove a Mustang. However, in today's official NASCAR records, the Mustang that Allison drove is listed as a bona fide Winston Cup victory for Ford. It is inconsistent for the Mustang driver to not be credited with his victory. Two years earlier, Grand American cars competed with the Winston Cuppers, and NASCAR officially credited all drivers with official starts—despite the fact that the Grand American drivers were not competing for points.

Lee Petty and Additional Discrepancies

Other discrepancies have surfaced in recent years. Sanctioning NASCAR properly gives Lee Petty credit for winning 54 Grand National events in his career. However, title sponsor R.J. Reynold's Winston Cup annual Media Guide credit Petty with 55 career wins, but the weekly updated Winston Cup guide, issued at every race, lists him with 54 victories. The same entity can't seem to agree on one set of numbers.

The fact is Lee Petty won 54 NASCAR Grand National races during his career, which spanned from 1949-1964. The additional victory Winston slipped in was a 25-mile exhibition event staged at Newark, New Jersey on November 5, 1950, which actually served as one of two "pilot" events for the Short Track Division that began in 1951. There were no championship points available, and it was not part of the 1950 NASCAR Grand National schedule. The two exhibition races, the other held in Buffalo, New York, were simply not part of NASCAR's premier racing series.

The two tracks were a quarter-mile in length, and the Grand National rules were that no championship events were to be staged on tracks smaller than a half mile. The NASCAR Short Track Division was introduced in 1951 because so many short track promoters wanted to stage races for the Grand National cars. It was a separate division entirely. To include a "pilot" race for another division that carried no championships points into the Grand National Series performance borders on the ridiculous.

Bobby Courtwright won the other exhibition race at Buffalo. NASCAR has never recognized Courtwright's victory in the 25-mile race as a Grand National win for the simple reason is that it was not an official, point-paying event. Winston, however, gives Courtwright credit for winning an official event. For the sake of documenting the sport of NASCAR Winston Cup and Grand National racing as consistently as possible, these events do not count as official Grand National races because they were not races that offered championship points. As Kyle Petty recently said, the new breed of racing people are merely "revisionists" who care little about the integrity of racing's past. "I'll say this until the day I die: Everybody over there in NASCAR-land is a revisionist. They don't want to tell the truth," Kyle said.

A number of other incidents in NASCAR's early years have been interpreted differently by NASCAR and Winston. In addition to Petty and Courtwright, NASCAR and Winston have different career win totals for the following drivers: Herb Thomas, Speedy Thompson, Tiny Lund, Joe Lee Johnson, Donald Thomas, Parnelli Jones, Whitey Norman, Al Keller, Darel Dieringer, Gwyn Staley, and Tommy Thompson. NASCAR even gives credit to Buddy Norton for a single victory when no one named Buddy Norton ever competed in an official event.

A meeting conducted in NASCAR's Charlotte offices in April, 2002 attempted to clean up the discrepancies. Personnel from NASCAR, Winston, this writer, and several other historians were present. At the conclusion of the meeting, everyone in the room agreed 100 percent with the numbers which appear in this offering, and the need for consistency in evaluating the findings. Unfortunately, the proper changes and adjustments in the name of consistency were never incorporated in NASCAR's or Winston's official records.

It is a shame that a major league sport such as NASCAR Winston Cup racing has so many different sets of statistical information tables available to the media and public. For this encyclopedia, we do make an conscientious effort to compile information with an underscored effort on consistency. A race that carried championship points toward the NASCAR Winston Cup/Grand National title is documented herein, and whoever won that race gets credit for a victory. And competitors receive credit for a start, if they started the race. This encyclopedia will no longer hand out victories to drivers who won exhibition races or events that were never NASCAR sanctioned.

Fixing Things Later—Partially

There are a number of gray areas that have surfaced in NASCAR's record keeping. Ray Elder won the 1971 500-miler at Riverside, California but was not originally credited with the victory. Elder was competing for Winston West points rather than Winston Cup (similar to Allison), and his victory was not credited until 1976, five years after he won the race. On-the-spot calculations by NASCAR in 1971 did not credit a race winner unless he was competing for Winston Cup points.

That was a direct turnaround from NASCAR's interpretation during the 1960s. A number of races had been won by Indy Car drivers (A. J. Foyt, Dan Gurney, Johnny Rutherford, Mario Andretti, etc.) who were not competing for Winston Cup points, but they received credit for winning a Winston Cup event when they indeed won the event. Many races have been won by drivers who failed to mail in an entry form and thus did not compete for Winston Cup points, but their victories also counted.

In 1971, the record keepers got lost in the gray areas. Ray Elder, Bobby Allison, and Tiny Lund won races when they were competing for points in divisions other than the Winston Cup. While Elder's victory was appropriately adjusted five years later, no adjustments were made for Bobby Allison and Tiny Lund, who won twice in Camaros. Lund's pair of wins currently count as Winston Cup wins for Chevrolet but not for the man who

won driving the Camaros. This discrepancy has been addressed in this encyclopedia. When a man won a race, he has been awarded credit for winning that race.

This is essentially the way NASCAR interprets its races today. At Phoenix, Arizona, and Sears Point, California, a number of drivers competing for Winston West points compete with the Winston Cup regulars. If a Winston West driver happened to win the Phoenix or Sears Point event, he received Winston West points, and he also received credit for winning a Winston Cup event.

Sweepstakes Races

In the late 1950s, NASCAR conducted a number of "Sweepstakes" races, which grouped two and sometimes three different divisions. The Grand National hardtops (today's Winston Cup), Convertibles, and NASCAR Short Track Division (a separate series that competed on tracks shorter than a half-mile) cars all competed together. NASCAR's interpretation during that era was to credit the winner of the race with a victory only if he was in a Grand National (Winston Cup) car. If a Convertible car won the race, the highest Grand National finisher (sometimes, but not always) received credit for the win. In 1957, Whitey Norman received credit for winning a Sweepstakes race at Langhorne, Pennsylvania, when he finished second to Gwyn Staley's Convertible. Norman's victory was credited in the 1958 NASCAR Record Book, but his win disappeared by 1959. Since Norman didn't actually win a race, NASCAR dropped his name from the victory list. And his name fails to show up anywhere in the Winston Cup kingdom as winning a race. Simply said, Whitey Norman finished second in the 1957 Langhorne race, and second place is what he is credited with in this encyclopedia. In NASCAR's official records, no driver is credited with winning the 1957 Langhorne event.

In a 1959 Sweepstakes event staged in California, Harlan Richardson was the highest-finishing Grand National (Winston Cup) driver, but he finished in 16th place, 94 laps behind Parnelli Jones, who won the race in a Short Track Division car. For this event, NASCAR immediately credited Jones with winning the race, not Richardson, who was the highest-finishing Grand National driver. Yet for another Sweepstakes race in the same year, Bob Welborn won at Weaverville, North Carolina, in a Convertible, but NASCAR failed to credit him with a victory. In the same year, different interpretations represent virtually identical situations.

Sound confusing? It has been, and interpretations today have contributed to that. In NASCAR's defense, there have been varying types of races throughout the years. In the 1950s, foreign cars were eligible in certain NASCAR Grand National (now Winston Cup) events. In fact, a Jaguar driven by Al Keller won NASCAR's first venture in road racing (on the airport runways at Linden, New Jersey, in 1954). A Volkswagen actually competed in an event at Langhorne. Corvettes, MGs, and Sprites also competed on occasion. NASCAR also had frequent personnel changes in its statistical department, and succeeding individuals had little definitive or historical background data to rely on. Thus, different evaluations in similar situations surfaced through the years. Understandably, a number of these discrepancies have crept into the charted and uncharted records.

NASCAR's annual Record Book did not begin publishing year-by-year driver records until 1969.

A Start is a Start

The NASCAR Encyclopedia has credited drivers with finish positions regardless of the points, if any, they were competing for. A start is a start, a win is a win, and all drivers receive credit accordingly.

Post-season winnings have been credited for all years in this Encyclopedia. In the first two decades of Winston Cup racing, post-season awards were not officially credited to a driver's statistical record by the sanctioning body—only the winnings earned in the actual races were credited. Beginning in 1971, the post-season Winston awards were counted in official NASCAR records but not the NASCAR point money or any other post-season awards. Special event winnings were not counted until the mid-1980s. When Dale Earnhardt won the Busch Clash in 1980, the $50,000 he won was not credited to his annual or career earnings. But, When Earnhardt won the 1988 Busch Clash, the $75,000 he won that day was credited to him in official NASCAR records. In an effort to maintain consistency, all post-season and special event earnings have been credited to the driver.

From 1976-78, NASCAR failed to credit contingency awards for each and every race to any driver. It seems odd that David Pearson could win a 500-mile race at Darlington as late as 1976 and only get credit for the $11,670 in official NASCAR winnings. With the predetermined contingency money added, Pearson actually won $17,570. This practice by NASCAR was effective for only three years. In this encyclopedia, the contingency money has been credited to the drivers during those years. Maintaining a consistent method of handling the numbers is paramount – not only for this project but for the sake of NASCAR stock car racing.

No other major league sport treats its time-honored statistical accounts so haphazardly.

And in 1956 . . .

An unusual and unprecedented incident occurred in the 1956 season that has only recently been uncovered. A 300-mile event was staged at Langhorne, Pennsylvania. Five hundred points were originally awarded for first place with a drop of 20 points for each descending position. After NASCAR had released the official box score, it was determined that the Langhorne contest should have awarded 620 points for the winner with a drop of 24 points for each place in the finishing order. Speedy Thompson finished in third place and was originally awarded 460 points. After the "clerical error" was detected by NASCAR, Thompson's new point total should have been 572 points, an increase of 112 points. When NASCAR updated the new point totals, Thompson was credited with only 112 points, instead of 572. The error resulted in Thompson finishing third in the final point standings rather than second. It is odd that this error was never detected at the time. In this encyclopedia, Thompson has been credited with finishing second in the final 1956 point standings.

In NASCAR's official final 1956 point standings, Tom Harbison was officially credited with 1,248 points, ranking him 39th overall. Harbison never competed in a Grand National (now Winston Cup) race and, accordingly, is not listed as ranking 39th in the 1956 season in this encyclopedia.

Rankings

Driver rankings in this encyclopedia reflect the driver's position in the final season point standings. Tiebreakers have been applied in all cases, but there are some instances where there have been absolute ties. For example, A. J. Foyt and Gary Bradberry tied for 70th in the 1994 final point standings. Each had one start and finished in 30th place, earning 73 points. That is regarded as an absolute tie.

In most cases, applying NASCAR's procedure for breaking ties will do just that—break the tie. If one or more drivers accumulate the same number of points, the driver with the highest finishing position gets the nod. If two drivers tie for the championship, the title goes to the driver who posts the most victories. If that number is the same, the procedure falls back to the driver finishing second the most times and so on.

Pole Winners

Pole winners have been credited per NASCAR's structure for awarding poles. The procedure—or interpretation—has changed only once during the history of Winston Cup Grand National racing. Since 1990, the driver who registered the fastest run under the clock during the first round of qualifying has earned the pole position. On a number of occasions since 1990, the pole-winning driver has had an incident in practice before the race that forced him and his team to unload a back-up car for the race. Prior to 1990, when a primary car was withdrawn from a race, the driver lost the pole.

The most memorable example of a driver losing the pole came in qualifying for the 1983 Daytona 500. Cale Yarborough zipped through the timing lights at 200.503 miles per hour on his first of two qualifying laps but flipped his Chevrolet on the second lap, destroying the car. His time, fastest in the first qualifying round, earned him the pole. However, the pole-winning car had suffered irreparable damage and team owner Harry Ranier made the decision to withdraw the car. The official pole for the 1983 Daytona 500 went to the second- fastest qualifier, Ricky Rudd, who had posted a 198.864 miles per hour lap. Yarborough had to requalify in the backup car, and he wound up winning the Daytona 500 six days later. But he didn't get credit for winning the pole.

Another similar ruling occurred in the inaugural Talladega 500 in 1969. Charlie Glotzbach had earned the pole with a qualifying lap of 199.466 miles per hour, but when his car was withdrawn in the driver's boycott of the event, Bobby Isaac went down on record as winning the pole with a speed of 196.386 miles per hour. Isaac had posted the seventh-fastest qualifying lap in the first round of time trials, but since the first six cars were withdrawn, Isaac officially wound up with the pole.

A Few Incompletes

During the formative years, record keeping for NASCAR Grand National (now Winston Cup) racing was not as thorough as it is today, and many of the records have been discarded. Our records are 99 percent complete, but some of the drivers' finishing positions for 1951 have not been determined. Often a top-ten finishing order was released, but other competitors who started the race were not assigned finishing positions in any particular order. On a few occasions, the number of drivers and the number of starters were not the same. Some positions have been left blank. For these events, a driver has simply been listed as competing in the race without a definite finish position.

Lap Leaders

NASCAR did not include lap leaders for the Winston Cup Grand National events until the early 1970s. Through years of research, most of the lap leaders in each race have been determined. Not surprisingly, statistics for the early years have been the most difficult to locate. In events where complete lap leaders are not available, the winning driver is credited with leading one lap—the last one. The final lap is the only one that is assured. Accordingly, the figures for lap leaders for the early years are quite low. Lee Petty, Herb Thomas, the Flock brothers, and many others certainly led more laps than are indicated, but until the missing links are found, there is little that can be done.

We have uncovered most of the race results from the beginning of NASCAR's elite stock car racing series, but we are interested in any additional information that you, the reader, may have. We not only invite you to contribute any additional information, we encourage it.

—Greg Fielden

ACKNOWLEDGMENTS

This book would not be complete without our acknowledgment of all the people who tirelessly worked to make this second edition a reality.

Neil Reshen and Dawn Reshen-Doty of Benay Enterprises, Inc., would like to thank Heather Edwards, Mary Ellen Cosentino, Rachael Mendela for all of their help, Merrilee Warholak, whose research and editorial contributions are truly appreciated, and to Chris Doty for his invaluable assistance. Special thanks to Ken Samelson for his tireless assistance.

Peter Golenbock wishes to thank the following for their many kindnesses: Betty Karlen, the chief librarian of the International Motorsport Hall of Fame, who worked so hard to supply the photos for this book. To Jim Freeman, the new president of the IM Hall of Fame, and to Ralph Earnhardt Karlen, who kept everyone company; to Bob Latford and Dick Berggren for their memories of drivers past; to Donna Freismuth, Tom Cotter, Humpy Wheeler, Jimmy Johnson, Ed Carroll, Ralph Moody, and the late Tim Flock for their long-time support and assistance, and to all those racers, crew chiefs, mechanics, and other friends in NASCAR who have been so kind to me over the years.

Greg Fielden expresses his special thanks to P J. Hollebrand and Allan E. Brown for their invaluable assistance with this project, and to Jon Mauk, Fletcher WIlliams, Tim and Frances Flock, Hank Schoolfield, Larry Jendras Jr., Doris Roberts, Dink Gardner, Tim Milecki, Bob Weeks, Lawson Diggett, Skeeter Austin, Houston Lawing, Patricia Fielden, Don O'Reilly, K.C. Breslauer, Halifax Historical Society, Morris and Jeanne Metcalfe, Paul Dalton, Dorothy Davis, Owen Kearns Jr., Mitzi Teague, Fred Bince, Dave Rodman, Larry Belewski, Ken Clapp, Chris Economaki, and Marty Little.

Russ Thompson would like to thank Skeeter Austin, Tom Cothron, Joyce Tucker, Bob Weeks, Noel Thompson, Thelma Thompson, Judd Pendergrass, Elowise Wright, Norm Partin, Lynn Haddock, Lloyd Hawn, Tom Crosby, Bob Ray, David Shankle, Jay Glynn, Megan Summers, his wife Cheryl, and son Ben.

INTRODUCTION
A Brief History of Stock Car Racing
By Peter Golenbock

It's been a half a dozen years since the inaugural *Stock Car Racing Encyclopedia*, and what a six years it has been. NASCAR has exploded exponentially in the numbers of fans it draws, the national exposure it gets on television, and in the money that is pouring into the sport from sponsors and race goers. If Big Bill France were alive today, even he would nod his head in wonder. His baby, born on the red clay of the Southland, has become a national passion that rivals, if not surpasses, the traditional American stick and ball sports. France would smile at the big rigs lined up side by side at the races bearing the logos of many of the biggest and best-known brands in the country. He would nod approvingly at the $5 million tab charged to these companies for sponsoring one of the Winston Cup race cars. He would shake his head sorrowfully knowing that a number of the smaller Carolina tracks that helped build NASCAR into the powerhouse it has become have had to be sacrificed as superspeedways have been built around the land in such locations as Texas, Nevada, and New Hampshire. NASCAR now runs at Indianapolis and in Japan. France would need only to think back to racing's roots, and he would marvel.

The Bootleggers

When the sport of stock car racing first began to organize itself in the late 1940s, the leading drivers were mostly bootleggers, men who ran whiskey from illegal stills to hundreds of markets across the Southeast. They were the real Dukes of Hazzard, only there was nothing funny about their business. Driving at high speeds at night, often with the police in pursuit was dangerous. Jail and loss of livelihood were the penalties for losing the race.

The bootleggers had faster cars. They could go 95 miles per hour in first gear, 115 in second. Few police cars could go faster than 95. The bootleggers' cars also had better equipment, notably special springs and shocks for handling on the turns. Parts were imported from California, where the hot rod was king.

The local sheriffs were intent on catching bootleggers not so much because selling untaxed whiskey was illegal, but because if the sheriff could catch his prey, he then could sell the car at auction and reap half the returns. Often the bootlegger bought back his own car, and the cat-and-mouse game began anew.

Sheriffs went to great lengths to corral the faster, better handling cars. Some tried attaching a cowcatcher-like device (like a large ice tongs) to the bumper. The trick was to catch a bootlegger with a full load going up a hill and clamp onto the car before he could get away. To combat the clamp, the bootleggers resorted to putting the bumpers on with coat-hanger wire. They'd latch on, the bootlegger would floor it, and the fender would roll under the front wheels of the revenuer's car and get tangled. By the time the revenuer got the bumper free, the whiskey runner was long gone.

Other sheriffs relied on their marksmanship, shooting the bootlegger's radiator with a shotgun. Some bootleggers countered by installing a steel plate to protect the radiator, others put the radiator in the trunk and ran air scoops from the front to cool the engine.

To keep the sheriffs from catching them, the bootleggers had tricks of their own. They made bootleg turns, spinning 180 degrees and driving off in the other direction; spilled oil on the roads; tried smokescreens; created roads where there were none; and devised a system of using a second car to block the sheriff while the car with the load got away. The old Burt Reynolds—Jackie Gleason Smokey and the Bandit movies weren't far off the mark. To stay in business, the kingpins also paid off the sheriffs, something even the movies didn't talk about.

Tim Flock, NASCAR champion in 1952 and 1955, came from a family of bootleggers-racers (along with brothers Fonty and Bob). Tim recalled that the first race among the bootleggers was held in the mid-1930s in a cow pasture in the town of Stockbridge, Georgia, about 15 miles outside Atlanta.

"We didn't have no tickets, no safety equipment, no fences, no nothing. Just a bunch of these bootleggers who'd been arguing all week about who had the fastest car would get together and prove it."

According to Flock, the participants formed a track by running around and around an oval about a half-mile round until the tires dug up enough dirt to make the course visible.

"These guys would run and bet against their own cars, betting who had the fastest car. That night they'd be hauling liquor in the same car. About 50 people saw this dust cloud and came up trying to see what was causing it." The next time, the crowd swelled to a hundred. Then it tripled. Before long, the cars were racing every Sunday. (According to Flock, the car owners would buy four tires from Sears Roebuck on Saturday, race them on Sunday, and bring them back on Monday. "Naw, I don't know how they got wore out so fast.") By the 1940s, a crowd of 5,000 at a stock car race was not uncommon.

Among the moonshine haulers famed for their racing skills were such racers as the three Flock brothers, who worked for their uncle; Peachtree Williams, one of the biggest bootleggers in the state of Georgia; Curtis Turner; Bob Smith; the Martin boys; Clay Earles, the owner of the Martinsville Speedway; Buddy Shuman, who was once shot in the neck while running moonshine; Wendell Scott, an African-American racer who was arrested when he had to swerve at high speed to avoid hitting a bunch of drunks walking on the highway and; and the most famous of them all, Junior Johnson, who drove hundreds of sorties delivering moonshine. Johnson, dubbed the Last American Hero by author Tom Wolfe, was often chased by the law but was never caught behind the wheel of a car.

"Making moonshine was a hand-me-down trade that came down through the generations," said Johnson. "By the time one was too old to make it, another had already picked it up. It was important that the location of the still be kept secret, because the revenuers were out there looking for it. Sometimes the moonshiners put [the stills] underground, and put them in buildings. They would be back in the woods where no one could see them or find them. There were a lot of ways to conceal them. It was a cat-and-mouse game."

The bootleggers knew the names of the revenuers and vice versa. Several years before he obtained a driver's license, Johnson was driving from his home in Ronda, North Carolina, to cities such as Lexington, High Point, Greensboro, Winston Salem, and Charlotte. Like the other bootleggers, Johnson learned how to make the motors fast and how to make the cars drive well. Two or three times a night, every night, Johnson and the others made their runs. "It was hard, dangerous, scary work," said Johnson. "I did that from the time I was thirteen until I was in the mid-twenties, three hundred sixty-five days a year, seven or eight times a week, probably more."

Johnson drove his first stock car race at age 16 at a North Wilkesboro dirt track in a race among the local bootleggers. His brother and he had fixed up the car, and when they got to the track his brother told him, "You drive." He did, with the same reckless abandon he had demonstrated on his moonshine runs.

Recalled Ralph Moody, "Back then the drivers were rough, boy. There was always some kind of fight going on. They'd wangbang out there, but if someone figured it was a little bit out of line, if the guy figured you were too rough, there was a fight."

Moody recalled the time Junior Johnson and Lee Petty were running at the old Fairgrounds at Charlotte. The race was 50 laps, and Johnson was winning about three-quarters of the way through. Petty couldn't catch him, so he kept banging into Johnson's left rear, trying to spin him out and knock him out of the way. Finally, Petty managed to cut Johnson's tire.

Johnson was driving for the Wood brothers, and when he came into pit, he told Glen and Leonard Wood, "Put a tire on it."

Glen said, "Oh, no. Oh, no." Moody, standing next to Glen, asked him, "Oh, no?" Said Glen, "We're in for it now."

Moody said, "They put a tire on it, and Junior went out there, and he sailed around there, and here came Lee Petty. Junior let Petty by and ran him down the end of the racetrack and never shut it down and ran him off the end of the big pigpen out there and over the wall. Petty went sailing clear out of the racetrack! The race was coming to an end, and Junior knocked him out just so Lee couldn't win it."

The first big race Johnson drove was at Darlington in 1952, a 200-mile Modified-Sportsman race hastily added to the NASCAR schedule to compete with an Indy Car race slated for Raleigh, North Carolina, on the July 4th weekend. The race lacked the flair of a late model event because Bill France, who ran NASCAR, the top racing body in the area, favored using new cars in his races. "He felt people could relate to the new cars," said Johnson. "If you were driving a fifty-one Ford, and a fifty-one Ford was running on the racetrack, you could relate to it better than to a thirty-four Ford modified to run. France was the one who started NASCAR, and he had a lot to do with everybody's career in racing. I don't think there's a single soul in racing today who Bill France Sr. wasn't a big booster in their career."

NASCAR's Founding Father

William Henry Getty France was 25 years old when he moved from Washington, D.C., to Daytona Beach, Florida, in 1934 to escape the ice and cold of the north. France had two middle names because his parents hoped the Getty name would bring their son riches. He had been into cars since high school, when he and a buddy named Hugh Ostermeyer built a canvas-covered race car with a Model T engine capable of running 90 miles per hour.

In Washington, D.C., he had worked in car garages and service stations, driven in sprint car races, won, and too often got burned by promoters who skipped out with the proceeds.

He remembered one race in 1930 in a town called Pikesville, Maryland, where a winning purse of $500 was trumpeted. He finished fourth. When he went for his prize money, he was told the winner got $50 and he $10. France, angry, wanted to know why, when the purse was supposed to be $500. He was told that the larger purse had been announced as a ploy to impress the fans.

He had been working for a service station, and during the winter his job was to venture out onto the street and restart dead batteries. France knew his future was in fixing cars, and he decided that if he were going to be lying on his back, he wanted to be where he could feel warm and comfortable. He had heard talk of how fast Florida was developing. Florida was his destination. Exactly where in Florida, however, he wasn't sure.

France, his wife, Annie, and their infant son, Bill Jr., headed south in his Hupmobile. On a beautiful fall day they stopped their car on the sands of Daytona Beach to go swimming. The beauty of the place charmed them. Bill and Annie decided to end their journey. They rented a little, one-bedroom, furnished house for $15 a month. France first got a job as a house painter and soon thereafter as a mechanic at J. Saxton Lloyd's Buick Pontiac-Cadillac garage.

In March 1935, with France in attendance, Sir Malcolm Campbell drove his supercharged V-8 to a land-speed record of 276 miles per hour on the sands of Daytona Beach. The problem for Campbell and other land-speed racers was that though the Daytona Beach sand was wide, flat, firm, and long enough for most races, Campbell's incredible speed made racing there too dangerous. He needed a longer, flatter, smoother, less windy course.

Later that year, Campbell took his Bluebird to the beds of Utah's Bonneville Salt Flats and broke the record at 301 miles per hour. Daytona Beach was abandoned forever as the landspeed capital.

In an effort to resuscitate the city's racing reputation and a flagging economy, Daytona city officials staged a AAA-sanctioned 250-mile stock car race for all comers on March 8, 1936. The man in charge was a well-known racing promoter named Sig Haugdahl. He devised a combination beach-road race with the backstretch and turns on the sand and the front straightaway on the paved street closest to the beach.

It was a handicap race with the slower qualifiers leaving the line first. Twenty-seven drivers entered, including France, who drove a Ford owned by a man named Glen Brooks. France started 10th, leaving about eight minutes after the slowest Willys.

The initial race had some problems. The worst was if you drove too slow, you got stuck in the sand; if you went too fast, you risked turning over.

The heaviest cars got stuck in the sand, and because speeds were slower than expected, the tide came in before the race was over. The north turn was completely blocked with stuck cars at around the 200-mile mark when the officials called it.

Shortened prematurely, it took several days for racing officials to figure out that Milt "Red" Marion had won. Bill France, who swore he passed Marion a couple of times, was awarded fifth place, twelve laps back. Marion won $1,700 in prize money and France received $375. At that time the minimum wage was $14.50 a week.

The other negative was that because there was no way to fence in the entire course, thousands of spectators watched the race without paying. The city fathers lost $22,000 on the promotion.

The following year the Elks Club took a crack at the promotion, running a 50-mile race to ensure the tides wouldn't be a factor. The crowd was so anemic the winning driver was awarded a purse of $43. The Elks were dissuaded from ever doing that again.

The Chamber of Commerce needed to find a person or group to promote the race. France, whose Pure Oil gas station on Main Street had become a headquarters for the local racers, was asked if he knew anyone who might be interested in putting on the race.

France had been racing a 1937 Ford coupe owned by a local restaurant owner named Charlie Reese on the weekends. Reese asked France if he would have an interest in taking on the promotion.

France foresaw that the race had a future if run right. He saw that when a motorcycle race was organized, fans flocked to see it. He figured the lack of success of the stock car event was a result of inadequate or inept promotion.

France told Reese, "I can get the cars and the drivers, but I don't have any money."

Reese replied, "I'll put up the money and you can do the work." France agreed, and that first year sold 4,500 tickets at fifty cents apiece. The next year they raised ticket prices to a dollar, and after donating 10 percent to the Bundles for Britain campaign, France and Reese split $2,000. The annual beach race at Daytona was saved.

Bill France Organizes

On December 12, 1947, Bill France gathered racing promoters from around the Southeast for a meeting at the Ebony Bar atop the Streamline Hotel in Daytona Beach. France saw the need to set up an organization of promoters, mechanics, and drivers to regulate the sport.

Acutely aware that unscrupulous promoters were negatively affecting the image of the sport, Bill France believed that an association of racing promoters was needed for the sport to grow. To enhance competition, France wanted to see a set of rules that would keep the cars and the competition uniform. His other goals were to provide insurance for the drivers and to inaugurate a point system so drivers could compete for a driving championship.

France had attempted to promote his beach race as a "national championship" only to be told he could not do that unless he had rules, a point championship, and an organization that crossed more than one state line. The rebuff likely was the impetus for his call to organize. Yet as far back as 1938, when France began promoting the race on the beach at Daytona, he had expressed his belief that the sport was in need of a set of rules to keep cars uniform and the competition equal.

At the end of that 1938 beach race, the first racer to cross the finish line was driver Smokey Purser. After Purser received the checkered flag, he drove away from the beach and out of sight. The race's technical director, Ed Parkinson, figured Purser was hiding something. Purser was promptly disqualified.

During the organization meeting France expressed his feeling that the first and foremost goal should be equal competition. He sought to codify the rules to help reduce cheating. If this was to be "stock" car racing, each car mechanic had to know what he could or could not do. France knew it wouldn't be possible to catch everyone, but he knew he had to at least try to curb the most flagrant abusers.

As part of the new organization, France said, he wanted the sport to be able to list its champions, to memorialize their records and their earnings. As a promoter, France was aware of the importance of records and statistics, and he kept records of who led after each lap as a clever way of involving local merchants in his races.

Among the prizes France had awarded in the 1938 race on the beach at Daytona to lap leaders were a bottle of rum, $2.50 credit at a local men's clothing store, a box of fancy Hav-a-Tampa cigars, a case of Pennzoil motor oil, a pair of $5 sunglasses from Walgreen's, two cases of Blue Ribbon beer, and a $25 credit on any automobile in Dick Rose's used car lot. This element of sponsor involvement has never changed. The only difference today is the amount awarded by sponsors.

France made one other proposal, one that was to distance and distinguish his new organization from all other racing groups. It was the notion of only allowing new cars in the races. France told the other promoters, "We need to think about our image. If you race a junky-looking automobile—even if you take a new Cadillac, take the bumpers off and let it get real dirty—then in people's minds it would still be a jalopy.

"We need to have races for the most modern automobiles available. Plain, ordinary working people have to be able to associate with the cars. Standard street stock cars are what we should be running."

France's reasoning bordered on genius. He could not have foreseen a day when the car manufacturers would pump millions of dollars into racing but, ultimately, that was the result of his thinking. When, in 1950, Joe Littlejohn drove his Olds 88 Rocket 98.840 miles per hour to win the pole in France's beach race, it gave a big boost to Olds 88 sales. No new cars were made during World War II (nor was there any auto racing; Bill France built sub chasers during the war) but once the war ended, the car manufacturers used racing to sell and promote their products as Hudsons, Chevys, Chryslers, and Fords vied on the NASCAR circuit. The dealers' slogan became, "Win on Sunday, sell on Monday."

At that historic meeting Bill France was named president of the organization. When a name for the organization was requested, the first suggestion was NSCRA, the National Stock

Car Racing Association. But a small group in Georgia already had the name, and so driver-mechanic Red Vogt suggested an alternative, the National Association for Stock Car Automobile Racing (NASCAR). There was some concern that NASCAR sounded a lot like Nash Car (Nash was a minor auto manufacturer), but the recommendation was seconded and passed.

The group needed money to incorporate. Louis Ossinsky, a Daytona Beach attorney who was a customer at Bill France's gas station, volunteered to do the work. The incorporation date was February 21, 1948. Its headquarters were located at 88 Main Street.

In order to give this new organization some publicity and clout, France hired the world-famous endurance record driver Erwin "Cannonball" Baker to be NASCAR's Commissioner of Racing. Baker, who knew cars, was known to be fair, and his authority gave the new organization needed prestige.

The First "New Car" Race

The first "new car" race was held at the Charlotte Speedway on June 19, 1949. It called for 200 laps over the three-quarter-mile dirt oval. Beside Fords, Oldsmobiles, Buicks, and Chryslers, there were Hudsons, Lincolns, a Mercury, and even a Kaiser. Under the new rules set down by Bill France and NASCAR, the cars had to come off the showroom floor. There could be no tampering, no souping up of the engines. For this season, the oldest a competing car could be was a 1946 model.

The Charlotte race, the first ever in the Grand National championship series, was won by Glenn Dunnaway in a 1947 Ford owned by Hubert Westmoreland. After the race inspectors discovered a wedge that had been placed to stiffen the rear springs of Dunnaway's car. The car had been used during the week for bootlegging. The use of a wedge was typical in bootleggers' cars, but it was in violation of NASCAR's rules. Dunnaway was disqualified; the victory and the $2,000 first-place prize money were given to Jim Roper, who drove a 1949 Lincoln.

The other drivers, among them Tim and Fonty Flock and Red Byron, were convinced that Dunnaway hadn't known about the wedge and chipped in part of their purses. Dunnaway went home richer than if he had won.

Car owner Hubert Westmoreland sued, claiming his car was stock and demanded his prize money. Discussing the illegal wedge in court, the lawyer for NASCAR kept repeating the term "bootlegger" over and over. NASCAR won the case.

The era during which most of the cars were owned by bootleggers had come to an end.

The Early Sponsors

In 1955 a millionaire by the name of Carl Kiekhaefer entered the sport. He owned the Mercury Outboard Motor Company, and he chose to race Chrysler cars. Kiekhaefer's initial reason for entering racing was to learn more about motors in order to improve his boat engines. He also advertised his product, writing "Mercury Outboards" on the side of his car in big block letters. When it became clear that Kiekhaefer's advertising was selling a lot of Mercury cars, he changed the lettering to read "Kiekhaefer Outboards."

Carl Kiekhaefer changed the face of racing. He spent a great deal of money preparing his car, paid his driver Tim Flock a lord's salary of $40,000 a year, and dominated the '55 season, winning 18 poles and 18 Grand National races.

The next year Kiekhaefer sponsored as many as six drivers, including Buck Baker, Tim Flock, Speedy Thompson, and Charlie Scott, the first African American to compete at NASCAR's elite level. Kiekhaefer's cars won 21 of the first 25 races in 1956. From March 25 through May 30, Kiekhaefer's cars won 16 consecutive races, still a record for a car owner. But Kiekhaefer made the lives of his drivers intolerable. He ordered them around, prevented them from sleeping with their wives the night before the race, and made them fill out reports after a race. When Tim Flock quit early in the 1956 season and his replacement, Herb Thomas, also quit Kiekhaefer late that summer, the team suffered during the last part of the season, winning only 4 of the final 20 starts. In two years Kiekhaefer's cars won 52 of the 90 races entered, but he had become disillusioned and he retired from racing forever at the end of 1956. Many years later, Kiekhaefer was elected to the Hall of Fame.

Because of Kiekhaefer success selling outboard motors (and Mercury cars) through his racing exposure, in 1957 General Motors and Ford decided to get involved in racing big time. The factories spent a lot of money preparing their cars. On the Chevy payroll were some of the top drivers, including Buck Baker, Speedy Thompson, Jack Smith, Rex White, and Frankie Schneider. Ford picked John Holman to run its team, and Holman hired as his drivers Fireball Roberts, Curtis Turner, Joe Weatherly, Bill Amick, Marvin Panch, and Ralph Moody. Driving for Pontiac were Banjo Matthews and Cotton Owens. Billy Myers and Jim Paschal drove for Mercury. Lee Petty and Ralph Earnhardt drove Oldsmobiles, and Johnny Allen drove for Plymouth. Everyone else ran independently on the cheap.

It was a very exciting time in racing, but the infusion of car factory money was short lived. On May 19, 1957, in a race at Martinsville, Billy Myers and Tom Pistone collided. Myers's Mercury hurtled the retaining wall and hit four spectators standing near a sign that read "No Spectators Allowed." Among the four spectators was eight-year-old Alvin Helsabeck, who had to undergo brain surgery. The headlines were on front pages across America. The car companies were horrified by the negative publicity.

Two weeks later, the car companies completely withdrew their sponsorship and support. The drivers suddenly found themselves the owners of their cars. The withdrawal of the factories was a shock, but Bill France was undeterred. NASCAR needed an infusion of excitement to hold the fans' interest, and France himself provided the electric jolt to the fortunes of NASCAR with the opening in February of 1959 of the Daytona International Speedway

The Age of the Superspeedway

During a poker game in 1949, stock car race promoter Harold Brasington proposed that an asphalt track be built near his home in Darlington, South Carolina. Brasington had visited the Indianapolis Speedway, and he envisioned building a similar track for stock cars.

Brasington took a huge risk but with the advance sale of $25,000 worth of tickets, he was able to complete construction. Brasington, who had competed in Bill France's beach races in Daytona, originally gave the race sanction to the Central States Racing Association, but when he found himself short on drivers, he called France and invited him to view the site. France, impressed, pledged his NASCAR drivers.

On September 4, 1950, Darlington International Raceway's first Southern 500 was staged, 400 laps around a mile-and-a-quarter paved track. Seventy-five cars competed. It took 15 days to qualify the field. There were few hotels to accommodate the crowds, but that first year 25,000 fans flocked to see the race.

The favorites were Red Byron and Curtis Turner, but the winner was Johnny "Madman" Mantz from Long Beach, California. Mantz qualified 43rd, but he won because his car was light and, through his Indy racing, he had connections with tire people in Dayton, Ohio, and was able to put heavy duty truck tires, similar to Indy-style tires, on his car.

During the race Mantz changed tires but three times. The cars using standard tires had to change tires as many as 24 times. Twenty-two cars had blowouts. Mantz averaged 75.25 miles per hour to win.

When he crossed the finish line, the second car, driven by Glenn "Fireball" Roberts, was nine laps back. The co-owners of Mantz's 1950 Plymouth, which was used to run business errands during the week, were mechanic Hubert Westmoreland, NASCAR starter and flagman Alvin Hawkins, and Bill France.

Bill France became enamored of the superspeedway concept. He had been trying to coerce the ruling political body of Daytona Beach to allow him to build a similar facility since 1949. He felt that stock car racing needed a track that was wide and banked so cars could run in different grooves and pass in the turns. Indy Car racing had been king up to that time, but France believed the Indy track too narrow for stock car racing; the cars would have to run single file around the turns, and because the track was flat, the wear on the cars would be too great.

France wanted to build a paved track at Daytona because he foresaw that the growth in popularity of his beach race would soon clash with the growth of the beach community. In anticipation of the day when he would be barred from staging his race, he began lobbying for a permanent facility in order to make sure Daytona Beach didn't lose motor sports racing.

A Racing and Recreation District was formed, land was bought, and France got a 99-year lease. The chairman of the commission was J. Saxton Lloyd, who owned the Buick and Cadillac dealership where France had worked when he first moved to Daytona Beach.

France sold 300,000 shares of stock at one dollar a share and then had to borrow $600,000 from oil millionaire Clint Murchison and his financial advisor, Howard Sluyter. France could have built a conventional track with the original money, but he was so committed to his vision of a banked track that he refused to compromise. He went deep into personal debt to see the realization of his dream.

France started selling tickets and used a lot of the ticket money for construction costs. His track was such a success that he paid off the original $600,000 loan only ten years after the Daytona International Speedway opened.

When the Daytona International Speedway opened in 1959, the drivers marveled. Where Darlington was a fast mile-and-three-eighths track, Daytona was two-and-a-half miles around, and with its long straightaways, breathtaking speeds of over 140 miles per hour were attainable.

Said Speedway President Jim Foster, "Mr. France had something that none of the others had and that was vision. Bill France was a visionary. He saw where the sport was going to go, and he believed in it strongly, risked every penny he had. When he built his Speedway, he went deep in debt, and for years afterward was besieged by creditors. And when the others were selling their Daytona Speedway stock, he bought. And Daytona was a huge success, and he built the Talladega track, and he bought Darlington, and he bought Watkins Glen, and it's all because Bill France had this vision. Bill France was the one who took on the risk. It's the risktakers who become wealthy. And mostly it's those who refused to take that risk who were left bitter and angry."

Concluded Foster, "Without Bill France, there would have been no NASCAR, would have been no racing as we know it today."

At Daytona, cars could go 30 to 40 miles per hour faster than they had driven before. All the drivers felt like rookies on the new track. Said driver Jimmy Thompson about the new track, "There have been other tracks that separated the men from the boys. This is the track that will separate the brave from the weak after the boys are gone."

When driver Lee Petty saw the huge track at Daytona for the first time, he realized that his world of short-track, dirt-track racing soon would be coming to an end.

"We knew stock car racing was never going to be the same again," he said.

The Early Legends

Smokey Yunick was a controversial owner-mechanic genius who was renowned for his innovative engine and chassis designs. His cars won scores of races with Herb Thomas, and later he won with drivers Paul Goldsmith, Fireball Roberts, and Marvin Panch.

Said Yunick about Thomas, who during the week was a dirt farmer, "Herb Thomas could really drive. He was smart in the race. He knew how to pace himself. He was as good as they came, and they have never given him enough credit for his ability."

Another of Yunick's favorites was old breed Buck Baker, driving champion in 1956 and 1957 (winner of forty-six races).

Said Yunick, "Buck was a wild son of a bitch. He had a nasty streak. When he got drunk, he'd show off. He was bad about fighting, and when he got drunk he was a nasty son of a bitch."

That's the way it was back then, rough and tumble. Ralph Moody, who began racing in the 1930s, remembers the old timers. An itinerant race driver, Moody settled in the Charlotte area in 1956. Moody became partners with a man named John Holman, and the new concern began under the name Holman-Moody, which quickly became the premier car-building firm in racing. At its peak in 1960 Holman-Moody built 400 racecars. Holman was the businessman, Moody the brains of the operation.

Driving for the Holman-Moody team were most of the legendary drivers of the period: Curtis Turner, Joe Weatherly, Marvin Panch, Fireball Roberts, Freddy Lorenzen, and Junior Johnson.

The stories told about these legendary racers reflect a period in America that today seems long gone. The Depression created a class of hungry, often fierce, competitive men without formal educations who dragged themselves up by their bootstraps and retained that inner drive, even after they attained success.

Lee Petty, who won 54 races, came from a farming background. During the Depression he sold biscuits and later had a small trucking business. He turned to racing and, like many before and after him, found out just how tough it was to be an independent owner-driver. Petty, unlike most of the others, was a family man and too serious about winning races to party late into the night. He was also a churlish despot who would do anything to win. One time in the mid-1950s, Petty put wing nuts and armor plating on the side of his Oldsmobile, so that anytime his car brushed against the side of another car he'd shred the opponent's sheet metal. Charlton Heston's enemy had done that to him during the chariot race in Ben Hur; Lee Petty did it for real.

One time during a race at High Point, Petty came into the pits. His son, Richard, a member of the pit crew, climbed up on the hood to wipe the mud off the windshield. The crew finished changing tires, and without saying a word to Richard, Lee Petty drove away, with a petrified Richard still on the car, hanging on. Lee drove one entire lap before he returned to the pit road to let Richard off. After the race, he cussed out the boy. When Richard himself began to race, there were times when Lee bumped him and caused him to crash, so great was Lee's desire to win.

Unlike the serious Petty, life for Curtis Turner (seventeen wins), Joe Weatherly (twenty-five wins), and Fireball Roberts (thirty-three wins) was a never-ending string of parties and competitions that ended in their early deaths.

On the track Turner was a fearsome competitor who would think nothing of forcing you off the track if you were in his way. Turner had a feel for how far he could push his racecar. He could get his car completely sideways at 135 miles per hour and save it, where other drivers would lose control.

Off the track Turner loved women, V.O. and 7-Up, and flying. He had a saying, "If you feel bad enough before you start a race, nothing can happen to bother you." Turner, the quintessential partier, wouldn't invite you back to his fourteen-acre home if you didn't get drunk at one of his parties, which might last a week. At one shindig Joe Weatherly was seen using a fire extinguisher to serve drinks in flower vases. Young girls dancing on tables. Guests lay on the floor passed out. Said Tim Flock "Curtis was a party man."

Turner was a businessman who made, and then lost, millions. He sold timber, owned movie theaters, and with Bruton Smith built the Charlotte Motor Speedway, before it went broke. Humpy Wheeler, who later became president of the Speedway, often said that Turner's mistake was trying to mix racing with business.

In 1961 Turner sought to organize the NASCAR drivers for the Teamsters Union. Turner wanted the drivers to receive 40 percent of the gate receipts. He was also hoping Teamster boss Jimmy Hoffa would help him save his failing track. But in return for their support, Hoffa had Turner ask for parimutuel betting on the races.

Turner had once teamed with NASCAR head Bill France in a Pan American Road Race, and he had saved their lives when he averted a plunge off a steep cliff by driving the car into the rocks on the other side of the road. Despite their shared past, France broke Turner's efforts, threatening to close the tracks, find new drivers and put the old ones out of work. Turner found himself isolated. France banned Turner from racing for life but after four years, Turner begged forgiveness, and France allowed him to return.

Turner, an expert pilot, often took businessmen up in his airplane to sell them timber. According to Tim Flock, he'd have them so scared they would be afraid to look out the window. Said Flock, "He would fly over the worst timber in the world and say, 'There's some damn fine timber down there,' and they'd say 'Okay. Okay. Can we go back down to the ground now? "And that's why he sold so much timber."

A jokester, Turner had the habit of turning off one of the two engines in mid-flight and pretending he didn't know what was wrong. He would say to a passenger who had never flown before, "Go ahead, you fly it."

Turner died on a Sunday afternoon in October 1970 when his Aerocommander crashed into a hill near Du Bois, Pennsylvania, twenty minutes after takeoff. His body was found a half-block away in the woods. The passenger, golf pro Clarence King, was strapped in the cockpit seat. Speculation was that while Curtis was sleeping off a toot in the back, King suffered a heart attack, and the plane crashed.

Turner's sidekick was Little Joe Weatherly. They were the Don Quixote and Sancho Panza of stock car racing, drinking buddies, hell raisers. Weatherly, who got his start driving motorcycles, loved to play practical jokes. He had a stuffed mongoose in a box, and he'd pop it open and scare the unsuspecting. He wore one suit that was half gray and half red.

Weatherly spoke in short, staccato bursts, and when he got excited ran his words together and talked "four thousand miles per hour," according to Humpy Wheeler, who recalled the night Weatherly bet Fireball Roberts that Roberts couldn't back up his brand-new, black and gold Pontiac at a high speed. Robert of course, took the bet. They marked a course, at the end which were three-foot-high wooden telephone poles that Weatherly had made invisible by painting them black.

Wheeler was sitting in the back seat when Roberts flew backward, hit an unseen pole, and bent the back of the car almost in half. Wheeler, who was lucky he wasn't killed, had sore neck for a week.

Because Weatherly was very superstitious, other drivers drove him crazy by throwing peanuts onto his seat before race. He also thought the color green brought him bad luck so of course, they were always bringing him something green.

Weatherly also loved to fly, even though he never learned how to make flight plans or use the instruments, including the radio. Sometimes he flew in a direction opposite of what he was intending. One time on a trip to Dayton, Ohio, he was quite surprised when he passed by the top of the Empire State

Building in New York. On another trip, from Darlington to Charlotte, he ended up in Spartanburg.

Joe Weatherly died on January 19, 1964, at Riverside. California, during the fifth race of the season. Little Joe was trying to catch the eventual winner, Dan Gurney, but the brakes of his Mercury failed, and Weatherly went wide into the dangerous turn six and hit the wall on the left side. He wasn't going more than 85 miles per hour, but the impact caused his head to fly out the driver's window, and his skull slapped against the concrete wall, killing him. His was the first death in a Grand National Race in seven years.

Glenn "Fireball" Roberts, perhaps the first superstar in stock car racing, received what proved to be fatal burns in a fiery crash at Charlotte on May 24, 1964, four months after Weatherly's fatal crash. Roberts, who had won 33 races in a career that began in 1947, was talking of retirement at the time of his death. He had started young and was able to beat all comers until a young driver named Fred Lorenzen challenged him and proved himself superior. On the day Roberts was severely burned, according to Lorenzen, Roberts didn't want to race. Weatherly's death still haunted him, and the fire to race had burned itself out. His desire was gone.

Banjo Matthews, then a driver and later one of the sport's most famous body fabricators until his death in October 1996 remembers that Roberts was losing his skills. He had spun out on superspeedways during practice a couple of times. Roberts, who had socked away a lot of money, talked to Matthews about retiring. He talked of going to work for a beer distributorship to do public relations. According to fellow driver and friend Neil Castles, he intended to become a radio broadcaster. He had been taking a course in public speaking.

The night before the accident, Roberts and Ned Jarrett sat poolside at a motel and talked. Roberts said his competitive edge was missing. He talked about quitting. For Roberts, the thrill was ebbing. His nerves were beginning to jangle.

The morning of Roberts' crash, Banjo Matthews helped Roberts put on his uniform. Roberts complained that the flame retardant fiberglass in the uniform made him break out in a rash. As a result, he cut his sleeves off. According to Matthews, Roberts told him he didn't feel up to racing.

"Glenn," said Mathews, "get your ass up and go get in your car and go home."

"I can't do that," said Roberts. Matthews wanted to know why.

"Because all these people are here to see me race," Roberts said. He said he also felt obligated to Ford and his sponsors.

During the race at Charlotte, Junior Johnson hooked the rear of Ned Jarrett's car, spinning out both cars. Roberts came down the straightaway, swerved to avoid Johnson and Jarrett and smashed into an opening in the concrete wall. After the car became airborn, it turned upside down and the fuel tank broke open, with the fuel cascading into the car. Back then there was no rubber bladder or fuel cell to prevent spilled gas. When the car came to a stop, the fuel began to pool around the car.

Suddenly, the lavender car with the white number "22" ignited. Fire raged. Roberts, strapped in the car, knew to hold his breath to keep the flames from searing his lungs. As the conflagration burned all around Roberts, Ned Jarrett tried to pull him out.

"My God, Ned," said Roberts, "help me. I'm on fire."

The heroic Jarrett finally did pull him out, burning his own hands. Once he got Roberts out, he began tearing off the driver's clothing. Roberts, still conscious, helped him. The rescue squad finished, and the racer was taken by helicopter to Charlotte Memorial Hospital. He was burned over 80 percent of his body.

For a while it looked like Roberts would make it, despite his third-degree burns. "He is a remarkable patient," announced his doctors, who after several weeks said he was improving. But after an operation to remove burned skin on June 30, his condition worsened. Pneumonia set in. He lapsed into a coma and never regained consciousness. Glenn "Fireball" Roberts died on July 2, 1964, of the burns, pneumonia, and blood poisoning.

After the funeral, a relative complained: "Want to hear about bad taste? Glenn gets burned to death, and the mortuary sends the family a smoked ham. That's the goddam South for you."

Two years after Roberts' death, Ned Jarrett, who won NASCAR's racing championship in 1961 and 1965, retired. In 13 years Jarrett had won 50 races, tied for seventh on the list with Junior Johnson. Ironically, it was Ned Jarrett who entered the broadcasting profession, where he has been an analyst for CBS, ESPN, and TNN ever since.

The King

On the heels of the deaths of Turner, Weatherly, and Roberts came a new generation of racers led by Lee Petty's son, Richard, whose driving skill would take stock car racing to its next plateau. Beginning in 1958, the year before his father won the initial Daytona 500 race, Richard would go on to become the Babe Ruth of stock car racing. Long before his retirement in 1992 he would be called simply The King. Over a driving career spanning 35 years, Richard Petty would win an incredible 200 NASCAR Winston Cup Grand National races and seven times be named driving champion (1964, 1967, 1971, 1972, 1974, 1975, and 1979).

Perhaps the most famous race Richard Petty didn't win came in the Daytona 500 in 1976 when he and rival David Pearson drove side by side toward the checkered flag. Coming out of turn two, Pearson shot his Mercury around Petty's Dodge. Pearson, in the lead, drifted high into turn three. Petty tried to duck down low and, as they came off turn four, were door to door, inches apart. Then they collided. Out of control, Pearson hit the wall nose first, clipping Petty's rear bumper. Both cars went skidding out of control.

Petty's Dodge stopped on the infield grass, a hundred yards from the finish line. His engine was dead. It could not be restarted. Pearson had come to a stop at the foot of the pit road, perhaps a couple of hundred yards from the finish.

Working the starter over and over, Pearson was able to get his car to jump ahead a foot or two at a time until he was able to cross the line. No other car was on the lead lap, so Petty was awarded second place even though he had completed but 199 laps. That race is considered the most dramatic finish in superspeedway history.

After the race Petty was asked what he was thinking while the crash was taking place.

"Well," he said in his most endearing manner, "I wasn't exactly hollering, 'Hooray for me.'"

Three years later Petty was the beneficiary of another renowned Daytona 500 crash, which occurred on the last lap when Cale Yarborough and Donnie Allison tangled and wrecked each other's cars, allowing Petty to roar across the finish line with the 1979 Daytona victory.

In all Richard Petty won the Daytona 500 in 1964, 1966, 1971, 1973, 1974, 1979, and 1981. He won roughly one-third of the races at Daytona during the years in which he dominated NASCAR racing.

And yet, despite his immense popularity, Richard Petty never shunned a request for an interview or for an autograph, as he became the unofficial ambassador of stock car racing. When interviewed in 1992, he said with a smile, "You know, there is no man on earth who has been interviewed more times than I have." Who else might have been in the running for such a distinction? Muhammad Ali? He retired a long time ago. Charles Lindbergh? Elvis? They were recluses much of their lives. John Wayne? Movie stars were kept from the press by agents and bodyguards. Other famous American athletes, like Mickey Mantle, Willie Mays, and Hank Aaron shunned the press whenever possible. Few of the newcomers in any sport seem to embrace the media and the fans. Even Michael Jordan, as great a player as he is, seems uncomfortable in an uncontrolled interview situation.

Richard Petty, the winningest stock car driver of all time, courted the press and repaid his legions of fans for their loyalty by allowing them easy access. Millions of Richard Petty autographs grace walls all across America. For all those reasons, he will always be regarded as The King.

The Crown Princes

Petty's duels with such drivers as David Pearson, Bobby Allison, and Cale Yarborough were classics. Pearson (105 NASCAR wins), Allison (85 wins), and Yarborough (83 wins) are currently ranked second, third, and fifth respectively in wins on the all time driver's list.

If Richard Petty was The King, David Pearson was Crown Prince, the winner of the NASCAR championship in 1966, 1968, and 1969. Said Petty, "David was the best I ever ran with." A quiet man who was uncomfortable in public, David Pearson was most at home behind the wheel of a racecar, and it didn't matter what sort of track it was. Said Petty, "David loved to drive the race car, but that's all he wanted to do with it. He wasn't interested in the PR part, wasn't interested in making anything out of it. All he loved was to drive the racecar, and he was super. He could win on quarter-mile dirt tracks, quarter-mile asphalts, superspeedways, road courses—it didn't make any difference." Pearson retired in 1987.

Bobby Allison, who came from Hueytown, Alabama, won the championship in 1983 and finished second five times, often by minuscule margins. Allison, who was one of the most popular drivers in racing history, was so infatuated with racing that he would run 40 to 50 short-track events in addition to his NASCAR duties. Racing has been his whole life. Allison's career was cut short in 1988 when he was T-boned at the door and suffered a severe blow to his head in a crash at Pocono. Had the accident not happened, Allison might well be driving today.

Cale Yarborough, champion in 1976, 1977, and 1978, was a down-home South Carolina farmer best known for his competitiveness. Like Turner and Weatherly, Yarborough loved flying and other thrilling things such as wrestling an alligator and skydiving. He also loved to fight, and his fistic confrontation with the Allison brothers, Bobby and Donnie, at the end of the 1979 Daytona 500 became the stuff of legends. The first driver to qualify at over 200 miles per hour at Daytona (in 1984), Yarborough ran so hard his crew chief had to tell him to slow down for him to run faster. If his car was loose, his crew learned it had better bring him in, or else he would keep driving hard, risking a collision with a wall. Regardless of how far back Yarborough might be in a race, he never gave up. Yarborough retired in 1988.

The Era of the Sponsors

Junior Johnson and Ralph Seagraves from R.J. Reynolds were good old mountain buddies, and after Johnson asked Seagraves if R.J. Reynolds would be interested in putting up $800,000 to sponsor his car, Seagraves told Johnson that R.J. Reynolds wanted to spend closer to $400 million, because the federal government had forbidden the tobacco company from placing its ads on TV and radio and in magazines, and it was looking for a new avenue for its advertising.

Johnson brought Seagraves to see Bill France Sr. After R.J. Reynolds sponsored the first Winston 500 at Talladega, and then the Winston Western 500 at Riverside, California, the company agreed to put up the prize money for the NASCAR point fund—the monetary prizes for the top drivers. After several years, the name of the competition was changed from the Winston Cup Grand National Championship to the Winston Cup Series, the name it was known by through the 2002 season.

Before R.J. Reynolds became involved, most of the sponsors had been automobile related: Champion spark plugs, Goodyear, Firestone, STP, Purolator, and service stations such as Pure Oil Company. Once Winston came in and started using racing in its marketing and had almost instant success, the beer companies such as Falstaff, Miller, and Coors got involved.

The real phenomenon came along about 1984. About then NASCAR made it known that 48 percent of older race fans were women. As a result, Gatorade came in as a sponsor, and they now sponsor the Gatorade circle of champions. At the same time Procter & Gamble came in, along with Crisco, Tide, Hanes Pantyhose, and even candy bars. From then on corporations brought store managers and presidents of chains to every major race and began entertaining them. As more and more sponsors saw the sales of their products soar because of their connection to NASCAR racing, the sport enjoyed a prosperity never equaled in its history.

Jaws

A young driver by the name of Dale Earnhardt surprised everyone when he became the first driver in NASCAR history to follow rookie-of-the-year honors (1979) with a driving championship (1980). But the newcomer who most rattled the older generation of racers and race fans was brash Darrell Waltrip, who arrived on the NASCAR scene from Nashville with a vocal message to the veterans, "Look out." In one race at North Wilkesboro in 1979, the cocky Waltrip kept ramming into the rear of Bobby Allison's car, warning the veteran driver to move out of his way. On the radio Waltrip's crew chief warned him not to do that, but an arrogant Waltrip, who was nicknamed "Jaws" by Cale Yarborough for his ability to run his mouth, replied, "He'll take it. There ain't nothing he can do about it." About that time Allison let off the gas and let Waltrip pass. Then the angry Allison put the youngster into the wall.

Waltrip would brag that he was better than his older competitors' and in time he was, breaking the monopoly of the older drivers by winning the NASCAR championship in 1981, 1982, and 1985. Though fans booed Waltrip and threw things at him, it was Darrell Waltrip who broke the hold of the older vets and led the way for the new generation of drivers who included Dale Earnhardt, Tim Richmond, Davey Allison, Terry Labonte (1996 and 1984 champion), Mark Martin, Rusty Wallace (1989 champion), Kyle Petty, and Ernie Irvan.

Another driver who began racing in the late 1970s and who made his mark is Bill Elliott, who earned the driving title in 1988. Elliott earned fame by winning The Winston Million—an award of $1 million for winning three of the Big Four races (Daytona 500, Winston 500, and Southern 500) in 1985. That year he also set the race speed mark of 186.288 miles per hour in winning at Talladega. Elliott, who is from Dawsonville, Georgia, is one of the most popular drivers in racing history.

The Intimidator

Dale Earnhardt, who is loved and hated by more racing fans than any other driver, is the son of Ralph Earnhardt, a champion dirt track racer. Like his father, Dale runs with a fearless intensity that can at times be intimidating. If a driver doesn't get out of his way, Earnhardt has been known to take the air off the offender's spoiler and send him into the wall. His father often told him, "Establish your territory." That's exactly what Earnhardt has done, winning the NASCAR driving championship in 1980, 1986, 1987, 1990, 1991, 1993, and 1994.

Tragedy

The race world was shocked and saddened when two of Earnhardt's top challengers, Alan Kulwicki and Davey Allison, met early deaths in 1993 in separate air accidents. The following year Neil Bonnett died in a crash at Daytona.

In 1990 Alan Kulwicki was offered $1 million to drive for car owner Junior Johnson, but the brash independent turned down the offer. Said Kulwicki, "I figured I could make pretty good money and be happy running my own team. If I drove for him, maybe I'd he happy and maybe I wouldn't."

Kulwicki, who began driving in 1985 with a used car and two crew members, believed he could win a championship as owner of his own race team. Everyone thought he was foolish not to take the money and run for Johnson. But Alan Kulwicki was a maverick, a racer who listened to his heart, who did things his way. Just two years later Kulwicki was battling Bill Elliott for the title. To win, he needed to finish the final race in Atlanta with

the most laps led, even if Elliott won the race. Elliott did win, but Kulwicki, who led the most laps and finished second, won the title by ten points over Elliott. Said Kulwicki after the race, "When I moved down South years ago, this was my dream. I came here in a pick-up truck and a trailer. I want to thank the many people who helped me along the way."

Alan Kulwicki was the toast of racing, but his reign was short-lived. One of the perks of Kulwicki's winning the championship was that he was given the use of a plane owned by his sponsor, Hooters restaurants. On April 1, 1993, his plane mysteriously crashed en route to the track in Bristol, Tennessee. Kulwicki and three others aboard were killed.

Davey Allison, who was NASCAR rookie-of-the-year in 1987 was well on his way to a driving championship in 1992 when, at Pocono in July, he and Darrell Waltrip collided and Allison's car shot off the track, flipped backwards, and tumbled wildly. He suffered two fractures of his right forearm and a broken right wrist and collarbone. Despite the serious injuries, a valiant Allison was in the car to start the race the following week at Talladega. He let Bobby Hillin take over after the first caution. Then on Friday, August 13, 1992, Davey's brother, Clifford, was killed in a crash at the Michigan International Speedway. Distraught and in mourning, Davey went to Michigan, drove the entire 400-mile race, and finished fifth. Going into the final race of the season in Atlanta, a top-five finish by Allison would have given him the championship, but a collision with Ernie Irvan late in the race eliminated him and allowed Alan Kulwicki to earn the 1992 driving title.

Allison was again in contention to win the championship in 1993, but on June 12, 1993, he was flying his helicopter to the Talledega track when he miscalculated on landing, the copter's back rotor hit a chain-link fence, and the machine fell sideways to the ground, killing him and badly injuring his close friend Red Farmer. The loss of Kulwicki and then Allison in such close proximity cast a pall over the entire sport.

Neil Bonnett, an Alabaman who was like family to the Allisons, began racing in 1973 and won 18 Winston Cup races before his 1990 retirement, which was prompted by a series of serious injuries that put him in the hospital seven years in a row. The crash that sent him into retirement occurred during the 1990 TranSouth 500 at Darlington. Head injuries prevented him from recognizing his family. When he recovered, Bonnett became an integral part of racing's coverage on CBS and TNN, but the lure of the track became too great. In 1993 Bonnett decided to return to racing. On February 11, 1994, while practicing for the Daytona 500, he apparently lost control of his car on the high-banked turn four, skidded almost sideways, and slammed into the outside wall nearly head-on. He suffered massive head injuries and died.

The racing world suffered another blow when Lee Petty died Wednesday, April 5, 2000. He is greatly missed as one of the celebrated legends of stock car racing.

Bonnett's death was particularly painful for his closest friend, Dale Earnhardt. When Earnhardt began the 1994 season, he said over and over again, "I want to dedicate this season to Neil Bonnett." When Earnhardt sped to an easy Winston Cup championship, his seventh, tying Richard Petty for the NASCAR record, he told reporters, "I can't even fish in my own lake anymore because Neil used to fish there all the time. I've tried and I can't do it."

Meanwhile, the popularity of Dale Earnhardt was transcending the sport. His fans were legendary, but so were his distracters, who took to waving banners that read, "Anybody but Earnhardt."

The Coming of Wonder Boy

If Earnhardt needed a White Knight to compete against his Black Knight image, he found one in 1995 when a 24-year-old cherub by the name of Jeff Gordon surprised everyone by winning the racing championship over the legendary Intimidator. Gordon, who began racing midgets at age five and who won his first national championship at age eight, became the second-youngest driver after 23-year old Bill Rexford to win a NASCAR driving championship.

Earnhardt heated the rivalry when he went on the Tonight Show with Jay Leno and bragged that he had been the first "man" to win the Brickyard 400.

"Didn't Jeff Gordon win it in the inaugural?" Leno asked.

"Well, Wonder Boy won it first," Earnhardt admitted.

Before the final race at Atlanta, a race that Gordon only had to finish anywhere but last to win the championship, Earnhardt drove past him and gave him the finger.

"I was telling him that he's number one," said Earnhardt. Earnhardt won the race and passed Gordon seventeen times. It didn't matter. Gordon was 1995 champion. Said Earnhardt, "I think they were drinking champagne during the pit stops."

Said Gordon, "I'm sorry if it happened to me too soon. But that's the way it happened. I'd be the first to say I'm blessed. I'm just living my life."

In 1996 Jeff Gordon proved that his ability to win races was no fluke when he won 10 races, but the championship went to his fellow Rick Hendrick teammate, the steadier Terry Labonte. Gordon had finished far back in a half dozen races and trailed Labonte by 47 points entering the final race at Atlanta. When Labonte finished fifth to clinch the racing title and younger brother Bobby won the race, the two brothers celebrated with a joint victory lap. At Atlanta, Gordon fell two laps back when his car began vibrating, then fought his way up to a gutsy third-place finish. A third Hendrick driver, Ken Schrader, finished 12th in the points standings. No other team owner ever had three cars finish so high. During the season Terry Labonte broke Richard Petty's record of competing in 536 straight races. It was 12 years after "The Iceman" won his first Winston Cup championship.

On July 28, 1996, Dale Earnhardt was involved in a horrific crash at Talladega. He suffered a broken sternum and collarbone. He was unable to drive in the Brickyard 500 the next week but returned at Watkins Glen and finished a heroic sixth. At the end of the season team owner Richard Childress made news when he lured Larry McReynolds from the Robert Yates team to be Earnhardt's crew chief. Earnhardt finished fourth in the standings but 330 points back.

Jeff Gordon regained his championship in 1997 at the final race at Atlanta. He needed to finish 18th in the race to win, but had to start the race with a backup car after a collision during practice. Starting 37th, Gordon drove cautiously, fearful that his right front tire might blow before the finish, and he cruised to a 17th-place finish, edging Dale Jarrett by 14 points and Mark Martin by 29. Gordon won 10 races but none after September 14 at Loudon.

The win by Gordon was particularly gratifying for the Hendrick team because earlier in the season car owner Rick Hendrick had been diagnosed with leukemia. Awaiting a bone marrow transplant, Rick Hendrick watched the race on TV from his home on Lake Norman.

The night before, Gordon told Hendrick, "I'm gonna win this race. I'm gonna make you smile tomorrow."

In 1997 Gordon added a $1 million bonus from RJ Reynolds for winning three of the big four races, the Daytona 500, the Coca-Cola 600, and the Southern 500. Only Bill Elliott had accomplish the feat before him. Before that only Lee Roy Yarbrough (1969) and David Pearson (1976) won Daytona, Charlotte, and Darlington in a single year.

The Intimidator No Longer

Before the 1997 Southern 500, Dale Earnhardt caused his team members concern when he twice fell asleep behind the wheel waiting for the signal to start the cars. Soon after the green flag dropped, he suffered what appeared to be a seizure and hit the concrete retaining wall. Disoriented, Earnhardt needed two laps to find the pit road. When asked what had happened, the 46-year old legend told owner Richard Childress, "I'm sorry. I saw two race tracks." He was rushed to the hospital, but doctors couldn't find anything wrong with him, and he was released.

Just as perplexing was Earnhardt's inability to win races. Earnhardt finished the season winless, the first time that had happened since 1981, two seasons before he began driving for Richard Childress. Earnhardt finished fifth in the points but 494 points out of first place.

Earnhardt fans wondered whether their hero's winning ways were over. At the same time they, and fans of other drivers, began to loudly voice their disapproval of Jeff Gordon, who was booed before every race. They resented his Generation X youth, were jealous that he was engaged to the beautiful Brooke Sealey, Miss Winston, and were contemptuous of his website that he advertised on the back of his driver's suit. A rival website was set up by the Jeff Gordon Haters of America.

Gordon, meanwhile, in 1998 established himself as the racer to beat when he won the Winston Cup championship for the third time in four years. This time he won in a walk, tying Richard Petty's modern mark of 13 wins in a 33-race season. The win also gave Hendrick Motorsports an unprecedented four straight titles.

"Jeff Gordon is one of the greatest race drivers who has ever been in a car," said Martin, the Winston Cup runner up.

Despite Gordon's dominance, the highlight of the 1998 season occurred at Daytona in February when Dale Earnhardt won the Daytona 500 after 19 frustrating years of trying. The win broke a 59-race streak dating back to March of 1996. Gordon looked like a sure winner until lap 123 when he hit a piece of debris on the track and damaged his front end, ruining the handling of his car. Earnhardt flew by him into the lead. Every fan at the track wondered, "Can he hang on?" So many times at Daytona Dale hadn't. But a crash near the end of the race ensured that Earnhardt would be the victor. As Earnhardt drove toward Victory Lane, the crews of every race team spilled out of the pits to greet him.

"This is it. This is it. There ain't nothin' gonna top this," Earnhardt said.

Earnhardt was taken to the press room high atop the Winston tower press box, where he watched hundreds of his fans picking up pieces of turf as souvenirs. He waved to them from high above, and they waved back. A few minutes later on the infield his fans arranged themselves into the number three. Then they formed an eight, signifying a wished-for eighth championship. But the Earnhardt-dubbed Wonder Boy, Jeff Gordon, had other ideas.

Gordon, who drove a Chevrolet Monte Carlo, was so dominant that he was criticized not only by rivals driving other brands but by Chevy owners as well. Said Chevy car owner Felix Sabates, "NASCAR should bring a Hummer and make Jeff Gordon drive it. Then the rest of us would have a chance." Jack Roush went so far as to accuse Gordon's race team of soaking his tires in an untraceable chemical to make the car go faster. Gordon's tires were impounded but nothing untoward was found.

Said Dale Jarrett, who finished third in the points standing, "Just the whole year [Gordon] was just too good."

The 1999 Daytona 500 was billed as a battle between the Old Guard and the Upstart, Gordon. The Upstart won, along with a purse of more than a million dollars.

When Gordon won again at Atlanta in mid-March, everyone was willing to concede him another championship, but a series of accidents leading to DNFs at Martinsville, Texas and Talladega put him so far behind Dale Jarrett that he was unable to catch up despite a late-season rush. Hurting the 24 team was an apparent rift between and Gordon and his long-time friend and crew chief Ray Evernham. In September 1999 Evernham suddenly left Hendrick Motorsports to run the Dodge reentry program into Winston Cup racing. The spin was that this was an opportunity Evernham couldn't pass up, but when the two also split up their Busch team, Gordon hinted that there may have been a serious problem between them.

Then on October 5, five members of the Rainbow Warrior pit crew left the team and went to work for Robert Yates Racing and Dale Jarrett. The defections left Gordon and his team unsettled in 2000, though morale rose when Gordon won his first two races at Martinsville and Charlotte under the leadership of Brian Whitesell. But that success was short-lived, and Whitesell was replaced by Robby Loomis, who for nine years was the crew chief for Richard Petty.

Joe Gibbs Wins A Title

When 36-year-old Bobby Labonte won the 2000 driving championship over seven-time winner Dale Earnhardt, he and Terry became the first brothers ever to win championships. Bobby was also the first Busch series champion ever to win the Winston Cup prize. His owner, Joe Gibbs, became the only person ever to win the Lombardi Trophy, given to the coach of a Super Bowl team, and the Winston Cup.

The highlight of the season for Labonte was his win at the Brickyard 400 in August when with 14 laps to go, he bumped aside leader Rusty Wallace in turn three, passed him, and won the race in record time.

Without Ray Evernham and much of his crew, Jeff Gordon was inconsistent and finished ninth.

A Dark Day

When Michael Waltrip crossed the finish line of the Daytona 500 on February 18, 2001, it was the happiest day of his life. Television viewers could see the tears streaming down his face as he and DEI teammate Dale Earnhardt Jr. finished the race one-two.

But behind him Dale Earnhardt's car collided with Sterling Marlin and after bouncing off Ken Schrader, slowly began aiming toward the outside wall. When the black number three Goodwrench Chevrolet hit the wall head-on, everyone held his breath. The ambulance drove onto the track. Crew members yelled for Dale to respond. All was silent. Earnhardt was considered invincible, a god. But it turned out he was only human. Experts said he died instantly. The sport would never be the same again . The entire NASCAR nation mourned, and it has not stopped mourning to this day.

By the end of the 2001 season NASCAR had mandated the HANS devise, a safer head restraint. The only complaint came from driver Tony Stewart, who said it was "ridiculous and unfair."

Seventeen different drivers won races in 2001. Jeff Gordon, at age 30, won his fourth driving championship. Only Richard Petty and Dale Earnhardt, with seven titles, had won more. Married to the former Miss Winston, NASCAR was hoping Gordon would take Earnhardt's role of ambassador at large. But that honor would be bestowed not on Gordon but on Dale Earnhardt Jr., who displayed the same charisma of his father, returning to Daytona and leaving not a dry eye in the house when he won the Firecracker 500. In 2001 Dale Jr. became the most popular driver on the circuit. Little E, as he is called, has made stock car racing "cool."

Tony Stewart, who finished second to Gordon in the point standings, was another of the young Turks. Stewart gave notice that he didn't believe in the old-school notions of willingly signing autographs for fans and answering questions from reporters. Stewart constantly complained about the fans in the garage area and once knocked a tape recorder out of a reporter's hand and gave it a kick. Times have changed. Richard Petty no longer is the role model. The King is dead. Long live the King.

The 2001 season was marked by an incident after the Bristol race when the hair-triggered Stewart plowed into Jeff Gordon on pit row. Gordon had spun Stewart to gain position, and Stewart was furious. NASCAR fined Stewart $10,000 and placed him on probation for the rest of the season.

In 2002 car owner Joe Gibbs proved that his win in 2000 with driver Bobby Labonte was no fluke when Stewart edged veteran Mark Martin for the driving championship. During the year Stewart twice was accused of assaulting photographers after races. He was placed on probation and fined $50,000 for one incident and cleared of the other by NASCAR officials. At the end of the season NASCAR announced it would limit access to the garage area by fans and media.

When Stewart began the season with a blown engine after only two laps at Daytona, then suffered through five DNFs, most everyone wrote him off. At midseason he wasn't even ranked in the top ten.

In late September, 10 drivers were still in the hunt for the championship. But then on September 29 points leader Sterling Marlin crashed and fractured his neck at Kansas City, and on October 6 Stewart took the points lead after the two drivers he was chasing, Martin and rookie Jimmie Johnson, collided on the pace lap before the green flag at Talladega. Stewart finished second that day to Dale Earnhardt Jr.

Stewart's main rival, Jeff Gordon, who was being sued for divorce by his wife Brooke, ended a 31-race winless streak at Bristol on August 24 and then won again at Darlington, and his fans wondered whether The Rainbow Warrior would make a late-season charge for the title.

Stewart went into the final race with a 89-point lead over Mark Martin. He had been aided by a 25-point penalty assessed to Martin's car after the race at Rockingham when inspectors discovered an unapproved spring. When Stewart finished 18th and Martin finished 4th at Homestead in the finale, Martin was 38 points short, and the reincarnation of A.J. Foyt, Stewart's boyhood hero, was the new champion.

As NASCAR enters the new millennium, the signs are everywhere that the financial stakes will continue to rise dramatically. Donald Trump bid $55 million to develop a site on eastern Long Island for a NASCAR superspeedway. Ted Turner won a $130 million contract to build a track in Kansas City. The biggest deal of them all was for $2.4 billion ($400 million for six years) in which NBC, Fox, and their cable partners will pay NASCAR to broadcast Winston Cup races. It quadruples what NASCAR had been paid in the past.

The only negative news was that RJ Reynolds announced it would soon end its long association with NASCAR. The company, which had injected hundreds of millions of dollars into the sport, announced it intended to go in a different direction. In mid-June 2002, the announcement was made that NEXTEL stepped up to the plate with a deal reported to be worth $75 million a year for 10 years to take over Winston's role as the primary sponsor of NASCAR.

PART 1
THE RECORDS

Key

Buick	Buick
Chev	Chevrolet
Chrys	Chrysler
Dodg	Dodge
Ford	Ford
Huds	Hudson
Jag	Jaguar
Linc	Lincoln
Mata	Matador (AMC)
Merc	Mercury
Nash	Nash
Olds	Oldsmobile
Plym	Plymouth
Pont	Pontiac
Stud	Studebaker

WINNERS BY CAR MANUFACTURER

YEAR	Buick	Chev	Chrys	Dodg	Ford	Huds	JAG	Linc	Mata	Merc	Nash	Olds	Plym	Pont	Stud	TOTAL
1949	0	0	0	0	0	0	0	2	0	0	0	5	1	0	0	8
1950	0	0	0	0	1	0	0	2	0	2	0	10	4	0	0	19
1951	0	0	1	0	0	12	0	0	0	2	1	20	2	0	3	41
1952	0	0	1	0	0	27	0	0	0	0	0	3	3	0	0	34
1953	0	0	0	6	0	22	0	0	0	0	0	9	0	0	0	37
1954	0	0	7	1	0	17	1	0	0	0	0	11	0	0	0	37
1955	2	2	27	1	2	1	0	0	0	0	0	10	0	0	0	45
1956	0	3	22	11	14	0	0	0	0	5	0	1	0	0	0	56
1957	0	21	0	0	26	0	0	0	0	0	0	4	0	2	0	53
1958	0	25	0	0	16	0	0	0	0	0	0	7	0	3	0	51
1959	0	16	0	0	16	0	0	0	0	0	0	4	7	1	0	44
1960	0	13	0	1	15	0	0	0	0	0	0	0	8	7	0	44
1961	0	11	1	0	7	0	0	0	0	0	0	0	3	30	0	52
1962	0	14	0	0	6	0	0	0	0	0	0	0	11	22	0	53
1963	0	8	0	0	23	0	0	0	0	1	0	0	19	4	0	55
1964	0	1	0	14	30	0	0	0	0	5	0	0	12	0	0	62
1965	0	0	0	2	48	0	0	0	0	1	0	0	4	0	0	55
1966	0	3	0	18	10	0	0	0	0	2	0	0	16	0	0	49
1967	0	3	0	5	10	0	0	0	0	0	0	0	31	0	0	49
1968	0	1	0	5	21	0	0	0	0	6	0	0	16	0	0	49
1969	0	0	0	22	26	0	0	0	0	4	0	0	2	0	0	54
1970	0	0	0	17	6	0	0	0	0	4	0	0	21	0	0	48
1971	0	3	0	7	4	0	0	0	0	12	0	0	22	0	0	48
1972	0	10	0	4	0	0	0	0	0	9	0	0	8	0	0	31
1973	0	7	0	8	0	0	0	0	1	11	0	0	1	0	0	28
1974	0	12	0	10	0	0	0	0	1	7	0	0	0	0	0	30
1975	0	6	0	14	4	0	0	0	3	3	0	0	0	0	0	30
1976	0	13	0	6	1	0	0	0	0	10	0	0	0	0	0	30
1977	0	21	0	7	0	0	0	0	0	2	0	0	0	0	0	30
1978	0	9	0	0	5	0	0	0	0	4	0	12	0	0	0	30
1979	0	19	0	0	5	0	0	0	0	3	0	4	0	0	0	31
1980	0	21	0	0	3	0	0	0	0	3	0	4	0	0	0	31
1981	22	1	0	0	7	0	0	0	0	0	0	0	0	1	0	31
1982	25	3	0	0	2	0	0	0	0	0	0	0	0	0	0	30
1983	6	15	0	0	4	0	0	0	0	0	0	0	0	5	0	30
1984	2	21	0	0	4	0	0	0	0	0	0	0	0	3	0	30
1985	0	14	0	0	14	0	0	0	0	0	0	0	0	0	0	28
1986	2	19	0	0	5	0	0	0	0	0	0	1	0	2	0	29
1987	1	15	0	0	11	0	0	0	0	0	0	0	0	2	0	29
1988	2	8	0	0	9	0	0	0	0	0	0	2	0	8	0	29
1989	1	13	0	0	8	0	0	0	0	0	0	1	0	6	0	29
1990	1	13	0	0	11	0	0	0	0	0	0	1	0	3	0	29
1991	0	11	0	0	10	0	0	0	0	0	0	5	0	3	0	29
1992	0	8	0	0	16	0	0	0	0	0	0	2	0	3	0	29
1993	0	9	0	0	10	0	0	0	0	0	0	0	0	11	0	30
1994	0	11	0	0	20	0	0	0	0	0	0	0	0	0	0	31
1995	0	21	0	0	8	0	0	0	0	0	0	0	0	2	0	31
1996	0	17	0	0	13	0	0	0	0	0	0	0	0	1	0	31
1997	0	11	0	0	19	0	0	0	0	0	0	0	0	2	0	32
1998	0	16	0	0	15	0	0	0	0	0	0	0	0	2	0	33
1999	0	12	0	0	13	0	0	0	0	0	0	0	0	9	0	34
2000	0	9	0	0	14	0	0	0	0	0	0	0	0	11	0	34
2001	0	16	0	4	11	0	0	0	0	0	0	0	0	5	0	36
2002	0	10	0	7	14	0	0	0	0	0	0	0	0	5	0	36
Total	64	515	59	170	537	79	1	4	5	96	1	116	191	153	3	1994

Derived from winning cars of each and every Winston Cup race from 1949–2002.

*All T-Bird victories count as Ford victories (T-Bird was listed separately in 1959).

**2 Camaro wins in 1971 count as Chevrolet; 1 Mustang win in 1971 counts as Ford.

CAREER RECORDS—DRIVERS

RACES STARTED

1.	Richard Petty	1,184
2.	Dave Marcis	883
3.	Darrell Waltrip	809
4.	Ricky Rudd	767
5.	Terry Labonte	745
6.	Bobby Allison	718
7.	Buddy Baker	699
8.	Bill Elliott	696
9.	Dale Earnhardt	676
10.	J.D. McDuffie	653
11.	Kyle Petty	645
12.	Buck Baker	636
13.	James Hylton	601
14.	Rusty Wallace	598
15.	David Pearson	574
16.	Sterling Marlin	568
17.	Geoffrey Bodine	564
18.	Ken Schrader	563
19.	Buddy Arrington	562
20.	Cale Yarborough	559
21.	Elmo Langley	536
22.	Michael Waltrip	534
23.	Mark Martin	530
24.	Benny Parsons	526
25.	Neil Castles	497
26.	Dale Jarrett	495
	Wendell Scott	495
28.	Morgan Shepherd	487
29.	Brett Bodine	474
	Harry Gant	474

WINS

1.	Richard Petty	200
2.	David Pearson	105
3.	Bobby Allison	85
4.	Darrell Waltrip	84
5.	Cale Yarborough	83
6.	Dale Earnhardt	76
7.	Jeff Gordon	61
8.	Lee Petty	54
	Rusty Wallace	54
10.	Ned Jarrett	50
	Junior Johnson	50
12.	Herb Thomas	48
13.	Buck Baker	46
14.	Bill Elliott	43
15.	Tim Flock	39
16.	Bobby Isaac	37
17.	Mark Martin	33
	Fireball Roberts	33
19.	Dale Jarrett	30
20.	Rex White	28
21.	Fred Lorenzen	26
22.	Jim Paschal	25
	Joe Weatherly	25
24.	Ricky Rudd	23
25.	Terry Labonte	21
	Benny Parsons	21
	Jack Smith	21
28.	Speedy Thompson	20
29.	Davey Allison	19
	Buddy Baker	19
	Fonty Flock	19
	Bobby Labonte	19
33.	Geoffrey Bodine	18
	Neil Bonnett	18
	Harry Gant	18
36.	Jeff Burton	17
	Marvin Panch	17
	Curtis Turner	17
39.	Ernie Irvan	15
	Tony Stewart	15
41.	Dick Hutcherson	14
	LeeRoy Yarbrough	14
43.	Dick Rathmann	13
	Tim Richmond	13
45.	Donnie Allison	10
	Sterling Marlin	10
47.	Paul Goldsmith	9
	Cotton Owens	9
	Bob Welborn	9
50.	Kyle Petty	8
51.	Darel Dieringer	7
	Dale Earnhardt, Jr.	7
	A.J. Foyt	7
	Jim Reed	7
	Marshall Teague	7
56.	Matt Kenseth	6
57.	Ward Burton	5
	Dan Gurney	5
	Alan Kulwicki	5
	Tiny Lund	5
	Dave Marcis	5
	Ralph Moody	5
63.	Kurt Busch	4
	Lloyd Dane	4
	Bob Flock	4
	Charlie Glotzbach	4
	Eddie Gray	4
	Pete Hamilton	4
	Bobby Hamilton	4
	Parnelli Jones	4
	Hershel McGriff	4
	Eddie Pagan	4
	Ken Schrader	4
	Morgan Shepherd	4
	Nelson Stacy	4
	Billy Wade	4
	Glen Wood	4
78.	Bill Blair	3
	Kevin Harvick	3
	Jimmie Johnson	3
	Dick Linder	3
	Jeremy Mayfield	3
	Frank Mundy	3
	Gwyn Staley	3
85.	John Andretti	2
	Johnny Beauchamp	2
	Red Byron	2
	Derrike Cope	2
	Ray Elder	2
	James Hylton	2
	Bobby Johns	2
	Joe Lee Johnson	2
	Al Keller	2
	Elmo Langley	2
	Danny Letner	2
	Billy Myers	2
	Joe Nemechek	2
	Jimmy Pardue	2
	Steve Park	2
	Tom Pistone	2
	Marvin Porter	2
	Gober Sosebee	2
	Jimmy Spencer	2
	Michael Waltrip	2
	Emanuel Zervakis	2
106.	Johnny Allen	1
	Bill Amick	1
	Mario Andretti	1
	Earl Balmer	1
	Johnny Benson, Jr.	1
	Brett Bodine	1
	Ron Bouchard	1
	Richard Brickhouse	1
	Dick Brooks	1
	Bob Burdick	1
	Marvin Burke	1
	Neil Cole	1
	Jim Cook	1
	Ricky Craven	1
	Mark Donohue	1
	Joe Eubanks	1
	Lou Figaro	1
	Jimmy Florian	1
	Larry Frank	1
	Robby Gordon	1
	Danny Graves	1
	Royce Haggerty	1
	Bobby Hillin	1
	Jim Hurtubise	1
	John Kieper	1
	Harold Kite	1
	Paul Lewis	1
	Johnny Mantz	1
	Jamie McMurray	1
	Sam McQuagg	1
	Lloyd Moore	1
	Jerry Nadeau	1
	Norm Nelson	1
	Ryan Newman	1
	Bill Norton	1
	Phil Parsons	1
	Dick Passwater	1
	Lennie Pond	1
	Bill Rexford	1
	Jody Ridley	1
	Shorty Rollins	1
	Jim Roper	1
	Earl Ross	1
	John Rostek	1
	Johnny Rutherford	1
	Greg Sacks	1
	Elliott Sadler	1
	Leon Sales	1
	Frankie Schneider	1
	Wendell Scott	1
	Buddy Shuman	1
	John Soares	1
	Lake Speed	1
	Chuck Stevenson	1

Donald Thomas	1	27. Ken Schrader	176	28. Mike Skinner	$10,986,209
Tommy Thompson	1	28. Bobby Isaac	170	29. Ricky Craven	$9,630,218
Art Watts	1	29. Kyle Petty	168	30. Steve Park	$9,375,347
Danny Weinberg	1	Morgan Shepherd	168		
Jack White	1				

Donald Thomas	1
Tommy Thompson	1
Art Watts	1
Danny Weinberg	1
Jack White	1

TOP 5 FINISHES

1.	Richard Petty	555
2.	Bobby Allison	336
3.	David Pearson	301
4.	Dale Earnhardt	281
5.	Darrell Waltrip	276
6.	Cale Yarborough	255
7.	Buck Baker	246
8.	Lee Petty	231
9.	Buddy Baker	202
10.	Mark Martin	200
11.	Benny Parsons	199
12.	Rusty Wallace	189
13.	Ricky Rudd	187
14.	Ned Jarrett	185
15.	Terry Labonte	177
16.	Bill Elliott	166
17.	Jeff Gordon	160
18.	Dale Jarrett	151
19.	Jim Paschal	149
20.	James Hylton	140
21.	Bobby Isaac	134
22.	Harry Gant	123
23.	Herb Thomas	122
24.	Junior Johnson	121
25.	Rex White	110
26.	Joe Weatherly	105
27.	Tim Flock	102
28.	Geoffrey Bodine	100
29.	Marvin Panch	96
30.	Jack Smith	95

TOP 10 FINISHES

1.	Richard Petty	712
2.	Bobby Allison	447
3.	Dale Earnhardt	428
4.	Darrell Waltrip	390
5.	Buck Baker	372
6.	David Pearson	366
7.	Ricky Rudd	356
8.	Terry Labonte	344
9.	Lee Petty	332
10.	Cale Yarborough	319
11.	Mark Martin	315
12.	Buddy Baker	311
13.	Rusty Wallace	309
14.	Bill Elliott	307
15.	James Hylton	301
16.	Benny Parsons	283
17.	Ned Jarrett	239
18.	Jim Paschal	230
19.	Dale Jarrett	228
20.	Dave Marcis	222
21.	Jeff Gordon	210
22.	Harry Gant	208
23.	Elmo Langley	193
24.	Sterling Marlin	192
25.	Geoffrey Bodine	190
26.	Neil Castles	178

27.	Ken Schrader	176
28.	Bobby Isaac	170
29.	Kyle Petty	168
	Morgan Shepherd	168

POLES

1.	Richard Petty	126
2.	David Pearson	113
3.	Cale Yarborough	70
4.	Darrell Waltrip	60
5.	Bobby Allison	59
6.	Bill Elliott	55
7.	Bobby Isaac	50
8.	Junior Johnson	47
9.	Jeff Gordon	45
10.	Buck Baker	44
11.	Mark Martin	42
12.	Buddy Baker	40
13.	Tim Flock	39
14.	Herb Thomas	38
15.	Geoffrey Bodine	37
16.	Rusty Wallace	36
	Rex White	36
18.	Ned Jarrett	35
	Fireball Roberts	35
20.	Fonty Flock	33
	Fred Lorenzen	33
22.	Terry Labonte	29
23.	Ricky Rudd	28
24.	Dale Earnhardt	26
25.	Alan Kulwicki	24
	Jack Smith	24
27.	Dick Hutcherson	23
	Ken Schrader	23
29.	Ernie Irvan	22
	Bobby Labonte	22

WINNINGS

1.	Jeff Gordon	$51,619,212
2.	Dale Earnhardt	$40,580,488
3.	Dale Jarrett	$36,991,472
4.	Mark Martin	$35,894,382
5.	Rusty Wallace	$33,855,508
6.	Bill Elliott	$31,274,371
7.	Terry Labonte	$29,728,770
8.	Ricky Rudd	$28,553,338
9.	Bobby Labonte	$26,808,749
10.	Jeff Burton	$26,353,220
11.	Sterling Marlin	$23,956,250
12.	Tony Stewart	$20,495,564
13.	Ken Schrader	$20,405,799
14.	Darrell Waltrip	$19,896,656
15.	Michael Waltrip	$18,017,605
16.	Ward Burton	$17,608,916
17.	Geoffrey Bodine	$16,001,307
18.	Kyle Petty	$15,563,953
19.	Bobby Hamilton	$15,170,875
20.	Jimmy Spencer	$14,801,024
21.	John Andretti	$14,474,639
22.	Jeremy Mayfield	$14,048,074
23.	Dale Earnhardt, Jr.	$13,570,067
24.	Brett Bodine	$13,212,988
25.	Johnny Benson, Jr.	$12,446,196
26.	Joe Nemechek	$12,121,684
27.	Ernie Irvan	$11,601,567

28.	Mike Skinner	$10,986,209
29.	Ricky Craven	$9,630,218
30.	Steve Park	$9,375,347

LAPS COMPLETED

1.	Richard Petty	307,848
2.	Darrell Waltrip	237,740
3.	Dave Marcis	231,400
4.	Ricky Rudd	221,474
5.	Terry Labonte	218,021
6.	Bill Elliott	203,702
7.	Dale Earnhardt	202,888
8.	Bobby Allison	196,838
9.	Kyle Petty	180,716
10.	Rusty Wallace	174,117
11.	Ken Schrader	163,646
12.	Sterling Marlin	161,182
13.	James Hylton	160,763
14.	Geoffrey Bodine	157,847
15.	Mark Martin	155,179
16.	Buddy Arrington	151,841
17.	J.D. McDuffie	151,764
18.	Michael Waltrip	151,218
19.	Buddy Baker	151,065
20.	Cale Yarborough	145,233
21.	Dale Jarrett	138,217
22.	Benny Parsons	135,073
23.	David Pearson	135,020
24.	Brett Bodine	134,201
25.	Harry Gant	133,695
26.	Morgan Shepherd	130,886
27.	Elmo Langley	119,808
28.	Jimmy Means	113,244
29.	Cecil Gordon	112,911
30.	Jimmy Spencer	112,808

LAPS LED

1.	Richard Petty	52,135
2.	Cale Yarborough	31,507
3.	Bobby Allison	27,516
4.	Dale Earnhardt	25,708
5.	David Pearson	25,444
6.	Darrell Waltrip	23,096
7.	Rusty Wallace	18,997
8.	Jeff Gordon	13,967
9.	Bobby Isaac	13,229
10.	Junior Johnson	12,644
11.	Bill Elliott	10,670
12.	Mark Martin	10,157
13.	Buddy Baker	9,589
14.	Ned Jarrett	9,402
15.	Geoffrey Bodine	8,685
16.	Harry Gant	8,456
17.	Fred Lorenzen	8,131
18.	Ricky Rudd	7,788
19.	Dale Jarrett	7,013
20.	Tim Flock	6,936
21.	Benny Parsons	6,851
22.	Terry Labonte	6,819
23.	Neil Bonnett	6,390
24.	Herb Thomas	6,195
25.	Fireball Roberts	5,977
26.	Buck Baker	5,773
27.	Ernie Irvan	5,481
28.	Davey Allison	5,028

29. Lee Petty		4,788
30. Curtis Turner		4,771

Races Led

1. Richard Petty	599
2. Bobby Allison	414
3. Dale Earnhardt	406
4. Darrell Waltrip	402
5. Cale Yarborough	340
6. David Pearson	329
7. Rusty Wallace	266
8. Mark Martin	261
9. Bill Elliott	254
10. Buddy Baker	242
11. Terry Labonte	238
12. Ricky Rudd	222
13. Geoffrey Bodine	220
14. Jeff Gordon	215
15. Dave Marcis	195
16. Harry Gant	192
Benny Parsons	192
18. Dale Jarrett	186
19. Sterling Marlin	156
20. Neil Bonnett	155
Bobby Isaac	155
22. Ken Schrader	138
23. Junior Johnson	137
24. Bobby Labonte	136
25. Ernie Irvan	124
26. Ned Jarrett	112
27. Jeff Burton	106
28. Donnie Allison	105
Buck Baker	105
30. Morgan Shepherd	104

Consecutive Races Won

1. Richard Petty	10	1967
2. Bobby Allison	5	1971
Richard Petty	5	1971
4. Dale Earnhardt	4	1987
Bill Elliott	4	1992
Harry Gant	4	1991
Jeff Gordon	4	1998
Mark Martin	4	1993
David Pearson	4	1966
David Pearson	4	1968
Billy Wade	4	1964
Darrell Waltrip	4	1981
Cale Yarborough	4	1976

Win Percent (100 Races Min.)

1. Tim Flock	21%
Herb Thomas	21%
3. Jeff Gordon	19%
4. David Pearson	18%
5. Richard Petty	17%
6. Junior Johnson	16%
Fred Lorenzen	16%
8. Fireball Roberts	16%
9. Cale Yarborough	15%
10. Dick Hutcherson	14%
Ned Jarrett	14%
12. Lee Petty	13%
13. Bobby Allison	12%
Fonty Flock	12%
Bobby Isaac	12%
Rex White	12%
17. Dale Earnhardt	11%
Tony Stewart	11%
Joe Weatherly	11%
20. Davey Allison	10%
Dick Rathmann	10%
Speedy Thompson	10%
Darrell Waltrip	10%
24. Curtis Turner	9%
Rusty Wallace	9%
26. Marvin Panch	8%
Jack Smith	8%
28. Buck Baker	7%
Paul Goldsmith	7%
Jim Reed	7%
Tim Richmond	7%
LeeRoy Yarbrough	7%

Average Finish (100 Races Min.)

1. Lee Petty	7.600
2. Dick Hutcherson	8.670
3. Rex White	8.983
4. Herb Thomas	9.017
5. Ned Jarrett	9.176
6. Tim Flock	9.564
7. Joe Weatherly	10.052
8. Dick Rathmann	10.734
9. David Pearson	11.033
10. Dale Earnhardt	11.061
11. Richard Petty	11.259
12. Buck Baker	11.378
13. Bobby Allison	11.494
14. Marvin Panch	11.676
15. Speedy Thompson	11.848
16. Jeff Gordon	11.894
17. Tony Stewart	11.964
18. Fonty Flock	12.175
19. Bob Welborn	12.317
20. Jack Smith	12.389
21. Jim Paschal	12.533
22. Cale Yarborough	12.608
23. Mark Martin	12.702
24. Bobby Isaac	12.854
25. Fireball Roberts	13.285
26. Larry Thomas	13.286
27. Cotton Owens	13.288
28. Fred Lorenzen	13.304
29. James Hylton	13.517
30. Junior Johnson	13.530

Performance Points (1949–2002)*

1. Richard Petty	3647
2. David Pearson	1954
3. Bobby Allison	1935
4. Darrell Waltrip	1647
5. Dale Earnhardt	1639
6. Cale Yarborough	1559
7. Lee Petty	1268
8. Buck Baker	1261
9. Rusty Wallace	1095
10. Ned Jarrett	1044
11. Jeff Gordon	1023
12. Mark Martin	1021
13. Bill Elliott	915
14. Buddy Baker	914
15. Benny Parsons	865
16. Ricky Rudd	843
17. Terry Labonte	842
18. Herb Thomas	797
19. Bobby Isaac	794
20. Junior Johnson	778
21. Dale Jarrett	775
22. Jim Paschal	755
23. Tim Flock	645
24. Rex White	637
25. Harry Gant	616
26. Joe Weatherly	590
27. Fireball Roberts	577
28. James Hylton	514
Marvin Panch	514
30. Geoffrey Bodine	509

* Points are based on an International point system on a 10-6-4-3-2-1 breakdown for the first six finishers in every event. It is the most effective method of ranking individuals based on performance.

Single Season Records— Drivers

Wins

1. Richard Petty	1967	27
2. Richard Petty	1971	21
3. Tim Flock	1955	18
4. Richard Petty	1970	18
5. Bobby Isaac	1969	17
6. David Pearson	1968	16
Richard Petty	1968	16
8. Ned Jarrett	1964	15
David Pearson	1966	15
10. Buck Baker	1956	14
Richard Petty	1963	14
12. Jeff Gordon	1998	13
Ned Jarrett	1965	13
Junior Johnson	1965	13
Richard Petty	1975	13
16. Herb Thomas	1953	12
Herb Thomas	1954	12
Darrell Waltrip	1981	12
Darrell Waltrip	1982	12
20. Bobby Allison	1971	11
Dale Earnhardt	1987	11
Bill Elliott	1985	11
Bobby Isaac	1970	11
David Pearson	1969	11
David Pearson	1973	11
Lee Petty	1959	11
27. Bobby Allison	1972	10
Buck Baker	1957	10
Jeff Gordon	1996	10
Jeff Gordon	1997	10
David Pearson	1976	10
Richard Petty	1969	10
Richard Petty	1974	10
Rusty Wallace	1993	10
Cale Yarborough	1974	10
Cale Yarborough	1978	10

Money

1. Jeff Gordon	2001	$10,879,757
2. Jeff Gordon	1998	$9,306,584

3.	Tony Stewart	2002	$9,163,761
4.	Mark Martin	2002	$7,004,893
5.	Dale Jarrett	1999	$6,649,596
6.	Jeff Gordon	1997	$6,375,658
7.	Jeff Gordon	2002	$6,154,475
8.	Jeff Gordon	1999	$5,858,633
9.	Dale Earnhardt, Jr.	2001	$5,827,542
10.	Jeff Burton	1999	$5,725,399
11.	Dale Jarrett	2001	$5,377,742
12.	Ryan Newman	2002	$5,346,651
13.	Dale Jarrett	2000	$5,225,499
14.	Jeff Burton	2000	$5,121,354
15.	Kurt Busch	2002	$5,105,394
16.	Dale Earnhardt, Jr.	2002	$4,970,034
17.	Tony Stewart	2001	$4,941,463
18.	Ward Burton	2002	$4,899,884
19.	Ricky Rudd	2001	$4,878,027
20.	Rusty Wallace	2001	$4,788,652
21.	Bobby Labonte	2001	$4,786,779
22.	Rusty Wallace	2002	$4,785,134
23.	Bobby Labonte	1999	$4,763,615
24.	Sterling Marlin	2001	$4,517,634
25.	Matt Kenseth	2002	$4,514,203
26.	Ricky Rudd	2002	$4,444,614
27.	Dale Jarrett	2002	$4,421,951
28.	Jeff Gordon	1995	$4,347,343
29.	Mark Martin	1998	$4,309,006
30.	Kevin Harvick	2001	$4,302,202

LAPS LED

1.	Richard Petty	1967	5,537
2.	Bobby Isaac	1969	5,072
3.	Richard Petty	1970	5,007
4.	Richard Petty	1971	4,932
5.	Bobby Allison	1972	4,343
6.	Richard Petty	1968	4,242
7.	Junior Johnson	1965	3,998
8.	David Pearson	1968	3,950
9.	Cale Yarborough	1976	3,771
10.	Bobby Allison	1971	3,599
11.	Cale Yarborough	1978	3,587
12.	Richard Petty	1964	3,534
13.	Cale Yarborough	1974	3,530
14.	Tim Flock	1955	3,495
15.	Dale Earnhardt	1987	3,358
16.	Ned Jarrett	1964	3,304
17.	Cale Yarborough	1977	3,218
18.	Richard Petty	1975	3,198
19.	Bobby Isaac	1970	3,188
20.	David Pearson	1966	3,174
21.	Cale Yarborough	1973	3,167
22.	Richard Petty	1974	3,100
23.	Darrell Waltrip	1982	3,027
24.	David Pearson	1969	3,018
25.	Richard Petty	1966	2,924
26.	Rusty Wallace	1993	2,861
27.	Cale Yarborough	1980	2,811
28.	Richard Petty	1969	2,778
29.	Dale Earnhardt	1989	2,730
30.	David Pearson	1973	2,658

MILES LED

1.	Bobby Allison	1971	4,073
2.	Bobby Allison	1972	4,063
3.	Cale Yarborough	1978	3,867
4.	Richard Petty	1971	3,725
5.	Richard Petty	1970	3,633

6.	Richard Petty	1967	3,607
7.	Cale Yarborough	1976	3,524
8.	Jeff Gordon	1995	3,463
9.	Dale Earnhardt	1987	3,399
10.	Richard Petty	1975	3,380
11.	Cale Yarborough	1974	3,290
12.	David Pearson	1973	3,282
13.	Bobby Allison	1982	3,217
14.	Dale Earnhardt	1990	3,205
15.	Bill Elliott	1985	3,188
16.	Cale Yarborough	1980	3,156
17.	Richard Petty	1964	3,063
18.	Richard Petty	1974	3,046
19.	Cale Yarborough	1977	3,044
20.	Jeff Gordon	2001	3,032
21.	Jeff Gordon	1998	2,746
22.	Cale Yarborough	1973	2,734
23.	Darrell Waltrip	1982	2,669
24.	Darrell Waltrip	1979	2,630
25.	Dale Earnhardt	1989	2,612
26.	Rusty Wallace	1989	2,548
27.	Dale Jarrett	1997	2,545
28.	Bobby Isaac	1969	2,521
29.	Richard Petty	1966	2,487
30.	Dale Earnhardt	1993	2,482

LAPS COMPLETED

1.	David Pearson	1969	14,270
2.	Richard Petty	1964	14,041
3.	Richard Petty	1971	13,739
4.	James Hylton	1969	13,540
5.	Ned Jarrett	1965	13,525
6.	Ned Jarrett	1964	13,325
7.	David Pearson	1964	13,225
8.	Neil Castles	1969	13,136
9.	David Pearson	1968	13,097
10.	Bobby Isaac	1968	12,947
11.	James Hylton	1971	12,785
12.	Richard Petty	1967	12,739
13.	Bobby Isaac	1970	12,726
14.	James Hylton	1970	12,712
15.	Richard Petty	1969	12,589
16.	Elmo Langley	1969	12,531
17.	Cecil Gordon	1971	12,468
18.	Bobby Allison	1970	12,452
19.	Joe Weatherly	1962	12,431
20.	Bobby Isaac	1969	12,308
21.	Richard Petty	1968	12,254
22.	Richard Petty	1963	12,183
23.	Jabe Thomas	1969	12,025
24.	Clyde Lynn	1968	12,013
25.	Wendell Scott	1969	11,856
26.	Ned Jarrett	1963	11,845
27.	Bobby Allison	1971	11,716
28.	John Sears	1969	11,620
29.	Dick Hutcherson	1965	11,610
30.	Richard Petty	1962	11,550

MILES DRIVEN

1.	Bobby Hamilton	2001	12,640
2.	Mike Skinner	2002	12,476
3.	Terry Labonte	2002	12,448
4.	Robby Gordon	2002	12,350
5.	Terry Labonte	2001	12,345
6.	Jerry Nadeau	1999	12,329
7.	Michael Waltrip	2001	12,323
8.	Brett Bodine	2001	12,257

9.	Stacy Compton	2001	12,151
10.	Jeremy Mayfield	2002	12,133
11.	James Hylton	1971	12,088
12.	Cecil Gordon	1971	12,041
13.	Casey Atwood	2002	12,002
14.	Ricky Craven	2001	11,992
15.	Joe Nemechek	1999	11,966
16.	Jimmy Spencer	2000	11,908
17.	Ken Schrader	2001	11,905
18.	Ken Schrader	1999	11,797
19.	Bill Elliott	1999	11,778
20.	Jerry Nadeau	2001	11,713
21.	Ward Burton	2001	11,701
22.	Ken Schrader	2002	11,657
23.	Darrell Waltrip	1994	11,627
24.	Elliott Sadler	2001	11,578
25.	Jeff Burton	2001	11,577
26.	Rick Mast	1999	11,544
27.	Michael Waltrip	1997	11,542
28.	Dave Blaney	2001	11,520
29.	Jimmy Spencer	1999	11,439
30.	Dave Blaney	2002	11,419

POLES

1.	Bobby Isaac	1969	20
2.	Richard Petty	1967	19
3.	Tim Flock	1955	18
4.	Richard Petty	1966	16
5.	David Pearson	1969	14
	Cale Yarborough	1980	14
7.	Bobby Isaac	1970	13
8.	Bobby Allison	1972	12
	Buck Baker	1956	12
	Fonty Flock	1951	12
	David Pearson	1964	12
	David Pearson	1968	12
	Richard Petty	1968	12
	Herb Thomas	1953	12
15.	Bill Elliott	1985	11
	David Pearson	1974	11
	Darrell Waltrip	1981	11
18.	Junior Johnson	1961	10
	Junior Johnson	1965	10
	Herb Thomas	1952	10

TOP 5 FINISHES

1.	Ned Jarrett	1965	42
	David Pearson	1969	42
3.	Ned Jarrett	1964	40
4.	Joe Weatherly	1962	39
5.	Richard Petty	1967	38
	Richard Petty	1971	38
7.	Richard Petty	1964	37
8.	David Pearson	1968	36
9.	Tim Flock	1955	32
	Dick Hutcherson	1965	32
	Bobby Isaac	1970	32
	Ned Jarrett	1963	32
	Richard Petty	1962	32
14.	Buck Baker	1956	31
	Richard Petty	1968	31
	Richard Petty	1969	31
17.	Bobby Allison	1970	30
	Buck Baker	1957	30
	Richard Petty	1963	30
20.	Bobby Isaac	1969	29
	David Pearson	1964	29

Rex White	1961	29
23. Lee Petty	1958	28
24. Bobby Allison	1971	27
James Hylton	1969	27
Bobby Isaac	1968	27
Lee Petty	1959	27
Richard Petty	1970	27
Jack Smith	1962	27
Herb Thomas	1953	27

TOP 10 FINISHES

1.	Ned Jarrett	1964	45
	Ned Jarrett	1965	45
	Joe Weatherly	1962	45
4.	David Pearson	1969	44
5.	Lee Petty	1958	43
	Richard Petty	1964	43
7.	David Pearson	1964	42
8.	Richard Petty	1971	41
9.	Richard Petty	1967	40
10.	Buck Baker	1956	39
	James Hylton	1967	39
	James Hylton	1969	39
	James Hylton	1970	39
	Ned Jarrett	1963	39
	Richard Petty	1962	39
	Richard Petty	1963	39
17.	Buck Baker	1957	38
	Bobby Isaac	1970	38
	David Pearson	1968	38
	Richard Petty	1969	38
	Rex White	1961	38
22.	Dick Hutcherson	1965	37
	James Hylton	1971	37
24.	Bobby Isaac	1968	36
	Herb Thomas	1956	36
26.	Bobby Allison	1970	35
	Buck Baker	1958	35
	Ned Jarrett	1962	35
	Lee Petty	1959	35
	Richard Petty	1968	35
	Jack Smith	1962	35
	Joe Weatherly	1963	35
	Rex White	1960	35

RACES LED

1.	Richard Petty	1967	41
	Richard Petty	1971	41
3.	David Pearson	1969	39
4.	Bobby Isaac	1969	38
5.	David Pearson	1968	37
6.	Bobby Isaac	1970	35
	Richard Petty	1968	35
8.	Tim Flock	1955	33
	Richard Petty	1964	33
10.	Richard Petty	1969	32
	Richard Petty	1970	32
12.	Bobby Allison	1971	31
	David Pearson	1964	31
14.	Bobby Allison	1972	30
	Ned Jarrett	1964	30
	Junior Johnson	1965	30
	Bobby Labonte	1999	30
	Richard Petty	1972	30
19.	Jeff Gordon	1995	29
	Richard Petty	1963	29

21.	Ned Jarrett	1965	28
	Darrell Waltrip	1980	28
	Cale Yarborough	1976	28
	Cale Yarborough	1977	28
	Cale Yarborough	1978	28
	Cale Yarborough	1980	28
27.	Dale Earnhardt	1987	27
	Darrell Waltrip	1981	27
	Darrell Waltrip	1982	27

WIN PERCENTAGE (MIN. 10 STARTS)

1.	David Pearson	1973	61%
2.	Fireball Roberts	1958	60%
3.	Richard Petty	1967	56%
4.	Fred Lorenzen	1964	50%
5.	Tim Flock	1955	46%
	Richard Petty	1971	46%
7.	David Pearson	1976	45%
	Richard Petty	1970	45%
9.	Richard Petty	1975	43%
10.	Darrell Waltrip	1982	40%
11.	Bill Elliott	1985	39%
	Jeff Gordon	1998	39%
	Darrell Waltrip	1981	39%
14.	Dale Earnhardt	1987	38%
15.	David Pearson	1974	37%
16.	Junior Johnson	1965	36%
	David Pearson	1966	36%
	Joe Weatherly	1961	36%
19.	David Pearson	1972	35%
	Herb Thomas	1954	35%
21.	Bobby Isaac	1969	34%
22.	David Pearson	1968	33%
	Richard Petty	1968	33%
	Richard Petty	1974	33%
	Marshall Teague	1951	33%
	Rusty Wallace	1993	33%
	Cale Yarborough	1974	33%
	Cale Yarborough	1978	33%
29.	Bobby Allison	1972	32%
	Jeff Gordon	1996	32%
	Herb Thomas	1953	32%

AVERAGE FINISH (MIN. 10 STARTS)

1.	Lloyd Dane	1957	3.800
2.	Marvin Panch	1963	3.833
3.	Richard Petty	1971	4.217
4.	Cale Yarborough	1977	4.500
5.	Tim Flock	1955	4.590
6.	Buck Baker	1957	4.675
7.	Richard Petty	1972	4.677
8.	Lee Petty	1953	4.833
9.	Ned Jarrett	1965	4.907
10.	Joe Weatherly	1962	4.962
11.	Fireball Roberts	1958	5.000
12.	Richard Petty	1967	5.021
13.	Herb Thomas	1953	5.216
14.	David Pearson	1969	5.275
15.	Bobby Allison	1972	5.323
16.	Rex White	1960	5.325
17.	Lee Petty	1954	5.647
18.	Jeff Gordon	1998	5.697
19.	Dick Rathmann	1954	5.750
20.	David Pearson	1968	5.833

21.	Dale Earnhardt	1987	5.931
22.	Cale Yarborough	1978	6.033
23.	Lee Petty	1959	6.167
24.	Lloyd Dane	1956	6.200
25.	Eddie Pagan	1957	6.267
26.	Lee Petty	1958	6.320
27.	David Pearson	1966	6.381
28.	Richard Petty	1979	6.387
29.	Curtis Turner	1954	6.500
30.	Mark Martin	1990	6.552

CAREER RECORDS—OWNERS

RACES STARTED

1.	Petty Enterprises	1841
2.	Wood Brothers	1098
3.	Bud Moore	918
4.	Richard Childress	847
5.	Junie Donlavey	842
6.	Junior Johnson	788
7.	Dave Marcis	715
8.	James Hylton	634
9.	Elmo Langley	632
10.	J.D. McDuffie	617
11.	Rick Hendrick	589
12.	Buddy Arrington	583
13.	RahMoc Enterprises	560
14.	Larry McClure	557
15.	Billy Hagan	546
16.	Buck Baker	523
17.	L.G. DeWitt	521
18.	D.K. Ulrich	498
19.	Roger Penske	481
20.	Jack Roush	473
21.	Wendell Scott	466
22.	Harry Melling	460
23.	Robert Yates	442
24.	Jimmy Means	438
25.	Henley Gray	429
26.	Don Robertson	428
27.	G.C. Spencer	424
28.	Stavola Brothers	409
29.	Cecil Gordon	406
30.	Chuck Rider	395

WINS

1.	Petty Enterprises	268
2.	Junior Johnson	132
3.	Rick Hendrick	109
4.	Wood Brothers	97
5.	Holman-Moody	96
6.	Richard Childress	73
7.	Bud Moore	63
8.	Jack Roush	59
9.	Robert Yates	53
10.	Carl Kiekhaefer	52
11.	Herb Thomas	44
12.	DiGard	43
13.	Nord Krauskopf	43
14.	Roger Penske	42
15.	Cotton Owens	38
16.	Joe Gibbs	36
17.	Harry Melling	34
18.	Bondy Long	29
19.	Rex White	26
20.	Harry Ranier	24

21. Frank Christian — 22
22. Peter DePaolo — 21
23. Richard Howard — 21
24. Raymond Beadle — 20
25. Ted Chester — 20
26. Jack Smith — 20
27. Ray Fox — 14
28. Larry McClure — 14
29. Buck Baker — 13
30. J.H. Petty — 13

TOP 5 FINISHES

1. Petty Enterprises — 885
2. Rick Hendrick — 443
3. Junior Johnson — 436
4. Jack Roush — 336
5. Wood Brothers — 328
6. Bud Moore — 298
7. Holman-Moody — 285
8. Richard Childress — 270
9. Robert Yates — 244
10. Roger Penske — 192
11. L.G. DeWitt — 177
12. Cotton Owens — 176
13. Nord Krauskopf — 171
14. Joe Gibbs — 161
15. Buck Baker — 160
16. DiGard — 158
17. Herb Thomas — 119
18. Carl Kiekhaefer — 116
19. Harry Melling — 114
20. Bondy Long — 113
21. Harry Ranier — 108
22. Billy Hagan — 101
23. James Hylton — 94
24. Rex White — 89
25. Jack Smith — 87
26. Frank Christian — 85
27. Peter DePaolo — 79
28. Raymond Beadle — 73
29. Bobby Allison — 68
    Hal Needham — 68
    J.H. Petty — 68

TOP 10 FINISHES

1. Petty Enterprises — 1248
2. Rick Hendrick — 746
3. Junior Johnson — 577
4. Jack Roush — 569
5. Richard Childress — 507
6. Wood Brothers — 498
7. Bud Moore — 463
8. Robert Yates — 352
9. Holman-Moody — 336
10. Buck Baker — 330
11. L.G. DeWitt — 315
12. Roger Penske — 289
13. Joe Gibbs — 263
14. Cotton Owens — 240
15. James Hylton — 237
16. Billy Hagan — 236
17. Junie Donlavey — 218
18. Nord Krauskopf — 214
19. DiGard — 212
20. Harry Melling — 180
21. Herb Thomas — 160
22. Harry Ranier — 151

23. Wendell Scott — 146
24. Larry McClure — 145
25. Carl Kiekhaefer — 139
26. Bondy Long — 133
27. G.C. Spencer — 131
28. Raymond Beadle — 130
    RahMoc Enterprises — 130

POLES

1. Petty Enterprises — 155
2. Junior Johnson — 118
3. Wood Brothers — 117
4. Rick Hendrick — 114
5. Holman-Moody — 85
6. Nord Krauskopf — 71
7. Jack Roush — 52
8. Carl Kiekhaefer — 50
9. Bud Moore — 45
10. Roger Penske — 41
11. Harry Melling — 40
    Robert Yates — 40
13. Harry Ranier — 39
14. Cotton Owens — 36
15. Herb Thomas — 35
16. Richard Childress — 34
17. Frank Christian — 32
18. Joe Gibbs — 29
19. Rex White — 28
20. Bondy Long — 26
    DiGard — 26
22. Alan Kulwicki — 24
23. Jack Smith — 23
24. Richard Howard — 22
25. Peter DePaolo — 18
    Ray Fox — 18
27. Buck Baker — 16
    Smokey Yunick — 16
29. Ted Chester — 15
    Billy Hagan — 15

LAPS COMPLETED

1. Petty Enterprises — 592,529
2. Rick Hendrick — 474,093
3. Jack Roush — 386,933
4. Richard Childress — 319,603
5. Junior Johnson — 303,480
6. Wood Brothers — 301,252
7. Bud Moore — 251,024
8. Junie Donlavey — 224,336
9. Robert Yates — 197,849
10. Dave Marcis — 186,749
11. James Hylton — 170,980
12. Felix Sabates — 163,426
13. Roger Penske — 156,946
14. RahMoc Enterprises — 156,342
15. Billy Hagan — 156,289
16. Elmo Langley — 156,231
17. Buddy Arrington — 155,723
18. Larry McClure — 152,796
19. Stavola Brothers — 148,182
20. Joe Gibbs — 143,591
21. J.D. McDuffie — 143,401
22. D.K. Ulrich — 139,271
23. Harry Melling — 135,985
24. L.G. DeWitt — 135,526
25. Buck Baker — 133,290
26. Travis Carter — 125,162

27. Holman-Moody — 122,353
28. Bill Davis — 118,201
29. Chuck Rider — 113,335
30. Don Robertson — 113,074

LAPS LED

1. Petty Enterprises — 61,022
2. Junior Johnson — 44,442
3. Rick Hendrick — 29,629
4. Holman-Moody — 24,897
5. Richard Childress — 24,522
6. Wood Brothers — 24,402
7. Jack Roush — 17,128
8. Bud Moore — 16,826
9. Roger Penske — 16,317
10. Nord Krauskopf — 15,705
11. Robert Yates — 15,123
12. DiGard — 14,346
13. Richard Howard — 10,157
14. Cotton Owens — 9,419
15. Carl Kiekhaefer — 8,257
16. Harry Melling — 8,026
17. Joe Gibbs — 7,342
18. Harry Ranier — 7,032
19. Bondy Long — 6,958
20. Raymond Beadle — 5,953
21. Herb Thomas — 5,809
22. Hal Needham — 4,987
23. Ray Fox — 4,599
24. L.G. DeWitt — 4,344
25. Frank Christian — 4,297
26. Felix Sabates — 4,210
27. Banjo Matthews — 4,106
28. Rex White — 3,810
29. Dale Earnhardt, Inc. — 3,630
30. Billy Hagan — 3,537

RACES LED

1. Petty Enterprises — 771
2. Junior Johnson — 542
3. Rick Hendrick — 460
4. Wood Brothers — 436
5. Richard Childress — 406
6. Bud Moore — 328
7. Jack Roush — 321
8. Robert Yates — 274
9. Holman-Moody — 249
10. Roger Penske — 245
11. DiGard — 228
12. Nord Krauskopf — 198
13. Joe Gibbs — 183
14. Cotton Owens — 154
15. Harry Melling — 153
16. Harry Ranier — 149
17. Billy Hagan — 146
18. Dave Marcis — 129
19. L.G. DeWitt — 128
20. Larry McClure — 126
21. Raymond Beadle — 116
22. Hal Needham — 113
23. Felix Sabates — 101
24. Hoss Ellington — 100
25. Bobby Allison — 87
26. RahMoc Enterprises — 87
27. Bondy Long — 83
28. Travis Carter — 80
29. Dale Earnhardt, Inc. — 80

WIN PERCENTAGE (50 STARTS MIN.)

1. Carl Kiekhaefer — 58%
2. Peter DePaolo — 34%
3. Holman-Moody — 26%
4. Herb Thomas — 21%
5. Ted Chester — 20%
   Richard Howard — 20%
7. Rick Hendrick — 19%
   Paul Spaulding — 19%
9. Junior Johnson — 17%
10. Bondy Long — 15%
    Petty Enterprises — 15%
    Rex White — 15%
13. Frank Christian — 14%
14. Nord Krauskopf — 13%
    Rex Lovette — 13%
    Smokey Yunick — 13%
17. Walt Chapman — 12%
    DiGard — 12%
    Jack Roush — 12%
    Robert Yates — 12%
21. John Eanes — 11%
    Ned Jarrett — 11%
    Cotton Owens — 11%
24. Joe Gibbs — 10%
    Speedy Thompson — 10%
26. Raymond Beadle — 9%
    Richard Childress — 9%
    Bobby Griffin — 9%
    Roger Penske — 9%
    J.H. Petty — 9%
    Harry Ranier — 9%
    Charles Robinson — 9%
    Jack Smith — 9%
    Wood Brothers — 9%
35. J.D. Bracken — 8%
    Ray Fox — 8%
    Eddie Pagan — 8%
    Jim Stephens — 8%
39. Friedkin Ent — 7%
    Harry Melling — 7%

AVERAGE FINISH (100 STARTS MIN.)

1. Rex White — 8.538
2. Bondy Long — 9.408
3. Charles Robinson — 9.673
4. Herb Thomas — 10.328
5. Bee Gee Holloway — 10.419
6. J.H. Petty — 10.511
7. Holman-Moody — 10.715
8. Richard Howard — 11.073
9. Cotton Owens — 11.525
10. Nord Krauskopf — 11.690
11. Jack Smith — 11.826
12. Frank Christian — 11.910
13. Junior Johnson — 12.807
14. L.G. DeWitt — 12.809
15. Herman Beam — 13.246
16. Raymond Beadle — 13.372
17. DiGard — 13.432
18. Langley-Woodfield — 13.584
19. Joe Gibbs — 13.815
20. Petty Enterprises — 13.837
21. Wade Younts — 13.903
22. Clyde Lynn — 14.168
23. Robert Yates — 14.254
24. Harry Ranier — 14.576
25. Wendell Scott — 14.696
26. Bud Moore — 14.714
27. Buck Baker — 14.722
28. L.D. Austin — 14.789
29. Richard Childress — 14.792
30. Roger Penske — 14.865

SINGLE SEASON RECORDS— OWNERS

WINS

1. Carl Kiekhaefer	1956	30
2. Petty Enterprises	1967	27
3. Carl Kiekhaefer	1955	22
Petty Enterprises	1971	22
5. Petty Enterprises	1963	19
Petty Enterprises	1970	19
7. Holman-Moody	1968	17
Nord Krauskopf	1969	17
9. Petty Enterprises	1968	16
10. Cotton Owens	1966	15
11. Rick Hendrick	1998	14
Bondy Long	1964	14
13. Holman-Moody	1965	13
Junior Johnson	1965	13
Bondy Long	1965	13
Petty Enterprises	1975	13
17. Rick Hendrick	1996	12
Junior Johnson	1981	12
Junior Johnson	1982	12
Herb Thomas	1953	12
Herb Thomas	1954	12
22. Richard Childress	1987	11
Rick Hendrick	1997	11
Holman-Moody	1963	11
Holman-Moody	1969	11
Holman-Moody	1971	11
Nord Krauskopf	1970	11
Harry Melling	1985	11
Petty Enterprises	1959	11
Petty Enterprises	1962	11
Wood Brothers	1973	11

LAPS LED

1. Petty Enterprises	1971	5,615
2. Petty Enterprises	1967	5,538
3. Petty Enterprises	1970	5,140
4. Nord Krauskopf	1969	5,072
5. Richard Howard	1972	4,343
6. Holman-Moody	1968	4,287
7. Petty Enterprises	1968	4,242
8. Carl Kiekhaefer	1956	4,228
9. Junior Johnson	1965	4,170
10. Carl Kiekhaefer	1955	4,029
11. Junior Johnson	1976	3,771
12. Petty Enterprises	1964	3,659
13. Junior Johnson	1978	3,587
14. Richard Childress	1987	3,358
15. Rick Hendrick	1996	3,332
16. Rick Hendrick	1995	3,284
17. Holman-Moody	1963	3,276
18. Junior Johnson	1977	3,218
19. Petty Enterprises	1975	3,198
20. Nord Krauskopf	1970	3,188
21. Cotton Owens	1966	3,174
22. Richard Howard	1973	3,169
23. Petty Enterprises	1974	3,100
24. Holman-Moody	1965	3,086
25. Bondy Long	1964	3,071
26. Petty Enterprises	1966	3,037
27. Junior Johnson	1982	3,028
28. Holman-Moody	1971	3,027
29. Holman-Moody	1969	3,025
30. Jack Roush	1998	2,867

MILES LED

1. Petty Enterprises	1971	4,629
2. Petty Enterprises	1970	4,282
3. Rick Hendrick	1995	4,162
4. Richard Howard	1972	4,063
5. Junior Johnson	1978	3,867
6. Holman-Moody	1971	3,843
7. Rick Hendrick	1996	3,684
8. Petty Enterprises	1967	3,610
9. Junior Johnson	1976	3,524
10. Rick Hendrick	1986	3,477
11. Jack Roush	1998	3,424
12. Richard Childress	1987	3,399
13. Petty Enterprises	1975	3,380
14. Petty Enterprises	1964	3,299
15. Rick Hendrick	2001	3,292
16. Wood Brothers	1973	3,282
17. DiGard	1982	3,217
18. Richard Childress	1990	3,205
19. Rick Hendrick	1998	3,203
20. Robert Yates	1997	3,191
21. Harry Melling	1985	3,188
22. Junior Johnson	1980	3,156
23. Wood Brothers	1972	3,121
24. Petty Enterprises	1974	3,046
25. Junior Johnson	1977	3,044
26. Joe Gibbs	1999	2,744
27. Richard Howard	1973	2,737
28. Carl Kiekhaefer	1956	2,718
29. Junior Johnson	1982	2,672
30. Petty Enterprises	1966	2,655

LAPS COMPLETE

1. Jack Roush	1999	48,254
2. Jack Roush	2000	46,694
3. Jack Roush	1998	45,924
4. Jack Roush	2001	39,907
5. Rick Hendrick	2002	39,889
6. Jack Roush	2002	39,633
7. Rick Hendrick	2001	32,174
8. Jack Roush	1997	32,050
9. Richard Childress	2002	30,675
10. Dale Earnhardt, Inc.	2001	30,148
11. Dale Earnhardt, Inc.	2002	30,137
12. Rick Hendrick	1990	29,816
13. Petty Enterprises	2002	29,638
14. Rick Hendrick	1999	28,460
15. Rick Hendrick	1998	28,440
16. Rick Hendrick	2000	28,320
17. Rick Hendrick	1994	28,130
18. Rick Hendrick	1989	27,905
19. Rick Hendrick	1996	27,823
20. Rick Hendrick	1995	27,351
21. Rick Hendrick	1997	27,227
22. Rick Hendrick	1988	27,185

23. Jack Roush	1996	27,007
24. Rick Hendrick	1993	26,059
25. Rick Hendrick	1987	25,176
26. Felix Sabates	1998	24,351
27. Petty Enterprises	2001	22,839
28. Petty Enterprises	1963	22,023
29. Richard Childress	2001	21,847
30. Buck Baker	1965	21,684

POLES

1. Carl Kiekhaefer	1955	25
Carl Kiekhaefer	1956	25
3. Nord Krauskopf	1969	20
4. Petty Enterprises	1967	19
5. Rick Hendrick	1986	16
Petty Enterprises	1966	16
7. Holman-Moody	1965	15
8. Holman-Moody	1969	14
Junior Johnson	1980	14
10. Frank Christian	1951	13
Nord Krauskopf	1970	13
12. Holman-Moody	1968	12
Cotton Owens	1964	12
Petty Enterprises	1968	12
15. Rick Hendrick	1995	11
Richard Howard	1972	11
Junior Johnson	1965	11
Junior Johnson	1981	11
Harry Melling	1985	11
Petty Enterprises	1970	11
Herb Thomas	1952	11
Herb Thomas	1953	11
Wood Brothers	1974	11
24. Nord Krauskopf	1972	10
Bondy Long	1965	10
Petty Enterprises	1971	10
J.H. Petty	1958	10
28. Peter DePaolo	1956	9
Ray Fox	1963	9
Rick Hendrick	1996	9
Holman-Moody	1963	9
Rex Lovette	1961	9
Roger Penske	2000	9
Petty Enterprises	1963	9
Petty Enterprises	1964	9
Rex White	1962	9
Wood Brothers	1971	9

TOP 5 FIINISHES

1. Carl Kiekhaefer	1956	74
2. Petty Enterprises	1963	51
3. Petty Enterprises	1971	50
4. Petty Enterprises	1964	49
5. Rick Hendrick	1996	45
Jack Roush	1998	45
7. Holman-Moody	1965	43
Petty Enterprises	1967	43
9. Holman-Moody	1969	42
Carl Kiekhaefer	1955	42

11. Peter DePaolo	1956	41
Bondy Long	1965	41
13. Petty Enterprises	1960	40
Petty Enterprises	1962	40
15. Cotton Owens	1964	39
Jack Roush	2002	39
17. Holman-Moody	1963	38
Holman-Moody	1968	38
Bondy Long	1964	38
Bud Moore	1962	38
Jack Roush	1999	38
22. Joe Gibbs	1999	35
23. Rick Hendrick	1997	34
Petty Enterprises	1970	34
Jack Roush	1997	34
26. Rick Hendrick	1989	33
Rick Hendrick	1995	33
Petty Enterprises	1959	33
Jack Roush	2000	33
30. Peter DePaolo	1957	32
Rick Hendrick	1998	32
Nord Krauskopf	1970	32

TOP 10 FIINISHES

1. Carl Kiekhaefer	1956	92
2. Jack Roush	1998	72
Jack Roush	2002	72
4. Petty Enterprises	1960	69
5. Petty Enterprises	1963	65
6. Peter DePaolo	1956	61
7. Petty Enterprises	1964	60
8. Cotton Owens	1964	59
9. Rick Hendrick	1996	58
Jack Roush	1999	58
11. Jack Roush	2000	57
12. Buck Baker	1965	56
Petty Enterprises	1971	56
14. Petty Enterprises	1962	54
15. Rick Hendrick	1995	50
Rick Hendrick	1997	50
Rick Hendrick	1998	50
Jack Roush	1997	50
19. Rick Hendrick	2002	49
Holman-Moody	1963	49
Holman-Moody	1965	49
22. Joe Gibbs	1999	47
Joe Gibbs	2000	47
Rick Hendrick	1988	47
Carl Kiekhaefer	1955	47
Petty Enterprises	1958	47
27. Rick Hendrick	1994	46
Bee Gee Holloway	1961	46
Jack Roush	2001	46
30. Rick Hendrick	1990	45
Bondy Long	1965	45
Petty Enterprises	1967	45

RACES LED

1. Petty Enterprises	1971	44
2. Petty Enterprises	1967	42

3. Holman-Moody	1969	40
Carl Kiekhaefer	1956	40
5. Holman-Moody	1968	38
Nord Krauskopf	1969	38
7. Petty Enterprises	1970	36
8. Carl Kiekhaefer	1955	35
Nord Krauskopf	1970	35
Petty Enterprises	1968	35
11. Jack Roush	2002	34
Holman-Moody	1965	34
Petty Enterprises	1964	34
14. Cotton Owens	1964	33
Petty Enterprises	1963	33
16. Joe Gibbs	1999	32
Petty Enterprises	1969	32
18. Rick Hendrick	1996	31
Junior Johnson	1965	31
Petty Enterprises	1972	31
21. Rick Hendrick	1995	30
Rick Hendrick	1999	30
Holman-Moody	1971	30
Richard Howard	1972	30
Jack Roush	2000	30
Jack Roush	2001	30
27. Rick Hendrick	1998	29

AVERAGE FINISH

1. Bobby Allison	1970	4.409
2. Junior Johnson	1977	4.500
3. Petty Enterprises	1953	4.757
4. Rex White	1960	4.919
5. Bondy Long	1965	5.037
6. Petty Enterprises	1971	5.094
7. Bud Moore	1962	5.096
8. Buck Baker	1957	5.500
9. Petty Enterprises	1967	5.818
10. Richard Childress	1987	5.931
11. Junior Johnson	1978	6.033
12. Holman-Moody	1969	6.113
13. Petty Enterprises	1954	6.257
14. Harry Ranier	1981	6.300
15. Jack Roush	1990	6.552
16. Petty Enterprises	1952	6.563
17. Harry Melling	1988	6.586
18. Petty Enterprises	1975	6.633
19. Richard Howard	1972	6.667
20. Nord Krauskopf	1970	6.809
21. Wood Brothers	1976	6.864
22. Rex White	1961	6.935
23. DiGard	1979	7.000
24. Raymond Beadle	1988	7.069
25. John Ditz	1954	7.114
26. Herb Thomas	1953	7.149
27. Walt Chapman	1953	7.303
28. Richard Childress	1986	7.379
29. Cotton Owens	1966	7.477
30. Petty Enterprises	1977	7.533

PART 2
YEAR BY YEAR

Driver	Starts	Poles	Finish						Laps	Laps Led	Races Led	Winston Cup Points	$
			1	2	3	4	5	6–10					

1970

	Driver	Starts	Poles	1	2	3	4	5	6–10	Laps	Laps Led	Races Led	Winston Cup Points	$
1.	Bobby Isaac	47	13	11	9	5	4	3	6	12,726	3,188	35	3,911	199,600
2.	Bobby Allison	46	5	3	15	8	4	0	5	12,452	1,246	22	3,860	149,745
3.	James Hylton	47	1	1	4	2	8	7	17	12,712	199	8	3,788	78,201
4.	Richard Petty	40	9	18	5	0	0	4	4	10,536	5,007	32	3,447	151,124
5.	Neil Castles	47	0	0	1	4	3	4	12	10,297	31	2	3,158	49,746

Key

STARTS	Number of starts that year
POLES	Number of poles that year
FINISH	
1	Number of first place finishes that year
2	Number of second place finishes that year
3	Number of third place finishes that year
4	Number of fourth place finishes that year
5	Number of fifth place finishes that year
6–10	Number of sixth through tenth place finishes that year
LAPS	Number of laps completed that year
LAPS LED	Number of laps led that year
RACES LED	Number of races led that year
WINSTON CUP POINTS	Winston Cup points that year
$	Winnings for that year
N/A	Information not available
NR	Not ranked, no points at season's end

The left-hand pages list the drivers ranked one through fifty for that year based on Winston Cup points. The right-hand page lists the top thirty leaders for that year in the following categories: laps completed, laps led, miles led, miles driven, and races led. Please note that some of the top thirty leaders in the preceding five categories may not have been ranked in the top fifty drivers (based on Winston Cup points) for that year.

*Please note that due to incomplete lap leader records for the years 1949–67, the figures for the Laps Led, Miles Led, and Races Led categories cannot be endorsed as absolute totals for those years. The statistics given here simply represent the most accurate figures given the information available.

Driver	Starts	Poles	Finish						Laps	Laps Led	Races Led	Winston Cup Points	$
			1	2	3	4	5	6–10					

1949

	Driver	Starts	Poles	1	2	3	4	5	6–10	Laps	Laps Led	Races Led	Winston Cup Points	$
1.	Red Byron	6	1	2	0	2	0	0	0	633	103	2	842.5	5,800
2.	Lee Petty	6	0	1	2	0	0	0	2	890	1	1	725	3,855
3.	Bob Flock	6	1	2	1	0	0	0	0	728	27	4	704	4,870
4.	Bill Blair	6	0	0	0	0	0	3	2	763	325	2	567.5	1,280
5.	Fonty Flock	6	0	0	1	1	1	0	0	304	85	1	554.5	2,015
6.	Curtis Turner	6	1	1	0	0	0	0	3	564	78	2	430	2,675
7.	Ray Erickson	4	0	0	1	1	0	0	1	713	0	0	422	1,460
8.	Tim Flock	5	0	0	1	0	0	1	1	347	0	0	421	1,510
9.	Glenn Dunnaway	6	0	0	0	1	0	0	2	594	1	1	384	810
10.	Frank Mundy	4	0	0	0	1	1	0	0	274	0	0	370	1,160
11.	Bill Snowden	4	0	0	0	0	0	1	2	182	0	0	315	660
12.	Bill Rexford	3	0	0	0	1	0	1	0	370	0	0	286	785
13.	Sara Christian	6	0	0	0	0	0	1	1	606	0	0	282	760
14.	Clyde Minter	2	0	0	0	0	2	0	0	386	0	0	280	760
15.	Gober Sosebee	3	1	0	1	0	0	0	1	170	34	1	265	1,305
16.	Jim Roper	2	0	1	0	0	0	0	0	197	47	1	253	2,130
17.	Sam Rice	2	0	0	0	0	2	0	0	192	0	0	231	680
18.	Jack White	1	0	1	0	0	0	0	0	200	66	1	200	1,580
19.	Dick Linder	3	0	0	1	0	0	0	0	416	0	0	180.5	830
20.	Billy Rafter	1	0	0	0	1	0	0	0	N/A	0	0	160	480
21.	Archie Smith	2	0	0	0	0	0	0	2	161	0	0	145	225
22.	Joe Littlejohn	1	0	0	0	0	1	0	0	40	0	0	140	300
23.	Jack Russell	3	0	0	0	0	0	0	2	178	0	0	140	175
24.	Mike Eagan	1	0	0	0	0	1	0	0	N/A	0	0	140	300
25.	Herb Thomas	4	0	0	0	0	0	1	0	197	0	0	132	225
26.	Sterling Long	2	0	0	0	0	0	0	1	N/A	0	0	100	150
27.	Frank Christian	1	0	0	0	0	0	0	1	N/A	0	0	100	175
28.	Frankie Schneider	1	0	0	0	0	0	0	1	N/A	0	0	100	150
29.	Lloyd Moore	1	0	0	0	0	0	0	1	186	0	0	100	150
30.	Roy Hall	1	0	0	0	0	0	0	1	196	0	0	100	150
31.	Slick Smith	4	0	0	0	0	0	0	1	277	0	0	99	275
32.	Al Keller	1	0	0	0	0	0	0	1	185	0	0	90	200
33.	John Wright	1	0	0	0	0	0	0	1	179	0	0	80	100
34.	Al Bonnell	2	1	0	0	0	0	0	1	183	0	0	80	150
35.	Otis Martin	4	0	0	0	0	0	0	1	66	0	0	69.5	200
36.	Jimmy Thompson	2	0	0	0	0	0	0	2	N/A	0	0	65	175
37.	Charles Muscatel	1	0	0	0	0	0	0	1	N/A	0	0	60	75
38.	Raymond Lewis	1	0	0	0	0	0	0	1	194	0	0	60	75
39.	Al Wagoner	1	0	0	0	0	0	0	1	178	0	0	60	75
40.	George Lewis	1	0	0	0	0	0	0	1	168	0	0	40	50
41.	Lou Volk	1	0	0	0	0	0	0	1	182	0	0	30	125
42.	Buddy Helms	1	0	0	0	0	0	0	1	N/A	0	0	27.5	75
43.	Bob Apperson	3	0	0	0	0	0	0	0	191	0	0	25	150
44.	Bill Bennett	1	0	0	0	0	0	0	0	181	0	0	24	100
45.	Ted Chamberlain	2	0	0	0	0	0	0	0	148	0	0	24	100
46.	Buck Baker	2	0	0	0	0	0	0	0	N/A	0	0	20	50
47.	Jack Etheridge	1	0	0	0	0	0	0	1	N/A	0	0	20	75
48.	Ellis Pearce	1	0	0	0	0	0	0	1	N/A	0	0	20	50
49.	Bobby Greene	2	0	0	0	0	0	0	0	148	0	0	19.5	50
50.	Ken Wagner	3	1	0	0	0	0	0	0	412	0	0	19	100

LAPS COMPLETED

1.	Lee Petty	890
2.	Bill Blair	763
3.	Bob Flock	728
4.	Ray Erickson	713
5.	Red Byron	633
6.	Sara Christian	606
7.	Glenn Dunnaway	594
8.	Curtis Turner	564
9.	Dick Linder	416
10.	Ken Wagner	412
11.	Clyde Minter	386
12.	Bill Rexford	370
13.	Tim Flock	347
14.	Fonty Flock	304
15.	Slick Smith	277
16.	Frank Mundy	274
17.	Jack White	200
18.	Jim Roper	197
	Herb Thomas	197
20.	Roy Hall	196
21.	Raymond Lewis	194
22.	Sam Rice	192
23.	Bob Apperson	191
24.	Lloyd Moore	186
25.	Al Keller	185
26.	Al Bonnell	183
27.	Bill Snowden	182
	Lou Volk	182
29.	Bill Bennett	181
30.	John Wright	179
31.	Jack Russell	178
	Al Wagoner	178
33.	Gober Sosebee	170
34.	George Lewis	168
35.	Archie Smith	161
36.	Ted Chamberlain	148
	Bobby Greene	148
38.	Otis Martin	66
39.	Joe Littlejohn	40

LAPS LED

1.	Bill Blair	325
2.	Red Byron	103
3.	Fonty Flock	85
4.	Curtis Turner	78
5.	Jack White	66
6.	Jim Roper	47
7.	Gober Sosebee	34
8.	Bob Flock	27
9.	Glenn Dunnaway	1
	Lee Petty	1

MILES LED

1.	Bill Blair	199
2.	Gober Sosebee	141
3.	Red Byron	73
4.	Curtis Turner	69
5.	Fonty Flock	43
6.	Jim Roper	35
7.	Jack White	33
8.	Bob Flock	15
9.	Glenn Dunnaway	1
	Lee Petty	1

MILES DRIVEN

1.	Bill Blair	663
2.	Red Byron	582
3.	Bob Flock	574
4.	Lee Petty	565
5.	Sara Christian	417
6.	Tim Flock	415
7.	Curtis Turner	382
8.	Frank Mundy	381
9.	Erick Erickson	357
10.	Glenn Dunnaway	347
11.	Dick Linder	289
12.	Bill Rexford	274
13.	Ken Wagner	206
14.	Clyde Minter	193
15.	Al Keller	185
16.	Al Bonnell	183
17.	Lou Volk	182
18.	Bill Bennett	181
19.	Budd Olsen	180
20.	Dick Zimmerman	178
21.	Erwin Blatt	176
22.	Louise Smith	175
23.	Don Cecchini	173
24.	Lee Schmidt	171
25.	Gober Sosebee	170
26.	Ed Tyson	169
	Ken Marriott	169
28.	Ken Schroeder	168
29.	Tommy Coates	167
30.	Wally Campbell	166
	Joe Littlejohn	166

RACES LED

1.	Bob Flock	4
2.	Red Byron	2
	Bill Blair	2
	Curtis Turner	2
5.	Glenn Dunnaway	1
	Fonty Flock	1
	Lee Petty	1
	Jim Roper	1
	Gober Sosebee	1
	Jack White	1

Driver	Starts	Poles	Finish 1	2	3	4	5	6–10	Laps	Laps Led	Races Led	Winston Cup Points	$

1950

Driver	Starts	Poles	1	2	3	4	5	6–10	Laps	Laps Led	Races Led	Winston Cup Points	$
1. Bill Rexford	17	0	1	0	1	2	1	6	1,302	98	2	1,959	5,750
2. Fireball Roberts	9	1	1	2	1	0	0	1	1,138	61	3	1,848.5	6,800
3. Lee Petty	17	0	1	1	2	3	2	4	1,558	43	1	1,590	7,120
4. Lloyd Moore	16	0	1	2	3	1	0	3	1,358	57	2	1,398	5,235
5. Curtis Turner	16	4	4	1	1	1	0	0	1,626	1,110	12	1,375.5	8,080
6. Johnny Mantz	3	0	1	0	0	0	0	1	400	351	1	1,282	10,810
7. Chuck Mahoney	11	1	0	1	1	0	1	3	705	18	1	1,217.5	2,250
8. Dick Linder	13	4	3	1	1	0	0	3	1,437	460	5	1,121	5,695
9. Jimmy Florian	10	1	1	0	1	1	0	3	1,060	40	1	801	2,730
10. Bill Blair	16	0	1	2	0	0	2	2	1,550	218	3	766	4,400
11. Herb Thomas	13	0	1	0	2	1	0	2	719	176	2	590.5	2,645
12. Buck Baker	9	1	0	1	1	0	0	3	587	10	1	531.5	2,145
13. Cotton Owens	3	0	0	0	0	0	0	1	511	23	1	500	1,100
14. Fonty Flock	7	2	1	0	0	1	0	1	951	369	4	458.5	2,195
15. Weldon Adams	4	0	0	0	1	0	1	1	560	0	0	440	1,205
16. Tim Flock	12	1	1	0	0	3	0	3	1,403	190	2	437.5	3,980
17. Clyde Minter	8	0	0	0	1	0	2	0	765	0	0	427	1,155
18. Dick Burns	8	0	0	0	0	1	1	1	323	0	0	341.5	780
19. Art Lamey	4	0	0	0	0	0	2	1	N/A	0	0	320	655
20. Bob Flock	4	0	0	1	0	0	0	2	595	5	1	314	1,155
21. George Hartley	8	0	0	0	0	0	0	2	371	0	0	298	875
22. Gayle Warren	10	0	0	0	0	0	1	1	429	10	1	287	550
23. Frank Mundy	8	0	0	0	0	0	0	3	310	0	0	275.5	550
24. Jim Paschal	6	0	0	1	0	0	0	1	669	0	0	220.5	850
25. Jack White	7	0	0	0	0	0	1	1	712	0	0	211.5	525
26. Roscoe Hough	4	0	0	0	0	0	0	2	296	0	0	207.5	325
27. Ray Duhigg	5	0	0	0	0	0	1	1	N/A	0	0	202.5	450
28. Leon Sales	2	0	1	0	0	0	0	0	227	18	1	200	1,000
29. Jimmy Thompson	4	0	0	0	0	0	0	3	522	0	0	200	525
30. Harold Kite	3	0	1	0	0	0	0	0	382	38	1	187	1,550
31. Neil Cole	2	0	0	0	0	0	1	0	N/A	0	0	183.5	300
32. Jack Smith	3	0	0	1	0	0	0	0	376	55	1	180	775
33. Bucky Sager	2	0	0	1	0	0	0	0	N/A	146	1	180	750
34. Red Harvey	1	0	0	1	0	0	0	0	N/A	1	1	180	750
35. Ted Swaim	1	0	0	1	0	0	0	0	200	0	0	180	750
36. Buck Barr	2	0	0	0	1	0	0	1	N/A	0	0	180	575
37. Pepper Cunningham	2	0	0	0	0	0	0	2	130	0	0	177.5	300
38. Ewell Weddle	3	0	0	0	1	0	0	0	158	0	0	173.5	600
39. Donald Thomas	2	0	0	0	0	0	0	2	141	0	0	164	300
40. Bill Snowden	4	0	0	0	0	0	1	1	532	0	0	163	325
41. Jimmie Lewallen	3	0	0	0	0	1	0	0	330	0	0	140	400
42. Chuck James	1	0	0	0	0	1	0	0	N/A	0	0	140	400
43. Dick Clothier	5	0	0	0	0	0	0	2	194	0	0	133.5	350
44. Paul Parks	6	0	0	0	0	0	0	1	95	0	0	124.5	375
45. Al Gross	3	0	0	0	0	1	0	0	182	0	0	124	550
46. Jack Reynolds	2	0	0	0	0	0	1	0	N/A	0	0	120	300
47. Jim Delaney	2	0	0	0	0	0	0	1	N/A	0	0	114	175
48. Carl Renner	2	0	0	0	0	0	0	1	N/A	0	0	108	250
49. Jack Holloway	2	0	0	0	0	0	0	2	192	0	0	107.5	225
50. Bob Dickson	6	0	0	0	0	0	0	2	627	0	0	105	275
51. J.C. VanLandingham	1	0	0	0	0	0	1	0	48	0	0	105	450

LAPS COMPLETED		LAPS LED		MILES LED		MILES DRIVEN		RACES LED	
1. Curtis Turner	1,626	1. Curtis Turner	1,110	1. Curtis Turner	689	1. Lee Petty	1,407	1. Curtis Turner	12
2. Lee Petty	1,558	2. Dick Linder	460	2. Johnny Mantz	439	2. Curtis Turner	1,390	2. Dick Linder	5
3. Bill Blair	1,550	3. Fonty Flock	369	3. Fonty Flock	326	3. Tim Flock	1,275	3. Fonty Flock	4
4. Dick Linder	1,437	4. Johnny Mantz	351	4. Dick Linder	230	4. Bill Blair	1,253	4. Bill Blair	3
5. Tim Flock	1,403	5. Bill Blair	218	5. Harold Kite	158	5. Bill Rexford	1,146	Fireball Roberts	3
6. Lloyd Moore	1,358	6. Tim Flock	190	6. Tim Flock	152	6. Fonty Flock	1,077	6. Tim Flock	2
7. Bill Rexford	1,302	7. Herb Thomas	176	7. Bill Blair	130	7. Fireball Roberts	1,065	Lloyd Moore	2
8. Fireball Roberts	1,138	8. Bucky Sager	146	8. Red Byron	94	8. Dick Linder	1,060	Bill Rexford	2
9. Jimmy Florian	1,060	9. Bill Rexford	98	9. Herb Thomas	88	9. Lloyd Moore	1,046	Herb Thomas	2
10. Fonty Flock	951	10. Fireball Roberts	61	10. Bucky Sager	73	10. Jack White	850	10. Buck Baker	1
11. Clyde Minter	765	11. Lloyd Moore	57	11. Bill Rexford	58	Jimmy Florian	850	Bob Flock	1
12. Herb Thomas	719	12. Jack Smith	55	12. Fireball Roberts	56	12. Red Byron	835	Jimmy Florian	1
13. Jack White	712	13. Lee Petty	43	13. Lee Petty	43	13. Bob Flock	781	Red Harvey	1
14. Chuck Mahoney	705	14. Jimmy Florian	40	14. Erick Erickson	31	14. Glenn Dunnaway	731	Harold Kite	1
15. Jim Paschal	669	15. Harold Kite	38	15. Cotton Owens	29	15. Cotton Owens	727	Johnny Mantz	1
16. Bob Dickson	627	16. Cotton Owens	23	Lloyd Moore	29	16. Clyde Minter	671	Chuck Mahoney	1
17. Bob Flock	595	17. Chuck Mahoney	18	17. Jack Smith	28	17. Chuck Mahoney	638	Cotton Owens	1
18. Buck Baker	587	Leon Sales	18	18. Jimmy Florian	20	18. Bob Apperson	631	Lee Petty	1
19. Weldon Adams	560	19. Buck Baker	10	19. Pee Wee Martin	12	19. Harold Kite	618	Bucky Sager	1
20. Bill Snowden	532	Gayle Warren	10	20. Leon Sales	11	20. Buck Baker	605	Leon Sales	1
21. Jimmy Thompson	522	21. Bob Flock	5	21. Chuck Mahoney	9	21. Jim Paschal	571	Jack Smith	1
22. Cotton Owens	511	22. Red Harvey	1	22. Gober Sosebee	5	22. Bill Snowden	568	Gayle Warren	1
23. Gayle Warren	429			Gayle Warren	5	23. Jack Smith	561		
24. Johnny Mantz	400			Buck Baker	5	24. Weldon Adams	555		
25. Harold Kite	382			25. Bob Flock	4	25. Billy Carden	548		
26. Jack Smith	376			26. Red Harvey	1	26. Gober Sosebee	543		
27. George Hartley	371					27. Johnny Grubb	541		
28. Jimmie Lewallen	330					28. Ted Chamberlain	539		
29. Dick Burns	323					29. Al Keller	538		
30. Frank Mundy	310					30. Elmer Wilson	519		
31. Roscoe Hough	296								
32. Leon Sales	227								
33. Ted Swaim	200								
34. Dick Clothier	194								
35. Jack Holloway	192								
36. Al Gross	182								
37. Ewell Weddle	158								
38. Donald Thomas	141								
39. Pepper Cunningham	130								
40. Paul Parks	95								
41. J.C. VanLandingham	48								

Driver	Starts	Poles	Finish 1	2	3	4	5	6–10	Laps	Laps Led	Races Led	Winston Cup Points	$

1951

Driver	Starts	Poles	1	2	3	4	5	6–10	Laps	Laps Led	Races Led	Winston Cup Points	$
1. Herb Thomas	35	4	7	1	3	4	1	2	2,159	954	10	4,208.5	20,850
2. Fonty Flock	34	13	8	2	4	5	1	2	2,788	2,068	21	4,062.3	15,200
3. Tim Flock	30	6	7	5	3	3	1	2	2,408	844	12	3,722.5	14,545
4. Lee Petty	32	0	1	4	2	1	3	8	1,248	99	1	2,392.3	7,340
5. Frank Mundy	26	4	3	2	1	2	1	3	874	445	5	1,963.5	7,085
6. Buddy Shuman	7	0	0	0	1	0	0	6	391	0	0	1,368.8	2,830
7. Jesse James Taylor	10	0	0	1	0	0	0	2	519	104	3	1,214	3,750
8. Dick Rathmann	15	0	0	3	1	0	0	3	231	0	0	1,040	3,225
9. Bill Snowden	12	0	0	0	0	2	1	6	383	0	0	1,009.3	2,640
10. Joe Eubanks	12	0	0	1	2	0	0	0	490	7	1	1,005.5	3,415
11. Lloyd Moore	22	0	0	0	1	0	3	4	322	0	0	996.5	2,600
12. Fireball Roberts	9	0	0	1	0	0	1	1	825	0	0	930	1,190
13. Jimmie Lewallen	12	0	0	0	2	0	2	4	613	0	0	874.3	2,430
14. Bob Flock	17	1	1	2	0	1	0	5	1,028	133	5	869	3,680
15. Jim Paschal	16	0	0	0	1	3	0	3	767	33	1	858.5	2,450
16. Bill Blair	18	0	0	1	1	2	0	3	815	0	0	840	2,710
17. Gober Sosebee	10	1	0	3	0	0	1	1	717	7	1	784	2,710
18. Erick Erickson	12	0	0	1	1	0	2	2	859	0	0	723.5	2,435
19. Tommy Thompson	5	0	1	0	0	0	0	1	398	58	1	755	5,510
20. Donald Thomas	17	0	0	0	1	0	3	4	479	0	0	743.5	2,060
21. Johnny Mantz	6	0	0	1	1	0	0	2	532	28	1	725	2,025
22. Lou Figaro	13	1	1	0	0	2	0	1	431	200	1	684.2	2,135
23. Buck Baker	11	0	0	0	1	0	3	1	338	0	0	644.5	1,650
24. Dick Meyer	6	0	0	1	0	0	2	1	N/A	82	1	626.5	1,650
25. Harold Kite	2	0	0	0	0	0	0	1	384	0	0	625	800
26. Billy Carden	11	1	0	0	1	1	0	3	519	58	1	509.8	1,460
27. Jimmy Florian	9	0	0	0	0	2	0	3	N/A	0	0	462.5	1,100
28. Jim Fiebelkorn	17	0	0	1	0	0	0	3	984	0	0	455	1,355
29. Ronnie Kohler	5	0	0	0	2	0	0	1	N/A	0	0	432	1,100
30. Danny Weinberg	6	0	1	0	0	0	1	1	297	1	1	423.5	1,470
31. Roscoe Hough	9	0	0	0	0	0	1	3	N/A	0	0	423	760
32. Woody Brown	3	0	0	0	1	0	1	0	14	0	0	421	1,125
33. Neil Cole	5	1	1	1	0	0	1	0	399	45	1	382	2,050
34. Paul Newkirk	1	0	0	0	0	0	1	0	241	0	0	375	500
35. John McGinley	6	0	0	1	0	1	0	0	224	0	0	372.5	1,300
36. Marvin Panch	3	0	0	1	0	0	0	1	N/A	0	0	371.5	1,075
37. Oda Greene	6	0	0	0	1	0	1	1	173	0	0	366.5	825
38. Jack Goodwin	3	0	0	0	0	0	0	1	617	0	0	362.5	725
39. Jack Smith	7	0	0	1	1	0	0	0	480	0	0	360.5	1,275
40. Bob Caswell	3	0	0	1	0	0	0	0	247	0	0	350	1,325
41. Lloyd Dane	7	0	0	0	1	1	0	1	447	0	0	323.5	975
42. Cotton Owens	5	0	0	0	0	0	1	2	370	0	0	312.5	225
43. Fred Steinbroner	6	0	0	0	0	1	1	1	198	0	0	306.5	700
44. Ewell Weddle	7	0	0	0	0	0	0	2	743	0	0	293.5	435
45. George Seeger	9	0	0	0	1	0	0	2	705	0	0	278	910
46. Sam Hawks	3	0	0	0	0	1	0	0	N/A	0	0	262.5	650
47. Don Bailey	10	0	0	0	0	1	0	1	151	0	0	239.5	625
48. Bud Farrell	5	0	0	0	0	1	0	1	373	0	0	227.5	700
49. Bud Riley	8	0	0	0	0	0	1	1	606	0	0	226.5	475
50. Fred Lee	5	0	0	0	0	1	0	1	98	0	0	224	450

LAPS COMPLETED

1.	Fonty Flock	2,788
2.	Tim Flock	2,408
3.	Herb Thomas	2,159
4.	Lee Petty	1,248
5.	Bob Flock	1,028
6.	Jim Fiebelkorn	984
7.	Frank Mundy	874
8.	Erick Erickson	859
9.	Fireball Roberts	825
10.	Bill Blair	815
11.	Jim Paschal	767
12.	Ewell Weddle	743
13.	Gober Sosebee	717
14.	George Seeger	705
15.	Jack Goodwin	617
16.	Jimmie Lewallen	613
17.	Bud Riley	606
18.	Johnny Mantz	532
19.	Billy Carden	519
	Jesse James Taylor	519
21.	Joe Eubanks	490
22.	Jack Smith	480
23.	Donald Thomas	479
24.	Lloyd Dane	447
25.	Lou Figaro	431
26.	Neil Cole	399
27.	Tommy Thompson	398
28.	Buddy Shuman	391
29.	Harold Kite	384
30.	Bill Snowden	383
31.	Bud Farrell	373
32.	Cotton Owens	370
33.	Buck Baker	338
34.	Lloyd Moore	322
35.	Danny Weinberg	297
36.	Bob Caswell	247
37.	Paul Newkirk	241
38.	Dick Rathmann	231
39.	John McGinley	224
40.	Fred Steinbroner	198
41.	Oda Greene	173
42.	Don Bailey	151
43.	Fred Lee	98
44.	Woody Brown	14

LAPS LED

1.	Fonty Flock	2,068
2.	Herb Thomas	954
3.	Tim Flock	844
4.	Frank Mundy	445
5.	Lou Figaro	200
6.	Bob Flock	133
7.	Jesse James Taylor	104
8.	Lee Petty	99
9.	Dick Meyer	82
10.	Billy Carden	58
	Tommy Thompson	58
12.	Neil Cole	45
13.	Jim Paschal	33
14.	Johnny Mantz	28
15.	Joe Eubanks	7
	Gober Sosebee	7
17.	Danny Weinberg	1

MILES LED

1.	Fonty Flock	855
2.	Herb Thomas	782
3.	Tim Flock	606
4.	Marshall Teague	531
5.	Curtis Turner	361
6.	Frank Mundy	261
7.	Lou Figaro	100
8.	Marvin Burke	98
9.	Bob Flock	82
10.	Tommy Thompson	58
11.	Jesse James Taylor	57
12.	Lee Petty	50
13.	Billy Carden	44
14.	Dick Meyer	41
15.	Jim Reed	29
16.	Neil Cole	23
17.	Jim Paschal	17
18.	Johnny Mantz	14
19.	Billy Myers	12
20.	Bill Norton	10
	Leonard Tippett	10
22.	Joe Eubanks	7
	Gober Sosebee	7
24.	Hershel McGriff	1
	John Soares	1
	Danny Weinberg	1

MILES DRIVEN

1.	Fonty Flock	2,068
2.	Herb Thomas	1,686
3.	Tim Flock	1,661
4.	Marshall Teague	1,417
5.	Lee Petty	1,059
6.	Curtis Turner	948
7.	Erick Erickson	922
8.	Jim Fiebelkorn	913
9.	Bob Flock	877
10.	Jim Paschal	846
11.	Ewell Weddle	799
12.	Bill Blair	755
13.	Fireball Roberts	738
14.	Jack Goodwin	712
15.	Gober Sosebee	711
16.	Billy Myers	702
17.	Red Byron	701
18.	George Seeger	697
19.	Jimmie Lewallen	671
20.	Iggy Katona	643
21.	Bud Riley	624
22.	Billy Carden	613
23.	Slick Smith	593
24.	Frank Mundy	579
25.	Jesse James Taylor	566
26.	Donald Thomas	563
27.	Hershel McGriff	561
28.	Jack Smith	552
29.	Tommy Melvin	551
30.	Leon Sales	548

RACES LED

1.	Fonty Flock	21
2.	Tim Flock	12
3.	Herb Thomas	10
4.	Bob Flock	5
	Frank Mundy	5
6.	Jesse James Taylor	3
7.	Billy Carden	1
	Neil Cole	1
	Joe Eubanks	1
	Lou Figaro	1
	Johnny Mantz	1
	Dick Meyer	1
	Jim Paschal	1
	Lee Petty	1
	Gober Sosebee	1
	Tommy Thompson	1
	Danny Weinberg	1

Driver	Starts	Poles	Finish 1	2	3	4	5	6–10	Laps	Laps Led	Races Led	Winston Cup Points	$

1952

Driver	Starts	Poles	1	2	3	4	5	6–10	Laps	Laps Led	Races Led	Winston Cup Points	$
1. Tim Flock	33	4	8	5	2	7	0	3	5,345	1,469	16	6,858.5	22,890
2. Herb Thomas	32	10	8	7	3	0	1	3	5,134	1,509	16	6,752.5	18,965
3. Lee Petty	32	0	3	6	5	5	2	6	5,094	193	7	6,498.5	16,876
4. Fonty Flock	29	7	2	6	2	2	2	3	3,943	984	10	5,183.5	19,112
5. Dick Rathmann	27	2	5	1	4	0	4	0	3,607	701	10	3,952.5	11,248
6. Bill Blair	19	1	1	3	4	2	0	3	2,463	120	4	3,449	7,899
7. Joe Eubanks	19	0	0	0	1	1	2	5	2,626	0	0	3,090.5	3,630
8. Ray Duhigg	18	0	0	0	2	1	1	6	2,823	0	0	2,986.5	3,811
9. Donald Thomas	21	1	1	1	1	1	1	9	2,623	9	1	2,574	4,477
10. Buddy Shuman	15	0	1	1	0	0	1	4	1,785	65	2	2,483	4,587
11. Ted Chamberlain	18	0	0	0	0	0	0	6	3,053	0	0	2,208	1,277
12. Buck Baker	14	2	1	0	0	2	0	3	1,550	139	3	2,159	3,187
13. Perk Brown	19	1	0	0	2	0	1	3	2,336	0	0	2,151.5	2,187
14. Jimmie Lewallen	20	0	0	0	0	1	1	5	2,327	0	0	2,033	2,052
15. Bub King	10	0	0	0	1	1	0	3	1,743	0	0	1,993	2,737
16. Herschel Buchanan	5	0	0	0	1	1	2	1	1,302	0	0	1,868	2,468
17. Johnny Patterson	5	0	0	1	0	0	1	0	1,054	0	0	1,708	3,618
18. Jim Paschal	15	0	0	0	0	1	0	6	1,705	0	0	1,694	1,483
19. Neil Cole	11	0	0	0	1	0	0	6	1,579	0	0	1,618	1,793
20. Lloyd Moore	8	0	0	1	0	1	0	2	1,457	0	0	1,513.5	2,193
21. Gene Comstock	8	0	0	0	0	1	0	2	1,496	0	0	1,339	785
22. Banjo Matthews	3	0	0	0	0	0	1	0	667	0	0	1,240	1,000
23. Ralph Liguori	12	0	0	0	0	1	0	5	1,671	0	0	1,230	920
24. Jack Reynolds	10	0	0	0	0	2	0	4	1,335	0	0	1,177.5	1,450
25. Dick Passwater	6	0	0	0	0	0	1	2	1,366	0	0	1,148	945
26. Bucky Sager	10	0	0	0	0	1	0	2	1,545	0	0	119.5	710
27. Frankie Schneider	6	0	0	0	1	2	0	1	411	0	0	931	1,350
28. Otis Martin	5	0	0	0	0	0	0	2	620	0	0	873.5	275
29. Coleman Lawrence	8	0	0	0	0	0	0	3	1,326	0	0	846	375
30. Ed Samples	8	0	0	1	1	0	0	2	614	0	0	827	1,535
31. Fred Dove	8	0	0	0	0	0	0	3	919	0	0	780	390
32. Slick Smith	5	0	0	0	0	0	0	3	613	0	0	746	725
33. Iggy Katona	5	0	0	0	0	0	0	2	1,067	0	0	742	525
34. Jack Smith	8	1	0	0	0	0	0	2	883	186	1	729	820
35. Tommy Moon	6	1	0	1	0	0	1	1	487	0	0	726	1,145
36. Rollin Smith	1	0	0	0	0	0	0	0	385	0	0	700	350
37. Speedy Thompson	2	0	0	0	0	0	0	0	409	0	0	656	305
38. Jimmy Thompson	1	0	0	0	0	0	0	0	383	0	0	650	300
39. Bud Farrell	6	0	0	0	0	0	0	2	881	0	0	648	325
40. Weldon Adams	6	0	0	0	0	0	0	2	708	0	0	634	275
41. Clyde Minter	5	0	0	0	0	0	0	3	620	0	0	632	375
42. Elton Hildreth	6	0	0	0	0	0	0	1	815	0	0	614	375
43. Dave Terrell	5	0	0	0	0	0	1	2	477	0	0	612	475
44. Tommy Thompson	5	0	0	0	0	0	0	1	589	20	1	602.5	525
45. Bob Moore	5	0	0	0	1	0	0	2	524	0	0	579.5	575
46. Jim Reed	7	0	0	0	0	0	1	2	597	0	0	567	475
47. E.C. Ramsey	7	0	0	0	0	0	0	0	826	0	0	560	260
48. Jimmy Florian	6	0	0	0	0	0	0	2	283	0	0	551	175
49. Ed Benedict	5	0	0	0	0	0	1	1	633	0	0	526	360
50. Curtis Turner	7	0	0	0	0	0	1	0	526	0	0	505	265

LAPS COMPLETED			LAPS LED			MILES LED			MILES DRIVEN			RACES LED	
1. Tim Flock	5,345		1. Herb Thomas	1,509		1. Fonty Flock	870		1. Tim Flock	3,564		1. Tim Flock	16
2. Herb Thomas	5,134		2. Tim Flock	1,469		2. Tim Flock	804		2. Herb Thomas	3,475		Herb Thomas	16
3. Lee Petty	5,094		3. Fonty Flock	984		3. Herb Thomas	754		3. Lee Petty	3,439		3. Fonty Flock	10
4. Fonty Flock	3,943		4. Dick Rathmann	701		4. Dick Rathmann	519		4. Fonty Flock	2,918		Dick Rathmann	10
5. Dick Rathmann	3,607		5. Lee Petty	193		5. Marshall Teague	248		5. Dick Rathmann	2,539		5. Lee Petty	7
6. Ted Chamberlain	3,053		6. Jack Smith	186		6. Lee Petty	141		6. Ted Chamberlain	2,181		6. Bill Blair	4
7. Ray Duhigg	2,823		7. Buck Baker	139		7. Gober Sosebee	119		7. Bill Blair	2,068		7. Buck Baker	3
8. Joe Eubanks	2,626		8. Bill Blair	120		8. Bill Blair	111		8. Joe Eubanks	2,066		8. Buddy Shuman	2
9. Donald Thomas	2,623		9. Buddy Shuman	65		9. Jack Smith	93		9. Ray Duhigg	2,029		9. Jack Smith	1
10. Bill Blair	2,463		10. Tommy Thompson	20		10. Buck Baker	91		10. Donald Thomas	1,928		Donald Thomas	1
11. Perk Brown	2,336		11. Donald Thomas	9		11. Buddy Shuman	33		11. Jimmie Lewallen	1,638		Tommy Thompson	1
12. Jimmie Lewallen	2,327					12. Tommy Thompson	25		12. Perk Brown	1,458			
13. Buddy Shuman	1,785					13. Fireball Roberts	19		13. Bub King	1,419			
14. Bub King	1,743					14. Roscoe Thompson	11		14. Buddy Shuman	1,413			
15. Jim Paschal	1,705					15. Donald Thomas	9		15. Buck Baker	1,273			
16. Ralph Liguori	1,671					16. George Gallup	7		16. Ralph Liguori	1,236			
17. Neil Cole	1,579					17. Curtis Turner	6		17. Gene Comstock	1,185			
18. Buck Baker	1,550					18. Bob Flock	1		18. Jim Paschal	1,109			
19. Bucky Sager	1,545								19. Dick Passwater	1,085			
20. Gene Comstock	1,496								20. Lloyd Moore	1,084			
21. Lloyd Moore	1,457								21. Herschel Buchanan	1,068			
22. Dick Passwater	1,366								Bucky Sager	1,068			
23. Jack Reynolds	1,335								23. Coleman Lawrence	1,045			
24. Coleman Lawrence	1,326								24. Neil Cole	982			
25. Herschel Buchanan	1,302								25. Pat Kirkwood	972			
26. Iggy Katona	1,067								26. Iggy Katona	925			
27. Johnny Patterson	1,054								27. Jack Reynolds	901			
28. Fred Dove	919								28. Johnny Patterson	879			
29. Jack Smith	883								29. Jack Smith	820			
30. Bud Farrell	881								30. Gober Sosebee	703			
31. E.C. Ramsey	826												
32. Elton Hildreth	815												
33. Weldon Adams	708												
34. Banjo Matthews	667												
35. Ed Benedict	633												
36. Otis Martin	620												
Clyde Minter	620												
38. Ed Samples	614												
39. Slick Smith	613												
40. Jim Reed	597												
41. Tommy Thompson	589												
42. Curtis Turner	526												
43. Bob Moore	524												
44. Tommy Moon	487												
45. Dave Terrell	477												
46. Frankie Schneider	411												
47. Speedy Thompson	409												
48. Rollin Smith	385												
49. Jimmy Thompson	383												
50. Jimmy Florian	283												

Driver	Starts	Poles	Finish						Laps	Laps Led	Races Led	Winston Cup Points	$
			1	2	3	4	5	6–10					

1953

	Driver	Starts	Poles	1	2	3	4	5	6–10	Laps	Laps Led	Races Led	Winston Cup Points	$
1.	Herb Thomas	37	11	12	8	3	3	1	4	4,292	1,420	23	8,460	28,910
2.	Lee Petty	36	0	5	4	10	4	3	6	3,021	209	6	7,814	18,447
3.	Dick Rathmann	34	2	5	12	1	2	1	3	2,545	542	8	7,362	20,245
4.	Buck Baker	33	4	4	2	3	4	3	9	1,619	564	9	6,713	18,167
5.	Fonty Flock	33	3	4	5	4	3	1	0	1,999	581	10	6,174	17,756
6.	Tim Flock	26	5	1	1	2	3	4	7	1,990	289	8	5,011	8,282
7.	Jim Paschal	24	1	1	0	1	2	2	3	1,179	73	1	4,211	5,571
8.	Joe Eubanks	24	1	0	1	2	4	0	8	718	82	2	3,603	5,254
9.	Jimmie Lewallen	22	0	0	1	2	0	4	6	908	0	0	3,508	4,222
10.	Curtis Turner	19	2	1	0	1	1	0	2	1,396	191	4	3,373	4,347
11.	Speedy Thompson	7	0	2	2	1	0	0	2	1,257	99	4	2,958	6,547
12.	Slick Smith	23	1	0	0	0	0	0	10	592	4	1	2,670	2,302
13.	Elton Hildreth	25	0	0	0	0	1	0	4	821	0	0	2,625	1,997
14.	Gober Sosebee	17	0	0	1	1	0	0	7	943	73	1	2,525	2,722
15.	Bill Blair	21	0	1	0	2	0	3	2	1,043	51	2	2,457	4,535
16.	Fred Dove	20	0	0	0	0	0	0	4	742	0	0	1,997	1,240
17.	Bub King	14	0	0	0	0	0	0	5	1,029	0	0	1,624	1,036
18.	Gene Comstock	13	0	0	0	0	0	0	3	756	0	0	1,519	990
19.	Donald Thomas	17	0	0	0	0	0	0	4	1,034	0	0	1,408	1,765
20.	Ralph Liguori	12	0	0	0	0	0	2	1	407	0	0	1,336	1,098
21.	Pop McGinnis	13	0	0	0	0	0	2	3	775	13	1	1,113	975
22.	Otis Martin	8	0	0	0	0	0	0	2	519	0	0	1,068	610
23.	Andy Winfree	7	0	0	0	0	0	0	3	277	0	0	954	300
24.	Bob Welborn	11	0	0	0	0	1	1	4	617	0	0	761	1,160
25.	Johnny Patterson	11	0	0	0	0	0	1	1	534	0	0	753	645
26.	Ted Chamberlain	9	0	0	0	0	0	0	3	572	0	0	738	500
27.	Neil Roberts	2	0	0	0	0	0	0	1	335	0	0	738	400
28.	Buddy Shuman	5	0	0	0	0	0	0	0	342	0	0	713	395
29.	Arden Mounts	10	0	0	0	0	0	0	1	792	0	0	644	395
30.	Bobby Myers	2	0	0	0	0	0	0	1	321	0	0	644	390
31.	Clyde Minter	8	0	0	0	0	0	0	3	591	0	0	636	405
32.	George Osborne	2	0	0	0	0	0	0	0	477	0	0	612	300
33.	Jim Reed	3	0	0	0	0	1	0	0	260	0	0	590	635
34.	Gorden Bracken	6	0	0	0	0	0	0	1	221	0	0	538	215
35.	Don Oldenberg	4	0	0	0	0	0	1	1	223	0	0	527	375
36.	C.H. Dingler	5	0	0	0	0	0	0	3	119	0	0	520	250
37.	Elbert Allen	4	0	0	0	0	0	0	2	N/A	0	0	488	250
38.	Mike Magill	3	0	0	0	0	0	0	0	244	0	0	486	235
39.	Lloyd Hulette	1	0	0	0	0	0	0	0	328	0	0	486	250
40.	Bill Harrison	3	0	0	0	0	0	0	3	N/A	0	0	480	450
41.	Tommy Thompson	3	0	0	0	1	0	0	0	39	0	0	463	865
42.	Coleman Lawrence	8	0	0	0	0	0	0	1	263	0	0	446	250
43.	Dub Livingston	6	0	0	0	0	0	0	1	309	0	0	435	225
44.	Buck Smith	5	0	0	0	0	0	0	1	N/A	0	0	400	175
45.	Jimmy Ayers	4	0	0	0	0	0	0	2	N/A	0	0	384	150
46.	Bob Walden	4	0	0	0	0	0	0	2	325	0	0	356	250
47.	Eddie Skinner	4	0	0	0	0	0	0	1	N/A	0	0	352	200
48.	Bill Adams	2	0	0	0	0	0	0	1	36	0	0	346	250
49.	Mel Krueger	3	0	0	0	0	0	0	1	N/A	0	0	336	175
50.	Johnny Beauchamp	3	0	0	0	0	0	0	1	N/A	0	0	328	150

LAPS COMPLETED

1.	Herb Thomas	4,292
2.	Lee Petty	3,021
3.	Dick Rathmann	2,545
4.	Fonty Flock	1,999
5.	Tim Flock	1,990
6.	Buck Baker	1,619
7.	Curtis Turner	1,396
8.	Speedy Thompson	1,257
9.	Jim Paschal	1,179
10.	Bill Blair	1,043
11.	Donald Thomas	1,034
12.	Bub King	1,029
13.	Gober Sosebee	943
14.	Jimmie Lewallen	908
15.	Elton Hildreth	821
16.	Arden Mounts	792
17.	Pop McGinnis	775
18.	Gene Comstock	756
19.	Fred Dove	742
20.	Joe Eubanks	718
21.	Bob Welborn	617
22.	Slick Smith	592
23.	Clyde Minter	591
24.	Ted Chamberlain	572
25.	Johnny Patterson	534
26.	Otis Martin	519
27.	George Osborne	477
28.	Ralph Liguori	407
29.	Buddy Shuman	342
30.	Neil Roberts	335
31.	Lloyd Hulette	328
32.	Bob Walden	325
33.	Bobby Myers	321
34.	Dub Livingston	309
35.	Andy Winfree	277
36.	Coleman Lawrence	263
37.	Jim Reed	260
38.	Mike Magill	244
39.	Don Oldenberg	223
40.	Gorden Bracken	221
41.	C.H. Dingler	119
42.	Tommy Thompson	39
43.	Bill Adams	36

LAPS LED

1.	Herb Thomas	1,420
2.	Fonty Flock	581
3.	Buck Baker	564
4.	Dick Rathmann	542
5.	Tim Flock	289
6.	Lee Petty	209
7.	Curtis Turner	191
8.	Speedy Thompson	99
9.	Joe Eubanks	82
10.	Jim Paschal	73
	Gober Sosebee	73
12.	Bill Blair	51
13.	Pop McGinnis	13
14.	Slick Smith	4

MILES LED

1.	Herb Thomas	790
2.	Fonty Flock	539
3.	Buck Baker	522
4.	Dick Rathmann	434
5.	Tim Flock	213
6.	Curtis Turner	149
7.	Lee Petty	117
8.	Hershel McGriff	101
9.	Speedy Thompson	77
10.	Fireball Roberts	56
11.	Bill Blair	54
12.	Joe Eubanks	41
13.	Jim Paschal	37
	Gober Sosebee	37
15.	Pop McGinnis	10
16.	Slick Smith	4
17.	Dick Passwater	2

MILES DRIVEN

1.	Herb Thomas	3,107
2.	Lee Petty	2,201
3.	Dick Rathmann	2,002
4.	Tim Flock	1,774
5.	Fonty Flock	1,626
6.	Buck Baker	1,550
7.	Curtis Turner	1,370
8.	Speedy Thompson	1,229
9.	Jim Paschal	1,218
10.	Dick Passwater	1,125
11.	Donald Thomas	1,119
12.	Bill Blair	1,100
13.	Bub King	1,013
14.	Gober Sosebee	928
15.	Gene Comstock	895
16.	Jimmie Lewallen	791
17.	Elton Hildreth	785
18.	Arden Mounts	759
19.	Slick Smith	755
20.	Fred Dove	720
21.	Pop McGinnis	664
22.	Otis Martin	608
23.	Joe Eubanks	588
24.	George Osborne	528
25.	Clyde Minter	519
26.	Dick Meyer	488
27.	Buddy Shuman	481
28.	Bob Welborn	466
29.	Neil Roberts	461
30.	Dick Allwine	456
	Herschel Buchanan	456

RACES LED

1.	Herb Thomas	23
2.	Fonty Flock	10
3.	Buck Baker	9
4.	Tim Flock	8
	Dick Rathmann	8
6.	Lee Petty	6
7.	Speedy Thompson	4
	Curtis Turner	4
9.	Bill Blair	2
	Joe Eubanks	2
11.	Pop McGinnis	1
	Jim Paschal	1
	Slick Smith	1
	Gober Sosebee	1

1954

Driver	Starts	Poles	Finish 1	2	3	4	5	6–10	Laps	Laps Led	Races Led	Winston Cup Points	$
1. Lee Petty	34	3	7	5	5	4	3	8	5,903	681	12	8,649	21,127
2. Herb Thomas	34	8	12	4	1	2	0	8	5,505	1,366	18	8,366	30,975
3. Buck Baker	34	7	4	7	6	3	3	5	5,726	768	14	6,893	19,368
4. Dick Rathmann	32	4	3	5	8	6	1	3	5,286	729	11	6,760	16,264
5. Joe Eubanks	33	0	0	1	2	5	3	13	5,167	0	0	5,467	8,559
6. Hershel McGriff	24	5	4	3	5	0	1	4	3,891	122	6	5,137	13,250
7. Jim Paschal	27	2	1	0	1	1	2	6	3,546	193	1	3,903	5,451
8. Jimmie Lewallen	22	0	0	2	0	0	3	5	2,963	0	0	3,233	4,694
9. Curtis Turner	10	1	1	1	2	1	2	1	1,678	277	3	2,994	10,120
10. Ralph Liguori	23	1	0	0	1	0	1	10	3,461	0	0	2,905	3,495
11. Blackie Pitt	27	0	0	0	0	0	0	6	3,731	0	0	2,661	1,925
12. Dave Terrell	30	0	0	0	0	0	0	8	3,876	0	0	2,645	2,225
13. Bill Blair	19	0	0	0	0	0	2	8	2,853	7	1	2,362	2,650
14. Laird Bruner	24	0	0	0	0	0	2	4	3,052	0	0	2,243	2,080
15. Gober Sosebee	18	1	1	0	1	1	1	3	1,970	170	2	2,114	3,150
16. John Soares	9	0	1	0	1	0	0	2	2,196	211	1	2,072	3,262
17. Marvin Panch	10	1	0	2	1	0	0	4	2,100	17	1	1,935	4,747
18. Eddie Skinner	16	0	0	0	0	0	0	1	2,044	0	0	1,794	1,017
19. Joel Million	9	0	0	0	0	0	0	1	1,298	0	0	1,779	1,092
20. Elton Hildreth	14	0	0	0	0	0	0	2	1,519	0	0	1,710	1,152
21. Arden Mounts	12	0	0	0	0	0	0	1	1,592	0	0	1,705	875
22. Fireball Roberts	5	0	0	0	0	0	0	2	811	0	0	1,648	1,080
23. Speedy Thompson	7	0	0	0	0	1	0	2	949	0	0	1,480	1,165
24. Johnny Patterson	4	0	0	0	0	1	0	0	582	0	0	1,417	1,240
25. Erick Erickson	6	0	0	0	0	0	1	2	1,398	0	0	1,337	1,365
26. Ray Duhigg	12	0	0	0	0	1	1	3	1,458	0	0	1,245	1,375
27. Slick Smith	6	0	0	0	0	1	0	1	698	0	0	1,122	950
28. Clyde Minter	12	0	0	0	0	0	0	6	1,653	0	0	1,116	900
29. Gwyn Staley	2	0	0	0	0	0	0	1	357	0	0	1,088	670
30. Lloyd Dane	4	0	0	1	0	0	2	1	1,268	180	1	984	1,600
31. Donald Thomas	9	0	0	1	0	1	1	1	1,175	53	1	980	1,675
32. Ted Chamberlain	10	0	0	0	0	0	0	1	1,596	0	0	920	475
33. Danny Letner	4	1	1	0	1	0	0	1	1,058	142	2	915	1,975
34. Elmo Langley	2	0	0	0	0	0	0	0	340	0	0	864	450
35. Tim Flock	5	1	0	1	0	0	0	2	800	180	1	860	1,050
36. Fred Dove	12	0	0	0	0	0	0	2	1,428	0	0	832	525
37. Dink Widenhouse	6	0	0	0	0	1	0	1	620	0	0	805	425
38. Gene Comstock	1	0	0	0	0	0	0	0	334	0	0	780	400
39. Walt Flinchum	8	0	0	0	0	0	0	2	1,123	0	0	756	425
40. Charlie Cregar	5	0	0	0	0	0	0	0	857	8	1	716	405
41. Bill Amick	6	0	0	1	0	0	0	0	884	9	1	700	250
42. Harvey Eakin	7	0	0	0	0	0	0	0	741	0	0	698	425
43. Lou Figaro	3	0	0	0	0	0	0	2	461	0	0	690	425
44. Ken Fisher	5	0	0	0	0	0	0	1	879	0	0	668	400
45. Jim Reed	9	0	0	0	0	0	2	1	1,083	0	0	631	965
46. Russ Hepler	6	0	0	0	0	1	0	0	691	0	0	624	525
46. Allen Adkins	2	0	0	0	1	1	0	0	545	0	0	624	1,150
48. Van Van Wey	3	0	0	0	0	0	0	0	629	0	0	602	495
49. Tony Nelson	3	0	0	0	0	0	0	1	995	0	0	568	325
50. John Dodd	3	0	0	0	0	0	0	2	463	0	0	552	150

Laps Completed

1.	Lee Petty	5,903
2.	Buck Baker	5,726
3.	Herb Thomas	5,505
4.	Dick Rathmann	5,286
5.	Joe Eubanks	5,167
6.	Hershel McGriff	3,891
7.	Dave Terrell	3,876
8.	Blackie Pitt	3,731
9.	Jim Paschal	3,546
10.	Ralph Liguori	3,461
11.	Laird Bruner	3,052
12.	Jimmie Lewallen	2,963
13.	Bill Blair	2,853
14.	John Soares	2,196
15.	Marvin Panch	2,100
16.	Eddie Skinner	2,044
17.	Gober Sosebee	1,970
18.	Curtis Turner	1,678
19.	Clyde Minter	1,653
20.	Ted Chamberlain	1,596
21.	Arden Mounts	1,592
22.	Elton Hildreth	1,519
23.	Ray Duhigg	1,458
24.	Fred Dove	1,428
25.	Erick Erickson	1,398
26.	Joel Million	1,298
27.	Lloyd Dane	1,268
28.	Donald Thomas	1,175
29.	Walt Flinchum	1,123
30.	Jim Reed	1,083
31.	Danny Letner	1,058
32.	Tony Nelson	995
33.	Speedy Thompson	949
34.	Bill Amick	884
35.	Ken Fisher	879
36.	Charlie Cregar	857
37.	Fireball Roberts	811
38.	Tim Flock	800
39.	Harvey Eakin	741
40.	Slick Smith	698
41.	Russ Hepler	691
42.	Van Van Wey	629
43.	Dink Widenhouse	620
44.	Johnny Patterson	582
45.	Allen Adkins	545
46.	John Dodd	463
47.	Lou Figaro	461
48.	Gwyn Staley	357
49.	Elmo Langley	340
50.	Gene Comstock	334

Laps Led

1.	Herb Thomas	1,366
2.	Buck Baker	768
3.	Dick Rathmann	729
4.	Lee Petty	681
5.	Curtis Turner	277
6.	John Soares	211
7.	Jim Paschal	193
8.	Lloyd Dane	180
	Tim Flock	180
10.	Gober Sosebee	170
11.	Danny Letner	142
12.	Hershel McGriff	122
13.	Donald Thomas	53
14.	Marvin Panch	17
15.	Bill Amick	9
16.	Charlie Cregar	8
17.	Bill Blair	7

Miles Led

1.	Herb Thomas	954
2.	Lee Petty	646
3.	Buck Baker	445
4.	Dick Rathmann	398
5.	Curtis Turner	376
6.	Al Keller	237
7.	John Soares	106
8.	Gober Sosebee	99
9.	Jim Paschal	97
10.	Lloyd Dane	90
	Tim Flock	90
12.	Hershel McGriff	80
13.	Danny Letner	72
14.	Donald Thomas	53
15.	Bill Amick	12
16.	Charlie Cregar	11
17.	Marvin Panch	10
18.	Fonty Flock	8
19.	Pop McGinnis	6
20.	Bill Blair	4

Miles Driven

1.	Lee Petty	4,060
2.	Herb Thomas	3,898
3.	Buck Baker	3,893
4.	Dick Rathmann	3,629
5.	Joe Eubanks	3,542
6.	Hershel McGriff	2,743
7.	Dave Terrell	2,608
8.	Blackie Pitt	2,507
9.	Jim Paschal	2,492
10.	Ralph Liguori	2,447
11.	Laird Bruner	2,338
12.	Jimmie Lewallen	2,206
13.	Bill Blair	1,893
14.	Marvin Panch	1,779
15.	Eddie Skinner	1,659
16.	John Soares	1,498
17.	Curtis Turner	1,497
18.	Ted Chamberlain	1,423
19.	Elton Hildreth	1,420
20.	Gober Sosebee	1,376
21.	Al Keller	1,372
22.	Joel Million	1,324
23.	Arden Mounts	1,317
24.	Erick Erickson	1,191
25.	Bill Widenhouse	999
26.	Fireball Roberts	975
27.	Speedy Thompson	942
28.	Ray Duhigg	938
29.	Harvey Eakin	915
30.	Charlie Cregar	877

Races Led

1.	Herb Thomas	18
2.	Buck Baker	14
3.	Lee Petty	12
4.	Dick Rathmann	11
5.	Hershel McGriff	6
6.	Curtis Turner	3
7.	Danny Letner	2
	Gober Sosebee	2
9.	Bill Amick	1
	Bill Blair	1
	Charlie Cregar	1
	Lloyd Dane	1
	Tim Flock	1
	Marvin Panch	1
	Jim Paschal	1
	John Soares	1
	Donald Thomas	1

Driver	Starts	Poles	Finish 1	2	3	4	5	6–10	Laps	Laps Led	Races Led	Winston Cup Points	$

1955

	Driver	Starts	Poles	1	2	3	4	5	6–10	Laps	Laps Led	Races Led	Winston Cup Points	$
1.	Tim Flock	39	20	18	5	5	1	3	1	6,208	3,495	33	9,596	37,780
2.	Buck Baker	43	2	3	6	6	4	5	10	6,850	808	9	8,088	19,771
3.	Lee Petty	42	1	6	4	5	4	1	10	6,328	769	6	7,194	18,920
4.	Bob Welborn	32	1	0	1	4	4	3	13	5,291	31	1	5,460	10,147
5.	Herb Thomas	23	2	3	3	3	3	2	1	3,248	250	7	5,186	18,024
6.	Junior Johnson	36	2	5	1	2	1	3	6	4,620	790	7	4,810	13,803
7.	Eddie Skinner	38	0	0	0	0	0	4	11	5,473	0	0	4,652	4,737
8.	Jim Paschal	36	2	3	3	3	2	1	8	4,751	306	7	4,572	10,586
9.	Jimmie Lewallen	33	1	0	2	0	4	2	8	4,028	0	0	4,526	6,440
10.	Gwyn Staley	24	1	0	1	2	2	2	7	3,196	33	1	4,360	6,547
11.	Fonty Flock	31	4	3	5	2	0	2	2	3,482	430	7	4,266	13,100
12.	Dave Terrell	25	0	0	0	2	0	1	7	3,199	9	1	3,170	3,655
13.	Jimmy Massey	11	0	0	0	1	1	2	4	1,906	0	0	2,924	3,510
14.	Marvin Panch	10	0	0	2	0	2	0	0	1,597	15	1	2,812	4,385
15.	Speedy Thompson	14	0	2	1	0	0	0	2	1,773	222	2	2,452	7,090
16.	Jim Reed	14	0	0	1	0	1	2	0	1,691	32	1	2,416	2,703
17.	Gene Simpson	22	0	0	0	0	0	1	6	2,667	0	0	2,388	2,158
18.	Dick Rathmann	20	3	0	2	2	3	0	1	2,296	176	5	2,298	4,368
19.	Ralph Liguori	12	0	0	0	0	0	0	6	1,402	0	0	2,124	1,973
20.	Joe Eubanks	14	0	0	0	0	0	0	4	1,607	0	0	2,028	2,008
21.	Blackie Pitt	20	0	0	0	0	0	0	7	2,532	0	0	1,992	1,785
22.	Harvey Henderson	17	0	0	0	0	0	1	5	2,284	0	0	1,930	1,810
23.	Banks Simpson	7	0	0	0	0	0	0	0	1,103	0	0	1,852	870
24.	Dink Widenhouse	15	1	0	0	0	0	0	6	1,743	0	0	1,752	1,660
25.	John Dodd, Jr.	12	0	0	0	0	0	1	6	1,585	0	0	1,496	1,695
26.	Bill Widenhouse	5	0	0	0	0	0	1	2	799	2	1	1,444	1,065
27.	Lou Spears	3	0	0	0	0	0	0	1	708	0	0	1,272	810
28.	Larry Flynn	1	0	0	0	0	0	1	0	359	0	0	1,260	1,175
29.	Cotton Owens	2	0	0	0	0	0	1	1	549	0	0	1,248	900
30.	Gordon Smith	15	0	0	0	0	0	0	2	1,584	0	0	1,212	975
31.	Billy Carden	13	0	0	0	0	2	0	1	1,589	0	0	1,172	1,340
32.	Arden Mounts	12	1	0	0	0	0	0	4	1,560	0	0	1,170	1,025
33.	Joel Million	8	0	0	1	0	1	0	4	973	0	0	1,136	1,685
34.	Curtis Turner	9	0	0	1	1	2	0	0	928	14	1	1,120	2,605
35.	John Lindsay	6	0	0	0	0	0	0	3	853	0	0	1,052	575
36.	Nace Mattingly	3	0	0	0	0	0	1	0	696	0	0	992	700
37.	Bill Blair	12	0	0	0	0	0	0	0	1,320	0	0	974	440
38.	Donald Thomas	10	0	0	0	0	2	0	2	1,320	0	0	932	1,240
39.	Ed Cole	13	0	0	0	0	0	0	0	1,433	0	0	924	645
40.	Mack Hanbury	8	0	0	0	0	0	0	2	807	0	0	900	575
41.	Danny Letner	4	0	1	0	1	0	0	0	614	34	1	892	1,780
42.	George Parrish	12	0	0	0	0	0	0	1	1,057	0	0	880	750
43.	Banjo Matthews	3	0	0	0	0	0	0	2	734	0	0	860	745
44.	Carl Krueger	7	0	0	0	0	0	1	1	955	0	0	748	585
45.	Ted Cannady	9	0	0	0	0	0	0	0	812	0	0	744	450
46.	Allen Adkins	4	0	0	1	0	0	1	0	601	79	1	740	1,160
47.	Joe Weatherly	6	0	0	0	0	1	0	3	994	140	1	724	2,575
48.	John McVitty	7	0	0	0	0	0	0	2	951	0	0	684	550
49.	Lloyd Dane	5	0	0	0	1	0	0	1	545	5	1	674	780
50.	Fred Dove	7	0	0	0	1	0	0	2	830	0	0	668	750

LAPS COMPLETED

1.	Buck Baker	6,850
2.	Lee Petty	6,328
3.	Tim Flock	6,208
4.	Eddie Skinner	5,473
5.	Bob Welborn	5,291
6.	Jim Paschal	4,751
7.	Junior Johnson	4,620
8.	Jimmie Lewallen	4,028
9.	Fonty Flock	3,482
10.	Herb Thomas	3,248
11.	Dave Terrell	3,199
12.	Gwyn Staley	3,196
13.	Gene Simpson	2,667
14.	Blackie Pitt	2,532
15.	Dick Rathmann	2,296
16.	Harvey Henderson	2,284
17.	Jimmy Massey	1,906
18.	Speedy Thompson	1,773
19.	Dink Widenhouse	1,743
20.	Jim Reed	1,691
21.	Joe Eubanks	1,607
22.	Marvin Panch	1,597
23.	Billy Carden	1,589
24.	John Dodd, Jr.	1,585
25.	Gordon Smith	1,584
26.	Arden Mounts	1,560
27.	Ed Cole	1,433
28.	Ralph Liguori	1,402
29.	Bill Blair	1,320
	Donald Thomas	1,320
31.	Banks Simpson	1,103
32.	George Parrish	1,057
33.	Joe Weatherly	994
34.	Joel Million	973
35.	Carl Krueger	955
36.	John McVitty	951
37.	Curtis Turner	928
38.	John Lindsay	853
39.	Fred Dove	830
40.	Ted Cannady	812
41.	Mack Hanbury	807
42.	Bill Widenhouse	799
43.	Banjo Matthews	734
44.	Lou Spears	708
45.	Nace Mattingly	696
46.	Danny Letner	614
47.	Allen Adkins	601
48.	Cotton Owens	549
49.	Lloyd Dane	545
50.	Larry Flynn	359

LAPS LED

1.	Tim Flock	3,495
2.	Buck Baker	808
3.	Junior Johnson	790
4.	Lee Petty	769
5.	Fonty Flock	430
6.	Jim Paschal	306
7.	Herb Thomas	250
8.	Speedy Thompson	222
9.	Dick Rathmann	176
10.	Joe Weatherly	140
11.	Allen Adkins	79
12.	Danny Letner	34
13.	Gwyn Staley	33
14.	Jim Reed	32
15.	Bob Welborn	31
16.	Marvin Panch	15
17.	Curtis Turner	14
18.	Dave Terrell	9
19.	Lloyd Dane	5
20.	Bill Widenhouse	2

MILES LED

1.	Tim Flock	1,775
2.	Fonty Flock	445
3.	Lee Petty	385
4.	Junior Johnson	383
5.	Buck Baker	359
6.	Speedy Thompson	269
7.	Herb Thomas	216
8.	Joe Weatherly	193
9.	Jim Paschal	178
10.	Dick Rathmann	122
11.	Norm Nelson	106
12.	John Kieper	89
13.	Allen Adkins	40
14.	Ed Brown	22
15.	Curtis Turner	19
16.	Danny Letner	17
17.	Jim Reed	16
	Bob Welborn	16
19.	Bill Amick	14
20.	Gwyn Staley	13
21.	Dave Terrell	9
22.	Marvin Panch	8
23.	Fireball Roberts	6
24.	Lloyd Dane	5
25.	Bill Widenhouse	3

MILES DRIVEN

1.	Buck Baker	4,762
2.	Tim Flock	4,556
3.	Lee Petty	4,403
4.	Bob Welborn	3,625
5.	Eddie Skinner	3,610
6.	Jim Paschal	3,202
7.	Junior Johnson	3,133
8.	Jimmie Lewallen	2,939
9.	Herb Thomas	2,707
10.	Fonty Flock	2,565
11.	Dave Terrell	2,433
12.	Gwyn Staley	2,230
13.	Gene Simpson	1,983
14.	Speedy Thompson	1,835
15.	Blackie Pitt	1,744
16.	Jimmy Massey	1,721
17.	Marvin Panch	1,654
18.	Dick Rathmann	1,587
19.	Joe Eubanks	1,487
20.	Ralph Liguori	1,422
21.	Banks Simpson	1,377
22.	Harvey Henderson	1,325
23.	Jim Reed	1,265
24.	Bill Blair	1,227
25.	Billy Carden	1,168
26.	Dink Widenhouse	1,166
27.	Arden Mounts	1,050
28.	Bobby Waddell	942
29.	John Dodd, Jr.	915
30.	Gordon Smith	910

RACES LED

1.	Tim Flock	33
2.	Buck Baker	9
3.	Fonty Flock	7
	Junior Johnson	7
	Jim Paschal	7
	Herb Thomas	7
7.	Lee Petty	6
8.	Dick Rathmann	5
9.	Speedy Thompson	2
10.	Allen Adkins	1
	Lloyd Dane	1
	Danny Letner	1
	Marvin Panch	1
	Jim Reed	1
	Gwyn Staley	1
	Dave Terrell	1
	Curtis Turner	1
	Joe Weatherly	1
	Bob Welborn	1
	Bill Widenhouse	1

Driver	Starts	Poles	Finish						Laps	Laps Led	Races Led	Winston Cup Points	$
			1	2	3	4	5	6–10					

1956

	Driver	Starts	Poles	1	2	3	4	5	6–10	Laps	Laps Led	Races Led	Winston Cup Points	$
1.	Buck Baker	48	12	14	7	3	4	3	8	8,495	1,401	23	9,252	34,077
2.	Speedy Thompson	42	7	8	5	5	4	2	5	6,957	2,023	23	8,788	27,169
3.	Herb Thomas	48	2	5	2	4	7	4	14	7,890	522	8	8,710	19,352
4.	Lee Petty	47	1	2	1	6	2	6	11	7,507	252	6	8,324	15,338
5.	Jim Paschal	42	1	1	8	2	4	2	10	6,626	212	6	7,878	17,204
6.	Billy Myers	42	1	2	6	3	1	1	9	6,270	103	4	6,976	15,830
7.	Fireball Roberts	33	3	5	1	2	7	2	5	5,695	470	10	5,794	14,742
8.	Ralph Moody	35	5	4	5	2	1	1	8	5,258	312	6	5,528	15,493
9.	Tim Flock	22	5	4	1	3	2	1	3	3,076	445	9	5,062	15,769
10.	Marvin Panch	20	1	1	2	5	2	0	3	3,298	150	6	4,680	11,520
11.	Rex White	24	1	0	0	2	0	1	11	4,240	0	0	4,642	5,334
12.	Johnny Allen	32	0	0	0	0	0	2	9	4,888	0	0	4,024	4,559
13.	Paul Goldsmith	9	0	1	0	0	2	1	2	2,292	182	1	3,788	8,569
14.	Gwyn Staley	22	0	0	0	0	2	3	8	3,506	0	0	3,550	5,159
15.	Joe Eubanks	26	2	0	0	3	0	4	6	3,398	107	2	3,284	5,584
16.	Joe Weatherly	17	1	0	1	1	3	1	6	2,745	20	1	3,084	5,251
17.	Bill Amick	13	0	0	1	3	1	2	3	2,446	10	2	3,048	5,381
18.	Jim Reed	11	2	0	1	1	2	1	0	1,542	286	3	5,890	5,077
19.	Tiny Lund	21	0	0	0	0	1	0	7	3,988	0	0	2,754	2,811
20.	Curtis Turner	13	0	1	3	0	0	0	1	1,967	287	3	2,580	14,541
21.	Jack Smith	15	0	1	0	0	0	0	5	2,669	234	2	2,320	3,825
22.	Billy Carden	23	0	0	0	0	0	0	4	2,831	0	0	2,108	2,175
23.	Lloyd Dane	10	0	2	0	1	2	0	4	1,706	91	2	2,106	4,370
24.	Frank Mundy	10	0	0	1	1	0	1	2	1,589	0	0	1,836	3,585
25.	Bobby Johns	9	0	0	0	0	0	0	3	1,537	0	0	1,832	1,450
26.	Blackie Pitt	27	0	0	0	0	0	0	5	2,702	0	0	1,760	1,545
27.	Harold Hardesty	9	0	0	1	0	0	1	4	1,761	0	0	1,724	2,380
28.	Al Watkins	14	0	0	0	0	0	0	4	2,065	0	0	1,710	1,185
29.	Chuck Meekins	7	0	0	1	1	1	0	3	1,241	43	3	1,656	2,815
30.	Harvey Henderson	18	0	0	0	0	0	0	4	2,520	0	0	1,634	1,360
31.	Bill Champion	14	0	0	0	0	0	0	4	2,297	0	0	1,632	1,570
32.	Eddie Pagan	8	2	1	1	0	0	2	0	1,366	31	2	1,598	4,095
33.	Pat Kirkwood	3	0	0	0	1	0	0	1	715	0	0	1,540	2,025
34.	Clyde Palmer	11	0	0	2	1	0	1	2	1,730	296	2	1,516	2,755
35.	John Kieper	8	2	1	1	1	1	0	3	1,479	67	2	1,506	3,250
36.	Johnny Dodson	11	0	0	0	0	0	0	4	1,842	0	0	1,488	1,450
37.	Bill Blair	9	0	0	0	0	0	0	4	1,275	0	0	1,284	1,005
38.	Junior Johnson	13	1	0	1	0	0	0	0	1,131	60	2	1,272	1,350
39.	Ed Cole	12	0	0	0	0	0	0	1	1,486	0	0	1,200	950
40.	Brownie King	15	0	0	0	0	0	0	0	1,994	0	0	1,140	925
41.	Scotty Cain	4	0	0	0	0	0	1	3	701	0	0	1,124	1,235
42.	Allen Adkins	6	0	0	0	0	0	1	2	1,016	0	0	1,104	1,465
43.	Bobby Keck	15	0	0	0	0	0	0	3	2,236	0	0	1,076	950
44.	Gordon Haines	7	0	0	1	0	1	0	2	1,067	66	1	1,066	1,500
45.	Bob Keefe	7	0	0	0	0	1	0	1	1,200	0	0	1,066	1,040
46.	Dick Beaty	15	0	0	0	0	0	0	3	1,513	0	0	1,036	910
47.	Jim Blomgren	6	0	0	0	0	0	0	1	841	0	0	992	475
48.	Ed Negre	5	0	0	0	0	1	1	2	936	200	2	952	1,225
49.	Jimmy Massey	7	0	0	0	0	1	2	1	1,140	0	0	950	1,545
50.	Fonty Flock	7	2	1	0	0	0	0	3	665	150	2	946	1,780

LAPS COMPLETED		LAPS LED		MILES LED		MILES DRIVEN		RACES LED	
1. Buck Baker	8,495	1. Speedy Thompson	2,023	1. Speedy Thompson	1,145	1. Buck Baker	5,460	1. Buck Baker	23
2. Herb Thomas	7,890	2. Buck Baker	1,401	2. Buck Baker	1,052	2. Herb Thomas	5,210	Speedy Thompson	23
3. Lee Petty	7,507	3. Herb Thomas	522	3. Tim Flock	454	3. Lee Petty	4,954	3. Fireball Roberts	10
4. Speedy Thompson	6,957	4. Fireball Roberts	470	4. Fireball Roberts	395	4. Speedy Thompson	4,646	4. Tim Flock	9
5. Jim Paschal	6,626	5. Tim Flock	445	5. Curtis Turner	340	5. Jim Paschal	4,544	5. Herb Thomas	8
6. Billy Myers	6,270	6. Ralph Moody	312	6. Herb Thomas	261	6. Billy Myers	4,231	6. Ralph Moody	6
7. Fireball Roberts	5,695	7. Clyde Palmer	296	7. Marvin Panch	247	7. Fireball Roberts	3,789	Marvin Panch	6
8. Ralph Moody	5,258	8. Curtis Turner	287	8. Jim Paschal	227	8. Ralph Moody	3,506	Jim Paschal	6
9. Johnny Allen	4,888	9. Jim Reed	286	9. Paul Goldsmith	182	9. Johnny Allen	3,349	Lee Petty	6
10. Rex White	4,240	10. Lee Petty	252	10. Ralph Moody	176	10. Rex White	2,978	10. Billy Myers	4
11. Tiny Lund	3,988	11. Jack Smith	234	11. Clyde Palmer	148	11. Tim Flock	2,696	11. Chuck Meekins	3
12. Gwyn Staley	3,506	12. Jim Paschal	212	12. Jim Reed	144	12. Joe Eubanks	2,529	Jim Reed	3
13. Joe Eubanks	3,398	13. Ed Negre	200	13. Chuck Stevenson	135	13. Marvin Panch	2,502	Curtis Turner	3
Marvin Panch	3,298	14. Paul Goldsmith	182	14. Lee Petty	127	14. Tiny Lund	2,466	14. Bill Amick	2
15. Tim Flock	3,076	15. Fonty Flock	150	15. Jack Smith	117	15. Gwyn Staley	2,404	Lloyd Dane	2
16. Billy Carden	2,831	Marvin Panch	150	16. Fonty Flock	109	16. Paul Goldsmith	2,040	Joe Eubanks	2
17. Joe Weatherly	2,745	17. Joe Eubanks	107	17. Ed Negre	100	17. Joe Weatherly	1,997	Fonty Flock	2
18. Blackie Pitt	2,702	18. Billy Myers	103	18. Lloyd Dane	59	18. Jack Smith	1,916	Junior Johnson	2
19. Jack Smith	2,669	19. Lloyd Dane	91	19. Joe Eubanks	56	19. Billy Carden	1,881	John Kieper	2
20. Harvey Henderson	2,520	20. John Kieper	67	20. Billy Myers	51	20. Blackie Pitt	1,754	Ed Negre	2
21. Bill Amick	2,446	21. Gordon Haines	66	21. John Kieper	43	21. Jim Reed	1,666	Eddie Pagan	2
22. Bill Champion	2,297	22. Junior Johnson	60	22. Royce Haggerty	36	22. Bill Amick	1,631	Clyde Palmer	2
23. Paul Goldsmith	2,292	23. Chuck Meekins	43	23. Chuck Meekins	35	23. Bill Champion	1,626	Jack Smith	2
24. Bobby Keck	2,236	24. Eddie Pagan	31	24. Gordon Haines	33	24. Harvey Henderson	1,618	24. Paul Goldsmith	1
25. Al Watkins	2,065	25. Joe Weatherly	20	25. Eddie Pagan	31	25. Frank Mundy	1,479	Gordon Haines	1
26. Brownie King	1,994	26. Bill Amick	10	26. Junior Johnson	28	26. Curtis Turner	1,431	Joe Weatherly	1
27. Curtis Turner	1,967			27. Joe Weatherly	10	27. Clyde Palmer	1,381		
28. Johnny Dodson	1,842			28. Ralph Earnhardt	6	28. Al Watkins	1,380		
29. Harold Hardesty	1,761			29. Bill Amick	5	29. Johnny Dodson	1,379		
30. Clyde Palmer	1,730			30. Bill Hyde	1	30. Harold Hardesty	1,350		
31. Lloyd Dane	1,706								
32. Frank Mundy	1,589								
33. Jim Reed	1,542								
34. Bobby Johns	1,537								
35. Dick Beaty	1,513								
36. Ed Cole	1,486								
37. John Kieper	1,479								
38. Eddie Pagan	1,366								
39. Bill Blair	1,275								
40. Chuck Meekins	1,241								
41. Bob Keefe	1,200								
42. Jimmy Massey	1,140								
43. Junior Johnson	1,131								
44. Gordon Haines	1,067								
45. Allen Adkins	1,016								
46. Ed Negre	936								
47. Jim Blomgren	841								
48. Pat Kirkwood	715								
49. Scotty Cain	701								
50. Fonty Flock	665								

31

1957

Driver	Starts	Poles	Finish 1	2	3	4	5	6–10	Laps	Laps Led	Races Led	Winston Cup Points	$
1. Buck Baker	40	6	10	7	4	5	4	8	8,058	858	15	10,716	30,764
2. Marvin Panch	42	4	6	3	6	6	1	5	6,890	449	12	9,956	24,307
3. Speedy Thompson	38	4	2	4	3	4	3	6	6,301	648	8	8,560	26,841
4. Lee Petty	41	3	4	4	3	3	6	13	7,466	449	11	8,528	18,326
5. Jack Smith	39	2	4	1	2	3	6	9	6,589	429	9	8,464	14,562
6. Fireball Roberts	42	4	8	6	2	1	4	6	6,891	1,107	16	8,268	19,829
7. Johnny Allen	42	1	0	0	1	1	2	13	6,033	0	0	7,068	9,815
8. L.D. Austin	40	0	0	0	0	0	1	12	6,920	0	0	6,532	6,485
9. Brownie King	36	0	0	0	0	0	1	15	5,756	0	0	5,740	5,589
10. Jim Paschal	35	0	0	1	2	3	3	8	4,999	0	0	5,124	7,079
11. Tiny Lund	32	3	0	0	3	1	2	9	4,922	209	2	4,848	6,424
12. Billy Myers	28	0	0	0	0	4	0	5	3,923	201	1	4,640	6,566
13. Paul Goldsmith	25	4	4	4	1	1	0	5	3,759	588	10	4,188	12,734
14. Cotton Owens	17	1	1	1	0	0	1	3	2,300	179	3	4,032	12,784
15. Eddie Pagan	15	2	3	3	3	1	1	0	2,611	3	3	3,612	7,274
16. Bill Amick	21	2	1	3	4	0	0	4	3,364	12	2	3,512	8,073
17. Dick Beaty	20	0	0	0	0	0	1	6	3,202	0	0	3,220	3,648
18. Jim Reed	6	0	0	0	1	1	0	1	892	11	2	2,836	3,408
19. Clarence DeZalia	25	0	0	0	0	0	0	6	4,059	0	0	2,828	3,308
20. Frankie Schneider	10	1	0	1	0	2	0	3	1,781	37	1	2,516	4,588
21. Rex White	9	1	0	1	0	3	0	2	1,585	193	2	2,508	3,870
22. Curtis Turner	10	1	0	2	0	0	0	2	1,397	109	4	2,356	4,830
23. George Green	17	0	0	0	0	1	0	3	2,668	0	0	2,216	2,240
24. Whitey Norman	13	0	0	1	0	0	0	3	2,437	0	0	1,920	3,990
25. Lloyd Dane	10	1	1	5	1	0	0	3	1,296	1	1	1,852	4,985
26. Jimmie Lewallen	7	0	0	0	0	0	0	0	895	0	0	1,796	1,030
27. Johnny Mackison	5	0	0	0	0	0	1	1	769	0	0	1,764	1,330
28. Bobby Keck	16	0	0	0	0	0	0	2	2,144	0	0	1,740	1,525
29. Billy Carden	3	0	0	0	0	0	0	2	625	0	0	1,600	1,675
30. Bill Benson	11	0	0	0	0	0	0	2	1,320	0	0	1,592	1,090
31. Dick Getty	10	0	0	0	0	0	3	5	1,174	0	0	1,504	1,890
32. Scotty Cain	11	0	0	0	0	3	0	4	1,151	0	0	1,492	1,165
33. Roy Tyner	10	0	0	0	0	0	0	2	1,705	0	0	1,468	1,020
34. T.A. Toomes	11	0	0	0	0	0	0	1	1,920	0	0	1,404	1,450
35. Possum Jones	6	0	0	0	0	0	0	4	1,443	0	0	1,360	2,375
36. Huck Spaulding	8	0	0	0	0	0	0	3	1,006	0	0	1,240	1,130
37. Ralph Earnhardt	9	0	0	0	0	0	0	3	1,465	0	0	1,180	1,150
38. George Seeger	6	0	0	1	3	1	0	0	764	19	1	1,108	2,740
39. Ken Rush	16	1	0	0	1	0	0	5	2,266	0	0	1,104	2,045
40. Peck Peckham	10	0	0	0	0	0	0	0	1,060	0	0	1,064	950
41. Bill Champion	10	0	0	0	0	0	0	1	1,663	0	0	956	1,125
42. Chuck Hansen	7	0	0	0	0	0	0	0	990	0	0	900	510
43. Danny Graves	7	1	1	0	1	0	1	1	787	1	1	880	1,895
44. Marvin Porter	6	0	1	1	0	0	0	1	771	1	1	872	1,770
45. Eddie Skinner	4	0	0	0	0	0	0	0	833	0	0	848	605
46. Jimmy Thompson	2	0	0	0	0	0	0	0	352	0	0	816	325
47. Parnelli Jones	10	1	1	0	0	0	0	2	743	1	1	812	1,625
48. Bobby Johns	1	0	0	0	0	0	0	0	335	0	0	800	225
49. Don Porter	6	0	0	0	0	0	0	4	722	0	0	784	810
50. Joe Weatherly	14	0	0	1	3	0	1	2	2,059	3	1	776	5,340

LAPS COMPLETED

1.	Buck Baker	8,058
2.	Lee Petty	7,466
3.	L.D. Austin	6,920
4.	Fireball Roberts	6,891
5.	Marvin Panch	6,890
6.	Jack Smith	6,589
7.	Speedy Thompson	6,301
8.	Johnny Allen	6,033
9.	Brownie King	5,756
10.	Jim Paschal	4,999
11.	Tiny Lund	4,922
12.	Clarence DeZalia	4,059
13.	Billy Myers	3,923
14.	Paul Goldsmith	3,759
15.	Bill Amick	3,364
16.	Dick Beaty	3,202
17.	George Green	2,668
18.	Eddie Pagan	2,611
19.	Whitey Norman	2,437
20.	Cotton Owens	2,300
21.	Ken Rush	2,266
22.	Bobby Keck	2,144
23.	Joe Weatherly	2,059
24.	T.A. Toomes	1,920
25.	Frankie Schneider	1,781
26.	Roy Tyner	1,705
27.	Bill Champion	1,663
28.	Rex White	1,585
29.	Ralph Earnhardt	1,465
30.	Possum Jones	1,443
31.	Curtis Turner	1,397
32.	Bill Benson	1,320
33.	Lloyd Dane	1,296
34.	Dick Getty	1,174
35.	Scotty Cain	1,151
36.	Peck Peckham	1,060
37.	Huck Spaulding	1,006
38.	Chuck Hansen	990
39.	Jimmie Lewallen	895
40.	Jim Reed	892
41.	Eddie Skinner	833
42.	Danny Graves	787
43.	Marvin Porter	771
44.	Johnny Mackison	769
45.	George Seeger	764
46.	Parnelli Jones	743
47.	Don Porter	722
48.	Billy Carden	625
49.	Jimmy Thompson	352
50.	Bobby Johns	335

LAPS LED

1.	Fireball Roberts	1,107
2.	Buck Baker	858
3.	Speedy Thompson	648
4.	Paul Goldsmith	588
5.	Marvin Panch	449
	Lee Petty	449
7.	Jack Smith	429
8.	Tiny Lund	209
9.	Billy Myers	201
10.	Rex White	193
11.	Cotton Owens	179
12.	Curtis Turner	109
13.	Frankie Schneider	37
14.	George Seeger	19
15.	Bill Amick	12
16.	Jim Reed	11
17.	Eddie Pagan	3
	Joe Weatherly	3
19.	Lloyd Dane	1
	Danny Graves	1
	Parnelli Jones	1
	Marvin Porter	1

MILES LED

1.	Fireball Roberts	697
2.	Speedy Thompson	503
3.	Buck Baker	500
4.	Paul Goldsmith	485
5.	Marvin Panch	299
6.	Jack Smith	275
7.	Bob Welborn	240
8.	Lee Petty	218
9.	Cotton Owens	213
10.	Gwyn Staley	133
	Curtis Turner	133
12.	Tiny Lund	105
13.	Billy Myers	101
14.	Rex White	97
15.	Ralph Moody	50
	Art Watts	50
17.	George Seeger	48
18.	Frankie Schneider	37
19.	Banjo Matthews	35
20.	Jim Reed	11
21.	Bill Amick	6
22.	Jimmy Massey	4
23.	Lloyd Dane	1
	Danny Graves	1
	Parnelli Jones	1
	Bobby Myers	1
	Eddie Pagan	1
	Marvin Porter	1
	Joe Weatherly	1

MILES DRIVEN

1.	Buck Baker	4,844
2.	Lee Petty	4,595
3.	Marvin Panch	4,401
4.	Fireball Roberts	4,269
5.	L.D. Austin	4,132
6.	Jack Smith	3,969
7.	Speedy Thompson	3,903
8.	Johnny Allen	3,876
9.	Brownie King	3,464
10.	Tiny Lund	3,024
11.	Jim Paschal	2,947
12.	Paul Goldsmith	2,495
13.	Billy Myers	2,441
14.	Clarence DeZalia	2,119
15.	Bill Amick	2,067
16.	Dick Beaty	2,061
17.	Eddie Pagan	1,802
18.	Cotton Owens	1,769
19.	Whitey Norman	1,614
20.	Gwyn Staley	1,516
21.	George Green	1,485
22.	Bobby Keck	1,419
23.	Ken Rush	1,397
24.	Possum Jones	1,395
25.	Joe Weatherly	1,350
26.	Curtis Turner	1,304
27.	Frankie Schneider	1,248
28.	Bill Champion	1,167
29.	Rex White	1,144
30.	Roy Tyner	1,099

RACES LED

1.	Fireball Roberts	16
2.	Buck Baker	15
3.	Marvin Panch	12
4.	Lee Petty	11
5.	Paul Goldsmith	10
6.	Jack Smith	9
7.	Speedy Thompson	8
8.	Curtis Turner	4
9.	Cotton Owens	3
	Eddie Pagan	3
11.	Bill Amick	2
	Tiny Lund	2
	Jim Reed	2
	Rex White	2
15.	Lloyd Dane	1
	Danny Graves	1
	Parnelli Jones	1
	Billy Myers	1
	Marvin Porter	1
	Frankie Schneider	1
	George Seeger	1
	Joe Weatherly	1

1958

	Driver	Starts	Poles	Finish 1	2	3	4	5	6–10	Laps	Laps Led	Races Led	Winston Cup Points	$
1.	Lee Petty	50	4	7	5	4	9	3	15	9,173	439	14	12,232	26,565
2.	Buck Baker	44	3	3	10	4	2	4	12	7,827	364	8	11,588	25,841
3.	Speedy Thompson	38	7	4	2	7	3	3	5	6,808	230	7	8,792	17,295
4.	Shorty Rollins	29	0	1	1	3	5	2	10	5,324	87	4	8,124	13,399
5.	Jack Smith	39	4	2	5	2	3	3	6	5,750	381	7	7,666	12,634
6.	L.D. Austin	46	0	0	0	0	0	0	10	6,903	0	0	6,972	6,246
7.	Rex White	22	7	2	4	6	0	1	4	3,848	471	7	6,552	12,233
8.	Junior Johnson	27	0	6	2	3	1	0	4	4,244	317	9	6,380	13,809
9.	Eddie Pagan	27	2	0	2	1	1	7	7	3,961	57	2	4,910	7,472
10.	Jim Reed	17	2	4	0	5	1	0	2	3,693	692	4	4,762	9,644
11.	Fireball Roberts	10	0	6	1	1	0	0	1	2,491	877	7	4,420	32,219
12.	Bobby Keck	30	0	0	0	0	0	0	7	4,345	0	0	4,240	3,459
13.	Herman Beam	20	0	0	0	0	0	0	1	3,651	0	0	4,224	2,599
14.	Herb Estes	11	0	0	0	0	0	0	4	2,202	0	0	4,048	2,509
15.	Clarence DeZalia	27	0	0	0	0	0	0	6	4,073	0	0	3,448	3,004
16.	Doug Cox	14	0	0	1	0	1	1	6	2,479	0	0	3,736	3,404
17.	Cotton Owens	29	2	1	4	2	1	0	9	3,700	241	5	3,716	6,579
18.	Marvin Panch	11	2	0	1	1	1	2	0	1,833	157	3	3,424	4,114
19.	Billy Rafter	19	0	0	0	0	0	1	7	3,160	0	0	2,916	2,799
20.	Curtis Turner	17	1	3	2	0	1	2	2	3,068	827	6	2,856	10,029
21.	Lloyd Dane	5	0	0	1	0	0	0	1	1,084	0	0	2,844	2,490
22.	Bob Duell	7	1	0	1	1	0	1	3	1,273	0	0	2,740	2,415
23.	Jimmy Thompson	7	0	0	0	0	1	0	1	923	0	0	2,540	3,275
24.	Fred Harb	25	0	0	0	1	2	1	3	3,651	0	0	2,484	3,315
25.	Tiny Lund	22	2	0	0	2	1	1	3	3,506	14	1	2,436	3,155
26.	Bill Poor	24	0	0	0	0	0	1	6	3,880	0	0	2,292	3,115
27.	Gene White	9	0	0	0	0	0	0	2	1,641	0	0	2,040	1,400
28.	Joe Weatherly	15	1	1	1	0	2	1	2	2,692	104	3	2,032	6,330
29.	Johnny Mackison	11	0	0	0	1	0	1	1	1,423	0	0	1,680	1,255
30.	Jim Parsley	10	0	0	0	0	0	0	4	1,720	0	0	1,488	1,135
31.	Al White	9	0	0	0	0	0	0	1	1,483	0	0	1,464	920
32.	Jimmy Massey	9	1	0	0	0	0	1	2	1,612	0	0	1,300	1,625
33.	Parnelli Jones	3	2	1	0	0	0	0	0	587	148	2	1,140	1,010
34.	Joe Eubanks	7	0	1	0	0	1	0	1	956	38	2	1,120	2,070
35.	Brownie King	24	0	0	0	0	0	0	5	3,926	0	0	1,116	3,045
36.	G.C. Spencer	1	0	0	0	0	0	0	0	343	0	0	1,040	315
37.	Richard Petty	9	0	0	0	0	0	0	1	977	0	0	1,016	760
38.	Billy Carden	13	0	0	0	0	0	0	2	1,469	0	0	1,012	815
39.	Elmo Langley	9	0	0	0	0	0	1	2	1,240	0	0	980	1,090
40.	Buzz Woodward	9	0	0	0	0	0	0	2	1,508	0	0	964	1,195
41.	Possum Jones	11	1	0	0	0	0	1	2	1,870	28	1	960	1,790
42.	Jim Paschal	6	1	1	0	0	1	0	2	1,105	150	1	928	1,670
43.	Chuck Hansen	7	0	0	0	0	0	0	1	1,011	0	0	916	580
44.	Eddie Gray	3	0	1	0	0	0	0	0	437	43	1	910	3,375
45.	Peck Peckham	11	0	0	0	0	0	0	0	1,263	0	0	868	835
46.	Lennie Page	8	0	0	0	0	0	0	2	901	0	0	836	760
47.	Bob Keefe	2	0	0	0	0	0	1	1	276	0	0	782	925
48.	R.L. Combs	9	0	0	0	0	0	0	1	1,062	0	0	760	805
49.	Volney Schulze	7	0	0	0	0	0	0	0	725	0	0	680	490
50.	Dean Layfield	7	0	0	0	0	0	0	0	522	0	0	664	370

LAPS COMPLETED

1. Lee Petty — 9,173
2. Buck Baker — 7,827
3. L.D. Austin — 6,903
4. Speedy Thompson — 6,808
5. Jack Smith — 5,750
6. Shorty Rollins — 5,324
7. Bobby Keck — 4,345
8. Junior Johnson — 4,244
9. Clarence DeZalia — 4,073
10. Eddie Pagan — 3,961
11. Brownie King — 3,926
12. Bill Poor — 3,880
13. Rex White — 3,848
14. Cotton Owens — 3,700
15. Jim Reed — 3,693
16. Herman Beam — 3,651
    Fred Harb — 3,651
18. Tiny Lund — 3,506
19. Billy Rafter — 3,160
20. Curtis Turner — 3,068
21. Joe Weatherly — 2,692
22. Fireball Roberts — 2,491
23. Doug Cox — 2,479
24. Herb Estes — 2,202
25. Possum Jones — 1,870
26. Marvin Panch — 1,833
27. Jim Parsley — 1,720
28. Gene White — 1,641
29. Jimmy Massey — 1,612
30. Buzz Woodward — 1,508
31. Al White — 1,483
32. Billy Carden — 1,469
33. Johnny Mackison — 1,423
34. Bob Duell — 1,273
35. Peck Peckham — 1,263
36. Elmo Langley — 1,240
37. Jim Paschal — 1,105
38. Lloyd Dane — 1,084
39. R.L. Combs — 1,062
40. Chuck Hansen — 1,011
41. Richard Petty — 977
42. Joe Eubanks — 956
43. Jimmy Thompson — 923
44. Lennie Page — 901
45. Volney Schulze — 725
46. Parnelli Jones — 587
47. Dean Layfield — 522
48. Eddie Gray — 437
49. G.C. Spencer — 343
50. Bob Keefe — 276

LAPS LED

1. Fireball Roberts — 877
2. Curtis Turner — 827
3. Jim Reed — 692
4. Rex White — 471
5. Lee Petty — 439
6. Jack Smith — 381
7. Buck Baker — 364
8. Junior Johnson — 317
9. Cotton Owens — 241
10. Speedy Thompson — 230
11. Marvin Panch — 157
12. Jim Paschal — 150
13. Parnelli Jones — 148
14. Joe Weatherly — 104
15. Shorty Rollins — 87
16. Eddie Pagan — 57
17. Eddie Gray — 43
18. Joe Eubanks — 38
19. Possum Jones — 28
20. Tiny Lund — 14

MILES LED

1. Fireball Roberts — 867
2. Curtis Turner — 534
3. Parnelli Jones — 388
4. Jack Smith — 254
5. Bob Welborn — 249
6. Jim Reed — 245
7. Buck Baker — 223
8. Junior Johnson — 207
9. Lee Petty — 187
10. Rex White — 186
11. Glen Wood — 184
12. Paul Goldsmith — 160
13. Cotton Owens — 148
14. Speedy Thompson — 140
15. Marvin Panch — 118
16. Eddie Gray — 113
17. Joe Weatherly — 53
18. Joe Eubanks — 47
19. Shorty Rollins — 43
20. Eddie Pagan — 40
    Frankie Schneider — 40
22. Jim Paschal — 38
23. Tim Flock — 25
24. Tiny Lund — 13
25. Possum Jones — 9
26. George Dunn — 3

MILES DRIVEN

1. Lee Petty — 5,671
2. Buck Baker — 4,726
3. Speedy Thompson — 4,437
4. L.D. Austin — 3,898
5. Jack Smith — 3,711
6. Shorty Rollins — 3,201
7. Junior Johnson — 2,797
8. Eddie Pagan — 2,607
9. Jim Reed — 2,474
10. Clarence DeZalia — 2,412
11. Herman Beam — 2,251
12. Bobby Keck — 2,219
13. Cotton Owens — 2,208
14. Fireball Roberts — 2,197
15. Curtis Turner — 2,190
    Bob Welborn — 2,190
17. Brownie King — 2,153
18. Rex White — 2,122
19. Joe Weatherly — 2,120
20. Tiny Lund — 1,991
21. Roy Tyner — 1,951
22. Bill Poor — 1,947
23. Fred Harb — 1,841
24. Herbert Estes — 1,658
25. Shep Langdon — 1,648
26. Doug Cox — 1,592
27. Marvin Panch — 1,576
28. Billy Rafter — 1,529
29. Johnny Allen — 1,483
30. Wilbur Rakestraw — 1,443

RACES LED

1. Lee Petty — 14
2. Junior Johnson — 9
3. Buck Baker — 8
4. Fireball Roberts — 7
   Jack Smith — 7
   Speedy Thompson — 7
   Rex White — 7
8. Curtis Turner — 6
9. Cotton Owens — 5
10. Jim Reed — 4
    Shorty Rollins — 4
12. Marvin Panch — 3
    Joe Weatherly — 3
14. Joe Eubanks — 2
    Parnelli Jones — 2
    Eddie Pagan — 2
17. Eddie Gray — 1
    Possum Jones — 1
    Tiny Lund — 1
    Jim Paschal — 1

35

1959

Driver	Starts	Poles	1	2	3	4	5	6–10	Laps	Laps Led	Races Led	Winston Cup Points	$
1. Lee Petty	42	2	11	5	7	4	0	8	8,278	1,011	16	11,792	49,220
2. Cotton Owens	37	2	1	4	2	2	4	9	6,633	209	4	9,962	14,640
3. Speedy Thompson	29	1	0	1	0	2	2	4	4,785	228	3	7,684	6,816
4. Herman Beam	30	0	0	0	0	0	1	11	6,024	0	0	7,396	6,380
5. Buck Baker	35	4	1	2	6	1	4	5	6,056	183	5	7,170	11,061
6. Tom Pistone	22	0	2	2	4	2	2	6	3,902	181	7	7,050	12,725
7. L.D. Austin	35	0	0	0	0	0	0	13	6,480	0	0	6,519	4,671
8. Jack Smith	21	3	4	1	2	2	0	3	3,594	222	7	6,150	13,290
9. Jim Reed	14	1	3	0	1	1	2	2	2,512	289	5	5,744	23,534
10. Rex White	23	5	5	2	2	1	1	2	4,744	826	9	5,526	12,360
11. Junior Johnson	28	1	5	1	3	3	2	1	4,433	166	7	4,864	9,675
12. Shep Langdon	21	0	0	0	0	0	0	6	3,976	0	0	4,768	3,526
13. G.C. Spencer	28	0	0	0	0	1	0	4	4,552	0	0	4,260	3,701
14. Tommy Irwin	25	1	0	1	2	3	4	6	4,409	174	2	3,876	9,190
15. Richard Petty	21	0	0	1	3	1	1	3	3,654	7	1	3,694	8,111
16. Fireball Roberts	8	3	1	0	0	0	0	3	1,445	147	3	3,676	10,661
17. Bob Welborn	29	5	3	1	3	3	0	3	3,895	176	7	3,588	6,491
18. Joe Weatherly	17	0	0	2	0	1	3	4	2,776	189	7	3,404	9,816
19. Bobby Johns	8	1	0	0	1	0	0	1	1,911	129	2	2,732	5,951
20. Tiny Lund	27	0	0	2	0	3	0	5	4,836	0	0	2,634	4,941
21. Bob Burdick	6	2	0	1	0	0	0	3	912	25	1	2,392	10,050
22. Larry Frank	15	0	0	1	0	1	2	5	3,300	39	1	2,256	5,993
23. Bobby Keck	18	0	0	0	0	0	0	0	2,484	0	0	2,186	1,270
24. Curtis Turner	10	1	2	1	0	1	0	0	1,293	438	5	2,088	3,845
25. Jim Paschal	6	0	0	2	0	0	1	1	1,485	0	0	1,792	2,980
26. Buddy Baker	12	0	0	0	0	1	0	4	1,639	0	0	1,692	1,705
27. Shorty Rollins	10	0	0	0	0	0	0	4	1,391	0	0	1,600	1,500
28. Elmo Langley	13	0	0	0	1	0	0	1	1,694	0	0	1,568	2,280
29. Jimmy Thompson	5	0	0	0	0	0	0	1	1,002	0	0	1,528	1,580
30. Brownie King	18	0	0	0	0	0	1	4	3,250	0	0	1,480	1,875
31. Tim Flock	2	0	0	0	0	0	0	1	223	0	0	1,464	850
32. Joe Eubanks	13	0	0	1	0	0	1	5	1,279	0	0	1,432	2,000
33. Roy Tyner	28	0	0	1	3	3	3	7	5,244	0	0	1,416	5,430
34. Charlie Cregar	3	0	0	0	0	0	0	0	496	0	0	1,408	560
35. Dick Freeman	3	0	0	0	0	0	0	0	695	0	0	1,352	475
36. Raul Cilloniz	2	0	0	0	0	0	0	0	229	0	0	1,272	550
37. Ned Jarrett	17	2	2	1	1	0	0	3	2,929	2	2	1,248	3,860
38. Dave White	5	0	0	0	0	0	0	1	1,253	0	0	1,228	660
39. Dick Joslin	4	0	0	0	0	0	0	0	338	0	0	1,224	485
40. Tommy Thompson	3	0	0	0	0	0	0	0	367	0	0	1,168	510
41. Harvey Hege	10	0	0	0	0	0	0	3	1,485	0	0	1,152	955
42. Eduardo Dibos	3	0	0	0	0	0	2	0	181	0	0	1,128	1,050
43. Bill Champion	1	0	0	0	0	0	0	0	343	0	0	1,120	500
44. Joe Caspolich	1	0	0	0	0	0	0	0	342	0	0	1,040	470
45. Jim Austin	5	0	0	0	0	0	0	0	784	0	0	1,016	440
46. Marvin Porter	7	0	0	0	1	1	0	2	1,696	0	0	984	1,940
47. Jim McGuirk	4	0	0	0	0	0	0	0	314	0	0	928	325
48. Harlan Richardson	10	0	0	0	0	0	0	2	1,893	0	0	924	1,120
49. Al White	5	0	0	0	0	0	0	0	826	0	0	872	575
50. Richard Riley	10	0	0	0	0	0	0	2	1,433	0	0	760	910

LAPS COMPLETED

1.	Lee Petty	8,278
2.	Cotton Owens	6,633
3.	L.D. Austin	6,480
4.	Buck Baker	6,056
5.	Herman Beam	6,024
6.	Roy Tyner	5,244
7.	Tiny Lund	4,836
8.	Speedy Thompson	4,785
9.	Rex White	4,744
10.	G.C. Spencer	4,552
11.	Junior Johnson	4,433
12.	Tommy Irwin	4,409
13.	Shep Langdon	3,976
14.	Tom Pistone	3,902
15.	Bob Welborn	3,895
16.	Richard Petty	3,654
17.	Jack Smith	3,594
18.	Larry Frank	3,300
19.	Brownie King	3,250
20.	Ned Jarrett	2,929
21.	Joe Weatherly	2,776
22.	Jim Reed	2,512
23.	Bobby Keck	2,484
24.	Bobby Johns	1,911
25.	Harlan Richardson	1,893
26.	Marvin Porter	1,696
27.	Elmo Langley	1,694
28.	Buddy Baker	1,639
29.	Harvey Hege	1,485
	Jim Paschal	1,485
31.	Fireball Roberts	1,445
32.	Richard Riley	1,433
33.	Shorty Rollins	1,391
34.	Curtis Turner	1,293
35.	Joe Eubanks	1,279
36.	Dave White	1,253
37.	Jimmy Thompson	1,002
38.	Bob Burdick	912
39.	Al White	826
40.	Jim Austin	784
41.	Dick Freeman	695
42.	Charlie Cregar	496
43.	Tommy Thompson	367
44.	Bill Champion	343
45.	Joe Caspolich	342
46.	Dick Joslin	338
47.	Jim McGuirk	314
48.	Raul Cilloniz	229
49.	Tim Flock	223
50.	Eduardo Dibos	181

LAPS LED

1.	Lee Petty	1,011
2.	Rex White	826
3.	Curtis Turner	438
4.	Jim Reed	289
5.	Speedy Thompson	228
6.	Jack Smith	222
7.	Cotton Owens	209
8.	Joe Weatherly	189
9.	Buck Baker	183
10.	Tom Pistone	181
11.	Bob Welborn	176
12.	Tommy Irwin	174
13.	Junior Johnson	166
14.	Fireball Roberts	147
15.	Bobby Johns	129
16.	Larry Frank	39
17.	Bob Burdick	25
18.	Richard Petty	7
19.	Ned Jarrett	2

MILES LED

1.	Lee Petty	616
2.	Fireball Roberts	320
3.	Jack Smith	296
4.	Jim Reed	267
5.	Curtis Turner	252
6.	Tom Pistone	241
7.	Rex White	220
8.	Johnny Beauchamp	175
9.	Cotton Owens	173
10.	Bob Welborn	154
11.	Bobby Johns	114
12.	Speedy Thompson	113
13.	Joe Weatherly	100
14.	Buck Baker	89
15.	Tommy Irwin	87
16.	Banjo Matthews	76
17.	Junior Johnson	73
18.	Glen Wood	49
19.	Bob Burdick	34
20.	Larry Frank	20
21.	Richard Petty	10
	Fritz Wilson	10
23.	Dick Bailey	1
	Russ Gemberling	1
	Eddie Gray	1
	Ned Jarrett	1
	Joe Lee Johnson	1

MILES DRIVEN

1.	Lee Petty	4,977
2.	Cotton Owens	4,347
3.	Herman Beam	4,006
4.	Buck Baker	3,606
5.	L.D. Austin	3,602
6.	Speedy Thompson	3,436
7.	Roy Tyner	3,410
8.	Rex White	3,039
9.	Tiny Lund	2,971
10.	Tom Pistone	2,966
11.	Tommy Irwin	2,847
12.	Junior Johnson	2,745
13.	Jack Smith	2,735
14.	Larry Frank	2,647
15.	G.C. Spencer	2,553
16.	Richard Petty	2,422
17.	Bob Welborn	2,364
18.	Glen Wood	2,292
19.	Shep Langdon	2,259
20.	Joe Weatherly	2,105
21.	Jim Reed	2,071
22.	Joe Lee Johnson	2,007
23.	George Green	1,966
24.	Brownie King	1,904
25.	Ken Rush	1,533
26.	Ned Jarrett	1,489
	Fireball Roberts	1,489
28.	Bobby Johns	1,440
29.	Gene White	1,319
30.	Elmo Langley	1,314

RACES LED

1.	Lee Petty	16
2.	Rex White	9
3.	Junior Johnson	7
	Tom Pistone	7
	Jack Smith	7
	Joe Weatherly	7
	Bob Welborn	7
8.	Buck Baker	5
	Jim Reed	5
	Curtis Turner	5
11.	Cotton Owens	4
12.	Fireball Roberts	3
	Speedy Thompson	3
14.	Tommy Irwin	2
	Ned Jarrett	2
	Bobby Johns	2
17.	Bob Burdick	1
	Larry Frank	1
	Richard Petty	1

Driver	Starts	Poles	Finish						Laps	Laps Led	Races Led	Winston Cup Points	$
			1	2	3	4	5	6–10					

1960

	Driver	Starts	Poles	1	2	3	4	5	6–10	Laps	Laps Led	Races Led	Winston Cup Points	$
1.	Rex White	40	3	6	6	7	4	2	10	8,921	541	11	21,164	57,550
2.	Richard Petty	40	2	3	6	3	3	1	14	8,189	447	6	17,228	41,873
3.	Bobby Johns	19	0	1	2	1	3	1	2	3,695	438	6	14,964	46,115
4.	Buck Baker	37	2	2	1	3	1	8	9	7,271	213	4	14,674	38,399
5.	Ned Jarrett	40	5	5	3	4	4	4	6	7,399	382	11	14,660	25,438
6.	Lee Petty	38	3	5	7	2	6	1	9	7,330	515	10	14,510	31,283
7.	Junior Johnson	34	3	3	2	4	2	3	4	5,096	320	7	9,932	38,990
8.	Emanuel Zervakis	14	1	0	0	1	1	0	8	3,382	0	0	9,720	12,124
9.	Jim Paschal	10	0	0	0	2	1	0	4	2,752	11	1	8,968	15,096
10.	Banjo Matthews	12	0	0	0	0	0	0	4	1,894	9	1	8,458	15,617
11.	Johnny Beauchamp	11	0	1	1	0	0	1	2	2,669	1	1	8,306	17,374
12.	Herman Beam	26	0	0	0	0	1	0	5	5,348	0	0	7,776	5,916
13.	Joe Lee Johnson	22	0	1	1	1	1	2	2	3,453	48	1	7,352	34,519
14.	Jack Smith	13	4	3	1	2	0	1	0	2,198	514	10	6,944	24,721
15.	Fred Lorenzen	10	0	0	0	2	0	1	2	2,086	93	1	6,764	9,136
16.	Bob Welborn	15	0	0	1	0	2	3	4	2,809	94	2	6,732	6,194
17.	Jimmy Pardue	29	0	0	0	0	0	1	9	4,566	0	0	6,682	5,610
18.	Tom Pistone	20	0	0	0	1	0	1	6	4,080	183	4	6,572	6,714
19.	Johnny Allen	10	0	0	1	0	0	1	3	1,820	0	0	6,506	14,789
20.	Joe Weatherly	24	0	3	2	0	2	0	4	4,294	246	6	6,380	21,624
21.	Doug Yates	24	1	0	0	2	1	0	5	4,030	39	1	6,374	5,205
22.	L.D. Austin	27	0	0	0	0	0	1	9	4,822	0	0	6,180	4,885
23.	David Pearson	22	1	0	1	0	1	1	4	3,885	0	0	5,956	5,030
24.	Gerald Duke	11	0	0	0	0	1	0	6	2,062	0	0	5,950	5,930
25.	Speedy Thompson	9	0	2	0	0	1	1	1	1,646	217	2	5,658	18,035
26.	Marvin Panch	11	0	0	0	0	0	0	1	1,482	22	1	5,268	3,225
27.	Paul Lewis	22	0	0	0	0	0	0	4	3,690	0	0	5,212	3,535
28.	Curtis Crider	24	0	0	0	0	0	0	2	3,985	0	0	4,720	3,645
29.	Fireball Roberts	9	6	2	0	0	0	0	1	1,338	578	9	4,700	19,895
30.	Shorty Rollins	4	0	0	0	0	0	0	1	952	0	0	4,374	2,120
31.	Possum Jones	13	0	0	3	1	0	0	1	2,594	0	0	4,270	6,330
32.	Tiny Lund	8	0	0	0	0	0	0	2	1,254	0	0	4,124	2,440
33.	G.C. Spencer	26	0	0	0	0	1	1	4	4,907	0	0	3,986	3,910
34.	Larry Frank	11	0	0	0	0	0	0	2	1,984	11	1	3,634	2,440
35.	Herb Tillman	9	0	0	0	0	0	0	0	1,705	0	0	3,504	2,695
36.	Curtis Turner	9	1	0	0	0	0	0	1	1,090	106	2	3,300	3,220
37.	Bunkie Blackburn	20	0	0	0	0	0	1	3	2,789	0	0	3,252	3,400
38.	Buddy Baker	15	0	0	0	0	0	0	1	2,149	0	0	3,070	1,745
39.	Cotton Owens	14	3	1	3	1	0	0	0	2,121	185	7	3,050	14,065
40.	Charley Griffith	5	0	0	0	0	0	0	0	599	0	0	2,684	1,300
41.	Wilbur Rakestraw	12	0	0	0	0	0	0	1	1,862	0	0	2,676	2,695
42.	Jimmy Massey	6	0	0	1	1	0	0	1	1,392	26	1	2,662	3,310
43.	Jimmy Thompson	9	0	0	0	0	0	0	0	1,944	0	0	2,472	1,940
44.	Jim Reed	8	0	0	0	1	0	0	0	1,175	28	1	2,340	2,240
45.	Jim Cook	3	1	1	0	0	0	0	0	560	0	0	2,178	1,600
46.	Ernie Gahan	2	0	0	0	0	0	0	0	818	0	0	2,080	625
47.	Elmo Henderson	6	0	0	0	0	0	0	0	870	0	0	2,072	1,425
48.	Bob Burdick	2	0	0	0	0	0	0	1	71	0	0	1,970	850
49.	Roz Howard	3	0	0	0	0	0	0	2	676	0	0	1,810	1,490
50.	Bob Potter	3	0	0	0	0	0	0	1	708	0	0	1,800	640

LAPS COMPLETED

1. Rex White — 8,921
2. Richard Petty — 8,189
3. Ned Jarrett — 7,399
4. Lee Petty — 7,330
5. Buck Baker — 7,271
6. Herman Beam — 5,348
7. Junior Johnson — 5,096
8. G.C. Spencer — 4,907
9. L.D. Austin — 4,822
10. Jimmy Pardue — 4,566
11. Joe Weatherly — 4,294
12. Tom Pistone — 4,080
13. Doug Yates — 4,030
14. Curtis Crider — 3,985
15. David Pearson — 3,885
16. Bobby Johns — 3,695
17. Paul Lewis — 3,690
18. Joe Lee Johnson — 3,453
19. Emanuel Zervakis — 3,382
20. Bob Welborn — 2,809
21. Bunkie Blackburn — 2,789
22. Jim Paschal — 2,752
23. Johnny Beauchamp — 2,669
24. Possum Jones — 2,594
25. Jack Smith — 2,198
26. Buddy Baker — 2,149
27. Cotton Owens — 2,121
28. Fred Lorenzen — 2,086
29. Gerald Duke — 2,062
30. Larry Frank — 1,984
31. Jimmy Thompson — 1,944
32. Banjo Matthews — 1,894
33. Wilbur Rakestraw — 1,862
34. Johnny Allen — 1,820
35. Herb Tillman — 1,705
36. Speedy Thompson — 1,646
37. Marvin Panch — 1,482
38. Jimmy Massey — 1,392
39. Fireball Roberts — 1,338
40. Tiny Lund — 1,254
41. Jim Reed — 1,175
42. Curtis Turner — 1,090
43. Shorty Rollins — 952
44. Elmo Henderson — 870
45. Ernie Gahan — 818
46. Bob Potter — 708
47. Roz Howard — 676
48. Charley Griffith — 599
49. Jim Cook — 560
50. Bob Burdick — 71

LAPS LED

1. Fireball Roberts — 578
2. Rex White — 541
3. Lee Petty — 515
4. Jack Smith — 514
5. Richard Petty — 447
6. Bobby Johns — 438
7. Ned Jarrett — 382
8. Junior Johnson — 320
9. Joe Weatherly — 246
10. Speedy Thompson — 217
11. Buck Baker — 213
12. Cotton Owens — 185
13. Tom Pistone — 183
14. Curtis Turner — 106
15. Bob Welborn — 94
16. Fred Lorenzen — 93
17. Joe Lee Johnson — 48
18. Doug Yates — 39
19. Jim Reed — 28
20. Jimmy Massey — 26
21. Marvin Panch — 22
22. Larry Frank — 11
    Jim Paschal — 11
24. Banjo Matthews — 9
25. Johnny Beauchamp — 1

MILES LED

1. Fireball Roberts — 918
2. Jack Smith — 786
3. Bobby Johns — 462
4. Richard Petty — 418
5. Lee Petty — 358
6. Junior Johnson — 307
7. Rex White — 296
8. Cotton Owens — 286
9. Joe Weatherly — 267
10. Buck Baker — 263
11. Tom Pistone — 161
12. Ned Jarrett — 143
13. Speedy Thompson — 139
14. Glen Wood — 133
15. Lloyd Dane — 125
16. Marvin Porter — 81
17. Curtis Turner — 74
18. Joe Lee Johnson — 72
    John Rostek — 72
20. Jim Reed — 56
21. Fred Lorenzen — 47
    Bob Welborn — 47
23. Scotty Cain — 27
24. Parnelli Jones — 25
25. Mel Larson — 24
26. Doug Yates — 20
27. Larry Frank — 17
28. Jimmy Thompson — 14
29. Jimmy Massey — 13
30. Marvin Panch — 11
    Frank Secrist — 11

MILES DRIVEN

1. Rex White — 6,916
2. Richard Petty — 6,015
3. Buck Baker — 5,854
4. Ned Jarrett — 5,479
5. Lee Petty — 5,389
6. Herman Beam — 4,730
7. L.D. Austin — 3,996
8. G.C. Spencer — 3,822
9. Bobby Johns — 3,815
10. Joe Weatherly — 3,804
11. Junior Johnson — 3,797
12. David Pearson — 3,768
13. Jimmy Pardue — 3,704
14. Tom Pistone — 3,699
15. Emanuel Zervakis — 3,457
16. Doug Yates — 3,262
17. Curtis Crider — 2,973
18. Banjo Matthews — 2,815
19. Jim Paschal — 2,713
20. Joe Lee Johnson — 2,651
21. Jack Smith — 2,570
22. Paul Lewis — 2,562
23. Bob Welborn — 2,533
24. Johnny Beauchamp — 2,530
25. Fred Lorenzen — 2,521
26. Johnny Allen — 2,501
27. Larry Frank — 2,408
28. Cotton Owens — 2,362
29. Marvin Panch — 2,322
30. Jimmy Thompson — 2,288

RACES LED

1. Ned Jarrett — 11
   Rex White — 11
3. Lee Petty — 10
   Jack Smith — 10
5. Fireball Roberts — 9
6. Junior Johnson — 7
   Cotton Owens — 7
8. Bobby Johns — 6
   Richard Petty — 6
   Joe Weatherly — 6
11. Buck Baker — 4
    Tom Pistone — 4
13. Speedy Thompson — 2
    Curtis Turner — 2
    Bob Welborn — 2
16. Johnny Beauchamp — 1
    Larry Frank — 1
    Joe Lee Johnson — 1
    Fred Lorenzen — 1
    Jimmy Massey — 1
    Banjo Matthews — 1
    Marvin Panch — 1
    Jim Paschal — 1
    Jim Reed — 1
    Doug Yates — 1

Driver	Starts	Poles	Finish 1	2	3	4	5	6–10	Laps	Laps Led	Races Led	Winston Cup Points	$
1961													
1. Ned Jarrett	46	4	1	4	8	4	6	11	9,813	606	9	27,272	41,056
2. Rex White	47	7	7	8	8	2	4	9	10,307	1,224	15	26,442	56,395
3. Emanuel Zervakis	38	1	2	1	3	5	8	9	9,198	386	2	22,312	27,281
4. Joe Weatherly	25	4	9	3	0	1	1	4	5,790	809	18	17,894	47,079
5. Fireball Roberts	22	6	2	4	2	2	3	1	5,075	1,002	13	17,600	50,267
6. Junior Johnson	41	10	7	3	2	3	1	6	7,016	2,373	23	17,178	28,541
7. Jack Smith	25	0	2	2	4	1	1	4	4,695	278	4	15,186	21,410
8. Richard Petty	42	2	2	4	4	5	3	5	7,866	703	7	14,984	25,239
9. Jim Paschal	23	1	2	4	1	2	3	4	5,464	209	4	13,922	18,100
10. Buck Baker	42	1	1	1	3	4	2	4	7,195	114	3	13,746	13,697
11. Jimmy Pardue	41	0	0	0	0	1	2	13	7,422	0	0	13,408	10,562
12. Johnny Allen	22	1	0	0	2	0	1	8	4,508	3	1	13,114	13,127
13. David Pearson	19	1	3	0	2	1	1	1	3,087	247	5	13,088	51,911
14. Bob Welborn	14	0	0	1	2	0	0	4	2,996	104	4	12,570	13,487
15. Herman Beam	41	0	0	0	0	1	0	13	8,827	0	0	11,382	9,392
16. Nelson Stacy	15	0	1	0	1	2	0	4	3,024	144	4	10,436	27,608
17. Ralph Earnhardt	8	0	0	1	1	0	0	3	1,664	90	3	10,182	11,473
18. Marvin Panch	9	1	1	1	0	1	0	3	1,517	129	2	9,392	30,478
19. Fred Lorenzen	15	4	3	1	0	1	1	0	2,567	781	10	9,316	30,395
20. G.C. Spencer	31	0	0	0	0	3	0	15	6,218	0	0	9,128	7,363
21. Curtis Crider	41	0	0	0	0	0	1	1	5,882	0	0	8,414	7,420
22. Cotton Owens	17	2	4	3	1	2	1	0	2,694	58	5	8,032	11,800
23. Tiny Lund	10	0	0	0	0	0	0	2	2,583	0	0	7,740	5,545
24. Bobby Johns	14	1	0	0	0	1	0	2	2,674	52	2	7,590	5,010
25. L.D. Austin	20	0	0	0	0	0	0	8	4,802	0	0	7,306	4,530
26. Tommy Irwin	26	0	0	2	0	1	0	5	3,748	166	1	7,300	7,170
27. Doug Yates	32	0	0	0	0	0	2	8	5,058	0	0	5,878	5,370
28. Paul Lewis	21	0	0	0	0	0	0	5	3,669	0	0	5,712	4,095
29. Bob Barron	31	0	0	0	0	0	0	5	5,005	0	0	5,412	3,825
30. Elmo Langley	15	0	0	0	0	0	1	4	2,826	0	0	5,376	3,530
31. Banjo Matthews	14	0	0	0	0	1	0	2	2,019	197	6	4,924	5,610
32. Wendell Scott	23	0	0	0	0	0	0	5	4,364	0	0	4,726	3,240
33. Jim Reed	8	0	0	2	0	0	1	1	1,735	32	1	4,705	3,350
34. Fred Harb	27	0	0	0	0	1	0	7	4,039	0	0	4,526	3,460
35. Darel Dieringer	7	0	0	0	0	0	1	1	1,008	0	0	4,416	3,150
36. Bob Burdick	5	0	1	0	0	1	0	1	1,086	44	2	4,382	18,750
37. Lee Reitzel	17	0	0	0	0	0	0	3	2,566	0	0	4,380	2,910
38. Tom Pistone	4	0	0	0	0	0	0	3	576	0	0	3,766	2,050
39. Buddy Baker	14	0	0	0	0	0	1	2	2,370	0	0	3,668	4,965
40. Roscoe Thompson	6	0	0	0	0	0	0	2	721	0	0	3,602	2,535
41. Woodie Wilson	5	0	0	0	0	0	0	1	828	0	0	3,580	2,625
42. Larry Frank	8	0	0	0	0	0	0	1	978	0	0	3,162	2,380
43. Larry Thomas	14	0	0	0	0	0	0	4	2,830	0	0	3,140	2,065
44. Harry Leake	15	0	0	0	0	0	0	7	3,295	0	0	3,092	2,000
45. Paul Goldsmith	2	0	0	0	1	0	0	1	239	0	0	2,930	6,050
46. Joe Lee Johnson	9	0	0	0	0	0	0	3	1,276	0	0	2,700	2,615
47. Bill Morgan	5	0	0	0	0	0	0	1	1,132	0	0	2,430	1,900
48. T.C. Hunt	7	0	0	0	0	0	0	0	940	0	0	2,430	2,750
49. Marvin Porter	8	0	0	0	0	0	1	0	1,096	0	0	2,326	2,070
50. Joe Eubanks	2	0	0	0	0	0	0	0	448	0	0	2,320	1,475

LAPS COMPLETED		LAPS LED		MILES LED		MILES DRIVEN		RACES LED	
1. Rex White	10,307	1. Junior Johnson	2,373	1. Fireball Roberts	1,650	1. Rex White	7,542	1. Junior Johnson	23
2. Ned Jarrett	9,813	2. Rex White	1,224	2. Junior Johnson	1,277	2. Ned Jarrett	7,184	2. Joe Weatherly	18
3. Emanuel Zervakis	9,198	3. Fireball Roberts	1,002	3. Fred Lorenzen	699	3. Emanuel Zervakis	6,664	3. Rex White	15
4. Herman Beam	8,827	4. Joe Weatherly	809	4. Rex White	627	4. Herman Beam	6,403	4. Fireball Roberts	13
5. Richard Petty	7,866	5. Fred Lorenzen	781	5. Joe Weatherly	547	5. Jimmy Pardue	5,628	5. Fred Lorenzen	10
6. Jimmy Pardue	7,422	6. Richard Petty	703	6. Richard Petty	456	6. Richard Petty	5,392	6. Ned Jarrett	9
7. Buck Baker	7,195	7. Ned Jarrett	606	7. Banjo Matthews	413	7. Joe Weatherly	5,329	7. Richard Petty	7
8. Junior Johnson	7,016	8. Emanuel Zervakis	386	8. David Pearson	381	8. Junior Johnson	5,228	8. Banjo Matthews	6
9. G.C. Spencer	6,218	9. Jack Smith	278	9. Ned Jarrett	317	9. Buck Baker	5,226	9. Cotton Owens	5
10. Curtis Crider	5,882	10. David Pearson	247	10. Nelson Stacy	214	10. Fireball Roberts	5,033	David Pearson	5
11. Joe Weatherly	5,790	11. Jim Paschal	209	11. Marvin Panch	207	11. Johnny Allen	4,493	11. Jim Paschal	4
12. Jim Paschal	5,464	12. Banjo Matthews	197	12. Curtis Turner	203	12. Curtis Crider	4,186	Jack Smith	4
13. Fireball Roberts	5,075	13. Tommy Irwin	166	13. Jack Smith	144	13. Jack Smith	4,098	Nelson Stacy	4
14. Doug Yates	5,058	14. Nelson Stacy	144	14. Ralph Earnhardt	134	14. G.C. Spencer	3,823	Bob Welborn	4
15. Bob Barron	5,005	15. Marvin Panch	129	15. Bob Welborn	129	15. Jim Paschal	3,665	15. Buck Baker	3
16. L.D. Austin	4,802	16. Buck Baker	114	16. Jim Paschal	117	16. David Pearson	3,449	Ralph Earnhardt	3
17. Jack Smith	4,695	17. Bob Welborn	104	17. Emanuel Zervakis	103	17. Bob Welborn	3,424	17. Bob Burdick	2
18. Johnny Allen	4,508	18. Ralph Earnhardt	90	18. Tommy Irwin	83	18. L.D. Austin	3,402	Bobby Johns	2
19. Wendell Scott	4,364	19. Cotton Owens	58	19. Eddie Gray	76	19. Nelson Stacy	3,281	Marvin Panch	2
20. Fred Harb	4,039	20. Bobby Johns	52	20. Bob Burdick	66	20. Tommy Irwin	3,235	Emanuel Zervakis	2
21. Tommy Irwin	3,748	21. Bob Burdick	44	21. Lee Petty	63	21. Bobby Johns	3,084	21. Johnny Allen	1
22. Paul Lewis	3,669	22. Jim Reed	32	22. Buck Baker	57	22. Elmo Langley	3,012	Tommy Irwin	1
23. Harry Leake	3,295	23. Johnny Allen	3	23. Cotton Owens	37	23. Banjo Matthews	3,010	Jim Reed	1
24. David Pearson	3,087			24. Glen Wood	35	24. Doug Yates	2,992		
25. Nelson Stacy	3,024			25. Bobby Johns	32	25. Bob Barron	2,870		
26. Bob Welborn	2,996			26. Bill Amick	25	26. Fred Lorenzen	2,815		
27. Larry Thomas	2,830			27. Jim Reed	8	27. Paul Lewis	2,803		
28. Elmo Langley	2,826			28. Johnny Allen	4	28. Tiny Lund	2,756		
29. Cotton Owens	2,694			29. Lloyd Dane	3	29. Marvin Panch	2,576		
30. Bobby Johns	2,674					30. Ralph Earnhardt	2,522		
31. Tiny Lund	2,583								
32. Fred Lorenzen	2,567								
33. Lee Reitzel	2,566								
34. Buddy Baker	2,370								
35. Banjo Matthews	2,019								
36. Jim Reed	1,735								
37. Ralph Earnhardt	1,664								
38. Marvin Panch	1,517								
39. Joe Lee Johnson	1,276								
40. Bill Morgan	1,132								
41. Marvin Porter	1,096								
42. Bob Burdick	1,086								
43. Darel Dieringer	1,008								
44. Larry Frank	978								
45. T.C. Hunt	940								
46. Woodie Wilson	828								
47. Roscoe Thompson	721								
48. Tom Pistone	576								
49. Joe Eubanks	448								
50. Paul Goldsmith	239								

Driver	Starts	Poles	Finish						Laps	Laps Led	Races Led	Winston Cup Points	$
			1	2	3	4	5	6–10					

1962

	Driver	Starts	Poles	1	2	3	4	5	6–10	Laps	Laps Led	Races Led	Winston Cup Points	$
1.	Joe Weatherly	52	7	9	12	10	3	5	6	12,431	1,014	17	30,836	70,743
2.	Richard Petty	52	5	8	9	8	5	2	7	11,550	1,396	19	28,440	60,764
3.	Ned Jarrett	52	4	6	2	3	3	5	16	10,998	866	11	25,336	43,444
4.	Jack Smith	51	7	5	6	5	8	3	8	10,781	894	9	22,870	34,748
5.	Rex White	37	9	8	3	3	1	3	5	7,683	1,129	15	19,424	36,246
6.	Jim Paschal	39	0	4	4	3	3	3	7	8,311	856	9	18,128	27,348
7.	Fred Lorenzen	19	3	2	2	4	1	2	1	4,435	471	9	17,554	46,100
8.	Fireball Roberts	19	9	3	3	0	2	1	3	4,312	960	12	16,380	66,152
9.	Marvin Panch	17	0	0	2	3	0	0	3	3,642	172	4	15,138	26,746
10.	David Pearson	12	0	0	0	0	1	0	6	2,690	280	4	14,404	19,032
11.	Herman Beam	51	1	0	0	0	0	0	18	11,217	0	0	13,650	12,571
12.	Curtis Crider	52	0	0	0	1	1	1	15	10,051	0	0	13,050	12,016
13.	Buck Baker	37	0	0	1	3	2	0	8	6,607	18	2	12,838	12,787
14.	Larry Frank	19	0	1	0	0	0	1	6	3,566	85	1	12,814	32,987
15.	Bob Welborn	25	0	0	1	0	2	2	7	5,654	0	0	12,368	10,347
16.	George Green	46	0	0	0	0	0	1	14	9,279	0	0	12,132	9,221
17.	Larry Thomas	37	0	0	0	0	2	1	9	7,268	0	0	11,946	9,486
18.	Thomas Cox	42	0	0	0	0	1	2	17	8,370	0	0	11,688	10,181
19.	Jimmy Pardue	29	0	1	1	1	1	1	11	7,274	200	3	11,414	12,066
20.	Junior Johnson	23	2	1	2	2	1	1	1	3,663	648	11	11,140	34,841
21.	Nelson Stacy	15	0	3	1	0	0	1	2	3,484	371	4	10,934	43,080
22.	Wendell Scott	41	1	0	0	2	1	1	15	8,542	0	0	9,906	7,133
23.	Buddy Baker	31	0	0	0	1	2	2	5	5,454	0	0	9,828	7,578
24.	G.C. Spencer	42	0	0	0	0	2	4	7	7,300	0	0	9,788	7,995
25.	Bunkie Blackburn	10	0	0	0	0	1	0	2	2,325	0	0	8,016	5,890
26.	Johnny Allen	20	1	1	0	0	3	1	3	4,094	288	4	7,602	7,230
27.	Emanuel Zervakis	11	0	0	0	0	0	0	2	2,151	5	1	6,406	4,545
28.	Bobby Johns	13	0	1	0	1	0	0	1	2,725	614	8	5,670	15,863
29.	Ralph Earnhardt	17	0	0	0	1	0	1	4	2,022	0	0	5,472	4,545
30.	Cotton Owens	16	1	0	2	2	2	1	1	2,000	36	2	4,984	5,905
31.	Banjo Matthews	5	2	0	1	0	0	0	1	523	145	3	4,956	11,375
32.	Sherman Utsman	12	0	0	0	0	0	1	3	3,293	0	0	4,896	3,580
33.	Darel Dieringer	14	1	0	0	0	0	1	2	3,179	17	1	4,548	4,880
34.	Tiny Lund	10	0	0	0	0	0	0	0	2,487	8	1	4,384	2,880
35.	Stick Elliott	21	0	0	0	0	0	0	2	3,027	0	0	4,254	3,928
36.	LeeRoy Yarbrough	12	0	0	0	0	0	1	0	1,478	0	0	4,240	3,485
37.	Tommy Irwin	20	0	0	1	0	1	0	7	2,982	10	1	3,980	3,305
38.	Ed Livingston	13	0	0	0	0	0	0	0	1,758	0	0	3,604	2,940
39.	Fred Harb	21	0	0	0	0	0	0	3	2,763	0	0	3,430	2,220
40.	Elmo Langley	6	0	0	0	0	0	0	0	774	0	0	2,556	1,795
41.	Bill Morton	5	0	0	0	0	0	0	2	1,359	0	0	2,522	1,350
42.	Speedy Thompson	3	0	0	0	0	0	0	1	443	0	0	2,522	1,400
43.	Jimmy Thompson	3	0	0	0	0	0	0	0	847	0	0	2,346	1,650
44.	Red Foote	4	0	0	0	0	0	0	0	939	0	0	2,274	1,600
45.	Ernie Gahan	3	0	0	0	0	0	0	1	284	0	0	2,092	725
46.	Billy Wade	4	0	0	0	0	0	0	2	1,054	0	0	2,008	1,350
47.	Jim Cushman	4	0	0	0	0	0	0	1	782	0	0	1,954	850
48.	Bill Wimble	2	0	0	0	0	0	0	0	231	0	0	1,944	675
49.	Troy Ruttman	1	0	0	0	0	0	1	0	218	0	0	1,890	1,750
50.	Cale Yarborough	8	0	0	0	0	0	0	1	727	0	0	1,884	2,725

LAPS COMPLETED

1.	Joe Weatherly	12,431
2.	Richard Petty	11,550
3.	Herman Beam	11,217
4.	Ned Jarrett	10,998
5.	Jack Smith	10,781
6.	Curtis Crider	10,051
7.	George Green	9,279
8.	Wendell Scott	8,542
9.	Thomas Cox	8,370
10.	Jim Paschal	8,311
11.	Rex White	7,683
12.	G.C. Spencer	7,300
13.	Jimmy Pardue	7,274
14.	Larry Thomas	7,268
15.	Buck Baker	6,607
16.	Bob Welborn	5,654
17.	Buddy Baker	5,454
18.	Fred Lorenzen	4,435
19.	Fireball Roberts	4,312
20.	Johnny Allen	4,094
21.	Junior Johnson	3,663
22.	Marvin Panch	3,642
23.	Larry Frank	3,566
24.	Nelson Stacy	3,484
25.	Sherman Utsman	3,293
26.	Darel Dieringer	3,179
27.	Stick Elliott	3,027
28.	Tommy Irwin	2,982
29.	Fred Harb	2,763
30.	Bobby Johns	2,725
31.	David Pearson	2,690
32.	Tiny Lund	2,487
33.	Bunkie Blackburn	2,325
34.	Emanuel Zervakis	2,151
35.	Ralph Earnhardt	2,022
36.	Cotton Owens	2,000
37.	Ed Livingston	1,758
38.	LeeRoy Yarbrough	1,478
39.	Bill Morton	1,359
40.	Billy Wade	1,054
41.	Red Foote	939
42.	Jimmy Thompson	847
43.	Jim Cushman	782
44.	Elmo Langley	774
45.	Cale Yarborough	727
46.	Banjo Matthews	523
47.	Speedy Thompson	443
48.	Ernie Gahan	284
49.	Bill Wimble	231
50.	Troy Ruttman	218

LAPS LED

1.	Richard Petty	1,396
2.	Rex White	1,129
3.	Joe Weatherly	1,014
4.	Fireball Roberts	960
5.	Jack Smith	894
6.	Ned Jarrett	866
7.	Jim Paschal	856
8.	Junior Johnson	648
9.	Bobby Johns	614
10.	Fred Lorenzen	471
11.	Nelson Stacy	371
12.	Johnny Allen	288
13.	David Pearson	280
14.	Jimmy Pardue	200
15.	Marvin Panch	172
16.	Banjo Matthews	145
17.	Larry Frank	85
18.	Cotton Owens	36
19.	Buck Baker	18
20.	Darel Dieringer	17
21.	Tommy Irwin	10
22.	Tiny Lund	8
23.	Emanuel Zervakis	5

MILES LED

1.	Fireball Roberts	1,130
2.	Richard Petty	804
3.	Joe Weatherly	642
4.	Junior Johnson	621
5.	Bobby Johns	501
6.	Rex White	447
7.	Jim Paschal	434
8.	David Pearson	413
9.	Fred Lorenzen	388
10.	Ned Jarrett	374
11.	Jack Smith	352
12.	Banjo Matthews	290
13.	Marvin Panch	235
14.	Nelson Stacy	212
15.	Jimmy Pardue	205
16.	Larry Frank	117
17.	Johnny Allen	104
18.	Darel Dieringer	23
19.	Cotton Owens	20
20.	Tiny Lund	12
21.	Buck Baker	9
22.	Emanuel Zervakis	8
23.	Tommy Irwin	5

MILES DRIVEN

1.	Joe Weatherly	8,001
2.	Richard Petty	7,561
3.	Herman Beam	7,140
4.	Jack Smith	7,110
5.	Ned Jarrett	7,064
6.	Curtis Crider	6,431
7.	George Green	5,896
8.	Jim Paschal	5,868
9.	Rex White	5,760
10.	Buck Baker	5,002
11.	Thomas Cox	4,990
12.	Larry Thomas	4,889
13.	Jimmy Pardue	4,855
14.	G.C. Spencer	4,791
15.	Bob Welborn	4,558
16.	Fred Lorenzen	4,372
17.	Wendell Scott	4,211
18.	Buddy Baker	4,139
19.	Fireball Roberts	4,068
20.	Marvin Panch	3,758
21.	David Pearson	3,552
22.	Larry Frank	3,506
23.	Johnny Allen	3,401
24.	Junior Johnson	3,224
25.	Nelson Stacy	3,171
26.	Darel Dieringer	2,986
27.	Bobby Johns	2,946
28.	Bunkie Blackburn	2,705
29.	Tiny Lund	2,580
30.	Emanuel Zervakis	2,357

RACES LED

1.	Richard Petty	19
2.	Joe Weatherly	17
3.	Rex White	15
4.	Fireball Roberts	12
5.	Ned Jarrett	11
	Junior Johnson	11
7.	Fred Lorenzen	9
	Jim Paschal	9
	Jack Smith	9
10.	Bobby Johns	8
11.	Johnny Allen	4
	Marvin Panch	4
	David Pearson	4
	Nelson Stacy	4
15.	Banjo Matthews	3
	Jimmy Pardue	3
17.	Buck Baker	2
	Cotton Owens	2
19.	Darel Dieringer	1
	Larry Frank	1
	Tommy Irwin	1
	Tiny Lund	1
	Emanuel Zervakis	1

Driver	Starts	Poles	Finish						Laps	Laps Led	Races Led	Winston Cup Points	$
			1	2	3	4	5	6–10					

1963

	Driver	Starts	Poles	1	2	3	4	5	6–10	Laps	Laps Led	Races Led	Winston Cup Points	$
1.	Joe Weatherly	53	6	3	5	5	5	2	15	11,343	878	12	33,398	74,624
2.	Richard Petty	54	8	14	9	2	4	1	9	12,183	2,316	29	31,170	55,964
3.	Fred Lorenzen	29	9	6	8	3	0	4	2	7,484	2,419	20	29,684	122,588
4.	Ned Jarrett	53	5	8	7	5	7	5	7	11,845	1,897	18	27,214	45,844
5.	Fireball Roberts	20	2	4	2	0	4	1	3	4,643	692	12	22,642	73,060
6.	Jimmy Pardue	46	1	1	0	1	3	1	11	9,719	74	3	22,228	20,359
7.	Darel Dieringer	20	0	1	0	1	3	2	8	5,513	84	3	21,418	29,725
8.	David Pearson	41	2	0	3	2	5	3	6	8,697	178	6	21,156	24,986
9.	Rex White	25	3	0	3	2	0	0	9	5,595	171	6	20,976	27,241
10.	Tiny Lund	22	0	1	1	1	1	2	6	5,093	127	5	19,624	49,397
11.	Buck Baker	47	0	1	3	6	2	5	13	9,505	63	2	18,114	18,616
12.	Junior Johnson	33	9	7	2	2	0	2	1	5,753	2,396	21	17,720	67,351
13.	Marvin Panch	12	3	1	2	5	1	0	3	3,510	291	6	17,156	39,102
14.	Nelson Stacy	12	0	0	0	1	2	1	5	2,816	76	2	14,974	18,266
15.	Wendell Scott	47	0	0	0	0	0	1	14	9,459	0	0	14,814	10,966
16.	Billy Wade	31	0	0	1	0	2	1	10	6,008	21	2	14,646	15,204
17.	Curtis Crider	49	0	0	0	1	0	1	13	8,859	0	0	13,996	11,644
18.	G.C. Spencer	31	0	0	1	1	1	1	8	4,888	30	3	13,744	13,514
19.	Jim Paschal	32	1	5	3	5	2	0	3	6,917	400	12	13,456	20,979
20.	Bobby Isaac	27	0	0	0	1	0	2	4	4,989	30	1	12,858	9,529
21.	Bobby Johns	12	0	0	0	1	0	2	3	2,433	84	3	12,652	15,915
22.	Larry Thomas	32	0	0	0	2	1	3	7	6,991	0	0	11,010	8,945
23.	Stick Elliott	29	0	0	0	0	0	0	7	4,703	0	0	9,582	6,285
24.	Jack Smith	28	2	0	0	0	1	3	7	5,290	25	2	8,218	8,645
25.	Cale Yarborough	18	0	0	0	0	0	3	4	4,519	0	0	8,062	5,550
26.	LeeRoy Yarbrough	14	1	0	0	0	0	1	4	2,564	8	1	7,872	6,680
27.	Herman Beam	25	0	0	0	0	0	0	6	5,061	0	0	7,742	5,255
28.	Larry Frank	11	0	0	0	1	1	0	0	2,392	5	1	7,582	5,450
29.	Larry Manning	22	0	0	0	0	1	0	8	5,060	0	0	6,952	5,405
30.	Ed Livingston	20	0	0	0	0	0	0	1	3,294	0	0	6,818	4,930
31.	Neil Castles	28	0	0	0	0	1	1	6	4,093	0	0	5,928	5,165
32.	Tommy Irwin	7	0	0	0	1	0	1	3	1,528	0	0	5,176	2,655
33.	Reb Wickersham	14	0	0	0	0	0	0	1	3,501	0	0	4,812	3,800
34.	Worth McMillion	15	0	0	0	0	0	0	4	4,177	0	0	4,614	3,145
35.	Bob James	10	0	0	0	0	0	0	0	1,414	0	0	4,316	3,375
36.	Roy Mayne	20	0	0	0	0	0	1	3	3,857	0	0	4,188	3,490
37.	Bob Cooper	9	0	0	0	0	0	0	1	1,559	0	0	4,164	3,115
38.	Jimmy Massey	10	0	0	0	0	1	0	5	1,904	0	0	4,016	2,870
39.	Elmo Langley	12	0	0	0	0	0	1	1	2,294	0	0	3,982	2,170
40.	Bob Welborn	11	0	0	1	2	1	0	0	2,221	0	0	3,484	4,830
41.	Fred Harb	16	0	0	1	0	1	0	5	2,563	0	0	3,286	2,720
42.	Dave MacDonald	2	0	0	1	0	0	0	0	323	92	1	2,944	5,330
43.	Major Melton	17	0	0	0	0	0	0	0	2,780	0	0	2,806	1,910
44.	Sal Tovella	3	0	0	0	0	0	0	0	346	0	0	2,570	1,300
45.	Ron Hornaday	2	0	0	0	0	0	0	1	316	0	0	2,520	1,600
46.	J.D. McDuffie	12	0	0	0	0	0	0	3	1,918	0	0	2,498	1,620
47.	Bob Perry	5	0	0	0	0	0	0	0	668	0	0	2,478	1,550
48.	Bunkie Blackburn	7	0	0	0	0	0	0	1	909	0	0	2,454	2,525
49.	Bill Foster	10	0	0	0	0	0	0	2	1,628	0	0	2,168	1,410
50.	Bud Harless	5	0	0	0	0	0	0	1	1,508	0	0	2,156	1,550

LAPS COMPLETED

1.	Richard Petty	12,183
2.	Ned Jarrett	11,845
3.	Joe Weatherly	11,343
4.	Jimmy Pardue	9,719
5.	Buck Baker	9,505
6.	Wendell Scott	9,459
7.	Curtis Crider	8,859
8.	David Pearson	8,697
9.	Fred Lorenzen	7,484
10.	Larry Thomas	6,991
11.	Jim Paschal	6,917
12.	Billy Wade	6,008
13.	Junior Johnson	5,753
14.	Rex White	5,595
15.	Darel Dieringer	5,513
16.	Jack Smith	5,290
17.	Tiny Lund	5,093
18.	Herman Beam	5,061
19.	Larry Manning	5,060
20.	Bobby Isaac	4,989
21.	G.C. Spencer	4,888
22.	Stick Elliott	4,703
23.	Fireball Roberts	4,643
24.	Cale Yarborough	4,519
25.	Worth McMillion	4,177
26.	Neil Castles	4,093
27.	Roy Mayne	3,857
28.	Marvin Panch	3,510
29.	Reb Wickersham	3,501
30.	Ed Livingston	3,294
31.	Nelson Stacy	2,816
32.	Major Melton	2,780
33.	LeeRoy Yarbrough	2,564
34.	Fred Harb	2,563
35.	Bobby Johns	2,433
36.	Larry Frank	2,392
37.	Elmo Langley	2,294
38.	Bob Welborn	2,221
39.	J.D. McDuffie	1,918
40.	Jimmy Massey	1,904
41.	Bill Foster	1,628
42.	Bob Cooper	1,559
43.	Tommy Irwin	1,528
44.	Bud Harless	1,508
45.	Bob James	1,414
46.	Bunkie Blackburn	909
47.	Bob Perry	668
48.	Sal Tovella	346
49.	Dave MacDonald	323
50.	Ron Hornaday	316

LAPS LED

1.	Fred Lorenzen	2,419
2.	Junior Johnson	2,396
3.	Richard Petty	2,316
4.	Ned Jarrett	1,897
5.	Joe Weatherly	878
6.	Fireball Roberts	692
7.	Jim Paschal	400
8.	Marvin Panch	291
9.	David Pearson	178
10.	Rex White	171
11.	Tiny Lund	127
12.	Dave MacDonald	92
13.	Darel Dieringer	84
	Bobby Johns	84
15.	Nelson Stacy	76
16.	Jimmy Pardue	74
17.	Buck Baker	63
18.	Bobby Isaac	30
	G.C. Spencer	30
20.	Jack Smith	25
21.	Billy Wade	21
22.	LeeRoy Yarbrough	8
23.	Larry Frank	5

MILES LED

1.	Junior Johnson	2,208
2.	Fred Lorenzen	1,540
3.	Richard Petty	1,201
4.	Ned Jarrett	785
5.	Fireball Roberts	621
6.	Joe Weatherly	530
7.	Dan Gurney	324
8.	Marvin Panch	312
9.	Dave MacDonald	248
10.	Jim Paschal	210
11.	Darel Dieringer	168
12.	Bobby Johns	148
13.	Rex White	138
14.	Parnelli Jones	105
	Tiny Lund	105
16.	A.J. Foyt	104
17.	David Pearson	84
18.	Glen Wood	67
19.	Nelson Stacy	65
20.	G.C. Spencer	57
21.	Paul Goldsmith	48
22.	Buck Baker	32
23.	Billy Wade	27
24.	Jimmy Pardue	19
25.	Bobby Isaac	15
	Johnny Rutherford	15
27.	Larry Frank	13
28.	Jack Smith	12
29.	LeeRoy Yarbrough	4

MILES DRIVEN

1.	Joe Weatherly	8,407
2.	Ned Jarrett	7,938
3.	Richard Petty	7,873
4.	Jimmy Pardue	7,295
5.	David Pearson	6,503
6.	Fred Lorenzen	6,472
7.	Wendell Scott	6,165
8.	Buck Baker	5,702
9.	Rex White	5,490
10.	Fireball Roberts	5,470
11.	Darel Dieringer	5,432
12.	Curtis Crider	5,402
13.	Billy Wade	4,989
14.	Tiny Lund	4,881
15.	Junior Johnson	4,789
16.	Jim Paschal	4,594
17.	Bobby Isaac	4,299
18.	Larry Thomas	4,209
19.	G.C. Spencer	4,004
20.	Stick Elliott	3,771
21.	Marvin Panch	3,742
22.	Jack Smith	3,620
23.	Herman Beam	3,476
24.	Bobby Johns	3,383
25.	Cale Yarborough	3,298
26.	Ed Livingston	3,196
27.	Nelson Stacy	3,179
28.	Larry Manning	2,931
29.	Larry Frank	2,735
30.	Reb Wickersham	2,577

RACES LED

1.	Richard Petty	29
2.	Junior Johnson	21
3.	Fred Lorenzen	20
4.	Ned Jarrett	18
5.	Jim Paschal	12
	Fireball Roberts	12
	Joe Weatherly	12
8.	Marvin Panch	6
	David Pearson	6
	Rex White	6
11.	Tiny Lund	5
12.	Darel Dieringer	3
	Bobby Johns	3
	Jimmy Pardue	3
	G.C. Spencer	3
16.	Buck Baker	2
	Jack Smith	2
	Nelson Stacy	2
	Billy Wade	2
20.	Larry Frank	1
	Bobby Isaac	1
	Dave MacDonald	1
	LeeRoy Yarbrough	1

Driver	Starts	Poles	Finish 1	2	3	4	5	6–10	Laps	Laps Led	Races Led	Winston Cup Points	$

1964

	Driver	Starts	Poles	1	2	3	4	5	6–10	Laps	Laps Led	Races Led	Winston Cup Points	$
1.	Richard Petty	61	9	9	14	12	0	2	6	14,041	3,534	33	40,252	114,772
2.	Ned Jarrett	60	9	15	7	5	7	6	5	13,325	3,304	30	34,950	71,925
3.	David Pearson	61	12	8	8	4	7	2	13	13,225	2,256	31	32,146	45,542
4.	Billy Wade	36	5	4	0	4	3	1	13	7,627	954	14	28,474	36,095
5.	Jimmy Pardue	50	2	0	2	4	4	4	10	9,412	237	5	26,570	41,598
6.	Curtis Crider	59	0	0	0	1	1	5	23	11,443	0	0	25,606	22,171
7.	Jim Paschal	22	0	1	3	1	2	3	5	6,030	155	4	25,450	60,116
8.	Larry Thomas	43	0	0	1	3	2	3	18	10,025	0	0	22,950	21,226
9.	Buck Baker	35	0	2	3	3	3	4	3	7,263	159	5	22,366	43,781
10.	Marvin Panch	31	4	3	7	3	4	1	3	6,499	648	10	21,480	34,836
11.	Darel Dieringer	27	1	1	0	1	2	2	7	5,662	238	5	19,972	20,685
12.	Wendell Scott	56	0	1	0	0	6	1	17	10,752	27	1	19,574	16,495
13.	Fred Lorenzen	16	7	8	1	0	1	0	0	4,426	2,375	11	18,098	73,860
14.	Junior Johnson	29	5	3	2	4	3	0	3	6,298	1,116	15	17,066	26,975
15.	LeeRoy Yarbrough	34	0	2	3	2	3	1	4	5,896	200	5	16,172	16,630
16.	Roy Tyner	46	0	0	0	0	0	0	17	7,327	0	0	13,922	11,488
17.	Neil Castles	58	0	0	0	0	0	1	23	8,336	0	0	13,372	14,318
18.	Bobby Isaac	19	0	1	3	0	1	0	2	3,163	134	6	13,252	26,733
19.	Cale Yarborough	24	0	0	0	0	0	2	7	4,990	10	1	12,618	10,378
20.	Tiny Lund	22	0	0	0	2	0	1	6	3,551	14	1	12,598	9,913
21.	Doug Cooper	39	0	0	0	1	2	1	7	5,549	0	0	11,942	10,445
22.	Paul Goldsmith	14	2	0	0	3	0	0	1	2,281	319	8	11,700	20,835
23.	J.T. Putney	17	0	0	0	1	0	0	5	4,226	0	0	10,744	7,295
24.	Larry Frank	12	0	0	0	0	0	0	3	1,483	0	0	10,314	7,830
25.	Jack Anderson	31	0	0	0	0	1	0	3	4,402	0	0	10,040	8,510
26.	G.C. Spencer	20	0	0	0	1	0	3	2	3,601	0	0	10,012	9,490
27.	Fireball Roberts	10	0	1	2	1	0	1	1	1,702	17	2	9,900	28,345
28.	Rex White	6	0	0	0	1	0	1	1	1,444	27	1	8,222	12,310
29.	Dave MacDonald	5	0	0	1	0	0	0	2	661	0	0	7,650	9,195
30.	Worth McMillion	18	0	0	0	0	0	0	6	4,681	0	0	7,586	4,710
31.	Buddy Baker	33	0	0	0	1	1	1	4	3,239	0	0	7,314	8,460
32.	Bunkie Blackburn	14	0	0	0	0	1	0	3	2,295	0	0	7,264	6,630
33.	Bill McMahan	20	0	0	0	0	0	1	3	4,134	0	0	7,240	7,205
34.	Buddy Arrington	28	0	0	0	0	0	2	7	5,172	0	0	6,364	4,715
35.	Earl Balmer	10	0	0	0	0	1	1	2	2,771	1	1	6,170	5,795
36.	Bob Derrington	18	0	0	0	0	0	0	2	1,897	1	1	5,896	2,755
37.	Bobby Johns	12	0	0	0	0	0	0	2	1,806	0	0	5,436	5,700
38.	E.J. Trivette	26	0	0	0	0	0	0	3	2,969	0	0	5,118	5,495
39.	Doug Moore	24	0	0	0	0	0	0	6	3,894	0	0	4,970	5,175
40.	Ken Spikes	6	0	0	0	0	0	0	1	1,018	0	0	4,934	3,100
41.	Earl Brooks	28	0	0	0	0	0	0	8	3,988	0	0	4,820	3,825
42.	Elmo Langley	14	0	0	0	0	0	0	5	2,739	0	0	4,400	3,905
43.	Roy Mayne	14	0	0	0	0	0	1	1	2,207	0	0	4,278	4,705
44.	Gene Hobby	18	0	0	0	0	0	0	3	4,013	0	0	4,054	2,795
45.	Doug Yates	16	1	0	1	0	0	2	4	2,573	9	1	3,778	3,340
46.	Ralph Earnhardt	11	0	0	0	0	1	0	0	1,107	0	0	3,720	3,290
47.	Bob Cooper	14	0	0	0	0	0	0	1	783	0	0	3,602	3,360
48.	Joe Weatherly	5	0	0	1	0	1	0	1	768	84	1	3,132	5,290
49.	Sam McQuagg	5	0	0	0	0	0	0	0	653	0	0	2,928	1,700
50.	Bobby Keck	10	0	0	0	0	1	1	3	2,137	0	0	2,754	2,850

LAPS COMPLETED

1. Richard Petty — 14,041
2. Ned Jarrett — 13,325
3. David Pearson — 13,225
4. Curtis Crider — 11,443
5. Wendell Scott — 10,752
6. Larry Thomas — 10,025
7. Jimmy Pardue — 9,412
8. Neil Castles — 8,336
9. Billy Wade — 7,627
10. Roy Tyner — 7,327
11. Buck Baker — 7,263
12. Marvin Panch — 6,499
13. Junior Johnson — 6,298
14. Jim Paschal — 6,030
15. LeeRoy Yarbrough — 5,896
16. Darel Dieringer — 5,662
17. Doug Cooper — 5,549
18. Buddy Arrington — 5,172
19. Cale Yarborough — 4,990
20. Worth McMillion — 4,681
21. Fred Lorenzen — 4,426
22. Jack Anderson — 4,402
23. J.T. Putney — 4,226
24. Bill McMahan — 4,134
25. Gene Hobby — 4,013
26. Earl Brooks — 3,988
27. Doug Moore — 3,894
28. G.C. Spencer — 3,601
29. Tiny Lund — 3,551
30. Buddy Baker — 3,239
31. Bobby Isaac — 3,163
32. E.J. Trivette — 2,969
33. Earl Balmer — 2,771
34. Elmo Langley — 2,739
35. Doug Yates — 2,573
36. Bunkie Blackburn — 2,295
37. Paul Goldsmith — 2,281
38. Roy Mayne — 2,207
39. Bobby Keck — 2,137
40. Bob Derrington — 1,897
41. Bobby Johns — 1,806
42. Fireball Roberts — 1,702
43. Larry Frank — 1,483
44. Rex White — 1,444
45. Ralph Earnhardt — 1,107
46. Ken Spikes — 1,018
47. Bob Cooper — 783
48. Joe Weatherly — 768
49. Dave MacDonald — 661
50. Sam McQuagg — 653

LAPS LED

1. Richard Petty — 3,534
2. Ned Jarrett — 3,304
3. Fred Lorenzen — 2,375
4. David Pearson — 2,256
5. Junior Johnson — 1,116
6. Billy Wade — 954
7. Marvin Panch — 648
8. Paul Goldsmith — 319
9. Darel Dieringer — 238
10. Jimmy Pardue — 237
11. LeeRoy Yarbrough — 200
12. Buck Baker — 159
13. Jim Paschal — 155
14. Bobby Isaac — 134
15. Joe Weatherly — 84
16. Wendell Scott — 27
    Rex White — 27
18. Fireball Roberts — 17
19. Tiny Lund — 14
20. Cale Yarborough — 10
21. Doug Yates — 9
22. Earl Balmer — 1
    Bob Derrington — 1

MILES LED

1. Richard Petty — 3,063
2. Fred Lorenzen — 1,651
3. Ned Jarrett — 1,467
4. David Pearson — 1,177
5. Billy Wade — 543
6. Junior Johnson — 509
7. Paul Goldsmith — 495
8. Marvin Panch — 397
9. Dan Gurney — 383
10. Bobby Isaac — 248
11. Jim Paschal — 229
12. Buck Baker — 203
13. Jimmy Pardue — 200
14. Darel Dieringer — 139
15. LeeRoy Yarbrough — 108
16. Bob Welborn — 63
17. Fireball Roberts — 47
18. Joe Weatherly — 42
19. Rex White — 41
20. A.J. Foyt — 40
21. Dick Hutcherson — 38
22. Cotton Owens — 27
23. Parnelli Jones — 24
24. Wendell Scott — 14
25. Jack Smith — 10
26. Tiny Lund — 7
27. Cale Yarborough — 5
    Doug Yates — 5
29. Earl Balmer — 3
    Bob Derrington — 3
    Jim Hurtubise — 3
32. Glen Wood — 1

MILES DRIVEN

1. Richard Petty — 9,480
2. David Pearson — 8,907
3. Ned Jarrett — 8,785
4. Curtis Crider — 7,872
5. Larry Thomas — 6,957
6. Billy Wade — 6,724
7. Jimmy Pardue — 6,613
8. Wendell Scott — 6,466
9. Buck Baker — 6,080
10. Jim Paschal — 5,531
11. Darel Dieringer — 5,364
12. Marvin Panch — 5,031
13. Roy Tyner — 4,641
14. LeeRoy Yarbrough — 4,477
15. Junior Johnson — 4,474
16. Fred Lorenzen — 4,181
17. Neil Castles — 4,158
18. Cale Yarborough — 4,121
19. Doug Cooper — 3,863
20. Tiny Lund — 3,662
21. J.T. Putney — 3,370
22. Jack Anderson — 3,365
23. Bobby Isaac — 3,360
24. Paul Goldsmith — 2,903
25. Bill McMahan — 2,897
26. G.C. Spencer — 2,803
27. Worth McMillion — 2,756
28. Buddy Arrington — 2,504
29. Larry Frank — 2,366
30. Bunkie Blackburn — 2,329

RACES LED

1. Richard Petty — 33
2. David Pearson — 31
3. Ned Jarrett — 30
4. Junior Johnson — 15
5. Billy Wade — 14
6. Fred Lorenzen — 11
7. Marvin Panch — 10
8. Paul Goldsmith — 8
9. Bobby Isaac — 6
10. Buck Baker — 5
    Darel Dieringer — 5
    Jimmy Pardue — 5
    LeeRoy Yarbrough — 5
14. Jim Paschal — 4
15. Fireball Roberts — 2
16. Earl Balmer — 1
    Bob Derrington — 1
    Tiny Lund — 1
    Wendell Scott — 1
    Joe Weatherly — 1
    Rex White — 1
    Cale Yarborough — 1
    Doug Yates — 1

Driver	Starts	Poles	Finish 1	2	3	4	5	6–10	Laps	Laps Led	Races Led	Winston Cup Points	$
1965													
1. Ned Jarrett	54	9	13	13	10	4	2	3	13,525	2,244	29	38,824	93,625
2. Dick Hutcherson	52	10	9	9	8	4	2	5	11,610	2,065	23	35,790	57,851
3. Darel Dieringer	35	2	1	4	2	3	0	5	6,845	737	10	24,696	52,214
4. G.C. Spencer	47	1	0	3	4	3	4	11	9,092	90	5	24,314	29,775
5. Marvin Panch	20	5	4	1	4	1	2	2	4,743	856	12	22,798	64,027
6. Bob Derrington	51	0	0	0	1	0	2	16	10,374	0	0	21,394	20,120
7. J.T. Putney	40	0	0	1	3	4	2	14	7,932	0	0	20,928	22,329
8. Neil Castles	51	0	0	0	1	1	4	22	9,768	0	0	20,848	22,329
9. Buddy Baker	42	0	0	2	4	2	4	5	6,969	0	0	20,672	26,837
10. Cale Yarborough	46	0	1	3	1	5	3	8	7,734	166	8	20,192	26,587
11. Wendell Scott	52	0	0	0	0	2	2	17	9,759	0	0	19,902	18,639
12. Junior Johnson	36	10	13	2	1	2	0	1	7,144	3,998	30	18,486	62,216
13. Fred Lorenzen	17	6	4	1	0	0	0	1	3,677	981	12	18,448	80,615
14. Paul Lewis	24	1	0	0	0	1	2	10	5,954	0	0	18,118	13,247
15. E.J. Trivette	39	0	0	0	0	0	0	7	7,485	0	0	13,450	13,248
16. Larry Hess	10	0	0	0	0	0	0	3	2,347	0	0	13,148	9,260
17. Buck Baker	31	0	0	2	0	0	1	9	5,266	0	0	13,136	21,580
18. Jimmy Helms	39	0	0	0	0	0	0	4	5,731	0	0	12,996	12,050
19. Doug Cooper	30	0	0	0	0	1	0	8	5,281	0	0	12,920	12,380
20. Bobby Johns	13	0	0	2	2	0	1	0	2,696	37	6	12,842	24,930
21. Tiny Lund	30	0	1	1	1	4	1	9	5,224	209	2	12,820	11,750
22. Buddy Arrington	31	0	0	0	1	1	4	4	5,274	0	0	11,744	11,600
23. Earl Balmer	9	0	0	1	0	1	0	2	1,320	32	6	11,636	19,045
24. Sam McQuagg	14	0	0	0	1	0	1	3	2,458	31	1	11,460	10,455
25. Elmo Langley	34	0	0	0	2	1	0	6	5,698	19	1	10,982	10,895
26. Henley Gray	38	0	0	0	0	0	1	6	5,291	0	0	9,552	8,320
27. Roy Mayne	14	0	0	0	0	1	0	4	2,463	0	0	8,838	9,060
28. Junior Spencer	21	0	0	0	0	0	1	6	4,062	0	0	8,436	9,345
29. H.B. Bailey	5	0	0	0	0	0	1	2	810	0	0	7,340	5,000
30. Wayne Smith	25	0	0	0	0	0	0	2	3,744	0	0	7,326	6,790
31. Donald Tucker	9	0	0	0	0	1	0	2	1,597	0	0	7,118	5,830
32. Tom Pistone	33	1	0	1	0	1	2	4	3,334	0	0	6,598	10,050
33. Bub Strickler	9	0	0	0	0	0	0	2	1,572	0	0	6,540	5,275
34. Bobby Allison	8	0	0	0	0	0	0	3	799	0	0	6,152	4,780
35. Jim Paschal	10	0	0	0	1	2	1	0	2,403	99	3	6,046	7,805
36. Roy Tyner	28	0	0	0	0	1	0	5	3,448	0	0	5,882	6,696
37. LeeRoy Yarbrough	14	0	0	0	0	1	1	1	1,747	42	2	5,852	5,905
38. Richard Petty	14	7	4	4	2	0	0	0	3,697	1,169	8	5,638	16,450
39. Curtis Turner	7	0	1	0	1	0	1	0	1,360	256	2	5,542	17,440
40. David Pearson	14	1	2	2	2	1	1	3	3,242	744	8	5,464	8,925
41. Clyde Lynn	24	0	0	0	0	0	0	9	4,522	0	0	5,414	4,545
42. Gene Black	18	0	0	0	0	0	0	4	4,167	0	0	4,970	6,080
43. Ned Setzer	8	0	0	0	0	0	0	3	862	0	0	4,828	4,805
44. Stick Elliott	15	0	0	1	0	1	0	1	2,082	0	0	4,332	4,985
45. Reb Wickersham	7	0	0	0	0	0	0	2	906	0	0	4,322	4,410
46. Frank Warren	4	0	0	0	0	0	0	1	769	0	0	3,814	2,880
47. Worth McMillion	10	0	0	0	0	0	0	2	2,290	0	0	3,794	2,590
48. Lionel Johnson	8	0	0	0	0	0	0	2	1,663	0	0	3,510	3,165
49. Paul Moore	14	1	0	1	1	1	0	4	1,687	93	2	3,216	3,435
50. Sonny Hutchins	10	0	0	0	0	0	1	1	2,272	0	0	3,118	3,780

LAPS COMPLETED

1.	Ned Jarrett	13,525
2.	Dick Hutcherson	11,610
3.	Bob Derrington	10,374
4.	Neil Castles	9,768
5.	Wendell Scott	9,759
6.	G.C. Spencer	9,092
7.	J.T. Putney	7,932
8.	Cale Yarborough	7,734
9.	E.J. Trivette	7,485
10.	Junior Johnson	7,144
11.	Buddy Baker	6,969
12.	Darel Dieringer	6,845
13.	Paul Lewis	5,954
14.	Jimmy Helms	5,731
15.	Elmo Langley	5,698
16.	Henley Gray	5,291
17.	Doug Cooper	5,281
18.	Buddy Arrington	5,274
19.	Buck Baker	5,266
20.	Tiny Lund	5,224
21.	Marvin Panch	4,743
22.	Clyde Lynn	4,522
23.	Gene Black	4,167
24.	Junior Spencer	4,062
25.	Wayne Smith	3,744
26.	Richard Petty	3,697
27.	Fred Lorenzen	3,677
28.	Roy Tyner	3,448
29.	Tom Pistone	3,334
30.	David Pearson	3,242
31.	Bobby Johns	2,696
32.	Roy Mayne	2,463
33.	Sam McQuagg	2,458
34.	Jim Paschal	2,403
35.	Larry Hess	2,347
36.	Worth McMillion	2,290
37.	Sonny Hutchins	2,272
38.	Stick Elliott	2,082
39.	LeeRoy Yarbrough	1,747
40.	Paul Moore	1,687
41.	Lionel Johnson	1,663
42.	Donald Tucker	1,597
43.	Bub Strickler	1,572
44.	Curtis Turner	1,360
45.	Earl Balmer	1,320
46.	Reb Wickersham	906
47.	Ned Setzer	862
48.	H.B. Bailey	810
49.	Bobby Allison	799
50.	Frank Warren	769

LAPS LED

1.	Junior Johnson	3,998
2.	Ned Jarrett	2,244
3.	Dick Hutcherson	2,065
4.	Richard Petty	1,169
5.	Fred Lorenzen	981
6.	Marvin Panch	856
7.	David Pearson	744
8.	Darel Dieringer	737
9.	Curtis Turner	256
10.	Tiny Lund	209
11.	Cale Yarborough	166
12.	Jim Paschal	99
13.	Paul Moore	93
14.	G.C. Spencer	90
15.	LeeRoy Yarbrough	42
16.	Bobby Johns	37
17.	Earl Balmer	32
18.	Sam McQuagg	31
19.	Elmo Langley	19

MILES LED

1.	Junior Johnson	2,449
2.	Ned Jarrett	1,097
3.	Dick Hutcherson	1,000
4.	Marvin Panch	985
5.	Fred Lorenzen	946
6.	Darel Dieringer	750
7.	Richard Petty	535
8.	David Pearson	380
9.	Dan Gurney	340
10.	A.J. Foyt	286
11.	Cale Yarborough	277
12.	Curtis Turner	265
13.	Tiny Lund	105
14.	Jim Paschal	98
15.	Parnelli Jones	97
16.	Bobby Isaac	68
17.	LeeRoy Yarbrough	63
18.	Larry Frank	50
19.	Paul Moore	47
20.	Earl Balmer	46
21.	Bobby Johns	43
	Sam McQuagg	43
23.	G.C. Spencer	38
24.	Neil Castles	33
25.	Elmo Langley	7
	Doug Yates	7

MILES DRIVEN

1.	Ned Jarrett	9,121
2.	Dick Hutcherson	8,131
3.	Bob Derrington	6,777
4.	Neil Castles	6,555
5.	G.C. Spencer	6,506
6.	Wendell Scott	6,451
7.	Darel Dieringer	5,806
8.	J.T. Putney	5,680
9.	Cale Yarborough	5,396
10.	Buddy Baker	5,394
11.	Paul Lewis	5,057
12.	Junior Johnson	5,040
13.	E.J. Trivette	4,935
14.	Marvin Panch	4,716
15.	Buck Baker	4,173
16.	Fred Lorenzen	3,998
17.	Jimmy Helms	3,987
18.	Doug Cooper	3,909
19.	Elmo Langley	3,816
20.	Buddy Arrington	3,545
21.	Larry Hess	3,543
22.	Tiny Lund	3,427
23.	Henley Gray	3,225
24.	Junior Spencer	3,127
25.	Gene Black	3,011
26.	Bobby Johns	2,941
27.	Sam McQuagg	2,922
28.	Wayne Smith	2,475
29.	Roy Mayne	2,449
30.	Jim Paschal	2,210

RACES LED

1.	Junior Johnson	30
2.	Ned Jarrett	29
3.	Dick Hutcherson	23
4.	Fred Lorenzen	12
	Marvin Panch	12
6.	Darel Dieringer	10
7.	David Pearson	8
	Richard Petty	8
	Cale Yarborough	8
10.	Earl Balmer	6
	Bobby Johns	6
12.	G.C. Spencer	5
13.	Jim Paschal	3
14.	Tiny Lund	2
	Paul Moore	2
	Curtis Turner	2
	LeeRoy Yarbrough	2
18.	Elmo Langley	1
	Sam McQuagg	1

49

Driver	Starts	Poles	1	2	3	4	5	6–10	Laps	Laps Led	Races Led	Winston Cup Points	$

1966

Driver	Starts	Poles	1	2	3	4	5	6–10	Laps	Laps Led	Races Led	Winston Cup Points	$
1. David Pearson	42	7	15	5	5	1	0	7	10,781	3,174	25	35,638	78,194
2. James Hylton	41	1	0	4	6	7	3	12	10,804	155	3	33,688	38,723
3. Richard Petty	39	16	8	9	3	0	0	2	8,737	2,924	26	22,952	94,666
4. Henley Gray	45	0	0	0	0	1	3	14	10,719	0	0	22,468	21,901
5. Paul Goldsmith	21	1	3	3	2	1	2	0	5,097	452	10	22,078	54,609
6. Wendell Scott	45	0	0	0	1	1	1	14	9,793	0	0	21,702	23,052
7. John Sears	46	0	0	1	1	4	5	19	9,981	109	2	21,432	25,192
8. J.T. Putney	39	0	0	1	2	1	0	5	7,836	32	2	21,208	18,653
9. Neil Castles	41	0	0	1	1	3	2	10	8,824	0	0	20,446	19,035
10. Bobby Allison	33	4	3	0	4	1	2	5	6,949	714	6	19,910	23,420
11. Elmo Langley	47	1	2	1	1	4	4	8	9,461	308	5	19,116	22,455
12. Darel Dieringer	25	0	3	3	0	1	0	2	4,818	515	8	18,214	52,530
13. Ned Jarrett	21	0	0	0	3	1	1	3	4,584	167	3	17,616	23,255
14. Jim Paschal	18	2	2	0	1	2	1	4	5,008	759	7	16,404	30,985
15. Sam McQuagg	16	0	1	0	1	0	2	3	3,575	175	3	0	29,530
16. Paul Lewis	21	0	1	1	6	1	0	5	6,260	67	2	15,352	17,827
17. Marvin Panch	14	0	1	0	1	2	0	2	2,808	183	5	15,308	38,432
18. Cale Yarborough	14	0	0	2	0	1	0	4	3,831	252	4	15,188	24,077
19. G.C. Spencer	20	0	0	3	0	0	3	3	4,711	2	1	15,028	26,722
20. Clyde Lynn	40	0	0	1	0	0	0	14	9,384	0	0	14,856	13,222
21. Buck Baker	36	0	0	3	0	2	2	7	6,725	0	0	14,504	13,860
22. Buddy Baker	41	1	0	1	0	0	0	6	6,361	142	4	14,302	21,325
23. Fred Lorenzen	11	2	2	1	0	1	2	0	3,066	782	7	12,454	36,310
24. Curtis Turner	21	2	0	1	1	3	0	1	3,697	385	11	12,266	16,890
25. Roy Mayne	18	0	0	0	0	0	1	4	4,052	0	0	11,074	9,940
26. LeeRoy Yarbrough	9	2	1	0	0	1	0	2	1,545	364	5	10,528	23,980
27. J.D. McDuffie	36	0	0	0	0	0	1	8	7,166	0	0	9,572	8,545
28. Dick Hutcherson	14	2	3	0	2	1	2	1	3,152	400	7	9,392	22,485
29. Tiny Lund	31	1	1	2	1	0	1	5	4,306	654	6	9,332	11,880
30. Blackie Watt	20	0	0	0	0	0	0	9	4,067	0	0	8,518	7,050
31. Frank Warren	11	0	0	0	0	0	0	1	1,989	0	0	8,334	6,740
32. Buddy Arrington	25	0	0	0	0	0	0	3	3,607	0	0	7,636	8,980
33. Wayne Smith	23	0	0	0	0	0	0	1	4,108	0	0	7,442	9,835
34. Jimmy Helms	29	0	0	0	0	0	0	0	3,186	0	0	6,530	5,915
35. Stick Elliott	19	0	0	0	0	1	0	2	3,285	0	0	6,358	7,335
36. Earl Balmer	9	0	1	0	0	0	1	0	1,388	4	2	5,794	7,935
37. Tom Pistone	28	4	0	3	1	0	2	0	4,090	385	8	5,788	7,775
38. Johnny Wynn	21	0	0	0	0	0	0	5	3,245	0	0	5,644	4,650
39. Larry Manning	13	0	0	0	0	1	0	0	2,769	0	0	4,964	3,920
40. Larry Hess	13	0	0	0	0	0	0	0	1,830	0	0	4,928	5,290
41. Roy Tyner	26	0	0	0	0	0	0	4	3,511	0	0	4,248	4,335
43. Bill Seifert	15	0	0	0	0	0	0	4	3,322	0	0	4,128	3,830
44. Bob Derrington	10	0	0	0	0	0	0	1	1,154	0	0	4,122	2,830
45. Joel Davis	21	0	0	0	0	1	0	2	2,977	0	0	4,066	4,885
46. Paul Connors	3	0	0	0	0	0	0	1	668	0	0	3,986	2,820
47. Jabe Thomas	13	0	0	0	0	0	0	0	1,559	0	0	3,820	3,480
48. Doug Cooper	21	0	0	0	1	1	1	1	3,177	0	0	3,808	5,185
49. Junior Johnson	7	3	0	0	0	0	1	0	1,813	467	6	3,750	3,610
50. Larry Frank	2	0	0	0	0	0	0	2	232	0	0	3,738	1,575

LAPS COMPLETED		LAPS LED		MILES LED		MILES DRIVEN		RACES LED	
1. James Hylton	10,804	1. David Pearson	3,174	1. Richard Petty	2,487	1. James Hylton	8,773	1. Richard Petty	26
2. David Pearson	10,781	2. Richard Petty	2,924	2. David Pearson	1,680	2. David Pearson	8,437	2. David Pearson	25
3. Henley Gray	10,719	3. Fred Lorenzen	782	3. Fred Lorenzen	642	3. Henley Gray	7,626	3. Curtis Turner	11
4. John Sears	9,981	4. Jim Paschal	759	4. LeeRoy Yarbrough	543	4. Wendell Scott	7,181	4. Paul Goldsmith	10
5. Wendell Scott	9,793	5. Bobby Allison	714	5. Paul Goldsmith	537	5. John Sears	6,845	5. Darel Dieringer	8
6. Elmo Langley	9,461	6. Tiny Lund	654	6. Jim Paschal	481	6. Richard Petty	6,733	Tom Pistone	8
7. Clyde Lynn	9,384	7. Darel Dieringer	515	7. Dan Gurney	400	7. J.T. Putney	6,708	7. Dick Hutcherson	7
8. Neil Castles	8,824	8. Junior Johnson	467	8. Sam McQuagg	373	8. Elmo Langley	6,640	Fred Lorenzen	7
9. Richard Petty	8,737	9. Paul Goldsmith	452	9. Darel Dieringer	369	9. Neil Castles	6,397	Jim Paschal	7
10. J.T. Putney	7,836	10. Dick Hutcherson	400	10. Curtis Turner	346	10. Clyde Lynn	6,033	10. Bobby Allison	6
11. J.D. McDuffie	7,166	11. Tom Pistone	385	11. Dick Hutcherson	321	11. Paul Goldsmith	5,382	Junior Johnson	6
12. Bobby Allison	6,949	Curtis Turner	385	12. Cale Yarborough	318	12. Bobby Allison	5,370	Tiny Lund	6
13. Buck Baker	6,725	13. LeeRoy Yarbrough	364	13. Bobby Allison	309	13. Jim Paschal	5,264	13. Elmo Langley	5
14. Buddy Baker	6,361	14. Elmo Langley	308	14. Tiny Lund	302	14. Buck Baker	4,939	Marvin Panch	5
15. Paul Lewis	6,260	15. Cale Yarborough	252	15. Jim Hurtubise	256	15. Buddy Baker	4,890	LeeRoy Yarbrough	5
16. Paul Goldsmith	5,097	16. Marvin Panch	183	16. Junior Johnson	244	16. Paul Lewis	4,742	16. Buddy Baker	4
17. Jim Paschal	5,008	17. Sam McQuagg	175	17. Marvin Panch	227	17. Darel Dieringer	4,545	Cale Yarborough	4
18. Darel Dieringer	4,818	18. Ned Jarrett	167	18. Buddy Baker	185	18. Ned Jarrett	4,336	18. James Hylton	3
19. G.C. Spencer	4,711	19. James Hylton	155	19. Tom Pistone	147	19. G.C. Spencer	4,277	Ned Jarrett	3
20. Ned Jarrett	4,584	20. Buddy Baker	142	20. John Sears	128	20. J.D. McDuffie	4,255	Sam McQuagg	3
21. Tiny Lund	4,306	21. John Sears	109	21. Elmo Langley	125	21. Curtis Turner	4,120	21. Earl Balmer	2
22. Wayne Smith	4,108	22. Paul Lewis	67	22. Ned Jarrett	72	22. Roy Mayne	4,051	Paul Lewis	2
23. Tom Pistone	4,090	23. J.T. Putney	32	23. James Hylton	48	23. Cale Yarborough	3,944	J.T. Putney	2
24. Blackie Watt	4,067	24. Earl Balmer	4	24. Paul Lewis	37	24. Sam McQuagg	3,906	John Sears	2
25. Roy Mayne	4,052	25. G.C. Spencer	2	25. Gordon Johncock	32	25. Marvin Panch	3,843	25. G.C. Spencer	1
26. Cale Yarborough	3,831			26. Bobby Isaac	16	26. Wayne Smith	3,655		
27. Curtis Turner	3,697			J.T. Putney	16	27. Tiny Lund	3,639		
28. Buddy Arrington	3,607			28. Don White	12	28. Fred Lorenzen	3,425		
29. Sam McQuagg	3,575			29. Bunkie Blackburn	10	29. Don White	3,199		
30. Roy Tyner	3,511			30. Earl Balmer	7	30. Buddy Arrington	3,054		
31. Bill Seifert	3,322								
32. Stick Elliott	3,285								
33. Johnny Wynn	3,245								
34. Jimmy Helms	3,186								
35. Doug Cooper	3,177								
36. Dick Hutcherson	3,152								
37. Fred Lorenzen	3,066								
38. Joel Davis	2,977								
39. Marvin Panch	2,808								
40. Larry Manning	2,769								
41. Frank Warren	1,989								
42. Larry Hess	1,830								
43. Junior Johnson	1,813								
44. Jabe Thomas	1,559								
45. LeeRoy Yarbrough	1,545								
46. Earl Balmer	1,388								
47. Bob Derrington	1,154								
48. Paul Connors	668								
49. Larry Frank	232								

Driver	Starts	Poles	Finish						Laps	Laps Led	Races Led	Winston Cup Points	$
			1	2	3	4	5	6–10					

1967

	Driver	Starts	Poles	1	2	3	4	5	6–10	Laps	Laps Led	Races Led	Winston Cup Points	$
1.	Richard Petty	48	19	27	7	2	1	1	2	12,739	5,537	41	42,472	150,197
2.	James Hylton	46	1	0	3	3	12	8	13	11,526	109	5	36,444	49,732
3.	Dick Hutcherson	33	9	2	9	7	3	1	3	8,893	1,455	21	33,658	85,160
4.	Bobby Allison	45	2	6	4	5	4	2	6	10,157	1,554	21	30,812	58,250
5.	John Sears	41	1	0	1	3	3	2	16	10,031	59	4	29,078	28,937
6.	Jim Paschal	45	1	4	5	5	3	3	5	9,402	1,074	16	27,624	60,123
7.	David Pearson	22	2	2	4	3	2	0	2	5,638	667	13	26,302	72,651
8.	Neil Castles	35	0	0	0	0	2	2	11	6,754	0	0	23,218	20,683
9.	Elmo Langley	45	0	0	1	3	2	4	14	9,652	0	0	22,286	23,898
10.	Wendell Scott	45	0	0	0	0	0	0	11	9,217	0	0	20,700	19,510
11.	Paul Goldsmith	21	0	0	2	3	1	1	1	4,851	398	7	20,402	38,732
12.	Darel Dieringer	19	6	1	3	3	0	1	1	4,537	765	11	20,194	34,710
13.	Clyde Lynn	44	0	0	0	0	2	3	17	9,556	0	0	20,016	19,520
14.	Bobby Isaac	12	0	0	1	0	0	2	2	2,625	65	3	19,698	24,475
15.	Buddy Baker	20	0	1	1	2	2	0	1	3,905	480	8	18,600	46,950
16.	Donnie Allison	20	0	0	1	0	2	1	3	4,336	158	2	18,298	17,614
17.	Henley Gray	43	0	0	0	0	0	0	10	7,864	0	0	17,502	15,987
18.	J.T. Putney	29	0	0	0	1	0	0	9	6,050	0	0	16,752	15,687
19.	Tiny Lund	19	0	0	0	0	1	3	1	3,587	36	3	16,292	17,332
20.	Cale Yarborough	17	4	2	3	1	1	0	2	4,114	908	9	16,228	57,912
21.	G.C. Spencer	29	0	0	0	3	0	2	5	4,947	0	0	15,240	20,225
22.	Bill Seifert	41	0	0	0	0	0	0	12	8,171	0	0	14,676	11,910
23.	Charlie Glotzbach	9	0	0	0	0	3	0	2	1,783	4	1	11,444	14,790
24.	Frank Warren	12	0	0	0	0	0	0	1	1,805	0	0	9,992	9,185
25.	Earl Brooks	34	1	0	0	0	0	0	8	5,373	24	1	9,952	8,610
26.	Buddy Arrington	15	0	0	0	0	0	1	4	2,972	0	0	9,768	7,820
27.	Buck Baker	21	0	0	0	0	0	0	5	4,544	0	0	9,450	7,560
28.	Wayne Smith	27	0	0	0	0	0	0	2	4,364	0	0	9,372	10,025
29.	Fred Lorenzen	5	0	1	1	0	0	0	0	895	23	4	9,268	17,875
30.	Roy Mayne	14	0	0	0	0	0	0	1	2,209	3	1	9,262	8,930
31.	Bobby Wawak	14	0	0	0	0	0	0	3	2,225	0	0	9,078	8,070
32.	Friday Hassler	21	0	0	0	0	1	2	6	4,309	12	1	8,820	10,270
33.	Paul Lewis	14	0	0	1	0	0	2	5	2,959	4	1	8,492	8,720
34.	Sonny Hutchins	7	0	0	0	0	0	0	2	998	0	0	8,448	6,385
35.	Paul Moore	6	0	0	0	0	0	2	1	1,351	0	0	7,812	7,200
36.	Sam McQuagg	15	0	0	0	0	2	1	0	2,244	11	3	7,400	9,845
37.	LeeRoy Yarbrough	15	0	1	0	2	0	0	1	2,647	34	4	7,012	15,325
38.	Don Biederman	22	0	0	0	0	0	0	1	2,679	0	0	5,850	5,935
39.	Ramo Stott	3	0	0	0	0	0	0	1	588	0	0	5,676	3,335
40.	George Davis	21	0	0	0	0	0	1	5	3,342	0	0	5,434	4,400
41.	Jack Harden	10	0	0	0	0	0	0	0	1,393	0	0	5,254	4,450
42.	Paul Dean Holt	24	0	0	0	0	0	0	1	3,165	0	0	5,006	4,220
43.	Roy Tyner	27	0	0	0	0	0	0	1	2,966	0	0	4,936	8,170
44.	Bill Champion	11	0	0	0	0	0	0	0	1,889	0	0	4,040	6,205
45.	Dick Johnson	23	0	0	0	0	0	0	0	2,636	0	0	3,954	5,070
46.	George Poulos	23	0	0	0	0	0	0	1	2,872	0	0	3,780	3,040
47.	Bill Dennis	3	0	0	0	0	0	0	0	1,012	0	0	3,730	2,335
48.	Doug Cooper	21	0	0	0	0	0	2	3	3,351	0	0	3,666	5,665
49.	Ed Negre	14	0	0	0	0	0	0	0	1,439	0	0	3,578	3,805
50.	H.B. Bailey	3	0	0	0	0	0	0	0	322	0	0	3,482	3,850

LAPS COMPLETED		LAPS LED		MILES LED		MILES DRIVEN		RACES LED	
1. Richard Petty	12,739	1. Richard Petty	5,537	1. Richard Petty	3,607	1. Richard Petty	9,387	1. Richard Petty	41
2. James Hylton	11,526	2. Bobby Allison	1,554	2. Cale Yarborough	1,035	2. James Hylton	8,534	2. Bobby Allison	21
3. Bobby Allison	10,157	3. Dick Hutcherson	1,455	3. Dick Hutcherson	902	3. Bobby Allison	7,686	Dick Hutcherson	21
4. John Sears	10,031	4. Jim Paschal	1,074	4. Jim Paschal	881	4. John Sears	7,468	4. Jim Paschal	16
5. Elmo Langley	9,652	5. Cale Yarborough	908	5. Bobby Allison	778	5. Dick Hutcherson	7,278	5. David Pearson	13
6. Clyde Lynn	9,556	6. Darel Dieringer	765	6. Buddy Baker	637	6. Jim Paschal	7,228	6. Darel Dieringer	11
7. Jim Paschal	9,402	7. David Pearson	667	7. David Pearson	576	7. Elmo Langley	6,781	7. Cale Yarborough	9
8. Wendell Scott	9,217	8. Buddy Baker	480	8. Darel Dieringer	570	8. Wendell Scott	6,639	8. Buddy Baker	8
9. Dick Hutcherson	8,893	9. Paul Goldsmith	398	9. Parnelli Jones	340	9. Clyde Lynn	6,551	9. Paul Goldsmith	7
10. Bill Seifert	8,171	10. Donnie Allison	158	10. Mario Andretti	337	10. David Pearson	5,940	10. Donnie Allison	5
11. Henley Gray	7,864	11. James Hylton	109	11. Paul Goldsmith	238	11. Henley Gray	5,859	11. Fred Lorenzen	4
12. Neil Castles	6,754	12. Bobby Isaac	65	12. Bobby Isaac	132	12. Neil Castles	5,508	John Sears	4
13. J.T. Putney	6,050	13. John Sears	59	13. A.J. Foyt	105	13. Paul Goldsmith	5,409	LeeRoy Yarbrough	4
14. David Pearson	5,638	14. Tiny Lund	36	14. Dan Gurney	97	14. Bill Seifert	5,133	14. Bobby Isaac	3
15. Earl Brooks	5,373	15. LeeRoy Yarbrough	34	15. Fred Lorenzen	55	15. Darel Dieringer	4,906	Tiny Lund	3
16. G.C. Spencer	4,947	16. Earl Brooks	24	16. Donnie Allison	54	16. J.T. Putney	4,817	Sam McQuagg	3
17. Paul Goldsmith	4,851	17. Fred Lorenzen	23	17. LeeRoy Yarbrough	39	17. Donnie Allison	4,537	17. Donnie Allison	2
18. Buck Baker	4,544	18. Friday Hassler	12	18. James Hylton	32	18. G.C. Spencer	4,156	18. Earl Brooks	1
19. Darel Dieringer	4,537	19. Sam McQuagg	11	19. Tiny Lund	24	19. Buddy Baker	4,135	Charlie Glotzbach	1
20. Wayne Smith	4,364	20. Charlie Glotzbach	4	20. John Sears	17	20. Bobby Isaac	3,927	Friday Hassler	1
21. Donnie Allison	4,336	Paul Lewis	4	21. Curtis Turner	15	21. Cale Yarborough	3,909	Paul Lewis	1
22. Friday Hassler	4,309	22. Roy Mayne	3	22. Earl Brooks	12	22. Wayne Smith	3,629	Roy Mayne	1
23. Cale Yarborough	4,114			23. Jack Bowsher	11	23. Earl Brooks	3,536		
24. Buddy Baker	3,905			24. Sam McQuagg	9	24. Tiny Lund	3,251		
25. Tiny Lund	3,587			25. Red Farmer	7	25. Buck Baker	3,156		
26. Doug Cooper	3,351			26. Charlie Glotzbach	6	26. Friday Hassler	3,091		
27. George Davis	3,342			Friday Hassler	6	27. LeeRoy Yarbrough	2,894		
28. Paul Dean Holt	3,165			Paul Lewis	6	28. Frank Warren	2,668		
29. Buddy Arrington	2,972			29. Whitey Gerkin	2	29. Buddy Arrington	2,635		
30. Roy Tyner	2,966			30. Gordon Johncock	1	30. Paul Lewis	2,593		
31. Paul Lewis	2,959			Roy Mayne	1				
32. George Poulos	2,872								
33. Don Biederman	2,679								
34. LeeRoy Yarbrough	2,647								
35. Dick Johnson	2,636								
36. Bobby Isaac	2,625								
37. Sam McQuagg	2,244								
38. Bobby Wawak	2,225								
39. Roy Mayne	2,209								
40. Bill Champion	1,889								
41. Frank Warren	1,805								
42. Charlie Glotzbach	1,783								
43. Ed Negre	1,439								
44. Jack Harden	1,393								
45. Paul Moore	1,351								
46. Bill Dennis	1,012								
47. Sonny Hutchins	998								
48. Fred Lorenzen	895								
49. Ramo Stott	588								
50. H.B. Bailey	322								

Driver	Starts	Poles	Finish 1	2	3	4	5	6–10	Laps	Laps Led	Races Led	Winston Cup Points	$

1968

	Driver	Starts	Poles	1	2	3	4	5	6–10	Laps	Laps Led	Races Led	Winston Cup Points	$
1.	David Pearson	48	12	16	12	4	2	2	2	13,097	3,950	37	3,499	133,065
2.	Bobby Isaac	49	3	3	9	7	4	4	9	12,947	1,384	20	3,373	60,342
3.	Richard Petty	49	12	16	6	5	2	2	4	12,254	4,542	35	3,123	99,535
4.	Clyde Lynn	49	0	0	0	0	1	1	23	12,013	0	0	3,041	29,226
5.	John Sears	49	0	0	0	1	1	3	19	11,077	0	0	3,017	29,179
6.	Elmo Langley	48	0	0	0	1	1	4	22	11,149	0	0	2,823	25,832
7.	James Hylton	41	0	0	1	4	8	3	12	10,058	15	3	2,719	32,608
8.	Jabe Thomas	48	0	0	0	0	0	1	14	11,194	0	0	2,687	21,166
9.	Wendell Scott	48	0	0	0	0	0	0	10	10,231	0	0	2,685	20,498
10.	Roy Tyner	48	0	0	0	0	2	2	10	8,789	0	0	2,504	20,247
11.	Bobby Allison	37	2	2	4	4	6	2	2	8,781	690	13	2,454	52,288
12.	Neil Castles	44	0	0	0	2	1	1	11	9,082	0	0	2,330	19,507
13.	Buddy Baker	38	4	1	4	6	3	2	2	7,949	564	12	2,310	56,023
14.	Bill Seifert	44	0	0	0	0	0	1	8	8,033	0	0	2,175	18,403
15.	Earl Brooks	40	0	0	0	0	0	0	5	6,507	0	0	1,957	14,233
16.	LeeRoy Yarbrough	26	6	2	3	6	1	3	1	6,423	1,300	14	1,894	87,920
17.	Cale Yarborough	21	4	6	2	1	0	3	0	5,661	1,215	16	1,804	138,052
18.	Paul Dean Holt	40	0	0	0	0	0	0	0	5,863	0	0	1,723	8,986
19.	Charlie Glotzbach	22	3	1	3	1	4	1	2	4,871	291	5	1,693	43,101
20.	Henley Gray	30	0	0	0	0	0	0	6	6,072	0	0	1,559	12,566
21.	Darel Dieringer	18	1	0	1	0	3	1	3	4,409	159	2	1,525	28,215
22.	Tiny Lund	17	0	0	0	1	1	3	5	4,547	1	1	1,443	17,785
23.	G.C. Spencer	26	0	0	0	0	1	0	5	4,380	0	0	1,401	10,110
24.	J.D. McDuffie	32	0	0	0	0	0	0	9	5,587	0	0	1,370	8,355
25.	Donnie Allison	13	1	1	1	3	0	0	3	3,829	284	6	1,307	50,815
26.	Stan Meserve	31	0	0	0	0	0	0	1	4,283	0	0	1,274	7,475
27.	Friday Hassler	20	0	0	0	0	2	1	5	5,012	0	0	1,224	12,000
28.	Bill Champion	18	0	0	0	0	0	0	2	3,505	0	0	1,155	10,170
29.	Paul Moore	16	0	0	1	0	1	0	7	3,399	51	2	1,086	12,325
30.	Paul Goldsmith	15	0	0	1	0	0	1	2	2,793	304	8	1,020	24,365
31.	Ed Negre	24	0	0	0	0	0	0	1	2,930	0	0	928	4,985
32.	Pete Hamilton	16	0	0	1	0	0	2	3	3,555	42	3	919	7,920
33.	Wayne Smith	18	0	0	0	0	0	0	1	2,456	0	0	901	7,235
34.	Dave Marcis	10	0	0	0	0	0	0	2	3,240	0	0	851	7,099
35.	Don Tarr	12	0	0	0	0	0	0	0	1,941	0	0	827	7,510
36.	E.J. Trivette	13	0	0	0	0	0	0	0	2,684	0	0	821	8,295
37.	Dick Johnson	11	0	0	0	0	0	0	0	2,187	0	0	735	5,920
38.	Bob Cooper	14	0	0	0	0	0	0	1	2,170	0	0	668	4,485
39.	Buck Baker	17	0	0	0	0	0	1	2	2,675	0	0	650	3,580
40.	William Gardner	14	0	0	0	0	0	0	2	3,546	0	0	640	4,275
41.	Larry Manning	12	0	0	0	0	0	0	0	2,151	0	0	640	6,995
42.	Frank Warren	10	0	0	0	0	0	0	1	1,643	0	0	611	5,365
43.	Jerry Grant	7	0	0	0	0	0	0	1	971	1	1	559	5,665
44.	Harold Fagan	12	0	0	0	0	0	0	1	1,808	0	0	531	3,680
45.	Richard Brickhouse	7	0	0	0	0	1	0	1	1,571	0	0	514	7,190
46.	Jim Hurtubise	6	0	0	0	0	0	0	1	982	0	0	504	4,490
47.	Curtis Turner	6	0	0	0	0	1	0	3	1,448	0	0	456	5,850
48.	Bobby Johns	7	0	0	0	0	0	0	0	750	0	0	453	5,010
49.	Eddie Yarboro	6	0	0	0	0	0	0	0	2,109	0	0	447	2,255
50.	Red Farmer	7	0	0	0	0	1	0	0	928	1	1	407	4,810

LAPS COMPLETED

1.	David Pearson	13,097
2.	Bobby Isaac	12,947
3.	Richard Petty	12,254
4.	Clyde Lynn	12,013
5.	Jabe Thomas	11,194
6.	Elmo Langley	11,149
7.	John Sears	11,077
8.	Wendell Scott	10,231
9.	James Hylton	10,058
10.	Neil Castles	9,082
11.	Roy Tyner	8,789
12.	Bobby Allison	8,781
13.	Bill Seifert	8,033
14.	Buddy Baker	7,949
15.	Earl Brooks	6,507
16.	LeeRoy Yarbrough	6,423
17.	Henley Gray	6,072
18.	Paul Dean Holt	5,863
19.	Cale Yarborough	5,661
20.	J.D. McDuffie	5,587
21.	Friday Hassler	5,012
22.	Charlie Glotzbach	4,871
23.	Tiny Lund	4,547
24.	Darel Dieringer	4,409
25.	G.C. Spencer	4,380
26.	Stan Meserve	4,283
27.	Donnie Allison	3,829
28.	Pete Hamilton	3,555
29.	William Gardner	3,546
30.	Bill Champion	3,505
31.	Paul Moore	3,399
32.	Dave Marcis	3,240
33.	Ed Negre	2,930
34.	Paul Goldsmith	2,793
35.	E.J. Trivette	2,684
36.	Buck Baker	2,675
37.	Wayne Smith	2,456
38.	Dick Johnson	2,187
39.	Bob Cooper	2,170
40.	Larry Manning	2,151
41.	Eddie Yarboro	2,109
42.	Don Tarr	1,941
43.	Harold Fagan	1,808
44.	Frank Warren	1,643
45.	Richard Brickhouse	1,571
46.	Curtis Turner	1,448
47.	Jim Hurtubise	982
48.	Jerry Grant	971
49.	Red Farmer	928
50.	Bobby Johns	750

LAPS LED

1.	Richard Petty	4,542
2.	David Pearson	3,950
3.	Bobby Isaac	1,384
4.	LeeRoy Yarbrough	1,300
5.	Cale Yarborough	1,215
6.	Bobby Allison	690
7.	Buddy Baker	564
8.	Paul Goldsmith	304
9.	Charlie Glotzbach	291
10.	Donnie Allison	284
11.	Darel Dieringer	159
12.	Paul Moore	51
13.	Pete Hamilton	42
14.	James Hylton	15
15.	Red Farmer	1
	Jerry Grant	1
	Tiny Lund	1

MILES LED

1.	David Pearson	2,328
2.	Richard Petty	2,115
3.	LeeRoy Yarbrough	1,409
4.	Cale Yarborough	1,403
5.	Bobby Isaac	731
6.	Buddy Baker	465
7.	Bobby Allison	450
8.	Donnie Allison	338
9.	Dan Gurney	335
10.	Charlie Glotzbach	283
11.	Paul Goldsmith	209
12.	Darel Dieringer	158
13.	Parnelli Jones	132
14.	Mario Andretti	51
15.	Paul Moore	50
16.	Buck Baker	37
17.	Pete Hamilton	30
18.	Tom Pistone	23
19.	Butch Hartman	18
20.	James Hylton	10
21.	Sam McQuagg	8
22.	Ray Hendrick	4
23.	Al Unser	3
24.	Red Farmer	2
	Jerry Grant	2
26.	Tiny Lund	1

MILES DRIVEN

1.	David Pearson	9,530
2.	Bobby Isaac	9,123
3.	Richard Petty	8,869
4.	Clyde Lynn	8,862
5.	John Sears	7,827
6.	Elmo Langley	7,750
7.	Bobby Allison	7,383
8.	Jabe Thomas	7,330
9.	Wendell Scott	7,314
10.	James Hylton	7,248
11.	LeeRoy Yarbrough	5,897
12.	Bill Seifert	5,857
13.	Roy Tyner	5,841
14.	Cale Yarborough	5,709
15.	Buddy Baker	5,690
16.	Neil Castles	5,447
17.	Darel Dieringer	4,972
18.	Charlie Glotzbach	4,791
19.	Henley Gray	4,580
20.	Earl Brooks	4,385
21.	Tiny Lund	4,381
22.	Friday Hassler	4,245
23.	Donnie Allison	4,107
24.	Bill Champion	3,531
25.	Paul Goldsmith	3,505
26.	Paul Dean Holt	3,473
27.	G.C. Spencer	3,276
28.	Paul Moore	3,219
29.	Dave Marcis	3,179
30.	J.D. McDuffie	3,018

RACES LED

1.	David Pearson	37
2.	Richard Petty	35
3.	Bobby Isaac	20
4.	Cale Yarborough	16
5.	LeeRoy Yarbrough	14
6.	Bobby Allison	13
7.	Buddy Baker	12
8.	Paul Goldsmith	8
9.	Donnie Allison	6
10.	Charlie Glotzbach	5
11.	Pete Hamilton	3
	James Hylton	3
13.	Darel Dieringer	2
	Paul Moore	2
15.	Red Farmer	1
	Jerry Grant	1
	Tiny Lund	1

Driver	Starts	Poles	Finish						Laps	Laps Led	Races Led	Winston Cup Points	$
			1	2	3	4	5	6–10					

1969

Driver	Starts	Poles	1	2	3	4	5	6–10	Laps	Laps Led	Races Led	Winston Cup Points	$
1. David Pearson	51	13	11	18	9	2	2	2	14,270	3,018	39	4,170	229,760
2. Richard Petty	50	6	10	9	9	0	3	7	12,589	2,778	32	3,813	129,906
3. James Hylton	52	0	0	4	9	8	6	12	13,540	162	12	3,750	114,416
4. Neil Castles	51	0	0	2	1	4	6	16	12,661	29	1	3,530	54,367
5. Elmo Langley	52	1	0	0	1	6	6	15	12,531	40	1	3,383	73,092
6. Bobby Isaac	50	21	17	3	5	3	1	4	12,308	5,072	38	3,301	92,074
7. John Sears	52	0	0	1	3	7	6	10	11,620	18	3	3,166	52,281
8. Jabe Thomas	51	0	0	0	0	0	0	12	12,025	0	0	3,103	44,989
9. Wendell Scott	51	0	0	0	0	0	0	11	11,856	0	0	3,015	47,451
10. Cecil Gordon	51	0	0	0	0	0	1	7	10,745	0	0	3,002	39,679
11. E.J. Trivette	49	0	0	0	0	0	0	15	11,110	0	0	2,988	35,896
12. Bill Champion	49	0	0	0	0	0	1	9	10,582	0	0	2,813	33,656
13. Bill Seifert	50	0	0	0	0	1	0	14	9,728	0	0	2,765	44,361
14. J.D. McDuffie	50	0	0	0	0	0	0	12	10,173	0	0	2,741	30,861
15. Ben Arnold	48	0	0	0	0	0	0	8	10,334	0	0	2,736	33,256
16. LeeRoy Yarbrough	30	0	7	2	0	6	1	5	8,190	1,155	17	2,712	193,211
17. Henley Gray	48	0	0	0	0	0	0	5	8,954	0	0	2,517	29,335
18. Earl Brooks	49	0	0	0	0	0	1	5	8,719	0	0	2,454	34,793
19. Dave Marcis	37	0	0	0	1	2	0	8	7,099	22	3	2,348	32,383
20. Bobby Allison	27	1	5	3	1	2	2	2	6,445	1,251	15	2,055	69,483
21. Dick Brooks	28	0	0	0	1	0	2	9	5,741	2	1	1,780	28,187
22. Buddy Baker	18	3	0	2	4	1	2	2	4,177	770	14	1,769	62,928
23. Cale Yarborough	19	6	2	2	1	2	0	1	4,341	946	16	1,715	74,240
24. Donnie Allison	16	2	1	2	4	1	2	1	3,893	400	10	1,662	78,055
25. Richard Brickhouse	24	0	1	0	0	0	1	7	3,629	34	2	1,660	45,637
26. G.C. Spencer	26	0	0	0	0	2	2	4	4,823	0	0	1,562	21,660
27. Ed Negre	31	0	0	0	0	0	0	4	4,556	0	0	1,465	15,160
28. Friday Hassler	18	0	0	0	0	0	0	7	4,607	3	1	1,421	17,690
29. Frank Warren	23	0	0	0	0	0	0	1	3,343	0	0	1,299	15,677
30. Hoss Ellington	15	0	0	0	0	0	0	4	2,988	0	0	1,210	16,552
31. Roy Tyner	21	0	0	0	0	0	0	1	3,285	0	0	1,191	12,302
32. Ed Hessert	16	0	0	0	0	0	0	4	2,635	1	1	1,113	17,690
33. Buddy Arrington	16	0	0	0	0	0	2	4	3,758	0	0	1,099	12,975
34. Dick Johnson	22	0	0	0	0	0	0	4	3,803	0	0	1,055	11,182
35. Buddy Young	21	0	0	0	0	0	1	5	4,510	0	0	981	15,422
36. Dub Simpson	20	0	0	0	0	0	0	0	2,923	0	0	959	12,915
37. Charlie Glotzbach	12	2	0	2	0	2	1	1	2,823	171	8	944	36,090
38. Roy Mayne	13	0	0	0	0	0	0	0	2,855	0	0	922	10,340
39. Wayne Smith	16	0	0	0	0	0	0	2	2,692	0	0	922	10,610
40. Paul Goldsmith	11	0	0	0	3	1	0	1	1,999	20	4	892	22,305
41. Don Tarr	12	0	0	0	0	0	0	3	1,754	6	1	855	13,720
42. Ken Meisenhelder	16	0	0	0	0	0	0	0	1,832	0	0	627	5,630
43. Pete Hazelwood	16	0	0	0	0	0	0	1	2,367	0	0	598	4,160
44. Sonny Hutchins	8	0	0	2	0	0	0	0	1,694	0	0	535	9,552
45. Wayne Gillette	16	0	0	0	0	0	0	0	887	0	0	509	5,827
46. Paul Dean Holt	14	0	0	0	0	0	0	0	1,408	0	0	485	4,442
47. Johnny Halford	8	0	0	0	0	0	0	0	1,881	0	0	465	4,200
48. Ray Elder	4	0	0	0	0	0	0	4	642	0	0	433	7,200
49. John Kennedy	9	0	0	0	0	0	0	0	1,085	0	0	417	6,462
50. Dick Poling	12	0	0	0	0	0	0	0	1,305	0	0	408	5,467

LAPS COMPLETED

1.	David Pearson	14,270
2.	James Hylton	13,540
3.	Neil Castles	12,661
4.	Richard Petty	12,589
5.	Elmo Langley	12,531
6.	Bobby Isaac	12,308
7.	Jabe Thomas	12,025
8.	Wendell Scott	11,856
9.	John Sears	11,620
10.	E.J. Trivette	11,110
11.	Cecil Gordon	10,745
12.	Bill Champion	10,582
13.	Ben Arnold	10,334
14.	J.D. McDuffie	10,173
15.	Bill Seifert	9,728
16.	Henley Gray	8,954
17.	Earl Brooks	8,719
18.	LeeRoy Yarbrough	8,190
19.	Dave Marcis	7,099
20.	Bobby Allison	6,445
21.	Dick Brooks	5,741
22.	G.C. Spencer	4,823
23.	Friday Hassler	4,607
24.	Ed Negre	4,556
25.	Buddy Young	4,510
26.	Cale Yarborough	4,341
27.	Buddy Baker	4,177
28.	Donnie Allison	3,893
29.	Dick Johnson	3,803
30.	Buddy Arrington	3,758
31.	Richard Brickhouse	3,629
32.	Frank Warren	3,343
33.	Roy Tyner	3,285
34.	Hoss Ellington	2,988
35.	Dub Simpson	2,923
36.	Roy Mayne	2,855
37.	Charlie Glotzbach	2,823
38.	Wayne Smith	2,692
39.	Ed Hessert	2,635
40.	Pete Hazelwood	2,367
41.	Paul Goldsmith	1,999
42.	Johnny Halford	1,881
43.	Ken Meisenhelder	1,832
44.	Don Tarr	1,754
45.	Sonny Hutchins	1,694
46.	Paul Dean Holt	1,408
47.	Dick Poling	1,305
48.	John Kennedy	1,085
49.	Wayne Gillette	887
50.	Ray Elder	642

LAPS LED

1.	Bobby Isaac	5,072
2.	David Pearson	3,018
3.	Richard Petty	2,778
4.	Bobby Allison	1,251
5.	LeeRoy Yarbrough	1,155
6.	Cale Yarborough	946
7.	Buddy Baker	770
8.	Donnie Allison	400
9.	Charlie Glotzbach	171
10.	James Hylton	162
11.	Elmo Langley	40
12.	Richard Brickhouse	34
13.	Neil Castles	29
14.	Dave Marcis	22
15.	Paul Goldsmith	20
16.	John Sears	18
17.	Don Tarr	6
18.	Friday Hassler	3
19.	Dick Brooks	2
20.	Ed Hessert	1

MILES LED

1.	Bobby Isaac	2,521
2.	David Pearson	1,985
3.	Richard Petty	1,930
4.	LeeRoy Yarbrough	1,728
5.	Cale Yarborough	1,289
6.	Bobby Allison	927
7.	Buddy Baker	896
8.	Donnie Allison	597
9.	Charlie Glotzbach	284
10.	Jim Vandiver	271
11.	A.J. Foyt	170
12.	James Hylton	92
13.	Richard Brickhouse	90
14.	Tiny Lund	74
15.	Paul Goldsmith	35
	Pete Hamilton	35
17.	Dave Marcis	23
18.	Elmo Langley	20
19.	Mario Andretti	19
20.	Dr. Don Tarr	16
21.	Neil Castles	12
22.	John Sears	11
	Ramo Stott	11
24.	Friday Hassler	6
25.	Dick Brooks	5
26.	Bobby Unser	3
27.	Dr. Ed Hessert	2

MILES DRIVEN

1.	David Pearson	11,269
2.	James Hylton	10,838
3.	Richard Petty	10,502
4.	Neil Castles	10,434
5.	Jabe Thomas	9,784
6.	Elmo Langley	9,719
7.	Bobby Isaac	9,230
8.	Wendell Scott	9,076
9.	E.J. Trivette	8,955
10.	Cecil Gordon	8,931
11.	John Sears	8,842
12.	LeeRoy Yarbrough	8,619
13.	Ben Arnold	8,474
14.	Bill Champion	7,977
15.	J.D. McDuffie	7,890
16.	Bill Seifert	7,473
17.	Henley Gray	7,293
18.	Earl Brooks	6,990
19.	Dave Marcis	6,833
20.	Bobby Allison	6,483
21.	Dick Brooks	6,162
22.	Cale Yarborough	5,482
23.	Buddy Baker	5,210
24.	Donnie Allison	5,106
25.	Friday Hassler	4,665
26.	Richard Brickhouse	4,535
27.	Hoss Ellington	4,136
28.	G.C. Spencer	3,980
29.	Charlie Glotzbach	3,957
30.	Buddy Young	3,845

RACES LED

1.	David Pearson	39
2.	Bobby Isaac	38
3.	Richard Petty	32
4.	LeeRoy Yarbrough	17
5.	Cale Yarborough	16
6.	Bobby Allison	15
7.	Buddy Baker	14
8.	James Hylton	12
9.	Donnie Allison	10
10.	Charlie Glotzbach	8
11.	Paul Goldsmith	4
12.	Dave Marcis	3
	John Sears	3
14.	Richard Brickhouse	2
15.	Dick Brooks	1
	Neil Castles	1
	Elmo Langley	1
	Friday Hassler	1
	Ed Hessert	1
	Don Tarr	1

Driver	Starts	Poles	Finish						Laps	Laps Led	Races Led	Winston Cup Points	$
			1	2	3	4	5	6–10					

1970

	Driver	Starts	Poles	1	2	3	4	5	6–10	Laps	Laps Led	Races Led	Winston Cup Points	$
1.	Bobby Isaac	47	13	11	9	5	4	3	6	12,726	3,188	35	3,911	199,600
2.	Bobby Allison	46	5	3	15	8	4	0	5	12,452	1,246	22	3,860	149,745
3.	James Hylton	47	1	1	4	2	8	7	17	12,712	199	8	3,788	78,201
4.	Richard Petty	40	9	18	5	0	0	4	4	10,536	5,007	32	3,447	151,124
5.	Neil Castles	47	0	0	1	4	3	4	12	10,297	31	2	3,158	49,746
6.	Elmo Langley	47	0	0	0	1	0	0	18	10,672	0	0	3,154	45,193
7.	Jabe Thomas	46	0	0	0	0	0	0	23	10,928	0	0	3,120	42,958
8.	Benny Parsons	45	1	0	1	2	4	5	11	9,164	164	6	2,993	59,402
9.	Dave Marcis	47	0	0	0	3	0	4	8	8,909	14	1	2,820	41,111
10.	Frank Warren	46	0	0	0	0	0	0	2	7,709	71	1	2,697	35,161
11.	Cecil Gordon	44	0	0	0	0	1	1	9	8,424	0	0	2,514	32,713
12.	John Sears	40	1	0	0	0	3	1	3	7,777	10	1	2,465	32,675
13.	Dick Brooks	34	0	0	2	5	4	4	3	6,821	194	6	2,460	53,754
14.	Wendell Scott	41	0	0	0	0	0	0	9	8,276	0	0	2,425	28,518
15.	Bill Champion	38	0	0	0	0	0	0	6	7,493	0	0	2,350	30,943
16.	J.D. McDuffie	36	0	0	0	0	0	1	9	8,461	0	0	2,079	24,905
17.	Ben Arnold	29	0	0	0	0	0	0	3	6,838	0	0	1,997	25,805
18.	Bill Seifert	39	0	0	0	0	0	1	3	5,189	0	0	1,962	25,647
19.	Henley Gray	34	0	0	0	0	0	0	2	6,134	0	0	1,871	23,130
20.	Friday Hassler	26	0	0	0	0	0	1	5	5,439	56	1	1,831	27,535
21.	Pete Hamilton	16	1	3	1	3	0	3	2	4,069	338	9	1,819	131,406
22.	Joe Frasson	21	0	0	0	0	0	0	2	4,866	0	0	1,723	20,172
23.	David Pearson	19	2	1	2	2	4	0	2	4,210	580	11	1,716	87,118
24.	Buddy Baker	18	1	1	2	0	1	2	2	3,611	485	11	1,555	63,510
25.	Bill Dennis	25	0	0	0	0	0	0	5	4,014	0	0	1,432	15,630
26.	Ed Negre	31	0	0	0	0	0	0	1	3,345	0	0	1,413	14,580
27.	G.C. Spencer	20	0	0	0	0	2	1	6	4,618	0	0	1,410	17,915
28.	Charlie Glotzbach	19	4	2	0	3	2	0	1	3,396	417	16	1,358	50,749
29.	Roy Mayne	16	0	0	0	0	0	0	3	3,731	0	0	1,333	16,910
30.	Bill Shirey	29	0	0	0	0	0	0	1	3,691	0	0	1,244	12,215
31.	Raymond Williams	21	0	0	0	0	0	0	0	3,641	0	0	1,204	12,535
32.	Larry Baumel	23	1	0	0	0	0	0	1	2,731	0	0	1,138	16,645
33.	Buddy Arrington	19	0	0	0	0	0	0	2	2,855	0	0	1,087	16,845
34.	Cale Yarborough	19	5	3	4	3	0	1	2	5,034	906	14	1,016	115,875
35.	Dr. Don Tarr	17	0	0	0	0	0	0	5	2,507	5	1	995	16,592
36.	Johnny Halford	25	0	0	0	0	0	0	0	3,619	16	1	975	15,654
37.	Earl Brooks	21	0	0	0	0	0	0	1	1,779	0	0	884	10,360
38.	Coo Coo Marlin	13	0	0	0	0	0	0	4	2,531	0	0	876	14,799
39.	Ron Keselowski	17	0	0	0	0	0	0	1	2,339	9	1	855	11,985
40.	Donnie Allison	19	0	3	0	2	3	2	2	5,252	697	10	841	96,081
41.	Ken Meisenhelder	19	0	0	0	0	0	0	2	2,717	0	0	812	7,020
42.	Roy Tyner	14	0	0	0	0	0	0	3	1,890	0	0	631	5,565
43.	LeeRoy Yarbrough	19	2	1	1	4	2	0	3	4,250	302	12	625	61,980
44.	Dick May	16	0	0	0	0	0	0	0	1,028	0	0	551	4,510
45.	Jim Vandiver	14	0	0	0	0	0	0	5	2,634	6	1	519	16,080
46.	John Kenney	11	0	0	0	0	0	0	0	1,385	0	0	457	4,115
47.	Dub Simpson	6	0	0	0	0	0	0	1	1,155	0	0	367	4,510
48.	Lee Roy Carrigg	9	0	0	0	0	0	0	0	1,002	0	0	355	4,130
49.	Joe Phipps	7	0	0	0	0	0	0	0	1,506	0	0	325	4,090
50.	Wayne Smith	8	0	0	0	0	0	0	0	593	0	0	300	4,505

#	LAPS COMPLETED	
1.	Bobby Isaac	12,726
2.	James Hylton	12,712
3.	Bobby Allison	12,452
4.	Jabe Thomas	10,928
5.	Elmo Langley	10,672
6.	Richard Petty	10,536
7.	Neil Castles	10,297
8.	Benny Parsons	9,164
9.	Dave Marcis	8,909
10.	J.D. McDuffie	8,461
11.	Cecil Gordon	8,424
12.	Wendell Scott	8,276
13.	John Sears	7,777
14.	Frank Warren	7,709
15.	Bill Champion	7,493
16.	Ben Arnold	6,838
17.	Dick Brooks	6,821
18.	Henley Gray	6,134
19.	Friday Hassler	5,439
20.	Donnie Allison	5,252
21.	Bill Seifert	5,189
22.	Cale Yarborough	5,034
23.	Joe Frasson	4,866
24.	G.C. Spencer	4,618
25.	LeeRoy Yarbrough	4,250
26.	David Pearson	4,210
27.	Pete Hamilton	4,069
28.	Bill Dennis	4,014
29.	Roy Mayne	3,731
30.	Bill Shirey	3,691
31.	Raymond Williams	3,641
32.	Johnny Halford	3,619
33.	Buddy Baker	3,611
34.	Charlie Glotzbach	3,396
35.	Ed Negre	3,345
36.	Buddy Arrington	2,855
37.	Larry Baumel	2,731
38.	Ken Meisenhelder	2,717
39.	Jim Vandiver	2,634
40.	Coo Coo Marlin	2,531
41.	Dr. Don Tarr	2,507
42.	Ron Keselowski	2,339
43.	Roy Tyner	1,890
44.	Earl Brooks	1,779
45.	Joe Phipps	1,506
46.	John Kenney	1,385
47.	Dub Simpson	1,155
48.	Dick May	1,028
49.	Lee Roy Carrigg	1,002
50.	Wayne Smith	593

#	LAPS LED	
1.	Richard Petty	5,007
2.	Bobby Isaac	3,188
3.	Bobby Allison	1,246
4.	Cale Yarborough	906
5.	Donnie Allison	697
6.	David Pearson	580
7.	Buddy Baker	485
8.	Charlie Glotzbach	417
9.	Pete Hamilton	338
10.	LeeRoy Yarbrough	302
11.	James Hylton	199
12.	Dick Brooks	194
13.	Benny Parsons	164
14.	Frank Warren	71
15.	Friday Hassler	56
16.	Neil Castles	31
17.	Johnny Halford	16
18.	Dave Marcis	14
19.	John Sears	10
20.	Ron Keselowski	9
21.	Jim Vandiver	6
22.	Dr. Don Tarr	5

#	MILES LED	
1.	Richard Petty	3,633
2.	Bobby Isaac	1,830
3.	Cale Yarborough	1,048
4.	Bobby Allison	970
5.	David Pearson	898
6.	Buddy Baker	883
7.	Donnie Allison	782
8.	Pete Hamilton	745
9.	Charlie Glotzbach	640
10.	LeeRoy Yarbrough	396
11.	Parnelli Jones	231
12.	James Hylton	126
13.	Dick Brooks	114
14.	Benny Parsons	112
15.	A.J. Foyt	92
16.	Fred Lorenzen	75
17.	Frank Warren	36
18.	Friday Hassler	33
19.	Tiny Lund	18
20.	Jim Paschal	17
21.	Dave Marcis	14
22.	Neil Castles	13
	Dr. Don Tarr	13
24.	Jim Vandiver	9
25.	Johnny Halford	8
26.	Richard Brickhouse	5
	Ron Keselowski	5
	Roger McCluskey	5
	John Sears	5
	Ramo Stott	5

#	MILES DRIVEN	
1.	Bobby Isaac	11,251
2.	James Hylton	11,223
3.	Bobby Allison	11,164
4.	Richard Petty	9,811
5.	Jabe Thomas	9,510
6.	Elmo Langley	9,319
7.	Neil Castles	9,154
8.	Benny Parsons	8,725
9.	Dave Marcis	8,041
10.	John Sears	7,939
11.	Frank Warren	7,763
12.	Dick Brooks	6,996
13.	Wendell Scott	6,949
14.	Cecil Gordon	6,872
15.	Bill Champion	6,864
16.	Ben Arnold	6,746
17.	Friday Hassler	6,518
18.	J.D. McDuffie	6,287
19.	Cale Yarborough	6,237
20.	Joe Frasson	6,230
21.	Pete Hamilton	6,210
22.	Buddy Baker	5,874
23.	David Pearson	5,815
24.	Donnie Allison	5,674
25.	LeeRoy Yarbrough	5,438
26.	Charlie Glotzbach	5,258
27.	Henley Gray	5,249
28.	Bill Seifert	5,196
29.	Roy Mayne	4,764
30.	G.C. Spencer	4,091

#	RACES LED	
1.	Bobby Isaac	35
2.	Richard Petty	32
3.	Bobby Allison	22
4.	Charlie Glotzbach	16
5.	Cale Yarborough	14
6.	LeeRoy Yarbrough	12
7.	Buddy Baker	11
	David Pearson	11
9.	Donnie Allison	10
10.	Pete Hamilton	9
11.	James Hylton	8
12.	Dick Brooks	6
	Benny Parsons	6
14.	Neil Castles	2
15.	Johnny Halford	1
	Friday Hassler	1
	Ron Keselowski	1
	Dave Marcis	1
	John Sears	1
	Dr. Don Tarr	1
	Jim Vandiver	1
	Frank Warren	1

Driver	Starts	Poles	Finish 1	2	3	4	5	6–10	Laps	Laps Led	Races Led	Winston Cup Points	$

1971

	Driver	Starts	Poles	1	2	3	4	5	6–10	Laps	Laps Led	Races Led	Winston Cup Points	$
1.	Richard Petty	46	9	21	8	7	2	0	3	13,739	4,932	41	4,435	351,071
2.	James Hylton	46	1	0	2	3	5	4	23	12,785	105	5	4,071	90,282
3.	Cecil Gordon	46	0	0	0	2	2	2	15	12,468	0	0	3,677	69,080
4.	Bobby Allison	42	9	11	7	3	5	1	4	11,716	3,589	31	3,636	254,316
5.	Elmo Langley	46	0	0	3	1	3	4	12	11,299	48	1	3,356	57,037
6.	Jabe Thomas	43	0	0	0	0	1	1	13	11,360	0	0	3,200	48,241
7.	Bill Champion	45	0	0	0	0	0	3	11	10,518	0	0	3,058	43,769
8.	Frank Warren	47	0	0	0	0	0	1	9	8,984	0	0	2,886	40,072
9.	J.D. McDuffie	43	0	0	0	1	0	1	6	9,359	5	1	2,862	35,578
10.	Walter Ballard	41	0	0	0	1	1	1	8	11,219	0	0	2,633	30,974
11.	Benny Parsons	35	0	1	2	5	1	4	5	7,981	144	4	2,611	55,896
12.	Ed Negre	43	0	0	0	0	0	0	2	8,359	0	0	2,528	29,738
13.	Bill Seifert	37	0	0	0	0	0	0	4	6,552	0	0	2,403	33,220
14.	Henley Gray	39	0	0	0	0	0	0	4	7,684	0	0	2,392	31,789
15.	Buddy Baker	19	1	1	6	5	0	1	3	4,817	727	15	2,358	115,150
16.	Friday Hassler	29	2	0	1	2	0	1	9	5,650	68	3	2,277	37,305
17.	Earl Brooks	35	0	0	0	0	1	0	3	6,757	0	0	2,205	25,360
18.	Bill Dennis	28	1	0	0	1	1	2	6	6,111	47	2	2,181	29,420
19.	Wendell Scott	37	0	0	0	0	0	0	4	7,791	0	0	2,180	21,701
20.	John Sears	37	0	0	0	0	0	0	3	7,512	0	0	2,167	26,735
21.	Dave Marcis	29	2	0	1	1	4	3	5	6,460	331	8	2,049	37,382
22.	Neil Castles	38	0	0	0	0	1	0	9	6,946	10	1	2,036	22,939
23.	Bobby Isaac	25	5	4	4	2	4	2	1	6,856	1,753	17	1,819	106,526
24.	Pete Hamilton	22	2	1	0	5	4	1	1	4,525	219	14	1,739	60,440
25.	Joe Frasson	17	0	0	0	0	0	1	3	3,752	0	0	1,619	20,975
26.	Ben Arnold	18	0	0	0	0	0	0	3	4,150	0	0	1,618	18,491
27.	Ron Keselowski	20	0	0	0	0	0	0	6	3,046	0	0	1,446	17,680
28.	Bill Shirey	27	0	0	0	0	0	0	2	3,667	0	0	1,303	9,160
29.	Donnie Allison	13	5	1	1	1	2	2	2	3,017	806	8	1,280	69,995
30.	Dean Dalton	19	0	0	0	0	0	0	1	3,487	0	0	1,276	13,910
31.	Raymond Williams	20	0	0	0	0	0	0	0	2,822	0	0	1,270	14,585
32.	Dick May	22	0	0	0	0	0	0	1	2,527	0	0	1,090	9,225
33.	Charlie Roberts	20	0	0	0	0	0	0	2	2,796	0	0	1,053	12,470
34.	G.C. Spencer	17	0	0	0	0	0	2	4	3,325	12	1	1,008	11,470
35.	Richard Brown	13	0	0	0	0	0	0	2	2,454	0	0	967	11,940
36.	Dick Brooks	20	0	0	1	5	0	3	3	4,495	16	5	939	32,921
37.	Larry Baumel	16	0	0	0	0	0	0	1	2,245	0	0	904	10,910
38.	Maynard Troyer	13	0	0	0	0	1	0	2	1,617	0	0	879	13,115
39.	Roy Mayne	11	0	0	0	0	0	0	1	1,918	0	0	852	10,330
40.	Ken Meisenhelder	15	0	0	0	0	0	0	1	2,194	0	0	797	5,405
41.	Tommy Gale	9	0	0	0	0	0	0	1	1,616	0	0	729	8,800
42.	Charlie Glotzbach	20	4	1	2	0	3	1	3	4,735	805	10	699	38,605
43.	Bill Hollar	11	0	0	0	0	0	0	1	2,095	0	0	644	4,275
44.	Marv Acton	11	0	0	0	0	0	0	0	1,421	0	0	627	8,620
45.	Fred Lorenzen	14	1	0	1	0	2	4	2	3,229	152	6	611	45,100
46.	Richard Childress	12	0	0	0	0	0	0	0	1,394	0	0	601	3,855
47.	Paul Tyler	10	0	0	0	0	0	0	0	1,521	0	0	561	6,360
48.	Jim Vandiver	7	0	0	0	0	0	1	3	1,423	0	0	553	13,575
49.	Coo Coo Marlin	12	0	0	0	0	0	0	0	1,495	0	0	527	9,085
50.	Eddie Yarboro	7	0	0	0	0	0	0	0	1,624	0	0	497	3,685

LAPS COMPLETED

1.	Richard Petty	13,739
2.	James Hylton	12,785
3.	Cecil Gordon	12,468
4.	Bobby Allison	11,716
5.	Jabe Thomas	11,360
6.	Elmo Langley	11,299
7.	Walter Ballard	11,219
8.	Bill Champion	10,518
9.	J.D. McDuffie	9,359
10.	Frank Warren	8,984
11.	Ed Negre	8,359
12.	Benny Parsons	7,981
13.	Wendell Scott	7,791
14.	Henley Gray	7,684
15.	John Sears	7,512
16.	Neil Castles	6,946
17.	Bobby Isaac	6,856
18.	Earl Brooks	6,757
19.	Bill Seifert	6,552
20.	Dave Marcis	6,460
21.	Bill Dennis	6,111
22.	Friday Hassler	5,650
23.	Buddy Baker	4,817
24.	Charlie Glotzbach	4,735
25.	Pete Hamilton	4,525
26.	Dick Brooks	4,495
27.	Ben Arnold	4,150
28.	Joe Frasson	3,752
29.	Bill Shirey	3,667
30.	Dean Dalton	3,487
31.	G.C. Spencer	3,325
32.	Fred Lorenzen	3,229
33.	Ron Keselowski	3,046
34.	Donnie Allison	3,017
35.	Raymond Williams	2,822
36.	Charlie Roberts	2,796
37.	Dick May	2,527
38.	Richard Brown	2,454
39.	Larry Baumel	2,245
40.	Ken Meisenhelder	2,194
41.	Bill Hollar	2,095
42.	Roy Mayne	1,918
43.	Eddie Yarboro	1,624
44.	Maynard Troyer	1,617
45.	Tommy Gale	1,616
46.	Paul Tyler	1,521
47.	Coo Coo Marlin	1,495
48.	Jim Vandiver	1,423
49.	Marv Acton	1,421
50.	Richard Childress	1,394

LAPS LED

1.	Richard Petty	4,932
2.	Bobby Allison	3,589
3.	Bobby Isaac	1,753
4.	Donnie Allison	806
5.	Charlie Glotzbach	805
6.	Buddy Baker	727
7.	Dave Marcis	331
8.	Pete Hamilton	219
9.	Fred Lorenzen	152
10.	Benny Parsons	144
11.	James Hylton	105
12.	Friday Hassler	68
13.	Elmo Langley	48
14.	Bill Dennis	47
15.	Dick Brooks	16
16.	G.C. Spencer	12
17.	Neil Castles	10
18.	J.D. McDuffie	5

MILES LED

1.	Bobby Allison	4,073
2.	Richard Petty	3,725
3.	Bobby Isaac	1,225
4.	Buddy Baker	1,008
5.	Donnie Allison	985
6.	A.J. Foyt	780
7.	Charlie Glotzbach	695
8.	Pete Hamilton	340
9.	David Pearson	257
10.	Dave Marcis	227
11.	Fred Lorenzen	225
12.	Ray Elder	183
13.	Tiny Lund	122
14.	Benny Parsons	79
15.	James Hylton	63
16.	Friday Hassler	44
17.	LeeRoy Yarbrough	32
18.	Jim Paschal	27
19.	Bill Dennis	25
20.	Dick Brooks	21
21.	Cale Yarborough	20
22.	Elmo Langley	16
23.	G.C. Spencer	12
24.	Hershel McGriff	10
25.	H.B. Bailey	6
26.	Neil Castles	4
27.	J.D. McDuffie	2

MILES DRIVEN

1.	Richard Petty	12,878
2.	James Hylton	12,725
3.	Bobby Allison	12,130
4.	Cecil Gordon	12,041
5.	Elmo Langley	10,490
6.	Jabe Thomas	9,822
7.	Bill Champion	9,721
8.	J.D. McDuffie	9,102
9.	Frank Warren	8,605
10.	Walter Ballard	8,041
11.	Buddy Baker	7,823
12.	Benny Parsons	7,640
13.	Bobby Isaac	7,604
14.	Ed Negre	7,549
15.	Henley Gray	7,511
16.	Bill Seifert	7,158
17.	Friday Hassler	7,137
18.	Bill Dennis	6,979
19.	Pete Hamilton	6,895
20.	Wendell Scott	6,826
21.	John Sears	6,818
22.	Dave Marcis	6,690
23.	Earl Brooks	6,654
24.	Ben Arnold	6,206
25.	Joe Frasson	5,699
26.	Neil Castles	5,622
27.	Fred Lorenzen	5,038
28.	Dick Brooks	4,784
29.	Charlie Glotzbach	4,702
30.	Donnie Allison	4,334

RACES LED

1.	Richard Petty	41
2.	Bobby Allison	31
3.	Bobby Isaac	17
4.	Buddy Baker	15
5.	Pete Hamilton	14
6.	Charlie Glotzbach	10
7.	Donnie Allison	8
	Dave Marcis	8
9.	Fred Lorenzen	6
10.	Dick Brooks	5
	James Hylton	5
12.	Benny Parsons	4
13.	Friday Hassler	3
14.	Bill Dennis	2
15.	Neil Castles	1
	Elmo Langley	1
	J.D. McDuffie	1
	G.C. Spencer	1

Driver	Starts	Poles	Finish 1	2	3	4	5	6–10	Laps	Laps Led	Races Led	Winston Cup Points	$

1972

	Driver	Starts	Poles	1	2	3	4	5	6–10	Laps	Laps Led	Races Led	Winston Cup Points	$
1.	Richard Petty	31	3	8	9	5	2	1	3	10,282	2,093	30	8,701	339,405
2.	Bobby Allison	31	11	10	12	2	1	0	2	10,063	4,343	30	8,573	348,939
3.	James Hylton	31	0	1	0	0	5	3	14	9,702	111	4	8,158	126,705
4.	Cecil Gordon	31	0	0	0	0	1	3	12	9,033	3	2	7,326	73,126
5.	Benny Parsons	31	0	0	1	0	8	1	9	7,922	19	2	6,844	102,043
6.	Walter Ballard	31	0	0	0	0	0	0	7	8,460	0	0	6,781	59,745
7.	Elmo Langley	30	0	0	0	0	0	1	8	8,150	0	0	6,656	59,644
8.	John Sears	28	0	0	0	0	0	2	5	7,882	0	0	6,298	51,314
9.	Dean Dalton	29	0	0	0	0	0	0	4	7,533	0	0	6,295	42,299
10.	Ben Arnold	26	0	0	0	0	0	0	7	6,976	0	0	6,179	44,547
11.	Frank Warren	30	0	0	0	0	0	0	2	7,091	0	0	5,788	45,048
12.	Jabe Thomas	28	0	0	0	0	0	0	4	7,132	0	0	5,772	43,438
13.	Bill Champion	29	0	0	0	0	0	0	4	7,044	0	0	5,740	42,242
14.	Raymond Williams	28	0	0	0	0	0	0	5	6,759	0	0	5,712	37,000
15.	Dave Marcis	27	0	0	0	2	1	2	6	6,708	4	2	5,459	45,012
16.	Charlie Roberts	26	0	0	0	0	0	0	1	6,437	0	0	5,354	32,488
17.	Henley Gray	28	0	0	0	0	0	0	2	6,121	0	0	5,093	38,461
18.	J.D. McDuffie	27	0	0	0	0	0	1	1	6,231	0	0	5,075	36,833
19.	Bobby Isaac	27	9	1	3	5	0	1	0	5,636	1,326	20	5,050	133,257
20.	David Pearson	17	4	6	1	3	2	0	1	4,902	1,571	16	4,718	142,440
21.	Ed Negre	26	0	0	0	0	0	0	0	5,755	0	0	4,696	30,538
22.	Buddy Arrington	20	0	0	0	0	0	1	9	5,503	0	0	4,555	28,700
23.	Larry Smith	23	0	0	0	0	0	0	7	4,320	0	0	4,173	24,215
24.	Buddy Baker	17	1	2	1	4	1	0	1	4,641	594	14	3,936	102,540
25.	Coo Coo Marlin	20	0	0	0	1	1	0	3	4,092	31	5	3,852	28,924
26.	David Ray Boggs	24	0	0	0	0	0	0	0	3,968	0	0	3,739	19,489
27.	Ron Keselowski	22	0	0	0	0	0	1	2	3,398	0	0	3,475	21,905
28.	Joe Frasson	16	0	0	0	1	0	0	3	3,013	9	2	3,152	21,570
29.	Richard Brown	16	0	0	0	0	0	1	0	3,403	0	0	2,939	19,283
30.	Neil Castles	21	0	0	0	0	0	0	1	4,075	0	0	2,789	18,760
31.	Jim Vandiver	16	0	0	0	2	0	0	1	2,871	6	1	2,514	27,983
32.	Clarence Lovell	12	0	0	0	0	0	0	0	2,202	0	0	2,360	10,770
33.	David Sisco	12	0	0	0	0	0	0	2	2,067	0	0	2,310	13,700
34.	LeeRoy Yarbrough	18	0	0	0	1	2	2	4	4,174	8	4	2,157	40,705
35.	George Altheide	11	0	0	0	0	0	0	0	1,578	0	0	1,916	10,405
36.	Donnie Allison	10	0	0	0	1	0	1	1	1,385	35	4	1,849	16,826
37.	Richard Childress	15	0	0	0	0	0	0	0	1,681	0	0	1,521	7,245
38.	Bill Shirey	13	0	0	0	0	0	0	0	1,812	0	0	1,468	8,070
39.	Fred Lorenzen	8	0	0	0	0	3	0	1	1,801	4	1	1,333	19,505
40.	Wendell Scott	6	0	0	0	0	0	0	0	1,763	0	0	1,317	5,830
41.	Tommy Gale	6	0	0	0	0	0	0	0	1,144	0	0	1,298	7,197
42.	Bill Dennis	11	0	0	0	1	0	1	0	2,327	2	1	1,279	9,604
43.	G.C. Spencer	10	0	0	0	0	0	0	1	1,492	0	0	1,238	8,040
44.	Dick May	6	0	0	0	0	0	0	1	955	0	0	1,229	5,370
45.	Hershel McGriff	4	0	0	0	0	0	2	1	727	3	1	1,199	12,290
46.	Les Covey	7	0	0	0	0	0	0	0	1,347	0	0	1,128	5,070
47.	Johnny Halford	5	0	0	0	0	0	0	1	1,032	0	0	1,103	4,955
48.	Pete Hamilton	5	0	0	0	0	0	1	0	1,044	8	2	1,083	8,005
49.	Dick Brooks	14	0	0	0	0	0	0	1	1,156	3	2	1,023	14,146
50.	Eddie Yarboro	6	0	0	0	0	0	0	0	1,728	0	0	1,007	3,435

LAPS COMPLETED

1.	Richard Petty	10,282
2.	Bobby Allison	10,063
3.	James Hylton	9,702
4.	Cecil Gordon	9,033
5.	Walter Ballard	8,460
6.	Elmo Langley	8,150
7.	Benny Parsons	7,922
8.	John Sears	7,882
9.	Dean Dalton	7,533
10.	Jabe Thomas	7,132
11.	Frank Warren	7,091
12.	Bill Champion	7,044
13.	Ben Arnold	6,976
14.	Raymond Williams	6,759
15.	Dave Marcis	6,708
16.	Charlie Roberts	6,437
17.	J.D. McDuffie	6,231
18.	Henley Gray	6,121
19.	Ed Negre	5,755
20.	Bobby Isaac	5,636
21.	Buddy Arrington	5,503
22.	David Pearson	4,902
23.	Buddy Baker	4,641
24.	Larry Smith	4,320
25.	LeeRoy Yarbrough	4,174
26.	Coo Coo Marlin	4,092
27.	Neil Castles	4,075
28.	David Ray Boggs	3,968
29.	Richard Brown	3,403
30.	Ron Keselowski	3,398
31.	Joe Frasson	3,013
32.	Jim Vandiver	2,871
33.	Bill Dennis	2,327
34.	Clarence Lovell	2,202
35.	David Sisco	2,067
36.	Bill Shirey	1,812
37.	Fred Lorenzen	1,801
38.	Wendell Scott	1,763
39.	Eddie Yarboro	1,728
40.	Richard Childress	1,681
41.	George Altheide	1,578
42.	G.C. Spencer	1,492
43.	Donnie Allison	1,385
44.	Les Covey	1,347
45.	Dick Brooks	1,156
46.	Tommy Gale	1,144
47.	Pete Hamilton	1,044
48.	Johnny Halford	1,032
49.	Dick May	955
50.	Hershel McGriff	727

LAPS LED

1.	Bobby Allison	4,343
2.	Richard Petty	2,093
3.	David Pearson	1,571
4.	Bobby Isaac	1,326
5.	Buddy Baker	594
6.	James Hylton	111
7.	Donnie Allison	35
8.	Coo Coo Marlin	31
9.	Benny Parsons	19
10.	Joe Frasson	9
11.	Pete Hamilton	8
	LeeRoy Yarbrough	8
13.	Jim Vandiver	6
14.	Fred Lorenzen	4
	Dave Marcis	4
16.	Dick Brooks	3
	Cecil Gordon	3
	Hershel McGriff	3
19.	Bill Dennis	2

MILES LED

1.	Bobby Allison	4,063
2.	David Pearson	2,292
3.	Richard Petty	2,287
4.	Bobby Isaac	1,515
5.	Buddy Baker	925
6.	A.J. Foyt	834
7.	James Hylton	287
8.	Ray Elder	131
9.	Donnie Allison	75
10.	Coo Coo Marlin	41
11.	Benny Parsons	39
12.	Pete Hamilton	21
13.	Darrell Waltrip	19
14.	Joe Frasson	18
15.	Fred Lorenzen	11
16.	Cale Yarborough	9
17.	H.B. Bailey	8
	Hershel McGriff	8
	Ramo Stott	8
	Jim Vandiver	8
21.	LeeRoy Yarbrough	7
22.	Dave Marcis	6
23.	Dick Brooks	4
	Cecil Gordon	4
25.	Bill Dennis	2

MILES DRIVEN

1.	Richard Petty	11,996
2.	Bobby Allison	11,801
3.	James Hylton	11,476
4.	Cecil Gordon	10,421
5.	Walter Ballard	9,748
6.	Benny Parsons	9,463
7.	Elmo Langley	9,460
8.	Dean Dalton	9,068
9.	John Sears	8,995
10.	Ben Arnold	8,935
11.	Frank Warren	8,404
12.	Jabe Thomas	8,207
13.	Bill Champion	8,122
14.	Raymond Williams	8,079
15.	Charlie Roberts	7,729
16.	Dave Marcis	7,522
17.	Henley Gray	7,308
18.	J.D. McDuffie	7,095
19.	Buddy Arrington	7,009
20.	Bobby Isaac	6,872
21.	Ed Negre	6,702
22.	David Pearson	6,593
23.	Buddy Baker	6,030
24.	Larry Smith	5,831
25.	Coo Coo Marlin	5,383
26.	David Ray Boggs	5,164
27.	Ron Keselowski	4,976
28.	LeeRoy Yarbrough	4,866
29.	Joe Frasson	4,638
30.	Richard D. Brown	4,190

RACES LED

1.	Bobby Allison	30
	Richard Petty	30
3.	Bobby Isaac	20
4.	David Pearson	16
5.	Buddy Baker	14
6.	Coo Coo Marlin	5
7.	Donnie Allison	4
	James Hylton	4
	LeeRoy Yarbrough	4
10.	Dick Brooks	2
	Joe Frasson	2
	Cecil Gordon	2
	Pete Hamilton	2
	Dave Marcis	2
	Benny Parsons	2
16.	Bill Dennis	1
	Fred Lorenzen	1
	Hershel McGriff	1
	Jim Vandiver	1

Driver	Starts	Poles	Finish 1	2	3	4	5	6–10	Laps	Laps Led	Races Led	Winston Cup Points	$
1973													
1. Benny Parsons	28	0	1	3	3	3	5	6	9,311	374	8	7,173	182,321
2. Cale Yarborough	28	5	4	6	4	1	1	3	9,314	3,167	21	7,106	267,513
3. Cecil Gordon	28	0	0	0	1	1	6	10	8,998	5	3	7,046	102,120
4. James Hylton	28	0	0	0	0	1	0	10	9,324	1	1	6,972	82,512
5. Richard Petty	28	3	6	6	1	2	0	2	8,644	1,815	16	6,877	234,389
6. Buddy Baker	27	5	2	4	6	4	0	4	8,369	975	14	6,327	190,531
7. Bobby Allison	27	6	2	2	6	4	1	1	8,072	870	20	6,272	161,818
8. Walter Ballard	28	0	0	0	0	0	0	4	8,048	5	1	5,955	53,875
9. Elmo Langley	27	0	0	0	0	0	0	4	8,016	0	0	5,826	49,542
10. J.D. McDuffie	27	0	0	0	0	0	3	7	7,388	11	2	5,743	56,140
11. Jabe Thomas	25	0	0	0	0	0	0	1	7,205	0	0	5,637	42,955
12. Buddy Arrington	26	0	0	0	0	0	1	3	7,917	0	0	5,483	40,877
13. David Pearson	18	8	11	2	1	0	0	0	5,338	2,658	16	5,382	228,408
14. Henley Gray	24	0	0	0	0	0	0	4	7,517	0	0	5,215	34,112
15. Richard Childress	25	0	0	0	0	1	0	1	6,918	1	1	5,169	37,880
16. Frank Warren	26	0	0	0	0	0	0	0	6,713	0	0	4,992	36,551
17. David Sisco	23	0	0	0	0	1	1	4	6,552	12	2	4,986	36,205
18. Ed Negre	24	0	0	0	0	0	1	1	6,230	0	0	4,942	34,235
19. Dean Dalton	26	0	0	0	0	0	0	2	5,889	0	0	4,712	35,954
20. Charlie Roberts	24	0	0	0	0	0	0	0	7,017	0	0	4,695	32,144
21. Bill Champion	26	0	0	0	0	0	0	1	5,103	0	0	4,447	31,828
22. Coo Coo Marlin	21	0	0	0	1	0	0	7	5,454	16	3	4,233	29,997
23. Lennie Pond	23	0	0	0	0	1	0	8	5,850	4	2	4,013	25,255
24. Dave Marcis	23	0	0	0	0	1	2	3	4,905	0	0	3,973	30,253
25. Raymond Williams	22	0	0	0	0	0	0	3	4,684	0	0	3,708	22,728
26. Bobby Isaac	19	0	0	2	1	2	0	1	4,177	62	7	3,352	84,550
27. Dick Brooks	14	0	1	0	1	0	1	6	3,448	25	3	3,200	55,369
28. Darrell Waltrip	19	0	0	1	0	0	0	4	3,783	50	3	2,968	42,466
29. Joe Frasson	14	0	0	0	1	1	0	2	2,732	1	1	2,952	25,884
30. Vic Parsons	18	0	0	0	0	0	0	6	3,498	0	0	2,929	18,200
31. Jim Vandiver	10	0	0	0	0	0	0	4	2,431	0	0	2,508	18,586
32. John Sears	17	0	0	0	0	0	0	0	3,568	0	0	2,465	16,890
33. Larry Smith	11	0	0	0	0	0	0	1	2,103	0	0	2,367	14,090
34. Rick Newsom	12	0	0	0	0	0	0	0	3,209	0	0	1,931	8,530
35. Donnie Allison	14	0	0	1	1	0	0	3	2,904	44	3	1,755	41,246
36. D.K. Ulrich	11	0	0	0	0	0	0	0	2,006	0	0	1,543	3,955
37. G.C. Spencer	10	0	0	0	0	0	0	1	1,459	0	0	1,503	12,013
38. Mel Larson	10	0	0	0	0	0	0	0	2,160	0	0	1,182	8,235
39. Johnny Barnes	8	0	0	0	0	0	0	0	1,416	0	0	1,174	8,585
40. Eddie Bond	6	0	0	0	0	0	0	0	1,407	0	0	1,163	6,901
41. Earle Canavan	5	0	0	0	0	0	0	0	1,223	0	0	1,144	4,980
42. Earl Brooks	9	0	0	0	0	0	0	0	2,267	0	0	1,075	4,880
43. Charlie Glotzbach	5	0	0	0	0	0	0	1	1,048	11	2	903	6,451
44. Randy Tissot	3	0	0	0	0	0	0	0	816	0	0	887	4,245
45. Ron Keselowski	5	0	0	0	0	0	1	0	733	0	0	879	6,060
46. Jimmy Crawford	4	0	0	0	0	0	0	0	1,053	0	0	846	4,059
47. Richard Brown	13	0	0	0	0	0	0	0	1,260	0	0	827	7,340
48. Clarence Lovell	4	0	0	0	0	1	0	1	661	0	0	813	9,175
49. Bill Dennis	4	0	0	0	0	0	0	2	1,430	0	0	809	4,225
50. Jack McCoy	3	0	0	0	0	0	1	2	797	0	0	793	5,270

LAPS COMPLETED	
1. James Hylton	9,324
2. Cale Yarborough	9,314
3. Benny Parsons	9,311
4. Cecil Gordon	8,998
5. Richard Petty	8,644
6. Buddy Baker	8,369
7. Bobby Allison	8,072
8. Walter Ballard	8,048
9. Elmo Langley	8,016
10. Buddy Arrington	7,917
11. Henley Gray	7,517
12. J.D. McDuffie	7,388
13. Jabe Thomas	7,205
14. Charlie Roberts	7,017
15. Richard Childress	6,918
16. Frank Warren	6,713
17. David Sisco	6,552
18. Ed Negre	6,230
19. Dean Dalton	5,889
20. Lennie Pond	5,850
21. Coo Coo Marlin	5,454
22. David Pearson	5,338
23. Bill Champion	5,103
24. Dave Marcis	4,905
25. Raymond Williams	4,684
26. Bobby Isaac	4,177
27. Darrell Waltrip	3,783
28. John Sears	3,568
29. Vic Parsons	3,498
30. Dick Brooks	3,448
31. Rick Newsom	3,209
32. Donnie Allison	2,904
33. Joe Frasson	2,732
34. Jim Vandiver	2,431
35. Earl Brooks	2,267
36. Mel Larson	2,160
37. Larry Smith	2,103
38. D.K. Ulrich	2,006
39. G.C. Spencer	1,459
40. Bill Dennis	1,430
41. Johnny Barnes	1,416
42. Eddie Bond	1,407
43. Richard Brown	1,260
44. Earle Canavan	1,223
45. Jimmy Crawford	1,053
46. Charlie Glotzbach	1,048
47. Randy Tissot	816
48. Jack McCoy	797
49. Ron Keselowski	733
50. Clarence Lovell	661

LAPS LED	
1. Cale Yarborough	3,167
2. David Pearson	2,658
3. Richard Petty	1,815
4. Buddy Baker	975
5. Bobby Allison	870
6. Benny Parsons	374
7. Bobby Isaac	62
8. Darrell Waltrip	50
9. Donnie Allison	44
10. Dick Brooks	25
11. Coo Coo Marlin	16
12. David Sisco	12
13. J.D. McDuffie	11
Charlie Glotzbach	11
15. Walter Ballard	5
Cecil Gordon	5
17. Lennie Pond	4
18. Richard Childress	1
Joe Frasson	1
James Hylton	1

MILES LED	
1. David Pearson	3,282
2. Cale Yarborough	2,734
3. Richard Petty	1,643
4. Buddy Baker	1,597
5. Bobby Allison	1,022
6. Mark Donohue	362
7. Benny Parsons	236
8. Donnie Allison	109
9. Darrell Waltrip	90
10. Bobby Isaac	82
11. Dick Brooks	65
12. Coo Coo Marlin	41
13. J.D. McDuffie	29
14. Charles Barrett	24
15. David Sisco	19
16. Charlie Glotzbach	15
17. Walter Ballard	13
18. Cecil Gordon	9
19. Lennie Pond	8
20. Richard Childress	3
James Hylton	3
Marty Robbins	3
Ramo Stott	3
Dick Trickle	3
25. Joe Frasson	2

MILES DRIVEN	
1. Benny Parsons	10,061
2. James Hylton	10,058
3. Cecil Gordon	10,004
4. Cale Yarborough	9,752
5. Richard Petty	9,292
6. Buddy Baker	8,918
7. Bobby Allison	8,653
8. Walter Ballard	8,640
9. Elmo Langley	8,385
10. J.D. McDuffie	8,137
11. Jabe Thomas	7,917
12. Buddy Arrington	7,890
13. Henley Gray	7,615
14. Richard Childress	7,469
15. David Pearson	7,197
16. Ed Negre	7,193
17. Frank Warren	7,185
18. David Sisco	7,146
19. Charlie Roberts	6,861
20. Dean Dalton	6,838
21. Bill Champion	6,375
22. Coo Coo Marlin	5,948
23. Lennie Pond	5,479
24. Dave Marcis	5,457
25. Darrell Waltrip	5,358
26. Raymond Williams	5,233
27. Dick Brooks	4,954
28. Bobby Isaac	4,545
29. Joe Frasson	4,390
30. Vic Parsons	4,021

RACES LED	
1. Cale Yarborough	21
2. Bobby Allison	20
3. David Pearson	16
Richard Petty	16
5. Buddy Baker	14
6. Benny Parsons	8
7. Bobby Isaac	7
8. Donnie Allison	3
Dick Brooks	3
Cecil Gordon	3
Coo Coo Marlin	3
Darrell Waltrip	3
13. Charlie Glotzbach	2
J.D. McDuffie	2
Lennie Pond	2
David Sisco	2
17. Walter Ballard	1
Richard Childress	1
Joe Frasson	1
James Hylton	1

Driver	Starts	Poles	Finish 1	2	3	4	5	6–10	Laps	Laps Led	Races Led	Winston Cup Points	$

1974

	Driver	Starts	Poles	1	2	3	4	5	6–10	Laps	Laps Led	Races Led	Winston Cup Points	$
1.	Richard Petty	30	7	10	8	4	0	0	1	9,097	3,100	24	5,037	432,020
2.	Cale Yarborough	30	3	10	4	5	1	1	1	9,398	3,530	26	4,470	363,782
3.	David Pearson	19	11	7	5	2	1	0	0	4,630	1,167	18	2,389	252,819
4.	Bobby Allison	27	3	2	3	5	2	5	0	7,523	899	20	2,019	178,437
5.	Benny Parsons	30	0	0	2	2	5	2	3	8,120	88	11	1,591	185,080
6.	Dave Marcis	30	0	0	0	0	2	4	12	8,658	12	2	1,378	83,377
7.	Buddy Baker	19	2	0	4	5	1	1	1	4,346	381	13	1,016	151,025
8.	Earl Ross	21	0	1	1	1	1	1	5	5,730	127	6	1,009	81,199
9.	Cecil Gordon	30	0	0	0	0	1	0	9	7,396	1	1	1,000	66,166
10.	David Sisco	28	0	0	0	1	1	0	7	7,483	43	4	956	58,313
11.	James Hylton	29	0	0	0	0	0	1	7	6,774	29	6	924	61,385
12.	J.D. McDuffie	30	0	0	0	0	0	0	7	8,283	1	1	920	59,535
13.	Frank Warren	29	0	0	0	0	0	1	1	7,342	0	0	820	55,779
14.	Richie Panch	28	0	0	0	1	0	1	5	6,257	1	1	775	52,713
15.	Walter Ballard	27	0	0	0	0	0	1	5	6,820	2	1	748	54,039
16.	Richard Childress	29	0	0	0	0	0	0	3	5,138	0	0	735	50,249
17.	Donnie Allison	21	2	0	1	1	2	2	4	5,101	183	10	728	60,315
18.	Lennie Pond	22	0	0	0	0	1	4	6	6,384	17	6	723	55,990
19.	Darrell Waltrip	16	1	0	1	3	2	1	4	4,649	103	5	609	67,775
20.	Tony Bettenhausen, Jr.	27	0	0	0	0	0	0	1	5,548	0	0	601	38,995
21.	Jackie Rogers	21	0	0	0	0	0	0	6	4,244	1	1	587	32,367
22.	Coo Coo Marlin	23	0	0	0	0	1	0	4	5,323	28	7	581	41,759
23.	Ed Negre	26	0	0	0	0	0	0	0	5,302	0	0	534	24,622
24.	Bob Burcham	20	0	0	0	0	1	0	4	4,819	2	1	445	27,923
25.	Elmo Langley	24	0	0	0	0	0	0	3	5,593	0	0	433	24,722
26.	Charlie Glotzbach	13	0	0	0	0	4	0	1	3,478	127	6	293	33,072
27.	Dick Brooks	16	0	0	0	0	0	0	3	2,951	1	1	267	22,760
28.	Joe Frasson	14	0	0	0	0	0	0	3	2,141	13	3	240	22,629
29.	George Follmer	13	1	0	0	0	1	2	2	3,086	27	2	230	53,780
30.	Buddy Arrington	17	0	0	0	0	0	0	4	4,782	0	0	221	21,510
31.	Bill Champion	18	0	0	0	0	0	0	0	2,324	0	0	207	13,480
32.	D.K. Ulrich	15	0	0	0	0	0	0	0	3,194	0	0	155	11,955
33.	Bobby Isaac	11	0	0	1	0	0	0	4	1,907	11	4	152	22,642
34.	Travis Tiller	13	0	0	0	0	0	0	0	2,180	0	0	146	11,410
35.	Roy Mayne	11	0	0	0	0	0	0	0	1,681	0	0	141	15,284
36.	Dean Dalton	14	0	0	0	0	0	0	0	2,414	6	1	125	12,375
37.	Neil Castles	14	0	0	0	0	0	0	0	1,422	0	0	123	12,479
38.	G.C. Spencer	10	0	0	0	0	0	0	1	1,205	3	1	96	12,985
39.	Ramo Stott	7	0	0	0	1	0	0	3	1,725	0	0	82	23,705
40.	Jim Vandiver	7	0	0	0	0	0	0	1	1,061	1	1	71	15,909
41.	Dan Daughtry	8	0	0	0	0	0	0	1	772	6	2	63	12,413
42.	Jabe Thomas	10	0	0	0	0	0	0	1	1,504	0	0	49	7,445
43.	Gary Bettenhausen	5	0	0	0	0	1	0	2	986	35	1	49	10,350
44.	A.J. Foyt	4	0	0	0	0	1	1	0	612	70	3	41	15,560
45.	Jerry Schild	5	0	0	0	0	0	0	1	1,142	0	0	35	8,396
46.	Earle Canavan	6	0	0	0	0	0	0	0	1,477	0	0	34	6,570
47.	Dick Trickle	3	0	0	0	0	0	0	3	1,201	0	0	24	10,828
48.	Marty Robbins	4	0	0	0	0	0	1	1	550	0	0	23	5,734
49.	Alton Jones	5	0	0	0	0	0	1	1	1,163	0	0	20	4,080
50.	Hershel McGriff	5	0	0	0	0	0	0	1	559	0	0	20	8,585

LAPS COMPLETED

1.	Cale Yarborough	9,398
2.	Richard Petty	9,097
3.	Dave Marcis	8,658
4.	J.D. McDuffie	8,283
5.	Benny Parsons	8,120
6.	Bobby Allison	7,523
7.	David Sisco	7,483
8.	Cecil Gordon	7,396
9.	Frank Warren	7,342
10.	Walter Ballard	6,820
11.	James Hylton	6,774
12.	Lennie Pond	6,384
13.	Richie Panch	6,257
14.	Earl Ross	5,730
15.	Elmo Langley	5,593
16.	Tony Bettenhausen, Jr.	5,548
17.	Coo Coo Marlin	5,323
18.	Ed Negre	5,302
19.	Richard Childress	5,138
20.	Donnie Allison	5,101
21.	Bob Burcham	4,819
22.	Buddy Arrington	4,782
23.	Darrell Waltrip	4,649
24.	David Pearson	4,630
25.	Buddy Baker	4,346
26.	Jackie Rogers	4,244
27.	Charlie Glotzbach	3,478
28.	D.K. Ulrich	3,194
29.	George Follmer	3,086
30.	Dick Brooks	2,951
31.	Dean Dalton	2,414
32.	Bill Champion	2,324
33.	Travis Tiller	2,180
34.	Joe Frasson	2,141
35.	Bobby Isaac	1,907
36.	Ramo Stott	1,725
37.	Roy Mayne	1,681
38.	Jabe Thomas	1,504
39.	Earle Canavan	1,477
40.	Neil Castles	1,422
41.	G.C. Spencer	1,205
42.	Dick Trickle	1,201
43.	Alton Jones	1,163
44.	Jerry Schild	1,142
45.	Jim Vandiver	1,061
46.	Gary Bettenhausen	986
47.	Dan Daughtry	772
48.	A.J. Foyt	612
49.	Hershel McGriff	559
50.	Marty Robbins	550

LAPS LED

1.	Cale Yarborough	3,530
2.	Richard Petty	3,100
3.	David Pearson	1,167
4.	Bobby Allison	899
5.	Buddy Baker	381
6.	Donnie Allison	183
7.	Charlie Glotzbach	127
	Earl Ross	127
9.	Darrell Waltrip	103
10.	Benny Parsons	88
11.	A.J. Foyt	70
12.	David Sisco	43
13.	Gary Bettenhausen	35
14.	James Hylton	29
15.	Coo Coo Marlin	28
16.	George Follmer	27
17.	Lennie Pond	17
18.	Joe Frasson	13
19.	Dave Marcis	12
20.	Bobby Isaac	11
21.	Dean Dalton	6
	Dan Daughtry	6
23.	G.C. Spencer	3
24.	Walter Ballard	2
	Bob Burcham	2
26.	Dick Brooks	1
	Cecil Gordon	1
	J.D. McDuffie	1
	Richie Panch	1
	Jackie Rogers	1
	Jim Vandiver	1

MILES LED

1.	Cale Yarborough	3,290
2.	Richard Petty	3,046
3.	David Pearson	1,874
4.	Bobby Allison	1,090
5.	Buddy Baker	657
6.	Donnie Allison	318
7.	Charlie Glotzbach	177
8.	A.J. Foyt	150
9.	Darrell Waltrip	138
10.	Gary Bettenhausen	93
11.	Earl Ross	93
12.	Benny Parsons	81
13.	George Follmer	72
14.	David Sisco	69
15.	Coo Coo Marlin	68
16.	James Hylton	61
17.	Sonny Hutchins	42
18.	Joe Frasson	25
19.	Bobby Isaac	23
20.	Randy Tissot	21
21.	Dave Marcis	16
22.	Dan Daughtry	15
23.	Grant Adcox	12
24.	Lennie Pond	11
25.	Jack McCoy	10
26.	Johnny Rutherford	7
27.	Walter Ballard	5
	Bob Burcham	5
	Jimmy Hensley	5
30.	G.C. Spencer	4

MILES DRIVEN

1.	Cale Yarborough	11,059
2.	Richard Petty	10,830
3.	Dave Marcis	9,967
4.	J.D. McDuffie	9,519
5.	Bobby Allison	9,154
6.	Cecil Gordon	9,080
7.	David Sisco	9,012
8.	Frank Warren	8,994
9.	Benny Parsons	8,866
10.	James Hylton	7,970
11.	David Pearson	7,746
12.	Earl Ross	7,467
13.	Walter Ballard	7,247
14.	Lennie Pond	7,013
15.	Richie Panch	6,873
16.	Richard Childress	6,484
17.	Bob Burcham	6,405
18.	Ed Negre	6,344
19.	Jackie Rogers	6,252
20.	Tony Bettenhausen, Jr.	6,151
21.	Coo Coo Marlin	6,082
22.	Darrell Waltrip	6,013
23.	Buddy Baker	5,891
24.	Elmo Langley	5,861
25.	Donnie Allison	5,761
26.	Buddy Arrington	4,798
27.	Dick Brooks	4,097
28.	Charlie Glotzbach	3,794
29.	George Follmer	3,748
30.	Joe Frasson	3,671

RACES LED

1.	Cale Yarborough	26
2.	Richard Petty	24
3.	Bobby Allison	20
4.	David Pearson	18
5.	Buddy Baker	13
6.	Benny Parsons	11
7.	Donnie Allison	10
8.	Coo Coo Marlin	7
9.	Charlie Glotzbach	6
	James Hylton	6
	Lennie Pond	6
	Earl Ross	6
13.	Darrell Waltrip	5
14.	Bobby Isaac	4
	David Sisco	4
16.	A.J. Foyt	3
	Joe Frasson	3
18.	Dan Daughtry	2
	George Follmer	2
	Dave Marcis	2
21.	Walter Ballard	1
	Gary Bettenhausen	1
	Bob Burcham	1
	Dick Brooks	1
	Dean Dalton	1
	Cecil Gordon	1
	J.D. McDuffie	1
	Richie Panch	1
	Jackie Rogers	1
	G.C. Spencer	1
	Jim Vandiver	1

Driver	Starts	Poles	Finish						Laps	Laps Led	Races Led	Winston Cup Points	$
			1	2	3	4	5	6–10					

1975

	Driver	Starts	Poles	1	2	3	4	5	6–10	Laps	Laps Led	Races Led	Winston Cup Points	$
1.	Richard Petty	30	3	13	5	3	0	0	3	9,082	3,198	26	4,783	481,751
2.	Dave Marcis	30	4	1	1	5	6	3	2	8,324	458	17	4,061	240,646
3.	James Hylton	30	0	0	0	0	1	1	14	9,650	11	4	3,914	113,642
4.	Benny Parsons	30	3	1	3	3	3	1	6	8,528	496	16	3,820	214,354
5.	Richard Childress	30	0	0	0	0	1	1	13	9,433	3	2	3,818	96,780
6.	Cecil Gordon	30	0	0	1	1	2	3	9	8,577	6	2	3,702	101,467
7.	Darrell Waltrip	28	2	2	2	2	3	2	3	7,240	562	13	3,462	160,192
8.	Elmo Langley	29	0	0	0	0	0	2	5	8,601	0	0	3,399	67,600
9.	Cale Yarborough	27	3	3	3	3	3	1	0	7,353	2,542	20	3,295	214,691
10.	Dick Brooks	25	0	0	1	2	3	0	9	7,344	60	4	3,182	93,001
11.	Walter Ballard	30	0	0	0	0	0	0	3	7,518	16	2	3,151	55,696
12.	Frank Warren	27	0	0	0	0	0	0	0	7,758	0	0	3,148	55,671
13.	David Sisco	28	0	0	0	1	0	1	5	7,572	37	4	3,116	62,186
14.	David Pearson	21	7	3	6	2	2	0	1	5,653	1,323	18	3,057	192,141
15.	Buddy Baker	23	3	4	2	4	1	1	1	6,281	748	18	3,050	136,351
16.	Bruce Hill	26	0	0	0	0	0	3	8	6,788	2	2	3,002	79,428
17.	Ed Negre	30	0	0	0	0	0	0	4	7,250	2	1	2,982	49,629
18.	J.D. McDuffie	26	0	0	0	0	0	1	5	5,832	0	0	2,745	50,937
19.	Buddy Arrington	25	0	0	0	0	0	0	3	7,786	0	0	2,654	45,893
20.	Coo Coo Marlin	23	0	0	0	1	0	3	7	5,199	25	5	2,584	60,013
21.	Lennie Pond	22	0	0	3	0	1	2	3	5,859	275	8	2,540	59,265
22.	Jabe Thomas	21	0	0	0	0	0	0	2	5,822	0	0	2,252	22,390
23.	Carl Adams	20	0	0	0	0	0	0	4	5,332	0	0	2,182	24,865
24.	Bobby Allison	19	3	3	3	1	2	1	0	4,268	578	14	2,181	122,435
25.	Bruce Jacobi	15	0	0	0	0	0	0	3	3,863	0	0	1,732	29,455
26.	Dean Dalton	16	0	0	0	0	0	0	3	3,800	0	0	1,486	19,430
27.	D.K. Ulrich	16	0	0	0	0	0	0	1	3,448	0	0	1,453	16,525
28.	Donnie Allison	14	2	0	0	2	0	1	3	2,819	33	5	1,376	45,595
29.	Richie Panch	14	0	0	0	0	0	1	3	2,276	8	3	1,243	32,585
30.	Jim Vandiver	13	0	0	0	0	1	0	3	2,929	1	1	1,228	24,200
31.	Bill Champion	13	0	0	0	0	0	0	0	2,690	0	0	1,218	11,340
32.	Earle Canavan	12	0	0	0	0	0	0	0	1,601	0	0	1,062	9,725
33.	Grant Adcox	12	0	0	0	0	0	0	1	1,721	0	0	1,020	17,525
34.	Joe Mihalic	10	0	0	0	0	0	0	1	1,939	0	0	957	12,910
35.	Joe Frasson	9	0	0	0	0	0	0	1	1,352	1	1	939	11,975
36.	Travis Tiller	10	0	0	0	0	0	0	0	1,958	0	0	922	7,780
37.	Rick Newsom	10	0	0	0	0	0	0	0	1,672	0	0	877	9,370
38.	Ferrel Harris	10	0	0	0	0	0	0	0	2,357	0	0	797	16,165
39.	Henley Gray	9	0	0	0	0	0	0	1	2,179	2	1	747	8,785
40.	G.C. Spencer	9	0	0	0	0	0	0	1	906	11	1	634	14,945
41.	Dick May	9	0	0	0	0	0	0	1	1,688	0	0	631	11,020
42.	Earl Brooks	7	0	0	0	0	0	0	0	1,229	0	0	534	4,900
43.	Neil Castles	7	0	0	0	0	0	0	0	578	0	0	529	4,190
44.	Jackie Rogers	8	0	0	0	0	0	0	1	913	2	1	502	11,000
45.	Harry Jefferson	5	0	0	0	0	0	0	2	1,036	0	0	455	11,395
46.	Tommy Gale	5	0	0	0	0	0	0	0	585	0	0	437	6,570
47.	Ricky Rudd	4	0	0	0	0	0	0	1	1,025	0	0	431	4,345
48.	Bobby Isaac	6	0	0	0	0	0	0	1	1,101	0	0	405	6,695
49.	Dick Skillen	5	0	0	0	0	0	0	0	1,052	0	0	389	4,865
50.	Ray Elder	3	0	0	0	0	1	0	0	368	1	1	372	8,020

LAPS COMPLETED

1.	James Hylton	9,650
2.	Richard Childress	9,433
3.	Richard Petty	9,082
4.	Elmo Langley	8,601
5.	Cecil Gordon	8,577
6.	Benny Parsons	8,528
7.	Dave Marcis	8,324
8.	Buddy Arrington	7,786
9.	Frank Warren	7,758
10.	David Sisco	7,572
11.	Walter Ballard	7,518
12.	Cale Yarborough	7,353
13.	Dick Brooks	7,344
14.	Ed Negre	7,250
15.	Darrell Waltrip	7,240
16.	Bruce Hill	6,788
17.	Buddy Baker	6,281
18.	Lennie Pond	5,859
19.	J.D. McDuffie	5,832
20.	Jabe Thomas	5,822
21.	David Pearson	5,653
22.	Carl Adams	5,332
23.	Coo Coo Marlin	5,199
24.	Bobby Allison	4,268
25.	Bruce Jacobi	3,863
26.	Dean Dalton	3,800
27.	D.K. Ulrich	3,448
28.	Jim Vandiver	2,929
29.	Donnie Allison	2,819
30.	Bill Champion	2,690
31.	Ferrel Harris	2,357
32.	Richie Panch	2,276
33.	Henley Gray	2,179
34.	Travis Tiller	1,958
35.	Joe Mihalic	1,939
36.	Grant Adcox	1,721
37.	Dick May	1,688
38.	Rick Newsom	1,672
39.	Earle Canavan	1,601
40.	Joe Frasson	1,352
41.	Earl Brooks	1,229
42.	Bobby Isaac	1,101
43.	Dick Skillen	1,052
44.	Harry Jefferson	1,036
45.	Ricky Rudd	1,025
46.	Jackie Rogers	913
47.	G.C. Spencer	906
48.	Tommy Gale	585
49.	Neil Castles	578
50.	Ray Elder	368

LAPS LED

1.	Richard Petty	3,198
2.	Cale Yarborough	2,542
3.	David Pearson	1,323
4.	Buddy Baker	748
5.	Bobby Allison	578
6.	Darrell Waltrip	562
7.	Benny Parsons	496
8.	Dave Marcis	458
9.	Lennie Pond	275
10.	Dick Brooks	60
11.	David Sisco	37
12.	Donnie Allison	33
13.	Coo Coo Marlin	25
14.	Walter Ballard	16
15.	James Hylton	11
	G.C. Spencer	11
17.	Richie Panch	8
18.	Cecil Gordon	6
19.	Richard Childress	3
20.	Henley Gray	2
	Bruce Hill	2
	Ed Negre	2
	Jackie Rogers	2
24.	Ray Elder	1
	Joe Frasson	1
	Jim Vandiver	1

MILES LED

1.	Richard Petty	3,380
2.	Cale Yarborough	2,075
3.	David Pearson	2,022
4.	Buddy Baker	1,584
5.	Bobby Allison	1,055
6.	Dave Marcis	420
7.	Benny Parsons	392
8.	Darrell Waltrip	367
9.	A.J. Foyt	299
10.	Lennie Pond	171
11.	Dick Brooks	103
12.	Donnie Allison	86
13.	David Sisco	72
14.	Coo Coo Marlin	52
15.	Jimmy Insolo	47
16.	Neil Bonnett	32
17.	James Hylton	27
18.	G.C. Spencer	15
19.	Walter Ballard	11
	Cecil Gordon	11
	Richie Panch	11
22.	Richard Childress	7
23.	Hershel McGriff	6
24.	Darel Dieringer	5
	Sonny Easley	5
	Marty Robbins	5
	Jackie Rogers	5
28.	Henley Gray	4
	Ed Negre	4

MILES DRIVEN

1.	James Hylton	11,032
2.	Richard Childress	10,926
3.	Richard Petty	10,847
4.	Elmo Langley	9,885
5.	Dave Marcis	9,790
6.	Cecil Gordon	9,684
7.	Frank Warren	9,124
8.	Benny Parsons	8,785
9.	David Pearson	8,580
10.	David Sisco	8,455
11.	Cale Yarborough	8,396
12.	Walter Ballard	8,255
13.	Buddy Arrington	8,170
14.	Buddy Baker	8,114
15.	Dick Brooks	8,053
16.	Ed Negre	7,816
17.	Bruce Hill	7,705
18.	Darrell Waltrip	7,426
19.	J.D. McDuffie	7,055
20.	Coo Coo Marlin	6,400
21.	Lennie Pond	6,361
22.	Bobby Allison	6,227
23.	Carl Adams	5,828
24.	Bruce Jacobi	5,767
25.	Jabe Thomas	5,662
26.	Dean Dalton	4,237
27.	D.K. Ulrich	4,093
28.	Donnie Allison	3,971
29.	Ferrel Harris	3,854
30.	Jim Vandiver	3,625

RACES LED

1.	Richard Petty	26
2.	Cale Yarborough	20
3.	Buddy Baker	18
	David Pearson	18
5.	Dave Marcis	17
6.	Benny Parsons	16
7.	Bobby Allison	14
8.	Darrell Waltrip	13
9.	Lennie Pond	8
10.	Donnie Allison	5
	Coo Coo Marlin	5
12.	Dick Brooks	4
	James Hylton	4
	David Sisco	4
15.	Richie Panch	3
16.	Walter Ballard	2
	Richard Childress	2
	Cecil Gordon	2
	Bruce Hill	2
20.	Ray Elder	1
	Joe Frasson	1
	Henley Gray	1
	Ed Negre	1
	Jackie Rogers	1
	G.C. Spencer	1
	Jim Vandiver	1

Driver	Starts	Poles	Finish						Laps	Laps Led	Races Led	Winston Cup Points	$
			1	2	3	4	5	6–10					

1976

	Driver	Starts	Poles	1	2	3	4	5	6–10	Laps	Laps Led	Races Led	Winston Cup Points	$
1.	Cale Yarborough	30	2	9	6	3	2	2	1	9,269	3,771	28	4,644	453,405
2.	Richard Petty	30	1	3	9	3	4	0	3	8,941	1,269	23	4,449	374,806
3.	Benny Parsons	30	2	2	2	7	2	5	5	8,679	455	15	4,304	270,043
4.	Bobby Allison	30	3	0	2	6	5	2	4	8,735	360	18	4,097	230,170
5.	Lennie Pond	30	0	0	2	0	4	4	9	8,182	217	10	3,930	159,701
6.	Dave Marcis	30	7	3	0	1	2	3	7	8,355	893	20	3,875	21,850
7.	Buddy Baker	30	2	1	3	1	4	7	0	7,335	1,028	15	3,745	239,922
8.	Darrell Waltrip	30	3	1	3	4	1	1	2	7,780	534	10	3,505	204,193
9.	David Pearson	22	8	10	3	2	1	0	2	6,194	1,233	19	3,483	346,890
10.	Dick Brooks	28	0	0	0	1	1	1	15	7,542	16	2	3,447	111,880
11.	Richard Childress	30	0	0	0	0	0	0	11	8,147	0	0	3,428	85,780
12.	J.D. McDuffie	30	0	0	0	0	0	1	7	7,954	0	0	3,400	82,240
13.	James Hylton	30	0	0	0	0	1	1	3	8,125	14	4	3,380	78,705
14.	D.K. Ulrich	30	0	0	0	0	0	0	2	8,489	0	0	3,280	69,435
15.	Cecil Gordon	30	0	0	0	0	0	0	5	7,387	7	3	3,247	73,830
16.	Frank Warren	30	0	0	0	0	0	0	3	8,063	0	0	3,240	67,732
17.	David Sisco	28	0	0	0	0	0	0	7	7,111	6	3	2,994	62,622
18.	Skip Manning	27	0	0	0	0	0	0	4	6,913	0	0	2,931	61,537
19.	Ed Negre	28	0	0	0	0	0	0	2	6,153	0	0	2,709	50,919
20.	Buddy Arrington	25	0	0	0	0	0	0	3	9,856	0	0	2,573	56,647
21.	Terry Bivins	18	0	0	0	0	0	1	5	5,237	6	1	2,099	44,070
22.	Bobby Wawak	19	0	0	0	0	0	0	9	4,888	0	0	2,062	31,415
23.	Bruce Hill	22	0	0	0	0	0	0	4	3,669	3	1	1,995	43,705
24.	Jimmy Means	19	0	0	0	0	0	0	0	4,336	1	1	1,752	20,945
25.	Dick May	19	0	0	0	0	0	0	0	4,643	0	0	1,719	29,425
26.	Walter Ballard	14	0	0	0	0	0	0	3	4,168	0	0	1,554	16,380
27.	Henley Gray	15	0	0	0	0	0	0	0	2,945	0	0	1,425	15,090
28.	Coo Coo Marlin	12	0	0	0	0	0	0	6	3,074	0	0	1,412	39,485
29.	Gary Myers	14	0	0	0	0	0	0	0	3,072	0	0	1,296	11,430
30.	Jackie Rogers	11	0	0	0	0	0	0	3	2,439	3	2	1,173	21,215
31.	Grant Adcox	11	0	0	0	0	0	0	2	3,326	0	0	1,163	25,715
32.	Neil Bonnett	13	0	0	0	0	0	1	3	2,174	1	1	1,130	31,800
33.	Tommy Gale	12	0	0	0	0	0	0	0	2,205	0	0	1,005	18,965
34.	Donnie Allison	9	0	1	0	1	0	0	3	2,178	104	4	988	48,445
35.	Joe Mihalic	9	0	0	0	0	0	0	0	2,171	0	0	981	12,925
36.	Elmo Langley	7	0	0	0	0	0	0	1	2,451	0	0	824	7,515
37.	Travis Tiller	9	0	0	0	0	0	0	0	2,012	0	0	816	6,310
38.	Sonny Easley	7	0	0	0	0	0	0	2	1,861	0	0	772	11,290
39.	Joe Frasson	9	0	0	0	0	0	0	1	863	1	1	707	12,075
40.	Jabe Thomas	6	0	0	0	0	0	0	0	1,944	0	0	648	6,160
41.	Bill Elliott	8	0	0	0	0	0	0	0	1,047	0	0	635	11,635
42.	Dean Dalton	6	0	0	0	0	0	0	0	1,433	0	0	633	7,245
43.	Earle Canavan	7	0	0	0	0	0	0	0	1,687	0	0	610	6,035
44.	Rick Newsom	7	0	0	0	0	0	0	0	1,604	0	0	607	5,520
45.	Tighe Scott	6	0	0	0	0	0	0	1	697	0	0	566	15,520
46.	Terry Ryan	5	0	0	0	0	0	1	2	603	1	1	558	29,940
47.	Darrell Bryant	8	0	0	0	0	0	0	1	1,678	0	0	546	11,925
48.	Buck Baker	8	0	0	0	0	0	0	1	1,977	0	0	513	12,655
49.	Chuck Bown	5	0	0	0	0	0	0	0	568	3	1	481	5,480
50.	Baxter Price	6	0	0	0	0	0	0	0	1,680	0	0	479	3,010

LAPS COMPLETED

1.	Buddy Arrington	9,856
2.	Cale Yarborough	9,269
3.	Richard Petty	8,941
4.	Bobby Allison	8,735
5.	Benny Parsons	8,679
6.	D.K. Ulrich	8,489
7.	Dave Marcis	8,355
8.	Lennie Pond	8,182
9.	Richard Childress	8,147
10.	James Hylton	8,125
11.	Frank Warren	8,063
12.	J.D. McDuffie	7,954
13.	Darrell Waltrip	7,780
14.	Dick Brooks	7,542
15.	Cecil Gordon	7,387
16.	Buddy Baker	7,335
17.	David Sisco	7,111
18.	Skip Manning	6,913
19.	David Pearson	6,194
20.	Ed Negre	6,153
21.	Terry Bivins	5,237
22.	Bobby Wawak	4,888
23.	Dick May	4,643
24.	Jimmy Means	4,336
25.	Walter Ballard	4,168
26.	Bruce Hill	3,669
27.	Grant Adcox	3,326
28.	Coo Coo Marlin	3,074
29.	Gary Myers	3,072
30.	Henley Gray	2,945
31.	Elmo Langley	2,451
32.	Jackie Rogers	2,439
33.	Tommy Gale	2,205
34.	Donnie Allison	2,178
35.	Neil Bonnett	2,174
36.	Joe Mihalic	2,171
37.	Travis Tiller	2,012
38.	Buck Baker	1,977
39.	Jabe Thomas	1,944
40.	Sonny Easley	1,861
41.	Earle Canavan	1,687
42.	Baxter Price	1,680
43.	Darrell Bryant	1,678
44.	Rick Newsom	1,604
45.	Dean Dalton	1,433
46.	Bill Elliott	1,047
47.	Joe Frasson	863
48.	Tighe Scott	697
49.	Terry Ryan	603
50.	Chuck Bown	568

LAPS LED

1.	Cale Yarborough	3,771
2.	Richard Petty	1,269
3.	David Pearson	1,233
4.	Buddy Baker	1,028
5.	Dave Marcis	893
6.	Darrell Waltrip	534
7.	Benny Parsons	455
8.	Bobby Allison	360
9.	Lennie Pond	217
10.	Donnie Allison	104
11.	Dick Brooks	16
12.	James Hylton	14
13.	Cecil Gordon	7
14.	Terry Bivins	6
	David Sisco	6
16.	Chuck Bown	3
	Bruce Hill	3
	Jackie Rogers	3
19.	Neil Bonnett	1
	Joe Frasson	1
	Jimmy Means	1
	Terry Ryan	1

MILES LED

1.	Cale Yarborough	3,524
2.	David Pearson	1,969
3.	Buddy Baker	1,537
4.	Richard Petty	1,453
5.	Dave Marcis	1,043
6.	Bobby Allison	544
7.	Benny Parsons	454
8.	Darrell Waltrip	341
9.	A.J. Foyt	199
10.	Lennie Pond	193
11.	Donnie Allison	150
12.	James Hylton	35
13.	Cecil Gordon	18
14.	Terry Bivins	15
15.	David Sisco	14
16.	Dick Brooks	10
17.	Chuck Bown	8
	Chuck Wahl	8
19.	Jackie Rogers	7
20.	Bruce Hill	6
21.	David Hobbs	5
22.	Jimmy Means	3
	Terry Ryan	3
24.	Neil Bonnett	2
	Joe Frasson	2

MILES DRIVEN

1.	Cale Yarborough	10,548
2.	Benny Parsons	10,404
3.	Richard Petty	10,346
4.	Bobby Allison	10,204
5.	Lennie Pond	10,056
6.	D.K. Ulrich	9,933
7.	Frank Warren	9,899
8.	Richard Childress	9,780
9.	Dave Marcis	9,733
10.	J.D. McDuffie	9,665
11.	James Hylton	9,331
12.	David Pearson	9,049
13.	Cecil Gordon	8,758
14.	Buddy Baker	8,610
15.	Dick Brooks	8,586
16.	Skip Manning	8,299
17.	David Sisco	8,102
18.	Darrell Waltrip	8,089
19.	Ed Negre	7,221
20.	Buddy Arrington	6,738
21.	Bobby Wawak	6,232
22.	Terry Bivins	5,816
23.	Dick May	5,486
24.	Bruce Hill	5,412
25.	Jimmy Means	5,118
26.	Grant Adcox	4,916
27.	Coo Coo Marlin	4,309
28.	Jackie Rogers	3,874
29.	Walter Ballard	3,543
30.	Henley Gray	3,479

RACES LED

1.	Cale Yarborough	28
2.	Richard Petty	23
3.	Dave Marcis	20
4.	David Pearson	19
5.	Bobby Allison	18
6.	Buddy Baker	15
	Benny Parsons	15
8.	Lennie Pond	10
	Darrell Waltrip	10
10.	Donnie Allison	4
	James Hylton	4
12.	Cecil Gordon	3
	David Sisco	3
14.	Dick Brooks	2
	Jackie Rogers	2
16.	Terry Bivins	1
	Neil Bonnett	1
	Chuck Bown	1
	Joe Frasson	1
	Bruce Hill	1
	Jimmy Means	1
	Terry Ryan	1

Driver	Starts	Poles	Finish						Laps	Laps Led	Races Led	Winston Cup Points	$
			1	2	3	4	5	6–10					

1977

	Driver	Starts	Poles	1	2	3	4	5	6–10	Laps	Laps Led	Races Led	Winston Cup Points	$
1.	Cale Yarborough	30	3	9	6	4	3	3	2	9,747	3,218	28	5,000	561,642
2.	Richard Petty	30	5	5	6	6	2	1	3	8,840	1,403	24	4,614	406,608
3.	Benny Parsons	30	3	4	3	10	0	3	2	9,410	1,398	25	4,570	359,341
4.	Darrell Waltrip	30	3	6	4	3	1	2	8	9,301	949	23	4,498	324,814
5.	Buddy Baker	30	0	0	0	2	4	3	11	8,084	52	7	3,961	224,847
6.	Dick Brooks	29	0	0	1	0	1	5	13	8,191	8	2	3,742	151,374
7.	James Hylton	30	0	0	0	0	0	0	11	8,375	3	1	3,476	108,392
8.	Bobby Allison	30	0	0	1	0	2	2	10	7,024	102	9	3,467	94,575
9.	Richard Childress	30	0	0	0	0	0	0	11	7,973	27	4	3,463	97,012
10.	Cecil Gordon	30	0	0	0	0	0	0	2	8,133	0	0	3,294	86,312
11.	Buddy Arrington	28	0	0	0	0	0	0	5	8,601	0	0	3,247	88,887
12.	J.D. McDuffie	30	0	0	0	0	0	0	4	8,252	1	1	3,236	85,227
13.	David Pearson	22	5	2	7	2	2	3	0	5,694	868	17	3,227	221,272
14.	Skip Manning	28	0	0	0	1	0	0	7	7,533	13	1	3,120	111,317
15.	D.K. Ulrich	30	0	0	0	0	0	0	0	6,735	0	0	2,901	69,677
16.	Frank Warren	29	0	0	0	0	0	0	1	6,466	1	1	2,876	67,945
17.	Ricky Rudd	25	0	0	0	0	1	0	9	6,233	13	3	2,810	75,905
18.	Neil Bonnett	23	6	2	0	1	1	1	4	5,993	493	11	2,649	122,615
19.	Jimmy Means	26	0	0	0	0	0	0	6	6,010	0	0	2,640	52,505
20.	Tighe Scott	26	0	0	0	0	0	1	0	6,134	0	0	2,628	63,225
21.	Sam Sommers	23	1	0	0	0	1	1	6	5,764	28	3	2,517	54,625
22.	Ed Negre	24	0	0	0	0	0	0	0	5,523	0	0	2,214	42,665
23.	Janet Guthrie	19	0	0	0	0	0	0	4	5,031	5	1	2,037	37,945
24.	Donnie Allison	17	3	2	2	1	4	0	1	4,133	1,163	13	1,970	146,435
25.	Dave Marcis	18	0	0	0	0	4	1	2	4,386	92	7	1,931	72,605
26.	Tommy Gale	18	0	0	0	0	0	0	0	4,493	0	0	1,689	39,190
27.	Dick May	12	0	0	0	0	0	0	0	3,557	0	0	1,324	21,690
28.	Henley Gray	14	0	0	0	0	0	0	0	3,289	0	0	1,214	18,610
29.	Bruce Hill	16	0	0	0	0	0	0	4	2,883	4	1	1,213	25,035
30.	Lennie Pond	14	0	0	0	0	2	2	2	3,154	5	3	1,193	49,440
31.	Butch Hartman	11	0	0	0	0	0	0	2	2,005	0	0	1,116	18,615
32.	Ferrel Harris	11	0	0	0	0	0	0	0	2,979	0	0	1,088	19,365
33.	Baxter Price	12	0	0	0	0	0	0	0	2,566	0	0	1,086	10,890
34.	Coo Coo Marlin	11	0	0	0	0	1	0	4	2,930	1	1	1,004	42,450
35.	Bill Elliott	10	0	0	0	0	0	0	2	2,082	0	0	926	20,075
36.	Gary Myers	10	0	0	0	0	0	0	0	2,648	0	0	888	10,975
37.	David Sisco	10	0	0	0	0	0	0	0	2,030	0	0	847	13,920
38.	Terry Bivins	8	0	0	0	0	0	0	1	1,972	0	0	841	14,920
39.	G.C. Spencer	8	0	0	0	0	0	0	1	1,817	0	0	785	15,755
40.	Terry Ryan	7	0	0	0	0	0	0	1	1,142	0	0	702	12,405
41.	Joe Mihalic	8	0	0	0	0	0	0	0	1,550	0	0	683	7,650
42.	Elmo Langley	7	0	0	0	0	0	0	0	1,395	0	0	634	5,855
43.	Dean Dalton	8	0	0	0	0	0	0	0	1,100	0	0	620	6,255
44.	Earl Brooks	6	0	0	0	0	0	0	0	1,260	0	0	552	3,045
45.	Bobby Wawak	8	0	0	0	0	0	0	0	1,633	0	0	522	13,455
46.	Harold Miller	6	0	0	0	0	0	0	0	1,267	0	0	470	8,480
47.	Junior Miller	5	0	0	0	0	0	0	0	1,028	0	0	467	2,475
48.	Ramo Stott	5	0	0	0	0	0	0	0	688	0	0	440	10,170
49.	Grant Adcox	6	0	0	0	0	0	0	0	776	0	0	413	8,750
50.	Sonny Easley	3	0	0	0	0	0	1	1	360	0	0	386	9,490

LAPS COMPLETED

1.	Cale Yarborough	9,747
2.	Benny Parsons	9,410
3.	Darrell Waltrip	9,301
4.	Richard Petty	8,840
5.	Buddy Arrington	8,601
6.	James Hylton	8,375
7.	J.D. McDuffie	8,252
8.	Dick Brooks	8,191
9.	Cecil Gordon	8,133
10.	Buddy Baker	8,084
11.	Richard Childress	7,973
12.	Skip Manning	7,533
13.	Bobby Allison	7,024
14.	D.K. Ulrich	6,735
15.	Frank Warren	6,466
16.	Ricky Rudd	6,233
17.	Tighe Scott	6,134
18.	Jimmy Means	6,010
19.	Neil Bonnett	5,993
20.	Sam Sommers	5,764
21.	David Pearson	5,694
22.	Ed Negre	5,523
23.	Janet Guthrie	5,031
24.	Tommy Gale	4,493
25.	Dave Marcis	4,386
26.	Donnie Allison	4,133
27.	Dick May	3,557
28.	Henley Gray	3,289
29.	Lennie Pond	3,154
30.	Ferrel Harris	2,979
31.	Coo Coo Marlin	2,930
32.	Bruce Hill	2,883
33.	Gary Myers	2,648
34.	Baxter Price	2,566
35.	Bill Elliott	2,082
36.	David Sisco	2,030
37.	Butch Hartman	2,005
38.	Terry Bivins	1,972
39.	G.C. Spencer	1,817
40.	Bobby Wawak	1,633
41.	Joe Mihalic	1,550
42.	Elmo Langley	1,395
43.	Harold Miller	1,267
44.	Earl Brooks	1,260
45.	Terry Ryan	1,142
46.	Dean Dalton	1,100
47.	Junior Miller	1,028
48.	Grant Adcox	776
49.	Ramo Stott	688
50.	Sonny Easley	360

LAPS LED

1.	Cale Yarborough	3,218
2.	Richard Petty	1,403
3.	Benny Parsons	1,398
4.	Donnie Allison	1,163
5.	Darrell Waltrip	949
6.	David Pearson	868
7.	Neil Bonnett	493
8.	Bobby Allison	102
9.	Dave Marcis	92
10.	Buddy Baker	52
11.	Sam Sommers	28
12.	Richard Childress	27
13.	Skip Manning	13
	Ricky Rudd	13
15.	Dick Brooks	8
16.	Janet Guthrie	5
	Lennie Pond	5
18.	Bruce Hill	4
19.	James Hylton	3
20.	Coo Coo Marlin	1
	J.D. McDuffie	1
	Frank Warren	1

MILES LED

1.	Cale Yarborough	3,044
2.	Richard Petty	1,985
3.	Benny Parsons	1,619
4.	Donnie Allison	1,612
5.	David Pearson	1,145
6.	Darrell Waltrip	1,006
7.	Neil Bonnett	485
8.	Dave Marcis	157
9.	Buddy Baker	123
10.	Bobby Allison	118
11.	A.J. Foyt	50
12.	Sam Sommers	48
13.	Skip Manning	35
14.	Ricky Rudd	27
15.	Richard Childress	22
16.	Janet Guthrie	13
17.	Bruce Hill	11
18.	Dick Brooks	10
19.	James Hylton	8
20.	Lennie Pond	4
21.	J.D. McDuffie	3
	Frank Warren	3
23.	Coo Coo Marlin	2

MILES DRIVEN

1.	Cale Yarborough	11,383
2.	Benny Parsons	10,756
3.	Darrell Waltrip	10,590
4.	Richard Petty	10,419
5.	Buddy Arrington	10,038
6.	Buddy Baker	9,877
7.	J.D. McDuffie	9,689
8.	Cecil Gordon	9,605
9.	James Hylton	9,592
10.	Dick Brooks	9,511
11.	Richard Childress	9,412
12.	Skip Manning	8,355
13.	David Pearson	8,181
14.	Frank Warren	8,108
15.	Bobby Allison	7,823
16.	D.K. Ulrich	7,649
17.	Ricky Rudd	7,509
18.	Tighe Scott	7,467
19.	Sam Sommers	7,081
20.	Jimmy Means	6,760
21.	Neil Bonnett	6,443
22.	Janet Guthrie	6,182
23.	Tommy Gale	6,072
24.	Ed Negre	6,040
25.	Donnie Allison	5,911
26.	Dave Marcis	5,499
27.	Bruce Hill	4,291
28.	Dick May	4,255
29.	Coo Coo Marlin	4,210
30.	Lennie Pond	3,714

RACES LED

1.	Cale Yarborough	28
2.	Benny Parsons	25
3.	Richard Petty	24
4.	Darrell Waltrip	23
5.	David Pearson	17
6.	Donnie Allison	13
7.	Neil Bonnett	11
8.	Bobby Allison	9
9.	Buddy Baker	7
	Dave Marcis	7
11.	Richard Childress	4
12.	Lennie Pond	3
	Ricky Rudd	3
	Sam Sommers	3
15.	Dick Brooks	2
	Janet Guthrie	1
	Bruce Hill	1
	James Hylton	1
	Skip Manning	1
	Coo Coo Marlin	1
	J.D. McDuffie	1
	Frank Warren	1

Driver	Starts	Poles	Finish						Laps	Laps Led	Races Led	Winston Cup Points	$
			1	2	3	4	5	6–10					

1978

	Driver	Starts	Poles	1	2	3	4	5	6–10	Laps	Laps Led	Races Led	Winston Cup Points	$
1.	Cale Yarborough	30	8	10	6	1	5	1	1	9,758	3,587	28	4,841	623,506
2.	Bobby Allison	30	1	5	3	4	0	2	8	9,283	1,043	19	4,367	411,517
3.	Darrell Waltrip	30	2	6	6	4	1	2	1	9,445	2,052	26	4,362	413,908
4.	Benny Parsons	30	2	3	3	6	2	1	6	9,709	824	21	4,350	329,993
5.	Dave Marcis	30	0	0	1	3	8	2	10	9,672	115	12	4,335	205,871
6.	Richard Petty	30	0	0	3	3	3	2	6	8,904	419	15	3,949	242,273
7.	Lennie Pond	28	5	1	2	2	1	5	8	8,443	318	12	3,794	181,096
8.	Dick Brooks	30	0	0	0	0	1	4	12	8,389	24	2	3,769	137,590
9.	Buddy Arrington	30	0	0	0	0	0	1	6	9,580	0	0	3,626	112,960
10.	Richard Childress	30	0	0	0	1	0	0	11	8,946	52	4	3,566	108,702
11.	J.D. McDuffie	30	1	0	0	0	0	1	5	7,300	15	4	3,255	86,857
12.	Neil Bonnett	30	3	0	1	1	2	3	5	6,278	316	6	3,129	162,742
13.	Tighe Scott	29	0	0	0	0	0	0	7	6,626	3	1	3,110	87,912
14.	Frank Warren	30	0	0	0	0	0	0	0	8,481	0	0	3,036	68,173
15.	Dick May	28	0	0	0	0	0	0	2	7,221	0	0	2,936	65,291
16.	David Pearson	22	7	4	2	1	1	3	0	5,375	757	13	2,756	198,775
17.	Jimmy Means	27	0	0	0	0	0	0	2	7,083	0	0	2,756	61,725
18.	Ronnie Thomas	27	0	0	0	0	0	0	2	7,287	0	0	2,733	75,815
19.	Cecil Gordon	26	0	0	0	0	0	0	1	6,773	0	0	2,641	53,815
20.	Tommy Gale	26	0	0	0	0	0	0	0	6,980	0	0	2,639	60,765
21.	Roger Hamby	26	0	0	0	0	0	0	2	7,181	0	0	2,617	41,315
22.	D.K. Ulrich	22	0	0	0	0	0	0	3	6,175	1	1	2,452	54,550
23.	Baxter Price	24	0	0	0	0	0	0	0	7,343	0	0	2,418	36,560
24.	Buddy Baker	19	1	0	1	1	1	1	4	4,319	354	10	2,130	111,765
25.	Donnie Allison	17	0	1	2	2	1	1	1	3,876	209	12	1,993	127,475
26.	James Hylton	19	0	0	0	0	0	0	4	5,774	16	2	1,965	48,045
27.	Gary Myers	19	0	0	0	0	0	0	0	5,524	0	0	1,915	22,140
28.	Ed Negre	21	0	0	0	0	0	0	1	4,826	0	0	1,857	28,995
29.	Skip Manning	17	0	0	0	0	1	0	3	4,410	0	0	1,802	55,470
30.	Grant Adcox	14	0	0	0	0	0	1	2	3,072	0	0	1,802	37,100
31.	Ricky Rudd	13	0	0	0	0	0	0	4	2,535	16	5	1,260	50,630
32.	Bruce Hill	14	0	0	0	0	0	0	2	2,802	0	0	1,214	25,770
33.	Bill Elliott	10	0	0	0	0	0	0	5	2,278	0	0	1,176	42,215
34.	Al Holbert	12	0	0	0	0	0	0	3	2,479	0	0	1,142	31,075
35.	Ferrel Harris	14	0	0	0	0	0	0	5	2,915	0	0	1,066	39,635
36.	Coo Coo Marlin	9	0	0	0	0	0	0	2	1,518	4	2	765	19,415
37.	Blackie Wangerin	10	0	0	0	0	0	0	0	1,342	0	0	760	13,515
38.	Bobby Wawak	7	0	0	0	0	0	0	0	1,298	0	0	680	5,870
39.	Terry Labonte	5	0	0	0	0	1	0	2	1,849	0	0	659	21,395
40.	Ralph Jones	7	0	0	0	0	0	0	0	1,871	0	0	634	6,305
41.	Janet Guthrie	7	0	0	0	0	0	0	1	1,147	0	0	592	17,120
42.	Earle Canavan	9	0	0	0	0	0	0	0	2,111	0	0	559	8,740
43.	Dale Earnhardt	5	0	0	0	0	1	0	1	1,359	0	0	558	20,745
44.	Roland Wlodyka	6	0	0	0	0	0	0	0	1,172	0	0	549	9,910
45.	Joe Frasson	5	0	0	0	0	0	0	0	1,436	0	0	533	9,210
46.	Nelson Oswald	6	0	0	0	0	0	0	0	1,103	0	0	501	2,955
47.	Joe Mihalic	6	0	0	0	0	0	0	0	1,216	0	0	419	6,030
48.	Jim Thirkettle	3	0	0	0	0	0	0	2	393	1	1	389	6,850
49.	Jimmy Insolo	3	0	0	0	0	0	0	2	345	5	2	369	8,665
50.	Satch Worley	4	0	0	0	0	0	0	1	1,298	0	0	368	6,205

LAPS COMPLETED

1.	Cale Yarborough	9,758
2.	Benny Parsons	9,709
3.	Dave Marcis	9,672
4.	Buddy Arrington	9,580
5.	Darrell Waltrip	9,445
6.	Bobby Allison	9,283
7.	Richard Childress	8,946
8.	Richard Petty	8,904
9.	Frank Warren	8,481
10.	Lennie Pond	8,443
11.	Dick Brooks	8,389
12.	Baxter Price	7,343
13.	J.D. McDuffie	7,300
14.	Ronnie Thomas	7,287
15.	Dick May	7,221
16.	Roger Hamby	7,181
17.	Jimmy Means	7,083
18.	Tommy Gale	6,980
19.	Cecil Gordon	6,773
20.	Tighe Scott	6,626
21.	Neil Bonnett	6,278
22.	D.K. Ulrich	6,175
23.	James Hylton	5,774
24.	Gary Myers	5,524
25.	David Pearson	5,375
26.	Ed Negre	4,826
27.	Skip Manning	4,410
28.	Buddy Baker	4,319
29.	Donnie Allison	3,876
30.	Grant Adcox	3,072
31.	Ferrel Harris	2,915
32.	Bruce Hill	2,802
33.	Ricky Rudd	2,535
34.	Al Holbert	2,479
35.	Bill Elliott	2,278
36.	Earle Canavan	2,111
37.	Ralph Jones	1,871
38.	Terry Labonte	1,849
39.	Coo Coo Marlin	1,518
40.	Joe Frasson	1,436
41.	Dale Earnhardt	1,359
42.	Blackie Wangerin	1,342
43.	Satch Worley	1,298
44.	Bobby Wawak	1,298
45.	Joe Mihalic	1,216
46.	Roland Wlodyka	1,172
47.	Janet Guthrie	1,147
48.	Nelson Oswald	1,103
49.	Jim Thirkettle	393
50.	Jimmy Insolo	345

LAPS LED

1.	Cale Yarborough	3,587
2.	Darrell Waltrip	2,052
3.	Bobby Allison	1,043
4.	Benny Parsons	824
5.	David Pearson	757
6.	Richard Petty	419
7.	Buddy Baker	354
8.	Lennie Pond	318
9.	Neil Bonnett	316
10.	Donnie Allison	209
11.	Dave Marcis	115
12.	Richard Childress	52
13.	Dick Brooks	24
14.	James Hylton	16
	Ricky Rudd	16
16.	J.D. McDuffie	15
17.	Jimmy Insolo	5
18.	Coo Coo Marlin	4
19.	Tighe Scott	3
20.	Jim Thirkettle	1
	D.K. Ulrich	1

MILES LED

1.	Cale Yarborough	3,867
2.	Darrell Waltrip	2,180
3.	Bobby Allison	1,509
4.	David Pearson	1,163
5.	Benny Parsons	762
6.	Buddy Baker	675
7.	Richard Petty	585
8.	Donnie Allison	338
9.	Lennie Pond	233
10.	Neil Bonnett	193
11.	Dave Marcis	134
12.	Richard Childress	30
13.	Ricky Rudd	26
14.	Dick Brooks	24
	Harry Gant	24
16.	J.D. McDuffie	18
17.	James Hylton	16
18.	Jimmy Insolo	13
19.	Coo Coo Marlin	6
20.	Richard White	5
21.	Tighe Scott	3
	Jim Thirkettle	3
23.	D.K. Ulrich	2

MILES DRIVEN

1.	Cale Yarborough	11,367
2.	Dave Marcis	10,993
3.	Benny Parsons	10,895
4.	Buddy Arrington	10,740
5.	Darrell Waltrip	10,542
6.	Bobby Allison	10,540
7.	Richard Petty	10,163
8.	Richard Childress	10,061
9.	Frank Warren	9,827
10.	Dick Brooks	9,723
11.	Lennie Pond	9,413
12.	Tommy Gale	8,867
13.	J.D. McDuffie	8,716
14.	Dick May	8,622
15.	Tighe Scott	8,224
16.	Jimmy Means	7,993
17.	Ronnie Thomas	7,770
18.	Roger Hamby	7,689
19.	Baxter Price	7,611
20.	David Pearson	7,603
21.	D.K. Ulrich	7,425
22.	Cecil Gordon	7,192
23.	Neil Bonnett	6,761
24.	Buddy Baker	6,594
25.	Gary Myers	6,134
26.	Donnie Allison	6,128
27.	Skip Manning	5,486
28.	James Hylton	5,019
29.	Ed Negre	4,951
30.	Grant Adcox	4,586

RACES LED

1.	Cale Yarborough	28
2.	Darrell Waltrip	26
3.	Benny Parsons	21
4.	Bobby Allison	19
5.	Richard Petty	15
6.	David Pearson	13
7.	Donnie Allison	12
	Dave Marcis	12
	Lennie Pond	12
10.	Buddy Baker	10
11.	Neil Bonnett	6
12.	Ricky Rudd	5
13.	Richard Childress	4
	J.D. McDuffie	4
15.	Dick Brooks	2
	James Hylton	2
	Jimmy Insolo	2
	Coo Coo Marlin	2
19.	Tighe Scott	1
	Jim Thirkettle	1
	D.K. Ulrich	1
22.	Buddy Arrington	
23.	Frank Warren	
24.	Dick May	
25.	Jimmy Means	
26.	Ronnie Thomas	
27.	Cecil Gordon	
28.	Tommy Gale	
29.	Roger Hamby	
30.	Baxter Price	
31.	Gary Myers	
32.	Ed Negre	
33.	Skip Manning	
34.	Grant Adcox	
35.	Bruce Hill	
36.	Bill Elliott	
37.	Al Holbert	
38.	Ferrel Harris	
39.	Blackie Wangerin	
40.	Bobby Wawak	
41.	Terry Labonte	
42.	Ralph Jones	
43.	Janet Guthrie	
44.	Earle Canavan	
45.	Dale Earnhardt	
46.	Roland Wlodyka	
47.	Joe Frasson	
48.	Nelson Oswald	
49.	Joe Mihalic	
50.	Satch Worley	

1979

Driver	Starts	Poles	Finish 1	2	3	4	5	6–10	Laps	Laps Led	Races Led	Winston Cup Points	$
1. Richard Petty	31	1	5	7	2	4	5	4	9,367	1,250	16	4,830	561,934
2. Darrell Waltrip	31	5	7	4	5	1	2	3	9,994	2,128	26	4,819	557,012
3. Bobby Allison	31	3	5	7	2	4	0	4	9,585	1,854	24	4,633	428,801
4. Cale Yarborough	31	1	4	2	6	4	3	3	9,677	1,323	22	4,604	440,129
5. Benny Parsons	31	1	2	2	2	5	5	5	9,335	736	12	4,256	264,930
6. Joe Millikan	31	1	0	1	1	0	3	15	9,122	188	8	4,014	229,713
7. Dale Earnhardt	27	4	1	1	3	4	2	6	8,340	604	16	3,749	274,810
8. Richard Childress	31	0	0	0	0	0	1	10	9,109	13	2	3,735	132,922
9. Ricky Rudd	28	0	0	0	2	0	2	13	8,836	22	4	3,642	150,898
10. Terry Labonte	31	0	0	0	1	0	1	11	8,766	8	4	3,615	134,653
11. Buddy Arrington	31	0	0	0	1	0	0	6	8,452	2	1	3,589	131,833
12. D.K. Ulrich	31	0	0	0	0	0	0	5	8,995	0	0	3,508	113,458
13. J.D. McDuffie	31	0	0	0	0	0	1	6	8,014	116	3	3,473	113,478
14. James Hylton	30	0	0	0	0	0	0	5	8,658	11	4	3,405	97,428
15. Buddy Baker	26	7	3	2	3	3	1	3	6,107	1,083	20	3,249	342,148
16. Frank Warren	31	0	0	0	0	0	0	3	8,477	0	0	3,199	94,539
17. Ronnie Thomas	30	0	0	0	0	0	0	3	6,928	1	1	2,912	100,079
18. Tommy Gale	27	0	0	0	0	0	0	1	7,054	0	0	2,795	72,809
19. Cecil Gordon	28	0	0	0	0	0	0	0	7,419	0	0	2,737	66,275
20. Dave Marcis	25	0	0	0	0	0	1	5	6,842	20	4	2,736	56,434
21. Harry Gant	25	1	0	0	0	0	0	5	6,226	29	4	2,664	47,185
22. Dick Brooks	27	0	0	0	1	0	0	7	6,307	16	1	2,622	61,985
23. Jimmy Means	27	0	0	0	0	0	0	1	5,131	0	0	2,575	55,560
24. Donnie Allison	20	1	0	2	1	2	2	3	4,891	293	9	2,508	144,770
25. Baxter Price	24	0	0	0	0	0	0	0	6,791	0	0	2,364	45,165
26. Neil Bonnett	21	4	3	0	0	1	0	2	4,213	568	14	2,223	151,235
27. Tighe Scott	17	0	0	0	0	1	0	6	3,834	0	0	1,879	88,010
28. Bill Elliott	14	0	0	1	0	0	0	4	3,691	8	3	1,548	58,200
29. Lennie Pond	15	0	0	0	0	0	0	2	3,043	14	2	1,415	42,970
30. Dick May	19	0	0	0	0	0	0	0	3,387	0	0	1,390	26,345
31. Roger Hamby	12	0	0	0	0	0	0	0	2,974	0	0	1,231	21,000
32. David Pearson	9	2	1	2	0	1	0	1	2,271	264	6	1,203	99,180
33. Coo Coo Marlin	7	0	0	0	0	0	0	2	907	0	0	613	27,540
34. Bruce Hill	7	0	0	0	0	0	0	0	1,352	0	0	594	17,265
35. Blackie Wangerin	7	0	0	0	0	0	0	0	894	0	0	571	14,300
36. Grant Adcox	6	0	0	0	0	0	0	0	1,132	5	1	560	15,290
37. Kyle Petty	5	0	0	0	0	0	0	1	1,069	0	0	559	10,810
38. Chuck Bown	7	0	0	0	0	0	0	2	1,388	0	0	523	31,380
39. John Anderson	4	0	0	0	0	0	1	0	1,263	1	1	496	11,210
40. Ralph Jones	6	0	0	0	0	0	0	0	729	0	0	477	12,785
41. Earle Canavan	8	0	0	0	0	0	0	0	734	0	0	456	6,675
42. Slick Johnson	4	0	0	0	0	0	0	1	1,039	0	0	431	5,360
43. Nelson Oswald	6	0	0	0	0	0	0	0	842	0	0	431	3,610
44. Dave Watson	4	0	0	0	0	0	0	1	1,092	7	2	413	7,170
45. Al Holbert	6	0	0	0	0	0	0	1	938	5	1	402	14,170
46. Bobby Wawak	4	0	0	0	0	0	0	1	740	0	0	376	7,295
47. Jody Ridley	3	0	0	0	0	0	1	1	787	0	0	374	11,245
48. Bill Hollar	5	0	0	0	0	0	0	0	542	0	0	371	2,545
49. Rick Newsom	4	0	0	0	0	0	0	0	484	0	0	355	5,530
50. Bill Schmitt	3	0	0	0	0	1	0	0	325	0	0	342	11,695

LAPS COMPLETED

1. Darrell Waltrip — 9,994
2. Cale Yarborough — 9,677
3. Bobby Allison — 9,585
4. Richard Petty — 9,367
5. Benny Parsons — 9,335
6. Joe Millikan — 9,122
7. Richard Childress — 9,109
8. D.K. Ulrich — 8,995
9. Ricky Rudd — 8,836
10. Terry Labonte — 8,766
11. James Hylton — 8,658
12. Frank Warren — 8,477
13. Buddy Arrington — 8,452
14. Dale Earnhardt — 8,340
15. J.D. McDuffie — 8,014
16. Cecil Gordon — 7,419
17. Tommy Gale — 7,054
18. Ronnie Thomas — 6,928
19. Dave Marcis — 6,842
20. Baxter Price — 6,791
21. Dick Brooks — 6,307
22. Harry Gant — 6,226
23. Buddy Baker — 6,107
24. Jimmy Means — 5,131
25. Donnie Allison — 4,891
26. Neil Bonnett — 4,213
27. Tighe Scott — 3,834
28. Bill Elliott — 3,691
29. Dick May — 3,387
30. Lennie Pond — 3,043
31. Roger Hamby — 2,974
32. David Pearson — 2,271
33. Chuck Bown — 1,388
34. Bruce Hill — 1,352
35. John Anderson — 1,263
36. Grant Adcox — 1,132
37. Dave Watson — 1,092
38. Kyle Petty — 1,069
39. Slick Johnson — 1,039
40. Al Holbert — 938
41. Coo Coo Marlin — 907
42. Blackie Wangerin — 894
43. Nelson Oswald — 842
44. Jody Ridley — 787
45. Bobby Wawak — 740
46. Earle Canavan — 734
47. Ralph Jones — 729
48. Bill Hollar — 542
49. Rick Newsom — 484
50. Bill Schmitt — 325

LAPS LED

1. Darrell Waltrip — 2,128
2. Bobby Allison — 1,854
3. Cale Yarborough — 1,323
4. Richard Petty — 1,250
5. Buddy Baker — 1,083
6. Benny Parsons — 736
7. Dale Earnhardt — 604
8. Neil Bonnett — 568
9. Donnie Allison — 293
10. David Pearson — 264
11. Joe Millikan — 188
12. J.D. McDuffie — 116
13. Harry Gant — 29
14. Ricky Rudd — 22
15. Dave Marcis — 20
16. Dick Brooks — 16
17. Lennie Pond — 14
18. Richard Childress — 13
19. James Hylton — 11
20. Bill Elliott — 8
    Terry Labonte — 8
22. Dave Watson — 7
23. Grant Adcox — 5
    Al Holbert — 5
25. Buddy Arrington — 2
26. John Anderson — 1
    Ronnie Thomas — 1

MILES LED

1. Darrell Waltrip — 2,630
2. Bobby Allison — 1,793
3. Cale Yarborough — 1,592
4. Buddy Baker — 1,276
5. Richard Petty — 1,151
6. Neil Bonnett — 1,056
7. Dale Earnhardt — 775
8. Benny Parsons — 769
9. Donnie Allison — 492
10. David Pearson — 359
11. Joe Millikan — 154
12. J.D. McDuffie — 70
13. Dick Brooks — 40
14. Harry Gant — 32
15. Ricky Rudd — 30
16. Lennie Pond — 23
17. A.J. Foyt — 18
18. Dave Marcis — 17
19. Terry Labonte — 16
20. Geoffrey Bodine — 15
21. Grant Adcox — 13
    Al Holbert — 13
    James Hylton — 13
24. Bill Elliott — 12
    Dave Watson — 12
26. Richard Childress — 10
27. Sterling Marlin — 7
28. Buddy Arrington — 5
29. Bill Green — 4

MILES DRIVEN

1. Darrell Waltrip — 11,769
2. Cale Yarborough — 11,193
3. Bobby Allison — 10,938
4. Richard Petty — 10,934
5. Benny Parsons — 10,575
6. Joe Millikan — 10,510
7. Richard Childress — 10,443
8. Buddy Arrington — 10,334
9. Frank Warren — 10,047
10. D.K. Ulrich — 10,044
11. Ricky Rudd — 9,918
12. Terry Labonte — 9,887
13. J.D. McDuffie — 9,634
14. James Hylton — 9,604
15. Dale Earnhardt — 9,357
16. Cecil Gordon — 8,164
17. Tommy Gale — 8,092
18. Ronnie Thomas — 7,841
19. Dave Marcis — 7,635
20. Dick Brooks — 7,423
21. Buddy Baker — 7,422
22. Harry Gant — 7,368
23. Baxter Price — 6,666
24. Donnie Allison — 6,420
25. Jimmy Means — 6,138
26. Neil Bonnett — 6,133
27. Tighe Scott — 5,684
28. Bill Elliott — 4,822
29. Lennie Pond — 3,864
30. Dick May — 3,714

RACES LED

1. Darrell Waltrip — 26
2. Bobby Allison — 24
3. Cale Yarborough — 22
4. Buddy Baker — 20
5. Dale Earnhardt — 16
   Richard Petty — 16
7. Neil Bonnett — 14
8. Benny Parsons — 12
9. Donnie Allison — 9
10. Joe Millikan — 8
11. David Pearson — 6
12. James Hylton — 4
    Harry Gant — 4
    Terry Labonte — 4
    Dave Marcis — 4
    Ricky Rudd — 4
17. Bill Elliott — 3
    J.D. McDuffie — 3
19. Richard Childress — 2
    Lennie Pond — 2
    Dave Watson — 2
22. Grant Adcox — 1
    John Anderson — 1
    Buddy Arrington — 1
    Dick Brooks — 1
    Al Holbert — 1
    Ronnie Thomas — 1

1980

Driver	Starts	Poles	1	2	3	4	5	6–10	Laps	Laps Led	Races Led	Winston Cup Points	$
1. Dale Earnhardt	31	0	5	3	4	3	4	5	9,615	1,185	25	4,661	671,991
2. Cale Yarborough	31	14	6	4	4	4	1	3	9,440	2,811	28	4,642	567,891
3. Benny Parsons	31	2	3	3	2	4	4	5	8,676	659	19	4,278	411,519
4. Richard Petty	31	0	2	4	3	2	4	4	9,314	713	23	4,255	397,318
5. Darrell Waltrip	31	5	5	3	2	6	0	1	9,015	2,023	28	4,239	405,711
6. Bobby Allison	31	2	4	2	4	1	1	6	8,244	948	18	4,019	378,970
7. Jody Ridley	31	0	0	0	0	0	2	16	9,579	2	2	3,972	204,883
8. Terry Labonte	31	0	1	0	1	1	3	10	8,760	46	6	3,766	222,502
9. Dave Marcis	31	0	0	0	1	2	1	10	9,012	94	14	3,745	150,165
10. Richard Childress	31	0	0	0	0	0	0	10	8,693	21	6	3,742	157,420
11. Harry Gant	31	0	0	3	2	2	2	5	7,986	263	10	3,703	177,150
12. Buddy Arrington	31	0	0	0	0	0	0	7	8,765	0	0	3,461	120,355
13. James Hylton	31	0	0	0	0	0	0	4	9,232	26	1	3,449	109,230
14. Ronnie Thomas	30	0	0	0	0	0	0	4	7,522	0	0	3,066	94,730
15. Cecil Gordon	29	0	0	0	0	0	0	3	7,864	0	0	2,993	83,300
16. J.D. McDuffie	31	0	0	0	0	0	0	3	6,044	0	0	2,968	82,402
17. Jimmy Means	28	0	0	0	0	0	0	0	7,684	0	0	2,947	105,628
18. Tommy Gale	29	0	0	0	0	0	0	0	7,605	0	0	2,885	84,279
19. Neil Bonnett	22	0	2	4	1	1	2	3	5,173	331	14	2,865	231,854
20. Roger Hamby	25	0	0	0	0	0	0	0	6,777	0	0	2,606	51,534
21. Buddy Baker	19	6	2	2	4	2	0	2	5,042	671	15	2,603	275,200
22. Lake Speed	19	0	0	0	0	0	0	5	4,019	2	1	1,853	69,670
23. Slick Johnson	18	0	0	0	0	0	0	5	4,724	7	2	1,851	35,460
24. John Anderson	20	0	0	0	0	0	0	2	4,282	0	0	1,805	48,265
25. Bobby Wawak	19	0	0	0	0	0	0	1	3,965	0	0	1,742	21,080
26. Donnie Allison	18	1	0	0	1	0	2	3	3,794	231	7	1,730	92,640
27. Dick Brooks	19	0	0	0	0	0	2	3	3,978	6	1	1,698	60,700
28. Kyle Petty	15	0	0	0	0	0	0	6	3,722	0	0	1,690	36,045
29. Baxter Price	18	0	0	0	0	0	0	0	4,890	0	0	1,689	26,615
30. Lennie Pond	18	0	0	0	1	1	0	5	3,861	68	6	1,558	62,265
31. Junior Miller	16	0	0	0	0	0	0	0	3,848	0	0	1,402	23,420
32. Dick May	21	0	0	0	0	0	0	2	5,767	0	0	1,323	42,945
33. Joe Millikan	12	0	0	0	0	1	1	4	2,796	5	3	1,274	74,765
34. Bill Elliott	12	0	0	0	0	0	0	4	2,572	4	4	1,232	42,545
35. Ricky Rudd	13	0	0	0	0	1	0	2	2,719	7	2	1,213	50,500
36. Bill Elswick	11	0	0	0	0	0	0	0	2,252	0	0	1,053	15,600
37. David Pearson	9	1	1	2	1	0	0	1	1,787	172	7	1,004	102,730
38. D.K. Ulrich	11	0	0	0	0	0	0	1	1,734	0	0	935	23,055
39. Tighe Scott	10	0	0	0	0	0	1	1	1,066	4	1	791	21,925
40. Frank Warren	7	0	0	0	0	0	0	0	1,591	0	0	559	18,375
41. Tim Richmond	5	0	0	0	0	0	0	0	1,359	0	0	527	14,925
42. Bill Schmitt	4	0	0	0	0	0	1	0	579	0	0	503	21,610
43. Buck Simmons	6	0	0	0	0	0	0	0	1,333	0	0	495	6,365
44. Rick Newsom	6	0	0	0	0	0	0	0	1,179	0	0	483	3,830
45. Dave Dion	4	0	0	0	0	0	0	1	1,075	0	0	441	5,015
46. Don Whittington	7	0	0	0	0	0	0	1	659	0	0	429	17,610
47. Steve Moore	4	0	0	0	0	0	0	0	735	0	0	412	9,040
48. Tommy Houston	4	0	0	0	0	0	0	0	1,170	10	1	396	5,020
49. Sterling Marlin	5	0	0	0	0	0	0	2	1,311	0	0	387	29,810
50. Bruce Hill	6	0	0	0	0	0	0	0	418	0	0	348	7,540

LAPS COMPLETED

1.	Dale Earnhardt	9,615
2.	Jody Ridley	9,579
3.	Cale Yarborough	9,440
4.	Richard Petty	9,314
5.	James Hylton	9,232
6.	Darrell Waltrip	9,015
7.	Dave Marcis	9,012
8.	Buddy Arrington	8,765
9.	Terry Labonte	8,760
10.	Richard Childress	8,693
11.	Benny Parsons	8,676
12.	Bobby Allison	8,244
13.	Harry Gant	7,986
14.	Cecil Gordon	7,864
15.	Jimmy Means	7,684
16.	Tommy Gale	7,605
17.	Ronnie Thomas	7,522
18.	Roger Hamby	6,777
19.	J.D. McDuffie	6,044
20.	Dick May	5,767
21.	Neil Bonnett	5,173
22.	Buddy Baker	5,042
23.	Baxter Price	4,890
24.	Slick Johnson	4,724
25.	John Anderson	4,282
26.	Lake Speed	4,019
27.	Dick Brooks	3,978
28.	Bobby Wawak	3,965
29.	Lennie Pond	3,861
30.	Junior Miller	3,848
31.	Donnie Allison	3,794
32.	Kyle Petty	3,722
33.	Joe Millikan	2,796
34.	Ricky Rudd	2,719
35.	Bill Elliott	2,572
36.	Bill Elswick	2,252
37.	David Pearson	1,787
38.	D.K. Ulrich	1,734
39.	Frank Warren	1,591
40.	Tim Richmond	1,359
41.	Buck Simmons	1,333
42.	Sterling Marlin	1,311
43.	Rick Newsom	1,179
44.	Tommy Houston	1,170
45.	Dave Dion	1,075
46.	Tighe Scott	1,066
47.	Steve Moore	735
48.	Don Whittington	659
49.	Bill Schmitt	579
50.	Bruce Hill	418

LAPS LED

1.	Cale Yarborough	2,811
2.	Darrell Waltrip	2,023
3.	Dale Earnhardt	1,185
4.	Bobby Allison	948
5.	Richard Petty	713
6.	Buddy Baker	671
7.	Benny Parsons	659
8.	Neil Bonnett	331
9.	Harry Gant	263
10.	Donnie Allison	231
11.	David Pearson	172
12.	Dave Marcis	94
13.	Lennie Pond	68
14.	Terry Labonte	46
15.	James Hylton	26
16.	Richard Childress	21
17.	Tommy Houston	10
18.	Slick Johnson	7
	Ricky Rudd	7
20.	Dick Brooks	6
21.	Joe Millikan	5
22.	Bill Elliott	4
	Tighe Scott	4
24.	Jody Ridley	2
	Lake Speed	2

MILES LED

1.	Cale Yarborough	3,156
2.	Darrell Waltrip	2,300
3.	Dale Earnhardt	1,316
4.	Buddy Baker	1,156
5.	Bobby Allison	930
6.	Benny Parsons	753
7.	Neil Bonnett	570
8.	Richard Petty	534
9.	David Pearson	273
10.	Donnie Allison	258
11.	Harry Gant	257
12.	Dave Marcis	106
13.	Terry Labonte	54
14.	Lennie Pond	45
15.	James Hylton	39
16.	Richard Childress	28
17.	Ricky Rudd	11
	Tighe Scott	11
19.	Dick Brooks	9
	Slick Johnson	9
21.	Bill Elliott	8
	Roy Smith	8
	Connie Saylor	8
24.	Tommy Houston	5
	Joe Millikan	5
	Lake Speed	5
27.	Kenny Hemphill	4
	Jody Ridley	4

MILES DRIVEN

1.	Dale Earnhardt	11,137
2.	Cale Yarborough	11,016
3.	Jody Ridley	10,977
4.	Richard Childress	10,693
5.	James Hylton	10,548
6.	Richard Petty	10,148
7.	Benny Parsons	10,036
8.	Terry Labonte	9,952
9.	Buddy Arrington	9,937
10.	Dave Marcis	9,791
11.	Darrell Waltrip	9,764
12.	Ronnie Thomas	9,082
13.	Bobby Allison	9,028
14.	Cecil Gordon	8,979
15.	Jimmy Means	8,891
16.	Tommy Gale	8,813
17.	Harry Gant	8,774
18.	Roger Hamby	7,837
19.	Neil Bonnett	7,504
20.	J.D. McDuffie	7,407
21.	Buddy Baker	6,953
22.	Dick May	6,361
23.	Lake Speed	6,271
24.	Donnie Allison	5,197
25.	Dick Brooks	5,107
26.	John Anderson	5,088
27.	Kyle Petty	4,942
28.	Baxter Price	4,930
29.	Lennie Pond	4,760
30.	Slick Johnson	4,731

RACES LED

1.	Darrell Waltrip	28
	Cale Yarborough	28
3.	Dale Earnhardt	25
4.	Richard Petty	23
5.	Benny Parsons	19
6.	Bobby Allison	18
7.	Buddy Baker	15
8.	Neil Bonnett	14
	Dave Marcis	14
10.	Harry Gant	10
11.	Donnie Allison	7
	David Pearson	7
13.	Richard Childress	6
	Terry Labonte	6
	Lennie Pond	6
16.	Bill Elliott	4
17.	Joe Millikan	3
18.	Slick Johnson	2
	Jody Ridley	2
	Ricky Rudd	2
21.	Dick Brooks	1
	Tommy Houston	1
	James Hylton	1
	Tighe Scott	1
	Lake Speed	1

Driver	Starts	Poles	Finish 1	2	3	4	5	6–10	Laps	Laps Led	Races Led	Winston Cup Points	$

1981

	Driver	Starts	Poles	1	2	3	4	5	6–10	Laps	Laps Led	Races Led	Winston Cup Points	$
1.	Darrell Waltrip	31	11	12	6	3	0	0	4	9,575	2,504	27	4,880	799,134
2.	Bobby Allison	31	2	5	7	4	3	2	5	10,098	1,142	23	4,827	680,957
3.	Harry Gant	31	3	0	7	1	4	1	5	9,132	1,169	20	4,210	280,047
4.	Terry Labonte	31	2	0	1	3	2	2	9	9,010	114	14	4,052	348,703
5.	Jody Ridley	31	0	1	0	0	1	1	15	8,971	28	6	4,002	267,605
6.	Ricky Rudd	31	3	0	3	4	3	4	3	8,942	441	12	3,988	395,685
7.	Dale Earnhardt	31	0	0	2	3	2	2	8	8,134	300	12	3,975	353,972
8.	Richard Petty	31	0	3	1	4	3	1	4	7,276	546	21	3,880	396,072
9.	Dave Marcis	31	1	0	0	2	1	1	5	8,004	178	15	3,507	162,213
10.	Benny Parsons	31	0	3	2	3	0	4	2	6,709	537	10	3,449	311,093
11.	Buddy Arrington	31	0	0	0	0	0	0	7	8,344	0	0	3,381	133,928
12.	Kyle Petty	31	0	0	0	0	0	1	9	7,402	20	3	3,335	117,453
13.	Morgan Shepherd	29	1	1	0	0	2	0	7	7,440	518	6	3,261	170,473
14.	Jimmy Means	30	0	0	0	0	0	0	2	8,647	0	0	3,142	105,628
15.	Tommy Gale	30	0	0	0	0	0	0	0	9,015	2	1	3,140	110,518
16.	Tim Richmond	29	0	0	0	0	0	0	6	8,266	24	2	3,091	96,448
17.	J.D. McDuffie	28	0	0	0	0	0	0	1	10,110	8	2	2,996	105,499
18.	Lake Speed	27	0	0	0	0	0	0	6	6,757	14	2	2,817	94,069
19.	James Hylton	28	0	0	0	0	0	0	0	7,051	12	2	2,753	87,305
20.	Joe Millikan	23	0	0	0	1	0	2	7	6,735	15	4	2,682	148,400
21.	Ron Bouchard	22	1	1	0	0	1	3	7	6,155	12	2	2,594	152,855
22.	Neil Bonnett	22	1	3	1	0	3	0	1	4,917	1,549	16	2,449	181,670
23.	Cecil Gordon	25	0	0	0	0	0	0	0	5,587	0	0	2,320	55,980
24.	Cale Yarborough	18	2	2	1	2	0	1	4	4,922	769	13	2,201	150,840
25.	Richard Childress	21	0	0	0	0	1	0	0	5,018	16	3	2,144	71,125
26.	Ronnie Thomas	23	0	0	0	0	0	0	0	5,756	0	0	2,138	53,605
27.	Buddy Baker	16	0	0	1	0	2	3	3	3,562	110	9	1,904	115,095
28.	Joe Ruttman	17	0	0	1	0	0	1	5	4,194	106	7	1,851	137,275
29.	Mike Alexander	19	0	0	0	0	0	0	3	4,340	4	1	1,784	34,055
30.	Bill Elliott	13	1	0	0	0	1	0	6	2,777	33	3	1,442	70,320
31.	Bobby Wawak	14	0	0	0	0	0	0	1	2,734	0	0	1,212	21,790
32.	D.K. Ulrich	15	0	0	0	0	1	0	0	4,504	0	0	1,191	38,095
33.	Johnny Rutherford	12	0	0	0	0	0	1	1	2,432	5	1	1,140	38,095
34.	Lennie Pond	12	0	0	0	0	0	0	0	3,083	0	0	1,100	29,045
35.	Elliott Forbes-Robinson	11	0	0	0	0	0	0	3	2,169	0	0	1,020	27,350
36.	Rick Newsom	9	0	0	0	0	0	0	0	1,676	0	0	768	8,625
37.	Dick May	9	0	0	0	0	0	0	1	1,843	0	0	754	26,280
38.	Stan Barrett	10	0	0	0	0	0	0	1	1,559	4	2	718	28,540
39.	Connie Saylor	7	0	0	0	0	0	0	0	4,177	0	0	664	19,715
40.	Gary Balough	10	0	0	0	0	0	0	1	2,267	1	1	656	34,430
41.	Rick Wilson	8	0	0	0	0	0	0	0	989	7	2	639	15,625
42.	Mark Martin	5	2	0	0	1	0	0	1	1,478	76	2	615	13,950
43.	Bruce Hill	8	0	0	0	0	0	0	0	880	0	0	596	15,485
44.	Donnie Allison	6	0	0	0	0	0	1	0	1,306	2	1	527	38,745
45.	Geoffrey Bodine	5	0	0	0	0	0	0	1	945	14	2	420	15,000
46.	Joe Fields	6	0	0	0	0	0	0	0	1,681	0	0	418	7,750
47.	Jack Ingram	5	0	0	0	0	0	0	1	822	0	0	377	9,965
48.	Randy Ogden	4	0	0	0	0	0	0	0	577	0	0	367	3,905
49.	Jim Robinson	3	0	0	0	0	0	0	2	264	0	0	351	9,505
50.	Don Waterman	3	0	0	0	0	0	0	1	301	1	1	351	8,570

LAPS COMPLETED

1.	J.D. McDuffie	10,110
2.	Bobby Allison	10,098
3.	Darrell Waltrip	9,575
4.	Harry Gant	9,132
5.	Tommy Gale	9,015
6.	Terry Labonte	9,010
7.	Jody Ridley	8,971
8.	Ricky Rudd	8,942
9.	Jimmy Means	8,647
10.	Buddy Arrington	8,344
11.	Tim Richmond	8,266
12.	Dale Earnhardt	8,134
13.	Dave Marcis	8,004
14.	Morgan Shepherd	7,440
15.	Kyle Petty	7,402
16.	Richard Petty	7,276
17.	James Hylton	7,051
18.	Lake Speed	6,757
19.	Joe Millikan	6,735
20.	Benny Parsons	6,709
21.	Ron Bouchard	6,155
22.	Ronnie Thomas	5,756
23.	Cecil Gordon	5,587
24.	Richard Childress	5,018
25.	Cale Yarborough	4,922
26.	Neil Bonnett	4,917
27.	D.K. Ulrich	4,504
28.	Mike Alexander	4,340
29.	Joe Ruttman	4,194
30.	Connie Saylor	4,177
31.	Buddy Baker	3,562
32.	Lennie Pond	3,083
33.	Bill Elliott	2,777
34.	Bobby Wawak	2,734
35.	Johnny Rutherford	2,432
36.	Gary Balough	2,267
37.	Elliott Forbes-Robinson	2,169
38.	Dick May	1,843
39.	Joe Fields	1,681
40.	Rick Newsom	1,676
41.	Stan Barrett	1,559
42.	Mark Martin	1,478
43.	Donnie Allison	1,306
44.	Rick Wilson	989
45.	Geoffrey Bodine	945
46.	Bruce Hill	880
47.	Jack Ingram	822
48.	Randy Ogden	577
49.	Don Waterman	301
50.	Jim Robinson	264

LAPS LED

1.	Darrell Waltrip	2,504
2.	Neil Bonnett	1,549
3.	Harry Gant	1,169
4.	Bobby Allison	1,142
5.	Cale Yarborough	769
6.	Richard Petty	546
7.	Benny Parsons	537
8.	Morgan Shepherd	518
9.	Ricky Rudd	441
10.	Dale Earnhardt	300
11.	Dave Marcis	178
12.	Terry Labonte	114
13.	Buddy Baker	110
14.	Joe Ruttman	106
15.	Mark Martin	76
16.	Bill Elliott	33
17.	Jody Ridley	28
18.	Tim Richmond	24
19.	Kyle Petty	20
20.	Richard Childress	16
21.	Joe Millikan	15
22.	Geoffrey Bodine	14
	Lake Speed	14
24.	Ron Bouchard	12
	James Hylton	12
26.	J.D. McDuffie	8
27.	Rick Wilson	7
28.	Johnny Rutherford	5
29.	Mike Alexander	4
	Stan Barrett	4
31.	Donnie Allison	2
	Tommy Gale	2
33.	Gary Balough	1
	Don Waterman	1

MILES LED

1.	Darrell Waltrip	2,323
2.	Neil Bonnett	2,055
3.	Bobby Allison	1,737
4.	Harry Gant	1,191
5.	Cale Yarborough	1,023
6.	Richard Petty	770
7.	Benny Parsons	519
8.	Dale Earnhardt	456
9.	Ricky Rudd	358
10.	Morgan Shepherd	288
11.	Buddy Baker	272
12.	Terry Labonte	217
13.	Joe Ruttman	157
14.	Dave Marcis	136
15.	David Pearson	55
16.	Bill Elliott	44
17.	Mark Martin	43
18.	Richard Childress	41
19.	Lake Speed	35
20.	Kyle Petty	33
21.	Jody Ridley	28
22.	James Hylton	27
23.	Tim Richmond	22
24.	Joe Millikan	21
25.	J.D. McDuffie	20
26.	Ron Bouchard	19
27.	Geoffrey Bodine	18
28.	Rick Wilson	17
29.	Butch Lindley	15
30.	Mike Alexander	10
	Stan Barrett	10
	Johnny Rutherford	10

MILES DRIVEN

1.	Bobby Allison	11,610
2.	Darrell Waltrip	10,975
3.	Jody Ridley	10,528
4.	Terry Labonte	10,363
5.	Harry Gant	10,284
6.	Dale Earnhardt	10,063
7.	Tommy Gale	9,927
8.	Ricky Rudd	9,879
9.	Buddy Arrington	9,444
10.	Jimmy Means	9,394
11.	Dave Marcis	9,256
12.	Tim Richmond	9,077
13.	J.D. McDuffie	8,871
14.	Richard Petty	8,602
15.	James Hylton	8,509
16.	Kyle Petty	8,484
17.	Morgan Shepherd	7,919
18.	Lake Speed	7,558
19.	Benny Parsons	7,515
20.	Joe Millikan	7,270
21.	Cale Yarborough	7,134
22.	Ron Bouchard	6,979
23.	Cecil Gordon	6,872
24.	Neil Bonnett	6,366
25.	Richard Childress	6,349
26.	Ronnie Thomas	5,928
27.	Buddy Baker	5,811
28.	Joe Ruttman	5,589
29.	Mike Alexander	4,886
30.	D.K. Ulrich	4,507

RACES LED

1.	Darrell Waltrip	27
2.	Bobby Allison	23
3.	Richard Petty	21
4.	Harry Gant	20
5.	Neil Bonnett	16
6.	Dave Marcis	15
7.	Terry Labonte	14
8.	Cale Yarborough	13
9.	Dale Earnhardt	12
	Ricky Rudd	12
11.	Benny Parsons	10
12.	Buddy Baker	9
13.	Joe Ruttman	7
14.	Jody Ridley	6
15.	Morgan Shepherd	6
16.	Joe Millikan	4
17.	Richard Childress	3
	Bill Elliott	3
	Kyle Petty	3
20.	Stan Barrett	2
	Geoffrey Bodine	2
	Ron Bouchard	2
	James Hylton	2
	Mark Martin	2
	J.D. McDuffie	2
	Tim Richmond	2
	Lake Speed	2
	Rick Wilson	2
29.	Donnie Allison	1
	Mike Alexander	1
	Gary Balough	1
	Tommy Gale	1
	Johnny Rutherford	1
	Don Waterman	1

Driver	Starts	Poles	Finish						Laps	Laps Led	Races Led	Winston Cup Points	$
			1	2	3	4	5	6–10					

1982

	Driver	Starts	Poles	1	2	3	4	5	6–10	Laps	Laps Led	Races Led	Winston Cup Points	$
1.	Darrell Waltrip	30	7	12	1	3	0	1	3	9,455	3,027	27	4,489	923,151
2.	Bobby Allison	30	1	8	2	1	2	1	6	9,184	2,423	24	4,417	795,078
3.	Terry Labonte	30	3	0	6	2	6	3	4	8,900	263	17	4,211	398,635
4.	Harry Gant	30	1	2	2	3	1	1	7	8,454	420	17	3,877	337,582
5.	Richard Petty	30	0	0	5	2	1	1	7	7,834	355	18	3,814	465,793
6.	Dave Marcis	30	0	1	1	0	0	0	12	8,370	56	10	3,666	249,027
7.	Buddy Arrington	30	0	0	0	0	0	0	8	9,236	5	3	3,642	178,159
8.	Ron Bouchard	30	1	0	0	2	1	0	12	8,048	1	1	3,545	375,759
9.	Ricky Rudd	30	2	0	2	0	3	1	7	7,753	140	8	3,537	217,140
10.	Morgan Shepherd	29	2	0	0	1	1	4	7	7,608	209	11	3,451	166,030
11.	Jimmy Means	30	0	0	0	0	0	0	2	8,837	2	1	3,423	154,460
12.	Dale Earnhardt	30	1	1	1	3	2	0	5	7,208	1,062	18	3,402	400,880
13.	Jody Ridley	30	0	0	0	0	0	0	10	7,983	4	4	3,333	308,664
14.	Mark Martin	30	0	0	0	0	0	2	6	7,449	4	3	3,042	142,710
15.	Kyle Petty	29	0	0	1	0	1	0	2	6,414	13	3	3,024	126,285
16.	Joe Ruttman	29	0	0	0	1	2	2	2	7,354	178	6	3,021	191,634
17.	Neil Bonnett	25	0	1	0	2	1	3	3	6,730	412	12	2,966	158,197
18.	Benny Parsons	23	3	0	0	4	3	3	3	5,631	253	8	2,892	252,267
19.	J.D. McDuffie	30	0	0	0	0	0	0	1	6,695	1	1	2,886	112,744
20.	Lake Speed	30	0	0	0	0	0	0	5	5,830	0	0	2,850	118,457
21.	Tommy Gale	26	0	0	0	0	0	0	0	7,566	1	1	2,698	101,485
22.	Geoffrey Bodine	25	2	0	0	1	2	1	6	6,518	118	6	2,654	247,750
23.	Buddy Baker	23	1	0	1	0	0	3	7	5,672	104	13	2,591	253,675
24.	D.K. Ulrich	25	0	0	0	0	0	0	1	7,102	0	0	2,566	78,130
25.	Bill Elliott	21	1	0	3	3	1	1	1	5,542	151	9	2,558	201,030
26.	Tim Richmond	26	1	2	2	0	1	2	5	6,834	319	12	2,497	175,980
27.	Cale Yarborough	16	2	3	2	1	2	0	0	3,439	379	12	2,022	231,590
28.	James Hylton	13	0	0	0	0	0	0	0	4,208	0	0	1,514	49,130
29.	Slick Johnson	17	0	0	0	0	0	0	1	3,826	3	2	1,261	44,190
30.	Ronnie Thomas	18	0	0	0	0	0	0	0	3,243	0	0	1,093	23,570
31.	Bobby Wawak	10	0	0	0	0	0	0	0	2,489	2	1	1,002	23,660
32.	Brad Teague	9	0	0	0	0	0	0	0	3,052	0	0	966	14,300
33.	Lennie Pond	13	0	0	0	0	0	0	2	2,490	1	1	756	45,715
34.	Rick Wilson	8	0	0	0	0	0	0	2	1,404	0	0	731	33,230
35.	Joe Millikan	8	0	0	0	0	0	0	2	2,408	5	1	678	56,230
36.	Rick Newsom	8	0	0	0	0	0	0	0	1,143	0	0	619	12,390
37.	David Pearson	6	2	0	0	1	0	1	0	1,019	7	2	613	55,945
38.	Gary Balough	5	0	0	0	0	0	0	1	1,359	0	0	564	35,735
39.	Lowell Cowell	5	0	0	0	0	0	0	0	862	0	0	554	26,215
40.	Philip Duffie	5	0	0	0	0	0	0	0	1,166	0	0	542	10,910
41.	H.B. Bailey	6	0	0	0	0	0	0	0	1,016	0	0	462	9,455
42.	Butch Lindley	4	0	0	1	0	0	0	0	1,020	165	2	435	16,695
43.	Dean Combs	5	0	0	0	0	0	0	0	639	0	0	431	7,940
44.	Delma Cowart	5	0	0	0	0	0	0	0	775	0	0	410	11,855
45.	Donnie Allison	9	0	0	0	0	0	0	3	1,818	1	1	406	38,180
46.	Bobby Hillin	5	0	0	0	0	0	0	0	917	0	0	379	9,830
47.	Roy Smith	3	0	0	0	0	0	0	2	394	0	0	375	26,770
48.	Dick Brooks	5	0	0	0	0	0	0	0	517	0	0	347	9,470
49.	Connie Saylor	7	0	0	0	0	0	0	0	1,450	3	1	335	16,225
50.	Darryl Sage	5	0	0	0	0	0	0	0	1,552	0	0	324	4,970

LAPS COMPLETED	
1. Darrell Waltrip	9,455
2. Buddy Arrington	9,236
3. Bobby Allison	9,184
4. Terry Labonte	8,900
5. Jimmy Means	8,837
6. Harry Gant	8,454
7. Dave Marcis	8,370
8. Ron Bouchard	8,048
9. Jody Ridley	7,983
10. Richard Petty	7,834
11. Ricky Rudd	7,753
12. Morgan Shepherd	7,608
13. Tommy Gale	7,566
14. Mark Martin	7,449
15. Joe Ruttman	7,354
16. Dale Earnhardt	7,208
17. D.K. Ulrich	7,102
18. Tim Richmond	6,834
19. Neil Bonnett	6,730
20. J.D. McDuffie	6,695
21. Geoffrey Bodine	6,518
22. Kyle Petty	6,414
23. Lake Speed	5,830
24. Buddy Baker	5,672
25. Benny Parsons	5,631
26. Bill Elliott	5,542
27. James Hylton	4,208
28. Slick Johnson	3,826
29. Cale Yarborough	3,439
30. Ronnie Thomas	3,243
31. Brad Teague	3,052
32. Lennie Pond	2,490
33. Bobby Wawak	2,489
34. Joe Millikan	2,408
35. Donnie Allison	1,818
36. Darryl Sage	1,552
37. Connie Saylor	1,450
38. Rick Wilson	1,404
39. Gary Balough	1,359
40. Philip Duffie	1,166
41. Rick Newsom	1,143
42. Butch Lindley	1,020
43. David Pearson	1,019
44. H.B. Bailey	1,016
45. Bobby Hillin	917
46. Lowell Cowell	862
47. Delma Cowart	775
48. Dean Combs	639
49. Dick Brooks	517
50. Roy Smith	394

LAPS LED	
1. Darrell Waltrip	3,027
2. Bobby Allison	2,423
3. Dale Earnhardt	1,062
4. Harry Gant	420
5. Neil Bonnett	412
6. Cale Yarborough	379
7. Richard Petty	355
8. Tim Richmond	319
9. Terry Labonte	263
10. Benny Parsons	253
11. Morgan Shepherd	209
12. Joe Ruttman	178
13. Butch Lindley	165
14. Bill Elliott	151
15. Ricky Rudd	140
16. Geoffrey Bodine	118
17. Buddy Baker	104
18. Dave Marcis	56
19. Kyle Petty	13
20. David Pearson	7
21. Buddy Arrington	5
Joe Millikan	5
23. Mark Martin	4
Jody Ridley	4
25. Slick Johnson	3
Connie Saylor	3
27. Jimmy Means	2
Bobby Wawak	2
29. Donnie Allison	1
Ron Bouchard	1
Tommy Gale	1
J.D. McDuffie	1
Lennie Pond	1

MILES LED	
1. Bobby Allison	3,217
2. Darrell Waltrip	2,669
3. Dale Earnhardt	1,176
4. Richard Petty	685
5. Cale Yarborough	639
6. Neil Bonnett	488
7. Tim Richmond	428
8. Harry Gant	420
9. Terry Labonte	371
10. Benny Parsons	362
11. Bill Elliott	222
12. Buddy Baker	176
13. Morgan Shepherd	157
14. Joe Ruttman	154
15. Geoffrey Bodine	125
16. Dave Marcis	88
17. Butch Lindley	87
18. Ricky Rudd	81
19. Kyle Petty	25
20. Jim Sauter	13
21. Buddy Arrington	11
Steve Moore	11
23. Mark Martin	10
David Pearson	10
25. Rodney Combs	8
26. Jody Ridley	6
27. Jimmy Means	5
Joe Millikan	5
29. Slick Johnson	4
Connie Saylor	4

MILES DRIVEN	
1. Bobby Allison	10,861
2. Buddy Arrington	10,705
3. Darrell Waltrip	10,598
4. Jimmy Means	10,274
5. Terry Labonte	10,259
6. Dave Marcis	9,642
7. Harry Gant	9,642
8. Richard Petty	9,025
9. Jody Ridley	8,790
10. Ricky Rudd	8,681
11. Tommy Gale	8,608
12. Ron Bouchard	8,544
13. Morgan Shepherd	8,468
14. Mark Martin	8,321
15. Tim Richmond	8,246
16. Joe Ruttman	8,034
17. Geoffrey Bodine	7,940
18. Neil Bonnett	7,903
19. Bill Elliott	7,887
20. J.D. McDuffie	7,851
21. Dale Earnhardt	7,787
22. Kyle Petty	7,720
23. D.K. Ulrich	7,587
24. Buddy Baker	7,393
25. Benny Parsons	7,314
26. Lake Speed	6,856
27. Cale Yarborough	5,642
28. James Hylton	4,332
29. Slick Johnson	4,230
30. Bobby Wawak	3,981

RACES LED	
1. Darrell Waltrip	27
2. Bobby Allison	24
3. Dale Earnhardt	18
Richard Petty	18
5. Harry Gant	17
Terry Labonte	17
7. Buddy Baker	13
8. Neil Bonnett	12
Tim Richmond	12
Cale Yarborough	12
11. Morgan Shepherd	11
12. Dave Marcis	10
13. Bill Elliott	9
14. Benny Parsons	8
Ricky Rudd	8
16. Geoffrey Bodine	6
Joe Ruttman	6
18. Jody Ridley	4
19. Buddy Arrington	3
Mark Martin	3
Kyle Petty	3
22. Slick Johnson	2
Butch Lindley	2
David Pearson	2
25. Donnie Allison	1
Ron Bouchard	1
Tommy Gale	1
J.D. McDuffie	1
Jimmy Means	1
Joe Millikan	1
Lennie Pond	1
Connie Saylor	1
Bobby Wawak	1

Driver	Starts	Poles	Finish 1	2	3	4	5	6–10	Laps	Laps Led	Races Led	Winston Cup Points	$

1983

Driver	Starts	Poles	1	2	3	4	5	6–10	Laps	Laps Led	Races Led	Winston Cup Points	$
1. Bobby Allison	30	0	6	5	6	1	0	7	10,038	1,755	25	4,667	883,010
2. Darrell Waltrip	30	7	6	8	4	2	2	3	9,403	2,362	22	4,620	865,185
3. Bill Elliott	30	0	1	4	1	3	3	10	9,536	174	15	4,279	514,030
4. Richard Petty	30	0	3	1	1	1	3	12	9,439	279	16	4,042	508,884
5. Terry Labonte	30	3	1	0	0	4	6	9	8,498	434	13	4,004	388,419
6. Neil Bonnett	30	4	2	1	2	5	0	7	9,418	659	15	3,842	453,586
7. Harry Gant	30	0	1	1	3	1	4	6	9,024	60	10	3,790	414,353
8. Dale Earnhardt	30	0	2	3	0	3	1	5	7,701	1,026	19	3,732	465,203
9. Ricky Rudd	30	4	2	1	1	1	2	7	8,581	871	13	3,693	275,400
10. Tim Richmond	30	4	1	1	4	1	3	5	7,176	590	15	3,612	262,139
11. Dave Marcis	30	0	0	0	0	0	0	7	7,771	24	6	3,361	306,355
12. Joe Ruttman	30	3	0	0	1	3	0	6	7,887	398	10	3,342	223,809
13. Kyle Petty	30	0	0	0	0	0	0	2	8,345	13	5	3,261	163,848
14. Dick Brooks	30	0	0	0	0	0	2	4	7,736	108	6	3,230	180,556
15. Buddy Arrington	30	0	0	0	0	0	0	2	8,933	1	1	3,158	138,429
16. Ron Bouchard	28	1	0	0	0	1	0	6	7,187	22	4	3,113	159,173
17. Geoffrey Bodine	28	1	0	1	0	2	2	4	7,042	490	13	3,019	209,611
18. Jimmy Means	28	0	0	0	0	0	0	3	7,968	2	1	2,983	132,915
19. Sterling Marlin	30	0	0	0	0	0	0	1	8,053	0	0	2,980	148,253
20. Morgan Shepherd	25	0	0	1	1	1	0	10	6,309	5	4	2,733	287,326
21. Buddy Baker	21	1	1	1	2	0	1	7	5,111	174	7	2,621	216,355
22. Ronnie Thomas	26	0	0	0	0	0	0	0	7,141	1	1	2,515	47,180
23. Tommy Gale	28	0	0	0	0	0	0	1	6,540	0	0	2,507	88,316
24. D.K. Ulrich	22	0	0	0	0	0	0	2	6,983	0	0	2,400	85,235
25. Trevor Boys	23	0	0	0	0	0	0	1	5,907	3	2	2,293	87,555
26. J.D. McDuffie	25	0	0	0	0	0	0	0	5,990	0	0	2,197	73,425
27. Lake Speed	18	0	0	0	1	1	0	3	4,933	22	2	2,114	78,220
28. Cale Yarborough	16	3	4	0	0	0	0	4	3,783	608	13	1,960	265,035
29. Benny Parsons	16	0	0	2	1	0	1	1	2,847	107	7	1,657	129,760
30. Mark Martin	16	0	0	0	1	0	0	2	4,130	1	1	1,627	99,055
31. Ronnie Hopkins	13	0	0	0	0	0	0	0	2,563	0	0	1,147	26,445
32. Jody Ridley	10	0	0	0	0	0	0	3	1,963	0	0	1,050	45,710
33. David Pearson	10	0	0	0	1	0	0	3	1,643	18	1	943	71,720
34. Lennie Pond	10	0	0	0	0	0	0	2	2,288	3	1	887	41,530
35. Ken Ragan	8	0	0	0	0	0	0	0	1,984	0	0	836	27,905
36. Bobby Wawak	9	0	0	0	0	0	0	0	2,167	0	0	825	19,130
37. Bobby Hillin	12	0	0	0	0	0	0	0	2,791	0	0	737	30,275
38. Slick Johnson	10	0	0	0	0	0	0	0	2,330	0	0	705	13,665
39. Mike Potter	11	0	0	0	0	0	0	0	1,916	0	0	662	20,375
40. Cecil Gordon	8	0	0	0	0	0	0	0	1,831	0	0	649	17,340
41. Rick Newsom	6	0	0	0	0	0	0	0	2,097	0	0	573	14,445
42. Dean Combs	5	0	0	0	0	0	0	1	1,296	0	0	500	21,370
43. Phil Parsons	5	0	0	0	0	0	0	0	887	0	0	458	23,850
44. Bob Senneker	5	0	0	0	0	0	0	0	1,317	0	0	436	11,335
45. Jerry Bowman	5	0	0	0	0	0	0	0	1,183	0	0	419	8,610
46. Clark Dwyer	5	0	0	0	0	0	0	1	851	0	0	411	14,570
47. Greg Sacks	5	0	0	0	0	0	0	0	638	0	0	359	8,060
48. Rick McCray	4	0	0	0	0	0	0	0	760	0	0	313	3,710
49. Delma Cowart	4	0	0	0	0	0	0	0	643	0	0	277	7,750
50. Philip Duffie	4	0	0	0	0	0	0	0	750	0	0	265	6,480

LAPS COMPLETED

1. Bobby Allison — 10,038
2. Bill Elliott — 9,536
3. Richard Petty — 9,439
4. Neil Bonnett — 9,418
5. Darrell Waltrip — 9,403
6. Harry Gant — 9,024
7. Buddy Arrington — 8,933
8. Ricky Rudd — 8,581
9. Terry Labonte — 8,498
10. Kyle Petty — 8,345
11. Sterling Marlin — 8,053
12. Jimmy Means — 7,968
13. Joe Ruttman — 7,887
14. Dave Marcis — 7,771
15. Dick Brooks — 7,736
16. Dale Earnhardt — 7,701
17. Ron Bouchard — 7,187
18. Tim Richmond — 7,176
19. Ronnie Thomas — 7,141
20. Geoffrey Bodine — 7,042
21. D.K. Ulrich — 6,983
22. Tommy Gale — 6,540
23. Morgan Shepherd — 6,309
24. J.D. McDuffie — 5,990
25. Trevor Boys — 5,907
26. Buddy Baker — 5,111
27. Lake Speed — 4,933
28. Mark Martin — 4,130
29. Cale Yarborough — 3,783
30. Benny Parsons — 2,847
31. Bobby Hillin — 2,791
32. Ronnie Hopkins — 2,563
33. Slick Johnson — 2,330
34. Lennie Pond — 2,288
35. Bobby Wawak — 2,167
36. Rick Newsom — 2,097
37. Ken Ragan — 1,984
38. Jody Ridley — 1,963
39. Mike Potter — 1,916
40. Cecil Gordon — 1,831
41. David Pearson — 1,643
42. Bob Senneker — 1,317
43. Dean Combs — 1,296
44. Jerry Bowman — 1,183
45. Phil Parsons — 887
46. Clark Dwyer — 851
47. Rick McCray — 760
48. Philip Duffie — 750
49. Delma Cowart — 643
50. Greg Sacks — 638

LAPS LED

1. Darrell Waltrip — 2,362
2. Bobby Allison — 1,755
3. Dale Earnhardt — 1,026
4. Ricky Rudd — 871
5. Neil Bonnett — 659
6. Cale Yarborough — 608
7. Tim Richmond — 590
8. Geoffrey Bodine — 490
9. Terry Labonte — 434
10. Joe Ruttman — 398
11. Richard Petty — 279
12. Buddy Baker — 174
    Bill Elliott — 174
14. Dick Brooks — 108
15. Benny Parsons — 107
16. Harry Gant — 60
17. Dave Marcis — 24
18. Ron Bouchard — 22
    Lake Speed — 22
20. David Pearson — 18
21. Kyle Petty — 13
22. Morgan Shepherd — 5
23. Trevor Boys — 3
    Lennie Pond — 3
25. Jimmy Means — 2
26. Buddy Arrington — 1
    Mark Martin — 1
    Ronnie Thomas — 1

MILES LED

1. Bobby Allison — 2,093
2. Darrell Waltrip — 1,814
3. Cale Yarborough — 993
4. Dale Earnhardt — 876
5. Tim Richmond — 861
6. Neil Bonnett — 781
7. Ricky Rudd — 708
8. Geoffrey Bodine — 699
9. Terry Labonte — 676
10. Richard Petty — 519
11. Joe Ruttman — 467
12. Buddy Baker — 375
13. Bill Elliott — 250
14. Benny Parsons — 215
15. Dick Brooks — 168
16. Harry Gant — 82
17. Ron Bouchard — 52
18. Lake Speed — 48
19. Dave Marcis — 39
20. Kyle Petty — 29
21. David Pearson — 25
22. Lennie Pond — 8
23. Morgan Shepherd — 7
24. Trevor Boys — 6
25. Jimmy Means — 5
26. Butch Lindley — 4
27. Ronnie Thomas — 3
28. Buddy Arrington — 2
29. Mark Martin — 1

MILES DRIVEN

1. Bobby Allison — 11,527
2. Bill Elliott — 11,272
3. Richard Petty — 10,697
4. Darrell Waltrip — 10,547
5. Neil Bonnett — 10,452
6. Harry Gant — 10,194
7. Buddy Arrington — 10,010
8. Ricky Rudd — 9,908
9. Terry Labonte — 9,775
10. Kyle Petty — 9,437
11. Dave Marcis — 9,171
12. Sterling Marlin — 9,167
13. Dale Earnhardt — 8,947
14. Joe Ruttman — 8,818
15. Jimmy Means — 8,816
16. Dick Brooks — 8,695
17. Ron Bouchard — 8,315
18. Tim Richmond — 8,218
19. D.K. Ulrich — 7,876
20. Tommy Gale — 7,815
21. Ronnie Thomas — 7,706
22. Morgan Shepherd — 7,613
23. Geoffrey Bodine — 7,328
24. Lake Speed — 6,929
25. Trevor Boys — 6,897
26. Buddy Baker — 6,816
27. J.D. McDuffie — 6,578
28. Cale Yarborough — 5,975
29. Mark Martin — 5,545
30. Benny Parsons — 5,285

RACES LED

1. Bobby Allison — 25
2. Darrell Waltrip — 22
3. Dale Earnhardt — 19
4. Richard Petty — 16
5. Neil Bonnett — 15
   Bill Elliott — 15
   Tim Richmond — 15
8. Geoffrey Bodine — 13
   Terry Labonte — 13
   Ricky Rudd — 13
   Cale Yarborough — 13
12. Harry Gant — 10
    Joe Ruttman — 10
14. Buddy Baker — 7
    Benny Parsons — 7
16. Dick Brooks — 6
    Dave Marcis — 6
18. Kyle Petty — 5
19. Ron Bouchard — 4
    Morgan Shepherd — 4
21. Trevor Boys — 2
    Lake Speed — 2
23. Buddy Arrington — 1
    Mark Martin — 1
    Jimmy Means — 1
    David Pearson — 1
    Lennie Pond — 1
    Ronnie Thomas — 1

Driver	Starts	Poles	Finish						Laps	Laps Led	Races Led	Winston Cup Points	$
			1	2	3	4	5	6–10					

1984

	Driver	Starts	Poles	1	2	3	4	5	6–10	Laps	Laps Led	Races Led	Winston Cup Points	$
1.	Terry Labonte	30	3	2	6	6	2	1	7	9,886	880	26	4,508	767,716
2.	Harry Gant	30	3	3	6	0	5	1	8	9,901	1,186	19	4,443	673,060
3.	Bill Elliott	30	4	3	1	4	4	1	11	9,848	570	17	4,377	680,344
4.	Dale Earnhardt	30	0	2	4	2	0	4	10	9,584	446	16	4,265	634,671
5.	Darrell Waltrip	30	4	7	2	3	1	0	7	9,464	2,030	22	4,230	731,023
6.	Bobby Allison	30	0	2	1	2	4	4	6	9,051	1,160	23	4,094	641,049
7.	Ricky Rudd	30	4	1	1	3	1	1	9	9,271	566	8	3,918	497,779
8.	Neil Bonnett	30	1	0	2	0	2	3	7	9,126	641	11	3,802	282,533
9.	Geoffrey Bodine	30	3	3	0	1	2	1	7	8,848	686	12	3,734	413,748
10.	Richard Petty	30	0	2	0	0	2	1	8	8,835	275	8	3,643	257,932
11.	Ron Bouchard	30	0	0	1	2	1	1	5	9,200	111	8	3,609	246,510
12.	Tim Richmond	30	0	1	3	0	0	2	5	8,225	58	7	3,505	345,848
13.	Dave Marcis	30	0	0	0	0	3	0	6	9,383	30	5	3,416	330,766
14.	Rusty Wallace	30	0	0	0	0	1	1	2	8,868	11	7	3,316	201,739
15.	Dick Brooks	30	0	0	0	1	0	0	4	8,157	185	3	3,265	192,407
16.	Kyle Petty	30	0	0	0	0	0	1	5	8,400	2	1	3,159	329,920
17.	Trevor Boys	30	0	0	0	0	0	0	1	8,619	20	3	3,040	165,376
18.	Joe Ruttman	29	1	0	0	0	0	0	8	6,635	55	4	2,945	168,433
19.	Greg Sacks	29	0	0	0	0	0	0	1	6,348	0	0	2,545	75,184
20.	Buddy Arrington	26	0	0	0	0	0	0	0	7,323	0	0	2,504	128,802
21.	Buddy Baker	21	1	0	1	2	0	1	8	6,216	84	2	2,477	151,635
22.	Cale Yarborough	16	4	3	1	3	1	2	0	4,387	736	12	2,448	403,853
23.	Clark Dwyer	26	0	0	0	0	0	0	0	7,025	1	1	2,374	114,355
24.	Phil Parsons	23	0	0	0	0	0	0	3	6,301	4	1	2,290	90,700
25.	Jimmy Means	22	0	0	0	0	0	0	0	7,044	0	0	2,218	105,105
26.	Lake Speed	19	0	0	0	1	0	1	5	4,814	122	5	2,023	98,320
27.	Benny Parsons	14	2	1	1	0	1	4	3	2,877	407	6	1,865	241,665
28.	Mike Alexander	19	0	0	0	0	0	0	1	4,656	0	0	1,862	94,820
29.	Morgan Shepherd	20	0	0	0	0	0	0	1	5,134	1	1	1,811	59,670
30.	Ronnie Thomas	21	0	0	0	0	0	0	0	4,976	2	1	1,775	79,325
31.	Tommy Ellis	20	0	0	0	0	0	0	1	5,010	1	1	1,738	44,315
32.	Bobby Hillin	16	0	0	0	0	0	0	0	3,452	0	0	1,477	45,020
33.	Tommy Gale	16	0	0	0	0	0	0	0	4,248	0	0	1,426	69,385
34.	J.D. McDuffie	16	0	0	0	0	0	0	0	4,064	0	0	1,366	50,320
35.	Jody Ridley	14	0	0	0	0	0	0	3	2,891	4	2	1,288	64,135
36.	Doug Heveron	16	0	0	0	0	0	0	0	3,553	7	1	1,265	39,950
37.	Sterling Marlin	14	0	0	0	0	0	0	2	2,737	0	0	1,207	54,355
38.	Lennie Pond	12	0	0	0	0	0	0	2	3,590	0	0	923	54,200
39.	Dean Combs	12	0	0	0	0	0	0	0	2,399	0	0	903	22,385
40.	Ken Ragan	10	0	0	0	0	0	0	0	1,839	1	1	873	37,045
41.	David Pearson	11	0	0	0	0	0	0	3	1,630	10	3	812	54,125
42.	D.K. Ulrich	9	0	0	0	0	0	0	0	2,565	0	0	810	31,040
43.	Connie Saylor	8	0	0	0	0	0	0	0	1,193	1	1	367	19,675
44.	Jerry Bowman	5	0	0	0	0	0	0	0	834	0	0	362	6,265
45.	Elliott Forbes-Robinson	5	0	0	0	0	0	0	0	895	0	0	349	11,335
46.	Jeff Hooker	4	0	0	0	0	0	0	0	980	0	0	322	4,495
47.	Bobby Wawak	4	0	0	0	0	0	0	0	874	0	0	307	8,575
48.	Dick May	3	0	0	0	0	0	0	0	1,274	0	0	300	5,325
49.	Dean Roper	3	0	0	0	0	0	0	0	500	0	0	294	19,150
50.	Bobby Gerhart	4	0	0	0	0	0	0	0	655	0	0	262	7,585

LAPS COMPLETED

1.	Harry Gant	9,901
2.	Terry Labonte	9,886
3.	Bill Elliott	9,848
4.	Dale Earnhardt	9,584
5.	Darrell Waltrip	9,464
6.	Dave Marcis	9,383
7.	Ricky Rudd	9,271
8.	Ron Bouchard	9,200
9.	Neil Bonnett	9,126
10.	Bobby Allison	9,051
11.	Rusty Wallace	8,868
12.	Geoffrey Bodine	8,848
13.	Richard Petty	8,835
14.	Trevor Boys	8,619
15.	Kyle Petty	8,400
16.	Tim Richmond	8,225
17.	Dick Brooks	8,157
18.	Buddy Arrington	7,323
19.	Jimmy Means	7,044
20.	Clark Dwyer	7,025
21.	Joe Ruttman	6,635
22.	Greg Sacks	6,348
23.	Phil Parsons	6,301
24.	Buddy Baker	6,216
25.	Morgan Shepherd	5,134
26.	Tommy Ellis	5,010
27.	Ronnie Thomas	4,976
28.	Lake Speed	4,814
29.	Mike Alexander	4,656
30.	Cale Yarborough	4,387
31.	Tommy Gale	4,248
32.	J.D. McDuffie	4,064
33.	Lennie Pond	3,590
34.	Doug Heveron	3,553
35.	Bobby Hillin	3,452
36.	Jody Ridley	2,891
37.	Benny Parsons	2,877
38.	Sterling Marlin	2,737
39.	D.K. Ulrich	2,565
40.	Dean Combs	2,399
41.	Ken Ragan	1,839
42.	David Pearson	1,630
43.	Dick May	1,274
44.	Connie Saylor	1,193
45.	Jeff Hooker	980
46.	Elliott Forbes-Robinson	895
47.	Bobby Wawak	874
48.	Jerry Bowman	834
49.	Bobby Gerhart	655
50.	Dean Roper	500

LAPS LED

1.	Darrell Waltrip	2,030
2.	Harry Gant	1,186
3.	Bobby Allison	1,160
4.	Terry Labonte	880
5.	Cale Yarborough	736
6.	Geoffrey Bodine	686
7.	Neil Bonnett	641
8.	Bill Elliott	570
9.	Ricky Rudd	566
10.	Dale Earnhardt	446
11.	Benny Parsons	407
12.	Richard Petty	275
13.	Dick Brooks	185
14.	Lake Speed	122
15.	Ron Bouchard	111
16.	Buddy Baker	84
17.	Tim Richmond	58
18.	Joe Ruttman	55
19.	Dave Marcis	30
20.	Trevor Boys	20
21.	Rusty Wallace	11
22.	David Pearson	10
23.	Doug Heveron	7
24.	Phil Parsons	4
	Jody Ridley	4
26.	Kyle Petty	2
	Ronnie Thomas	2
28.	Clark Dwyer	1
	Tommy Ellis	1
	Ken Ragan	1
	Connie Saylor	1
	Morgan Shepherd	1

MILES LED

1.	Darrell Waltrip	1,577
2.	Harry Gant	1,511
3.	Cale Yarborough	1,485
4.	Bobby Allison	1,216
5.	Terry Labonte	1,139
6.	Bill Elliott	814
7.	Benny Parsons	709
8.	Dale Earnhardt	663
9.	Geoffrey Bodine	562
10.	Richard Petty	458
11.	Neil Bonnett	409
12.	Ricky Rudd	338
13.	Buddy Baker	223
14.	Dick Brooks	188
15.	Lake Speed	147
16.	Ron Bouchard	142
17.	Tim Richmond	63
18.	Dave Marcis	46
19.	Joe Ruttman	36
20.	David Pearson	24
21.	Trevor Boys	23
22.	Doug Heveron	18
23.	Rusty Wallace	12
24.	Phil Parsons	11
25.	Jim Bown	10
26.	Jody Ridley	6
27.	Kyle Petty	5
28.	Clark Dwyer	3
	Tommy Ellis	3
	Hershel McGriff	3
	Ken Ragan	3

MILES DRIVEN

1.	Harry Gant	11,396
2.	Bill Elliott	11,385
3.	Terry Labonte	11,236
4.	Dale Earnhardt	10,850
5.	Ricky Rudd	10,584
6.	Bobby Allison	10,545
7.	Ron Bouchard	10,504
8.	Neil Bonnett	10,460
9.	Darrell Waltrip	10,440
10.	Dave Marcis	10,387
11.	Geoffrey Bodine	10,064
12.	Rusty Wallace	10,024
13.	Richard Petty	9,917
14.	Trevor Boys	9,704
15.	Tim Richmond	9,416
16.	Dick Brooks	9,320
17.	Kyle Petty	9,302
18.	Buddy Arrington	8,295
19.	Joe Ruttman	8,161
20.	Clark Dwyer	8,059
21.	Phil Parsons	7,802
22.	Greg Sacks	7,781
23.	Jimmy Means	7,482
24.	Buddy Baker	7,451
25.	Cale Yarborough	7,140
26.	Lake Speed	6,752
27.	Ronnie Thomas	5,761
28.	Mike Alexander	5,694
29.	Bobby Hillin	5,655
30.	Morgan Shepherd	5,478

RACES LED

1.	Terry Labonte	26
2.	Bobby Allison	23
3.	Darrell Waltrip	22
4.	Harry Gant	19
5.	Bill Elliott	17
6.	Dale Earnhardt	16
7.	Geoffrey Bodine	12
	Cale Yarborough	12
9.	Neil Bonnett	11
10.	Ron Bouchard	8
	Ricky Rudd	8
	Richard Petty	8
13.	Tim Richmond	7
	Rusty Wallace	7
15.	Benny Parsons	6
16.	Dave Marcis	5
	Lake Speed	5
18.	Joe Ruttman	4
19.	Trevor Boys	3
	Dick Brooks	3
	David Pearson	3
22.	Buddy Baker	2
	Jody Ridley	2
24.	Clark Dwyer	1
	Tommy Ellis	1
	Doug Heveron	1
	Phil Parsons	1
	Kyle Petty	1
	Ken Ragan	1
	Connie Saylor	1
	Morgan Shepherd	1
	Ronnie Thomas	1

Driver	Starts	Poles	Finish						Laps	Laps Led	Races Led	Winston Cup Points	$
			1	2	3	4	5	6–10					

1985

1.	Darrell Waltrip	28	5	3	6	6	2	1	3	8,931	969	21	4,292	1,318,375
2.	Bill Elliott	28	11	11	2	0	2	1	2	8,724	1,920	19	4,191	2,433,187
3.	Harry Gant	28	3	3	5	3	1	2	5	8,805	1,271	20	4,033	804,287
4.	Neil Bonnett	28	1	2	2	3	1	3	7	8,675	618	15	3,902	530,145
5.	Geoffrey Bodine	28	3	0	3	3	2	2	4	8,719	692	18	3,862	565,868
6.	Ricky Rudd	28	0	1	2	1	5	4	6	8,474	329	6	3,857	512,441
7.	Terry Labonte	28	4	1	2	3	1	1	9	7,973	563	14	3,683	694,510
8.	Dale Earnhardt	28	1	4	0	0	4	2	6	8,231	1,237	17	3,561	546,596
9.	Kyle Petty	28	0	0	1	1	1	4	5	8,796	75	6	3,528	296,367
10.	Lake Speed	28	0	0	1	0	1	0	12	8,572	8	4	3,507	300,326
11.	Tim Richmond	28	0	0	1	1	1	0	10	8,199	377	12	3,413	290,284
12.	Bobby Allison	28	0	0	0	3	3	1	4	7,656	422	14	3,312	272,536
13.	Ron Bouchard	28	0	0	1	1	2	1	7	7,723	77	5	3,267	240,304
14.	Richard Petty	28	0	0	0	1	0	0	12	7,767	105	7	3,140	306,142
15.	Bobby Hillin	28	0	0	0	0	0	0	5	8,636	2	2	3,091	145,070
16.	Ken Schrader	28	0	0	0	0	0	0	3	7,786	4	1	3,024	211,523
17.	Buddy Baker	28	0	0	0	0	2	0	5	6,226	4	2	2,986	235,480
18.	Dave Marcis	28	0	0	0	0	0	0	5	7,319	30	4	2,871	173,467
19.	Rusty Wallace	28	0	0	0	0	0	2	6	7,271	28	1	2,867	233,670
20.	Buddy Arrington	26	0	0	0	0	0	0	1	7,809	1	1	2,780	153,222
21.	Phil Parsons	28	0	0	0	0	0	0	4	6,678	1	1	2,740	104,840
22.	Clark Dwyer	28	0	0	0	0	0	0	0	7,205	0	0	2,641	128,710
23.	Jimmy Means	28	0	0	0	0	0	0	0	6,774	0	0	2,548	132,130
24.	Eddie Bierschwale	26	0	0	0	0	0	0	0	6,559	0	0	2,396	102,650
25.	Greg Sacks	20	0	1	0	0	0	0	4	4,855	36	3	1,944	234,141
26.	Cale Yarborough	16	0	2	2	2	0	0	1	3,450	664	11	1,861	310,465
27.	J.D. McDuffie	23	0	0	0	0	0	0	0	4,667	0	0	1,853	84,965
28.	Trevor Boys	20	0	0	0	0	0	0	0	3,973	3	1	1,461	76,325
29.	Benny Parsons	14	0	0	0	0	0	1	5	2,230	8	3	1,427	94,450
30.	Joe Ruttman	16	0	0	0	0	0	1	3	3,378	5	1	1,410	81,425
31.	Morgan Shepherd	16	0	0	0	0	0	1	1	2,951	1	1	1,406	55,985
32.	Bobby Wawak	14	0	0	0	0	0	0	0	3,157	0	0	1,226	42,165
33.	Lennie Pond	12	0	0	0	0	0	0	0	2,831	3	2	1,107	70,640
34.	Tommy Ellis	14	0	0	0	0	0	0	1	2,853	0	0	1,100	27,695
35.	Mike Alexander	11	0	0	0	0	0	0	0	2,336	0	0	1,046	43,765
36.	David Pearson	12	0	0	0	0	0	0	1	1,418	2	1	879	55,625
37.	Sterling Marlin	8	0	0	0	0	0	0	0	1,321	1	1	645	31,155
38.	Don Hume	7	0	0	0	0	0	0	0	2,057	0	0	637	22,230
39.	Ronnie Thomas	7	0	0	0	0	0	0	0	1,510	0	0	631	10,505
40.	Alan Kulwicki	5	0	0	0	0	0	0	0	1,843	0	0	509	10,290
41.	Rick Newsom	6	0	0	0	0	0	0	0	834	0	0	450	8,690
42.	Mike Potter	6	0	0	0	0	0	0	0	1,434	0	0	443	10,855
43.	Jerry Bowman	5	0	0	0	0	0	0	0	1,326	0	0	434	8,665
44.	Bobby Gerhart	5	0	0	0	0	0	0	0	1,166	0	0	422	7,400
45.	A.J. Foyt	7	0	0	0	0	0	1	0	966	2	2	410	29,750
46.	Phil Good	4	0	0	0	0	0	0	0	1,239	0	0	406	6,870
47.	Ken Ragan	7	0	0	0	0	0	0	0	1,359	0	0	356	35,995
48.	Slick Johnson	6	0	0	0	0	0	0	0	1,608	0	0	343	24,995
49.	Connie Saylor	5	0	0	0	0	0	0	0	456	0	0	296	8,915
50.	Jim Sauter	3	0	0	0	0	0	0	0	565	0	0	267	15,465

LAPS COMPLETED

1. Darrell Waltrip — 8,931
2. Harry Gant — 8,805
3. Kyle Petty — 8,796
4. Bill Elliott — 8,724
5. Geoffrey Bodine — 8,719
6. Neil Bonnett — 8,675
7. Bobby Hillin — 8,636
8. Lake Speed — 8,572
9. Ricky Rudd — 8,474
10. Dale Earnhardt — 8,231
11. Tim Richmond — 8,199
12. Terry Labonte — 7,973
13. Buddy Arrington — 7,809
14. Ken Schrader — 7,786
15. Richard Petty — 7,767
16. Ron Bouchard — 7,723
17. Bobby Allison — 7,656
18. Dave Marcis — 7,319
19. Rusty Wallace — 7,271
20. Clark Dwyer — 7,205
21. Jimmy Means — 6,774
22. Phil Parsons — 6,678
23. Eddie Bierschwale — 6,559
24. Buddy Baker — 6,226
25. Greg Sacks — 4,855
26. J.D. McDuffie — 4,667
27. Trevor Boys — 3,973
28. Cale Yarborough — 3,450
29. Joe Ruttman — 3,378
30. Bobby Wawak — 3,157
31. Morgan Shepherd — 2,951
32. Tommy Ellis — 2,853
33. Lennie Pond — 2,831
34. Mike Alexander — 2,336
35. Benny Parsons — 2,230
36. Don Hume — 2,057
37. Alan Kulwicki — 1,843
38. Slick Johnson — 1,608
39. Ronnie Thomas — 1,510
40. Mike Potter — 1,434
41. David Pearson — 1,418
42. Ken Ragan — 1,359
43. Jerry Bowman — 1,326
44. Sterling Marlin — 1,321
45. Phil Good — 1,239
46. Bobby Gerhart — 1,166
47. A.J. Foyt — 966
48. Rick Newsom — 834
49. Jim Sauter — 565
50. Connie Saylor — 456

LAPS LED

1. Bill Elliott — 1,920
2. Harry Gant — 1,271
3. Dale Earnhardt — 1,237
4. Darrell Waltrip — 969
5. Geoffrey Bodine — 692
6. Cale Yarborough — 664
7. Neil Bonnett — 618
8. Terry Labonte — 563
9. Bobby Allison — 422
10. Tim Richmond — 377
11. Ricky Rudd — 329
12. Richard Petty — 105
13. Ron Bouchard — 77
14. Kyle Petty — 75
15. Greg Sacks — 36
16. Dave Marcis — 30
17. Rusty Wallace — 28
18. Benny Parsons — 8
    Lake Speed — 8
20. Joe Ruttman — 5
21. Buddy Baker — 4
    Ken Schrader — 4
23. Trevor Boys — 3
    Lennie Pond — 3
25. A.J. Foyt — 2
    Bobby Hillin — 2
    David Pearson — 2
28. Buddy Arrington — 1
    Sterling Marlin — 1
    Phil Parsons — 1
    Morgan Shepherd — 1

MILES LED

1. Bill Elliott — 3,188
2. Harry Gant — 1,267
3. Cale Yarborough — 1,141
4. Dale Earnhardt — 1,093
5. Darrell Waltrip — 1,006
6. Geoffrey Bodine — 856
7. Terry Labonte — 727
8. Neil Bonnett — 722
9. Tim Richmond — 305
10. Bobby Allison — 292
11. Ricky Rudd — 288
12. Greg Sacks — 90
13. Ron Bouchard — 87
14. Kyle Petty — 82
15. Richard Petty — 77
16. Dave Marcis — 27
17. Benny Parsons — 20
18. Rusty Wallace — 15
19. Lake Speed — 14
20. Joe Ruttman — 13
21. Trevor Boys — 8
22. Lennie Pond — 7
23. A.J. Foyt — 5
    David Pearson — 5
25. Buddy Baker — 4
26. Buddy Arrington — 3
    Ken Schrader — 3
28. Bobby Hillin — 2
29. Sterling Marlin — 1
    Phil Parsons — 1
    Morgan Shepherd — 1

MILES DRIVEN

1. Darrell Waltrip — 10,917
2. Bill Elliott — 10,736
3. Geoffrey Bodine — 10,720
4. Kyle Petty — 10,384
5. Neil Bonnett — 10,358
6. Ricky Rudd — 10,288
7. Bobby Hillin — 10,212
8. Harry Gant — 10,185
9. Lake Speed — 10,087
10. Buddy Arrington — 9,653
11. Terry Labonte — 9,612
12. Tim Richmond — 9,497
13. Ken Schrader — 9,364
14. Bobby Allison — 9,339
15. Dale Earnhardt — 9,157
16. Ron Bouchard — 8,969
17. Richard Petty — 8,863
18. Dave Marcis — 8,737
19. Clark Dwyer — 8,558
20. Rusty Wallace — 8,384
21. Buddy Baker — 8,075
22. Eddie Bierschwale — 7,761
23. Phil Parsons — 7,611
24. Jimmy Means — 7,521
25. Greg Sacks — 6,434
26. Cale Yarborough — 5,675
27. J.D. McDuffie — 5,539
28. Joe Ruttman — 4,599
29. Bobby Wawak — 4,457
30. Trevor Boys — 4,408

RACES LED

1. Darrell Waltrip — 21
2. Harry Gant — 20
3. Bill Elliott — 19
4. Geoffrey Bodine — 18
5. Dale Earnhardt — 17
6. Neil Bonnett — 15
7. Bobby Allison — 14
   Terry Labonte — 14
9. Tim Richmond — 12
10. Cale Yarborough — 11
11. Richard Petty — 7
12. Kyle Petty — 6
13. Ricky Rudd — 6
14. Ron Bouchard — 5
15. Dave Marcis — 4
    Lake Speed — 4
17. Benny Parsons — 3
    Greg Sacks — 3
19. Buddy Baker — 2
    A.J. Foyt — 2
    Bobby Hillin — 2
    Lennie Pond — 2
23. Buddy Arrington — 1
    Trevor Boys — 1
    Sterling Marlin — 1
    Phil Parsons — 1
    David Pearson — 1
    Joe Ruttman — 1
    Ken Schrader — 1
    Morgan Shepherd — 1
    Rusty Wallace — 1

Driver	Starts	Poles	Finish 1	2	3	4	5	6–10	Laps	Laps Led	Races Led	Winston Cup Points	$

1986

Driver	Starts	Poles	Finish 1	2	3	4	5	6–10	Laps	Laps Led	Races Led	Winston Cup Points	$
1. Dale Earnhardt	29	1	5	5	3	1	2	7	9,212	2,127	26	4,468	1,768,880
2. Darrell Waltrip	29	1	3	2	4	6	6	1	8,327	573	21	4,180	1,099,735
3. Tim Richmond	29	8	7	4	0	1	1	4	8,544	1,006	21	4,174	973,221
4. Bill Elliott	29	4	2	0	2	1	3	8	8,549	511	15	3,844	1,049,142
5. Ricky Rudd	29	1	2	4	2	3	0	6	7,950	525	7	3,823	671,548
6. Rusty Wallace	29	0	2	0	0	2	0	12	8,486	417	8	3,762	557,354
7. Bobby Allison	29	0	1	2	1	1	1	9	8,391	127	11	3,698	503,095
8. Geoffrey Bodine	29	9	2	2	5	1	0	5	7,791	1,676	25	3,678	795,111
9. Bobby Hillin	29	0	1	0	1	2	0	10	8,121	25	4	3,546	448,452
10. Kyle Petty	29	0	1	0	1	0	2	10	8,446	17	6	3,537	403,242
11. Harry Gant	29	2	0	3	1	3	2	4	7,965	656	17	3,498	583,024
12. Terry Labonte	29	1	1	2	2	0	0	5	7,984	565	10	3,473	522,235
13. Neil Bonnett	28	0	1	1	1	1	2	6	7,691	323	16	3,369	485,930
14. Richard Petty	29	0	0	1	2	1	0	7	7,639	153	7	3,314	280,657
15. Joe Ruttman	29	0	0	2	0	0	3	9	7,732	55	5	3,295	259,263
16. Ken Schrader	29	0	0	0	0	0	0	4	8,047	2	2	3,052	235,904
17. Dave Marcis	29	0	0	0	0	0	1	3	7,316	63	11	2,912	220,461
18. Morgan Shepherd	27	0	1	0	1	2	0	4	6,358	357	13	2,896	244,146
19. Michael Waltrip	28	0	0	0	0	0	0	0	7,852	6	4	2,853	108,767
20. Buddy Arrington	26	0	0	0	0	0	0	0	8,152	4	1	2,776	186,588
21. Alan Kulwicki	23	0	0	0	0	1	0	3	7,898	14	6	2,705	94,450
22. Jimmy Means	26	0	0	0	0	0	0	0	6,472	5	3	2,495	157,940
23. Tommy Ellis	24	0	0	0	0	0	0	3	6,559	50	5	2,393	78,310
24. Buddy Baker	17	0	0	0	1	2	3	0	3,964	45	5	1,924	138,600
25. Eddie Bierschwale	24	0	0	0	0	0	0	0	5,558	1	1	1,860	98,110
26. J.D. McDuffie	20	0	0	0	0	0	0	0	4,750	1	1	1,825	106,115
27. Phil Parsons	17	0	0	0	0	0	1	4	3,404	1	1	1,742	84,680
28. Rick Wilson	17	0	0	0	0	0	0	4	3,265	7	1	1,698	88,820
29. Cale Yarborough	16	1	0	0	2	0	0	3	3,467	110	4	1,642	137,010
30. Benny Parsons	16	1	0	0	0	0	2	2	2,620	13	7	1,555	176,985
31. Ron Bouchard	17	0	0	0	0	0	0	2	3,654	1	1	1,553	106,825
32. Chet Fillip	17	0	0	0	0	0	0	0	3,276	0	0	1,433	36,110
33. Jody Ridley	12	0	0	0	0	0	0	1	3,183	0	0	1,213	84,380
34. Trevor Boys	14	0	0	0	0	0	0	0	3,210	2	1	1,064	74,645
35. Doug Heveron	13	0	0	0	0	0	0	0	2,536	1	1	1,052	74,030
36. Sterling Marlin	10	0	0	1	0	1	0	2	1,738	21	3	989	113,070
37. D.K. Ulrich	9	0	0	0	0	0	0	0	2,014	0	0	804	47,795
38. Pancho Carter	9	0	0	0	0	0	0	0	1,423	3	2	706	56,355
39. Ken Ragan	7	0	0	0	0	0	0	0	1,284	1	1	627	33,890
40. Lake Speed	5	0	0	0	0	0	0	2	1,779	10	2	608	82,800
41. Greg Sacks	8	0	0	0	0	0	0	1	1,181	0	0	579	64,810
42. Ronnie Thomas	6	0	0	0	0	0	0	0	973	0	0	504	25,215
43. Bobby Wawak	6	0	0	0	0	0	0	0	1,170	0	0	480	10,155
44. Rodney Combs	5	0	0	0	0	0	0	0	909	4	1	421	12,180
45. Derrike Cope	5	0	0	0	0	0	0	1	1,101	0	0	400	8,025
46. James Hylton	4	0	0	0	0	0	0	0	544	0	0	386	22,090
47. Davey Allison	5	0	0	0	0	0	0	1	1,435	13	1	364	24,190
48. Mark Martin	5	0	0	0	0	0	0	0	1,342	0	0	364	20,515
49. Jim Sauter	9	0	0	0	0	0	0	0	1,430	2	1	361	52,020
50. A.J. Foyt	5	0	0	0	0	0	0	0	640	1	1	355	24,135

LAPS COMPLETED

1.	Dale Earnhardt	9,212
2.	Bill Elliott	8,549
3.	Tim Richmond	8,544
4.	Rusty Wallace	8,486
5.	Kyle Petty	8,446
6.	Bobby Allison	8,391
7.	Darrell Waltrip	8,327
8.	Buddy Arrington	8,152
9.	Bobby Hillin	8,121
10.	Ken Schrader	8,047
11.	Terry Labonte	7,984
12.	Harry Gant	7,965
13.	Ricky Rudd	7,950
14.	Alan Kulwicki	7,898
15.	Michael Waltrip	7,852
16.	Geoffrey Bodine	7,791
17.	Joe Ruttman	7,732
18.	Neil Bonnett	7,691
19.	Richard Petty	7,639
20.	Dave Marcis	7,316
21.	Tommy Ellis	6,559
22.	Jimmy Means	6,472
23.	Morgan Shepherd	6,358
24.	Eddie Bierschwale	5,558
25.	J.D. McDuffie	4,750
26.	Buddy Baker	3,964
27.	Ron Bouchard	3,654
28.	Cale Yarborough	3,467
29.	Phil Parsons	3,404
30.	Chet Fillip	3,276
31.	Rick Wilson	3,265
32.	Trevor Boys	3,210
33.	Jody Ridley	3,183
34.	Benny Parsons	2,620
35.	Doug Heveron	2,536
36.	D.K. Ulrich	2,014
37.	Lake Speed	1,779
38.	Sterling Marlin	1,738
39.	Davey Allison	1,435
40.	Jim Sauter	1,430
41.	Pancho Carter	1,423
42.	Mark Martin	1,342
43.	Ken Ragan	1,284
44.	Greg Sacks	1,181
45.	Bobby Wawak	1,170
46.	Derrike Cope	1,101
47.	Ronnie Thomas	973
48.	Rodney Combs	909
49.	A.J. Foyt	640
50.	James Hylton	544

LAPS LED

1.	Dale Earnhardt	2,127
2.	Geoffrey Bodine	1,676
3.	Tim Richmond	1,006
4.	Harry Gant	656
5.	Darrell Waltrip	573
6.	Terry Labonte	565
7.	Ricky Rudd	525
8.	Bill Elliott	511
9.	Rusty Wallace	417
10.	Morgan Shepherd	357
11.	Neil Bonnett	323
12.	Richard Petty	153
13.	Bobby Allison	127
14.	Cale Yarborough	110
15.	Dave Marcis	63
16.	Joe Ruttman	55
17.	Tommy Ellis	50
18.	Buddy Baker	45
19.	Bobby Hillin	25
20.	Sterling Marlin	21
21.	Kyle Petty	17
22.	Alan Kulwicki	14
23.	Davey Allison	13
	Benny Parsons	13
25.	Lake Speed	10
26.	Rick Wilson	7
27.	Michael Waltrip	6
28.	Jimmy Means	5
29.	Buddy Arrington	4
	Rodney Combs	4
31.	Pancho Carter	3
32.	Trevor Boys	2
	Jim Sauter	2
	Ken Schrader	2
35.	Eddie Bierschwale	1
	Ron Bouchard	1
	A.J. Foyt	1
	Doug Heveron	1
	J.D. McDuffie	1
	Phil Parsons	1
	Ken Ragan	1

MILES LED

1.	Dale Earnhardt	2,439
2.	Geoffrey Bodine	2,056
3.	Tim Richmond	1,592
4.	Bill Elliott	972
5.	Harry Gant	796
6.	Terry Labonte	596
7.	Darrell Waltrip	550
8.	Morgan Shepherd	418
9.	Neil Bonnett	369
10.	Ricky Rudd	366
11.	Rusty Wallace	247
12.	Bobby Allison	171
13.	Cale Yarborough	164
14.	Richard Petty	128
15.	Buddy Baker	107
16.	Bobby Hillin	60
17.	Dave Marcis	50
18.	Sterling Marlin	39
19.	Joe Ruttman	38
20.	Tommy Ellis	37
21.	Davey Allison	35
22.	Kyle Petty	28
23.	Benny Parsons	25
24.	Alan Kulwicki	22
25.	Rick Wilson	19
26.	Lake Speed	13
27.	Rodney Combs	11
	Michael Waltrip	11
29.	Buddy Arrington	10
30.	Phil Barkdoll	8
	Pancho Carter	8

MILES DRIVEN

1.	Dale Earnhardt	11,166
2.	Bill Elliott	10,593
3.	Tim Richmond	10,528
4.	Rusty Wallace	10,418
5.	Kyle Petty	10,204
6.	Bobby Hillin	9,980
7.	Darrell Waltrip	9,948
8.	Bobby Allison	9,930
9.	Ricky Rudd	9,743
10.	Ken Schrader	9,699
11.	Harry Gant	9,565
12.	Buddy Arrington	9,459
13.	Terry Labonte	9,431
14.	Geoffrey Bodine	9,361
15.	Michael Waltrip	9,147
16.	Neil Bonnett	8,992
17.	Richard Petty	8,951
18.	Joe Ruttman	8,708
19.	Alan Kulwicki	8,667
20.	Dave Marcis	8,522
21.	Morgan Shepherd	8,348
22.	Jimmy Means	8,104
23.	Tommy Ellis	7,334
24.	Eddie Bierschwale	6,985
25.	Buddy Baker	6,465
26.	Phil Parsons	6,153
27.	Cale Yarborough	5,828
28.	Rick Wilson	5,310
29.	Benny Parsons	5,100
30.	Ron Bouchard	5,093

RACES LED

1.	Dale Earnhardt	26
2.	Geoffrey Bodine	25
3.	Tim Richmond	21
	Darrell Waltrip	21
5.	Harry Gant	17
6.	Neil Bonnett	16
7.	Bill Elliott	15
8.	Morgan Shepherd	13
9.	Bobby Allison	11
	Dave Marcis	11
11.	Terry Labonte	10
12.	Rusty Wallace	8
13.	Benny Parsons	7
	Richard Petty	7
	Ricky Rudd	7
16.	Alan Kulwicki	6
	Kyle Petty	6
18.	Buddy Baker	5
	Tommy Ellis	5
	Joe Ruttman	5
21.	Bobby Hillin	4
	Michael Waltrip	4
	Cale Yarborough	4
24.	Sterling Marlin	3
	Jimmy Means	3
26.	Pancho Carter	2
	Ken Schrader	2
	Lake Speed	2
29.	Davey Allison	1
	Buddy Arrington	1
	Eddie Bierschwale	1
	Ron Bouchard	1
	Trevor Boys	1
	Rodney Combs	1
	A.J. Foyt	1
	Doug Heveron	1
	J.D. McDuffie	1
	Phil Parsons	1
	Ken Ragan	1
	Jim Sauter	1
	Rick Wilson	1

Driver	Starts	Poles	Finish 1	2	3	4	5	6–10	Laps	Laps Led	Races Led	Winston Cup Points	$
1987													
1. Dale Earnhardt	29	1	11	5	1	2	2	3	9,043	3,358	27	4,696	2,069,243
2. Bill Elliott	29	8	6	3	1	5	1	4	8,902	1,339	22	4,207	1,599,210
3. Terry Labonte	29	4	1	2	2	5	3	9	8,609	592	16	4,007	805,054
4. Darrell Waltrip	29	0	1	1	1	2	1	10	8,996	311	14	3,911	511,768
5. Rusty Wallace	29	1	2	3	2	1	1	7	8,323	462	16	3,818	690,652
6. Ricky Rudd	29	0	2	2	4	1	1	3	8,206	493	11	3,742	653,508
7. Kyle Petty	29	0	1	1	4	0	0	8	8,523	103	7	3,737	544,437
8. Richard Petty	29	0	0	1	3	2	3	5	8,306	38	8	3,708	445,227
9. Bobby Allison	29	1	1	1	0	1	1	9	7,662	331	10	3,530	515,894
10. Ken Schrader	29	1	0	0	0	0	1	9	8,162	154	10	3,405	375,918
11. Sterling Marlin	29	0	0	0	1	2	1	4	8,356	68	6	3,381	306,412
12. Neil Bonnett	26	0	0	0	4	1	0	10	7,834	120	10	3,352	401,541
13. Geoffrey Bodine	29	2	0	1	1	0	1	7	7,738	342	13	3,328	449,816
14. Phil Parsons	29	0	0	0	0	1	0	6	8,216	18	2	3,327	180,261
15. Alan Kulwicki	29	3	0	1	0	1	1	6	7,758	102	8	3,238	369,889
16. Benny Parsons	29	0	0	3	0	1	2	3	7,075	87	9	3,215	566,484
17. Morgan Shepherd	29	1	0	1	1	1	4	4	6,510	167	8	3,099	317,034
18. Dave Marcis	29	0	0	0	2	0	0	5	6,880	84	9	3,080	256,354
19. Bobby Hillin	29	0	0	0	0	0	1	3	6,989	1	1	3,027	246,735
20. Michael Waltrip	29	0	0	0	0	0	0	1	7,790	0	0	2,840	205,370
21. Davey Allison	22	5	2	3	0	0	4	1	5,511	710	11	2,824	361,060
22. Harry Gant	29	1	0	0	0	0	0	4	6,494	71	3	2,725	197,645
23. Jimmy Means	28	0	0	0	0	0	0	1	6,239	21	1	2,483	154,055
24. Buddy Baker	20	0	0	1	1	1	0	7	4,509	91	7	2,373	255,320
25. Buddy Arrington	20	0	0	0	0	0	0	0	5,746	0	0	1,885	115,300
26. Dale Jarrett	24	0	0	0	0	0	0	2	4,788	0	0	1,840	143,405
27. Steve Christman	20	0	0	0	0	0	0	0	4,404	0	0	1,727	54,965
28. Rick Wilson	19	0	0	0	0	0	0	1	3,530	20	1	1,723	65,935
29. Cale Yarborough	16	0	0	0	0	1	1	2	2,671	11	2	1,450	111,025
30. J.D. McDuffie	17	0	0	0	0	0	0	0	3,459	0	0	1,361	45,555
31. Lake Speed	13	0	0	0	1	0	0	4	2,591	1	1	1,345	110,810
32. Brett Bodine	14	0	0	0	0	0	0	0	2,908	20	3	1,271	71,460
33. Greg Sacks	16	0	0	0	0	0	0	0	2,705	1	1	1,200	54,815
34. Eddie Bierschwale	14	0	0	0	0	0	0	0	3,560	0	0	1,162	66,790
35. Rodney Combs	14	0	0	0	0	0	0	0	2,752	0	0	1,098	90,990
36. Tim Richmond	8	1	2	0	0	1	0	1	1,199	161	6	1,063	151,850
37. Derrike Cope	11	0	0	0	0	0	0	0	1,631	0	0	797	33,750
38. Mark Stahl	9	0	0	0	0	0	0	0	1,635	0	0	687	32,850
39. Bobby Wawak	8	0	0	0	0	0	0	0	1,648	0	0	638	22,505
40. D.K. Ulrich	7	0	0	0	0	0	0	0	1,876	0	0	625	30,915
41. Ken Ragan	6	0	0	0	0	0	0	0	1,259	0	0	549	30,575
42. Connie Saylor	10	0	0	0	0	0	0	0	1,775	0	0	486	59,455
43. Jerry Cranmer	5	0	0	0	0	0	0	0	1,914	0	0	482	20,660
44. Trevor Boys	10	0	0	0	0	0	0	0	2,312	5	2	460	59,240
45. Mike Potter	5	0	0	0	0	0	0	0	994	0	0	456	13,290
46. Slick Johnson	8	0	0	0	0	0	0	0	2,113	3	2	444	40,630
47. Ron Bouchard	5	0	0	0	0	0	0	1	917	0	0	440	24,105
48. H.B. Bailey	5	0	0	0	0	0	0	0	1,150	0	0	428	18,885
49. A.J. Foyt	6	0	0	0	0	0	0	0	748	2	2	409	21,075
50. Larry Pearson	4	0	0	0	0	0	0	1	1,162	1	1	401	18,555

LAPS COMPLETED		LAPS LED		MILES LED		MILES DRIVEN		RACES LED	
1. Dale Earnhardt	9,043	1. Dale Earnhardt	3,358	1. Dale Earnhardt	3,399	1. Darrell Waltrip	11,036	1. Dale Earnhardt	27
2. Darrell Waltrip	8,996	2. Bill Elliott	1,339	2. Bill Elliott	1,950	2. Dale Earnhardt	10,900	2. Bill Elliott	22
3. Bill Elliott	8,902	3. Davey Allison	710	3. Davey Allison	1,152	3. Bill Elliott	10,423	3. Terry Labonte	16
4. Terry Labonte	8,609	4. Terry Labonte	592	4. Rusty Wallace	671	4. Kyle Petty	10,401	Rusty Wallace	16
5. Kyle Petty	8,523	5. Ricky Rudd	493	5. Terry Labonte	585	5. Sterling Marlin	10,305	5. Darrell Waltrip	14
6. Sterling Marlin	8,356	6. Rusty Wallace	462	6. Ricky Rudd	524	6. Terry Labonte	10,159	6. Geoffrey Bodine	13
7. Rusty Wallace	8,323	7. Geoffrey Bodine	342	7. Geoffrey Bodine	448	7. Richard Petty	9,987	7. Davey Allison	11
8. Richard Petty	8,306	8. Bobby Allison	331	8. Bobby Allison	422	8. Ken Schrader	9,902	Ricky Rudd	11
9. Phil Parsons	8,216	9. Darrell Waltrip	311	9. Tim Richmond	404	9. Ricky Rudd	9,893	9. Bobby Allison	10
10. Ricky Rudd	8,206	10. Morgan Shepherd	167	10. Ken Schrader	242	10. Phil Parsons	9,674	Neil Bonnett	10
11. Ken Schrader	8,162	11. Tim Richmond	161	11. Darrell Waltrip	187	11. Rusty Wallace	9,670	Ken Schrader	10
12. Neil Bonnett	7,834	12. Ken Schrader	154	12. Buddy Baker	176	12. Bobby Allison	9,296	12. Dave Marcis	9
13. Michael Waltrip	7,790	13. Neil Bonnett	120	13. Morgan Shepherd	156	13. Alan Kulwicki	9,121	Benny Parsons	9
14. Alan Kulwicki	7,758	14. Kyle Petty	103	14. Dave Marcis	122	14. Neil Bonnett	9,073	14. Alan Kulwicki	8
15. Geoffrey Bodine	7,738	15. Alan Kulwicki	102	15. Neil Bonnett	120	15. Benny Parsons	8,921	Richard Petty	8
16. Bobby Allison	7,662	16. Buddy Baker	91	16. Benny Parsons	116	16. Michael Waltrip	8,850	Morgan Shepherd	8
17. Benny Parsons	7,075	17. Benny Parsons	87	17. Kyle Petty	114	17. Geoffrey Bodine	8,817	17. Buddy Baker	7
18. Bobby Hillin	6,989	18. Dave Marcis	84	18. Alan Kulwicki	70	18. Dave Marcis	8,751	Kyle Petty	7
19. Dave Marcis	6,880	19. Harry Gant	71	19. Richard Petty	69	19. Bobby Hillin	8,615	19. Sterling Marlin	6
20. Morgan Shepherd	6,510	20. Sterling Marlin	68	20. Sterling Marlin	46	20. Davey Allison	8,520	Tim Richmond	6
21. Harry Gant	6,494	21. Richard Petty	38	21. Harry Gant	38	21. Morgan Shepherd	8,039	21. Brett Bodine	3
22. Jimmy Means	6,239	22. Jimmy Means	21	22. Brett Bodine	33	22. Harry Gant	7,921	Harry Gant	3
23. Buddy Arrington	5,746	23. Brett Bodine	20	23. Rick Wilson	30	23. Jimmy Means	7,184	23. Trevor Boys	2
24. Davey Allison	5,511	Rick Wilson	20	24. Brad Teague	26	24. Buddy Baker	7,165	A.J. Foyt	2
25. Dale Jarrett	4,788	25. Phil Parsons	18	25. George Follmer	21	25. Buddy Arrington	6,793	Slick Johnson	2
26. Buddy Baker	4,509	26. Cale Yarborough	11	Cale Yarborough	21	26. Dale Jarrett	5,681	Phil Parsons	2
27. Steve Christman	4,404	27. Trevor Boys	5	27. Phil Parsons	16	27. Rick Wilson	5,577	Cale Yarborough	2
28. Eddie Bierschwale	3,560	28. Slick Johnson	3	28. Trevor Boys	12	28. Steve Christman	5,101	28. Bobby Hillin	1
29. Rick Wilson	3,530	29. A.J. Foyt	2	29. Jimmy Means	11	29. Cale Yarborough	4,519	Jimmy Means	1
30. J.D. McDuffie	3,459	30. Bobby Hillin	1	30. Slick Johnson	6	30. Brett Bodine	4,485	Larry Pearson	1
31. Brett Bodine	2,908	Larry Pearson	1					Greg Sacks	1
32. Rodney Combs	2,752	Greg Sacks	1					Lake Speed	1
33. Greg Sacks	2,705	Lake Speed	1					Michael Waltrip	1
34. Cale Yarborough	2,671	Michael Waltrip	1					Rick Wilson	1
35. Lake Speed	2,591								
36. Trevor Boys	2,312								
37. Slick Johnson	2,113								
38. Jerry Cranmer	1,914								
39. D.K. Ulrich	1,876								
40. Connie Saylor	1,775								
41. Bobby Wawak	1,648								
42. Mark Stahl	1,635								
43. Derrike Cope	1,631								
44. Ken Ragan	1,259								
45. Tim Richmond	1,199								
46. Larry Pearson	1,162								
47. H.B. Bailey	1,150								
48. Mike Potter	994								
49. Ron Bouchard	917								
50. A.J. Foyt	748								

Driver	Starts	Poles	Finish 1	2	3	4	5	6–10	Laps	Laps Led	Races Led	Winston Cup Points	$

1988

	Driver	Starts	Poles	1	2	3	4	5	6–10	Laps	Laps Led	Races Led	Winston Cup Points	$
1.	Bill Elliott	29	6	6	2	2	4	1	7	9,647	1,559	20	4,488	1,554,639
2.	Rusty Wallace	29	2	6	5	4	2	2	4	9,222	891	19	4,484	1,411,567
3.	Dale Earnhardt	29	0	3	2	3	3	2	6	9,561	1,808	20	4,256	1,214,089
4.	Terry Labonte	29	1	1	2	3	4	1	7	9,206	208	17	4,007	950,781
5.	Ken Schrader	29	2	1	1	0	1	1	13	9,095	151	13	3,858	631,544
6.	Geoffrey Bodine	29	3	1	1	4	1	3	6	8,995	463	15	3,799	570,643
7.	Darrell Waltrip	29	2	2	1	1	2	4	4	9,065	520	18	3,764	731,659
8.	Davey Allison	29	3	2	2	3	2	3	4	8,333	650	14	3,631	844,532
9.	Phil Parsons	29	0	1	1	2	1	1	9	8,494	108	10	3,630	532,043
10.	Sterling Marlin	29	0	0	1	1	0	4	7	8,798	332	13	3,621	521,464
11.	Ricky Rudd	29	2	1	3	1	1	0	5	8,867	695	16	3,547	410,954
12.	Bobby Hillin	29	0	0	0	1	0	0	6	9,383	70	4	3,446	300,217
13.	Kyle Petty	29	0	0	0	0	0	2	6	8,883	66	3	3,296	377,092
14.	Alan Kulwicki	29	4	1	2	1	1	2	2	8,149	134	8	3,176	448,547
15.	Mark Martin	29	1	0	1	0	2	0	7	7,595	120	4	3,142	223,630
16.	Neil Bonnett	27	0	2	0	0	1	0	4	8,017	324	7	3,040	440,139
17.	Lake Speed	29	0	1	1	0	1	1	3	7,005	368	6	2,984	260,500
18.	Michael Waltrip	29	0	0	1	0	0	0	2	7,734	6	2	2,949	240,400
19.	Dave Marcis	29	0	0	0	0	0	0	2	8,278	62	7	2,854	212,485
20.	Brett Bodine	29	0	0	0	1	1	0	3	7,789	200	5	2,828	433,658
21.	Rick Wilson	28	1	0	1	0	1	0	3	6,870	145	3	2,762	209,925
22.	Richard Petty	29	0	0	0	1	0	0	4	6,207	12	3	2,644	190,155
23.	Dale Jarrett	29	0	0	0	0	0	0	1	6,556	5	2	2,622	118,640
24.	Benny Parsons	27	0	0	0	0	0	0	1	7,423	82	3	2,559	210,755
25.	Ken Bouchard	24	0	0	0	0	0	0	1	7,281	4	1	2,378	109,410
26.	Ernie Irvan	25	0	0	0	0	0	0	0	7,337	1	1	2,319	96,370
27.	Harry Gant	24	0	0	0	0	0	0	3	5,896	343	8	2,266	173,325
28.	Morgan Shepherd	23	2	0	1	0	1	0	4	4,601	127	5	2,193	197,425
29.	Buddy Baker	17	0	0	0	0	0	0	7	4,445	42	7	2,056	184,200
30.	Jimmy Means	27	0	0	0	0	0	0	0	5,172	12	4	2,045	139,290
31.	Derrike Cope	26	0	0	0	0	0	0	0	4,772	0	0	1,985	132,835
32.	Mike Alexander	16	0	0	0	1	0	1	4	4,677	51	5	1,931	200,709
33.	Bobby Allison	13	0	1	1	0	0	1	3	4,303	104	4	1,654	409,295
34.	Eddie Bierschwale	20	0	0	0	0	0	0	0	4,106	0	0	1,481	59,355
35.	Rodney Combs	19	0	0	0	0	0	0	0	3,693	0	0	1,468	54,150
36.	Brad Noffsinger	17	0	0	0	0	0	0	0	3,555	1	1	1,316	54,645
37.	Greg Sacks	15	0	0	0	0	0	0	3	3,543	1	1	1,237	105,579
38.	Cale Yarborough	10	0	0	0	0	0	0	3	1,653	6	2	940	66,065
39.	Joe Ruttman	12	0	0	0	0	0	0	1	1,899	0	0	803	46,455
40.	Brad Teague	13	0	0	0	0	0	0	0	3,408	0	0	802	53,105
41.	Jimmy Horton	8	0	0	0	0	0	0	0	2,007	0	0	647	23,575
42.	A.J. Foyt	7	0	0	0	0	0	0	0	920	9	3	523	29,660
43.	H.B. Bailey	7	0	0	0	0	0	0	0	1,180	0	0	478	15,775
44.	Jim Sauter	9	0	0	0	0	0	0	0	2,413	6	1	463	35,040
45.	Chad Little	4	0	0	0	0	0	0	0	1,089	3	1	405	14,225
46.	Buddy Arrington	4	0	0	0	0	0	0	0	760	0	0	352	22,165
47.	Ken Ragan	5	0	0	0	0	0	0	0	731	0	0	314	15,755
48.	Dana Patten	4	0	0	0	0	0	0	0	1,059	0	0	313	9,595
49.	Rick Jeffery	4	0	0	0	0	0	0	0	978	0	0	307	25,535
50.	Mickey Gibbs	5	0	0	0	0	0	0	0	636	2	1	283	12,850

LAPS COMPLETED		LAPS LED		MILES LED		MILES DRIVEN		RACES LED	
1. Bill Elliott	9,647	1. Dale Earnhardt	1,808	1. Bill Elliott	1,817	1. Bill Elliott	11,531	1. Dale Earnhardt	20
2. Dale Earnhardt	9,561	2. Bill Elliott	1,559	2. Dale Earnhardt	1,792	2. Dale Earnhardt	11,325	Bill Elliott	20
3. Bobby Hillin	9,383	3. Rusty Wallace	891	3. Rusty Wallace	1,260	3. Rusty Wallace	11,191	3. Rusty Wallace	19
4. Rusty Wallace	9,222	4. Ricky Rudd	695	4. Darrell Waltrip	879	4. Bobby Hillin	11,188	4. Darrell Waltrip	18
5. Terry Labonte	9,206	5. Davey Allison	650	5. Geoffrey Bodine	794	5. Terry Labonte	11,043	5. Terry Labonte	17
6. Ken Schrader	9,095	6. Darrell Waltrip	520	6. Davey Allison	713	6. Ken Schrader	11,033	6. Ricky Rudd	16
7. Darrell Waltrip	9,065	7. Geoffrey Bodine	463	7. Ricky Rudd	559	7. Darrell Waltrip	10,792	7. Geoffrey Bodine	15
8. Geoffrey Bodine	8,995	8. Lake Speed	368	8. Lake Speed	382	8. Geoffrey Bodine	10,566	8. Davey Allison	14
9. Kyle Petty	8,883	9. Harry Gant	343	9. Sterling Marlin	333	9. Kyle Petty	10,524	9. Sterling Marlin	13
10. Ricky Rudd	8,867	10. Sterling Marlin	332	10. Ken Schrader	323	10. Ricky Rudd	10,438	Ken Schrader	13
11. Sterling Marlin	8,798	11. Neil Bonnett	324	11. Neil Bonnett	283	11. Sterling Marlin	10,389	11. Phil Parsons	10
12. Phil Parsons	8,494	12. Terry Labonte	208	12. Brett Bodine	274	12. Phil Parsons	10,297	12. Harry Gant	8
13. Davey Allison	8,333	13. Brett Bodine	200	13. Phil Parsons	252	13. Michael Waltrip	10,050	Alan Kulwicki	8
14. Dave Marcis	8,278	14. Ken Schrader	151	14. Bobby Allison	241	14. Davey Allison	9,749	14. Buddy Baker	7
15. Alan Kulwicki	8,149	15. Rick Wilson	145	15. Terry Labonte	233	15. Dave Marcis	9,618	Neil Bonnett	7
16. Neil Bonnett	8,017	16. Alan Kulwicki	134	16. Harry Gant	229	16. Alan Kulwicki	9,325	Dave Marcis	7
17. Brett Bodine	7,789	17. Morgan Shepherd	127	17. Rick Wilson	215	17. Mark Martin	9,182	17. Lake Speed	6
18. Michael Waltrip	7,734	18. Mark Martin	120	18. Morgan Shepherd	139	18. Brett Bodine	9,163	18. Mike Alexander	5
19. Mark Martin	7,595	19. Phil Parsons	108	19. Mark Martin	132	19. Neil Bonnett	9,140	Brett Bodine	5
20. Benny Parsons	7,423	20. Bobby Allison	104	20. Benny Parsons	121	20. Ernie Irvan	8,855	Morgan Shepherd	5
21. Ernie Irvan	7,337	21. Benny Parsons	82	21. Alan Kulwicki	120	21. Benny Parsons	8,761	21. Bobby Allison	4
22. Ken Bouchard	7,281	22. Bobby Hillin	70	22. Bobby Hillin	66	22. Rick Wilson	8,713	Bobby Hillin	4
23. Lake Speed	7,005	23. Kyle Petty	66	23. Buddy Baker	61	23. Lake Speed	8,542	Mark Martin	4
24. Rick Wilson	6,870	24. Dave Marcis	62	24. Tom Kendall	60	24. Ken Bouchard	8,490	Jimmy Means	4
25. Dale Jarrett	6,556	25. Mike Alexander	51	25. Mike Alexander	58	25. Dale Jarrett	8,167	25. A.J. Foyt	3
26. Richard Petty	6,207	26. Buddy Baker	42	26. Dave Marcis	44	26. Richard Petty	7,628	Benny Parsons	3
27. Harry Gant	5,896	27. Jimmy Means	12	27. Kyle Petty	37	27. Harry Gant	6,877	Kyle Petty	3
28. Jimmy Means	5,172	Richard Petty	12	28. Richard Petty	29	28. Jimmy Means	6,592	Richard Petty	3
29. Derrike Cope	4,772	29. A.J. Foyt	9	29. A.J. Foyt	17	29. Derrike Cope	6,539	Rick Wilson	3
30. Mike Alexander	4,677	30. Jim Sauter	6	Jimmy Means	17	30. Buddy Baker	6,481	30. Dale Jarrett	2
31. Morgan Shepherd	4,601	Michael Waltrip	6					Michael Waltrip	2
32. Buddy Baker	4,445	Cale Yarborough	6					Cale Yarborough	2
33. Bobby Allison	4,303	33. Dale Jarrett	5					33. Ken Bouchard	1
34. Eddie Bierschwale	4,106	34. Ken Bouchard	4					Mickey Gibbs	1
35. Rodney Combs	3,693	35. Chad Little	3					Ernie Irvan	1
36. Brad Noffsinger	3,555	36. Mickey Gibbs	2					Chad Little	1
37. Greg Sacks	3,543	37. Ernie Irvan	1					Brad Noffsinger	1
38. Brad Teague	3,408	Brad Noffsinger	1					Greg Sacks	1
39. Jim Sauter	2,413	Greg Sacks	1					Jim Sauter	1
40. Jimmy Horton	2,007								
41. Joe Ruttman	1,899								
42. Cale Yarborough	1,653								
43. H.B. Bailey	1,180								
44. Chad Little	1,089								
45. Dana Patten	1,059								
46. Rick Jeffery	978								
47. A.J. Foyt	920								
48. Buddy Arrington	760								
49. Ken Ragan	731								
50. Mickey Gibbs	636								

Driver	Starts	Poles	Finish 1	2	3	4	5	6–10	Laps	Laps Led	Races Led	Winston Cup Points	$

1989

	Driver	Starts	Poles	1	2	3	4	5	6–10	Laps	Laps Led	Races Led	Winston Cup Points	$
1.	Rusty Wallace	29	4	6	4	0	2	1	7	9,104	2,020	23	4,176	2,237,950
2.	Dale Earnhardt	29	2	5	3	5	1	0	5	9,112	2,730	22	4,164	1,432,230
3.	Mark Martin	29	6	1	5	6	1	1	4	9,010	480	16	4,053	1,016,850
4.	Darrell Waltrip	29	0	6	2	2	2	2	4	9,333	858	17	3,971	1,312,479
5.	Ken Schrader	29	4	1	1	3	4	1	4	8,675	356	17	3,786	1,037,941
6.	Bill Elliott	29	2	3	0	1	3	1	6	9,037	380	11	3,774	849,370
7.	Harry Gant	29	0	1	3	1	2	2	5	8,627	439	11	3,610	639,792
8.	Ricky Rudd	29	0	1	0	2	3	1	8	9,326	247	7	3,608	533,624
9.	Geoffrey Bodine	29	3	1	1	3	3	1	2	9,051	510	14	3,600	619,494
10.	Terry Labonte	29	0	2	2	1	1	3	2	8,306	104	10	3,569	703,806
11.	Davey Allison	29	1	2	1	0	2	2	6	8,287	253	13	3,481	640,956
12.	Sterling Marlin	29	0	0	1	1	0	2	9	8,840	29	6	3,422	473,267
13.	Morgan Shepherd	29	1	0	2	0	1	2	8	7,590	139	6	3,403	544,255
14.	Alan Kulwicki	29	6	0	4	0	0	1	4	8,324	564	14	3,236	501,295
15.	Dick Trickle	28	0	0	0	3	1	2	3	8,604	80	8	3,203	343,728
16.	Bobby Hillin	28	0	0	0	0	0	1	6	8,377	26	4	3,139	283,181
17.	Rick Wilson	29	0	0	0	0	1	1	5	8,004	29	5	3,119	312,402
18.	Michael Waltrip	29	0	0	0	0	0	0	5	8,372	9	4	3,057	249,233
19.	Brett Bodine	29	0	0	0	0	0	1	5	8,202	2	2	3,051	281,274
20.	Neil Bonnett	26	0	0	0	0	0	0	11	7,795	23	6	2,995	271,628
21.	Phil Parsons	29	0	0	0	1	0	1	1	7,735	39	4	2,933	285,012
22.	Ernie Irvan	29	0	0	0	0	0	0	4	8,286	69	4	2,919	155,329
23.	Larry Pearson	29	0	0	0	0	0	0	2	7,993	5	2	2,860	156,060
24.	Dale Jarrett	29	0	0	0	0	0	2	3	7,798	99	3	2,789	232,317
25.	Dave Marcis	27	0	0	0	0	0	0	1	7,866	16	5	2,715	196,161
26.	Hut Stricklin	27	0	0	0	0	1	0	3	7,557	3	1	2,705	152,504
27.	Lake Speed	24	0	0	0	0	0	1	4	7,028	11	4	2,550	201,977
28.	Derrike Cope	23	0	0	0	0	0	0	4	5,382	5	3	2,180	125,630
29.	Richard Petty	25	0	0	0	0	0	0	0	5,567	9	1	2,148	133,050
30.	Kyle Petty	19	0	0	0	0	1	0	4	5,207	16	1	2,099	117,027
31.	Jimmy Means	22	0	0	0	0	0	0	0	4,868	4	1	1,698	65,005
32.	Greg Sacks	20	0	0	0	0	0	0	2	4,955	110	4	1,565	113,535
33.	Jim Sauter	17	0	0	0	0	0	0	2	3,974	8	1	1,510	73,832
34.	Jimmy Spencer	17	0	0	0	0	0	0	3	3,544	0	0	1,445	121,065
35.	Rick Mast	13	0	0	0	0	0	0	1	4,160	14	2	1,315	128,102
36.	Eddie Bierschwale	16	0	0	0	0	0	0	1	3,829	2	1	1,306	82,695
37.	Ben Hess	9	0	0	0	0	0	0	0	3,194	0	0	921	48,490
38.	Chad Little	8	0	0	0	0	0	0	0	2,036	0	0	602	44,690
39.	Butch Miller	9	0	0	0	0	0	0	0	1,129	0	0	576	22,520
40.	A.J. Foyt	7	0	0	0	0	0	0	0	860	6	2	527	31,995
41.	Mickey Gibbs	7	0	0	0	0	0	0	0	1,363	0	0	508	27,040
42.	Rodney Combs	9	0	0	0	0	0	0	0	1,657	0	0	470	36,090
43.	Joe Ruttman	9	0	0	0	0	0	0	1	1,704	0	0	469	64,645
44.	J.D. McDuffie	7	0	0	0	0	0	0	0	1,381	0	0	457	27,720
45.	Phil Barkdoll	4	0	0	0	0	0	0	0	658	2	1	378	29,050
46.	Jimmy Horton	5	0	0	0	0	0	0	0	955	0	0	377	19,232
47.	Dick Johnson	4	0	0	0	0	0	0	0	497	0	0	322	11,515
48.	Ken Bouchard	4	0	0	0	0	0	0	0	911	0	0	313	33,930
49.	Terry Byers	3	0	0	0	0	0	0	0	773	0	0	306	15,400
50.	Darin Brassfield	3	0	0	0	0	0	0	0	275	0	0	306	10,852

LAPS COMPLETED

1.	Darrell Waltrip	9,333
2.	Ricky Rudd	9,326
3.	Dale Earnhardt	9,112
4.	Rusty Wallace	9,104
5.	Geoffrey Bodine	9,051
6.	Bill Elliott	9,037
7.	Mark Martin	9,010
8.	Sterling Marlin	8,840
9.	Ken Schrader	8,675
10.	Harry Gant	8,627
11.	Dick Trickle	8,604
12.	Bobby Hillin	8,377
13.	Michael Waltrip	8,372
14.	Alan Kulwicki	8,324
15.	Terry Labonte	8,306
16.	Davey Allison	8,287
17.	Ernie Irvan	8,286
18.	Brett Bodine	8,202
19.	Rick Wilson	8,004
20.	Larry Pearson	7,993
21.	Dave Marcis	7,866
22.	Dale Jarrett	7,798
23.	Neil Bonnett	7,795
24.	Phil Parsons	7,735
25.	Morgan Shepherd	7,590
26.	Hut Stricklin	7,557
27.	Lake Speed	7,028
28.	Richard Petty	5,567
29.	Derrike Cope	5,382
30.	Kyle Petty	5,207
31.	Greg Sacks	4,955
32.	Jimmy Means	4,868
33.	Rick Mast	4,160
34.	Jim Sauter	3,974
35.	Eddie Bierschwale	3,829
36.	Jimmy Spencer	3,544
37.	Ben Hess	3,194
38.	Chad Little	2,036
39.	Joe Ruttman	1,704
40.	Rodney Combs	1,657
41.	J.D. McDuffie	1,381
42.	Mickey Gibbs	1,363
43.	Butch Miller	1,129
44.	Jimmy Horton	955
45.	Ken Bouchard	911
46.	A.J. Foyt	860
47.	Terry Byers	773
48.	Phil Barkdoll	658
49.	Dick Johnson	497
50.	Darin Brassfield	275

LAPS LED

1.	Dale Earnhardt	2,730
2.	Rusty Wallace	2,020
3.	Darrell Waltrip	858
4.	Alan Kulwicki	564
5.	Geoffrey Bodine	510
6.	Mark Martin	480
7.	Harry Gant	439
8.	Bill Elliott	380
9.	Ken Schrader	356
10.	Davey Allison	253
11.	Ricky Rudd	247
12.	Morgan Shepherd	139
13.	Greg Sacks	110
14.	Terry Labonte	104
15.	Dale Jarrett	99
16.	Dick Trickle	80
17.	Ernie Irvan	69
18.	Phil Parsons	39
19.	Sterling Marlin	29
	Rick Wilson	29
21.	Bobby Hillin	26
22.	Neil Bonnett	23
23.	Dave Marcis	16
	Kyle Petty	16
25.	Rick Mast	14
26.	Lake Speed	11
27.	Richard Petty	9
	Michael Waltrip	9
29.	Jim Sauter	8
30.	A.J. Foyt	6
31.	Derrike Cope	5
	Larry Pearson	5
33.	Jimmy Means	4
34.	Hut Stricklin	3
35.	Eddie Bierschwale	2
	Brett Bodine	2
	Phil Barkdoll	2

MILES LED

1.	Dale Earnhardt	2,612
2.	Rusty Wallace	2,548
3.	Darrell Waltrip	819
4.	Ken Schrader	711
5.	Alan Kulwicki	610
6.	Mark Martin	604
7.	Harry Gant	575
8.	Bill Elliott	573
9.	Davey Allison	464
10.	Geoffrey Bodine	450
11.	Ricky Rudd	364
12.	Morgan Shepherd	351
13.	Terry Labonte	240
14.	Dick Trickle	108
15.	Greg Sacks	65
16.	Dale Jarrett	55
17.	Phil Parsons	54
18.	Bobby Hillin	53
19.	Rick Wilson	52
20.	Sterling Marlin	40
	Kyle Petty	40
22.	Ernie Irvan	38
23.	Neil Bonnett	37
24.	Dave Marcis	26
25.	Rick Mast	25
26.	Lake Speed	21
27.	Michael Waltrip	19
28.	Richard Petty	14
29.	A.J. Foyt	13
30.	Jimmy Means	11

MILES DRIVEN

1.	Ricky Rudd	11,076
2.	Darrell Waltrip	10,986
3.	Bill Elliott	10,836
4.	Dale Earnhardt	10,798
5.	Rusty Wallace	10,783
6.	Ken Schrader	10,782
7.	Mark Martin	10,718
8.	Sterling Marlin	10,580
9.	Geoffrey Bodine	10,535
10.	Brett Bodine	10,356
11.	Bobby Hillin	10,298
12.	Harry Gant	10,295
13.	Dick Trickle	10,129
14.	Davey Allison	10,113
	Michael Waltrip	10,113
16.	Rick Wilson	9,992
17.	Dave Marcis	9,986
18.	Ernie Irvan	9,963
19.	Morgan Shepherd	9,910
20.	Terry Labonte	9,773
21.	Larry Pearson	9,737
22.	Alan Kulwicki	9,560
23.	Neil Bonnett	9,488
24.	Phil Parsons	9,321
25.	Hut Stricklin	9,287
26.	Dale Jarrett	9,180
27.	Lake Speed	8,245
28.	Richard Petty	7,929
29.	Kyle Petty	7,345
30.	Derrike Cope	6,863

RACES LED

1.	Rusty Wallace	23
2.	Dale Earnhardt	22
3.	Ken Schrader	17
	Darrell Waltrip	17
5.	Mark Martin	16
6.	Geoffrey Bodine	14
	Alan Kulwicki	14
8.	Davey Allison	13
9.	Bill Elliott	11
	Harry Gant	11
11.	Terry Labonte	10
12.	Dick Trickle	8
13.	Ricky Rudd	7
14.	Neil Bonnett	6
	Sterling Marlin	6
	Morgan Shepherd	6
17.	Dave Marcis	5
	Rick Wilson	5
19.	Bobby Hillin	4
	Ernie Irvan	4
	Phil Parsons	4
	Greg Sacks	4
	Lake Speed	4
	Michael Waltrip	4
25.	Derrike Cope	3
	Dale Jarrett	3
27.	Brett Bodine	2
	A.J. Foyt	2
	Larry Pearson	2
	Rick Mast	2
31.	Phil Barkdoll	1
	Eddie Bierschwale	1
	Jimmy Means	1
	Kyle Petty	1
	Richard Petty	1
	Jim Sauter	1
	Hut Stricklin	1

Driver	Starts	Poles	1	2	3	4	5	6–10	Laps	Laps Led	Races Led	Winston Cup Points	$

1990

#	Driver	Starts	Poles	1	2	3	4	5	6–10	Laps	Laps Led	Races Led	Winston Cup Points	$
1.	Dale Earnhardt	29	5	9	3	3	1	2	5	9,162	2,437	22	4,430	3,308,056
2.	Mark Martin	29	4	3	5	4	2	2	7	9,636	451	15	4,404	1,302,958
3.	Geoffrey Bodine	29	2	3	3	2	3	0	8	8,852	976	21	4,017	1,131,222
4.	Bill Elliott	29	2	1	4	1	5	1	4	9,349	1,182	13	3,999	1,090,730
5.	Morgan Shepherd	29	0	1	2	2	0	2	9	8,794	201	7	3,689	666,915
6.	Rusty Wallace	29	2	2	3	2	0	2	7	8,459	1,138	16	3,676	954,129
7.	Ricky Rudd	29	2	1	0	3	2	2	7	8,664	180	7	3,601	573,650
8.	Alan Kulwicki	29	1	1	1	1	1	1	8	8,635	400	10	3,599	550,936
9.	Ernie Irvan	29	3	1	2	1	1	1	7	9,001	280	10	3,593	535,280
10.	Ken Schrader	29	3	0	2	2	1	2	7	8,649	242	12	3,572	769,934
11.	Kyle Petty	29	2	1	0	0	1	0	12	8,485	852	12	3,501	746,326
12.	Brett Bodine	29	1	1	0	2	2	0	4	9,097	216	7	3,440	442,681
13.	Davey Allison	29	0	2	0	1	0	2	5	9,154	222	8	3,423	640,684
14.	Sterling Marlin	29	0	0	0	1	1	3	5	8,263	71	6	3,387	369,167
15.	Terry Labonte	29	0	0	1	0	3	0	5	8,518	9	3	3,371	450,230
16.	Michael Waltrip	29	0	0	0	1	2	2	5	8,226	17	4	3,251	395,507
17.	Harry Gant	28	0	1	0	1	1	3	3	7,441	53	9	3,182	522,519
18.	Derrike Cope	29	0	2	0	0	0	0	4	7,881	109	6	3,140	569,451
19.	Bobby Hillin	29	0	0	0	0	0	1	3	8,299	60	5	3,048	339,366
20.	Darrell Waltrip	23	0	0	1	1	2	1	7	8,138	297	9	3,013	520,420
21.	Dave Marcis	29	0	0	0	0	0	0	0	8,940	8	4	2,944	242,724
22.	Dick Trickle	29	1	0	0	1	0	1	2	8,291	82	4	2,863	350,990
23.	Rick Wilson	29	0	0	0	0	0	1	2	8,036	0	0	2,666	242,067
24.	Jimmy Spencer	26	0	0	0	0	0	0	2	7,576	10	5	2,579	219,775
25.	Dale Jarrett	24	0	0	0	0	1	0	6	6,801	74	5	2,558	214,495
26.	Richard Petty	29	0	0	0	0	0	0	1	7,438	5	1	2,556	169,465
27.	Butch Miller	23	0	0	0	0	0	0	1	6,891	4	4	2,377	151,941
28.	Hut Stricklin	24	0	0	0	0	0	0	2	6,037	1	1	2,316	169,199
29.	Jimmy Means	27	0	0	0	0	0	0	0	7,419	0	0	2,271	135,165
30.	Rob Moroso	25	0	0	0	0	0	0	1	5,666	9	3	2,184	162,002
31.	Rick Mast	20	0	0	0	0	0	0	1	5,335	0	0	1,719	112,875
32.	Greg Sacks	16	1	0	2	0	0	0	2	3,790	107	4	1,663	216,148
33.	Chad Little	18	0	0	0	0	0	0	0	4,840	0	0	1,632	80,140
34.	Jack Pennington	14	0	0	0	0	0	0	0	3,450	7	2	1,278	95,860
35.	Larry Pearson	9	0	0	0	0	0	0	0	2,871	0	0	822	72,305
36.	Jimmy Horton	9	0	0	0	0	0	0	0	2,264	0	0	756	72,375
37.	Mickey Gibbs	9	0	0	0	0	0	0	0	1,837	1	1	755	38,665
38.	Mike Alexander	7	0	0	0	0	0	0	0	2,392	0	0	682	41,080
39.	Phil Parsons	9	0	0	0	0	0	0	0	2,240	0	0	632	90,010
40.	J.D. McDuffie	8	0	0	0	0	0	0	0	1,301	0	0	557	26,170
41.	Buddy Baker	8	0	0	0	0	0	0	0	1,326	1	1	498	40,085
42.	Lake Speed	6	0	0	0	0	0	0	0	835	3	1	479	75,537
43.	Neil Bonnett	5	0	0	0	0	0	0	0	1,179	0	0	455	62,600
44.	Mark Stahl	5	0	0	0	0	0	0	0	1,268	0	0	371	18,470
45.	Bill Venturini	4	0	0	0	0	0	0	0	702	0	0	349	22,970
46.	Rodney Combs	5	0	0	0	0	0	0	0	988	0	0	323	23,365
47.	Irv Hoerr	2	0	0	0	0	0	0	2	164	3	1	281	14,775
48.	Tom Kendall	3	0	0	0	0	0	0	1	613	4	1	281	14,120
49.	Ted Musgrave	4	0	0	0	0	0	0	0	786	0	0	280	17,190
50.	Chuck Bown	3	0	0	0	0	0	0	0	951	0	0	276	10,150

LAPS COMPLETED

1.	Mark Martin	9,636
2.	Bill Elliott	9,349
3.	Dale Earnhardt	9,162
4.	Davey Allison	9,154
5.	Brett Bodine	9,097
6.	Ernie Irvan	9,001
7.	Dave Marcis	8,940
8.	Geoffrey Bodine	8,852
9.	Morgan Shepherd	8,794
10.	Ricky Rudd	8,664
11.	Ken Schrader	8,649
12.	Alan Kulwicki	8,635
13.	Terry Labonte	8,518
14.	Kyle Petty	8,485
15.	Rusty Wallace	8,459
16.	Bobby Hillin	8,299
17.	Dick Trickle	8,291
18.	Sterling Marlin	8,263
19.	Michael Waltrip	8,226
20.	Darrell Waltrip	8,138
21.	Rick Wilson	8,036
22.	Derrike Cope	7,881
23.	Jimmy Spencer	7,576
24.	Harry Gant	7,441
25.	Richard Petty	7,438
26.	Jimmy Means	7,419
27.	Butch Miller	6,891
28.	Dale Jarrett	6,801
29.	Hut Stricklin	6,037
30.	Rob Moroso	5,666
31.	Rick Mast	5,335
32.	Chad Little	4,840
33.	Greg Sacks	3,790
34.	Jack Pennington	3,450
35.	Larry Pearson	2,871
36.	Mike Alexander	2,392
37.	Jimmy Horton	2,264
38.	Phil Parsons	2,240
39.	Mickey Gibbs	1,837
40.	Buddy Baker	1,326
41.	J.D. McDuffie	1,301
42.	Mark Stahl	1,268
43.	Neil Bonnett	1,179
44.	Rodney Combs	988
45.	Chuck Bown	951
46.	Lake Speed	835
47.	Ted Musgrave	786
48.	Bill Venturini	702
49.	Tom Kendall	613
50.	Irv Hoerr	164

LAPS LED

1.	Dale Earnhardt	2,437
2.	Bill Elliott	1,182
3.	Rusty Wallace	1,138
4.	Geoffrey Bodine	976
5.	Kyle Petty	852
6.	Mark Martin	451
7.	Alan Kulwicki	400
8.	Darrell Waltrip	297
9.	Ernie Irvan	280
10.	Ken Schrader	242
11.	Davey Allison	222
12.	Brett Bodine	216
13.	Morgan Shepherd	201
14.	Ricky Rudd	180
15.	Derrike Cope	109
16.	Greg Sacks	107
17.	Dick Trickle	82
18.	Dale Jarrett	74
19.	Sterling Marlin	71
20.	Bobby Hillin	60
21.	Harry Gant	53
22.	Michael Waltrip	17
23.	Jimmy Spencer	10
24.	Terry Labonte	9
	Rob Moroso	9
26.	Dave Marcis	8
27.	Jack Pennington	7
28.	Richard Petty	5
29.	Tom Kendall	4
	Butch Miller	4
31.	Irv Hoerr	3
	Lake Speed	3
33.	Buddy Baker	1
	Mickey Gibbs	1
	Hut Stricklin	1

MILES LED

1.	Dale Earnhardt	3,205
2.	Bill Elliott	1,512
3.	Rusty Wallace	1,316
4.	Geoffrey Bodine	1,200
5.	Kyle Petty	846
6.	Mark Martin	557
7.	Alan Kulwicki	396
8.	Ken Schrader	286
	Morgan Shepherd	286
10.	Ernie Irvan	284
11.	Greg Sacks	272
12.	Davey Allison	253
13.	Darrell Waltrip	212
14.	Ricky Rudd	182
15.	Brett Bodine	168
16.	Derrike Cope	129
17.	Sterling Marlin	97
18.	Harry Gant	81
	Dick Trickle	81
20.	Bobby Hillin	70
21.	Dale Jarrett	46
22.	Michael Waltrip	30
23.	Jimmy Spencer	21
	Terry Labonte	21
25.	Jack Pennington	18
26.	Rob Moroso	13
27.	A.J. Foyt	11
28.	Mike Chase	10
	Tom Kendall	10
	Richard Petty	10

MILES DRIVEN

1.	Mark Martin	11,589
2.	Bill Elliott	11,189
3.	Dale Earnhardt	11,057
4.	Brett Bodine	10,980
5.	Davey Allison	10,918
6.	Alan Kulwicki	10,757
7.	Geoffrey Bodine	10,748
8.	Dave Marcis	10,732
9.	Morgan Shepherd	10,638
10.	Ernie Irvan	10,512
11.	Ricky Rudd	10,494
12.	Kyle Petty	10,250
13.	Terry Labonte	10,245
14.	Michael Waltrip	10,223
15.	Bobby Hillin	10,200
16.	Rusty Wallace	10,174
17.	Sterling Marlin	10,079
18.	Ken Schrader	10,050
19.	Dick Trickle	9,908
20.	Harry Gant	9,771
21.	Derrike Cope	9,595
22.	Rick Wilson	9,383
23.	Darrell Waltrip	9,288
24.	Richard Petty	9,165
25.	Jimmy Spencer	9,029
26.	Butch Miller	8,750
27.	Jimmy Means	8,749
28.	Hut Stricklin	8,118
29.	Dale Jarrett	7,800
30.	Rob Moroso	6,971

RACES LED

1.	Dale Earnhardt	22
2.	Geoffrey Bodine	21
3.	Rusty Wallace	16
4.	Mark Martin	15
5.	Bill Elliott	13
6.	Kyle Petty	12
	Ken Schrader	12
8.	Ernie Irvan	10
	Alan Kulwicki	10
10.	Harry Gant	9
	Darrell Waltrip	9
12.	Davey Allison	8
13.	Brett Bodine	7
	Ricky Rudd	7
	Morgan Shepherd	7
16.	Derrike Cope	6
	Sterling Marlin	6
18.	Bobby Hillin	5
	Dale Jarrett	5
	Jimmy Spencer	5
21.	Dave Marcis	4
	Butch Miller	4
	Greg Sacks	4
	Dick Trickle	4
	Michael Waltrip	4
26.	Terry Labonte	3
	Rob Moroso	3
28.	Jack Pennington	2
29.	Buddy Baker	1
	Mickey Gibbs	1
	Irv Hoerr	1
	Tom Kendall	1
	Richard Petty	1
	Lake Speed	1
	Hut Stricklin	1
	Rick Wilson	

1991

Driver	Starts	Poles	Finish 1	2	3	4	5	6–10	Laps	Laps Led	Races Led	Winston Cup Points	$
1. Dale Earnhardt	29	0	4	3	4	1	2	7	9,541	1,133	20	4,287	2,416,685
2. Ricky Rudd	29	1	1	3	0	2	3	8	9,561	425	13	4,092	1,093,765
3. Davey Allison	29	3	5	4	2	1	0	4	8,770	1,528	23	4,088	1,712,924
4. Harry Gant	29	1	5	2	3	4	1	2	9,428	1,684	17	3,985	1,194,033
5. Ernie Irvan	29	1	2	3	0	4	2	8	8,770	584	16	3,925	1,079,017
6. Mark Martin	29	5	1	1	5	4	3	3	8,903	663	15	3,914	1,039,991
7. Sterling Marlin	29	2	0	2	1	1	3	9	9,205	201	8	3,839	633,690
8. Darrell Waltrip	29	0	2	2	1	0	0	12	9,229	203	12	3,711	604,854
9. Ken Schrader	29	0	2	2	2	1	3	8	8,331	440	16	3,690	772,434
10. Rusty Wallace	29	2	2	0	3	2	2	5	8,316	524	14	3,582	502,073
11. Bill Elliott	29	2	1	2	1	0	2	6	9,020	203	6	3,535	705,605
12. Morgan Shepherd	29	0	0	0	2	2	0	10	9,023	86	5	3,438	521,147
13. Alan Kulwicki	29	4	1	0	1	1	1	7	8,447	233	9	3,354	595,614
14. Geoffrey Bodine	27	2	1	2	1	1	1	6	7,997	152	12	3,277	625,256
15. Michael Waltrip	29	2	0	0	1	0	3	8	8,394	292	11	3,254	440,812
16. Hut Stricklin	29	0	0	1	0	2	0	4	8,813	69	7	3,199	426,524
17. Dale Jarrett	29	0	1	0	0	0	2	5	7,767	47	7	3,124	444,256
18. Terry Labonte	29	1	0	0	0	0	1	6	7,989	52	2	3,024	348,898
19. Brett Bodine	29	1	0	1	0	1	0	4	7,873	163	3	2,980	376,220
20. Joe Ruttman	29	0	0	0	1	0	0	3	8,974	11	1	2,938	361,661
21. Rick Mast	29	0	0	0	0	1	0	2	8,901	32	3	2,918	344,020
22. Bobby Hamilton	28	0	0	0	0	0	0	4	8,214	7	3	2,915	259,105
23. Ted Musgrave	29	0	0	0	0	0	0	0	9,074	6	5	2,841	200,910
24. Richard Petty	29	0	0	0	0	0	0	1	8,341	1	1	2,817	268,035
25. Jimmy Spencer	29	0	0	0	1	0	0	5	7,627	330	6	2,790	283,620
26. Rick Wilson	29	0	0	0	0	0	0	0	7,966	10	1	2,723	241,375
27. Chad Little	28	0	0	0	0	0	0	1	7,784	21	3	2,678	184,190
28. Derrike Cope	28	0	0	0	0	1	0	1	6,784	0	0	2,516	419,380
29. Dave Marcis	27	0	0	0	0	0	0	1	7,211	3	3	2,374	219,760
30. Bobby Hillin	22	0	0	0	0	0	0	1	6,152	10	1	2,317	251,645
31. Kyle Petty	18	2	1	1	0	0	0	2	6,622	553	7	2,078	413,727
32. Lake Speed	20	0	0	0	0	0	0	0	4,513	0	0	1,742	149,300
33. Jimmy Means	20	0	0	0	0	0	0	0	4,425	3	3	1,562	111,210
34. Mickey Gibbs	15	0	0	0	0	0	0	0	4,078	0	0	1,401	100,360
35. Dick Trickle	14	0	0	0	0	0	0	1	3,650	0	0	1,258	129,125
36. Stanley Smith	12	0	0	0	0	0	0	0	1,932	12	1	893	56,915
37. Larry Pearson	11	0	0	0	0	0	0	0	1,543	0	0	848	56,570
38. Wally Dallenbach	11	0	0	0	0	0	0	0	2,070	0	0	803	54,020
39. Greg Sacks	11	0	0	0	0	0	0	0	2,101	0	0	791	84,215
40. Buddy Baker	6	0	0	0	0	0	0	0	845	0	0	552	58,060
41. Jimmy Hensley	4	0	0	0	0	0	0	1	1,708	0	0	488	32,125
42. Eddie Bierschwale	5	0	0	0	0	0	0	0	1,112	0	0	431	55,025
43. Jim Sauter	6	0	0	0	0	0	0	0	1,012	0	0	423	47,395
44. Kenny Wallace	5	0	0	0	0	0	0	0	1,544	1	1	412	58,325
45. Jeff Purvis	6	0	0	0	0	0	0	0	888	0	0	399	42,910
46. Phil Barkdoll	4	0	0	0	0	0	0	0	646	0	0	364	41,655
47. Mike Chase	5	0	0	0	0	0	0	0	804	0	0	356	22,700
48. J.D. McDuffie	5	0	0	0	0	0	0	0	732	0	0	335	19,795
49. Bill Sedgwick	3	0	0	0	0	0	0	0	848	0	0	324	15,150
50. Randy LaJoie	4	0	0	0	0	0	0	0	1,080	0	0	304	23,875

LAPS COMPLETED		LAPS LED		MILES LED		MILES DRIVEN		RACES LED	
1. Ricky Rudd	9,561	1. Harry Gant	1,684	1. Davey Allison	1,877	1. Dale Earnhardt	11,438	1. Davey Allison	23
2. Dale Earnhardt	9,541	2. Davey Allison	1,528	2. Dale Earnhardt	1,537	2. Ricky Rudd	11,429	2. Dale Earnhardt	20
3. Harry Gant	9,428	3. Dale Earnhardt	1,133	3. Harry Gant	1,477	3. Sterling Marlin	11,210	3. Harry Gant	17
4. Darrell Waltrip	9,229	4. Mark Martin	663	4. Mark Martin	926	4. Harry Gant	11,127	4. Ernie Irvan	16
5. Sterling Marlin	9,205	5. Ernie Irvan	584	5. Ernie Irvan	918	5. Darrell Waltrip	10,903	Ken Schrader	16
6. Ted Musgrave	9,074	6. Kyle Petty	553	6. Ken Schrader	667	6. Bill Elliott	10,818	6. Mark Martin	15
7. Morgan Shepherd	9,023	7. Rusty Wallace	524	7. Kyle Petty	667	7. Mark Martin	10,777	7. Rusty Wallace	14
8. Bill Elliott	9,020	8. Ken Schrader	440	8. Rusty Wallace	509	8. Joe Ruttman	10,776	8. Ricky Rudd	13
9. Joe Ruttman	8,974	9. Ricky Rudd	425	9. Ricky Rudd	416	9. Rick Mast	10,691	9. Geoffrey Bodine	12
10. Mark Martin	8,903	10. Jimmy Spencer	330	10. Michael Waltrip	404	10. Davey Allison	10,613	Darrell Waltrip	12
11. Rick Mast	8,901	11. Michael Waltrip	292	11. Bill Elliott	341	11. Ted Musgrave	10,581	11. Michael Waltrip	11
12. Hut Stricklin	8,813	12. Alan Kulwicki	233	12. Sterling Marlin	335	12. Ernie Irvan	10,494	12. Alan Kulwicki	9
13. Davey Allison	8,770	13. Bill Elliott	203	13. Darrell Waltrip	227	13. Morgan Shepherd	10,485	13. Sterling Marlin	8
14. Ernie Irvan	8,770	Darrell Waltrip	203	14. Geoffrey Bodine	211	14. Hut Stricklin	10,436	14. Dale Jarrett	7
15. Alan Kulwicki	8,447	15. Sterling Marlin	201	Jimmy Spencer	211	15. Rusty Wallace	10,150	Kyle Petty	7
16. Michael Waltrip	8,394	16. Brett Bodine	163	16. Alan Kulwicki	152	16. Bobby Hamilton	10,141	Hut Stricklin	7
17. Richard Petty	8,341	17. Geoffrey Bodine	152	17. Hut Stricklin	130	17. Alan Kulwicki	9,998	17. Bill Elliott	6
18. Ken Schrader	8,331	18. Morgan Shepherd	86	18. Brett Bodine	96	18. Ken Schrader	9,843	Jimmy Spencer	6
19. Rusty Wallace	8,316	19. Hut Stricklin	69	19. Morgan Shepherd	89	19. Michael Waltrip	9,759	19. Ted Musgrave	5
20. Bobby Hamilton	8,214	20. Terry Labonte	52	20. Dale Jarrett	80	20. Rick Wilson	9,697	Morgan Shepherd	5
21. Geoffrey Bodine	7,997	21. Dale Jarrett	47	21. Rick Mast	73	21. Richard Petty	9,646	21. Brett Bodine	3
22. Terry Labonte	7,989	22. Rick Mast	32	22. Terry Labonte	64	22. Terry Labonte	9,617	Bobby Hamilton	3
23. Rick Wilson	7,966	23. Chad Little	21	23. Tom Kendall	30	23. Geoffrey Bodine	9,591	Chad Little	3
24. Brett Bodine	7,873	24. Stanley Smith	12	24. Joe Ruttman	28	24. Chad Little	9,530	Dave Marcis	3
25. Chad Little	7,784	25. Joe Ruttman	11	25. Chad Little	26	25. Dale Jarrett	9,440	Rick Mast	3
26. Dale Jarrett	7,767	26. Bobby Hillin	10	26. Bobby Hillin	15	26. Brett Bodine	9,050	Jimmy Means	3
27. Jimmy Spencer	7,627	Rick Wilson	10	27. Ted Musgrave	12	27. Dave Marcis	9,024	27. Terry Labonte	2
28. Dave Marcis	7,211	28. Bobby Hamilton	7	Stanley Smith	12	28. Jimmy Spencer	8,583	28. Bobby Hillin	1
29. Derrike Cope	6,784	29. Ted Musgrave	6	29. Rick Wilson	10	29. Derrike Cope	8,451	Richard Petty	1
30. Kyle Petty	6,622	30. Dave Marcis	3	30. Bobby Hamilton	9	30. Bobby Hillin	8,353	Joe Ruttman	1
31. Bobby Hillin	6,152	Jimmy Means	3					Stanley Smith	1
32. Lake Speed	4,513	32. Richard Petty	1					Kenny Wallace	1
33. Jimmy Means	4,425	Kenny Wallace	1					Rick Wilson	1
34. Mickey Gibbs	4,078								
35. Dick Trickle	3,650								
36. Greg Sacks	2,101								
37. Wally Dallenbach	2,070								
38. Stanley Smith	1,932								
39. Jimmy Hensley	1,708								
40. Kenny Wallace	1,544								
41. Larry Pearson	1,543								
42. Eddie Bierschwale	1,112								
43. Randy LaJoie	1,080								
44. Jim Sauter	1,012								
45. Jeff Purvis	888								
46. Bill Sedgwick	848								
47. Buddy Baker	845								
48. Mike Chase	804								
49. J.D. McDuffie	732								
50. Phil Barkdoll	646								

1992

Driver	Starts	Poles	Finish 1	2	3	4	5	6–10	Laps	Laps Led	Races Led	Winston Cup Points	$
1. Alan Kulwicki	29	6	2	3	2	2	2	6	8,991	1,235	20	4,078	2,322,561
2. Bill Elliott	29	2	5	2	3	1	3	3	9,115	1,272	18	4,068	1,692,381
3. Davey Allison	29	2	5	1	1	5	3	2	8,976	1,377	18	4,015	1,955,628
4. Harry Gant	29	0	2	3	2	0	3	5	9,197	407	15	3,955	1,122,776
5. Kyle Petty	29	3	2	0	4	3	0	8	9,058	971	8	3,945	1,107,063
6. Mark Martin	29	1	2	5	2	1	0	7	8,954	533	17	3,887	1,000,571
7. Ricky Rudd	29	1	1	0	2	3	3	9	8,968	331	9	3,735	793,903
8. Terry Labonte	29	0	0	1	0	2	1	12	8,912	43	4	3,674	600,381
9. Darrell Waltrip	29	1	3	2	3	0	2	3	8,706	513	14	3,659	876,492
10. Sterling Marlin	29	5	0	3	0	1	2	7	8,462	218	8	3,603	649,048
11. Ernie Irvan	29	3	3	2	1	2	1	2	8,561	477	17	3,580	996,885
12. Dale Earnhardt	29	1	1	2	2	1	0	9	8,694	487	10	3,574	915,463
13. Rusty Wallace	29	1	1	2	1	1	0	7	8,761	673	11	3,556	657,925
14. Morgan Shepherd	29	0	0	2	0	0	1	8	9,093	60	3	3,549	634,222
15. Brett Bodine	29	1	0	0	1	1	0	11	8,807	237	11	3,491	495,224
16. Geoffrey Bodine	29	0	2	0	2	2	1	4	8,222	474	5	3,437	716,583
17. Ken Schrader	29	1	0	0	2	1	1	7	8,425	83	5	3,404	639,679
18. Ted Musgrave	29	0	0	0	0	0	1	6	9,253	11	3	3,315	449,121
19. Dale Jarrett	29	0	0	1	1	0	0	6	8,586	99	5	3,251	418,648
20. Dick Trickle	29	0	0	0	0	0	3	6	8,259	5	2	3,097	429,521
21. Derrike Cope	29	0	0	0	0	0	0	3	8,483	0	0	3,033	277,215
22. Rick Mast	29	1	0	0	0	0	0	1	8,121	0	0	2,830	350,740
23. Michael Waltrip	29	0	0	0	0	1	0	1	8,474	3	1	2,825	410,545
24. Wally Dallenbach	29	0	0	0	0	0	1	0	8,105	0	0	2,799	220,245
25. Bobby Hamilton	29	0	0	0	0	0	0	2	8,998	0	0	2,787	367,065
26. Richard Petty	29	0	0	0	0	0	0	0	7,977	5	1	2,731	348,870
27. Hut Stricklin	28	0	0	0	0	0	0	4	7,928	60	2	2,689	336,965
28. Jimmy Hensley	22	0	0	0	0	0	0	4	6,804	22	3	2,410	247,660
29. Dave Marcis	29	0	0	0	0	0	0	0	6,759	0	0	2,348	218,045
30. Greg Sacks	20	0	0	0	0	0	0	0	4,926	6	1	1,759	178,120
31. Chad Little	19	0	0	0	0	0	0	1	5,114	0	0	1,669	145,805
32. Jimmy Means	22	0	0	0	0	0	0	0	4,370	0	0	1,531	133,160
33. Jimmy Spencer	12	0	0	0	0	2	1	0	3,803	1	1	1,284	183,585
34. Bobby Hillin	13	0	0	0	0	0	0	0	2,770	0	0	1,135	102,160
35. Stanley Smith	14	0	0	0	0	0	0	0	2,685	0	0	959	89,650
36. Mike Potter	11	0	0	0	0	0	0	0	1,869	0	0	806	74,710
37. Jim Sauter	9	0	0	0	0	0	0	0	2,829	0	0	729	56,045
38. Lake Speed	9	0	0	0	0	0	0	0	2,248	0	0	726	49,545
39. Jimmy Horton	9	0	0	0	0	0	0	0	2,194	0	0	660	50,125
40. Bob Schacht	9	0	0	0	0	0	0	0	1,363	2	1	611	58,815
41. Charlie Glotzbach	7	0	0	0	0	0	0	0	1,528	0	0	592	48,060
42. James Hylton	8	0	0	0	0	0	0	0	611	0	0	476	37,910
43. Andy Belmont	8	0	0	0	0	0	0	0	779	0	0	467	39,820
44. Jeff Purvis	6	0	0	0	0	0	0	0	1,418	0	0	453	45,545
45. Dave Mader III	5	0	0	0	0	0	0	0	1,387	7	1	436	69,635
46. Jerry O'Neil	6	0	0	0	0	0	0	0	958	0	0	429	32,370
47. Eddie Bierschwale	4	0	0	0	0	0	0	0	628	0	0	277	25,995
48. Buddy Baker	3	0	0	0	0	0	0	0	547	0	0	255	49,500
49. Rich Bickle	3	0	0	0	0	0	0	0	816	0	0	252	13,370
50. Mike Wallace	3	0	0	0	0	0	0	0	1,042	0	0	249	17,415

LAPS COMPLETED		LAPS LED		MILES LED		MILES DRIVEN		RACES LED	
1. Ted Musgrave	9,253	1. Davey Allison	1,377	1. Davey Allison	2,315	1. Harry Gant	11,221	1. Alan Kulwicki	20
2. Harry Gant	9,197	2. Bill Elliott	1,272	2. Bill Elliott	1,231	2. Bill Elliott	11,125	2. Davey Allison	18
3. Bill Elliott	9,115	3. Alan Kulwicki	1,235	3. Alan Kulwicki	1,159	3. Davey Allison	10,999	Bill Elliott	18
4. Morgan Shepherd	9,093	4. Kyle Petty	971	4. Kyle Petty	1,071	4. Ted Musgrave	10,989	4. Ernie Irvan	17
5. Kyle Petty	9,058	5. Rusty Wallace	673	5. Ernie Irvan	800	5. Kyle Petty	10,938	Mark Martin	17
6. Bobby Hamilton	8,998	6. Mark Martin	533	6. Mark Martin	690	6. Alan Kulwicki	10,853	6. Harry Gant	15
7. Alan Kulwicki	8,991	7. Darrell Waltrip	513	7. Rusty Wallace	572	7. Morgan Shepherd	10,840	7. Darrell Waltrip	14
8. Davey Allison	8,976	8. Dale Earnhardt	487	8. Harry Gant	499	8. Bobby Hamilton	10,737	8. Brett Bodine	11
9. Ricky Rudd	8,968	9. Ernie Irvan	477	9. Dale Earnhardt	466	9. Mark Martin	10,671	Rusty Wallace	11
10. Mark Martin	8,954	10. Geoffrey Bodine	474	10. Sterling Marlin	436	10. Terry Labonte	10,613	10. Dale Earnhardt	10
11. Terry Labonte	8,912	11. Harry Gant	407	11. Darrell Waltrip	392	11. Rusty Wallace	10,452	11. Ricky Rudd	9
12. Brett Bodine	8,807	12. Ricky Rudd	331	12. Ricky Rudd	390	12. Dale Jarrett	10,295	12. Sterling Marlin	8
13. Rusty Wallace	8,761	13. Brett Bodine	237	13. Geoffrey Bodine	288	13. Sterling Marlin	10,287	Kyle Petty	8
14. Darrell Waltrip	8,706	14. Sterling Marlin	218	14. Brett Bodine	177	14. Ernie Irvan	10,280	14. Geoffrey Bodine	5
15. Dale Earnhardt	8,694	15. Dale Jarrett	99	15. Dale Jarrett	150	15. Ricky Rudd	10,270	Dale Jarrett	5
16. Dale Jarrett	8,586	16. Ken Schrader	83	16. Ken Schrader	126	16. Darrell Waltrip	10,249	Ken Schrader	5
17. Ernie Irvan	8,561	17. Morgan Shepherd	60	17. Terry Labonte	78	17. Brett Bodine	10,248	17. Terry Labonte	4
18. Derrike Cope	8,483	18. Hut Stricklin	60	18. Morgan Shepherd	71	18. Dale Earnhardt	10,198	18. Jimmy Hensley	3
19. Michael Waltrip	8,474	19. Terry Labonte	43	19. Hut Stricklin	61	19. Michael Waltrip	10,184	Ted Musgrave	3
20. Sterling Marlin	8,462	20. Jimmy Hensley	22	20. Jimmy Hensley	32	20. Derrike Cope	10,175	Morgan Shepherd	3
21. Ken Schrader	8,425	21. Ted Musgrave	11	21. Ted Musgrave	23	21. Rick Mast	9,984	21. Hut Stricklin	2
22. Dick Trickle	8,259	22. Dave Mader III	7	22. Richard Petty	13	22. Dick Trickle	9,883	Dick Trickle	2
23. Geoffrey Bodine	8,222	23. Greg Sacks	6	23. Dick Trickle	10	23. Ken Schrader	9,816	23. Dave Mader III	1
24. Rick Mast	8,121	24. Richard Petty	5	24. Greg Sacks	9	24. Geoffrey Bodine	9,780	Richard Petty	1
25. Wally Dallenbach	8,105	Dick Trickle	5	25. Michael Waltrip	8	25. Wally Dallenbach	9,682	Greg Sacks	1
26. Richard Petty	7,977	26. Michael Waltrip	3	26. Dave Mader III	4	26. Richard Petty	9,624	Bob Schacht	1
27. Hut Stricklin	7,928	27. Bob Schacht	2	27. Bob Schacht	3	27. Hut Stricklin	9,261	Jimmy Spencer	1
28. Jimmy Hensley	6,804	28. Jimmy Spencer	1	28. Jimmy Spencer	2	28. Dave Marcis	8,498	Michael Waltrip	1
29. Dave Marcis	6,759					29. Jimmy Hensley	8,492		
30. Chad Little	5,114					30. Chad Little	6,707		
31. Greg Sacks	4,926								
32. Jimmy Means	4,370								
33. Jimmy Spencer	3,803								
34. Jim Sauter	2,829								
35. Bobby Hillin	2,770								
36. Stanley Smith	2,685								
37. Lake Speed	2,248								
38. Jimmy Horton	2,194								
39. Mike Potter	1,869								
40. Charlie Glotzbach	1,528								
41. Jeff Purvis	1,418								
42. Dave Mader III	1,387								
43. Bob Schacht	1,363								
44. Mike Wallace	1,042								
45. Jerry O'Neil	958								
46. Rich Bickle	816								
47. Andy Belmont	779								
48. Eddie Bierschwale	628								
49. James Hylton	611								
50. Buddy Baker	547								

Driver	Starts	Poles	Finish 1	2	3	4	5	6–10	Laps	Laps Led	Races Led	Winston Cup Points	$

1993

	Driver	Starts	Poles	1	2	3	4	5	6–10	Laps	Laps Led	Races Led	Winston Cup Points	$
1.	Dale Earnhardt	30	3	6	5	3	3	0	4	9,787	1,474	21	4,526	3,353,789
2.	Rusty Wallace	30	3	10	4	2	1	2	2	9,641	2,861	20	4,446	1,702,154
3.	Mark Martin	30	5	5	3	1	1	2	7	9,381	1,388	20	4,150	1,657,662
4.	Dale Jarrett	30	0	1	1	4	5	2	5	9,149	264	15	4,000	1,242,394
5.	Kyle Petty	30	1	1	1	2	2	3	6	9,259	527	13	3,860	914,662
6.	Ernie Irvan	30	4	3	4	3	0	2	2	8,234	1,120	19	3,834	1,400,468
7.	Morgan Shepherd	30	0	1	1	0	1	0	12	9,442	92	9	3,807	682,532
8.	Bill Elliott	30	2	0	1	2	2	1	9	9,349	15	4	3,774	955,859
9.	Ken Schrader	30	6	0	2	2	3	2	6	8,877	285	14	3,715	952,748
10.	Ricky Rudd	30	0	1	1	1	3	3	5	8,635	137	7	3,644	752,562
11.	Harry Gant	30	1	0	0	1	2	1	8	8,843	266	8	3,524	772,832
12.	Jimmy Spencer	30	0	0	1	2	2	0	5	8,867	64	4	3,496	686,026
13.	Darrell Waltrip	30	0	0	0	2	1	1	6	9,194	151	9	3,479	746,646
14.	Jeff Gordon	30	1	0	2	1	1	3	4	8,390	189	14	3,447	765,168
15.	Sterling Marlin	30	0	0	1	0	0	0	7	9,153	345	7	3,355	628,835
16.	Geoffrey Bodine	30	1	1	0	1	0	0	7	8,496	102	11	3,338	783,762
17.	Michael Waltrip	30	0	0	0	0	0	0	5	9,378	39	6	3,291	529,923
18.	Terry Labonte	30	0	0	0	0	0	0	10	8,866	55	3	3,280	531,717
19.	Bobby Labonte	30	1	0	0	0	0	0	6	9,295	33	7	3,221	395,660
20.	Brett Bodine	29	2	0	1	0	0	2	6	8,120	102	7	3,183	582,014
21.	Rick Mast	30	0	0	0	0	0	1	4	8,488	31	4	3,001	568,095
22.	Wally Dallenbach	30	0	0	1	0	0	0	3	8,411	3	2	2,978	474,340
23.	Kenny Wallace	30	0	0	0	0	0	0	3	8,806	1	1	2,893	330,325
24.	Hut Stricklin	30	0	0	0	0	1	0	1	8,356	99	3	2,866	494,600
25.	Ted Musgrave	29	0	0	0	0	0	2	3	8,530	8	3	2,853	458,615
26.	Derrike Cope	30	0	0	0	0	0	0	1	8,406	38	3	2,787	402,515
27.	Bobby Hillin	30	0	0	0	0	0	0	0	8,343	3	1	2,717	263,540
28.	Rick Wilson	29	0	0	0	0	0	0	1	8,117	1	1	2,647	299,725
29.	Phil Parsons	26	0	0	0	0	0	0	2	6,331	3	1	2,454	293,725
30.	Dick Trickle	26	0	0	0	0	0	1	1	7,003	3	1	2,224	245,065
31.	Davey Allison	16	0	1	1	2	1	1	2	5,061	275	9	2,104	513,585
32.	Jimmy Hensley	21	0	0	0	0	0	0	2	5,843	1	1	2,001	368,150
33.	Dave Marcis	23	0	0	0	0	0	0	0	6,233	14	3	1,970	202,305
34.	Lake Speed	21	0	0	0	0	0	0	1	5,852	2	1	1,956	319,800
35.	Greg Sacks	19	0	0	0	0	0	0	1	5,251	1	1	1,730	168,055
36.	Jimmy Means	18	0	0	0	0	0	0	0	4,765	2	2	1,471	148,205
37.	Bobby Hamilton	15	0	0	0	0	0	0	1	3,996	0	0	1,348	142,740
38.	Jimmy Horton	13	0	0	0	0	0	0	0	2,198	0	0	841	115,105
39.	Jeff Purvis	8	0	0	0	0	0	0	0	2,491	3	2	774	108,545
40.	Todd Bodine	10	0	0	0	0	0	0	0	2,393	0	0	715	63,245
41.	Alan Kulwicki	5	0	0	0	1	1	0	1	1,588	4	2	625	165,470
42.	P.J. Jones	6	0	0	0	0	0	0	1	710	0	0	498	53,370
43.	Joe Ruttman	5	0	0	0	0	0	1	0	1,133	0	0	417	70,700
44.	Joe Nemechek	5	0	0	0	0	0	0	0	1,114	0	0	389	56,580
45.	Loy Allen, Jr.	5	0	0	0	0	0	0	0	878	0	0	362	34,695
46.	Mike Wallace	4	0	0	0	0	0	0	0	1,287	0	0	343	30,125
47.	Jim Sauter	4	0	0	0	0	0	0	0	769	0	0	295	48,860
48.	Rich Bickle	5	0	0	0	0	0	0	0	842	1	1	292	36,095
49.	Rick Carelli	3	0	0	0	0	0	0	0	499	0	0	258	19,650
50.	John Andretti	4	0	0	0	0	0	0	0	904	0	0	250	24,915

LAPS COMPLETED

1. Dale Earnhardt — 9,787
2. Rusty Wallace — 9,641
3. Morgan Shepherd — 9,442
4. Mark Martin — 9,381
5. Michael Waltrip — 9,378
6. Bill Elliott — 9,349
7. Bobby Labonte — 9,295
8. Kyle Petty — 9,259
9. Darrell Waltrip — 9,194
10. Sterling Marlin — 9,153
11. Dale Jarrett — 9,149
12. Ken Schrader — 8,877
13. Jimmy Spencer — 8,867
14. Terry Labonte — 8,866
15. Harry Gant — 8,843
16. Kenny Wallace — 8,806
17. Ricky Rudd — 8,635
18. Ted Musgrave — 8,530
19. Geoffrey Bodine — 8,496
20. Rick Mast — 8,488
21. Wally Dallenbach — 8,411
22. Derrike Cope — 8,406
23. Jeff Gordon — 8,390
24. Hut Stricklin — 8,356
25. Bobby Hillin — 8,343
26. Ernie Irvan — 8,234
27. Brett Bodine — 8,120
28. Rick Wilson — 8,117
29. Dick Trickle — 7,003
30. Phil Parsons — 6,331
31. Dave Marcis — 6,233
32. Lake Speed — 5,852
33. Jimmy Hensley — 5,843
34. Greg Sacks — 5,251
35. Davey Allison — 5,061
36. Jimmy Means — 4,765
37. Bobby Hamilton — 3,996
38. Jeff Purvis — 2,491
39. Todd Bodine — 2,393
40. Jimmy Horton — 2,198
41. Alan Kulwicki — 1,588
42. Mike Wallace — 1,287
43. Joe Ruttman — 1,133
44. Joe Nemechek — 1,114
45. John Andretti — 904
46. Loy Allen, Jr. — 878
47. Rich Bickle — 842
48. Jim Sauter — 769
49. P.J. Jones — 710
50. Rick Carelli — 499

LAPS LED

1. Rusty Wallace — 2,861
2. Dale Earnhardt — 1,474
3. Mark Martin — 1,388
4. Ernie Irvan — 1,120
5. Kyle Petty — 527
6. Sterling Marlin — 345
7. Ken Schrader — 285
8. Davey Allison — 275
9. Harry Gant — 266
10. Dale Jarrett — 264
11. Jeff Gordon — 189
12. Darrell Waltrip — 151
13. Ricky Rudd — 137
14. Brett Bodine — 102
    Geoffrey Bodine — 102
16. Hut Stricklin — 99
17. Morgan Shepherd — 92
18. Jimmy Spencer — 64
19. Terry Labonte — 55
20. Michael Waltrip — 39
21. Derrike Cope — 38
22. Bobby Labonte — 33
23. Rick Mast — 31
24. Bill Elliott — 15
25. Dave Marcis — 14
26. Ted Musgrave — 8
27. Alan Kulwicki — 4
28. Wally Dallenbach — 3
    Bobby Hillin — 3
    Phil Parsons — 3
    Jeff Purvis — 3
    Dick Trickle — 3
33. Jimmy Means — 2
    Lake Speed — 2
35. Rich Bickle — 1
    Jimmy Hensley — 1
    Greg Sacks — 1
    Kenny Wallace — 1
    Rick Wilson — 1

MILES LED

1. Dale Earnhardt — 2,482
2. Rusty Wallace — 2,334
3. Mark Martin — 1,827
4. Ernie Irvan — 1,248
5. Kyle Petty — 834
6. Dale Jarrett — 469
7. Harry Gant — 340
8. Sterling Marlin — 323
9. Ken Schrader — 320
10. Jeff Gordon — 262
11. Davey Allison — 253
12. Ricky Rudd — 239
13. Geoffrey Bodine — 161
14. Darrell Waltrip — 149
15. Brett Bodine — 122
16. Morgan Shepherd — 117
17. Derrike Cope — 89
18. Hut Stricklin — 70
19. Jimmy Spencer — 63
20. Michael Waltrip — 48
21. Terry Labonte — 35
22. Bobby Labonte — 26
23. Bill Elliott — 23
    Rick Mast — 23
25. Dave Marcis — 16
26. Ted Musgrave — 13
27. Bobby Hillin — 8
28. Alan Kulwicki — 5
    Phil Parsons — 5

MILES DRIVEN

1. Dale Earnhardt — 11,809
2. Morgan Shepherd — 11,407
3. Bill Elliott — 11,351
4. Dale Jarrett — 11,336
5. Rusty Wallace — 11,232
6. Sterling Marlin — 11,222
7. Kyle Petty — 11,187
8. Michael Waltrip — 11,146
9. Mark Martin — 11,107
10. Ken Schrader — 10,995
11. Bobby Labonte — 10,938
12. Harry Gant — 10,868
13. Jimmy Spencer — 10,837
14. Darrell Waltrip — 10,818
15. Terry Labonte — 10,642
16. Kenny Wallace — 10,552
17. Ted Musgrave — 10,397
18. Rick Wilson — 10,330
19. Ricky Rudd — 10,266
20. Hut Stricklin — 10,212
21. Geoffrey Bodine — 10,199
22. Ernie Irvan — 10,160
23. Jeff Gordon — 10,067
24. Wally Dallenbach — 10,056
25. Derrike Cope — 9,966
26. Rick Mast — 9,803
27. Bobby Hillin — 9,769
28. Brett Bodine — 9,383
29. Dick Trickle — 8,376
30. Phil Parsons — 8,042

RACES LED

1. Dale Earnhardt — 21
2. Mark Martin — 20
   Rusty Wallace — 20
4. Ernie Irvan — 19
5. Dale Jarrett — 15
6. Jeff Gordon — 14
   Ken Schrader — 14
8. Kyle Petty — 13
9. Geoffrey Bodine — 11
10. Davey Allison — 9
    Morgan Shepherd — 9
    Darrell Waltrip — 9
13. Harry Gant — 8
14. Brett Bodine — 7
    Bobby Labonte — 7
    Sterling Marlin — 7
    Ricky Rudd — 7
18. Michael Waltrip — 6
19. Bill Elliott — 4
    Rick Mast — 4
    Jimmy Spencer — 4
22. Derrike Cope — 3
    Terry Labonte — 3
    Dave Marcis — 3
    Ted Musgrave — 3
    Hut Stricklin — 3
27. Wally Dallenbach — 2
    Alan Kulwicki — 2
    Jimmy Means — 2
    Jeff Purvis — 2
31. Rich Bickle — 1
    Jimmy Hensley — 1
    Bobby Hillin — 1
    Phil Parsons — 1
    Greg Sacks — 1
    Lake Speed — 1
    Dick Trickle — 1
    Kenny Wallace — 1
    Rick Wilson — 1

Driver	Starts	Poles	Finish 1	2	3	4	5	6–10	Laps	Laps Led	Races Led	Winston Cup Points	$

1994

Driver	Starts	Poles	1	2	3	4	5	6–10	Laps	Laps Led	Races Led	Winston Cup Points	$
1. Dale Earnhardt	31	2	4	7	6	1	2	5	9,546	1,015	23	4,694	3,400,733
2. Mark Martin	31	1	2	4	2	4	3	5	9,549	726	18	4,250	1,678,906
3. Rusty Wallace	31	2	8	3	1	4	1	3	9,281	2,143	19	4,207	1,959,072
4. Ken Schrader	31	0	0	1	2	4	2	9	9,704	223	9	4,060	1,211,062
5. Ricky Rudd	31	1	1	0	0	3	2	9	9,728	192	10	4,050	1,079,441
6. Morgan Shepherd	31	0	0	2	2	1	4	7	9,788	81	10	4,029	1,119,038
7. Terry Labonte	31	0	3	1	1	0	1	8	9,149	486	8	3,876	1,150,921
8. Jeff Gordon	31	1	2	1	1	2	1	7	9,277	446	17	3,776	1,799,523
9. Darrell Waltrip	31	0	0	0	2	2	0	9	9,905	60	8	3,688	854,280
10. Bill Elliott	31	1	1	1	3	0	1	6	9,173	62	8	3,617	951,679
11. Lake Speed	31	0	0	0	1	1	2	5	9,111	39	5	3,565	845,963
12. Michael Waltrip	31	0	0	0	1	0	1	8	9,508	8	5	3,512	720,426
13. Ted Musgrave	31	3	0	0	0	0	1	7	9,237	50	4	3,477	669,687
14. Sterling Marlin	31	1	1	1	1	0	2	6	9,184	144	11	3,443	1,140,683
15. Kyle Petty	31	0	0	0	0	1	1	5	9,076	7	2	3,339	818,832
16. Dale Jarrett	30	0	1	0	0	2	1	5	8,410	55	8	3,298	893,754
17. Geoffrey Bodine	31	5	3	1	1	1	1	3	8,149	1,746	20	3,297	1,287,626
18. Rick Mast	31	1	0	1	3	0	0	6	8,756	166	8	3,238	733,361
19. Brett Bodine	31	0	0	1	0	0	0	5	8,931	55	6	3,159	801,944
20. Todd Bodine	30	0	0	0	1	0	1	5	8,475	60	5	3,048	504,316
21. Bobby Labonte	31	0	0	0	0	0	1	1	8,541	3	2	3,038	550,305
22. Ernie Irvan	20	5	3	6	2	0	2	2	5,357	1,783	17	3,026	1,311,522
23. Bobby Hamilton	30	0	0	0	0	0	0	1	8,337	24	4	2,749	514,520
24. Jeff Burton	30	0	0	0	0	2	0	1	7,781	122	4	2,726	594,700
25. Harry Gant	30	1	0	0	0	0	0	7	7,347	94	3	2,720	556,020
26. Hut Stricklin	29	0	0	0	0	0	0	1	8,562	26	2	2,711	333,495
27. Joe Nemechek	29	0	0	0	1	0	0	2	7,953	22	2	2,673	386,315
28. Steve Grissom	28	0	0	0	0	0	0	3	8,394	1	1	2,660	300,915
29. Jimmy Spencer	29	1	2	0	0	1	0	1	6,904	47	6	2,613	479,235
30. Derrike Cope	30	0	0	0	0	0	0	2	8,506	11	2	2,612	398,436
31. Greg Sacks	31	1	0	0	0	0	0	3	8,346	38	8	2,593	411,728
32. John Andretti	29	0	0	0	0	0	0	0	7,508	41	4	2,299	391,920
33. Mike Wallace	22	0	0	0	0	0	1	0	6,672	13	1	2,191	265,115
34. Dick Trickle	25	0	0	0	0	0	0	1	6,422	1	1	2,019	244,806
35. Ward Burton	26	1	0	1	0	0	0	1	5,320	73	5	1,971	304,700
36. Dave Marcis	23	0	0	0	0	0	0	1	5,914	17	4	1,910	261,650
37. Jeremy Mayfield	20	0	0	0	0	0	0	0	5,581	0	0	1,673	226,265
38. Wally Dallenbach	14	0	0	0	0	1	0	2	3,568	1	1	1,493	241,492
39. Loy Allen, Jr.	19	3	0	0	0	0	0	0	4,446	12	3	1,468	216,751
40. Kenny Wallace	12	0	0	0	0	1	0	2	4,426	4	3	1,413	235,005
41. Jimmy Hensley	17	0	0	0	0	0	0	0	3,861	4	3	1,394	203,520
42. Chuck Bown	13	1	0	0	0	0	0	1	3,694	0	0	1,211	225,260
43. Rich Bickle	12	0	0	0	0	0	0	0	2,087	0	0	849	115,575
44. Bobby Hillin	9	0	0	0	0	0	0	0	2,007	2	1	749	125,340
45. Brad Teague	8	0	0	0	0	0	0	0	1,959	0	0	548	59,900
46. Jeff Purvis	7	0	0	0	0	0	0	0	1,081	0	0	484	78,755
47. Billy Standridge	8	0	0	0	0	0	0	0	1,260	0	0	404	56,405
48. Randy LaJoie	3	0	0	0	0	0	0	0	1,010	0	0	312	30,565
49. Rick Carelli	4	0	0	0	0	0	0	0	958	0	0	283	31,975
50. Phil Parsons	3	0	0	0	0	0	0	0	757	0	0	243	21,415

LAPS COMPLETED

1.	Darrell Waltrip	9,905
2.	Morgan Shepherd	9,788
3.	Ricky Rudd	9,728
4.	Ken Schrader	9,704
5.	Mark Martin	9,549
6.	Dale Earnhardt	9,546
7.	Michael Waltrip	9,508
8.	Rusty Wallace	9,281
9.	Jeff Gordon	9,277
10.	Ted Musgrave	9,237
11.	Sterling Marlin	9,184
12.	Bill Elliott	9,173
13.	Terry Labonte	9,149
14.	Lake Speed	9,111
15.	Kyle Petty	9,076
16.	Brett Bodine	8,931
17.	Rick Mast	8,756
18.	Hut Stricklin	8,562
19.	Bobby Labonte	8,541
20.	Derrike Cope	8,506
21.	Todd Bodine	8,475
22.	Dale Jarrett	8,410
23.	Steve Grissom	8,394
24.	Greg Sacks	8,346
25.	Bobby Hamilton	8,337
26.	Geoffrey Bodine	8,149
27.	Joe Nemechek	7,953
28.	Jeff Burton	7,781
29.	John Andretti	7,508
30.	Harry Gant	7,347
31.	Jimmy Spencer	6,904
32.	Mike Wallace	6,672
33.	Dick Trickle	6,422
34.	Dave Marcis	5,914
35.	Jeremy Mayfield	5,581
36.	Ernie Irvan	5,357
37.	Ward Burton	5,320
38.	Loy Allen, Jr.	4,446
39.	Kenny Wallace	4,426
40.	Jimmy Hensley	3,861
41.	Chuck Bown	3,694
42.	Wally Dallenbach	3,568
43.	Rich Bickle	2,087
44.	Bobby Hillin	2,007
45.	Brad Teague	1,959
46.	Billy Standridge	1,260
47.	Jeff Purvis	1,081
48.	Randy LaJoie	1,010
49.	Rick Carelli	958
50.	Phil Parsons	757

LAPS LED

1.	Rusty Wallace	2,143
2.	Ernie Irvan	1,783
3.	Geoffrey Bodine	1,746
4.	Dale Earnhardt	1,015
5.	Mark Martin	726
6.	Terry Labonte	486
7.	Jeff Gordon	446
8.	Ken Schrader	223
9.	Ricky Rudd	192
10.	Rick Mast	166
11.	Sterling Marlin	144
12.	Jeff Burton	122
13.	Harry Gant	94
14.	Morgan Shepherd	81
15.	Ward Burton	73
16.	Bill Elliott	62
17.	Todd Bodine	60
	Darrell Waltrip	60
19.	Brett Bodine	55
	Dale Jarrett	55
21.	Ted Musgrave	50
22.	Jimmy Spencer	47
23.	John Andretti	41
24.	Lake Speed	39
25.	Greg Sacks	38
26.	Hut Stricklin	26
27.	Bobby Hamilton	24
28.	Joe Nemechek	22
29.	Dave Marcis	17
30.	Mike Wallace	13
31.	Loy Allen, Jr.	12
32.	Derrike Cope	11
33.	Michael Waltrip	8
34.	Kyle Petty	7
35.	Jimmy Hensley	4
	Kenny Wallace	4
37.	Bobby Labonte	3
38.	Bobby Hillin	2
39.	Wally Dallenbach	1
	Steve Grissom	1
	Dick Trickle	1

MILES LED

1.	Ernie Irvan	2,421
2.	Rusty Wallace	2,114
3.	Geoffrey Bodine	2,030
4.	Dale Earnhardt	1,327
5.	Mark Martin	919
6.	Jeff Gordon	657
7.	Terry Labonte	441
8.	Ken Schrader	295
9.	Sterling Marlin	235
10.	Ricky Rudd	226
11.	Rick Mast	196
12.	Jeff Burton	187
13.	Todd Bodine	109
	Ward Burton	109
	Jimmy Spencer	109
16.	Bill Elliott	105
17.	Morgan Shepherd	95
18.	Brett Bodine	85
19.	Darrell Waltrip	77
20.	Dale Jarrett	69
21.	Greg Sacks	63
22.	John Andretti	62
	Harry Gant	62
24.	Lake Speed	56
25.	Ted Musgrave	42
26.	Loy Allen, Jr.	27
	Dave Marcis	27
28.	Derrike Cope	24
29.	Bobby Hamilton	23
30.	Mike Wallace	20

MILES DRIVEN

1.	Ricky Rudd	12,047
2.	Darrell Waltrip	12,027
3.	Morgan Shepherd	11,951
4.	Ken Schrader	11,741
5.	Michael Waltrip	11,667
6.	Jeff Gordon	11,549
7.	Dale Earnhardt	11,410
8.	Mark Martin	11,404
9.	Bill Elliott	11,382
10.	Terry Labonte	11,314
11.	Lake Speed	11,291
12.	Kyle Petty	11,100
13.	Sterling Marlin	10,842
14.	Ted Musgrave	10,818
15.	Brett Bodine	10,773
16.	Rick Mast	10,754
17.	Rusty Wallace	10,731
18.	Hut Stricklin	10,587
19.	Todd Bodine	10,479
20.	Bobby Labonte	10,456
21.	Dale Jarrett	10,442
22.	Jeff Burton	10,240
23.	Bobby Hamilton	10,221
24.	Steve Grissom	10,169
25.	Greg Sacks	10,092
26.	Geoffrey Bodine	9,771
27.	Derrike Cope	9,719
28.	Harry Gant	9,598
29.	Joe Nemechek	9,488
30.	John Andretti	8,921

RACES LED

1.	Dale Earnhardt	23
2.	Geoffrey Bodine	20
3.	Rusty Wallace	19
4.	Mark Martin	18
5.	Jeff Gordon	17
	Ernie Irvan	17
7.	Sterling Marlin	11
8.	Ricky Rudd	10
	Morgan Shepherd	10
10.	Ken Schrader	9
11.	Bill Elliott	8
	Dale Jarrett	8
	Terry Labonte	8
	Rick Mast	8
	Greg Sacks	8
	Darrell Waltrip	8
17.	Brett Bodine	6
	Jimmy Spencer	6
19.	Todd Bodine	5
	Ward Burton	5
	Lake Speed	5
	Michael Waltrip	5
23.	John Andretti	4
	Jeff Burton	4
	Bobby Hamilton	4
	Dave Marcis	4
	Ted Musgrave	4
28.	Loy Allen, Jr.	3
	Harry Gant	3
	Jimmy Hensley	3
	Kenny Wallace	3
32.	Derrike Cope	2
	Bobby Labonte	2
	Joe Nemechek	2
	Kyle Petty	2
	Hut Stricklin	2
37.	Wally Dallenbach	1
	Steve Grissom	1
	Bobby Hillin	1
	Dick Trickle	1
	Mike Wallace	1

Driver	Starts	Poles	Finish 1	2	3	4	5	6–10	Laps	Laps Led	Races Led	Winston Cup Points	$

1995

	Driver	Starts	Poles	1	2	3	4	5	6–10	Laps	Laps Led	Races Led	Winston Cup Points	$
1.	Jeff Gordon	31	9	7	4	5	0	1	6	9,405	2,610	29	4,614	4,347,343
2.	Dale Earnhardt	31	3	5	6	5	1	2	4	9,625	1,574	24	4,580	3,154,241
3.	Sterling Marlin	31	1	3	2	0	3	1	13	9,729	475	12	4,361	2,253,502
4.	Mark Martin	31	4	4	1	4	1	3	9	9,393	739	14	4,320	1,893,519
5.	Rusty Wallace	31	0	2	4	6	2	1	4	9,497	1,093	17	4,240	1,642,837
6.	Terry Labonte	31	1	3	4	2	3	2	3	9,076	437	11	4,146	1,558,659
7.	Ted Musgrave	31	1	0	2	2	2	1	6	9,290	43	6	3,949	1,147,445
8.	Bill Elliott	31	2	0	0	0	2	2	7	9,349	124	8	3,746	996,816
9.	Ricky Rudd	31	2	1	0	1	4	4	6	8,813	368	11	3,734	1,337,703
10.	Bobby Labonte	31	2	3	3	0	0	1	7	9,018	277	14	3,718	1,413,682
11.	Morgan Shepherd	31	0	0	1	1	1	1	6	9,274	32	8	3,618	996,374
12.	Michael Waltrip	31	0	0	0	1	0	1	6	9,221	45	11	3,601	898,338
13.	Dale Jarrett	31	1	1	1	2	1	4	5	8,671	324	8	3,584	1,363,158
14.	Bobby Hamilton	31	0	0	1	0	2	1	6	9,409	129	7	3,576	804,505
15.	Derrike Cope	31	0	0	1	0	0	1	6	9,335	70	4	3,384	683,075
16.	Geoffrey Bodine	31	0	0	0	0	0	1	3	9,257	14	4	3,357	1,011,090
17.	Ken Schrader	31	1	0	0	1	1	0	8	8,550	237	9	3,221	886,566
18.	John Andretti	31	1	0	0	0	1	0	4	8,402	69	8	3,140	593,542
19.	Darrell Waltrip	31	1	0	0	1	3	0	4	8,222	168	8	3,078	850,632
20.	Brett Bodine	31	0	0	0	0	0	0	2	9,159	6	1	2,988	893,029
21.	Rick Mast	31	1	0	0	0	0	0	3	8,559	143	3	2,984	749,550
22.	Ward Burton	29	0	1	0	0	1	1	3	7,745	173	4	2,926	634,655
23.	Lake Speed	31	0	0	0	0	0	0	2	9,073	17	1	2,921	529,435
24.	Ricky Craven	31	0	0	0	0	0	0	4	8,711	5	4	2,883	597,054
25.	Dick Trickle	31	0	0	0	0	0	0	1	8,940	5	1	2,875	694,920
26.	Jimmy Spencer	29	0	0	0	0	0	0	4	8,664	4	2	2,809	504,560
27.	Steve Grissom	29	0	0	0	0	0	1	3	8,279	17	2	2,757	509,047
28.	Joe Nemechek	29	0	0	0	0	1	0	3	8,502	1	1	2,742	428,925
29.	Robert Pressley	31	0	0	0	0	0	0	1	8,181	37	3	2,663	695,875
30.	Kyle Petty	30	0	1	0	0	0	0	4	8,127	311	4	2,638	698,875
31.	Jeremy Mayfield	27	0	0	0	0	0	0	1	7,943	79	3	2,637	436,805
32.	Jeff Burton	29	0	0	0	0	0	1	1	8,050	3	2	2,556	628,270
33.	Todd Bodine	28	0	0	0	0	1	0	2	6,683	19	2	2,372	664,620
34.	Mike Wallace	26	0	0	0	0	0	0	1	6,819	2	2	2,178	428,006
35.	Dave Marcis	28	0	0	0	0	0	0	0	7,318	3	2	2,126	337,853
36.	Hut Stricklin	24	1	0	0	0	1	1	3	5,513	45	4	2,082	486,065
37.	Bobby Hillin	18	0	0	0	0	0	0	1	4,411	2	2	1,686	244,270
38.	Elton Sawyer	20	0	0	0	0	0	0	0	4,573	0	0	1,499	416,490
39.	Greg Sacks	20	0	0	0	0	0	0	0	4,682	0	0	1,349	323,720
40.	Randy LaJoie	14	0	0	0	0	0	0	0	3,606	0	0	1,133	281,945
41.	Loy Allen, Jr.	11	0	0	0	0	0	0	1	2,707	18	1	890	186,670
42.	Kenny Wallace	11	0	0	0	0	0	0	0	3,127	0	0	878	151,700
43.	Chuck Bown	9	0	0	0	0	0	0	0	2,068	0	0	618	99,995
44.	Jimmy Hensley	9	0	0	0	0	0	0	0	1,512	0	0	558	161,025
45.	Rich Bickle	8	0	0	0	0	0	0	0	1,995	3	1	538	153,250
46.	Davy Jones	7	0	0	0	0	0	0	0	1,680	0	0	520	109,925
47.	Jeff Purvis	7	0	0	0	0	0	0	0	951	0	0	391	93,875
48.	Ernie Irvan	3	0	0	0	0	0	0	2	924	142	2	354	54,875
49.	Steve Kinser	5	0	0	0	0	0	0	0	958	0	0	287	105,224
50.	Wally Dallenbach	2	0	0	1	0	0	0	0	131	21	1	221	63,900

LAPS COMPLETED

1.	Sterling Marlin	9,729
2.	Dale Earnhardt	9,625
3.	Rusty Wallace	9,497
4.	Bobby Hamilton	9,409
5.	Jeff Gordon	9,405
6.	Mark Martin	9,393
7.	Bill Elliott	9,349
8.	Derrike Cope	9,335
9.	Ted Musgrave	9,290
10.	Morgan Shepherd	9,274
11.	Geoffrey Bodine	9,257
12.	Michael Waltrip	9,221
13.	Brett Bodine	9,159
14.	Terry Labonte	9,076
15.	Lake Speed	9,073
16.	Bobby Labonte	9,018
17.	Dick Trickle	8,940
18.	Ricky Rudd	8,813
19.	Ricky Craven	8,711
20.	Dale Jarrett	8,671
21.	Jimmy Spencer	8,664
22.	Rick Mast	8,559
23.	Ken Schrader	8,550
24.	Joe Nemechek	8,502
25.	John Andretti	8,402
26.	Steve Grissom	8,279
27.	Darrell Waltrip	8,222
28.	Robert Pressley	8,181
29.	Kyle Petty	8,127
30.	Jeff Burton	8,050
31.	Jeremy Mayfield	7,943
32.	Ward Burton	7,745
33.	Dave Marcis	7,318
34.	Mike Wallace	6,819
35.	Todd Bodine	6,683
36.	Hut Stricklin	5,513
37.	Greg Sacks	4,682
38.	Elton Sawyer	4,573
39.	Bobby Hillin	4,411
40.	Randy LaJoie	3,606
41.	Kenny Wallace	3,127
42.	Loy Allen, Jr.	2,707
43.	Chuck Bown	2,068
44.	Rich Bickle	1,995
45.	Davy Jones	1,680
46.	Jimmy Hensley	1,512
47.	Steve Kinser	958
48.	Jeff Purvis	951
49.	Ernie Irvan	924
50.	Wally Dallenbach	131

LAPS LED

1.	Jeff Gordon	2,610
2.	Dale Earnhardt	1,574
3.	Rusty Wallace	1,093
4.	Mark Martin	739
5.	Sterling Marlin	475
6.	Terry Labonte	437
7.	Ricky Rudd	368
8.	Dale Jarrett	324
9.	Kyle Petty	311
10.	Bobby Labonte	277
11.	Ken Schrader	237
12.	Ward Burton	173
13.	Darrell Waltrip	168
14.	Rick Mast	143
15.	Ernie Irvan	142
16.	Bobby Hamilton	129
17.	Bill Elliott	124
18.	Jeremy Mayfield	79
19.	Derrike Cope	70
20.	John Andretti	69
21.	Hut Stricklin	45
	Michael Waltrip	45
23.	Ted Musgrave	43
24.	Robert Pressley	37
25.	Morgan Shepherd	32
26.	Wally Dallenbach	21
27.	Todd Bodine	19
28	Loy Allen, Jr.	18
29.	Steve Grissom	17
	Lake Speed	17
31.	Geoffrey Bodine	14
32.	Brett Bodine	6
33.	Ricky Craven	5
	Dick Trickle	5
35.	Jimmy Spencer	4
36.	Rich Bickle	3
	Jeff Burton	3
	Dave Marcis	3
39.	Bobby Hillin	2
	Mike Wallace	2
41.	Joe Nemechek	1

MILES LED

1.	Jeff Gordon	3,463
2.	Dale Earnhardt	1,734
3.	Mark Martin	1,013
4.	Rusty Wallace	985
5.	Sterling Marlin	969
6.	Ricky Rudd	511
7.	Bobby Labonte	412
8.	Ken Schrader	397
9.	Terry Labonte	334
10.	Dale Jarrett	306
11.	Kyle Petty	293
12.	Bill Elliott	261
13.	Ward Burton	196
14.	Rick Mast	147
15.	Ernie Irvan	130
	Bobby Hamilton	130
17.	Darrell Waltrip	110
18.	John Andretti	86
19.	Hut Stricklin	66
20.	Michael Waltrip	65
21.	Jeremy Mayfield	60
22.	Ted Musgrave	56
23.	Derrike Cope	54
	Morgan Shepherd	54
25.	Wally Dallenbach	51
26.	Loy Allen, Jr.	48
27.	Todd Bodine	27
	Robert Pressley	27
29.	Geoffrey Bodine	25
30.	Steve Grissom	12

MILES DRIVEN

1.	Sterling Marlin	11,939
2.	Dale Earnhardt	11,715
3.	Jeff Gordon	11,609
4.	Geoffrey Bodine	11,572
5.	Rusty Wallace	11,564
6.	Bobby Hamilton	11,550
7.	Morgan Shepherd	11,547
8.	Bill Elliott	11,434
9.	Mark Martin	11,428
10.	Michael Waltrip	11,400
11.	Ted Musgrave	11,381
12.	Terry Labonte	11,376
13.	Lake Speed	11,197
14.	Dick Trickle	11,094
15.	Ricky Craven	11,087
16.	Brett Bodine	11,084
17.	Derrike Cope	11,040
18.	Bobby Labonte	10,975
19.	Ricky Rudd	10,834
20.	Rick Mast	10,600
21.	Jimmy Spencer	10,475
22.	Jeremy Mayfield	10,441
23.	Dale Jarrett	10,418
24.	Steve Grissom	10,300
25.	Joe Nemechek	10,221
26.	Jeff Burton	10,193
27.	John Andretti	10,174
28.	Ken Schrader	10,167
29.	Kyle Petty	10,077
30.	Robert Pressley	9,996

RACES LED

1.	Jeff Gordon	29
2.	Dale Earnhardt	24
3.	Rusty Wallace	17
4.	Bobby Labonte	14
	Mark Martin	14
6.	Sterling Marlin	12
7.	Terry Labonte	11
	Ricky Rudd	11
	Michael Waltrip	11
10.	Ken Schrader	9
11.	John Andretti	8
	Bill Elliott	8
	Dale Jarrett	8
	Morgan Shepherd	8
	Darrell Waltrip	8
16.	Bobby Hamilton	7
17.	Ted Musgrave	6
18.	Geoffrey Bodine	4
	Ward Burton	4
	Derrike Cope	4
	Ricky Craven	4
	Kyle Petty	4
	Hut Stricklin	4
24.	Rick Mast	3
	Jeremy Mayfield	3
	Robert Pressley	3
27.	Todd Bodine	2
	Jeff Burton	2
	Steve Grissom	2
	Bobby Hillin	2
	Ernie Irvan	2
	Dave Marcis	2
	Jimmy Spencer	2
	Mike Wallace	2
35.	Loy Allen, Jr.	1
	Rich Bickle	1
	Brett Bodine	1
	Wally Dallenbach	1
	Joe Nemechek	1
	Lake Speed	1
	Dick Trickle	1

Driver	Starts	Poles	Finish 1	2	3	4	5	6–10	Laps	Laps Led	Races Led	Winston Cup Points	$

1996

	Driver	Starts	Poles	1	2	3	4	5	6–10	Laps	Laps Led	Races Led	Winston Cup Points	$
1.	Terry Labonte	31	4	2	7	5	1	6	3	9,443	972	22	4,657	4,030,648
2.	Jeff Gordon	31	5	10	3	4	2	2	3	8,972	2,315	25	4,620	3,428,485
3.	Dale Jarrett	31	2	4	7	4	2	0	4	9,307	743	20	4,568	2,985,418
4.	Dale Earnhardt	31	2	2	3	3	4	1	4	9,530	617	18	4,327	2,285,926
5.	Mark Martin	31	4	0	4	5	3	2	9	9,064	701	16	4,278	1,887,396
6.	Ricky Rudd	31	0	1	2	1	1	0	11	9,281	150	12	3,845	1,503,025
7.	Rusty Wallace	31	0	5	1	0	1	1	10	8,383	965	13	3,717	1,665,315
8.	Sterling Marlin	31	0	2	0	1	1	1	5	8,877	331	10	3,682	1,588,425
9.	Bobby Hamilton	31	2	1	0	1	0	1	8	9,153	648	11	3,639	1,151,235
10.	Ernie Irvan	31	1	2	2	0	6	2	4	8,617	383	15	3,632	1,683,313
11.	Bobby Labonte	31	4	1	1	0	1	2	9	8,916	330	13	3,590	1,475,196
12.	Ken Schrader	31	0	0	0	1	1	1	7	9,408	45	7	3,540	1,089,603
13.	Jeff Burton	30	1	0	0	1	3	2	6	8,592	208	7	3,538	884,303
14.	Michael Waltrip	31	0	0	0	0	0	1	10	9,279	18	5	3,535	1,182,811
15.	Jimmy Spencer	31	0	0	0	0	1	1	7	9,339	156	7	3,476	1,090,876
16.	Ted Musgrave	31	1	0	0	1	1	0	5	9,351	3	2	3,466	961,512
17.	Geoffrey Bodine	31	0	1	0	1	0	0	4	8,918	90	7	3,218	1,031,762
18.	Rick Mast	31	0	0	0	0	1	0	4	8,972	1	1	3,190	924,559
19.	Morgan Shepherd	31	0	0	0	0	0	1	4	8,976	55	4	3,133	719,059
20.	Ricky Craven	31	2	0	0	2	0	1	2	8,551	136	9	3,078	941,959
21.	Johnny Benson	30	1	0	0	0	0	1	5	8,507	105	4	3,004	947,080
22.	Hut Stricklin	31	0	0	1	0	0	0	0	8,620	163	3	2,854	631,055
23.	Lake Speed	31	0	0	0	0	0	0	2	8,493	10	3	2,834	817,175
24.	Brett Bodine	30	0	0	0	0	0	0	1	8,732	3	2	2,814	767,716
25.	Wally Dallenbach	30	0	0	0	1	0	0	2	8,191	0	0	2,786	837,001
26.	Jeremy Mayfield	30	1	0	0	0	1	1	0	7,914	20	4	2,721	592,853
27.	Kyle Petty	28	0	0	0	0	0	0	2	8,081	72	5	2,696	689,041
28.	Kenny Wallace	30	0	0	0	0	0	0	2	8,415	7	2	2,694	457,665
29.	Darrell Waltrip	31	0	0	0	0	0	0	2	7,766	2	2	2,657	740,185
30.	Bill Elliott	24	0	0	0	0	0	0	6	7,439	109	7	2,627	716,506
31.	John Andretti	30	0	0	0	0	0	2	1	7,850	32	5	2,621	688,511
32.	Robert Pressley	30	0	0	0	0	1	1	1	7,948	110	7	2,485	690,465
33.	Ward Burton	27	1	0	0	0	0	0	4	6,544	54	4	2,411	873,619
34.	Joe Nemechek	29	0	0	0	0	0	0	2	8,110	2	1	2,391	666,247
35.	Derrike Cope	29	0	0	0	0	0	0	3	7,329	28	2	2,374	675,781
36.	Dick Trickle	26	0	0	0	0	0	0	1	6,694	2	1	2,131	404,927
37.	Bobby Hillin	26	0	0	0	0	0	0	0	7,164	4	1	2,128	395,224
38.	Dave Marcis	27	0	0	0	0	0	0	0	7,202	20	8	2,047	435,177
39.	Steve Grissom	13	0	0	0	0	0	1	1	3,169	12	1	1,188	314,983
40.	Todd Bodine	10	0	0	0	0	0	0	1	3,210	1	1	991	198,525
41.	Mike Wallace	11	0	0	0	0	0	0	0	2,877	3	1	799	169,082
42.	Greg Sacks	9	0	0	0	0	0	0	0	2,196	3	1	710	207,755
43.	Elton Sawyer	9	0	0	0	0	0	0	0	2,448	0	0	705	129,618
44.	Chad Little	9	0	0	0	0	0	0	0	1,816	0	0	627	164,752
45.	Loy Allen, Jr.	9	0	0	0	0	0	0	0	1,439	0	0	603	130,667
46.	Gary Bradberry	8	0	0	0	0	0	0	0	1,867	0	0	591	155,785
47.	Mike Skinner	5	0	0	0	0	0	0	0	1,459	10	1	529	65,850
48.	Jeff Purvis	4	0	0	0	0	0	0	0	532	0	0	328	91,127
49.	Jeff Green	4	0	0	0	0	0	0	0	813	0	0	247	46,875
50.	Randy MacDonald	3	0	0	0	0	0	0	0	680	0	0	228	31,610

LAPS COMPLETED

1.	Dale Earnhardt	9,530
2.	Terry Labonte	9,443
3.	Ken Schrader	9,408
4.	Ted Musgrave	9,351
5.	Jimmy Spencer	9,339
6.	Dale Jarrett	9,307
7.	Ricky Rudd	9,281
8.	Michael Waltrip	9,279
9.	Bobby Hamilton	9,153
10.	Mark Martin	9,064
11.	Morgan Shepherd	8,976
12.	Jeff Gordon	8,972
13.	Rick Mast	8,972
14.	Geoffrey Bodine	8,918
15.	Bobby Labonte	8,916
16.	Sterling Marlin	8,877
17.	Brett Bodine	8,732
18.	Hut Stricklin	8,620
19.	Ernie Irvan	8,617
20.	Jeff Burton	8,592
21.	Ricky Craven	8,551
22.	Johnny Benson	8,507
23.	Lake Speed	8,493
24.	Kenny Wallace	8,415
25.	Rusty Wallace	8,383
26.	Wally Dallenbach	8,191
27.	Joe Nemechek	8,110
28.	Kyle Petty	8,081
29.	Robert Pressley	7,948
30.	Jeremy Mayfield	7,914
31.	John Andretti	7,850
32.	Darrell Waltrip	7,766
33.	Bill Elliott	7,439
34.	Derrike Cope	7,329
35.	Dave Marcis	7,202
36.	Bobby Hillin	7,164
37.	Dick Trickle	6,694
38.	Ward Burton	6,544
39.	Todd Bodine	3,210
40.	Steve Grissom	3,169
41.	Mike Wallace	2,877
42.	Elton Sawyer	2,448
43.	Greg Sacks	2,196
44.	Gary Bradberry	1,867
45.	Chad Little	1,816
46.	Mike Skinner	1,459
47.	Loy Allen, Jr.	1,439
48.	Jeff Green	813
49.	Randy MacDonald	680
50.	Jeff Purvis	532

LAPS LED

1.	Jeff Gordon	2,315
2.	Terry Labonte	972
3.	Rusty Wallace	965
4.	Dale Jarrett	743
5.	Mark Martin	701
6.	Bobby Hamilton	648
7.	Dale Earnhardt	617
8.	Ernie Irvan	383
9.	Sterling Marlin	331
10.	Bobby Labonte	330
11.	Jeff Burton	208
12.	Hut Stricklin	163
13.	Jimmy Spencer	156
14.	Ricky Rudd	150
15.	Ricky Craven	136
16.	Robert Pressley	110
17.	Bill Elliott	109
18.	Johnny Benson	105
19.	Geoffrey Bodine	90
20.	Kyle Petty	72
21.	Morgan Shepherd	55
22.	Ward Burton	54
23.	Ken Schrader	45
24.	John Andretti	32
25.	Derrike Cope	28
26.	Dave Marcis	20
	Jeremy Mayfield	20
28.	Michael Waltrip	18
29.	Steve Grissom	12
30.	Mike Skinner	10
	Lake Speed	10
32.	Kenny Wallace	7
33.	Bobby Hillin	4
34.	Brett Bodine	3
	Ted Musgrave	3
	Greg Sacks	3
	Mike Wallace	3
38.	Joe Nemechek	2
	Dick Trickle	2
	Darrell Waltrip	2
41.	Todd Bodine	1
	Rick Mast	1

MILES LED

1.	Jeff Gordon	2,387
2.	Terry Labonte	1,207
3.	Mark Martin	1,091
4.	Dale Jarrett	996
5.	Dale Earnhardt	911
6.	Rusty Wallace	789
7.	Sterling Marlin	646
8.	Ernie Irvan	486
	Bobby Labonte	486
10.	Bobby Hamilton	460
11.	Hut Stricklin	245
12.	Johnny Benson, Jr.	215
13.	Ricky Rudd	185
14.	Ricky Craven	181
15.	Jeff Burton	178
16.	Jimmy Spencer	174
17.	Bill Elliott	134
18.	Geoffrey Bodine	127
19.	Robert Pressley	108
20.	Morgan Shepherd	104
21.	Ken Schrader	95
22.	John Andretti	73
23.	Derrike Cope	66
24.	Ward Burton	62
25.	Jeremy Mayfield	45
26.	Kyle Petty	43
	Michael Waltrip	43
28.	Dave Marcis	37
29.	Steve Grissom	32
30.	Lake Speed	21

MILES DRIVEN

1.	Dale Earnhardt	11,524
2.	Terry Labonte	11,523
3.	Ken Schrader	11,500
4.	Ricky Rudd	11,401
5.	Ted Musgrave	11,387
6.	Jimmy Spencer	11,239
7.	Dale Jarrett	11,181
8.	Michael Waltrip	11,166
9.	Geoffrey Bodine	11,068
10.	Mark Martin	11,067
11.	Rick Mast	10,937
12.	Bobby Hamilton	10,897
13.	Morgan Shepherd	10,721
14.	Brett Bodine	10,718
15.	Hut Stricklin	10,633
16.	Sterling Marlin	10,583
17.	Bobby Labonte	10,571
18.	Jeff Burton	10,552
19.	Jeff Gordon	10,518
20.	Johnny Benson, Jr.	10,484
21.	Wally Dallenbach	10,417
22.	Ernie Irvan	10,218
23.	Ricky Craven	10,215
24.	Rusty Wallace	10,160
25.	Lake Speed	10,028
26.	John Andretti	9,912
27.	Kenny Wallace	9,897
28.	Joe Nemechek	9,711
29.	Kyle Petty	9,683
30.	Robert Pressley	9,678

RACES LED

1.	Jeff Gordon	25
2.	Terry Labonte	22
3.	Dale Jarrett	20
4.	Dale Earnhardt	18
5.	Mark Martin	16
6.	Ernie Irvan	15
7.	Bobby Labonte	13
	Rusty Wallace	13
9.	Ricky Rudd	12
10.	Bobby Hamilton	11
11.	Sterling Marlin	10
12.	Ricky Craven	9
13.	Dave Marcis	8
14.	Geoffrey Bodine	7
	Jeff Burton	7
	Bill Elliott	7
	Robert Pressley	7
	Ken Schrader	7
	Jimmy Spencer	7
20.	John Andretti	5
	Kyle Petty	5
	Michael Waltrip	5
23.	Johnny Benson	4
	Ward Burton	4
	Jeremy Mayfield	4
	Morgan Shepherd	4
27.	Lake Speed	3
	Hut Stricklin	3
29.	Brett Bodine	2
	Derrike Cope	2
	Ted Musgrave	2
	Kenny Wallace	2
	Darrell Waltrip	2
34.	Todd Bodine	1
	Steve Grissom	1
	Bobby Hillin	1
	Rick Mast	1
	Joe Nemechek	1
	Greg Sacks	1
	Mike Skinner	1
	Dick Trickle	1
	Mike Wallace	1

Driver	Starts	Poles	Finish 1	2	3	4	5	6–10	Laps	Laps Led	Races Led	Winston Cup Points	$

1997

Driver	Starts	Poles	1	2	3	4	5	6–10	Laps	Laps Led	Races Led	Winston Cup Points	$
1. Jeff Gordon	32	1	10	3	2	4	3	1	9,276	1,645	24	4,710	6,375,658
2. Dale Jarrett	32	3	7	4	4	2	3	3	9,769	2,086	22	4,696	3,240,542
3. Mark Martin	32	3	4	2	4	2	4	8	9,599	796	20	4,681	2,532,484
4. Jeff Burton	32	0	3	3	3	2	2	5	9,275	685	17	4,285	2,296,614
5. Dale Earnhardt	32	0	0	4	1	1	1	9	9,693	215	10	4,216	2,151,909
6. Terry Labonte	32	1	1	3	2	2	0	12	9,605	256	11	4,177	2,270,144
7. Bobby Labonte	32	3	1	3	2	2	1	9	9,482	484	12	4,101	2,217,999
8. Bill Elliott	32	1	0	1	0	3	1	9	9,610	442	11	3,836	1,607,827
9. Rusty Wallace	32	1	1	3	2	0	2	4	8,747	778	11	3,598	1,705,625
10. Ken Schrader	32	2	0	0	0	2	0	6	9,612	46	7	3,576	1,355,292
11. Johnny Benson	32	1	0	0	0	0	0	8	9,648	19	7	3,575	1,256,457
12. Ted Musgrave	32	0	0	1	1	3	0	3	9,266	131	6	3,556	1,256,680
13. Jeremy Mayfield	32	0	0	0	0	1	2	5	9,541	3	2	3,547	1,067,203
14. Ernie Irvan	32	2	1	2	0	1	1	8	8,757	439	15	3,534	1,614,281
15. Kyle Petty	32	0	0	0	1	0	1	7	9,192	210	6	3,455	984,314
16. Bobby Hamilton	32	2	1	1	3	0	1	2	9,535	416	9	3,450	1,478,843
17. Ricky Rudd	32	0	2	0	1	1	2	5	9,094	77	4	3,330	1,975,981
18. Michael Waltrip	32	0	0	0	0	0	0	6	9,277	11	5	3,173	1,138,599
19. Ricky Craven	30	0	0	0	2	0	2	3	7,806	280	9	3,108	1,259,550
20. Jimmy Spencer	32	0	0	0	0	0	1	3	8,665	70	8	3,079	1,073,779
21. Steve Grissom	31	0	0	0	0	2	1	3	8,800	2	1	3,061	1,074,374
22. Geoffrey Bodine	29	2	0	2	0	1	0	7	8,224	68	12	3,046	1,092,734
23. John Andretti	32	1	1	0	1	1	0	0	9,333	135	5	3,019	1,143,725
24. Ward Burton	31	1	0	0	0	0	0	7	8,976	140	4	2,987	1,004,944
25. Sterling Marlin	32	0	0	0	1	0	1	4	8,584	71	7	2,954	1,301,370
26. Darrell Waltrip	31	0	0	0	0	0	1	3	8,427	17	6	2,942	958,679
27. Derrike Cope	31	0	0	0	0	0	1	1	8,557	4	2	2,901	707,404
28. Joe Nemechek	30	2	0	0	0	0	0	3	8,861	108	6	2,754	732,194
29. Brett Bodine	31	0	0	0	0	0	0	2	8,666	4	3	2,716	936,694
30. Mike Skinner	31	2	0	0	0	0	0	3	8,389	34	8	2,669	900,569
31. Dick Trickle	28	0	0	0	1	0	1	0	8,476	0	0	2,629	656,189
32. Rick Mast	29	0	0	0	0	0	0	2	8,415	1	1	2,569	829,336
33. Kenny Wallace	31	2	0	0	0	0	0	2	8,333	0	0	2,462	939,001
34. Hut Stricklin	29	0	0	0	0	0	0	1	8,494	6	1	2,423	802,904
35. Lake Speed	25	0	0	0	0	0	0	0	7,494	3	1	2,301	715,074
36. Chad Little	27	0	0	0	0	0	0	1	7,732	7	1	2,081	555,914
37. David Green	26	0	0	0	0	0	0	0	7,282	1	1	2,038	512,583
38. Morgan Shepherd	23	0	0	0	1	0	0	2	6,398	12	2	2,033	662,999
39. Jeff Green	20	0	0	0	0	1	0	1	5,524	18	2	1,624	434,685
40. Robby Gordon	20	1	0	0	0	1	0	0	4,395	42	1	1,495	622,439
41. Wally Dallenbach	22	0	0	0	0	0	0	1	4,598	21	3	1,475	471,479
42. Dave Marcis	19	0	0	0	0	0	0	0	5,246	0	0	1,405	427,364
43. Robert Pressley	14	0	0	0	0	0	0	0	3,941	9	2	984	252,478
44. Gary Bradberry	16	0	0	0	0	0	0	0	4,207	0	0	868	251,930
45. Greg Sacks	12	0	0	0	0	0	0	0	2,456	8	2	778	320,714
46. Mike Wallace	7	0	0	0	0	0	0	0	1,845	0	0	541	159,303
47. Bobby Hillin	10	0	0	0	0	0	0	0	1,781	0	0	511	211,978
48. Lance Hooper	6	0	0	0	0	0	0	0	1,380	0	0	402	145,000
49. Kenny Irwin, Jr.	4	0	0	0	0	0	0	1	1,283	12	1	390	71,730
50. Billy Standridge	6	0	0	0	0	0	0	0	1,199	0	0	366	149,824

LAPS COMPLETED

1.	Dale Jarrett	9,769
2.	Dale Earnhardt	9,693
3.	Johnny Benson	9,648
4.	Ken Schrader	9,612
5.	Bill Elliott	9,610
6.	Terry Labonte	9,605
7.	Mark Martin	9,599
8.	Jeremy Mayfield	9,541
9.	Bobby Hamilton	9,535
10.	Bobby Labonte	9,482
11.	John Andretti	9,333
12.	Michael Waltrip	9,277
13.	Jeff Gordon	9,276
14.	Jeff Burton	9,275
15.	Ted Musgrave	9,266
16.	Kyle Petty	9,192
17.	Ricky Rudd	9,094
18.	Ward Burton	8,976
19.	Joe Nemechek	8,861
20.	Steve Grissom	8,800
21.	Ernie Irvan	8,757
22.	Rusty Wallace	8,747
23.	Brett Bodine	8,666
24.	Jimmy Spencer	8,665
25.	Sterling Marlin	8,584
26.	Derrike Cope	8,557
27.	Hut Stricklin	8,494
28.	Dick Trickle	8,476
29.	Darrell Waltrip	8,427
30.	Rick Mast	8,415
31.	Mike Skinner	8,389
32.	Kenny Wallace	8,333
33.	Geoffrey Bodine	8,224
34.	Ricky Craven	7,806
35.	Chad Little	7,732
36.	Lake Speed	7,494
37.	David Green	7,282
38.	Morgan Shepherd	6,398
39.	Jeff Green	5,524
40.	Dave Marcis	5,246
41.	Wally Dallenbach	4,598
42.	Robby Gordon	4,395
43.	Gary Bradberry	4,207
44.	Robert Pressley	3,941
45.	Greg Sacks	2,456
46.	Mike Wallace	1,845
47.	Bobby Hillin	1,781
48.	Lance Hooper	1,380
49.	Kenny Irwin, Jr.	1,283
50.	Billy Standridge	1,199

LAPS LED

1.	Dale Jarrett	2,086
2.	Jeff Gordon	1,645
3.	Mark Martin	796
4.	Rusty Wallace	778
5.	Jeff Burton	685
6.	Bobby Labonte	484
7.	Bill Elliott	442
8.	Ernie Irvan	439
9.	Bobby Hamilton	416
10.	Ricky Craven	280
11.	Terry Labonte	256
12.	Dale Earnhardt	215
13.	Kyle Petty	210
14.	Ward Burton	140
15.	John Andretti	135
16.	Ted Musgrave	131
17.	Joe Nemechek	108
18.	Ricky Rudd	77
19.	Sterling Marlin	71
20.	Jimmy Spencer	70
21.	Geoffrey Bodine	68
22.	Ken Schrader	46
23.	Robby Gordon	42
24.	Mike Skinner	34
25.	Wally Dallenbach	21
26.	Johnny Benson	19
27.	Jeff Green	18
28.	Darrell Waltrip	17
29.	Kenny Irwin, Jr.	12
	Morgan Shepherd	12
31.	Michael Waltrip	11
32.	Robert Pressley	9
33.	Greg Sacks	8
34.	Chad Little	7
35.	Hut Stricklin	6
36.	Brett Bodine	4
	Derrike Cope	4
38.	Jeremy Mayfield	3
	Lake Speed	3
40.	Steve Grissom	2
41.	David Green	1
	Rick Mast	1

MILES LED

1.	Dale Jarrett	2,545
2.	Jeff Gordon	1,837
3.	Mark Martin	1,250
4.	Jeff Burton	736
5.	Bobby Labonte	679
6.	Ernie Irvan	646
7.	Bill Elliott	575
8.	Rusty Wallace	573
9.	Terry Labonte	489
10.	Dale Earnhardt	485
11.	Bobby Hamilton	389
12.	John Andretti	339
13.	Ricky Craven	307
14.	Ted Musgrave	270
15.	Kyle Petty	222
16.	Ward Burton	213
17.	Joe Nemechek	149
18.	Sterling Marlin	143
19.	Ricky Rudd	120
20.	Geoffrey Bodine	102
21.	Jimmy Spencer	76
22.	Ken Schrader	74
23.	Robby Gordon	64
24.	Mike Skinner	61
25.	Wally Dallenbach	50
26.	Jeff Green	42
27.	Darrell Waltrip	38
28.	Johnny Benson, Jr.	34
29.	Michael Waltrip	23
30.	Greg Sacks	21

MILES DRIVEN

1.	Dale Jarrett	12,646
2.	Johnny Benson, Jr.	12,504
3.	Dale Earnhardt	12,503
4.	Bill Elliott	12,429
5.	Bobby Labonte	12,368
6.	Ken Schrader	12,364
7.	Mark Martin	12,354
8.	Jeff Burton	12,346
9.	Jeremy Mayfield	12,326
10.	Terry Labonte	12,297
11.	Bobby Hamilton	12,266
12.	Ted Musgrave	12,095
13.	Michael Waltrip	12,041
14.	Jeff Gordon	11,983
15.	John Andretti	11,965
16.	Kyle Petty	11,957
17.	Ricky Rudd	11,619
18.	Ernie Irvan	11,592
19.	Brett Bodine	11,317
20.	Steve Grissom	11,299
21.	Joe Nemechek	11,285
22.	Jimmy Spencer	11,233
23.	Ward Burton	11,109
24.	Darrell Waltrip	10,978
25.	Rusty Wallace	10,954
26.	Dick Trickle	10,896
27.	Kenny Wallace	10,868
28.	Derrike Cope	10,852
29.	Sterling Marlin	10,836
30.	Mike Skinner	10,486

RACES LED

1.	Jeff Gordon	24
2.	Dale Jarrett	22
3.	Mark Martin	20
4.	Jeff Burton	17
5.	Ernie Irvan	15
6.	Geoffrey Bodine	12
	Bobby Labonte	12
8.	Bill Elliott	11
	Terry Labonte	11
	Rusty Wallace	11
11.	Dale Earnhardt	10
12.	Ricky Craven	9
	Bobby Hamilton	9
14.	Jimmy Spencer	8
	Mike Skinner	8
16.	Johnny Benson	7
	Sterling Marlin	7
	Ken Schrader	7
19.	Ted Musgrave	6
	Joe Nemechek	6
	Kyle Petty	6
	Darrell Waltrip	6
23.	John Andretti	5
	Michael Waltrip	5
25.	Ward Burton	4
	Ricky Rudd	4
27.	Brett Bodine	3
	Wally Dallenbach	3
29.	Derrike Cope	2
	Jeff Green	2
	Jeremy Mayfield	2
	Robert Pressley	2
	Greg Sacks	2
	Morgan Shepherd	2
35.	Robby Gordon	1
	David Green	1
	Steve Grissom	1
	Kenny Irwin, Jr.	1
	Chad Little	1
	Rick Mast	1
	Lake Speed	1
	Hut Stricklin	1

1998

Driver	Starts	Poles	Finish 1	2	3	4	5	6–10	Laps	Laps Led	Races Led	Winston Cup Points	$
1. Jeff Gordon	33	7	13	6	3	1	3	2	9,818	1,706	26	5,328	9,306,584
2. Mark Martin	33	3	7	6	4	3	2	4	9,830	1,731	23	4,964	4,309,006
3. Dale Jarrett	33	2	3	5	6	2	3	3	9,475	831	22	4,619	4,019,657
4. Rusty Wallace	33	4	1	2	5	3	4	6	9,603	946	19	4,501	2,667,889
5. Jeff Burton	33	0	2	4	2	5	5	5	9,488	974	13	4,415	2,626,987
6. Bobby Labonte	33	3	2	3	2	4	0	7	9,512	182	13	4,180	2,980,052
7. Jeremy Mayfield	33	1	1	1	3	2	5	4	9,745	476	9	4,157	2,332,034
8. Dale Earnhardt	33	0	1	0	1	2	1	8	9,459	274	14	3,928	2,990,749
9. Terry Labonte	33	0	1	1	2	1	0	10	9,573	338	12	3,901	2,054,163
10. Bobby Hamilton	33	1	1	1	0	1	0	5	9,840	443	6	3,786	2,089,566
11. John Andretti	33	1	0	0	2	0	1	7	9,181	136	4	3,682	1,838,379
12. Ken Schrader	33	2	0	0	0	3	0	8	9,238	60	4	3,675	1,887,339
13. Sterling Marlin	32	0	0	0	0	0	0	6	9,154	342	6	3,530	1,350,161
14. Jimmy Spencer	31	0	0	1	0	2	0	5	8,934	117	11	3,464	1,741,012
15. Chad Little	32	0	0	1	0	0	0	6	9,081	69	8	3,423	1,449,659
16. Ward Burton	33	2	0	1	0	0	0	4	9,551	132	9	3,352	1,516,183
17. Michael Waltrip	32	0	0	0	0	0	0	5	9,519	14	7	3,340	1,508,680
18. Bill Elliott	32	0	0	0	0	0	0	5	8,865	40	8	3,305	1,618,421
19. Ernie Irvan	30	3	0	0	0	0	0	11	8,153	193	5	3,262	1,600,452
20. Johnny Benson	32	0	0	0	0	1	2	7	8,565	93	10	3,160	1,360,335
21. Mike Skinner	30	0	0	0	2	1	1	5	8,425	112	5	3,153	1,518,901
22. Ricky Rudd	33	0	1	0	0	0	0	4	9,127	255	3	3,131	1,602,895
23. Ted Musgrave	32	0	0	1	0	0	1	3	8,298	0	0	3,124	1,253,626
24. Darrell Waltrip	33	0	0	0	0	0	1	1	8,994	16	4	2,957	1,056,475
25. Brett Bodine	33	0	0	0	0	0	0	0	9,462	17	6	2,907	1,281,673
26. Joe Nemechek	32	0	0	0	0	1	0	3	8,771	41	5	2,897	1,343,991
27. Geoffrey Bodine	32	0	0	0	0	0	1	4	8,745	33	4	2,864	1,247,255
28. Kenny Irwin, Jr.	32	1	0	0	0	0	1	3	8,182	129	4	2,760	1,459,967
29. Dick Trickle	32	0	0	0	0	0	0	1	8,671	4	2	2,678	1,208,771
30. Kyle Petty	33	0	0	0	0	0	0	2	8,464	0	0	2,675	1,287,731
31. Kenny Wallace	31	0	0	0	0	0	0	7	7,076	59	4	2,615	1,019,861
32. Robert Pressley	30	0	0	0	1	0	0	0	7,224	3	2	2,388	996,721
33. Rick Mast	30	1	0	0	0	0	0	1	7,667	61	2	2,296	894,327
34. Steve Grissom	27	0	0	0	0	0	0	2	7,119	8	1	2,215	1,030,041
35. Kevin Lepage	27	0	0	0	0	0	0	2	7,198	0	0	2,196	852,721
36. Jerry Nadeau	30	0	0	0	0	0	0	0	8,132	0	0	2,121	804,867
37. Derrike Cope	28	0	0	0	0	0	0	0	7,526	16	3	2,065	956,980
38. Wally Dallenbach	23	0	0	0	0	0	0	3	5,939	13	2	1,832	807,856
39. Rich Bickle	21	0	0	0	0	1	0	0	5,691	0	0	1,773	682,255
40. Jeff Green	22	0	0	0	0	0	0	0	6,088	0	0	1,687	589,841
41. Todd Bodine	14	0	0	0	0	0	1	1	4,846	47	2	1,322	378,766
42. Steve Park	17	0	0	0	0	0	0	0	4,595	0	0	1,322	487,265
43. Lake Speed	16	0	0	0	0	0	0	0	4,790	0	0	1,297	552,521
44. David Green	15	0	0	0	0	0	0	0	3,500	0	0	1,014	441,121
45. Dave Marcis	13	0	0	0	0	0	0	0	3,378	13	3	949	444,946
46. Ricky Craven	11	1	0	0	0	0	0	1	2,687	19	2	907	506,230
47. Morgan Shepherd	12	0	0	0	0	0	0	0	2,796	0	0	843	364,541
48. Gary Bradberry	13	0	0	0	0	0	0	0	3,398	0	0	787	341,307
49. Randy LaJoie	9	0	0	0	0	0	1	2	2,750	0	0	768	336,905
50. Hut Stricklin	14	0	0	0	0	0	0	0	3,188	0	0	700	337,106

LAPS COMPLETED

1.	Bobby Hamilton	9,840
2.	Mark Martin	9,830
3.	Jeff Gordon	9,818
4.	Jeremy Mayfield	9,745
5.	Rusty Wallace	9,603
6.	Terry Labonte	9,573
7.	Ward Burton	9,551
8.	Michael Waltrip	9,519
9.	Bobby Labonte	9,512
10.	Jeff Burton	9,488
11.	Dale Jarrett	9,475
12.	Brett Bodine	9,462
13.	Dale Earnhardt	9,459
14.	Ken Schrader	9,238
15.	John Andretti	9,181
16.	Sterling Marlin	9,154
17.	Ricky Rudd	9,127
18.	Chad Little	9,081
19.	Darrell Waltrip	8,994
20.	Jimmy Spencer	8,934
21.	Bill Elliott	8,865
22.	Joe Nemechek	8,771
23.	Geoffrey Bodine	8,745
24.	Dick Trickle	8,671
25.	Johnny Benson	8,565
26.	Kyle Petty	8,464
27.	Mike Skinner	8,425
28.	Ted Musgrave	8,298
29.	Kenny Irwin, Jr.	8,182
30.	Ernie Irvan	8,153
31.	Jerry Nadeau	8,132
32.	Rick Mast	7,667
33.	Derrike Cope	7,526
34.	Robert Pressley	7,224
35.	Kevin Lepage	7,198
36.	Steve Grissom	7,119
37.	Kenny Wallace	7,076
38.	Jeff Green	6,088
39.	Wally Dallenbach	5,939
40.	Rich Bickle	5,691
41.	Todd Bodine	4,846
42.	Lake Speed	4,790
43.	Steve Park	4,595
44.	David Green	3,500
45.	Gary Bradberry	3,398
46.	Dave Marcis	3,378
47.	Hut Stricklin	3,188
48.	Morgan Shepherd	2,796
49.	Randy LaJoie	2,750
50.	Ricky Craven	2,687

LAPS LED

1.	Mark Martin	1,731
2.	Jeff Gordon	1,706
3.	Jeff Burton	974
4.	Rusty Wallace	946
5.	Dale Jarrett	831
6.	Jeremy Mayfield	476
7.	Bobby Hamilton	443
8.	Sterling Marlin	342
9.	Terry Labonte	338
10.	Dale Earnhardt	274
11.	Ricky Rudd	255
12.	Ernie Irvan	193
13.	Bobby Labonte	182
14.	John Andretti	136
15.	Ward Burton	132
16.	Kenny Irwin, Jr.	129
17.	Jimmy Spencer	117
18.	Mike Skinner	112
19.	Johnny Benson	93
20.	Chad Little	69
21.	Rick Mast	61
22.	Ken Schrader	60
23.	Kenny Wallace	59
24.	Todd Bodine	47
25.	Joe Nemechek	41
26.	Bill Elliott	40
27.	Geoffrey Bodine	33
28.	Ricky Craven	19
29.	Brett Bodine	17
30.	Derrike Cope	16
	Darrell Waltrip	16
32.	Michael Waltrip	14
33.	Wally Dallenbach	13
	Dave Marcis	13
35.	Steve Grissom	8
36.	Dick Trickle	4
37.	Robert Pressley	3

MILES LED

1.	Jeff Gordon	2,746
2.	Mark Martin	2,164
3.	Jeff Burton	1,143
4.	Dale Jarrett	1,130
5.	Rusty Wallace	899
6.	Jeremy Mayfield	672
7.	Dale Earnhardt	537
8.	Terry Labonte	429
9.	Bobby Labonte	373
10.	Ernie Irvan	341
11.	Mike Skinner	271
12.	Bobby Hamilton	260
13.	Sterling Marlin	252
14.	Kenny Irwin, Jr.	211
15.	Ward Burton	163
16.	Ricky Rudd	154
17.	Jimmy Spencer	125
18.	John Andretti	108
19.	Johnny Benson, Jr.	99
20.	Chad Little	94
21.	Joe Nemechek	75
22.	Todd Bodine	72
23.	Kenny Wallace	68
24.	Rick Mast	63
25.	Ken Schrader	57
26.	Geoffrey Bodine	40
27.	Bill Elliott	35
28.	Darrell Waltrip	33
29.	Derrike Cope	31
	Wally Dallenbach	31

MILES DRIVEN

1.	Jeff Gordon	12,784
2.	Bobby Hamilton	12,759
3.	Mark Martin	12,744
4.	Jeremy Mayfield	12,584
5.	Ward Burton	12,509
6.	Michael Waltrip	12,493
7.	Bobby Labonte	12,376
8.	Terry Labonte	12,372
9.	Dale Jarrett	12,360
10.	Brett Bodine	12,346
11.	Rusty Wallace	12,308
12.	Dale Earnhardt	12,277
13.	Jeff Burton	12,141
14.	John Andretti	12,037
15.	Sterling Marlin	12,012
16.	Joe Nemechek	11,909
17.	Darrell Waltrip	11,885
18.	Chad Little	11,828
19.	Jimmy Spencer	11,827
20.	Ken Schrader	11,800
21.	Ricky Rudd	11,589
22.	Bill Elliott	11,443
23.	Dick Trickle	11,433
24.	Kyle Petty	11,239
25.	Johnny Benson, Jr.	11,108
26.	Ted Musgrave	11,068
27.	Geoffrey Bodine	11,016
28.	Mike Skinner	10,856
29.	Ernie Irvan	10,649
30.	Kenny Irwin, Jr.	10,548

RACES LED

1.	Jeff Gordon	26
2.	Mark Martin	23
3.	Dale Jarrett	22
4.	Rusty Wallace	19
5.	Dale Earnhardt	14
6.	Jeff Burton	13
	Bobby Labonte	13
8.	Terry Labonte	12
9.	Jimmy Spencer	11
10.	Johnny Benson	10
11.	Ward Burton	9
	Jeremy Mayfield	9
13.	Bill Elliott	8
	Chad Little	8
15.	Michael Waltrip	7
16.	Brett Bodine	6
	Bobby Hamilton	6
	Sterling Marlin	6
19.	Ernie Irvan	5
	Joe Nemechek	5
	Mike Skinner	5
22.	John Andretti	4
	Geoffrey Bodine	4
	Kenny Irwin, Jr.	4
	Ken Schrader	4
	Kenny Wallace	4
	Darrell Waltrip	4
28.	Derrike Cope	3
	Dave Marcis	3
	Ricky Rudd	3
31.	Todd Bodine	2
	Ricky Craven	2
	Wally Dallenbach	2
	Rick Mast	2
	Robert Pressley	2
	Dick Trickle	2
37.	Steve Grissom	1

1999

Driver	Starts	Poles	Finish 1	2	3	4	5	6–10	Laps	Laps Led	Races Led	Winston Cup Points	$
1. Dale Jarrett	34	0	4	6	4	5	5	5	9,900	1,100	22	5,262	6,649,596
2. Bobby Labonte	34	5	5	6	7	1	4	3	10,011	1,201	30	5,061	4,763,615
3. Mark Martin	34	1	2	4	5	5	3	7	9,903	701	25	4,943	3,509,744
4. Tony Stewart	34	2	3	2	1	4	2	9	9,908	1,213	17	4,774	3,190,149
5. Jeff Burton	34	1	6	2	3	4	3	5	9,878	1,063	18	4,733	5,725,399
6. Jeff Gordon	34	7	7	4	5	1	1	3	9,384	1,320	26	4,620	5,858,633
7. Dale Earnhardt	34	0	3	3	0	0	1	14	9,751	230	8	4,492	3,048,236
8. Rusty Wallace	34	4	1	0	1	3	2	9	9,592	1,009	11	4,155	2,454,050
9. Ward Burton	34	1	0	3	0	2	1	10	9,828	243	13	4,062	2,405,913
10. Mike Skinner	34	2	0	0	1	4	0	9	9,732	465	14	4,003	2,499,877
11. Jeremy Mayfield	34	0	0	1	2	0	2	7	9,870	221	11	3,743	2,125,227
12. Terry Labonte	34	0	1	0	0	0	0	6	9,325	350	11	3,580	2,475,365
13. Bobby Hamilton	34	0	0	0	0	1	0	9	9,774	3	2	3,564	2,019,255
14. Steve Park	34	0	0	0	0	0	0	5	9,575	166	6	3,481	1,767,690
15. Ken Schrader	34	1	0	0	0	0	0	6	9,676	8	3	3,479	1,939,147
16. Sterling Marlin	34	1	0	0	0	2	0	3	9,711	56	9	3,397	1,797,416
17. John Andretti	34	1	1	0	1	1	0	7	8,526	238	10	3,394	2,001,832
18. Wally Dallenbach	34	0	0	0	0	0	1	5	9,751	13	4	3,367	1,741,176
19. Kenny Irwin, Jr.	34	2	0	0	1	0	1	4	9,445	35	3	3,338	2,125,810
20. Jimmy Spencer	34	0	0	1	0	0	1	2	9,579	43	5	3,312	1,752,299
21. Bill Elliott	34	0	0	0	0	0	1	1	9,764	15	3	3,246	1,624,101
22. Kenny Wallace	34	0	0	1	0	0	2	2	8,805	56	1	3,210	1,416,208
23. Chad Little	34	0	0	0	0	0	0	5	9,465	3	3	3,193	1,623,976
24. Elliott Sadler	34	0	0	0	0	0	0	1	9,851	5	3	3,191	1,589,221
25. Kevin Lepage	34	1	0	0	0	0	1	1	9,646	20	2	3,185	1,587,841
26. Kyle Petty	32	0	0	0	0	0	0	9	8,708	11	4	3,103	1,278,953
27. Geoffrey Bodine	34	0	0	0	1	0	0	1	9,535	8	3	3,053	1,257,494
28. Johnny Benson	34	0	0	0	0	0	0	2	9,362	8	3	3,012	1,567,668
29. Michael Waltrip	34	0	0	0	0	0	1	2	9,022	48	6	2,974	1,701,160
30. Joe Nemechek	34	3	1	0	0	0	0	2	9,410	158	6	2,851	1,634,946
31. Ricky Rudd	34	1	0	0	2	0	1	2	9,230	21	3	2,922	1,632,011
32. Rick Mast	34	0	0	0	0	0	0	2	9,487	25	3	2,845	1,290,143
33. Ted Musgrave	32	0	0	0	0	0	0	2	9,063	5	2	2,689	1,162,403
34. Jerry Nadeau	34	0	0	0	0	0	1	1	9,476	9	1	2,686	1,370,229
35. Brett Bodine	32	0	0	0	0	0	0	0	8,940	4	3	2,351	1,321,396
36. David Green	32	1	0	0	0	0	0	0	8,273	7	1	2,320	1,079,536
37. Darrell Waltrip	27	0	0	0	0	0	0	0	7,204	3	2	2,158	973,133
38. Rich Bickle	24	0	0	0	0	0	0	2	6,343	1	1	2,149	892,456
39. Robert Pressley	28	0	0	0	0	0	0	0	7,785	3	3	2,050	1,033,223
40. Ernie Irvan	21	0	0	0	0	0	0	5	5,009	9	2	1,915	1,073,775
41. Ricky Craven	24	0	0	0	0	0	0	0	5,965	2	2	1,513	853,835
42. Dave Marcis	20	0	0	0	0	0	0	0	5,354	9	4	1,324	731,221
43. Hut Stricklin	10	0	0	0	0	0	0	1	3,091	0	0	918	378,942
44. Derrike Cope	15	0	0	0	0	0	0	0	3,489	0	0	915	617,976
45. Buckshot Jones	10	0	0	0	0	0	0	0	2,529	0	0	676	345,128
46. Todd Bodine	7	0	0	0	0	0	0	0	2,008	0	0	529	208,382
47. Dick Trickle	9	0	0	0	0	0	0	0	2,357	0	0	528	275,364
48. Dale Earnhardt, Jr.	5	0	0	0	0	0	0	1	1,363	1	1	500	162,095
49. Matt Kenseth	5	0	0	0	0	1	0	0	1,358	0	0	434	143,561
50. Steve Grissom	6	0	0	0	0	0	0	0	1,509	0	0	336	193,529

LAPS COMPLETED

1. Bobby Labonte — 10,011
2. Tony Stewart — 9,908
3. Mark Martin — 9,903
4. Dale Jarrett — 9,900
5. Jeff Burton — 9,878
6. Jeremy Mayfield — 9,870
7. Elliott Sadler — 9,851
8. Ward Burton — 9,828
9. Bobby Hamilton — 9,774
10. Bill Elliott — 9,764
11. Wally Dallenbach — 9,751
    Dale Earnhardt — 9,751
13. Mike Skinner — 9,732
14. Sterling Marlin — 9,711
15. Ken Schrader — 9,676
16. Kevin Lepage — 9,646
17. Rusty Wallace — 9,592
18. Jimmy Spencer — 9,579
19. Steve Park — 9,575
20. Geoffrey Bodine — 9,535
21. Rick Mast — 9,487
22. Jerry Nadeau — 9,476
23. Chad Little — 9,465
24. Kenny Irwin, Jr. — 9,445
25. Joe Nemechek — 9,410
26. Jeff Gordon — 9,384
27. Johnny Benson — 9,362
28. Terry Labonte — 9,325
29. Ricky Rudd — 9,230
30. Ted Musgrave — 9,063
31. Michael Waltrip — 9,022
32. Brett Bodine — 8,940
33. Kenny Wallace — 8,805
34. Kyle Petty — 8,708
35. John Andretti — 8,526
36. David Green — 8,273
37. Robert Pressley — 7,785
38. Darrell Waltrip — 7,204
39. Rich Bickle — 6,343
40. Ricky Craven — 5,965
41. Dave Marcis — 5,354
42. Ernie Irvan — 5,009
43. Derrike Cope — 3,489
44. Hut Stricklin — 3,091
45. Buckshot Jones — 2,529
46. Dick Trickle — 2,357
47. Todd Bodine — 2,008
48. Steve Grissom — 1,509
49. Dale Earnhardt, Jr. — 1,363
50. Matt Kenseth — 1,358

LAPS LED

1. Jeff Gordon — 1,320
2. Tony Stewart — 1,213
3. Bobby Labonte — 1,201
4. Dale Jarrett — 1,100
5. Jeff Burton — 1,063
6. Rusty Wallace — 1,009
7. Mark Martin — 701
8. Mike Skinner — 465
9. Terry Labonte — 350
10. Ward Burton — 243
11. John Andretti — 238
12. Dale Earnhardt — 230
13. Jeremy Mayfield — 221
14. Steve Park — 166
15. Joe Nemechek — 158
16. Sterling Marlin — 56
    Kenny Wallace — 56
18. Michael Waltrip — 48
19. Jimmy Spencer — 43
20. Kenny Irwin, Jr. — 35
21. Rick Mast — 25
22. Ricky Rudd — 21
23. Kevin Lepage — 20
24. Bill Elliott — 15
25. Wally Dallenbach — 13
26. Kyle Petty — 11
27. Ernie Irvan — 9
    Dave Marcis — 9
    Jerry Nadeau — 9
30. Johnny Benson — 8
    Geoffrey Bodine — 8
    Ken Schrader — 8
33. David Green — 7
34. Ted Musgrave — 5
    Elliott Sadler — 5
36. Brett Bodine — 4
37. Chad Little — 3
    Bobby Hamilton — 3
    Robert Pressley — 3
    Darrell Waltrip — 3
41. Ricky Craven — 2
42. Rich Bickle — 1
    Dale Earnhardt, Jr. — 1

MILES LED

1. Jeff Gordon — 1,921
2. Dale Jarrett — 1,852
3. Bobby Labonte — 1,689
4. Jeff Burton — 1,255
5. Tony Stewart — 1,059
6. Rusty Wallace — 1,013
7. Mark Martin — 879
8. Mike Skinner — 620
9. Dale Earnhardt — 394
10. Terry Labonte — 372
11. Ward Burton — 361
12. Jeremy Mayfield — 336
13. John Andretti — 281
14. Steve Park — 256
15. Joe Nemechek — 136
16. Michael Waltrip — 108
17. Sterling Marlin — 82
18. Jimmy Spencer — 78
19. Kenny Irwin, Jr. — 52
20. Ricky Rudd — 49
21. Rick Mast — 44
22. Bill Elliott — 35
23. Kevin Lepage — 34
24. Wally Dallenbach — 32
25. Kenny Wallace — 29
26. Jerry Nadeau — 22
    Boris Said III — 22
28. Ken Schrader — 17
29. Geoffrey Bodine — 16
    Ernie Irvan — 16

MILES DRIVEN

1. Bobby Labonte — 13,133
2. Tony Stewart — 12,998
3. Dale Jarrett — 12,987
4. Jeremy Mayfield — 12,931
5. Bobby Hamilton — 12,914
6. Elliott Sadler — 12,855
7. Mark Martin — 12,848
8. Jeff Burton — 12,784
9. Bill Elliott — 12,776
10. Dale Earnhardt — 12,760
11. Ken Schrader — 12,695
12. Wally Dallenbach — 12,640
13. Mike Skinner — 12,639
14. Sterling Marlin — 12,635
15. Kevin Lepage — 12,630
16. Ward Burton — 12,608
17. Rick Mast — 12,542
18. Jimmy Spencer — 12,333
19. Jerry Nadeau — 12,329
20. Geoffrey Bodine — 12,256
21. Steve Park — 12,243
22. Kenny Irwin, Jr. — 12,234
23. Terry Labonte — 12,221
24. Chad Little — 12,160
25. Rusty Wallace — 12,158
26. Jeff Gordon — 12,131
27. Ricky Rudd — 12,031
28. Joe Nemechek — 11,966
29. Johnny Benson, Jr. — 11,902
30. Michael Waltrip — 11,896

RACES LED

1. Bobby Labonte — 30
2. Jeff Gordon — 26
3. Mark Martin — 25
4. Dale Jarrett — 22
5. Jeff Burton — 18
6. Tony Stewart — 17
7. Mike Skinner — 14
8. Ward Burton — 13
9. Terry Labonte — 11
   Jeremy Mayfield — 11
   Rusty Wallace — 11
12. John Andretti — 10
13. Sterling Marlin — 9
14. Dale Earnhardt — 8
15. Joe Nemechek — 6
    Steve Park — 6
    Michael Waltrip — 6
18. Jimmy Spencer — 5
19. Wally Dallenbach — 4
    Dave Marcis — 4
    Kyle Petty — 4
22. Johnny Benson — 3
    Brett Bodine — 3
    Geoffrey Bodine — 3
    Bill Elliott — 3
    Kenny Irwin, Jr. — 3
    Chad Little — 3
    Rick Mast — 3
    Robert Pressley — 3
    Ricky Rudd — 3
    Elliott Sadler — 3
    Ken Schrader — 3
33. Ricky Craven — 2
    Bobby Hamilton — 2
    Ernie Irvan — 2
    Kevin Lepage — 2
    Ted Musgrave — 2
    Darrell Waltrip — 2
39. Rich Bickle — 1
    Dale Earnhardt, Jr. — 1
    David Green — 1
    Jerry Nadeau — 1
    Kenny Wallace — 1

Driver	Starts	Poles	Finish 1	2	3	4	5	6–10	Laps	Laps Led	Races Led	Winston Cup Points	$

2000

	Driver	Starts	Poles	1	2	3	4	5	6–10	Laps	Laps Led	Races Led	Winston Cup Points	$
1.	Bobby Labonte	34	3	4	4	4	2	5	5	10,158	464	23	5,130	4,041,746
2.	Dale Earnhardt	34	0	2	5	4	2	0	11	10,005	353	17	4,865	3,701,391
3.	Jeff Burton	34	1	4	5	2	1	3	7	9,656	1,131	22	4,836	5,121,354
4.	Dale Jarrett	34	3	2	3	1	5	4	9	9,750	333	15	4,684	5,225,499
5.	Ricky Rudd	34	2	0	1	5	3	3	7	10,048	362	14	4,575	2,385,404
6.	Tony Stewart	34	2	6	2	0	3	1	11	9,335	1,211	16	4,570	3,200,191
7.	Rusty Wallace	34	9	4	1	1	3	3	8	9,925	1,731	21	4,544	3,037,721
8.	Mark Martin	34	0	1	1	7	1	3	7	9,240	494	18	4,410	2,763,536
9.	Jeff Gordon	34	3	3	1	1	4	2	11	9,897	425	15	4,361	2,703,586
10.	Ward Burton	34	0	1	0	3	0	0	13	9,097	506	10	4,152	2,385,326
11.	Steve Park	34	2	1	0	1	3	1	7	9,925	290	11	3,934	2,052,827
12.	Mike Skinner	34	1	0	1	0	0	0	10	9,640	349	12	3,898	1,985,594
13.	Johnny Benson	33	0	0	2	0	0	1	4	9,451	62	5	3,716	1,627,874
14.	Matt Kenseth	34	0	1	1	1	0	1	7	9,466	161	7	3,711	2,150,764
15.	Joe Nemechek	34	1	0	1	1	0	1	6	9,467	8	3	3,534	1,907,281
16.	Dale Earnhardt, Jr.	34	2	2	0	0	1	0	2	9,644	426	10	3,516	2,610,396
17.	Terry Labonte	32	1	0	1	0	0	2	3	9,335	33	3	3,433	2,043,094
18.	Ken Schrader	34	0	0	0	0	0	0	2	9,954	33	5	3,398	1,530,844
19.	Sterling Marlin	34	0	0	1	0	0	0	6	9,459	82	6	3,363	1,819,644
20.	Jerry Nadeau	34	0	1	0	0	2	0	2	8,839	357	10	3,273	2,038,669
21.	Bill Elliott	32	0	0	0	2	1	0	4	8,636	111	8	3,267	2,447,788
22.	Jimmy Spencer	34	0	0	0	0	0	2	3	9,363	46	8	3,188	1,858,762
23.	John Andretti	34	0	0	0	0	0	0	2	9,217	11	6	3,169	1,964,402
24.	Jeremy Mayfield	32	4	2	3	0	1	0	6	8,268	850	17	3,156	2,090,501
25.	Robert Pressley	34	0	0	0	0	0	1	0	9,183	14	4	3,055	1,427,817
26.	Kenny Wallace	34	0	0	1	0	0	0	0	8,900	17	2	2,874	1,723,966
27.	Michael Waltrip	34	0	0	0	1	0	0	0	8,704	5	5	2,797	1,689,421
28.	Kevin Lepage	32	0	0	0	0	0	1	2	8,743	38	9	2,795	1,679,186
29.	Elliott Sadler	33	0	0	0	0	0	0	1	8,644	6	5	2,762	1,578,356
30.	Bobby Hamilton	34	0	0	0	0	0	0	2	8,903	64	4	2,715	1,619,775
31.	Dave Blaney	33	0	0	0	0	0	0	2	8,329	4	1	2,656	1,272,689
32.	Chad Little	27	0	0	0	0	0	0	1	7,178	7	5	2,634	1,418,884
33.	Rick Mast	29	0	0	0	0	0	0	2	8,185	1	1	2,366	1,156,427
34.	Wally Dallenbach	30	0	0	0	0	0	0	1	8,226	2	1	2,344	1,169,069
35.	Brett Bodine	29	0	0	0	0	0	0	0	8,336	5	2	2,145	1,020,659
36.	Darrell Waltrip	29	0	0	0	0	0	0	0	6,988	5	4	1,981	1,246,280
37.	Scott Pruett	28	0	0	0	0	0	0	1	6,216	23	2	1,879	1,135,854
38.	Stacy Compton	27	0	0	0	0	0	0	0	6,912	4	3	1,857	1,069,649
39.	Mike Bliss	25	0	0	0	0	0	0	1	5,492	4	1	1,748	953,948
40.	Ted Musgrave	18	0	0	0	0	0	0	0	4,951	7	6	1,614	827,216
41.	Kyle Petty	19	0	0	0	0	0	0	1	4,988	8	2	1,441	894,911
42.	Kenny Irwin, Jr.	17	0	0	0	0	1	0	0	4,304	2	2	1,440	949,436
43.	Robby Gordon	17	0	0	0	0	1	0	1	3,933	14	3	1,309	620,781
44.	Ricky Craven	16	0	0	0	0	0	0	0	4,153	64	2	1,175	636,522
45.	Geoffrey Bodine	14	0	0	0	0	0	0	0	2,780	20	1	1,039	704,981
46.	Dave Marcis	11	0	0	0	0	0	0	0	3,172	14	2	723	405,572
47.	Ed Berrier	10	0	0	0	0	0	0	0	2,086	0	0	628	417,144
48.	Kurt Busch	7	0	0	0	0	0	0	0	2,411	0	0	613	311,915
49.	Todd Bodine	5	0	0	0	0	0	0	1	881	0	0	456	234,065
50.	Hut Stricklin	7	0	0	0	0	0	0	0	1,248	0	0	436	255,200

LAPS COMPLETED

1.	Bobby Labonte	10,158
2.	Ricky Rudd	10,048
3.	Dale Earnhardt	10,005
4.	Ken Schrader	9,954
5.	Steve Park	9,925
	Rusty Wallace	9,925
7.	Jeff Gordon	9,897
8.	Dale Jarrett	9,750
9.	Jeff Burton	9,656
10.	Dale Earnhardt, Jr.	9,644
11.	Mike Skinner	9,640
12.	Joe Nemechek	9,467
13.	Matt Kenseth	9,466
14.	Sterling Marlin	9,459
15.	Johnny Benson	9,451
16.	Jimmy Spencer	9,363
17.	Terry Labonte	9,335
	Tony Stewart	9,335
19.	Mark Martin	9,240
20.	John Andretti	9,217
21.	Robert Pressley	9,183
22.	Ward Burton	9,097
23.	Bobby Hamilton	8,903
24.	Kenny Wallace	8,900
25.	Jerry Nadeau	8,839
26.	Kevin Lepage	8,743
27.	Michael Waltrip	8,704
28.	Elliott Sadler	8,644
29.	Bill Elliott	8,636
30.	Brett Bodine	8,336
31.	Dave Blaney	8,329
32.	Jeremy Mayfield	8,268
33.	Wally Dallenbach	8,226
34.	Rick Mast	8,185
35.	Chad Little	7,178
36.	Darrell Waltrip	6,988
37.	Stacy Compton	6,912
38.	Scott Pruett	6,216
39.	Mike Bliss	5,492
40.	Kyle Petty	4,988
41.	Ted Musgrave	4,951
42.	Kenny Irwin, Jr.	4,304
43.	Ricky Craven	4,153
44.	Robby Gordon	3,933
45.	Dave Marcis	3,172
46.	Geoffrey Bodine	2,780
47.	Kurt Busch	2,411
48.	Ed Berrier	2,086
49.	Hut Stricklin	1,248
50.	Todd Bodine	881

LAPS LED

1.	Rusty Wallace	1,731
2.	Tony Stewart	1,211
3.	Jeff Burton	1,131
4.	Jeremy Mayfield	850
5.	Ward Burton	506
6.	Mark Martin	494
7.	Bobby Labonte	464
8	Dale Earnhardt, Jr.	426
9.	Jeff Gordon	425
10.	Ricky Rudd	362
11.	Jerry Nadeau	357
12.	Dale Earnhardt	353
13.	Mike Skinner	349
14.	Dale Jarrett	333
15.	Steve Park	290
16.	Matt Kenseth	161
17.	Bill Elliott	111
18.	Sterling Marlin	82
19.	Ricky Craven	64
	Bobby Hamilton	64
21.	Johnny Benson	62
22.	Jimmy Spencer	46
23.	Kevin Lepage	38
24.	Terry Labonte	33
	Ken Schrader	33
26.	Scott Pruett	23
27.	Geoffrey Bodine	20
28.	Kenny Wallace	17
29.	Robby Gordon	14
	Dave Marcis	14
	Robert Pressley	14
32.	John Andretti	11
33.	Joe Nemechek	8
	Kyle Petty	8
35.	Chad Little	7
	Ted Musgrave	7
37.	Elliott Sadler	6
38.	Brett Bodine	5
	Darrell Waltrip	5
	Michael Waltrip	5
41.	Dave Blaney	4
	Mike Bliss	4
	Stacy Compton	4
44.	Wally Dallenbach	2
	Kenny Irwin, Jr.	2
46.	Rick Mast	1

MILES LED

1.	Rusty Wallace	1,866
2.	Tony Stewart	1,248
3.	Jeff Burton	1,104
4.	Jeremy Mayfield	1,069
5.	Mark Martin	768
6.	Dale Jarrett	691
7.	Dale Earnhardt, Jr.	648
8.	Ward Burton	637
9.	Bobby Labonte	630
10.	Ricky Rudd	547
11.	Jerry Nadeau	540
12.	Mike Skinner	539
13.	Dale Earnhardt	506
14.	Jeff Gordon	477
15.	Steve Park	327
16.	Matt Kenseth	300
17.	Bill Elliott	265
18.	Johnny Benson, Jr.	143
19.	Sterling Marlin	125
20.	Jimmy Spencer	83
21.	Bobby Hamilton	77
22.	Ricky Craven	67
23.	Kevin Lepage	56
24.	Terry Labonte	35
25.	Ken Schrader	34
26.	Kenny Wallace	33
27.	Robby Gordon	24
28.	Robert Pressley	23
29.	Geoffrey Bodine	21
30.	Dave Marcis	20
	Scott Pruett	20

MILES DRIVEN

1.	Bobby Labonte	13,270
2.	Dale Earnhardt	13,186
3.	Ricky Rudd	13,013
4.	Ken Schrader	12,920
5.	Rusty Wallace	12,902
6.	Steve Park	12,877
7.	Jeff Gordon	12,849
8.	Dale Jarrett	12,714
9.	Dale Earnhardt, Jr.	12,633
10.	Jeff Burton	12,626
	Mike Skinner	12,626
12.	Matt Kenseth	12,553
13.	Jimmy Spencer	12,308
14.	Tony Stewart	12,296
15.	Ward Burton	12,290
16.	Joe Nemechek	12,281
17.	Robert Pressley	12,260
18.	Johnny Benson, Jr.	12,195
19.	Sterling Marlin	12,097
20.	Terry Labonte	11,932
21.	Kenny Wallace	11,822
22.	Mark Martin	11,758
23.	John Andretti	11,656
24.	Dave Blaney	11,571
25.	Jerry Nadeau	11,508
26.	Bill Elliott	11,422
27.	Bobby Hamilton	11,304
28.	Michael Waltrip	11,244
29.	Rick Mast	11,055
30.	Elliott Sadler	11,045

RACES LED

1.	Bobby Labonte	23
2.	Jeff Burton	22
3.	Rusty Wallace	21
4.	Mark Martin	18
5.	Dale Earnhardt	17
	Jeremy Mayfield	17
7.	Tony Stewart	16
8.	Jeff Gordon	15
	Dale Jarrett	15
10.	Ricky Rudd	14
11.	Mike Skinner	12
12.	Steve Park	11
13.	Ward Burton	10
	Dale Earnhardt, Jr.	10
	Jerry Nadeau	10
16.	Kevin Lepage	9
17.	Bill Elliott	8
	Jimmy Spencer	8
19.	Matt Kenseth	7
20.	John Andretti	6
	Sterling Marlin	6
	Ted Musgrave	6
23.	Johnny Benson	5
	Chad Little	5
	Elliott Sadler	5
	Ken Schrader	5
	Michael Waltrip	5
28.	Bobby Hamilton	4
	Robert Pressley	4
	Darrell Waltrip	4
31.	Stacy Compton	3
	Robby Gordon	3
	Terry Labonte	3
	Joe Nemechek	3
35.	Brett Bodine	2
	Ricky Craven	2
	Kenny Irwin, Jr.	2
	Dave Marcis	2
	Kyle Petty	2
	Scott Pruett	2
	Kenny Wallace	2
42.	Dave Blaney	1
	Mike Bliss	1
	Geoffrey Bodine	1
	Wally Dallenbach	1
	Rick Mast	1

Driver	Starts	Poles	Finish						Laps	Laps Led	Races Led	Winston Cup Points	$
			1	2	3	4	5	6–10					

2001

#	Driver	Starts	Poles	1	2	3	4	5	6–10	Laps	Laps Led	Races Led	Winston Cup Points	$
1.	Jeff Gordon	36	6	6	6	3	2	1	6	10,638	2,322	25	5,112	10,879,757
2.	Tony Stewart	36	0	3	3	2	3	4	7	10,429	465	12	4,763	4,941,463
3.	Sterling Marlin	36	1	2	3	2	1	4	8	10,723	567	24	4,741	4,517,634
4.	Ricky Rudd	36	1	2	2	5	4	1	8	10,536	568	16	4,706	4,878,027
5.	Dale Jarrett	36	4	4	2	1	4	1	7	10,744	511	17	4,612	5,377,742
6.	Bobby Labonte	36	1	2	1	2	1	3	11	10,361	228	17	4,561	4,786,779
7.	Rusty Wallace	36	0	1	0	2	2	3	6	10,138	1,105	11	4,481	4,788,652
8.	Dale Earnhardt, Jr.	36	2	3	2	3	1	0	6	10,302	767	16	4,460	5,827,542
9.	Kevin Harvick	35	0	2	3	1	0	0	10	10,561	374	12	4,406	4,302,202
10.	Jeff Burton	36	0	2	1	2	1	2	8	10,463	401	10	4,394	4,230,737
11.	Johnny Benson	36	0	0	0	3	1	2	8	10,049	101	10	4,152	2,894,903
12.	Mark Martin	36	2	0	0	0	2	1	12	10,138	190	19	4,095	3,797,006
13.	Matt Kenseth	36	0	0	0	0	4	0	5	10,341	100	14	3,982	2,565,579
14.	Ward Burton	36	0	1	0	2	1	2	4	10,158	178	7	3,846	3,583,692
15.	Bill Elliott	36	2	1	0	1	1	2	4	9,915	171	9	3,824	3,618,017
16.	Jimmy Spencer	36	2	0	0	0	2	1	5	10,259	214	11	3,782	2,669,638
17.	Jerry Nadeau	36	0	0	1	1	1	1	6	10,238	180	7	3,675	2,507,827
18.	Bobby Hamilton	36	0	1	0	0	1	1	4	10,750	239	4	3,575	2,527,310
19.	Ken Schrader	36	0	0	0	0	0	0	5	10,534	10	3	3,480	2,418,181
20.	Elliott Sadler	36	0	1	0	1	0	0	0	10,392	125	8	3,471	2,683,225
21.	Ricky Craven	36	1	1	1	0	1	1	3	9,670	170	9	3,379	1,996,981
22.	Dave Blaney	35	0	0	0	0	0	0	6	9,872	71	2	3,303	1,827,896
23.	Terry Labonte	36	0	0	0	0	0	1	2	10,517	0	0	3,280	3,011,901
24.	Michael Waltrip	36	0	1	2	0	0	0	0	9,527	88	8	3,159	3,411,644
25.	Robert Pressley	34	0	0	1	0	0	0	4	9,154	5	4	3,156	2,171,520
26.	Casey Atwood	35	1	0	0	1	0	0	2	9,473	137	4	3,132	1,979,111
27.	Kurt Busch	35	1	0	0	1	1	1	3	8,965	160	5	3,081	2,170,629
28.	Joe Nemechek	31	0	1	0	0	0	0	3	8,706	227	6	2,994	2,510,723
29.	Todd Bodine	35	3	0	0	0	0	2	0	9,161	110	11	2,960	1,740,315
30.	Brett Bodine	36	0	0	0	0	0	0	2	9,968	3	3	2,948	1,740,526
31.	John Andretti	35	0	0	1	0	0	0	1	9,994	53	2	2,943	2,873,184
32.	Steve Park	24	0	1	3	0	1	0	7	6,368	477	8	2,859	2,385,971
33.	Stacy Compton	35	2	0	0	0	0	0	1	9,605	29	5	2,752	1,704,962
34.	Mike Wallace	29	0	0	1	0	0	0	5	8,684	61	4	2,693	2,075,044
35.	Jeremy Mayfield	28	0	0	0	3	1	1	2	7,286	60	3	2,651	2,682,603
36.	Kevin Lepage	29	0	0	0	0	0	0	1	8,557	13	2	2,461	1,424,852
37.	Jason Leffler	30	1	0	0	0	0	0	1	7,983	15	3	2,413	1,724,692
38.	Ron Hornaday, Jr.	32	0	0	0	0	0	0	1	8,659	29	3	2,305	1,435,857
39.	Kenny Wallace	24	1	0	1	0	0	0	1	7,334	104	4	2,054	1,507,922
40.	Mike Skinner	23	0	0	0	0	0	0	1	6,718	46	3	2,029	1,921,186
41.	Buckshot Jones	30	0	0	0	0	0	0	0	7,819	2	2	1,939	1,631,488
42.	Hut Stricklin	22	0	0	0	0	0	0	1	6,215	0	0	1,770	1,006,021
43.	Kyle Petty	24	0	0	0	0	0	0	0	5,026	1	1	1,673	1,008,919
44.	Robby Gordon	17	0	1	1	0	0	0	1	4,401	50	3	1,552	1,371,900
45.	Rick Mast	17	0	0	0	0	0	0	0	4,543	0	0	1,187	680,321
46.	Andy Houston	17	0	0	0	0	0	0	0	3,612	1	1	1,123	865,263
47.	Bobby Hamilton, Jr.	10	0	0	0	0	0	0	0	2,577	0	0	748	546,847
48.	Jeff Green	8	1	0	0	0	0	0	1	1,758	71	1	539	441,449
49.	Ryan Newman	7	1	0	1	0	0	1	0	1,478	13	2	497	465,276
50.	Boris Said III	2	0	0	0	0	0	0	1	202	0	0	272	124,340

LAPS COMPLETED

1. Bobby Hamilton — 10,750
2. Dale Jarrett — 10,744
3. Sterling Marlin — 10,723
4. Jeff Gordon — 10,638
5. Kevin Harvick — 10,561
6. Ricky Rudd — 10,536
7. Ken Schrader — 10,534
8. Terry Labonte — 10,517
9. Jeff Burton — 10,463
10. Tony Stewart — 10,429
11. Elliott Sadler — 10,392
12. Bobby Labonte — 10,361
13. Matt Kenseth — 10,341
14. Dale Earnhardt, Jr. — 10,302
15. Jimmy Spencer — 10,259
16. Jerry Nadeau — 10,238
17. Ward Burton — 10,158
18. Mark Martin — 10,138
    Rusty Wallace — 10,138
20. Johnny Benson — 10,049
21. John Andretti — 9,994
22. Brett Bodine — 9,968
23. Bill Elliott — 9,915
24. Dave Blaney — 9,872
25. Ricky Craven — 9,670
26. Stacy Compton — 9,605
27. Michael Waltrip — 9,527
28. Casey Atwood — 9,473
29. Todd Bodine — 9,161
30. Robert Pressley — 9,154
31. Kurt Busch — 8,965
32. Joe Nemechek — 8,706
33. Mike Wallace — 8,684
34. Ron Hornaday, Jr. — 8,659
35. Kevin Lepage — 8,557
36. Jason Leffler — 7,983
37. Buckshot Jones — 7,819
38. Kenny Wallace — 7,334
39. Jeremy Mayfield — 7,286
40. Mike Skinner — 6,718
41. Steve Park — 6,368
42. Hut Stricklin — 6,215
43. Kyle Petty — 5,026
44. Rick Mast — 4,543
45. Robby Gordon — 4,401
46. Andy Houston — 3,612
47. Bobby Hamilton, Jr. — 2,577
48. Jeff Green — 1,758
49. Ryan Newman — 1,478
50. Boris Said III — 202

LAPS LED

1. Jeff Gordon — 2,322
2. Rusty Wallace — 1,105
3. Dale Earnhardt, Jr. — 767
4. Ricky Rudd — 568
5. Sterling Marlin — 567
6. Dale Jarrett — 511
7. Steve Park — 477
8. Tony Stewart — 465
9. Jeff Burton — 401
10. Kevin Harvick — 374
11. Bobby Hamilton — 239
12. Bobby Labonte — 228
13. Joe Nemechek — 227
14. Jimmy Spencer — 214
15. Mark Martin — 190
16. Jerry Nadeau — 180
17. Ward Burton — 178
18. Bill Elliott — 171
19. Ricky Craven — 170
20. Kurt Busch — 160
21. Casey Atwood — 137
22. Elliott Sadler — 125
23. Todd Bodine — 110
24. Kenny Wallace — 104
25. Johnny Benson — 101
26. Matt Kenseth — 100
27. Michael Waltrip — 88
28. Dave Blaney — 71
    Jeff Green — 71
30. Mike Wallace — 61
31. Jeremy Mayfield — 60
32. John Andretti — 53
33. Robby Gordon — 50
34. Mike Skinner — 46
35. Stacy Compton — 29
36. Ron Hornaday, Jr. — 29
37. Jason Leffler — 15
38. Kevin Lepage — 13
    Ryan Newman — 13
40. Ken Schrader — 10
41. Robert Pressley — 5
42. Brett Bodine — 3
43. Buckshot Jones — 2
44. Andy Houston — 1
    Kyle Petty — 1

MILES LED

1. Jeff Gordon — 3,032
2. Dale Earnhardt, Jr. — 1,354
3. Sterling Marlin — 905
4. Rusty Wallace — 878
5. Dale Jarrett — 756
6. Ricky Rudd — 695
7. Steve Park — 600
8. Tony Stewart — 589
9. Jeff Burton — 466
10. Kevin Harvick — 420
11. Jimmy Spencer — 375
12. Bobby Labonte — 351
13. Bill Elliott — 295
14. Ward Burton — 279
15. Jerry Nadeau — 261
16. Joe Nemechek — 255
17. Michael Waltrip — 222
18. Mark Martin — 215
19. Kurt Busch — 175
20. Johnny Benson, Jr. — 173
21. Casey Atwood — 164
22. Bobby Hamilton — 162
23. Todd Bodine — 159
24. Matt Kenseth — 144
25. Ricky Craven — 119
26. Dave Blaney — 109
27. Kenny Wallace — 105
28. Mike Skinner — 102
29. Robby Gordon — 89
30. Elliott Sadler — 88

MILES DRIVEN

1. Sterling Marlin — 14,102
2. Bobby Hamilton — 14,100
3. Dale Jarrett — 14,047
4. Jeff Gordon — 14,026
5. Ken Schrader — 13,997
6. Tony Stewart — 13,978
7. Jeff Burton — 13,937
8. Terry Labonte — 13,909
9. Ricky Rudd — 13,843
10. Dale Earnhardt, Jr. — 13,685
11. Mark Martin — 13,681
12. Kevin Harvick — 13,667
13. Bobby Labonte — 13,579
14. Matt Kenseth — 13,568
15. Elliott Sadler — 13,541
16. Jerry Nadeau — 13,511
17. Brett Bodine — 13,469
18. Bill Elliott — 13,458
19. Johnny Benson, Jr. — 13,414
20. Jimmy Spencer — 13,330
21. Rusty Wallace — 13,219
22. Ward Burton — 13,166
23. John Andretti — 12,997
24. Michael Waltrip — 12,823
25. Dave Blaney — 12,821
26. Stacy Compton — 12,810
27. Ricky Craven — 12,787
28. Robert Pressley — 12,464
29. Kurt Busch — 11,994
30. Todd Bodine — 11,981

RACES LED

1. Jeff Gordon — 25
2. Sterling Marlin — 24
3. Mark Martin — 19
4. Dale Jarrett — 17
   Bobby Labonte — 17
6. Dale Earnhardt, Jr. — 16
   Ricky Rudd — 16
8. Matt Kenseth — 14
9. Kevin Harvick — 12
   Tony Stewart — 12
11. Todd Bodine — 11
    Jimmy Spencer — 11
    Rusty Wallace — 11
14. Johnny Benson — 10
    Jeff Burton — 10
16. Ricky Craven — 9
    Bill Elliott — 9
18. Steve Park — 8
    Elliott Sadler — 8
    Michael Waltrip — 8
21. Ward Burton — 7
    Jerry Nadeau — 7
23. Joe Nemechek — 6
24. Kurt Busch — 5
    Stacy Compton — 5
26. Casey Atwood — 4
    Bobby Hamilton — 4
    Robert Pressley — 4
    Kenny Wallace — 4
    Mike Wallace — 4
31. Brett Bodine — 3
    Robby Gordon — 3
    Ron Hornaday, Jr. — 3
    Jason Leffler — 3
    Jeremy Mayfield — 3
    Ken Schrader — 3
    Mike Skinner — 3
38. John Andretti — 2
    Dave Blaney — 2
    Kevin Lepage — 2
    Buckshot Jones — 2
    Ryan Newman — 2
43. Jeff Green — 1
    Andy Houston — 1
    Kyle Petty — 1

121

2002

Driver	Starts	Poles	Finish 1	2	3	4	5	6–10	Laps	Laps Led	Races Led	Winston Cup Points	$
1. Tony Stewart	36	4	3	3	4	2	3	6	10,181	746	17	4,800	9,163,761
2. Mark Martin	36	0	1	3	2	3	3	10	10,517	363	15	4,762	7,004,893
3. Kurt Busch	36	1	4	3	2	3	0	8	10,259	933	20	4,641	5,105,394
4. Jeff Gordon	36	3	3	2	1	2	5	7	10,201	989	14	4,607	6,154,475
5. Jimmie Johnson	36	5	3	0	2	1	0	15	10,521	838	14	4,600	3,788,268
6. Ryan Newman	36	6	1	5	1	3	4	8	9,871	753	22	4,593	5,346,651
7. Rusty Wallace	36	1	0	4	1	1	1	10	10,591	202	9	4,574	4,785,134
8. Matt Kenseth	36	1	5	2	1	2	1	8	10,303	692	16	4,432	4,514,203
9. Dale Jarrett	36	1	2	1	3	2	2	8	9,881	441	15	4,415	4,421,951
10. Ricky Rudd	36	1	1	0	4	2	1	4	10,195	357	11	4,323	4,444,614
11. Dale Earnhardt, Jr.	36	2	2	1	1	4	3	5	10,344	1,068	22	4,270	4,970,034
12. Jeff Burton	36	0	0	0	3	2	0	9	9,980	124	13	4,259	4,244,856
13. Bill Elliott	36	4	2	1	1	1	1	7	10,352	275	13	4,158	4,122,699
14. Michael Waltrip	36	0	1	1	0	1	1	6	9,928	180	12	3,985	3,185,969
15. Ricky Craven	36	2	0	0	1	0	2	6	10,054	382	11	3,888	2,838,087
16. Bobby Labonte	36	0	1	1	1	0	2	2	10,135	123	5	3,810	4,183,715
17. Jeff Green	36	0	0	1	1	0	2	2	10,325	120	5	3,704	2,531,339
18. Sterling Marlin	29	2	2	1	2	2	1	6	7,844	451	12	3,703	4,228,889
19. Dave Blaney	36	0	0	0	0	0	0	5	10,305	65	9	3,670	2,978,593
20. Robby Gordon	36	0	0	0	1	0	0	4	10,294	44	4	3,632	3,342,703
21. Kevin Harvick	35	1	1	0	2	1	1	3	9,566	178	8	3,501	3,849,216
22. Kyle Petty	36	0	0	0	0	0	0	1	10,423	22	4	3,501	2,198,073
23. Elliott Sadler	36	0	0	2	0	0	0	5	9,789	29	8	3,418	3,491,694
24. Terry Labonte	36	0	0	0	1	0	0	3	9,966	11	1	3,417	3,244,240
25. Ward Burton	36	1	2	0	0	0	1	5	8,931	371	11	3,362	4,899,884
26. Jeremy Mayfield	36	0	0	1	0	0	1	2	10,117	30	5	3,309	2,494,583
27. Jimmy Spencer	34	0	0	1	0	1	0	4	9,684	174	3	3,187	2,136,792
28. John Andretti	36	0	0	0	0	0	1	9,743	22	5	3,161	2,954,229
29. Johnny Benson	31	0	1	1	0	1	0	4	8,310	116	6	3,132	2,791,879
30. Ken Schrader	36	0	0	0	0	0	0	0	9,812	46	1	2,954	2,460,140
31. Mike Skinner	36	0	0	0	0	0	0	1	10,074	2	2	2,886	2,094,232
32. Bobby Hamilton	31	0	0	0	0	0	0	3	8,824	57	3	2,832	2,196,956
33. Steve Park	32	0	0	0	0	0	0	2	8,721	50	2	2,694	2,681,594
34. Joe Nemechek	33	0	0	2	0	1	0	0	8,165	178	4	2,682	2,454,482
35. Casey Atwood	35	0	0	0	0	0	0	0	9,454	0	0	2,621	1,988,254
36. Brett Bodine	32	0	0	0	0	0	0	0	8,817	3	3	2,276	1,766,820
37. Jerry Nadeau	28	0	0	0	0	0	0	1	7,347	102	4	2,250	1,806,133
38. Todd Bodine	24	1	0	0	0	0	1	3	5,552	19	3	1,987	1,879,767
39. Kenny Wallace	21	0	0	0	0	0	0	1	5,742	4	2	1,868	1,379,803
40. Hut Stricklin	22	0	0	0	0	0	0	0	5,936	5	2	1,781	1,313,548
41. Mike Wallace	21	0	0	0	0	0	0	1	5,267	1	1	1,551	1,274,703
42. Stacy Compton	21	0	0	0	0	0	0	0	5,282	5	3	1,527	1,185,709
43. Geoffrey Bodine	10	0	0	0	1	0	0	1	1,832	5	1	837	1,224,501
44. Steve Grissom	10	0	0	0	0	0	0	1	3,070	0	0	769	529,781
45. Hermie Sadler	10	0	0	0	0	0	0	0	3,458	0	0	688	473,290
46. Jamie McMurray	6	0	1	0	0	0	0	1	1,680	97	2	679	717,942
47. Rick Mast	9	0	0	0	0	0	0	0	3,033	0	0	576	469,843
48. Greg Biffle	7	0	0	0	0	0	0	0	1,914	12	1	570	394,773
49. Buckshot Jones	7	0	0	0	0	0	0	0	2,218	0	0	559	394,223
50. Ted Musgrave	5	0	0	0	0	0	0	0	1,537	0	0	452	283,770

Laps Completed		Laps Led		Miles Led		Miles Driven		Races Led	
1. Rusty Wallace	10,591	1. Dale Earnhardt, Jr.	1,068	1. Dale Earnhardt, Jr.	1,362	1. Jimmie Johnson	13,915	1. Dale Earnhardt, Jr.	22
2. Jimmie Johnson	10,521	2. Jeff Gordon	989	2. Kurt Busch	1,203	2. Mark Martin	13,838	Ryan Newman	22
3. Mark Martin	10,517	3. Kurt Busch	933	3. Jeff Gordon	1,156	3. Rusty Wallace	13,824	3. Kurt Busch	20
4. Kyle Petty	10,423	4. Jimmie Johnson	838	4. Jimmie Johnson	1,130	4. Kyle Petty	13,701	4. Tony Stewart	17
5. Bill Elliott	10,352	5. Ryan Newman	753	5. Tony Stewart	918	5. Bill Elliott	13,665	5. Matt Kenseth	16
6. Dale Earnhardt, Jr.	10,344	6. Tony Stewart	746	6. Ryan Newman	905	6. Jeff Green	13,561	6. Dale Jarrett	15
7. Jeff Green	10,325	7. Matt Kenseth	692	7. Matt Kenseth	862	7. Ricky Rudd	13,559	Mark Martin	15
8. Dave Blaney	10,305	8. Sterling Marlin	451	8. Sterling Marlin	845	8. Jeff Gordon	13,552	8. Jeff Gordon	14
9. Matt Kenseth	10,303	9. Dale Jarrett	441	9. Dale Jarrett	698	9. Robby Gordon	13,548	Jimmie Johnson	14
10. Robby Gordon	10,294	10. Ricky Craven	382	10. Bill Elliott	573	10. Dale Earnhardt, Jr.	13,525	10. Jeff Burton	13
11. Kurt Busch	10,259	11. Ward Burton	371	11. Ricky Rudd	490	11. Dave Blaney	13,517	Bill Elliott	13
12. Jeff Gordon	10,201	12. Mark Martin	363	12. Mark Martin	456	12. Matt Kenseth	13,428	12. Sterling Marlin	12
13. Ricky Rudd	10,195	13. Ricky Rudd	357	13. Michael Waltrip	364	13. Bobby Labonte	13,355	Michael Waltrip	12
14. Tony Stewart	10,181	14. Bill Elliott	275	14. Ricky Craven	332	14. Terry Labonte	13,248	14. Ward Burton	11
15. Bobby Labonte	10,135	15. Rusty Wallace	202	15. Ward Burton	282	15. Jeff Burton	13,205	Ricky Craven	11
16. Jeremy Mayfield	10,117	16. Michael Waltrip	180	16. Joe Nemechek	280	16. Elliott Sadler	13,183	Ricky Rudd	11
17. Mike Skinner	10,074	17. Kevin Harvick	178	17. Kevin Harvick	271	17. Michael Waltrip	13,175	17. Dave Blaney	9
18. Ricky Craven	10,054	Joe Nemechek	178	18. Rusty Wallace	221	18. Mike Skinner	13,136	Rusty Wallace	9
19. Jeff Burton	9,980	19. Jimmy Spencer	174	19. Jeff Burton	213	19. Tony Stewart	13,134	19. Kevin Harvick	8
20. Terry Labonte	9,966	20. Jeff Burton	124	20. Jimmy Spencer	153	20. Ricky Craven	13,110	Elliott Sadler	8
21. Michael Waltrip	9,928	21. Bobby Labonte	123	21. Jamie McMurray	145	21. Ryan Newman	13,101	21. Johnny Benson	6
22. Dale Jarrett	9,881	22. Jeff Green	120	22. Bobby Labonte	126	22. Kurt Busch	13,099	22. John Andretti	5
23. Ryan Newman	9,871	23. Johnny Benson	116	23. Jeff Green	120	23. Dale Jarrett	13,041	Jeff Green	5
24. Ken Schrader	9,812	24. Jerry Nadeau	102	24. Ken Schrader	115	24. Jeremy Mayfield	12,934	Bobby Labonte	5
25. Elliott Sadler	9,789	25. Jamie McMurray	97	25. Robby Gordon	111	25. John Andretti	12,881	Jeremy Mayfield	5
26. John Andretti	9,743	26. Dave Blaney	65	26. Jerry Nadeau	108	26. Kevin Harvick	12,777	26. Robby Gordon	4
27. Jimmy Spencer	9,684	27. Bobby Hamilton	57	27. Johnny Benson, Jr.	105	27. Jimmy Spencer	12,576	Jerry Nadeau	4
28. Kevin Harvick	9,566	28. Steve Park	50	28. Dave Blaney	88	28. Casey Atwood	12,402	Joe Nemechek	4
29. Casey Atwood	9,454	29. Ken Schrader	46	29. Jeremy Mayfield	58	29. Ken Schrader	12,323	Kyle Petty	4
30. Ward Burton	8,931	30. Robby Gordon	44	30. Steve Park	49	30. Bobby Hamilton	11,617	30. Brett Bodine	3
31. Bobby Hamilton	8,824	31. Jeremy Mayfield	30					Todd Bodine	3
32. Brett Bodine	8,817	32. Elliott Sadler	29					Stacy Compton	3
33. Steve Park	8,721	33. John Andretti	22					Bobby Hamilton	3
34. Johnny Benson	8,310	Kyle Petty	22					Jimmy Spencer	3
35. Joe Nemechek	8,165	35. Todd Bodine	19					35. Steve Park	2
36. Sterling Marlin	7,844	36. Greg Biffle	12					Jamie McMurray	2
37. Jerry Nadeau	7,347	37. Terry Labonte	11					Mike Skinner	2
38. Hut Stricklin	5,936	38. Geoffrey Bodine	5					Hut Stricklin	2
39. Kenny Wallace	5,742	Stacy Compton	5					Kenny Wallace	2
40. Todd Bodine	5,552	Hut Stricklin	5					40. Greg Biffle	1
41. Stacy Compton	5,282	41. Kenny Wallace	4					Geoffrey Bodine	1
42. Mike Wallace	5,267	42. Brett Bodine	3					Terry Labonte	1
43. Hermie Sadler	3,458	43. Mike Skinner	2					Ken Schrader	1
44. Steve Grissom	3,070	44. Mike Wallace	1					Mike Wallace	1
45. Rick Mast	3,033								
46. Buckshot Jones	2,218								
47. Greg Biffle	1,914								
48. Geoffrey Bodine	1,832								
49. Jamie McMurray	1,680								
50. Ted Musgrave	1,537								

PART 3
THE DRIVERS

Year	Rank	Starts	Poles	Finish						Laps	Laps Led	Races Led	Miles	$
				1	2	3	4	5	6–10					

Richard Petty

Richard Lee Petty (The King)
B: 7/2/1937
Racing Hometown: Randleman, NC

Year	Rank	Starts	Poles	1	2	3	4	5	6–10	Laps	Laps Led	Races Led	Miles	$
1958	37	9	0	0	0	0	0	0	1	977	0	0	410	760
1959	15	21	0	0	1	3	1	1	3	3,654	7	1	2,422	8,111
1960	2	40	2	3	6	3	3	1	14	8,189	418	5	6,015	41,873
1961	8	42	2	2	4	4	5	3	5	7,866	703	7	5,392	15,096
1990	26	29	0	0	0	0	0	0	1	7,438	5	1	9,165	169,465
1991	24	29	0	0	0	0	0	0	1	8,341	1	1	9,646	268,035
1992	26	29	0	0	0	0	0	0	0	7,977	5	1	9,624	348,870
Lifetime		1184	127	200	157	104	52	42	157	307,848	50,572	594	304,035	$8,515,325

Key

RANK	Rank that year as according to Winston Cup Points
STARTS	Number of starts that year
POLES	Number of poles that year
FINISH	
1	Number of first place finishes that year
2	Number of second place finishes that year
3	Number of third place finishes that year
4	Number of fourth place finishes that year
5	Number of fifth place finishes that year
6–10	Number of sixth through tenth place finishes that year
LAPS	Number of laps completed that year (a blank entry indicates that the information is not available or incomplete)
LAPS LED	Number of laps led that year
RACES LED	Number of races led that year
MILES	Number of miles driven that year (a blank entry indicates that the information is not available or incomplete)
$	Winnings for that year (includes post-season and special event earnings)
N/A	Information not available or incomplete
NR	Not ranked, no points at season's end

*Please note a driver will occasionally win money without having any starts. The winnings were derived from special events which were not part of the official NASCAR Winston Cup schedule.

*Please also note that the above record is incomplete and shown here for example purposes only.

Year	Rank	Starts	Poles	1	2	3	Finish 4	5	6–10	Laps	Laps Led	Races Led	Miles	$

Paul Aars

Paul Aars
Racing Hometown: San Mateo, CA

Year	Rank	Starts	Poles	1	2	3	4	5	6–10	Laps	Laps Led	Races Led	Miles	$
1958	67	1	0	0	0	0	0	0	1	168	0	0	442	200
Lifetime		1	0	0	0	0	0	0	1	168	0	0	442	$200

Bobby Abel

Robert Abel
B: 4/20/1930   D: 1/31/1995
Racing Hometown: Wrightsville, PA

Year	Rank	Starts	Poles	1	2	3	4	5	6–10	Laps	Laps Led	Races Led	Miles	$
1957	NR	1	0	0	0	0	0	0	0	57	0	0	57	0
Lifetime		1	0	0	0	0	0	0	0	57	0	0	57	$0

Marv Acton

Marv Acton
B: 2/3/1944
Racing Hometown: Porterville, CA

Year	Rank	Starts	Poles	1	2	3	4	5	6–10	Laps	Laps Led	Races Led	Miles	$
1971	44	11	0	0	0	0	0	0	0	1,421	0	0	2,399	8,620
1974	NR	1	0	0	0	0	0	0	0	66	0	0	41	365
1977	92	2	0	0	0	0	0	0	0	359	0	0	202	945
Lifetime		14	0	0	0	0	0	0	0	1,846	0	0	2,642	$9,930

Bill Adams

William Adams
Racing Hometown: Ambridge, PA

Year	Rank	Starts	Poles	1	2	3	4	5	6–10	Laps	Laps Led	Races Led	Miles	$
1953	48	2	0	0	0	0	0	0	1	36	0	0	148	250
Lifetime		2	0	0	0	0	0	0	1	36	0	0	148	$250

Boyd Adams

Boyd Adams
Racing Hometown: Nashville, TN

Year	Rank	Starts	Poles	1	2	3	4	5	6–10	Laps	Laps Led	Races Led	Miles	$
1965	135	1	0	0	0	0	0	0	0	15	0	0	8	100
Lifetime		1	0	0	0	0	0	0	0	15	0	0	8	$100

Carl Adams

Carl Adams
B: 4/24/1942
Racing Hometown: National City, CA

Year	Rank	Starts	Poles	1	2	3	4	5	6–10	Laps	Laps Led	Races Led	Miles	$
1972	75	2	0	0	0	0	0	0	1	320	0	0	818	3,170
1973	69	2	0	0	0	0	0	0	0	290	0	0	760	2,030
1974	51	5	0	0	0	0	0	0	0	732	0	0	1,478	5,705
1975	23	20	0	0	0	0	0	0	4	5,332	0	0	5,828	24,865
Lifetime		29	0	0	0	0	0	0	5	6,674	0	0	8,883	$35,770

Serge Adams

Serge Adams
Racing Hometown: Montreal, Que, Canada

Year	Rank	Starts	Poles	1	2	3	4	5	6–10	Laps	Laps Led	Races Led	Miles	$
1968	68	3	0	0	0	0	0	0	0	368	0	0	440	1,260
Lifetime		3	0	0	0	0	0	0	0	368	0	0	440	$1,260

Weldon Adams

Weldon Adams
B: 1938   D: 5/9/1995
Racing Hometown: Augusta, GA

Year	Rank	Starts	Poles	1	2	3	4	5	6–10	Laps	Laps Led	Races Led	Miles	$
1950	15	4	0	0	0	1	0	1	1	560	0	0	555	1,205
1951	N/A	11	0	0	0	0	0	0	2	246	0	0	237	425
1952	40	6	0	0	0	0	0	0	2	708	0	0	537	275
1953	150	2	0	0	0	0	0	0	0	217	0	0	298	135
1962	115	1	0	0	0	0	0	0	0	90	0	0	45	85
1964	129	1	0	0	0	0	0	0	0	2	0	0	6	525
Lifetime		25	0	0	0	1	0	1	5	1,823	0	0	1,678	$2,650

Grant Adcox

Grant Adcox
B: 1/2/1950   D: 11/19/1989   *Killed in Atlanta NASCAR race.*
Racing Hometown: Chattanooga, TN

Year	Rank	Starts	Poles	1	2	3	4	5	6–10	Laps	Laps Led	Races Led	Miles	$
1974	54	4	0	0	0	0	0	0	0	979	8	1	1,375	5,935
1975	33	11	0	0	0	0	0	0	1	1,652	0	0	2,884	17,525
1976	31	11	0	0	0	0	0	0	2	3,326	0	0	4,916	25,715
1977	49	6	0	0	0	0	0	0	0	776	0	0	1,482	8,750

Year	Rank	Starts	Poles	Finish 1	2	3	4	5	6–10	Laps	Laps Led	Races Led	Miles	$

Grant Adcox *continued*

Year	Rank	Starts	Poles	1	2	3	4	5	6–10	Laps	Laps Led	Races Led	Miles	$
1978	30	14	0	0	0	0	0	1	2	3,072	0	0	4,586	37,100
1979	36	6	0	0	0	0	0	0	0	1,132	5	1	2,104	15,290
1983	95T	1	0	0	0	0	0	0	0	1	0	0	3	1,790
1984	91T	1	0	0	0	0	0	0	0	1	0	0	3	1,800
1985	70	2	0	0	0	0	0	0	0	169	0	0	426	4,590
1986	101T	1	0	0	0	0	0	0	0	154	0	0	385	2,195
1989	51	3	0	0	0	0	0	0	0	541	0	0	1,188	11,815
Lifetime		60	0	0	0	0	0	1	5	11,803	13	2	19,352	$132,505

Allen Adkins

Allen Adkins
B: 3/29/1929
Racing Hometown: Clovis, CA

Year	Rank	Starts	Poles	1	2	3	4	5	6–10	Laps	Laps Led	Races Led	Miles	$
1954	46	2	0	0	0	1	1	0	0	545	0	0	397	1,150
1955	46	4	0	0	1	0	0	1	0	601	80	1	502	1,160
1956	42	6	0	0	0	0	0	1	2	1,016	0	0	1,101	1,465
1957	95	2	0	0	0	0	0	0	1	252	0	0	193	350
Lifetime		14	0	0	1	1	1	2	3	2,414	80	1	2,192	$4,125

Blair Aiken

Blair Aiken
B: 9/2/1956
Racing Hometown: Lakeport, CA

Year	Rank	Starts	Poles	1	2	3	4	5	6–10	Laps	Laps Led	Races Led	Miles	$
1985	72	2	0	0	0	0	0	0	0	135	0	0	354	2,020
Lifetime		2	0	0	0	0	0	0	0	135	0	0	354	$2,020

Thomas Aiken

Thomas Aiken
Racing Hometown: Atlanta, GA

Year	Rank	Starts	Poles	1	2	3	4	5	6–10	Laps	Laps Led	Races Led	Miles	$
1958	121	1	0	0	0	0	0	0	0	93	0	0	93	110
Lifetime		1	0	0	0	0	0	0	0	93	0	0	93	$110

Chuck Akerblade

Chuck Akerblade
Racing Hometown: Portland, OR

Year	Rank	Starts	Poles	1	2	3	4	5	6–10	Laps	Laps Led	Races Led	Miles	$
1956	169	1	0	0	0	0	0	0	0	238	0	0	119	100
Lifetime		1	0	0	0	0	0	0	0	238	0	0	119	$100

Will Albright

Will Albright
Racing Hometown: Graham, NC

Year	Rank	Starts	Poles	1	2	3	4	5	6–10	Laps	Laps Led	Races Led	Miles	$
1950	136	1	0	0	0	0	0	0	0	43	0	0	179	50
Lifetime		1	0	0	0	0	0	0	0	43	0	0	179	$50

Ronnie Alderman

Ronnie Alderman

Year	Rank	Starts	Poles	1	2	3	4	5	6–10	Laps	Laps Led	Races Led	Miles	$
1973	118	1	0	0	0	0	0	0	0	34	0	0	89	655
Lifetime		1	0	0	0	0	0	0	0	34	0	0	89	$655

John Alexander

John Alexander
B: 5/22/1954
Racing Hometown: Elmira, NY

Year	Rank	Starts	Poles	1	2	3	4	5	6–10	Laps	Laps Led	Races Led	Miles	$
1990	101	1	0	0	0	0	0	0	0	35	0	0	86	2,210
Lifetime		1	0	0	0	0	0	0	0	35	0	0	86	$2,210

Mike Alexander

Michael Alexander
B: 7/31/1957
Racing Hometown: Franklin, TN

Year	Rank	Starts	Poles	1	2	3	4	5	6–10	Laps	Laps Led	Races Led	Miles	$
1980	NR	1	0	0	0	0	0	0	1	409	0	0	244	3,130
1981	29	19	0	0	0	0	0	0	3	4,340	4	1	4,886	34,055
1984	28	19	0	0	0	0	0	0	1	4,656	0	0	5,694	94,820
1985	35	11	0	0	0	0	0	0	0	2,336	0	0	3,410	43,765
1988	32	16	0	0	0	1	0	1	4	4,677	51	5	6,015	200,709
1989	81T	1	0	0	0	0	0	0	0	188	0	0	470	16,275
1990	38	7	0	0	0	0	0	0	0	2,392	0	0	2,325	41,080
Lifetime		74	0	0	0	1	0	1	9	18,998	55	6	23,043	$433,834

Year	Rank	Starts	Poles	1	2	3	Finish 4	5	6–10	Laps	Laps Led	Races Led	Miles	$

Elbert Allen

Elbert Allen
Racing Hometown: Atlanta, GA

Year	Rank	Starts	Poles	1	2	3	4	5	6–10	Laps	Laps Led	Races Led	Miles	$
1953	37	4	0	0	0	0	0	0	2	0	0	0	0	250
1954	79	4	0	0	0	0	0	0	0	472	0	0	401	100
Lifetime		8	0	0	0	0	0	0	2	472	0	0	401	$350

Johnny Allen

John Harold Allen
B: 9/17/1934
Racing Hometown: Greenville, SC

Year	Rank	Starts	Poles	1	2	3	4	5	6–10	Laps	Laps Led	Races Led	Miles	$
1955	114	1	0	0	0	0	0	0	0	169	0	0	254	195
1956	12	32	0	0	0	0	0	2	9	4,888	0	0	3,349	4,559
1957	7	42	1	0	0	1	1	2	13	6,033	0	0	3,876	9,815
1958	NR	22	0	0	0	1	0	1	4	2,613	0	0	1,483	2,240
1959	NR	5	0	0	0	1	0	0	0	522	0	0	883	2,525
1960	19	10	0	0	1	0	0	1	3	1,820	0	0	2,501	14,789
1961	12	22	1	0	0	2	0	1	8	4,508	3	1	4,493	34,519
1962	26	20	1	1	0	0	3	1	3	4,094	288	4	3,401	7,230
1963	59	8	0	0	0	0	0	0	1	743	0	0	951	2,325
1964	60	4	0	0	0	0	0	0	1	484	0	0	586	1,775
1965	82	2	0	0	0	0	0	0	0	120	0	0	300	1,235
1966	68	3	0	0	0	0	0	0	0	598	0	0	633	1,585
1967	104	2	0	0	0	0	0	0	0	137	0	0	170	1,565
Lifetime		173	3	1	1	5	4	8	42	26,729	291	5	22,880	$84,357

Loy Allen Jr.

Loy Allen Jr.
B: 4/7/1966
Racing Hometown: Raleigh, NC

Year	Rank	Starts	Poles	1	2	3	4	5	6–10	Laps	Laps Led	Races Led	Miles	$
1993	45	5	0	0	0	0	0	0	0	878	0	0	1,537	34,695
1994	39	19	3	0	0	0	0	0	0	4,446	12	3	6,776	216,751
1995	41	11	0	0	0	0	0	0	1	2,707	18	1	4,182	186,670
1996	45	9	0	0	0	0	0	0	0	1,439	0	0	2,772	130,667
1997	58	2	0	0	0	0	0	0	0	266	0	0	564	67,300
1999	62	2	0	0	0	0	0	0	0	306	0	0	668	53,135
Lifetime		48	3	0	0	0	0	0	1	10,042	30	4	16,498	$689,218

Olin Allen

Olin Allen
Racing Hometown: Macon, GA

Year	Rank	Starts	Poles	1	2	3	4	5	6–10	Laps	Laps Led	Races Led	Miles	$
1952	108	1	0	0	0	0	0	0	0	182	0	0	91	25
Lifetime		1	0	0	0	0	0	0	0	182	0	0	91	$25

Bobby Allison

Robert Arthur Allison
B: 12/3/1937
Racing Hometown: Hueytown, AL

Year	Rank	Starts	Poles	1	2	3	4	5	6–10	Laps	Laps Led	Races Led	Miles	$
1961	106	4	0	0	0	0	0	0	0	359	0	0	751	650
1965	34	8	0	0	0	0	0	0	3	799	0	0	1,324	4,780
1966	10	33	4	3	0	4	1	2	5	6,949	477	6	5,370	23,420
1967	4	45	2	6	4	5	4	2	6	10,157	1,481	20	7,686	58,250
1968	11	37	2	2	4	4	6	2	2	8,781	721	13	7,383	52,288
1969	20	27	1	5	3	1	2	2	2	6,445	1,251	15	6,483	69,483
1970	2	46	5	3	15	8	4	0	5	12,452	1,246	22	11,164	149,745
1971	4	42	9	11	7	3	5	1	4	11,716	3,589	31	12,130	254,316
1972	2	31	11	10	12	2	1	0	2	10,063	4,343	30	11,801	348,939
1973	7	27	6	2	2	6	4	1	1	8,072	870	20	8,653	161,818
1974	4	27	3	2	3	5	2	5	0	7,523	899	20	9,154	178,437
1975	24	19	3	3	3	1	2	1	0	4,268	578	14	6,227	122,435
1976	4	30	3	0	2	6	5	2	4	8,735	360	18	10,204	230,170
1977	8	30	0	0	1	0	2	2	10	7,024	102	9	7,823	94,575
1978	2	30	1	5	3	4	0	2	8	9,283	1,043	19	10,540	411,517
1979	3	31	3	5	7	2	4	0	4	9,585	1,854	24	10,938	428,801
1980	6	31	2	4	2	4	1	1	6	8,244	948	18	9,028	378,970
1981	2	31	2	5	7	4	3	2	5	10,098	1,142	23	11,610	680,957
1982	2	30	1	8	2	1	2	1	6	9,184	2,423	24	10,861	795,078
1983	1	30	0	6	5	6	1	0	7	10,038	1,755	25	11,527	883,010
1984	6	30	0	2	1	2	4	4	6	9,051	1,160	23	10,545	641,049
1985	12	28	0	0	0	3	3	1	4	7,656	422	14	9,339	272,536
1986	7	29	0	1	2	1	1	1	9	8,391	127	11	9,930	503,095

Year	Rank	Starts	Poles	Finish 1	2	3	4	5	6–10	Laps	Laps Led	Races Led	Miles	$

Bobby Allison *continued*

Year	Rank	Starts	Poles	1	2	3	4	5	6–10	Laps	Laps Led	Races Led	Miles	$
1987	9	29	1	1	1	0	1	1	9	7,662	331	10	9,296	515,894
1988	33	13	0	1	1	0	0	1	3	4,303	104	4	4,762	409,295
Lifetime		718	59	85	87	72	58	34	111	196,838	27,226	413	214,527	$7,669,508

Davey Allison

David Carl Allison
B: 2/25/1961   D: 7/13/1993   *Killed @ Talladega in helicopter mishap.*
Racing Hometown: Hueytown, AL

Year	Rank	Starts	Poles	1	2	3	4	5	6–10	Laps	Laps Led	Races Led	Miles	$
1985	71	3	0	0	0	0	0	0	1	539	0	0	1,025	10,615
1986	47	5	0	0	0	0	0	0	1	1,435	13	1	1,368	24,190
1987	21	22	5	2	3	0	0	4	1	5,511	710	11	8,520	361,060
1988	8	29	3	2	2	3	2	3	4	8,333	650	14	9,749	844,532
1989	11	29	1	2	1	0	2	2	6	8,287	253	13	10,113	560,904
1990	13	29	0	2	0	1	0	2	5	9,154	222	8	10,918	640,684
1991	3	29	3	5	4	2	1	0	4	8,770	1,528	23	10,613	1,712,924
1992	3	29	2	5	1	1	5	3	2	8,976	1,377	18	10,999	1,955,628
1993	31	16	0	1	1	2	1	1	2	5,061	275	9	6,215	513,585
Lifetime		191	14	19	12	9	11	15	26	56,066	5,028	97	69,518	$6,624,122

Donnie Allison

Donald Joseph Allison
B: 9/7/1939
Racing Hometown: Hueytown, AL

Year	Rank	Starts	Poles	1	2	3	4	5	6–10	Laps	Laps Led	Races Led	Miles	$
1966	64	2	0	0	0	0	0	0	1	664	0	0	757	2,180
1967	16	20	0	0	1	0	2	1	3	4,336	158	2	4,537	17,614
1968	25	13	1	1	1	3	0	0	3	3,829	283	6	4,107	50,815
1969	24	16	2	1	2	4	1	2	1	3,893	400	10	5,106	78,055
1970	40	19	0	3	0	2	3	2	2	5,252	697	10	5,674	96,081
1971	29	13	5	1	1	1	2	2	2	3,017	806	8	4,334	69,995
1972	36	10	0	0	0	1	0	1	1	1,385	35	4	2,667	16,826
1973	35	14	0	0	1	1	0	0	3	2,904	44	3	3,697	41,246
1974	17	21	2	0	1	1	2	2	4	5,101	183	10	5,761	60,315
1975	28	14	2	0	0	2	0	1	3	2,819	33	5	3,971	45,595
1976	34	9	0	1	0	1	0	0	3	2,178	104	4	3,254	48,445
1977	24	17	3	2	2	1	4	0	1	4,133	1,163	13	5,911	146,435
1978	25	17	0	1	2	2	1	1	1	3,876	209	12	6,128	127,475
1979	24	20	1	0	2	1	2	2	3	4,891	293	9	6,420	144,770
1980	26	18	1	0	0	1	0	2	3	3,794	231	7	5,197	92,640
1981	44	6	0	0	0	0	0	1	0	1,306	2	1	2,082	38,745
1982	41	9	0	0	0	0	0	0	3	1,818	1	1	2,541	38,180
1983	NR	2	0	0	0	0	0	0	0	138	0	0	339	6,375
1986	114T	1	0	0	0	0	0	0	0	131	0	0	179	1,840
1988	81	1	0	0	0	0	0	0	0	114	0	0	228	3,000
Lifetime		242	17	10	13	21	17	17	37	55,579	4,642	105	72,890	$1,126,627

Dick Allwine

Richard Allwine
Racing Hometown: Greensburg, PA

Year	Rank	Starts	Poles	1	2	3	4	5	6–10	Laps	Laps Led	Races Led	Miles	$
1953	52	3	0	0	0	0	0	0	1	382	0	0	456	605
1955	202	1	0	0	0	0	0	0	0	202	0	0	278	50
1956	95	2	0	0	0	0	0	0	0	294	0	0	294	200
Lifetime		6	0	0	0	0	0	0	1	878	0	0	1,028	$855

Dave Alonzo

David Alonzo
Racing Hometown: Mt. View, CA

Year	Rank	Starts	Poles	1	2	3	4	5	6–10	Laps	Laps Led	Races Led	Miles	$
1969	72	2	0	0	0	0	0	0	0	486	0	0	504	1,555
1970	67	2	0	0	0	0	0	0	0	160	0	0	420	2,260
Lifetime		4	0	0	0	0	0	0	0	646	0	0	924	$3,815

George Alsobrook

George L. Alsobrook
B: 2/23/1934
Racing Hometown: Hiram, GA

Year	Rank	Starts	Poles	1	2	3	4	5	6–10	Laps	Laps Led	Races Led	Miles	$
1958	123	1	0	0	0	0	0	0	0	54	0	0	27	70
1959	NR	4	0	0	0	0	0	0	1	936	0	0	723	1,150
1961	69	8	0	0	0	0	0	0	1	938	0	0	736	1,825
1962	69	5	0	0	0	0	0	0	1	406	0	0	723	925
Lifetime		18	0	0	0	0	0	0	3	2,334	0	0	2,209	$3,970

Year	Rank	Starts	Poles	Finish 1	2	3	4	5	6–10	Laps	Laps Led	Races Led	Miles	$

George Altheide

George J. Altheide
B: 1/6/1933
Racing Hometown: Morritown, TN

Year	Rank	Starts	Poles	1	2	3	4	5	6–10	Laps	Laps Led	Races Led	Miles	$
1971	55	5	0	0	0	0	0	0	0	840	0	0	1,857	4,620
1972	35	11	0	0	0	0	0	0	0	1,578	0	0	2,760	10,405
Lifetime		16	0	0	0	0	0	0	0	2,418	0	0	4,617	$15,025

Bernard Alvarez

Bernard V. Alvarez
B: 12/14/1939
Racing Hometown: Jacksonville, FL

Year	Rank	Starts	Poles	1	2	3	4	5	6–10	Laps	Laps Led	Races Led	Miles	$
1964	90	7	0	0	0	0	0	0	0	162	0	0	127	650
1965	115	2	0	0	0	0	0	0	0	9	0	0	7	600
Lifetime		9	0	0	0	0	0	0	0	171	0	0	134	$1,250

Pancho Alvarez

Pancho Alvarez
Racing Hometown: Tampa, FL

Year	Rank	Starts	Poles	1	2	3	4	5	6–10	Laps	Laps Led	Races Led	Miles	$
1952	191T	1	0	0	0	0	0	0	0		0	0		25
Lifetime		1	0	0	0	0	0	0	0		0	0		$25

Bill Amberg

William Amberg

Year	Rank	Starts	Poles	1	2	3	4	5	6–10	Laps	Laps Led	Races Led	Miles	$
1951	NR	1	0	0	0	0	0	0	0	94	0	0	59	25
Lifetime		1	0	0	0	0	0	0	0	94	0	0	59	$25

Bill Amick

William Amick
B: 11/16/1925
Racing Hometown: Portland, OR

Year	Rank	Starts	Poles	1	2	3	4	5	6–10	Laps	Laps Led	Races Led	Miles	$
1954	41	6	0	0	1	0	0	0	0	884	9	1	867	1,750
1955	76	4	2	0	0	0	1	1	0	485	28	1	388	710
1956	17	13	0	0	1	3	1	2	3	2,446	9	1	1,631	5,381
1957	16	21	2	1	3	4	0	0	4	3,364	12	2	2,067	8,073
1961	187	1	1	0	0	0	0	0	0	25	25	1	25	25
1963	67	1	0	0	0	0	0	0	1	142	0	0	383	1,000
1964	52	1	0	0	0	0	1	0	0	181	0	0	489	2,470
1965	72	1	0	0	0	0	0	0	0	95	0	0	257	620
Lifetime		48	5	1	5	7	3	3	8	7,622	83	6	6,107	$20,029

Art Anderson

Arthur Anderson
Racing Hometown: Syracuse, NY

Year	Rank	Starts	Poles	1	2	3	4	5	6–10	Laps	Laps Led	Races Led	Miles	$
1957	NR	1	0	0	0	0	0	0	0	14	0	0	14	50
Lifetime		1	0	0	0	0	0	0	0	14	0	0	14	$50

Axel Anderson

Axel Anderson
B: 7/21/1921   D: 9/14/1994
Racing Hometown: Patchogue, NY

Year	Rank	Starts	Poles	1	2	3	4	5	6–10	Laps	Laps Led	Races Led	Miles	$
1955	133	2	0	0	0	0	0	0	0	152	0	0	267	225
1958	100	3	0	0	0	0	0	0	0	203	0	0	178	155
Lifetime		5	0	0	0	0	0	0	0	355	0	0	445	$380

Carl Anderson

Carl Anderson
Racing Hometown: Arlington, VA

Year	Rank	Starts	Poles	1	2	3	4	5	6–10	Laps	Laps Led	Races Led	Miles	$
1956	165	1	0	0	0	0	0	0	1	173	0	0	87	200
1957	198T	1	0	0	0	0	0	0	0	56	0	0	28	0
Lifetime		2	0	0	0	0	0	0	1	229	0	0	115	$200

Dave Anderson

David Anderson
Racing Hometown: Birmingham, AL

Year	Rank	Starts	Poles	1	2	3	4	5	6–10	Laps	Laps Led	Races Led	Miles	$
1951	N/A	1	0	0	0	0	0	0	0	335	0	0	419	50
Lifetime		1	0	0	0	0	0	0	0	335	0	0	419	$50

Year	Rank	Starts	Poles	Finish 1	2	3	4	5	6–10	Laps	Laps Led	Races Led	Miles	$

Eddie Anderson

Edward Anderson
B: 1927   D: 5/1/1995
Racing Hometown: Blue Island, IL

Year	Rank	Starts	Poles	1	2	3	4	5	6–10	Laps	Laps Led	Races Led	Miles	$
1951	N/A	5	0	0	0	0	0	0	0	8	0	0	6	110
Lifetime		5	0	0	0	0	0	0	0	8	0	0	6	$110

Fuzzy Anderson

Fuzzy Anderson

Year	Rank	Starts	Poles	1	2	3	4	5	6–10	Laps	Laps Led	Races Led	Miles	$
1951	N/A	3	0	0	0	0	0	0	0		0	0		75
Lifetime		3	0	0	0	0	0	0	0		0	0		$75

Jack Anderson

Jack Anderson
B: 7/26/1936
Racing Hometown: Pearisburg, VA

Year	Rank	Starts	Poles	1	2	3	4	5	6–10	Laps	Laps Led	Races Led	Miles	$
1963	98	3	0	0	0	0	0	0	0	532	0	0	231	475
1964	25	31	0	0	0	0	1	0	3	4,402	0	0	3,365	8,510
1965	90	2	0	0	0	0	0	0	0	18	0	0	45	1,220
Lifetime		36	0	0	0	0	1	0	3	4,952	0	0	3,641	$10,205

Jess Anderson

Jess Anderson
Racing Hometown: Burbank, CA

Year	Rank	Starts	Poles	1	2	3	4	5	6–10	Laps	Laps Led	Races Led	Miles	$
1951	N/A	1	0	0	0	0	0	0	0		0	0		25
Lifetime		1	0	0	0	0	0	0	0		0	0		$25

John Anderson

John B. Anderson
B: 4/20/1944   D: 7/31/1986   *Killed in highway crash in Charlotte, NC.*
Racing Hometown: Massilon, OH

Year	Rank	Starts	Poles	1	2	3	4	5	6–10	Laps	Laps Led	Races Led	Miles	$
1979	39	4	0	0	0	0	0	1	0	1,263	1	1	1,757	11,210
1980	24	20	0	0	0	0	0	0	2	4,282	0	0	5,088	48,265
1981	NR	3	0	0	0	0	0	0	0	583	0	0	772	7,800
1982	83	4	0	0	0	0	0	0	0	625	0	0	1,108	11,855
1983	NR	1	0	0	0	0	0	0	0	317	0	0	476	1,350
Lifetime		32	0	0	0	0	0	1	2	7,070	1	1	9,200	$80,480

Johnny Anderson

John Anderson
B: 7/24/1942
Racing Hometown: Palmdale, CA

Year	Rank	Starts	Poles	1	2	3	4	5	6–10	Laps	Laps Led	Races Led	Miles	$
1971	NR	1	0	0	0	0	0	0	0	34	0	0	89	690
1972	67	4	0	0	0	0	0	0	0	385	0	0	969	4,600
1973	80	2	0	0	0	0	0	0	0	186	0	0	487	1,840
1974	84	2	0	0	0	0	0	0	0	154	0	0	403	2,130
Lifetime		9	0	0	0	0	0	0	0	759	0	0	1,949	$9,260

Ken Anderson

Kenneth Anderson
Racing Hometown: Mt. Croghan, SC

Year	Rank	Starts	Poles	1	2	3	4	5	6–10	Laps	Laps Led	Races Led	Miles	$
1964	89	3	0	0	0	0	0	0	0	848	0	0	463	450
Lifetime		3	0	0	0	0	0	0	0	848	0	0	463	$450

Ole Anderson

Ole Anderson

Year	Rank	Starts	Poles	1	2	3	4	5	6–10	Laps	Laps Led	Races Led	Miles	$
1956	272T	1	0	0	0	0	0	0	0	9	0	0	9	40
Lifetime		1	0	0	0	0	0	0	0	9	0	0	9	$40

John Andretti

John Andrew Andretti
B: 3/12/1963
Racing Hometown: Bethlehem, PA

Year	Rank	Starts	Poles	1	2	3	4	5	6–10	Laps	Laps Led	Races Led	Miles	$
1993	50	4	0	0	0	0	0	0	0	904	0	0	925	24,915
1994	32	29	0	0	0	0	0	0	0	7,508	41	4	8,921	391,920
1995	18	31	1	0	0	0	1	0	4	8,402	69	8	10,174	593,542
1996	31	30	0	0	0	0	0	2	1	7,850	32	5	9,912	688,511
1997	23	32	1	1	0	1	1	0	0	9,333	135	5	11,965	1,143,725
1998	11	33	1	0	0	2	0	1	7	9,181	136	4	12,037	1,838,379

Year	Rank	Starts	Poles	Finish 1	2	3	4	5	6–10	Laps	Laps Led	Races Led	Miles	$

John Andretti *continued*

Year	Rank	Starts	Poles	1	2	3	4	5	6–10	Laps	Laps Led	Races Led	Miles	$
1999	17	34	1	1	0	1	1	0	7	8,526	238	10	11,246	2,001,832
2000	23	34	0	0	0	0	0	0	2	9,217	11	6	11,656	1,964,402
2001	31	35	0	0	1	0	0	0	1	9,994	53	2	12,997	2,873,184
2002	28	36	0	0	0	0	0	0	1	9,743	22	5	12,881	2,954,229
Lifetime		298	4	2	1	4	3	3	23	80,658	737	49	102,713	$14,474,639

Mario Andretti

Mario Gabriel Andretti
B: 2/28/1940
Racing Hometown: Nazareth, PA

Year	Rank	Starts	Poles	1	2	3	4	5	6–10	Laps	Laps Led	Races Led	Miles	$
1966	NR	4	0	0	0	0	0	0	0	300	1	1	781	2,140
1967	NR	6	0	1	0	0	0	0	2	867	137	3	1,757	52,165
1968	NR	3	0	0	0	0	0	0	0	297	20	2	751	2,845
1969	NR	1	0	0	0	0	0	0	0	132	7	1	356	925
Lifetime		14	0	1	0	0	0	0	2	1,596	165	7	3,645	$58,075

Ed Andrews

Edward Andrews
Racing Hometown: San Francisco, CA

Year	Rank	Starts	Poles	1	2	3	4	5	6–10	Laps	Laps Led	Races Led	Miles	$
1960	92	1	0	0	0	0	0	0	0	150	0	0	210	350
Lifetime		1	0	0	0	0	0	0	0	150	0	0	210	$350

Tommy Andrews

Thomas Andrews
B: 3/15/1936
Racing Hometown: Huntsville, AL

Year	Rank	Starts	Poles	1	2	3	4	5	6–10	Laps	Laps Led	Races Led	Miles	$
1971	NR	2	0	0	0	0	0	0	0	251	0	0	79	450
Lifetime		2	0	0	0	0	0	0	0	251	0	0	79	$450

Wayne Andrews

Wayne Earl Andrews
B: 8/18/1938
Racing Hometown: Siler City, NC

Year	Rank	Starts	Poles	1	2	3	4	5	6–10	Laps	Laps Led	Races Led	Miles	$
1971	NR	5	0	0	0	0	0	1	2	1,372	0	0	600	1,780
1973	125	1	0	0	0	0	0	0	0	5	0	0	8	1,005
Lifetime		6	0	0	0	0	0	1	2	1,377	0	0	608	$2,785

Don Angel

Donald Angel
Racing Hometown: Miami, FL

Year	Rank	Starts	Poles	1	2	3	4	5	6–10	Laps	Laps Led	Races Led	Miles	$
1958	NR	3	0	0	0	0	0	0	0	401	0	0	241	210
1959	NR	2	0	0	0	0	0	0	0	167	0	0	100	100
Lifetime		5	0	0	0	0	0	0	0	568	0	0	341	$310

Bob Apperson

Robert Apperson
Racing Hometown: Charlottesville, VA

Year	Rank	Starts	Poles	1	2	3	4	5	6–10	Laps	Laps Led	Races Led	Miles	$
1949	43	3	0	0	0	0	0	0	0	191	0	0	96	150
1950	67	7	0	0	0	0	0	0	0	573	0	0	631	200
1952	197	1	0	0	0	0	0	0	0		0	0		25
Lifetime		11	0	0	0	0	0	0	0	764	0	0	726	$375

Nelson Applegate

Nelson Applegate
B: 1925   D: 1979
Racing Hometown: Denville, NJ

Year	Rank	Starts	Poles	1	2	3	4	5	6–10	Laps	Laps Led	Races Led	Miles	$
1951	N/A	3	0	0	0	0	0	0	0		0	0		50
1952	89	2	0	0	0	0	0	0	1	313	0	0	219	160
Lifetime		5	0	0	0	0	0	0	1	313	0	0	219	$210

Sam Ard

Samuel J. Ard
B: 2/14/1939
Racing Hometown: Asheboro, NC

Year	Rank	Starts	Poles	1	2	3	4	5	6–10	Laps	Laps Led	Races Led	Miles	$
1984	NR	1	0	0	0	0	0	0	0	1	0	0	1	1,100
Lifetime		1	0	0	0	0	0	0	0	1	0	0	1	$1,100

Year	Rank	Starts	Poles	Finish						Laps	Laps Led	Races Led	Miles	$
				1	2	3	4	5	6–10	Laps	Led	Led	Miles	$

Frank Arford

Frank Arford
D: 6/20/1953 *Killed qualifying for Langborne NASCAR race.*
Racing Hometown: Indianapolis, IN

Year	Rank	Starts	Poles	1	2	3	4	5	6–10	Laps	Laps Led	Races Led	Miles	$
1953	NR	4	0	0	0	0	0	0	0	255	0	0	261	100
Lifetime		4	0	0	0	0	0	0	0	255	0	0	261	$100

Russell Armentrout

Russell Armentrout

Year	Rank	Starts	Poles	1	2	3	4	5	6–10	Laps	Laps Led	Races Led	Miles	$
1953	NR	2	0	0	0	0	0	0	0	60	0	0	60	50
Lifetime		2	0	0	0	0	0	0	0	60	0	0	60	$50

Ben Arnold

Ben Robert Arnold
B: 7/30/1936
Racing Hometown: Fairfield, AL

Year	Rank	Starts	Poles	1	2	3	4	5	6–10	Laps	Laps Led	Races Led	Miles	$
1968	51	10	0	0	0	0	0	0	0	1,413	0	0	1,203	2,785
1969	15	48	0	0	0	0	0	0	8	10,334	0	0	8,474	33,256
1970	17	29	0	0	0	0	0	0	3	6,838	0	0	6,746	25,805
1971	26	18	0	0	0	0	0	0	3	4,150	0	0	6,206	18,491
1972	10	26	0	0	0	0	0	0	7	6,976	0	0	8,935	44,547
1973	127	1	0	0	0	0	0	0	0	9	0	0	24	580
Lifetime		132	0	0	0	0	0	0	21	29,720	0	0	31,588	$125,464

Pete Arnold

Peter Andrew Arnold
B: 8/31/1943
Racing Hometown: Bellaire, TX

Year	Rank	Starts	Poles	1	2	3	4	5	6–10	Laps	Laps Led	Races Led	Miles	$
1971	85	1	0	0	0	0	0	0	0	58	0	0	29	340
Lifetime		1	0	0	0	0	0	0	0	58	0	0	29	$340

Ralph Arnold

Ralph Arnold
Racing Hometown: Macon, GA

Year	Rank	Starts	Poles	1	2	3	4	5	6–10	Laps	Laps Led	Races Led	Miles	$
1969	NR	1	0	0	0	0	0	0	0	43	0	0	116	765
Lifetime		1	0	0	0	0	0	0	0	43	0	0	116	$765

Buddy Arrington

Buddy Rogers Arrington
B: 7/26/1938
Racing Hometown: Martinsville, VA

Year	Rank	Starts	Poles	1	2	3	4	5	6–10	Laps	Laps Led	Races Led	Miles	$
1964	34	28	0	0	0	0	0	2	7	5,172	0	0	2,504	4,715
1965	22	31	0	0	0	1	1	4	4	5,274	0	0	3,545	11,600
1966	32	25	0	0	0	0	0	0	3	3,607	0	0	3,054	8,980
1967	26	15	0	0	0	0	0	1	4	2,972	0	0	2,635	7,820
1968	NR	1	0	0	0	0	0	0	0	186	0	0	465	2,350
1969	33	16	0	0	0	0	0	2	4	3,758	0	0	3,557	12,975
1970	33	19	0	0	0	0	0	0	2	2,855	0	0	3,638	16,845
1971	NR	1	0	0	0	0	0	0	0	472	0	0	248	650
1972	22	20	0	0	0	0	0	1	9	5,503	0	0	7,009	28,700
1973	12	26	0	0	0	0	0	1	3	7,917	0	0	8,153	40,877
1974	30	17	0	0	0	0	0	0	4	4,782	0	0	4,798	21,510
1975	19	25	0	0	0	0	0	0	3	7,786	0	0	8,170	45,893
1976	20	25	0	0	0	0	0	0	3	9,856	0	0	8,689	56,647
1977	11	28	0	0	0	0	0	0	5	8,601	0	0	10,038	88,887
1978	9	30	0	0	0	0	0	1	6	9,580	0	0	10,740	112,960
1979	11	31	0	0	0	1	0	0	6	8,452	2	1	10,334	131,833
1980	12	31	0	0	0	0	0	0	7	8,765	0	0	9,937	120,355
1981	11	31	0	0	0	0	0	0	7	8,344	0	0	9,444	133,928
1982	7	30	0	0	0	0	0	0	8	9,236	5	3	10,705	178,159
1983	15	30	0	0	0	0	0	0	2	8,933	1	1	10,010	138,429
1984	20	26	0	0	0	0	0	0	0	7,323	0	0	8,295	128,802
1985	20	26	0	0	0	0	0	0	1	7,809	1	1	9,653	153,222
1986	20	26	0	0	0	0	0	0	0	8,152	4	1	9,459	186,588
1987	25	20	0	0	0	0	0	0	0	5,746	0	0	6,793	115,300
1988	46	4	0	0	0	0	0	0	0	760	0	0	1,549	22,165
Lifetime		562	0	0	0	2	1	12	88	151,841	13	7	163,421	$1,770,190

Year	Rank	Starts	Poles	Finish						Laps	Laps Led	Races Led	Miles	$
				1	2	3	4	5	6–10					

Joey Arrington

Joseph Arrington
B: 7/25/1956
Racing Hometown: Rocky Mount, VA

Year	Rank	Starts	Poles	1	2	3	4	5	6–10	Laps	Laps Led	Races Led	Miles	$
1974	97	1	0	0	0	0	0	0	0	341	0	0	213	525
1975	99	2	0	0	0	0	0	0	0	91	0	0	87	1,060
1978	60	3	0	0	0	0	0	0	0	690	0	0	706	2,790
1979	109	1	0	0	0	0	0	0	0	42	0	0	42	650
1980	84T	1	0	0	0	0	0	0	0	368	0	0	199	2,030
Lifetime		8	0	0	0	0	0	0	0	1,532	0	0	1,248	$7,055

Woody Arrington

Woodrow Arrington
Racing Hometown: Aberdeen, NC

Year	Rank	Starts	Poles	1	2	3	4	5	6–10	Laps	Laps Led	Races Led	Miles	$
1955	240T	1	0	0	0	0	0	0	0	4	0	0	4	0
Lifetime		1	0	0	0	0	0	0	0	4	0	0	4	$0

Bob Ashbrook

Robert Harold Ashbrook
B: 3/20/1929
Racing Hometown: Akron, OH

Year	Rank	Starts	Poles	1	2	3	4	5	6–10	Laps	Laps Led	Races Led	Miles	$
1969	57	2	0	0	0	0	0	0	0	200	0	0	399	1,587
1970	108T	1	0	0	0	0	0	0	0	44	0	0	110	220
Lifetime		3	0	0	0	0	0	0	0	244	0	0	509	$1,807

George Ashbrook

George Ashbrook
Racing Hometown: Akron, OH

Year	Rank	Starts	Poles	1	2	3	4	5	6–10	Laps	Laps Led	Races Led	Miles	$
1969	75T	1	0	0	0	0	0	0	0	262	0	0	262	540
Lifetime		1	0	0	0	0	0	0	0	262	0	0	262	$540

Bruce Atchley

Bruce H. Atchley
Racing Hometown: Loudon, TN

Year	Rank	Starts	Poles	1	2	3	4	5	6–10	Laps	Laps Led	Races Led	Miles	$
1952	60	6	0	0	0	0	0	0	0	307	0	0	187	200
Lifetime		6	0	0	0	0	0	0	0	307	0	0	187	$200

Irv Atkinson

Irv Atkinson
Racing Hometown: Grand Rapids, MI

Year	Rank	Starts	Poles	1	2	3	4	5	6–10	Laps	Laps Led	Races Led	Miles	$
1954	NR	1	0	0	0	0	0	0	0	35	0	0	18	0
Lifetime		1	0	0	0	0	0	0	0	35	0	0	18	$0

Ray Atkinson

Raymond Atkinson
Racing Hometown: Indianapolis, IN

Year	Rank	Starts	Poles	1	2	3	4	5	6–10	Laps	Laps Led	Races Led	Miles	$
1952	NR	1	0	0	0	0	0	0	0	255	0	0	128	25
Lifetime		1	0	0	0	0	0	0	0	255	0	0	128	$25

W.H. Atkinson

W.H. Atkinson III
Racing Hometown: Bunnell, FL

Year	Rank	Starts	Poles	1	2	3	4	5	6–10	Laps	Laps Led	Races Led	Miles	$
1956	276	1	0	0	0	0	0	0	0		0	0		0
Lifetime		1	0	0	0	0	0	0	0		0	0		$0

Roger Attard

Roger Attard
Racing Hometown: Highland Park, MI

Year	Rank	Starts	Poles	1	2	3	4	5	6–10	Laps	Laps Led	Races Led	Miles	$
1952	185	1	0	0	0	0	0	0	0	25	0	0	25	0
Lifetime		1	0	0	0	0	0	0	0	25	0	0	25	$0

Casey Atwood

Casey Atwood
B: 8/25/1980
Racing Hometown: Antioch, TN

Year	Rank	Starts	Poles	1	2	3	4	5	6–10	Laps	Laps Led	Races Led	Miles	$
2000	54	3	0	0	0	0	0	0	1	1,160	0	0	960	97,030
2001	26	35	1	0	0	1	0	0	2	9,473	137	4	11,904	1,979,111
2002	35	35	0	0	0	0	0	0	0	9,454	0	0	12,402	1,988,254
Lifetime		73	1	0	0	1	0	0	3	20,087	137	4	25,266	$4,064,395

Year	Rank	Starts	Poles	Finish 1	2	3	4	5	6–10	Laps	Laps Led	Races Led	Miles	$

Buzz Auckland

Buzz Auckland
Racing Hometown: Southampton, PA

Year	Rank	Starts	Poles	1	2	3	4	5	6–10	Laps	Laps Led	Races Led	Miles	$
1956	290	1	0	0	0	0	0	0	0	43	0	0	43	0
Lifetime		1	0	0	0	0	0	0	0	43	0	0	43	$0

Reggie Ausmus

Reginald Ausmus

Year	Rank	Starts	Poles	1	2	3	4	5	6–10	Laps	Laps Led	Races Led	Miles	$
1956	266T	1	0	0	0	0	0	0	0	138	0	0	138	40
1957	114T	2	0	0	0	0	0	0	0	256	0	0	128	150
Lifetime		3	0	0	0	0	0	0	0	394	0	0	266	$190

Gene Austin

Gene Austin
Racing Hometown: Mexico, NY

Year	Rank	Starts	Poles	1	2	3	4	5	6–10	Laps	Laps Led	Races Led	Miles	$
1950	52	2	0	0	0	0	0	0	1		0	0		175
Lifetime		2	0	0	0	0	0	0	1		0	0		$175

Jack Austin

Jack Austin
Racing Hometown: Gardena, CA

Year	Rank	Starts	Poles	1	2	3	4	5	6–10	Laps	Laps Led	Races Led	Miles	$
1959	NR	1	0	0	0	0	0	0	0	54	0	0	54	75
Lifetime		1	0	0	0	0	0	0	0	54	0	0	54	$75

Jim Austin

James Austin
Racing Hometown: Boynton Beach, FL

Year	Rank	Starts	Poles	1	2	3	4	5	6–10	Laps	Laps Led	Races Led	Miles	$
1959	45	5	0	0	0	0	0	0	0	784	0	0	413	440
1960	97	2	0	0	0	0	0	0	0	199	0	0	124	310
Lifetime		7	0	0	0	0	0	0	0	983	0	0	537	$750

L.D. Austin

L.D. Austin
B: 8/17/1918 *Deceased.*
Racing Hometown: Greenville, SC

Year	Rank	Starts	Poles	1	2	3	4	5	6–10	Laps	Laps Led	Races Led	Miles	$
1957	8	40	0	0	0	0	0	1	12	6,920	0	0	4,132	6,485
1958	6	46	0	0	0	0	0	0	10	6,903	0	0	3,898	6,246
1959	7	35	0	0	0	0	0	0	13	6,480	0	0	3,602	4,671
1960	22	27	0	0	0	0	0	1	9	4,822	0	0	3,996	4,885
1961	25	20	0	0	0	0	0	0	8	4,802	0	0	3,402	4,530
1962	NR	1	0	0	0	0	0	0	0	53	0	0	27	0
Lifetime		169	0	0	0	0	0	2	52	29,980	0	0	19,057	$26,817

Paul Austin

Paul Austin
Racing Hometown: Asheville, NC

Year	Rank	Starts	Poles	1	2	3	4	5	6–10	Laps	Laps Led	Races Led	Miles	$
1951	N/A	1	0	0	0	0	0	0	0		0	0		25
Lifetime		1	0	0	0	0	0	0	0		0	0		$25

Scott Autrey

Scott Autrey
B: 7/9/1953
Racing Hometown: San Angelo, TX

Year	Rank	Starts	Poles	1	2	3	4	5	6–10	Laps	Laps Led	Races Led	Miles	$
1985	88T	1	0	0	0	0	0	0	0	79	0	0	207	1,125
Lifetime		1	0	0	0	0	0	0	0	79	0	0	207	$1,125

Jimmy Ayers

James Ayers
B: 4/2/1917
Racing Hometown: Gardendale, AL

Year	Rank	Starts	Poles	1	2	3	4	5	6–10	Laps	Laps Led	Races Led	Miles	$
1950	NR	1	0	0	0	0	0	0	0		0	0		0
1951	71	7	0	0	0	0	0	0	5	225	0	0	281	475
1952	101	3	0	0	0	0	0	0	0	179	0	0	90	85
1953	45	4	0	0	0	0	0	0	2		0	0		150
1954	171	2	0	0	0	0	0	0	0	219	0	0	178	75
1955	72	2	0	0	0	0	0	0	1	277	0	0	292	350
Lifetime		19	0	0	0	0	0	0	8	900	0	0	840	$1,135

Year	Rank	Starts	Poles	Finish 1	2	3	4	5	6–10	Laps	Laps Led	Races Led	Miles	$

Bill Bade

William Bade
Racing Hometown: Redondo Beach, CA

Year	Rank	Starts	Poles	1	2	3	4	5	6–10	Laps	Laps Led	Races Led	Miles	$
1954	85	3	0	0	0	0	0	0	1	832	0	0	488	190
1956	224	1	0	0	0	0	0	0	0	214	0	0	214	40
1957	146	2	0	0	0	0	0	0	0	194	0	0	97	90
1958	171	1	0	0	0	0	0	0	0	28	0	0	28	25
Lifetime		7	0	0	0	0	0	0	1	1,268	0	0	827	$345

George Bagnell

George Bagnell
B: 1926

Year	Rank	Starts	Poles	1	2	3	4	5	6–10	Laps	Laps Led	Races Led	Miles	$
1950	NR	1	0	0	0	0	0	0	0		0	0		0
Lifetime		1	0	0	0	0	0	0	0		0	0		$0

Dick Bailey

Richard Bailey
B: 1922
Racing Hometown: Grove City, PA

Year	Rank	Starts	Poles	1	2	3	4	5	6–10	Laps	Laps Led	Races Led	Miles	$
1951	N/A	2	0	0	0	0	0	0	0		0	0		25
1958	118	1	0	0	0	0	0	0	0	33	0	0	135	75
1959	NR	1	1	0	0	0	0	0	0	54	3	1	14	50
Lifetime		4	1	0	0	0	0	0	0	87	3	1	149	$150

Don Bailey

Donald Bailey
B: 1927
Racing Hometown: Brockway, PA

Year	Rank	Starts	Poles	1	2	3	4	5	6–10	Laps	Laps Led	Races Led	Miles	$
1951	47	10	0	0	0	0	1	0	1	151	0	0	76	625
1956	270T	1	0	0	0	0	0	0	0		0	0		25
1957	160T	1	0	0	0	0	0	0	0	62	0	0	62	75
Lifetime		12	0	0	0	0	1	0	1	213	0	0	138	$725

H.B. Bailey

Herring Burl Bailey
B: 11/15/1936   D: 4/17/2003   *Heart failure.*
Racing Hometown: Houston, TX

Year	Rank	Starts	Poles	1	2	3	4	5	6–10	Laps	Laps Led	Races Led	Miles	$
1962	128	1	0	0	0	0	0	0	0	101	0	0	152	300
1963	53	2	0	0	0	0	0	0	0	226	0	0	565	775
1964	136	2	0	0	0	0	0	0	0	141	0	0	195	900
1965	29	5	0	0	0	0	0	1	2	810	0	0	1,338	5,000
1966	66	4	0	0	0	0	0	0	0	450	0	0	671	2,745
1967	50	3	0	0	0	0	0	0	0	322	0	0	676	3,850
1968	81	2	0	0	0	0	0	0	0	187	0	0	264	1,250
1969	53	6	0	0	0	0	0	0	1	638	0	0	1,303	5,880
1970	NR	1	0	0	0	0	0	0	0	180	0	0	246	995
1971	NR	5	0	0	0	0	0	0	0	723	11	1	656	2,865
1972	58	5	0	0	0	0	0	1	0	1,167	6	1	1,654	8,010
1973	77	2	0	0	0	0	0	0	0	243	0	0	483	1,935
1975	114T	1	0	0	0	0	0	0	0	1	0	0	1	1,015
1977	NR	1	0	0	0	0	0	0	1	187	0	0	497	8,450
1979	56	4	0	0	0	0	0	0	0	738	0	0	1,175	5,835
1981	54	4	0	0	0	0	0	0	0	605	0	0	989	7,125
1982	42	6	0	0	0	0	0	0	0	1,016	0	0	1,612	9,455
1983	61	2	0	0	0	0	0	0	0	684	0	0	1,033	4,110
1984	58	2	0	0	0	0	0	0	0	529	0	0	770	5,640
1985	88T	2	0	0	0	0	0	0	0	206	0	0	299	3,065
1986	52	4	0	0	0	0	0	0	0	918	1	1	1,289	9,225
1987	48	5	0	0	0	0	0	0	0	1,150	0	0	1,691	18,885
1988	43	7	0	0	0	0	0	0	0	1,180	0	0	1,788	15,775
1989	60	2	0	0	0	0	0	0	0	487	0	0	787	6,595
1990	65	3	0	0	0	0	0	0	0	421	0	0	608	9,525
1991	53	3	0	0	0	0	0	0	0	545	0	0	981	13,095
1992	95T	1	0	0	0	0	0	0	0	8	0	0	16	5,355
1993	60	2	0	0	0	0	0	0	0	238	0	0	442	12,750
Lifetime		87	0	0	0	0	0	2	4	14,101	18	3	22,178	$170,405

Year	Rank	Starts	Poles	Finish						Laps	Laps Led	Races Led	Miles	$
				1	2	3	4	5	6–10					

Buck Baity

Buck Baity
Racing Hometown: Yadkinsville, NC

Year	Rank	Starts	Poles	1	2	3	4	5	6–10	Laps	Laps Led	Races Led	Miles	$
1951	N/A	1	0	0	0	0	0	0	0	248	0	0	310	0
Lifetime		1	0	0	0	0	0	0	0	248	0	0	310	$0

Bill Baker

William Baker
B: 6/19/1931
Racing Hometown: Pismo Beach, CA

Year	Rank	Starts	Poles	1	2	3	4	5	6–10	Laps	Laps Led	Races Led	Miles	$
1977	69	2	0	0	0	0	0	0	0	142	0	0	372	2,540
1978	101	1	0	0	0	0	0	0	0	20	0	0	52	550
Lifetime		3	0	0	0	0	0	0	0	162	0	0	424	$3,090

Bobby Baker

Robert Baker
Racing Hometown: Lakeland, FL

Year	Rank	Starts	Poles	1	2	3	4	5	6–10	Laps	Laps Led	Races Led	Miles	$
1987	80	1	0	0	0	0	0	0	0	380	0	0	238	3,500
Lifetime		1	0	0	0	0	0	0	0	380	0	0	238	$3,500

Brian Baker

Brian Scott Baker
B: 6/8/1961
Racing Hometown: Charlotte, NC

Year	Rank	Starts	Poles	1	2	3	4	5	6–10	Laps	Laps Led	Races Led	Miles	$
1986	107T	1	0	0	0	0	0	0	0	252	0	0	252	3,985
Lifetime		1	0	0	0	0	0	0	0	252	0	0	252	$3,985

Buck Baker

Elzie Wylie Baker
B: 3/4/1919   D: 4/14/2002
Racing Hometown: Charlotte, NC

Year	Rank	Starts	Poles	1	2	3	4	5	6–10	Laps	Laps Led	Races Led	Miles	$
1949	48	2	0	0	0	0	0	0	0		0	0		50
1950	12	9	1	0	1	1	0	0	3	587	10	1	605	2,145
1951	23	11	0	0	0	1	0	3	1	338	0	0	407	1,650
1952	12	14	2	1	0	0	2	0	3	1,550	139	3	1,273	3,187
1953	4	33	4	4	2	3	4	3	9	1,619	564	9	1,550	18,167
1954	3	34	7	4	7	6	3	3	5	5,726	768	14	3,893	19,368
1955	2	42	2	3	6	6	4	5	10	6,705	708	8	4,762	19,771
1956	1	48	12	14	7	3	4	3	8	8,495	1,401	23	5,460	34,077
1957	1	40	6	10	7	4	5	4	8	8,058	858	15	4,844	30,764
1958	2	44	3	3	10	4	2	4	12	7,827	364	8	4,726	25,841
1959	5	35	4	1	2	6	1	4	5	6,056	183	5	3,606	11,061
1960	4	37	2	2	1	3	1	8	9	7,271	213	4	5,854	38,399
1961	10	42	1	1	1	3	4	2	4	7,195	114	3	5,226	17,374
1962	13	37	0	0	1	3	2	0	8	6,607	18	2	5,002	12,787
1963	11	47	0	1	3	6	2	5	13	9,505	62	1	5,702	18,616
1964	9	35	0	2	3	3	3	4	3	7,263	159	5	6,080	43,781
1965	17	31	0	0	2	0	0	1	9	5,266	0	0	4,173	21,580
1966	21	36	0	0	3	0	2	2	7	6,725	0	0	4,939	13,860
1967	27	21	0	0	0	0	0	0	5	4,544	0	0	3,156	7,560
1968	39	17	0	0	0	0	0	1	2	2,675	110	1	1,560	3,580
1969	NR	1	0	0	0	0	0	0	0	108	0	0	287	1,300
1970	NR	1	0	0	0	0	0	0	0	267	0	0	267	610
1971	NR	6	0	0	0	0	1	0	1	1,775	0	0	835	2,345
1972	NR	5	0	0	0	0	0	0	0	660	0	0	722	3,255
1973	101	1	0	0	0	0	0	0	0	357	0	0	363	670
1976	48	8	0	0	0	0	0	0	1	1,977	0	0	2,678	12,655
Lifetime		637	44	46	56	52	40	52	126	109,156	5,671	102	77,968	$364,453

Buddy Baker

Elzie Wylie Baker Jr.
B: 1/25/1941
Racing Hometown: Charlotte, NC

Year	Rank	Starts	Poles	1	2	3	4	5	6–10	Laps	Laps Led	Races Led	Miles	$
1959	26	12	0	0	0	0	1	0	4	1,639	0	0	876	1,705
1960	38	15	0	0	0	0	0	0	1	2,149	0	0	1,881	1,745
1961	39	14	0	0	0	0	0	1	2	2,370	0	0	2,434	4,965
1962	23	31	0	0	0	1	2	2	5	5,454	0	0	4,139	7,578
1963	52	8	0	0	0	0	1	0	1	1,478	0	0	1,098	2,665
1964	31	33	0	0	0	1	1	1	4	3,239	0	0	2,246	8,460
1965	9	42	0	0	2	4	2	4	5	6,969	0	0	5,394	26,837

Year	Rank	Starts	Poles	Finish						Laps	Laps Led	Races Led	Miles	$
				1	2	3	4	5	6–10					

Buddy Baker *continued*

Year	Rank	Starts	Poles	1	2	3	4	5	6–10	Laps	Laps Led	Races Led	Miles	$
1966	22	41	1	0	1	0	0	0	6	6,361	142	4	4,890	21,325
1967	15	20	0	1	1	2	2	0	1	3,905	480	8	4,135	46,950
1968	13	38	4	1	4	6	3	2	2	7,949	454	11	5,690	56,023
1969	22	18	3	0	2	4	1	2	2	4,177	770	14	5,210	62,928
1970	24	18	1	1	2	0	1	2	2	3,611	485	11	5,874	63,510
1971	15	19	1	1	6	5	0	1	3	4,817	727	15	7,823	115,150
1972	24	17	1	2	1	4	1	0	1	4,641	594	14	6,030	102,540
1973	6	27	5	2	4	6	4	0	4	8,369	975	14	8,918	190,531
1974	7	19	2	0	4	5	1	1	1	4,346	381	13	5,891	151,025
1975	15	23	3	4	2	4	1	1	1	6,281	748	18	8,114	136,351
1976	7	30	2	1	3	1	4	7	0	7,335	1,028	15	8,610	239,922
1977	5	30	0	0	0	2	4	3	11	8,084	52	7	9,877	224,847
1978	24	19	1	0	1	1	1	1	4	4,319	354	10	6,594	111,765
1979	15	26	7	3	2	3	3	1	3	6,107	1,083	20	7,422	342,148
1980	21	19	6	2	2	4	2	0	2	5,042	671	15	6,953	275,200
1981	27	16	0	0	1	0	2	3	3	3,562	110	9	5,811	115,095
1982	23	23	1	0	1	0	0	3	7	5,672	104	13	7,393	253,675
1983	21	21	1	1	1	2	0	1	7	5,111	174	7	6,816	216,355
1984	21	21	1	0	1	2	0	1	8	6,216	84	2	7,451	151,635
1985	17	28	0	0	0	0	2	0	5	6,226	4	2	8,075	235,480
1986	24	17	0	0	0	1	2	3	0	3,964	45	5	6,465	138,600
1987	24	20	0	0	1	1	1	0	7	4,509	91	7	7,165	255,320
1988	29	17	0	0	0	0	0	0	7	4,445	42	7	6,481	184,200
1990	41	8	0	0	0	0	0	0	0	1,326	1	1	2,353	40,085
1991	40	6	0	0	0	0	0	0	0	845	0	0	1,958	58,060
1992	48	3	0	0	0	0	0	0	0	547	0	0	1,227	49,500
Lifetime		699	40	19	42	59	42	40	109	151,065	9,599	242	181,292	$3,892,175

Charlie Baker

Charles Baker Jr.
B: 5/4/1952
Racing Hometown: New Oxford, PA

Year	Rank	Starts	Poles	1	2	3	4	5	6–10	Laps	Laps Led	Races Led	Miles	$
1982	NR	3	0	0	0	0	0	0	0	444	0	0	1,025	5,235
1986	92T	1	0	0	0	0	0	0	0	457	0	0	465	2,500
1987	68	3	0	0	0	0	0	0	0	901	0	0	1,138	6,560
1988	87T	1	0	0	0	0	0	0	0	136	0	0	138	1,590
1989	57	3	0	0	0	0	0	0	0	255	0	0	611	16,370
1990	77	2	0	0	0	0	0	0	0	84	0	0	85	5,325
Lifetime		13	0	0	0	0	0	0	0	2,277	0	0	3,462	$37,580

Gary Baker

Gary Baker
B: 5/28/1946
Racing Hometown: Nashville, TN

Year	Rank	Starts	Poles	1	2	3	4	5	6–10	Laps	Laps Led	Races Led	Miles	$
1980	NR	1	0	0	0	0	0	0	0	145	0	0	386	3,440
Lifetime		1	0	0	0	0	0	0	0	145	0	0	386	$3,440

Jim Baker

James Baker
Racing Hometown: Atlanta, GA

Year	Rank	Starts	Poles	1	2	3	4	5	6–10	Laps	Laps Led	Races Led	Miles	$
1953	117T	1	0	0	0	0	0	0	0		0	0		25
Lifetime		1	0	0	0	0	0	0	0		0	0		$25

Randy Baker

Randall Baker
B: 5/14/1958
Racing Hometown: Charlotte, NC

Year	Rank	Starts	Poles	1	2	3	4	5	6–10	Laps	Laps Led	Races Led	Miles	$
1982	84T	1	0	0	0	0	0	0	0	347	0	0	353	1,300
1984	54	3	0	0	0	0	0	0	0	553	0	0	826	6,400
1985	NR	1	0	0	0	0	0	0	0	453	0	0	461	2,025
1986	83	2	0	0	0	0	0	0	0	328	0	0	499	2,790
1987	NR	2	0	0	0	0	0	0	0	653	0	0	986	8,060
1988	82	1	0	0	0	0	0	0	0	135	0	0	184	2,055
1991	58	2	0	0	0	0	0	0	0	689	0	0	941	8,055
1992	75	1	0	0	0	0	0	0	0	459	0	0	467	8,700
1996	67	1	0	0	0	0	0	0	0	51	0	0	78	12,550
Lifetime		14	0	0	0	0	0	0	0	3,668	0	0	4,794	$51,935

Year	Rank	Starts	Poles	Finish 1	2	3	4	5	6–10	Laps	Laps Led	Races Led	Miles	$

W.E. Baker

William E. Baker (Bill)
Racing Hometown: New Zion, SC

Year	Rank	Starts	Poles	1	2	3	4	5	6–10	Laps	Laps Led	Races Led	Miles	$
1952	82	1	0	0	0	0	0	0	0	368	0	0	460	90
1952	82	1	0	0	0	0	0	0	0	368	0	0	460	90
Lifetime		2	0	0	0	0	0	0	0	736	0	0	920	$180

Ivan Baldwin

Ivan Baldwin
B: 8/26/1946
Racing Hometown: Modesto, CA

Year	Rank	Starts	Poles	1	2	3	4	5	6–10	Laps	Laps Led	Races Led	Miles	$
1971	NR	3	0	0	0	0	0	0	0	272	0	0	692	3,535
1972	98	1	0	0	0	0	0	0	0	123	0	0	322	1,120
1975	112	2	0	0	0	0	0	0	0	9	0	0	24	1,040
Lifetime		6	0	0	0	0	0	0	0	404	0	0	1,038	$5,695

Rick Baldwin

Richard Baldwin
B: 6/10/1955 D: 6/12/1997 *Comatose since 6/14/87 in Michigan qualifying crash.*
Racing Hometown: Corpus Christi, TX

Year	Rank	Starts	Poles	1	2	3	4	5	6–10	Laps	Laps Led	Races Led	Miles	$
1981	NR	1	0	0	0	0	0	0	0	149	0	0	298	1,550
1982	76	1	0	0	0	0	0	0	0	323	0	0	485	6,065
1983	69	5	0	0	0	0	0	0	0	818	0	0	1,222	15,140
1985	64	2	0	0	0	0	0	0	0	458	0	0	765	3,035
1986	NR	2	0	0	0	0	0	0	0	393	0	0	260	6,905
Lifetime		11	0	0	0	0	0	0	0	2,141	0	0	3,030	$32,695

Roger Baldwin

Roger Baldwin
Racing Hometown: Belmont, NC

Year	Rank	Starts	Poles	1	2	3	4	5	6–10	Laps	Laps Led	Races Led	Miles	$
1957	NR	2	0	0	0	0	0	0	0	337	0	0	337	200
Lifetime		2	0	0	0	0	0	0	0	337	0	0	337	$200

F. Ballantine

F. Ballantine

Year	Rank	Starts	Poles	1	2	3	4	5	6–10	Laps	Laps Led	Races Led	Miles	$
1954	NR	1	0	0	0	0	0	0	0	9	0	0	18	25
Lifetime		1	0	0	0	0	0	0	0	9	0	0	18	$25

Walter Ballard

Walter H. Ballard
B: 1/12/1933
Racing Hometown: Houston, TX

Year	Rank	Starts	Poles	1	2	3	4	5	6–10	Laps	Laps Led	Races Led	Miles	$
1966	72	1	0	0	0	0	0	0	0	234	0	0	322	525
1971	10	41	0	0	0	1	1	1	8	11,219	0	0	10,781	30,974
1972	6	31	0	0	0	0	0	0	7	8,460	0	0	9,748	59,745
1973	8	28	0	0	0	0	0	0	4	8,048	5	1	8,640	53,875
1974	15	27	0	0	0	0	0	1	5	6,820	2	1	7,247	54,039
1975	11	30	0	0	0	0	0	0	3	7,518	16	2	8,255	55,696
1976	26	14	0	0	0	0	0	0	3	4,168	0	0	3,543	16,380
1977	54	3	0	0	0	0	0	0	0	752	0	0	738	5,175
1978	96T	1	0	0	0	0	0	0	0	0	0	0	0	505
Lifetime		176	0	0	0	1	1	2	30	47,219	23	4	49,274	$276,914

Claude Ballot-Lena

Claude Ballot-Lena
Racing Hometown: Paris, France

Year	Rank	Starts	Poles	1	2	3	4	5	6–10	Laps	Laps Led	Races Led	Miles	$
1978	NR	5	0	0	0	0	0	0	1	776	0	0	1,667	11,780
1979	NR	2	0	0	0	0	0	0	0	251	0	0	463	2,080
Lifetime		7	0	0	0	0	0	0	1	1,027	0	0	2,130	$13,860

Earl Balmer

Earl Franklin Balmer
B: 12/13/1935
Racing Hometown: Floyds Knob, IN

Year	Rank	Starts	Poles	1	2	3	4	5	6–10	Laps	Laps Led	Races Led	Miles	$
1959	54	2	0	0	0	0	0	0	0	436	0	0	423	250
1964	35	10	0	0	0	0	1	1	2	2,771	1	1	2,052	5,795
1965	23	9	0	0	1	0	1	0	2	1,320	32	6	2,174	19,045
1966	36	9	0	1	0	0	0	1	0	1,388	4	2	2,097	7,935
1967	100	1	0	0	0	0	0	0	0	102	0	0	140	625
1968	NR	1	0	0	0	0	0	0	0	59	0	0	89	1,075
Lifetime		32	0	1	1	0	2	2	4	6,076	37	9	6,974	$34,725

Year	Rank	Starts	Poles	Finish 1	2	3	4	5	6–10	Laps	Laps Led	Races Led	Miles	$

Gary Balough

Gary Balough
B: 9/16/1947
Racing Hometown: Ft. Lauderdale, FL

Year	Rank	Starts	Poles	1	2	3	4	5	6–10	Laps	Laps Led	Races Led	Miles	$
1979	89	3	0	0	0	0	0	0	0	216	0	0	540	6,015
1980	108	1	0	0	0	0	0	0	0	16	0	0	24	610
1981	40	10	0	0	0	0	0	0	1	2,267	1	1	3,232	34,430
1982	38	5	0	0	0	0	0	0	1	1,359	0	0	1,608	35,735
1991	74T	2	0	0	0	0	0	0	0	44	0	0	68	6,410
1992	93T	1	0	0	0	0	0	0	0	131	0	0	197	5,100
Lifetime		22	0	0	0	0	0	0	2	4,033	1	1	5,669	$88,300

John Banks

John Banks
Racing Hometown: Windsor, Ont, Canada

Year	Rank	Starts	Poles	1	2	3	4	5	6–10	Laps	Laps Led	Races Led	Miles	$
1974	NR	1	0	0	0	0	0	0	0	14	0	0	28	835
1975	86T	3	0	0	0	0	0	0	0	478	0	0	816	2,760
Lifetime		4	0	0	0	0	0	0	0	492	0	0	844	$3,595

Ron Barfield Jr.

Ron Barfield Jr.
B: 4/20/1971
Racing Hometown: Florence, SC

Year	Rank	Starts	Poles	1	2	3	4	5	6–10	Laps	Laps Led	Races Led	Miles	$
1997	59	1	0	0	0	0	0	0	0	160	0	0	400	64,935
Lifetime		1	0	0	0	0	0	0	0	160	0	0	400	$64,935

Phil Barkdoll

Phillip Barkdoll
B: 9/9/1937
Racing Hometown: Phoenix, AZ

Year	Rank	Starts	Poles	1	2	3	4	5	6–10	Laps	Laps Led	Races Led	Miles	$
1984	65	2	0	0	0	0	0	0	0	212	0	0	564	5,075
1985	69	2	0	0	0	0	0	0	0	200	0	0	532	5,525
1986	103	2	0	0	0	0	0	0	0	249	3	2	662	6,045
1987	98T	1	0	0	0	0	0	0	0	27	0	0	72	3,150
1988	52	3	0	0	0	0	0	0	0	465	0	0	1,220	17,145
1989	45	4	0	0	0	0	0	0	0	658	2	1	1,702	29,050
1990	64	3	0	0	0	0	0	0	0	202	0	0	524	24,160
1991	46	4	0	0	0	0	0	0	0	646	0	0	1,674	41,655
1992	55	2	0	0	0	0	0	0	0	354	0	0	885	33,255
Lifetime		23	0	0	0	0	0	0	0	3,013	5	3	7,836	$165,060

Bill Barker

William Barker
Racing Hometown: Greenville, PA

Year	Rank	Starts	Poles	1	2	3	4	5	6–10	Laps	Laps Led	Races Led	Miles	$
1952	79	2	0	0	0	0	0	0	0	376	0	0	301	75
1954	99	4	0	0	0	0	0	0	0	364	0	0	279	35
Lifetime		6	0	0	0	0	0	0	0	740	0	0	580	$110

Curley Barker

Curley Barker
Racing Hometown: Tillemook, OR

Year	Rank	Starts	Poles	1	2	3	4	5	6–10	Laps	Laps Led	Races Led	Miles	$
1956	58	4	0	0	0	2	0	1	1	840	0	0	420	1,395
Lifetime		4	0	0	0	2	0	1	1	840	0	0	420	$1,395

John Barker

John Barker
Racing Hometown: Hickory, NC

Year	Rank	Starts	Poles	1	2	3	4	5	6–10	Laps	Laps Led	Races Led	Miles	$
1949	66	1	0	0	0	0	0	0	0		0	0		50
1951	N/A	7	0	0	0	0	0	0	0	471	0	0	526	175
Lifetime		8	0	0	0	0	0	0	0	471	0	0	526	$225

Johnny Barnes

John Barnes
B: 4/24/1942
Racing Hometown: Port Charlotte, FL

Year	Rank	Starts	Poles	1	2	3	4	5	6–10	Laps	Laps Led	Races Led	Miles	$
1971	NR	1	0	0	0	0	0	0	0	23	0	0	61	615
1973	39	8	0	0	0	0	0	0	0	1,416	0	0	2,181	8,585
1974	65	4	0	0	0	0	0	0	0	135	0	0	171	2,515
Lifetime		13	0	0	0	0	0	0	0	1,574	0	0	2,413	$11,715

Year	Rank	Starts	Poles	Finish 1	2	3	4	5	6–10	Laps	Laps Led	Races Led	Miles	$

Jerry Barnett

Jerry Barnett
B: 12/17/1951
Racing Hometown: Bonita, CA

Year	Rank	Starts	Poles	1	2	3	4	5	6–10	Laps	Laps Led	Races Led	Miles	$
1971	NR	2	0	0	0	0	0	0	0	118	0	0	256	1,260
Lifetime		2	0	0	0	0	0	0	0	118	0	0	256	$1,260

Dick Baron

Richard Baron
Racing Hometown: Sacramento, CA

Year	Rank	Starts	Poles	1	2	3	4	5	6–10	Laps	Laps Led	Races Led	Miles	$
1961	189	1	0	0	0	0	0	0	0	5	0	0	5	25
Lifetime		1	0	0	0	0	0	0	0	5	0	0	5	$25

Buck Barr

Buck Barr
Racing Hometown: Zanesville, OH

Year	Rank	Starts	Poles	1	2	3	4	5	6–10	Laps	Laps Led	Races Led	Miles	$
1950	36	2	0	0	0	1	0	0	1		0	0		575
Lifetime		2	0	0	0	1	0	0	1		0	0		$575

Charles Barrett

Charles Barrett
B: 11/28/1944
Racing Hometown: Cleveland, GA

Year	Rank	Starts	Poles	1	2	3	4	5	6–10	Laps	Laps Led	Races Led	Miles	$
1973	65	4	0	0	0	0	0	0	1	726	9	1	1,305	5,610
Lifetime		4	0	0	0	0	0	0	1	726	9	1	1,305	$5,610

Stan Barrett

Stanley Barrett
B: 6/26/1943
Racing Hometown: Bishop, CA

Year	Rank	Starts	Poles	1	2	3	4	5	6–10	Laps	Laps Led	Races Led	Miles	$
1980	NR	3	0	0	0	0	0	0	1	987	0	0	1,454	13,760
1981	38	10	0	0	0	0	0	0	1	1,559	4	2	3,265	28,540
1982	96	1	0	0	0	0	0	0	0	65	0	0	163	5,585
1989	61	4	0	0	0	0	0	0	0	391	0	0	615	11,500
1990	74	1	0	0	0	0	0	0	0	74	0	0	186	3,850
Lifetime		19	0	0	0	0	0	0	2	3,076	4	2	5,682	$63,235

Stanton Barrett

Stanton Barrett
B: 12/1/1972
Racing Hometown: Bishop, CA

Year	Rank	Starts	Poles	1	2	3	4	5	6–10	Laps	Laps Led	Races Led	Miles	$
1999	57	2	0	0	0	0	0	0	0	454	0	0	876	84,665
Lifetime		2	0	0	0	0	0	0	0	454	0	0	876	$84,665

Bob Barron

Dr. Robert Barron
B: 1/13/1921
Racing Hometown: Bradenton, FL

Year	Rank	Starts	Poles	1	2	3	4	5	6–10	Laps	Laps Led	Races Led	Miles	$
1960	140	1	0	0	0	0	0	0	0	186	0	0	279	900
1961	29	31	0	0	0	0	0	0	5	5,005	0	0	2,870	3,825
Lifetime		32	0	0	0	0	0	0	5	5,191	0	0	3,149	$4,725

Chester Barron

Charles Barron
Racing Hometown: Cornelia, GA

Year	Rank	Starts	Poles	1	2	3	4	5	6–10	Laps	Laps Led	Races Led	Miles	$
1956	144	2	0	0	0	0	0	0	1	207	0	0	152	150
1958	NR	1	0	0	0	0	0	0	0	49	0	0	49	75
1959	NR	3	0	0	0	0	0	0	1	271	0	0	175	275
Lifetime		6	0	0	0	0	0	0	2	527	0	0	376	$500

Paul Barrow

Paul Barrow
Racing Hometown: Sycanore, IL

Year	Rank	Starts	Poles	1	2	3	4	5	6–10	Laps	Laps Led	Races Led	Miles	$
1962	64	2	0	0	0	0	0	0	0	189	0	0	473	500
Lifetime		2	0	0	0	0	0	0	0	189	0	0	473	$500

Charles Barry

Charles Barry
D: 2/1970
Racing Hometown: Syracuse, NY

Year	Rank	Starts	Poles	1	2	3	4	5	6–10	Laps	Laps Led	Races Led	Miles	$
1952	78	3	0	0	0	0	0	0	0	312	0	0	162	75

Year	Rank	Starts	Poles	1	2	3	Finish 4	5	6–10	Laps	Laps Led	Races Led	Miles	$

Charles Barry *continued*

Year	Rank	Starts	Poles	1	2	3	4	5	6–10	Laps	Laps Led	Races Led	Miles	$
1953	NR	1	0	0	0	0	0	0	1		0	0		100
Lifetime		4	0	0	0	0	0	0	1	312	0	0	162	$175

Darrell Basham

Darrell Basham
B: 3/17/1949
Racing Hometown: Jeffersonville, IN

Year	Rank	Starts	Poles	1	2	3	4	5	6–10	Laps	Laps Led	Races Led	Miles	$
1979	NR	1	0	0	0	0	0	0	0	101	0	0	60	385
Lifetime		1	0	0	0	0	0	0	0	101	0	0	60	$385

Paul Bass

Paul Bass
Racing Hometown: Indianapolis, IN

Year	Rank	Starts	Poles	1	2	3	4	5	6–10	Laps	Laps Led	Races Led	Miles	$
1959	NR	1	0	0	0	0	0	0	0	52	0	0	130	100
Lifetime		1	0	0	0	0	0	0	0	52	0	0	130	$100

Mike Batinick

Michael Batinick
Racing Hometown: Campbell, CA

Year	Rank	Starts	Poles	1	2	3	4	5	6–10	Laps	Laps Led	Races Led	Miles	$
1958	62	2	0	0	0	0	0	0	0	257	0	0	528	240
Lifetime		2	0	0	0	0	0	0	0	257	0	0	528	$240

George Bauer

George Bauer
Racing Hometown: Covington, KY

Year	Rank	Starts	Poles	1	2	3	4	5	6–10	Laps	Laps Led	Races Led	Miles	$
1969	NR	2	0	0	0	0	0	0	0	203	0	0	508	2,410
Lifetime		2	0	0	0	0	0	0	0	203	0	0	508	$2,410

Ed Baugess

Edward Baugess

Year	Rank	Starts	Poles	1	2	3	4	5	6–10	Laps	Laps Led	Races Led	Miles	$
1983	90T	1	0	0	0	0	0	0	0	13	0	0	8	725
Lifetime		1	0	0	0	0	0	0	0	13	0	0	8	$725

Larry Baumel

Larry Allan Baumel
B: 5/26/1944
Racing Hometown: Sparta, WI

Year	Rank	Starts	Poles	1	2	3	4	5	6–10	Laps	Laps Led	Races Led	Miles	$
1969	59	6	0	0	0	0	0	0	0	964	0	0	682	2,760
1970	32	23	1	0	0	0	0	0	1	2,731	0	0	3,697	16,645
1971	37	16	0	0	0	0	0	0	1	2,245	0	0	2,998	10,910
Lifetime		45	1	0	0	0	0	0	2	5,940	0	0	7,376	$30,315

Ray Baxter

Raymond Baxter
Racing Hometown: Bronx, NY

Year	Rank	Starts	Poles	1	2	3	4	5	6–10	Laps	Laps Led	Races Led	Miles	$
1956	239T	1	0	0	0	0	0	0	0	55	0	0	55	50
Lifetime		1	0	0	0	0	0	0	0	55	0	0	55	$50

Hal Beal

Harold Beal (Hal)
Racing Hometown: Portland, OR

Year	Rank	Starts	Poles	1	2	3	4	5	6–10	Laps	Laps Led	Races Led	Miles	$
1956	66	5	0	0	0	0	1	0	2	781	0	0	398	915
1957	69	4	0	0	0	0	0	0	1	429	0	0	236	400
1963	83	1	0	0	0	0	0	0	0	164	0	0	443	425
Lifetime		10	0	0	0	0	1	0	3	1,374	0	0	1,077	$1,740

Herman Beam

Herman Beam
B: 12/11/1929   D: 8/27/1980
Racing Hometown: Johnson City, TN

Year	Rank	Starts	Poles	1	2	3	4	5	6–10	Laps	Laps Led	Races Led	Miles	$
1957	NR	1	0	0	0	0	0	0	0		0	0		50
1958	13	20	0	0	0	0	0	0	1	3,651	0	0	2,251	2,599
1959	4	30	0	0	0	0	0	1	11	6,024	0	0	4,006	6,380
1960	12	26	0	0	0	0	1	0	5	5,348	0	0	4,730	5,916
1961	15	41	0	0	0	0	1	0	13	8,827	0	0	6,403	6,194
1962	11	51	1	0	0	0	0	0	18	11,217	0	0	7,140	12,571
1963	27	25	0	0	0	0	0	0	6	5,061	0	0	3,476	5,255
Lifetime		194	1	0	0	0	2	1	54	40,128	0	0	28,005	$38,965

Year	Rank	Starts	Poles	Finish						Laps	Laps Led	Races Led	Miles	$
				1	2	3	4	5	6–10					

Nix Beard

Nix Beard
Racing Hometown: Germantown, OH

Year	Rank	Starts	Poles	1	2	3	4	5	6–10	Laps	Laps Led	Races Led	Miles	$
1950	126T	1	0	0	0	0	0	0	0		0	0		0
Lifetime		1	0	0	0	0	0	0	0		0	0		$0

Byron Beatty

Byron Beatty

Year	Rank	Starts	Poles	1	2	3	4	5	6–10	Laps	Laps Led	Races Led	Miles	$
1950	NR	1	0	0	0	0	0	0	0	351	0	0	439	0
Lifetime		1	0	0	0	0	0	0	0	351	0	0	439	$0

Dick Beaty

Richard Beaty
B: 12/16/1924
Racing Hometown: Charlotte, NC

Year	Rank	Starts	Poles	1	2	3	4	5	6–10	Laps	Laps Led	Races Led	Miles	$
1955	203	1	0	0	0	0	0	0	0	184	0	0	253	50
1956	46	15	0	0	0	0	0	0	3	1,513	0	0	1,091	910
1957	17	20	0	0	0	0	0	1	6	3,202	0	0	2,061	3,648
1958	89	2	0	0	0	0	0	0	0	448	0	0	224	150
Lifetime		38	0	0	0	0	0	1	9	5,347	0	0	3,628	$4,758

Johnny Beauchamp

John Beauchamp
B: 3/23/1923   D: 4/17/1981
Racing Hometown: Harlan, IA

Year	Rank	Starts	Poles	1	2	3	4	5	6–10	Laps	Laps Led	Races Led	Miles	$
1953	50	3	0	0	0	0	0	0	1		0	0		150
1957	66	1	0	0	1	0	0	0	0		0	0		2,450
1959	NR	7	0	1	2	0	0	0	0	1,107	130	2	1,146	10,465
1960	11	11	0	1	1	0	0	1	2	2,669	1	1	2,530	17,374
1961	166	1	0	0	0	0	0	0	0	37	0	0	93	75
Lifetime		23	0	2	4	0	0	1	3	3,813	131	3	3,768	$30,514

Bob Beck

Robert Beck
Racing Hometown: Buffalo, NY

Year	Rank	Starts	Poles	1	2	3	4	5	6–10	Laps	Laps Led	Races Led	Miles	$
1955	158	2	0	0	0	0	0	0	0	223	0	0	144	75
Lifetime		2	0	0	0	0	0	0	0	223	0	0	144	$75

Randy Becker

Randall Becker
B: 10/2/1952
Racing Hometown: Highland, CA

Year	Rank	Starts	Poles	1	2	3	4	5	6–10	Laps	Laps Led	Races Led	Miles	$
1982	103	2	0	0	0	0	0	0	0	116	0	0	304	1,640
1983	70	2	0	0	0	0	0	0	0	139	0	0	364	3,650
Lifetime		4	0	0	0	0	0	0	0	255	0	0	668	$5,290

Christine Beckers

Christine Beckers

Year	Rank	Starts	Poles	1	2	3	4	5	6–10	Laps	Laps Led	Races Led	Miles	$
1977	NR	1	0	0	0	0	0	0	0	33	0	0	83	695
Lifetime		1	0	0	0	0	0	0	0	33	0	0	83	$695

Troy Beebe

Troy Beebe
B: 1/5/1962
Racing Hometown: Modesto, CA

Year	Rank	Starts	Poles	1	2	3	4	5	6–10	Laps	Laps Led	Races Led	Miles	$
1989	75T	1	0	0	0	0	0	0	0	72	0	0	181	2,605
1990	71	4	0	0	0	0	0	0	0	584	0	0	1,001	19,675
Lifetime		5	0	0	0	0	0	0	0	656	0	0	1,182	$22,280

Earl Beer

Earl Beer
Racing Hometown: Brooklyn, NY

Year	Rank	Starts	Poles	1	2	3	4	5	6–10	Laps	Laps Led	Races Led	Miles	$
1954	NR	1	0	0	0	0	0	0	0	46	0	0	92	100
Lifetime		1	0	0	0	0	0	0	0	46	0	0	92	$100

George Behlman

George Behlman
B: 4/22/1944
Racing Hometown: Lemon Grove, CA

Year	Rank	Starts	Poles	1	2	3	4	5	6–10	Laps	Laps Led	Races Led	Miles	$
1973	100	1	0	0	0	0	0	0	0	137	0	0	359	875

Year	Rank	Starts	Poles	1	2	Finish 3	4	5	6–10	Laps	Laps Led	Races Led	Miles	$

George Behlman *continued*

Year	Rank	Starts	Poles	1	2	3	4	5	6–10	Laps	Laps Led	Races Led	Miles	$
1974	124	1	0	0	0	0	0	0	0	25	0	0	66	695
Lifetime		2	0	0	0	0	0	0	0	162	0	0	424	$1,570

Leo Beiethaupt

Leo Beiethaupt
Racing Hometown: Los Angeles, CA

Year	Rank	Starts	Poles	1	2	3	4	5	6–10	Laps	Laps Led	Races Led	Miles	$
1951	N/A	1	0	0	0	0	0	0	1		0	0		100
Lifetime		1	0	0	0	0	0	0	1		0	0		$100

Sam Beler

Samuel Beler
Racing Hometown: Lakewood, CA

Year	Rank	Starts	Poles	1	2	3	4	5	6–10	Laps	Laps Led	Races Led	Miles	$
1976	109T	1	0	0	0	0	0	0	0	15	0	0	39	585
Lifetime		1	0	0	0	0	0	0	0	15	0	0	39	$585

John Belgard

John E. Belgard
Racing Hometown: Hyattsville, MD

Year	Rank	Starts	Poles	1	2	3	4	5	6–10	Laps	Laps Led	Races Led	Miles	$
1949	NR	1	0	0	0	0	0	0	0		0	0		0
Lifetime		1	0	0	0	0	0	0	0		0	0		$0

Joe Bell

Joseph Bell
D: 8/20/66   *Died of heart attack while in car @ Saugus, CA.*
Racing Hometown: N. Tarrytown, NY

Year	Rank	Starts	Poles	1	2	3	4	5	6–10	Laps	Laps Led	Races Led	Miles	$
1954	186	1	0	0	0	0	0	0	0	48	0	0	48	0
Lifetime		1	0	0	0	0	0	0	0	48	0	0	48	$0

Phillips Bell

Phillips Bell
Racing Hometown: Manasquan, NJ

Year	Rank	Starts	Poles	1	2	3	4	5	6–10	Laps	Laps Led	Races Led	Miles	$
1954	NR	1	0	0	0	0	0	0	0	45	0	0	90	75
Lifetime		1	0	0	0	0	0	0	0	45	0	0	90	$75

Joe Bellinato

Joseph Bellinato
B: 1922   D: 7/7/1992
Racing Hometown: Singac, NJ

Year	Rank	Starts	Poles	1	2	3	4	5	6–10	Laps	Laps Led	Races Led	Miles	$
1951	224	1	0	0	0	0	0	0	0		0	0		25
Lifetime		1	0	0	0	0	0	0	0		0	0		$25

Andy Belmont

Andrew Belmont
B: 11/20/1957
Racing Hometown: Langhorne, PA

Year	Rank	Starts	Poles	1	2	3	4	5	6–10	Laps	Laps Led	Races Led	Miles	$
1989	86	1	0	0	0	0	0	0	0	373	0	0	373	2,150
1991	89	1	0	0	0	0	0	0	0	11	0	0	11	3,450
1992	43	8	0	0	0	0	0	0	0	779	0	0	1,535	39,820
Lifetime		10	0	0	0	0	0	0	0	1,163	0	0	1,919	$45,420

Ed Benedict

Edward Benedict
Racing Hometown: Miamisburg, OH

Year	Rank	Starts	Poles	1	2	3	4	5	6–10	Laps	Laps Led	Races Led	Miles	$
1951	88	6	0	0	0	0	0	0	1	445	0	0	538	300
1952	49	5	0	0	0	0	0	1	1	633	0	0	380	360
1953	73	1	0	0	0	0	0	0	1	189	0	0	95	125
Lifetime		12	0	0	0	0	0	1	3	1,267	0	0	1,012	$785

Corey Benjamin

Corey Benjamin
Racing Hometown: Rising Sun, MD

Year	Rank	Starts	Poles	1	2	3	4	5	6–10	Laps	Laps Led	Races Led	Miles	$
1956	261	1	0	0	0	0	0	0	0	34	0	0	34	50
Lifetime		1	0	0	0	0	0	0	0	34	0	0	34	$50

Jerry Benjamin

Jerry Benjamin
Racing Hometown: Rising Sun, MD

Year	Rank	Starts	Poles	1	2	3	4	5	6–10	Laps	Laps Led	Races Led	Miles	$
1955	226	1	0	0	0	0	0	0	0	71	0	0	71	50

Year	Rank	Starts	Poles	Finish 1	2	3	4	5	6–10	Laps	Laps Led	Races Led	Miles	$

Jerry Benjamin *continued*

Year	Rank	Starts	Poles	1	2	3	4	5	6–10	Laps	Laps Led	Races Led	Miles	$
1957	191	3	0	0	0	0	0	0	0	200	0	0	157	125
1958	173	1	0	0	0	0	0	0	0	26	0	0	13	10
Lifetime		5	0	0	0	0	0	0	0	297	0	0	241	$185

Arnold Bennett

Arnold Bennett
Racing Hometown: Battle Creek, MI

Year	Rank	Starts	Poles	1	2	3	4	5	6–10	Laps	Laps Led	Races Led	Miles	$
1970	113	1	0	0	0	0	0	0	0	1	0	0	3	0
Lifetime		1	0	0	0	0	0	0	0	1	0	0	3	$0

Bill Bennett

William Bennett
Racing Hometown: Rehoboth Beach, NJ

Year	Rank	Starts	Poles	1	2	3	4	5	6–10	Laps	Laps Led	Races Led	Miles	$
1949	45	1	0	0	0	0	0	0	0	181	0	0	181	100
Lifetime		1	0	0	0	0	0	0	0	181	0	0	181	$100

Bud Bennett

Bud Bennett
Racing Hometown: Grand Rapids, MI

Year	Rank	Starts	Poles	1	2	3	4	5	6–10	Laps	Laps Led	Races Led	Miles	$
1954	NR	1	0	0	0	0	0	0	0	167	0	0	84	25
Lifetime		1	0	0	0	0	0	0	0	167	0	0	84	$25

Harry Bennett

Harry Bennett
Racing Hometown: St.Claire Shores, MI

Year	Rank	Starts	Poles	1	2	3	4	5	6–10	Laps	Laps Led	Races Led	Miles	$
1953	169	1	0	0	0	0	0	0	0		0	0		25
Lifetime		1	0	0	0	0	0	0	0		0	0		$25

Jim Bennett

James M. Bennett
D: 11/11/199
Racing Hometown: Jonesboro, GA

Year	Rank	Starts	Poles	1	2	3	4	5	6–10	Laps	Laps Led	Races Led	Miles	$
1961	82	2	0	0	0	0	0	0	0	170	0	0	351	500
1962	63	5	0	0	0	0	0	1	1	402	0	0	341	950
Lifetime		7	0	0	0	0	0	1	1	572	0	0	692	$1,450

Russell Bennett

Russell Horace Bennett
B: 12/29/1920
Racing Hometown: Milford, DE

Year	Rank	Starts	Poles	1	2	3	4	5	6–10	Laps	Laps Led	Races Led	Miles	$
1950	90	2	0	0	0	0	0	0	0	123	0	0	123	100
Lifetime		2	0	0	0	0	0	0	0	123	0	0	123	$100

Norm Benning

Norman Benning
B: 1/16/1952
Racing Hometown: Level Green, PA

Year	Rank	Starts	Poles	1	2	3	4	5	6–10	Laps	Laps Led	Races Led	Miles	$
1989	53	3	0	0	0	0	0	0	0	653	0	0	880	6,875
1993	87T	1	0	0	0	0	0	0	0	1	0	0	1	5,410
Lifetime		4	0	0	0	0	0	0	0	654	0	0	881	$12,285

Bill Benson

William Benson
Racing Hometown: Far Rockaway, NY

Year	Rank	Starts	Poles	1	2	3	4	5	6–10	Laps	Laps Led	Races Led	Miles	$
1957	30	11	0	0	0	0	0	0	2	1,320	0	0	827	1,090
1958	53	5	0	0	0	0	0	0	0	549	0	0	375	220
Lifetime		16	0	0	0	0	0	0	2	1,869	0	0	1,202	$1,310

Johnny Benson Sr.

Johnny Benson, Sr.
B: 4/24/1937
Racing Hometown: Grand Rapids, MI

Year	Rank	Starts	Poles	1	2	3	4	5	6–10	Laps	Laps Led	Races Led	Miles	$
1973	97	1	0	0	0	0	0	0	0	185	0	0	370	850
Lifetime		1	0	0	0	0	0	0	0	185	0	0	370	$850

Year	Rank	Starts	Poles	Finish						Laps	Laps Led	Races Led	Miles	$
				1	2	3	4	5	6–10					

Johnny Benson Jr.

Johnny Benson Jr.
B: 6/27/1963
Racing Hometown: Grand Rapids, MI

Year	Rank	Starts	Poles	1	2	3	4	5	6–10	Laps	Laps Led	Races Led	Miles	$
1996	21	30	1	0	0	0	0	1	5	8,507	105	4	10,484	947,080
1997	11	32	1	0	0	0	0	0	8	9,648	19	7	12,504	1,256,457
1998	20	32	0	0	0	0	1	2	7	8,565	93	10	11,108	1,360,335
1999	28	34	0	0	0	0	0	0	2	9,362	8	3	11,902	1,567,668
2000	13	33	0	0	2	0	0	1	4	9,451	62	5	12,195	1,627,874
2001	11	36	0	0	0	3	1	2	8	10,049	101	10	13,414	2,894,903
2002	29	31	0	1	1	0	1	0	4	8,310	116	6	11,081	2,791,879
Lifetime		228	2	1	3	3	3	6	38	63,892	504	45	82,688	$12,446,196

Tiny Benson

Tiny Benson
Racing Hometown: Syracuse, NY

Year	Rank	Starts	Poles	1	2	3	4	5	6–10	Laps	Laps Led	Races Led	Miles	$
1958	73	4	0	0	0	0	0	0	2	445	0	0	182	450
1959	NR	2	0	0	0	0	0	0	2	298	0	0	205	350
Lifetime		6	0	0	0	0	0	0	4	743	0	0	387	$800

Roy Bentley

Roy Bentley   *Killed in highway crash.*
Racing Hometown: Florence, SC

Year	Rank	Starts	Poles	1	2	3	4	5	6–10	Laps	Laps Led	Races Led	Miles	$
1950	NR	1	0	0	0	0	0	0	0	319	0	0	399	0
1953	161	1	0	0	0	0	0	0	0	220	0	0	220	25
1955	197	1	0	0	0	0	0	0	0	317	0	0	436	60
1956	139	3	0	0	0	0	0	0	0	329	0	0	292	200
Lifetime		6	0	0	0	0	0	0	0	1,185	0	0	1,347	$285

Clarence Benton

Clarence Benton
Racing Hometown: N.Wilkesboro, NC

Year	Rank	Starts	Poles	1	2	3	4	5	6–10	Laps	Laps Led	Races Led	Miles	$
1949	NR	1	0	0	0	0	0	0	0		0	0		0
Lifetime		1	0	0	0	0	0	0	0		0	0		$0

Ben Benz

Ben Benz (Real Name: Bernard Friedland)
Racing Hometown: Far Rockaway, NY

Year	Rank	Starts	Poles	1	2	3	4	5	6–10	Laps	Laps Led	Races Led	Miles	$
1958	82	4	0	0	0	0	0	0	2	831	0	0	408	400
1959	62	5	0	0	0	0	0	0	2	665	0	0	740	625
Lifetime		9	0	0	0	0	0	0	4	1,496	0	0	1,148	$1,025

Leo Bergeron

Leo Bergeron
Racing Hometown: Montreal, Que, Canada

Year	Rank	Starts	Poles	1	2	3	4	5	6–10	Laps	Laps Led	Races Led	Miles	$
1953	121	2	0	0	0	0	0	0	0		0	0		65
Lifetime		2	0	0	0	0	0	0	0		0	0		$65

Ed Bergin

Edward Bergin

Year	Rank	Starts	Poles	1	2	3	4	5	6–10	Laps	Laps Led	Races Led	Miles	$
1955	198	1	0	0	0	0	0	0	0	302	0	0	415	160
Lifetime		1	0	0	0	0	0	0	0	302	0	0	415	$160

Gene Bergin

Eugene Bergin
B: 1933
Racing Hometown: Enfield, CT

Year	Rank	Starts	Poles	1	2	3	4	5	6–10	Laps	Laps Led	Races Led	Miles	$
1956	219	2	0	0	0	0	0	0	0	384	0	0	500	310
Lifetime		2	0	0	0	0	0	0	0	384	0	0	500	$310

Ed Berrier

Edward Berrier
B: 11/8/1961
Racing Hometown: Winston-Salem, NC

Year	Rank	Starts	Poles	1	2	3	4	5	6–10	Laps	Laps Led	Races Led	Miles	$
1995	57	1	0	0	0	0	0	0	0	358	0	0	489	13,460
1996	66	1	0	0	0	0	0	0	0	57	0	0	78	9,895
1997	55	3	0	0	0	0	0	0	0	1,119	0	0	909	87,895
1999	53	4	0	0	0	0	0	0	0	1,050	0	0	1,587	120,325
2000	47	10	0	0	0	0	0	0	0	2,086	0	0	3,797	417,144
Lifetime		19	0	0	0	0	0	0	0	4,670	0	0	6,860	$648,719

Year	Rank	Starts	Poles	Finish 1	2	3	4	5	6–10	Laps	Laps Led	Races Led	Miles	$

Max Berrier

Max Berrier
B: 2/1/1936
Racing Hometown: Wallburg, NC

Year	Rank	Starts	Poles	1	2	3	4	5	6–10	Laps	Laps Led	Races Led	Miles	$
1955	NR	2	0	0	0	0	0	0	0	232	0	0	116	100
1957	129	2	0	0	0	0	0	0	0	0	0	0	0	50
1959	NR	2	0	0	0	0	0	0	0	214	0	0	64	110
1972	NR	1	0	0	0	0	0	0	0	349	0	0	218	740
Lifetime		7	0	0	0	0	0	0	0	795	0	0	398	$1,000

Robert Berrier

Robert Berrier
Racing Hometown: Winston-Salem, NC

Year	Rank	Starts	Poles	1	2	3	4	5	6–10	Laps	Laps Led	Races Led	Miles	$
1961	NR	1	0	0	0	0	0	0	0	137	0	0	34	110
1962	NR	1	0	0	0	0	0	0	0	100	0	0	25	250
Lifetime		2	0	0	0	0	0	0	0	237	0	0	59	$360

Joe Bessey

Joseph Bessey
B: 6/25/1961
Racing Hometown: Portland, ME

Year	Rank	Starts	Poles	1	2	3	4	5	6–10	Laps	Laps Led	Races Led	Miles	$
2000	65	1	0	0	0	0	0	0	0	297	0	0	314	48,975
Lifetime		1	0	0	0	0	0	0	0	297	0	0	314	$48,975

Randy Bethea

Randolph Bethea
Racing Hometown: Johnson City, TN

Year	Rank	Starts	Poles	1	2	3	4	5	6–10	Laps	Laps Led	Races Led	Miles	$
1975	109T	1	0	0	0	0	0	0	0	251	0	0	377	1,055
Lifetime		1	0	0	0	0	0	0	0	251	0	0	377	$1,055

Fred Bethune

Frederick Bethune
Racing Hometown: Wyandotte, MI

Year	Rank	Starts	Poles	1	2	3	4	5	6–10	Laps	Laps Led	Races Led	Miles	$
1952	63	2	0	0	0	0	0	0	1	377	0	0	293	125
Lifetime		2	0	0	0	0	0	0	1	377	0	0	293	$125

Gary Bettenhausen

Gary Clyde Bettenhausen
B: 11/18/1941
Racing Hometown: Monrovia, IN

Year	Rank	Starts	Poles	1	2	3	4	5	6–10	Laps	Laps Led	Races Led	Miles	$
1967	NR	3	0	0	0	0	0	0	1	124	0	0	310	1,680
1974	43	5	0	0	0	0	1	0	2	986	35	1	2,100	10,350
Lifetime		8	0	0	0	0	1	0	3	1,110	35	1	2,410	$12,030

Tony Bettenhausen Jr.

Tony Lee Bettenhausen Jr.
B: 10/31/1950   D: 2/15/2000   Plane crash.
Racing Hometown: Indianapolis, IN

Year	Rank	Starts	Poles	1	2	3	4	5	6–10	Laps	Laps Led	Races Led	Miles	$
1973	54	5	0	0	0	0	0	0	0	863	0	0	1,319	5,015
1974	20	27	0	0	0	0	0	0	1	5,548	0	0	6,151	38,995
1982	NR	1	0	0	0	0	0	0	0	139	0	0	278	3,215
Lifetime		33	0	0	0	0	0	0	1	6,550	0	0	7,748	$47,225

Jim Bickerstaff

James Bickerstaff
Racing Hometown: Pittsburgh, PA

Year	Rank	Starts	Poles	1	2	3	4	5	6–10	Laps	Laps Led	Races Led	Miles	$
1959	NR	1	0	0	0	0	0	0	0	12	0	0	3	50
Lifetime		1	0	0	0	0	0	0	0	12	0	0	3	$50

Rich Bickle

Richard Bickle Jr.
B: 5/13/1961
Racing Hometown: Edgerton, WI

Year	Rank	Starts	Poles	1	2	3	4	5	6–10	Laps	Laps Led	Races Led	Miles	$
1989	62	2	0	0	0	0	0	0	0	355	0	0	540	4,185
1990	84T	1	0	0	0	0	0	0	0	195	0	0	488	19,120
1991	51	3	0	0	0	0	0	0	0	1,118	0	0	1,404	13,425
1992	49	3	0	0	0	0	0	0	0	816	0	0	881	13,370
1993	48	5	0	0	0	0	0	0	0	842	1	1	1,356	36,095
1994	43	12	0	0	0	0	0	0	0	2,087	0	0	3,616	115,575

Year	Rank	Starts	Poles	Finish						Laps	Laps Led	Races Led	Miles	$
				1	2	3	4	5	6–10					

Rich Bickle *continued*

Year	Rank	Starts	Poles	1	2	3	4	5	6–10	Laps	Laps Led	Races Led	Miles	$
1995	45	8	0	0	0	0	0	0	0	1,995	3	1	2,400	153,250
1997	65	1	0	0	0	0	0	0	0	153	0	0	383	56,410
1998	39	21	0	0	0	0	1	0	0	5,691	0	0	6,938	682,255
1999	38	24	0	0	0	0	0	0	2	6,343	1	1	9,099	892,456
2000	56	3	0	0	0	0	0	0	0	989	0	0	1,067	135,960
2001	65	1	0	0	0	0	0	0	0	494	0	0	259	30,300
Lifetime		84	0	0	0	0	1	0	2	21,078	5	3	28,430	$2,152,401

Andy Biddle

Andrew Biddle
Racing Hometown: Grand Rapids, MI

Year	Rank	Starts	Poles	1	2	3	4	5	6–10	Laps	Laps Led	Races Led	Miles	$
1954	NR	1	0	0	0	0	0	0	0	142	0	0	71	25
Lifetime		1	0	0	0	0	0	0	0	142	0	0	71	$25

Don Biederman

Donald Biederman
Racing Hometown: Port Credit, Ont, Canada

Year	Rank	Starts	Poles	1	2	3	4	5	6–10	Laps	Laps Led	Races Led	Miles	$
1966	58	14	0	0	0	0	0	0	0	2,169	0	0	1,285	2,215
1967	38	22	0	0	0	0	0	0	1	2,679	0	0	2,231	5,935
1968	77	2	0	0	0	0	0	0	0	252	0	0	372	1,210
1969	88	4	0	0	0	0	0	0	1	566	0	0	687	1,960
Lifetime		42	0	0	0	0	0	0	2	5,666	0	0	4,576	$11,320

Eddie Bierschwale

Edward Bierschwale
B: 6/29/1959
Racing Hometown: San Antonio, TX

Year	Rank	Starts	Poles	1	2	3	4	5	6–10	Laps	Laps Led	Races Led	Miles	$
1983	51	3	0	0	0	0	0	0	0	524	0	0	888	3,665
1984	66	2	0	0	0	0	0	0	0	317	0	0	583	3,495
1985	24	26	0	0	0	0	0	0	0	6,559	0	0	7,761	102,650
1986	25	24	0	0	0	0	0	0	0	5,558	1	1	6,985	98,110
1987	34	14	0	0	0	0	0	0	0	3,560	0	0	4,062	66,790
1988	34	20	0	0	0	0	0	0	0	4,106	0	0	6,121	59,355
1989	36	16	0	0	0	0	0	0	1	3,829	2	1	4,974	82,695
1990	54	3	0	0	0	0	0	0	0	665	0	0	1,264	28,540
1991	42	5	0	0	0	0	0	0	0	1,112	0	0	2,127	55,025
1992	47	4	0	0	0	0	0	0	0	628	0	0	1,092	25,995
Lifetime		117	0	0	0	0	0	0	1	26,858	3	2	35,855	$526,320

Greg Biffle

Greg Biffle
B: 12/23/1969
Racing Hometown: Vancouver, WA

Year	Rank	Starts	Poles	1	2	3	4	5	6–10	Laps	Laps Led	Races Led	Miles	$
2002	48	7	0	0	0	0	0	0	0	1,914	12	1	2,271	394,773
Lifetime		7	0	0	0	0	0	0	0	1,914	12	1	2,271	$394,773

Tom Bigelow

Thomas Allan Bigelow
B: 10/31/1939
Racing Hometown: Winchester, IN

Year	Rank	Starts	Poles	1	2	3	4	5	6–10	Laps	Laps Led	Races Led	Miles	$
1986	121T	1	0	0	0	0	0	0	0	58	0	0	88	985
Lifetime		1	0	0	0	0	0	0	0	58	0	0	88	$985

Art Binkley

Arthur Binkley
B: 12/19/1920 *Comatose after 6/21/57 crash @ Ft. Wayne*
Racing Hometown: New Albany, IN

Year	Rank	Starts	Poles	1	2	3	4	5	6–10	Laps	Laps Led	Races Led	Miles	$
1954	NR	1	0	0	0	0	0	0	0	21	0	0	86	0
1956	NR	1	0	0	0	0	0	0	0	349	0	0	175	150
1957	NR	3	0	0	0	0	0	0	0	690	0	0	495	390
Lifetime		5	0	0	0	0	0	0	0	1,060	0	0	755	$540

Gordon Birkett

Gordon Birkett
Racing Hometown: Tappahannock, VA

Year	Rank	Starts	Poles	1	2	3	4	5	6–10	Laps	Laps Led	Races Led	Miles	$
1971	NR	2	0	0	0	0	0	0	0	263	0	0	123	635
Lifetime		2	0	0	0	0	0	0	0	263	0	0	123	$635

Year	Rank	Starts	Poles	Finish						Laps	Laps Led	Races Led	Miles	$
				1	2	3	4	5	6–10					

Gordon Bishop

Gordon Bishop
Racing Hometown: Anniston, AL

Year	Rank	Starts	Poles	1	2	3	4	5	6–10	Laps	Laps Led	Races Led	Miles	$
1952	125	2	0	0	0	0	0	0	0		0	0		25
Lifetime		2	0	0	0	0	0	0	0		0	0		$25

Terry Bivins

Terry Bivins
B: 9/13/1943
Racing Hometown: Shawnee Mission, KS

Year	Rank	Starts	Poles	1	2	3	4	5	6–10	Laps	Laps Led	Races Led	Miles	$
1975	78	2	0	0	0	0	0	0	1	562	0	0	758	2,735
1976	21	18	0	0	0	0	0	1	5	5,237	6	1	5,816	44,070
1977	38	8	0	0	0	0	0	0	1	1,972	0	0	2,115	14,920
Lifetime		28	0	0	0	0	0	1	7	7,771	6	1	8,690	$61,725

Don Black

Donald Black
Racing Hometown: Parker, PA

Year	Rank	Starts	Poles	1	2	3	4	5	6–10	Laps	Laps Led	Races Led	Miles	$
1951	N/A	1	0	0	0	0	0	0	0		0	0		25
Lifetime		1	0	0	0	0	0	0	0		0	0		$25

Gene Black

Francis Eugene Black, II
B: 9/23/1943
Racing Hometown: Arden, NC

Year	Rank	Starts	Poles	1	2	3	4	5	6–10	Laps	Laps Led	Races Led	Miles	$
1965	42	18	0	0	0	0	0	0	4	4,167	0	0	3,011	6,080
1966	55	12	0	0	0	0	0	0	2	1,713	0	0	1,216	3,765
1968	65	7	0	0	0	0	0	0	0	762	0	0	336	805
Lifetime		37	0	0	0	0	0	0	6	6,642	0	0	4,563	$10,650

Sonny Black

Robert Black
B: 1926   D: 9/18/1964   *Killed in practice @ 5-Flags Speedway in Pensacola, FL.*
Racing Hometown: Forrest Park, GA

Year	Rank	Starts	Poles	1	2	3	4	5	6–10	Laps	Laps Led	Races Led	Miles	$
1951	N/A	4	0	0	0	0	0	0	2	73	0	0	91	175
1955	170T	1	0	0	0	0	0	0	0	181	0	0	91	50
1956	209T	1	0	0	0	0	0	0	0	79	0	0	79	50
Lifetime		6	0	0	0	0	0	0	2	333	0	0	261	$275

Bunkie Blackburn

James Ronald Blackburn
B: 4/22/1936
Racing Hometown: Fayetteville, NC

Year	Rank	Starts	Poles	1	2	3	4	5	6–10	Laps	Laps Led	Races Led	Miles	$
1960	37	20	0	0	0	0	0	1	3	2,789	0	0	2,110	3,400
1961	108	5	0	0	0	0	0	0	0	478	0	0	485	1,175
1962	25	10	0	0	0	0	1	0	2	2,325	0	0	2,705	5,890
1963	48	7	0	0	0	0	0	0	1	909	0	0	1,220	2,525
1964	32	14	0	0	0	0	1	0	3	2,295	0	0	2,329	6,630
1965	70	6	0	0	0	0	0	0	1	371	0	0	637	3,420
1966	57	8	0	0	0	0	1	0	0	770	4	1	1,151	5,900
1970	NR	1	0	0	0	0	0	0	0	35	0	0	36	620
Lifetime		71	0	0	0	0	3	1	10	9,972	4	1	10,673	$29,560

Gene Blackburn

Gene Blackburn
Racing Hometown: Bristol, TN

Year	Rank	Starts	Poles	1	2	3	4	5	6–10	Laps	Laps Led	Races Led	Miles	$
1961	178	1	0	0	0	0	0	0	0	117	0	0	59	100
1962	113	1	0	0	0	0	0	0	0	274	0	0	137	150
Lifetime		2	0	0	0	0	0	0	0	391	0	0	196	$250

Glenn Blackman

Glenn Blackman
Racing Hometown: Columbia, SC

Year	Rank	Starts	Poles	1	2	3	4	5	6–10	Laps	Laps Led	Races Led	Miles	$
1955	212	1	0	0	0	0	0	0	0		0	0		0
Lifetime		1	0	0	0	0	0	0	0		0	0		$0

Bill Blackwell

William Blackwell

Year	Rank	Starts	Poles	1	2	3	4	5	6–10	Laps	Laps Led	Races Led	Miles	$
1954	NR	1	0	0	0	0	0	0	0	4	0	0	2	0
Lifetime		1	0	0	0	0	0	0	0	4	0	0	2	$0

Year	Rank	Starts	Poles	Finish 1	2	3	4	5	6–10	Laps	Laps Led	Races Led	Miles	$

Dick Blackwell

Samuel Richard Blackwell
B: 1920
Racing Hometown: Startex, SC

Year	Rank	Starts	Poles	1	2	3	4	5	6–10	Laps	Laps Led	Races Led	Miles	$
1956	159	3	0	0	0	0	0	0	0	192	0	0	154	60
1959	80	3	0	0	0	0	0	0	0	544	0	0	487	250
Lifetime		6	0	0	0	0	0	0	0	736	0	0	641	$310

Bill Blair

William Ivey Blair
B: 7/14/1911 D: 11/2/1995
Racing Hometown: High Point, NC

Year	Rank	Starts	Poles	1	2	3	4	5	6–10	Laps	Laps Led	Races Led	Miles	$
1949	4	6	0	0	0	0	0	3	2	763	325	2	663	1,280
1950	10	16	0	1	2	0	0	2	2	1,550	218	3	1,253	4,400
1951	16	18	0	0	1	1	2	0	3	815	0	0	755	2,710
1952	6	19	1	1	3	4	2	0	3	2,463	120	4	2,068	7,899
1953	15	21	0	1	0	2	0	3	2	1,043	51	2	1,100	4,535
1954	13	19	0	0	0	0	0	2	8	2,853	7	1	1,893	2,650
1955	37	12	0	0	0	0	0	0	0	1,320	0	0	1,227	440
1956	37	9	0	0	0	0	0	0	4	1,275	0	0	1,164	1,005
1957	157	1	0	0	0	0	0	0	0	63	0	0	87	100
1958	NR	2	0	0	0	0	0	0	0	147	0	0	137	200
Lifetime		123	1	3	6	7	4	10	24	12,292	721	12	10,346	$25,219

Gene Blair

Gene Blair
B: 1933 D: 8/18/1962 *Killed in Midget race @ Cattaraugus Fairgrounds in Little Valley, NY.*
Racing Hometown: Buffalo, NY

Year	Rank	Starts	Poles	1	2	3	4	5	6–10	Laps	Laps Led	Races Led	Miles	$
1957	NR	1	0	0	0	0	0	0	0	32	0	0	74	110
Lifetime		1	0	0	0	0	0	0	0	32	0	0	74	$110

T.L. Blakely

Terrance L. Blakely (Terry)
Racing Hometown: Birmingham, MI

Year	Rank	Starts	Poles	1	2	3	4	5	6–10	Laps	Laps Led	Races Led	Miles	$
1966	148	1	0	0	0	0	0	0	0	10	0	0	25	0
Lifetime		1	0	0	0	0	0	0	0	10	0	0	25	$0

Pug Blalock

Silas Blalock
Racing Hometown: Decatur, GA

Year	Rank	Starts	Poles	1	2	3	4	5	6–10	Laps	Laps Led	Races Led	Miles	$
1951	N/A	3	0	0	0	0	0	0	1		0	0		100
Lifetime		3	0	0	0	0	0	0	1		0	0		$100

Leonard Blanchard

Charles Leonard Blanchard
B: 11/20/1936
Racing Hometown: Jackson, KY

Year	Rank	Starts	Poles	1	2	3	4	5	6–10	Laps	Laps Led	Races Led	Miles	$
1970	NR	2	0	0	0	0	0	0	0	92	0	0	230	1,135
1971	86	1	0	0	0	0	0	0	0	46	0	0	115	255
Lifetime		3	0	0	0	0	0	0	0	138	0	0	345	$1,390

Dave Blaney

David Blaney
B: 10/24/1962
Racing Hometown: Hartford, OH

Year	Rank	Starts	Poles	1	2	3	4	5	6–10	Laps	Laps Led	Races Led	Miles	$
1992	79T	1	0	0	0	0	0	0	0	371	0	0	377	4,500
1999	51	5	0	0	0	0	0	0	0	996	0	0	1,676	212,170
2000	31	33	0	0	0	0	0	0	2	8,329	4	1	11,571	1,272,689
2001	22	35	0	0	0	0	0	0	6	9,872	71	2	12,821	1,827,896
2002	19	36	0	0	0	0	0	0	5	10,305	65	9	13,517	2,978,593
Lifetime		110	0	0	0	0	0	0	13	29,873	140	12	39,962	$6,295,848

Lem Blankenship

Lem Blankenship
B: 2/6/1945
Racing Hometown: Keokuk, IA

Year	Rank	Starts	Poles	1	2	3	4	5	6–10	Laps	Laps Led	Races Led	Miles	$
1972	NR	1	0	0	0	0	0	0	0	50	0	0	76	855
Lifetime		1	0	0	0	0	0	0	0	50	0	0	76	$855

Year	Rank	Starts	Poles	Finish 1	2	3	4	5	6–10	Laps	Laps Led	Races Led	Miles	$

Charlie Blanton
Charles Ken Blanton
B: 12/29/1935
Racing Hometown: Gaffney, SC

1973	87	1	0	0	0	0	0	0	0	351	0	0	527	1,825
1974	129T	1	0	0	0	0	0	0	0	231	0	0	235	720
1978	NR	1	0	0	0	0	0	0	0	52	0	0	53	590
Lifetime		3	0	0	0	0	0	0	0	634	0	0	814	$3,135

Erwin Blatt
Erwin W. Blatt
Racing Hometown: Hamburg, PA

1949	60	1	0	0	0	0	0	0	0	176	0	0	176	50
1952	68	2	0	0	0	0	0	0	0	566	0	0	650	160
1958	132T	1	0	0	0	0	0	0	0	28	0	0	80	85
Lifetime		4	0	0	0	0	0	0	0	770	0	0	906	$295

Chuck Blewitt
Charles Blewitt (Chuck)
Racing Hometown: Brooklyn, NY

1954	142	1	0	0	0	0	0	0	0	207	0	0	207	50
1956	93	2	0	0	0	0	0	0	0	411	0	0	327	200
1957	141	3	0	0	0	0	0	0	0	205	0	0	107	150
Lifetime		6	0	0	0	0	0	0	0	823	0	0	640	$400

Mike Bliss
Michael Bliss
B: 4/5/1965
Racing Hometown: Milwaukie, OR

1998	58	2	0	0	0	0	0	0	0	743	0	0	510	32,520
1999	58	2	0	0	0	0	0	0	0	766	0	0	539	42,475
2000	39	25	0	0	0	0	0	0	1	5,492	4	1	8,161	953,948
2002	64	1	0	0	0	0	0	0	0	500	0	0	263	81,942
Lifetime		30	0	0	0	0	0	0	1	7,501	4	1	9,472	$1,110,885

Bill Block
William Block
Racing Hometown: Winston-Salem, NC

| 1962 | NR | 1 | 0 | 0 | 0 | 0 | 0 | 0 | 0 | 32 | 0 | 0 | 8 | 75 |
| Lifetime | | 1 | 0 | 0 | 0 | 0 | 0 | 0 | 0 | 32 | 0 | 0 | 8 | $75 |

Bruce Blodgett
Bruce Blodgett
B: 11/25/1945
Racing Hometown: Fresno, CA

| 1976 | NR | 1 | 0 | 0 | 0 | 0 | 0 | 0 | 0 | 447 | 0 | 0 | 235 | 800 |
| Lifetime | | 1 | 0 | 0 | 0 | 0 | 0 | 0 | 0 | 447 | 0 | 0 | 235 | $800 |

Jim Blomgren
James Blomgren
Racing Hometown: El Monte, CA

1956	47	6	0	0	0	0	0	0	1	841	0	0	820	475
1957	71	4	0	0	0	0	0	1	0	356	0	0	320	520
1958	179	1	0	0	0	0	0	0	0	8	0	0	8	0
1959	109	1	0	0	0	0	0	0	0	49	0	0	49	50
1960	84	3	0	0	0	0	0	0	2	288	0	0	332	400
1961	92	4	0	0	0	0	1	0	1	401	0	0	406	590
1964	104	1	0	0	0	0	0	0	0	94	0	0	254	500
Lifetime		20	0	0	0	0	1	1	4	2,037	0	0	2,187	$2,535

Larry Bock
Lawrence Bock
Racing Hometown: Miskawaka, IN

| 1969 | NR | 1 | 0 | 0 | 0 | 0 | 0 | 0 | 0 | 85 | 0 | 0 | 226 | 1,225 |
| Lifetime | | 1 | 0 | 0 | 0 | 0 | 0 | 0 | 0 | 85 | 0 | 0 | 226 | $1,225 |

Brett Bodine
Brett E. Bodine
B: 1/11/1959
Racing Hometown: Chemung, NY

| 1986 | 92T | 1 | 0 | 0 | 0 | 0 | 0 | 0 | 0 | 394 | 0 | 0 | 591 | 10,100 |
| 1987 | 32 | 14 | 0 | 0 | 0 | 0 | 0 | 0 | 0 | 2,908 | 20 | 3 | 4,485 | 71,460 |

Year	Rank	Starts	Poles	Finish 1	2	3	4	5	6–10	Laps	Laps Led	Races Led	Miles	$

Brett Bodine *continued*

Year	Rank	Starts	Poles	1	2	3	4	5	6–10	Laps	Laps Led	Races Led	Miles	$
1988	20	29	0	0	0	1	1	0	3	7,789	200	5	9,163	433,658
1989	19	29	0	0	0	0	0	1	5	8,202	2	2	10,356	233,182
1990	12	29	1	1	0	2	2	0	4	9,097	216	7	10,980	442,681
1991	19	29	1	0	1	0	1	0	4	7,873	163	3	9,050	376,220
1992	15	29	1	0	0	1	1	0	11	8,807	237	11	10,248	495,224
1993	20	29	2	0	1	0	0	2	6	8,120	102	7	9,383	582,014
1994	19	31	0	0	1	0	0	0	5	8,931	55	6	10,773	801,944
1995	20	31	0	0	0	0	0	0	2	9,159	6	1	11,084	893,029
1996	24	30	0	0	0	0	0	0	1	8,732	3	2	10,718	767,716
1997	29	31	0	0	0	0	0	0	2	8,666	4	3	11,317	936,694
1998	25	33	0	0	0	0	0	0	0	9,462	17	6	12,346	1,281,673
1999	35	32	0	0	0	0	0	0	0	8,940	4	3	11,365	1,321,396
2000	35	29	0	0	0	0	0	0	0	8,336	5	2	10,220	1,020,659
2001	30	36	0	0	0	0	0	0	2	9,968	3	3	13,469	1,740,526
2002	36	32	0	0	0	0	0	0	0	8,817	3	3	11,506	1,766,820
Lifetime		474	5	1	3	4	5	3	45	134,201	1,040	67	167,054	$13,174,996

Geoffrey Bodine

Geoffrey Bodine
B: 4/18/1949
Racing Hometown: Chemung, NY

Year	Rank	Starts	Poles	1	2	3	4	5	6–10	Laps	Laps Led	Races Led	Miles	$
1979	81	3	0	0	0	0	0	0	0	443	6	1	631	4,820
1981	45	5	0	0	0	0	0	0	1	945	14	2	1,388	15,000
1982	22	25	2	0	0	1	2	1	6	6,518	118	6	7,940	247,750
1983	17	28	1	0	1	0	2	2	4	7,042	490	13	7,328	209,611
1984	9	30	3	3	0	1	2	1	7	8,848	686	12	10,064	413,748
1985	5	28	3	0	3	3	2	2	4	8,719	692	18	10,720	565,868
1986	8	29	9	2	2	5	1	0	5	7,791	1,676	25	9,361	795,111
1987	13	29	2	0	1	1	0	1	7	7,738	342	13	8,817	449,816
1988	6	29	3	1	1	4	1	3	6	8,995	463	15	10,566	570,643
1989	9	29	3	1	1	3	3	1	2	9,051	510	14	10,535	521,300
1990	3	29	2	3	3	2	3	0	8	8,852	976	21	10,748	1,131,222
1991	14	27	2	1	2	1	1	1	6	7,997	152	12	9,591	625,256
1992	16	29	0	2	0	2	2	1	4	8,222	474	5	9,780	716,583
1993	16	30	1	1	0	1	0	0	7	8,496	102	11	10,199	783,762
1994	17	31	5	3	1	1	1	1	3	8,149	1,746	20	9,771	1,287,626
1995	16	31	0	0	0	0	0	1	3	9,257	14	4	11,572	1,011,090
1996	17	31	0	1	0	1	0	0	4	8,918	90	7	11,068	1,031,762
1997	22	29	2	0	2	0	1	0	7	8,224	68	12	9,905	1,092,734
1998	27	32	0	0	0	0	0	1	4	8,745	33	4	11,016	1,247,255
1999	27	34	0	0	0	1	0	0	1	9,535	8	3	12,256	1,257,494
2000	45	14	0	0	0	0	0	0	0	2,780	20	1	3,829	704,981
2001	57	2	0	0	0	0	0	0	0	750	0	0	658	80,855
2002	43	10	0	0	0	1	0	0	1	1,832	5	1	3,059	1,224,501
Lifetime		564	38	18	17	28	21	16	90	157,847	8,685	220	190,802	$15,988,788

Todd Bodine

Todd Bodine
B: 2/27/1964
Racing Hometown: Chemung, NY

Year	Rank	Starts	Poles	1	2	3	4	5	6–10	Laps	Laps Led	Races Led	Miles	$
1992	87T	1	0	0	0	0	0	0	0	16	0	0	39	3,485
1993	40	10	0	0	0	0	0	0	0	2,393	0	0	2,311	63,245
1994	20	30	0	0	0	1	0	1	5	8,475	60	5	10,479	504,316
1995	33	28	0	0	0	0	1	0	2	6,683	19	2	9,058	664,620
1996	40	10	0	0	0	0	0	0	1	3,210	1	1	4,184	198,525
1997	52	5	1	0	0	0	0	0	0	753	9	1	1,211	125,845
1998	41	14	0	0	0	0	0	1	1	4,846	47	2	5,085	378,766
1999	46	7	0	0	0	0	0	0	0	2,008	0	0	2,007	208,382
2000	49	5	0	0	0	0	0	0	1	881	0	0	1,504	234,065
2001	29	35	3	0	0	0	0	2	0	9,161	110	11	11,981	1,740,315
2002	38	24	1	0	0	0	0	1	3	5,552	19	3	7,674	1,879,767
Lifetime		169	5	0	0	1	1	5	13	43,978	265	25	55,532	$6,001,331

Tommy Boger

Thomas Boger
B: 1925
Racing Hometown: Concord, NC

Year	Rank	Starts	Poles	1	2	3	4	5	6–10	Laps	Laps Led	Races Led	Miles	$
1953	174	1	0	0	0	0	0	0	0	32	0	0	131	25
Lifetime		1	0	0	0	0	0	0	0	32	0	0	131	$25

Year	Rank	Starts	Poles	Finish 1	2	3	4	5	6–10	Laps	Laps Led	Races Led	Miles	$

David Ray Boggs

David Ray Boggs
B: 9/8/1943
Racing Hometown: Morrisville, NC

Year	Rank	Starts	Poles	1	2	3	4	5	6–10	Laps	Laps Led	Races Led	Miles	$
1971	55	7	0	0	0	0	0	0	2	1,985	0	0	1,711	4,969
1972	26	24	0	0	0	0	0	0	0	3,968	0	0	5,164	19,489
1973	NR	1	0	0	0	0	0	0	0	116	0	0	158	1,235
Lifetime		32	0	0	0	0	0	0	2	6,069	0	0	7,034	$25,693

Fred Boggs

Fred J. Boggs
Racing Hometown: Warsaw, IN

Year	Rank	Starts	Poles	1	2	3	4	5	6–10	Laps	Laps Led	Races Led	Miles	$
1957	180	1	0	0	0	0	0	0	0		0	0		25
Lifetime		1	0	0	0	0	0	0	0		0	0		$25

Pete Boland

Peter Boland
Racing Hometown: Charleston, SC

Year	Rank	Starts	Poles	1	2	3	4	5	6–10	Laps	Laps Led	Races Led	Miles	$
1961	139	2	0	0	0	0	0	0	0	217	0	0	126	110
1964	116	3	0	0	0	0	0	0	0	7	0	0	6	200
Lifetime		5	0	0	0	0	0	0	0	224	0	0	132	$310

Bill Boldt

William Boldt
Racing Hometown: Torrance, CA

Year	Rank	Starts	Poles	1	2	3	4	5	6–10	Laps	Laps Led	Races Led	Miles	$
1958	98	2	0	0	0	0	0	0	1	244	0	0	490	210
1965	123	1	0	0	0	0	0	0	0	19	0	0	51	500
Lifetime		3	0	0	0	0	0	0	1	263	0	0	542	$710

Aubrey Boles

Aubrey Boles
Racing Hometown: High Point, NC

Year	Rank	Starts	Poles	1	2	3	4	5	6–10	Laps	Laps Led	Races Led	Miles	$
1959	NR	4	0	0	0	0	0	0	1	796	0	0	398	300
1960	150	1	0	0	0	0	0	0	0	97	0	0	49	50
Lifetime		5	0	0	0	0	0	0	1	893	0	0	447	$350

Fred Boles

Fred Boles
Racing Hometown: Greenville, SC

Year	Rank	Starts	Poles	1	2	3	4	5	6–10	Laps	Laps Led	Races Led	Miles	$
1959	NR	1	0	0	0	0	0	0	0	165	0	0	83	85
Lifetime		1	0	0	0	0	0	0	0	165	0	0	83	$85

Bob Bolheimer

Robert Bolheimer
Racing Hometown: Raleigh, NC

Year	Rank	Starts	Poles	1	2	3	4	5	6–10	Laps	Laps Led	Races Led	Miles	$
1958	139	2	0	0	0	0	0	0	0	209	0	0	215	100
Lifetime		2	0	0	0	0	0	0	0	209	0	0	215	$100

Al Bolinger

Al Bolinger

Year	Rank	Starts	Poles	1	2	3	4	5	6–10	Laps	Laps Led	Races Led	Miles	$
1954	NR	1	0	0	0	0	0	0	0	103	0	0	52	25
Lifetime		1	0	0	0	0	0	0	0	103	0	0	52	$25

Lee Bolton

Lee Roy Bolton (Lefty)
Racing Hometown: Gastonia, NC

Year	Rank	Starts	Poles	1	2	3	4	5	6–10	Laps	Laps Led	Races Led	Miles	$
1964	140	1	0	0	0	0	0	0	0	48	0	0	24	0
1966	87	3	0	0	0	0	0	0	2	455	0	0	217	880
Lifetime		4	0	0	0	0	0	0	2	503	0	0	241	$880

Les Bomar

Les Bomar
Racing Hometown: Los Angeles, CA

Year	Rank	Starts	Poles	1	2	3	4	5	6–10	Laps	Laps Led	Races Led	Miles	$
1951	N/A	4	0	0	0	0	0	0	0		0	0		100
Lifetime		4	0	0	0	0	0	0	0		0	0		$100

Year	Rank	Starts	Poles	Finish						Laps	Laps Led	Races Led	Miles	$
				1	2	3	4	5	6–10					

Tony Bonadies

Anthony Bonadies
B: 12/29/1916   D: 7/5/1964   *Killed in ARDC Midget race @ Williams Grove, PA.*
Racing Hometown: Bronx, NY

Year	Rank	Starts	Poles	1	2	3	4	5	6–10	Laps	Laps Led	Races Led	Miles	$
1952	145	2	0	0	0	0	0	0	0	523	0	0	611	360
Lifetime		2	0	0	0	0	0	0	0	523	0	0	611	$360

Crash Bond

Lowell E. Bond
Racing Hometown: Nashville, TN

Year	Rank	Starts	Poles	1	2	3	4	5	6–10	Laps	Laps Led	Races Led	Miles	$
1961	132	1	0	0	0	0	0	0	0	367	0	0	184	150
Lifetime		1	0	0	0	0	0	0	0	367	0	0	184	$150

Eddie Bond

Edward Bond
B: 11/12/1930
Racing Hometown: Bedford, IN

Year	Rank	Starts	Poles	1	2	3	4	5	6–10	Laps	Laps Led	Races Led	Miles	$
1973	40	6	0	0	0	0	0	0	0	1,407	0	0	2,287	6,901
Lifetime		6	0	0	0	0	0	0	0	1,407	0	0	2,287	$6,901

Bob Bondurant

Robert L. Bondurant
B: 4/27/1933
Racing Hometown: Sonoma, CA

Year	Rank	Starts	Poles	1	2	3	4	5	6–10	Laps	Laps Led	Races Led	Miles	$
1963	149	1	0	0	0	0	0	0	0	44	0	0	119	200
1965	105	1	0	0	0	0	0	0	0	47	0	0	127	520
1981	80	2	0	0	0	0	0	0	0	207	0	0	542	2,430
Lifetime		4	0	0	0	0	0	0	0	298	0	0	788	$3,150

Al Bonnell

Al Bonnell
B: 1/26/1909   D: 1/12/1980
Racing Hometown: Erie, PA

Year	Rank	Starts	Poles	1	2	3	4	5	6–10	Laps	Laps Led	Races Led	Miles	$
1949	34	2	1	0	0	0	0	0	1	183	0	0	183	150
Lifetime		2	1	0	0	0	0	0	1	183	0	0	183	$150

Bill Bonner

William Bonner
Racing Hometown: Los Angeles, CA

Year	Rank	Starts	Poles	1	2	3	4	5	6–10	Laps	Laps Led	Races Led	Miles	$
1950	112T	1	0	0	0	0	0	0	0		0	0		0
Lifetime		1	0	0	0	0	0	0	0		0	0		$0

Neil Bonnett

Lawrence Neil Bonnett
B: 7/30/1946   D: 2/11/1994   *Killed in practice for Daytona 500.*
Racing Hometown: Bessemer, AL

Year	Rank	Starts	Poles	1	2	3	4	5	6–10	Laps	Laps Led	Races Led	Miles	$
1974	87	2	0	0	0	0	0	0	0	97	0	0	258	2,560
1975	NR	2	0	0	0	0	0	0	0	474	12	1	483	2,705
1976	32	13	0	0	0	0	0	1	3	2,174	1	1	3,213	31,800
1977	18	23	6	2	0	1	1	1	4	5,993	493	11	6,443	122,615
1978	12	30	3	0	1	1	2	3	5	6,278	316	6	6,761	162,742
1979	26	21	4	3	0	0	1	0	2	4,213	568	14	6,133	151,235
1980	19	22	0	2	4	1	1	2	3	5,173	331	14	7,504	231,854
1981	22	22	1	3	1	0	3	0	1	4,917	1,549	16	6,366	181,670
1982	17	25	0	1	0	2	1	3	3	6,730	412	12	7,903	158,197
1983	6	30	4	2	1	2	5	0	7	9,418	659	15	10,452	453,586
1984	8	30	1	0	2	0	2	3	7	9,126	641	11	10,460	282,533
1985	4	28	1	2	2	3	1	3	7	8,675	618	15	10,358	530,145
1986	13	28	0	1	1	1	1	2	6	7,691	323	16	8,992	485,930
1987	12	26	0	0	0	4	1	0	10	7,834	120	10	9,073	401,541
1988	16	27	0	2	0	0	1	0	4	8,017	324	7	9,140	440,139
1989	20	26	0	0	0	0	0	0	11	7,795	23	6	9,488	227,052
1990	43	5	0	0	0	0	0	0	0	1,179	0	0	1,635	62,600
1993	67T	2	0	0	0	0	0	0	0	134	0	0	353	14,515
Lifetime		362	20	18	12	15	20	18	73	95,918	6,390	155	115,015	$3,943,419

Year	Rank	Starts	Poles	Finish 1	2	3	4	5	6–10	Laps	Laps Led	Races Led	Miles	$

Joe Booher

Joseph Booher
B: 2/22/1941   D: 2/12/1993   *Killed in Dash race @ Daytona.*
Racing Hometown: W. Lafayette, IN

Year	Rank	Starts	Poles	1	2	3	4	5	6–10	Laps	Laps Led	Races Led	Miles	$
1978	NR	3	0	0	0	0	0	0	0	595	0	0	769	3,205
1980	56	6	0	0	0	0	0	0	0	1,273	0	0	1,674	15,930
1981	82	4	0	0	0	0	0	0	0	581	0	0	1,259	4,995
1982	NR	2	0	0	0	0	0	0	0	371	0	0	832	3,300
1983	NR	1	0	0	0	0	0	0	0	2	0	0	3	935
1985	65	2	0	0	0	0	0	0	0	358	0	0	801	3,685
1986	71	2	0	0	0	0	0	0	0	556	0	0	556	8,930
1988	87T	1	0	0	0	0	0	0	0	272	0	0	272	1,495
Lifetime		21	0	0	0	0	0	0	0	4,008	0	0	6,165	$42,475

Bud Boone

Bud Boone
Racing Hometown: Warren, OH

Year	Rank	Starts	Poles	1	2	3	4	5	6–10	Laps	Laps Led	Races Led	Miles	$
1950	68T	1	0	0	0	0	0	0	1		0	0		75
Lifetime		1	0	0	0	0	0	0	1		0	0		$75

Ernie Boost

Ernie Boost
Racing Hometown: Cleveland, OH

Year	Rank	Starts	Poles	1	2	3	4	5	6–10	Laps	Laps Led	Races Led	Miles	$
1952	NR	3	0	0	0	0	0	0	1	381	0	0	232	100
Lifetime		3	0	0	0	0	0	0	1	381	0	0	232	$100

Bobby Booth

Robert Booth
Racing Hometown: Hapeville, GA

Year	Rank	Starts	Poles	1	2	3	4	5	6–10	Laps	Laps Led	Races Led	Miles	$
1951	N/A	3	0	0	0	0	0	0	0	156	0	0	169	25
Lifetime		3	0	0	0	0	0	0	0	156	0	0	169	$25

John Borden

John Borden
Racing Hometown: Lancaster, NY

Year	Rank	Starts	Poles	1	2	3	4	5	6–10	Laps	Laps Led	Races Led	Miles	$
1950	82	2	0	0	0	0	0	0	0		0	0		50
Lifetime		2	0	0	0	0	0	0	0		0	0		$50

John Borneman

John Borneman Jr.
B: 4/19/1949
Racing Hometown: El Cajon, CA

Year	Rank	Starts	Poles	1	2	3	4	5	6–10	Laps	Laps Led	Races Led	Miles	$
1977	96T	1	0	0	0	0	0	0	0	150	0	0	375	1,200
1978	61	3	0	0	0	0	0	0	0	305	0	0	777	3,320
1979	98T	1	0	0	0	0	0	0	0	79	0	0	207	1,305
1980	81	2	0	0	0	0	0	0	0	84	0	0	220	1,250
1981	73T	1	0	0	0	0	0	0	0	116	0	0	304	3,140
Lifetime		8	0	0	0	0	0	0	0	734	0	0	1,883	$10,215

Joe Bossard

Joseph Bossard
Racing Hometown: Little Falls, NJ

Year	Rank	Starts	Poles	1	2	3	4	5	6–10	Laps	Laps Led	Races Led	Miles	$
1954	91	2	0	0	0	0	0	0	0	206	0	0	168	50
Lifetime		2	0	0	0	0	0	0	0	206	0	0	168	$50

Jim Bossic

James Bossic
Racing Hometown: Montgomery, AL

Year	Rank	Starts	Poles	1	2	3	4	5	6–10	Laps	Laps Led	Races Led	Miles	$
1955	NR	1	0	0	0	0	0	0	0	0	0	0	0	25
Lifetime		1	0	0	0	0	0	0	0	0	0	0	0	$25

Tommy Bostick

Thomas P. Bostick
Racing Hometown: Bennettsville, SC

Year	Rank	Starts	Poles	1	2	3	4	5	6–10	Laps	Laps Led	Races Led	Miles	$
1966	122	1	0	0	0	0	0	0	0	42	0	0	42	500
Lifetime		1	0	0	0	0	0	0	0	42	0	0	42	$500

Rodney Bottinger

Rodney Bottinger
Racing Hometown: Charleston, SC

Year	Rank	Starts	Poles	1	2	3	4	5	6–10	Laps	Laps Led	Races Led	Miles	$
1964	NR	3	0	0	0	0	0	0	0	17	0	0	9	300
Lifetime		3	0	0	0	0	0	0	0	17	0	0	9	$300

Year	Rank	Starts	Poles	Finish						Laps	Laps Led	Races Led	Miles	$
				1	2	3	4	5	6–10					

Ken Bouchard

Kenneth P. Bouchard
B: 4/6/1955
Racing Hometown: Fitchburg, MA

Year	Rank	Starts	Poles	1	2	3	4	5	6–10	Laps	Laps Led	Races Led	Miles	$
1987	93	1	0	0	0	0	0	0	0	158	0	0	316	2,075
1988	25	24	0	0	0	0	0	0	1	7,281	4	1	8,490	109,410
1989	48	4	0	0	0	0	0	0	0	911	0	0	1,373	33,930
1993	52	3	0	0	0	0	0	0	0	503	0	0	849	25,785
1994	69	1	0	0	0	0	0	0	0	280	0	0	426	6,675
Lifetime		33	0	0	0	0	0	0	1	9,133	4	1	11,455	$177,875

Ron Bouchard

Ronald Bouchard
B: 11/23/1948
Racing Hometown: Fitchburg, MA

Year	Rank	Starts	Poles	1	2	3	4	5	6–10	Laps	Laps Led	Races Led	Miles	$
1981	21	22	1	1	0	0	1	3	7	6,155	12	2	6,979	152,855
1982	8	30	1	0	0	2	1	0	12	8,048	1	1	8,544	375,759
1983	16	28	1	0	0	0	1	0	6	7,187	22	4	8,315	159,173
1984	11	30	0	0	1	2	1	1	5	9,200	111	8	10,504	246,510
1985	13	28	0	0	1	1	2	1	7	7,723	77	5	8,969	240,304
1986	31	17	0	0	0	0	0	0	2	3,654	1	1	5,093	106,825
1987	47	5	0	0	0	0	0	0	1	917	0	0	1,446	24,105
Lifetime		160	3	1	2	5	6	5	40	42,884	224	21	49,850	$1,305,531

Nathan Boutwell

Nathan Boutwell
D: 9/29/1993
Racing Hometown: Pelham, NH

Year	Rank	Starts	Poles	1	2	3	4	5	6–10	Laps	Laps Led	Races Led	Miles	$
1964	62	2	0	0	0	0	0	0	0	217	0	0	543	1,100
Lifetime		2	0	0	0	0	0	0	0	217	0	0	543	$1,100

Eliso Bowie

Eliso Bowie
Racing Hometown: San Mateo, CA

Year	Rank	Starts	Poles	1	2	3	4	5	6–10	Laps	Laps Led	Races Led	Miles	$
1955	223	1	0	0	0	0	0	0	0	172	0	0	172	90
Lifetime		1	0	0	0	0	0	0	0	172	0	0	172	$90

Bill Bowman

William Bowman
Racing Hometown: Aberdeen, MD

Year	Rank	Starts	Poles	1	2	3	4	5	6–10	Laps	Laps Led	Races Led	Miles	$
1955	81	3	0	0	0	0	0	0	2	675	0	0	610	610
1956	176T	1	0	0	0	0	0	0	1	181	0	0	91	100
1957	60	4	0	0	0	0	0	0	1	817	0	0	463	510
Lifetime		8	0	0	0	0	0	0	4	1,673	0	0	1,163	$1,220

Jerry Bowman

Jerry Bowman
B: 3/9/1962
Racing Hometown: Havere D' Grace, MD

Year	Rank	Starts	Poles	1	2	3	4	5	6–10	Laps	Laps Led	Races Led	Miles	$
1982	NR	1	0	0	0	0	0	0	0	53	0	0	81	765
1983	45	5	0	0	0	0	0	0	0	1,183	0	0	1,553	8,610
1984	44	5	0	0	0	0	0	0	0	834	0	0	1,000	6,265
1985	43	5	0	0	0	0	0	0	0	1,326	0	0	1,632	8,665
1986	85	2	0	0	0	0	0	0	0	255	0	0	255	2,125
1987	92	1	0	0	0	0	0	0	0	161	0	0	161	1,450
Lifetime		19	0	0	0	0	0	0	0	3,812	0	0	4,682	$27,880

Dick Bown

Richard Bown
B: 8/12/1928
Racing Hometown: Portland, OR

Year	Rank	Starts	Poles	1	2	3	4	5	6–10	Laps	Laps Led	Races Led	Miles	$
1963	143	1	0	0	0	0	0	0	0	166	0	0	448	425
1965	98	1	0	0	0	0	0	0	0	47	0	0	127	525
1969	NR	1	0	0	0	0	0	0	0	160	0	0	432	1,230
1970	51	6	0	0	0	0	0	0	1	836	0	0	1,187	4,275
1971	NR	4	0	0	0	0	0	0	0	414	0	0	941	4,500
1972	59	3	0	0	0	0	0	0	0	459	0	0	1,181	4,465
1973	75	2	0	0	0	0	0	0	0	196	0	0	514	1,860
1974	90	1	0	0	0	0	0	0	0	24	0	0	63	935
1975	104	1	0	0	0	0	0	0	0	17	0	0	45	775
Lifetime		20	0	0	0	0	0	0	1	2,319	0	0	4,936	$18,990

Year	Rank	Starts	Poles	Finish 1	2	3	4	5	6–10	Laps	Laps Led	Races Led	Miles	$

Jim Bown

James Bown
B: 6/24/1960
Racing Hometown: Portland, OR

Year	Rank	Starts	Poles	1	2	3	4	5	6–10	Laps	Laps Led	Races Led	Miles	$
1981	75	2	0	0	0	0	0	0	0	48	0	0	126	1,415
1982	56	2	0	0	0	0	0	0	1	204	0	0	534	4,490
1983	74	2	0	0	0	0	0	0	0	118	0	0	309	2,125
1984	69	2	0	0	0	0	0	0	0	132	4	1	346	2,330
1985	59	2	0	0	0	0	0	0	0	185	0	0	485	4,860
1986	112	1	0	0	0	0	0	0	0	81	0	0	212	1,175
1987	91	2	0	0	0	0	0	0	0	264	0	0	668	8,850
1988	76	2	0	0	0	0	0	0	0	86	0	0	122	3,325
1989	59	4	0	0	0	0	0	0	0	664	0	0	786	8,100
1990	61	4	0	0	0	0	0	0	0	910	0	0	1,058	18,330
Lifetime		23	0	0	0	0	0	0	1	2,692	4	1	4,646	$55,000

Chuck Bown

Richard Charles Bown
B: 2/22/1954
Racing Hometown: Portland, OR

Year	Rank	Starts	Poles	1	2	3	4	5	6–10	Laps	Laps Led	Races Led	Miles	$
1972	69	3	0	0	0	0	0	0	0	391	0	0	1,005	3,710
1973	73	2	0	0	0	0	0	0	1	204	0	0	534	2,305
1974	93	3	0	0	0	0	0	0	0	104	0	0	271	2,070
1975	57	5	0	0	0	0	0	0	0	415	0	0	634	5,160
1976	49	5	0	0	0	0	0	0	0	568	3	1	1,192	5,480
1977	59	3	0	0	0	0	0	0	0	180	0	0	468	7,270
1978	56	4	0	0	0	0	0	0	0	539	0	0	732	3,585
1979	38	7	0	0	0	0	0	0	2	1,388	0	0	2,143	31,380
1980	51	8	0	0	0	0	0	0	0	1,060	0	0	1,905	13,145
1981	67	3	0	0	0	0	0	0	0	631	0	0	860	4,725
1990	50	3	0	0	0	0	0	0	0	951	0	0	1,280	10,150
1991	76	1	0	0	0	0	0	0	0	391	0	0	244	5,225
1993	71	1	0	0	0	0	0	0	0	306	0	0	306	6,610
1994	42	13	1	0	0	0	0	0	1	3,694	0	0	4,164	225,260
1995	43	9	0	0	0	0	0	0	0	2,068	0	0	3,026	99,995
1996	53	3	0	0	0	0	0	0	0	338	0	0	723	23,270
Lifetime		73	1	0	0	0	0	0	4	13,228	3	1	19,488	$449,340

Jack Bowsher

Jack Bowsher
B: 10/2/1930
Racing Hometown: Springfield, OH

Year	Rank	Starts	Poles	1	2	3	4	5	6–10	Laps	Laps Led	Races Led	Miles	$
1966	NR	2	0	0	0	0	0	0	0	775	0	0	932	1,710
1967	NR	2	0	0	0	0	0	0	0	207	11	1	302	1,705
Lifetime		4	0	0	0	0	0	0	0	982	11	1	1,234	$3,415

Jim Boyd

James Boyd
B: 3/31/1920
Racing Hometown: Cottonwood, CA

Year	Rank	Starts	Poles	1	2	3	4	5	6–10	Laps	Laps Led	Races Led	Miles	$
1975	71	2	0	0	0	0	0	0	0	203	0	0	524	2,335
Lifetime		2	0	0	0	0	0	0	0	203	0	0	524	$2,335

Frank Boylan

Frank Boylan
Racing Hometown: Ashtabula, OH

Year	Rank	Starts	Poles	1	2	3	4	5	6–10	Laps	Laps Led	Races Led	Miles	$
1950	92	2	0	0	0	0	0	0	0	196	0	0	98	50
Lifetime		2	0	0	0	0	0	0	0	196	0	0	98	$50

Bobby Boyles

Robert Boyles

Year	Rank	Starts	Poles	1	2	3	4	5	6–10	Laps	Laps Led	Races Led	Miles	$
1970	NR	1	0	0	0	0	0	0	0	3	0	0	1	200
Lifetime		1	0	0	0	0	0	0	0	3	0	0	1	$200

Buddie Boys

Buddie Boys
B: 1926
Racing Hometown: Alsa Craig, Ont, Canada

Year	Rank	Starts	Poles	1	2	3	4	5	6–10	Laps	Laps Led	Races Led	Miles	$
1984	84	1	0	0	0	0	0	0	0	178	0	0	181	1,055
1986	98	2	0	0	0	0	0	0	0	91	0	0	168	2,480
Lifetime		3	0	0	0	0	0	0	0	269	0	0	349	$3,535

Year	Rank	Starts	Poles	Finish						Laps	Laps Led	Races Led	Miles	$
				1	2	3	4	5	6–10					

Trevor Boys

Trevor Boys
B: 11/3/1957
Racing Hometown: Alsa Craig, Ont, Canada

Year	Rank	Starts	Poles	1	2	3	4	5	6–10	Laps	Laps Led	Races Led	Miles	$
1982	86	1	0	0	0	0	0	0	0	105	0	0	275	1,200
1983	25	23	0	0	0	0	0	0	1	5,907	3	2	6,897	87,555
1984	17	30	0	0	0	0	0	0	1	8,619	20	3	9,704	165,376
1985	28	20	0	0	0	0	0	0	0	3,973	3	1	5,158	76,325
1986	34	14	0	0	0	0	0	0	0	3,210	2	1	3,501	74,645
1987	44	10	0	0	0	0	0	0	0	2,312	5	2	3,133	59,240
1988	65	2	0	0	0	0	0	0	0	505	0	0	804	17,960
1989	NR	1	0	0	0	0	0	0	0	118	2	1	295	2,575
1993	79	1	0	0	0	0	0	0	0	38	1	1	95	6,540
Lifetime		102	0	0	0	0	0	0	2	24,787	36	11	29,861	$491,416

Geoff Brabham

Geoffrey Brabham
B: 3/20/1952
Racing Hometown: Sydney, Australia

Year	Rank	Starts	Poles	1	2	3	4	5	6–10	Laps	Laps Led	Races Led	Miles	$
1994	76T	1	0	0	0	0	0	0	0	127	0	0	318	27,400
Lifetime		1	0	0	0	0	0	0	0	127	0	0	318	$27,400

Johnny Frank

Johnny Frank
Racing Hometown: Far Rockaway, NY

Year	Rank	Starts	Poles	1	2	3	4	5	6–10	Laps	Laps Led	Races Led	Miles	$
1957	NR	1	0	0	0	0	0	0	0	111	0	0	111	75
Lifetime		1	0	0	0	0	0	0	0	111	0	0	111	$75

Bobby Brack

Robert Frederick Brack
B: 8/20/1938
Racing Hometown: Miami, FL

Year	Rank	Starts	Poles	1	2	3	4	5	6–10	Laps	Laps Led	Races Led	Miles	$
1971	58	5	0	0	0	0	0	0	0	946	0	0	1,616	4,608
1979	122	1	0	0	0	0	0	0	0	70	1	1	105	930
Lifetime		6	0	0	0	0	0	0	0	1,016	1	1	1,721	$5,538

Gordon Bracken

Gordon W. Bracken Jr.
Racing Hometown: Barnesville, GA

Year	Rank	Starts	Poles	1	2	3	4	5	6–10	Laps	Laps Led	Races Led	Miles	$
1953	34	6	0	0	0	0	0	0	1	221	0	0	221	215
Lifetime		6	0	0	0	0	0	0	1	221	0	0	221	$215

Gary Bradberry

Gary Bradberry
B: 1/27/1961
Racing Hometown: Chelsea, AL

Year	Rank	Starts	Poles	1	2	3	4	5	6–10	Laps	Laps Led	Races Led	Miles	$
1994	70T	1	0	0	0	0	0	0	0	276	0	0	420	6,600
1995	NR	4	0	0	0	0	0	0	0	604	0	0	803	33,575
1996	46	9	0	0	0	0	0	0	0	2,212	0	0	2,827	155,785
1997	44	16	0	0	0	0	0	0	0	4,207	0	0	5,004	251,930
1998	49	13	0	0	0	0	0	0	0	3,398	0	0	4,525	336,905
1999	66	1	0	0	0	0	0	0	0	233	0	0	359	33,705
2000	63	2	0	0	0	0	0	0	0	642	0	0	498	63,700
2002	84T	1	0	0	0	0	0	0	0	72	0	0	144	40,399
Lifetime		47	0	0	0	0	0	0	0	11,644	0	0	14,581	$922,599

Melvin Bradley

Melvin Bradley
Racing Hometown: Richmond, VA

Year	Rank	Starts	Poles	1	2	3	4	5	6–10	Laps	Laps Led	Races Led	Miles	$
1962	59	3	0	0	0	0	1	0	1	1,007	0	0	445	990
1967	85	3	0	0	0	0	0	0	1	549	0	0	321	525
Lifetime		6	0	0	0	0	1	0	2	1,556	0	0	766	$1,515

Eddie Bradshaw

Edward Bradshaw
B: 7/15/1934
Racing Hometown: Bakersfield, CA

Year	Rank	Starts	Poles	1	2	3	4	5	6–10	Laps	Laps Led	Races Led	Miles	$
1974	105	1	0	0	0	0	0	0	1	123	0	0	322	1,375
1975	96	1	0	0	0	0	0	0	0	63	0	0	165	820
1976	70	2	0	0	0	0	0	0	0	224	0	0	587	2,685
1977	72	2	0	0	0	0	0	0	1	152	0	0	394	2,920

Year	Rank	Starts	Poles	Finish						Laps	Laps Led	Races Led	Miles	$
				1	2	3	4	5	6–10					

Eddie Bradshaw *continued*

Year	Rank	Starts	Poles	1	2	3	4	5	6–10	Laps	Laps Led	Races Led	Miles	$
1978	100	1	0	0	0	0	0	0	0	15	0	0	39	600
Lifetime		7	0	0	0	0	0	0	2	577	0	0	1,507	$8,400

Art Brady

Arthur Brady
  Racing Hometown: Peoria, IL

1962	71	2	0	0	0	0	0	0	0	179	0	0	448	450
Lifetime		2	0	0	0	0	0	0	0	179	0	0	448	$450

Lonnie Bragg

Lonnie Bragg
  Racing Hometown: Terre Haute, IN

1953	NR	1	0	0	0	0	0	0	0	149	0	0	205	105
Lifetime		1	0	0	0	0	0	0	0	149	0	0	205	$105

Al Brand

Clarence Brand
  Racing Hometown: Inglewood, CA

1961	111	3	0	0	0	0	0	0	0	205	0	0	179	155
1963	152	1	0	0	0	0	0	0	0	1	0	0	3	200
1964	133	1	0	0	0	0	0	0	0	7	0	0	19	500
Lifetime		5	0	0	0	0	0	0	0	213	0	0	201	$855

Don Branson

Donald Branson
  Racing Hometown: Chaelston, SC

1964	92	8	0	0	0	0	0	0	0	271	0	0	116	660
Lifetime		8	0	0	0	0	0	0	0	271	0	0	116	$660

Wally Branston

Walter Branston
  Racing Hometown: Toronto, Ont, Canada

1954	211	1	0	0	0	0	0	0	0	52	0	0	26	0
Lifetime		1	0	0	0	0	0	0	0	52	0	0	26	$0

Bruce Brantley

Bruce Brantley
  Racing Hometown: Chamblee, GA

1962	126	1	0	0	0	0	0	0	0	139	0	0	209	275
1963	91	4	0	0	0	0	0	0	1	231	0	0	146	840
Lifetime		5	0	0	0	0	0	0	1	370	0	0	354	$1,115

Frank Brantley

Frank Meyer Brantley
B: 11/10/1932
  Racing Hometown: Savannah, GA

1962	NR	1	0	0	0	0	0	0	0	164	0	0	82	85
1964	101	2	0	0	0	0	0	0	0	262	0	0	131	290
Lifetime		3	0	0	0	0	0	0	0	426	0	0	213	$375

Everett Brashear

Everett Brashear
  Racing Hometown: Beaumont, TX

1957	183	1	0	0	0	0	0	0	0		0	0		25
Lifetime		1	0	0	0	0	0	0	0		0	0		$25

Darin Brassfield

Darin Brassfield
B: 9/16/1960
  Racing Hometown: Los Gatos, CA

1989	50	3	0	0	0	0	0	0	0	275	0	0	488	10,852
Lifetime		3	0	0	0	0	0	0	0	275	0	0	488	$10,852

Bill Braun

William Braun
  Racing Hometown: Paterson, NJ

1951	139T	1	0	0	0	0	0	0	1		0	0		50
Lifetime		1	0	0	0	0	0	0	1		0	0		$50

Year	Rank	Starts	Poles	Finish 1	2	3	4	5	6–10	Laps	Laps Led	Races Led	Miles	$

Jim Bray

James Charles Bray
B: 2/8/1933
Racing Hometown: Long Branch, Ont, Canada

Year	Rank	Starts	Poles	1	2	3	4	5	6–10	Laps	Laps Led	Races Led	Miles	$
1962	76	3	0	0	0	0	0	0	0	362	0	0	175	300
1963	109	2	0	0	0	0	0	0	0	377	0	0	120	225
1964	69	4	0	0	0	0	0	0	0	167	0	0	452	1,875
1965	93	2	0	0	0	0	0	0	0	6	0	0	15	1,190
1974	62	2	0	0	0	0	0	0	0	319	0	0	322	1,445
Lifetime		13	0	0	0	0	0	0	0	1,231	0	0	1,085	$5,035

Victor Brenzelli

Victor Brenzelli
Racing Hometown: Atlanta, GA

Year	Rank	Starts	Poles	1	2	3	4	5	6–10	Laps	Laps Led	Races Led	Miles	$
1951	N/A	1	0	0	0	0	0	0	0		0	0		25
Lifetime		1	0	0	0	0	0	0	0		0	0		$25

Bobby Brewer

George Robert Brewer
B: 8/11/1929
Racing Hometown: Winston-Salem, NC

Year	Rank	Starts	Poles	1	2	3	4	5	6–10	Laps	Laps Led	Races Led	Miles	$
1969	NR	1	0	0	0	0	0	0	0	9	0	0	24	975
Lifetime		1	0	0	0	0	0	0	0	9	0	0	24	$975

E.J. Brewer

Emery J. Brewer
Racing Hometown: Winston-Salem, NC

Year	Rank	Starts	Poles	1	2	3	4	5	6–10	Laps	Laps Led	Races Led	Miles	$
1957	NR	1	0	0	0	0	0	0	0	138	0	0	69	110
1958	129	5	0	0	0	0	0	0	1	486	0	0	390	490
Lifetime		6	0	0	0	0	0	0	1	624	0	0	459	$600

Richard Brickhouse

Richard Fleming Brickhouse
B: 10/27/1939
Racing Hometown: Rocky Point, NC

Year	Rank	Starts	Poles	1	2	3	4	5	6–10	Laps	Laps Led	Races Led	Miles	$
1968	45	7	0	0	0	0	1	0	1	1,571	0	0	1,977	7,190
1969	25	24	0	1	0	0	0	1	7	3,629	34	2	4,535	45,637
1970	58	5	0	0	0	0	0	1	1	409	2	1	902	6,925
1979	126T	1	0	0	0	0	0	0	0	15	0	0	23	870
1982	89	2	0	0	0	0	0	0	0	557	0	0	673	2,610
Lifetime		39	0	1	0	0	1	2	9	6,181	36	3	8,109	$63,232

Kenneth Bridge

Kenneth Bridge
Racing Hometown: Thompsonville, CT

Year	Rank	Starts	Poles	1	2	3	4	5	6–10	Laps	Laps Led	Races Led	Miles	$
1954	190	1	0	0	0	0	0	0	0	5	0	0	5	0
Lifetime		1	0	0	0	0	0	0	0	5	0	0	5	$0

Johnny Bridgers

John F. Bridgers
Racing Hometown: Rowland, NC

Year	Rank	Starts	Poles	1	2	3	4	5	6–10	Laps	Laps Led	Races Led	Miles	$
1952	163	1	0	0	0	0	0	0	0	244	0	0	305	0
1953	151	1	0	0	0	0	0	0	0	279	0	0	384	120
Lifetime		2	0	0	0	0	0	0	0	523	0	0	689	$120

Buck Brigance

Buck Brigance
Racing Hometown: Charlotte, NC

Year	Rank	Starts	Poles	1	2	3	4	5	6–10	Laps	Laps Led	Races Led	Miles	$
1958	NR	1	0	0	0	0	0	0	0	109	0	0	55	70
1959	87	13	0	0	0	0	0	0	1	1,865	0	0	919	891
1960	NR	2	0	0	0	0	0	0	1	297	0	0	149	210
Lifetime		16	0	0	0	0	0	0	2	2,271	0	0	1,122	$1,171

Mason Bright

Mason Bright
B: 1929
Racing Hometown: Detroit, MI

Year	Rank	Starts	Poles	1	2	3	4	5	6–10	Laps	Laps Led	Races Led	Miles	$
1953	171	1	0	0	0	0	0	0	0	33	0	0	135	25
1954	NR	2	0	0	0	0	0	0	0	200	0	0	226	50
Lifetime		3	0	0	0	0	0	0	0	233	0	0	361	$75

Year	Rank	Starts	Poles	Finish						Laps	Laps Led	Races Led	Miles	$
				1	2	3	4	5	6–10	Laps	Led	Led	Miles	$

Kenny Brightbill

Kenneth Brightbill
B: 1946
Racing Hometown: Sinking Springs, PA

Year	Rank	Starts	Poles	1	2	3	4	5	6–10	Laps	Laps Led	Races Led	Miles	$
1974	106	2	0	0	0	0	0	0	2	663	0	0	944	3,950
1975	77	1	0	0	0	0	0	0	1	480	0	0	480	2,000
1977	77	2	0	0	0	0	0	0	0	206	0	0	497	1,950
1978	NR	1	0	0	0	0	0	0	0	177	0	0	443	1,130
Lifetime		6	0	0	0	0	0	0	3	1,526	0	0	2,363	$9,030

Charles Brinkley

Charles Brinkley
Racing Hometown: Memphis, TN

Year	Rank	Starts	Poles	1	2	3	4	5	6–10	Laps	Laps Led	Races Led	Miles	$
1954	NR	2	0	0	0	0	0	0	0	319	0	0	445	100
Lifetime		2	0	0	0	0	0	0	0	319	0	0	445	$100

Maudis Brissette

Maudis Brissette
Racing Hometown: Bailey, NC

Year	Rank	Starts	Poles	1	2	3	4	5	6–10	Laps	Laps Led	Races Led	Miles	$
1951	209T	1	0	0	0	0	0	0	0		0	0		25
Lifetime		1	0	0	0	0	0	0	0		0	0		$25

Ronnie Bristow

Ronald Bristow
Racing Hometown: Aberdeen, CA

Year	Rank	Starts	Poles	1	2	3	4	5	6–10	Laps	Laps Led	Races Led	Miles	$
1963	121	2	0	0	0	0	0	0	0	112	0	0	48	485
Lifetime		2	0	0	0	0	0	0	0	112	0	0	48	$485

Leonard Brock

Leonard Brock (Lee)
Racing Hometown: Niota, TN

Year	Rank	Starts	Poles	1	2	3	4	5	6–10	Laps	Laps Led	Races Led	Miles	$
1968	94	3	0	0	0	0	0	0	0	17	0	0	8	175
Lifetime		3	0	0	0	0	0	0	0	17	0	0	8	$175

Pete Brock

Peter Brock
Racing Hometown: Riverside, CA

Year	Rank	Starts	Poles	1	2	3	4	5	6–10	Laps	Laps Led	Races Led	Miles	$
1963	89	1	0	0	0	0	0	0	0	134	0	0	362	350
Lifetime		1	0	0	0	0	0	0	0	134	0	0	362	$350

Barry Brooks

Barry Brooks
Racing Hometown: Ft. Mill, SC

Year	Rank	Starts	Poles	1	2	3	4	5	6–10	Laps	Laps Led	Races Led	Miles	$
1965	87	4	0	0	0	0	0	0	0	131	0	0	76	1,450
Lifetime		4	0	0	0	0	0	0	0	131	0	0	76	$1,450

Dick Brooks

Richard Brooks
B: 4/14/1942
Racing Hometown: Porterville, CA

Year	Rank	Starts	Poles	1	2	3	4	5	6–10	Laps	Laps Led	Races Led	Miles	$
1969	21	28	0	0	0	1	0	2	9	5,741	2	1	6,162	28,187
1970	13	34	0	0	2	5	4	4	3	6,821	194	6	6,996	53,754
1971	36	20	0	0	1	5	0	3	3	4,495	16	5	4,784	32,921
1972	49	14	0	0	0	0	0	0	1	1,156	3	2	2,169	14,146
1973	27	14	0	1	0	1	0	1	6	3,448	25	3	4,954	55,369
1974	27	16	0	0	0	0	0	0	3	2,951	1	1	4,097	22,760
1975	10	25	0	0	1	2	3	0	9	7,344	60	4	8,053	93,001
1976	10	28	0	0	0	1	1	1	15	7,542	16	2	8,586	111,880
1977	6	29	0	0	1	0	1	5	13	8,191	8	2	9,511	151,374
1978	8	30	0	0	0	0	1	4	12	8,389	24	2	9,723	137,590
1979	22	27	0	0	0	1	0	0	7	6,307	16	1	7,423	61,985
1980	27	19	0	0	0	0	0	2	3	3,978	6	1	5,107	60,700
1981	61	5	0	0	0	0	0	0	0	1,397	1	1	2,065	14,845
1982	48	5	0	0	0	0	0	0	0	517	0	0	688	9,470
1983	14	30	0	0	0	0	0	2	4	7,736	108	6	8,695	180,556
1984	15	30	0	0	0	1	0	0	4	8,157	185	3	9,320	192,407
1985	53	4	0	0	0	0	0	0	1	1,076	0	0	1,572	29,340
Lifetime		358	0	1	5	17	10	24	93	85,246	665	40	99,905	$1,250,285

Year	Rank	Starts	Poles	Finish 1	2	3	4	5	6–10	Laps	Laps Led	Races Led	Miles	$

Earl Brooks

Earl Lee Brooks
B: 8/11/1929
Racing Hometown: Lynchburg, VA

Year	Rank	Starts	Poles	1	2	3	4	5	6–10	Laps	Laps Led	Races Led	Miles	$
1962	58	8	0	0	0	0	0	0	3	946	0	0	451	745
1963	93	3	0	0	0	0	0	1	0	783	0	0	354	725
1964	41	28	0	0	0	0	0	0	8	3,988	0	0	1,834	3,825
1965	139	1	0	0	0	0	0	0	0	0	0	0	0	100
1966	63	9	0	0	0	0	0	0	1	1,769	0	0	1,198	3,470
1967	25	34	1	0	0	0	0	0	8	5,373	24	1	3,536	8,610
1968	15	40	0	0	0	0	0	0	5	6,507	0	0	4,385	14,233
1969	18	49	0	0	0	0	0	1	5	8,719	0	0	6,990	34,793
1970	37	21	0	0	0	0	0	0	1	1,779	0	0	1,891	10,360
1971	17	35	0	0	0	0	1	0	3	6,757	0	0	6,654	25,360
1972	73	6	0	0	0	0	0	0	0	609	0	0	593	3,215
1973	42	9	0	0	0	0	0	0	0	2,267	0	0	1,397	4,880
1974	115	1	0	0	0	0	0	0	0	1	0	0	1	1,100
1975	42	8	0	0	0	0	0	0	0	1,534	0	0	1,681	4,900
1976	63	4	0	0	0	0	0	0	0	1,230	0	0	1,340	5,225
1977	44	6	0	0	0	0	0	0	0	1,260	0	0	949	3,045
1979	NR	1	0	0	0	0	0	0	0	79	0	0	49	405
Lifetime		263	1	0	0	0	1	2	34	43,601	24	1	33,302	$124,991

Gary Brooks

Gary Brooks

Year	Rank	Starts	Poles	1	2	3	4	5	6–10	Laps	Laps Led	Races Led	Miles	$
1991	87T	1	0	0	0	0	0	0	0	11	0	0	11	3,425
Lifetime		1	0	0	0	0	0	0	0	11	0	0	11	$3,425

Tex Brooks

Tex Brooks
Racing Hometown: Yonkers, NY

Year	Rank	Starts	Poles	1	2	3	4	5	6–10	Laps	Laps Led	Races Led	Miles	$
1954	100	2	0	0	0	0	0	0	0	57	0	0	93	35
Lifetime		2	0	0	0	0	0	0	0	57	0	0	93	$35

Willard Brooks

Willard Brooks
Racing Hometown: Mobile, AL

Year	Rank	Starts	Poles	1	2	3	4	5	6–10	Laps	Laps Led	Races Led	Miles	$
1951	N/A	1	0	0	0	0	0	0	0		0	0		25
Lifetime		1	0	0	0	0	0	0	0		0	0		$25

Wayne Broome

Wayne Broome
Racing Hometown: Mt. Gilead, NC

Year	Rank	Starts	Poles	1	2	3	4	5	6–10	Laps	Laps Led	Races Led	Miles	$
1979	115	2	0	0	0	0	0	0	0	125	0	0	318	2,140
Lifetime		2	0	0	0	0	0	0	0	125	0	0	318	$2,140

Bill Brown

William Brown
Racing Hometown: Chicago, IL

Year	Rank	Starts	Poles	1	2	3	4	5	6–10	Laps	Laps Led	Races Led	Miles	$
1952	154T	1	0	0	0	0	0	0	0	111	0	0	56	25
1952	154T	1	0	0	0	0	0	0	0	111	0	0	56	25
1954	NR	1	0	0	0	0	0	0	0	41	0	0	21	0
1954	NR	1	0	0	0	0	0	0	0	41	0	0	21	0
1955	166T	1	0	0	0	0	0	0	0	169	0	0	85	60
1955	166T	1	0	0	0	0	0	0	0	169	0	0	85	60
1959	NR	1	0	0	0	0	0	0	1	183	0	0	46	165
1959	NR	1	0	0	0	0	0	0	1	183	0	0	46	165
Lifetime		8	0	0	0	0	0	0	2	1,008	0	0	413	$500

Bob Brown

Robert Sydney Brown
B: 7/4/1943
Racing Hometown: Milan, TN

Year	Rank	Starts	Poles	1	2	3	4	5	6–10	Laps	Laps Led	Races Led	Miles	$
1971	61	5	0	0	0	0	0	0	0	462	0	0	335	1,335
1972	103	2	0	0	0	0	0	0	0	324	0	0	175	710
1973	106	2	0	0	0	0	0	0	0	353	0	0	210	590
Lifetime		9	0	0	0	0	0	0	0	1,139	0	0	721	$2,635

Year	Rank	Starts	Poles	Finish 1	2	3	4	5	6–10	Laps	Laps Led	Races Led	Miles	$

Brownie Brown

T. T. Brown
Racing Hometown: Las Vegas, NV

Year	Rank	Starts	Poles	1	2	3	4	5	6–10	Laps	Laps Led	Races Led	Miles	$
1960	NR	1	0	0	0	0	0	0	0	12	0	0	17	0
1961	NR	1	0	0	0	0	0	0	0	6	0	0	8	0
Lifetime		2	0	0	0	0	0	0	0	18	0	0	25	$0

Cannonball Brown

Thomas Brown
Racing Hometown: Atlanta, GA

Year	Rank	Starts	Poles	1	2	3	4	5	6–10	Laps	Laps Led	Races Led	Miles	$
1958	NR	2	0	0	0	0	0	0	0	104	0	0	99	50
Lifetime		2	0	0	0	0	0	0	0	104	0	0	99	$50

Chester Brown

Chester Brown
Racing Hometown: Greenville, SC

Year	Rank	Starts	Poles	1	2	3	4	5	6–10	Laps	Laps Led	Races Led	Miles	$
1955	NR	1	0	0	0	0	0	0	0	20	0	0	10	0
Lifetime		1	0	0	0	0	0	0	0	20	0	0	10	$0

Ed Brown

Edwin Brown
B: 3/15/1920
Racing Hometown: Merridian, CA

Year	Rank	Starts	Poles	1	2	3	4	5	6–10	Laps	Laps Led	Races Led	Miles	$
1955	53	4	0	0	0	0	0	0	2	584	44	1	488	450
1956	244	1	0	0	0	0	0	0	0	72	0	0	180	55
1957	142	1	0	0	0	0	0	0	0	52	0	0	130	115
1961	151	1	0	0	0	0	0	0	0	74	0	0	74	50
1965	64	1	0	0	0	0	0	0	0	151	0	0	408	605
1968	88	1	0	0	0	0	0	0	0	73	0	0	197	615
Lifetime		9	0	0	0	0	0	0	2	1,006	44	1	1,477	$1,890

Len Brown

Leonard Brown
Racing Hometown: Lambertville, NJ

Year	Rank	Starts	Poles	1	2	3	4	5	6–10	Laps	Laps Led	Races Led	Miles	$
1949	NR	1	0	0	0	0	0	0	0	158	0	0	158	25
1950	81	3	0	0	0	0	0	0	0	290	0	0	205	175
1951	N/A	1	0	0	0	0	0	0	0		0	0		0
Lifetime		5	0	0	0	0	0	0	0	448	0	0	363	$200

Merritt Brown

Merritt L. Brown
Racing Hometown: Daytona Beach, FL

Year	Rank	Starts	Poles	1	2	3	4	5	6–10	Laps	Laps Led	Races Led	Miles	$
1952	169	1	0	0	0	0	0	0	0	28	0	0	35	0
1953	NR	1	0	0	0	0	0	0	0	20	0	0	28	100
Lifetime		2	0	0	0	0	0	0	0	48	0	0	63	$100

Mike Brown

Michael A. Brown (Nick)
Racing Hometown: Royal Oak, MI

Year	Rank	Starts	Poles	1	2	3	4	5	6–10	Laps	Laps Led	Races Led	Miles	$
1954	122	2	0	0	0	0	0	0	0	149	0	0	201	50
Lifetime		2	0	0	0	0	0	0	0	149	0	0	201	$50

Perk Brown

(Real Name: Jack B. Thomasson)
B: 2/10/1925   D: 7/7/1999
Racing Hometown: Spray, NC

Year	Rank	Starts	Poles	1	2	3	4	5	6–10	Laps	Laps Led	Races Led	Miles	$
1952	13	19	1	0	0	2	0	1	3	2,336	0	0	1,458	2,187
1953	NR	2	0	0	0	0	0	0	0	14	0	0	57	25
1954	115	3	0	0	0	0	0	0	0	346	0	0	212	75
1955	131	2	0	0	0	0	0	0	1	275	0	0	138	150
1963	112	2	0	0	0	0	0	0	1	233	0	0	69	300
Lifetime		28	1	0	0	2	0	1	5	3,204	0	0	1,933	$2,737

Richard Brown

Richard D. Brown
B: 4/9/1940
Racing Hometown: Claremont, NC

Year	Rank	Starts	Poles	1	2	3	4	5	6–10	Laps	Laps Led	Races Led	Miles	$
1954	NR	1	0	0	0	0	0	0	0	118	0	0	59	0
1954	NR	1	0	0	0	0	0	0	0	118	0	0	59	0
1961	77	1	0	0	0	0	0	0	0	133	0	0	186	250
1961	77	1	0	0	0	0	0	0	0	133	0	0	186	250
Lifetime		4	0	0	0	0	0	0	0	502	0	0	490	$500

Year	Rank	Starts	Poles	Finish 1	2	3	4	5	6–10	Laps	Laps Led	Races Led	Miles	$

Woody Brown

Woodward Brown
　　Racing Hometown: Oakland, CA

Year	Rank	Starts	Poles	1	2	3	4	5	6–10	Laps	Laps Led	Races Led	Miles	$
1951	32	3	0	0	0	1	0	1	0	14	0	0	7	1,125
1954	60	4	0	0	0	0	0	0	0	991	0	0	613	175
Lifetime		7	0	0	0	1	0	1	0	1,005	0	0	620	$1,300

Richard Brownlee

Richard Brownlee
　　Racing Hometown: Greensboro, NC

Year	Rank	Starts	Poles	1	2	3	4	5	6–10	Laps	Laps Led	Races Led	Miles	$
1954	NR	1	0	0	0	0	0	0	0	74	0	0	37	25
1955	57	7	0	0	0	0	0	0	0	681	0	0	359	315
Lifetime		8	0	0	0	0	0	0	0	755	0	0	396	$340

Rodney Bruce

Rodney Bruce
　　Racing Hometown: Hampton, VA

Year	Rank	Starts	Poles	1	2	3	4	5	6–10	Laps	Laps Led	Races Led	Miles	$
1970	NR	1	0	0	0	0	0	0	0	261	0	0	103	225
Lifetime		1	0	0	0	0	0	0	0	261	0	0	103	$225

Laird Bruner

Laird Bruner
　　Racing Hometown: Rockwood, PA

Year	Rank	Starts	Poles	1	2	3	4	5	6–10	Laps	Laps Led	Races Led	Miles	$
1953	152	1	0	0	0	0	0	0	0	142	0	0	195	105
1954	14	24	0	0	0	0	0	2	4	3,052	0	0	2,338	2,080
Lifetime		25	0	0	0	0	0	2	4	3,194	0	0	2,533	$2,185

Andy Bruni

Andrew Bruni
　　Racing Hometown: Grand Rapids, MI

Year	Rank	Starts	Poles	1	2	3	4	5	6–10	Laps	Laps Led	Races Led	Miles	$
1954	NR	1	0	0	0	0	0	0	0	34	0	0	17	0
Lifetime		1	0	0	0	0	0	0	0	34	0	0	17	$0

Darrell Bryant

Darrell Bryant
　　B: 10/6/1940
　　Racing Hometown: Thomasville, NC

Year	Rank	Starts	Poles	1	2	3	4	5	6–10	Laps	Laps Led	Races Led	Miles	$
1964	95	5	0	0	0	0	0	0	1	366	0	0	177	725
1965	91	3	0	0	0	0	0	0	0	102	0	0	69	755
1966	100	2	0	0	0	0	0	0	0	243	0	0	139	670
1976	47	8	0	0	0	0	0	0	1	1,678	0	0	2,105	11,925
Lifetime		18	0	0	0	0	0	0	2	2,389	0	0	2,490	$14,075

Kirk Bryant

Kirk Bryant
　　B: 4/27/1962
　　Racing Hometown: Thomasville, NC

Year	Rank	Starts	Poles	1	2	3	4	5	6–10	Laps	Laps Led	Races Led	Miles	$
1986	58	4	0	0	0	0	0	0	0	842	0	0	978	26,335
1987	95	1	0	0	0	0	0	0	0	205	0	0	208	1,415
Lifetime		5	0	0	0	0	0	0	0	1,047	0	0	1,187	$27,750

Herschel Buchanan

Herschel Buchanan
　　B: 1908 D: 5/11/1985
　　Racing Hometown: Shreveport, LA

Year	Rank	Starts	Poles	1	2	3	4	5	6–10	Laps	Laps Led	Races Led	Miles	$
1950	53	2	0	0	0	0	0	0	1	3	0	0	13	200
1951	N/A	1	0	0	0	0	0	0	0		0	0		0
1952	16	5	0	0	0	1	1	2	1	1,302	0	0	1,068	2,468
1953	NR	14	0	0	0	1	2	1	2	506	0	0	456	2,050
1954	53	1	0	0	0	0	0	1	0	160	0	0	240	500
Lifetime		23	0	0	0	2	3	4	4	1,971	0	0	1,776	$5,218

Julian Buesink

Julian Buesink
　　B: 1910
　　Racing Hometown: Findlay Park, NY

Year	Rank	Starts	Poles	1	2	3	4	5	6–10	Laps	Laps Led	Races Led	Miles	$
1951	N/A	1	0	0	0	0	0	0	0		0	0		0
Lifetime		1	0	0	0	0	0	0	0		0	0		$0

Year	Rank	Starts	Poles	Finish 1	2	3	4	5	6–10	Laps	Laps Led	Races Led	Miles	$

Andy Buffington

Andrew Buffington
Racing Hometown: Forrest Park, GA

Year	Rank	Starts	Poles	1	2	3	4	5	6–10	Laps	Laps Led	Races Led	Miles	$
1964	106	1	0	0	0	0	0	0	1	173	0	0	87	175
Lifetime		1	0	0	0	0	0	0	1	173	0	0	87	$175

George Bumgardner

George Bumgardner
Racing Hometown: Sarasota Springs, NY

Year	Rank	Starts	Poles	1	2	3	4	5	6–10	Laps	Laps Led	Races Led	Miles	$
1957	NR	1	0	0	0	0	0	0	0	111	0	0	111	100
Lifetime		1	0	0	0	0	0	0	0	111	0	0	111	$100

Paul Bumhaver

Paul Bumhaver
Racing Hometown: Mansfield, OH

Year	Rank	Starts	Poles	1	2	3	4	5	6–10	Laps	Laps Led	Races Led	Miles	$
1966	108	2	0	0	0	0	0	0	0	548	0	0	274	500
Lifetime		2	0	0	0	0	0	0	0	548	0	0	274	$500

Hully Bunn

Hully Bunn
B: 4/14/1920
Racing Hometown: Bristol, CT

Year	Rank	Starts	Poles	1	2	3	4	5	6–10	Laps	Laps Led	Races Led	Miles	$
1951	N/A	1	0	0	0	0	0	0	0		0	0		25
Lifetime		1	0	0	0	0	0	0	0		0	0		$25

Ann Bunselmeyer

Ann Bunselmeyer
B: 1916
Racing Hometown: Elmsford, NY

Year	Rank	Starts	Poles	1	2	3	4	5	6–10	Laps	Laps Led	Races Led	Miles	$
1950	126T	1	0	0	0	0	0	0	0		0	0		0
Lifetime		1	0	0	0	0	0	0	0		0	0		$0

Clarence Burch

Clarence Burch
Racing Hometown: Durham, NC

Year	Rank	Starts	Poles	1	2	3	4	5	6–10	Laps	Laps Led	Races Led	Miles	$
1954	194	1	0	0	0	0	0	0	0	58	0	0	58	50
Lifetime		1	0	0	0	0	0	0	0	58	0	0	58	$50

Bob Burcham

Robert Burcham
B: 8/22/1935
Racing Hometown: Rossville, GA

Year	Rank	Starts	Poles	1	2	3	4	5	6–10	Laps	Laps Led	Races Led	Miles	$
1968	103	2	0	0	0	0	0	0	0	366	0	0	183	515
1969	NR	1	0	0	0	0	0	0	0	2	0	0	5	900
1974	24	20	0	0	0	0	1	0	4	4,819	2	1	6,405	27,923
1975	55	3	0	0	0	0	0	0	0	733	0	0	1,289	6,895
1976	55	5	0	0	0	0	0	0	0	621	0	0	1,108	6,465
1977	68	3	0	0	0	0	0	0	1	588	0	0	1,082	15,095
1978	86T	1	0	0	0	0	0	0	0	243	0	0	332	2,790
1979	65	2	0	0	0	0	0	0	0	356	0	0	826	6,565
Lifetime		37	0	0	0	0	1	0	5	7,728	2	1	11,229	$67,148

Bob Burdick

Robert Burdick
B: 10/20/1936
Racing Hometown: Omaha, NE

Year	Rank	Starts	Poles	1	2	3	4	5	6–10	Laps	Laps Led	Races Led	Miles	$
1959	21	6	2	0	1	0	0	0	3	912	25	1	1,000	10,050
1960	93	2	0	0	0	0	0	0	1	71	0	0	178	475
1961	36	5	0	1	0	0	1	0	1	1,086	44	2	1,798	18,750
1962	85	2	0	0	0	0	0	0	1	95	0	0	238	625
Lifetime		15	2	1	1	0	1	0	6	2,164	69	3	3,213	$29,900

Bud Burdick

Bud Burdick
Racing Hometown: Omaha, NE

Year	Rank	Starts	Poles	1	2	3	4	5	6–10	Laps	Laps Led	Races Led	Miles	$
1960	48	2	0	0	0	0	0	0	1	236	0	0	590	850
Lifetime		2	0	0	0	0	0	0	1	236	0	0	590	$850

Year	Rank	Starts	Poles	1	2	3	4	5	6–10	Laps	Laps Led	Races Led	Miles	$

Marvin Burke
Marvin Burke
Racing Hometown: Pittsburg, CA

Year	Rank	Starts	Poles	1	2	3	4	5	6–10	Laps	Laps Led	Races Led	Miles	$
1951	N/A	1	0	1	0	0	0	0	0	250	156	1	156	1,875
Lifetime		1	0	1	0	0	0	0	0	250	156	1	156	$1,875

Bob Burkhart
Robert Burkhart

Year	Rank	Starts	Poles	1	2	3	4	5	6–10	Laps	Laps Led	Races Led	Miles	$
1950	NR	1	0	0	0	0	0	0	0		0	0		0
Lifetime		1	0	0	0	0	0	0	0		0	0		$0

Charles Burnett
Charles Burnett
Racing Hometown: Warner Robbins, GA

Year	Rank	Starts	Poles	1	2	3	4	5	6–10	Laps	Laps Led	Races Led	Miles	$
1968	66	2	0	0	0	0	0	0	0	215	0	0	469	1,765
Lifetime		2	0	0	0	0	0	0	0	215	0	0	469	$1,765

Frank Burnett
Frank Burnett
Racing Hometown: Modesto, CA

Year	Rank	Starts	Poles	1	2	3	4	5	6–10	Laps	Laps Led	Races Led	Miles	$
1967	93	1	0	0	0	0	0	0	0	60	0	0	162	500
1968	85	1	0	0	0	0	0	0	0	92	0	0	248	640
1969	NR	1	0	0	0	0	0	0	0	80	0	0	216	785
Lifetime		3	0	0	0	0	0	0	0	232	0	0	626	$1,925

Jerry Burnett
Jerry Burnett
Racing Hometown: New Ellington, SC

Year	Rank	Starts	Poles	1	2	3	4	5	6–10	Laps	Laps Led	Races Led	Miles	$
1962	116T	1	0	0	0	0	0	0	0	143	0	0	57	75
Lifetime		1	0	0	0	0	0	0	0	143	0	0	57	$75

Dick Burns
Richard Burns
Racing Hometown: Braddock, PA

Year	Rank	Starts	Poles	1	2	3	4	5	6–10	Laps	Laps Led	Races Led	Miles	$
1950	18	8	0	0	0	0	1	1	1	323	0	0	162	780
1956	209T	1	0	0	0	0	0	0	0	148	0	0	74	50
Lifetime		9	0	0	0	0	1	1	1	471	0	0	236	$830

Herbert Burns
Herbert Burns
Racing Hometown: Tampa, FL

Year	Rank	Starts	Poles	1	2	3	4	5	6–10	Laps	Laps Led	Races Led	Miles	$
1950	58	2	0	0	0	0	0	0	2		0	0		150
Lifetime		2	0	0	0	0	0	0	2		0	0		$150

Carl Burris
Carl E. Burris
B: 1924
Racing Hometown: Leaksville, NC

Year	Rank	Starts	Poles	1	2	3	4	5	6–10	Laps	Laps Led	Races Led	Miles	$
1953	NR	2	0	0	0	0	0	1	0	194	0	0	97	225
1954	156T	1	0	0	0	0	0	0	0	150	0	0	75	0
1958	NR	4	0	0	0	0	0	0	1	502	0	0	257	375
1959	113	1	0	0	0	0	0	0	0	2	0	0	3	150
1960	143	2	0	0	0	0	0	0	0	81	0	0	151	200
Lifetime		10	0	0	0	0	0	1	1	929	0	0	582	$950

Clarence Burris
Clarence Burris
Racing Hometown: Heidelberg, PA

Year	Rank	Starts	Poles	1	2	3	4	5	6–10	Laps	Laps Led	Races Led	Miles	$
1949	53	1	0	0	0	0	0	0	0	165	0	0	83	50
Lifetime		1	0	0	0	0	0	0	0	165	0	0	83	$50

Bill Burton
William Burton
Racing Hometown: Marcy, NY

Year	Rank	Starts	Poles	1	2	3	4	5	6–10	Laps	Laps Led	Races Led	Miles	$
1950	129T	1	0	0	0	0	0	0	0		0	0		0
Lifetime		1	0	0	0	0	0	0	0		0	0		$0

Year	Rank	Starts	Poles	Finish 1	2	3	4	5	6–10	Laps	Laps Led	Races Led	Miles	$

Jeff Burton

Jeff Burton
B: 6/29/1967
Racing Hometown: South Boston, VA

Year	Rank	Starts	Poles	1	2	3	4	5	6–10	Laps	Laps Led	Races Led	Miles	$
1993	83T	1	0	0	0	0	0	0	0	86	0	0	91	9,550
1994	24	30	0	0	0	0	2	0	1	7,781	122	4	10,240	594,700
1995	32	29	0	0	0	0	0	1	1	8,050	3	2	10,193	628,270
1996	13	30	1	0	0	1	3	2	6	8,592	208	7	10,552	884,303
1997	4	32	0	3	3	3	2	2	5	9,275	685	17	12,346	2,296,614
1998	5	33	0	2	4	2	5	5	5	9,488	974	13	12,141	2,626,987
1999	5	34	1	6	2	3	4	3	5	9,878	1,063	18	12,784	5,725,399
2000	3	34	1	4	5	2	1	3	7	9,656	1,131	22	12,626	5,121,354
2001	10	36	0	2	1	2	1	2	8	10,463	401	10	13,937	4,230,737
2002	12	36	0	0	0	3	2	0	9	9,980	124	13	13,205	4,244,856
Lifetime		295	3	17	15	16	20	18	47	83,249	4,711	106	108,115	$26,362,770

Ward Burton

Ward Burton
B: 10/25/1961
Racing Hometown: South Boston, VA

Year	Rank	Starts	Poles	1	2	3	4	5	6–10	Laps	Laps Led	Races Led	Miles	$
1994	35	26	1	0	1	0	0	0	1	5,320	73	5	6,303	304,700
1995	22	29	0	1	0	0	1	1	3	7,745	173	4	9,892	634,655
1996	33	27	1	0	0	0	0	0	4	6,544	54	4	8,845	873,619
1997	24	31	1	0	0	0	0	0	7	8,976	140	4	11,109	1,004,944
1998	16	33	2	0	1	0	0	0	4	9,551	132	9	12,509	1,516,183
1999	9	34	1	0	3	0	2	1	10	9,828	243	13	12,608	2,405,913
2000	10	34	0	1	0	3	0	0	13	9,097	506	10	12,290	2,385,326
2001	14	36	0	1	0	2	1	2	4	10,158	178	7	13,166	3,583,692
2002	25	35	1	2	0	0	0	1	5	8,673	371	11	11,358	4,899,884
Lifetime		285	7	5	5	5	4	5	51	75,892	1,870	67	98,079	$17,608,916

Kurt Busch

Kurt Busch
B: 8/4/1978
Racing Hometown: Las Vegas, NV

Year	Rank	Starts	Poles	1	2	3	4	5	6–10	Laps	Laps Led	Races Led	Miles	$
2000	48	7	0	0	0	0	0	0	0	2,411	0	0	2,702	311,915
2001	27	35	1	0	0	1	1	1	3	8,965	160	5	11,994	2,170,629
2002	3	36	1	4	3	2	3	0	8	10,259	933	20	13,099	5,105,394
Lifetime		78	2	4	3	3	4	1	11	21,635	1,093	25	27,794	$7,587,938

George Bush

George Bush
Racing Hometown: Hamburg, NY

Year	Rank	Starts	Poles	1	2	3	4	5	6–10	Laps	Laps Led	Races Led	Miles	$
1952	52	5	0	0	0	0	0	0	3	598	0	0	488	330
Lifetime		5	0	0	0	0	0	0	3	598	0	0	488	$330

Bill Butts

William Butts
B: 9/3/1937
Racing Hometown: El Cajon, CA

Year	Rank	Starts	Poles	1	2	3	4	5	6–10	Laps	Laps Led	Races Led	Miles	$
1972	76	2	0	0	0	0	0	0	0	313	0	0	798	3,060
Lifetime		2	0	0	0	0	0	0	0	313	0	0	798	$3,060

Terry Byers

Terry Byers
B: 1/23/1950
Racing Hometown: Wollongong, Australia

Year	Rank	Starts	Poles	1	2	3	4	5	6–10	Laps	Laps Led	Races Led	Miles	$
1989	49	3	0	0	0	0	0	0	0	773	0	0	1,554	15,400
1990	103	2	0	0	0	0	0	0	0	41	0	0	63	7,525
Lifetime		5	0	0	0	0	0	0	0	814	0	0	1,616	$22,925

Danny Byrd

Daniel Byrd
B: 8/3/1937
Racing Hometown: Taylor, MI

Year	Rank	Starts	Poles	1	2	3	4	5	6–10	Laps	Laps Led	Races Led	Miles	$
1965	85	4	0	0	0	0	0	1	0	294	0	0	210	1,075
Lifetime		4	0	0	0	0	0	1	0	294	0	0	210	$1,075

Year	Rank	Starts	Poles	1	2	3	4	5	6–10	Laps	Laps Led	Races Led	Miles	$

Jim Byrd
James Byrd
Racing Hometown: Los Angeles, CA

Year	Rank	Starts	Poles	1	2	3	4	5	6–10	Laps	Laps Led	Races Led	Miles	$
1951	N/A	3	0	0	0	0	0	0	1		0	0		150
Lifetime		3	0	0	0	0	0	0	1		0	0		$150

Red Byron
Robert North Byron Jr.
B: 3/12/1915   D: 11/11/1960   *Died in hotel @ Chicago.*
Racing Hometown: Anniston, AL

Year	Rank	Starts	Poles	1	2	3	4	5	6–10	Laps	Laps Led	Races Led	Miles	$
1949	1	6	1	2	0	2	0	0	0	633	103	2	582	5,800
1950	NR	4	1	0	1	1	1	0	0	634	85	3	835	3,325
1951	NR	5	0	0	0	0	1	0	1	609	0	0	701	975
Lifetime		15	2	2	1	3	2	0	1	1,876	188	5	2,117	$10,100

Scotty Cain
Scott Cain
B: 8/11/1920
Racing Hometown: Venice, CA

Year	Rank	Starts	Poles	1	2	3	4	5	6–10	Laps	Laps Led	Races Led	Miles	$
1956	41	4	0	0	0	0	0	1	3	701	0	0	698	1,235
1957	32	11	0	0	0	0	3	0	4	1,151	0	0	782	1,165
1958	NR	1	0	0	0	0	0	0	1	176	0	0	463	275
1959	79	2	0	0	1	0	0	0	0	467	0	0	247	700
1960	79	4	0	0	1	1	0	0	0	351	19	1	324	1,225
1961	91	4	0	0	0	0	0	0	1	218	0	0	335	705
1963	84	2	0	0	0	0	0	0	0	229	0	0	618	575
1965	57	1	0	0	0	0	0	0	1	172	0	0	464	1,175
1966	127	1	0	0	0	0	0	0	0	20	0	0	54	525
1967	59	1	0	0	0	0	0	0	1	171	0	0	462	1,400
1968	74	1	0	0	0	0	0	0	1	167	0	0	451	1,150
1969	63	1	0	0	0	0	0	0	1	170	0	0	459	1,450
1970	111	2	0	0	0	0	0	0	0	60	0	0	157	1,495
1971	NR	1	0	0	0	0	0	0	1	143	0	0	375	1,270
Lifetime		36	0	0	2	1	3	1	14	4,196	19	1	5,888	$14,345

Leo Caldwell
Leo Caldwell
B: 1926   D: 11/8/1996
Racing Hometown: Perrysburg, OH

Year	Rank	Starts	Poles	1	2	3	4	5	6–10	Laps	Laps Led	Races Led	Miles	$
1950	84T	1	0	0	0	0	0	0	0		0	0		50
1951	NR	1	0	0	0	0	0	0	0		0	0		25
1952	87	2	0	0	0	0	0	0	0		0	0		75
Lifetime		4	0	0	0	0	0	0	0		0	0		$150

John Callis
John C. Callis
B: 5/31/1949
Racing Hometown: Orlando, FL

Year	Rank	Starts	Poles	1	2	3	4	5	6–10	Laps	Laps Led	Races Led	Miles	$
1980	91	2	0	0	0	0	0	0	0	464	0	0	472	1,500
1982	58	3	0	0	0	0	0	0	0	352	0	0	507	2,675
1983	72	2	0	0	0	0	0	0	0	525	0	0	671	2,775
Lifetime		7	0	0	0	0	0	0	0	1,341	0	0	1,649	$6,950

Austin Cameron
Austin Cameron
B: 1/27/1977
Racing Hometown: El Cajon, CA

Year	Rank	Starts	Poles	1	2	3	4	5	6–10	Laps	Laps Led	Races Led	Miles	$
2002	81T	1	0	0	0	0	0	0	0	24	0	0	47	46,945
Lifetime		1	0	0	0	0	0	0	0	24	0	0	47	$46,945

Bob Cameron
Robert Cameron
B: 12/18/1927
Racing Hometown: Kenmore, NY

Year	Rank	Starts	Poles	1	2	3	4	5	6–10	Laps	Laps Led	Races Led	Miles	$
1949	62T	1	0	0	0	0	0	0	0		0	0		50
1953	NR	1	0	0	0	0	0	0	1		0	0		150
Lifetime		2	0	0	0	0	0	0	1		0	0		$200

Year	Rank	Starts	Poles	Finish 1	2	3	4	5	6–10	Laps	Laps Led	Races Led	Miles	$

Gordon Campbell

Gordon Campbell

Year	Rank	Starts	Poles	1	2	3	4	5	6–10	Laps	Laps Led	Races Led	Miles	$
1956	171	1	0	0	0	0	0	0	0	74	0	0	185	75
Lifetime		1	0	0	0	0	0	0	0	74	0	0	185	$75

Kim Campbell

Kim Campbell

Year	Rank	Starts	Poles	1	2	3	4	5	6–10	Laps	Laps Led	Races Led	Miles	$
1991	79	1	0	0	0	0	0	0	0	64	0	0	157	3,725
Lifetime		1	0	0	0	0	0	0	0	64	0	0	157	$3,725

Ray Campbell

Raymond Campbell
B: 1929
Racing Hometown: Tonawanda, NY

Year	Rank	Starts	Poles	1	2	3	4	5	6–10	Laps	Laps Led	Races Led	Miles	$
1957	NR	1	0	0	0	0	0	0	0	77	0	0	77	135
1958	134T	1	0	0	0	0	0	0	0	150	0	0	75	70
Lifetime		2	0	0	0	0	0	0	0	227	0	0	152	$205

Wally Campbell

Wally Campbell
B: 7/16/1926   D: 7/17/1954   *Killed in Sprint Car @ Salem, IN during practice.*
Racing Hometown: Trenton, NJ

Year	Rank	Starts	Poles	1	2	3	4	5	6–10	Laps	Laps Led	Races Led	Miles	$
1949	NR	1	0	0	0	0	0	0	0	166	0	0	166	25
1950	NR	2	1	0	0	0	0	0	0	309	0	0	386	175
1951	NR	5	0	0	0	0	0	0	0	21	0	0	11	75
1953	NR	3	0	0	0	0	0	0	0	4	0	0	16	50
Lifetime		11	1	0	0	0	0	0	0	500	0	0	579	$325

Ed Camrud

Edward Camrud

Year	Rank	Starts	Poles	1	2	3	4	5	6–10	Laps	Laps Led	Races Led	Miles	$
1951	N/A	1	0	0	0	0	0	0	1		0	0		100
Lifetime		1	0	0	0	0	0	0	1		0	0		$100

Frank Canale

Frank Canale
Racing Hometown: Toledo, OH

Year	Rank	Starts	Poles	1	2	3	4	5	6–10	Laps	Laps Led	Races Led	Miles	$
1950	NR	1	0	0	0	0	0	0	0	74	0	0	37	0
Lifetime		1	0	0	0	0	0	0	0	74	0	0	37	$0

Earle Canavan

Earle Samuel Canavan
B: 12/5/1938
Racing Hometown: Ft. Johnson, NY

Year	Rank	Starts	Poles	1	2	3	4	5	6–10	Laps	Laps Led	Races Led	Miles	$
1969	NR	1	0	0	0	0	0	0	0	62	0	0	165	1,100
1971	63	5	0	0	0	0	0	0	0	375	0	0	483	2,530
1972	62	7	0	0	0	0	0	0	0	777	0	0	1,027	5,858
1973	41	5	0	0	0	0	0	0	0	1,223	0	0	1,681	4,980
1974	46	6	0	0	0	0	0	0	0	1,477	0	0	2,106	6,570
1975	32	12	0	0	0	0	0	0	0	1,601	0	0	1,861	9,725
1976	43	7	0	0	0	0	0	0	0	1,687	0	0	1,609	6,035
1977	56	5	0	0	0	0	0	0	0	646	0	0	783	4,390
1978	42	9	0	0	0	0	0	0	0	2,111	0	0	2,451	8,740
1979	41	8	0	0	0	0	0	0	0	734	0	0	1,122	6,675
1982	102	3	0	0	0	0	0	0	0	88	0	0	140	2,905
1985	91T	1	0	0	0	0	0	0	0	53	0	0	53	875
1986	114T	1	0	0	0	0	0	0	0	165	0	0	168	1,475
Lifetime		70	0	0	0	0	0	0	0	10,999	0	0	13,648	$61,858

Ted Cannady

Theodore H. Cannady
Racing Hometown: Collinsville, VA

Year	Rank	Starts	Poles	1	2	3	4	5	6–10	Laps	Laps Led	Races Led	Miles	$
1955	45	9	0	0	0	0	0	0	0	812	0	0	705	450
1956	92	6	0	0	0	0	0	0	0	814	0	0	484	260
Lifetime		15	0	0	0	0	0	0	0	1,626	0	0	1,189	$710

Year	Rank	Starts	Poles	Finish						Laps	Laps Led	Races Led	Miles	$
				1	2	3	4	5	6–10					

Ben Cannaziaro

Benjamin Cannaziaro
B: 5/17/1910
Racing Hometown: Trenton, NJ

Year	Rank	Starts	Poles	1	2	3	4	5	6–10	Laps	Laps Led	Races Led	Miles	$
1949	NR	1	0	0	0	0	0	0	0	159	0	0	159	25
Lifetime		1	0	0	0	0	0	0	0	159	0	0	159	$25

Billy Cantrell

William Cantrell
B: 1915
Racing Hometown: Anaheim, CA

Year	Rank	Starts	Poles	1	2	3	4	5	6–10	Laps	Laps Led	Races Led	Miles	$
1957	122	1	0	0	0	0	0	0	0	53	0	0	133	110
1965	NR	1	0	0	0	0	0	0	0	2	0	0	5	500
Lifetime		2	0	0	0	0	0	0	0	55	0	0	138	$610

Jimmy Lee Capps

Jimmy Lee Capps
B: 3/12/1938
Racing Hometown: Jacksonville, FL

Year	Rank	Starts	Poles	1	2	3	4	5	6–10	Laps	Laps Led	Races Led	Miles	$
1964	123	1	0	0	0	0	0	0	0	50	0	0	25	50
1976	54	4	0	0	0	0	0	0	1	505	0	0	1,229	6,950
1977	57	3	0	0	0	0	0	0	0	815	0	0	1,097	4,800
1978	63	3	0	0	0	0	0	0	0	586	0	0	701	3,880
Lifetime		11	0	0	0	0	0	0	1	1,956	0	0	3,052	$15,680

John Capps

John Capps
Racing Hometown: Greensboro, NC

Year	Rank	Starts	Poles	1	2	3	4	5	6–10	Laps	Laps Led	Races Led	Miles	$
1955	NR	1	0	0	0	0	0	0	0	17	0	0	17	25
Lifetime		1	0	0	0	0	0	0	0	17	0	0	17	$25

Billy Carden

Williamy Carden
B: 4/1/1924
Racing Hometown: Mableton, GA

Year	Rank	Starts	Poles	1	2	3	4	5	6–10	Laps	Laps Led	Races Led	Miles	$
1949	72	1	0	0	0	0	0	0	0		0	0		50
1950	93	3	0	0	0	0	0	0	0	368	0	0	548	75
1951	26	11	1	0	0	1	1	0	3	519	58	1	613	1,460
1952	74	3	0	0	0	0	0	0	0	186	0	0	93	50
1955	31	13	0	0	0	0	2	0	1	1,589	0	0	1,168	1,340
1956	22	23	0	0	0	0	0	0	4	2,831	0	0	1,881	2,175
1957	29	3	0	0	0	0	0	0	2	625	0	0	751	1,675
1958	38	13	0	0	0	0	0	0	2	1,469	0	0	804	815
1959	NR	3	0	0	0	0	0	0	1	364	0	0	574	375
Lifetime		73	1	0	0	1	3	0	13	7,951	58	1	6,432	$8,015

Pete Cardenas

Peter Cardenas
Racing Hometown: Long Beach, CA

Year	Rank	Starts	Poles	1	2	3	4	5	6–10	Laps	Laps Led	Races Led	Miles	$
1957	201T	1	0	0	0	0	0	0	0	9	0	0	9	0
Lifetime		1	0	0	0	0	0	0	0	9	0	0	9	$0

Rick Carelli

Richard Carelli
B: 11/9/1955
Racing Hometown: Arvada, CO

Year	Rank	Starts	Poles	1	2	3	4	5	6–10	Laps	Laps Led	Races Led	Miles	$
1992	74	2	0	0	0	0	0	0	0	58	0	0	145	9,005
1993	49	3	0	0	0	0	0	0	0	499	0	0	671	19,650
1994	49	4	0	0	0	0	0	0	0	958	0	0	1,165	31,975
Lifetime		9	0	0	0	0	0	0	0	1,515	0	0	1,980	$60,630

Frank Carlin

Frank Carlin

Year	Rank	Starts	Poles	1	2	3	4	5	6–10	Laps	Laps Led	Races Led	Miles	$
1951	N/A	1	0	0	0	0	0	0	0		0	0		0
Lifetime		1	0	0	0	0	0	0	0		0	0		$0

Year	Rank	Starts	Poles	Finish						Laps	Laps Led	Races Led	Miles	$
				1	2	3	4	5	6–10					

Harold Carmac
Harold Carmac
Racing Hometown: Ramseur, NC

Year	Rank	Starts	Poles	1	2	3	4	5	6–10	Laps	Laps Led	Races Led	Miles	$
1962	75	2	0	0	0	0	0	0	1	172	0	0	86	525
Lifetime		2	0	0	0	0	0	0	1	172	0	0	86	$525

Bob Carpenter
Robert Carpenter
Racing Hometown: Wabash, IN

Year	Rank	Starts	Poles	1	2	3	4	5	6–10	Laps	Laps Led	Races Led	Miles	$
1951	N/A	1	0	0	0	0	0	0	0		0	0		25
Lifetime		1	0	0	0	0	0	0	0		0	0		$25

Erwin Carpenter
Erwin Carpenter
Racing Hometown: Rock Hill, SC

Year	Rank	Starts	Poles	1	2	3	4	5	6–10	Laps	Laps Led	Races Led	Miles	$
1959	NR	1	0	0	0	0	0	0	0	299	0	0	150	75
Lifetime		1	0	0	0	0	0	0	0	299	0	0	150	$75

Don Carr
Donald Carr
Racing Hometown: Detroit, MI

Year	Rank	Starts	Poles	1	2	3	4	5	6–10	Laps	Laps Led	Races Led	Miles	$
1956	129	5	0	0	0	0	0	0	0	499	0	0	364	210
Lifetime		5	0	0	0	0	0	0	0	499	0	0	364	$210

Jack Carr
Jack Carr
Racing Hometown: Atlanta, GA

Year	Rank	Starts	Poles	1	2	3	4	5	6–10	Laps	Laps Led	Races Led	Miles	$
1950	NR	2	0	0	0	0	0	0	0	52	0	0	65	0
Lifetime		2	0	0	0	0	0	0	0	52	0	0	65	$0

Lee Roy Carrigg
Lee Roy Carrigg
B: 2/22/1942
Racing Hometown: Elloree, SC

Year	Rank	Starts	Poles	1	2	3	4	5	6–10	Laps	Laps Led	Races Led	Miles	$
1970	48	9	0	0	0	0	0	0	0	1,002	0	0	1,021	4,130
Lifetime		9	0	0	0	0	0	0	0	1,002	0	0	1,021	$4,130

Bob Carroll
Robert Carroll

Year	Rank	Starts	Poles	1	2	3	4	5	6–10	Laps	Laps Led	Races Led	Miles	$
1956	NR	1	0	0	0	0	0	0	0	62	0	0	31	50
Lifetime		1	0	0	0	0	0	0	0	62	0	0	31	$50

Lynn Carroll
Lynn Carroll

Year	Rank	Starts	Poles	1	2	3	4	5	6–10	Laps	Laps Led	Races Led	Miles	$
1978	NR	1	0	0	0	0	0	0	0	445	0	0	237	650
Lifetime		1	0	0	0	0	0	0	0	445	0	0	237	$650

Jim Carrusso
James Carrusso
Racing Hometown: Sewickley, PA

Year	Rank	Starts	Poles	1	2	3	4	5	6–10	Laps	Laps Led	Races Led	Miles	$
1949	NR	2	0	0	0	0	0	0	0	67	0	0	34	25
Lifetime		2	0	0	0	0	0	0	0	67	0	0	34	$25

Hank Carruthers
Rankin Carruthers
Racing Hometown: Haw River, NC

Year	Rank	Starts	Poles	1	2	3	4	5	6–10	Laps	Laps Led	Races Led	Miles	$
1952	147T	1	0	0	0	0	0	0	0	18	0	0	18	25
Lifetime		1	0	0	0	0	0	0	0	18	0	0	18	$25

Crash Carson
Crash Carson

Year	Rank	Starts	Poles	1	2	3	4	5	6–10	Laps	Laps Led	Races Led	Miles	$
1955	227T	1	0	0	0	0	0	0	0	8	0	0	8	40
Lifetime		1	0	0	0	0	0	0	0	8	0	0	8	$40

Dick Carter
Richard Carter
B: 1935   D: 8/14/1965   *Killed @ Grand Rapids, MI Super Modified race.*
Racing Hometown: San Leandro, CA

Year	Rank	Starts	Poles	1	2	3	4	5	6–10	Laps	Laps Led	Races Led	Miles	$
1954	132	3	0	0	0	0	0	0	0	376	0	0	265	65

Year	Rank	Starts	Poles	Finish 1	2	3	4	5	6–10	Laps	Laps Led	Races Led	Miles	$

Dick Carter *continued*

Year	Rank	Starts	Poles	1	2	3	4	5	6–10	Laps	Laps Led	Races Led	Miles	$
1958	144	1	0	0	0	0	0	0	0	86	0	0	86	50
1959	115	2	0	0	0	0	0	0	0	269	0	0	131	125
1961	NR	1	0	0	0	0	0	0	0	119	0	0	167	100
Lifetime		7	0	0	0	0	0	0	0	850	0	0	649	$340

Duane Carter

Duane C. Carter
B: 5/5/1913   D: 3/7/1993
Racing Hometown: Fresno, CA

Year	Rank	Starts	Poles	1	2	3	4	5	6–10	Laps	Laps Led	Races Led	Miles	$
1950	56T	1	0	0	0	0	0	0	1		0	0		125
1985	NR	1	0	0	0	0	0	0	0	336	0	0	459	2,755
1986	38	9	0	0	0	0	0	0	0	1,423	3	2	2,690	56,355
1990	90	1	0	0	0	0	0	0	0	298	0	0	454	3,040
1992	82	1	0	0	0	0	0	0	0	297	0	0	446	3,735
1994	60	1	0	0	0	0	0	0	0	322	0	0	490	9,130
1995	63T	1	0	0	0	0	0	0	0	180	0	0	450	8,475
Lifetime		15	0	0	0	0	0	0	1	2,856	3	2	4,988	$83,615

Rags Carter

Allen Carter
B: 12/2/1928   D: 5/23/1993
Racing Hometown: Miami Springs, FL

Year	Rank	Starts	Poles	1	2	3	4	5	6–10	Laps	Laps Led	Races Led	Miles	$
1952	NR	1	0	0	0	0	0	0	1	183	0	0	92	150
Lifetime		1	0	0	0	0	0	0	1	183	0	0	92	$150

Raymond Carter

Raymond Carter
Racing Hometown: Henry, VA

Year	Rank	Starts	Poles	1	2	3	4	5	6–10	Laps	Laps Led	Races Led	Miles	$
1964	114T	1	0	0	0	0	0	0	0	37	0	0	12	100
1965	62	9	0	0	0	0	0	0	2	638	0	0	617	2,145
Lifetime		10	0	0	0	0	0	0	2	675	0	0	629	$2,245

Mario Caruso

Mario Caruso
D: 10/2/1993
Racing Hometown: Shrewsburg, MA

Year	Rank	Starts	Poles	1	2	3	4	5	6–10	Laps	Laps Led	Races Led	Miles	$
1966	114	1	0	0	0	0	0	0	0	167	0	0	56	130
1967	122	1	0	0	0	0	0	0	0	96	0	0	32	100
Lifetime		2	0	0	0	0	0	0	0	263	0	0	88	$230

Jerry Carver

Gerald Carver
Racing Hometown: Canfield, OH

Year	Rank	Starts	Poles	1	2	3	4	5	6–10	Laps	Laps Led	Races Led	Miles	$
1951	N/A	2	0	0	0	0	0	0	0		0	0		50
Lifetime		2	0	0	0	0	0	0	0		0	0		$50

Joe Carver

Joseph Carver

Year	Rank	Starts	Poles	1	2	3	4	5	6–10	Laps	Laps Led	Races Led	Miles	$
1951	N/A	1	0	0	0	0	0	0	0		0	0		25
Lifetime		1	0	0	0	0	0	0	0		0	0		$25

Walt Carver

Walter Carver

Year	Rank	Starts	Poles	1	2	3	4	5	6–10	Laps	Laps Led	Races Led	Miles	$
1952	NR	1	0	0	0	0	0	0	1	188	0	0	94	50
Lifetime		1	0	0	0	0	0	0	1	188	0	0	94	$50

Joe Caspolich

Joseph Caspolich
B: 7/20/1929
Racing Hometown: Gulfport, MS

Year	Rank	Starts	Poles	1	2	3	4	5	6–10	Laps	Laps Led	Races Led	Miles	$
1957	156	1	0	0	0	0	0	0	0	66	0	0	91	200
1959	44	1	0	0	0	0	0	0	0	342	0	0	470	470
1960	51	5	0	0	0	0	0	0	0	838	0	0	1,542	1,965
1961	160	1	0	0	0	0	0	0	0	50	0	0	69	200
Lifetime		8	0	0	0	0	0	0	0	1,296	0	0	2,172	$2,835

Year	Rank	Starts	Poles	1	2	3	4	5	6–10	Laps	Laps Led	Races Led	Miles	$

Neil Castles

Henry Neil Castles (Soapy)
B: 10/1/1934
Racing Hometown: Charlotte, NC

Year	Rank	Starts	Poles	1	2	3	4	5	6–10	Laps	Laps Led	Races Led	Miles	$
1957	123	5	0	0	0	0	0	0	0	492	0	0	359	475
1958	NR	15	0	0	0	0	0	0	0	1,797	0	0	993	805
1959	77	5	0	0	0	0	0	0	0	754	0	0	458	410
1960	145	18	0	0	0	0	0	0	5	2,293	0	0	1,162	2,125
1962	NR	8	0	0	0	0	0	0	1	547	0	0	240	620
1963	31	28	0	0	0	0	1	1	6	4,093	0	0	2,330	5,165
1964	17	58	0	0	0	0	0	1	23	8,336	0	0	4,158	14,318
1965	8	51	0	0	0	1	1	4	22	9,768	66	1	6,555	22,329
1966	9	41	0	0	1	1	3	2	10	8,824	0	0	6,397	19,035
1967	8	35	0	0	0	0	2	2	11	6,754	0	0	5,508	20,683
1968	12	44	0	0	0	2	1	1	11	9,082	0	0	5,447	19,507
1969	4	52	0	0	2	1	5	6	16	13,136	29	1	10,434	54,367
1970	5	47	0	0	1	4	3	4	12	10,297	31	2	9,154	49,746
1971	22	38	0	0	0	0	1	0	9	6,946	10	1	5,622	22,939
1972	30	21	0	0	0	0	0	0	1	4,075	0	0	3,936	18,760
1973	55	8	0	0	0	0	0	0	0	869	0	0	803	7,074
1974	37	14	0	0	0	0	0	0	0	1,422	0	0	1,303	12,479
1975	43	7	0	0	0	0	0	0	0	578	0	0	513	4,190
1976	NR	3	0	0	0	0	0	0	0	350	0	0	210	1,405
Lifetime		498	0	0	4	9	17	21	127	90,413	136	5	65,582	$276,432

Bob Caswell

Robert E. Caswell (Bill)
Racing Hometown: Walnut Creek, CA

Year	Rank	Starts	Poles	1	2	3	4	5	6–10	Laps	Laps Led	Races Led	Miles	$
1951	40	3	0	0	1	0	0	0	0	247	0	0	154	1,325
1953	122T	1	0	0	0	0	0	0	0		0	0		25
1954	59	3	0	0	0	0	0	0	1	751	0	0	498	225
Lifetime		7	0	0	1	0	0	0	1	998	0	0	652	$1,575

Larry Caudill

Lawrence Caudill
B: 6/29/1948
Racing Hometown: N.Wilkesboro, NC

Year	Rank	Starts	Poles	1	2	3	4	5	6–10	Laps	Laps Led	Races Led	Miles	$
1987	NR	1	0	0	0	0	0	0	0	470	0	0	470	4,725
Lifetime		1	0	0	0	0	0	0	0	470	0	0	470	$4,725

Charlie Causey

Charles Causey
Racing Hometown: Rome, GA

Year	Rank	Starts	Poles	1	2	3	4	5	6–10	Laps	Laps Led	Races Led	Miles	$
1952	187	1	0	0	0	0	0	0	0	7	0	0	7	25
1953	104	3	0	0	0	0	0	0	0	35	0	0	144	50
Lifetime		4	0	0	0	0	0	0	0	42	0	0	151	$75

George Cavana

George A. Cavana
Racing Hometown: S. Glastonbury, CT

Year	Rank	Starts	Poles	1	2	3	4	5	6–10	Laps	Laps Led	Races Led	Miles	$
1951	N/A	1	0	0	0	0	0	0	0		0	0		25
Lifetime		1	0	0	0	0	0	0	0		0	0		$25

Don Cecchini

Donald Cecchini
Racing Hometown: Philadelphia, PA

Year	Rank	Starts	Poles	1	2	3	4	5	6–10	Laps	Laps Led	Races Led	Miles	$
1949	69	1	0	0	0	0	0	0	0	173	0	0	173	50
1950	N/A	1	0	0	0	0	0	0	0		0	0		0
Lifetime		2	0	0	0	0	0	0	0	173	0	0	173	$50

Bud Chaddock

Bud Chaddock
Racing Hometown: Parkersburg, WV

Year	Rank	Starts	Poles	1	2	3	4	5	6–10	Laps	Laps Led	Races Led	Miles	$
1954	177	1	0	0	0	0	0	0	0	66	0	0	99	50
Lifetime		1	0	0	0	0	0	0	0	66	0	0	99	$50

Floyd Chaddock

Floyd Chaddock
Racing Hometown: Parkersburg, WV

Year	Rank	Starts	Poles	1	2	3	4	5	6–10	Laps	Laps Led	Races Led	Miles	$
1955	231	1	0	0	0	0	0	0	0	35	0	0	144	35
Lifetime		1	0	0	0	0	0	0	0	35	0	0	144	$35

Year	Rank	Starts	Poles	Finish						Laps	Laps Led	Races Led	Miles	$
				1	2	3	4	5	6–10					

Hank Chaffee

Hank Chaffee
Racing Hometown: Dundee, NY

Year	Rank	Starts	Poles	1	2	3	4	5	6–10	Laps	Laps Led	Races Led	Miles	$
1954	156T	1	0	0	0	0	0	0	0	157	0	0	79	0
Lifetime		1	0	0	0	0	0	0	0	157	0	0	79	$0

Ray Chaike

Ramon Chaike
Racing Hometown: Mt. Healthy, OH

Year	Rank	Starts	Poles	1	2	3	4	5	6–10	Laps	Laps Led	Races Led	Miles	$
1955	180	1	0	0	0	0	0	0	0	37	0	0	152	50
1956	74	3	0	0	0	0	0	0	0	554	0	0	339	225
Lifetime		4	0	0	0	0	0	0	0	591	0	0	491	$275

Gerald Chamberlain

Gerald Chamberlain
Racing Hometown: Everett, PA

Year	Rank	Starts	Poles	1	2	3	4	5	6–10	Laps	Laps Led	Races Led	Miles	$
1969	89	2	0	0	0	0	0	0	1	324	0	0	453	2,225
Lifetime		2	0	0	0	0	0	0	1	324	0	0	453	$2,225

Ted Chamberlain

Theodore Carl Chamberlain
B: 5/15/1906   D: 1968
Racing Hometown: St.Petersburg, FL

Year	Rank	Starts	Poles	1	2	3	4	5	6–10	Laps	Laps Led	Races Led	Miles	$
1949	44	2	0	0	0	0	0	0	0	148	0	0	74	100
1950	61	5	0	0	0	0	0	0	2	541	0	0	539	225
1951	N/A	3	0	0	0	0	0	0	1	340	0	0	425	175
1952	11	18	0	0	0	0	0	0	6	3,053	0	0	2,181	1,277
1953	26	9	0	0	0	0	0	0	3	572	0	0	442	500
1954	32	10	0	0	0	0	0	0	1	1,596	0	0	1,423	475
1955	227T	1	0	0	0	0	0	0	0	67	0	0	67	50
1957	NR	5	0	0	0	0	0	0	1	903	0	0	738	550
1958	51	9	0	0	0	0	0	0	1	809	0	0	403	680
1959	NR	1	0	0	0	0	0	0	0	68	0	0	17	50
Lifetime		63	0	0	0	0	0	0	15	8,097	0	0	6,309	$4,082

Charlie Chamblee

Charles Chamblee
Racing Hometown: Arab, AL

Year	Rank	Starts	Poles	1	2	3	4	5	6–10	Laps	Laps Led	Races Led	Miles	$
1980	NR	1	0	0	0	0	0	0	0	298	0	0	454	2,825
1981	NR	1	0	0	0	0	0	0	0	10	0	0	6	830
Lifetime		2	0	0	0	0	0	0	0	308	0	0	460	$3,655

Bill Champion

William Champion
B: 10/16/1921   D: 5/20/1991
Racing Hometown: Norfolk, VA

Year	Rank	Starts	Poles	1	2	3	4	5	6–10	Laps	Laps Led	Races Led	Miles	$
1951	N/A	1	0	0	0	0	0	0	1		0	0		50
1955	80	1	0	0	0	0	0	0	0	346	0	0	476	195
1956	31	14	0	0	0	0	0	0	4	2,297	0	0	1,626	1,570
1957	41	10	0	0	0	0	0	0	1	1,663	0	0	1,167	1,125
1959	43	1	0	0	0	0	0	0	0	343	0	0	472	500
1962	121	2	0	0	0	0	0	0	0	55	0	0	41	400
1965	116	1	0	0	0	0	0	0	0	109	0	0	36	100
1966	61	9	0	0	0	0	0	0	0	1,120	0	0	1,220	3,735
1967	44	11	0	0	0	0	0	0	0	1,889	0	0	2,027	6,205
1968	28	18	0	0	0	0	0	0	2	3,505	0	0	3,531	10,170
1969	12	49	0	0	0	0	0	1	9	9,982	0	0	7,977	33,656
1970	15	38	0	0	0	0	0	0	6	7,493	0	0	6,864	30,943
1971	7	45	0	0	0	0	0	3	11	10,518	0	0	9,721	43,769
1972	13	29	0	0	0	0	0	0	4	7,044	0	0	8,122	42,242
1973	21	26	0	0	0	0	0	0	1	5,103	0	0	6,375	31,828
1974	31	18	0	0	0	0	0	0	0	2,324	0	0	2,263	13,480
1975	31	13	0	0	0	0	0	0	0	2,690	0	0	2,777	11,340
1976	64	3	0	0	0	0	0	0	0	530	0	0	317	2,185
Lifetime		289	0	0	0	0	0	4	39	57,011	0	0	55,010	$233,493

Charlie Chapman

Charles Chapman
Racing Hometown: Compton, CA

Year	Rank	Starts	Poles	1	2	3	4	5	6–10	Laps	Laps Led	Races Led	Miles	$
1960	89	1	0	0	0	0	0	0	0	152	0	0	213	400

Year	Rank	Starts	Poles	Finish 1	2	3	4	5	6–10	Laps	Laps Led	Races Led	Miles	$

Charlie Chapman *continued*

Year	Rank	Starts	Poles	1	2	3	4	5	6–10	Laps	Laps Led	Races Led	Miles	$
1961	81	6	0	0	0	0	0	0	0	702	0	0	515	610
Lifetime		7	0	0	0	0	0	0	0	854	0	0	727	$1,010

Hank Chapman

Hank Chapman
    Racing Hometown: Aurora, IL

Year	Rank	Starts	Poles	1	2	3	4	5	6–10	Laps	Laps Led	Races Led	Miles	$
1957	182	1	0	0	0	0	0	0	0		0	0		25
Lifetime		1	0	0	0	0	0	0	0		0	0		$25

Johnny Chapman

Johnny Dale Chapman
    B: 12/14/1967
    Racing Hometown: Stoney Point, NC

Year	Rank	Starts	Poles	1	2	3	4	5	6–10	Laps	Laps Led	Races Led	Miles	$
1993	81T	1	0	0	0	0	0	0	0	368	0	0	374	6,526
Lifetime		1	0	0	0	0	0	0	0	368	0	0	374	$6,526

J.R. Charbonneau

Jean R. Charbonneau

Year	Rank	Starts	Poles	1	2	3	4	5	6–10	Laps	Laps Led	Races Led	Miles	$
1982	NR	1	0	0	0	0	0	0	0	118	0	0	118	650
Lifetime		1	0	0	0	0	0	0	0	118	0	0	118	$650

Rene Charland

Joseph Maurice Charland
    B: 11/13/1928
    Racing Hometown: Agawam, MA

Year	Rank	Starts	Poles	1	2	3	4	5	6–10	Laps	Laps Led	Races Led	Miles	$
1964	119	1	0	0	0	0	0	0	0	9	0	0	2	100
1965	108	2	0	0	0	0	0	0	0	26	0	0	30	1,005
1966	83	5	0	0	0	1	0	0	0	452	0	0	185	1,590
1971	NR	1	0	0	0	0	0	0	0	33	0	0	12	100
Lifetime		9	0	0	0	1	0	0	0	520	0	0	229	$2,795

Mike Chase

Michael Chase
    B: 4/17/1952
    Racing Hometown: Bakersfield, CA

Year	Rank	Starts	Poles	1	2	3	4	5	6–10	Laps	Laps Led	Races Led	Miles	$
1990	57	3	0	0	0	0	0	0	0	340	4	1	647	11,500
1991	47	5	0	0	0	0	0	0	0	804	0	0	1,505	22,700
1992	84T	1	0	0	0	0	0	0	0	69	0	0	174	6,330
1993	87T	1	0	0	0	0	0	0	0	87	0	0	87	6,015
1994	56	3	0	0	0	0	0	0	0	463	0	0	706	36,090
Lifetime		13	0	0	0	0	0	0	0	1,763	4	1	3,119	$82,635

Ray Chase

Raymond Chase
    Racing Hometown: Portland, OR

Year	Rank	Starts	Poles	1	2	3	4	5	6–10	Laps	Laps Led	Races Led	Miles	$
1951	N/A	6	0	0	0	0	0	0	0	354	0	0	399	100
1952	137	1	0	0	0	0	0	0	0	173	0	0	173	25
Lifetime		7	0	0	0	0	0	0	0	527	0	0	572	$125

Bob Chauncey

Robert Chauncey

Year	Rank	Starts	Poles	1	2	3	4	5	6–10	Laps	Laps Led	Races Led	Miles	$
1956	246T	1	0	0	0	0	0	0	0	78	0	0	39	50
Lifetime		1	0	0	0	0	0	0	0	78	0	0	39	$50

Tru Cheek

Truceson Burgess Cheek
    B: 6/11/1937
    Racing Hometown: Sylmar, CA

Year	Rank	Starts	Poles	1	2	3	4	5	6–10	Laps	Laps Led	Races Led	Miles	$
1971	NR	1	0	0	0	0	0	0	0	57	0	0	149	750
1972	NR	1	0	0	0	0	0	0	0	12	0	0	31	645
Lifetime		2	0	0	0	0	0	0	0	69	0	0	181	$1,395

Bill Cheesbourg

William Cheesbourg
    B: 6/12/1927   D: 11/6/1995
    Racing Hometown: Tucson, AZ

Year	Rank	Starts	Poles	1	2	3	4	5	6–10	Laps	Laps Led	Races Led	Miles	$
1951	N/A	2	0	0	0	0	0	0	0		0	0		50
Lifetime		2	0	0	0	0	0	0	0		0	0		$50

Year	Rank	Starts	Poles	Finish						Laps	Laps Led	Races Led	Miles	$
				1	2	3	4	5	6–10					

Tom Cherry

Thomas Cherry
B: 1911   D: 7/6/1990
Racing Hometown: Muncie, IN

Year	Rank	Starts	Poles	1	2	3	4	5	6–10	Laps	Laps Led	Races Led	Miles	$
1953	58	1	0	0	0	0	0	0	1	38	0	0	156	180
Lifetime		1	0	0	0	0	0	0	1	38	0	0	156	$180

Ann Chester

Ann Chester
Racing Hometown: Buffalo, NY

Year	Rank	Starts	Poles	1	2	3	4	5	6–10	Laps	Laps Led	Races Led	Miles	$
1950	NR	2	0	0	0	0	0	0	0	92	0	0	46	0
Lifetime		2	0	0	0	0	0	0	0	92	0	0	46	$0

Bill Chevalier

William J. Chevalier
B: 2/14/1922
Racing Hometown: Sayerville, NJ

Year	Rank	Starts	Poles	1	2	3	4	5	6–10	Laps	Laps Led	Races Led	Miles	$
1954	NR	2	0	0	0	0	0	0	0	66	0	0	99	25
1971	NR	1	0	0	0	0	0	0	1	188	0	0	282	620
Lifetime		3	0	0	0	0	0	0	1	254	0	0	381	$645

Lloyd Chick

Lloyd Chick
Racing Hometown: Chicago, IL

Year	Rank	Starts	Poles	1	2	3	4	5	6–10	Laps	Laps Led	Races Led	Miles	$
1954	175	1	0	0	0	0	0	0	0	94	0	0	141	50
1955	113	2	0	0	0	0	0	0	1	245	0	0	123	125
Lifetime		3	0	0	0	0	0	0	1	339	0	0	264	$175

Richard Childress

Richard Reed Childress
B: 9/21/1945
Racing Hometown: Winston-Salem, NC

Year	Rank	Starts	Poles	1	2	3	4	5	6–10	Laps	Laps Led	Races Led	Miles	$
1969	NR	1	0	0	0	0	0	0	0	80	0	0	213	1,175
1971	46	12	0	0	0	0	0	0	0	1,394	0	0	1,006	3,855
1972	37	15	0	0	0	0	0	0	0	1,681	0	0	1,652	7,245
1973	15	25	0	0	0	0	1	0	1	6,918	1	1	7,469	37,880
1974	16	29	0	0	0	0	0	0	3	5,138	0	0	6,484	50,249
1975	5	30	0	0	0	0	1	1	13	9,433	3	2	10,926	96,780
1976	11	30	0	0	0	0	0	0	11	8,147	0	0	9,780	85,780
1977	9	30	0	0	0	0	0	0	11	7,973	27	4	9,412	97,012
1978	10	30	0	0	0	1	0	0	11	8,946	52	4	10,061	108,702
1979	8	31	0	0	0	0	0	1	10	9,109	13	2	10,443	132,922
1980	10	31	0	0	0	0	0	0	10	8,693	21	6	10,693	157,420
1981	25	21	0	0	0	0	1	0	0	5,018	16	3	6,349	71,125
Lifetime		285	0	0	0	1	3	2	70	72,530	133	22	84,487	$850,145

Ronnie Childress

Ronald Childress
Racing Hometown: Winston-Salem, NC

Year	Rank	Starts	Poles	1	2	3	4	5	6–10	Laps	Laps Led	Races Led	Miles	$
1974	139	1	0	0	0	0	0	0	0	43	0	0	27	325
Lifetime		1	0	0	0	0	0	0	0	43	0	0	27	$325

Jack Choquette

Jack Choquette
B: 1928
Racing Hometown: Montclaire, NJ

Year	Rank	Starts	Poles	1	2	3	4	5	6–10	Laps	Laps Led	Races Led	Miles	$
1955	54	4	0	0	1	0	0	0	0	469	0	0	371	825
1956	164	2	0	0	0	0	0	0	1	173	0	0	87	100
Lifetime		6	0	0	1	0	0	0	1	642	0	0	458	$925

Frank Christian

Frank E. Christian
Racing Hometown: Atlanta, GA

Year	Rank	Starts	Poles	1	2	3	4	5	6–10	Laps	Laps Led	Races Led	Miles	$
1949	26T	1	0	0	0	0	0	0	1		0	0		175
Lifetime		1	0	0	0	0	0	0	1		0	0		$175

Sara Christian

Sara Christian
B: 1920
Racing Hometown: Atlanta, GA

Year	Rank	Starts	Poles	1	2	3	4	5	6–10	Laps	Laps Led	Races Led	Miles	$
1949	13	6	0	0	0	0	0	1	1	606	0	0	417	760

Year	Rank	Starts	Poles	1	2	3	Finish 4	5	6–10	Laps	Laps Led	Races Led	Miles	$

Sara Christian *continued*

Year	Rank	Starts	Poles	1	2	3	4	5	6–10	Laps	Laps Led	Races Led	Miles	$
1950	107T	1	0	0	0	0	0	0	0		0	0		50
Lifetime		7	0	0	0	0	0	1	1	606	0	0	417	$810

Steve Christman

Steve Christman
B: 9/22/1947
Racing Hometown: Ft. Wayne, IN

Year	Rank	Starts	Poles	1	2	3	4	5	6–10	Laps	Laps Led	Races Led	Miles	$
1987	27	20	0	0	0	0	0	0	0	4,404	0	0	5,101	54,965
Lifetime		20	0	0	0	0	0	0	0	4,404	0	0	5,101	$54,965

J. Christopher

J. Christopher

Year	Rank	Starts	Poles	1	2	3	4	5	6–10	Laps	Laps Led	Races Led	Miles	$
1954	NR	1	0	0	0	0	0	0	0	23	0	0	46	0
Lifetime		1	0	0	0	0	0	0	0	23	0	0	46	$0

Ted Christopher

Ted Christopher
B: 6/5/1958
Racing Hometown: Plainville, CT

Year	Rank	Starts	Poles	1	2	3	4	5	6–10	Laps	Laps Led	Races Led	Miles	$
1999	64	1	0	0	0	0	0	0	0	89	0	0	218	22,360
Lifetime		1	0	0	0	0	0	0	0	89	0	0	218	$22,360

Ronnie Chumley

Ronald B. Chumley
B: 1/18/1935
Racing Hometown: Houston, TX

Year	Rank	Starts	Poles	1	2	3	4	5	6–10	Laps	Laps Led	Races Led	Miles	$
1964	NR	2	0	0	0	0	0	0	0	59	0	0	148	850
1966	105	2	0	0	0	0	0	0	0	42	0	0	105	1,130
1971	70	2	0	0	0	0	0	0	0	291	0	0	378	990
1972	94	1	0	0	0	0	0	0	0	200	0	0	400	645
Lifetime		7	0	0	0	0	0	0	0	592	0	0	1,031	$3,615

Obie Chupp

Obie Chupp
Racing Hometown: Columbus, GA

Year	Rank	Starts	Poles	1	2	3	4	5	6–10	Laps	Laps Led	Races Led	Miles	$
1953	NR	1	0	0	0	0	0	0	0	36	0	0	148	50
Lifetime		1	0	0	0	0	0	0	0	36	0	0	148	$50

Jerry Churchill

Gerald Eugene Churchill
B: 9/18/1938
Racing Hometown: Dearborne, MI

Year	Rank	Starts	Poles	1	2	3	4	5	6–10	Laps	Laps Led	Races Led	Miles	$
1971	68	6	0	0	0	0	0	0	0	664	0	0	299	1,815
1984	85T	1	0	0	0	0	0	0	0	118	0	0	118	870
Lifetime		7	0	0	0	0	0	0	0	782	0	0	417	$2,685

Raul Cilloniz

Raul Cilloniz
Racing Hometown: Lima, Peru

Year	Rank	Starts	Poles	1	2	3	4	5	6–10	Laps	Laps Led	Races Led	Miles	$
1959	36	2	0	0	0	0	0	0	0	229	0	0	573	550
Lifetime		2	0	0	0	0	0	0	0	229	0	0	573	$550

Bill Cintia

William Cintia
Racing Hometown: Waterbury, CT

Year	Rank	Starts	Poles	1	2	3	4	5	6–10	Laps	Laps Led	Races Led	Miles	$
1951	N/A	1	0	0	0	0	0	0	1		0	0		50
Lifetime		1	0	0	0	0	0	0	1		0	0		$50

Buck Clardy

Buck Clardy
B: 6/22/1925
Racing Hometown: Greenville, SC

Year	Rank	Starts	Poles	1	2	3	4	5	6–10	Laps	Laps Led	Races Led	Miles	$
1951	N/A	1	0	0	0	0	0	0	0		0	0		25
Lifetime		1	0	0	0	0	0	0	0		0	0		$25

Year	Rank	Starts	Poles	Finish 1	2	3	4	5	6–10	Laps	Laps Led	Races Led	Miles	$

Bill Claren

William Claren
B: 5/31/1925
Racing Hometown: Montclair, NJ

Year	Rank	Starts	Poles	1	2	3	4	5	6–10	Laps	Laps Led	Races Led	Miles	$
1954	NR	1	0	0	0	0	0	0	1	49	0	0	98	275
Lifetime		1	0	0	0	0	0	0	1	49	0	0	98	$275

George Clark

George Clark
Racing Hometown: Hartford, CT

Year	Rank	Starts	Poles	1	2	3	4	5	6–10	Laps	Laps Led	Races Led	Miles	$
1951	N/A	1	0	0	0	0	0	0	0		0	0		25
1953	96	1	0	0	0	0	0	0	0		0	0		35
1954	81	1	0	0	0	0	0	0	0	179	0	0	90	25
Lifetime		3	0	0	0	0	0	0	0	179	0	0	90	$85

Jim Clark

James Clark
Racing Hometown: Ft. Worth, TX

Year	Rank	Starts	Poles	1	2	3	4	5	6–10	Laps	Laps Led	Races Led	Miles	$
1952	104T	1	0	0	0	0	0	0	0	135	0	0	68	25
1954	52	6	0	0	0	0	0	0	1	721	0	0	508	400
Lifetime		7	0	0	0	0	0	0	1	856	0	0	576	$425

Jimmy Clark

Jimmy Clark
B: 3/14/1936   D: 4/7/1968   *Killed in Formula 2 race @ Hockenheim, W.Germany.*
Racing Hometown: Duns, Scotland

Year	Rank	Starts	Poles	1	2	3	4	5	6–10	Laps	Laps Led	Races Led	Miles	$
1967	NR	1	0	0	0	0	0	0	0	144	0	0	144	665
Lifetime		1	0	0	0	0	0	0	0	144	0	0	144	$665

Joe Clark

Joseph Clark
Racing Hometown: Neptune Beach, CA

Year	Rank	Starts	Poles	1	2	3	4	5	6–10	Laps	Laps Led	Races Led	Miles	$
1961	164	2	0	0	0	0	0	0	0	56	0	0	61	25
1964	84	6	0	0	0	0	0	0	0	272	0	0	208	2,250
1965	120	1	0	0	0	0	0	0	0	41	0	0	111	500
1966	132	1	0	0	0	0	0	0	0	4	0	0	11	500
1967	97	1	0	0	0	0	0	0	0	52	0	0	140	500
1968	114	1	0	0	0	0	0	0	0	0	0	0	0	500
1970	NR	1	0	0	0	0	0	0	1	136	0	0	356	1,215
1971	NR	1	0	0	0	0	0	0	0	21	0	0	55	1,065
Lifetime		14	0	0	0	0	0	0	1	582	0	0	942	$6,555

Paul Clark

Paul Clark
Racing Hometown: Mansfield, OH

Year	Rank	Starts	Poles	1	2	3	4	5	6–10	Laps	Laps Led	Races Led	Miles	$
1963	96	4	0	0	0	0	0	0	0	470	0	0	370	875
Lifetime		4	0	0	0	0	0	0	0	470	0	0	370	$875

Ray Clark

Raymond Clark
B: 1922   D: 8/24/1958   *Killed in race @ Ferndale, CA Fairgrounds.*
Racing Hometown: Tucson, AZ

Year	Rank	Starts	Poles	1	2	3	4	5	6–10	Laps	Laps Led	Races Led	Miles	$
1955	128	2	0	0	0	0	0	0	0	193	0	0	142	50
Lifetime		2	0	0	0	0	0	0	0	193	0	0	142	$50

Sherman Clark

Sherman Clark
Racing Hometown: Yuba Linda, CA

Year	Rank	Starts	Poles	1	2	3	4	5	6–10	Laps	Laps Led	Races Led	Miles	$
1955	103	2	0	0	0	0	1	0	0	214	0	0	214	380
1956	80	5	0	0	0	0	0	0	2	405	0	0	428	425
1957	112	1	0	0	0	0	0	0	0	54	0	0	135	115
Lifetime		8	0	0	0	0	1	0	2	673	0	0	777	$920

Allan Clarke

Allan Clarke
Racing Hometown: Miami, FL

Year	Rank	Starts	Poles	1	2	3	4	5	6–10	Laps	Laps Led	Races Led	Miles	$
1952	73	3	0	0	0	0	0	0	1	170	0	0	85	125
1953	144T	1	0	0	0	0	0	0	0	76	0	0	38	25
1954	NR	1	0	0	0	0	0	0	0	166	0	0	83	25
1955	166T	1	0	0	0	0	0	0	0	179	0	0	90	25
Lifetime		6	0	0	0	0	0	0	1	591	0	0	296	$200

Year	Rank	Starts	Poles	Finish 1	2	3	4	5	6–10	Laps	Laps Led	Races Led	Miles	$

George Clarke

George Clarke
Racing Hometown: E.Hartford, CT

Year	Rank	Starts	Poles	1	2	3	4	5	6–10	Laps	Laps Led	Races Led	Miles	$
1953	NR	1	0	0	0	0	0	0	0		0	0		25
1954	NR	1	0	0	0	0	0	0	0	44	0	0	88	25
Lifetime		2	0	0	0	0	0	0	0	44	0	0	88	$50

Jack Clarke

Jack Clarke

Year	Rank	Starts	Poles	1	2	3	4	5	6–10	Laps	Laps Led	Races Led	Miles	$
1954	NR	3	0	0	0	0	0	0	0	401	0	0	268	65
Lifetime		3	0	0	0	0	0	0	0	401	0	0	268	$65

Johnny Clements

John Clements
Racing Hometown: Burlington, NC

Year	Rank	Starts	Poles	1	2	3	4	5	6–10	Laps	Laps Led	Races Led	Miles	$
1963	128	1	0	0	0	0	0	0	0	132	0	0	66	100
Lifetime		1	0	0	0	0	0	0	0	132	0	0	66	$100

Roger Clemmens

Roger Clemmens
Racing Hometown: Greensboro, NC

Year	Rank	Starts	Poles	1	2	3	4	5	6–10	Laps	Laps Led	Races Led	Miles	$
1957	NR	1	0	0	0	0	0	0	0		0	0		0
Lifetime		1	0	0	0	0	0	0	0		0	0		$0

Bill Cleveland

William Cleveland
Racing Hometown: Teaneck, NJ

Year	Rank	Starts	Poles	1	2	3	4	5	6–10	Laps	Laps Led	Races Led	Miles	$
1953	77	2	0	0	0	0	0	0	1		0	0		50
1954	167	2	0	0	0	0	0	0	0	224	0	0	187	60
Lifetime		4	0	0	0	0	0	0	1	224	0	0	187	$110

June Cleveland

Glen Cleveland
D: 9/28/1991
Racing Hometown: McBean, GA

Year	Rank	Starts	Poles	1	2	3	4	5	6–10	Laps	Laps Led	Races Led	Miles	$
1950	102	2	0	0	0	0	0	0	0	130	0	0	251	50
1951	N/A	1	0	0	0	0	0	0	0		0	0		25
1952	56	5	0	0	0	0	1	0	1	655	0	0	517	510
1953	158	1	0	0	0	0	0	0	0		0	0		25
Lifetime		9	0	0	0	0	1	0	1	785	0	0	768	$610

Bill Clifton

William Clifton
Racing Hometown: San Fernando, CA

Year	Rank	Starts	Poles	1	2	3	4	5	6–10	Laps	Laps Led	Races Led	Miles	$
1964	NR	1	0	0	0	0	0	0	0	150	0	0	405	525
Lifetime		1	0	0	0	0	0	0	0	150	0	0	405	$525

Fuzzy Clifton

Donald R. Clifton
Racing Hometown: King, NC

Year	Rank	Starts	Poles	1	2	3	4	5	6–10	Laps	Laps Led	Races Led	Miles	$
1959	NR	1	0	0	0	0	0	0	1	214	0	0	86	140
Lifetime		1	0	0	0	0	0	0	1	214	0	0	86	$140

Ernie Cline

Ernest Cline
Racing Hometown: Winston-Salem, NC

Year	Rank	Starts	Poles	1	2	3	4	5	6–10	Laps	Laps Led	Races Led	Miles	$
1980	NR	1	0	0	0	0	0	0	0	74	0	0	75	610
1981	97	1	0	0	0	0	0	0	0	77	0	0	41	550
1982	94	1	0	0	0	0	0	0	0	154	0	0	157	900
1983	94	1	0	0	0	0	0	0	0	35	0	0	36	910
Lifetime		4	0	0	0	0	0	0	0	340	0	0	309	$2,970

Gene Cline

Gene Cline
B: 5/30/1930
Racing Hometown: Rome, GA

Year	Rank	Starts	Poles	1	2	3	4	5	6–10	Laps	Laps Led	Races Led	Miles	$
1966	59	13	0	0	0	0	0	0	2	2,125	0	0	1,451	3,945
Lifetime		13	0	0	0	0	0	0	2	2,125	0	0	1,451	$3,945

Year	Rank	Starts	Poles	Finish 1	2	3	4	5	6–10	Laps	Laps Led	Races Led	Miles	$

Bill Clinton
William Clinton
Racing Hometown: San Fernando, CA

Year	Rank	Starts	Poles	1	2	3	4	5	6–10	Laps	Laps Led	Races Led	Miles	$
1961	126	3	0	0	0	0	0	0	0	183	0	0	102	145
1963	76	2	0	0	0	0	0	0	0	247	0	0	667	725
Lifetime		5	0	0	0	0	0	0	0	430	0	0	768	$870

Dick Clothier
Richard Clothier
Racing Hometown: Fulton, NJ

Year	Rank	Starts	Poles	1	2	3	4	5	6–10	Laps	Laps Led	Races Led	Miles	$
1950	43	5	0	0	0	0	0	0	2	194	0	0	115	350
Lifetime		5	0	0	0	0	0	0	2	194	0	0	115	$350

Byron Clouse
Byron Clouse

Year	Rank	Starts	Poles	1	2	3	4	5	6–10	Laps	Laps Led	Races Led	Miles	$
1953	NR	1	0	0	0	0	0	0	1		0	0		125
Lifetime		1	0	0	0	0	0	0	1		0	0		$125

Tommy Coates
Thomas Coates
Racing Hometown: Trenton, NJ

Year	Rank	Starts	Poles	1	2	3	4	5	6–10	Laps	Laps Led	Races Led	Miles	$
1949	77	1	0	0	0	0	0	0	0	167	0	0	167	50
1950	N/A	1	0	0	0	0	0	0	0		0	0		50
1951	NR	1	0	0	0	0	0	0	0		0	0		0
Lifetime		3	0	0	0	0	0	0	0	167	0	0	167	$100

Shelly Colby
Sheldon Colby

Year	Rank	Starts	Poles	1	2	3	4	5	6–10	Laps	Laps Led	Races Led	Miles	$
1954	NR	1	0	0	0	0	0	0	0	82	0	0	41	0
Lifetime		1	0	0	0	0	0	0	0	82	0	0	41	$0

Ed Cole
Edward Cole Jr.
Racing Hometown: Pinehurst, NC

Year	Rank	Starts	Poles	1	2	3	4	5	6–10	Laps	Laps Led	Races Led	Miles	$
1955	39	13	0	0	0	0	0	0	0	1,433	0	0	779	695
1956	39	12	0	0	0	0	0	0	1	1,486	0	0	1,012	950
1957	144	1	0	0	0	0	0	0	0	163	0	0	82	100
Lifetime		26	0	0	0	0	0	0	1	3,082	0	0	1,873	$1,745

Fred Cole
Fred Cole

Year	Rank	Starts	Poles	1	2	3	4	5	6–10	Laps	Laps Led	Races Led	Miles	$
1954	NR	1	0	0	0	0	0	0	0	44	0	0	88	100
Lifetime		1	0	0	0	0	0	0	0	44	0	0	88	$100

George Cole
George Cole
Racing Hometown: Rhinebeck, NY

Year	Rank	Starts	Poles	1	2	3	4	5	6–10	Laps	Laps Led	Races Led	Miles	$
1954	154T	1	0	0	0	0	0	0	0	159	0	0	80	25
Lifetime		1	0	0	0	0	0	0	0	159	0	0	80	$25

Hal Cole
Harold Cole
Racing Hometown: South Gate, CA

Year	Rank	Starts	Poles	1	2	3	4	5	6–10	Laps	Laps Led	Races Led	Miles	$
1951	N/A	3	0	0	0	0	0	0	1		0	0		200
Lifetime		3	0	0	0	0	0	0	1		0	0		$200

Neil Cole
Neil Cole
B: 5/27/1926
Racing Hometown: Oakland, NJ

Year	Rank	Starts	Poles	1	2	3	4	5	6–10	Laps	Laps Led	Races Led	Miles	$
1950	31	2	0	0	0	0	0	1	0		0	0		300
1951	33	5	1	1	1	0	0	1	0	399	45	1	200	2,050
1952	19	11	0	0	0	1	0	0	6	1,579	0	0	982	1,793
1953	165T	1	0	0	0	0	0	0	0		0	0		25
Lifetime		19	1	1	1	1	0	2	6	1,978	45	1	1,181	$4,168

Bob Coleman
Robert Coleman

Year	Rank	Starts	Poles	1	2	3	4	5	6–10	Laps	Laps Led	Races Led	Miles	$
1955	150	1	0	0	0	0	0	0	0	152	0	0	228	95
Lifetime		1	0	0	0	0	0	0	0	152	0	0	228	$95

Year	Rank	Starts	Poles	Finish						Laps	Laps Led	Races Led	Miles	$
				1	2	3	4	5	6–10					

Earl Coleman

Earl H. Coleman Jr.
    Racing Hometown: Atlanta, GA

Year	Rank	Starts	Poles	1	2	3	4	5	6–10	Laps	Laps Led	Races Led	Miles	$
1951	N/A	1	0	0	0	0	0	0	0		0	0		0
Lifetime		1	0	0	0	0	0	0	0		0	0		$0

Bob Collins

Robert Collins
    Racing Hometown: Norton, VA

Year	Rank	Starts	Poles	1	2	3	4	5	6–10	Laps	Laps Led	Races Led	Miles	$
1950	84T	1	0	0	0	0	0	0	0	133	0	0	67	50
Lifetime		1	0	0	0	0	0	0	0	133	0	0	67	$50

Gary Collins

Gary Collins
    B: 1/24/1960
    Racing Hometown: Bakersfield, CA

Year	Rank	Starts	Poles	1	2	3	4	5	6–10	Laps	Laps Led	Races Led	Miles	$
1988	80	1	0	0	0	0	0	0	0	212	0	0	212	2,525
1990	91T	1	0	0	0	0	0	0	0	280	0	0	280	3,125
1991	91	1	0	0	0	0	0	0	0	61	0	0	61	3,250
1994	79	1	0	0	0	0	0	0	0	43	0	0	108	7,350
Lifetime		4	0	0	0	0	0	0	0	596	0	0	661	$16,250

Roy Collins

Roy Collins
    Racing Hometown: Garden City, MI

Year	Rank	Starts	Poles	1	2	3	4	5	6–10	Laps	Laps Led	Races Led	Miles	$
1971	NR	1	0	0	0	0	0	0	0	7	0	0	18	1,040
Lifetime		1	0	0	0	0	0	0	0	7	0	0	18	$1,040

Leland Colvin Jr.

Leland Colvin Jr.
    Racing Hometown: Camden, SC

Year	Rank	Starts	Poles	1	2	3	4	5	6–10	Laps	Laps Led	Races Led	Miles	$
1964	114T	1	0	0	0	0	0	0	0	118	0	0	59	100
Lifetime		1	0	0	0	0	0	0	0	118	0	0	59	$100

Leland Colvin

Leland Colvin, Sr.
    B: 8/17/1914
    Racing Hometown: Darlington, SC

Year	Rank	Starts	Poles	1	2	3	4	5	6–10	Laps	Laps Led	Races Led	Miles	$
1951	N/A	4	0	0	0	0	0	0	1		0	0		150
Lifetime		4	0	0	0	0	0	0	1		0	0		$150

Sam Colvin

Samuel Eugene Colvin
    B: 7/21/1934
    Racing Hometown: Greenville, SC

Year	Rank	Starts	Poles	1	2	3	4	5	6–10	Laps	Laps Led	Races Led	Miles	$
1958	117	1	0	0	0	0	0	0	0	185	0	0	93	125
Lifetime		1	0	0	0	0	0	0	0	185	0	0	93	$125

Dean Combs

Dean Combs
    B: 2/23/1952
    Racing Hometown: N.Wilkesboro, NC

Year	Rank	Starts	Poles	1	2	3	4	5	6–10	Laps	Laps Led	Races Led	Miles	$
1981	NR	2	0	0	0	0	0	0	0	183	0	0	149	1,155
1982	44	5	0	0	0	0	0	0	0	639	0	0	1,100	7,940
1983	42	5	0	0	0	0	0	0	1	1,296	0	0	1,995	21,370
1984	39	12	0	0	0	0	0	0	0	2,399	0	0	3,152	22,385
Lifetime		24	0	0	0	0	0	0	1	4,517	0	0	6,396	$52,850

George Combs

George Combs

Year	Rank	Starts	Poles	1	2	3	4	5	6–10	Laps	Laps Led	Races Led	Miles	$
1955	170T	1	0	0	0	0	0	0	0	27	0	0	14	50
Lifetime		1	0	0	0	0	0	0	0	27	0	0	14	$50

R.L. Combs

R.L. Combs
    Racing Hometown: N.Wilkesboro, NC

Year	Rank	Starts	Poles	1	2	3	4	5	6–10	Laps	Laps Led	Races Led	Miles	$
1957	138	3	0	0	0	0	0	0	0	123	0	0	62	210
1958	48	9	0	0	0	0	0	0	1	1,062	0	0	473	805
1959	104	9	0	0	0	0	0	0	1	1,476	0	0	664	735
Lifetime		21	1	0	0	0	0	0	2	2,661	0	0	1,199	$1,750

Year	Rank	Starts	Poles	1	2	3	Finish 4	5	6–10	Laps	Laps Led	Races Led	Miles	$

Rodney Combs

Rodney Combs
B: 3/27/1950
Racing Hometown: Cincinnati, OH

Year	Rank	Starts	Poles	1	2	3	4	5	6–10	Laps	Laps Led	Races Led	Miles	$
1982	71	1	0	0	0	0	0	0	1	325	5	1	495	2,900
1983	87	1	0	0	0	0	0	0	0	320	0	0	480	1,725
1984	NR	1	0	0	0	0	0	0	0	192	0	0	384	1,750
1986	44	5	0	0	0	0	0	0	0	909	4	1	1,767	12,180
1987	35	14	0	0	0	0	0	0	0	2,752	0	0	4,411	90,990
1988	35	19	0	0	0	0	0	0	0	3,693	0	0	4,909	54,150
1989	42	9	0	0	0	0	0	0	0	1,657	0	0	2,109	36,090
1990	46	5	0	0	0	0	0	0	0	988	0	0	1,407	23,365
Lifetime		55	0	0	0	0	0	0	1	10,836	9	2	15,963	$223,150

Stacy Compton

Stacy Compton
B: 5/26/1967
Racing Hometown: Lynchburg, VA

Year	Rank	Starts	Poles	1	2	3	4	5	6–10	Laps	Laps Led	Races Led	Miles	$
1996	56	2	0	0	0	0	0	0	0	756	0	0	398	18,115
1999	55	3	0	0	0	0	0	0	0	951	0	0	1,092	92,600
2000	38	27	0	0	0	0	0	0	0	6,912	4	3	9,188	1,069,649
2001	33	35	2	0	0	0	0	0	1	9,605	29	5	12,810	1,704,962
2002	42	21	0	0	0	0	0	0	0	5,282	5	3	7,598	1,185,709
Lifetime		88	2	0	0	0	0	0	1	23,506	38	11	31,085	$4,071,035

Gene Comstock

Gene Comstock
B: 2/21/1909   D: 2/1/1980
Racing Hometown: Chesapeake, OH

Year	Rank	Starts	Poles	1	2	3	4	5	6–10	Laps	Laps Led	Races Led	Miles	$
1950	NR	1	0	0	0	0	0	0	0	355	0	0	444	0
1951	N/A	4	0	0	0	0	0	0	0	357	0	0	446	125
1952	21	8	0	0	0	0	1	0	2	1,496	0	0	1,185	785
1953	18	13	0	0	0	0	0	0	3	756	0	0	895	990
1954	38	1	0	0	0	0	0	0	0	334	0	0	459	400
1955	183	2	0	0	0	0	0	0	0	239	0	0	380	250
Lifetime		29	0	0	0	0	1	0	5	3,537	0	0	3,809	$2,550

Doug Congden

Douglas Congden

Year	Rank	Starts	Poles	1	2	3	4	5	6–10	Laps	Laps Led	Races Led	Miles	$
1952	NR	1	0	0	0	0	0	0	0	30	0	0	15	25
Lifetime		1	0	0	0	0	0	0	0	30	0	0	15	$25

Jack Conley

Jack Conley
Racing Hometown: Brighton, MI

Year	Rank	Starts	Poles	1	2	3	4	5	6–10	Laps	Laps Led	Races Led	Miles	$
1954	NR	1	0	0	0	0	0	0	0	37	0	0	152	50
Lifetime		1	0	0	0	0	0	0	0	37	0	0	152	$50

Lee Connell

Lee Connell
Racing Hometown: Monroe, NC

Year	Rank	Starts	Poles	1	2	3	4	5	6–10	Laps	Laps Led	Races Led	Miles	$
1951	N/A	1	0	0	0	0	0	0	0	58	0	0	73	0
Lifetime		1	0	0	0	0	0	0	0	58	0	0	73	$0

Bob Connor

Robert Connor
Racing Hometown: Saugus, CA

Year	Rank	Starts	Poles	1	2	3	4	5	6–10	Laps	Laps Led	Races Led	Miles	$
1957	192	1	0	0	0	0	0	0	0	88	0	0	44	25
1965	69	1	0	0	0	0	0	0	0	115	0	0	311	580
Lifetime		2	0	0	0	0	0	0	0	203	0	0	355	$605

Paul Connors

Paul H. Connors Jr.
Racing Hometown: W. Palm Beach, FL

Year	Rank	Starts	Poles	1	2	3	4	5	6–10	Laps	Laps Led	Races Led	Miles	$
1966	46	3	0	0	0	0	0	0	1	668	0	0	737	2,820
1969	82	1	0	0	0	0	0	0	0	31	0	0	78	635
1970	84	1	0	0	0	0	0	0	0	134	0	0	183	890
Lifetime		5	0	0	0	0	0	0	1	833	0	0	997	$4,345

Year	Rank	Starts	Poles	Finish 1	2	3	4	5	6–10	Laps	Laps Led	Races Led	Miles	$

Al Conroy

Al Conroy
   Racing Hometown: Chicago, IL

Year	Rank	Starts	Poles	1	2	3	4	5	6–10	Laps	Laps Led	Races Led	Miles	$
1952	161	1	0	0	0	0	0	0	0	308	0	0	385	150
Lifetime		1	0	0	0	0	0	0	0	308	0	0	385	$150

Jim Conway

James Conway
   Racing Hometown: Greenville, SC

Year	Rank	Starts	Poles	1	2	3	4	5	6–10	Laps	Laps Led	Races Led	Miles	$
1965	131	1	0	0	0	0	0	0	0	1	0	0	2	500
1967	101	1	0	0	0	0	0	0	0	215	0	0	108	100
Lifetime		2	0	0	0	0	0	0	0	216	0	0	109	$600

Bill Cook

William Cook

Year	Rank	Starts	Poles	1	2	3	4	5	6–10	Laps	Laps Led	Races Led	Miles	$
1960	NR	1	0	0	0	0	0	0	0	137	0	0	192	200
Lifetime		1	0	0	0	0	0	0	0	137	0	0	192	$200

Dick Cook

Richard Cook
   Racing Hometown: Lakewood, CA

Year	Rank	Starts	Poles	1	2	3	4	5	6–10	Laps	Laps Led	Races Led	Miles	$
1961	96	3	0	0	0	0	0	0	0	273	0	0	353	490
Lifetime		3	0	0	0	0	0	0	0	273	0	0	353	$490

James V. Cook

James V. Cook
   B: 8/15/1922
   Racing Hometown: High Point, NC

Year	Rank	Starts	Poles	1	2	3	4	5	6–10	Laps	Laps Led	Races Led	Miles	$
1950	NR	1	0	0	0	0	0	0	0		0	0		0
Lifetime		1	0	0	0	0	0	0	0		0	0		$0

Jim Cook

James Cook
   Racing Hometown: Norwalk, CA

Year	Rank	Starts	Poles	1	2	3	4	5	6–10	Laps	Laps Led	Races Led	Miles	$
1954	82	4	0	0	0	0	0	0	1	985	0	0	585	165
1955	225	1	0	0	0	0	0	0	0	110	0	0	110	40
1956	87	6	0	0	0	0	0	1	0	663	0	0	638	540
1957	NR	5	0	0	0	0	0	0	0	371	0	0	335	290
1958	72	2	0	0	0	0	1	0	0	258	0	0	519	455
1959	90	2	0	0	0	0	0	0	1	357	0	0	195	325
1960	45	3	1	1	0	0	0	0	0	560	1	1	778	1,600
1961	75	4	0	0	0	0	1	0	1	314	0	0	421	925
1963	75	2	0	0	0	0	0	0	0	274	0	0	740	625
1964	55	4	0	0	0	0	0	0	0	396	0	0	580	1,550
1965	121	1	0	0	0	0	0	0	0	36	0	0	97	550
1966	129	1	0	0	0	0	0	0	0	14	0	0	38	500
1967	77	1	0	0	0	0	0	0	0	92	0	0	248	530
1968	75	1	0	0	0	0	0	0	0	162	0	0	437	1,000
1969	NR	1	0	0	0	0	0	0	0	3	0	0	8	750
1970	86	1	0	0	0	0	0	0	0	94	0	0	246	925
Lifetime		39	1	1	0	0	2	1	3	4,689	1	1	5,975	$10,770

Mel Cook

Mel Cook
   Racing Hometown: Cincinnati, OH

Year	Rank	Starts	Poles	1	2	3	4	5	6–10	Laps	Laps Led	Races Led	Miles	$
1952	NR	1	0	0	0	0	0	0	0	38	0	0	19	25
Lifetime		1	0	0	0	0	0	0	0	38	0	0	19	$25

Smokey Cook

Fred Cook
   Racing Hometown: Winston-Salem, NC

Year	Rank	Starts	Poles	1	2	3	4	5	6–10	Laps	Laps Led	Races Led	Miles	$
1960	126	1	0	0	0	0	0	0	0	1	0	0	0	140
1963	NR	1	0	0	0	0	0	0	0	12	0	0	3	75
Lifetime		2	0	0	0	0	0	0	0	13	0	0	3	$215

Bill Cooper

William Cooper
   B: 8/22/1946
   Racing Hometown: Phoenix, AZ

Year	Rank	Starts	Poles	1	2	3	4	5	6–10	Laps	Laps Led	Races Led	Miles	$
1989	96T	1	0	0	0	0	0	0	0	61	0	0	154	2,360
Lifetime		1	0	0	0	0	0	0	0	61	0	0	154	$2,360

Year	Rank	Starts	Poles	Finish						Laps	Laps Led	Races Led	Miles	$
				1	2	3	4	5	6–10					

Bob Cooper

Robert Eugene Cooper
B: 11/13/1935
Racing Hometown: Gastonia, NC

Year	Rank	Starts	Poles	1	2	3	4	5	6–10	Laps	Laps Led	Races Led	Miles	$
1962	52	13	0	0	0	0	0	0	1	1,644	0	0	883	1,300
1963	37	9	0	0	0	0	0	0	1	1,559	0	0	1,889	3,115
1964	47	14	0	0	0	0	0	0	1	783	0	0	803	3,360
1965	84	4	0	0	0	0	0	0	1	697	0	0	252	600
1966	86	2	0	0	0	0	0	0	1	634	0	0	317	500
1967	64	7	0	0	0	0	0	0	2	1,195	0	0	743	2,345
1968	38	14	0	0	0	0	0	0	1	2,170	0	0	1,415	4,485
1969	98	1	0	0	0	0	0	0	0	55	0	0	83	675
Lifetime		64	0	0	0	0	0	0	8	8,737	0	0	6,385	$16,380

Doug Cooper

Ben Douglas Cooper
B: 9/9/1938   D: 9/3/1987
Racing Hometown: Gastonia, NC

Year	Rank	Starts	Poles	1	2	3	4	5	6–10	Laps	Laps Led	Races Led	Miles	$
1963	95	2	0	0	0	1	0	0	0	154	0	0	139	750
1964	21	39	0	0	0	1	1	2	7	5,549	0	0	3,863	10,445
1965	19	30	0	0	0	0	1	0	8	5,281	0	0	3,909	12,380
1966	48	21	0	0	0	1	1	1	1	3,177	0	0	2,097	5,185
1967	48	21	0	0	0	0	0	2	3	3,351	0	0	2,091	5,665
1968	112	1	0	0	0	0	0	0	0	206	0	0	103	275
Lifetime		114	0	0	0	3	3	5	19	17,718	0	0	12,202	$34,700

Edward Cooper

Edward Cooper
B: 12/26/1946
Racing Hometown: Clark Lake, MI

Year	Rank	Starts	Poles	1	2	3	4	5	6–10	Laps	Laps Led	Races Led	Miles	$
1985	91T	1	0	0	0	0	0	0	0	7	0	0	14	1,375
1990	76	2	0	0	0	0	0	0	0	94	0	0	188	8,225
Lifetime		3	0	0	0	0	0	0	0	101	0	0	202	$9,600

Elmer Cooper

Elmer Cooper
Racing Hometown: Winston-Salem, NC

Year	Rank	Starts	Poles	1	2	3	4	5	6–10	Laps	Laps Led	Races Led	Miles	$
1953	NR	1	0	0	0	0	0	0	0	271	0	0	373	110
Lifetime		1	0	0	0	0	0	0	0	271	0	0	373	$110

Jim Cooper

James Cooper
Racing Hometown: Winston-Salem, NC

Year	Rank	Starts	Poles	1	2	3	4	5	6–10	Laps	Laps Led	Races Led	Miles	$
1954	209	1	0	0	0	0	0	0	0	141	0	0	71	0
Lifetime		1	0	0	0	0	0	0	0	141	0	0	71	$0

Derrike Cope

Derrike Cope
B: 11/3/1958
Racing Hometown: Spanaway, WA

Year	Rank	Starts	Poles	1	2	3	4	5	6–10	Laps	Laps Led	Races Led	Miles	$
1982	101	1	0	0	0	0	0	0	0	42	0	0	110	625
1984	57	3	0	0	0	0	0	0	0	370	0	0	631	9,200
1985	55	2	0	0	0	0	0	0	0	206	0	0	540	7,100
1986	45	5	0	0	0	0	0	0	1	1,101	0	0	1,349	8,025
1987	37	11	0	0	0	0	0	0	0	1,631	0	0	1,978	33,750
1988	31	26	0	0	0	0	0	0	0	4,772	0	0	6,539	132,835
1989	29	23	0	0	0	0	0	0	4	5,382	5	3	6,863	121,780
1990	18	29	0	2	0	0	0	0	4	7,881	109	6	9,595	569,451
1991	28	28	0	0	0	0	1	0	1	6,784	0	0	8,451	419,380
1992	21	29	0	0	0	0	0	0	3	8,483	0	0	10,175	277,215
1993	26	30	0	0	0	0	0	0	1	8,406	38	3	9,966	402,515
1994	30	30	0	0	0	0	0	0	2	8,506	11	2	9,719	398,436
1995	15	31	0	0	1	0	0	1	6	9,335	70	4	11,040	683,075
1996	35	29	0	0	0	0	0	0	3	7,329	28	2	8,831	675,781
1997	27	31	0	0	0	0	0	1	1	8,557	4	2	10,852	707,404
1998	37	28	1	0	0	0	0	0	0	7,526	16	3	9,641	956,980
1999	44	15	0	0	0	0	0	0	0	3,489	0	0	4,913	617,976
2000	57	3	0	0	0	0	0	0	0	638	0	0	1,139	161,630
2001	60	1	0	0	0	0	0	0	0	263	0	0	395	47,500
2002	53	7	0	0	0	0	0	0	0	1,503	0	0	2,302	301,490
Lifetime		362	1	2	1	0	1	2	26	92,204	281	25	115,027	$6,532,148

Year	Rank	Starts	Poles	Finish						Laps	Laps Led	Races Led	Miles	$
				1	2	3	4	5	6–10	Laps	Led	Led	Miles	$

Ernie Cope

Ernest Cope
B: 7/16/1969

Year	Rank	Starts	Poles	1	2	3	4	5	6–10	Laps	Laps Led	Races Led	Miles	$
1995	71	1	0	0	0	0	0	0	0	19	0	0	19	8,605
Lifetime		1	0	0	0	0	0	0	0	19	0	0	19	$8,605

Marvin Copple

Marvin Copple
Racing Hometown: Lincoln, NE

Year	Rank	Starts	Poles	1	2	3	4	5	6–10	Laps	Laps Led	Races Led	Miles	$
1953	69T	1	0	0	0	0	0	1	0		0	0		200
1955	136	1	0	0	0	0	0	0	0	37	0	0	152	85
Lifetime		2	0	0	0	0	0	1	0	37	0	0	152	$285

Guy Cork

George Cork (Guy)
Racing Hometown: Newark, NJ

Year	Rank	Starts	Poles	1	2	3	4	5	6–10	Laps	Laps Led	Races Led	Miles	$
1956	75	4	0	0	0	0	0	0	0	905	0	0	619	375
Lifetime		4	0	0	0	0	0	0	0	905	0	0	619	$375

Bill Corley

William Corley
Racing Hometown: Jackson, MS

Year	Rank	Starts	Poles	1	2	3	4	5	6–10	Laps	Laps Led	Races Led	Miles	$
1958	176	1	0	0	0	0	0	0	0	7	0	0	29	0
Lifetime		1	0	0	0	0	0	0	0	7	0	0	29	$0

Bill Cornwall

William Cornwall
Racing Hometown: Harvey, IL

Year	Rank	Starts	Poles	1	2	3	4	5	6–10	Laps	Laps Led	Races Led	Miles	$
1954	203	1	0	0	0	0	0	0	0	18	0	0	74	0
Lifetime		1	0	0	0	0	0	0	0	18	0	0	74	$0

Tony Correnti

Anthony Correnti
Racing Hometown: Newark, NJ

Year	Rank	Starts	Poles	1	2	3	4	5	6–10	Laps	Laps Led	Races Led	Miles	$
1951	N/A	1	0	0	0	0	0	0	0		0	0		0
Lifetime		1	0	0	0	0	0	0	0		0	0		$0

Joe Cote

Joseph Cote
Racing Hometown: N.Charleston, SC

Year	Rank	Starts	Poles	1	2	3	4	5	6–10	Laps	Laps Led	Races Led	Miles	$
1964	118	4	0	0	0	0	0	0	0	23	0	0	12	350
Lifetime		4	0	0	0	0	0	0	0	23	0	0	12	$350

Vince Cougineri

Vince Cougineri

Year	Rank	Starts	Poles	1	2	3	4	5	6–10	Laps	Laps Led	Races Led	Miles	$
1956	103	1	0	0	0	0	0	0	0	256	0	0	256	150
Lifetime		1	0	0	0	0	0	0	0	256	0	0	256	$150

Bobby Courtwright

Robert Courtwright
B: 11/6/1923   D: 9/6/1988
Racing Hometown: Butler, NJ

Year	Rank	Starts	Poles	1	2	3	4	5	6–10	Laps	Laps Led	Races Led	Miles	$
1950	62T	1	0	0	0	0	0	0	1	189	0	0	95	125
1952	55	4	0	0	0	0	0	1	0	424	0	0	218	275
1954	95	1	0	0	0	0	0	0	0	107	0	0	107	25
Lifetime		6	0	0	0	0	0	1	1	720	0	0	419	$425

Les Covey

Les Fred Covey
B: 5/5/1939
Racing Hometown: Paris, Ont, Canada

Year	Rank	Starts	Poles	1	2	3	4	5	6–10	Laps	Laps Led	Races Led	Miles	$
1972	46	7	0	0	0	0	0	0	0	1,347	0	0	1,540	5,070
Lifetime		7	0	0	0	0	0	0	0	1,347	0	0	1,540	$5,070

Delma Cowart

Clinton Cowart
B: 7/6/1941
Racing Hometown: Savannah, GA

Year	Rank	Starts	Poles	1	2	3	4	5	6–10	Laps	Laps Led	Races Led	Miles	$
1981	NR	1	0	0	0	0	0	0	0	315	0	0	479	1,940
1982	45	5	0	0	0	0	0	0	0	775	0	0	1,466	11,855
1983	49	4	0	0	0	0	0	0	0	643	0	0	1,141	7,750
1984	64	2	0	0	0	0	0	0	0	533	0	0	803	4,170

Year	Rank	Starts	Poles	Finish						Laps	Laps Led	Races Led	Miles	$
				1	2	3	4	5	6–10					

Delma Cowart *continued*

Year	Rank	Starts	Poles	1	2	3	4	5	6–10	Laps	Laps Led	Races Led	Miles	$
1985	79	2	0	0	0	0	0	0	0	71	0	0	183	9,930
1986	60	3	0	0	0	0	0	0	0	403	0	0	977	7,595
1987	NR	1	0	0	0	0	0	0	0	180	0	0	479	3,130
1992	54	3	0	0	0	0	0	0	0	498	0	0	950	33,470
Lifetime		21	0	0	0	0	0	0	0	3,418	0	0	6,477	$79,840

Lowell Cowell

Lowell Cowell
B: 10/10/1945
Racing Hometown: Morganton, WV

Year	Rank	Starts	Poles	1	2	3	4	5	6–10	Laps	Laps Led	Races Led	Miles	$
1981	55	4	0	0	0	0	0	0	0	812	0	0	1,220	8,055
1982	39	5	0	0	0	0	0	0	0	862	0	0	2,210	26,215
1983	NR	1	0	0	0	0	0	0	0	93	0	0	247	3,335
Lifetime		10	0	0	0	0	0	0	0	1,767	0	0	3,677	$37,605

A.J. Cox

Aubrey Johnson Cox
B: 9/8/1927
Racing Hometown: Wilmington, DE

Year	Rank	Starts	Poles	1	2	3	4	5	6–10	Laps	Laps Led	Races Led	Miles	$
1971	81	1	0	0	0	0	0	0	0	82	0	0	82	615
1972	NR	1	0	0	0	0	0	0	0	2	0	0	3	325
Lifetime		2	0	0	0	0	0	0	0	84	0	0	85	$940

Buddy Cox

Buddy Cox

Year	Rank	Starts	Poles	1	2	3	4	5	6–10	Laps	Laps Led	Races Led	Miles	$
1952	NR	1	0	0	0	0	0	0	0	29	0	0	15	25
Lifetime		1	0	0	0	0	0	0	0	29	0	0	15	$25

Doug Cox

William Douglas Cox
Racing Hometown: Greenville, SC

Year	Rank	Starts	Poles	1	2	3	4	5	6–10	Laps	Laps Led	Races Led	Miles	$
1955	139	1	0	0	0	0	0	0	0	181	0	0	91	50
1956	111	3	1	0	0	0	0	1	1	511	0	0	231	460
1957	84	3	0	0	0	0	0	1	0	230	0	0	176	460
1958	16	14	0	0	1	0	1	1	6	2,479	0	0	1,592	3,404
1959	NR	4	0	0	0	0	0	0	2	532	0	0	266	380
1961	88	5	0	0	0	0	0	0	0	367	0	0	190	510
Lifetime		30	1	0	1	0	1	3	9	4,300	0	0	2,544	$5,264

Dutch Cox

Dutch Cox

Year	Rank	Starts	Poles	1	2	3	4	5	6–10	Laps	Laps Led	Races Led	Miles	$
1955	NR	1	0	0	0	0	0	0	0	225	0	0	309	150
Lifetime		1	0	0	0	0	0	0	0	225	0	0	309	$150

James Cox

James Cox
B: 12/13/1945
Racing Hometown: Radford, VA

Year	Rank	Starts	Poles	1	2	3	4	5	6–10	Laps	Laps Led	Races Led	Miles	$
1969	60	8	0	0	0	0	0	0	0	606	0	0	299	1,935
1970	64	7	0	0	0	0	0	0	0	318	0	0	210	2,755
1971	75	5	0	0	0	0	0	0	0	531	0	0	327	1,650
1972	105	2	0	0	0	0	0	0	0	527	0	0	323	1,220
Lifetime		22	0	0	0	0	0	0	0	1,982	0	0	1,159	$7,560

Thomas Cox

Thomas Clarkston Cox
B: 2/24/1936   D: 1999
Racing Hometown: Asheboro, NC

Year	Rank	Starts	Poles	1	2	3	4	5	6–10	Laps	Laps Led	Races Led	Miles	$
1962	18	42	0	0	0	0	1	2	17	8,370	0	0	4,990	10,181
1963	133	2	0	0	0	0	0	0	0	8	0	0	12	700
Lifetime		44	0	0	0	0	1	2	17	8,378	0	0	5,002	$10,881

Johnny Coy

John Coy
B: 1925
Racing Hometown: Merrick, NY

Year	Rank	Starts	Poles	1	2	3	4	5	6–10	Laps	Laps Led	Races Led	Miles	$
1956	194	1	0	0	0	0	0	0	0	197	0	0	197	175
1984	NR	1	0	0	0	0	0	0	0	416	0	0	416	1,090

Year	Rank	Starts	Poles	1	2	3	4	5	6–10	Laps	Laps Led	Races Led	Miles	$

Johnny Coy *continued*

| 1986 | 73 | 2 | 0 | 0 | 0 | 0 | 0 | 0 | 0 | 591 | 0 | 0 | 593 | 9,200 |
| Lifetime | | 4 | 0 | 0 | 0 | 0 | 0 | 0 | 0 | 1,204 | 0 | 0 | 1,206 | $10,465 |

Gene Coyle

Gene Coyle
B: 1955 D: 5/13/1991
Racing Hometown: Piscataway, NJ

| 1984 | NR | 2 | 0 | 0 | 0 | 0 | 0 | 0 | 0 | 619 | 0 | 0 | 895 | 4,840 |
| Lifetime | | 2 | 0 | 0 | 0 | 0 | 0 | 0 | 0 | 619 | 0 | 0 | 895 | $4,840 |

Lamar Crabtree

Lamar Crabtree
Racing Hometown: Pensacola, FL

1951	84T	1	0	0	0	0	0	0	1		0	0		200
1952	110	2	0	0	0	0	0	0	0	349	0	0	365	25
1953	97T	1	0	0	0	0	0	0	0		0	0		25
Lifetime		4	0	0	0	0	0	0	1	349	0	0	365	$250

Herb Craig

Herbert Craig
Racing Hometown: Keithville, LA

| 1950 | 120T | 1 | 0 | 0 | 0 | 0 | 0 | 0 | 0 | | 0 | 0 | | 0 |
| Lifetime | | 1 | 0 | 0 | 0 | 0 | 0 | 0 | 0 | | 0 | 0 | | $0 |

Jim Cramblitt

James Cramblitt
Racing Hometown: Baltimore, MD

| 1955 | 162 | 2 | 0 | 0 | 0 | 0 | 0 | 0 | 0 | 200 | 0 | 0 | 111 | 75 |
| Lifetime | | 2 | 0 | 0 | 0 | 0 | 0 | 0 | 0 | 200 | 0 | 0 | 111 | $75 |

Pappy Crane

H.T. Crane
Racing Hometown: Long Beach, MS

| 1960 | 99 | 2 | 0 | 0 | 0 | 0 | 0 | 0 | 1 | 270 | 0 | 0 | 313 | 340 |
| Lifetime | | 2 | 0 | 0 | 0 | 0 | 0 | 0 | 1 | 270 | 0 | 0 | 313 | $340 |

Willie Crane

Willie Crane
Racing Hometown: Springfield, MO

| 1968 | 87 | 1 | 0 | 0 | 0 | 0 | 0 | 0 | 0 | 300 | 0 | 0 | 450 | 875 |
| Lifetime | | 1 | 0 | 0 | 0 | 0 | 0 | 0 | 0 | 300 | 0 | 0 | 450 | $875 |

Jerry Cranmer

Gerald Cranmer
Racing Hometown: Atlantic City, NJ

1986	56	5	0	0	0	0	0	0	0	1,727	0	0	1,771	23,510
1987	43	5	0	0	0	0	0	0	0	1,914	0	0	1,278	20,660
Lifetime		10	0	0	0	0	0	0	0	3,641	0	0	3,050	$44,170

Ricky Craven

Richard Craven
B: 5/24/1966
Racing Hometown: Newburgh, ME

1991	82T	1	0	0	0	0	0	0	0	221	0	0	225	3,750
1995	24	31	0	0	0	0	0	0	4	8,711	5	4	11,087	597,054
1996	20	31	2	0	0	2	0	1	2	8,551	136	9	10,215	941,959
1997	19	30	0	0	0	2	0	2	3	7,806	280	9	10,468	1,259,550
1998	46	11	1	0	0	0	0	0	1	2,687	19	2	4,017	506,230
1999	41	24	0	0	0	0	0	0	0	5,965	2	2	7,064	853,835
2000	44	16	0	0	0	0	0	0	0	4,153	64	2	4,922	636,522
2001	21	36	1	1	1	0	1	1	3	9,670	170	9	12,787	1,996,981
2002	15	36	2	0	0	1	0	2	6	10,054	382	11	13,110	2,838,087
Lifetime		216	6	1	1	5	1	6	19	57,818	1,058	48	73,894	$9,633,968

Freddie Crawford

Fred Crawford

| 1990 | NR | 1 | 0 | 0 | 0 | 0 | 0 | 0 | 0 | 6 | 0 | 0 | 6 | 2,775 |
| Lifetime | | 1 | 0 | 0 | 0 | 0 | 0 | 0 | 0 | 6 | 0 | 0 | 6 | $2,775 |

Year	Rank	Starts	Poles	Finish						Laps	Laps Led	Races Led	Miles	$
				1	2	3	4	5	6–10					

Herb Crawford

Herbert Crawford
Racing Hometown: San Diego, CA

Year	Rank	Starts	Poles	1	2	3	4	5	6–10	Laps	Laps Led	Races Led	Miles	$
1955	135	3	0	0	0	0	0	0	1	338	0	0	251	150
1956	288	1	0	0	0	0	0	0	0	63	0	0	158	40
Lifetime		4	0	0	0	0	0	0	1	401	0	0	409	$190

Jimmy Crawford

James Harrison Crawford
B: 7/12/1944
Racing Hometown: East Point, GA

Year	Rank	Starts	Poles	1	2	3	4	5	6–10	Laps	Laps Led	Races Led	Miles	$
1970	69	3	0	0	0	0	0	0	0	292	0	0	526	1,795
1971	74	2	0	0	0	0	0	0	0	44	0	0	108	200
1972	89	1	0	0	0	0	0	0	0	181	0	0	481	1,695
1973	46	4	0	0	0	0	0	0	0	1,053	0	0	1,228	4,059
1974	56	4	0	0	0	0	0	0	0	559	0	0	903	5,965
Lifetime		14	0	0	0	0	0	0	0	2,129	0	0	3,246	$13,714

Spook Crawford

Ankrum Crawford
Racing Hometown: Fayetteville, NC

Year	Rank	Starts	Poles	1	2	3	4	5	6–10	Laps	Laps Led	Races Led	Miles	$
1956	NR	1	0	0	0	0	0	0	0	13	0	0	7	50
1957	NR	1	0	0	0	0	0	0	0	34	0	0	78	125
1958	132T	1	0	0	0	0	0	0	0	152	0	0	76	85
1960	88	3	0	0	0	0	0	0	1	439	0	0	212	320
Lifetime		6	0	0	0	0	0	0	1	638	0	0	373	$580

Walt Crawford

Walter Crawford
Racing Hometown: Greenville, SC

Year	Rank	Starts	Poles	1	2	3	4	5	6–10	Laps	Laps Led	Races Led	Miles	$
1950	104	1	0	0	0	0	0	0	0	358	0	0	448	0
Lifetime		1	0	0	0	0	0	0	0	358	0	0	448	$0

Charlie Cregar

Charles Cregar
Racing Hometown: Bloomsbury, NJ

Year	Rank	Starts	Poles	1	2	3	4	5	6–10	Laps	Laps Led	Races Led	Miles	$
1954	40	5	0	0	0	0	0	0	0	857	8	1	877	405
1955	213	2	0	0	0	0	0	0	0	47	0	0	56	0
1956	232	2	0	0	0	0	0	0	0	74	0	0	37	0
1957	57	3	0	0	0	0	0	0	3	356	0	0	178	500
1958	156	1	0	0	0	0	0	0	0	127	0	0	127	100
1959	34	3	0	0	0	0	0	0	0	496	0	0	725	560
Lifetime		16	0	0	0	0	0	0	3	1,957	8	1	2,000	$1,565

Curtis Crider

Curtis Wade Crider (Crawfish)
B: 10/7/1930
Racing Hometown: Abbeyville, SC

Year	Rank	Starts	Poles	1	2	3	4	5	6–10	Laps	Laps Led	Races Led	Miles	$
1959	NR	4	0	0	0	0	0	0	1	453	0	0	227	375
1960	28	24	0	0	0	0	0	0	2	3,985	0	0	2,973	3,645
1961	21	41	0	0	0	0	0	1	1	5,882	0	0	4,186	7,420
1962	12	52	0	0	0	1	1	1	15	10,051	0	0	6,431	12,016
1963	17	49	0	0	0	1	0	1	13	8,859	0	0	5,402	11,644
1964	6	59	0	0	0	1	1	5	23	11,443	0	0	7,872	22,171
1965	NR	3	0	0	0	0	1	0	1	785	0	0	455	1,200
Lifetime		232	0	0	0	3	3	8	56	41,458	0	0	27,546	$58,471

Bud Crothers

Bud Crothers
Racing Hometown: Piedmont, SC

Year	Rank	Starts	Poles	1	2	3	4	5	6–10	Laps	Laps Led	Races Led	Miles	$
1959	60	3	0	0	0	0	0	0	1	867	0	0	712	475
Lifetime		3	0	0	0	0	0	0	1	867	0	0	712	$475

Ray Crowley

Raymond Crowley

Year	Rank	Starts	Poles	1	2	3	4	5	6–10	Laps	Laps Led	Races Led	Miles	$
1956	294T	1	0	0	0	0	0	0	0	36	0	0	18	100
Lifetime		1	0	0	0	0	0	0	0	36	0	0	18	$100

Year	Rank	Starts	Poles	Finish 1	2	3	4	5	6–10	Laps	Laps Led	Races Led	Miles	$

Ronnie Croy

Ronald Croy
Racing Hometown: Pearisburg, VA

Year	Rank	Starts	Poles	1	2	3	4	5	6–10	Laps	Laps Led	Races Led	Miles	$
1964	141	1	0	0	0	0	0	0	0	11	0	0	6	150
Lifetime		1	0	0	0	0	0	0	0	11	0	0	6	$150

Tommie Crozier

Thomas Crozier
Racing Hometown: Roanoke, VA

Year	Rank	Starts	Poles	1	2	3	4	5	6–10	Laps	Laps Led	Races Led	Miles	$
1984	80T	1	0	0	0	0	0	0	0	277	0	0	277	990
1985	54	3	0	0	0	0	0	0	0	516	0	0	560	4,895
1986	86	2	0	0	0	0	0	0	0	354	0	0	359	2,475
1989	70	2	0	0	0	0	0	0	0	112	0	0	136	4,600
Lifetime		8	0	0	0	0	0	0	0	1,259	0	0	1,332	$12,960

Jack Culpepper

Jack Culpepper
Racing Hometown: W. Palm Beach, FL

Year	Rank	Starts	Poles	1	2	3	4	5	6–10	Laps	Laps Led	Races Led	Miles	$
1953	NR	1	0	0	0	0	0	0	0	119	0	0	60	25
Lifetime		1	0	0	0	0	0	0	0	119	0	0	60	$25

Jack Cumiford

Jack Cumiford

Year	Rank	Starts	Poles	1	2	3	4	5	6–10	Laps	Laps Led	Races Led	Miles	$
1954	NR	1	0	0	0	0	0	0	0	170	0	0	85	25
Lifetime		1	0	0	0	0	0	0	0	170	0	0	85	$25

Richard Cummings

Richard Cummings (Red)
B: 2/26/1924
Racing Hometown: Beverley, MA

Year	Rank	Starts	Poles	1	2	3	4	5	6–10	Laps	Laps Led	Races Led	Miles	$
1950	NR	1	0	0	0	0	0	0	0		0	0		0
Lifetime		1	0	0	0	0	0	0	0		0	0		$0

Pepper Cunningham

William Cunningham
Racing Hometown: Trenton, NJ

Year	Rank	Starts	Poles	1	2	3	4	5	6–10	Laps	Laps Led	Races Led	Miles	$
1949	NR	1	0	0	0	0	0	0	0	134	0	0	134	0
1950	37	2	0	0	0	0	0	0	2	130	0	0	130	300
1951	N/A	4	0	0	0	0	0	0	0		0	0		75
1952	NR	1	0	0	0	0	0	0	0		0	0		25
1953	56	1	0	0	0	0	0	0	0		0	0		50
1954	NR	1	0	0	0	0	0	0	0	0	0	0	0	0
1955	237	1	0	0	0	0	0	0	0	3	0	0	3	0
Lifetime		11	0	0	0	0	0	0	2	267	0	0	267	$450

Danny Curley

Daniel Curley

Year	Rank	Starts	Poles	1	2	3	4	5	6–10	Laps	Laps Led	Races Led	Miles	$
1954	NR	1	0	0	0	0	0	0	0	125	0	0	63	25
Lifetime		1	0	0	0	0	0	0	0	125	0	0	63	$25

Floyd Curtis

Floyd Curtis
Racing Hometown: Rossville, GA

Year	Rank	Starts	Poles	1	2	3	4	5	6–10	Laps	Laps Led	Races Led	Miles	$
1954	88	2	0	0	0	0	0	0	1	270	0	0	181	125
1955	219	1	0	0	0	0	0	0	0	10	0	0	15	40
Lifetime		3	0	0	0	0	0	0	1	280	0	0	196	$165

Jim Cushman

James Cushman
Racing Hometown: Lansing, MI

Year	Rank	Starts	Poles	1	2	3	4	5	6–10	Laps	Laps Led	Races Led	Miles	$
1956	264T	1	0	0	0	0	0	0	0		0	0		50
1962	47	4	0	0	0	0	0	0	1	782	0	0	883	850
1963	62	2	0	0	0	0	0	0	0	211	0	0	528	625
Lifetime		7	0	0	0	0	0	0	1	993	0	0	1,411	$1,525

Steve Dabb

Steve Dabb

Year	Rank	Starts	Poles	1	2	3	4	5	6–10	Laps	Laps Led	Races Led	Miles	$
1951	N/A	1	0	0	0	0	0	0	0		0	0		25
Lifetime		1	0	0	0	0	0	0	0		0	0		$25

Year	Rank	Starts	Poles	Finish 1	2	3	4	5	6–10	Laps	Laps Led	Races Led	Miles	$

Fred Dagavar

Fred Dagavar
  Racing Hometown: Philadelphia, PA

Year	Rank	Starts	Poles	1	2	3	4	5	6–10	Laps	Laps Led	Races Led	Miles	$
1950	118	1	0	0	0	0	0	0	0		0	0		50
Lifetime		1	0	0	0	0	0	0	0		0	0		$50

Clyde Dagit

Clyde A. Dagit
  Racing Hometown: Pekin, IL

Year	Rank	Starts	Poles	1	2	3	4	5	6–10	Laps	Laps Led	Races Led	Miles	$
1974	117	1	0	0	0	0	0	0	0	183	0	0	366	1,020
1975	82T	1	0	0	0	0	0	0	0	418	0	0	425	1,400
Lifetime		2	0	0	0	0	0	0	0	601	0	0	791	$2,420

Don Dahle

Donald Dahle
  Racing Hometown: Clarion, PA

Year	Rank	Starts	Poles	1	2	3	4	5	6–10	Laps	Laps Led	Races Led	Miles	$
1959	NR	1	0	0	0	0	0	0	1	192	0	0	48	200
Lifetime		1	0	0	0	0	0	0	1	192	0	0	48	$200

Chuck Daigh

Charles George Daigh
  Racing Hometown: Long Beach, CA

Year	Rank	Starts	Poles	1	2	3	4	5	6–10	Laps	Laps Led	Races Led	Miles	$
1963	131	1	0	0	0	0	0	0	0	37	0	0	93	75
1964	125T	1	0	0	0	0	0	0	0	62	0	0	167	500
Lifetime		2	0	0	0	0	0	0	0	99	0	0	260	$575

Darrell Dake

Darrell Dake
  B: 8/11/1927
  Racing Hometown: Cedar Rapids, IA

Year	Rank	Starts	Poles	1	2	3	4	5	6–10	Laps	Laps Led	Races Led	Miles	$
1960	56	2	0	0	0	0	0	0	1	235	0	0	588	575
1961	157	2	0	0	0	0	0	0	0	54	0	0	135	200
Lifetime		4	0	0	0	0	0	0	1	289	0	0	723	$775

Wally Dallenbach, Sr.

Wallace Paul Dallenbach, Sr.
  B: 12/12/1936
  Racing Hometown: E.Brunswick, NJ

Year	Rank	Starts	Poles	1	2	3	4	5	6–10	Laps	Laps Led	Races Led	Miles	$
1974	NR	1	0	0	0	0	0	0	0	125	0	0	188	1,395
Lifetime		1	0	0	0	0	0	0	0	125	0	0	188	$1,395

Wally Dallenbach

Wallace Paul Dallenbach Jr.
  B: 5/23/1963
  Racing Hometown: Basalt, CO

Year	Rank	Starts	Poles	1	2	3	4	5	6–10	Laps	Laps Led	Races Led	Miles	$
1962	81	2	0	0	0	0	0	0	1	92	0	0	230	650
1964	112	1	0	0	0	0	0	0	0	142	0	0	71	110
1991	38	11	0	0	0	0	0	0	0	2,070	0	0	3,246	54,020
1992	24	29	0	0	0	0	0	1	0	8,105	0	0	9,682	220,245
1993	22	30	0	0	1	0	0	0	3	8,411	3	2	10,056	474,340
1994	38	14	0	0	0	0	1	0	2	3,568	1	1	5,323	241,492
1995	50	2	0	0	1	0	0	0	0	131	21	1	324	63,900
1996	25	30	0	0	0	1	0	0	2	8,191	0	0	10,417	837,001
1997	41	22	0	0	0	0	0	0	1	4,598	21	3	6,793	471,479
1998	38	23	0	0	0	0	0	0	3	5,939	13	2	8,448	807,856
1999	18	34	0	0	0	0	0	1	5	9,751	13	4	12,640	1,741,176
2000	34	30	0	0	0	0	0	0	1	8,226	2	1	10,783	1,169,069
2001	63	1	0	0	0	0	0	0	0	198	0	0	495	64,410
Lifetime		229	0	0	2	1	1	2	18	59,422	74	14	78,508	$6,145,748

Dean Dalton

Dean Dalton
  B: 6/18/1945
  Racing Hometown: Asheville, NC

Year	Rank	Starts	Poles	1	2	3	4	5	6–10	Laps	Laps Led	Races Led	Miles	$
1971	30	19	0	0	0	0	0	0	1	3,487	0	0	4,311	13,910
1972	9	29	0	0	0	0	0	0	4	7,533	0	0	9,068	42,299
1973	19	26	0	0	0	0	0	0	2	5,889	0	0	6,838	35,954
1974	36	14	0	0	0	0	0	0	0	2,414	6	1	2,303	12,375
1975	26	16	0	0	0	0	0	0	3	3,800	0	0	4,237	19,430
1976	42	6	0	0	0	0	0	0	0	1,433	0	0	1,853	7,245
1977	43	8	0	0	0	0	0	0	0	1,100	0	0	1,304	6,255

Year	Rank	Starts	Poles	1	2	3	Finish 4	5	6–10	Laps	Laps Led	Races Led	Miles	$

Dean Dalton *continued*

Year	Rank	Starts	Poles	1	2	3	4	5	6–10	Laps	Laps Led	Races Led	Miles	$
Lifetime		118	0	0	0	0	0	0	10	25,656	6	1	29,915	$137,468

Roxy Dancy

Roxy R. Dancy
Racing Hometown: Shreveport, LA

Year	Rank	Starts	Poles	1	2	3	4	5	6–10	Laps	Laps Led	Races Led	Miles	$
1953	NR	1	0	0	0	0	0	0	0		0	0		25
Lifetime		1	0	0	0	0	0	0	0		0	0		$25

Lloyd Dane

Lloyd Dane
B: 8/9/1925
Racing Hometown: Eldon, MO

Year	Rank	Starts	Poles	1	2	3	4	5	6–10	Laps	Laps Led	Races Led	Miles	$
1951	41	7	0	0	0	1	1	0	1	447	0	0	421	975
1954	30	4	0	0	1	0	0	2	1	1,268	180	1	756	1,600
1955	49	5	0	0	0	1	0	0	1	545	5	1	446	780
1956	23	10	0	2	0	1	2	0	4	1,706	66	2	1,257	4,370
1957	25	10	1	1	5	1	0	0	3	1,296	1	1	863	4,985
1958	21	5	0	0	1	0	0	0	1	1,084	0	0	1,198	2,490
1959	86	2	0	0	1	0	0	0	1	578	0	0	286	1,100
1960	75	3	0	0	0	1	0	1	0	323	89	1	375	950
1961	74	4	0	1	0	0	0	0	1	396	1	1	443	1,390
1963	90	2	0	0	0	0	0	0	0	139	0	0	375	550
1964	79	1	0	0	0	0	0	0	0	154	0	0	416	525
Lifetime		53	1	4	8	5	3	3	13	7,936	342	7	6,836	$19,715

Clayton Danello

Clayton Danello
Racing Hometown: Hartford, CT

Year	Rank	Starts	Poles	1	2	3	4	5	6–10	Laps	Laps Led	Races Led	Miles	$
1955	93	2	0	0	0	0	0	0	0	335	0	0	274	225
Lifetime		2	0	0	0	0	0	0	0	335	0	0	274	$225

Dan Danello

Daniel Danello

Year	Rank	Starts	Poles	1	2	3	4	5	6–10	Laps	Laps Led	Races Led	Miles	$
1954	181	1	0	0	0	0	0	0	0	199	0	0	199	50
Lifetime		1	0	0	0	0	0	0	0	199	0	0	199	$50

Dan Daniels

Daniel Daniels
Racing Hometown: Batavia, NY

Year	Rank	Starts	Poles	1	2	3	4	5	6–10	Laps	Laps Led	Races Led	Miles	$
1951	N/A	2	0	0	0	0	0	0	0		0	0		50
Lifetime		2	0	0	0	0	0	0	0		0	0		$50

Quinton Daniels

Quinton Daniels
Racing Hometown: Tyler, TX

Year	Rank	Starts	Poles	1	2	3	4	5	6–10	Laps	Laps Led	Races Led	Miles	$
1951	108	7	0	0	0	0	0	0	1		0	0		250
Lifetime		7	0	0	0	0	0	0	1		0	0		$250

J.C. Danielson

James C. Danielson
B: 12/11/1930
Racing Hometown: Chico, CA

Year	Rank	Starts	Poles	1	2	3	4	5	6–10	Laps	Laps Led	Races Led	Miles	$
1972	80	1	0	0	0	0	0	0	0	184	0	0	460	2,120
1973	86	1	0	0	0	0	0	0	1	176	0	0	461	1,520
1974	104	1	0	0	0	0	0	0	0	178	0	0	466	1,425
1976	99T	1	0	0	0	0	0	0	0	39	0	0	102	890
Lifetime		4	0	0	0	0	0	0	1	577	0	0	1,490	$5,955

Bay Darnell

Wilbur Darnell
B: 2/4/1931
Racing Hometown: Lake Bluff, IL

Year	Rank	Starts	Poles	1	2	3	4	5	6–10	Laps	Laps Led	Races Led	Miles	$
1954	NR	1	0	0	0	0	0	0	0	18	0	0	9	0
1964	NR	1	0	0	0	0	0	0	0	205	0	0	308	625
1967	117	1	0	0	0	0	0	0	0	123	0	0	185	600
Lifetime		3	0	0	0	0	0	0	0	346	0	0	501	$1,225

Year	Rank	Starts	Poles	Finish 1	2	3	4	5	6–10	Laps	Laps Led	Races Led	Miles	$

Gene Darragh

Eugene Darragh
Racing Hometown: Tampa, FL

Year	Rank	Starts	Poles	1	2	3	4	5	6–10	Laps	Laps Led	Races Led	Miles	$
1950	NR	1	0	0	0	0	0	0	0	323	0	0	404	0
1951	N/A	1	0	0	0	0	0	0	0	309	0	0	386	50
1952	103	3	0	0	0	0	0	0	0	237	0	0	228	60
1953	NR	1	0	0	0	0	0	0	0		0	0		0
Lifetime		6	0	0	0	0	0	0	0	869	0	0	1,018	$110

Hugh Darragh

Hugh Darragh
Racing Hometown: Ebenezer, NY

Year	Rank	Starts	Poles	1	2	3	4	5	6–10	Laps	Laps Led	Races Led	Miles	$
1950	106	3	0	0	0	0	0	0	0	142	0	0	71	0
Lifetime		3	0	0	0	0	0	0	0	142	0	0	71	$0

Dan Daughtry

Daniel Daughtry
B: 4/10/1940
Racing Hometown: Punta Gorda, FL

Year	Rank	Starts	Poles	1	2	3	4	5	6–10	Laps	Laps Led	Races Led	Miles	$
1974	41	8	0	0	0	0	0	0	1	772	6	2	1,321	12,413
1975	103	2	0	0	0	0	0	0	0	9	0	0	23	2,530
Lifetime		10	0	0	0	0	0	0	1	781	6	2	1,344	$14,943

Bill Davis

William Davis
B: 3/22/1932
Racing Hometown: West Palm Beach, FL

Year	Rank	Starts	Poles	1	2	3	4	5	6–10	Laps	Laps Led	Races Led	Miles	$
1952	96	1	0	0	0	0	0	0	1		0	0		75
Lifetime		1	0	0	0	0	0	0	1		0	0		$75

Bob Davis

Robert W. Davis
B: 3/21/1925
Racing Hometown: Lighthouse Point, FL

Year	Rank	Starts	Poles	1	2	3	4	5	6–10	Laps	Laps Led	Races Led	Miles	$
1973	111	1	0	0	0	0	0	0	0	93	0	0	247	1,140
Lifetime		1	0	0	0	0	0	0	0	93	0	0	247	$1,140

Gene Davis

Gene Davis
Racing Hometown: Santa Monica, CA

Year	Rank	Starts	Poles	1	2	3	4	5	6–10	Laps	Laps Led	Races Led	Miles	$
1963	129	1	0	0	0	0	0	0	0	95	0	0	257	200
1965	55	1	0	0	0	0	0	1	0	177	0	0	478	1,850
Lifetime		2	0	0	0	0	0	1	0	272	0	0	734	$2,050

George Davis

George Davis
B: 5/29/1938
Racing Hometown: Adelphix, MD

Year	Rank	Starts	Poles	1	2	3	4	5	6–10	Laps	Laps Led	Races Led	Miles	$
1967	40	21	0	0	0	0	0	1	5	3,342	0	0	1,866	4,400
1968	56	6	0	0	0	0	0	0	1	576	0	0	362	1,915
1969	NR	1	0	0	0	0	0	0	0	24	0	0	24	400
Lifetime		28	0	0	0	0	0	1	6	3,942	0	0	2,252	$6,715

Jeff Davis

Jeffrey Davis
B: 1/29/1959
Racing Hometown: Anaheim, CA

Year	Rank	Starts	Poles	1	2	3	4	5	6–10	Laps	Laps Led	Races Led	Miles	$
1992	76	1	0	0	0	0	0	0	0	299	0	0	299	4,785
1993	93T	1	0	0	0	0	0	0	0	46	0	0	116	6,560
1997	66	1	0	0	0	0	0	0	0	60	0	0	151	30,745
Lifetime		3	0	0	0	0	0	0	0	405	0	0	566	$42,090

Joel Davis

Joel Davis
B: 1/25/1941
Racing Hometown: Tenneville, GA

Year	Rank	Starts	Poles	1	2	3	4	5	6–10	Laps	Laps Led	Races Led	Miles	$
1963	102	3	0	0	0	0	0	0	0	280	0	0	140	245
1966	45	21	0	0	0	0	1	0	2	2,977	0	0	1,690	4,885
1967	60	6	0	0	0	0	0	0	2	888	0	0	773	1,825
Lifetime		30	0	0	0	0	1	0	4	4,145	0	0	2,604	$6,955

Year	Rank	Starts	Poles	Finish						Laps	Laps Led	Races Led	Miles	$
				1	2	3	4	5	6–10					

Keith Davis

Keith Davis
Racing Hometown: Hueytown, AL

Year	Rank	Starts	Poles	1	2	3	4	5	6–10	Laps	Laps Led	Races Led	Miles	$
1979	90	2	0	0	0	0	0	0	0	45	0	0	103	2,310
Lifetime		2	0	0	0	0	0	0	0	45	0	0	103	$2,310

Ray Davis

Raymond Davis

Year	Rank	Starts	Poles	1	2	3	4	5	6–10	Laps	Laps Led	Races Led	Miles	$
1957	167	1	0	0	0	0	0	0	0	78	0	0	39	50
Lifetime		1	0	0	0	0	0	0	0	78	0	0	39	$50

Walt Davis

Walter Davis

Year	Rank	Starts	Poles	1	2	3	4	5	6–10	Laps	Laps Led	Races Led	Miles	$
1951	N/A	2	0	0	0	0	0	0	2		0	0		150
Lifetime		2	0	0	0	0	0	0	2		0	0		$150

Bob Dawson

Robert Dawson
Racing Hometown: Orlando, FL

Year	Rank	Starts	Poles	1	2	3	4	5	6–10	Laps	Laps Led	Races Led	Miles	$
1955	110	2	0	0	0	0	0	0	0	190	0	0	228	75
Lifetime		2	0	0	0	0	0	0	0	190	0	0	228	$75

Chick Dawson

Chick Dawson

Year	Rank	Starts	Poles	1	2	3	4	5	6–10	Laps	Laps Led	Races Led	Miles	$
1955	244	1	0	0	0	0	0	0	0	11	0	0	6	0
Lifetime		1	0	0	0	0	0	0	0	11	0	0	6	$0

Tom Dawson

Thomas Dawson
Racing Hometown: Philadelphia, PA

Year	Rank	Starts	Poles	1	2	3	4	5	6–10	Laps	Laps Led	Races Led	Miles	$
1952	84T	1	0	0	0	0	0	0	1	134	0	0	134	150
Lifetime		1	0	0	0	0	0	0	1	134	0	0	134	$150

Bill Deakin

William Deakin

Year	Rank	Starts	Poles	1	2	3	4	5	6–10	Laps	Laps Led	Races Led	Miles	$
1952	97	1	0	0	0	0	0	0	0	225	0	0	225	50
Lifetime		1	0	0	0	0	0	0	0	225	0	0	225	$50

Dizzy Dean

Dizzy Dean
Racing Hometown: Millers, MD

Year	Rank	Starts	Poles	1	2	3	4	5	6–10	Laps	Laps Led	Races Led	Miles	$
1954	215T	1	0	0	0	0	0	0	0	1	0	0	1	0
Lifetime		1	0	0	0	0	0	0	0	1	0	0	1	$0

O.A. Dean

O.A. Dean
Racing Hometown: Mobile, AL

Year	Rank	Starts	Poles	1	2	3	4	5	6–10	Laps	Laps Led	Races Led	Miles	$
1951	N/A	1	0	0	0	0	0	0	0		0	0		25
Lifetime		1	0	0	0	0	0	0	0		0	0		$25

Al DeAngelo

Al DeAngelo
B: 1927
Racing Hometown: Flushing, NY

Year	Rank	Starts	Poles	1	2	3	4	5	6–10	Laps	Laps Led	Races Led	Miles	$
1966	143	1	0	0	0	0	0	0	0	23	0	0	5	0
Lifetime		1	0	0	0	0	0	0	0	23	0	0	5	$0

Billy DeCoster

William DeCoster
B: 1938
Racing Hometown: Basking Ridge, NJ

Year	Rank	Starts	Poles	1	2	3	4	5	6–10	Laps	Laps Led	Races Led	Miles	$
1965	61	2	0	0	0	0	0	0	0	252	0	0	378	800
Lifetime		2	0	0	0	0	0	0	0	252	0	0	378	$800

Bob Deehan

Robert Deehan

Year	Rank	Starts	Poles	1	2	3	4	5	6–10	Laps	Laps Led	Races Led	Miles	$
1954	NR	1	0	0	0	0	0	0	0	213	0	0	213	40
Lifetime		1	0	0	0	0	0	0	0	213	0	0	213	$40

Year	Rank	Starts	Poles	Finish 1	2	3	4	5	6–10	Laps	Laps Led	Races Led	Miles	$

Frank Deiny

Frank Deiny
D: 1986
Racing Hometown: Los Angeles, CA

Year	Rank	Starts	Poles	1	2	3	4	5	6–10	Laps	Laps Led	Races Led	Miles	$
1963	NR	1	0	0	0	0	0	0	0	44	0	0	119	200
1964	NR	1	0	0	0	0	0	0	0	9	0	0	24	500
1970	NR	1	0	0	0	0	0	0	0	4	0	0	10	800
Lifetime		3	0	0	0	0	0	0	0	57	0	0	154	$1,500

Bill Delaney

William Delaney

Year	Rank	Starts	Poles	1	2	3	4	5	6–10	Laps	Laps Led	Races Led	Miles	$
1962	NR	1	0	0	0	0	0	0	0	3	0	0	1	60
Lifetime		1	0	0	0	0	0	0	0	3	0	0	1	$60

Jim Delaney

James William Delaney
B: 1929   D: 4/5/1991
Racing Hometown: Lyndhurst, NJ

Year	Rank	Starts	Poles	1	2	3	4	5	6–10	Laps	Laps Led	Races Led	Miles	$
1949	NR	1	0	0	0	0	0	0	0		0	0		0
1950	47	2	0	0	0	0	0	0	1		0	0		175
1951	64	7	0	0	0	0	0	1	1	494	0	0	468	425
1957	135	1	0	0	0	0	0	0	0		0	0		75
Lifetime		11	0	0	0	0	0	1	2	494	0	0	468	$675

Rex DeLewis

Rex DeLewis
Racing Hometown: Dayton, OH

Year	Rank	Starts	Poles	1	2	3	4	5	6–10	Laps	Laps Led	Races Led	Miles	$
1955	185	1	0	0	0	0	0	0	0	42	0	0	42	0
Lifetime		1	0	0	0	0	0	0	0	42	0	0	42	$0

Rick DeLewis

Richard DeLewis
Racing Hometown: Dearborne, MI

Year	Rank	Starts	Poles	1	2	3	4	5	6–10	Laps	Laps Led	Races Led	Miles	$
1955	189	2	0	0	0	0	0	0	0	122	0	0	105	50
Lifetime		2	0	0	0	0	0	0	0	122	0	0	105	$50

Joe Deloach

Joseph Deloach
Racing Hometown: Blackville, SC

Year	Rank	Starts	Poles	1	2	3	4	5	6–10	Laps	Laps Led	Races Led	Miles	$
1952	104T	1	0	0	0	0	0	0	0	135	0	0	68	50
Lifetime		1	0	0	0	0	0	0	0	135	0	0	68	$50

Mal Delometer

Mal Delometer

Year	Rank	Starts	Poles	1	2	3	4	5	6–10	Laps	Laps Led	Races Led	Miles	$
1963	NR	1	0	0	0	0	0	0	0	183	0	0	92	120
Lifetime		1	0	0	0	0	0	0	0	183	0	0	92	$120

Matthew DeMatthews

Matthew DeMatthews

Year	Rank	Starts	Poles	1	2	3	4	5	6–10	Laps	Laps Led	Races Led	Miles	$
1962	NR	1	0	0	0	0	0	0	0	2	0	0	3	400
Lifetime		1	0	0	0	0	0	0	0	2	0	0	3	$400

Phil Demola

Phillip Demola
Racing Hometown: Nutley, NJ

Year	Rank	Starts	Poles	1	2	3	4	5	6–10	Laps	Laps Led	Races Led	Miles	$
1953	134T	1	0	0	0	0	0	0	0		0	0		25
Lifetime		1	0	0	0	0	0	0	0		0	0		$25

Dick Denise

Richard Denise
Racing Hometown: Rochester, NY

Year	Rank	Starts	Poles	1	2	3	4	5	6–10	Laps	Laps Led	Races Led	Miles	$
1956	NR	1	0	0	0	0	0	0	0	41	0	0	21	50
Lifetime		1	0	0	0	0	0	0	0	41	0	0	21	$50

Jack Deniston

Jack Deniston
Racing Hometown: Arlington, VA

Year	Rank	Starts	Poles	1	2	3	4	5	6–10	Laps	Laps Led	Races Led	Miles	$
1962	127	1	0	0	0	0	0	0	0	81	0	0	27	50

Year	Rank	Starts	Poles	Finish						Laps	Laps Led	Races Led	Miles	$
				1	2	3	4	5	6–10					

Jack Deniston *continued*

1963	125	1	0	0	0	0	0	0	0	187	0	0	47	135
Lifetime		2	0	0	0	0	0	0	0	268	0	0	74	$185

Arnold Denley

Arnold Denley

1956	266T	1	0	0	0	0	0	0	0	5	0	0	8	150
Lifetime		1	0	0	0	0	0	0	0	5	0	0	8	$150

F.L. Denney

F.L. Denney
Racing Hometown: Ft. Worth, TX

1950	107T	1	0	0	0	0	0	0	0		0	0		50
Lifetime		1	0	0	0	0	0	0	0		0	0		$50

Bill Dennis

William C. Dennis
B: 12/9/1935
Racing Hometown: Glen Allen, VA

1962	107	1	0	0	0	0	0	0	0	268	0	0	134	150
1967	47	3	0	0	0	0	0	0	0	1,012	0	0	1,160	2,335
1969	62	3	0	0	0	0	0	0	0	276	0	0	209	1,655
1970	25	25	0	0	0	0	0	0	5	4,014	0	0	3,748	15,630
1971	18	28	1	0	0	1	1	2	6	6,111	47	2	6,979	29,420
1972	42	11	0	0	0	1	0	1	0	2,327	2	1	2,249	9,604
1973	49	4	0	0	0	0	0	0	2	1,430	0	0	1,115	4,225
1974	60	3	0	0	0	0	0	0	2	1,118	0	0	1,147	7,775
1976	92T	1	0	0	0	0	0	0	0	313	0	0	470	1,385
1978	105T	1	0	0	0	0	0	0	0	66	0	0	99	1,560
1979	70	2	0	0	0	0	0	0	0	387	0	0	777	12,645
1981	81	1	0	0	0	0	0	0	0	327	0	0	491	3,200
Lifetime		83	1	0	0	2	1	3	15	17,649	49	3	18,577	$89,584

Lloyd Dennis

Lloyd Dennis
Racing Hometown: Salisbury, NC

1951	N/A	1	0	0	0	0	0	0	0	39	0	0	29	10
Lifetime		1	0	0	0	0	0	0	0	39	0	0	29	$10

Jim Derhaag

James Derhaag
Racing Hometown: Chaska, MN

1991	69	1	0	0	0	0	0	0	0	88	0	0	216	5,120
Lifetime		1	0	0	0	0	0	0	0	88	0	0	216	$5,120

Zeke DeRose

Zeke DeRose
Racing Hometown: Paterson, NJ

1952	133T	1	0	0	0	0	0	0	0	168	0	0	84	25
Lifetime		1	0	0	0	0	0	0	0	168	0	0	84	$25

Benny DeRosier

Benoit DeRosier
Racing Hometown: New Brittain, CT

1956	132	4	0	0	0	0	0	0	0	236	0	0	236	200
Lifetime		4	0	0	0	0	0	0	0	236	0	0	236	$200

Ernie Derr

Ernie Derr
B: 11/29/1921
Racing Hometown: Keokuk, IA

1953	NR	1	0	0	0	0	0	0	0		0	0		25
Lifetime		1	0	0	0	0	0	0	0		0	0		$25

Bob Derrington

Robert Elbert Derrington
B: 11/22/1930
Racing Hometown: Houston, TX

1964	36	18	0	0	0	0	0	0	2	1,897	1	1	1,819	2,755
1965	6	51	0	0	0	1	0	2	16	10,374	0	0	6,777	20,120

Year	Rank	Starts	Poles	Finish 1	2	3	4	5	6–10	Laps	Laps Led	Races Led	Miles	$

Bob Derrington *continued*

Year	Rank	Starts	Poles	1	2	3	4	5	6–10	Laps	Laps Led	Races Led	Miles	$
1966	44	10	0	0	0	0	0	0	1	1,154	0	0	1,274	2,830
Lifetime		79	0	0	0	1	0	2	19	13,425	1	1	9,870	$25,705

Leroy DeShields

Leroy DeShields
    Racing Hometown: Oklahoma City, OK

Year	Rank	Starts	Poles	1	2	3	4	5	6–10	Laps	Laps Led	Races Led	Miles	$
1956	291	1	0	0	0	0	0	0	0	75	0	0	75	35
Lifetime		1	0	0	0	0	0	0	0	75	0	0	75	$35

Geoffrey Dessault

Geoffrey Dessault
    Racing Hometown: Victoriaville, Ont, Canada

Year	Rank	Starts	Poles	1	2	3	4	5	6–10	Laps	Laps Led	Races Led	Miles	$
1953	NR	1	0	0	0	0	0	0	0		0	0		50
Lifetime		1	0	0	0	0	0	0	0		0	0		$50

Tony DeStafano

Anthony DeStafano

Year	Rank	Starts	Poles	1	2	3	4	5	6–10	Laps	Laps Led	Races Led	Miles	$
1955	169	1	0	0	0	0	0	0	0	103	0	0	103	25
Lifetime		1	0	0	0	0	0	0	0	103	0	0	103	$25

Dennis DeVea

Dennis DeVea
    B: 3/15/1948
    Racing Hometown: Joliet, IL

Year	Rank	Starts	Poles	1	2	3	4	5	6–10	Laps	Laps Led	Races Led	Miles	$
1982	NR	1	0	0	0	0	0	0	0	185	1	1	370	1,670
Lifetime		1	0	0	0	0	0	0	0	185	1	1	370	$1,670

Bob Devine

Robert Devine
    Racing Hometown: New Fairfield, CT

Year	Rank	Starts	Poles	1	2	3	4	5	6–10	Laps	Laps Led	Races Led	Miles	$
1961	128	1	0	0	0	0	0	0	0	92	0	0	23	150
1962	80	2	0	0	0	0	0	0	0	453	0	0	151	240
Lifetime		3	0	0	0	0	0	0	0	545	0	0	174	$390

Ed DeWolff

Edward DeWolff
    Racing Hometown: Lodi, NJ

Year	Rank	Starts	Poles	1	2	3	4	5	6–10	Laps	Laps Led	Races Led	Miles	$
1953	59	3	0	0	0	0	0	0	1		0	0		110
1954	166	2	0	0	0	0	0	0	0	95	0	0	49	10
Lifetime		5	0	0	0	0	0	0	1	95	0	0	49	$120

Clarence DeZalia

Clarence DeZalia
    B: 10/1/1919
    Racing Hometown: Aberdeen, MD

Year	Rank	Starts	Poles	1	2	3	4	5	6–10	Laps	Laps Led	Races Led	Miles	$
1955	94	5	0	0	0	0	0	0	0	691	0	0	610	200
1957	19	25	0	0	0	0	0	0	6	4,059	0	0	2,119	3,308
1958	15	27	0	0	0	0	0	0	6	4,073	0	0	2,412	3,004
1959	102	1	0	0	0	0	0	0	0	136	0	0	45	60
Lifetime		58	0	0	0	0	0	0	12	8,959	0	0	5,185	$6,572

Oliver Dial

Oliver Dial
    Racing Hometown: S.Norfolk, VA

Year	Rank	Starts	Poles	1	2	3	4	5	6–10	Laps	Laps Led	Races Led	Miles	$
1951	N/A	2	0	0	0	0	0	0	0	355	0	0	444	100
Lifetime		2	0	0	0	0	0	0	0	355	0	0	444	$100

Bud Diamond

Bud Diamond
    Racing Hometown: Long Beach, CA

Year	Rank	Starts	Poles	1	2	3	4	5	6–10	Laps	Laps Led	Races Led	Miles	$
1954	131	2	0	0	0	0	0	0	0	277	0	0	139	25
Lifetime		2	0	0	0	0	0	0	0	277	0	0	139	$25

Eduardo Dibos

Eduardo Dibos (Chi Chi)
    Deceased.
    Racing Hometown: Lima, Peru

Year	Rank	Starts	Poles	1	2	3	4	5	6–10	Laps	Laps Led	Races Led	Miles	$
1959	42	3	0	0	0	0	0	2	0	181	0	0	453	1,050
Lifetime		3	0	0	0	0	0	2	0	181	0	0	453	$1,050

Year	Rank	Starts	Poles	Finish						Laps	Laps Led	Races Led	Miles	$
				1	2	3	4	5	6–10					

Duke DiBrizzi

Duke DiBrizzi
B: 3/13/1928
Racing Hometown: Jamesburg, NY

Year	Rank	Starts	Poles	1	2	3	4	5	6–10	Laps	Laps Led	Races Led	Miles	$
1957	94	2	0	0	0	0	0	0	0	432	0	0	173	225
Lifetime		2	0	0	0	0	0	0	0	432	0	0	173	$225

Eddie Dickerson

Edward Dickerson
B: 7/17/1955
Racing Hometown: Milford, DE

Year	Rank	Starts	Poles	1	2	3	4	5	6–10	Laps	Laps Led	Races Led	Miles	$
1980	73	2	0	0	0	0	0	0	0	787	0	0	632	1,590
Lifetime		2	0	0	0	0	0	0	0	787	0	0	632	$1,590

Larry Dickson

Larrence Dickson
B: 9/8/1938
Racing Hometown: Marietta, OH

Year	Rank	Starts	Poles	1	2	3	4	5	6–10	Laps	Laps Led	Races Led	Miles	$
1972	NR	1	0	0	0	0	0	0	0	103	0	0	258	1,535
Lifetime		1	0	0	0	0	0	0	0	103	0	0	258	$1,535

Bob Dickson

Robert Dickson
Racing Hometown: Salem, NJ

Year	Rank	Starts	Poles	1	2	3	4	5	6–10	Laps	Laps Led	Races Led	Miles	$
1950	51	6	0	0	0	0	0	0	2	627	0	0	380	275
1951	N/A	1	0	0	0	0	0	0	0		0	0		25
Lifetime		7	0	0	0	0	0	0	2	627	0	0	380	$300

Darel Dieringer

Darel E. Dieringer
B: 6/1/1926   D: 10/28/1989
Racing Hometown: Indianapolis, IN

Year	Rank	Starts	Poles	1	2	3	4	5	6–10	Laps	Laps Led	Races Led	Miles	$
1957	59	9	0	0	0	0	0	0	3	1,262	0	0	849	1,210
1958	131	2	0	0	0	0	0	0	0	125	0	0	102	110
1961	35	7	0	0	0	0	0	1	1	1,008	0	0	1,735	3,150
1962	33	14	1	0	0	0	0	1	2	3,179	17	1	2,986	4,880
1963	7	20	0	1	0	1	3	2	8	5,513	70	2	5,432	29,725
1964	11	27	1	1	0	1	2	2	7	5,662	238	5	5,364	20,685
1965	3	35	2	1	4	2	3	0	5	6,845	656	10	5,806	52,214
1966	12	25	0	3	3	0	1	0	2	4,818	517	8	4,545	52,530
1967	12	19	6	1	3	3	0	1	1	4,537	765	11	4,906	34,710
1968	21	18	1	0	1	0	3	1	3	4,409	160	2	4,972	28,215
1969	NR	1	0	0	0	0	0	0	0	119	0	0	60	250
1975	54	4	0	0	0	0	0	0	2	923	2	1	1,629	10,530
Lifetime		181	11	7	11	7	12	8	34	38,400	2,425	40	38,385	$238,209

Bob Dietrich

Robert Dietrich
Racing Hometown: Pittsburgh, PA

Year	Rank	Starts	Poles	1	2	3	4	5	6–10	Laps	Laps Led	Races Led	Miles	$
1951	68	2	0	0	0	0	0	0	2		0	0		225
Lifetime		2	0	0	0	0	0	0	2		0	0		$225

Ernie Dietzman

Ernest Dietzman

Year	Rank	Starts	Poles	1	2	3	4	5	6–10	Laps	Laps Led	Races Led	Miles	$
1951	N/A	1	0	0	0	0	0	0	0		0	0		25
Lifetime		1	0	0	0	0	0	0	0		0	0		$25

Tom Dill

Thomas Dill
Racing Hometown: Harbor Creek, PA

Year	Rank	Starts	Poles	1	2	3	4	5	6–10	Laps	Laps Led	Races Led	Miles	$
1961	71	3	0	0	0	0	0	0	0	273	0	0	631	630
Lifetime		3	0	0	0	0	0	0	0	273	0	0	631	$630

Mike Dillon

Michael Dillon
B: 2/1/1965
Racing Hometown: Welcome, NC

Year	Rank	Starts	Poles	1	2	3	4	5	6–10	Laps	Laps Led	Races Led	Miles	$
1998	66	1	0	0	0	0	0	0	0	239	0	0	478	28,050
Lifetime		1	0	0	0	0	0	0	0	239	0	0	478	$28,050

Year	Rank	Starts	Poles	Finish						Laps	Laps Led	Races Led	Miles	$
				1	2	3	4	5	6–10					

Jim Dimeo

James Dimeo
Racing Hometown: Gastonia, NC

Year	Rank	Starts	Poles	1	2	3	4	5	6–10	Laps	Laps Led	Races Led	Miles	$
1964	97	3	0	0	0	0	0	0	1	368	0	0	136	385
Lifetime		3	0	0	0	0	0	0	1	368	0	0	136	$385

Chick DiNatale

Chick DiNatale
Racing Hometown: Trenton, NJ

Year	Rank	Starts	Poles	1	2	3	4	5	6–10	Laps	Laps Led	Races Led	Miles	$
1949	NR	1	0	0	0	0	0	0	0	96	0	0	96	0
Lifetime		1	0	0	0	0	0	0	0	96	0	0	96	$0

Rocky DiNatale

Rocky DiNatale
Racing Hometown: Trenton, NJ

Year	Rank	Starts	Poles	1	2	3	4	5	6–10	Laps	Laps Led	Races Led	Miles	$
1951	NR	1	0	0	0	0	0	0	0		0	0		25
Lifetime		1	0	0	0	0	0	0	0		0	0		$25

John Dineen

John Dineen
B: 4/3/1946
Racing Hometown: El Cajon, CA

Year	Rank	Starts	Poles	1	2	3	4	5	6–10	Laps	Laps Led	Races Led	Miles	$
1976	95	1	0	0	0	0	0	0	0	73	0	0	191	1,040
1977	84T	1	0	0	0	0	0	0	0	89	0	0	233	1,400
Lifetime		2	0	0	0	0	0	0	0	162	0	0	424	$2,440

C.H. Dingler

Charles H. Dingler (Charlie)
Racing Hometown: Birmingham, AL

Year	Rank	Starts	Poles	1	2	3	4	5	6–10	Laps	Laps Led	Races Led	Miles	$
1951	N/A	3	0	0	0	0	0	0	0		0	0		100
1952	153	1	0	0	0	0	0	0	0	160	0	0	80	35
1953	36	5	0	0	0	0	0	0	3	119	0	0	60	250
1954	118	3	0	0	0	0	0	0	1	383	0	0	348	175
1955	NR	1	0	0	0	0	0	0	0	8	0	0	4	0
1956	96	3	0	0	0	0	0	0	0	181	0	0	239	200
Lifetime		16	0	0	0	0	0	0	4	851	0	0	730	$760

Harry Dinwiddie

Harry Dinwiddie
B: 1/25/1954
Racing Hometown: Oneida, TN

Year	Rank	Starts	Poles	1	2	3	4	5	6–10	Laps	Laps Led	Races Led	Miles	$
1980	82	1	0	0	0	0	0	0	0	173	0	0	460	5,250
Lifetime		1	0	0	0	0	0	0	0	173	0	0	460	$5,250

Dave Dion

David F. Dion
B: 11/30/1943
Racing Hometown: Hudson, NH

Year	Rank	Starts	Poles	1	2	3	4	5	6–10	Laps	Laps Led	Races Led	Miles	$
1978	69	4	0	0	0	0	0	0	0	335	0	0	314	2,285
1979	72	2	0	0	0	0	0	0	0	528	0	0	284	1,265
1980	45	4	0	0	0	0	0	0	1	1,075	0	0	1,171	5,015
1981	94	1	0	0	0	0	0	0	0	143	0	0	78	615
1983	90T	1	0	0	0	0	0	0	0	50	0	0	27	700
Lifetime		12	0	0	0	0	0	0	1	2,131	0	0	1,873	$9,880

Sam DiRusso

Samuel DiRusso
Racing Hometown: Sandbury, MA

Year	Rank	Starts	Poles	1	2	3	4	5	6–10	Laps	Laps Led	Races Led	Miles	$
1951	NR	1	0	0	0	0	0	0	0		0	0		25
1953	NR	2	0	0	0	0	0	0	1	213	0	0	225	75
Lifetime		3	0	0	0	0	0	0	1	213	0	0	225	$100

Al Disney

Al Disney
Racing Hometown: Silver Spring, MD

Year	Rank	Starts	Poles	1	2	3	4	5	6–10	Laps	Laps Led	Races Led	Miles	$
1961	142	1	0	0	0	0	0	0	0	214	0	0	107	125
Lifetime		1	0	0	0	0	0	0	0	214	0	0	107	$125

Year	Rank	Starts	Poles	Finish						Laps	Laps Led	Races Led	Miles	$
				1	2	3	4	5	6–10					

Pete Diviney

Peter Diviney
  Racing Hometown: St. Claire Shores, MI

Year	Rank	Starts	Poles	1	2	3	4	5	6–10	Laps	Laps Led	Races Led	Miles	$
1956	125	2	0	0	0	0	0	0	0	378	0	0	189	150
1957	200	1	0	0	0	0	0	0	0	13	0	0	13	0
Lifetime		3	0	0	0	0	0	0	0	391	0	0	202	$150

Ben Dixon

Benjamin Dixon
  Racing Hometown: Shelby, NC

Year	Rank	Starts	Poles	1	2	3	4	5	6–10	Laps	Laps Led	Races Led	Miles	$
1951	N/A	1	0	0	0	0	0	0	0		0	0		0
1953	NR	1	0	0	0	0	0	0	0	187	0	0	257	105
Lifetime		2	0	0	0	0	0	0	0	187	0	0	257	$105

Dick Dixon

Richard Dixon
  B: 1929   D: 5/28/1967   *Killed in Modified race @ Thompson, CT.*
  Racing Hometown: Warehouse Point, CT

Year	Rank	Starts	Poles	1	2	3	4	5	6–10	Laps	Laps Led	Races Led	Miles	$
1960	119	2	0	0	0	0	0	0	0	181	0	0	453	250
1962	NR	1	0	0	0	0	0	0	0	23	0	0	12	75
1965	NR	8	0	0	0	2	1	2	2	2,029	0	0	733	2,215
Lifetime		11	0	0	0	2	1	2	2	2,233	0	0	1,197	$2,540

John Dodd, Sr.

John Dodd, Sr.
  B: 1913
  Racing Hometown: Glen Burnie, MD

Year	Rank	Starts	Poles	1	2	3	4	5	6–10	Laps	Laps Led	Races Led	Miles	$
1953	NR	1	0	0	0	0	0	0	0		0	0		35
1954	50	1	0	0	0	0	0	0	1	161	0	0	81	150
1954	207	2	0	0	0	0	0	0	1	302	0	0	271	300
1955	25	13	0	0	0	0	0	1	6	1,653	0	0	915	1,695
1955	164T	2	0	0	0	0	0	0	0	292	0	0	160	100
1956	158	4	0	0	0	0	0	0	1	372	0	0	180	100
1956	297T	1	0	0	0	0	0	0	0	28	0	0	14	0
1957	NR	1	0	0	0	0	0	0	0	67	0	0	34	25
1957	130	1	0	0	0	0	0	0	1	189	0	0	95	140
1958	83	1	0	0	0	0	0	0	0	290	0	0	290	150
1959	NR	3	0	0	0	0	0	0	1	704	0	0	352	540
1960	NR	2	0	0	0	0	0	0	0	51	0	0	54	50
1962	108	2	0	0	0	0	0	0	0	78	0	0	127	625
Lifetime		34	0	0	0	0	0	1	11	4,187	0	0	2,571	$3,910

Randy Dodd

Randall Dodd
  Racing Hometown: Newhall, CA

Year	Rank	Starts	Poles	1	2	3	4	5	6–10	Laps	Laps Led	Races Led	Miles	$
1967	108	1	0	0	0	0	0	0	0	47	0	0	127	500
1969	NR	1	0	0	0	0	0	0	0	143	0	0	386	950
1970	83	2	0	0	0	0	0	0	0	183	0	0	479	1,715
Lifetime		4	0	0	0	0	0	0	0	373	0	0	992	$3,165

Johnny Dodson

Johnny Frank Dodson
  B: 4/24/1931
  Racing Hometown: King, NC

Year	Rank	Starts	Poles	1	2	3	4	5	6–10	Laps	Laps Led	Races Led	Miles	$
1956	36	11	0	0	0	0	0	0	4	1,842	0	0	1,379	1,450
1957	121	4	0	0	0	0	0	0	1	404	0	0	326	715
Lifetime		15	0	0	0	0	0	0	5	2,246	0	0	1,706	$2,165

Russ Dohlen

Russell Dohlen

Year	Rank	Starts	Poles	1	2	3	4	5	6–10	Laps	Laps Led	Races Led	Miles	$
1957	NR	1	0	0	0	0	0	0	0	0	0	0	0	0
Lifetime		1	0	0	0	0	0	0	0	0	0	0	0	$0

Johnny Dollar

John Dollar
  Racing Hometown: Bay Shore, NY

Year	Rank	Starts	Poles	1	2	3	4	5	6–10	Laps	Laps Led	Races Led	Miles	$
1960	144	2	0	0	0	0	0	0	0	8	0	0	17	200
Lifetime		2	0	0	0	0	0	0	0	8	0	0	17	$200

Year	Rank	Starts	Poles	Finish 1	2	3	4	5	6–10	Laps	Laps Led	Races Led	Miles	$

Jack Donohue

Jack Donohue
B: 1945
Racing Hometown: Nobleton, Ont, Canada

Year	Rank	Starts	Poles	1	2	3	4	5	6–10	Laps	Laps Led	Races Led	Miles	$
1974	98	2	0	0	0	0	0	0	0	333	0	0	237	1,020
1976	65	3	0	0	0	0	0	0	0	888	0	0	896	2,680
Lifetime		5	0	0	0	0	0	0	0	1,221	0	0	1,132	$3,700

Mark Donohue

Mark Donohue
B: 3/18/1937   D: 8/19/1975   *Killed in practice for Austrian Grand Prix.*
Racing Hometown: Newtown Square, PA

Year	Rank	Starts	Poles	1	2	3	4	5	6–10	Laps	Laps Led	Races Led	Miles	$
1972	NR	4	0	0	0	0	0	0	0	390	0	0	669	5,580
1973	NR	2	0	1	0	0	0	0	0	393	138	1	808	16,120
Lifetime		6	0	1	0	0	0	0	0	783	138	1	1,477	$21,700

Jim Donovan

James Donovan
Racing Hometown: Chicago, IL

Year	Rank	Starts	Poles	1	2	3	4	5	6–10	Laps	Laps Led	Races Led	Miles	$
1956	151	2	0	0	0	0	0	0	0	247	0	0	152	200
Lifetime		2	0	0	0	0	0	0	0	247	0	0	152	$200

Paul Dorrity

Paul Dorrity
B: 10/19/1943
Racing Hometown: Modesto, CA

Year	Rank	Starts	Poles	1	2	3	4	5	6–10	Laps	Laps Led	Races Led	Miles	$
1968	99	1	0	0	0	0	0	0	0	28	0	0	76	500
1969	NR	1	0	0	0	0	0	0	0	129	0	0	348	850
1970	77	2	0	0	0	0	0	0	0	143	0	0	375	1,690
1971	NR	2	0	0	0	0	0	0	0	74	0	0	194	1,685
1972	84	2	0	0	0	0	0	0	0	208	0	0	545	1,860
Lifetime		8	0	0	0	0	0	0	0	582	0	0	1,537	$6,585

Frank Douglas

Frank Douglas
Racing Hometown: Albuquerque, NM

Year	Rank	Starts	Poles	1	2	3	4	5	6–10	Laps	Laps Led	Races Led	Miles	$
1955	178T	1	0	0	0	0	0	0	0	89	0	0	89	25
Lifetime		1	0	0	0	0	0	0	0	89	0	0	89	$25

Red Douglass

R.W. Douglass
B: 1920
Racing Hometown: New Albany, OH

Year	Rank	Starts	Poles	1	2	3	4	5	6–10	Laps	Laps Led	Races Led	Miles	$
1953	163	1	0	0	0	0	0	0	0	33	0	0	135	25
Lifetime		1	0	0	0	0	0	0	0	33	0	0	135	$25

Fred Dove

Fred Dove
Racing Hometown: Martinsville, VA

Year	Rank	Starts	Poles	1	2	3	4	5	6–10	Laps	Laps Led	Races Led	Miles	$
1952	31	8	0	0	0	0	0	0	3	919	0	0	692	390
1953	16	20	0	0	0	0	0	0	4	742	0	0	720	1,240
1954	36	12	0	0	0	0	0	0	2	1,428	0	0	869	525
1955	50	7	0	0	0	1	0	0	2	830	0	0	398	750
Lifetime		47	0	0	0	1	0	0	11	3,919	0	0	2,678	$2,905

Red Dowdy

Red Dowdy
Racing Hometown: Dallas, TX

Year	Rank	Starts	Poles	1	2	3	4	5	6–10	Laps	Laps Led	Races Led	Miles	$
1953	NR	1	0	0	0	0	0	0	0		0	0		25
Lifetime		1	0	0	0	0	0	0	0		0	0		$25

Fred Drake

Fred Drake

Year	Rank	Starts	Poles	1	2	3	4	5	6–10	Laps	Laps Led	Races Led	Miles	$
1972	NR	1	0	0	0	0	0	0	0	93	0	0	140	345
Lifetime		1	0	0	0	0	0	0	0	93	0	0	140	$345

Tom Drake

Thomas Drake

Year	Rank	Starts	Poles	1	2	3	4	5	6–10	Laps	Laps Led	Races Led	Miles	$
1954	NR	1	0	0	0	0	0	0	0	444	0	0	222	50
Lifetime		1	0	0	0	0	0	0	0	444	0	0	222	$50

Year	Rank	Starts	Poles	1	2	3	4	5	6–10	Laps	Laps Led	Races Led	Miles	$

Jerry Draper

Jerry Draper
Racing Hometown: Silvis, IL

Year	Rank	Starts	Poles	1	2	3	4	5	6–10	Laps	Laps Led	Races Led	Miles	$
1953	102	1	0	0	0	0	0	0	0		0	0		25
1958	141	3	0	0	0	0	0	0	0	488	0	0	430	250
1959	NR	6	0	0	0	0	0	0	3	1,049	0	0	503	640
Lifetime		10	0	0	0	0	0	0	3	1,537	0	0	932	$915

John DuBoise

John DuBoise
B: 4/26/1919
Racing Hometown: Paterson, NJ

Year	Rank	Starts	Poles	1	2	3	4	5	6–10	Laps	Laps Led	Races Led	Miles	$
1950	73	2	0	0	0	0	0	0	0	367	0	0	459	250
1951	66	3	0	0	0	0	1	0	0	211	0	0	179	350
1952	159	2	0	0	0	0	0	0	0	203	0	0	128	50
Lifetime		7	0	0	0	0	1	0	0	781	0	0	766	$650

Don Duckworth

Donald Duckworth
B: 1928 *Severely injured in 1955 Darlington.*
Racing Hometown: Graycourt, SC

Year	Rank	Starts	Poles	1	2	3	4	5	6–10	Laps	Laps Led	Races Led	Miles	$
1955	204	1	0	0	0	0	0	0	0	147	0	0	202	50
Lifetime		1	0	0	0	0	0	0	0	147	0	0	202	$50

Bob Duell

Robert Duell
Racing Hometown: Warren, PA

Year	Rank	Starts	Poles	1	2	3	4	5	6–10	Laps	Laps Led	Races Led	Miles	$
1956	78	6	0	0	0	0	0	1	0	642	0	0	443	670
1957	76	5	0	0	0	0	0	0	0	503	0	0	476	260
1958	22	7	1	0	1	1	0	1	3	1,273	0	0	969	2,415
1959	108	4	0	0	0	0	0	0	0	672	0	0	578	650
1960	64	6	0	0	0	0	0	0	1	422	0	0	531	935
Lifetime		28	1	0	1	1	0	2	4	3,512	0	0	2,997	$4,930

Philip Duffie

Philip Duffie
Racing Hometown: Augusta, GA

Year	Rank	Starts	Poles	1	2	3	4	5	6–10	Laps	Laps Led	Races Led	Miles	$
1982	40	5	0	0	0	0	0	0	0	1,166	0	0	2,273	10,910
1983	50	4	0	0	0	0	0	0	0	750	0	0	1,168	6,480
1988	77T	1	0	0	0	0	0	0	0	332	0	0	454	2,540
1990	68	2	0	0	0	0	0	0	0	191	0	0	419	8,030
Lifetime		12	0	0	0	0	0	0	0	2,439	0	0	4,314	$27,960

Art Dugan

Arthur Dugan

Year	Rank	Starts	Poles	1	2	3	4	5	6–10	Laps	Laps Led	Races Led	Miles	$
1954	NR	1	0	0	0	0	0	0	0	165	0	0	83	25
Lifetime		1	0	0	0	0	0	0	0	165	0	0	83	$25

Bobby Dugan

Robert Dugan
Racing Hometown: Waukegan, IL

Year	Rank	Starts	Poles	1	2	3	4	5	6–10	Laps	Laps Led	Races Led	Miles	$
1952	77	2	0	0	0	0	0	0	0	275	0	0	138	75
Lifetime		2	0	0	0	0	0	0	0	275	0	0	138	$75

Yvon DuHamel

Yvon DuHamel
B: 1939
Racing Hometown: Villa LaSalle, Que, Canada

Year	Rank	Starts	Poles	1	2	3	4	5	6–10	Laps	Laps Led	Races Led	Miles	$
1973	109	1	0	0	0	0	0	0	1	381	0	0	238	800
Lifetime		1	0	0	0	0	0	0	1	381	0	0	238	$800

Ray Duhigg

Raymond Duhigg
B: 1929   D: 10/9/1955   *Killed in race @ Salem, IN.*
Racing Hometown: Toledo, OH

Year	Rank	Starts	Poles	1	2	3	4	5	6–10	Laps	Laps Led	Races Led	Miles	$
1950	27	5	0	0	0	0	0	1	1	0	0	0	0	450
1951	N/A	6	0	0	0	0	0	0	0	213	0	0	190	150
1952	8	18	0	0	0	2	1	1	6	2,823	0	0	2,029	3,811
1953	NR	12	0	0	0	2	2	0	4	489	0	0	411	2,765
1954	26	12	0	0	0	0	1	1	3	1,458	0	0	938	1,375

Year	Rank	Starts	Poles	Finish 1	2	3	4	5	6–10	Laps	Laps Led	Races Led	Miles	$

Ray Duhigg *continued*

Year	Rank	Starts	Poles	1	2	3	4	5	6–10	Laps	Laps Led	Races Led	Miles	$
1955	86	1	0	0	0	1	0	0	0	39	0	0	160	1,000
Lifetime		54	0	0	0	5	4	3	14	5,022	0	0	3,727	$9,551

Gerald Duke

Gerald Duke
B: 1928
Racing Hometown: College Park, GA

Year	Rank	Starts	Poles	1	2	3	4	5	6–10	Laps	Laps Led	Races Led	Miles	$
1959	51	1	0	0	0	0	0	0	0	249	0	0	125	125
1960	24	11	0	0	0	0	1	0	6	2,062	0	0	2,017	5,930
1961	176	1	0	0	0	0	0	0	0	39	0	0	20	50
1962	84	4	0	0	0	0	0	0	0	607	0	0	754	800
Lifetime		17	0	0	0	0	1	0	6	2,957	0	0	2,915	$6,905

George Dunn

George Dunn
B: 1931
Racing Hometown: Raleigh, NC

Year	Rank	Starts	Poles	1	2	3	4	5	6–10	Laps	Laps Led	Races Led	Miles	$
1958	75	10	1	0	1	0	1	1	3	1,747	10	1	939	1,880
1959	NR	1	0	0	0	0	0	0	0	145	0	0	48	130
1962	92	1	0	0	0	0	1	0	0	108	0	0	27	305
Lifetime		12	1	0	1	0	2	1	3	2,000	10	1	1,015	$2,315

Huey Dunn

Huey Dunn
Racing Hometown: Charlotte, NC

Year	Rank	Starts	Poles	1	2	3	4	5	6–10	Laps	Laps Led	Races Led	Miles	$
1950	75	1	0	0	0	0	0	0	1	172	0	0	129	75
Lifetime		1	0	0	0	0	0	0	1	172	0	0	129	$75

Jim Dunn

James Dunn
Racing Hometown: Beaverdam, VA

Year	Rank	Starts	Poles	1	2	3	4	5	6–10	Laps	Laps Led	Races Led	Miles	$
1958	163	1	0	0	0	0	0	0	0	21	0	0	55	100
Lifetime		1	0	0	0	0	0	0	0	21	0	0	55	$100

Glenn Dunnaway

Henry Glenn Dunnaway
B: 1915   D: 3/15/1964   *Killed @ train crossing in Camden, SC.*
Racing Hometown: Gastonia, NC

Year	Rank	Starts	Poles	1	2	3	4	5	6–10	Laps	Laps Led	Races Led	Miles	$
1949	9	6	0	0	0	1	0	0	2	594	0	0	347	810
1950	NR	7	0	0	1	0	1	0	1	866	0	0	731	1,275
1951	89	6	0	0	0	0	0	0	2		0	0		275
Lifetime		19	0	0	1	1	1	0	5	1,460	0	0	1,078	$2,360

Harold Dunnaway

Harold Dunnaway
B: 10/7/1933
Racing Hometown: Gastonia, NC

Year	Rank	Starts	Poles	1	2	3	4	5	6–10	Laps	Laps Led	Races Led	Miles	$
1966	123	1	0	0	0	0	0	0	0	14	0	0	14	560
Lifetime		1	0	0	0	0	0	0	0	14	0	0	14	$560

Gary DuPuis

Gary DuPuis
Racing Hometown: Deland, FL

Year	Rank	Starts	Poles	1	2	3	4	5	6–10	Laps	Laps Led	Races Led	Miles	$
1970	89	1	0	0	0	0	0	0	0	78	0	0	195	735
Lifetime		1	0	0	0	0	0	0	0	78	0	0	195	$735

Ralph Dutton

Ralph Dutton
Racing Hometown: Chilhowie, VA

Year	Rank	Starts	Poles	1	2	3	4	5	6–10	Laps	Laps Led	Races Led	Miles	$
1953	125	4	0	0	0	0	0	0	0	46	0	0	23	100
1954	145T	1	0	0	0	0	0	0	0	70	0	0	44	25
Lifetime		5	0	0	0	0	0	0	0	116	0	0	67	$125

Red Duvall

Duane Michael Duvall
B: 10/7/1923   D: 12/12/199
Racing Hometown: Hammond, IN

Year	Rank	Starts	Poles	1	2	3	4	5	6–10	Laps	Laps Led	Races Led	Miles	$
1951	52	2	0	0	0	1	0	0	1		0	0		550

Year	Rank	Starts	Poles	Finish						Laps	Laps Led	Races Led	Miles	$
				1	2	3	4	5	6–10	Laps				

Red Duvall *continued*

Year	Rank	Starts	Poles	1	2	3	4	5	6–10	Laps	Laps Led	Races Led	Miles	$
1952	54	4	0	0	0	0	0	0	2	538	0	0	372	275
1953	72	1	0	0	0	0	0	0	0	37	0	0	152	75
1954	NR	1	0	0	0	0	0	0	0	49	0	0	25	0
Lifetime		8	0	0	0	1	0	0	3	624	0	0	548	$900

Clark Dwyer

Clark Dwyer
B: 1/12/1964
Racing Hometown: Littleton, CO

Year	Rank	Starts	Poles	1	2	3	4	5	6–10	Laps	Laps Led	Races Led	Miles	$
1983	46	5	0	0	0	0	0	0	1	851	0	0	1,412	14,570
1984	23	26	0	0	0	0	0	0	0	7,025	1	1	8,059	114,355
1985	22	28	0	0	0	0	0	0	0	7,205	0	0	8,558	128,710
Lifetime		59	0	0	0	0	0	0	1	15,081	1	1	18,029	$257,635

Carson Dyer

Carson Dyer
Racing Hometown: Atlanta, GA

Year	Rank	Starts	Poles	1	2	3	4	5	6–10	Laps	Laps Led	Races Led	Miles	$
1950	NR	1	0	0	0	0	0	0	0	310	0	0	388	0
1951	N/A	2	0	0	0	0	0	0	0		0	0		50
1952	84T	1	0	0	0	0	0	0	1	283	0	0	142	170
Lifetime		4	0	0	0	0	0	0	1	593	0	0	529	$220

Charles Dyer

Charles Dyer
B: 11/10/1917   D: 5/24/1957   *Died of heart attack in late model race @ Fredericksburg, VA.*
Racing Hometown: N.Bergen, NJ

Year	Rank	Starts	Poles	1	2	3	4	5	6–10	Laps	Laps Led	Races Led	Miles	$
1951	NR	1	0	0	0	0	0	0	0		0	0		0
1955	70	3	0	0	0	0	0	0	2	446	0	0	268	350
Lifetime		4	0	0	0	0	0	0	2	446	0	0	268	$350

Ralph Dyer

Ralph Dyer
Racing Hometown: Shreveport, LA

Year	Rank	Starts	Poles	1	2	3	4	5	6–10	Laps	Laps Led	Races Led	Miles	$
1950	94T	1	0	0	0	0	0	0	0		0	0		50
1953	NR	6	0	0	0	0	0	0	3	480	0	0	384	600
Lifetime		7	0	0	0	0	0	0	3	480	0	0	384	$650

Dick Eagan

Clayton Richard Eagan
B: 6/12/1919
Racing Hometown: Springdale, CT

Year	Rank	Starts	Poles	1	2	3	4	5	6–10	Laps	Laps Led	Races Led	Miles	$
1950	NR	1	0	0	0	0	0	0	0		0	0		0
1951	51	3	0	0	0	1	0	0	1		0	0		625
1952	NR	2	0	0	0	0	0	0	1		0	0		100
Lifetime		6	0	0	0	1	0	0	2		0	0		$725

Mike Eagan

Michael P. Eagan
B: 8/2/1926
Racing Hometown: Dunkirk, NY

Year	Rank	Starts	Poles	1	2	3	4	5	6–10	Laps	Laps Led	Races Led	Miles	$
1949	22T	1	0	0	0	0	1	0	0		0	0		300
Lifetime		1	0	0	0	0	1	0	0		0	0		$300

Harvey Eakin

Harvey E. Eakin
Racing Hometown: Baltimore, MD

Year	Rank	Starts	Poles	1	2	3	4	5	6–10	Laps	Laps Led	Races Led	Miles	$
1954	42	7	0	0	0	0	0	0	0	741	0	0	915	425
1955	106	3	0	0	0	0	0	0	0	307	0	0	416	210
1956	175	2	0	0	0	0	0	0	0	278	0	0	278	100
1957	56	5	0	0	0	0	0	0	0	763	0	0	575	375
Lifetime		17	0	0	0	0	0	0	0	2,089	0	0	2,184	$1,110

Danny Eames

Daniel Eames
B: 1918
Racing Hometown: Long Beach, CA

Year	Rank	Starts	Poles	1	2	3	4	5	6–10	Laps	Laps Led	Races Led	Miles	$
1958	NR	1	0	0	0	0	0	0	0	147	0	0	387	185
Lifetime		1	0	0	0	0	0	0	0	147	0	0	387	$185

Year	Rank	Starts	Poles	Finish 1	2	3	4	5	6–10	Laps	Laps Led	Races Led	Miles	$

Jerry Earl

Jerry Earl
  Racing Hometown: Rochester, NY

Year	Rank	Starts	Poles	1	2	3	4	5	6–10	Laps	Laps Led	Races Led	Miles	$
1953	80T	1	0	0	0	0	0	0	1		0	0		100
Lifetime		1	0	0	0	0	0	0	1		0	0		$100

Dale Earnhardt

Ralph Dale Earnhardt
  B: 4/29/1951   D: 2/18/2001   *Killed in Daytona 500.*
  Racing Hometown: Kannapolis, NC

Year	Rank	Starts	Poles	1	2	3	4	5	6–10	Laps	Laps Led	Races Led	Miles	$
1975	NR	1	0	0	0	0	0	0	0	355	0	0	533	2,425
1976	103	2	0	0	0	0	0	0	0	416	0	0	630	3,085
1977	117	1	0	0	0	0	0	0	0	25	0	0	38	1,375
1978	43	5	0	0	0	0	1	0	1	1,359	0	0	2,370	20,745
1979	7	27	4	1	1	3	4	2	6	8,340	604	16	9,357	274,810
1980	1	31	0	5	3	4	3	4	5	9,615	1,185	25	11,137	671,991
1981	7	31	0	0	2	3	2	2	8	8,134	300	12	10,063	353,972
1982	12	30	1	1	1	3	2	0	5	7,208	1,062	18	7,787	400,880
1983	8	30	0	2	3	0	3	1	5	7,701	1,026	19	8,947	465,203
1984	4	30	0	2	4	2	0	4	10	9,584	446	16	10,850	634,671
1985	8	28	1	4	0	0	4	2	6	8,231	1,237	17	9,157	546,596
1986	1	29	1	5	5	3	1	2	7	9,212	2,127	26	11,166	1,768,880
1987	1	29	1	11	5	1	2	2	3	9,043	3,358	27	10,900	2,069,243
1988	3	29	0	3	2	3	3	2	6	9,561	1,808	20	11,325	1,214,089
1989	2	29	2	5	3	5	1	0	5	9,112	2,730	22	10,798	885,050
1990	1	29	5	9	3	3	1	2	5	9,162	2,437	22	11,057	3,308,056
1991	1	29	0	4	3	4	1	2	7	9,541	1,133	20	11,438	2,416,685
1992	12	29	1	1	2	2	1	0	9	8,694	487	10	10,198	915,463
1993	1	30	3	6	5	3	3	0	4	9,787	1,474	21	11,809	3,353,789
1994	1	31	2	4	7	6	1	2	5	9,546	1,015	23	11,410	3,400,733
1995	2	31	3	5	6	5	1	2	4	9,625	1,574	24	11,715	3,154,241
1996	4	31	2	2	3	3	4	1	4	9,530	617	18	11,524	2,285,926
1997	5	32	0	0	4	1	1	1	9	9,693	215	10	12,503	2,151,909
1998	8	33	0	1	0	1	2	1	8	9,459	274	14	12,277	2,990,749
1999	7	34	0	3	3	0	0	1	14	9,751	230	8	12,760	3,048,236
2000	2	34	0	2	5	4	2	0	11	10,005	353	17	13,186	3,701,391
2001	58	1	0	0	0	0	0	0	0	199	16	1	498	194,111
Lifetime		676	26	76	70	59	43	33	147	202,888	25,708	406	245,429	$40,234,304

Dale Earnhardt Jr.

Ralph Dale Earnhardt Jr.
  B: 10/10/1974
  Racing Hometown: Kannapolis, NC

Year	Rank	Starts	Poles	1	2	3	4	5	6–10	Laps	Laps Led	Races Led	Miles	$
1999	48	5	0	0	0	0	0	0	1	1,363	1	1	1,838	162,095
2000	16	34	2	2	0	0	1	0	2	9,644	426	10	12,633	2,610,396
2001	8	36	2	3	2	3	1	0	6	10,302	767	16	13,685	5,827,542
2002	11	36	2	2	1	1	4	3	5	10,344	1,068	22	13,525	4,970,034
Lifetime		111	6	7	3	4	6	3	14	31,653	2,262	49	41,681	$13,570,067

Kerry Earnhardt

Kerry Earnhardt
  B: 12/8/1969
  Racing Hometown: Kannapolis, NC

Year	Rank	Starts	Poles	1	2	3	4	5	6–10	Laps	Laps Led	Races Led	Miles	$
2000	73T	1	0	0	0	0	0	0	0	5	0	0	10	21,830
Lifetime		1	0	0	0	0	0	0	0	5	0	0	10	$21,830

Ralph Earnhardt

Ralph Lee Earnhardt
  B: 2/29/1928   D: 9/26/1973   *Heart attack.*
  Racing Hometown: Kannapolis, NC

Year	Rank	Starts	Poles	1	2	3	4	5	6–10	Laps	Laps Led	Races Led	Miles	$
1956	148	1	1	0	1	0	0	0	0	250	15	1	100	625
1957	37	9	0	0	0	0	0	0	3	1,465	0	0	764	1,150
1961	17	8	0	0	1	1	0	0	3	1,664	90	3	2,522	6,714
1962	29	17	0	0	0	1	0	1	4	2,022	0	0	2,159	4,545
1963	94	5	0	0	0	0	0	0	0	491	0	0	767	1,995
1964	46	11	0	0	0	0	1	0	0	1,107	0	0	1,055	3,290
Lifetime		51	1	0	2	2	1	1	10	6,999	105	4	7,366	$18,319

Sonny Easley

Lynwood Easley
  B: 6/5/1939   D: 1/15/1978   *Killed @ Riverside, CA.*
  Racing Hometown: Van Nuys, CA

Year	Rank	Starts	Poles	1	2	3	4	5	6–10	Laps	Laps Led	Races Led	Miles	$
1972	113	1	0	0	0	0	0	0	0	35	0	0	92	670

Year	Rank	Starts	Poles	Finish						Laps	Laps Led	Races Led	Miles	$
				1	2	3	4	5	6–10					

Sonny Easley *continued*

Year	Rank	Starts	Poles	1	2	3	4	5	6–10	Laps	Laps Led	Races Led	Miles	$
1973	90	2	0	0	0	0	0	0	0	144	0	0	377	2,015
1974	61	3	0	0	0	0	0	0	1	415	0	0	1,074	4,800
1975	66	3	0	0	0	0	0	0	0	136	2	1	355	2,405
1976	38	7	0	0	0	0	0	0	2	1,861	0	0	2,137	11,290
1977	50	3	0	0	0	0	0	1	1	360	0	0	925	9,490
Lifetime		19	0	0	0	0	0	1	4	2,951	2	1	4,960	$30,670

Doug Easton

Douglas Easton
B: 3/12/1931
Racing Hometown: Horse Cave, NY

Year	Rank	Starts	Poles	1	2	3	4	5	6–10	Laps	Laps Led	Races Led	Miles	$
1969	NR	1	0	0	0	0	0	0	0	0	0	0	0	875
Lifetime		1	0	0	0	0	0	0	0	0	0	0	0	$875

Tom Edmonds

Thomas Edmonds

Year	Rank	Starts	Poles	1	2	3	4	5	6–10	Laps	Laps Led	Races Led	Miles	$
1959	NR	1	0	0	0	0	0	0	0	239	0	0	96	75
Lifetime		1	0	0	0	0	0	0	0	239	0	0	96	$75

Frank Edwards

Frank Edwards
Racing Hometown: Chicago, IL

Year	Rank	Starts	Poles	1	2	3	4	5	6–10	Laps	Laps Led	Races Led	Miles	$
1956	195T	1	0	0	0	0	0	0	0	182	0	0	91	100
Lifetime		1	0	0	0	0	0	0	0	182	0	0	91	$100

J.D. Edwards

J.D. Edwards
Racing Hometown: Albemarle, NC

Year	Rank	Starts	Poles	1	2	3	4	5	6–10	Laps	Laps Led	Races Led	Miles	$
1949	54	1	0	0	0	0	0	0	0		0	0		50
Lifetime		1	0	0	0	0	0	0	0		0	0		$50

Jonathan Edwards

Jonathan Lee Edwards
B: 1958
Racing Hometown: Lake Wylie, SC

Year	Rank	Starts	Poles	1	2	3	4	5	6–10	Laps	Laps Led	Races Led	Miles	$
1985	68	2	0	0	0	0	0	0	0	633	0	0	644	3,220
1986	53	4	0	0	0	0	0	0	0	1,114	0	0	1,405	8,030
1987	78	2	0	0	0	0	0	0	0	226	0	0	309	3,055
Lifetime		8	0	0	0	0	0	0	0	1,973	0	0	2,358	$14,305

Marion Edwards

Marion Edwards
D: 1973
Racing Hometown: Hialeah, FL

Year	Rank	Starts	Poles	1	2	3	4	5	6–10	Laps	Laps Led	Races Led	Miles	$
1952	NR	1	0	0	0	0	0	1	0	183	0	0	92	200
1953	116	2	0	0	0	0	0	0	0	197	0	0	210	50
1955	NR	1	0	0	0	0	0	0	0	180	0	0	90	25
Lifetime		4	0	0	0	0	0	1	0	560	0	0	392	$275

Howard Elder

Howard Elder

Year	Rank	Starts	Poles	1	2	3	4	5	6–10	Laps	Laps Led	Races Led	Miles	$
1949	NR	1	0	0	0	0	0	0	0		0	0		25
Lifetime		1	0	0	0	0	0	0	0		0	0		$25

Ray Elder

Raymond Marvin Elder
B: 8/19/1942
Racing Hometown: Carruthers, CA

Year	Rank	Starts	Poles	1	2	3	4	5	6–10	Laps	Laps Led	Races Led	Miles	$
1967	114	1	0	0	0	0	0	0	0	23	0	0	62	500
1968	96	1	0	0	0	0	0	0	0	37	0	0	100	500
1969	48	4	0	0	0	0	0	0	4	642	0	0	1,523	7,200
1970	53	4	0	0	0	0	0	0	1	441	0	0	1,127	4,570
1971	NR	4	0	1	1	0	0	0	1	564	70	2	1,439	30,595
1972	52	3	0	1	0	0	1	1	0	493	50	2	1,268	23,165
1973	58	3	0	0	0	1	0	0	0	381	0	0	977	9,225
1974	95	2	0	0	0	0	0	0	0	37	0	0	94	1,435
1975	50	3	0	0	0	0	1	0	0	368	1	1	956	8,020
1976	58	2	0	0	0	0	2	0	0	284	0	0	744	11,715

Year	Rank	Starts	Poles	Finish 1	2	3	4	5	6–10	Laps	Laps Led	Races Led	Miles	$

Ray Elder *continued*

Year	Rank	Starts	Poles	1	2	3	4	5	6–10	Laps	Laps Led	Races Led	Miles	$
1977	105	1	0	0	0	0	0	0	0	14	0	0	37	625
1978	64	3	0	0	0	0	0	0	1	108	0	0	283	5,305
Lifetime		31	0	2	1	1	4	1	7	3,392	121	5	8,609	$102,855

Vic Elford

Victor Elford
B: 6/10/1935
Racing Hometown: South London, England

Year	Rank	Starts	Poles	1	2	3	4	5	6–10	Laps	Laps Led	Races Led	Miles	$
1969	NR	2	0	0	0	0	0	0	0	236	0	0	590	2,950
1971	NR	1	0	0	0	0	0	0	0	46	0	0	115	220
1972	NR	1	0	0	0	0	0	0	1	182	0	0	455	3,445
Lifetime		4	0	0	0	0	0	0	1	464	0	0	1,160	$6,615

Hoss Ellington

Charles Everett Ellington
B: 5/12/1935
Racing Hometown: Wilmington, NC

Year	Rank	Starts	Poles	1	2	3	4	5	6–10	Laps	Laps Led	Races Led	Miles	$
1968	61	3	0	0	0	0	0	0	0	494	0	0	703	2,395
1969	30	15	0	0	0	0	0	0	4	2,988	0	0	4,136	16,552
1970	55	3	0	0	0	0	0	0	0	728	0	0	875	3,133
Lifetime		21	0	0	0	0	0	0	4	4,210	0	0	5,714	$22,080

Bill Elliott

William Clyde Elliott
B: 10/8/1955
Racing Hometown: Dawsonville, GA

Year	Rank	Starts	Poles	1	2	3	4	5	6–10	Laps	Laps Led	Races Led	Miles	$
1976	41	8	0	0	0	0	0	0	0	1,047	0	0	1,452	11,635
1977	35	10	0	0	0	0	0	0	2	2,082	0	0	3,319	20,075
1978	33	10	0	0	0	0	0	0	5	2,278	0	0	4,099	42,215
1979	28	14	0	0	1	0	0	0	4	3,691	8	3	4,822	58,200
1980	34	11	0	0	0	0	0	0	4	2,106	4	4	4,076	42,545
1981	30	13	1	0	0	0	1	0	6	2,777	33	3	4,444	70,320
1982	25	21	1	0	3	3	1	1	1	5,542	151	9	7,887	201,030
1983	3	30	0	1	4	1	3	3	10	9,536	174	15	11,272	514,030
1984	3	30	4	3	1	4	4	1	11	9,848	570	17	11,385	680,344
1985	2	28	11	11	2	0	2	1	2	8,724	1,920	19	10,736	2,433,187
1986	4	29	4	2	0	2	1	3	8	8,549	511	15	10,593	1,049,142
1987	2	29	8	6	3	1	5	1	4	8,902	1,339	22	10,423	1,599,210
1988	1	29	6	6	2	2	4	1	7	9,647	1,559	20	11,531	1,554,639
1989	6	29	2	3	0	1	3	1	6	9,037	380	11	10,836	694,962
1990	4	29	2	1	4	1	5	1	4	9,349	1,182	13	11,189	1,090,730
1991	11	29	2	1	2	1	0	2	6	9,020	203	6	10,818	705,605
1992	2	29	2	5	2	3	1	3	3	9,115	1,272	18	11,125	1,692,381
1993	8	30	2	0	1	2	2	1	9	9,349	15	4	11,351	955,859
1994	10	31	1	1	1	3	0	1	6	9,173	62	8	11,382	951,679
1995	8	31	2	0	0	0	2	2	7	9,349	124	8	11,434	996,816
1996	30	24	0	0	0	0	0	0	6	7,439	109	7	8,642	716,506
1997	8	32	1	0	1	0	3	1	9	9,610	442	11	12,429	1,607,827
1998	18	32	0	0	0	0	0	0	5	8,865	40	8	11,443	1,618,421
1999	21	34	0	0	0	0	0	1	1	9,764	15	3	12,776	1,624,101
2000	21	32	0	0	0	2	1	0	4	8,636	111	8	11,421	2,447,788
2001	15	36	2	1	0	1	1	2	4	9,915	171	9	13,458	3,618,017
2002	13	36	4	2	1	1	1	1	7	10,352	275	13	13,665	4,122,699
Lifetime		696	55	43	28	28	40	27	141	203,702	10,670	254	258,009	$31,119,963

Brent Elliott

Brent Elliott
B: 5/2/1959
Racing Hometown: Denton, NC

Year	Rank	Starts	Poles	1	2	3	4	5	6–10	Laps	Laps Led	Races Led	Miles	$
1984	80T	1	0	0	0	0	0	0	0	203	0	0	127	835
1985	63	3	0	0	0	0	0	0	0	837	0	0	469	3,210
1986	100	1	0	0	0	0	0	0	0	325	0	0	203	950
Lifetime		5	0	0	0	0	0	0	0	1,365	0	0	799	$4,995

Stick Elliott

Gene Hampton Elliott
B: 7/27/1934   D: 11/1/1980
Racing Hometown: Shelby, NC

Year	Rank	Starts	Poles	1	2	3	4	5	6–10	Laps	Laps Led	Races Led	Miles	$
1962	35	21	0	0	0	0	0	0	2	3,027	0	0	2,317	3,928

Year	Rank	Starts	Poles	Finish 1	2	3	4	5	6–10	Laps	Laps Led	Races Led	Miles	$

Stick Elliott *continued*

Year	Rank	Starts	Poles	1	2	3	4	5	6–10	Laps	Laps Led	Races Led	Miles	$
1963	23	29	0	0	0	0	0	0	7	4,703	0	0	3,771	6,285
1964	91	7	0	0	0	0	0	0	0	211	0	0	244	1,450
1965	44	15	0	0	1	0	1	0	1	2,082	0	0	1,562	4,985
1966	35	19	0	0	0	0	1	0	2	3,285	0	0	2,716	7,335
1967	58	1	0	0	0	0	0	0	0	370	0	0	555	1,650
1971	NR	2	0	0	0	0	0	0	0	598	0	0	687	1,818
Lifetime		94	0	0	1	0	2	0	12	14,276	0	0	11,851	$27,451

Tommie Elliott

Thomas D. Elliott
B: 12/27/1935   D: 6/18/1989
Racing Hometown: Bloomfield, NJ

Year	Rank	Starts	Poles	1	2	3	4	5	6–10	Laps	Laps Led	Races Led	Miles	$
1951	152	2	0	0	0	0	0	0	0		0	0		50
1954	62	3	0	0	0	0	0	0	3	546	0	0	273	400
1957	NR	1	0	0	0	0	0	0	1	281	0	0	281	500
1958	172	1	0	0	0	0	0	0	0	40	0	0	20	0
Lifetime		7	0	0	0	0	0	0	4	867	0	0	574	$950

James Ellis

James Ellis
Racing Hometown: Mobile, AL

Year	Rank	Starts	Poles	1	2	3	4	5	6–10	Laps	Laps Led	Races Led	Miles	$
1951	160T	1	0	0	0	0	0	0	0		0	0		25
Lifetime		1	0	0	0	0	0	0	0		0	0		$25

Tommy Ellis

Thomas W. Ellis
B: 8/8/1947
Racing Hometown: Richmond, VA

Year	Rank	Starts	Poles	1	2	3	4	5	6–10	Laps	Laps Led	Races Led	Miles	$
1976	92T	1	0	0	0	0	0	0	0	429	0	0	429	1,335
1981	62	4	0	0	0	0	1	0	0	651	2	2	767	13,475
1982	75	2	0	0	0	0	0	0	0	642	0	0	348	3,220
1983	79	1	0	0	0	0	0	0	0	386	0	0	579	4,350
1984	31	20	0	0	0	0	0	0	1	5,010	1	1	5,356	44,315
1985	34	14	0	0	0	0	0	0	1	2,853	0	0	3,511	27,695
1986	23	24	0	0	0	0	0	0	3	6,559	50	5	7,334	78,310
1987	55	4	0	0	0	0	0	0	0	564	0	0	661	16,535
1988	91	2	0	0	0	0	0	0	0	178	0	0	267	3,125
1989	66	3	0	0	0	0	0	0	0	996	0	0	885	15,385
1990	NR	1	0	0	0	0	0	0	0	285	0	0	285	3,050
1991	70	2	0	0	0	0	0	0	0	887	0	0	1,085	13,250
Lifetime		78	0	0	0	0	1	0	5	19,440	53	8	21,506	$224,045

Pee Wee Ellwanger

Ronald Gene Ellwanger
B: 8/12/1935
Racing Hometown: Roanoke, VA

Year	Rank	Starts	Poles	1	2	3	4	5	6–10	Laps	Laps Led	Races Led	Miles	$
1965	83	4	0	0	0	0	0	0	0	345	0	0	173	575
1966	138	1	0	0	0	0	0	0	0	127	0	0	64	250
Lifetime		5	0	0	0	0	0	0	0	472	0	0	236	$825

Al Elmore

Al Elmore
Racing Hometown: Bishopville, SC

Year	Rank	Starts	Poles	1	2	3	4	5	6–10	Laps	Laps Led	Races Led	Miles	$
1979	87T	1	0	0	0	0	0	0	0	389	0	0	232	1,265
1983	NR	4	0	0	0	0	0	0	0	1,151	0	0	1,384	13,155
Lifetime		5	0	0	0	0	0	0	0	1,540	0	0	1,616	$14,420

Bill Elswick

William Elswick
B: 2/23/1948
Racing Hometown: N.Miami, FL

Year	Rank	Starts	Poles	1	2	3	4	5	6–10	Laps	Laps Led	Races Led	Miles	$
1979	62	3	0	0	0	0	0	0	0	1,112	0	0	842	3,400
1980	36	11	0	0	0	0	0	0	0	2,252	0	0	2,115	15,600
1981	85	3	0	0	0	0	0	0	0	662	0	0	1,345	20,100
Lifetime		17	0	0	0	0	0	0	0	4,026	0	0	4,302	$39,100

Year	Rank	Starts	Poles	Finish						Laps	Laps Led	Races Led	Miles	$
				1	2	3	4	5	6–10	Laps				

Jack Ely

Jack Ely
B: 7/21/1957
Racing Hometown: Bethel, CT

Year	Rank	Starts	Poles	1	2	3	4	5	6–10	Laps	Laps Led	Races Led	Miles	$
1986	94	2	0	0	0	0	0	0	0	329	0	0	823	5,145
1989	96T	1	0	0	0	0	0	0	0	204	0	0	204	1,800
Lifetime		3	0	0	0	0	0	0	0	533	0	0	1,027	$6,945

Bun Emery

Laurice Emery
Racing Hometown: Chicago, IL

Year	Rank	Starts	Poles	1	2	3	4	5	6–10	Laps	Laps Led	Races Led	Miles	$
1956	225T	1	0	0	0	0	0	0	0	364	0	0	182	200
Lifetime		1	0	0	0	0	0	0	0	364	0	0	182	$200

Vallie Engelauf

Vallie Engelauf
Racing Hometown: Riverside, CA

Year	Rank	Starts	Poles	1	2	3	4	5	6–10	Laps	Laps Led	Races Led	Miles	$
1968	93	1	0	0	0	0	0	0	0	38	0	0	103	505
Lifetime		1	0	0	0	0	0	0	0	38	0	0	103	$505

Bob England

Robert England
B: 1/29/1935
Racing Hometown: Daly City, CA

Year	Rank	Starts	Poles	1	2	3	4	5	6–10	Laps	Laps Led	Races Led	Miles	$
1969	NR	1	0	0	0	0	0	0	0	1	0	0	3	750
1970	112	2	0	0	0	0	0	0	0	126	0	0	330	1,740
1971	NR	4	0	0	0	0	0	0	0	477	0	0	1,160	4,105
Lifetime		7	0	0	0	0	0	0	0	604	0	0	1,493	$6,595

George England

George England
Racing Hometown: Dallas, TX

Year	Rank	Starts	Poles	1	2	3	4	5	6–10	Laps	Laps Led	Races Led	Miles	$
1966	76	1	0	0	0	0	0	0	0	293	0	0	440	745
1967	73	5	0	0	0	0	0	0	1	748	0	0	780	3,050
1968	100	1	0	0	0	0	0	0	0	235	0	0	118	275
1974	81	3	0	0	0	0	0	0	0	184	0	0	178	1,485
Lifetime		10	0	0	0	0	0	0	1	1,460	0	0	1,515	$5,555

Bud Erb

Herbert Erb
Racing Hometown: Mobile, AL

Year	Rank	Starts	Poles	1	2	3	4	5	6–10	Laps	Laps Led	Races Led	Miles	$
1951	N/A	3	0	0	0	0	0	0	0		0	0		100
1956	NR	1	0	0	0	0	0	0	0	116	0	0	58	50
1957	NR	4	0	0	0	0	0	0	3	479	0	0	269	629
Lifetime		8	0	0	0	0	0	0	3	595	0	0	327	$779

Erick Erickson

Erick Erickson
B: 11/8/1916
Racing Hometown: Lancaster, CA

Year	Rank	Starts	Poles	1	2	3	4	5	6–10	Laps	Laps Led	Races Led	Miles	$
1950	NR	2	0	0	0	0	0	0	0	137	31	1	131	50
1951	18	15	0	0	1	1	0	2	2	979	0	0	922	2,435
1952	NR	2	0	0	0	0	0	0	0	184	0	0	184	60
1953	NR	1	0	0	0	0	0	0	0		0	0		25
1954	25	6	0	0	0	0	0	1	2	1,398	0	0	1,191	1,365
1955	211	2	0	0	0	0	0	0	0	74	0	0	74	30
1956	72	5	0	0	0	0	0	0	1	736	0	0	639	365
Lifetime		33	0	0	1	1	0	3	5	3,508	31	1	3,140	$4,330

John Erickson

John Erickson
Racing Hometown: Jackson, MS

Year	Rank	Starts	Poles	1	2	3	4	5	6–10	Laps	Laps Led	Races Led	Miles	$
1954	96	1	0	0	0	0	0	0	0	137	0	0	206	100
Lifetime		1	0	0	0	0	0	0	0	137	0	0	206	$100

Ray Erickson

Raymond Erickson
B: 4/15/1918
Racing Hometown: Chicago, IL

Year	Rank	Starts	Poles	1	2	3	4	5	6–10	Laps	Laps Led	Races Led	Miles	$
1949	7	4	0	0	1	1	0	0	1	713	0	0	357	1,460
Lifetime		4	0	0	1	1	0	0	1	713	0	0	357	$1,460

Year	Rank	Starts	Poles	Finish 1	2	3	4	5	6–10	Laps	Laps Led	Races Led	Miles	$

Mike Ernest

Michael Ernest
  Racing Hometown: Wadsworth, OH

Year	Rank	Starts	Poles	1	2	3	4	5	6–10	Laps	Laps Led	Races Led	Miles	$
1951	N/A	1	0	0	0	0	0	0	0		0	0		0
1952	NR	1	0	0	0	0	0	0	0	168	0	0	84	50
Lifetime		2	0	0	0	0	0	0	0	168	0	0	84	$50

Bill Ervin

William Ervin
  Racing Hometown: Tellico Plains, TN

Year	Rank	Starts	Poles	1	2	3	4	5	6–10	Laps	Laps Led	Races Led	Miles	$
1967	57	18	0	0	0	0	0	0	0	1,804	0	0	926	2,005
1968	64	5	0	0	0	0	0	0	0	785	0	0	393	700
1969	NR	1	0	0	0	0	0	0	0	161	0	0	81	100
Lifetime		24	0	0	0	0	0	0	0	2,750	0	0	1,399	$2,805

Wimpy Ervin

Paul Ervin
  B: 12/24/1917
  Racing Hometown: Bloomfield, NJ

Year	Rank	Starts	Poles	1	2	3	4	5	6–10	Laps	Laps Led	Races Led	Miles	$
1951	N/A	4	0	0	0	0	0	0	1		0	0		175
1952	171	2	0	0	0	0	0	0	0	217	0	0	217	35
1953	NR	2	0	0	0	0	0	0	1		0	0		110
1954	NR	2	0	0	0	0	0	0	0	132	0	0	164	25
Lifetime		10	0	0	0	0	0	0	2	349	0	0	381	$345

Larry Esau

Larry George Esau
  B: 5/8/1947
  Racing Hometown: San Diego, CA

Year	Rank	Starts	Poles	1	2	3	4	5	6–10	Laps	Laps Led	Races Led	Miles	$
1972	102	1	0	0	0	0	0	0	0	118	0	0	309	1,080
1974	120	1	0	0	0	0	0	0	0	47	0	0	123	825
1975	82T	1	0	0	0	0	0	0	0	135	0	0	354	1,535
1976	86T	1	0	0	0	0	0	0	0	169	0	0	443	1,745
Lifetime		4	0	0	0	0	0	0	0	469	0	0	1,229	$5,185

Ron Esau

Ronald Esau
  B: 10/9/1954
  Racing Hometown: Lakeside, CA

Year	Rank	Starts	Poles	1	2	3	4	5	6–10	Laps	Laps Led	Races Led	Miles	$
1975	91T	1	0	0	0	0	0	0	0	96	0	0	252	1,125
1976	77	2	0	0	0	0	0	0	0	160	0	0	419	2,310
1983	83	2	0	0	0	0	0	0	0	70	0	0	183	1,575
1984	62	2	0	0	0	0	0	0	0	170	0	0	445	2,660
1985	100	1	0	0	0	0	0	0	0	10	0	0	26	2,925
1986	113	2	0	0	0	0	0	0	0	168	0	0	440	8,475
1987	NR	1	0	0	0	0	0	0	0	90	0	0	236	4,165
1988	69	2	0	0	0	0	0	0	0	231	0	0	596	9,335
1989	71	3	0	0	0	0	0	0	0	326	0	0	543	8,670
1990	80	1	0	0	0	0	0	0	0	383	0	0	287	3,050
Lifetime		17	0	0	0	0	0	0	0	1,704	0	0	3,428	$44,290

Bob Esposito

Robert Esposito

Year	Rank	Starts	Poles	1	2	3	4	5	6–10	Laps	Laps Led	Races Led	Miles	$
1956	184T	1	0	0	0	0	0	0	0	189	0	0	95	100
Lifetime		1	0	0	0	0	0	0	0	189	0	0	95	$100

Curtis Estes

Curtis Estes
  Racing Hometown: Norfolk, VA

Year	Rank	Starts	Poles	1	2	3	4	5	6–10	Laps	Laps Led	Races Led	Miles	$
1953	108T	1	0	0	0	0	0	0	0		0	0		25
Lifetime		1	0	0	0	0	0	0	0		0	0		$25

Herbert Estes

Herbert Estes (Tootle)
  D: 8/20/1982   *Died 2 hours after winning Late Model race at Bulls Gap, TN.*
  Racing Hometown: Knoxville, TN

Year	Rank	Starts	Poles	1	2	3	4	5	6–10	Laps	Laps Led	Races Led	Miles	$
1956	184T	1	0	0	0	0	0	0	0	178	0	0	89	100
1958	14	11	0	0	0	0	0	0	4	2,202	0	0	1,658	2,509
Lifetime		12	0	0	0	0	0	0	4	2,380	0	0	1,747	$2,609

Year	Rank	Starts	Poles	Finish						Laps	Laps Led	Races Led	Miles	$
				1	2	3	4	5	6–10	Laps	Led	Led	Miles	$

Jack Etheridge

Jack A. Etheridge
B: 4/24/1916
Racing Hometown: Jacksonville, FL

Year	Rank	Starts	Poles	1	2	3	4	5	6–10	Laps	Laps Led	Races Led	Miles	$
1949	46T	1	0	0	0	0	0	0	1		0	0		75
1967	95	3	0	0	0	0	0	0	0	160	0	0	84	645
1969	94T	1	0	0	0	0	0	0	0	7	0	0	4	100
Lifetime		5	0	0	0	0	0	0	1	167	0	0	88	$820

Joe Eubanks

Joseph F. Eubanks
B: 8/9/1925   D: 6/21/1971
Racing Hometown: Spartanburg, SC

Year	Rank	Starts	Poles	1	2	3	4	5	6–10	Laps	Laps Led	Races Led	Miles	$
1950	91	1	0	0	0	0	0	0	0	259	0	0	324	0
1951	10	12	0	0	1	2	0	0	0	490	7	1	513	3,415
1952	7	19	0	0	0	1	1	2	5	2,626	0	0	2,066	3,630
1953	8	24	1	0	1	2	4	0	8	718	82	2	588	5,254
1954	5	33	0	0	1	2	5	3	13	5,167	0	0	3,542	8,559
1955	20	14	0	0	0	0	0	0	4	1,607	0	0	1,487	2,008
1956	15	26	2	0	0	3	0	4	6	3,398	107	2	2,529	5,584
1957	124	1	0	0	0	0	0	0	1	180	0	0	90	100
1958	34	7	0	1	0	0	1	0	1	956	38	2	737	2,070
1959	32	13	0	0	1	0	0	1	5	1,279	0	0	945	2,000
1960	57	7	0	0	0	0	0	1	1	822	0	0	687	1,310
1961	50	2	0	0	0	0	0	0	0	448	0	0	672	1,475
Lifetime		159	3	1	4	10	11	11	44	17,950	234	7	14,178	$35,405

Rod Eulenfeld

Ludwig Everard Eulenfeld
B: 12/20/1935
Racing Hometown: Jacksonville, FL

Year	Rank	Starts	Poles	1	2	3	4	5	6–10	Laps	Laps Led	Races Led	Miles	$
1964	139	1	0	0	0	0	0	0	0	1	0	0	1	50
1965	110T	1	0	0	0	0	0	0	0	0	0	0	0	100
1968	67	2	0	0	0	0	0	0	0	229	0	0	464	2,150
1970	99	1	0	0	0	0	0	0	0	80	0	0	44	390
1971	79	1	0	0	0	0	0	0	0	293	0	0	446	1,135
Lifetime		6	0	0	0	0	0	0	0	603	0	0	955	$3,825

Ernest Eury

Ernest Eury
Racing Hometown: Conford, NC

Year	Rank	Starts	Poles	1	2	3	4	5	6–10	Laps	Laps Led	Races Led	Miles	$
1966	74	8	0	0	0	0	0	0	1	1,221	0	0	660	1,190
1971	87	1	0	0	0	0	0	0	0	1	0	0	1	200
Lifetime		9	0	0	0	0	0	0	1	1,222	0	0	660	$1,390

Jim Ewing

James Ewing
Racing Hometown: Akron, OH

Year	Rank	Starts	Poles	1	2	3	4	5	6–10	Laps	Laps Led	Races Led	Miles	$
1954	145T	1	0	0	0	0	0	0	0	100	0	0	50	25
Lifetime		1	0	0	0	0	0	0	0	100	0	0	50	$25

Ben Eyerly

Benjamin Eyerly

Year	Rank	Starts	Poles	1	2	3	4	5	6–10	Laps	Laps Led	Races Led	Miles	$
1957	171	1	0	0	0	0	0	0	0	41	0	0	21	50
Lifetime		1	0	0	0	0	0	0	0	41	0	0	21	$50

David Ezell

David Ezell
B: 6/19/1928
Racing Hometown: Jacksonville, FL

Year	Rank	Starts	Poles	1	2	3	4	5	6–10	Laps	Laps Led	Races Led	Miles	$
1952	86	1	0	0	0	1	0	0	0	153	0	0	77	450
1956	268	1	0	0	0	0	0	0	0		0	0		50
1961	172	1	0	0	0	0	0	0	0	87	0	0	44	50
Lifetime		3	0	0	0	1	0	0	0	240	0	0	120	$550

Art Faber

Arthur Faber
Racing Hometown: Parsippany, NJ

Year	Rank	Starts	Poles	1	2	3	4	5	6–10	Laps	Laps Led	Races Led	Miles	$
1954	208	1	0	0	0	0	0	0	0	61	0	0	31	10
Lifetime		1	0	0	0	0	0	0	0	61	0	0	31	$10

Year	Rank	Starts	Poles	Finish						Laps	Laps Led	Races Led	Miles	$
				1	2	3	4	5	6–10					

Fred Faber

Fred Faber
  Racing Hometown: Rochester, NY

Year	Rank	Starts	Poles	1	2	3	4	5	6–10	Laps	Laps Led	Races Led	Miles	$
1951	N/A	1	0	0	0	0	0	0	0		0	0		25
Lifetime		1	0	0	0	0	0	0	0		0	0		$25

Harold Fagan

Harold P. Fagan
  B: 3/11/1940 D: 8/6/1993
  Racing Hometown: Willowdale, Ont, Canada

Year	Rank	Starts	Poles	1	2	3	4	5	6–10	Laps	Laps Led	Races Led	Miles	$
1967	101	5	0	0	0	0	0	0	0	309	0	0	210	600
1968	44	12	0	0	0	0	0	0	1	1,808	0	0	1,343	3,680
1970	96	2	0	0	0	0	0	0	0	179	0	0	466	1,925
1971	89	1	0	0	0	0	0	0	0	1	0	0	0	100
Lifetime		20	0	0	0	0	0	0	1	2,297	0	0	2,019	$6,305

Joy Fair

Joy Fair
  B: 9/11/1930
  Racing Hometown: Pontiac Springs, MI

Year	Rank	Starts	Poles	1	2	3	4	5	6–10	Laps	Laps Led	Races Led	Miles	$
1956	163	2	0	0	0	0	0	0	1	192	0	0	96	100
Lifetime		2	0	0	0	0	0	0	1	192	0	0	96	$100

Cy Fairchild

Cyrus Fairchild
  B: 10/11/1936
  Racing Hometown: Saginaw, MI

Year	Rank	Starts	Poles	1	2	3	4	5	6–10	Laps	Laps Led	Races Led	Miles	$
1966	146T	1	0	0	0	0	0	0	0	18	0	0	45	0
Lifetime		1	0	0	0	0	0	0	0	18	0	0	45	$0

Len Fanelli

Leonard Fanelli
  B: 7/1/1912
  Racing Hometown: New Rochelle, NY

Year	Rank	Starts	Poles	1	2	3	4	5	6–10	Laps	Laps Led	Races Led	Miles	$
1951	N/A	1	0	0	0	0	0	0	0		0	0		50
Lifetime		1	0	0	0	0	0	0	0		0	0		$50

Ray Fanning

Raymond Fanning
  Racing Hometown: Baltimore, MD

Year	Rank	Starts	Poles	1	2	3	4	5	6–10	Laps	Laps Led	Races Led	Miles	$
1958	NR	1	0	0	0	0	0	0	1	157	0	0	79	130
1959	97	1	0	0	0	0	0	0	0	117	0	0	59	60
Lifetime		2	0	0	0	0	0	0	1	274	0	0	137	$190

Al Farmer

Al Farmer
  Critically injured @ Pikes Peak hill climb.
  Racing Hometown: New Ellington, SC

Year	Rank	Starts	Poles	1	2	3	4	5	6–10	Laps	Laps Led	Races Led	Miles	$
1964	108	2	0	0	0	0	0	0	0	289	0	0	136	260
Lifetime		2	0	0	0	0	0	0	0	289	0	0	136	$260

Freddie Farmer

Fred Farmer
  Racing Hometown: Los Angeles, CA

Year	Rank	Starts	Poles	1	2	3	4	5	6–10	Laps	Laps Led	Races Led	Miles	$
1951	102T	5	0	0	0	0	0	0	1	447	0	0	540	250
Lifetime		5	0	0	0	0	0	0	1	447	0	0	540	$250

Red Farmer

Charles Lawrence Farmer
  B: 10/15/1932
  Racing Hometown: Hialeah, Fl

Year	Rank	Starts	Poles	1	2	3	4	5	6–10	Laps	Laps Led	Races Led	Miles	$
1953	176	1	0	0	0	0	0	0	0	12	0	0	49	0
1956	154	3	0	0	0	0	0	0	0	324	0	0	162	125
1960	131	2	0	0	0	0	0	0	0	103	0	0	258	250
1962	90	2	0	0	0	0	0	0	0	72	0	0	180	535
1965	104	1	0	0	0	0	0	0	0	3	0	0	8	1,070
1967	54	4	0	0	0	0	0	0	0	610	7	1	749	2,925
1968	50	7	0	0	0	0	1	0	0	928	1	1	849	4,810
1969	92	1	0	0	0	0	0	0	0	101	0	0	51	100
1971	NR	3	0	0	0	0	0	0	1	213	0	0	533	2,835

Year	Rank	Starts	Poles	Finish 1	2	3	4	5	6–10	Laps	Laps Led	Races Led	Miles	$

Red Farmer *continued*

Year	Rank	Starts	Poles	1	2	3	4	5	6–10	Laps	Laps Led	Races Led	Miles	$
1972	63	5	0	0	0	0	1	0	0	474	0	0	1,101	9,575
1973	72	3	0	0	0	0	0	0	0	247	0	0	647	4,235
1974	76	2	0	0	0	0	0	0	0	329	0	0	875	2,860
1975	97	2	0	0	0	0	0	0	0	44	0	0	117	1,875
Lifetime		36	0	0	0	0	2	0	1	3,460	8	2	5,577	$31,195

Jack Farnell

Jack Farnell
Racing Hometown: College Park, NY

Year	Rank	Starts	Poles	1	2	3	4	5	6–10	Laps	Laps Led	Races Led	Miles	$
1954	NR	1	0	0	0	0	0	0	0	10	0	0	20	25
Lifetime		1	0	0	0	0	0	0	0	10	0	0	20	$25

Bubba Farr

Marion Farr
B: 1921
Racing Hometown: Aususta, GA

Year	Rank	Starts	Poles	1	2	3	4	5	6–10	Laps	Laps Led	Races Led	Miles	$
1962	116T	1	0	0	0	0	0	0	0	22	0	0	11	75
1963	120	2	0	0	0	0	0	0	0	34	0	0	85	550
Lifetime		3	0	0	0	0	0	0	0	56	0	0	96	$625

Bud Farrell

George Farrell
Racing Hometown: Red Bank, NJ

Year	Rank	Starts	Poles	1	2	3	4	5	6–10	Laps	Laps Led	Races Led	Miles	$
1951	48	5	0	0	0	0	1	0	1	373	0	0	466	700
1952	39	6	0	0	0	0	0	0	2	881	0	0	621	325
Lifetime		11	0	0	0	0	1	0	3	1,254	0	0	1,087	$1,025

Jack Farris

Jack Farris
B: 1929
Racing Hometown: New Paris, OH

Year	Rank	Starts	Poles	1	2	3	4	5	6–10	Laps	Laps Led	Races Led	Miles	$
1955	232	1	0	0	0	0	0	0	0	30	0	0	123	25
Lifetime		1	0	0	0	0	0	0	0	30	0	0	123	$25

Lew Fattman

Lew Fattman
Racing Hometown: Greenville, PA

Year	Rank	Starts	Poles	1	2	3	4	5	6–10	Laps	Laps Led	Races Led	Miles	$
1950	NR	1	0	0	0	0	0	0	0	53	0	105	0	0
Lifetime		1	0	0	0	0	0	0	0	53	0	105	0	0

Lee Faulk

Lee Faulk

Year	Rank	Starts	Poles	1	2	3	4	5	6–10	Laps	Laps Led	Races Led	Miles	$
1988	66	3	0	0	0	0	0	0	0	841	0	0	858	9,320
Lifetime		3	0	0	0	0	0	0	0	841	0	0	858	$9,320

Bill Faulkner

William Faulkner

Year	Rank	Starts	Poles	1	2	3	4	5	6–10	Laps	Laps Led	Races Led	Miles	$
1962	NR	1	0	0	0	0	0	0	0	43	0	0	11	125
Lifetime		1	0	0	0	0	0	0	0	43	0	0	11	$125

Doc Faustina

Dr. Leonard Manuel Faustina
B: 2/1/1939
Racing Hometown: Las Vegas, NC

Year	Rank	Starts	Poles	1	2	3	4	5	6–10	Laps	Laps Led	Races Led	Miles	$
1971	65	3	0	0	0	0	0	0	0	402	0	0	864	2,745
1972	61	5	0	0	0	0	0	0	0	607	0	0	1,161	3,635
1975	91T	1	0	0	0	0	0	0	0	116	0	0	290	880
1976	96T	1	0	0	0	0	0	0	0	378	0	0	378	735
Lifetime		10	0	0	0	0	0	0	0	1,503	0	0	2,693	$7,995

Lou Faver

Louis Faver
Racing Hometown: Irvington, NJ

Year	Rank	Starts	Poles	1	2	3	4	5	6–10	Laps	Laps Led	Races Led	Miles	$
1953	182	1	0	0	0	0	0	0	0	12	0	0	12	25
Lifetime		1	0	0	0	0	0	0	0	12	0	0	12	$25

Year	Rank	Starts	Poles	Finish 1	2	3	4	5	6–10	Laps	Laps Led	Races Led	Miles	$

Pat Fay

Patrick Fay
B: 3/31/1944
Racing Hometown: Gustine, CA

Year	Rank	Starts	Poles	1	2	3	4	5	6–10	Laps	Laps Led	Races Led	Miles	$
1970	NR	1	0	0	0	0	0	0	0	24	0	0	63	655
1971	NR	3	0	0	0	0	0	0	1	248	0	0	636	3,635
Lifetime		4	0	0	0	0	0	0	1	272	0	0	699	$4,290

Gary Fedewa

Gary Fedewa
B: 1/1/1944
Racing Hometown: Lansing, MI

Year	Rank	Starts	Poles	1	2	3	4	5	6–10	Laps	Laps Led	Races Led	Miles	$
1986	51	4	0	0	0	0	0	0	0	819	0	0	1,229	7,230
1987	86	1	0	0	0	0	0	0	0	355	0	0	355	1,650
Lifetime		5	0	0	0	0	0	0	0	1,174	0	0	1,584	$8,880

Tim Fedewa

Timothy Fedewa
B: 5/9/1967
Racing Hometown: Holt, MI

Year	Rank	Starts	Poles	1	2	3	4	5	6–10	Laps	Laps Led	Races Led	Miles	$
1994	64	1	0	0	0	0	0	0	0	487	0	0	487	8,565
Lifetime		1	0	0	0	0	0	0	0	487	0	0	487	$8,565

Paul Feldner

Paul J. Feldner
B: 2/14/1935
Racing Hometown: Richfield, WI

Year	Rank	Starts	Poles	1	2	3	4	5	6–10	Laps	Laps Led	Races Led	Miles	$
1970	NR	2	0	0	0	0	0	0	1	214	0	0	535	1,490
1972	NR	1	0	0	0	0	0	0	0	198	0	0	396	750
Lifetime		3	0	0	0	0	0	0	1	412	0	0	931	$2,240

Dick Fellows

Richard Fellows
Racing Hometown: Minneapolis, MN

Year	Rank	Starts	Poles	1	2	3	4	5	6–10	Laps	Laps Led	Races Led	Miles	$
1953	86T	1	0	0	0	0	0	0	1		0	0		75
Lifetime		1	0	0	0	0	0	0	1		0	0		$75

Ron Fellows

Ronald Fellows
B: 9/28/1959
Racing Hometown: Toronto, Ont, Canada

Year	Rank	Starts	Poles	1	2	3	4	5	6–10	Laps	Laps Led	Races Led	Miles	$
1995	63T	1	0	0	0	0	0	0	0	40	0	0	98	9,035
1998	63	2	0	0	0	0	0	0	0	355	0	0	472	46,310
1999	52	1	0	0	1	0	0	0	0	90	3	1	221	67,270
2000	73T	1	0	0	0	0	0	0	0	21	0	0	51	24,725
2001	59	2	0	0	0	0	0	0	0	137	23	2	285	72,055
2002	70	1	0	0	0	0	0	0	0	110	0	0	215	47,930
Lifetime		8	0	0	1	0	0	0	0	753	26	3	1,341	$267,325

Gene Felton

Gene Felton
B: 5/11/1936
Racing Hometown: Marietta, GA

Year	Rank	Starts	Poles	1	2	3	4	5	6–10	Laps	Laps Led	Races Led	Miles	$
1976	88T	1	0	0	0	0	0	0	0	308	0	0	469	1,635
Lifetime		1	0	0	0	0	0	0	0	308	0	0	469	$1,635

Ed Ferree

Edward Ferree
B: 3/16/1952
Racing Hometown: Saxonburg, PA

Year	Rank	Starts	Poles	1	2	3	4	5	6–10	Laps	Laps Led	Races Led	Miles	$
1992	77T	1	0	0	0	0	0	0	0	50	0	0	123	4,035
1993	58	2	0	0	0	0	0	0	0	507	0	0	561	12,865
Lifetime		3	0	0	0	0	0	0	0	557	0	0	684	$16,900

Bill Ferrier

William Ferrier
Racing Hometown: Fillmore, CA

Year	Rank	Starts	Poles	1	2	3	4	5	6–10	Laps	Laps Led	Races Led	Miles	$
1961	118	2	0	0	0	0	0	0	0	214	0	0	148	130
Lifetime		2	0	0	0	0	0	0	0	214	0	0	148	$130

Year	Rank	Starts	Poles	Finish						Laps	Laps Led	Races Led	Miles	$
				1	2	3	4	5	6–10	Laps				

Paul Fess

Paul Fess
Racing Hometown: Mt. Pleasant, PA

Year	Rank	Starts	Poles	1	2	3	4	5	6–10	Laps	Laps Led	Races Led	Miles	$
1978	NR	1	0	0	0	0	0	0	0	75	0	0	188	835
1979	76	2	0	0	0	0	0	0	0	232	0	0	532	4,860
Lifetime		3	0	0	0	0	0	0	0	307	0	0	719	$5,695

Jim Fiebelkorn

James Fiebelkorn
Racing Hometown: Randolph, NY

Year	Rank	Starts	Poles	1	2	3	4	5	6–10	Laps	Laps Led	Races Led	Miles	$
1951	28	17	0	0	1	0	0	0	3	984	0	0	913	1,355
1952	183	1	0	0	0	0	0	0	0	35	0	0	35	0
Lifetime		18	0	0	1	0	0	0	3	1,019	0	0	948	$1,355

Wayne Fielden

Wayne Fielden
Racing Hometown: Knoxville, TN

Year	Rank	Starts	Poles	1	2	3	4	5	6–10	Laps	Laps Led	Races Led	Miles	$
1956	130T	2	0	0	0	0	0	0	1	361	0	0	181	200
Lifetime		2	0	0	0	0	0	0	1	361	0	0	181	$200

Bo Fields

Elmer Fields
Racing Hometown: Alger, AL

Year	Rank	Starts	Poles	1	2	3	4	5	6–10	Laps	Laps Led	Races Led	Miles	$
1954	105	1	0	0	0	0	0	0	0	137	0	0	206	200
1955	124	3	0	0	0	0	0	0	0	347	0	0	292	100
Lifetime		4	0	0	0	0	0	0	0	484	0	0	498	$300

Joe Fields

Joe Fields (Real Name: J.E. Liesfeld Jr.)
B: 6/26/1945
Racing Hometown: Montpeliar, VA

Year	Rank	Starts	Poles	1	2	3	4	5	6–10	Laps	Laps Led	Races Led	Miles	$
1979	NR	1	0	0	0	0	0	0	0	379	0	0	205	1,385
1981	46	6	0	0	0	0	0	0	0	1,681	0	0	1,160	7,750
1982	91	3	0	0	0	0	0	0	0	738	0	0	397	2,610
1983	78	3	0	0	0	0	0	0	0	1,064	0	0	787	4,315
1984	63	2	0	0	0	0	0	0	0	661	0	0	661	1,915
1986	NR	1	0	0	0	0	0	0	0	0	0	0	0	875
Lifetime		16	0	0	0	0	0	0	0	4,523	0	0	3,211	$18,850

L.D. Fields

Lawrence D. Fields (Junior)

Year	Rank	Starts	Poles	1	2	3	4	5	6–10	Laps	Laps Led	Races Led	Miles	$
1971	83	1	0	0	0	0	0	0	0	31	0	0	31	570
Lifetime		1	0	0	0	0	0	0	0	31	0	0	31	$570

Wade Fields

Wade Fields
Racing Hometown: Sanford, NC

Year	Rank	Starts	Poles	1	2	3	4	5	6–10	Laps	Laps Led	Races Led	Miles	$
1951	N/A	6	0	0	0	0	0	0	0	268	0	0	335	175
1956	237	1	0	0	0	0	0	0	0	244	0	0	336	50
Lifetime		7	0	0	0	0	0	0	0	512	0	0	671	$225

Lou Figaro

Lou Figaro
B: 10/12/1917   D: 10/25/195   *Died after crash in 10/24/54 NASCAR Grand National Race @ North Wilkesboro.*
Racing Hometown: Inglewood, CA

Year	Rank	Starts	Poles	1	2	3	4	5	6–10	Laps	Laps Led	Races Led	Miles	$
1951	22	13	1	1	0	0	2	0	1	431	200	1	331	2,135
1954	43	3	0	0	0	0	0	0	2	461	0	0	403	425
Lifetime		16	1	1	0	0	2	0	3	892	200	1	734	$2,560

Chet Fillip

Chet Fillip
B: 4/4/1957
Racing Hometown: San Angelo, TX

Year	Rank	Starts	Poles	1	2	3	4	5	6–10	Laps	Laps Led	Races Led	Miles	$
1985	80	1	0	0	0	0	0	0	0	308	0	0	469	1,425
1986	32	17	0	0	0	0	0	0	0	3,276	0	0	4,552	36,110
1987	56	6	0	0	0	0	0	0	0	895	0	0	1,624	30,065
Lifetime		24	0	0	0	0	0	0	0	4,479	0	0	6,645	$67,600

Year	Rank	Starts	Poles	Finish 1	2	3	4	5	6–10	Laps	Laps Led	Races Led	Miles	$

Bob Finale

Robert Finale

Year	Rank	Starts	Poles	1	2	3	4	5	6–10	Laps	Laps Led	Races Led	Miles	$
1958	NR	1	0	0	0	0	0	0	1	138	0	0	46	165
Lifetime		1	0	0	0	0	0	0	1	138	0	0	46	$165

John Findlay

John Findlay

Year	Rank	Starts	Poles	1	2	3	4	5	6–10	Laps	Laps Led	Races Led	Miles	$
1957	91	3	0	0	0	0	0	0	1	382	0	0	191	320
1958	61	4	0	0	0	0	0	1	0	674	0	0	320	530
1959	NR	1	0	0	0	0	0	0	0	116	0	0	58	50
Lifetime		8	0	0	0	0	0	1	1	1,172	0	0	569	$900

Jimmy Finger

James Finger
Racing Hometown: Austin, TX

Year	Rank	Starts	Poles	1	2	3	4	5	6–10	Laps	Laps Led	Races Led	Miles	$
1971	NR	1	0	0	0	0	0	0	0	18	0	0	36	530
1972	83	2	0	0	0	0	0	0	0	214	0	0	535	3,830
1979	64	3	0	0	0	0	0	0	0	152	0	0	398	5,020
1980	84T	1	0	0	0	0	0	0	0	181	0	0	362	2,200
Lifetime		7	0	0	0	0	0	0	0	565	0	0	1,331	$11,580

Phil Finney

Phillip W. Finney
B: 4/20/1950
Racing Hometown: Merritt Island, FL

Year	Rank	Starts	Poles	1	2	3	4	5	6–10	Laps	Laps Led	Races Led	Miles	$
1971	71	1	0	0	0	0	0	0	0	357	0	0	193	400
1972	107	1	0	0	0	0	0	0	0	321	0	0	174	450
1973	NR	1	0	0	0	0	0	0	0	55	0	0	146	910
1974	114	1	0	0	0	0	0	0	0	100	0	0	266	1,010
1977	110T	1	0	0	0	0	0	0	0	148	0	0	225	645
1980	78T	2	0	0	0	0	0	0	0	188	0	0	476	3,125
Lifetime		7	0	0	0	0	0	0	0	1,169	0	0	1,481	$6,540

Ed Fiola

Edward Fiola
B: 1928
Racing Hometown: Turtle Creek, PA

Year	Rank	Starts	Poles	1	2	3	4	5	6–10	Laps	Laps Led	Races Led	Miles	$
1957	106	2	0	0	0	0	0	0	0	127	0	0	127	75
Lifetime		2	0	0	0	0	0	0	0	127	0	0	127	$75

B. Fisher

B. Fisher

Year	Rank	Starts	Poles	1	2	3	4	5	6–10	Laps	Laps Led	Races Led	Miles	$
1954	NR	1	0	0	0	0	0	0	0	29	0	0	58	0
Lifetime		1	0	0	0	0	0	0	0	29	0	0	58	$0

Bobby Fisher

Robert D. Fisher
Racing Hometown: Vero Beach, FL

Year	Rank	Starts	Poles	1	2	3	4	5	6–10	Laps	Laps Led	Races Led	Miles	$
1978	109	2	0	0	0	0	0	0	0	33	0	0	22	1,410
1979	116T	1	0	0	0	0	0	0	0	136	0	0	204	1,465
Lifetime		3	0	0	0	0	0	0	0	169	0	0	226	$2,875

Cal Fisher

Cal Fisher
Racing Hometown: Lexington, NE

Year	Rank	Starts	Poles	1	2	3	4	5	6–10	Laps	Laps Led	Races Led	Miles	$
1951	N/A	1	0	0	0	0	0	0	0		0	0		25
Lifetime		1	0	0	0	0	0	0	0		0	0		$25

Jack Fisher

Jack Fisher
Racing Hometown: Moline, IL

Year	Rank	Starts	Poles	1	2	3	4	5	6–10	Laps	Laps Led	Races Led	Miles	$
1952	111	2	0	0	0	0	0	0	0	307	0	0	307	60
Lifetime		2	0	0	0	0	0	0	0	307	0	0	307	$60

Ken Fisher

Kenneth Fisher
Racing Hometown: Hamburg, NY

Year	Rank	Starts	Poles	1	2	3	4	5	6–10	Laps	Laps Led	Races Led	Miles	$
1954	44	5	0	0	0	0	0	0	1	879	0	0	657	400
1955	73	9	0	0	0	0	0	0	1	453	0	0	287	175
Lifetime		14	0	0	0	0	0	0	2	1,332	0	0	944	$575

Year	Rank	Starts	Poles	Finish 1	2	3	4	5	6–10	Laps	Laps Led	Races Led	Miles	$

Terry Fisher

Terry Fisher
B: 5/24/1962
Racing Hometown: Sandy, OR

Year	Rank	Starts	Poles	1	2	3	4	5	6–10	Laps	Laps Led	Races Led	Miles	$
1989	79	1	0	0	0	0	0	0	0	72	0	0	181	2,825
1990	72	1	0	0	0	0	0	0	0	74	0	0	186	4,575
1993	83T	1	0	0	0	0	0	0	0	132	0	0	132	6,040
1995	67	1	0	0	0	0	0	0	0	57	0	0	144	9,760
Lifetime		4	0	0	0	0	0	0	0	335	0	0	644	$23,200

Woody Fisher

Woodrow Fisher
Racing Hometown: Ormond Beach, FL

Year	Rank	Starts	Poles	1	2	3	4	5	6–10	Laps	Laps Led	Races Led	Miles	$
1978	66	3	0	0	0	0	0	0	0	383	0	0	510	4,135
Lifetime		3	0	0	0	0	0	0	0	383	0	0	510	$4,135

John Fite

John Fite
Racing Hometown: Liberty, SC

Year	Rank	Starts	Poles	1	2	3	4	5	6–10	Laps	Laps Led	Races Led	Miles	$
1956	152	3	0	0	0	0	0	0	0	388	0	0	218	200
Lifetime		3	0	0	0	0	0	0	0	388	0	0	218	$200

Christian Fittipaldi

Christian Fittipaldi
B: 1/18/1971
Racing Hometown: Sao Paulo, Brazil

Year	Rank	Starts	Poles	1	2	3	4	5	6–10	Laps	Laps Led	Races Led	Miles	$
2002	79T	1	0	0	0	0	0	0	0	252	0	0	252	39,600
Lifetime		1	0	0	0	0	0	0	0	252	0	0	252	$39,600

Jim Fitzgerald

James Fitzgerald
B: 12/1/1921   D: 11/8/1987   *Killed in Trans-Am race, St. Petersburg, FL.*
Racing Hometown: Pittsburgh, PA

Year	Rank	Starts	Poles	1	2	3	4	5	6–10	Laps	Laps Led	Races Led	Miles	$
1986	120	1	0	0	0	0	0	0	0	28	0	0	73	925
1987	77	1	0	0	0	0	0	0	0	93	0	0	244	1,675
Lifetime		2	0	0	0	0	0	0	0	121	0	0	317	$2,600

Pat Flaherty

George Francis Patrick Flaherty
B: 1/6/1926   D: 4/9/2002
Racing Hometown: Chicago, IL

Year	Rank	Starts	Poles	1	2	3	4	5	6–10	Laps	Laps Led	Races Led	Miles	$
1951	N/A	1	0	0	0	0	0	0	0	13	0	0	13	0
Lifetime		1	0	0	0	0	0	0	0	13	0	0	13	$0

Walt Flanders

Walter Flanders
Racing Hometown: Detroit, MI

Year	Rank	Starts	Poles	1	2	3	4	5	6–10	Laps	Laps Led	Races Led	Miles	$
1951	N/A	1	0	0	0	0	0	0	0	145	0	0	145	10
Lifetime		1	0	0	0	0	0	0	0	145	0	0	145	$10

Bill Flatcher

William Flatcher

Year	Rank	Starts	Poles	1	2	3	4	5	6–10	Laps	Laps Led	Races Led	Miles	$
1951	N/A	1	0	0	0	0	0	0	0		0	0		25
Lifetime		1	0	0	0	0	0	0	0		0	0		$25

Al Fleming

Al Fleming
Racing Hometown: Richmond, VA

Year	Rank	Starts	Poles	1	2	3	4	5	6–10	Laps	Laps Led	Races Led	Miles	$
1952	160	1	0	0	0	0	0	0	0	336	0	0	420	210
Lifetime		1	0	0	0	0	0	0	0	336	0	0	420	$210

Bobby Fleming

Robert Winfield Fleming
B: 3/20/1941
Racing Hometown: Danville, VA

Year	Rank	Starts	Poles	1	2	3	4	5	6–10	Laps	Laps Led	Races Led	Miles	$
1969	NR	1	0	0	0	0	0	0	0	146	0	0	388	1,400
1974	96	2	0	0	0	0	0	0	0	394	0	0	210	1,025
Lifetime		3	0	0	0	0	0	0	0	540	0	0	598	$2,425

Year	Rank	Starts	Poles	Finish						Laps	Laps Led	Races Led	Miles	$
				1	2	3	4	5	6–10					

George Fleming

George Fleming
Racing Hometown: Bristol, PA

Year	Rank	Starts	Poles	1	2	3	4	5	6–10	Laps	Laps Led	Races Led	Miles	$
1952	200	1	0	0	0	0	0	0	0		0	0		0
1953	172	1	0	0	0	0	0	0	0	33	0	0	135	25
1957	NR	1	0	0	0	0	0	0	0	174	0	0	87	135
Lifetime		3	0	0	0	0	0	0	0	207	0	0	222	$160

Jack Fleming

Jack Fleming
Racing Hometown: Panama, NY

Year	Rank	Starts	Poles	1	2	3	4	5	6–10	Laps	Laps Led	Races Led	Miles	$
1951	N/A	1	0	0	0	0	0	0	0		0	0		0
Lifetime		1	0	0	0	0	0	0	0		0	0		$0

Eddie Flemke

Edward A. Flemke
B: 8/12/1930   D: 3/30/1984
Racing Hometown: Ne Brittain, CT

Year	Rank	Starts	Poles	1	2	3	4	5	6–10	Laps	Laps Led	Races Led	Miles	$
1961	120	1	0	0	0	0	0	0	0	231	0	0	58	175
Lifetime		1	0	0	0	0	0	0	0	231	0	0	58	$175

Walt Flinchum

Walter Flinchum
Racing Hometown: Summerfield, NC

Year	Rank	Starts	Poles	1	2	3	4	5	6–10	Laps	Laps Led	Races Led	Miles	$
1954	39	8	0	0	0	0	0	0	2	1,123	0	0	689	425
Lifetime		8	0	0	0	0	0	0	2	1,123	0	0	689	$425

Bob Flock

Robert Newman Flock
B: 4/16/1918   D: 5/16/1964
Racing Hometown: Atlanta, GA

Year	Rank	Starts	Poles	1	2	3	4	5	6–10	Laps	Laps Led	Races Led	Miles	$
1949	3	6	1	2	1	0	0	0	0	728	26	3	574	4,870
1950	20	4	0	0	1	0	0	0	2	595	5	1	781	1,155
1951	14	17	1	1	2	0	1	0	5	978	133	5	877	3,680
1952	73	2	0	1	0	0	0	0	0	538	1	1	523	1,060
1954	NR	2	0	0	0	0	0	0	0	167	0	0	84	25
1955	62	1	0	0	0	0	0	1	0	195	0	0	293	650
1956	77	4	0	0	0	0	0	1	0	442	0	0	397	485
Lifetime		36	2	4	4	0	1	2	7	3,643	165	10	3,526	$11,925

Fonty Flock

Truman Fontello Flock
B: 3/21/1921   D: 7/15/1972
Racing Hometown: Decatur, GA

Year	Rank	Starts	Poles	1	2	3	4	5	6–10	Laps	Laps Led	Races Led	Miles	$
1949	5	6	0	0	1	1	1	0	0	304	85	1	153	2,015
1950	14	7	2	1	0	0	1	0	1	951	369	4	1,077	2,195
1951	2	34	13	8	2	4	5	1	2	2,788	1,503	20	2,068	15,200
1952	4	29	7	2	6	2	2	2	3	3,943	954	10	2,918	19,112
1953	5	33	3	4	5	4	3	1	0	1,999	581	10	1,626	17,756
1954	NR	5	0	0	1	0	0	1	0	657	15	1	425	1,000
1955	11	31	4	3	5	2	0	2	2	3,482	430	7	2,565	13,100
1956	50	7	2	1	0	0	0	0	3	665	134	1	638	1,780
1957	63	2	0	0	0	1	0	0	0	18	0	0	25	1,600
Lifetime		154	31	19	20	14	12	7	11	14,807	4,071	54	11,495	$73,758

Tim Flock

Julius Timothy Flock
B: 5/11/1924   D: 3/31/1998
Racing Hometown: Atlanta, GA

Year	Rank	Starts	Poles	1	2	3	4	5	6–10	Laps	Laps Led	Races Led	Miles	$
1949	8	5	0	0	1	0	0	1	1	347	0	0	415	1,510
1950	16	13	1	1	0	0	3	0	3	1,403	190	2	1,275	3,980
1951	3	30	6	7	5	3	3	1	2	2,259	681	13	1,661	14,545
1952	1	33	4	8	5	2	7	0	3	5,345	1,164	15	3,564	22,890
1953	6	26	5	1	1	2	3	4	7	1,990	289	8	1,774	8,282
1954	35	5	1	0	1	0	0	0	2	800	180	1	791	1,050
1955	1	39	20	18	5	5	1	3	1	6,208	3,368	33	4,556	37,780
1956	9	22	5	4	1	3	2	1	3	3,076	445	9	2,696	15,769
1957	93	1	0	0	0	0	0	0	0		0	0		135
1958	NR	3	0	0	0	0	0	0	0	167	25	1	176	410
1959	31	2	0	0	0	0	0	0	1	223	0	0	558	850

Year	Rank	Starts	Poles	Finish						Laps	Laps Led	Races Led	Miles	$
				1	2	3	4	5	6–10					

Tim Flock *continued*

Year	Rank	Starts	Poles	1	2	3	4	5	6–10	Laps	Laps Led	Races Led	Miles	$
1960	63	2	0	0	0	0	0	0	1	235	0	0	348	850
1961	NR	7	0	0	0	0	0	0	3	1,227	0	0	1,398	1,605
Lifetime		188	42	39	19	15	19	10	27	23,280	6,342	82	19,211	$109,656

Jimmy Florian

James Frank Florian
  B: 9/25/1923
    Racing Hometown: Cleveland, OH

Year	Rank	Starts	Poles	1	2	3	4	5	6–10	Laps	Laps Led	Races Led	Miles	$
1950	9	10	1	1	0	1	1	0	3	1,060	40	1	850	2,730
1951	27	9	0	0	0	0	2	0	3		0	0		1,100
1952	48	6	0	0	0	0	0	0	2	283	0	0	188	175
1954	NR	1	0	0	0	0	0	0	0	34	0	0	139	25
Lifetime		26	1	1	0	1	3	0	8	1,377	40	1	1,178	$4,030

Bill Flowers

William Flowers
  B: 3/3/1959
    Racing Hometown: Power Springs, GA

Year	Rank	Starts	Poles	1	2	3	4	5	6–10	Laps	Laps Led	Races Led	Miles	$
1989	96T	1	0	0	0	0	0	0	0	2	0	0	2	1,800
Lifetime		1	0	0	0	0	0	0	0	2	0	0	2	$1,800

Jack Flynn

Jack Flynn

Year	Rank	Starts	Poles	1	2	3	4	5	6–10	Laps	Laps Led	Races Led	Miles	$
1951	80	2	0	0	0	0	0	0	1		0	0		225
Lifetime		2	0	0	0	0	0	0	1		0	0		$225

Larry Flynn

Lawrence Flynn
  Racing Hometown: Holly Hill, FL

Year	Rank	Starts	Poles	1	2	3	4	5	6–10	Laps	Laps Led	Races Led	Miles	$
1955	28	1	0	0	0	0	0	1	0	359	0	0	494	1,175
1956	153	2	0	0	0	0	0	0	0	402	0	0	395	250
1959	53	4	0	0	0	0	0	0	0	206	0	0	283	275
1961	101	1	0	0	0	0	0	0	0	195	0	0	268	200
Lifetime		8	0	0	0	0	0	1	0	1,162	0	0	1,440	$1,900

Sonny Fogle

Samuel Fogle
  Racing Hometown: Columbia, SC

Year	Rank	Starts	Poles	1	2	3	4	5	6–10	Laps	Laps Led	Races Led	Miles	$
1963	66	8	0	0	0	0	0	0	0	779	0	0	382	600
Lifetime		8	0	0	0	0	0	0	0	779	0	0	382	$600

Dick Foley

Richard A. Foley Jr.
  Racing Hometown: Montreal, Que, Canada

Year	Rank	Starts	Poles	1	2	3	4	5	6–10	Laps	Laps Led	Races Led	Miles	$
1957	186	1	0	0	0	0	0	0	0		0	0		0
1958	111	1	0	0	0	0	0	0	0	34	0	0	139	75
1959	55	3	0	0	0	0	0	0	0	226	0	0	565	250
1960	101	2	0	0	0	0	0	0	0	69	0	0	173	325
Lifetime		7	0	0	0	0	0	0	0	329	0	0	877	$650

George Follmer

George Follmer
  B: 1/27/1934
    Racing Hometown: Arcadia, CA

Year	Rank	Starts	Poles	1	2	3	4	5	6–10	Laps	Laps Led	Races Led	Miles	$
1972	120	1	0	0	0	0	0	0	0	4	0	0	10	1,440
1974	29	13	1	0	0	0	1	2	2	3,086	27	2	3,748	53,780
1975	75	2	0	0	0	0	0	0	0	105	0	0	267	2,370
1986	76	2	0	0	0	0	0	0	0	130	0	0	326	3,885
1987	69	2	0	0	0	0	0	0	0	122	8	1	320	2,880
Lifetime		20	1	0	0	0	1	2	2	3,447	35	3	4,670	$64,355

Ronnie Fones

Ralston Fones
  Racing Hometown: Landover, MD

Year	Rank	Starts	Poles	1	2	3	4	5	6–10	Laps	Laps Led	Races Led	Miles	$
1961	144	2	0	0	0	0	0	0	0	217	0	0	75	185
1962	88T	2	0	0	0	0	0	0	0	434	0	0	145	200
Lifetime		4	0	0	0	0	0	0	0	651	0	0	219	$385

Red Foote

Melvin K. Foote
B: 11/27/1927
Racing Hometown: Southington, CT

Year	Rank	Starts	Poles	1	2	3	4	5	6–10	Laps	Laps Led	Races Led	Miles	$
1962	44	4	0	0	0	0	0	0	0	939	0	0	1,367	1,600
1963	80	3	0	0	0	0	0	0	0	316	0	0	625	950
1965	134	3	0	0	0	0	0	0	0	181	0	0	88	420
Lifetime		10	0	0	0	0	0	0	0	1,436	0	0	2,080	$2,970

Elliott Forbes-Robinson

Elliott Forbes-Robinson
B: 10/31/1943
Racing Hometown: LaCresenta, CA

Year	Rank	Starts	Poles	1	2	3	4	5	6–10	Laps	Laps Led	Races Led	Miles	$
1977	67	3	0	0	0	0	0	0	0	571	0	0	716	3,575
1981	35	11	0	0	0	0	0	0	3	2,169	0	0	3,495	27,350
1982	68	2	0	0	0	0	0	0	0	174	0	0	447	7,985
1983	101T	1	0	0	0	0	0	0	0	36	0	0	90	5,550
1984	45	5	0	0	0	0	0	0	0	895	0	0	1,513	11,335
Lifetime		22	0	0	0	0	0	0	3	3,845	0	0	6,261	$55,795

Henry Ford

Henry Ford
Racing Hometown: Memphis, TN

Year	Rank	Starts	Poles	1	2	3	4	5	6–10	Laps	Laps Led	Races Led	Miles	$
1955	66	5	0	0	0	0	0	0	0	579	0	0	336	190
Lifetime		5	0	0	0	0	0	0	0	579	0	0	336	$190

John Ford

John Ford
Racing Hometown: Harrisburg, PA

Year	Rank	Starts	Poles	1	2	3	4	5	6–10	Laps	Laps Led	Races Led	Miles	$
1954	183	1	0	0	0	0	0	0	0	198	0	0	198	50
Lifetime		1	0	0	0	0	0	0	0	198	0	0	198	$50

Nick Fornoro

Nofri Samuel Fornoro
B: 10/23/1920
Racing Hometown: Danbury, CT

Year	Rank	Starts	Poles	1	2	3	4	5	6–10	Laps	Laps Led	Races Led	Miles	$
1953	NR	1	0	0	0	0	0	0	1	181	0	0	181	200
Lifetime		1	0	0	0	0	0	0	1	181	0	0	181	$200

Roy Forsythe

Roy Forsythe

Year	Rank	Starts	Poles	1	2	3	4	5	6–10	Laps	Laps Led	Races Led	Miles	$
1951	N/A	1	0	0	0	0	0	0	0		0	0		25
Lifetime		1	0	0	0	0	0	0	0		0	0		$25

Curt Foss

Curt Foss
Racing Hometown: South Wales, NY

Year	Rank	Starts	Poles	1	2	3	4	5	6–10	Laps	Laps Led	Races Led	Miles	$
1949	NR	1	0	0	0	0	0	0	0	68	0	0	34	0
1950	129T	1	0	0	0	0	0	0	0	158	0	0	79	0
Lifetime		2	0	0	0	0	0	0	0	226	0	0	113	$0

Bill Foster

William Foster
B: 9/15/1934
Racing Hometown: High Point, NC

Year	Rank	Starts	Poles	1	2	3	4	5	6–10	Laps	Laps Led	Races Led	Miles	$
1961	170	1	0	0	0	0	0	0	0	61	0	0	61	25
1962	68	5	0	0	0	0	0	0	1	1,230	0	0	740	800
1963	49	10	0	0	0	0	0	0	2	1,628	0	0	1,049	1,410
Lifetime		16	0	0	0	0	0	0	3	2,919	0	0	1,850	$2,235

Billy Foster

William Foster
B: 9/18/1937 D: 1/20/1967 *Killed in practice for NASCAR Riverside race after earning the 9th starting position.*
Racing Hometown: Victoria, B.C., Canada

Year	Rank	Starts	Poles	1	2	3	4	5	6–10	Laps	Laps Led	Races Led	Miles	$
1966	NR	1	0	0	0	0	0	0	1	181	0	0	489	1,275
Lifetime		1	0	0	0	0	0	0	1	181	0	0	489	$1,275

Year	Rank	Starts	Poles	Finish						Laps	Laps Led	Races Led	Miles	$
				1	2	3	4	5	6–10					

Earl Foushee

Earl Foushee
  Racing Hometown: Durham, NC

Year	Rank	Starts	Poles	1	2	3	4	5	6–10	Laps	Laps Led	Races Led	Miles	$
1953	160	1	0	0	0	0	0	0	0	256	0	0	256	50
Lifetime		1	0	0	0	0	0	0	0	256	0	0	256	$50

Bobby Fox

Robert Fox
  B: 3/12/1948
  Racing Hometown: Bremerton, WA

Year	Rank	Starts	Poles	1	2	3	4	5	6–10	Laps	Laps Led	Races Led	Miles	$
1984	79	1	0	0	0	0	0	0	0	352	0	0	358	1,495
Lifetime		1	0	0	0	0	0	0	0	352	0	0	358	$1,495

George Fox

George Fox
  Racing Hometown: Wilkesboro, NC

Year	Rank	Starts	Poles	1	2	3	4	5	6–10	Laps	Laps Led	Races Led	Miles	$
1962	138	1	0	0	0	0	0	0	0	3	0	0	2	50
Lifetime		1	0	0	0	0	0	0	0	3	0	0	2	$50

Jackie Fox

Jack Fox
  Racing Hometown: Asheville, NC

Year	Rank	Starts	Poles	1	2	3	4	5	6–10	Laps	Laps Led	Races Led	Miles	$
1967	120	2	0	0	0	0	0	0	0	57	0	0	23	0
Lifetime		2	0	0	0	0	0	0	0	57	0	0	23	$0

Jim Fox

James Fox
  Racing Hometown: Rochester, NY

Year	Rank	Starts	Poles	1	2	3	4	5	6–10	Laps	Laps Led	Races Led	Miles	$
1953	NR	1	0	0	0	0	0	0	0		0	0		25
Lifetime		1	0	0	0	0	0	0	0		0	0		$25

Leon Fox

Leon Fox
  B: 12/17/1937
  Racing Hometown: Bremerton, WA

Year	Rank	Starts	Poles	1	2	3	4	5	6–10	Laps	Laps Led	Races Led	Miles	$
1973	96	1	0	0	0	0	0	0	0	139	0	0	364	925
1974	112	1	0	0	0	0	0	0	0	113	0	0	296	1,210
Lifetime		2	0	0	0	0	0	0	0	252	0	0	660	$2,135

Stan Fox

Stan Fox (Real Name: Stanley Cole Fuchs)
  B: 7/7/1952   D: 12/18/2000   Killed in highway accident in Australia.
  Racing Hometown: Janesville, WI

Year	Rank	Starts	Poles	1	2	3	4	5	6–10	Laps	Laps Led	Races Led	Miles	$
1992	68	2	0	0	0	0	0	0	0	146	0	0	359	11,750
Lifetime		2	0	0	0	0	0	0	0	146	0	0	359	$11,750

A.J. Foyt

Anthony Joseph Foyt Jr.
  B: 1/16/1935
  Racing Hometown: Houston, TX

Year	Rank	Starts	Poles	1	2	3	4	5	6–10	Laps	Laps Led	Races Led	Miles	$
1963	NR	5	0	0	1	1	0	0	0	639	64	3	1,509	8,850
1964	NR	6	0	1	0	0	1	0	0	851	16	2	1,785	15,950
1965	NR	4	0	1	0	0	0	0	2	685	161	3	1,390	12,040
1966	NR	4	0	0	0	0	0	0	0	141	0	0	350	2,390
1967	NR	7	0	0	1	0	1	0	0	1,060	57	5	1,534	8,035
1968	NR	4	0	0	0	0	0	0	1	572	0	0	1,105	4,975
1969	NR	4	1	0	1	0	2	0	0	522	63	2	1,254	17,375
1970	NR	3	0	1	0	0	0	0	0	298	35	1	768	21,210
1971	NR	7	4	2	1	1	0	0	0	1,134	392	4	2,124	88,574
1972	NR	6	3	2	2	0	1	0	0	1,417	344	6	2,778	101,340
1973	NR	3	0	0	0	0	1	0	0	467	0	0	947	8,555
1974	44	4	0	0	0	0	1	1	0	612	70	3	1,360	15,560
1975	NR	7	0	0	0	0	0	1	0	1,420	186	5	2,462	18,055
1976	NR	5	1	0	0	0	1	0	0	581	79	3	1,335	15,610
1977	NR	6	1	0	0	0	0	1	2	1,058	20	3	2,165	29,200
1978	NR	2	0	0	0	1	0	0	0	255	0	0	667	24,875
1979	NR	2	0	0	0	1	0	0	1	356	7	2	890	41,690
1980	101	1	0	0	0	0	0	0	0	69	0	0	173	3,575
1981	59	3	0	0	0	0	0	0	1	530	0	0	1,007	9,210

Year	Rank	Starts	Poles	Finish						Laps	Laps Led	Races Led	Miles	$
				1	2	3	4	5	6–10	Laps	Led	Led	Miles	$

A.J. Foyt *continued*

Year	Rank	Starts	Poles	1	2	3	4	5	6–10	Laps	Laps Led	Races Led	Miles	$
1982	70	2	0	0	0	0	0	0	0	162	0	0	388	9,405
1983	76	3	0	0	0	0	0	0	0	406	0	0	890	22,935
1984	76	3	0	0	0	0	0	0	0	224	0	0	418	8,830
1985	45	7	0	0	0	0	0	1	0	966	2	2	1,781	29,750
1986	50	5	0	0	0	0	0	0	0	640	1	1	1,220	24,135
1987	49	6	0	0	0	0	0	0	0	748	2	2	1,274	21,075
1988	42	7	0	0	0	0	0	0	0	920	9	3	1,992	29,660
1989	40	7	0	0	0	0	0	0	0	860	6	2	1,869	31,995
1990	62	3	0	0	0	0	0	0	0	301	4	1	782	26,725
1992	70	1	0	0	0	0	0	0	0	195	0	0	488	23,055
1994	70T	1	0	0	0	0	0	0	0	156	0	0	390	29,000
Lifetime		128	10	7	6	4	8	4	7	18,245	1,518	53	37,097	$703,634

Len Fraker

Leon Fraker
Racing Hometown: Puente, CA

Year	Rank	Starts	Poles	1	2	3	4	5	6–10	Laps	Laps Led	Races Led	Miles	$
1956	NR	1	0	0	0	0	0	0	0	10	0	0	25	30
Lifetime		1	0	0	0	0	0	0	0	10	0	0	25	$30

Glenn Francis

Glenn Francis
B: 5/22/1942
Racing Hometown: Bakersfield, CA

Year	Rank	Starts	Poles	1	2	3	4	5	6–10	Laps	Laps Led	Races Led	Miles	$
1970	NR	1	0	0	0	0	0	0	0	95	0	0	249	805
1971	NR	1	0	0	0	0	0	0	0	27	0	0	71	1,015
Lifetime		2	0	0	0	0	0	0	0	122	0	0	320	$1,820

Tom Francis

Thomas Francis

Year	Rank	Starts	Poles	1	2	3	4	5	6–10	Laps	Laps Led	Races Led	Miles	$
1955	146	1	0	0	0	0	0	0	0	95	0	0	95	90
1956	287	1	0	0	0	0	0	0	0	68	0	0	170	40
Lifetime		2	0	0	0	0	0	0	0	163	0	0	265	$130

Bob Francy

Robert Francy
Racing Hometown: Phoenix, AZ

Year	Rank	Starts	Poles	1	2	3	4	5	6–10	Laps	Laps Led	Races Led	Miles	$
1956	246T	1	0	0	0	0	0	0	0	91	0	0	46	0
Lifetime		1	0	0	0	0	0	0	0	91	0	0	46	$0

Larry Frank

Larry S. Frank
B: 4/29/1931
Racing Hometown: Indianapolis, IN

Year	Rank	Starts	Poles	1	2	3	4	5	6–10	Laps	Laps Led	Races Led	Miles	$
1956	NR	1	0	0	0	0	0	0	0	77	0	0	39	50
1957	NR	4	0	0	0	0	0	0	0	1,113	0	0	935	995
1958	137	11	0	0	0	1	0	0	3	2,099	0	0	1,259	2,590
1959	22	15	0	0	1	0	1	2	5	3,300	39	1	2,647	5,993
1960	34	11	0	0	0	0	0	0	2	1,984	11	1	2,408	2,440
1961	42	8	0	0	0	0	0	0	1	978	0	0	1,585	2,380
1962	14	19	0	1	0	0	0	1	6	3,566	85	1	3,506	32,987
1963	28	11	0	0	0	1	1	0	0	2,392	5	1	2,735	5,450
1964	24	12	0	0	0	0	0	0	3	1,483	0	0	2,366	7,830
1965	53	9	0	0	0	0	1	0	0	1,009	33	1	1,200	5,080
1966	50	2	0	0	0	0	0	0	2	232	0	0	580	1,575
Lifetime		103	0	1	1	2	3	3	22	18,233	173	5	19,259	$67,370

Allen Franklin

Allen Franklin
Racing Hometown: Skygusty, WV

Year	Rank	Starts	Poles	1	2	3	4	5	6–10	Laps	Laps Led	Races Led	Miles	$
1961	173	2	0	0	0	0	0	0	0	8	0	0	4	225
Lifetime		2	0	0	0	0	0	0	0	8	0	0	4	$225

Ray Franklin

Raymond Franklin
Racing Hometown: Hawthorne, CA

Year	Rank	Starts	Poles	1	2	3	4	5	6–10	Laps	Laps Led	Races Led	Miles	$
1957	173	1	0	0	0	0	0	0	0	42	0	0	105	60
Lifetime		1	0	0	0	0	0	0	0	42	0	0	105	$60

Year	Rank	Starts	Poles	1	2	3	4	5	6–10	Laps	Laps Led	Races Led	Miles	$

Joe Frasson

Joseph R. Frasson
B: 9/3/1935
Racing Hometown: Golden Valley, MN

Year	Rank	Starts	Poles	1	2	3	4	5	6–10	Laps	Laps Led	Races Led	Miles	$
1969	NR	1	0	0	0	0	0	0	0	3	0	0	8	825
1970	22	21	0	0	0	0	0	0	2	4,866	0	0	6,230	20,172
1971	25	17	0	0	0	0	0	1	3	3,752	0	0	5,699	20,975
1972	28	16	0	0	0	1	0	0	3	3,013	9	2	4,638	21,570
1973	29	14	0	0	0	1	1	0	2	2,732	1	1	4,390	25,884
1974	28	14	0	0	0	0	0	0	3	2,141	13	3	3,671	22,629
1975	35	9	0	0	0	0	0	0	1	1,352	1	1	2,018	11,975
1976	39	9	0	0	0	0	0	0	1	863	1	1	1,510	12,075
1977	93T	1	0	0	0	0	0	0	0	126	0	0	335	2,050
1978	45	5	0	0	0	0	0	0	0	1,436	0	0	1,878	9,210
Lifetime		107	0	0	0	2	1	1	15	20,284	25	8	30,379	$147,365

Pete Frazee

Peter Frazee
B: 11/2/1926
Racing Hometown: Rahway, N J

Year	Rank	Starts	Poles	1	2	3	4	5	6–10	Laps	Laps Led	Races Led	Miles	$
1958	66	2	0	0	0	0	0	0	0	517	0	0	432	310
Lifetime		2	0	0	0	0	0	0	0	517	0	0	432	$310

Fred Frazier

Fred Frazier
Racing Hometown: Weldon, NC

Year	Rank	Starts	Poles	1	2	3	4	5	6–10	Laps	Laps Led	Races Led	Miles	$
1956	130T	2	0	0	0	0	0	0	1	288	0	0	144	200
Lifetime		2	0	0	0	0	0	0	1	288	0	0	144	$200

Dick Freeman

Richard Freeman
B: 1931
Racing Hometown: Dayton, OH

Year	Rank	Starts	Poles	1	2	3	4	5	6–10	Laps	Laps Led	Races Led	Miles	$
1954	NR	1	0	0	0	0	0	0	0	20	0	0	10	0
1959	35	3	0	0	0	0	0	0	0	695	0	0	800	475
1960	124	2	0	0	0	0	0	0	0	41	0	0	103	250
Lifetime		6	0	0	0	0	0	0	0	756	0	0	912	$725

Doug French

Douglas French
B: 5/16/1959
Racing Hometown: Howell, NJ

Year	Rank	Starts	Poles	1	2	3	4	5	6–10	Laps	Laps Led	Races Led	Miles	$
1987	87	1	0	0	0	0	0	0	0	75	0	0	41	895
Lifetime		1	0	0	0	0	0	0	0	75	0	0	41	$895

Jim Frey

James Frey

Year	Rank	Starts	Poles	1	2	3	4	5	6–10	Laps	Laps Led	Races Led	Miles	$
1954	NR	1	0	0	0	0	0	0	0	52	0	0	33	0
Lifetime		1	0	0	0	0	0	0	0	52	0	0	33	$0

Lamoine Frey

Lamoine Frey

Year	Rank	Starts	Poles	1	2	3	4	5	6–10	Laps	Laps Led	Races Led	Miles	$
1957	85	1	0	0	0	0	0	0	1	191	0	0	96	200
Lifetime		1	0	0	0	0	0	0	1	191	0	0	96	$200

Billy Fritts

Williamy Fritts
Racing Hometown: Chester, NJ

Year	Rank	Starts	Poles	1	2	3	4	5	6–10	Laps	Laps Led	Races Led	Miles	$
1953	122T	1	0	0	0	0	0	0	0		0	0		25
Lifetime		1	0	0	0	0	0	0	0		0	0		$25

Ted Fritz

Theodore Fritz
B: 5/13/1936
Racing Hometown: Modesto, CA

Year	Rank	Starts	Poles	1	2	3	4	5	6–10	Laps	Laps Led	Races Led	Miles	$
1975	109T	1	0	0	0	0	0	0	0	10	0	0	26	620
Lifetime		1	0	0	0	0	0	0	0	10	0	0	26	$620

Year	Rank	Starts	Poles	Finish 1	2	3	4	5	6–10	Laps	Laps Led	Races Led	Miles	$

Steve Froines

Steve Froines
Racing Hometown: Lafayette, CA

Year	Rank	Starts	Poles	1	2	3	4	5	6–10	Laps	Laps Led	Races Led	Miles	$
1970	88	2	0	0	0	0	0	0	0	86	0	0	225	1,520
Lifetime		2	0	0	0	0	0	0	0	86	0	0	225	$1,520

Dudley Froy

Dudley Froy
Racing Hometown: Tucson, AZ

Year	Rank	Starts	Poles	1	2	3	4	5	6–10	Laps	Laps Led	Races Led	Miles	$
1951	N/A	2	0	0	0	0	0	0	0		0	0		50
Lifetime		2	0	0	0	0	0	0	0		0	0		$50

Herb Fry

Herbert Fry
Racing Hometown: Wayne, WV

Year	Rank	Starts	Poles	1	2	3	4	5	6–10	Laps	Laps Led	Races Led	Miles	$
1952	94	1	0	0	0	0	0	0	0	366	0	0	458	95
Lifetime		1	0	0	0	0	0	0	0	366	0	0	458	$95

Freddy Fryar

Freddy George Fryar
B: 2/15/1936
Racing Hometown: Baton Rouge, LA

Year	Rank	Starts	Poles	1	2	3	4	5	6–10	Laps	Laps Led	Races Led	Miles	$
1956	209T	1	0	0	0	0	0	0	0	183	0	0	92	100
1959	NR	1	0	0	0	0	0	0	0	53	0	0	27	0
1961	168	1	0	0	0	0	0	0	0	116	0	0	174	200
1970	68	1	0	0	0	0	0	0	1	182	0	0	484	3,000
1971	NR	2	0	0	0	0	0	0	0	238	0	0	595	2,010
Lifetime		6	0	0	0	0	0	0	1	772	0	0	1,371	$5,310

Harold Fryar

Harold Fryar
Racing Hometown: Chattanooga, TN

Year	Rank	Starts	Poles	1	2	3	4	5	6–10	Laps	Laps Led	Races Led	Miles	$
1962	110T	1	0	0	0	0	0	0	0	187	0	0	62	110
Lifetime		1	0	0	0	0	0	0	0	187	0	0	62	$110

George Tet

George Tet
B: 4/1/1923
Racing Hometown: Ozone Park, NY

Year	Rank	Starts	Poles	1	2	3	4	5	6–10	Laps	Laps Led	Races Led	Miles	$
1960	NR	1	0	0	0	0	0	0	0	171	0	0	257	200
1961	NR	2	0	0	0	0	0	0	0	60	0	0	150	250
Lifetime		3	0	0	0	0	0	0	0	231	0	0	407	$450

Stan Fox

Stanley Cole Fuchs
B: 7/7/1952   *Killed in highway accident.*
Racing Hometown: Janesville, WI

Year	Rank	Starts	Poles	1	2	3	4	5	6–10	Laps	Laps Led	Races Led	Miles	$
1992	68	2	0	0	0	0	0	0	0	146	0	0	359	11,750
Lifetime		2	0	0	0	0	0	0	0	146	0	0	359	$11,750

Hideo Fukuyama

Hideo Fukuyama
B: 8/13/1955
Racing Hometown: Suzuka City, Japan

Year	Rank	Starts	Poles	1	2	3	4	5	6–10	Laps	Laps Led	Races Led	Miles	$
2002	73	2	0	0	0	0	0	0	0	643	0	0	453	79,005
Lifetime		2	0	0	0	0	0	0	0	643	0	0	453	$79,005

Dusty Fuller

Dusty Fuller

Year	Rank	Starts	Poles	1	2	3	4	5	6–10	Laps	Laps Led	Races Led	Miles	$
1955	NR	1	0	0	0	0	0	0	0	197	0	0	197	40
Lifetime		1	0	0	0	0	0	0	0	197	0	0	197	$40

Jeff Fuller

Jeffrey Carl Fuller
B: 3/27/1957
Racing Hometown: Auburn, MA

Year	Rank	Starts	Poles	1	2	3	4	5	6–10	Laps	Laps Led	Races Led	Miles	$
1992	77T	1	0	0	0	0	0	0	0	386	0	0	290	4,000
2000	53	7	0	0	0	0	0	0	0	1,798	1	1	2,116	208,720
Lifetime		8	0	0	0	0	0	0	0	2,184	1	1	2,406	$212,720

Year	Rank	Starts	Poles	Finish						Laps	Laps Led	Races Led	Miles	$
				1	2	3	4	5	6–10					

Buck Fulp

John Fulp
B: 1938
Racing Hometown: Anderson, SC

Year	Rank	Starts	Poles	1	2	3	4	5	6–10	Laps	Laps Led	Races Led	Miles	$
1961	122	1	0	0	0	0	0	0	1	65	0	0	98	175
Lifetime		1	0	0	0	0	0	0	1	65	0	0	98	$175

Al Funderburk

Alfred W. Funderburk
D: 2/21/1997
Racing Hometown: Tampa, FL

Year	Rank	Starts	Poles	1	2	3	4	5	6–10	Laps	Laps Led	Races Led	Miles	$
1952	NR	1	0	0	0	0	0	0	1		0	0		50
Lifetime		1	0	0	0	0	0	0	1		0	0		$50

Troy Funk

Troy Funk

Year	Rank	Starts	Poles	1	2	3	4	5	6–10	Laps	Laps Led	Races Led	Miles	$
1958	148	1	0	0	0	0	0	0	0	64	0	0	32	50
Lifetime		1	0	0	0	0	0	0	0	64	0	0	32	$50

Niles Gage

Niles Henry Gage Jr.
B: 11/23/1934
Racing Hometown: Milton, ME

Year	Rank	Starts	Poles	1	2	3	4	5	6–10	Laps	Laps Led	Races Led	Miles	$
1968	117	1	0	0	0	0	0	0	0	274	0	0	91	155
Lifetime		1	0	0	0	0	0	0	0	274	0	0	91	$155

Ernie Gahan

Ernest E. Gahan
B: 10/12/1926
Racing Hometown: Dover, NH

Year	Rank	Starts	Poles	1	2	3	4	5	6–10	Laps	Laps Led	Races Led	Miles	$
1960	46	2	0	0	0	0	0	0	0	818	0	0	759	625
1961	90	5	0	0	0	0	0	0	1	707	0	0	348	750
1962	45	3	0	0	0	0	0	0	1	284	0	0	604	725
1966	119T	1	0	0	0	0	0	0	0	114	0	0	38	115
Lifetime		11	0	0	0	0	0	0	2	1,923	0	0	1,749	$2,215

Harry Gailey

James Harry Gailey
B: 2/24/1936
Racing Hometown: Clermont, GA

Year	Rank	Starts	Poles	1	2	3	4	5	6–10	Laps	Laps Led	Races Led	Miles	$
1971	NR	1	0	0	0	0	0	0	0	141	0	0	375	990
Lifetime		1	0	0	0	0	0	0	0	141	0	0	375	$990

Dexter Gainey

Dexter L. Gainey
B: 11/3/1930
Racing Hometown: Taylors, SC

Year	Rank	Starts	Poles	1	2	3	4	5	6–10	Laps	Laps Led	Races Led	Miles	$
1968	123	2	0	0	0	0	0	0	0	142	0	0	92	650
Lifetime		2	0	0	0	0	0	0	0	142	0	0	92	$650

Bill Galdarisi

William Galdarisi
Racing Hometown: Hermosa Beach, CA

Year	Rank	Starts	Poles	1	2	3	4	5	6–10	Laps	Laps Led	Races Led	Miles	$
1954	110	1	0	0	0	0	0	0	0	445	0	0	223	100
Lifetime		1	0	0	0	0	0	0	0	445	0	0	223	$100

Tommy Gale

Thomas J. Gale
B: 9/10/1934
Racing Hometown: McKeesport, PA

Year	Rank	Starts	Poles	1	2	3	4	5	6–10	Laps	Laps Led	Races Led	Miles	$
1968	NR	1	0	0	0	0	0	0	0	172	0	0	172	760
1969	90	1	0	0	0	0	0	0	0	46	0	0	115	290
1970	52	5	0	0	0	0	0	0	1	391	0	0	659	3,135
1971	41	9	0	0	0	0	0	0	1	1,616	0	0	2,969	8,800
1972	41	6	0	0	0	0	0	0	0	1,144	0	0	1,959	7,197
1973	57	5	0	0	0	0	0	0	0	451	0	0	983	5,680
1975	46	5	0	0	0	0	0	0	0	585	0	0	1,104	6,570
1976	33	12	0	0	0	0	0	0	0	2,205	0	0	3,202	18,965

Year	Rank	Starts	Poles	Finish 1	2	3	4	5	6–10	Laps	Laps Led	Races Led	Miles	$

Tommy Gale *continued*

Year	Rank	Starts	Poles	1	2	3	4	5	6–10	Laps	Laps Led	Races Led	Miles	$
1977	26	18	0	0	0	0	0	0	0	4,493	0	0	6,163	39,190
1978	20	26	0	0	0	0	0	0	0	6,980	0	0	8,867	60,765
1979	18	27	0	0	0	0	0	0	1	7,054	0	0	8,092	72,809
1980	18	29	0	0	0	0	0	0	0	7,605	0	0	8,813	84,279
1981	15	30	0	0	0	0	0	0	0	9,015	2	1	9,927	110,518
1982	21	26	0	0	0	0	0	0	0	7,566	1	1	8,608	101,485
1983	23	28	0	0	0	0	0	0	1	6,540	0	0	7,815	88,316
1984	33	16	0	0	0	0	0	0	0	4,248	0	0	5,268	69,385
1986	NR	1	0	0	0	0	0	0	0	175	0	0	466	5,845
Lifetime		245	0	0	0	0	0	0	4	60,286	3	2	75,180	$683,989

Homer Galloway

Homer Galloway
Racing Hometown: Hartsville, SC

Year	Rank	Starts	Poles	1	2	3	4	5	6–10	Laps	Laps Led	Races Led	Miles	$
1961	140T	1	0	0	0	0	0	0	0	127	0	0	42	110
Lifetime		1	0	0	0	0	0	0	0	127	0	0	42	$110

George Gallup

George L Gallup
D: 1960   *Killed while flagging short track race @ Menands NY (Empire Raceway).*
Racing Hometown: Oneonta, NJ

Year	Rank	Starts	Poles	1	2	3	4	5	6–10	Laps	Laps Led	Races Led	Miles	$
1952	72	4	0	0	0	0	0	0	1	441	13	1	356	175
1953	NR	1	0	0	0	0	0	0	0	36	0	0	148	50
Lifetime		5	0	0	0	0	0	0	1	477	13	1	504	$225

Dan Galullo

Daniel Galullo

Year	Rank	Starts	Poles	1	2	3	4	5	6–10	Laps	Laps Led	Races Led	Miles	$
1956	246T	1	0	0	0	0	0	0	0	34	0	0	17	25
Lifetime		1	0	0	0	0	0	0	0	34	0	0	17	$25

Harry Gant

Harry Phil Gant
B: 1/10/1940
Racing Hometown: Taylorsville, NC

Year	Rank	Starts	Poles	1	2	3	4	5	6–10	Laps	Laps Led	Races Led	Miles	$
1973	85	1	0	0	0	0	0	0	0	307	0	0	461	2,260
1974	64	3	0	0	0	0	0	0	1	790	0	0	846	4,784
1975	105T	1	0	0	0	0	0	0	0	306	0	0	459	1,130
1976	84	1	0	0	0	0	0	0	1	387	0	0	581	5,430
1977	100T	1	0	0	0	0	0	0	0	266	0	0	399	1,460
1978	53	5	0	0	0	0	0	0	1	873	45	1	1,230	14,150
1979	21	25	1	0	0	0	0	0	5	6,226	29	4	7,368	47,185
1980	11	31	0	0	3	2	2	2	5	7,986	263	10	8,774	177,150
1981	3	31	3	0	7	1	4	1	5	9,132	1,169	20	10,284	280,047
1982	4	30	1	2	2	3	1	1	7	8,454	420	17	9,642	337,582
1983	7	30	0	1	1	3	1	4	6	9,024	60	10	10,194	414,353
1984	2	30	3	3	6	0	5	1	8	9,901	1,186	19	11,396	673,060
1985	3	28	3	3	5	3	1	2	5	8,805	1,271	20	10,185	804,287
1986	11	29	2	0	3	1	3	2	4	7,965	656	17	9,565	583,024
1987	22	29	1	0	0	0	0	0	4	6,494	71	3	7,921	197,645
1988	27	24	0	0	0	0	0	0	3	5,896	343	8	6,877	173,325
1989	7	29	0	1	3	1	2	2	5	8,627	439	11	10,295	487,202
1990	17	28	0	1	0	1	1	3	3	7,441	53	9	9,771	522,519
1991	4	29	1	5	2	3	4	1	2	9,428	1,684	17	11,127	1,194,033
1992	4	29	0	2	3	2	0	3	5	9,197	407	15	11,221	1,122,776
1993	11	30	1	0	0	1	2	1	8	8,843	266	8	10,868	772,832
1994	25	30	1	0	0	0	0	0	7	7,347	94	3	9,598	556,020
Lifetime		474	17	18	35	21	26	23	85	133,695	8,456	192	159,060	$8,372,254

Ruben Garcia

Ruben Garcia
B: 4/1/1946
Racing Hometown: South El Monte, CA

Year	Rank	Starts	Poles	1	2	3	4	5	6–10	Laps	Laps Led	Races Led	Miles	$
1984	70	2	0	0	0	0	0	0	0	121	0	0	317	1,885
1985	56	2	0	0	0	0	0	0	0	196	0	0	514	6,525
1986	72	2	0	0	0	0	0	0	0	169	0	0	443	4,530
1987	70	2	0	0	0	0	0	0	0	116	0	0	304	4,180
1988	89T	1	0	0	0	0	0	0	0	27	0	0	71	3,380
Lifetime		9	0	0	0	0	0	0	0	629	0	0	1,648	$20,500

Year	Rank	Starts	Poles	1	2	3	4	5	6–10	Laps	Laps Led	Races Led	Miles	$

Arnold Gardner

Arnold Gardner
B: 12/25/1926   D: 2/10/1994
Racing Hometown: Batavia, IL

Year	Rank	Starts	Poles	1	2	3	4	5	6–10	Laps	Laps Led	Races Led	Miles	$
1960	96	4	0	0	0	0	0	0	0	614	0	0	904	575
Lifetime		4	0	0	0	0	0	0	0	614	0	0	904	$575

Bud Gardner

Bud Gardner

Year	Rank	Starts	Poles	1	2	3	4	5	6–10	Laps	Laps Led	Races Led	Miles	$
1958	NR	1	0	0	0	0	0	0	0	127	0	0	42	100
Lifetime		1	0	0	0	0	0	0	0	127	0	0	42	$100

Frank Gardner

Frank Gardner
Racing Hometown: Sydney, Australia

Year	Rank	Starts	Poles	1	2	3	4	5	6–10	Laps	Laps Led	Races Led	Miles	$
1968	NR	1	0	0	0	0	0	0	0	1	0	0	1	515
Lifetime		1	0	0	0	0	0	0	0	1	0	0	1	$515

Johnny Gardner

John Gardner
Racing Hometown: Rock Hill, SC

Year	Rank	Starts	Poles	1	2	3	4	5	6–10	Laps	Laps Led	Races Led	Miles	$
1958	146	14	0	0	0	0	0	0	0	1,510	0	0	894	780
Lifetime		14	0	0	0	0	0	0	0	1,510	0	0	894	$780

Slick Gardner

Slick Gardner
B: 12/24/1946
Racing Hometown: Buellton, CA

Year	Rank	Starts	Poles	1	2	3	4	5	6–10	Laps	Laps Led	Races Led	Miles	$
1973	126	1	0	0	0	0	0	0	0	9	0	0	24	990
Lifetime		1	0	0	0	0	0	0	0	9	0	0	24	$990

Walson Gardner

William Walson Gardner
B: 8/21/1932
Racing Hometown: Laurinburg, NC

Year	Rank	Starts	Poles	1	2	3	4	5	6–10	Laps	Laps Led	Races Led	Miles	$
1965	107	2	0	0	0	0	0	0	0	61	0	0	31	200
1967	NR	1	0	0	0	0	0	0	0	47	0	0	24	150
1968	40	14	0	0	0	0	0	0	2	3,546	0	0	2,174	4,275
1969	55	7	0	0	0	0	0	0	0	1,299	0	0	650	2,115
Lifetime		24	0	0	0	0	0	0	2	4,953	0	0	2,878	$6,740

Nick Garin

Nick Garin
Racing Hometown: Oakdale, PA

Year	Rank	Starts	Poles	1	2	3	4	5	6–10	Laps	Laps Led	Races Led	Miles	$
1949	62	1	0	0	0	0	0	0	0	142	0	0	71	50
1951	NR	1	0	0	0	0	0	0	0		0	0		0
Lifetime		2	0	0	0	0	0	0	0	142	0	0	71	$50

Dick Garlington

Richard Garlington
Racing Hometown: Atlanta, GA

Year	Rank	Starts	Poles	1	2	3	4	5	6–10	Laps	Laps Led	Races Led	Miles	$
1954	192T	2	0	0	0	0	0	0	0	46	0	0	155	25
Lifetime		2	0	0	0	0	0	0	0	46	0	0	155	$25

Cliff Garner

Clifford Garner
B: 1937
Racing Hometown: Los Angeles, CA

Year	Rank	Starts	Poles	1	2	3	4	5	6–10	Laps	Laps Led	Races Led	Miles	$
1966	88	1	0	0	0	0	0	0	0	98	0	0	265	500
1967	113	1	0	0	0	0	0	0	0	25	0	0	68	500
1969	NR	1	0	0	0	0	0	0	0	48	0	0	130	775
1972	NR	1	0	0	0	0	0	0	0	185	0	0	463	1,495
Lifetime		4	0	0	0	0	0	0	0	356	0	0	924	$3,270

Reitzel Garner

Reitzel Garner
Racing Hometown: Asheboro, NC

Year	Rank	Starts	Poles	1	2	3	4	5	6–10	Laps	Laps Led	Races Led	Miles	$
1956	135	2	0	0	0	0	0	0	0	657	0	0	437	325
Lifetime		2	0	0	0	0	0	0	0	657	0	0	437	$325

Year	Rank	Starts	Poles	Finish 1	2	3	4	5	6–10	Laps	Laps Led	Races Led	Miles	$

Chuck Garrett

Chuck Garrett
Racing Hometown: Sharon, PA

Year	Rank	Starts	Poles	1	2	3	4	5	6–10	Laps	Laps Led	Races Led	Miles	$
1950	62T	1	0	0	0	0	0	0	1		0	0		100
1952	NR	1	0	0	0	0	0	0	0	109	0	0	109	0
1954	NR	1	0	0	0	0	0	0	1	149	0	0	75	200
Lifetime		3	0	0	0	0	0	0	2	258	0	0	184	$300

Steve Garrett

Steve Garrett

Year	Rank	Starts	Poles	1	2	3	4	5	6–10	Laps	Laps Led	Races Led	Miles	$
1962	NR	1	0	0	0	0	0	0	0	40	0	0	10	75
Lifetime		1	0	0	0	0	0	0	0	40	0	0	10	$75

Charles Gattalia

Charles Gattalia
Racing Hometown: New Haven, CT

Year	Rank	Starts	Poles	1	2	3	4	5	6–10	Laps	Laps Led	Races Led	Miles	$
1951	54	6	0	0	1	0	0	0	0		0	0		750
1952	NR	8	0	0	0	0	0	0	3	810	0	0	565	485
Lifetime		14	0	0	1	0	0	0	3	810	0	0	565	$1,235

Louis Gatto

Louis Gatto
Racing Hometown: Bloomfield, NJ

Year	Rank	Starts	Poles	1	2	3	4	5	6–10	Laps	Laps Led	Races Led	Miles	$
1978	102T	1	0	0	0	0	0	0	0	5	0	0	5	500
1979	83	2	0	0	0	0	0	0	0	31	0	0	39	1,445
Lifetime		3	0	0	0	0	0	0	0	36	0	0	44	$1,945

Ron Gautsche

Rolland Gautsche
B: 7/6/1935
Racing Hometown: Truckee, CA

Year	Rank	Starts	Poles	1	2	3	4	5	6–10	Laps	Laps Led	Races Led	Miles	$
1971	NR	3	0	0	0	0	0	0	0	176	0	0	460	2,935
1972	87	2	0	0	0	0	0	0	0	215	0	0	544	2,735
Lifetime		5	0	0	0	0	0	0	0	391	0	0	1,004	$5,670

Scott Gaylord

Scott Gaylord
B: 8/12/1958
Racing Hometown: Lakewood, CO

Year	Rank	Starts	Poles	1	2	3	4	5	6–10	Laps	Laps Led	Races Led	Miles	$
1991	80T	1	0	0	0	0	0	0	0	61	0	0	154	3,625
1992	87T	1	0	0	0	0	0	0	0	124	0	0	124	4,265
1993	74T	1	0	0	0	0	0	0	0	75	0	0	184	5,935
1996	65	1	0	0	0	0	0	0	0	67	0	0	169	10,095
Lifetime		4	0	0	0	0	0	0	0	327	0	0	630	$23,920

Jack Gaynor

Jack Gaynor
Racing Hometown: Los Angeles, CA

Year	Rank	Starts	Poles	1	2	3	4	5	6–10	Laps	Laps Led	Races Led	Miles	$
1951	N/A	1	0	0	0	0	0	0	0		0	0		25
Lifetime		1	0	0	0	0	0	0	0		0	0		$25

Bill Gazaway

William Gazaway
B: 4/13/1935
Racing Hometown: Atlanta, GA

Year	Rank	Starts	Poles	1	2	3	4	5	6–10	Laps	Laps Led	Races Led	Miles	$
1960	NR	1	0	0	0	0	0	0	0	1	0	0	2	200
Lifetime		1	0	0	0	0	0	0	0	1	0	0	2	$200

Bud Geiselman

Bud Geiselman
Racing Hometown: Raleigh, NC

Year	Rank	Starts	Poles	1	2	3	4	5	6–10	Laps	Laps Led	Races Led	Miles	$
1955	206T	1	0	0	0	0	0	0	0	164	0	0	82	50
1956	205	2	0	0	0	0	0	0	0	173	0	0	173	50
Lifetime		3	0	0	0	0	0	0	0	337	0	0	255	$100

Victor Geisler

Victor Geisler
Racing Hometown: Cullman, AL

Year	Rank	Starts	Poles	1	2	3	4	5	6–10	Laps	Laps Led	Races Led	Miles	$
1954	206	1	0	0	0	0	0	0	0	2	0	0	8	0
Lifetime		1	0	0	0	0	0	0	0	2	0	0	8	$0

Year	Rank	Starts	Poles	Finish 1	2	3	4	5	6–10	Laps	Laps Led	Races Led	Miles	$

Roy Gemberling

Roy Gemberling
B: 1923
Racing Hometown: Kent, OH

Year	Rank	Starts	Poles	1	2	3	4	5	6–10	Laps	Laps Led	Races Led	Miles	$
1964	117	1	0	0	0	0	0	0	0	34	0	0	85	100
Lifetime		1	0	0	0	0	0	0	0	34	0	0	85	$100

Russ Gemberling

Russell Gemberling
Racing Hometown: Kent, OH

Year	Rank	Starts	Poles	1	2	3	4	5	6–10	Laps	Laps Led	Races Led	Miles	$
1959	117	1	0	0	0	0	0	0	0	127	3	1	32	85
Lifetime		1	0	0	0	0	0	0	0	127	3	1	32	$85

Tony Genove

Tony Genove

Year	Rank	Starts	Poles	1	2	3	4	5	6–10	Laps	Laps Led	Races Led	Miles	$
1949	NR	1	0	0	0	0	0	0	0		0	0		0
Lifetime		1	0	0	0	0	0	0	0		0	0		$0

J.W. Gentry

J.W. Gentry

Year	Rank	Starts	Poles	1	2	3	4	5	6–10	Laps	Laps Led	Races Led	Miles	$
1953	NR	1	0	0	0	0	0	0	0		0	0		25
Lifetime		1	0	0	0	0	0	0	0		0	0		$25

Doug George

Douglas George
B: 11/5/1960
Racing Hometown: Atwater, CA

Year	Rank	Starts	Poles	1	2	3	4	5	6–10	Laps	Laps Led	Races Led	Miles	$
1995	NR	2	0	0	0	0	0	0	0	251	0	0	362	18,610
Lifetime		2	0	0	0	0	0	0	0	251	0	0	362	$18,610

Benny Georgeson

Benjamin Georgeson
Racing Hometown: Ft. Lauderdale, FL

Year	Rank	Starts	Poles	1	2	3	4	5	6–10	Laps	Laps Led	Races Led	Miles	$
1949	NR	1	0	0	0	0	0	0	0		0	0		0
Lifetime		1	0	0	0	0	0	0	0		0	0		$0

Bobby Gerhart

Robert Gerhart
B: 7/21/1958
Racing Hometown: Lebanon, PA

Year	Rank	Starts	Poles	1	2	3	4	5	6–10	Laps	Laps Led	Races Led	Miles	$
1983	82	2	0	0	0	0	0	0	0	69	0	0	173	2,550
1984	50	4	0	0	0	0	0	0	0	655	0	0	813	7,585
1985	44	5	0	0	0	0	0	0	0	1,166	0	0	1,503	7,400
1986	57	4	0	0	0	0	0	0	0	575	0	0	1,178	6,535
1987	74	2	0	0	0	0	0	0	0	169	0	0	423	3,665
1988	55	2	0	0	0	0	0	0	0	377	0	0	943	5,050
1989	72	1	0	0	0	0	0	0	0	193	0	0	483	2,975
1990	91T	1	0	0	0	0	0	0	0	151	0	0	151	2,950
1992	57	3	0	0	0	0	0	0	0	350	0	0	904	15,810
Lifetime		24	0	0	0	0	0	0	0	3,705	0	0	6,569	$54,520

Whitey Gerkin

William Thomas Gerkin
B: 5/26/1930   D: 10/8/1973   *Died from injuries at Illiana Speedway.*
Racing Hometown: Melrose Park, IL

Year	Rank	Starts	Poles	1	2	3	4	5	6–10	Laps	Laps Led	Races Led	Miles	$
1960	59	2	0	0	0	0	0	0	0	233	0	0	583	400
1963	140	1	0	0	0	0	0	0	0	23	0	0	58	75
1967	NR	2	0	0	0	0	0	0	0	407	2	1	408	1,410
Lifetime		5	0	0	0	0	0	0	0	663	2	1	1,048	$1,885

Wally Gervais

Wally Gervais

Year	Rank	Starts	Poles	1	2	3	4	5	6–10	Laps	Laps Led	Races Led	Miles	$
1956	162	3	0	0	0	0	0	0	0	110	0	0	82	140
Lifetime		3	0	0	0	0	0	0	0	110	0	0	82	$140

Ernie Gesell

Ernest Gesell

Year	Rank	Starts	Poles	1	2	3	4	5	6–10	Laps	Laps Led	Races Led	Miles	$
1959	NR	1	0	0	0	0	0	0	1	115	0	0	115	200
Lifetime		1	0	0	0	0	0	0	1	115	0	0	115	$200

Year	Rank	Starts	Poles	Finish 1	2	3	4	5	6–10	Laps	Laps Led	Races Led	Miles	$

Dick Getty

Richard Getty
Racing Hometown: Van Nuys, CA

Year	Rank	Starts	Poles	1	2	3	4	5	6–10	Laps	Laps Led	Races Led	Miles	$
1956	201	3	0	0	0	0	0	0	0	186	0	0	217	90
1957	31	10	0	0	0	0	0	3	5	1,174	0	0	786	1,890
1959	121	2	0	0	0	0	0	0	0	138	0	0	59	175
1960	135	2	0	0	0	0	0	0	0	198	0	0	254	385
1961	93	4	0	0	0	0	0	0	0	310	0	0	331	500
1962	60	5	0	0	0	0	0	0	2	525	0	0	213	675
Lifetime		26	0	0	0	0	0	3	7	2,531	0	0	1,860	$3,715

Vince Giamformaggio

Vincent Giamformaggio
Racing Hometown: Santa Fe Springs, CA

Year	Rank	Starts	Poles	1	2	3	4	5	6–10	Laps	Laps Led	Races Led	Miles	$
1977	106T	1	0	0	0	0	0	0	0	93	0	0	233	850
1978	93T	1	0	0	0	0	0	0	0	41	0	0	107	805
1979	74	2	0	0	0	0	0	0	0	139	0	0	361	4,295
1980	90	1	0	0	0	0	0	0	0	109	0	0	286	2,260
Lifetime		5	0	0	0	0	0	0	0	382	0	0	987	$8,210

Mickey Gibbs

Mickey Gibbs
B: 3/15/1958
Racing Hometown: Glencoe, AL

Year	Rank	Starts	Poles	1	2	3	4	5	6–10	Laps	Laps Led	Races Led	Miles	$
1988	50	5	0	0	0	0	0	0	0	636	2	1	1,134	12,850
1989	41	7	0	0	0	0	0	0	0	1,363	0	0	1,927	27,040
1990	37	9	0	0	0	0	0	0	0	1,837	1	1	2,541	38,665
1991	34	15	0	0	0	0	0	0	0	4,078	0	0	5,308	100,360
Lifetime		36	0	0	0	0	0	0	0	7,914	3	2	10,910	$178,915

Shorty Gibbs

Sidney Gibbs
Racing Hometown: Greenville, SC

Year	Rank	Starts	Poles	1	2	3	4	5	6–10	Laps	Laps Led	Races Led	Miles	$
1952	99	2	0	0	0	0	0	0	0	87	0	0	53	50
Lifetime		2	0	0	0	0	0	0	0	87	0	0	53	$50

Herb Gibson

Herbert Gibson

Year	Rank	Starts	Poles	1	2	3	4	5	6–10	Laps	Laps Led	Races Led	Miles	$
1956	264T	1	0	0	0	0	0	0	0	21	0	0	32	50
1957	165T	1	0	0	0	0	0	0	0	0	0	0	0	75
Lifetime		2	0	0	0	0	0	0	0	21	0	0	32	$125

Mark Gibson

Mark Gibson
B: 8/14/1957
Racing Hometown: Daytona Beach, FL

Year	Rank	Starts	Poles	1	2	3	4	5	6–10	Laps	Laps Led	Races Led	Miles	$
1987	96T	1	0	0	0	0	0	0	0	204	0	0	204	1,300
1989	91T	1	0	0	0	0	0	0	0	100	0	0	250	2,880
Lifetime		2	0	0	0	0	0	0	0	304	0	0	454	$4,180

Tom Gifford

Thomas Gifford
Racing Hometown: Providence, RI

Year	Rank	Starts	Poles	1	2	3	4	5	6–10	Laps	Laps Led	Races Led	Miles	$
1951	N/A	1	0	0	0	0	0	0	0		0	0		0
1952	157	3	0	0	0	0	0	0	0	53	0	0	27	50
Lifetime		4	0	0	0	0	0	0	0	53	0	0	27	$50

Art Gill

Arthur Gill
Racing Hometown: Mantua, OH

Year	Rank	Starts	Poles	1	2	3	4	5	6–10	Laps	Laps Led	Races Led	Miles	$
1950	70	3	0	0	0	0	0	0	0	360	0	0	180	125
Lifetime		3	0	0	0	0	0	0	0	360	0	0	180	$125

Jim Gillette

James Gillette
Racing Hometown: Roanoke, VA

Year	Rank	Starts	Poles	1	2	3	4	5	6–10	Laps	Laps Led	Races Led	Miles	$
1954	108	2	0	0	0	0	0	0	0	441	0	0	477	140
Lifetime		2	0	0	0	0	0	0	0	441	0	0	477	$140

Year	Rank	Starts	Poles	Finish						Laps	Laps Led	Races Led	Miles	$
				1	2	3	4	5	6–10					

Mel Gillette

Mel Gillette
Racing Hometown: Howell, MI

Year	Rank	Starts	Poles	1	2	3	4	5	6–10	Laps	Laps Led	Races Led	Miles	$
1969	NR	1	0	0	0	0	0	0	0	50	0	0	100	720
Lifetime		1	0	0	0	0	0	0	0	50	0	0	100	$720

Wayne Gillette

Elias Wayne Gillette
B: 7/17/1938
Racing Hometown: Atlanta, Ga

Year	Rank	Starts	Poles	1	2	3	4	5	6–10	Laps	Laps Led	Races Led	Miles	$
1969	45	16	0	0	0	0	0	0	0	887	0	0	981	5,827
Lifetime		16	0	0	0	0	0	0	0	887	0	0	981	$5,827

Elmer Gilliam

Elmer Gilliam
Racing Hometown: Morristown, TN

Year	Rank	Starts	Poles	1	2	3	4	5	6–10	Laps	Laps Led	Races Led	Miles	$
1965	NR	1	0	0	0	0	0	0	0	1	0	0	1	100
1967	NR	3	0	0	0	0	0	0	0	9	0	0	6	325
Lifetime		4	0	0	0	0	0	0	0	10	0	0	6	$425

Jim Gilliam

James Gilliam
Racing Hometown: N.Hollywood, CA

Year	Rank	Starts	Poles	1	2	3	4	5	6–10	Laps	Laps Led	Races Led	Miles	$
1974	113	1	0	0	0	0	0	0	0	76	0	0	199	1,025
Lifetime		1	0	0	0	0	0	0	0	76	0	0	199	$1,025

Butch Gilliland

Butch Gilliland
B: 2/25/1958
Racing Hometown: Anaheim, CA

Year	Rank	Starts	Poles	1	2	3	4	5	6–10	Laps	Laps Led	Races Led	Miles	$
1990	84T	1	0	0	0	0	0	0	0	71	0	0	179	4,200
1991	78	1	0	0	0	0	0	0	0	299	0	0	299	3,750
1992	65	2	0	0	0	0	0	0	0	347	0	0	431	10,990
1993	78	1	0	0	0	0	0	0	0	71	0	0	179	6,765
1994	67	1	0	0	0	0	0	0	0	72	0	0	181	7,755
1995	69	1	0	0	0	0	0	0	0	19	0	0	48	9,760
1997	60	1	0	0	0	0	0	0	0	74	0	0	186	21,410
1998	64	1	0	0	0	0	0	0	0	112	0	0	218	28,625
1999	68T	1	0	0	0	0	0	0	0	3	0	0	6	25,415
Lifetime		10	0	0	0	0	0	0	0	1,068	0	0	1,727	$118,670

Joe Gillow

Joseph Gillow

Year	Rank	Starts	Poles	1	2	3	4	5	6–10	Laps	Laps Led	Races Led	Miles	$
1952	NR	1	0	0	0	0	0	0	0	20	0	0	10	25
Lifetime		1	0	0	0	0	0	0	0	20	0	0	10	$25

Dick Girvin

Richard Girvin
Racing Hometown: South Norfolk, VA

Year	Rank	Starts	Poles	1	2	3	4	5	6–10	Laps	Laps Led	Races Led	Miles	$
1953	140T	1	0	0	0	0	0	0	0		0	0		25
Lifetime		1	0	0	0	0	0	0	0		0	0		$25

Frank Gise

Frank Gise
Racing Hometown: New Point, IN

Year	Rank	Starts	Poles	1	2	3	4	5	6–10	Laps	Laps Led	Races Led	Miles	$
1951	N/A	2	0	0	0	0	0	0	1	215	0	0	269	100
Lifetime		2	0	0	0	0	0	0	1	215	0	0	269	$100

Don Glass

Donald Glass

Year	Rank	Starts	Poles	1	2	3	4	5	6–10	Laps	Laps Led	Races Led	Miles	$
1953	NR	1	0	0	0	0	0	0	0		0	0		75
Lifetime		1	0	0	0	0	0	0	0		0	0		$75

Charlie Glotzbach

Charles Lee Glotzbach
B: 6/19/1938
Racing Hometown: Edwardsville, IN

Year	Rank	Starts	Poles	1	2	3	4	5	6–10	Laps	Laps Led	Races Led	Miles	$
1960	136	2	0	0	0	0	0	0	0	266	0	0	399	400
1961	56	4	0	0	0	0	0	0	0	344	0	0	653	755

Year	Rank	Starts	Poles	Finish						Laps	Laps Led	Races Led	Miles	$
				1	2	3	4	5	6–10					

Charlie Glotzbach *continued*

Year	Rank	Starts	Poles	1	2	3	4	5	6–10	Laps	Laps Led	Races Led	Miles	$
1967	23	9	0	0	0	0	3	0	2	1,783	4	1	2,461	14,790
1968	19	22	3	1	3	1	4	1	2	4,871	291	5	4,791	43,101
1969	37	12	2	0	2	0	2	1	1	2,823	169	8	3,957	36,090
1970	28	19	4	2	0	3	2	0	1	3,396	417	16	5,258	50,749
1971	42	20	4	1	2	0	3	1	3	4,735	805	10	4,702	38,605
1972	65	3	0	0	1	1	0	0	0	709	0	0	1,150	26,175
1973	43	5	0	0	0	0	0	0	1	1,048	11	2	1,307	6,451
1974	26	13	0	0	0	0	4	0	1	3,478	127	6	3,794	33,072
1975	111	2	0	0	0	0	0	0	1	454	1	1	681	6,390
1976	109T	1	0	0	0	0	0	0	0	121	0	0	182	1,535
1981	88T	1	0	0	0	0	0	0	0	218	0	0	327	1,275
1990	70	3	0	0	0	0	0	0	0	651	0	0	649	15,355
1992	41	7	0	0	0	0	0	0	0	1,528	0	0	2,564	48,060
Lifetime		123	13	4	8	5	18	3	12	26,425	1,825	49	32,873	$322,803

Gene Glover

Eugene Glover
B: 11/20/1934
Racing Hometown: Kingsport, TN

Year	Rank	Starts	Poles	1	2	3	4	5	6–10	Laps	Laps Led	Races Led	Miles	$
1957	150	1	0	0	0	0	0	0	0	104	0	0	52	100
Lifetime		1	0	0	0	0	0	0	0	104	0	0	52	$100

Fred Goad

Fred Goad
Racing Hometown: Woodlawn, VA

Year	Rank	Starts	Poles	1	2	3	4	5	6–10	Laps	Laps Led	Races Led	Miles	$
1965	118	2	0	0	0	0	0	0	0	9	0	0	11	515
Lifetime		2	0	0	0	0	0	0	0	9	0	0	11	$515

P.E. Godfrey

P.E. Godfrey
Racing Hometown: Charlotte, NC

Year	Rank	Starts	Poles	1	2	3	4	5	6–10	Laps	Laps Led	Races Led	Miles	$
1950	NR	1	0	0	0	0	0	0	0	278	0	0	348	0
Lifetime		1	0	0	0	0	0	0	0	278	0	0	348	$0

Paul Goldsmith

Paul Goldsmith
B: 10/2/1927
Racing Hometown: St.Claire Shores, MI

Year	Rank	Starts	Poles	1	2	3	4	5	6–10	Laps	Laps Led	Races Led	Miles	$
1956	13	9	0	1	0	0	2	1	2	2,292	177	1	2,090	8,569
1957	13	25	4	4	4	1	1	0	5	3,759	642	11	2,495	12,734
1958	NR	2	1	1	0	0	0	0	1	178	39	1	206	4,690
1961	45	2	0	0	0	1	0	0	1	239	0	0	598	6,050
1962	51	1	0	0	0	0	0	0	1	218	0	0	327	1,375
1963	NR	6	1	0	1	0	0	0	0	545	22	3	1,058	4,170
1964	22	14	2	0	0	3	0	0	1	2,281	319	8	2,903	20,835
1966	5	21	1	3	3	2	1	2	0	5,097	440	10	5,382	54,609
1967	11	21	0	0	2	3	1	1	1	4,851	397	7	5,409	38,732
1968	30	15	0	0	1	0	0	1	2	2,793	304	8	3,505	24,365
1969	40	11	0	0	0	3	1	0	1	1,999	20	4	2,970	22,305
Lifetime		127	9	9	11	13	6	5	15	24,252	2,360	53	26,943	$198,434

Tubby Gonzales

Elar Gonzales
B: 10/21/1919
Racing Hometown: Houston, TX

Year	Rank	Starts	Poles	1	2	3	4	5	6–10	Laps	Laps Led	Races Led	Miles	$
1961	84	5	0	0	0	0	1	0	0	598	0	0	889	1,300
1962	NR	4	0	0	0	0	0	0	0	422	0	0	629	1,050
Lifetime		9	0	0	0	0	1	0	0	1,020	0	0	1,518	$2,350

Phil Good

Phillip Good
B: 1/27/1955
Racing Hometown: Williamsburg, VA

Year	Rank	Starts	Poles	1	2	3	4	5	6–10	Laps	Laps Led	Races Led	Miles	$
1984	NR	1	0	0	0	0	0	0	0	331	0	0	331	1,065
1985	46	4	0	0	0	0	0	0	0	1,239	0	0	1,081	6,870
1986	81	2	0	0	0	0	0	0	0	439	0	0	254	2,825
1987	101T	1	0	0	0	0	0	0	0	10	0	0	25	1,435
Lifetime		8	0	0	0	0	0	0	0	2,019	0	0	1,690	$12,195

Year	Rank	Starts	Poles	Finish						Laps	Laps Led	Races Led	Miles	$
				1	2	3	4	5	6–10					

Dick Goode

Richard Goode
B: 12/1/1927   D: 11/5/1992
Racing Hometown: Mishawaka, IN

Year	Rank	Starts	Poles	1	2	3	4	5	6–10	Laps	Laps Led	Races Led	Miles	$
1963	100	2	0	0	0	0	0	0	1	107	0	0	268	700
Lifetime		2	0	0	0	0	0	0	1	107	0	0	268	$700

Gene Goodman

Gene Goodman

Year	Rank	Starts	Poles	1	2	3	4	5	6–10	Laps	Laps Led	Races Led	Miles	$
1956	146	1	0	0	0	0	0	0	0	130	0	0	195	75
Lifetime		1	0	0	0	0	0	0	0	130	0	0	195	$75

Jack Goodwin

Jack Goodwin
Racing Hometown: Berkeley, CA

Year	Rank	Starts	Poles	1	2	3	4	5	6–10	Laps	Laps Led	Races Led	Miles	$
1951	38	3	0	0	0	0	0	0	1	617	0	0	712	725
1952	195	1	0	0	0	0	0	0	0		0	0		25
1965	141	1	0	0	0	0	0	0	0	0	0	0	0	0
1966	121	1	0	0	0	0	0	0	0	35	0	0	88	100
Lifetime		6	0	0	0	0	0	0	1	652	0	0	800	$850

Clyde Goons

Clyde Goons

Year	Rank	Starts	Poles	1	2	3	4	5	6–10	Laps	Laps Led	Races Led	Miles	$
1958	NR	1	0	0	0	0	0	0	0	69	0	0	23	85
Lifetime		1	0	0	0	0	0	0	0	69	0	0	23	$85

Cecil Gordon

Cecil Owen Gordon
B: 6/21/1941
Racing Hometown: Horse Shoe, NC

Year	Rank	Starts	Poles	1	2	3	4	5	6–10	Laps	Laps Led	Races Led	Miles	$
1968	55	9	0	0	0	0	0	0	0	1,144	0	0	729	2,295
1969	10	51	0	0	0	0	0	1	7	10,745	0	0	8,931	39,679
1970	11	44	0	0	0	0	1	1	9	8,424	0	0	6,872	32,713
1971	3	46	0	0	0	2	2	2	15	12,468	0	0	12,041	69,080
1972	4	31	0	0	0	0	1	3	12	9,033	3	2	10,421	73,126
1973	3	28	0	0	0	1	1	6	10	8,998	5	3	10,004	102,120
1974	9	30	0	0	0	0	1	0	9	7,396	1	1	9,080	66,166
1975	6	30	0	0	1	1	2	3	9	8,577	6	2	9,684	101,467
1976	15	30	0	0	0	0	0	0	5	7,387	7	3	8,758	73,830
1977	10	30	0	0	0	0	0	0	2	8,133	0	0	9,605	86,312
1978	19	26	0	0	0	0	0	0	1	6,773	0	0	7,192	53,815
1979	19	28	0	0	0	0	0	0	0	7,419	0	0	8,164	66,275
1980	15	29	0	0	0	0	0	0	3	7,864	0	0	8,979	83,300
1981	23	25	0	0	0	0	0	0	0	5,587	0	0	6,872	55,980
1982	82	4	0	0	0	0	0	0	0	1,125	0	0	1,445	13,920
1983	40	8	0	0	0	0	0	0	0	1,831	0	0	3,021	17,340
1985	NR	1	0	0	0	0	0	0	0	7	0	0	4	2,640
Lifetime		450	0	0	1	4	8	16	82	112,911	22	11	121,802	$940,058

Jeff Gordon

Jeffrey Michael Gordon
B: 8/4/1971
Racing Hometown: Pittsboro, IN

Year	Rank	Starts	Poles	1	2	3	4	5	6–10	Laps	Laps Led	Races Led	Miles	$
1992	79T	1	0	0	0	0	0	0	0	164	0	0	250	6,285
1993	14	30	1	0	2	1	1	3	4	8,390	189	14	10,067	765,168
1994	8	31	1	2	1	1	2	1	7	9,277	446	17	11,549	1,799,523
1995	1	31	9	7	4	5	0	1	6	9,405	2,610	29	11,609	4,347,343
1996	2	31	5	10	3	4	2	2	3	8,972	2,315	25	10,518	3,428,485
1997	1	32	1	10	3	2	4	3	1	9,276	1,645	24	11,983	6,375,658
1998	1	33	7	13	6	3	1	3	2	9,818	1,706	26	12,784	9,306,584
1999	6	34	7	7	4	5	1	1	3	9,384	1,320	26	12,131	5,858,633
2000	9	34	3	3	1	1	4	2	11	9,897	425	15	12,849	2,703,586
2001	1	36	8	6	6	3	2	1	6	10,638	2,322	25	14,026	10,879,757
2002	4	36	3	3	2	1	2	5	7	10,201	989	14	13,552	6,154,475
Lifetime		329	45	61	32	26	19	22	50	95,422	13,967	215	121,317	$51,625,497

Lee Gordon

Donald Lee Gordon
B: 2/4/1936
Racing Hometown: Horse Shoe, NC

Year	Rank	Starts	Poles	1	2	3	4	5	6–10	Laps	Laps Led	Races Led	Miles	$
1969	NR	1	0	0	0	0	0	0	0	160	0	0	80	100

Year	Rank	Starts	Poles	Finish 1	2	3	4	5	6–10	Laps	Laps Led	Races Led	Miles	$

Lee Gordon *continued*

Year	Rank	Starts	Poles	1	2	3	4	5	6–10	Laps	Laps Led	Races Led	Miles	$
1970	NR	7	0	0	0	0	0	0	0	755	0	0	354	1,970
Lifetime		8	0	0	0	0	0	0	0	915	0	0	434	$2,070

Robby Gordon

Robert Gordon
B: 1/2/1969
Racing Hometown: Cerritos, CA

Year	Rank	Starts	Poles	1	2	3	4	5	6–10	Laps	Laps Led	Races Led	Miles	$
1991	55	2	0	0	0	0	0	0	0	584	0	0	781	27,265
1993	93T	1	0	0	0	0	0	0	0	55	0	0	146	7,665
1994	76T	1	0	0	0	0	0	0	0	69	0	0	138	7,965
1996	57	3	0	0	0	0	0	0	0	344	0	0	447	23,365
1997	40	20	1	0	0	0	1	0	0	4,395	42	1	5,848	622,439
1998	67	1	0	0	0	0	0	0	0	102	1	1	199	24,765
2000	43	17	0	0	0	0	1	0	1	3,933	14	3	5,219	620,781
2001	44	17	0	1	1	0	0	0	1	4,401	50	3	6,202	1,371,900
2002	20	36	0	0	0	1	0	0	4	10,294	44	4	13,548	3,342,703
Lifetime		98	1	1	1	1	2	0	6	24,177	151	12	32,529	$6,048,848

Wally Gore

Wally Gore
Racing Hometown: Arlington, VA

Year	Rank	Starts	Poles	1	2	3	4	5	6–10	Laps	Laps Led	Races Led	Miles	$
1957	NR	1	0	0	0	0	0	0	0	203	0	0	81	110
Lifetime		1	0	0	0	0	0	0	0	203	0	0	81	$110

Bob Gossett

Robert Gossett

Year	Rank	Starts	Poles	1	2	3	4	5	6–10	Laps	Laps Led	Races Led	Miles	$
1961	177	1	0	0	0	0	0	0	0	19	0	0	10	0
Lifetime		1	0	0	0	0	0	0	0	19	0	0	10	$0

Herb Gott

Herbert Gott
Racing Hometown: Toledo, OH

Year	Rank	Starts	Poles	1	2	3	4	5	6–10	Laps	Laps Led	Races Led	Miles	$
1951	N/A	1	0	0	0	0	0	0	0		0	0		25
Lifetime		1	0	0	0	0	0	0	0		0	0		$25

Ken Goudermoat

Kenneth Goudermoat

Year	Rank	Starts	Poles	1	2	3	4	5	6–10	Laps	Laps Led	Races Led	Miles	$
1955	208	1	0	0	0	0	0	0	0	118	0	0	59	50
Lifetime		1	0	0	0	0	0	0	0	118	0	0	59	$50

Junie Gough

Junie Gough
B: 4/19/1925
Racing Hometown: Rising Sun, MD

Year	Rank	Starts	Poles	1	2	3	4	5	6–10	Laps	Laps Led	Races Led	Miles	$
1955	206T	1	0	0	0	0	0	0	0	150	0	0	75	50
Lifetime		1	0	0	0	0	0	0	0	150	0	0	75	$50

Harry Goularte

Harry Goularte
B: 7/29/1956
Racing Hometown: Morgan Hill, CA

Year	Rank	Starts	Poles	1	2	3	4	5	6–10	Laps	Laps Led	Races Led	Miles	$
1977	91	1	0	0	0	0	0	0	0	81	0	0	212	900
1978	76	2	0	0	0	0	0	0	0	185	0	0	473	1,930
1979	104T	1	0	0	0	0	0	0	0	82	0	0	215	1,460
1984	61	2	0	0	0	0	0	0	0	172	0	0	451	3,490
1987	65	2	0	0	0	0	0	0	0	171	0	0	448	4,770
Lifetime		8	0	0	0	0	0	0	0	691	0	0	1,799	$12,550

Bob Gould

Robert Gould
Racing Hometown: Andalusia, AL

Year	Rank	Starts	Poles	1	2	3	4	5	6–10	Laps	Laps Led	Races Led	Miles	$
1955	161	2	0	0	0	0	0	0	0	102	0	0	94	75
Lifetime		2	0	0	0	0	0	0	0	102	0	0	94	$75

Year	Rank	Starts	Poles	Finish						Laps	Laps Led	Races Led	Miles	$
				1	2	3	4	5	6–10					

Johnny Gouveia

Johnny Gouveia
B: 7/23/1927
Racing Hometown: New Bedford, MA

Year	Rank	Starts	Poles	1	2	3	4	5	6–10	Laps	Laps Led	Races Led	Miles	$
1952	168	1	0	0	0	0	0	0	0	61	0	0	76	0
1955	82	4	0	0	0	0	0	0	1	614	0	0	307	260
Lifetime		5	0	0	0	0	0	0	1	675	0	0	383	$260

Scott Gow

Scott Gow

Year	Rank	Starts	Poles	1	2	3	4	5	6–10	Laps	Laps Led	Races Led	Miles	$
1952	NR	1	0	0	0	0	0	0	0	46	0	0	23	25
Lifetime		1	0	0	0	0	0	0	0	46	0	0	23	$25

Ron Grable

Ronald Grable
Racing Hometown: Belmont, CA

Year	Rank	Starts	Poles	1	2	3	4	5	6–10	Laps	Laps Led	Races Led	Miles	$
1971	NR	1	0	0	0	0	0	0	0	77	0	0	202	1,160
Lifetime		1	0	0	0	0	0	0	0	77	0	0	202	$1,160

Don Graham

Donald Graham
B: 10/5/1943
Racing Hometown: Rio Linda, CA

Year	Rank	Starts	Poles	1	2	3	4	5	6–10	Laps	Laps Led	Races Led	Miles	$
1977	100T	1	0	0	0	0	0	0	0	118	0	0	295	1,000
1978	86T	1	0	0	0	0	0	0	0	75	0	0	197	875
1979	101T	1	0	0	0	0	0	0	0	100	0	0	262	1,495
Lifetime		3	0	0	0	0	0	0	0	293	0	0	754	$3,370

Frank Graham

Frank Graham
B: 7/27/1940
Racing Hometown: Charleston Heights, SC

Year	Rank	Starts	Poles	1	2	3	4	5	6–10	Laps	Laps Led	Races Led	Miles	$
1961	175	1	0	0	0	0	0	0	0	140	0	0	210	300
1962	100T	1	0	0	0	0	0	0	1	178	0	0	89	175
1963	111	3	0	0	0	0	0	0	0	99	0	0	245	1,050
1964	NR	3	0	0	0	0	0	0	0	410	0	0	206	820
Lifetime		8	0	0	0	0	0	0	1	827	0	0	750	$2,345

Jim Graham

James Graham
Racing Hometown: Rockville, MD

Year	Rank	Starts	Poles	1	2	3	4	5	6–10	Laps	Laps Led	Races Led	Miles	$
1954	56	2	0	0	0	0	0	0	1	530	0	0	385	400
1956	105	3	0	0	0	1	0	0	0	317	0	0	173	595
Lifetime		5	0	0	0	1	0	0	1	847	0	0	558	$995

Russ Graham

Russell Graham (Bud)
Racing Hometown: Murrayville, PA

Year	Rank	Starts	Poles	1	2	3	4	5	6–10	Laps	Laps Led	Races Led	Miles	$
1955	59	5	0	0	0	0	0	0	0	735	0	0	702	375
1956	124	2	0	0	0	0	0	0	0	153	0	0	163	100
Lifetime		7	0	0	0	0	0	0	0	888	0	0	865	$475

Ron Grana

Ronald Ciro Grana
B: 3/4/1940
Racing Hometown: Farmington, MI

Year	Rank	Starts	Poles	1	2	3	4	5	6–10	Laps	Laps Led	Races Led	Miles	$
1969	67	1	0	0	0	0	0	0	0	162	0	0	324	1,275
1970	87	3	0	0	0	0	0	0	1	243	0	0	546	2,165
1971	NR	1	0	0	0	0	0	0	0	187	0	0	381	920
1972	NR	1	0	0	0	0	0	0	0	31	0	0	62	690
Lifetime		6	0	0	0	0	0	0	1	623	0	0	1,313	$5,050

C.L. Grant

Coleman L. Grant (Crash)
B: 1924   D: 3/23/1997
Racing Hometown: High Point, NC

Year	Rank	Starts	Poles	1	2	3	4	5	6–10	Laps	Laps Led	Races Led	Miles	$
1950	NR	1	0	0	0	0	0	0	0		0	0		0
1951	237T	1	0	0	0	0	0	0	0		0	0		25
1952	70	4	0	0	0	0	0	0	0	421	0	0	263	100
Lifetime		6	0	0	0	0	0	0	0	421	0	0	263	$125

Year	Rank	Starts	Poles	Finish 1	2	3	4	5	6–10	Laps	Laps Led	Races Led	Miles	$

Jerry Grant

Jerry Grant
B: 1/23/1935
Racing Hometown: Escondido, CA

Year	Rank	Starts	Poles	1	2	3	4	5	6–10	Laps	Laps Led	Races Led	Miles	$
1965	54	3	0	0	0	0	0	0	1	327	0	0	851	2,150
1966	65	3	0	0	0	0	0	1	0	433	1	1	854	3,180
1967	NR	4	0	0	0	0	0	1	0	312	0	0	727	5,520
1968	43	7	0	0	0	0	0	0	1	971	1	1	1,312	5,665
1973	NR	1	0	0	0	0	0	0	0	4	0	0	10	1,015
1974	121	1	0	0	0	0	0	0	0	45	0	0	118	775
Lifetime		19	0	0	0	0	0	2	2	2,092	2	2	3,873	$18,305

Danny Graves

Danny Graves (Real Name: Frank Danley)
D: 1987 *Killed in bar room brawl.*
Racing Hometown: Modesto, CA

Year	Rank	Starts	Poles	1	2	3	4	5	6–10	Laps	Laps Led	Races Led	Miles	$
1957	43	7	1	1	0	1	0	1	1	787	1	1	473	1,895
1958	150	2	0	0	0	0	0	0	0	90	0	0	198	125
Lifetime		9	1	1	0	1	0	1	1	877	1	1	671	$2,020

Bob Gray

Robert Gray
Racing Hometown: Charleston, SC

Year	Rank	Starts	Poles	1	2	3	4	5	6–10	Laps	Laps Led	Races Led	Miles	$
1964	135	1	0	0	0	0	0	0	0	2	0	0	3	400
Lifetime		1	0	0	0	0	0	0	0	2	0	0	3	$400

Don Gray

Donald Gray
D: 8/21/1994 Suffered heart attack while competing in race @ St. Charles (MO)
Racing Hometown: Indianapolis, IN

Year	Rank	Starts	Poles	1	2	3	4	5	6–10	Laps	Laps Led	Races Led	Miles	$
1957	NR	3	0	0	0	0	0	0	0	549	0	0	604	325
1958	125	2	0	0	0	0	0	0	0	264	0	0	120	115
Lifetime		5	0	0	0	0	0	0	0	813	0	0	724	$440

Eddie Gray

Edward Gray
B: 1920   D: 10/25/1969 *Died of heart attack; had suffered ailment in*
Sportsman race @ Riverside 1/18/69.
Racing Hometown: Gardena, CA

Year	Rank	Starts	Poles	1	2	3	4	5	6–10	Laps	Laps Led	Races Led	Miles	$
1957	55	5	0	0	0	0	0	1	1	525	0	0	421	755
1958	44	3	0	1	0	0	0	0	0	437	43	1	807	3,375
1959	76	2	0	1	0	0	0	0	0	317	1	1	187	875
1960	76	4	0	0	0	0	0	0	1	279	0	0	395	580
1961	64	4	1	2	1	0	0	0	0	509	76	2	532	3,485
1963	103	1	0	0	0	0	0	0	0	131	0	0	354	225
1964	63	1	0	0	0	0	0	0	0	174	0	0	470	650
1965	56	1	0	0	0	0	0	0	1	176	0	0	475	1,300
1966	110	1	0	0	0	0	0	0	0	43	0	0	116	500
Lifetime		22	1	4	1	0	0	1	3	2,591	120	4	3,756	$11,745

Henley Gray

Clarence Henley Gray
B: 1/3/1933
Racing Hometown: Rome, GA

Year	Rank	Starts	Poles	1	2	3	4	5	6–10	Laps	Laps Led	Races Led	Miles	$
1964	NR	1	0	0	0	0	0	0	0	126	0	0	63	100
1965	26	38	0	0	0	0	0	1	6	5,291	0	0	3,225	8,320
1966	4	45	0	0	0	0	1	3	14	10,719	0	0	7,626	21,901
1967	17	43	0	0	0	0	0	0	10	7,864	0	0	5,859	15,987
1968	20	30	0	0	0	0	0	0	6	6,072	0	0	4,580	12,566
1969	17	48	0	0	0	0	0	0	5	8,954	0	0	7,293	29,335
1970	19	34	0	0	0	0	0	0	2	6,134	0	0	5,249	23,130
1971	14	39	0	0	0	0	0	0	4	7,684	0	0	7,511	31,789
1972	17	28	0	0	0	0	0	0	2	6,121	0	0	7,308	38,461
1973	14	24	0	0	0	0	0	0	4	7,517	0	0	7,615	34,112
1974	55	5	0	0	0	0	0	0	1	1,342	0	0	1,193	5,185
1975	39	9	0	0	0	0	0	0	1	2,179	2	1	2,472	8,785
1976	27	15	0	0	0	0	0	0	0	2,945	0	0	3,479	15,090
1977	28	14	0	0	0	0	0	0	0	3,289	0	0	2,613	18,610
Lifetime		373	0	0	0	0	1	4	55	76,237	2	1	66,087	$263,371

Year	Rank	Starts	Poles	Finish 1	2	3	4	5	6–10	Laps	Laps Led	Races Led	Miles	$

Steve Gray

Steve Gray
B: 8/11/1956
Racing Hometown: Rome, GA

Year	Rank	Starts	Poles	1	2	3	4	5	6–10	Laps	Laps Led	Races Led	Miles	$
1979	126T	1	0	0	0	0	0	0	0	1	0	0	3	1,305
1980	NR	1	0	0	0	0	0	0	0	35	0	0	35	450
1982	90	1	0	0	0	0	0	0	0	103	0	0	258	1,250
1983	86	3	0	0	0	0	0	0	0	853	0	0	853	3,525
1984	83	1	0	0	0	0	0	0	0	178	0	0	445	1,675
1985	NR	1	0	0	0	0	0	0	0	151	0	0	378	1,970
Lifetime		8	0	0	0	0	0	0	0	1,321	0	0	1,971	$10,175

Vince Gray

Vincent Gray

Year	Rank	Starts	Poles	1	2	3	4	5	6–10	Laps	Laps Led	Races Led	Miles	$
1954	NR	1	0	0	0	0	0	0	0	34	0	0	68	0
Lifetime		1	0	0	0	0	0	0	0	34	0	0	68	$0

Bob Greeley

Robert Greeley
Racing Hometown: Auburn, ME

Year	Rank	Starts	Poles	1	2	3	4	5	6–10	Laps	Laps Led	Races Led	Miles	$
1972	100	1	0	0	0	0	0	0	0	182	0	0	273	500
Lifetime		1	0	0	0	0	0	0	0	182	0	0	273	$500

Bill Green

William Green
B: 1946
Racing Hometown: Edgewood, KY

Year	Rank	Starts	Poles	1	2	3	4	5	6–10	Laps	Laps Led	Races Led	Miles	$
1978	96T	1	0	0	0	0	0	0	0	0	0	0	0	400
1979	NR	1	0	0	0	0	0	0	0	76	2	1	152	980
Lifetime		2	0	0	0	0	0	0	0	76	2	1	152	$1,380

David Green

David Allen Green
B: 1/28/1958
Racing Hometown: Owensboro, KY

Year	Rank	Starts	Poles	1	2	3	4	5	6–10	Laps	Laps Led	Races Led	Miles	$
1997	37	26	0	0	0	0	0	0	0	7,282	1	1	9,404	512,583
1998	44	15	0	0	0	0	0	0	0	3,500	0	0	4,563	441,121
1999	36	32	1	0	0	0	0	0	0	8,273	7	1	10,757	1,079,536
2000	59	2	0	0	0	0	0	0	0	740	0	0	664	78,850
Lifetime		75	1	0	0	0	0	0	0	19,795	8	2	25,389	$2,112,090

George Green

George Green
B: 9/15/1927
Racing Hometown: Johnson City, TN

Year	Rank	Starts	Poles	1	2	3	4	5	6–10	Laps	Laps Led	Races Led	Miles	$
1956	76	6	0	0	0	0	0	0	0	867	0	0	468	550
1957	23	17	0	0	0	0	1	0	3	2,668	0	0	1,485	2,240
1958	NR	12	0	0	0	0	0	0	0	1,304	0	0	563	655
1959	107	18	0	0	0	0	0	0	5	3,337	0	0	1,966	2,385
1960	98	3	0	0	0	0	0	0	0	237	0	0	327	360
1961	52	11	0	0	0	0	1	0	2	1,926	0	0	1,186	1,635
1962	16	46	0	0	0	0	0	1	14	9,279	0	0	5,896	9,221
1963	88	3	0	0	0	0	0	0	2	569	0	0	198	425
Lifetime		116	0	0	0	0	2	1	26	20,187	0	0	12,088	$17,471

Jeff Green

Jeff Green
B: 9/6/1962
Racing Hometown: Owensboro, KY

Year	Rank	Starts	Poles	1	2	3	4	5	6–10	Laps	Laps Led	Races Led	Miles	$
1994	51	3	0	0	0	0	0	0	0	717	0	0	741	20,270
1996	49	4	0	0	0	0	0	0	0	813	0	0	966	46,875
1997	39	20	0	0	0	0	1	0	1	5,524	18	2	7,146	434,685
1998	40	22	0	0	0	0	0	0	0	6,088	0	0	7,189	589,841
1999	60	1	0	0	0	0	0	0	0	199	0	0	498	31,415
2001	48	8	1	0	0	0	0	0	1	1,758	71	1	2,778	441,449
2002	17	36	0	0	1	1	0	2	2	10,325	120	5	13,561	2,531,339
Lifetime		94	1	0	1	1	1	2	4	25,424	209	8	32,878	$4,095,874

Year	Rank	Starts	Poles	Finish 1	2	3	4	5	6–10	Laps	Laps Led	Races Led	Miles	$

Jerry Green

Jerry Green

Year	Rank	Starts	Poles	1	2	3	4	5	6–10	Laps	Laps Led	Races Led	Miles	$
1958	NR	1	0	0	0	0	0	0	0	154	0	0	77	65
Lifetime		1	0	0	0	0	0	0	0	154	0	0	77	$65

Bobby Greene

Robert Greene
B: 6/12/1925
Racing Hometown: Siler City, NC

Year	Rank	Starts	Poles	1	2	3	4	5	6–10	Laps	Laps Led	Races Led	Miles	$
1949	49	2	0	0	0	0	0	0	0	148	0	0	74	50
Lifetime		2	0	0	0	0	0	0	0	148	0	0	74	$50

Oda Greene

Oda Greene
B: 9/23/1928
Racing Hometown: Toledo, OH

Year	Rank	Starts	Poles	1	2	3	4	5	6–10	Laps	Laps Led	Races Led	Miles	$
1951	37	6	0	0	0	1	0	1	1	173	0	0	173	825
1952	NR	1	0	0	0	0	0	0	0	134	0	0	67	25
Lifetime		7	0	0	0	1	0	1	1	307	0	0	240	$850

John Greenwood

John Greenwood
B: 1945
Racing Hometown: Troy, MI

Year	Rank	Starts	Poles	1	2	3	4	5	6–10	Laps	Laps Led	Races Led	Miles	$
1980	NR	2	0	0	0	0	0	0	0	174	0	0	411	2,730
Lifetime		2	0	0	0	0	0	0	0	174	0	0	411	$2,730

Bob Greer

Robert Greer
Racing Hometown: Hubbard, OH

Year	Rank	Starts	Poles	1	2	3	4	5	6–10	Laps	Laps Led	Races Led	Miles	$
1950	NR	1	0	0	0	0	0	0	0	56	0	0	28	0
1951	N/A	5	0	0	0	0	0	0	0	126	0	0	126	50
Lifetime		6	0	0	0	0	0	0	0	182	0	0	154	$50

Bill Greever

William Greever
Racing Hometown: Bluefield, WV

Year	Rank	Starts	Poles	1	2	3	4	5	6–10	Laps	Laps Led	Races Led	Miles	$
1949	75	1	0	0	0	0	0	0	0	134	0	0	67	0
1950	120T	1	0	0	0	0	0	0	0	128	0	0	64	0
Lifetime		2	0	0	0	0	0	0	0	262	0	0	131	$0

Peter Gregg

Peter Holden Gregg
B: 5/4/1940   D: 12/16/1980   *Suicide.*
Racing Hometown: Jacksonville, FL

Year	Rank	Starts	Poles	1	2	3	4	5	6–10	Laps	Laps Led	Races Led	Miles	$
1973	120	1	0	0	0	0	0	0	0	34	0	0	51	775
Lifetime		1	0	0	0	0	0	0	0	34	0	0	51	$775

Ben Gregory

Benjamin Gregory
Racing Hometown: Crockett, CA

Year	Rank	Starts	Poles	1	2	3	4	5	6–10	Laps	Laps Led	Races Led	Miles	$
1951	NR	1	0	0	0	0	0	0	0		0	0		50
1954	NR	4	0	0	0	0	2	0	0	1,232	0	0	730	825
1955	142	1	0	0	0	0	0	0	1	96	0	0	96	200
Lifetime		6	0	0	0	0	2	0	1	1,328	0	0	826	$1,075

Buzz Gregory

Buzz Gregory
B: 1903   D: 9/10/1993
Racing Hometown: Speedway City, IN

Year	Rank	Starts	Poles	1	2	3	4	5	6–10	Laps	Laps Led	Races Led	Miles	$
1966	96	2	0	0	0	0	0	0	0	563	0	0	282	500
Lifetime		2	0	0	0	0	0	0	0	563	0	0	282	$500

George Gregory

George Gregory

Year	Rank	Starts	Poles	1	2	3	4	5	6–10	Laps	Laps Led	Races Led	Miles	$
1955	240T	1	0	0	0	0	0	0	0	82	0	0	41	25
Lifetime		1	0	0	0	0	0	0	0	82	0	0	41	$25

Year	Rank	Starts	Poles	Finish 1	2	3	4	5	6–10	Laps	Laps Led	Races Led	Miles	$

Allan Grice

Allan Grice
B: 1943

Year	Rank	Starts	Poles	1	2	3	4	5	6–10	Laps	Laps Led	Races Led	Miles	$
1987	NR	1	0	0	0	0	0	0	0	161	0	0	242	1,700
1989	93T	1	0	0	0	0	0	0	0	294	0	0	441	1,900
Lifetime		2	0	0	0	0	0	0	0	455	0	0	683	$3,600

Dick Grice

Richard Grice

Year	Rank	Starts	Poles	1	2	3	4	5	6–10	Laps	Laps Led	Races Led	Miles	$
1954	NR	1	0	0	0	0	0	0	0	52	0	0	26	0
Lifetime		1	0	0	0	0	0	0	0	52	0	0	26	$0

Charley Griffin

Charles Griffin
B: 9/4/1929   D: 11/1999
Racing Hometown: Chattanooga, TN

Year	Rank	Starts	Poles	1	2	3	4	5	6–10	Laps	Laps Led	Races Led	Miles	$
1958	65	2	0	0	0	0	0	0	0	211	0	0	150	215
1959	NR	6	0	0	0	1	0	0	2	438	0	0	697	4,955
1960	40	5	0	0	0	0	0	0	0	599	0	0	921	1,300
1962	87	3	0	0	0	0	0	0	0	229	0	0	299	625
1963	135	1	0	0	0	0	0	0	0	182	0	0	91	60
Lifetime		17	0	0	0	1	0	0	2	1,659	0	0	2,157	$7,155

Charlie Griffin

Charles Griffin
Racing Hometown: Roanoke, VA

Year	Rank	Starts	Poles	1	2	3	4	5	6–10	Laps	Laps Led	Races Led	Miles	$
1975	76	2	0	0	0	0	0	0	0	82	0	0	51	720
Lifetime		2	0	0	0	0	0	0	0	82	0	0	51	$720

Jerry Griffin

Jerry Griffin

Year	Rank	Starts	Poles	1	2	3	4	5	6–10	Laps	Laps Led	Races Led	Miles	$
1970	NR	1	0	0	0	0	0	0	0	94	0	0	246	790
Lifetime		1	0	0	0	0	0	0	0	94	0	0	246	$790

Jimmy Griggs

James Griggs
D: 12/17/1998
Racing Hometown: Donelson, TN

Year	Rank	Starts	Poles	1	2	3	4	5	6–10	Laps	Laps Led	Races Led	Miles	$
1963	117	1	0	0	0	0	0	0	0	304	0	0	152	240
Lifetime		1	0	0	0	0	0	0	0	304	0	0	152	$240

Al Grinnan

Alfred Grinnan
B: 1931
Racing Hometown: Fredericksburg, VA

Year	Rank	Starts	Poles	1	2	3	4	5	6–10	Laps	Laps Led	Races Led	Miles	$
1971	NR	1	0	0	0	0	0	0	0	459	0	0	249	495
Lifetime		1	0	0	0	0	0	0	0	459	0	0	249	$495

Steve Grissom

Stephen Todd Grissom
B: 6/26/1963
Racing Hometown: Gadsden, AL

Year	Rank	Starts	Poles	1	2	3	4	5	6–10	Laps	Laps Led	Races Led	Miles	$
1990	78T	1	0	0	0	0	0	0	0	322	0	0	490	4,275
1993	74T	1	0	0	0	0	0	0	0	300	0	0	300	6,485
1994	28	28	0	0	0	0	0	0	3	8,394	1	1	10,169	300,915
1995	27	29	0	0	0	0	0	1	3	8,279	17	2	10,300	509,047
1996	39	13	0	0	0	0	0	1	1	3,169	12	1	4,302	314,983
1997	21	31	0	0	0	0	2	1	3	8,800	2	1	11,299	1,074,374
1998	34	27	0	0	0	0	0	0	2	7,119	8	1	10,247	1,030,041
1999	50	6	0	0	0	0	0	0	0	1,509	0	0	1,705	193,529
2000	52	5	0	0	0	0	0	0	0	1,569	0	0	1,916	246,785
2002	44	10	0	0	0	0	0	0	1	3,070	0	0	4,122	529,781
Lifetime		151	0	0	0	0	2	3	13	42,531	40	6	54,850	$4,210,215

Pat Grogan

Patrick Grogan
Racing Hometown: Kinston, NC

Year	Rank	Starts	Poles	1	2	3	4	5	6–10	Laps	Laps Led	Races Led	Miles	$
1956	270T	2	0	0	0	0	0	0	0	223	0	0	299	50
Lifetime		2	0	0	0	0	0	0	0	223	0	0	299	$50

Year	Rank	Starts	Poles	Finish 1	2	3	4	5	6–10	Laps	Laps Led	Races Led	Miles	$

Jerry Groh

Jerry Groh

Year	Rank	Starts	Poles	1	2	3	4	5	6–10	Laps	Laps Led	Races Led	Miles	$
1951	N/A	2	0	0	0	0	0	0	0		0	0		50
Lifetime		2	0	0	0	0	0	0	0		0	0		$50

Al Gross

Al Gross
Racing Hometown: Tampa, FL

Year	Rank	Starts	Poles	1	2	3	4	5	6–10	Laps	Laps Led	Races Led	Miles	$
1950	45	3	0	0	0	0	1	0	0	182	0	0	267	550
Lifetime		3	0	0	0	0	1	0	0	182	0	0	267	$550

Bill Gross

William Gross
Racing Hometown: Philadelphia, PA

Year	Rank	Starts	Poles	1	2	3	4	5	6–10	Laps	Laps Led	Races Led	Miles	$
1955	127	3	0	0	0	0	0	0	0	352	0	0	220	125
Lifetime		3	0	0	0	0	0	0	0	352	0	0	220	$125

Bob Grossman

Robert Grossman
B: 1912
Racing Hometown: West Nyack, NY

Year	Rank	Starts	Poles	1	2	3	4	5	6–10	Laps	Laps Led	Races Led	Miles	$
1954	NR	1	0	0	0	0	1	0	0	49	0	0	98	400
1965	NR	1	0	0	0	0	0	0	0	13	0	0	30	175
Lifetime		2	0	0	0	0	1	0	0	62	0	0	128	$575

Johnny Grubb

John R. Grubb
B: 4/23/1914
Racing Hometown: Beckley, WV

Year	Rank	Starts	Poles	1	2	3	4	5	6–10	Laps	Laps Led	Races Led	Miles	$
1950	55	4	0	0	0	0	0	0	1	530	0	0	541	575
1951	192T	1	0	0	0	0	0	0	0		0	0		25
Lifetime		5	0	0	0	0	0	0	1	530	0	0	541	$600

Cecil Grubbs

Cecil Grubbs

Year	Rank	Starts	Poles	1	2	3	4	5	6–10	Laps	Laps Led	Races Led	Miles	$
1958	NR	1	0	0	0	0	0	0	0	79	0	0	49	50
Lifetime		1	0	0	0	0	0	0	0	79	0	0	49	$50

Tom Guffy

Thomas Guffy

Year	Rank	Starts	Poles	1	2	3	4	5	6–10	Laps	Laps Led	Races Led	Miles	$
1961	184	1	0	0	0	0	0	0	0	29	0	0	41	0
Lifetime		1	0	0	0	0	0	0	0	29	0	0	41	$0

Joe Guide

Joseph Guide Jr.
Racing Hometown: Memphis, TN

Year	Rank	Starts	Poles	1	2	3	4	5	6–10	Laps	Laps Led	Races Led	Miles	$
1952	152	2	0	0	0	0	0	0	0	200	0	0	250	0
1953	106	2	0	0	0	0	0	0	0	147	0	0	300	150
1954	162	2	0	0	0	0	0	0	0	160	0	0	331	75
1955	77	2	0	0	0	0	0	0	0	275	0	0	413	360
1956	140T	1	0	0	0	0	0	0	0	141	0	0	212	200
Lifetime		9	0	0	0	0	0	0	0	923	0	0	1,505	$785

Dick Gulstrand

Richard Gulstrand
Racing Hometown: Manhattan Beach, CA

Year	Rank	Starts	Poles	1	2	3	4	5	6–10	Laps	Laps Led	Races Led	Miles	$
1965	68	1	0	0	0	0	0	0	0	151	0	0	408	615
1966	94	1	0	0	0	0	0	0	0	65	0	0	176	500
1970	NR	2	0	0	0	0	0	1	1	309	0	0	810	3,890
1971	NR	2	0	0	0	0	0	0	0	251	0	0	637	2,775
1972	115	1	0	0	0	0	0	0	0	28	0	0	73	740
Lifetime		7	0	0	0	0	0	1	1	804	0	0	2,103	$8,520

John Gunn

John Gunn

Year	Rank	Starts	Poles	1	2	3	4	5	6–10	Laps	Laps Led	Races Led	Miles	$
1981	87	1	0	0	0	0	0	0	0	67	0	0	176	2,225
Lifetime		1	0	0	0	0	0	0	0	67	0	0	176	$2,225

Year	Rank	Starts	Poles	Finish						Laps	Laps Led	Races Led	Miles	$
				1	2	3	4	5	6–10	Laps	Led	Led	Miles	$

Larry Gunselman

Lawrence Gunselman
B: 12/1/1964
Racing Hometown: Belfair, WA

Year	Rank	Starts	Poles	1	2	3	4	5	6–10	Laps	Laps Led	Races Led	Miles	$
1996	62	1	0	0	0	0	0	0	0	70	0	0	176	10,200
1997	67	1	0	0	0	0	0	0	0	60	0	0	151	20,720
Lifetime		2	0	0	0	0	0	0	0	130	0	0	328	$30,920

Dan Gurney

Daniel Sexton Gurney
B: 4/13/1931
Racing Hometown: Costa Mesa, CA

Year	Rank	Starts	Poles	1	2	3	4	5	6–10	Laps	Laps Led	Races Led	Miles	$
1962	77	2	0	0	0	0	1	0	0	174	0	0	435	700
1963	NR	3	0	1	0	0	0	2	0	424	120	1	1,097	18,250
1964	NR	4	0	1	0	0	0	0	1	433	142	1	1,103	14,770
1965	NR	1	0	1	0	0	0	0	0	185	126	1	500	13,625
1966	NR	1	0	1	0	0	0	0	0	185	148	1	500	18,445
1967	NR	1	0	0	0	0	0	0	0	143	36	1	386	990
1968	NR	1	1	1	0	0	0	0	0	186	124	1	502	21,250
1969	NR	1	0	0	0	0	0	0	0	66	0	0	178	980
1970	NR	1	1	0	0	0	0	0	1	180	0	0	472	2,400
1980	NR	1	0	0	0	0	0	0	0	79	0	0	207	1,105
Lifetime		16	2	5	0	0	1	2	2	2,055	696	6	5,379	$92,515

Janet Guthrie

Janet Guthrie
B: 3/7/1938
Racing Hometown: New York, NY

Year	Rank	Starts	Poles	1	2	3	4	5	6–10	Laps	Laps Led	Races Led	Miles	$
1976	NR	5	0	0	0	0	0	0	0	1,183	0	0	2,015	8,179
1977	23	19	0	0	0	0	0	0	4	5,031	5	1	6,182	37,945
1978	41	7	0	0	0	0	0	0	1	1,147	0	0	2,406	17,120
1980	69	2	0	0	0	0	0	0	0	327	0	0	818	15,065
Lifetime		33	0	0	0	0	0	0	5	7,688	5	1	11,420	$78,309

Alton Haddock

John Alton Haddock
B: 8/16/1915
Racing Hometown: Greenville, SC

Year	Rank	Starts	Poles	1	2	3	4	5	6–10	Laps	Laps Led	Races Led	Miles	$
1950	NR	2	0	0	0	0	0	0	0	139	0	0	293	125
1951	N/A	2	0	0	0	0	0	0	1	136	0	0	136	100
Lifetime		4	0	0	0	0	0	0	1	275	0	0	429	$225

Bob Haden

Robert Haden
Racing Hometown: Scottsville, NY

Year	Rank	Starts	Poles	1	2	3	4	5	6–10	Laps	Laps Led	Races Led	Miles	$
1954	212	1	0	0	0	0	0	0	0	23	0	0	12	0
Lifetime		1	0	0	0	0	0	0	0	23	0	0	12	$0

Billy Hagan

William Joseph Hagan
B: 3/22/1932
Racing Hometown: Lafayette, LA

Year	Rank	Starts	Poles	1	2	3	4	5	6–10	Laps	Laps Led	Races Led	Miles	$
1969	NR	1	0	0	0	0	0	0	1	155	0	0	412	1,750
1975	84T	1	0	0	0	0	0	0	0	175	0	0	466	1,770
1979	94T	1	0	0	0	0	0	0	0	185	0	0	370	3,280
Lifetime		3	0	0	0	0	0	0	1	515	0	0	1,248	$6,800

Budd Hagelin

Budd Hagelin
B: 12/8/1944
Racing Hometown: Camden, NJ

Year	Rank	Starts	Poles	1	2	3	4	5	6–10	Laps	Laps Led	Races Led	Miles	$
1974	NR	1	0	0	0	0	0	0	0	44	0	0	115	720
1976	82	1	0	0	0	0	0	0	0	409	0	0	409	1,040
Lifetime		2	0	0	0	0	0	0	0	453	0	0	524	$1,760

Al Hager

Al Hager
Racing Hometown: Florissant, MO

Year	Rank	Starts	Poles	1	2	3	4	5	6–10	Laps	Laps Led	Races Led	Miles	$
1955	92	1	0	0	0	0	0	0	0	176	0	0	264	125
Lifetime		1	0	0	0	0	0	0	0	176	0	0	264	$125

Year	Rank	Starts	Poles	Finish 1	2	3	4	5	6–10	Laps	Laps Led	Races Led	Miles	$

Dick Hagey
Richard Hagey
Racing Hometown: Philadelphia, PA

Year	Rank	Starts	Poles	1	2	3	4	5	6–10	Laps	Laps Led	Races Led	Miles	$
1953	NR	1	0	0	0	0	0	0	0		0	0		40
Lifetime		1	0	0	0	0	0	0	0		0	0		$40

Royce Haggerty
Royce C. Haggerty
Racing Hometown: Portland, OR

Year	Rank	Starts	Poles	1	2	3	4	5	6–10	Laps	Laps Led	Races Led	Miles	$
1955	111	1	0	0	0	0	0	0	0	228	0	0	228	100
1956	59	6	0	1	0	0	0	0	1	1,017	72	2	610	1,720
1957	143	2	0	0	0	0	0	0	0	172	0	0	86	185
Lifetime		9	0	1	0	0	0	0	1	1,417	72	2	924	$2,005

Neil Haight
Neil Haight

Year	Rank	Starts	Poles	1	2	3	4	5	6–10	Laps	Laps Led	Races Led	Miles	$
1958	113	2	0	0	0	0	0	0	0	132	0	0	39	195
Lifetime		2	0	0	0	0	0	0	0	132	0	0	39	$195

Jimmy Hailey
James Hailey
Racing Hometown: Winston-Salem, NC

Year	Rank	Starts	Poles	1	2	3	4	5	6–10	Laps	Laps Led	Races Led	Miles	$
1974	131	1	0	0	0	0	0	0	0	421	0	0	228	615
Lifetime		1	0	0	0	0	0	0	0	421	0	0	228	$615

Gordon Haines
Gordon Haines
Racing Hometown: Yakima, WA

Year	Rank	Starts	Poles	1	2	3	4	5	6–10	Laps	Laps Led	Races Led	Miles	$
1956	44	7	0	0	1	0	1	0	2	1,067	66	1	715	1,500
Lifetime		7	0	0	1	0	1	0	2	1,067	66	1	715	$1,500

Ted Hairfield
Theodore Hairfield
B: 12/18/1931
Racing Hometown: Richmond, VA

Year	Rank	Starts	Poles	1	2	3	4	5	6–10	Laps	Laps Led	Races Led	Miles	$
1963	106	2	0	0	0	0	0	0	0	50	0	0	125	675
Lifetime		2	0	0	0	0	0	0	0	50	0	0	125	$675

Ed Hale
Edward Hale
Racing Hometown: Lakeside, CA

Year	Rank	Starts	Poles	1	2	3	4	5	6–10	Laps	Laps Led	Races Led	Miles	$
1979	87T	1	0	0	0	0	0	0	0	85	0	0	223	2,045
1980	99	1	0	0	0	0	0	0	0	37	0	0	97	1,200
Lifetime		2	0	0	0	0	0	0	0	122	0	0	320	$3,245

Bob Hale
Robert Hale (Bob)
Racing Hometown: Tucson, AZ

Year	Rank	Starts	Poles	1	2	3	4	5	6–10	Laps	Laps Led	Races Led	Miles	$
1969	NR	1	0	0	0	0	0	0	0	24	0	0	65	750
1970	NR	1	0	0	0	0	0	0	0	120	0	0	314	890
Lifetime		2	0	0	0	0	0	0	0	144	0	0	379	$1,640

Johnny Halford
Johnny Lain Halford
B: 10/15/1930
Racing Hometown: Spartanburg, SC

Year	Rank	Starts	Poles	1	2	3	4	5	6–10	Laps	Laps Led	Races Led	Miles	$
1969	47	8	0	0	0	0	0	0	0	1,881	0	0	1,494	4,200
1970	36	25	0	0	0	0	0	0	0	3,619	16	1	4,057	15,654
1971	NR	2	0	0	0	0	0	0	0	308	0	0	513	1,719
1972	47	5	0	0	0	0	0	0	1	1,032	0	0	1,574	4,955
1978	NR	1	0	0	0	0	0	0	0	84	0	0	85	610
Lifetime		41	0	0	0	0	0	0	1	6,924	16	1	7,723	$27,138

Bill Hall
William Hall
Racing Hometown: Haw River, NC

Year	Rank	Starts	Poles	1	2	3	4	5	6–10	Laps	Laps Led	Races Led	Miles	$
1957	198T	1	0	0	0	0	0	0	0	25	0	0	13	50
Lifetime		1	0	0	0	0	0	0	0	25	0	0	13	$50

Year	Rank	Starts	Poles	Finish 1	2	3	4	5	6–10	Laps	Laps Led	Races Led	Miles	$

Buck Hall
Buck Hall
Racing Hometown: Burlington, NC

Year	Rank	Starts	Poles	1	2	3	4	5	6–10	Laps	Laps Led	Races Led	Miles	$
1956	253	1	0	0	0	0	0	0	0	11	0	0	10	25
Lifetime		1	0	0	0	0	0	0	0	11	0	0	10	$25

Dana Hall
Dana Hall
Racing Hometown: Gastonia, NC

Year	Rank	Starts	Poles	1	2	3	4	5	6–10	Laps	Laps Led	Races Led	Miles	$
1965	129	1	0	0	0	0	0	0	0	1	0	0	3	500
Lifetime		1	0	0	0	0	0	0	0	1	0	0	3	$500

Don Hall
Donald Hall
B: 9/2/1943
Racing Hometown: Puyallup, WA

Year	Rank	Starts	Poles	1	2	3	4	5	6–10	Laps	Laps Led	Races Led	Miles	$
1974	116	1	0	0	0	0	0	0	0	102	0	0	255	1,100
1975	80	1	0	0	0	0	0	0	0	188	0	0	470	2,225
Lifetime		2	0	0	0	0	0	0	0	290	0	0	725	$3,325

Roy Hall
Roy Hall
B: 1921   D: 3/14/1991
Racing Hometown: Atlanta, GA

Year	Rank	Starts	Poles	1	2	3	4	5	6–10	Laps	Laps Led	Races Led	Miles	$
1949	26T	1	0	0	0	0	0	0	1	196	0	0	98	150
1952	165	1	0	0	0	0	0	0	0	182	0	0	228	0
Lifetime		2	0	0	0	0	0	0	1	378	0	0	326	$150

Shane Hall
Shane Hall
B: 8/25/1969
Racing Hometown: Simpsonville, SC

Year	Rank	Starts	Poles	1	2	3	4	5	6–10	Laps	Laps Led	Races Led	Miles	$
1995	65T	1	0	0	0	0	0	0	0	205	0	0	208	13,975
Lifetime		1	0	0	0	0	0	0	0	205	0	0	208	$13,975

Richard Hallock
Richard M. Hallock
Racing Hometown: Walden, NY

Year	Rank	Starts	Poles	1	2	3	4	5	6–10	Laps	Laps Led	Races Led	Miles	$
1950	NR	1	0	0	0	0	0	0	0	0	0	0	0	0
1954	133	3	0	0	0	0	0	0	0	388	0	0	342	150
1955	134	3	0	0	0	0	0	0	1	321	0	0	245	150
Lifetime		7	0	0	0	0	0	0	1	709	0	0	586	$300

Roy Hallquist
Roy Hallquist
Racing Hometown: Stratford, CT

Year	Rank	Starts	Poles	1	2	3	4	5	6–10	Laps	Laps Led	Races Led	Miles	$
1962	120T	1	0	0	0	0	0	0	1	183	0	0	46	175
1963	122T	1	0	0	0	0	0	0	0	34	0	0	97	130
1966	78	4	0	0	0	0	2	0	0	547	0	0	335	895
1968	113	1	0	0	0	0	0	0	0	51	0	0	51	250
1969	58	3	0	0	0	0	0	0	0	260	0	0	224	1,070
Lifetime		10	0	0	0	0	2	0	1	1,075	0	0	752	$2,520

Joe Halton
Joseph Halton
Racing Hometown: High Point, NC

Year	Rank	Starts	Poles	1	2	3	4	5	6–10	Laps	Laps Led	Races Led	Miles	$
1959	NR	6	0	0	0	0	0	0	1	898	0	0	365	465
Lifetime		6	0	0	0	0	0	0	1	898	0	0	365	$465

Jeff Halverson
Jeffrey Halverson
Racing Hometown: Three Rivers, MI

Year	Rank	Starts	Poles	1	2	3	4	5	6–10	Laps	Laps Led	Races Led	Miles	$
1979	123T	1	0	0	0	0	0	0	0	1	0	0	1	490
Lifetime		1	0	0	0	0	0	0	0	1	0	0	1	$490

Ed Hamanard
Edward Hamanard
Racing Hometown: Rome, NY

Year	Rank	Starts	Poles	1	2	3	4	5	6–10	Laps	Laps Led	Races Led	Miles	$
1950	NR	1	0	0	0	0	0	0	0	68	0	0	34	0
Lifetime		1	0	0	0	0	0	0	0	68	0	0	34	$0

Year	Rank	Starts	Poles	Finish						Laps	Laps Led	Races Led	Miles	$
				1	2	3	4	5	6–10	Laps	Led	Led	Miles	$

J.V. Hamby
John V. Hamby
Racing Hometown: Columbia, SC

Year	Rank	Starts	Poles	1	2	3	4	5	6–10	Laps	Laps Led	Races Led	Miles	$
1958	NR	2	0	0	0	0	0	0	1	237	0	0	119	200
1961	105	4	0	0	0	0	0	0	0	745	0	0	382	450
1962	79	2	0	0	0	0	0	0	0	203	0	0	82	190
1964	87	5	0	0	0	0	0	0	1	484	0	0	173	735
Lifetime		13	0	0	0	0	0	0	2	1,669	0	0	755	$1,575

Roger Hamby
Roger Hamby
B: 7/2/1943
Racing Hometown: Ferguson, NC

Year	Rank	Starts	Poles	1	2	3	4	5	6–10	Laps	Laps Led	Races Led	Miles	$
1977	89	2	0	0	0	0	0	0	0	614	0	0	605	2,275
1978	21	26	0	0	0	0	0	0	2	7,181	0	0	7,689	41,315
1979	31	12	0	0	0	0	0	0	0	2,974	0	0	2,736	21,000
1980	20	26	0	0	0	0	0	0	0	7,243	0	0	7,837	51,534
1981	90	1	0	0	0	0	0	0	0	72	0	0	144	2,450
Lifetime		67	0	0	0	0	0	0	2	18,084	0	0	19,011	$118,574

Bobby Hamilton
Robert Hamilton
B: 5/29/1957
Racing Hometown: Nashville, TN

Year	Rank	Starts	Poles	1	2	3	4	5	6–10	Laps	Laps Led	Races Led	Miles	$
1989	89	1	0	0	0	0	0	0	0	215	5	1	215	3,075
1990	66	3	0	0	0	0	0	0	0	407	0	0	611	10,665
1991	22	28	0	0	0	0	0	0	4	8,214	7	3	10,141	259,105
1992	25	29	0	0	0	0	0	0	2	8,998	0	0	10,737	367,065
1993	37	15	0	0	0	0	0	0	1	3,996	0	0	5,281	142,740
1994	23	30	0	0	0	0	0	0	1	8,337	24	4	10,221	514,520
1995	14	31	0	0	1	0	2	1	6	9,409	129	7	11,550	804,505
1996	9	31	2	1	0	1	0	1	8	9,153	648	11	10,897	1,151,235
1997	16	32	2	1	1	3	0	1	2	9,535	416	9	12,266	1,478,843
1998	10	33	1	1	1	0	1	0	5	9,840	443	6	12,759	2,089,566
1999	13	34	0	0	0	0	1	0	9	9,774	3	2	12,914	2,019,255
2000	60	2	0	0	0	0	0	0	0	580	0	0	885	82,390
2000	30	34	0	0	0	0	0	0	2	8,903	64	4	11,304	1,619,775
2001	18	36	0	1	0	0	1	1	4	10,750	239	4	14,100	2,527,310
2001	47	10	0	0	0	0	0	0	0	2,577	0	0	3,701	546,847
2002	32	31	0	0	0	0	0	0	3	8,824	57	3	11,617	2,196,956
Lifetime		380	5	4	3	4	5	4	47	109,512	2,035	54	139,201	$15,813,852

Bobby Hamilton Jr.
Robert Hamilton
B: 1/8/1977
Racing Hometown: Mt. Juliet, TN

Year	Rank	Starts	Poles	1	2	3	4	5	6–10	Laps	Laps Led	Races Led	Miles	$
2001		2	0	0	0	0	0	0	0		0	0		
2001		10	0	0	0	0	0	0	0		0	0		
Lifetime		12	0	0	0	0	0	0	0					$

Don Hamilton
Donald Hamilton
Racing Hometown: Portland, OR

Year	Rank	Starts	Poles	1	2	3	4	5	6–10	Laps	Laps Led	Races Led	Miles	$
1956	243	2	0	0	0	0	0	0	0	70	0	0	35	0
Lifetime		2	0	0	0	0	0	0	0	70	0	0	35	$0

Pete Hamilton
Peter Goodwill Hamilton
B: 7/20/1942
Racing Hometown: Dedham, MA

Year	Rank	Starts	Poles	1	2	3	4	5	6–10	Laps	Laps Led	Races Led	Miles	$
1968	32	16	0	0	1	0	0	2	3	3,555	33	2	2,592	7,920
1969	NR	3	0	0	0	0	0	1	1	421	14	1	724	5,435
1970	21	16	1	3	1	3	0	3	2	4,069	338	9	6,210	131,406
1971	24	22	2	1	0	5	4	1	1	4,525	219	14	6,895	60,440
1972	48	5	0	0	0	0	0	1	0	1,044	8	2	1,630	8,005
1973	114	2	0	0	0	0	0	0	0	71	0	0	140	2,905
Lifetime		64	3	4	2	8	4	8	7	13,685	612	28	18,191	$216,111

Year	Rank	Starts	Poles	1	2	3	Finish 4	5	6–10	Laps	Laps Led	Races Led	Miles	$

Bill Hammersly

William Hammersly (Red)
B: 5/30/1908   D: 3/1970
Racing Hometown: Mariners Harbor, NY

Year	Rank	Starts	Poles	1	2	3	4	5	6–10	Laps	Laps Led	Races Led	Miles	$
1952	129T	1	0	0	0	0	0	0	0	172	0	0	86	25
1953	179	1	0	0	0	0	0	0	0		0	0		25
Lifetime		2	0	0	0	0	0	0	0	172	0	0	86	$50

Carl Hammill

Carl Hammill
Racing Hometown: Santa Rosa, CA

Year	Rank	Starts	Poles	1	2	3	4	5	6–10	Laps	Laps Led	Races Led	Miles	$
1955	224	1	0	0	0	0	0	0	0	144	0	0	144	40
1956	97	2	0	0	0	0	0	0	0	321	0	0	321	160
Lifetime		3	0	0	0	0	0	0	0	465	0	0	465	$200

Art Hammond

Arthur Hammond
Racing Hometown: Rome, NY

Year	Rank	Starts	Poles	1	2	3	4	5	6–10	Laps	Laps Led	Races Led	Miles	$
1950	129T	1	0	0	0	0	0	0	0		0	0		0
Lifetime		1	0	0	0	0	0	0	0		0	0		$0

Keith Hamner

Keith Hamner
Racing Hometown: Elkin, WV

Year	Rank	Starts	Poles	1	2	3	4	5	6–10	Laps	Laps Led	Races Led	Miles	$
1952	61	1	0	0	0	0	0	0	0	375	0	0	469	90
1953	84	2	0	0	0	0	0	0	1	33	0	0	135	75
Lifetime		3	0	0	0	0	0	0	1	408	0	0	604	$165

Andy Hampton

Andrew T. Hampton
B: 11/30/1928
Racing Hometown: Louisville, KY

Year	Rank	Starts	Poles	1	2	3	4	5	6–10	Laps	Laps Led	Races Led	Miles	$
1959	67	1	0	0	0	0	0	0	0	76	0	0	38	50
1968	NR	1	0	0	0	0	0	0	1	193	0	0	483	2,525
1969	NR	2	0	0	0	0	0	0	1	197	0	0	493	2,500
Lifetime		4	0	0	0	0	0	0	2	466	0	0	1,013	$5,075

John Hamson

John Hamson
Racing Hometown: Santa Barbara, CA

Year	Rank	Starts	Poles	1	2	3	4	5	6–10	Laps	Laps Led	Races Led	Miles	$
1976	105T	1	0	0	0	0	0	0	0	26	0	0	68	790
Lifetime		1	0	0	0	0	0	0	0	26	0	0	68	$790

Mack Hanbury

Mack Hanbury
Racing Hometown: Hyattsville, MD

Year	Rank	Starts	Poles	1	2	3	4	5	6–10	Laps	Laps Led	Races Led	Miles	$
1955	40	8	0	0	0	0	0	0	2	807	0	0	584	575
1966	107	2	0	0	0	0	0	0	0	220	0	0	78	225
Lifetime		10	0	0	0	0	0	0	2	1,027	0	0	662	$800

Richard Hancock

Richard Hancock

Year	Rank	Starts	Poles	1	2	3	4	5	6–10	Laps	Laps Led	Races Led	Miles	$
1951	N/A	1	0	0	0	0	0	0	0		0	0		25
Lifetime		1	0	0	0	0	0	0	0		0	0		$25

Jeff Handy

H.L. Handy
Racing Hometown: Charlotte, NC

Year	Rank	Starts	Poles	1	2	3	4	5	6–10	Laps	Laps Led	Races Led	Miles	$
1975	86T	1	0	0	0	0	0	0	0	174	0	0	463	1,820
1976	NR	1	0	0	0	0	0	0	0	3	0	0	2	370
Lifetime		2	0	0	0	0	0	0	0	177	0	0	465	$2,190

Chuck Hansen

Charles H. Hansen
Racing Hometown: Whiteford, MD

Year	Rank	Starts	Poles	1	2	3	4	5	6–10	Laps	Laps Led	Races Led	Miles	$
1954	72	6	0	0	0	0	0	0	1	694	0	0	520	225
1955	61	5	0	0	0	0	0	0	2	733	0	0	421	275
1956	269	1	0	0	0	0	0	0	0	66	0	0	66	50

Year	Rank	Starts	Poles	Finish 1	2	3	4	5	6–10	Laps	Laps Led	Races Led	Miles	$

Chuck Hansen *continued*

Year	Rank	Starts	Poles	1	2	3	4	5	6–10	Laps	Laps Led	Races Led	Miles	$
1957	42	7	0	0	0	0	0	0	0	990	0	0	734	510
1958	43	7	0	0	0	0	0	0	1	1,011	0	0	659	580
Lifetime		26	0	0	0	0	0	0	4	3,494	0	0	2,400	$1,640

Jerry Hansen

Jerry Hansen
Racing Hometown: Bremen, GA

Year	Rank	Starts	Poles	1	2	3	4	5	6–10	Laps	Laps Led	Races Led	Miles	$
1974	69	3	0	0	0	0	0	0	0	221	0	0	543	3,230
Lifetime		3	0	0	0	0	0	0	0	221	0	0	543	$3,230

Walt Hansgen

Walter Hansgen
B: 10/28/1919   D: 4/7/1966   *Died from injuries suffered 4/2/66 while practicing for LeMans 24-Hour race.*
Racing Hometown: Westfield, NJ

Year	Rank	Starts	Poles	1	2	3	4	5	6–10	Laps	Laps Led	Races Led	Miles	$
1964	NR	2	0	0	0	2	0	0	0	113	0	0	286	1,100
1965	NR	1	0	0	0	0	0	0	1	58	0	0	133	355
Lifetime		3	0	0	0	2	0	0	1	171	0	0	420	$1,455

Fred Harb

Fareed Joseph Harb Jr.
B: 6/14/1930
Racing Hometown: High Point, NC

Year	Rank	Starts	Poles	1	2	3	4	5	6–10	Laps	Laps Led	Races Led	Miles	$
1955	109	2	0	0	0	0	0	0	0	276	0	0	185	135
1956	217	3	0	0	0	0	0	0	0	231	0	0	101	100
1957	NR	3	0	0	0	0	0	0	0	322	0	0	161	360
1958	24	25	0	0	0	1	2	1	3	3,651	0	0	1,840	3,315
1959	106	19	1	0	0	1	0	1	4	2,689	0	0	1,277	1,875
1960	60	20	0	0	0	0	0	2	5	3,269	0	0	1,467	2,780
1961	34	27	0	0	0	0	1	0	7	4,039	0	0	2,022	3,460
1962	39	21	0	0	0	0	0	0	3	2,763	0	0	1,190	2,220
1963	41	16	0	0	1	0	1	0	5	2,563	0	0	1,053	2,720
1964	99	3	0	0	0	0	0	1	1	550	0	0	138	555
1965	71	5	0	0	0	0	0	1	1	766	0	0	291	840
Lifetime		144	1	0	1	2	4	6	29	21,119	0	0	9,724	$18,360

Jack Harden

Jack W. Harden
B: 4/23/1934
Racing Hometown: Huntsville, AL

Year	Rank	Starts	Poles	1	2	3	4	5	6–10	Laps	Laps Led	Races Led	Miles	$
1967	41	10	0	0	0	0	0	0	0	1,393	0	0	1,958	4,450
Lifetime		10	0	0	0	0	0	0	0	1,393	0	0	1,958	$4,450

Harold Hardesty

Harold Hardesty
Racing Hometown: Pasco, WA

Year	Rank	Starts	Poles	1	2	3	4	5	6–10	Laps	Laps Led	Races Led	Miles	$
1956	27	9	0	0	1	0	0	1	4	1,761	0	0	1,350	2,380
1957	105	4	0	0	0	0	0	0	0	303	0	0	166	205
1958	109	1	0	0	0	0	0	1	0	98	0	0	98	300
1968	89	1	0	0	0	0	0	0	0	67	0	0	181	575
1969	NR	1	0	0	0	0	0	0	1	163	0	0	440	1,250
Lifetime		16	0	0	1	0	0	2	5	2,392	0	0	2,235	$4,710

J.E. Hardie

J.E. Hardie
Racing Hometown: Tabor City, NC

Year	Rank	Starts	Poles	1	2	3	4	5	6–10	Laps	Laps Led	Races Led	Miles	$
1950	NR	1	0	0	0	0	0	0	0	317	0	0	396	0
1951	N/A	1	0	0	0	0	0	0	0	339	0	0	424	50
1952	119	2	0	0	0	0	0	0	0	69	0	0	86	25
Lifetime		4	0	0	0	0	0	0	0	725	0	0	906	$75

Charles Hardiman

Charles Hardiman
Racing Hometown: Goodlettesville, TN

Year	Rank	Starts	Poles	1	2	3	4	5	6–10	Laps	Laps Led	Races Led	Miles	$
1954	74	1	0	0	0	0	0	0	0	146	0	0	219	200
Lifetime		1	0	0	0	0	0	0	0	146	0	0	219	$200

Year	Rank	Starts	Poles	1	2	3	Finish 4	5	6–10	Laps	Laps Led	Races Led	Miles	$

John Hardy

John Hardy

Year	Rank	Starts	Poles	1	2	3	4	5	6–10	Laps	Laps Led	Races Led	Miles	$
1962	NR	1	0	0	0	0	0	0	0	435	0	0	218	125
Lifetime		1	0	0	0	0	0	0	0	435	0	0	218	$125

John Harkins

John Harkins

Year	Rank	Starts	Poles	1	2	3	4	5	6–10	Laps	Laps Led	Races Led	Miles	$
1975	NR	1	0	0	0	0	0	0	0	382	0	0	382	800
Lifetime		1	0	0	0	0	0	0	0	382	0	0	382	$800

Bud Harless

Pearley Jackson Harless
B: 1/21/1924
Racing Hometown: Gilbert, WV

Year	Rank	Starts	Poles	1	2	3	4	5	6–10	Laps	Laps Led	Races Led	Miles	$
1953	134T	1	0	0	0	0	0	0	0	168	0	0	84	25
1954	75	5	0	0	0	0	0	0	0	482	0	0	364	75
1955	98	4	0	0	0	0	0	0	1	324	0	0	294	210
1963	50	5	0	0	0	0	0	0	1	1,508	0	0	958	1,550
1964	67	8	0	0	0	0	0	0	0	1,373	0	0	712	2,330
1965	77	5	0	0	0	0	0	0	0	849	0	0	621	2,065
Lifetime		28	0	0	0	0	0	0	2	4,704	0	0	3,032	$6,255

Marshall Harless

Marshall Harless
Racing Hometown: Gilbert, WV

Year	Rank	Starts	Poles	1	2	3	4	5	6–10	Laps	Laps Led	Races Led	Miles	$
1954	154T	1	0	0	0	0	0	0	0	82	0	0	82	25
Lifetime		1	0	0	0	0	0	0	0	82	0	0	82	$25

Allan Harley

Allan Harley
Racing Hometown: Bristol, VA

Year	Rank	Starts	Poles	1	2	3	4	5	6–10	Laps	Laps Led	Races Led	Miles	$
1962	130	2	0	0	0	0	0	0	0	15	0	0	8	150
Lifetime		2	0	0	0	0	0	0	0	15	0	0	8	$150

Rock Harn

Otis A. Harn
B: 7/29/1924
Racing Hometown: North Augusta, SC

Year	Rank	Starts	Poles	1	2	3	4	5	6–10	Laps	Laps Led	Races Led	Miles	$
1962	129	1	0	0	0	0	0	0	0	2	0	0	1	50
1965	101	1	0	0	0	0	0	0	0	1	0	0	2	445
1966	145	1	0	0	0	0	0	0	0	33	0	0	83	0
Lifetime		3	0	0	0	0	0	0	0	36	0	0	85	$495

Leon Harrell

Leon Harrell
Racing Hometown: Asheville, NC

Year	Rank	Starts	Poles	1	2	3	4	5	6–10	Laps	Laps Led	Races Led	Miles	$
1951	N/A	1	0	0	0	0	0	0	0		0	0		25
Lifetime		1	0	0	0	0	0	0	0		0	0		$25

Red Harrelson

Raymond Harrelson
Racing Hometown: Pensacola, FL

Year	Rank	Starts	Poles	1	2	3	4	5	6–10	Laps	Laps Led	Races Led	Miles	$
1951	N/A	1	1	0	0	0	0	0	0		0	0		25
1952	98	2	0	0	0	0	0	0	0	73	0	0	39	75
Lifetime		3	1	0	0	0	0	0	0	73	0	0	39	$100

Bob Harris

Robert Harris
B: 9/11/1926
Racing Hometown: Greensboro, NC

Year	Rank	Starts	Poles	1	2	3	4	5	6–10	Laps	Laps Led	Races Led	Miles	$
1953	NR	1	0	0	0	0	0	0	0		0	0		35
Lifetime		1	0	0	0	0	0	0	0		0	0		$35

Ferrel Harris

Ferrel Harris
B: 10/8/1940   D: 5/ /2000
Racing Hometown: Pikeville, KY

Year	Rank	Starts	Poles	1	2	3	4	5	6–10	Laps	Laps Led	Races Led	Miles	$
1975	38	10	0	0	0	0	0	0	0	2,357	0	0	3,854	16,165
1976	80	2	0	0	0	0	0	0	0	217	0	0	565	2,950
1977	32	11	0	0	0	0	0	0	0	2,979	0	0	2,560	19,365

Year	Rank	Starts	Poles	1	2	3	Finish 4	5	6–10	Laps	Laps Led	Races Led	Miles	$

Ferrel Harris *continued*

Year	Rank	Starts	Poles	1	2	3	4	5	6–10	Laps	Laps Led	Races Led	Miles	$
1978	35	14	0	0	0	0	0	0	5	2,915	0	0	4,372	39,635
1979	NR	1	0	0	0	0	0	0	0	2	0	0	3	1,260
1980	NR	2	0	0	0	0	0	0	0	359	0	0	512	4,025
1982	NR	1	0	0	0	0	0	0	0	146	0	0	388	2,625
Lifetime		41	0	0	0	0	0	0	5	8,975	0	0	12,255	$86,025

Runt Harris

Gayther Wallace Harris
B: 6/4/1927   D: 6/30/1990
Racing Hometown: Fredericksburg, VA

Year	Rank	Starts	Poles	1	2	3	4	5	6–10	Laps	Laps Led	Races Led	Miles	$
1950	129T	1	0	0	0	0	0	0	0	41	0	0	21	0
1957	158	1	0	0	0	0	0	0	0	50	0	0	69	100
1959	NR	1	0	0	0	0	0	1	0	193	0	0	97	250
1960	109	3	0	0	0	0	0	0	0	391	0	0	233	350
1962	109	2	0	0	0	0	0	0	0	130	0	0	51	100
Lifetime		8	0	0	0	0	0	1	0	805	0	0	470	$800

Bill Harrison

William J. Harrison
B: 9/2/1910   D: 11/1993
Racing Hometown: Topeka, KS

Year	Rank	Starts	Poles	1	2	3	4	5	6–10	Laps	Laps Led	Races Led	Miles	$
1949	NR	1	0	0	0	0	0	0	0		0	0		25
1950	135	2	0	0	0	0	0	0	0	38	0	0	29	0
1951	N/A	1	0	0	0	0	0	0	0	133	0	0	100	25
1953	40	3	0	0	0	0	0	0	3		0	0		450
1954	210	1	0	0	0	0	0	0	0		0	0		0
1955	108	2	0	0	0	0	0	0	1	279	0	0	140	125
Lifetime		10	0	0	0	0	0	0	4	450	0	0	268	$625

Jack Harrison

Jack Harrison
B: 1930   D: 11/11/1956   *Died of ulcers @ age 26.*
Racing Hometown: W. Newton, IN

Year	Rank	Starts	Poles	1	2	3	4	5	6–10	Laps	Laps Led	Races Led	Miles	$
1952	NR	1	0	0	0	0	0	0	0	277	0	0	139	50
1954	NR	1	0	0	0	0	0	0	0	19	0	0	19	25
Lifetime		2	0	0	0	0	0	0	0	296	0	0	158	$75

Joe Harrison

Joseph Harrison
Racing Hometown: Syracuse, NY

Year	Rank	Starts	Poles	1	2	3	4	5	6–10	Laps	Laps Led	Races Led	Miles	$
1950	NR	1	0	0	0	0	0	0	0	3	0	0	13	25
Lifetime		1	0	0	0	0	0	0	0	3	0	0	13	$25

Tubby Harrison

Tubby Harrison
Racing Hometown: Topeka, KS

Year	Rank	Starts	Poles	1	2	3	4	5	6–10	Laps	Laps Led	Races Led	Miles	$
1953	53T	2	0	0	0	0	0	0	2		0	0		150
Lifetime		2	0	0	0	0	0	0	2		0	0		$150

Jack Hart

Jack Hart
B: 1926
Racing Hometown: Boothwyn, PA

Year	Rank	Starts	Poles	1	2	3	4	5	6–10	Laps	Laps Led	Races Led	Miles	$
1960	116	1	0	0	0	0	0	0	0	76	0	0	19	145
1961	NR	1	0	0	0	0	0	0	0	52	0	0	13	60
Lifetime		2	0	0	0	0	0	0	0	128	0	0	32	$205

Jim Hart

James Hart
Racing Hometown: Newark, NJ

Year	Rank	Starts	Poles	1	2	3	4	5	6–10	Laps	Laps Led	Races Led	Miles	$
1951	N/A	1	0	0	0	0	0	0	0		0	0		25
Lifetime		1	0	0	0	0	0	0	0		0	0		$25

George Hartley

George Hartley
Racing Hometown: Erie, PA

Year	Rank	Starts	Poles	1	2	3	4	5	6–10	Laps	Laps Led	Races Led	Miles	$
1950	21	8	0	0	0	0	0	0	2	371	0	0	464	875
Lifetime		8	0	0	0	0	0	0	2	371	0	0	464	$875

Year	Rank	Starts	Poles	Finish 1	2	3	4	5	6–10	Laps	Laps Led	Races Led	Miles	$

Butch Hartman

Larry Hartman
B: 5/11/1940   D: 12/22/1994
Racing Hometown: Zanesville, OH

Year	Rank	Starts	Poles	1	2	3	4	5	6–10	Laps	Laps Led	Races Led	Miles	$
1966	NR	1	0	0	0	0	0	0	0	307	0	0	461	875
1968	NR	5	0	0	0	0	0	0	2	1,458	10	2	2,278	6,455
1972	NR	1	0	0	0	0	0	1	0	326	0	0	489	3,570
1977	31	11	0	0	0	0	0	0	2	2,005	0	0	3,690	18,615
1978	104	1	0	0	0	0	0	0	0	121	0	0	184	640
1979	86	1	0	0	0	0	0	0	0	351	0	0	479	2,225
Lifetime		20	0	0	0	0	0	1	4	4,568	10	2	7,581	$32,380

Walt Hartman

Walter Hartman
Racing Hometown: Chattanooga, TN

Year	Rank	Starts	Poles	1	2	3	4	5	6–10	Laps	Laps Led	Races Led	Miles	$
1951	N/A	3	0	0	0	0	0	0	0		0	0		75
Lifetime		3	0	0	0	0	0	0	0		0	0		$75

Billie Harvey

William Harvey
B: 1950
Racing Hometown: Delray Beach, FL

Year	Rank	Starts	Poles	1	2	3	4	5	6–10	Laps	Laps Led	Races Led	Miles	$
1980	87	4	0	0	0	0	0	0	0	805	0	0	1,691	7,995
1981	91	2	0	0	0	0	0	0	0	60	0	0	150	3,915
1982	104T	1	0	0	0	0	0	0	0	6	0	0	15	3,875
1983	NR	1	0	0	0	0	0	0	0	1	0	0	3	1,730
Lifetime		8	0	0	0	0	0	0	0	872	0	0	1,859	$17,515

Gordon Harvey

Gordon Harvey
B: 1920
Racing Hometown: Sayerville, NJ

Year	Rank	Starts	Poles	1	2	3	4	5	6–10	Laps	Laps Led	Races Led	Miles	$
1951	N/A	1	0	0	0	0	0	0	0		0	0		0
Lifetime		1	0	0	0	0	0	0	0		0	0		$0

Red Harvey

Red Harvey
Racing Hometown: Dayton, OH

Year	Rank	Starts	Poles	1	2	3	4	5	6–10	Laps	Laps Led	Races Led	Miles	$
1950	34T	1	0	0	1	0	0	0	0	0	1	1	0	750
1951	N/A	1	0	0	0	0	0	0	1		0	0		100
Lifetime		2	0	0	1	0	0	0	1	0	1	1	0	$850

Walt Harvey

Walter Harvey
Racing Hometown: Greenboro, NC

Year	Rank	Starts	Poles	1	2	3	4	5	6–10	Laps	Laps Led	Races Led	Miles	$
1954	150	1	0	0	0	0	0	0	0	284	0	0	391	120
Lifetime		1	0	0	0	0	0	0	0	284	0	0	391	$120

Kevin Harvick

Kevin Harvick
B: 12/8/1975
Racing Hometown: Bakersfield, CA

Year	Rank	Starts	Poles	1	2	3	4	5	6–10	Laps	Laps Led	Races Led	Miles	$
2001	9	35	0	2	3	1	0	0	10	10,561	374	12	13,667	4,302,202
2002	21	35	1	1	0	2	1	1	3	9,566	178	8	12,777	3,849,216
Lifetime		70	1	3	3	3	1	1	13	20,127	552	20	26,444	$8,151,418

Bill Hasley

William Hasley

Year	Rank	Starts	Poles	1	2	3	4	5	6–10	Laps	Laps Led	Races Led	Miles	$
1958	143	2	0	0	0	0	0	0	0	154	0	0	322	125
Lifetime		2	0	0	0	0	0	0	0	154	0	0	322	$125

Friday Hassler

Raymond Hassler
B: 6/29/1935   D: 2/17/1972   *Killed in 125-mile qualifying race @ Daytona.*
Racing Hometown: Chattanooga, TN

Year	Rank	Starts	Poles	1	2	3	4	5	6–10	Laps	Laps Led	Races Led	Miles	$
1960	87	2	0	0	0	0	0	0	0	251	0	0	377	425
1961	53	7	0	0	0	0	0	0	1	939	0	0	1,513	2,175
1962	114	2	0	0	0	0	0	0	0	257	0	0	321	300
1966	56	9	0	0	0	0	0	1	2	2,431	0	0	1,797	4,290
1967	32	21	0	0	0	0	1	2	6	4,309	1	1	3,091	10,270

Year	Rank	Starts	Poles	Finish 1	2	3	4	5	6–10	Laps	Laps Led	Races Led	Miles	$

Friday Hassler *continued*

Year	Rank	Starts	Poles	1	2	3	4	5	6–10	Laps	Laps Led	Races Led	Miles	$
1968	27	20	0	0	0	0	2	1	5	5,012	0	0	4,245	12,000
1969	28	18	0	0	0	0	0	0	7	4,607	3	1	4,665	17,690
1970	20	26	0	0	0	0	0	1	5	5,439	56	1	6,518	27,535
1971	16	29	2	0	1	2	0	1	9	5,650	68	3	7,137	37,305
1972	93	1	0	0	0	0	0	0	1	137	0	0	359	2,020
Lifetime		135	2	0	1	2	3	6	36	29,032	128	6	30,022	$114,010

Barney Hatchell

Barney Hatchell

Year	Rank	Starts	Poles	1	2	3	4	5	6–10	Laps	Laps Led	Races Led	Miles	$
1958	103	2	0	0	0	0	0	0	0	281	0	0	141	160
Lifetime		2	0	0	0	0	0	0	0	281	0	0	141	$160

Jake Hatcher

Joseph C. Hatcher
Racing Hometown: Pensacola, FL

Year	Rank	Starts	Poles	1	2	3	4	5	6–10	Laps	Laps Led	Races Led	Miles	$
1956	184T	1	0	0	0	0	0	0	0	172	0	0	86	100
Lifetime		1	0	0	0	0	0	0	0	172	0	0	86	$100

Ewell Hatfield

Ewell Hatfield
Racing Hometown: Wharncliffe, WV

Year	Rank	Starts	Poles	1	2	3	4	5	6–10	Laps	Laps Led	Races Led	Miles	$
1955	196	1	0	0	0	0	0	0	0	319	0	0	439	60
1956	NR	2	0	0	0	0	0	0	0	191	0	0	156	150
Lifetime		3	0	0	0	0	0	0	0	510	0	0	595	$210

Jack Hauher

Jack Hauher
Racing Hometown: Buffalo, NY

Year	Rank	Starts	Poles	1	2	3	4	5	6–10	Laps	Laps Led	Races Led	Miles	$
1952	140T	1	0	0	0	0	0	0	0	26	0	0	13	25
Lifetime		1	0	0	0	0	0	0	0	26	0	0	13	$25

Ted Hauser

Theodore Hauser

Year	Rank	Starts	Poles	1	2	3	4	5	6–10	Laps	Laps Led	Races Led	Miles	$
1957	NR	1	0	0	0	0	0	0	0	43	0	0	43	100
Lifetime		1	0	0	0	0	0	0	0	43	0	0	43	$100

Bob Havenmann

Robert Havenmann
Racing Hometown: Eureka, CA

Year	Rank	Starts	Poles	1	2	3	4	5	6–10	Laps	Laps Led	Races Led	Miles	$
1954	68	2	0	0	0	0	0	0	1	694	0	0	347	275
1955	69	3	0	0	0	0	0	0	2	506	0	0	410	400
1956	107	4	0	0	0	0	0	0	1	496	0	0	366	290
1957	136T	1	0	0	0	0	0	0	0	117	0	0	73	100
1958	130	1	0	0	0	0	0	0	0	91	0	0	91	100
Lifetime		11	0	0	0	0	0	0	4	1,904	0	0	1,287	$1,165

John Haver

John Haver
Racing Hometown: Weimar, TX

Year	Rank	Starts	Poles	1	2	3	4	5	6–10	Laps	Laps Led	Races Led	Miles	$
1976	107T	1	0	0	0	0	0	0	0	49	0	0	98	780
1979	NR	1	0	0	0	0	0	0	0	36	0	0	72	950
Lifetime		2	0	0	0	0	0	0	0	85	0	0	170	$1,730

Jeff Hawkins

Jeffrey Hawkins
Racing Hometown: Greenville, SC

Year	Rank	Starts	Poles	1	2	3	4	5	6–10	Laps	Laps Led	Races Led	Miles	$
1965	81	6	0	0	0	0	0	0	0	322	0	0	261	2,160
1966	79	2	0	0	0	0	0	1	1	360	0	0	180	425
1968	119	1	0	0	0	0	0	0	0	107	0	0	54	100
Lifetime		9	0	0	0	0	0	1	1	789	0	0	495	$2,685

Lewis Hawkins

Lewis Hawkins
Racing Hometown: Spartanburg, SC

Year	Rank	Starts	Poles	1	2	3	4	5	6–10	Laps	Laps Led	Races Led	Miles	$
1950	124	1	0	0	0	0	0	0	0		0	0		50
Lifetime		1	0	0	0	0	0	0	0		0	0		$50

Year	Rank	Starts	Poles	1	2	Finish 3	4	5	6–10	Laps	Laps Led	Races Led	Miles	$

Sam Hawks

Samuel Hawks
Racing Hometown: Modesto, CA

Year	Rank	Starts	Poles	1	2	3	4	5	6–10	Laps	Laps Led	Races Led	Miles	$
1951	46	3	0	0	0	0	1	0	0		0	0		650
1954	87	3	0	0	0	0	0	0	1	677	0	0	440	265
Lifetime		6	0	0	0	0	1	0	1	677	0	0	440	$915

J.T. Hayes

James Terry Hayes
Racing Hometown: Corinth, MS

Year	Rank	Starts	Poles	1	2	3	4	5	6–10	Laps	Laps Led	Races Led	Miles	$
1990	102	1	0	0	0	0	0	0	0	10	0	0	10	2,700
Lifetime		1	0	0	0	0	0	0	0	10	0	0	10	$2,700

Ronnie Hayes

Ronald Hayes

Year	Rank	Starts	Poles	1	2	3	4	5	6–10	Laps	Laps Led	Races Led	Miles	$
1954	NR	1	0	0	0	0	0	0	0	43	0	0	22	0
Lifetime		1	0	0	0	0	0	0	0	43	0	0	22	$0

Stew Hayes

Stewart Hayes
Racing Hometown: Rochester, NY

Year	Rank	Starts	Poles	1	2	3	4	5	6–10	Laps	Laps Led	Races Led	Miles	$
1952	133T	1	0	0	0	0	0	0	0	156	0	0	78	25
Lifetime		1	0	0	0	0	0	0	0	156	0	0	78	$25

Bill Hazel

William Hazel

Year	Rank	Starts	Poles	1	2	3	4	5	6–10	Laps	Laps Led	Races Led	Miles	$
1957	81	1	0	0	0	0	0	0	0	96	0	0	144	175
Lifetime		1	0	0	0	0	0	0	0	96	0	0	144	$175

Pete Hazelwood

Charles Hazelwood
Racing Hometown: Cartersville, GA

Year	Rank	Starts	Poles	1	2	3	4	5	6–10	Laps	Laps Led	Races Led	Miles	$
1969	43	16	0	0	0	0	0	0	1	2,367	0	0	1,163	4,160
1970	81	3	0	0	0	0	0	0	0	51	0	0	26	620
Lifetime		19	0	0	0	0	0	0	1	2,418	0	0	1,189	$4,780

Louis Headley

Louis M. Headley
Racing Hometown: Plymouth Meeting, PA

Year	Rank	Starts	Poles	1	2	3	4	5	6–10	Laps	Laps Led	Races Led	Miles	$
1955	234	1	0	0	0	0	0	0	0	3	0	0	12	0
1956	294T	1	0	0	0	0	0	0	0	1	0	0	1	25
Lifetime		2	0	0	0	0	0	0	0	4	0	0	13	$25

Gil Hearne

Gilbert Hearne
B: 6/18/1939
Racing Hometown: Wrightstown, NJ

Year	Rank	Starts	Poles	1	2	3	4	5	6–10	Laps	Laps Led	Races Led	Miles	$
1965	112T	1	0	0	0	0	0	0	0	172	0	0	57	100
1966	117	2	0	0	0	0	0	0	0	319	0	0	160	100
Lifetime		3	0	0	0	0	0	0	0	491	0	0	217	$200

Allen Heath

Allen Fred Heath
B: 1/18/1918
Racing Hometown: Saskatoon, Sask, Canada

Year	Rank	Starts	Poles	1	2	3	4	5	6–10	Laps	Laps Led	Races Led	Miles	$
1951	N/A	4	0	0	0	0	0	0	0		0	0		75
1954	NR	1	0	0	0	0	0	0	0	52	0	0	26	0
Lifetime		5	0	0	0	0	0	0	0	52	0	0	26	$75

Jim Heath

James Heath
Racing Hometown: Oakland, CA

Year	Rank	Starts	Poles	1	2	3	4	5	6–10	Laps	Laps Led	Races Led	Miles	$
1954	101	2	0	0	0	0	0	0	1	436	0	0	323	140
Lifetime		2	0	0	0	0	0	0	1	436	0	0	323	$140

Jay Hedgecock

Wesley Hedgecock
B: 2/28/1955
Racing Hometown: High Point, NC

Year	Rank	Starts	Poles	1	2	3	4	5	6–10	Laps	Laps Led	Races Led	Miles	$
1993	72T	1	0	0	0	0	0	0	0	372	0	0	233	4,780

Year	Rank	Starts	Poles	Finish 1	2	3	4	5	6–10	Laps	Laps Led	Races Led	Miles	$

Jay Hedgecock *continued*

Year	Rank	Starts	Poles	1	2	3	4	5	6–10	Laps	Laps Led	Races Led	Miles	$
1994	58	2	0	0	0	0	0	0	0	537	0	0	288	9,475
Lifetime		3	0	0	0	0	0	0	0	909	0	0	520	$14,255

Jason Hedlesky

Jason Hedlesky
B: 2/20/1974
Racing Hometown: Clinton, MI

2002	84T	1	0	0	0	0	0	0	0	31	0	0	47	39,160
Lifetime		1	0	0	0	0	0	0	0	31	0	0	47	$39,160

Gene Hege

Gene Hege

1958	154	1	0	0	0	0	0	0	0	85	0	0	43	0
Lifetime		1	0	0	0	0	0	0	0	85	0	0	43	$0

Harvey Hege

Harvey Hege
Racing Hometown: Thomasville, NC

1958	152	13	0	0	0	0	0	0	2	1,498	0	0	786	1,200
1959	41	10	0	0	0	0	0	0	3	1,485	0	0	765	955
1960	NR	1	0	0	0	0	0	0	0	62	0	0	31	100
1961	145	1	0	0	0	0	0	0	0	166	0	0	42	100
Lifetime		25	0	0	0	0	0	0	5	3,211	0	0	1,624	$2,355

Marvin Heinis

Marvin Heinis
Racing Hometown: Sylmar, CA

1961	137	2	0	0	0	0	0	0	0	132	0	0	187	200
Lifetime		2	0	0	0	0	0	0	0	132	0	0	187	$200

Greg Heller

Gregory Heller
Racing Hometown: Dubois, PA

1977	98T	1	0	0	0	0	0	0	0	110	0	0	275	680
1978	NR	1	0	0	0	0	0	0	0	250	0	0	250	575
Lifetime		2	0	0	0	0	0	0	0	360	0	0	525	$1,255

Buddy Helms

Buddy Helms
Racing Hometown: Charlotte, NC

1949	42	1	0	0	0	0	0	0	1		0	0		75
1950	NR	3	0	0	0	0	0	0	0	36	0	0	18	0
1951	N/A	1	0	0	0	0	0	0	0	132	0	0	99	25
Lifetime		5	0	0	0	0	0	0	1	168	0	0	117	$100

Jimmy Helms

James Helms
B: 8/7/1935
Racing Hometown: Charlotte, NC

1964	54	18	0	0	0	0	0	0	2	750	0	0	386	4,180
1965	18	39	0	0	0	0	0	0	4	5,731	0	0	3,987	12,050
1966	34	29	0	0	0	0	0	0	0	3,186	0	0	2,785	5,915
1967	78	2	0	0	0	0	0	0	1	607	0	0	304	640
Lifetime		88	0	0	0	0	0	0	7	10,274	0	0	7,461	$22,785

Kenny Hemphill

Kenneth Hemphill
B: 1951
Racing Hometown: Vandergrift, PA

1980	62	5	0	0	0	0	0	0	1	884	4	1	1,493	8,970
Lifetime		5	0	0	0	0	0	0	1	884	4	1	1,493	$8,970

Elmo Henderson

Elmo Henderson
Racing Hometown: Spartanburg, SC

1959	81	2	0	0	0	0	0	0	0	176	0	0	102	200
1960	47	6	0	0	0	0	0	0	0	870	0	0	1,083	1,425

Year	Rank	Starts	Poles	1	2	3	4	5	6–10	Laps	Laps Led	Races Led	Miles	$

Elmo Henderson *continued*

Year	Rank	Starts	Poles	1	2	3	4	5	6–10	Laps	Laps Led	Races Led	Miles	$
1961	77	4	0	0	0	0	0	0	1	583	0	0	782	835
1964	59	8	0	0	0	0	0	1	2	661	0	0	362	2,175
1965	99	1	0	0	0	0	0	0	0	101	0	0	51	130
Lifetime		21	0	0	0	0	0	1	3	2,391	0	0	2,378	$4,765

Harvey Henderson

Harvey Henderson
Racing Hometown: Beltsville, MD

Year	Rank	Starts	Poles	1	2	3	4	5	6–10	Laps	Laps Led	Races Led	Miles	$
1952	120T	1	0	0	0	0	0	0	0		0	0		25
1955	22	17	0	0	0	0	0	1	5	2,284	0	0	1,325	1,810
1956	30	18	0	0	0	0	0	0	4	2,520	0	0	1,618	1,360
1957	NR	1	0	0	0	0	0	0	0	172	0	0	86	100
1958	120	2	0	0	0	0	0	0	0	160	0	0	58	125
1961	163	1	0	0	0	0	0	0	0	153	0	0	77	75
Lifetime		40	0	0	0	0	0	1	9	5,289	0	0	3,164	$3,495

Rick Henderson

Richard Henderson
Racing Hometown: Petaluma, CA

Year	Rank	Starts	Poles	1	2	3	4	5	6–10	Laps	Laps Led	Races Led	Miles	$
1954	109	3	0	0	0	0	0	0	0	609	0	0	404	65
Lifetime		3	0	0	0	0	0	0	0	609	0	0	404	$65

Ray Hendrick

Raymond D. Hendrick
B: 4/1/1929   D: 9/28/1990
Racing Hometown: Richmond, VA

Year	Rank	Starts	Poles	1	2	3	4	5	6–10	Laps	Laps Led	Races Led	Miles	$
1956	228	2	0	0	0	0	0	0	0	177	0	0	231	100
1962	83	2	0	0	0	0	0	0	0	714	0	0	357	275
1963	87	2	0	0	0	0	0	1	1	573	0	0	238	625
1967	112	1	0	0	0	0	0	0	0	107	0	0	54	175
1968	95	4	0	0	0	0	0	1	3	1,295	7	1	590	1,470
1969	75T	1	0	0	0	0	0	0	0	351	0	0	176	490
1971	NR	1	0	0	0	0	0	0	0	295	0	0	300	665
1972	NR	1	0	0	0	0	0	0	0	311	0	0	164	625
1973	88	2	0	0	0	0	0	0	0	613	0	0	325	1,950
1974	128	1	0	0	0	0	0	0	0	179	0	0	94	620
Lifetime		17	0	0	0	0	0	2	4	4,615	7	1	2,528	$6,995

Rick Hendrick

Joseph R. Hendrick, III
B: 7/12/1949
Racing Hometown: Charlotte, NC

Year	Rank	Starts	Poles	1	2	3	4	5	6–10	Laps	Laps Led	Races Led	Miles	$
1987	NR	1	0	0	0	0	0	0	0	75	0	0	197	1,150
1988	63	1	0	0	0	0	0	0	0	94	0	0	246	2,550
Lifetime		2	0	0	0	0	0	0	0	169	0	0	443	$3,700

Roy Lee Hendrick

Roy Lee Hendrick
B: 12/25/1953
Racing Hometown: Richmond, VA

Year	Rank	Starts	Poles	1	2	3	4	5	6–10	Laps	Laps Led	Races Led	Miles	$
1986	119	1	0	0	0	0	0	0	0	91	0	0	91	875
Lifetime		1	0	0	0	0	0	0	0	91	0	0	91	$875

Jim Hendrickson

James Hendrickson
B: 12/24/1924   D: 2/2/1997
Racing Hometown: Deer Park, NY

Year	Rank	Starts	Poles	1	2	3	4	5	6–10	Laps	Laps Led	Races Led	Miles	$
1961	117	2	0	0	0	0	0	0	0	208	0	0	349	275
Lifetime		2	0	0	0	0	0	0	0	208	0	0	349	$275

J.C. Hendrix

J.C. Hendrix
D: 4/16/1963   Killed in Stock car race @ Cleveland, TN.
Racing Hometown: Griffin, GA

Year	Rank	Starts	Poles	1	2	3	4	5	6–10	Laps	Laps Led	Races Led	Miles	$
1959	52	3	1	0	0	0	0	0	1	361	0	0	274	360
1961	67	2	0	0	0	0	0	0	1	456	0	0	684	1,175
1962	94	1	0	0	0	0	0	0	0	379	0	0	237	250
Lifetime		6	1	0	0	0	0	0	2	1,196	0	0	1,194	$1,785

Year	Rank	Starts	Poles	Finish						Laps	Laps Led	Races Led	Miles	$
				1	2	3	4	5	6–10					

Jimmy Hensley

James Hensley Jr.
B: 10/11/1945
Racing Hometown: Ridgeway, VA

Year	Rank	Starts	Poles	1	2	3	4	5	6–10	Laps	Laps Led	Races Led	Miles	$
1972	99	2	0	0	0	0	0	1	0	548	0	0	288	1,900
1973	103	1	0	0	0	0	0	0	1	485	0	0	255	1,550
1974	83	2	0	0	0	0	0	0	1	668	9	1	351	2,260
1975	98	2	0	0	0	0	0	0	1	534	0	0	281	1,860
1976	68	2	0	0	0	0	0	0	1	474	0	0	249	2,150
1977	60	2	0	0	0	0	0	0	1	812	0	0	427	2,680
1981	NR	1	0	0	0	0	0	0	1	487	0	0	256	4,650
1982	NR	3	0	0	0	0	0	0	1	791	0	0	418	3,205
1984	NR	4	0	0	0	0	0	0	0	1,484	0	0	793	12,895
1986	54	3	0	0	0	0	0	0	0	1,194	0	0	634	11,755
1988	NR	1	0	0	0	0	0	0	0	290	0	0	153	4,245
1990	88	2	0	0	0	0	0	0	0	692	0	0	820	7,475
1991	41	4	0	0	0	0	0	0	1	1,708	0	0	1,491	32,125
1992	28	22	0	0	0	0	0	0	4	6,804	22	3	8,492	247,660
1993	32	21	0	0	0	0	0	0	2	5,843	1	1	6,930	368,150
1994	41	17	0	0	0	0	0	0	0	3,861	4	3	5,751	203,520
1995	44	9	0	0	0	0	0	0	0	1,512	0	0	2,434	161,025
Lifetime		98	0	0	0	0	0	1	14	28,187	36	8	30,023	$1,069,105

Bill Henson

William Henson
Racing Hometown: Birmingham, AL

Year	Rank	Starts	Poles	1	2	3	4	5	6–10	Laps	Laps Led	Races Led	Miles	$
1950	NR	1	0	0	0	0	0	0	0	200	0	0	250	100
Lifetime		1	0	0	0	0	0	0	0	200	0	0	250	$100

Bernie Hentges

Bernard Hentges
Racing Hometown: Anoka, MN

Year	Rank	Starts	Poles	1	2	3	4	5	6–10	Laps	Laps Led	Races Led	Miles	$
1957	187	1	0	0	0	0	0	0	0		0	0		0
1959	78	2	0	0	0	0	0	0	0	176	0	0	440	210
Lifetime		3	0	0	0	0	0	0	0	176	0	0	440	$210

Russ Hepler

Russell Hepler
B: 1923
Racing Hometown: Clarion, PA

Year	Rank	Starts	Poles	1	2	3	4	5	6–10	Laps	Laps Led	Races Led	Miles	$
1951	N/A	1	0	0	0	0	0	0	1		0	0		50
1952	113	2	0	0	0	0	0	0	0	166	0	0	97	25
1954	47	6	0	0	0	0	1	0	0	691	0	0	510	525
1957	90	4	1	0	0	0	0	0	0	365	0	0	206	345
Lifetime		13	1	0	0	0	1	0	1	1,222	0	0	812	$945

Tommy Herbert

Thomas Herbert
B: 1922
Racing Hometown: Delray Beach, FL

Year	Rank	Starts	Poles	1	2	3	4	5	6–10	Laps	Laps Led	Races Led	Miles	$
1956	275	1	0	0	0	0	0	0	0		0	0		0
1960	127	2	0	0	0	0	0	0	0	155	0	0	388	250
Lifetime		3	0	0	0	0	0	0	0	155	0	0	388	$250

Terry Herman

Terry Herman
Racing Hometown: Sonora, CA

Year	Rank	Starts	Poles	1	2	3	4	5	6–10	Laps	Laps Led	Races Led	Miles	$
1981	NR	2	0	0	0	0	0	0	0	188	0	0	500	7,035
1982	NR	1	0	0	0	0	0	0	0	113	0	0	296	4,220
Lifetime		3	0	0	0	0	0	0	0	301	0	0	796	$11,255

Ronnie Herra

Ronald Herra

Year	Rank	Starts	Poles	1	2	3	4	5	6–10	Laps	Laps Led	Races Led	Miles	$
1956	260	1	0	0	0	0	0	0	0	34	0	0	34	50
Lifetime		1	0	0	0	0	0	0	0	34	0	0	34	$50

Year	Rank	Starts	Poles	Finish 1	2	3	4	5	6–10	Laps	Laps Led	Races Led	Miles	$

Skimp Hersey

John Edward Hersey
B: 2/8/1913   D: 6/12/1950   *Died from burns suffered @ Lakewood Speedway 6/11/50.*
Racing Hometown: St. Augustine, FL

Year	Rank	Starts	Poles	1	2	3	4	5	6–10	Laps	Laps Led	Races Led	Miles	$
1949	NR	1	0	0	0	0	0	0	0		0	0		25
Lifetime		1	0	0	0	0	0	0	0		0	0		$25

Ben Hess

Benjamin Hess
B: 12/20/1964
Racing Hometown: Dayton, OH

Year	Rank	Starts	Poles	1	2	3	4	5	6–10	Laps	Laps Led	Races Led	Miles	$
1988	67	1	0	0	0	0	0	0	0	472	0	0	480	3,370
1989	37	9	0	0	0	0	0	0	0	3,194	0	0	3,818	48,490
1990	89	1	0	0	0	0	0	0	0	169	0	0	338	4,275
1995	59	1	0	0	0	0	0	0	0	196	0	0	490	35,785
Lifetime		12	0	0	0	0	0	0	0	4,031	0	0	5,126	$91,920

Larry Hess

Lawrence Hess
B: 5/3/1935
Racing Hometown: Oil City, PA

Year	Rank	Starts	Poles	1	2	3	4	5	6–10	Laps	Laps Led	Races Led	Miles	$
1965	16	10	0	0	0	0	0	0	3	2,347	0	0	3,543	9,260
1966	40	13	0	0	0	0	0	0	0	1,830	0	0	2,160	5,290
1967	109	2	0	0	0	0	0	0	0	58	0	0	82	900
1968	109	1	0	0	0	0	0	0	0	0	0	0	0	460
1969	81	1	0	0	0	0	0	0	0	122	0	0	183	1,325
Lifetime		27	0	0	0	0	0	0	3	4,357	0	0	5,968	$17,235

Dr. Ed Hessert

Dr. Edmond C. Hessert
B: 6/25/1932   *Deceased.*
Racing Hometown: Trenton, NJ

Year	Rank	Starts	Poles	1	2	3	4	5	6–10	Laps	Laps Led	Races Led	Miles	$
1969	32	16	0	0	0	0	0	0	4	2,635	1	1	3,208	17,690
1970	82	2	0	0	0	0	0	0	0	105	0	0	203	495
1971	82	2	0	0	0	0	0	0	0	108	0	0	55	415
1972	114	2	0	0	0	0	0	0	0	157	0	0	343	1,505
Lifetime		22	0	0	0	0	0	0	4	3,005	1	1	3,808	$20,105

Tom Hessert

Thomas Hessert
B: 4/1/1951
Racing Hometown: Trenton, NJ

Year	Rank	Starts	Poles	1	2	3	4	5	6–10	Laps	Laps Led	Races Led	Miles	$
1982	100	1	0	0	0	0	0	0	0	8	0	0	20	950
Lifetime		1	0	0	0	0	0	0	0	8	0	0	20	$950

Doug Heveron

Douglas Heveron
B: 3/29/1964
Racing Hometown: Liverpool, NY

Year	Rank	Starts	Poles	1	2	3	4	5	6–10	Laps	Laps Led	Races Led	Miles	$
1984	36	16	0	0	0	0	0	0	0	3,553	7	1	4,864	39,950
1985	97	2	0	0	0	0	0	0	0	238	0	0	595	11,015
1986	35	13	0	0	0	0	0	0	0	2,536	1	1	3,409	74,030
Lifetime		31	0	0	0	0	0	0	0	6,327	8	2	8,868	$124,995

Bud Hickey

Bud Hickey

Year	Rank	Starts	Poles	1	2	3	4	5	6–10	Laps	Laps Led	Races Led	Miles	$
1985	95T	1	0	0	0	0	0	0	0	40	0	0	105	950
Lifetime		1	0	0	0	0	0	0	0	40	0	0	105	$950

Lester Hicks

Lester Hicks
Racing Hometown: Bristol, VA

Year	Rank	Starts	Poles	1	2	3	4	5	6–10	Laps	Laps Led	Races Led	Miles	$
1962	119	2	0	0	0	0	0	0	0	264	0	0	132	150
Lifetime		2	0	0	0	0	0	0	0	264	0	0	132	$150

Bill Hidden

William Hidden

Year	Rank	Starts	Poles	1	2	3	4	5	6–10	Laps	Laps Led	Races Led	Miles	$
1957	114T	2	0	0	0	0	0	0	0	121	0	0	89	150
Lifetime		2	0	0	0	0	0	0	0	121	0	0	89	$150

Year	Rank	Starts	Poles	Finish 1	2	3	4	5	6–10	Laps	Laps Led	Races Led	Miles	$

Boyce Hildreth

Boyce Hildreth
Racing Hometown: Greensboro, NC

Year	Rank	Starts	Poles	1	2	3	4	5	6–10	Laps	Laps Led	Races Led	Miles	$
1955	214	2	0	0	0	0	0	0	0	46	0	0	24	50
Lifetime		2	0	0	0	0	0	0	0	46	0	0	24	$50

Don Hildreth

Donald Hildreth
Racing Hometown: Portland, OR

Year	Rank	Starts	Poles	1	2	3	4	5	6–10	Laps	Laps Led	Races Led	Miles	$
1956	214T	1	0	0	0	0	0	0	0	140	0	0	70	50
Lifetime		1	0	0	0	0	0	0	0	140	0	0	70	$50

Elton Hildreth

Elton C. Hildreth
B: 1918
Racing Hometown: Bridgeton, NJ

Year	Rank	Starts	Poles	1	2	3	4	5	6–10	Laps	Laps Led	Races Led	Miles	$
1952	42	6	0	0	0	0	0	0	1	815	0	0	608	375
1953	13	25	0	0	0	0	1	0	4	821	0	0	785	1,997
1954	20	14	0	0	0	0	0	0	2	1,519	0	0	1,420	1,152
1955	156	3	0	0	0	0	0	0	0	130	0	0	79	100
1956	257	1	0	0	0	0	0	0	0	122	0	0	122	75
1957	88	2	0	0	0	0	0	0	0	153	0	0	153	150
Lifetime		51	0	0	0	0	1	0	7	3,560	0	0	3,167	$3,849

Bruce Hill

Bruce Hill
B: 7/9/1949
Racing Hometown: Topeka, KS

Year	Rank	Starts	Poles	1	2	3	4	5	6–10	Laps	Laps Led	Races Led	Miles	$
1974	101	1	0	0	0	0	0	0	0	189	0	0	473	1,575
1975	16	26	0	0	0	0	0	3	8	6,788	2	2	7,705	79,428
1976	23	22	0	0	0	0	0	0	4	3,669	3	1	5,412	43,705
1977	29	16	0	0	0	0	0	0	4	2,883	4	1	4,291	25,035
1978	32	14	0	0	0	0	0	0	2	2,802	0	0	3,790	25,770
1979	34	7	0	0	0	0	0	0	0	1,352	0	0	2,693	17,265
1980	50	6	0	0	0	0	0	0	0	418	0	0	808	7,540
1981	43	8	0	0	0	0	0	0	0	880	0	0	1,514	15,485
Lifetime		100	0	0	0	0	0	3	18	18,981	9	4	26,685	$215,803

Charlie Hill

Charles Hill
Racing Hometown: Winston-Salem, NC

Year	Rank	Starts	Poles	1	2	3	4	5	6–10	Laps	Laps Led	Races Led	Miles	$
1952	NR	1	0	0	0	0	0	0	0	217	0	0	217	50
Lifetime		1	0	0	0	0	0	0	0	217	0	0	217	$50

Cliff Hill

Clifford Hill

Year	Rank	Starts	Poles	1	2	3	4	5	6–10	Laps	Laps Led	Races Led	Miles	$
1961	152	1	0	0	0	0	0	0	0	31	0	0	80	50
Lifetime		1	0	0	0	0	0	0	0	31	0	0	80	$50

Frank Hill

Frank Hill

Year	Rank	Starts	Poles	1	2	3	4	5	6–10	Laps	Laps Led	Races Led	Miles	$
1978	NR	1	0	0	0	0	0	0	0	37	0	0	98	1,280
Lifetime		1	0	0	0	0	0	0	0	37	0	0	98	$1,280

Fred Hill

Fred Hill

Year	Rank	Starts	Poles	1	2	3	4	5	6–10	Laps	Laps Led	Races Led	Miles	$
1971	NR	1	0	0	0	0	0	0	0	116	0	0	58	350
Lifetime		1	0	0	0	0	0	0	0	116	0	0	58	$350

Herb Hill

Herbert Hill

Year	Rank	Starts	Poles	1	2	3	4	5	6–10	Laps	Laps Led	Races Led	Miles	$
1955	187	1	0	0	0	0	0	0	0	70	0	0	70	40
Lifetime		1	0	0	0	0	0	0	0	70	0	0	70	$40

Jerry Hill

Jerry Hill
B: 7/25/1961
Racing Hometown: Brandywine, MD

Year	Rank	Starts	Poles	1	2	3	4	5	6–10	Laps	Laps Led	Races Led	Miles	$
1991	72	2	0	0	0	0	0	0	0	52	0	0	52	6,975

Year	Rank	Starts	Poles	Finish 1	2	3	4	5	6–10	Laps	Laps Led	Races Led	Miles	$

Jerry Hill *continued*

Year	Rank	Starts	Poles	1	2	3	4	5	6–10	Laps	Laps Led	Races Led	Miles	$
1992	51	4	0	0	0	0	0	0	0	520	0	0	554	17,705
1993	68T	2	0	0	0	0	0	0	0	353	0	0	359	12,885
Lifetime		8	0	0	0	0	0	0	0	925	0	0	965	$37,565

Morris Hill

Morris Hill
Racing Hometown: Montgomery, AL

Year	Rank	Starts	Poles	1	2	3	4	5	6–10	Laps	Laps Led	Races Led	Miles	$
1955	NR	1	0	0	0	0	0	0	0	0	0	0	0	25
Lifetime		1	0	0	0	0	0	0	0	0	0	0	0	$25

Ray Hill

Raymond Hill
B: 9/20/1931
Racing Hometown: Concord, NC

Year	Rank	Starts	Poles	1	2	3	4	5	6–10	Laps	Laps Led	Races Led	Miles	$
1966	73	6	0	0	0	0	0	0	3	1,430	0	0	604	1,045
1966	73	6	0	0	0	0	0	0	3	1,430	0	0	604	1,045
1967	123	1	0	0	0	0	0	0	0	91	0	0	46	275
1967	123	1	0	0	0	0	0	0	0	91	0	0	46	275
1968	NR	1	0	0	0	0	0	0	0	1	0	0	1	100
1968	NR	1	0	0	0	0	0	0	0	1	0	0	1	100
Lifetime		16	0	0	0	0	0	0	6	3,044	0	0	1,300	$2,840

Andy Hillenburg

Andrew Hillenburg
B: 4/30/1963
Racing Hometown: Indianapolis, IN

Year	Rank	Starts	Poles	1	2	3	4	5	6–10	Laps	Laps Led	Races Led	Miles	$
1991	64T	2	0	0	0	0	0	0	0	320	0	0	484	7,520
1993	91T	1	0	0	0	0	0	0	0	242	0	0	363	4,365
1995	65T	1	0	0	0	0	0	0	0	157	0	0	393	17,320
1998	54	4	0	0	0	0	0	0	0	836	0	0	1,697	175,505
1999	68T	1	0	0	0	0	0	0	0	50	0	0	133	32,736
2002	84T	1	0	0	0	0	0	0	0	12	0	0	16	34,598
Lifetime		10	0	0	0	0	0	0	0	1,617	0	0	3,086	$272,044

Harvey Hilligas

Harvey Hilligas
Racing Hometown: Philadelphia, PA

Year	Rank	Starts	Poles	1	2	3	4	5	6–10	Laps	Laps Led	Races Led	Miles	$
1949	NR	1	0	0	0	0	0	0	0	162	0	0	162	25
Lifetime		1	0	0	0	0	0	0	0	162	0	0	162	$25

Bobby Hillin

Robert Hillin Jr.
B: 6/5/1964
Racing Hometown: Midland, TX

Year	Rank	Starts	Poles	1	2	3	4	5	6–10	Laps	Laps Led	Races Led	Miles	$
1982	46	5	0	0	0	0	0	0	0	917	0	0	1,515	9,830
1983	37	12	0	0	0	0	0	0	0	2,791	0	0	4,199	30,275
1984	32	16	0	0	0	0	0	0	0	3,452	0	0	5,655	45,020
1985	15	28	0	0	0	0	0	0	5	8,636	2	2	10,212	145,070
1986	9	29	0	1	0	1	2	0	10	8,121	25	4	9,980	448,452
1987	19	29	0	0	0	0	0	1	3	6,989	1	1	8,615	246,735
1988	12	29	0	0	0	1	0	0	6	9,383	70	4	11,188	300,217
1989	16	28	0	0	0	0	0	1	6	8,377	26	4	10,298	232,204
1990	19	29	0	0	0	0	0	1	3	8,299	60	5	10,200	339,366
1991	30	22	0	0	0	0	0	0	1	6,152	10	1	8,353	251,645
1992	34	13	0	0	0	0	0	0	0	2,770	0	0	4,686	102,160
1993	27	30	0	0	0	0	0	0	0	8,343	3	1	9,769	263,540
1994	44	9	0	0	0	0	0	0	0	2,007	2	1	3,171	125,340
1995	37	18	0	0	0	0	0	0	1	4,411	2	2	6,353	244,270
1996	37	26	0	0	0	0	0	0	0	7,164	4	1	8,870	395,224
1997	47	10	0	0	0	0	0	0	0	1,781	0	0	2,292	211,978
2000	70	1	0	0	0	0	0	0	0	314	0	0	167	27,525
Lifetime		334	0	1	0	2	2	3	35	89,907	205	26	115,525	$3,418,851

Jimmy Hindman

James Hindman

Year	Rank	Starts	Poles	1	2	3	4	5	6–10	Laps	Laps Led	Races Led	Miles	$
1979	NR	1	0	0	0	0	0	0	0	2	0	0	1	350
Lifetime		1	0	0	0	0	0	0	0	2	0	0	1	$350

Year	Rank	Starts	Poles		Finish						Laps	Laps Led	Races Led	Miles	$
				1	2	3	4	5	6–10		Laps	Led	Led	Miles	$

Joe Hines

Joseph Charleton Hines Jr.
B: 8/24/1937
Racing Hometown: Statesboro, GA

Year	Rank	Starts	Poles	1	2	3	4	5	6–10	Laps	Laps Led	Races Led	Miles	$
1969	NR	1	0	0	0	0	0	0	0	38	0	0	76	800
1970	107	1	0	0	0	0	0	0	0	43	0	0	108	245
1971	90	1	0	0	0	0	0	0	0	1	0	0	3	0
Lifetime		3	0	0	0	0	0	0	0	82	0	0	186	$1,045

Rudy Hires

Rudolph Hires
Racing Hometown: Norfolk, VA

Year	Rank	Starts	Poles	1	2	3	4	5	6–10	Laps	Laps Led	Races Led	Miles	$
1951	N/A	1	0	0	0	0	0	0	0	82	0	0	103	0
1952	162	1	0	0	0	0	0	0	0	267	0	0	334	50
Lifetime		2	0	0	0	0	0	0	0	349	0	0	436	$50

Butch Hirst

John Hirst
B: 8/29/1940
Racing Hometown: Orange City, FL

Year	Rank	Starts	Poles	1	2	3	4	5	6–10	Laps	Laps Led	Races Led	Miles	$
1970	56	5	0	0	0	0	0	0	0	663	0	0	1,398	5,414
1971	NR	1	0	0	0	0	0	0	0	2	0	0	5	0
Lifetime		6	0	0	0	0	0	0	0	665	0	0	1,403	$5,414

Mike Hiss

Michael Hiss
B: 7/7/1941
Racing Hometown: Norwalk, CT

Year	Rank	Starts	Poles	1	2	3	4	5	6–10	Laps	Laps Led	Races Led	Miles	$
1976	NR	1	0	0	0	0	0	0	0	169	0	0	423	1,365
Lifetime		1	0	0	0	0	0	0	0	169	0	0	423	$1,365

George Hixon

George Hixon

Year	Rank	Starts	Poles	1	2	3	4	5	6–10	Laps	Laps Led	Races Led	Miles	$
1967	NR	1	0	0	0	0	0	0	0	187	0	0	94	120
Lifetime		1	0	0	0	0	0	0	0	187	0	0	94	$120

Dutch Hoag

Donald Hoag
B: 11/2/1926
Racing Hometown: Penn Yan, NY

Year	Rank	Starts	Poles	1	2	3	4	5	6–10	Laps	Laps Led	Races Led	Miles	$
1952	114T	1	0	0	0	0	0	0	0	163	0	0	82	25
1955	112	2	0	0	0	0	0	0	1	285	0	0	143	200
1957	NR	1	0	0	0	0	0	0	0	85	0	0	85	0
Lifetime		4	0	0	0	0	0	0	1	533	0	0	309	$225

Chuck Hobbs

Charles Hobbs
Racing Hometown: Gibson, OH

Year	Rank	Starts	Poles	1	2	3	4	5	6–10	Laps	Laps Led	Races Led	Miles	$
1957	181	1	0	0	0	0	0	0	0		0	0		25
Lifetime		1	0	0	0	0	0	0	0		0	0		$25

David Hobbs

David Wishart Hobbs
B: 6/9/1939
Racing Hometown: Upper Boddington, England

Year	Rank	Starts	Poles	1	2	3	4	5	6–10	Laps	Laps Led	Races Led	Miles	$
1976	NR	2	0	0	0	0	0	0	0	255	2	1	544	3,030
Lifetime		2	0	0	0	0	0	0	0	255	2	1	544	$3,030

Gene Hobby

Eugene Hobby
B: 10/17/1937
Racing Hometown: Henderson, NC

Year	Rank	Starts	Poles	1	2	3	4	5	6–10	Laps	Laps Led	Races Led	Miles	$
1964	44	18	0	0	0	0	0	0	3	4,013	0	0	1,804	2,795
1965	51	15	0	0	0	0	1	0	1	1,979	0	0	971	2,560
1966	135	2	0	0	0	0	0	0	0	34	0	0	12	0
Lifetime		35	0	0	0	0	1	0	4	6,026	0	0	2,788	$5,355

Year	Rank	Starts	Poles	Finish 1	2	3	4	5	6–10	Laps	Laps Led	Races Led	Miles	$

Cotton Hodges

James Elmer Hodges
B: 5/12/1926
Racing Hometown: Hollywood, FL

Year	Rank	Starts	Poles	1	2	3	4	5	6–10	Laps	Laps Led	Races Led	Miles	$
1953	173	1	0	0	0	0	0	0	0	32	0	0	131	25
1954	NR	1	0	0	0	0	0	0	0	164	0	0	82	25
1963	145	1	0	0	0	0	0	0	0	9	0	0	5	50
Lifetime		3	0	0	0	0	0	0	0	205	0	0	218	$100

Irv Hoerr

Irv Hoerr
B: 11/14/1946
Racing Hometown: Peoria, IL

Year	Rank	Starts	Poles	1	2	3	4	5	6–10	Laps	Laps Led	Races Led	Miles	$
1987	NR	1	0	0	0	0	0	0	0	114	0	0	299	1,705
1990	47	2	0	0	0	0	0	0	2	164	3	1	407	14,775
1991	52	3	0	0	0	0	0	0	0	243	0	0	608	11,125
1992	95T	1	0	0	0	0	0	0	0	22	0	0	55	4,725
Lifetime		7	0	0	0	0	0	0	2	543	3	1	1,369	$32,330

Charlie Hoff

Charles Hoff
Racing Hometown: Bloomfield, NJ

Year	Rank	Starts	Poles	1	2	3	4	5	6–10	Laps	Laps Led	Races Led	Miles	$
1953	127T	1	0	0	0	0	0	0	0		0	0		25
Lifetime		1	0	0	0	0	0	0	0		0	0		$25

Dick Hoffman

Richard Hoffman

Year	Rank	Starts	Poles	1	2	3	4	5	6–10	Laps	Laps Led	Races Led	Miles	$
1957	164	1	0	0	0	0	0	0	0	50	0	0	125	60
Lifetime		1	0	0	0	0	0	0	0	50	0	0	125	$60

Don Hoffman

Donald Hoffman
Racing Hometown: Des Moines, IA

Year	Rank	Starts	Poles	1	2	3	4	5	6–10	Laps	Laps Led	Races Led	Miles	$
1975	NR	1	0	0	0	0	0	0	0	178	0	0	445	1,650
Lifetime		1	0	0	0	0	0	0	0	178	0	0	445	$1,650

John Hoffman

John Hoffman
Racing Hometown: Charlotte, NC

Year	Rank	Starts	Poles	1	2	3	4	5	6–10	Laps	Laps Led	Races Led	Miles	$
1963	146	1	0	0	0	0	0	0	0	51	0	0	13	100
Lifetime		1	0	0	0	0	0	0	0	51	0	0	13	$100

Bob Hogle

Robert Hogle
B: 1934   *Killed @ Ascot.*
Racing Hometown: Buena Park, CA

Year	Rank	Starts	Poles	1	2	3	4	5	6–10	Laps	Laps Led	Races Led	Miles	$
1959	NR	2	0	0	0	0	0	0	0	429	0	0	184	165
1960	149	1	0	0	0	0	0	0	0	3	0	0	4	0
Lifetime		3	0	0	0	0	0	0	0	432	0	0	188	$165

Al Holbert

Alvah R. Holbert
B: 11/11/1946   D: 9/30/1988   *Killed in private plane crash.*
Racing Hometown: Warrington, PA

Year	Rank	Starts	Poles	1	2	3	4	5	6–10	Laps	Laps Led	Races Led	Miles	$
1976	NR	1	0	0	0	0	0	0	0	7	0	0	11	855
1978	34	12	0	0	0	0	0	0	3	2,479	0	0	3,919	31,075
1979	45	6	0	0	0	0	0	0	1	938	5	1	1,620	14,170
Lifetime		19	0	0	0	0	0	0	4	3,424	5	1	5,549	$46,100

Gene Holcomb

Gene Holcomb
Racing Hometown: Aberdeen, MD

Year	Rank	Starts	Poles	1	2	3	4	5	6–10	Laps	Laps Led	Races Led	Miles	$
1954	161	2	0	0	0	0	0	0	0	369	0	0	283	50
1955	145	2	0	0	0	0	0	0	0	188	0	0	147	25
Lifetime		4	0	0	0	0	0	0	0	557	0	0	430	$75

Jerry Holden

Jerry Holden
Racing Hometown: Springfield, MO

Year	Rank	Starts	Poles	1	2	3	4	5	6–10	Laps	Laps Led	Races Led	Miles	$
1986	NR	1	0	0	0	0	0	0	0	100	0	0	100	1,200

Year	Rank	Starts	Poles		Finish					Laps	Laps Led	Races Led	Miles	$
				1	2	3	4	5	6–10					

Jerry Holden *continued*

Year	Rank	Starts	Poles	1	2	3	4	5	6–10	Laps	Laps Led	Races Led	Miles	$
1987	105	2	0	0	0	0	0	0	0	141	0	0	362	4,100
Lifetime		3	0	0	0	0	0	0	0	241	0	0	462	$5,300

Joe Holder

Joseph Holder
Racing Hometown: Franklinton, NC

Year	Rank	Starts	Poles	1	2	3	4	5	6–10	Laps	Laps Led	Races Led	Miles	$
1965	114	2	0	0	0	0	0	0	0	135	0	0	47	200
1966	146T	1	0	0	0	0	0	0	0	2	0	0	1	0
Lifetime		3	0	0	0	0	0	0	0	137	0	0	48	$200

Bill Holland

William A. Holland
B: 12/18/1907   D: 5/19/1984
Racing Hometown: Bridgeport, CT

Year	Rank	Starts	Poles	1	2	3	4	5	6–10	Laps	Laps Led	Races Led	Miles	$
1951	55	7	0	0	0	0	1	0	1	224	0	0	191	425
1952	179	1	0	0	0	0	0	0	0	123	0	0	123	25
Lifetime		8	0	0	0	0	1	0	1	347	0	0	314	$450

Bill Hollar

William Mack Hollar
B: 9/6/1938
Racing Hometown: Burlington, NC

Year	Rank	Starts	Poles	1	2	3	4	5	6–10	Laps	Laps Led	Races Led	Miles	$
1970	66	3	0	0	0	0	0	0	1	792	0	0	414	970
1971	43	11	0	0	0	0	0	0	1	2,095	0	0	1,602	4,275
1972	112	1	0	0	0	0	0	0	0	64	0	0	128	705
1973	89	1	0	0	0	0	0	0	0	419	0	0	419	1,060
1975	60	3	0	0	0	0	0	0	0	1,107	0	0	777	1,865
1976	115T	1	0	0	0	0	0	0	0	2	0	0	5	540
1978	72	3	0	0	0	0	0	0	0	90	0	0	62	1,360
1979	48	5	0	0	0	0	0	0	0	542	0	0	376	2,545
1980	92T	1	0	0	0	0	0	0	0	281	0	0	152	600
Lifetime		29	0	0	0	0	0	0	2	5,392	0	0	3,934	$13,920

Armond Holley

Armond Holley
B: 7/17/1934
Racing Hometown: Columbus, MS

Year	Rank	Starts	Poles	1	2	3	4	5	6–10	Laps	Laps Led	Races Led	Miles	$
1967	69	5	0	0	0	0	0	0	0	378	0	0	451	2,775
Lifetime		5	0	0	0	0	0	0	0	378	0	0	451	$2,775

Claude Holliday

Sterling Claude Holliday (Buck)
Racing Hometown: Waddington, NY

Year	Rank	Starts	Poles	1	2	3	4	5	6–10	Laps	Laps Led	Races Led	Miles	$
1957	NR	1	0	0	0	0	0	0	0	12	0	0	28	50
Lifetime		1	0	0	0	0	0	0	0	12	0	0	28	$50

Red Hollingsworth

Red Hollingsworth
Racing Hometown: Chattanooga, TN

Year	Rank	Starts	Poles	1	2	3	4	5	6–10	Laps	Laps Led	Races Led	Miles	$
1961	154	3	0	0	0	0	0	0	0	70	0	0	173	450
Lifetime		3	0	0	0	0	0	0	0	70	0	0	173	$450

Jack Holloway

Jack Holloway
Racing Hometown: Winston-Salem, NC

Year	Rank	Starts	Poles	1	2	3	4	5	6–10	Laps	Laps Led	Races Led	Miles	$
1950	49	2	0	0	0	0	0	0	2	192	0	0	96	225
1951	N/A	3	0	0	0	0	0	0	0		0	0		75
1952	205	1	0	0	0	0	0	0	0	12	0	0	6	25
Lifetime		6	0	0	0	0	0	0	2	204	0	0	102	$325

Bill Holluck

William Holluck
Racing Hometown: Martinsville, VA

Year	Rank	Starts	Poles	1	2	3	4	5	6–10	Laps	Laps Led	Races Led	Miles	$
1951	N/A	1	0	0	0	0	0	0	0		0	0		25
Lifetime		1	0	0	0	0	0	0	0		0	0		$25

Year	Rank	Starts	Poles	Finish						Laps	Laps Led	Races Led	Miles	$
				1	2	3	4	5	6–10					

Elgin Holmes

Elgin Holmes
Racing Hometown: Miami, FL

Year	Rank	Starts	Poles	1	2	3	4	5	6–10	Laps	Laps Led	Races Led	Miles	$
1956	254	1	0	0	0	0	0	0	0	71	0	0	178	50
1957	195	1	0	0	0	0	0	0	0	14	0	0	35	35
1958	134T	1	0	0	0	0	0	0	0	91	0	0	91	75
Lifetime		3	0	0	0	0	0	0	0	176	0	0	304	$160

Harland Holmes

Harland Holmes
Racing Hometown: Lewiston, NY

Year	Rank	Starts	Poles	1	2	3	4	5	6–10	Laps	Laps Led	Races Led	Miles	$
1950	100	3	0	0	0	0	0	0	0	177	0	0	89	50
Lifetime		3	0	0	0	0	0	0	0	177	0	0	89	$50

Hop Holmes

Preston Holmes
B: 1937   D: 7/4/1989
Racing Hometown: Loris, SC

Year	Rank	Starts	Poles	1	2	3	4	5	6–10	Laps	Laps Led	Races Led	Miles	$
1965	109	1	0	0	0	0	0	0	0	71	0	0	36	100
Lifetime		1	0	0	0	0	0	0	0	71	0	0	36	$100

Paul Dean Holt

Paul Dean Holt
B: 3/30/1936
Racing Hometown: Sweetwater, TN

Year	Rank	Starts	Poles	1	2	3	4	5	6–10	Laps	Laps Led	Races Led	Miles	$
1966	98	4	0	0	0	0	0	0	0	213	0	0	87	475
1967	42	24	0	0	0	0	0	0	1	3,165	0	0	1,962	4,220
1968	18	40	0	0	0	0	0	0	0	5,863	0	0	3,473	8,986
1969	46	14	0	0	0	0	0	0	0	1,408	0	0	1,015	4,442
1975	96	2	0	0	0	0	0	0	0	120	0	0	72	685
1977	96T	1	0	0	0	0	0	0	0	49	0	0	29	275
Lifetime		85	0	0	0	0	0	0	1	10,818	0	0	6,638	$19,083

Willard Holt

Willard Holt
Racing Hometown: Cincinnati, OH

Year	Rank	Starts	Poles	1	2	3	4	5	6–10	Laps	Laps Led	Races Led	Miles	$
1955	157	1	0	0	0	0	0	0	0	37	0	0	152	50
Lifetime		1	0	0	0	0	0	0	0	37	0	0	152	$50

Frank Holzhauer

Frank Holzhauer
Racing Hometown: Lakewood, NJ

Year	Rank	Starts	Poles	1	2	3	4	5	6–10	Laps	Laps Led	Races Led	Miles	$
1951	N/A	1	0	0	0	0	0	0	0		0	0		25
Lifetime		1	0	0	0	0	0	0	0		0	0		$25

Hooker Hood

Clarence Caldwell Hood
B: 4/9/1926
Racing Hometown: Memphis, TN

Year	Rank	Starts	Poles	1	2	3	4	5	6–10	Laps	Laps Led	Races Led	Miles	$
1954	112	2	0	0	0	0	0	0	0	248	0	0	244	75
1955	75	3	0	0	0	0	0	0	0	256	0	0	420	175
Lifetime		5	0	0	0	0	0	0	0	504	0	0	665	$250

Jeff Hooker

Jeffrey Hooker
Racing Hometown: Valley City, OH

Year	Rank	Starts	Poles	1	2	3	4	5	6–10	Laps	Laps Led	Races Led	Miles	$
1984	46	4	0	0	0	0	0	0	0	980	0	0	861	4,495
1985	NR	1	0	0	0	0	0	0	0	11	0	0	15	1,100
Lifetime		5	0	0	0	0	0	0	0	991	0	0	876	$5,595

Lance Hooper

Lance Hooper
B: 6/1/1967
Racing Hometown: Palmdale, CA

Year	Rank	Starts	Poles	1	2	3	4	5	6–10	Laps	Laps Led	Races Led	Miles	$
1996	61	1	0	0	0	0	0	0	0	302	0	0	302	9,645
1997	48	6	0	0	0	0	0	0	0	1,380	0	0	1,509	145,000
2001	70T	1	0	0	0	0	0	0	0	104	0	0	160	47,700
2002	75	1	0	0	0	0	0	0	0	488	0	0	260	51,840
Lifetime		9	0	0	0	0	0	0	0	2,274	0	0	2,232	$254,185

Year	Rank	Starts	Poles	Finish 1	2	3	4	5	6–10	Laps	Laps Led	Races Led	Miles	$

Carl Hoover

Carl Hoover

Year	Rank	Starts	Poles	1	2	3	4	5	6–10	Laps	Laps Led	Races Led	Miles	$
1955	238	1	0	0	0	0	0	0	0	35	0	0	35	20
Lifetime		1	0	0	0	0	0	0	0	35	0	0	35	$20

Ronnie Hopkins

Ronald Hopkins Jr.
B: 5/9/1962
Racing Hometown: Greenville, SC

Year	Rank	Starts	Poles	1	2	3	4	5	6–10	Laps	Laps Led	Races Led	Miles	$
1983	31	13	0	0	0	0	0	0	0	2,563	0	0	3,101	26,445
Lifetime		13	0	0	0	0	0	0	0	2,563	0	0	3,101	$26,445

Jim Hopkinson

James Hopkinson
B: 12/13/1942
Racing Hometown: Carmichael, CA

Year	Rank	Starts	Poles	1	2	3	4	5	6–10	Laps	Laps Led	Races Led	Miles	$
1980	95	1	0	0	0	0	0	0	0	42	0	0	110	750
Lifetime		1	0	0	0	0	0	0	0	42	0	0	110	$750

O.E. Horn

O.E. Horn

Year	Rank	Starts	Poles	1	2	3	4	5	6–10	Laps	Laps Led	Races Led	Miles	$
1965	NR	1	0	0	0	0	0	0	0	330	0	0	165	300
Lifetime		1	0	0	0	0	0	0	0	330	0	0	165	$300

Ron Hornaday

Ronald Lee Hornaday
B: 1930
Racing Hometown: San Fernando, CA

Year	Rank	Starts	Poles	1	2	3	4	5	6–10	Laps	Laps Led	Races Led	Miles	$
1955	175T	1	0	0	0	0	0	0	0	90	0	0	90	25
1957	132T	1	0	0	0	0	0	0	0	95	0	0	95	100
1958	145	2	0	0	0	0	0	0	0	53	0	0	60	125
1959	NR	1	0	0	0	0	0	0	0	325	0	0	130	75
1960	83	3	0	0	0	0	1	0	0	283	0	0	328	610
1961	103	4	0	0	0	0	0	1	0	283	0	0	219	325
1963	45	2	0	0	0	0	0	0	1	316	0	0	853	1,600
1966	62	1	0	0	0	0	0	0	1	171	0	0	462	900
1971	NR	1	0	0	0	0	0	0	0	177	0	0	443	1,750
1973	113	1	0	0	0	0	0	0	0	62	0	0	162	685
Lifetime		17	0	0	0	0	1	1	2	1,855	0	0	2,841	$6,195

Ron Hornaday Jr.

Ronald Lee Hornaday Jr.
B: 6/20/1958
Racing Hometown: Palmdale, CA

Year	Rank	Starts	Poles	1	2	3	4	5	6–10	Laps	Laps Led	Races Led	Miles	$
1992	64	2	0	0	0	0	0	0	0	373	0	0	482	11,290
1993	69	1	0	0	0	0	0	0	0	307	0	0	307	6,660
1994	61	2	0	0	0	0	0	0	0	350	1	1	431	13,710
1995	58	1	0	0	0	0	0	0	0	307	0	0	307	9,660
1998	60	1	0	0	0	0	0	0	0	112	0	0	218	27,850
1999	63	1	0	0	0	0	0	0	0	396	0	0	297	22,810
2000	61	1	0	0	0	0	0	0	0	90	0	0	221	47,020
2001	38	32	0	0	0	0	0	0	1	8,659	29	3	11,102	1,435,857
2002	58	3	0	0	0	0	0	0	0	843	0	0	1,327	149,285
Lifetime		44	0	0	0	0	0	0	1	11,437	30	4	14,691	$1,724,142

Jimmy Horton

James Horton
B: 7/3/1956
Racing Hometown: Folsom, N J

Year	Rank	Starts	Poles	1	2	3	4	5	6–10	Laps	Laps Led	Races Led	Miles	$
1987	67	2	0	0	0	0	0	0	0	256	0	0	640	4,405
1988	41	8	0	0	0	0	0	0	0	2,007	0	0	2,894	23,575
1989	46	5	0	0	0	0	0	0	0	955	0	0	1,391	19,232
1990	36	9	0	0	0	0	0	0	0	2,264	0	0	3,545	72,375
1992	39	9	0	0	0	0	0	0	0	2,194	0	0	2,930	50,125
1993	38	13	0	0	0	0	0	0	0	2,198	0	0	3,632	115,105
1994	62	1	0	0	0	0	0	0	0	199	0	0	498	33,485
1995	61T	1	0	0	0	0	0	0	0	192	0	0	480	16,550
Lifetime		48	0	0	0	0	0	0	0	10,265	0	0	16,009	$334,852

Year	Rank	Starts	Poles	Finish						Laps	Laps Led	Races Led	Miles	$
				1	2	3	4	5	6–10					

Lee Hough

Lee Hough
    Racing Hometown: Princetown, NJ

Year	Rank	Starts	Poles	1	2	3	4	5	6–10	Laps	Laps Led	Races Led	Miles	$
1950	NR	2	0	0	0	0	0	0	0	60	0	0	30	0
Lifetime		2	0	0	0	0	0	0	0	60	0	0	30	$0

Pappy Hough

Roscoe Morris Hough
    B: 11/22/1902   *Deceased.*
    Racing Hometown: Paterson, N J

Year	Rank	Starts	Poles	1	2	3	4	5	6–10	Laps	Laps Led	Races Led	Miles	$
1950	26	5	0	0	0	0	0	0	2	296	0	0	215	325
1951	31	9	0	0	0	0	0	1	3		0	0		760
1952	NR	4	1	0	0	0	0	0	1	565	0	0	393	250
1955	85	3	0	0	0	0	0	0	0	422	0	0	256	160
Lifetime		21	1	0	0	0	0	1	6	1,283	0	0	864	$1,495

Kevin Housby

Kevin Housby
    B: 4/26/1956
    Racing Hometown: Des Moines, IA

Year	Rank	Starts	Poles	1	2	3	4	5	6–10	Laps	Laps Led	Races Led	Miles	$
1979	92T	1	0	0	0	0	0	0	0	149	0	0	396	3,190
1980	75	3	0	0	0	0	0	0	0	524	0	0	1,006	6,165
1981	103	1	0	0	0	0	0	0	0	53	0	0	133	2,480
Lifetime		5	0	0	0	0	0	0	0	726	0	0	1,535	$11,835

Chuck Housley

Chuck Housley
    Racing Hometown: Columbus, GA

Year	Rank	Starts	Poles	1	2	3	4	5	6–10	Laps	Laps Led	Races Led	Miles	$
1953	65	2	0	0	0	0	0	0	0		0	0		50
Lifetime		2	0	0	0	0	0	0	0		0	0		$50

Andy Houston

Andy Houston
    B: 11/7/1970
    Racing Hometown: Hickory, NC

Year	Rank	Starts	Poles	1	2	3	4	5	6–10	Laps	Laps Led	Races Led	Miles	$
2000	55	5	0	0	0	0	0	0	0	1,209	0	0	1,549	141,850
2001	46	17	0	0	0	0	0	0	0	3,612	1	1	4,812	865,263
Lifetime		22	0	0	0	0	0	0	0	4,821	1	1	6,362	$1,007,113

Tommy Houston

Thomas C. Houston
    B: 1/29/1945
    Racing Hometown: Hickory, NC

Year	Rank	Starts	Poles	1	2	3	4	5	6–10	Laps	Laps Led	Races Led	Miles	$
1980	48	4	0	0	0	0	0	0	0	1,170	10	1	949	5,020
1981	51	7	0	0	0	0	0	0	0	2,219	0	0	1,903	20,760
1982	88	1	0	0	0	0	0	0	0	238	0	0	129	875
1985	91T	1	0	0	0	0	0	0	0	47	0	0	64	1,645
Lifetime		13	0	0	0	0	0	0	0	3,674	10	1	3,045	$28,300

Roz Howard

Roz Howard
    Racing Hometown: Macon, GA

Year	Rank	Starts	Poles	1	2	3	4	5	6–10	Laps	Laps Led	Races Led	Miles	$
1956	57	1	0	0	0	0	0	0	0	343	0	0	472	250
1958	NR	2	0	0	0	0	0	0	1	300	0	0	150	215
1960	49	3	0	0	0	0	0	0	2	676	0	0	535	1,490
Lifetime		6	0	0	0	0	0	0	0	3	1,319	0	0	1,157	$1,955

Zane Howell

Zane Howell

Year	Rank	Starts	Poles	1	2	3	4	5	6–10	Laps	Laps Led	Races Led	Miles	$
1952	NR	1	0	0	0	0	0	0	0	109	0	0	55	25
Lifetime		1	0	0	0	0	0	0	0	109	0	0	55	$25

Augie Howerton

August Howerton
    Racing Hometown: Tulsa, OK

Year	Rank	Starts	Poles	1	2	3	4	5	6–10	Laps	Laps Led	Races Led	Miles	$
1956	NR	1	0	0	0	0	0	0	1	181	0	0	91	150
Lifetime		1	0	0	0	0	0	0	0	1	181	0	0	91	$150

Year	Rank	Starts	Poles	Finish 1	2	3	4	5	6–10	Laps	Laps Led	Races Led	Miles	$

Ed Howland

Edward Howland

Year	Rank	Starts	Poles	1	2	3	4	5	6–10	Laps	Laps Led	Races Led	Miles	$
1970	NR	1	0	0	0	0	0	0	0	91	0	0	238	760
Lifetime		1	0	0	0	0	0	0	0	91	0	0	238	$760

John Hren

John Hren
Racing Hometown: Bloomington, CA

Year	Rank	Starts	Poles	1	2	3	4	5	6–10	Laps	Laps Led	Races Led	Miles	$
1972	110	1	0	0	0	0	0	0	0	45	0	0	118	720
1973	115	1	0	0	0	0	0	0	0	58	0	0	152	1,020
Lifetime		2	0	0	0	0	0	0	0	103	0	0	270	$1,740

Jack Hubbard

Jack Hubbard

Year	Rank	Starts	Poles	1	2	3	4	5	6–10	Laps	Laps Led	Races Led	Miles	$
1955	210	1	0	0	0	0	0	0	0	56	0	0	84	50
Lifetime		1	0	0	0	0	0	0	0	56	0	0	84	$50

Tom Hubert

Tom Hubert

Year	Rank	Starts	Poles	1	2	3	4	5	6–10	Laps	Laps Led	Races Led	Miles	$
1997	61	1	0	0	0	0	0	0	0	73	0	0		21,350
1998	61	2	0	0	0	0	0	0	0	166	0	0	368	42,430
1999	56	2	0	0	0	0	0	0	0	372	0	0	608	74,120
2000	66	1	0	0	0	0	0	0	0	90	0	0	221	33,175
2002	69	1	0	0	0	0	0	0	0	90	0	0	221	41,925
Lifetime		7	0	0	0	0	0	0	0	791	0	0	1,416	$213,000

Chuck Huckabee

Chuck Huckabee (Huck)
Racing Hometown: Chattanooga, TN

Year	Rank	Starts	Poles	1	2	3	4	5	6–10	Laps	Laps Led	Races Led	Miles	$
1963	105	3	0	0	0	0	0	0	1	171	0	0	86	450
1964	NR	9	0	0	0	0	0	0	0	788	0	0	306	830
Lifetime		12	0	0	0	0	0	0	1	959	0	0	391	$1,280

Cliff Hucul

Clifford Hucul
B: 8/21/1948
Racing Hometown: Prince George, B.C., Canada

Year	Rank	Starts	Poles	1	2	3	4	5	6–10	Laps	Laps Led	Races Led	Miles	$
1986	91	2	0	0	0	0	0	0	0	229	0	0	232	2,325
Lifetime		2	0	0	0	0	0	0	0	229	0	0	232	$2,325

Skip Hudson

Skip Hudson
Racing Hometown: Arlington, CA

Year	Rank	Starts	Poles	1	2	3	4	5	6–10	Laps	Laps Led	Races Led	Miles	$
1963	147	1	0	0	0	0	0	0	0	75	0	0	203	275
1964	57	1	0	0	0	0	0	0	1	178	0	0	481	1,075
1965	79	1	0	0	0	0	0	0	0	90	0	0	243	635
1966	126	1	0	0	0	0	0	0	0	30	0	0	81	500
Lifetime		4	0	0	0	0	0	0	1	373	0	0	1,007	$2,485

Jerry Hufflin

Jerry Calvin Hufflin
B: 6/4/1944
Racing Hometown: Greenville, SC

Year	Rank	Starts	Poles	1	2	3	4	5	6–10	Laps	Laps Led	Races Led	Miles	$
1974	100	2	0	0	0	0	0	0	0	262	0	0	155	900
1990	98T	1	0	0	0	0	0	0	0	130	0	0	130	2,750
Lifetime		3	0	0	0	0	0	0	0	392	0	0	285	$3,650

Stuart Huffman

Alan Stuart Huffman
Killed in ARCA race @ Atlanta.
Racing Hometown: Newton, NC

Year	Rank	Starts	Poles	1	2	3	4	5	6–10	Laps	Laps Led	Races Led	Miles	$
1980	96T	2	0	0	0	0	0	0	0	517	0	0	535	1,310
Lifetime		2	0	0	0	0	0	0	0	517	0	0	535	$1,310

George Hufford

George Hufford
Racing Hometown: McKeesport, PA

Year	Rank	Starts	Poles	1	2	3	4	5	6–10	Laps	Laps Led	Races Led	Miles	$
1952	151	3	0	0	0	0	0	0	0	192	0	0	96	75
Lifetime		3	0	0	0	0	0	0	0	192	0	0	96	$75

Year	Rank	Starts	Poles	Finish						Laps	Laps Led	Races Led	Miles	$
				1	2	3	4	5	6–10					

Ray Hughes

Raymond Hughes
Racing Hometown: Asheboro, NC

Year	Rank	Starts	Poles	1	2	3	4	5	6–10	Laps	Laps Led	Races Led	Miles	$
1962	56	6	0	0	0	0	0	0	2	1,289	0	0	536	965
1963	126T	1	0	0	0	0	0	0	0	183	0	0	46	110
Lifetime		7	0	0	0	0	0	0	2	1,472	0	0	582	$1,075

Lloyd Hulette

Lloyd Hulette
Racing Hometown: Cincinnati, OH

Year	Rank	Starts	Poles	1	2	3	4	5	6–10	Laps	Laps Led	Races Led	Miles	$
1953	39	1	0	0	0	0	0	0	0	328	0	0	451	250
Lifetime		1	0	0	0	0	0	0	0	328	0	0	451	$250

Jim Hull

James Hull
B: 1952
Racing Hometown: Clarkston, MI

Year	Rank	Starts	Poles	1	2	3	4	5	6–10	Laps	Laps Led	Races Led	Miles	$
1985	86T	1	0	0	0	0	0	0	0	68	0	0	136	1,570
1986	99	1	0	0	0	0	0	0	0	191	0	0	382	5,390
Lifetime		2	0	0	0	0	0	0	0	259	0	0	518	$6,960

Don Hume

Donald Hume
B: 5/8/1938
Racing Hometown: Belvidere, NJ

Year	Rank	Starts	Poles	1	2	3	4	5	6–10	Laps	Laps Led	Races Led	Miles	$
1964	137	2	0	0	0	0	0	0	0	18	0	0	26	900
1965	66	4	0	0	0	0	0	0	0	640	0	0	916	2,720
1981	NR	1	0	0	0	0	0	0	0	101	0	0	103	590
1984	NR	1	0	0	0	0	0	0	0	299	0	0	455	1,595
1985	38	7	0	0	0	0	0	0	0	2,057	0	0	1,907	22,230
Lifetime		15	0	0	0	0	0	0	0	3,115	0	0	3,406	$28,035

Lee Humphers

Lee Humphers
Racing Hometown: San Pablo, CA

Year	Rank	Starts	Poles	1	2	3	4	5	6–10	Laps	Laps Led	Races Led	Miles	$
1957	152T	1	0	0	0	0	0	0	0	91	0	0	91	50
Lifetime		1	0	0	0	0	0	0	0	91	0	0	91	$50

Dave Humphrey

David Humphrey

Year	Rank	Starts	Poles	1	2	3	4	5	6–10	Laps	Laps Led	Races Led	Miles	$
1951	N/A	1	0	0	0	0	0	0	0		0	0		0
Lifetime		1	0	0	0	0	0	0	0		0	0		$0

Bob Hundley

Robert Hundley

Year	Rank	Starts	Poles	1	2	3	4	5	6–10	Laps	Laps Led	Races Led	Miles	$
1959	NR	1	0	0	0	0	0	0	0	141	0	0	71	100
Lifetime		1	0	0	0	0	0	0	0	141	0	0	71	$100

Curtis Hunt

Curtis Hunt

Year	Rank	Starts	Poles	1	2	3	4	5	6–10	Laps	Laps Led	Races Led	Miles	$
1951	N/A	1	0	0	0	0	0	0	0	15	0	0	15	25
Lifetime		1	0	0	0	0	0	0	0	15	0	0	15	$25

Fred Hunt

Fred Hunt
Racing Hometown: Tracy, CA

Year	Rank	Starts	Poles	1	2	3	4	5	6–10	Laps	Laps Led	Races Led	Miles	$
1956	182	2	0	0	0	0	0	0	0	118	0	0	99	100
1957	195	1	0	0	0	0	0	0	0	20	0	0	50	50
Lifetime		3	0	0	0	0	0	0	0	138	0	0	149	$150

T.C. Hunt

Theodore C. Hunt
B: 4/7/1926   D: 3/1/1995
Racing Hometown: Atlanta, GA

Year	Rank	Starts	Poles	1	2	3	4	5	6–10	Laps	Laps Led	Races Led	Miles	$
1960	100	3	0	0	0	0	0	0	0	353	0	0	497	600
1961	48	7	0	0	0	0	0	0	0	940	0	0	1,445	2,750
1962	62	9	0	0	0	0	0	0	2	920	0	0	614	1,340
1963	60	3	0	0	0	0	0	0	0	754	0	0	947	865
1965	78	1	0	0	0	0	0	0	0	214	0	0	321	550

Year	Rank	Starts	Poles	Finish 1	2	3	4	5	6–10	Laps	Laps Led	Races Led	Miles	$

T.C. Hunt *continued*

Year	Rank	Starts	Poles	1	2	3	4	5	6–10	Laps	Laps Led	Races Led	Miles	$
1969	NR	1	0	0	0	0	0	0	0	53	0	0	141	1,050
Lifetime		24	0	0	0	0	0	0	2	3,234	0	0	3,966	$7,155

Bob Hunter

Robert Hunter
   Racing Hometown: Indianapolis, IN

Year	Rank	Starts	Poles	1	2	3	4	5	6–10	Laps	Laps Led	Races Led	Miles	$
1953	NR	1	0	0	0	0	0	0	0	210	0	0	289	105
Lifetime		1	0	0	0	0	0	0	0	210	0	0	289	$105

Jim Hunter

James Hunter
   B: 1936
   Racing Hometown: Knoxville, TN

Year	Rank	Starts	Poles	1	2	3	4	5	6–10	Laps	Laps Led	Races Led	Miles	$
1965	96	1	0	0	0	0	1	0	0	191	0	0	96	300
1966	139	1	0	0	0	0	0	0	0	8	0	0	4	0
1967	91	3	1	0	0	1	0	0	0	382	0	0	191	720
Lifetime		5	1	0	0	1	1	0	0	581	0	0	291	$1,020

Jim Hurlbert

James Hurlbert
   Racing Hometown: Mahomet, IL

Year	Rank	Starts	Poles	1	2	3	4	5	6–10	Laps	Laps Led	Races Led	Miles	$
1979	106T	1	0	0	0	0	0	0	0	150	0	0	300	1,400
1980	107	1	0	0	0	0	0	0	0	33	0	0	83	2,950
1982	NR	1	0	0	0	0	0	0	0	1	0	0	3	1,430
Lifetime		3	0	0	0	0	0	0	0	184	0	0	385	$5,780

Mark Hurley

Harry Mark Hurley
   B: 12/12/1936
   Racing Hometown: Johnson City, TN

Year	Rank	Starts	Poles	1	2	3	4	5	6–10	Laps	Laps Led	Races Led	Miles	$
1961	135	1	0	0	0	0	0	0	0	224	0	0	90	125
1962	99	3	0	0	0	0	0	0	0	289	0	0	145	100
1963	92	3	0	0	0	0	1	0	0	568	0	0	224	635
1964	71	9	0	0	0	0	0	0	1	1,082	0	0	504	1,770
Lifetime		16	0	0	0	0	1	0	1	2,163	0	0	961	$2,630

Bob Hurt

Robert Hurt

Year	Rank	Starts	Poles	1	2	3	4	5	6–10	Laps	Laps Led	Races Led	Miles	$
1963	NR	1	0	0	0	0	0	0	0	144	0	0	48	75
Lifetime		1	0	0	0	0	0	0	0	144	0	0	48	$75

Jim Hurtubise

James Ernest Hurtubise
   B: 12/5/1932   D: 1/6/1989
   Racing Hometown: N.Tonawanda, NY

Year	Rank	Starts	Poles	1	2	3	4	5	6–10	Laps	Laps Led	Races Led	Miles	$
1957	99	2	0	0	0	0	0	0	1	244	0	0	122	210
1963	NR	4	0	0	0	0	0	0	0	583	0	0	1,196	1,300
1964	NR	1	0	0	0	0	0	0	0	77	2	1	116	585
1966	NR	6	0	1	1	0	0	1	2	1,215	158	4	2,434	25,010
1967	NR	2	0	0	0	0	0	0	1	196	0	0	490	2,600
1968	46	6	0	0	0	0	0	0	1	982	0	0	1,520	4,490
1969	NR	1	0	0	0	0	0	0	0	63	0	0	168	1,125
1970	63	2	0	0	0	0	0	0	1	211	0	0	528	2,575
1971	84	3	0	0	0	0	0	0	1	290	0	0	682	4,100
1972	NR	2	0	0	0	0	0	0	1	271	0	0	705	3,515
1974	78	2	0	0	0	0	0	0	0	344	0	0	633	5,200
1976	88T	1	0	0	0	0	0	0	0	180	0	0	450	3,975
1977	58	4	0	0	0	0	0	0	0	235	0	0	570	5,110
Lifetime		36	0	1	1	0	0	1	8	4,891	160	5	9,612	$59,795

Joe Dean Huss

Joseph Dean Huss
   B: 3/8/1939
   Racing Hometown: Roanoke Rapids, NC

Year	Rank	Starts	Poles	1	2	3	4	5	6–10	Laps	Laps Led	Races Led	Miles	$
1971	NR	3	0	0	0	0	0	0	0	1,242	0	0	671	1,435
Lifetime		3	0	0	0	0	0	0	0	1,242	0	0	671	$1,435

Year	Rank	Starts	Poles	1	2	3	4	5	6–10	Laps	Laps Led	Races Led	Miles	$

Dick Hutcherson

Richard Leon Hutcherson
B: 11/30/1931
Racing Hometown: Keokuk, IA

Year	Rank	Starts	Poles	1	2	3	4	5	6–10	Laps	Laps Led	Races Led	Miles	$
1964	76	4	2	0	1	0	0	1	0	592	75	2	362	1,585
1965	2	52	10	9	9	8	4	2	5	11,610	2,065	23	8,131	57,851
1966	28	14	2	3	0	2	1	2	1	3,152	400	7	3,042	22,485
1967	3	33	9	2	9	7	3	1	3	8,893	1,325	20	7,278	85,160
Lifetime		103	23	14	19	17	8	6	9	24,247	3,865	52	18,812	$167,081

Ron Hutcherson

Ronald Hutcherson
B: 4/24/1943
Racing Hometown: Keokuk, IA

Year	Rank	Starts	Poles	1	2	3	4	5	6–10	Laps	Laps Led	Races Led	Miles	$
1972	NR	1	0	0	0	0	0	0	0	29	0	0	29	550
1977	NR	4	0	0	0	0	0	0	0	917	0	0	1,578	17,760
1978	68	3	0	0	0	0	1	0	0	388	0	0	870	24,720
1979	NR	1	0	0	0	0	0	0	0	0	0	0	0	1,165
Lifetime		9	0	0	0	0	1	0	0	1,334	0	0	2,477	$44,195

Sonny Hutchins

Ernest Lloyd Hutchins
B: 5/17/1929
Racing Hometown: Richmond, VA

Year	Rank	Starts	Poles	1	2	3	4	5	6–10	Laps	Laps Led	Races Led	Miles	$
1955	242T	1	0	0	0	0	0	0	0	15	0	0	8	0
1965	50	10	0	0	0	0	0	1	1	2,272	0	0	1,332	3,780
1966	83	4	0	0	0	0	0	0	0	222	0	0	318	2,190
1967	34	7	0	0	0	0	0	0	2	998	0	0	1,711	6,385
1968	62	4	0	0	0	0	0	0	0	420	0	0	528	2,810
1969	44	8	0	0	2	0	0	0	0	1,694	0	0	1,608	9,552
1970	78	2	0	0	0	0	0	1	0	722	0	0	612	2,575
1973	112	1	0	0	0	0	0	0	0	254	0	0	138	440
1974	132	1	0	0	0	0	0	0	0	150	79	1	79	590
Lifetime		38	0	0	2	0	0	2	3	6,747	79	1	6,333	$28,322

Randy Hutchison

Ivan Randall Hutchison
B: 8/25/1948
Racing Hometown: Newport News, VA

Year	Rank	Starts	Poles	1	2	3	4	5	6–10	Laps	Laps Led	Races Led	Miles	$
1971	NR	6	0	0	0	0	0	0	1	1,233	0	0	556	2,010
1974	134	1	0	0	0	0	0	0	0	66	0	0	35	730
Lifetime		7	0	0	0	0	0	0	1	1,299	0	0	590	$2,740

Bill Hyde

William Hyde
Racing Hometown: Portland, OR

Year	Rank	Starts	Poles	1	2	3	4	5	6–10	Laps	Laps Led	Races Led	Miles	$
1955	102	1	0	0	1	0	0	0	0	109	0	0	109	820
1956	55	6	0	0	0	0	0	0	3	770	1	1	644	910
Lifetime		7	0	0	1	0	0	0	3	879	1	1	753	$1,730

James Hylton

James Harvey Hylton
B: 8/26/1935
Racing Hometown: Inman, SC

Year	Rank	Starts	Poles	1	2	3	4	5	6–10	Laps	Laps Led	Races Led	Miles	$
1964	NR	3	0	0	0	0	0	0	0	47	0	0	72	350
1966	2	41	1	0	4	6	7	3	12	10,804	152	2	8,773	38,723
1967	2	46	1	0	3	3	12	8	13	11,526	108	4	8,534	49,732
1968	7	41	0	0	1	4	8	3	12	10,058	10	2	7,248	32,608
1969	3	52	0	0	4	9	8	6	12	13,540	162	12	10,838	114,416
1970	3	47	1	1	4	2	8	7	17	12,712	199	8	11,223	78,201
1971	2	46	1	0	2	3	5	4	23	12,785	105	5	12,725	90,282
1972	3	31	0	1	0	0	5	3	14	9,702	111	4	11,476	126,705
1973	4	28	0	0	0	0	1	0	10	9,324	1	1	10,058	82,512
1974	11	29	0	0	0	0	0	1	7	6,774	29	6	7,970	61,385
1975	3	30	0	0	0	0	1	1	14	9,650	11	4	11,032	113,642
1976	13	30	0	0	0	0	1	1	3	8,125	14	4	9,331	78,705
1977	7	30	0	0	0	0	0	0	11	8,375	3	1	9,592	108,392
1978	26	19	0	0	0	0	0	0	4	5,774	16	2	5,019	48,045
1979	14	30	0	0	0	0	0	0	5	8,658	11	4	9,604	97,428
1980	13	31	0	0	0	0	0	0	4	9,232	26	1	10,548	109,230
1981	19	28	0	0	0	0	0	0	0	7,051	12	2	8,509	87,305

Year	Rank	Starts	Poles	Finish						Laps	Laps Led	Races Led	Miles	$
				1	2	3	4	5	6–10	Laps	Led	Led	Miles	$

James Hylton *continued*

Year	Rank	Starts	Poles	1	2	3	4	5	6–10	Laps	Laps Led	Races Led	Miles	$
1982	28	13	0	0	0	0	0	0	0	4,208	0	0	4,332	49,130
1983	NR	2	0	0	0	0	0	0	0	556	0	0	662	12,105
1985	NR	1	0	0	0	0	0	0	0	201	0	0	201	3,945
1986	46	4	0	0	0	0	0	0	0	544	0	0	578	22,090
1987	79	2	0	0	0	0	0	0	0	93	0	0	99	2,550
1989	74	2	0	0	0	0	0	0	0	38	0	0	43	3,775
1990	NR	1	0	0	0	0	0	0	0	202	0	0	202	2,800
1991	54	4	0	0	0	0	0	0	0	87	0	0	113	14,190
1992	42	8	0	0	0	0	0	0	0	611	0	0	1,100	37,910
1993	64T	2	0	0	0	0	0	0	0	86	0	0	109	11,945
Lifetime		601	4	2	18	27	56	37	161	160,763	970	62	159,992	$1,478,101

Jimmy Ingalls

James Ingalls
Racing Hometown: Boca Raton, FL

Year	Rank	Starts	Poles	1	2	3	4	5	6–10	Laps	Laps Led	Races Led	Miles	$
1983	81	2	0	0	0	0	0	0	0	901	0	0	901	3,080
1984	68	3	0	0	0	0	0	0	0	491	0	0	597	8,865
Lifetime		5	0	0	0	0	0	0	0	1,392	0	0	1,498	$11,945

Jim Inglebright

James Inglebright
B: 11/18/1961
Racing Hometown: Fairfield, CA

Year	Rank	Starts	Poles	1	2	3	4	5	6–10	Laps	Laps Led	Races Led	Miles	$
2002	76	1	0	0	0	0	0	0	0	109	0	0	213	47,190
Lifetime		1	0	0	0	0	0	0	0	109	0	0	213	$47,190

Bill Ingram

William Ingram
Racing Hometown: Acworth, GA

Year	Rank	Starts	Poles	1	2	3	4	5	6–10	Laps	Laps Led	Races Led	Miles	$
1989	78	1	0	0	0	0	0	0	0	181	0	0	481	3,875
Lifetime		1	0	0	0	0	0	0	0	181	0	0	481	$3,875

Jack Ingram

Jack Ingram
B: 12/28/1936
Racing Hometown: Asheville, NC

Year	Rank	Starts	Poles	1	2	3	4	5	6–10	Laps	Laps Led	Races Led	Miles	$
1965	140	1	0	0	0	0	0	0	0	4	0	0	2	100
1966	119T	1	0	0	0	0	0	0	0	14	0	0	5	100
1967	87	4	0	0	1	0	0	0	0	506	0	0	218	1,165
1968	63	4	0	0	0	0	0	0	2	805	0	0	385	1,150
1979	63	4	0	0	0	0	0	0	0	532	0	0	661	4,240
1981	47	5	0	0	0	0	0	0	1	822	0	0	1,285	9,965
Lifetime		19	0	0	1	0	0	0	3	2,683	0	0	2,556	$16,720

Jim Ingram

James Ingram
Racing Hometown: Cheraw, SC

Year	Rank	Starts	Poles	1	2	3	4	5	6–10	Laps	Laps Led	Races Led	Miles	$
1980	86	1	0	0	0	0	0	0	0	437	0	0	437	1,435
Lifetime		1	0	0	0	0	0	0	0	437	0	0	437	$1,435

Jimmy Ingram

James Ingram
Racing Hometown: Jacksonville, FL

Year	Rank	Starts	Poles	1	2	3	4	5	6–10	Laps	Laps Led	Races Led	Miles	$
1951	N/A	1	0	0	0	0	0	0	0		0	0		25
1952	166	1	0	0	0	0	0	0	0	91	0	0	114	0
Lifetime		2	0	0	0	0	0	0	0	91	0	0	114	$25

Tommy Ingram

Thomas Ingram
D: 4/17/1995
Racing Hometown: Asheville, NC

Year	Rank	Starts	Poles	1	2	3	4	5	6–10	Laps	Laps Led	Races Led	Miles	$
1967	106	2	0	0	0	0	0	0	0	58	0	0	73	1,060
Lifetime		2	0	0	0	0	0	0	0	58	0	0	73	$1,060

Jimmy Insolo

James Edward Insolo
B: 2/4/1943
Racing Hometown: Mission Hills, CA

Year	Rank	Starts	Poles	1	2	3	4	5	6–10	Laps	Laps Led	Races Led	Miles	$
1970	85	2	0	0	0	0	0	0	0	137	0	0	359	1,635

Year	Rank	Starts	Poles	Finish						Laps	Laps Led	Races Led	Miles	$
				1	2	3	4	5	6–10					

Jimmy Insolo *continued*

Year	Rank	Starts	Poles	1	2	3	4	5	6–10	Laps	Laps Led	Races Led	Miles	$
1971	NR	3	0	0	0	0	0	0	0	349	0	0	892	3,790
1972	97	1	0	0	0	0	0	0	0	130	0	0	341	835
1973	62	2	0	0	0	0	1	1	0	335	0	0	878	6,295
1974	67	3	0	0	0	0	0	0	0	338	1	1	867	3,360
1975	53	4	0	0	0	0	0	0	1	296	18	1	717	5,640
1976	61	3	0	0	0	1	0	0	1	454	0	0	1,169	12,105
1977	109	2	0	0	0	0	1	0	0	97	0	0	254	4,490
1978	49	3	0	0	0	0	0	0	2	345	5	2	880	8,665
1979	55	2	0	0	0	0	0	0	0	156	0	0	409	5,080
1981	NR	1	0	0	0	0	0	0	0	41	0	0	107	755
1982	NR	1	0	0	0	0	0	0	0	89	0	0	233	2,470
1983	104	1	0	0	0	0	0	0	0	1	0	0	3	840
Lifetime		28	0	0	0	1	2	1	4	2,768	24	4	7,109	$55,960

Bubba Into

James Into
B: 1938
Racing Hometown: Hardeeville, SC

Year	Rank	Starts	Poles	1	2	3	4	5	6–10	Laps	Laps Led	Races Led	Miles	$
1964	134	2	0	0	0	0	0	0	0	185	0	0	93	210
Lifetime		2	0	0	0	0	0	0	0	185	0	0	93	$210

Innes Ireland

Robert MacGregor Innes Ireland
B: 6/12/1930   D: 10/23/1993
Racing Hometown: Prestiegne Rads, United Kingdom

Year	Rank	Starts	Poles	1	2	3	4	5	6–10	Laps	Laps Led	Races Led	Miles	$
1967	NR	2	0	0	0	0	0	0	1	165	0	0	413	1,265
Lifetime		2	0	0	0	0	0	0	1	165	0	0	413	$1,265

Ernie Irvan

Ernie Irvan
B: 1/13/1959
Racing Hometown: Modesto, CA

Year	Rank	Starts	Poles	1	2	3	4	5	6–10	Laps	Laps Led	Races Led	Miles	$
1987	52	5	0	0	0	0	0	0	1	1,341	1	1	1,311	23,050
1988	26	25	0	0	0	0	0	0	0	7,337	1	1	8,855	96,370
1989	22	29	0	0	0	0	0	0	4	8,286	69	4	9,963	144,347
1990	9	29	3	1	2	1	1	1	7	9,001	280	10	10,512	535,280
1991	5	29	1	2	3	0	4	2	8	8,770	584	16	10,494	1,079,017
1992	11	29	3	3	2	1	2	1	2	8,561	477	17	10,280	996,885
1993	6	30	4	3	4	3	0	2	2	8,234	1,120	19	10,160	1,400,468
1994	22	20	5	3	6	2	0	2	2	5,357	1,783	17	7,644	1,311,522
1995	48	3	0	0	0	0	0	0	2	924	142	2	945	54,875
1996	10	31	1	2	2	0	6	2	4	8,617	383	15	10,218	1,683,313
1997	14	32	2	1	2	0	1	1	8	8,757	439	15	11,592	1,614,281
1998	19	30	3	0	0	0	0	0	11	8,153	193	5	10,649	1,600,452
1999	40	21	0	0	0	0	0	0	5	5,009	9	2	7,385	1,073,775
Lifetime		313	22	15	21	7	14	11	56	88,347	5,481	124	110,007	$11,613,635

Billy Irvin

William Irvin
Racing Hometown: Baltimore, MD

Year	Rank	Starts	Poles	1	2	3	4	5	6–10	Laps	Laps Led	Races Led	Miles	$
1954	NR	7	0	0	0	0	0	0	0	846	0	0	585	125
Lifetime		7	0	0	0	0	0	0	0	846	0	0	585	$125

Kenny Irwin Jr.

Kenny Irwin Jr.
B: 8/5/1969
Racing Hometown: Indianapolis, IN

Year	Rank	Starts	Poles	1	2	3	4	5	6–10	Laps	Laps Led	Races Led	Miles	$
1997	49	4	0	0	0	0	0	0	1	1,283	12	1	1,227	71,730
1998	28	32	1	0	0	0	0	1	3	8,182	129	4	10,548	1,459,967
1999	19	34	2	0	0	1	0	1	4	9,445	35	3	12,234	2,125,810
2000	42	17	0	0	0	0	1	0	0	4,304	2	2	6,138	949,436
Lifetime		87	3	0	0	1	1	2	8	23,214	178	10	30,147	$4,606,943

Tommy Irwin

Tommy Irwin
B: 4/27/1928
Racing Hometown: Keyesville, VA

Year	Rank	Starts	Poles	1	2	3	4	5	6–10	Laps	Laps Led	Races Led	Miles	$
1958	NR	5	0	0	0	1	1	0	1	1,255	0	0	689	1,280
1959	14	25	1	0	1	2	3	4	6	4,409	174	2	2,847	9,190

Year	Rank	Starts	Poles	Finish 1	2	3	4	5	6–10	Laps	Laps Led	Races Led	Miles	$

Tommy Irwin *continued*

Year	Rank	Starts	Poles	1	2	3	4	5	6–10	Laps	Laps Led	Races Led	Miles	$
1960	55	16	1	0	0	0	3	1	7	2,659	0	0	1,641	2,805
1961	26	26	0	0	2	0	1	0	5	3,748	166	1	3,235	7,170
1962	37	20	0	0	1	0	1	0	7	2,982	10	1	1,637	3,305
1963	32	7	0	0	0	1	0	1	3	1,528	0	0	1,105	2,655
Lifetime		99	2	0	4	4	9	6	29	16,581	350	4	11,154	$26,405

Bobby Isaac

Robert Vance Isaac
B: 8/1/1932   D: 8/14/1977
Racing Hometown: Catawba, NC

Year	Rank	Starts	Poles	1	2	3	4	5	6–10	Laps	Laps Led	Races Led	Miles	$
1961	158T	1	0	0	0	0	0	0	0	2	0	0	3	50
1963	20	27	0	0	0	1	0	2	4	4,989	30	1	4,299	9,529
1964	18	19	0	1	3	0	1	0	2	3,163	134	6	3,360	26,733
1965	75	4	1	0	1	0	0	0	0	699	67	2	472	1,860
1966	53	9	0	0	1	1	0	0	1	1,387	21	2	1,388	5,530
1967	14	12	0	0	1	0	0	2	2	2,625	65	3	3,927	24,475
1968	2	49	3	3	9	7	4	4	9	12,947	1,111	19	9,123	60,342
1969	6	50	21	17	3	5	3	1	4	12,308	5,072	38	9,230	92,074
1970	1	47	13	11	9	5	4	3	6	12,726	3,188	35	11,251	199,600
1971	23	25	5	4	4	2	4	2	1	6,856	1,753	17	7,604	106,526
1972	19	27	9	1	3	5	0	1	0	5,636	1,326	20	6,872	133,257
1973	26	19	0	0	2	1	2	0	1	4,177	62	7	4,545	84,550
1974	33	11	0	0	1	0	0	0	4	1,907	11	4	2,490	22,642
1975	48	6	0	0	0	0	0	0	1	1,101	0	0	1,214	6,695
1976	114	2	0	0	0	0	0	0	1	512	0	0	540	4,190
Lifetime		308	52	37	37	27	18	15	36	71,035	12,840	154	66,316	$778,053

Larry Isley

Lawrence Isley
Racing Hometown: Burlington, NC

Year	Rank	Starts	Poles	1	2	3	4	5	6–10	Laps	Laps Led	Races Led	Miles	$
1979	101T	1	0	0	0	0	0	0	0	256	0	0	160	925
Lifetime		1	0	0	0	0	0	0	0	256	0	0	160	$925

Don Israel

Donald Israel
Racing Hometown: Asheville, NC

Year	Rank	Starts	Poles	1	2	3	4	5	6–10	Laps	Laps Led	Races Led	Miles	$
1966	106	1	0	0	0	0	0	0	1	188	0	0	94	150
Lifetime		1	0	0	0	0	0	0	1	188	0	0	94	$150

Ed Jacken

Edward Jacken
Racing Hometown: Syracuse, NY

Year	Rank	Starts	Poles	1	2	3	4	5	6–10	Laps	Laps Led	Races Led	Miles	$
1957	NR	1	0	0	0	0	0	0	0	72	0	0	72	110
Lifetime		1	0	0	0	0	0	0	0	72	0	0	72	$110

Wayne Jacks

Wayne Jacks
B: 2/21/1949
Racing Hometown: Las Vegas, NV

Year	Rank	Starts	Poles	1	2	3	4	5	6–10	Laps	Laps Led	Races Led	Miles	$
1993	91T	1	0	0	0	0	0	0	0	48	0	0	48	5,980
Lifetime		1	0	0	0	0	0	0	0	48	0	0	48	$5,980

Burt Jackson

Burt Jackson
Racing Hometown: Los Angeles, CA

Year	Rank	Starts	Poles	1	2	3	4	5	6–10	Laps	Laps Led	Races Led	Miles	$
1951	N/A	1	0	0	0	0	0	0	1		0	0		100
Lifetime		1	0	0	0	0	0	0	1		0	0		$100

Charlie Jackson

Charles Jackson
Racing Hometown: Indianapolis, IN

Year	Rank	Starts	Poles	1	2	3	4	5	6–10	Laps	Laps Led	Races Led	Miles	$
1956	90	5	0	0	0	0	0	0	2	635	0	0	336	260
Lifetime		5	0	0	0	0	0	0	2	635	0	0	336	$260

Lacy Jackson

Lacy Jackson
Racing Hometown: N.Augusta, SC

Year	Rank	Starts	Poles	1	2	3	4	5	6–10	Laps	Laps Led	Races Led	Miles	$
1953	149	1	0	0	0	0	0	0	0	288	0	0	396	130
Lifetime		1	0	0	0	0	0	0	0	288	0	0	396	$130

Year	Rank	Starts	Poles	Finish						Laps	Laps Led	Races Led	Miles	$
				1	2	3	4	5	6–10					

Bruce Jacobi

Bruce Jacobi
B: 6/23/1935   D: 2/4/1987   *Died of injuries suffered @ Daytona 1983.*
Racing Hometown: Indianapolis, IN

Year	Rank	Starts	Poles	1	2	3	4	5	6–10	Laps	Laps Led	Races Led	Miles	$
1975	25	15	0	0	0	0	0	0	3	3,863	0	0	5,767	29,455
1976	73	3	0	0	0	0	0	0	0	621	0	0	788	3,385
1980	92T	1	0	0	0	0	0	0	0	189	0	0	378	985
1981	NR	1	0	0	0	0	0	0	0	117	0	0	293	955
Lifetime		20	0	0	0	0	0	0	3	4,790	0	0	7,226	$34,780

Al Jacobs

Al Jacobs
Racing Hometown: Gardena, CA

Year	Rank	Starts	Poles	1	2	3	4	5	6–10	Laps	Laps Led	Races Led	Miles	$
1951	N/A	3	0	0	0	0	0	0	0		0	0		100
Lifetime		3	0	0	0	0	0	0	0		0	0		$100

Jake Jacobs

Warren Jacobs
B: 1928
Racing Hometown: Providence, RI

Year	Rank	Starts	Poles	1	2	3	4	5	6–10	Laps	Laps Led	Races Led	Miles	$
1957	116	1	0	0	0	0	0	0	0	58	0	0	58	100
Lifetime		1	0	0	0	0	0	0	0	58	0	0	58	$100

Lawrence Jacquelin

Lawrence Jacquelin
Racing Hometown: New Haven, CT

Year	Rank	Starts	Poles	1	2	3	4	5	6–10	Laps	Laps Led	Races Led	Miles	$
1952	190	1	0	0	0	0	0	0	0	34	0	0	34	0
Lifetime		1	0	0	0	0	0	0	0	34	0	0	34	$0

Carl Jaemar

Carl Jaemar

Year	Rank	Starts	Poles	1	2	3	4	5	6–10	Laps	Laps Led	Races Led	Miles	$
1961	129	1	0	0	0	0	0	0	1	95	0	0	95	100
Lifetime		1	0	0	0	0	0	0	1	95	0	0	95	$100

Bill James

William James
Racing Hometown: Lectonia, OH

Year	Rank	Starts	Poles	1	2	3	4	5	6–10	Laps	Laps Led	Races Led	Miles	$
1952	117	1	0	0	0	0	0	0	0	117	0	0	117	25
Lifetime		1	0	0	0	0	0	0	0	117	0	0	117	$25

Bob James

Robert James
D: 10/25/200
Racing Hometown: Cuyahoga Falls, OH

Year	Rank	Starts	Poles	1	2	3	4	5	6–10	Laps	Laps Led	Races Led	Miles	$
1951	N/A	1	0	0	0	0	0	0	0	55	0	0	28	25
1963	35	10	0	0	0	0	0	0	0	1,414	0	0	2,068	3,375
Lifetime		11	0	0	0	0	0	0	0	1,469	0	0	2,096	$3,400

Chuck James

Charles James
Racing Hometown: Columbiana, OH

Year	Rank	Starts	Poles	1	2	3	4	5	6–10	Laps	Laps Led	Races Led	Miles	$
1950	42	1	0	0	0	0	1	0	0		0	0		400
Lifetime		1	0	0	0	0	1	0	0		0	0		$400

Dave James

David James
Racing Hometown: Venice, CA

Year	Rank	Starts	Poles	1	2	3	4	5	6–10	Laps	Laps Led	Races Led	Miles	$
1958	52	2	0	0	0	0	0	0	2	262	0	0	538	300
1959	116	2	0	0	0	0	0	0	1	493	0	0	221	400
1964	124	1	0	0	0	0	0	0	0	79	0	0	213	500
1966	131	1	0	0	0	0	0	0	0	4	0	0	11	500
1968	72	1	0	0	0	0	0	0	1	171	0	0	462	1,250
1969	NR	1	0	0	0	0	0	0	0	5	0	0	14	850
Lifetime		8	0	0	0	0	0	0	4	1,014	0	0	1,458	$3,800

Frank James

Frank Edwin James
B: 3/19/1938
Racing Hometown: Bakersfield, CA

Year	Rank	Starts	Poles	1	2	3	4	5	6–10	Laps	Laps Led	Races Led	Miles	$
1970	79	2	0	0	0	0	0	0	0	257	0	0	673	1,915
1971	NR	3	0	0	0	0	0	0	1	409	0	0	1,050	3,890

Year	Rank	Starts	Poles	Finish 1	2	3	4	5	6–10	Laps	Laps Led	Races Led	Miles	$

Frank James *continued*

Year	Rank	Starts	Poles	1	2	3	4	5	6–10	Laps	Laps Led	Races Led	Miles	$
1972	79	2	0	0	0	0	0	0	1	259	0	0	679	2,195
Lifetime		7	0	0	0	0	0	0	2	925	0	0	2,402	$8,000

Mike James

Markey L. James
B: 11/4/1941
Racing Hometown: Medford, OR

Year	Rank	Starts	Poles	1	2	3	4	5	6–10	Laps	Laps Led	Races Led	Miles	$
1971	NR	1	0	0	0	0	0	0	0	1	0	0	3	615
1972	88	2	0	0	0	0	0	0	0	180	0	0	450	2,620
1973	102	1	0	0	0	0	0	0	0	129	0	0	338	1,065
1974	119	1	0	0	0	0	0	0	0	103	0	0	270	995
Lifetime		5	0	0	0	0	0	0	0	413	0	0	1,061	$5,295

Walt James

Walter James
B: 1923
Racing Hometown: Saucier, MS

Year	Rank	Starts	Poles	1	2	3	4	5	6–10	Laps	Laps Led	Races Led	Miles	$
1957	196	1	0	0	0	0	0	0	0	14	0	0	35	35
Lifetime		1	0	0	0	0	0	0	0	14	0	0	35	$35

Frank Jamison

Frank Jamison
Racing Hometown: Quarryville, PA

Year	Rank	Starts	Poles	1	2	3	4	5	6–10	Laps	Laps Led	Races Led	Miles	$
1956	122	3	0	0	0	0	0	0	1	315	0	0	229	350
1957	139	2	0	0	0	0	0	0	0	87	0	0	81	150
Lifetime		5	0	0	0	0	0	0	1	402	0	0	309	$500

Roy Janelle

Roy Janelle
B: 1918
Racing Hometown: Depew, NY

Year	Rank	Starts	Poles	1	2	3	4	5	6–10	Laps	Laps Led	Races Led	Miles	$
1951	NR	1	0	0	0	0	0	0	0		0	0		0
1952	146	1	0	0	0	0	0	0	0		0	0		25
Lifetime		2	0	0	0	0	0	0	0		0	0		$25

Bill Jarick

William Jarick
Racing Hometown: Westchester, CA

Year	Rank	Starts	Poles	1	2	3	4	5	6–10	Laps	Laps Led	Races Led	Miles	$
1957	125	2	0	0	0	0	0	0	1	115	0	0	106	100
1958	106	2	0	0	0	0	0	0	1	111	0	0	137	250
1959	119	2	1	0	0	0	0	0	0	360	0	0	152	100
Lifetime		6	1	0	0	0	0	0	2	586	0	0	395	$450

Dale Jarrett

Dale Arnold Jarrett
B: 11/26/1956
Racing Hometown: Hickory, NC

Year	Rank	Starts	Poles	1	2	3	4	5	6–10	Laps	Laps Led	Races Led	Miles	$
1984	72	3	0	0	0	0	0	0	0	796	0	0	798	7,345
1986	107T	1	0	0	0	0	0	0	0	69	0	0	37	990
1987	26	24	0	0	0	0	0	0	2	4,788	0	0	5,681	143,405
1988	23	29	0	0	0	0	0	0	1	6,556	5	2	8,167	118,640
1989	24	29	0	0	0	0	0	2	3	7,798	99	3	9,180	215,317
1990	25	24	0	0	0	0	1	0	6	6,801	74	5	7,800	214,495
1991	17	29	0	1	0	0	0	2	5	7,767	47	7	9,440	444,256
1992	19	29	0	0	1	1	0	0	6	8,586	99	5	10,295	418,648
1993	4	30	0	1	1	4	5	2	5	9,149	264	15	11,336	1,242,394
1994	16	30	0	1	0	0	2	1	5	8,410	55	8	10,442	893,754
1995	13	31	1	1	1	2	1	4	5	8,671	324	8	10,418	1,363,158
1996	3	31	2	4	7	4	2	0	4	9,307	743	20	11,181	2,985,418
1997	2	32	3	7	4	4	2	3	3	9,769	2,086	22	12,646	3,240,542
1998	3	33	2	3	5	6	2	3	3	9,475	831	22	12,360	4,019,657
1999	1	34	0	4	6	4	5	5	5	9,900	1,100	22	12,987	6,649,596
2000	4	34	3	2	3	1	5	4	9	9,750	333	15	12,714	5,225,499
2001	5	36	5	4	2	1	4	1	7	10,744	512	17	14,047	5,377,742
2002	9	36	1	2	1	3	2	2	8	9,881	441	15	13,041	4,421,951
Lifetime		495	17	30	31	30	31	29	77	138,217	7,013	186	172,571	$36,982,807

Year	Rank	Starts	Poles	Finish 1	2	3	4	5	6–10	Laps	Laps Led	Races Led	Miles	$

Glenn Jarrett

Glenn Ned Jarrett
B: 8/11/1950
Racing Hometown: Conover, NC

Year	Rank	Starts	Poles	1	2	3	4	5	6–10	Laps	Laps Led	Races Led	Miles	$
1978	85	1	0	0	0	0	0	0	0	317	0	0	476	2,940
1979	118T	2	0	0	0	0	0	0	0	330	0	0	416	2,745
1980	NR	2	0	0	0	0	0	0	0	209	0	0	502	4,435
1981	58	3	0	0	0	0	0	0	0	679	0	0	864	12,650
1982	104T	1	0	0	0	0	0	0	0	35	0	0	53	735
1983	95T	1	0	0	0	0	0	0	0	24	0	0	60	1,200
Lifetime		10	0	0	0	0	0	0	0	1,594	0	0	2,370	$24,705

Ned Jarrett

Ned Miller Jarrett
B: 10/12/1932
Racing Hometown: Newton, NC

Year	Rank	Starts	Poles	1	2	3	4	5	6–10	Laps	Laps Led	Races Led	Miles	$
1953	68	2	0	0	0	0	0	0	0	8	0	0	11	125
1954	147	2	0	0	0	0	0	0	0	273	0	0	151	25
1955	173	3	0	0	0	0	0	0	0	403	0	0	491	260
1956	166	2	0	0	0	0	0	0	0	244	0	0	140	60
1957	169	1	0	0	0	0	0	0	0	7	0	0	4	50
1959	37	17	2	2	1	1	0	0	3	2,929	2	2	1,489	3,860
1960	5	40	5	5	3	4	4	4	6	7,399	380	9	5,479	25,438
1961	1	46	4	1	4	8	4	6	11	9,813	606	9	7,184	41,873
1962	3	52	4	6	2	3	3	5	16	10,998	866	11	7,064	43,444
1963	4	53	5	8	7	5	7	5	7	11,845	1,685	18	7,938	45,844
1964	2	60	9	15	7	5	7	6	5	13,325	3,083	30	8,785	71,925
1965	1	54	9	13	13	10	4	2	3	13,525	2,051	28	9,121	93,625
1966	13	21	0	0	0	3	1	1	3	4,584	167	3	4,336	23,255
Lifetime		353	38	50	37	39	30	29	54	75,353	8,840	110	52,192	$349,784

Dr. Bob Jarvis

Dr. Robert D. Jarvis
Racing Hometown: Greenville, SC

Year	Rank	Starts	Poles	1	2	3	4	5	6–10	Laps	Laps Led	Races Led	Miles	$
1982	92	2	0	0	0	0	0	0	0	192	0	0	204	2,895
Lifetime		2	0	0	0	0	0	0	0	192	0	0	204	$2,895

Harry Jefferson

Harry Jefferson
B: 11/2/1946
Racing Hometown: Naches, WA

Year	Rank	Starts	Poles	1	2	3	4	5	6–10	Laps	Laps Led	Races Led	Miles	$
1973	117	1	0	0	0	0	0	0	0	37	0	0	97	1,015
1974	52	4	0	0	0	0	0	0	1	457	0	0	775	6,083
1975	45	5	0	0	0	0	0	0	2	1,036	0	0	1,787	11,395
1976	111T	1	0	0	0	0	0	0	0	14	0	0	37	535
1977	88	1	0	0	0	0	0	0	0	195	0	0	488	1,600
Lifetime		12	0	0	0	0	0	0	3	1,739	0	0	3,183	$20,628

Rick Jeffrey

Richard Jeffrey
B: 6/9/1951
Racing Hometown: Prospect, KY

Year	Rank	Starts	Poles	1	2	3	4	5	6–10	Laps	Laps Led	Races Led	Miles	$
1988	49	4	0	0	0	0	0	0	0	978	0	0	1,767	25,535
Lifetime		4	0	0	0	0	0	0	0	978	0	0	1,767	$25,535

Bob Jeffries

Robert Jeffries
Racing Hometown: Detroit, MI

Year	Rank	Starts	Poles	1	2	3	4	5	6–10	Laps	Laps Led	Races Led	Miles	$
1951	N/A	2	0	0	0	0	0	0	0	225	0	0	225	25
Lifetime		2	0	0	0	0	0	0	0	225	0	0	225	$25

Dick Jennette

Richard Jennette
Career ended 9/11/55 @ Detroit, MI Fairgrounds.
Racing Hometown: Whitmore Lake, MI

Year	Rank	Starts	Poles	1	2	3	4	5	6–10	Laps	Laps Led	Races Led	Miles	$
1954	NR	1	0	0	0	0	0	0	0	115	0	0	58	25
Lifetime		1	0	0	0	0	0	0	0	115	0	0	58	$25

Year	Rank	Starts	Poles	1	2	3	Finish 4	5	6–10	Laps	Laps Led	Races Led	Miles	$

John Jennings

John Jennings
Racing Hometown: Fayetteville, NC

Year	Rank	Starts	Poles	1	2	3	4	5	6–10	Laps	Laps Led	Races Led	Miles	$
1970	71	6	0	0	0	0	0	0	0	610	0	0	281	1,515
Lifetime		6	0	0	0	0	0	0	0	610	0	0	281	$1,515

Bill Jennings

William Jennings
B: 3/27/1926
Racing Hometown: Syracuse, NY

Year	Rank	Starts	Poles	1	2	3	4	5	6–10	Laps	Laps Led	Races Led	Miles	$
1953	86T	1	0	0	0	0	0	0	1		0	0		75
Lifetime		1	0	0	0	0	0	0	1		0	0		$75

Joe Jernigan

Joseph Stanley Jernigan (Little Joe)
B: 5/23/1915   D: 6/23/1951   *Killed at Royal Speedway in Richmond, VA.*
Racing Hometown: Norfolk, VA

Year	Rank	Starts	Poles	1	2	3	4	5	6–10	Laps	Laps Led	Races Led	Miles	$
1950	87	2	0	0	0	0	0	0	0	166	0	0	296	100
1951	N/A	2	0	0	0	0	0	0	0		0	0		25
Lifetime		4	0	0	0	0	0	0	0	166	0	0	296	$125

Dick Jerrett

Richard Jerrett
Racing Hometown: Mexico, NY

Year	Rank	Starts	Poles	1	2	3	4	5	6–10	Laps	Laps Led	Races Led	Miles	$
1950	NR	3	0	0	0	0	0	0	2	184	0	0	92	175
Lifetime		3	0	0	0	0	0	0	2	184	0	0	92	$175

Tom Jerris

Thomas Jerris
Racing Hometown: Pittsburgh, PA

Year	Rank	Starts	Poles	1	2	3	4	5	6–10	Laps	Laps Led	Races Led	Miles	$
1951	76	1	0	0	0	0	0	1	0		0	0		250
Lifetime		1	0	0	0	0	0	1	0		0	0		$250

Paul Jett

Paul Jett
Racing Hometown: San Antonio, TX

Year	Rank	Starts	Poles	1	2	3	4	5	6–10	Laps	Laps Led	Races Led	Miles	$
1972	727	1	0	0	0	0	0	0	0	220	0	0	440	680
Lifetime		1	0	0	0	0	0	0	0	220	0	0	440	$680

Fran Jischke

Francis Jischke
Racing Hometown: Rochester, NY

Year	Rank	Starts	Poles	1	2	3	4	5	6–10	Laps	Laps Led	Races Led	Miles	$
1951	N/A	1	0	0	0	0	0	0	0		0	0		25
1952	129T	1	0	0	0	0	0	0	0	158	0	0	79	25
1954	217	1	0	0	0	0	0	0	0	22	0	0	11	0
Lifetime		3	0	0	0	0	0	0	0	180	0	0	90	$50

Gordon Johncock

Gordon Walter Johncock
B: 8/5/1936
Racing Hometown: Coldwater, MI

Year	Rank	Starts	Poles	1	2	3	4	5	6–10	Laps	Laps Led	Races Led	Miles	$
1966	NR	5	0	0	0	0	1	0	1	1,139	21	2	1,673	5,485
1967	NR	6	0	0	0	0	0	1	0	685	1	1	930	4,945
1972	NR	2	0	0	0	0	0	0	0	226	0	0	430	1,384
1973	NR	6	1	0	0	0	1	0	0	1,307	0	0	1,809	10,600
1975	NR	1	0	0	0	0	0	0	0	47	0	0	125	1,230
1976	NR	1	0	0	0	0	0	0	0	41	0	0	62	870
Lifetime		21	1	0	0	0	2	1	1	3,445	22	3	5,029	$24,514

Bobby Johns

Robert James Johns
B: 5/22/1934
Racing Hometown: Miami, Fl

Year	Rank	Starts	Poles	1	2	3	4	5	6–10	Laps	Laps Led	Races Led	Miles	$
1956	25	9	0	0	0	0	0	0	3	1,537	0	0	1,091	1,450
1957	48	1	0	0	0	0	0	0	0	335	0	0	461	225
1958	NR	3	0	0	0	0	1	0	0	894	0	0	835	1,625
1959	19	8	1	0	0	1	0	0	1	1,911	129	2	1,440	5,951
1960	3	19	0	1	2	1	3	1	2	3,695	416	5	3,815	46,115
1961	24	14	1	0	0	0	1	0	2	2,674	52	2	3,084	5,010
1962	28	13	0	1	0	1	0	0	1	2,725	614	8	2,946	15,863
1963	21	12	0	0	0	1	0	2	3	2,433	84	3	3,383	15,915

Year	Rank	Starts	Poles	Finish						Laps	Laps Led	Races Led	Miles	$
				1	2	3	4	5	6–10					

Bobby Johns *continued*

Year	Rank	Starts	Poles	1	2	3	4	5	6–10	Laps	Laps Led	Races Led	Miles	$
1964	37	12	0	0	0	0	0	0	2	1,806	0	0	1,859	5,700
1965	20	13	0	0	2	2	0	1	0	2,696	37	6	2,941	24,930
1966	60	11	0	0	0	0	0	0	1	1,419	0	0	1,236	5,245
1967	62	11	0	0	0	0	0	0	0	1,279	0	0	1,301	6,405
1968	48	7	0	0	0	0	0	0	0	750	0	0	1,108	5,010
1969	54	8	0	0	0	0	0	0	0	1,075	0	0	1,185	5,875
Lifetime		141	2	2	4	6	5	4	15	25,229	1,332	26	26,684	$145,319

Don Johns

Donald Johns
B: 1934   D: 8/25/1962   *Killed in race @ Minnesota Fairgrounds in St.Paul, MN.*
Racing Hometown: Bellflower, CA

Year	Rank	Starts	Poles	1	2	3	4	5	6–10	Laps	Laps Led	Races Led	Miles	$
1957	111	2	0	0	0	0	0	0	1	255	0	0	128	200
Lifetime		2	0	0	0	0	0	0	1	255	0	0	128	$200

Ken Johns

Kenneth Johns
Racing Hometown: Ft. Worth, TX

Year	Rank	Starts	Poles	1	2	3	4	5	6–10	Laps	Laps Led	Races Led	Miles	$
1955	58	2	0	0	0	0	0	0	2	249	0	0	326	300
Lifetime		2	0	0	0	0	0	0	2	249	0	0	326	$300

Squirt Johns

Squirt Johns
Racing Hometown: Bradford, PA

Year	Rank	Starts	Poles	1	2	3	4	5	6–10	Laps	Laps Led	Races Led	Miles	$
1958	NR	2	0	0	0	0	0	0	0	105	0	0	35	90
Lifetime		2	0	0	0	0	0	0	0	105	0	0	35	$90

Amos Johnson

Amos Neill Johnson Jr.
B: 4/9/1941
Racing Hometown: Raleigh, NC

Year	Rank	Starts	Poles	1	2	3	4	5	6–10	Laps	Laps Led	Races Led	Miles	$
1969	NR	1	0	0	0	0	0	0	0	147	0	0	391	1,450
Lifetime		1	0	0	0	0	0	0	0	147	0	0	391	$1,450

Bob Johnson

Robert Johnson
Racing Hometown: Tampa, FL

Year	Rank	Starts	Poles	1	2	3	4	5	6–10	Laps	Laps Led	Races Led	Miles	$
1951	N/A	1	0	0	0	0	0	0	0	214	0	0	268	0
Lifetime		1	0	0	0	0	0	0	0	214	0	0	268	$0

Cal Johnson

Cal Johnson
Racing Hometown: Ashland, VA

Year	Rank	Starts	Poles	1	2	3	4	5	6–10	Laps	Laps Led	Races Led	Miles	$
1951	86	2	0	0	0	0	0	0	2		0	0		150
Lifetime		2	0	0	0	0	0	0	2		0	0		$150

Dick Johnson

Richard Myron Johnson
B: 1/9/1928
Racing Hometown: Elverta, CA

Year	Rank	Starts	Poles	1	2	3	4	5	6–10	Laps	Laps Led	Races Led	Miles	$
1967	45	23	0	0	0	0	0	0	0	2,636	0	0	1,647	5,070
1968	37	11	0	0	0	0	0	0	0	2,187	0	0	2,040	5,920
1969	34	22	0	0	0	0	0	0	4	3,803	0	0	2,910	11,182
Lifetime		56	0	0	0	0	0	0	4	8,626	0	0	6,596	$22,172

Dick Johnson

Richard Johnson
B: 1945
Racing Hometown: Brisbane, Australia

Year	Rank	Starts	Poles	1	2	3	4	5	6–10	Laps	Laps Led	Races Led	Miles	$
1989	47	4	0	0	0	0	0	0	0	497	0	0	1,270	11,515
1990	63	3	0	0	0	0	0	0	0	166	0	0	304	8,950
Lifetime		7	0	0	0	0	0	0	0	663	0	0	1,574	$20,465

Don Johnson

Donald Johnson

Year	Rank	Starts	Poles	1	2	3	4	5	6–10	Laps	Laps Led	Races Led	Miles	$
1954	NR	1	0	0	0	0	0	0	0	39	0	0	78	0
Lifetime		1	0	0	0	0	0	0	0	39	0	0	78	$0

Year	Rank	Starts	Poles	Finish 1	2	3	4	5	6–10	Laps	Laps Led	Races Led	Miles	$

Fred Johnson

Fred Johnson
B: 12/9/1929
Racing Hometown: Hamptonville, NC

Year	Rank	Starts	Poles	1	2	3	4	5	6–10	Laps	Laps Led	Races Led	Miles	$
1949	NR	2	0	0	0	0	0	0	0		0	0		0
1950	60	2	0	0	0	0	0	0	1	244	0	0	197	125
1955	186	2	0	0	0	0	0	0	0	258	0	0	345	460
1956	106	1	0	0	0	0	0	0	1	60	0	0	246	325
Lifetime		7	0	0	0	0	0	0	2	562	0	0	787	$910

Gary Johnson

Gary Johnson
B: 5/12/1940
Racing Hometown: Modesto, CA

Year	Rank	Starts	Poles	1	2	3	4	5	6–10	Laps	Laps Led	Races Led	Miles	$
1976	79	1	0	0	0	0	0	0	0	72	0	0	189	840
1977	74	2	0	0	0	0	0	0	0	126	0	0	330	2,445
1978	102T	1	0	0	0	0	0	0	0	3	0	0	8	500
Lifetime		4	0	0	0	0	0	0	0	201	0	0	527	$3,785

Hubert Johnson

Hubert Johnson

Year	Rank	Starts	Poles	1	2	3	4	5	6–10	Laps	Laps Led	Races Led	Miles	$
1960	NR	1	0	0	0	0	0	0	0	105	0	0	53	50
Lifetime		1	0	0	0	0	0	0	0	105	0	0	53	$50

Jerry Johnson

Jerry Johnson
Racing Hometown: Torrance, CA

Year	Rank	Starts	Poles	1	2	3	4	5	6–10	Laps	Laps Led	Races Led	Miles	$
1958	NR	1	0	0	0	0	0	0	0	93	0	0	93	100
Lifetime		1	0	0	0	0	0	0	0	93	0	0	93	$100

Jimmie Johnson

Jimmie Johnson
B: 9/17/1975
Racing Hometown: El Cajon, CA

Year	Rank	Starts	Poles	1	2	3	4	5	6–10	Laps	Laps Led	Races Led	Miles	$
2001	53	3	0	0	0	0	0	0	0	781	0	0	1,187	122,320
2002	5	36	5	3	0	2	1	0	15	10,521	838	14	13,915	3,788,268
Lifetime		39	5	3	0	2	1	0	15	11,302	838	14	15,102	$3,910,588

Joe Lee Johnson

Joseph Lee Johnson
B: 9/11/1929
Racing Hometown: Chattanooga, TN

Year	Rank	Starts	Poles	1	2	3	4	5	6–10	Laps	Laps Led	Races Led	Miles	$
1957	92	2	0	0	0	0	0	0	0	63	0	0	95	175
1958	91	6	0	0	0	0	0	1	2	989	0	0	732	1,210
1959	70	12	0	1	0	0	1	1	3	2,743	1	1	2,007	6,807
1960	13	22	0	1	1	1	1	2	2	3,453	48	1	2,651	34,519
1961	46	9	0	0	0	0	0	0	3	1,276	0	0	1,461	2,615
1962	93	4	0	0	0	0	0	0	0	381	0	0	191	340
Lifetime		55	0	2	1	1	2	4	10	8,905	49	2	7,137	$45,666

Junior Johnson

Robert Glenn Johnson
B: 6/28/1931
Racing Hometown: Ronda, NC

Year	Rank	Starts	Poles	1	2	3	4	5	6–10	Laps	Laps Led	Races Led	Miles	$
1953	NR	1	0	0	0	0	0	0	0	222	0	0	305	110
1954	55	4	1	0	0	0	0	1	0	535	0	0	389	550
1955	6	36	2	5	1	2	1	3	6	4,620	790	7	3,133	13,803
1956	38	13	1	0	1	0	0	0	0	1,131	60	2	955	1,350
1957	154	1	0	0	0	0	0	0	0	102	0	0	64	50
1958	8	27	0	6	2	3	1	0	4	4,244	317	9	2,797	13,809
1959	11	28	1	5	1	3	3	2	1	4,433	166	7	2,745	9,675
1960	7	34	3	3	2	4	2	3	4	5,096	254	7	3,797	38,990
1961	6	41	10	7	3	2	3	1	6	7,016	2,365	22	5,228	38,990
1962	20	23	2	1	2	2	1	1	1	3,663	641	10	3,224	34,841
1963	12	33	9	7	2	2	0	2	1	5,753	2,299	21	4,789	67,351
1964	14	29	5	3	2	4	3	0	3	6,298	1,116	15	4,474	26,975
1965	12	36	10	13	2	1	2	0	1	7,144	3,998	30	5,040	62,216
1966	49	7	3	0	0	0	0	1	0	1,813	467	6	1,160	3,610
Lifetime		313	47	50	18	23	16	14	27	52,070	12,473	136	38,100	$312,320

Year	Rank	Starts	Poles	Finish						Laps	Laps Led	Races Led	Miles	$
				1	2	3	4	5	6–10	Laps	Led	Led	Miles	$

Ken Johnson

Kenneth Johnson
  Racing Hometown: Jamestown, NY

Year	Rank	Starts	Poles	1	2	3	4	5	6–10	Laps	Laps Led	Races Led	Miles	$
1956	NR	1	0	0	0	0	0	0	0	127	0	0	64	100
1958	NR	1	0	0	0	1	0	0	0	149	0	0	50	375
1959	59	4	0	0	0	0	0	0	1	408	0	0	366	370
1960	NR	4	0	0	0	0	0	0	0	317	0	0	721	460
1961	154	2	0	0	0	0	0	0	0	36	0	0	90	250
Lifetime		12	0	0	0	1	0	0	1	1,037	0	0	1,290	$1,555

Lionel Johnson

Lionel Barbour Johnson
  B: 10/16/1928
  Racing Hometown: Unionville, VA

Year	Rank	Starts	Poles	1	2	3	4	5	6–10	Laps	Laps Led	Races Led	Miles	$
1965	48	8	0	0	0	0	0	0	2	1,663	0	0	1,338	3,165
1966	91	5	0	0	0	0	0	0	0	328	0	0	274	1,895
Lifetime		13	0	0	0	0	0	0	2	1,991	0	0	1,611	$5,060

Lou Johnson

Lou Johnson
  B: 11/25/1924
  Racing Hometown: Wilmington, DE

Year	Rank	Starts	Poles	1	2	3	4	5	6–10	Laps	Laps Led	Races Led	Miles	$
1953	78	2	0	0	0	0	0	0	0		0	0		50
Lifetime		2	0	0	0	0	0	0	0		0	0		$50

Slick Johnson

Julius David Johnson, III
  B: 2/23/1948   D: 2/14/1990   *Killed in ARCA 200 @ Daytona.*
  Racing Hometown: Florence, SC

Year	Rank	Starts	Poles	1	2	3	4	5	6–10	Laps	Laps Led	Races Led	Miles	$
1979	42	4	0	0	0	0	0	0	1	1,039	0	0	1,134	5,360
1980	23	18	0	0	0	0	0	0	5	4,724	7	2	4,731	35,460
1981	65	4	0	0	0	0	0	0	0	611	0	0	752	4,150
1982	29	17	0	0	0	0	0	0	1	3,826	3	2	4,230	44,190
1983	38	10	0	0	0	0	0	0	0	2,330	0	0	2,501	13,665
1984	NR	1	0	0	0	0	0	0	0	70	0	0	96	1,495
1985	48	6	0	0	0	0	0	0	0	1,608	0	0	2,327	24,995
1987	46	8	0	0	0	0	0	0	0	2,113	3	2	1,839	40,630
Lifetime		68	0	0	0	0	0	0	7	16,321	13	6	17,610	$169,945

Ray Johnstone

Raymond Johnstone
  B: 6/19/1928
  Racing Hometown: San Bernadino, CA

Year	Rank	Starts	Poles	1	2	3	4	5	6–10	Laps	Laps Led	Races Led	Miles	$
1969	NR	1	0	0	0	0	0	0	0	163	0	0	440	1,225
1970	NR	1	0	0	0	0	0	0	0	26	0	0	68	660
1971	NR	3	0	0	0	0	0	0	0	211	0	0	541	3,405
1972	109	1	0	0	0	0	0	0	0	62	0	0	162	725
Lifetime		6	0	0	0	0	0	0	0	462	0	0	1,212	$6,015

Carl Joiner

Carl Joiner
  B: 5/12/1924
  Racing Hometown: Portland, OR

Year	Rank	Starts	Poles	1	2	3	4	5	6–10	Laps	Laps Led	Races Led	Miles	$
1957	NR	1	0	0	0	0	0	0	0	18	0	0	9	100
1961	109	1	0	0	0	0	0	0	0	125	0	0	175	100
1963	104	1	0	0	0	0	0	0	0	143	0	0	386	375
1966	125	1	0	0	0	0	0	0	0	41	0	0	111	500
1968	111	1	0	0	0	0	0	0	0	3	0	0	8	500
1970	104T	1	0	0	0	0	0	0	0	23	0	0	60	800
1971	NR	3	0	0	0	0	0	0	1	385	0	0	987	4,250
1972	77	2	0	0	0	0	0	1	0	283	0	0	741	3,420
1973	116	1	0	0	0	0	0	0	0	46	0	0	121	1,015
1975	91T	1	0	0	0	0	0	0	0	87	0	0	228	895
1976	78	2	0	0	0	0	0	0	0	227	0	0	581	2,155
1977	102T	1	0	0	0	0	0	0	0	10	0	0	26	740
Lifetime		16	0	0	0	0	0	1	1	1,391	0	0	3,433	$14,850

Year	Rank	Starts	Poles	Finish 1	2	3	4	5	6–10	Laps	Laps Led	Races Led	Miles	$

Jerry Jolly

Jerry Jolly
B: 8/12/1941
Racing Hometown: Denver, CO

Year	Rank	Starts	Poles	1	2	3	4	5	6–10	Laps	Laps Led	Races Led	Miles	$
1978	70	3	0	0	0	0	0	0	0	307	0	0	652	5,740
1979	101T	1	0	0	0	0	0	0	0	99	0	0	263	2,440
1984	89	1	0	0	0	0	0	0	0	10	0	0	26	715
Lifetime		5	0	0	0	0	0	0	0	416	0	0	941	$8,895

Alton Jones

Alton Jones
B: 8/27/1941
Racing Hometown: Pleasant Grove, AL

Year	Rank	Starts	Poles	1	2	3	4	5	6–10	Laps	Laps Led	Races Led	Miles	$
1970	NR	1	0	0	0	0	0	0	0	155	0	0	412	1,485
1973	74	5	0	0	0	0	0	0	1	686	0	0	807	4,195
1974	49	5	0	0	0	0	0	1	1	1,163	0	0	1,095	4,080
1975	62	2	0	0	0	0	0	0	1	790	0	0	471	1,935
Lifetime		13	0	0	0	0	0	1	3	2,794	0	0	2,785	$11,695

Bill Jones

William Jones

Year	Rank	Starts	Poles	1	2	3	4	5	6–10	Laps	Laps Led	Races Led	Miles	$
1958	NR	1	0	0	0	0	0	0	0	160	0	0	421	195
Lifetime		1	0	0	0	0	0	0	0	160	0	0	421	$195

Britton Jones

Britton Jones
Racing Hometown: Las Vegas, NV

Year	Rank	Starts	Poles	1	2	3	4	5	6–10	Laps	Laps Led	Races Led	Miles	$
1955	239	1	0	0	0	0	0	0	0	11	0	0	11	20
Lifetime		1	0	0	0	0	0	0	0	11	0	0	11	$20

Buckshot Jones

Roy Jones
B: 7/23/1970
Racing Hometown: Norcross, GA

Year	Rank	Starts	Poles	1	2	3	4	5	6–10	Laps	Laps Led	Races Led	Miles	$
1997	70	1	0	0	0	0	0	0	0	38	0	0	58	20,875
1998	52	5	0	0	0	0	0	0	1	1,025	0	0	1,769	162,435
1999	45	10	0	0	0	0	0	0	0	2,529	0	0	3,947	345,128
2000	68	1	0	0	0	0	0	0	0	277	0	0	427	35,275
2001	41	30	0	0	0	0	0	0	0	7,819	2	2	10,352	1,631,488
2002	49	7	0	0	0	0	0	0	0	2,218	0	0	2,399	394,223
Lifetime		54	0	0	0	0	0	0	1	13,906	2	2	18,951	$2,589,424

Bud Jones

Bud Jones
Racing Hometown: Wilkesboro, NC

Year	Rank	Starts	Poles	1	2	3	4	5	6–10	Laps	Laps Led	Races Led	Miles	$
1953	NR	1	0	0	0	0	0	0	0	36	0	0	23	25
Lifetime		1	0	0	0	0	0	0	0	36	0	0	23	$25

Davy Jones

Duane Davy Jones
B: 6/1/1964
Racing Hometown: Chicago, IL

Year	Rank	Starts	Poles	1	2	3	4	5	6–10	Laps	Laps Led	Races Led	Miles	$
1995	46	7	0	0	0	0	0	0	0	1,680	0	0	2,359	109,925
Lifetime		7	0	0	0	0	0	0	0	1,680	0	0	2,359	$109,925

Frank Jones

Frank Jones
Racing Hometown: Seattle, WA

Year	Rank	Starts	Poles	1	2	3	4	5	6–10	Laps	Laps Led	Races Led	Miles	$
1968	90	1	0	0	0	0	0	0	0	55	0	0	149	520
Lifetime		1	0	0	0	0	0	0	0	55	0	0	149	$520

Guy Jones

Guy Jones
Racing Hometown: South Gate, CA

Year	Rank	Starts	Poles	1	2	3	4	5	6–10	Laps	Laps Led	Races Led	Miles	$
1968	NR	1	0	0	0	0	0	0	0	109	0	0	294	650
1969	NR	1	0	0	0	0	0	0	0	8	0	0	22	800
Lifetime		2	0	0	0	0	0	0	0	117	0	0	316	$1,450

Year	Rank	Starts	Poles		Finish					Laps	Laps Led	Races Led	Miles	$
				1	2	3	4	5	6–10					

Hap Jones

Vivien S. Jones
B: 4/18/1927
Racing Hometown: Jackson Center, PA

Year	Rank	Starts	Poles	1	2	3	4	5	6–10	Laps	Laps Led	Races Led	Miles	$
1951	84T	1	0	0	0	0	0	0	1		0	0		200
1954	NR	1	0	0	0	0	0	0	0	31	0	0	127	0
Lifetime		2	0	0	0	0	0	0	1	31	0	0	127	$200

Harvey Jones

Harvey Jones
B: 1924
Racing Hometown: Tallahassee, FL

Year	Rank	Starts	Poles	1	2	3	4	5	6–10	Laps	Laps Led	Races Led	Miles	$
1965	97	1	0	0	0	0	0	1	0	195	0	0	98	275
1965	97	1	0	0	0	0	0	1	0	195	0	0	98	275
Lifetime		2	0	0	0	0	0	2	0	390	0	0	195	$550

Henry Jones

Henry F. Jones
B: 9/13/1950
Racing Hometown: Manhattan, KS

Year	Rank	Starts	Poles	1	2	3	4	5	6–10	Laps	Laps Led	Races Led	Miles	$
1979	58	3	0	0	0	0	0	0	0	77	0	0	43	1,160
1980	106	4	0	0	0	0	0	0	0	376	0	0	850	4,725
1981	79	1	0	0	0	0	0	0	0	363	0	0	197	765
Lifetime		8	0	0	0	0	0	0	0	816	0	0	1,090	$6,650

James Jones

James Jones
Racing Hometown: Goldsboro, NC

Year	Rank	Starts	Poles	1	2	3	4	5	6–10	Laps	Laps Led	Races Led	Miles	$
1956	214T	1	0	0	0	0	0	0	0	169	0	0	85	100
1958	NR	1	0	0	0	0	0	0	0	212	0	0	212	100
Lifetime		2	0	0	0	0	0	0	0	381	0	0	297	$200

Jim Jones

James Jones
B: 1922
Racing Hometown: Osceola, AR

Year	Rank	Starts	Poles	1	2	3	4	5	6–10	Laps	Laps Led	Races Led	Miles	$
1954	NR	1	0	0	0	0	0	0	0	7	0	0	4	0
Lifetime		1	0	0	0	0	0	0	0	7	0	0	4	$0

Joe Jones

Joseph Jones
Racing Hometown: Winston-Salem, NC

Year	Rank	Starts	Poles	1	2	3	4	5	6–10	Laps	Laps Led	Races Led	Miles	$
1961	70	9	0	0	0	0	0	0	0	895	0	0	639	1,065
1962	103	2	0	0	0	0	0	0	0	250	0	0	125	100
1963	122T	1	0	0	0	0	0	0	0	186	0	0	47	130
Lifetime		12	0	0	0	0	0	0	0	1,331	0	0	810	$1,295

Owen Jones

Owen Jones
Racing Hometown: Cleveland, OH

Year	Rank	Starts	Poles	1	2	3	4	5	6–10	Laps	Laps Led	Races Led	Miles	$
1951	N/A	2	0	0	0	0	0	0	0		0	0		50
Lifetime		2	0	0	0	0	0	0	0		0	0		$50

P.J. Jones

P.J. Jones
B: 4/23/1969
Racing Hometown: Rolling Hills, CA

Year	Rank	Starts	Poles	1	2	3	4	5	6–10	Laps	Laps Led	Races Led	Miles	$
1993	42	6	0	0	0	0	0	0	1	710	0	0	1,447	53,370
1994	59	2	0	0	0	0	0	0	0	370	0	0	467	13,065
2000	58	2	0	0	0	0	0	0	0	479	0	0	804	70,900
2002	60	1	0	0	0	0	1	0	0	90	0	0	221	65,950
Lifetime		11	0	0	0	0	1	0	1	1,649	0	0	2,939	$203,285

Parnelli Jones

Rufus Parnell Jones
B: 8/12/1933
Racing Hometown: Torrance, CA

Year	Rank	Starts	Poles	1	2	3	4	5	6–10	Laps	Laps Led	Races Led	Miles	$
1956	67	3	0	0	1	0	0	0	0	591	0	0	564	1,705
1957	47	10	1	1	0	0	0	0	2	743	1	1	582	1,625

Year	Rank	Starts	Poles	Finish 1	2	3	4	5	6–10	Laps	Laps Led	Races Led	Miles	$

Parnelli Jones *continued*

Year	Rank	Starts	Poles	1	2	3	4	5	6–10	Laps	Laps Led	Races Led	Miles	$
1958	33	3	2	1	0	0	0	0	0	587	148	2	954	1,010
1959	94	2	0	1	0	0	0	0	0	560	1	1	268	1,905
1960	91	3	0	0	0	0	0	0	1	204	25	1	371	465
1963	NR	4	0	0	0	0	0	0	1	444	39	1	993	2,000
1964	NR	4	0	0	0	0	0	0	1	202	9	1	502	2,110
1965	NR	1	0	0	0	0	0	0	0	37	36	1	100	980
1967	NR	1	0	1	0	0	0	0	0	185	126	1	500	18,720
1968	NR	1	0	0	0	1	0	0	0	186	49	1	502	5,600
1969	NR	1	0	0	0	0	0	0	0	22	0	0	59	770
1970	NR	1	0	0	0	0	0	0	0	168	88	1	440	1,275
Lifetime		34	3	4	1	1	0	0	5	3,929	522	11	5,834	$38,165

Pee Wee Jones

Phillip Jones
B: 3/31/1928
Racing Hometown: Clemmons, NC

Year	Rank	Starts	Poles	1	2	3	4	5	6–10	Laps	Laps Led	Races Led	Miles	$
1955	148T	2	0	0	0	0	0	0	0	204	0	0	102	50
1956	128	3	0	0	0	0	0	0	0	549	0	0	327	125
1957	NT	1	0	0	0	0	0	0	0	262	0	0	262	225
1959	NT	1	0	0	0	0	0	0	0	150	0	0	38	50
Lifetime		7	0	0	0	0	0	0	0	1,165	0	0	729	$450

Possum Jones

Lewis V. Jones
B: 1/16/1932
Racing Hometown: Mango, FL

Year	Rank	Starts	Poles	1	2	3	4	5	6–10	Laps	Laps Led	Races Led	Miles	$
1952	164	1	0	0	0	0	0	0	0	193	0	0	241	0
1955	199	1	0	0	0	0	0	0	0	276	0	0	380	60
1956	137	1	0	0	0	0	0	0	0	336	0	0	462	110
1957	35	6	0	0	0	0	0	0	4	1,443	0	0	1,395	2,375
1958	41	11	1	0	0	0	0	1	2	1,870	28	1	1,254	1,790
1959	112	1	0	0	0	0	0	0	0	74	0	0	102	295
1960	31	13	0	0	3	1	0	0	1	2,594	0	0	2,127	6,330
1963	61	7	0	0	0	0	0	0	1	917	0	0	763	1,880
1964	94	5	0	0	0	0	0	0	0	531	0	0	227	740
1965	136	1	0	0	0	0	0	0	0	0	0	0	0	100
Lifetime		47	1	0	3	1	0	1	8	8,234	28	1	6,951	$13,680

Ralph Jones

Ralph Jones
B: 1/20/1944
Racing Hometown: Upton, KY

Year	Rank	Starts	Poles	1	2	3	4	5	6–10	Laps	Laps Led	Races Led	Miles	$
1977	51	4	0	0	0	0	0	0	0	871	0	0	645	3,395
1978	40	7	0	0	0	0	0	0	0	1,871	0	0	1,856	6,305
1979	40	6	0	0	0	0	0	0	0	729	0	0	1,171	12,785
1980	94	2	0	0	0	0	0	0	0	547	0	0	780	3,495
1988	74	1	0	0	0	0	0	0	0	190	0	0	475	10,595
Lifetime		20	0	0	0	0	0	0	0	4,208	0	0	4,928	$36,575

Richard Jones

Richard Jones

Year	Rank	Starts	Poles	1	2	3	4	5	6–10	Laps	Laps Led	Races Led	Miles	$
1954	NR	1	0	0	0	0	0	0	0	1	0	0	2	0
Lifetime		1	0	0	0	0	0	0	0	1	0	0	2	$0

Ed Jordan

Edward Jordan
Racing Hometown: Houston, TX

Year	Rank	Starts	Poles	1	2	3	4	5	6–10	Laps	Laps Led	Races Led	Miles	$
1966	104	3	0	0	0	0	0	0	0	147	0	0	76	460
Lifetime		3	0	0	0	0	0	0	0	147	0	0	76	$460

Bill Joslin

William Joslin
Racing Hometown: Fayettevile, NC

Year	Rank	Starts	Poles	1	2	3	4	5	6–10	Laps	Laps Led	Races Led	Miles	$
1950	110	2	0	0	0	0	0	0	0		0	0		25
1951	N/A	4	0	0	0	0	0	0	0	108	0	0	54	100
Lifetime		6	0	0	0	0	0	0	0	108	0	0	54	$125

| Year | Rank | Starts | Poles | Finish | | | | | | Laps | Laps Led | Races Led | Miles | $ |
				1	2	3	4	5	6–10					

Dick Joslin

Richard Joslin
B: 9/18/1926   D: 1/23/1972
Racing Hometown: Orlando, FL

Year	Rank	Starts	Poles	1	2	3	4	5	6–10	Laps	Laps Led	Races Led	Miles	$
1955	95	1	0	0	0	0	0	0	1	38	0	0	156	425
1957	128	1	0	0	0	0	0	0	1	48	0	0	77	100
1958	177	1	0	0	0	0	0	0	0	6	0	0	25	0
1959	39	4	0	0	0	0	0	0	0	338	0	0	793	485
1960	73	3	0	0	0	0	0	0	0	302	0	0	755	535
Lifetime		10	0	0	0	0	0	0	2	732	0	0	1,805	$1,545

Claude Joyce

Claude Joyce
Racing Hometown: Kernersville, NC

Year	Rank	Starts	Poles	1	2	3	4	5	6–10	Laps	Laps Led	Races Led	Miles	$
1951	N/A	1	0	0	0	0	0	0	0		0	0		25
Lifetime		1	0	0	0	0	0	0	0		0	0		$25

Stuart Joyce

Stuart Joyce
B: 1917   D: 1/11/1981
Racing Hometown: Wannamaker, IN

Year	Rank	Starts	Poles	1	2	3	4	5	6–10	Laps	Laps Led	Races Led	Miles	$
1952	53	1	0	0	0	0	0	0	1	229	0	0	229	200
Lifetime		1	0	0	0	0	0	0	1	229	0	0	229	$200

J.L. Justice

J.L. Justice
Racing Hometown: Raleigh, NC

Year	Rank	Starts	Poles	1	2	3	4	5	6–10	Laps	Laps Led	Races Led	Miles	$
1953	126	3	0	0	0	0	0	0	0	226	0	0	307	145
Lifetime		3	0	0	0	0	0	0	0	226	0	0	307	$145

Jack Kabat

Jack Kabat
Racing Hometown: Cleveland, OH

Year	Rank	Starts	Poles	1	2	3	4	5	6–10	Laps	Laps Led	Races Led	Miles	$
1950	56T	1	0	0	0	0	0	0	1	0	0	0	0	125
1951	N/A	1	0	0	0	0	0	0	0		0	0		25
Lifetime		2	0	0	0	0	0	0	1	0	0	0	0	$150

Dick Kable

Richard Kable
Racing Hometown: Cleveland, OH

Year	Rank	Starts	Poles	1	2	3	4	5	6–10	Laps	Laps Led	Races Led	Miles	$
1954	NR	1	0	0	0	0	0	0	0	168	0	0	84	0
Lifetime		1	0	0	0	0	0	0	0	168	0	0	84	$0

Hoss Kagle

Ralph Kagle
B: 1928
Racing Hometown: Mt. Ranier, MD

Year	Rank	Starts	Poles	1	2	3	4	5	6–10	Laps	Laps Led	Races Led	Miles	$
1956	NR	1	0	0	0	0	0	0	0	135	0	0	135	100
1961	136	1	0	0	0	0	0	0	0	2	0	0	1	125
Lifetime		2	0	0	0	0	0	0	0	137	0	0	136	$225

Reds Kagle

Richard H. Kagle
B: 4/20/1932
Racing Hometown: Greenbelt, MD

Year	Rank	Starts	Poles	1	2	3	4	5	6–10	Laps	Laps Led	Races Led	Miles	$
1954	86	1	0	0	0	0	0	0	0	220	0	0	220	175
1956	191	2	0	0	0	0	0	0	0	202	0	0	85	60
1957	172	1	0	0	0	0	0	0	0	23	0	0	12	25
1958	NR	14	0	0	0	0	0	2	5	1,642	0	0	896	1,750
1959	91	4	0	0	0	0	1	0	0	627	0	0	340	525
1961	54	3	0	0	0	0	0	0	1	720	0	0	963	1,495
Lifetime		25	0	0	0	0	1	2	6	3,434	0	0	2,515	$4,030

H.R. Kahl

H.R. Kahl
Racing Hometown: Cathedral City, CA

Year	Rank	Starts	Poles	1	2	3	4	5	6–10	Laps	Laps Led	Races Led	Miles	$
1954	135	2	0	0	0	0	0	0	0	225	0	0	113	25
Lifetime		2	0	0	0	0	0	0	0	225	0	0	113	$25

Year	Rank	Starts	Poles	Finish						Laps	Laps Led	Races Led	Miles	$
				1	2	3	4	5	6–10	Laps				

Red Kalajainen

Red Kalajainen

Year	Rank	Starts	Poles	1	2	3	4	5	6–10	Laps	Laps Led	Races Led	Miles	$
1958	155	1	0	0	0	0	0	0	0	68	0	0	27	25
Lifetime		1	0	0	0	0	0	0	0	68	0	0	27	$25

Frank Kapack

Frank Kapack

Year	Rank	Starts	Poles	1	2	3	4	5	6–10	Laps	Laps Led	Races Led	Miles	$
1953	NR	1	0	0	0	0	0	0	0		0	0		25
Lifetime		1	0	0	0	0	0	0	0		0	0		$25

Iggy Katona

Egnatius Katona
B: 8/16/1916
Racing Hometown: Willis, MI

Year	Rank	Starts	Poles	1	2	3	4	5	6–10	Laps	Laps Led	Races Led	Miles	$
1951	131	5	0	0	0	0	0	0	0	559	0	0	643	150
1952	33	5	0	0	0	0	0	0	2	1,067	0	0	925	525
1965	65	1	0	0	0	0	0	0	1	251	0	0	377	850
1966	81	1	0	0	0	0	0	0	0	286	0	0	429	715
1974	102	1	0	0	0	0	0	0	0	181	0	0	481	1,675
Lifetime		13	0	0	0	0	0	0	3	2,344	0	0	2,855	$3,915

Frank Katucka

Frank Katucka

Year	Rank	Starts	Poles	1	2	3	4	5	6–10	Laps	Laps Led	Races Led	Miles	$
1953	NR	1	0	0	0	0	0	0	0		0	0		25
Lifetime		1	0	0	0	0	0	0	0		0	0		$25

Bob Kauf

Robert C. Kauf
B: 4/1/1942
Racing Hometown: Pacoima, CA

Year	Rank	Starts	Poles	1	2	3	4	5	6–10	Laps	Laps Led	Races Led	Miles	$
1971	NR	2	0	0	0	0	0	0	0	64	0	0	168	1,675
1972	90	2	0	0	0	0	0	0	0	178	0	0	445	2,500
1973	NR	1	0	0	0	0	0	0	0	9	0	0	24	1,015
Lifetime		5	0	0	0	0	0	0	0	251	0	0	637	$5,190

Blaine Kauffman

Blaine Kauffman
Racing Hometown: Burton, OH

Year	Rank	Starts	Poles	1	2	3	4	5	6–10	Laps	Laps Led	Races Led	Miles	$
1966	136	1	0	0	0	0	0	0	0	33	0	0	83	0
1968	70	2	0	0	0	0	0	0	0	710	0	0	480	750
Lifetime		3	0	0	0	0	0	0	0	743	0	0	562	$750

William Kearney

William Kearney
Racing Hometown: Calumet, IL

Year	Rank	Starts	Poles	1	2	3	4	5	6–10	Laps	Laps Led	Races Led	Miles	$
1954	NR	1	0	0	0	0	0	0	0	28	0	0	115	0
Lifetime		1	0	0	0	0	0	0	0	28	0	0	115	$0

Bobby Keck

Robert Keck
Racing Hometown: Graham, NC

Year	Rank	Starts	Poles	1	2	3	4	5	6–10	Laps	Laps Led	Races Led	Miles	$
1956	43	15	0	0	0	0	0	0	3	2,236	0	0	1,309	950
1957	28	16	0	0	0	0	0	0	2	2,144	0	0	1,419	1,525
1958	12	30	0	0	0	0	0	0	7	4,345	0	0	2,219	3,459
1959	23	18	0	0	0	0	0	0	0	2,484	0	0	1,152	1,270
1963	65	9	0	0	0	0	0	0	2	935	0	0	458	1,530
1964	50	10	0	0	0	0	1	1	3	2,137	0	0	1,407	2,850
Lifetime		98	0	0	0	0	1	1	17	14,281	0	0	7,963	$11,584

Bob Keefe

Robert Keefe
Racing Hometown: Yakima, WA

Year	Rank	Starts	Poles	1	2	3	4	5	6–10	Laps	Laps Led	Races Led	Miles	$
1956	45	7	0	0	0	0	1	0	1	1,200	0	0	779	1,040
1957	97	3	0	0	0	0	0	0	1	367	0	0	184	440
1958	47	2	0	0	0	0	0	1	1	276	0	0	571	925
1959	NR	1	0	0	0	0	0	1	0	459	0	0	184	500
Lifetime		13	0	0	0	0	1	2	3	2,302	0	0	1,717	$2,905

Year	Rank	Starts	Poles	Finish 1	2	3	4	5	6–10	Laps	Laps Led	Races Led	Miles	$

Dick Keene

Richard Keene

Year	Rank	Starts	Poles	1	2	3	4	5	6–10	Laps	Laps Led	Races Led	Miles	$
1954	NR	1	0	0	0	0	0	0	0	31	0	0	62	0
Lifetime		1	0	0	0	0	0	0	0	31	0	0	62	$0

Tex Keene

Tex Keene
B: 12/26/1917
Racing Hometown: Marietta, GA

Year	Rank	Starts	Poles	1	2	3	4	5	6–10	Laps	Laps Led	Races Led	Miles	$
1950	NR	2	0	0	0	0	0	0	0	229	0	0	286	0
Lifetime		2	0	0	0	0	0	0	0	229	0	0	286	$0

Al Keller

Al Keller
B: 4/11/1920   D: 11/19/1961   *Killed in Indy Car race @ Phoenix Fairgrounds.*
Racing Hometown: Buffalo, NY

Year	Rank	Starts	Poles	1	2	3	4	5	6–10	Laps	Laps Led	Races Led	Miles	$
1949	32	1	0	0	0	0	0	0	1	185	0	0	185	200
1950	125	3	0	0	0	0	0	0	0	328	0	0	538	50
1952	64	4	0	0	0	0	0	0	0	328	0	0	164	125
1953	107	4	0	0	0	0	0	0	0	73	0	0	37	115
1954	NR	13	1	2	2	0	2	0	3	1,811	195	5	1,372	5,135
1956	69	4	0	0	1	0	0	0	1	482	0	0	395	1,300
Lifetime		29	1	2	3	0	2	0	5	3,207	195	5	2,691	$6,925

Duke Keller

Duke Keller

Year	Rank	Starts	Poles	1	2	3	4	5	6–10	Laps	Laps Led	Races Led	Miles	$
1952	206T	1	0	0	0	0	0	0	0	6	0	0	3	25
Lifetime		1	0	0	0	0	0	0	0	6	0	0	3	$25

Frank Keller

Frank Keller

Year	Rank	Starts	Poles	1	2	3	4	5	6–10	Laps	Laps Led	Races Led	Miles	$
1950	94T	1	0	0	0	0	0	0	0		0	0		50
Lifetime		1	0	0	0	0	0	0	0		0	0		$50

Pete Keller

Peter Keller
B: 11/13/1929
Racing Hometown: Columbia, SC

Year	Rank	Starts	Poles	1	2	3	4	5	6–10	Laps	Laps Led	Races Led	Miles	$
1950	NR	1	0	0	0	0	0	0	0	281	0	0	351	0
Lifetime		1	0	0	0	0	0	0	0	281	0	0	351	$0

Calvin Kelly

Calvin Kelly
Racing Hometown: Greenville, SC

Year	Rank	Starts	Poles	1	2	3	4	5	6–10	Laps	Laps Led	Races Led	Miles	$
1966	NR	2	0	0	0	0	0	0	0	41	0	0	103	1,120
Lifetime		2	0	0	0	0	0	0	0	41	0	0	103	$1,120

Joe Kelly

Joe Kelly (Real Name: Dave Haupt)
Critically injured @ Flemington 8/15/70.
Racing Hometown: Quakertown, PA

Year	Rank	Starts	Poles	1	2	3	4	5	6–10	Laps	Laps Led	Races Led	Miles	$
1961	87	2	0	0	0	0	0	0	0	200	0	0	500	300
1963	130	1	0	0	0	0	0	0	0	120	0	0	60	85
Lifetime		3	0	0	0	0	0	0	0	320	0	0	560	$385

Pete Kelly

Peter Kelly
Racing Hometown: Columbus, GA

Year	Rank	Starts	Poles	1	2	3	4	5	6–10	Laps	Laps Led	Races Led	Miles	$
1952	132	2	0	0	0	0	0	0	0	231	0	0	237	35
1959	NR	2	0	0	0	0	0	0	0	44	0	0	95	150
Lifetime		4	0	0	0	0	0	0	0	275	0	0	332	$185

Ray Kelly

Raymond Kelly
B: 12/29/1946   D: 4/17/1992
Racing Hometown: West Covina, CA

Year	Rank	Starts	Poles	1	2	3	4	5	6–10	Laps	Laps Led	Races Led	Miles	$
1986	116T	1	0	0	0	0	0	0	0	36	0	0	94	850
Lifetime		1	0	0	0	0	0	0	0	36	0	0	94	$850

Year	Rank	Starts	Poles	Finish 1	2	3	4	5	6–10	Laps	Laps Led	Races Led	Miles	$

Jerry Kemp

Jerry Kemp
D: 1/14/1995
Racing Hometown: St. Louis, MO

Year	Rank	Starts	Poles	1	2	3	4	5	6–10	Laps	Laps Led	Races Led	Miles	$
1950	NR	1	0	0	0	0	0	0	0	315	0	0	394	0
Lifetime		1	0	0	0	0	0	0	0	315	0	0	394	$0

Mike Kempton

Michael John Kempton
B: 1/21/1947
Racing Hometown: Merriam, KS

Year	Rank	Starts	Poles	1	2	3	4	5	6–10	Laps	Laps Led	Races Led	Miles	$
1977	75	2	0	0	0	0	0	0	0	336	0	0	450	2,555
1979	73	2	0	0	0	0	0	0	0	499	0	0	487	1,605
Lifetime		4	0	0	0	0	0	0	0	835	0	0	937	$4,160

Tom Kendall

Thomas Kendall
B: 10/17/1966
Racing Hometown: LeCanada, CA

Year	Rank	Starts	Poles	1	2	3	4	5	6–10	Laps	Laps Led	Races Led	Miles	$
1987	NR	1	0	0	0	0	0	0	0	26	0	0	68	950
1988	64	1	0	0	0	0	0	0	0	94	23	1	246	3,400
1989	NR	1	0	0	0	0	0	0	0	79	1	1	194	3,015
1990	48	3	0	0	0	0	0	0	1	613	4	1	822	14,120
1991	63	1	0	0	0	0	0	0	0	74	12	1	186	12,450
1992	66	1	0	0	0	0	0	0	0	74	0	0	186	6,755
1993	54	2	0	0	0	0	0	0	0	158	0	0	392	32,190
1994	63	1	0	0	0	0	0	0	0	88	0	0	216	9,435
1996	60	1	0	0	0	0	0	0	0	73	4	1	184	20,730
1998	56	2	0	0	0	0	0	0	0	202	2	1	439	53,205
Lifetime		14	0	0	0	0	0	0	1	1,481	46	6	2,933	$156,250

Bob Kennedy

Robert Kennedy
Racing Hometown: Philipsburg, NJ

Year	Rank	Starts	Poles	1	2	3	4	5	6–10	Laps	Laps Led	Races Led	Miles	$
1954	179	1	0	0	0	0	0	0	0	46	0	0	46	0
Lifetime		1	0	0	0	0	0	0	0	46	0	0	46	$0

John Kennedy

John Kennedy
Racing Hometown: Villa Park, IL

Year	Rank	Starts	Poles	1	2	3	4	5	6–10	Laps	Laps Led	Races Led	Miles	$
1969	49	9	0	0	0	0	0	0	0	1,085	0	0	1,675	6,462
1977	106T	1	0	0	0	0	0	0	0	66	0	0	132	880
1978	51	5	0	0	0	0	0	0	0	296	0	0	350	2,900
1979	52	5	0	0	0	0	0	0	0	600	0	0	942	4,515
Lifetime		20	0	0	0	0	0	0	0	2,047	0	0	3,099	$14,757

Ted Kennedy

Theodore Kennedy

Year	Rank	Starts	Poles	1	2	3	4	5	6–10	Laps	Laps Led	Races Led	Miles	$
1986	74	2	0	0	0	0	0	0	0	172	0	0	451	3,255
1990	104	1	0	0	0	0	0	0	0	11	0	0	28	3,225
Lifetime		6	0	0	0	0	0	0	0	183	0	0	478	$6,450

John Kenney

John Golden Kenney Jr.
B: 2/28/1943
Racing Hometown: Poqouson, VA

Year	Rank	Starts	Poles	1	2	3	4	5	6–10	Laps	Laps Led	Races Led	Miles	$
1969	97	1	0	0	0	0	0	0	0	4	0	0	6	1,050
1970	46	11	0	0	0	0	0	0	0	1,385	0	0	675	4,115
Lifetime		12	0	0	0	0	0	0	0	1,389	0	0	681	$5,165

Matt Kenseth

Matt Kenseth
B: 3/10/1972
Racing Hometown: Cambridge, WI

Year	Rank	Starts	Poles	1	2	3	4	5	6–10	Laps	Laps Led	Races Led	Miles	$
1998	57	1	0	0	0	0	0	0	1	400	0	0	400	42,340
1999	49	5	0	0	0	0	1	0	0	1,358	0	0	1,733	143,561
2000	14	34	0	1	1	1	0	1	7	9,466	161	7	12,553	2,150,764
2001	13	36	0	0	0	0	4	0	5	10,341	100	14	13,568	2,565,579
2002	8	36	1	5	2	1	2	1	8	10,303	692	16	13,428	4,514,203
Lifetime		112	1	6	3	2	7	2	21	31,868	953	37	41,683	$9,416,447

Year	Rank	Starts	Poles	Finish 1	2	3	4	5	6–10	Laps	Laps Led	Races Led	Miles	$

Al Kent

Al Kent
   Racing Hometown: Richmond, VA

Year	Rank	Starts	Poles	1	2	3	4	5	6–10	Laps	Laps Led	Races Led	Miles	$
1953	117T	1	0	0	0	0	0	0	0		0	0		25
Lifetime		1	0	0	0	0	0	0	0		0	0		$25

Don Kent

Donald Kent

Year	Rank	Starts	Poles	1	2	3	4	5	6–10	Laps	Laps Led	Races Led	Miles	$
1952	NR	1	0	0	0	0	0	0	0	255	0	0	128	25
Lifetime		1	0	0	0	0	0	0	0	255	0	0	128	$25

Gary Kershaw

Gary Kershaw

Year	Rank	Starts	Poles	1	2	3	4	5	6–10	Laps	Laps Led	Races Led	Miles	$
1981	73T	1	0	0	0	0	0	0	0	117	0	0	307	1,800
Lifetime		1	0	0	0	0	0	0	0	117	0	0	307	$1,800

Bob Keselowski

Robert Keselowski
   B: 8/1/1951
   Racing Hometown: Rochester Hills, CA

Year	Rank	Starts	Poles	1	2	3	4	5	6–10	Laps	Laps Led	Races Led	Miles	$
1994	81T	1	0	0	0	0	0	0	0	17	0	0	43	7,150
Lifetime		1	0	0	0	0	0	0	0	17	0	0	43	$7,150

Ron Keselowski

Ronald William Keselowski
   B: 9/12/1946
   Racing Hometown: Troy, MI

Year	Rank	Starts	Poles	1	2	3	4	5	6–10	Laps	Laps Led	Races Led	Miles	$
1970	39	17	0	0	0	0	0	0	1	2,339	9	1	2,842	11,985
1971	27	20	0	0	0	0	0	0	6	3,046	0	0	4,255	17,680
1972	27	22	0	0	0	0	0	1	2	3,398	0	0	4,976	21,905
1973	45	5	0	0	0	0	0	1	0	733	0	0	1,297	6,060
1974	59	4	0	0	0	0	0	0	0	456	0	0	797	5,160
Lifetime		68	0	0	0	0	0	2	9	9,972	9	1	14,168	$62,790

Tip R. Key

Tip R. Key
   Racing Hometown: Hannibal, MO

Year	Rank	Starts	Poles	1	2	3	4	5	6–10	Laps	Laps Led	Races Led	Miles	$
1951	N/A	1	0	0	0	0	0	0	0		0	0		25
Lifetime		1	0	0	0	0	0	0	0		0	0		$25

Jerry Keyes

Jerry Keyes

Year	Rank	Starts	Poles	1	2	3	4	5	6–10	Laps	Laps Led	Races Led	Miles	$
1954	NR	1	0	0	0	0	0	0	0	338	0	0	169	25
Lifetime		1	0	0	0	0	0	0	0	338	0	0	169	$25

John Kieper

John Kieper
   B: 2/2/1932
   Racing Hometown: Portland, OR

Year	Rank	Starts	Poles	1	2	3	4	5	6–10	Laps	Laps Led	Races Led	Miles	$
1954	NR	1	0	0	0	0	0	0	0	420	0	0	210	25
1955	56	2	0	0	1	0	0	0	0	323	66	1	323	1,500
1956	35	8	2	1	1	1	1	0	3	1,479	49	1	917	3,250
1957	152T	1	0	0	0	0	0	0	0	6	0	0	3	50
1975	86T	2	0	0	0	0	0	0	0	191	0	0	490	2,110
1976	111T	1	0	0	0	0	0	0	0	62	0	0	155	710
1977	113T	1	0	0	0	0	0	0	0	50	0	0	125	740
Lifetime		16	2	1	2	1	1	0	3	2,531	115	2	2,223	$8,385

Jay Kilgore

J. Kilgore
   Racing Hometown: Verona, NJ

Year	Rank	Starts	Poles	1	2	3	4	5	6–10	Laps	Laps Led	Races Led	Miles	$
1954	NR	1	0	0	0	0	0	0	0	45	0	0	90	130
Lifetime		1	0	0	0	0	0	0	0	45	0	0	90	$130

Glenn Killian

Glenn Killian
   Racing Hometown: Hickory, NC

Year	Rank	Starts	Poles	1	2	3	4	5	6–10	Laps	Laps Led	Races Led	Miles	$
1962	133	1	0	0	0	0	0	0	0	3	0	0	1	50
Lifetime		1	0	0	0	0	0	0	0	3	0	0	1	$50

Year	Rank	Starts	Poles	Finish 1	2	3	4	5	6–10	Laps	Laps Led	Races Led	Miles	$

Don Kimberling

Donald Kimberling
Racing Hometown: Tyronne, PA

Year	Rank	Starts	Poles	1	2	3	4	5	6–10	Laps	Laps Led	Races Led	Miles	$
1958	140	1	0	0	0	0	0	0	0	7	0	0	10	100
Lifetime		1	0	0	0	0	0	0	0	7	0	0	10	$100

Oma Kimbrough

Oma Kimbrough
B: 3/29/1951
Racing Hometown: Tyronne, PA

Year	Rank	Starts	Poles	1	2	3	4	5	6–10	Laps	Laps Led	Races Led	Miles	$
1989	87T	1	0	0	0	0	0	0	0	64	0	0	157	2,135
1990	98T	1	0	0	0	0	0	0	0	40	0	0	98	2,240
1991	73	1	0	0	0	0	0	0	0	80	0	0	196	3,620
Lifetime		3	0	0	0	0	0	0	0	184	0	0	451	$7,995

Bill Kimmel

William J. Kimmel
B: 9/13/1928
Racing Hometown: Clarksville, IN

Year	Rank	Starts	Poles	1	2	3	4	5	6–10	Laps	Laps Led	Races Led	Miles	$
1969	NR	2	0	0	0	0	0	0	0	39	0	0	98	1,100
1970	108T	1	0	0	0	0	0	0	0	41	0	0	103	220
Lifetime		3	0	0	0	0	0	0	0	80	0	0	200	$1,320

Frank Kimmell

Frank Kimmell
B: 4/30/1962
Racing Hometown: Croydon, IN

Year	Rank	Starts	Poles	1	2	3	4	5	6–10	Laps	Laps Led	Races Led	Miles	$
1998	65	1	0	0	0	0	0	0	0	197	0	0	394	28,065
Lifetime		1	0	0	0	0	0	0	0	197	0	0	394	$28,065

Marty Kinerk

Marty Kinerk
Racing Hometown: South Gate, CA

Year	Rank	Starts	Poles	1	2	3	4	5	6–10	Laps	Laps Led	Races Led	Miles	$
1969	NR	1	0	0	0	0	0	0	0	40	0	0	108	755
1971	NR	1	0	0	0	0	0	0	0	91	0	0	228	1,450
Lifetime		2	0	0	0	0	0	0	0	131	0	0	336	$2,205

Al King

Al King
Racing Hometown: St.Louis, MO

Year	Rank	Starts	Poles	1	2	3	4	5	6–10	Laps	Laps Led	Races Led	Miles	$
1951	N/A	1	0	0	0	0	0	0	0		0	0		25
Lifetime		1	0	0	0	0	0	0	0		0	0		$25

Brownie King

Herman H. King
B: 1/31/1934
Racing Hometown: Johnson City, TN

Year	Rank	Starts	Poles	1	2	3	4	5	6–10	Laps	Laps Led	Races Led	Miles	$
1956	40	15	0	0	0	0	0	0	0	1,994	0	0	1,322	925
1957	9	36	0	0	0	0	0	1	15	5,756	0	0	3,464	5,589
1958	35	24	0	0	0	0	0	0	5	3,926	0	0	2,153	3,045
1959	30	18	0	0	0	0	0	1	4	3,250	0	0	1,904	1,875
1960	113	3	0	0	0	0	0	0	1	410	0	0	647	465
1961	183	1	0	0	0	0	0	0	0	442	0	0	221	250
Lifetime		97	0	0	0	0	0	2	25	15,778	0	0	9,711	$12,149

Bub King

T.L. King
Racing Hometown: Corbin, KY

Year	Rank	Starts	Poles	1	2	3	4	5	6–10	Laps	Laps Led	Races Led	Miles	$
1950	NR	1	0	0	0	0	0	0	0	329	0	0	411	0
1951	60	9	0	0	0	0	0	0	2	247	0	0	260	450
1952	15	10	0	0	0	1	1	0	3	1,743	0	0	1,419	2,737
1953	17	14	0	0	0	0	0	0	5	1,029	0	0	1,013	1,036
1954	141	1	0	0	0	0	0	0	0	34	0	0	17	25
Lifetime		35	0	0	0	1	1	0	10	3,382	0	0	3,120	$4,248

Byron King

Byron King
Racing Hometown: Orlando, FL

Year	Rank	Starts	Poles	1	2	3	4	5	6–10	Laps	Laps Led	Races Led	Miles	$
1954	NR	1	0	0	0	0	0	0	0	37	0	0	152	60
Lifetime		1	0	0	0	0	0	0	0	37	0	0	152	$60

Year	Rank	Starts	Poles	Finish 1	2	3	4	5	6–10	Laps	Laps Led	Races Led	Miles	$

J.W. King

J.W. King
Racing Hometown: Atlanta, GA

Year	Rank	Starts	Poles	1	2	3	4	5	6–10	Laps	Laps Led	Races Led	Miles	$
1969	NR	1	0	0	0	0	0	0	0	26	0	0	69	1,000
Lifetime		1	0	0	0	0	0	0	0	26	0	0	69	$1,000

Max King

Max King
B: 6/4/1913
Racing Hometown: Cartersville, GA

Year	Rank	Starts	Poles	1	2	3	4	5	6–10	Laps	Laps Led	Races Led	Miles	$
1953	134T	1	0	0	0	0	0	0	0		0	0		25
Lifetime		1	0	0	0	0	0	0	0		0	0		$25

Steve Kinser

Steve Kinser
B: 6/4/1954
Racing Hometown: Bloomington, IN

Year	Rank	Starts	Poles	1	2	3	4	5	6–10	Laps	Laps Led	Races Led	Miles	$
1995	49	5	0	0	0	0	0	0	0	958	0	0	948	105,224
Lifetime		5	0	0	0	0	0	0	0	958	0	0	948	$105,224

Stuart Kirby

Stuart Kirby
B: 5/9/1981
Racing Hometown: Bowling Green, KY

Year	Rank	Starts	Poles	1	2	3	4	5	6–10	Laps	Laps Led	Races Led	Miles	$
2001	70T	1	0	0	0	0	0	0	0	46	0	0	69	32,605
2002	71	2	0	0	0	0	0	0	0	168	0	0	252	105,503
Lifetime		3	0	0	0	0	0	0	0	214	0	0	321	$138,108

Pat Kirkwood

Patrick Kirkwood
Racing Hometown: Ft. Worth, TX

Year	Rank	Starts	Poles	1	2	3	4	5	6–10	Laps	Laps Led	Races Led	Miles	$
1949	NR	1	0	0	0	0	0	0	0		0	0		0
1952	NR	4	1	0	0	1	0	1	0	764	0	0	972	1,215
1956	33	3	0	0	0	1	0	0	1	715	0	0	928	2,025
1957	178	1	0	0	0	0	0	0	0		0	0		50
Lifetime		9	1	0	0	2	0	1	1	1,479	0	0	1,900	$3,290

Ken Kiser

Kenneth Kiser

Year	Rank	Starts	Poles	1	2	3	4	5	6–10	Laps	Laps Led	Races Led	Miles	$
1954	NR	1	0	0	0	0	0	0	0	164	0	0	82	25
Lifetime		1	0	0	0	0	0	0	0	164	0	0	82	$25

Harold Kite

Harold Kite
B: 11/12/1921   D: 10/17/1965   *Killed in NASCAR race @ Charlotte, NC.*
Racing Hometown: East Point, GA

Year	Rank	Starts	Poles	1	2	3	4	5	6–10	Laps	Laps Led	Races Led	Miles	$
1950	30	3	0	1	0	0	0	0	0	382	38	1	618	1,550
1951	25	2	0	0	0	0	0	0	1	384	0	0	480	800
1955	181	2	0	0	0	0	0	0	0	279	0	0	387	110
1956	184T	1	0	0	0	0	0	0	0	178	0	0	89	110
1965	133	1	0	0	0	0	0	0	0	1	0	0	2	410
Lifetime		9	0	1	0	0	0	0	1	1,224	38	1	1,575	$2,980

Mike Kittlekow

Michael Kittlekow

Year	Rank	Starts	Poles	1	2	3	4	5	6–10	Laps	Laps Led	Races Led	Miles	$
1971	NR	1	0	0	0	0	0	0	0	38	0	0	100	1,015
Lifetime		1	0	0	0	0	0	0	0	38	0	0	100	$1,015

Dick Klank

Richard Klank

Year	Rank	Starts	Poles	1	2	3	4	5	6–10	Laps	Laps Led	Races Led	Miles	$
1957	131	7	0	0	0	0	0	0	1	942	0	0	631	565
Lifetime		7	0	0	0	0	0	0	1	942	0	0	631	$565

Mike Klapak

Michael Klapak
B: 3/8/1913   D: 3/13/1997
Racing Hometown: Warren, OH

Year	Rank	Starts	Poles	1	2	3	4	5	6–10	Laps	Laps Led	Races Led	Miles	$
1950	98	4	0	0	0	0	0	0	0	158	0	0	79	50
1951	N/A	5	0	0	0	0	0	0	1		0	0		150

Year	Rank	Starts	Poles	Finish						Laps	Laps Led	Races Led	Miles	$
				1	2	3	4	5	6–10					

Mike Klapak *continued*

Year	Rank	Starts	Poles	1	2	3	4	5	6–10	Laps	Laps Led	Races Led	Miles	$
1952	199	1	0	0	0	0	0	0	0		0	0		0
1953	NR	2	0	0	0	0	0	0	2		0	0		250
Lifetime		12	0	0	0	0	0	0	3	158	0	0	79	$450

Charles Kleber

Charles Kleber

Year	Rank	Starts	Poles	1	2	3	4	5	6–10	Laps	Laps Led	Races Led	Miles	$
1951	209T	1	0	0	0	0	0	0	0		0	0		25
Lifetime		1	0	0	0	0	0	0	0		0	0		$25

Ken Klutz

Kenneth Klutz
Racing Hometown: Salisbury, NC

Year	Rank	Starts	Poles	1	2	3	4	5	6–10	Laps	Laps Led	Races Led	Miles	$
1951	N/A	1	0	0	0	0	0	0	0	95	0	0	71	25
Lifetime		1	0	0	0	0	0	0	0	95	0	0	71	$25

Peter Knab

Peter C. Knab
B: 1938
Racing Hometown: Dayton, OH

Year	Rank	Starts	Poles	1	2	3	4	5	6–10	Laps	Laps Led	Races Led	Miles	$
1977	78	3	0	0	0	0	0	0	0	507	0	0	1,017	6,865
Lifetime		3	0	0	0	0	0	0	0	507	0	0	1,017	$6,865

Fred Knapp

Fred Knapp
D: 6/2000
Racing Hometown: Jamestown, NY

Year	Rank	Starts	Poles	1	2	3	4	5	6–10	Laps	Laps Led	Races Led	Miles	$
1957	120	2	0	0	0	0	0	0	1	216	0	0	128	240
Lifetime		2	0	0	0	0	0	0	1	216	0	0	128	$240

Art Knoll

Arthur Knoll
Racing Hometown: Pitsburgh, PA

Year	Rank	Starts	Poles	1	2	3	4	5	6–10	Laps	Laps Led	Races Led	Miles	$
1951	NR	1	0	0	0	0	0	0	0		0	0		25
Lifetime		1	0	0	0	0	0	0	0		0	0		$25

Rick Knoop

Richard Knoop
B: 7/8/1953
Racing Hometown: Atherton, CA

Year	Rank	Starts	Poles	1	2	3	4	5	6–10	Laps	Laps Led	Races Led	Miles	$
1981	NR	1	0	0	0	0	0	0	0	197	0	0	394	3,405
1986	95	1	0	0	0	0	0	0	0	88	0	0	216	6,995
1987	81	3	0	0	0	0	0	0	0	686	0	0	1,027	17,375
Lifetime		5	0	0	0	0	0	0	0	971	0	0	1,636	$27,775

Barry Knowlton

Barry Knowlton

Year	Rank	Starts	Poles	1	2	3	4	5	6–10	Laps	Laps Led	Races Led	Miles	$
1957	174	1	0	0	0	0	0	0	0	73	0	0	37	50
Lifetime		1	0	0	0	0	0	0	0	73	0	0	37	$50

Red Knuter

Red Knuter
Racing Hometown: North Platte, NE

Year	Rank	Starts	Poles	1	2	3	4	5	6–10	Laps	Laps Led	Races Led	Miles	$
1953	108T	1	0	0	0	0	0	0	0		0	0		25
Lifetime		1	0	0	0	0	0	0	0		0	0		$25

Bud Koehler

Bud Koehler
B: 2/15/1921
Racing Hometown: Blue Island, IL

Year	Rank	Starts	Poles	1	2	3	4	5	6–10	Laps	Laps Led	Races Led	Miles	$
1952	176	1	0	0	0	0	0	0	0	140	0	0	140	25
Lifetime		1	0	0	0	0	0	0	0	140	0	0	140	$25

Ronnie Kohler

Ronald W. Kohler
B: 5/28/1927
Racing Hometown: Paterson, NJ

Year	Rank	Starts	Poles	1	2	3	4	5	6–10	Laps	Laps Led	Races Led	Miles	$
1951	29	5	0	0	0	2	0	0	1		0	0		1,100
1952	80	2	0	0	0	0	0	1	0	253	0	0	127	225

Year	Rank	Starts	Poles	Finish 1	2	3	4	5	6–10	Laps	Laps Led	Races Led	Miles	$

Ronnie Kohler *continued*

Year	Rank	Starts	Poles	1	2	3	4	5	6–10	Laps	Laps Led	Races Led	Miles	$
1953	NR	4	0	0	0	0	0	1	0		0	0		425
1954	103	2	0	0	0	0	0	0	1	368	0	0	276	150
Lifetime		13	0	0	0	2	0	2	2	621	0	0	403	$1,900

Bob Korf

Robert Korf
Racing Hometown: Long Beach, CA

Year	Rank	Starts	Poles	1	2	3	4	5	6–10	Laps	Laps Led	Races Led	Miles	$
1956	101	1	0	0	0	0	0	0	1	36	0	0	148	400
Lifetime		1	0	0	0	0	0	0	1	36	0	0	148	$400

Bob Kosiski

Robert Kosiski
Racing Hometown: Omaha, NE

Year	Rank	Starts	Poles	1	2	3	4	5	6–10	Laps	Laps Led	Races Led	Miles	$
1960	110	2	0	0	0	0	0	0	0	163	0	0	408	250
Lifetime		2	0	0	0	0	0	0	0	163	0	0	408	$250

Buddy Krebs

Buddy Krebs
Killed in Modified race @ Oswego, NY.
Racing Hometown: E.Hartford, CT

Year	Rank	Starts	Poles	1	2	3	4	5	6–10	Laps	Laps Led	Races Led	Miles	$
1953	117T	1	0	0	0	0	0	0	0		0	0		25
1955	NR	1	0	0	0	0	0	0	0	50	0	0	50	50
1956	282	1	0	0	0	0	0	0	0	1	0	0	4	0
Lifetime		3	0	0	0	0	0	0	0	51	0	0	54	$75

John Krebs

John Krebs
B: 10/1/1950
Racing Hometown: Roseville, CA

Year	Rank	Starts	Poles	1	2	3	4	5	6–10	Laps	Laps Led	Races Led	Miles	$
1982	67	2	0	0	0	0	0	0	0	127	0	0	333	1,750
1983	92	1	0	0	0	0	0	0	0	60	0	0	157	1,100
1984	78	2	0	0	0	0	0	0	0	54	0	0	141	1,790
1985	81T	1	0	0	0	0	0	0	0	73	0	0	191	2,250
1986	87	2	0	0	0	0	0	0	0	94	0	0	246	2,075
1987	88T	1	0	0	0	0	0	0	0	80	0	0	210	1,125
1988	73	1	0	0	0	0	0	0	0	92	0	0	241	1,600
1989	91T	1	0	0	0	0	0	0	0	65	0	0	164	3,000
1990	67	2	0	0	0	0	0	0	0	366	0	0	477	8,435
1991	84	1	0	0	0	0	0	0	0	57	1	1	144	3,525
1992	61	2	0	0	0	0	0	0	0	380	0	0	489	12,990
1993	61	2	0	0	0	0	0	0	0	154	0	0	386	13,955
1994	80	1	0	0	0	0	0	0	0	18	1	1	45	8,100
Lifetime		19	0	0	0	0	0	0	0	1,620	2	2	3,225	$61,695

Ed Kretz

Ed Kretz
Racing Hometown: Monterey, CA

Year	Rank	Starts	Poles	1	2	3	4	5	6–10	Laps	Laps Led	Races Led	Miles	$
1956	279	1	0	0	0	0	0	0	0	11	0	0	45	0
Lifetime		1	0	0	0	0	0	0	0	11	0	0	45	$0

Jeff Krogh

Jeffrey Krogh
B: 3/21/1972
Racing Hometown: Kamiah, ID

Year	Rank	Starts	Poles	1	2	3	4	5	6–10	Laps	Laps Led	Races Led	Miles	$
1996	59	2	0	0	0	0	0	0	0	222	0	0	330	19,680
Lifetime		2	0	0	0	0	0	0	0	222	0	0	330	$19,680

Stan Kross

Stanley Kross
B: 1910
Racing Hometown: Salem, IN

Year	Rank	Starts	Poles	1	2	3	4	5	6–10	Laps	Laps Led	Races Led	Miles	$
1954	66	5	0	0	0	0	0	0	1	135	0	0	215	150
Lifetime		5	0	0	0	0	0	0	1	135	0	0	215	$150

Carl Krueger

Carl Krueger
Racing Hometown: Newton, PA

Year	Rank	Starts	Poles	1	2	3	4	5	6–10	Laps	Laps Led	Races Led	Miles	$
1955	44	7	0	0	0	0	0	1	1	955	0	0	534	585
Lifetime		7	0	0	0	0	0	1	1	955	0	0	534	$585

Year	Rank	Starts	Poles	Finish 1	2	3	4	5	6–10	Laps	Laps Led	Races Led	Miles	$

Mel Krueger

Mel Krueger
Racing Hometown: Anita, IA

Year	Rank	Starts	Poles	1	2	3	4	5	6–10	Laps	Laps Led	Races Led	Miles	$
1953	49	3	0	0	0	0	0	0	1		0	0		175
1954	117	2	0	0	0	0	0	0	0	208	0	0	226	50
Lifetime		5	0	0	0	0	0	0	1	208	0	0	226	$225

Alan Kulwicki

Alan Dennis Kulwicki
B: 12/14/1954 D: 4/1/1993 *Killed in private plane crash en route to Bristol.*
Racing Hometown: Greenfield, WI

Year	Rank	Starts	Poles	1	2	3	4	5	6–10	Laps	Laps Led	Races Led	Miles	$
1985	40	5	0	0	0	0	0	0	0	1,843	0	0	1,998	10,290
1986	21	23	0	0	0	0	1	0	3	7,898	14	6	8,667	94,450
1987	15	29	3	0	1	0	1	1	6	7,758	102	8	9,121	369,889
1988	14	29	4	1	2	1	1	2	2	8,149	134	8	9,325	448,547
1989	14	29	6	0	4	0	0	1	4	8,324	564	14	9,560	425,500
1990	8	29	1	1	1	1	1	1	8	8,635	400	10	10,757	550,936
1991	13	29	4	1	0	1	1	1	7	8,447	233	9	9,998	595,614
1992	1	29	6	2	3	2	2	2	6	8,991	1,235	20	10,853	2,322,561
1993	41	5	0	0	0	1	1	0	1	1,588	4	2	1,995	165,470
Lifetime		207	24	5	11	6	8	8	37	61,633	2,686	77	72,273	$4,983,257

Joe Kusler

Joseph Kusler
Racing Hometown: Franklin, NJ

Year	Rank	Starts	Poles	1	2	3	4	5	6–10	Laps	Laps Led	Races Led	Miles	$
1955	147T	1	0	0	0	0	0	0	0	164	0	0	82	25
Lifetime		1	0	0	0	0	0	0	0	164	0	0	82	$25

Bud Kutina

Bud Kutina
Racing Hometown: Rochester, MN

Year	Rank	Starts	Poles	1	2	3	4	5	6–10	Laps	Laps Led	Races Led	Miles	$
1955	118	1	0	0	0	0	0	0	0	38	0	0	156	140
Lifetime		1	0	0	0	0	0	0	0	38	0	0	156	$140

Kuzie Kuzmanich

Kuzie Kuzmanich
Racing Hometown: Portland, OR

Year	Rank	Starts	Poles	1	2	3	4	5	6–10	Laps	Laps Led	Races Led	Miles	$
1960	106	2	0	0	0	0	0	0	1	115	0	0	124	350
1961	125	1	0	0	0	0	0	0	1	97	0	0	97	150
Lifetime		3	0	0	0	0	0	0	2	212	0	0	221	$500

Bobby Labonte

Robert Allen Labonte
B: 5/8/1964
Racing Hometown: Corpus Christi, TX

Year	Rank	Starts	Poles	1	2	3	4	5	6–10	Laps	Laps Led	Races Led	Miles	$
1991	66	2	0	0	0	0	0	0	0	128	0	0	168	8,350
1993	19	30	1	0	0	0	0	0	6	9,295	33	7	10,938	395,660
1994	21	31	0	0	0	0	0	1	1	8,541	3	2	10,456	550,305
1995	10	31	2	3	3	0	0	1	7	9,018	277	14	10,975	1,413,682
1996	11	31	4	1	1	0	1	2	9	8,916	330	13	10,571	1,475,196
1997	7	32	3	1	3	2	2	1	9	9,482	484	12	12,368	2,217,999
1998	6	33	3	2	3	2	4	0	7	9,512	182	13	12,376	2,980,052
1999	2	34	5	5	6	7	1	4	3	10,011	1,201	30	13,133	4,763,615
2000	1	34	3	4	4	4	2	5	5	10,158	464	23	13,270	4,041,746
2001	6	36	1	2	1	2	1	3	11	10,361	228	17	13,579	4,786,779
2002	16	36	0	1	1	1	0	2	2	10,135	123	5	13,355	4,183,715
Lifetime		330	22	19	22	18	11	19	60	95,557	3,325	136	121,189	$26,817,099

Terry Labonte

Terrence Lee Labonte
B: 11/16/1956
Racing Hometown: Corpus Christi, TX

Year	Rank	Starts	Poles	1	2	3	4	5	6–10	Laps	Laps Led	Races Led	Miles	$
1978	39	5	0	0	0	0	1	0	2	1,849	0	0	1,879	21,395
1979	10	31	0	0	0	1	0	1	11	8,766	8	4	9,887	134,653
1980	8	31	0	1	0	1	1	3	10	8,760	46	6	9,952	222,502
1981	4	31	2	0	1	3	2	2	9	9,010	114	14	10,363	348,703
1982	3	30	3	0	6	2	6	3	4	8,900	263	17	10,259	398,635
1983	5	30	3	1	0	0	4	6	9	8,498	434	13	9,775	388,419
1984	1	30	3	2	6	6	2	1	7	9,886	880	26	11,236	767,716
1985	7	28	4	1	2	3	1	1	9	7,973	563	14	9,612	694,510

Year	Rank	Starts	Poles	1	2	3	4	5	6–10	Laps	Laps Led	Races Led	Miles	$

Terry Labonte *continued*

Year	Rank	Starts	Poles	1	2	3	4	5	6–10	Laps	Laps Led	Races Led	Miles	$
1986	12	29	1	1	2	2	0	0	5	7,984	565	10	9,431	522,235
1987	3	29	4	1	2	2	5	3	9	8,609	592	16	10,159	805,054
1988	4	29	1	1	2	3	4	1	7	9,206	208	17	11,043	950,781
1989	10	29	0	2	2	1	1	3	2	8,306	104	10	9,773	565,702
1990	15	29	0	0	1	0	3	0	5	8,518	9	3	10,245	450,230
1991	18	29	1	0	0	0	0	1	6	7,989	52	2	9,617	348,898
1992	8	29	0	0	1	0	2	1	12	8,912	43	4	10,613	600,381
1993	18	30	0	0	0	0	0	0	10	8,866	55	3	10,642	531,717
1994	7	31	0	3	1	1	0	1	8	9,149	486	8	11,314	1,150,921
1995	6	31	1	3	4	2	3	2	3	9,076	437	11	11,376	1,558,659
1996	1	31	4	2	7	5	1	6	3	9,443	972	22	11,523	4,030,648
1997	6	32	1	1	3	2	2	0	12	9,605	256	11	12,297	2,270,144
1998	9	33	0	1	1	2	1	0	10	9,573	338	12	12,372	2,054,163
1999	12	34	0	1	0	0	0	0	6	9,325	350	11	12,221	2,475,365
2000	17	32	1	0	1	0	0	2	3	9,335	33	3	11,932	2,043,094
2001	23	36	0	0	0	0	0	1	2	10,517	0	0	13,909	3,011,901
2002	24	36	0	0	0	1	0	0	3	9,966	11	1	13,248	3,244,240
Lifetime		745	29	21	42	37	39	38	167	218,021	6,819	238	264,680	$29,590,666

Rick Lach

Rick Lach

Year	Rank	Starts	Poles	1	2	3	4	5	6–10	Laps	Laps Led	Races Led	Miles	$
1986	121T	1	0	0	0	0	0	0	0	20	0	0	52	825
Lifetime		1	0	0	0	0	0	0	0	20	0	0	52	$825

Jim Lacy

James Lacy
B: 1926
Racing Hometown: N. Bellmore, NY

Year	Rank	Starts	Poles	1	2	3	4	5	6–10	Laps	Laps Led	Races Led	Miles	$
1953	66	3	0	0	0	0	0	0	0		0	0		125
1954	NR	1	0	0	0	0	0	0	0	3	0	0	3	0
Lifetime		4	0	0	0	0	0	0	0	3	0	0	3	$125

Arnold Ladd

Arnold Ladd

Year	Rank	Starts	Poles	1	2	3	4	5	6–10	Laps	Laps Led	Races Led	Miles	$
1954	NR	1	0	0	0	0	0	0	0	41	0	0	82	45
Lifetime		1	0	0	0	0	0	0	0	41	0	0	82	$45

Scott Lagasse

Scott Lagasse
B: 2/20/1959
Racing Hometown: St.Augustine, FL

Year	Rank	Starts	Poles	1	2	3	4	5	6–10	Laps	Laps Led	Races Led	Miles	$
1993	59	1	0	0	0	0	0	0	0	90	0	0	221	7,800
1994	75	1	0	0	0	0	0	0	0	65	0	0	159	6,055
Lifetime		2	0	0	0	0	0	0	0	155	0	0	380	$13,855

Bill LaGrance

William LaGrance
Racing Hometown: Greensboro, NC

Year	Rank	Starts	Poles	1	2	3	4	5	6–10	Laps	Laps Led	Races Led	Miles	$
1951	NR	1	0	0	0	0	0	0	0		0	0		25
Lifetime		1	0	0	0	0	0	0	0		0	0		$25

Randy LaJoie

Randall LaJoie
B: 8/28/1961
Racing Hometown: Norwalk, CT

Year	Rank	Starts	Poles	1	2	3	4	5	6–10	Laps	Laps Led	Races Led	Miles	$
1985	NR	1	0	0	0	0	0	0	0	319	0	0	486	2,925
1986	107T	1	0	0	0	0	0	0	0	144	0	0	360	1,815
1988	NR	1	0	0	0	0	0	0	0	89	0	0	89	1,460
1989	83T	1	0	0	0	0	0	0	0	178	0	0	445	2,725
1990	73	2	0	0	0	0	0	0	0	177	0	0	443	6,675
1991	50	4	0	0	0	0	0	0	0	1,080	0	0	1,447	23,875
1994	48	3	0	0	0	0	0	0	0	1,010	0	0	1,390	30,565
1995	40	14	0	0	0	0	0	0	0	3,606	0	0	4,490	281,945
1998	50	9	0	0	0	0	0	1	2	2,750	0	0	3,138	337,106
1999	61	2	0	0	0	0	0	0	0	436	0	0	528	71,200
Lifetime		38	0	0	0	0	0	1	2	9,789	0	0	12,816	$760,291

Year	Rank	Starts	Poles	Finish 1	2	3	4	5	6–10	Laps	Laps Led	Races Led	Miles	$

Ben Lalomia

Ben Lalomia
B: 3/29/1919
Racing Hometown: Buffalo, NY

Year	Rank	Starts	Poles	1	2	3	4	5	6–10	Laps	Laps Led	Races Led	Miles	$
1951	N/A	1	0	0	0	0	0	0	0		0	0		25
Lifetime		1	0	0	0	0	0	0	0		0	0		$25

Morris Lamb

Morris Lamb
Racing Hometown: Germantown, OH

Year	Rank	Starts	Poles	1	2	3	4	5	6–10	Laps	Laps Led	Races Led	Miles	$
1950	137T	1	0	0	0	0	0	0	0		0	0		0
Lifetime		1	0	0	0	0	0	0	0		0	0		$0

Art Lamey

Arthur Lamey
D: 8/30/1983
Racing Hometown: Racine, WI

Year	Rank	Starts	Poles	1	2	3	4	5	6–10	Laps	Laps Led	Races Led	Miles	$
1950	19	4	0	0	0	0	0	2	1	0	0	0	0	655
Lifetime		4	0	0	0	0	0	2	1	0	0	0	0	$655

Sam Lamm

Sam Lamm (Real Name: Fred Bince) *Also raced as Fred Lee.*
B: 9/28/1923
Racing Hometown: Los Angeles, CA

Year	Rank	Starts	Poles	1	2	3	4	5	6–10	Laps	Laps Led	Races Led	Miles	$
1951	NR	1	0	0	0	0	0	0	0		0	0		25
1954	NR	2	0	0	0	0	0	0	0	426	0	0	326	50
1956	NR	1	0	0	0	0	0	0	0	3	0	0	8	30
Lifetime		4	0	0	0	0	0	0	0	429	0	0	334	$105

Sonny Lamphear

Hugh Lamphear
Racing Hometown: Charlotte, NC

Year	Rank	Starts	Poles	1	2	3	4	5	6–10	Laps	Laps Led	Races Led	Miles	$
1966	75	13	0	0	0	0	0	0	1	622	0	0	379	2,270
Lifetime		13	0	0	0	0	0	0	1	622	0	0	379	$2,270

Jim Lamport

James Lamport
Racing Hometown: Pittsburg, CA

Year	Rank	Starts	Poles	1	2	3	4	5	6–10	Laps	Laps Led	Races Led	Miles	$
1959	NR	1	0	0	0	0	0	0	0	414	0	0	166	150
Lifetime		1	0	0	0	0	0	0	0	414	0	0	166	$150

Furman Lancaster

Furman Lancaster
Racing Hometown: Atlanta, GA

Year	Rank	Starts	Poles	1	2	3	4	5	6–10	Laps	Laps Led	Races Led	Miles	$
1951	N/A	1	0	0	0	0	0	0	1	140	0	0	140	100
Lifetime		1	0	0	0	0	0	0	1	140	0	0	140	$100

Junie Lancaster

Junie Lancaster

Year	Rank	Starts	Poles	1	2	3	4	5	6–10	Laps	Laps Led	Races Led	Miles	$
1954	NR	1	0	0	0	0	0	0	0	202	0	0	202	50
Lifetime		1	0	0	0	0	0	0	0	202	0	0	202	$50

Tommy Lane

Thomas Lane

Year	Rank	Starts	Poles	1	2	3	4	5	6–10	Laps	Laps Led	Races Led	Miles	$
1951	138	2	0	0	0	0	0	0	1		0	0		125
Lifetime		2	0	0	0	0	0	0	1		0	0		$125

Shep Langdon

Shepard Langdon
Racing Hometown: Angier, NC

Year	Rank	Starts	Poles	1	2	3	4	5	6–10	Laps	Laps Led	Races Led	Miles	$
1957	NR	2	0	0	0	0	0	0	0	268	0	0	268	0
1958	NR	18	0	0	0	0	0	0	1	3,220	0	0	1,648	1,645
1959	12	21	0	0	0	0	0	0	6	3,976	0	0	2,259	3,526
1960	65	4	0	0	0	0	0	0	1	588	0	0	756	635
Lifetime		45	0	0	0	0	0	0	8	8,052	0	0	4,931	$5,806

Year	Rank	Starts	Poles	Finish						Laps	Laps Led	Races Led	Miles	$
				1	2	3	4	5	6–10					

Elmo Langley

Elmo Harrell Langley
B: 8/22/1929   D: 11/21/1996
Racing Hometown: Landover, MD

Year	Rank	Starts	Poles	1	2	3	4	5	6–10	Laps	Laps Led	Races Led	Miles	$
1954	34	2	0	0	0	0	0	0	0	340	0	0	466	450
1955	100	4	0	0	0	0	0	0	1	518	0	0	370	350
1956	NR	1	0	0	0	0	0	0	0	338	0	0	465	140
1957	132T	1	0	0	0	0	0	0	0	189	0	0	95	150
1958	39	9	0	0	0	0	0	1	2	1,240	0	0	874	1,090
1959	28	13	0	0	0	1	0	0	1	1,694	0	0	1,314	2,280
1960	54	11	0	0	0	0	0	0	0	1,234	0	0	1,195	1,640
1961	30	15	0	0	0	0	0	1	4	2,826	0	0	3,012	3,530
1962	40	6	0	0	0	0	0	0	0	774	0	0	1,086	1,795
1963	39	12	0	0	0	0	0	1	1	2,294	0	0	1,562	2,170
1964	42	14	0	0	0	0	0	0	5	2,739	0	0	1,658	3,905
1965	25	34	0	0	0	2	1	0	6	5,698	0	0	3,816	10,895
1966	11	47	1	2	1	1	4	4	8	9,461	276	5	6,640	22,455
1967	9	45	0	0	1	3	2	4	14	9,652	0	0	6,781	23,898
1968	6	48	0	0	0	1	1	4	22	11,149	0	0	7,750	25,832
1969	5	52	1	0	0	1	6	6	15	12,531	40	1	9,719	73,092
1970	6	47	0	0	0	1	0	0	18	10,672	0	0	9,319	45,193
1971	5	46	0	0	3	1	3	4	12	11,299	48	1	10,490	57,037
1972	7	30	0	0	0	0	0	1	8	8,150	0	0	9,460	59,644
1973	9	27	0	0	0	0	0	0	4	8,016	0	0	8,385	49,542
1974	25	24	0	0	0	0	0	0	3	5,593	0	0	5,861	24,722
1975	8	29	0	0	0	0	0	2	5	8,601	0	0	9,885	67,600
1976	36	7	0	0	0	0	0	0	1	2,451	0	0	1,368	7,515
1977	42	7	0	0	0	0	0	0	0	1,395	0	0	812	5,855
1978	65	3	0	0	0	0	0	0	0	482	0	0	326	2,765
1979	82	3	0	0	0	0	0	0	0	466	0	0	253	3,010
1981	69	1	0	0	0	0	0	0	0	6	0	0	6	575
Lifetime		538	2	2	5	11	17	28	130	119,808	364	7	102,966	$497,130

John Lansaw

John Lansaw
Racing Hometown: Anaheim, CA

Year	Rank	Starts	Poles	1	2	3	4	5	6–10	Laps	Laps Led	Races Led	Miles	$
1955	168	1	0	0	0	0	0	0	0	74	0	0	74	50
1956	242	2	0	0	0	0	0	0	0	133	0	0	124	35
Lifetime		3	0	0	0	0	0	0	0	207	0	0	198	$85

Nick Lari

Nicholas Lari
Racing Hometown: Santa Monica, CA

Year	Rank	Starts	Poles	1	2	3	4	5	6–10	Laps	Laps Led	Races Led	Miles	$
1956	229	1	0	0	0	0	0	0	0	155	0	0	78	50
Lifetime		1	0	0	0	0	0	0	0	155	0	0	78	$50

Glen Larsen

Glen G. Larsen
Racing Hometown: Aurora, IL

Year	Rank	Starts	Poles	1	2	3	4	5	6–10	Laps	Laps Led	Races Led	Miles	$
1952	91T	1	0	0	0	0	0	0	1	171	0	0	86	125
Lifetime		1	0	0	0	0	0	0	1	171	0	0	86	$125

Mel Larson

Mel Larson
B: 10/1/1929
Racing Hometown: Phoenix, AZ

Year	Rank	Starts	Poles	1	2	3	4	5	6–10	Laps	Laps Led	Races Led	Miles	$
1955	143	2	0	0	0	0	0	0	1	230	0	0	135	150
1956	99	6	0	0	0	0	0	0	1	504	0	0	471	385
1957	119	11	1	0	0	0	0	1	5	1,295	0	0	761	1,235
1958	68	4	0	0	0	0	0	0	1	546	0	0	412	280
1959	92	2	0	0	0	0	0	0	2	529	0	0	258	350
1960	66	4	1	0	1	0	0	0	1	465	19	2	835	1,325
1970	NR	1	0	0	0	0	0	0	1	133	0	0	348	1,115
1972	95	4	0	0	0	0	0	0	0	609	0	0	1,336	3,630
1973	38	10	0	0	0	0	0	0	0	2,160	0	0	2,000	8,235
1975	NR	1	0	0	0	0	0	0	0	36	0	0	72	665
1978	77	2	0	0	0	0	0	0	0	169	0	0	407	2,290
Lifetime		47	2	0	1	0	0	1	12	6,676	19	2	7,035	$19,660

Year	Rank	Starts	Poles	Finish						Laps	Laps Led	Races Led	Miles	$
				1	2	3	4	5	6–10					

Eddie LaRue
Edward LaRue

Year	Rank	Starts	Poles	1	2	3	4	5	6–10	Laps	Laps Led	Races Led	Miles	$
1951	N/A	1	0	0	0	0	0	0	0		0	0		25
Lifetime		1	0	0	0	0	0	0	0		0	0		$25

Roland LaRue
Roland LaRue
Racing Hometown: Mantica, OH

Year	Rank	Starts	Poles	1	2	3	4	5	6–10	Laps	Laps Led	Races Led	Miles	$
1954	126T	1	0	0	0	0	0	0	0	118	0	0	59	25
Lifetime		1	0	0	0	0	0	0	0	118	0	0	59	$25

Cecil Lassiter
Cecil Lassiter

Year	Rank	Starts	Poles	1	2	3	4	5	6–10	Laps	Laps Led	Races Led	Miles	$
1956	115	1	0	0	0	0	0	0	0	235	0	0	235	100
Lifetime		1	0	0	0	0	0	0	0	235	0	0	235	$100

Bill Latham
William Latham
Racing Hometown: Birmingham, AL

Year	Rank	Starts	Poles	1	2	3	4	5	6–10	Laps	Laps Led	Races Led	Miles	$
1961	124	1	0	0	0	0	0	0	0	440	0	0	220	250
1966	NR	2	0	0	0	0	0	0	0	160	0	0	54	200
Lifetime		3	0	0	0	0	0	0	0	600	0	0	274	$450

Patrick Latimer
Patrick Latimer

Year	Rank	Starts	Poles	1	2	3	4	5	6–10	Laps	Laps Led	Races Led	Miles	$
1987	103T	1	0	0	0	0	0	0	0	38	0	0	39	1,250
Lifetime		1	0	0	0	0	0	0	0	38	0	0	39	$1,250

Glenn Laughlin
Glenn Laughlin
Racing Hometown: Akron, OH

Year	Rank	Starts	Poles	1	2	3	4	5	6–10	Laps	Laps Led	Races Led	Miles	$
1954	156T	1	0	0	0	0	0	0	0	54	0	0	27	0
Lifetime		1	0	0	0	0	0	0	0	54	0	0	27	$0

Ray Laughlin
Raymond Laughlin

Year	Rank	Starts	Poles	1	2	3	4	5	6–10	Laps	Laps Led	Races Led	Miles	$
1954	NR	1	0	0	0	0	0	0	0	40	0	0	80	0
Lifetime		1	0	0	0	0	0	0	0	40	0	0	80	$0

Harry LaVois
Harry LaVois
Racing Hometown: Newark, NJ

Year	Rank	Starts	Poles	1	2	3	4	5	6–10	Laps	Laps Led	Races Led	Miles	$
1954	NR	1	0	0	0	0	0	1	0	49	0	0	98	275
Lifetime		1	0	0	0	0	0	1	0	49	0	0	98	$275

Clare Lawicki
Clare Lawicki
Racing Hometown: Roseville, MI

Year	Rank	Starts	Poles	1	2	3	4	5	6–10	Laps	Laps Led	Races Led	Miles	$
1954	NR	1	0	0	0	0	0	0	0	175	0	0	88	25
Lifetime		1	0	0	0	0	0	0	0	175	0	0	88	$25

Bill Lawrence
William Lawrence
Racing Hometown: Martinsville, VA

Year	Rank	Starts	Poles	1	2	3	4	5	6–10	Laps	Laps Led	Races Led	Miles	$
1951	N/A	1	0	0	0	0	0	0	0		0	0		25
Lifetime		1	0	0	0	0	0	0	0		0	0		$25

Coleman Lawrence
Coleman Lawrence
Racing Hometown: Martinsville, VA

Year	Rank	Starts	Poles	1	2	3	4	5	6–10	Laps	Laps Led	Races Led	Miles	$
1951	78	6	0	0	0	0	0	0	2	130	0	0	130	250
1952	29	8	0	0	0	0	0	0	3	1,326	0	0	1,045	375
1953	42	8	0	0	0	0	0	0	1	263	0	0	263	250
Lifetime		22	0	0	0	0	0	0	6	1,719	0	0	1,438	$875

Dick Lawrence
Richard Lawrence

Year	Rank	Starts	Poles	1	2	3	4	5	6–10	Laps	Laps Led	Races Led	Miles	$
1969	NR	1	0	0	0	0	0	0	0	108	0	0	287	1,275
Lifetime		1	0	0	0	0	0	0	0	108	0	0	287	$1,275

Year	Rank	Starts	Poles	Finish 1	2	3	4	5	6–10	Laps	Laps Led	Races Led	Miles	$

Jack Lawrence

Jack Lawrence
B: 10/13/1941
Racing Hometown: Grand Rapids, MI

Year	Rank	Starts	Poles	1	2	3	4	5	6–10	Laps	Laps Led	Races Led	Miles	$
1953	90	2	0	0	0	0	0	0	0	101	0	0	51	50
1958	116	1	0	0	0	0	0	0	1	177	0	0	89	140
Lifetime		3	0	0	0	0	0	0	1	278	0	0	139	$190

Leonard Lawrence

Leonard Lawrence
Racing Hometown: Tampa, FL

Year	Rank	Starts	Poles	1	2	3	4	5	6–10	Laps	Laps Led	Races Led	Miles	$
1953	113	2	0	0	0	0	0	0	0		0	0		50
Lifetime		2	0	0	0	0	0	0	0		0	0		$50

Mike Laws

Michael Laws
B: 10/7/1957
Racing Hometown: Orlando, FL

Year	Rank	Starts	Poles	1	2	3	4	5	6–10	Laps	Laps Led	Races Led	Miles	$
1986	78	2	0	0	0	0	0	0	0	422	0	0	698	3,095
Lifetime		2	0	0	0	0	0	0	0	422	0	0	698	$3,095

Dean Layfield

Dean Layfield
B: 4/6/1919   D: 8/25/1961   *Died of injuries from 8/20/61 Super Modified race @ Perry Raceway in Perry, NY.*
Racing Hometown: Wellsville, NY

Year	Rank	Starts	Poles	1	2	3	4	5	6–10	Laps	Laps Led	Races Led	Miles	$
1957	NR	1	0	0	0	0	1	0	0	97	0	0	97	295
1958	50	7	0	0	0	0	0	0	0	522	0	0	433	370
Lifetime		8	0	0	0	0	1	0	0	619	0	0	530	$665

Anthony Lazzaro

Anthony Lazzaro
B: 8/23/1963
Racing Hometown: Acworth, GA

Year	Rank	Starts	Poles	1	2	3	4	5	6–10	Laps	Laps Led	Races Led	Miles	$
2001	68T	1	0	0	0	0	0	0	0	88	0	0	216	32,265
Lifetime		1	0	0	0	0	0	0	0	88	0	0	216	$32,265

Harry Leake

Harry Leake
Racing Hometown: Lewisville, NC

Year	Rank	Starts	Poles	1	2	3	4	5	6–10	Laps	Laps Led	Races Led	Miles	$
1958	NR	2	0	0	0	0	0	0	0	336	0	0	123	115
1961	44	15	0	0	0	0	0	0	7	3,295	0	0	1,935	2,000
1962	61	5	0	0	0	0	0	0	1	669	0	0	278	525
Lifetime		22	0	0	0	0	0	0	8	4,300	0	0	2,335	$2,640

Dawson Lechlider

F. Dawson Lechlider
Racing Hometown: Silver Spring, MD

Year	Rank	Starts	Poles	1	2	3	4	5	6–10	Laps	Laps Led	Races Led	Miles	$
1951	N/A	4	0	0	0	0	0	0	0	49	0	0	49	75
Lifetime		4	0	0	0	0	0	0	0	49	0	0	49	$75

Bill Ledbetter

William Ledbetter
Racing Hometown: Los Angeles, CA

Year	Rank	Starts	Poles	1	2	3	4	5	6–10	Laps	Laps Led	Races Led	Miles	$
1951	81	3	0	0	0	0	0	0	1		0	0		250
Lifetime		3	0	0	0	0	0	0	1		0	0		$250

Max Ledbetter

Max Ledbetter
Racing Hometown: Franklin, NC

Year	Rank	Starts	Poles	1	2	3	4	5	6–10	Laps	Laps Led	Races Led	Miles	$
1966	70	9	0	0	0	0	0	0	1	1,752	0	0	882	1,110
1967	53	10	0	0	0	0	0	0	4	2,394	0	0	1,171	2,325
1968	102T	1	0	0	0	0	0	0	0	134	0	0	67	100
1969	NR	1	0	0	0	0	0	0	0	91	0	0	46	260
Lifetime		21	0	0	0	0	0	0	5	4,371	0	0	2,165	$3,795

Bobby Lee

Robert Lee
Racing Hometown: Sumter, SC

Year	Rank	Starts	Poles	1	2	3	4	5	6–10	Laps	Laps Led	Races Led	Miles	$
1958	64	5	0	0	0	0	0	0	0	532	0	0	568	285
Lifetime		5	0	0	0	0	0	0	0	532	0	0	568	$285

Year	Rank	Starts	Poles	1	2	3	Finish 4	5	6–10	Laps	Laps Led	Races Led	Miles	$

Doc Lee

Doc Lee

Year	Rank	Starts	Poles	1	2	3	4	5	6–10	Laps	Laps Led	Races Led	Miles	$
1961	NR	1	0	0	0	0	0	0	0	135	0	0	34	75
Lifetime		1	0	0	0	0	0	0	0	135	0	0	34	$75

Fred Lee

Fred Lee (Real Name: Fred Bince) *Also raced as Sam Lamm.*
B: 9/28/1923
Racing Hometown: Los Angeles, CA

Year	Rank	Starts	Poles	1	2	3	4	5	6–10	Laps	Laps Led	Races Led	Miles	$
1951	50	5	0	0	0	0	1	0	1	98	0	0	49	450
Lifetime		5	0	0	0	0	1	0	1	98	0	0	49	$450

Hank Lee

Edward Franklin Lee
B: 1928 D: 6/4/1952 *Died of heart attack @ age 24.*
Racing Hometown: Mobile, AL

Year	Rank	Starts	Poles	1	2	3	4	5	6–10	Laps	Laps Led	Races Led	Miles	$
1951	N/A	1	0	0	0	0	0	0	0		0	0		25
1952	NR	2	0	0	0	0	0	0	0	114	0	0	104	50
Lifetime		3	0	0	0	0	0	0	0	114	0	0	104	$75

Jim Lee

James Lee
Racing Hometown: Vista, CA

Year	Rank	Starts	Poles	1	2	3	4	5	6–10	Laps	Laps Led	Races Led	Miles	$
1974	127	1	0	0	0	0	0	0	0	21	0	0	55	650
1982	69	2	0	0	0	0	0	0	0	125	0	0	328	1,760
Lifetime		3	0	0	0	0	0	0	0	146	0	0	383	$2,410

Russ Lee

Russell Lee
Racing Hometown: Robbinsdale, MN

Year	Rank	Starts	Poles	1	2	3	4	5	6–10	Laps	Laps Led	Races Led	Miles	$
1950	NR	1	0	0	0	0	0	0	0	38	0	0	158	25
Lifetime		1	0	0	0	0	0	0	0	38	0	0	158	$25

Ted Lee

Theodore Lee
Racing Hometown: Encino, CA

Year	Rank	Starts	Poles	1	2	3	4	5	6–10	Laps	Laps Led	Races Led	Miles	$
1953	79	4	0	0	0	0	0	0	0	294	0	0	387	125
1954	NR	2	0	0	0	0	0	0	0	492	0	0	328	65
Lifetime		6	0	0	0	0	0	0	0	786	0	0	715	$190

Marion Leech

Marion Leech
Racing Hometown: Evansville, IN

Year	Rank	Starts	Poles	1	2	3	4	5	6–10	Laps	Laps Led	Races Led	Miles	$
1952	NR	1	0	0	0	0	0	0	0	117	0	0	59	25
Lifetime		1	0	0	0	0	0	0	0	117	0	0	59	$25

Jason Leffler

Jason Leffler
B: 9/16/1975
Racing Hometown: Indianapolis, IN

Year	Rank	Starts	Poles	1	2	3	4	5	6–10	Laps	Laps Led	Races Led	Miles	$
2001	37	30	1	0	0	0	0	0	1	7,983	15	3	11,049	1,724,692
2002	63	2	0	0	0	0	0	0	0	572	0	0	706	78,500
Lifetime		32	1	0	0	0	0	0	1	8,555	15	3	11,756	$1,803,192

Herb Legg

Herbert Legg
Racing Hometown: Rochester, NY

Year	Rank	Starts	Poles	1	2	3	4	5	6–10	Laps	Laps Led	Races Led	Miles	$
1952	147T	1	0	0	0	0	0	0	0	133	0	0	67	25
Lifetime		1	0	0	0	0	0	0	0	133	0	0	67	$25

Irv Leitch

Irving Leitch
Racing Hometown: Glenshaw, PA

Year	Rank	Starts	Poles	1	2	3	4	5	6–10	Laps	Laps Led	Races Led	Miles	$
1950	NR	1	0	0	0	0	0	0	0	113	0	0	57	0
1951	N/A	1	0	0	0	0	0	0	0		0	0		25
Lifetime		2	0	0	0	0	0	0	0	113	0	0	57	$25

Year	Rank	Starts	Poles	Finish 1	2	3	4	5	6–10	Laps	Laps Led	Races Led	Miles	$

Butch Leitzinger

Butch Leitzinger
B: 2/8/1969
Racing Hometown: State College, PA

Year	Rank	Starts	Poles	1	2	3	4	5	6–10	Laps	Laps Led	Races Led	Miles	$
1994	72T	1	0	0	0	0	0	0	0	81	0	0	198	6,330
1995	54	1	0	0	0	0	0	0	0	90	0	0	221	17,060
1996	58	1	0	0	0	0	0	0	0	90	0	0	221	22,705
Lifetime		3	0	0	0	0	0	0	0	261	0	0	639	$46,095

Larry LeMay

Lawrence LeMay
B: 10/25/1949
Racing Hometown: Mt. Clemens, MI

Year	Rank	Starts	Poles	1	2	3	4	5	6–10	Laps	Laps Led	Races Led	Miles	$
1976	75	2	0	0	0	0	0	0	0	460	0	0	280	975
1977	79	2	0	0	0	0	0	0	0	288	0	0	177	710
Lifetime		4	0	0	0	0	0	0	0	748	0	0	457	$1,685

Albert Lemieux

Albert Lemieux
Racing Hometown: Montreal, Que., Canada

Year	Rank	Starts	Poles	1	2	3	4	5	6–10	Laps	Laps Led	Races Led	Miles	$
1952	NR	1	0	0	0	0	0	0	1	121	0	0	61	50
Lifetime		1	0	0	0	0	0	0	1	121	0	0	61	$50

Eddie Lenz

Edward Lenz
Racing Hometown: Colden, NY

Year	Rank	Starts	Poles	1	2	3	4	5	6–10	Laps	Laps Led	Races Led	Miles	$
1951	N/A	1	0	0	0	0	0	0	0		0	0		25
1952	N/A	1	0	0	0	0	0	0	0	55	0	0	28	25
Lifetime		2	0	0	0	0	0	0	0	55	0	0	28	$50

Joe Leonard

Joseph Paul Leonard
B: 8/4/1934
Racing Hometown: San Diego, CA

Year	Rank	Starts	Poles	1	2	3	4	5	6–10	Laps	Laps Led	Races Led	Miles	$
1969	NR	1	0	0	0	0	0	0	0	47	0	0	118	720
Lifetime		1	0	0	0	0	0	0	0	47	0	0	118	$720

Kevin Lepage

Kevin Lepage
B: 6/26/1962
Racing Hometown: Shelburne, VT

Year	Rank	Starts	Poles	1	2	3	4	5	6–10	Laps	Laps Led	Races Led	Miles	$
1997	56	3	0	0	0	0	0	0	0	624	0	0	1,161	57,720
1998	35	27	0	0	0	0	0	0	2	7,198	0	0	8,876	852,721
1999	25	34	1	0	0	0	0	1	1	9,646	20	2	12,630	1,587,841
2000	28	32	0	0	0	0	0	1	2	8,743	38	9	10,936	1,679,186
2001	36	29	0	0	0	0	0	0	1	8,557	13	2	10,552	1,424,852
2002	62	3	0	0	0	0	0	0	0	494	0	0	526	142,459
Lifetime		128	1	0	0	0	0	2	6	35,262	71	13	44,680	$5,744,779

Tracy Leslie

Tracy Leslie
B: 10/24/1957
Racing Hometown: Mt. Clemens, MI

Year	Rank	Starts	Poles	1	2	3	4	5	6–10	Laps	Laps Led	Races Led	Miles	$
1989	56	2	0	0	0	0	0	0	0	557	0	0	934	8,800
1990	69	3	0	0	0	0	0	0	0	316	0	0	504	11,740
Lifetime		5	0	0	0	0	0	0	0	873	0	0	1,438	$20,540

Danny Letner

Daniel Letner
Racing Hometown: Downey, CA

Year	Rank	Starts	Poles	1	2	3	4	5	6–10	Laps	Laps Led	Races Led	Miles	$
1951	87	5	0	0	0	0	0	0	2	153	0	0	153	225
1954	33	4	1	1	0	1	0	0	1	1,058	142	2	674	1,975
1955	41	4	0	1	0	1	0	0	0	614	34	1	514	1,780
1956	127	6	0	0	0	0	0	0	0	585	0	0	705	410
1957	70	5	0	0	0	0	0	0	1	546	0	0	350	500
1959	NR	1	0	0	0	0	0	0	0	224	0	0	90	100
1961	NR	1	0	0	0	1	0	0	0	175	0	0	245	750
1963	55	1	0	0	0	0	0	0	1	179	0	0	483	950
Lifetime		27	1	2	0	3	0	0	5	3,534	176	3	3,214	$6,690

Year	Rank	Starts	Poles	1	2	Finish 3	4	5	6–10	Laps	Laps Led	Races Led	Miles	$

Jimmie Lewallen

James Edward Lewallen
B: 8/22/1919   D: 10/16/1995
Racing Hometown: Archdale, NC

Year	Rank	Starts	Poles	1	2	3	4	5	6–10	Laps	Laps Led	Races Led	Miles	$
1949	NR	3	0	0	0	0	0	0	0		0	0		25
1950	41	3	0	0	0	0	1	0	0	330	0	0	413	400
1951	13	12	0	0	0	2	0	2	4	613	0	0	671	2,430
1952	14	20	0	0	0	0	1	1	5	2,327	0	0	1,638	2,052
1953	9	22	0	0	1	2	0	4	6	908	0	0	791	4,222
1954	8	22	0	0	2	0	0	3	5	2,963	0	0	2,206	4,694
1955	9	33	1	0	2	0	4	2	8	4,028	0	0	2,939	6,440
1956	56	11	0	0	0	0	1	0	0	779	0	0	565	1,150
1957	26	7	0	0	0	0	0	0	0	895	0	0	865	1,030
1958	NR	1	0	0	0	0	0	0	0	389	0	0	195	210
1959	NR	6	0	0	0	0	0	0	1	509	0	0	198	350
1960	NR	2	0	0	0	0	0	0	0	63	0	0	16	215
Lifetime		142	1	0	5	4	7	12	29	13,804	0	0	10,495	$23,218

Emory Lewis

Emory Lewis
Racing Hometown: Winchester, KY

Year	Rank	Starts	Poles	1	2	3	4	5	6–10	Laps	Laps Led	Races Led	Miles	$
1953	NR	2	0	0	0	0	0	0	1	387	0	0	364	255
1954	NR	5	0	0	0	0	0	0	2	422	0	0	378	475
Lifetime		7	0	0	0	0	0	0	3	809	0	0	742	$730

Skip Lewis

George Lewis
Racing Hometown: Dayton, NY

Year	Rank	Starts	Poles	1	2	3	4	5	6–10	Laps	Laps Led	Races Led	Miles	$
1949	40	1	0	0	0	0	0	0	1	168	0	0	84	50
Lifetime		1	0	0	0	0	0	0	1	168	0	0	84	$50

Herb Lewis

Herbert Lewis
Racing Hometown: Nashville, TN

Year	Rank	Starts	Poles	1	2	3	4	5	6–10	Laps	Laps Led	Races Led	Miles	$
1959	65	1	0	0	0	0	0	0	0	221	0	0	111	100
Lifetime		1	0	0	0	0	0	0	0	221	0	0	111	$100

Paul Lewis

William Paul Lewis
B: 9/28/1932
Racing Hometown: Johnson City, TN

Year	Rank	Starts	Poles	1	2	3	4	5	6–10	Laps	Laps Led	Races Led	Miles	$
1960	27	22	0	0	0	0	0	0	4	3,690	0	0	2,562	3,535
1961	28	21	0	0	0	0	0	0	5	3,669	0	0	2,803	4,095
1962	55	6	0	0	0	0	0	0	0	945	0	0	989	1,695
1963	138	1	0	0	0	0	0	0	0	2	0	0	3	500
1964	142	1	0	0	0	0	0	0	0	27	0	0	17	150
1965	14	24	1	0	0	0	1	2	10	5,954	0	0	5,057	13,247
1966	16	21	0	1	1	6	1	0	5	6,260	67	2	4,742	17,827
1967	33	14	0	0	1	0	0	2	5	2,959	4	1	2,593	8,720
1968	71	4	0	0	0	0	0	1	0	584	0	0	571	3,100
Lifetime		114	1	1	2	6	2	5	29	24,090	71	3	19,337	$52,869

Raymond Lewis

Raymond Lewis
Racing Hometown: War, WV

Year	Rank	Starts	Poles	1	2	3	4	5	6–10	Laps	Laps Led	Races Led	Miles	$
1949	37T	1	0	0	0	0	0	0	1	194	0	0	97	75
Lifetime		1	0	0	0	0	0	0	1	194	0	0	97	$75

Frank Lies

Frank Lies
Racing Hometown: Wichita, KS

Year	Rank	Starts	Poles	1	2	3	4	5	6–10	Laps	Laps Led	Races Led	Miles	$
1958	158	1	0	0	0	0	0	0	0	33	0	0	33	100
Lifetime		1	0	0	0	0	0	0	0	33	0	0	33	$100

Ralph Liguori

Ralph Liguori
B: 10/10/1926
Racing Hometown: Bronx, NY

Year	Rank	Starts	Poles	1	2	3	4	5	6–10	Laps	Laps Led	Races Led	Miles	$
1951	N/A	1	0	0	0	0	0	0	0	20	0	0	10	0

Year	Rank	Starts	Poles	Finish 1	2	3	4	5	6–10	Laps	Laps Led	Races Led	Miles	$

Ralph Liguori *continued*

Year	Rank	Starts	Poles	1	2	3	4	5	6–10	Laps	Laps Led	Races Led	Miles	$
1952	23	12	0	0	0	0	1	0	5	1,671	0	0	1,236	920
1953	20	12	0	0	0	0	0	2	1	407	0	0	377	1,098
1954	10	23	1	0	0	1	0	1	10	3,461	0	0	2,447	3,495
1955	19	12	0	0	0	0	0	0	6	1,402	0	0	1,422	1,973
1956	51	16	0	0	0	0	0	0	3	1,382	0	0	1,093	1,210
Lifetime		76	1	0	0	1	1	3	25	8,343	0	0	6,585	$8,696

Bill Lillenthal

William Lillenthal
Racing Hometown: East Randolph, NY

Year	Rank	Starts	Poles	1	2	3	4	5	6–10	Laps	Laps Led	Races Led	Miles	$
1951	N/A	1	0	0	0	0	0	0	0		0	0		50
Lifetime		1	0	0	0	0	0	0	0		0	0		$50

Dick Linder

Richard R. Linder
B: 4/6/1923   D: 4/19/1959   *Killed in Indy Car race @ Trenton, NJ.*
Racing Hometown: Pittsburgh, PA

Year	Rank	Starts	Poles	1	2	3	4	5	6–10	Laps	Laps Led	Races Led	Miles	$
1949	19	3	0	0	1	0	0	0	0	416	0	0	289	830
1950	8	13	4	3	1	1	0	0	3	1,437	460	5	1,060	5,695
1951	N/A	10	0	0	0	0	0	0	2	21	0	0	11	375
1953	97T	1	0	0	0	0	0	0	0	176	0	0	88	25
1956	281	1	0	0	0	0	0	0	0		0	0		0
Lifetime		28	4	3	2	1	0	0	5	2,050	460	5	1,447	$6,925

Gus Linder

Gus Linder
Racing Hometown: Pittsburgh, PA

Year	Rank	Starts	Poles	1	2	3	4	5	6–10	Laps	Laps Led	Races Led	Miles	$
1951	219T	1	0	0	0	0	0	0	0		0	0		25
Lifetime		1	0	0	0	0	0	0	0		0	0		$25

Butch Lindley

Clyde Lindley
B: 3/25/1948   D: 6/6/1990   *Died from injuries in All Pro race @ Bradenton, FL.*
Racing Hometown: Greenville, SC

Year	Rank	Starts	Poles	1	2	3	4	5	6–10	Laps	Laps Led	Races Led	Miles	$
1979	111T	1	0	0	0	0	0	0	0	82	0	0	43	570
1981	60	3	0	0	0	0	0	0	0	559	28	2	323	2,375
1982	43	4	0	0	1	0	0	0	0	1,020	165	2	548	16,695
1983	56	2	0	0	0	0	0	0	0	518	7	1	279	3,535
1985	NR	1	0	0	0	0	0	0	0	352	0	0	191	1,365
Lifetime		11	0	0	1	0	0	0	0	2,531	200	5	1,384	$24,540

John Lindsay

John Lindsay
Racing Hometown: Jersey City, NJ

Year	Rank	Starts	Poles	1	2	3	4	5	6–10	Laps	Laps Led	Races Led	Miles	$
1954	NR	1	0	0	0	0	0	0	0	197	0	0	197	50
1955	35	6	0	0	0	0	0	0	3	853	0	0	630	575
1956	63	5	0	0	0	0	0	0	1	715	0	0	585	425
1958	85	3	0	0	0	0	0	0	1	476	0	0	262	310
Lifetime		15	0	0	0	0	0	0	5	2,241	0	0	1,673	$1,360

Jim Lineberger

James Lineberger
Racing Hometown: Hickory, NC

Year	Rank	Starts	Poles	1	2	3	4	5	6–10	Laps	Laps Led	Races Led	Miles	$
1969	83T	1	0	0	0	0	0	0	0	131	0	0	197	925
Lifetime		1	0	0	0	0	0	0	0	131	0	0	197	$925

Bob Link

Robert Link
Racing Hometown: Walnut Creek, VA

Year	Rank	Starts	Poles	1	2	3	4	5	6–10	Laps	Laps Led	Races Led	Miles	$
1968	105	1	0	0	0	0	0	0	0	14	0	0	38	500
Lifetime		1	0	0	0	0	0	0	0	14	0	0	38	$500

Robert Link

Robert Link
Racing Hometown: Macon, GA

Year	Rank	Starts	Poles	1	2	3	4	5	6–10	Laps	Laps Led	Races Led	Miles	$
1969	NR	1	0	0	0	0	0	0	0	62	0	0	167	775
Lifetime		1	0	0	0	0	0	0	0	62	0	0	167	$775

Year	Rank	Starts	Poles	Finish 1	2	3	4	5	6–10	Laps	Laps Led	Races Led	Miles	$

Terry Link

Terry Link
B: 8/13/1952
Racing Hometown: Daytona Beach, FL

Year	Rank	Starts	Poles	1	2	3	4	5	6–10	Laps	Laps Led	Races Led	Miles	$
1974	86	2	0	0	0	0	0	0	0	146	0	0	388	2,185
1975	117	1	0	0	0	0	0	0	0	6	0	0	16	595
Lifetime		3	0	0	0	0	0	0	0	152	0	0	404	$2,780

Jim Linke

James Linke
Racing Hometown: Jamesburg, NY

Year	Rank	Starts	Poles	1	2	3	4	5	6–10	Laps	Laps Led	Races Led	Miles	$
1957	72	4	0	0	0	0	0	0	1	361	0	0	282	400
1958	80	3	0	0	0	0	0	0	0	397	0	0	308	170
Lifetime		7	0	0	0	0	0	0	1	758	0	0	590	$570

Bennis Listman

Bennis Listman

Year	Rank	Starts	Poles	1	2	3	4	5	6–10	Laps	Laps Led	Races Led	Miles	$
1971	NR	1	0	0	0	0	0	0	0	6	0	0	1	100
Lifetime		1	0	0	0	0	0	0	0	6	0	0	1	$100

Chad Little

Chad Little
B: 4/29/1963
Racing Hometown: Spokane, WA

Year	Rank	Starts	Poles	1	2	3	4	5	6–10	Laps	Laps Led	Races Led	Miles	$
1986	70	2	0	0	0	0	0	0	0	145	0	0	380	6,065
1987	59	2	0	0	0	0	0	0	0	211	0	0	553	8,810
1988	45	4	0	0	0	0	0	0	0	1,089	3	1	1,435	14,225
1989	38	8	0	0	0	0	0	0	0	2,036	0	0	2,794	44,690
1990	33	18	0	0	0	0	0	0	0	4,840		0	6,429	80,140
1991	27	28	0	0	0	0	0	0	1	7,784	21	3	9,530	184,190
1992	31	19	0	0	0	0	0	0	1	5,114		0	6,707	145,805
1993	51	3	0	0	0	0	0	0	0	775	0	0	1,361	39,340
1994	68	1	0	0	0	0	0	0	0	196	1	1	490	30,805
1995	53	2	0	0	0	0	0	0	0	195	0	0	508	20,425
1996	44	9	0	0	0	0	0	0	0	1,816	0	0	2,396	164,752
1997	36	27	0	0	0	0	0	0	1	7,732	7	1	9,152	555,914
1998	15	32	0	0	1	0	0	0	6	9,081	69	8	11,828	1,449,659
1999	23	34	0	0	0	0	0	0	5	9,465	3	3	12,160	1,623,976
2000	32	27	0	0	0	0	0	0	1	7,178	7	5	10,055	1,418,884
2002	77T	1	0	0	0	0	0	0	0	395	0	0	395	49,745
Lifetime		217	0	0	1	0	0	0	15	58,052	111	22	76,174	$5,837,425

Chuck Little

Charles M. Little
B: 6/1/1944
Racing Hometown: Spokane, WA

Year	Rank	Starts	Poles	1	2	3	4	5	6–10	Laps	Laps Led	Races Led	Miles	$
1975	100T	1	0	0	0	0	0	0	0	35	0	0	92	875
Lifetime		1	0	0	0	0	0	0	0	35	0	0	92	$875

Joe Little

Joe Little

Year	Rank	Starts	Poles	1	2	3	4	5	6–10	Laps	Laps Led	Races Led	Miles	$
1951	N/A	1	0	0	0	0	0	0	1		0	0		100
Lifetime		1	0	0	0	0	0	0	1		0	0		$100

Mike Little

Michael Little
B: 1914
Racing Hometown: Johnstown, PA

Year	Rank	Starts	Poles	1	2	3	4	5	6–10	Laps	Laps Led	Races Led	Miles	$
1951	N/A	1	0	0	0	0	0	0	0		0	0		25
1952	191T	1	0	0	0	0	0	0	0	62	0	0	31	25
Lifetime		2	0	0	0	0	0	0	0	62	0	0	31	$50

Joe Littlejohn

Joseph Littlejohn
B: 1/3/1908   D: 7/29/1989
Racing Hometown: Spartanburg, SC

Year	Rank	Starts	Poles	1	2	3	4	5	6–10	Laps	Laps Led	Races Led	Miles	$
1949	22T	1	0	0	0	0	1	0	0	40	0	0	166	300
1950	NR	1	1	0	0	0	0	0	0	7	0	0	29	25
Lifetime		2	1	0	0	0	1	0	0	47	0	0	195	$325

Year	Rank	Starts	Poles	Finish						Laps	Laps Led	Races Led	Miles	$
				1	2	3	4	5	6–10					

Virgil Livengood

Virgil Livengood
Racing Hometown: Mankota, MN

Year	Rank	Starts	Poles	1	2	3	4	5	6–10	Laps	Laps Led	Races Led	Miles	$
1950	NR	1	0	0	0	0	0	0	0	338	0	0	423	0
1953	57	3	0	0	0	0	0	0	1	7	0	0	4	100
1954	199	1	0	0	0	0	0	0	0	35	0	0	144	25
Lifetime		5	0	0	0	0	0	0	1	380	0	0	570	$125

Dub Livingston

Dub Livingston
Racing Hometown: Gadsden, AL

Year	Rank	Starts	Poles	1	2	3	4	5	6–10	Laps	Laps Led	Races Led	Miles	$
1952	NR	1	0	0	0	0	0	0	0	152	0	0	76	25
1953	43	6	0	0	0	0	0	0	1	309	0	0	252	225
Lifetime		7	0	0	0	0	0	0	1	461	0	0	328	$250

Ed Livingston

Edward Livingston
B: 10/17/1935
Racing Hometown: Follly Beach, SC

Year	Rank	Starts	Poles	1	2	3	4	5	6–10	Laps	Laps Led	Races Led	Miles	$
1961	62	10	0	0	0	0	0	0	0	1,467	0	0	2,187	1,945
1962	38	13	0	0	0	0	0	0	0	1,758	0	0	2,146	2,940
1963	30	20	0	0	0	0	0	0	1	3,294	0	0	3,196	4,930
1964	93	4	0	0	0	0	1	0	0	213	0	0	116	1,375
Lifetime		47	0	0	0	0	1	0	1	6,732	0	0	7,645	$11,190

Jim Locke

James Locke
Racing Hometown: Circleville, OH

Year	Rank	Starts	Poles	1	2	3	4	5	6–10	Laps	Laps Led	Races Led	Miles	$
1962	125	1	0	0	0	0	0	0	0	140	0	0	210	225
Lifetime		1	0	0	0	0	0	0	0	140	0	0	210	$225

Les Loeser

Lester Loeser
Racing Hometown: Modesto, CA

Year	Rank	Starts	Poles	1	2	3	4	5	6–10	Laps	Laps Led	Races Led	Miles	$
1970	94T	1	0	0	0	0	0	0	0	38	0	0	100	830
1972	96	1	0	0	0	0	0	0	0	164	0	0	410	1,745
Lifetime		2	0	0	0	0	0	0	0	202	0	0	510	$2,575

Owen Loggins

Owen Loggins
Racing Hometown: Lafayette, CA

Year	Rank	Starts	Poles	1	2	3	4	5	6–10	Laps	Laps Led	Races Led	Miles	$
1955	90	3	0	0	0	0	0	0	0	341	0	0	326	150
1956	300	1	0	0	0	0	0	0	0	0	0	0	0	0
1958	167	1	0	0	0	0	0	0	0	25	0	0	66	175
1959	103	1	0	0	0	0	0	0	0	57	0	0	57	100
1960	112	1	0	0	0	0	0	0	0	126	0	0	176	100
Lifetime		7	0	0	0	0	0	0	0	549	0	0	625	$525

Lella Lombardi

Maria Grazia Lombardi
B: 3/26/1943   D: 3/3/1992   *Cancer.*
Racing Hometown: Frugarolo, Italy

Year	Rank	Starts	Poles	1	2	3	4	5	6–10	Laps	Laps Led	Races Led	Miles	$
1977	NR	1	0	0	0	0	0	0	0	103	0	0	258	785
Lifetime		1	0	0	0	0	0	0	0	103	0	0	258	$785

Bill Lone

William Raymond Lone
Racing Hometown: Glen Burnie, MD

Year	Rank	Starts	Poles	1	2	3	4	5	6–10	Laps	Laps Led	Races Led	Miles	$
1954	NR	1	0	0	0	0	0	0	0	209	0	0	209	150
1957	NR	1	0	0	0	0	0	0	0	167	0	0	84	100
Lifetime		2	0	0	0	0	0	0	0	376	0	0	293	$250

Bill Long

W.G. Long
Racing Hometown: Charlotte, NC

Year	Rank	Starts	Poles	1	2	3	4	5	6–10	Laps	Laps Led	Races Led	Miles	$
1950	54	1	0	0	0	0	0	0	1	141	0	0	71	175
Lifetime		1	0	0	0	0	0	0	1	141	0	0	71	$175

Year	Rank	Starts	Poles	1	2	3	Finish 4	5	6–10	Laps	Laps Led	Races Led	Miles	$

Carl Long

Carl Long
B: 9/20/1967
Racing Hometown: Roxboro, NC

Year	Rank	Starts	Poles	1	2	3	4	5	6–10	Laps	Laps Led	Races Led	Miles	$
2000	62	2	0	0	0	0	0	0	0	353	0	0	359	67,625
2001	56	3	0	0	0	0	0	0	0	513	0	0	688	117,514
2002	72	2	0	0	0	0	0	0	0	255	0	0	410	88,975
Lifetime		7	0	0	0	0	0	0	0	1,121	0	0	1,457	$274,114

Gene Long

Gene Long
Racing Hometown: Artesia, CA

Year	Rank	Starts	Poles	1	2	3	4	5	6–10	Laps	Laps Led	Races Led	Miles	$
1957	113	1	0	0	0	0	0	0	1	112	0	0	56	250
Lifetime		1	0	0	0	0	0	0	1	112	0	0	56	$250

Lucky Long

William G. Long
Racing Hometown: Lakewood, CA

Year	Rank	Starts	Poles	1	2	3	4	5	6–10	Laps	Laps Led	Races Led	Miles	$
1956	209T	1	0	0	0	0	0	0	0	180	0	0	90	50
1957	201T	1	0	0	0	0	0	0	0	24	0	0	12	0
1958	63	2	0	0	0	0	0	0	0	252	0	0	524	300
1959	83	2	0	0	0	0	0	1	1	554	0	0	280	700
Lifetime		6	0	0	0	0	0	1	1	1,010	0	0	906	$1,050

Sterling Long

Sterling Long
Racing Hometown: Charlotte, NC

Year	Rank	Starts	Poles	1	2	3	4	5	6–10	Laps	Laps Led	Races Led	Miles	$
1949	30	2	0	0	0	0	0	0	1		0	0		150
1950	NR	1	0	0	0	0	0	0	0		0	0		0
Lifetime		3	0	0	0	0	0	0	1		0	0		$150

Jimmy Longo

James Longo
Racing Hometown: Hubbard, OH

Year	Rank	Starts	Poles	1	2	3	4	5	6–10	Laps	Laps Led	Races Led	Miles	$
1951	N/A	1	0	0	0	0	0	0	0		0	0		25
Lifetime		1	0	0	0	0	0	0	0		0	0		$25

Al Loquasto

Al Loquasto
B: 6/21/1943   D: 8/7/1991   *Killed in private plane crash.*
Racing Hometown: Easton, PA

Year	Rank	Starts	Poles	1	2	3	4	5	6–10	Laps	Laps Led	Races Led	Miles	$
1981	NR	1	0	0	0	0	0	0	0	184	0	0	460	2,345
1982	81	5	0	0	0	0	0	0	0	519	0	0	1,228	14,090
Lifetime		6	0	0	0	0	0	0	0	703	0	0	1,688	$16,435

Fred Lorenzen

Fred Lorenzen
B: 12/30/1934
Racing Hometown: Elmhurst, IL

Year	Rank	Starts	Poles	1	2	3	4	5	6–10	Laps	Laps Led	Races Led	Miles	$
1956	120	7	0	0	0	0	0	0	0	778	0	0	420	235
1960	15	10	0	0	0	2	0	1	2	2,086	93	1	2,521	9,136
1961	19	15	4	3	1	0	1	1	0	2,567	729	9	2,815	21,624
1962	7	19	3	2	2	4	1	2	1	4,435	436	8	4,372	46,100
1963	3	29	9	6	8	3	0	4	2	7,484	2,384	19	6,472	122,588
1964	13	16	7	8	1	0	1	0	0	4,426	2,375	11	4,181	73,860
1965	13	17	6	4	1	0	0	0	1	3,677	981	12	3,998	80,615
1966	23	11	2	2	1	0	1	2	0	3,066	782	7	3,425	36,310
1967	29	5	0	1	1	0	0	0	0	895	23	4	1,411	17,875
1970	54	7	1	0	0	1	0	0	0	1,165	50	2	1,720	12,610
1971	45	14	1	0	1	0	2	4	2	3,229	152	6	5,038	45,100
1972	39	8	0	0	0	0	3	0	1	1,801	4	1	2,833	19,505
Lifetime		158	33	26	16	10	9	14	9	35,609	8,009	80	39,204	$485,558

Ken Love

Kenneth Love
Racing Hometown: Chicago Heights, IL

Year	Rank	Starts	Poles	1	2	3	4	5	6–10	Laps	Laps Led	Races Led	Miles	$
1956	192	3	0	0	0	0	0	0	0	278	0	0	328	200
1957	177	1	0	0	0	0	0	0	0		0	0		60
1958	78	3	0	0	0	0	0	0	0	125	0	0	156	135
Lifetime		7	0	0	0	0	0	0	0	403	0	0	484	$395

Year	Rank	Starts	Poles	1	2	3	4	5	6–10	Laps	Laps Led	Races Led	Miles	$

Gene Lovelace

Gene Lovelace
D: 7/3/1970 *Died of heart attack during race at Southside Speedway in Richmond, VA.*
Racing Hometown: Newport News, VA

Year	Rank	Starts	Poles	1	2	3	4	5	6–10	Laps	Laps Led	Races Led	Miles	$
1964	110	1	0	0	0	0	0	0	0	125	0	0	50	130
Lifetime		1	0	0	0	0	0	0	0	125	0	0	50	$130

Clarence Lovell

Clarence Lovell
B: 6/19/1946   D: 5/11/1973   *Killed in highway crash.*
Racing Hometown: San Antonio, TX

Year	Rank	Starts	Poles	1	2	3	4	5	6–10	Laps	Laps Led	Races Led	Miles	$
1972	32	12	0	0	0	0	0	0	0	2,202	0	0	3,586	10,770
1973	48	4	0	0	0	0	1	0	1	661	0	0	1,169	9,175
Lifetime		16	0	0	0	0	1	0	1	2,863	0	0	4,755	$19,945

Bosco Lowe

William B. Lowe
B: 3/27/1943
Racing Hometown: Fairview, NC

Year	Rank	Starts	Poles	1	2	3	4	5	6–10	Laps	Laps Led	Races Led	Miles	$
1967	96	2	0	0	0	0	0	0	1	333	0	0	143	340
1968	91	2	0	0	0	0	0	0	0	258	0	0	136	225
1982	NR	1	0	0	0	0	0	0	0	381	0	0	572	3,900
1983	100	1	0	0	0	0	0	0	0	36	0	0	90	5,350
1985	NR	1	0	0	0	0	0	0	0	171	0	0	455	6,825
Lifetime		7	0	0	0	0	0	0	1	1,179	0	0	1,396	$16,640

Harold Lucas

Harold Lucas

Year	Rank	Starts	Poles	1	2	3	4	5	6–10	Laps	Laps Led	Races Led	Miles	$
1951	N/A	1	0	0	0	0	0	0	0		0	0		25
Lifetime		1	0	0	0	0	0	0	0		0	0		$25

Keith Lucas

Keith Lucas
Racing Hometown: Sperry, IA

Year	Rank	Starts	Poles	1	2	3	4	5	6–10	Laps	Laps Led	Races Led	Miles	$
1953	91T	1	0	0	0	0	0	0	1		0	0		50
Lifetime		1	0	0	0	0	0	0	1		0	0		$50

Glenn Luce

Glenn Luce
Racing Hometown: Strong, ME

Year	Rank	Starts	Poles	1	2	3	4	5	6–10	Laps	Laps Led	Races Led	Miles	$
1968	120T	1	0	0	0	0	0	0	0	223	0	0	74	125
Lifetime		1	0	0	0	0	0	0	0	223	0	0	74	$125

Jim Luke

James Luke
Racing Hometown: Utica, NY

Year	Rank	Starts	Poles	1	2	3	4	5	6–10	Laps	Laps Led	Races Led	Miles	$
1954	163	1	0	0	0	0	0	0	0	154	0	0	77	0
Lifetime		1	0	0	0	0	0	0	0	154	0	0	77	$0

Tiny Lund

DeWayne Louis Lund
B: 3/3/1936   D: 8/17/1975   *Killed in Talladega 500.*
Racing Hometown: Cross, SC

Year	Rank	Starts	Poles	1	2	3	4	5	6–10	Laps	Laps Led	Races Led	Miles	$
1955	217	1	0	0	0	0	0	0	0	65	0	0	98	60
1956	19	21	0	0	0	0	1	0	7	3,988	0	0	2,466	2,811
1957	11	32	3	0	0	3	1	2	9	4,922	209	2	3,024	6,424
1958	25	22	2	0	0	2	1	1	3	3,506	14	1	1,991	3,155
1959	20	27	0	0	2	0	3	0	5	4,836	0	0	2,971	4,941
1960	32	8	0	0	0	0	0	0	2	1,254	0	0	1,706	2,440
1961	23	10	0	0	0	0	0	0	2	2,583	0	0	2,756	5,545
1962	34	10	0	0	0	0	0	0	0	2,487	8	1	2,580	2,880
1963	10	22	0	1	1	1	1	1	7	5,093	127	5	4,881	49,397
1964	20	22	0	0	0	2	0	1	6	3,551	14	1	3,662	9,913
1965	21	30	0	1	1	1	4	1	9	5,224	209	2	3,427	11,750
1966	29	31	1	1	2	1	0	1	5	4,306	592	5	3,639	11,880
1967	19	19	0	0	0	0	1	3	1	3,587	36	3	3,251	17,332
1968	22	17	0	0	0	1	1	3	5	4,547	1	1	4,381	17,785
1969	NR	1	0	0	0	0	0	0	1	152	28	1	404	1,675
1970	NR	5	0	0	0	0	2	0	0	819	7	2	1,540	11,365
1971	NR	15	0	2	3	0	1	0	3	3,783	258	7	3,255	18,965

Year	Rank	Starts	Poles	Finish 1	2	3	4	5	6–10	Laps	Laps Led	Races Led	Miles	$

Tiny Lund *continued*

Year	Rank	Starts	Poles	1	2	3	4	5	6–10	Laps	Laps Led	Races Led	Miles	$
1972	104	4	0	0	0	0	0	0	0	638	0	0	704	2,345
1973	94	5	0	0	0	0	0	0	0	388	0	0	410	4,420
1975	116	1	0	0	0	0	0	0	0	6	0	0	16	620
Lifetime		303	6	5	9	11	16	13	65	55,735	1,503	31	47,161	$185,703

Dave Lundman

David Lundman
    Racing Hometown: Libertyville, IL

Year	Rank	Starts	Poles	1	2	3	4	5	6–10	Laps	Laps Led	Races Led	Miles	$
1956	207	1	0	0	0	0	0	0	0		0	0		60
Lifetime		1	0	0	0	0	0	0	0		0	0		$60

Leon Lundy

Leon Lundy
    Racing Hometown: Philadelphia, PA

Year	Rank	Starts	Poles	1	2	3	4	5	6–10	Laps	Laps Led	Races Led	Miles	$
1953	71	1	0	0	0	0	0	0	0		0	0		75
1954	184	1	0	0	0	0	0	0	0	192	0	0	192	50
1955	NR	1	0	0	0	0	0	0	0	193	0	0	193	150
Lifetime		3	0	0	0	0	0	0	0	385	0	0	385	$275

Tom Lupo

Thomas Lupo
    Racing Hometown: Green Sea, SC

Year	Rank	Starts	Poles	1	2	3	4	5	6–10	Laps	Laps Led	Races Led	Miles	$
1956	235	1	0	0	0	0	0	0	0	313	0	0	430	50
Lifetime		1	0	0	0	0	0	0	0	313	0	0	430	$50

Frank Luptow

Frank Luptow
    B: 1914   D: 9/21/1952   *Killed at Lakewood Speedway in Atlanta during AAA Stock car race.*
    Racing Hometown: Tampa, FL

Year	Rank	Starts	Poles	1	2	3	4	5	6–10	Laps	Laps Led	Races Led	Miles	$
1950	128	1	0	0	0	0	0	0	0	43	0	0	179	50
1951	69	4	0	0	0	0	0	1	0	161	0	0	125	250
Lifetime		5	0	0	0	0	0	1	0	204	0	0	305	$300

Louis Luther

Louis Luther

Year	Rank	Starts	Poles	1	2	3	4	5	6–10	Laps	Laps Led	Races Led	Miles	$
1951	N/A	1	0	0	0	0	0	0	0		0	0		25
Lifetime		1	0	0	0	0	0	0	0		0	0		$25

Bill Lutz

William F. Lutz
    B: 4/30/1929
    Racing Hometown: Louisville, KY

Year	Rank	Starts	Poles	1	2	3	4	5	6–10	Laps	Laps Led	Races Led	Miles	$
1956	NR	1	0	0	0	0	0	0	0	63	0	0	32	50
1957	75	1	0	0	0	0	0	0	1		0	0		600
1960	129	2	0	0	0	0	0	0	0	88	0	0	220	250
Lifetime		4	0	0	0	0	0	0	1	151	0	0	252	$900

Harold Lutz

Harold Lutz
    Killed in highway crash 10/1/56 age 36.
    Racing Hometown: Louisville, KY

Year	Rank	Starts	Poles	1	2	3	4	5	6–10	Laps	Laps Led	Races Led	Miles	$
1954	NR	1	0	0	0	0	0	0	0	11	0	0	17	50
Lifetime		1	0	0	0	0	0	0	0	11	0	0	17	$50

Ralph Lyden

Ralph Lyden
    Racing Hometown: Indianapolis, IN

Year	Rank	Starts	Poles	1	2	3	4	5	6–10	Laps	Laps Led	Races Led	Miles	$
1950	129T	1	0	0	0	0	0	0	0		0	0		0
Lifetime		1	0	0	0	0	0	0	0		0	0		$0

Norman Lynch

Norman Lynch
    Racing Hometown: Columbus, OH

Year	Rank	Starts	Poles	1	2	3	4	5	6–10	Laps	Laps Led	Races Led	Miles	$
1952	178	1	0	0	0	0	0	0	0	130	0	0	130	25
Lifetime		1	0	0	0	0	0	0	0	130	0	0	130	$25

Year	Rank	Starts	Poles	Finish 1	2	3	4	5	6–10	Laps	Laps Led	Races Led	Miles	$

Sandy Lynch

Sandy Neal Lynch
B: 5/24/1922
Racing Hometown: Atlanta, GA

Year	Rank	Starts	Poles	1	2	3	4	5	6–10	Laps	Laps Led	Races Led	Miles	$
1951	N/A	2	0	0	0	0	0	0	0	215	0	0	269	25
Lifetime		2	0	0	0	0	0	0	0	215	0	0	269	$25

L. Lyndstrom

L. Lyndstrom

Year	Rank	Starts	Poles	1	2	3	4	5	6–10	Laps	Laps Led	Races Led	Miles	$
1951	NR	1	0	0	0	0	0	0	0	99	0	0	25	60
Lifetime		1	0	0	0	0	0	0	0	99	0	0	25	$60

Clyde Lynn

Clyde Lynn
B: 3/3/1936
Racing Hometown: Christiansburg, VA

Year	Rank	Starts	Poles	1	2	3	4	5	6–10	Laps	Laps Led	Races Led	Miles	$
1965	41	24	0	0	0	0	0	0	9	4,522	0	0	2,067	4,545
1966	20	40	0	0	1	0	0	0	14	9,384	0	0	6,033	13,222
1967	13	44	0	0	0	0	2	3	17	9,556	0	0	6,551	19,520
1968	4	49	0	0	0	0	1	1	23	12,013	0	0	8,862	29,226
1969	87	3	0	0	0	0	0	0	1	688	0	0	386	1,915
1970	NR	1	0	0	0	0	0	0	1	386	0	0	241	625
1971	80	3	0	0	0	0	0	0	0	508	0	0	271	1,080
1976	96T	1	0	0	0	0	0	0	0	123	0	0	66	735
Lifetime		165	0	0	1	0	3	4	65	37,180	0	0	24,476	$70,868

John Lyons

John Lyons

Year	Rank	Starts	Poles	1	2	3	4	5	6–10	Laps	Laps Led	Races Led	Miles	$
1971	NR	1	0	0	0	0	0	0	0	35	0	0	92	700
Lifetime		1	0	0	0	0	0	0	0	35	0	0	92	$700

Paul Lyons

Paul Lyons

Year	Rank	Starts	Poles	1	2	3	4	5	6–10	Laps	Laps Led	Races Led	Miles	$
1961	NR	1	0	0	0	0	0	0	0	4	0	0	1	0
1962	NR	1	0	0	0	0	0	0	0	9	0	0	2	25
Lifetime		2	0	0	0	0	0	0	0	13	0	0	3	$25

Art MacBurney

Arthur MacBurney

Year	Rank	Starts	Poles	1	2	3	4	5	6–10	Laps	Laps Led	Races Led	Miles	$
1955	122	1	0	0	0	0	0	0	0	204	0	0	204	175
Lifetime		1	0	0	0	0	0	0	0	204	0	0	204	$175

Dave MacDonald

David MacDonald
B: 7/23/1937   D: 5/30/1964   *Killed in Indianapolis 500.*
Racing Hometown: El Monte, CA

Year	Rank	Starts	Poles	1	2	3	4	5	6–10	Laps	Laps Led	Races Led	Miles	$
1963	42	2	0	0	1	0	0	0	0	323	92	1	872	5,330
1964	29	5	0	0	1	0	0	0	2	661	0	0	1,599	9,195
Lifetime		7	0	0	2	0	0	0	2	984	92	1	2,471	$14,525

Eddie MacDonald

Edward MacDonald
Racing Hometown: Tifton, GA

Year	Rank	Starts	Poles	1	2	3	4	5	6–10	Laps	Laps Led	Races Led	Miles	$
1966	54	3	0	0	0	0	0	0	1	492	0	0	870	2,110
Lifetime		3	0	0	0	0	0	0	1	492	0	0	870	$2,110

Randy MacDonald

Randall MacDonald
B: 7/26/1962
Racing Hometown: Oshawa, Ont, Canada

Year	Rank	Starts	Poles	1	2	3	4	5	6–10	Laps	Laps Led	Races Led	Miles	$
1994	65	1	0	0	0	0	0	0	0	466	0	0	474	8,200
1996	50	3	0	0	0	0	0	0	0	680	0	0	1,285	31,610
1997	69	1	0	0	0	0	0	0	0	148	0	0	157	18,600
Lifetime		5	0	0	0	0	0	0	0	1,294	0	0	1,915	$58,410

Year	Rank	Starts	Poles	Finish 1	2	3	4	5	6–10	Laps	Laps Led	Races Led	Miles	$

Johnny Mackison

John Mackison
B: 9/27/1935
Racing Hometown: Delta, PA

Year	Rank	Starts	Poles	1	2	3	4	5	6–10	Laps	Laps Led	Races Led	Miles	$
1957	27	5	0	0	0	0	0	1	1	769	0	0	693	1,330
1958	29	11	0	0	0	1	0	1	1	1,423	0	0	1,074	1,255
Lifetime		16	0	0	0	1	0	2	2	2,192	0	0	1,766	$2,585

Dave Mader

David Mader Jr.
B: 10/19/1930
Racing Hometown: Birmingham, AL

Year	Rank	Starts	Poles	1	2	3	4	5	6–10	Laps	Laps Led	Races Led	Miles	$
1961	61	6	0	0	0	0	0	0	0	638	0	0	791	880
Lifetime		6	0	0	0	0	0	0	0	638	0	0	791	$880

Dave Mader III

David Mader III
B: 6/30/1955
Racing Hometown: Maylene, AL

Year	Rank	Starts	Poles	1	2	3	4	5	6–10	Laps	Laps Led	Races Led	Miles	$
1988	72	1	0	0	0	0	0	0	0	271	0	0	144	1,565
1989	75T	1	0	0	0	0	0	0	0	480	0	0	488	2,675
1990	75	1	0	0	0	0	0	0	0	323	0	0	492	4,525
1991	61	2	0	0	0	0	0	0	0	515	0	0	753	7,910
1992	45	5	0	0	0	0	0	0	0	1,387	7	1	1,389	69,635
Lifetime		10	0	0	0	0	0	0	0	2,976	7	1	3,266	$86,310

Paul Magee

Paul Magee
Racing Hometown: Scio, OH

Year	Rank	Starts	Poles	1	2	3	4	5	6–10	Laps	Laps Led	Races Led	Miles	$
1952	114T	1	0	0	0	0	0	0	0	173	0	0	87	25
Lifetime		1	0	0	0	0	0	0	0	173	0	0	87	$25

Jocko Maggiacomo

Chauncey Maggiacomo
B: 11/30/1947
Racing Hometown: Poukeepsie, NY

Year	Rank	Starts	Poles	1	2	3	4	5	6–10	Laps	Laps Led	Races Led	Miles	$
1977	80	3	0	0	0	0	0	0	0	467	0	0	806	2,080
1978	105T	1	0	0	0	0	0	0	0	45	0	0	113	815
1979	106T	1	0	0	0	0	0	0	0	172	0	0	430	1,105
1980	80	2	0	0	0	0	0	0	0	280	0	0	283	1,615
1981	98T	1	0	0	0	0	0	0	0	189	0	0	189	540
1982	61	4	0	0	0	0	0	0	0	411	0	0	546	3,525
1983	60	3	0	0	0	0	0	0	0	312	0	0	722	3,850
1986	96	2	0	0	0	0	0	0	0	14	0	0	35	2,695
1987	62	3	0	0	0	0	0	0	0	233	0	0	583	4,885
1988	57	3	0	0	0	0	0	0	0	125	0	0	321	4,755
Lifetime		23	0	0	0	0	0	0	0	2,248	0	0	4,027	$25,865

Mike Magill

Michael Magill
B: 2/8/1920
Racing Hometown: Haddonville, NJ

Year	Rank	Starts	Poles	1	2	3	4	5	6–10	Laps	Laps Led	Races Led	Miles	$
1952	NR	2	0	0	0	0	0	0	0	50	0	0	50	25
1953	38	3	0	0	0	0	0	0	0	244	0	0	336	235
Lifetime		5	0	0	0	0	0	0	0	294	0	0	386	$260

Emory Mahon

Emory Mahon
Racing Hometown: Warren, PA

Year	Rank	Starts	Poles	1	2	3	4	5	6–10	Laps	Laps Led	Races Led	Miles	$
1955	117	2	0	0	0	0	0	0	1	256	0	0	165	200
1957	NR	1	0	0	0	0	0	0	0	3	0	0	3	50
1958	NR	2	0	0	0	0	1	0	0	149	0	0	50	270
Lifetime		5	0	0	0	0	1	0	1	408	0	0	218	$520

Chuck Mahoney

Charles Mahoney
B: 3/3/1920   D: 7/20/1999
Racing Hometown: Rome, NY

Year	Rank	Starts	Poles	1	2	3	4	5	6–10	Laps	Laps Led	Races Led	Miles	$
1949	71	1	0	0	0	0	0	0	0		0	0		0
1950	7	11	1	0	1	1	0	1	3	705	18	1	638	2,250

Year	Rank	Starts	Poles	Finish						Laps	Laps Led	Races Led	Miles	$
				1	2	3	4	5	6–10					

Chuck Mahoney *continued*

Year	Rank	Starts	Poles	1	2	3	4	5	6–10	Laps	Laps Led	Races Led	Miles	$
1951	N/A	1	0	0	0	0	0	0	1		0	0		100
1952	203	1	0	0	0	0	0	0	0		0	0		25
1956	167	2	0	0	0	0	0	0	0	219	0	0	110	200
Lifetime		16	1	0	1	1	0	1	4	924	18	1	748	$2,575

Jimmy Mairs

James Mairs
Racing Hometown: Wheaton, MD

Year	Rank	Starts	Poles	1	2	3	4	5	6–10	Laps	Laps Led	Races Led	Miles	$
1956	283	1	0	0	0	0	0	0	0		0	0		0
1959	NR	1	0	0	0	0	0	0	0	202	0	0	101	75
1961	89	3	0	0	0	0	0	0	0	293	0	0	73	510
Lifetime		5	0	0	0	0	0	0	0	495	0	0	174	$585

Bill Majot

William E. Majot
Racing Hometown: Toledo, OH

Year	Rank	Starts	Poles	1	2	3	4	5	6–10	Laps	Laps Led	Races Led	Miles	$
1951	N/A	3	0	0	0	0	0	0	0	233	0	0	233	75
Lifetime		3	0	0	0	0	0	0	0	233	0	0	233	$75

Jim Malloy

James Malloy
B: 5/23/1932   D: 5/18/1972   *Died of injuries suffered practicing for Indy 500 (5/14/72).*
Racing Hometown: Denver, CO

Year	Rank	Starts	Poles	1	2	3	4	5	6–10	Laps	Laps Led	Races Led	Miles	$
1966	NR	1	0	0	0	0	0	0	0	37	0	0	93	100
Lifetime		1	0	0	0	0	0	0	0	37	0	0	93	$100

Art Malone

Arthur Malone
B: 6/3/1936
Racing Hometown: Lutz, FL

Year	Rank	Starts	Poles	1	2	3	4	5	6–10	Laps	Laps Led	Races Led	Miles	$
1961	100	1	0	0	0	0	0	0	1	484	0	0	242	500
1962	65	1	0	0	0	0	0	0	1	95	0	0	238	600
Lifetime		2	0	0	0	0	0	0	2	579	0	0	480	$1,100

Bob Malzahn

Robert Malzahn
B: 1931
Racing Hometown: Miami, FL

Year	Rank	Starts	Poles	1	2	3	4	5	6–10	Laps	Laps Led	Races Led	Miles	$
1958	NR	1	0	0	0	0	0	0	0	33	0	0	33	0
Lifetime		1	0	0	0	0	0	0	0	33	0	0	33	$0

Bill Mann

William Mann
Racing Hometown: Gothenburg, NE

Year	Rank	Starts	Poles	1	2	3	4	5	6–10	Laps	Laps Led	Races Led	Miles	$
1953	97T	1	0	0	0	0	0	0	0		0	0		25
Lifetime		1	0	0	0	0	0	0	0		0	0		$25

Larry Mann

Lawrence Mann
D: 9/14/1952   *Killed in NASCAR race @ Langhorne*
Racing Hometown: Yonkers, NY

Year	Rank	Starts	Poles	1	2	3	4	5	6–10	Laps	Laps Led	Races Led	Miles	$
1952	NR	6	0	0	0	0	0	0	0	767	0	0	632	135
Lifetime		6	0	0	0	0	0	0	0	767	0	0	632	$135

John Manning

John Manning
Racing Hometown: Axton, VA

Year	Rank	Starts	Poles	1	2	3	4	5	6–10	Laps	Laps Led	Races Led	Miles	$
1950	112T	1	0	0	0	0	0	0	0	95	0	0	48	0
Lifetime		1	0	0	0	0	0	0	0	95	0	0	48	$0

Larry Manning

Lawrence N. Manning
B: 10/4/1942
Racing Hometown: Salisbury, NC

Year	Rank	Starts	Poles	1	2	3	4	5	6–10	Laps	Laps Led	Races Led	Miles	$
1963	29	22	0	0	0	0	1	0	8	5,060	0	0	2,931	5,405
1964	75	5	0	0	0	0	0	0	3	971	0	0	438	910
1965	NR	10	0	0	0	0	0	0	1	1,683	0	0	1,062	2,465
1966	39	13	0	0	0	0	1	0	0	2,769	0	0	1,689	3,920

Year	Rank	Starts	Poles	Finish 1	2	3	4	5	6–10	Laps	Laps Led	Races Led	Miles	$

Larry Manning *continued*

Year	Rank	Starts	Poles	1	2	3	4	5	6–10	Laps	Laps Led	Races Led	Miles	$
1967	79	6	0	0	0	0	0	0	0	630	0	0	508	2,575
1968	41	12	0	0	0	0	0	0	0	2,151	0	0	2,257	6,995
1970	100	1	0	0	0	0	0	0	0	83	0	0	52	755
1974	135	1	0	0	0	0	0	0	0	1	0	0	1	580
Lifetime		70	0	0	0	0	2	0	12	13,348	0	0	8,937	$23,605

Skip Manning

Skip Manning
B: 4/23/1945
Racing Hometown: Bogalusa, LA

Year	Rank	Starts	Poles	1	2	3	4	5	6–10	Laps	Laps Led	Races Led	Miles	$
1975	61	5	0	0	0	0	0	0	0	995	0	0	1,794	9,705
1976	18	27	0	0	0	0	0	0	4	6,913	0	0	8,299	61,537
1977	14	28	0	0	0	1	0	0	7	7,533	13	1	8,355	111,317
1978	29	17	0	0	0	0	1	0	3	4,410	0	0	5,486	55,470
1979	91	2	0	0	0	0	0	0	0	182	0	0	326	5,880
Lifetime		79	0	0	0	1	1	0	14	20,033	13	1	24,260	$243,909

George Mantooth

George Edward Mantooth
B: 6/7/1925   D: 4/9/1995
Racing Hometown: Concord, NC

Year	Rank	Starts	Poles	1	2	3	4	5	6–10	Laps	Laps Led	Races Led	Miles	$
1949	NR	1	0	0	0	0	0	0	0		0	0		0
1956	302	1	0	0	0	0	0	0	0	43	0	0	22	0
Lifetime		2	0	0	0	0	0	0	0	43	0	0	22	$0

Johnny Mantz

John Mantz
B: 9/18/1918   D: 10/25/1972   *Killed in highway crash.*
Racing Hometown: Long Beach, CA

Year	Rank	Starts	Poles	1	2	3	4	5	6–10	Laps	Laps Led	Races Led	Miles	$
1950	6	3	0	1	0	0	0	0	1	400	351	1	500	10,810
1951	21	6	0	0	1	1	0	0	2	532	28	1	454	2,025
1955	116	2	0	0	0	0	0	0	1	148	0	0	171	245
1956	98	1	0	0	0	1	0	0	0	79	0	0	198	1,130
Lifetime		12	0	1	1	2	0	0	4	1,159	379	2	1,323	$14,210

Dave Marburger

David Marburger

Year	Rank	Starts	Poles	1	2	3	4	5	6–10	Laps	Laps Led	Races Led	Miles	$
1959	NR	1	0	0	0	0	0	0	0	22	0	0	11	0
Lifetime		1	0	0	0	0	0	0	0	22	0	0	11	$0

Dave Marcis

David A. Marcis
B: 3/1/1941
Racing Hometown: Wausau, WI

Year	Rank	Starts	Poles	1	2	3	4	5	6–10	Laps	Laps Led	Races Led	Miles	$
1968	34	10	0	0	0	0	0	0	2	3,240	0	0	3,179	7,099
1969	19	37	0	0	0	1	2	0	8	7,099	22	3	6,833	32,383
1970	9	47	0	0	0	3	0	4	8	8,909	14	1	8,041	41,111
1971	21	29	2	0	1	1	4	3	5	6,460	331	8	6,690	37,382
1972	15	27	0	0	0	2	1	2	6	6,708	4	2	7,522	45,012
1973	24	23	0	0	0	0	1	2	3	4,905	0	0	5,457	30,253
1974	6	30	0	0	0	0	2	4	12	8,658	12	2	9,967	83,377
1975	2	30	4	1	1	5	6	3	2	8,324	458	17	9,790	240,646
1976	6	30	7	3	0	1	2	3	7	8,355	893	20	9,733	21,850
1977	25	18	0	0	0	0	4	1	2	4,386	92	7	5,499	72,605
1978	5	30	0	0	1	3	8	2	10	9,672	115	12	10,993	205,871
1979	20	25	0	0	0	0	0	1	5	6,842	20	4	7,635	56,434
1980	9	31	0	0	0	1	2	1	10	9,012	94	14	9,791	150,165
1981	9	31	1	0	0	2	1	1	5	8,004	178	15	9,256	162,213
1982	6	30	0	1	1	0	0	0	12	8,370	56	10	9,642	249,027
1983	11	30	0	0	0	0	0	0	7	7,771	24	6	9,171	306,355
1984	13	30	0	0	0	0	3	0	6	9,383	30	5	10,387	330,766
1985	18	28	0	0	0	0	0	0	5	7,319	30	4	8,737	173,467
1986	17	29	0	0	0	0	0	1	3	7,316	63	11	8,522	220,461
1987	18	29	0	0	0	2	0	0	5	6,880	84	9	8,751	256,354
1988	19	29	0	0	0	0	0	0	2	8,278	62	7	9,618	212,485
1989	25	27	0	0	0	0	0	0	1	7,866	16	5	9,986	195,161
1990	21	29	0	0	0	0	0	0	0	8,940	8	4	10,732	242,724
1991	29	27	0	0	0	0	0	0	1	7,211	3	3	9,024	219,760

Year	Rank	Starts	Poles	Finish 1	2	3	4	5	6–10	Laps	Laps Led	Races Led	Miles	$

Dave Marcis *continued*

Year	Rank	Starts	Poles	1	2	3	4	5	6–10	Laps	Laps Led	Races Led	Miles	$
1992	29	29	0	0	0	0	0	0	0	6,759	0	0	8,498	218,045
1993	33	23	0	0	0	0	0	0	0	6,233	14	3	7,819	202,305
1994	36	23	0	0	0	0	0	0	1	5,914	17	4	7,762	261,650
1995	35	28	0	0	0	0	0	0	0	7,318	3	2	9,225	337,853
1996	38	27	0	0	0	0	0	0	0	7,202	20	8	8,699	435,177
1997	42	19	0	0	0	0	0	0	0	5,246	0	0	6,703	427,364
1998	45	13	0	0	0	0	0	0	0	3,378	13	3	4,688	444,946
1999	42	20	0	0	0	0	0	0	0	5,354	9	4	7,362	731,221
2000	46	11	0	0	0	0	0	0	0	3,172	14	2	4,059	405,572
2001	54	3	0	0	0	0	0	0	0	837	0	0	1,149	118,700
2002	81T	1	0	0	0	0	0	0	0	79	0	0	198	112,575
Lifetime		883	14	5	4	21	36	28	128	231,400	2,699	195	271,118	$7,288,369

Howard Mark

Howard Mark
  Racing Hometown: Deland, FL

Year	Rank	Starts	Poles	1	2	3	4	5	6–10	Laps	Laps Led	Races Led	Miles	$
1986	116T	1	0	0	0	0	0	0	0	14	0	0	14	875
Lifetime		1	0	0	0	0	0	0	0	14	0	0	14	$875

Curtis Markham

Curtis Markham
  B: 9/21/1959
  Racing Hometown: Fredericksburg, VA

Year	Rank	Starts	Poles	1	2	3	4	5	6–10	Laps	Laps Led	Races Led	Miles	$
1987	90	3	0	0	0	0	0	0	0	578	0	0	488	8,245
1994	78	1	0	0	0	0	0	0	0	32	0	0	49	8,325
Lifetime		4	0	0	0	0	0	0	0	610	0	0	536	$16,570

Peck Markota

Peck Markota
  Racing Hometown: Gardena, CA

Year	Rank	Starts	Poles	1	2	3	4	5	6–10	Laps	Laps Led	Races Led	Miles	$
1958	87	1	0	0	0	0	0	0	0	98	0	0	258	100
Lifetime		1	0	0	0	0	0	0	0	98	0	0	258	$100

Coo Coo Marlin

Clifton Burton Marlin
  B: 1/3/1932
  Racing Hometown: Columbia, TN

Year	Rank	Starts	Poles	1	2	3	4	5	6–10	Laps	Laps Led	Races Led	Miles	$
1966	103	1	0	0	0	0	0	0	1	375	0	0	188	375
1967	88	3	0	0	0	0	0	0	0	158	0	0	155	755
1969	52	7	0	0	0	0	0	0	2	993	0	0	1,285	5,680
1970	38	13	0	0	0	0	0	0	4	2,531	0	0	3,825	14,799
1971	49	12	0	0	0	0	0	0	0	1,495	0	0	2,336	9,085
1972	25	20	0	0	0	1	1	0	3	4,092	31	5	5,383	28,924
1973	22	21	0	0	0	1	0	0	7	5,454	16	3	5,948	29,997
1974	22	23	0	0	0	0	1	0	4	5,323	28	7	6,082	41,759
1975	20	23	0	0	0	1	0	3	7	5,199	25	5	6,400	60,013
1976	28	12	0	0	0	0	0	0	6	3,074	0	0	4,309	39,485
1977	34	11	0	0	0	0	1	0	4	2,930	1	1	4,210	42,450
1978	36	9	0	0	0	0	0	0	2	1,518	4	2	2,372	19,415
1979	33	7	0	0	0	0	0	0	2	907	0	0	1,989	27,540
1980	54	3	0	0	0	0	0	0	0	377	0	0	978	8,400
Lifetime		165	0	0	0	3	3	3	42	34,426	105	23	45,460	$328,677

Jack Marlin

Jack Marlin

Year	Rank	Starts	Poles	1	2	3	4	5	6–10	Laps	Laps Led	Races Led	Miles	$
1968	NR	1	0	0	0	0	0	0	1	237	0	0	119	300
Lifetime		1	0	0	0	0	0	0	1	237	0	0	119	$300

Sterling Marlin

Sterling Marlin
  B: 6/30/1957
  Racing Hometown: Columbia, TN

Year	Rank	Starts	Poles	1	2	3	4	5	6–10	Laps	Laps Led	Races Led	Miles	$
1976	101	1	0	0	0	0	0	0	0	55	0	0	33	565
1978	67	2	0	0	0	0	0	0	1	591	0	0	708	10,320
1979	85	1	0	0	0	0	0	0	0	341	11	1	203	505
1980	49	5	0	0	0	0	0	0	2	1,311	0	0	1,762	29,810
1981	93	2	0	0	0	0	0	0	0	437	0	0	435	1,955
1982	NR	1	0	0	0	0	0	0	0	256	0	0	384	3,615

Year	Rank	Starts	Poles	Finish						Laps	Laps Led	Races Led	Miles	$
				1	2	3	4	5	6–10					

Sterling Marlin *continued*

Year	Rank	Starts	Poles	1	2	3	4	5	6–10	Laps	Laps Led	Races Led	Miles	$
1983	19	30	0	0	0	0	0	0	1	8,053	0	0	9,167	148,253
1984	37	14	0	0	0	0	0	0	2	2,737	0	0	3,983	54,355
1985	37	8	0	0	0	0	0	0	0	1,321	1	1	2,348	31,155
1986	36	10	0	0	1	0	1	0	2	1,738	21	3	3,225	113,070
1987	11	29	0	0	0	1	2	1	4	8,356	68	6	10,305	306,412
1988	10	29	0	0	1	1	0	4	7	8,798	332	13	10,389	521,464
1989	12	29	0	0	1	1	0	2	9	8,840	29	6	10,580	369,900
1990	14	29	0	0	0	1	1	3	5	8,263	71	6	10,079	369,167
1991	7	29	2	0	2	1	1	3	9	9,205	201	8	11,210	633,690
1992	10	29	5	0	3	0	1	2	7	8,462	218	8	10,287	649,048
1993	15	30	0	0	1	0	0	0	7	9,153	345	7	11,222	628,835
1994	14	31	1	1	1	1	0	2	6	9,184	144	11	10,842	1,140,683
1995	3	31	1	3	2	0	3	1	13	9,729	475	12	11,939	2,253,502
1996	8	31	0	2	0	1	1	1	5	8,877	331	10	10,583	1,588,425
1997	25	32	0	0	0	1	0	1	4	8,584	71	7	10,836	1,301,370
1998	13	32	0	0	0	0	0	0	6	9,154	342	6	12,012	1,350,161
1999	16	34	1	0	0	0	2	0	3	9,711	56	9	12,635	1,797,416
2000	19	34	0	0	1	0	0	0	6	9,459	82	6	12,097	1,819,644
2001	3	36	1	2	3	2	1	4	8	10,723	567	24	14,102	4,517,634
2002	18	29	2	2	1	2	2	1	6	7,844	451	12	10,650	4,228,889
Lifetime		568	13	10	17	12	15	25	113	161,182	3,816	156	202,017	$23,869,843

Gene Marmor

Gene Marmor
  Racing Hometown: Northlake, IL

Year	Rank	Starts	Poles	1	2	3	4	5	6–10	Laps	Laps Led	Races Led	Miles	$
1960	67	4	0	0	0	0	0	0	1	732	0	0	836	775
Lifetime		4	0	0	0	0	0	0	1	732	0	0	836	$775

Ken Marriott

Kenneth Marriott
  B: 1920
  Racing Hometown: Baltimore, MD

Year	Rank	Starts	Poles	1	2	3	4	5	6–10	Laps	Laps Led	Races Led	Miles	$
1949	73	1	0	0	0	0	0	0	0	169	0	0	169	50
1950	NR	1	0	0	0	0	0	0	0		0	0		0
1953	NR	1	0	0	0	0	0	0	0		0	0		40
1957	NR	1	0	0	0	0	0	0	1	281	0	0	281	600
1959	NR	1	0	0	0	0	0	0	0	1	0	0	3	100
Lifetime		5	0	0	0	0	0	0	1	451	0	0	453	$790

Jack Marsh

Jack Marsh

Year	Rank	Starts	Poles	1	2	3	4	5	6–10	Laps	Laps Led	Races Led	Miles	$
1957	79	3	0	0	0	0	0	0	1	489	0	0	262	365
Lifetime		3	0	0	0	0	0	0	1	489	0	0	262	$365

Sam Marshall

Samuel Marshall
  Racing Hometown: Jacksonville, FL

Year	Rank	Starts	Poles	1	2	3	4	5	6–10	Laps	Laps Led	Races Led	Miles	$
1949	NR	1	0	0	0	0	0	0	0		0	0		0
Lifetime		1	0	0	0	0	0	0	0		0	0		$0

Bobby Marshman

Robert Marshman
  B: 9/24/1936 D: 12/4/1964 *Killed in test session @ Phoenix Int'l Raceway.*
  Racing Hometown: Pottstown, PA

Year	Rank	Starts	Poles	1	2	3	4	5	6–10	Laps	Laps Led	Races Led	Miles	$
1964	NR	2	0	0	0	0	0	0	1	56	0	0	140	925
Lifetime		2	0	0	0	0	0	0	1	56	0	0	140	$925

Dick Martin

Richard Martin
  Racing Hometown: Toledo, OH

Year	Rank	Starts	Poles	1	2	3	4	5	6–10	Laps	Laps Led	Races Led	Miles	$
1952	109	2	0	0	0	0	0	0	0	72	0	0	36	50
Lifetime		2	0	0	0	0	0	0	0	72	0	0	36	$50

Joe Martin

Joseph H. Martin
  Racing Hometown: Lewis, DE

Year	Rank	Starts	Poles	1	2	3	4	5	6–10	Laps	Laps Led	Races Led	Miles	$
1954	NR	1	0	0	0	0	0	0	0	85	0	0	85	0
Lifetime		1	0	0	0	0	0	0	0	85	0	0	85	$0

Year	Rank	Starts	Poles	Finish 1	2	3	4	5	6–10	Laps	Laps Led	Races Led	Miles	$

John Martin

John Martin
B: 3/20/1939
Racing Hometown: Irvine, CA

Year	Rank	Starts	Poles	1	2	3	4	5	6–10	Laps	Laps Led	Races Led	Miles	$
1967	NR	2	0	0	0	0	0	0	0	154	0	0	363	1,120
1974	58	4	0	0	0	0	0	0	0	283	0	0	639	4,465
1975	NR	1	0	0	0	0	0	0	0	53	0	0	133	850
Lifetime		7	0	0	0	0	0	0	0	490	0	0	1,134	$6,435

Mark Martin

Mark Martin
B: 1/9/1959
Racing Hometown: Batesville, AR

Year	Rank	Starts	Poles	1	2	3	4	5	6–10	Laps	Laps Led	Races Led	Miles	$
1981	42	5	2	0	0	1	0	0	1	1,478	76	2	829	13,950
1982	14	30	0	0	0	0	0	2	6	7,449	4	3	8,321	142,710
1983	30	16	0	0	0	1	0	0	2	4,130	1	1	5,545	99,055
1986	48	5	0	0	0	0	0	0	0	1,342	0	0	1,955	20,515
1987	101T	1	0	0	0	0	0	0	0	68	0	0	102	3,550
1988	15	29	1	0	1	0	2	0	7	7,595	120	4	9,182	223,630
1989	3	29	6	1	5	6	1	1	4	9,010	480	16	10,718	622,878
1990	2	29	4	3	5	4	2	2	7	9,636	451	15	11,589	1,302,958
1991	6	29	5	1	1	5	4	3	3	8,903	663	15	10,777	1,039,991
1992	6	29	1	2	5	2	1	0	7	8,954	533	17	10,671	1,000,571
1993	3	30	5	5	3	1	1	2	7	9,381	1,388	20	11,107	1,657,662
1994	2	31	1	2	4	2	4	3	5	9,549	726	18	11,404	1,678,906
1995	4	31	4	4	1	4	1	3	9	9,393	739	14	11,428	1,893,519
1996	5	31	4	0	4	5	3	2	9	9,064	701	16	11,067	1,887,396
1997	3	32	3	4	2	4	2	4	8	9,599	796	20	12,354	2,532,484
1998	2	33	3	7	6	4	3	2	4	9,830	1,731	23	12,744	4,309,006
1999	3	34	1	2	4	5	5	3	7	9,903	701	25	12,848	3,509,744
2000	8	34	0	1	1	7	1	3	7	9,240	494	18	11,758	2,763,536
2001	12	36	2	0	0	0	2	1	12	10,138	190	19	13,681	3,797,006
2002	2	36	0	1	3	2	3	3	10	10,517	363	15	13,838	7,004,893
Lifetime		530	42	33	45	53	35	34	115	155,179	10,157	261	191,916	$35,503,960

Otis Martin

Otis Mason Martin
B: 3/1/1918
Racing Hometown: Bassett, VA

Year	Rank	Starts	Poles	1	2	3	4	5	6–10	Laps	Laps Led	Races Led	Miles	$
1949	35	4	0	0	0	0	0	0	1	66	0	0	33	200
1950	66	1	0	0	0	0	0	0	1	47	0	0	196	175
1951	N/A	2	0	0	0	0	0	0	0		0	0		50
1952	28	5	0	0	0	0	0	0	2	620	0	0	560	275
1953	22	8	0	0	0	0	0	0	2	519	0	0	608	610
1954	123	3	0	0	0	0	0	0	0	414	0	0	637	225
Lifetime		23	0	0	0	0	0	0	6	1,666	0	0	2,035	$1,535

Pee Wee Martin

Leonard Martin
B: 6/29/1922
Racing Hometown: Bassett, VA

Year	Rank	Starts	Poles	1	2	3	4	5	6–10	Laps	Laps Led	Races Led	Miles	$
1949	NR	1	0	0	0	0	0	0	0		0	0		0
1950	83	2	0	0	0	0	0	0	0	344	12	1	430	150
Lifetime		3	0	0	0	0	0	0	0	344	12	1	430	$150

Virgil Martin

Virgil Martin

Year	Rank	Starts	Poles	1	2	3	4	5	6–10	Laps	Laps Led	Races Led	Miles	$
1955	194	1	0	0	0	0	0	0	0	62	0	0	62	20
Lifetime		1	0	0	0	0	0	0	0	62	0	0	62	$20

Larry Marx

Lawrence Marx
Racing Hometown: Buffalo, NY

Year	Rank	Starts	Poles	1	2	3	4	5	6–10	Laps	Laps Led	Races Led	Miles	$
1956	NR	1	0	0	0	0	0	0	0	78	0	0	39	100
Lifetime		1	0	0	0	0	0	0	0	78	0	0	39	$100

George Masker

George Masker

Year	Rank	Starts	Poles	1	2	3	4	5	6–10	Laps	Laps Led	Races Led	Miles	$
1950	NR	1	0	0	0	0	0	0	0		0	0		0
Lifetime		1	0	0	0	0	0	0	0		0	0		0

Year	Rank	Starts	Poles	Finish 1	2	3	4	5	6–10	Laps	Laps Led	Races Led	Miles	$

Buck Mason

Buck Mason
Racing Hometown: Richmond, VA

Year	Rank	Starts	Poles	1	2	3	4	5	6–10	Laps	Laps Led	Races Led	Miles	$
1953	62	2	0	0	0	0	0	0	0		0	0		75
1954	151T	1	0	0	0	0	0	0	0	283	0	0	389	110
Lifetime		3	0	0	0	0	0	0	0	283	0	0	389	$185

Bill Massey

William Carl Massey
B: 1929   D: 8/22/1965   *Killed when hit in head with chair leg in tavern.*
Racing Hometown: Rural Hall, NC

Year	Rank	Starts	Poles	1	2	3	4	5	6–10	Laps	Laps Led	Races Led	Miles	$
1956	203T	1	0	0	0	0	0	0	0	176	0	0	88	100
1957	147	2	0	0	0	0	0	0	0	215	0	0	124	200
1960	120	1	0	0	0	0	0	0	0	71	0	0	18	130
Lifetime		4	0	0	0	0	0	0	0	462	0	0	229	$430

Ed Massey

Edsel Massey
Racing Hometown: Birmingham, AL

Year	Rank	Starts	Poles	1	2	3	4	5	6–10	Laps	Laps Led	Races Led	Miles	$
1951	N/A	3	0	0	0	0	0	0	1		0	0		150
1953	139	2	0	0	0	0	0	0	0		0	0		50
1954	172	1	0	0	0	0	0	0	0	127	0	0	191	50
1956	294T	1	0	0	0	0	0	0	0	76	0	0	38	0
Lifetime		7	0	0	0	0	0	0	1	203	0	0	229	$250

Jimmy Massey

James Massey
B: 12/1/1929
Racing Hometown: Mebane, NC

Year	Rank	Starts	Poles	1	2	3	4	5	6–10	Laps	Laps Led	Races Led	Miles	$
1955	13	11	0	0	0	1	1	2	4	1,906	0	0	1,721	3,510
1956	49	7	0	0	0	0	1	2	1	1,140	0	0	717	1,545
1957	NR	2	0	0	1	0	0	0	1	652	7	1	345	2,115
1958	32	9	1	0	0	0	0	1	2	1,612	0	0	1,114	1,625
1960	42	6	0	0	1	1	0	0	1	1,392	26	1	1,299	3,310
1963	38	15	0	0	0	0	1	0	7	3,179	0	0	1,433	2,870
1964	143	1	0	0	0	0	0	0	0		0	0		0
Lifetime		51	1	0	2	2	3	5	16	9,881	33	2	6,629	$14,975

Sam Massey

Samuel Massey
Racing Hometown: Atlanta, GA

Year	Rank	Starts	Poles	1	2	3	4	5	6–10	Laps	Laps Led	Races Led	Miles	$
1959	NR	1	0	0	0	0	0	0	0	73	0	0	73	110
Lifetime		1	0	0	0	0	0	0	0	73	0	0	73	$110

Bill Massuch

William Massuch
Racing Hometown: Lansing, MI

Year	Rank	Starts	Poles	1	2	3	4	5	6–10	Laps	Laps Led	Races Led	Miles	$
1969	74	1	0	0	0	0	0	0	0	157	0	0	314	1,075
Lifetime		1	0	0	0	0	0	0	0	157	0	0	314	$1,075

Rick Mast

Richard K. Mast
B: 3/4/1957
Racing Hometown: Rockbridge Baths, VA

Year	Rank	Starts	Poles	1	2	3	4	5	6–10	Laps	Laps Led	Races Led	Miles	$
1988	NR	2	0	0	0	0	0	0	0	512	2	1	527	9,190
1989	35	13	0	0	0	0	0	0	1	4,160	14	2	4,439	128,102
1990	31	20	0	0	0	0	0	0	1	5,335	0	0	5,842	112,875
1991	21	29	0	0	0	0	1	0	2	8,901	32	3	10,691	344,020
1992	22	29	1	0	0	0	0	0	1	8,121	0	0	9,984	350,740
1993	21	30	0	0	0	0	0	1	4	8,488	31	4	9,803	568,095
1994	18	31	1	0	1	3	0	0	6	8,756	166	8	10,754	733,361
1995	21	31	1	0	0	0	0	0	3	8,559	143	3	10,600	749,550
1996	18	31	0	0	0	0	1	0	4	8,972	1	1	10,937	924,559
1997	32	29	0	0	0	0	0	0	2	8,415	1	1	10,471	829,336
1998	33	30	1	0	0	0	0	0	1	7,667	61	2	9,655	894,327
1999	32	34	0	0	0	0	0	0	2	9,487	25	3	12,542	1,290,143
2000	33	29	0	0	0	0	0	0	2	8,185	1	1	11,055	1,156,427
2001	45	17	0	0	0	0	0	0	0	4,543	0	0	5,651	680,321
2002	47	9	0	0	0	0	0	0	0	3,033	0	0	3,364	469,843
Lifetime		364	4	0	1	3	2	1	29	103,134	477	29	126,316	$9,240,889

Year	Rank	Starts	Poles	Finish 1	2	3	4	5	6–10	Laps	Laps Led	Races Led	Miles	$

Gary Mathews

Gary Mathews
Racing Hometown: Fresno, CA

Year	Rank	Starts	Poles	1	2	3	4	5	6–10	Laps	Laps Led	Races Led	Miles	$
1974	123	1	0	0	0	0	0	0	0	37	0	0	97	725
1975	64	2	0	0	0	0	0	0	1	298	0	0	781	3,795
1976	90	2	0	0	0	0	0	0	0	209	0	0	548	2,410
1977	93T	1	0	0	0	0	0	0	0	91	0	0	238	1,225
Lifetime		6	0	0	0	0	0	0	1	635	0	0	1,664	$8,155

Gary Mathieson

Gary Mathieson
Racing Hometown: Norwalk, CT

Year	Rank	Starts	Poles	1	2	3	4	5	6–10	Laps	Laps Led	Races Led	Miles	$
1954	92	1	0	0	0	0	0	0	1	114	0	0	114	100
Lifetime		1	0	0	0	0	0	0	1	114	0	0	114	$100

Lyle Matlock

Lyle Matlock
Racing Hometown: Los Altos, CA

Year	Rank	Starts	Poles	1	2	3	4	5	6–10	Laps	Laps Led	Races Led	Miles	$
1956	222	2	1	0	0	0	0	0	0	142	0	0	73	50
1957	201T	1	0	0	0	0	0	0	0	47	0	0	24	0
Lifetime		3	1	0	0	0	0	0	0	189	0	0	97	$50

Bob Matson

Robert Matson (Bud)
Racing Hometown: Cleveland Heights, OH

Year	Rank	Starts	Poles	1	2	3	4	5	6–10	Laps	Laps Led	Races Led	Miles	$
1951	N/A	1	0	0	0	0	0	0	0		0	0		25
Lifetime		1	0	0	0	0	0	0	0		0	0		$25

Banjo Matthews

Edwin Keith Matthews
B: 2/14/1932
Racing Hometown: Asheville, NC

Year	Rank	Starts	Poles	1	2	3	4	5	6–10	Laps	Laps Led	Races Led	Miles	$
1952	22	3	0	0	0	0	0	1	0	667	0	0	628	1,000
1955	43	3	0	0	0	0	0	0	2	734	0	0	672	745
1956	117	1	0	0	0	0	0	0	0	149	0	0	224	200
1957	58	5	1	0	0	1	0	0	0	713	56	1	404	855
1958	95	3	0	0	0	0	0	0	0	90	0	0	93	190
1959	61	4	0	0	0	0	0	0	0	654	55	1	483	1,990
1960	10	12	0	0	0	0	0	0	4	1,894	9	1	2,815	15,617
1961	31	14	0	0	0	0	1	0	2	2,019	196	5	3,010	5,610
1962	31	5	2	0	1	0	0	0	1	532	145	3	1,098	11,375
1963	57	1	0	0	0	0	0	0	0	358	0	0	537	700
Lifetime		51	3	0	1	1	1	1	9	7,810	461	11	9,963	$38,282

Frank Matthews

Frank Matthews
Racing Hometown: Dallas, TX

Year	Rank	Starts	Poles	1	2	3	4	5	6–10	Laps	Laps Led	Races Led	Miles	$
1949	59	1	0	0	0	0	0	0	0		0	0		50
Lifetime		1	0	0	0	0	0	0	0		0	0		$50

Nace Mattingly

P.A. Mattingly
Racing Hometown: Leonardtown, MD

Year	Rank	Starts	Poles	1	2	3	4	5	6–10	Laps	Laps Led	Races Led	Miles	$
1955	36	3	0	0	0	0	0	1	0	696	0	0	653	700
1956	231	3	0	0	0	0	0	1	0	311	0	0	219	410
1957	103	4	0	0	0	0	0	0	0	658	0	0	614	400
1958	119	4	0	0	0	0	0	0	1	325	0	0	145	285
1960	NR	2	0	0	0	0	0	0	1	361	0	0	181	285
1963	108	1	0	0	0	0	0	0	1	288	0	0	108	240
Lifetime		17	0	0	0	0	0	2	3	2,639	0	0	1,921	$2,320

Bobby Mausgrover

Robert H. Mausgrover
B: 3/27/1940
Racing Hometown: Keokuk, IA

Year	Rank	Starts	Poles	1	2	3	4	5	6–10	Laps	Laps Led	Races Led	Miles	$
1967	90	4	0	0	0	0	0	0	1	610	0	0	448	1,800
1968	73	4	0	0	0	0	0	0	0	298	0	0	173	1,235
1969	51	13	0	0	0	0	0	0	0	1,192	0	0	995	5,305
1970	65	3	0	0	0	0	0	0	0	103	0	0	179	2,710
1971	52	12	0	0	0	0	0	0	0	1,418	0	0	1,562	6,140

Year	Rank	Starts	Poles	Finish 1	2	3	4	5	6–10	Laps	Laps Led	Races Led	Miles	$
Bobby Mausgrover *continued*														
1972	55	6	0	0	0	0	0	0	0	655	0	0	1,214	5,100
1973	60	4	0	0	0	0	0	0	0	678	0	0	1,000	3,510
Lifetime		46	0	0	0	0	0	0	1	4,954	0	0	5,571	$25,800

Dick May

Richard Shelton May
B: 11/7/1930
Racing Hometown: Watertown, NY

Year	Rank	Starts	Poles	1	2	3	4	5	6–10	Laps	Laps Led	Races Led	Miles	$
1970	44	16	0	0	0	0	0	0	0	1,028	0	0	689	4,510
1971	32	22	0	0	0	0	0	0	1	2,527	0	0	2,524	9,225
1972	44	6	0	0	0	0	0	0	1	955	0	0	1,793	5,370
1973	71	4	0	0	0	0	0	0	0	337	0	0	566	3,605
1974	75	2	0	0	0	0	0	0	0	350	0	0	924	3,310
1975	41	9	0	0	0	0	0	0	1	1,688	0	0	2,344	11,020
1976	25	19	0	0	0	0	0	0	0	4,643	0	0	5,486	29,425
1977	27	12	0	0	0	0	0	0	0	3,557	0	0	4,255	21,690
1978	15	28	0	0	0	0	0	0	2	7,221	0	0	8,622	65,291
1979	30	19	0	0	0	0	0	0	0	3,387	0	0	3,714	26,345
1980	32	21	0	0	0	0	0	0	2	5,767	0	0	6,361	42,945
1981	37	9	0	0	0	0	0	0	1	1,843	0	0	3,173	26,280
1982	55	8	0	0	0	0	0	0	0	1,930	0	0	2,522	16,810
1983	64	6	0	0	0	0	0	0	0	1,103	0	0	1,392	8,090
1984	48	3	0	0	0	0	0	0	0	1,274	0	0	1,282	5,325
1985	NR	2	0	0	0	0	0	0	0	665	0	0	636	2,825
Lifetime		186	0	0	0	0	0	0	8	38,275	0	0	46,282	$282,066

Gary Mayeda

Gary Mayeda
B: 1/19/1954
Racing Hometown: Riverside, CA

Year	Rank	Starts	Poles	1	2	3	4	5	6–10	Laps	Laps Led	Races Led	Miles	$
1984	NR	1	0	0	0	0	0	0	0	21	0	0	55	2,215
Lifetime		1	0	0	0	0	0	0	0	21	0	0	55	$2,215

Jim Mayes

James Mayes
Racing Hometown: Princeton, IN

Year	Rank	Starts	Poles	1	2	3	4	5	6–10	Laps	Laps Led	Races Led	Miles	$
1951	N/A	1	0	0	0	0	0	0	0		0	0		50
1952	196	1	0	0	0	0	0	0	0		0	0		25
Lifetime		2	0	0	0	0	0	0	0		0	0		$75

Jeremy Mayfield

Jeremy Mayfield
B: 5/27/1969
Racing Hometown: Owensboro, KY

Year	Rank	Starts	Poles	1	2	3	4	5	6–10	Laps	Laps Led	Races Led	Miles	$
1993	74T	1	0	0	0	0	0	0	0	324	0	0	486	4,830
1994	37	20	0	0	0	0	0	0	0	5,581	0	0	7,313	226,265
1995	31	27	0	0	0	0	0	0	1	7,943	79	3	10,441	436,805
1996	26	30	1	0	0	0	1	1	0	7,914	20	4	9,509	592,853
1997	13	32	0	0	0	0	1	2	5	9,541	3	2	12,326	1,067,203
1998	7	33	1	1	1	3	2	5	4	9,745	476	9	12,584	2,332,034
1999	11	34	0	0	1	2	0	2	7	9,870	221	11	12,931	2,125,227
2000	24	32	4	2	3	0	1	0	6	8,268	850	17	10,587	2,090,501
2001	35	28	0	0	0	3	1	1	2	7,286	60	3	9,906	2,682,603
2002	26	36	0	0	1	0	0	1	2	10,117	30	5	12,934	2,494,583
Lifetime		273	6	3	6	8	6	12	27	76,589	1,739	54	99,017	$14,052,904

Roy Mayne

Roy Elwood Mayne
B: 5/16/1935
Racing Hometown: Sumter, SC

Year	Rank	Starts	Poles	1	2	3	4	5	6–10	Laps	Laps Led	Races Led	Miles	$
1963	36	20	0	0	0	0	0	1	3	3,857	0	0	1,944	3,490
1964	43	14	0	0	0	0	0	1	1	2,207	0	0	1,457	4,705
1965	27	14	0	0	0	0	1	0	4	2,463	0	0	2,449	9,060
1966	25	18	0	0	0	0	0	1	4	4,052	0	0	4,051	9,940
1967	30	14	0	0	0	0	0	0	1	2,209	3	1	2,574	8,930
1968	115	1	0	0	0	0	0	0	0	77	0	0	116	775
1969	38	13	0	0	0	0	0	0	0	2,855	0	0	2,788	10,340

Year	Rank	Starts	Poles	Finish 1	2	3	4	5	6–10	Laps	Laps Led	Races Led	Miles	$

Roy Mayne *continued*

Year	Rank	Starts	Poles	1	2	3	4	5	6–10	Laps	Laps Led	Races Led	Miles	$
1970	29	16	0	0	0	0	0	0	3	3,731	0	0	4,764	16,910
1971	39	11	0	0	0	0	0	0	1	1,918	0	0	2,662	10,330
1972	86	4	0	0	0	0	0	0	0	362	0	0	518	2,990
1973	93	3	0	0	0	0	0	0	1	658	0	0	1,095	5,470
1974	35	11	0	0	0	0	0	0	0	1,681	0	0	2,856	15,284
Lifetime		139	0	0	0	0	1	3	18	26,070	3	1	27,274	$98,224

Lucky Mays

Harold Mays (Lucky)
Racing Hometown: Augusta, GA

Year	Rank	Starts	Poles	1	2	3	4	5	6–10	Laps	Laps Led	Races Led	Miles	$
1951	147T	1	0	0	0	0	0	0	0		0	0		50
1952	174	2	0	0	0	0	0	0	0	1	0	0	1	60
Lifetime		3	0	0	0	0	0	0	0	1	0	0	1	$110

George McBride

George McBride
Racing Hometown: Livingston, NJ

Year	Rank	Starts	Poles	1	2	3	4	5	6–10	Laps	Laps Led	Races Led	Miles	$
1954	NR	1	0	0	0	0	0	0	0	35	0	0	70	30
Lifetime		1	0	0	0	0	0	0	0	35	0	0	70	$30

Hub McBride

Hub McBride
Racing Hometown: Decatur, GA

Year	Rank	Starts	Poles	1	2	3	4	5	6–10	Laps	Laps Led	Races Led	Miles	$
1950	NR	1	0	0	0	0	0	0	0	341	0	0	426	0
1953	NR	1	0	0	0	0	0	0	0	29	0	0	119	25
Lifetime		2	0	0	0	0	0	0	0	370	0	0	545	$25

Robin McCall

Robin McCall
B: 1/20/1964
Racing Hometown: San Antonio, TX

Year	Rank	Starts	Poles	1	2	3	4	5	6–10	Laps	Laps Led	Races Led	Miles	$
1982	74	2	0	0	0	0	0	0	0	154	0	0	308	2,395
Lifetime		2	0	0	0	0	0	0	0	154	0	0	308	$2,395

Buzz McCann

Harold McCann
Racing Hometown: St.Paul, MN

Year	Rank	Starts	Poles	1	2	3	4	5	6–10	Laps	Laps Led	Races Led	Miles	$
1960	NR	1	0	0	0	0	0	0	0	8	0	0	20	0
1961	190	1	0	0	0	0	0	0	0	1	0	0	3	0
Lifetime		2	0	0	0	0	0	0	0	9	0	0	23	$0

Buck McCardell

Buck McCardell
Racing Hometown: Conowingo, MD

Year	Rank	Starts	Poles	1	2	3	4	5	6–10	Laps	Laps Led	Races Led	Miles	$
1950	NR	1	0	0	0	0	0	0	0		0	0		0
1952	144	3	0	0	0	0	0	0	0	49	0	0	49	60
Lifetime		4	0	0	0	0	0	0	0	49	0	0	49	$60

Norm McCarthy

Norm McCarthy
B: 1924   D: 7/26/1992
Racing Hometown: Bedford, OH

Year	Rank	Starts	Poles	1	2	3	4	5	6–10	Laps	Laps Led	Races Led	Miles	$
1951	N/A	3	0	0	0	0	0	0	1		0	0		125
Lifetime		3	0	0	0	0	0	0	1		0	0		$125

Jack McClure

Jack McClure
Racing Hometown: Columbia, SC

Year	Rank	Starts	Poles	1	2	3	4	5	6–10	Laps	Laps Led	Races Led	Miles	$
1951	N/A	2	0	0	0	0	0	0	0		0	0		25
Lifetime		2	0	0	0	0	0	0	0		0	0		$25

Jeff McClure

Jeff McClure
B: 1/22/1967
Racing Hometown: Harrisburg, NC

Year	Rank	Starts	Poles	1	2	3	4	5	6–10	Laps	Laps Led	Races Led	Miles	$
1992	79T	1	0	0	0	0	0	0	0	173	0	0	346	5,990
Lifetime		1	0	0	0	0	0	0	0	173	0	0	346	$5,990

Year	Rank	Starts	Poles	Finish						Laps	Laps Led	Races Led	Miles	$
				1	2	3	4	5	6–10					

Roger McCluskey

Roger F. McCluskey
B: 8/24/1930   D: 8/29/1993
Racing Hometown: Tucson, AZ

Year	Rank	Starts	Poles	1	2	3	4	5	6–10	Laps	Laps Led	Races Led	Miles	$
1969	NR	1	0	0	0	0	0	0	0	100	0	0	270	825
1970	NR	1	0	0	1	0	0	0	0	193	2	1	506	9,000
1972	NR	1	0	0	0	0	0	0	0	241	0	0	362	1,586
1977	NR	1	0	0	0	0	0	0	0	20	0	0	50	700
Lifetime		4	0	0	1	0	0	0	0	554	2	1	1,187	$12,111

Jim McCorkindale

James McCorkindale

Year	Rank	Starts	Poles	1	2	3	4	5	6–10	Laps	Laps Led	Races Led	Miles	$
1958	165	1	0	0	0	0	0	0	0	120	0	0	316	110
Lifetime		1	0	0	0	0	0	0	0	120	0	0	316	$110

Jack McCoy

Jack McCoy
B: 3/24/1938
Racing Hometown: Bakersfield, CA

Year	Rank	Starts	Poles	1	2	3	4	5	6–10	Laps	Laps Led	Races Led	Miles	$
1963	150	1	0	0	0	0	0	0	0	1	0	0	3	200
1966	80	1	0	0	0	0	0	0	0	123	0	0	332	540
1967	82	1	0	0	0	0	0	0	0	88	0	0	238	575
1968	82T	1	0	0	0	0	0	0	0	118	0	0	319	725
1969	NR	2	0	0	0	0	0	0	1	257	0	0	533	2,750
1970	92	2	0	0	0	0	0	0	1	207	0	0	542	2,740
1971	NR	3	0	0	0	0	0	0	0	443	0	0	1,138	4,315
1972	82	3	0	0	0	0	0	0	0	228	0	0	575	4,070
1973	50	3	0	0	0	0	0	1	2	797	0	0	1,106	5,270
1974	72	3	0	0	0	0	0	0	0	175	4	1	453	3,390
Lifetime		20	0	0	0	0	0	1	4	2,437	4	1	5,238	$24,575

Jack D. McCoy

Jack D. McCoy
Racing Hometown: Ashland, OR

Year	Rank	Starts	Poles	1	2	3	4	5	6–10	Laps	Laps Led	Races Led	Miles	$
1956	227	1	0	0	0	0	0	0	0	125	0	0	125	50
1957	68	5	0	0	0	0	0	1	0	553	0	0	277	520
1958	54	2	0	0	0	0	0	0	1	198	0	0	493	550
1959	114	1	0	0	0	0	0	0	0	42	0	0	42	50
Lifetime		9	0	0	0	0	0	1	1	918	0	0	937	$1,170

Rick McCray

Richard McCray
B: 6/12/1956
Racing Hometown: Bloomington, CA

Year	Rank	Starts	Poles	1	2	3	4	5	6–10	Laps	Laps Led	Races Led	Miles	$
1978	57	3	0	0	0	0	0	0	0	220	0	0	575	4,585
1979	110	1	0	0	0	0	0	0	0	31	0	0	81	750
1980	66	3	0	0	0	0	0	0	0	238	0	0	601	3,415
1981	88T	1	0	0	0	0	0	0	0	66	0	0	173	1,655
1982	54	2	0	0	0	0	0	0	0	151	0	0	396	3,355
1983	48	4	0	0	0	0	0	0	0	760	0	0	629	3,710
1984	71	2	0	0	0	0	0	0	0	102	0	0	267	2,170
1985	99	2	0	0	0	0	0	0	0	47	0	0	123	1,665
1986	84	2	0	0	0	0	0	0	0	123	0	0	322	4,910
1987	72	3	0	0	0	0	0	0	0	277	0	0	587	10,675
1988	83T	1	0	0	0	0	0	0	0	46	0	0	121	1,140
1989	83T	1	0	0	0	0	0	0	0	72	0	0	181	3,200
Lifetime		25	0	0	0	0	0	0	0	2,133	0	0	4,056	$41,230

Tex McCullough

Tex McCullough
Racing Hometown: Asheville, NC

Year	Rank	Starts	Poles	1	2	3	4	5	6–10	Laps	Laps Led	Races Led	Miles	$
1966	124	1	0	0	0	0	0	0	0	5	0	0	5	535
Lifetime		1	0	0	0	0	0	0	0	5	0	0	5	$535

John McDaniel

John L. McDaniel
Racing Hometown: W. Palm Beach, FL

Year	Rank	Starts	Poles	1	2	3	4	5	6–10	Laps	Laps Led	Races Led	Miles	$
1958	86	3	0	0	0	0	0	0	0	279	0	0	167	100
Lifetime		3	0	0	0	0	0	0	0	279	0	0	167	$100

Year	Rank	Starts	Poles	1	2	3	4	5	6–10	Laps	Laps Led	Races Led	Miles	$

Bill McDonald

William A. McDonald
Racing Hometown: Buffalo, NY

Year	Rank	Starts	Poles	1	2	3	4	5	6–10	Laps	Laps Led	Races Led	Miles	$
1961	181	1	0	0	0	0	0	0	0	180	0	0	90	100
1962	112	2	0	0	0	0	0	0	0	121	0	0	61	100
Lifetime		3	0	0	0	0	0	0	0	301	0	0	151	$200

Eddie McDonald

Edward McDonald
Racing Hometown: Gainesville, FL

Year	Rank	Starts	Poles	1	2	3	4	5	6–10	Laps	Laps Led	Races Led	Miles	$
1958	NR	1	0	0	0	0	0	0	0	177	0	0	89	100
Lifetime		1	0	0	0	0	0	0	0	177	0	0	89	$100

Neil McDonald

Neil McDonald
Racing Hometown: Ridgefield, NJ

Year	Rank	Starts	Poles	1	2	3	4	5	6–10	Laps	Laps Led	Races Led	Miles	$
1953	NR	1	0	0	0	0	0	0	0		0	0		25
Lifetime		1	0	0	0	0	0	0	0		0	0		$25

Stewart McDonald

Stewart McDonald
Racing Hometown: Mac Dill Field, FL

Year	Rank	Starts	Poles	1	2	3	4	5	6–10	Laps	Laps Led	Races Led	Miles	$
1953	103	1	0	0	0	0	0	0	0	271	0	0	271	50
Lifetime		1	0	0	0	0	0	0	0	271	0	0	271	$50

Charles McDuffie

Charles McDuffie
Racing Hometown: Yorktown Heights, NY

Year	Rank	Starts	Poles	1	2	3	4	5	6–10	Laps	Laps Led	Races Led	Miles	$
1954	197	2	0	0	0	0	0	0	0	150	0	0	75	0
Lifetime		2	0	0	0	0	0	0	0	150	0	0	75	$0

Glenn McDuffie

Glenn McDuffie
Racing Hometown: Raleigh, NC

Year	Rank	Starts	Poles	1	2	3	4	5	6–10	Laps	Laps Led	Races Led	Miles	$
1975	NR	1	0	0	0	0	0	0	0	431	0	0	438	1,130
1976	98	1	0	0	0	0	0	0	0	205	0	0	208	730
Lifetime		2	0	0	0	0	0	0	0	636	0	0	647	$1,860

J.D. McDuffie

John Delphus McDuffie
B: 12/5/1938   D: 8/11/1991   *Killed at Watkins Glen.*
Racing Hometown: Sanford, NC

Year	Rank	Starts	Poles	1	2	3	4	5	6–10	Laps	Laps Led	Races Led	Miles	$
1963	46	12	0	0	0	0	0	0	3	1,918	0	0	765	1,620
1966	27	36	0	0	0	0	0	1	8	7,166	0	0	4,255	8,545
1967	NR	1	0	0	0	0	0	0	0	137	0	0	69	150
1968	24	32	0	0	0	0	0	0	9	5,587	0	0	3,018	8,355
1969	14	50	0	0	0	0	0	0	12	10,173	0	0	7,890	30,861
1970	16	36	0	0	0	0	0	1	9	8,461	0	0	6,287	24,905
1971	9	43	0	0	0	1	0	1	6	9,359	5	1	9,102	35,578
1972	18	27	0	0	0	0	0	1	1	6,231	0	0	7,095	36,833
1973	10	27	0	0	0	0	0	3	7	7,388	11	2	8,137	56,140
1974	12	30	0	0	0	0	0	0	7	8,283	1	1	9,519	59,535
1975	18	26	0	0	0	0	0	1	5	5,832	0	0	7,055	50,937
1976	12	30	0	0	0	0	0	1	7	7,954	0	0	9,665	82,240
1977	12	30	0	0	0	0	0	0	4	8,252	1	1	9,689	85,227
1978	11	30	1	0	0	0	0	1	5	7,300	15	4	8,716	86,857
1979	13	31	0	0	0	0	0	1	6	8,014	116	3	9,634	113,478
1980	16	31	0	0	0	0	0	0	3	6,044	0	0	7,407	82,402
1981	17	28	0	0	0	0	0	0	1	10,110	8	2	13,371	105,499
1982	19	30	0	0	0	0	0	0	1	6,695	1	1	7,851	112,744
1983	26	25	0	0	0	0	0	0	0	5,990	0	0	6,578	73,425
1984	34	16	0	0	0	0	0	0	0	4,064	0	0	3,422	50,320
1985	27	23	0	0	0	0	0	0	0	4,667	0	0	5,539	84,965
1986	26	20	0	0	0	0	0	0	0	4,750	1	1	5,085	106,115
1987	30	17	0	0	0	0	0	0	0	3,459	0	0	4,062	45,555
1988	61	2	0	0	0	0	0	0	0	516	1	1	574	3,750
1989	44	7	0	0	0	0	0	0	0	1,381	0	0	1,847	27,720
1990	40	8	0	0	0	0	0	0	0	1,301	0	0	1,659	26,170
1991	48	5	0	0	0	0	0	0	0	732	0	0	1,143	19,795
Lifetime		653	1	0	0	1	0	11	94	151,764	160	17	159,433	$1,419,721

Year	Rank	Starts	Poles	Finish 1	2	3	4	5	6–10	Laps	Laps Led	Races Led	Miles	$

Jeff McDuffie

Jeff McDuffie
B: 3/31/1962
Racing Hometown: Sanford, NC

Year	Rank	Starts	Poles	1	2	3	4	5	6–10	Laps	Laps Led	Races Led	Miles	$
1980	53	3	0	0	0	0	0	0	0	1,138	0	0	869	2,725
1982	80	1	0	0	0	0	0	0	0	377	0	0	236	1,005
1985	NR	1	0	0	0	0	0	0	0	445	0	0	453	1,875
Lifetime		5	0	0	0	0	0	0	0	1,960	0	0	1,557	$5,605

Bob McElee

Robert McElee

Year	Rank	Starts	Poles	1	2	3	4	5	6–10	Laps	Laps Led	Races Led	Miles	$
1981	NR	2	0	0	0	0	0	0	1	803	0	0	461	5,450
Lifetime		2	0	0	0	0	0	0	1	803	0	0	461	$5,450

Jim McElreath

Jim McElreath
B: 2/18/1928
Racing Hometown: Arlington, TX

Year	Rank	Starts	Poles	1	2	3	4	5	6–10	Laps	Laps Led	Races Led	Miles	$
1964	NR	3	0	0	0	0	0	0	0	336	0	0	667	1,350
1971	NR	1	0	0	0	0	0	0	0	88	0	0	220	1,440
Lifetime		4	0	0	0	0	0	0	0	424	0	0	887	$2,790

John McFadden

John McFadden
B: 11/4/1951
Racing Hometown: Forrest City, NC

Year	Rank	Starts	Poles	1	2	3	4	5	6–10	Laps	Laps Led	Races Led	Miles	$
1982	87	1	0	0	0	0	0	0	0	368	0	0	196	655
1983	57	3	0	0	0	0	0	0	0	289	0	0	181	2,260
1989	67	2	0	0	0	0	0	0	0	213	0	0	291	5,279
1992	52	5	0	0	0	0	0	0	0	37	0	0	53	21,810
Lifetime		11	0	0	0	0	0	0	0	907	0	0	721	$30,004

Bill McGee

William McGee
Racing Hometown: Zanesville, OH

Year	Rank	Starts	Poles	1	2	3	4	5	6–10	Laps	Laps Led	Races Led	Miles	$
1950	NR	1	0	0	0	0	0	0	0		0	0		0
Lifetime		1	0	0	0	0	0	0	0		0	0		$0

Ron McGee

Ronald McGee
B: 12/27/1947
Racing Hometown: Sunnyvale, CA

Year	Rank	Starts	Poles	1	2	3	4	5	6–10	Laps	Laps Led	Races Led	Miles	$
1977	102T	1	0	0	0	0	0	0	0	103	0	0	258	950
Lifetime		1	0	0	0	0	0	0	0	103	0	0	258	$950

John McGinley

John McGinley
B: 1925
Racing Hometown: Chicora, PA

Year	Rank	Starts	Poles	1	2	3	4	5	6–10	Laps	Laps Led	Races Led	Miles	$
1951	35	6	0	0	1	0	1	0	0	224	0	0	224	1,300
1954	70	4	0	0	0	0	0	0	1	435	0	0	249	350
1955	NR	1	0	0	0	0	0	0	0	157	0	0	79	60
Lifetime		11	0	0	1	0	1	0	1	816	0	0	552	$1,710

Billy McGinnis

William McGinnis
Racing Hometown: Griffin, GA

Year	Rank	Starts	Poles	1	2	3	4	5	6–10	Laps	Laps Led	Races Led	Miles	$
1976	NR	1	0	0	0	0	0	0	0	15	0	0	23	805
1977	NR	1	0	0	0	0	0	0	0	264	0	0	402	1,570
1978	92	1	0	0	0	0	0	0	0	221	0	0	336	875
Lifetime		3	0	0	0	0	0	0	0	500	0	0	761	$3,250

Pop McGinnis

Glenn McGinnis
Racing Hometown: Huntington, WV

Year	Rank	Starts	Poles	1	2	3	4	5	6–10	Laps	Laps Led	Races Led	Miles	$
1952	91T	1	0	0	0	0	0	0	1	180	0	0	90	125
1953	21	13	0	0	0	0	0	2	3	775	13	1	664	975
1954	78	4	0	0	0	0	0	0	1	536	4	1	618	315
1955	140	2	0	0	0	0	0	0	0	201	0	0	116	100
1964	138	1	0	0	0	0	0	0	0	238	0	0	104	200

Year	Rank	Starts	Poles	Finish 1	2	3	4	5	6–10	Laps	Laps Led	Races Led	Miles	$

Pop McGinnis *continued*

Year	Rank	Starts	Poles	1	2	3	4	5	6–10	Laps	Laps Led	Races Led	Miles	$
1970	103	1	0	0	0	0	0	0	1	274	0	0	120	330
Lifetime		22	0	0	0	0	0	2	6	2,204	17	2	1,712	$2,045

John McGorrien

John McGorrien

Year	Rank	Starts	Poles	1	2	3	4	5	6–10	Laps	Laps Led	Races Led	Miles	$
1953	NR	1	0	0	0	0	0	0	0		0	0		50
Lifetime		1	0	0	0	0	0	0	0		0	0		$50

Steve McGrath

Steve McGrath
B: 4/28/1924
Racing Hometown: New Canaan, CT

Year	Rank	Starts	Poles	1	2	3	4	5	6–10	Laps	Laps Led	Races Led	Miles	$
1953	75	3	0	0	0	0	0	0	0		0	0		90
1960	133	1	0	0	0	0	0	0	0	188	0	0	259	200
Lifetime		4	0	0	0	0	0	0	0	188	0	0	259	$290

Joe Bill McGraw

Joseph William McGraw
Racing Hometown: Syracuse, NY

Year	Rank	Starts	Poles	1	2	3	4	5	6–10	Laps	Laps Led	Races Led	Miles	$
1956	NR	5	0	0	0	0	0	0	1	424	0	0	211	500
Lifetime		5	0	0	0	0	0	0	1	424	0	0	211	$500

Mickey McGreevey

Mickey McGreevey (Mike)
B: 1/3/1926
Racing Hometown: Hayward, CA

Year	Rank	Starts	Poles	1	2	3	4	5	6–10	Laps	Laps Led	Races Led	Miles	$
1955	101	1	0	0	0	0	0	0	0	232	0	0	232	150
1957	87	3	0	0	0	0	0	0	0	189	0	0	205	235
Lifetime		4	0	0	0	0	0	0	0	421	0	0	437	$385

Hershel McGriff

Hershel McGriff
B: 12/14/1927
Racing Hometown: Bridal Veil, OR

Year	Rank	Starts	Poles	1	2	3	4	5	6–10	Laps	Laps Led	Races Led	Miles	$
1950	NR	1	0	0	0	0	0	0	1	374	0	0	468	500
1951	N/A	4	0	0	0	0	1	0	0	463	1	1	561	1,260
1952	NR	2	0	0	0	0	0	0	1	283	0	0	261	325
1953	51	2	0	0	0	0	0	0	0	274	101	1	274	125
1954	6	24	5	4	3	5	0	1	4	3,891	122	6	2,743	13,250
1971	NR	3	0	0	0	0	0	0	0	397	4	2	1,021	3,860
1972	45	4	0	0	0	0	0	2	1	727	3	1	1,728	12,290
1973	51	3	0	0	0	0	0	1	1	426	0	0	1,093	8,690
1974	50	5	0	0	0	0	0	0	1	559	0	0	1,198	8,585
1975	70	5	0	0	0	0	0	0	1	652	4	1	1,353	7,995
1976	102	2	0	0	0	0	0	0	0	179	0	0	456	1,655
1977	65	2	0	0	0	0	0	0	1	120	0	0	314	3,240
1978	83	2	0	0	0	0	0	0	1	208	0	0	545	4,490
1980	59	2	0	0	0	0	0	0	0	149	0	0	390	1,780
1981	66	3	0	0	0	0	0	0	0	80	1	1	210	2,170
1982	73	2	0	0	0	0	0	0	0	115	0	0	301	1,545
1983	53	2	0	0	0	0	0	0	1	191	0	0	500	5,650
1984	67	2	0	0	0	0	0	0	1	149	1	1	390	3,815
1985	66	2	0	0	0	0	0	0	0	178	0	0	466	2,835
1986	77	2	0	0	0	0	0	0	0	170	0	0	445	4,080
1987	66	4	0	0	0	0	0	0	0	367	0	0	896	12,985
1988	53	3	0	0	0	0	0	0	0	316	0	0	526	5,960
1989	65	1	0	0	0	0	0	0	0	74	0	0	186	5,075
1990	105	1	0	0	0	0	0	0	0	2	0	0	5	3,225
1991	60	2	0	0	0	0	0	0	0	361	0	0	454	7,475
1992	97	1	0	0	0	0	0	0	0	19	0	0	48	4,725
1993	95	1	0	0	0	0	0	0	0	27	0	0	68	6,560
Lifetime		87	5	4	3	5	1	4	14	10,751	237	14	16,901	$134,145

Norman McGriff

Norman McGriff
B: 9/6/1933
Racing Hometown: Portland, OR

Year	Rank	Starts	Poles	1	2	3	4	5	6–10	Laps	Laps Led	Races Led	Miles	$
1957	65	3	0	0	0	0	0	0	2	342	0	0	198	370
Lifetime		3	0	0	0	0	0	0	2	342	0	0	198	$370

Year	Rank	Starts	Poles	Finish 1	2	3	4	5	6–10	Laps	Laps Led	Races Led	Miles	$

Jim McGuirk

James McGuirk
Racing Hometown: Vero Beach, FL

Year	Rank	Starts	Poles	1	2	3	4	5	6–10	Laps	Laps Led	Races Led	Miles	$
1959	47	4	0	0	0	0	0	0	0	314	0	0	590	325
1962	82	2	0	0	0	0	0	0	0	196	0	0	490	500
1963	58	3	0	0	0	0	0	0	0	212	0	0	530	1,200
Lifetime		9	0	0	0	0	0	0	0	722	0	0	1,610	$2,025

Sumner McKnight

Sumner McKnight
B: 9/9/1946
Racing Hometown: Newport Beach, CA

Year	Rank	Starts	Poles	1	2	3	4	5	6–10	Laps	Laps Led	Races Led	Miles	$
1977	102T	1	0	0	0	0	0	0	0	15	0	0	39	650
1983	55	2	0	0	0	0	0	0	0	204	0	0	534	5,275
1984	56	2	0	0	0	0	0	0	0	192	0	0	503	5,140
1985	73	1	0	0	0	0	0	0	0	91	0	0	238	3,985
Lifetime		6	0	0	0	0	0	0	0	502	0	0	1,315	$15,050

Jim McLain

James McLain
Racing Hometown: Wilkesboro, NC

Year	Rank	Starts	Poles	1	2	3	4	5	6–10	Laps	Laps Led	Races Led	Miles	$
1954	174	1	0	0	0	0	0	0	0	112	0	0	168	50
1955	123	3	0	0	0	0	0	0	0	118	0	0	271	110
Lifetime		4	0	0	0	0	0	0	0	230	0	0	439	$160

Mike McLaughlin

Michael McLaughlin
B: 10/6/1956
Racing Hometown: Waterloo, NY

Year	Rank	Starts	Poles	1	2	3	4	5	6–10	Laps	Laps Led	Races Led	Miles	$
1994	55	2	0	0	0	0	0	0	0	386	0	0	529	17,975
Lifetime		2	0	0	0	0	0	0	0	386	0	0	529	$17,975

Don McLeish

Donald McLeish

Year	Rank	Starts	Poles	1	2	3	4	5	6–10	Laps	Laps Led	Races Led	Miles	$
1951	N/A	1	0	0	0	0	0	0	0		0	0		25
Lifetime		1	0	0	0	0	0	0	0		0	0		$25

Bill McMahan

William McMahan
Racing Hometown: Dandridge, TN

Year	Rank	Starts	Poles	1	2	3	4	5	6–10	Laps	Laps Led	Races Led	Miles	$
1964	33	20	0	0	0	0	0	1	3	4,134	0	0	2,897	7,205
1965	119	1	0	0	0	0	0	0	0	0	0	0	0	100
Lifetime		21	0	0	0	0	0	1	3	4,134	0	0	2,897	$7,305

Alan McMillion

Alan McMillion
Racing Hometown: Amelia, VA

Year	Rank	Starts	Poles	1	2	3	4	5	6–10	Laps	Laps Led	Races Led	Miles	$
1965	103	1	0	0	0	0	0	0	0	236	0	0	79	110
1966	NR	1	0	0	0	0	0	0	0	250	0	0	125	150
Lifetime		2	0	0	0	0	0	0	0	486	0	0	204	$260

Worth McMillion

Hollingsworth McMillion
B: 10/8/1926
Racing Hometown: Amelia, VA

Year	Rank	Starts	Poles	1	2	3	4	5	6–10	Laps	Laps Led	Races Led	Miles	$
1962	72	4	0	0	0	0	0	0	0	1,105	0	0	517	675
1963	34	15	0	0	0	0	0	0	4	4,177	0	0	2,412	3,145
1964	30	18	0	0	0	0	0	0	6	4,681	0	0	2,756	4,710
1965	47	10	0	0	0	0	0	0	2	2,290	0	0	1,289	2,590
1966	52	9	0	0	0	0	0	0	3	2,311	0	0	1,450	2,440
1967	83	2	0	0	0	0	0	0	2	497	0	0	249	775
1968	NR	3	0	0	0	0	0	1	0	772	0	0	444	875
1969	77	1	0	0	0	0	0	0	0	328	0	0	164	480
Lifetime		62	0	0	0	0	0	1	17	16,161	0	0	9,281	$15,690

Jamie McMurray

Jamie McMurray
B: 6/3/1976
Racing Hometown: Joplin, MO

Year	Rank	Starts	Poles	1	2	3	4	5	6–10	Laps	Laps Led	Races Led	Miles	$
2002	46	6	0	1	0	0	0	0	1	1,680	97	2	2,434	717,942
Lifetime		6	0	1	0	0	0	0	1	1,680	97	2	2,434	$717,942

Year	Rank	Starts	Poles	Finish 1	2	3	4	5	6–10	Laps	Laps Led	Races Led	Miles	$

Sam McQuagg

Samuel David McQuagg
B: 11/11/1937
Racing Hometown: Columbus, GA

Year	Rank	Starts	Poles	1	2	3	4	5	6–10	Laps	Laps Led	Races Led	Miles	$
1962	106	1	0	0	0	0	0	0	0	51	0	0	26	120
1964	49	5	0	0	0	0	0	0	0	653	0	0	842	1,700
1965	24	14	0	0	0	1	0	1	3	2,458	31	1	2,922	10,455
1966	15	16	0	1	0	1	0	2	3	3,575	175	3	3,906	29,530
1967	36	15	0	0	0	0	2	1	0	2,244	17	3	2,508	9,845
1968	54	5	0	0	0	0	0	0	2	1,045	5	1	1,566	4,960
1969	70	3	0	0	0	0	0	0	2	1,056	0	0	845	2,625
1974	56	3	0	0	0	0	0	0	2	698	1	1	1,221	6,100
Lifetime		62	0	1	0	2	2	4	12	11,780	229	9	13,834	$65,335

John McVitty

John McVitty
B: 1925   D: 4/21/1956   *Killed at Langhorne qualifying.*
Racing Hometown: Mamaroneck, NY

Year	Rank	Starts	Poles	1	2	3	4	5	6–10	Laps	Laps Led	Races Led	Miles	$
1955	48	7	0	0	0	0	0	0	2	951	0	0	559	550
1956	116	4	0	0	0	0	0	0	1	431	0	0	228	250
Lifetime		11	0	0	0	0	0	0	3	1,382	0	0	787	$800

Bill Meacham

William Meacham
B: 4/13/1960
Racing Hometown: Pineville, NC

Year	Rank	Starts	Poles	1	2	3	4	5	6–10	Laps	Laps Led	Races Led	Miles	$
1990	94T	1	0	0	0	0	0	0	0	87	0	0	65	2,425
1991	68	2	0	0	0	0	0	0	0	146	0	0	159	6,535
Lifetime		3	0	0	0	0	0	0	0	233	0	0	225	$8,960

Leon Meadows

Leon Meadows
Racing Hometown: Kokomo, IN

Year	Rank	Starts	Poles	1	2	3	4	5	6–10	Laps	Laps Led	Races Led	Miles	$
1952	181	1	0	0	0	0	0	0	0	67	0	0	67	25
Lifetime		1	0	0	0	0	0	0	0	67	0	0	67	$25

Jimmy Means

James Means
B: 5/29/1950
Racing Hometown: Huntsville, AL

Year	Rank	Starts	Poles	1	2	3	4	5	6–10	Laps	Laps Led	Races Led	Miles	$
1976	24	19	0	0	0	0	0	0	0	4,336	1	1	5,118	20,945
1977	19	26	0	0	0	0	0	0	6	6,010	0	0	6,760	52,505
1978	17	27	0	0	0	0	0	0	2	7,083	0	0	7,993	61,725
1979	23	27	0	0	0	0	0	0	1	5,131	0	0	6,138	55,560
1980	17	28	0	0	0	0	0	0	0	7,684	0	0	8,891	105,628
1981	14	30	0	0	0	0	0	0	2	8,647	0	0	9,394	105,628
1982	11	30	0	0	0	0	0	0	2	8,837	2	1	10,274	154,460
1983	18	28	0	0	0	0	0	0	3	7,968	2	1	8,816	132,915
1984	25	22	0	0	0	0	0	0	0	7,044	0	0	7,482	105,105
1985	23	28	0	0	0	0	0	0	0	6,774	0	0	7,521	132,130
1986	22	26	0	0	0	0	0	0	0	6,472	5	3	8,104	157,940
1987	23	28	0	0	0	0	0	0	1	6,239	21	1	7,184	154,055
1988	30	27	0	0	0	0	0	0	0	5,172	12	4	6,592	139,290
1989	31	22	0	0	0	0	0	0	0	4,868	4	1	6,289	60,705
1990	29	27	0	0	0	0	0	0	0	7,419	0	0	8,749	135,165
1991	33	20	0	0	0	0	0	0	0	4,425	3	3	6,580	111,210
1992	32	22	0	0	0	0	0	0	0	4,370	0	0	5,165	133,160
1993	36	18	0	0	0	0	0	0	0	4,765	2	2	5,644	148,205
Lifetime		455	0	0	0	0	0	0	17	113,244	52	17	132,693	$1,966,331

Bill Meazell

William Meazell
Racing Hometown: Nacogdoches, TX

Year	Rank	Starts	Poles	1	2	3	4	5	6–10	Laps	Laps Led	Races Led	Miles	$
1979	118T	1	0	0	0	0	0	0	0	46	0	0	92	1,000
Lifetime		1	0	0	0	0	0	0	0	46	0	0	92	$1,000

Chuck Meekins

Charles Meekins
Racing Hometown: Los Angeles, CA

Year	Rank	Starts	Poles	1	2	3	4	5	6–10	Laps	Laps Led	Races Led	Miles	$
1951	58	5	0	0	1	0	0	0	0	202	0	0	102	675
1954	NR	3	0	0	0	0	0	0	1	719	0	0	479	300

Year	Rank	Starts	Poles	Finish 1	2	3	4	5	6–10	Laps	Laps Led	Races Led	Miles	$

Chuck Meekins *continued*

Year	Rank	Starts	Poles	1	2	3	4	5	6–10	Laps	Laps Led	Races Led	Miles	$
1955	230	3	0	0	0	0	1	0	0	467	0	0	369	450
1956	29	7	0	0	1	1	1	0	3	1,241	17	2	1,015	2,815
1957	51	6	0	0	0	1	2	0	1	563	0	0	434	1,280
Lifetime		24	0	0	2	2	4	0	5	3,192	17	2	2,398	$5,520

John Meekins

John Meekins
Racing Hometown: Los Angeles, CA

Year	Rank	Starts	Poles	1	2	3	4	5	6–10	Laps	Laps Led	Races Led	Miles	$
1950	NR	1	0	0	0	0	0	0	0		0	0		0
Lifetime		1	0	0	0	0	0	0	0		0	0		$0

John Meggers

John Charles Meggers
B: 12/8/1928
Racing Hometown: Washington, DC

Year	Rank	Starts	Poles	1	2	3	4	5	6–10	Laps	Laps Led	Races Led	Miles	$
1953	NR	5	0	0	0	0	0	0	3		0	0		350
Lifetime		5	0	0	0	0	0	0	3		0	0		$350

Ken Meisenhelder

Kenneth Anthony Meisenhelder
B: 12/17/1942
Racing Hometown: Springfield, MA

Year	Rank	Starts	Poles	1	2	3	4	5	6–10	Laps	Laps Led	Races Led	Miles	$
1968	118	1	0	0	0	0	0	0	0	103	0	0	93	100
1969	42	16	0	0	0	0	0	0	0	1,832	0	0	1,285	5,630
1970	41	19	0	0	0	0	0	0	2	2,717	0	0	1,842	7,020
1971	40	15	0	0	0	0	0	0	1	2,194	0	0	1,544	5,405
Lifetime		51	0	0	0	0	0	0	3	6,846	0	0	4,763	$18,155

Johnny Mello

John Mello
Racing Hometown: Hanford, CA

Year	Rank	Starts	Poles	1	2	3	4	5	6–10	Laps	Laps Led	Races Led	Miles	$
1960	148	1	0	0	0	0	0	0	0	22	0	0	31	0
Lifetime		1	0	0	0	0	0	0	0	22	0	0	31	$0

Major Melton

Major Melton
B: 1/25/1930
Racing Hometown: Laurinburg, NC

Year	Rank	Starts	Poles	1	2	3	4	5	6–10	Laps	Laps Led	Races Led	Miles	$
1963	43	17	0	0	0	0	0	0	0	2,780	0	0	1,287	1,910
1964	58	3	0	0	0	0	0	0	1	737	0	0	648	1,100
Lifetime		20	0	0	0	0	0	0	1	3,517	0	0	1,935	$3,010

Tommy Melvin

Thomas Melvin
Racing Hometown: Oconomowoc, WI

Year	Rank	Starts	Poles	1	2	3	4	5	6–10	Laps	Laps Led	Races Led	Miles	$
1950	88	1	0	0	0	0	0	0	0		0	0		50
1951	NR	3	0	0	0	0	0	0	0	459	0	0	551	75
Lifetime		4	0	0	0	0	0	0	0	459	0	0	551	$125

Joe Merola

Joseph Merola
Racing Hometown: Wilkensberg, PA

Year	Rank	Starts	Poles	1	2	3	4	5	6–10	Laps	Laps Led	Races Led	Miles	$
1949	55T	1	0	0	0	0	0	0	0	161	0	0	81	50
1950	NR	2	0	0	0	0	0	0	0	0	0	0	0	0
1951	N/A	4	0	0	0	0	0	0	1	472	0	0	522	175
Lifetime		7	0	0	0	0	0	0	1	633	0	0	602	$225

Charles Merrill

Charles Merrill
Racing Hometown: Mobile, AL

Year	Rank	Starts	Poles	1	2	3	4	5	6–10	Laps	Laps Led	Races Led	Miles	$
1954	139	1	0	0	0	0	0	0	0	129	0	0	194	50
Lifetime		1	0	0	0	0	0	0	0	129	0	0	194	$50

Stan Meserve

Stanley Rexford Meserve
B: 8/23/1941
Racing Hometown: Winslow, ME

Year	Rank	Starts	Poles	1	2	3	4	5	6–10	Laps	Laps Led	Races Led	Miles	$
1968	26	31	0	0	0	0	0	0	1	4,283	0	0	2,759	7,475
Lifetime		31	0	0	0	0	0	0	1	4,283	0	0	2,759	$7,475

Year	Rank	Starts	Poles	Finish 1	2	3	4	5	6–10	Laps	Laps Led	Races Led	Miles	$

Chuck Mesler

Chuck Mesler
Racing Hometown: Ecorse, MI

Year	Rank	Starts	Poles	1	2	3	4	5	6–10	Laps	Laps Led	Races Led	Miles	$
1956	209T	1	0	0	0	0	0	0	0	175	0	0	88	100
Lifetime		1	0	0	0	0	0	0	0	175	0	0	88	$100

Al Metz

Al Metz Jr.
Racing Hometown: Masury, OH

Year	Rank	Starts	Poles	1	2	3	4	5	6–10	Laps	Laps Led	Races Led	Miles	$
1954	113T	1	0	0	0	0	0	0	0	131	0	0	66	25
Lifetime		1	0	0	0	0	0	0	0	131	0	0	66	$25

Jim Metzler

James Metzler
B: 3/10/1912   Deceased.
Racing Hometown: Pottersville, NJ

Year	Rank	Starts	Poles	1	2	3	4	5	6–10	Laps	Laps Led	Races Led	Miles	$
1951	N/A	1	0	0	0	0	0	0	0		0	0		0
Lifetime		1	0	0	0	0	0	0	0		0	0		$0

Bill Meyer

William Meyer
Racing Hometown: Anaheim, CA

Year	Rank	Starts	Poles	1	2	3	4	5	6–10	Laps	Laps Led	Races Led	Miles	$
1965	124	1	0	0	0	0	0	0	0	19	0	0	51	500
Lifetime		1	0	0	0	0	0	0	0	19	0	0	51	$500

Dick Meyer

Richard Meyer
D: 9/16/1953   *Killed in highway crash en route from Detroit race to pregnant wife.*
Racing Hometown: Porterville, CA

Year	Rank	Starts	Poles	1	2	3	4	5	6–10	Laps	Laps Led	Races Led	Miles	$
1951	24	6	0	0	1	0	0	2	1		82	1		1,650
1952	112	1	0	0	0	0	0	0	0		0	0		50
1953	NR	1	0	0	0	0	1	0	0	355	0	0	488	1,000
Lifetime		8	0	0	1	0	1	2	1	355	82	1	488	$2,700

Hylan Micka

Hylan Micka

Year	Rank	Starts	Poles	1	2	3	4	5	6–10	Laps	Laps Led	Races Led	Miles	$
1958	NR	1	0	0	0	0	0	0	0	66	0	0	174	150
Lifetime		1	0	0	0	0	0	0	0	66	0	0	174	$150

Joe Mihalic

Joseph Mihalic
B: 11/8/1926
Racing Hometown: Pittsburgh, PA

Year	Rank	Starts	Poles	1	2	3	4	5	6–10	Laps	Laps Led	Races Led	Miles	$
1974	53	5	0	0	0	0	0	0	1	1,725	0	0	1,570	7,595
1975	34	10	0	0	0	0	0	0	1	1,939	0	0	2,695	12,910
1976	35	9	0	0	0	0	0	0	0	2,171	0	0	3,129	12,925
1977	41	8	0	0	0	0	0	0	0	1,550	0	0	2,137	7,650
1978	47	6	0	0	0	0	0	0	0	1,216	0	0	1,537	6,030
Lifetime		38	0	0	0	0	0	0	2	8,601	0	0	11,067	$47,110

Walter Milczarski

Walter Milczarski

Year	Rank	Starts	Poles	1	2	3	4	5	6–10	Laps	Laps Led	Races Led	Miles	$
1954	NR	1	0	0	0	0	0	0	0	142	0	0	71	0
Lifetime		1	0	0	0	0	0	0	0	142	0	0	71	$0

Ken Miles

Kenneth Miles
B: 11/1/1918   D: 8/17/1966   *Killed @ Riverside testing Ford Formula J car.*
Racing Hometown: Hollywood, CA

Year	Rank	Starts	Poles	1	2	3	4	5	6–10	Laps	Laps Led	Races Led	Miles	$
1963	NR	1	0	0	0	0	0	0	0	139	0	0	375	710
Lifetime		1	0	0	0	0	0	0	0	139	0	0	375	$710

Jim Millard

James Millard
Racing Hometown: Hollywood, FL

Year	Rank	Starts	Poles	1	2	3	4	5	6–10	Laps	Laps Led	Races Led	Miles	$
1952	91T	1	0	0	0	0	0	0	1		0	0		100
Lifetime		1	0	0	0	0	0	0	1		0	0		$100

325

Year	Rank	Starts	Poles	1	2	3	Finish 4	5	6–10	Laps	Laps Led	Races Led	Miles	$

Al Miller

Al Miller
Racing Hometown: Detroit, MI

Year	Rank	Starts	Poles	1	2	3	4	5	6–10	Laps	Laps Led	Races Led	Miles	$
1951	N/A	1	0	0	0	0	0	0	0	115	0	0	115	0
Lifetime		1	0	0	0	0	0	0	0	115	0	0	115	$0

Bill Miller

William Miller
B: 1915   D: 12/31/195
Racing Hometown: Evansville, IN

Year	Rank	Starts	Poles	1	2	3	4	5	6–10	Laps	Laps Led	Races Led	Miles	$
1951	65	6	0	0	0	0	0	0	2		0	0		350
1952	83	4	0	0	0	0	0	0	0	547	0	0	562	125
Lifetime		10	0	0	0	0	0	0	2	547	0	0	562	$475

Butch Miller

Henry Miller
B: 6/5/1952
Racing Hometown: Medallion, OH

Year	Rank	Starts	Poles	1	2	3	4	5	6–10	Laps	Laps Led	Races Led	Miles	$
1986	75	3	0	0	0	0	0	0	0	799	0	0	891	5,085
1987	100	2	0	0	0	0	0	0	0	215	0	0	307	3,145
1988	NR	2	0	0	0	0	0	0	0	790	18	1	497	5,905
1989	39	9	0	0	0	0	0	0	0	1,129	0	0	1,194	22,520
1990	27	23	0	0	0	0	0	0	1	6,891	4	4	8,750	151,941
1994	53	2	0	0	0	0	0	0	0	842	0	0	982	17,335
Lifetime		41	0	0	0	0	0	0	1	10,666	22	5	12,621	$205,931

Charlie Miller

Charles Miller
B: 1912   D: 9/24/1955   *Killed in Sprint Car race @ Shelby, NC.*
Racing Hometown: Allentown, PA

Year	Rank	Starts	Poles	1	2	3	4	5	6–10	Laps	Laps Led	Races Led	Miles	$
1953	NR	1	0	0	0	0	0	0	0		0	0		100
Lifetime		1	0	0	0	0	0	0	0		0	0		$100

Chris Miller

Christopher Miller
Racing Hometown: Seven Valleys, PA

Year	Rank	Starts	Poles	1	2	3	4	5	6–10	Laps	Laps Led	Races Led	Miles	$
1954	185	1	0	0	0	0	0	0	0	126	0	0	126	0
Lifetime		1	0	0	0	0	0	0	0	126	0	0	126	$0

Dick Miller

Richard Miller
Racing Hometown: Los Angeles, CA

Year	Rank	Starts	Poles	1	2	3	4	5	6–10	Laps	Laps Led	Races Led	Miles	$
1961	NR	2	0	0	0	0	0	0	0	134	0	0	136	140
Lifetime		2	0	0	0	0	0	0	0	134	0	0	136	$140

Jim Miller

James Miller

Year	Rank	Starts	Poles	1	2	3	4	5	6–10	Laps	Laps Led	Races Led	Miles	$
1951	N/A	1	0	0	0	0	0	0	0		0	0		0
Lifetime		1	0	0	0	0	0	0	0		0	0		$0

Johnny Miller

John Miller
Racing Hometown: Kannapolis, NC

Year	Rank	Starts	Poles	1	2	3	4	5	6–10	Laps	Laps Led	Races Led	Miles	$
1960	118	2	0	0	0	0	0	0	0	207	0	0	307	500
Lifetime		2	0	0	0	0	0	0	0	207	0	0	307	$500

Junior Miller

Junior Miller
B: 4/26/1951
Racing Hometown: Winston-Salem, NC

Year	Rank	Starts	Poles	1	2	3	4	5	6–10	Laps	Laps Led	Races Led	Miles	$
1976	67	2	0	0	0	0	0	0	0	744	0	0	465	1,325
1977	46	5	0	0	0	0	0	0	0	1,028	0	0	648	2,475
1978	71	2	0	0	0	0	0	0	0	498	0	0	359	2,110
1980	31	16	0	0	0	0	0	0	0	3,848	0	0	3,140	23,420
1981	68	2	0	0	0	0	0	0	0	276	0	0	190	3,130
Lifetime		27	0	0	0	0	0	0	0	6,394	0	0	4,802	$32,460

Kirby Miller

Kirby Miller
Racing Hometown: Canoga Park, CA

Year	Rank	Starts	Poles	1	2	3	4	5	6–10	Laps	Laps Led	Races Led	Miles	$
1958	126	1	0	0	0	0	0	0	0	152	0	0	400	110

Year	Rank	Starts	Poles	Finish						Laps	Laps Led	Races Led	Miles	$
				1	2	3	4	5	6–10					

Kirby Miller *continued*

Year	Rank	Starts	Poles	1	2	3	4	5	6–10	Laps	Laps Led	Races Led	Miles	$
1959	NR	1	0	0	0	0	0	0	0	47	0	0	19	150
Lifetime		2	0	0	0	0	0	0	0	199	0	0	419	$260

Larry Miller

Larry Martin Miller
B: 8/22/1934
Racing Hometown: Taylors, SC

Year	Rank	Starts	Poles	1	2	3	4	5	6–10	Laps	Laps Led	Races Led	Miles	$
1967	52	15	0	0	0	0	0	0	1	1,558	0	0	704	2,075
Lifetime		15	0	0	0	0	0	0	1	1,558	0	0	704	$2,075

Mike Miller

Michael Miller
Racing Hometown: Wisconsin Rapids, WI

Year	Rank	Starts	Poles	1	2	3	4	5	6–10	Laps	Laps Led	Races Led	Miles	$
1980	83	2	0	0	0	0	0	0	0	176	0	0	267	2,145
1989	93T	1	0	0	0	0	0	0	0	137	0	0	274	3,075
Lifetime		3	0	0	0	0	0	0	0	313	0	0	541	$5,220

Nels Miller

Nels Miller

Year	Rank	Starts	Poles	1	2	3	4	5	6–10	Laps	Laps Led	Races Led	Miles	$
1973	119	1	0	0	0	0	0	0	0	19	0	0	50	900
Lifetime		1	0	0	0	0	0	0	0	19	0	0	50	$900

Scott Miller

Scott Miller
B: 8/23/1957
Racing Hometown: Garden Grove, CA

Year	Rank	Starts	Poles	1	2	3	4	5	6–10	Laps	Laps Led	Races Led	Miles	$
1981	95	1	0	0	0	0	0	0	0	69	0	0	181	805
1982	77	1	0	0	0	0	0	0	0	90	0	0	236	1,495
1983	71	2	0	0	0	0	0	0	0	173	0	0	453	2,400
1984	73	2	0	0	0	0	0	0	0	98	0	0	257	1,815
Lifetime		6	0	0	0	0	0	0	0	430	0	0	1,127	$6,515

T.R. Miller

T.R. Miller
Racing Hometown: High Point, NC

Year	Rank	Starts	Poles	1	2	3	4	5	6–10	Laps	Laps Led	Races Led	Miles	$
1961	148	1	0	0	0	0	0	0	0	96	0	0	24	75
Lifetime		1	0	0	0	0	0	0	0	96	0	0	24	$75

V.E. Miller

V.E. Miller

Year	Rank	Starts	Poles	1	2	3	4	5	6–10	Laps	Laps Led	Races Led	Miles	$
1951	N/A	1	0	0	0	0	0	0	0		0	0		25
Lifetime		1	0	0	0	0	0	0	0		0	0		$25

Harold Miller

William Miller
B: 10/19/1950
Racing Hometown: Emerson, GA

Year	Rank	Starts	Poles	1	2	3	4	5	6–10	Laps	Laps Led	Races Led	Miles	$
1975	52	2	0	0	0	0	0	0	0	247	0	0	494	1,625
1976	57	3	0	0	0	0	0	0	0	499	0	0	1,184	4,885
1977	46	6	0	0	0	0	0	0	0	1,267	0	0	2,276	8,480
Lifetime		11	0	0	0	0	0	0	0	2,013	0	0	3,954	$14,990

Ken Milligan

Kenneth Milligan
Racing Hometown: Knoxville, TN

Year	Rank	Starts	Poles	1	2	3	4	5	6–10	Laps	Laps Led	Races Led	Miles	$
1956	79	4	0	0	0	0	0	0	1	347	0	0	267	300
Lifetime		4	0	0	0	0	0	0	1	347	0	0	267	$300

Joe Millikan

Joseph Millikan
B: 4/30/1950
Racing Hometown: Randleman, NC

Year	Rank	Starts	Poles	1	2	3	4	5	6–10	Laps	Laps Led	Races Led	Miles	$
1974	NR	1	0	0	0	0	0	0	0	456	0	0	464	1,150
1979	6	31	1	0	1	1	0	3	15	9,122	188	8	10,510	229,713
1980	33	12	0	0	0	0	1	1	4	2,796	5	3	2,937	74,765
1981	20	23	0	0	0	1	0	2	7	6,735	15	4	7,270	148,400
1982	35	8	0	0	0	0	0	0	2	2,408	5	1	2,453	62,325
1983	NR	1	0	0	0	0	0	0	0	384	0	0	240	1,075

Year	Rank	Starts	Poles	Finish 1	2	3	4	5	6–10	Laps	Laps Led	Races Led	Miles	$

Joe Millikan *continued*

Year	Rank	Starts	Poles	1	2	3	4	5	6–10	Laps	Laps Led	Races Led	Miles	$
1984	75	2	0	0	0	0	0	0	0	512	0	0	606	5,645
1986	88	2	0	0	0	0	0	0	0	59	0	0	56	1,950
Lifetime		80	1	0	1	2	1	6	28	22,472	213	16	24,535	$525,023

Joel Million

Joel Million
Racing Hometown: Richmond, KY

Year	Rank	Starts	Poles	1	2	3	4	5	6–10	Laps	Laps Led	Races Led	Miles	$
1954	19	9	0	0	0	0	0	0	1	1,298	0	0	1,324	1,092
1955	33	8	0	0	1	0	1	0	4	973	0	0	605	1,685
1956	218	2	0	0	0	0	0	0	0	175	0	0	88	50
Lifetime		19	0	0	1	0	1	0	5	2,446	0	0	2,016	$2,827

Curley Mills

Curley Mills
Racing Hometown: Charlotte, NC

Year	Rank	Starts	Poles	1	2	3	4	5	6–10	Laps	Laps Led	Races Led	Miles	$
1967	81	4	0	0	0	0	0	0	2	500	0	0	243	580
Lifetime		4	0	0	0	0	0	0	2	500	0	0	243	$580

Charlie Mincey

Charles Mincey
Racing Hometown: Acworth, GA

Year	Rank	Starts	Poles	1	2	3	4	5	6–10	Laps	Laps Led	Races Led	Miles	$
1954	107	1	0	0	0	0	0	0	1	184	0	0	92	100
Lifetime		1	0	0	0	0	0	0	1	184	0	0	92	$100

Billy Minter

William Minter
Racing Hometown: Martinsville, VA

Year	Rank	Starts	Poles	1	2	3	4	5	6–10	Laps	Laps Led	Races Led	Miles	$
1954	104	4	0	0	0	0	0	0	0	412	0	0	248	75
Lifetime		4	0	0	0	0	0	0	0	412	0	0	248	$75

Clyde Minter

Clyde Minter
B: 10/15/1921   D: 12/21/197
Racing Hometown: Martinsville, VA

Year	Rank	Starts	Poles	1	2	3	4	5	6–10	Laps	Laps Led	Races Led	Miles	$
1949	14	2	0	0	0	0	2	0	0	386	0	0	193	760
1950	17	8	0	0	0	1	0	2	0	765	0	0	671	1,155
1951	N/A	6	0	0	0	0	0	0	1	81	0	0	66	150
1952	41	5	0	0	0	0	0	0	3	620	0	0	442	375
1953	31	8	0	0	0	0	0	0	3	591	0	0	519	405
1954	28	12	0	0	0	0	0	0	6	1,653	0	0	870	900
1955	152T	1	0	0	0	0	0	0	1	178	0	0	89	100
Lifetime		42	0	0	0	1	2	2	14	4,274	0	0	2,850	$3,845

Pat Mintey

Patrick N Mintey
B: 5/25/1947
Racing Hometown: Arleta, CA

Year	Rank	Starts	Poles	1	2	3	4	5	6–10	Laps	Laps Led	Races Led	Miles	$
1981	101	1	0	0	0	0	0	0	0	40	0	0	105	850
1983	77	1	0	0	0	0	0	0	0	73	0	0	191	1,175
Lifetime		2	0	0	0	0	0	0	0	113	0	0	296	$2,025

Walter Minx

Walter Minx

Year	Rank	Starts	Poles	1	2	3	4	5	6–10	Laps	Laps Led	Races Led	Miles	$
1949	NR	1	0	0	0	0	0	0	0	25	0	0	25	0
Lifetime		1	0	0	0	0	0	0	0	25	0	0	25	$0

Artie Mitchell

Artie Mitchell
Racing Hometown: Savannah, GA

Year	Rank	Starts	Poles	1	2	3	4	5	6–10	Laps	Laps Led	Races Led	Miles	$
1954	156T	1	0	0	0	0	0	0	0	9	0	0	5	0
Lifetime		1	0	0	0	0	0	0	0	9	0	0	5	$0

Bill Mitchell

William Mitchell

Year	Rank	Starts	Poles	1	2	3	4	5	6–10	Laps	Laps Led	Races Led	Miles	$
1958	166	1	0	0	0	0	0	0	0	107	0	0	282	100
Lifetime		1	0	0	0	0	0	0	0	107	0	0	282	$100

Year	Rank	Starts	Poles	Finish						Laps	Laps Led	Races Led	Miles	$
				1	2	3	4	5	6–10					

Clyde Mitchell

Clyde Mitchell
Racing Hometown: Los Angeles, CA

Year	Rank	Starts	Poles	1	2	3	4	5	6–10	Laps	Laps Led	Races Led	Miles	$
1956	173T	1	0	0	0	0	0	0	0	216	0	0	216	50
1957	160T	1	0	0	0	0	0	0	0	50	0	0	125	60
1960	NR	2	0	0	0	0	0	0	1	135	0	0	135	190
Lifetime		4	0	0	0	0	0	0	1	401	0	0	476	$300

Dick Mitchell

Richard Mitchell
Racing Hometown: Torrance, CA

Year	Rank	Starts	Poles	1	2	3	4	5	6–10	Laps	Laps Led	Races Led	Miles	$
1963	107	1	0	0	0	0	0	0	0	126	0	0	340	200
1964	82	1	0	0	0	0	0	0	0	152	0	0	410	525
Lifetime		2	0	0	0	0	0	0	0	278	0	0	751	$725

Mike Mitchell

Michael Mitchell
Racing Hometown: Los Angeles, CA

Year	Rank	Starts	Poles	1	2	3	4	5	6–10	Laps	Laps Led	Races Led	Miles	$
1961	NR	1	0	0	0	0	0	0	0	5	0	0	13	50
Lifetime		1	0	0	0	0	0	0	0	5	0	0	13	$50

Herk Moak

Herbert Moak
Racing Hometown: Mt. Albany, NY

Year	Rank	Starts	Poles	1	2	3	4	5	6–10	Laps	Laps Led	Races Led	Miles	$
1955	190T	1	0	0	0	0	0	0	0	132	0	0	66	50
Lifetime		1	0	0	0	0	0	0	0	132	0	0	66	$50

Ethel Mobley

Ethel Mobley
B: 3/8/1920   D: 6/26/1984
Racing Hometown: Atlanta, GA

Year	Rank	Starts	Poles	1	2	3	4	5	6–10	Laps	Laps Led	Races Led	Miles	$
1949	52	2	0	0	0	0	0	0	0		0	0		50
Lifetime		2	0	0	0	0	0	0	0		0	0		$50

Butch Mock

Royce Mock, III
B: 4/8/1952
Racing Hometown: N. Miami, FL

Year	Rank	Starts	Poles	1	2	3	4	5	6–10	Laps	Laps Led	Races Led	Miles	$
1978	89	2	0	0	0	0	0	0	0	564	0	0	853	2,390
1979	126T	1	0	0	0	0	0	0	0	38	0	0	95	2,165
Lifetime		3	0	0	0	0	0	0	0	602	0	0	948	$4,555

Johnny Mock

John Mock
Racing Hometown: Eureka, KS

Year	Rank	Starts	Poles	1	2	3	4	5	6–10	Laps	Laps Led	Races Led	Miles	$
1955	152T	1	0	0	0	0	0	0	1	183	0	0	92	100
Lifetime		1	0	0	0	0	0	0	1	183	0	0	92	$100

Dick Moffitt

Richard Moffitt

Year	Rank	Starts	Poles	1	2	3	4	5	6–10	Laps	Laps Led	Races Led	Miles	$
1951	N/A	4	0	0	0	0	0	0	2	142	0	0	71	300
Lifetime		4	0	0	0	0	0	0	2	142	0	0	71	$300

Patty Moise

Patricia Moise
B: 12/19/1960
Racing Hometown: Jacksonville, FL

Year	Rank	Starts	Poles	1	2	3	4	5	6–10	Laps	Laps Led	Races Led	Miles	$
1987	94	1	0	0	0	0	0	0	0	53	0	0	130	1,690
1988	59	2	0	0	0	0	0	0	0	241	0	0	598	4,870
1989	69	2	0	0	0	0	0	0	0	33	0	0	88	6,180
Lifetime		5	0	0	0	0	0	0	0	327	0	0	816	$12,740

Chris Monoleos

Christopher Monoleos
B: 4/26/1938
Racing Hometown: Burbank, CA

Year	Rank	Starts	Poles	1	2	3	4	5	6–10	Laps	Laps Led	Races Led	Miles	$
1979	121	1	0	0	0	0	0	0	0	2	0	0	5	550
Lifetime		1	0	0	0	0	0	0	0	2	0	0	5	$550

Year	Rank	Starts	Poles	Finish						Laps	Laps Led	Races Led	Miles	$
				1	2	3	4	5	6–10					

Phil Montague

Philip Montague

Year	Rank	Starts	Poles	1	2	3	4	5	6–10	Laps	Laps Led	Races Led	Miles	$
1969	NR	1	0	0	0	0	0	0	0	8	0	0	8	230
Lifetime		1	0	0	0	0	0	0	0	8	0	0	8	$230

Jack Montgangelo

Jack Montgangelo

Year	Rank	Starts	Poles	1	2	3	4	5	6–10	Laps	Laps Led	Races Led	Miles	$
1956	161	1	0	0	0	0	0	0	0	206	0	0	206	100
Lifetime		1	0	0	0	0	0	0	0	206	0	0	206	$100

Henry Montgomery

Henry Montgomery
Racing Hometown: Tampa, FL

Year	Rank	Starts	Poles	1	2	3	4	5	6–10	Laps	Laps Led	Races Led	Miles	$
1963	134	1	0	0	0	0	0	0	0	166	0	0	50	75
Lifetime		1	0	0	0	0	0	0	0	166	0	0	50	$75

Ralph Moody

Ralph Moody
B: 9/10/1917
Racing Hometown: Taunton, MA

Year	Rank	Starts	Poles	1	2	3	4	5	6–10	Laps	Laps Led	Races Led	Miles	$
1956	8	35	5	4	5	2	1	1	8	5,258	312	6	3,506	15,493
1957	NR	10	0	1	0	2	2	0	0	1,039	100	1	560	2,905
1959	NR	1	0	0	0	0	0	0	1	197	0	0	99	200
1962	137	1	0	0	0	0	0	0	0	1	0	0	1	75
Lifetime		47	5	5	5	4	3	1	9	6,495	412	7	4,165	$18,673

Tommy Moon

Thomas Moon
B: 4/16/1925   D: 2002
Racing Hometown: Jacksonville, FL

Year	Rank	Starts	Poles	1	2	3	4	5	6–10	Laps	Laps Led	Races Led	Miles	$
1951	83	2	0	0	0	0	0	0	1		0	0		200
1952	35	6	1	0	1	0	0	1	1	487	0	0	428	1,145
1953	178	1	0	0	0	0	0	0	0	5	0	0	21	0
1954	111	1	0	0	0	0	0	0	1	179	0	0	90	100
Lifetime		10	1	0	1	0	0	1	3	671	0	0	538	$1,445

Bill Moore

William Moore
Racing Hometown: Phoenix, AZ

Year	Rank	Starts	Poles	1	2	3	4	5	6–10	Laps	Laps Led	Races Led	Miles	$
1954	NR	1	0	0	0	0	0	0	1	183	0	0	92	100
1956	88	6	0	0	0	0	0	0	2	633	0	0	574	485
1957	197	1	0	0	0	0	0	0	0	7	0	0	18	35
Lifetime		8	0	0	0	0	0	0	3	823	0	0	683	$620

Bob Moore

Robert F. Moore
B: 6/1/1921
Racing Hometown: Kent, OH

Year	Rank	Starts	Poles	1	2	3	4	5	6–10	Laps	Laps Led	Races Led	Miles	$
1950	NR	2	0	0	0	0	0	0	0		0	0		
1952	N/A	2	0	0	0	0	0	0	0		0	0		25
1952	45	5	0	0	0	1	0	0	2	524	0	0	270	575
Lifetime		9	0	0	0	1	0	0	2	524	0	0	270	$600

Bob Moore

Robert Moore
Racing Hometown: Tampa, FL

Year	Rank	Starts	Poles	1	2	3	4	5	6–10	Laps	Laps Led	Races Led	Miles	$
1952	NR	1	0	0	0	0	0	0	1		0	0		50
Lifetime		1	0	0	0	0	0	0	1		0	0		$50

Bob Moore

Robert Moore
Racing Hometown: Macon, GA

Year	Rank	Starts	Poles	1	2	3	4	5	6–10	Laps	Laps Led	Races Led	Miles	$
1968	58	4	0	0	0	0	0	0	1	1,033	0	0	1,057	2,745
Lifetime		4	0	0	0	0	0	0	1	1,033	0	0	1,057	$2,745

Bud Moore

Paul Moore (Little Bud)
B: 12/7/1941
Racing Hometown: Charleston, SC

Year	Rank	Starts	Poles	1	2	3	4	5	6–10	Laps	Laps Led	Races Led	Miles	$
1964	102	3	0	0	0	0	0	0	0	209	0	0	229	700

Year	Rank	Starts	Poles	Finish 1	2	3	4	5	6–10	Laps	Laps Led	Races Led	Miles	$

Bud Moore *continued*

Year	Rank	Starts	Poles	1	2	3	4	5	6–10	Laps	Laps Led	Races Led	Miles	$
1965	49	14	1	0	1	1	1	0	4	1,687	93	2	804	3,435
1966	115	1	0	0	0	0	0	0	0	35	0	0	18	100
1967	35	6	0	0	0	0	0	2	1	1,351	0	0	1,681	7,200
1968	29	16	0	0	1	0	1	0	7	3,399	51	2	3,219	12,325
1973	110	1	0	0	0	0	0	0	0	174	0	0	238	1,225
Lifetime		41	1	0	2	1	2	2	12	6,855	144	4	6,188	$24,985

Bunk Moore

Samuel Marion Moore
B: 1925   *Died circa 1987.*
Racing Hometown: Indian Trail, NC

Year	Rank	Starts	Poles	1	2	3	4	5	6–10	Laps	Laps Led	Races Led	Miles	$
1955	148T	2	0	0	0	0	0	0	0	199	0	0	100	50
1956	62	5	0	0	0	0	0	1	1	736	0	0	416	845
1958	NR	1	0	0	0	0	0	0	0	141	0	0	88	70
1959	73	10	0	0	0	0	0	0	0	1,350	0	0	684	530
1960	115	3	0	0	0	0	0	0	0	416	0	0	411	285
1961	153	2	0	0	0	0	0	0	0	273	0	0	137	150
1966	111T	1	0	0	0	0	0	0	0	101	0	0	51	100
Lifetime		24	0	0	0	0	0	1	1	3,216	0	0	1,886	$2,030

Charles Moore

Charles Moore
Racing Hometown: West Asheville, NC

Year	Rank	Starts	Poles	1	2	3	4	5	6–10	Laps	Laps Led	Races Led	Miles	$
1951	N/A	1	0	0	0	0	0	0	0		0	0		25
Lifetime		1	0	0	0	0	0	0	0		0	0		$25

Doug Moore

Douglas Beall Moore
Racing Hometown: Chattanooga, TN

Year	Rank	Starts	Poles	1	2	3	4	5	6–10	Laps	Laps Led	Races Led	Miles	$
1964	39	24	0	0	0	0	0	0	6	3,894	0	0	1,870	5,175
1965	67	5	0	0	0	0	0	0	0	664	0	0	452	1,160
Lifetime		29	0	0	0	0	0	0	6	4,558	0	0	2,322	$6,335

Fred Moore

Fred Moore (Red)
Racing Hometown: Pensacola, FL

Year	Rank	Starts	Poles	1	2	3	4	5	6–10	Laps	Laps Led	Races Led	Miles	$
1951	N/A	1	0	0	0	0	0	0	0	112	0	0	140	0
1953	63	2	0	0	0	0	0	0	1		0	0		75
Lifetime		3	0	0	0	0	0	0	1	112	0	0	140	$75

Lloyd Moore

Lloyd D. Moore
B: 6/8/1912
Racing Hometown: Frewsburg, NY

Year	Rank	Starts	Poles	1	2	3	4	5	6–10	Laps	Laps Led	Races Led	Miles	$
1949	26T	1	0	0	0	0	0	0	1	186	0	0	93	150
1950	4	16	0	1	2	3	1	0	3	1,358	57	2	1,046	5,235
1951	11	22	0	0	0	1	0	3	4	322	0	0	332	2,600
1952	20	8	0	0	1	0	1	0	2	1,457	0	0	1,084	2,193
1955	91	2	0	0	0	0	0	0	0	439	0	0	567	235
Lifetime		49	0	1	3	4	2	3	10	3,762	57	2	3,122	$10,413

Pat Moore

Murray Moore
Racing Hometown: Clymer, NY

Year	Rank	Starts	Poles	1	2	3	4	5	6–10	Laps	Laps Led	Races Led	Miles	$
1960	151	1	0	0	0	0	0	0	0	72	0	0	36	50
Lifetime		1	0	0	0	0	0	0	0	72	0	0	36	$50

Steve Moore

Steve Moore
B: 11/6/1958
Racing Hometown: Carrollton, GA

Year	Rank	Starts	Poles	1	2	3	4	5	6–10	Laps	Laps Led	Races Led	Miles	$
1977	NR	1	0	0	0	0	0	0	0	139	0	0	370	2,165
1978	90	1	0	0	0	0	0	0	0	150	0	0	399	1,590
1979	94T	1	0	0	0	0	0	0	0	170	0	0	452	2,415
1980	47	4	0	0	0	0	0	0	0	735	0	0	1,469	9,040
1982	59	4	0	0	0	0	0	0	0	456	4	1	727	6,625
1983	65	2	0	0	0	0	0	0	0	316	0	0	714	5,215

Year	Rank	Starts	Poles	Finish						Laps	Laps Led	Races Led	Miles	$
				1	2	3	4	5	6–10					

Steve Moore *continued*

Year	Rank	Starts	Poles	1	2	3	4	5	6–10	Laps	Laps Led	Races Led	Miles	$
1984	60	2	0	0	0	0	0	0	0	237	0	0	622	5,095
1988	51	3	0	0	0	0	0	0	0	726	0	0	1,069	18,790
Lifetime		18	0	0	0	0	0	0	0	2,929	4	1	5,822	$50,935

Rocky Moran

William James Moran (Rocky)
B: 2/3/1951
Racing Hometown: Arcadia, CA

Year	Rank	Starts	Poles	1	2	3	4	5	6–10	Laps	Laps Led	Races Led	Miles	$
1978	62	3	0	0	0	0	0	0	0	289	0	0	735	3,195
Lifetime		3	0	0	0	0	0	0	0	289	0	0	735	$3,195

Harold Morese

Harold Morese
D: 2/22/1953 *Killed in AAA race at Carrell Speedway, Gardena, CA*

Year	Rank	Starts	Poles	1	2	3	4	5	6–10	Laps	Laps Led	Races Led	Miles	$
1952	NR	1	0	0	0	0	0	0	0	186	0	0	93	25
Lifetime		1	0	0	0	0	0	0	0	186	0	0	93	$25

Jerry Morese

Jerry Morese
Racing Hometown: Newark, NJ

Year	Rank	Starts	Poles	1	2	3	4	5	6–10	Laps	Laps Led	Races Led	Miles	$
1951	70	2	0	0	0	0	0	1	0		0	0		275
1956	184T	1	0	0	0	0	0	0	0	184	0	0	92	100
Lifetime		3	0	0	0	0	0	1	0	184	0	0	92	$375

Tony Moretti

Anthony Moretti

Year	Rank	Starts	Poles	1	2	3	4	5	6–10	Laps	Laps Led	Races Led	Miles	$
1957	170	1	0	0	0	0	0	0	0	19	0	0	10	50
Lifetime		1	0	0	0	0	0	0	0	19	0	0	10	$50

Bill Morgan

Herbert William Morgan
Racing Hometown: Fairfax, VA

Year	Rank	Starts	Poles	1	2	3	4	5	6–10	Laps	Laps Led	Races Led	Miles	$
1953	86T	1	0	0	0	0	0	0	1	185	0	0	93	100
1954	187	1	0	0	0	0	0	0	0	44	0	0	44	0
1957	101	1	0	0	0	0	0	0	0	223	0	0	223	100
1960	125	1	0	0	0	0	0	0	1	183	0	0	92	130
1961	47	5	0	0	0	0	0	0	1	1,132	0	0	1,179	1,900
Lifetime		9	0	0	0	0	0	0	3	1,767	0	0	1,630	$2,230

Lee Morgan

Lee Morgan

Year	Rank	Starts	Poles	1	2	3	4	5	6–10	Laps	Laps Led	Races Led	Miles	$
1950	NR	1	0	0	0	0	0	0	0	342	0	0	428	0
Lifetime		1	0	0	0	0	0	0	0	342	0	0	428	$0

Sonny Morgan

Sonny Morgan
B: 1935
Racing Hometown: Beaumont, TX

Year	Rank	Starts	Poles	1	2	3	4	5	6–10	Laps	Laps Led	Races Led	Miles	$
1957	184	1	0	0	0	0	0	0	0		0	0		25
Lifetime		1	0	0	0	0	0	0	0		0	0		$25

Wayne Morgan

Wayne Morgan

Year	Rank	Starts	Poles	1	2	3	4	5	6–10	Laps	Laps Led	Races Led	Miles	$
1978	82	2	0	0	0	0	0	0	0	19	0	0	12	785
Lifetime		2	0	0	0	0	0	0	0	19	0	0	12	$785

Wes Morgan

Wister Lewis Morgan
B: 11/22/1922
Racing Hometown: Alexandria, VA

Year	Rank	Starts	Poles	1	2	3	4	5	6–10	Laps	Laps Led	Races Led	Miles	$
1960	74	2	0	0	0	0	0	0	0	277	0	0	378	350
1961	107	3	0	0	0	0	0	0	1	493	0	0	573	405
Lifetime		5	0	0	0	0	0	0	1	770	0	0	950	$755

Year	Rank	Starts	Poles	Finish						Laps	Laps Led	Races Led	Miles	$
				1	2	3	4	5	6–10					

Rob Moroso

Robert Moroso
B: 9/28/1968   D: 9/30/1990   *Killed in highway crash.*
Racing Hometown: Madison, CT

Year	Rank	Starts	Poles	1	2	3	4	5	6–10	Laps	Laps Led	Races Led	Miles	$
1988	54	2	0	0	0	0	0	0	0	473	0	0	585	5,750
1989	63	2	0	0	0	0	0	0	0	583	0	0	671	4,725
1990	30	25	0	0	0	0	0	0	1	5,666	9	3	6,971	162,002
Lifetime		29	0	0	0	0	0	0	1	6,722	9	3	8,227	$172,477

Buckshot Morris

Riley Morris
Racing Hometown: Atlanta, GA

Year	Rank	Starts	Poles	1	2	3	4	5	6–10	Laps	Laps Led	Races Led	Miles	$
1949	NR	2	0	0	0	0	0	0	0		0	0		0
Lifetime		2	0	0	0	0	0	0	0		0	0		$0

Bill Morton

Robert William Morton
B: 7/22/1938   D: 10/29/200
Racing Hometown: Church Hill, TN

Year	Rank	Starts	Poles	1	2	3	4	5	6–10	Laps	Laps Led	Races Led	Miles	$
1955	144	2	0	0	0	0	0	0	0	288	0	0	267	110
1957	77	5	0	0	0	0	0	0	4	653	0	0	365	600
1958	110	8	0	0	0	0	0	0	0	1,370	0	0	917	1,045
1959	71	3	0	0	0	0	0	0	0	398	0	0	218	100
1961	60	6	0	0	0	0	0	0	3	1,879	0	0	932	7,015
1962	41	5	0	0	0	0	0	0	2	1,359	0	0	1,255	1,350
1963	155	1	0	0	0	0	0	0	0	115	0	0	58	125
1965	58	5	0	0	0	0	0	0	0	601	0	0	832	2,590
Lifetime		35	0	0	0	0	0	0	9	6,663	0	0	4,842	$12,935

Walt Mortz

Walter Mortz

Year	Rank	Starts	Poles	1	2	3	4	5	6–10	Laps	Laps Led	Races Led	Miles	$
1957	NR	1	0	0	0	0	0	0	0	15	0	0	35	100
Lifetime		1	0	0	0	0	0	0	0	15	0	0	35	$100

Earl Mosbach

Earl Mosbach

Year	Rank	Starts	Poles	1	2	3	4	5	6–10	Laps	Laps Led	Races Led	Miles	$
1957	165T	1	0	0	0	0	0	0	0	55	0	0	28	50
Lifetime		1	0	0	0	0	0	0	0	55	0	0	28	$50

Earl Moss

Earl Moss
B: 7/28/1925   D: 9/23/1994
Racing Hometown: Creedmoor, NC

Year	Rank	Starts	Poles	1	2	3	4	5	6–10	Laps	Laps Led	Races Led	Miles	$
1951	N/A	5	0	0	0	0	0	0	1	479	0	0	515	310
1952	104T	1	0	0	0	0	0	0	0	162	0	0	81	25
1953	162	1	0	0	0	0	0	0	0	190	0	0	190	25
1956	198	2	0	0	0	0	0	0	0	84	0	0	67	125
1959	NR	2	0	0	0	0	0	0	1	279	0	0	140	140
Lifetime		11	0	0	0	0	0	0	2	1,194	0	0	992	$625

David Mote

David George Mote
B: 10/3/1940
Racing Hometown: Siler City, NC

Year	Rank	Starts	Poles	1	2	3	4	5	6–10	Laps	Laps Led	Races Led	Miles	$
1968	76	7	0	0	0	0	0	0	0	396	0	0	376	1,150
Lifetime		7	0	0	0	0	0	0	0	396	0	0	376	$1,150

Lothar Motschenbacher

Lothar Motschenbacher
B: 11/19/1938
Racing Hometown: Cologne, W.Germany

Year	Rank	Starts	Poles	1	2	3	4	5	6–10	Laps	Laps Led	Races Led	Miles	$
1970	NR	1	0	0	0	0	0	0	0	7	0	0	18	800
Lifetime		1	0	0	0	0	0	0	0	7	0	0	18	$800

Arden Mounts

Arden Mounts
Deceased.
Racing Hometown: Gilbert, WV

Year	Rank	Starts	Poles	1	2	3	4	5	6–10	Laps	Laps Led	Races Led	Miles	$
1953	29	10	0	0	0	0	0	0	1	792	0	0	759	395

Year	Rank	Starts	Poles	Finish 1	2	3	4	5	6–10	Laps	Laps Led	Races Led	Miles	$

Arden Mounts *continued*

Year	Rank	Starts	Poles	1	2	3	4	5	6–10	Laps	Laps Led	Races Led	Miles	$
1954	21	12	0	0	0	0	0	0	1	1,592	0	0	1,317	875
1955	32	12	1	0	0	0	0	0	4	1,560	0	0	1,050	1,025
1956	136	3	0	0	0	0	0	0	0	545	0	0	381	210
Lifetime		37	1	0	0	0	0	0	6	4,489	0	0	3,506	$2,505

Pete Moxley

Peter Moxley
Racing Hometown: Delta, PA

Year	Rank	Starts	Poles	1	2	3	4	5	6–10	Laps	Laps Led	Races Led	Miles	$
1954	196	2	0	0	0	0	0	0	0	149	0	0	75	10
Lifetime		2	0	0	0	0	0	0	0	149	0	0	75	$10

Larry Moyer

Lawrence Moyer
Racing Hometown: Ft. Wayne, IN

Year	Rank	Starts	Poles	1	2	3	4	5	6–10	Laps	Laps Led	Races Led	Miles	$
1988	79	1	0	0	0	0	0	0	0	148	0	0	370	2,355
Lifetime		1	0	0	0	0	0	0	0	148	0	0	370	$2,355

Roy Mulligan

Roy Mulligan
B: 1940   D: 6/30/1975   *Electrocuted.*
Racing Hometown: Birmingham, AL

Year	Rank	Starts	Poles	1	2	3	4	5	6–10	Laps	Laps Led	Races Led	Miles	$
1971	NR	1	0	0	0	0	0	0	0	83	0	0	221	1,450
Lifetime		1	0	0	0	0	0	0	0	83	0	0	221	$1,450

Jack Mulrain

Jack Mulrain
Racing Hometown: Elizabeth, NJ

Year	Rank	Starts	Poles	1	2	3	4	5	6–10	Laps	Laps Led	Races Led	Miles	$
1952	120T	1	0	0	0	0	0	0	0	173	0	0	87	25
Lifetime		1	0	0	0	0	0	0	0	173	0	0	87	$25

Frank Mundy

Frank Mundy (Real Name: Francisco Melendez)
B: 6/18/1918
Racing Hometown: Atlanta, GA

Year	Rank	Starts	Poles	1	2	3	4	5	6–10	Laps	Laps Led	Races Led	Miles	$
1949	10	4	0	0	0	1	1	0	0	274	0	0	381	1,160
1950	23	8	0	0	0	0	0	0	3	310	0	0	283	550
1951	NR	26	4	3	2	1	2	1	3	874	445	5	579	6,460
1952	NR	5	0	0	0	0	0	0	2	536	0	0	462	275
1956	24	9	0	0	1	1	0	1	2	1,589	0	0	1,479	3,585
Lifetime		52	4	3	3	3	3	2	10	3,583	445	5	3,185	$12,030

Jim Mundy

James Mundy
Racing Hometown: Columbia, SC

Year	Rank	Starts	Poles	1	2	3	4	5	6–10	Laps	Laps Led	Races Led	Miles	$
1956	239T	1	0	0	0	0	0	0	0	104	0	0	78	50
Lifetime		1	0	0	0	0	0	0	0	104	0	0	78	$50

Dutch Munsinger

Dutch Munsinger
Racing Hometown: Tabor, IA

Year	Rank	Starts	Poles	1	2	3	4	5	6–10	Laps	Laps Led	Races Led	Miles	$
1954	178	1	0	0	0	0	0	0	0	46	0	0	69	0
1955	125	2	0	0	0	0	0	0	1	145	0	0	121	150
1956	292	1	0	0	0	0	0	0	0	69	0	0	69	25
Lifetime		4	0	0	0	0	0	0	1	260	0	0	259	$175

Terry Murchison

Terry Murchison
Racing Hometown: Rome, GA

Year	Rank	Starts	Poles	1	2	3	4	5	6–10	Laps	Laps Led	Races Led	Miles	$
1965	138	1	0	0	0	0	0	0	0	2	0	0	1	250
Lifetime		1	0	0	0	0	0	0	0	2	0	0	1	$250

Jim Murray

James Murray
Racing Hometown: Illinois

Year	Rank	Starts	Poles	1	2	3	4	5	6–10	Laps	Laps Led	Races Led	Miles	$
1955	105	2	0	0	0	0	0	1	0	165	0	0	197	330
Lifetime		2	0	0	0	0	0	1	0	165	0	0	197	$330

Year	Rank	Starts	Poles	Finish						Laps	Laps Led	Races Led	Miles	$
				1	2	3	4	5	6–10					

Ralph Murray

Ralph Murray

Year	Rank	Starts	Poles	1	2	3	4	5	6–10	Laps	Laps Led	Races Led	Miles	$
1956	301	1	0	0	0	0	0	0	0	2	0	0	1	0
Lifetime		1	0	0	0	0	0	0	0	2	0	0	1	$0

David Murry

David Murry
B: 1/29/1957
Racing Hometown: New Orleans, LA

Year	Rank	Starts	Poles	1	2	3	4	5	6–10	Laps	Laps Led	Races Led	Miles	$
1999	67	1	0	0	0	0	0	0	0	78	0	0	191	21,965
Lifetime		1	0	0	0	0	0	0	0	78	0	0	191	$21,965

Charles Muscatel

Charles Muscatel
Racing Hometown: Lambertville, NJ

Year	Rank	Starts	Poles	1	2	3	4	5	6–10	Laps	Laps Led	Races Led	Miles	$
1949	37T	1	0	0	0	0	0	0	1		0	0		75
1950	NR	1	0	0	0	0	0	0	0	26	0	0	26	0
Lifetime		2	0	0	0	0	0	0	1	26	0	0	26	$75

Elmer Musclow

Elmer Musclow
Racing Hometown: Rochester, NY

Year	Rank	Starts	Poles	1	2	3	4	5	6–10	Laps	Laps Led	Races Led	Miles	$
1953	127T	1	0	0	0	0	0	0	0		0	0		25
1954	134	1	0	0	0	0	0	0	0	171	0	0	86	25
Lifetime		2	0	0	0	0	0	0	0	171	0	0	86	$50

Ted Musgrave

Ted Musgrave
B: 12/18/1955
Racing Hometown: Franklin, WI

Year	Rank	Starts	Poles	1	2	3	4	5	6–10	Laps	Laps Led	Races Led	Miles	$
1990	49	4	0	0	0	0	0	0	0	786	0	0	1,019	17,190
1991	23	29	0	0	0	0	0	0	0	9,074	6	5	10,581	200,910
1992	18	29	0	0	0	0	0	1	6	9,253	11	3	10,989	449,121
1993	25	29	0	0	0	0	0	2	3	8,530	8	3	10,397	458,615
1994	13	31	3	0	0	0	0	1	7	9,237	50	4	10,818	669,687
1995	7	31	1	0	2	2	2	1	6	9,290	43	6	11,381	1,147,445
1996	16	31	1	0	0	1	1	0	5	9,351	3	2	11,387	961,512
1997	12	32	0	0	1	1	3	0	3	9,266	131	6	12,095	1,256,680
1998	23	31	0	0	1	0	0	1	3	8,298	0	0	11,068	1,253,626
1999	33	32	0	0	0	0	0	0	2	9,063	5	2	11,670	1,162,403
2000	40	18	0	0	0	0	0	0	0	4,951	7	6	6,248	827,216
2001	64	1	0	0	0	0	0	0	0	198	0	0	495	43,565
2002	50	5	0	0	0	0	0	0	0	1,537	0	0	1,943	283,770
Lifetime		303	5	0	4	4	6	6	35	88,834	264	37	110,092	$8,731,740

Billy Myers

William Wade Myers
B: 10/19/1924   D: 4/12/1958   *Died of heart attack while racing @ Winston-Salem.*
Racing Hometown: Germanton, NC

Year	Rank	Starts	Poles	1	2	3	4	5	6–10	Laps	Laps Led	Races Led	Miles	$
1951	59	8	0	0	0	1	0	0	1	609	23	1	702	925
1952	NR	1	0	0	0	0	0	0	0	220	0	0	220	50
1955	78	3	0	0	0	0	0	0	1	512	0	0	555	240
1956	6	42	1	2	6	3	1	1	9	6,270	204	4	4,231	15,830
1957	12	28	0	0	0	0	4	0	5	3,923	201	1	2,441	6,566
1958	162	2	0	0	0	0	0	0	0	28	0	0	115	50
Lifetime		84	1	2	6	4	5	1	16	11,562	428	6	8,265	$23,661

Bob Myers

Robert Myers
Racing Hometown: Calumet City, IL

Year	Rank	Starts	Poles	1	2	3	4	5	6–10	Laps	Laps Led	Races Led	Miles	$
1951	164	1	0	0	0	0	0	0	0	230	0	0	230	50
Lifetime		1	0	0	0	0	0	0	0	230	0	0	230	$50

Bobby Myers

Robert Harris Myers
B: 6/27/1927   D: 9/2/1957   *Killed in Darlington's Southern 500.*
Racing Hometown: Winston-Salem, NC

Year	Rank	Starts	Poles	1	2	3	4	5	6–10	Laps	Laps Led	Races Led	Miles	$
1951	208	2	0	0	0	0	0	0	0	199	0	0	199	50
1952	158	1	0	0	0	0	0	0	0	145	0	0	181	0
1953	30	2	0	0	0	0	0	0	1	321	0	0	441	390

Year	Rank	Starts	Poles	1	2	3	Finish 4	5	6–10	Laps	Laps Led	Races Led	Miles	$

Bobby Myers *continued*

Year	Rank	Starts	Poles	1	2	3	4	5	6–10	Laps	Laps Led	Races Led	Miles	$
1956	61	8	0	0	0	0	0	0	2	980	0	0	714	600
1957	126	2	0	0	0	0	0	0	0	53	1	1	50	335
Lifetime		15	0	0	0	0	0	0	3	1,698	1	1	1,585	$1,375

Gary Myers

Gary Myers
B: 2/20/1940
Racing Hometown: Huntsville, AL

Year	Rank	Starts	Poles	1	2	3	4	5	6–10	Laps	Laps Led	Races Led	Miles	$
1974	125	2	0	0	0	0	0	0	0	35	0	0	36	1,425
1974	125	2	0	0	0	0	0	0	0	35	0	0	36	1,425
1976	29	14	0	0	0	0	0	0	0	3,072	0	0	2,795	11,430
1976	29	14	0	0	0	0	0	0	0	3,072	0	0	2,795	11,430
1977	36	10	0	0	0	0	0	0	0	2,648	0	0	2,691	10,975
1977	36	10	0	0	0	0	0	0	0	2,648	0	0	2,691	10,975
1978	27	19	0	0	0	0	0	0	0	5,524	0	0	6,134	22,140
1978	27	19	0	0	0	0	0	0	0	5,524	0	0	6,134	22,140
Lifetime		90	0	0	0	0	0	0	0	22,558	0	0	23,311	$91,940

Randy Myers

Randall Myers
Racing Hometown: Walnut Grove, NC

Year	Rank	Starts	Poles	1	2	3	4	5	6–10	Laps	Laps Led	Races Led	Miles	$
1977	NR	1	0	0	0	0	0	0	0	377	0	0	383	1,000
Lifetime		1	0	0	0	0	0	0	0	377	0	0	383	$1,000

Ronny Myers

Ronald Myers
Racing Hometown: Los Angeles, CA

Year	Rank	Starts	Poles	1	2	3	4	5	6–10	Laps	Laps Led	Races Led	Miles	$
1959	NR	1	0	0	0	0	0	0	0	369	0	0	148	100
Lifetime		1	0	0	0	0	0	0	0	369	0	0	148	$100

Jerry Nadeau

Jerry Nadeau
B: 9/9/1969
Racing Hometown: Danbury, CT

Year	Rank	Starts	Poles	1	2	3	4	5	6–10	Laps	Laps Led	Races Led	Miles	$
1997	54	5	0	0	0	0	0	0	0	997	0	0	1,907	108,645
1998	36	30	0	0	0	0	0	0	0	8,132	0	0	10,523	804,867
1999	34	34	0	0	0	0	0	1	1	9,476	9	1	12,329	1,370,229
2000	20	34	0	1	0	0	2	0	2	8,839	357	10	11,508	2,038,669
2001	17	36	0	0	1	1	1	1	6	10,238	170	7	13,511	2,507,827
2002	37	29	0	0	0	0	0	0	1	7,605	102	4	10,231	1,806,133
Lifetime		168	0	1	1	1	3	2	10	45,287	638	22	60,010	$8,636,370

Joe Nagle

Joseph Nagle
Racing Hometown: Dayton, OH

Year	Rank	Starts	Poles	1	2	3	4	5	6–10	Laps	Laps Led	Races Led	Miles	$
1950	68T	1	0	0	0	0	0	0	1	0	0	0	0	75
Lifetime		1	0	0	0	0	0	0	1	0	0	0	0	$75

Burrhead Nantz

Homer Nantz
Racing Hometown: Mooresville, NC

Year	Rank	Starts	Poles	1	2	3	4	5	6–10	Laps	Laps Led	Races Led	Miles	$
1960	117	3	0	0	0	0	0	0	0	66	0	0	133	300
Lifetime		3	0	0	0	0	0	0	0	66	0	0	133	$300

Harold Nash

Harold Nash
Racing Hometown: Atlanta, GA

Year	Rank	Starts	Poles	1	2	3	4	5	6–10	Laps	Laps Led	Races Led	Miles	$
1953	180	2	0	0	0	0	0	0	0		0	0		50
1954	192T	2	0	0	0	0	0	0	0	27	0	0	111	0
Lifetime		4	0	0	0	0	0	0	0	27	0	0	111	$50

Johnny Nave

John Nave
Racing Hometown: Jonesboro, GA

Year	Rank	Starts	Poles	1	2	3	4	5	6–10	Laps	Laps Led	Races Led	Miles	$
1958	NR	1	0	0	0	0	0	0	0	70	0	0	63	70
1962	132	2	0	0	0	0	0	0	0	170	0	0	106	200
1964	NR	1	0	0	0	0	0	0	0	2	0	0	1	250
Lifetime		4	0	0	0	0	0	0	0	242	0	0	170	$520

Year	Rank	Starts	Poles	Finish 1	2	3	4	5	6–10	Laps	Laps Led	Races Led	Miles	$

Brian Naylor

Brian Naylor
B: 1926
Racing Hometown: Stockport, England

Year	Rank	Starts	Poles	1	2	3	4	5	6–10	Laps	Laps Led	Races Led	Miles	$
1961	156	2	0	0	0	0	0	0	0	86	0	0	215	200
Lifetime		2	0	0	0	0	0	0	0	86	0	0	215	$200

Al Neal

Al Neal
Racing Hometown: N. Lithonium, MD

Year	Rank	Starts	Poles	1	2	3	4	5	6–10	Laps	Laps Led	Races Led	Miles	$
1954	189	1	0	0	0	0	0	0	0	13	0	0	13	0
1954	189	1	0	0	0	0	0	0	0	13	0	0	13	0
Lifetime		2	0	0	0	0	0	0	0	26	0	0	26	$0

Chuck Neale

Charles Neale
Racing Hometown: Grand Rapids, MI

Year	Rank	Starts	Poles	1	2	3	4	5	6–10	Laps	Laps Led	Races Led	Miles	$
1954	NR	1	0	0	0	0	0	0	0	170	0	0	85	25
Lifetime		1	0	0	0	0	0	0	0	170	0	0	85	$25

Ed Negre

Ed Charles Negre
B: 7/16/1929
Racing Hometown: Kelso, WA

Year	Rank	Starts	Poles	1	2	3	4	5	6–10	Laps	Laps Led	Races Led	Miles	$
1955	83T	1	0	0	0	0	0	0	1	239	0	0	239	200
1956	48	5	0	0	0	0	1	1	2	936	207	2	597	1,225
1957	NR	6	0	0	0	0	0	1	2	519	0	0	307	825
1961	113	2	0	0	0	0	0	0	1	308	0	0	258	260
1967	49	14	0	0	0	0	0	0	0	1,439	0	0	1,100	3,805
1968	31	24	0	0	0	0	0	0	1	2,930	0	0	1,467	4,985
1969	27	31	0	0	0	0	0	0	4	4,556	0	0	3,474	15,160
1970	26	31	0	0	0	0	0	0	1	3,345	0	0	2,702	14,580
1971	12	43	0	0	0	0	0	0	2	8,359	0	0	7,549	29,738
1972	21	26	0	0	0	0	0	0	0	5,755	0	0	6,702	30,538
1973	18	24	0	0	0	0	0	1	1	6,230	0	0	7,193	34,235
1974	23	26	0	0	0	0	0	0	0	5,302	0	0	6,344	24,622
1975	17	30	0	0	0	0	0	0	4	7,250	2	1	7,816	49,629
1976	19	28	0	0	0	0	0	0	2	6,153	0	0	7,221	50,919
1977	22	24	0	0	0	0	0	0	0	5,523	0	0	6,040	42,665
1978	28	21	0	0	0	0	0	0	1	4,826	0	0	4,951	28,995
1979	51	3	0	0	0	0	0	0	0	849	0	0	1,387	11,215
Lifetime		339	0	0	0	0	1	3	22	64,519	209	3	65,349	$343,596

Jess Nelson

Jess Nelson
Racing Hometown: Sacramento, CA

Year	Rank	Starts	Poles	1	2	3	4	5	6–10	Laps	Laps Led	Races Led	Miles	$
1956	214T	1	0	0	0	0	0	0	0	88	0	0	88	50
Lifetime		1	0	0	0	0	0	0	0	88	0	0	88	$50

Norm Nelson

Norm Nelson
B: 1/30/1923   D: 11/8/1988
Racing Hometown: Racine, WI

Year	Rank	Starts	Poles	1	2	3	4	5	6–10	Laps	Laps Led	Races Led	Miles	$
1955	68	2	1	1	0	0	0	0	0	273	106	1	354	1,420
1966	NR	1	0	0	0	0	0	0	1	176	0	0	475	1,000
1967	NR	1	0	0	0	1	0	0	0	183	0	0	494	5,250
1968	NR	1	0	0	0	0	0	0	0	87	0	0	235	720
Lifetime		5	1	1	0	1	0	0	1	719	106	1	1,558	$8,390

Tony Nelson

Tony Nelson
Racing Hometown: Ventura, CA

Year	Rank	Starts	Poles	1	2	3	4	5	6–10	Laps	Laps Led	Races Led	Miles	$
1954	49	3	0	0	0	0	0	0	1	995	0	0	616	325
Lifetime		3	0	0	0	0	0	0	1	995	0	0	616	$325

Joe Nemechek

Joseph Frank Nemechek, III
B: 9/26/1963
Racing Hometown: Naples, FL

Year	Rank	Starts	Poles	1	2	3	4	5	6–10	Laps	Laps Led	Races Led	Miles	$
1993	44	5	0	0	0	0	0	0	0	1,114	0	0	1,516	56,580

Year	Rank	Starts	Poles	Finish						Laps	Laps Led	Races Led	Miles	$
				1	2	3	4	5	6–10					

Joe Nemechek *continued*

Year	Rank	Starts	Poles	1	2	3	4	5	6–10	Laps	Laps Led	Races Led	Miles	$
1994	27	29	0	0	0	1	0	0	2	7,953	22	2	9,488	386,315
1995	28	29	0	0	0	0	1	0	3	8,502	1	1	10,221	428,925
1996	34	29	0	0	0	0	0	0	2	8,110	2	1	9,711	666,247
1997	28	30	2	0	0	0	0	0	3	8,861	108	6	11,285	732,194
1998	26	32	0	0	0	0	1	0	3	8,771	41	5	11,909	1,343,991
1999	30	34	3	1	0	0	0	0	2	9,410	158	6	11,966	1,634,946
2000	15	34	1	0	1	1	0	1	6	9,467	8	3	12,281	1,907,281
2001	28	31	0	1	0	0	0	0	3	8,706	227	6	11,369	2,510,723
2002	34	33	0	0	2	0	1	0	0	8,165	178	4	10,877	2,454,482
Lifetime		286	6	2	3	2	3	1	24	79,059	745	34	100,624	$12,121,684

Archie Nepstad

Archie Nepstad
Racing Hometown: Rochester, MN

Year	Rank	Starts	Poles	1	2	3	4	5	6–10	Laps	Laps Led	Races Led	Miles	$
1955	235	1	0	0	0	0	0	0	0	41	0	0	41	25
Lifetime		1	0	0	0	0	0	0	0	41	0	0	41	$25

Joe Edd Neubert

Joe Edd Neubert
Racing Hometown: Knoxville, TN

Year	Rank	Starts	Poles	1	2	3	4	5	6–10	Laps	Laps Led	Races Led	Miles	$
1967	99	3	0	0	0	0	0	0	1	254	0	0	127	465
Lifetime		3	0	0	0	0	0	0	1	254	0	0	127	$465

Al Neves

Al Neves
Racing Hometown: Oakland, CA

Year	Rank	Starts	Poles	1	2	3	4	5	6–10	Laps	Laps Led	Races Led	Miles	$
1954	137	2	0	0	0	0	0	0	0	455	0	0	333	65
Lifetime		2	0	0	0	0	0	0	0	455	0	0	333	$65

Paul Newkirk

Paul Newkirk
Racing Hometown: Cedar Rapids, IA

Year	Rank	Starts	Poles	1	2	3	4	5	6–10	Laps	Laps Led	Races Led	Miles	$
1951	34	1	0	0	0	0	0	1	0	241	0	0	241	500
1952	184	1	0	0	0	0	0	0	0	27	0	0	27	0
1953	112	1	0	0	0	0	0	0	0		0	0		25
Lifetime		3	0	0	0	0	0	1	0	268	0	0	268	$525

Homer Newland

Homer Newland
B: 2/17/1930
Racing Hometown: Dearborne, MI

Year	Rank	Starts	Poles	1	2	3	4	5	6–10	Laps	Laps Led	Races Led	Miles	$
1955	215	1	0	0	0	0	0	0	0	120	0	0	60	25
1969	65	2	0	0	0	0	0	0	0	179	0	0	393	1,875
Lifetime		3	0	0	0	0	0	0	0	299	0	0	453	$1,900

Gus Newman

Gus Newman
Racing Hometown: Las Vegas, NV

Year	Rank	Starts	Poles	1	2	3	4	5	6–10	Laps	Laps Led	Races Led	Miles	$
1961	130	2	0	0	0	0	0	0	0	40	0	0	93	130
Lifetime		2	0	0	0	0	0	0	0	40	0	0	93	$130

Ryan Newman

Ryan Newman
B: 12/8/1977
Racing Hometown: South Bend, IN

Year	Rank	Starts	Poles	1	2	3	4	5	6–10	Laps	Laps Led	Races Led	Miles	$
2000	71	1	0	0	0	0	0	0	0	176	0	0	176	37,825
2001	49	7	1	0	1	0	0	1	0	1,478	13	2	2,350	465,276
2002	6	36	6	1	5	1	3	4	8	9,871	753	22	13,101	5,346,651
Lifetime		44	7	1	6	1	3	5	8	11,525	766	24	15,626	$5,849,752

Rick Newsom

Rickey Lyle Newsom
B: 3/19/1950   D: 8/16/1988   *Killed in private plane crash.*
Racing Hometown: Ft. Mill, SC

Year	Rank	Starts	Poles	1	2	3	4	5	6–10	Laps	Laps Led	Races Led	Miles	$
1972	91	1	0	0	0	0	0	0	0	231	0	0	462	800
1973	34	12	0	0	0	0	0	0	0	3,209	0	0	2,559	8,530
1974	92	3	0	0	0	0	0	0	0	801	0	0	773	2,370
1975	37	10	0	0	0	0	0	0	0	1,672	0	0	1,695	9,370

Year	Rank	Starts	Poles	1	2	3	4	5	6–10	Laps	Laps Led	Races Led	Miles	$

Rick Newsom *continued*

Year	Rank	Starts	Poles	1	2	3	4	5	6–10	Laps	Laps Led	Races Led	Miles	$
1976	44	7	0	0	0	0	0	0	0	1,604	0	0	1,393	5,520
1977	NR	7	0	0	0	0	0	0	0	1,240	0	0	888	3,260
1979	49	4	0	0	0	0	0	0	0	484	0	0	1,236	5,530
1980	44	6	0	0	0	0	0	0	0	1,179	0	0	790	3,830
1981	36	9	0	0	0	0	0	0	0	1,676	0	0	1,741	8,625
1982	36	8	0	0	0	0	0	0	0	1,143	0	0	1,931	12,390
1983	41	6	0	0	0	0	0	0	0	2,097	0	0	1,699	14,445
1984	82	1	0	0	0	0	0	0	0	242	0	0	246	1,235
1985	41	6	0	0	0	0	0	0	0	834	0	0	1,105	8,690
1986	69	3	0	0	0	0	0	0	0	358	0	0	447	4,185
Lifetime		83	0	0	0	0	0	0	0	16,770	0	0	16,964	$88,780

A.F. Nichols

A.F. Nichols
Racing Hometown: Atlanta, GA

Year	Rank	Starts	Poles	1	2	3	4	5	6–10	Laps	Laps Led	Races Led	Miles	$
1962	NR	1	0	0	0	0	0	0	0	1	0	0	2	200
Lifetime		1	0	0	0	0	0	0	0	1	0	0	2	$200

Nick Nicolette

Nicholas Nicolette
Racing Hometown: Belleville, NJ

Year	Rank	Starts	Poles	1	2	3	4	5	6–10	Laps	Laps Led	Races Led	Miles	$
1951	N/A	1	0	0	0	0	0	0	0		0	0		0
1953	115	2	0	0	0	0	0	0	0		0	0		65
Lifetime		3	0	0	0	0	0	0	0		0	0		$65

Wayne Niedecken

Wayne Niedecken
B: 4/8/1931   D: 3/22/1993
Racing Hometown: Pensacola, FL

Year	Rank	Starts	Poles	1	2	3	4	5	6–10	Laps	Laps Led	Races Led	Miles	$
1953	NR	1	0	0	0	0	0	0	0		0	0		25
Lifetime		1	0	0	0	0	0	0	0		0	0		$25

Stan Noble

Stanley Noble
Racing Hometown: Gardena, CA

Year	Rank	Starts	Poles	1	2	3	4	5	6–10	Laps	Laps Led	Races Led	Miles	$
1951	N/A	3	0	0	0	0	0	0	0		0	0		75
Lifetime		3	0	0	0	0	0	0	0		0	0		$75

Don Noel

Donald E. Noel
B: 6/29/1929
Racing Hometown: Arletto, CA

Year	Rank	Starts	Poles	1	2	3	4	5	6–10	Laps	Laps Led	Races Led	Miles	$
1960	71	3	0	0	0	0	0	1	0	240	0	0	309	900
1961	66	4	0	0	2	0	0	1	0	493	0	0	518	1,705
1963	86	2	0	0	0	0	0	0	0	259	0	0	699	800
1964	NR	1	0	0	0	0	0	0	0	10	0	0	27	500
1967	74	1	0	0	0	0	0	0	0	131	0	0	354	625
1968	98	1	0	0	0	0	0	0	0	31	0	0	84	575
1970	106	2	0	0	0	0	0	0	0	38	0	0	100	1,450
1971	NR	3	0	0	0	0	0	0	0	164	0	0	425	3,235
1972	92	2	0	0	0	0	0	0	0	159	0	0	413	2,585
1973	104	1	0	0	0	0	0	0	0	119	0	0	312	770
1977	110T	1	0	0	0	0	0	0	0	0	0	0	0	500
1978	91	2	0	0	0	0	0	0	0	180	0	0	453	1,765
1979	116T	1	0	0	0	0	0	0	0	15	0	0	39	700
Lifetime		24	0	0	2	0	0	2	0	1,839	0	0	3,732	$16,110

Brad Noffsinger

Brad Noffsinger
B: 8/29/1960
Racing Hometown: Huntington Beach, CA

Year	Rank	Starts	Poles	1	2	3	4	5	6–10	Laps	Laps Led	Races Led	Miles	$
1988	36	17	0	0	0	0	0	0	0	3,555	1	1	5,518	54,645
Lifetime		17	0	0	0	0	0	0	0	3,555	1	1	5,518	$54,645

G.T. Nolan

G.Thomas Nolan (Tommy)
Racing Hometown: Jetersville, VA

Year	Rank	Starts	Poles	1	2	3	4	5	6–10	Laps	Laps Led	Races Led	Miles	$
1965	74	8	0	0	0	0	0	0	1	1,018	0	0	563	1,165

Year	Rank	Starts	Poles	Finish 1	2	3	4	5	6–10	Laps	Laps Led	Races Led	Miles	$

G.T. Nolan *continued*

Year	Rank	Starts	Poles	1	2	3	4	5	6–10	Laps	Laps Led	Races Led	Miles	$
1966	93	3	0	0	0	0	0	0	0	486	0	0	199	305
1967	105	1	0	0	0	0	0	0	0	144	0	0	130	100
1968	122	1	0	0	0	0	0	0	0	123	0	0	62	110
Lifetime		13	0	0	0	0	0	0	1	1,771	0	0	952	$1,680

Whitey Norman

William G. Norman
B: 4/14/1926
Racing Hometown: Winston-Salem, NC

Year	Rank	Starts	Poles	1	2	3	4	5	6–10	Laps	Laps Led	Races Led	Miles	$
1956	180T	1	0	0	0	0	0	0	1	150	0	0	94	100
1957	24	13	0	0	1	0	0	0	3	2,437	0	0	1,614	3,990
1958	138	9	0	0	0	0	2	0	1	1,348	0	0	752	1,635
1959	NR	6	0	0	0	0	0	0	0	899	0	0	403	445
Lifetime		29	0	0	1	0	2	0	5	4,834	0	0	2,862	$6,170

Ed Normi

Edward Normi
B: 6/27/0   D: 1993
Racing Hometown: Petaluma, CA

Year	Rank	Starts	Poles	1	2	3	4	5	6–10	Laps	Laps Led	Races Led	Miles	$
1954	124	2	0	0	0	0	0	0	0	313	0	0	176	65
1955	NR	1	0	0	0	0	0	0	0	237	0	0	237	250
Lifetime		3	0	0	0	0	0	0	0	550	0	0	413	$315

Chick Norris

Chick Norris
Racing Hometown: Pittsburgh, PA

Year	Rank	Starts	Poles	1	2	3	4	5	6–10	Laps	Laps Led	Races Led	Miles	$
1955	178T	1	0	0	0	0	0	0	0	10	0	0	5	50
Lifetime		1	0	0	0	0	0	0	0	10	0	0	5	$50

Paul Norris

Paul Norris
Racing Hometown: Concord, NC

Year	Rank	Starts	Poles	1	2	3	4	5	6–10	Laps	Laps Led	Races Led	Miles	$
1960	139	1	0	0	0	0	0	0	0	1	0	0	2	200
Lifetime		1	0	0	0	0	0	0	0	1	0	0	2	$200

Bill Norton

William Norton
Racing Hometown: Gardena, CA

Year	Rank	Starts	Poles	1	2	3	4	5	6–10	Laps	Laps Led	Races Led	Miles	$
1951	N/A	3	0	1	0	1	0	0	1	200	19	1	100	1,675
1953	NR	1	0	0	0	0	0	0	0	241	0	0	331	110
Lifetime		4	0	1	0	1	0	0	1	441	19	1	431	$1,785

George Norton

George Norton
Racing Hometown: Pacoima, CA

Year	Rank	Starts	Poles	1	2	3	4	5	6–10	Laps	Laps Led	Races Led	Miles	$
1957	109	3	0	0	0	0	0	0	1	192	0	0	116	235
1958	79	2	0	0	0	0	0	0	0	248	0	0	512	170
1959	NR	1	0	0	0	0	0	0	0	73	0	0	29	50
Lifetime		6	0	0	0	0	0	0	1	513	0	0	657	$455

Jack Norton

James Norton
Racing Hometown: Long Beach, CA

Year	Rank	Starts	Poles	1	2	3	4	5	6–10	Laps	Laps Led	Races Led	Miles	$
1960	130	1	0	0	0	0	0	0	0	65	0	0	65	100
1961	83	4	0	0	0	0	0	0	1	352	0	0	418	590
1963	118	1	0	0	0	0	0	0	0	140	0	0	378	325
Lifetime		6	0	0	0	0	0	0	1	557	0	0	861	$1,015

James Norton

James Norton
Racing Hometown: Dallas, GA

Year	Rank	Starts	Poles	1	2	3	4	5	6–10	Laps	Laps Led	Races Led	Miles	$
1960	NR	5	0	0	0	0	0	0	1	814	0	0	352	540
1963	142	1	0	0	0	0	0	0	0	84	0	0	126	275
Lifetime		6	0	0	0	0	0	0	1	898	0	0	478	$815

George Norvath

George Norvath

Year	Rank	Starts	Poles	1	2	3	4	5	6–10	Laps	Laps Led	Races Led	Miles	$
1954	NR	1	0	0	0	0	0	0	0	143	0	0	72	10
Lifetime		1	0	0	0	0	0	0	0	143	0	0	72	$10

Year	Rank	Starts	Poles	Finish 1	2	3	4	5	6–10	Laps	Laps Led	Races Led	Miles	$

Tom Nundy

Thomas Nundy

Year	Rank	Starts	Poles	1	2	3	4	5	6–10	Laps	Laps Led	Races Led	Miles	$
1958	NR	1	0	0	0	0	0	0	0	34	0	0	11	65
Lifetime		1	0	0	0	0	0	0	0	34	0	0	11	$65

Jack O'Brien

Jack O'Brien
Racing Hometown: Pittsburgh, PA

Year	Rank	Starts	Poles	1	2	3	4	5	6–10	Laps	Laps Led	Races Led	Miles	$
1949	NR	2	0	0	0	0	0	0	0	115	0	0	58	0
Lifetime		2	0	0	0	0	0	0	0	115	0	0	58	$0

Dan Obrist

Daniel Obrist
B: 9/27/1946
Racing Hometown: Portland, OR

Year	Rank	Starts	Poles	1	2	3	4	5	6–10	Laps	Laps Led	Races Led	Miles	$
1995	70	1	0	0	0	0	0	0	0	7	0	0	18	9,760
Lifetime		1	0	0	0	0	0	0	0	7	0	0	18	$9,760

Don O'Dell

Donald O'Dell
Racing Hometown: Blue Island, IL

Year	Rank	Starts	Poles	1	2	3	4	5	6–10	Laps	Laps Led	Races Led	Miles	$
1960	142	1	0	0	0	0	0	0	0	90	0	0	135	200
1961	127	2	0	0	0	0	0	0	1	48	0	0	120	340
Lifetime		3	0	0	0	0	0	0	1	138	0	0	255	$540

Joe Bill O'Dell

Joseph William O'Dell
Racing Hometown: Baltimore, MD

Year	Rank	Starts	Poles	1	2	3	4	5	6–10	Laps	Laps Led	Races Led	Miles	$
1953	96	5	0	0	0	0	0	0	1	183	0	0	92	210
1954	94	4	0	0	0	0	0	0	0	556	0	0	382	75
1956	269	1	0	0	0	0	0	0	0	37	0	0	19	60
1957	104	1	0	0	0	0	0	0	0	222	0	0	222	0
Lifetime		11	0	0	0	0	0	0	1	998	0	0	714	$345

Rick O'Dell

Richard O'Dell
B: 10/26/1948
Racing Hometown: Victoria, B.C., Canada

Year	Rank	Starts	Poles	1	2	3	4	5	6–10	Laps	Laps Led	Races Led	Miles	$
1981	76	1	0	0	0	0	0	0	0	86	0	0	225	2,145
Lifetime		1	0	0	0	0	0	0	0	86	0	0	225	$2,145

Larry Odo

Lawrence Odo
B: 9/28/1922
Racing Hometown: Chicago, IL

Year	Rank	Starts	Poles	1	2	3	4	5	6–10	Laps	Laps Led	Races Led	Miles	$
1956	NR	1	0	0	0	0	0	0	0	361	0	0	181	150
1959	NR	1	0	0	0	0	0	0	0	3	0	0	8	100
Lifetime		2	0	0	0	0	0	0	0	364	0	0	188	$250

Randy Ogden

Randall Ogden
B: 9/23/1958
Racing Hometown: Woodward, OK

Year	Rank	Starts	Poles	1	2	3	4	5	6–10	Laps	Laps Led	Races Led	Miles	$
1979	NR	3	0	0	0	0	0	0	0	473	0	0	737	2,465
1980	72	3	0	0	0	0	0	0	0	135	0	0	267	2,385
1981	58	4	0	0	0	0	0	0	0	577	0	0	762	3,905
Lifetime		10	0	0	0	0	0	0	0	1,185	0	0	1,766	$8,755

Don Oldenberg

Donald Oldenberg
B: 12/18/1922   D: 12/13/1983
Racing Hometown: Highland, IN

Year	Rank	Starts	Poles	1	2	3	4	5	6–10	Laps	Laps Led	Races Led	Miles	$
1951	62	3	0	0	0	0	0	1	1		0	0		375
1952	186	1	0	0	0	0	0	0	0		0	0		25
1953	35	4	0	0	0	0	0	1	1	223	0	0	245	375
1954	NR	6	0	0	0	0	0	0	3	806	0	0	715	900
1955	88	2	0	0	0	0	0	0	2	260	0	0	178	350
1956	206	3	0	0	0	0	0	0	0	495	0	0	341	200
1957	98	1	0	0	0	0	0	0	0		0	0		100
Lifetime		20	0	0	0	0	0	2	7	1,784	0	0	1,479	$2,325

341

Year	Rank	Starts	Poles	Finish 1	2	3	4	5	6–10	Laps	Laps Led	Races Led	Miles	$

Jack Oldenhage

Jack Oldenhage
  Racing Hometown: Merced, CA

Year	Rank	Starts	Poles	1	2	3	4	5	6–10	Laps	Laps Led	Races Led	Miles	$
1957	86	3	0	0	0	0	0	0	1	354	0	0	177	250
Lifetime		3	0	0	0	0	0	0	1	354	0	0	177	$250

Barney Oldfield

Bernard Oldfield
  Racing Hometown: Asheboro, NC

Year	Rank	Starts	Poles	1	2	3	4	5	6–10	Laps	Laps Led	Races Led	Miles	$
1957	118	1	0	0	0	0	0	0	0	356	0	0	178	150
Lifetime		1	0	0	0	0	0	0	0	356	0	0	178	$150

Charles Oldham

Charles T. Oldham
  Racing Hometown: Manning, SC

Year	Rank	Starts	Poles	1	2	3	4	5	6–10	Laps	Laps Led	Races Led	Miles	$
1956	272T	1	0	0	0	0	0	0	0		0	0		25
Lifetime		1	0	0	0	0	0	0	0		0	0		$25

Jackie Oliver

Jack Keith Oliver
  B: 8/14/1943
  Racing Hometown: Walton-on-Thames, England

Year	Rank	Starts	Poles	1	2	3	4	5	6–10	Laps	Laps Led	Races Led	Miles	$
1971	NR	1	0	0	0	0	0	0	0	117	0	0	234	605
1972	NR	7	0	0	0	0	1	0	0	1,034	0	0	1,486	11,575
Lifetime		8	0	0	0	0	1	0	0	1,151	0	0	1,720	$12,180

Jerry Oliver

Jerry Dennis Oliver
  B: 1/18/1944
  Racing Hometown: Concord, CA

Year	Rank	Starts	Poles	1	2	3	4	5	6–10	Laps	Laps Led	Races Led	Miles	$
1966	77	1	0	0	0	0	0	0	0	144	0	0	389	560
1967	65	1	0	0	0	0	0	0	0	160	0	0	432	800
1968	92	1	0	0	0	0	0	0	0	39	0	0	105	510
1969	NR	1	0	0	0	0	0	0	0	48	0	0	130	770
1970	70	2	0	0	0	0	0	0	1	268	0	0	702	2,175
1971	NR	2	0	0	0	0	0	1	0	192	0	0	503	2,970
1972	NR	1	0	0	0	0	0	0	0	122	0	0	320	1,100
Lifetime		9	0	0	0	0	0	1	1	973	0	0	2,581	$8,885

Budd Olsen

Budd Olsen
  B: 10/16/1924   D: 12/26/199
  Racing Hometown: Paulsboro, NJ

Year	Rank	Starts	Poles	1	2	3	4	5	6–10	Laps	Laps Led	Races Led	Miles	$
1949	51	1	0	0	0	0	0	0	0	180	0	0	180	75
1961	NR	1	0	0	0	0	0	0	0	168	0	0	42	175
Lifetime		2	0	0	0	0	0	0	0	348	0	0	222	$250

Bill Olson

William Olson

Year	Rank	Starts	Poles	1	2	3	4	5	6–10	Laps	Laps Led	Races Led	Miles	$
1958	88	1	0	0	0	0	0	0	0	162	0	0	426	130
Lifetime		1	0	0	0	0	0	0	0	162	0	0	426	$130

Keith Olson

Keith Olson

Year	Rank	Starts	Poles	1	2	3	4	5	6–10	Laps	Laps Led	Races Led	Miles	$
1957	NR	1	0	0	0	0	0	0	0	17	0	0	9	100
Lifetime		1	0	0	0	0	0	0	0	17	0	0	9	$100

Ollie Olson

A. A. Olson
  Racing Hometown: Richmond, VA

Year	Rank	Starts	Poles	1	2	3	4	5	6–10	Laps	Laps Led	Races Led	Miles	$
1953	165T	1	0	0	0	0	0	0	0		0	0		25
Lifetime		1	0	0	0	0	0	0	0		0	0		$25

Jerry O'Neil

Jerry O'Neil
  B: 3/28/1956
  Racing Hometown: Auburn, NY

Year	Rank	Starts	Poles	1	2	3	4	5	6–10	Laps	Laps Led	Races Led	Miles	$
1989	52	4	0	0	0	0	0	0	0	1,026	0	0	1,255	9,165
1990	51	4	0	0	0	0	0	0	0	423	0	0	1,054	27,580

Year	Rank	Starts	Poles	Finish 1	2	3	4	5	6–10	Laps	Laps Led	Races Led	Miles	$

Jerry O'Neil *continued*

Year	Rank	Starts	Poles	1	2	3	4	5	6–10	Laps	Laps Led	Races Led	Miles	$
1992	46	6	0	0	0	0	0	0	0	958	0	0	1,644	32,370
1993	64T	2	0	0	0	0	0	0	0	340	0	0	506	13,700
Lifetime		16	0	0	0	0	0	0	0	2,747	0	0	4,459	$82,815

Jan Opperman

Jan Opperman
B: 2/9/1939 D: 9/4/1997
Racing Hometown: Beaver Crossing, NE

Year	Rank	Starts	Poles	1	2	3	4	5	6–10	Laps	Laps Led	Races Led	Miles	$
1974	103	1	0	0	0	0	0	0	1	188	0	0	470	1,850
Lifetime		1	0	0	0	0	0	0	1	188	0	0	470	$1,850

Jim Ord

James Ord

Year	Rank	Starts	Poles	1	2	3	4	5	6–10	Laps	Laps Led	Races Led	Miles	$
1955	87	2	0	0	0	0	0	0	1	217	0	0	192	225
Lifetime		2	0	0	0	0	0	0	1	217	0	0	192	$225

Bobby Ore

Robert Ore
Racing Hometown: Gunter, TX

Year	Rank	Starts	Poles	1	2	3	4	5	6–10	Laps	Laps Led	Races Led	Miles	$
1974	137	1	0	0	0	0	0	0	0	297	0	0	177	440
Lifetime		1	0	0	0	0	0	0	0	297	0	0	177	$440

Gibb Orr

Gibb Orr
B: 1918
Racing Hometown: Niles, OH

Year	Rank	Starts	Poles	1	2	3	4	5	6–10	Laps	Laps Led	Races Led	Miles	$
1952	95	2	0	0	0	0	0	0	0	197	0	0	120	25
Lifetime		2	0	0	0	0	0	0	0	197	0	0	120	$25

Phil Orr

Phillip Orr
Racing Hometown: Winter Park, FL

Year	Rank	Starts	Poles	1	2	3	4	5	6–10	Laps	Laps Led	Races Led	Miles	$
1957	96	1	0	0	0	0	0	0	0		0	0		110
1958	84	1	0	0	0	0	0	0	0	31	0	0	127	50
Lifetime		2	0	0	0	0	0	0	0	31	0	0	127	$160

Red Ortwein

Myron Ortwein
Racing Hometown: San Lorenzo, CA

Year	Rank	Starts	Poles	1	2	3	4	5	6–10	Laps	Laps Led	Races Led	Miles	$
1954	170	2	0	0	0	0	0	0	0	338	0	0	241	40
Lifetime		2	0	0	0	0	0	0	0	338	0	0	241	$40

Bill Osborne

William Osborne
Racing Hometown: Pensacola, FL

Year	Rank	Starts	Poles	1	2	3	4	5	6–10	Laps	Laps Led	Races Led	Miles	$
1950	NR	1	0	0	0	0	0	0	0	311	0	0	389	100
1951	67	1	0	0	0	0	1	0	0	148	0	0	111	300
1956	155	1	0	0	0	0	0	0	0	128	0	0	192	75
Lifetime		3	0	0	0	0	1	0	0	587	0	0	692	$475

Bill Osborne

William Osborne
B: 11/24/1946
Racing Hometown: Rialto, CA

Year	Rank	Starts	Poles	1	2	3	4	5	6–10	Laps	Laps Led	Races Led	Miles	$
1971	NR	2	0	0	0	0	0	0	0	61	0	0	157	1,870
1972	117	1	0	0	0	0	0	0	0	36	0	0	90	1,440
1974	85	2	0	0	0	0	0	0	0	164	0	0	418	1,875
1975	73T	2	0	0	0	0	0	0	0	192	0	0	503	2,230
1977	NR	1	0	0	0	0	0	0	0	188	0	0	470	1,350
1980	88	2	0	0	0	0	0	0	0	42	0	0	75	1,075
1985	60	2	0	0	0	0	0	0	0	198	0	0	519	3,605
1986	NR	1	0	0	0	0	0	0	0	38	0	0	100	850
Lifetime		13	0	0	0	0	0	0	0	658	0	0	2,332	$14,295

Bob Osborne

Robert Osborne

Year	Rank	Starts	Poles	1	2	3	4	5	6–10	Laps	Laps Led	Races Led	Miles	$
1957	82	2	0	0	0	0	0	0	0	80	0	0	158	135

Year	Rank	Starts	Poles	Finish 1	2	3	4	5	6–10	Laps	Laps Led	Races Led	Miles	$

Bob Osborne *continued*

Year	Rank	Starts	Poles	1	2	3	4	5	6–10	Laps	Laps Led	Races Led	Miles	$
1958	168	1	0	0	0	0	0	0	0	16	0	0	42	100
Lifetime		3	0	0	0	0	0	0	0	96	0	0	200	$235

George Osborne

George Osborne
Racing Hometown: Winchester, KY

Year	Rank	Starts	Poles	1	2	3	4	5	6–10	Laps	Laps Led	Races Led	Miles	$
1953	32	2	0	0	0	0	0	0	0	477	0	0	528	300
1954	204	1	0	0	0	0	0	0	0	16	0	0	66	0
Lifetime		3	0	0	0	0	0	0	0	493	0	0	594	$300

Johnny Osteen

John Osteen
Racing Hometown: Orlando, FL

Year	Rank	Starts	Poles	1	2	3	4	5	6–10	Laps	Laps Led	Races Led	Miles	$
1956	280	1	0	0	0	0	0	0	0		0	0		0
Lifetime		1	0	0	0	0	0	0	0		0	0		$0

Don Ostendorf

Donald Ostendorf
Racing Hometown: N.Platte, NE

Year	Rank	Starts	Poles	1	2	3	4	5	6–10	Laps	Laps Led	Races Led	Miles	$
1953	127T	1	0	0	0	0	0	0	0		0	0		25
Lifetime		1	0	0	0	0	0	0	0		0	0		$25

Billy Oswald

Williamy Oswald
Racing Hometown: New York, NY

Year	Rank	Starts	Poles	1	2	3	4	5	6–10	Laps	Laps Led	Races Led	Miles	$
1953	NR	1	0	0	0	0	0	0	1	174	0	0	174	150
1963	135T	1	0	0	0	0	0	0	0	61	0	0	31	60
Lifetime		2	0	0	0	0	0	0	1	235	0	0	205	$210

Nelson Oswald

Nelson Oswald
Racing Hometown: Jamestown, NC

Year	Rank	Starts	Poles	1	2	3	4	5	6–10	Laps	Laps Led	Races Led	Miles	$
1978	46	6	0	0	0	0	0	0	0	1,103	0	0	781	2,955
1979	43	6	0	0	0	0	0	0	0	842	0	0	1,000	3,610
1980	78T	2	0	0	0	0	0	0	0	184	0	0	374	2,520
Lifetime		14	0	0	0	0	0	0	0	2,129	0	0	2,154	$9,085

L.D. Ottinger

Lloyd Dolph Ottinger
B: 12/30/1938
Racing Hometown: Newport, TN

Year	Rank	Starts	Poles	1	2	3	4	5	6–10	Laps	Laps Led	Races Led	Miles	$
1966	144	1	0	0	0	0	0	0	0	32	0	0	16	0
1973	56	3	0	0	1	0	0	0	1	813	0	0	955	7,452
1974	62	4	0	0	0	0	0	0	0	290	0	0	395	4,985
1984	77	2	0	0	0	0	0	0	0	695	0	0	714	7,650
Lifetime		10	0	0	1	0	0	0	1	1,830	0	0	2,080	$20,087

Frank Oviado

Frank Oviado
Racing Hometown: Phoenix, AZ

Year	Rank	Starts	Poles	1	2	3	4	5	6–10	Laps	Laps Led	Races Led	Miles	$
1951	NR	1	0	0	0	0	0	0	0		0	0		0
Lifetime		1	0	0	0	0	0	0	0		0	0		0

Cotton Owens

Everett Owens
B: 5/21/1924
Racing Hometown: Spartanburg, SC

Year	Rank	Starts	Poles	1	2	3	4	5	6–10	Laps	Laps Led	Races Led	Miles	$
1950	13	3	0	0	0	0	0	0	1	511	23	1	727	1,100
1951	42	5	0	0	0	0	0	1	2	370	0	0	463	225
1952	65	4	0	0	0	0	0	0	1	391	0	0	202	200
1953	76	1	0	0	0	0	0	0	0	274	0	0	274	50
1954	84	4	0	0	0	0	0	0	1	530	0	0	475	175
1955	29	2	0	0	0	0	0	1	1	549	0	0	584	900
1956	52	8	0	0	0	0	0	1	3	1,137	0	0	709	870
1957	14	17	1	1	1	0	0	1	3	2,300	179	3	1,769	12,784
1958	17	29	2	1	4	2	1	0	9	3,700	208	3	2,208	6,579
1959	2	37	2	1	4	2	2	4	9	6,633	209	4	4,347	14,640
1960	39	14	3	1	3	1	0	0	0	2,121	184	6	2,362	14,065
1961	22	17	2	4	3	1	2	1	0	2,694	57	4	2,124	11,800

Year	Rank	Starts	Poles	Finish 1	2	3	4	5	6–10	Laps	Laps Led	Races Led	Miles	$

Cotton Owens *continued*

Year	Rank	Starts	Poles	1	2	3	4	5	6–10	Laps	Laps Led	Races Led	Miles	$
1962	30	16	1	0	2	2	2	1	1	2,000	36	2	1,515	5,905
1963	114T	1	0	0	0	0	0	0	1	170	0	0	85	175
1964	80	2	0	1	1	0	0	0	0	466	54	1	299	3,400
Lifetime		160	11	9	18	8	7	10	32	23,846	950	24	18,143	$72,868

Augie Pabst

August Pabst
B: 1933
Racing Hometown: Milwaukee, WI

Year	Rank	Starts	Poles	1	2	3	4	5	6–10	Laps	Laps Led	Races Led	Miles	$
1963	NR	1	0	0	0	0	0	0	0	18	0	0	49	250
Lifetime		1	0	0	0	0	0	0	0	18	0	0	49	$250

Ken Pace

Kenneth Pace
Racing Hometown: Martinsville, VA

Year	Rank	Starts	Poles	1	2	3	4	5	6–10	Laps	Laps Led	Races Led	Miles	$
1954	NR	2	0	0	0	0	0	0	0	258	0	0	144	25
1955	155	2	0	0	0	0	0	0	0	160	0	0	80	25
Lifetime		4	0	0	0	0	0	0	0	418	0	0	224	$50

Sammy Packard

Samuel Packard
D: 2003
Racing Hometown: Barrington, RI

Year	Rank	Starts	Poles	1	2	3	4	5	6–10	Laps	Laps Led	Races Led	Miles	$
1951	N/A	2	0	0	0	0	0	0	0		0	0		50
1961	115	1	0	0	0	0	0	0	1	444	0	0	111	275
1962	NR	1	0	0	0	0	0	0	0	45	0	0	23	110
Lifetime		4	0	0	0	0	0	0	1	489	0	0	134	$435

Eddie Pagan

Edward L. Pagan
B: 8/1/1918   D: 8/1/1984
Racing Hometown: Lynwood, CA

Year	Rank	Starts	Poles	1	2	3	4	5	6–10	Laps	Laps Led	Races Led	Miles	$
1954	80	2	0	0	0	0	0	0	0	682	0	0	453	140
1955	107	2	0	0	0	0	0	0	0	287	0	0	287	120
1956	32	8	2	1	1	0	0	2	0	1,366	1	1	1,037	4,095
1957	15	15	2	3	3	3	1	1	0	2,611	3	3	1,802	7,274
1958	9	27	2	0	2	1	1	7	7	3,961	57	2	2,607	7,472
1959	NR	1	0	0	0	0	0	0	1	439	0	0	176	375
1961	68	5	0	0	0	0	0	1	3	581	0	0	657	985
1962	98	1	0	0	0	0	0	0	0	354	0	0	177	250
1963	132	1	0	0	0	0	0	0	0	137	0	0	370	325
Lifetime		62	6	4	6	4	2	11	11	10,418	61	6	7,564	$21,036

Marian Pagan

Marian Pagan (Mopsie)
Racing Hometown: Lynwood, CA

Year	Rank	Starts	Poles	1	2	3	4	5	6–10	Laps	Laps Led	Races Led	Miles	$
1954	NR	1	0	0	0	0	0	0	0	261	0	0	131	25
Lifetime		1	0	0	0	0	0	0	0	261	0	0	131	$25

Arthur Page

Arthur Page
Racing Hometown: Charlotte, NC

Year	Rank	Starts	Poles	1	2	3	4	5	6–10	Laps	Laps Led	Races Led	Miles	$
1965	112T	1	0	0	0	0	0	0	0	43	0	0	22	100
Lifetime		1	0	0	0	0	0	0	0	43	0	0	22	$100

Lenny Page

Lenny Plewniak
Racing Hometown: Buffalo, NY

Year	Rank	Starts	Poles	1	2	3	4	5	6–10	Laps	Laps Led	Races Led	Miles	$
1956	NR	1	0	0	0	0	0	0	1	180	0	0	90	250
1957	73	4	0	0	0	0	0	0	1	396	0	0	332	410
1959	72	2	0	0	0	0	0	0	1	251	0	0	143	280
1960	61	5	0	0	0	0	0	0	2	774	0	0	616	1,050
Lifetime		12	0	0	0	0	0	0	5	1,601	0	0	1,180	$1,990

Mike Page

Michael Page
Racing Hometown: Richmond, VA

Year	Rank	Starts	Poles	1	2	3	4	5	6–10	Laps	Laps Led	Races Led	Miles	$
1966	109	1	0	0	0	0	0	0	0	132	0	0	119	100
Lifetime		1	0	0	0	0	0	0	0	132	0	0	119	$100

Year	Rank	Starts	Poles		Finish					Laps	Laps Led	Races Led	Miles	$
				1	2	3	4	5	6–10					

Pete Page

Peter Page
Racing Hometown: Nashville, TN

Year	Rank	Starts	Poles	1	2	3	4	5	6–10	Laps	Laps Led	Races Led	Miles	$
1951	N/A	1	0	0	0	0	0	0	0		0	0		25
Lifetime		1	0	0	0	0	0	0	0		0	0		$25

Harold Painter

William Harold Painter
Racing Hometown: Greenvville, NC

Year	Rank	Starts	Poles	1	2	3	4	5	6–10	Laps	Laps Led	Races Led	Miles	$
1965	132	1	0	0	0	0	0	0	0	0	0	0	0	100
Lifetime		1	0	0	0	0	0	0	0	0	0	0	0	$100

Bud Palmer

Bud Palmer
Racing Hometown: Nassau, NY

Year	Rank	Starts	Poles	1	2	3	4	5	6–10	Laps	Laps Led	Races Led	Miles	$
1955	188	1	0	0	0	0	0	0	0	36	0	0	148	35
1956	274	1	0	0	0	0	0	0	0		0	0		0
Lifetime		2	0	0	0	0	0	0	0	36	0	0	148	$35

Clyde Palmer

Clyde Palmer
B: 1923
Racing Hometown: Monte Vista, CA

Year	Rank	Starts	Poles	1	2	3	4	5	6–10	Laps	Laps Led	Races Led	Miles	$
1954	NR	2	0	0	0	0	1	0	1	526	0	0	263	450
1955	115	2	0	0	0	1	0	0	0	154	0	0	154	470
1956	34	11	0	0	2	1	0	1	2	1,730	296	2	1,381	2,755
1957	67	6	0	0	0	1	0	0	0	578	0	0	380	795
1961	188	1	0	0	0	0	0	0	0	16	0	0	16	25
Lifetime		22	0	0	2	3	1	1	3	3,004	296	2	2,193	$4,495

Ernest Palmer

Ernest C. Palmer
Racing Hometown: Nassau, NY

Year	Rank	Starts	Poles	1	2	3	4	5	6–10	Laps	Laps Led	Races Led	Miles	$
1954	202	1	0	0	0	0	0	0	0	20	0	0	82	0
Lifetime		1	0	0	0	0	0	0	0	20	0	0	82	$0

Norm Palmer

Norm Palmer
B: 5/30/1940   *Killed in late 1980s. Drove off cliff, then struck by Mack truck after climbing to safety.*
Racing Hometown: Torrance, CA

Year	Rank	Starts	Poles	1	2	3	4	5	6–10	Laps	Laps Led	Races Led	Miles	$
1977	55	3	0	0	0	0	0	0	1	239	0	0	620	4,560
1978	73	2	0	0	0	0	0	0	0	119	0	0	312	2,100
1979	79T	1	0	0	0	0	0	0	1	91	0	0	238	2,500
1985	98	1	0	0	0	0	0	0	0	22	0	0	58	745
Lifetime		7	0	0	0	0	0	0	2	471	0	0	1,227	$9,905

Marvin Panch

Marvin Richard Panch
B: 5/28/1926
Racing Hometown: Oakland, CA

Year	Rank	Starts	Poles	1	2	3	4	5	6–10	Laps	Laps Led	Races Led	Miles	$
1951	36	3	0	0	1	0	0	0	1		0	0		1,075
1953	60	2	0	0	0	0	0	0	0	275	0	0	378	160
1954	17	10	1	0	2	1	0	0	4	2,100	17	1	1,779	4,747
1955	14	10	0	0	2	0	2	0	0	1,597	15	1	1,654	4,385
1956	10	20	1	1	2	5	2	0	3	3,298	150	6	2,502	11,520
1957	2	42	4	6	3	6	6	1	5	6,890	396	11	4,401	24,307
1958	18	11	2	0	1	1	1	2	0	1,833	157	3	1,576	4,114
1959	66	4	0	0	0	0	0	0	0	640	0	0	860	1,050
1960	26	11	0	0	0	0	0	0	1	1,482	22	1	2,322	3,225
1961	18	9	1	1	1	0	1	0	3	1,517	57	2	2,576	14,789
1962	9	17	0	0	2	3	0	0	3	3,642	172	4	3,758	26,746
1963	13	12	3	1	2	5	1	0	3	3,510	280	6	3,742	39,102
1964	10	31	4	3	7	3	4	1	3	6,499	593	9	5,031	34,836
1965	5	20	5	4	1	4	1	2	2	4,743	856	12	4,716	64,027
1966	17	14	0	1	0	1	2	0	2	2,808	183	5	3,843	38,432
Lifetime		216	21	17	24	29	20	6	30	40,834	2,898	61	39,135	$272,515

Year	Rank	Starts	Poles	Finish						Laps	Laps Led	Races Led	Miles	$
				1	2	3	4	5	6–10					

Richie Panch

Richard Panch
B: 5/28/1954   D: 9/2/1985   *Killed in private plane crash.*
Racing Hometown: Daytona Beach, FL

Year	Rank	Starts	Poles	1	2	3	4	5	6–10	Laps	Laps Led	Races Led	Miles	$
1973	70	4	0	0	0	0	0	0	0	510	0	0	654	4,510
1974	14	28	0	0	0	1	0	1	5	6,257	1	1	6,873	52,713
1975	29	14	0	0	0	0	0	1	3	2,276	8	3	3,133	32,585
1976	92T	1	0	0	0	0	0	0	0	252	0	0	384	1,035
Lifetime		47	0	0	0	1	0	2	8	9,295	9	4	11,043	$90,843

Jimmy Pardue

James Mansfield Pardue
B: 10/26/1930   D: 9/22/1964   *Killed @ Charlotte in Goodyear tire test.*
Racing Hometown: N.Wilkesboro, NC

Year	Rank	Starts	Poles	1	2	3	4	5	6–10	Laps	Laps Led	Races Led	Miles	$
1955	245	1	0	0	0	0	0	0	0	10	0	0	5	0
1956	145	2	0	0	0	0	0	0	0	170	0	0	85	200
1959	NR	7	0	0	0	0	0	0	1	657	0	0	308	515
1960	17	32	0	0	0	0	0	1	10	5,004	0	0	3,704	5,610
1961	11	44	0	0	0	0	1	2	13	7,757	0	0	5,628	5,916
1962	19	29	0	1	1	1	1	1	11	7,274	200	3	4,855	12,066
1963	6	52	1	1	0	1	4	1	13	9,719	74	3	7,295	20,359
1964	5	50	2	0	2	4	4	4	10	9,412	237	5	6,613	41,598
Lifetime		217	3	2	3	6	10	9	58	40,003	511	11	28,493	$86,264

Dan Pardus

Dan Pardus
B: 4/2/1963
Racing Hometown: Daytona Beach, FL

Year	Rank	Starts	Poles	1	2	3	4	5	6–10	Laps	Laps Led	Races Led	Miles	$
1998	68	1	0	0	0	0	0	0	0	99	0	0	248	25,425
Lifetime		1	0	0	0	0	0	0	0	99	0	0	248	$25,425

Steve Park

Steve Park
B: 8/23/1967
Racing Hometown: E. Northport, NY

Year	Rank	Starts	Poles	1	2	3	4	5	6–10	Laps	Laps Led	Races Led	Miles	$
1997	51	5	0	0	0	0	0	0	0	1,235	0	0	1,443	74,480
1998	42	17	0	0	0	0	0	0	0	4,595	0	0	5,626	487,265
1999	14	34	0	0	0	0	0	0	5	9,575	166	6	12,243	1,767,690
2000	11	34	2	1	0	1	3	1	7	9,925	290	11	12,877	2,052,827
2001	32	24	0	1	3	0	1	0	7	6,368	477	8	8,777	2,385,971
2002	33	32	0	0	0	0	0	0	2	8,721	50	2	10,951	2,681,594
Lifetime		146	2	2	3	1	4	1	21	40,419	983	27	51,918	$9,449,827

Hank Parker Jr.

Hank Parker Jr.
B: 10/7/1975
Racing Hometown: Denver, NC

Year	Rank	Starts	Poles	1	2	3	4	5	6–10	Laps	Laps Led	Races Led	Miles	$
2002	79T	1	0	0	0	0	0	0	0	389	0	0	396	39,625
Lifetime		1	0	0	0	0	0	0	0	389	0	0	396	$39,625

Stan Parker

Stanley L. Parker
Racing Hometown: Maitland, FL

Year	Rank	Starts	Poles	1	2	3	4	5	6–10	Laps	Laps Led	Races Led	Miles	$
1963	NR	1	0	0	0	0	0	0	0	59	0	0	18	0
Lifetime		1	0	0	0	0	0	0	0	59	0	0	18	$0

Bill Parks

William Parks

Year	Rank	Starts	Poles	1	2	3	4	5	6–10	Laps	Laps Led	Races Led	Miles	$
1956	193	2	0	0	0	0	0	0	0	205	0	0	205	110
Lifetime		2	0	0	0	0	0	0	0	205	0	0	205	$110

Paul Parks

Paul Parks
Racing Hometown: Columbus, OH

Year	Rank	Starts	Poles	1	2	3	4	5	6–10	Laps	Laps Led	Races Led	Miles	$
1950	44	6	0	0	0	0	0	0	1	95	0	0	95	375
1951	N/A	1	0	0	0	0	0	0	0		0	0		25
1953	181	1	0	0	0	0	0	0	0	33	0	0	17	25
1960	NR	3	0	0	0	0	0	0	0	273	0	0	537	250

Year	Rank	Starts	Poles	1	2	3	4	5	6–10	Laps	Laps Led	Races Led	Miles	$

Paul Parks *continued*

Year	Rank	Starts	Poles	1	2	3	4	5	6–10	Laps	Laps Led	Races Led	Miles	$
1961	155	2	0	0	0	0	0	0	0	208	0	0	520	200
Lifetime		13	0	0	0	0	0	0	1	609	0	0	1,168	$875

Bud Parnell

William Parnell
    Racing Hometown: College Park, GA

Year	Rank	Starts	Poles	1	2	3	4	5	6–10	Laps	Laps Led	Races Led	Miles	$
1960	85	4	0	0	0	0	0	0	1	407	0	0	204	280
Lifetime		4	0	0	0	0	0	0	1	407	0	0	204	$280

Stan Parnell

Stanley Parnell
    Racing Hometown: Albany, GA

Year	Rank	Starts	Poles	1	2	3	4	5	6–10	Laps	Laps Led	Races Led	Miles	$
1952	126T	1	0	0	0	0	0	0	0	159	0	0	80	50
Lifetime		1	0	0	0	0	0	0	0	159	0	0	80	$50

Wendell Parnell

Wendell Parnell

Year	Rank	Starts	Poles	1	2	3	4	5	6–10	Laps	Laps Led	Races Led	Miles	$
1969	NR	1	0	0	0	0	0	0	0	87	0	0	235	795
Lifetime		1	0	0	0	0	0	0	0	87	0	0	235	$795

Dick Parran

Richard Parran
    Racing Hometown: Raleigh, NC

Year	Rank	Starts	Poles	1	2	3	4	5	6–10	Laps	Laps Led	Races Led	Miles	$
1958	169	1	0	0	0	0	0	0	0	22	0	0	22	0
Lifetime		1	0	0	0	0	0	0	0	22	0	0	22	$0

Lee Parris

Lee Parris

Year	Rank	Starts	Poles	1	2	3	4	5	6–10	Laps	Laps Led	Races Led	Miles	$
1960	NR	1	0	0	0	0	0	0	0	129	0	0	65	100
Lifetime		1	0	0	0	0	0	0	0	129	0	0	65	$100

George Parrish

George W. Parrish
    Racing Hometown: Henderson, NC

Year	Rank	Starts	Poles	1	2	3	4	5	6–10	Laps	Laps Led	Races Led	Miles	$
1954	73	3	0	0	0	0	0	0	0	440	0	0	482	185
1955	42	12	0	0	0	0	0	0	1	1,057	0	0	596	750
1957	108	5	0	0	0	0	0	0	0	483	0	0	472	525
1958	136	1	0	0	0	0	0	0	0	7	0	0	2	50
Lifetime		21	0	0	0	0	0	0	1	1,987	0	0	1,552	$1,510

Frank Parry

Frank Parry

Year	Rank	Starts	Poles	1	2	3	4	5	6–10	Laps	Laps Led	Races Led	Miles	$
1955	NR	1	0	0	0	0	0	0	0	205	0	0	205	50
Lifetime		1	0	0	0	0	0	0	0	205	0	0	205	$50

Gene Parry

Gene Parry

Year	Rank	Starts	Poles	1	2	3	4	5	6–10	Laps	Laps Led	Races Led	Miles	$
1953	NR	1	0	0	0	0	0	0	0		0	0		25
Lifetime		1	0	0	0	0	0	0	0		0	0		$25

Jim Parsley

James Parsley
    Racing Hometown: Wheaton, MD

Year	Rank	Starts	Poles	1	2	3	4	5	6–10	Laps	Laps Led	Races Led	Miles	$
1958	30	10	0	0	0	0	0	0	4	1,720	0	0	760	1,135
1959	NR	1	0	0	0	0	0	0	1	177	0	0	89	150
Lifetime		11	0	0	0	0	0	0	5	1,897	0	0	848	$1,285

Benny Parsons

Benny Parsons
B: 7/12/1941
    Racing Hometown: Ellerbe, NC

Year	Rank	Starts	Poles	1	2	3	4	5	6–10	Laps	Laps Led	Races Led	Miles	$
1964	120	1	0	0	0	0	0	0	0	258	0	0	129	250
1969	56	4	0	0	0	1	0	1	1	568	0	0	1,259	7,650
1970	8	45	1	0	1	2	4	5	11	9,164	164	6	8,725	59,402
1971	11	35	0	1	2	5	1	4	5	7,981	144	4	7,640	55,896
1972	5	31	0	0	1	0	8	1	9	7,922	19	2	9,463	102,043

Year	Rank	Starts	Poles	Finish						Laps	Laps Led	Races Led	Miles	$
				1	2	3	4	5	6–10					

Benny Parsons *continued*

Year	Rank	Starts	Poles	1	2	3	4	5	6–10	Laps	Laps Led	Races Led	Miles	$
1973	1	28	0	1	3	3	3	5	6	9,311	374	8	10,061	182,321
1974	5	30	0	0	2	2	5	2	3	8,120	88	11	8,866	185,080
1975	4	30	3	1	3	3	3	1	6	8,528	496	16	8,785	214,354
1976	3	30	2	2	2	7	2	5	5	8,679	455	15	10,404	270,043
1977	3	30	3	4	3	10	0	3	2	9,410	1,398	25	10,756	359,341
1978	4	30	2	3	3	6	2	1	6	9,709	824	21	10,895	329,993
1979	5	31	1	2	2	2	5	5	5	9,335	736	12	10,575	264,930
1980	3	31	2	3	3	2	4	4	5	8,676	659	19	10,036	411,519
1981	10	31	0	3	0	3	0	4	2	6,709	537	10	7,515	311,093
1982	18	23	3	0	0	4	3	3	3	5,631	253	8	7,314	252,267
1983	29	16	0	0	2	1	0	1	1	2,847	107	7	5,285	129,760
1984	27	14	2	1	1	0	1	4	3	2,877	407	6	5,451	241,665
1985	29	14	0	0	0	0	0	1	5	2,230	8	3	4,279	94,450
1986	30	16	1	0	0	0	0	2	2	2,620	13	7	5,100	176,985
1987	16	29	0	0	3	0	1	2	3	7,075	87	9	8,921	566,484
1988	24	27	0	0	0	0	0	0	1	7,423	82	3	8,761	210,755
Lifetime		526	20	21	31	51	42	54	84	135,073	6,851	192	160,219	$4,426,281

Goldie Parsons

Gloria Parsons
B: 1941
Racing Hometown: Clemmons, NC

Year	Rank	Starts	Poles	1	2	3	4	5	6–10	Laps	Laps Led	Races Led	Miles	$
1965	NR	1	0	0	0	0	0	0	0	242	0	0	81	100
Lifetime		1	0	0	0	0	0	0	0	242	0	0	81	$100

Phil Parsons

Phillip Parsons
B: 6/21/1957
Racing Hometown: Denver, NC

Year	Rank	Starts	Poles	1	2	3	4	5	6–10	Laps	Laps Led	Races Led	Miles	$
1983	43	5	0	0	0	0	0	0	0	887	0	0	1,696	23,850
1984	24	23	0	0	0	0	0	0	3	6,301	4	1	7,801	90,700
1985	21	28	0	0	0	0	0	0	4	6,678	1	1	7,611	104,840
1986	27	17	0	0	0	0	0	1	4	3,404	1	1	6,153	84,680
1987	14	29	0	0	0	0	1	0	6	8,216	18	2	9,674	180,261
1988	9	29	0	1	1	2	1	1	9	8,494	108	10	10,297	532,043
1989	21	29	0	0	0	1	0	1	1	7,735	39	4	9,321	269,012
1990	39	9	0	0	0	0	0	0	0	2,240	0	0	2,767	90,010
1992	53	2	0	0	0	0	0	0	1	567	0	0	872	58,475
1993	29	26	0	0	0	0	0	0	2	6,331	3	1	8,042	293,725
1994	50	3	0	0	0	0	0	0	0	757	0	0	922	21,415
1995	60	2	0	0	0	0	0	0	0	36	0	0	81	41,450
1997	62T	1	0	0	0	0	0	0	0	289	0	0	395	12,845
Lifetime		203	0	1	1	3	2	3	30	51,935	174	20	65,632	$1,803,306

Vic Parsons

Victor Arthur Parsons
B: 11/29/1939
Racing Hometown: Willowdale, Ont, Canada

Year	Rank	Starts	Poles	1	2	3	4	5	6–10	Laps	Laps Led	Races Led	Miles	$
1972	NR	1	0	0	0	0	0	0	1	380	0	0	238	800
1973	30	18	0	0	0	0	0	0	6	3,498	0	0	4,021	18,200
Lifetime		19	0	0	0	0	0	0	7	3,878	0	0	4,259	$19,000

Jim Paschal

James Roy Paschal
B: 12/5/1926
Racing Hometown: High Point, NC

Year	Rank	Starts	Poles	1	2	3	4	5	6–10	Laps	Laps Led	Races Led	Miles	$
1949	NR	1	0	0	0	0	0	0	0		0	0		0
1950	24	6	0	0	1	0	0	0	1	669	0	0	571	850
1951	15	16	0	0	0	1	3	0	3	767	33	1	846	2,450
1952	18	15	0	0	0	0	1	0	6	1,705	0	0	1,109	1,483
1953	7	24	1	1	0	1	2	2	3	1,179	173	1	1,218	5,571
1954	7	27	2	1	0	1	1	2	6	3,546	193	1	2,492	5,451
1955	8	36	2	3	3	3	2	1	8	4,751	306	7	3,202	10,586
1956	5	42	1	1	8	2	4	2	10	6,626	212	6	4,544	17,204
1957	10	35	0	0	1	2	3	3	8	4,999	0	0	2,947	7,079
1958	42	6	1	1	0	0	1	0	2	1,105	150	1	918	1,670
1959	25	6	0	0	2	0	0	1	1	1,485	0	0	1,012	2,980
1960	9	10	0	0	0	2	1	0	4	2,752	11	1	2,713	15,096

Year	Rank	Starts	Poles	Finish 1	2	3	4	5	6–10	Laps	Laps Led	Races Led	Miles	$

Jim Paschal *continued*

Year	Rank	Starts	Poles	1	2	3	4	5	6–10	Laps	Laps Led	Races Led	Miles	$
1961	9	23	1	2	4	1	2	3	4	5,464	203	3	3,665	15,617
1962	6	39	0	4	4	3	3	3	7	8,311	819	8	5,868	27,348
1963	19	32	1	5	3	5	2	0	3	6,917	392	11	4,594	20,979
1964	7	22	0	1	3	1	2	3	5	6,030	155	4	5,531	60,116
1965	35	10	0	0	0	1	2	1	0	2,403	93	2	2,210	7,805
1966	14	18	2	2	0	1	2	1	4	5,008	759	7	5,264	30,985
1967	6	45	1	4	5	5	3	3	5	9,402	1,072	15	7,228	60,123
1968	104	1	0	0	0	0	0	0	0	171	0	0	91	275
1970	NR	1	0	0	0	0	0	0	0	325	11	1	488	1,800
1971	NR	6	0	0	0	2	0	0	1	1,746	50	2	1,153	4,215
1972	NR	1	0	0	0	0	0	0	0	338	0	0	507	1,825
Lifetime		422	12	25	34	31	34	25	81	75,699	4,632	71	58,170	$301,508

John Paschall

John Paschall
Racing Hometown: Hibernia, NJ

Year	Rank	Starts	Poles	1	2	3	4	5	6–10	Laps	Laps Led	Races Led	Miles	$
1959	68	1	0	0	0	0	0	0	0	67	0	0	168	100
Lifetime		1	0	0	0	0	0	0	0	67	0	0	168	$100

Ed Paskovich

Edward Paskovich
Racing Hometown: Hackensack, NJ

Year	Rank	Starts	Poles	1	2	3	4	5	6–10	Laps	Laps Led	Races Led	Miles	$
1953	NR	2	0	0	0	0	0	0	0		0	0		50
1954	168	3	0	0	0	0	0	0	0	260	0	0	179	10
1955	89	5	0	0	0	0	0	0	1	333	0	0	346	300
Lifetime		10	0	0	0	0	0	0	1	593	0	0	525	$360

Dick Passwater

Richard Passwater
B: 1926
Racing Hometown: Indianapolis, IN

Year	Rank	Starts	Poles	1	2	3	4	5	6–10	Laps	Laps Led	Races Led	Miles	$
1952	25	6	0	0	0	0	0	1	2	1,366	0	0	1,085	945
1953	NR	14	0	1	0	0	3	2	5	993	3	1	1,125	4,555
Lifetime		20	0	1	0	0	3	3	7	2,359	3	1	2,210	$5,500

Dana Patten

Dana Patten
Racing Hometown: Enfield, NH

Year	Rank	Starts	Poles	1	2	3	4	5	6–10	Laps	Laps Led	Races Led	Miles	$
1988	48	4	0	0	0	0	0	0	0	1,059	0	0	1,446	9,595
Lifetime		4	0	0	0	0	0	0	0	1,059	0	0	1,446	$9,595

Johnny Patterson

John Patterson
B: 1931   D: 7/5/1969
Racing Hometown: Huntington, WV

Year	Rank	Starts	Poles	1	2	3	4	5	6–10	Laps	Laps Led	Races Led	Miles	$
1952	17	5	0	0	1	0	0	1	0	1,054	0	0	879	3,618
1953	25	11	0	0	0	0	0	1	1	534	0	0	410	645
1954	24	4	0	0	0	0	1	0	0	582	0	0	759	1,240
1955	104	1	0	0	0	0	0	0	0	342	0	0	470	225
1956	53	3	0	0	0	0	0	0	1	563	0	0	582	425
1959	111	1	0	0	0	0	0	0	0	180	0	0	248	150
Lifetime		25	0	0	1	0	1	2	2	3,255	0	0	3,347	$6,303

Don Patton

Donald Patton

Year	Rank	Starts	Poles	1	2	3	4	5	6–10	Laps	Laps Led	Races Led	Miles	$
1969	NR	1	0	0	0	0	0	0	0	441	0	0	242	500
Lifetime		1	0	0	0	0	0	0	0	441	0	0	242	$500

Donny Paul

Donald Paul
B: 1/2/1961
Racing Hometown: Berrien Springs, MI

Year	Rank	Starts	Poles	1	2	3	4	5	6–10	Laps	Laps Led	Races Led	Miles	$
1984	93	1	0	0	0	0	0	0	0	1	0	0	2	1,005
1985	90	1	0	0	0	0	0	0	0	156	0	0	234	1,120
1987	98T	1	0	0	0	0	0	0	0	104	0	0	208	1,915
Lifetime		3	0	0	0	0	0	0	0	261	0	0	444	$4,040

Year	Rank	Starts	Poles	Finish						Laps	Laps Led	Races Led	Miles	$
				1	2	3	4	5	6–10	Laps	Led	Led	Miles	$

John Paul Jr.

John Paul Jr.
B: 2/19/1960
Racing Hometown: Lawrenceville, GA

Year	Rank	Starts	Poles	1	2	3	4	5	6–10	Laps	Laps Led	Races Led	Miles	$
1991	56	2	0	0	0	0	0	0	0	167	0	0	413	8,460
Lifetime		2	0	0	0	0	0	0	0	167	0	0	413	$8,460

Ellis Pearce

Ellis Pearce (Buttercup)
Racing Hometown: Jacksonville, FL

Year	Rank	Starts	Poles	1	2	3	4	5	6–10	Laps	Laps Led	Races Led	Miles	$
1949	46T	1	0	0	0	0	0	0	1		0	0		50
Lifetime		1	0	0	0	0	0	0	1		0	0		$50

Kenny Paulsen

Kenny Paulsen
Racing Hometown: Stone Park, IL

Year	Rank	Starts	Poles	1	2	3	4	5	6–10	Laps	Laps Led	Races Led	Miles	$
1956	284	1	0	0	0	0	0	0	0	40	0	0	20	50
Lifetime		1	0	0	0	0	0	0	0	40	0	0	20	$50

David Pearson

David Gene Pearson
B: 12/22/1934
Racing Hometown: Speartanburg, SC

Year	Rank	Starts	Poles	1	2	3	4	5	6–10	Laps	Laps Led	Races Led	Miles	$
1960	23	22	1	0	1	0	1	1	4	3,885	0	0	3,768	5,030
1961	13	19	1	3	0	2	1	1	1	3,087	247	5	3,449	24,721
1962	10	12	0	0	0	0	1	0	6	2,690	280	4	3,552	19,032
1963	8	41	2	0	3	2	5	3	6	8,697	178	6	6,503	24,986
1964	3	61	12	8	8	4	7	2	13	13,225	2,127	30	8,906	45,542
1965	40	14	1	2	2	2	1	1	3	3,242	575	7	1,803	8,925
1966	1	42	7	15	5	5	1	0	7	10,781	3,174	25	8,437	78,194
1967	7	22	2	2	4	3	2	0	2	5,638	661	13	5,940	72,651
1968	1	48	12	16	12	4	2	2	2	13,097	3,710	36	9,530	133,065
1969	1	51	13	11	18	9	2	2	2	14,270	3,003	39	11,269	229,760
1970	23	19	2	1	2	2	4	0	2	4,210	580	11	5,815	87,118
1971	51	17	2	2	4	0	2	0	1	2,998	252	10	3,118	32,010
1972	20	17	4	6	1	3	2	0	1	4,902	1,571	16	6,593	142,440
1973	13	18	8	11	2	1	0	0	0	5,338	2,658	16	7,197	228,408
1974	3	19	11	7	5	2	1	0	0	4,630	1,167	18	7,746	252,819
1975	14	21	7	3	6	2	2	0	1	5,653	1,323	18	8,580	192,141
1976	9	22	8	10	3	2	1	0	2	6,194	1,233	19	9,049	346,890
1977	13	22	5	2	7	2	2	3	0	5,694	868	17	8,181	221,272
1978	16	22	7	4	2	1	1	3	0	5,375	757	13	7,603	198,775
1979	32	9	2	1	2	0	1	0	1	2,271	264	6	3,228	99,180
1980	37	9	1	1	2	1	0	0	1	1,787	172	7	3,252	102,730
1981	70	6	1	0	0	0	0	0	2	1,309	48	3	1,876	17,150
1982	37	6	2	0	0	1	0	1	0	1,019	7	2	1,721	55,945
1983	33	10	0	0	0	1	0	0	3	1,643	18	1	3,094	71,720
1984	41	11	0	0	0	0	0	0	3	1,630	10	3	2,949	54,125
1985	36	12	0	0	0	0	0	0	1	1,418	2	1	2,641	55,625
1986	82	2	0	0	0	0	0	0	1	337	0	0	605	8,405
Lifetime		574	111	105	89	49	39	19	65	135,020	24,885	326	146,406	$2,808,659

Dell Pearson

Dell Pearson
Racing Hometown: Portland, OR

Year	Rank	Starts	Poles	1	2	3	4	5	6–10	Laps	Laps Led	Races Led	Miles	$
1951	73	8	0	0	1	0	0	0	2	310	0	0	310	900
Lifetime		8	0	0	1	0	0	0	2	310	0	0	310	$900

Hugh Pearson

Hugh Pearson
B: 4/15/1947
Racing Hometown: Bakersfield, CA

Year	Rank	Starts	Poles	1	2	3	4	5	6–10	Laps	Laps Led	Races Led	Miles	$
1973	105	2	0	0	0	0	0	0	0	94	0	0	246	1,720
1974	91	2	0	0	0	0	0	0	0	116	0	0	302	1,385
1975	72	2	0	0	0	0	0	0	0	218	0	0	553	2,550
1976	81	2	0	0	0	0	0	0	0	115	0	0	301	1,930
1977	83	1	0	0	0	0	0	0	1	114	0	0	299	2,490
Lifetime		9	0	0	0	0	0	0	1	657	0	0	1,701	$10,075

Year	Rank	Starts	Poles	Finish 1	2	3	4	5	6–10	Laps	Laps Led	Races Led	Miles	$

Larry Pearson

Larwrence Pearson
B: 11/2/1953
Racing Hometown: Spartanburg, SC

Year	Rank	Starts	Poles	1	2	3	4	5	6–10	Laps	Laps Led	Races Led	Miles	$
1986	79	2	0	0	0	0	0	0	0	358	0	0	566	14,310
1987	50	4	0	0	0	0	0	0	1	1,162	1	1	1,435	18,555
1988	62	2	0	0	0	0	0	0	0	281	0	0	427	3,705
1989	23	29	0	0	0	0	0	0	2	7,993	5	2	9,737	148,232
1990	35	9	0	0	0	0	0	0	0	2,871	0	0	3,220	72,305
1991	37	11	0	0	0	0	0	0	0	1,543	0	0	2,662	56,570
Lifetime		57	0	0	0	0	0	0	3	14,208	6	3	18,047	$313,677

Sam Pearson

Samuel Pearson

Year	Rank	Starts	Poles	1	2	3	4	5	6–10	Laps	Laps Led	Races Led	Miles	$
1954	NR	1	0	0	0	0	0	0	0	150	0	0	75	25
Lifetime		1	0	0	0	0	0	0	0	150	0	0	75	$25

Peck Peckham

Sewell Peckham
Racing Hometown: Old Bridge, NJ

Year	Rank	Starts	Poles	1	2	3	4	5	6–10	Laps	Laps Led	Races Led	Miles	$
1954	97	3	0	0	0	0	0	0	0	354	0	0	239	35
1956	150	3	0	0	0	0	0	0	0	301	0	0	225	225
1957	40	10	0	0	0	0	0	0	0	1,060	0	0	716	950
1958	45	11	0	0	0	0	0	0	0	1,263	0	0	834	835
Lifetime		27	0	0	0	0	0	0	0	2,978	0	0	2,013	$2,045

Ken Pedersen

Kenneth Pedersen
B: 1959
Racing Hometown: San Rafael, CA

Year	Rank	Starts	Poles	1	2	3	4	5	6–10	Laps	Laps Led	Races Led	Miles	$
1995	68	1	0	0	0	0	0	0	0	25	0	0	63	9,760
Lifetime		1	0	0	0	0	0	0	0	25	0	0	63	$9,760

Nestor Peles

Nestor Peles
Racing Hometown: Glen Campbell, PA

Year	Rank	Starts	Poles	1	2	3	4	5	6–10	Laps	Laps Led	Races Led	Miles	$
1977	110T	2	0	0	0	0	0	0	0	209	0	0	473	1,330
1978	56	3	0	0	0	0	0	0	0	979	0	0	1,249	2,880
1979	96T	1	0	0	0	0	0	0	0	465	0	0	465	1,000
1980	96T	1	0	0	0	0	0	0	0	207	0	0	207	600
Lifetime		7	0	0	0	0	0	0	0	1,860	0	0	2,394	$5,810

Steve Peles

Steve Peles
B: 1961
Racing Hometown: Glen Campbell, PA

Year	Rank	Starts	Poles	1	2	3	4	5	6–10	Laps	Laps Led	Races Led	Miles	$
1979	69	2	0	0	0	0	0	0	0	641	0	0	922	2,180
Lifetime		2	0	0	0	0	0	0	0	641	0	0	922	$2,180

Gene Peltier

Gene Peltier
Racing Hometown: South Gate, CA

Year	Rank	Starts	Poles	1	2	3	4	5	6–10	Laps	Laps Led	Races Led	Miles	$
1959	NR	1	0	0	0	0	0	0	0	36	0	0	14	50
Lifetime		1	0	0	0	0	0	0	0	36	0	0	14	$50

Dean Pelton

Dean Pelton
Racing Hometown: Takoma Park, MD

Year	Rank	Starts	Poles	1	2	3	4	5	6–10	Laps	Laps Led	Races Led	Miles	$
1954	69	3	0	0	0	0	0	0	0	620	0	0	605	155
Lifetime		3	0	0	0	0	0	0	0	620	0	0	605	$155

Charles Pemberton

Charles Pemberton
Racing Hometown: San Jose, CA

Year	Rank	Starts	Poles	1	2	3	4	5	6–10	Laps	Laps Led	Races Led	Miles	$
1954	63	2	0	0	0	0	0	0	1	525	0	0	381	200
Lifetime		2	0	0	0	0	0	0	1	525	0	0	381	$200

Year	Rank	Starts	Poles	Finish 1	2	3	4	5	6–10	Laps	Laps Led	Races Led	Miles	$

Joe Penland

Joseph Penland
B: 1935   D: 7/27/1997
Racing Hometown: Caycee, SC

Year	Rank	Starts	Poles	1	2	3	4	5	6–10	Laps	Laps Led	Races Led	Miles	$
1962	102	3	0	0	0	0	0	0	0	379	0	0	190	235
1964	125T	1	0	0	0	0	0	0	0	4	0	0	12	525
1965	89	3	0	0	0	0	0	0	0	112	0	0	60	1,260
Lifetime		7	0	0	0	0	0	0	0	495	0	0	262	$2,020

Jack Pennington

Jack Pennington
B: 9/3/1953
Racing Hometown: Augusta, GA

Year	Rank	Starts	Poles	1	2	3	4	5	6–10	Laps	Laps Led	Races Led	Miles	$
1989	75T	2	0	0	0	0	0	0	0	580	0	0	743	4,475
1990	34	14	0	0	0	0	0	0	0	3,450	7	2	5,902	95,860
Lifetime		16	0	0	0	0	0	0	0	4,030	7	2	6,645	$100,335

Bob Penrod

Robert Penrod
B: 11/7/1946
Racing Hometown: Atlanta, GA

Year	Rank	Starts	Poles	1	2	3	4	5	6–10	Laps	Laps Led	Races Led	Miles	$
1984	90	1	0	0	0	0	0	0	0	55	0	0	84	955
Lifetime		1	0	0	0	0	0	0	0	55	0	0	84	$955

Buck Peralta

Buck Peralta
B: 11/11/1934
Racing Hometown: Lake Oswego, OR

Year	Rank	Starts	Poles	1	2	3	4	5	6–10	Laps	Laps Led	Races Led	Miles	$
1974	107	1	0	0	0	0	0	0	0	121	0	0	317	1,250
Lifetime		1	0	0	0	0	0	0	0	121	0	0	317	$1,250

Bob Perry

Robert Perry
D: 1992
Racing Hometown: Hawthorne, CA

Year	Rank	Starts	Poles	1	2	3	4	5	6–10	Laps	Laps Led	Races Led	Miles	$
1957	89	1	0	0	0	0	0	0	0	71	0	0	71	50
1958	128	2	0	0	0	0	0	0	0	121	0	0	317	200
1959	75	3	0	0	0	0	0	0	1	509	0	0	317	500
1960	78	3	0	0	0	0	0	0	1	256	0	0	314	475
1961	76	4	0	0	0	0	0	1	2	424	0	0	452	840
1963	47	5	0	0	0	0	0	0	0	668	0	0	1,325	1,550
Lifetime		18	0	0	0	0	0	1	4	2,049	0	0	2,797	$3,615

Dale Perry

Dale Perry
B: 6/18/1937

Year	Rank	Starts	Poles	1	2	3	4	5	6–10	Laps	Laps Led	Races Led	Miles	$
1985	84T	1	0	0	0	0	0	0	0	57	0	0	149	880
Lifetime		1	0	0	0	0	0	0	0	57	0	0	149	$880

Rod Perry

Marion Perry
B: 1924   D: 5/5/1992
Racing Hometown: Miami, FL

Year	Rank	Starts	Poles	1	2	3	4	5	6–10	Laps	Laps Led	Races Led	Miles	$
1957	NR	1	0	0	0	0	0	0	0		0	0		100
Lifetime		1	0	0	0	0	0	0	0		0	0		$100

Steve Perry

Steve Perry
B: 4/22/1955
Racing Hometown: Dallas, TX

Year	Rank	Starts	Poles	1	2	3	4	5	6–10	Laps	Laps Led	Races Led	Miles	$
1991	77	1	0	0	0	0	0	0	0	244	0	0	244	4,150
Lifetime		1	0	0	0	0	0	0	0	244	0	0	244	$4,150

Dominic Persicketti

Dominic Persicketti
Racing Hometown: Trenton, NJ

Year	Rank	Starts	Poles	1	2	3	4	5	6–10	Laps	Laps Led	Races Led	Miles	$
1954	188	1	0	0	0	0	0	0	0	25	0	0	25	0
1959	74	2	0	0	0	0	0	0	1	581	0	0	359	450
1961	NR	1	0	0	0	0	0	0	1	450	0	0	113	300
1963	141	1	0	0	0	0	0	0	0	16	0	0	8	50
Lifetime		5	0	0	0	0	0	0	2	1,072	0	0	505	$800

Year	Rank	Starts	Poles	Finish 1	2	3	4	5	6–10	Laps	Laps Led	Races Led	Miles	$

Natz Peters

Ronald Nathen Peters
Racing Hometown: Pinellas Park, FL

Year	Rank	Starts	Poles	1	2	3	4	5	6–10	Laps	Laps Led	Races Led	Miles	$
1983	93	1	0	0	0	0	0	0	0	103	0	0	103	800
Lifetime		1	0	0	0	0	0	0	0	103	0	0	103	$800

M.R. Peterson

M.R. Peterson (Eric)
Racing Hometown: Brooklyn, NY

Year	Rank	Starts	Poles	1	2	3	4	5	6–10	Laps	Laps Led	Races Led	Miles	$
1954	NR	1	0	0	0	0	0	0	0	6	0	0	12	0
Lifetime		1	0	0	0	0	0	0	0	6	0	0	12	$0

Terry Petris

Terry Petris
B: 6/28/1951
Racing Hometown: Bakersfield, CA

Year	Rank	Starts	Poles	1	2	3	4	5	6–10	Laps	Laps Led	Races Led	Miles	$
1986	80	2	0	0	0	0	0	0	0	149	0	0	390	3,110
1988	NR	1	0	0	0	0	0	0	0	52	0	0	136	1,150
Lifetime		3	0	0	0	0	0	0	0	201	0	0	527	$4,260

Gene Petro

Eugene Petro
Racing Hometown: Columbus, IN

Year	Rank	Starts	Poles	1	2	3	4	5	6–10	Laps	Laps Led	Races Led	Miles	$
1966	NR	1	0	0	0	0	0	0	0	35	0	0	88	100
Lifetime		1	0	0	0	0	0	0	0	35	0	0	88	$100

Paul Pettitt

Paul Pettitt
Racing Hometown: Danbury, CT

Year	Rank	Starts	Poles	1	2	3	4	5	6–10	Laps	Laps Led	Races Led	Miles	$
1950	NR	1	0	0	0	0	0	0	0		0	0		0
1951	191	4	0	0	0	0	0	0	0		0	0		50
1952	NR	3	0	0	0	0	0	0	0	198	0	0	116	60
1954	77	2	0	0	0	0	0	1	0	166	0	0	149	325
1955	154	2	0	0	0	0	0	0	0	50	0	0	25	100
Lifetime		12	0	0	0	0	0	1	0	414	0	0	290	$535

Adam Petty

Adam Petty
B: 7/10/1980 D: 5/12/2000 *Practice crash for BGN race—Loudon, NH.*
Racing Hometown: High Point, NC

Year	Rank	Starts	Poles	1	2	3	4	5	6–10	Laps	Laps Led	Races Led	Miles	$
2000	69	1	0	0	0	0	0	0	0	215	0	0	323	38,675
Lifetime		1	0	0	0	0	0	0	0	215	0	0	323	$38,675

Julian Petty

Julian H. Petty (Julie)
Racing Hometown: Greensboro, NC

Year	Rank	Starts	Poles	1	2	3	4	5	6–10	Laps	Laps Led	Races Led	Miles	$
1952	NR	1	0	0	0	0	0	0	1	193	0	0	97	125
1955	182	2	0	0	0	0	0	0	0	5	0	0	3	75
Lifetime		3	0	0	0	0	0	0	1	198	0	0	99	$200

Kyle Petty

Kyle Petty
B: 6/2/1960
Racing Hometown: Randleman, NC

Year	Rank	Starts	Poles	1	2	3	4	5	6–10	Laps	Laps Led	Races Led	Miles	$
1979	37	5	0	0	0	0	0	0	1	1,069	0	0	2,111	10,810
1980	28	15	0	0	0	0	0	0	6	3,722	0	0	4,942	36,045
1981	12	31	0	0	0	0	0	1	9	7,402	20	3	8,484	117,453
1982	15	29	0	0	1	0	1	0	2	6,414	13	3	7,720	126,285
1983	13	30	0	0	0	0	0	0	2	8,345	13	5	9,437	163,848
1984	16	30	0	0	0	0	0	1	5	8,400	2	1	9,302	329,920
1985	9	28	0	0	1	1	1	4	5	8,796	75	6	10,384	296,367
1986	10	29	0	1	0	1	0	2	10	8,446	17	6	10,204	403,242
1987	7	29	0	1	1	4	0	0	8	8,523	103	7	10,401	544,437
1988	13	29	0	0	0	0	0	2	6	8,883	66	3	10,524	377,092
1989	30	19	0	0	0	0	1	0	4	5,207	16	1	7,345	98,977
1990	11	29	2	1	0	0	1	0	12	8,485	852	12	10,250	746,326
1991	31	18	2	1	1	0	0	0	2	6,622	553	7	6,547	413,727
1992	5	29	3	2	0	4	3	0	8	9,058	971	8	10,938	1,107,063
1993	5	30	1	1	1	2	2	3	6	9,259	527	13	11,187	914,662
1994	15	31	0	0	0	0	1	1	5	9,076	7	2	11,100	818,832

Year	Rank	Starts	Poles	Finish						Laps	Laps Led	Races Led	Miles	$
				1	2	3	4	5	6–10					

Kyle Petty *continued*

Year	Rank	Starts	Poles	1	2	3	4	5	6–10	Laps	Laps Led	Races Led	Miles	$
1995	30	30	0	1	0	0	0	0	4	8,127	311	4	10,077	698,875
1996	27	28	0	0	0	0	0	0	2	8,081	72	5	9,683	689,041
1997	15	32	0	0	0	1	0	1	7	9,192	210	6	11,957	984,314
1998	30	33	0	0	0	0	0	0	2	8,464	0	0	11,239	1,287,731
1999	26	32	0	0	0	0	0	0	9	8,708	11	4	11,206	1,278,953
2000	41	19	0	0	0	0	0	0	1	4,988	8	2	6,389	894,911
2001	43	24	0	0	0	0	0	0	0	5,026	1	1	7,569	1,008,919
2002	22	36	0	0	0	0	0	0	1	10,423	22	4	13,701	2,198,073
Lifetime		645	8	8	5	13	10	15	117	180,716	3,870	103	222,696	$15,545,903

Lee Petty

Lee Arnold Petty
B: 3/14/1914   D: 4/5/2000
Racing Hometown: Randleman, NC

Year	Rank	Starts	Poles	1	2	3	4	5	6–10	Laps	Laps Led	Races Led	Miles	$
1949	2	6	0	1	2	0	0	0	2	890	1	1	565	3,855
1950	3	17	0	1	1	2	3	2	4	1,558	43	1	1,407	7,120
1951	4	32	0	1	4	2	1	3	8	1,103	99	1	1,059	7,340
1952	3	32	0	3	6	5	5	2	6	5,094	193	7	3,439	16,876
1953	2	36	0	5	4	10	4	3	6	3,021	210	7	2,201	18,447
1954	1	34	3	7	5	5	4	3	8	5,903	676	11	4,060	21,127
1955	3	42	1	6	4	5	4	1	10	6,328	769	6	4,403	18,920
1956	4	47	1	2	1	6	2	6	11	7,507	252	6	4,954	15,338
1957	4	41	3	4	4	3	3	6	13	7,466	449	11	4,595	18,326
1958	1	50	4	7	5	4	9	3	15	9,173	409	14	5,671	26,565
1959	1	42	2	11	5	7	4	0	8	8,278	1,000	15	4,977	49,220
1960	6	39	3	5	7	2	6	1	9	7,518	500	8	5,389	31,283
1961	104	3	1	1	0	1	0	0	0	433	126	2	291	1,260
1962	73	1	0	0	0	0	0	1	0	499	0	0	250	750
1963	82	3	0	0	0	0	1	0	1	291	0	0	179	600
1964	109	2	0	0	0	0	0	0	0	28	0	0	30	250
Lifetime		427	18	54	48	52	46	31	101	65,090	4,727	90	43,469	$237,277

Maurice Petty

Maurice Petty
B: 3/27/1939
Racing Hometown: Randleman, NC

Year	Rank	Starts	Poles	1	2	3	4	5	6–10	Laps	Laps Led	Races Led	Miles	$
1960	94	2	0	0	0	0	0	0	2	375	0	0	142	290
1961	59	9	0	0	0	1	1	0	2	1,207	0	0	611	1,460
1962	57	5	0	0	0	0	1	1	1	800	0	0	443	965
1963	74	4	0	0	0	0	0	1	1	654	0	0	238	575
1964	61	6	0	0	0	0	1	1	3	1,130	0	0	587	1,540
Lifetime		26	0	0	0	1	3	3	9	4,166	0	0	2,021	$4,830

Richard Petty

Richard Lee Petty (The King)
B: 7/2/1937
Racing Hometown: Randleman, NC

Year	Rank	Starts	Poles	1	2	3	4	5	6–10	Laps	Laps Led	Races Led	Miles	$
1958	37	9	0	0	0	0	0	0	1	977	0	0	410	760
1959	15	21	0	0	1	3	1	1	3	3,654	7	1	2,422	8,111
1960	2	40	2	3	6	3	3	1	14	8,189	418	5	6,015	41,873
1961	8	42	2	2	4	4	5	3	5	7,866	703	7	5,392	15,096
1962	2	52	5	8	9	8	5	2	7	11,550	1,396	19	7,561	60,764
1963	2	54	8	14	9	2	4	1	9	12,183	2,024	28	7,873	55,964
1964	1	61	9	9	14	12	0	2	6	14,041	3,302	31	9,480	114,772
1965	38	14	7	4	4	2	0	0	0	3,697	852	9	1,693	16,450
1966	3	39	16	8	9	3	0	0	2	8,737	2,739	26	6,733	94,666
1967	1	48	19	27	7	2	1	1	2	12,739	5,178	40	9,387	150,197
1968	3	49	12	16	6	5	2	2	4	12,254	4,198	34	8,869	99,535
1969	2	50	6	10	9	9	0	3	7	12,589	2,773	32	10,502	129,906
1970	4	40	9	18	5	0	0	4	4	10,536	5,007	32	9,811	151,124
1971	1	46	9	21	8	7	2	0	3	13,739	4,932	41	12,878	351,071
1972	1	31	3	8	9	5	2	1	3	10,282	2,093	30	11,996	339,405
1973	5	28	3	6	6	1	2	0	2	8,644	1,815	16	9,292	234,389
1974	1	30	7	10	8	4	0	0	1	9,097	3,100	24	10,830	432,020
1975	1	30	3	13	5	3	0	0	3	9,082	3,198	26	10,847	481,751
1976	2	30	1	3	9	3	4	0	3	8,941	1,269	23	10,346	374,806
1977	2	30	5	5	6	6	2	1	3	8,840	1,403	24	10,419	406,608
1978	6	30	0	0	3	3	3	2	6	8,904	419	15	10,163	242,273

Year	Rank	Starts	Poles	Finish 1	2	3	4	5	6–10	Laps	Laps Led	Races Led	Miles	$

Richard Petty *continued*

Year	Rank	Starts	Poles	1	2	3	4	5	6–10	Laps	Laps Led	Races Led	Miles	$
1979	1	31	1	5	7	2	4	5	4	9,367	1,250	16	10,934	561,934
1980	4	31	0	2	4	3	2	4	4	9,314	713	23	10,148	397,318
1981	8	31	0	3	1	4	3	1	4	7,276	546	21	8,602	396,072
1982	5	30	0	0	5	2	1	1	7	7,834	355	18	9,025	465,793
1983	4	30	0	3	1	1	1	3	12	9,439	279	16	10,697	508,884
1984	10	30	0	2	0	0	2	1	8	8,835	275	8	9,917	257,932
1985	14	28	0	0	0	1	0	0	12	7,767	105	7	8,863	306,142
1986	14	29	0	0	1	2	1	0	7	7,639	153	7	8,951	280,657
1987	8	29	0	0	1	3	2	3	5	8,306	38	8	9,987	445,227
1988	22	29	0	0	0	1	0	0	4	6,207	12	3	7,628	190,155
1989	29	25	0	0	0	0	0	0	0	5,567	9	1	7,929	117,300
1990	26	29	0	0	0	0	0	0	1	7,438	5	1	9,165	169,465
1991	24	29	0	0	0	0	0	0	1	8,341	1	1	9,646	268,035
1992	26	29	0	0	0	0	0	0	0	7,977	5	1	9,624	348,870
Lifetime		1184	127	200	157	104	52	42	157	307,848	50,572	594	304,035	$8,515,325

Ritchie Petty

Ritchie Petty
B: 6/20/1968
Racing Hometown: Randleman, NC

Year	Rank	Starts	Poles	1	2	3	4	5	6–10	Laps	Laps Led	Races Led	Miles	$
1993	53	3	0	0	0	0	0	0	0	364	0	0	950	22,990
1994	81T	1	0	0	0	0	0	0	0	73	0	0	183	8,705
Lifetime		4	0	0	0	0	0	0	0	437	0	0	1,133	$31,695

Eddie Pettyjohn

Edward Pettyjohn
Racing Hometown: Milton, DE

Year	Rank	Starts	Poles	1	2	3	4	5	6–10	Laps	Laps Led	Races Led	Miles	$
1973	76	2	0	0	0	0	0	0	1	491	0	0	491	2,145
1974	94	3	0	0	0	0	0	0	0	401	1	1	453	4,210
Lifetime		5	0	0	0	0	0	0	1	892	1	1	944	$6,355

Steve Pfeifer

Steve Pfeifer
B: 10/4/1938
Racing Hometown: San Francisco, CA

Year	Rank	Starts	Poles	1	2	3	4	5	6–10	Laps	Laps Led	Races Led	Miles	$
1978	99	1	0	0	0	0	0	0	0	98	0	0	245	955
1979	84	3	0	0	0	0	0	0	0	368	0	0	565	4,220
1980	77	2	0	0	0	0	0	0	0	157	0	0	411	1,805
1981	86	2	0	0	0	0	0	0	0	175	0	0	459	4,135
Lifetime		8	0	0	0	0	0	0	0	798	0	0	1,679	$11,115

Howard Phillippi

Howard Phillippi
Racing Hometown: Torrance, CA

Year	Rank	Starts	Poles	1	2	3	4	5	6–10	Laps	Laps Led	Races Led	Miles	$
1954	NR	2	0	0	0	0	0	0	0	264	0	0	232	40
1956	157	4	0	0	0	0	0	0	0	501	0	0	398	125
1957	100	3	0	0	0	0	0	0	1	334	0	0	167	200
1958	92	2	0	0	0	0	0	0	1	190	0	0	55	320
Lifetime		11	0	0	0	0	0	0	2	1,289	0	0	852	$685

Larry Phillips

Larry Gene Phillips
B: 7/3/1942
Racing Hometown: Springfield, MO

Year	Rank	Starts	Poles	1	2	3	4	5	6–10	Laps	Laps Led	Races Led	Miles	$
1976	NR	1	0	0	0	0	0	0	0	188	0	0	470	1,990
Lifetime		1	0	0	0	0	0	0	0	188	0	0	470	$1,990

Joe Phipps

Joseph D. Phipps
Racing Hometown: Newark, DE

Year	Rank	Starts	Poles	1	2	3	4	5	6–10	Laps	Laps Led	Races Led	Miles	$
1970	49	7	0	0	0	0	0	0	0	1,506	0	0	1,583	4,090
1971	77	2	0	0	0	0	0	0	0	73	0	0	53	920
Lifetime		9	0	0	0	0	0	0	0	1,579	0	0	1,635	$5,010

Paul Phipps

Paul Phipps

Year	Rank	Starts	Poles	1	2	3	4	5	6–10	Laps	Laps Led	Races Led	Miles	$
1954	NR	1	0	0	0	0	0	0	0	167	0	0	84	25
Lifetime		1	0	0	0	0	0	0	0	167	0	0	84	$25

Year	Rank	Starts	Poles	1	2	Finish 3	4	5	6–10	Laps	Laps Led	Races Led	Miles	$

Bob Pickell

Robert Pickell
  Racing Hometown: Flemington, NJ

Year	Rank	Starts	Poles	1	2	3	4	5	6–10	Laps	Laps Led	Races Led	Miles	$
1967	76	3	0	0	0	0	0	0	0	467	0	0	304	1,600
Lifetime		3	0	0	0	0	0	0	0	467	0	0	304	$1,600

Wilbur Pickett

Dr. Wilbur Pickett
  B: 1/1/1930   D: 10/6/1974   *Killed in private plane crash.*
  Racing Hometown: Daytona Beach, FL

Year	Rank	Starts	Poles	1	2	3	4	5	6–10	Laps	Laps Led	Races Led	Miles	$
1969	NR	1	0	0	0	0	0	0	0	92	0	0	245	1,250
Lifetime		1	0	0	0	0	0	0	0	92	0	0	245	$1,250

Andy Pierce

Andrew Pierce
  Racing Hometown: Gardena, CA

Year	Rank	Starts	Poles	1	2	3	4	5	6–10	Laps	Laps Led	Races Led	Miles	$
1951	N/A	3	1	0	0	0	0	0	0	98	0	0	49	50
Lifetime		3	1	0	0	0	0	0	0	98	0	0	49	$50

Jug Pierce

Jug Pierce

Year	Rank	Starts	Poles	1	2	3	4	5	6–10	Laps	Laps Led	Races Led	Miles	$
1958	NR	1	0	0	0	0	0	0	0	53	0	0	18	50
Lifetime		1	0	0	0	0	0	0	0	53	0	0	18	$50

Ed Pimm

Edward George Pimm
  B: 5/3/1956
  Racing Hometown: Newburg, NY

Year	Rank	Starts	Poles	1	2	3	4	5	6–10	Laps	Laps Led	Races Led	Miles	$
1987	63	3	0	0	0	0	0	0	0	243	1	1	595	6,810
1988	60	2	0	0	0	0	0	0	0	502	0	0	794	13,350
Lifetime		5	0	0	0	0	0	0	0	745	1	1	1,388	$20,160

Tom Pistone

Thomas Pistone (Tiger)
  B: 3/17/1929
  Racing Hometown: Chicago, IL

Year	Rank	Starts	Poles	1	2	3	4	5	6–10	Laps	Laps Led	Races Led	Miles	$
1955	NR	1	0	0	0	0	0	0	0	28	0	0	18	0
1956	252	3	0	0	0	0	0	0	0	355	0	0	158	125
1957	61	2	0	0	0	1	0	0	0	588	0	0	294	1,260
1959	6	22	0	2	2	4	2	2	6	3,902	181	7	2,966	12,725
1960	18	20	0	0	0	1	0	1	6	4,080	157	3	3,699	6,714
1961	38	4	0	0	0	0	0	0	3	576	0	0	1,081	2,050
1962	131	1	0	0	0	0	0	0	0	2	0	0	5	250
1965	32	33	1	0	1	0	1	2	4	3,334	0	0	1,906	10,050
1966	37	28	4	0	3	1	0	2	0	4,090	373	7	2,489	7,775
1967	68	9	0	0	0	1	0	0	4	1,455	0	0	753	2,495
1968	52	7	0	0	0	1	1	1	1	1,531	43	2	747	2,250
Lifetime		130	5	2	6	9	4	8	24	19,941	754	19	14,115	$45,694

Ted Pitcher

Ted Pitcher

Year	Rank	Starts	Poles	1	2	3	4	5	6–10	Laps	Laps Led	Races Led	Miles	$
1955	120	2	0	0	0	0	0	0	0	219	0	0	110	110
Lifetime		2	0	0	0	0	0	0	0	219	0	0	110	$110

Blackie Pitt

William H. Pitt
  B: 3/18/1925
  Racing Hometown: Rocky Mount, NC

Year	Rank	Starts	Poles	1	2	3	4	5	6–10	Laps	Laps Led	Races Led	Miles	$
1954	11	27	0	0	0	0	0	0	6	3,731	0	0	2,507	1,925
1955	21	20	0	0	0	0	0	0	7	2,532	0	0	1,744	1,785
1956	26	27	0	0	0	0	0	0	5	2,702	0	0	1,754	1,545
1958	69	7	0	0	0	0	0	0	1	361	0	0	217	315
Lifetime		81	0	0	0	0	0	0	19	9,326	0	0	6,222	$5,570

Brownie Pitt

Brownie Pitt

Year	Rank	Starts	Poles	1	2	3	4	5	6–10	Laps	Laps Led	Races Led	Miles	$
1956	NR	1	0	0	0	0	0	0	0	49	0	0	44	100
Lifetime		1	0	0	0	0	0	0	0	49	0	0	44	$100

Year	Rank	Starts	Poles	Finish 1	2	3	4	5	6–10	Laps	Laps Led	Races Led	Miles	$

Chuck Pittinger

Chuck Pittinger

Year	Rank	Starts	Poles	1	2	3	4	5	6–10	Laps	Laps Led	Races Led	Miles	$
1981	NR	1	0	0	0	0	0	0	0	80	0	0	210	1,155
Lifetime		1	0	0	0	0	0	0	0	80	0	0	210	$1,155

Clyde Pittinger

Clyde Pittinger
Racing Hometown: Newton, NJ

| 1952 | NR | 3 | 0 | 0 | 0 | 0 | 0 | 0 | 0 | 703 | 0 | 0 | 633 | 140 |
| **Lifetime** | | 3 | 0 | 0 | 0 | 0 | 0 | 0 | 0 | 703 | 0 | 0 | 633 | $140 |

Art Plas

Arthur Plas
Racing Hometown: Eryia, OH

1951	N/A	1	0	0	0	0	0	0	0		0	0		25
1952	NR	1	0	0	0	0	0	0	0	46	0	0	23	25
Lifetime		2	0	0	0	0	0	0	0	46	0	0	23	$50

Ray Platte

Raymond Platte
B: 1926   D: 7/21/1963   *Died from injuries @ S. Boston, Va 7/20/63.*
Racing Hometown: Norfolk, VA

| 1955 | 195 | 1 | 0 | 0 | 0 | 0 | 0 | 0 | 0 | 339 | 0 | 0 | 466 | 100 |
| **Lifetime** | | 1 | 0 | 0 | 0 | 0 | 0 | 0 | 0 | 339 | 0 | 0 | 466 | $100 |

Dave Pletcher

David Pletcher
B: 1/26/1952
Racing Hometown: Clearwater, FL

1987	73	2	0	0	0	0	0	0	0	210	0	0	548	4,915
1988	77T	1	0	0	0	0	0	0	0	464	0	0	472	2,015
Lifetime		3	0	0	0	0	0	0	0	674	0	0	1,020	$6,930

Jerry Plotts

Jerry Plotts
Racing Hometown: Sacramento, CA

| 1961 | 186 | 1 | 0 | 0 | 0 | 0 | 0 | 0 | 0 | 30 | 0 | 0 | 30 | 25 |
| **Lifetime** | | 1 | 0 | 0 | 0 | 0 | 0 | 0 | 0 | 30 | 0 | 0 | 30 | $25 |

Charles Poalillo

Charles Poalillo
Racing Hometown: Pennsylvania

1984	NR	1	0	0	0	0	0	0	0	159	0	0	398	2,050
1985	NR	1	0	0	0	0	0	0	0	22	0	0	55	1,395
Lifetime		2	0	0	0	0	0	0	0	181	0	0	453	$3,445

Bill Polich

William Polich
Racing Hometown: Dana Point, CA

| 1976 | 74 | 2 | 0 | 0 | 0 | 0 | 0 | 0 | 0 | 167 | 0 | 0 | 438 | 2,155 |
| **Lifetime** | | 2 | 0 | 0 | 0 | 0 | 0 | 0 | 0 | 167 | 0 | 0 | 438 | $2,155 |

Dick Poling

Richard Poling
Racing Hometown: Sumter, SC

1969	50	12	0	0	0	0	0	0	0	1,305	0	0	1,630	5,467
1971	66	3	0	0	0	0	0	0	0	249	0	0	398	915
Lifetime		15	0	0	0	0	0	0	0	1,554	0	0	2,027	$6,382

Tony Polito

Tony Polito
Racing Hometown: Pompton Lake, NJ

| 1953 | 144T | 1 | 0 | 0 | 0 | 0 | 0 | 0 | 0 | | 0 | 0 | | 25 |
| **Lifetime** | | 1 | 0 | 0 | 0 | 0 | 0 | 0 | 0 | | 0 | 0 | | $25 |

Hank Pollard

Hank Pollard

| 1952 | NR | 1 | 0 | 0 | 0 | 0 | 0 | 0 | 0 | 4 | 0 | 0 | 2 | 25 |
| **Lifetime** | | 1 | 0 | 0 | 0 | 0 | 0 | 0 | 0 | 4 | 0 | 0 | 2 | $25 |

Year	Rank	Starts	Poles	Finish 1	2	3	4	5	6–10	Laps	Laps Led	Races Led	Miles	$

Larry Pollard

Lawrence Pollard
B: 5/5/1954
Racing Hometown: Victoria, B.C., Canada

Year	Rank	Starts	Poles	1	2	3	4	5	6–10	Laps	Laps Led	Races Led	Miles	$
1987	NR	4	0	0	0	0	0	0	0	1,415	0	0	1,324	19,130
Lifetime		4	0	0	0	0	0	0	0	1,415	0	0	1,324	$19,130

Al Pombo

Al Pombo
B: 1928
Racing Hometown: Fresno, CA

Year	Rank	Starts	Poles	1	2	3	4	5	6–10	Laps	Laps Led	Races Led	Miles	$
1956	199	2	0	0	0	0	0	0	0	334	0	0	273	90
1960	134	1	0	0	0	0	0	0	0	52	0	0	52	50
Lifetime		3	0	0	0	0	0	0	0	386	0	0	325	$140

Lennie Pond

Lennie Pond
B: 8/11/1940
Racing Hometown: Ettrick, VA

Year	Rank	Starts	Poles	1	2	3	4	5	6–10	Laps	Laps Led	Races Led	Miles	$
1969	83T	1	0	0	0	0	0	0	0	73	0	0	74	650
1970	NR	1	0	0	0	0	0	0	0	88	0	0	134	1,020
1973	23	23	0	0	0	0	1	0	8	5,850	4	2	5,479	25,255
1974	18	22	0	0	0	0	1	4	6	6,384	17	6	7,013	55,990
1975	21	22	0	0	3	0	1	2	3	5,859	275	8	6,361	59,265
1976	5	30	0	0	2	0	4	4	9	8,182	217	10	10,055	159,701
1977	30	14	0	0	0	0	2	2	2	3,154	5	3	3,714	49,440
1978	7	28	5	1	2	2	1	5	8	8,443	318	12	9,413	181,096
1979	29	15	0	0	0	0	0	0	2	3,043	14	2	3,864	42,970
1980	30	18	0	0	0	1	1	0	5	3,861	68	6	4,760	62,265
1981	34	12	0	0	0	0	0	0	0	3,083	0	0	3,446	29,045
1982	33	13	0	0	0	0	0	0	2	2,490	1	1	3,193	45,715
1983	34	10	0	0	0	0	0	0	2	2,288	3	1	2,911	41,530
1984	38	12	0	0	0	0	0	0	2	3,590	0	0	3,350	54,200
1985	33	12	0	0	0	0	0	0	0	2,831	3	2	4,320	70,640
1988	NR	1	0	0	0	0	0	0	0	383	0	0	208	2,375
1989	64	1	0	0	0	0	0	0	0	394	0	0	296	3,475
Lifetime		235	5	1	7	3	11	17	49	59,996	925	53	68,591	$884,632

Bobby Poole

Robert Poole

Year	Rank	Starts	Poles	1	2	3	4	5	6–10	Laps	Laps Led	Races Led	Miles	$
1973	NR	1	0	0	0	0	0	0	0	2	0	0	1	250
Lifetime		1	0	0	0	0	0	0	0	2	0	0	1	$250

Junior Pooler

Junior Pooler

Year	Rank	Starts	Poles	1	2	3	4	5	6–10	Laps	Laps Led	Races Led	Miles	$
1951	N/A	1	0	0	0	0	0	0	0		0	0		25
Lifetime		1	0	0	0	0	0	0	0		0	0		$25

Bill Poor

C. William Poor Jr.
Racing Hometown: Wheaton, MO

Year	Rank	Starts	Poles	1	2	3	4	5	6–10	Laps	Laps Led	Races Led	Miles	$
1956	NR	1	0	0	0	0	0	0	0	364	0	0	182	200
1957	NR	2	0	0	0	0	0	0	0	167	0	0	84	160
1958	26	24	0	0	0	0	0	1	6	3,880	0	0	1,947	3,115
1959	93	4	0	0	0	0	0	0	0	484	0	0	219	190
Lifetime		31	0	0	0	0	0	1	6	4,895	0	0	2,431	$3,665

Don Porter

Donald Porter
B: 1927   D: 7/13/1958   *Killed in race @ Portland, OR.*
Racing Hometown: Redding, CA

Year	Rank	Starts	Poles	1	2	3	4	5	6–10	Laps	Laps Led	Races Led	Miles	$
1956	160	3	1	0	0	0	0	0	0	179	0	0	140	100
1957	49	6	0	0	0	0	0	0	4	722	0	0	456	810
Lifetime		9	1	0	0	0	0	0	4	901	0	0	596	$910

Lloyd Porter

Lloyd Porter

Year	Rank	Starts	Poles	1	2	3	4	5	6–10	Laps	Laps Led	Races Led	Miles	$
1951	N/A	3	0	0	0	0	0	0	0		0	0		25
Lifetime		3	0	0	0	0	0	0	0		0	0		$25

Year	Rank	Starts	Poles	Finish 1	2	3	4	5	6–10	Laps	Laps Led	Races Led	Miles	$

Marvin Porter

Marvin Porter
B: 1924   D: 2002
Racing Hometown: Lakewood, CA

Year	Rank	Starts	Poles	1	2	3	4	5	6–10	Laps	Laps Led	Races Led	Miles	$
1957	44	6	0	1	1	0	0	0	1	771	1	1	632	1,770
1958	NR	6	0	0	0	0	0	0	2	542	0	0	433	565
1959	46	7	0	0	0	1	1	0	2	1,696	0	0	706	1,940
1960	69	3	0	1	0	0	0	0	0	223	61	2	295	3,800
1961	49	8	0	0	0	0	0	1	0	1,096	0	0	1,252	2,070
1963	79	2	0	0	0	0	0	0	0	202	0	0	545	1,100
1964	56	1	0	0	0	0	0	0	1	179	0	0	483	1,150
1967	115	1	0	0	0	0	0	0	0	15	0	0	41	500
Lifetime		34	0	2	1	1	1	1	6	4,724	62	3	4,387	$12,895

Randy Porter

Randall Porter
B: 7/6/1964
Racing Hometown: Greenville, SC

Year	Rank	Starts	Poles	1	2	3	4	5	6–10	Laps	Laps Led	Races Led	Miles	$
1992	62T	2	0	0	0	0	0	0	0	502	0	0	962	12,475
Lifetime		2	0	0	0	0	0	0	0	502	0	0	962	$12,475

Sam Posey

Samuel Posey
B: 5/26/1944
Racing Hometown: Sharon, CT

Year	Rank	Starts	Poles	1	2	3	4	5	6–10	Laps	Laps Led	Races Led	Miles	$
1970	NR	1	0	0	0	0	0	0	0	82	0	0	215	900
Lifetime		1	0	0	0	0	0	0	0	82	0	0	215	$900

Bob Potter

Robert Potter
Racing Hometown: Duluth, MN

Year	Rank	Starts	Poles	1	2	3	4	5	6–10	Laps	Laps Led	Races Led	Miles	$
1959	105	2	0	0	0	0	0	0	0	46	0	0	115	150
1960	50	3	0	0	0	0	0	0	1	708	0	0	822	640
Lifetime		5	0	0	0	0	0	0	1	754	0	0	937	$790

John Potter

John Potter
Racing Hometown: Inglewood, CA

Year	Rank	Starts	Poles	1	2	3	4	5	6–10	Laps	Laps Led	Races Led	Miles	$
1959	85	2	0	0	0	0	0	0	2	549	0	0	277	550
1960	114	2	0	0	0	0	0	0	0	126	0	0	158	150
Lifetime		4	0	0	0	0	0	0	2	675	0	0	435	$700

Mike Potter

Michael Potter
B: 7/4/1949
Racing Hometown: Johnson City, TN

Year	Rank	Starts	Poles	1	2	3	4	5	6–10	Laps	Laps Led	Races Led	Miles	$
1979	67	4	0	0	0	0	0	0	0	1,021	0	0	835	3,165
1980	64	3	0	0	0	0	0	0	0	450	0	0	535	2,370
1981	92	6	0	0	0	0	0	0	0	1,051	0	0	1,351	14,500
1982	97	2	0	0	0	0	0	0	0	322	0	0	645	3,535
1983	39	11	0	0	0	0	0	0	0	1,916	0	0	2,322	20,175
1984	NR	1	0	0	0	0	0	0	0	9	0	0	9	710
1985	42	6	0	0	0	0	0	0	0	1,434	0	0	1,729	10,855
1986	67	3	0	0	0	0	0	0	0	470	0	0	476	5,890
1987	45	5	0	0	0	0	0	0	0	994	0	0	947	13,290
1988	83T	1	0	0	0	0	0	0	0	44	0	0	110	1,700
1989	93T	1	0	0	0	0	0	0	0	137	0	0	187	2,455
1990	60	3	0	0	0	0	0	0	0	463	0	0	747	9,775
1992	36	11	0	0	0	0	0	0	0	1,869	0	0	3,151	74,710
1993	66	2	0	0	0	0	0	0	0	236	0	0	241	11,915
Lifetime		59	0	0	0	0	0	0	0	10,416	0	0	13,285	$175,045

George Poulos

George Poulos
B: 5/21/1932
Racing Hometown: Charlotte, NC

Year	Rank	Starts	Poles	1	2	3	4	5	6–10	Laps	Laps Led	Races Led	Miles	$
1967	46	23	0	0	0	0	0	0	1	2,872	0	0	1,457	3,040
Lifetime		23	0	0	0	0	0	0	1	2,872	0	0	1,457	$3,040

Year	Rank	Starts	Poles	Finish						Laps	Laps Led	Races Led	Miles	$
				1	2	3	4	5	6–10					

Charles Powell

Charles Powell
Racing Hometown: Paramont, CA

Year	Rank	Starts	Poles	1	2	3	4	5	6–10	Laps	Laps Led	Races Led	Miles	$
1965	127	1	0	0	0	0	0	0	0	1	0	0	3	500
1966	134	1	0	0	0	0	0	0	0	1	0	0	3	500
Lifetime		2	0	0	0	0	0	0	0	2	0	0	5	$1,000

Floyd Powell

John Floyd Powell
B: 1931   D: 8/23/1963   *Killed by brother-in-law Melvin Easler.*
Racing Hometown: Chesnee, SC

Year	Rank	Starts	Poles	1	2	3	4	5	6–10	Laps	Laps Led	Races Led	Miles	$
1962	110T	1	0	0	0	0	0	0	0	142	0	0	71	110
1963	69	5	0	0	0	0	0	0	2	543	0	0	667	1,315
Lifetime		6	0	0	0	0	0	0	2	685	0	0	738	$1,425

Frank Powell

Frank Powell
Racing Hometown: Pittsburgh, PA

Year	Rank	Starts	Poles	1	2	3	4	5	6–10	Laps	Laps Led	Races Led	Miles	$
1955	175T	1	0	0	0	0	0	0	0	23	0	0	12	50
Lifetime		1	0	0	0	0	0	0	0	23	0	0	12	$50

Macon Powers

Macon Powers
Racing Hometown: Vinton, VA

Year	Rank	Starts	Poles	1	2	3	4	5	6–10	Laps	Laps Led	Races Led	Miles	$
1950	129T	1	0	0	0	0	0	0	0	125	0	0	63	0
Lifetime		1	0	0	0	0	0	0	0	125	0	0	63	$0

Bill Pratt

William Pratt

Year	Rank	Starts	Poles	1	2	3	4	5	6–10	Laps	Laps Led	Races Led	Miles	$
1970	NR	1	0	0	0	0	0	0	0	5	0	0	13	630
Lifetime		1	0	0	0	0	0	0	0	5	0	0	13	$630

Hal Prentice

Hal Prentice
Racing Hometown: Ferndale, MI

Year	Rank	Starts	Poles	1	2	3	4	5	6–10	Laps	Laps Led	Races Led	Miles	$
1955	220	1	0	0	0	0	0	0	0	197	0	0	197	90
Lifetime		1	0	0	0	0	0	0	0	197	0	0	197	$90

Bob Presnell

Robert Presnell
Racing Hometown: Lenoir, NC

Year	Rank	Starts	Poles	1	2	3	4	5	6–10	Laps	Laps Led	Races Led	Miles	$
1961	99	5	0	0	0	0	0	0	1	494	0	0	201	520
Lifetime		5	0	0	0	0	0	0	1	494	0	0	201	$520

Robert Pressley

Robert E. Pressley
B: 4/8/1959
Racing Hometown: Asheville, NC

Year	Rank	Starts	Poles	1	2	3	4	5	6–10	Laps	Laps Led	Races Led	Miles	$
1994	57	3	0	0	0	0	0	0	0	587	0	0	947	39,485
1995	29	31	0	0	0	0	0	0	1	8,181	37	3	9,996	695,875
1996	32	30	0	0	0	0	1	1	1	7,948	110	7	9,678	690,465
1997	43	14	0	0	0	0	0	0	0	3,941	9	2	4,205	252,478
1998	32	30	0	0	0	1	0	0	0	7,224	3	2	10,244	996,721
1999	39	28	0	0	0	0	0	0	0	7,785	3	3	9,898	1,033,223
2000	25	34	0	0	0	0	0	1	0	9,183	14	4	12,260	1,427,817
2001	25	34	0	0	1	0	0	0	4	9,154	5	4	12,464	2,171,520
2002	68	1	0	0	0	0	0	0	0	190	0	0	475	147,709
Lifetime		205	0	0	1	1	1	2	6	54,193	181	25	70,168	$7,455,293

Albert Price

Albert Price
Racing Hometown: Greensboro, NC

Year	Rank	Starts	Poles	1	2	3	4	5	6–10	Laps	Laps Led	Races Led	Miles	$
1952	NR	1	0	0	0	0	0	0	0	37	0	0	37	25
Lifetime		1	0	0	0	0	0	0	0	37	0	0	37	$25

Baxter Price

Baxter Larry Price
B: 11/29/1938
Racing Hometown: Monroe, NC

Year	Rank	Starts	Poles	1	2	3	4	5	6–10	Laps	Laps Led	Races Led	Miles	$
1973	122	1	0	0	0	0	0	0	0	3	0	0	2	325

Year	Rank	Starts	Poles	Finish 1	2	3	4	5	6–10	Laps	Laps Led	Races Led	Miles	$

Baxter Price *continued*

Year	Rank	Starts	Poles	1	2	3	4	5	6–10	Laps	Laps Led	Races Led	Miles	$
1975	59	3	0	0	0	0	0	0	0	331	0	0	548	1,685
1976	50	6	0	0	0	0	0	0	0	1,680	0	0	1,432	3,010
1977	33	12	0	0	0	0	0	0	0	2,566	0	0	2,706	10,890
1978	23	24	0	0	0	0	0	0	0	7,343	0	0	7,611	36,560
1979	25	24	0	0	0	0	0	0	0	6,791	0	0	6,666	45,165
1980	29	18	0	0	0	0	0	0	0	4,890	0	0	4,930	26,615
1981	96	2	0	0	0	0	0	0	0	17	0	0	11	1,400
Lifetime		90	0	0	0	0	0	0	0	23,621	0	0	23,905	$125,650

Bob Price

Robert Price
Racing Hometown: Burbank, CA

Year	Rank	Starts	Poles	1	2	3	4	5	6–10	Laps	Laps Led	Races Led	Miles	$
1958	159	2	0	0	0	0	0	0	0	146	0	0	382	110
1959	120	2	0	0	0	0	0	0	0	427	0	0	176	225
1960	80	3	0	0	0	0	0	0	0	258	0	0	314	445
1961	114	2	0	0	0	0	0	0	1	204	0	0	150	180
Lifetime		9	0	0	0	0	0	0	1	1,035	0	0	1,022	$960

Don Price

Donald Price
Racing Hometown: Trevose, PA

Year	Rank	Starts	Poles	1	2	3	4	5	6–10	Laps	Laps Led	Races Led	Miles	$
1952	126T	1	0	0	0	0	0	0	0	116	0	0	116	25
1953	143	1	0	0	0	0	0	0	0		0	0		50
Lifetime		2	0	0	0	0	0	0	0	116	0	0	116	$75

Frank Price

Frank Price
Racing Hometown: Pittston, PA

Year	Rank	Starts	Poles	1	2	3	4	5	6–10	Laps	Laps Led	Races Led	Miles	$
1953	NR	2	0	0	0	0	0	0	0		0	0		125
Lifetime		2	0	0	0	0	0	0	0		0	0		$125

Mike Price

Michael Price
Racing Hometown: Atlanta, GA

Year	Rank	Starts	Poles	1	2	3	4	5	6–10	Laps	Laps Led	Races Led	Miles	$
1959	NR	1	0	0	0	0	0	0	0	72	0	0	72	50
Lifetime		1	0	0	0	0	0	0	0	72	0	0	72	$50

Walt Price

Walter Price
B: 3/15/1935
Racing Hometown: San Fernando, CA

Year	Rank	Starts	Poles	1	2	3	4	5	6–10	Laps	Laps Led	Races Led	Miles	$
1964	128	1	0	0	0	0	0	0	0	43	0	0	116	500
1966	73	1	0	0	0	0	0	0	0	154	0	0	416	575
1967	103	1	0	0	0	0	0	0	0	51	0	0	138	500
1974	89	2	0	0	0	0	0	0	0	136	0	0	349	1,800
Lifetime		5	0	0	0	0	0	0	0	384	0	0	1,019	$3,375

Charles Prickett

Charles Prickett
Racing Hometown: Sanger, CA

Year	Rank	Starts	Poles	1	2	3	4	5	6–10	Laps	Laps Led	Races Led	Miles	$
1967	63	1	0	0	0	0	0	0	1	162	0	0	437	1,000
Lifetime		1	0	0	0	0	0	0	1	162	0	0	437	$1,000

Clyde Prickett

Clyde Prickett
Racing Hometown: Fresno, CA

Year	Rank	Starts	Poles	1	2	3	4	5	6–10	Laps	Laps Led	Races Led	Miles	$
1966	130	1	0	0	0	0	0	0	0	11	0	0	30	500
1967	75	1	0	0	0	0	0	0	0	104	0	0	281	610
1968	80	1	0	0	0	0	0	0	0	140	0	0	378	700
Lifetime		3	0	0	0	0	0	0	0	255	0	0	689	$1,810

Cotton Priddy

Thomas Priddy
B: 1929   D: 6/1956   *Killed in NASCAR Race @ LeHi, Ark.*
Racing Hometown: Lousiville, KY

Year	Rank	Starts	Poles	1	2	3	4	5	6–10	Laps	Laps Led	Races Led	Miles	$
1953	131	2	0	0	0	0	0	0	0	35	0	0	144	75
1956	250T	1	0	0	0	0	0	0	0	38	0	0	57	50
Lifetime		3	0	0	0	0	0	0	0	73	0	0	201	$125

Year	Rank	Starts	Poles	Finish 1	2	3	4	5	6–10	Laps	Laps Led	Races Led	Miles	$

Bob Prince

Robert Prince
Racing Hometown: Detroit, MI

Year	Rank	Starts	Poles	1	2	3	4	5	6–10	Laps	Laps Led	Races Led	Miles	$
1951	N/A	1	0	0	0	0	0	0	0	199	0	0	199	25
Lifetime		1	0	0	0	0	0	0	0	199	0	0	199	$25

Talmadge Prince

Talmadge Prince (Tab)
B: 2/1937   D: 2/19/1970   *Killed in Daytona 125-mile qualifying race.*
Racing Hometown: Dublin, GA

Year	Rank	Starts	Poles	1	2	3	4	5	6–10	Laps	Laps Led	Races Led	Miles	$
1970	NR	1	0	0	0	0	0	0	0	18	0	0	45	0
Lifetime		1	0	0	0	0	0	0	0	18	0	0	45	$0

Joe Prismo

Joseph Prismo

Year	Rank	Starts	Poles	1	2	3	4	5	6–10	Laps	Laps Led	Races Led	Miles	$
1956	149	1	0	0	0	0	0	0	1	246	0	0	123	200
Lifetime		1	0	0	0	0	0	0	1	246	0	0	123	$200

Clem Proctor

Clem Proctor
B: 10/16/1928   D: 1/1995
Racing Hometown: Compton, CA

Year	Rank	Starts	Poles	1	2	3	4	5	6–10	Laps	Laps Led	Races Led	Miles	$
1960	NR	1	0	0	0	0	0	0	0	338	0	0	465	500
1961	112	2	0	0	0	0	0	0	1	100	0	0	105	250
1963	72	2	0	0	0	0	0	0	0	260	0	0	702	850
1964	130	1	0	0	0	0	0	0	0	15	0	0	41	500
1966	82	1	0	0	0	0	0	0	0	114	0	0	308	600
1972	111	1	0	0	0	0	0	0	0	37	0	0	97	685
1973	124	1	0	0	0	0	0	0	0	5	0	0	13	1,015
Lifetime		9	0	0	0	0	0	0	1	869	0	0	1,730	$4,400

Bob Pronger

Robert Pronger
B: 1/22/1922   D: 6/17/1971   *Declared missing after disappearing at the hands of mafia agents.*
Racing Hometown: Blue Island, IL

Year	Rank	Starts	Poles	1	2	3	4	5	6–10	Laps	Laps Led	Races Led	Miles	$
1951	N/A	1	0	0	0	0	0	0	0	332	0	0	415	50
1952	139	2	0	0	0	0	0	0	0	189	0	0	224	25
1953	177	1	1	0	0	0	0	0	0	5	0	0	21	0
1958	151	2	0	0	0	0	0	0	0	16	0	0	66	25
1959	84	2	0	0	0	0	0	0	0	156	0	0	390	125
1961	165	1	0	0	0	0	0	0	0	37	0	0	93	85
Lifetime		9	1	0	0	0	0	0	0	735	0	0	1,208	$310

Oren Prosser

Oren Prosser
B: 1941
Racing Hometown: Granada Hills, CA

Year	Rank	Starts	Poles	1	2	3	4	5	6–10	Laps	Laps Led	Races Led	Miles	$
1961	161T	1	0	0	0	0	0	0	0	73	0	0	73	50
1963	137	1	0	0	0	0	0	0	0	95	0	0	257	200
1964	113	1	0	0	0	0	0	0	0	87	0	0	235	500
Lifetime		3	0	0	0	0	0	0	0	255	0	0	564	$750

Scott Pruett

Scott Pruett
B: 3/24/1960
Racing Hometown: Roseville, CA

Year	Rank	Starts	Poles	1	2	3	4	5	6–10	Laps	Laps Led	Races Led	Miles	$
2000	37	28	0	0	0	0	0	0	1	6,216	23	2	8,744	1,135,854
2001	51	2	0	0	0	0	0	0	0	202	3	1	439	134,045
2002	61	1	0	0	0	0	0	0	1	90	0	0	221	66,690
Lifetime		31	0	0	0	0	0	0	2	6,508	26	3	9,403	$1,336,589

Bill Pruitt

William Pruitt
Racing Hometown: Detroit, Mi

Year	Rank	Starts	Poles	1	2	3	4	5	6–10	Laps	Laps Led	Races Led	Miles	$
1952	NR	1	0	0	0	0	0	0	0	169	0	0	169	25
Lifetime		1	0	0	0	0	0	0	0	169	0	0	169	$25

Year	Rank	Starts	Poles	Finish 1	2	3	4	5	6–10	Laps	Laps Led	Races Led	Miles	$

Don Pruitt

Donald Pruitt
Racing Hometown: Burbank, CA

Year	Rank	Starts	Poles	1	2	3	4	5	6–10	Laps	Laps Led	Races Led	Miles	$
1974	126	1	0	0	0	0	0	0	0	28	0	0	73	670
Lifetime		1	0	0	0	0	0	0	0	28	0	0	73	$670

Ervin Pruitt

Ervin Pruitt
B: 5/11/1940
Racing Hometown: Spartanburg, SC

Year	Rank	Starts	Poles	1	2	3	4	5	6–10	Laps	Laps Led	Races Led	Miles	$
1968	79	5	0	0	0	0	0	0	1	1,376	0	0	733	1,930
1969	64	4	0	0	0	0	0	0	1	565	0	0	371	850
Lifetime		9	0	0	0	0	0	0	2	1,941	0	0	1,104	$2,780

Ray Pruitt

Raymond Pruitt
Racing Hometown: Yorktown, PA

Year	Rank	Starts	Poles	1	2	3	4	5	6–10	Laps	Laps Led	Races Led	Miles	$
1951	N/A	2	0	0	0	0	0	0	0	93	0	0	70	25
Lifetime		2	0	0	0	0	0	0	0	93	0	0	70	$25

Smokey Purser

Carl Daniel Purser
B: Late 1800s   D: 5/30/1964
Racing Hometown: Lumber City, GA

Year	Rank	Starts	Poles	1	2	3	4	5	6–10	Laps	Laps Led	Races Led	Miles	$
1952	NR	1	0	0	0	0	0	0	0	1	0	0	4	0
Lifetime		1	0	0	0	0	0	0	0	1	0	0	4	$0

Jeff Purvis

Jeffrey Thomas Purvis
B: 2/19/1959
Racing Hometown: Clarksville, TN

Year	Rank	Starts	Poles	1	2	3	4	5	6–10	Laps	Laps Led	Races Led	Miles	$
1990	56	5	0	0	0	0	0	0	0	918	0	0	765	40,930
1991	45	6	0	0	0	0	0	0	0	888	0	0	1,486	42,910
1992	44	6	0	0	0	0	0	0	0	1,418	0	0	1,281	45,545
1993	39	8	0	0	0	0	0	0	0	2,491	3	2	2,742	108,545
1994	46	7	0	0	0	0	0	0	0	1,081	0	0	2,259	78,755
1995	47	7	0	0	0	0	0	0	0	951	0	0	1,928	93,875
1996	48	4	0	0	0	0	0	0	0	532	0	0	1,364	91,127
1997	57	3	0	0	0	0	0	0	0	376	1	1	661	80,526
2001	55	4	0	0	0	0	0	0	0	409	0	0	1,066	238,985
Lifetime		50	0	0	0	0	0	0	0	9,064	4	3	13,552	$821,198

Don Puskarich

Donald Puskarich
B: 2/26/1939
Racing Hometown: Garden Grove, CA

Year	Rank	Starts	Poles	1	2	3	4	5	6–10	Laps	Laps Led	Races Led	Miles	$
1975	65	3	0	0	0	0	0	0	0	184	0	0	480	3,060
1976	62	3	0	0	0	0	0	0	0	343	0	0	876	3,770
1977	82	2	0	0	0	0	0	0	0	51	0	0	134	1,520
1978	98	1	0	0	0	0	0	0	0	36	0	0	94	700
1979	111T	1	0	0	0	0	0	0	0	47	0	0	123	855
1980	61	3	0	0	0	0	0	0	0	201	0	0	526	3,835
1981	57	3	0	0	0	0	0	0	0	211	0	0	553	4,770
1982	84T	1	0	0	0	0	0	0	0	87	0	0	228	1,870
Lifetime		17	0	0	0	0	0	0	0	1,160	0	0	3,014	$20,380

J.T. Putney

Julian Taylor Putney
B: 10/5/1928   D: 4/11/2001
Racing Hometown: Arden, NC

Year	Rank	Starts	Poles	1	2	3	4	5	6–10	Laps	Laps Led	Races Led	Miles	$
1964	23	17	0	0	0	1	0	0	5	4,226	0	0	3,370	7,295
1965	7	40	0	0	1	3	4	2	14	7,932	0	0	5,680	22,329
1966	8	39	0	0	1	2	1	0	5	7,836	32	2	6,708	18,653
1967	18	29	0	0	0	1	0	0	9	6,050	0	0	4,817	15,687
Lifetime		125	0	0	2	7	5	2	33	26,044	32	2	20,576	$63,964

Bud Rackley

Bud Rackley
Racing Hometown: Houston, TX

Year	Rank	Starts	Poles	1	2	3	4	5	6–10	Laps	Laps Led	Races Led	Miles	$
1955	NR	1	0	0	0	0	0	0	0	44	0	0	61	50
Lifetime		1	0	0	0	0	0	0	0	44	0	0	61	$50

Year	Rank	Starts	Poles	Finish						Laps	Laps Led	Races Led	Miles	$
				1	2	3	4	5	6–10					

Francis Radaker

Francis Neale Radaker
Racing Hometown: DuBoise, PA

Year	Rank	Starts	Poles	1	2	3	4	5	6–10	Laps	Laps Led	Races Led	Miles	$
1952	204	1	0	0	0	0	0	0	0	64	0	0	32	25
Lifetime		1	0	0	0	0	0	0	0	64	0	0	32	$25

Paul Radford

James Paul Radford
B: 9/29/1931
Racing Hometown: Ferrum, VA

Year	Rank	Starts	Poles	1	2	3	4	5	6–10	Laps	Laps Led	Races Led	Miles	$
1974	136	1	0	0	0	0	0	0	0	20	0	0	11	750
Lifetime		1	0	0	0	0	0	0	0	20	0	0	11	$750

Jack Radtke

Jack Radtke
Racing Hometown: Grays Lake, IL

Year	Rank	Starts	Poles	1	2	3	4	5	6–10	Laps	Laps Led	Races Led	Miles	$
1955	109	1	0	0	0	0	0	0	1	38	0	0	156	150
1956	123	1	0	0	0	0	0	0	0		0	0		110
Lifetime		2	0	0	0	0	0	0	1	38	0	0	156	$260

Billy Rafter

William Fred Rafter
B: 7/31/1929
Racing Hometown: Clarence Center, NY

Year	Rank	Starts	Poles	1	2	3	4	5	6–10	Laps	Laps Led	Races Led	Miles	$
1949	20	1	0	0	0	1	0	0	0		0	0		480
1953	144T	1	0	0	0	0	0	0	0		0	0		25
1954	201	1	0	0	0	0	0	0	0	32	0	0	131	0
1956	73	9	0	0	0	0	0	0	1	1,140	0	0	623	975
1957	127	4	0	0	0	0	0	0	1	250	0	0	304	440
1958	19	19	0	0	0	0	0	1	7	3,160	0	0	1,529	2,799
Lifetime		35	0	0	0	1	0	1	9	4,582	0	0	2,587	$4,719

Ken Ragan

Kenneth Ragan
B: 9/12/1950
Racing Hometown: Unadilla, GA

Year	Rank	Starts	Poles	1	2	3	4	5	6–10	Laps	Laps Led	Races Led	Miles	$
1983	35	8	0	0	0	0	0	0	0	1,984	0	0	3,526	27,905
1984	40	10	0	0	0	0	0	0	0	1,839	1	1	3,467	37,045
1985	47	7	0	0	0	0	0	0	0	1,359	0	0	2,255	35,995
1986	39	7	0	0	0	0	0	0	0	1,284	1	1	2,503	33,890
1987	41	6	0	0	0	0	0	0	0	1,259	0	0	2,354	30,575
1988	47	5	0	0	0	0	0	0	0	731	0	0	1,426	15,755
1989	54	3	0	0	0	0	0	0	0	550	0	0	922	7,295
1990	55	4	0	0	0	0	0	0	0	398	0	0	840	15,720
Lifetime		50	0	0	0	0	0	0	0	9,404	2	2	17,295	$204,180

Walt Ragan

Walter Ragan
Racing Hometown: Conowingo, MD

Year	Rank	Starts	Poles	1	2	3	4	5	6–10	Laps	Laps Led	Races Led	Miles	$
1952	NR	2	0	0	0	0	0	0	0	238	0	0	238	75
1955	—	1	0	0	0	0	0	0	0	162	0	0	81	50
Lifetime		3	0	0	0	0	0	0	0	400	0	0	319	$125

Lloyd Ragon

Lloyd M. Ragon
Racing Hometown: Syracuse, NY

Year	Rank	Starts	Poles	1	2	3	4	5	6–10	Laps	Laps Led	Races Led	Miles	$
1958	77	2	0	0	0	0	0	0	1	34	0	0	139	230
Lifetime		2	0	0	0	0	0	0	1	34	0	0	139	$230

Buddy Ragsdale

Buddy Ragsdale

Year	Rank	Starts	Poles	1	2	3	4	5	6–10	Laps	Laps Led	Races Led	Miles	$
1958	NR	1	0	0	0	0	0	0	0	130	0	0	130	150
Lifetime		1	0	0	0	0	0	0	0	130	0	0	130	$150

Bobby Rahal

Robert Woodward Rahal
B: 1/10/1953
Racing Hometown: Medina, OH

Year	Rank	Starts	Poles	1	2	3	4	5	6–10	Laps	Laps Led	Races Led	Miles	$
1984	91T	1	0	0	0	0	0	0	0	44	0	0	115	875
Lifetime		1	0	0	0	0	0	0	0	44	0	0	115	$875

					Finish							Laps	Races		
Year	Rank	Starts	Poles	1	2	3	4	5	6–10		Laps	Led	Led	Miles	$

Tony Raines

Tony Raines
B: 4/14/1964
Racing Hometown: LaPorte, IN

Year	Rank	Starts	Poles	1	2	3	4	5	6–10	Laps	Laps Led	Races Led	Miles	$
2002	51	7	0	0	0	0	0	0	0	1,586	0	0	1,921	282,787
Lifetime		7	0	0	0	0	0	0	0	1,586	0	0	1,921	$282,787

Ansel Rakestraw

Ansel Rakestraw
Racing Hometown: Hiram, GA

Year	Rank	Starts	Poles	1	2	3	4	5	6–10	Laps	Laps Led	Races Led	Miles	$
1956	NR	1	0	0	0	0	0	0	0	48	0	0	197	100
1957	NR	2	0	0	0	0	0	0	0	276	0	0	138	200
Lifetime		3	0	0	0	0	0	0	0	324	0	0	335	$300

Benny Rakestraw

Benjamin Rakestraw
Racing Hometown: Dallas, GA

Year	Rank	Starts	Poles	1	2	3	4	5	6–10	Laps	Laps Led	Races Led	Miles	$
1956	NR	1	0	0	0	0	0	0	1	156	0	0	78	100
1958	174	5	0	0	0	0	0	0	1	756	0	0	384	400
1959	NR	7	0	0	0	0	1	0	0	1,144	0	0	774	1,165
Lifetime		13	0	0	0	0	1	0	2	2,056	0	0	1,236	$1,665

Tyre Rakestraw

Tyrell Rakestraw
Racing Hometown: Hiram, GA

Year	Rank	Starts	Poles	1	2	3	4	5	6–10	Laps	Laps Led	Races Led	Miles	$
1953	NR	1	0	0	0	0	0	0	0	308	0	0	424	160
Lifetime		1	0	0	0	0	0	0	0	308	0	0	424	$160

Wilbur Rakestraw

Wilbur Carlton Rakestraw
B: 6/6/1928
Racing Hometown: Dallas, GA

Year	Rank	Starts	Poles	1	2	3	4	5	6–10	Laps	Laps Led	Races Led	Miles	$
1956	NR	1	0	0	0	0	0	0	0	29	0	0	15	100
1958	NR	9	0	0	0	0	1	0	2	1,688	0	0	1,443	1,655
1959	NR	3	0	0	0	0	0	0	1	413	0	0	815	1,025
1960	41	12	0	0	0	0	0	0	1	1,862	0	0	2,038	2,695
1961	95	5	0	0	0	0	0	0	1	360	0	0	306	635
Lifetime		30	0	0	0	0	1	0	5	4,352	0	0	4,616	$6,110

Tom Raley

Thomas E. Raley
B: 12/16/1936
Racing Hometown: North Beach, MD

Year	Rank	Starts	Poles	1	2	3	4	5	6–10	Laps	Laps Led	Races Led	Miles	$
1967	84	9	0	0	0	0	0	0	0	632	0	0	363	925
Lifetime		9	0	0	0	0	0	0	0	632	0	0	363	$925

Ted Rambo

Theodore Rambo
Racing Hometown: New Bloomington, OH

Year	Rank	Starts	Poles	1	2	3	4	5	6–10	Laps	Laps Led	Races Led	Miles	$
1954	71	5	0	0	0	0	0	0	1	296	0	0	260	200
Lifetime		5	0	0	0	0	0	0	1	296	0	0	260	$200

Nick Rampling

Nicholas Rampling
Racing Hometown: Cooksville, Ont., Canada

Year	Rank	Starts	Poles	1	2	3	4	5	6–10	Laps	Laps Led	Races Led	Miles	$
1966	97	3	0	0	0	0	0	0	0	472	0	0	209	230
Lifetime		3	0	0	0	0	0	0	0	472	0	0	209	$230

E.C. Ramsey

E.C. Ramsey
Racing Hometown: Greenville, SC

Year	Rank	Starts	Poles	1	2	3	4	5	6–10	Laps	Laps Led	Races Led	Miles	$
1952	47	7	0	0	0	0	0	0	0	826	0	0	693	260
Lifetime		7	0	0	0	0	0	0	0	826	0	0	693	$260

Darvin Randahl

Darvin Randahl
Racing Hometown: Rio, WI

Year	Rank	Starts	Poles	1	2	3	4	5	6–10	Laps	Laps Led	Races Led	Miles	$
1956	65	7	0	0	0	0	0	0	1	528	0	0	448	710
Lifetime		7	0	0	0	0	0	0	1	528	0	0	448	$710

Year	Rank	Starts	Poles	Finish						Laps	Laps Led	Races Led	Miles	$
				1	2	3	4	5	6–10					

Maurice Randall

Maurice Randall
B: 11/28/1952
Racing Hometown: Charlotte, MI

Year	Rank	Starts	Poles	1	2	3	4	5	6–10	Laps	Laps Led	Races Led	Miles	$
1984	NR	1	0	0	0	0	0	0	0	50	0	0	30	1,010
1985	67	3	0	0	0	0	0	0	0	104	0	0	107	3,450
Lifetime		4	0	0	0	0	0	0	0	154	0	0	137	$4,460

Roscoe Rann

Roscoe Rann
Racing Hometown: Memphis, TN

Year	Rank	Starts	Poles	1	2	3	4	5	6–10	Laps	Laps Led	Races Led	Miles	$
1954	NR	1	0	0	0	0	0	0	0	33	0	0	50	100
1955	97	2	0	0	0	0	0	0	0	271	0	0	407	110
Lifetime		3	0	0	0	0	0	0	0	304	0	0	456	$210

Jim Raptis

James Al Raptis
B: 6/21/1947
Racing Hometown: Woodstock, GA

Year	Rank	Starts	Poles	1	2	3	4	5	6–10	Laps	Laps Led	Races Led	Miles	$
1977	95	3	0	0	0	0	0	0	0	116	0	0	252	2,530
Lifetime		3	0	0	0	0	0	0	0	116	0	0	252	$2,530

Dick Rathmann

Richard R. Rathmann   Born as: Jim Rathmann (swapped identities with brother in 1940s)
B: 1/6/1924   D: 2/1/2000
Racing Hometown: Los Angeles, CA

Year	Rank	Starts	Poles	1	2	3	4	5	6–10	Laps	Laps Led	Races Led	Miles	$
1951	8	15	0	0	3	1	0	0	3	231	0	0	131	3,225
1952	5	27	2	5	1	4	0	4	0	3,607	701	10	2,539	11,248
1953	3	34	2	5	12	1	2	1	3	2,545	542	8	2,002	20,245
1954	4	32	4	3	5	8	6	1	3	5,286	729	11	3,629	16,264
1955	18	20	3	0	2	2	3	0	1	2,296	176	5	1,587	4,368
Lifetime		128	11	13	23	16	11	6	10	13,965	2,148	34	9,888	$55,350

Jim Rathmann

James Rathmann   Born as: Dick Rathmann (swapped identities with brother in 1940s)
B: 7/16/1928
Racing Hometown: Alhambra, CA

Year	Rank	Starts	Poles	1	2	3	4	5	6–10	Laps	Laps Led	Races Led	Miles	$
1949	NR	1	0	0	0	0	0	0	0		0	0		0
1950	89	1	0	0	0	0	0	0	0	46	0	0	192	50
1951	N/A	1	0	0	0	0	0	0	0	76	0	0	76	0
Lifetime		3	0	0	0	0	0	0	0	122	0	0	268	$50

Ken Rauch

Kenneth Rauch

Year	Rank	Starts	Poles	1	2	3	4	5	6–10	Laps	Laps Led	Races Led	Miles	$
1952	NR	1	0	0	0	0	0	0	0	133	0	0	67	25
Lifetime		1	0	0	0	0	0	0	0	133	0	0	67	$25

Bob Rauscher

Robert Rauscher

Year	Rank	Starts	Poles	1	2	3	4	5	6–10	Laps	Laps Led	Races Led	Miles	$
1957	83	3	0	0	0	0	0	1	1	329	0	0	195	435
Lifetime		3	0	0	0	0	0	1	1	329	0	0	195	$435

John Ray

John Ray
Racing Hometown: Los Angeles, CA

Year	Rank	Starts	Poles	1	2	3	4	5	6–10	Laps	Laps Led	Races Led	Miles	$
1953	NR	1	0	0	0	0	0	0	0	202	0	0	202	25
Lifetime		1	0	0	0	0	0	0	0	202	0	0	202	$25

Johnny Ray

John Ray
B: 3/25/1937
Racing Hometown: Eastaboga, AL

Year	Rank	Starts	Poles	1	2	3	4	5	6–10	Laps	Laps Led	Races Led	Miles	$
1974	80	2	0	0	0	0	0	0	0	252	0	0	670	2,435
1975	69	4	0	0	0	0	0	0	0	247	0	0	577	3,435
1976	83	2	0	0	0	0	0	0	0	145	0	0	367	3,005
Lifetime		8	0	0	0	0	0	0	0	644	0	0	1,614	$8,875

Year	Rank	Starts	Poles	Finish						Laps	Laps Led	Races Led	Miles	$
				1	2	3	4	5	6–10					

Joie Ray

Joie Ray
Racing Hometown: Portland, OR

Year	Rank	Starts	Poles	1	2	3	4	5	6–10	Laps	Laps Led	Races Led	Miles	$
1952	NR	1	0	0	0	0	0	0	0		0	0		0
Lifetime		1	0	0	0	0	0	0	0		0	0		$0

Leo Ray

Leo Ray
Racing Hometown: Rapid City, SD

Year	Rank	Starts	Poles	1	2	3	4	5	6–10	Laps	Laps Led	Races Led	Miles	$
1953	80T	1	0	0	0	0	0	0	1		0	0		100
Lifetime		1	0	0	0	0	0	0	1		0	0		$100

Lee Raymond

Lee Raymond
B: 10/2/1954
Racing Hometown: Dayton, OH

Year	Rank	Starts	Poles	1	2	3	4	5	6–10	Laps	Laps Led	Races Led	Miles	$
1989	NR	1	0	0	0	0	0	0	0	189	0	0	473	13,530
Lifetime		1	0	0	0	0	0	0	0	189	0	0	473	$13,530

Bob Read

Robert Read
Seriously burned 8/12/51 @ Delaware Valley Speedway, Stroudsburg, NJ.
Racing Hometown: Blairstown, N J

Year	Rank	Starts	Poles	1	2	3	4	5	6–10	Laps	Laps Led	Races Led	Miles	$
1950	NR	1	0	0	0	0	0	0	0		0	0		25
1951	N/A	1	0	0	0	0	0	0	0		0	0		0
Lifetime		2	0	0	0	0	0	0	0		0	0		$25

Jim Reed

James Reed
B: 2/21/1926
Racing Hometown: Peekskill, NY

Year	Rank	Starts	Poles	1	2	3	4	5	6–10	Laps	Laps Led	Races Led	Miles	$
1951	56	4	0	0	1	0	0	0	0	199	58	1	100	675
1952	46	7	0	0	0	0	0	1	2	597	0	0	336	475
1953	33	3	0	0	0	0	1	0	0	260	0	0	358	635
1954	45	9	0	0	0	0	0	2	1	1,083	0	0	815	965
1955	16	14	0	0	1	0	1	2	0	1,691	32	1	1,265	2,703
1956	18	11	2	0	1	1	2	1	0	1,542	286	3	1,666	5,077
1957	18	6	0	0	0	1	1	0	1	892	11	2	980	3,408
1958	10	17	2	4	0	5	1	0	2	3,693	692	4	2,474	9,644
1959	9	14	1	3	0	1	1	2	2	2,512	289	5	2,071	23,534
1960	44	8	0	0	0	1	0	0	0	1,175	28	1	1,670	2,240
1961	33	8	0	0	2	0	0	1	1	1,735	32	1	1,717	3,350
1962	70	4	0	0	0	0	0	1	0	919	0	0	781	1,030
1963	139	1	0	0	0	0	0	0	0	29	0	0	15	50
Lifetime		106	5	7	5	9	7	10	9	16,327	1,428	18	14,247	$53,786

Mark Reed

Mark Reed
Racing Hometown: Phoenix, AZ

Year	Rank	Starts	Poles	1	2	3	4	5	6–10	Laps	Laps Led	Races Led	Miles	$
1990	94T	1	0	0	0	0	0	0	0	269	0	0	269	3,100
1991	82T	1	0	0	0	0	0	0	0	177	0	0	177	3,375
Lifetime		2	0	0	0	0	0	0	0	446	0	0	446	$6,475

Bo Reeder

Bo Reeder
Racing Hometown: Compton, CA

Year	Rank	Starts	Poles	1	2	3	4	5	6–10	Laps	Laps Led	Races Led	Miles	$
1967	66	1	0	0	0	0	0	0	0	159	0	0	429	700
1968	108	1	0	0	0	0	0	0	0	4	0	0	11	500
Lifetime		2	0	0	0	0	0	0	0	163	0	0	440	$1,200

Ken Reeder

Kenneth Reeder
Racing Hometown: McConnellsburg, PA

Year	Rank	Starts	Poles	1	2	3	4	5	6–10	Laps	Laps Led	Races Led	Miles	$
1954	126T	1	0	0	0	0	0	0	0	179	0	0	90	25
Lifetime		1	0	0	0	0	0	0	0	179	0	0	90	$25

Nat Reeder

Nat Reeder
Racing Hometown: Hollywood, CA

Year	Rank	Starts	Poles	1	2	3	4	5	6–10	Laps	Laps Led	Races Led	Miles	$
1965	63	1	0	0	0	0	0	0	0	100	0	0	270	625
Lifetime		1	0	0	0	0	0	0	0	100	0	0	270	$625

Year	Rank	Starts	Poles	1	2	3	4	5	6–10	Laps	Laps Led	Races Led	Miles	$

Walt Regan
Walter Regan

Year	Rank	Starts	Poles	1	2	3	4	5	6–10	Laps	Laps Led	Races Led	Miles	$
1952	88	1	0	0	0	0	0	0	0	225	0	0	225	50
1955	190T	1	0	0	0	0	0	0	0	162	0	0	81	50
Lifetime		2	0	0	0	0	0	0	0	387	0	0	306	$100

Jim Reich
James Reich
B: 11/5/1942
Racing Hometown: Turlock, CA

Year	Rank	Starts	Poles	1	2	3	4	5	6–10	Laps	Laps Led	Races Led	Miles	$
1982	57	2	0	0	0	0	0	0	1	202	0	0	529	4,865
Lifetime		2	0	0	0	0	0	0	1	202	0	0	529	$4,865

Hassell Reid
Hassell Reid
Racing Hometown: Winston-Salem, NC

Year	Rank	Starts	Poles	1	2	3	4	5	6–10	Laps	Laps Led	Races Led	Miles	$
1954	143	3	0	0	0	0	0	0	0	262	0	0	141	100
Lifetime		3	0	0	0	0	0	0	0	262	0	0	141	$100

Dave Reiley
David Reiley

Year	Rank	Starts	Poles	1	2	3	4	5	6–10	Laps	Laps Led	Races Led	Miles	$
1951	N/A	1	0	0	0	0	0	0	0		0	0		0
Lifetime		1	0	0	0	0	0	0	0		0	0		$0

Lee Reitzel
Dr. Lee L. Reitzel
B: 9/14/1932   D: 9/24/1965
Racing Hometown: Charlotte, NC

Year	Rank	Starts	Poles	1	2	3	4	5	6–10	Laps	Laps Led	Races Led	Miles	$
1961	37	17	0	0	0	0	0	0	3	2,566	0	0	2,039	2,910
1962	66	8	0	0	0	0	0	0	1	1,056	0	0	863	1,205
1963	99	4	0	0	0	0	0	0	0	496	0	0	275	875
Lifetime		29	0	0	0	0	0	0	4	4,118	0	0	3,177	$4,990

Bill Remaly
William Remaly

Year	Rank	Starts	Poles	1	2	3	4	5	6–10	Laps	Laps Led	Races Led	Miles	$
1951	N/A	1	0	0	0	0	0	0	0	80	0	0	80	25
Lifetime		1	0	0	0	0	0	0	0	80	0	0	80	$25

B.E. Renfro
B.E. Renfro
Racing Hometown: Charlotte, NC

Year	Rank	Starts	Poles	1	2	3	4	5	6–10	Laps	Laps Led	Races Led	Miles	$
1949	NR	2	0	0	0	0	0	0	0		0	0		25
Lifetime		2	0	0	0	0	0	0	0		0	0		$25

Randy Renfrow
Randy Renfrow
B: 1/28/1958
Racing Hometown: Wilson, NC

Year	Rank	Starts	Poles	1	2	3	4	5	6–10	Laps	Laps Led	Races Led	Miles	$
2002	84T	1	0	0	0	0	0	0	0	58	0	0	44	39,667
Lifetime		1	0	0	0	0	0	0	0	58	0	0	44	$39,667

Carl Renner
Carl Renner
Racing Hometown: Toledo, OH

Year	Rank	Starts	Poles	1	2	3	4	5	6–10	Laps	Laps Led	Races Led	Miles	$
1950	48	2	0	0	0	0	0	0	1	0	0	0	0	225
Lifetime		2	0	0	0	0	0	0	1	0	0	0	0	$225

A.J. Reno
Arthur J. Reno
Racing Hometown: Dawsonville, VA

Year	Rank	Starts	Poles	1	2	3	4	5	6–10	Laps	Laps Led	Races Led	Miles	$
1974	NR	1	0	0	0	0	0	0	0	15	0	0	40	760
1975	90	1	0	0	0	0	0	0	0	170	0	0	452	1,670
Lifetime		2	0	0	0	0	0	0	0	185	0	0	492	$2,430

Bob Reuther
Robert Reuther
B: 9/12/1927
Racing Hometown: Nashville, TN

Year	Rank	Starts	Poles	1	2	3	4	5	6–10	Laps	Laps Led	Races Led	Miles	$
1951	NR	1	0	0	0	0	0	0	0		0	0		0

Year	Rank	Starts	Poles	Finish 1	2	3	4	5	6–10	Laps	Laps Led	Races Led	Miles	$

Bob Reuther *continued*

Year	Rank	Starts	Poles	1	2	3	4	5	6–10	Laps	Laps Led	Races Led	Miles	$
1959	58	1	0	0	0	0	0	0	1	284	0	0	142	250
1960	NR	1	0	0	0	0	0	0	0	285	0	0	143	140
Lifetime		3	0	0	0	0	0	0	1	569	0	0	285	$390

Buzzie Reutimann

Emile Reutimann
B: 5/7/1941
Racing Hometown: Harrisburg, PA

Year	Rank	Starts	Poles	1	2	3	4	5	6–10	Laps	Laps Led	Races Led	Miles	$
1963	119	1	0	0	0	0	0	0	1	192	0	0	58	140
Lifetime		1	0	0	0	0	0	0	1	192	0	0	58	$140

Melvin Revis

Melvin W. Revis
B: 1947
Racing Hometown: Spartanburg, SC

Year	Rank	Starts	Poles	1	2	3	4	5	6–10	Laps	Laps Led	Races Led	Miles	$
1979	NR	1	0	0	0	0	0	0	0	76	0	0	41	410
1980	104	1	0	0	0	0	0	0	0	23	0	0	31	1,115
Lifetime		2	0	0	0	0	0	0	0	99	0	0	72	$1,525

Bill Rexford

William J. Rexford
B: 3/14/1927   D: 4/18/1994
Racing Hometown: Conowango Valley, NY

Year	Rank	Starts	Poles	1	2	3	4	5	6–10	Laps	Laps Led	Races Led	Miles	$
1949	12	3	0	0	0	1	0	1	0	370	0	0	274	785
1950	1	17	0	1	0	1	2	1	6	1,302	98	2	1,146	5,750
1951	72	11	1	0	0	0	0	0	1	354	0	0	308	450
1952	NR	3	0	0	0	0	0	0	1	396	0	0	239	150
1953	NR	2	0	0	0	0	0	1	1	173	0	0	173	350
Lifetime		36	1	1	0	2	2	3	9	2,595	98	2	2,140	$7,485

Don Reynolds

Donald Reynolds
Racing Hometown: Cabazon, CA

Year	Rank	Starts	Poles	1	2	3	4	5	6–10	Laps	Laps Led	Races Led	Miles	$
1974	76	2	0	0	0	0	0	0	1	303	0	0	772	2,600
1975	86T	1	0	0	0	0	0	0	0	110	0	0	288	1,230
1976	91	1	0	0	0	0	0	0	0	83	0	0	217	1,140
Lifetime		4	0	0	0	0	0	0	1	496	0	0	1,278	$4,970

Jack Reynolds

Jack Reynolds
B: 4/17/1928
Racing Hometown: Hathorne, NJ

Year	Rank	Starts	Poles	1	2	3	4	5	6–10	Laps	Laps Led	Races Led	Miles	$
1950	46	2	0	0	0	0	0	1	0		0	0		300
1951	79	2	0	0	0	0	0	0	1		0	0		225
1952	24	10	0	0	0	0	2	0	4	1,335	0	0	901	1,450
Lifetime		14	0	0	0	0	2	1	5	1,335	0	0	901	$1,975

Tom Reynolds

Tom Reynolds

Year	Rank	Starts	Poles	1	2	3	4	5	6–10	Laps	Laps Led	Races Led	Miles	$
1975	—	2	0	0	0	0	0	0	0	203	0	0	524	2,195
Lifetime		2	0	0	0	0	0	0	0	203	0	0	524	$2,195

John Rezek

John Rezek
Racing Hometown: Alvin, TX

Year	Rank	Starts	Poles	1	2	3	4	5	6–10	Laps	Laps Led	Races Led	Miles	$
1978	—	1	0	0	0	0	0	0	0	214	0	0	218	675
1979	66	4	0	0	0	0	0	0	0	584	0	0	1,012	5,035
Lifetime		5	0	0	0	0	0	0	0	798	0	0	1,229	$5,710

Jim Rhoades

James Rhoades
Racing Hometown: Hanover, MD

Year	Rank	Starts	Poles	1	2	3	4	5	6–10	Laps	Laps Led	Races Led	Miles	$
1956	112	5	0	0	0	0	0	0	1	454	0	0	340	335
1958	94	1	0	0	0	0	0	0	0	208	0	0	208	150
Lifetime		6	0	0	0	0	0	0	1	662	0	0	548	$485

Year	Rank	Starts	Poles	Finish 1	2	3	4	5	6–10	Laps	Laps Led	Races Led	Miles	$

Willy T. Ribbs

Willy Theodore Ribbs
B: 1/3/1956
Racing Hometown: San Jose, CA

Year	Rank	Starts	Poles	1	2	3	4	5	6–10	Laps	Laps Led	Races Led	Miles	$
1986	65	3	0	0	0	0	0	0	0	516	0	0	540	3,520
Lifetime		3	0	0	0	0	0	0	0	516	0	0	540	$3,520

Hank Ribet

Henry Ribet
Racing Hometown: Palm Beach, FL

1953	168	1	0	0	0	0	0	0	0	68	0	0	34	25
Lifetime		1	0	0	0	0	0	0	0	68	0	0	34	$25

Ken Rice

Kenneth Rice

1967	NR	3	0	0	0	0	0	0	0	22	0	0	8	200
Lifetime		3	0	0	0	0	0	0	0	22	0	0	8	$200

Sam Rice

John Sam Rice
Racing Hometown: Martinsville, VA

1949	17	2	0	0	0	0	2	0	0	192	0	0	96	680
Lifetime		2	0	0	0	0	2	0	0	192	0	0	96	$680

Leo Richards

Leo Richards
Racing Hometown: Gardner, MA

1952	133T	1	0	0	0	0	0	0	0		0	0		25
Lifetime		1	0	0	0	0	0	0	0		0	0		$25

Harlan Richardson

Harlan Richardson
Racing Hometown: Houston, TX

1959	48	10	0	0	0	0	0	0	2	1,893	0	0	948	1,120
1961	134	4	0	0	0	0	0	0	0	284	0	0	640	525
1962	NR	1	0	0	0	0	0	0	0	17	0	0	43	50
Lifetime		15	0	0	0	0	0	0	2	2,194	0	0	1,630	$1,695

Jack Richardson

Jack Richardson
Racing Hometown: Phoenix, AZ

1955	184	1	0	0	0	0	0	0	0	50	0	0	25	25
1956	297T	1	0	0	0	0	0	0	0	8	0	0	4	0
Lifetime		2	0	0	0	0	0	0	0	58	0	0	29	$25

Larry Richardson

Lawrence Richardson
Racing Hometown: Gunter, TX

1974	129T	1	0	0	0	0	0	0	0	36	0	0	90	670
Lifetime		1	0	0	0	0	0	0	0	36	0	0	90	$670

Paul Richardson

Paul Richardson

1952	NR	1	0	0	0	0	0	0	0	39	0	0	24	25
Lifetime		1	0	0	0	0	0	0	0	39	0	0	24	$25

Cliff Richmond

Clifford Richmond
Racing Hometown: San Luis Obispo, CA

1955	126	2	0	0	0	0	0	0	0	246	0	0	167	50
Lifetime		2	0	0	0	0	0	0	0	246	0	0	167	$50

Tim Richmond

Timothy Richmond
B: 6/7/1955   D: 8/13/1989   *Died of AIDS.*
Racing Hometown: Ashland, OH

1980	41	5	0	0	0	0	0	0	0	1,359	0	0	1,650	14,925
1981	16	29	0	0	0	0	0	0	6	8,266	24	2	9,077	96,448
1982	26	26	1	2	2	0	1	2	5	6,834	319	12	8,246	175,980
1983	10	30	4	1	1	4	1	3	5	7,176	590	15	8,218	262,139

Year	Rank	Starts	Poles	Finish 1	2	3	4	5	6–10	Laps	Laps Led	Races Led	Miles	$

Tim Richmond *continued*

Year	Rank	Starts	Poles	1	2	3	4	5	6–10	Laps	Laps Led	Races Led	Miles	$
1984	12	30	0	1	3	0	0	2	5	8,225	58	7	9,416	345,848
1985	11	28	0	0	1	1	1	0	10	8,199	377	12	9,497	290,284
1986	3	29	8	7	4	0	1	1	4	8,544	1,006	21	10,528	973,221
1987	36	8	1	2	0	0	1	0	1	1,199	161	6	2,860	151,850
Lifetime		185	14	13	11	5	5	8	36	49,802	2,535	75	59,493	$2,310,695

Woody Richmond

Woody Richmond
Racing Hometown: Jacksonville, FL

Year	Rank	Starts	Poles	1	2	3	4	5	6–10	Laps	Laps Led	Races Led	Miles	$
1955	—	1	0	0	0	0	0	0	0	33	0	0	17	25
Lifetime		1	0	0	0	0	0	0	0	33	0	0	17	$25

Dick Richter

Bertram Langley Gurley
B: 2/28/1925   D: 1958

Year	Rank	Starts	Poles	1	2	3	4	5	6–10	Laps	Laps Led	Races Led	Miles	$
1951	NR	1	0	0	0	0	0	0	0		0	0		0
Lifetime		1	0	0	0	0	0	0	0		0	0		$0

Judge Rider

Judge Rider
Racing Hometown: Dahlonega, GA

Year	Rank	Starts	Poles	1	2	3	4	5	6–10	Laps	Laps Led	Races Led	Miles	$
1956	236	1	0	0	0	0	0	0	0	258	0	0	355	50
Lifetime		1	0	0	0	0	0	0	0	258	0	0	355	$50

Sam Rider

Samuel Rider

Year	Rank	Starts	Poles	1	2	3	4	5	6–10	Laps	Laps Led	Races Led	Miles	$
1949	NR	1	0	0	0	0	0	0	0		0	0		50
Lifetime		1	0	0	0	0	0	0	0		0	0		$50

Jody Ridley

Jody Ridley
B: 5/19/1942
Racing Hometown: Chatsworth, GA

Year	Rank	Starts	Poles	1	2	3	4	5	6–10	Laps	Laps Led	Races Led	Miles	$
1973	59	3	0	0	0	0	0	1	0	690	0	0	989	7,120
1974	88	2	0	0	0	0	0	0	0	163	0	0	205	2,935
1975	NR	3	0	0	0	0	0	0	0	421	0	0	631	3,315
1977	86	1	0	0	0	0	0	0	0	316	0	0	481	2,080
1979	47	3	0	0	0	0	0	1	1	787	0	0	1,403	11,245
1980	7	31	0	0	0	0	0	2	16	9,579	2	2	10,977	204,883
1981	5	31	0	1	0	0	1	1	15	8,971	28	6	10,528	267,605
1982	13	30	0	0	0	0	0	0	10	7,983	4	4	8,790	308,664
1983	32	10	0	0	0	0	0	0	3	1,963	0	0	3,494	45,710
1984	35	14	0	0	0	0	0	0	3	2,891	4	2	4,810	64,135
1986	33	12	0	0	0	0	0	0	1	3,183	0	0	4,055	84,380
Lifetime		140	0	1	0	0	1	5	49	36,947	38	14	46,363	$1,002,072

Hilly Rife

Hillen Rife
Racing Hometown: New Oxford, PA

Year	Rank	Starts	Poles	1	2	3	4	5	6–10	Laps	Laps Led	Races Led	Miles	$
1954	179T	1	0	0	0	0	0	0	0	174	0	0	87	0
Lifetime		1	0	0	0	0	0	0	0	174	0	0	87	$0

John Riggi

John Riggi
Racing Hometown: Heidelberg, PA

Year	Rank	Starts	Poles	1	2	3	4	5	6–10	Laps	Laps Led	Races Led	Miles	$
1949	NR	1	0	0	0	0	0	0	0	33	0	0	17	0
Lifetime		1	0	0	0	0	0	0	0	33	0	0	17	$0

Tommy Riggins

Thomas Riggins
B: 10/10/1951
Racing Hometown: Jacksonville, FL

Year	Rank	Starts	Poles	1	2	3	4	5	6–10	Laps	Laps Led	Races Led	Miles	$
1986	89	1	0	0	0	0	0	0	0	89	0	0	218	3,525
1990	53	4	0	0	0	0	0	0	0	469	0	0	1,013	12,140
Lifetime		5	0	0	0	0	0	0	0	558	0	0	1,231	$15,665

Year	Rank	Starts	Poles	Finish						Laps	Laps Led	Races Led	Miles	$
				1	2	3	4	5	6–10					

L.C. Rigsby

L.C. Rigsby
Racing Hometown: Orlando, FL

Year	Rank	Starts	Poles	1	2	3	4	5	6–10	Laps	Laps Led	Races Led	Miles	$
1952	202	1	0	0	0	0	0	0	0		0	0		0
Lifetime		1	0	0	0	0	0	0	0		0	0		$0

Eddie Riker

Edward Riker
Racing Hometown: Boonton, NJ

Year	Rank	Starts	Poles	1	2	3	4	5	6–10	Laps	Laps Led	Races Led	Miles	$
1953	67	2	0	0	0	0	0	0	1		0	0		185
1954	NR	4	0	0	0	0	0	0	0	455	0	0	411	235
1960	108	1	0	0	0	0	0	0	0	61	0	0	122	110
Lifetime		7	0	0	0	0	0	0	1	516	0	0	533	$530

Bob Riley

Robert Riley
Racing Hometown: Norwalk, CT

Year	Rank	Starts	Poles	1	2	3	4	5	6–10	Laps	Laps Led	Races Led	Miles	$
1980	NR	2	0	0	0	0	0	0	0	196	0	0	408	1,625
1981	72	3	0	0	0	0	0	0	0	139	0	0	265	1,975
1983	62	3	0	0	0	0	0	0	0	329	0	0	491	3,530
1984	NR	1	0	0	0	0	0	0	0	179	0	0	448	1,735
1985	NR	1	0	0	0	0	0	0	0	449	0	0	449	2,100
Lifetime		10	0	0	0	0	0	0	0	1,292	0	0	2,060	$10,965

Bud Riley

Harvey Riley
Racing Hometown: Los Angeles, CA

Year	Rank	Starts	Poles	1	2	3	4	5	6–10	Laps	Laps Led	Races Led	Miles	$
1951	49	8	0	0	0	0	0	1	1	606	0	0	624	475
Lifetime		8	0	0	0	0	0	1	1	606	0	0	624	$475

Richard Riley

Richard Riley
Racing Hometown: Charlotte, NC

Year	Rank	Starts	Poles	1	2	3	4	5	6–10	Laps	Laps Led	Races Led	Miles	$
1956	180T	1	0	0	0	0	0	0	1	141	0	0	71	100
1959	50	10	0	0	0	0	0	0	2	1,433	0	0	767	910
1960	81	4	0	0	0	0	0	0	1	609	0	0	563	600
Lifetime		15	0	0	0	0	0	0	4	2,183	0	0	1,400	$1,610

Bud Rinaldo

Bud Rinaldo
Racing Hometown: Shreveport, LA

Year	Rank	Starts	Poles	1	2	3	4	5	6–10	Laps	Laps Led	Races Led	Miles	$
1953	NR	1	0	0	0	0	0	0	0		0	0		25
Lifetime		1	0	0	0	0	0	0	0		0	0		$25

Tommy Ringstaff

Thomas Ringstaff
Racing Hometown: Catlettsburg, KY

Year	Rank	Starts	Poles	1	2	3	4	5	6–10	Laps	Laps Led	Races Led	Miles	$
1955	99	3	0	0	0	0	0	0	1	225	0	0	199	125
Lifetime		3	0	0	0	0	0	0	1	225	0	0	199	$125

Gene Riniker

Gene Riniker
Racing Hometown: Riverside, CA

Year	Rank	Starts	Poles	1	2	3	4	5	6–10	Laps	Laps Led	Races Led	Miles	$
1975	79	1	0	0	0	0	0	0	1	138	0	0	362	1,735
Lifetime		1	0	0	0	0	0	0	1	138	0	0	362	$1,735

Laurent Rioux

Laurent Rioux
Racing Hometown: Montreal, Canada

Year	Rank	Starts	Poles	1	2	3	4	5	6–10	Laps	Laps Led	Races Led	Miles	$
1983	NR	2	0	0	0	0	0	0	0	884	0	0	674	2,555
1984	NR	1	0	0	0	0	0	0	0	424	0	0	431	1,695
Lifetime		3	0	0	0	0	0	0	0	1,308	0	0	1,105	$4,250

Michael Ritch

Michael Ritch
B: 2/24/1973
Racing Hometown: High Point, NC

Year	Rank	Starts	Poles	1	2	3	4	5	6–10	Laps	Laps Led	Races Led	Miles	$
1995	61T	1	0	0	0	0	0	0	0	226	0	0	226	12,655
Lifetime		1	0	0	0	0	0	0	0	226	0	0	226	$12,655

Year	Rank	Starts	Poles	Finish 1	2	3	4	5	6–10	Laps	Laps Led	Races Led	Miles	$

Tom Rivers

Thomas Rivers
Racing Hometown: Oakhurst, NJ

Year	Rank	Starts	Poles	1	2	3	4	5	6–10	Laps	Laps Led	Races Led	Miles	$
1954	NR	1	0	0	0	0	0	0	0	45	0	0	90	175
Lifetime		1	0	0	0	0	0	0	0	45	0	0	90	$175

Hank Rivet

Henry Rivet
Racing Hometown: Roanoke, VA

Year	Rank	Starts	Poles	1	2	3	4	5	6–10	Laps	Laps Led	Races Led	Miles	$
1953	NR	1	0	0	0	0	0	0	0	32	0	0	131	25
Lifetime		1	0	0	0	0	0	0	0	32	0	0	131	$25

Tom Roa

Thomas Roa
Racing Hometown: Compton, CA

Year	Rank	Starts	Poles	1	2	3	4	5	6–10	Laps	Laps Led	Races Led	Miles	$
1967	116	1	0	0	0	0	0	0	0	9	0	0	24	500
Lifetime		1	0	0	0	0	0	0	0	9	0	0	24	$500

Bert Robbins

Bertrand B. Robbins
B: 3/6/1931
Racing Hometown: Washington, DC

Year	Rank	Starts	Poles	1	2	3	4	5	6–10	Laps	Laps Led	Races Led	Miles	$
1964	86	2	0	0	0	0	0	1	0	918	0	0	401	600
1965	80	5	0	0	0	0	0	0	2	479	0	0	241	1,240
Lifetime		7	0	0	0	0	0	1	2	1,397	0	0	641	$1,840

Marty Robbins

Martin David Robbins (Real Last Name: Robinson)
B: 9/26/1925   D: 12/8/1982
Racing Hometown: Glendale, AZ

Year	Rank	Starts	Poles	1	2	3	4	5	6–10	Laps	Laps Led	Races Led	Miles	$
1966	140	1	0	0	0	0	0	0	0	48	0	0	24	100
1968	78	1	0	0	0	0	0	0	0	312	0	0	468	1,525
1970	94T	1	0	0	0	0	0	0	0	105	0	0	158	1,160
1971	69	5	0	0	0	0	0	0	1	1,295	0	0	1,991	7,152
1972	54	5	0	0	0	0	0	0	2	1,096	0	0	1,864	7,950
1973	83	4	0	0	0	0	0	0	1	334	1	1	829	5,395
1974	48	4	0	0	0	0	0	1	1	550	0	0	1,343	5,734
1975	81	2	0	0	0	0	0	0	0	65	2	1	172	3,160
1977	76	2	0	0	0	0	0	0	0	229	0	0	482	2,590
1978	84	1	0	0	0	0	0	0	0	171	0	0	455	2,240
1979	68	3	0	0	0	0	0	0	0	235	0	0	520	3,120
1980	71	4	0	0	0	0	0	0	0	529	0	0	1,188	7,520
1982	79	2	0	0	0	0	0	0	0	134	0	0	248	2,055
Lifetime		35	0	0	0	0	0	1	5	5,103	3	2	9,741	$49,701

Bob Roberts

Robert Roberts

Year	Rank	Starts	Poles	1	2	3	4	5	6–10	Laps	Laps Led	Races Led	Miles	$
1960	NR	1	0	0	0	0	0	0	0	10	0	0	5	50
Lifetime		1	0	0	0	0	0	0	0	10	0	0	5	$50

Charlie Roberts

Charles Douglas Roberts
B: 10/28/1940
Racing Hometown: Anniston, AL

Year	Rank	Starts	Poles	1	2	3	4	5	6–10	Laps	Laps Led	Races Led	Miles	$
1971	33	20	0	0	0	0	0	0	2	2,796	0	0	3,688	12,470
1972	16	26	0	0	0	0	0	0	1	6,437	0	0	7,729	32,488
1973	20	24	0	0	0	0	0	0	0	7,017	0	0	6,861	32,144
1974	71	3	0	0	0	0	0	0	0	226	0	0	471	3,940
Lifetime		73	0	0	0	0	0	0	3	16,476	0	0	18,749	$81,042

Cliff Roberts

Clifford Roberts
Racing Hometown: Oakland, CA

Year	Rank	Starts	Poles	1	2	3	4	5	6–10	Laps	Laps Led	Races Led	Miles	$
1954	71	2	0	0	0	0	0	0	0	616	0	0	308	50
Lifetime		2	0	0	0	0	0	0	0	616	0	0	308	$50

Fireball Roberts

Edward Glenn Roberts
B: 1/20/1929   D: 7/2/1964   *Died of injuries @ Charlotte (5/24/64).*
Racing Hometown: Daytona Beach, FL

Year	Rank	Starts	Poles	1	2	3	4	5	6–10	Laps	Laps Led	Races Led	Miles	$
1950	2	9	1	1	2	1	0	0	1	1,138	61	3	1,065	6,800

Year	Rank	Starts	Poles	Finish 1	2	3	4	5	6–10	Laps	Laps Led	Races Led	Miles	$

Fireball Roberts *continued*

Year	Rank	Starts	Poles	1	2	3	4	5	6–10	Laps	Laps Led	Races Led	Miles	$
1951	12	9	0	0	1	0	0	1	1	825	0	0	738	1,190
1952	59	7	1	0	0	0	0	0	1	443	15	1	436	199
1953	132	2	0	0	0	0	0	0	0	352	41	1	426	365
1954	22	5	0	0	0	0	0	0	2	811	0	0	975	1,080
1955	201	2	1	0	0	0	0	0	0	69	4	1	201	140
1956	7	33	3	5	1	2	7	2	5	5,695	470	10	3,789	14,742
1957	6	42	4	8	6	2	1	4	6	6,891	1,107	16	4,269	19,829
1958	11	10	0	6	1	1	0	0	1	2,491	876	6	2,197	32,219
1959	16	8	3	1	0	0	0	0	3	1,445	147	3	1,489	10,661
1960	29	9	6	2	0	0	0	0	1	1,338	559	8	2,072	19,895
1961	5	22	6	2	4	2	2	3	1	5,075	978	13	5,033	31,283
1962	8	19	9	3	3	0	2	1	3	4,312	967	12	4,068	66,152
1963	5	20	2	4	2	0	4	1	3	4,643	692	12	5,470	73,060
1964	27	10	0	1	2	1	0	1	1	1,702	17	2	2,013	28,345
Lifetime		207	36	33	22	9	16	13	29	37,230	5,934	88	34,242	$305,960

Gene Roberts

Gene Roberts
Racing Hometown: Rochelle Park, NJ

Year	Rank	Starts	Poles	1	2	3	4	5	6–10	Laps	Laps Led	Races Led	Miles	$
1954	136	1	0	0	0	0	0	0	0	168	0	0	84	25
Lifetime		1	0	0	0	0	0	0	0	168	0	0	84	$25

Johnny Roberts

Johnny Roberts
B: 5/31/1924   D: 7/25/1965   *Killed @ Lincoln Speedway in New Oxford, PA in Modified race.*
Racing Hometown: Brooklyn, MD

Year	Rank	Starts	Poles	1	2	3	4	5	6–10	Laps	Laps Led	Races Led	Miles	$
1953	167	2	0	0	0	0	0	0	0	33	0	0	135	50
1954	148	2	0	0	0	0	0	0	0	160	0	0	159	25
1955	60	4	0	0	0	0	0	0	1	600	0	0	406	250
1956	114	4	0	0	0	0	0	0	0	461	0	0	215	210
1961	167	1	0	0	0	0	0	0	0	113	0	0	57	75
Lifetime		13	0	0	0	0	0	0	1	1,367	0	0	972	$610

Neil Roberts

Neil Roberts
Racing Hometown: Atlanta, GA

Year	Rank	Starts	Poles	1	2	3	4	5	6–10	Laps	Laps Led	Races Led	Miles	$
1951	N/A	1	0	0	0	0	0	0	0		0	0		50
1953	27	2	0	0	0	0	0	0	1	335	0	0	461	400
Lifetime		3	0	0	0	0	0	0	1	335	0	0	461	$450

Ralph Roberts

Ralph Roberts

Year	Rank	Starts	Poles	1	2	3	4	5	6–10	Laps	Laps Led	Races Led	Miles	$
1958	NR	1	0	0	0	0	0	0	0	160	0	0	421	120
Lifetime		1	0	0	0	0	0	0	0	160	0	0	421	$120

Odie Robertson

Odie Robertson
Racing Hometown: Littleton, CO

Year	Rank	Starts	Poles	1	2	3	4	5	6–10	Laps	Laps Led	Races Led	Miles	$
1974	111	1	0	0	0	0	0	0	0	89	0	0	233	1,075
Lifetime		1	0	0	0	0	0	0	0	89	0	0	233	$1,075

Jim Robinson

James Robinson
B: 1/28/1946   D: 12/1996   *Severely injured @ Phoenix 2/7/88.*
Racing Hometown: N.Hollywood, CA

Year	Rank	Starts	Poles	1	2	3	4	5	6–10	Laps	Laps Led	Races Led	Miles	$
1979	57	3	0	0	0	0	0	0	0	193	0	0	493	3,005
1980	58	3	0	0	0	0	0	0	0	288	0	0	742	4,300
1981	59	3	0	0	0	0	0	0	2	264	0	0	692	9,505
1982	66	2	0	0	0	0	0	0	0	150	0	0	393	2,220
1983	52	2	0	0	0	0	0	0	0	204	0	0	534	6,075
1984	55	2	0	0	0	0	0	0	0	189	0	0	495	7,560
1985	52	2	0	0	0	0	0	0	0	209	0	0	548	10,820
1986	66	2	0	0	0	0	0	0	0	192	0	0	503	9,300
1987	64	2	0	0	0	0	0	0	0	157	0	0	411	5,685
Lifetime		21	0	0	0	0	0	0	2	1,846	0	0	4,812	$58,470

Year	Rank	Starts	Poles	Finish						Laps	Laps Led	Races Led	Miles	$
				1	2	3	4	5	6-10					

Robbie Robinson

Robert Robinson
Racing Hometown: Fleming, OH

Year	Rank	Starts	Poles	1	2	3	4	5	6-10	Laps	Laps Led	Races Led	Miles	$
1952	NR	4	0	0	0	0	0	0	0	300	0	0	160	75
Lifetime		4	0	0	0	0	0	0	0	300	0	0	160	$75

Shawna Robinson

Shawna Robinson
B: 11/30/1964
Racing Hometown: Des Moines, IA

Year	Rank	Starts	Poles	1	2	3	4	5	6-10	Laps	Laps Led	Races Led	Miles	$
2001	68T	1	0	0	0	0	0	0	0	197	0	0	394	35,190
2002	52	7	0	0	0	0	0	0	0	1,210	0	0	2,127	425,469
Lifetime		8	0	0	0	0	0	0	0	1,407	0	0	2,521	$460,659

Pedro Rodriguez

Pedro Rodriguez
B: 1/18/1940   D: 7/11/1971   *Killed in West German Interstate Race.*
Racing Hometown: Mexico City, Mexico

Year	Rank	Starts	Poles	1	2	3	4	5	6-10	Laps	Laps Led	Races Led	Miles	$
1959	NR	1	0	0	0	0	0	0	1	144	0	0	144	300
1963	NR	1	0	0	0	0	0	0	0	54	0	0	135	400
1965	NR	1	0	0	0	0	0	1	0	391	0	0	587	3,425
1971	NR	3	0	0	0	0	0	0	0	228	0	0	570	3,150
Lifetime		6	0	0	0	0	0	1	1	817	0	0	1,436	$7,275

Robert Roeber

Robert Roeber (Bob)
Racing Hometown: Posen, IL

Year	Rank	Starts	Poles	1	2	3	4	5	6-10	Laps	Laps Led	Races Led	Miles	$
1961	133	2	0	0	0	0	0	0	0	208	0	0	520	315
Lifetime		2	0	0	0	0	0	0	0	208	0	0	520	$315

Jerry Roedell

Jerry Roedell
Racing Hometown: Peoria, IL

Year	Rank	Starts	Poles	1	2	3	4	5	6-10	Laps	Laps Led	Races Led	Miles	$
1960	141	1	0	0	0	0	0	0	0	168	0	0	252	200
Lifetime		1	0	0	0	0	0	0	0	168	0	0	252	$200

Don Rogala

Donald Rogala
Racing Hometown: Erie, PA

Year	Rank	Starts	Poles	1	2	3	4	5	6-10	Laps	Laps Led	Races Led	Miles	$
1949	NR	1	0	0	0	0	0	0	0	167	0	0	84	50
Lifetime		1	0	0	0	0	0	0	0	167	0	0	84	$50

Jackie Rogers

Julius Franklin Rogers, III
B: 5/6/1943
Racing Hometown: Wilmington, NC

Year	Rank	Starts	Poles	1	2	3	4	5	6-10	Laps	Laps Led	Races Led	Miles	$
1974	21	21	0	0	0	0	0	0	6	4,244	1	1	6,252	32,367
1975	44	8	0	0	0	0	0	0	1	913	2	1	1,746	11,000
1976	30	11	0	0	0	0	0	0	3	2,439	3	2	3,874	21,215
Lifetime		40	0	0	0	0	0	0	10	7,596	6	4	11,873	$64,582

Joe Rogers

Joseph Rogers
D: 6/24/1951   *Killed at Arlington Downs Speeday in Texas.*
Racing Hometown: Tampa, FL

Year	Rank	Starts	Poles	1	2	3	4	5	6-10	Laps	Laps Led	Races Led	Miles	$
1951	N/A	1	0	0	0	0	0	0	0		0	0		25
Lifetime		1	0	0	0	0	0	0	0		0	0		$25

John Rogers

John A. Rogers (Buck)
Racing Hometown: Crystal Lake, IL

Year	Rank	Starts	Poles	1	2	3	4	5	6-10	Laps	Laps Led	Races Led	Miles	$
1962	124	1	0	0	0	0	0	0	0	35	0	0	88	50
1963	110	2	0	0	0	0	0	0	0	109	0	0	273	625
Lifetime		3	0	0	0	0	0	0	0	144	0	0	360	$675

Johnny Rogers

John Rogers
Racing Hometown: Trenton, NJ

Year	Rank	Starts	Poles	1	2	3	4	5	6-10	Laps	Laps Led	Races Led	Miles	$
1949	NR	1	0	0	0	0	0	0	0		0	0		0
Lifetime		1	0	0	0	0	0	0	0		0	0		$0

Year	Rank	Starts	Poles	1	2	3	4	5	6–10	Laps	Laps Led	Races Led	Miles	$

George Rogge

George Rogge
  Racing Hometown: Palo Alto, CA

Year	Rank	Starts	Poles	1	2	3	4	5	6–10	Laps	Laps Led	Races Led	Miles	$
1954	NR	1	0	0	0	0	0	0	0	64	0	0	64	40
Lifetime		1	0	0	0	0	0	0	0	64	0	0	64	$40

Jimmy Roland

James Roland
  Racing Hometown: Newberry, SC

Year	Rank	Starts	Poles	1	2	3	4	5	6–10	Laps	Laps Led	Races Led	Miles	$
1955	129	2	0	0	0	0	0	0	1	324	0	0	282	150
Lifetime		2	0	0	0	0	0	0	1	324	0	0	282	$150

Joe Roletto

Joseph Roletto

Year	Rank	Starts	Poles	1	2	3	4	5	6–10	Laps	Laps Led	Races Led	Miles	$
1955	159T	1	0	0	0	0	0	0	0	212	0	0	212	50
Lifetime		1	0	0	0	0	0	0	0	212	0	0	212	$50

Shorty Rollins

Lloyd George Rollins
  B: 4/3/1929   D: 12/28/199
  Racing Hometown: Corpus Christi, TX

Year	Rank	Starts	Poles	1	2	3	4	5	6–10	Laps	Laps Led	Races Led	Miles	$
1958	4	29	0	1	1	3	5	2	10	5,324	187	4	3,201	13,399
1959	27	10	0	0	0	0	0	0	4	1,391	0	0	1,122	1,500
1960	30	4	0	0	0	0	0	0	1	952	0	0	1,480	2,120
Lifetime		43	0	1	1	3	5	2	15	7,667	187	4	5,803	$17,019

Gene Romero

Gene Romero
  B: 1946
  Racing Hometown: San Luis Obispo, CA

Year	Rank	Starts	Poles	1	2	3	4	5	6–10	Laps	Laps Led	Races Led	Miles	$
1972	106	1	0	0	0	0	0	0	0	105	0	0	263	1,620
Lifetime		1	0	0	0	0	0	0	0	105	0	0	263	$1,620

Jim Romine

James Romine
  Racing Hometown: Youngstown, OH

Year	Rank	Starts	Poles	1	2	3	4	5	6–10	Laps	Laps Led	Races Led	Miles	$
1951	N/A	3	0	0	0	0	0	0	1		0	0		150
1954	NR	1	0	0	0	0	0	0	0	25	0	0	103	0
Lifetime		4	0	0	0	0	0	0	1	25	0	0	103	$150

Slim Rominger

Slim Rominger
  Racing Hometown: Clemmons, NC

Year	Rank	Starts	Poles	1	2	3	4	5	6–10	Laps	Laps Led	Races Led	Miles	$
1953	148	2	0	0	0	0	0	0	0	153	0	0	147	125
Lifetime		2	0	0	0	0	0	0	0	153	0	0	147	$125

Ed Rooney

Edward Rooney Jr.
  Racing Hometown: Somerville, NJ

Year	Rank	Starts	Poles	1	2	3	4	5	6–10	Laps	Laps Led	Races Led	Miles	$
1951	N/A	1	0	0	0	0	0	0	0		0	0		25
Lifetime		1	0	0	0	0	0	0	0		0	0		$25

Dean Roper

Dean Roper
  B: 12/26/1938   D: 8/17/2001   *Killed in ARCA race @ Springfield, IL.*
  Racing Hometown: Fair Grove, MO

Year	Rank	Starts	Poles	1	2	3	4	5	6–10	Laps	Laps Led	Races Led	Miles	$
1983	54	2	0	0	0	0	0	0	0	364	0	0	937	16,485
1984	49	3	0	0	0	0	0	0	0	500	0	0	1,274	19,150
Lifetime		5	0	0	0	0	0	0	0	864	0	0	2,211	$35,635

Jim Roper

James Chris Roper
  B: 8/13/1916   D: 6/23/2000
  Racing Hometown: Halstead, KS

Year	Rank	Starts	Poles	1	2	3	4	5	6–10	Laps	Laps Led	Races Led	Miles	$
1949	16	2	0	1	0	0	0	0	0	197	47	1	148	2,130
Lifetime		2	0	1	0	0	0	0	0	197	47	1	148	$2,130

Frank Ropp

Frank Ropp

Year	Rank	Starts	Poles	1	2	3	4	5	6–10	Laps	Laps Led	Races Led	Miles	$
1954	NR	1	0	0	0	0	0	0	0	163	0	0	82	25
Lifetime		1	0	0	0	0	0	0	0	163	0	0	82	$25

Year	Rank	Starts	Poles	Finish						Laps	Laps Led	Races Led	Miles	$
				1	2	3	4	5	6–10					

Mickey Rorer

Mickey Rorer
Racing Hometown: Quakertown, PA

Year	Rank	Starts	Poles	1	2	3	4	5	6–10	Laps	Laps Led	Races Led	Miles	$
1953	85	2	0	0	0	0	0	0	0		0	0		60
Lifetime		2	0	0	0	0	0	0	0		0	0		$60

Bobby Rose

Robert Rose
Racing Hometown: Inglewood, CA

Year	Rank	Starts	Poles	1	2	3	4	5	6–10	Laps	Laps Led	Races Led	Miles	$
1954	NR	1	0	0	0	0	0	0	0	393	0	0	197	25
1957	NR	2	0	0	0	0	0	0	0	195	0	0	145	175
1959	56	3	0	0	0	0	0	0	0	182	0	0	441	150
Lifetime		6	0	0	0	0	0	0	0	770	0	0	782	$350

Gene Rose

Gene Rose

Year	Rank	Starts	Poles	1	2	3	4	5	6–10	Laps	Laps Led	Races Led	Miles	$
1955	137	1	0	0	0	0	0	0	0	160	0	0	240	95
Lifetime		1	0	0	0	0	0	0	0	160	0	0	240	$95

Howard Rose

Howard Rose
B: 12/18/1963
Racing Hometown: Ashland, KY

Year	Rank	Starts	Poles	1	2	3	4	5	6–10	Laps	Laps Led	Races Led	Miles	$
1986	110	1	0	0	0	0	0	0	0	241	0	0	241	1,200
Lifetime		1	0	0	0	0	0	0	0	241	0	0	241	$1,200

Ralph Rose

Ralph Rose
Racing Hometown: S.Norfolk, VA

Year	Rank	Starts	Poles	1	2	3	4	5	6–10	Laps	Laps Led	Races Led	Miles	$
1953	53T	2	0	0	0	0	0	0	2		0	0		150
Lifetime		2	0	0	0	0	0	0	2		0	0		$150

Sam Rose

Samuel Rose
Racing Hometown: San Bernadino, CA

Year	Rank	Starts	Poles	1	2	3	4	5	6–10	Laps	Laps Led	Races Led	Miles	$
1968	86	1	0	0	0	0	0	0	0	92	0	0	248	630
1969	NR	1	0	0	0	0	0	0	0	65	0	0	176	775
1970	74	1	0	0	0	0	0	0	0	157	0	0	411	1,175
Lifetime		3	0	0	0	0	0	0	0	314	0	0	835	$2,580

H.G. Rosier

Howard G. Rosier Jr.
Racing Hometown: N.Augusta, SC

Year	Rank	Starts	Poles	1	2	3	4	5	6–10	Laps	Laps Led	Races Led	Miles	$
1962	53	5	0	0	0	0	0	0	1	772	0	0	807	1,505
1963	97	3	0	0	0	0	1	0	0	228	0	0	172	850
Lifetime		8	0	0	0	0	1	0	1	1,000	0	0	979	$2,355

Bob Ross

Robert Ross
Racing Hometown: Lakewood, CA

Year	Rank	Starts	Poles	1	2	3	4	5	6–10	Laps	Laps Led	Races Led	Miles	$
1956	68	3	0	0	0	0	0	0	2	601	0	0	418	575
1957	53	3	0	0	0	0	0	0	3	396	0	0	314	720
1958	96	2	0	0	1	0	0	0	0	135	0	0	192	600
1959	82	2	0	0	0	0	2	0	0	582	0	0	293	935
1960	105	3	0	0	0	0	0	0	0	105	0	0	117	250
1961	110	2	1	0	1	0	0	0	0	112	0	0	117	800
1963	70	2	0	0	0	0	0	0	1	315	0	0	851	1,525
Lifetime		17	1	0	2	0	2	0	6	2,246	0	0	2,302	$5,405

Brian Ross

Brian J. Ross
B: 9/4/1944
Racing Hometown: Ballston Spa, NY

Year	Rank	Starts	Poles	1	2	3	4	5	6–10	Laps	Laps Led	Races Led	Miles	$
1990	83	1	0	0	0	0	0	0	0	175	0	0	438	3,775
1991	87T	1	0	0	0	0	0	0	0	37	0	0	37	3,475
Lifetime		2	0	0	0	0	0	0	0	212	0	0	475	$7,250

Year	Rank	Starts	Poles	Finish 1	2	3	4	5	6–10	Laps	Laps Led	Races Led	Miles	$

Dick Ross

Richard Ross
Racing Hometown: Harve De Grace, MD

Year	Rank	Starts	Poles	1	2	3	4	5	6–10	Laps	Laps Led	Races Led	Miles	$
1954	165	2	0	0	0	0	0	0	0	341	0	0	271	50
Lifetime		2	0	0	0	0	0	0	0	341	0	0	271	$50

Earl Ross

Earl Ross
B: 9/4/1941
Racing Hometown: Alsa Craig, Ont, Canada

Year	Rank	Starts	Poles	1	2	3	4	5	6–10	Laps	Laps Led	Races Led	Miles	$
1973	68	3	0	0	0	0	0	0	0	335	0	0	797	4,005
1974	8	21	0	1	1	1	1	1	5	5,730	127	6	7,467	81,199
1975	NR	1	0	0	0	0	0	0	0	372	0	0	558	2,965
1976	115T	1	0	0	0	0	0	0	0	28	0	0	70	2,025
Lifetime		26	0	1	1	1	1	1	5	6,465	127	6	8,892	$90,194

Jim Ross

James Ross
Racing Hometown: Detroit, MI

Year	Rank	Starts	Poles	1	2	3	4	5	6–10	Laps	Laps Led	Races Led	Miles	$
1951	N/A	2	0	0	0	0	0	0	0		0	0		25
Lifetime		2	0	0	0	0	0	0	0		0	0		$25

John Ross

John Ross
Racing Hometown: Syracuse, NY

Year	Rank	Starts	Poles	1	2	3	4	5	6–10	Laps	Laps Led	Races Led	Miles	$
1953	NR	1	0	0	0	0	0	0	0		0	0		25
Lifetime		1	0	0	0	0	0	0	0		0	0		$25

Mario Rossi

Mario Joseph Rossi
B: 11/17/1932   *Declared missing on 1/1/83. Presumed lost in private plane crash.*
Racing Hometown: Trenton, NJ

Year	Rank	Starts	Poles	1	2	3	4	5	6–10	Laps	Laps Led	Races Led	Miles	$
1955	83T	1	0	0	0	0	0	0	1	223	0	0	223	200
1956	258	1	0	0	0	0	0	0	0	97	0	0	97	60
1958	60	2	0	0	0	0	0	0	0	501	0	0	475	220
Lifetime		4	0	0	0	0	0	0	1	821	0	0	795	$480

John Rostek

John Rostek
B: 11/12/1925
Racing Hometown: Ft. Collins, Co

Year	Rank	Starts	Poles	1	2	3	4	5	6–10	Laps	Laps Led	Races Led	Miles	$
1960	NR	5	1	1	0	1	0	0	1	658	65	2	688	2,060
1963	68	1	0	0	0	0	0	0	0	172	0	0	464	500
Lifetime		6	1	1	0	1	0	0	1	830	65	2	1,152	$2,560

Dr. Gil Roth

Dr. Gilbert Roth

Year	Rank	Starts	Poles	1	2	3	4	5	6–10	Laps	Laps Led	Races Led	Miles	$
1982	99	1	0	0	0	0	0	0	0	91	0	0	91	615
Lifetime		1	0	0	0	0	0	0	0	91	0	0	91	$615

Tom Rotsell

Thomas Rotsell

Year	Rank	Starts	Poles	1	2	3	4	5	6–10	Laps	Laps Led	Races Led	Miles	$
1986	101T	1	0	0	0	0	0	0	0	84	0	0	206	2,080
1987	84T	1	0	0	0	0	0	0	0	84	0	0	206	2,110
1988	71	1	0	0	0	0	0	0	0	90	0	0	221	2,470
Lifetime		3	0	0	0	0	0	0	0	258	0	0	632	$6,660

Jack Rounds

Jack Rounds
B: 12/2/1930
Racing Hometown: Huntington, WV

Year	Rank	Starts	Poles	1	2	3	4	5	6–10	Laps	Laps Led	Races Led	Miles	$
1958	71	1	0	0	0	0	0	0	0	167	0	0	439	150
Lifetime		1	0	0	0	0	0	0	0	167	0	0	439	$150

Year	Rank	Starts	Poles	Finish						Laps	Laps Led	Races Led	Miles	$
				1	2	3	4	5	6–10					

Lloyd Ruby

Lloyd Ruby
B: 1/12/1928
Racing Hometown: Wichita Falls, TX

Year	Rank	Starts	Poles	1	2	3	4	5	6–10	Laps	Laps Led	Races Led	Miles	$
1967	NR	1	0	0	0	0	0	0	0	96	0	0	259	565
Lifetime		1	0	0	0	0	0	0	0	96	0	0	259	$565

Al Rudd Jr.

Al Rudd Jr.
Racing Hometown: Chesapeake, VA

Year	Rank	Starts	Poles	1	2	3	4	5	6–10	Laps	Laps Led	Races Led	Miles	$
1979	NR	1	0	0	0	0	0	0	0	39	0	0	78	740
Lifetime		1	0	0	0	0	0	0	0	39	0	0	78	$740

Ricky Rudd

Richard Lee Rudd
B: 9/12/1956
Racing Hometown: Chesapeake, VA

Year	Rank	Starts	Poles	1	2	3	4	5	6–10	Laps	Laps Led	Races Led	Miles	$
1975	47	4	0	0	0	0	0	0	1	1,025	0	0	886	4,345
1976	53	4	0	0	0	0	0	0	1	876	0	0	1,527	7,175
1977	17	25	0	0	0	0	1	0	9	6,233	13	3	7,509	75,905
1978	31	13	0	0	0	0	0	0	4	2,535	16	5	4,334	50,630
1979	9	28	0	0	0	2	0	2	13	8,836	22	4	9,918	150,898
1980	35	13	0	0	0	0	1	0	2	2,719	7	2	4,149	50,500
1981	6	31	3	0	3	4	3	4	3	8,942	441	12	9,879	395,685
1982	9	30	2	0	2	0	3	1	7	7,753	140	8	8,681	217,140
1983	9	30	4	2	1	1	1	2	7	8,581	871	13	9,908	275,400
1984	7	30	4	1	1	3	1	1	9	9,271	566	8	10,584	497,779
1985	6	28	0	1	2	1	5	4	6	8,474	329	6	10,288	512,441
1986	5	29	1	2	4	2	3	0	6	7,950	525	7	9,743	671,548
1987	6	29	0	2	2	4	1	1	3	8,206	493	11	9,893	653,508
1988	11	29	2	1	3	1	1	0	5	8,867	695	16	10,438	410,954
1989	8	29	0	1	0	2	3	1	8	9,326	247	7	11,076	409,352
1990	7	29	2	1	0	3	2	2	7	8,664	180	7	10,494	573,650
1991	2	29	1	1	3	0	2	3	8	9,561	425	13	11,429	1,093,765
1992	7	29	1	1	0	2	3	3	9	8,968	331	9	10,270	793,903
1993	10	30	0	1	1	1	3	3	5	8,635	137	7	10,266	752,562
1994	5	31	1	1	0	0	3	2	9	9,728	192	10	12,047	1,079,441
1995	9	31	2	1	0	1	4	4	6	8,813	368	11	10,834	1,337,703
1996	6	31	0	1	2	1	1	0	11	9,281	150	12	11,401	1,503,025
1997	17	32	0	2	0	1	1	2	5	9,094	77	4	11,619	1,975,981
1998	22	33	0	1	0	0	0	0	4	9,127	255	3	11,589	1,602,895
1999	31	34	1	0	0	2	0	1	2	9,230	21	3	12,031	1,632,011
2000	5	34	2	0	1	5	3	3	7	10,048	362	14	13,013	2,385,404
2001	4	36	1	2	2	5	4	1	8	10,536	568	16	13,843	4,878,027
2002	10	36	1	1	0	4	2	1	4	10,195	357	11	13,559	4,444,614
Lifetime		767	28	23	27	45	51	41	169	221,474	7,788	222	271,212	$28,436,241

Charlie Rudolph

Charles Rudolph
B: 1958
Racing Hometown: Newark, NJ

Year	Rank	Starts	Poles	1	2	3	4	5	6–10	Laps	Laps Led	Races Led	Miles	$
1987	51	2	0	0	0	0	0	0	0	658	0	0	952	4,540
Lifetime		2	0	0	0	0	0	0	0	658	0	0	952	$4,540

Don Rudolph

Donald Rudolph
Racing Hometown: Newark, NJ

Year	Rank	Starts	Poles	1	2	3	4	5	6–10	Laps	Laps Led	Races Led	Miles	$
1951	N/A	1	0	0	0	0	0	0	0		0	0		0
1952	180	1	0	0	0	0	0	0	0	82	0	0	82	25
Lifetime		2	0	0	0	0	0	0	0	82	0	0	82	$25

Bob Ruppert

Robert Ruppert
Racing Hometown: Las Vegas, NV

Year	Rank	Starts	Poles	1	2	3	4	5	6–10	Laps	Laps Led	Races Led	Miles	$
1955	121	1	0	0	0	0	0	0	1	102	0	0	102	200
1956	138	2	0	0	0	0	0	0	0	164	0	0	278	150
Lifetime		3	0	0	0	0	0	0	1	266	0	0	380	$350

Year	Rank	Starts	Poles	Finish						Laps	Laps Led	Races Led	Miles	$
				1	2	3	4	5	6–10					

Dan Rush

Daniel Rush
Racing Hometown: Rome, GA

Year	Rank	Starts	Poles	1	2	3	4	5	6–10	Laps	Laps Led	Races Led	Miles	$
1951	N/A	1	0	0	0	0	0	0	0		0	0		25
Lifetime		1	0	0	0	0	0	0	0		0	0		$25

Ermon Rush

Ermon Rush
Racing Hometown: Thomasville, NC

Year	Rank	Starts	Poles	1	2	3	4	5	6–10	Laps	Laps Led	Races Led	Miles	$
1953	74	3	0	0	0	0	0	0	0		0	0		75
1959	NR	1	0	0	0	0	0	0	0	188	0	0	47	140
Lifetime		4	0	0	0	0	0	0	0	188	0	0	47	$215

Ken Rush

Samuel Kenneth Rush
B: 9/14/1931
Racing Hometown: High Point, NC

Year	Rank	Starts	Poles	1	2	3	4	5	6–10	Laps	Laps Led	Races Led	Miles	$
1957	39	16	1	0	0	1	0	0	5	2,266	0	0	1,397	2,045
1958	160	11	1	0	0	0	0	0	3	1,625	0	0	828	1,640
1959	NR	12	1	0	1	0	1	0	1	2,388	0	0	1,533	2,095
1961	51	6	0	0	0	0	0	1	1	1,586	0	0	1,065	2,325
1962	104	1	0	0	0	0	0	0	0	463	0	0	232	150
1964	70	8	0	0	0	0	1	0	1	768	0	0	398	1,640
1971	NR	1	0	0	0	0	0	0	0	117	0	0	29	240
1972	NR	1	0	0	0	0	0	0	0	149	0	0	224	1,625
Lifetime		56	3	0	1	1	2	1	11	9,362	0	0	5,706	$11,760

Rusty Rushton

Russell Rushton
Racing Hometown: Patuckett, RI

Year	Rank	Starts	Poles	1	2	3	4	5	6–10	Laps	Laps Led	Races Led	Miles	$
1951	N/A	2	0	0	0	0	0	0	0		0	0		50
Lifetime		2	0	0	0	0	0	0	0		0	0		$50

Hank Russ

Hank Russ
Racing Hometown: Saginaw, MI

Year	Rank	Starts	Poles	1	2	3	4	5	6–10	Laps	Laps Led	Races Led	Miles	$
1951	N/A	1	0	0	0	0	0	0	0		0	0		25
1954	N/A	1	0	0	0	0	0	0	0	165	0	0	83	25
Lifetime		2	0	0	0	0	0	0	0	165	0	0	83	$50

Fred Russell

Fred Russell
Racing Hometown: Oakland, CA

Year	Rank	Starts	Poles	1	2	3	4	5	6–10	Laps	Laps Led	Races Led	Miles	$
1951	N/A	1	0	0	0	0	0	0	1		0	0		75
Lifetime		1	0	0	0	0	0	0	1		0	0		$75

Jack Russell

Jack Russell
Racing Hometown: Erie, PA

Year	Rank	Starts	Poles	1	2	3	4	5	6–10	Laps	Laps Led	Races Led	Miles	$
1949	24	3	0	0	0	0	0	0	2	178	0	0	89	175
1950	116T	1	0	0	0	0	0	0	0	0	0	0	0	0
1958	NR	1	0	0	0	0	0	0	0	74	0	0	74	100
Lifetime		5	0	0	0	0	0	0	2	252	0	0	163	$275

Jim Russell

James Russell
Racing Hometown: Odessa, TX

Year	Rank	Starts	Poles	1	2	3	4	5	6–10	Laps	Laps Led	Races Led	Miles	$
1957	190	4	0	0	0	0	0	0	0	263	0	0	148	150
Lifetime		4	0	0	0	0	0	0	0	263	0	0	148	$150

Jerry Russo

Jerry Russo

Year	Rank	Starts	Poles	1	2	3	4	5	6–10	Laps	Laps Led	Races Led	Miles	$
1951	N/A	1	0	0	0	0	0	0	0		0	0		25
Lifetime		1	0	0	0	0	0	0	0		0	0		$25

Johnny Rutherford

John Sherman Rutherford, III
B: 3/12/1938
Racing Hometown: Ft. Worth, TX

Year	Rank	Starts	Poles	1	2	3	4	5	6–10	Laps	Laps Led	Races Led	Miles	$
1963	NR	2	0	1	0	0	0	0	1	236	6	1	590	2,350

Year	Rank	Starts	Poles	Finish						Laps	Laps Led	Races Led	Miles	$
				1	2	3	4	5	6–10					

Johnny Rutherford *continued*

Year	Rank	Starts	Poles	1	2	3	4	5	6–10	Laps	Laps Led	Races Led	Miles	$
1964	NR	3	0	0	0	0	0	0	1	280	0	0	700	2,175
1965	NR	1	0	0	0	0	0	0	0	298	0	0	447	650
1966	NR	2	0	0	0	0	0	0	0	150	0	0	375	1,210
1972	NR	1	0	0	0	0	0	0	0	224	0	0	448	1,280
1973	NR	1	0	0	0	0	0	0	0	471	0	0	479	1,325
1974	82	3	0	0	0	0	0	0	0	325	3	2	611	5,164
1975	NR	4	0	0	0	0	0	0	0	189	0	0	337	4,925
1976	NR	2	0	0	0	0	0	0	0	347	0	0	660	2,745
1977	NR	3	0	0	0	0	0	0	0	193	0	0	452	4,150
1981	33	12	0	0	0	0	0	1	1	2,432	5	1	3,793	38,095
1988	89T	1	0	0	0	0	0	0	0	155	0	0	155	3,775
Lifetime		35	0	1	0	0	0	1	3	5,300	14	4	9,045	$67,844

Joe Ruttman

Joseph Ruttman
B: 10/28/1944
Racing Hometown: Upland, CA

Year	Rank	Starts	Poles	1	2	3	4	5	6–10	Laps	Laps Led	Races Led	Miles	$
1963	56	1	0	0	0	0	0	0	1	176	0	0	475	850
1964	127	1	0	0	0	0	0	0	0	46	0	0	124	500
1977	84T	1	0	0	0	0	0	0	0	196	0	0	490	2,035
1980	NR	1	0	0	0	0	0	0	0	29	0	0	73	1,055
1981	28	17	0	0	1	0	0	1	5	4,194	106	7	5,589	137,275
1982	16	29	0	0	0	1	2	2	2	7,354	178	6	8,034	191,634
1983	12	30	3	0	0	1	3	0	6	7,887	398	10	8,818	223,809
1984	18	29	1	0	0	0	0	0	8	6,635	55	4	8,161	168,433
1985	30	16	0	0	0	0	0	1	3	3,378	5	1	4,599	81,425
1986	15	29	0	0	2	0	0	3	9	7,732	55	5	8,708	259,263
1987	NR	4	0	0	0	0	0	0	2	963	0	0	1,380	28,405
1988	39	12	0	0	0	0	0	0	1	1,899	0	0	3,425	46,455
1989	43	9	0	0	0	0	0	0	1	1,704	0	0	2,673	64,645
1990	81T	1	0	0	0	0	0	0	0	196	0	0	490	22,950
1991	20	29	0	0	0	1	0	0	3	8,974	11	1	10,776	361,661
1992	84T	1	0	0	0	0	0	0	0	213	0	0	320	5,250
1993	43	5	0	0	0	0	0	1	0	1,133	0	0	1,597	70,700
1994	54	2	0	0	0	0	0	0	0	527	0	0	990	39,695
1995	56	1	0	0	0	0	0	0	0	200	0	0	500	39,135
Lifetime		218	4	0	3	3	5	8	41	53,436	808	34	67,219	$1,745,175

Troy Ruttman

Troy Ruttman
B: 3/11/1930   D: 5/19/1997   *Cancer.*
Racing Hometown: Mooreland, OK

Year	Rank	Starts	Poles	1	2	3	4	5	6–10	Laps	Laps Led	Races Led	Miles	$
1962	49	1	0	0	0	0	0	1	0	218	0	0	327	1,750
1963	NR	5	0	0	0	1	0	0	2	796	0	0	1,699	6,430
1964	NR	1	0	0	0	0	0	0	1	177	0	0	478	850
Lifetime		7	0	0	0	1	0	1	3	1,191	0	0	2,504	$9,030

Hal Ruyle

Hal Ruyle
Racing Hometown: St. Louis, MO

Year	Rank	Starts	Poles	1	2	3	4	5	6–10	Laps	Laps Led	Races Led	Miles	$
1954	NR	1	0	0	0	0	0	0	0	178	0	0	89	25
Lifetime		1	0	0	0	0	0	0	0	178	0	0	89	$25

Kelly Ryan

Kelly Ryan

Year	Rank	Starts	Poles	1	2	3	4	5	6–10	Laps	Laps Led	Races Led	Miles	$
1962	NR	1	0	0	0	0	0	0	0	34	0	0	9	75
Lifetime		1	0	0	0	0	0	0	0	34	0	0	9	$75

Terry Ryan

Terry Ryan
B: 5/13/1938
Racing Hometown: Davenport, IA

Year	Rank	Starts	Poles	1	2	3	4	5	6–10	Laps	Laps Led	Races Led	Miles	$
1976	46	5	0	0	0	0	0	1	2	603	1	1	1,516	29,940
1977	40	7	0	0	0	0	0	0	1	1,142	0	0	2,240	12,405
Lifetime		12	0	0	0	0	0	1	3	1,745	1	1	3,756	$42,345

Year	Rank	Starts	Poles	Finish						Laps	Laps Led	Races Led	Miles	$
				1	2	3	4	5	6–10					

Red Ryder
Samuel Ryder
Racing Hometown: Athol Springs, NY

Year	Rank	Starts	Poles	1	2	3	4	5	6–10	Laps	Laps Led	Races Led	Miles	$
1950	55T	1	0	0	0	0	0	0	0		0	0		0
1951	N/A	1	0	0	0	0	0	0	0		0	0		25
Lifetime		2	0	0	0	0	0	0	0		0	0		$25

Mike Saathoff
Michael Saathoff
Racing Hometown: Los Angeles, CA

Year	Rank	Starts	Poles	1	2	3	4	5	6–10	Laps	Laps Led	Races Led	Miles	$
1961	149	1	0	0	0	0	0	0	0	129	0	0	181	200
Lifetime		1	0	0	0	0	0	0	0	129	0	0	181	$200

Greg Sacks
Gregory Sacks
B: 11/3/1952
Racing Hometown: Mattituck, NY

Year	Rank	Starts	Poles	1	2	3	4	5	6–10	Laps	Laps Led	Races Led	Miles	$
1983	47	5	0	0	0	0	0	0	0	638	0	0	1,202	8,060
1984	19	29	0	0	0	0	0	0	1	6,348	0	0	7,781	75,184
1985	25	20	0	1	0	0	0	0	4	4,855	36	3	6,434	234,141
1986	41	8	0	0	0	0	0	0	1	1,181	0	0	1,743	64,810
1987	33	16	0	0	0	0	0	0	0	2,705	1	1	4,254	54,815
1988	37	15	0	0	0	0	0	0	3	3,543	1	1	4,507	105,579
1989	32	20	0	0	0	0	0	0	2	4,955	110	4	5,692	96,035
1990	32	16	1	0	2	0	0	0	2	3,790	107	4	5,470	216,148
1991	39	11	0	0	0	0	0	0	0	2,101	0	0	3,161	84,215
1992	30	20	0	0	0	0	0	0	0	4,926	6	1	6,502	178,120
1993	35	19	0	0	0	0	0	0	1	5,251	1	1	7,220	168,055
1994	31	31	1	0	0	0	0	0	3	8,346	38	8	10,092	411,728
1995	39	20	0	0	0	0	0	0	0	4,682	0	0	5,633	323,720
1996	42	9	0	0	0	0	0	0	0	2,196	3	1	3,614	207,755
1997	45	12	0	0	0	0	0	0	0	2,456	8	2	3,990	320,714
1998	53	7	0	0	0	0	0	0	0	1,821	0	0	2,312	280,130
Lifetime		258	2	1	2	0	0	0	17	59,794	311	26	79,607	$2,829,209

Elliott Sadler
Elliott Sadler
B: 4/24/1975
Racing Hometown: Emporia, VA

Year	Rank	Starts	Poles	1	2	3	4	5	6–10	Laps	Laps Led	Races Led	Miles	$
1998	59	2	0	0	0	0	0	0	0	705	0	0	577	45,325
1999	24	34	0	0	0	0	0	0	1	9,851	5	3	12,855	1,589,221
2000	29	33	0	0	0	0	0	0	1	8,644	6	5	11,045	1,578,356
2001	20	36	0	1	0	1	0	0	0	10,392	125	8	13,541	2,683,225
2002	23	36	0	0	2	0	0	0	5	9,789	29	8	13,183	3,491,694
Lifetime		141	0	1	2	1	0	0	7	39,381	165	24	51,199	$9,387,821

Hermie Sadler
Herman Sadler
B: 4/24/1968
Racing Hometown: Emporia, VA

Year	Rank	Starts	Poles	1	2	3	4	5	6–10	Laps	Laps Led	Races Led	Miles	$
1996	63T	1	0	0	0	0	0	0	0	349	0	0	349	13,055
2001	52	3	0	0	0	0	0	0	0	1,206	0	0	1,141	121,865
2002	45	10	0	0	0	0	0	0	0	3,458	0	0	3,145	473,290
Lifetime		14	0	0	0	0	0	0	0	5,013	0	0	4,635	$608,210

Darryl Sage
Darryl Sage
B: 5/8/1965
Racing Hometown: Murfreesboro, TN

Year	Rank	Starts	Poles	1	2	3	4	5	6–10	Laps	Laps Led	Races Led	Miles	$
1982	50	5	0	0	0	0	0	0	0	1,552	0	0	1,137	4,970
1983	85	3	0	0	0	0	0	0	0	638	0	0	675	3,060
Lifetime		8	0	0	0	0	0	0	0	2,190	0	0	1,812	$8,030

Bucky Sager
John Sager
Racing Hometown: Toledo, OH

Year	Rank	Starts	Poles	1	2	3	4	5	6–10	Laps	Laps Led	Races Led	Miles	$
1950	33	2	0	0	1	0	0	0	0		146	1		750
1951	N/A	1	0	0	0	0	0	0	0		0	0		25
1952	26	10	0	0	0	0	1	0	2	1,545	0	0	1,068	710

Year	Rank	Starts	Poles	Finish 1	2	3	4	5	6–10	Laps	Laps Led	Races Led	Miles	$

Bucky Sager *continued*

Year	Rank	Starts	Poles	1	2	3	4	5	6–10	Laps	Laps Led	Races Led	Miles	$
1954	NR	3	0	0	0	0	0	0	0	190	0	0	221	50
Lifetime		16	0	0	1	0	1	0	2	1,735	146	1	1,289	$1,535

Bob Said

Robert Said
B: 1922   D: 2002
Racing Hometown: Greenwich, CT

Year	Rank	Starts	Poles	1	2	3	4	5	6–10	Laps	Laps Led	Races Led	Miles	$
1959	NR	1	0	0	0	0	0	0	0	42	0	0	105	100
Lifetime		1	0	0	0	0	0	0	0	42	0	0	105	$100

Boris Said III

Boris Said, III
B: 9/18/1962
Racing Hometown: Carlsbad, CA

Year	Rank	Starts	Poles	1	2	3	4	5	6–10	Laps	Laps Led	Races Led	Miles	$
1999	59	2	0	0	0	0	0	0	0	310	9	1	513	59,260
2000	72	1	0	0	0	0	0	0	0	26	0	0	51	36,940
2001	50	2	0	0	0	0	0	0	1	202	0	0	439	124,340
2002	59	2	0	0	0	0	0	0	0	172	0	0	380	87,400
Lifetime		7	0	0	0	0	0	0	1	710	9	1	1,383	$307,940

Gary Sain

Gary L. Sain
Racing Hometown: Hickory, NC

Year	Rank	Starts	Poles	1	2	3	4	5	6–10	Laps	Laps Led	Races Led	Miles	$
1962	74	5	0	0	0	0	0	0	0	986	0	0	533	1,000
1963	64	7	0	0	0	0	0	0	1	994	0	0	523	700
1967	86	4	0	0	0	0	0	0	1	399	0	0	271	2,335
Lifetime		16	0	0	0	0	0	0	2	2,379	0	0	1,327	$4,035

Leon Sales

Leon J. Sales
B: 10/4/1923   D: 4/27/1981
Racing Hometown: Winston-Salem, NC

Year	Rank	Starts	Poles	1	2	3	4	5	6–10	Laps	Laps Led	Races Led	Miles	$
1950	28	2	0	1	0	0	0	0	0	227	18	1	139	1,000
1951	N/A	4	0	0	0	0	0	0	2	452	0	0	548	850
1952	188	2	0	0	0	0	0	0	0		0	0		25
Lifetime		8	0	1	0	0	0	0	2	679	18	1	687	$1,875

Ed Samples

Edward Samples
B: 1/31/1921   D: 6/10/1991
Racing Hometown: Atlanta, GA

Year	Rank	Starts	Poles	1	2	3	4	5	6–10	Laps	Laps Led	Races Led	Miles	$
1951	61	4	0	0	0	0	0	0	2	15	0	0	11	285
1952	30	8	0	0	1	1	0	0	2	614	0	0	370	1,535
1954	NR	1	0	0	0	0	0	0	0	36	0	0	148	40
Lifetime		13	0	0	1	1	0	0	4	665	0	0	529	$1,860

Jesse Samples

Jesse Samples
Racing Hometown: Atlanta, GA

Year	Rank	Starts	Poles	1	2	3	4	5	6–10	Laps	Laps Led	Races Led	Miles	$
1965	106	1	0	0	0	0	0	0	0	198	0	0	297	495
Lifetime		1	0	0	0	0	0	0	0	198	0	0	297	$495

Jesse Samples Jr.

Jesse Samples Jr.
B: 1968
Racing Hometown: Atlanta, GA

Year	Rank	Starts	Poles	1	2	3	4	5	6–10	Laps	Laps Led	Races Led	Miles	$
1987	76	2	0	0	0	0	0	0	0	164	0	0	106	2,410
Lifetime		2	0	0	0	0	0	0	0	164	0	0	106	$2,410

Bob Sampson

Robert Sampson
Racing Hometown: Levittown, PA

Year	Rank	Starts	Poles	1	2	3	4	5	6–10	Laps	Laps Led	Races Led	Miles	$
1953	NR	1	0	0	0	0	0	0	0	172	0	0	86	25
1954	200	1	0	0	0	0	0	0	0	32	0	0	131	0
Lifetime		2	0	0	0	0	0	0	0	204	0	0	217	$25

Year	Rank	Starts	Poles	Finish						Laps	Laps Led	Races Led	Miles	$
				1	2	3	4	5	6–10					

Charles Sanchez

Charles Sanchez
Racing Hometown: Ripon, CA

Year	Rank	Starts	Poles	1	2	3	4	5	6–10	Laps	Laps Led	Races Led	Miles	$
1958	109	1	0	0	0	0	0	0	1	98	0	0	98	250
1959	117	1	0	0	0	0	0	0	0	35	0	0	35	25
Lifetime		2	0	0	0	0	0	0	1	133	0	0	133	$275

August Sand

August Sand
Racing Hometown: Pittsburgh, PA

Year	Rank	Starts	Poles	1	2	3	4	5	6–10	Laps	Laps Led	Races Led	Miles	$
1959	NR	1	0	0	0	0	0	0	0	133	0	0	33	100
Lifetime		1	0	0	0	0	0	0	0	133	0	0	33	$100

Ronnie Sanders

Ronald Sanders
B: 12/5/1945
Racing Hometown: Fayetteville, GA

Year	Rank	Starts	Poles	1	2	3	4	5	6–10	Laps	Laps Led	Races Led	Miles	$
1981	77	1	0	0	0	0	0	0	0	191	0	0	478	7,635
1987	NR	1	0	0	0	0	0	0	0	195	0	0	488	13,930
1989	83T	1	0	0	0	0	0	0	0	184	0	0	460	12,570
Lifetime		3	0	0	0	0	0	0	0	570	0	0	1,425	$34,135

Rusty Sanders

Rusty Sanders
Racing Hometown: Bakersfield, CA

Year	Rank	Starts	Poles	1	2	3	4	5	6–10	Laps	Laps Led	Races Led	Miles	$
1976	104	1	0	0	0	0	0	0	0	29	0	0	76	815
Lifetime		1	0	0	0	0	0	0	0	29	0	0	76	$815

Scott Sandman

Scott Sandman
Racing Hometown: Pittsburgh, PA

Year	Rank	Starts	Poles	1	2	3	4	5	6–10	Laps	Laps Led	Races Led	Miles	$
1959	NR	1	0	0	0	0	0	0	0	20	0	0	5	50
Lifetime		1	0	0	0	0	0	0	0	20	0	0	5	$50

Bobby Sands

Robert Sands
Racing Hometown: Henryville, IN

Year	Rank	Starts	Poles	1	2	3	4	5	6–10	Laps	Laps Led	Races Led	Miles	$
1980	100	1	0	0	0	0	0	0	0	2	0	0	1	450
Lifetime		1	0	0	0	0	0	0	0	2	0	0	1	$450

Dick Sanford

Richard Sanford
Racing Hometown: Ramsey, NJ

Year	Rank	Starts	Poles	1	2	3	4	5	6–10	Laps	Laps Led	Races Led	Miles	$
1954	119T	1	0	0	0	0	0	0	0	180	0	0	90	25
Lifetime		1	0	0	0	0	0	0	0	180	0	0	90	$25

Ed Sanger

Edward Sanger
B: 1940
Racing Hometown: Waterloo, IA

Year	Rank	Starts	Poles	1	2	3	4	5	6–10	Laps	Laps Led	Races Led	Miles	$
1985	81T	1	0	0	0	0	0	0	0	358	0	0	224	910
Lifetime		1	0	0	0	0	0	0	0	358	0	0	224	$910

Dick Santee

Richard Santee
Racing Hometown: Fullerton, CA

Year	Rank	Starts	Poles	1	2	3	4	5	6–10	Laps	Laps Led	Races Led	Miles	$
1959	NR	1	0	0	0	0	0	0	0	407	0	0	163	130
1961	116	1	0	0	0	0	0	0	0	159	0	0	223	400
Lifetime		2	0	0	0	0	0	0	0	566	0	0	385	$530

Marshall Sargent

Marshall Sargent
D: 10/19/199
Racing Hometown: Salinas, CA

Year	Rank	Starts	Poles	1	2	3	4	5	6–10	Laps	Laps Led	Races Led	Miles	$
1957	64	5	0	0	0	0	0	0	2	541	0	0	334	575
1958	164	1	0	0	0	0	0	0	0	135	0	0	355	110
1960	146	1	0	0	0	0	0	0	0	1	0	0	1	25
1961	86	3	0	0	0	0	0	0	0	369	0	0	690	450
1963	NR	1	0	0	0	0	0	0	0	157	0	0	424	375
1964	107	1	0	0	0	0	0	0	1	77	0	0	39	150
Lifetime		12	0	0	0	0	0	0	3	1,280	0	0	1,842	$1,685

Year	Rank	Starts	Poles	Finish						Laps	Laps Led	Races Led	Miles	$
				1	2	3	4	5	6–10					

Don Satterfield

Donald Satterfield
B: 11/9/1953
Racing Hometown: Spartanburg, SC

Year	Rank	Starts	Poles	1	2	3	4	5	6–10	Laps	Laps Led	Races Led	Miles	$
1981	NR	1	0	0	0	0	0	0	0	1	0	0	1	450
1983	NR	3	0	0	0	0	0	0	0	645	0	0	359	2,555
Lifetime		4	0	0	0	0	0	0	0	646	0	0	359	$3,005

Sandy Satullo

S. Sandy Satullo, II
B: 1954
Racing Hometown: Fairview Park, OH

Year	Rank	Starts	Poles	1	2	3	4	5	6–10	Laps	Laps Led	Races Led	Miles	$
1979	77	2	0	0	0	0	0	0	0	210	0	0	429	2,360
1981	98T	1	0	0	0	0	0	0	0	68	0	0	181	1,500
Lifetime		3	0	0	0	0	0	0	0	278	0	0	610	$3,860

Joe Saunders

Joseph Saunders
Racing Hometown: Syracuse, NY

Year	Rank	Starts	Poles	1	2	3	4	5	6–10	Laps	Laps Led	Races Led	Miles	$
1957	NR	1	0	0	0	0	0	0	0	19	0	0	19	50
Lifetime		1	0	0	0	0	0	0	0	19	0	0	19	$50

Jim Sauter

James Sauter
B: 6/1/1943
Racing Hometown: Necedah, WI

Year	Rank	Starts	Poles	1	2	3	4	5	6–10	Laps	Laps Led	Races Led	Miles	$
1980	109	1	0	0	0	0	0	0	0	33	0	0	50	900
1982	62	3	0	0	0	0	0	0	1	511	5	1	961	23,270
1983	68	5	0	0	0	0	0	0	0	1,414	0	0	1,830	26,910
1984	88	3	0	0	0	0	0	0	0	737	0	0	1,152	18,015
1985	50	3	0	0	0	0	0	0	0	565	0	0	1,107	15,465
1986	49	9	0	0	0	0	0	0	0	1,430	2	1	3,067	58,420
1987	53	3	0	0	0	0	0	0	1	781	0	0	1,364	14,855
1988	44	9	0	0	0	0	0	0	0	2,413	6	1	3,204	35,040
1989	33	17	0	0	0	0	0	0	2	3,974	8	1	5,118	73,832
1990	58	3	0	0	0	0	0	0	0	712	0	0	1,172	11,875
1991	43	6	0	0	0	0	0	0	0	1,012	0	0	1,843	47,395
1992	37	9	0	0	0	0	0	0	0	2,829	0	0	2,435	56,045
1993	47	4	0	0	0	0	0	0	0	769	0	0	1,505	48,860
1996	52	2	0	0	0	0	0	0	0	633	0	0	631	47,700
Lifetime		77	0	0	0	0	0	0	4	17,813	21	4	25,440	$478,582

Jay Sauter

Jay Sauter
B: 6/22/1962
Racing Hometown: Necedah, WI

Year	Rank	Starts	Poles	1	2	3	4	5	6–10	Laps	Laps Led	Races Led	Miles	$
2002	65	3	0	0	0	0	0	0	0	368	0	0	597	130,087
Lifetime		3	0	0	0	0	0	0	0	368	0	0	597	$130,087

Tim Sauter

Tim Sauter
B: 10/13/1964
Racing Hometown: Necedah, WI

Year	Rank	Starts	Poles	1	2	3	4	5	6–10	Laps	Laps Led	Races Led	Miles	$
2002	66	2	0	0	0	0	0	0	0	607	0	0	553	85,060
Lifetime		2	0	0	0	0	0	0	0	607	0	0	553	$85,060

Swede Savage

David Earle Savage Jr.
B: 8/26/1946   D: 7/2/1973   *Died from injuries in 1973 Indy 500.*
Racing Hometown: Santa Ana, CA

Year	Rank	Starts	Poles	1	2	3	4	5	6–10	Laps	Laps Led	Races Led	Miles	$
1967	70	3	0	0	0	0	0	0	2	1,091	0	0	571	1,275
1968	84	2	0	0	0	1	0	0	0	841	0	0	592	2,635
1969	NR	4	0	0	0	0	0	1	1	924	0	0	1,074	5,120
Lifetime		9	0	0	0	1	0	1	3	2,856	0	0	2,237	$9,030

Elton Sawyer

Everett Elton Sawyer
B: 11/5/1959
Racing Hometown: Chesapeake, VA

Year	Rank	Starts	Poles	1	2	3	4	5	6–10	Laps	Laps Led	Races Led	Miles	$
1995	38	20	0	0	0	0	0	0	0	4,573	0	0	6,186	416,490

Year	Rank	Starts	Poles	Finish						Laps	Laps Led	Races Led	Miles	$
				1	2	3	4	5	6–10					

Elton Sawyer *continued*

Year	Rank	Starts	Poles	1	2	3	4	5	6–10	Laps	Laps Led	Races Led	Miles	$
1996	43	9	0	0	0	0	0	0	0	2,448	0	0	3,330	129,618
Lifetime		29	0	0	0	0	0	0	0	7,021	0	0	9,516	$546,108

Lucky Sawyer

Richard Sawyer
   Racing Hometown: Baltimore, MD

Year	Rank	Starts	Poles	1	2	3	4	5	6–10	Laps	Laps Led	Races Led	Miles	$
1952	131	3	0	0	0	0	0	0	0	333	0	0	315	110
1953	105	4	0	0	0	0	0	0	0	27	0	0	96	75
1957	193	2	0	0	0	0	0	0	0	81	0	0	49	50
1958	178	1	0	0	0	0	0	0	0	12	0	0	6	10
Lifetime		10	0	0	0	0	0	0	0	453	0	0	465	$245

Connie Saylor

Connie Saylor
   B: 6/3/1940   D: 2/4/1993
   Racing Hometown: Johnson City, TN

Year	Rank	Starts	Poles	1	2	3	4	5	6–10	Laps	Laps Led	Races Led	Miles	$
1978	54	2	0	0	0	0	0	0	0	504	0	0	756	5,105
1979	75	2	0	0	0	0	0	0	0	262	0	0	565	4,435
1980	67	5	0	0	0	0	0	0	0	1,171	5	2	1,729	9,350
1981	39	7	0	0	0	0	0	0	0	4,177	0	0	6,568	19,715
1982	49	7	0	0	0	0	0	0	0	1,450	3	1	1,704	16,225
1983	101T	2	0	0	0	0	0	0	0	175	0	0	441	6,860
1984	43	8	0	0	0	0	0	0	0	1,193	1	1	2,166	19,675
1985	49	5	0	0	0	0	0	0	0	456	0	0	871	8,915
1986	59	7	0	0	0	0	0	0	0	1,760	0	0	2,846	33,770
1987	42	10	0	0	0	0	0	0	0	1,775	0	0	2,776	59,455
1988	68	2	0	0	0	0	0	0	0	496	0	0	552	12,210
Lifetime		57	0	0	0	0	0	0	0	13,419	9	4	20,974	$195,715

John Scarfo

John Scarfo
   Racing Hometown: Detroit, MI

Year	Rank	Starts	Poles	1	2	3	4	5	6–10	Laps	Laps Led	Races Led	Miles	$
1952	177	1	0	0	0	0	0	0	0	135	0	0	135	25
Lifetime		1	0	0	0	0	0	0	0	135	0	0	135	$25

Bob Schacht

Robert Schacht
   B: 1/24/1950
   Racing Hometown: Lombard, IL

Year	Rank	Starts	Poles	1	2	3	4	5	6–10	Laps	Laps Led	Races Led	Miles	$
1981	71	2	0	0	0	0	0	0	0	241	0	0	263	1,290
1982	52	3	0	0	0	0	0	0	0	576	0	0	318	2,880
1988	70	3	0	0	0	0	0	0	0	165	0	0	171	5,170
1989	57	2	0	0	0	0	0	0	0	602	0	0	818	5,475
1992	40	9	0	0	0	0	0	0	0	1,363	2	1	2,320	58,815
1993	55	4	0	0	0	0	0	0	0	272	0	0	365	26,075
1994	83	1	0	0	0	0	0	0	0	11	0	0	28	7,560
Lifetime		24	0	0	0	0	0	0	0	3,230	2	1	4,283	$107,265

Bill Schade

William C. Schade
   Racing Hometown: Irwin, PA

Year	Rank	Starts	Poles	1	2	3	4	5	6–10	Laps	Laps Led	Races Led	Miles	$
1951	N/A	2	0	0	0	0	0	0	0		0	0		50
Lifetime		2	0	0	0	0	0	0	0		0	0		$50

John Schelesky

John Schelesky
   Racing Hometown: Pittsburgh, PA

Year	Rank	Starts	Poles	1	2	3	4	5	6–10	Laps	Laps Led	Races Led	Miles	$
1950	NR	1	0	0	0	0	0	0	0		0	0		25
Lifetime		1	0	0	0	0	0	0	0		0	0		$25

Milford Schell

Milford Schell
   Racing Hometown: Erie, PA

Year	Rank	Starts	Poles	1	2	3	4	5	6–10	Laps	Laps Led	Races Led	Miles	$
1950	NR	1	0	0	0	0	0	0	0	104	0	0	52	0
Lifetime		1	0	0	0	0	0	0	0	104	0	0	52	$0

Year	Rank	Starts	Poles	Finish 1	2	3	4	5	6–10	Laps	Laps Led	Races Led	Miles	$

Norman Schihl

Norman Schihl
Racing Hometown: Toronto, Ont, Canada

Year	Rank	Starts	Poles	1	2	3	4	5	6–10	Laps	Laps Led	Races Led	Miles	$
1956	NR	1	0	0	0	0	0	0	0	349	0	0	175	150
Lifetime		1	0	0	0	0	0	0	0	349	0	0	175	$150

Jerry Schild

Jerry Schild
Racing Hometown: Houston, TX

Year	Rank	Starts	Poles	1	2	3	4	5	6–10	Laps	Laps Led	Races Led	Miles	$
1974	45	5	0	0	0	0	0	0	1	1,142	0	0	1,750	8,396
Lifetime		5	0	0	0	0	0	0	1	1,142	0	0	1,750	$8,396

Robin Schildnecht

Robin Schildnecht
B: 12/24/1953
Racing Hometown: Louisville, KY

Year	Rank	Starts	Poles	1	2	3	4	5	6–10	Laps	Laps Led	Races Led	Miles	$
1977	87	2	0	0	0	0	0	0	0	581	0	0	344	1,575
Lifetime		2	0	0	0	0	0	0	0	581	0	0	344	$1,575

Harry Schilling

Harry Schilling
Racing Hometown: Iseton, CA

Year	Rank	Starts	Poles	1	2	3	4	5	6–10	Laps	Laps Led	Races Led	Miles	$
1971	NR	3	0	0	0	0	0	0	0	222	0	0	561	3,395
1972	71	3	0	0	0	0	0	0	0	587	0	0	923	2,399
1974	122	1	0	0	0	0	0	0	0	65	0	0	170	1,005
Lifetime		7	0	0	0	0	0	0	0	874	0	0	1,654	$6,799

Don Schissler

Donald Schissler
B: 1934
Racing Hometown: Detroit, MI

Year	Rank	Starts	Poles	1	2	3	4	5	6–10	Laps	Laps Led	Races Led	Miles	$
1967	94	2	0	0	0	0	0	0	0	176	0	0	124	1,015
1969	NR	1	0	0	0	0	0	0	0	0	0	0	0	850
Lifetime		3	0	0	0	0	0	0	0	176	0	0	124	$1,865

Joe Schlesser

Joseph Schlesser
B: 5/18/1928   D: 7/7/1968   *Killed in 1968 French Grand Prix.*
Racing Hometown: Neuilly-Sur-Seine, France

Year	Rank	Starts	Poles	1	2	3	4	5	6–10	Laps	Laps Led	Races Led	Miles	$
1964	NR	2	0	0	0	0	0	0	1	231	0	0	578	1,350
Lifetime		2	0	0	0	0	0	0	1	231	0	0	578	$1,350

Lee Schmidt

Lee Schmidt
B: 2/5/1919
Racing Hometown: Milwaukee, WI

Year	Rank	Starts	Poles	1	2	3	4	5	6–10	Laps	Laps Led	Races Led	Miles	$
1949	70	1	0	0	0	0	0	0	0	171	0	0	171	50
1950	NR	1	0	0	0	0	0	0	0	40	0	0	167	25
Lifetime		2	0	0	0	0	0	0	0	211	0	0	338	$75

Bill Schmitt

William Schmitt
B: 2/13/1936
Racing Hometown: Redding, CA

Year	Rank	Starts	Poles	1	2	3	4	5	6–10	Laps	Laps Led	Races Led	Miles	$
1975	58	3	0	0	0	0	0	0	1	293	0	0	764	3,970
1976	72	2	0	0	0	0	0	0	1	318	0	0	816	3,360
1977	64	3	0	0	0	0	0	0	0	144	0	0	375	3,285
1978	52	3	0	0	0	0	0	0	1	304	0	0	773	8,430
1979	50	3	0	0	0	0	1	0	0	325	0	0	828	11,695
1980	42	4	0	0	0	0	0	1	0	579	0	0	1,473	21,610
1981	52	3	0	0	0	0	0	0	0	257	1	1	673	6,610
1982	64	2	0	0	0	0	0	0	0	186	0	0	487	2,210
1983	67	2	0	0	0	0	0	0	1	107	0	0	280	4,520
1984	59	2	0	0	0	0	0	0	0	125	0	0	328	5,270
1985	61	2	0	0	0	0	0	0	0	157	0	0	411	5,640
1986	64	2	0	0	0	0	0	0	0	207	0	0	542	7,840
1987	75	2	0	0	0	0	0	0	0	99	0	0	259	2,500
1988	56	2	0	0	0	0	0	0	0	252	0	0	406	6,245
1989	55	2	0	0	0	0	0	0	0	380	0	0	491	7,920
1990	59	2	0	0	0	0	0	0	0	384	0	0	496	11,525

Year	Rank	Starts	Poles	Finish						Laps	Laps Led	Races Led	Miles	$
				1	2	3	4	5	6–10					

Bill Schmitt *continued*

Year	Rank	Starts	Poles	1	2	3	4	5	6–10	Laps	Laps Led	Races Led	Miles	$
1991	57	2	0	0	0	0	0	0	0	210	0	0	322	10,605
1992	62T	2	0	0	0	0	0	0	0	282	0	0	393	13,095
1993	77	1	0	0	0	0	0	0	0	71	0	0	179	6,815
Lifetime		44	0	0	0	0	1	1	4	4,680	1	1	10,299	$143,145

Frankie Schneider

Franklin Schneider
B: 8/11/1926
Racing Hometown: Lambertville, NJ

Year	Rank	Starts	Poles	1	2	3	4	5	6–10	Laps	Laps Led	Races Led	Miles	$
1949	26T	1	0	0	0	0	0	0	1		0	0		150
1950	80	1	0	0	0	0	0	0	0		0	0		50
1951	N/A	1	0	0	0	0	0	0	0		0	0		0
1952	27	6	0	0	0	1	2	0	1	411	0	0	211	1,350
1953	NR	1	0	0	0	0	0	0	0		0	0		100
1957	20	10	1	0	1	0	2	0	3	1,781	37	1	1,248	4,588
1958	NR	7	0	1	1	0	3	0	0	1,215	106	1	606	1,970
Lifetime		27	1	1	2	1	7	0	5	3,407	143	2	2,064	$8,208

Lee Schneider

Lee Schneider
Racing Hometown: Glenshaw, PA

Year	Rank	Starts	Poles	1	2	3	4	5	6–10	Laps	Laps Led	Races Led	Miles	$
1951	N/A	1	0	0	0	0	0	0	0	64	0	0	48	25
Lifetime		1	0	0	0	0	0	0	0	64	0	0	48	$25

Terry Schoonover

Terry L. Schoonover
D: 11/11/1984 *Killed in Atlanta 500.*
Racing Hometown: Royal Palm Beach, FL

Year	Rank	Starts	Poles	1	2	3	4	5	6–10	Laps	Laps Led	Races Led	Miles	$
1984	85T	2	0	0	0	0	0	0	0	543	0	0	614	2,585
Lifetime		2	0	0	0	0	0	0	0	543	0	0	614	$2,585

Ken Schrader

Ken Schrader
B: 5/29/1955
Racing Hometown: Fenton, MO

Year	Rank	Starts	Poles	1	2	3	4	5	6–10	Laps	Laps Led	Races Led	Miles	$
1984	53	5	0	0	0	0	0	0	0	1,508	0	0	1,632	16,425
1985	16	28	0	0	0	0	0	0	3	7,786	4	1	9,364	211,523
1986	16	29	0	0	0	0	0	0	4	8,047	2	2	9,699	235,904
1987	10	29	1	0	0	0	0	1	9	8,162	154	10	9,902	375,918
1988	5	29	2	1	1	0	1	1	13	9,095	151	13	11,033	631,544
1989	5	29	4	1	1	3	4	1	4	8,675	356	17	10,782	702,615
1990	10	29	3	0	2	2	1	2	7	8,649	242	12	10,050	769,934
1991	9	29	0	2	2	2	1	3	8	8,331	440	16	9,843	772,434
1992	17	29	1	0	0	2	1	1	7	8,425	83	5	9,816	639,679
1993	9	30	6	0	2	2	3	2	6	8,877	285	14	10,995	952,748
1994	4	31	0	0	1	2	4	2	9	9,704	223	9	11,741	1,211,062
1995	17	31	1	0	0	1	1	0	8	8,550	237	9	10,167	886,566
1996	12	31	0	0	0	1	1	1	7	9,408	45	7	11,500	1,089,603
1997	10	32	2	0	0	0	2	0	6	9,612	46	7	12,364	1,355,292
1998	12	33	2	0	0	0	3	0	8	9,238	60	4	11,800	1,887,339
1999	15	34	1	0	0	0	0	0	6	9,676	8	3	12,695	1,939,147
2000	18	34	0	0	0	0	0	0	2	9,954	33	5	12,919	1,530,844
2001	19	36	0	0	0	0	0	0	5	10,534	10	3	13,997	2,418,181
2002	30	35	0	0	0	0	0	0	0	9,415	46	1	12,322	2,460,140
Lifetime		563	23	4	9	15	22	14	112	163,646	2,425	138	202,623	$20,086,898

Chuck Schroedel

Chuck Schroedel

Year	Rank	Starts	Poles	1	2	3	4	5	6–10	Laps	Laps Led	Races Led	Miles	$
1987	103T	1	0	0	0	0	0	0	0	8	0	0	20	1,375
Lifetime		1	0	0	0	0	0	0	0	8	0	0	20	$1,375

Dorsey Schroeder

Dorsey Schroeder
B: 2/5/1953
Racing Hometown: Baldwin, MO

Year	Rank	Starts	Poles	1	2	3	4	5	6–10	Laps	Laps Led	Races Led	Miles	$
1991	59	2	0	0	0	0	0	0	0	92	3	1	224	11,945
1992	60	2	0	0	0	0	0	0	0	372	0	0	758	36,105

Year	Rank	Starts	Poles	Finish						Laps	Laps Led	Races Led	Miles	$
				1	2	3	4	5	6–10	Laps	Led	Led	Miles	$

Dorsey Schroeder *continued*

Year	Rank	Starts	Poles	1	2	3	4	5	6–10	Laps	Laps Led	Races Led	Miles	$
1993	62	2	0	0	0	0	0	0	0	69	0	0	174	13,615
1996	55	1	0	0	0	0	0	0	0	90	2	1	221	22,745
1997	62T	1	0	0	0	0	0	0	0	89	0	0	218	11,630
2001	62	1	0	0	0	0	0	0	0	112		0	218	52,805
Lifetime		9	0	0	0	0	0	0	0	824	5	2	1,812	$148,845

Ken Schroeder

Kenneth Schroeder
Racing Hometown: Jamestown, NY

Year	Rank	Starts	Poles	1	2	3	4	5	6–10	Laps	Laps Led	Races Led	Miles	$
1949	76	1	0	0	0	0	0	0	0	168	0	0	168	50
Lifetime		1	0	0	0	0	0	0	0	168	0	0	168	$50

Walt Schubert

Walter Schubert
Racing Hometown: Cold Spring, NY

Year	Rank	Starts	Poles	1	2	3	4	5	6–10	Laps	Laps Led	Races Led	Miles	$
1955	159T	1	0	0	0	0	0	0	0	196	0	0	196	75
1956	86	4	0	0	0	0	0	0	1	413	0	0	324	375
Lifetime		5	0	0	0	0	0	0	1	609	0	0	520	$450

Larry Schultz

Lawrence Schultz
Racing Hometown: Highland Falls, NY

Year	Rank	Starts	Poles	1	2	3	4	5	6–10	Laps	Laps Led	Races Led	Miles	$
1953	NR	2	0	0	0	0	0	0	0		0	0		65
Lifetime		2	0	0	0	0	0	0	0		0	0		$65

Fritz Schulz

Fritz Schulz
B: 1936
Racing Hometown: Adenau, Germany

Year	Rank	Starts	Poles	1	2	3	4	5	6–10	Laps	Laps Led	Races Led	Miles	$
1971	NR	1	0	0	0	0	0	0	0	45	0	0	113	205
Lifetime		1	0	0	0	0	0	0	0	45	0	0	113	$205

Volney Schulze

Volney E. Schulze
Racing Hometown: Silver Spring, MD

Year	Rank	Starts	Poles	1	2	3	4	5	6–10	Laps	Laps Led	Races Led	Miles	$
1954	214	1	0	0	0	0	0	0	0	46	0	0	23	0
1955	67	6	0	0	0	0	0	0	1	674	0	0	456	300
1957	78	3	0	0	0	0	0	0	1	530	0	0	380	340
1958	49	7	0	0	0	0	0	0	0	725	0	0	370	490
Lifetime		17	0	0	0	0	0	0	2	1,975	0	0	1,228	$1,130

Bobby Schuyler

Robert Schuyler
Racing Hometown: Islip, NY

Year	Rank	Starts	Poles	1	2	3	4	5	6–10	Laps	Laps Led	Races Led	Miles	$
1964	NR	1	0	0	0	0	0	0	0	3	0	0	1	100
Lifetime		1	0	0	0	0	0	0	0	3	0	0	1	$100

Bob Schwingle

Robert Schwingle
Racing Hometown: Naples, NJ

Year	Rank	Starts	Poles	1	2	3	4	5	6–10	Laps	Laps Led	Races Led	Miles	$
1952	140T	1	0	0	0	0	0	0	0	142	0	0	71	25
1954	140	1	0	0	0	0	0	0	0	165	0	0	83	25
Lifetime		2	0	0	0	0	0	0	0	307	0	0	154	$50

Bill Scott

William Scott
Racing Hometown: Winston-Salem, NC

Year	Rank	Starts	Poles	1	2	3	4	5	6–10	Laps	Laps Led	Races Led	Miles	$
1959	69	6	0	0	0	0	0	0	2	805	0	0	452	430
Lifetime		6	0	0	0	0	0	0	2	805	0	0	452	$430

Bill Scott

William Scott
B: 10/10/1948
Racing Hometown: San Bernadino, CA

Year	Rank	Starts	Poles	1	2	3	4	5	6–10	Laps	Laps Led	Races Led	Miles	$
1970	NR	1	0	0	0	0	0	0	0	6	0	0	16	635
Lifetime		1	0	0	0	0	0	0	0	6	0	0	16	$635

Year	Rank	Starts	Poles	Finish 1	2	3	4	5	6–10	Laps	Laps Led	Races Led	Miles	$

Bill Scott

William Scott
Racing Hometown: Brevard, NC

Year	Rank	Starts	Poles	1	2	3	4	5	6–10	Laps	Laps Led	Races Led	Miles	$
1982	93	1	0	0	0	0	0	0	0	75	0	0	200	2,825
1983	—	0												1,900
1985	NR	1	0	0	0	0	0	0	0	71	0	0	178	1,615
Lifetime		1	0	0	0	0	0	0	0	146	0	0	378	$6,340

Billy Scott

William Scott
B: 8/1935
Racing Hometown: Union, SC

Year	Rank	Starts	Poles	1	2	3	4	5	6–10	Laps	Laps Led	Races Led	Miles	$
1973	84	1	0	0	0	0	0	0	0	340	0	0	510	1,850
1974	109	1	0	0	0	0	0	0	0	262	0	0	393	1,625
Lifetime		2	0	0	0	0	0	0	0	602	0	0	903	$3,475

Bob Scott

Robert Scott
B: 10/4/1928   D: 7/5/1954   *Killed in Indy Car race @ Darlington.*
Racing Hometown: Los Angeles, CA

Year	Rank	Starts	Poles	1	2	3	4	5	6–10	Laps	Laps Led	Races Led	Miles	$
1950	137T	1	0	0	0	0	0	0	0		0	0		0
Lifetime		1	0	0	0	0	0	0	0		0	0		$0

Charlie Scott

Charles Scott
Racing Hometown: College Park, GA

Year	Rank	Starts	Poles	1	2	3	4	5	6–10	Laps	Laps Led	Races Led	Miles	$
1956	173T	1	0	0	0	0	0	0	0		0	0		75
Lifetime		1	0	0	0	0	0	0	0		0	0		$75

Fifi Scott

FiFi Scott
Racing Hometown: W. Sacramento, CA

Year	Rank	Starts	Poles	1	2	3	4	5	6–10	Laps	Laps Led	Races Led	Miles	$
1955	216	2	0	0	0	0	0	0	0	216	0	0	145	25
Lifetime		2	0	0	0	0	0	0	0	216	0	0	145	$25

Harry Scott

Harry Scott

Year	Rank	Starts	Poles	1	2	3	4	5	6–10	Laps	Laps Led	Races Led	Miles	$
1951	N/A	1	0	0	0	0	0	0	1		0	0		100
Lifetime		1	0	0	0	0	0	0	1		0	0		$100

Lyle Scott

Lyle Scott
Racing Hometown: Port Washington, NY

Year	Rank	Starts	Poles	1	2	3	4	5	6–10	Laps	Laps Led	Races Led	Miles	$
1950	59	6	0	0	0	0	0	0	1	380	0	0	223	175
1951	N/A	2	0	0	0	0	0	0	1		0	0		125
1953	91T	1	0	0	0	0	0	0	1		0	0		50
1956	233T	1	0	0	0	0	0	0	0		0	0		60
Lifetime		10	0	0	0	0	0	0	3	380	0	0	223	$410

Tighe Scott

Tighe Scott
B: 6/2/1949
Racing Hometown: Pen Argyle, PA

Year	Rank	Starts	Poles	1	2	3	4	5	6–10	Laps	Laps Led	Races Led	Miles	$
1976	45	6	0	0	0	0	0	0	1	697	0	0	1,703	15,520
1977	20	26	0	0	0	0	0	1	0	6,134	0	0	7,467	63,225
1978	13	29	0	0	0	0	0	0	7	6,626	3	1	8,224	87,912
1979	27	17	0	0	0	0	1	0	6	3,834	0	0	5,684	88,010
1980	39	10	0	0	0	0	0	1	1	1,066	4	1	1,968	21,925
1982	NR	1	0	0	0	0	0	0	0	81	0	0	203	5,050
Lifetime		89	0	0	0	0	1	2	15	18,438	7	2	25,249	$281,642

Wendell Scott

Wendell Oliver Scott
B: 8/29/1921   D: 12/23/199
Racing Hometown: Danville, VA

Year	Rank	Starts	Poles	1	2	3	4	5	6–10	Laps	Laps Led	Races Led	Miles	$
1961	32	23	0	0	0	0	0	0	5	4,364	0	0	2,217	3,240
1962	22	41	1	0	0	2	1	1	15	8,542	0	0	4,211	7,133
1963	15	47	0	0	0	0	0	1	14	9,459	0	0	6,165	10,966
1964	12	56	0	1	0	0	6	1	17	10,752	27	1	6,466	16,495
1965	11	52	0	0	0	0	2	2	17	9,759	0	0	6,451	18,639

Year	Rank	Starts	Poles	1	2	3	Finish 4	5	6–10	Laps	Laps Led	Races Led	Miles	$

Wendell Scott *continued*

Year	Rank	Starts	Poles	1	2	3	4	5	6–10	Laps	Laps Led	Races Led	Miles	$
1966	6	45	0	0	0	1	1	1	14	9,793	0	0	7,181	23,052
1967	10	45	0	0	0	0	0	0	11	9,217	0	0	6,639	19,510
1968	9	48	0	0	0	0	0	0	10	10,231	0	0	7,314	20,498
1969	9	51	0	0	0	0	0	0	11	11,856	0	0	9,076	47,451
1970	14	41	0	0	0	0	0	0	9	8,276	0	0	6,949	28,518
1971	19	37	0	0	0	0	0	0	4	7,791	0	0	6,826	21,701
1972	40	6	0	0	0	0	0	0	0	1,763	0	0	1,926	5,830
1973	61	3	0	0	0	0	0	0	0	632	0	0	915	3,530
Lifetime		495	1	1	0	3	10	6	127	102,435	27	1	72,336	$226,563

Arley Scranton

Arley Scranton
Racing Hometown: Compton, CA

Year	Rank	Starts	Poles	1	2	3	4	5	6–10	Laps	Laps Led	Races Led	Miles	$
1954	NR	1	0	0	0	0	0	0	0	413	0	0	207	25
1956	NR	1	0	0	0	0	0	0	0	9	0	0	23	20
1957	175T	1	0	0	0	0	0	0	0	25	0	0	25	25
1958	158	2	0	0	0	0	0	0	0	17	0	0	17	100
1959	118	2	0	0	0	0	0	0	0	361	0	0	158	100
1961	NR	1	0	0	0	0	0	0	0	3	0	0	8	0
1966	133	1	0	0	0	0	0	0	0	3	0	0	8	500
Lifetime		9	0	0	0	0	0	0	0	831	0	0	444	$770

Rick Scribner

Richard Scribner
B: 2/10/1952
Racing Hometown: Orangevale, CA

Year	Rank	Starts	Poles	1	2	3	4	5	6–10	Laps	Laps Led	Races Led	Miles	$
1992	72	2	0	0	0	0	0	0	0	75	0	0	178	9,025
Lifetime		2	0	0	0	0	0	0	0	75	0	0	178	$9,025

Ed Sczech

Edward Sczech
B: 2/1/1944
Racing Hometown: San Antonio, TX

Year	Rank	Starts	Poles	1	2	3	4	5	6–10	Laps	Laps Led	Races Led	Miles	$
1973	53	4	0	0	0	0	0	0	0	558	0	0	1,141	4,270
1973	53	4	0	0	0	0	0	0	0	558	0	0	1,141	4,270
Lifetime		8	0	0	0	0	0	0	0	1,116	0	0	2,282	$8,540

James Sears

James Sidney Sears
B: 11/11/1940   D: 8/3/1973   *Killed at Starlite Speedway in Monroe, NC.*
Racing Hometown: Rockingham, NC

Year	Rank	Starts	Poles	1	2	3	4	5	6–10	Laps	Laps Led	Races Led	Miles	$
1967	NR	1	0	0	0	0	0	0	0	72	0	0	72	505
1968	110	1	0	0	0	0	0	0	0	92	0	0	92	710
1969	83T	1	0	0	0	0	0	0	0	247	0	0	247	725
1970	102	2	0	0	0	0	0	0	2	641	0	0	552	1,665
1971	NR	1	0	0	0	0	0	0	0	9	0	0	9	545
Lifetime		6	0	0	0	0	0	0	2	1,061	0	0	972	$4,150

John Sears

John Hamilton Sears
B: 5/9/1936   D: 11/1/1999
Racing Hometown: Ellerbe, NC

Year	Rank	Starts	Poles	1	2	3	4	5	6–10	Laps	Laps Led	Races Led	Miles	$
1964	65	6	0	0	0	0	0	0	3	1,200	0	0	581	1,130
1965	95	2	0	0	0	0	0	0	1	281	0	0	94	650
1966	7	46	0	0	1	1	4	5	19	9,981	73	1	6,845	25,192
1967	5	41	1	0	1	3	3	2	16	10,031	62	4	7,468	28,937
1968	5	49	0	0	0	1	1	3	19	11,077	0	0	7,827	29,179
1969	7	52	0	0	1	3	7	6	10	11,620	18	3	8,842	52,281
1970	12	40	1	0	0	0	3	1	3	7,777	10	1	7,939	32,675
1971	20	37	0	0	0	0	0	0	3	7,512	0	0	6,818	26,735
1972	8	28	0	0	0	0	0	2	5	7,882	0	0	8,995	51,314
1973	32	17	0	0	0	0	0	0	0	3,568	0	0	3,335	16,890
Lifetime		318	2	0	3	8	18	19	79	70,929	163	9	58,744	$264,983

Frank Secrist

Frank Secrist
B: 1930
Racing Hometown: Oildale, CA

Year	Rank	Starts	Poles	1	2	3	4	5	6–10	Laps	Laps Led	Races Led	Miles	$
1956	250T	1	0	0	0	0	0	0	0	207	0	0	207	40

Year	Rank	Starts	Poles	Finish						Laps	Laps Led	Races Led	Miles	$
				1	2	3	4	5	6–10					

Frank Secrist *continued*

1957	168	2	0	0	0	0	0	0	0	104	0	0	100	95
1960	122	2	1	0	0	0	0	0	0	105	8	1	123	175
1961	97	3	0	0	0	0	1	0	0	249	0	0	313	750
Lifetime		8	1	0	0	0	1	0	0	665	8	1	743	$1,060

Bill Sedgwick

William Sedgwick
B: 3/19/1955
Racing Hometown: Granada Hills, CA

1989	99	1	0	0	0	0	0	0	0	170	0	0	170	3,525
1990	52	3	0	0	0	0	0	0	0	730	0	0	653	11,355
1991	49	3	0	0	0	0	0	0	0	848	0	0	740	15,150
1992	56	2	0	0	0	0	0	0	0	373	0	0	485	16,365
1993	72T	1	0	0	0	0	0	0	0	73	0	0	184	8,140
Lifetime		10	0	0	0	0	0	0	0	2,194	0	0	2,232	$54,535

George Seeger

George Seeger
Racing Hometown: Whittier, CA

1951	45	9	0	0	0	1	0	0	2	705	0	0	697	910
1954	NR	2	0	0	0	0	0	1	0	669	0	0	335	350
1956	89	2	0	0	0	0	0	0	1	205	0	0	322	400
1957	38	6	0	0	1	3	1	0	0	764	19	1	520	2,740
Lifetime		19	0	0	1	4	1	1	3	2,343	19	1	1,874	$4,400

John Seeley

John Seeley
Racing Hometown: Frewsburg, NY

1958	NR	1	0	0	0	0	0	1	0	143	0	0	48	245
1959	89	1	0	0	0	0	0	0	0	160	0	0	80	125
Lifetime		2	0	0	0	0	0	1	0	303	0	0	128	$370

Bob Seharns

Robert Seharns

1958	NR	1	0	0	0	0	0	0	0	131	0	0	44	130
Lifetime		1	0	0	0	0	0	0	0	131	0	0	44	$130

Ken Seibel

Ken Seibel
Racing Hometown: Syracuse, NY

1956	—	1	0	0	0	0	0	0	0	134	0	0	134	100
Lifetime		1	0	0	0	0	0	0	0	134	0	0	134	$100

Bill Seifert

William John Seifert
B: 7/2/1939
Racing Hometown: Skyland, NC

1966	43	15	0	0	0	0	0	0	4	3,322	0	0	1,920	3,830
1967	22	41	0	0	0	0	0	0	12	8,171	0	0	5,133	11,910
1968	14	44	0	0	0	0	0	1	8	8,033	0	0	5,857	18,403
1969	13	50	0	0	0	0	0	1	14	9,728	0	0	7,473	44,361
1970	18	39	0	0	0	0	0	1	3	5,189	0	0	5,196	25,647
1971	13	37	0	0	0	0	0	0	4	6,552	0	0	7,158	33,220
1972	74	6	0	0	0	0	0	0	1	472	0	0	652	7,290
1977	71	2	0	0	0	0	0	0	0	346	0	0	540	2,270
1979	123T	1	0	0	0	0	0	0	0	32	0	0	64	960
Lifetime		235	0	0	0	0	0	3	46	41,845	0	0	33,993	$147,891

Al Self

Al Self
Racing Hometown: Venice, CA

1960	77	2	0	0	0	0	0	0	1	227	0	0	290	550
1963	151	1	0	0	0	0	0	0	0	1	0	0	3	200
1964	132	1	0	0	0	0	0	0	0	9	0	0	24	500
1965	92	1	0	0	0	0	0	0	0	49	0	0	132	500
Lifetime		5	0	0	0	0	0	0	1	286	0	0	449	$1,750

Year	Rank	Starts	Poles	Finish						Laps	Laps Led	Races Led	Miles	$
				1	2	3	4	5	6–10	Laps	Led	Led	Miles	$

Jack Sellers

Jack Sellers
B: 7/27/1944
Racing Hometown: Sacramento, CA

Year	Rank	Starts	Poles	1	2	3	4	5	6–10	Laps	Laps Led	Races Led	Miles	$
1990	NR	1	0	0	0	0	0	0	0	41	0	0	103	3,225
1992	93T	1	0	0	0	0	0	0	0	48	0	0	121	4,725
Lifetime		2	0	0	0	0	0	0	0	89	0	0	224	$7,950

Mark Sellers

Mark Sellers
Racing Hometown: Spartanburg, SC

Year	Rank	Starts	Poles	1	2	3	4	5	6–10	Laps	Laps Led	Races Led	Miles	$
1969	78	3	0	0	0	0	0	0	0	164	0	0	82	450
Lifetime		3	0	0	0	0	0	0	0	164	0	0	82	$450

Bob Senneker

Robert Senneker
B: 1945
Racing Hometown: Dorr, MI

Year	Rank	Starts	Poles	1	2	3	4	5	6–10	Laps	Laps Led	Races Led	Miles	$
1968	NR	1	0	0	0	0	0	0	0	182	0	0	455	3,200
1970	80	1	0	0	0	0	0	0	0	175	0	0	357	775
1981	NR	1	0	0	0	0	0	0	0	256	0	0	384	1,975
1983	44	5	0	0	0	0	0	0	0	1,317	0	0	2,186	11,335
Lifetime		8	0	0	0	0	0	0	0	1,930	0	0	3,382	$17,285

Harry Sents

Harry Sents
Racing Hometown: Glen Aubrey, NY

Year	Rank	Starts	Poles	1	2	3	4	5	6–10	Laps	Laps Led	Races Led	Miles	$
1950	105	2	0	0	0	0	0	0	0	145	0	0	73	25
Lifetime		2	0	0	0	0	0	0	0	145	0	0	73	$25

Frank Sessoms

Frank Marvin Sessoms
B: 1/29/1933
Racing Hometown: Darlington, SC

Year	Rank	Starts	Poles	1	2	3	4	5	6–10	Laps	Laps Led	Races Led	Miles	$
1962	88T	2	0	0	0	0	0	0	0	319	0	0	160	185
1969	NR	1	0	0	0	0	0	0	0	128	0	0	340	1,325
1971	NR	2	0	0	0	0	0	0	2	852	0	0	496	1,180
Lifetime		5	0	0	0	0	0	0	2	1,299	0	0	996	$2,690

Dennis Setzer

Dennis Setzer
B: 2/27/1960
Racing Hometown: Newton, NC

Year	Rank	Starts	Poles	1	2	3	4	5	6–10	Laps	Laps Led	Races Led	Miles	$
1998	51	7	0	0	0	0	0	0	0	2,142	0	0	2,361	150,495
Lifetime		7	0	0	0	0	0	0	0	2,142	0	0	2,361	$150,495

Ned Setzer

Ned Setzer
D: 7/29/1975
Racing Hometown: Claremont, NC

Year	Rank	Starts	Poles	1	2	3	4	5	6–10	Laps	Laps Led	Races Led	Miles	$
1965	43	8	0	0	0	0	0	0	3	862	0	0	859	4,805
1966	101	2	0	0	0	0	0	0	0	147	0	0	368	1,200
Lifetime		10	0	0	0	0	0	0	3	1,009	0	0	1,227	$6,005

Leland Sewell

Leland Sewell
Racing Hometown: Memphis, TN

Year	Rank	Starts	Poles	1	2	3	4	5	6–10	Laps	Laps Led	Races Led	Miles	$
1954	176	1	0	0	0	0	0	0	0	84	0	0	126	50
1955	96	1	0	0	0	0	0	0	0	176	0	0	264	125
Lifetime		2	0	0	0	0	0	0	0	260	0	0	390	$175

Buster Sexton

Buster Sexton
Racing Hometown: Duncan, SC

Year	Rank	Starts	Poles	1	2	3	4	5	6–10	Laps	Laps Led	Races Led	Miles	$
1966	111T	1	0	0	0	0	0	0	0	183	0	0	92	100
1967	124	1	0	0	0	0	0	0	0	15	0	0	8	100
1969	94T	1	0	0	0	0	0	0	0	9	0	0	5	0
Lifetime		3	0	0	0	0	0	0	0	207	0	0	104	$200

Year	Rank	Starts	Poles	Finish						Laps	Laps Led	Races Led	Miles	$
				1	2	3	4	5	6–10					

Ralph Shaffer

Ralph Shaffer
Racing Hometown: Monticello, IL

Year	Rank	Starts	Poles	1	2	3	4	5	6–10	Laps	Laps Led	Races Led	Miles	$
1955	233	1	0	0	0	0	0	0	0	16	0	0	66	0
Lifetime		1	0	0	0	0	0	0	0	16	0	0	66	$0

Herb Shannon

Herbert Shannon
B: 9/1/1931
Racing Hometown: Peoria, IL

Year	Rank	Starts	Poles	1	2	3	4	5	6–10	Laps	Laps Led	Races Led	Miles	$
1960	NR	1	0	0	0	0	0	0	0	184	0	0	276	350
1965	NR	2	0	0	0	0	0	0	0	110	0	0	275	1,130
Lifetime		3	0	0	0	0	0	0	0	294	0	0	551	$1,480

Scott Sharp

Scott Sharp
B: 2/14/1968
Racing Hometown: E.Norwalk, CT

Year	Rank	Starts	Poles	1	2	3	4	5	6–10	Laps	Laps Led	Races Led	Miles	$
1992	69	1	0	0	0	0	0	0	0	51	0	0	125	7,155
Lifetime		1	0	0	0	0	0	0	0	51	0	0	125	$7,155

Bob Shaw

William B. Shaw
Racing Hometown: Warren, OH

Year	Rank	Starts	Poles	1	2	3	4	5	6–10	Laps	Laps Led	Races Led	Miles	$
1951	N/A	1	0	0	0	0	0	0	0		0	0		0
1952	172	1	0	0	0	0	0	0	0	112	0	0	56	25
Lifetime		2	0	0	0	0	0	0	0	112	0	0	56	$25

Ernie Shaw

Ernest Anthony Shaw
B: 10/9/1942
Racing Hometown: Winston-Salem, NC

Year	Rank	Starts	Poles	1	2	3	4	5	6–10	Laps	Laps Led	Races Led	Miles	$
1969	NR	1	0	0	0	0	0	0	0	149	0	0	396	1,500
1971	NR	2	0	0	0	0	0	0	1	578	0	0	312	775
1974	68	4	0	0	0	0	0	0	0	842	0	0	538	2,280
1976	NR	1	0	0	0	0	0	0	0	372	0	0	202	700
1979	92T	1	0	0	0	0	0	0	0	368	0	0	230	625
Lifetime		9	0	0	0	0	0	0	1	2,309	0	0	1,677	$5,880

Graham Shaw

J. Graham Shaw
B: 7/8/1937
Racing Hometown: Columbia, SC

Year	Rank	Starts	Poles	1	2	3	4	5	6–10	Laps	Laps Led	Races Led	Miles	$
1964	66	2	0	0	0	0	0	0	0	127	0	0	379	1,000
Lifetime		2	0	0	0	0	0	0	0	127	0	0	379	$1,000

Lloyd Shaw

Lloyd Shaw
Racing Hometown: Toronto, Ont, Canada

Year	Rank	Starts	Poles	1	2	3	4	5	6–10	Laps	Laps Led	Races Led	Miles	$
1953	NR	1	1	0	0	0	0	0	0		0	0		40
Lifetime		1	1	0	0	0	0	0	0		0	0		$40

Ace Shearer

Ace Shearer
Racing Hometown: Erie, PA

Year	Rank	Starts	Poles	1	2	3	4	5	6–10	Laps	Laps Led	Races Led	Miles	$
1950	137T	1	0	0	0	0	0	0	0	129	0	0	65	0
Lifetime		1	0	0	0	0	0	0	0	129	0	0	65	$0

Eddie Sheeler

Eddie Sheeler
Racing Hometown: Chicago, IL

Year	Rank	Starts	Poles	1	2	3	4	5	6–10	Laps	Laps Led	Races Led	Miles	$
1951	N/A	2	0	0	0	0	0	0	0		0	0		75
Lifetime		2	0	0	0	0	0	0	0		0	0		$75

Ralph Sheeler

Ralph Sheeler
B: 11/10/1910
Racing Hometown: Paterson, NJ

Year	Rank	Starts	Poles	1	2	3	4	5	6–10	Laps	Laps Led	Races Led	Miles	$
1953	61	3	0	0	0	0	0	0	0		0	0		85
Lifetime		3	0	0	0	0	0	0	0		0	0		$85

Year	Rank	Starts	Poles	1	2	3	Finish 4	5	6–10	Laps	Laps Led	Races Led	Miles	$

Kirk Shelmerdine

Kirk Shelmerdine
B: 3/8/1958
Racing Hometown: Philadelphia, PA

Year	Rank	Starts	Poles	1	2	3	4	5	6–10	Laps	Laps Led	Races Led	Miles	$
1981	NR	1	0	0	0	0	0	0	0	2	0	0	4	950
1994	66	1	0	0	0	0	0	0	0	179	0	0	476	11,265
2002	74	2	0	0	0	0	0	0	0	91	0	0	213	76,965
Lifetime		4	0	0	0	0	0	0	0	272	0	0	693	$89,180

Ron Shephard

Ronald Shephard

Year	Rank	Starts	Poles	1	2	3	4	5	6–10	Laps	Laps Led	Races Led	Miles	$
1986	104T	1	0	0	0	0	0	0	0	282	0	0	153	3,145
1987	71	2	0	0	0	0	0	0	0	198	0	0	462	3,745
Lifetime		3	0	0	0	0	0	0	0	480	0	0	615	$6,890

Morgan Shepherd

Clay Morgan Shepherd
B: 10/21/1941
Racing Hometown: Conover, NC

Year	Rank	Starts	Poles	1	2	3	4	5	6–10	Laps	Laps Led	Races Led	Miles	$
1970	90	3	0	0	0	0	0	0	0	522	0	0	241	965
1977	53	3	0	0	0	0	0	0	1	1,114	0	0	1,433	6,915
1978	75	2	0	0	0	0	0	0	0	397	0	0	604	8,115
1981	13	29	1	1	0	0	2	0	7	7,440	518	6	7,919	170,473
1982	10	29	2	0	0	1	1	4	7	7,608	209	11	8,468	166,030
1983	20	25	0	0	1	1	1	0	10	6,309	5	4	7,613	287,326
1984	29	20	0	0	0	0	0	0	1	5,134	1	1	5,478	59,670
1985	31	16	0	0	0	0	0	1	1	2,951	1	1	4,062	55,985
1986	18	27	0	1	0	1	2	0	4	6,358	357	13	8,348	244,146
1987	17	29	1	0	1	1	1	4	4	6,510	167	8	8,039	317,034
1988	28	23	2	0	1	0	1	0	4	4,601	127	5	6,087	197,425
1989	13	29	1	0	2	0	1	2	8	7,590	139	6	9,910	471,037
1990	5	29	0	1	2	2	0	2	9	8,794	201	7	10,638	666,915
1991	12	29	0	0	0	2	2	0	10	9,023	86	5	10,485	521,147
1992	14	29	0	0	2	0	0	1	8	9,093	60	3	10,840	634,222
1993	7	30	0	1	1	0	1	0	12	9,442	92	9	11,407	682,532
1994	6	31	0	0	2	2	1	4	7	9,788	81	10	11,951	1,119,038
1995	11	31	0	0	1	1	1	1	6	9,274	32	8	11,547	996,374
1996	19	31	0	0	0	0	0	1	4	8,976	55	4	10,721	719,059
1997	38	23	0	0	0	1	0	0	2	6,398	12	2	9,150	662,999
1998	47	12	0	0	0	0	0	0	0	2,796	0	0	3,317	364,541
1999	65	1	0	0	0	0	0	0	0	388	0	0	395	29,400
2001	66	1	0	0	0	0	0	0	0	159	0	0	398	84,610
2002	55	5	0	0	0	0	0	0	0	221	4	1	335	171,570
Lifetime		487	7	4	13	12	14	20	105	130,886	2,147	104	159,384	$8,637,528

Joe Sheppard

Joseph Sheppard
B: 1929
Racing Hometown: Trenton, NJ

Year	Rank	Starts	Poles	1	2	3	4	5	6–10	Laps	Laps Led	Races Led	Miles	$
1954	151T	1	0	0	0	0	0	0	0	215	0	0	296	75
Lifetime		1	0	0	0	0	0	0	0	215	0	0	296	$75

Lou Sherman

Louis Sherman
Racing Hometown: Portland, OR

Year	Rank	Starts	Poles	1	2	3	4	5	6–10	Laps	Laps Led	Races Led	Miles	$
1956	64	5	0	0	0	1	0	0	1	837	0	0	531	810
Lifetime		5	0	0	0	1	0	0	1	837	0	0	531	$810

Ray Sherman

Raymond Sherman
Racing Hometown: Shermont, DE

Year	Rank	Starts	Poles	1	2	3	4	5	6–10	Laps	Laps Led	Races Led	Miles	$
1953	NR	1	0	0	0	0	0	0	0		0	0		40
Lifetime		1	0	0	0	0	0	0	0		0	0		$40

James Shields

James Shields
Racing Hometown: Richester, NY

Year	Rank	Starts	Poles	1	2	3	4	5	6–10	Laps	Laps Led	Races Led	Miles	$
1951	N/A	1	0	0	0	0	0	0	0		0	0		25
Lifetime		1	0	0	0	0	0	0	0		0	0		$25

Year	Rank	Starts	Poles	Finish 1	2	3	4	5	6–10	Laps	Laps Led	Races Led	Miles	$

Harry Shipe

Harry Shipe
Racing Hometown: Silver Spring, MD

Year	Rank	Starts	Poles	1	2	3	4	5	6–10	Laps	Laps Led	Races Led	Miles	$
1970	97	2	0	0	0	0	0	0	0	45	0	0	65	450
Lifetime		2	0	0	0	0	0	0	0	45	0	0	65	$450

Bill Shirey

William L. Shirey
B: 2/28/1932
Racing Hometown: Detroit, MI

Year	Rank	Starts	Poles	1	2	3	4	5	6–10	Laps	Laps Led	Races Led	Miles	$
1969	61	3	0	0	0	0	0	0	0	418	0	0	332	1,315
1970	30	29	0	0	0	0	0	0	1	3,691	0	0	2,542	12,215
1971	28	27	0	0	0	0	0	0	2	3,667	0	0	2,574	9,160
1972	38	13	0	0	0	0	0	0	0	1,812	0	0	1,951	8,070
Lifetime		72	0	0	0	0	0	0	3	9,588	0	0	7,399	$30,760

Barney Shore

Bernard Shore
Racing Hometown: Lewisville, NC

Year	Rank	Starts	Poles	1	2	3	4	5	6–10	Laps	Laps Led	Races Led	Miles	$
1958	170	12	0	0	0	0	0	1	2	1,741	0	0	835	1,320
1959	NR	6	0	0	0	0	0	0	2	628	0	0	212	425
1960	NR	1	0	0	0	0	0	0	0	93	0	0	47	50
Lifetime		19	0	0	0	0	0	1	4	2,462	0	0	1,094	$1,795

Chuck Shove

Charles Shove
Racing Hometown: Portland, OR

Year	Rank	Starts	Poles	1	2	3	4	5	6–10	Laps	Laps Led	Races Led	Miles	$
1963	148	1	0	0	0	0	0	0	0	74	0	0	200	200
Lifetime		1	0	0	0	0	0	0	0	74	0	0	200	$200

Dick Shuebruk

Richard Shuebruk
Racing Hometown: Boston, MA

Year	Rank	Starts	Poles	1	2	3	4	5	6–10	Laps	Laps Led	Races Led	Miles	$
1950	NR	1	0	0	0	0	0	0	0		0	0		0
Lifetime		1	0	0	0	0	0	0	0		0	0		$0

Buddy Shuman

Lewis Grier Shuman
B: 9/8/1915   D: 11/13/1955   *Died in a hotel fire in Hickory, NC.*
Racing Hometown: Charlotte, NC

Year	Rank	Starts	Poles	1	2	3	4	5	6–10	Laps	Laps Led	Races Led	Miles	$
1951	6	7	0	0	0	1	0	0	6	391	0	0	489	2,830
1952	10	15	0	1	1	0	0	1	4	1,785	2	2	1,413	4,587
1953	28	5	0	0	0	0	0	0	0	342	0	0	481	395
1955	138	2	0	0	0	0	0	0	2	379	0	0	170	350
Lifetime		29	0	1	1	1	0	1	12	2,897	2	2	2,553	$8,162

Larry Shurter

Larry Shurter
B: 9/27/1917
Racing Hometown: West Shokan, NY

Year	Rank	Starts	Poles	1	2	3	4	5	6–10	Laps	Laps Led	Races Led	Miles	$
1950	NR	1	0	0	0	0	0	0	0	37	0	0	154	25
1952	69	4	0	0	0	0	0	0	0	138	0	0	107	125
Lifetime		5	0	0	0	0	0	0	0	175	0	0	261	$150

Leo Sigmon

Leo Sigmon
Racing Hometown: Marion, VA

Year	Rank	Starts	Poles	1	2	3	4	5	6–10	Laps	Laps Led	Races Led	Miles	$
1951	N/A	2	0	0	0	0	0	0	0		0	0		50
Lifetime		2	0	0	0	0	0	0	0		0	0		$50

Jim Sills

James Sills
Racing Hometown: Rio Linda, CA

Year	Rank	Starts	Poles	1	2	3	4	5	6–10	Laps	Laps Led	Races Led	Miles	$
1956	133	1	0	0	0	0	0	0	0	76	0	0	190	150
Lifetime		1	0	0	0	0	0	0	0	76	0	0	190	$150

Don Simkins

Donald Simkins
Racing Hometown: Orcutt, CA

Year	Rank	Starts	Poles	1	2	3	4	5	6–10	Laps	Laps Led	Races Led	Miles	$
1970	NR	1	0	0	0	0	0	0	0	127	0	0	333	965
Lifetime		1	0	0	0	0	0	0	0	127	0	0	333	$965

Year	Rank	Starts	Poles	Finish 1	2	3	4	5	6–10	Laps	Laps Led	Races Led	Miles	$

David Simko

David Simko
B: 11/26/1954
Racing Hometown: Clarkston, MI

Year	Rank	Starts	Poles	1	2	3	4	5	6–10	Laps	Laps Led	Races Led	Miles	$
1982	106	2	0	0	0	0	0	0	0	100	0	0	203	2,700
1983	98T	1	0	0	0	0	0	0	0	154	0	0	234	1,315
1984	NR	1	0	0	0	0	0	0	0	189	0	0	378	1,800
1986	104T	1	0	0	0	0	0	0	0	170	0	0	340	1,625
1987	54	4	0	0	0	0	0	0	0	1,050	0	0	1,611	7,330
1988	NR	1	0	0	0	0	0	0	0	9	0	0	18	2,450
Lifetime		10	0	0	0	0	0	0	0	1,672	0	0	2,784	$17,220

Buck Simmons

Buck Simmons
B: 7/31/1946
Racing Hometown: Baldwin, GA

Year	Rank	Starts	Poles	1	2	3	4	5	6–10	Laps	Laps Led	Races Led	Miles	$
1979	71	2	0	0	0	0	0	0	0	438	0	0	787	3,025
1980	43	6	0	0	0	0	0	0	0	1,333	0	0	1,308	6,365
Lifetime		8	0	0	0	0	0	0	0	1,771	0	0	2,095	$9,390

Brian Simo

Brian Simo
B: 10/1/1959
Racing Hometown: Carlsbad, CA

Year	Rank	Starts	Poles	1	2	3	4	5	6–10	Laps	Laps Led	Races Led	Miles	$
2000	67	1	0	0	0	0	0	0	0	95	0	0	185	37,110
2001	61	2	0	0	0	0	0	0	0	113	0	0	262	72,175
Lifetime		3	0	0	0	0	0	0	0	208	0	0	447	$109,285

Dick Simon

Richard Raymond Simon
B: 9/21/1933
Racing Hometown: San Juan Capristano, CA

Year	Rank	Starts	Poles	1	2	3	4	5	6–10	Laps	Laps Led	Races Led	Miles	$
1973	NR	2	0	0	0	0	0	0	1	264	0	0	689	3,700
1974	NR	1	0	0	0	0	0	0	0	96	0	0	240	3,410
Lifetime		3	0	0	0	0	0	0	1	360	0	0	929	$7,110

Rick Simon

Richard Simon
Racing Hometown: Portland, OR

Year	Rank	Starts	Poles	1	2	3	4	5	6–10	Laps	Laps Led	Races Led	Miles	$
1957	NR	1	0	0	0	0	0	0	0	23	0	0	12	100
Lifetime		1	0	0	0	0	0	0	0	23	0	0	12	$100

Banks Simpson

Banks Simpson
B: 11/4/1916
Racing Hometown: Concord, NC

Year	Rank	Starts	Poles	1	2	3	4	5	6–10	Laps	Laps Led	Races Led	Miles	$
1955	23	7	0	0	0	0	0	0	0	1,103	0	0	1,377	870
Lifetime		7	0	0	0	0	0	0	0	1,103	0	0	1,377	$870

Dub Simpson

Clifford Walker Simpson
B: 1936
Racing Hometown: Charlotte, NC

Year	Rank	Starts	Poles	1	2	3	4	5	6–10	Laps	Laps Led	Races Led	Miles	$
1967	NR	1	0	0	0	0	0	0	0	89	0	0	134	865
1968	57	4	0	0	0	0	0	1	0	721	0	0	589	1,850
1969	36	20	0	0	0	0	0	0	0	2,923	0	0	2,997	12,915
1970	47	6	0	0	0	0	0	0	1	1,155	0	0	1,111	4,510
1971	59	11	0	0	0	0	0	0	0	621	0	0	655	6,300
1972	78	5	0	0	0	0	0	0	0	563	0	0	637	3,525
1974	—	1	0	0	0	0	0	0	0	157	0	0	94	340
Lifetime		48	0	0	0	0	0	1	1	6,229	0	0	6,217	$30,305

Gene Simpson

Gene Simpson
Racing Hometown: Meadville, PA

Year	Rank	Starts	Poles	1	2	3	4	5	6–10	Laps	Laps Led	Races Led	Miles	$
1955	17	22	0	0	0	0	0	1	6	2,667	0	0	1,983	2,158
1956	140T	1	0	0	0	0	0	0	0		0	0		100
Lifetime		23	0	0	0	0	0	1	6	2,667	0	0	1,983	$2,258

Year	Rank	Starts	Poles	Finish						Laps	Laps Led	Races Led	Miles	$
				1	2	3	4	5	6–10	Laps	Led	Led	Miles	$

Jack Simpson

Jack Simpson
B: 6/5/1948
Racing Hometown: Montreal, Que, Canada

Year	Rank	Starts	Poles	1	2	3	4	5	6–10	Laps	Laps Led	Races Led	Miles	$
1973	108	1	0	0	0	0	0	0	0	104	0	0	272	725
1974	118	1	0	0	0	0	0	0	0	105	0	0	275	875
1978	86T	1	0	0	0	0	0	0	0	74	0	0	194	1,105
Lifetime		3	0	0	0	0	0	0	0	283	0	0	741	$2,705

Wallace Simpson

Wallace Simpson
Racing Hometown: Macon, GA

Year	Rank	Starts	Poles	1	2	3	4	5	6–10	Laps	Laps Led	Races Led	Miles	$
1954	NR	1	0	0	0	0	0	0	0	143	0	0	72	25
Lifetime		1	0	0	0	0	0	0	0	143	0	0	72	$25

Wimpy Sipple

Elwin Sipple
Racing Hometown: Fairport, NY

Year	Rank	Starts	Poles	1	2	3	4	5	6–10	Laps	Laps Led	Races Led	Miles	$
1953	140T	1	0	0	0	0	0	0	0		0	0		25
Lifetime		1	0	0	0	0	0	0	0		0	0		$25

David Sisco

David Sisco
B: 6/26/1937
Racing Hometown: Nashville, TN

Year	Rank	Starts	Poles	1	2	3	4	5	6–10	Laps	Laps Led	Races Led	Miles	$
1971	57	4	0	0	0	0	0	0	0	853	0	0	1,019	3,625
1972	33	12	0	0	0	0	0	0	2	2,067	0	0	3,269	13,700
1973	17	23	0	0	0	0	1	1	4	6,552	12	2	7,146	36,205
1974	10	28	0	0	0	1	1	0	7	7,483	43	4	9,012	58,313
1975	13	28	0	0	0	1	0	1	5	7,572	37	4	8,455	62,186
1976	17	28	0	0	0	0	0	0	7	7,111	6	3	8,102	62,622
1977	37	10	0	0	0	0	0	0	0	2,030	0	0	2,186	13,920
Lifetime		133	0	0	0	2	2	2	25	33,668	98	13	39,189	$250,571

Jerry Sisco

Jerry Lee Sisco
B: 8/1/1941
Racing Hometown: Nashville, TN

Year	Rank	Starts	Poles	1	2	3	4	5	6–10	Laps	Laps Led	Races Led	Miles	$
1974	NR	1	0	0	0	0	0	0	0	142	0	0	85	295
1976	60	3	0	0	0	0	0	0	0	781	0	0	797	3,070
Lifetime		4	0	0	0	0	0	0	0	923	0	0	882	$3,365

Marvin Sjolin

Marvin Sjolin
Racing Hometown: Highland, CA

Year	Rank	Starts	Poles	1	2	3	4	5	6–10	Laps	Laps Led	Races Led	Miles	$
1969	NR	1	0	0	0	0	0	0	0	132	0	0	356	925
Lifetime		1	0	0	0	0	0	0	0	132	0	0	356	$925

Buren Skeen

Buren Skeen
B: 1937   D: 9/13/1965   *Died from Injuries suffered @ Darlington.*
Racing Hometown: Denton, NC

Year	Rank	Starts	Poles	1	2	3	4	5	6–10	Laps	Laps Led	Races Led	Miles	$
1965	60	8	0	0	0	0	0	1	2	1,319	0	0	676	2,875
Lifetime		8	0	0	0	0	0	1	2	1,319	0	0	676	$2,875

Dick Skillen

Dr. Richard Skillen
B: 8/5/1945
Racing Hometown: Claremont, NH

Year	Rank	Starts	Poles	1	2	3	4	5	6–10	Laps	Laps Led	Races Led	Miles	$
1974	66	3	0	0	0	0	0	0	0	1,324	0	0	1,560	2,595
1975	49	5	0	0	0	0	0	0	0	1,052	0	0	1,333	4,865
1976	51	5	0	0	0	0	0	0	0	810	0	0	1,716	8,250
1977	113T	1	0	0	0	0	0	0	0	38	0	0	101	1,305
1980	96T	1	0	0	0	0	0	0	0	76	0	0	202	2,785
1983	101T	1	0	0	0	0	0	0	0	1	0	0	3	1,450
1985	75	1	0	0	0	0	0	0	0	167	0	0	444	3,920
Lifetime		17	0	0	0	0	0	0	0	3,468	0	0	5,359	$25,170

Year	Rank	Starts	Poles	1	2	3	4	5	6–10	Laps	Laps Led	Races Led	Miles	$

Eddie Skinner

Edward Skinner
Racing Hometown: Yerrington, NV

Year	Rank	Starts	Poles	1	2	3	4	5	6–10	Laps	Laps Led	Races Led	Miles	$
1953	47	4	0	0	0	0	0	0	1		0	0		200
1954	18	16	0	0	0	0	0	0	1	2,044	0	0	1,659	1,017
1955	7	38	0	0	0	0	0	4	11	5,473	0	0	3,610	4,738
1956	118	6	0	0	0	0	0	0	0	427	0	0	242	200
1957	45	4	0	0	0	0	0	0	0	833	0	0	534	605
1958	58	5	0	0	0	0	0	0	0	750	0	0	440	420
Lifetime		73	0	0	0	0	0	4	13	9,527	0	0	6,485	$7,180

J.R. Skinner

J.R. Skinner
Racing Hometown: Northridge, CA

Year	Rank	Starts	Poles	1	2	3	4	5	6–10	Laps	Laps Led	Races Led	Miles	$
1971	NR	1	0	0	0	0	0	0	0	17	0	0	45	640
Lifetime		1	0	0	0	0	0	0	0	17	0	0	45	$640

Mike Skinner

Michael Curtis Skinner
B: 6/28/1957
Racing Hometown: Ontario, CA

Year	Rank	Starts	Poles	1	2	3	4	5	6–10	Laps	Laps Led	Races Led	Miles	$
1986	61	3	0	0	0	0	0	0	0	807	0	0	635	4,255
1990	96	1	0	0	0	0	0	0	0	230	0	0	234	2,825
1991	64T	2	0	0	0	0	0	0	0	350	0	0	362	7,005
1992	59	2	0	0	0	0	0	0	0	929	0	0	945	11,050
1993	82	1	0	0	0	0	0	0	0	145	0	0	198	5,180
1994	72T	1	0	0	0	0	0	0	0	469	0	0	477	9,550
1996	47	5	0	0	0	0	0	0	0	1,459	10	1	1,742	65,850
1997	30	31	2	0	0	0	0	0	3	8,389	34	8	10,486	900,569
1998	21	30	0	0	0	2	1	1	5	8,425	112	5	10,856	1,518,901
1999	10	34	2	0	0	1	4	0	9	9,732	465	14	12,639	2,499,877
2000	12	34	1	0	1	0	0	0	10	9,640	349	12	12,626	1,985,594
2001	40	23	0	0	0	0	0	0	1	6,718	46	3	8,627	1,921,186
2002	31	36	0	0	0	0	0	0	1	10,074	2	2	13,136	2,094,232
Lifetime		203	5	0	1	3	5	1	29	57,367	1,018	45	72,964	$11,026,074

Otis Skinner

Otis Skinner
Racing Hometown: Riverside, CA

Year	Rank	Starts	Poles	1	2	3	4	5	6–10	Laps	Laps Led	Races Led	Miles	$
1958	57	1	0	0	0	0	0	0	1	178	0	0	468	325
Lifetime		1	0	0	0	0	0	0	1	178	0	0	468	$325

Joe Skovron

Joseph Skovron
Racing Hometown: Greenville, RI

Year	Rank	Starts	Poles	1	2	3	4	5	6–10	Laps	Laps Led	Races Led	Miles	$
1951	N/A	1	0	0	0	0	0	0	0		0	0		0
Lifetime		1	0	0	0	0	0	0	0		0	0		$0

Ann Slaasted

Ann Slaasted
Racing Hometown: Racine, WI

Year	Rank	Starts	Poles	1	2	3	4	5	6–10	Laps	Laps Led	Races Led	Miles	$
1950	NR	1	0	0	0	0	0	0	0		0	0		0
Lifetime		1	0	0	0	0	0	0	0		0	0		$0

Sandy Slack

Everett S. Slack Jr.
Racing Hometown: N. Platte, NE

Year	Rank	Starts	Poles	1	2	3	4	5	6–10	Laps	Laps Led	Races Led	Miles	$
1953	91T	1	0	0	0	0	0	0	1		0	0		50
Lifetime		1	0	0	0	0	0	0	1		0	0		$50

Wayne Slark

Wayne Slark

Year	Rank	Starts	Poles	1	2	3	4	5	6–10	Laps	Laps Led	Races Led	Miles	$
1986	116T	1	0	0	0	0	0	0	0	96	0	0	98	4,055
Lifetime		1	0	0	0	0	0	0	0	96	0	0	98	$4,055

Bob Slawinski

Robert Slawinski
Racing Hometown: Harper Woods, MI

Year	Rank	Starts	Poles	1	2	3	4	5	6–10	Laps	Laps Led	Races Led	Miles	$
1982	98	1	0	0	0	0	0	0	0	56	0	0	149	1,745
Lifetime		1	0	0	0	0	0	0	0	56	0	0	149	$1,745

Year	Rank	Starts	Poles			Finish				Laps	Laps Led	Races Led	Miles	$
				1	2	3	4	5	6–10					

Robert Slensby
Robert C. Slensby
Racing Hometown: Pensacola, FL

Year	Rank	Starts	Poles	1	2	3	4	5	6–10	Laps	Laps Led	Races Led	Miles	$
1954	173	1	0	0	0	0	0	0	0	117	0	0	176	50
1956	195T	1	0	0	0	0	0	0	0	117	0	0	59	100
Lifetime		2	0	0	0	0	0	0	0	234	0	0	234	$150

Bill Small
William Small
Racing Hometown: Newhall, CA

Year	Rank	Starts	Poles	1	2	3	4	5	6–10	Laps	Laps Led	Races Led	Miles	$
1968	102	1	0	0	0	0	0	0	0	16	0	0	43	500
Lifetime		1	0	0	0	0	0	0	0	16	0	0	43	$500

Jason Small
Jason Small
B: 6/7/1979
Racing Hometown: Bakersfield, CA

Year	Rank	Starts	Poles	1	2	3	4	5	6–10	Laps	Laps Led	Races Led	Miles	$
2002	77T	1	0	0	0	0	0	0	0	160	0	0	320	41,130
Lifetime		1	0	0	0	0	0	0	0	160	0	0	320	$41,130

Al Smith
Al Smith
B: 1/30/1929
Racing Hometown: Daytona, OH

Year	Rank	Starts	Poles	1	2	3	4	5	6–10	Laps	Laps Led	Races Led	Miles	$
1952	NR	1	0	0	0	0	0	0	0	125	0	0	63	25
Lifetime		1	0	0	0	0	0	0	0	125	0	0	63	$25

Archie Smith
Archie Smith
Racing Hometown: Denton, NC

Year	Rank	Starts	Poles	1	2	3	4	5	6–10	Laps	Laps Led	Races Led	Miles	$
1949	21	2	0	0	0	0	0	0	2	161	0	0	81	225
Lifetime		2	0	0	0	0	0	0	2	161	0	0	81	$225

Barney Smith
Barney Smith
Racing Hometown: Macon, GA

Year	Rank	Starts	Poles	1	2	3	4	5	6–10	Laps	Laps Led	Races Led	Miles	$
1950	77	1	0	0	0	0	0	0	0	366	0	0	458	275
1951	N/A	2	0	0	0	0	0	0	0		0	0		75
1952	58	3	0	0	0	0	0	0	2	647	0	0	324	285
Lifetime		6	0	0	0	0	0	0	2	1,013	0	0	781	$635

Bill Smith
William Smith
Racing Hometown: Hillside, NJ

Year	Rank	Starts	Poles	1	2	3	4	5	6–10	Laps	Laps Led	Races Led	Miles	$
1954	NR	3	0	0	0	0	0	0	1	828	0	0	456	340
Lifetime		3	0	0	0	0	0	0	1	828	0	0	456	$340

Bill Smith
William Smith
Racing Hometown: Kannapolis, NC

Year	Rank	Starts	Poles	1	2	3	4	5	6–10	Laps	Laps Led	Races Led	Miles	$
1954	NR	3	0	0	0	0	0	0	0	60	0	0	30	200
Lifetime		3	0	0	0	0	0	0	0	60	0	0	30	$200

Billy Smith
William Smith
Racing Hometown: Hampton, VA

Year	Rank	Starts	Poles	1	2	3	4	5	6–10	Laps	Laps Led	Races Led	Miles	$
1979	120	1	0	0	0	0	0	0	0	179	0	0	245	1,575
Lifetime		1	0	0	0	0	0	0	0	179	0	0	245	$1,575

Bob Smith
Robert Smith
Racing Hometown: Rinet, VA

Year	Rank	Starts	Poles	1	2	3	4	5	6–10	Laps	Laps Led	Races Led	Miles	$
1949	NR	2	0	0	0	0	0	0	0		0	0		25
1950	NR	2	0	0	0	0	0	0	0	419	0	0	458	0
Lifetime		4	0	0	0	0	0	0	0	419	0	0	458	$25

Buck Smith
James Smith
Racing Hometown: Martinsville, VA

Year	Rank	Starts	Poles	1	2	3	4	5	6–10	Laps	Laps Led	Races Led	Miles	$
1953	44	5	0	0	0	0	0	0	1		0	0		175
Lifetime		5	0	0	0	0	0	0	1		0	0		$175

Year	Rank	Starts	Poles	Finish 1	2	3	4	5	6–10	Laps	Laps Led	Races Led	Miles	$

Dick Smith

Richard Smith
Racing Hometown: Lakewood, CA

Year	Rank	Starts	Poles	1	2	3	4	5	6–10	Laps	Laps Led	Races Led	Miles	$
1960	NR	2	0	0	0	0	0	0	2	262	0	0	330	850
1961	95	3	0	0	0	1	0	0	0	191	0	0	218	475
Lifetime		5	0	0	0	1	0	0	2	453	0	0	548	$1,325

Frank Smith

Frank Smith
B: 12/16/1901
Racing Hometown: Denton, NC

Year	Rank	Starts	Poles	1	2	3	4	5	6–10	Laps	Laps Led	Races Led	Miles	$
1949	61	2	0	0	0	0	0	0	0		0	0		50
Lifetime		2	0	0	0	0	0	0	0		0	0		$50

Frank Smith

Frank Smith
Racing Hometown: Memphis, TN

Year	Rank	Starts	Poles	1	2	3	4	5	6–10	Laps	Laps Led	Races Led	Miles	$
1954	83	1	0	0	0	0	0	0	0	144	0	0	216	100
Lifetime		1	0	0	0	0	0	0	0	144	0	0	216	$100

Freddy Smith

William Freddy Smith
B: 12/22/1946
Racing Hometown: Kings Mountain, NC

Year	Rank	Starts	Poles	1	2	3	4	5	6–10	Laps	Laps Led	Races Led	Miles	$
1979	NR	2	0	0	0	0	0	0	0	765	0	0	936	2,950
Lifetime		2	0	0	0	0	0	0	0	765	0	0	936	$2,950

Garland Smith

Garland Smith

Year	Rank	Starts	Poles	1	2	3	4	5	6–10	Laps	Laps Led	Races Led	Miles	$
1949	NR	1	0	0	0	0	0	0	0		0	0		25
Lifetime		1	0	0	0	0	0	0	0		0	0		$25

Gordon Smith

Gordon Smith
Racing Hometown: Enfield, NC

Year	Rank	Starts	Poles	1	2	3	4	5	6–10	Laps	Laps Led	Races Led	Miles	$
1955	30	15	0	0	0	0	0	0	2	1,584	0	0	910	975
Lifetime		15	0	0	0	0	0	0	2	1,584	0	0	910	$975

Harold Smith

Harold Wayne Smith
B: 1927
Racing Hometown: Dayton, OH

Year	Rank	Starts	Poles	1	2	3	4	5	6–10	Laps	Laps Led	Races Led	Miles	$
1959	64	2	0	0	0	0	0	0	0	194	0	0	485	160
1960	NR	2	0	0	0	0	0	0	0	105	0	0	263	200
1966	51	3	0	0	0	0	1	0	0	703	0	0	962	4,195
1968	82T	1	0	0	0	0	0	0	0	244	0	0	366	1,850
1970	98	1	0	0	0	0	0	0	0	30	0	0	60	635
Lifetime		9	0	0	0	0	1	0	0	1,276	0	0	2,135	$7,040

Jack Smith

Jack Thomas Smith
B: 5/24/1924   D: 10/17/200
Racing Hometown: Sandy Springs, GA

Year	Rank	Starts	Poles	1	2	3	4	5	6–10	Laps	Laps Led	Races Led	Miles	$
1949	58	1	0	0	0	0	0	0	0		0	0		50
1950	32	3	0	0	1	0	0	0	0	376	55	1	561	775
1951	39	7	0	0	1	1	0	0	0	480	0	0	552	1,275
1952	34	8	1	0	0	0	0	0	2	883	186	1	820	820
1954	64	6	0	0	0	0	0	0	1	381	0	0	423	500
1955	141	2	0	0	0	0	0	0	2	386	0	0	193	400
1956	21	15	0	1	0	0	0	0	5	2,669	234	2	1,916	3,825
1957	5	39	2	4	1	2	3	7	8	6,589	429	9	3,969	14,562
1958	5	39	4	2	5	2	3	3	6	5,750	381	7	3,711	12,634
1959	8	21	3	4	1	2	2	0	3	3,594	222	7	2,735	13,290
1960	14	13	4	3	1	2	0	1	0	2,198	498	8	2,570	24,721
1961	7	25	0	2	2	4	1	1	4	4,695	278	4	4,098	12,124
1962	4	51	7	5	6	5	8	3	8	10,781	894	9	7,110	34,748
1963	24	28	2	0	0	0	1	3	7	5,290	25	2	3,620	8,645
1964	81	4	1	0	1	1	0	0	0	459	20	1	240	1,575
Lifetime		262	24	21	19	19	18	18	46	44,531	3,222	51	32,516	$129,944

Year	Rank	Starts	Poles	Finish						Laps	Laps Led	Races Led	Miles	$
				1	2	3	4	5	6–10					

Jack Smith

Jack Smith
Racing Hometown: New Jersey

Year	Rank	Starts	Poles	1	2	3	4	5	6–10	Laps	Laps Led	Races Led	Miles	$
1953	N/A	1	0	0	0	0	0	0	0		0	0		25
Lifetime		1	0	0	0	0	0	0	0		0	0		$25

Jerry Smith

Jerry Smith
Racing Hometown: Chattanooga, TN

Year	Rank	Starts	Poles	1	2	3	4	5	6–10	Laps	Laps Led	Races Led	Miles	$
1959	NR	2	0	0	0	0	0	0	0	644	0	0	322	215
1962	NR	1	0	0	0	0	0	0	0	109	0	0	36	60
Lifetime		3	0	0	0	0	0	0	0	753	0	0	358	$275

John Smith

John W. Smith
Racing Hometown: Baltimore, MD

Year	Rank	Starts	Poles	1	2	3	4	5	6–10	Laps	Laps Led	Races Led	Miles	$
1954	113T	1	0	0	0	0	0	0	0	174	0	0	87	25
Lifetime		1	0	0	0	0	0	0	0	174	0	0	87	$25

John Smith

John Smith
Racing Hometown: San Jose, CA

Year	Rank	Starts	Poles	1	2	3	4	5	6–10	Laps	Laps Led	Races Led	Miles	$
1957	163	1	0	0	0	0	0	0	0	61	0	0	31	50
Lifetime		1	0	0	0	0	0	0	0	61	0	0	31	$50

Larry Smith

Larry Grayson Smith
B: 6/16/1942   D: 8/12/1973   *Killed in Talladega 500.*
Racing Hometown: Lenoir, NC

Year	Rank	Starts	Poles	1	2	3	4	5	6–10	Laps	Laps Led	Races Led	Miles	$
1971	54	4	0	0	0	0	0	0	1	896	0	0	1,699	5,058
1972	23	23	0	0	0	0	0	0	7	4,320	0	0	5,831	24,215
1973	33	11	0	0	0	0	0	0	1	2,103	0	0	3,576	14,090
Lifetime		38	0	0	0	0	0	0	9	7,319	0	0	11,105	$43,363

Louise Smith

Louise Smith
B: 7/31/1916
Racing Hometown: Greenville, SC

Year	Rank	Starts	Poles	1	2	3	4	5	6–10	Laps	Laps Led	Races Led	Miles	$
1949	67	3	0	0	0	0	0	0	0	175	0	0	175	75
1950	109	5	0	0	0	0	0	0	0	84	0	0	84	25
1952	173	3	0	0	0	0	0	0	0	118	0	0	101	85
Lifetime		11	0	0	0	0	0	0	0	377	0	0	360	$185

Paul Smith

Paul Smith
Racing Hometown: Dayton, OH

Year	Rank	Starts	Poles	1	2	3	4	5	6–10	Laps	Laps Led	Races Led	Miles	$
1950	74	3	0	0	0	0	0	0	1	0	0	0	0	50
Lifetime		3	0	0	0	0	0	0	1	0	0	0	0	$50

Perry Smith

Perry Smith
D: 12/8/1951   *Killed in private plane crash while flying an 80 year-old lady to Chicago for medical treatment.*
Racing Hometown: W. Columbia, SC

Year	Rank	Starts	Poles	1	2	3	4	5	6–10	Laps	Laps Led	Races Led	Miles	$
1951	N/A	1	0	0	0	0	1	0	0		0	0		300
Lifetime		1	0	0	0	0	1	0	0		0	0		$300

R.K. Smith

R.K. Smith

Year	Rank	Starts	Poles	1	2	3	4	5	6–10	Laps	Laps Led	Races Led	Miles	$
1991	92	1	0	0	0	0	0	0	0	2	0	0	5	3,457
1992	83	1	0	0	0	0	0	0	0	70	0	0	176	4,880
Lifetime		2	0	0	0	0	0	0	0	72	0	0	181	$8,337

Ralph Smith

Ralph Smith
Racing Hometown: Roswell, GA

Year	Rank	Starts	Poles	1	2	3	4	5	6–10	Laps	Laps Led	Races Led	Miles	$
1962	96	2	0	0	0	0	0	0	0	684	0	0	342	300
Lifetime		2	0	0	0	0	0	0	0	684	0	0	342	$300

Year	Rank	Starts	Poles	1	2	3	4	5	6–10	Laps	Laps Led	Races Led	Miles	$

Rollin Smith

Rollin Smith
Racing Hometown: N.Manchester, IN

Year	Rank	Starts	Poles	1	2	3	4	5	6–10	Laps	Laps Led	Races Led	Miles	$
1950	NR	1	0	0	0	0	0	0	0	208	0	0	260	0
1952	36	1	0	0	0	0	0	0	0	385	0	0	481	350
Lifetime		2	0	0	0	0	0	0	0	593	0	0	741	$350

Roy Smith

Wilroy Clarence Smith
B: 8/6/1944
Racing Hometown: Victoria, B.C., Canada

Year	Rank	Starts	Poles	1	2	3	4	5	6–10	Laps	Laps Led	Races Led	Miles	$
1975	NR	1	0	0	0	0	0	0	0	62	0	0	155	900
1976	69	3	0	0	0	0	0	0	0	225	0	0	569	4,285
1977	62	3	0	0	0	0	0	0	0	205	0	0	532	5,365
1978	78	1	0	0	0	0	0	0	1	115	0	0	301	2,300
1979	100	1	0	0	0	0	0	0	0	193	0	0	483	2,690
1980	60	3	0	0	0	0	0	0	0	223	3	1	576	3,775
1981	56	3	0	0	0	0	0	0	1	178	0	0	466	8,695
1982	47	3	0	0	0	0	0	0	2	394	0	0	1,009	26,770
1983	95T	1	0	0	0	0	0	0	0	36	0	0	94	2,025
1984	NR	1	0	0	0	0	0	0	0	70	0	0	183	2,475
1987	83	2	0	0	0	0	0	0	0	29	0	0	76	2,325
1988	58	2	0	0	0	0	0	0	0	303	1	1	441	4,550
1989	80	2	0	0	0	0	0	0	0	86	0	0	156	7,820
Lifetime		26	0	0	0	0	0	0	4	2,119	4	2	5,041	$73,975

Ruel Smith

Ruel Smith
Racing Hometown: Mobile, AL

Year	Rank	Starts	Poles	1	2	3	4	5	6–10	Laps	Laps Led	Races Led	Miles	$
1950	NR	2	0	0	0	0	0	0	0	336	0	0	385	0
1951	N/A	1	0	0	0	0	0	0	0		0	0		25
Lifetime		3	0	0	0	0	0	0	0	336	0	0	385	$25

Sam Smith

Sam Smith
Racing Hometown: Greensboro, NC

Year	Rank	Starts	Poles	1	2	3	4	5	6–10	Laps	Laps Led	Races Led	Miles	$
1954	126T	1	0	0	0	0	0	0	0	137	0	0	69	25
Lifetime		1	0	0	0	0	0	0	0	137	0	0	69	$25

Samuel Smith

Samuel Hollis Smith (Sam)
B: 1936   D: 5/7/1982
Racing Hometown: Union, SC

Year	Rank	Starts	Poles	1	2	3	4	5	6–10	Laps	Laps Led	Races Led	Miles	$
1965	102	1	0	0	0	0	0	0	0	108	0	0	54	110
Lifetime		1	0	0	0	0	0	0	0	108	0	0	54	$110

Slick Smith

Ebenezer Smith
Deceased.
Racing Hometown: Atlanta, GA

Year	Rank	Starts	Poles	1	2	3	4	5	6–10	Laps	Laps Led	Races Led	Miles	$
1949	31	4	0	0	0	0	0	0	1	277	0	0	139	275
1950	103	5	0	0	0	0	0	0	0	375	0	0	457	25
1951	90	4	0	0	0	0	0	0	0	529	0	0	593	315
1952	32	5	0	0	0	0	0	0	3	613	0	0	516	725
1953	12	23	1	0	0	0	0	0	10	592	4	1	755	2,302
1954	27	6	0	0	0	0	1	0	1	698	0	0	688	950
1955	193	3	0	0	0	0	0	0	2	424	0	0	434	525
Lifetime		50	1	0	0	0	1	0	17	3,508	4	1	3,581	$5,117

Snuffy Smith

Snuffy Smith
Racing Hometown: Hickory, NC

Year	Rank	Starts	Poles	1	2	3	4	5	6–10	Laps	Laps Led	Races Led	Miles	$
1953	122T	1	0	0	0	0	0	0	0		0	0		25
Lifetime		1	0	0	0	0	0	0	0		0	0		$25

Stanley Smith

Stanley Smith
B: 9/29/1949
Racing Hometown: Chelsea, AL

Year	Rank	Starts	Poles	1	2	3	4	5	6–10	Laps	Laps Led	Races Led	Miles	$
1990	98T	1	0	0	0	0	0	0	0	54	0	0	144	4,285

Year	Rank	Starts	Poles	Finish 1	2	3	4	5	6–10	Laps	Laps Led	Races Led	Miles	$

Stanley Smith *continued*

Year	Rank	Starts	Poles	1	2	3	4	5	6–10	Laps	Laps Led	Races Led	Miles	$
1991	36	12	0	0	0	0	0	0	0	1,932	12	1	3,201	56,915
1992	35	14	0	0	0	0	0	0	0	2,685	0	0	4,009	89,650
1993	89T	1	0	0	0	0	0	0	0	68	0	0	181	7,690
Lifetime		28	0	0	0	0	0	0	0	4,739	12	1	7,534	$158,540

Wayne Smith

Howard Wayne Smith
B: 4/12/1939
Racing Hometown: Advance, NC

Year	Rank	Starts	Poles	1	2	3	4	5	6–10	Laps	Laps Led	Races Led	Miles	$
1965	30	25	0	0	0	0	0	0	2	3,744	0	0	2,475	6,790
1966	33	23	0	0	0	0	0	0	1	4,108	0	0	3,655	9,835
1967	28	27	0	0	0	0	0	0	2	4,364	0	0	3,629	10,025
1968	33	18	0	0	0	0	0	0	1	2,456	0	0	1,985	7,235
1969	39	16	0	0	0	0	0	0	2	2,692	0	0	2,951	10,610
1970	50	8	0	0	0	0	0	0	0	593	0	0	813	4,505
1971	67	2	0	0	0	0	0	0	0	67	0	0	39	660
1972	81	3	0	0	0	0	0	0	1	270	0	0	624	3,445
Lifetime		122	0	0	0	0	0	0	9	18,294	0	0	16,172	$53,105

Tom Sneva

Thomas E. Sneva
B: 6/1/1948
Racing Hometown: Spokane, WA

Year	Rank	Starts	Poles	1	2	3	4	5	6–10	Laps	Laps Led	Races Led	Miles	$
1977	NR	1	0	0	0	0	0	0	0	194	0	0	291	1,150
1982	53	3	0	0	0	0	0	0	0	520	0	0	840	15,585
1983	75	2	0	0	0	0	0	0	1	274	0	0	648	29,740
1985	NR	1	0	0	0	0	0	0	0	138	0	0	210	1,455
1987	88T	1	0	0	0	0	0	0	0	182	0	0	455	11,135
Lifetime		8	0	0	0	0	0	0	1	1,308	0	0	2,444	$59,065

Les Snow

Leslie Snow Jr.
B: 9/20/1925
Racing Hometown: Bloomington, IL

Year	Rank	Starts	Poles	1	2	3	4	5	6–10	Laps	Laps Led	Races Led	Miles	$
1951	77	2	0	0	0	0	0	0	1	222	0	0	222	375
1969	NR	1	0	0	0	0	0	0	0	2	0	0	5	925
Lifetime		3	0	0	0	0	0	0	1	224	0	0	227	$1,300

Bill Snowden

William Snowden
B: 5/11/1910   D: 1/1959
Racing Hometown: St.Augustine, FL

Year	Rank	Starts	Poles	1	2	3	4	5	6–10	Laps	Laps Led	Races Led	Miles	$
1949	11	4	0	0	0	0	0	1	2	182	0	0	91	660
1950	40	4	0	0	0	0	0	1	1	532	0	0	568	325
1951	9	12	0	0	0	0	2	1	6	383	0	0	479	2,640
1952	62	4	0	0	0	0	0	0	1	384	0	0	237	290
Lifetime		24	0	0	0	0	2	3	10	1,481	0	0	1,375	$3,915

John Soares

John Soares
Racing Hometown: Oakland, CA

Year	Rank	Starts	Poles	1	2	3	4	5	6–10	Laps	Laps Led	Races Led	Miles	$
1951	N/A	3	0	0	0	0	0	0	1		1	1		125
1954	16	9	0	1	0	1	0	0	2	2,196	211	1	1,498	3,262
1955	209	1	0	0	0	0	0	0	0	86	0	0	86	25
Lifetime		13	0	1	0	1	0	0	3	2,282	212	2	1,584	$3,412

John Soares Jr.

John Soares Jr.
B: 5/18/1942
Racing Hometown: Hayward, CA

Year	Rank	Starts	Poles	1	2	3	4	5	6–10	Laps	Laps Led	Races Led	Miles	$
1970	NR	1	0	0	0	0	1	0	0	141	0	0	369	3,415
1971	NR	4	0	0	0	0	0	0	1	764	0	0	1,280	4,855
1972	70	3	0	0	0	0	0	0	0	337	0	0	861	4,315
1973	99	2	0	0	0	0	0	0	0	122	0	0	320	1,980
1975	105T	1	0	0	0	0	0	0	0	18	0	0	47	670
1985	62	2	0	0	0	0	0	0	0	192	0	0	503	3,100
Lifetime		13	0	0	0	0	1	0	1	1,574	0	0	3,379	$18,335

Year	Rank	Starts	Poles	Finish						Laps	Laps Led	Races Led	Miles	$
				1	2	3	4	5	6–10					

Jay Sommers

Jay Sommers
Racing Hometown: Mt. Clemens, MI

Year	Rank	Starts	Poles	1	2	3	4	5	6–10	Laps	Laps Led	Races Led	Miles	$
1988	83T	1	0	0	0	0	0	0	0	280	0	0	280	1,510
Lifetime		1	0	0	0	0	0	0	0	280	0	0	280	$1,510

Joe Sommers

Joseph Sommers
Racing Hometown: Newark, NJ

Year	Rank	Starts	Poles	1	2	3	4	5	6–10	Laps	Laps Led	Races Led	Miles	$
1951	N/A	1	0	0	0	0	0	0	1		0	0		75
Lifetime		1	0	0	0	0	0	0	1		0	0		$75

Sam Sommers

Cecil Franklin Sommers
B: 9/17/1939
Racing Hometown: Savannah, GA

Year	Rank	Starts	Poles	1	2	3	4	5	6–10	Laps	Laps Led	Races Led	Miles	$
1976	52	5	0	0	0	0	0	0	1	1,000	0	0	1,534	8,930
1977	21	23	1	0	0	0	1	1	6	5,764	28	3	7,081	54,625
1978	81	2	0	0	0	0	0	0	0	512	0	0	748	3,190
Lifetime		30	1	0	0	0	1	1	7	7,276	28	3	9,363	$66,745

Dick Soper

Richard Soper

Year	Rank	Starts	Poles	1	2	3	4	5	6–10	Laps	Laps Led	Races Led	Miles	$
1950	NR	1	0	0	0	0	0	0	0	282	0	0	353	0
Lifetime		1	0	0	0	0	0	0	0	282	0	0	353	$0

Jack Soper

Jack George Soper
Racing Hometown: Charlotte, NC

Year	Rank	Starts	Poles	1	2	3	4	5	6–10	Laps	Laps Led	Races Led	Miles	$
1966	142	1	0	0	0	0	0	0	0	25	0	0	5	0
Lifetime		1	0	0	0	0	0	0	0	25	0	0	5	$0

David Sosebee

David Sosebee
B: 12/8/1955
Racing Hometown: Dawsonville, GA

Year	Rank	Starts	Poles	1	2	3	4	5	6–10	Laps	Laps Led	Races Led	Miles	$
1979	78	3	0	0	0	0	0	0	0	547	0	0	892	2,910
1986	90	2	0	0	0	0	0	0	0	267	0	0	404	2,310
1987	61	3	0	0	0	0	0	0	0	570	0	0	1,013	25,030
1988	75	2	0	0	0	0	0	0	0	289	0	0	499	4,960
Lifetime		10	0	0	0	0	0	0	0	1,673	0	0	2,807	$35,210

Gober Sosebee

Gober Sosebee
B: 10/15/1915
Racing Hometown: Atlanta, GA

Year	Rank	Starts	Poles	1	2	3	4	5	6–10	Laps	Laps Led	Races Led	Miles	$
1949	15	3	1	0	1	0	0	0	1	170	34	1	170	1,305
1950	NR	2	0	0	0	0	0	0	0	385	4	1	543	315
1951	17	10	1	0	3	0	0	1	1	717	7	1	711	2,710
1952	90	9	0	1	0	0	0	3	1	780	62	3	703	2,125
1953	14	17	0	0	1	1	0	0	7	943	73	1	928	2,722
1954	15	18	1	1	0	1	1	1	3	1,970	170	2	1,376	3,150
1955	64	6	0	0	0	0	2	0	0	344	0	0	218	775
1958	112	5	1	0	0	0	0	0	3	692	0	0	476	695
1959	NR	1	0	0	0	0	0	0	0	44	0	0	110	100
Lifetime		71	4	2	5	2	3	5	16	6,045	350	9	5,235	$13,897

Jim Southard

James Southard
B: 1934
Racing Hometown: Marietta, GA

Year	Rank	Starts	Poles	1	2	3	4	5	6–10	Laps	Laps Led	Races Led	Miles	$
1984	51	4	0	0	0	0	0	0	0	1,113	0	0	1,653	6,965
1985	NR	1	0	0	0	0	0	0	0	431	0	0	438	1,970
Lifetime		5	0	0	0	0	0	0	0	1,544	0	0	2,091	$8,935

Leland Sowell

Leland Sowell
Racing Hometown: Memphis, TN

Year	Rank	Starts	Poles	1	2	3	4	5	6–10	Laps	Laps Led	Races Led	Miles	$
1954	—	1	0	0	0	0	0	0	0	84	0	0	126	50

Year	Rank	Starts	Poles	Finish 1	2	3	4	5	6–10	Laps	Laps Led	Races Led	Miles	$

Leland Sowell *continued*

Year	Rank	Starts	Poles	1	2	3	4	5	6–10	Laps	Laps Led	Races Led	Miles	$
1955	—	1	0	0	0	0	0	0	0	176	0	0	264	125
Lifetime		2	0	0	0	0	0	0	0	260	0	0	390	$175

Nick Spano

Nicholas Spano
Racing Hometown: Montclair, NJ

Year	Rank	Starts	Poles	1	2	3	4	5	6–10	Laps	Laps Led	Races Led	Miles	$
1954	156T	1	0	0	0	0	0	0	0	147	0	0	74	10
Lifetime		1	0	0	0	0	0	0	0	147	0	0	74	$10

Tony Spanos

Anthony Spanos
B: 5/19/1954

Year	Rank	Starts	Poles	1	2	3	4	5	6–10	Laps	Laps Led	Races Led	Miles	$
1987	NR	1	0	0	0	0	0	0	0	386	0	0	203	1,555
Lifetime		1	0	0	0	0	0	0	0	386	0	0	203	$1,555

Huck Spaulding

Huck Spaulding
Racing Hometown: Coxsackie, NY

Year	Rank	Starts	Poles	1	2	3	4	5	6–10	Laps	Laps Led	Races Led	Miles	$
1957	36	8	0	0	0	0	0	0	3	1,006	0	0	659	1,130
1958	153	1	0	0	0	0	0	0	0		0	0		50
Lifetime		9	0	0	0	0	0	0	3	1,006	0	0	659	$1,180

Jack Spearman

Jack Spearman

Year	Rank	Starts	Poles	1	2	3	4	5	6–10	Laps	Laps Led	Races Led	Miles	$
1954	NR	1	0	0	0	0	0	0	0	39	0	0	78	0
Lifetime		1	0	0	0	0	0	0	0	39	0	0	78	$0

Lou Spears

Louis Spears
Racing Hometown: Ardmore, PA

Year	Rank	Starts	Poles	1	2	3	4	5	6–10	Laps	Laps Led	Races Led	Miles	$
1955	27	3	0	0	0	0	0	0	1	708	0	0	748	810
1956	208	3	0	0	0	0	0	0	0	406	0	0	495	175
1957	NR	3	0	0	0	0	0	0	0	351	0	0	172	235
Lifetime		9	0	0	0	0	0	0	1	1,465	0	0	1,416	$1,220

Lake Speed

Lake Chambers Speed
B: 1/17/1948
Racing Hometown: Jackson, MS

Year	Rank	Starts	Poles	1	2	3	4	5	6–10	Laps	Laps Led	Races Led	Miles	$
1980	22	19	0	0	0	0	0	0	5	4,019	2	1	6,271	69,670
1981	18	27	0	0	0	0	0	0	6	6,757	14	2	7,558	94,069
1982	20	30	0	0	0	0	0	0	5	5,830	0	0	6,856	118,457
1983	27	18	0	0	0	1	1	0	3	4,933	22	2	6,929	78,220
1984	26	19	0	0	0	1	0	1	5	4,814	122	5	6,752	98,320
1985	10	28	0	0	1	0	1	0	12	8,572	8	4	10,087	300,326
1986	40	5	0	0	0	0	0	0	2	1,779	10	2	2,271	82,800
1987	31	13	0	0	0	1	0	0	4	2,591	1	1	4,433	110,810
1988	17	29	0	1	1	0	1	1	3	7,005	368	6	8,542	260,500
1989	27	24	0	0	0	0	0	1	4	7,028	11	4	8,245	185,227
1990	42	6	0	0	0	0	0	0	0	835	3	1	1,753	75,537
1991	32	20	0	0	0	0	0	0	0	4,513	0	0	5,053	149,300
1992	38	9	0	0	0	0	0	0	0	2,248	0	0	3,200	49,545
1993	34	21	0	0	0	0	0	0	1	5,852	2	1	7,218	319,800
1994	11	31	0	0	0	1	1	2	5	9,111	39	5	11,291	845,963
1995	23	31	0	0	0	0	0	0	2	9,073	17	1	11,197	529,435
1996	23	31	0	0	0	0	0	0	2	8,493	10	3	10,028	817,175
1997	35	25	0	0	0	0	0	0	0	7,494	3	1	9,424	715,074
1998	43	16	0	0	0	0	0	0	0	4,790	0	0	6,357	552,521
Lifetime		402	0	1	2	4	4	5	59	105,737	632	39	133,465	$5,452,749

Sam Speers

Samuel Speers

Year	Rank	Starts	Poles	1	2	3	4	5	6–10	Laps	Laps Led	Races Led	Miles	$
1956	176T	1	0	0	0	0	0	0	1	119	0	0	74	125
Lifetime		1	0	0	0	0	0	0	1	119	0	0	74	$125

Year	Rank	Starts	Poles	1	2	3	4	5	6–10	Laps	Laps Led	Races Led	Miles	$

Cy Spencer

Cyrus Spencer

Year	Rank	Starts	Poles	1	2	3	4	5	6–10	Laps	Laps Led	Races Led	Miles	$
1956	225T	1	0	0	0	0	0	0	0	34	0	0	17	50
Lifetime		1	0	0	0	0	0	0	0	34	0	0	17	$50

Ed Spencer

Edward Spencer
Racing Hometown: Nanticolte, PA

Year	Rank	Starts	Poles	1	2	3	4	5	6–10	Laps	Laps Led	Races Led	Miles	$
1953	153	1	0	0	0	0	0	0	0		0	0		25
Lifetime		1	0	0	0	0	0	0	0		0	0		$25

G.C. Spencer

Grover Clifton Spencer
B: 7/9/1925
Racing Hometown: Jonesboro, TN

Year	Rank	Starts	Poles	1	2	3	4	5	6–10	Laps	Laps Led	Races Led	Miles	$
1958	36	1	0	0	0	0	0	0	0	343	0	0	472	315
1959	13	28	0	0	0	0	1	0	4	4,552	0	0	2,553	3,701
1960	33	26	0	0	0	0	1	1	4	4,907	0	0	3,822	3,910
1961	20	31	0	0	0	0	3	0	15	6,218	0	0	3,823	5,205
1962	24	42	0	0	0	0	2	4	7	7,300	0	0	4,791	7,995
1963	18	31	0	0	1	1	1	1	8	4,888	30	3	4,004	13,514
1964	26	20	0	0	0	1	0	3	2	3,601	0	0	2,803	9,490
1965	4	47	1	0	3	4	3	4	11	9,092	90	5	6,506	29,775
1966	19	20	0	0	3	0	0	3	3	4,711	2	1	4,277	26,722
1967	21	29	0	0	0	3	0	2	5	4,947	0	0	4,156	20,225
1968	23	26	0	0	0	0	1	0	5	4,380	0	0	3,276	10,110
1969	26	26	0	0	0	0	2	2	4	4,823	0	0	3,980	21,660
1970	27	20	0	0	0	0	2	1	6	4,618	0	0	4,091	17,915
1971	34	17	0	0	0	0	0	2	4	3,325	12	1	2,873	11,470
1972	43	10	0	0	0	0	0	0	1	1,492	0	0	1,611	8,040
1973	37	10	0	0	0	0	0	0	1	1,459	0	0	2,043	12,013
1974	38	10	0	0	0	0	0	0	1	1,205	3	1	1,721	12,985
1975	40	9	0	0	0	0	0	0	1	906	11	1	1,663	14,945
1976	59	4	0	0	0	0	0	0	0	501	0	0	941	4,965
1977	39	8	0	0	0	0	0	0	1	1,817	0	0	2,908	15,755
Lifetime		415	1	0	7	9	16	23	83	75,085	148	12	62,314	$250,710

Jimmy Spencer

James Peter Spencer
B: 2/15/1957
Racing Hometown: Berwick, PA

Year	Rank	Starts	Poles	1	2	3	4	5	6–10	Laps	Laps Led	Races Led	Miles	$
1989	34	17	0	0	0	0	0	0	3	3,544	0	0	4,560	121,065
1990	24	26	0	0	0	0	0	0	2	7,576	10	5	9,029	219,775
1991	25	29	0	0	0	1	0	0	5	7,627	330	6	8,583	283,620
1992	33	12	0	0	0	0	2	1	0	3,803	1	1	4,176	183,585
1993	12	30	0	0	1	2	2	0	5	8,867	64	4	10,837	686,026
1994	29	29	1	2	0	0	1	0	1	6,904	47	6	8,733	479,235
1995	26	29	0	0	0	0	0	0	4	8,664	4	2	10,475	504,560
1996	15	31	0	0	0	0	1	1	7	9,339	156	7	11,239	1,090,876
1997	20	32	0	0	0	0	0	1	3	8,665	70	8	11,233	1,073,779
1998	14	31	0	0	1	0	2	0	5	8,934	117	11	11,827	1,741,012
1999	20	34	0	0	1	0	0	1	2	9,579	43	5	12,333	1,752,299
2000	22	34	0	0	0	0	0	2	3	9,363	46	8	12,308	1,858,762
2001	16	36	2	0	0	0	2	1	5	10,259	214	11	13,330	2,669,638
2002	27	34	0	0	1	0	1	0	4	9,684	174	3	12,576	2,136,792
Lifetime		404	3	2	4	3	11	7	49	112,808	1,276	77	141,237	$14,801,024

Junior Spencer

Henry Spencer
B: 8/27/1937
Racing Hometown: Hamlin, WV

Year	Rank	Starts	Poles	1	2	3	4	5	6–10	Laps	Laps Led	Races Led	Miles	$
1964	83	3	0	0	0	0	0	0	0	1,172	0	0	558	670
1965	28	21	0	0	0	0	0	1	6	4,062	0	0	3,127	9,345
1971	NR	1	0	0	0	0	0	0	0	112	0	0	51	310
Lifetime		25	0	0	0	0	0	1	6	5,346	0	0	3,736	$10,325

Steve Spencer

Steve Spencer
B: 12/5/1945
Racing Hometown: Old Hickory, TN

Year	Rank	Starts	Poles	1	2	3	4	5	6–10	Laps	Laps Led	Races Led	Miles	$
1979	59	2	0	0	0	0	0	0	0	556	0	0	331	2,270

Year	Rank	Starts	Poles	1	2	3	4	5	6–10	Laps	Laps Led	Races Led	Miles	$

Steve Spencer *continued*

1980	NR	3	0	0	0	0	0	0	0	599	0	0	344	2,050
1981	78	3	0	0	0	0	0	0	0	1,038	0	0	747	5,805
Lifetime		8	0	0	0	0	0	0	0	2,193	0	0	1,422	$10,125

Craig Spetman

Craig Spetman
B: 11/10/1951
Racing Hometown: Council Bluffs, IA

| 1985 | 94 | 1 | 0 | 0 | 0 | 0 | 0 | 0 | 0 | 188 | 0 | 0 | 191 | 1,150 |
| Lifetime | | 1 | 0 | 0 | 0 | 0 | 0 | 0 | 0 | 188 | 0 | 0 | 191 | $1,150 |

Ken Spikes

Kenneth Spikes
Racing Hometown: Cordele, GA

1964	40	6	0	0	0	0	0	0	1	1,018	0	0	1,570	3,100
1967	72	9	0	0	0	0	0	0	0	621	0	0	817	4,245
1970	104T	1	0	0	0	0	0	0	0	116	0	0	309	890
Lifetime		16	0	0	0	0	0	0	1	1,755	0	0	2,695	$8,235

Richard Spittle

Richard Spittle
Racing Hometown: Mineral Springs, NC

| 1958 | 142 | 1 | 0 | 0 | 0 | 0 | 0 | 0 | 0 | 125 | 0 | 0 | 63 | 50 |
| Lifetime | | 1 | 0 | 0 | 0 | 0 | 0 | 0 | 0 | 125 | 0 | 0 | 63 | $50 |

J.C. Spradley

J.C. Spradley
Racing Hometown: Gloverville, SC

| 1969 | 72 | 1 | 0 | 0 | 0 | 0 | 0 | 0 | 0 | 203 | 0 | 0 | 279 | 1,075 |
| Lifetime | | 1 | 0 | 0 | 0 | 0 | 0 | 0 | 0 | 203 | 0 | 0 | 279 | $1,075 |

Dean Sprague

Dean Sprague
Racing Hometown: Belmont, NY

| 1951 | N/A | 1 | 0 | 0 | 0 | 0 | 0 | 0 | 0 | 46 | 0 | 0 | 35 | 25 |
| Lifetime | | 1 | 0 | 0 | 0 | 0 | 0 | 0 | 0 | 46 | 0 | 0 | 35 | $25 |

Jack Sprague

Jack Sprague
B: 8/8/1964
Racing Hometown: Spring Lake, MI

1996	54	2	0	0	0	0	0	0	0	333	2	1	345	22,720
1997	68	1	0	0	0	0	0	0	0	256	0	0	136	18,650
2002	57	3	0	0	0	0	0	0	0	747		0	937	132,000
Lifetime		6	0	0	0	0	0	0	0	1,336	2	1	1,418	$173,370

Robert Sprague

Robert Sprague
Racing Hometown: New York

| 1950 | 84T | 1 | 0 | 0 | 0 | 0 | 0 | 0 | 0 | | 0 | 0 | | 50 |
| Lifetime | | 1 | 0 | 0 | 0 | 0 | 0 | 0 | 0 | | 0 | 0 | | $50 |

Robert Sprague

Robert Sprague
B: 12/26/1959
Racing Hometown: North Bend, OR

| 1991 | 86 | 1 | 0 | 0 | 0 | 0 | 0 | 0 | 0 | 54 | 1 | 1 | 136 | 3,500 |
| Lifetime | | 1 | 0 | 0 | 0 | 0 | 0 | 0 | 0 | 54 | 1 | 1 | 136 | $3,500 |

Walt Sprague

Walter D. Sprague
B: 1936 D: 8/24/1951   Killed @ Monroe County Fairgrounds in Rochester, NY.
Racing Hometown: Wellsville, NY

| 1951 | N/A | 7 | 0 | 0 | 0 | 0 | 0 | 0 | 2 | 113 | 0 | 0 | 113 | 385 |
| Lifetime | | 7 | 0 | 0 | 0 | 0 | 0 | 0 | 2 | 113 | 0 | 0 | 113 | $385 |

Ray Springer

Raymond Springer
Racing Hometown: Freeport, IL

Year	Rank	Starts	Poles	1	2	3	4	5	6–10	Laps	Laps Led	Races Led	Miles	$
1953	97T	1	0	0	0	0	0	0	0		0	0		25
Lifetime		1	0	0	0	0	0	0	0		0	0		$25

Don Sprouse

Donald W. Sprouse
B: 4/22/1941
Racing Hometown: Greenville, SC

Year	Rank	Starts	Poles	1	2	3	4	5	6–10	Laps	Laps Led	Races Led	Miles	$
1980	55	4	0	0	0	0	0	0	0	1,312	0	0	745	2,880
1981	63	2	0	0	0	0	0	0	0	570	0	0	663	6,850
Lifetime		6	0	0	0	0	0	0	0	1,882	0	0	1,408	$9,730

Dick Stacey

Richard Stacey
Racing Hometown: Detroit, MI

Year	Rank	Starts	Poles	1	2	3	4	5	6–10	Laps	Laps Led	Races Led	Miles	$
1952	118	1	0	0	0	0	0	0	0	175	0	0	175	25
Lifetime		1	0	0	0	0	0	0	0	175	0	0	175	$25

Bill Stacy

William Stacy
Racing Hometown: Garden Grove, CA

Year	Rank	Starts	Poles	1	2	3	4	5	6–10	Laps	Laps Led	Races Led	Miles	$
1956	286	1	0	0	0	0	0	0	0	70	0	0	175	50
Lifetime		1	0	0	0	0	0	0	0	70	0	0	175	$50

Nelson Stacy

William Nelson Stacy
B: 12/28/1921   D: 5/14/1986
Racing Hometown: Cincinnati, OH

Year	Rank	Starts	Poles	1	2	3	4	5	6–10	Laps	Laps Led	Races Led	Miles	$
1952	NR	1	0	0	0	0	0	0	0	277	0	0	139	50
1961	16	15	0	1	0	1	2	0	4	3,024	144	4	3,281	5,610
1962	21	15	0	3	1	0	0	1	2	3,484	371	4	3,171	43,080
1963	14	12	0	0	0	1	2	1	5	2,816	56	1	3,179	18,266
1964	NR	1	0	0	0	0	0	0	0	5	0	0	7	500
1965	94	1	0	0	0	0	0	0	0	83	0	0	208	480
Lifetime		45	0	4	1	2	4	2	11	9,689	571	9	9,984	$67,986

Mark Stahl

Mark Stahl
B: 8/12/1951
Racing Hometown: San Diego, CA

Year	Rank	Starts	Poles	1	2	3	4	5	6–10	Laps	Laps Led	Races Led	Miles	$
1981	84	1	0	0	0	0	0	0	0	109	0	0	286	1,080
1982	72	2	0	0	0	0	0	0	0	109	0	0	286	4,240
1983	66	2	0	0	0	0	0	0	0	622	0	0	363	1,970
1984	52	3	0	0	0	0	0	0	0	842	0	0	892	4,035
1985	77	1	0	0	0	0	0	0	0	375	0	0	563	3,800
1986	62	3	0	0	0	0	0	0	0	719	0	0	889	5,890
1987	38	9	0	0	0	0	0	0	0	1,635	0	0	2,643	32,850
1988	83T	1	0	0	0	0	0	0	0	233	0	0	237	1,615
1989	81T	1	0	0	0	0	0	0	0	176	0	0	468	3,785
1990	44	5	0	0	0	0	0	0	0	1,268	0	0	1,890	18,470
1991	67	2	0	0	0	0	0	0	0	30	0	0	35	7,105
Lifetime		30	0	0	0	0	0	0	0	6,118	0	0	8,552	$84,840

Gwyn Staley

Gwyn Edward Staley
B: 7/6/1927   D: 3/23/1958   *Killed in NASCAR Convertible race @ Richmond.*
Racing Hometown: Burlington, NC

Year	Rank	Starts	Poles	1	2	3	4	5	6–10	Laps	Laps Led	Races Led	Miles	$
1951	N/A	2	0	0	0	0	0	0	0	303	0	0	379	75
1952	166	1	0	0	0	0	0	0	0	74	0	0	93	0
1953	144T	1	0	0	0	0	0	0	0		0	0		25
1954	29	2	0	0	0	0	0	0	1	357	0	0	480	670
1955	10	24	1	0	1	2	2	2	7	3,196	33	1	2,230	6,547
1956	14	22	0	0	0	0	2	3	8	3,506	0	0	2,404	5,159
1957	151	13	2	3	1	0	2	1	2	2,449	196	4	1,516	9,080
1958	55	4	0	0	1	0	2	1	0	336	0	0	255	1,730
Lifetime		69	3	3	3	2	8	7	18	10,221	229	5	7,355	$23,286

Year	Rank	Starts	Poles	Finish						Laps	Laps Led	Races Led	Miles	$
				1	2	3	4	5	6–10					

Willard Stamey

Willard Stamey
Racing Hometown: Greenville, SC

Year	Rank	Starts	Poles	1	2	3	4	5	6–10	Laps	Laps Led	Races Led	Miles	$
1955	NR	1	0	0	0	0	0	0	0	187	0	0	94	60
Lifetime		1	0	0	0	0	0	0	0	187	0	0	94	$60

Bill Stammer

William Stammer
Racing Hometown: Pasadena, CA

Year	Rank	Starts	Poles	1	2	3	4	5	6–10	Laps	Laps Led	Races Led	Miles	$
1951	N/A	4	0	0	0	0	0	0	2		0	0		200
1954	93	2	0	0	0	0	0	0	0	631	0	0	316	75
1955	63	2	0	0	0	0	0	0	2	338	0	0	338	400
1956	200	2	0	0	0	0	0	0	0	131	0	0	241	140
Lifetime		10	0	0	0	0	0	0	4	1,100	0	0	894	$815

Bob Stanclift

Robert Stanclift
Racing Hometown: Long Beach, CA

Year	Rank	Starts	Poles	1	2	3	4	5	6–10	Laps	Laps Led	Races Led	Miles	$
1955	130	2	0	0	0	0	0	0	1	135	0	0	135	140
1956	230	1	0	0	0	0	0	0	0	72	0	0	180	40
Lifetime		3	0	0	0	0	0	0	1	207	0	0	315	$180

Billy Standridge

William Standridge
B: 11/27/1953
Racing Hometown: Shelby, NC

Year	Rank	Starts	Poles	1	2	3	4	5	6–10	Laps	Laps Led	Races Led	Miles	$
1994	47	8	0	0	0	0	0	0	0	1,260	0	0	1,706	56,405
1995	51	2	0	0	0	0	0	0	0	594	0	0	859	20,345
1996	51	3	0	0	0	0	0	0	0	789	0	0	1,123	27,780
1997	50	6	0	0	0	0	0	0	0	1,199	0	0	2,000	149,824
1998	55	4	0	0	0	0	0	0	0	568	0	0	1,476	147,640
Lifetime		23	0	0	0	0	0	0	0	4,410	0	0	7,164	$401,994

Paul Stanley

Paul Stanley
Racing Hometown: Martinsville, VA

Year	Rank	Starts	Poles	1	2	3	4	5	6–10	Laps	Laps Led	Races Led	Miles	$
1951	N/A	2	0	0	0	0	0	0	0		0	0		50
Lifetime		2	0	0	0	0	0	0	0		0	0		$50

Sam Stanley

Samuel Stanley
B: 5/30/1934
Racing Hometown: Newhall, CA

Year	Rank	Starts	Poles	1	2	3	4	5	6–10	Laps	Laps Led	Races Led	Miles	$
1965	59	1	0	0	0	0	0	0	1	172	0	0	464	1,050
1972	116	1	0	0	0	0	0	0	0	17	0	0	45	655
Lifetime		2	0	0	0	0	0	0	1	189	0	0	509	$1,705

Don Stanyer

Donald Stanyer

Year	Rank	Starts	Poles	1	2	3	4	5	6–10	Laps	Laps Led	Races Led	Miles	$
1956	285	1	0	0	0	0	0	0	0	70	0	0	175	40
Lifetime		1	0	0	0	0	0	0	0	70	0	0	175	$40

Jim Stapley

James Stapley
Racing Hometown: Phoenix, AZ

Year	Rank	Starts	Poles	1	2	3	4	5	6–10	Laps	Laps Led	Races Led	Miles	$
1956	293	1	0	0	0	0	0	0	0	51	0	0	51	0
Lifetime		1	0	0	0	0	0	0	0	51	0	0	51	$0

Charles Stark

Charles Stark
Racing Hometown: Tampa, FL

Year	Rank	Starts	Poles	1	2	3	4	5	6–10	Laps	Laps Led	Races Led	Miles	$
1952	154T	1	0	0	0	0	0	0	0		0	0		25
Lifetime		1	0	0	0	0	0	0	0		0	0		$25

Fred Starr

Fred Starr
Racing Hometown: Brooklyn, NH

Year	Rank	Starts	Poles	1	2	3	4	5	6–10	Laps	Laps Led	Races Led	Miles	$
1954	116	2	0	0	0	0	0	0	0	169	0	0	85	35
Lifetime		2	0	0	0	0	0	0	0	169	0	0	85	$35

Year	Rank	Starts	Poles	Finish						Laps	Laps Led	Races Led	Miles	$
				1	2	3	4	5	6–10					

Stan Starr Jr.

Stanley Monroe Starr Jr.
B: 8/11/1943
Racing Hometown: Madison, TN

Year	Rank	Starts	Poles	1	2	3	4	5	6–10	Laps	Laps Led	Races Led	Miles	$
1969	NR	1	0	0	0	0	0	0	0	82	0	0	218	1,200
Lifetime		1	0	0	0	0	0	0	0	82	0	0	218	$1,200

J.O. Staton

Joseph O. Staton
Racing Hometown: Greenville, SC

Year	Rank	Starts	Poles	1	2	3	4	5	6–10	Laps	Laps Led	Races Led	Miles	$
1952	67	7	0	0	0	0	0	0	1	331	0	0	185	250
Lifetime		7	0	0	0	0	0	0	1	331	0	0	185	$250

Al Stearn

Al Stearn
Racing Hometown: Syracuse, NY

Year	Rank	Starts	Poles	1	2	3	4	5	6–10	Laps	Laps Led	Races Led	Miles	$
1957	NR	1	0	0	0	0	0	0	0	57	0	0	57	100
Lifetime		1	0	0	0	0	0	0	0	57	0	0	57	$100

Johnny Steele

John Steele
B: 12/20/1934
Racing Hometown: Carmichael, CA

Year	Rank	Starts	Poles	1	2	3	4	5	6–10	Laps	Laps Led	Races Led	Miles	$
1965	125	1	0	0	0	0	0	0	0	16	0	0	43	500
1966	69	2	0	0	0	0	0	0	0	325	0	0	523	900
1967	92	5	0	0	0	0	0	0	0	402	0	0	254	900
1968	97	1	0	0	0	0	0	0	0	33	0	0	89	500
1969	NR	1	0	0	0	0	0	0	0	3	0	0	8	750
1971	NR	1	0	0	0	0	0	0	0	79	0	0	198	1,375
Lifetime		11	0	0	0	0	0	0	0	858	0	0	1,115	$4,925

Tim Steele

Timothy Steele
B: 3/1/1968
Racing Hometown: Coopersville, MI

Year	Rank	Starts	Poles	1	2	3	4	5	6–10	Laps	Laps Led	Races Led	Miles	$
1994	52	5	0	0	0	0	0	0	0	391	0	0	807	65,000
Lifetime		5	0	0	0	0	0	0	0	391	0	0	807	$65,000

Fred Steinbroner

Fred Steinbroner
Racing Hometown: Los Angeles, CA

Year	Rank	Starts	Poles	1	2	3	4	5	6–10	Laps	Laps Led	Races Led	Miles	$
1951	43	6	0	0	0	0	1	1	1	198	0	0	99	700
1955	151	1	0	0	0	0	0	0	0	84	0	0	84	80
1956	223	1	0	0	0	0	0	0	0	72	0	0	180	40
Lifetime		8	0	0	0	0	1	1	1	354	0	0	363	$820

Lyle Stelter

Lyle Stelter
Racing Hometown: Phoenix, AZ

Year	Rank	Starts	Poles	1	2	3	4	5	6–10	Laps	Laps Led	Races Led	Miles	$
1960	NR	2	0	0	0	0	0	0	0	130	0	0	164	160
1963	116	2	0	0	0	0	0	0	0	304	0	0	85	175
1966	NR	2	0	0	0	0	0	0	0	38	0	0	35	0
Lifetime		6	0	0	0	0	0	0	0	472	0	0	285	$335

Tommy Stenger

Thomas Stenger
Racing Hometown: Dayton, OH

Year	Rank	Starts	Poles	1	2	3	4	5	6–10	Laps	Laps Led	Races Led	Miles	$
1951	N/A	1	0	0	0	0	0	0	0		0	0		25
Lifetime		1	0	0	0	0	0	0	0		0	0		$25

Dirk Stephens

Dirk Stephens
B: 6/13/1963
Racing Hometown: Tumwater, WA

Year	Rank	Starts	Poles	1	2	3	4	5	6–10	Laps	Laps Led	Races Led	Miles	$
1993	63	2	0	0	0	0	0	0	0	106	0	0	215	12,880
Lifetime		2	0	0	0	0	0	0	0	106	0	0	215	$12,880

Tojo Stephens

Tojo Stephens
Racing Hometown: Dunn, NC

Year	Rank	Starts	Poles	1	2	3	4	5	6–10	Laps	Laps Led	Races Led	Miles	$
1955	NR	1	0	0	0	0	0	0	0	291	0	0	400	60
Lifetime		1	0	0	0	0	0	0	0	291	0	0	400	$60

Year	Rank	Starts	Poles	Finish 1	2	3	4	5	6–10	Laps	Laps Led	Races Led	Miles	$

Nero Steptoe

Nero Steptoe
Racing Hometown: Albany, GA

Year	Rank	Starts	Poles	1	2	3	4	5	6–10	Laps	Laps Led	Races Led	Miles	$
1953	NR	1	0	0	0	0	0	0	0		0	0		25
1954	NR	1	0	0	0	0	0	0	0	35	0	0	144	25
1962	86	3	0	0	0	0	0	0	0	168	0	0	64	275
Lifetime		5	0	0	0	0	0	0	0	203	0	0	208	$325

Glenn Steurer

Glenn Steurer
B: 6/3/1955
Racing Hometown: Canoga Park, CA

Year	Rank	Starts	Poles	1	2	3	4	5	6–10	Laps	Laps Led	Races Led	Miles	$
1985	51	2	0	0	0	0	0	0	0	211	0	0	553	6,850
1986	63	2	0	0	0	0	0	0	0	210	0	0	550	10,755
1987	NR	1	0	0	0	0	0	0	0	19	0	0	50	925
Lifetime		5	0	0	0	0	0	0	0	440	0	0	1,153	$18,530

Bugs Stevens

Bugs Stevens (Real Name: Carl S. Berghman)
B: 5/11/1934
Racing Hometown: Rehoboth, MA

Year	Rank	Starts	Poles	1	2	3	4	5	6–10	Laps	Laps Led	Races Led	Miles	$
1970	61	3	0	0	0	0	0	0	1	458	0	0	682	6,145
Lifetime		3	0	0	0	0	0	0	1	458	0	0	682	$6,145

Chuck Stevenson

Charles J. Stevenson
B: 10/15/1917   D: 8/1/1995
Racing Hometown: Sidney, MT

Year	Rank	Starts	Poles	1	2	3	4	5	6–10	Laps	Laps Led	Races Led	Miles	$
1955	218	1	0	0	0	0	0	0	0	43	0	0	65	60
1956	94	1	0	1	0	0	0	0	0	80	54	1	200	1,570
Lifetime		2	0	1	0	0	0	0	0	123	54	1	265	$1,630

Jim Stewart

James Stewart
Racing Hometown: Sacramento, CA

Year	Rank	Starts	Poles	1	2	3	4	5	6–10	Laps	Laps Led	Races Led	Miles	$
1961	140T	1	0	0	0	0	0	0	0	93	0	0	93	100
Lifetime		1	0	0	0	0	0	0	0	93	0	0	93	$100

Joe Stewart

Joseph Stewart
Racing Hometown: Memphis, TN

Year	Rank	Starts	Poles	1	2	3	4	5	6–10	Laps	Laps Led	Races Led	Miles	$
1956	233T	1	0	0	0	0	0	0	0	57	0	0	86	50
Lifetime		1	0	0	0	0	0	0	0	57	0	0	86	$50

Pete Stewart

Marvin Peter Stewart
B: 8/12/1931
Racing Hometown: Statesville, NC

Year	Rank	Starts	Poles	1	2	3	4	5	6–10	Laps	Laps Led	Races Led	Miles	$
1953	NR	1	0	0	0	0	0	0	0	20	0	0	13	25
1954	195	1	0	0	0	0	0	0	0	77	0	0	39	0
1956	108	3	0	0	0	0	0	0	0	756	0	0	356	235
1957	NR	1	0	0	0	0	0	0	0	25	0	0	13	0
1963	124	2	0	0	0	0	0	0	0	78	0	0	109	150
1964	51	7	0	0	0	0	0	0	0	1,243	0	0	879	2,365
1965	100	2	0	0	0	0	0	0	0	2	0	0	5	1,165
Lifetime		17	0	0	0	0	0	0	0	2,201	0	0	1,412	$3,940

Tony Stewart

Tony Stewart
B: 5/20/1971
Racing Hometown: Rushville, IN

Year	Rank	Starts	Poles	1	2	3	4	5	6–10	Laps	Laps Led	Races Led	Miles	$
1999	4	34	2	3	2	1	4	2	9	9,908	1,213	17	12,998	3,190,149
2000	6	34	2	6	2	0	3	1	11	9,335	1,211	16	12,296	3,200,191
2001	2	36	0	3	3	2	3	4	7	10,429	465	12	13,978	4,941,463
2002	1	36	4	3	3	4	2	3	6	10,181	746	17	13,134	9,163,761
Lifetime		140	8	15	10	7	12	10	33	39,853	3,635	62	52,406	$20,495,564

H.F. Stickleather

H.F. Stickleather
Racing Hometown: Charlotte, NC

Year	Rank	Starts	Poles	1	2	3	4	5	6–10	Laps	Laps Led	Races Led	Miles	$
1949	62T	1	0	0	0	0	0	0	0	167	0	0	84	50
Lifetime		1	0	0	0	0	0	0	0	167	0	0	84	$50

Year	Rank	Starts	Poles	Finish						Laps	Laps Led	Races Led	Miles	$
				1	2	3	4	5	6–10					

Bill Stickler
William Stickler
Racing Hometown: Gardena, CA

Year	Rank	Starts	Poles	1	2	3	4	5	6–10	Laps	Laps Led	Races Led	Miles	$
1951	N/A	2	0	0	0	0	0	0	0		0	0		50
Lifetime		2	0	0	0	0	0	0	0		0	0		$50

Ernie Stierly
Ernest Stierly
B: 12/29/1930
Racing Hometown: Vancouver, WA

Year	Rank	Starts	Poles	1	2	3	4	5	6–10	Laps	Laps Led	Races Led	Miles	$
1976	107T	1	0	0	0	0	0	0	0	21	0	0	55	765
1977	81	2	0	0	0	0	0	0	0	137	0	0	352	1,805
1978	74	2	0	0	0	0	0	0	0	141	0	0	369	2,520
Lifetime		5	0	0	0	0	0	0	0	299	0	0	777	$5,090

Billy Stiles
William Stiles
Racing Hometown: Charlotte, NC

Year	Rank	Starts	Poles	1	2	3	4	5	6–10	Laps	Laps Led	Races Led	Miles	$
1966	141	1	0	0	0	0	0	0	0	4	0	0	1	0
Lifetime		1	0	0	0	0	0	0	0	4	0	0	1	$0

Chuck Stimus
Charles Stimus
Racing Hometown: Rochester, NY

Year	Rank	Starts	Poles	1	2	3	4	5	6–10	Laps	Laps Led	Races Led	Miles	$
1951	N/A	1	0	0	0	0	0	0	1		0	0		150
Lifetime		1	0	0	0	0	0	0	1		0	0		$150

Don Stives
Donald Stives
Racing Hometown: Highstown, NJ

Year	Rank	Starts	Poles	1	2	3	4	5	6–10	Laps	Laps Led	Races Led	Miles	$
1967	98	3	0	0	0	0	0	0	1	188	0	0	49	510
Lifetime		3	0	0	0	0	0	0	1	188	0	0	49	$510

Harold Stockton
Harold Stockton
Racing Hometown: Franklin, NC

Year	Rank	Starts	Poles	1	2	3	4	5	6–10	Laps	Laps Led	Races Led	Miles	$
1967	80	6	0	0	0	0	0	0	0	626	0	0	287	705
Lifetime		6	0	0	0	0	0	0	0	626	0	0	287	$705

Virgil Stockton
Virgil Stockton
Racing Hometown: Melvindale, MI

Year	Rank	Starts	Poles	1	2	3	4	5	6–10	Laps	Laps Led	Races Led	Miles	$
1953	127T	1	0	0	0	0	0	0	0		0	0		25
1954	NR	4	0	0	0	0	0	0	1	463	0	0	232	175
Lifetime		5	0	0	0	0	0	0	1	463	0	0	232	$200

Mike Stolarcyk
Michael Stolarcyk

Year	Rank	Starts	Poles	1	2	3	4	5	6–10	Laps	Laps Led	Races Led	Miles	$
1985	86T	1	0	0	0	0	0	0	0	116	0	0	290	1,615
Lifetime		1	0	0	0	0	0	0	0	116	0	0	290	$1,615

Steve Stolarek
Steve Stolarek
Racing Hometown: Minneapolis, MN

Year	Rank	Starts	Poles	1	2	3	4	5	6–10	Laps	Laps Led	Races Led	Miles	$
1977	113T	1	0	0	0	0	0	0	0	21	0	0	21	490
Lifetime		1	0	0	0	0	0	0	0	21	0	0	21	$490

Rolf Stommelen
Rolf-Johann Stommelen
B: 7/11/1943   D: 4/24/1983   *Killed @ Riverside, CA.*
Racing Hometown: Siegen, W. Germany

Year	Rank	Starts	Poles	1	2	3	4	5	6–10	Laps	Laps Led	Races Led	Miles	$
1971	NR	1	0	0	0	0	0	0	0	53	0	0	141	790
Lifetime		1	0	0	0	0	0	0	0	53	0	0	141	$790

Charlie Stone
Charles Stone
Racing Hometown: Austell, GA

Year	Rank	Starts	Poles	1	2	3	4	5	6–10	Laps	Laps Led	Races Led	Miles	$
1958	93	1	0	0	0	0	0	0	0	35	0	0	144	100
Lifetime		1	0	0	0	0	0	0	0	35	0	0	144	$100

Year	Rank	Starts	Poles	Finish						Laps	Laps Led	Races Led	Miles	$
				1	2	3	4	5	6–10					

Dick Stone

Richard Stone
Racing Hometown: Novelty, OH

Year	Rank	Starts	Poles	1	2	3	4	5	6–10	Laps	Laps Led	Races Led	Miles	$
1951	N/A	4	0	0	0	0	0	0	1		0	0		125
1954	163T	1	0	0	0	0	0	0	0	12	0	0	6	0
Lifetime		5	0	0	0	0	0	0	1	12	0	0	6	$125

Roland Stone

Roland Stone
Racing Hometown: Galax, VA

Year	Rank	Starts	Poles	1	2	3	4	5	6–10	Laps	Laps Led	Races Led	Miles	$
1950	NR	1	0	0	0	0	0	0	0		0	0		0
Lifetime		1	0	0	0	0	0	0	0		0	0		$0

Ramo Stott

Ramo E. Stott
B: 4/6/1934
Racing Hometown: Keokuk, IA

Year	Rank	Starts	Poles	1	2	3	4	5	6–10	Laps	Laps Led	Races Led	Miles	$
1967	39	3	0	0	0	0	0	0	1	588	0	0	1,082	3,335
1969	69	3	0	0	0	1	0	0	1	375	4	1	968	8,785
1970	60	3	0	0	0	0	0	0	3	424	2	1	1,089	4,875
1971	64	3	0	0	0	0	0	0	1	476	0	0	1,075	3,715
1972	66	5	0	0	1	1	0	0	1	1,113	3	1	1,965	19,655
1973	52	4	0	0	0	0	0	0	2	488	1	1	1,109	8,440
1974	39	7	0	0	0	1	0	0	3	1,725	0	0	2,906	23,705
1975	68	2	0	0	0	0	0	1	0	259	0	0	657	13,030
1976	NR	1	1	0	0	0	0	0	0	113	0	0	283	6,830
1977	48	5	0	0	0	0	0	0	0	688	0	0	1,438	10,170
Lifetime		36	1	0	1	3	0	1	12	6,249	10	4	12,570	$102,540

Joel Stowe

Joel Stowe
Racing Hometown: Waxhaw, NC

Year	Rank	Starts	Poles	1	2	3	4	5	6–10	Laps	Laps Led	Races Led	Miles	$
1980	89	2	0	0	0	0	0	0	0	835	0	0	694	4,685
1981	NR	1	0	0	0	0	0	0	0	14	0	0	7	540
1982	NR	1	0	0	0	0	0	0	0	57	0	0	36	705
Lifetime		4	0	0	0	0	0	0	0	906	0	0	737	$5,930

Don Strain

Donald Strain
Racing Hometown: Pittsburgh, PA

Year	Rank	Starts	Poles	1	2	3	4	5	6–10	Laps	Laps Led	Races Led	Miles	$
1959	NR	1	0	0	0	0	0	0	1	181	0	0	45	140
Lifetime		1	0	0	0	0	0	0	1	181	0	0	45	$140

Harold Strapp

Harold Strapp

Year	Rank	Starts	Poles	1	2	3	4	5	6–10	Laps	Laps Led	Races Led	Miles	$
1951	N/A	1	0	0	0	0	0	0	0		0	0		0
Lifetime		1	0	0	0	0	0	0	0		0	0		$0

Victor Strassburg

Victor Strassburg
Racing Hometown: Niagara Falls, NY

Year	Rank	Starts	Poles	1	2	3	4	5	6–10	Laps	Laps Led	Races Led	Miles	$
1953	156	1	0	0	0	0	0	0	0		0	0		25
Lifetime		1	0	0	0	0	0	0	0		0	0		$25

Al Straub

Allen Straub
B: 11/9/1940
Racing Hometown: Louisville, KY

Year	Rank	Starts	Poles	1	2	3	4	5	6–10	Laps	Laps Led	Races Led	Miles	$
1969	NR	1	0	0	0	0	0	0	0	9	0	0	24	950
1971	NR	1	0	0	0	0	0	0	0	48	0	0	22	300
Lifetime		2	0	0	0	0	0	0	0	57	0	0	46	$1,250

Jim Street

James Street
Racing Hometown: Winston-Salem, NC

Year	Rank	Starts	Poles	1	2	3	4	5	6–10	Laps	Laps Led	Races Led	Miles	$
1962	NR	1	0	0	0	0	0	0	0	8	0	0	2	50
Lifetime		1	0	0	0	0	0	0	0	8	0	0	2	$50

Year	Rank	Starts	Poles	1	2	3	Finish 4	5	6–10	Laps	Laps Led	Races Led	Miles	$

Bub Strickler

Early Harry Strickler
B: 12/18/1938
Racing Hometown: Timberville, VA

Year	Rank	Starts	Poles	1	2	3	4	5	6–10	Laps	Laps Led	Races Led	Miles	$
1965	33	9	0	0	0	0	0	0	2	1,572	0	0	1,909	5,275
1966	NR	4	0	0	0	0	0	0	0	232	0	0	244	1,595
1970	91	1	0	0	0	0	0	0	0	316	0	0	198	455
1971	NR	1	0	0	0	0	0	0	0	1	0	0	3	1,000
1979	123T	1	0	0	0	0	0	0	0	67	0	0	68	550
1980	NR	5	0	0	0	0	0	0	0	1,199	0	0	733	3,200
Lifetime		21	0	0	0	0	0	0	2	3,387	0	0	3,154	$12,075

Hut Stricklin

Waymond Lane Stricklin Jr.
B: 6/24/1961
Racing Hometown: Calera, AL

Year	Rank	Starts	Poles	1	2	3	4	5	6–10	Laps	Laps Led	Races Led	Miles	$
1987	58	3	0	0	0	0	0	0	0	912	0	0	1,009	6,085
1989	26	27	0	0	0	0	1	0	3	7,557	3	1	9,287	137,054
1990	28	24	0	0	0	0	0	0	2	6,037	1	1	8,118	169,199
1991	16	29	0	0	1	0	2	0	4	8,813	69	7	10,436	426,524
1992	27	28	0	0	0	0	0	0	4	7,928	60	2	9,261	336,965
1993	24	30	0	0	0	0	1	0	1	8,356	99	3	10,212	494,600
1994	26	29	0	0	0	0	0	0	1	8,562	26	2	10,587	333,495
1995	36	24	1	0	0	0	1	1	3	5,513	45	4	7,311	486,065
1996	22	31	0	0	1	0	0	0	0	8,620	163	3	10,633	631,055
1997	34	29	0	0	0	0	0	0	1	8,494	6	1	10,241	802,904
1998	48	14	0	0	0	0	0	0	0	3,188	0	0	3,482	341,307
1999	43	10	0	0	0	0	0	0	1	3,091	0	0	3,683	378,942
2000	50	7	0	0	0	0	0	0	0	1,248	0	0	1,617	255,200
2001	42	22	0	0	0	0	0	0	1	6,215		0	9,123	1,006,021
2002	40	22	0	0	0	0	0	0	0	5,936	5	2	8,027	1,313,548
Lifetime		329	1	0	2	0	5	1	21	90,470	477	26	113,027	$7,118,964

D. Wayne Strout

D. Wayne Strout
B: 1951
Racing Hometown: Dallas, TX

Year	Rank	Starts	Poles	1	2	3	4	5	6–10	Laps	Laps Led	Races Led	Miles	$
1987	84T	1	0	0	0	0	0	0	0	381	0	0	381	1,700
Lifetime		1	0	0	0	0	0	0	0	381	0	0	381	$1,700

Don Stumpf

Donald Stumpf
B: 1927   D: 12/11/199
Racing Hometown: Ridgefield Park, NJ

Year	Rank	Starts	Poles	1	2	3	4	5	6–10	Laps	Laps Led	Races Led	Miles	$
1953	153	1	0	0	0	0	0	0	0		0	0		25
Lifetime		1	0	0	0	0	0	0	0		0	0		$25

Frank Stutts

Frank Stutts
Racing Hometown: Mooresville, NC

Year	Rank	Starts	Poles	1	2	3	4	5	6–10	Laps	Laps Led	Races Led	Miles	$
1954	NR	3	0	0	0	0	0	0	0	426	0	0	452	125
Lifetime		3	0	0	0	0	0	0	0	426	0	0	452	$125

Johnny Suddreth

John Morgan Suddreth
B: 7/11/1929
Racing Hometown: Atlanta, GA

Year	Rank	Starts	Poles	1	2	3	4	5	6–10	Laps	Laps Led	Races Led	Miles	$
1960	86	3	0	0	0	0	0	0	0	351	0	0	676	515
1961	169	1	0	0	0	0	0	0	0	22	0	0	33	200
1962	95	3	0	0	0	0	0	0	0	261	0	0	392	895
1963	143	1	0	0	0	0	0	0	0	16	0	0	24	250
Lifetime		8	0	0	0	0	0	0	0	650	0	0	1,124	$1,860

Tom Suligoy

Thomas Suligoy
Racing Hometown: Joilet, IL

Year	Rank	Starts	Poles	1	2	3	4	5	6–10	Laps	Laps Led	Races Led	Miles	$
1951	N/A	1	0	0	0	0	0	0	0	115	0	0	115	0
Lifetime		1	0	0	0	0	0	0	0	115	0	0	115	$0

Year	Rank	Starts	Poles	Finish						Laps	Laps Led	Races Led	Miles	$
				1	2	3	4	5	6–10					

Bill Sullivan
William Sullivan

Year	Rank	Starts	Poles	1	2	3	4	5	6–10	Laps	Laps Led	Races Led	Miles	$
1956	156	2	0	0	0	0	0	0	0	278	0	0	154	100
Lifetime		2	0	0	0	0	0	0	0	278	0	0	154	$100

Danny Sullivan
Daniel John Sullivan, III
B: 3/9/1950
Racing Hometown: Louisville, KY

Year	Rank	Starts	Poles	1	2	3	4	5	6–10	Laps	Laps Led	Races Led	Miles	$
1994	74	1	0	0	0	0	0	0	0	152	0	0	380	22,750
Lifetime		1	0	0	0	0	0	0	0	152	0	0	380	$22,750

Ross Surgenor
Ross Surgenor
Racing Hometown: Victoria, B.C., Canada

Year	Rank	Starts	Poles	1	2	3	4	5	6–10	Laps	Laps Led	Races Led	Miles	$
1974	99	2	0	0	0	0	0	0	0	134	0	0	351	2,095
Lifetime		2	0	0	0	0	0	0	0	134	0	0	351	$2,095

Parks Surratt
Parks Surratt
Racing Hometown: Gaffney, SC

Year	Rank	Starts	Poles	1	2	3	4	5	6–10	Laps	Laps Led	Races Led	Miles	$
1953	114	3	0	0	0	0	0	0	0	271	0	0	153	75
1954	76	4	0	0	0	0	0	0	0	649	0	0	325	100
Lifetime		7	0	0	0	0	0	0	0	920	0	0	478	$175

Len Sutton
Leonard Sutton
B: 8/9/1925
Racing Hometown: Portland, OR

Year	Rank	Starts	Poles	1	2	3	4	5	6–10	Laps	Laps Led	Races Led	Miles	$
1956	168	1	0	0	0	0	0	0	0	238	0	0	119	150
1963	NR	4	0	0	0	0	0	0	0	274	0	0	570	1,175
Lifetime		5	0	0	0	0	0	0	0	512	0	0	689	$1,325

Lem Svajian
Lem Svajian
Racing Hometown: Detroit, MI

Year	Rank	Starts	Poles	1	2	3	4	5	6–10	Laps	Laps Led	Races Led	Miles	$
1957	179	1	0	0	0	0	0	0	0		0	0		50
Lifetime		1	0	0	0	0	0	0	0		0	0		$50

Ted Swaim
Ted Swaim
Racing Hometown: Winston-Salem, NC

Year	Rank	Starts	Poles	1	2	3	4	5	6–10	Laps	Laps Led	Races Led	Miles	$
1950	34T	1	0	0	1	0	0	0	0	200	0	0	100	600
1951	N/A	2	0	0	0	0	0	0	0	360	0	0	450	75
1952	175	1	0	0	0	0	0	0	0	65	0	0	65	25
Lifetime		4	0	0	1	0	0	0	0	625	0	0	615	$700

Ted Sweeney
Ted Sweeney
Racing Hometown: Portland, OR

Year	Rank	Starts	Poles	1	2	3	4	5	6–10	Laps	Laps Led	Races Led	Miles	$
1956	134	3	0	0	0	0	0	0	0	377	0	0	196	150
Lifetime		3	0	0	0	0	0	0	0	377	0	0	196	$150

Nolan Swift
Nolan Swift
B: 1923
Racing Hometown: Syracuse, NY

Year	Rank	Starts	Poles	1	2	3	4	5	6–10	Laps	Laps Led	Races Led	Miles	$
1956	119	2	0	0	0	0	0	0	1	174	0	0	156	175
Lifetime		2	0	0	0	0	0	0	1	174	0	0	156	$175

Jeff Swindell
Jeffrey Swindell
B: 1960
Racing Hometown: Memphis, TN

Year	Rank	Starts	Poles	1	2	3	4	5	6–10	Laps	Laps Led	Races Led	Miles	$
1986	111	1	0	0	0	0	0	0	0	227	0	0	345	1,160
1987	96T	1	0	0	0	0	0	0	0	102	0	0	271	5,230
Lifetime		2	0	0	0	0	0	0	0	329	0	0	617	$6,390

Year	Rank	Starts	Poles	Finish 1	2	3	4	5	6–10	Laps	Laps Led	Races Led	Miles	$

Sammy Swindell

Samuel Alan Swindell
B: 10/26/1955
Racing Hometown: Bartlett, TN

Year	Rank	Starts	Poles	1	2	3	4	5	6–10	Laps	Laps Led	Races Led	Miles	$
1985	84T	1	0	0	0	0	0	0	0	242	0	0	368	1,175
1991	90	1	0	0	0	0	0	0	0	28	0	0	70	16,500
Lifetime		2	0	0	0	0	0	0	0	270	0	0	438	$17,675

Joe Sykes

Joseph Sykes
Racing Hometown: Buffalo, NY

Year	Rank	Starts	Poles	1	2	3	4	5	6–10	Laps	Laps Led	Races Led	Miles	$
1955	NR	1	0	0	0	0	0	0	0	69	0	0	69	0
1956	NR	1	0	0	0	0	0	0	0	166	0	0	83	100
Lifetime		2	0	0	0	0	0	0	0	235	0	0	152	$100

G.T. Tallas

George T. Tallas
B: 1/31/1944
Racing Hometown: Sun Valley, CA

Year	Rank	Starts	Poles	1	2	3	4	5	6–10	Laps	Laps Led	Races Led	Miles	$
1970	93	2	0	0	0	0	0	0	0	139	0	0	364	1,585
1971	NR	2	0	0	0	0	0	0	0	189	0	0	491	2,490
1972	108	1	0	0	0	0	0	0	0	88	0	0	220	1,620
1975	102	1	0	0	0	0	0	0	0	28	0	0	73	825
Lifetime		6	0	0	0	0	0	0	0	444	0	0	1,149	$6,520

Bill Tanner

William Tanner
Racing Hometown: Newton, PA

Year	Rank	Starts	Poles	1	2	3	4	5	6–10	Laps	Laps Led	Races Led	Miles	$
1954	191	1	0	0	0	0	0	0	0	4	0	0	4	0
1955	71	5	0	0	0	0	0	0	1	423	0	0	425	475
1956	202	2	0	0	0	0	0	0	0	230	0	0	230	75
Lifetime		8	0	0	0	0	0	0	1	657	0	0	659	$550

Frank Tanner

Frank Tanner
Racing Hometown: Charleston, SC

Year	Rank	Starts	Poles	1	2	3	4	5	6–10	Laps	Laps Led	Races Led	Miles	$
1964	103	4	0	0	0	0	0	0	0	9	0	0	7	300
Lifetime		4	0	0	0	0	0	0	0	9	0	0	7	$300

Tony Tantarelli

Anthony Tantarelli
Racing Hometown: Columbus, OH

Year	Rank	Starts	Poles	1	2	3	4	5	6–10	Laps	Laps Led	Races Led	Miles	$
1968	101	1	0	0	0	0	0	0	0	74	0	0	111	650
Lifetime		1	0	0	0	0	0	0	0	74	0	0	111	$650

Gene Tapia

Gene Tapia
Racing Hometown: Mobile, AL

Year	Rank	Starts	Poles	1	2	3	4	5	6–10	Laps	Laps Led	Races Led	Miles	$
1951	181	3	0	0	0	0	0	0	0		0	0		75
1953	134T	1	0	0	0	0	0	0	0		0	0		25
Lifetime		4	0	0	0	0	0	0	0		0	0		$100

Dr. Don Tarr

Dr. Donald F. Tarr
B: 5/4/1929
Racing Hometown: Miami Beach, FL

Year	Rank	Starts	Poles	1	2	3	4	5	6–10	Laps	Laps Led	Races Led	Miles	$
1967	89	3	0	0	0	0	0	0	0	621	0	0	506	1,580
1968	35	12	0	0	0	0	0	0	0	1,941	0	0	2,415	7,510
1969	41	12	0	0	0	0	0	0	3	1,754	6	1	3,122	13,720
1970	35	17	0	0	0	0	0	0	5	2,507	5	1	3,429	16,592
1971	62	4	0	0	0	0	0	0	1	496	0	0	771	3,995
Lifetime		48	0	0	0	0	0	0	9	7,319	11	2	10,244	$43,397

Robert Tartaglia

Robert Tartaglia
B: 4/19/1959
Racing Hometown: Reedley, CA

Year	Rank	Starts	Poles	1	2	3	4	5	6–10	Laps	Laps Led	Races Led	Miles	$
1979	106T	1	0	0	0	0	0	0	0	47	0	0	123	825
1981	102	1	0	0	0	0	0	0	0	4	0	0	10	500
Lifetime		2	0	0	0	0	0	0	0	51	0	0	134	$1,325

Year	Rank	Starts	Poles	Finish 1	2	3	4	5	6–10	Laps	Laps Led	Races Led	Miles	$

Al Tasnady

Alex Tasnady
B: 3/4/1929   D: 12/1988
Racing Hometown: Vineland, NJ

Year	Rank	Starts	Poles	1	2	3	4	5	6–10	Laps	Laps Led	Races Led	Miles	$
1957	188	1	0	0	0	0	0	0	0		0	0		0
1960	NR	1	0	0	0	0	0	0	0	172	0	0	86	110
1967	119	1	0	0	0	0	0	0	0	89	0	0	89	275
Lifetime		3	0	0	0	0	0	0	0	261	0	0	175	$385

Jim Tatum

James Tatum
Racing Hometown: Jacksonville, FL

Year	Rank	Starts	Poles	1	2	3	4	5	6–10	Laps	Laps Led	Races Led	Miles	$
1965	NR	1	0	0	0	0	0	0	0	103	0	0	34	100
1966	85	4	0	0	0	0	0	0	0	351	0	0	174	445
Lifetime		5	0	0	0	0	0	0	0	454	0	0	208	$545

Bill Taylor

William L. Taylor
Racing Hometown: Concord, NC

Year	Rank	Starts	Poles	1	2	3	4	5	6–10	Laps	Laps Led	Races Led	Miles	$
1957	NR	1	0	0	0	0	0	0	0	223	0	0	223	100
1959	NR	3	0	0	0	0	0	0	0	827	0	0	433	240
Lifetime		4	0	0	0	0	0	0	0	1,050	0	0	656	$340

Billy Taylor

William Taylor
Racing Hometown: Yanceville, NC

Year	Rank	Starts	Poles	1	2	3	4	5	6–10	Laps	Laps Led	Races Led	Miles	$
1969	86	2	0	0	0	0	0	0	0	65	0	0	163	1,140
Lifetime		2	0	0	0	0	0	0	0	65	0	0	163	$1,140

Don Taylor

Donald Taylor
Racing Hometown: Torrance, CA

Year	Rank	Starts	Poles	1	2	3	4	5	6–10	Laps	Laps Led	Races Led	Miles	$
1959	98	2	0	0	0	0	0	0	0	430	0	0	214	200
Lifetime		2	0	0	0	0	0	0	0	430	0	0	214	$200

Graham Taylor

Graham Taylor
B: 2/3/1939
Racing Hometown: Port Royal, PA

Year	Rank	Starts	Poles	1	2	3	4	5	6–10	Laps	Laps Led	Races Led	Miles	$
1992	71	2	0	0	0	0	0	0	0	17	0	0	17	8,595
1993	89T	1	0	0	0	0	0	0	0	3	0	0	8	6,210
Lifetime		3	0	0	0	0	0	0	0	20	0	0	25	$14,805

Jesse James Taylor

Jesse James Taylor
B: 1929
Racing Hometown: Macon, GA

Year	Rank	Starts	Poles	1	2	3	4	5	6–10	Laps	Laps Led	Races Led	Miles	$
1950	NR	1	0	0	0	0	0	0	0	329	0	0	411	0
1951	7	10	0	0	1	0	0	0	2	519	104	3	566	3,750
1956	126	3	0	0	0	0	0	0	0	269	0	0	186	250
1958	NR	1	0	0	0	0	0	0	0	95	0	0	131	100
1961	171	1	0	0	0	0	0	0	0	10	0	0	15	250
Lifetime		16	0	0	1	0	0	0	2	1,222	104	3	1,309	$4,350

Ken Taylor

Kenneth Taylor
Racing Hometown: Louisville, KY

Year	Rank	Starts	Poles	1	2	3	4	5	6–10	Laps	Laps Led	Races Led	Miles	$
1954	NR	1	0	0	0	0	0	0	0	137	0	0	69	25
Lifetime		1	0	0	0	0	0	0	0	137	0	0	69	$25

T.W. Taylor

T.W. Taylor
B: 1/25/1955
Racing Hometown: Chester, VA

Year	Rank	Starts	Poles	1	2	3	4	5	6–10	Laps	Laps Led	Races Led	Miles	$
1992	84T	1	0	0	0	0	0	0	0	138	0	0	367	6,045
1993	56	3	0	0	0	0	0	0	0	280	1	1	391	19,205
Lifetime		4	0	0	0	0	0	0	0	418	1	1	758	$25,250

Year	Rank	Starts	Poles	Finish						Laps	Laps Led	Races Led	Miles	$
				1	2	3	4	5	6–10					

Brad Teague

Brad Teague
B: 12/9/1947
Racing Hometown: Johnson City, TN

Year	Rank	Starts	Poles	1	2	3	4	5	6–10	Laps	Laps Led	Races Led	Miles	$
1982	32	9	0	0	0	0	0	0	0	3,052	0	0	2,611	14,300
1986	68	3	0	0	0	0	0	0	0	419	0	0	321	3,860
1987	57	5	0	0	0	0	0	0	0	915	17	1	1,176	15,045
1988	40	13	0	0	0	0	0	0	0	3,408	0	0	3,647	53,105
1989	68	2	0	0	0	0	0	0	0	733	0	0	628	4,830
1991	71	1	0	0	0	0	0	0	0	322	0	0	483	4,175
1992	58	2	0	0	0	0	0	0	0	603	0	0	611	12,280
1993	85T	1	0	0	0	0	0	0	0	13	0	0	18	5,010
1994	45	8	0	0	0	0	0	0	0	1,959	0	0	2,095	59,900
Lifetime		44	0	0	0	0	0	0	0	11,424	17	1	11,588	$172,505

Kerry Teague

Kerry Teague
B: 1/12/1961
Racing Hometown: Concord, NC

Year	Rank	Starts	Poles	1	2	3	4	5	6–10	Laps	Laps Led	Races Led	Miles	$
1991	85	1	0	0	0	0	0	0	0	124	0	0	186	3,125
1992	67	2	0	0	0	0	0	0	0	137	0	0	325	26,235
1993	57	2	0	0	0	0	0	0	0	223	0	0	558	14,400
Lifetime		5	0	0	0	0	0	0	0	484	0	0	1,069	$43,760

Marshall Teague

Marshall Teague
B: 2/17/1922   D: 2/11/1959   *Killed in test session @ Daytona.*
Racing Hometown: Daytona Beach, FL

Year	Rank	Starts	Poles	1	2	3	4	5	6–10	Laps	Laps Led	Races Led	Miles	$
1949	62T	1	0	0	0	0	0	0	0		0	0		50
1950	119	3	0	0	0	0	0	0	0	240	0	0	329	50
1951	NR	15	1	5	0	2	0	0	2	1,611	539	8	1,417	7,410
1952	NR	4	1	2	0	0	0	0	0	317	236	2	299	2,550
Lifetime		23	2	7	0	2	0	0	2	2,168	775	10	2,045	$10,060

Ted Tedrow

Theodore Tedrow
Racing Hometown: Mobile, AL

Year	Rank	Starts	Poles	1	2	3	4	5	6–10	Laps	Laps Led	Races Led	Miles	$
1951	N/A	1	0	0	0	0	0	0	0		0	0		25
Lifetime		1	0	0	0	0	0	0	0		0	0		$25

Dave Terrell

David Terrell
B: 2/21/1931
Racing Hometown: Newton, PA

Year	Rank	Starts	Poles	1	2	3	4	5	6–10	Laps	Laps Led	Races Led	Miles	$
1952	43	5	0	0	0	0	0	1	2	477	0	0	306	475
1954	12	30	0	0	0	0	0	0	8	3,876	0	0	2,608	2,225
1955	12	25	0	0	0	2	0	1	7	3,199	9	1	2,433	3,655
1956	121	5	0	0	0	0	0	0	1	363	0	0	235	260
1957	NR	2	0	0	0	0	0	0	1	290	0	0	290	750
1958	NR	1	0	0	0	0	0	0	0	113	0	0	57	50
Lifetime		68	0	0	0	2	0	2	19	8,318	9	1	5,927	$7,415

Kevin Terris

Kevin Terris
B: 10/27/1944
Racing Hometown: Hermosa Beach, CA

Year	Rank	Starts	Poles	1	2	3	4	5	6–10	Laps	Laps Led	Races Led	Miles	$
1970	72	2	0	0	0	0	0	0	0	169	0	0	443	1,875
1971	NR	4	0	0	0	0	0	0	2	519	0	0	1,361	5,965
1972	60	4	0	0	0	0	0	0	1	651	0	0	1,562	5,695
1984	NR	1	0	0	0	0	0	0	0	78	0	0	204	1,275
Lifetime		11	0	0	0	0	0	0	3	1,417	0	0	3,570	$14,810

George Tet

Tetsuo Fuchigami
B: 4/1/1923
Racing Hometown: Ozone Park, NY

Year	Rank	Starts	Poles	1	2	3	4	5	6–10	Laps	Laps Led	Races Led	Miles	$
1960	NR	1	0	0	0	0	0	0	0	171	0	0	257	200
1961	NR	2	0	0	0	0	0	0	0	60	0	0	150	250
Lifetime		3	0	0	0	0	0	0	0	231	0	0	407	$450

Year	Rank	Starts	Poles	Finish						Laps	Laps Led	Races Led	Miles	$
				1	2	3	4	5	6–10					

Ash Tharrett

Ashton Tharrett
Racing Hometown: Rochester, NY

Year	Rank	Starts	Poles	1	2	3	4	5	6–10	Laps	Laps Led	Races Led	Miles	$
1954	179T	1	0	0	0	0	0	0	0	153	0	0	77	0
Lifetime		1	0	0	0	0	0	0	0	153	0	0	77	$0

Rod Therrian

Roderick Therrian
Racing Hometown: Atlanta, GA

Year	Rank	Starts	Poles	1	2	3	4	5	6–10	Laps	Laps Led	Races Led	Miles	$
1951	N/A	1	0	0	0	0	0	0	0		0	0		25
Lifetime		1	0	0	0	0	0	0	0		0	0		$25

Jim Thirkettle

James Thirkettle
B: 3/9/1945
Racing Hometown: Sylmar, CA

Year	Rank	Starts	Poles	1	2	3	4	5	6–10	Laps	Laps Led	Races Led	Miles	$
1975	107T	1	0	0	0	0	0	0	0	50	0	0	125	750
1976	85	2	0	0	0	0	0	0	0	133	0	0	334	1,730
1977	66	2	0	0	0	0	0	0	0	154	0	0	403	2,265
1978	48	3	0	0	0	0	0	0	2	393	1	1	1,006	6,850
1979	79T	1	0	0	0	0	0	0	1	117	0	0	307	2,450
Lifetime		9	0	0	0	0	0	0	3	847	1	1	2,175	$14,045

Donald Thomas

Donald Thomas
B: 7/10/1932   D: 12/16/1977
Racing Hometown: Olivia, NC

Year	Rank	Starts	Poles	1	2	3	4	5	6–10	Laps	Laps Led	Races Led	Miles	$
1950	39	2	0	0	0	0	0	0	2	141	0	0	71	300
1951	20	17	0	0	0	1	0	3	4	479	0	0	563	2,060
1952	9	21	1	1	1	1	1	1	9	2,623	9	1	1,928	4,477
1953	19	17	0	0	0	0	0	0	4	1,034	0	0	1,119	1,765
1954	31	9	0	0	1	0	1	1	1	1,175	53	1	689	1,675
1955	38	10	0	0	0	0	2	0	2	1,320	0	0	855	1,240
1956	110	3	0	0	0	0	0	0	1	165	0	0	114	200
Lifetime		79	1	1	2	2	4	5	23	6,937	62	2	5,338	$11,717

Hank Thomas

Henry C. Thomas
Racing Hometown: Winston-Salem, NC

Year	Rank	Starts	Poles	1	2	3	4	5	6–10	Laps	Laps Led	Races Led	Miles	$
1963	126T	1	0	0	0	0	0	0	0	44	0	0	11	125
1966	42	14	0	0	0	1	0	2	4	3,114	0	0	1,482	3,630
Lifetime		15	0	0	0	1	0	2	4	3,158	0	0	1,493	$3,755

Herb Thomas

Herbert Watson Thomas
B: 4/6/1923   D: 8/9/2000
Racing Hometown: Olivia, NC

Year	Rank	Starts	Poles	1	2	3	4	5	6–10	Laps	Laps Led	Races Led	Miles	$
1949	25	4	0	0	0	0	0	1	0	197	0	0	99	225
1950	11	13	0	1	0	2	1	0	2	719	176	2	438	2,645
1951	1	35	4	7	1	3	4	1	2	2,159	1,004	10	1,686	20,850
1952	2	32	10	8	7	3	0	1	3	5,134	982	15	3,475	18,965
1953	1	37	11	12	8	3	3	1	4	4,292	1,222	23	3,107	28,910
1954	2	34	8	12	4	1	2	0	8	5,505	1,257	17	3,898	30,975
1955	5	23	2	3	3	3	3	2	1	3,248	151	7	2,707	18,024
1956	3	48	2	5	2	4	7	4	14	7,890	340	8	5,210	19,352
1957	148	2	0	0	0	0	0	0	0	146	0	0	123	25
1962	97	1	0	0	0	0	0	0	0	377	0	0	236	200
Lifetime		229	37	48	25	19	20	10	34	29,667	5,132	82	20,978	$140,171

Hildrey Thomas

Hildrey M. Thomas
Racing Hometown: Chocowinity, NC

Year	Rank	Starts	Poles	1	2	3	4	5	6–10	Laps	Laps Led	Races Led	Miles	$
1953	108T	1	0	0	0	0	0	0	0		0	0		25
Lifetime		1	0	0	0	0	0	0	0		0	0		$25

Jabe Thomas

Cerry Ezra Thomas
B: 5/12/1930
Racing Hometown: Chriatiansburg, VA

Year	Rank	Starts	Poles	1	2	3	4	5	6–10	Laps	Laps Led	Races Led	Miles	$
1965	52	10	0	0	0	0	0	0	1	2,161	0	0	1,764	4,250
1966	47	13	0	0	0	0	0	0	0	1,559	0	0	1,406	3,480

Year	Rank	Starts	Poles	Finish						Laps	Laps Led	Races Led	Miles	$
				1	2	3	4	5	6–10					

Jabe Thomas *continued*

Year	Rank	Starts	Poles	1	2	3	4	5	6–10	Laps	Laps Led	Races Led	Miles	$
1967	51	20	0	0	0	0	0	0	3	2,408	0	0	1,847	7,055
1968	8	48	0	0	0	0	0	1	14	11,194	0	0	7,330	21,166
1969	8	51	0	0	0	0	0	0	12	12,025	0	0	9,784	44,989
1970	7	46	0	0	0	0	0	0	23	10,928	0	0	9,510	42,958
1971	6	43	0	0	0	0	1	1	13	11,360	0	0	9,822	48,241
1972	12	28	0	0	0	0	0	0	4	7,132	0	0	8,207	43,438
1973	11	25	0	0	0	0	0	0	1	7,205	0	0	7,917	42,955
1974	42	10	0	0	0	0	0	0	1	1,504	0	0	1,007	7,445
1975	22	21	0	0	0	0	0	0	2	5,822	0	0	5,662	22,390
1976	40	6	0	0	0	0	0	0	0	1,944	0	0	1,291	6,160
1978	105T	1	0	0	0	0	0	0	0	1	0	0	1	480
Lifetime		322	0	0	0	0	1	2	74	75,243	0	0	65,548	$295,007

Larry Thomas

Larry Thomas
B: 4/13/1936 D: 1/25/1965 *Killed in highway crash @ Tifton, GA.*
Racing Hometown: Thomasville, NC

Year	Rank	Starts	Poles	1	2	3	4	5	6–10	Laps	Laps Led	Races Led	Miles	$
1961	43	14	0	0	0	0	0	0	4	2,830	0	0	1,256	2,065
1962	17	37	0	0	0	0	2	1	9	7,268	0	0	4,889	9,486
1963	22	32	0	0	0	2	1	3	7	6,991	0	0	4,209	8,945
1964	8	43	0	0	1	3	2	3	18	10,025	0	0	6,957	21,226
Lifetime		126	0	0	1	5	5	7	38	27,114	0	0	17,311	$41,722

Lou Thomas

Louis Thomas
Racing Hometown: Linthicum Heights, MD

Year	Rank	Starts	Poles	1	2	3	4	5	6–10	Laps	Laps Led	Races Led	Miles	$
1953	155	1	0	0	0	0	0	0	0		0	0		35
Lifetime		1	0	0	0	0	0	0	0		0	0		$35

Ronnie Thomas

Ronald Thomas
B: 3/8/1955
Racing Hometown: Chriatiansburg, VA

Year	Rank	Starts	Poles	1	2	3	4	5	6–10	Laps	Laps Led	Races Led	Miles	$
1977	52	4	0	0	0	0	0	0	0	821	0	0	715	4,590
1978	18	27	0	0	0	0	0	0	2	7,287	0	0	7,770	75,815
1979	17	30	0	0	0	0	0	0	3	6,928	1	1	7,841	100,079
1980	14	30	0	0	0	0	0	0	4	7,522	0	0	9,082	94,730
1981	26	23	0	0	0	0	0	0	0	5,756	0	0	5,928	53,605
1982	30	18	0	0	0	0	0	0	0	3,243	0	0	3,288	23,570
1983	22	26	0	0	0	0	0	0	0	7,141	1	1	7,706	47,180
1984	30	21	0	0	0	0	0	0	0	4,976	2	1	5,761	79,325
1985	39	7	0	0	0	0	0	0	0	1,510	0	0	1,157	10,505
1986	42	6	0	0	0	0	0	0	0	973	0	0	1,547	25,215
1987	60	4	0	0	0	0	0	0	0	874	0	0	694	5,020
1989	73	1	0	0	0	0	0	0	0	196	0	0	392	3,925
Lifetime		197	0	0	0	0	0	0	9	47,227	4	3	51,882	$523,559

Ted Thomas

Theodore Thomas

Year	Rank	Starts	Poles	1	2	3	4	5	6–10	Laps	Laps Led	Races Led	Miles	$
1989	90	1	0	0	0	0	0	0	0	55	0	0	135	1,975
Lifetime		1	0	0	0	0	0	0	0	55	0	0	135	$1,975

Bob Thompson

Robert Thompson
Racing Hometown: Buena Park, CA

Year	Rank	Starts	Poles	1	2	3	4	5	6–10	Laps	Laps Led	Races Led	Miles	$
1965	122	1	0	0	0	0	0	0	0	26	0	0	70	500
Lifetime		1	0	0	0	0	0	0	0	26	0	0	70	$500

Chet Thompson

Chester Thompson
Racing Hometown: Oakland, CA

Year	Rank	Starts	Poles	1	2	3	4	5	6–10	Laps	Laps Led	Races Led	Miles	$
1955	NR	1	0	0	0	0	0	0	0	199	0	0	199	40
1956	203T	1	0	0	0	0	0	0	0	94	0	0	94	50
Lifetime		2	0	0	0	0	0	0	0	293	0	0	293	$90

Year	Rank	Starts	Poles	Finish						Laps	Laps Led	Races Led	Miles	$
				1	2	3	4	5	6–10					

Chuck Thompson

Charles H. Thompson
Racing Hometown: Holly Hill, FL

Year	Rank	Starts	Poles	1	2	3	4	5	6–10	Laps	Laps Led	Races Led	Miles	$
1957	136T	1	0	0	0	0	0	0	0	47	0	0	75	100
Lifetime		1	0	0	0	0	0	0	0	47	0	0	75	$100

Frank Thompson

Frank Thompson
Racing Hometown: Shewsbury, PA

Year	Rank	Starts	Poles	1	2	3	4	5	6–10	Laps	Laps Led	Races Led	Miles	$
1958	101	3	0	0	0	0	0	0	0	285	0	0	161	150
Lifetime		3	0	0	0	0	0	0	0	285	0	0	161	$150

Fred Thompson

Fred Thompson

Year	Rank	Starts	Poles	1	2	3	4	5	6–10	Laps	Laps Led	Races Led	Miles	$
1951	N/A	1	0	0	0	0	0	0	0		0	0		25
1953	114T	1	0	0	0	0	0	0	1	186	0	0	93	175
Lifetime		2	0	0	0	0	0	0	1	186	0	0	93	$200

Jerry Thompson

Gerald Thompson
Racing Hometown: Clauson, MI

Year	Rank	Starts	Poles	1	2	3	4	5	6–10	Laps	Laps Led	Races Led	Miles	$
1973	91	1	0	0	0	0	0	0	0	162	0	0	424	1,195
Lifetime		1	0	0	0	0	0	0	0	162	0	0	424	$1,195

Jim Thompson

James Thompson
Racing Hometown: Huntington, WV

Year	Rank	Starts	Poles	1	2	3	4	5	6–10	Laps	Laps Led	Races Led	Miles	$
1955	163	2	0	0	0	0	0	0	0	357	0	0	340	200
Lifetime		2	0	0	0	0	0	0	0	357	0	0	340	$200

Jimmy Thompson

James Thompson
B: 2/1/1924   D: 9/26/1964
Racing Hometown: Monroe, NC

Year	Rank	Starts	Poles	1	2	3	4	5	6–10	Laps	Laps Led	Races Led	Miles	$
1949	36	2	0	0	0	0	0	0	2		0	0		175
1950	29	4	0	0	0	0	0	0	3	522	0	0	510	525
1951	N/A	3	0	0	0	0	0	0	0	236	0	0	295	25
1952	38	1	0	0	0	0	0	0	0	383	0	0	479	300
1954	153	1	0	0	0	0	0	0	0	4	0	0	6	75
1955	65	6	0	0	0	0	0	0	1	883	0	0	739	650
1957	46	2	0	0	0	0	0	0	0	352	0	0	489	325
1958	23	7	0	0	0	0	1	0	1	923	0	0	609	3,275
1959	29	5	0	0	0	0	0	0	1	1,002	0	0	1,145	1,580
1960	43	9	0	0	0	0	0	0	0	1,944	9	1	2,288	1,940
1961	121	3	0	0	0	0	0	0	0	267	0	0	301	450
1962	43	3	0	0	0	0	0	0	0	847	0	0	1,271	1,650
Lifetime		46	0	0	0	0	1	0	8	7,363	9	1	8,131	$10,970

Johnny Thompson

John Thompson
B: 9/9/1922
Racing Hometown: Jacksonville, FL

Year	Rank	Starts	Poles	1	2	3	4	5	6–10	Laps	Laps Led	Races Led	Miles	$
1951	N/A	2	0	0	0	0	0	0	0		0	0		50
1952	136	3	0	0	0	0	0	0	0		0	0		50
Lifetime		5	0	0	0	0	0	0	0		0	0		$100

Mark Thompson

Mark Thompson
B: 7/9/1951
Racing Hometown: Cartersville, GA

Year	Rank	Starts	Poles	1	2	3	4	5	6–10	Laps	Laps Led	Races Led	Miles	$
1992	90T	1	0	0	0	0	0	0	0	8	0	0	20	4,370
1992	90T	1	0	0	0	0	0	0	0	8	0	0	20	4,370
Lifetime		2	0	0	0	0	0	0	0	16	0	0	40	$8,740

Ray Thompson

Raymond Thompson
Racing Hometown: Orlando, FL

Year	Rank	Starts	Poles	1	2	3	4	5	6–10	Laps	Laps Led	Races Led	Miles	$
1951	N/A	1	0	0	0	0	0	0	0		0	0		25

Year	Rank	Starts	Poles	Finish 1	2	3	4	5	6–10	Laps	Laps Led	Races Led	Miles	$

Ray Thompson *continued*

Year	Rank	Starts	Poles	1	2	3	4	5	6–10	Laps	Laps Led	Races Led	Miles	$
1956	255	2	0	0	0	0	0	0	0	12	0	0	12	50
Lifetime		3	0	0	0	0	0	0	0	12	0	0	12	$75

Roscoe Thompson

Roscoe A. Thompson
B: 7/5/1922
Racing Hometown: Forrest Park, GA

Year	Rank	Starts	Poles	1	2	3	4	5	6–10	Laps	Laps Led	Races Led	Miles	$
1950	97	2	0	0	0	0	0	0	0	69	0	0	218	50
1951	N/A	3	0	0	0	0	0	0	0	64	0	0	64	75
1952	170	7	0	0	0	0	0	0	0	332	11	1	228	240
1953	82	2	0	0	0	0	0	0	0		0	0		50
1958	90	1	0	0	0	0	0	0	0	44	0	0	44	75
1959	96	2	0	0	0	0	0	0	0	96	0	0	138	100
1960	58	2	0	0	0	0	0	0	0	402	0	0	603	710
1961	40	6	0	0	0	0	0	0	2	721	0	0	1,341	2,535
1962	54	4	0	0	0	0	0	0	0	305	0	0	495	1,605
Lifetime		29	0	0	0	0	0	0	2	2,033	11	1	3,130	$5,440

Sam Thompson

Samuel Thompson
Racing Hometown: Pittsburgh, PA

Year	Rank	Starts	Poles	1	2	3	4	5	6–10	Laps	Laps Led	Races Led	Miles	$
1951	N/A	1	0	0	0	0	0	0	0	52	0	0	26	25
Lifetime		1	0	0	0	0	0	0	0	52	0	0	26	$25

Speedy Thompson

Alfred B. Thompson
B: 4/3/1926   D: 4/2/1972   *Died of heart attack while competing @ Metrolina Speeday in Charlotte, NC.*
Racing Hometown: Monroe, NC

Year	Rank	Starts	Poles	1	2	3	4	5	6–10	Laps	Laps Led	Races Led	Miles	$
1950	NR	1	0	0	0	0	0	0	0		0	0		0
1951	75	3	0	0	0	0	0	1	0	39	0	0	29	325
1952	37	2	0	0	0	0	0	0	0	409	0	0	511	305
1953	11	7	0	2	2	1	0	0	2	1,257	98	3	1,229	6,547
1954	23	7	0	0	0	0	1	0	2	949	0	0	942	1,165
1955	15	15	0	2	1	0	0	0	2	1,918	222	2	1,835	7,090
1956	2	42	7	8	5	5	4	2	5	6,957	2,030	23	4,646	27,169
1957	3	38	4	2	4	3	4	3	6	6,301	648	8	3,903	26,841
1958	3	38	7	4	2	7	3	3	5	6,808	230	7	4,437	17,295
1959	3	29	1	0	1	0	2	2	4	4,785	228	3	3,436	6,816
1960	25	9	0	2	0	0	1	1	1	1,646	208	2	2,129	18,035
1961	63	3	0	0	0	0	0	0	0	440	0	0	660	1,100
1962	42	3	0	0	0	0	0	0	1	443	0	0	850	1,400
1971	NR	1	0	0	0	0	0	0	0	376	0	0	564	1,800
Lifetime		198	19	20	15	16	15	12	28	32,328	3,664	48	25,170	$115,888

Tommy Thompson

Howard W. Thompson
B: 4/22/1922
Racing Hometown: Louisville, KY

Year	Rank	Starts	Poles	1	2	3	4	5	6–10	Laps	Laps Led	Races Led	Miles	$
1950	79	3	0	0	0	0	0	0	0	272	0	0	439	75
1951	19	5	0	1	0	0	0	0	1	398	58	1	435	5,510
1952	44	5	0	0	0	0	0	0	1	589	20	1	547	525
1953	41	3	0	0	0	1	0	0	0	39	0	0	160	865
1954	205	1	0	0	0	0	0	0	0	15	0	0	62	0
1955	205	1	0	0	0	0	0	0	0	41	0	0	56	50
1956	278	1	0	0	0	0	0	0	0		0	0		0
1959	40	3	0	0	0	0	0	0	0	367	0	0	422	510
Lifetime		22	0	1	0	1	0	0	2	1,721	78	2	2,121	$7,535

Gene Thonesen

Gene Thonesen
B: 12/1/1953   D: 8/4/1993   *Killed on tractor.*
Racing Hometown: Readley, CA

Year	Rank	Starts	Poles	1	2	3	4	5	6–10	Laps	Laps Led	Races Led	Miles	$
1981	83	1	0	0	0	0	0	0	0	110	0	0	288	2,125
Lifetime		1	0	0	0	0	0	0	0	110	0	0	288	$2,125

Year	Rank	Starts	Poles	Finish 1	2	3	4	5	6–10	Laps	Laps Led	Races Led	Miles	$

Bill Thorp

William Thorp
Racing Hometown: Gardena, CA

Year	Rank	Starts	Poles	1	2	3	4	5	6–10	Laps	Laps Led	Races Led	Miles	$
1958	104	1	0	0	0	0	0	0	0	154	0	0	405	110
Lifetime		1	0	0	0	0	0	0	0	154	0	0	405	$110

Marv Thorpe

Marvin Thorpe

Year	Rank	Starts	Poles	1	2	3	4	5	6–10	Laps	Laps Led	Races Led	Miles	$
1958	NR	1	0	0	0	0	0	0	0	67	0	0	22	100
Lifetime		1	0	0	0	0	0	0	0	67	0	0	22	$100

Ruben Thrash

Ruben Thrash
Racing Hometown: Inglewood, CA

Year	Rank	Starts	Poles	1	2	3	4	5	6–10	Laps	Laps Led	Races Led	Miles	$
1958	122	2	0	0	0	0	0	0	0	133	0	0	202	200
Lifetime		2	0	0	0	0	0	0	0	133	0	0	202	$200

Ray Throckmorton

Raymond Throckmorton
Racing Hometown: Richmond, VA

Year	Rank	Starts	Poles	1	2	3	4	5	6–10	Laps	Laps Led	Races Led	Miles	$
1951	N/A	1	0	0	0	0	0	0	0		0	0		50
Lifetime		1	0	0	0	0	0	0	0		0	0		$50

Bill Thurber

William Thurber
Racing Hometown: Palm Beach, FL

Year	Rank	Starts	Poles	1	2	3	4	5	6–10	Laps	Laps Led	Races Led	Miles	$
1956	184T	1	0	0	0	0	0	0	0	173	0	0	87	75
Lifetime		1	0	0	0	0	0	0	0	173	0	0	87	$75

Billy Tibbett

William Tibbett
Racing Hometown: Natick, MA

Year	Rank	Starts	Poles	1	2	3	4	5	6–10	Laps	Laps Led	Races Led	Miles	$
1951	N/A	2	0	0	0	0	0	0	0	318	0	0	398	75
Lifetime		2	0	0	0	0	0	0	0	318	0	0	398	$75

Al Tibbetts

Al Tibbetts
Racing Hometown: Newportville, PA

Year	Rank	Starts	Poles	1	2	3	4	5	6–10	Laps	Laps Led	Races Led	Miles	$
1950	NR	1	0	0	0	0	0	0	0	48	0	0	48	0
Lifetime		1	0	0	0	0	0	0	0	48	0	0	48	$0

Charles Tidwell

Charles Tidwell
Racing Hometown: Macon, GA

Year	Rank	Starts	Poles	1	2	3	4	5	6–10	Laps	Laps Led	Races Led	Miles	$
1950	NR	2	0	0	0	0	0	0	0	300	0	0	375	100
Lifetime		2	0	0	0	0	0	0	0	300	0	0	375	$100

Travis Tiller

Travis Branton Tiller
B: 5/15/1937
Racing Hometown: Triangle, VA

Year	Rank	Starts	Poles	1	2	3	4	5	6–10	Laps	Laps Led	Races Led	Miles	$
1974	34	13	0	0	0	0	0	0	0	2,180	0	0	2,299	11,410
1975	36	10	0	0	0	0	0	0	0	1,958	0	0	2,178	7,780
1976	37	9	0	0	0	0	0	0	0	2,012	0	0	1,787	6,310
1977	61	3	0	0	0	0	0	0	0	250	0	0	183	1,615
1979	60	5	0	0	0	0	0	0	0	218	0	0	336	5,065
1980	65	4	0	0	0	0	0	0	0	830	0	0	733	3,050
1981	100	1	0	0	0	0	0	0	0	111	0	0	169	850
1982	51	4	0	0	0	0	0	0	0	557	0	0	1,107	6,395
1983	73	2	0	0	0	0	0	0	0	338	0	0	463	4,360
Lifetime		51	0	0	0	0	0	0	0	8,454	0	0	9,256	$46,835

Don Tilley

William Donald Tilley
Racing Hometown: Huntersvile, NC

Year	Rank	Starts	Poles	1	2	3	4	5	6–10	Laps	Laps Led	Races Led	Miles	$
1964	105	2	0	0	0	0	0	0	0	275	0	0	164	250
1965	76	2	0	0	0	0	0	0	0	119	0	0	298	1,240
1966	118	2	0	0	0	0	0	0	0	63	0	0	56	505
Lifetime		6	0	0	0	0	0	0	0	457	0	0	517	$1,995

Year	Rank	Starts	Poles	Finish						Laps	Laps Led	Races Led	Miles	$
				1	2	3	4	5	6–10					

Hank Tillman

Harvey Tillman

Year	Rank	Starts	Poles	1	2	3	4	5	6–10	Laps	Laps Led	Races Led	Miles	$
1952	120T	1	0	0	0	0	0	0	0	160	0	0	80	25
1961	147	1	0	0	0	0	0	0	0	146	0	0	219	300
Lifetime		2	0	0	0	0	0	0	0	306	0	0	299	$325

Herb Tillman

Herbert Tillman
B: 1/8/1929
Racing Hometown: Miami, FL

Year	Rank	Starts	Poles	1	2	3	4	5	6–10	Laps	Laps Led	Races Led	Miles	$
1953	133	2	0	0	0	0	0	0	0	122	0	0	126	50
1960	35	9	0	0	0	0	0	0	0	1,705	0	0	2,244	2,695
1961	72	5	0	0	0	0	0	0	0	609	0	0	587	1,000
1962	118	1	0	0	0	0	0	0	0	194	0	0	291	500
Lifetime		17	0	0	0	0	0	0	0	2,630	0	0	3,248	$4,245

Cliff Timberman

Clifford Timberman
Racing Hometown: Charlotte, NC

Year	Rank	Starts	Poles	1	2	3	4	5	6–10	Laps	Laps Led	Races Led	Miles	$
1959	NR	1	0	0	0	0	0	0	0	2	0	0	1	0
Lifetime		1	0	0	0	0	0	0	0	2	0	0	1	$0

Leonard Tippett

Leonard Tippett
Racing Hometown: Greenville, SC

Year	Rank	Starts	Poles	1	2	3	4	5	6–10	Laps	Laps Led	Races Led	Miles	$
1951	N/A	8	0	0	1	0	0	0	1	359	19	1	270	850
1952	57	5	0	0	0	0	0	0	0	221	0	0	134	150
Lifetime		13	0	0	1	0	0	0	1	580	19	1	403	$1,000

Randy Tissot

Randall Tissot
B: 3/30/1944
Racing Hometown: Hollywood, FL

Year	Rank	Starts	Poles	1	2	3	4	5	6–10	Laps	Laps Led	Races Led	Miles	$
1973	44	3	0	0	0	0	0	0	0	816	0	0	1,390	4,245
1974	70	3	0	0	0	0	0	0	0	473	8	1	839	3,750
1975	51	7	0	0	0	0	0	0	0	1,121	0	0	1,657	10,030
Lifetime		13	0	0	0	0	0	0	0	2,410	8	1	3,886	$18,025

Jerry Titus

Jerry Titus
B: 10/24/1928   D: 8/5/1970   *Died of injuries suffered @ Elkhart Lake 7/20/70.*
Racing Hometown: Tarzana, CA

Year	Rank	Starts	Poles	1	2	3	4	5	6–10	Laps	Laps Led	Races Led	Miles	$
1968	106	1	0	0	0	0	0	0	0	5	0	0	14	500
Lifetime		1	0	0	0	0	0	0	0	5	0	0	14	$500

Toby Tobias

Richard Lincoln Tobias
B: 2/12/1932   D: 6/23/1978   *Killed @ Flemington, NJ.*
Racing Hometown: Lebanon, PA

Year	Rank	Starts	Poles	1	2	3	4	5	6–10	Laps	Laps Led	Races Led	Miles	$
1973	121	1	0	0	0	0	0	0	0	50	0	0	50	680
Lifetime		1	0	0	0	0	0	0	0	50	0	0	50	$680

Don Tomberlin

Donald Tomberlin
Racing Hometown: Warner Robbins, GA

Year	Rank	Starts	Poles	1	2	3	4	5	6–10	Laps	Laps Led	Races Led	Miles	$
1968	NR	1	0	0	0	0	0	0	0	181	0	0	91	100
1969	68	2	0	0	0	0	0	0	0	215	0	0	233	1,025
Lifetime		3	0	0	0	0	0	0	0	396	0	0	323	$1,125

Chuck Tombs

Charles Tombs
Racing Hometown: Jeffersonville, IN

Year	Rank	Starts	Poles	1	2	3	4	5	6–10	Laps	Laps Led	Races Led	Miles	$
1959	100	1	0	0	0	0	0	0	0	134	0	0	67	0
1960	102	2	0	0	0	0	0	0	0	227	0	0	114	100
Lifetime		3	0	0	0	0	0	0	0	361	0	0	181	$100

Year	Rank	Starts	Poles	Finish 1	2	3	4	5	6–10	Laps	Laps Led	Races Led	Miles	$

Red Tomlinson

Norman Tomlinson
D: 7/18/54
Racing Hometown: Edgely, PA

Year	Rank	Starts	Poles	1	2	3	4	5	6–10	Laps	Laps Led	Races Led	Miles	$
1952	128	2	0	0	0	0	0	0	0	311	0	0	311	60
Lifetime		2	0	0	0	0	0	0	0	311	0	0	311	$60

T.A. Toomes

T.A. Toomes
B: 12/18/1930
Racing Hometown: Asheboro, NC

Year	Rank	Starts	Poles	1	2	3	4	5	6–10	Laps	Laps Led	Races Led	Miles	$
1957	34	11	0	0	0	0	0	0	1	1,920	0	0	1,040	1,450
Lifetime		11	0	0	0	0	0	0	1	1,920	0	0	1,040	$1,450

Warren Tope

Warren Tope
B: 4/24/1947   D: 7/5/1975   *Killed in practice for a street race.*
Racing Hometown: Troy, MI

Year	Rank	Starts	Poles	1	2	3	4	5	6–10	Laps	Laps Led	Races Led	Miles	$
1975	114T	2	0	0	0	0	0	0	0	305	0	0	467	3,170
Lifetime		2	0	0	0	0	0	0	0	305	0	0	467	$3,170

Pete Torres

Peter Torres
B: 4/17/1944
Racing Hometown: Alhambra, CA

Year	Rank	Starts	Poles	1	2	3	4	5	6–10	Laps	Laps Led	Races Led	Miles	$
1971	NR	1	0	0	0	0	0	0	0	19	0	0	50	645
1975	73T	2	0	0	0	0	0	0	0	162	0	0	424	2,035
Lifetime		3	0	0	0	0	0	0	0	181	0	0	474	$2,680

John Torrese

John Torrese
Racing Hometown: Ira, NY

Year	Rank	Starts	Poles	1	2	3	4	5	6–10	Laps	Laps Led	Races Led	Miles	$
1953	NR	1	0	0	0	0	0	0	0		0	0		25
Lifetime		1	0	0	0	0	0	0	0		0	0		$25

Pete Toth

Peter Toth
Racing Hometown: Toledo, OH

Year	Rank	Starts	Poles	1	2	3	4	5	6–10	Laps	Laps Led	Races Led	Miles	$
1952	140T	1	0	0	0	0	0	0	0	125	0	0	63	25
Lifetime		1	0	0	0	0	0	0	0	125	0	0	63	$25

Sal Tovella

Salvatore Tovella
B: 8/14/1928
Racing Hometown: Chicago, IL

Year	Rank	Starts	Poles	1	2	3	4	5	6–10	Laps	Laps Led	Races Led	Miles	$
1956	221	1	0	0	0	0	0	0	0	142	0	0	71	100
1960	107	2	0	0	0	0	0	0	0	43	0	0	108	275
1961	58	4	0	0	0	0	0	0	0	393	0	0	808	850
1962	105	2	0	0	0	0	0	0	0	77	0	0	193	450
1963	44	3	0	0	0	0	0	0	0	346	0	0	888	1,300
1964	73	2	0	0	0	0	0	0	0	167	0	0	418	850
Lifetime		14	0	0	0	0	0	0	0	1,168	0	0	2,484	$3,825

Ward Towers

Ward Towers
Racing Hometown: Cornith, NY

Year	Rank	Starts	Poles	1	2	3	4	5	6–10	Laps	Laps Led	Races Led	Miles	$
1958	97	1	0	0	0	0	0	0	0	34	0	0	139	90
Lifetime		1	0	0	0	0	0	0	0	34	0	0	139	$90

Chuck Townsen

Charles Townsen
Racing Hometown: Hawthorne, CA

Year	Rank	Starts	Poles	1	2	3	4	5	6–10	Laps	Laps Led	Races Led	Miles	$
1958	115	1	0	0	0	0	0	0	0	152	0	0	400	110
Lifetime		1	0	0	0	0	0	0	0	152	0	0	400	$110

Year	Rank	Starts	Poles	Finish						Laps	Laps Led	Races Led	Miles	$
				1	2	3	4	5	6–10					

Roy Trantham

Roy Musten Trantham
B: 10/2/1941
Racing Hometown: Asheville, NC

Year	Rank	Starts	Poles	1	2	3	4	5	6–10	Laps	Laps Led	Races Led	Miles	$
1968	60	5	0	0	0	0	0	0	1	968	0	0	671	2,285
Lifetime		5	0	0	0	0	0	0	1	968	0	0	671	$2,285

Frank Travers

Frank Travers

Year	Rank	Starts	Poles	1	2	3	4	5	6–10	Laps	Laps Led	Races Led	Miles	$
1951	N/A	1	0	0	0	0	0	0	0		0	0		0
Lifetime		1	0	0	0	0	0	0	0		0	0		$0

Slow Poke Travis

Tom Travis (Slow Poke)
Racing Hometown: Lexington, KY

Year	Rank	Starts	Poles	1	2	3	4	5	6–10	Laps	Laps Led	Races Led	Miles	$
1953	170	1	0	0	0	0	0	0	0	33	0	0	135	25
Lifetime		1	0	0	0	0	0	0	0	33	0	0	135	$25

Hank Trice

Hank Trice

Year	Rank	Starts	Poles	1	2	3	4	5	6–10	Laps	Laps Led	Races Led	Miles	$
1956	NR	1	0	0	0	0	0	0	0	73	0	0	37	50
Lifetime		1	0	0	0	0	0	0	0	73	0	0	37	$50

Dick Trickle

Richard Trickle
B: 10/27/1941
Racing Hometown: Winsonsin Rapids, WI

Year	Rank	Starts	Poles	1	2	3	4	5	6–10	Laps	Laps Led	Races Led	Miles	$
1970	NR	2	0	0	0	0	0	0	0	176	0	0	440	1,415
1973	81	1	0	0	0	0	0	1	0	327	2	1	491	3,385
1974	47	3	0	0	0	0	0	0	3	1,201	0	0	1,568	10,828
1975	113	1	0	0	0	0	0	0	0	3	0	0	8	1,705
1976	105T	1	0	0	0	0	0	0	0	142	0	0	213	1,225
1977	98T	1	0	0	0	0	0	0	0	141	0	0	212	1,100
1978	108	1	0	0	0	0	0	0	0	24	0	0	36	910
1984	87	1	0	0	0	0	0	0	0	53	0	0	133	7,500
1985	55	3	0	0	0	0	0	0	1	452	0	0	778	8,650
1986	55	2	0	0	0	0	0	0	0	676	0	0	975	19,175
1989	15	28	0	0	0	3	1	2	3	8,604	80	8	10,129	273,432
1990	22	29	1	0	0	1	0	1	2	8,291	82	4	9,908	350,990
1991	35	14	0	0	0	0	0	0	1	3,650	0	0	4,274	129,125
1992	20	29	0	0	0	0	0	3	6	8,259	5	2	9,883	429,521
1993	30	26	0	0	0	0	0	1	1	7,003	3	1	8,376	245,065
1994	34	25	0	0	0	0	0	0	1	6,422	1	1	7,107	244,806
1995	25	31	0	0	0	0	0	0	1	8,940	5	1	11,094	694,920
1996	36	26	0	0	0	0	0	0	1	6,694	2	1	8,352	404,927
1997	31	28	0	0	0	1	0	1	0	8,476	0	0	10,896	656,189
1998	29	32	0	0	0	0	0	0	1	8,671	4	2	11,433	1,208,771
1999	47	9	0	0	0	0	0	0	0	2,357	0	0	2,328	275,364
2000	51	6	0	0	0	0	0	0	0	1,807	0	0	2,469	233,865
2001	67	1	0	0	0	0	0	0	0	389	0	0	396	33,850
2002	67	3	0	0	0	0	0	0	0	587	0	0	572	136,830
Lifetime		303	1	0	0	5	1	9	21	83,345	184	21	102,068	$5,373,548

Herb Trimble

Herbert Trimble
Racing Hometown: Middletown, OH

Year	Rank	Starts	Poles	1	2	3	4	5	6–10	Laps	Laps Led	Races Led	Miles	$
1951	N/A	2	0	0	0	0	0	0	1	198	0	0	248	50
Lifetime		2	0	0	0	0	0	0	1	198	0	0	248	$50

Charles Triplett

Charles Triplett
Racing Hometown: N. Wilkesboro, NC

Year	Rank	Starts	Poles	1	2	3	4	5	6–10	Laps	Laps Led	Races Led	Miles	$
1966	116	1	0	0	0	0	0	0	0	85	0	0	43	100
Lifetime		1	0	0	0	0	0	0	0	85	0	0	43	$100

E.J. Trivette

E.J. Trivette
B: 6/6/1936
Racing Hometown: Deep Gap, NC

Year	Rank	Starts	Poles	1	2	3	4	5	6–10	Laps	Laps Led	Races Led	Miles	$
1959	NR	4	0	0	0	0	0	0	0	534	0	0	285	175

Year	Rank	Starts	Poles	Finish						Laps	Laps Led	Races Led	Miles	$
				1	2	3	4	5	6–10					

E.J. Trivette *continued*

Year	Rank	Starts	Poles	1	2	3	4	5	6–10	Laps	Laps Led	Races Led	Miles	$
1960	62	9	0	0	0	0	0	0	0	1,000	0	0	532	940
1961	80	6	0	0	0	0	0	0	1	667	0	0	360	700
1962	135	1	0	0	0	0	0	0	0	29	0	0	15	100
1963	51	11	0	0	0	0	0	0	2	1,996	0	0	1,368	1,965
1964	38	26	0	0	0	0	0	0	3	2,969	0	0	1,903	5,495
1965	15	39	0	0	0	0	0	0	7	7,485	0	0	4,935	13,248
1966	84	3	0	0	0	0	0	0	0	187	0	0	279	1,445
1967	55	7	0	0	0	0	0	0	1	1,418	0	0	1,155	2,360
1968	36	13	0	0	0	0	0	0	0	2,684	0	0	2,746	8,295
1969	11	49	0	0	0	0	0	0	15	11,110	0	0	8,955	35,896
1970	62	4	0	0	0	0	0	0	0	188	0	0	347	2,840
1971	60	5	0	0	0	0	0	0	0	914	0	0	759	1,895
Lifetime		177	0	0	0	0	0	0	29	31,181	0	0	23,637	$75,354

Maynard Troyer

Maynard Ray Troyer
B: 11/22/1938
Racing Hometown: Spencerport, NY

Year	Rank	Starts	Poles	1	2	3	4	5	6–10	Laps	Laps Led	Races Led	Miles	$
1971	38	13	0	0	0	0	1	0	2	1,617	0	0	2,884	13,115
1973	98	1	0	0	0	0	0	0	0	150	0	0	375	1,825
Lifetime		14	0	0	0	0	1	0	2	1,767	0	0	3,259	$14,940

Russ Truelove

Russ E. Truelove
Racing Hometown: Waterbury, CT

Year	Rank	Starts	Poles	1	2	3	4	5	6–10	Laps	Laps Led	Races Led	Miles	$
1953	86T	1	0	0	0	0	0	0	1		0	0		75
1955	51	6	0	0	0	0	0	0	2	738	0	0	689	585
1956	60	5	0	0	0	0	0	0	2	545	0	0	574	450
1957	189	1	0	0	0	0	0	0	0		0	0		0
Lifetime		13	0	0	0	0	0	0	5	1,283	0	0	1,263	$1,110

Jimmy Trull

James Trull
B: 1953
Racing Hometown: Ft. Mill, SC

Year	Rank	Starts	Poles	1	2	3	4	5	6–10	Laps	Laps Led	Races Led	Miles	$
1966	137	1	0	0	0	0	0	0	0	247	0	0	124	247
Lifetime		1	0	0	0	0	0	0	0	247	0	0	124	$247

Donald Tucker

Donald Tucker
Racing Hometown: Greensboro, NC

Year	Rank	Starts	Poles	1	2	3	4	5	6–10	Laps	Laps Led	Races Led	Miles	$
1965	31	9	0	0	0	0	1	0	2	1,597	0	0	1,703	5,830
Lifetime		9	0	0	0	0	1	0	2	1,597	0	0	1,703	$5,830

Reino Tulonen

Reino Tulonen
B: 8/20/1924
Racing Hometown: Fitchburg, MA

Year	Rank	Starts	Poles	1	2	3	4	5	6–10	Laps	Laps Led	Races Led	Miles	$
1951	74	4	0	0	0	0	0	1	0	353	0	0	441	400
Lifetime		4	0	0	0	0	0	1	0	353	0	0	441	$400

Dick Turcott

Richard Turcott
Racing Hometown: Brewerton, NY

Year	Rank	Starts	Poles	1	2	3	4	5	6–10	Laps	Laps Led	Races Led	Miles	$
1952	140T	1	0	0	0	0	0	0	0	163	0	0	82	25
Lifetime		1	0	0	0	0	0	0	0	163	0	0	82	$25

Rod Turcott

Rod Turcott
Racing Hometown: Brewerton, NY

Year	Rank	Starts	Poles	1	2	3	4	5	6–10	Laps	Laps Led	Races Led	Miles	$
1952	138	1	0	0	0	0	0	0	0	167	0	0	84	25
Lifetime		1	0	0	0	0	0	0	0	167	0	0	84	$25

Curtis Turner

Curtis Morton Turner (Pops)
B: 4/12/1924   D: 10/4/1970   *Killed in private plane crash with Clarence King.*
Racing Hometown: Roanoke, VA

Year	Rank	Starts	Poles	1	2	3	4	5	6–10	Laps	Laps Led	Races Led	Miles	$
1949	6	6	1	1	0	0	0	0	3	564	78	2	382	2,675

Year	Rank	Starts	Poles	Finish						Laps	Laps Led	Races Led	Miles	$
				1	2	3	4	5	6–10					

Curtis Turner *continued*

Year	Rank	Starts	Poles	1	2	3	4	5	6–10	Laps	Laps Led	Races Led	Miles	$
1950	5	16	4	4	1	1	1	0	0	1,626	1,110	12	1,390	8,080
1951	NR	12	0	3	0	0	0	0	2	1,164	513	6	948	3,980
1952	50	7	0	0	0	0	0	1	0	526	12	1	427	265
1953	10	19	2	1	0	1	1	0	2	1,396	191	4	1,370	4,347
1954	9	10	1	1	1	2	1	2	1	1,678	277	3	1,497	10,120
1955	34	9	0	0	1	1	2	0	0	928	14	1	832	2,605
1956	20	13	0	1	3	0	0	0	1	1,967	286	2	1,431	14,541
1957	22	10	1	0	2	0	0	0	2	1,397	109	4	1,304	4,830
1958	20	17	1	3	2	0	1	2	2	3,068	827	6	2,190	10,029
1959	24	10	1	2	1	0	1	0	0	1,293	438	5	1,175	3,845
1960	36	9	1	0	0	0	0	0	1	1,090	106	2	1,694	3,220
1961	NR	8	0	0	1	0	0	0	1	1,182	151	5	1,257	6,090
1965	39	7	0	1	0	1	0	1	0	1,360	256	2	1,288	17,440
1966	24	21	2	0	1	1	3	0	1	3,697	385	11	4,120	16,890
1967	71	4	2	0	0	0	0	0	0	241	6	1	524	7,875
1968	47	6	0	0	0	0	1	0	3	1,448	0	0	1,542	5,850
Lifetime		184	16	17	13	7	11	6	19	24,625	4,759	67	23,370	$122,682

Danny Turner

Daniel Turner
Racing Hometown: Atlanta, GA

Year	Rank	Starts	Poles	1	2	3	4	5	6–10	Laps	Laps Led	Races Led	Miles	$
1969	66	3	0	0	0	0	0	0	0	285	0	0	150	1,040
Lifetime		3	0	0	0	0	0	0	0	285	0	0	150	$1,040

E.J. Turner

E.J. Turner
Racing Hometown: Glenolden, PA

Year	Rank	Starts	Poles	1	2	3	4	5	6–10	Laps	Laps Led	Races Led	Miles	$
1954	182	1	0	0	0	0	0	0	0	199	0	0	199	50
1955	172	1	0	0	0	0	0	0	0	194	0	0	194	50
Lifetime		2	0	0	0	0	0	0	0	393	0	0	393	$100

Bill Tuten

William Tuten
Racing Hometown: Hialeah, FL

Year	Rank	Starts	Poles	1	2	3	4	5	6–10	Laps	Laps Led	Races Led	Miles	$
1954	NR	1	0	0	0	0	0	0	0	179	0	0	90	25
Lifetime		1	0	0	0	0	0	0	0	179	0	0	90	$25

Jack Tykarski

Jack Tykarski
Racing Hometown: Trenton, NJ

Year	Rank	Starts	Poles	1	2	3	4	5	6–10	Laps	Laps Led	Races Led	Miles	$
1956	109	1	0	0	0	0	0	0	0	250	0	0	250	225
Lifetime		1	0	0	0	0	0	0	0	250	0	0	250	$225

Carl Tyler

Carl Tyler
B: 1927   D: 1/6/1993
Racing Hometown: Bradford, PA

Year	Rank	Starts	Poles	1	2	3	4	5	6–10	Laps	Laps Led	Races Led	Miles	$
1958	70	10	0	0	0	0	0	0	0	1,016	0	0	843	745
1959	99	2	0	0	0	0	0	0	0	63	0	0	158	150
Lifetime		12	0	0	0	0	0	0	0	1,079	0	0	1,001	$895

Cliff Tyler

Cliff Tyler Jr.
Racing Hometown: Cotchogue, NY

Year	Rank	Starts	Poles	1	2	3	4	5	6–10	Laps	Laps Led	Races Led	Miles	$
1970	73	4	0	0	0	0	0	0	0	455	0	0	393	1,315
Lifetime		4	0	0	0	0	0	0	0	455	0	0	393	$1,315

Paul Tyler

Paul John Tyler, II
B: 2/10/1942
Racing Hometown: Palo Alto, CA

Year	Rank	Starts	Poles	1	2	3	4	5	6–10	Laps	Laps Led	Races Led	Miles	$
1971	47	10	0	0	0	0	0	0	0	1,521	0	0	1,684	6,360
1972	53	4	0	0	0	0	0	0	1	1,125	0	0	1,312	4,200
1973	67	6	0	0	0	0	0	0	0	702	0	0	954	6,575
Lifetime		20	0	0	0	0	0	0	1	3,348	0	0	3,950	$17,135

Year	Rank	Starts	Poles	Finish 1	2	3	4	5	6–10	Laps	Laps Led	Races Led	Miles	$

Roy Tyner

William Leroy Tyner
B: 1/13/1937 D: 2/23/1989 *Shot in truck in Conover, NC; truck set afire.*
Racing Hometown: Red Springs, NC

Year	Rank	Starts	Poles	1	2	3	4	5	6–10	Laps	Laps Led	Races Led	Miles	$
1957	33	10	0	0	0	0	0	0	2	1,705	0	0	1,099	1,020
1958	59	22	0	0	0	0	0	1	2	3,148	0	0	1,951	2,550
1959	33	28	0	0	1	0	3	3	7	5,244	0	0	3,410	5,430
1960	52	23	0	0	0	0	1	0	4	2,076	0	0	1,808	2,930
1961	57	10	0	0	0	0	0	0	1	1,480	0	0	1,354	1,560
1963	85	8	0	0	0	0	0	0	0	381	0	0	193	1,345
1964	16	46	0	0	0	0	0	0	17	7,327	0	0	4,641	11,488
1965	36	28	0	0	0	0	1	0	5	3,448	0	0	2,171	6,696
1966	41	26	0	0	0	0	0	0	4	3,511	0	0	2,046	4,335
1967	43	27	0	0	0	0	0	0	1	2,966	0	0	2,300	8,170
1968	10	48	0	0	0	0	2	2	10	8,789	0	0	5,841	20,247
1969	31	21	0	0	0	0	0	0	1	3,285	0	0	3,030	12,302
1970	42	14	0	0	0	0	0	0	3	1,890	0	0	1,197	5,565
Lifetime		311	0	0	1	0	7	6	57	45,250	0	0	31,041	$83,638

Ed Tyson

Edward Tyson
Racing Hometown: Langhorne, PA

Year	Rank	Starts	Poles	1	2	3	4	5	6–10	Laps	Laps Led	Races Led	Miles	$
1949	74	1	0	0	0	0	0	0	0	169	0	0	169	50
Lifetime		1	0	0	0	0	0	0	0	169	0	0	169	$50

D.K. Ulrich

Donald Keith Ulrich
B: 4/10/1944
Racing Hometown: Woodbury, NJ

Year	Rank	Starts	Poles	1	2	3	4	5	6–10	Laps	Laps Led	Races Led	Miles	$
1971	53	12	0	0	0	0	0	0	0	1,526	0	0	1,064	3,955
1972	64	4	0	0	0	0	0	0	0	1,001	0	0	1,041	2,695
1973	36	11	0	0	0	0	0	0	0	2,006	0	0	2,125	3,955
1974	32	15	0	0	0	0	0	0	0	3,194	0	0	3,606	11,955
1975	27	16	0	0	0	0	0	0	1	3,448	0	0	4,093	16,525
1976	14	30	0	0	0	0	0	0	2	8,489	0	0	9,933	69,435
1977	15	30	0	0	0	0	0	0	0	6,735	0	0	7,649	69,677
1978	22	22	0	0	0	0	0	0	3	6,175	1	1	7,425	54,550
1979	12	31	0	0	0	0	0	0	5	8,995	0	0	10,044	113,458
1980	38	11	0	0	0	0	0	0	1	1,734	0	0	1,898	23,055
1981	32	15	0	0	0	0	1	0	0	4,504	0	0	4,507	38,095
1982	24	25	0	0	0	0	0	0	1	7,102	0	0	7,587	78,130
1983	24	22	0	0	0	0	0	0	2	6,983	0	0	7,876	85,235
1984	42	9	0	0	0	0	0	0	0	2,565	0	0	2,513	31,040
1985	NR	1	0	0	0	0	0	0	0	286	0	0	291	1,350
1986	37	9	0	0	0	0	0	0	0	2,014	0	0	2,191	47,795
1987	40	7	0	0	0	0	0	0	0	1,876	0	0	1,844	30,915
1990	91T	1	0	0	0	0	0	0	0	185	0	0	139	4,265
1992	90T	1	0	0	0	0	0	0	0	21	0	0	21	4,165
Lifetime		272	0	0	0	0	1	0	15	68,839	1	1	75,846	$690,250

Al Unser

Alfred Unser
B: 5/29/1939
Racing Hometown: Albuquerque, NM

Year	Rank	Starts	Poles	1	2	3	4	5	6–10	Laps	Laps Led	Races Led	Miles	$
1968	NR	2	0	0	0	0	1	0	1	382	1	1	991	7,800
1969	NR	1	0	0	0	0	1	0	0	183	0	0	494	3,825
1986	106	2	0	0	0	0	0	0	0	171	0	0	438	4,275
Lifetime		5	0	0	0	0	2	0	1	736	1	1	1,923	$15,900

Al Unser Jr.

Alfred Unser Jr.
B: 4/19/1962
Racing Hometown: Albuquerque, NM

Year	Rank	Starts	Poles	1	2	3	4	5	6–10	Laps	Laps Led	Races Led	Miles	$
1993	81T	1	0	0	0	0	0	0	0	157	0	0	393	23,005
Lifetime		1	0	0	0	0	0	0	0	157	0	0	393	$23,005

Bobby Unser

Robert William Unser
B: 2/20/1934
Racing Hometown: Albuquerque, NM

Year	Rank	Starts	Poles	1	2	3	4	5	6–10	Laps	Laps Led	Races Led	Miles	$
1969	NR	2	0	0	0	0	1	0	0	106	2	2	265	1,900

Year	Rank	Starts	Poles	Finish 1	2	3	4	5	6–10	Laps	Laps Led	Races Led	Miles	$

Bobby Unser *continued*

Year	Rank	Starts	Poles	1	2	3	4	5	6–10	Laps	Laps Led	Races Led	Miles	$
1972	NR	1	0	0	0	0	0	0	0	8	0	0	12	603
1973	NR	1	0	0	0	0	1	0	0	186	0	0	487	4,520
Lifetime		4	0	0	0	0	2	0	0	300	2	2	764	$7,023

Tom Usry

Thomas R. Usry
B: 2/9/1937
Racing Hometown: Sanford, NC

Year	Rank	Starts	Poles	1	2	3	4	5	6–10	Laps	Laps Led	Races Led	Miles	$
1970	NR	1	0	0	0	0	0	0	0	226	0	0	82	255
Lifetime		1	0	0	0	0	0	0	0	226	0	0	82	$255

Dub Utsman

Dub Utsman
Racing Hometown: Bluff City, TN

Year	Rank	Starts	Poles	1	2	3	4	5	6–10	Laps	Laps Led	Races Led	Miles	$
1961	179	1	0	0	0	0	0	0	0	200	0	0	100	125
Lifetime		1	0	0	0	0	0	0	0	200	0	0	100	$125

John A. Utsman

John A. Utsman
B: 12/7/1939
Racing Hometown: Bluff City, TN

Year	Rank	Starts	Poles	1	2	3	4	5	6–10	Laps	Laps Led	Races Led	Miles	$
1973	64	3	0	0	0	0	0	0	1	775	0	0	780	2,965
1976	56	4	0	0	0	0	0	0	0	1,276	0	0	1,859	8,185
1978	59	4	0	0	0	0	0	0	0	612	0	0	1,026	7,040
1979	111T	1	0	0	0	0	0	0	0	101	0	0	253	2,850
1980	76	2	0	0	0	0	0	0	0	613	0	0	620	4,035
Lifetime		14	0	0	0	0	0	0	1	3,377	0	0	4,537	$25,075

Layman Utsman

Layman Utsman
B: 5/5/1933
Racing Hometown: Bluff City, TN

Year	Rank	Starts	Poles	1	2	3	4	5	6–10	Laps	Laps Led	Races Led	Miles	$
1959	NR	2	0	0	0	0	0	0	0	235	0	0	131	50
1961	180	1	0	0	0	0	0	0	0	35	0	0	18	100
Lifetime		3	0	0	0	0	0	0	0	270	0	0	149	$150

Sherman Utsman

Sherman Utsman
B: 4/15/1932
Racing Hometown: Bluff City, TN

Year	Rank	Starts	Poles	1	2	3	4	5	6–10	Laps	Laps Led	Races Led	Miles	$
1956	82	5	0	0	0	0	0	0	1	948	0	0	801	475
1961	102	1	0	0	0	0	0	0	1	481	0	0	241	450
1962	32	12	0	0	0	0	0	1	3	3,293	0	0	2,314	3,580
1963	78	3	0	0	0	0	0	0	3	582	0	0	204	555
Lifetime		21	0	0	0	0	0	1	8	5,304	0	0	3,559	$5,060

Pete Vail

Peter Vail
Racing Hometown: Ossining, NY

Year	Rank	Starts	Poles	1	2	3	4	5	6–10	Laps	Laps Led	Races Led	Miles	$
1952	156	2	0	0	0	0	0	0	0	152	0	0	76	50
Lifetime		2	0	0	0	0	0	0	0	152	0	0	76	$50

Joe Valente

Joseph Valente
Racing Hometown: Berkeley, CA

Year	Rank	Starts	Poles	1	2	3	4	5	6–10	Laps	Laps Led	Races Led	Miles	$
1954	54	4	0	0	0	0	0	0	1	1,066	0	0	650	275
Lifetime		4	0	0	0	0	0	0	1	1,066	0	0	650	$275

Sarel van der Merwe

Sarel van der Merwe
B: 12/5/1946
Racing Hometown: Port Elizabeth, S.Africa

Year	Rank	Starts	Poles	1	2	3	4	5	6–10	Laps	Laps Led	Races Led	Miles	$
1990	78T	1	0	0	0	0	0	0	0	77	0	0	189	12,070
Lifetime		1	0	0	0	0	0	0	0	77	0	0	189	$12,070

Carl Van Horn

Carl Van Horn
Racing Hometown: Belvidere, NJ

Year	Rank	Starts	Poles	1	2	3	4	5	6–10	Laps	Laps Led	Races Led	Miles	$
1975	94	1	0	0	0	0	0	0	0	110	0	0	275	1,355
Lifetime		1	0	0	0	0	0	0	0	110	0	0	275	$1,355

Year	Rank	Starts	Poles	Finish						Laps	Laps Led	Races Led	Miles	$
				1	2	3	4	5	6–10					

Eddie Van Horn

Edward Van Horn
Racing Hometown: Clifton, NJ

Year	Rank	Starts	Poles	1	2	3	4	5	6–10	Laps	Laps Led	Races Led	Miles	$
1952	NR	3	0	0	0	0	0	0	1	501	0	0	383	110
1953	140T	1	0	0	0	0	0	0	0		0	0		25
1954	121	2	0	0	0	0	0	0	0	197	0	0	111	25
Lifetime		6	0	0	0	0	0	0	1	698	0	0	494	$160

J.C. Van Landingham

J. C. Van Landingham
Racing Hometown: Deland, FL

Year	Rank	Starts	Poles	1	2	3	4	5	6–10	Laps	Laps Led	Races Led	Miles	$
1950	50	1	0	0	0	0	0	1	0	48	0	0	200	450
Lifetime		1	0	0	0	0	0	1	0	48	0	0	200	$450

Van Van Wey

Van Van Wey
Racing Hometown: W. Terre Haute, IN

Year	Rank	Starts	Poles	1	2	3	4	5	6–10	Laps	Laps Led	Races Led	Miles	$
1954	48	3	0	0	0	0	0	0	0	629	0	0	801	495
1955	200	1	0	0	0	0	0	0	0	247	0	0	340	60
Lifetime		4	0	0	0	0	0	0	0	876	0	0	1,141	$555

Bill Vanderhoff

William Vanderhoff
Racing Hometown: Roseland, NJ

Year	Rank	Starts	Poles	1	2	3	4	5	6–10	Laps	Laps Led	Races Led	Miles	$
1967	110T	1	0	0	0	0	0	0	0	114	0	0	57	100
1968	53	11	0	0	0	0	0	0	0	939	0	0	440	2,050
Lifetime		12	0	0	0	0	0	0	0	1,053	0	0	497	$2,150

Jim Vandiver

James Enoch Vandiver
B: 12/13/1939
Racing Hometown: Huntersville, NC

Year	Rank	Starts	Poles	1	2	3	4	5	6–10	Laps	Laps Led	Races Led	Miles	$
1968	124	1	0	0	0	0	0	0	0	5	0	0	2	100
1969	96	3	0	0	1	0	0	0	1	726	102	1	833	13,925
1970	45	14	0	0	0	0	0	0	5	2,634	6	1	3,671	16,080
1971	48	7	0	0	0	0	0	1	3	1,423	0	0	2,566	13,575
1972	31	16	0	0	0	2	0	0	1	2,871	6	1	3,462	27,983
1973	31	10	0	0	0	0	0	0	4	2,431	0	0	3,841	18,586
1974	40	7	0	0	0	0	0	0	1	1,061	1	1	1,996	15,909
1975	30	13	0	0	0	0	1	0	3	2,929	1	1	3,625	24,200
1976	86T	1	0	0	0	0	0	0	0	176	0	0	468	3,735
1977	90	1	0	0	0	0	0	0	0	137	0	0	343	3,520
1978	80	2	0	0	0	0	0	0	0	362	0	0	562	3,530
1979	61	4	0	0	0	0	0	0	0	716	1	1	1,069	8,015
1980	52	4	0	0	0	0	0	0	1	610	0	0	1,136	13,185
1983	88	2	0	0	0	0	0	0	0	448	0	0	674	4,810
Lifetime		85	0	0	1	2	1	1	19	16,529	117	6	24,248	$167,153

Keith VanHoughten

Keith VanHoughten

Year	Rank	Starts	Poles	1	2	3	4	5	6–10	Laps	Laps Led	Races Led	Miles	$
1991	NR	1	0	0	0	0	0	0	0	13	0	0	13	3,475
Lifetime		1	0	0	0	0	0	0	0	13	0	0	13	$3,475

Joe Varde

Joseph Varde
Racing Hometown: Tampa, FL

Year	Rank	Starts	Poles	1	2	3	4	5	6–10	Laps	Laps Led	Races Led	Miles	$
2002	81T	1	0	0	0	0	0	0	0	49	0	0	120	37,610
Lifetime		1	0	0	0	0	0	0	0	49	0	0	120	$37,610

Bud Vaughn

Bud Vaughn
Racing Hometown: Inglewood, CA

Year	Rank	Starts	Poles	1	2	3	4	5	6–10	Laps	Laps Led	Races Led	Miles	$
1957	117	2	0	0	0	0	0	0	0	265	0	0	133	145
1965	NR	4	0	0	0	0	0	0	1	164	0	0	72	840
Lifetime		6	0	0	0	0	0	0	1	429	0	0	205	$985

Jimmy Vaughn

James Dotson Vaughn
B: 3/20/1942
Racing Hometown: Greenville, SC

Year	Rank	Starts	Poles	1	2	3	4	5	6–10	Laps	Laps Led	Races Led	Miles	$
1965	NR	4	0	0	0	0	0	0	0	135	0	0	68	420
1969	NR	1	0	0	0	0	0	0	1	159	0	0	423	2,000

Year	Rank	Starts	Poles	Finish 1	2	3	4	5	6–10	Laps	Laps Led	Races Led	Miles	$

Jimmy Vaughn *continued*

Year	Rank	Starts	Poles	1	2	3	4	5	6–10	Laps	Laps Led	Races Led	Miles	$
1971	NR	3	0	0	0	0	0	0	0	575	0	0	294	1,015
Lifetime		8	0	0	0	0	0	0	1	869	0	0	784	$3,435

Robert Vaughn

Robert Vaughn
Racing Hometown: Jackson, NJ

Year	Rank	Starts	Poles	1	2	3	4	5	6–10	Laps	Laps Led	Races Led	Miles	$
1965	73	2	0	0	0	0	0	0	0	5	0	0	13	1,160
Lifetime		2	0	0	0	0	0	0	0	5	0	0	13	$1,160

Billy Vee

William Vee
D: 1/8/1996
Racing Hometown: Rochester, NY

Year	Rank	Starts	Poles	1	2	3	4	5	6–10	Laps	Laps Led	Races Led	Miles	$
1954	NR	1	0	0	0	0	0	0	0	168	0	0	84	25
Lifetime		1	0	0	0	0	0	0	0	168	0	0	84	$25

Bill Venturini

William Venturini
B: 2/14/1953
Racing Hometown: Chicago, IL

Year	Rank	Starts	Poles	1	2	3	4	5	6–10	Laps	Laps Led	Races Led	Miles	$
1989	100	1	0	0	0	0	0	0	0	80	0	0	160	2,975
1990	45	4	0	0	0	0	0	0	0	702	0	0	1,647	22,970
1991	74T	2	0	0	0	0	0	0	0	71	0	0	146	7,925
Lifetime		7	0	0	0	0	0	0	0	853	0	0	1,952	$33,870

Dick Vermillion

Richard Vermillion
Racing Hometown: Corbin, KY

Year	Rank	Starts	Poles	1	2	3	4	5	6–10	Laps	Laps Led	Races Led	Miles	$
1954	130	1	0	0	0	0	0	0	0	139	0	0	70	25
Lifetime		1	0	0	0	0	0	0	0	139	0	0	70	$25

Don Vershure

Donald Vershure
Racing Hometown: Atlanta, GA

Year	Rank	Starts	Poles	1	2	3	4	5	6–10	Laps	Laps Led	Races Led	Miles	$
1953	157	3	0	0	0	0	0	0	0	86	0	0	66	75
Lifetime		3	0	0	0	0	0	0	0	86	0	0	66	$75

Bill Vesler

William Vesler
Racing Hometown: Chicago, IL

Year	Rank	Starts	Poles	1	2	3	4	5	6–10	Laps	Laps Led	Races Led	Miles	$
1956	256	1	0	0	0	0	0	0	0	50	0	0	25	41
Lifetime		1	0	0	0	0	0	0	0	50	0	0	25	$41

Lou Volk

Louis Volk
B: 12/2/1910
Racing Hometown: Paterson, NJ

Year	Rank	Starts	Poles	1	2	3	4	5	6–10	Laps	Laps Led	Races Led	Miles	$
1949	41	1	0	0	0	0	0	0	1	182	0	0	182	125
1951	N/A	1	0	0	0	0	0	0	0		0	0		25
Lifetime		2	0	0	0	0	0	0	1	182	0	0	182	$150

Eli Vukovich

Eli Vukovich
B: 5/26/1916   D: 8/23/2001
Racing Hometown: Fresno, CA

Year	Rank	Starts	Poles	1	2	3	4	5	6–10	Laps	Laps Led	Races Led	Miles	$
1954	NR	1	0	0	0	0	0	0	0	262	0	0	131	25
Lifetime		1	0	0	0	0	0	0	0	262	0	0	131	$25

Bobby Waddell

Robert Waddell
Racing Hometown: N. Wilkesboro, NC

Year	Rank	Starts	Poles	1	2	3	4	5	6–10	Laps	Laps Led	Races Led	Miles	$
1955	55	7	0	0	0	0	0	0	0	992	0	0	942	385
1956	91	8	0	0	0	0	0	0	0	490	0	0	299	335
1957	175T	1	0	0	0	0	0	0	0	39	0	0	20	50
1959	88	7	0	0	0	0	0	0	0	512	0	0	262	360
1960	NR	1	0	0	0	0	0	0	0	168	0	0	84	50
1961	55	7	0	0	0	0	0	0	2	951	0	0	864	1,025
1962	91	6	0	0	0	0	0	0	0	303	0	0	161	470
Lifetime		37	0	0	0	0	0	0	2	3,455	0	0	2,633	$2,675

Year	Rank	Starts	Poles	Finish						Laps	Laps Led	Races Led	Miles	$
				1	2	3	4	5	6–10					

Billy Wade

Billy Drew Wade
B: 2/28/1930   D: 1/5/1965   *Killed in tire test @ Daytona.*
Racing Hometown: Houston, TX

Year	Rank	Starts	Poles	1	2	3	4	5	6–10	Laps	Laps Led	Races Led	Miles	$
1962	46	4	0	0	0	0	0	0	2	1,054	0	0	938	1,350
1963	16	31	0	0	1	0	2	1	10	6,008	21	2	4,989	15,204
1964	4	36	5	4	0	4	3	1	13	7,627	954	14	6,724	36,095
Lifetime		71	5	4	1	4	5	2	25	14,689	975	16	12,651	$52,649

Jack Wade

Jack Wade
Racing Hometown: Charlottesville, VA

Year	Rank	Starts	Poles	1	2	3	4	5	6–10	Laps	Laps Led	Races Led	Miles	$
1951	N/A	2	0	0	0	0	0	0	0		0	0		50
Lifetime		2	0	0	0	0	0	0	0		0	0		$50

Pat Wade

Patrick Wade

Year	Rank	Starts	Poles	1	2	3	4	5	6–10	Laps	Laps Led	Races Led	Miles	$
1951	N/A	1	0	0	0	0	0	0	0		0	0		25
Lifetime		1	0	0	0	0	0	0	0		0	0		$25

Ken Wagner

Kenneth W. Wagner
B: 9/19/1917
Racing Hometown: Pennington, NJ

Year	Rank	Starts	Poles	1	2	3	4	5	6–10	Laps	Laps Led	Races Led	Miles	$
1949	50	3	1	0	0	0	0	0	0	412	0	0	206	100
1950	72	3	0	0	0	0	0	0	1	274	0	0	313	250
1956	170	3	0	0	0	0	0	0	0	112	0	0	64	60
Lifetime		9	1	0	0	0	0	0	1	798	0	0	583	$410

Al Wagoner

Al Wagoner
Racing Hometown: Winston-Salem, NC

Year	Rank	Starts	Poles	1	2	3	4	5	6–10	Laps	Laps Led	Races Led	Miles	$
1949	37T	1	0	0	0	0	0	0	1	178	0	0	89	75
Lifetime		1	0	0	0	0	0	0	1	178	0	0	89	$75

Chuck Wahl

Chuck Wahl
B: 12/20/1950
Racing Hometown: Burbank, CA

Year	Rank	Starts	Poles	1	2	3	4	5	6–10	Laps	Laps Led	Races Led	Miles	$
1973	123	1	0	0	0	0	0	0	0	7	0	0	18	630
1974	74	2	0	0	0	0	0	0	1	275	0	0	702	2,870
1975	56	3	0	0	0	0	0	0	1	299	0	0	780	4,020
1976	71	2	0	0	0	0	0	0	0	182	3	1	477	2,705
1977	70	2	0	0	0	0	0	0	0	155	0	0	406	2,420
1978	79	2	0	0	0	0	0	0	0	102	0	0	262	1,520
1980	NR	1	0	0	0	0	0	0	0	88	0	0	231	1,005
Lifetime		13	0	0	0	0	0	0	2	1,108	3	1	2,876	$15,170

Frank Waite

Frank Waite
Racing Hometown: Tucker, GA

Year	Rank	Starts	Poles	1	2	3	4	5	6–10	Laps	Laps Led	Races Led	Miles	$
1963	81	4	0	0	0	0	0	0	0	617	0	0	309	425
Lifetime		4	0	0	0	0	0	0	0	617	0	0	309	$425

Augie Walackas

Augie Walackas
Racing Hometown: Brockston, MA

Year	Rank	Starts	Poles	1	2	3	4	5	6–10	Laps	Laps Led	Races Led	Miles	$
1950	NR	1	0	0	0	0	0	0	0		0	0		0
1951	53	4	0	0	0	1	0	0	2		0	0		575
Lifetime		5	0	0	0	1	0	0	2		0	0		$575

Bob Walden

Robert Walden
Racing Hometown: High Point, NC

Year	Rank	Starts	Poles	1	2	3	4	5	6–10	Laps	Laps Led	Races Led	Miles	$
1953	46	4	0	0	0	0	0	0	2	325	0	0	180	250
1958	56	14	0	0	0	0	1	0	8	2,104	0	0	1,167	1,810
Lifetime		18	0	0	0	0	1	0	10	2,429	0	0	1,347	$2,060

Year	Rank	Starts	Poles	Finish 1	2	3	4	5	6–10	Laps	Laps Led	Races Led	Miles	$

Lennie Waldo

Lennie Frank Waldo
B: 2/3/1944
Racing Hometown: Columbus, OH

Year	Rank	Starts	Poles	1	2	3	4	5	6–10	Laps	Laps Led	Races Led	Miles	$
1968	59	4	0	0	0	0	0	0	0	671	0	0	1,091	3,620
Lifetime		4	0	0	0	0	0	0	0	671	0	0	1,091	$3,620

Sam Waldrop

Samuel Waldrop
Racing Hometown: Charlotte, NC

Year	Rank	Starts	Poles	1	2	3	4	5	6–10	Laps	Laps Led	Races Led	Miles	$
1968	116	1	0	0	0	0	0	0	0	171	0	0	86	130
Lifetime		1	0	0	0	0	0	0	0	171	0	0	86	$130

Robert Wales

Robert E. Wales (Paddlefoot)
Racing Hometown: Pleasant Grove, AL

Year	Rank	Starts	Poles	1	2	3	4	5	6–10	Laps	Laps Led	Races Led	Miles	$
1972	118	2	0	0	0	0	0	0	0	14	0	0	37	1,510
Lifetime		2	0	0	0	0	0	0	0	14	0	0	37	$1,510

Bill Walker

William Walker
Racing Hometown: Springfield, MA

Year	Rank	Starts	Poles	1	2	3	4	5	6–10	Laps	Laps Led	Races Led	Miles	$
1956	83	2	0	0	0	0	0	0	1	418	0	0	328	600
1957	54	3	0	0	0	1	0	0	1	355	0	0	371	950
1958	NR	1	0	0	0	0	0	0	0	160	0	0	53	85
Lifetime		6	0	0	0	1	0	0	2	933	0	0	752	$1,635

Don Walker

Donald Walker
Racing Hometown: Palmer, WA

Year	Rank	Starts	Poles	1	2	3	4	5	6–10	Laps	Laps Led	Races Led	Miles	$
1964	98	1	0	0	0	0	0	0	0	106	0	0	286	525
1965	126	1	0	0	0	0	0	0	0	14	0	0	38	500
1966	71	1	0	0	0	0	0	0	0	154	0	0	416	590
Lifetime		3	0	0	0	0	0	0	0	274	0	0	740	$1,615

Jimmy Walker

James Walker
B: 4/26/1939

Year	Rank	Starts	Poles	1	2	3	4	5	6–10	Laps	Laps Led	Races Led	Miles	$
1982	60	3	0	0	0	0	0	0	0	131	0	0	130	2,320
1983	89	2	0	0	0	0	0	0	0	289	0	0	179	1,505
1985	83	1	0	0	0	0	0	0	0	180	0	0	180	1,350
Lifetime		6	0	0	0	0	0	0	0	600	0	0	489	$5,175

John Walker

John Walker

Year	Rank	Starts	Poles	1	2	3	4	5	6–10	Laps	Laps Led	Races Led	Miles	$
1958	NR	1	0	0	0	0	0	0	1	135	0	0	45	155
Lifetime		1	0	0	0	0	0	0	1	135	0	0	45	$155

Mitch Walker

Mitchell Walker

Year	Rank	Starts	Poles	1	2	3	4	5	6–10	Laps	Laps Led	Races Led	Miles	$
1964	NR	1	0	0	0	0	0	0	0	174	0	0	87	130
Lifetime		1	0	0	0	0	0	0	0	174	0	0	87	$130

Murrace Walker

Murrace Walker
Racing Hometown: Whiteville, NC

Year	Rank	Starts	Poles	1	2	3	4	5	6–10	Laps	Laps Led	Races Led	Miles	$
1950	111	1	0	0	0	0	0	0	0	358	0	0	448	0
1951	N/A	1	0	0	0	0	0	0	0	104	0	0	130	0
Lifetime		2	0	0	0	0	0	0	0	462	0	0	578	$0

Bryant Wallace

Hugh Bryant Wallace
Racing Hometown: Concord, NC

Year	Rank	Starts	Poles	1	2	3	4	5	6–10	Laps	Laps Led	Races Led	Miles	$
1961	146	2	0	0	0	0	0	0	0	81	0	0	40	100
1966	113	1	0	0	0	0	0	0	0	39	0	0	20	100
1968	NR	1	0	0	0	0	0	0	0	118	0	0	59	100
Lifetime		4	0	0	0	0	0	0	0	238	0	0	118	$300

Year	Rank	Starts	Poles	Finish 1	2	3	4	5	6–10	Laps	Laps Led	Races Led	Miles	$

Cotton Wallace

Carl Wallace
Racing Hometown: Atlanta, GA

Year	Rank	Starts	Poles	1	2	3	4	5	6–10	Laps	Laps Led	Races Led	Miles	$
1965	NR	1	0	0	0	0	0	0	0	5	0	0	8	500
Lifetime		1	0	0	0	0	0	0	0	5	0	0	8	$500

Kenny Wallace

Kenneth Wallace
B: 8/23/1963
Racing Hometown: St.Louis, MO

Year	Rank	Starts	Poles	1	2	3	4	5	6–10	Laps	Laps Led	Races Led	Miles	$
1990	81T	1	0	0	0	0	0	0	0	315	0	0	197	2,550
1991	44	5	0	0	0	0	0	0	0	1,544	1	1	1,823	58,325
1993	23	30	0	0	0	0	0	0	3	8,806	1	1	10,552	330,325
1994	40	12	0	0	0	0	1	0	2	4,426	4	3	4,686	235,005
1995	42	11	0	0	0	0	0	0	0	3,127	0	0	4,071	151,700
1996	28	30	0	0	0	0	0	0	2	8,415	7	2	9,897	457,665
1997	33	31	2	0	0	0	0	0	2	8,333	0	0	10,868	939,001
1998	31	31	0	0	0	0	0	0	7	7,076	59	4	9,349	1,019,861
1999	22	34	0	0	1	0	0	2	2	8,805	56	1	11,514	1,416,208
2000	26	34	0	0	1	0	0	0	0	8,900	17	2	11,822	1,723,966
2001	39	24	1	0	1	0	0	0	1	7,334	104	4	8,864	1,507,922
2002	39	21	0	0	0	0	0	0	1	5,742	4	2	7,874	1,379,803
Lifetime		264	3	0	3	0	1	2	20	72,823	253	20	91,517	$9,222,331

Mike Wallace

Michael Wallace
B: 3/10/1959
Racing Hometown: St. Louis, MO

Year	Rank	Starts	Poles	1	2	3	4	5	6–10	Laps	Laps Led	Races Led	Miles	$
1991	62	2	0	0	0	0	0	0	0	315	0	0	351	7,000
1992	50	3	0	0	0	0	0	0	0	1,042	0	0	1,347	17,415
1993	46	4	0	0	0	0	0	0	0	1,287	0	0	1,819	30,125
1994	33	22	0	0	0	0	0	1	0	6,672	13	1	8,629	265,115
1995	34	26	0	0	0	0	0	0	1	6,819	2	2	8,808	428,006
1996	41	11	0	0	0	0	0	0	0	2,877	3	1	3,628	169,082
1997	46	7	0	0	0	0	0	0	0	1,845	0	0	2,394	159,303
1998	62	1	0	0	0	0	0	0	0	199	0	0	498	85,405
1999	54	2	0	0	0	0	0	0	0	596	0	0	795	135,261
2001	34	29	0	0	1	0	0	0	5	8,684	61	4	10,901	2,075,044
2002	41	22	0	0	0	0	0	0	1	5,664	1	1	7,134	1,274,703
Lifetime		129	0	0	1	0	0	1	7	36,000	80	9	46,303	$4,646,459

Rusty Wallace

Russell William Wallace
B: 8/14/1956
Racing Hometown: St.Louis, MO

Year	Rank	Starts	Poles	1	2	3	4	5	6–10	Laps	Laps Led	Races Led	Miles	$
1980	57	2	0	0	1	0	0	0	0	653	0	0	987	22,860
1981	64	4	0	0	0	0	0	0	1	838	0	0	1,431	10,895
1982	65	3	0	0	0	0	0	0	0	418	0	0	669	7,655
1984	14	30	0	0	0	0	1	1	2	8,868	11	7	10,024	201,739
1985	19	28	0	0	0	0	0	2	6	7,271	28	1	8,384	233,670
1986	6	29	0	2	0	0	2	0	12	8,486	417	8	10,418	557,354
1987	5	29	1	2	3	2	1	1	7	8,323	462	16	9,670	690,652
1988	2	29	2	6	5	4	2	2	4	9,222	891	19	11,191	1,411,567
1989	1	29	4	6	4	0	2	1	7	9,104	2,020	23	10,783	860,990
1990	6	29	2	2	3	2	0	2	7	8,459	1,138	16	10,174	954,129
1991	10	29	2	2	0	3	2	2	5	8,316	524	14	10,150	502,073
1992	13	29	1	1	2	1	1	0	7	8,761	673	11	10,452	657,925
1993	2	30	3	10	4	2	1	2	2	9,641	2,861	20	11,232	1,702,154
1994	3	31	2	8	3	1	4	1	3	9,281	2,143	19	10,731	1,959,072
1995	5	31	0	2	4	6	2	1	4	9,497	1,093	17	11,564	1,642,837
1996	7	31	0	5	1	0	1	1	10	8,383	965	13	10,160	1,665,315
1997	9	32	1	1	3	2	0	2	4	8,747	778	11	10,954	1,705,625
1998	4	33	4	1	2	5	3	4	6	9,603	946	19	12,308	2,667,889
1999	8	34	4	1	0	1	3	2	9	9,592	1,009	11	12,158	2,454,050
2000	7	34	9	4	1	1	3	3	8	9,925	1,731	21	12,902	3,037,721
2001	7	36	0	1	0	2	2	3	6	10,138	1,105	11	13,219	4,788,652
2002	7	36	1	0	4	1	1	1	10	10,591	202	9	13,824	4,785,134
Lifetime		598	36	54	40	33	31	31	120	174,117	18,997	266	213,383	$32,519,958

Year	Rank	Starts	Poles	Finish 1	2	3	4	5	6–10	Laps	Laps Led	Races Led	Miles	$

Walter Wallace

Walter Wallace
Racing Hometown: Nashville, TN

Year	Rank	Starts	Poles	1	2	3	4	5	6–10	Laps	Laps Led	Races Led	Miles	$
1966	95	1	0	0	0	0	0	0	0	379	0	0	190	300
1967	125	1	0	0	0	0	0	0	0	11	0	0	6	100
1976	76	2	0	0	0	0	0	0	0	437	0	0	260	775
Lifetime		4	0	0	0	0	0	0	0	827	0	0	455	$1,175

Edgar Wallen

Edgar Wallen
Racing Hometown: Richmond, VA

Year	Rank	Starts	Poles	1	2	3	4	5	6–10	Laps	Laps Led	Races Led	Miles	$
1966	90	3	0	0	0	0	0	0	0	524	0	0	238	360
Lifetime		3	0	0	0	0	0	0	0	524	0	0	238	$360

Guy Waller

Guy Waller (Crash)
B: 2/9/1919
Racing Hometown: Atlanta, GA

Year	Rank	Starts	Poles	1	2	3	4	5	6–10	Laps	Laps Led	Races Led	Miles	$
1951	N/A	1	0	0	0	0	0	0	0	52	0	0	39	25
Lifetime		1	0	0	0	0	0	0	0	52	0	0	39	$25

Claude Wallington

Claude Wallington

Year	Rank	Starts	Poles	1	2	3	4	5	6–10	Laps	Laps Led	Races Led	Miles	$
1951	82	2	0	0	0	0	0	0	1		0	0		225
Lifetime		2	0	0	0	0	0	0	1		0	0		$225

Bob Walters

Robert William Walters
Racing Hometown: Salisbury, NC

Year	Rank	Starts	Poles	1	2	3	4	5	6–10	Laps	Laps Led	Races Led	Miles	$
1951	N/A	6	0	0	0	0	0	0	0	151	0	0	124	125
Lifetime		6	0	0	0	0	0	0	0	151	0	0	124	$125

Dan Walters

Daniel Walters
Racing Hometown: Griffen, IN

Year	Rank	Starts	Poles	1	2	3	4	5	6–10	Laps	Laps Led	Races Led	Miles	$
1953	NR	1	0	0	0	0	0	0	0	15	0	0	62	0
Lifetime		1	0	0	0	0	0	0	0	15	0	0	62	$0

Dick Walters

Richard Walters

Year	Rank	Starts	Poles	1	2	3	4	5	6–10	Laps	Laps Led	Races Led	Miles	$
1955	177	1	0	0	0	0	0	0	0	78	0	0	78	100
1957	NR	3	0	0	0	0	0	0	1	499	0	0	327	290
1958	99	4	0	0	0	0	0	0	0	305	0	0	129	290
Lifetime		8	0	0	0	0	0	0	1	882	0	0	534	$680

Lucky Walters

Lucky Walters

Year	Rank	Starts	Poles	1	2	3	4	5	6–10	Laps	Laps Led	Races Led	Miles	$
1954	NR	1	0	0	0	0	0	0	0	18	0	0	27	0
Lifetime		1	0	0	0	0	0	0	0	18	0	0	27	$0

Nook Walters

H.H. Walters
D: 12/24/198
Racing Hometown: Niles, OH

Year	Rank	Starts	Poles	1	2	3	4	5	6–10	Laps	Laps Led	Races Led	Miles	$
1951	N/A	2	0	0	0	0	0	0	0		0	0		50
1952	120T	1	0	0	0	0	0	0	0	171	0	0	86	25
1960	NR	1	0	0	0	0	1	0	0	179	0	0	90	275
Lifetime		4	0	0	0	0	1	0	0	350	0	0	175	$350

Sonny Walters

K. Sonny Walters
Racing Hometown: Syracuse, NY

Year	Rank	Starts	Poles	1	2	3	4	5	6–10	Laps	Laps Led	Races Led	Miles	$
1954	NR	1	0	0	0	0	0	0	0	134	0	0	67	0
1956	245	1	0	0	0	0	0	0	0	20	0	0	20	50
Lifetime		2	0	0	0	0	0	0	0	154	0	0	87	$50

Year	Rank	Starts	Poles	Finish 1	2	3	4	5	6–10	Laps	Laps Led	Races Led	Miles	$

Salt Walther

David Walther
B: 11/22/1947
Racing Hometown: Dayton, OH

Year	Rank	Starts	Poles	1	2	3	4	5	6–10	Laps	Laps Led	Races Led	Miles	$
1975	NR	2	0	0	0	0	0	0	0	240	0	0	506	2,330
1976	NR	2	0	0	0	0	0	0	0	192	0	0	473	6,485
1977	NR	1	0	0	0	0	0	0	0	114	0	0	285	2,725
Lifetime		5	0	0	0	0	0	0	0	546	0	0	1,264	$11,540

Chuck Walton

Chuck Walton

Year	Rank	Starts	Poles	1	2	3	4	5	6–10	Laps	Laps Led	Races Led	Miles	$
1985	95T	1	0	0	0	0	0	0	0	5	0	0	5	875
Lifetime		1	0	0	0	0	0	0	0	5	0	0	5	$875

Paul Walton

Paul Walton
Racing Hometown: High Point, NC

Year	Rank	Starts	Poles	1	2	3	4	5	6–10	Laps	Laps Led	Races Led	Miles	$
1958	NR	1	0	0	0	0	0	0	0	144	0	0	36	130
1959	NR	1	0	0	0	0	0	0	0	112	0	0	70	60
Lifetime		2	0	0	0	0	0	0	0	256	0	0	106	$190

Darrell Waltrip

Darrell Waltrip
B: 2/5/1947
Racing Hometown: Franklin, TN

Year	Rank	Starts	Poles	1	2	3	4	5	6–10	Laps	Laps Led	Races Led	Miles	$
1972	56	5	0	0	0	1	0	0	2	1,211	7	1	1,653	8,615
1973	28	19	0	0	1	0	0	0	4	3,783	50	3	5,358	42,466
1974	19	16	1	0	1	3	2	1	4	4,649	103	5	6,013	67,775
1975	7	28	2	2	2	2	3	2	3	7,240	562	13	7,426	160,192
1976	8	30	3	1	3	4	1	1	2	7,780	534	10	8,089	204,193
1977	4	30	3	6	4	3	1	2	8	9,301	949	23	10,590	324,814
1978	3	30	2	6	6	4	1	2	1	9,445	2,052	26	10,542	413,908
1979	2	31	5	7	4	5	1	2	3	9,994	2,128	26	11,769	557,012
1980	5	31	5	5	3	2	6	0	1	9,015	2,023	28	9,764	405,711
1981	1	31	11	12	6	3	0	0	4	9,575	2,504	27	10,975	799,134
1982	1	30	7	12	1	3	0	1	3	9,455	3,027	27	10,598	923,151
1983	2	30	7	6	8	4	2	2	3	9,403	2,362	22	10,547	865,185
1984	5	30	4	7	2	3	1	0	7	9,464	2,030	22	10,440	731,023
1985	1	28	5	3	6	6	2	1	3	8,931	969	21	10,917	1,318,375
1986	2	29	1	3	2	4	6	6	1	8,327	573	21	9,948	1,099,735
1987	4	29	0	1	1	1	2	1	10	8,996	311	14	11,036	511,768
1988	7	29	2	2	1	1	2	4	4	9,065	520	18	10,792	731,659
1989	4	29	0	6	2	2	2	2	4	9,333	858	17	10,986	949,535
1990	20	23	0	0	1	1	2	1	7	8,138	297	9	9,288	520,420
1991	8	29	0	2	2	1	0	0	12	9,229	203	12	10,903	604,854
1992	9	29	1	3	2	3	0	2	3	8,706	513	14	10,249	876,492
1993	13	30	0	0	0	2	1	1	6	9,194	151	9	10,818	746,646
1994	9	31	0	0	0	2	2	0	9	9,905	60	8	12,027	854,280
1995	19	31	1	0	0	1	3	0	4	8,222	168	8	9,582	850,632
1996	29	31	0	0	0	0	0	0	2	7,766	2	2	8,972	740,185
1997	26	31	0	0	0	0	0	1	3	8,427	17	6	10,978	958,679
1998	24	33	0	0	0	0	0	1	1	8,994	16	4	11,885	1,056,475
1999	37	27	0	0	0	0	0	0	0	7,204	3	2	8,937	973,133
2000	36	29	0	0	0	0	0	0	0	6,988	5	4	9,685	1,246,280
Lifetime		809	60	84	58	61	40	33	114	237,740	22,997	402	280,767	$19,542,327

Michael Waltrip

Michael Waltrip
B: 4/30/1963
Racing Hometown: Owensboro, KY

Year	Rank	Starts	Poles	1	2	3	4	5	6–10	Laps	Laps Led	Races Led	Miles	$
1985	57	5	0	0	0	0	0	0	0	1,013	0	0	1,583	9,540
1986	19	28	0	0	0	0	0	0	0	7,852	6	4	9,147	108,767
1987	20	29	0	0	0	0	0	0	1	7,790	1	1	8,850	205,370
1988	18	29	0	0	1	0	0	0	2	7,734	6	2	10,050	240,400
1989	18	29	0	0	0	0	0	0	5	8,372	9	4	10,113	215,480
1990	16	29	0	0	0	1	2	2	5	8,226	17	4	10,223	395,507
1991	15	29	2	0	0	1	0	3	8	8,394	292	11	9,759	440,812
1992	23	29	0	0	0	0	1	0	1	8,474	3	1	10,184	410,545
1993	17	30	0	0	0	0	0	0	5	9,378	39	6	11,146	529,923

Year	Rank	Starts	Poles	Finish						Laps	Laps Led	Races Led	Miles	$
				1	2	3	4	5	6–10					

Michael Waltrip *continued*

Year	Rank	Starts	Poles	1	2	3	4	5	6–10	Laps	Laps Led	Races Led	Miles	$
1994	12	31	0	0	0	1	0	1	8	9,508	8	5	11,667	720,426
1995	12	31	0	0	0	1	0	1	6	9,221	45	11	11,400	898,338
1996	14	31	0	0	0	0	0	1	10	9,279	18	5	11,166	1,182,811
1997	18	32	0	0	0	0	0	0	6	9,277	11	5	12,041	1,138,599
1998	17	32	0	0	0	0	0	0	5	9,519	14	7	12,493	1,508,680
1999	29	34	0	0	0	0	0	1	2	9,022	48	6	11,896	1,701,160
2000	27	34	0	0	0	1	0	0	0	8,704	5	5	11,244	1,689,421
2001	24	36	0	1	2	0	0	0	0	9,527	88	8	12,823	3,411,644
2002	14	36	0	1	1	0	1	1	6	9,928	180	12	13,175	3,185,969
Lifetime		534	2	2	4	5	4	10	70	151,218	790	97	188,962	$17,993,392

Blackie Wangerin

Ervin Wangerin
B: 4/4/1935
Racing Hometown: Bloomington, MN

Year	Rank	Starts	Poles	1	2	3	4	5	6–10	Laps	Laps Led	Races Led	Miles	$
1971	NR	1	0	0	0	0	0	0	0	16	0	0	40	0
1977	NR	1	0	0	0	0	0	0	0	260	0	0	396	885
1978	37	10	0	0	0	0	0	0	0	1,342	0	0	2,522	13,515
1979	35	7	0	0	0	0	0	0	0	894	0	0	1,750	14,300
1980	63	3	0	0	0	0	0	0	0	548	0	0	808	6,920
1981	104	1	0	0	0	0	0	0	0	17	0	0	43	2,750
1982	95	1	0	0	0	0	0	0	0	73	0	0	183	1,600
1983	80	2	0	0	0	0	0	0	0	48	0	0	62	1,860
1984	NR	1	0	0	0	0	0	0	0	0	0	0	0	960
Lifetime		27	0	0	0	0	0	0	0	3,198	0	0	5,803	$42,790

Bill Ward

William Ward
B: 8/8/1930
Racing Hometown: Anniston, AL

Year	Rank	Starts	Poles	1	2	3	4	5	6–10	Laps	Laps Led	Races Led	Miles	$
1969	NR	1	0	0	0	0	0	0	0	149	0	0	396	1,550
1971	72	2	0	0	0	0	0	0	0	281	0	0	747	2,865
1972	119	1	0	0	0	0	0	0	0	10	0	0	27	770
1973	87	2	0	0	0	0	0	0	0	188	0	0	500	2,275
1975	100T	1	0	0	0	0	0	0	0	145	0	0	386	1,320
Lifetime		7	0	0	0	0	0	0	0	773	0	0	2,056	$8,780

Glen Ward

Glen Ward
B: 10/2/1946
Racing Hometown: Ashland, OR

Year	Rank	Starts	Poles	1	2	3	4	5	6–10	Laps	Laps Led	Races Led	Miles	$
1980	105	1	0	0	0	0	0	0	0	77	0	0	193	875
Lifetime		1	0	0	0	0	0	0	0	77	0	0	193	$875

James Ward

James Ward
Racing Hometown: Atlanta, GA

Year	Rank	Starts	Poles	1	2	3	4	5	6–10	Laps	Laps Led	Races Led	Miles	$
1951	N/A	1	0	0	0	0	0	0	0	55	0	0	41	25
Lifetime		1	0	0	0	0	0	0	0	55	0	0	41	$25

Rodger Ward

Rodger Ward
B: 1/10/1921
Racing Hometown: Los Angeles, CA

Year	Rank	Starts	Poles	1	2	3	4	5	6–10	Laps	Laps Led	Races Led	Miles	$
1963	NR	2	0	0	0	0	0	0	0	251	0	0	386	325
1964	NR	1	0	0	0	0	0	0	0	24	0	0	65	525
Lifetime		3	0	0	0	0	0	0	0	275	0	0	450	$850

Jimmy Warden

James Warden
Racing Hometown: Bluff City, TN

Year	Rank	Starts	Poles	1	2	3	4	5	6–10	Laps	Laps Led	Races Led	Miles	$
1951	N/A	1	0	0	0	0	0	0	0	314	0	0	393	50
Lifetime		1	0	0	0	0	0	0	0	314	0	0	393	$50

Rick Ware

Richard Ware
B: 7/13/1960
Racing Hometown: High Point, NC

Year	Rank	Starts	Poles	1	2	3	4	5	6–10	Laps	Laps Led	Races Led	Miles	$
1990	97	1	0	0	0	0	0	0	0	42	0	0	103	2,295
Lifetime		1	0	0	0	0	0	0	0	42	0	0	103	$2,295

Year	Rank	Starts	Poles	Finish						Laps	Laps Led	Races Led	Miles	$
				1	2	3	4	5	6–10					

Daniel Warlick

Daniel Warlick
Racing Hometown: Shelby, NC

Year	Rank	Starts	Poles	1	2	3	4	5	6–10	Laps	Laps Led	Races Led	Miles	$
1965	NR	2	0	0	0	0	0	0	1	432	0	0	168	250
Lifetime		2	0	0	0	0	0	0	1	432	0	0	168	$250

Ken Warmington

Kenneth Warmington
Racing Hometown: Buffalo, NY

Year	Rank	Starts	Poles	1	2	3	4	5	6–10	Laps	Laps Led	Races Led	Miles	$
1950	90	3	0	0	0	0	0	0	0	177	0	0	89	25
Lifetime		3	0	0	0	0	0	0	0	177	0	0	89	$25

David Warren

David Warren
Racing Hometown: Cleveland, NC

Year	Rank	Starts	Poles	1	2	3	4	5	6–10	Laps	Laps Led	Races Led	Miles	$
1965	110T	1	0	0	0	0	0	0	0	32	0	0	16	100
Lifetime		1	0	0	0	0	0	0	0	32	0	0	16	$100

Frank Warren

Frank Warren
B: 9/8/1937
Racing Hometown: Augusta, GA

Year	Rank	Starts	Poles	1	2	3	4	5	6–10	Laps	Laps Led	Races Led	Miles	$
1963	101	2	0	0	0	0	0	0	1	373	0	0	187	260
1964	68	2	0	0	0	0	0	0	0	266	0	0	446	735
1965	46	4	0	0	0	0	0	0	1	769	0	0	1,088	2,880
1966	31	11	0	0	0	0	0	0	1	1,989	0	0	2,803	6,740
1967	24	12	0	0	0	0	0	0	1	1,805	0	0	2,668	9,185
1968	42	10	0	0	0	0	0	0	1	1,643	0	0	1,900	5,365
1969	29	23	0	0	0	0	0	0	1	3,343	0	0	3,822	15,677
1970	10	46	0	0	0	0	0	0	2	7,709	71	1	7,763	35,161
1971	8	47	0	0	0	0	0	1	9	8,984	0	0	8,605	40,072
1972	11	30	0	0	0	0	0	0	2	7,091	0	0	8,404	45,048
1973	16	26	0	0	0	0	0	0	0	6,713	0	0	7,185	36,551
1974	13	29	0	0	0	0	0	1	1	7,342	0	0	8,994	55,779
1975	12	27	0	0	0	0	0	0	0	7,758	0	0	9,124	55,671
1976	16	30	0	0	0	0	0	0	3	8,063	0	0	9,899	67,732
1977	16	29	0	0	0	0	0	0	1	6,466	1	1	8,108	67,945
1978	14	30	0	0	0	0	0	0	0	8,481	0	0	9,827	68,173
1979	16	31	0	0	0	0	0	0	3	8,477	0	0	10,047	94,539
1980	40	7	0	0	0	0	0	0	0	1,591	0	0	2,561	18,375
Lifetime		396	0	0	0	0	0	2	27	88,863	72	2	103,430	$625,888

Gayle Warren

Gayle Warren
Racing Hometown: Marion, VA

Year	Rank	Starts	Poles	1	2	3	4	5	6–10	Laps	Laps Led	Races Led	Miles	$
1950	22	10	0	0	0	0	0	1	1	429	10	1	356	550
1951	N/A	3	0	0	0	0	0	0	0	370	0	0	463	150
1953	83	2	0	0	0	0	0	0	0	327	0	0	348	150
Lifetime		15	0	0	0	0	0	1	1	1,126	10	1	1,166	$850

Jerome Warren

Jerome Warren
Racing Hometown: Charlotte, NC

Year	Rank	Starts	Poles	1	2	3	4	5	6–10	Laps	Laps Led	Races Led	Miles	$
1963	113	5	0	0	0	0	0	0	0	171	0	0	89	435
Lifetime		5	0	0	0	0	0	0	0	171	0	0	89	$435

Wayne Watercutter

Wayne Watercutter
Racing Hometown: Sidney, OH

Year	Rank	Starts	Poles	1	2	3	4	5	6–10	Laps	Laps Led	Races Led	Miles	$
1979	NR	3	0	0	0	0	0	0	0	681	0	0	722	2,380
1980	70	2	0	0	0	0	0	0	0	378	0	0	756	2,525
Lifetime		5	0	0	0	0	0	0	0	1,059	0	0	1,478	$4,905

Don Waterman

Donald Waterman
B: 4/15/1950
Racing Hometown: Portland, OR

Year	Rank	Starts	Poles	1	2	3	4	5	6–10	Laps	Laps Led	Races Led	Miles	$
1980	74	2	0	0	0	0	0	0	0	250	0	0	633	3,555
1981	50	3	0	0	0	0	0	0	1	301	1	1	789	8,570
1982	63	2	0	0	0	0	0	0	0	156	1	1	409	3,805
1983	63	2	0	0	0	0	0	0	0	189	0	0	495	3,355
Lifetime		9	0	0	0	0	0	0	1	896	2	2	2,325	$19,285

Year	Rank	Starts	Poles	Finish						Laps	Laps Led	Races Led	Miles	$
				1	2	3	4	5	6–10					

Richard Waters

Richard Waters

Year	Rank	Starts	Poles	1	2	3	4	5	6–10	Laps	Laps Led	Races Led	Miles	$
1978	NR	1	0	0	0	0	0	0	0	13	0	0	8	265
Lifetime		1	0	0	0	0	0	0	0	13	0	0	8	$265

Al Watkins

Al Watkins
Racing Hometown: Gardendale, AL

Year	Rank	Starts	Poles	1	2	3	4	5	6–10	Laps	Laps Led	Races Led	Miles	$
1954	NR	1	0	0	0	0	0	0	0	159	0	0	80	25
1955	74	3	0	0	0	0	0	0	0	491	0	0	386	300
1956	28	14	0	0	0	0	0	0	4	2,065	0	0	1,380	1,185
Lifetime		18	0	0	0	0	0	0	4	2,715	0	0	1,845	$1,510

Jim Watkins

James Watkins
Racing Hometown: Detroit, MI

Year	Rank	Starts	Poles	1	2	3	4	5	6–10	Laps	Laps Led	Races Led	Miles	$
1956	NR	3	0	0	0	0	0	0	0	156	0	0	69	300
Lifetime		3	0	0	0	0	0	0	0	156	0	0	69	$300

Bobby Watson

Robert Lee Watson
B: 4/22/1936
Racing Hometown: Prestonburg, KY

Year	Rank	Starts	Poles	1	2	3	4	5	6–10	Laps	Laps Led	Races Led	Miles	$
1970	101	1	0	0	0	0	0	0	0	11	0	0	6	430
Lifetime		1	0	0	0	0	0	0	0	11	0	0	6	$430

Dave Watson

David Watson
B: 11/7/1945
Racing Hometown: Milton, WI

Year	Rank	Starts	Poles	1	2	3	4	5	6–10	Laps	Laps Led	Races Led	Miles	$
1978	NR	1	0	0	0	0	0	0	0	316	0	0	481	1,600
1979	44	4	0	0	0	0	0	0	1	1,092	7	2	1,161	7,170
Lifetime		5	0	0	0	0	0	0	1	1,408	7	2	1,642	$8,770

Dick Watson

Richard Watson
Racing Hometown: Clinton, CT

Year	Rank	Starts	Poles	1	2	3	4	5	6–10	Laps	Laps Led	Races Led	Miles	$
1969	91	1	0	0	0	0	0	0	0	171	0	0	107	370
Lifetime		1	0	0	0	0	0	0	0	171	0	0	107	$370

Jimmy Watson

James Watson

Year	Rank	Starts	Poles	1	2	3	4	5	6–10	Laps	Laps Led	Races Led	Miles	$
1970	NR	1	0	0	0	0	0	0	0	451	0	0	247	505
1971	NR	1	0	0	0	0	0	0	0	29	0	0	16	350
Lifetime		2	0	0	0	0	0	0	0	480	0	0	263	$855

Blackie Watt

William O. Watt
B: 12/6/1933
Racing Hometown: New Alexandria, PA

Year	Rank	Starts	Poles	1	2	3	4	5	6–10	Laps	Laps Led	Races Led	Miles	$
1966	30	20	0	0	0	0	0	0	9	4,067	0	0	3,003	7,050
1967	67	4	0	0	0	0	0	0	0	330	0	0	540	2,235
Lifetime		24	0	0	0	0	0	0	9	4,397	0	0	3,543	$9,285

Art Watts

Arthur Watts
Racing Hometown: Portland, OR

Year	Rank	Starts	Poles	1	2	3	4	5	6–10	Laps	Laps Led	Races Led	Miles	$
1954	58	4	0	0	0	0	0	0	0	848	0	0	797	240
1956	71	6	0	0	0	0	0	0	2	935	0	0	552	525
1957	52	5	5	1	0	1	0	0	1	689	100	1	377	1,755
1958	76	1	0	0	0	0	0	0	1	165	0	0	434	140
1960	82	1	0	0	0	0	0	0	1	168	0	0	235	525
1961	NR	1	0	0	0	0	0	0	0	85	0	0	119	100
1963	71	1	0	0	0	0	0	0	0	171	0	0	462	475
Lifetime		19	5	1	0	1	0	0	4	3,061	100	1	2,975	$3,760

Bobby Wawak

Robert L. Wawak
B: 9/4/1939
Racing Hometown: Villa Park, IL

Year	Rank	Starts	Poles	1	2	3	4	5	6–10	Laps	Laps Led	Races Led	Miles	$
1965	117	1	0	0	0	0	0	0	0	46	0	0	63	560

Year	Rank	Starts	Poles	Finish 1	2	3	4	5	6–10	Laps	Laps Led	Races Led	Miles	$

Bobby Wawak *continued*

Year	Rank	Starts	Poles	1	2	3	4	5	6–10	Laps	Laps Led	Races Led	Miles	$
1967	31	14	0	0	0	0	0	0	3	2,225	0	0	2,320	8,070
1969	80	1	0	0	0	0	0	0	0	74	0	0	148	657
1971	76	2	0	0	0	0	0	0	0	615	0	0	891	2,665
1976	22	19	0	0	0	0	0	0	9	4,888	0	0	6,232	31,415
1977	45	8	0	0	0	0	0	0	0	1,633	0	0	2,407	13,455
1978	38	7	0	0	0	0	0	0	0	1,298	0	0	1,056	5,870
1979	46	4	0	0	0	0	0	0	0	740	0	0	855	7,295
1980	25	19	0	0	0	0	0	0	1	3,965	0	0	4,170	21,080
1981	31	14	0	0	0	0	0	0	1	2,734	0	0	3,485	21,790
1982	31	10	0	0	0	0	0	0	0	2,489	2	1	3,981	23,660
1983	36	9	0	0	0	0	0	0	0	2,167	0	0	3,262	19,130
1984	47	4	0	0	0	0	0	0	0	874	0	0	1,433	8,575
1985	32	14	0	0	0	0	0	0	0	3,157	0	0	4,457	42,165
1986	43	6	0	0	0	0	0	0	0	1,170	0	0	1,634	10,155
1987	39	8	0	0	0	0	0	0	0	1,648	0	0	2,343	22,505
Lifetime		140	0	0	0	0	0	0	14	29,723	2	1	38,737	$239,047

Bob Weatherly

Robert Weatherly
Racing Hometown: Timmonsville, SC

Year	Rank	Starts	Poles	1	2	3	4	5	6–10	Laps	Laps Led	Races Led	Miles	$
1953	NR	1	0	0	0	0	0	0	0	289	0	0	397	140
Lifetime		1	0	0	0	0	0	0	0	289	0	0	397	$140

Joe Weatherly

Joe Herbert Weatherly
B: 5/29/1922   D: 1/19/1964   *Killed @ Riverside, CA*
Racing Hometown: Norfolk, VA

Year	Rank	Starts	Poles	1	2	3	4	5	6–10	Laps	Laps Led	Races Led	Miles	$
1952	51	1	0	0	0	0	0	0	0	376	0	0	470	150
1954	102	1	0	0	0	0	0	0	1	196	0	0	98	200
1955	47	6	0	0	0	0	1	0	3	994	140	1	873	2,575
1956	16	17	1	0	1	1	3	1	6	2,745	20	1	1,997	5,251
1957	50	14	0	0	1	3	0	1	2	2,059	3	1	1,350	5,340
1958	28	15	1	1	1	0	2	1	2	2,692	104	3	2,120	6,330
1959	18	17	0	0	2	0	1	3	4	2,776	189	7	2,105	9,816
1960	20	24	0	3	2	0	2	0	4	4,294	245	5	3,804	21,624
1961	4	25	4	9	3	0	1	1	4	5,790	609	17	5,329	25,438
1962	1	52	7	9	12	10	3	5	6	12,431	592	16	8,001	70,743
1963	1	53	6	3	5	5	5	2	15	11,343	790	11	8,407	74,624
1964	48	5	0	0	1	0	1	0	1	768	84	1	916	5,290
Lifetime		230	19	25	28	19	19	14	48	46,464	2,776	63	35,470	$227,381

Marshall Weatherly

Marshall Weatherly
Racing Hometown: Charlotte, NC

Year	Rank	Starts	Poles	1	2	3	4	5	6–10	Laps	Laps Led	Races Led	Miles	$
1951	N/A	4	0	0	0	0	0	0	0		0	0		100
Lifetime		4	0	0	0	0	0	0	0		0	0		$100

Frank Weathers

Frank Weathers
Racing Hometown: Maiden, NC

Year	Rank	Starts	Poles	1	2	3	4	5	6–10	Laps	Laps Led	Races Led	Miles	$
1964	122	2	0	0	0	0	0	0	0	53	0	0	22	500
1965	86	5	0	0	0	0	0	0	1	620	0	0	314	640
Lifetime		7	0	0	0	0	0	0	1	673	0	0	336	$1,140

Louis Weathersbee

Louis Weathersbee
Racing Hometown: N.Charleston, SC

Year	Rank	Starts	Poles	1	2	3	4	5	6–10	Laps	Laps Led	Races Led	Miles	$
1964	77	4	0	0	0	0	0	0	0	385	0	0	314	610
Lifetime		4	0	0	0	0	0	0	0	385	0	0	314	$610

Al Weaver

Al Weaver

Year	Rank	Starts	Poles	1	2	3	4	5	6–10	Laps	Laps Led	Races Led	Miles	$
1950	NR	1	0	0	0	0	0	0	0	119	0	0	60	0
Lifetime		1	0	0	0	0	0	0	0	119	0	0	60	$0

Chuck Webb

Chuck Webb
Racing Hometown: Sacramento, CA

Year	Rank	Starts	Poles	1	2	3	4	5	6–10	Laps	Laps Led	Races Led	Miles	$
1959	101	1	0	0	0	0	0	0	0	63	0	0	63	100

Year	Rank	Starts	Poles	1	2	3	Finish 4	5	6–10	Laps	Laps Led	Races Led	Miles	$

Chuck Webb *continued*

Year	Rank	Starts	Poles	1	2	3	4	5	6–10	Laps	Laps Led	Races Led	Miles	$
1961	119	2	0	0	0	0	0	0	1	120	0	0	129	200
Lifetime		3	0	0	0	0	0	0	1	183	0	0	192	$300

Al Weber
Al Weber
    Racing Hometown: Akron, OH

Year	Rank	Starts	Poles	1	2	3	4	5	6–10	Laps	Laps Led	Races Led	Miles	$
1955	119	2	0	0	0	0	0	0	1	201	0	0	101	150
Lifetime		2	0	0	0	0	0	0	1	201	0	0	101	$150

Ewell Weddle
Ewell H. Weddle
    Racing Hometown: Winston-Salem, NC

Year	Rank	Starts	Poles	1	2	3	4	5	6–10	Laps	Laps Led	Races Led	Miles	$
1950	38	3	0	0	0	1	0	0	0	158	0	0	79	600
1951	44	7	0	0	0	0	0	0	2	743	0	0	799	435
1952	66	3	0	0	0	0	0	0	0	465	0	0	316	125
1953	55	4	0	0	0	0	0	0	1		0	0		125
Lifetime		17	0	0	0	1	0	0	3	1,366	0	0	1,194	$1,285

F. Weichman
F. Weichman

Year	Rank	Starts	Poles	1	2	3	4	5	6–10	Laps	Laps Led	Races Led	Miles	$
1950	120T	1	0	0	0	0	0	0	0		0	0		0
Lifetime		1	0	0	0	0	0	0	0		0	0		$0

Charles Weidler
Charles Weidler
    Racing Hometown: Williamsport, PA

Year	Rank	Starts	Poles	1	2	3	4	5	6–10	Laps	Laps Led	Races Led	Miles	$
1952	76	5	0	0	0	0	0	0	0	639	0	0	549	125
1953	164	2	0	0	0	0	0	0	0	9	0	0	37	25
Lifetime		7	0	0	0	0	0	0	0	648	0	0	586	$150

Ernie Weidler
Ernest Weidler

Year	Rank	Starts	Poles	1	2	3	4	5	6–10	Laps	Laps Led	Races Led	Miles	$
1953	NR	1	0	0	0	0	0	0	0		0	0		25
Lifetime		1	0	0	0	0	0	0	0		0	0		$25

Bill Weiman
William Weiman

Year	Rank	Starts	Poles	1	2	3	4	5	6–10	Laps	Laps Led	Races Led	Miles	$
1954	NR	1	0	0	0	0	0	0	0	20	0	0	10	0
Lifetime		1	0	0	0	0	0	0	0	20	0	0	10	$0

Danny Weinberg
Daniel Weinberg
    Racing Hometown: Downey, CA

Year	Rank	Starts	Poles	1	2	3	4	5	6–10	Laps	Laps Led	Races Led	Miles	$
1951	30	6	0	1	0	0	0	1	1	297	1	1	149	1,470
1958	102	1	0	0	0	1	0	0	0	99	0	0	99	425
1959	NR	1	0	0	0	1	0	0	0	100	0	0	100	425
1960	90	3	0	0	0	0	0	1	0	216	0	0	231	525
1961	73	4	1	0	0	2	0	0	1	446	0	0	453	1,185
1963	144	1	0	0	0	0	0	0	0	27	0	0	73	300
1964	131	1	0	0	0	0	0	0	0	9	0	0	24	500
Lifetime		17	1	1	0	4	0	2	2	1,194	1	1	1,129	$4,830

Robert Weisemeyer
Robert L. Weisemeyer
    Racing Hometown: Hepzibah, GA

Year	Rank	Starts	Poles	1	2	3	4	5	6–10	Laps	Laps Led	Races Led	Miles	$
1952	191T	1	0	0	0	0	0	0	0	9	0	0	9	25
Lifetime		1	0	0	0	0	0	0	0	9	0	0	9	$25

Bob Welborn
Robert Joe Welborn
    B: 5/5/1928   D: 8/10/1997
    Racing Hometown: Denton, NC

Year	Rank	Starts	Poles	1	2	3	4	5	6–10	Laps	Laps Led	Races Led	Miles	$
1952	81	3	0	0	0	0	0	0	0	324	0	0	195	90
1953	24	11	0	0	0	0	1	1	4	617	0	0	466	1,160
1954	51	12	0	0	0	1	0	0	2	1,251	0	0	794	1,125
1955	4	32	1	0	1	4	4	3	13	5,291	31	1	3,625	10,147
1956	84	6	0	0	0	0	0	0	2	974	0	0	474	650
1957	NR	4	0	1	0	0	0	2	0	1,152	457	2	968	5,000

Year	Rank	Starts	Poles	Finish						Laps	Laps Led	Races Led	Miles	$
				1	2	3	4	5	6–10					

Bob Welborn *continued*

Year	Rank	Starts	Poles	1	2	3	4	5	6–10	Laps	Laps Led	Races Led	Miles	$
1958	149	18	1	5	3	2	0	0	5	3,770	579	7	2,190	13,270
1959	17	29	5	3	1	3	3	0	3	3,895	176	7	2,364	6,491
1960	16	15	0	0	1	0	2	3	4	2,809	94	2	2,533	6,194
1961	14	14	0	0	1	2	0	0	4	2,996	104	4	3,424	9,136
1962	15	25	0	0	1	0	2	2	7	5,654	0	0	4,558	10,347
1963	40	11	0	0	1	2	1	0	0	2,221	0	0	1,741	4,830
1964	78	3	0	0	0	0	0	2	0	506	125	1	286	805
Lifetime		183	7	9	9	14	13	13	44	31,460	1,566	24	23,617	$69,245

Don Welch

Donald Welch
Racing Hometown: Rochester, NY

Year	Rank	Starts	Poles	1	2	3	4	5	6–10	Laps	Laps Led	Races Led	Miles	$
1954	126T	1	0	0	0	0	0	0	0	175	0	0	88	25
Lifetime		1	0	0	0	0	0	0	0	175	0	0	88	$25

Doug Wells

Douglas Wells
Racing Hometown: Fort Valley, GA

Year	Rank	Starts	Poles	1	2	3	4	5	6–10	Laps	Laps Led	Races Led	Miles	$
1953	175	1	0	0	0	0	0	0	0	13	0	0	53	0
Lifetime		1	0	0	0	0	0	0	0	13	0	0	53	$0

Tommy Wells

Thomas Wells
Racing Hometown: Guntersville, AL

Year	Rank	Starts	Poles	1	2	3	4	5	6–10	Laps	Laps Led	Races Led	Miles	$
1951	N/A	3	0	0	0	0	0	0	0	81	0	0	41	75
1961	98	4	0	0	0	0	0	1	0	727	0	0	507	750
Lifetime		7	0	0	0	0	0	1	0	808	0	0	547	$825

Phil Wendt

Philip Wendt
Racing Hometown: Irvington, AL

Year	Rank	Starts	Poles	1	2	3	4	5	6–10	Laps	Laps Led	Races Led	Miles	$
1968	69	3	0	0	0	0	0	0	0	418	0	0	445	1,980
Lifetime		3	0	0	0	0	0	0	0	418	0	0	445	$1,980

Paul Wensink

Harold Paul Wensink
B: 11/5/1929
Racing Hometown: Deshler, OH

Year	Rank	Starts	Poles	1	2	3	4	5	6–10	Laps	Laps Led	Races Led	Miles	$
1952	114T	1	0	0	0	0	0	0	0	127	0	0	64	25
Lifetime		1	0	0	0	0	0	0	0	127	0	0	64	$25

Pee Wee Wentz

James Elmo Wentz
B: 5/26/1941
Racing Hometown: Danville, VA

Year	Rank	Starts	Poles	1	2	3	4	5	6–10	Laps	Laps Led	Races Led	Miles	$
1971	NR	1	0	0	0	0	0	0	0	100	0	0	46	300
1973	78	2	0	0	0	0	0	0	0	594	0	0	499	1,315
1974	73	3	0	0	0	0	0	0	1	540	0	0	624	3,705
Lifetime		6	0	0	0	0	0	0	1	1,234	0	0	1,168	$5,320

Jim Wesley

James Wesley

Year	Rank	Starts	Poles	1	2	3	4	5	6–10	Laps	Laps Led	Races Led	Miles	$
1950	120T	1	0	0	0	0	0	0	0	0	0	0	0	0
Lifetime		1	0	0	0	0	0	0	0	0	0	0	0	$0

Bill West

William West
Racing Hometown: Downey, CA

Year	Rank	Starts	Poles	1	2	3	4	5	6–10	Laps	Laps Led	Races Led	Miles	$
1954	65	3	0	0	0	0	0	0	1	888	0	0	557	250
1955	52	3	0	0	0	1	0	0	1	374	0	0	374	910
1956	113	2	0	0	0	0	0	0	0	291	0	0	405	150
Lifetime		8	0	0	0	1	0	0	2	1,553	0	0	1,336	$1,310

George West

George West
Racing Hometown: St.Paul, Va

Year	Rank	Starts	Poles	1	2	3	4	5	6–10	Laps	Laps Led	Races Led	Miles	$
1957	185	1	0	0	0	0	0	0	0		0	0		0
Lifetime		1	0	0	0	0	0	0	0		0	0		$0

Year	Rank	Starts	Poles	Finish 1	2	3	4	5	6–10	Laps	Laps Led	Races Led	Miles	$

Vernon West

Vernon West

Year	Rank	Starts	Poles	1	2	3	4	5	6–10	Laps	Laps Led	Races Led	Miles	$
1958	NR	1	0	0	0	0	0	0	0	1	0	0	0	50
Lifetime		1	0	0	0	0	0	0	0	1	0	0	0	$50

Ed Westveer

Edward Westveer
Racing Hometown: Detroit, MI

Year	Rank	Starts	Poles	1	2	3	4	5	6–10	Laps	Laps Led	Races Led	Miles	$
1952	182	1	0	0	0	0	0	0	0	45	0	0	45	25
Lifetime		1	0	0	0	0	0	0	0	45	0	0	45	$25

Dick Whalen

Richard Whalen
B: 4/7/1935
Racing Hometown: San Jose, CA

Year	Rank	Starts	Poles	1	2	3	4	5	6–10	Laps	Laps Led	Races Led	Miles	$
1979	96T	1	0	0	0	0	0	0	0	81	0	0	212	950
Lifetime		1	0	0	0	0	0	0	0	81	0	0	212	$950

Buster Whaley

Buster Whaley
Racing Hometown: Sylacauga, AL

Year	Rank	Starts	Poles	1	2	3	4	5	6–10	Laps	Laps Led	Races Led	Miles	$
1954	119T	1	0	0	0	0	0	0	0	171	0	0	86	25
Lifetime		1	0	0	0	0	0	0	0	171	0	0	86	$25

Doug Wheeler

Stephen Douglas Wheeler
B: 6/17/1946

Year	Rank	Starts	Poles	1	2	3	4	5	6–10	Laps	Laps Led	Races Led	Miles	$
1983	58	2	0	0	0	0	0	0	0	203	0	0	532	4,625
Lifetime		2	0	0	0	0	0	0	0	203	0	0	532	$4,625

Legs Whitcomb

David Whitcomb
Racing Hometown: Valparaiso, IN

Year	Rank	Starts	Poles	1	2	3	4	5	6–10	Laps	Laps Led	Races Led	Miles	$
1954	NR	1	0	0	0	0	0	0	0	97	0	0	49	0
Lifetime		1	0	0	0	0	0	0	0	97	0	0	49	$0

Al White

Al White (Real Name: Al Gristermacher)
Racing Hometown: Buffalo, NY

Year	Rank	Starts	Poles	1	2	3	4	5	6–10	Laps	Laps Led	Races Led	Miles	$
1956	220	2	0	0	0	0	0	0	0	330	0	0	165	200
1957	107	3	0	0	0	0	0	0	1	161	0	0	200	200
1958	31	9	0	0	0	0	0	0	1	1,483	0	0	1,030	920
1959	49	5	0	0	0	0	0	0	0	826	0	0	644	575
1960	NR	2	0	0	0	0	0	0	1	643	0	0	322	450
1962	123	1	0	0	0	0	0	0	0	233	0	0	117	125
1963	154	1	0	0	0	0	0	0	0	211	0	0	106	150
1964	64	7	0	0	0	0	0	0	3	1,484	0	0	655	1,030
1965	NR	4	0	0	0	0	0	0	1	348	0	0	262	545
1966	99	2	0	0	0	0	0	0	0	449	0	0	142	230
Lifetime		36	0	0	0	0	0	0	7	6,168	0	0	3,643	$4,425

Bob White

Robert White

Year	Rank	Starts	Poles	1	2	3	4	5	6–10	Laps	Laps Led	Races Led	Miles	$
1951	N/A	1	0	0	0	0	0	0	0		0	0		0
Lifetime		1	0	0	0	0	0	0	0		0	0		$0

Dave White

David White
Racing Hometown: Silver Spring, MD

Year	Rank	Starts	Poles	1	2	3	4	5	6–10	Laps	Laps Led	Races Led	Miles	$
1958	74	2	0	0	0	0	0	0	1	205	0	0	266	150
1959	38	5	0	0	0	0	0	0	1	1,253	0	0	533	660
Lifetime		7	0	0	0	0	0	0	2	1,458	0	0	799	$810

Don White

Donald White
B: 6/24/1926
Racing Hometown: Keokuk, IA

Year	Rank	Starts	Poles	1	2	3	4	5	6–10	Laps	Laps Led	Races Led	Miles	$
1954	90	1	0	0	0	0	0	0	0	38	0	0	156	90
1954	90	1	0	0	0	0	0	0	0	38	0	0	156	90
1955	79	3	0	0	2	1	0	0	0	296	0	0	198	1,750

Year	Rank	Starts	Poles	Finish						Laps	Laps Led	Races Led	Miles	$
				1	2	3	4	5	6–10					

Don White *continued*

Year	Rank	Starts	Poles	1	2	3	4	5	6–10	Laps	Laps Led	Races Led	Miles	$
1955	79	3	0	0	2	1	0	0	0	296	0	0	198	1,750
1964	NR	1	0	0	0	0	0	0	0	176	0	0	475	825
1964	NR	1	0	0	0	0	0	0	0	176	0	0	475	825
1966	NR	8	0	0	1	2	0	0	2	1,961	8	1	3,199	19,670
1966	NR	8	0	0	1	2	0	0	2	1,961	8	1	3,199	19,670
1967	NR	6	0	0	0	0	1	0	2	997	0	0	1,691	8,410
1967	NR	6	0	0	0	0	1	0	2	997	0	0	1,691	8,410
1968	NR	2	0	0	0	0	0	0	1	585	0	0	738	2,105
1968	NR	2	0	0	0	0	0	0	1	585	0	0	738	2,105
1969	NR	1	0	0	0	0	0	0	0	41	0	0	111	835
1969	NR	1	0	0	0	0	0	0	0	41	0	0	111	835
1970	NR	1	0	0	0	0	0	0	0	16	0	0	42	880
1970	NR	1	0	0	0	0	0	0	0	16	0	0	42	880
1972	NR	1	0	0	0	0	0	0	0	114	0	0	285	1,745
1972	NR	1	0	0	0	0	0	0	0	114	0	0	285	1,745
Lifetime		48	0	0	6	6	2	0	10	8,448	16	2	13,789	$72,620

Gene White

Gene White
B: 5/12/1931   D: 4/15/1986
Racing Hometown: Marietta, GA

Year	Rank	Starts	Poles	1	2	3	4	5	6–10	Laps	Laps Led	Races Led	Miles	$
1956	277	1	0	0	0	0	0	0	0		0	0		0
1958	27	9	0	0	0	0	0	0	2	1,641	0	0	1,295	1,400
1959	95	9	0	0	0	0	0	0	2	1,457	0	0	1,319	2,060
1960	104	3	0	0	0	0	0	0	0	321	0	0	652	400
1961	138	1	0	0	0	0	0	0	0	147	0	0	221	300
Lifetime		23	0	0	0	0	0	0	4	3,566	0	0	3,487	$4,160

J.C. White

John C. White
Racing Hometown: Hildebran, NC

Year	Rank	Starts	Poles	1	2	3	4	5	6–10	Laps	Laps Led	Races Led	Miles	$
1951	N/A	4	0	0	0	0	0	0	0	128	0	0	128	150
1952	104T	1	0	0	0	0	0	0	0	164	0	0	103	25
Lifetime		5	0	0	0	0	0	0	0	292	0	0	231	$175

Jack White

Jack White
Racing Hometown: Lockport, NY

Year	Rank	Starts	Poles	1	2	3	4	5	6–10	Laps	Laps Led	Races Led	Miles	$
1949	18	1	0	1	0	0	0	0	0	200	66	1	100	1,580
1950	25	7	0	0	0	0	0	1	1	712	0	0	850	525
1951	N/A	4	0	0	0	0	0	0	0	158	0	0	158	75
Lifetime		12	0	1	0	0	0	1	1	1,070	66	1	1,108	$2,180

Jesse White

Jesse White
Racing Hometown: Hickory, NC

Year	Rank	Starts	Poles	1	2	3	4	5	6–10	Laps	Laps Led	Races Led	Miles	$
1951	195T	1	0	0	0	0	0	0	0		0	0		25
Lifetime		1	0	0	0	0	0	0	0		0	0		$25

Ken White

Kenneth White

Year	Rank	Starts	Poles	1	2	3	4	5	6–10	Laps	Laps Led	Races Led	Miles	$
1965	NR	1	0	0	0	0	0	0	0	0	0	0	0	400
Lifetime		1	0	0	0	0	0	0	0	0	0	0	0	$400

Pap White

John C. White
B: 6/26/1922
Racing Hometown: High Point, NC

Year	Rank	Starts	Poles	1	2	3	4	5	6–10	Laps	Laps Led	Races Led	Miles	$
1950	65	1	0	0	0	0	0	0	0		0	0		25
1951	62	1	0	0	0	0	0	0	1	383	0	0	479	400
Lifetime		2	0	0	0	0	0	0	1	383	0	0	479	$425

Rex White

Rex Allen White
B: 8/17/1929
Racing Hometown: Spartanburg, SC

Year	Rank	Starts	Poles	1	2	3	4	5	6–10	Laps	Laps Led	Races Led	Miles	$
1956	11	24	1	0	0	2	0	1	11	4,240	0	0	2,978	5,334
1957	21	9	1	0	1	0	3	0	2	1,585	193	2	1,144	3,870

Year	Rank	Starts	Poles	Finish 1	2	3	4	5	6–10	Laps	Laps Led	Races Led	Miles	$

Rex White *continued*

Year	Rank	Starts	Poles	1	2	3	4	5	6–10	Laps	Laps Led	Races Led	Miles	$
1958	7	22	7	2	4	6	0	1	4	3,848	471	7	2,122	12,233
1959	10	23	5	5	2	2	1	1	2	4,744	824	7	3,039	12,360
1960	1	40	3	6	6	7	4	2	10	8,921	332	9	6,916	57,550
1961	2	47	7	7	8	8	2	4	9	10,307	1,224	15	7,542	46,115
1962	5	37	9	8	3	3	1	3	5	7,683	1,124	14	5,760	36,246
1963	9	25	3	0	3	2	0	0	9	5,595	171	6	5,490	27,241
1964	28	6	0	0	0	1	0	1	1	1,444	27	1	1,683	12,310
Lifetime		233	36	28	27	31	11	13	53	48,367	4,366	61	36,674	$213,259

Richard White

Richard White
B: 12/17/1939
Racing Hometown: Escondido, CA

Year	Rank	Starts	Poles	1	2	3	4	5	6–10	Laps	Laps Led	Races Led	Miles	$
1973	63	2	0	0	0	0	0	0	2	329	0	0	862	3,370
1974	108	1	0	0	0	0	0	0	0	139	0	0	364	1,200
1975	84T	1	0	0	0	0	0	0	0	117	0	0	307	1,285
1977	73	2	0	0	0	0	0	0	0	251	0	0	637	2,375
1978	55	3	0	0	0	0	0	0	0	346	2	1	884	4,550
1979	54	3	0	0	0	0	0	0	0	234	0	0	599	4,070
Lifetime		12	0	0	0	0	0	0	2	1,416	2	1	3,652	$16,850

Bill Whitley

William L. Whitley
Racing Hometown: Winston-Salem, NC

Year	Rank	Starts	Poles	1	2	3	4	5	6–10	Laps	Laps Led	Races Led	Miles	$
1960	123	1	0	0	0	0	0	0	0	6	0	0	2	145
1961	NR	1	0	0	0	0	0	0	0	39	0	0	10	50
1962	NR	1	0	0	0	0	0	0	0	171	0	0	43	370
1963	NR	2	0	0	0	0	0	0	0	5	0	0	2	100
1964	96	6	0	0	0	0	0	0	0	455	0	0	195	700
Lifetime		11	0	0	0	0	0	0	0	676	0	0	251	$1,365

Bob Whitlow

Robert Whitlow
B: 2/15/1936
Racing Hometown: Pontiac, MI

Year	Rank	Starts	Poles	1	2	3	4	5	6–10	Laps	Laps Led	Races Led	Miles	$
1973	92	1	0	0	0	0	0	0	0	204	0	0	408	980
1974	NR	1	0	0	0	0	0	0	0	183	0	0	366	1,055
Lifetime		2	0	0	0	0	0	0	0	387	0	0	774	$2,035

Jim Whitman

James Whitman
B: 1/19/1937
Racing Hometown: Paramus, NJ

Year	Rank	Starts	Poles	1	2	3	4	5	6–10	Laps	Laps Led	Races Led	Miles	$
1960	53	5	0	0	0	0	0	0	0	567	0	0	1,055	1,450
Lifetime		5	0	0	0	0	0	0	0	567	0	0	1,055	$1,450

Russ Whitman

Russell Whitman

Year	Rank	Starts	Poles	1	2	3	4	5	6–10	Laps	Laps Led	Races Led	Miles	$
1959	NR	1	0	0	0	0	0	0	0	27	0	0	7	50
Lifetime		1	0	0	0	0	0	0	0	27	0	0	7	$50

Bob Whitmire

Robert Whitmire
Racing Hometown: Ft. Lauderdale, FL

Year	Rank	Starts	Poles	1	2	3	4	5	6–10	Laps	Laps Led	Races Led	Miles	$
1951	N/A	1	0	0	0	0	0	0	0		0	0		0
1957	149	1	0	0	0	0	0	0	0	153	0	0	77	100
Lifetime		2	0	0	0	0	0	0	0	153	0	0	77	$100

Jim Whitt

James Whitt
Racing Hometown: El Cajon, CA

Year	Rank	Starts	Poles	1	2	3	4	5	6–10	Laps	Laps Led	Races Led	Miles	$
1972	57	2	0	0	0	0	0	0	0	410	0	0	909	2,735
1973	95	2	0	0	0	0	0	0	0	124	0	0	325	1,780
Lifetime		4	0	0	0	0	0	0	0	534	0	0	1,234	$4,515

Year	Rank	Starts	Poles	Finish 1	2	3	4	5	6–10	Laps	Laps Led	Races Led	Miles	$

Bill Whittington

William Whittington
B: 9/11/1949
Racing Hometown: Ft. Lauderdale, FL

Year	Rank	Starts	Poles	1	2	3	4	5	6–10	Laps	Laps Led	Races Led	Miles	$
1980	102T	2	0	0	0	0	0	0	1	183	0	0	472	7,385
Lifetime		2	0	0	0	0	0	0	1	183	0	0	472	$7,385

Don Whittington

Donald Whittington
B: 1/23/1946
Racing Hometown: Lubbock, TX

Year	Rank	Starts	Poles	1	2	3	4	5	6–10	Laps	Laps Led	Races Led	Miles	$
1980	46	7	0	0	0	0	0	0	1	659	0	0	1,512	17,610
1981	53	3	0	0	0	0	0	0	0	346	0	0	883	13,685
Lifetime		10	0	0	0	0	0	0	1	1,005	0	0	2,395	$31,295

Reb Wickersham

Charles Allmond Wickersham
B: 1/11/1934
Racing Hometown: Long Boat Key, FL

Year	Rank	Starts	Poles	1	2	3	4	5	6–10	Laps	Laps Led	Races Led	Miles	$
1960	70	7	0	0	0	0	0	0	0	1,119	0	0	1,948	2,575
1961	79	8	0	0	0	0	0	0	1	1,343	0	0	1,199	1,345
1962	134	1	0	0	0	0	0	0	0	133	0	0	67	0
1963	33	14	0	0	0	0	0	0	1	3,501	0	0	2,577	3,800
1964	53	4	0	0	0	0	0	0	0	330	0	0	639	1,675
1965	45	7	0	0	0	0	0	0	2	906	0	0	1,198	4,410
Lifetime		41	0	0	0	0	0	0	4	7,332	0	0	7,627	$13,805

Bill Widenhouse

William Widenhouse
B: 6/17/1929
Racing Hometown: Midland, NC

Year	Rank	Starts	Poles	1	2	3	4	5	6–10	Laps	Laps Led	Races Led	Miles	$
1950	140	1	0	0	0	0	0	0	0	350	0	0	438	0
1951	55	4	0	0	0	0	0	0	0	371	0	0	464	225
1952	100	2	0	0	0	0	0	0	0	181	0	0	105	50
1953	NR	1	0	0	0	0	0	0	0	234	0	0	322	110
1954	37	6	0	0	0	0	0	0	0	987	0	0	999	425
1955	26	5	0	0	0	0	0	1	2	799	2	1	780	1,065
1956	100	6	0	0	0	0	0	1	0	511	0	0	411	460
1963	63	5	0	0	0	0	0	0	1	575	0	0	535	850
1964	NR	1	0	0	0	0	0	0	0	153	0	0	77	90
Lifetime		31	0	0	0	0	0	2	3	4,161	2	1	4,129	$3,275

Dink Widenhouse

David Widenhouse
B: 1/1/1932
Racing Hometown: Concord, NC

Year	Rank	Starts	Poles	1	2	3	4	5	6–10	Laps	Laps Led	Races Led	Miles	$
1954	61	6	0	0	0	0	1	0	1	620	0	0	401	625
1955	24	15	1	0	0	0	0	0	6	1,743	0	0	1,166	1,660
1956	70	7	0	0	0	0	1	0	2	734	0	0	535	940
Lifetime		28	1	0	0	0	2	0	9	3,097	0	0	2,102	$3,225

Earl Wilcox

Earl Wilcox
Racing Hometown: Asheville, NC

Year	Rank	Starts	Poles	1	2	3	4	5	6–10	Laps	Laps Led	Races Led	Miles	$
1961	182	1	0	0	0	0	0	0	0	81	0	0	41	0
Lifetime		1	0	0	0	0	0	0	0	81	0	0	41	$0

Harold Wilcox

Harold Wilcox
Racing Hometown: Bangor, ME

Year	Rank	Starts	Poles	1	2	3	4	5	6–10	Laps	Laps Led	Races Led	Miles	$
1961	123	1	0	0	0	0	0	0	0	112	0	0	28	150
Lifetime		1	0	0	0	0	0	0	0	112	0	0	28	$150

Carl Wilkerson

Carl Wilkerson
Racing Hometown: Youngstown, OH

Year	Rank	Starts	Poles	1	2	3	4	5	6–10	Laps	Laps Led	Races Led	Miles	$
1950	NR	1	0	0	0	0	0	0	0	72	0	0	36	0
Lifetime		1	0	0	0	0	0	0	0	72	0	0	36	$0

Year	Rank	Starts	Poles	Finish 1	2	3	4	5	6–10	Laps	Laps Led	Races Led	Miles	$

Felix Wilkes

Felix Wilkes
Racing Hometown: Annendale, NJ

Year	Rank	Starts	Poles	1	2	3	4	5	6–10	Laps	Laps Led	Races Led	Miles	$
1949	NR	3	0	0	0	0	0	0	0	38	0	0	38	0
1950	NR	1	0	0	0	0	0	0	0		0	0		0
1951	N/A	2	0	0	0	0	0	0	0	18	0	0	14	10
1952	189	1	0	0	0	0	0	0	0	141	0	0	141	35
Lifetime		7	0	0	0	0	0	0	0	197	0	0	193	$45

Keith Wilkinson

Keith Wilkinson
Racing Hometown: Sacramento, CA

Year	Rank	Starts	Poles	1	2	3	4	5	6–10	Laps	Laps Led	Races Led	Miles	$
1961	158T	1	0	0	0	0	0	0	0	74	0	0	74	50
Lifetime		1	0	0	0	0	0	0	0	74	0	0	74	$50

Bill Williams

William Williams
Racing Hometown: Oakland, CA

Year	Rank	Starts	Poles	1	2	3	4	5	6–10	Laps	Laps Led	Races Led	Miles	$
1954	NR	1	0	0	0	0	0	0	0	113	0	0	57	0
1955	221	1	0	0	0	0	0	0	0	195	0	0	195	40
Lifetime		2	0	0	0	0	0	0	0	308	0	0	252	$40

Bob Williams

Robert Williams
B: 6/1/1937
Racing Hometown: Jackson, MS

Year	Rank	Starts	Poles	1	2	3	4	5	6–10	Laps	Laps Led	Races Led	Miles	$
1971	NR	2	0	0	0	0	0	0	0	475	0	0	283	835
Lifetime		2	0	0	0	0	0	0	0	475	0	0	283	$835

Buster Williams

Buster Williams
Racing Hometown: Philadelphia, PA

Year	Rank	Starts	Poles	1	2	3	4	5	6–10	Laps	Laps Led	Races Led	Miles	$
1950	NR	1	0	0	0	0	0	0	0		0	0		0
Lifetime		1	0	0	0	0	0	0	0		0	0		$0

Chet Williams

Chester Williams
Racing Hometown: Detroit, MI

Year	Rank	Starts	Poles	1	2	3	4	5	6–10	Laps	Laps Led	Races Led	Miles	$
1953	94	2	0	0	0	0	0	0	0	374	0	0	429	135
Lifetime		2	0	0	0	0	0	0	0	374	0	0	429	$135

Chub Williams

Chub Williams

Year	Rank	Starts	Poles	1	2	3	4	5	6–10	Laps	Laps Led	Races Led	Miles	$
1956	179	1	0	0	0	0	0	0	0	225	0	0	113	75
Lifetime		1	0	0	0	0	0	0	0	225	0	0	113	$75

Dale Williams

Dale Williams
Racing Hometown: North Wilkesboro, NC

Year	Rank	Starts	Poles	1	2	3	4	5	6–10	Laps	Laps Led	Races Led	Miles	$
1951	N/A	1	0	0	0	0	0	0	1		0	0		100
Lifetime		1	0	0	0	0	0	0	1		0	0		$100

Jack Williams

Jack Williams

Year	Rank	Starts	Poles	1	2	3	4	5	6–10	Laps	Laps Led	Races Led	Miles	$
1956	NR	1	0	0	0	0	0	0	0	94	0	0	59	50
Lifetime		1	0	0	0	0	0	0	0	94	0	0	59	$50

Raymond Williams

Raymond M. Williams
B: 4/15/1939
Racing Hometown: Chapel Hill, NC

Year	Rank	Starts	Poles	1	2	3	4	5	6–10	Laps	Laps Led	Races Led	Miles	$
1970	31	21	0	0	0	0	0	0	0	3,641	0	0	3,844	12,535
1971	31	20	0	0	0	0	0	0	0	2,822	0	0	4,072	14,585
1972	14	28	0	0	0	0	0	0	5	6,759	0	0	8,079	37,000
1973	25	22	0	0	0	0	0	0	3	4,684	0	0	5,233	22,728
1977	113T	1	0	0	0	0	0	0	0	0	0	0	0	490
1978	93T	1	0	0	0	0	0	0	0	74	0	0	185	1,290
Lifetime		93	0	0	0	0	0	0	8	17,980	0	0	21,413	$88,628

Year	Rank	Starts	Poles	Finish						Laps	Laps Led	Races Led	Miles	$
				1	2	3	4	5	6–10					

Rodney Williams

Rodney Williams
Racing Hometown: Chesnee, SC

Year	Rank	Starts	Poles	1	2	3	4	5	6–10	Laps	Laps Led	Races Led	Miles	$
1964	121	2	0	0	0	0	0	0	0	115	0	0	68	550
Lifetime		2	0	0	0	0	0	0	0	115	0	0	68	$550

Tom Williams

Thomas Williams
B: 9/7/1943
Racing Hometown: Schertz, TX

Year	Rank	Starts	Poles	1	2	3	4	5	6–10	Laps	Laps Led	Races Led	Miles	$
1976	113	1	0	0	0	0	0	0	0	41	0	0	103	1,615
Lifetime		1	0	0	0	0	0	0	0	41	0	0	103	$1,615

Charles Williamson

Charles Williamson
Racing Hometown: Roanoke, VA

Year	Rank	Starts	Poles	1	2	3	4	5	6–10	Laps	Laps Led	Races Led	Miles	$
1961	161T	1	0	0	0	0	0	0	0	107	0	0	27	30
Lifetime		1	0	0	0	0	0	0	0	107	0	0	27	$30

Mooney Williamson

Mooney Williamson
Racing Hometown: Norfolk, VA

Year	Rank	Starts	Poles	1	2	3	4	5	6–10	Laps	Laps Led	Races Led	Miles	$
1952	201	1	0	0	0	0	0	0	0		0	0		0
Lifetime		1	0	0	0	0	0	0	0		0	0		$0

Tim Williamson

Timothy Williamson
B: 1/13/1956   D: 1/12/1980   *Killed @ Riverside, CA in Grand American race.*
Racing Hometown: Seaside, CA

Year	Rank	Starts	Poles	1	2	3	4	5	6–10	Laps	Laps Led	Races Led	Miles	$
1979	53	3	0	0	0	0	0	0	1	340	0	0	868	5,580
Lifetime		3	0	0	0	0	0	0	1	340	0	0	868	$5,580

Andy Wilson

Andrew Wilson

Year	Rank	Starts	Poles	1	2	3	4	5	6–10	Laps	Laps Led	Races Led	Miles	$
1956	239T	1	0	0	0	0	0	0	0	59	0	0	30	50
Lifetime		1	0	0	0	0	0	0	0	59	0	0	30	$50

Baldy Wilson

C.L. Wilson
Racing Hometown: Roanoke, VA

Year	Rank	Starts	Poles	1	2	3	4	5	6–10	Laps	Laps Led	Races Led	Miles	$
1950	78	1	0	0	0	0	0	0	0	127	0	0	127	75
Lifetime		1	0	0	0	0	0	0	0	127	0	0	127	$75

Bob Wilson

Robert Wilson
Racing Hometown: Toledo, OH

Year	Rank	Starts	Poles	1	2	3	4	5	6–10	Laps	Laps Led	Races Led	Miles	$
1950	116T	1	0	0	0	0	0	0	0	150	0	0	75	0
Lifetime		1	0	0	0	0	0	0	0	150	0	0	75	$0

Buzz Wilson

Charles Wilson
Racing Hometown: Parkton, MD

Year	Rank	Starts	Poles	1	2	3	4	5	6–10	Laps	Laps Led	Races Led	Miles	$
1957	109	1	0	0	0	0	0	0	0	114	0	0	114	75
1958	134	4	0	0	0	0	0	0	0	386	0	0	189	250
Lifetime		5	0	0	0	0	0	0	0	500	0	0	303	$325

Denny Wilson

Dennis Wilson

Year	Rank	Starts	Poles	1	2	3	4	5	6–10	Laps	Laps Led	Races Led	Miles	$
1992	89	1	0	0	0	0	0	0	0	9	0	0	22	3,450
Lifetime		1	0	0	0	0	0	0	0	9	0	0	22	$3,450

Doug Wilson

Doug Wilson
Racing Hometown: Greensboro, NC

Year	Rank	Starts	Poles	1	2	3	4	5	6–10	Laps	Laps Led	Races Led	Miles	$
1964	88	4	0	0	0	0	0	0	0	1,086	0	0	523	750
Lifetime		4	0	0	0	0	0	0	0	1,086	0	0	523	$750

Year	Rank	Starts	Poles	Finish 1	2	3	4	5	6–10	Laps	Laps Led	Races Led	Miles	$

Elmer Wilson

Elmer Wilson
Racing Hometown: Toledo, OH

Year	Rank	Starts	Poles	1	2	3	4	5	6–10	Laps	Laps Led	Races Led	Miles	$
1950	71	4	0	0	0	0	0	0	0	497	0	0	519	200
1951	N/A	3	0	0	0	0	0	0	0	80	0	0	80	25
Lifetime		7	0	0	0	0	0	0	0	577	0	0	599	$225

Fritz Wilson

Fritz Wilson
Racing Hometown: Denver, CO

Year	Rank	Starts	Poles	1	2	3	4	5	6–10	Laps	Laps Led	Races Led	Miles	$
1959	63	7	0	0	1	0	0	0	1	651	4	1	460	880
1960	68	4	0	0	0	0	2	0	0	284	0	0	367	1,100
1965	NR	1	0	0	0	0	0	0	0	84	0	0	227	550
Lifetime		12	0	0	1	0	2	0	1	1,019	4	1	1,054	$2,530

Gus Wilson

Gus Wilson
Racing Hometown: Baltimore, MD

Year	Rank	Starts	Poles	1	2	3	4	5	6–10	Laps	Laps Led	Races Led	Miles	$
1957	162	2	0	0	0	0	0	0	0	260	0	0	130	150
1958	124	3	0	0	0	0	0	0	0	359	0	0	163	175
1959	NR	1	0	0	0	0	0	0	0	100	0	0	50	50
Lifetime		6	0	0	0	0	0	0	0	719	0	0	343	$375

Jim Wilson

James Wilson
Racing Hometown: Springfield, Ont, Canada

Year	Rank	Starts	Poles	1	2	3	4	5	6–10	Laps	Laps Led	Races Led	Miles	$
1955	174	1	0	0	0	0	0	0	0	37	0	0	152	50
1956	183	2	0	0	0	0	0	0	0	181	0	0	94	50
Lifetime		3	0	0	0	0	0	0	0	218	0	0	246	$100

Paul Wilson

Paul Wilson

Year	Rank	Starts	Poles	1	2	3	4	5	6–10	Laps	Laps Led	Races Led	Miles	$
1958	NR	1	0	0	0	0	0	0	0	58	0	0	19	60
Lifetime		1	0	0	0	0	0	0	0	58	0	0	19	$60

Rick Wilson

Richard Wilson
B: 1/31/1953
Racing Hometown: Bartow, FL

Year	Rank	Starts	Poles	1	2	3	4	5	6–10	Laps	Laps Led	Races Led	Miles	$
1980	62	3	0	0	0	0	0	0	0	262	0	0	595	5,510
1981	41	8	0	0	0	0	0	0	0	989	7	2	1,713	15,625
1982	34	8	0	0	0	0	0	0	2	1,404	0	0	2,612	33,230
1983	98T	1	0	0	0	0	0	0	0	55	0	0	146	2,135
1985	74	2	0	0	0	0	0	0	0	432	0	0	784	4,460
1986	28	17	0	0	0	0	0	0	4	3,265	7	1	5,310	88,820
1987	28	19	0	0	0	0	0	0	1	3,530	20	1	5,577	65,935
1988	21	28	1	0	1	0	1	0	3	6,870	145	3	8,713	209,925
1989	17	29	0	0	0	0	1	1	5	8,004	29	5	9,992	265,605
1990	23	29	0	0	0	0	0	1	2	8,036	0	0	9,383	242,067
1991	26	29	0	0	0	0	0	0	0	7,966	10	1	9,697	241,375
1992	73	1	0	0	0	0	0	0	0	195	0	0	488	24,045
1993	28	29	0	0	0	0	0	0	1	8,117	1	1	10,330	299,725
1997	53	3	0	0	0	0	0	0	0	690	0	0	1,295	96,785
Lifetime		206	1	0	1	0	2	2	18	49,815	219	14	66,635	$1,595,242

Woodie Wilson

Woodrow Wilson
B: 8/8/1925   D: 9/13/1994
Racing Hometown: Mobile, AL

Year	Rank	Starts	Poles	1	2	3	4	5	6–10	Laps	Laps Led	Races Led	Miles	$
1949	NR	1	0	0	0	0	0	0	0		0	0		25
1955	NR	1	0	0	0	0	0	0	0	18	0	0	27	50
1961	41	5	0	0	0	0	0	0	1	828	0	0	1,324	2,625
1962	78	3	0	0	0	0	0	0	1	70	0	0	144	750
Lifetime		10	0	0	0	0	0	0	2	916	0	0	1,495	$3,450

George Wiltshire

George Wiltshire
B: 5/10/1939
Racing Hometown: Corona, NY

Year	Rank	Starts	Poles	1	2	3	4	5	6–10	Laps	Laps Led	Races Led	Miles	$
1971	NR	1	0	0	0	0	0	0	0	2	0	0	0	100

Year	Rank	Starts	Poles	Finish 1	2	3	4	5	6–10	Laps	Laps Led	Races Led	Miles	$

George Wiltshire *continued*

Year	Rank	Starts	Poles	1	2	3	4	5	6–10	Laps	Laps Led	Races Led	Miles	$
1975	107T	1	0	0	0	0	0	0	0	15	0	0	38	630
Lifetime		2	0	0	0	0	0	0	0	17	0	0	38	$730

Jerry Wimbish

Jerry Wimbish
  Racing Hometown: Atlanta, GA

Year	Rank	Starts	Poles	1	2	3	4	5	6–10	Laps	Laps Led	Races Led	Miles	$
1950	62T	1	0	0	0	0	0	0	1		0	0		100
1951	N/A	2	0	0	0	0	0	0	1	51	0	0	51	75
1952	71	4	0	0	0	0	0	1	0	222	0	0	113	395
1953	69T	1	0	0	0	0	0	1	0		0	0		200
1954	NR	1	0	0	0	0	0	0	0	92	0	0	92	25
Lifetime		9	0	0	0	0	0	2	2	365	0	0	256	$795

Bill Wimble

William Wimble
  B: 1/11/1932
  Racing Hometown: Lisbon, N Y

Year	Rank	Starts	Poles	1	2	3	4	5	6–10	Laps	Laps Led	Races Led	Miles	$
1958	114	2	0	0	0	0	0	0	0	241	0	0	121	100
1962	48	2	0	0	0	0	0	0	0	231	0	0	578	675
Lifetime		4	0	0	0	0	0	0	0	472	0	0	698	$775

Scott Wimmer

Scott Wimmer
  B: 1/26/1976
  Racing Hometown: Wausau, WI

Year	Rank	Starts	Poles	1	2	3	4	5	6–10	Laps	Laps Led	Races Led	Miles	$
2000	64	1	0	0	0	0	0	0	0	322	9	1	496	37,780
2002	56	3	0	0	0	0	0	0	0	482	0	0	717	143,110
Lifetime		4	0	0	0	0	0	0	0	804	9	1	1,213	$180,890

Doug Wimpy

Douglas Wimpy
  Racing Hometown: Mobile, AL

Year	Rank	Starts	Poles	1	2	3	4	5	6–10	Laps	Laps Led	Races Led	Miles	$
1951	N/A	1	0	0	0	0	0	0	0		0	0		25
Lifetime		1	0	0	0	0	0	0	0		0	0		$25

Andy Winfree

Andrew Winfree
  Racing Hometown: Greensboro, NC

Year	Rank	Starts	Poles	1	2	3	4	5	6–10	Laps	Laps Led	Races Led	Miles	$
1953	23	7	0	0	0	0	0	0	3	277	0	0	277	300
1954	NR	3	0	0	0	0	0	0	1	301	0	0	216	175
Lifetime		10	0	0	0	0	0	0	4	578	0	0	493	$475

Don Wingier

Donald Wingier

Year	Rank	Starts	Poles	1	2	3	4	5	6–10	Laps	Laps Led	Races Led	Miles	$
1968	—	3	0	0	0	0	0	0	0	381	0	0	94	320
Lifetime		3	0	0	0	0	0	0	0	381	0	0	94	$320

Dorus Wisecraver

Dorus Seymour Wisecraver
  B: 1936
  Racing Hometown: Zanesville, OH

Year	Rank	Starts	Poles	1	2	3	4	5	6–10	Laps	Laps Led	Races Led	Miles	$
1967	NR	2	0	0	0	0	0	0	0	219	0	0	548	2,325
Lifetime		2	0	0	0	0	0	0	0	219	0	0	548	$2,325

Roland Wlodyka

Roland Wlodyka
  B: 10/15/1938
  Racing Hometown: Boston, MA

Year	Rank	Starts	Poles	1	2	3	4	5	6–10	Laps	Laps Led	Races Led	Miles	$
1977	63	5	0	0	0	0	0	0	0	501	0	0	1,100	5,520
1978	44	6	0	0	0	0	0	0	0	1,172	0	0	1,707	9,910
Lifetime		11	0	0	0	0	0	0	0	1,673	0	0	2,807	$15,430

Johnny Wohlfiel

John Wohlfiel
  Racing Hometown: Drayton Plains, MI

Year	Rank	Starts	Poles	1	2	3	4	5	6–10	Laps	Laps Led	Races Led	Miles	$
1951	N/A	1	0	0	0	0	0	0	0	27	0	0	27	0
Lifetime		1	0	0	0	0	0	0	0	27	0	0	27	$0

Year	Rank	Starts	Poles	1	2	3	4	5	6–10	Laps	Laps Led	Races Led	Miles	$

Johnny Wolford
John Wolford
Racing Hometown: Circleville, OH

| 1960 | NR | 1 | 0 | 0 | 0 | 0 | 0 | 0 | 0 | 5 | 0 | 0 | 8 | 200 |
| Lifetime | | 1 | 0 | 0 | 0 | 0 | 0 | 0 | 0 | 5 | 0 | 0 | 8 | $200 |

Bob Wood
Robert Wood
Racing Hometown: Portland, OR

| 1957 | NR | 1 | 0 | 0 | 0 | 0 | 0 | 0 | 0 | 18 | 0 | 0 | 9 | 100 |
| Lifetime | | 1 | 0 | 0 | 0 | 0 | 0 | 0 | 0 | 18 | 0 | 0 | 9 | $100 |

Gifford Wood
Gifford Wood
Racing Hometown: Collinsville, VA

1953	NR	2	0	0	0	0	0	0	0	136	0	0	68	50
1954	144	1	0	0	0	0	0	0	0	152	0	0	76	25
Lifetime		3	0	0	0	0	0	0	0	288	0	0	144	$75

Glen Wood
Glen Wood
B: 7/18/1925
Racing Hometown: Stuart, VA

1953	64	2	0	0	0	0	0	0	0	274	0	0	274	125
1954	215T	1	0	0	0	0	0	0	0	33	0	0	17	0
1955	242T	1	0	0	0	0	0	0	0	55	0	0	28	0
1956	246T	2	0	0	0	0	0	0	0	177	0	0	89	50
1957	74	6	0	0	0	0	0	0	1	1,062	0	0	847	1,670
1958	NR	10	3	0	1	0	0	0	6	2,348	360	4	1,331	3,120
1959	57	20	3	0	5	1	1	2	4	4,186	98	2	2,292	6,875
1960	103	9	4	3	0	2	0	1	1	2,206	766	5	973	5,260
1961	65	6	1	0	2	1	0	0	0	1,101	138	1	445	2,000
1963	73	3	2	1	0	1	0	0	0	571	268	2	143	1,070
1964	100	2	1	0	0	1	0	0	0	305	5	1	76	530
Lifetime		62	14	4	8	6	1	3	12	12,318	1,635	15	6,513	$20,700

Rich Woodland
Richard Woodland Jr.
B: 8/5/1970
Racing Hometown: Templeton, CA

1993	85T	1	0	0	0	0	0	0	0	114	0	0	114	6,030
1996	63T	1	0	0	0	0	0	0	0	68	0	0	171	10,095
Lifetime		2	0	0	0	0	0	0	0	182	0	0	285	$16,125

Sean Woodside
Sean Woodside
B: 10/16/1970
Racing Hometown: Saugus, CA

| 1997 | 64 | 1 | 0 | 0 | 0 | 0 | 0 | 0 | 0 | 69 | 0 | 0 | 174 | 20,905 |
| Lifetime | | 1 | 0 | 0 | 0 | 0 | 0 | 0 | 0 | 69 | 0 | 0 | 174 | $20,905 |

Cliff Woodson
Clifford Woodson

| 1951 | N/A | 1 | 0 | 0 | 0 | 0 | 0 | 0 | 0 | 1 | 0 | 0 | 1 | 10 |
| Lifetime | | 1 | 0 | 0 | 0 | 0 | 0 | 0 | 0 | 1 | 0 | 0 | 1 | $10 |

Buzz Woodward
Benton H. Woodward
B: 1937
Racing Hometown: Coatesville, PA

1956	172	1	0	0	0	0	0	0	0	120	0	0	120	50
1957	NR	1	0	0	0	0	0	0	1	87	0	0	87	165
1958	40	9	0	0	0	0	0	0	2	1,508	0	0	1,028	1,195
1959	NR	1	0	0	0	0	0	1	0	191	0	0	96	225
1961	NR	1	0	0	0	0	0	0	1	459	0	0	115	400
Lifetime		13	0	0	0	0	0	1	4	2,365	0	0	1,446	$2,035

Year	Rank	Starts	Poles	Finish 1	2	3	4	5	6–10	Laps	Laps Led	Races Led	Miles	$

Wayne Woodward

Wayne Woodward
B: 8/26/1934   D: 10/11/199
Racing Hometown: Ringgold, GA

Year	Rank	Starts	Poles	1	2	3	4	5	6–10	Laps	Laps Led	Races Led	Miles	$
1966	67	7	0	0	0	0	0	0	0	1,194	0	0	876	1,930
Lifetime		7	0	0	0	0	0	0	0	1,194	0	0	876	$1,930

Bill Woolkin

William Woolkin

Year	Rank	Starts	Poles	1	2	3	4	5	6–10	Laps	Laps Led	Races Led	Miles	$
1959	NR	1	0	0	0	0	0	0	0	109	0	0	27	70
Lifetime		1	0	0	0	0	0	0	0	109	0	0	27	$70

Satch Worley

Donald A. Worley Jr.
B: 6/2/1948
Racing Hometown: Rocky Mount, VA

Year	Rank	Starts	Poles	1	2	3	4	5	6–10	Laps	Laps Led	Races Led	Miles	$
1974	110	1	0	0	0	0	0	0	1	431	0	0	227	1,300
1978	50	4	0	0	0	0	0	0	1	1,298	0	0	1,590	6,205
Lifetime		5	0	0	0	0	0	0	2	1,729	0	0	1,817	$7,505

Bruce Worrell

Bruce Worrell
Racing Hometown: Lakewood, CA

Year	Rank	Starts	Poles	1	2	3	4	5	6–10	Laps	Laps Led	Races Led	Miles	$
1960	72	3	0	0	0	0	0	0	2	333	0	0	394	650
1961	85	4	0	0	0	0	0	0	2	391	0	0	379	540
1963	153	1	0	0	0	0	0	0	0	1	0	0	3	200
1964	72	1	0	0	0	0	0	0	0	161	0	0	435	575
1965	128	1	0	0	0	0	0	0	0	1	0	0	3	500
1966	128	1	0	0	0	0	0	0	0	15	0	0	41	500
1967	56	1	0	0	0	0	0	0	1	174	0	0	470	1,650
Lifetime		12	0	0	0	0	0	0	5	1,076	0	0	1,723	$4,615

Whitey Worton

Whitey Worton

Year	Rank	Starts	Poles	1	2	3	4	5	6–10	Laps	Laps Led	Races Led	Miles	$
1951	N/A	1	0	0	0	0	0	0	0		0	0		25
Lifetime		1	0	0	0	0	0	0	0		0	0		$25

Cecil Wray

Cecil Wray
Racing Hometown: Middletown, OH

Year	Rank	Starts	Poles	1	2	3	4	5	6–10	Laps	Laps Led	Races Led	Miles	$
1958	105	1	0	0	0	0	0	0	0	34	0	0	139	75
Lifetime		1	0	0	0	0	0	0	0	34	0	0	139	$75

Cliff Wright

Clifford Wright

Year	Rank	Starts	Poles	1	2	3	4	5	6–10	Laps	Laps Led	Races Led	Miles	$
1955	222	1	0	0	0	0	0	0	0	178	0	0	178	40
Lifetime		1	0	0	0	0	0	0	0	178	0	0	178	$40

Gary Wright

Gary Wright
B: 12/19/1958
Racing Hometown: Hooks, TN

Year	Rank	Starts	Poles	1	2	3	4	5	6–10	Laps	Laps Led	Races Led	Miles	$
1991	81T	1	0	0	0	0	0	0	0	63	0	0	158	3,750
Lifetime		1	0	0	0	0	0	0	0	63	0	0	158	$3,750

Harold Wright

Harold Wright
Racing Hometown: Syracuse, NY

Year	Rank	Starts	Poles	1	2	3	4	5	6–10	Laps	Laps Led	Races Led	Miles	$
1952	120T	1	0	0	0	0	0	0	0	162	0	0	81	25
Lifetime		1	0	0	0	0	0	0	0	162	0	0	81	$25

Jim Wright

James Wright
Racing Hometown: Richmond, VA

Year	Rank	Starts	Poles	1	2	3	4	5	6–10	Laps	Laps Led	Races Led	Miles	$
1967	121	1	0	0	0	0	0	0	0	9	0	0	5	125
Lifetime		1	0	0	0	0	0	0	0	9	0	0	5	$125

Year	Rank	Starts	Poles	Finish 1	2	3	4	5	6–10	Laps	Laps Led	Races Led	Miles	$

John Wright

John C. Wright
B: 2/14/1923
Racing Hometown: Ransomville, NY

Year	Rank	Starts	Poles	1	2	3	4	5	6–10	Laps	Laps Led	Races Led	Miles	$
1949	33	1	0	0	0	0	0	0	1	179	0	0	90	100
Lifetime		1	0	0	0	0	0	0	1	179	0	0	90	$100

L.W. Wright

L.W. Wright
Racing Hometown: Nashville, TN

Year	Rank	Starts	Poles	1	2	3	4	5	6–10	Laps	Laps Led	Races Led	Miles	$
1982	NR	1	0	0	0	0	0	0	0	13	0	0	35	1,545
Lifetime		1	0	0	0	0	0	0	0	13	0	0	35	$1,545

Millard Wright

Millard Wright
Racing Hometown: Montclair, NJ

Year	Rank	Starts	Poles	1	2	3	4	5	6–10	Laps	Laps Led	Races Led	Miles	$
1955	132	2	0	0	0	0	0	0	0	225	0	0	113	110
1956	NR	1	0	0	0	0	0	0	0	178	0	0	89	50
Lifetime		3	0	0	0	0	0	0	0	403	0	0	202	$160

Ted Wright

Theodore Wright
Racing Hometown: Greensburg, PA

Year	Rank	Starts	Poles	1	2	3	4	5	6–10	Laps	Laps Led	Races Led	Miles	$
1954	NR	1	0	0	0	0	0	0	0	132	0	0	66	25
Lifetime		1	0	0	0	0	0	0	0	132	0	0	66	$25

Bailey Wynkoop

Bailey Wynkoop
Racing Hometown: Falls Church, VA

Year	Rank	Starts	Poles	1	2	3	4	5	6–10	Laps	Laps Led	Races Led	Miles	$
1958	127	2	0	0	0	0	0	0	0	153	0	0	59	170
Lifetime		2	0	0	0	0	0	0	0	153	0	0	59	$170

Johnny Wynn

John Wynn (Jack)
B: 10/14/1931
Racing Hometown: Grand Rapids, MI

Year	Rank	Starts	Poles	1	2	3	4	5	6–10	Laps	Laps Led	Races Led	Miles	$
1966	38	21	0	0	0	0	0	0	5	3,245	0	0	2,491	4,650
Lifetime		21	0	0	0	0	0	0	5	3,245	0	0	2,491	$4,650

Eddie Yarboro

Edward James Yarboro
B: 7/7/1938
Racing Hometown: Elkin, NC

Year	Rank	Starts	Poles	1	2	3	4	5	6–10	Laps	Laps Led	Races Led	Miles	$
1966	102	3	0	0	0	0	0	0	1	457	0	0	184	165
1967	61	9	0	0	0	0	0	0	3	1,680	0	0	820	1,745
1968	49	6	0	0	0	0	0	0	0	2,109	0	0	1,347	2,255
1970	NR	1	0	0	0	0	0	0	1	338	0	0	201	800
1971	50	7	0	0	0	0	0	0	0	1,624	0	0	1,310	3,685
1972	50	6	0	0	0	0	0	0	0	1,728	0	0	1,336	3,435
1973	128	1	0	0	0	0	0	0	0	4	0	0	11	610
Lifetime		33	0	0	0	0	0	0	5	7,940	0	0	5,209	$12,695

Cale Yarborough

William Caleb Yarborough
B: 3/27/1939
Racing Hometown: Timmonsville, SC

Year	Rank	Starts	Poles	1	2	3	4	5	6–10	Laps	Laps Led	Races Led	Miles	$
1957	159	1	0	0	0	0	0	0	0	31	0	0	43	100
1959	110	1	0	0	0	0	0	0	0	219	0	0	301	150
1960	132	1	0	0	0	0	0	0	0	114	0	0	57	85
1961	NR	1	0	0	0	0	0	0	0	135	0	0	186	200
1962	50	8	0	0	0	0	0	0	1	727	0	0	1,046	2,725
1963	25	18	0	0	0	0	0	3	4	4,519	0	0	3,298	5,550
1964	19	24	0	0	0	0	0	2	7	4,990	10	1	4,121	10,378
1965	10	46	0	1	3	1	5	3	8	7,734	166	8	5,396	26,587
1966	18	14	0	0	2	0	1	0	4	3,831	252	4	3,944	24,077
1967	20	17	4	2	3	1	1	0	2	4,114	908	9	3,909	57,912
1968	17	21	4	6	2	1	0	3	0	5,661	1,065	16	5,709	138,052
1969	23	19	6	2	2	1	2	0	1	4,341	946	16	5,482	74,240
1970	34	19	5	3	4	3	0	1	2	5,034	906	14	6,237	115,875
1971	NR	4	0	0	0	0	0	0	1	564	13	1	961	3,844
1972	51	5	0	0	0	0	0	1	3	1,196	9	1	1,968	11,667
1973	2	28	5	4	6	4	1	1	3	9,314	3,167	21	9,752	267,513

Year	Rank	Starts	Poles	Finish						Laps	Laps Led	Races Led	Miles	$
				1	2	3	4	5	6–10					

Cale Yarborough *continued*

Year	Rank	Starts	Poles	1	2	3	4	5	6–10	Laps	Laps Led	Races Led	Miles	$
1974	2	30	3	10	4	5	1	1	1	9,398	3,530	26	11,059	363,782
1975	9	28	3	3	3	3	3	1	0	7,648	2,542	20	8,395	214,691
1976	1	30	2	9	6	3	2	2	1	9,269	3,771	28	10,548	453,405
1977	1	30	3	9	6	4	3	3	2	9,747	3,218	28	11,383	561,642
1978	1	30	8	10	6	1	5	1	1	9,758	3,587	28	11,367	623,506
1979	4	31	1	4	2	6	4	3	3	9,677	1,323	22	11,193	440,129
1980	2	31	14	6	4	4	4	1	3	9,440	2,811	28	11,016	567,891
1981	24	18	2	2	1	2	0	1	4	4,922	769	13	7,134	150,840
1982	27	16	2	3	2	1	2	0	0	3,439	379	12	5,642	231,590
1983	28	16	3	4	0	0	0	0	4	3,783	608	13	5,975	265,035
1984	22	16	4	3	1	3	1	2	0	4,387	736	12	7,140	403,853
1985	26	16	0	2	2	2	0	0	1	3,450	664	11	5,675	310,465
1986	29	16	1	0	0	2	0	0	3	3,467	110	4	5,828	137,010
1987	29	16	0	0	0	0	1	1	2	2,671	11	2	4,519	111,025
1988	38	10	0	0	0	0	0	0	3	1,653	6	2	3,169	66,065
Lifetime		561	70	83	59	47	36	30	64	145,233	31,507	340	172,454	$5,639,884

J.C. Yarborough

Julian C. Yarborough
Racing Hometown: Timmonsville, SC

Year	Rank	Starts	Poles	1	2	3	4	5	6–10	Laps	Laps Led	Races Led	Miles	$
1969	79	2	0	0	0	0	0	0	0	318	0	0	159	415
Lifetime		2	0	0	0	0	0	0	0	318	0	0	159	$415

Eldon Yarbrough

Eldon Yarbrough
Racing Hometown: Jacksonville, FL

Year	Rank	Starts	Poles	1	2	3	4	5	6–10	Laps	Laps Led	Races Led	Miles	$
1966	NR	1	0	0	0	0	0	0	0	74	0	0	111	500
1967	118	1	0	0	0	0	0	0	0	46	0	0	69	580
1969	NR	1	0	0	0	0	0	1	0	194	0	0	97	325
Lifetime		3	0	0	0	0	0	1	0	314	0	0	277	$1,405

LeeRoy Yarbrough

Lonnie LeeRoy Yarbrough
B: 9/17/1938   D: 12/7/1984   *Died in Mental Institution.*
Racing Hometown: Jacksonville, FL

Year	Rank	Starts	Poles	1	2	3	4	5	6–10	Laps	Laps Led	Races Led	Miles	$
1960	137	1	0	0	0	0	0	0	0	60	0	0	90	225
1962	36	12	0	0	0	0	0	1	0	1,478	0	0	1,730	3,485
1963	26	14	1	0	0	0	0	1	4	2,564	8	1	2,433	6,680
1964	15	34	0	2	3	2	3	1	4	5,896	186	5	4,477	16,630
1965	37	14	0	0	0	0	1	1	1	1,747	42	2	1,748	5,905
1966	26	9	2	1	0	0	1	0	2	1,545	364	5	2,546	23,980
1967	37	15	0	1	0	2	0	0	1	2,647	34	4	2,894	15,325
1968	16	26	6	2	3	6	1	3	1	6,423	1,302	14	5,897	87,920
1969	16	30	0	7	2	0	6	1	5	8,190	1,153	17	8,619	193,211
1970	43	19	2	1	1	4	2	0	3	4,250	302	12	5,438	61,980
1971	73	6	0	0	0	0	1	0	2	1,144	26	2	1,779	9,260
1972	34	18	0	0	0	1	2	2	4	4,174	8	4	4,866	40,705
Lifetime		198	11	14	9	15	17	10	27	40,118	3,425	66	42,515	$465,306

Jack Yardley

Jack Yardley
Racing Hometown: Haddonfield, NJ

Year	Rank	Starts	Poles	1	2	3	4	5	6–10	Laps	Laps Led	Races Led	Miles	$
1950	NR	1	0	0	0	0	0	0	0	89	0	0	111	0
Lifetime		1	0	0	0	0	0	0	0	89	0	0	111	$0

Doug Yates

Alfred Doug Yates
B: 1/5/1925
Racing Hometown: Chapel Hill, N C

Year	Rank	Starts	Poles	1	2	3	4	5	6–10	Laps	Laps Led	Races Led	Miles	$
1952	198	1	0	0	0	0	0	0	0		0	0		25
1956	178	2	0	0	0	0	0	0	0	86	0	0	90	150
1958	175	1	0	0	0	0	0	0	0	16	0	0	66	25
1960	21	24	1	0	0	2	1	0	5	4,030	39	1	3,262	5,205
1961	27	32	0	0	0	0	0	2	8	5,058	0	0	2,992	5,370
1962	67	7	0	0	0	0	0	0	2	883	0	0	510	1,090
1964	45	16	1	0	1	0	0	2	4	2,573	9	1	1,172	3,340
1965	88	4	0	0	0	0	0	0	1	271	13	1	150	550
Lifetime		87	2	0	1	2	1	4	20	12,917	61	3	8,241	$15,755

Year	Rank	Starts	Poles	Finish						Laps	Laps Led	Races Led	Miles	$
				1	2	3	4	5	6–10					

Cliff Yiskis

Clifford Yiskis
Racing Hometown: Cupertino, CA

Year	Rank	Starts	Poles	1	2	3	4	5	6–10	Laps	Laps Led	Races Led	Miles	$
1957	110	1	0	0	0	0	1	0	0	140	0	0	88	365
Lifetime		1	0	0	0	0	1	0	0	140	0	0	88	$365

Shorty York

Aaron Ransom York Jr.
B: 1/13/1924   D: 12/24/1970   *Suicide.*
Racing Hometown: Mocksville, NC

Year	Rank	Starts	Poles	1	2	3	4	5	6–10	Laps	Laps Led	Races Led	Miles	$
1950	96	1	0	0	0	0	0	0	0	358	0	0	448	0
1951	57	5	0	0	1	0	0	0	0	363	0	0	454	725
1956	102	1	0	0	0	0	0	0	0	336	0	0	462	130
1957	155	2	0	0	0	0	0	0	0	188	0	0	163	350
1959	NR	1	0	0	0	0	0	0	0	185	0	0	46	120
1960	95	2	0	0	0	0	0	0	0	434	0	0	412	325
Lifetime		12	0	0	1	0	0	0	0	1,864	0	0	1,985	$1,650

Ernie Yorton

Ernest Yorton
Racing Hometown: Fairport, NY

Year	Rank	Starts	Poles	1	2	3	4	5	6–10	Laps	Laps Led	Races Led	Miles	$
1951	N/A	1	0	0	0	0	0	0	1		0	0		100
Lifetime		1	0	0	0	0	0	0	1		0	0		$100

Buddy Young

Nicholas C. Young
B: 1/13/1943
Racing Hometown: Fairfax, VA

Year	Rank	Starts	Poles	1	2	3	4	5	6–10	Laps	Laps Led	Races Led	Miles	$
1969	35	21	0	0	0	0	0	1	5	4,510	0	0	3,845	15,422
1970	59	2	0	0	0	0	0	0	1	501	0	0	569	1,980
Lifetime		23	0	0	0	0	0	1	6	5,011	0	0	4,414	$17,402

Clay Young

Clay Young
B: 6/9/1947
Racing Hometown: Smyrna, GA

Year	Rank	Starts	Poles	1	2	3	4	5	6–10	Laps	Laps Led	Races Led	Miles	$
1980	NR	1	0	0	0	0	0	0	0	265	0	0	403	1,150
1986	97	1	0	0	0	0	0	0	0	90	0	0	236	1,400
1992	90T	1	0	0	0	0	0	0	0	40	0	0	106	5,690
1993	70	2	0	0	0	0	0	0	0	60	0	0	143	14,370
Lifetime		5	0	0	0	0	0	0	0	455	0	0	889	$22,610

Ernie Young

Ernest Young
Racing Hometown: Lakewood, CA

Year	Rank	Starts	Poles	1	2	3	4	5	6–10	Laps	Laps Led	Races Led	Miles	$
1954	138	3	0	0	0	0	0	0	0	739	0	0	459	65
1955	NR	3	0	0	0	0	0	0	1	311	0	0	249	150
1956	85	5	0	0	0	0	0	0	0	419	0	0	443	330
1957	102	2	0	0	0	0	1	0	0	153	0	0	97	375
1958	81	1	0	0	0	0	0	0	0	165	0	0	434	130
Lifetime		14	0	0	0	0	1	0	1	1,787	0	0	1,680	$1,050

Leslie Young

Leslie Young (Real Name: Ray Elston)
Racing Hometown: Wilkes Barre, PA

Year	Rank	Starts	Poles	1	2	3	4	5	6–10	Laps	Laps Led	Races Led	Miles	$
1954	NR	1	0	0	0	0	0	0	0	5	0	0	5	0
1955	236	1	0	0	0	0	0	0	0	21	0	0	21	25
Lifetime		2	0	0	0	0	0	0	0	26	0	0	26	$25

Steve Young

Steve Young
Racing Hometown: Charlotte, NC

Year	Rank	Starts	Poles	1	2	3	4	5	6–10	Laps	Laps Led	Races Led	Miles	$
1964	74	9	0	0	0	0	0	0	1	991	0	0	513	1,375
Lifetime		9	0	0	0	0	0	0	1	991	0	0	513	$1,375

Johnny Yountz

John Yountz
Racing Hometown: Liberty, NC

Year	Rank	Starts	Poles	1	2	3	4	5	6–10	Laps	Laps Led	Races Led	Miles	$
1951	N/A	1	0	0	0	0	0	0	0	361	0	0	451	50
Lifetime		1	0	0	0	0	0	0	0	361	0	0	451	$50

Year	Rank	Starts	Poles	Finish						Laps	Laps Led	Races Led	Miles	$
				1	2	3	4	5	6–10					

Pete Yow

Pete Yow
  Racing Hometown: Sanford, NC

Year	Rank	Starts	Poles	1	2	3	4	5	6–10	Laps	Laps Led	Races Led	Miles	$
1956	54	11	0	0	0	0	0	0	2	1,221	0	0	680	700
Lifetime		11	0	0	0	0	0	0	2	1,221	0	0	680	$700

Smokey Yunick

Henry Yunick
  B: 5/25/1923   D: 5/9/2001
  Racing Hometown: Daytona Beach, FL

Year	Rank	Starts	Poles	1	2	3	4	5	6–10	Laps	Laps Led	Races Led	Miles	$
1952	147T	1	0	0	0	0	0	0	0	7	0	0	4	25
Lifetime		1	0	0	0	0	0	0	0	7	0	0	4	$25

Johnny Zeke

John Zeke
  B: 11/20/1920
  Racing Hometown: Levitown, NY

Year	Rank	Starts	Poles	1	2	3	4	5	6–10	Laps	Laps Led	Races Led	Miles	$
1953	159	2	0	0	0	0	0	0	0	84	0	0	84	65
1954	213	1	0	0	0	0	0	0	0	6	0	0	3	10
1956	297T	1	0	0	0	0	0	0	0	49	0	0	25	0
Lifetime		4	0	0	0	0	0	0	0	139	0	0	112	$75

Emanuel Zervakis

Emanuel Zervakis (Manny)
  B: 1/23/1930
  Racing Hometown: Richmond, VA

Year	Rank	Starts	Poles	1	2	3	4	5	6–10	Laps	Laps Led	Races Led	Miles	$
1956	81	6	0	0	0	0	0	0	0	773	0	0	831	475
1957	140	5	0	0	0	0	0	0	0	1,032	0	0	739	675
1958	161	6	0	0	0	0	0	0	0	457	0	0	378	465
1960	8	14	1	0	0	1	1	0	8	3,382	0	0	3,457	12,124
1961	3	38	1	2	1	3	5	8	9	9,198	386	2	6,664	38,399
1962	27	11	0	0	0	0	0	0	2	2,151	5	1	2,357	4,545
1963	54	3	0	0	0	0	0	0	0	436	0	0	586	1,400
Lifetime		83	2	2	1	4	6	8	19	17,429	391	3	15,011	$58,083

Dennis Zimmerman

Dennis Zimmerman (Denny)
  B: 12/14/1940
  Racing Hometown: Glastonburg, CT

Year	Rank	Starts	Poles	1	2	3	4	5	6–10	Laps	Laps Led	Races Led	Miles	$
1964	111	1	0	0	0	0	0	0	0	209	0	0	78	100
Lifetime		1	0	0	0	0	0	0	0	209	0	0	78	$100

Dick Zimmerman

Richard C. Zimmerman
  B: 12/17/1918   *Killed as flagman @ Grand Rapids, MI.*
  Racing Hometown: Milwaukee, WI

Year	Rank	Starts	Poles	1	2	3	4	5	6–10	Laps	Laps Led	Races Led	Miles	$
1949	57	1	0	0	0	0	0	0	0	178	0	0	178	50
1954	149	2	0	0	0	0	0	0	0	350	0	0	236	40
1955	147	2	0	0	0	0	0	0	0	222	0	0	150	25
Lifetime		5	0	0	0	0	0	0	0	750	0	0	563	$115

Earl Zindahl

Earl Zindahl

Year	Rank	Starts	Poles	1	2	3	4	5	6–10	Laps	Laps Led	Races Led	Miles	$
1952	NR	1	0	0	0	0	0	0	0	88	0	0	44	25
Lifetime		1	0	0	0	0	0	0	0	88	0	0	44	$25

Jack Zink

John Smith Zink Jr.
  B: 1929
  Racing Hometown: Tulsa, OK

Year	Rank	Starts	Poles	1	2	3	4	5	6–10	Laps	Laps Led	Races Led	Miles	$
1956	195T	1	0	0	0	0	0	0	0	10	0	0	5	100
Lifetime		1	0	0	0	0	0	0	0	10	0	0	5	$100

Pat Zocano

Pat Zocano
  Racing Hometown: Detroit, MI

Year	Rank	Starts	Poles	1	2	3	4	5	6–10	Laps	Laps Led	Races Led	Miles	$
1956	263	1	0	0	0	0	0	0	0		0	0		60
Lifetime		1	0	0	0	0	0	0	0		0	0		$60

Ralph Zrimsek

Ralph Zrimsek
B: 1/30/1918
Racing Hometown: Canonsburg, PA

Year	Rank	Starts	Poles	Finish						Laps	Laps Led	Races Led	Miles	$
				1	2	3	4	5	6–10					
1949	NR	1	0	0	0	0	0	0	0	59	0	0	30	0
Lifetime		1	0	0	0	0	0	0	0	59	0	0	30	$0

PART 4
THE OWNERS

Year	Driver	Starts	Poles	Finish						Laps	Laps Led	Races Led	Miles	$
				1	2	3	4	5	6–10	Laps	Led	Led	Miles	$

Petty Enterprises (Statistics represent the Petty Enterprises team, which has had a number of partnerships and owners, including Lee, Richard, Kyle and Maurice Petty.)

Year	Driver	Starts	Poles	1	2	3	4	5	6–10	Laps	Laps Led	Races Led	Miles	$
1949	Lee Petty	6	0	1	2	0	0	0	2	890	1	1	565	3,375
1950	Lee Petty	17	0	1	1	2	3	2	4	1,558	43	1	1,407	5,775
1951	Lee Petty	32	0	1	4	2	1	3	8	1,103	99	1	1,059	7,300
1952	Lee Petty	32	0	3	6	5	5	2	6	5,094	193	7	3,439	15,670
1953	Jimmie Lewallen	1	0	0	1	0	0	0	0	198	0	0	99	700
2002	Ted Musgrave	1	0	0	0	0	0	0	0	246	0	0	379	58,450
Lifetime		2458	155	268	225	184	114	94	363	592,529	61,022	826	619,315	$33,295,961

Key

STARTS	Number of starts that year; owners are only credited with one start per race, regardless of how many drivers competed in a particular race for that owner
POLES	Number of poles that year
FINISH	
1	Number of first place finishes that year
2	Number of second place finishes that year
3	Number of third place finishes that year
4	Number of fourth place finishes that year
5	Number of fifth place finishes that year
6–10	Number of sixth through tenth place finishes that year
LAPS	Number of laps completed that year
LAPS LED	Number of laps led that year
RACES LED	Number of races led that year; owners with more than one driver leading in the same race are only credited with one race led
MILES	Number of miles driven that year
$	Winnings for that year

Please note that the above record is incomplete and shown here for example purposes only.

Year	Driver	Starts	Poles	Finish 1	2	3	4	5	6–10	Laps	Laps Led	Races Led	Miles	$

Van Acker

Year	Driver	Starts	Poles	1	2	3	4	5	6–10	Laps	Laps Led	Races Led	Miles	$
1959	Eduardo Dibos	3	0	0	0	0	0	2	0	181	0	0	453	1,050
Lifetime		3	0	0	0	0	0	2	0	181	0	0	453	$1,050

Ed Ackerman

Year	Driver	Starts	Poles	1	2	3	4	5	6–10	Laps	Laps Led	Races Led	Miles	$
1966	Gil Hearne	1	0	0	0	0	0	0	0	90	0	0	45	100
1966	Rene Charland	5	0	0	0	1	0	0	0	452	0	0	185	1,590
Lifetime		6	0	0	0	1	0	0	0	542	0	0	230	$1,690

Bill Adams

Year	Driver	Starts	Poles	1	2	3	4	5	6–10	Laps	Laps Led	Races Led	Miles	$
1953	Mike Klapak	2	0	0	0	0	0	0	2		0	0		250
1953	Bill Adams	2	0	0	0	0	0	0	1	36	0	0	148	250
Lifetime		4	0	0	0	0	0	0	3	36	0	0	148	$500

Bob Adams

Year	Driver	Starts	Poles	1	2	3	4	5	6–10	Laps	Laps Led	Races Led	Miles	$
1963	Elmo Langley	3	0	0	0	0	0	0	0	779	0	0	654	900
1963	Larry Manning	20	0	0	0	0	1	0	7	4,898	0	0	2,780	4,480
1964	Larry Manning	1	0	0	0	0	0	0	1	229	0	0	115	200
1966	Larry Manning	9	0	0	0	0	1	0	0	1,810	0	0	981	2,330
1967	Dr. Don Tarr	1	0	0	0	0	0	0	0	404	0	0	202	360
1967	Larry Manning	3	0	0	0	0	0	0	0	162	0	0	127	1,125
1967	Melvin Bradley	3	0	0	0	0	0	0	1	549	0	0	321	525
1967	Bill Dennis	3	0	0	0	0	0	0	0	1,012	0	0	1,160	2,335
Lifetime		43	0	0	0	0	2	0	9	9,843	0	0	6,339	$12,255

Joe Bill Adams

Year	Driver	Starts	Poles	1	2	3	4	5	6–10	Laps	Laps Led	Races Led	Miles	$
1965	Wendell Scott	1	0	0	0	0	0	0	0	179	0	0	269	950
1965	Joe Bill Adams	2	0	0	0	0	0	0	1	244	0	0	99	450
1965	Fred Goad	2	0	0	0	0	0	0	0	9	0	0	11	515
Lifetime		5	0	0	0	0	0	0	1	432	0	0	378	$1,915

Robert Adams

Year	Driver	Starts	Poles	1	2	3	4	5	6–10	Laps	Laps Led	Races Led	Miles	$
1963	Larry Manning	1	0	0	0	0	0	0	1	151	0	0	136	225
Lifetime		1	0	0	0	0	0	0	1	151	0	0	136	$225

Weldon Adams

Year	Driver	Starts	Poles	1	2	3	4	5	6–10	Laps	Laps Led	Races Led	Miles	$
1950	Weldon Adams	2	0	0	0	0	0	1	1	193	0	0	97	400
1952	Weldon Adams	6	0	0	0	0	0	0	2	708	0	0	537	275
1953	Weldon Adams	1	0	0	0	0	0	0	0	217	0	0	298	110
Lifetime		9	0	0	0	0	0	1	3	1,118	0	0	931	$785

Herb Adcox

Year	Driver	Starts	Poles	1	2	3	4	5	6–10	Laps	Laps Led	Races Led	Miles	$
1961	Freddy Fryar	1	0	0	0	0	0	0	0	116	0	0	174	200
1974	Grant Adcox	4	0	0	0	0	0	0	0	979	8	1	1,375	5,935
1975	Grant Adcox	10	0	0	0	0	0	0	0	1,516	0	0	2,530	15,985
1976	Grant Adcox	11	0	0	0	0	0	0	2	3,326	0	0	4,916	25,715
1977	Grant Adcox	6	0	0	0	0	0	0	0	776	0	0	1,482	8,750
1978	Grant Adcox	14	0	0	0	0	0	1	2	3,072	0	0	4,586	36,350
1979	Grant Adcox	6	0	0	0	0	0	0	0	1,132	5	1	2,104	15,290
1983	Grant Adcox	1	0	0	0	0	0	0	0	1	0	0	3	1,790
1984	Grant Adcox	1	0	0	0	0	0	0	0	1	0	0	3	1,800
1984	Connie Saylor	1	0	0	0	0	0	0	0	186	0	0	465	6,900
1985	Grant Adcox	2	0	0	0	0	0	0	0	169	0	0	426	4,590
1986	Ken Ragan	1	0	0	0	0	0	0	0	184	0	0	460	11,870
1986	Grant Adcox	1	0	0	0	0	0	0	0	154	0	0	385	2,195
1989	Grant Adcox	3	0	0	0	0	0	0	0	541	0	0	1,188	11,815
Lifetime		62	0	0	0	0	0	1	5	12,156	13	2	20,097	$149,185

Bob Akins / Brad Sutton

Year	Driver	Starts	Poles	1	2	3	4	5	6–10	Laps	Laps Led	Races Led	Miles	$
1993	Bobby Hamilton	2	0	0	0	0	0	0	1	694	0	0	993	21,715
Lifetime		2	0	0	0	0	0	0	1	694	0	0	993	$21,715

Year	Driver	Starts	Poles	Finish 1	2	3	4	5	6–10	Laps	Laps Led	Races Led	Miles	$

Will Albright

Year	Driver	Starts	Poles	1	2	3	4	5	6–10	Laps	Laps Led	Races Led	Miles	$
1950	Will Albright	1	0	0	0	0	0	0	0	43	0	0	179	50
Lifetime		1	0	0	0	0	0	0	0	43	0	0	179	$50

Claude Alexander

Year	Driver	Starts	Poles	1	2	3	4	5	6–10	Laps	Laps Led	Races Led	Miles	$
1952	Ed Samples	8	0	0	1	1	0	0	2	614	0	0	370	1,535
1954	Ed Samples	1	0	0	0	0	0	0	0	36	0	0	148	40
Lifetime		9	0	0	1	1	0	0	2	650	0	0	517	$1,575

Chester Alford

Year	Driver	Starts	Poles	1	2	3	4	5	6–10	Laps	Laps Led	Races Led	Miles	$
1950	Russ Lee	1	0	0	0	0	0	0	0	38	0	0	158	25
Lifetime		1	0	0	0	0	0	0	0	38	0	0	158	$25

Ken Allen

Year	Driver	Starts	Poles	1	2	3	4	5	6–10	Laps	Laps Led	Races Led	Miles	$
1986	Ron Shephard	1	0	0	0	0	0	0	0	282	0	0	153	3,145
1987	Eddie Bierschwale	1	0	0	0	0	0	0	0	192	0	0	262	2,760
1987	Jesse Samples, Jr.	2	0	0	0	0	0	0	0	164	0	0	106	2,410
1988	Connie Saylor	1	0	0	0	0	0	0	0	464	0	0	472	2,565
1988	Rodney Combs	1	0	0	0	0	0	0	0	220	0	0	335	1,760
1989	Rodney Combs	3	0	0	0	0	0	0	0	696	0	0	794	6,135
1989	Jim Bown	1	0	0	0	0	0	0	0	195	0	0	198	1,900
1991	Dick Trickle	4	0	0	0	0	0	0	0	714	0	0	433	14,235
Lifetime		14	0	0	0	0	0	0	0	2,927	0	0	2,753	$34,910

Loy Allen

Year	Driver	Starts	Poles	1	2	3	4	5	6–10	Laps	Laps Led	Races Led	Miles	$
1993	Loy Allen, Jr.	4	0	0	0	0	0	0	0	573	0	0	1,232	28,135
Lifetime		4	0	0	0	0	0	0	0	573	0	0	1,232	$28,135

Bobby Allison

Year	Driver	Starts	Poles	1	2	3	4	5	6–10	Laps	Laps Led	Races Led	Miles	$
1969	Bobby Allison	2	0	0	0	0	0	0	1	423	0	0	212	790
1970	Dave Marcis	1	0	0	0	0	0	0	1	195	0	0	293	795
1970	Bobby Allison	21	2	2	8	4	2	0	2	6,115	841	9	2,883	26,330
1971	Bobby Allison	17	2	1	1	0	3	1	3	3,977	484	8	3,662	24,210
1973	Bobby Allison	27	6	2	2	6	4	1	1	8,072	870	20	8,653	138,580
1974	Neil Bonnett	1	0	0	0	0	0	0	0	46	0	0	122	1,110
1974	Bobby Allison	20	3	1	3	5	1	2	0	5,598	712	15	6,289	111,875
1975	Neil Bonnett	2	0	0	0	0	0	0	0	474	12	1	483	2,705
1977	Bobby Allison	30	0	0	1	0	2	2	10	7,024	102	9	7,823	77,605
1985	Bobby Allison	13	0	0	0	0	1	0	1	3,153	51	4	3,793	33,915
1990	Mike Alexander	7	0	0	0	0	0	0	0	2,392	0	0	2,325	41,080
1990	Hut Stricklin	21	0	0	0	0	0	0	2	5,681	1	1	7,403	130,759
1990	Jeff Purvis	1	0	0	0	0	0	0	0	247	0	0	130	3,300
1991	Hut Stricklin	29	0	0	1	0	2	0	4	8,813	69	7	10,436	346,030
1992	Jeff Purvis	4	0	0	0	0	0	0	0	1,080	0	0	746	34,920
1992	Hut Stricklin	21	0	0	0	0	0	0	4	5,577	60	2	7,224	262,935
1992	Jimmy Spencer	4	0	0	0	0	2	1	0	1,463	0	0	1,810	103,905
1993	Jimmy Spencer	30	0	0	1	2	2	0	5	8,867	64	4	10,837	583,750
1994	Derrike Cope	12	0	0	0	0	0	0	2	3,889	4	1	3,800	178,140
1994	Tim Steele	5	0	0	0	0	0	0	0	391	0	0	807	65,000
1994	Chuck Bown	13	1	0	0	0	0	0	1	3,694	0	0	4,164	233,660
1995	Derrike Cope	31	0	0	1	0	0	0	6	9,335	70	4	11,040	598,840
1996	Derrike Cope	29	0	0	0	0	0	1	3	7,329	28	2	8,831	674,081
Lifetime		341	14	6	18	17	19	8	46	93,835	3,368	87	103,763	$3,674,315

Dave Alonzo

Year	Driver	Starts	Poles	1	2	3	4	5	6–10	Laps	Laps Led	Races Led	Miles	$
1969	Dave Alonzo	2	0	0	0	0	0	0	0	486	0	0	504	1,555
1970	Dave Alonzo	2	0	0	0	0	0	0	0	160	0	0	420	2,260
Lifetime		4	0	0	0	0	0	0	0	646	0	0	924	$3,815

George Alsobrook

Year	Driver	Starts	Poles	1	2	3	4	5	6–10	Laps	Laps Led	Races Led	Miles	$
1962	George Alsobrook	1	0	0	0	0	0	0	0	32	0	0	16	100
Lifetime		1	0	0	0	0	0	0	0	32	0	0	16	$100

Year	Driver	Starts	Poles	Finish 1	2	3	4	5	6–10	Laps	Laps Led	Races Led	Miles	$

George Altheide

Year	Driver	Starts	Poles	1	2	3	4	5	6–10	Laps	Laps Led	Races Led	Miles	$
1972	G.C. Spencer	1	0	0	0	0	0	0	0	95	0	0	143	785
1972	J.D. McDuffie	1	0	0	0	0	0	0	0	318	0	0	434	1,515
Lifetime		2	0	0	0	0	0	0	0	413	0	0	577	$2,300

Bernard Alvarez

Year	Driver	Starts	Poles	1	2	3	4	5	6–10	Laps	Laps Led	Races Led	Miles	$
1964	Larry Thomas	1	0	0	0	0	0	0	1	254	0	0	381	825
1964	Rene Charland	1	0	0	0	0	0	0	0	9	0	0	2	100
1964	Buddy Baker	6	0	0	0	0	0	0	1	604	0	0	471	1,750
1964	Bernard Alvarez	6	0	0	0	0	0	0	0	89	0	0	95	650
1966	Ned Jarrett	9	0	0	0	1	0	0	0	1,584	27	1	1,082	4,820
Lifetime		23	0	0	0	1	0	0	2	2,540	27	1	2,031	$8,145

Pancho Alvarez

Year	Driver	Starts	Poles	1	2	3	4	5	6–10	Laps	Laps Led	Races Led	Miles	$
1952	Pancho Alvarez	1	0	0	0	0	0	0	0		0	0		25
Lifetime		1	0	0	0	0	0	0	0		0	0		$25

Carmen Amica

Year	Driver	Starts	Poles	1	2	3	4	5	6–10	Laps	Laps Led	Races Led	Miles	$
1954	Curtis Turner	1	0	0	0	1	0	0	0	198	0	0	99	450
1954	Bill Amick	1	0	0	0	0	0	0	0	124	0	0	62	0
1954	Laird Bruner	20	0	0	0	0	0	1	4	2,620	0	0	2,050	1,380
Lifetime		22	0	0	0	1	0	1	4	2,942	0	0	2,211	$1,830

Bill Amick

Year	Driver	Starts	Poles	1	2	3	4	5	6–10	Laps	Laps Led	Races Led	Miles	$
1957	Bill Amick	15	2	1	3	3	0	0	3	2,718	12	2	1,744	6,870
Lifetime		15	2	1	3	3	0	0	3	2,718	12	2	1,744	$6,870

Bill Andersen

Year	Driver	Starts	Poles	1	2	3	4	5	6–10	Laps	Laps Led	Races Led	Miles	$
1970	Glenn Francis	1	0	0	0	0	0	0	0	95	0	0	249	805
1971	Glenn Francis	1	0	0	0	0	0	0	0	27	0	0	71	1,015
Lifetime		2	0	0	0	0	0	0	0	122	0	0	320	$1,820

Axel Anderson

Year	Driver	Starts	Poles	1	2	3	4	5	6–10	Laps	Laps Led	Races Led	Miles	$
1955	Axel Anderson	2	0	0	0	0	0	0	0	152	0	0	267	225
1957	Art Anderson	1	0	0	0	0	0	0	0	14	0	0	14	50
Lifetime		3	0	0	0	0	0	0	0	166	0	0	281	$275

Carl Anderson

Year	Driver	Starts	Poles	1	2	3	4	5	6–10	Laps	Laps Led	Races Led	Miles	$
1985	Craig Spetman	1	0	0	0	0	0	0	0	188	0	0	191	1,150
Lifetime		1	0	0	0	0	0	0	0	188	0	0	191	$1,150

Eddie Anderson

Year	Driver	Starts	Poles	1	2	3	4	5	6–10	Laps	Laps Led	Races Led	Miles	$
1951	Eddie Anderson	4	0	0	0	0	0	0	0	8	0	0	6	110
Lifetime		4	0	0	0	0	0	0	0	8	0	0	6	$110

Jack Anderson

Year	Driver	Starts	Poles	1	2	3	4	5	6–10	Laps	Laps Led	Races Led	Miles	$
1964	Jack Anderson	2	0	0	0	0	0	0	2	591	0	0	654	1,800
Lifetime		2	0	0	0	0	0	0	2	591	0	0	654	$1,800

M.C. Anderson

Year	Driver	Starts	Poles	1	2	3	4	5	6–10	Laps	Laps Led	Races Led	Miles	$
1976	Sam Sommers	5	0	0	0	0	0	0	1	1,000	0	0	1,534	8,930
1977	Sam Sommers	22	1	0	0	0	1	1	6	5,387	28	3	6,845	53,975
1978	Buddy Baker	19	1	0	1	1	1	1	4	4,319	354	10	6,594	111,015
1979	Benny Parsons	31	1	2	2	2	5	5	5	9,335	736	12	10,575	207,150
1980	Marty Robbins	1	0	0	0	0	0	0	0	171	0	0	257	1,000
1980	Benny Parsons	31	2	3	3	2	4	4	5	8,676	659	19	10,036	345,260
1981	Cale Yarborough	18	2	2	1	2	0	1	4	4,922	769	13	7,134	150,090
1982	Cale Yarborough	16	2	3	2	1	2	0	0	3,439	379	12	5,642	219,340
Lifetime		143	9	10	9	8	13	12	25	37,249	2,925	69	48,616	$1,096,760

Year	Driver	Starts	Poles	Finish 1	2	3	4	5	6–10	Laps	Laps Led	Races Led	Miles	$

Tommy Andrews

Year	Driver	Starts	Poles	1	2	3	4	5	6–10	Laps	Laps Led	Races Led	Miles	$
1971	Tommy Andrews	2	0	0	0	0	0	0	0	251	0	0	79	450
Lifetime		2	0	0	0	0	0	0	0	251	0	0	79	$450

Don Angel

Year	Driver	Starts	Poles	1	2	3	4	5	6–10	Laps	Laps Led	Races Led	Miles	$
1958	Tiny Lund	12	0	0	0	1	1	0	3	2,439	0	0	1,145	1,890
1958	Jim Paschal	1	0	0	0	0	0	0	1	193	0	0	97	165
1958	Eddie Pagan	1	0	0	0	0	0	0	0	77	0	0	19	45
1958	Don Angel	3	0	0	0	0	0	0	0	401	0	0	241	210
1959	Don Angel	2	0	0	0	0	0	0	0	167	0	0	100	100
1959	Marvin Panch	1	0	0	0	0	0	0	0	37	0	0	19	50
1959	Speedy Thompson	1	0	0	0	0	0	0	0	190	0	0	48	100
1960	Tommy Herbert	2	0	0	0	0	0	0	0	155	0	0	388	250
Lifetime		23	0	0	0	1	1	0	4	3,659	0	0	2,056	$2,810

Bob Apperson

Year	Driver	Starts	Poles	1	2	3	4	5	6–10	Laps	Laps Led	Races Led	Miles	$
1949	Bob Apperson	3	0	0	0	0	0	0	0	191	0	0	96	150
1950	Bob Apperson	7	0	0	0	0	0	0	0	573	0	0	631	200
1952	Bob Apperson	1	0	0	0	0	0	0	0		0	0		25
Lifetime		11	0	0	0	0	0	0	0	764	0	0	726	$375

Bill Appleton

Year	Driver	Starts	Poles	1	2	3	4	5	6–10	Laps	Laps Led	Races Led	Miles	$
1949	Marshall Teague	1	0	0	0	0	0	0	0		0	0		50
Lifetime		1	0	0	0	0	0	0	0		0	0		$50

Sam Arakalian

Year	Driver	Starts	Poles	1	2	3	4	5	6–10	Laps	Laps Led	Races Led	Miles	$
1977	Vince Giamformaggio	1	0	0	0	0	0	0	0	93	0	0	233	850
1978	Vince Giamformaggio	1	0	0	0	0	0	0	0	41	0	0	107	805
Lifetime		2	0	0	0	0	0	0	0	134	0	0	340	$1,655

Sam Arena

Year	Driver	Starts	Poles	1	2	3	4	5	6–10	Laps	Laps Led	Races Led	Miles	$
1954	Bill Bade	2	0	0	0	0	0	0	1	688	0	0	344	150
1957	Bill Bade	2	0	0	0	0	0	0	0	194	0	0	97	90
1959	Bobby Rose	3	0	0	0	0	0	0	0	182	0	0	441	150
Lifetime		7	0	0	0	0	0	0	1	1,064	0	0	882	$390

Frank Arford

Year	Driver	Starts	Poles	1	2	3	4	5	6–10	Laps	Laps Led	Races Led	Miles	$
1952	Dick Passwater	6	0	0	0	0	0	1	2	1,366	0	0	1,085	945
1953	Frank Arford	4	0	0	0	0	0	0	0	255	0	0	261	100
1953	Slick Smith	1	0	0	0	0	0	0	0		0	0		40
1953	Dick Passwater	13	0	1	0	0	3	2	4	643	3	1	644	3,925
Lifetime		24	0	1	0	0	3	3	6	2,264	3	1	1,990	$5,010

Ted Armstrong

Year	Driver	Starts	Poles	1	2	3	4	5	6–10	Laps	Laps Led	Races Led	Miles	$
1978	Gary Johnson	1	0	0	0	0	0	0	0	3	0	0	8	500
Lifetime		1	0	0	0	0	0	0	0	3	0	0	8	$500

Ben Arnold

Year	Driver	Starts	Poles	1	2	3	4	5	6–10	Laps	Laps Led	Races Led	Miles	$
1967	Red Farmer	2	0	0	0	0	0	0	0	58	0	0	145	1,000
1970	Ben Arnold	28	0	0	0	0	0	0	3	6,772	0	0	6,720	22,108
1971	Ben Arnold	17	0	0	0	0	0	0	3	4,117	0	0	6,156	17,701
1972	Ben Arnold	26	0	0	0	0	0	0	7	6,976	0	0	8,935	37,625
1973	Ben Arnold	1	0	0	0	0	0	0	0	9	0	0	24	580
Lifetime		74	0	0	0	0	0	0	13	17,932	0	0	21,980	$79,014

Alan Aroneck

Year	Driver	Starts	Poles	1	2	3	4	5	6–10	Laps	Laps Led	Races Led	Miles	$
1989	Jerry O'Neil	4	0	0	0	0	0	0	0	1,026	0	0	1,255	9,165
1990	Jerry O'Neil	3	0	0	0	0	0	0	0	349	0	0	873	24,605
1992	D.K. Ulrich	1	0	0	0	0	0	0	0	21	0	0	21	4,165
1992	Jerry O'Neil	6	0	0	0	0	0	0	0	958	0	0	1,644	27,970

Year	Driver	Starts	Poles	Finish 1	2	3	4	5	6–10	Laps	Laps Led	Races Led	Miles	$

Alan Aroneck *continued*

Year	Driver	Starts	Poles	1	2	3	4	5	6–10	Laps	Laps Led	Races Led	Miles	$
1993	Jerry O'Neil	1	0	0	0	0	0	0	0	9	0	0	10	9,250
Lifetime		15	0	0	0	0	0	0	0	2,363	0	0	3,802	$75,155

Buddy Arrington

Year	Driver	Starts	Poles	1	2	3	4	5	6–10	Laps	Laps Led	Races Led	Miles	$
1964	Buddy Arrington	28	0	0	0	0	0	2	7	5,172	0	0	2,504	5,315
1965	Darrell Bryant	1	0	0	0	0	0	0	0	1	0	0	1	100
1965	Raymond Carter	9	0	0	0	0	0	0	2	638	0	0	617	2,145
1965	Buddy Arrington	29	0	0	0	1	1	4	3	4,784	0	0	2,810	10,100
1965	Billy DeCoster	1	0	0	0	0	0	0	0	252	0	0	378	700
1965	Pee Wee Ellwanger	4	0	0	0	0	0	0	0	345	0	0	173	575
1966	Buddy Arrington	18	0	0	0	0	0	0	3	2,456	0	0	2,133	7,050
1966	Darrell Bryant	1	0	0	0	0	0	0	0	17	0	0	26	445
1966	E.J. Trivette	1	0	0	0	0	0	0	0	2	0	0	3	525
1967	Larry Manning	1	0	0	0	0	0	0	0	4	0	0	2	275
1967	Buddy Arrington	15	0	0	0	0	0	1	4	2,972	0	0	2,635	7,820
1967	Larry Hess	1	0	0	0	0	0	0	0	53	0	0	80	800
1968	Buddy Arrington	1	0	0	0	0	0	0	0	186	0	0	465	2,350
1969	Buddy Arrington	16	0	0	0	0	0	0	4	3,758	0	0	3,557	12,975
1970	Larry Manning	1	0	0	0	0	0	0	0	83	0	0	52	755
1970	Buddy Arrington	19	0	0	0	0	0	0	2	2,855	0	0	3,638	16,845
1971	Buddy Arrington	1	0	0	0	0	0	0	0	472	0	0	248	650
1972	Ed Negre	1	0	0	0	0	0	0	0	167	0	0	104	425
1972	Buddy Arrington	20	0	0	0	0	0	1	9	5,503	0	0	7,009	29,050
1973	Buddy Arrington	26	0	0	0	0	0	1	3	7,917	0	0	8,153	34,010
1974	Pee Wee Wentz	1	0	0	0	0	0	0	1	342	0	0	467	2,500
1974	Joey Arrington	1	0	0	0	0	0	0	0	341	0	0	213	525
1974	Satch Worley	1	0	0	0	0	0	0	1	431	0	0	227	1,300
1974	John Martin	1	0	0	0	0	0	0	0	16	0	0	40	1,045
1974	Joe Millikan	1	0	0	0	0	0	0	0	456	0	0	464	1,150
1974	Buddy Arrington	17	0	0	0	0	0	0	4	4,782	0	0	4,798	22,565
1974	Larry Manning	1	0	0	0	0	0	0	0	1	0	0	1	580
1975	Buddy Arrington	25	0	0	0	0	0	0	3	7,786	0	0	8,170	40,065
1975	Joey Arrington	2	0	0	0	0	0	0	0	91	0	0	87	1,060
1976	Buddy Arrington	25	0	0	0	0	0	0	3	9,856	0	0	8,689	51,112
1977	Buddy Arrington	28	0	0	0	0	0	0	5	8,601	0	0	10,038	76,310
1978	Joey Arrington	2	0	0	0	0	0	0	0	326	0	0	509	1,990
1978	Buddy Arrington	30	0	0	0	0	0	1	6	9,580	0	0	10,740	96,940
1978	Ed Negre	1	0	0	0	0	0	0	0	3	0	0	2	405
1979	Buddy Arrington	31	0	0	0	1	0	0	6	8,452	2	1	10,334	118,390
1979	Earl Brooks	1	0	0	0	0	0	0	0	79	0	0	49	405
1979	Joey Arrington	1	0	0	0	0	0	0	0	42	0	0	42	650
1980	Eddie Dickerson	2	0	0	0	0	0	0	0	787	0	0	632	1,590
1980	Dick May	1	0	0	0	0	0	0	0	4	0	0	2	380
1980	Buddy Arrington	31	0	0	0	0	0	0	7	8,765	0	0	9,937	105,945
1981	Buddy Arrington	30	0	0	0	0	0	0	6	7,930	0	0	9,197	115,245
1982	Randy Becker	1	0	0	0	0	0	0	0	31	0	0	81	575
1982	Buddy Arrington	30	0	0	0	0	0	0	8	9,236	5	3	10,705	147,795
1983	Buddy Arrington	30	0	0	0	0	0	0	2	8,933	1	1	10,010	120,265
1984	Buddy Arrington	25	0	0	0	0	0	0	0	7,256	0	0	8,253	113,375
1985	Morgan Shepherd	1	0	0	0	0	0	0	0	190	0	0	475	15,300
1985	Phil Good	1	0	0	0	0	0	0	0	362	0	0	196	1,470
1985	Buddy Arrington	26	0	0	0	0	0	0	1	7,809	1	1	9,653	136,425
1986	Buddy Arrington	26	0	0	0	0	0	0	0	8,152	4	1	9,459	150,310
1987	Mike Potter	1	0	0	0	0	0	0	0	74	0	0	181	1,890
1987	Eddie Bierschwale	7	0	0	0	0	0	0	0	1,901	0	0	1,989	43,635
1987	Buddy Arrington	18	0	0	0	0	0	0	0	4,865	0	0	6,324	103,305
1987	Chet Fillip	2	0	0	0	0	0	0	0	275	0	0	728	12,190
1988	Brad Teague	4	0	0	0	0	0	0	0	1,389	0	0	1,326	18,925
1988	Jimmy Hensley	1	0	0	0	0	0	0	0	290	0	0	153	4,245
1988	Dale Jarrett	1	0	0	0	0	0	0	0	27	0	0	41	4,200
1988	Buddy Arrington	4	0	0	0	0	0	0	0	760	0	0	1,549	19,665
1988	Ron Esau	2	0	0	0	0	0	0	0	231	0	0	596	9,335
1988	Rick Jeffrey	2	0	0	0	0	0	0	0	652	0	0	952	11,310
1988	Ken Schrader	1	0	0	0	0	0	0	0	395	0	0	214	4,610
1989	Brad Teague	1	0	0	0	0	0	0	0	488	0	0	260	2,480
Lifetime		611	0	0	0	2	1	12	90	159,624	13	7	172,367	$1,694,367

Year	Driver	Starts	Poles	1	2	3	4	5	6–10	Laps	Laps Led	Races Led	Miles	$

Bruce Atchley

Year	Driver	Starts	Poles	1	2	3	4	5	6–10	Laps	Laps Led	Races Led	Miles	$
1952	Bruce Atchley	6	0	0	0	0	0	0	0	307	0	0	187	200
1952	Dick Rathmann	1	0	0	0	0	0	0	0	48	0	0	48	25
Lifetime		7	0	0	0	0	0	0	0	355	0	0	235	$225

H.W. Atkinson

Year	Driver	Starts	Poles	1	2	3	4	5	6–10	Laps	Laps Led	Races Led	Miles	$
1956	W.H. Atkinson	1	0	0	0	0	0	0	0		0	0		0
Lifetime		1	0	0	0	0	0	0	0		0	0		$0

Roger Attard

Year	Driver	Starts	Poles	1	2	3	4	5	6–10	Laps	Laps Led	Races Led	Miles	$
1952	Roger Attard	1	0	0	0	0	0	0	0	25	0	0	25	0
Lifetime		1	0	0	0	0	0	0	0	25	0	0	25	$0

George Augustine

Year	Driver	Starts	Poles	1	2	3	4	5	6–10	Laps	Laps Led	Races Led	Miles	$
1958	Axel Anderson	3	0	0	0	0	0	0	0	203	0	0	178	155
Lifetime		3	0	0	0	0	0	0	0	203	0	0	178	$155

L.D. Austin

Year	Driver	Starts	Poles	1	2	3	4	5	6–10	Laps	Laps Led	Races Led	Miles	$
1957	L.D. Austin	40	0	0	0	0	0	1	12	6,920	0	0	4,132	5,275
1958	L.D. Austin	45	0	0	0	0	0	0	10	6,585	0	0	3,739	4,625
1959	L.D. Austin	32	0	0	0	0	0	0	12	5,659	0	0	3,192	3,630
1960	Rex White	1	0	0	0	0	0	1	1	182	0	0	46	140
1960	Buck Baker	1	0	0	0	0	0	0	1	189	0	0	47	175
1960	L.D. Austin	26	0	0	0	0	0	0	9	4,820	0	0	3,995	4,825
1961	L.D. Austin	20	0	0	0	0	0	0	8	4,802	0	0	3,402	7,460
1962	L.D. Austin	1	0	0	0	0	0	0	0	53	0	0	27	
Lifetime		166	0	0	0	0	0	2	53	29,210	0	0	18,580	$26,130

George Avery

Year	Driver	Starts	Poles	1	2	3	4	5	6–10	Laps	Laps Led	Races Led	Miles	$
1975	A.J. Reno	1	0	0	0	0	0	0	0	170	0	0	452	1,670
Lifetime		1	0	0	0	0	0	0	0	170	0	0	452	$1,670

Jimmy Ayers

Year	Driver	Starts	Poles	1	2	3	4	5	6–10	Laps	Laps Led	Races Led	Miles	$
1950	Jimmy Ayers	1	0	0	0	0	0	0	0		0	0		0
1951	Jimmy Ayers	7	0	0	0	0	0	0	5	225	0	0	281	475
1952	Jimmy Ayers	3	0	0	0	0	0	0	0	179	0	0	90	85
1953	Jimmy Ayers	4	0	0	0	0	0	0	2		0	0		175
1954	Jimmy Ayers	2	0	0	0	0	0	0	0	219	0	0	178	75
1955	Jimmy Ayers	2	0	0	0	0	0	0	1	277	0	0	292	350
Lifetime		19	0	0	0	0	0	0	8	900	0	0	840	$1,160

Hugh Babb

Year	Driver	Starts	Poles	1	2	3	4	5	6–10	Laps	Laps Led	Races Led	Miles	$
1956	Billy Myers	2	0	0	0	1	0	0	1	390	0	0	176	575
1957	Danny Graves	1	0	0	0	0	0	0	0	17	0	0	9	50
1957	Clyde Palmer	1	0	0	0	1	0	0	0	149	0	0	75	470
1957	Buck Baker	15	2	4	3	2	1	2	3	2,825	487	6	1,506	10,025
1957	Jack Smith	15	0	1	1	1	1	1	5	2,534	115	1	1,345	3,855
1957	Johnny Beauchamp	1	0	0	1	0	0	0	0		0	0		2,450
1957	Rex White	2	0	0	0	0	0	0	1	24	0	0	12	300
1957	Frankie Schneider	2	0	0	0	0	1	0	0	194	0	0	97	355
1957	Speedy Thompson	15	1	0	2	3	0	2	2	2,347	55	2	1,280	4,540
1957	Tom Pistone	2	0	0	0	1	0	0	0	588	0	0	294	1,260
Lifetime		56	3	5	7	9	3	5	12	9,068	657	9	4,793	$23,880

Dick Bahre

Year	Driver	Starts	Poles	1	2	3	4	5	6–10	Laps	Laps Led	Races Led	Miles	$
1981	Charlie Glotzbach	1	0	0	0	0	0	0	0	218	0	0	327	1,275
1981	Geoffrey Bodine	2	0	0	0	0	0	0	0	267	0	0	567	6,390
1982	Geoffrey Bodine	1	0	0	0	0	0	0	0	3	0	0	8	3,450
1983	Bill Elliott	1	0	0	0	0	0	0	0	36	0	0	90	5,550
1984	Gene Coyle	2	0	0	0	0	0	0	0	619	0	0	895	4,840
1984	Don Hume	1	0	0	0	0	0	0	0	299	0	0	455	1,595
1984	Connie Saylor	2	0	0	0	0	0	0	0	262	0	0	378	2,935

Year	Driver	Starts	Poles	Finish						Laps	Laps Led	Races Led	Miles	$
				1	2	3	4	5	6–10	Laps	Led	Led	Miles	$

Dick Bahre *continued*

Year	Driver	Starts	Poles	1	2	3	4	5	6–10	Laps	Laps Led	Races Led	Miles	$
1984	Sterling Marlin	1	0	0	0	0	0	0	0	1	0	0	1	1,085
1984	Morgan Shepherd	4	0	0	0	0	0	0	0	689	0	0	965	7,450
1985	Dick May	1	0	0	0	0	0	0	0	368	0	0	230	985
1985	Morgan Shepherd	1	0	0	0	0	0	0	0	61	0	0	62	1,150
1985	Michael Waltrip	5	0	0	0	0	0	0	0	1,013	0	0	1,583	9,540
1985	Elton Dotson	1	0	0	0	0	0	0	0	10	0	0	25	1,675
1985	Jim Hull	1	0	0	0	0	0	0	0	68	0	0	136	1,570
1988	Dave Mader III	1	0	0	0	0	0	0	0	271	0	0	144	1,565
1989	Dave Mader III	1	0	0	0	0	0	0	0	480	0	0	488	2,675
1990	Dave Mader III	1	0	0	0	0	0	0	0	323	0	0	492	4,525
1991	Dave Mader III	2	0	0	0	0	0	0	0	515	0	0	753	7,910
1992	Denny Wilson	1	0	0	0	0	0	0	0	9	0	0	22	3,450
1993	Johnny Chapman	1	0	0	0	0	0	0	0	368	0	0	374	6,526
Lifetime		31	0	0	0	0	0	0	0	5,880	0	0	7,995	$76,141

Dick Bailey

Year	Driver	Starts	Poles	1	2	3	4	5	6–10	Laps	Laps Led	Races Led	Miles	$
1958	Dick Bailey	1	0	0	0	0	0	0	0	33	0	0	135	75
Lifetime		1	0	0	0	0	0	0	0	33	0	0	135	$75

Don Bailey

Year	Driver	Starts	Poles	1	2	3	4	5	6–10	Laps	Laps Led	Races Led	Miles	$
1956	Don Bailey	1	0	0	0	0	0	0	0		0	0		25
Lifetime		1	0	0	0	0	0	0	0		0	0		$25

H.B. Bailey

Year	Driver	Starts	Poles	1	2	3	4	5	6–10	Laps	Laps Led	Races Led	Miles	$
1962	H.B. Bailey	1	0	0	0	0	0	0	0	101	0	0	152	300
1963	H.B. Bailey	2	0	0	0	0	0	0	0	226	0	0	565	775
1964	H.B. Bailey	1	0	0	0	0	0	0	0	135	0	0	186	500
1965	H.B. Bailey	5	0	0	0	0	0	1	2	810	0	0	1,338	5,000
1966	H.B. Bailey	4	0	0	0	0	0	0	0	450	0	0	671	2,745
1967	H.B. Bailey	3	0	0	0	0	0	0	0	322	0	0	676	3,850
1968	H.B. Bailey	2	0	0	0	0	0	0	0	187	0	0	264	1,250
1969	H.B. Bailey	6	0	0	0	0	0	0	1	638	0	0	1,303	5,880
1969	Buck Baker	1	0	0	0	0	0	0	0	108	0	0	287	1,300
1970	H.B. Bailey	1	0	0	0	0	0	0	0	180	0	0	246	995
1971	Frank Warren	1	0	0	0	0	0	1	0	289	0	0	145	650
1971	H.B. Bailey	4	0	0	0	0	0	0	0	606	11	1	422	2,265
1973	H.B. Bailey	2	0	0	0	0	0	0	0	243	0	0	483	1,935
1975	H.B. Bailey	1	0	0	0	0	0	0	0	1	0	0	1	1,015
1977	H.B. Bailey	1	0	0	0	0	0	0	1	187	0	0	497	8,450
1979	H.B. Bailey	4	0	0	0	0	0	0	0	738	0	0	1,175	5,835
1981	H.B. Bailey	4	0	0	0	0	0	0	0	605	0	0	989	7,125
1982	H.B. Bailey	6	0	0	0	0	0	0	0	1,016	0	0	1,612	9,455
1982	Dick May	1	0	0	0	0	0	0	0	260	0	0	396	2,430
1983	H.B. Bailey	2	0	0	0	0	0	0	0	684	0	0	1,033	4,110
1984	H.B. Bailey	2	0	0	0	0	0	0	0	529	0	0	770	5,640
1985	H.B. Bailey	2	0	0	0	0	0	0	0	206	0	0	299	3,065
1986	H.B. Bailey	4	0	0	0	0	0	0	0	918	1	1	1,289	9,225
1987	H.B. Bailey	5	0	0	0	0	0	0	0	1,150	0	0	1,691	12,885
1988	H.B. Bailey	7	0	0	0	0	0	0	0	1,180	0	0	1,788	15,775
1989	H.B. Bailey	2	0	0	0	0	0	0	0	487	0	0	787	6,595
1990	H.B. Bailey	3	0	0	0	0	0	0	0	421	0	0	608	9,525
1991	H.B. Bailey	3	0	0	0	0	0	0	0	545	0	0	981	13,095
1992	H.B. Bailey	1	0	0	0	0	0	0	0	8	0	0	16	5,355
1993	H.B. Bailey	2	0	0	0	0	0	0	0	238	0	0	442	12,750
Lifetime		83	0	0	0	0	0	2	4	13,468	12	2	21,108	$159,775

Gary Baird

Year	Driver	Starts	Poles	1	2	3	4	5	6–10	Laps	Laps Led	Races Led	Miles	$
1971	E.J. Trivette	5	0	0	0	0	0	0	0	914	0	0	759	1,895
Lifetime		5	0	0	0	0	0	0	0	914	0	0	759	$1,895

R.L. Baird

Year	Driver	Starts	Poles	1	2	3	4	5	6–10	Laps	Laps Led	Races Led	Miles	$
1960	Bud Parnell	4	0	0	0	0	0	0	1	407	0	0	204	280
Lifetime		4	0	0	0	0	0	0	1	407	0	0	204	$280

Year	Driver	Starts	Poles	Finish 1	2	3	4	5	6–10	Laps	Laps Led	Races Led	Miles	$

Buck Baity

Year	Driver	Starts	Poles	1	2	3	4	5	6–10	Laps	Laps Led	Races Led	Miles	$
1951	Buck Baity	1	0	0	0	0	0	0	0	248	0	0	310	0
Lifetime		1	0	0	0	0	0	0	0	248	0	0	310	$0

Bill Baker

Year	Driver	Starts	Poles	1	2	3	4	5	6–10	Laps	Laps Led	Races Led	Miles	$
1977	Bill Baker	2	0	0	0	0	0	0	0	142	0	0	372	2,540
1978	Bill Baker	1	0	0	0	0	0	0	0	20	0	0	52	550
Lifetime		3	0	0	0	0	0	0	0	162	0	0	424	$3,090

Buck Baker

Year	Driver	Starts	Poles	1	2	3	4	5	6–10	Laps	Laps Led	Races Led	Miles	$
1950	Buck Baker	5	1	0	1	0	0	0	2	213	10	1	286	1,400
1951	Buck Baker	6	0	0	0	1	0	1	1	63	0	0	63	925
1952	Buck Baker	2	0	0	0	0	0	0	0	49	0	0	38	25
1954	Tim Flock	2	1	0	1	0	0	0	1	389	180	1	195	750
1955	Banks Simpson	1	0	0	0	0	0	0	0	172	0	0	258	95
1955	Buck Baker	9	0	1	0	1	0	3	3	1,688	40	2	1,525	4,525
1957	Fireball Roberts	1	0	0	0	0	0	0	0	482	0	0	241	350
1957	Buck Baker	25	4	6	4	2	4	2	5	5,233	371	9	3,338	14,690
1958	Buck Baker	44	3	3	10	4	2	4	12	7,827	364	8	4,726	22,740
1958	Jack Smith	1	0	0	0	0	0	1	0	155	0	0	97	225
1958	Possum Jones	1	0	0	0	0	0	0	1	246	0	0	246	575
1958	G.C. Spencer	1	0	0	0	0	0	0	1	343	0	0	472	315
1958	Tiny Lund	1	1	0	0	0	0	0	0	46	14	1	41	0
1958	Gwyn Staley	1	0	0	0	0	0	1	0	38	0	0	156	700
1959	Buck Baker	23	3	0	2	4	1	4	2	3,027	182	4	1,735	5,245
1959	Tiny Lund	3	0	0	0	0	0	0	1	227	0	0	414	350
1959	Shorty Rollins	1	0	0	0	0	0	0	0	15	0	0	8	50
1959	Buddy Baker	6	0	0	0	0	0	0	3	781	0	0	391	680
1959	Fireball Roberts	1	0	0	0	0	0	0	1	148	0	0	148	525
1960	Buddy Baker	1	0	0	0	0	0	0	0	136	0	0	187	200
1960	Buck Baker	34	1	1	1	2	1	8	8	6,520	3	2	5,207	13,615
1961	Herb Tillman	2	0	0	0	0	0	0	0	91	0	0	137	550
1961	Buddy Baker	13	0	0	0	0	0	1	2	2,311	0	0	2,405	4,915
1961	Buck Baker	42	1	1	1	3	4	2	4	7,195	114	3	5,226	12,425
1962	Buck Baker	36	0	0	1	3	2	0	7	6,344	18	2	4,607	10,310
1962	Buddy Baker	31	0	0	0	1	2	2	5	5,454	0	0	4,139	7,578
1962	Darel Dieringer	1	0	0	0	0	0	0	0	36	0	0	18	85
1962	Junior Johnson	1	0	0	0	0	0	0	0	8	0	0	4	50
1962	Thomas Cox	1	0	0	0	0	0	0	0	11	0	0	17	250
1963	Curtis Crider	1	0	0	0	0	0	0	1	171	0	0	86	175
1963	Ronnie Bristow	2	0	0	0	0	0	0	0	112	0	0	48	485
1963	Neil Castles	28	0	0	0	0	1	1	6	4,093	0	0	2,330	5,590
1963	Buck Baker	45	0	1	3	6	2	5	12	9,082	64	3	5,112	15,400
1963	Buddy Baker	3	0	0	0	0	1	0	0	574	0	0	434	1,095
1963	Fred Harb	1	0	0	0	0	0	0	0	94	0	0	85	100
1964	Neil Castles	58	0	0	0	0	0	1	23	8,336	0	0	4,158	13,335
1964	Jimmy Helms	17	0	0	0	0	0	0	1	532	0	0	299	4,040
1964	Buddy Baker	1	0	0	0	0	0	0	1	127	0	0	381	1,050
1964	Steve Young	9	0	0	0	0	0	0	1	991	0	0	513	1,375
1964	Buck Baker	3	0	0	1	0	0	0	0	509	0	0	255	805
1964	Bob Gray	1	0	0	0	0	0	0	0	2	0	0	3	400
1964	Bill McMahan	1	0	0	0	0	0	0	0	348	0	0	174	270
1965	Neil Castles	49	0	0	0	1	1	4	22	9,409	66	1	6,225	16,155
1965	Ken White	1	0	0	0	0	0	0	0	0	0	0	0	400
1965	Goldie Parsons	1	0	0	0	0	0	0	0	242	0	0	81	100
1965	Darrell Bryant	1	0	0	0	0	0	0	0	57	0	0	57	555
1965	Buddy Baker	38	0	0	2	4	2	4	4	6,710	0	0	5,280	24,865
1965	Buck Baker	31	0	0	2	0	0	1	9	5,266	0	0	4,173	20,835
1966	Ray Hill	6	0	0	0	0	0	0	3	1,430	0	0	604	1,045
1966	Neil Castles	40	0	0	1	1	3	2	10	8,804	0	0	6,389	16,220
1966	Doug Cooper	1	0	0	0	0	0	0	0	167	0	0	84	150
1966	Eddie MacDonald	2	0	0	0	0	0	0	1	348	0	0	510	1,525
1966	Max Ledbetter	1	0	0	0	0	0	0	0	140	0	0	70	110
1966	Buddy Baker	10	0	0	0	0	0	0	1	1,819	0	0	1,505	4,105
1966	Paul Connors	2	0	0	0	0	0	0	1	630	0	0	642	2,720
1966	Darel Dieringer	2	0	0	0	0	0	0	0	277	0	0	139	200
1966	Buck Baker	36	0	0	3	0	2	2	7	6,725	0	0	4,939	14,900
1967	Ken Rice	3	0	0	0	0	0	0	0	22	0	0	8	200

Year	Driver	Starts	Poles	Finish 1	2	3	4	5	6–10	Laps	Laps Led	Races Led	Miles	$

Buck Baker *continued*

Year	Driver	Starts	Poles	1	2	3	4	5	6–10	Laps	Laps Led	Races Led	Miles	$
1967	J.T. Putney	1	0	0	0	0	0	0	0	307	0	0	307	710
1967	Neil Castles	3	0	0	0	0	0	1	0	417	0	0	191	540
1967	Doug Cooper	8	0	0	0	0	0	0	1	1,569	0	0	1,088	2,625
1967	Buddy Baker	3	0	0	0	0	0	0	0	257	0	0	83	330
1967	Buck Baker	21	0	0	0	0	0	0	5	4,544	0	0	3,156	7,730
1967	Al Tasnady	1	0	0	0	0	0	0	0	89	0	0	89	275
1968	Bobby Mausgrover	3	0	0	0	0	0	0	0	247	0	0	103	630
1968	Buck Baker	16	0	0	0	0	0	1	2	2,645	110	1	1,545	3,455
1968	Dub Simpson	3	0	0	0	0	0	0	0	721	0	0	589	1,350
1968	George England	1	0	0	0	0	0	1	0	235	0	0	118	275
1968	Neil Castles	1	0	0	0	0	0	0	0	4	0	0	6	430
1968	Sam Waldrop	1	0	0	0	0	0	0	0	171	0	0	86	130
1968	Serge Adams	1	0	0	0	0	0	0	0	109	0	0	55	100
1968	Ken Meisenhelder	1	0	0	0	0	0	0	0	103	0	0	93	100
1971	Buck Baker	6	0	0	0	0	1	0	1	1,775	0	0	835	2,345
1982	J.R. Charbonneau	1	0	0	0	0	0	0	0	118	0	0	118	650
1982	Randy Baker	1	0	0	0	0	0	0	0	347	0	0	353	1,300
1982	Tom Hessert	1	0	0	0	0	0	0	0	8	0	0	20	950
1984	Randy Baker	3	0	0	0	0	0	0	0	553	0	0	826	6,400
1985	Randy Baker	1	0	0	0	0	0	0	0	453	0	0	461	2,025
1986	Randy Baker	2	0	0	0	0	0	0	0	328	0	0	499	2,790
1987	Patrick Latimer	1	0	0	0	0	0	0	0	38	0	0	39	1,250
1987	Randy Baker	2	0	0	0	0	0	0	0	653	0	0	986	8,060
1988	Randy Baker	1	0	0	0	0	0	0	0	135	0	0	184	2,055
1991	Randy Baker	2	0	0	0	0	0	0	0	689	0	0	941	8,055
1992	Randy Baker	1	0	0	0	0	0	0	0	459	0	0	467	8,700
1996	Randy Baker	1	0	0	0	0	0	0	0	51	0	0	78	12,550
Lifetime		777	15	13	33	33	29	52	170	133,290	1,536	38	94,214	$328,158

Buddy Baker / Danny Schiff

Year	Driver	Starts	Poles	1	2	3	4	5	6–10	Laps	Laps Led	Races Led	Miles	$
1985	Buddy Baker	28	0	0	0	0	2	0	5	6,226	4	2	8,075	203,680
1986	Al Unser	1	0	0	0	0	0	3	0	61	0	0	149	1,915
1986	Buddy Baker	17	0	0	0	1	2	0	0	3,964	45	5	6,465	124,600
1987	Buddy Baker	20	0	0	1	1	1	0	7	4,509	91	7	7,165	204,325
1987	Irv Hoerr	1	0	0	0	0	0	0	0	114	0	0	299	1,705
1988	Rick Mast	2	0	0	0	0	0	0	0	512	2	1	527	9,190
1988	Buddy Baker	17	0	0	0	0	0	0	7	4,445	42	7	6,481	167,450
1988	Morgan Shepherd	3	0	0	0	0	1	0	1	661	6	1	992	36,770
1988	Greg Sacks	7	0	0	0	0	0	0	1	2,349	1	1	2,087	42,930
1989	Greg Sacks	10	0	0	0	0	0	0	2	3,053	108	3	3,470	69,590
1989	Jimmy Spencer	17	0	0	0	0	0	0	3	3,544	0	0	4,560	121,065
1989	Joe Ruttman	1	0	0	0	0	0	0	1	74	0	0	186	11,350
Lifetime		124	0	0	1	2	6	3	27	29,512	299	27	40,456	$994,570

Jimmy Baker

Year	Driver	Starts	Poles	1	2	3	4	5	6–10	Laps	Laps Led	Races Led	Miles	$
1962	LeeRoy Yarbrough	2	0	0	0	0	0	0	0	79	0	0	119	500
1962	Roscoe Thompson	3	0	0	0	0	0	0	0	293	0	0	477	1,280
1963	LeeRoy Yarbrough	1	0	0	0	0	0	0	0	114	0	0	57	50
Lifetime		6	0	0	0	0	0	0	0	486	0	0	652	$1,830

W.E. Baker

Year	Driver	Starts	Poles	1	2	3	4	5	6–10	Laps	Laps Led	Races Led	Miles	$
1952	W.E. Baker	1	0	0	0	0	0	0	0	368	0	0	460	90
Lifetime		1	0	0	0	0	0	0	0	368	0	0	460	$90

Ivan Baldwin

Year	Driver	Starts	Poles	1	2	3	4	5	6–10	Laps	Laps Led	Races Led	Miles	$
1971	Ivan Baldwin	3	0	0	0	0	0	0	0	272	0	0	692	3,535
1972	Ivan Baldwin	1	0	0	0	0	0	0	0	123	0	0	322	1,120
1980	Bill Osborne	1	0	0	0	0	0	0	0	20	0	0	52	500
1982	Jim Reich	2	0	0	0	0	0	0	1	202	0	0	529	4,865
Lifetime		7	0	0	0	0	0	0	1	617	0	0	1,596	$10,020

Rick Baldwin

Year	Driver	Starts	Poles	1	2	3	4	5	6–10	Laps	Laps Led	Races Led	Miles	$
1982	Rick Baldwin	1	0	0	0	0	0	0	0	323	0	0	485	6,065

Year	Driver	Starts	Poles	Finish 1	2	3	4	5	6–10	Laps	Laps Led	Races Led	Miles	$

Rick Baldwin *continued*

Year	Driver	Starts	Poles	1	2	3	4	5	6–10	Laps	Laps Led	Races Led	Miles	$
1983	Rick Baldwin	4	0	0	0	0	0	0	0	811	0	0	1,204	13,155
1985	Rick Baldwin	1	0	0	0	0	0	0	0	142	0	0	284	1,550
Lifetime		6	0	0	0	0	0	0	0	1,276	0	0	1,972	$20,770

Roger Baldwin

Year	Driver	Starts	Poles	1	2	3	4	5	6–10	Laps	Laps Led	Races Led	Miles	$
1957	Roger Baldwin	2	0	0	0	0	0	0	0	337	0	0	337	200
Lifetime		2	0	0	0	0	0	0	0	337	0	0	337	$200

Ralph Ball

Year	Driver	Starts	Poles	1	2	3	4	5	6–10	Laps	Laps Led	Races Led	Miles	$
1985	Connie Saylor	5	0	0	0	0	0	0	0	456	0	0	871	8,915
1986	Tom Bigelow	1	0	0	0	0	0	0	0	58	0	0	88	985
1986	Connie Saylor	1	0	0	0	0	0	0	0	114	0	0	303	2,575
1986	Brad Teague	3	0	0	0	0	0	0	0	419	0	0	321	3,860
1987	Brad Teague	2	0	0	0	0	0	0	0	51	0	0	82	3,455
1987	Joe Ruttman	1	0	0	0	0	0	0	0	27	0	0	72	3,125
1988	Connie Saylor	1	0	0	0	0	0	0	0	32	0	0	80	9,645
1988	Dale Jarrett	1	0	0	0	0	0	0	0	164	0	0	250	2,175
1991	Brad Teague	1	0	0	0	0	0	0	0	322	0	0	483	4,175
1992	Brad Teague	1	0	0	0	0	0	0	0	147	0	0	368	5,200
1993	Brad Teague	1	0	0	0	0	0	0	0	13	0	0	18	5,010
Lifetime		18	0	0	0	0	0	0	0	1,803	0	0	2,935	$49,120

Vic Ballard

Year	Driver	Starts	Poles	1	2	3	4	5	6–10	Laps	Laps Led	Races Led	Miles	$
1971	Walter Ballard	41	0	0	0	1	1	1	8	11,219	0	0	10,781	25,573
1972	Walter Ballard	30	0	0	0	0	0	0	7	8,293	0	0	9,578	42,374
1973	Walter Ballard	28	0	0	0	0	0	0	4	8,048	5	1	8,640	40,985
1974	Walter Ballard	26	0	0	0	0	0	1	5	6,788	2	1	7,167	45,782
1974	Kenny Brightbill	1	0	0	0	0	0	0	1	187	0	0	468	2,125
Lifetime		126	0	0	0	1	1	2	25	34,535	7	2	36,633	$156,839

Walter Ballard

Year	Driver	Starts	Poles	1	2	3	4	5	6–10	Laps	Laps Led	Races Led	Miles	$
1966	Walter Ballard	1	0	0	0	0	0	0	0	234	0	0	322	525
1973	Dick May	1	0	0	0	0	0	0	0	139	0	0	370	1,530
1975	Bill Champion	1	0	0	0	0	0	0	0	41	0	0	22	1,055
1975	Carl Van Horn	1	0	0	0	0	0	0	0	110	0	0	275	1,355
1975	Salt Walther	1	0	0	0	0	0	0	0	52	0	0	130	1,325
1975	Walter Ballard	27	0	0	0	0	0	0	3	7,148	16	2	7,504	42,975
1976	Walter Ballard	8	0	0	0	0	0	0	3	2,906	0	0	2,218	10,470
1976	Salt Walther	1	0	0	0	0	0	0	0	5	0	0	5	605
1976	Dale Earnhardt	1	0	0	0	0	0	0	0	156	0	0	234	1,725
1976	Bruce Hill	2	0	0	0	0	0	0	1	659	0	0	949	5,670
1976	Terry Bivins	10	0	0	0	0	0	0	3	3,295	0	0	2,955	21,495
1976	Tighe Scott	6	0	0	0	0	0	0	1	697	0	0	1,703	15,520
1977	Tighe Scott	25	0	0	0	0	0	1	0	5,936	0	0	7,197	56,395
1977	Walter Ballard	2	0	0	0	0	0	0	0	527	0	0	616	4,700
1978	Tighe Scott	29	0	0	0	0	0	0	7	6,626	3	1	8,224	75,480
1979	Tighe Scott	17	0	0	0	0	1	0	6	3,834	0	0	5,684	87,300
1979	Bruce Hill	7	0	0	0	0	0	0	0	1,352	0	0	2,693	17,265
1980	Bruce Hill	6	0	0	0	0	0	0	0	418	0	0	808	7,540
1980	Tighe Scott	10	0	0	0	0	0	1	1	1,066	4	1	1,968	21,925
Lifetime		156	0	0	0	0	1	2	25	35,201	23	4	43,877	$374,855

Jack Balmer

Year	Driver	Starts	Poles	1	2	3	4	5	6–10	Laps	Laps Led	Races Led	Miles	$
1971	Joe Dean Huss	3	0	0	0	0	0	0	0	1,242	0	0	671	1,435
Lifetime		3	0	0	0	0	0	0	0	1,242	0	0	671	$1,435

Steve Balogh

Year	Driver	Starts	Poles	1	2	3	4	5	6–10	Laps	Laps Led	Races Led	Miles	$
1992	Mike Potter	10	0	0	0	0	0	0	0	1,862	0	0	3,144	67,035
1994	Bob Schacht	1	0	0	0	0	0	0	0	11	0	0	28	7,560
Lifetime		11	0	0	0	0	0	0	0	1,873	0	0	3,171	$74,595

Year	Driver	Starts	Poles	Finish 1	2	3	4	5	6–10	Laps	Laps Led	Races Led	Miles	$

Patricia Bandyul

Year	Driver	Starts	Poles	1	2	3	4	5	6–10	Laps	Laps Led	Races Led	Miles	$
1992	Jeff Fuller	1	0	0	0	0	0	0	0	386	0	0	290	4,000
Lifetime		1	0	0	0	0	0	0	0	386	0	0	290	$4,000

Jim Bangsberry

Year	Driver	Starts	Poles	1	2	3	4	5	6–10	Laps	Laps Led	Races Led	Miles	$
1966	T.L. Blakely	1	0	0	0	0	0	0	0	10	0	0	25	0
1966	Bunkie Blackburn	1	0	0	0	0	0	0	0	53	0	0	53	550
Lifetime		2	0	0	0	0	0	0	0	63	0	0	78	$550

Scott Barbour

Year	Driver	Starts	Poles	1	2	3	4	5	6–10	Laps	Laps Led	Races Led	Miles	$
1999	Hut Stricklin	9	0	0	0	0	0	0	1	2,700	0	0	3,096	331,840
1999	Ricky Craven	12	0	0	0	0	0	0	0	3,297	2	2	3,997	424,799
1999	Loy Allen Jr.	2	0	0	0	0	0	0	0	306	0	0	668	53,135
Lifetime		23	0	0	0	0	0	0	1	6,303	2	2	7,760	$809,774

Phil Barkdoll

Year	Driver	Starts	Poles	1	2	3	4	5	6–10	Laps	Laps Led	Races Led	Miles	$
1984	Phil Barkdoll	2	0	0	0	0	0	0	0	212	0	0	564	5,075
1984	Morgan Shepherd	1	0	0	0	0	0	0	0	196	0	0	392	2,250
1984	Joe Ruttman	1	0	0	0	0	0	0	0	8	0	0	12	1,005
1986	Phil Barkdoll	2	0	0	0	0	0	0	0	249	3	2	662	6,045
1987	Phil Barkdoll	1	0	0	0	0	0	0	0	27	0	0	72	3,150
1988	Joe Ruttman	2	0	0	0	0	0	0	0	171	0	0	224	3,275
1988	Phil Barkdoll	3	0	0	0	0	0	0	0	465	0	0	1,220	17,145
1989	Phil Barkdoll	4	0	0	0	0	0	0	0	658	2	1	1,702	26,950
1990	Phil Barkdoll	3	0	0	0	0	0	0	0	202	0	0	524	24,160
1990	Phil Parsons	1	0	0	0	0	0	0	0	101	0	0	269	4,600
1991	Phil Barkdoll	3	0	0	0	0	0	0	0	461	0	0	1,182	35,030
1992	Phil Barkdoll	2	0	0	0	0	0	0	0	354	0	0	885	33,255
1998	Mike Wallace	1	0	0	0	0	0	0	0	199	0	0	498	85,405
Lifetime		26	0	0	0	0	0	0	0	3,303	5	3	8,206	$247,345

M.C. Barlow

Year	Driver	Starts	Poles	1	2	3	4	5	6–10	Laps	Laps Led	Races Led	Miles	$
1955	Ed Bergin	1	0	0	0	0	0	0	0	302	0	0	415	160
Lifetime		1	0	0	0	0	0	0	0	302	0	0	415	$160

Malcomb Barlow

Year	Driver	Starts	Poles	1	2	3	4	5	6–10	Laps	Laps Led	Races Led	Miles	$
1956	Gene Bergin	2	0	0	0	0	0	0	0	384	0	0	500	310
Lifetime		2	0	0	0	0	0	0	0	384	0	0	500	$310

James Barnes

Year	Driver	Starts	Poles	1	2	3	4	5	6–10	Laps	Laps Led	Races Led	Miles	$
1952	Bill Pruitt	1	0	0	0	0	0	0	0	169	0	0	169	25
Lifetime		1	0	0	0	0	0	0	0	169	0	0	169	$25

Dean Barnicle

Year	Driver	Starts	Poles	1	2	3	4	5	6–10	Laps	Laps Led	Races Led	Miles	$
1971	Kevin Terris	4	0	0	0	0	0	0	2	519	0	0	1,361	5,965
1972	Kevin Terris	4	0	0	0	0	0	0	1	651	0	0	1,562	5,695
1973	Richard White	2	0	0	0	0	0	0	2	329	0	0	862	3,370
1974	Richard White	1	0	0	0	0	0	0	0	139	0	0	364	1,200
Lifetime		11	0	0	0	0	0	0	5	1,638	0	0	4,149	$16,230

Bob Barron

Year	Driver	Starts	Poles	1	2	3	4	5	6–10	Laps	Laps Led	Races Led	Miles	$
1960	Jimmy Pardue	5	0	0	0	0	0	0	1	589	0	0	486	805
1960	Bob Barron	1	0	0	0	0	0	0	0	186	0	0	279	900
1961	Bobby Waddell	1	0	0	0	0	0	0	0	22	0	0	30	220
1961	Bob Barron	30	0	0	0	0	0	0	4	4,848	0	0	2,792	3,685
Lifetime		37	0	0	0	0	0	0	5	5,645	0	0	3,587	$5,610

Chester Barron

Year	Driver	Starts	Poles	1	2	3	4	5	6–10	Laps	Laps Led	Races Led	Miles	$
1958	Chester Barron	1	0	0	0	0	0	0	0	49	0	0	49	75
1959	Ken Rush	2	0	0	0	0	0	0	0	650	0	0	280	200

Year	Driver	Starts	Poles	Finish 1	2	3	4	5	6–10	Laps	Laps Led	Races Led	Miles	$

Chester Barron *continued*

Year	Driver	Starts	Poles	1	2	3	4	5	6–10	Laps	Laps Led	Races Led	Miles	$
1959	Joe Lee Johnson	1	0	0	0	0	0	0	0	58	0	0	80	150
1959	Chester Barron	3	0	0	0	0	0	0	1	271	0	0	175	275
Lifetime		7	0	0	0	0	0	0	1	1,028	0	0	583	$700

Bud Barry

Year	Driver	Starts	Poles	1	2	3	4	5	6–10	Laps	Laps Led	Races Led	Miles	$
1952	Leo Caldwell	2	0	0	0	0	0	0	0		0	0		75
Lifetime		2	0	0	0	0	0	0	0		0	0		$75

H.B. Bassett

Year	Driver	Starts	Poles	1	2	3	4	5	6–10	Laps	Laps Led	Races Led	Miles	$
1957	Jim Cook	2	0	0	0	0	0	0	0	133	0	0	67	80
Lifetime		2	0	0	0	0	0	0	0	133	0	0	67	$80

Lorrin Bates

Year	Driver	Starts	Poles	1	2	3	4	5	6–10	Laps	Laps Led	Races Led	Miles	$
1956	Jim Blomgren	5	0	0	0	0	0	0	1	700	0	0	679	560
1957	Jim Cook	2	0	0	0	0	0	0	0	187	0	0	141	125
1957	Jim Blomgren	1	0	0	0	0	0	0	0	53	0	0	133	110
Lifetime		8	0	0	0	0	0	0	1	940	0	0	952	$795

Doug Bawel

Year	Driver	Starts	Poles	1	2	3	4	5	6–10	Laps	Laps Led	Races Led	Miles	$
1996	Bobby Hillin	25	0	0	0	0	0	0	0	6,673	4	1	8,608	350,899
1997	Bobby Hillin	10	0	0	0	0	0	0	0	1,781	0	0	2,292	199,339
1997	Robert Pressley	7	0	0	0	0	0	0	0	1,774	0	0	2,097	103,970
1997	Morgan Shepherd	5	0	0	0	0	0	0	0	1,065	0	0	2,033	84,475
1998	Robert Pressley	30	0	0	0	1	0	0	0	7,224	3	2	10,244	984,525
1998	Hut Stricklin	2	0	0	0	0	0	0	0	889	0	0	652	47,265
1999	Robert Pressley	28	0	0	0	0	0	0	0	7,785	3	3	9,898	999,226
2000	Robert Pressley	34	0	0	0	0	0	1	0	9,183	14	4	12,260	1,393,778
2001	Robert Pressley	34	0	0	1	0	0	0	4	9,154	5	4	12,464	2,012,083
2001	Boris Said III	2	0	0	0	0	0	0	1	202	0	0	439	124,340
2002	Boris Said III	2	0	0	0	0	0	0	0	172	0	0	380	87,400
2002	Dave Blaney	36	0	0	0	0	0	0	5	10,305	65	9	13,517	2,586,573
Lifetime		215	0	0	1	1	0	1	10	56,207	94	23	74,885	$8,973,873

Herman Beach

Year	Driver	Starts	Poles	1	2	3	4	5	6–10	Laps	Laps Led	Races Led	Miles	$
1965	J.T. Putney	1	0	0	0	1	0	0	0	199	0	0	100	400
Lifetime		1	0	0	0	1	0	0	0	199	0	0	100	$400

Raymond Beadle

Year	Driver	Starts	Poles	1	2	3	4	5	6–10	Laps	Laps Led	Races Led	Miles	$
1983	Tim Richmond	30	4	1	1	4	1	3	5	7,176	590	15	8,218	226,966
1984	Tim Richmond	30	0	1	3	0	0	2	5	8,225	58	7	9,416	314,830
1985	Sammy Swindell	1	0	0	0	0	0	0	0	242	0	0	368	1,175
1985	Tim Richmond	28	0	0	1	1	1	0	10	8,199	377	12	9,497	230,220
1986	Rusty Wallace	29	0	2	0	0	2	0	12	8,486	417	8	10,418	386,220
1987	Rusty Wallace	29	1	2	3	2	1	1	7	8,323	462	16	9,670	528,760
1988	Rusty Wallace	29	2	6	5	4	2	2	4	9,222	891	19	11,191	940,135
1989	Rusty Wallace	29	4	6	4	0	2	1	7	9,104	2,020	23	10,783	860,990
1990	Rusty Wallace	29	2	2	3	2	0	2	7	8,459	1,138	16	10,174	794,014
Lifetime		234	13	20	20	13	9	11	57	67,436	5,953	116	79,734	$4,283,310

Robert Beadle

Year	Driver	Starts	Poles	1	2	3	4	5	6–10	Laps	Laps Led	Races Led	Miles	$
1980	Roy Smith	2	0	0	0	0	0	0	0	109	3	1	277	2,075
1981	Roy Smith	3	0	0	0	0	0	0	1	178	0	0	466	8,695
Lifetime		5	0	0	0	0	0	0	1	287	3	1	744	$10,770

Wayne Beahr

Year	Driver	Starts	Poles	1	2	3	4	5	6–10	Laps	Laps Led	Races Led	Miles	$
1983	Morgan Shepherd	1	0	0	0	0	0	0	0	50	0	0	27	850
1983	Joe Millikan	1	0	0	0	0	0	0	0	384	0	0	240	1,075
1983	Dick May	4	0	0	0	0	0	0	0	768	0	0	896	5,070
1984	Dick May	3	0	0	0	0	0	0	0	1,274	0	0	1,282	5,325
1985	Dick May	1	0	0	0	0	0	0	0	297	0	0	406	1,840

Year	Driver	Starts	Poles	Finish 1	2	3	4	5	6–10	Laps	Laps Led	Races Led	Miles	$

Wayne Beahr *continued*

Year	Driver	Starts	Poles	1	2	3	4	5	6–10	Laps	Laps Led	Races Led	Miles	$
1985	J.D. McDuffie	1	0	0	0	0	0	0	0	203	0	0	203	3,565
1985	Morgan Shepherd	1	0	0	0	0	0	0	0	123	0	0	125	1,075
1986	Roy Lee Hendrick	1	0	0	0	0	0	0	0	91	0	0	91	875
1986	Joe Fields	1	0	0	0	0	0	0	0	0	0	0	0	875
1986	Joe Millikan	2	0	0	0	0	0	0	0	59	0	0	56	1,950
1987	Curtis Markham	1	0	0	0	0	0	0	0	29	0	0	29	1,175
Lifetime		17	0	0	0	0	0	0	0	3,278	0	0	3,355	$23,675

Herman Beam

Year	Driver	Starts	Poles	1	2	3	4	5	6–10	Laps	Laps Led	Races Led	Miles	$
1957	Herman Beam	1	0	0	0	0	0	0	0		0	0		50
1958	Herman Beam	20	0	0	0	0	0	0	1	3,651	0	0	2,251	2,135
1959	Herman Beam	30	0	0	0	0	0	1	11	6,024	0	0	4,006	4,130
1960	Herman Beam	26	0	0	0	0	1	0	5	4,785	0	0	4,730	5,348
1961	Herman Beam	41	0	0	0	0	1	0	13	8,827	0	0	6,403	8,055
1962	Herman Beam	51	1	0	0	0	0	0	18	11,217	0	0	7,140	9,935
1963	Ned Jarrett	1	0	0	0	0	0	1	0	195	0	0	98	275
1963	Larry Thomas	1	0	0	0	0	0	0	0	373	0	0	560	1,000
1963	Herman Beam	25	0	0	0	0	0	0	6	5,061	0	0	3,476	5,205
1963	Cale Yarborough	14	0	0	0	0	0	3	4	3,926	0	0	2,389	4,100
1964	Tiny Lund	1	0	0	0	0	0	1	0	196	0	0	98	275
1964	Cale Yarborough	17	0	0	0	0	0	2	4	3,194	10	1	2,591	5,515
1964	H.B. Bailey	1	0	0	0	0	0	0	0	6	0	0	9	400
1964	Larry Frank	1	0	0	0	0	0	0	0	12	0	0	11	0
1964	Larry Thomas	10	0	0	1	1	2	1	4	3,712	0	0	2,189	7,350
1965	J.T. Putney	27	0	0	1	2	4	2	10	6,415	0	0	4,885	15,755
1966	J.T. Putney	1	0	0	0	0	0	0	0	102	0	0	51	0
Lifetime		268	1	0	2	3	8	11	76	58,259	10	1	40,884	$68,965

Fred Bear

Year	Driver	Starts	Poles	1	2	3	4	5	6–10	Laps	Laps Led	Races Led	Miles	$
1969	Buddy Young	21	0	0	0	0	0	1	5	4,510	0	0	3,845	15,422
Lifetime		21	0	0	0	0	0	1	5	4,510	0	0	3,845	$15,422

Joe Bearscheck

Year	Driver	Starts	Poles	1	2	3	4	5	6–10	Laps	Laps Led	Races Led	Miles	$
1954	Danny Letner	4	1	1	0	1	0	0	1	1,058	143	2	674	1,975
Lifetime		4	1	1	0	1	0	0	1	1,058	143	2	674	$1,975

Byron Beatty

Year	Driver	Starts	Poles	1	2	3	4	5	6–10	Laps	Laps Led	Races Led	Miles	$
1950	Byron Beatty	1	0	0	0	0	0	0	0	351	0	0	439	0
Lifetime		1	0	0	0	0	0	0	0	351	0	0	439	$0

Dick Beaty

Year	Driver	Starts	Poles	1	2	3	4	5	6–10	Laps	Laps Led	Races Led	Miles	$
1957	Bill Amick	1	0	0	0	0	0	0	1	189	0	0	95	210
1957	Dick Beaty	19	0	0	0	0	0	1	6	3,061	0	0	1,990	3,175
1957	Speedy Thompson	1	0	0	0	0	0	0	0	144	0	0	72	100
1957	Fireball Roberts	1	0	0	0	0	0	1	0	195	0	0	98	270
1958	Dick Beaty	2	0	0	0	0	0	0	0	448	0	0	224	150
1958	Junior Johnson	1	0	0	0	0	0	0	1	148	0	0	37	215
1958	Joe Weatherly	1	0	0	0	0	0	0	0	144	0	0	36	120
Lifetime		26	0	0	0	0	0	2	8	4,329	0	0	2,551	$4,240

Joe Beccue

Year	Driver	Starts	Poles	1	2	3	4	5	6–10	Laps	Laps Led	Races Led	Miles	$
1951	Bud Riley	7	0	0	0	0	0	0	1	457	0	0	549	550
Lifetime		7	0	0	0	0	0	1	1	457	0	0	549	$550

Gary Bechtel

Year	Driver	Starts	Poles	1	2	3	4	5	6–10	Laps	Laps Led	Races Led	Miles	$
1990	Bobby Hamilton	1	0	0	0	0	0	0	0	102	0	0	153	4,540
1990	Phil Parsons	3	0	0	0	0	0	0	0	586	0	0	959	14,755
1992	John Krebs	2	0	0	0	0	0	0	0	380	0	0	489	12,990
1993	Andy Hillenburg	1	0	0	0	0	0	0	0	242	0	0	363	4,365
1993	John Krebs	2	0	0	0	0	0	0	0	154	0	0	386	13,955
1993	Steve Grissom	1	0	0	0	0	0	0	0	300	0	0	300	6,485

Year	Driver	Starts	Poles	Finish 1	2	3	4	5	6–10	Laps	Laps Led	Races Led	Miles	$

Gary Bechtel *continued*

Year	Driver	Starts	Poles	1	2	3	4	5	6–10	Laps	Laps Led	Races Led	Miles	$
1994	John Krebs	1	0	0	0	0	0	0	0	18	1	1	45	8,100
1994	Steve Grissom	28	0	0	0	0	0	0	3	8,394	1	1	10,169	292,815
1995	Steve Grissom	29	0	0	0	0	0	1	3	8,279	17	2	10,300	514,747
1996	Chad Little	4	0	0	0	0	0	0	0	889	0	0	785	84,525
1996	Robert Pressley	3	0	0	0	0	0	0	0	854	0	0	1,017	55,650
1996	Steve Grissom	13	0	0	0	0	0	1	1	3,169	12	1	4,302	308,183
1996	Jeff Green	2	0	0	0	0	0	0	0	722	0	0	738	30,040
1996	Greg Sacks	6	0	0	0	0	0	0	0	1,059	3	1	2,142	161,425
1996	Butch Leitzinger	1	0	0	0	0	0	0	0	90	0	0	221	22,705
1997	Robert Pressley	7	0	0	0	0	0	0	0	2,167	9	2	2,108	137,479
1997	Jeff Green	20	0	0	0	0	1	0	1	5,524	18	2	7,146	434,685
1998	Elliott Sadler	2	0	0	0	0	0	0	0	705	0	0	577	45,325
1998	Jeff Green	3	0	0	0	0	0	0	0	943	0	0	1,187	81,125
Lifetime		129	0	0	0	0	1	2	8	34,577	61	10	43,388	$2,233,894

Bob Beck

Year	Driver	Starts	Poles	1	2	3	4	5	6–10	Laps	Laps Led	Races Led	Miles	$
1955	Bob Beck	2	0	0	0	0	0	0	0	223	0	0	144	75
Lifetime		2	0	0	0	0	0	0	0	223	0	0	144	$75

Tom Beck

Year	Driver	Starts	Poles	1	2	3	4	5	6–10	Laps	Laps Led	Races Led	Miles	$
1983	Lennie Pond	3	0	0	0	0	0	0	1	405	3	1	913	19,490
Lifetime		3	0	0	0	0	0	0	1	405	3	1	913	$19,490

Randy Becker

Year	Driver	Starts	Poles	1	2	3	4	5	6–10	Laps	Laps Led	Races Led	Miles	$
1983	Randy Becker	1	0	0	0	0	0	0	0	116	0	0	304	1,950
Lifetime		1	0	0	0	0	0	0	0	116	0	0	304	$1,950

Allen Beebe

Year	Driver	Starts	Poles	1	2	3	4	5	6–10	Laps	Laps Led	Races Led	Miles	$
1990	Troy Beebe	2	0	0	0	0	0	0	0	333	0	0	439	6,560
Lifetime		2	0	0	0	0	0	0	0	333	0	0	439	$6,560

Jack Beebe

Year	Driver	Starts	Poles	1	2	3	4	5	6–10	Laps	Laps Led	Races Led	Miles	$
1978	Satch Worley	4	0	0	0	0	0	0	1	1,298	0	0	1,590	6,205
1979	Geoffrey Bodine	3	0	0	0	0	0	0	0	443	6	1	631	4,820
1979	Harry Gant	22	1	0	0	0	0	0	4	5,927	29	4	6,771	40,560
1980	Harry Gant	28	0	0	3	2	2	2	3	7,584	262	9	7,840	140,550
1981	Harry Gant	4	0	0	1	0	0	0	1	1,329	112	2	1,587	46,920
1981	Ron Bouchard	22	1	1	0	0	1	3	7	6,155	12	2	6,979	139,585
1982	Ron Bouchard	30	1	0	0	2	1	0	12	8,048	1	1	8,544	309,825
1983	Ron Bouchard	28	1	0	0	0	1	0	6	7,187	22	4	8,315	131,045
1984	Ron Bouchard	30	0	0	1	2	1	1	5	9,200	111	8	10,504	215,245
1985	Ron Bouchard	28	0	0	1	1	2	1	7	7,723	77	5	8,969	212,265
1986	Morgan Shepherd	12	0	1	0	0	2	0	3	2,782	130	6	4,776	129,915
Lifetime		211	4	2	6	7	10	7	49	57,676	762	42	66,507	$1,376,935

Troy Beebe

Year	Driver	Starts	Poles	1	2	3	4	5	6–10	Laps	Laps Led	Races Led	Miles	$
1989	Troy Beebe	1	0	0	0	0	0	0	0	72	0	0	181	2,605
Lifetime		1	0	0	0	0	0	0	0	72	0	0	181	$2,605

B.S. Beeson

Year	Driver	Starts	Poles	1	2	3	4	5	6–10	Laps	Laps Led	Races Led	Miles	$
1950	Shorty York	1	0	0	0	0	0	0	0	358	0	0	448	0
Lifetime		1	0	0	0	0	0	0	0	358	0	0	448	$0

Torsten Behn

Year	Driver	Starts	Poles	1	2	3	4	5	6–10	Laps	Laps Led	Races Led	Miles	$
1981	Rick O'Dell	1	0	0	0	0	0	0	0	86	0	0	225	2,145
Lifetime		1	0	0	0	0	0	0	0	86	0	0	225	$2,145

John Belgard

Year	Driver	Starts	Poles	1	2	3	4	5	6–10	Laps	Laps Led	Races Led	Miles	$
1949	John Belgard	1	0	0	0	0	0	0	0		0	0		0
Lifetime		1	0	0	0	0	0	0	0		0	0		$0

Year	Driver	Starts	Poles	Finish 1	2	3	4	5	6–10	Laps	Laps Led	Races Led	Miles	$

Charles Bell

Year	Driver	Starts	Poles	1	2	3	4	5	6–10	Laps	Laps Led	Races Led	Miles	$
1967	Jack McCoy	1	0	0	0	0	0	0	0	88	0	0	238	575
1968	Jack McCoy	1	0	0	0	0	0	0	0	118	0	0	319	725
Lifetime		2	0	0	0	0	0	0	0	206	0	0	556	$1,300

Ed Benedict

Year	Driver	Starts	Poles	1	2	3	4	5	6–10	Laps	Laps Led	Races Led	Miles	$
1952	Ed Benedict	2	0	0	0	0	0	0	1	413	0	0	207	125
1952	Bucky Sager	9	0	0	0	0	1	0	2	1,394	0	0	993	685
Lifetime		11	0	0	0	0	1	0	3	1,807	0	0	1,199	$810

Ron Benfield

Year	Driver	Starts	Poles	1	2	3	4	5	6–10	Laps	Laps Led	Races Led	Miles	$
1981	Morgan Shepherd	3	0	0	0	0	0	0	0	390	43	2	428	2,405
1981	Johnny Rutherford	12	0	0	0	0	0	1	1	2,432	5	1	3,793	38,095
1981	Rusty Wallace	2	0	0	0	0	0	0	0	351	0	0	697	2,245
1982	Morgan Shepherd	29	2	0	0	1	1	4	7	7,608	209	11	8,468	134,920
1983	Joe Ruttman	30	3	0	0	1	3	0	6	7,887	398	10	8,818	202,806
1984	Morgan Shepherd	3	0	0	0	0	0	0	1	926	1	1	1,285	17,300
1984	L.D. Ottinger	2	0	0	0	0	0	0	0	695	0	0	714	7,650
1984	Joe Ruttman	25	1	0	0	0	0	0	7	6,233	54	3	7,504	133,620
1985	Trevor Boys	6	0	0	0	0	0	0	0	542	0	0	695	21,980
Lifetime		112	6	0	0	2	4	5	22	27,064	710	28	32,402	$561,021

Mike Bennett

Year	Driver	Starts	Poles	1	2	3	4	5	6–10	Laps	Laps Led	Races Led	Miles	$
1973	Bill Ward	2	0	0	0	0	0	0	0	188	0	0	500	2,275
Lifetime		2	0	0	0	0	0	0	0	188	0	0	500	$2,275

Bill Benson

Year	Driver	Starts	Poles	1	2	3	4	5	6–10	Laps	Laps Led	Races Led	Miles	$
1957	Bill Benson	11	0	0	0	0	0	0	2	1,320	0	0	827	1,090
1958	Bill Benson	5	0	0	0	0	0	0	0	549	0	0	375	220
Lifetime		16	0	0	0	0	0	0	2	1,869	0	0	1,202	$1,310

Tiny Benson

Year	Driver	Starts	Poles	1	2	3	4	5	6–10	Laps	Laps Led	Races Led	Miles	$
1958	Tiny Benson	3	0	0	0	0	0	0	2	310	0	0	115	400
1959	Tiny Benson	2	0	0	0	0	0	0	2	298	0	0	205	350
Lifetime		5	0	0	0	0	0	0	4	608	0	0	319	$750

Roy Bentley

Year	Driver	Starts	Poles	1	2	3	4	5	6–10	Laps	Laps Led	Races Led	Miles	$
1950	Roy Bentley	1	0	0	0	0	0	0	0	319	0	0	399	0
Lifetime		1	0	0	0	0	0	0	0	319	0	0	399	$0

Clarence Benton

Year	Driver	Starts	Poles	1	2	3	4	5	6–10	Laps	Laps Led	Races Led	Miles	$
1949	Clarence Benton	1	0	0	0	0	0	0	0		0	0		0
Lifetime		1	0	0	0	0	0	0	0		0	0		$0

John Berejoski

Year	Driver	Starts	Poles	1	2	3	4	5	6–10	Laps	Laps Led	Races Led	Miles	$
1964	Elmo Langley	10	0	0	0	0	0	0	3	2,123	0	0	1,353	3,290
Lifetime		10	0	0	0	0	0	0	3	2,123	0	0	1,353	$3,290

Mellie Bernard

Year	Driver	Starts	Poles	1	2	3	4	5	6–10	Laps	Laps Led	Races Led	Miles	$
1953	Ned Jarrett	1	0	0	0	0	0	0	0		0	0		25
1954	Ned Jarrett	2	0	0	0	0	0	0	0	273	0	0	151	25
1955	Ned Jarrett	2	0	0	0	0	0	0	0	333	0	0	447	260
Lifetime		5	0	0	0	0	0	0	0	606	0	0	598	$310

Kenny Bernstein

Year	Driver	Starts	Poles	1	2	3	4	5	6–10	Laps	Laps Led	Races Led	Miles	$
1986	Joe Ruttman	29	0	0	2	0	0	3	9	7,732	55	5	8,708	209,040
1987	Morgan Shepherd	29	1	0	1	1	1	4	4	6,510	167	8	8,039	276,430
1988	Ricky Rudd	29	2	1	3	1	1	0	5	8,867	695	16	10,438	361,590
1989	Ricky Rudd	29	0	1	0	2	3	1	8	9,326	247	7	11,076	409,352
1990	Brett Bodine	29	1	1	0	2	2	0	4	9,097	216	7	10,980	377,724

Year	Driver	Starts	Poles	Finish 1	2	3	4	5	6–10	Laps	Laps Led	Races Led	Miles	$

Kenny Bernstein *continued*

Year	Driver	Starts	Poles	1	2	3	4	5	6–10	Laps	Laps Led	Races Led	Miles	$
1991	Brett Bodine	29	1	0	1	0	1	0	4	7,873	163	3	9,050	310,550
1992	Brett Bodine	29	1	0	0	1	1	0	11	8,807	237	11	10,248	425,530
1993	Dick Trickle	1	0	0	0	0	0	0	0	407	0	0	407	12,755
1993	Brett Bodine	29	2	0	1	0	0	2	6	8,120	102	7	9,383	489,410
1994	Brett Bodine	31	0	0	1	0	0	0	5	8,931	55	6	10,773	691,380
1995	Hut Stricklin	24	1	0	0	0	1	1	3	5,513	45	4	7,311	486,065
1995	Steve Kinser	5	0	0	0	0	0	0	0	958	0	0	948	105,224
Lifetime		293	9	3	9	7	10	11	59	82,141	1,982	74	97,361	$4,155,050

Ed Berrier

Year	Driver	Starts	Poles	1	2	3	4	5	6–10	Laps	Laps Led	Races Led	Miles	$
1996	Ed Berrier	1	0	0	0	0	0	0	0	57	0	0	78	9,895
Lifetime		1	0	0	0	0	0	0	0	57	0	0	78	$9,895

Max Berrier

Year	Driver	Starts	Poles	1	2	3	4	5	6–10	Laps	Laps Led	Races Led	Miles	$
1955	Max Berrier	2	0	0	0	0	0	0	0	232	0	0	116	100
1959	Max Berrier	2	0	0	0	0	0	0	0	214	0	0	64	110
Lifetime		4	0	0	0	0	0	0	0	446	0	0	180	$210

Joe Bessey

Year	Driver	Starts	Poles	1	2	3	4	5	6–10	Laps	Laps Led	Races Led	Miles	$
1999	Geoffrey Bodine	34	0	0	0	1	0	0	1	9,535	8	3	12,256	1,484,394
2000	Geoffrey Bodine	12	0	0	0	0	0	0	0	2,738	20	1	3,765	577,715
2000	Joe Bessey	1	0	0	0	0	0	0	0	297	0	0	314	48,975
2000	Rich Bickle	3	0	0	0	0	0	0	0	989	0	0	1,067	135,960
2000	Ted Musgrave	5	0	0	0	0	0	0	0	1,012	1	1	1,303	205,491
2000	Dick Trickle	4	0	0	0	0	0	0	0	1,024	0	0	1,812	181,715
Lifetime		59	0	0	0	1	0	0	1	15,595	29	5	20,518	$2,634,250

Fred Bethune

Year	Driver	Starts	Poles	1	2	3	4	5	6–10	Laps	Laps Led	Races Led	Miles	$
1952	Fred Bethune	2	0	0	0	0	0	0	1	377	0	0	293	125
Lifetime		2	0	0	0	0	0	0	1	377	0	0	293	$125

Larry Bettinger

Year	Driver	Starts	Poles	1	2	3	4	5	6–10	Laps	Laps Led	Races Led	Miles	$
1951	Bill Norton	3	0	1	0	1	0	0	1	200	19	1	100	1,675
Lifetime		3	0	1	0	1	0	0	1	200	19	1	100	$1,675

Jack Beumer

Year	Driver	Starts	Poles	1	2	3	4	5	6–10	Laps	Laps Led	Races Led	Miles	$
1954	Ed Normi	1	0	0	0	0	0	0	0	39	0	0	39	40
1954	Sam Hawks	1	0	0	0	0	0	0	1	230	0	0	115	200
Lifetime		2	0	0	0	0	0	0	1	269	0	0	154	$240

Tim Beverley

Year	Driver	Starts	Poles	1	2	3	4	5	6–10	Laps	Laps Led	Races Led	Miles	$
1998	Darrell Waltrip	15	0	0	0	0	0	0	0	4,391	2	1	5,363	377,050
1998	Ron Hornaday Jr.	1	0	0	0	0	0	0	0	112	0	0	218	27,850
1999	David Green	9	1	0	0	0	0	0	0	2,351	7	1	2,853	293,790
1999	Rich Bickle	19	0	0	0	0	0	0	2	4,897	0	0	7,578	740,449
2000	Johnny Benson Jr.	33	0	0	2	0	0	1	4	9,451	62	5	12,195	1,584,785
Lifetime		77	1	0	2	0	0	1	6	21,202	71	7	28,208	$3,023,924

Rich Bickle

Year	Driver	Starts	Poles	1	2	3	4	5	6–10	Laps	Laps Led	Races Led	Miles	$
1989	Rich Bickle	2	0	0	0	0	0	0	0	355	0	0	540	4,185
1990	Rich Bickle	1	0	0	0	0	0	0	0	195	0	0	488	19,120
Lifetime		3	0	0	0	0	0	0	0	550	0	0	1,027	$23,305

Don Bierschwale (Statistics include shared ownerships with several different partners during the Bierschwale's tenure in NASCAR.)

Year	Driver	Starts	Poles	1	2	3	4	5	6–10	Laps	Laps Led	Races Led	Miles	$
1971	Jimmy Finger	1	0	0	0	0	0	0	0	18	0	0	36	530
1972	Jimmy Finger	2	0	0	0	0	0	0	0	214	0	0	535	3,830

Year	Driver	Starts	Poles	Finish						Laps	Laps Led	Races Led	Miles	$
				1	2	3	4	5	6–10					
1972	Clarence Lovell	12	0	0	0	0	0	0	0	2,202	0	0	3,586	10,770
1973	Johnny Rutherford	1	0	0	0	0	0	0	0	471	0	0	479	1,325
1973	Ed Sczech	4	0	0	0	0	0	0	0	558	0	0	1,141	4,270
1973	Dick Brooks	1	0	0	0	0	0	0	1	351	0	0	479	2,880
1973	Clarence Lovell	4	0	0	0	0	1	0	1	661	0	0	1,169	9,175
1974	Johnny Rutherford	2	0	0	0	0	0	0	0	123	2	1	308	4,415
1974	Iggy Katona	1	0	0	0	0	0	0	0	181	0	0	481	1,675
1979	Jimmy Finger	3	0	0	0	0	0	0	0	152	0	0	398	5,020
1983	Eddie Bierschwale	3	0	0	0	0	0	0	0	524	0	0	888	3,665
1984	Eddie Bierschwale	2	0	0	0	0	0	0	0	317	0	0	583	3,495
1988	Eddie Bierschwale	20	0	0	0	0	0	0	0	4,106	0	0	6,121	57,555
1989	Eddie Bierschwale	14	0	0	0	0	0	0	1	3,740	2	1	4,752	67,910
1990	Eddie Bierschwale	2	0	0	0	0	0	0	0	474	0	0	787	8,415
1991	Eddie Bierschwale	3	0	0	0	0	0	0	0	621	0	0	1,174	41,785
1992	Eddie Bierschwale	4	0	0	0	0	0	0	0	628	0	0	1,092	23,045
1992	A.J. Foyt	1	0	0	0	0	0	0	0	195	0	0	488	23,055
Lifetime		80	0	0	0	0	1	0	3	15,536	4	2	24,495	$272,815

George Bignotti

Year	Driver	Starts	Poles	Finish						Laps	Laps Led	Races Led	Miles	$
1954	Jim Graham	2	0	0	0	0	0	0	1	530	0	0	385	400
Lifetime		2	0	0	0	0	0	0	1	530	0	0	385	$400

Robert Bilby

Year	Driver	Starts	Poles	Finish						Laps	Laps Led	Races Led	Miles	$
1989	Phil Parsons	1	0	0	0	0	0	0	0	394	0	0	246	2,245
1989	Mike Miller	1	0	0	0	0	0	0	0	137	0	0	274	3,075
Lifetime		2	0	0	0	0	0	0	0	531	0	0	520	$5,320

Fred Bince

Year	Driver	Starts	Poles	Finish						Laps	Laps Led	Races Led	Miles	$
1951	Fred Lee	3	0	0	0	0	0	0	1		0	0		150
1954	Sam Lamm	2	0	0	0	0	0	0	0	426	0	0	326	50
1955	Owen Loggins	3	0	0	0	0	0	0	0	341	0	0	326	150
Lifetime		8	0	0	0	0	0	0	1	767	0	0	652	$350

Art Binkley

Year	Driver	Starts	Poles	Finish						Laps	Laps Led	Races Led	Miles	$
1956	Art Binkley	1	0	0	0	0	0	0	0	349	0	0	175	150
1957	Art Binkley	3	0	0	0	0	0	0	0	690	0	0	495	390
Lifetime		4	0	0	0	0	0	0	0	1,039	0	0	669	$540

Jack Birmingham

Year	Driver	Starts	Poles	Finish						Laps	Laps Led	Races Led	Miles	$
1999	Todd Bodine	7	0	0	0	0	0	0	0	2,008	0	0	2,007	208,382
1999	Mike Bliss	2	0	0	0	0	0	0	0	766	0	0	539	42,475
1999	Buckshot Jones	1	0	0	0	0	0	0	0	187	0	0	497	32,915
2000	Jeff Fuller	6	0	0	0	0	0	0	0	1,683	1	1	1,944	186,650
2000	Mike Bliss	24	0	0	0	0	0	0	1	5,296	4	1	7,671	835,134
2001	Rick Mast	5	0	0	0	0	0	0	0	1,059	0	0	1,343	150,525
2001	Kenny Wallace	12	0	0	0	0	0	0	0	3,383	1	1	4,202	583,489
Lifetime		57	0	0	0	0	0	0	1	14,382	6	3	18,202	$2,039,570

Martin Birrane

Year	Driver	Starts	Poles	Finish						Laps	Laps Led	Races Led	Miles	$
1991	John Paul Jr.	2	0	0	0	0	0	0	0	167	0	0	413	8,460
1991	Bobby Hillin	2	0	0	0	0	0	0	0	554	10	1	836	10,975
1992	Bobby Hillin	10	0	0	0	0	0	0	0	2,091	0	0	3,958	79,930
Lifetime		14	0	0	0	0	0	0	0	2,812	10	1	5,207	$99,365

Gordon Bishop

Year	Driver	Starts	Poles	Finish						Laps	Laps Led	Races Led	Miles	$
1952	Gordon Bishop	2	0	0	0	0	0	0	0		0	0		25
Lifetime		2	0	0	0	0	0	0	0		0	0		$25

Bobby Black

Year	Driver	Starts	Poles	Finish						Laps	Laps Led	Races Led	Miles	$
1974	Bobby Ore	1	0	0	0	0	0	0	0	297	0	0	177	440
Lifetime		1	0	0	0	0	0	0	0	297	0	0	177	$440

Year	Driver	Starts	Poles	Finish 1	2	3	4	5	6–10	Laps	Laps Led	Races Led	Miles	$

Gene Black

Year	Driver	Starts	Poles	1	2	3	4	5	6–10	Laps	Laps Led	Races Led	Miles	$
1966	Henley Gray	2	0	0	0	0	1	0	0	679	0	0	636	1,265
1966	Paul Moore	1	0	0	0	0	0	0	0	35	0	0	18	100
1966	Earl Brooks	8	0	0	0	0	0	0	1	1,677	0	0	1,060	2,595
1966	Elmo Langley	1	0	0	0	1	0	0	0	192	0	0	96	400
1966	Gene Black	11	0	0	0	0	0	0	2	1,709	0	0	1,205	3,265
1966	Buddy Baker	1	0	0	0	0	0	0	0	317	0	0	198	225
1966	Bill Seifert	1	0	0	0	0	0	0	0	63	0	0	32	100
1966	Don Israel	1	0	0	0	0	0	0	1	188	0	0	94	150
1966	Buster Sexton	1	0	0	0	0	0	0	0	183	0	0	92	100
1966	Bunkie Blackburn	1	0	0	0	0	0	0	0	1	0	0	2	580
1967	Jackie Fox	2	0	0	0	0	0	0	0	57	0	0	23	0
1967	Bob Cooper	1	0	0	0	0	0	0	0	24	0	0	33	565
1967	Earl Brooks	14	0	0	0	0	0	0	4	1,804	0	0	937	2,395
1967	Jimmy Helms	1	0	0	0	0	0	0	1	177	0	0	89	150
1968	Gene Black	7	0	0	0	0	0	0	0	762	0	0	336	805
1968	Bryant Wallace	1	0	0	0	0	0	0	0	118	0	0	59	100
1968	Earl Brooks	1	0	0	0	0	0	0	0	89	0	0	223	1,085
1968	Bill Seifert	1	0	0	0	0	0	0	0	53	0	0	18	100
Lifetime		56	0	0	0	1	1	0	9	8,128	0	0	5,148	$13,980

John Black

Year	Driver	Starts	Poles	1	2	3	4	5	6–10	Laps	Laps Led	Races Led	Miles	$
1964	Henley Gray	1	0	0	0	0	0	0	0	126	0	0	63	100
1964	John Sears	6	0	0	0	0	0	0	3	1,200	0	0	581	1,130
Lifetime		7	0	0	0	0	0	0	3	1,326	0	0	644	$1,230

M.J. Black

Year	Driver	Starts	Poles	1	2	3	4	5	6–10	Laps	Laps Led	Races Led	Miles	$
1960	Jimmy Pardue	2	0	0	0	0	0	0	1	478	0	0	548	530
1960	E.J. Trivette	9	0	0	0	0	0	0	0	1,000	0	0	532	940
1960	Curtis Crider	1	0	0	0	0	0	0	0	45	0	0	41	50
1961	E.J. Trivette	5	0	0	0	0	0	0	1	611	0	0	276	600
1961	Jimmy Pardue	2	0	0	0	0	0	0	0	238	0	0	119	200
1961	Bobby Waddell	1	0	0	0	0	0	0	0	3	0	0	5	50
1961	George Green	7	0	0	0	0	0	0	2	1,130	0	0	613	685
Lifetime		27	0	0	0	0	0	0	4	3,505	0	0	2,133	$3,055

Melvin Black

Year	Driver	Starts	Poles	1	2	3	4	5	6–10	Laps	Laps Led	Races Led	Miles	$
1961	Charlie Glotzbach	4	0	0	0	0	0	0	0	344	0	0	653	755
Lifetime		4	0	0	0	0	0	0	0	344	0	0	653	$755

Sonny Black

Year	Driver	Starts	Poles	1	2	3	4	5	6–10	Laps	Laps Led	Races Led	Miles	$
1951	Sonny Black	4	0	0	0	0	0	0	2	73	0	0	91	175
1955	Sonny Black	1	0	0	0	0	0	0	0	181	0	0	91	50
Lifetime		5	0	0	0	0	0	0	2	254	0	0	182	$225

A.J. Blackwelder

Year	Driver	Starts	Poles	1	2	3	4	5	6–10	Laps	Laps Led	Races Led	Miles	$
1959	Shorty Rollins	1	0	0	0	0	0	0	0	90	0	0	225	300
1959	Bunk Moore	1	0	0	0	0	0	0	0	24	0	0	24	0
1960	Carl Burris	2	0	0	0	0	0	0	0	81	0	0	151	200
1960	Curtis Crider	1	0	0	0	0	0	0	0	110	0	0	28	125
Lifetime		5	0	0	0	0	0	0	0	305	0	0	427	$625

Clay Blackwell

Year	Driver	Starts	Poles	1	2	3	4	5	6–10	Laps	Laps Led	Races Led	Miles	$
1975	Johnny Ray	4	0	0	0	0	0	0	0	247	0	0	577	3,435
1975	Bill Champion	1	0	0	0	0	0	0	0	144	0	0	197	1,340
1976	Johnny Ray	1	0	0	0	0	0	0	0	111	0	0	278	2,270
Lifetime		6	0	0	0	0	0	0	0	502	0	0	1,052	$7,045

Bill Blair

Year	Driver	Starts	Poles	1	2	3	4	5	6–10	Laps	Laps Led	Races Led	Miles	$
1950	Bill Blair	1	0	0	0	0	0	1	0		0	0		300
1951	Bill Blair	15	0	0	0	1	2	0	2	616	0	0	656	2,000
1953	Bill Blair	21	0	1	0	2	0	3	2	1,043	51	2	1,100	3,995

Year	Driver	Starts	Poles	Finish 1	2	3	4	5	6–10	Laps	Laps Led	Races Led	Miles	$

Bill Blair *continued*

Year	Driver	Starts	Poles	1	2	3	4	5	6–10	Laps	Laps Led	Races Led	Miles	$
1954	Bill Blair	16	0	0	0	0	0	2	8	2,426	7	1	1,679	2,300
1955	Jim Paschal	1	0	0	0	0	0	0	0	83	0	0	83	50
1955	Bill Blair	5	0	0	0	0	0	0	0	844	0	0	919	365
1956	Bill Blair	2	0	0	0	0	0	0	1	360	0	0	341	500
1958	Bill Blair	1	0	0	0	0	0	0	0	104	0	0	94	125
Lifetime		62	0	1	0	3	2	6	13	5,476	58	3	4,871	$9,635

David Blair

Year	Driver	Starts	Poles	1	2	3	4	5	6–10	Laps	Laps Led	Races Led	Miles	$
1996	Elton Sawyer	8	0	0	0	0	0	0	0	2,121	0	0	2,833	112,303
1996	Todd Bodine	3	0	0	0	0	0	0	0	1,092	1	1	1,293	32,800
1997	Kenny Irwin Jr.	4	0	0	0	0	0	0	1	1,283	12	1	1,227	61,230
1997	Rick Wilson	3	0	0	0	0	0	0	0	690	0	0	1,295	96,785
Lifetime		18	0	0	0	0	0	0	1	5,186	13	2	6,647	$303,118

Joe Blair

Year	Driver	Starts	Poles	1	2	3	4	5	6–10	Laps	Laps Led	Races Led	Miles	$
1954	Jimmie Lewallen	10	0	0	2	0	0	1	2	1,602	0	0	1,031	2,400
1954	Ray Duhigg	1	0	0	0	0	0	0	0	43	0	0	65	0
1955	Richard Brownlee	7	0	0	0	0	0	0	0	681	0	0	359	315
1955	Perk Brown	2	0	0	0	0	0	0	1	275	0	0	138	150
1955	Jimmie Lewallen	9	0	0	0	0	0	2	3	1,041	0	0	573	1,325
1956	Fred Harb	1	0	0	0	0	0	0	0	31	0	0	16	50
1956	Bill Blair	5	0	0	0	0	0	0	2	353	0	0	280	280
Lifetime		35	0	0	2	0	0	3	8	4,026	0	0	2,459	$4,520

Pug Blalock

Year	Driver	Starts	Poles	1	2	3	4	5	6–10	Laps	Laps Led	Races Led	Miles	$
1951	Pug Blalock	2	0	0	0	0	0	0	1		0	0		75
Lifetime		2	0	0	0	0	0	0	1		0	0		$75

Leonard Blanchard

Year	Driver	Starts	Poles	1	2	3	4	5	6–10	Laps	Laps Led	Races Led	Miles	$
1970	Leonard Blanchard	2	0	0	0	0	0	0	0	92	0	0	230	1,135
1971	Leonard Blanchard	1	0	0	0	0	0	0	0	46	0	0	115	255
Lifetime		3	0	0	0	0	0	0	0	138	0	0	345	$1,390

F.J. Bland

Year	Driver	Starts	Poles	1	2	3	4	5	6–10	Laps	Laps Led	Races Led	Miles	$
1950	Cotton Owens	1	0	0	0	0	0	0	1	380	23	1	475	930
1951	Cotton Owens	4	0	0	0	0	0	0	2	370	0	0	463	425
Lifetime		5	0	0	0	0	0	0	3	750	23	1	938	$1,355

Vernon Blank

Year	Driver	Starts	Poles	1	2	3	4	5	6–10	Laps	Laps Led	Races Led	Miles	$
1972	Dick Brooks	1	0	0	0	0	0	0	0	21	0	0	29	575
1972	Fred Drake	1	0	0	0	0	0	0	0	93	0	0	140	345
1972	H.B. Bailey	3	0	0	0	0	0	0	0	687	6	1	1,151	6,245
Lifetime		5	0	0	0	0	0	1	0	801	6	1	1,320	$7,165

Erwin Blatt

Year	Driver	Starts	Poles	1	2	3	4	5	6–10	Laps	Laps Led	Races Led	Miles	$
1952	Erwin Blatt	2	0	0	0	0	0	0	0	566	0	0	650	160
Lifetime		2	0	0	0	0	0	0	0	566	0	0	650	$160

Earl Blevins

Year	Driver	Starts	Poles	1	2	3	4	5	6–10	Laps	Laps Led	Races Led	Miles	$
1951	Gayle Warren	3	0	0	0	0	0	0	0	370	0	0	463	150
Lifetime		3	0	0	0	0	0	0	0	370	0	0	463	$150

Jim Blomgren

Year	Driver	Starts	Poles	1	2	3	4	5	6–10	Laps	Laps Led	Races Led	Miles	$
1957	Jim Blomgren	2	0	0	0	0	0	0	0	183	0	0	127	360
1958	Jim Blomgren	1	0	0	0	0	0	0	0	8	0	0	8	0
Lifetime		3	0	0	0	0	0	1	0	191	0	0	135	$360

Year	Driver	Starts	Poles	Finish 1	2	3	4	5	6–10	Laps	Laps Led	Races Led	Miles	$

Brett Bodine

Year	Driver	Starts	Poles	1	2	3	4	5	6–10	Laps	Laps Led	Races Led	Miles	$
1996	Brett Bodine	30	0	0	0	0	0	0	1	8,732	3	2	10,718	732,716
1997	Brett Bodine	31	0	0	0	0	0	0	2	8,666	4	3	11,317	926,705
1998	Brett Bodine	33	0	0	0	0	0	0	0	9,462	17	6	12,346	1,216,677
1999	Brett Bodine	32	0	0	0	0	0	0	0	8,940	4	3	11,365	1,310,199
2000	Brett Bodine	29	0	0	0	0	0	0	0	8,336	5	2	10,220	990,740
2001	Geoffrey Bodine	2	0	0	0	0	0	0	0	750	0	0	658	80,855
2001	Brett Bodine	36	0	0	0	0	0	0	2	9,968	3	3	13,469	1,692,415
2002	Brett Bodine	32	0	0	0	0	0	0	0	8,817	3	3	11,506	1,688,444
Lifetime		225	0	0	0	0	0	0	5	63,671	39	22	81,599	$8,638,751

Geoffrey Bodine

Year	Driver	Starts	Poles	1	2	3	4	5	6–10	Laps	Laps Led	Races Led	Miles	$
1993	Geoffrey Bodine	7	0	0	0	0	0	0	1	1,974	32	1	1,831	124,730
1994	Geoffrey Bodine	31	5	3	1	1	1	0	3	8,149	1,746	20	9,771	854,988
1995	Geoffrey Bodine	31	0	0	0	0	0	0	3	9,257	14	4	11,572	921,905
1996	Geoffrey Bodine	31	0	1	0	1	0	0	4	8,918	90	7	11,068	919,970
1997	Geoffrey Bodine	29	2	0	2	0	1	0	7	8,224	68	12	9,905	992,575
1997	Todd Bodine	1	0	0	0	0	0	0	0	47	0	0	71	25,400
Lifetime		130	7	4	3	2	2	2	18	36,569	1,950	44	44,217	$3,839,568

Buzzy Boehmen

Year	Driver	Starts	Poles	1	2	3	4	5	6–10	Laps	Laps Led	Races Led	Miles	$
1949	Buck Baker	1	0	0	0	0	0	0	0		0	0		0
Lifetime		1	0	0	0	0	0	0	0		0	0		$0

Tommy Boger

Year	Driver	Starts	Poles	1	2	3	4	5	6–10	Laps	Laps Led	Races Led	Miles	$
1953	Tommy Boger	1	0	0	0	0	0	0	0	32	0	0	131	25
Lifetime		1	0	0	0	0	0	0	0	32	0	0	131	$25

David Ray Boggs

Year	Driver	Starts	Poles	1	2	3	4	5	6–10	Laps	Laps Led	Races Led	Miles	$
1971	David Ray Boggs	7	0	0	0	0	0	0	2	1,985	0	0	1,711	4,969
1972	David Ray Boggs	23	0	0	0	0	0	0	0	3,664	0	0	4,708	18,575
1972	Bill Shirey	1	0	0	0	0	0	0	0	212	0	0	424	765
Lifetime		31	0	0	0	0	0	0	2	5,861	0	0	6,843	$24,309

Fred Boggs

Year	Driver	Starts	Poles	1	2	3	4	5	6–10	Laps	Laps Led	Races Led	Miles	$
1957	Fred Boggs	1	0	0	0	0	0	0	0		0	0		25
Lifetime		1	0	0	0	0	0	0	0		0	0		$25

Pete Boland

Year	Driver	Starts	Poles	1	2	3	4	5	6–10	Laps	Laps Led	Races Led	Miles	$
1961	Pete Boland	1	0	0	0	0	0	0	0	32	0	0	80	0
1961	Tiny Lund	2	0	0	0	0	0	0	0	279	0	0	140	170
Lifetime		3	0	0	0	0	0	0	0	311	0	0	220	$170

Aubrey Boles

Year	Driver	Starts	Poles	1	2	3	4	5	6–10	Laps	Laps Led	Races Led	Miles	$
1959	Aubrey Boles	4	0	0	0	0	0	0	1	796	0	0	398	300
1960	Aubrey Boles	1	0	0	0	0	0	0	0	97	0	0	49	50
Lifetime		5	0	0	0	0	0	0	1	893	0	0	447	$350

Toy Bolton

Year	Driver	Starts	Poles	1	2	3	4	5	6–10	Laps	Laps Led	Races Led	Miles	$
1962	Bob Cooper	2	0	0	0	0	0	0	0	205	0	0	103	180
1962	Stick Elliott	20	0	0	0	0	0	0	2	2,686	0	0	1,805	3,528
1963	Cale Yarborough	1	0	0	0	0	0	0	0	336	0	0	504	500
1963	Stick Elliott	23	0	0	0	0	0	0	7	3,560	0	0	2,418	4,310
1964	Stick Elliott	6	0	0	0	0	0	0	0	210	0	0	243	1,050
1964	Lee Bolton	1	0	0	0	0	0	0	0	48	0	0	24	0
1965	Jim Paschal	3	0	0	0	0	0	0	0	454	0	0	657	2,160
1965	Ned Setzer	7	0	0	0	0	0	0	3	792	0	0	796	4,695
1965	Stick Elliott	15	0	0	1	0	1	0	1	2,082	0	0	1,562	5,235
1965	Darel Dieringer	1	0	0	0	0	0	0	0	24	0	0	8	0
1966	Ned Setzer	2	0	0	0	0	0	0	0	147	0	0	368	1,200
1966	Stick Elliott	19	0	0	0	0	1	0	2	3,285	0	0	2,716	7,335
1966	Lee Bolton	3	0	0	0	0	0	0	2	455	0	0	217	880

Year	Driver	Starts	Poles	Finish 1	2	3	4	5	6–10	Laps	Laps Led	Races Led	Miles	$

Toy Bolton *continued*

Year	Driver	Starts	Poles	1	2	3	4	5	6–10	Laps	Laps Led	Races Led	Miles	$
1966	Joel Davis	8	0	0	0	0	0	0	0	1,222	0	0	569	1,225
1966	Darel Dieringer	1	0	0	0	0	0	0	1	293	0	0	147	425
1966	Curtis Turner	5	1	0	0	0	1	0	1	1,056	80	1	577	2,270
1967	Joel Davis	1	0	0	0	0	0	0	0	129	0	0	65	100
1967	Stick Elliott	1	0	0	0	0	0	0	0	370	0	0	555	1,650
1967	Buddy Baker	1	0	0	0	0	1	0	0	191	0	0	96	300
Lifetime		120	1	0	1	0	4	0	19	17,545	80	1	13,428	$37,043

Les Bomar

Year	Driver	Starts	Poles	1	2	3	4	5	6–10	Laps	Laps Led	Races Led	Miles	$
1951	Les Bomar	4	0	0	0	0	0	0	0		0	0		100
Lifetime		4	0	0	0	0	0	0	0		0	0		$100

Tony Bonadies

Year	Driver	Starts	Poles	1	2	3	4	5	6–10	Laps	Laps Led	Races Led	Miles	$
1952	Tony Bonadies	1	0	0	0	0	0	0	0	350	0	0	438	325
Lifetime		1	0	0	0	0	0	0	0	350	0	0	438	$325

Eddie Bond

Year	Driver	Starts	Poles	1	2	3	4	5	6–10	Laps	Laps Led	Races Led	Miles	$
1973	Frank Warren	1	0	0	0	0	0	0	0	167	0	0	89	415
1973	Eddie Bond	6	0	0	0	0	0	0	0	1,407	0	0	2,287	6,901
Lifetime		7	0	0	0	0	0	0	0	1,574	0	0	2,376	$7,316

Bob Bondurant

Year	Driver	Starts	Poles	1	2	3	4	5	6–10	Laps	Laps Led	Races Led	Miles	$
1963	Bob Bondurant	1	0	0	0	0	0	0	0	44	0	0	119	200
1981	Bob Bondurant	1	0	0	0	0	0	0	0	93	0	0	244	1,130
Lifetime		2	0	0	0	0	0	0	0	137	0	0	362	$1,330

Neil Bonnett

Year	Driver	Starts	Poles	1	2	3	4	5	6–10	Laps	Laps Led	Races Led	Miles	$
1976	Neil Castles	1	0	0	0	0	0	0	0	203	0	0	110	475
1976	Neil Bonnett	13	0	0	0	0	0	0	3	2,174	1	1	3,213	31,800
Lifetime		14	0	0	0	0	0	1	3	2,377	1	1	3,323	$32,275

Joe Booher

Year	Driver	Starts	Poles	1	2	3	4	5	6–10	Laps	Laps Led	Races Led	Miles	$
1980	Joe Booher	1	0	0	0	0	0	0	0	81	0	0	123	880
1988	Joe Booher	1	0	0	0	0	0	0	0	272	0	0	272	1,495
Lifetime		2	0	0	0	0	0	0	0	353	0	0	395	$2,375

Kay Borland

Year	Driver	Starts	Poles	1	2	3	4	5	6–10	Laps	Laps Led	Races Led	Miles	$
1975	John Harkins	1	0	0	0	0	0	0	0	382	0	0	382	800
Lifetime		1	0	0	0	0	0	0	0	382	0	0	382	$800

John Borneman

Year	Driver	Starts	Poles	1	2	3	4	5	6–10	Laps	Laps Led	Races Led	Miles	$
1978	John Borneman	2	0	0	0	0	0	0	0	255	0	0	646	2,295
1979	John Borneman	1	0	0	0	0	0	0	0	79	0	0	207	1,305
1979	Jim Robinson	1	0	0	0	0	0	0	0	17	0	0	45	755
1980	John Borneman	2	0	0	0	0	0	0	0	84	0	0	220	1,250
1981	John Borneman	1	0	0	0	0	0	0	0	116	0	0	304	3,140
Lifetime		7	0	0	0	0	0	0	0	551	0	0	1,422	$8,745

Nelson Bowers

Year	Driver	Starts	Poles	1	2	3	4	5	6–10	Laps	Laps Led	Races Led	Miles	$
1997	Derrike Cope	31	0	0	0	0	0	1	1	8,557	4	2	10,852	691,015
1998	Ernie Irvan	30	3	0	0	0	0	0	11	8,153	193	5	10,649	1,434,541
1998	Ricky Craven	3	0	0	0	0	0	0	0	835	0	0	960	84,030
1999	Jerry Nadeau	12	0	0	0	0	0	0	0	3,811	0	0	3,897	441,945
1999	Dick Trickle	1	0	0	0	0	0	0	0	178	0	0	356	27,620
1999	Ernie Irvan	21	0	0	0	0	0	0	5	5,009	9	2	7,385	1,033,275
2000	Ken Schrader	34	0	0	0	0	0	0	2	9,954	33	5	12,919	1,471,625
2001	Ken Schrader	36	0	0	0	0	0	0	5	10,534	10	3	13,997	2,140,311
2001	Johnny Benson Jr.	36	0	0	0	3	1	2	8	10,049	101	10	13,414	2,434,264

Year	Driver	Starts	Poles	Finish 1	2	3	4	5	6–10	Laps	Laps Led	Races Led	Miles	$

Nelson Bowers *continued*

Year	Driver	Starts	Poles	1	2	3	4	5	6–10	Laps	Laps Led	Races Led	Miles	$
2002	Mike Wallace	1	0	0	0	0	0	0	0	172	0	0	258	80,150
2002	Ken Schrader	35	0	0	0	0	0	0	0	9,415	46	1	12,322	2,267,124
2002	Jerry Nadeau	3	0	0	0	0	0	0	0	1,092	37	1	1,307	238,355
2002	Joe Nemechek	1	0	0	0	0	0	0	0	400	0	0	300	74,710
2002	Johnny Benson Jr.	31	0	1	1	0	1	0	4	8,310	116	6	11,081	2,627,731
Lifetime		275	3	1	1	3	2	3	36	76,469	549	35	99,698	$15,046,696

R.L. Bowling

Year	Driver	Starts	Poles	1	2	3	4	5	6–10	Laps	Laps Led	Races Led	Miles	$
1953	Curtis Turner	1	0	0	0	0	0	0	1	38	0	0	156	300
Lifetime		1	0	0	0	0	0	0	1	38	0	0	156	$300

Bill Bowman

Year	Driver	Starts	Poles	1	2	3	4	5	6–10	Laps	Laps Led	Races Led	Miles	$
1955	Bill Bowman	3	0	0	0	0	0	0	2	675	0	0	610	610
1956	Bill Bowman	1	0	0	0	0	0	0	1	181	0	0	91	100
1957	Bill Bowman	4	0	0	0	0	0	0	1	817	0	0	463	510
Lifetime		8	0	0	0	0	0	0	4	1,673	0	0	1,163	$1,220

Jerry Bowman

Year	Driver	Starts	Poles	1	2	3	4	5	6–10	Laps	Laps Led	Races Led	Miles	$
1982	Jerry Bowman	1	0	0	0	0	0	0	0	53	0	0	81	765
1983	Jerry Bowman	5	0	0	0	0	0	0	0	1,183	0	0	1,553	8,610
1985	Jerry Bowman	5	0	0	0	0	0	0	0	1,326	0	0	1,632	8,665
1986	Jerry Bowman	2	0	0	0	0	0	0	0	255	0	0	255	2,125
1987	Jerry Bowman	1	0	0	0	0	0	0	0	161	0	0	161	1,450
Lifetime		14	0	0	0	0	0	0	0	2,978	0	0	3,682	$21,615

Oscar Bowman

Year	Driver	Starts	Poles	1	2	3	4	5	6–10	Laps	Laps Led	Races Led	Miles	$
1965	Rod Eulenfeld	1	0	0	0	0	0	0	0	0	0	0	0	100
Lifetime		1	0	0	0	0	0	0	0	0	0	0	0	$100

Dick Bown

Year	Driver	Starts	Poles	1	2	3	4	5	6–10	Laps	Laps Led	Races Led	Miles	$
1972	Chuck Bown	3	0	0	0	0	0	0	0	391	0	0	1,005	3,710
1973	Chuck Bown	2	0	0	0	0	0	0	1	204	0	0	534	2,305
1974	Chuck Bown	3	0	0	0	0	0	0	0	104	0	0	271	2,070
1975	Chuck Bown	3	0	0	0	0	0	0	0	55	0	0	143	2,065
1981	Jim Bown	2	0	0	0	0	0	0	0	48	0	0	126	1,415
1981	Chuck Bown	2	0	0	0	0	0	0	0	513	0	0	683	2,775
1982	Jim Bown	2	0	0	0	0	0	0	1	204	0	0	534	4,490
1988	Jim Bown	2	0	0	0	0	0	0	0	86	0	0	122	3,325
1989	Jim Bown	3	0	0	0	0	0	0	0	469	0	0	587	6,200
Lifetime		22	0	0	0	0	0	0	2	2,074	0	0	4,005	$28,355

Jack Bowsher

Year	Driver	Starts	Poles	1	2	3	4	5	6–10	Laps	Laps Led	Races Led	Miles	$
1966	Jack Bowsher	2	0	0	0	0	0	0	0	775	0	0	932	1,710
1967	Jack Bowsher	2	0	0	0	0	0	0	0	207	11	1	302	1,705
1969	A.J. Foyt	4	1	0	1	0	2	0	0	522	63	2	1,254	17,375
1970	A.J. Foyt	3	0	1	0	0	0	0	0	298	35	1	768	21,210
Lifetime		11	1	1	1	0	2	0	0	1,802	109	4	3,256	$42,000

Elmer Boxton

Year	Driver	Starts	Poles	1	2	3	4	5	6–10	Laps	Laps Led	Races Led	Miles	$
1968	Dexter Gainey	2	0	0	0	0	0	0	0	142	0	0	92	650
1968	Bobby Mausgrover	1	0	0	0	0	0	0	0	51	0	0	70	605
1968	Lennie Waldo	3	0	0	0	0	0	0	0	592	0	0	972	2,770
1968	Jabe Thomas	1	0	0	0	0	0	0	0	53	0	0	80	580
Lifetime		7	0	0	0	0	0	0	0	838	0	0	1,213	$4,605

James Boyd

Year	Driver	Starts	Poles	1	2	3	4	5	6–10	Laps	Laps Led	Races Led	Miles	$
1973	George Behlman	1	0	0	0	0	0	0	0	137	0	0	359	875
1974	George Behlman	1	0	0	0	0	0	0	0	25	0	0	66	695
Lifetime		2	0	0	0	0	0	0	0	162	0	0	424	$1,570

Year	Driver	Starts	Poles	Finish						Laps	Laps Led	Races Led	Miles	$
				1	2	3	4	5	6–10	Laps	Led	Led	Miles	$

Jim Boyd

Year	Driver	Starts	Poles	1	2	3	4	5	6–10	Laps	Led	Led	Miles	$
1975	Jim Boyd	2	0	0	0	0	0	0	0	203	0	0	524	2,335
Lifetime		2	0	0	0	0	0	0	0	203	0	0	524	$2,335

Ray Boynton

Year	Driver	Starts	Poles	1	2	3	4	5	6–10	Laps	Led	Led	Miles	$
1960	Dick Dixon	2	0	0	0	0	0	0	0	181	0	0	453	250
Lifetime		2	0	0	0	0	0	0	0	181	0	0	453	$250

Buddie Boys

Year	Driver	Starts	Poles	1	2	3	4	5	6–10	Laps	Led	Led	Miles	$
1984	Buddie Boys	1	0	0	0	0	0	0	0	178	0	0	181	1,055
1985	Trevor Boys	1	0	0	0	0	0	0	0	14	0	0	37	925
1988	Trevor Boys	1	0	0	0	0	0	0	0	306	0	0	306	2,875
Lifetime		3	0	0	0	0	0	0	0	498	0	0	524	$4,855

Trevor Boys

Year	Driver	Starts	Poles	1	2	3	4	5	6–10	Laps	Led	Led	Miles	$
1982	Trevor Boys	1	0	0	0	0	0	0	0	105	0	0	275	1,200
Lifetime		1	0	0	0	0	0	0	0	105	0	0	275	$1,200

Gordon Bracken

Year	Driver	Starts	Poles	1	2	3	4	5	6–10	Laps	Led	Led	Miles	$
1953	Fred Moore	1	0	0	0	0	0	0	0		0	0		25
1953	Gordon Bracken	6	0	0	0	0	0	0	1	221	0	0	221	215
Lifetime		7	0	0	0	0	0	0	1	221	0	0	221	$240

J.D. Bracken

Year	Driver	Starts	Poles	1	2	3	4	5	6–10	Laps	Led	Led	Miles	$
1966	Bobby Allison	21	4	3	0	2	0	2	3	4,496	714	6	2,708	11,115
1967	Sam McQuagg	1	0	0	0	0	0	0	0	63	0	0	32	125
1967	Bobby Allison	27	1	3	2	2	2	2	4	5,642	1,077	14	3,125	12,285
1967	Donnie Allison	8	0	0	1	0	1	1	0	1,185	157	1	555	2,320
1967	Paul Lewis	1	0	0	0	0	0	2	0	5	0	0	3	150
1968	Paul Lewis	3	0	0	0	0	0	1	0	337	0	0	201	1,200
1968	Bobby Allison	22	0	1	2	3	3	2	2	5,113	42	3	3,387	21,260
1969	Red Farmer	1	0	0	0	0	2	0	0	101	0	0	51	100
Lifetime		84	5	7	5	7	6	10	9	16,942	1,990	24	10,060	$48,555

Charles Bradberry

Year	Driver	Starts	Poles	1	2	3	4	5	6–10	Laps	Led	Led	Miles	$
1995	Gary Bradberry	2	0	0	0	0	0	0	0	32	0	0	61	14,295
Lifetime		2	0	0	0	0	0	0	0	32	0	0	61	$14,295

Melvin Bradley

Year	Driver	Starts	Poles	1	2	3	4	5	6–10	Laps	Led	Led	Miles	$
1962	Melvin Bradley	3	0	0	0	0	1	0	1	1,007	0	0	445	990
1962	Doug Yates	2	0	0	0	0	0	0	0	106	0	0	159	525
1962	Tommy Irwin	11	0	0	1	0	1	0	4	1,867	0	0	855	2,300
Lifetime		16	0	0	1	0	2	0	5	2,980	0	0	1,459	$3,815

Les Brand

Year	Driver	Starts	Poles	1	2	3	4	5	6–10	Laps	Led	Led	Miles	$
1954	Paul Phipps	1	0	0	0	0	0	0	0	167	0	0	84	25
1954	Dick Zimmerman	2	0	0	0	0	0	0	0	350	0	0	236	40
1955	Dick Zimmerman	2	0	0	0	0	0	0	0	222	0	0	150	25
Lifetime		5	0	0	0	0	0	0	0	739	0	0	469	$90

Bruce Brantley

Year	Driver	Starts	Poles	1	2	3	4	5	6–10	Laps	Led	Led	Miles	$
1963	Bruce Brantley	4	0	0	0	0	0	0	1	231	0	0	146	840
Lifetime		4	0	0	0	0	0	0	1	231	0	0	146	$840

Darin Brassfield

Year	Driver	Starts	Poles	1	2	3	4	5	6–10	Laps	Led	Led	Miles	$
1989	Darin Brassfield	3	0	0	0	0	0	0	0	275	0	0	488	10,852
Lifetime		3	0	0	0	0	0	0	0	275	0	0	488	$10,852

Year	Driver	Starts	Poles	Finish						Laps	Laps Led	Races Led	Miles	$
				1	2	3	4	5	6–10					

J.D. Braswell

Year	Driver	Starts	Poles	1	2	3	4	5	6–10	Laps	Laps Led	Races Led	Miles	$
1960	Don O'Dell	1	0	0	0	0	0	0	0	90	0	0	135	200
1961	Don O'Dell	2	0	0	0	0	0	0	1	48	0	0	120	340
1961	Fireball Roberts	1	0	1	0	0	0	0	0	178	178	1	249	2,000
1961	Red Hollingsworth	1	0	0	0	0	0	0	0	2	0	0	3	200
1961	Tiny Lund	3	0	0	0	0	0	0	1	682	0	0	638	950
Lifetime		8	0	1	0	0	0	0	2	1,000	178	1	1,145	$3,690

Joseph Braun

Year	Driver	Starts	Poles	1	2	3	4	5	6–10	Laps	Laps Led	Races Led	Miles	$
1953	George Fleming	1	0	0	0	0	0	0	0	33	0	0	135	25
Lifetime		1	0	0	0	0	0	0	0	33	0	0	135	$25

Dan Bray

Year	Driver	Starts	Poles	1	2	3	4	5	6–10	Laps	Laps Led	Races Led	Miles	$
1974	Jim Hurtubise	1	0	0	0	0	0	0	0	112	0	0	280	3,600
Lifetime		1	0	0	0	0	0	0	0	112	0	0	280	$3,600

Jim Bray

Year	Driver	Starts	Poles	1	2	3	4	5	6–10	Laps	Laps Led	Races Led	Miles	$
1963	Jim Bray	1	0	0	0	0	0	0	0	171	0	0	43	100
1974	Jim Bray	2	0	0	0	0	0	0	0	319	0	0	322	1,445
Lifetime		3	0	0	0	0	0	0	0	490	0	0	365	$1,545

E.J. Brewer

Year	Driver	Starts	Poles	1	2	3	4	5	6–10	Laps	Laps Led	Races Led	Miles	$
1957	E.J. Brewer	1	0	0	0	0	0	0	0	138	0	0	69	110
1958	Cecil Grubbs	1	0	0	0	0	0	0	0	79	0	0	49	50
1958	E.J. Brewer	4	0	0	0	0	0	0	1	249	0	0	153	240
Lifetime		6	0	0	0	0	0	0	1	466	0	0	271	$400

Johnny Bridges

Year	Driver	Starts	Poles	1	2	3	4	5	6–10	Laps	Laps Led	Races Led	Miles	$
1952	Johnny Bridgers	1	0	0	0	0	0	0	0	244	0	0	305	0
1953	Johnny Bridgers	1	0	0	0	0	0	0	0	279	0	0	384	120
Lifetime		2	0	0	0	0	0	0	0	523	0	0	689	$120

Harley J. Briggs

Year	Driver	Starts	Poles	1	2	3	4	5	6–10	Laps	Laps Led	Races Led	Miles	$
1951	Andy Pierce	1	0	0	0	0	0	0	0		0	0		25
Lifetime		1	0	0	0	0	0	0	0		0	0		$25

Ralph Briggs

Year	Driver	Starts	Poles	1	2	3	4	5	6–10	Laps	Laps Led	Races Led	Miles	$
1956	Sam Lamm	1	0	0	0	0	0	0	0	3	0	0	8	30
Lifetime		1	0	0	0	0	0	0	0	3	0	0	8	$30

Mason Bright

Year	Driver	Starts	Poles	1	2	3	4	5	6–10	Laps	Laps Led	Races Led	Miles	$
1953	Mason Bright	1	0	0	0	0	0	0	0	33	0	0	135	25
1954	Mason Bright	2	0	0	0	0	0	0	0	200	0	0	226	50
Lifetime		3	0	0	0	0	0	0	0	233	0	0	361	$75

Bob Bristol

Year	Driver	Starts	Poles	1	2	3	4	5	6–10	Laps	Laps Led	Races Led	Miles	$
1958	Lucky Long	1	0	0	0	0	0	0	0	167	0	0	439	250
1959	Lucky Long	2	0	0	0	0	0	1	1	554	0	0	280	700
1967	Bruce Worrell	1	0	0	0	0	0	0	1	174	0	0	470	1,650
1968	Harold Hardesty	1	0	0	0	0	0	0	0	67	0	0	181	575
1969	Harold Hardesty	1	0	0	0	0	0	0	1	163	0	0	440	1,250
Lifetime		6	0	0	0	0	0	1	3	1,125	0	0	1,810	$4,425

Manley Britt

Year	Driver	Starts	Poles	1	2	3	4	5	6–10	Laps	Laps Led	Races Led	Miles	$
1958	Larry Frank	3	0	0	0	0	0	0	1	315	0	0	257	435
1958	George Dunn	10	1	0	1	0	1	1	3	1,747	10	1	939	1,880
1959	Gene White	1	0	0	0	0	0	0	0	155	0	0	78	0
1959	Bill Taylor	1	0	0	0	0	0	0	0	439	0	0	220	125
1959	Earl Moss	2	0	0	0	0	0	0	1	279	0	0	140	140

Year	Driver	Starts	Poles	Finish						Laps	Laps Led	Races Led	Miles	$
				1	2	3	4	5	6–10					

Manley Britt *continued*

Year	Driver	Starts	Poles	1	2	3	4	5	6–10	Laps	Laps Led	Races Led	Miles	$
1959	Pee Wee Jones	1	0	0	0	0	0	0	0	150	0	0	38	50
1959	Ken Rush	5	1	0	1	0	0	0	1	680	0	0	743	1,220
1959	George Dunn	1	0	0	0	0	0	0	0	145	0	0	48	130
Lifetime		24	2	0	2	0	1	1	6	3,910	10	1	2,462	$3,980

Allan Brooke

Year	Driver	Starts	Poles	1	2	3	4	5	6–10	Laps	Laps Led	Races Led	Miles	$
1973	Earl Ross	3	0	0	0	0	0	0	0	335	0	0	797	4,005
1974	Earl Ross	6	0	0	1	0	0	1	0	1,429	6	1	2,428	22,865
Lifetime		9	0	0	1	0	0	1	0	1,764	6	1	3,225	$26,870

H.J. Brooking

Year	Driver	Starts	Poles	1	2	3	4	5	6–10	Laps	Laps Led	Races Led	Miles	$
1972	Bill Dennis	3	0	0	0	1	0	0	0	915	2	1	803	3,714
1973	Bill Dennis	4	0	0	0	0	0	0	2	1,430	0	0	1,115	4,225
Lifetime		7	0	0	0	1	0	0	2	2,345	2	1	1,917	$7,939

Dick Brooks

Year	Driver	Starts	Poles	1	2	3	4	5	6–10	Laps	Laps Led	Races Led	Miles	$
1969	Dick Brooks	28	0	0	0	1	0	2	9	5,741	2	1	6,162	28,187
1970	Dick Brooks	32	0	0	2	5	4	4	3	6,787	194	6	6,910	47,877
1970	Pete Hamilton	1	0	0	0	1	0	0	0	299	0	0	118	600
1971	Bill Dennis	1	0	0	0	0	0	0	0	328	0	0	175	545
1971	Dick Brooks	1	0	0	0	0	0	0	0	279	0	0	153	495
1971	Marv Acton	11	0	0	0	0	0	0	0	1,421	0	0	2,399	8,620
1972	Johnny Halford	5	0	0	0	0	0	0	1	1,032	0	0	1,574	4,710
1973	Dick Brooks	2	0	0	0	0	0	0	1	532	1	1	565	3,644
1974	Dick Brooks	16	0	0	0	0	0	0	3	2,951	1	1	4,097	22,580
1994	Bobby Hamilton	7	0	0	0	0	0	0	0	2,550	0	0	2,491	96,010
1995	Butch Leitzinger	1	0	0	0	0	0	0	0	90	0	0	221	17,060
1995	Randy LaJoie	1	0	0	0	0	0	0	0	96	0	0	255	16,175
1995	Shane Hall	1	0	0	0	0	0	0	0	205	0	0	208	13,975
1995	Rich Bickle	8	0	0	0	0	0	0	0	1,995	3	1	2,400	148,250
1995	Greg Sacks	10	0	0	0	0	0	0	0	2,795	0	0	3,137	179,730
1995	Andy Hillenburg	1	0	0	0	0	0	0	0	157	0	0	393	17,320
Lifetime		126	0	0	2	7	4	6	17	27,258	201	10	31,258	$605,778

Earl Brooks

Year	Driver	Starts	Poles	1	2	3	4	5	6–10	Laps	Laps Led	Races Led	Miles	$
1962	Earl Brooks	5	0	0	0	0	0	0	3	831	0	0	394	595
1968	Clyde Lynn	1	0	0	0	0	0	0	0	235	0	0	353	1,425
1968	Earl Brooks	19	0	0	0	0	0	0	3	2,513	0	0	1,207	3,220
1969	Earl Brooks	42	0	0	0	0	0	1	5	7,300	0	0	5,672	21,327
1970	Earl Brooks	20	0	0	0	0	0	0	1	1,750	0	0	1,851	9,545
1970	Wendell Scott	2	0	0	0	0	0	0	0	233	0	0	205	860
1970	Dave Marcis	6	0	0	0	0	0	0	1	1,531	0	0	781	2,190
1971	Ed Negre	1	0	0	0	0	0	0	0	243	0	0	152	460
1971	Earl Brooks	30	0	0	0	0	1	0	2	5,495	0	0	5,235	17,702
1971	Bill Hollar	11	0	0	0	0	0	0	1	2,095	0	0	1,602	4,275
1972	Earl Brooks	6	0	0	0	0	0	0	0	609	0	0	593	3,215
1973	Dick May	1	0	0	0	0	0	0	0	61	0	0	36	250
1973	Earl Brooks	9	0	0	0	0	0	0	0	2,267	0	0	1,397	4,880
Lifetime		153	0	0	0	0	1	1	16	25,163	0	0	19,479	$69,944

Elmer Brooks

Year	Driver	Starts	Poles	1	2	3	4	5	6–10	Laps	Laps Led	Races Led	Miles	$
1954	Slick Smith	1	0	0	0	0	0	0	0	38	0	0	19	25
1954	Charlie Mincey	1	0	0	0	0	0	0	1	184	0	0	92	100
1954	Bill Blair	2	0	0	0	0	0	0	0	334	0	0	167	25
1954	Gober Sosebee	1	0	0	0	0	0	0	1	153	0	0	230	300
1954	Tim Flock	1	0	0	0	0	0	0	1	243	0	0	243	250
1954	Curtis Turner	4	1	1	1	0	0	0	0	886	277	3	842	7,320
Lifetime		10	1	1	1	0	0	0	3	1,838	277	3	1,592	$8,020

Gary Brooks

Year	Driver	Starts	Poles	1	2	3	4	5	6–10	Laps	Laps Led	Races Led	Miles	$
1991	Gary Brooks	1	0	0	0	0	0	0	0	11	0	0	11	3,425
Lifetime		1	0	0	0	0	0	0	0	11	0	0	11	$3,425

489

Year	Driver	Starts	Poles	Finish 1	2	3	4	5	6–10	Laps	Laps Led	Races Led	Miles	$

Woody Brougher

Year	Driver	Starts	Poles	1	2	3	4	5	6–10	Laps	Laps Led	Races Led	Miles	$
1956	Dick Linder	1	0	0	0	0	0	0	0		0	0		0
Lifetime		1	0	0	0	0	0	0	0		0	0		$0

Allan Brown

Year	Driver	Starts	Poles	1	2	3	4	5	6–10	Laps	Laps Led	Races Led	Miles	$
1971	Bob Brown	5	0	0	0	0	0	0	0	462	0	0	335	1,335
1972	Bob Brown	2	0	0	0	0	0	0	0	324	0	0	175	710
1973	Bob Brown	2	0	0	0	0	0	0	0	353	0	0	210	590
Lifetime		9	0	0	0	0	0	0	0	1,139	0	0	721	$2,635

Cannonball Brown

Year	Driver	Starts	Poles	1	2	3	4	5	6–10	Laps	Laps Led	Races Led	Miles	$
1958	Cannonball Brown	2	0	0	0	0	0	0	0	104	0	0	99	50
Lifetime		2	0	0	0	0	0	0	0	104	0	0	99	$50

Ed Brown

Year	Driver	Starts	Poles	1	2	3	4	5	6–10	Laps	Laps Led	Races Led	Miles	$
1955	Ed Brown	4	0	0	0	0	0	0	2	584	44	1	488	450
1956	Ed Brown	1	0	0	0	0	0	0	0	72	0	0	180	55
1957	Ed Brown	1	0	0	0	0	0	0	0	52	0	0	130	115
1961	Ed Brown	1	0	0	0	0	0	0	0	74	0	0	74	50
Lifetime		7	0	0	0	0	0	0	2	782	44	1	872	$670

James Brown

Year	Driver	Starts	Poles	1	2	3	4	5	6–10	Laps	Laps Led	Races Led	Miles	$
1968	Bob Moore	1	0	0	0	0	0	0	1	227	0	0	114	200
1968	Charles Burnett	1	0	0	0	0	0	0	0	69	0	0	104	630
1968	Don Biederman	1	0	0	0	0	0	0	0	123	0	0	308	1,110
Lifetime		3	0	0	0	0	0	0	1	419	0	0	525	$1,940

Jerry Brown

Year	Driver	Starts	Poles	1	2	3	4	5	6–10	Laps	Laps Led	Races Led	Miles	$
1973	Richard D. Brown	12	0	0	0	0	0	0	0	911	0	0	582	6,915
1973	Ed Negre	1	0	0	0	0	0	0	0	183	0	0	275	13,385
1974	Richard D. Brown	1	0	0	0	0	0	0	0	51	0	0	51	595
1975	Richard D. Brown	4	0	0	0	0	0	0	0	365	0	0	218	1,660
1976	Richard D. Brown	3	0	0	0	0	0	0	0	591	0	0	340	1,310
Lifetime		21	0	0	0	0	0	0	0	2,101	0	0	1,465	$23,865

Len Brown

Year	Driver	Starts	Poles	1	2	3	4	5	6–10	Laps	Laps Led	Races Led	Miles	$
1949	Len Brown	1	0	0	0	0	0	0	0	158	0	0	158	25
1950	Len Brown	1	0	0	0	0	0	0	0	171	0	0	86	50
1951	Len Brown	1	0	0	0	0	0	0	0		0	0		0
Lifetime		3	0	0	0	0	0	0	0	329	0	0	244	$75

Richard Brown

Year	Driver	Starts	Poles	1	2	3	4	5	6–10	Laps	Laps Led	Races Led	Miles	$
1970	Butch Hirst	1	0	0	0	0	0	0	0	224	0	0	336	1,499
1970	Bugs Stevens	3	0	0	0	0	0	0	1	458	0	0	682	6,145
1970	Dr. Don Tarr	1	0	0	0	0	0	0	1	157	0	0	393	2,050
1970	Roy Mayne	1	0	0	0	0	0	0	0	420	0	0	427	795
Lifetime		6	0	0	0	0	0	0	2	1,259	0	0	1,838	$10,489

Spencer Brown

Year	Driver	Starts	Poles	1	2	3	4	5	6–10	Laps	Laps Led	Races Led	Miles	$
1982	Bill Scott (BNC)	1	0	0	0	0	0	0	0	75	0	0	200	2,175
Lifetime		1	0	0	0	0	0	0	0	75	0	0	200	$2,175

Frank Bruner

Year	Driver	Starts	Poles	1	2	3	4	5	6–10	Laps	Laps Led	Races Led	Miles	$
1956	Robert Slensby	1	0	0	0	0	0	0	0	117	0	0	59	100
Lifetime		1	0	0	0	0	0	0	0	117	0	0	59	$100

Laird Bruner

Year	Driver	Starts	Poles	1	2	3	4	5	6–10	Laps	Laps Led	Races Led	Miles	$
1953	Laird Bruner	1	0	0	0	0	0	0	0	142	0	0	195	105
Lifetime		1	0	0	0	0	0	0	0	142	0	0	195	$105

Year	Driver	Starts	Poles	Finish						Laps	Laps Led	Races Led	Miles	$
				1	2	3	4	5	6–10					

James Bryan

Year	Driver	Starts	Poles	1	2	3	4	5	6–10	Laps	Laps Led	Races Led	Miles	$
1960	Bobby Johns	7	0	0	0	0	0	0	2	915	0	0	566	1,765
Lifetime		7	0	0	0	0	0	0	2	915	0	0	566	$1,765

Darrell Bryant

Year	Driver	Starts	Poles	1	2	3	4	5	6–10	Laps	Laps Led	Races Led	Miles	$
1987	Kirk Bryant	1	0	0	0	0	0	0	0	205	0	0	208	1,415
Lifetime		1	0	0	0	0	0	0	0	205	0	0	208	$1,415

Henry Bryant

Year	Driver	Starts	Poles	1	2	3	4	5	6–10	Laps	Laps Led	Races Led	Miles	$
1953	Lamar Crabtree	1	0	0	0	0	0	0	0		0	0		25
Lifetime		1	0	0	0	0	0	0	0		0	0		$25

James Bryant

Year	Driver	Starts	Poles	1	2	3	4	5	6–10	Laps	Laps Led	Races Led	Miles	$
1973	L.D. Ottinger	3	0	0	1	0	0	0	1	813	0	0	955	7,452
Lifetime		3	0	0	1	0	0	0	1	813	0	0	955	$7,452

Herschel Buchanan

Year	Driver	Starts	Poles	1	2	3	4	5	6–10	Laps	Laps Led	Races Led	Miles	$
1950	Herschel Buchanan	2	0	0	0	0	0	0	1	3	0	0	13	200
1951	Herschel Buchanan	1	0	0	0	0	0	0	0		0	0		0
1952	Herschel Buchanan	4	0	0	0	1	0	2	1	1,116	0	0	975	1,850
1953	Herschel Buchanan	14	0	0	0	1	2	1	2	506	0	0	456	2,050
1954	Herschel Buchanan	1	0	0	0	0	0	1	0	160	0	0	240	500
Lifetime		22	0	0	0	2	2	4	4	1,785	0	0	1,683	$4,600

Buck McCardell

Year	Driver	Starts	Poles	1	2	3	4	5	6–10	Laps	Laps Led	Races Led	Miles	$
1952	Buck McCardell	2	0	0	0	0	0	0	0	49	0	0	49	35
Lifetime		2	0	0	0	0	0	0	0	49	0	0	49	$35

Ray Buckner

Year	Driver	Starts	Poles	1	2	3	4	5	6–10	Laps	Laps Led	Races Led	Miles	$
1968	Charles Burnett	1	0	0	0	0	0	0	0	146	0	0	365	1,135
1968	Don Tomberlin	1	0	0	0	0	0	0	0	181	0	0	91	100
1968	Bob Moore	3	0	0	0	0	0	0	0	806	0	0	943	2,545
1969	Don Tomberlin	2	0	0	0	0	0	0	0	215	0	0	233	1,025
Lifetime		7	0	0	0	0	0	0	0	1,348	0	0	1,631	$4,805

Julian Buesink

Year	Driver	Starts	Poles	1	2	3	4	5	6–10	Laps	Laps Led	Races Led	Miles	$
1949	Lloyd Moore	1	0	0	0	0	0	0	1	186	0	0	93	150
1949	Bill Rexford	3	0	0	0	1	0	1	0	370	0	0	274	625
1950	Lloyd Moore	16	0	1	2	3	1	0	3	1,358	57	2	1,046	5,055
1950	Jim Paschal	1	0	0	0	0	0	0	0	307	0	0	384	0
1950	Bill Rexford	17	0	1	0	1	2	1	6	1,302	98	2	1,146	4,800
1950	George Hartley	8	0	0	0	0	0	0	2	371	0	0	464	850
1951	Ted Swaim	1	0	0	0	0	0	0	0		0	0		25
1951	Lloyd Moore	22	0	0	0	1	0	3	4	322	0	0	332	2,335
1951	Julian Buesink	1	0	0	0	0	0	0	0		0	0		0
1951	Jimmie Lewallen	1	0	0	0	0	0	0	1		0	0		150
1951	Jim Paschal	13	0	0	0	1	3	0	2	414	33	1	404	1,985
1951	Harold Kite	2	0	0	0	0	0	0	1	384	0	0	480	800
1951	Dean Sprague	1	0	0	0	0	0	0	0	46	0	0	35	25
1951	Bill Rexford	5	1	0	0	0	0	0	1	115	0	0	58	325
1952	Bill Rexford	1	0	0	0	0	0	0	0	131	0	0	66	25
1952	Jim Paschal	6	0	0	0	0	0	0	4	582	0	0	338	515
1952	Lloyd Moore	8	0	0	1	0	1	0	2	1,457	0	0	1,084	1,925
1953	Bill Rexford	2	0	0	0	0	0	1	1	173	0	0	173	350
1955	Tommy Thompson	1	0	0	0	0	0	0	0	41	0	0	56	50
1955	Lloyd Moore	2	0	0	0	0	0	0	0	439	0	0	567	235
1956	Bob Duell	6	0	0	0	0	0	1	0	642	0	0	443	670
1957	Bob Duell	5	0	0	0	0	0	0	0	503	0	0	476	260
1958	Bob Duell	7	1	0	1	1	0	1	3	1,273	0	0	969	2,415
1959	Bob Duell	4	0	0	0	0	0	0	0	672	0	0	578	650
1959	Buddy Baker	1	0	0	0	0	0	0	0	64	0	0	88	150
1960	Bob Duell	6	0	0	0	0	0	0	1	422	0	0	531	935
1961	Cale Yarborough	1	0	0	0	0	0	0	0	135	0	0	186	200

Year	Driver	Starts	Poles	Finish						Laps	Laps Led	Races Led	Miles	$
				1	2	3	4	5	6–10					

Julian Buesink *continued*

Year	Driver	Starts	Poles	1	2	3	4	5	6–10	Laps	Laps Led	Races Led	Miles	$
1961	Tom Dill	3	0	0	0	0	0	0	0	273	0	0	631	630
1962	Cale Yarborough	4	0	0	0	0	0	0	1	336	0	0	520	1,340
1963	Cale Yarborough	2	0	0	0	0	0	0	0	248	0	0	383	675
Lifetime		151	2	2	4	8	7	8	33	12,566	188	5	11,803	$28,150

Bill Bumgardner

Year	Driver	Starts	Poles	1	2	3	4	5	6–10	Laps	Laps Led	Races Led	Miles	$
2002	Chad Little	1	0	0	0	0	0	0	0	395	0	0	395	49,745
2002	Joe Varde	1	0	0	0	0	0	0	0	49	0	0	120	37,610
2002	Tony Raines	7	0	0	0	0	0	0	0	1,586	0	0	1,921	282,787
Lifetime		9	0	0	0	0	0	0	0	2,030	0	0	2,436	370,142

A.L. Bumgarner

Year	Driver	Starts	Poles	1	2	3	4	5	6–10	Laps	Laps Led	Races Led	Miles	$
1956	Fonty Flock	1	0	0	0	0	0	0	1	97	0	0	97	200
1956	Tiny Lund	2	0	0	0	0	0	0	0	631	0	0	316	150
1956	Jack Smith	1	0	0	0	0	0	0	1	127	0	0	95	100
1956	Junior Johnson	8	1	0	0	0	0	0	0	381	17	1	233	200
1957	Tiny Lund	20	3	0	0	2	0	0	7	3,129	209	2	1,938	3,490
1957	Junior Johnson	1	0	0	0	0	0	0	0	102	0	0	64	50
1958	Banjo Matthews	1	0	0	0	0	0	0	0	54	0	0	14	115
1958	Jerry Draper	1	0	0	0	0	0	0	0	10	0	0	5	50
1958	Jimmy Thompson	3	0	0	0	0	0	0	0	85	0	0	172	200
1958	Tiny Lund	1	0	0	0	0	0	0	0	27	0	0	27	0
1958	Jimmy Massey	7	1	0	0	0	0	0	1	1,006	0	0	607	870
Lifetime		46	5	0	0	2	0	0	10	5,649	226	3	3,568	$5,425

Bob Bunselmeyer

Year	Driver	Starts	Poles	1	2	3	4	5	6–10	Laps	Laps Led	Races Led	Miles	$
1956	Walt Schubert	4	0	0	0	0	0	0	1	413	0	0	324	375
Lifetime		4	0	0	0	0	0	0	1	413	0	0	324	$375

Clarence Burbank

Year	Driver	Starts	Poles	1	2	3	4	5	6–10	Laps	Laps Led	Races Led	Miles	$
1951	Tommy Melvin	1	0	0	0	0	0	0	0	367	0	0	459	50
Lifetime		1	0	0	0	0	0	0	0	367	0	0	459	$50

Paul Burchard

Year	Driver	Starts	Poles	1	2	3	4	5	6–10	Laps	Laps Led	Races Led	Miles	$
1972	Carl Adams	2	0	0	0	0	0	0	1	320	0	0	818	3,170
Lifetime		2	0	0	0	0	0	0	1	320	0	0	818	$3,170

Roy Burdick

Year	Driver	Starts	Poles	1	2	3	4	5	6–10	Laps	Laps Led	Races Led	Miles	$
1959	Bob Burdick	6	2	0	1	0	0	0	3	912	25	1	1,000	10,040
1959	Johnny Beauchamp	4	0	1	1	0	0	0	0	430	130	2	741	8,625
1960	Herb Shannon	1	0	0	0	0	0	0	0	184	0	0	276	350
1960	Jimmy Thompson	1	0	0	0	0	0	0	0	303	0	0	455	300
1960	Jerry Roedell	1	0	0	0	0	0	0	0	168	0	0	252	200
1960	Bud Burdick	2	0	0	0	0	0	0	1	236	0	0	590	750
1960	Bob Burdick	2	0	0	0	0	0	0	1	71	0	0	178	475
1961	Bob Burdick	5	0	1	0	0	1	0	1	1,086	44	2	1,798	18,750
1962	Bob Burdick	2	0	0	0	0	0	0	1	95	0	0	238	625
Lifetime		24	2	2	2	0	1	0	7	3,485	199	5	5,527	$40,115

Harold Burke

Year	Driver	Starts	Poles	1	2	3	4	5	6–10	Laps	Laps Led	Races Led	Miles	$
1986	Gary Fedewa	4	0	0	0	0	0	0	0	819	0	0	1,229	7,230
1987	Gary Fedewa	1	0	0	0	0	0	0	0	355	0	0	355	1,650
Lifetime		5	0	0	0	0	0	0	0	1,174	0	0	1,584	$8,880

Frank Burnett

Year	Driver	Starts	Poles	1	2	3	4	5	6–10	Laps	Laps Led	Races Led	Miles	$
1967	Frank Burnett	1	0	0	0	0	0	0	0	60	0	0	162	500
Lifetime		1	0	0	0	0	0	0	0	60	0	0	162	$500

Year	Driver	Starts	Poles	Finish						Laps	Laps Led	Races Led	Miles	$
				1	2	3	4	5	6–10					

Carl Burris

Year	Driver	Starts	Poles	1	2	3	4	5	6–10	Laps	Laps Led	Races Led	Miles	$
1958	Carl Burris	4	0	0	0	0	0	0	1	502	0	0	257	375
Lifetime		4	0	0	0	0	0	0	1	502	0	0	257	$375

Terry Byers

Year	Driver	Starts	Poles	1	2	3	4	5	6–10	Laps	Laps Led	Races Led	Miles	$
1989	Terry Byers	3	0	0	0	0	0	0	0	773	0	0	1,554	11,400
1990	Terry Byers	2	0	0	0	0	0	0	0	41	0	0	63	7,525
Lifetime		5	0	0	0	0	0	0	0	814	0	0	1,616	$18,925

C & M Motorsports

Year	Driver	Starts	Poles	1	2	3	4	5	6–10	Laps	Laps Led	Races Led	Miles	$
1986	Eddie Bierschwale	3	0	0	0	0	0	0	0	463	0	0	467	3,710
1986	Trevor Boys	1	0	0	0	0	0	0	0	473	0	0	473	2,350
1986	Doug Heveron	1	0	0	0	0	0	0	0	185	0	0	492	4,940
1986	Morgan Shepherd	1	0	0	0	0	0	0	0	381	0	0	200	1,525
Lifetime		6	0	0	0	0	0	0	0	1,502	0	0	1,632	$12,525

Scotty Cain

Year	Driver	Starts	Poles	1	2	3	4	5	6–10	Laps	Laps Led	Races Led	Miles	$
1956	Scotty Cain	4	0	0	0	0	0	1	3	701	0	0	698	1,235
1957	Scotty Cain	11	0	0	0	0	3	0	4	1,151	0	0	782	2,005
1958	Scotty Cain	1	0	0	0	0	0	0	1	176	0	0	463	275
1959	Scotty Cain	2	0	0	1	0	0	0	0	467	0	0	247	700
1960	Rex White	1	0	0	0	0	0	0	1	162	0	0	227	500
1960	Scotty Cain	4	0	0	1	1	0	0	0	351	19	1	324	1,225
1961	Scotty Cain	4	0	0	0	0	0	0	1	218	0	0	335	705
1963	Scotty Cain	2	0	0	0	0	0	0	0	229	0	0	618	575
Lifetime		29	0	0	2	1	3	1	10	3,455	19	1	3,693	$7,220

James Calder

Year	Driver	Starts	Poles	1	2	3	4	5	6–10	Laps	Laps Led	Races Led	Miles	$
1971	Frank James	2	0	0	0	0	0	0	0	274	0	0	697	2,870
1972	Frank James	2	0	0	0	0	0	0	1	259	0	0	679	2,195
Lifetime		4	0	0	0	0	0	0	1	533	0	0	1,375	$5,065

Jim Calder

Year	Driver	Starts	Poles	1	2	3	4	5	6–10	Laps	Laps Led	Races Led	Miles	$
1970	Frank James	2	0	0	0	0	0	0	0	257	0	0	673	1,915
1971	Mike James	1	0	0	0	0	0	0	0	1	0	0	3	615
1971	Frank James	1	0	0	0	0	0	0	1	135	0	0	354	1,020
Lifetime		4	0	0	0	0	0	0	1	393	0	0	1,030	$3,550

Cliff Caldwell

Year	Driver	Starts	Poles	1	2	3	4	5	6–10	Laps	Laps Led	Races Led	Miles	$
1951	Sam Lamm	1	0	0	0	0	0	0	0		0	0		25
1951	Fred Lee	1	0	0	0	0	0	0	0	98	0	0	49	25
Lifetime		2	0	0	0	0	0	0	0	98	0	0	49	$50

John Callis

Year	Driver	Starts	Poles	1	2	3	4	5	6–10	Laps	Laps Led	Races Led	Miles	$
1980	John Callis	2	0	0	0	0	0	0	0	464	0	0	472	1,500
1982	John Callis	3	0	0	0	0	0	0	0	352	0	0	507	2,675
1983	John Callis	2	0	0	0	0	0	0	0	525	0	0	671	2,775
Lifetime		7	0	0	0	0	0	0	0	1,341	0	0	1,649	$6,950

Bill Caltrider

Year	Driver	Starts	Poles	1	2	3	4	5	6–10	Laps	Laps Led	Races Led	Miles	$
1951	Jack Goodwin	2	0	0	0	0	0	0	1	617	0	0	712	700
1951	Dave Anderson	1	0	0	0	0	0	0	0	335	0	0	419	50
Lifetime		3	0	0	0	0	0	0	1	952	0	0	1,130	$750

W.A. Caltrider

Year	Driver	Starts	Poles	1	2	3	4	5	6–10	Laps	Laps Led	Races Led	Miles	$
1952	Ted Chamberlain	2	0	0	0	0	0	0	1	350	0	0	350	125
1952	Iggy Katona	3	0	0	0	0	0	0	1	887	0	0	835	400
Lifetime		5	0	0	0	0	0	0	2	1,237	0	0	1,185	$525

Year	Driver	Starts	Poles	Finish 1	2	3	4	5	6–10	Laps	Laps Led	Races Led	Miles	$

J.W. Campbell

Year	Driver	Starts	Poles	1	2	3	4	5	6–10	Laps	Laps Led	Races Led	Miles	$
1955	Russ Truelove	6	0	0	0	0	0	0	2	738	0	0	689	585
Lifetime		6	0	0	0	0	0	0	2	738	0	0	689	$585

S.T. Campbell

Year	Driver	Starts	Poles	1	2	3	4	5	6–10	Laps	Laps Led	Races Led	Miles	$
1957	Joe Lee Johnson	2	0	0	0	0	0	0	0	63	0	0	95	175
1958	Joe Lee Johnson	4	0	0	0	0	0	1	0	650	0	0	490	485
1959	Joe Lee Johnson	1	0	0	0	0	0	0	1	147	0	0	49	170
Lifetime		7	0	0	0	0	0	1	1	860	0	0	633	$830

W.E. Campbell

Year	Driver	Starts	Poles	1	2	3	4	5	6–10	Laps	Laps Led	Races Led	Miles	$
1955	Bud Palmer	1	0	0	0	0	0	0	0	36	0	0	148	35
1956	Bud Palmer	1	0	0	0	0	0	0	0		0	0		0
Lifetime		2	0	0	0	0	0	0	0	36	0	0	148	$35

Earl Canavan

Year	Driver	Starts	Poles	1	2	3	4	5	6–10	Laps	Laps Led	Races Led	Miles	$
1971	Earle Canavan	5	0	0	0	0	0	0	0	375	0	0	483	2,530
1972	Earle Canavan	7	0	0	0	0	0	0	0	777	0	0	1,027	5,858
1973	Earle Canavan	5	0	0	0	0	0	0	0	1,223	0	0	1,681	4,980
1974	Earle Canavan	6	0	0	0	0	0	0	0	1,477	0	0	2,106	6,570
1975	Earle Canavan	12	0	0	0	0	0	0	0	1,601	0	0	1,861	9,725
1976	Earle Canavan	7	0	0	0	0	0	0	0	1,687	0	0	1,609	6,035
1977	Earle Canavan	5	0	0	0	0	0	0	0	646	0	0	783	4,390
1978	Earle Canavan	9	0	0	0	0	0	0	0	2,111	0	0	2,451	8,740
1979	Earle Canavan	8	0	0	0	0	0	0	0	734	0	0	1,122	8,500
1982	Earle Canavan	3	0	0	0	0	0	0	0	88	0	0	140	2,905
1985	Earle Canavan	1	0	0	0	0	0	0	0	53	0	0	53	875
1986	Earle Canavan	1	0	0	0	0	0	0	0	165	0	0	168	1,475
Lifetime		69	0	0	0	0	0	0	0	10,937	0	0	13,483	$62,583

Earle Canavan

Year	Driver	Starts	Poles	1	2	3	4	5	6–10	Laps	Laps Led	Races Led	Miles	$
1969	Earle Canavan	1	0	0	0	0	0	0	0	62	0	0	165	1,100
Lifetime		1	0	0	0	0	0	0	0	62	0	0	165	$1,100

Bob Cancro

Year	Driver	Starts	Poles	1	2	3	4	5	6–10	Laps	Laps Led	Races Led	Miles	$
1954	Ted Rambo	5	0	0	0	0	0	0	1	296	0	0	260	200
Lifetime		5	0	0	0	0	0	0	1	296	0	0	260	$200

Ted Cannady

Year	Driver	Starts	Poles	1	2	3	4	5	6–10	Laps	Laps Led	Races Led	Miles	$
1955	Ted Cannady	9	0	0	0	0	0	0	0	812	0	0	705	450
1956	Ted Cannady	6	0	0	0	0	0	0	0	814	0	0	484	260
Lifetime		15	0	0	0	0	0	0	0	1,626	0	0	1,189	$710

Ron Caraglas

Year	Driver	Starts	Poles	1	2	3	4	5	6–10	Laps	Laps Led	Races Led	Miles	$
1987	Doug French	1	0	0	0	0	0	0	0	75	0	0	41	895
Lifetime		1	0	0	0	0	0	0	0	75	0	0	41	$895

Frank Carlini

Year	Driver	Starts	Poles	1	2	3	4	5	6–10	Laps	Laps Led	Races Led	Miles	$
1951	Jack Goodwin	1	0	0	0	0	0	0	0		0	0		25
Lifetime		1	0	0	0	0	0	0	0		0	0		$25

Bob Carpenter

Year	Driver	Starts	Poles	1	2	3	4	5	6–10	Laps	Laps Led	Races Led	Miles	$
1951	Fred Steinbroner	6	0	0	0	0	1	1	1	198	0	0	99	650
1951	Bob Carpenter	1	0	0	0	0	0	0	0		0	0		25
Lifetime		7	0	0	0	0	1	1	1	198	0	0	99	$675

Leslie Carr

Year	Driver	Starts	Poles	1	2	3	4	5	6–10	Laps	Laps Led	Races Led	Miles	$
1956	Buzz Auckland	1	0	0	0	0	0	0	0	43	0	0	43	0
Lifetime		1	0	0	0	0	0	0	0	43	0	0	43	$0

Year	Driver	Starts	Poles	Finish 1	2	3	4	5	6–10	Laps	Laps Led	Races Led	Miles	$

Dick Carter

Year	Driver	Starts	Poles	1	2	3	4	5	6–10	Laps	Laps Led	Races Led	Miles	$
1954	Dick Carter	3	0	0	0	0	0	0	0	376	0	0	265	65
Lifetime		3	0	0	0	0	0	0	0	376	0	0	265	$65

Travis Carter (Statistics represent teams owned by Travis Carter along with severalother teams with shared ownership.)

Year	Driver	Starts	Poles	1	2	3	4	5	6–10	Laps	Laps Led	Races Led	Miles	$
1990	Butch Miller	23	0	0	0	0	0	0	1	6,891	4	4	8,750	144,941
1990	Rick Mast	6	0	0	0	0	0	0	1	1,400	0	0	1,667	26,625
1991	Jimmy Spencer	29	0	0	0	1	0	0	5	7,627	330	6	8,583	280,320
1992	Jimmy Spencer	7	0	0	0	0	0	0	0	1,853	1	1	2,107	66,055
1994	Hut Stricklin	29	0	0	0	0	0	0	1	8,562	26	2	10,587	325,295
1995	Jimmy Spencer	29	0	0	0	0	0	0	4	8,664	4	2	10,475	504,560
1996	Jimmy Spencer	31	0	0	0	0	1	0	7	9,339	156	7	11,239	891,255
1997	Jimmy Spencer	32	0	0	0	0	0	1	3	8,665	70	8	11,233	962,020
1998	Ted Musgrave	1	0	0	0	0	0	1	0	498	0	0	265	35,310
1998	Frank Kimmell	1	0	0	0	0	0	0	0	197	0	0	394	28,065
1998	Jimmy Spencer	31	0	0	1	0	2	1	5	8,934	117	11	11,827	1,500,640
1999	Darrell Waltrip	27	0	0	0	0	0	0	0	7,204	3	2	8,937	954,133
1999	Jimmy Spencer	34	0	0	1	0	0	2	2	9,579	43	5	12,333	1,588,231
2000	Darrell Waltrip	28	0	0	0	0	0	0	0	6,602	5	4	9,106	1,136,671
2000	Todd Bodine	1	0	0	0	0	0	0	0	324	0	0	499	39,300
2000	Jimmy Spencer	34	0	0	0	0	0	1	3	9,363	46	8	12,308	1,763,355
2001	Todd Bodine	35	3	0	0	0	0	2	0	9,161	110	11	11,981	2,083,769
2001	Jimmy Spencer	36	2	0	0	0	2	1	5	10,259	214	11	13,330	2,305,562
2002	Joe Nemechek	7	0	0	0	0	0	0	0	1,831	0	0	2,645	609,812
2002	Hideo Fukuyama	2	0	0	0	0	0	0	0	643	0	0	453	79,005
2002	Geoffrey Bodine	4	0	0	0	0	0	0	0	621	0	0	1,186	241,980
2002	Todd Bodine	24	1	0	0	0	0	1	3	5,552	19	3	7,674	1,773,349
Lifetime		451	6	0	2	1	5	9	40	123,769	1,148	85	157,578	$17,340,253

Bob Casperson

Year	Driver	Starts	Poles	1	2	3	4	5	6–10	Laps	Laps Led	Races Led	Miles	$
1968	Dick Johnson	2	0	0	0	0	0	0	0	401	0	0	327	1,405
Lifetime		2	0	0	0	0	0	0	0	401	0	0	327	$1,405

Neil Castles

Year	Driver	Starts	Poles	1	2	3	4	5	6–10	Laps	Laps Led	Races Led	Miles	$
1957	Neil Castles	4	0	0	0	0	0	0	0	441	0	0	333	375
1958	Neil Castles	11	0	0	0	0	0	0	0	1,568	0	0	874	570
1959	Erwin Carpenter	1	0	0	0	0	0	0	0	299	0	0	150	75
1959	Neil Castles	2	0	0	0	0	0	0	0	299	0	0	150	110
1960	Neil Castles	18	0	0	0	0	0	0	5	2,293	0	0	1,162	2,125
1962	Neil Castles	7	0	0	0	0	0	0	1	486	0	0	209	535
1962	Jim Bray	1	0	0	0	0	0	0	0	34	0	0	11	75
1967	Jim Conway	1	0	0	0	0	0	0	0	215	0	0	108	100
1967	Elmer Gilliam	3	0	0	0	0	0	0	0	9	0	0	6	325
1967	Walter Wallace	1	0	0	0	0	0	0	0	11	0	0	6	100
1967	Neil Castles	24	0	0	0	0	1	1	9	4,978	0	0	3,866	11,505
1967	Mario Caruso	1	0	0	0	0	0	0	0	96	0	0	32	100
1967	Cale Yarborough	1	0	0	0	0	0	0	1	386	0	0	241	600
1968	Buck Baker	1	0	0	0	0	0	0	0	30	0	0	15	125
1968	Dub Simpson	1	0	0	0	0	0	0	0	0	0	0	0	500
1968	Neil Castles	42	0	0	0	1	1	1	11	8,926	0	0	5,305	15,215
1968	Ray Hill	1	0	0	0	0	0	0	0	1	0	0	1	100
1969	Dub Simpson	1	0	0	0	0	0	0	0	243	0	0	243	775
1969	Ed Negre	3	0	0	0	0	0	0	0	24	0	0	18	875
1969	Les Snow	1	0	0	0	0	0	0	0	2	0	0	5	925
1969	Neil Castles	50	0	0	2	1	5	6	16	12,881	29	1	10,065	37,062
1969	Bill Champion	1	0	0	0	0	0	0	0	3	0	0	2	250
1970	Roy Tyner	1	0	0	0	0	0	0	0	26	0	0	53	645
1970	Neil Castles	46	0	0	1	4	3	4	12	9,952	31	2	8,938	34,883
1970	Buddy Baker	1	0	0	0	0	0	0	0	7	0	0	3	225
1971	Dr. Ed Hessert	1	0	0	0	0	0	0	0	94	0	0	34	100
1971	Neil Castles	36	0	0	0	0	1	0	9	6,830	10	1	5,448	21,290
1971	Buddy Baker	1	0	0	1	0	0	0	0	200	34	1	300	2,980
1971	Bobby Mausgrover	11	0	0	0	0	0	0	0	1,379	0	0	1,465	6,140
1971	Harold Fagan	1	0	0	0	0	0	0	0	1	0	0	0	100
1971	Frank Warren	1	0	0	0	0	0	0	1	273	0	0	99	275
1971	Bill Champion	1	0	0	0	0	0	0	0	141	0	0	353	740

Year	Driver	Starts	Poles	Finish 1	2	3	4	5	6–10	Laps	Laps Led	Races Led	Miles	$

Neil Castles *continued*

Year	Driver	Starts	Poles	1	2	3	4	5	6–10	Laps	Laps Led	Races Led	Miles	$
1972	Dr. Ed Hessert	1	0	0	0	0	0	0	0	107	0	0	268	1,170
1972	Dave Marcis	1	0	0	0	0	0	0	1	382	0	0	239	650
1972	Neil Castles	21	0	0	0	0	0	0	1	4,075	0	0	3,936	18,760
1973	Neil Castles	8	0	0	0	0	0	0	0	869	0	0	803	7,074
1974	Neil Castles	13	0	0	0	0	0	0	0	1,401	0	0	1,282	11,699
1975	Neil Castles	7	0	0	0	0	0	0	0	578	0	0	513	4,190
1975	Harry Gant	1	0	0	0	0	0	0	0	306	0	0	459	1,130
1976	Neil Castles	1	0	0	0	0	0	0	0	22	0	0	22	505
1976	Bobby Isaac	1	0	0	0	0	0	0	0	39	0	0	59	910
Lifetime		330	0	0	4	6	11	12	67	59,907	104	5	47,074	$185,888

Charlie Causey

Year	Driver	Starts	Poles	1	2	3	4	5	6–10	Laps	Laps Led	Races Led	Miles	$
1953	Charlie Causey	3	0	0	0	0	0	0	0	35	0	0	144	50
Lifetime		3	0	0	0	0	0	0	0	35	0	0	144	$50

Ted Chamberlain

Year	Driver	Starts	Poles	1	2	3	4	5	6–10	Laps	Laps Led	Races Led	Miles	$
1949	Ted Chamberlain	2	0	0	0	0	0	0	0	148	0	0	74	100
1950	Ted Chamberlain	5	0	0	0	0	0	0	2	541	0	0	539	225
1951	Ted Chamberlain	2	0	0	0	0	0	0	1		0	0		125
1952	Ted Chamberlain	16	0	0	0	0	0	0	5	2,703	0	0	1,831	850
1953	Ted Chamberlain	9	0	0	0	0	0	0	3	572	0	0	442	500
1954	Slick Smith	1	0	0	0	0	0	0	0	114	0	0	86	25
1954	Ted Chamberlain	10	0	0	0	0	0	0	1	1,596	0	0	1,423	475
1957	Ted Chamberlain	5	0	0	0	0	0	0	1	903	0	0	738	550
1958	Ted Chamberlain	9	0	0	0	0	0	0	1	809	0	0	403	680
1959	Ted Chamberlain	1	0	0	0	0	0	0	0	68	0	0	17	50
Lifetime		60	0	0	0	0	0	0	14	7,454	0	0	5,552	$3,580

Bill Champion

Year	Driver	Starts	Poles	1	2	3	4	5	6–10	Laps	Laps Led	Races Led	Miles	$
1956	Bill Champion	1	0	0	0	0	0	0	1	187	0	0	94	100
1957	Neil Castles	1	0	0	0	0	0	0	0	51	0	0	26	100
1957	Bill Champion	5	0	0	0	0	0	0	0	859	0	0	419	535
1965	Neil Castles	1	0	0	0	0	0	0	0	173	0	0	238	595
1966	Bill Champion	9	0	0	0	0	0	0	0	1,120	0	0	1,220	3,735
1967	Bill Champion	11	0	0	0	0	0	0	0	1,889	0	0	2,027	6,205
1967	Dick Johnson	3	0	0	0	0	0	0	0	428	0	0	206	330
1968	Elmo Langley	1	0	0	0	0	0	0	1	239	0	0	96	175
1968	Bill Champion	18	0	0	0	0	0	0	2	3,505	0	0	3,531	10,170
1969	Bill Champion	48	0	0	0	0	0	1	9	9,979	0	0	7,976	25,125
1969	Elmo Langley	1	0	0	0	0	0	0	0	304	0	0	309	930
1969	Jabe Thomas	1	0	0	0	0	0	0	0	56	0	0	56	410
1969	John Kennedy	1	0	0	0	0	0	0	0	1	0	0	1	345
1969	Phil Montague	1	0	0	0	0	0	0	0	8	0	0	8	230
1969	John Kenney	1	0	0	0	0	0	0	0	4	0	0	6	1,050
1970	Bill Champion	38	0	0	0	0	0	0	6	7,493	0	0	6,864	25,735
1971	Bill Champion	43	0	0	0	0	0	3	11	10,336	0	0	9,266	29,694
1972	Dick Brooks	1	0	0	0	0	0	0	0	232	0	0	464	930
1972	Bill Champion	29	0	0	0	0	0	0	4	7,044	0	0	8,122	37,645
1973	Bill Champion	26	0	0	0	0	0	0	1	5,103	0	0	6,375	31,326
1974	Elmo Langley	1	0	0	0	0	0	0	0	51	0	0	77	1,037
1974	Bill Champion	18	0	0	0	0	0	0	0	2,324	0	0	2,263	13,480
1974	Randy Hutchison	1	0	0	0	0	0	0	0	66	0	0	35	730
1975	Bill Champion	10	0	0	0	0	0	0	0	2,504	0	0	2,558	9,165
1975	Ed Negre	1	0	0	0	0	0	0	0	338	0	0	178	625
1975	Elmo Langley	1	0	0	0	0	0	0	1	393	0	0	234	835
1975	Ricky Rudd	4	0	0	0	0	0	0	1	1,025	0	0	886	4,345
1975	Tommy Gale	4	0	0	0	0	0	0	0	502	0	0	897	4,345
1975	Walter Ballard	1	0	0	0	0	0	0	0	89	0	0	48	640
1976	Tommy Ellis	1	0	0	0	0	0	0	0	429	0	0	429	1,335
1976	Bill Elliott	4	0	0	0	0	0	0	0	628	0	0	812	6,765
1976	Bruce Jacobi	1	0	0	0	0	0	0	0	59	0	0	81	1,670
1976	Clyde Lynn	1	0	0	0	0	0	0	0	123	0	0	66	735
1976	Earl Brooks	1	0	0	0	0	0	0	0	250	0	0	250	1,065
1976	Johnny Ray	1	0	0	0	0	0	0	0	34	0	0	89	735
1976	Terry Bivins	1	0	0	0	0	0	0	0	192	0	0	384	2,875

Year	Driver	Starts	Poles	1	2	3	4	5	6–10	Laps	Laps Led	Races Led	Miles	$

Bill Champion *continued*

Year	Driver	Starts	Poles	1	2	3	4	5	6–10	Laps	Laps Led	Races Led	Miles	$
1976	Bill Champion	3	0	0	0	0	0	0	0	530	0	0	317	2,185
1977	Dean Dalton	1	0	0	0	0	0	0	0	391	0	0	398	1,100
1977	Raymond Williams	1	0	0	0	0	0	0	0	0	0	0	0	490
1977	Dick May	1	0	0	0	0	0	0	0	169	0	0	231	1,400
1978	Jimmy Means	1	0	0	0	0	0	0	0	151	0	0	402	1,685
1979	Billy Smith	1	0	0	0	0	0	0	0	179	0	0	245	1,575
Lifetime		299	0	0	0	0	0	4	37	59,438	0	0	58,177	234,182

Ralph Chaney

Year	Driver	Starts	Poles	1	2	3	4	5	6–10	Laps	Laps Led	Races Led	Miles	$
1950	Jim Paschal	1	0	0	0	0	0	0	1	188	0	0	94	75
1951	Tommy Moon	1	0	0	0	0	0	0	0		0	0		0
1951	John Barker	3	0	0	0	0	0	0	0	40	0	0	30	75
1951	Doug Wimpy	1	0	0	0	0	0	0	0		0	0		25
Lifetime		6	0	0	0	0	0	0	1	228	0	0	124	$175

Ed Chann

Year	Driver	Starts	Poles	1	2	3	4	5	6–10	Laps	Laps Led	Races Led	Miles	$
1957	Lyle Matlock	1	0	0	0	0	0	0	0	47	0	0	24	0
Lifetime		1	0	0	0	0	0	0	0	47	0	0	24	$0

Bob Chapman

Year	Driver	Starts	Poles	1	2	3	4	5	6–10	Laps	Laps Led	Races Led	Miles	$
1960	Bill Lutz	2	0	0	0	0	0	0	0	88	0	0	220	250
Lifetime		2	0	0	0	0	0	0	0	88	0	0	220	$250

Charles Chapman

Year	Driver	Starts	Poles	1	2	3	4	5	6–10	Laps	Laps Led	Races Led	Miles	$
1960	Eddie Gray	1	0	0	0	0	0	0	0	36	0	0	90	0
1960	Bob Ross	1	0	0	0	0	0	0	0	1	0	0	1	50
1960	Charlie Chapman	1	0	0	0	0	0	0	0	152	0	0	213	400
1960	Clem Proctor	1	0	0	0	0	0	0	0	338	0	0	465	500
1960	Jim Cook	1	0	0	0	0	0	0	0	343	0	0	515	400
1961	Clem Proctor	1	0	0	0	0	0	0	1	97	0	0	97	250
1961	Charlie Chapman	6	0	0	0	0	0	0	0	702	0	0	515	610
1961	Elmo Henderson	1	0	0	0	0	0	0	0	184	0	0	460	200
Lifetime		13	0	0	0	0	0	0	1	1,853	0	0	2,355	$2,410

Hank Chapman

Year	Driver	Starts	Poles	1	2	3	4	5	6–10	Laps	Laps Led	Races Led	Miles	$
1957	Hank Chapman	1	0	0	0	0	0	0	0		0	0		25
Lifetime		1	0	0	0	0	0	0	0		0	0		$25

Walt Chapman

Year	Driver	Starts	Poles	1	2	3	4	5	6–10	Laps	Laps Led	Races Led	Miles	$
1951	John McGinley	6	0	0	1	0	1	0	0	224	0	0	224	1,175
1951	Dick Rathmann	14	0	0	3	1	0	0	2	231	0	0	131	2,700
1952	Jack Smith	1	0	0	0	0	0	0	1	98	0	0	98	150
1952	Dick Rathmann	24	1	5	1	4	0	4	0	3,300	701	10	2,319	10,214
1952	Frank Mundy	1	0	0	0	0	0	0	0	225	0	0	225	50
1953	Dick Rathmann	33	2	5	12	1	2	1	3	2,545	542	8	2,002	19,155
1954	Russ Hepler	6	0	0	0	0	1	0	0	691	0	0	510	525
1954	John McGinley	1	0	0	0	0	0	0	0	36	0	0	50	75
1955	Herb Thomas	1	0	0	0	0	0	0	0	22	0	0	90	0
Lifetime		87	3	10	17	6	4	5	6	7,372	1,243	18	5,649	$34,044

Jack Chatenay

Year	Driver	Starts	Poles	1	2	3	4	5	6–10	Laps	Laps Led	Races Led	Miles	$
1956	Clyde Palmer	2	0	0	0	0	0	0	1	418	0	0	364	200
1956	Don Stanyer	1	0	0	0	0	0	0	0	70	0	0	175	40
1956	Herb Thomas	1	0	0	0	0	0	0	0	20	0	0	20	90
1956	Jim Graham	1	0	0	0	0	0	0	0		0	0		0
1957	Pete Cardenas	1	0	0	0	0	0	0	0	9	0	0	9	0
1957	Marvin Porter	3	0	0	0	0	0	0	1	334	0	0	170	320
1957	Clyde Palmer	1	0	0	0	0	0	0	0	33	0	0	83	80
1958	Owen Loggins	1	0	0	0	0	0	0	0	25	0	0	66	175
1959	Owen Loggins	1	0	0	0	0	0	0	0	57	0	0	57	100
1959	Bob Keefe	1	0	0	0	0	0	1	0	459	0	0	184	500

Year	Driver	Starts	Poles	1	2	3	4	5	6–10	Laps	Laps Led	Races Led	Miles	$

Jack Chatenay *continued*

Year	Driver	Starts	Poles	1	2	3	4	5	6–10	Laps	Laps Led	Races Led	Miles	$
1960	Marshall Sargent	1	0	0	0	0	0	0	0	1	0	0	1	25
1960	Owen Loggins	1	0	0	0	0	0	0	0	126	0	0	176	100
1961	Oren Prosser	1	0	0	0	0	0	0	0	73	0	0	73	50
1961	Dick Cook	3	0	0	0	0	0	0	0	273	0	0	353	490
1961	Jim Stewart	1	0	0	0	0	0	0	0	93	0	0	93	100
1961	Dick Carter	1	0	0	0	0	0	0	0	119	0	0	167	100
1961	Cliff Hill	1	0	0	0	0	0	0	0	31	0	0	80	50
Lifetime		22	0	0	0	0	0	1	2	2,141	0	0	2,070	$2,420

J.L. Cheatham

Year	Driver	Starts	Poles	1	2	3	4	5	6–10	Laps	Laps Led	Races Led	Miles	$
1961	Tiny Lund	1	0	0	0	0	0	0	0	234	0	0	351	550
1961	Friday Hassler	3	0	0	0	0	0	0	1	549	0	0	821	1,625
1961	Johnny Allen	2	0	0	0	0	0	0	0	265	0	0	229	400
1961	Elmo Langley	2	0	0	0	0	0	0	0	349	0	0	524	660
1961	Dave Mader	2	0	0	0	0	0	0	0	114	0	0	57	75
1961	Bill Morgan	1	0	0	0	0	0	0	0	237	0	0	119	225
Lifetime		11	0	0	0	0	0	0	1	1,748	0	0	2,099	$3,535

Tom Cherry

Year	Driver	Starts	Poles	1	2	3	4	5	6–10	Laps	Laps Led	Races Led	Miles	$
1953	Tom Cherry	1	0	0	0	0	0	0	1	38	0	0	156	180
Lifetime		1	0	0	0	0	0	0	1	38	0	0	156	$180

Marshall Chesrown

Year	Driver	Starts	Poles	1	2	3	4	5	6–10	Laps	Laps Led	Races Led	Miles	$
1992	Rick Carelli	2	0	0	0	0	0	0	0	58	0	0	145	9,005
1993	Rick Carelli	3	0	0	0	0	0	0	0	499	0	0	671	19,650
1994	Rick Carelli	4	0	0	0	0	0	0	0	958	0	0	1,165	31,975
Lifetime		9	0	0	0	0	0	0	0	1,515	0	0	1,980	$60,630

David Chester

Year	Driver	Starts	Poles	1	2	3	4	5	6–10	Laps	Laps Led	Races Led	Miles	$
1949	Billy Carden	1	0	0	0	0	0	0	0		0	0		50
Lifetime		1	0	0	0	0	0	0	0		0	0		$50

Leon Chester

Year	Driver	Starts	Poles	1	2	3	4	5	6–10	Laps	Laps Led	Races Led	Miles	$
1949	Gober Sosebee	3	1	0	1	0	0	0	1	170	34	1	170	1,225
Lifetime		3	1	0	1	0	0	0	1	170	34	1	170	$1,225

Ted Chester

Year	Driver	Starts	Poles	1	2	3	4	5	6–10	Laps	Laps Led	Races Led	Miles	$
1950	Gober Sosebee	1	0	0	0	0	0	0	0	21	0	0	88	25
1951	Fonty Flock	1	0	1	0	0	0	0	0	200	118	1	125	1,000
1951	Frank Mundy	1	0	1	0	0	0	0	0	200	114	1	100	1,000
1951	Bob Flock	16	1	1	2	0	1	0	4	978	133	5	877	3,325
1951	Tim Flock	29	5	7	4	3	3	1	2	2,259	815	11	1,661	13,060
1952	Tim Flock	33	4	8	5	2	7	0	3	5,345	1,470	16	3,564	20,210
1952	Roscoe Thompson	3	0	0	0	0	0	0	0	13	0	0	16	75
1952	Bob Flock	2	0	1	0	0	0	0	0	538	1	1	523	1,060
1952	Jack Smith	1	0	0	0	0	0	0	0	387	0	0	484	420
1952	Frank Mundy	4	0	0	0	0	0	0	2	311	0	0	237	225
1953	Tim Flock	26	5	1	1	2	3	4	7	1,990	289	8	1,774	7,365
1956	Jack Smith	7	0	0	0	0	0	0	4	1,582	49	1	1,353	1,100
1957	Jack Smith	1	0	0	0	0	0	0	0	97	0	0	49	50
Lifetime		125	15	20	12	7	14	5	22	13,921	2,989	44	10,850	$48,915

Kennie Childers

Year	Driver	Starts	Poles	1	2	3	4	5	6–10	Laps	Laps Led	Races Led	Miles	$
1978	Harry Gant	4	0	0	0	0	0	0	1	872	45	1	1,227	12,175
1979	Jack Ingram	4	0	0	0	0	0	0	0	532	0	0	661	4,240
1979	Harry Gant	3	0	0	0	0	0	0	1	299	0	0	597	5,875
1979	Lennie Pond	8	0	0	0	0	0	0	2	1,287	12	1	1,935	16,350
1979	Neil Bonnett	1	0	0	0	0	0	0	0	352	0	0	481	2,300
1979	Butch Lindley	1	0	0	0	0	0	0	0	82	0	0	43	570
1979	Buck Simmons	2	0	0	0	0	0	0	0	438	0	0	787	3,025
1980	Lennie Pond	1	0	0	0	0	0	0	0	12	0	0	18	1,220

Year	Driver	Starts	Poles	Finish 1	2	3	4	5	6–10	Laps	Laps Led	Races Led	Miles	$

Kennie Childers *continued*

Year	Driver	Starts	Poles	1	2	3	4	5	6–10	Laps	Laps Led	Races Led	Miles	$
1980	Donnie Allison	13	1	0	0	1	0	1	2	2,639	196	5	3,355	34,585
1980	Buck Simmons	6	0	0	0	0	0	0	0	1,333	0	0	1,308	6,365
1981	Donnie Allison	3	0	0	0	0	0	0	0	493	0	0	886	14,320
1981	Tim Richmond	8	0	0	0	0	0	0	2	1,888	0	0	2,488	15,430
1981	David Pearson	1	1	0	0	0	0	0	0	57	41	1	57	2,675
1981	Harry Gant	3	0	0	0	0	1	1	0	1,174	204	1	677	10,780
1981	Buddy Baker	1	0	0	0	0	0	0	0	43	0	0	23	610
Lifetime		59	2	0	0	1	1	2	8	11,501	498	9	14,543	$130,520

Richard Childress

Year	Driver	Starts	Poles	1	2	3	4	5	6–10	Laps	Laps Led	Races Led	Miles	$
1969	Richard Childress	1	0	0	0	0	0	0	0	80	0	0	213	1,175
1972	Richard Childress	14	0	0	0	0	0	0	0	1,502	0	0	1,294	6,365
1976	Richard Childress	30	0	0	0	0	0	0	11	0	0	9,780	72,105	8,147
1977	Richard Childress	30	0	0	0	0	0	0	11	8,346	27	4	9,412	82,485
1978	Richard Childress	30	0	0	0	1	0	0	11	7,973	52	4	10,061	93,670
1979	Richard Childress	31	0	0	0	0	0	1	10	9,109	13	2	10,443	111,405
1980	Richard Childress	31	0	0	0	0	0	0	10	8,693	21	6	10,693	139,990
1981	Dale Earnhardt	11	0	0	0	0	2	1	4	3,082	18	2	3,426	69,905
1981	Richard Childress	20	0	0	0	0	1	0	0	5,013	16	3	6,336	69,915
1982	Ricky Rudd	30	2	0	2	0	3	1	7	7,753	140	8	8,681	182,075
1983	Ricky Rudd	30	4	2	1	1	1	2	7	8,581	871	13	9,908	235,565
1984	Dale Earnhardt	30	0	2	4	2	0	4	10	9,584	446	16	10,850	509,805
1985	Dale Earnhardt	28	1	4	0	0	4	2	6	8,231	1,237	17	9,157	457,658
1986	Dale Earnhardt	29	1	5	5	3	1	2	7	9,212	2,127	26	11,166	868,100
1987	Dale Earnhardt	29	1	11	5	1	2	2	3	9,043	3,358	27	10,900	1,041,125
1988	Rodney Combs	1	0	0	0	0	0	0	0	4	0	0	4	1,500
1988	Dale Earnhardt	29	0	3	2	3	3	2	6	9,561	1,808	20	11,325	739,175
1989	Dale Earnhardt	29	2	5	3	5	1	0	5	9,112	2,730	22	10,798	885,050
1990	Dale Earnhardt	29	5	9	3	3	1	2	5	9,162	2,437	22	11,057	1,307,830
1991	Dale Earnhardt	29	0	4	3	4	1	2	7	9,541	1,133	20	11,438	1,029,065
1992	Dale Earnhardt	29	1	1	2	2	1	0	9	8,694	487	10	10,198	838,385
1993	Neil Bonnett	2	0	0	0	0	0	0	0	134	0	0	353	14,515
1993	Dale Earnhardt	30	3	6	5	3	3	0	4	9,787	1,474	21	11,809	1,324,240
1994	Dale Earnhardt	31	2	4	7	6	1	2	5	9,546	1,015	23	11,410	1,467,825
1995	Dale Earnhardt	31	3	5	6	5	1	2	4	9,625	1,574	24	11,715	2,378,200
1996	Dale Earnhardt	31	2	2	3	3	4	1	4	9,530	617	18	11,524	1,589,396
1996	Mike Skinner	5	0	0	0	0	0	0	0	1,459	10	1	1,742	62,200
1997	Dale Earnhardt	32	0	0	4	1	1	1	9	9,693	215	10	12,503	1,538,430
1997	Mike Skinner	31	2	0	0	0	0	0	3	8,389	34	8	10,486	869,430
1998	Mike Skinner	30	0	0	0	2	1	1	5	8,425	112	5	10,856	1,176,685
1998	Morgan Shepherd	2	0	0	0	0	0	0	0	644	0	0	648	50,140
1998	Mike Dillon	1	0	0	0	0	0	0	0	239	0	0	478	28,050
1998	Dale Earnhardt	33	0	1	0	1	2	1	8	9,459	274	14	12,277	2,900,828
1999	Mike Skinner	34	2	0	0	1	4	0	9	9,732	465	14	12,639	2,126,624
1999	Dale Earnhardt	34	0	3	3	0	0	1	14	9,751	230	8	12,760	2,682,049
2000	Dale Earnhardt	34	0	2	5	4	2	0	11	10,005	353	17	13,186	2,624,635
2000	Mike Skinner	34	1	0	1	0	0	0	10	9,640	349	12	12,626	1,912,355
2001	Robby Gordon	10	0	1	0	0	0	0	1	2,611	30	2	3,508	917,020
2001	Dale Earnhardt	1	0	0	0	0	0	0	0	199	16	1	498	194,111
2001	Jeff Green	8	1	0	0	0	0	0	1	1,758	71	1	2,778	407,249
2001	Mike Skinner	23	0	0	0	0	0	0	1	6,718	46	3	8,627	1,800,258
2001	Kevin Harvick	35	0	2	3	1	0	0	10	10,561	374	12	13,667	3,557,016
2002	Jeff Green	36	0	0	1	1	0	2	2	10,325	120	5	13,561	2,012,989
2002	Robby Gordon	36	0	0	0	1	0	0	4	10,294	44	4	13,548	2,928,969
2002	Kevin Harvick	35	1	1	0	2	1	1	3	9,566	178	8	12,777	3,611,061
2002	Kenny Wallace	1	0	0	0	0	0	0	0	490	0	0	257	82,678
Lifetime		1100	34	73	68	56	41	32	237	319,603	24,522	433	393,373	$46,999,301

John Childs

Year	Driver	Starts	Poles	1	2	3	4	5	6–10	Laps	Laps Led	Races Led	Miles	$
1981	Rusty Wallace	2	0	0	0	0	0	0	1	487	0	0	734	8,650
1982	Rusty Wallace	3	0	0	0	0	0	0	0	418	0	0	669	7,655
Lifetime		5	0	0	0	0	0	0	1	905	0	0	1,402	$16,305

Gordon Chilson

Year	Driver	Starts	Poles	1	2	3	4	5	6–10	Laps	Laps Led	Races Led	Miles	$
1986	Tom Rotsell	1	0	0	0	0	0	0	0	84	0	0	206	2,080

Year	Driver	Starts	Poles	1	2	3	4	5	6–10	Laps	Laps Led	Races Led	Miles	$

Gordon Chilson *continued*

Year	Driver	Starts	Poles	1	2	3	4	5	6–10	Laps	Laps Led	Races Led	Miles	$
1987	Tom Rotsell	1	0	0	0	0	0	0	0	84	0	0	206	2,110
1988	Tom Rotsell	1	0	0	0	0	0	0	0	90	0	0	221	2,470
1988	Bob Schacht	2	0	0	0	0	0	0	0	27	0	0	68	3,520
Lifetime		5	0	0	0	0	0	0	0	285	0	0	700	$10,180

Chet Chiroso

Year	Driver	Starts	Poles	1	2	3	4	5	6–10	Laps	Laps Led	Races Led	Miles	$
1954	Sam Hawks	2	0	0	0	0	0	0	0	447	0	0	325	65
1954	Marvin Panch	1	0	0	0	0	0	0	1	186	0	0	93	100
1954	Cliff Roberts	1	0	0	0	0	0	0	0	194	0	0	97	25
Lifetime		4	0	0	0	0	0	0	1	827	0	0	515	$190

Keith Christensen

Year	Driver	Starts	Poles	1	2	3	4	5	6–10	Laps	Laps Led	Races Led	Miles	$
1971	Paul Tyler	1	0	0	0	0	0	0	0	11	0	0	5	300
Lifetime		1	0	0	0	0	0	0	0	11	0	0	5	$300

Frank Christian

Year	Driver	Starts	Poles	1	2	3	4	5	6–10	Laps	Laps Led	Races Led	Miles	$
1949	Sara Christian	5	0	0	0	0	0	1	1	606	0	0	417	575
1949	Joe Littlejohn	1	0	0	0	0	1	0	0	40	0	0	166	300
1949	Bob Flock	4	0	2	1	0	0	0	0	690	22	3	545	4,550
1949	Frank Christian	1	0	0	0	0	0	0	1		0	0		175
1949	Curtis Turner	2	1	0	0	0	0	0	2	364	18	1	182	100
1949	Buckshot Morris	2	0	0	0	0	0	0	0		0	0		0
1950	Sara Christian	1	0	0	0	0	0	0	0		0	0		50
1950	Fonty Flock	5	2	1	0	0	1	0	0	875	369	4	863	1,900
1950	Tim Flock	1	0	0	0	0	0	0	0		0	0		0
1950	Bob Flock	4	0	0	1	0	0	0	2	595	5	1	781	1,075
1951	Slick Smith	1	0	0	0	0	0	0	0	379	0	0	474	240
1951	Billy Carden	1	0	0	0	0	0	0	0		0	0		25
1951	Fonty Flock	33	13	7	2	4	5	1	2	2,588	1,952	20	1,943	13,535
1952	Roscoe Thompson	2	0	0	0	0	0	0	0	83	11	1	77	80
1952	Herschel Buchanan	1	0	0	0	0	1	0	0	186	0	0	93	350
1952	Gober Sosebee	1	0	0	0	0	0	0	0		39	1		25
1952	Fonty Flock	28	7	2	6	2	2	2	2	3,780	984	10	2,837	17,915
1952	Slick Smith	5	0	0	0	0	0	0	3	613	0	0	516	725
1953	Fonty Flock	33	3	4	5	4	3	1	0	1,999	581	10	1,626	16,465
1953	Slick Smith	20	1	0	0	0	0	0	9	392	4	1	480	1,635
1953	Roscoe Thompson	1	0	0	0	0	0	0	0		0	0		25
1953	Curtis Turner	2	1	1	0	1	0	0	0	459	100	1	594	2,500
1954	Hershel McGriff	21	4	4	3	5	0	1	4	3,688	122	6	2,453	11,520
1954	Fonty Flock	3	0	0	1	0	0	0	0	545	15	1	273	700
1954	Dick Rathmann	1	0	0	0	0	0	0	0	148	0	0	74	25
1954	Dick Garlington	1	0	0	0	0	0	0	0	11	0	0	11	0
1954	Curtis Turner	5	0	0	0	1	1	2	1	594	0	0	556	2,050
1954	Bill Amick	4	0	0	0	0	0	0	0	510	9	1	555	250
1954	Slick Smith	3	0	0	0	0	1	0	1	321	0	0	358	750
1954	Pop McGinnis	1	0	0	0	0	0	0	1	123	0	0	92	150
1955	Slick Smith	3	0	0	0	0	0	0	2	424	0	0	434	525
1955	Fonty Flock	8	0	1	0	1	0	2	0	680	66	1	584	2,485
1955	Buck Baker	1	0	0	1	0	0	0	0	200	0	0	100	650
1955	Banjo Matthews	2	0	0	0	0	0	0	2	386	0	0	193	500
1955	Buddy Shuman	1	0	0	0	0	0	0	1	193	0	0	77	100
1955	Speedy Thompson	2	0	0	0	0	0	0	0	134	0	0	67	125
Lifetime		210	32	22	20	18	15	10	34	21,606	4,297	62	17,420	$82,075

Ted Christopher

Year	Driver	Starts	Poles	1	2	3	4	5	6–10	Laps	Laps Led	Races Led	Miles	$
1999	Ted Christopher	1	0	0	0	0	0	0	0	89	0	0	218	22,360
Lifetime		1	0	0	0	0	0	0	0	89	0	0	218	$22,360

Bill Church

Year	Driver	Starts	Poles	1	2	3	4	5	6–10	Laps	Laps Led	Races Led	Miles	$
1966	Wayne Woodward	1	0	0	0	0	0	0	0	258	0	0	387	640
1966	E.J. Trivette	1	0	0	0	0	0	0	0	2	0	0	1	300
Lifetime		2	0	0	0	0	0	0	0	260	0	0	388	$940

Year	Driver	Starts	Poles	Finish 1	2	3	4	5	6–10	Laps	Laps Led	Races Led	Miles	$

William Church

Year	Driver	Starts	Poles	1	2	3	4	5	6–10	Laps	Laps Led	Races Led	Miles	$
1962	E.J. Trivette	1	0	0	0	0	0	0	0	29	0	0	15	100
1963	E.J. Trivette	4	0	0	0	0	0	0	2	846	0	0	418	555
1963	Billy Wade	1	0	0	0	0	0	0	0	10	0	0	3	95
Lifetime		6	0	0	0	0	0	0	2	885	0	0	435	$750

Jerry Churchill

Year	Driver	Starts	Poles	1	2	3	4	5	6–10	Laps	Laps Led	Races Led	Miles	$
1984	Jerry Churchill	1	0	0	0	0	0	0	0	118	0	0	118	870
Lifetime		1	0	0	0	0	0	0	0	118	0	0	118	$870

Cicci-Welliver

Year	Driver	Starts	Poles	1	2	3	4	5	6–10	Laps	Laps Led	Races Led	Miles	$
1992	Todd Bodine	1	0	0	0	0	0	0	0	16	0	0	39	3,485
1997	Todd Bodine	1	1	0	0	0	0	0	0	87	0	0	213	16,465
2000	Todd Bodine	1	0	0	0	0	0	0	0	31	0	0	76	24,760
Lifetime		3	1	0	0	0	0	0	0	134	0	0	328	$44,710

Raul Cilloniz

Year	Driver	Starts	Poles	1	2	3	4	5	6–10	Laps	Laps Led	Races Led	Miles	$
1959	Raul Cilloniz	2	0	0	0	0	0	0	0	229	0	0	573	550
Lifetime		2	0	0	0	0	0	0	0	229	0	0	573	$550

Albert Clark

Year	Driver	Starts	Poles	1	2	3	4	5	6–10	Laps	Laps Led	Races Led	Miles	$
1976	Gary Johnson	1	0	0	0	0	0	0	0	72	0	0	189	840
1977	Gary Johnson	2	0	0	0	0	0	0	0	126	0	0	330	2,445
Lifetime		3	0	0	0	0	0	0	0	198	0	0	519	$3,285

Bob Clark

Year	Driver	Starts	Poles	1	2	3	4	5	6–10	Laps	Laps Led	Races Led	Miles	$
1987	Brad Teague	2	0	0	0	0	0	0	0	648	17	1	979	8,135
1988	Joe Ruttman	9	0	0	0	0	0	0	1	1,657	0	0	3,129	41,630
1988	Brad Teague	8	0	0	0	0	0	0	0	1,959	0	0	2,230	29,155
1988	Butch Miller	2	0	0	0	0	0	0	0	790	18	1	497	5,905
1988	Donnie Allison	1	0	0	0	0	0	0	0	114	0	0	228	3,000
1988	Lee Faulk	3	0	0	0	0	0	0	0	841	0	0	858	9,320
1988	Johnny Rutherford	1	0	0	0	0	0	0	0	155	0	0	155	3,775
1988	Jim Sauter	4	0	0	0	0	0	0	0	1,376	6	1	1,651	14,280
1989	Jim Sauter	8	0	0	0	0	0	0	1	2,076	0	0	2,400	31,480
Lifetime		38	0	0	0	0	0	0	2	9,616	41	3	12,127	$146,680

Ed Clark

Year	Driver	Starts	Poles	1	2	3	4	5	6–10	Laps	Laps Led	Races Led	Miles	$
1975	Bob Burcham	1	0	0	0	0	0	0	0	184	0	0	460	4,320
1975	Red Farmer	2	0	0	0	0	0	0	0	44	0	0	117	1,875
Lifetime		3	0	0	0	0	0	0	0	228	0	0	577	$6,195

Fred Clark

Year	Driver	Starts	Poles	1	2	3	4	5	6–10	Laps	Laps Led	Races Led	Miles	$
1961	Bob Welborn	1	0	0	0	0	0	0	0	112	0	0	56	150
1961	Elmo Langley	1	0	0	0	0	0	0	0	341	0	0	469	500
1961	Friday Hassler	3	0	0	0	0	0	0	0	275	0	0	635	450
1961	Gene White	1	0	0	0	0	0	0	0	147	0	0	221	300
1961	Tiny Lund	3	0	0	0	0	0	0	1	1,065	0	0	1,184	3,225
1961	J.C. Hendrix	1	0	0	0	0	0	0	1	254	0	0	381	875
1962	Johnny Suddeth	2	0	0	0	0	0	0	0	256	0	0	384	575
1962	Tiny Lund	6	0	0	0	0	0	0	0	1,748	8	1	1,765	1,870
1962	J.C. Hendrix	1	0	0	0	0	0	0	0	379	0	0	237	250
1963	Bunkie Blackburn	1	0	0	0	0	0	0	0	194	0	0	291	450
1963	Johnny Suddeth	1	0	0	0	0	0	0	0	16	0	0	24	250
Lifetime		21	0	0	0	0	0	0	2	4,787	8	1	5,645	$8,895

Paul Clark

Year	Driver	Starts	Poles	1	2	3	4	5	6–10	Laps	Laps Led	Races Led	Miles	$
1963	Paul Clark	4	0	0	0	0	0	0	0	470	0	0	370	875
Lifetime		4	0	0	0	0	0	0	0	470	0	0	370	$875

Year	Driver	Starts	Poles	Finish 1	2	3	4	5	6–10	Laps	Laps Led	Races Led	Miles	$

Sherman Clark

Year	Driver	Starts	Poles	1	2	3	4	5	6–10	Laps	Laps Led	Races Led	Miles	$
1955	Sherman Clark	2	0	0	0	0	1	0	0	214	0	0	214	380
1956	Sherman Clark	5	0	0	0	0	0	0	2	405	0	0	428	425
1957	Sherman Clark	1	0	0	0	0	0	0	0	54	0	0	135	115
Lifetime		8	0	0	0	0	1	0	2	673	0	0	777	$920

Harry Clary

Year	Driver	Starts	Poles	1	2	3	4	5	6–10	Laps	Laps Led	Races Led	Miles	$
1978	Bruce Hill	14	0	0	0	0	0	0	2	2,802	0	0	3,790	25,870
Lifetime		14	0	0	0	0	0	0	2	2,802	0	0	3,790	$25,870

Edgar Clay

Year	Driver	Starts	Poles	1	2	3	4	5	6–10	Laps	Laps Led	Races Led	Miles	$
1953	Bud Harless	1	0	0	0	0	0	0	0	168	0	0	84	25
1954	Bud Harless	5	0	0	0	0	0	0	0	482	0	0	364	75
1955	Bud Harless	4	0	0	0	0	0	0	1	324	0	0	294	210
Lifetime		10	0	0	0	0	0	0	1	974	0	0	741	$310

Paul Clayton

Year	Driver	Starts	Poles	1	2	3	4	5	6–10	Laps	Laps Led	Races Led	Miles	$
1963	Bunkie Blackburn	1	0	0	0	0	0	0	0	339	0	0	466	800
1963	Floyd Powell	4	0	0	0	0	0	0	1	389	0	0	529	1,040
1964	G.C. Spencer	1	0	0	0	0	0	0	0	95	0	0	48	50
Lifetime		6	0	0	0	0	0	0	1	823	0	0	1,042	$1,890

Crawford Clements

Year	Driver	Starts	Poles	1	2	3	4	5	6–10	Laps	Laps Led	Races Led	Miles	$
1986	Buddie Boys	2	0	0	0	0	0	0	0	91	0	0	168	2,480
Lifetime		2	0	0	0	0	0	0	0	91	0	0	168	$2,480

Louis Clements

Year	Driver	Starts	Poles	1	2	3	4	5	6–10	Laps	Laps Led	Races Led	Miles	$
1964	Rex White	1	0	0	0	0	0	0	0	17	0	0	51	575
Lifetime		1	0	0	0	0	0	0	0	17	0	0	51	$575

June Cleveland

Year	Driver	Starts	Poles	1	2	3	4	5	6–10	Laps	Laps Led	Races Led	Miles	$
1953	June Cleveland	1	0	0	0	0	0	0	0		0	0		25
Lifetime		1	0	0	0	0	0	0	0		0	0		$25

Dub Clewis

Year	Driver	Starts	Poles	1	2	3	4	5	6–10	Laps	Laps Led	Races Led	Miles	$
1968	Richard Brickhouse	7	0	0	0	0	1	0	1	1,571	0	0	1,977	7,190
1969	Richard Brickhouse	16	0	0	0	0	0	1	4	2,388	0	0	2,781	13,822
1969	Bill Shirey	2	0	0	0	0	0	0	0	336	0	0	168	450
1969	Joe Hines	1	0	0	0	0	0	0	0	38	0	0	76	800
Lifetime		26	0	0	0	0	1	1	5	4,333	0	0	5,001	$22,262

Ebart Clifton

Year	Driver	Starts	Poles	1	2	3	4	5	6–10	Laps	Laps Led	Races Led	Miles	$
1960	Jimmy Pardue	25	0	0	0	0	0	0	8	3,937	0	0	2,670	3,520
Lifetime		25	0	0	0	0	0	1	8	3,937	0	0	2,670	$3,520

Ernie Cline

Year	Driver	Starts	Poles	1	2	3	4	5	6–10	Laps	Laps Led	Races Led	Miles	$
1980	Ernie Cline	1	0	0	0	0	0	0	0	74	0	0	75	610
1981	Ernie Cline	1	0	0	0	0	0	0	0	77	0	0	41	550
1983	Ernie Cline	1	0	0	0	0	0	0	0	35	0	0	36	910
Lifetime		3	0	0	0	0	0	0	0	186	0	0	152	$2,070

Gene Cline

Year	Driver	Starts	Poles	1	2	3	4	5	6–10	Laps	Laps Led	Races Led	Miles	$
1965	Jimmy Helms	2	0	0	0	0	0	0	0	435	0	0	435	885
1965	Henley Gray	38	0	0	0	0	0	1	6	5,291	0	0	3,225	8,320
1965	E.J. Trivette	1	0	0	0	0	0	0	0	72	0	0	36	275
1966	Henley Gray	3	0	0	0	0	0	0	0	548	0	0	274	250
1966	Jim Hunter	1	0	0	0	0	0	0	0	8	0	0	4	0
1966	Bill Seifert	2	0	0	0	0	0	0	1	578	0	0	312	365
1966	Gene Cline	13	0	0	0	0	0	0	2	2,125	0	0	1,451	3,945
1966	E.J. Trivette	1	0	0	0	0	0	0	0	183	0	0	275	620

Year	Driver	Starts	Poles	Finish 1	2	3	4	5	6–10	Laps	Laps Led	Races Led	Miles	$

Gene Cline *continued*

Year	Driver	Starts	Poles	1	2	3	4	5	6–10	Laps	Laps Led	Races Led	Miles	$
1966	Clyde Lynn	1	0	0	0	0	0	0	1	440	0	0	220	400
1966	Jeff Hawkins	1	0	0	0	0	0	0	1	168	0	0	84	150
Lifetime		63	0	0	0	0	0	1	11	9,848	0	0	6,316	$15,210

Bill Clinton

Year	Driver	Starts	Poles	1	2	3	4	5	6–10	Laps	Laps Led	Races Led	Miles	$
1959	Eddie Pagan	1	0	0	0	0	0	0	1	439	0	0	176	375
1960	Dick Getty	2	0	0	0	0	0	0	0	198	0	0	254	385
1961	Eddie Pagan	4	0	0	0	0	0	1	3	492	0	0	523	985
1961	Bill Clinton	3	0	0	0	0	0	0	0	183	0	0	102	145
1963	Bill Clinton	2	0	0	0	0	0	0	0	247	0	0	667	725
1967	Scotty Cain	1	0	0	0	0	0	0	1	171	0	0	462	1,400
1968	Scotty Cain	1	0	0	0	0	0	0	1	167	0	0	451	1,150
1969	Scotty Cain	1	0	0	0	0	0	0	1	170	0	0	459	1,450
1970	Scotty Cain	2	0	0	0	0	0	0	0	60	0	0	157	1,495
Lifetime		17	0	0	0	0	0	1	7	2,127	0	0	3,251	$8,110

Derick Close

Year	Driver	Starts	Poles	1	2	3	4	5	6–10	Laps	Laps Led	Races Led	Miles	$
1989	Jack Pennington	2	0	0	0	0	0	0	0	580	0	0	743	4,475
1990	Jack Pennington	14	0	0	0	0	0	0	0	3,450	7	2	5,902	93,660
1991	Rich Bickle	3	0	0	0	0	0	0	0	1,118	0	0	1,404	13,425
1991	Greg Sacks	10	0	0	0	0	0	0	0	2,081	0	0	3,111	46,765
1992	Buddy Baker	3	0	0	0	0	0	0	0	547	0	0	1,227	49,500
Lifetime		32	0	0	0	0	0	0	0	7,776	7	2	12,387	$207,825

Dick Clothier

Year	Driver	Starts	Poles	1	2	3	4	5	6–10	Laps	Laps Led	Races Led	Miles	$
1950	Dick Clothier	4	0	0	0	0	0	0	1	194	0	0	115	250
Lifetime		4	0	0	0	0	0	0	1	194	0	0	115	$250

Millard Clothier

Year	Driver	Starts	Poles	1	2	3	4	5	6–10	Laps	Laps Led	Races Led	Miles	$
1949	Jim Roper	1	0	0	0	0	0	0	0		0	0		50
Lifetime		1	0	0	0	0	0	0	0		0	0		$50

George Clugston

Year	Driver	Starts	Poles	1	2	3	4	5	6–10	Laps	Laps Led	Races Led	Miles	$
1954	George Seeger	1	0	0	0	0	0	0	0	183	0	0	92	0
Lifetime		1	0	0	0	0	0	0	0	183	0	0	92	$0

Tommy Coates

Year	Driver	Starts	Poles	1	2	3	4	5	6–10	Laps	Laps Led	Races Led	Miles	$
1950	Tommy Coates	1	0	0	0	0	0	0	0		0	0		50
Lifetime		1	0	0	0	0	0	0	0		0	0		$50

Talmadge Cochrane

Year	Driver	Starts	Poles	1	2	3	4	5	6–10	Laps	Laps Led	Races Led	Miles	$
1958	Benny Rakestraw	4	0	0	0	0	0	0	0	567	0	0	290	250
1959	Wilbur Rakestraw	1	0	0	0	0	0	0	0	87	0	0	218	300
1960	Wilbur Rakestraw	12	0	0	0	0	0	0	1	1,862	0	0	2,038	2,695
Lifetime		17	0	0	0	0	0	0	1	2,516	0	0	2,545	$3,245

Ed Cole

Year	Driver	Starts	Poles	1	2	3	4	5	6–10	Laps	Laps Led	Races Led	Miles	$
1956	Ed Cole	6	0	0	0	0	0	0	1	777	0	0	563	650
1957	Ed Cole	1	0	0	0	0	0	0	0	163	0	0	82	100
Lifetime		7	0	0	0	0	0	0	1	940	0	0	644	$750

Grady Cole / Bruce Griffin

Year	Driver	Starts	Poles	1	2	3	4	5	6–10	Laps	Laps Led	Races Led	Miles	$
1949	Fonty Flock	1	0	0	1	0	0	0	0		0	0		1,000
Lifetime		1	0	0	1	0	0	0	0		0	0		$1,000

Neil Cole

Year	Driver	Starts	Poles	1	2	3	4	5	6–10	Laps	Laps Led	Races Led	Miles	$
1952	Neil Cole	5	0	0	0	0	0	0	2	591	0	0	361	375
Lifetime		5	0	0	0	0	0	0	2	591	0	0	361	$375

Year	Driver	Starts	Poles	Finish 1	2	3	4	5	6–10	Laps	Laps Led	Races Led	Miles	$

R.H. Coleman

Year	Driver	Starts	Poles	1	2	3	4	5	6–10	Laps	Laps Led	Races Led	Miles	$
1956	Jake Hatcher	1	0	0	0	0	0	0	0	172	0	0	86	100
1956	Bill Osborne (FL)	1	0	0	0	0	0	0	0	128	0	0	192	75
Lifetime		2	0	0	0	0	0	0	0	300	0	0	278	$175

Frank Coletto

Year	Driver	Starts	Poles	1	2	3	4	5	6–10	Laps	Laps Led	Races Led	Miles	$
1974	Bill Osborne	1	0	0	0	0	0	0	0	96	0	0	240	900
1975	Pete Torres	1	0	0	0	0	0	0	0	122	0	0	320	1,060
1975	Bill Osborne	1	0	0	0	0	0	0	0	67	0	0	176	795
Lifetime		3	0	0	0	0	0	0	0	285	0	0	735	$2,755

Harold Collins

Year	Driver	Starts	Poles	1	2	3	4	5	6–10	Laps	Laps Led	Races Led	Miles	$
1967	Roy Tyner	2	0	0	0	0	0	0	0	185	0	0	272	1,235
1967	Ken Spikes	7	0	0	0	0	0	0	0	316	0	0	394	2,920
Lifetime		9	0	0	0	0	0	0	0	501	0	0	666	$4,155

Marion Collins

Year	Driver	Starts	Poles	1	2	3	4	5	6–10	Laps	Laps Led	Races Led	Miles	$
1988	Gary Collins	1	0	0	0	0	0	0	0	212	0	0	212	2,525
1990	Gary Collins	1	0	0	0	0	0	0	0	280	0	0	280	3,125
1991	Gary Collins	1	0	0	0	0	0	0	0	61	0	0	61	3,250
Lifetime		3	0	0	0	0	0	0	0	553	0	0	553	$8,900

Bob Colvin

Year	Driver	Starts	Poles	1	2	3	4	5	6–10	Laps	Laps Led	Races Led	Miles	$
1954	Dave Terrell	1	0	0	0	0	0	0	0	18	0	0	27	100
1954	Carl Burris	1	0	0	0	0	0	0	0	150	0	0	75	0
Lifetime		2	0	0	0	0	0	0	0	168	0	0	102	$100

Leland Colvin

Year	Driver	Starts	Poles	1	2	3	4	5	6–10	Laps	Laps Led	Races Led	Miles	$
1950	Jimmy Thompson	4	0	0	0	0	0	0	3	522	0	0	510	450
1951	Jimmy Thompson	2	0	0	0	0	0	0	0		0	0		25
1951	Weldon Adams	3	0	0	0	0	0	0	0	104	0	0	130	50
1951	Leland Colvin	4	0	0	0	0	0	0	1		0	0		150
1951	Speedy Thompson	2	0	0	0	0	0	1	0	39	0	0	29	75
1953	Fireball Roberts	1	0	0	0	0	0	0	0	198	41	1	272	340
1954	Fireball Roberts	5	0	0	0	0	0	0	2	811	0	0	975	1,055
1955	Bill Champion	1	0	0	0	0	0	0	0	346	0	0	476	195
1956	Doug Yates	1	0	0	0	0	0	0	0	54	0	0	74	50
1956	Bill Brown (Ch)	1	0	0	0	0	0	0	0	235	0	0	323	250
1958	J.V. Hamby	2	0	0	0	0	0	0	1	237	0	0	119	200
1963	Bill Widenhouse	5	0	0	0	0	0	0	1	575	0	0	535	850
1963	H.G. Rosier	1	0	0	0	0	0	0	0	66	0	0	91	500
1963	Stan Parker	1	0	0	0	0	0	0	0	59	0	0	18	0
1964	Bill Widenhouse	1	0	0	0	0	0	0	0	153	0	0	77	90
1964	Bobby Keck	1	0	0	0	0	0	0	0	155	0	0	140	425
Lifetime		35	0	0	0	0	0	1	8	3,554	41	1	3,768	$4,705

R.L. Combs

Year	Driver	Starts	Poles	1	2	3	4	5	6–10	Laps	Laps Led	Races Led	Miles	$
1957	R.L. Combs	3	0	0	0	0	0	0	0	123	0	0	62	210
1958	R.L. Combs	9	0	0	0	0	0	0	1	1,062	0	0	473	785
1959	R.L. Combs	9	1	0	0	0	0	0	1	1,476	0	0	664	735
Lifetime		21	1	0	0	0	0	0	2	2,661	0	0	1,199	$1,730

Lucky Compton

Year	Driver	Starts	Poles	1	2	3	4	5	6–10	Laps	Laps Led	Races Led	Miles	$
1988	Ralph Jones	1	0	0	0	0	0	0	0	190	0	0	475	10,595
1988	David Sosebee	2	0	0	0	0	0	0	0	289	0	0	499	4,960
1989	Ronnie Thomas	1	0	0	0	0	0	0	0	196	0	0	392	3,925
1989	Lee Raymond	1	0	0	0	0	0	0	0	189	0	0	473	13,530
Lifetime		5	0	0	0	0	0	0	0	864	0	0	1,839	$33,010

Gene Comstock

Year	Driver	Starts	Poles	1	2	3	4	5	6–10	Laps	Laps Led	Races Led	Miles	$
1950	Gene Comstock	1	0	0	0	0	0	0	0	355	0	0	444	0
1951	Gene Comstock	4	0	0	0	0	0	0	0	357	0	0	446	125

Year	Driver	Starts	Poles	Finish						Laps	Laps Led	Races Led	Miles	$
				1	2	3	4	5	6–10	Laps	Led	Led	Miles	$

Gene Comstock *continued*

Year	Driver	Starts	Poles	1	2	3	4	5	6–10	Laps	Laps Led	Races Led	Miles	$
1952	Gene Comstock	8	0	0	0	0	1	0	2	1,496	0	0	1,185	785
1953	Arden Mounts	10	0	0	0	0	0	0	1	792	0	0	759	395
1953	Gene Comstock	13	0	0	0	0	0	0	3	756	0	0	895	725
1954	Gene Comstock	1	0	0	0	0	0	0	0	334	0	0	459	400
1954	Dick Rathmann	1	0	0	0	0	0	0	0	115	0	0	86	25
1954	Arden Mounts	11	0	0	0	0	0	0	1	1,552	0	0	1,287	850
1955	Arden Mounts	3	0	0	0	0	0	0	2	411	0	0	328	385
1955	Bill Blair	1	0	0	0	0	0	0	0	43	0	0	22	25
1955	Gene Comstock	2	0	0	0	0	0	0	0	239	0	0	380	250
Lifetime		55	0	0	0	0	1	0	9	6,450	0	0	6,290	$3,965

Cos Concilla

Year	Driver	Starts	Poles	1	2	3	4	5	6–10	Laps	Laps Led	Races Led	Miles	$
1951	Ben Gregory	1	0	0	0	0	0	0	0		0	0		50
1954	Ben Gregory	2	0	0	0	0	2	0	0	782	0	0	391	750
1955	Danny Letner	3	0	1	0	1	0	0	0	523	34	1	423	1,755
1956	Danny Letner	1	0	0	0	0	0	0	0	75	0	0	188	110
1963	Bob Perry	3	0	0	0	0	0	0	0	381	0	0	551	775
1963	Bruce Worrell	1	0	0	0	0	0	0	0	1	0	0	3	200
1967	Jim Cook	1	0	0	0	0	0	0	0	92	0	0	248	530
1968	Jim Cook	1	0	0	0	0	0	0	0	162	0	0	437	1,000
1969	Ray Johnstone	1	0	0	0	0	0	0	0	163	0	0	440	1,225
1970	Jerry Oliver	2	0	0	0	0	0	0	1	268	0	0	702	2,175
1971	Jerry Oliver	2	0	0	0	0	0	1	0	192	0	0	503	2,970
1972	Jerry Oliver	1	0	0	0	0	0	0	0	122	0	0	320	1,100
1972	Ray Johnstone	1	0	0	0	0	0	0	0	62	0	0	162	725
Lifetime		20	0	1	0	1	2	1	1	2,823	34	1	4,368	$13,365

Ernie Conn

Year	Driver	Starts	Poles	1	2	3	4	5	6–10	Laps	Laps Led	Races Led	Miles	$
1969	Jack McCoy	2	0	0	0	0	0	0	1	257	0	0	533	2,750
1970	Jack McCoy	2	0	0	0	0	0	0	1	207	0	0	542	2,740
1971	Jack McCoy	3	0	0	0	0	0	0	0	443	0	0	1,138	4,315
1972	Jack McCoy	3	0	0	0	0	0	0	0	228	0	0	575	4,070
1973	Jack McCoy	3	0	0	0	0	0	1	2	797	0	0	1,106	5,270
1974	Jack McCoy	3	0	0	0	0	0	0	0	175	4	1	453	3,390
1975	Ivan Baldwin	2	0	0	0	0	0	0	0	9	0	0	24	1,040
Lifetime		18	0	0	0	0	0	1	4	2,116	4	1	4,371	$23,575

Cal Connell

Year	Driver	Starts	Poles	1	2	3	4	5	6–10	Laps	Laps Led	Races Led	Miles	$
1951	Bill Holland	1	0	0	0	0	0	0	0	80	0	0	80	0
Lifetime		1	0	0	0	0	0	0	0	80	0	0	80	$0

Lee Connell

Year	Driver	Starts	Poles	1	2	3	4	5	6–10	Laps	Laps Led	Races Led	Miles	$
1951	Lee Connell	1	0	0	0	0	0	0	0	58	0	0	73	0
Lifetime		1	0	0	0	0	0	0	0	58	0	0	73	$0

James Cook

Year	Driver	Starts	Poles	1	2	3	4	5	6–10	Laps	Laps Led	Races Led	Miles	$
1968	Wayne Smith	1	0	0	0	0	0	0	0	106	0	0	42	100
Lifetime		1	0	0	0	0	0	0	0	106	0	0	42	$100

Lee Coonis

Year	Driver	Starts	Poles	1	2	3	4	5	6–10	Laps	Laps Led	Races Led	Miles	$
1951	Clyde Minter	1	0	0	0	0	0	0	0		0	0		25
Lifetime		1	0	0	0	0	0	0	0		0	0		$25

Bob Cooper

Year	Driver	Starts	Poles	1	2	3	4	5	6–10	Laps	Laps Led	Races Led	Miles	$
1962	Bob Cooper	11	0	0	0	0	0	0	1	1,439	0	0	780	1,120
1963	Doug Cooper	2	0	0	0	1	0	0	0	154	0	0	139	750
1963	Bob Cooper	9	0	0	0	0	0	0	1	1,559	0	0	1,889	3,115
1964	Doug Cooper	38	0	0	0	1	1	2	7	5,492	0	0	3,835	9,945
1964	Bob Cooper	9	0	0	0	0	0	0	1	491	0	0	620	3,090
1965	Darel Dieringer	1	0	0	0	0	0	0	0	4	0	0	2	100
1965	Sam McQuagg	1	0	0	0	0	0	1	0	249	0	0	374	545

Year	Driver	Starts	Poles	Finish 1	2	3	4	5	6–10	Laps	Laps Led	Races Led	Miles	$

Bob Cooper *continued*

Year	Driver	Starts	Poles	1	2	3	4	5	6–10	Laps	Laps Led	Races Led	Miles	$
1965	Barry Brooks	4	0	0	0	0	0	0	0	131	0	0	76	1,450
1965	Bob Cooper	4	0	0	0	0	0	0	1	697	0	0	252	600
1965	Daniel Warlick	1	0	0	0	0	0	0	0	51	0	0	26	0
1965	Doug Cooper	28	0	0	0	0	1	0	8	4,959	0	0	3,575	10,400
1966	Paul Goldsmith	3	0	0	1	0	0	1	0	497	16	1	224	975
1966	Bob Cooper	1	0	0	0	0	0	1	0	375	0	0	188	200
1966	Doug Cooper	18	0	0	0	1	1	0	1	2,969	0	0	1,929	4,625
1967	Doug Cooper	13	0	0	0	0	0	2	2	1,782	0	0	1,003	3,040
1967	Bob Cooper	6	0	0	0	0	0	0	2	1,171	0	0	710	1,780
1968	Bob Cooper	14	0	0	0	0	0	0	1	2,170	0	0	1,415	4,540
1968	William Gardner	2	0	0	0	0	0	0	0	128	0	0	64	350
Lifetime		165	0	0	1	3	3	6	25	24,318	16	1	17,099	$46,625

Ed Cooper

Year	Driver	Starts	Poles	1	2	3	4	5	6–10	Laps	Laps Led	Races Led	Miles	$
1985	Edward Cooper	1	0	0	0	0	0	0	0	7	0	0	14	1,375
1990	Edward Cooper	2	0	0	0	0	0	0	0	94	0	0	188	8,225
Lifetime		3	0	0	0	0	0	0	0	101	0	0	202	$9,600

W.T. Coppedge

Year	Driver	Starts	Poles	1	2	3	4	5	6–10	Laps	Laps Led	Races Led	Miles	$
1960	Larry Frank	2	0	0	0	0	0	0	1	175	0	0	88	180
1960	Junior Johnson	1	0	0	0	0	0	0	0	113	0	0	57	110
1960	Tommy Irwin	1	0	0	0	0	0	0	1	196	0	0	98	175
1960	Tom Pistone	16	0	0	0	1	0	1	4	3,328	183	4	2,839	4,880
Lifetime		20	0	0	0	1	0	1	6	3,812	183	4	3,081	$5,345

Jim B. Copperheat

Year	Driver	Starts	Poles	1	2	3	4	5	6–10	Laps	Laps Led	Races Led	Miles	$
1952	Bill Rexford	1	0	0	0	0	0	0	0	82	0	0	82	25
Lifetime		1	0	0	0	0	0	0	0	82	0	0	82	$25

Ken Corman

Year	Driver	Starts	Poles	1	2	3	4	5	6–10	Laps	Laps Led	Races Led	Miles	$
1958	Johnny Mackison	8	0	0	0	1	0	1	1	897	0	0	585	965
Lifetime		8	0	0	0	1	0	1	1	897	0	0	585	$965

Vincent Cornella

Year	Driver	Starts	Poles	1	2	3	4	5	6–10	Laps	Laps Led	Races Led	Miles	$
1954	John Kieper	1	0	0	0	0	0	0	0	420	0	0	210	25
Lifetime		1	0	0	0	0	0	0	0	420	0	0	210	$25

Fred Correa

Year	Driver	Starts	Poles	1	2	3	4	5	6–10	Laps	Laps Led	Races Led	Miles	$
1982	John Krebs	1	0	0	0	0	0	0	0	40	0	0	105	600
Lifetime		1	0	0	0	0	0	0	0	40	0	0	105	$600

Ron Cory

Year	Driver	Starts	Poles	1	2	3	4	5	6–10	Laps	Laps Led	Races Led	Miles	$
1965	Jack Anderson	2	0	0	0	0	0	0	0	18	0	0	45	1,220
Lifetime		2	0	0	0	0	0	0	0	18	0	0	45	$1,220

Luther Costales

Year	Driver	Starts	Poles	1	2	3	4	5	6–10	Laps	Laps Led	Races Led	Miles	$
1962	Harlan Richardson	1	0	0	0	0	0	0	0	17	0	0	43	50
1962	Billy Wade	1	0	0	0	0	0	0	0	182	0	0	455	425
Lifetime		2	0	0	0	0	0	0	0	199	0	0	498	$475

Howard Coulter

Year	Driver	Starts	Poles	1	2	3	4	5	6–10	Laps	Laps Led	Races Led	Miles	$
1957	Russ Hepler	4	1	0	0	0	0	0	0	365	0	0	206	345
Lifetime		4	1	0	0	0	0	0	0	365	0	0	206	$345

Bobby Courtwright

Year	Driver	Starts	Poles	1	2	3	4	5	6–10	Laps	Laps Led	Races Led	Miles	$
1952	Bobby Courtwright	4	0	0	0	0	0	1	0	424	0	0	218	275
1954	Bobby Courtwright	1	0	0	0	0	0	0	0	107	0	0	107	25
Lifetime		5	0	0	0	0	0	1	0	531	0	0	325	$300

Year	Driver	Starts	Poles	Finish						Laps	Laps Led	Races Led	Miles	$
				1	2	3	4	5	6–10	Laps	Led	Led	Miles	$

A.J. Cox

Year	Driver	Starts	Poles	1	2	3	4	5	6–10	Laps	Led	Led	Miles	$
1971	A.J. Cox	1	0	0	0	0	0	0	0	82	0	0	82	615
1972	A.J. Cox	1	0	0	0	0	0	0	0	2	0	0	3	325
1972	Jim Vandiver	1	0	0	0	0	0	0	0	299	0	0	299	875
Lifetime		3	0	0	0	0	0	0	0	383	0	0	384	$1,815

Doug Cox

Year	Driver	Starts	Poles	1	2	3	4	5	6–10	Laps	Led	Led	Miles	$
1955	Doug Cox	1	0	0	0	0	0	0	0	181	0	0	91	50
1958	Doug Cox	14	0	0	1	0	1	1	6	2,479	0	0	1,592	3,095
1959	Doug Cox	4	0	0	0	0	0	0	2	532	0	0	266	380
1961	Doug Cox	5	0	0	0	0	0	0	0	367	0	0	190	510
Lifetime		24	0	0	1	0	1	1	8	3,559	0	0	2,138	$4,035

Marion Cox

Year	Driver	Starts	Poles	1	2	3	4	5	6–10	Laps	Led	Led	Miles	$
1955	Roy Bentley	1	0	0	0	0	0	0	0	317	0	0	436	60
1956	Roy Bentley	3	0	0	0	0	0	0	0	329	0	0	292	200
Lifetime		4	0	0	0	0	0	0	0	646	0	0	728	$260

Owen Cox

Year	Driver	Starts	Poles	1	2	3	4	5	6–10	Laps	Led	Led	Miles	$
1955	Pop McGinnis	2	0	0	0	0	0	0	0	201	0	0	116	100
Lifetime		2	0	0	0	0	0	0	0	201	0	0	116	$100

Paul Cox

Year	Driver	Starts	Poles	1	2	3	4	5	6–10	Laps	Led	Led	Miles	$
1950	Marshall Teague	3	0	0	0	0	0	0	0	240	0	0	329	50
Lifetime		3	0	0	0	0	0	0	0	240	0	0	329	$50

Paul Craig Jr.

Year	Driver	Starts	Poles	1	2	3	4	5	6–10	Laps	Led	Led	Miles	$
1958	Cecil Wray	1	0	0	0	0	0	0	0	34	0	0	139	75
Lifetime		1	0	0	0	0	0	0	0	34	0	0	139	$75

Tom Craigen

Year	Driver	Starts	Poles	1	2	3	4	5	6–10	Laps	Led	Led	Miles	$
1993	Dirk Stephens	2	0	0	0	0	0	0	0	106	0	0	215	12,880
Lifetime		2	0	0	0	0	0	0	0	106	0	0	215	$12,880

Gerald Craker

Year	Driver	Starts	Poles	1	2	3	4	5	6–10	Laps	Led	Led	Miles	$
1974	Don Hall	1	0	0	0	0	0	0	0	102	0	0	255	1,100
1975	Don Hall	1	0	0	0	0	0	0	0	188	0	0	470	2,225
1976	Chuck Bown	5	0	0	0	0	0	0	0	568	3	1	1,192	5,480
1977	Chuck Bown	3	0	0	0	0	0	0	0	180	0	0	468	7,270
1978	Jimmy Insolo	2	0	0	0	0	0	0	1	147	5	2	385	5,025
1979	Jimmy Insolo	2	0	0	0	0	0	0	0	156	0	0	409	5,080
1981	Hershel McGriff	3	0	0	0	0	0	0	0	80	1	1	210	2,170
Lifetime		17	0	0	0	0	0	0	1	1,421	9	4	3,389	$28,350

Bill Cramer

Year	Driver	Starts	Poles	1	2	3	4	5	6–10	Laps	Led	Led	Miles	$
1951	George Seeger	1	0	0	0	1	0	0	0	199	0	0	100	400
Lifetime		1	0	0	0	1	0	0	0	199	0	0	100	$400

Gill Cramer

Year	Driver	Starts	Poles	1	2	3	4	5	6–10	Laps	Led	Led	Miles	$
1973	Bobby Mausgrover	1	0	0	0	0	0	0	0	58	0	0	88	915
Lifetime		1	0	0	0	0	0	0	0	58	0	0	88	$915

Pappy Crane

Year	Driver	Starts	Poles	1	2	3	4	5	6–10	Laps	Led	Led	Miles	$
1957	Joe Caspolich	1	0	0	0	0	0	0	0	66	0	0	91	200
1958	Bill Corley	1	0	0	0	0	0	0	0	7	0	0	29	0
1960	Pappy Crane	1	0	0	0	0	0	0	1	181	0	0	91	140
Lifetime		3	0	0	0	0	0	0	1	254	0	0	210	$340

Year	Driver	Starts	Poles	Finish 1	2	3	4	5	6–10	Laps	Laps Led	Races Led	Miles	$

Crawford Enterprises

Year	Driver	Starts	Poles	1	2	3	4	5	6–10	Laps	Laps Led	Races Led	Miles	$
1970	E.J. Trivette	1	0	0	0	0	0	0	0	68	0	0	37	395
1970	Jimmy Crawford	3	0	0	0	0	0	0	0	292	0	0	526	1,795
1971	Jimmy Crawford	2	0	0	0	0	0	0	0	44	0	0	108	200
1972	Donnie Allison	1	0	0	0	0	0	0	0	61	19	1	162	2,090
1972	Gordon Johncock	2	0	0	0	0	0	0	0	226	0	0	430	1,384
1972	Jimmy Crawford	1	0	0	0	0	0	0	0	181	0	0	481	1,695
1973	Dick Brooks	2	0	1	0	0	0	0	0	295	24	2	785	22,620
1973	Jimmy Crawford	4	0	0	0	0	0	0	0	1,053	0	0	1,228	4,059
1973	Pete Hamilton	1	0	0	0	0	0	0	0	38	0	0	58	905
1974	Jimmy Crawford	4	0	0	0	0	0	0	0	559	0	0	903	5,965
Lifetime		21	0	1	0	0	0	0	0	2,817	43	3	4,718	$41,108

C.L. Crawford

Year	Driver	Starts	Poles	1	2	3	4	5	6–10	Laps	Laps Led	Races Led	Miles	$
1965	J.T. Putney	2	0	0	0	0	0	0	1	224	0	0	112	300
1965	Gene Black	18	0	0	0	0	0	0	4	4,167	0	0	3,011	6,080
1965	Darel Dieringer	1	0	0	0	0	0	0	0	420	0	0	210	330
Lifetime		21	0	0	0	0	0	0	5	4,811	0	0	3,333	$6,710

J H Crawford

Year	Driver	Starts	Poles	1	2	3	4	5	6–10	Laps	Laps Led	Races Led	Miles	$
1966	Bunkie Blackburn	2	0	0	0	0	0	0	0	81	0	0	151	860
1966	Friday Hassler	1	0	0	0	0	0	0	0	256	0	0	128	150
Lifetime		3	0	0	0	0	0	0	0	337	0	0	279	$1,010

Spook Crawford

Year	Driver	Starts	Poles	1	2	3	4	5	6–10	Laps	Laps Led	Races Led	Miles	$
1955	Johnny Allen	1	0	0	0	0	0	0	0	169	0	0	254	195
1956	Spook Crawford	1	0	0	0	0	0	0	0	13	0	0	7	50
1956	Johnny Allen	32	0	0	0	0	0	2	9	4,888	0	0	3,349	4,190
1957	Johnny Allen	42	1	0	0	1	1	2	13	6,033	0	0	3,876	7,975
1957	Spook Crawford	1	0	0	0	0	0	0	0	34	0	0	78	125
1958	Shorty Rollins	2	0	0	0	0	0	0	0	327	0	0	181	275
1958	Roy Tyner	20	0	0	0	0	0	1	2	2,865	0	0	1,810	2,215
1958	Vernon West	1	0	0	0	0	0	0	0	1	0	0	0	50
1958	Spook Crawford	1	0	0	0	0	0	0	0	152	0	0	76	85
1958	Johnny Allen	18	0	0	0	1	0	1	3	2,214	0	0	1,206	1,950
1958	Neil Castles	1	0	0	0	0	0	0	0	141	0	0	88	50
1959	Jimmy Pardue	1	0	0	0	0	0	0	0	131	0	0	44	50
1959	Benny Rakestraw	6	0	0	0	0	1	0	0	962	0	0	683	1,095
1959	Tiny Lund	4	0	0	0	0	0	0	0	1,059	0	0	723	430
1960	Tiny Lund	1	0	0	0	0	0	0	1	187	0	0	94	140
1960	Buddy Baker	4	0	0	0	0	0	0	0	576	0	0	751	720
1960	Bunkie Blackburn	20	0	0	0	0	0	1	3	2,789	0	0	2,110	3,600
1960	Curtis Crider	2	0	0	0	0	0	0	0	417	0	0	626	650
1960	Spook Crawford	3	0	0	0	0	0	0	1	439	0	0	212	320
1960	Bob Reuther	1	0	0	0	0	0	0	0	285	0	0	143	140
1960	L.D. Austin	1	0	0	0	0	0	0	0	2	0	0	1	60
1960	G.C. Spencer	1	0	0	0	0	0	0	0	301	0	0	414	200
1961	Johnny Suddeth	1	0	0	0	0	0	0	0	22	0	0	33	200
1961	Paul Parks	2	0	0	0	0	0	0	0	208	0	0	520	200
Lifetime		167	1	0	0	2	2	7	32	24,215	0	0	17,276	$24,965

Walt Crawford

Year	Driver	Starts	Poles	1	2	3	4	5	6–10	Laps	Laps Led	Races Led	Miles	$
1950	Walt Crawford	1	0	0	0	0	0	0	0	358	0	0	448	0
Lifetime		1	0	0	0	0	0	0	0	358	0	0	448	$0

Charlie Cregar

Year	Driver	Starts	Poles	1	2	3	4	5	6–10	Laps	Laps Led	Races Led	Miles	$
1956	Charlie Cregar	2	0	0	0	0	0	0	0	74	0	0	37	0
1957	Charlie Cregar	3	0	0	0	0	0	0	3	356	0	0	178	500
1958	Charlie Cregar	1	0	0	0	0	0	0	0	127	0	0	127	100
Lifetime		6	0	0	0	0	0	0	3	557	0	0	342	$600

J.C. Crews

Year	Driver	Starts	Poles	1	2	3	4	5	6–10	Laps	Laps Led	Races Led	Miles	$
1971	H.B. Bailey	1	0	0	0	0	0	0	0	117	0	0	234	600

Year	Driver	Starts	Poles	Finish 1	2	3	4	5	6–10	Laps	Laps Led	Races Led	Miles	$

J.C. Crews *continued*

Year	Driver	Starts	Poles	1	2	3	4	5	6–10	Laps	Laps Led	Races Led	Miles	$
1971	Bobby Brack	5	0	0	0	0	0	0	0	946	0	0	1,616	4,608
1971	Rod Eulenfeld	1	0	0	0	0	0	0	0	293	0	0	446	1,135
1972	H.B. Bailey	2	0	0	0	0	0	0	0	480	0	0	502	1,765
1972	Bobby Mausgrover	2	0	0	0	0	0	0	0	334	0	0	549	1,545
1972	Bill Ward	1	0	0	0	0	0	0	0	10	0	0	27	770
1972	Dick May	4	0	0	0	0	0	0	0	636	0	0	1,067	3,330
1973	Bobby Mausgrover	1	0	0	0	0	0	0	0	9	0	0	24	560
1973	Johnny Barnes	8	0	0	0	0	0	0	0	1,416	0	0	2,181	8,585
1974	Johnny Barnes	1	0	0	0	0	0	0	0	1	0	0	3	750
Lifetime		26	0	0	0	0	0	0	0	4,242	0	0	6,650	$23,648

Curtis Crider

Year	Driver	Starts	Poles	1	2	3	4	5	6–10	Laps	Laps Led	Races Led	Miles	$
1960	Curtis Crider	20	0	0	0	0	0	0	2	3,413	0	0	2,279	2,820
1960	Richard Riley	1	0	0	0	0	0	0	0	143	0	0	215	200
1961	Charles Williamson	1	0	0	0	0	0	0	0	107	0	0	27	30
1961	Homer Galloway	1	0	0	0	0	0	0	0	127	0	0	42	110
1961	Bob Barron	1	0	0	0	0	0	0	1	157	0	0	79	140
1961	Bob Presnell	1	0	0	0	0	0	0	0	1	0	0	0	50
1961	Curtis Crider	41	0	0	0	0	0	1	1	5,882	0	0	4,186	7,420
1961	David Ezell	1	0	0	0	0	0	0	0	87	0	0	44	50
1961	Pete Boland	1	0	0	0	0	0	0	0	185	0	0	46	110
1961	Ed Livingston	9	0	0	0	0	0	0	0	1,290	0	0	1,944	1,745
1962	Curtis Crider	52	0	0	0	1	1	1	15	10,051	0	0	6,431	9,490
1962	Earl Brooks	1	0	0	0	0	0	0	0	2	0	0	1	150
1962	Ed Livingston	2	0	0	0	0	0	0	0	320	0	0	160	175
1962	Glenn Killian	1	0	0	0	0	0	0	0	3	0	0	1	50
1962	Frank Brantley	1	0	0	0	0	0	0	0	164	0	0	82	85
1962	Jerry Smith	1	0	0	0	0	0	0	0	109	0	0	36	60
1962	John Hardy	1	0	0	0	0	0	0	0	435	0	0	218	125
1962	H.G. Rosier	1	0	0	0	0	0	0	0	119	0	0	60	65
1962	Runt Harris	2	0	0	0	0	0	0	0	130	0	0	51	100
1963	Jerome Warren	1	0	0	0	0	0	0	0	25	0	0	13	100
1963	Chuck Huckabee	3	0	0	0	0	0	0	1	171	0	0	86	450
1963	Curtis Crider	43	0	0	0	1	0	1	11	7,618	0	0	4,653	9,300
1964	Ed Livingston	1	0	0	0	0	0	0	0	2	0	0	3	500
1964	Curtis Crider	58	0	0	0	1	1	5	23	11,411	0	0	7,786	17,250
1964	Darrell Bryant	4	0	0	0	0	0	0	1	365	0	0	177	450
1964	Rodney Bottinger	2	0	0	0	0	0	0	0	9	0	0	5	200
1964	Frank Graham	1	0	0	0	0	0	0	0	1	0	0	1	500
1964	Roy Mayne	2	0	0	0	0	0	0	0	43	0	0	66	930
1964	Stick Elliott	1	0	0	0	0	0	0	0	1	0	0	2	400
1964	Chuck Huckabee	9	0	0	0	0	0	0	0	788	0	0	306	830
1964	Buddy Baker	2	0	0	0	0	0	0	0	56	0	0	33	235
1964	Joe Cote	4	0	0	0	0	0	0	0	23	0	0	12	350
1964	Pete Boland	3	0	0	0	0	0	0	0	7	0	0	6	200
1964	Wally Dallenbach	1	0	0	0	0	0	0	0	142	0	0	71	110
1964	Gene Lovelace	1	0	0	0	0	0	0	0	125	0	0	50	130
1964	J.V. Hamby	4	0	0	0	0	0	0	1	479	0	0	170	460
1964	Bob Cooper	5	0	0	0	0	0	0	0	292	0	0	183	1,420
1964	Frank Tanner	1	0	0	0	0	0	0	0	2	0	0	1	100
1965	Darel Dieringer	1	0	0	0	0	0	0	0	119	0	0	107	100
1965	Curtis Crider	1	0	0	0	0	1	0	0	238	0	0	119	600
Lifetime		287	0	0	0	3	3	8	56	44,642	0	0	29,749	$57,590

Will Cronkrite

Year	Driver	Starts	Poles	1	2	3	4	5	6–10	Laps	Laps Led	Races Led	Miles	$
1978	Baxter Price	1	0	0	0	0	0	0	0	179	0	0	269	1,165
1978	Dale Earnhardt	4	0	0	0	0	0	0	1	1,032	0	0	1,872	13,245
1979	Jim Hurlbert	1	0	0	0	0	0	0	0	150	0	0	300	1,400
1979	Jerry Jolly	1	0	0	0	0	0	0	0	99	0	0	263	2,440
1979	Ferrel Harris	1	0	0	0	0	0	0	0	2	0	0	3	1,260
1982	John McFadden	1	0	0	0	0	0	0	0	368	0	0	196	655
1982	Bill Elliott	2	0	0	0	0	0	0	0	174	0	0	447	7,985
1983	Jimmy Walker	2	0	0	0	0	0	0	0	289	0	0	179	1,505
1983	Rick Baldwin	1	0	0	0	0	0	0	0	7	0	0	19	1,985
Lifetime		14	0	0	0	0	0	0	1	2,300	0	0	3,547	$31,640

Year	Driver	Starts	Poles	Finish						Laps	Laps Led	Races Led	Miles	$
				1	2	3	4	5	6–10					

Don Culpepper

Year	Driver	Starts	Poles	1	2	3	4	5	6–10	Laps	Laps Led	Races Led	Miles	$
1967	Earl Brooks	19	1	0	0	0	0	0	4	3,354	24	1	2,464	5,990
1967	Tiny Lund	3	0	0	0	0	0	0	0	981	0	0	536	690
1967	Roy Tyner	1	0	0	0	0	0	0	0	260	0	0	390	1,200
1968	Ben Arnold	9	0	0	0	0	0	0	0	1,129	0	0	812	1,960
1968	Tiny Lund	2	0	0	0	0	0	0	1	287	0	0	144	440
1968	James Sears	1	0	0	0	0	0	0	0	92	0	0	92	710
1968	Stan Meserve	1	0	0	0	0	0	0	0	346	0	0	216	275
1968	Roy Tyner	17	0	0	0	0	0	1	4	2,835	0	0	2,255	7,735
1968	Earl Brooks	2	0	0	0	0	0	0	0	529	0	0	252	400
Lifetime		55	1	0	0	0	0	1	9	9,813	24	1	7,162	$19,400

Red Culpepper

Year	Driver	Starts	Poles	1	2	3	4	5	6–10	Laps	Laps Led	Races Led	Miles	$
1969	Tommy Gale	1	0	0	0	0	0	0	0	46	0	0	115	290
1969	Ben Arnold	45	0	0	0	0	0	0	7	9,858	0	0	7,914	24,712
Lifetime		46	0	0	0	0	0	0	7	9,904	0	0	8,029	$25,002

Clayton Cunningham

Year	Driver	Starts	Poles	1	2	3	4	5	6–10	Laps	Laps Led	Races Led	Miles	$
1994	Ken Bouchard	1	0	0	0	0	0	0	0	280	0	0	426	6,675
Lifetime		1	0	0	0	0	0	0	0	280	0	0	426	$6,675

H.B. Cunningham

Year	Driver	Starts	Poles	1	2	3	4	5	6–10	Laps	Laps Led	Races Led	Miles	$
1967	Coo Coo Marlin	1	0	0	0	0	0	0	0	120	0	0	60	130
1969	Coo Coo Marlin	7	0	0	0	0	0	0	2	993	0	0	1,285	5,680
1970	Coo Coo Marlin	13	0	0	0	0	0	0	4	2,531	0	0	3,825	14,799
1971	Coo Coo Marlin	12	0	0	0	0	0	0	0	1,495	0	0	2,336	9,135
1971	Jabe Thomas	1	0	0	0	0	0	0	0	292	0	0	438	1,230
1971	Wendell Scott	1	0	0	0	0	0	0	0	64	0	0	96	714
1972	Coo Coo Marlin	20	0	0	0	1	1	0	3	4,092	31	5	5,383	28,924
1973	Coo Coo Marlin	21	0	0	0	1	0	0	7	5,454	16	3	5,948	29,997
1974	Coo Coo Marlin	23	0	0	0	0	1	0	4	5,323	28	7	6,082	41,944
1975	Coo Coo Marlin	23	0	0	0	1	0	0	7	5,199	25	5	6,400	54,240
1976	Charlie Glotzbach	1	0	0	0	0	0	0	0	121	0	0	182	1,535
1976	Coo Coo Marlin	12	0	0	0	0	0	3	6	3,074	0	0	4,309	39,485
1976	Sterling Marlin	1	0	0	0	0	0	0	0	55	0	0	33	565
1976	Walter Wallace	1	0	0	0	0	0	0	0	59	0	0	35	325
1977	Coo Coo Marlin	11	0	0	0	0	1	0	4	2,930	1	1	4,210	42,450
1978	Coo Coo Marlin	9	0	0	0	0	0	0	2	1,518	4	2	2,372	19,415
1978	Sterling Marlin	2	0	0	0	0	0	0	1	591	0	0	708	10,320
1979	Sterling Marlin	1	0	0	0	0	0	0	0	341	11	1	203	505
1979	Jimmy Means	1	0	0	0	0	0	0	0	1	0	0	2	855
1979	Coo Coo Marlin	7	0	0	0	0	0	0	2	907	0	0	1,989	27,540
1980	Coo Coo Marlin	3	0	0	0	0	0	0	0	377	0	0	978	8,400
1980	Sterling Marlin	2	0	0	0	0	0	0	1	332	0	0	692	18,750
Lifetime		173	0	0	0	3	3	3	43	35,869	116	24	47,566	$356,938

J.B. Cunningham

Year	Driver	Starts	Poles	1	2	3	4	5	6–10	Laps	Laps Led	Races Led	Miles	$
1955	Tommy Ringstaff	3	0	0	0	0	0	0	1	225	0	0	199	125
Lifetime		3	0	0	0	0	0	0	1	225	0	0	199	$125

Pepper Cunningham

Year	Driver	Starts	Poles	1	2	3	4	5	6–10	Laps	Laps Led	Races Led	Miles	$
1949	Pepper Cunningham	1	0	0	0	0	0	0	0	134	0	0	134	0
1950	Pepper Cunningham	2	0	0	0	0	0	0	2	130	0	0	130	300
1951	Pepper Cunningham	4	0	0	0	0	0	0	0		0	0		75
1953	Pepper Cunningham	1	0	0	0	0	0	0	0		0	0		50
1954	Pepper Cunningham	1	0	0	0	0	0	0	0	0	0	0	0	0
1955	Pepper Cunningham	1	0	0	0	0	0	0	0	3	0	0	3	0
Lifetime		10	0	0	0	0	0	0	2	267	0	0	267	$425

Mike Curb

Year	Driver	Starts	Poles	1	2	3	4	5	6–10	Laps	Laps Led	Races Led	Miles	$
1984	Richard Petty	30	0	2	0	0	2	1	8	8,835	275	8	9,917	232,520
1985	Tom Sneva	1	0	0	0	0	0	0	0	138	0	0	210	1,455
1985	Richard Petty	28	0	0	0	1	0	0	12	7,767	105	7	8,863	268,585
1986	Ron Bouchard	17	0	0	0	0	0	0	2	3,654	1	1	5,093	106,825

Year	Driver	Starts	Poles	Finish 1	2	3	4	5	6–10	Laps	Laps Led	Races Led	Miles	$

Mike Curb continued

Year	Driver	Starts	Poles	1	2	3	4	5	6–10	Laps	Laps Led	Races Led	Miles	$
1986	Dale Jarrett	1	0	0	0	0	0	0	0	69	0	0	37	990
1987	Ed Pimm	3	0	0	0	0	0	0	0	243	1	1	595	6,810
1988	Ed Pimm	2	0	0	0	0	0	0	0	502	0	0	794	13,350
1988	Brad Noffsinger	17	0	0	0	0	0	0	0	3,555	1	1	5,518	50,645
Lifetime		99	0	2	0	1	2	1	22	24,763	383	18	31,026	$681,180

Dick Curry

Year	Driver	Starts	Poles	1	2	3	4	5	6–10	Laps	Laps Led	Races Led	Miles	$
1953	Dick Allwine	1	0	0	0	0	0	0	0	198	0	0	272	105
Lifetime		1	0	0	0	0	0	0	0	198	0	0	272	$105

Jim Cushman

Year	Driver	Starts	Poles	1	2	3	4	5	6–10	Laps	Laps Led	Races Led	Miles	$
1956	Nolan Swift	2	0	0	0	0	0	0	1	174	0	0	156	175
1956	Jim Cushman	1	0	0	0	0	0	0	0		0	0		50
Lifetime		3	0	0	0	0	0	0	1	174	0	0	156	$225

Clyde Dagit

Year	Driver	Starts	Poles	1	2	3	4	5	6–10	Laps	Laps Led	Races Led	Miles	$
1974	Clyde Dagit	1	0	0	0	0	0	0	0	183	0	0	366	1,020
1975	Clyde Dagit	1	0	0	0	0	0	0	0	418	0	0	425	1,400
Lifetime		2	0	0	0	0	0	0	0	601	0	0	791	$2,420

Dean Dalton

Year	Driver	Starts	Poles	1	2	3	4	5	6–10	Laps	Laps Led	Races Led	Miles	$
1971	Dean Dalton	19	0	0	0	0	0	0	1	3,487	0	0	4,311	13,690
1971	Bill Dennis	1	0	0	0	0	0	0	0	434	0	0	228	675
1971	Ed Negre	1	0	0	0	0	0	0	0	106	0	0	56	435
1972	Dean Dalton	29	0	0	0	0	0	0	4	7,533	0	0	9,068	34,716
1973	Dean Dalton	23	0	0	0	0	0	0	2	4,942	0	0	6,238	30,830
1974	Dean Dalton	12	0	0	0	0	0	0	0	2,073	6	1	2,102	11,575
1974	Henley Gray	1	0	0	0	0	0	0	0	332	0	0	198	550
1974	Jackie Rogers	1	0	0	0	0	0	0	0	9	0	0	5	515
1975	Walter Ballard	1	0	0	0	0	0	0	0	187	0	0	468	1,425
1975	Ed Negre	2	0	0	0	0	0	0	0	528	0	0	408	2,030
1975	Dean Dalton	14	0	0	0	0	0	0	3	3,777	0	0	4,178	17,960
1976	Jack Donohue	3	0	0	0	0	0	0	0	888	0	0	896	2,680
1976	Frank Warren	1	0	0	0	0	0	0	0	320	0	0	168	1,700
1976	Ed Negre	1	0	0	0	0	0	0	0	16	0	0	40	825
1976	Dean Dalton	6	0	0	0	0	0	0	0	1,433	0	0	1,853	7,245
1976	Cecil Gordon	1	0	0	0	0	0	0	0	385	0	0	229	565
1976	D.K. Ulrich	1	0	0	0	0	0	0	0	378	0	0	567	2,965
1977	Dean Dalton	5	0	0	0	0	0	0	0	417	0	0	488	2,685
Lifetime		122	0	0	0	0	0	0	10	27,245	6	1	31,502	$133,066

Carl Dane

Year	Driver	Starts	Poles	1	2	3	4	5	6–10	Laps	Laps Led	Races Led	Miles	$
1954	George Seeger	1	0	0	0	0	0	1	0	486	0	0	243	350
1956	Chuck Stevenson	1	0	1	0	0	0	0	0	80	54	1	200	1,570
1959	Danny Weinberg	1	0	0	0	1	0	0	0	100	0	0	100	425
1960	Danny Weinberg	3	0	0	0	0	0	1	0	216	0	0	231	525
1963	Danny Weinberg	1	0	0	0	0	0	0	0	27	0	0	73	300
1963	Joe Ruttman	1	0	0	0	0	0	0	1	176	0	0	475	850
1967	Marvin Porter	1	0	0	0	0	0	0	0	15	0	0	41	500
Lifetime		9	0	1	0	1	0	2	1	1,100	54	1	1,362	$4,520

Jim Dane

Year	Driver	Starts	Poles	1	2	3	4	5	6–10	Laps	Laps Led	Races Led	Miles	$
1954	Lloyd Dane	1	0	0	1	0	0	0	0	495	180	1	248	800
1955	Bill West	2	0	0	0	1	0	0	1	350	0	0	350	910
1956	Bill West	1	0	0	0	0	0	0	0	76	0	0	190	110
Lifetime		4	0	0	1	1	0	0	1	921	180	1	788	$1,820

Lloyd Dane

Year	Driver	Starts	Poles	1	2	3	4	5	6–10	Laps	Laps Led	Races Led	Miles	$
1951	Lloyd Dane	7	0	0	0	1	1	0	1	447	0	0	421	1,000
1954	Lloyd Dane	3	0	0	0	0	0	2	1	773	0	0	509	800
1955	Lloyd Dane	3	0	0	0	1	0	0	0	303	5	1	204	505

Year	Driver	Starts	Poles	Finish 1	2	3	4	5	6–10	Laps	Laps Led	Races Led	Miles	$

Lloyd Dane continued

Year	Driver	Starts	Poles	1	2	3	4	5	6–10	Laps	Laps Led	Races Led	Miles	$
1956	Lloyd Dane	10	0	2	0	1	2	0	4	1,706	91	2	1,257	4,370
1957	Lloyd Dane	10	1	1	5	1	0	0	3	1,296	1	1	863	4,985
1958	Lloyd Dane	4	0	0	0	0	0	0	1	894	0	0	698	640
1959	Lloyd Dane	2	0	0	1	0	0	0	1	578	0	0	286	1,100
1960	Lloyd Dane	3	0	0	0	1	0	1	0	323	89	1	375	950
1961	Lloyd Dane	4	0	1	0	0	0	0	1	396	1	1	443	1,390
1963	Lloyd Dane	1	0	0	0	0	0	0	0	8	0	0	22	300
Lifetime		47	1	4	6	5	3	3	12	6,724	187	6	5,077	$16,040

Tom Daniels

Year	Driver	Starts	Poles	1	2	3	4	5	6–10	Laps	Laps Led	Races Led	Miles	$
1960	Possum Jones	12	0	0	3	1	0	0	1	2,303	0	0	1,691	6,055
1960	Tommy Irwin	1	0	0	0	0	0	0	0	300	0	0	450	260
1961	Tommy Irwin	22	0	0	1	0	1	0	5	2,988	0	0	2,452	5,925
Lifetime		35	0	0	4	1	1	0	6	5,591	0	0	4,593	$12,240

J.C. Danielson

Year	Driver	Starts	Poles	1	2	3	4	5	6–10	Laps	Laps Led	Races Led	Miles	$
1972	J.C. Danielson	1	0	0	0	0	0	0	0	184	0	0	460	2,120
Lifetime		1	0	0	0	0	0	0	0	184	0	0	460	$2,120

B.J. Dantone

Year	Driver	Starts	Poles	1	2	3	4	5	6–10	Laps	Laps Led	Races Led	Miles	$
1951	Red Byron	4	0	0	0	0	1	0	1	609	0	0	701	925
1951	Jack Smith	1	0	0	0	0	0	0	0	123	0	0	123	0
1951	Bill Miller	4	0	0	0	0	0	0	2		0	0		275
1952	Bill Miller	4	0	0	0	0	0	0	0	547	0	0	562	125
Lifetime		13	0	0	0	0	1	0	3	1,279	0	0	1,386	$1,325

Bay Darnell

Year	Driver	Starts	Poles	1	2	3	4	5	6–10	Laps	Laps Led	Races Led	Miles	$
1983	Tom Sneva	2	0	0	0	0	0	0	1	274	0	0	648	29,740
Lifetime		2	0	0	0	0	0	0	1	274	0	0	648	$29,740

Mason Darnell

Year	Driver	Starts	Poles	1	2	3	4	5	6–10	Laps	Laps Led	Races Led	Miles	$
1953	Keith Hamner	2	0	0	0	0	0	0	1	33	0	0	135	75
Lifetime		2	0	0	0	0	0	0	1	33	0	0	135	$75

Gene Darragh

Year	Driver	Starts	Poles	1	2	3	4	5	6–10	Laps	Laps Led	Races Led	Miles	$
1952	Gene Darragh	3	0	0	0	0	0	0	0	237	0	0	228	60
1953	Gene Darragh	1	0	0	0	0	0	0	0		0	0		0
Lifetime		4	0	0	0	0	0	0	0	237	0	0	228	$60

Anthony Davella

Year	Driver	Starts	Poles	1	2	3	4	5	6–10	Laps	Laps Led	Races Led	Miles	$
1949	Johnny Rogers	1	0	0	0	0	0	0	0		0	0		0
Lifetime		1	0	0	0	0	0	0	0		0	0		$0

Bill Davis

Year	Driver	Starts	Poles	1	2	3	4	5	6–10	Laps	Laps Led	Races Led	Miles	$
1993	Bobby Labonte	30	1	0	0	0	0	0	6	9,295	33	7	10,938	353,575
1994	Bobby Labonte	31	0	0	0	0	0	1	1	8,541	3	2	10,456	512,005
1995	Wally Dallenbach	1	0	0	1	0	0	0	0	90	21	1	221	54,140
1995	Ward Burton	9	0	1	0	0	1	1	1	3,173	130	3	3,202	274,525
1995	Randy LaJoie	13	0	0	0	0	0	0	0	3,510	0	0	4,235	265,770
1995	Jimmy Hensley	5	0	0	0	0	0	0	0	741	0	0	1,705	129,595
1996	Ward Burton	27	1	0	0	0	0	0	4	6,544	54	4	8,845	840,119
1997	Ward Burton	31	1	0	0	0	0	0	7	8,976	140	4	11,109	924,155
1998	Ward Burton	33	2	0	1	0	0	0	4	9,551	132	9	12,509	1,367,012
1999	Dave Blaney	5	0	0	0	0	0	0	0	996	0	0	1,676	212,170
1999	Ward Burton	34	1	0	3	0	2	1	10	9,828	243	13	12,608	2,062,824
2000	Ward Burton	34	0	1	0	3	0	0	13	9,097	506	10	12,290	2,299,795
2000	Dave Blaney	33	0	0	0	0	0	0	2	8,329	4	1	11,571	1,238,275
2000	Scott Wimmer	1	0	0	0	0	0	0	0	322	9	1	496	37,780
2001	Dave Blaney	35	0	0	0	0	0	0	6	9,872	71	2	12,821	1,683,729
2001	Hut Stricklin	1	0	0	0	0	0	0	0	325	0	0	501	54,950

Year	Driver	Starts	Poles	Finish 1	2	3	4	5	6–10	Laps	Laps Led	Races Led	Miles	$

Bill Davis *continued*

Year	Driver	Starts	Poles	1	2	3	4	5	6–10	Laps	Laps Led	Races Led	Miles	$
2001	Ward Burton	36	0	1	0	2	1	2	4	10,158	178	7	13,166	3,168,234
2002	Ward Burton	35	1	2	0	0	0	1	5	8,673	371	11	11,358	4,595,379
2002	Geoffrey Bodine	1	0	0	0	0	0	0	0	497	5	1	261	35,615
2002	Hut Stricklin	22	0	0	0	0	0	0	0	5,936	5	2	8,027	1,255,910
2002	Kenny Wallace	10	0	0	0	0	0	0	0	3,175	3	1	3,792	454,320
2002	Scott Wimmer	3	0	0	0	0	0	0	0	482	0	0	717	143,110
2002	Tom Hubert	1	0	0	0	0	0	0	0	90	0	0	221	41,925
Lifetime		431	7	5	5	5	4	6	63	118,201	1,908	79	152,722	$22,004,912

Bob Davis

Year	Driver	Starts	Poles	1	2	3	4	5	6–10	Laps	Laps Led	Races Led	Miles	$
1970	Bobby Mausgrover	3	0	0	0	0	0	0	0	103	0	0	179	2,710
1970	Raymond Williams	1	0	0	0	0	0	0	0	14	0	0	14	460
1971	Freddy Fryar	2	0	0	0	0	0	0	0	238	0	0	595	2,010
1971	Ed Negre	1	0	0	0	0	0	0	0	354	0	0	531	1,525
1971	Bobby Mausgrover	1	0	0	0	0	0	0	0	39	0	0	98	0
Lifetime		8	0	0	0	0	0	0	0	748	0	0	1,416	$6,705

Buster Davis

Year	Driver	Starts	Poles	1	2	3	4	5	6–10	Laps	Laps Led	Races Led	Miles	$
1972	Dick May	1	0	0	0	0	0	0	0	178	0	0	356	790
1973	Frank Warren	1	0	0	0	0	0	0	0	78	0	0	107	680
1973	Tony Bettenhausen,	1	0	0	0	0	0	0	0	9	0	0	14	900
1973	Johnny Benson Sr.	1	0	0	0	0	0	0	0	185	0	0	370	850
1973	Bob Davis	1	0	0	0	0	0	0	0	93	0	0	247	1,140
1974	Johnny Ray	2	0	0	0	0	0	0	0	252	0	0	670	2,435
Lifetime		7	0	0	0	0	0	0	0	795	0	0	1,764	$6,795

George Davis

Year	Driver	Starts	Poles	1	2	3	4	5	6–10	Laps	Laps Led	Races Led	Miles	$
1967	George Davis	21	0	0	0	0	0	1	5	3,342	0	0	1,866	4,360
1967	Bobby Allison	1	0	0	0	0	1	0	0	290	0	0	145	575
1968	George Davis	6	0	0	0	0	0	0	1	576	0	0	362	1,915
Lifetime		28	0	0	0	0	1	1	6	4,208	0	0	2,373	$6,850

Gus Davis

Year	Driver	Starts	Poles	1	2	3	4	5	6–10	Laps	Laps Led	Races Led	Miles	$
1954	Allen Adkins	2	0	0	0	1	1	0	0	545	0	0	397	1,150
1955	Allen Adkins	3	0	0	1	0	0	1	0	368	79	1	269	1,000
1956	Allen Adkins	2	0	0	0	0	0	1	0	215	0	0	332	495
Lifetime		7	0	0	1	1	1	2	0	1,128	79	1	998	$2,645

Jeff Davis

Year	Driver	Starts	Poles	1	2	3	4	5	6–10	Laps	Laps Led	Races Led	Miles	$
1992	Jeff Davis	1	0	0	0	0	0	0	0	299	0	0	299	4,785
1993	Jeff Davis	1	0	0	0	0	0	0	0	46	0	0	116	6,560
Lifetime		2	0	0	0	0	0	0	0	345	0	0	415	$11,345

Jim Davis

Year	Driver	Starts	Poles	1	2	3	4	5	6–10	Laps	Laps Led	Races Led	Miles	$
1950	Fireball Roberts	1	0	0	0	0	0	0	0	8	0	0	33	25
Lifetime		1	0	0	0	0	0	0	0	8	0	0	33	$25

Joel Davis

Year	Driver	Starts	Poles	1	2	3	4	5	6–10	Laps	Laps Led	Races Led	Miles	$
1963	Joel Davis	3	0	0	0	0	0	0	0	280	0	0	140	245
1963	Curtis Crider	1	0	0	0	0	0	0	0	90	0	0	45	75
Lifetime		4	0	0	0	0	0	0	0	370	0	0	185	$320

Keith Davis

Year	Driver	Starts	Poles	1	2	3	4	5	6–10	Laps	Laps Led	Races Led	Miles	$
1979	Keith Davis	2	0	0	0	0	0	0	0	45	0	0	103	2,310
Lifetime		2	0	0	0	0	0	0	0	45	0	0	103	$2,310

Morris Davis

Year	Driver	Starts	Poles	1	2	3	4	5	6–10	Laps	Laps Led	Races Led	Miles	$
1970	Gary DuPuis	1	0	0	0	0	0	0	0	78	0	0	195	735
1970	Butch Hirst	4	0	0	0	0	0	0	0	439	0	0	1,062	3,915

Year	Driver	Starts	Poles	Finish 1	2	3	4	5	6–10	Laps	Laps Led	Races Led	Miles	$

Morris Davis *continued*

Year	Driver	Starts	Poles	1	2	3	4	5	6–10	Laps	Laps Led	Races Led	Miles	$
1970	Rod Eulenfeld	1	0	0	0	0	0	0	0	80	0	0	44	390
1974	Dan Daughtry	8	0	0	0	0	0	0	1	772	6	2	1,321	12,413
1975	Dan Daughtry	2	0	0	0	0	0	0	0	9	0	0	23	2,530
1975	Darel Dieringer	3	0	0	0	0	0	0	2	550	2	1	1,069	7,515
1977	Jim Hurtubise	1	0	0	0	0	0	0	0	0	0	0	0	535
Lifetime		20	0	0	0	0	0	0	3	1,928	8	3	3,714	$28,033

Ralph Davis

Year	Driver	Starts	Poles	1	2	3	4	5	6–10	Laps	Laps Led	Races Led	Miles	$
1971	Dick May	3	0	0	0	0	0	0	0	441	0	0	857	2,495
Lifetime		3	0	0	0	0	0	0	0	441	0	0	857	$2,495

Hanley Dawson

Year	Driver	Starts	Poles	1	2	3	4	5	6–10	Laps	Laps Led	Races Led	Miles	$
1960	Johnny Allen	10	0	0	1	0	0	1	3	1,820	0	0	2,501	14,035
Lifetime		10	0	0	1	0	0	1	3	1,820	0	0	2,501	$14,035

Russ Dawson

Year	Driver	Starts	Poles	1	2	3	4	5	6–10	Laps	Laps Led	Races Led	Miles	$
1969	Benny Parsons	4	0	0	0	1	0	1	1	568	0	0	1,259	7,650
Lifetime		4	0	0	0	1	0	1	1	568	0	0	1,259	$7,650

Charles Dean

Year	Driver	Starts	Poles	1	2	3	4	5	6–10	Laps	Laps Led	Races Led	Miles	$
1977	Peter Knab	3	0	0	0	0	0	0	0	507	0	0	1,017	6,865
1977	Lella Lombardi	1	0	0	0	0	0	0	0	103	0	0	258	785
1978	Jerry Jolly	3	0	0	0	0	0	0	0	307	0	0	652	5,740
1978	Bill Green	1	0	0	0	0	0	0	0	0	0	0	0	400
1979	Bill Green	1	0	0	0	0	0	0	0	76	2	1	152	980
1979	Glenn Jarrett	1	0	0	0	0	0	0	0	166	0	0	249	1,630
Lifetime		10	0	0	0	0	0	0	0	1,159	2	1	2,327	$16,400

Donald Dean

Year	Driver	Starts	Poles	1	2	3	4	5	6–10	Laps	Laps Led	Races Led	Miles	$
1977	Harry Goularte	1	0	0	0	0	0	0	0	81	0	0	212	900
Lifetime		1	0	0	0	0	0	0	0	81	0	0	212	$900

Larry DeBeau

Year	Driver	Starts	Poles	1	2	3	4	5	6–10	Laps	Laps Led	Races Led	Miles	$
1966	Cy Fairchild	1	0	0	0	0	0	0	0	18	0	0	45	0
1966	Tiny Lund	1	0	0	0	0	0	0	0	267	0	0	267	725
Lifetime		2	0	0	0	0	0	0	0	285	0	0	312	$725

J.R. DeLotto

Year	Driver	Starts	Poles	1	2	3	4	5	6–10	Laps	Laps Led	Races Led	Miles	$
1976	D.K. Ulrich	28	0	0	0	0	0	0	2	7,943	0	0	8,919	54,010
1977	D.K. Ulrich	30	0	0	0	0	0	0	0	6,735	0	0	7,649	59,790
Lifetime		58	0	0	0	0	0	0	2	14,678	0	113,800	16,568	

J.A. Delvecchio

Year	Driver	Starts	Poles	1	2	3	4	5	6–10	Laps	Laps Led	Races Led	Miles	$
1973	John Soares Jr.	2	0	0	0	0	0	0	0	122	0	0	320	1,980
Lifetime		2	0	0	0	0	0	0	0	122	0	0	320	$1,980

Matthew DeMatthews

Year	Driver	Starts	Poles	1	2	3	4	5	6–10	Laps	Laps Led	Races Led	Miles	$
1960	Johnny Dollar	2	0	0	0	0	0	0	0	8	0	0	17	200
1960	Johnny Wolford	1	0	0	0	0	0	0	0	5	0	0	8	200
1961	Roy Tyner	2	0	0	0	0	0	0	0	158	0	0	245	600
1962	John Dodd Jr.	2	0	0	0	0	0	0	0	78	0	0	127	625
1962	Sammy Packard	1	0	0	0	0	0	0	0	45	0	0	23	110
1962	Woodie Wilson	2	0	0	0	0	0	0	0	31	0	0	47	525
1962	Matthew DeMatthews	1	0	0	0	0	0	0	0	2	0	0	3	400
1962	G.C. Spencer	3	0	0	0	0	0	0	0	95	0	0	187	650
1963	Bob Hurt	1	0	0	0	0	0	0	0	144	0	0	48	75
Lifetime		15	0	0	0	0	0	0	0	566	0	0	703	$3,385

Year	Driver	Starts	Poles	Finish						Laps	Laps Led	Races Led	Miles	$
				1	2	3	4	5	6–10	Laps	Led	Led	Miles	$

Bill Dennis

Year	Driver	Starts	Poles	1	2	3	4	5	6–10	Laps	Led	Led	Miles	$
1969	Bill Dennis	3	0	0	0	0	0	0	0	276	0	0	209	1,655
1969	Ben Arnold	1	0	0	0	0	0	0	0	105	0	0	107	665
1970	Ben Arnold	1	0	0	0	0	0	0	0	66	0	0	26	200
1970	Bill Dennis	21	0	0	0	0	0	0	5	3,471	0	0	2,807	12,070
1972	Bill Dennis	1	0	0	0	0	0	0	0	105	0	0	55	250
Lifetime		27	0	0	0	0	0	0	5	4,023	0	0	3,204	$14,840

Lloyd Dennis

Year	Driver	Starts	Poles	1	2	3	4	5	6–10	Laps	Led	Led	Miles	$
1951	Bob Walters	3	0	0	0	0	0	0	0		0	0		50
1951	Lloyd Dennis	1	0	0	0	0	0	0	0	39	0	0	29	10
Lifetime		4	0	0	0	0	0	0	0	39	0	0	29	$60

Peter DePaolo

Year	Driver	Starts	Poles	1	2	3	4	5	6–10	Laps	Led	Led	Miles	$
1955	Buck Baker	7	1	1	1	1	0	1	3	1,142	337	2	884	3,410
1955	Speedy Thompson	2	0	1	0	0	0	0	0	270	158	1	370	2,900
1955	Marvin Panch	4	0	0	1	0	0	0	0	535	0	0	520	1,600
1955	Chuck Stevenson	1	0	0	0	0	0	0	0	43	0	0	65	60
1955	Joe Weatherly	1	0	0	0	0	0	0	0	29	0	0	44	60
1955	Johnny Mantz	1	0	0	0	0	0	0	0	46	0	0	69	60
1956	Fonty Flock	1	0	0	0	0	0	0	1	194	0	0	78	150
1956	Jack Smith	1	0	0	0	0	0	0	0	109	0	0	55	100
1956	Joe Weatherly	2	0	0	1	0	0	0	1	594	20	1	297	1,175
1956	Junior Johnson	2	0	0	0	0	0	0	0	211	43	1	88	200
1956	Fireball Roberts	33	3	5	1	2	7	2	5	5,695	470	10	3,789	13,760
1956	Curtis Turner	2	0	0	0	0	0	0	0	320	0	0	236	200
1956	Marvin Panch	1	0	0	0	1	0	0	0	359	43	1	494	3,370
1956	Billy Carden	5	0	0	0	0	0	0	2	622	0	0	310	550
1956	Speedy Thompson	1	0	0	0	0	0	1	0	193	67	1	97	310
1956	Bill Amick	13	0	0	1	3	1	2	3	2,446	9	1	1,631	5,135
1956	Bob Flock	1	0	0	0	0	0	0	0	52	0	0	52	50
1956	Ralph Moody	35	5	4	5	2	1	1	8	5,258	312	6	3,506	14,695
1956	Ralph Earnhardt	1	1	0	1	0	0	0	0	250	15	1	100	625
1957	Joe Weatherly	4	0	0	0	0	0	0	1	248	0	0	143	525
1957	Allen Adkins	1	0	0	0	0	0	0	1	158	0	0	99	250
1957	Bill Amick	3	0	0	0	1	0	0	0	199	0	0	100	480
1957	Curtis Turner	5	1	0	2	0	0	0	1	617	2	1	370	3,045
1957	Jim Reed	1	0	0	0	0	0	0	0		0	0		0
1957	Marvin Panch	18	4	3	1	3	3	1	1	2,496	295	7	1,539	7,375
1957	Paul Goldsmith	5	0	1	1	0	0	0	1	673	95	2	357	1,775
1957	Ralph Earnhardt	1	0	0	0	0	0	0	0	164	0	0	82	100
1957	Fireball Roberts	17	3	5	4	0	1	1	2	2,795	744	10	1,649	8,905
1957	Ralph Moody	9	0	1	0	2	2	0	0	1,014	100	1	548	2,830
Lifetime		178	18	21	19	15	15	9	30	26,732	2,710	46	17,567	$73,695

Ernie Derr

Year	Driver	Starts	Poles	1	2	3	4	5	6–10	Laps	Led	Led	Miles	$
1953	Ernie Derr	1	0	0	0	0	0	0	0		0	0		25
Lifetime		1	0	0	0	0	0	0	0		0	0		$25

Bob Derrington

Year	Driver	Starts	Poles	1	2	3	4	5	6–10	Laps	Led	Led	Miles	$
1964	Bob Derrington	1	0	0	0	0	0	0	0	8	0	0	4	120
1965	Bob Derrington	51	0	0	0	1	0	2	16	10,374	0	0	6,777	14,580
1966	Bob Derrington	6	0	0	0	0	0	0	0	864	0	0	1,057	2,215
1966	Bunk Moore	1	0	0	0	0	0	0	0	101	0	0	51	100
1966	Larry Manning	1	0	0	0	0	0	0	0	322	0	0	483	1,370
Lifetime		60	0	0	0	1	0	2	16	11,669	0	0	8,372	$18,385

B.R. DeWitt

Year	Driver	Starts	Poles	1	2	3	4	5	6–10	Laps	Led	Led	Miles	$
1992	Bobby Hillin	1	0	0	0	0	0	0	0	51	0	0	125	4,420
Lifetime		1	0	0	0	0	0	0	0	51	0	0	125	$4,420

L.G. DeWitt

Year	Driver	Starts	Poles	1	2	3	4	5	6–10	Laps	Led	Led	Miles	$
1965	John Sears	2	0	0	0	0	0	0	1	281	0	0	94	650

Year	Driver	Starts	Poles	Finish						Laps	Laps Led	Races Led	Miles	$
				1	2	3	4	5	6–10					

L.G. DeWitt *continued*

Year	Driver	Starts	Poles	1	2	3	4	5	6–10	Laps	Laps Led	Races Led	Miles	$
1966	John Sears	46	0	0	1	1	4	5	19	9,981	109	2	6,845	19,965
1967	Elmo Langley	2	0	0	0	1	0	1	0	491	0	0	246	975
1967	John Sears	41	1	0	1	3	3	2	16	10,031	59	4	7,468	21,305
1967	James Sears	1	0	0	0	0	0	0	0	72	0	0	72	505
1967	Henley Gray	1	0	0	0	0	0	0	0	266	0	0	399	1,175
1968	John Sears	49	0	0	0	1	1	3	19	11,077	0	0	7,827	20,960
1969	Jim Hurtubise	1	0	0	0	0	0	0	0	63	0	0	168	1,125
1969	John Sears	51	0	0	1	3	7	6	10	11,617	18	3	8,837	34,417
1969	LeeRoy Yarbrough	1	0	0	0	0	0	1	0	196	2	1	196	675
1970	James Sears	1	0	0	0	0	0	0	1	448	0	0	456	1,390
1970	Benny Parsons	43	1	0	1	2	4	5	10	8,929	164	6	8,137	50,300
1970	John Sears	1	0	0	0	0	0	0	0	40	0	0	20	200
1970	Buddy Young	2	0	0	0	0	0	0	1	501	0	0	569	1,980
1971	Benny Parsons	35	0	1	2	5	1	4	5	7,981	144	4	7,640	48,495
1971	Ray Hendrick	1	0	0	0	0	0	0	0	295	0	0	300	665
1972	Benny Parsons	31	0	0	1	0	8	1	9	7,922	19	2	9,463	75,318
1973	Benny Parsons	28	0	1	3	3	3	5	6	9,311	374	8	10,061	91,845
1974	Jan Opperman	1	0	0	0	0	0	0	1	188	0	0	470	1,850
1974	Benny Parsons	30	0	0	2	2	5	2	3	8,120	88	11	8,866	159,510
1975	Benny Parsons	30	3	1	3	3	3	1	6	8,528	496	16	8,785	178,800
1976	Benny Parsons	30	2	2	2	7	2	5	5	8,679	455	15	10,404	223,089
1976	Earl Ross	1	0	0	0	0	0	0	0	28	0	0	70	2,025
1976	David Hobbs	1	0	0	0	0	0	0	0	68	2	1	170	1,900
1977	Benny Parsons	30	3	4	3	10	0	3	2	9,410	1,398	25	10,756	314,550
1978	Benny Parsons	30	2	3	3	6	2	1	6	9,709	824	21	10,895	291,390
1979	Joe Millikan	31	1	0	1	1	0	3	15	9,122	188	8	10,510	199,460
1980	Joe Millikan	9	0	0	0	0	1	1	3	2,172	4	2	1,894	59,240
Lifetime		530	13	12	24	48	44	49	138	135,526	4,344	129	131,617	$1,803,759

Ray & Dianne DeWitt (Statistics represent teams with primary ownership of DeWitt, plus a shared ownership with D.K. Ulrich.)

Year	Driver	Starts	Poles	1	2	3	4	5	6–10	Laps	Laps Led	Races Led	Miles	$
1992	Ted Musgrave	29	0	0	0	0	0	1	6	9,253	11	3	10,989	407,610
1993	Ted Musgrave	29	0	0	0	0	0	2	3	8,530	8	3	10,397	424,315
1994	Tim Fedewa	1	0	0	0	0	0	0	0	487	0	0	487	8,565
1994	Butch Miller	2	0	0	0	0	0	0	0	842	0	0	982	17,335
1994	Jimmy Hensley	15	0	0	0	0	0	0	0	3,460	2	2	5,142	184,460
1995	Ben Hess	1	0	0	0	0	0	0	0	196	0	0	490	35,785
Lifetime		77	0	0	0	0	0	3	9	22,768	21	8	28,488	$1,078,070

Clarence DeZalia

Year	Driver	Starts	Poles	1	2	3	4	5	6–10	Laps	Laps Led	Races Led	Miles	$
1955	Woody Arrington	1	0	0	0	0	0	0	0	4	0	0	4	0
1955	Clarence DeZalia	5	0	0	0	0	0	0	0	691	0	0	610	200
1955	Ed Cole	7	0	0	0	0	0	0	0	850	0	0	408	335
1956	Ed Cole	5	0	0	0	0	0	0	0	594	0	0	363	250
1957	Clarence DeZalia	25	0	0	0	0	0	0	6	4,059	0	0	2,119	2,945
1958	Clarence DeZalia	27	0	0	0	0	0	0	6	4,073	0	0	2,412	2,540
1959	Clarence DeZalia	1	0	0	0	0	0	0	0	136	0	0	45	60
Lifetime		71	0	0	0	0	0	0	12	10,407	0	0	5,961	$6,330

George DiBidart

Year	Driver	Starts	Poles	1	2	3	4	5	6–10	Laps	Laps Led	Races Led	Miles	$
2002	Kenny Wallace	2	0	0	0	0	0	0	0	240	1	1	596	131,775
Lifetime		2	0	0	0	0	0	0	0	240	1	1	596	$131,775

William Dickenson

Year	Driver	Starts	Poles	1	2	3	4	5	6–10	Laps	Laps Led	Races Led	Miles	$
1958	Dean Layfield	7	0	0	0	0	0	0	0	522	0	0	433	370
Lifetime		7	0	0	0	0	0	0	0	522	0	0	433	$370

R L Diestler

Year	Driver	Starts	Poles	1	2	3	4	5	6–10	Laps	Laps Led	Races Led	Miles	$
1967	Gordon Johncock	4	0	0	0	0	0	0	0	160	0	0	391	2,350
1967	John Martin	1	0	0	0	0	0	0	0	44	0	0	66	500
Lifetime		5	0	0	0	0	0	0	0	204	0	0	457	$2,850

Year	Driver	Starts	Poles	Finish 1	2	3	4	5	6–10	Laps	Laps Led	Races Led	Miles	$

DiGard (Principal owner was Bill Gardner. Statistics represent the entire tenure of the DiGard Racing Team, including R&D cars, and shared ownership with Mike DiProspero and Jim Gardner.)

Year	Driver	Starts	Poles	1	2	3	4	5	6–10	Laps	Laps Led	Races Led	Miles	$
1973	Donnie Allison	14	0	0	1	1	0	0	3	2,904	44	3	3,697	31,246
1974	Donnie Allison	21	2	0	1	1	2	2	4	5,101	182	10	5,761	54,825
1975	Darrell Waltrip	11	0	1	0	2	0	0	1	2,760	271	5	2,355	43,630
1975	Donnie Allison	10	2	0	0	1	0	1	2	1,935	9	3	2,652	35,495
1975	Johnny Rutherford	1	0	0	0	0	0	0	0	51	0	0	128	2,075
1976	Darrell Waltrip	30	3	1	3	4	1	1	2	7,780	534	10	8,089	186,210
1977	Darrell Waltrip	30	3	6	4	3	1	2	8	9,301	949	23	10,590	286,615
1978	Darrell Waltrip	30	2	6	6	4	1	2	1	9,445	2,151	26	10,542	360,013
1979	Darrell Waltrip	30	5	7	4	5	1	2	2	9,794	2,066	25	11,269	448,155
1980	Don Whittington	1	0	0	0	0	0	0	1	117	0	0	307	2,300
1980	Darrell Waltrip	30	5	5	3	2	5	0	1	8,815	1,956	27	9,364	345,015
1981	Ricky Rudd	31	3	0	3	4	3	4	3	8,942	441	12	9,879	352,980
1982	Bobby Allison	30	1	8	2	1	2	1	6	9,184	2,423	24	10,861	574,545
1983	Jimmy Insolo	1	0	0	0	0	0	0	0	1	0	0	3	840
1983	Bobby Allison	30	0	6	5	6	1	0	7	10,038	1,755	25	11,527	608,700
1984	Bobby Allison	30	0	2	1	2	4	4	6	9,051	1,160	23	10,545	589,125
1985	Greg Sacks	14	0	1	0	0	0	0	2	3,501	34	2	4,203	155,350
1985	Bobby Allison	15	0	0	0	3	2	1	3	4,503	371	10	5,546	202,690
1985	Dick Trickle	1	0	0	0	0	0	0	1	199	0	0	398	5,850
1985	Ken Ragan	1	0	0	0	0	0	0	0	224	0	0	336	1,475
1986	Greg Sacks	8	0	0	0	0	0	0	1	1,181	0	0	1,743	54,810
1986	Willy T. Ribbs	3	0	0	0	0	0	0	0	516	0	0	540	3,520
1986	Trevor Boys	1	0	0	0	0	0	0	0	111	0	0	113	1,175
1986	Jeff Swindell	1	0	0	0	0	0	0	0	227	0	0	345	1,160
1987	Rodney Combs	3	0	0	0	0	0	0	0	621	0	0	786	19,065
Lifetime		377	26	43	33	39	23	20	54	106,302	14,346	228	121,577	$4,366,864

Alan Dillard

Year	Driver	Starts	Poles	1	2	3	4	5	6–10	Laps	Laps Led	Races Led	Miles	$
1994	Ward Burton	26	1	0	1	0	0	0	1	5,320	73	5	6,303	271,250
1995	Gary Bradberry	2	0	0	0	0	0	0	0	572	0	0	742	19,280
1995	Ward Burton	20	0	0	0	0	0	0	2	4,572	43	1	6,690	334,330
1995	Jimmy Hensley	2	0	0	0	0	0	0	0	501	0	0	407	13,780
1995	Greg Sacks	3	0	0	0	0	0	0	0	874	0	0	727	34,640
Lifetime		53	1	0	1	0	0	0	3	11,839	116	6	14,869	$673,280

C.H. Dingler

Year	Driver	Starts	Poles	1	2	3	4	5	6–10	Laps	Laps Led	Races Led	Miles	$
1951	C.H. Dingler	3	0	0	0	0	0	0	0		0	0		100
1952	C.H. Dingler	1	0	0	0	0	0	0	0	160	0	0	80	35
1953	C.H. Dingler	5	0	0	0	0	0	0	3	119	0	0	60	275
1954	C.H. Dingler	3	0	0	0	0	0	0	1	383	0	0	348	175
1955	C.H. Dingler	1	0	0	0	0	0	0	0	8	0	0	4	0
1956	C.H. Dingler	3	0	0	0	0	0	0	0	181	0	0	239	200
Lifetime		16	0	0	0	0	0	0	4	851	0	0	730	$785

Dingman Brothers

Year	Driver	Starts	Poles	1	2	3	4	5	6–10	Laps	Laps Led	Races Led	Miles	$
1986	Al Unser	1	0	0	0	0	0	0	0	110	0	0	288	2,360
1986	Tommy Riggins	1	0	0	0	0	0	0	0	89	0	0	218	3,525
1987	Greg Sacks	16	0	0	0	0	0	0	0	2,705	1	1	4,254	44,815
1988	Greg Sacks	8	0	0	0	0	0	0	2	1,194	0	0	2,420	44,500
1989	Mickey Gibbs	2	0	0	0	0	0	0	0	505	0	0	969	6,535
1989	Jim Sauter	1	0	0	0	0	0	0	0	5	0	0	13	2,715
Lifetime		29	0	0	0	0	0	0	2	4,608	1	1	8,161	$104,450

Harry Dinwiddle

Year	Driver	Starts	Poles	1	2	3	4	5	6–10	Laps	Laps Led	Races Led	Miles	$
1981	Lake Speed	1	0	0	0	0	0	0	0	125	0	0	75	1,360
Lifetime		1	0	0	0	0	0	0	0	125	0	0	75	$1,360

Dave Dion

Year	Driver	Starts	Poles	1	2	3	4	5	6–10	Laps	Laps Led	Races Led	Miles	$
1978	Dave Dion	4	0	0	0	0	0	0	0	335	0	0	314	2,285
1979	Dave Dion	1	0	0	0	0	0	0	0	380	0	0	206	675
1980	Dave Dion	4	0	0	0	0	0	0	1	1,075	0	0	1,171	5,015

Year	Driver	Starts	Poles	Finish 1	2	3	4	5	6–10	Laps	Laps Led	Races Led	Miles	$

Dave Dion *continued*

Year	Driver	Starts	Poles	1	2	3	4	5	6–10	Laps	Laps Led	Races Led	Miles	$
1981	Dave Dion	1	0	0	0	0	0	0	0	143	0	0	78	615
1983	Dave Dion	1	0	0	0	0	0	0	0	50	0	0	27	700
Lifetime		11	0	0	0	0	0	0	1	1,983	0	0	1,795	$9,290

Sam DiRusso

Year	Driver	Starts	Poles	1	2	3	4	5	6–10	Laps	Laps Led	Races Led	Miles	$
1953	Sam DiRusso	2	0	0	0	0	0	0	1	213	0	0	225	75
Lifetime		2	0	0	0	0	0	0	1	213	0	0	225	$75

John Ditz

Year	Driver	Starts	Poles	1	2	3	4	5	6–10	Laps	Laps Led	Races Led	Miles	$
1954	Donald Thomas	6	0	0	1	0	1	0	1	772	53	1	469	1,350
1954	Dick Rathmann	28	4	2	5	7	6	1	3	4,524	621	10	3,094	12,960
1954	Arden Mounts	1	0	0	0	0	0	0	0	40	0	0	30	25
1955	Dick Rathmann	17	3	0	2	2	3	0	1	1,985	176	5	1,158	4,020
Lifetime		52	7	2	8	9	10	1	5	7,321	850	16	4,751	$18,355

J.I. Divers

Year	Driver	Starts	Poles	1	2	3	4	5	6–10	Laps	Laps Led	Races Led	Miles	$
1961	Bill Morton	1	0	0	0	0	0	0	0	182	0	0	46	125
1961	Wes Morgan	3	0	0	0	0	0	0	1	493	0	0	573	405
1961	Harvey Henderson	1	0	0	0	0	0	0	0	153	0	0	77	75
Lifetime		5	0	0	0	0	0	0	1	828	0	0	695	$605

Robert Dixon

Year	Driver	Starts	Poles	1	2	3	4	5	6–10	Laps	Laps Led	Races Led	Miles	$
1949	Raymond Lewis	1	0	0	0	0	0	0	1	194	0	0	97	75
Lifetime		1	0	0	0	0	0	0	1	194	0	0	97	$75

Thee Dixon

Year	Driver	Starts	Poles	1	2	3	4	5	6–10	Laps	Laps Led	Races Led	Miles	$
1990	Mike Skinner	1	0	0	0	0	0	0	0	230	0	0	234	2,825
1991	Mike Skinner	2	0	0	0	0	0	0	0	350	0	0	362	7,005
1992	Mike Skinner	2	0	0	0	0	0	0	0	929	0	0	945	11,050
1992	Bob Schacht	1	0	0	0	0	0	0	0	23	0	0	35	5,225
1993	Ken Bouchard	3	0	0	0	0	0	0	0	503	0	0	849	25,785
1993	Jim Sauter	1	0	0	0	0	0	0	0	265	0	0	398	4,380
Lifetime		10	0	0	0	0	0	0	0	2,300	0	0	2,822	$56,270

John Dodd Sr.

Year	Driver	Starts	Poles	1	2	3	4	5	6–10	Laps	Laps Led	Races Led	Miles	$
1954	John Dodd Jr.	1	0	0	0	0	0	0	1	161	0	0	81	150
1954	John Dodd Sr.	1	0	0	0	0	0	0	1	240	0	0	240	300
1955	John Dodd Sr.	2	0	0	0	0	0	0	0	292	0	0	160	100
1955	Elmo Langley	1	0	0	0	0	0	0	0	174	0	0	87	50
1955	John Dodd Jr.	13	0	0	0	0	0	1	6	1,653	0	0	915	1,695
1956	John Dodd Jr.	4	0	0	0	0	0	0	1	372	0	0	180	100
1956	John Dodd Sr.	1	0	0	0	0	0	0	0	28	0	0	14	0
1957	John Dodd Jr.	1	0	0	0	0	0	0	0	67	0	0	34	25
1957	John Dodd Sr.	1	0	0	0	0	0	0	1	189	0	0	95	140
1958	John Dodd Sr.	1	0	0	0	0	0	0	0	290	0	0	290	150
1959	Ralph Moody	1	0	0	0	0	0	0	1	197	0	0	99	200
1959	John Dodd Sr.	3	0	0	0	0	0	0	1	704	0	0	352	540
1960	John Dodd Jr.	2	0	0	0	0	0	0	0	51	0	0	54	50
Lifetime		32	0	0	0	0	0	1	12	4,418	0	0	2,599	$3,500

Frank Dodge

Year	Driver	Starts	Poles	1	2	3	4	5	6–10	Laps	Laps Led	Races Led	Miles	$
1953	Eddie Skinner	4	0	0	0	0	0	0	1		0	0		200
1954	Bill Amick	1	0	0	1	0	0	0	0	250	0	0	250	1,500
1954	Bill Blair	1	0	0	0	0	0	0	0	93	0	0	47	0
1954	Blackie Pitt	1	0	0	0	0	0	0	0	119	0	0	60	25
1954	Eddie Skinner	16	0	0	0	0	0	0	1	2,044	0	0	1,659	800
1954	Laird Bruner	3	0	0	0	0	0	1	0	370	0	0	195	325
1955	Eddie Skinner	38	0	0	0	0	0	4	11	5,473	0	0	3,610	4,055
1956	Eddie Skinner	4	0	0	0	0	0	0	0	335	0	0	150	100
Lifetime		68	0	0	1	0	0	5	13	8,684	0	0	5,970	$7,005

Year	Driver	Starts	Poles	Finish						Laps	Laps Led	Races Led	Miles	$
				1	2	3	4	5	6–10					

Johnny Dodson

Year	Driver	Starts	Poles	1	2	3	4	5	6–10	Laps	Laps Led	Races Led	Miles	$
1956	Johnny Dodson	11	0	0	0	0	0	0	4	1,842	0	0	1,379	1,450
1957	Johnny Dodson	2	0	0	0	0	0	0	1	141	0	0	71	240
Lifetime		13	0	0	0	0	0	0	5	1,983	0	0	1,450	$1,690

Jack Doering

Year	Driver	Starts	Poles	1	2	3	4	5	6–10	Laps	Laps Led	Races Led	Miles	$
1974	Dick Trickle	1	0	0	0	0	0	0	1	389	0	0	584	3,825
Lifetime		1	0	0	0	0	0	0	1	389	0	0	584	$3,825

Junie Donlavey

Year	Driver	Starts	Poles	1	2	3	4	5	6–10	Laps	Laps Led	Races Led	Miles	$
1952	Joe Weatherly	1	0	0	0	0	0	0	0	376	0	0	470	150
1957	Emanuel Zervakis	3	0	0	0	0	0	0	0	892	0	0	669	525
1957	Runt Harris	1	0	0	0	0	0	0	0	50	0	0	69	100
1958	Buzz Woodward	1	0	0	0	0	0	0	0	72	0	0	36	60
1958	Emanuel Zervakis	6	0	0	0	0	0	0	0	457	0	0	378	465
1959	Runt Harris	1	0	0	0	0	0	1	0	193	0	0	97	250
1960	Runt Harris	3	0	0	0	0	0	0	0	391	0	0	233	350
1960	Speedy Thompson	3	0	0	0	0	0	0	0	589	0	0	870	1,450
1960	Tiny Lund	1	0	0	0	0	0	0	0	52	0	0	78	250
1961	Johnny Roberts	1	0	0	0	0	0	0	0	113	0	0	57	75
1965	Sonny Hutchins	10	0	0	0	0	0	1	1	2,272	0	0	1,332	3,585
1966	Sonny Hutchins	4	0	0	0	0	0	0	0	222	0	0	318	2,190
1967	Sonny Hutchins	7	0	0	0	0	0	0	2	998	0	0	1,711	6,385
1968	Sonny Hutchins	4	0	0	0	0	0	0	0	420	0	0	528	2,810
1969	Sonny Hutchins	8	0	0	2	0	0	0	0	1,694	0	0	1,608	9,565
1970	Sonny Hutchins	2	0	0	0	0	0	1	0	722	0	0	612	2,575
1970	Bill Dennis	3	0	0	0	0	0	0	0	385	0	0	521	2,460
1970	LeeRoy Yarbrough	1	0	0	0	0	0	0	0	22	0	0	33	320
1971	Bill Dennis	26	1	0	0	1	1	2	6	5,349	47	2	6,577	25,883
1972	Johnny Rutherford	1	0	0	0	0	0	0	0	224	0	0	448	1,280
1972	Dick Brooks	4	0	0	0	0	0	0	1	334	0	0	785	5,885
1972	Bill Dennis	2	0	0	0	0	0	1	0	570	0	0	475	3,520
1972	Bobby Isaac	1	0	0	0	0	0	0	0	19	0	0	10	250
1972	Butch Hartman	1	0	0	0	0	0	1	0	326	0	0	489	3,570
1972	David Pearson	1	0	0	0	0	0	0	0	86	1	1	47	680
1972	Fred Lorenzen	1	0	0	0	0	1	0	0	197	0	0	296	1,475
1972	Jackie Oliver	7	0	0	0	0	1	0	0	1,034	0	0	1,486	11,575
1972	Jimmy Hensley	2	0	0	0	0	0	1	0	548	0	0	288	1,900
1972	LeeRoy Yarbrough	2	0	0	0	0	0	1	0	334	2	1	506	5,495
1972	Ron Hutcherson	1	0	0	0	0	0	0	0	29	0	0	29	550
1972	Max Berrier	1	0	0	0	0	0	0	0	349	0	0	218	740
1972	Ramo Stott	2	0	0	1	1	0	0	0	674	3	1	986	14,390
1972	Richard D. Brown	1	0	0	0	0	0	0	0	48	0	0	72	663
1973	Dick Brooks	8	0	0	0	0	0	1	4	2,073	0	0	2,632	16,425
1973	Eddie Pettyjohn	2	0	0	0	0	0	0	1	491	0	0	491	2,145
1973	Jody Ridley	2	0	0	0	0	0	1	0	396	0	0	690	6,175
1973	Yvon DuHamel	1	0	0	0	0	0	0	1	381	0	0	238	800
1973	Charlie Glotzbach	1	0	0	0	0	0	0	1	483	0	0	491	2,625
1973	Ramo Stott	2	0	0	0	0	0	0	1	202	0	0	506	5,650
1973	Richie Panch	3	0	0	0	0	0	0	0	509	0	0	652	3,620
1973	Ray Hendrick	2	0	0	0	0	0	0	0	613	0	0	325	1,950
1973	Harry Gant	1	0	0	0	0	0	0	0	307	0	0	461	2,260
1973	Paul Moore	1	0	0	0	0	0	0	0	174	0	0	238	1,225
1973	Jimmy Hensley	1	0	0	0	0	0	0	1	485	0	0	255	1,550
1974	Jody Ridley	2	0	0	0	0	0	0	0	163	0	0	205	2,935
1974	Jimmy Hensley	1	0	0	0	0	0	0	1	489	0	0	257	1,650
1974	Bill Dennis	3	0	0	0	0	0	0	2	1,118	0	0	1,147	7,775
1974	Bobby Isaac	1	0	0	0	0	0	0	0	59	0	0	81	1,115
1974	George Follmer	1	0	0	0	0	0	0	0	50	0	0	125	1,500
1974	Eddie Pettyjohn	3	0	0	0	0	0	0	0	401	1	1	453	4,210
1974	Richie Panch	1	0	0	0	0	0	0	0	96	0	0	51	795
1974	Harry Gant	1	0	0	0	0	0	0	1	387	0	0	242	1,055
1974	Charlie Glotzbach	10	0	0	0	0	3	0	1	2,627	117	5	2,696	22,722
1974	Paul Radford	1	0	0	0	0	0	0	0	20	0	0	11	750
1975	Kenny Brightbill	1	0	0	0	0	0	0	1	480	0	0	480	2,000
1975	Dick May	1	0	0	0	0	0	0	0	8	0	0	8	505
1975	Earl Ross	1	0	0	0	0	0	0	0	372	0	0	558	2,965
1975	Dick Brooks	25	0	0	1	2	3	0	9	7,344	60	4	8,053	80,185

Year	Driver	Starts	Poles	Finish 1	2	3	4	5	6–10	Laps	Laps Led	Races Led	Miles	$

Junie Donlavey *continued*

Year	Driver	Starts	Poles	1	2	3	4	5	6–10	Laps	Laps Led	Races Led	Miles	$
1975	Jody Ridley	2	0	0	0	0	0	0	0	410	0	0	624	3,000
1976	Buck Baker	1	0	0	0	0	0	0	1	360	0	0	492	3,670
1976	Dick Brooks	26	0	0	0	1	1	1	15	7,479	16	2	8,512	96,605
1976	Gene Felton	1	0	0	0	0	0	0	0	308	0	0	469	1,635
1976	David Hobbs	1	0	0	0	0	0	0	0	187	0	0	374	1,130
1976	Dick Trickle	1	0	0	0	0	0	0	0	142	0	0	213	1,225
1977	Christine Beckers	1	0	0	0	0	0	0	0	33	0	0	83	695
1977	Dick Brooks	27	0	0	1	0	1	5	13	7,833	8	2	9,118	122,825
1978	Dick Brooks	27	0	0	0	0	1	4	12	7,824	24	2	9,026	111,260
1979	Jody Ridley	3	0	0	0	0	0	1	1	787	0	0	1,403	11,245
1979	Ricky Rudd	28	0	0	0	2	0	2	13	8,836	22	4	9,918	135,605
1980	Jody Ridley	31	0	0	0	0	0	2	16	9,579	2	2	10,977	166,000
1981	Jody Ridley	30	0	1	0	0	1	1	15	8,528	28	6	10,078	215,925
1982	Jody Ridley	30	0	0	0	0	0	0	10	7,983	4	4	8,790	294,905
1983	Dick Brooks	30	0	0	0	0	0	2	4	7,736	108	6	8,695	159,565
1984	Dick Brooks	30	0	0	0	1	0	0	4	8,157	185	3	9,320	173,880
1985	Ken Schrader	28	0	0	0	0	0	0	3	7,786	4	1	9,364	178,595
1986	Ken Schrader	29	0	0	0	0	0	0	4	8,047	2	2	9,699	204,210
1987	Ken Schrader	29	1	0	0	0	0	1	9	8,162	154	10	9,902	291,540
1988	Jimmy Means	1	0	0	0	0	0	0	0	394	0	0	246	3,650
1988	Benny Parsons	27	0	0	0	0	0	0	1	7,423	82	3	8,761	185,755
1989	Chad Little	8	0	0	0	0	0	0	0	2,036	0	0	2,794	33,690
1989	Lennie Pond	1	0	0	0	0	0	0	0	394	0	0	296	3,475
1989	Stan Barrett	4	0	0	0	0	0	0	0	391	0	0	615	11,500
1990	J.T. Hayes	1	0	0	0	0	0	0	0	10	0	0	10	2,700
1990	Charlie Glotzbach	1	0	0	0	0	0	0	0	394	0	0	296	3,100
1990	Buddy Baker	8	0	0	0	0	0	0	0	1,326	1	1	2,353	38,385
1990	Ernie Irvan	3	0	0	0	0	0	0	0	993	0	0	1,199	37,605
1991	Robby Gordon	2	0	0	0	0	0	0	0	584	0	0	781	27,265
1991	Steve Perry	1	0	0	0	0	0	0	0	244	0	0	244	4,150
1991	Wally Dallenbach	11	0	0	0	0	0	0	0	2,070	0	0	3,246	49,520
1992	Dorsey Schroeder	1	0	0	0	0	0	0	0	196	0	0	490	25,720
1992	Hut Stricklin	4	0	0	0	0	0	0	0	1,734	0	0	1,267	18,810
1992	Kerry Teague	1	0	0	0	0	0	0	0	15	0	0	20	3,790
1992	Charlie Glotzbach	7	0	0	0	0	0	0	0	1,528	0	0	2,564	44,760
1992	Bobby Hillin	1	0	0	0	0	0	0	0	235	0	0	358	4,350
1992	Pancho Carter	1	0	0	0	0	0	0	0	297	0	0	446	3,735
1993	Bobby Hillin	30	0	0	0	0	0	0	0	8,343	3	1	9,769	250,720
1994	Mike Wallace	22	0	0	0	0	0	1	0	6,672	13	1	8,629	261,925
1994	Bobby Hillin	3	0	0	0	0	0	0	0	1,044	0	0	1,251	48,455
1995	Mike Wallace	26	0	0	0	0	0	0	1	6,819	2	2	8,808	427,456
1996	Mike Wallace	10	0	0	0	0	0	0	0	2,678	3	1	3,230	147,607
1996	Dick Trickle	17	0	0	0	0	0	0	0	4,336	2	1	5,441	268,905
1997	Dorsey Schroeder	1	0	0	0	0	0	0	0	89	0	0	218	11,630
1997	Dick Trickle	28	0	0	0	1	0	1	0	8,476	0	0	10,896	642,300
1998	Dick Trickle	32	0	0	0	0	0	0	1	8,671	4	2	11,433	1,171,375
1999	Ed Berrier	4	0	0	0	0	0	0	0	1,050	0	0	1,587	120,325
1999	Stanton Barrett	2	0	0	0	0	0	0	0	454	0	0	876	84,665
1999	Morgan Shepherd	1	0	0	0	0	0	0	0	388	0	0	395	29,400
1999	Mike Wallace	1	0	0	0	0	0	0	0	199	0	0	498	111,806
1999	Hut Stricklin	1	0	0	0	0	0	0	0	391	0	0	587	37,515
2000	Hut Stricklin	7	0	0	0	0	0	0	0	1,248	0	0	1,617	255,200
2000	Brian Simo	1	0	0	0	0	0	0	0	95	0	0	185	37,110
2000	Ed Berrier	10	0	0	0	0	0	0	0	2,086	0	0	3,797	387,030
2001	Brian Simo	2	0	0	0	0	0	0	0	113	0	0	262	72,175
2001	Hut Stricklin	21	0	0	0	0	0	0	1	5,890	0	0	8,622	915,800
2001	Rick Mast	3	0	0	0	0	0	0	0	871	0	0	1,022	113,725
2002	Rick Mast	9	0	0	0	0	0	0	0	3,033	0	0	3,364	417,580
2002	Gary Bradberry	1	0	0	0	0	0	0	0	72	0	0	144	40,399
2002	Lance Hooper	1	0	0	0	0	0	0	0	488	0	0	260	51,840
2002	Hermie Sadler	2	0	0	0	0	0	0	0	589	0	0	1,077	93,915
2002	Jason Hedlesky	1	0	0	0	0	0	0	0	31	0	0	47	39,160
Lifetime		863	2	1	5	9	13	32	158	224,336	898	71	270,729	$8,999,501

Glen Dorrity

Year	Driver	Starts	Poles	1	2	3	4	5	6–10	Laps	Laps Led	Races Led	Miles	$
1968	Paul Dorrity	1	0	0	0	0	0	0	0	28	0	0	76	500
1969	Paul Dorrity	1	0	0	0	0	0	0	0	129	0	0	348	850
1970	Paul Dorrity	2	0	0	0	0	0	0	0	143	0	0	375	1,690

Year	Driver	Starts	Poles	Finish						Laps	Laps Led	Races Led	Miles	$
				1	2	3	4	5	6–10					

Glen Dorrity *continued*

Year	Driver	Starts	Poles	1	2	3	4	5	6–10	Laps	Laps Led	Races Led	Miles	$
1971	Paul Dorrity	2	0	0	0	0	0	0	0	74	0	0	194	1,685
1972	Paul Dorrity	1	0	0	0	0	0	0	0	130	0	0	341	845
Lifetime		7	0	0	0	0	0	0	0	504	0	0	1,333	$5,570

Larry Dorsey

Year	Driver	Starts	Poles	1	2	3	4	5	6–10	Laps	Laps Led	Races Led	Miles	$
1954	Chuck Meekins	3	0	0	0	0	0	0	1	719	0	0	479	300
1955	Chuck Meekins	2	0	0	0	0	1	0	0	241	0	0	143	350
Lifetime		5	0	0	0	0	1	0	1	960	0	0	622	$650

Dan Dostinich

Year	Driver	Starts	Poles	1	2	3	4	5	6–10	Laps	Laps Led	Races Led	Miles	$
1967	Charles Prickett	1	0	0	0	0	0	0	1	162	0	0	437	1,000
1967	Clyde Prickett	1	0	0	0	0	0	0	0	104	0	0	281	610
1968	Clyde Prickett	1	0	0	0	0	0	0	0	140	0	0	378	700
1969	Jim Cook	1	0	0	0	0	0	0	0	3	0	0	8	750
Lifetime		4	0	0	0	0	0	0	1	409	0	0	1,104	$3,060

R.W. Douglass

Year	Driver	Starts	Poles	1	2	3	4	5	6–10	Laps	Laps Led	Races Led	Miles	$
1953	Red Douglass	1	0	0	0	0	0	0	0	33	0	0	135	25
Lifetime		1	0	0	0	0	0	0	0	33	0	0	135	$25

Fred Dove

Year	Driver	Starts	Poles	1	2	3	4	5	6–10	Laps	Laps Led	Races Led	Miles	$
1952	Fred Dove	5	0	0	0	0	0	0	2	610	0	0	453	250
1953	Fred Dove	19	0	0	0	0	0	0	4	734	0	0	687	975
1954	Fred Dove	10	0	0	0	0	0	0	2	1,245	0	0	770	525
1955	Fred Dove	5	0	0	0	1	0	0	2	788	0	0	376	725
Lifetime		39	0	0	0	1	0	0	10	3,377	0	0	2,286	$2,475

Russ Draime

Year	Driver	Starts	Poles	1	2	3	4	5	6–10	Laps	Laps Led	Races Led	Miles	$
1979	John Anderson	4	0	0	0	0	0	1	0	1,263	1	1	1,757	11,210
1980	John Anderson	1	0	0	0	0	0	0	0	183	0	0	458	9,135
Lifetime		5	0	0	0	0	0	1	0	1,446	1	1	2,214	$20,345

Gary Drake

Year	Driver	Starts	Poles	1	2	3	4	5	6–10	Laps	Laps Led	Races Led	Miles	$
1954	Blackie Pitt	26	0	0	0	0	0	0	6	3,612	0	0	2,448	1,690
1954	Lee Petty	1	0	0	0	0	1	0	0	196	0	0	98	350
1955	Blackie Pitt	1	0	0	0	0	0	0	1	189	0	0	95	200
Lifetime		28	0	0	0	0	1	0	7	3,997	0	0	2,640	$2,240

Jerry Draper

Year	Driver	Starts	Poles	1	2	3	4	5	6–10	Laps	Laps Led	Races Led	Miles	$
1959	Roy Tyner	1	0	0	0	0	0	0	0	141	0	0	141	250
1959	Jerry Draper	6	0	0	0	0	0	0	3	1,049	0	0	503	640
1959	Bob Welborn	1	0	0	0	0	1	0	0	199	0	0	100	250
Lifetime		8	0	0	0	0	1	0	3	1,389	0	0	743	$1,140

John DuBoise

Year	Driver	Starts	Poles	1	2	3	4	5	6–10	Laps	Laps Led	Races Led	Miles	$
1950	John DuBoise	2	0	0	0	0	0	0	0	367	0	0	459	250
1951	John DuBoise	2	0	0	0	0	1	0	0	127	0	0	95	325
Lifetime		4	0	0	0	0	1	0	0	494	0	0	554	$575

Philip Duffie

Year	Driver	Starts	Poles	1	2	3	4	5	6–10	Laps	Laps Led	Races Led	Miles	$
1982	Philip Duffie	5	0	0	0	0	0	0	0	1,166	0	0	2,273	13,755
1983	Philip Duffie	4	0	0	0	0	0	0	0	750	0	0	1,168	6,480
1988	Philip Duffie	1	0	0	0	0	0	0	0	332	0	0	454	2,540
Lifetime		10	0	0	0	0	0 ~	0	0	2,248	0	0	3,895	$22,775

Ray Duhigg

Year	Driver	Starts	Poles	1	2	3	4	5	6–10	Laps	Laps Led	Races Led	Miles	$
1951	Ray Duhigg	5	0	0	0	0	0	0	0	46	0	0	23	125
Lifetime		5	0	0	0	0	0	0	0	46	0	0	23	$125

Year	Driver	Starts	Poles	Finish 1	2	3	4	5	6–10	Laps	Laps Led	Races Led	Miles	$

Gerald Duke

Year	Driver	Starts	Poles	1	2	3	4	5	6–10	Laps	Laps Led	Races Led	Miles	$
1959	Gerald Duke	1	0	0	0	0	0	0	0	249	0	0	125	125
1959	Possum Jones	1	0	0	0	0	0	0	0	74	0	0	102	295
1959	Speedy Thompson	1	0	0	0	0	0	0	0	75	0	0	38	0
1959	Jack Smith	1	0	0	0	0	1	0	0	196	0	0	98	275
1960	Gerald Duke	11	0	0	0	0	1	0	6	2,062	0	0	2,017	5,930
1960	Elmo Langley	1	0	0	0	0	0	0	0	25	0	0	34	220
1960	Charley Griffin	2	0	0	0	0	0	0	0	22	0	0	55	100
1961	Gerald Duke	1	0	0	0	0	0	0	0	39	0	0	20	50
Lifetime		19	0	0	0	0	2	0	6	2,742	0	0	2,487	$6,995

J.R. Dunberry

Year	Driver	Starts	Poles	1	2	3	4	5	6–10	Laps	Laps Led	Races Led	Miles	$
1953	Buddy Shuman	1	0	0	0	0	0	0	0	4	0	0	16	0
Lifetime		1	0	0	0	0	0	0	0	4	0	0	16	$0

Glenn Dunnaway

Year	Driver	Starts	Poles	1	2	3	4	5	6–10	Laps	Laps Led	Races Led	Miles	$
1949	Glenn Dunnaway	5	0	0	0	1	0	0	2	394	1	1	197	650
1950	Glenn Dunnaway	6	0	0	1	0	1	0	1	866	0	0	731	1,275
1951	Glenn Dunnaway	5	0	0	0	0	0	0	2		0	0		250
Lifetime		16	0	0	1	1	1	0	5	1,260	1	1	928	$2,175

Roy Dutton

Year	Driver	Starts	Poles	1	2	3	4	5	6–10	Laps	Laps Led	Races Led	Miles	$
1967	E.J. Trivette	6	0	0	0	0	0	0	1	1,289	0	0	961	1,810
1967	Henley Gray	2	0	0	0	0	0	0	0	302	0	0	448	1,545
Lifetime		8	0	0	0	0	0	0	1	1,591	0	0	1,409	$3,355

Duane Duvall

Year	Driver	Starts	Poles	1	2	3	4	5	6–10	Laps	Laps Led	Races Led	Miles	$
1953	Red Duvall	1	0	0	0	0	0	0	0	37	0	0	152	75
Lifetime		1	0	0	0	0	0	0	0	37	0	0	152	$75

Carson Dyer

Year	Driver	Starts	Poles	1	2	3	4	5	6–10	Laps	Laps Led	Races Led	Miles	$
1950	Carson Dyer	1	0	0	0	0	0	0	0	310	0	0	388	0
1951	Carson Dyer	2	0	0	0	0	0	0	0		0	0		50
Lifetime		3	0	0	0	0	0	0	0	310	0	0	388	$50

Charles Dyer

Year	Driver	Starts	Poles	1	2	3	4	5	6–10	Laps	Laps Led	Races Led	Miles	$
1951	Charles Dyer	1	0	0	0	0	0	0	0		0	0		0
Lifetime		1	0	0	0	0	0	0	0		0	0		$0

Ralph Dyer

Year	Driver	Starts	Poles	1	2	3	4	5	6–10	Laps	Laps Led	Races Led	Miles	$
1953	Ralph Dyer	6	0	0	0	0	0	0	3	480	0	0	384	600
Lifetime		6	0	0	0	0	0	0	3	480	0	0	384	$600

Dick Eagan

Year	Driver	Starts	Poles	1	2	3	4	5	6–10	Laps	Laps Led	Races Led	Miles	$
1952	Dick Eagan	2	0	0	0	0	0	0	1		0	0		100
Lifetime		2	0	0	0	0	0	0	1		0	0		$100

Harvey Eakin

Year	Driver	Starts	Poles	1	2	3	4	5	6–10	Laps	Laps Led	Races Led	Miles	$
1954	Harvey Eakin	7	0	0	0	0	0	0	0	741	0	0	915	425
1955	Harvey Eakin	3	0	0	0	0	0	0	0	307	0	0	416	210
1956	Harvey Eakin	2	0	0	0	0	0	0	0	278	0	0	278	100
1957	Harvey Eakin	5	0	0	0	0	0	0	0	763	0	0	575	375
Lifetime		17	0	0	0	0	0	0	0	2,089	0	0	2,184	$1,110

John Eanes

Year	Driver	Starts	Poles	1	2	3	4	5	6–10	Laps	Laps Led	Races Led	Miles	$
1950	Pee Wee Martin	1	0	0	0	0	0	0	0	344	0	0	430	100
1950	Curtis Turner	15	4	4	1	1	1	0	0	1,580	1,110	12	1,198	8,265
1951	Curtis Turner	8	0	2	0	0	0	0	1	1,014	409	5	836	2,680
1952	Jim Paschal	2	0	0	0	0	0	0	2	261	0	0	187	200

Year	Driver	Starts	Poles	Finish						Laps	Laps Led	Races Led	Miles	$
				1	2	3	4	5	6–10	Laps	Led	Led	Miles	$

John Eanes *continued*

Year	Driver	Starts	Poles	1	2	3	4	5	6–10	Laps	Laps Led	Races Led	Miles	$
1952	Curtis Turner	7	0	0	0	0	0	1	0	526	12	1	427	290
1952	Jimmie Lewallen	2	0	0	0	0	0	0	0	100	0	0	82	25
1953	Curtis Turner	16	1	0	0	0	1	0	1	899	91	3	621	1,175
1953	Jimmie Lewallen	3	0	0	0	0	0	0	2		0	0		190
1954	Dick Garlington	1	0	0	0	0	0	0	0	35	0	0	144	25
1955	Ralph Shaffer	1	0	0	0	0	0	0	0	16	0	0	66	0
Lifetime		56	5	6	1	1	2	1	6	4,775	1,622	21	3,989	$12,950

Dale Earnhardt, Inc. (Statistics represent the DEI team, founded by Dale Earnhardt and currently owned by Teresa Earnhardt.)

Year	Driver	Starts	Poles	1	2	3	4	5	6–10	Laps	Laps Led	Races Led	Miles	$
1996	Robby Gordon	1	0	0	0	0	0	0	0	206	0	0	309	4,800
1996	Jeff Green	2	0	0	0	0	0	0	0	91	0	0	228	16,835
1997	Steve Park	4	0	0	0	0	0	0	0	1,037	0	0	1,339	60,405
1998	Darrell Waltrip	13	0	0	0	0	0	1	1	3,596	14	3	4,909	737,615
1998	Steve Park	17	0	0	0	0	0	0	0	4,595	0	0	5,626	488,415
1999	Dale Earnhardt Jr.	5	0	0	0	0	0	0	0	1,363	1	1	1,838	162,095
1999	Steve Park	34	0	0	0	0	0	0	5	9,575	166	6	12,243	1,568,811
2000	Dale Earnhardt Jr.	34	2	2	0	0	1	0	2	9,644	426	10	12,633	2,067,065
2000	Steve Park	34	2	1	0	1	3	1	7	9,925	290	11	12,877	1,956,635
2001	Michael Waltrip	36	0	1	2	0	0	0	0	9,527	88	8	12,823	3,285,364
2001	Dale Earnhardt Jr.	36	2	3	2	3	1	0	6	10,302	767	16	13,685	5,203,852
2001	Kenny Wallace	12	1	0	1	0	0	0	1	3,951	103	3	4,661	838,923
2001	Steve Park	24	0	1	3	0	1	0	7	6,368	477	8	8,777	2,324,849
2002	Steve Park	32	0	0	0	0	0	0	2	8,721	50	2	10,951	2,573,149
2002	Michael Waltrip	36	0	1	1	0	1	1	6	9,928	180	12	13,175	2,721,604
2002	Dale Earnhardt Jr.	36	2	2	1	1	4	3	5	10,344	1068	22	13,525	4,229,036
2002	Kenny Wallace	4	0	0	0	0	0	0	1	1,144	0	0	1,700	415,354
Lifetime		360	9	11	10	5	11	6	44	100,317	3,630	102	131,301	$28,654,807

Sonny Easley

Year	Driver	Starts	Poles	1	2	3	4	5	6–10	Laps	Laps Led	Races Led	Miles	$
1977	Sonny Easley	2	0	0	0	0	0	0	1	245	0	0	624	3,200
Lifetime		2	0	0	0	0	0	0	1	245	0	0	624	$3,200

Herb Eberhart

Year	Driver	Starts	Poles	1	2	3	4	5	6–10	Laps	Laps Led	Races Led	Miles	$
1956	Bob Stanclift	1	0	0	0	0	0	0	0	72	0	0	180	40
1956	Bill Hyde	1	0	0	0	0	0	0	0	67	0	0	34	50
1956	Clyde Palmer	1	0	0	0	0	0	0	0	225	0	0	225	100
1956	Gordon Haines	7	0	0	1	0	1	0	2	1,067	66	1	715	1,500
Lifetime		10	0	0	1	0	1	0	2	1,431	66	1	1,154	$1,690

J.D. Edgett

Year	Driver	Starts	Poles	1	2	3	4	5	6–10	Laps	Laps Led	Races Led	Miles	$
1981	Gary Kershaw	1	0	0	0	0	0	0	0	117	0	0	307	1,800
1982	Roy Smith	2	0	0	0	0	0	0	1	198	0	0	519	7,795
1983	Roy Smith	1	0	0	0	0	0	0	0	36	0	0	94	2,025
Lifetime		4	0	0	0	0	0	0	1	351	0	0	920	$11,620

John Edgett

Year	Driver	Starts	Poles	1	2	3	4	5	6–10	Laps	Laps Led	Races Led	Miles	$
1982	Roy Smith	1	0	0	0	0	0	0	1	196	0	0	490	18,975
Lifetime		1	0	0	0	0	0	0	1	196	0	0	490	$18,975

Jimmy Edwards

Year	Driver	Starts	Poles	1	2	3	4	5	6–10	Laps	Laps Led	Races Led	Miles	$
1978	Glenn Jarrett	1	0	0	0	0	0	0	0	317	0	0	476	2,940
1979	Richard Brickhouse	1	0	0	0	0	0	0	0	15	0	0	23	870
Lifetime		2	0	0	0	0	0	0	0	332	0	0	498	$3,810

Jonathon Edwards

Year	Driver	Starts	Poles	1	2	3	4	5	6–10	Laps	Laps Led	Races Led	Miles	$
1985	Jonathan Edwards	2	0	0	0	0	0	0	0	633	0	0	644	3,220
1986	Jonathan Edwards	4	0	0	0	0	0	0	0	1,114	0	0	1,405	8,030
1987	Jonathan Edwards	2	0	0	0	0	0	0	0	226	0	0	309	3,055
Lifetime		8	0	0	0	0	0	0	0	1,973	0	0	2,358	$14,305

Year	Driver	Starts	Poles	Finish						Laps	Laps Led	Races Led	Miles	$
				1	2	3	4	5	6–10	Laps	Led	Led	Miles	$

Fred Elder

Year	Driver	Starts	Poles	1	2	3	4	5	6–10	Laps	Laps Led	Races Led	Miles	$
1968	Ray Elder	1	0	0	0	0	0	0	0	37	0	0	100	500
1969	Ray Elder	4	0	0	0	0	0	0	4	642	0	0	1,523	7,200
1970	Ray Elder	4	0	0	0	0	0	0	1	441	0	0	1,127	4,570
1971	Ray Elder	4	0	1	1	0	0	0	1	564	70	2	1,439	30,595
1972	Ray Elder	3	0	1	0	0	1	1	0	493	50	2	1,268	23,165
1973	Ray Elder	3	0	0	0	1	0	0	0	381	0	0	977	9,225
1974	Ray Elder	2	0	0	0	0	0	0	0	37	0	0	94	1,435
1975	Ray Elder	3	0	0	0	0	1	0	0	368	1	1	956	8,020
1976	Ray Elder	2	0	0	0	0	2	0	0	284	0	0	744	11,715
Lifetime		26	0	2	1	1	4	1	6	3,247	121	5	8,228	$96,425

Ray Elder

Year	Driver	Starts	Poles	1	2	3	4	5	6–10	Laps	Laps Led	Races Led	Miles	$
1967	Ray Elder	1	0	0	0	0	0	0	0	23	0	0	62	500
Lifetime		1	0	0	0	0	0	0	0	23	0	0	62	$500

Ronnie Elder

Year	Driver	Starts	Poles	1	2	3	4	5	6–10	Laps	Laps Led	Races Led	Miles	$
1973	Lennie Pond	23	0	0	0	0	1	0	8	5,850	4	2	5,479	25,255
1974	Lennie Pond	22	0	0	0	0	1	4	6	6,384	17	6	7,013	49,155
1975	Lennie Pond	22	0	0	3	0	1	2	3	5,859	275	8	6,361	54,865
1976	Lennie Pond	30	0	0	2	0	4	4	9	8,182	217	10	10,055	129,515
1977	Lennie Pond	14	0	0	0	0	2	2	2	3,154	5	3	3,714	49,440
Lifetime		111	0	0	5	0	9	12	28	29,429	518	29	32,622	$308,230

Bobby Eller

Year	Driver	Starts	Poles	1	2	3	4	5	6–10	Laps	Laps Led	Races Led	Miles	$
1986	Trevor Boys	2	0	0	0	0	0	0	0	430	0	0	691	3,725
Lifetime		2	0	0	0	0	0	0	0	430	0	0	691	$3,725

Hoss Ellington

Year	Driver	Starts	Poles	1	2	3	4	5	6–10	Laps	Laps Led	Races Led	Miles	$
1968	Hoss Ellington	3	0	0	0	0	0	0	0	494	0	0	703	2,395
1969	Hoss Ellington	15	0	0	0	0	0	0	4	2,988	0	0	4,136	16,552
1970	Hoss Ellington	3	0	0	0	0	0	0	0	728	0	0	875	3,133
1972	Cale Yarborough	3	0	0	0	0	0	0	2	812	9	1	1,106	4,857
1972	Fred Lorenzen	7	0	0	0	0	2	0	1	1,604	4	1	2,538	18,030
1972	John Sears	1	0	0	0	0	0	1	0	388	0	0	243	950
1973	Charlie Glotzbach	4	0	0	0	0	0	0	0	565	11	2	816	3,826
1973	Ramo Stott	1	0	0	0	0	0	0	0	46	1	1	122	740
1973	Gordon Johncock	6	1	0	0	0	1	0	0	1,307	0	0	1,809	10,600
1974	A.J. Foyt	2	0	0	0	0	1	0	0	369	64	2	753	7,905
1974	Bobby Isaac	7	0	0	0	0	0	0	3	1,070	9	3	1,527	9,300
1974	Charlie Glotzbach	3	0	0	0	0	1	0	0	851	10	1	1,098	10,125
1974	Sam McQuagg	3	0	0	0	0	0	0	2	698	1	1	1,221	6,100
1975	Gordon Johncock	1	0	0	0	0	0	0	0	47	0	0	125	1,230
1975	A.J. Foyt	7	0	0	0	0	0	0	0	1,420	186	5	2,462	18,055
1975	Donnie Allison	2	0	0	0	1	0	0	0	306	23	1	679	10,100
1975	Charlie Glotzbach	1	0	0	0	0	0	0	1	395	0	0	593	5,355
1975	Bobby Isaac	1	0	0	0	0	0	0	0	113	79	0	115	600
1976	A.J. Foyt	5	1	0	0	0	1	1	0	581	79	3	1,335	15,610
1976	Donnie Allison	9	0	1	0	1	0	0	3	2,178	104	4	3,254	48,445
1977	Donnie Allison	17	3	2	2	1	4	0	1	4,133	1,163	13	5,911	145,935
1978	Donnie Allison	14	0	1	2	2	1	1	0	3,232	209	12	5,300	123,530
1979	Donnie Allison	20	1	0	2	1	2	2	3	4,891	293	9	6,420	142,620
1980	David Pearson	9	1	1	2	1	0	0	1	1,787	172	7	3,252	94,330
1980	Donnie Allison	3	0	0	0	0	0	1	1	894	35	2	1,303	44,285
1981	David Pearson	1	0	0	0	0	0	0	1	365	0	0	499	4,850
1981	Buddy Baker	15	0	0	1	0	2	3	3	3,519	110	9	5,788	113,735
1982	Donnie Allison	1	0	0	0	0	0	0	0	36	0	0	55	745
1982	Buddy Baker	7	1	0	0	0	0	1	1	1,491	19	7	2,511	68,605
1982	Benny Parsons	2	0	0	0	0	0	0	0	149	1	1	231	2,430
1982	Kyle Petty	6	0	0	0	0	0	0	0	974	0	0	1,745	12,105
1983	Lake Speed	18	0	0	0	1	1	1	3	4,933	22	2	6,929	78,220
1984	Lake Speed	17	0	0	0	1	0	1	5	4,372	122	5	6,245	90,705
1985	Rick Wilson	1	0	0	0	0	0	0	0	321	0	0	489	1,945
1985	Pancho Carter	1	0	0	0	0	0	0	0	336	0	0	459	2,755
1985	David Pearson	8	0	0	0	0	0	0	1	1,215	2	1	2,270	38,090

Year	Driver	Starts	Poles	1	2	3	4	5	6–10	Laps	Laps Led	Races Led	Miles	$

Hoss Ellington *continued*

Year	Driver	Starts	Poles	1	2	3	4	5	6–10	Laps	Laps Led	Races Led	Miles	$
1985	Davey Allison	3	0	0	0	0	0	0	1	539	0	0	1,025	10,615
1986	Sterling Marlin	10	0	0	1	0	1	0	2	1,738	21	3	3,225	113,070
1987	Brett Bodine	14	0	0	0	0	0	0	0	2,908	20	3	4,485	40,145
1987	Ron Bouchard	5	0	0	0	0	0	0	1	917	0	0	1,446	24,105
1988	Dale Jarrett	8	0	0	0	0	0	0	0	1,004	1	1	2,363	44,656
Lifetime		264	8	5	10	9	17	11	40	56,714	2,691	100	87,458	$1,391,384

Bill Elliott (Statistics include partnerships and shared ownership with Dan Marino and Charles Hardy.)

Year	Driver	Starts	Poles	1	2	3	4	5	6–10	Laps	Laps Led	Races Led	Miles	$
1995	Bill Elliott	31	2	0	0	0	2	2	7	9,349	124	8	11,434	799,549
1996	Bill Elliott	24	0	0	0	0	0	0	6	7,439	109	7	8,642	690,006
1996	Tom Kendall	1	0	0	0	0	0	0	0	73	4	1	184	20,730
1996	Todd Bodine	4	0	0	0	0	0	0	1	1,104	0	0	1,708	92,945
1996	Dorsey Schroeder	1	0	0	0	0	0	0	0	90	2	1	221	22,745
1996	Bobby Hillin	1	0	0	0	0	0	0	0	491	0	0	262	25,735
1997	Ron Barfield Jr.	1	0	0	0	0	0	0	0	160	0	0	400	64,935
1997	Bill Elliott	32	1	0	1	0	3	1	9	9,610	442	11	12,429	1,286,518
1998	Wally Dallenbach	2	0	0	0	0	0	0	0	300	0	0	750	94,535
1998	Dennis Setzer	7	0	0	0	0	0	0	0	2,142	0	150,495	2,361	
1998	Jerry Nadeau	14	0	0	0	0	0	0	0	3,878	0	366,816	5,124	
1998	Matt Kenseth	1	0	0	0	0	0	0	1	400	0	0	400	42,340
1998	Bill Elliott	32	0	0	0	0	0	0	5	8,865	40	8	11,443	1,348,865
1998	Ted Musgrave	7	0	0	0	0	0	1	0	1,847	0	166,110	2,597	
1998	Tom Hubert	1	0	0	0	0	0	0	0	88	0	0	216	17,745
1999	Bill Elliott	34	0	0	0	0	0	1	1	9,764	15	3	12,776	2,440,826
2000	David Green	2	0	0	0	0	0	0	0	740	0	0	664	78,850
2000	Bill Elliott	32	0	0	0	2	1	0	4	8,636	111	8	11,421	2,220,957
Lifetime		227	3	0	1	2	6	5	34	64,976	847	47	83,031	$9,930,702

Buddy Elliott

Year	Driver	Starts	Poles	1	2	3	4	5	6–10	Laps	Laps Led	Races Led	Miles	$
1949	Tim Flock	5	0	0	1	0	0	1	1	347	0	0	415	1,350
1950	Tim Flock	4	0	0	0	0	1	0	0	730	0	0	643	875
Lifetime		9	0	0	1	0	1	1	1	1,077	0	0	1,057	$2,225

George Elliott

Year	Driver	Starts	Poles	1	2	3	4	5	6–10	Laps	Laps Led	Races Led	Miles	$
1966	Don Tilley	1	0	0	0	0	0	0	0	48	0	0	48	505
1973	Charles Barrett	4	0	0	0	0	0	0	1	726	9	1	1,305	5,610
1973	Jody Ridley	1	0	0	0	0	0	0	0	294	0	0	299	945
1974	A.J. Reno	1	0	0	0	0	0	0	0	15	0	0	40	760
1976	Bill Elliott	4	0	0	0	0	0	0	0	419	0	0	640	4,870
1976	Al Holbert	1	0	0	0	0	0	0	0	7	0	0	11	855
1977	Bill Elliott	10	0	0	0	0	0	0	2	2,082	0	0	3,319	20,075
1978	Bill Elliott	10	0	0	0	0	0	0	5	2,278	0	0	4,099	42,215
1979	Bill Elliott	10	0	0	1	0	0	0	3	2,061	8	3	3,763	49,605
1980	Bill Elliott	11	0	0	0	0	0	0	4	2,106	4	4	4,076	42,545
1981	Bill Elliott	13	1	0	0	0	1	0	6	2,777	33	3	4,444	68,570
Lifetime		66	1	0	1	0	1	0	21	12,813	54	11	22,043	$236,555

Kermit Elliott

Year	Driver	Starts	Poles	1	2	3	4	5	6–10	Laps	Laps Led	Races Led	Miles	$
1984	Brent Elliott	1	0	0	0	0	0	0	0	203	0	0	127	835
1985	Brent Elliott	3	0	0	0	0	0	0	0	837	0	0	469	3,210
1986	Brent Elliott	1	0	0	0	0	0	0	0	325	0	0	203	950
Lifetime		5	0	0	0	0	0	0	0	1,365	0	0	799	$4,995

Bill Ellis

Year	Driver	Starts	Poles	1	2	3	4	5	6–10	Laps	Laps Led	Races Led	Miles	$
1969	Sam McQuagg	3	0	0	0	0	0	0	2	1,056	0	0	845	2,625
1969	Richard Brickhouse	6	0	0	0	0	0	0	3	1,000	1	1	1,148	6,395
1969	Ramo Stott	1	0	0	0	1	0	0	0	188	4	1	500	7,050
1970	Freddy Fryar	1	0	0	0	0	0	0	1	182	0	0	484	3,000
1970	Richard Brickhouse	2	0	0	0	0	0	1	1	247	0	0	618	3,625
1971	Jim Paschal	1	0	0	0	0	0	0	0	386	0	0	579	2,050
1971	Pedro Rodriguez	1	0	0	0	0	0	0	0	16	0	0	40	0
Lifetime		15	0	0	0	1	0	1	7	3,075	5	2	4,214	$24,745

Year	Driver	Starts	Poles	1	2	3	4	5	6–10	Laps	Laps Led	Races Led	Miles	$

Tommy Ellis

Year	Driver	Starts	Poles	1	2	3	4	5	6–10	Laps	Laps Led	Races Led	Miles	$
1981	Tommy Ellis	4	0	0	0	0	1	0	0	651	2	2	767	13,475
1982	Tommy Ellis	2	0	0	0	0	0	0	0	642	0	0	348	3,220
Lifetime		6	0	0	0	0	1	0	0	1,293	2	2	1,115	$16,695

Ray Elston

Year	Driver	Starts	Poles	1	2	3	4	5	6–10	Laps	Laps Led	Races Led	Miles	$
1955	Leslie Young	1	0	0	0	0	0	0	0	21	0	0	21	25
Lifetime		1	0	0	0	0	0	0	0	21	0	0	21	$25

Adele Emerson

Year	Driver	Starts	Poles	1	2	3	4	5	6–10	Laps	Laps Led	Races Led	Miles	$
1990	Ted Kennedy	1	0	0	0	0	0	0	0	11	0	0	28	3,225
1990	Jack Sellers	1	0	0	0	0	0	0	0	41	0	0	103	3,225
1992	Jack Sellers	1	0	0	0	0	0	0	0	48	0	0	121	4,725
Lifetime		3	0	0	0	0	0	0	0	100	0	0	252	$11,175

Ray & Ernestine Emerson

Year	Driver	Starts	Poles	1	2	3	4	5	6–10	Laps	Laps Led	Races Led	Miles	$
1977	Jim Hurtubise	1	0	0	0	0	0	0	0	154	0	0	385	2,065
1978	Harry Gant	1	0	0	0	0	0	0	0	1	0	0	3	1,975
Lifetime		2	0	0	0	0	0	0	0	155	0	0	388	$4,040

Bob England

Year	Driver	Starts	Poles	1	2	3	4	5	6–10	Laps	Laps Led	Races Led	Miles	$
1969	Bob England	1	0	0	0	0	0	0	0	1	0	0	3	750
1970	Bob England	2	0	0	0	0	0	0	0	126	0	0	330	1,740
1971	Bob England	4	0	0	0	0	0	0	0	477	0	0	1,160	4,105
Lifetime		7	0	0	0	0	0	0	0	604	0	0	1,493	$6,595

George England

Year	Driver	Starts	Poles	1	2	3	4	5	6–10	Laps	Laps Led	Races Led	Miles	$
1974	George England	3	0	0	0	0	0	0	0	184	0	0	178	1,485
Lifetime		3	0	0	0	0	0	0	0	184	0	0	178	$1,485

Erick Erickson

Year	Driver	Starts	Poles	1	2	3	4	5	6–10	Laps	Laps Led	Races Led	Miles	$
1951	Erick Erickson	3	0	0	0	1	0	0	0		0	0		550
1954	Erick Erickson	5	0	0	0	0	0	1	1	921	0	0	952	1,115
1955	Erick Erickson	2	0	0	0	0	0	0	0	74	0	0	74	30
1956	Erick Erickson	5	0	0	0	0	0	0	1	736	0	0	639	365
Lifetime		15	0	0	0	1	0	1	2	1,731	0	0	1,665	$2,060

Ray Erickson

Year	Driver	Starts	Poles	1	2	3	4	5	6–10	Laps	Laps Led	Races Led	Miles	$
1954	Dick Rathmann	1	0	1	0	0	0	0	0	250	108	1	125	1,000
Lifetime		1	0	1	0	0	0	0	0	250	108	1	125	$1,000

Ron Esau

Year	Driver	Starts	Poles	1	2	3	4	5	6–10	Laps	Laps Led	Races Led	Miles	$
1976	Ron Esau	2	0	0	0	0	0	0	0	160	0	0	419	2,310
Lifetime		2	0	0	0	0	0	0	0	160	0	0	419	$2,310

Clay Esteridge

Year	Driver	Starts	Poles	1	2	3	4	5	6–10	Laps	Laps Led	Races Led	Miles	$
1965	Wendell Scott	1	0	0	0	0	0	0	1	320	0	0	440	900
1965	Lionel Johnson	8	0	0	0	0	0	0	2	1,663	0	0	1,338	3,165
1966	Lionel Johnson	5	0	0	0	0	0	0	0	328	0	0	274	1,895
Lifetime		14	0	0	0	0	0	0	3	2,311	0	0	2,051	$5,960

Herb Estes

Year	Driver	Starts	Poles	1	2	3	4	5	6–10	Laps	Laps Led	Races Led	Miles	$
1958	Herbert Estes	10	0	0	0	0	0	0	3	2,010	0	0	1,562	1,895
1958	Tiny Lund	2	0	0	0	0	0	0	0	152	0	0	99	185
Lifetime		12	0	0	0	0	0	0	3	2,162	0	0	1,661	$2,080

Jack Etheridge

Year	Driver	Starts	Poles	1	2	3	4	5	6–10	Laps	Laps Led	Races Led	Miles	$
1949	Jack Etheridge	1	0	0	0	0	0	0	1		0	0		75
1967	Jack Etheridge	3	0	0	0	0	0	0	0	160	0	0	84	645
Lifetime		4	0	0	0	0	0	0	1	160	0	0	84	$720

Year	Driver	Starts	Poles	Finish						Laps	Laps Led	Races Led	Miles	$
				1	2	3	4	5	6–10	Laps	Led	Led	Miles	$

Joe Eubanks

Year	Driver	Starts	Poles	1	2	3	4	5	6–10	Laps	Laps Led	Races Led	Miles	$
1950	Joe Eubanks	1	0	0	0	0	0	0	0	259	0	0	324	0
Lifetime		1	0	0	0	0	0	0	0	259	0	0	324	$0

Gene Evans

Year	Driver	Starts	Poles	1	2	3	4	5	6–10	Laps	Laps Led	Races Led	Miles	$
1974	Johnny Barnes	1	0	0	0	0	0	0	0	116	0	0	158	700
Lifetime		1	0	0	0	0	0	0	0	116	0	0	158	$700

David Everett

Year	Driver	Starts	Poles	1	2	3	4	5	6–10	Laps	Laps Led	Races Led	Miles	$
1956	Wayne Fielden	2	0	0	0	0	0	0	1	361	0	0	181	200
1956	Herbert Estes	1	0	0	0	0	0	0	0	178	0	0	89	100
1956	Ken Milligan	4	0	0	0	0	0	0	1	347	0	0	267	300
Lifetime		7	0	0	0	0	0	0	2	886	0	0	536	$600

Ray Evernham

Year	Driver	Starts	Poles	1	2	3	4	5	6–10	Laps	Laps Led	Races Led	Miles	$
2000	Casey Atwood	3	0	0	0	0	0	0	1	1,160	0	0	960	97,030
2001	Bill Elliott	36	2	1	0	1	1	2	4	9,915	171	9	13,458	3,203,071
2001	Casey Atwood	35	1	0	0	1	0	0	2	9,473	137	4	11,904	1,744,669
2002	Jeremy Mayfield	36	0	0	1	0	0	1	2	10,117	30	5	12,934	2,336,116
2002	Hank Parker Jr.	1	0	0	0	0	0	0	0	389	0	0	396	39,625
2002	Casey Atwood	1	0	0	0	0	0	0	0	261	0	0	394	37,175
2002	Bill Elliott	36	4	2	1	1	1	1	7	10,352	275	13	13,665	3,537,783
Lifetime		148	7	3	2	3	2	4	16	41,667	613	31	53,711	$10,995,469

Don Every

Year	Driver	Starts	Poles	1	2	3	4	5	6–10	Laps	Laps Led	Races Led	Miles	$
1959	Elmo Henderson	1	0	0	0	0	0	0	0	16	0	0	22	150
1959	Cotton Owens	5	0	0	0	1	0	0	2	940	0	0	375	915
1959	Joe Eubanks	12	0	0	1	0	0	1	5	1,253	0	0	910	1,810
1960	Joe Eubanks	7	0	0	0	0	0	1	1	822	0	0	687	1,310
1961	Joe Eubanks	2	0	0	0	0	0	0	0	448	0	0	672	1,475
Lifetime		27	0	0	1	1	0	2	8	3,479	0	0	2,666	$5,660

David Ezell

Year	Driver	Starts	Poles	1	2	3	4	5	6–10	Laps	Laps Led	Races Led	Miles	$
1952	David Ezell	1	0	0	0	1	0	0	0	153	0	0	77	450
Lifetime		1	0	0	0	1	0	0	0	153	0	0	77	$450

Joe Falk

Year	Driver	Starts	Poles	1	2	3	4	5	6–10	Laps	Laps Led	Races Led	Miles	$
1997	Kevin Lepage	3	0	0	0	0	0	0	0	624	0	0	1,161	57,720
1997	Greg Sacks	1	0	0	0	0	0	0	0	158	0	0	395	57,410
1998	Morgan Shepherd	6	0	0	0	0	0	0	0	1,146	0	0	1,476	206,835
1998	Andy Hillenburg	3	0	0	0	0	0	0	0	638	0	0	1,202	96,000
1998	Todd Bodine	7	0	0	0	0	0	1	0	2,402	1	1	2,359	194,865
1998	Tom Kendall	1	0	0	0	0	0	0	0	112	2	1	218	33,800
1998	Kevin Lepage	13	0	0	0	0	0	0	0	3,185	0	0	4,579	373,645
1999	Steve Grissom	2	0	0	0	0	0	0	0	502	0	0	567	67,450
1999	Dick Trickle	7	0	0	0	0	0	0	0	1,950	0	0	1,628	195,060
1999	Andy Hillenburg	1	0	0	0	0	0	0	0	50	0	0	133	32,736
2000	Todd Bodine	2	0	0	0	0	0	0	1	367	0	0	532	52,745
Lifetime		46	0	0	0	0	0	1	1	11,134	3	2	14,251	$1,368,266

Freddie Farmer

Year	Driver	Starts	Poles	1	2	3	4	5	6–10	Laps	Laps Led	Races Led	Miles	$
1951	Freddie Farmer	3	0	0	0	0	0	0	0	447	0	0	540	125
Lifetime		3	0	0	0	0	0	0	0	447	0	0	540	$125

Red Farmer

Year	Driver	Starts	Poles	1	2	3	4	5	6–10	Laps	Laps Led	Races Led	Miles	$
1968	Red Farmer	7	0	0	0	0	1	0	0	928	1	1	849	4,810
Lifetime		7	0	0	0	0	1	0	0	928	1	1	849	$4,810

Dudley Farrell

Year	Driver	Starts	Poles	1	2	3	4	5	6–10	Laps	Laps Led	Races Led	Miles	$
1961	Nelson Stacy	15	0	1	0	1	2	0	4	3,024	144	4	3,281	26,760
Lifetime		15	0	1	0	1	2	0	4	3,024	144	4	3,281	$26,760

Year	Driver	Starts	Poles	Finish 1	2	3	4	5	6–10	Laps	Laps Led	Races Led	Miles	$

T.B. Faucett

Year	Driver	Starts	Poles	1	2	3	4	5	6–10	Laps	Laps Led	Races Led	Miles	$
1961	Ralph Earnhardt	1	0	0	0	0	0	0	0	62	0	0	93	250
1961	Woodie Wilson	5	0	0	0	0	0	0	1	828	0	0	1,324	2,625
1962	Woodie Wilson	1	0	0	0	0	0	0	1	39	0	0	98	225
1962	Stick Elliott	1	0	0	0	0	0	0	0	341	0	0	512	350
Lifetime		8	0	0	0	0	0	0	2	1,270	0	0	2,026	$3,450

Tinker Faulkner

Year	Driver	Starts	Poles	1	2	3	4	5	6–10	Laps	Laps Led	Races Led	Miles	$
1966	George England	1	0	0	0	0	0	0	0	293	0	0	440	745
Lifetime		1	0	0	0	0	0	0	0	293	0	0	440	$745

Doc Faustina

Year	Driver	Starts	Poles	1	2	3	4	5	6–10	Laps	Laps Led	Races Led	Miles	$
1971	Doc Faustina	3	0	0	0	0	0	0	0	402	0	0	864	2,745
1971	Richard Childress	1	0	0	0	0	0	0	0	180	0	0	180	645
1971	Dave Marcis	2	0	0	0	0	0	0	0	146	0	0	360	1,555
1971	Jim Vandiver	1	0	0	0	0	0	0	0	10	0	0	15	640
1971	Earl Brooks	2	0	0	0	0	0	0	0	450	0	0	662	2,095
1971	Dick May	1	0	0	0	0	0	0	0	268	0	0	408	590
1972	Mel Larson	1	0	0	0	0	0	0	0	209	0	0	418	760
1972	J.D. McDuffie	1	0	0	0	0	0	0	0	3	0	0	2	275
1972	Doc Faustina	5	0	0	0	0	0	0	0	607	0	0	1,161	3,635
1973	Dick Simon	2	0	0	0	0	0	0	1	264	0	0	689	3,700
1973	Wendell Scott	1	0	0	0	0	0	0	0	305	0	0	458	1,800
1973	Charlie Blanton	1	0	0	0	0	0	0	0	351	0	0	527	1,825
1974	Neil Castles	1	0	0	0	0	0	0	0	21	0	0	21	780
1974	Earl Brooks	1	0	0	0	0	0	0	0	1	0	0	1	1,100
1974	Harry Gant	2	0	0	0	0	0	0	0	403	0	0	605	3,729
1974	John Martin	3	0	0	0	0	0	0	0	267	0	0	599	3,420
1974	Charlie Blanton	1	0	0	0	0	0	0	0	231	0	0	235	720
1974	Dick Simon	1	0	0	0	0	0	0	0	96	0	0	240	3,410
1975	Doc Faustina	1	0	0	0	0	0	0	0	116	0	0	290	880
1976	Doc Faustina	1	0	0	0	0	0	0	0	378	0	0	378	735
1976	James Hylton	1	0	0	0	0	0	0	0	171	0	0	174	655
1976	Bruce Blodgett	1	0	0	0	0	0	0	0	447	0	0	235	800
1976	Neil Castles	1	0	0	0	0	0	0	0	125	0	0	78	425
Lifetime		35	0	0	0	0	0	0	1	5,451	0	0	8,600	$36,919

Martin Fay

Year	Driver	Starts	Poles	1	2	3	4	5	6–10	Laps	Laps Led	Races Led	Miles	$
1970	Pat Fay	1	0	0	0	0	0	0	0	24	0	0	63	655
Lifetime		1	0	0	0	0	0	0	0	24	0	0	63	$655

Ross Ferguson

Year	Driver	Starts	Poles	1	2	3	4	5	6–10	Laps	Laps Led	Races Led	Miles	$
1971	Dick Brooks	3	0	0	0	0	0	0	0	250	0	0	212	1,821
Lifetime		3	0	0	0	0	0	0	0	250	0	0	212	$1,821

John Fernandez

Year	Driver	Starts	Poles	1	2	3	4	5	6–10	Laps	Laps Led	Races Led	Miles	$
1954	Marvin Panch	1	0	0	0	0	0	0	1	244	0	0	244	200
Lifetime		1	0	0	0	0	0	0	1	244	0	0	244	$200

Gayle Ferree

Year	Driver	Starts	Poles	1	2	3	4	5	6–10	Laps	Laps Led	Races Led	Miles	$
1992	Ed Ferree	1	0	0	0	0	0	0	0	50	0	0	123	4,035
1993	Ed Ferree	2	0	0	0	0	0	0	0	507	0	0	561	12,865
Lifetime		3	0	0	0	0	0	0	0	557	0	0	684	$16,900

Lynda Ferreri

Year	Driver	Starts	Poles	1	2	3	4	5	6–10	Laps	Laps Led	Races Led	Miles	$
1976	Janet Guthrie	5	0	0	0	0	0	0	0	1,183	0	0	2,015	8,179
1977	Janet Guthrie	19	0	0	0	0	0	0	4	5,031	5	1	6,182	38,045
1978	Janet Guthrie	7	0	0	0	0	0	0	1	1,147	0	0	2,406	18,120
Lifetime		31	0	0	0	0	0	0	5	7,361	5	1	10,603	$64,344

Jim Fiebelkorn

Year	Driver	Starts	Poles	1	2	3	4	5	6–10	Laps	Laps Led	Races Led	Miles	$
1951	Jim Fiebelkorn	17	0	0	1	0	0	0	3	984	0	0	913	1,275
Lifetime		17	0	0	1	0	0	0	3	984	0	0	913	$1,275

Year	Driver	Starts	Poles	Finish 1	2	3	4	5	6–10	Laps	Laps Led	Races Led	Miles	$

Joe Fields

Year	Driver	Starts	Poles	1	2	3	4	5	6–10	Laps	Laps Led	Races Led	Miles	$
1981	Joe Fields	6	0	0	0	0	0	0	0	1,681	0	0	1,160	7,750
1982	Joe Fields	3	0	0	0	0	0	0	0	738	0	0	397	2,610
1983	Joe Fields	3	0	0	0	0	0	0	0	1,064	0	0	787	4,315
1984	Joe Fields	2	0	0	0	0	0	0	0	661	0	0	661	1,915
Lifetime		14	0	0	0	0	0	0	0	4,144	0	0	3,005	$16,590

Junior Fields

Year	Driver	Starts	Poles	1	2	3	4	5	6–10	Laps	Laps Led	Races Led	Miles	$
1971	J.D. McDuffie	1	0	0	0	0	0	0	0	2	0	0	3	645
1971	Bill Chevalier	1	0	0	0	0	0	0	1	188	0	0	282	620
1971	Charlie Glotzbach	2	0	0	0	0	0	0	0	42	0	0	36	1,045
1971	Ed Negre	4	0	0	0	0	0	0	1	1,004	0	0	788	2,708
1971	Speedy Thompson	1	0	0	0	0	0	0	0	376	0	0	564	1,800
1971	Richard D. Brown	8	0	0	0	0	0	0	2	1,675	0	0	2,264	7,830
1971	Pete Hamilton	2	0	0	0	0	0	0	0	118	5	1	37	200
1971	L.D. Fields	1	0	0	0	0	0	0	0	31	0	0	31	570
Lifetime		20	0	0	0	0	0	0	4	3,436	5	1	4,005	$15,418

Wade Fields

Year	Driver	Starts	Poles	1	2	3	4	5	6–10	Laps	Laps Led	Races Led	Miles	$
1951	Wade Fields	1	0	0	0	0	0	0	0		0	0		25
Lifetime		1	0	0	0	0	0	0	0		0	0		$25

Lou Figaro

Year	Driver	Starts	Poles	1	2	3	4	5	6–10	Laps	Laps Led	Races Led	Miles	$
1954	Lou Figaro	3	0	0	0	0	0	0	2	461	0	0	403	425
Lifetime		3	0	0	0	0	0	0	2	461	0	0	403	$425

Frank Filizer

Year	Driver	Starts	Poles	1	2	3	4	5	6–10	Laps	Laps Led	Races Led	Miles	$
1960	Sal Tovella	2	0	0	0	0	0	0	0	43	0	0	108	275
Lifetime		2	0	0	0	0	0	0	0	43	0	0	108	$275

Corey Fillip

Year	Driver	Starts	Poles	1	2	3	4	5	6–10	Laps	Laps Led	Races Led	Miles	$
1987	Slick Johnson	1	0	0	0	0	0	0	0	11	0	0	7	1,125
1987	Eddie Bierschwale	1	0	0	0	0	0	0	0	392	0	0	245	1,430
1987	Buddy Arrington	2	0	0	0	0	0	0	0	881	0	0	470	3,995
1987	Chet Fillip	4	0	0	0	0	0	0	0	620	0	0	896	17,875
1987	Mike Potter	4	0	0	0	0	0	0	0	920	0	0	766	5,955
Lifetime		12	0	0	0	0	0	0	0	2,824	0	0	2,384	$30,380

James Finch

Year	Driver	Starts	Poles	1	2	3	4	5	6–10	Laps	Laps Led	Races Led	Miles	$
1990	Jeff Purvis	4	0	0	0	0	0	0	0	671	0	0	635	37,630
1991	Jeff Purvis	6	0	0	0	0	0	0	0	888	0	0	1,486	41,110
1992	Jeff Purvis	2	0	0	0	0	0	0	0	338	0	0	535	10,625
1993	Jeff Purvis	3	0	0	0	0	0	0	0	378	0	0	980	24,675
1994	Jeff Purvis	6	0	0	0	0	0	0	0	942	0	0	1,981	67,440
1995	Jeff Purvis	6	0	0	0	0	0	0	0	631	0	0	1,441	86,505
1996	Jeff Purvis	4	0	0	0	0	0	0	0	532	0	0	1,364	91,127
2001	Jeff Purvis	4	0	0	0	0	0	0	0	409	0	0	1,066	238,985
2002	Geoffrey Bodine	5	0	0	0	1	0	0	1	714	0	0	1,612	902,452
Lifetime		40	0	0	0	1	0	0	1	5,503	0	1,500,549	11,101	

John Findlay

Year	Driver	Starts	Poles	1	2	3	4	5	6–10	Laps	Laps Led	Races Led	Miles	$
1957	John Findlay	3	0	0	0	0	0	0	1	382	0	0	191	320
1958	John Findlay	3	0	0	0	0	0	0	0	485	0	0	225	305
Lifetime		6	0	0	0	0	0	0	1	867	0	0	416	$625

Jim Findley

Year	Driver	Starts	Poles	1	2	3	4	5	6–10	Laps	Laps Led	Races Led	Miles	$
1958	John Findlay	1	0	0	0	0	0	1	0	189	0	0	95	225
1959	John Findlay	1	0	0	0	0	0	0	0	116	0	0	58	50
Lifetime		2	0	0	0	0	0	1	0	305	0	0	153	$275

Phil Finney

Year	Driver	Starts	Poles	1	2	3	4	5	6–10	Laps	Laps Led	Races Led	Miles	$
1971	Phil Finney	1	0	0	0	0	0	0	0	357	0	0	193	400

Year	Driver	Starts	Poles	Finish 1	2	3	4	5	6–10	Laps	Laps Led	Races Led	Miles	$

Phil Finney *continued*

Year	Driver	Starts	Poles	1	2	3	4	5	6–10	Laps	Laps Led	Races Led	Miles	$
1974	Phil Finney	1	0	0	0	0	0	0	0	100	0	0	266	1,010
1977	Phil Finney	1	0	0	0	0	0	0	0	148	0	0	225	645
1980	Phil Finney	2	0	0	0	0	0	0	0	188	0	0	476	3,125
Lifetime		5	0	0	0	0	0	0	0	793	0	0	1,161	$5,180

Lonnie Fish

Year	Driver	Starts	Poles	1	2	3	4	5	6–10	Laps	Laps Led	Races Led	Miles	$
1956	Larry Frank	1	0	0	0	0	0	0	0	77	0	0	39	50
1957	George West	1	0	0	0	0	0	0	0		0	0		0
1957	Shep Langdon	2	0	0	0	0	0	0	0	268	0	0	268	0
1957	Larry Frank	4	0	0	0	0	0	0	0	1,113	0	0	935	995
1957	Don Gray	3	0	0	0	0	0	0	0	549	0	0	604	325
1957	George Green	11	0	0	0	0	0	0	2	1,779	0	0	928	1,435
1958	Tiny Lund	1	0	0	0	1	0	0	0	149	0	0	50	380
Lifetime		23	0	0	0	1	0	0	2	3,935	0	0	2,822	$3,185

Bob Fish

Year	Driver	Starts	Poles	1	2	3	4	5	6–10	Laps	Laps Led	Races Led	Miles	$
1955	Fireball Roberts	2	1	0	0	0	0	0	0	69	4	1	201	140
1956	Tommy Thompson	1	0	0	0	0	0	0	0		0	0		0
1958	Fireball Roberts	1	0	0	0	0	0	0	1	37	0	0	152	250
Lifetime		4	1	0	0	0	0	0	1	106	4	1	353	$390

Bob Fisher

Year	Driver	Starts	Poles	1	2	3	4	5	6–10	Laps	Laps Led	Races Led	Miles	$
1992	Ron Hornaday Jr.	2	0	0	0	0	0	0	0	373	0	0	482	11,290
Lifetime		2	0	0	0	0	0	0	0	373	0	0	482	$11,290

Bobby Fisher

Year	Driver	Starts	Poles	1	2	3	4	5	6–10	Laps	Laps Led	Races Led	Miles	$
1978	Bobby Fisher	2	0	0	0	0	0	0	0	33	0	0	22	1,410
1979	Bobby Fisher	1	0	0	0	0	0	0	0	136	0	0	204	1,465
Lifetime		3	0	0	0	0	0	0	0	169	0	0	226	$2,875

Jack Fisher

Year	Driver	Starts	Poles	1	2	3	4	5	6–10	Laps	Laps Led	Races Led	Miles	$
1952	Dick Stacey	1	0	0	0	0	0	0	0	175	0	0	175	25
1952	Jack Fisher	2	0	0	0	0	0	0	0	307	0	0	307	60
Lifetime		3	0	0	0	0	0	0	0	482	0	0	482	$85

Joe Fisher

Year	Driver	Starts	Poles	1	2	3	4	5	6–10	Laps	Laps Led	Races Led	Miles	$
1954	Art Watts	2	0	0	0	0	0	0	0	336	0	0	168	25
Lifetime		2	0	0	0	0	0	0	0	336	0	0	168	$25

Ken Fisher

Year	Driver	Starts	Poles	1	2	3	4	5	6–10	Laps	Laps Led	Races Led	Miles	$
1954	Ken Fisher	5	0	0	0	0	0	0	1	879	0	0	657	400
1955	Ken Fisher	9	0	0	0	0	0	0	1	453	0	0	287	175
Lifetime		14	0	0	0	0	0	0	2	1,332	0	0	944	$575

Terry Fisher

Year	Driver	Starts	Poles	1	2	3	4	5	6–10	Laps	Laps Led	Races Led	Miles	$
1995	Terry Fisher	1	0	0	0	0	0	0	0	57	0	0	144	9,760
Lifetime		1	0	0	0	0	0	0	0	57	0	0	144	$9,760

Armando Fitz / Terry Bradshaw

Year	Driver	Starts	Poles	1	2	3	4	5	6–10	Laps	Laps Led	Races Led	Miles	$
2002	Ron Hornaday Jr.	1	0	0	0	0	0	0	0	307	0	0	307	40,275
Lifetime		1	0	0	0	0	0	0	0	307	0	0	307	$40,275

J.M. Fitzgibbons

Year	Driver	Starts	Poles	1	2	3	4	5	6–10	Laps	Laps Led	Races Led	Miles	$
1955	Sonny Hutchins	1	0	0	0	0	0	0	0	15	0	0	8	0
1955	Millard Wright	1	0	0	0	0	0	0	0	43	0	0	22	50
1955	Bill Blair	5	0	0	0	0	0	0	0	427	0	0	262	175
1955	Blackie Pitt	7	0	0	0	0	0	0	2	806	0	0	443	660
1956	Red Farmer	3	0	0	0	0	0	0	0	324	0	0	162	125

Year	Driver	Starts	Poles	Finish 1	2	3	4	5	6–10	Laps	Laps Led	Races Led	Miles	$

J.M. Fitzgibbons *continued*

Year	Driver	Starts	Poles	1	2	3	4	5	6–10	Laps	Laps Led	Races Led	Miles	$
1956	Bobby Johns	1	0	0	0	0	0	0	1	349	0	0	480	700
Lifetime		18	0	0	0	0	0	0	3	1,964	0	0	1,376	$1,710

Tommy Fleming

Year	Driver	Starts	Poles	1	2	3	4	5	6–10	Laps	Laps Led	Races Led	Miles	$
1969	Bobby Fleming	1	0	0	0	0	0	0	0	146	0	0	388	1,400
Lifetime		1	0	0	0	0	0	0	0	146	0	0	388	$1,400

Ray Fletcher

Year	Driver	Starts	Poles	1	2	3	4	5	6–10	Laps	Laps Led	Races Led	Miles	$
1955	Van Van Wey	1	0	0	0	0	0	0	0	247	0	0	340	60
Lifetime		1	0	0	0	0	0	0	0	247	0	0	340	$60

Sam Fletcher

Year	Driver	Starts	Poles	1	2	3	4	5	6–10	Laps	Laps Led	Races Led	Miles	$
1965	Iggy Katona	1	0	0	0	0	0	0	1	251	0	0	377	850
1965	Nelson Stacy	1	0	0	0	0	0	0	0	83	0	0	208	480
1965	Johnny Allen	2	0	0	0	0	0	0	0	120	0	0	300	1,235
1965	Bunkie Blackburn	2	0	0	0	0	0	0	0	155	0	0	220	925
1965	Curtis Turner	1	0	0	0	0	0	0	0	51	0	0	70	545
Lifetime		7	0	0	0	0	0	0	1	660	0	0	1,174	$4,035

Ruby Flock

Year	Driver	Starts	Poles	1	2	3	4	5	6–10	Laps	Laps Led	Races Led	Miles	$
1949	Sara Christian	1	0	0	0	0	0	0	0		0	0		25
Lifetime		1	0	0	0	0	0	0	0		0	0		$25

Tim Flock

Year	Driver	Starts	Poles	1	2	3	4	5	6–10	Laps	Laps Led	Races Led	Miles	$
1958	Tim Flock	1	0	0	0	0	0	0	0	66	25	1	66	310
Lifetime		1	0	0	0	0	0	0	0	66	25	1	66	$310

Jimmy Florian

Year	Driver	Starts	Poles	1	2	3	4	5	6–10	Laps	Laps Led	Races Led	Miles	$
1950	Jimmy Florian	9	1	1	0	1	1	0	2	1,060	40	1	850	2,510
1951	Jimmy Florian	6	0	0	0	0	1	0	2		0	0		575
1952	Jimmy Florian	6	0	0	0	0	0	0	2	283	0	0	188	175
1954	Jimmy Florian	1	0	0	0	0	0	0	0	34	0	0	139	25
Lifetime		22	1	1	0	1	2	0	6	1,377	40	1	1,178	$3,285

Larry Flynn

Year	Driver	Starts	Poles	1	2	3	4	5	6–10	Laps	Laps Led	Races Led	Miles	$
1959	Larry Flynn	4	0	0	0	0	0	0	0	206	0	0	283	275
Lifetime		4	0	0	0	0	0	0	0	206	0	0	283	$275

Sam Fogle

Year	Driver	Starts	Poles	1	2	3	4	5	6–10	Laps	Laps Led	Races Led	Miles	$
1965	Possum Jones	1	0	0	0	0	0	0	0	0	0	0	0	100
1965	Darel Dieringer	3	0	0	0	0	0	0	0	129	0	0	65	320
1965	Samuel Smith	1	0	0	0	0	0	0	0	108	0	0	54	110
1965	Doug Cooper	1	0	0	0	0	0	0	0	124	0	0	62	110
1965	J.T. Putney	1	0	0	0	0	0	0	1	233	0	0	47	175
1965	Curtis Crider	1	0	0	0	0	0	0	1	157	0	0	141	225
1965	LeeRoy Yarbrough	3	0	0	0	0	0	0	0	234	0	0	109	120
1965	Cale Yarborough	11	0	0	0	0	0	0	5	1,593	3	1	736	2,105
1965	Harvey Jones	1	0	0	0	0	0	1	0	195	0	0	98	275
1965	Bob Grossman	1	0	0	0	0	0	0	0	13	0	0	30	175
1965	Paul Moore	1	0	0	0	0	0	0	1	376	0	0	141	225
1965	Ned Setzer	1	0	0	0	0	0	0	0	70	0	0	63	110
1965	Elmo Henderson	1	0	0	0	0	0	0	0	101	0	0	51	130
Lifetime		27	0	0	0	0	0	1	8	3,333	3	1	1,595	$4,180

Dick Foley

Year	Driver	Starts	Poles	1	2	3	4	5	6–10	Laps	Laps Led	Races Led	Miles	$
1957	Dick Foley	1	0	0	0	0	0	0	0		0	0		0
1958	Dick Foley	1	0	0	0	0	0	0	0	34	0	0	139	75
1959	Dick Foley	3	0	0	0	0	0	0	0	226	0	0	565	250

Year	Driver	Starts	Poles	Finish 1	2	3	4	5	6–10	Laps	Laps Led	Races Led	Miles	$

Dick Foley *continued*

Year	Driver	Starts	Poles	1	2	3	4	5	6–10	Laps	Laps Led	Races Led	Miles	$
1960	Dick Foley	2	0	0	0	0	0	0	0	69	0	0	173	325
Lifetime		7	0	0	0	0	0	0	0	329	0	0	877	$650

Clint Folsom

Year	Driver	Starts	Poles	1	2	3	4	5	6–10	Laps	Laps Led	Races Led	Miles	$
1992	Stan Fox	2	0	0	0	0	0	0	0	146	0	0	359	11,750
Lifetime		2	0	0	0	0	0	0	0	146	0	0	359	$11,750

Henry Ford

Year	Driver	Starts	Poles	1	2	3	4	5	6–10	Laps	Laps Led	Races Led	Miles	$
1955	Junior Johnson	1	0	0	0	0	0	0	0	75	0	0	75	50
1955	Buck Baker	5	0	0	0	1	1	1	0	715	8	1	358	1,160
1955	Henry Ford	5	0	0	0	0	0	0	0	579	0	0	336	190
Lifetime		11	0	0	0	1	1	1	0	1,369	8	1	769	$1,400

John Foster

Year	Driver	Starts	Poles	1	2	3	4	5	6–10	Laps	Laps Led	Races Led	Miles	$
1956	Tim Flock	4	2	0	0	0	0	0	0	670	73	3	637	740
1956	Doug Cox	3	1	0	0	0	0	1	1	511	0	0	231	460
1957	Doug Cox	3	0	0	0	0	0	1	0	230	0	0	176	460
Lifetime		10	3	0	0	0	0	2	1	1,411	73	3	1,043	$1,660

Earl Foushee

Year	Driver	Starts	Poles	1	2	3	4	5	6–10	Laps	Laps Led	Races Led	Miles	$
1953	Earl Foushee	1	0	0	0	0	0	0	0	256	0	0	256	50
Lifetime		1	0	0	0	0	0	0	0	256	0	0	256	$50

James Fowler

Year	Driver	Starts	Poles	1	2	3	4	5	6–10	Laps	Laps Led	Races Led	Miles	$
1953	Cotton Hodges	1	0	0	0	0	0	0	0	32	0	0	131	25
1983	Ed Baugess	1	0	0	0	0	0	0	0	13	0	0	8	725
Lifetime		2	0	0	0	0	0	0	0	45	0	0	139	$750

Bobby Fox

Year	Driver	Starts	Poles	1	2	3	4	5	6–10	Laps	Laps Led	Races Led	Miles	$
1984	Bobby Fox	1	0	0	0	0	0	0	0	352	0	0	358	1,495
Lifetime		1	0	0	0	0	0	0	0	352	0	0	358	$1,495

Leon Fox

Year	Driver	Starts	Poles	1	2	3	4	5	6–10	Laps	Laps Led	Races Led	Miles	$
1974	Leon Fox	1	0	0	0	0	0	0	0	113	0	0	296	1,210
Lifetime		1	0	0	0	0	0	0	0	113	0	0	296	$1,210

Ray Fox

Year	Driver	Starts	Poles	1	2	3	4	5	6–10	Laps	Laps Led	Races Led	Miles	$
1962	Darel Dieringer	1	1	0	0	0	0	0	0	3	0	0	8	50
1962	David Pearson	7	0	0	0	0	0	0	5	1,284	278	3	2,028	10,390
1962	Junior Johnson	6	1	1	1	0	0	0	0	1,347	332	4	1,297	22,385
1963	Jim Paschal	2	0	0	0	0	0	0	0	231	8	1	408	1,300
1963	Buck Baker	1	0	0	0	0	0	0	0	67	0	0	101	450
1963	G.C. Spencer	5	0	0	0	1	0	0	1	604	21	1	568	1,400
1963	Junior Johnson	32	9	7	2	2	0	1	1	5,608	2,396	21	4,398	64,090
1964	Bobby Schuyler	1	0	0	0	0	0	0	0	3	0	0	1	100
1964	LeeRoy Yarbrough	11	0	0	1	0	1	1	1	2,175	8	1	2,586	7,935
1964	Junior Johnson	11	0	1	1	0	3	0	2	2,284	16	2	2,148	8,940
1964	Buck Baker	23	0	2	1	3	2	3	2	4,940	138	4	4,022	33,890
1964	Buddy Baker	2	0	0	0	0	0	0	0	10	0	0	4	200
1965	Bunkie Blackburn	2	0	0	0	0	0	0	0	129	0	0	200	1,130
1965	LeeRoy Yarbrough	6	0	0	0	0	0	1	0	860	42	2	1,313	4,745
1966	Bunkie Blackburn	1	0	0	0	0	1	0	0	283	0	0	389	2,225
1966	Buddy Baker	6	0	0	1	0	0	0	1	1,155	106	3	1,625	13,930
1966	Earl Balmer	2	0	1	0	0	0	0	0	61	1	1	153	2,045
1967	Innes Ireland	2	0	0	0	0	0	0	1	165	0	0	413	1,265
1967	Buddy Baker	11	0	1	1	1	1	0	1	2,403	480	8	3,349	42,550
1968	Buddy Baker	37	4	1	4	6	3	2	2	7,890	454	11	5,531	54,075
1969	Jim Vandiver	2	0	0	1	0	0	0	0	252	102	1	596	13,225
1969	Buddy Baker	6	2	0	0	0	1	1	0	911	191	4	1,097	13,440

				Finish							Laps	Races		
Year	Driver	Starts	Poles	1	2	3	4	5	6–10	Laps	Led	Led	Miles	$

Ray Fox continued

Year	Driver	Starts	Poles	1	2	3	4	5	6–10	Laps	Laps Led	Races Led	Miles	$
1969	Charlie Glotzbach	1	0	0	0	0	0	0	0	46	4	1	115	740
1969	Dr. Don Tarr	6	0	0	0	0	0	0	3	1,160	6	1	2,121	10,485
1969	Neil Castles	2	0	0	0	0	0	0	0	255	0	0	370	2,085
1969	Paul Goldsmith	1	0	0	0	0	0	0	0	40	0	0	20	465
1970	Fred Lorenzen	4	1	0	0	1	0	0	0	656	3	1	1,031	9,295
1970	Jim Vandiver	3	0	0	0	0	0	0	1	324	0	0	555	2,640
1971	Cale Yarborough	3	0	0	0	0	0	0	1	355	13	1	648	2,790
1972	Cale Yarborough	1	0	0	0	0	0	0	1	188	0	0	470	4,660
1974	Wally Dallenbach,	1	0	0	0	0	0	0	0	125	0	0	188	1,395
Lifetime		199	18	14	13	14	12	9	23	35,814	4,599	71	37,750	$334,315

A.J. Foyt

Year	Driver	Starts	Poles	1	2	3	4	5	6–10	Laps	Laps Led	Races Led	Miles	$
1973	A.J. Foyt	3	0	0	0	0	1	0	0	467	0	0	947	8,555
1974	A.J. Foyt	2	0	0	0	0	0	1	0	243	6	1	608	9,205
1977	Johnny Rutherford	1	0	0	0	0	0	0	0	114	0	0	303	1,865
1977	A.J. Foyt	6	1	0	0	0	0	1	2	1,058	20	3	2,165	29,200
1978	Ron Hutcherson	3	0	0	0	0	1	0	0	388	0	0	870	24,720
1978	A.J. Foyt	2	0	0	0	1	0	0	0	255	0	0	667	24,875
1979	A.J. Foyt	2	0	0	0	1	0	0	1	356	7	2	890	41,690
1980	A.J. Foyt	1	0	0	0	0	0	0	0	69	0	0	173	3,575
1980	Don Whittington	1	0	0	0	0	0	0	0	61	0	0	93	830
1981	A.J. Foyt	3	0	0	0	0	0	0	1	530	0	0	1,007	9,210
1982	A.J. Foyt	2	0	0	0	0	0	0	0	162	0	0	388	9,405
1983	A.J. Foyt	3	0	0	0	0	0	0	0	406	0	0	890	22,935
1984	A.J. Foyt	3	0	0	0	0	0	0	0	224	0	0	418	8,830
1985	A.J. Foyt	7	0	0	0	0	0	1	0	966	2	2	1,781	29,750
1986	A.J. Foyt	5	0	0	0	0	0	0	0	640	1	1	1,220	24,135
1987	A.J. Foyt	5	0	0	0	0	0	0	0	738	2	2	1,249	13,205
1988	A.J. Foyt	7	0	0	0	0	0	0	0	920	9	3	1,992	29,660
1989	Tracy Leslie	2	0	0	0	0	0	0	0	557	0	0	934	8,800
1989	A.J. Foyt	7	0	0	0	0	0	0	0	860	6	2	1,869	31,995
1990	A.J. Foyt	3	0	0	0	0	0	0	0	301	4	1	782	26,725
1991	Mike Chase	4	0	0	0	0	0	0	0	751	0	0	1,371	19,225
1994	A.J. Foyt	1	0	0	0	0	0	0	0	156	0	0	390	29,000
2000	Dick Trickle	2	0	0	0	0	0	0	0	783	0	0	656	52,150
2000	Rick Mast	24	0	0	0	0	0	0	2	6,530	1	1	9,030	896,825
2000	Mike Bliss	1	0	0	0	0	0	0	0	196	0	0	490	88,875
2001	Ron Hornaday Jr.	32	0	0	0	0	0	0	1	8,659	29	3	11,102	1,383,330
2002	Stacy Compton	18	0	0	0	0	0	0	0	4,808	2	2	6,569	989,783
2002	P.J. Jones	1	0	0	0	0	1	0	0	90	0	0	221	65,950
2002	Mike Wallace	17	0	0	0	0	0	0	1	4,766	1	1	5,462	805,323
Lifetime		168	1	0	0	2	3	3	8	36,054	90	24	54,541	$4,689,626

Bill France

Year	Driver	Starts	Poles	1	2	3	4	5	6–10	Laps	Laps Led	Races Led	Miles	$
1969	Tiny Lund	1	0	0	0	0	0	0	1	152	28	1	404	1,675
Lifetime		1	0	0	0	0	0	0	1	152	28	1	404	$1,675

O.C. Francis

Year	Driver	Starts	Poles	1	2	3	4	5	6–10	Laps	Laps Led	Races Led	Miles	$
1952	Charles Barry	3	0	0	0	0	0	0	0	312	0	0	162	75
1953	Charles Barry	1	0	0	0	0	0	0	1		0	0		100
Lifetime		4	0	0	0	0	0	0	1	312	0	0	162	$175

Larry Frank

Year	Driver	Starts	Poles	1	2	3	4	5	6–10	Laps	Laps Led	Races Led	Miles	$
1958	Larry Frank	7	0	0	0	1	0	0	2	1,713	0	0	904	1,880
1959	Larry Frank	14	0	0	1	0	1	2	5	3,210	39	1	2,602	5,918
1964	Larry Frank	6	0	0	0	0	0	0	1	1,052	0	0	1,469	4,680
1965	Larry Frank	9	0	0	0	0	1	0	0	1,009	33	1	1,200	5,080
Lifetime		36	0	0	1	1	2	2	8	6,984	72	2	6,175	$17,558

Walt Frank

Year	Driver	Starts	Poles	1	2	3	4	5	6–10	Laps	Laps Led	Races Led	Miles	$
1949	Budd Olsen	1	0	0	0	0	0	0	0	180	0	0	180	75
Lifetime		1	0	0	0	0	0	0	0	180	0	0	180	$75

Year	Driver	Starts	Poles	Finish 1	2	3	4	5	6–10	Laps	Laps Led	Races Led	Miles	$

Warren Fraser

Year	Driver	Starts	Poles	1	2	3	4	5	6–10	Laps	Laps Led	Races Led	Miles	$
1951	Danny Weinberg	1	0	0	0	0	0	0	0		0	0		25
1951	Dick Rathmann	1	0	0	0	0	0	0	1		0	0		150
1951	George Seeger	1	0	0	0	0	0	0	1		0	0		50
Lifetime		3	0	0	0	0	0	0	2		0	0		$225

Joe Frasson

Year	Driver	Starts	Poles	1	2	3	4	5	6–10	Laps	Laps Led	Races Led	Miles	$
1970	Joe Frasson	19	0	0	0	0	0	0	2	4,358	0	0	5,995	19,095
1971	Joe Frasson	17	0	0	0	0	0	1	3	3,752	0	0	5,699	20,950
1972	George Follmer	1	0	0	0	0	0	0	0	4	0	0	10	1,440
1972	Joe Frasson	16	0	0	0	1	0	0	3	3,013	9	2	4,638	21,645
1973	Joe Frasson	14	0	0	0	1	1	0	2	2,732	1	1	4,390	25,884
1974	Joe Frasson	14	0	0	0	0	0	0	3	2,141	13	3	3,671	22,629
1975	Joe Frasson	9	0	0	0	0	0	0	1	1,352	1	1	2,018	10,710
1976	Harry Gant	1	0	0	0	0	0	0	1	387	0	0	581	5,430
1976	Joe Frasson	9	0	0	0	0	0	0	1	863	1	1	1,510	13,565
1976	Buck Baker	1	0	0	0	0	0	0	0	32	0	0	80	830
1977	Joe Frasson	1	0	0	0	0	0	0	0	126	0	0	335	2,050
1977	Dick Trickle	1	0	0	0	0	0	0	0	141	0	0	212	1,100
1978	Joe Frasson	5	0	0	0	0	0	0	0	1,436	0	0	1,878	8,560
Lifetime		108	0	0	0	2	1	1	16	20,337	25	8	31,018	$153,888

Fred Frazier

Year	Driver	Starts	Poles	1	2	3	4	5	6–10	Laps	Laps Led	Races Led	Miles	$
1956	Lee Petty	1	0	0	0	0	0	0	0	340	0	0	468	175
1956	Joe Weatherly	1	0	0	0	0	0	0	1	170	0	0	68	100
1956	Bunk Moore	3	0	0	0	0	0	1	1	537	0	0	311	745
1956	Fred Frazier	2	0	0	0	0	0	0	1	288	0	0	144	200
1956	Glen Wood	1	0	0	0	0	0	0	0	67	0	0	34	50
Lifetime		8	0	0	0	0	0	1	3	1,402	0	0	1,024	$1,270

Joe Frazier

Year	Driver	Starts	Poles	1	2	3	4	5	6–10	Laps	Laps Led	Races Led	Miles	$
1957	George Parrish	5	0	0	0	0	0	0	0	483	0	0	472	525
1958	George Parrish	1	0	0	0	0	0	0	0	7	0	0	2	50
Lifetime		6	0	0	0	0	0	0	0	490	0	0	474	$575

Ray Frederick

Year	Driver	Starts	Poles	1	2	3	4	5	6–10	Laps	Laps Led	Races Led	Miles	$
1974	Jackie Rogers	20	0	0	0	0	0	0	6	4,235	1	1	6,248	30,332
1975	Jackie Rogers	1	0	0	0	0	0	0	0	370	0	0	555	2,815
Lifetime		21	0	0	0	0	0	0	6	4,605	1	1	6,803	$33,147

Eric Freedlander

Year	Driver	Starts	Poles	1	2	3	4	5	6–10	Laps	Laps Led	Races Led	Miles	$
1985	Tommy Ellis	14	0	0	0	0	0	0	1	2,853	0	0	3,511	27,695
1986	Tommy Ellis	24	0	0	0	0	0	0	3	6,559	50	5	7,334	77,310
1987	Tommy Ellis	4	0	0	0	0	0	0	0	564	0	0	661	16,535
1987	Dale Jarrett	24	0	0	0	0	0	0	2	4,788	0	0	5,681	132,655
Lifetime		66	0	0	0	0	0	0	6	14,764	50	5	17,187	$254,195

Bob Freeman

Year	Driver	Starts	Poles	1	2	3	4	5	6–10	Laps	Laps Led	Races Led	Miles	$
1970	Roy Mayne	1	0	0	0	0	0	0	0	405	0	0	222	465
1970	John Kenney	11	0	0	0	0	0	0	0	1,385	0	0	675	4,115
1971	Charlie Roberts	3	0	0	0	0	0	0	1	651	0	0	925	3,715
Lifetime		15	0	0	0	0	0	0	1	2,441	0	0	1,822	$8,295

Dick Freeman

Year	Driver	Starts	Poles	1	2	3	4	5	6–10	Laps	Laps Led	Races Led	Miles	$
1959	Dick Freeman	3	0	0	0	0	0	0	0	695	0	0	800	475
1960	Cotton Owens	1	0	0	0	0	0	0	0	137	0	0	86	60
1960	George Tet	1	0	0	0	0	0	0	0	171	0	0	257	200
1960	Dick Freeman	2	0	0	0	0	0	0	0	41	0	0	103	250
Lifetime		7	0	0	0	0	0	0	0	1,044	0	0	1,244	$985

Pat Freeman

Year	Driver	Starts	Poles	1	2	3	4	5	6–10	Laps	Laps Led	Races Led	Miles	$
1954	Dick Freeman	1	0	0	0	0	0	0	0	20	0	0	10	0
Lifetime		1	0	0	0	0	0	0	0	20	0	0	10	$0

Year	Driver	Starts	Poles	Finish						Laps	Laps Led	Races Led	Miles	$
				1	2	3	4	5	6–10	Laps	Led	Led	Miles	$

Charles French

Year	Driver	Starts	Poles	1	2	3	4	5	6–10	Laps	Laps Led	Races Led	Miles	$
1960	Ken Johnson	4	0	0	0	0	0	0	0	317	0	0	721	460
1961	Ken Johnson	1	0	0	0	0	0	0	0	33	0	0	83	50
1961	Jim Hendrickson	2	0	0	0	0	0	0	0	208	0	0	349	275
Lifetime		7	0	0	0	0	0	0	0	558	0	0	1,152	$785

James French

Year	Driver	Starts	Poles	1	2	3	4	5	6–10	Laps	Laps Led	Races Led	Miles	$
1961	Ken Johnson	1	0	0	0	0	0	0	0	3	0	0	8	200
Lifetime		1	0	0	0	0	0	0	0	3	0	0	8	$200

Bernard Friedland

Year	Driver	Starts	Poles	1	2	3	4	5	6–10	Laps	Laps Led	Races Led	Miles	$
1958	Ben Benz	4	0	0	0	0	0	0	2	831	0	0	408	400
1959	Johnny Patterson	1	0	0	0	0	0	0	0	180	0	0	248	150
1959	Ben Benz	5	0	0	0	0	0	0	2	665	0	0	740	625
Lifetime		10	0	0	0	0	0	0	4	1,676	0	0	1,396	$1,175

Rodney Friesen

Year	Driver	Starts	Poles	1	2	3	4	5	6–10	Laps	Laps Led	Races Led	Miles	$
1978	Don Graham	1	0	0	0	0	0	0	0	75	0	0	197	875
1979	Don Graham	1	0	0	0	0	0	0	0	100	0	0	262	1,495
Lifetime		2	0	0	0	0	0	0	0	175	0	0	459	$2,370

Ken Friez

Year	Driver	Starts	Poles	1	2	3	4	5	6–10	Laps	Laps Led	Races Led	Miles	$
1974	David Sisco	1	0	0	0	0	0	0	0	315	0	0	473	2,793
1975	Hershel McGriff	2	0	0	0	0	0	0	0	63	0	0	158	2,200
1975	Darel Dieringer	1	0	0	0	0	0	0	0	373	0	0	560	3,015
Lifetime		4	0	0	0	0	0	0	0	751	0	0	1,190	$8,008

Ted Fritz

Year	Driver	Starts	Poles	1	2	3	4	5	6–10	Laps	Laps Led	Races Led	Miles	$
1975	Ted Fritz	1	0	0	0	0	0	0	0	10	0	0	26	620
Lifetime		1	0	0	0	0	0	0	0	10	0	0	26	$620

Herb Fry

Year	Driver	Starts	Poles	1	2	3	4	5	6–10	Laps	Laps Led	Races Led	Miles	$
1952	Herb Fry	1	0	0	0	0	0	0	0	366	0	0	458	95
Lifetime		1	0	0	0	0	0	0	0	366	0	0	458	$95

Irving Frye

Year	Driver	Starts	Poles	1	2	3	4	5	6–10	Laps	Laps Led	Races Led	Miles	$
1952	Pop McGinnis	1	0	0	0	0	0	0	1	180	0	0	90	125
1953	Pop McGinnis	13	0	0	0	0	0	2	3	775	13	1	664	975
1954	Pop McGinnis	3	0	0	0	0	0	0	0	413	4	1	526	165
Lifetime		17	0	0	0	0	0	2	4	1,368	17	2	1,280	$1,265

Tetsuo Fuchigami

Year	Driver	Starts	Poles	1	2	3	4	5	6–10	Laps	Laps Led	Races Led	Miles	$
1961	George Tet	2	0	0	0	0	0	0	0	60	0	0	150	250
Lifetime		2	0	0	0	0	0	0	0	60	0	0	150	$250

Harold Furr

Year	Driver	Starts	Poles	1	2	3	4	5	6–10	Laps	Laps Led	Races Led	Miles	$
1971	Richard D. Brown	5	0	0	0	0	0	0	0	779	0	0	823	3,910
1971	Dub Simpson	2	0	0	0	0	0	0	0	109	0	0	222	1,305
1972	Buck Baker	4	0	0	0	0	0	0	0	503	0	0	507	2,320
Lifetime		11	0	0	0	0	0	0	0	1,391	0	0	1,552	$7,535

Ernie Gahan

Year	Driver	Starts	Poles	1	2	3	4	5	6–10	Laps	Laps Led	Races Led	Miles	$
1960	Ernie Gahan	2	0	0	0	0	0	0	0	818	0	0	759	625
Lifetime		2	0	0	0	0	0	0	0	818	0	0	759	$625

Tommy Gale

Year	Driver	Starts	Poles	1	2	3	4	5	6–10	Laps	Laps Led	Races Led	Miles	$
1973	Tommy Gale	5	0	0	0	0	0	0	0	451	0	0	983	5,680
Lifetime		5	0	0	0	0	0	0	0	451	0	0	983	$5,680

Year	Driver	Starts	Poles	Finish 1	2	3	4	5	6–10	Laps	Laps Led	Races Led	Miles	$

Bill Galearisi

Year	Driver	Starts	Poles	1	2	3	4	5	6–10	Laps	Laps Led	Races Led	Miles	$
1954	Bill Galdarisi	1	0	0	0	0	0	0	0	445	0	0	223	100
Lifetime		1	0	0	0	0	0	0	0	445	0	0	223	$100

Don Gallagher

Year	Driver	Starts	Poles	1	2	3	4	5	6–10	Laps	Laps Led	Races Led	Miles	$
1949	Dick Zimmerman	1	0	0	0	0	0	0	0	178	0	0	178	50
Lifetime		1	0	0	0	0	0	0	0	178	0	0	178	$50

Dennis Gallion

Year	Driver	Starts	Poles	1	2	3	4	5	6–10	Laps	Laps Led	Races Led	Miles	$
1970	John Sears	4	0	0	0	0	0	0	0	623	0	0	1,361	4,635
1970	Dick Brooks	2	0	0	0	0	0	0	0	34	0	0	86	1,390
Lifetime		6	0	0	0	0	0	0	0	657	0	0	1,447	$6,025

George Gallup

Year	Driver	Starts	Poles	1	2	3	4	5	6–10	Laps	Laps Led	Races Led	Miles	$
1952	George Gallup	4	0	0	0	0	0	0	1	441	13	1	356	175
1953	George Gallup	1	0	0	0	0	0	0	0	36	0	0	148	50
Lifetime		5	0	0	0	0	0	0	1	477	13	1	504	$225

Richard Gallup

Year	Driver	Starts	Poles	1	2	3	4	5	6–10	Laps	Laps Led	Races Led	Miles	$
1956	Ken Love	1	0	0	0	0	0	0	0	134	0	0	184	50
1957	Ken Love	1	0	0	0	0	0	0	0		0	0		60
Lifetime		2	0	0	0	0	0	0	0	134	0	0	184	$110

Frank Galpin

Year	Driver	Starts	Poles	1	2	3	4	5	6–10	Laps	Laps Led	Races Led	Miles	$
1958	Jack D. McCoy	1	0	0	0	0	0	0	1	181	0	0	476	550
1958	Harold Hardesty	1	0	0	0	0	0	0	0	98	0	0	98	300
1960	Ron Hornaday	3	0	0	0	0	1	0	0	283	0	0	328	610
1961	Ron Hornaday	4	0	0	0	0	0	1	0	283	0	0	219	325
1963	Ron Hornaday	2	0	0	0	0	0	0	1	316	0	0	853	1,600
1963	Don Noel	1	0	0	0	0	0	0	0	133	0	0	359	350
Lifetime		12	0	0	0	0	1	2	2	1,294	0	0	2,333	$3,735

Chip Ganassi

Year	Driver	Starts	Poles	1	2	3	4	5	6–10	Laps	Laps Led	Races Led	Miles	$
2001	Jason Leffler	30	1	0	0	0	0	0	1	7,983	15	3	11,049	1,662,200
2001	Dorsey Schroeder	1	0	0	0	0	0	0	0	112	0	0	218	52,805
2001	Scott Pruett	1	0	0	0	0	0	0	0	90	3	1	221	57,025
2001	Sterling Marlin	36	1	2	3	2	1	4	8	10,723	567	24	14,102	3,303,745
2002	Mike Bliss	1	0	0	0	0	0	0	0	500	0	0	263	81,942
2002	Scott Pruett	1	0	0	0	0	0	0	1	90	0	0	221	66,690
2002	Sterling Marlin	29	2	2	1	2	2	1	6	7,844	451	12	10,650	3,495,738
2002	Jimmy Spencer	34	0	0	1	0	1	0	4	9,684	174	3	12,576	2,039,346
2002	Jamie McMurray	6	0	1	0	0	0	0	1	1,680	97	2	2,434	669,097
Lifetime		139	4	5	5	4	4	5	21	38,706	1,307	45	51,733	$11,428,588

Johnny Gardner

Year	Driver	Starts	Poles	1	2	3	4	5	6–10	Laps	Laps Led	Races Led	Miles	$
1958	Johnny Gardner	14	0	0	0	0	0	0	0	1,510	0	0	894	780
Lifetime		14	0	0	0	0	0	0	0	1,510	0	0	894	$780

Slick Gardner

Year	Driver	Starts	Poles	1	2	3	4	5	6–10	Laps	Laps Led	Races Led	Miles	$
1973	Slick Gardner	1	0	0	0	0	0	0	0	9	0	0	24	990
Lifetime		1	0	0	0	0	0	0	0	9	0	0	24	$990

William Gardner

Year	Driver	Starts	Poles	1	2	3	4	5	6–10	Laps	Laps Led	Races Led	Miles	$
1967	William Gardner	1	0	0	0	0	0	0	0	47	0	0	24	150
1968	William Gardner	12	0	0	0	0	0	0	2	3,418	0	0	2,110	3,925
1969	William Gardner	7	0	0	0	0	0	0	0	1,299	0	0	650	2,115
Lifetime		20	0	0	0	0	0	0	2	4,764	0	0	2,783	$6,190

Tom Garn

Year	Driver	Starts	Poles	1	2	3	4	5	6–10	Laps	Laps Led	Races Led	Miles	$
1971	Richard Childress	11	0	0	0	0	0	0	0	1,214	0	0	826	3,210

Year	Driver	Starts	Poles	Finish 1	2	3	4	5	6–10	Laps	Laps Led	Races Led	Miles	$

Tom Garn *continued*

Year	Driver	Starts	Poles	1	2	3	4	5	6–10	Laps	Laps Led	Races Led	Miles	$
1971	Wendell Scott	1	0	0	0	0	0	0	0	153	0	0	407	1,115
1973	Richard Childress	25	0	0	0	0	1	0	1	6,918	1	1	7,469	35,110
1974	Richard Childress	29	0	0	0	0	0	0	3	5,138	0	0	6,484	44,964
1975	Richard Childress	30	0	0	0	0	1	1	13	9,433	3	2	10,926	67,635
Lifetime		96	0	0	0	0	2	1	17	22,856	4	3	26,112	$152,034

Reitzel Garner

Year	Driver	Starts	Poles	1	2	3	4	5	6–10	Laps	Laps Led	Races Led	Miles	$
1956	Reitzel Garner	2	0	0	0	0	0	0	0	657	0	0	437	325
1957	Barney Oldfield	1	0	0	0	0	0	0	0	356	0	0	178	150
Lifetime		3	0	0	0	0	0	0	0	1,013	0	0	615	$475

Chick Garno

Year	Driver	Starts	Poles	1	2	3	4	5	6–10	Laps	Laps Led	Races Led	Miles	$
1956	Bud Geiselman	1	0	0	0	0	0	0	0	112	0	0	112	50
Lifetime		1	0	0	0	0	0	0	0	112	0	0	112	$50

Charles Gattalia

Year	Driver	Starts	Poles	1	2	3	4	5	6–10	Laps	Laps Led	Races Led	Miles	$
1951	Charles Gattalia	2	0	0	0	0	0	0	0		0	0		75
1952	Charles Gattalia	8	0	0	0	0	0	0	3	810	0	0	565	485
Lifetime		10	0	0	0	0	0	0	3	810	0	0	565	$560

Roland Gautsche

Year	Driver	Starts	Poles	1	2	3	4	5	6–10	Laps	Laps Led	Races Led	Miles	$
1974	Jimmy Insolo	1	0	0	0	0	0	0	0	71	0	0	186	785
Lifetime		1	0	0	0	0	0	0	0	71	0	0	186	$785

Ron Gautsche

Year	Driver	Starts	Poles	1	2	3	4	5	6–10	Laps	Laps Led	Races Led	Miles	$
1971	Ron Gautsche	3	0	0	0	0	0	0	0	176	0	0	460	2,935
1972	Ron Gautsche	2	0	0	0	0	0	0	0	215	0	0	544	2,735
Lifetime		5	0	0	0	0	0	0	0	391	0	0	1,004	$5,670

Scott Gaylord

Year	Driver	Starts	Poles	1	2	3	4	5	6–10	Laps	Laps Led	Races Led	Miles	$
1996	Scott Gaylord	1	0	0	0	0	0	0	0	67	0	0	169	10,095
Lifetime		1	0	0	0	0	0	0	0	67	0	0	169	$10,095

Jack Gaynor

Year	Driver	Starts	Poles	1	2	3	4	5	6–10	Laps	Laps Led	Races Led	Miles	$
1951	Jack Gaynor	1	0	0	0	0	0	0	0		0	0		25
1951	Lou Figaro	11	1	1	0	0	2	0	1	431	200	1	331	2,150
Lifetime		12	1	1	0	0	2	0	1	431	200	1	331	$2,175

Bill Gazaway

Year	Driver	Starts	Poles	1	2	3	4	5	6–10	Laps	Laps Led	Races Led	Miles	$
1960	Joe Caspolich	2	0	0	0	0	0	0	0	526	0	0	762	1,425
1960	Tiny Lund	4	0	0	0	0	0	0	0	586	0	0	945	650
1960	Bill Gazaway	1	0	0	0	0	0	0	0	1	0	0	2	200
Lifetime		7	0	0	0	0	0	0	0	1,113	0	0	1,709	$2,275

Robert Gee

Year	Driver	Starts	Poles	1	2	3	4	5	6–10	Laps	Laps Led	Races Led	Miles	$
1978	Skip Manning	1	0	0	0	0	0	0	0	59	0	0	89	1,525
1978	Ferrel Harris	10	0	0	0	0	0	0	3	2,079	0	0	3,152	21,245
Lifetime		11	0	0	0	0	0	0	3	2,138	0	0	3,240	$22,770

Frank Geiselman

Year	Driver	Starts	Poles	1	2	3	4	5	6–10	Laps	Laps Led	Races Led	Miles	$
1955	Bud Geiselman	1	0	0	0	0	0	0	0	164	0	0	82	50
Lifetime		1	0	0	0	0	0	0	0	164	0	0	82	$50

Romeo Gelsi

Year	Driver	Starts	Poles	1	2	3	4	5	6–10	Laps	Laps Led	Races Led	Miles	$
1957	Al Tasnady	1	0	0	0	0	0	0	0		0	0		0
Lifetime		1	0	0	0	0	0	0	0		0	0		$0

Year	Driver	Starts	Poles	Finish 1	2	3	4	5	6–10	Laps	Laps Led	Races Led	Miles	$

Eldon George

Year	Driver	Starts	Poles	1	2	3	4	5	6–10	Laps	Laps Led	Races Led	Miles	$
1995	Doug George	2	0	0	0	0	0	0	0	251	0	0	362	18,610
Lifetime		2	0	0	0	0	0	0	0	251	0	0	362	$18,610

Jay George

Year	Driver	Starts	Poles	1	2	3	4	5	6–10	Laps	Laps Led	Races Led	Miles	$
1958	Bill Thorp	1	0	0	0	0	0	0	0	154	0	0	405	110
1959	Jack Austin	1	0	0	0	0	0	0	0	54	0	0	54	75
1960	Bill Cook	1	0	0	0	0	0	0	0	137	0	0	192	200
1960	Brownie Brown	1	0	0	0	0	0	0	0	12	0	0	17	0
1961	Brownie Brown	1	0	0	0	0	0	0	0	6	0	0	8	0
Lifetime		5	0	0	0	0	0	0	0	363	0	0	676	$385

Joe George

Year	Driver	Starts	Poles	1	2	3	4	5	6–10	Laps	Laps Led	Races Led	Miles	$
1956	Herb Gibson	1	0	0	0	0	0	0	0	21	0	0	32	50
Lifetime		1	0	0	0	0	0	0	0	21	0	0	32	$50

Benny Georgeson

Year	Driver	Starts	Poles	1	2	3	4	5	6–10	Laps	Laps Led	Races Led	Miles	$
1949	Benny Georgeson	1	0	0	0	0	0	0	0		0	0		0
Lifetime		1	0	0	0	0	0	0	0		0	0		$0

Bobby Gerhart / Billy Gerhart

Year	Driver	Starts	Poles	1	2	3	4	5	6–10	Laps	Laps Led	Races Led	Miles	$
1984	Bobby Gerhart	4	0	0	0	0	0	0	0	655	0	0	813	7,585
1985	Bobby Gerhart	5	0	0	0	0	0	0	0	1,166	0	0	1,503	7,400
1986	Bobby Gerhart	4	0	0	0	0	0	0	0	575	0	0	1,178	6,535
1987	Bobby Gerhart	2	0	0	0	0	0	0	0	169	0	0	423	3,665
1988	Bobby Gerhart	2	0	0	0	0	0	0	0	377	0	0	943	5,050
1989	Bobby Gerhart	1	0	0	0	0	0	0	0	193	0	0	483	2,975
1990	Bobby Gerhart	1	0	0	0	0	0	0	0	151	0	0	151	2,950
1992	Bobby Gerhart	3	0	0	0	0	0	0	0	350	0	0	904	15,810
Lifetime		22	0	0	0	0	0	0	0	3,636	0	0	6,396	$51,970

James Gess

Year	Driver	Starts	Poles	1	2	3	4	5	6–10	Laps	Laps Led	Races Led	Miles	$
1954	Charlie Cregar	2	0	0	0	0	0	0	0	441	8	1	558	280
1955	Charlie Cregar	2	0	0	0	0	0	0	0	47	0	0	56	0
Lifetime		4	0	0	0	0	0	0	0	488	8	1	614	$280

Betty Getty

Year	Driver	Starts	Poles	1	2	3	4	5	6–10	Laps	Laps Led	Races Led	Miles	$
1957	Dick Getty	1	0	0	0	0	0	1	0	194	0	0	97	255
Lifetime		1	0	0	0	0	0	1	0	194	0	0	97	$255

Dick Getty

Year	Driver	Starts	Poles	1	2	3	4	5	6–10	Laps	Laps Led	Races Led	Miles	$
1956	Dick Getty	3	0	0	0	0	0	0	0	186	0	0	217	90
1957	Dick Getty	9	0	0	0	0	0	2	5	980	0	0	689	1,635
1959	Dick Getty	2	0	0	0	0	0	0	0	138	0	0	59	175
1961	Dick Getty	4	0	0	0	0	0	0	0	310	0	0	331	500
1962	Dick Getty	5	0	0	0	0	0	0	2	525	0	0	213	675
1962	Eddie Pagan	1	0	0	0	0	0	0	0	354	0	0	177	250
1963	Eddie Pagan	1	0	0	0	0	0	0	0	137	0	0	370	325
Lifetime		25	0	0	0	0	0	2	7	2,630	0	0	2,055	$3,650

Richard Giachetti

Year	Driver	Starts	Poles	1	2	3	4	5	6–10	Laps	Laps Led	Races Led	Miles	$
1968	Jack Ingram	2	0	0	0	0	0	0	0	82	0	0	48	250
1969	Dub Simpson	3	0	0	0	0	0	0	0	277	0	0	638	2,425
1969	Bob Ashbrook	2	0	0	0	0	0	0	0	200	0	0	399	1,587
1969	George Ashbrook	1	0	0	0	0	0	0	0	262	0	0	262	540
1969	Lennie Pond	1	0	0	0	0	0	0	0	73	0	0	74	650
1970	Harold Fagan	2	0	0	0	0	0	0	0	179	0	0	466	1,925
1970	Harold Smith	1	0	0	0	0	0	0	0	30	0	0	60	635
1970	Bob Ashbrook	1	0	0	0	0	0	0	0	44	0	0	110	220
1971	Red Farmer	2	0	0	0	0	0	0	1	140	0	0	350	1,510
1971	Tommy Gale	1	0	0	0	0	0	0	0	185	0	0	377	1,045
1971	David Pearson	1	0	0	1	0	0	0	0	275	1	1	100	1,500

Year	Driver	Starts	Poles	Finish 1	2	3	4	5	6–10	Laps	Laps Led	Races Led	Miles	$

Richard Giachetti *continued*

Year	Driver	Starts	Poles	1	2	3	4	5	6–10	Laps	Laps Led	Races Led	Miles	$
1971	James Sears	1	0	0	0	0	0	0	0	9	0	0	9	545
1972	Bill Seifert	1	0	0	0	0	0	0	0	1	0	0	2	705
1972	Larry Dickson	1	0	0	0	0	0	0	0	103	0	0	258	1,535
Lifetime		20	0	0	1	0	0	0	1	1,860	1	1	3,153	$15,072

Don Gibbs

Year	Driver	Starts	Poles	1	2	3	4	5	6–10	Laps	Laps Led	Races Led	Miles	$
1988	Mickey Gibbs	5	0	0	0	0	0	0	0	636	2	1	1,134	12,850
1989	Mickey Gibbs	1	0	0	0	0	0	0	0	37	0	0	56	1,935
Lifetime		6	0	0	0	0	0	0	0	673	2	1	1,190	$14,785

Joe Gibbs

Year	Driver	Starts	Poles	1	2	3	4	5	6–10	Laps	Laps Led	Races Led	Miles	$
1992	Dale Jarrett	29	0	0	1	1	0	0	6	8,586	99	5	10,295	363,465
1993	Dale Jarrett	30	0	1	1	4	5	2	5	9,149	264	15	11,336	964,025
1994	Dale Jarrett	30	0	1	0	0	2	1	5	8,410	55	8	10,442	780,605
1995	Bobby Labonte	31	2	3	3	0	0	1	7	9,018	277	14	10,975	1,293,200
1996	Bobby Labonte	31	4	1	1	0	1	2	9	8,916	330	13	10,571	1,317,420
1997	Bobby Labonte	32	3	1	3	2	2	1	9	9,482	484	12	12,368	1,794,250
1998	Bobby Labonte	33	3	2	3	2	4	0	7	9,512	182	13	12,376	2,520,370
1999	Bobby Labonte	34	5	5	6	7	1	4	3	10,011	1,201	30	13,133	3,413,741
1999	Tony Stewart	34	2	3	2	1	4	2	9	9,908	1,213	17	12,998	2,452,939
2000	Bobby Labonte	34	3	4	4	4	2	5	5	10,158	464	23	13,270	3,961,915
2000	Tony Stewart	34	2	6	2	0	3	1	11	9,335	1211	16	12,296	3,105,060
2001	Tony Stewart	36	0	3	3	2	3	4	7	10,429	465	12	13,978	3,118,146
2001	Bobby Labonte	36	1	2	1	2	1	3	11	10,361	228	17	13,579	3,941,397
2002	Bobby Labonte	36	0	1	1	1	0	2	2	10,135	123	5	13,355	3,674,309
2002	Tony Stewart	36	4	3	3	4	2	3	6	10,181	746	17	13,134	4,288,962
Lifetime		496	29	36	34	30	30	31	102	143,591	7,342	217	184,107	$36,989,804

Shorty Gibbs

Year	Driver	Starts	Poles	1	2	3	4	5	6–10	Laps	Laps Led	Races Led	Miles	$
1952	Shorty Gibbs	2	0	0	0	0	0	0	0	87	0	0	53	50
Lifetime		2	0	0	0	0	0	0	0	87	0	0	53	$50

Bo Gibson

Year	Driver	Starts	Poles	1	2	3	4	5	6–10	Laps	Laps Led	Races Led	Miles	$
1987	Mark Gibson	1	0	0	0	0	0	0	0	204	0	0	204	1,300
Lifetime		1	0	0	0	0	0	0	0	204	0	0	204	$1,300

Ed Gibson

Year	Driver	Starts	Poles	1	2	3	4	5	6–10	Laps	Laps Led	Races Led	Miles	$
1975	Bobby Isaac	3	0	0	0	0	0	0	1	740	0	0	727	4,135
1975	Charlie Glotzbach	1	0	0	0	0	0	0	0	59	1	1	89	1,035
Lifetime		4	0	0	0	0	0	0	1	799	1	1	815	$5,170

Kyle Gibson

Year	Driver	Starts	Poles	1	2	3	4	5	6–10	Laps	Laps Led	Races Led	Miles	$
1966	Johnny Steele	2	0	0	0	0	0	0	0	325	0	0	523	900
1968	Johnny Steele	1	0	0	0	0	0	0	0	33	0	0	89	500
Lifetime		3	0	0	0	0	0	0	0	358	0	0	612	$1,400

Tom Gifford

Year	Driver	Starts	Poles	1	2	3	4	5	6–10	Laps	Laps Led	Races Led	Miles	$
1952	Tom Gifford	3	0	0	0	0	0	0	0	53	0	0	27	50
Lifetime		3	0	0	0	0	0	0	0	53	0	0	27	$50

Boyce Gillette

Year	Driver	Starts	Poles	1	2	3	4	5	6–10	Laps	Laps Led	Races Led	Miles	$
1952	Al Funderburk	1	0	0	0	0	0	0	1		0	0		50
Lifetime		1	0	0	0	0	0	0	1		0	0		$50

Emory Gilliam

Year	Driver	Starts	Poles	1	2	3	4	5	6–10	Laps	Laps Led	Races Led	Miles	$
1967	Paul Moore	1	0	0	0	0	0	0	0	33	0	0	17	100
1967	Paul Lewis	4	0	0	0	0	0	1	2	644	0	0	307	690
1967	Neil Castles	5	0	0	0	0	1	0	1	841	0	0	987	4,660
1967	Bill Vanderhoff	1	0	0	0	0	0	0	0	114	0	0	57	100

Year	Driver	Starts	Poles	1	2	3	4	5	6–10	Laps	Laps Led	Races Led	Miles	$

Emory Gilliam *continued*

Year	Driver	Starts	Poles	1	2	3	4	5	6–10	Laps	Laps Led	Races Led	Miles	$
1967	Armond Holley	1	0	0	0	0	0	0	0	31	0	0	47	775
Lifetime		12	0	0	0	0	1	1	3	1,663	0	0	1,414	$6,325

Joe Gilliam

Year	Driver	Starts	Poles	1	2	3	4	5	6–10	Laps	Laps Led	Races Led	Miles	$
1956	Joe Bill O'Dell	1	0	0	0	0	0	0	0	37	0	0	19	60
Lifetime		1	0	0	0	0	0	0	0	37	0	0	19	$60

Butch Gilliland

Year	Driver	Starts	Poles	1	2	3	4	5	6–10	Laps	Laps Led	Races Led	Miles	$
1990	Butch Gilliland	1	0	0	0	0	0	0	0	71	0	0	179	4,200
1990	Butch Gilliland	1	0	0	0	0	0	0	0	71	0	0	179	4,200
1992	Butch Gilliland	1	0	0	0	0	0	0	0	55	0	0	139	4,780
1992	Butch Gilliland	1	0	0	0	0	0	0	0	55	0	0	139	4,780
1994	Butch Gilliland	1	0	0	0	0	0	0	0	72	0	0	181	7,755
1994	Butch Gilliland	1	0	0	0	0	0	0	0	72	0	0	181	7,755
Lifetime		6	0	0	0	0	0	0	0	396	0	0	998	$33,470

Laurie Gilliland

Year	Driver	Starts	Poles	1	2	3	4	5	6–10	Laps	Laps Led	Races Led	Miles	$
1992	Butch Gilliland	1	0	0	0	0	0	0	0	292	0	0	292	6,210
1993	Butch Gilliland	1	0	0	0	0	0	0	0	71	0	0	179	6,765
Lifetime		2	0	0	0	0	0	0	0	363	0	0	471	$12,975

Bob Gilreath

Year	Driver	Starts	Poles	1	2	3	4	5	6–10	Laps	Laps Led	Races Led	Miles	$
1967	Harold Fagan	5	0	0	0	0	0	0	0	309	0	0	210	600
Lifetime		5	0	0	0	0	0	0	0	309	0	0	210	$600

Arthur Godfrey

Year	Driver	Starts	Poles	1	2	3	4	5	6–10	Laps	Laps Led	Races Led	Miles	$
1977	John Borneman	1	0	0	0	0	0	0	0	150	0	0	375	1,200
1978	John Borneman	1	0	0	0	0	0	0	0	50	0	0	131	1,025
Lifetime		2	0	0	0	0	0	0	0	200	0	0	506	$2,225

Tom Goff

Year	Driver	Starts	Poles	1	2	3	4	5	6–10	Laps	Laps Led	Races Led	Miles	$
1974	Dick Skillen	3	0	0	0	0	0	0	0	1,324	0	0	1,560	2,595
1975	Dick Skillen	5	0	0	0	0	0	0	0	1,052	0	0	1,333	4,865
1976	Dick Skillen	5	0	0	0	0	0	0	0	810	0	0	1,716	8,250
1977	Dick Skillen	1	0	0	0	0	0	0	0	38	0	0	101	1,305
1982	Richard Brickhouse	2	0	0	0	0	0	0	0	557	0	0	673	2,610
1983	Dick Skillen	1	0	0	0	0	0	0	0	1	0	0	3	1,450
1985	Dick Skillen	1	0	0	0	0	0	0	0	167	0	0	444	3,920
Lifetime		18	0	0	0	0	0	0	0	3,949	0	0	5,830	$24,995

John Golabek

Year	Driver	Starts	Poles	1	2	3	4	5	6–10	Laps	Laps Led	Races Led	Miles	$
1951	Neil Cole	5	1	1	1	0	0	1	0	399	45	1	200	1,950
1952	Neil Cole	6	0	0	0	1	0	0	4	988	0	0	621	1,150
1953	Ronnie Kohler	3	0	0	0	0	0	1	0		0	0		350
1953	Neil Cole	1	0	0	0	0	0	0	0		0	0		25
Lifetime		15	1	1	1	1	0	2	4	1,387	45	1	820	$3,475

Tubby Gonzales

Year	Driver	Starts	Poles	1	2	3	4	5	6–10	Laps	Laps Led	Races Led	Miles	$
1961	Darel Dieringer	1	0	0	0	0	0	0	0	45	0	0	62	300
1961	Tubby Gonzales	5	0	0	0	0	1	0	0	598	0	0	889	1,300
1961	Fred Lorenzen	1	0	0	0	0	1	0	0	198	0	0	495	3,825
1962	Tubby Gonzales	4	0	0	0	0	0	0	0	422	0	0	629	1,050
Lifetime		11	0	0	0	0	2	0	0	1,263	0	0	2,075	$6,475

James Good

Year	Driver	Starts	Poles	1	2	3	4	5	6–10	Laps	Laps Led	Races Led	Miles	$
1970	Dick Gulstrand	2	0	0	0	0	0	1	1	309	0	0	810	3,890
1971	Dick Gulstrand	2	0	0	0	0	0	0	0	251	0	0	637	2,775
Lifetime		4	0	0	0	0	0	1	1	560	0	0	1,446	$6,665

Year	Driver	Starts	Poles	Finish						Laps	Laps Led	Races Led	Miles	$
				1	2	3	4	5	6–10					

Phil Good

Year	Driver	Starts	Poles	1	2	3	4	5	6–10	Laps	Laps Led	Races Led	Miles	$
1984	Phil Good	1	0	0	0	0	0	0	0	331	0	0	331	1,065
1985	Phil Good	3	0	0	0	0	0	0	0	877	0	0	885	5,400
1986	Phil Good	2	0	0	0	0	0	0	0	439	0	0	254	2,825
1987	Phil Good	1	0	0	0	0	0	0	0	10	0	0	25	1,435
Lifetime		7	0	0	0	0	0	0	0	1,657	0	0	1,494	$10,725

Dick Goode

Year	Driver	Starts	Poles	1	2	3	4	5	6–10	Laps	Laps Led	Races Led	Miles	$
1963	Dick Goode	2	0	0	0	0	0	0	1	107	0	0	268	700
Lifetime		2	0	0	0	0	0	0	1	107	0	0	268	$700

J.O. Goode

Year	Driver	Starts	Poles	1	2	3	4	5	6–10	Laps	Laps Led	Races Led	Miles	$
1951	Jimmie Lewallen	2	0	0	0	0	0	0	1		0	0		100
1952	Bob Welborn	2	0	0	0	0	0	0	0	187	0	0	127	65
1952	Jimmie Lewallen	6	0	0	0	0	0	0	1	510	0	0	258	300
1952	Ray Duhigg	8	0	0	0	1	0	0	3	1,458	0	0	1,270	1,825
1953	Bob Welborn	8	0	0	0	0	1	1	2	617	0	0	466	935
1953	Ray Duhigg	1	0	0	0	0	0	0	1		0	0		100
1954	Jimmie Lewallen	2	0	0	0	0	0	0	1	190	0	0	114	125
1954	Ray Duhigg	6	0	0	0	0	1	1	3	1,036	0	0	684	1,325
1955	Ray Duhigg	1	0	0	0	1	0	0	0	39	0	0	160	1,000
Lifetime		36	0	0	0	2	2	2	12	4,037	0	0	3,078	$5,775

Jack Goodwin

Year	Driver	Starts	Poles	1	2	3	4	5	6–10	Laps	Laps Led	Races Led	Miles	$
1956	Jack Goodwin (MI)	1	0	0	0	0	0	0	0	58	0	0	238	200
Lifetime		1	0	0	0	0	0	0	0	58	0	0	238	$200

Cecil Gordon

Year	Driver	Starts	Poles	1	2	3	4	5	6–10	Laps	Laps Led	Races Led	Miles	$
1970	Henley Gray	1	0	0	0	0	0	0	0	24	0	0	9	220
1970	Bill Dennis	1	0	0	0	0	0	0	0	158	0	0	420	1,140
1970	Cecil Gordon	44	0	0	0	0	1	1	9	8,424	0	0	6,872	27,480
1970	Dave Marcis	2	0	0	0	0	0	1	0	420	0	0	158	665
1970	Jim Vandiver	1	0	0	0	0	0	0	0	281	0	0	111	240
1970	Lee Gordon	6	0	0	0	0	0	0	0	729	0	0	346	1,745
1971	Cecil Gordon	46	0	0	0	2	2	2	15	12,468	0	0	12,041	42,925
1972	Cecil Gordon	31	0	0	0	0	1	3	12	9,033	3	2	10,421	50,170
1973	Cecil Gordon	28	0	0	0	1	1	6	10	8,998	5	3	10,004	57,490
1974	Cecil Gordon	30	0	0	0	0	1	0	9	7,396	1	1	9,080	53,589
1975	Cecil Gordon	30	0	0	1	1	2	3	9	8,577	6	2	9,684	77,930
1976	Cecil Gordon	28	0	0	0	0	0	0	5	6,637	7	3	7,981	59,985
1977	Cecil Gordon	30	0	0	0	0	0	0	2	8,133	0	0	9,605	72,635
1978	Cecil Gordon	25	0	0	0	0	0	0	1	6,647	0	0	7,113	45,925
1978	Junior Miller	1	0	0	0	0	0	0	0	376	0	0	235	1,480
1979	D.K. Ulrich	1	0	0	0	0	0	0	0	383	0	0	228	1,135
1979	Cecil Gordon	26	0	0	0	0	0	0	0	6,907	0	0	7,708	59,195
1980	Cecil Gordon	26	0	0	0	0	0	0	3	7,353	0	0	8,513	72,320
1980	Lake Speed	1	0	0	0	0	0	0	0	79	0	0	207	1,305
1981	Cecil Gordon	18	0	0	0	0	0	0	0	4,470	0	0	5,831	50,650
1981	Jimmy Hensley	1	0	0	0	0	0	0	1	487	0	0	256	4,650
1981	Lennie Pond	1	0	0	0	0	0	0	0	388	0	0	582	8,100
1981	Morgan Shepherd	7	0	0	0	0	0	0	2	2,155	104	1	2,278	28,925
1981	Steve Spencer	1	0	0	0	0	0	0	0	400	0	0	238	1,890
1982	John Anderson	1	0	0	0	0	0	0	0	305	0	0	458	6,100
1982	Tony Bettenhausen,	1	0	0	0	0	0	0	0	139	0	0	278	3,215
1982	Lennie Pond	10	0	0	0	0	0	0	1	1,425	1	1	1,820	30,175
1982	J.D. McDuffie	1	0	0	0	0	0	0	0	422	0	0	222	2,655
1982	Dick May	1	0	0	0	0	0	0	0	193	0	0	386	4,445
1982	Cecil Gordon	4	0	0	0	0	0	0	0	1,125	0	0	1,445	13,920
1982	Ronnie Thomas	2	0	0	0	0	0	0	0	344	0	0	542	5,690
1983	Jim Vandiver	2	0	0	0	0	0	0	0	448	0	0	674	4,810
1983	Cecil Gordon	8	0	0	0	0	0	0	0	1,831	0	0	3,021	17,340
Lifetime		416	0	0	1	4	8	16	79	107,155	127	13	118,767	$810,139

Harry Goularte

Year	Driver	Starts	Poles	1	2	3	4	5	6–10	Laps	Laps Led	Races Led	Miles	$
1978	Harry Goularte	2	0	0	0	0	0	0	0	185	0	0	473	1,930

Year	Driver	Starts	Poles	Finish 1	2	3	4	5	6–10	Laps	Laps Led	Races Led	Miles	$

Harry Goularte *continued*

Year	Driver	Starts	Poles	1	2	3	4	5	6–10	Laps	Laps Led	Races Led	Miles	$
1979	Harry Goularte	1	0	0	0	0	0	0	0	82	0	0	215	1,460
1984	Harry Goularte	2	0	0	0	0	0	0	0	172	0	0	451	3,490
1987	Harry Goularte	2	0	0	0	0	0	0	0	171	0	0	448	4,770
Lifetime		7	0	0	0	0	0	0	0	610	0	0	1,587	$11,650

Mel Gould

Year	Driver	Starts	Poles	1	2	3	4	5	6–10	Laps	Laps Led	Races Led	Miles	$
1954	Bill Tanner	1	0	0	0	0	0	0	0	4	0	0	4	0
Lifetime		1	0	0	0	0	0	0	0	4	0	0	4	$0

Johnny Gouveia

Year	Driver	Starts	Poles	1	2	3	4	5	6–10	Laps	Laps Led	Races Led	Miles	$
1952	Johnny Gouveia	1	0	0	0	0	0	0	0	61	0	0	76	0
1955	Johnny Gouveia	4	0	0	0	0	0	0	1	614	0	0	307	260
Lifetime		5	0	0	0	0	0	0	1	675	0	0	383	$260

Matt Gowen

Year	Driver	Starts	Poles	1	2	3	4	5	6–10	Laps	Laps Led	Races Led	Miles	$
1953	Larry Schultz	1	0	0	0	0	0	0	0		0	0		40
1953	Stewart McDonald	1	0	0	0	0	0	0	0	271	0	0	271	50
Lifetime		2	0	0	0	0	0	0	0	271	0	0	271	$90

Ed Grady

Year	Driver	Starts	Poles	1	2	3	4	5	6–10	Laps	Laps Led	Races Led	Miles	$
1965	Bobby Allison	4	0	0	0	0	0	0	2	528	0	0	1,007	3,350
Lifetime		4	0	0	0	0	0	0	2	528	0	0	1,007	$3,350

C.J. Grana

Year	Driver	Starts	Poles	1	2	3	4	5	6–10	Laps	Laps Led	Races Led	Miles	$
1969	Ron Grana	1	0	0	0	0	0	0	0	162	0	0	324	1,275
1970	Ron Grana	3	0	0	0	0	0	0	1	243	0	0	546	2,165
1971	Ron Grana	1	0	0	0	0	0	0	0	187	0	0	381	920
Lifetime		5	0	0	0	0	0	0	1	592	0	0	1,251	$4,360

Ron Grana

Year	Driver	Starts	Poles	1	2	3	4	5	6–10	Laps	Laps Led	Races Led	Miles	$
1972	Ron Grana	1	0	0	0	0	0	0	0	31	0	0	62	690
Lifetime		1	0	0	0	0	0	0	0	31	0	0	62	$690

Danny Graves

Year	Driver	Starts	Poles	1	2	3	4	5	6–10	Laps	Laps Led	Races Led	Miles	$
1957	Danny Graves	6	1	1	0	1	0	1	1	770	1	1	465	1,845
1958	Danny Graves	2	0	0	0	0	0	0	0	90	0	0	198	125
Lifetime		8	1	1	0	1	0	1	1	860	1	1	662	$1,970

Bill Gray

Year	Driver	Starts	Poles	1	2	3	4	5	6–10	Laps	Laps Led	Races Led	Miles	$
1976	Jimmy Means	19	0	0	0	0	0	0	0	4,336	1	1	5,118	20,945
1977	Jimmy Means	25	0	0	0	0	0	0	6	5,972	0	0	6,659	45,645
Lifetime		44	0	0	0	0	0	0	6	10,308	1	1	11,776	$66,590

Don Gray

Year	Driver	Starts	Poles	1	2	3	4	5	6–10	Laps	Laps Led	Races Led	Miles	$
1958	Don Gray	2	0	0	0	0	0	0	0	264	0	0	120	115
Lifetime		2	0	0	0	0	0	0	0	264	0	0	120	$115

Eddie Gray

Year	Driver	Starts	Poles	1	2	3	4	5	6–10	Laps	Laps Led	Races Led	Miles	$
1961	Eddie Gray	4	1	2	1	0	0	0	0	509	76	2	532	3,485
Lifetime		4	1	2	1	0	0	0	0	509	76	2	532	$3,485

Henley Gray

Year	Driver	Starts	Poles	1	2	3	4	5	6–10	Laps	Laps Led	Races Led	Miles	$
1966	Ned Jarrett	2	0	0	0	0	0	0	1	512	0	0	618	2,575
1966	Coo Coo Marlin	1	0	0	0	0	0	0	1	375	0	0	188	375
1966	G.C. Spencer	1	0	0	0	0	0	1	0	193	0	0	97	275
1966	Henley Gray	40	0	0	0	0	0	3	14	9,492	0	0	6,716	13,475

Year	Driver	Starts	Poles	Finish						Laps	Laps Led	Races Led	Miles	$
				1	2	3	4	5	6–10	Laps	Led	Led	Miles	$

Henley Gray *continued*

Year	Driver	Starts	Poles	1	2	3	4	5	6–10	Laps	Laps Led	Races Led	Miles	$
1967	Henley Gray	40	0	0	0	0	0	0	10	7,296	0	0	5,012	12,055
1967	Red Farmer	2	0	0	0	0	0	0	0	552	7	1	604	1,925
1968	Henley Gray	30	0	0	0	0	0	0	6	6,072	0	0	4,580	11,250
1968	Cecil Gordon	5	0	0	0	0	0	0	0	717	0	0	352	670
1968	Harold Fagan	11	0	0	0	0	0	0	1	1,805	0	0	1,340	3,430
1968	Jeff Hawkins	1	0	0	0	0	0	0	0	107	0	0	54	100
1968	Paul Dean Holt	4	0	0	0	0	0	0	0	504	0	0	263	535
1968	Wendell Scott	1	0	0	0	0	0	0	0	115	0	0	173	650
1968	Doug Cooper	1	0	0	0	0	0	0	0	206	0	0	103	275
1969	Henley Gray	2	0	0	0	0	0	0	2	631	0	0	316	700
1970	Henley Gray	32	0	0	0	0	0	0	2	5,816	0	0	4,799	19,545
1970	Lee Gordon	1	0	0	0	0	0	0	0	26	0	0	9	225
1971	Henley Gray	38	0	0	0	0	0	0	4	7,565	0	0	7,448	25,188
1972	Charlie Roberts	2	0	0	0	0	0	0	0	226	0	0	484	2,740
1972	Henley Gray	26	0	0	0	0	0	0	2	5,983	0	0	7,199	34,433
1973	Jabe Thomas	1	0	0	0	0	0	0	0	315	0	0	430	1,605
1973	Henley Gray	24	0	0	0	0	0	0	4	7,517	0	0	7,615	27,870
1974	Dick May	1	0	0	0	0	0	0	0	176	0	0	461	1,825
1974	Henley Gray	4	0	0	0	0	0	0	1	1,010	0	0	996	4,635
1974	Bob Burcham	7	0	0	0	0	0	0	1	1,730	2	1	2,632	8,653
1974	Dean Dalton	2	0	0	0	0	0	0	0	341	0	0	201	910
1975	Dick May	1	0	0	0	0	0	0	0	139	0	0	348	1,085
1975	Henley Gray	7	0	0	0	0	0	0	1	1,497	2	1	1,824	7,060
1975	Bob Burcham	2	0	0	0	0	0	0	0	549	0	0	829	2,575
1975	Jabe Thomas	1	0	0	0	0	0	0	0	177	0	0	471	1,910
1976	Frank Warren	1	0	0	0	0	0	0	0	434	0	0	441	835
1976	Henley Gray	14	0	0	0	0	0	0	0	2,944	0	0	3,478	14,505
1976	Ed Negre	2	0	0	0	0	0	0	0	78	0	0	203	1,960
1976	Tommy Gale	1	0	0	0	0	0	0	0	70	0	0	175	990
1976	Bill Dennis	1	0	0	0	0	0	0	0	313	0	0	470	1,385
1976	Dick May	1	0	0	0	0	0	0	0	48	0	0	120	690
1976	Cecil Gordon	1	0	0	0	0	0	0	0	365	0	0	548	2,605
1977	Bobby Wawak	1	0	0	0	0	0	0	0	319	0	0	436	2,465
1977	Henley Gray	12	0	0	0	0	0	0	0	2,898	0	0	2,338	16,410
1977	Dick May	5	0	0	0	0	0	0	0	1,664	0	0	1,338	6,815
1977	Dave Marcis	1	0	0	0	0	0	0	0	382	0	0	239	1,600
1977	Bob Burcham	3	0	0	0	0	0	0	1	588	0	0	1,082	15,095
1978	Bill Dennis	1	0	0	0	0	0	0	0	66	0	0	99	1,560
1978	Bob Burcham	1	0	0	0	0	0	0	0	243	0	0	332	2,790
1978	Dick May	18	0	0	0	0	0	0	0	4,185	0	0	4,804	31,035
1978	Joe Booher	1	0	0	0	0	0	0	0	178	0	0	445	1,775
1978	Woody Fisher	3	0	0	0	0	0	0	0	383	0	0	510	4,135
1978	Elmo Langley	2	0	0	0	0	0	0	0	93	0	0	94	1,600
1978	Joey Arrington	1	0	0	0	0	0	0	0	364	0	0	197	800
1979	Billy Hagan	1	0	0	0	0	0	0	0	185	0	0	370	3,280
1979	Glenn Jarrett	1	0	0	0	0	0	0	0	164	0	0	167	1,115
1979	Joe Fields	1	0	0	0	0	0	0	0	379	0	0	205	1,385
1979	Dick May	9	0	0	0	0	0	0	0	2,329	0	0	2,137	14,305
1979	Bill Dennis	2	0	0	0	0	0	0	0	387	0	0	777	12,645
1979	Bob Burcham	2	0	0	0	0	0	0	0	356	0	0	826	6,565
1979	Steve Gray	1	0	0	0	0	0	0	0	1	0	0	3	1,305
1979	Steve Spencer	2	0	0	0	0	0	0	0	556	0	0	331	2,270
1979	Cecil Gordon	2	0	0	0	0	0	0	0	512	0	0	456	3,015
1979	Lennie Pond	5	0	0	0	0	0	0	0	1,286	0	0	1,512	11,895
1979	Vince Giamformaggio	2	0	0	0	0	0	0	0	139	0	0	361	4,295
1980	Cecil Gordon	1	0	0	0	0	0	0	0	166	0	0	253	1,860
1980	J.D. McDuffie	1	0	0	0	0	0	0	0	150	0	0	375	4,290
1980	James Hylton	1	0	0	0	0	0	0	0	312	0	0	468	3,425
1980	John A. Utsman	1	0	0	0	0	0	0	0	464	0	0	247	1,340
1980	John Anderson	8	0	0	0	0	0	0	0	1,499	0	0	2,097	21,585
1980	Steve Gray	1	0	0	0	0	0	0	0	35	0	0	35	450
1980	Steve Spencer	3	0	0	0	0	0	0	0	599	0	0	344	2,050
1980	Vince Giamformaggio	1	0	0	0	0	0	0	0	109	0	0	286	2,260
1980	Dick May	6	0	0	0	0	0	0	1	1,443	0	0	2,148	18,260
1981	Bill Dennis	1	0	0	0	0	0	0	0	327	0	0	491	3,200
1981	Cecil Gordon	1	0	0	0	0	0	0	0	189	0	0	378	905
1981	Dick May	3	0	0	0	0	0	0	0	274	0	0	712	4,960

Year	Driver	Starts	Poles	Finish 1	2	3	4	5	6–10	Laps	Laps Led	Races Led	Miles	$

Henley Gray *continued*

Year	Driver	Starts	Poles	1	2	3	4	5	6–10	Laps	Laps Led	Races Led	Miles	$
1981	Ronnie Sanders	1	0	0	0	0	0	0	0	191	0	0	478	7,635
1982	Dick May	2	0	0	0	0	0	0	0	404	0	0	560	4,680
1982	John Anderson	3	0	0	0	0	0	0	0	320	0	0	650	5,755
1982	Steve Gray	1	0	0	0	0	0	0	0	103	0	0	258	1,250
1982	Dennis DeVea	1	0	0	0	0	0	0	0	185	1	1	370	1,670
1982	Charlie Baker	3	0	0	0	0	0	0	0	444	0	0	1,025	5,235
1982	Benny Parsons	1	0	0	0	0	0	0	0	100	0	0	250	1,730
1982	Buddy Baker	1	0	0	0	0	0	0	0	51	0	0	27	820
1983	Bobby Gerhart	2	0	0	0	0	0	0	0	69	0	0	173	2,550
1983	J.D. McDuffie	1	0	0	0	0	0	0	0	177	0	0	269	1,030
1983	John Anderson	1	0	0	0	0	0	0	0	317	0	0	476	1,350
1983	Steve Gray	3	0	0	0	0	0	0	0	853	0	0	853	3,525
1983	Billie Harvey	1	0	0	0	0	0	0	0	1	0	0	3	1,730
1984	Charles Poalillo	1	0	0	0	0	0	0	0	159	0	0	398	2,050
1985	Bobby Wawak	1	0	0	0	0	0	0	0	175	0	0	466	3,210
1985	Charles Poalillo	1	0	0	0	0	0	0	0	22	0	0	55	1,395
1985	Steve Gray	1	0	0	0	0	0	0	0	151	0	0	378	1,970
1985	Slick Johnson	1	0	0	0	0	0	0	0	175	0	0	438	11,210
1986	Eddie Bierschwale	5	0	0	0	0	0	0	0	610	0	0	1,296	18,195
1986	Donnie Allison	1	0	0	0	0	0	0	0	131	0	0	179	1,840
1987	Chuck Schroedel	1	0	0	0	0	0	0	0	8	0	0	20	1,375
1989	Bill Ingram	1	0	0	0	0	0	0	0	181	0	0	481	3,875
1989	Ronnie Sanders	1	0	0	0	0	0	0	0	184	0	0	460	12,570
1992	Mark Thompson	1	0	0	0	0	0	0	0	8	0	0	20	4,370
1993	Mike Potter	1	0	0	0	0	0	0	0	232	0	0	236	6,475
Lifetime		453	0	0	0	0	0	4	52	94,371	12	4	98,300	$531,754

Steve Gray

Year	Driver	Starts	Poles	1	2	3	4	5	6–10	Laps	Laps Led	Races Led	Miles	$
1984	Steve Gray	1	0	0	0	0	0	0	0	178	0	0	445	1,675
Lifetime		1	0	0	0	0	0	0	0	178	0	0	445	$1,675

Bob Greeley

Year	Driver	Starts	Poles	1	2	3	4	5	6–10	Laps	Laps Led	Races Led	Miles	$
1972	Bob Greeley	1	0	0	0	0	0	0	0	182	0	0	273	500
Lifetime		1	0	0	0	0	0	0	0	182	0	0	273	$500

Charles Green

Year	Driver	Starts	Poles	1	2	3	4	5	6–10	Laps	Laps Led	Races Led	Miles	$
1957	Eddie Gray	5	0	0	0	0	0	1	1	525	0	0	421	755
Lifetime		5	0	0	0	0	0	1	1	525	0	0	421	$755

Donald Green

Year	Driver	Starts	Poles	1	2	3	4	5	6–10	Laps	Laps Led	Races Led	Miles	$
1976	Walter Wallace	1	0	0	0	0	0	0	0	378	0	0	225	450
Lifetime		1	0	0	0	0	0	0	0	378	0	0	225	$450

George Green

Year	Driver	Starts	Poles	1	2	3	4	5	6–10	Laps	Laps Led	Races Led	Miles	$
1956	George Green	6	0	0	0	0	0	0	0	867	0	0	468	550
1957	George Green	2	0	0	0	0	0	0	1	307	0	0	154	250
Lifetime		8	0	0	0	0	0	0	1	1,174	0	0	622	$800

Sherrill Green

Year	Driver	Starts	Poles	1	2	3	4	5	6–10	Laps	Laps Led	Races Led	Miles	$
1977	Harry Gant	1	0	0	0	0	0	0	0	266	0	0	399	1,460
Lifetime		1	0	0	0	0	0	0	0	266	0	0	399	$1,460

Bobby Greene

Year	Driver	Starts	Poles	1	2	3	4	5	6–10	Laps	Laps Led	Races Led	Miles	$
1949	Bobby Greene	2	0	0	0	0	0	0	0	148	0	0	74	50
Lifetime		2	0	0	0	0	0	0	0	148	0	0	74	$50

Oda Greene

Year	Driver	Starts	Poles	1	2	3	4	5	6–10	Laps	Laps Led	Races Led	Miles	$
1952	Oda Greene	1	0	0	0	0	0	0	0	134	0	0	67	25
Lifetime		1	0	0	0	0	0	0	0	134	0	0	67	$25

Year	Driver	Starts	Poles	Finish 1	2	3	4	5	6–10	Laps	Laps Led	Races Led	Miles	$

Bob Greer

Year	Driver	Starts	Poles	1	2	3	4	5	6–10	Laps	Laps Led	Races Led	Miles	$
1951	Bob Greer	5	0	0	0	0	0	0	0	126	0	0	126	50
Lifetime		5	0	0	0	0	0	0	0	126	0	0	126	$50

Bobby Griffin

Year	Driver	Starts	Poles	1	2	3	4	5	6–10	Laps	Laps Led	Races Led	Miles	$
1950	Buck Baker	4	0	0	0	1	0	0	1	374	0	0	319	625
1951	Buck Baker	3	0	0	0	0	0	2	0		0	0		800
1951	Gene Darragh	1	0	0	0	0	0	0	0	309	0	0	386	50
1952	Buck Baker	1	0	0	0	0	0	0	0		0	0		25
1953	Slick Smith	1	0	0	0	0	0	0	0	200	0	0	275	105
1953	Buck Baker	30	4	4	2	3	4	3	7	1,582	564	9	1,398	15,945
1954	Bob Welborn	1	0	0	0	1	0	0	0	196	0	0	98	450
1954	Buck Baker	19	1	2	6	3	2	1	2	3,085	336	6	2,217	12,315
1954	Jim Paschal	5	1	1	0	1	0	1	0	704	193	1	407	1,800
1954	Ray Duhigg	2	0	0	0	0	0	0	0	80	0	0	40	50
1955	Speedy Thompson	5	0	0	1	0	0	0	0	743	0	0	900	1,955
1955	Buddy Shuman	1	0	0	0	0	0	0	1	186	0	0	93	250
1955	Buck Baker	18	1	1	4	3	3	0	2	2,628	423	4	1,564	6,995
Lifetime		91	7	8	13	12	9	7	13	10,087	1,516	20	7,696	$41,365

Charles Griffin

Year	Driver	Starts	Poles	1	2	3	4	5	6–10	Laps	Laps Led	Races Led	Miles	$
1960	Johnny Miller	1	0	0	0	0	0	0	0	181	0	0	272	300
Lifetime		1	0	0	0	0	0	0	0	181	0	0	272	$300

Pee Wee Griffin

Year	Driver	Starts	Poles	1	2	3	4	5	6–10	Laps	Laps Led	Races Led	Miles	$
1978	Donnie Allison	3	0	0	0	0	0	0	1	644	0	0	829	3,380
Lifetime		3	0	0	0	0	0	0	1	644	0	0	829	$3,380

Charley Griffith

Year	Driver	Starts	Poles	1	2	3	4	5	6–10	Laps	Laps Led	Races Led	Miles	$
1959	Charley Griffin	6	0	0	0	1	0	0	2	438	0	0	697	4,955
1959	Jerry Smith	2	0	0	0	0	0	0	0	644	0	0	322	215
1959	Freddy Fryar	1	0	0	0	0	0	0	0	53	0	0	27	0
Lifetime		9	0	0	0	1	0	0	2	1,135	0	0	1,046	$5,170

Pat Grogan

Year	Driver	Starts	Poles	1	2	3	4	5	6–10	Laps	Laps Led	Races Led	Miles	$
1956	Pat Grogan	1	0	0	0	0	0	0	0	202	0	0	278	50
Lifetime		1	0	0	0	0	0	0	0	202	0	0	278	$50

Heyward Grooms

Year	Driver	Starts	Poles	1	2	3	4	5	6–10	Laps	Laps Led	Races Led	Miles	$
1981	Delma Cowart	1	0	0	0	0	0	0	0	315	0	0	479	1,940
1982	Delma Cowart	2	0	0	0	0	0	0	0	308	0	0	517	5,065
Lifetime		3	0	0	0	0	0	0	0	623	0	0	996	$7,005

Bill Groves

Year	Driver	Starts	Poles	1	2	3	4	5	6–10	Laps	Laps Led	Races Led	Miles	$
1965	Gene Davis	1	0	0	0	0	0	1	0	177	0	0	478	1,850
Lifetime		1	0	0	0	0	0	1	0	177	0	0	478	$1,850

Johnny Grubb

Year	Driver	Starts	Poles	1	2	3	4	5	6–10	Laps	Laps Led	Races Led	Miles	$
1950	Johnny Grubb	4	0	0	0	0	0	0	1	530	0	0	541	575
1951	Johnny Grubb	1	0	0	0	0	0	0	0		0	0		25
Lifetime		5	0	0	0	0	0	0	1	530	0	0	541	$600

Sally Guide

Year	Driver	Starts	Poles	1	2	3	4	5	6–10	Laps	Laps Led	Races Led	Miles	$
1952	Joe Guide	2	0	0	0	0	0	0	0	200	0	0	250	0
1953	Joe Guide	2	0	0	0	0	0	0	0	147	0	0	300	150
1954	Joe Guide	2	0	0	0	0	0	0	0	160	0	0	331	75
1955	Joe Guide	2	0	0	0	0	0	0	0	275	0	0	413	360
1956	Joe Guide	1	0	0	0	0	0	0	0	141	0	0	212	200
Lifetime		9	0	0	0	0	0	0	0	923	0	0	1,505	$785

Year	Driver	Starts	Poles	Finish 1	2	3	4	5	6–10	Laps	Laps Led	Races Led	Miles	$

Dick Gulstrand

Year	Driver	Starts	Poles	1	2	3	4	5	6–10	Laps	Laps Led	Races Led	Miles	$
1972	Dick Gulstrand	1	0	0	0	0	0	0	0	28	0	0	73	740
Lifetime		1	0	0	0	0	0	0	0	28	0	0	73	$740

William Gundaker

Year	Driver	Starts	Poles	1	2	3	4	5	6–10	Laps	Laps Led	Races Led	Miles	$
1951	Bud Farrell	4	0	0	0	0	0	0	1	373	0	0	466	325
1952	Bud Farrell	6	0	0	0	0	0	0	2	881	0	0	621	325
Lifetime		10	0	0	0	0	0	0	3	1,254	0	0	1,087	$650

Gerry Gunderman

Year	Driver	Starts	Poles	1	2	3	4	5	6–10	Laps	Laps Led	Races Led	Miles	$
1986	Mark Martin	5	0	0	0	0	0	0	0	1,342	0	0	1,955	20,515
Lifetime		5	0	0	0	0	0	0	0	1,342	0	0	1,955	$20,515

Don Guy

Year	Driver	Starts	Poles	1	2	3	4	5	6–10	Laps	Laps Led	Races Led	Miles	$
1979	Robert Tartaglia	1	0	0	0	0	0	0	0	47	0	0	123	825
1980	Steve Pfeifer	1	0	0	0	0	0	0	0	82	0	0	215	905
Lifetime		2	0	0	0	0	0	0	0	129	0	0	338	$1,730

John Gwinn

Year	Driver	Starts	Poles	1	2	3	4	5	6–10	Laps	Laps Led	Races Led	Miles	$
1976	Bobby Wawak	19	0	0	0	0	0	0	9	4,888	0	0	6,232	30,415
1977	Ron Hutcherson	3	0	0	0	0	0	0	0	832	0	0	1,365	13,235
1977	Bobby Wawak	3	0	0	0	0	0	0	0	202	0	0	332	5,770
Lifetime		25	0	0	0	0	0	0	9	5,922	0	0	7,929	$49,420

Ted Haak

Year	Driver	Starts	Poles	1	2	3	4	5	6–10	Laps	Laps Led	Races Led	Miles	$
1960	Al Self	2	0	0	0	0	0	0	1	227	0	0	290	550
Lifetime		2	0	0	0	0	0	0	1	227	0	0	290	$550

Bob Haas

Year	Driver	Starts	Poles	1	2	3	4	5	6–10	Laps	Laps Led	Races Led	Miles	$
1982	Ernie Cline	1	0	0	0	0	0	0	0	154	0	0	157	900
Lifetime		1	0	0	0	0	0	0	0	154	0	0	157	$900

Alton Haddock

Year	Driver	Starts	Poles	1	2	3	4	5	6–10	Laps	Laps Led	Races Led	Miles	$
1950	Alton Haddock	1	0	0	0	0	0	0	0	98	0	0	123	100
Lifetime		1	0	0	0	0	0	0	0	98	0	0	123	$100

Billy Hagan

Year	Driver	Starts	Poles	1	2	3	4	5	6–10	Laps	Laps Led	Races Led	Miles	$
1969	Billy Hagan	1	0	0	0	0	0	0	1	155	0	0	412	1,750
1975	Skip Manning	5	0	0	0	0	0	0	0	995	0	0	1,794	9,705
1975	Billy Hagan	1	0	0	0	0	0	0	0	175	0	0	466	1,770
1976	Skip Manning	25	0	0	0	0	0	0	4	6,446	0	0	7,806	42,965
1977	Skip Manning	28	0	0	0	1	0	0	7	7,533	13	1	8,355	100,030
1978	Terry Labonte	5	0	0	0	0	1	0	2	1,849	0	0	1,879	20,995
1978	Skip Manning	15	0	0	0	0	1	0	3	4,043	0	0	4,929	51,145
1978	Mel Larson	1	0	0	0	0	0	0	0	31	0	0	62	1,175
1978	Dick May	2	0	0	0	0	0	0	1	956	0	0	964	6,780
1979	Terry Labonte	31	0	0	0	1	0	1	11	8,766	8	4	9,887	122,700
1980	Terry Labonte	31	0	1	0	1	1	3	10	8,760	46	6	9,952	199,825
1981	Terry Labonte	31	2	0	1	3	2	2	9	9,010	114	14	10,363	276,970
1982	Terry Labonte	30	3	0	6	2	6	3	4	8,900	263	17	10,259	297,595
1983	Terry Labonte	30	3	1	0	0	4	6	9	8,498	434	13	9,775	258,650
1984	Terry Labonte	30	3	2	6	6	2	1	7	9,886	880	26	11,236	417,293
1984	Joe Millikan	1	0	0	0	0	0	0	0	53	0	0	139	900
1985	Terry Labonte	28	4	1	2	3	1	1	9	7,973	563	14	9,612	476,850
1986	Terry Labonte	29	1	1	2	2	0	0	5	7,984	565	10	9,431	443,690
1987	Sterling Marlin	29	0	0	0	1	2	1	4	8,356	68	6	10,305	261,665
1988	Sterling Marlin	29	0	0	1	1	0	4	7	8,798	332	13	10,389	333,910
1989	Sterling Marlin	29	0	0	1	1	0	2	9	8,840	29	6	10,580	369,900
1990	Sterling Marlin	29	0	0	0	1	1	3	5	8,263	71	6	10,079	311,477
1991	Terry Labonte	29	1	0	0	0	0	1	6	7,989	52	2	9,617	302,020
1992	Terry Labonte	29	0	0	1	0	2	1	12	8,912	43	4	10,613	472,570

Year	Driver	Starts	Poles	Finish 1	2	3	4	5	6–10	Laps	Laps Led	Races Led	Miles	$

Billy Hagan *continued*

Year	Driver	Starts	Poles	1	2	3	4	5	6–10	Laps	Laps Led	Races Led	Miles	$
1993	Terry Labonte	30	0	0	0	0	0	0	10	8,866	55	3	10,642	461,865
1994	Randy MacDonald	1	0	0	0	0	0	0	0	466	0	0	474	8,200
1994	John Andretti	18	0	0	0	0	0	0	0	3,786	1	1	5,130	272,495
Lifetime		547	17	6	20	23	23	29	135	156,289	3,537	146	185,152	$5,524,890

Budd Hagelin

Year	Driver	Starts	Poles	1	2	3	4	5	6–10	Laps	Laps Led	Races Led	Miles	$
1974	Budd Hagelin	1	0	0	0	0	0	0	0	44	0	0	115	720
1976	Budd Hagelin	1	0	0	0	0	0	0	0	409	0	0	409	1,040
Lifetime		2	0	0	0	0	0	0	0	453	0	0	524	$1,760

George Hakes

Year	Driver	Starts	Poles	1	2	3	4	5	6–10	Laps	Laps Led	Races Led	Miles	$
1989	Bob Schacht	1	0	0	0	0	0	0	0	139	0	0	348	2,775
1989	Andy Belmont	1	0	0	0	0	0	0	0	373	0	0	373	2,150
1990	Tommy Riggins	4	0	0	0	0	0	0	0	469	0	0	1,013	12,140
1991	Jim Derhaag	1	0	0	0	0	0	0	0	88	0	0	216	5,120
Lifetime		7	0	0	0	0	0	0	0	1,069	0	0	1,949	$22,185

Ed Hale

Year	Driver	Starts	Poles	1	2	3	4	5	6–10	Laps	Laps Led	Races Led	Miles	$
1980	Ed Hale	1	0	0	0	0	0	0	0	37	0	0	97	1,200
Lifetime		1	0	0	0	0	0	0	0	37	0	0	97	$1,200

D.G. Hall

Year	Driver	Starts	Poles	1	2	3	4	5	6–10	Laps	Laps Led	Races Led	Miles	$
1950	June Cleveland	2	0	0	0	0	0	0	0	130	0	0	251	50
1951	June Cleveland	1	0	0	0	0	0	0	0		0	0		25
Lifetime		3	0	0	0	0	0	0	0	130	0	0	251	$75

Ray Hall

Year	Driver	Starts	Poles	1	2	3	4	5	6–10	Laps	Laps Led	Races Led	Miles	$
1957	Bob Perry	1	0	0	0	0	0	0	0	71	0	0	71	50
Lifetime		1	0	0	0	0	0	0	0	71	0	0	71	$50

Roy Hallquist

Year	Driver	Starts	Poles	1	2	3	4	5	6–10	Laps	Laps Led	Races Led	Miles	$
1963	Roy Hallquist	1	0	0	0	0	0	0	0	34	0	0	97	130
Lifetime		1	0	0	0	0	0	0	0	34	0	0	97	$130

Joel Halpern

Year	Driver	Starts	Poles	1	2	3	4	5	6–10	Laps	Laps Led	Races Led	Miles	$
1980	Darrell Waltrip	1	0	0	0	0	1	0	0	200	67	1	400	6,050
1980	Chuck Bown	4	0	0	0	0	0	0	0	496	0	0	904	4,270
1980	Donnie Allison	1	0	0	0	0	0	0	0	127	0	0	338	2,125
1981	David Pearson	4	0	0	0	0	0	0	1	887	7	2	1,320	9,625
Lifetime		10	0	0	0	0	1	0	1	1,710	74	3	2,962	$22,070

Jeff Halverson

Year	Driver	Starts	Poles	1	2	3	4	5	6–10	Laps	Laps Led	Races Led	Miles	$
1979	Jeff Halverson	1	0	0	0	0	0	0	0	1	0	0	1	490
1983	Dick May	1	0	0	0	0	0	0	0	34	0	0	85	1,350
1984	Johnny Coy Jr.	1	0	0	0	0	0	0	0	416	0	0	416	1,090
Lifetime		3	0	0	0	0	0	0	0	451	0	0	502	$2,930

John V. Hamby

Year	Driver	Starts	Poles	1	2	3	4	5	6–10	Laps	Laps Led	Races Led	Miles	$
1961	J.V. Hamby	2	0	0	0	0	0	0	0	515	0	0	273	225
Lifetime		2	0	0	0	0	0	0	0	515	0	0	273	$225

Roger Hamby

Year	Driver	Starts	Poles	1	2	3	4	5	6–10	Laps	Laps Led	Races Led	Miles	$
1977	Roger Hamby	2	0	0	0	0	0	0	0	614	0	0	605	2,275
1978	Roger Hamby	26	0	0	0	0	0	0	2	7,181	0	0	7,689	41,565
1979	Jim Vandiver	1	0	0	0	0	0	0	0	240	0	0	328	1,800
1979	Steve Pfeifer	2	0	0	0	0	0	0	0	360	0	0	544	3,595
1979	Roger Hamby	12	0	0	0	0	0	0	0	2,974	0	0	2,736	19,365

Year	Driver	Starts	Poles	Finish 1	2	3	4	5	6–10	Laps	Laps Led	Races Led	Miles	$

Roger Hamby *continued*

Year	Driver	Starts	Poles	1	2	3	4	5	6–10	Laps	Laps Led	Races Led	Miles	$
1979	Skip Manning	2	0	0	0	0	0	0	0	182	0	0	326	5,880
1979	Bill Elliott	4	0	0	0	0	0	0	1	1,630	0	0	1,059	8,610
1980	Don Whittington	1	0	0	0	0	0	0	0	187	0	0	468	9,510
1980	Glenn Jarrett	1	0	0	0	0	0	0	0	195	0	0	488	3,850
1980	Roger Hamby	26	0	0	0	0	0	0	0	7,243	0	0	7,837	43,830
1981	Tommy Houston	7	0	0	0	0	0	0	0	2,219	0	0	1,903	20,760
1981	Glenn Jarrett	3	0	0	0	0	0	0	0	679	0	0	864	12,650
1981	Harry Gant	1	0	0	0	0	0	0	0	114	0	0	299	3,120
1981	John Anderson	2	0	0	0	0	0	0	0	542	0	0	711	6,835
1981	Lake Speed	1	0	0	0	0	0	0	0	115	0	0	301	3,345
1981	Lowell Cowell	4	0	0	0	0	0	0	0	812	0	0	1,220	8,055
1981	Mike Potter	6	0	0	0	0	0	0	0	1,051	0	0	1,351	14,500
1981	Roger Hamby	1	0	0	0	0	0	0	0	72	0	0	144	2,450
1981	Steve Pfeifer	1	0	0	0	0	0	0	0	92	0	0	241	3,080
1981	Steve Spencer	2	0	0	0	0	0	0	0	638	0	0	508	3,915
1982	Lowell Cowell	5	0	0	0	0	0	0	0	862	0	0	2,210	26,215
1982	Mike Potter	2	0	0	0	0	0	0	0	322	0	0	645	3,535
1982	Lake Speed	29	0	0	0	0	0	0	5	5,827	0	0	6,848	103,960
1983	Sterling Marlin	30	0	0	0	0	0	0	1	8,053	0	0	9,167	119,375
1983	Clark Dwyer	5	0	0	0	0	0	0	1	851	0	0	1,412	14,570
1984	Morgan Shepherd	6	0	0	0	0	0	0	0	1,658	0	0	1,412	19,035
1984	Lake Speed	2	0	0	0	0	0	0	0	442	0	0	508	7,615
1984	Sterling Marlin	1	0	0	0	0	0	0	0	197	0	0	493	15,150
1984	Clark Dwyer	20	0	0	0	0	0	0	0	5,286	1	1	6,359	90,975
1985	Ken Ragan	6	0	0	0	0	0	0	0	1,135	0	0	1,919	34,520
1985	Lennie Pond	7	0	0	0	0	0	0	0	1,271	3	2	2,759	38,595
1985	Phil Parsons	14	0	0	0	0	0	0	1	4,491	0	0	3,480	55,065
1985	Bosco Lowe	1	0	0	0	0	0	0	0	171	0	0	455	6,825
1986	Phil Parsons	2	0	0	0	0	0	0	0	245	0	0	241	7,870
1986	Pancho Carter	6	0	0	0	0	0	0	0	751	3	2	1,810	33,805
1986	Jim Hull	1	0	0	0	0	0	0	0	191	0	0	382	5,390
1986	Eddie Bierschwale	9	0	0	0	0	0	0	0	3,399	0	0	3,076	41,960
1986	Doug Heveron	10	0	0	0	0	0	0	0	1,854	0	0	2,440	62,285
1987	Slick Johnson	7	0	0	0	0	0	0	0	2,102	3	2	1,832	36,505
1987	Trevor Boys	4	0	0	0	0	0	0	0	822	4	1	1,199	21,065
1987	Rodney Combs	1	0	0	0	0	0	0	0	43	0	0	65	4,490
1987	Mark Martin	1	0	0	0	0	0	0	0	68	0	0	102	3,550
1987	Larry Pollard	4	0	0	0	0	0	0	0	1,415	0	0	1,324	19,130
1987	Brad Teague	1	0	0	0	0	0	0	0	216	0	0	115	3,455
1987	David Sosebee	3	0	0	0	0	0	0	0	570	0	0	1,013	25,030
1987	Jeff Swindell	1	0	0	0	0	0	0	0	102	0	0	271	5,230
1987	Jim Bown	2	0	0	0	0	0	0	0	264	0	0	668	8,850
1987	Larry Caudill	1	0	0	0	0	0	0	0	470	0	0	470	4,725
1988	Lennie Pond	1	0	0	0	0	0	0	0	383	0	0	208	2,375
1988	Steve Moore	3	0	0	0	0	0	0	0	726	0	0	1,069	18,790
Lifetime		290	0	0	0	0	0	0	11	71,327	14	8	83,571	$1,058,930

Bobby Hamilton

Year	Driver	Starts	Poles	1	2	3	4	5	6–10	Laps	Laps Led	Races Led	Miles	$
2000	Bobby Hamilton Jr.	1	0	0	0	0	0	0	0	261	0	0	394	35,500
Lifetime		1	0	0	0	0	0	0	0	261	0	0	394	$35,500

Hubert Hamilton

Year	Driver	Starts	Poles	1	2	3	4	5	6–10	Laps	Laps Led	Races Led	Miles	$
1951	Jimmie Lewallen	7	0	0	0	2	0	2	2	367	0	0	459	1,825
1952	Ray Duhigg	1	0	0	0	0	0	0	0		0	0		25
Lifetime		8	0	0	0	2	0	2	2	367	0	0	459	$1,850

Margo Hamm

Year	Driver	Starts	Poles	1	2	3	4	5	6–10	Laps	Laps Led	Races Led	Miles	$
1968	Stan Meserve	29	0	0	0	0	0	0	1	3,769	0	0	2,459	7,100
Lifetime		29	0	0	0	0	0	0	1	3,769	0	0	2,459	$7,100

Richard Hammond

Year	Driver	Starts	Poles	1	2	3	4	5	6–10	Laps	Laps Led	Races Led	Miles	$
1972	Jim Hurtubise	2	0	0	0	0	0	0	1	271	0	0	705	3,515
Lifetime		2	0	0	0	0	0	0	1	271	0	0	705	$3,515

Year	Driver	Starts	Poles	Finish						Laps	Laps Led	Races Led	Miles	$
				1	2	3	4	5	6–10	Laps	Led	Led	Miles	$

Mack Hanbury

Year	Driver	Starts	Poles	1	2	3	4	5	6–10	Laps	Laps Led	Races Led	Miles	$
1955	Mack Hanbury	8	0	0	0	0	0	0	2	807	0	0	584	575
Lifetime		8	0	0	0	0	0	0	2	807	0	0	584	$575

Bob Hancher

Year	Driver	Starts	Poles	1	2	3	4	5	6–10	Laps	Laps Led	Races Led	Miles	$
1998	Wally Dallenbach	1	0	0	0	0	0	0	0	245	0	0	490	29,225
1998	Gary Bradberry	1	0	0	0	0	0	0	0	118	0	0	125	29,200
1998	Todd Bodine	7	0	0	0	0	0	0	1	2,444	46	1	2,725	142,825
Lifetime		9	0	0	0	0	0	0	1	2,807	46	1	3,340	$201,250

Mark Handley

Year	Driver	Starts	Poles	1	2	3	4	5	6–10	Laps	Laps Led	Races Led	Miles	$
1954	Kenneth Bridge	1	0	0	0	0	0	0	0	5	0	0	5	0
Lifetime		1	0	0	0	0	0	0	0	5	0	0	5	$0

Hiram Handy

Year	Driver	Starts	Poles	1	2	3	4	5	6–10	Laps	Laps Led	Races Led	Miles	$
1975	Dick May	4	0	0	0	0	0	0	1	1,248	0	0	1,449	6,575
1975	Elmo Langley	1	0	0	0	0	0	0	0	310	0	0	472	1,500
1976	Earl Brooks	2	0	0	0	0	0	0	0	667	0	0	662	2,170
1976	Dick May	3	0	0	0	0	0	0	0	818	0	0	1,003	4,790
1976	Buck Baker	5	0	0	0	0	0	0	0	1,284	0	0	1,655	6,920
1977	Earl Brooks	5	0	0	0	0	0	0	0	1,129	0	0	867	2,645
Lifetime		20	0	0	0	0	0	0	1	5,456	0	0	6,108	$24,600

Jeff Handy

Year	Driver	Starts	Poles	1	2	3	4	5	6–10	Laps	Laps Led	Races Led	Miles	$
1966	Jabe Thomas	12	0	0	0	0	0	0	0	1,327	0	0	1,290	3,480
1966	Doug Cooper	1	0	0	0	0	0	0	0	16	0	0	22	460
1966	Buddy Baker	1	0	0	0	0	0	0	0	149	0	0	75	120
1967	Jabe Thomas	1	0	0	0	0	0	0	1	269	0	0	135	200
1975	Jeff Handy	1	0	0	0	0	0	0	0	174	0	0	463	1,820
1976	Jeff Handy	1	0	0	0	0	0	0	0	3	0	0	2	370
1976	J.D. McDuffie	1	0	0	0	0	0	0	0	389	0	0	396	735
Lifetime		18	0	0	0	0	0	0	1	2,327	0	0	2,381	$7,185

James Hanley

Year	Driver	Starts	Poles	1	2	3	4	5	6–10	Laps	Laps Led	Races Led	Miles	$
1970	Friday Hassler	26	0	0	0	0	0	1	5	5,439	56	1	6,518	25,755
Lifetime		26	0	0	0	0	0	1	5	5,439	56	1	6,518	$25,755

Chuck Hansen

Year	Driver	Starts	Poles	1	2	3	4	5	6–10	Laps	Laps Led	Races Led	Miles	$
1955	Chuck Hansen	1	0	0	0	0	0	0	0	109	0	0	109	25
1957	Chuck Hansen	7	0	0	0	0	0	0	0	990	0	0	734	510
1958	Chuck Hansen	7	0	0	0	0	0	0	1	1,011	0	0	659	580
Lifetime		15	0	0	0	0	0	0	1	2,110	0	0	1,502	$1,115

Fred Harb

Year	Driver	Starts	Poles	1	2	3	4	5	6–10	Laps	Laps Led	Races Led	Miles	$
1955	Fred Harb	1	0	0	0	0	0	0	0	183	0	0	92	75
1956	Fred Harb	2	0	0	0	0	0	0	0	200	0	0	85	50
1957	Billy Myers	1	0	0	0	0	0	0	0	160	0	0	80	100
1957	Fred Harb	3	0	0	0	0	0	0	0	322	0	0	161	360
1957	Shorty York	1	0	0	0	0	0	0	0	109	0	0	55	50
1958	Fred Harb	25	0	0	0	1	2	1	3	3,651	0	0	1,840	3,315
1959	Fred Harb	17	1	0	0	1	0	1	3	2,324	0	0	1,094	1,625
1960	Harvey Hege	1	0	0	0	0	0	0	0	62	0	0	31	100
1960	Shorty York	2	0	0	0	0	0	0	0	434	0	0	412	325
1960	Fred Harb	19	0	0	0	0	0	2	5	2,899	0	0	1,282	2,505
1960	Buddy Baker	2	0	0	0	0	0	0	0	302	0	0	189	160
1961	Fred Harb	27	0	0	0	0	1	0	7	4,039	0	0	2,022	3,460
1961	Buddy Baker	1	0	0	0	0	0	0	0	59	0	0	30	50
1962	Joe Weatherly	1	0	0	0	0	1	0	0	197	0	0	66	290
1962	Fred Harb	20	0	0	0	0	0	0	3	2,703	0	0	1,160	2,220
1963	Bob Welborn	3	0	0	0	1	0	0	0	845	0	0	446	875
1963	Fred Harb	11	0	0	1	0	0	0	5	2,104	0	0	793	2,040
1963	Ralph Earnhardt	1	0	0	0	0	0	0	0	88	0	0	121	570
1963	Bunkie Blackburn	1	0	0	0	0	0	0	0	161	0	0	242	325

Year	Driver	Starts	Poles	Finish 1	2	3	4	5	6–10	Laps	Laps Led	Races Led	Miles	$

Fred Harb *continued*

Year	Driver	Starts	Poles	1	2	3	4	5	6–10	Laps	Laps Led	Races Led	Miles	$
1964	Fred Harb	1	0	0	0	0	0	0	1	188	0	0	47	180
Lifetime		140	1	0	1	3	4	4	27	21,030	0	0	10,246	$18,675

Bud Harbaugh

Year	Driver	Starts	Poles	1	2	3	4	5	6–10	Laps	Laps Led	Races Led	Miles	$
1956	Gene Simpson	1	0	0	0	0	0	0	0		0	0		100
Lifetime		1	0	0	0	0	0	0	0		0	0		$100

Tom Harbison

Year	Driver	Starts	Poles	1	2	3	4	5	6–10	Laps	Laps Led	Races Led	Miles	$
1956	Marvin Panch	19	1	1	2	4	2	0	3	2,939	107	5	2,008	7,475
1956	Allen Adkins	2	0	0	0	0	0	0	2	304	0	0	245	400
1956	Danny Letner	4	0	0	0	0	0	0	0	510	0	0	518	300
1957	Danny Letner	1	0	0	0	0	0	0	0	22	0	0	55	65
1957	Jim Delaney	1	0	0	0	0	0	0	0		0	0		75
1957	Mickey McGreevey	1	0	0	0	0	0	0	0	55	0	0	138	135
Lifetime		28	1	1	2	4	2	0	5	3,830	107	5	2,963	$8,450

J.E. Hardie

Year	Driver	Starts	Poles	1	2	3	4	5	6–10	Laps	Laps Led	Races Led	Miles	$
1951	J.E. Hardie	1	0	0	0	0	0	0	0	339	0	0	424	50
1952	J.E. Hardie	2	0	0	0	0	0	0	0	69	0	0	86	25
Lifetime		3	0	0	0	0	0	0	0	408	0	0	510	$75

Bud Harless

Year	Driver	Starts	Poles	1	2	3	4	5	6–10	Laps	Laps Led	Races Led	Miles	$
1965	Bud Harless	1	0	0	0	0	0	0	0	222	0	0	305	605
Lifetime		1	0	0	0	0	0	0	0	222	0	0	305	$605

Fred Harless

Year	Driver	Starts	Poles	1	2	3	4	5	6–10	Laps	Laps Led	Races Led	Miles	$
1963	Bud Harless	5	0	0	0	0	0	0	1	1,508	0	0	958	1,550
Lifetime		5	0	0	0	0	0	0	1	1,508	0	0	958	$1,550

Marshall Harless

Year	Driver	Starts	Poles	1	2	3	4	5	6–10	Laps	Laps Led	Races Led	Miles	$
1954	Marshall Harless	1	0	0	0	0	0	0	0	82	0	0	82	25
Lifetime		1	0	0	0	0	0	0	0	82	0	0	82	$25

Robert Harper

Year	Driver	Starts	Poles	1	2	3	4	5	6–10	Laps	Laps Led	Races Led	Miles	$
1966	Donnie Allison	2	0	0	0	0	0	0	1	664	0	0	757	2,180
1967	Armond Holley	4	0	0	0	0	0	0	0	347	0	0	404	2,000
1967	Donnie Allison	5	0	0	0	0	0	0	1	1,282	0	0	1,397	5,255
Lifetime		11	0	0	0	0	0	0	2	2,293	0	0	2,558	$9,435

Red Harrelson

Year	Driver	Starts	Poles	1	2	3	4	5	6–10	Laps	Laps Led	Races Led	Miles	$
1952	Lamar Crabtree	1	0	0	0	0	0	0	0	254	0	0	318	0
Lifetime		1	0	0	0	0	0	0	0	254	0	0	318	$0

Robert Harrington

Year	Driver	Starts	Poles	1	2	3	4	5	6–10	Laps	Laps Led	Races Led	Miles	$
1984	Elliott	5	0	0	0	0	0	0	0	895	0	0	1,513	11,335
1984	Morgan Shepherd	1	0	0	0	0	0	0	0	397	0	0	215	1,735
1984	Rodney Combs	1	0	0	0	0	0	0	0	192	0	0	384	1,750
1986	Rodney Combs	5	0	0	0	0	0	0	0	909	4	1	1,767	12,180
Lifetime		12	0	0	0	0	0	0	0	2,393	4	1	3,880	$27,000

Ferrel Harris

Year	Driver	Starts	Poles	1	2	3	4	5	6–10	Laps	Laps Led	Races Led	Miles	$
1975	Ferrel Harris	10	0	0	0	0	0	0	0	2,357	0	0	3,854	16,165
1975	Hershel McGriff	1	0	0	0	0	0	0	0	310	4	1	465	2,625
1976	Ferrel Harris	2	0	0	0	0	0	0	0	217	0	0	565	2,950
1976	Skip Manning	1	0	0	0	0	0	0	0	107	0	0	268	1,835
1977	Elliott	1	0	0	0	0	0	0	0	44	0	0	110	2,025
1980	Dick May	1	0	0	0	0	0	0	0	323	0	0	485	3,700
1980	Ferrel Harris	1	0	0	0	0	0	0	0	342	0	0	467	2,675
Lifetime		17	0	0	0	0	0	0	0	3,700	4	1	6,213	$31,975

Year	Driver	Starts	Poles	Finish						Laps	Laps Led	Races Led	Miles	$
				1	2	3	4	5	6–10					

Bill Harrison

Year	Driver	Starts	Poles	1	2	3	4	5	6–10	Laps	Laps Led	Races Led	Miles	$
1951	Bill Harrison	1	0	0	0	0	0	0	0	133	0	0	100	25
Lifetime		1	0	0	0	0	0	0	0	133	0	0	100	$25

Donald Harrison

Year	Driver	Starts	Poles	1	2	3	4	5	6–10	Laps	Laps Led	Races Led	Miles	$
1962	Cale Yarborough	3	0	0	0	0	0	0	0	179	0	0	208	1,010
1962	Gerald Duke	4	0	0	0	0	0	0	0	607	0	0	754	800
1963	LeeRoy Yarbrough	1	0	0	0	0	0	0	0	19	0	0	26	630
Lifetime		8	0	0	0	0	0	0	0	805	0	0	988	$2,440

Greg Harrison

Year	Driver	Starts	Poles	1	2	3	4	5	6–10	Laps	Laps Led	Races Led	Miles	$
1976	John Hamson	1	0	0	0	0	0	0	0	26	0	0	68	790
Lifetime		1	0	0	0	0	0	0	0	26	0	0	68	$790

Joe Harrison

Year	Driver	Starts	Poles	1	2	3	4	5	6–10	Laps	Laps Led	Races Led	Miles	$
1950	Joe Harrison	1	0	0	0	0	0	0	0	3	0	0	13	25
Lifetime		1	0	0	0	0	0	0	0	3	0	0	13	$25

Steve Harrison

Year	Driver	Starts	Poles	1	2	3	4	5	6–10	Laps	Laps Led	Races Led	Miles	$
1982	Dick Brooks	1	0	0	0	0	0	0	0	239	0	0	359	1,515
Lifetime		1	0	0	0	0	0	0	0	239	0	0	359	$1,515

W.M. Harrison

Year	Driver	Starts	Poles	1	2	3	4	5	6–10	Laps	Laps Led	Races Led	Miles	$
1963	LeeRoy Yarbrough	1	0	0	0	0	0	0	0	130	0	0	179	420
1963	Bubba Farr	2	0	0	0	0	0	0	0	34	0	0	85	550
Lifetime		3	0	0	0	0	0	0	0	164	0	0	264	$970

George Harrivel

Year	Driver	Starts	Poles	1	2	3	4	5	6–10	Laps	Laps Led	Races Led	Miles	$
1976	John Haver	1	0	0	0	0	0	0	0	49	0	0	98	780
Lifetime		1	0	0	0	0	0	0	0	49	0	0	98	$780

Bud Hartje

Year	Driver	Starts	Poles	1	2	3	4	5	6–10	Laps	Laps Led	Races Led	Miles	$
1966	James Hylton	41	1	0	4	6	7	3	12	10,804	155	3	8,773	29,575
1967	James Hylton	46	1	0	3	3	12	8	139	11,526	10	5	8,534	38,930
Lifetime		87	2	0	7	9	19	11	25	22,330	264	8	17,307	$68,505

George Hartley

Year	Driver	Starts	Poles	1	2	3	4	5	6–10	Laps	Laps Led	Races Led	Miles	$
1951	Bill Rexford	1	0	0	0	0	0	0	0	143	0	0	179	0
Lifetime		1	0	0	0	0	0	0	0	143	0	0	179	$0

Butch Hartman

Year	Driver	Starts	Poles	1	2	3	4	5	6–10	Laps	Laps Led	Races Led	Miles	$
1966	Butch Hartman	1	0	0	0	0	0	0	0	307	0	0	461	875
1968	Butch Hartman	5	0	0	0	0	0	0	2	1,458	10	2	2,278	6,455
1977	Butch Hartman	11	0	0	0	0	0	0	2	2,005	0	0	3,690	18,615
1978	Butch Hartman	1	0	0	0	0	0	0	0	121	0	0	184	640
1979	Butch Hartman	1	0	0	0	0	0	0	0	351	0	0	479	2,225
Lifetime		19	0	0	0	0	0	0	4	4,242	10	2	7,092	$28,810

Billie Harvey

Year	Driver	Starts	Poles	1	2	3	4	5	6–10	Laps	Laps Led	Races Led	Miles	$
1977	Billy McGinnis	1	0	0	0	0	0	0	0	264	0	0	402	1,570
1978	Billy McGinnis	1	0	0	0	0	0	0	0	221	0	0	336	875
1979	Gary Balough	3	0	0	0	0	0	0	0	216	0	0	540	6,015
1979	Dick May	1	0	0	0	0	0	0	0	0	0	0	0	1,050
1980	Billie Harvey	4	0	0	0	0	0	0	0	805	0	0	1,691	7,995
1980	Gary Balough	1	0	0	0	0	0	0	0	16	0	0	24	610
1981	Billie Harvey	2	0	0	0	0	0	0	0	60	0	0	150	3,915
1982	Tim Richmond	1	0	0	0	0	0	0	0	112	0	0	114	820
1982	Billie Harvey	1	0	0	0	0	0	0	0	6	0	0	15	3,875
Lifetime		15	0	0	0	0	0	0	0	1,700	0	0	3,272	$26,725

Year	Driver	Starts	Poles	Finish 1	2	3	4	5	6–10	Laps	Laps Led	Races Led	Miles	$

Friday Hassler

Year	Driver	Starts	Poles	1	2	3	4	5	6–10	Laps	Laps Led	Races Led	Miles	$
1969	Friday Hassler	17	0	0	0	0	0	0	6	4,145	3	1	4,434	17,275
1969	John Sears	1	0	0	0	0	0	0	0	3	0	0	5	725
1971	Friday Hassler	29	2	0	1	2	0	1	9	5,650	68	3	7,137	32,200
1972	Friday Hassler	1	0	0	0	0	0	0	1	137	0	0	359	2,020
Lifetime		48	2	0	1	2	0	1	16	9,935	71	4	11,934	$52,220

Ed Hastings

Year	Driver	Starts	Poles	1	2	3	4	5	6–10	Laps	Laps Led	Races Led	Miles	$
1949	Erick Erickson	4	0	0	1	1	0	0	1	713	0	0	357	1,300
1950	Erick Erickson	2	0	0	0	0	0	0	0	137	31	1	131	50
1951	Dale Williams	1	0	0	0	0	0	0	1		0	0		100
1951	Erick Erickson	2	0	0	0	0	0	0	0	120	0	0	90	25
1956	Danny Letner	1	0	0	0	0	0	0	0		0	0		0
Lifetime		10	0	0	1	1	0	0	2	970	31	1	578	$1,475

Bob Havenmann

Year	Driver	Starts	Poles	1	2	3	4	5	6–10	Laps	Laps Led	Races Led	Miles	$
1954	Bob Havenmann	2	0	0	0	0	0	0	1	694	0	0	347	275
1955	Bob Havenmann	3	0	0	0	0	0	0	2	506	0	0	410	400
1956	Bob Havenmann	4	0	0	0	0	0	0	1	496	0	0	366	290
1957	Bob Havenmann	1	0	0	0	0	0	0	0	117	0	0	73	100
1958	Bob Havenmann	1	0	0	0	0	0	0	0	91	0	0	91	100
Lifetime		11	0	0	0	0	0	0	4	1,904	0	0	1,287	$1,165

John Haver

Year	Driver	Starts	Poles	1	2	3	4	5	6–10	Laps	Laps Led	Races Led	Miles	$
1979	John Haver	1	0	0	0	0	0	0	0	36	0	0	72	950
Lifetime		1	0	0	0	0	0	0	0	36	0	0	72	$950

Ronald Hawk

Year	Driver	Starts	Poles	1	2	3	4	5	6–10	Laps	Laps Led	Races Led	Miles	$
1962	Paul Barrow	2	0	0	0	0	0	0	0	189	0	0	473	500
Lifetime		2	0	0	0	0	0	0	0	189	0	0	473	$500

Butch Hawkersmith

Year	Driver	Starts	Poles	1	2	3	4	5	6–10	Laps	Laps Led	Races Led	Miles	$
1973	Alton Jones	5	0	0	0	0	0	0	1	686	0	0	807	4,195
1974	Alton Jones	5	0	0	0	0	0	1	1	1,163	0	0	1,095	4,395
1975	Alton Jones	2	0	0	0	0	0	0	1	790	0	0	471	1,935
Lifetime		12	0	0	0	0	0	1	3	2,639	0	0	2,373	$10,525

Bobby Hawkins

Year	Driver	Starts	Poles	1	2	3	4	5	6–10	Laps	Laps Led	Races Led	Miles	$
1981	Dick Brooks	2	0	0	0	0	0	0	0	702	0	0	877	3,175
1981	Jack Ingram	5	0	0	0	0	0	0	1	822	0	0	1,285	9,965
1982	Dick Brooks	4	0	0	0	0	0	0	0	278	0	0	330	7,955
1982	David Pearson	6	2	0	0	1	0	1	0	1,019	7	2	1,721	47,945
1983	David Pearson	10	0	0	0	1	0	0	3	1,643	18	1	3,094	59,720
1984	David Pearson	11	0	0	0	0	0	0	3	1,630	10	3	2,949	54,125
1985	Butch Lindley	1	0	0	0	0	0	0	0	352	0	0	191	1,365
1985	Morgan Shepherd	4	0	0	0	0	0	1	1	820	0	0	1,099	18,575
Lifetime		43	2	0	0	2	0	2	8	7,266	35	6	11,545	$202,825

Joe Hawkins

Year	Driver	Starts	Poles	1	2	3	4	5	6–10	Laps	Laps Led	Races Led	Miles	$
1952	Billy Myers	1	0	0	0	0	0	0	0	220	0	0	220	50
1952	Buddy Shuman	1	0	0	0	0	0	0	0	376	0	0	470	100
Lifetime		2	0	0	0	0	0	0	0	596	0	0	690	$150

Tom Hawkins

Year	Driver	Starts	Poles	1	2	3	4	5	6–10	Laps	Laps Led	Races Led	Miles	$
1962	Sal Tovella	2	0	0	0	0	0	0	0	77	0	0	193	450
Lifetime		2	0	0	0	0	0	0	0	77	0	0	193	$450

Tom Hawkinson

Year	Driver	Starts	Poles	1	2	3	4	5	6–10	Laps	Laps Led	Races Led	Miles	$
1963	Sal Tovella	3	0	0	0	0	0	0	0	346	0	0	888	1,300
Lifetime		3	0	0	0	0	0	0	0	346	0	0	888	$1,300

Year	Driver	Starts	Poles	Finish 1	2	3	4	5	6–10	Laps	Laps Led	Races Led	Miles	$

Ed Hawks

Year	Driver	Starts	Poles	1	2	3	4	5	6–10	Laps	Laps Led	Races Led	Miles	$
1974	Bobby Fleming	1	0	0	0	0	0	0	0	341	0	0	182	525
1974	Walter Ballard	1	0	0	0	0	0	0	0	32	0	0	80	645
1974	Johnny Barnes	2	0	0	0	0	0	0	0	18	0	0	10	1,065
1974	Ernie Shaw	4	0	0	0	0	0	0	0	842	0	0	538	2,280
Lifetime		8	0	0	0	0	0	0	0	1,233	0	0	809	$4,515

D. Nienberg Hay

Year	Driver	Starts	Poles	1	2	3	4	5	6–10	Laps	Laps Led	Races Led	Miles	$
1976	Bill Polich	1	0	0	0	0	0	0	0	86	0	0	225	1,165
Lifetime		1	0	0	0	0	0	0	0	86	0	0	225	$1,165

Johnny Hayes

Year	Driver	Starts	Poles	1	2	3	4	5	6–10	Laps	Laps Led	Races Led	Miles	$
1982	Benny Parsons	6	0	0	0	0	0	3	2	1,803	2	1	2,645	29,165
1983	Benny Parsons	16	0	0	2	1	0	1	1	2,847	107	7	5,285	119,760
1983	Phil Parsons	5	0	0	0	0	0	0	0	887	0	0	1,696	23,850
1984	Benny Parsons	14	2	1	1	0	1	4	3	2,877	407	6	5,451	211,665
1984	Phil Parsons	23	0	0	0	0	0	0	3	6,301	4	1	7,801	92,165
Lifetime		64	2	1	3	1	1	8	9	14,715	520	15	22,878	$476,605

Frank Hayworth

Year	Driver	Starts	Poles	1	2	3	4	5	6–10	Laps	Laps Led	Races Led	Miles	$
1956	Bill Blair	2	0	0	0	0	0	0	1	562	0	0	544	225
1956	Jim Paschal	36	1	1	8	2	3	1	7	5,404	110	4	3,488	12,710
1957	Max Berrier	2	0	0	0	0	0	0	0	0	0	0	0	50
1957	Jim Paschal	6	0	0	0	1	1	0	2	822	0	0	636	1,605
1957	Ken Rush	13	0	0	0	0	0	0	4	1,878	0	0	1,203	1,505
Lifetime		59	1	1	8	3	4	1	14	8,666	110	4	5,871	$16,095

Louis Headley

Year	Driver	Starts	Poles	1	2	3	4	5	6–10	Laps	Laps Led	Races Led	Miles	$
1955	Louis Headley	1	0	0	0	0	0	0	0	3	0	0	12	0
1956	Louis Headley	1	0	0	0	0	0	0	0	1	0	0	1	25
Lifetime		2	0	0	0	0	0	0	0	4	0	0	13	$25

Allen Heath

Year	Driver	Starts	Poles	1	2	3	4	5	6–10	Laps	Laps Led	Races Led	Miles	$
1951	Allen Heath	3	0	0	0	0	0	0	0		0	0		50
1954	Jim Heath	1	0	0	0	0	0	0	0	210	0	0	210	40
1954	Allen Heath	1	0	0	0	0	0	0	0	52	0	0	26	0
Lifetime		5	0	0	0	0	0	0	0	262	0	0	236	$90

Charles Heckert

Year	Driver	Starts	Poles	1	2	3	4	5	6–10	Laps	Laps Led	Races Led	Miles	$
1972	Sonny Easley	1	0	0	0	0	0	0	0	35	0	0	92	670
Lifetime		1	0	0	0	0	0	0	0	35	0	0	92	$670

Larry Hedrick

Year	Driver	Starts	Poles	1	2	3	4	5	6–10	Laps	Laps Led	Races Led	Miles	$
1990	Larry Pearson	4	0	0	0	0	0	0	0	1,676	0	0	1,750	17,865
1991	Larry Pearson	11	0	0	0	0	0	0	0	1,543	0	0	2,662	53,570
1992	Dave Marcis	7	0	0	0	0	0	0	0	2,097	0	0	1,717	43,060
1992	Hut Stricklin	2	0	0	0	0	0	0	0	312	0	0	313	13,670
1992	Greg Sacks	20	0	0	0	0	0	0	0	4,926	6	1	6,502	162,870
1993	Phil Parsons	25	0	0	0	0	0	0	1	6,003	0	0	7,542	271,000
1993	Dick Trickle	5	0	0	0	0	0	1	1	1,741	3	1	1,958	61,790
1994	Joe Nemechek	29	0	0	0	1	0	0	2	7,953	22	2	9,488	356,815
1995	Ricky Craven	31	0	0	0	0	0	0	4	8,711	5	4	11,087	549,304
1996	Ricky Craven	31	2	0	0	2	0	1	2	8,551	136	9	10,215	860,340
1997	Steve Grissom	31	0	0	0	0	2	0	3	8,800	2	1	11,299	1,018,335
1998	David Green	4	0	0	0	0	0	0	0	864	0	0	988	100,595
1998	Steve Grissom	24	0	0	0	0	0	1	2	6,546	8	1	9,061	952,140
1999	Dick Trickle	1	0	0	0	0	0	0	0	229	0	0	344	19,675
1999	Gary Bradberry	1	0	0	0	0	0	0	0	233	0	0	359	33,950
1999	David Green	23	0	0	0	0	0	0	0	5,922	0	0	7,904	761,990
1999	Derrike Cope	3	0	0	0	0	0	0	0	758	0	0	1,042	91,225
2000	Gary Bradberry	2	0	0	0	0	0	0	0	642	0	0	498	63,700
2000	Rick Mast	5	0	0	0	0	0	0	0	1,655	0	0	2,025	200,520
Lifetime		259	2	0	0	3	2	3	15	69,162	182	19	86,753	$5,632,169

Year	Driver	Starts	Poles	Finish						Laps	Laps Led	Races Led	Miles	$
				1	2	3	4	5	6–10	Laps	Led	Led	Miles	$

Gene Hege

Year	Driver	Starts	Poles	1	2	3	4	5	6–10	Laps	Laps Led	Races Led	Miles	$
1958	Gene Hege	1	0	0	0	0	0	0	0	85	0	0	43	0
Lifetime		1	0	0	0	0	0	0	0	85	0	0	43	$0

Harvey Hege

Year	Driver	Starts	Poles	1	2	3	4	5	6–10	Laps	Laps Led	Races Led	Miles	$
1958	Eddie Pagan	1	0	0	0	0	0	0	0	4	0	0	2	0
1958	Harvey Hege	13	0	0	0	0	0	0	2	1,498	0	0	786	1,200
1958	Buck Brigance	1	0	0	0	0	0	0	0	109	0	0	55	70
1958	Shep Langdon	2	0	0	0	0	0	0	0	586	0	0	293	300
1959	Shorty York	1	0	0	0	0	0	0	0	185	0	0	46	120
1959	Neil Castles	2	0	0	0	0	0	0	0	363	0	0	182	150
1959	Harvey Hege	10	0	0	0	0	0	0	3	1,485	0	0	765	955
1959	Fred Harb	2	0	0	0	0	0	0	1	365	0	0	183	250
Lifetime		32	0	0	0	0	0	0	6	4,595	0	0	2,311	$3,045

Greg Heller

Year	Driver	Starts	Poles	1	2	3	4	5	6–10	Laps	Laps Led	Races Led	Miles	$
1977	Greg Heller	1	0	0	0	0	0	0	0	110	0	0	275	680
1978	Bobby Wawak	1	0	0	0	0	0	0	0	65	0	0	163	850
1978	Greg Heller	1	0	0	0	0	0	0	0	250	0	0	250	575
Lifetime		3	0	0	0	0	0	0	0	425	0	0	688	$2,105

Buddy Helms

Year	Driver	Starts	Poles	1	2	3	4	5	6–10	Laps	Laps Led	Races Led	Miles	$
1949	Buddy Helms	1	0	0	0	0	0	0	1		0	0		75
1949	Slick Smith	3	0	0	0	0	0	0	0	277	0	0	139	150
1950	Buddy Helms	3	0	0	0	0	0	0	0	36	0	0	18	0
1951	Buddy Helms	1	0	0	0	0	0	0	0	132	0	0	99	25
Lifetime		8	0	0	0	0	0	0	1	445	0	0	256	$250

C.W. Henderson

Year	Driver	Starts	Poles	1	2	3	4	5	6–10	Laps	Laps Led	Races Led	Miles	$
1982	Brad Teague	9	0	0	0	0	0	0	0	3,052	0	0	2,611	14,300
1983	Ronnie Hopkins	13	0	0	0	0	0	0	0	2,563	0	0	3,101	26,445
1984	Morgan Shepherd	2	0	0	0	0	0	0	0	667	0	0	353	1,700
Lifetime		24	0	0	0	0	0	0	0	6,282	0	0	6,066	$42,445

Elmo Henderson

Year	Driver	Starts	Poles	1	2	3	4	5	6–10	Laps	Laps Led	Races Led	Miles	$
1959	Elmo Henderson	1	0	0	0	0	0	0	0	160	0	0	80	50
1961	Joe Weatherly	1	0	0	0	0	0	0	0	189	0	0	76	70
Lifetime		2	0	0	0	0	0	0	0	349	0	0	156	$120

Harvey Henderson

Year	Driver	Starts	Poles	1	2	3	4	5	6–10	Laps	Laps Led	Races Led	Miles	$
1952	Harvey Henderson	1	0	0	0	0	0	0	0		0	0		25
1955	Harvey Henderson	17	0	0	0	0	0	1	5	2,284	0	0	1,325	1,810
1956	Harvey Henderson	18	0	0	0	0	0	0	4	2,520	0	0	1,618	1,360
1957	Harvey Henderson	1	0	0	0	0	0	0	0	172	0	0	86	100
1958	Harvey Henderson	2	0	0	0	0	0	0	0	160	0	0	58	125
Lifetime		39	0	0	0	0	0	1	9	5,136	0	0	3,088	$3,420

Ray Henderson

Year	Driver	Starts	Poles	1	2	3	4	5	6–10	Laps	Laps Led	Races Led	Miles	$
1954	Rick Henderson	3	0	0	0	0	0	0	0	609	0	0	404	65
Lifetime		3	0	0	0	0	0	0	0	609	0	0	404	$65

Rick Hendrick (Statistics include principal owner Rick Hendrick's partnerships with Jeff Gordon, Paul Newman & others.)

Year	Driver	Starts	Poles	1	2	3	4	5	6–10	Laps	Laps Led	Races Led	Miles	$
1984	Geoffrey Bodine	30	3	3	0	1	2	1	7	8,848	686	12	10,064	351,900
1985	Geoffrey Bodine	28	3	0	3	3	2	2	4	8,719	692	18	10,720	461,900
1985	Dick Brooks	1	0	0	0	0	0	0	1	393	0	0	590	9,000
1986	Geoffrey Bodine	29	9	2	2	5	1	0	5	7,791	1,676	25	9,361	669,605
1986	Tim Richmond	29	8	7	4	0	1	1	4	8,544	1,006	21	10,528	657,670
1986	Brett Bodine	1	0	0	0	0	0	0	0	394	0	0	591	10,100
1987	Darrell Waltrip	29	0	1	1	1	2	1	10	8,996	311	14	11,036	293,770
1987	Jim Fitzgerald	1	0	0	0	0	0	0	0	93	0	0	244	1,675
1987	Geoffrey Bodine	29	2	0	1	1	0	1	7	7,738	342	13	8,817	353,640

Year	Driver	Starts	Poles	Finish 1	2	3	4	5	6–10	Laps	Laps Led	Races Led	Miles	$

Rick Hendrick *continued*

Year	Driver	Starts	Poles	1	2	3	4	5	6–10	Laps	Laps Led	Races Led	Miles	$
1987	Tim Richmond	8	1	2	0	0	1	0	1	1,199	161	6	2,860	111,850
1987	Rick Hendrick	1	0	0	0	0	0	0	0	75	0	0	197	1,150
1987	Benny Parsons	29	0	0	3	0	1	2	3	7,075	87	9	8,921	514,330
1988	Rick Hendrick	1	0	0	0	0	0	0	0	94	0	0	246	2,550
1988	Ken Schrader	28	2	1	1	0	1	1	13	8,700	151	13	10,819	481,080
1988	Geoffrey Bodine	29	3	1	1	4	1	3	6	8,995	463	15	10,566	424,450
1988	Darrell Waltrip	29	2	2	1	1	2	4	4	9,065	520	18	10,792	618,435
1988	Rob Moroso	1	0	0	0	0	0	0	0	331	0	0	497	4,500
1989	Ken Schrader	29	4	1	1	3	4	1	4	8,675	356	17	10,782	702,615
1989	Kyle Petty	1	0	0	0	0	0	0	0	392	0	0	588	6,000
1989	Greg Sacks	1	0	0	0	0	0	0	0	160	0	0	160	2,895
1989	Geoffrey Bodine	29	3	1	1	3	3	1	2	9,051	510	14	10,535	521,300
1989	Darrell Waltrip	29	0	6	2	2	2	2	4	9,333	858	17	10,986	949,535
1989	Bobby Hamilton	1	0	0	0	0	0	0	0	215	5	1	215	3,075
1989	Tom Kendall	1	0	0	0	0	0	0	0	79	1	1	194	3,015
1990	Hut Stricklin	1	0	0	0	0	0	0	0	82	0	0	112	2,765
1990	Ken Schrader	29	3	0	2	2	1	2	7	8,649	242	12	10,050	529,975
1990	Darrell Waltrip	23	0	0	1	1	2	1	7	8,138	297	9	9,288	431,732
1990	Ricky Rudd	29	2	1	0	3	2	2	7	8,664	180	7	10,494	444,662
1990	Sarel van der Merwe	1	0	0	0	0	0	0	0	77	0	0	189	12,070
1990	Stan Barrett	1	0	0	0	0	0	0	0	74	0	0	186	3,850
1990	Jimmy Horton	2	0	0	0	0	0	0	0	342	0	0	885	30,475
1990	Greg Sacks	16	1	0	2	0	0	0	2	3,790	107	4	5,470	190,348
1991	Ricky Rudd	29	1	1	3	0	2	3	8	9,561	425	13	11,429	638,455
1991	Ken Schrader	29	0	2	2	2	1	3	8	8,331	440	16	9,843	584,550
1992	Jeff Gordon	1	0	0	0	0	0	0	0	164	0	0	250	6,285
1992	Ken Schrader	29	1	0	0	2	1	1	7	8,425	83	5	9,816	548,240
1992	Ricky Rudd	29	1	1	0	2	3	3	9	8,968	331	9	10,270	629,285
1993	Ken Schrader	30	6	0	2	2	3	2	6	8,877	285	14	10,995	721,165
1993	Jeff Gordon	30	1	0	2	1	1	3	4	8,390	189	14	10,067	624,035
1993	Al Unser Jr.	1	0	0	0	0	0	0	0	157	0	0	393	23,005
1993	Ricky Rudd	30	0	1	1	1	3	3	5	8,635	137	7	10,266	638,105
1994	Ken Schrader	31	0	0	1	2	4	2	9	9,704	223	9	11,741	776,335
1994	Jeff Gordon	31	1	2	1	1	2	1	7	9,277	446	17	11,549	1,507,010
1994	Terry Labonte	31	0	3	1	1	0	1	8	9,149	486	8	11,314	959,695
1995	Jeff Purvis	1	0	0	0	0	0	0	0	320	0	0	487	7,370
1995	Jeff Gordon	31	9	7	4	5	0	1	6	9,405	2,610	29	11,609	2,430,460
1995	Terry Labonte	31	1	3	4	2	3	2	3	9,076	437	11	11,376	1,327,295
1995	Ken Schrader	31	1	0	0	1	1	0	8	8,550	237	9	10,167	806,830
1996	Jeff Gordon	31	5	10	3	4	2	2	3	8,972	2,315	25	10,518	2,391,518
1996	Terry Labonte	31	4	2	7	5	1	6	3	9,443	972	22	11,523	1,866,713
1996	Ken Schrader	31	0	0	0	1	1	1	7	9,408	45	7	11,500	953,287
1997	Jack Sprague	1	0	0	0	0	0	0	0	256	0	0	136	18,650
1997	Ricky Craven	30	0	0	0	2	0	2	3	7,806	280	9	10,468	1,055,471
1997	Todd Bodine	1	0	0	0	0	0	0	0	284	9	1	426	58,550
1997	Jeff Gordon	32	1	10	3	2	4	3	1	9,276	1,645	24	11,983	2,914,138
1997	Terry Labonte	32	1	1	3	2	2	0	12	9,605	256	11	12,297	1,841,855
1998	Terry Labonte	33	0	1	1	2	1	0	10	9,573	338	12	12,372	1,797,805
1998	Jeff Gordon	33	7	13	6	3	1	3	2	9,818	1,706	26	12,784	5,074,942
1998	Randy LaJoie	9	0	0	0	0	0	1	2	2,750	0	0	3,138	336,905
1998	Ricky Craven	8	1	0	0	0	0	0	1	1,852	19	2	3,057	421,500
1998	Wally Dallenbach	16	0	0	0	0	0	0	3	4,447	13	2	5,577	508,300
1999	Jeff Gordon	34	7	7	4	5	1	1	3	9,384	1,320	26	12,131	4,074,101
1999	Terry Labonte	34	0	1	0	0	0	0	6	9,325	350	11	12,221	2,090,646
1999	Wally Dallenbach	34	0	0	0	0	0	1	5	9,751	13	4	12,640	1,588,381
2000	Terry Labonte	32	1	0	1	0	0	2	3	9,335	33	3	11,932	1,960,025
2000	Ron Hornaday Jr.	1	0	0	0	0	0	0	0	90	0	0	221	47,020
2000	Jerry Nadeau	34	0	1	0	0	2	0	2	8,839	357	10	11,508	1,917,470
2000	Jeff Gordon	34	3	3	1	1	4	2	11	9,897	425	15	12,849	2,588,455
2000	Todd Bodine	1	0	0	0	0	0	0	0	159	0	0	398	117,260
2001	Jerry Nadeau	36	0	0	1	1	1	1	6	10,238	170	7	13,511	2,157,094
2001	Jeff Gordon	36	8	6	6	3	2	1	6	10,638	2,322	25	14,026	4,999,537
2001	Jimmie Johnson	3	0	0	0	0	0	0	0	781	0	0	1,187	122,320
2001	Terry Labonte	36	0	0	0	0	0	1	2	10,517	0	0	13,909	2,844,629
2002	Jerry Nadeau	11	0	0	0	0	0	0	1	3,267	45	2	4,207	751,424
2002	Joe Nemechek	25	0	0	2	0	1	0	0	5,934	178	4	7,932	1,667,437
2002	Jeff Gordon	36	3	3	2	1	2	5	7	10,201	989	14	13,552	4,687,138
2002	Jimmie Johnson	36	5	3	0	2	1	0	15	10,521	838	14	13,915	2,637,793

Year	Driver	Starts	Poles	Finish 1	2	3	4	5	6–10	Laps	Laps Led	Races Led	Miles	$

Rick Hendrick *continued*

Year	Driver	Starts	Poles	1	2	3	4	5	6–10	Laps	Laps Led	Races Led	Miles	$
2002	Terry Labonte	36	0	0	0	1	0	0	3	9,966	11	1	13,248	2,988,922
Lifetime		1638	114	109	87	87	78	82	303	474,093	29,629	684	593,718	$77,509,323

Don Henison

Year	Driver	Starts	Poles	1	2	3	4	5	6–10	Laps	Laps Led	Races Led	Miles	$
1958	Ruben Thrash	2	0	0	0	0	0	0	0	133	0	0	202	200
Lifetime		2	0	0	0	0	0	0	0	133	0	0	202	$200

R.G. Henschel

Year	Driver	Starts	Poles	1	2	3	4	5	6–10	Laps	Laps Led	Races Led	Miles	$
1961	Robert Roeber	1	0	0	0	0	0	0	0	38	0	0	95	115
Lifetime		1	0	0	0	0	0	0	0	38	0	0	95	$115

Casper Hensley

Year	Driver	Starts	Poles	1	2	3	4	5	6–10	Laps	Laps Led	Races Led	Miles	$
1964	Bunkie Blackburn	12	0	0	0	0	1	0	3	2,294	0	0	2,327	5,780
1964	Bill McMahan	19	0	0	0	0	0	1	3	3,786	0	0	2,723	6,935
1965	Bill McMahan	1	0	0	0	0	0	0	0	0	0	0	0	100
1965	Bunkie Blackburn	2	0	0	0	0	0	0	1	87	0	0	218	1,365
1965	Jim Hunter	1	0	0	0	0	1	0	0	191	0	0	96	300
Lifetime		35	0	0	0	0	2	1	7	6,358	0	0	5,363	$14,480

Jimmy Hensley

Year	Driver	Starts	Poles	1	2	3	4	5	6–10	Laps	Laps Led	Races Led	Miles	$
1977	Jimmy Hensley	1	0	0	0	0	0	0	1	491	0	0	258	2,050
Lifetime		1	0	0	0	0	0	0	1	491	0	0	258	$2,050

Bernie Hentges

Year	Driver	Starts	Poles	1	2	3	4	5	6–10	Laps	Laps Led	Races Led	Miles	$
1959	Bernie Hentges	2	0	0	0	0	0	0	0	176	0	0	440	210
Lifetime		2	0	0	0	0	0	0	0	176	0	0	440	$210

Ray Herlocker

Year	Driver	Starts	Poles	1	2	3	4	5	6–10	Laps	Laps Led	Races Led	Miles	$
1962	Thomas Cox	33	0	0	0	0	1	1	15	6,344	0	0	4,020	6,635
1962	Harold Carmac	2	0	0	0	0	0	0	1	172	0	0	86	525
1962	Ray Hughes	6	0	0	0	0	0	0	2	1,289	0	0	536	965
1963	Ray Hughes	1	0	0	0	0	0	0	0	183	0	0	46	110
Lifetime		42	0	0	0	0	1	1	18	7,988	0	0	4,687	$8,235

John Hernandez

Year	Driver	Starts	Poles	1	2	3	4	5	6–10	Laps	Laps Led	Races Led	Miles	$
1955	Marvin Panch	1	0	0	0	0	1	0	0	247	0	0	247	650
Lifetime		1	0	0	0	0	1	0	0	247	0	0	247	$650

Skimp Hersey

Year	Driver	Starts	Poles	1	2	3	4	5	6–10	Laps	Laps Led	Races Led	Miles	$
1949	Skimp Hersey	1	0	0	0	0	0	0	0		0	0		25
Lifetime		1	0	0	0	0	0	0	0		0	0		$25

Ben Hess

Year	Driver	Starts	Poles	1	2	3	4	5	6–10	Laps	Laps Led	Races Led	Miles	$
1988	Ben Hess	1	0	0	0	0	0	0	0	472	0	0	480	3,370
1989	Ben Hess	9	0	0	0	0	0	0	0	3,194	0	0	3,818	43,490
Lifetime		10	0	0	0	0	0	0	0	3,666	0	0	4,298	$46,860

Larry Hess

Year	Driver	Starts	Poles	1	2	3	4	5	6–10	Laps	Laps Led	Races Led	Miles	$
1965	Larry Hess	10	0	0	0	0	0	0	3	2,347	0	0	3,543	8,295
1965	Jim Tatum	1	0	0	0	0	0	0	0	103	0	0	34	100
1966	Larry Hess	13	0	0	0	0	0	0	0	1,830	0	0	2,160	5,290
1967	Larry Hess	1	0	0	0	0	0	0	0	5	0	0	3	100
1968	Larry Hess	1	0	0	0	0	0	0	0	0	0	0	0	460
Lifetime		26	0	0	0	0	0	0	3	4,285	0	0	5,740	$14,245

Dr. Ed Hessert

Year	Driver	Starts	Poles	1	2	3	4	5	6–10	Laps	Laps Led	Races Led	Miles	$
1969	Dr. Ed Hessert	14	0	0	0	0	0	0	4	2,535	1	1	3,158	11,667

Year	Driver	Starts	Poles	Finish						Laps	Laps Led	Races Led	Miles	$
				1	2	3	4	5	6–10	Laps	Led	Led	Miles	$

Dr. Ed Hessert *continued*

Year	Driver	Starts	Poles	1	2	3	4	5	6–10	Laps	Laps Led	Races Led	Miles	$
1970	Dr. Ed Hessert	1	0	0	0	0	0	0	0	45	0	0	113	255
1971	Dr. Ed Hessert	1	0	0	0	0	0	0	0	14	0	0	21	315
Lifetime		16	0	0	0	0	0	0	4	2,594	1	1	3,292	$12,237

Tom Heveron

Year	Driver	Starts	Poles	1	2	3	4	5	6–10	Laps	Laps Led	Races Led	Miles	$
1984	Doug Heveron	14	0	0	0	0	0	0	0	2,960	7	1	4,320	32,305
1985	Doug Heveron	1	0	0	0	0	0	0	0	44	0	0	110	8,460
Lifetime		15	0	0	0	0	0	0	0	3,004	7	1	4,430	$40,765

Hal Hicks & Mike Witter

Year	Driver	Starts	Poles	1	2	3	4	5	6–10	Laps	Laps Led	Races Led	Miles	$
1998	Dan Pardus	1	0	0	0	0	0	0	0	99	0	0	248	25,425
1999	Ricky Craven	12	0	0	0	0	0	0	0	2,668	0	0	3,067	396,339
2000	Ricky Craven	16	0	0	0	0	0	0	0	4,153	64	2	4,922	577,385
2001	Rick Mast	9	0	0	0	0	0	0	0	2,613	0	0	3,286	346,340
Lifetime		38	0	0	0	0	0	0	0	9,533	64	2	11,523	$1,345,489

George Hicks

Year	Driver	Starts	Poles	1	2	3	4	5	6–10	Laps	Laps Led	Races Led	Miles	$
1951	George Seeger	1	0	0	0	0	0	0	0		0	0		25
Lifetime		1	0	0	0	0	0	0	0		0	0		$25

Elton Hildreth

Year	Driver	Starts	Poles	1	2	3	4	5	6–10	Laps	Laps Led	Races Led	Miles	$
1952	Elton Hildreth	6	0	0	0	0	0	0	1	815	0	0	608	375
1953	Elton Hildreth	25	0	0	0	0	1	0	4	821	0	0	785	1,600
1954	Elton Hildreth	14	0	0	0	0	0	0	2	1,519	0	0	1,420	960
1955	Boyce Hildreth	1	0	0	0	0	0	0	0	5	0	0	3	0
1955	Elton Hildreth	3	0	0	0	0	0	0	0	130	0	0	79	100
1956	Elton Hildreth	1	0	0	0	0	0	0	0	122	0	0	122	75
1957	Elton Hildreth	2	0	0	0	0	0	0	0	153	0	0	153	150
Lifetime		52	0	0	0	0	1	0	7	3,565	0	0	3,170	$3,260

Bruce Hill

Year	Driver	Starts	Poles	1	2	3	4	5	6–10	Laps	Laps Led	Races Led	Miles	$
1974	Bruce Hill	1	0	0	0	0	0	0	0	189	0	0	473	1,575
1975	Bruce Hill	26	0	0	0	0	0	3	8	6,788	2	2	7,705	53,175
1976	Bruce Hill	20	0	0	0	0	0	0	3	3,010	3	1	4,463	38,035
1977	Bruce Hill	16	0	0	0	0	0	0	4	2,883	4	1	4,291	25,035
1981	Bruce Hill	7	0	0	0	0	0	0	0	826	0	0	1,379	12,035
Lifetime		70	0	0	0	0	0	3	15	13,696	9	4	18,310	$129,855

Charlie Hill

Year	Driver	Starts	Poles	1	2	3	4	5	6–10	Laps	Laps Led	Races Led	Miles	$
1952	Charlie Hill	1	0	0	0	0	0	0	0	217	0	0	217	50
Lifetime		1	0	0	0	0	0	0	0	217	0	0	217	$50

Dave Hill

Year	Driver	Starts	Poles	1	2	3	4	5	6–10	Laps	Laps Led	Races Led	Miles	$
1977	Ray Elder	1	0	0	0	0	0	0	0	14	0	0	37	625
1977	Gary Mathews	1	0	0	0	0	0	0	0	91	0	0	238	1,225
1978	Ray Elder	3	0	0	0	0	0	0	1	108	0	0	283	5,305
Lifetime		5	0	0	0	0	0	0	1	213	0	0	558	$7,155

Jerry Hill

Year	Driver	Starts	Poles	1	2	3	4	5	6–10	Laps	Laps Led	Races Led	Miles	$
1991	Jerry Hill	1	0	0	0	0	0	0	0	13	0	0	13	3,475
Lifetime		1	0	0	0	0	0	0	0	13	0	0	13	$3,475

Andy Hillenburg

Year	Driver	Starts	Poles	1	2	3	4	5	6–10	Laps	Laps Led	Races Led	Miles	$
1991	Andy Hillenburg	2	0	0	0	0	0	0	0	320	0	0	484	7,520
Lifetime		2	0	0	0	0	0	0	0	320	0	0	484	$7,520

Bobby Hillin Sr.

Year	Driver	Starts	Poles	1	2	3	4	5	6–10	Laps	Laps Led	Races Led	Miles	$
1982	Bobby Hillin	5	0	0	0	0	0	0	0	917	0	0	1,515	9,830

Year	Driver	Starts	Poles	Finish 1	2	3	4	5	6–10	Laps	Laps Led	Races Led	Miles	$

Bobby Hillin Sr. *continued*

Year	Driver	Starts	Poles	1	2	3	4	5	6–10	Laps	Laps Led	Races Led	Miles	$
1983	Bobby Hillin	12	0	0	0	0	0	0	0	2,791	0	0	4,199	30,275
Lifetime		17	0	0	0	0	0	0	0	3,708	0	0	5,715	$40,105

Jimmy Hindman

Year	Driver	Starts	Poles	1	2	3	4	5	6–10	Laps	Laps Led	Races Led	Miles	$
1979	Jimmy Hindman	1	0	0	0	0	0	0	0	2	0	0	1	350
Lifetime		1	0	0	0	0	0	0	0	2	0	0	1	$350

John Hines

Year	Driver	Starts	Poles	1	2	3	4	5	6–10	Laps	Laps Led	Races Led	Miles	$
1960	Fireball Roberts	9	6	2	0	0	0	0	1	1,338	578	9	2,072	19,895
Lifetime		9	6	2	0	0	0	0	1	1,338	578	9	2,072	$19,895

Joe Hines Jr.

Year	Driver	Starts	Poles	1	2	3	4	5	6–10	Laps	Laps Led	Races Led	Miles	$
1970	Joe Hines	1	0	0	0	0	0	0	0	43	0	0	108	245
1971	Joe Hines	1	0	0	0	0	0	0	0	1	0	0	3	0
Lifetime		2	0	0	0	0	0	0	0	44	0	0	110	$245

James Hinnant

Year	Driver	Starts	Poles	1	2	3	4	5	6–10	Laps	Laps Led	Races Led	Miles	$
1951	Wade Fields	3	0	0	0	0	0	0	0	268	0	0	335	100
Lifetime		3	0	0	0	0	0	0	0	268	0	0	335	$100

Rocky Hinton

Year	Driver	Starts	Poles	1	2	3	4	5	6–10	Laps	Laps Led	Races Led	Miles	$
1962	Ernie Gahan	3	0	0	0	0	0	0	1	284	0	0	604	725
1962	Red Foote	4	0	0	0	0	0	0	0	939	0	0	1,367	1,600
1963	Red Foote	3	0	0	0	0	0	0	0	316	0	0	625	950
1964	Nathan Boutwell	2	0	0	0	0	0	0	0	217	0	0	543	1,100
1968	Pete Hamilton	10	0	0	1	0	0	2	1	2,064	14	1	1,346	3,800
Lifetime		22	0	0	1	0	0	2	2	3,820	14	1	4,485	$8,175

Rudy Hires

Year	Driver	Starts	Poles	1	2	3	4	5	6–10	Laps	Laps Led	Races Led	Miles	$
1951	Rudy Hires	1	0	0	0	0	0	0	0	82	0	0	103	0
1952	Rudy Hires	1	0	0	0	0	0	0	0	267	0	0	334	50
Lifetime		2	0	0	0	0	0	0	0	349	0	0	436	$50

Tom Hixon

Year	Driver	Starts	Poles	1	2	3	4	5	6–10	Laps	Laps Led	Races Led	Miles	$
1967	George England	5	0	0	0	0	0	0	1	748	0	0	780	3,050
1967	George Hixon	1	0	0	0	0	0	0	0	187	0	0	94	120
Lifetime		6	0	0	0	0	0	0	1	935	0	0	874	$3,170

Chuck Hobbs

Year	Driver	Starts	Poles	1	2	3	4	5	6–10	Laps	Laps Led	Races Led	Miles	$
1957	Chuck Hobbs	1	0	0	0	0	0	0	0		0	0		25
Lifetime		1	0	0	0	0	0	0	0		0	0		$25

Gene Hobby

Year	Driver	Starts	Poles	1	2	3	4	5	6–10	Laps	Laps Led	Races Led	Miles	$
1965	Joe Holder	2	0	0	0	0	0	0	0	135	0	0	47	200
1965	J.T. Putney	1	0	0	0	0	0	0	0	1	0	0	1	100
1965	Gene Hobby	15	0	0	0	0	1	0	1	1,979	0	0	971	2,560
1965	Darrell Bryant	1	0	0	0	0	0	0	0	44	0	0	11	100
1965	Buddy Baker	1	0	0	0	0	0	0	0	16	0	0	8	100
1965	LeeRoy Yarbrough	1	0	0	0	0	0	0	0	25	0	0	13	100
1966	Gene Hobby	2	0	0	0	0	0	0	0	34	0	0	12	0
Lifetime		23	0	0	0	0	1	0	1	2,234	0	0	1,063	$3,160

Rudy Hoerr

Year	Driver	Starts	Poles	1	2	3	4	5	6–10	Laps	Laps Led	Races Led	Miles	$
1968	Al Unser	1	0	0	0	0	0	0	1	182	0	0	491	1,550
1969	Al Unser	1	0	0	0	0	1	0	0	183	0	0	494	3,825
Lifetime		2	0	0	0	0	1	0	1	365	0	0	986	$5,375

Year	Driver	Starts	Poles	Finish 1	2	3	4	5	6–10	Laps	Laps Led	Races Led	Miles	$

Al Holbert

Year	Driver	Starts	Poles	1	2	3	4	5	6–10	Laps	Laps Led	Races Led	Miles	$
1979	Al Holbert	6	0	0	0	0	0	0	1	938	5	1	1,620	14,170
Lifetime		6	0	0	0	0	0	0	1	938	5	1	1,620	$14,170

Don Holcomb

Year	Driver	Starts	Poles	1	2	3	4	5	6–10	Laps	Laps Led	Races Led	Miles	$
1956	Al Watkins	12	0	0	0	0	0	0	4	1,812	0	0	1,254	1,035
1956	Allen Adkins	1	0	0	0	0	0	0	0	315	0	0	433	50
Lifetime		13	0	0	0	0	0	0	4	2,127	0	0	1,687	$1,085

Grimes Holcomb

Year	Driver	Starts	Poles	1	2	3	4	5	6–10	Laps	Laps Led	Races Led	Miles	$
1984	Jerry Bowman	1	0	0	0	0	0	0	0	470	0	0	470	1,550
Lifetime		1	0	0	0	0	0	0	0	470	0	0	470	$1,550

Jerry Holden

Year	Driver	Starts	Poles	1	2	3	4	5	6–10	Laps	Laps Led	Races Led	Miles	$
1985	Don Hume	1	0	0	0	0	0	0	0	63	0	0	158	1,370
1986	Jerry Holden	1	0	0	0	0	0	0	0	100	0	0	100	1,200
1987	Jerry Holden	1	0	0	0	0	0	0	0	8	0	0	8	1,250
Lifetime		3	0	0	0	0	0	0	0	171	0	0	266	$3,820

Bill Hollar

Year	Driver	Starts	Poles	1	2	3	4	5	6–10	Laps	Laps Led	Races Led	Miles	$
1972	Henley Gray	1	0	0	0	0	0	0	0	57	0	0	58	565
1972	Bill Hollar	1	0	0	0	0	0	0	0	64	0	0	128	705
1973	Dick May	2	0	0	0	0	0	0	0	137	0	0	160	1,825
1973	Dean Dalton	1	0	0	0	0	0	0	0	138	0	0	138	700
1973	Bill Hollar	1	0	0	0	0	0	0	0	419	0	0	419	1,060
1975	Bill Hollar	3	0	0	0	0	0	0	0	1,107	0	0	777	1,865
1976	Walter Ballard	2	0	0	0	0	0	0	0	382	0	0	586	2,750
1976	Bill Hollar	1	0	0	0	0	0	0	0	2	0	0	5	540
1978	Bill Hollar	3	0	0	0	0	0	0	0	90	0	0	62	1,360
1978	Cecil Gordon	1	0	0	0	0	0	0	0	126	0	0	79	465
1979	Bill Hollar	5	0	0	0	0	0	0	0	542	0	0	376	2,545
1979	Dick May	2	0	0	0	0	0	0	0	354	0	0	390	1,615
1980	Dick May	6	0	0	0	0	0	0	0	1,847	0	0	1,364	4,880
1980	Bill Hollar	1	0	0	0	0	0	0	0	281	0	0	152	600
1980	D.K. Ulrich	1	0	0	0	0	0	0	0	2	0	0	2	510
Lifetime		31	0	0	0	0	0	0	0	5,548	0	0	4,695	$21,985

Red Hollingsworth

Year	Driver	Starts	Poles	1	2	3	4	5	6–10	Laps	Laps Led	Races Led	Miles	$
1960	Charlie Glotzbach	2	0	0	0	0	0	0	0	266	0	0	399	400
1961	Red Hollingsworth	2	0	0	0	0	0	0	0	68	0	0	170	250
Lifetime		4	0	0	0	0	0	0	0	334	0	0	569	$650

Bee Gee Holloway

Year	Driver	Starts	Poles	1	2	3	4	5	6–10	Laps	Laps Led	Races Led	Miles	$
1960	Tom Pistone	2	0	0	0	0	0	0	1	484	0	0	726	900
1961	Johnny Allen	14	1	0	0	1	0	1	5	2,530	3	1	2,566	6,685
1961	Ned Jarrett	44	4	1	4	8	4	6	11	9,686	606	9	7,121	27,125
1961	Fireball Roberts	1	0	0	0	0	0	0	0	144	0	0	72	0
1961	Tiny Lund	1	0	0	0	0	0	0	0	323	0	0	444	650
1961	Tom Pistone	4	0	0	0	0	0	0	3	576	0	0	1,081	2,050
1961	Ken Rush	5	0	0	0	0	0	0	1	1,254	0	0	899	2,200
1962	Ralph Earnhardt	1	0	0	0	0	0	0	0	94	0	0	47	50
1962	Bob Welborn	1	0	0	0	0	0	0	0	213	0	0	320	750
1962	Johnny Allen	2	0	0	0	0	0	0	0	222	0	0	555	750
1962	Fred Harb	1	0	0	0	0	0	1	0	60	0	0	30	0
1962	Ned Jarrett	51	4	6	2	3	3	5	15	10,802	866	11	7,015	34,780
1963	Ned Jarrett	2	0	0	0	0	0	1	0	280	0	0	122	200
Lifetime		129	9	7	6	12	7	14	36	26,668	1,475	21	20,996	$76,140

Jack Holloway

Year	Driver	Starts	Poles	1	2	3	4	5	6–10	Laps	Laps Led	Races Led	Miles	$
1952	Jack Holloway	1	0	0	0	0	0	0	0	12	0	0	6	25
Lifetime		1	0	0	0	0	0	0	0	12	0	0	6	$25

Holman-Moody

Year	Driver	Starts	Poles	Finish 1	2	3	4	5	6–10	Laps	Laps Led	Races Led	Miles	$
1957	Bill Amick	2	0	0	0	0	0	0	0	258	0	0	129	150
1957	Joe Weatherly	10	0	0	1	3	0	1	1	1,811	3	1	1,207	4,815
1957	Curtis Turner	3	0	0	0	0	0	0	1	434	56	2	458	675
1958	Possum Jones	1	0	0	0	0	0	0	0	169	0	0	85	125
1958	Joe Weatherly	11	1	1	1	0	1	1	1	1,909	104	3	1,690	4,935
1958	Curtis Turner	14	1	3	2	0	1	2	2	2,628	827	6	1,878	9,320
1960	Curtis Turner	6	1	0	0	0	0	0	1	817	106	2	1,341	2,770
1960	Joe Weatherly	17	0	3	1	0	1	0	2	3,194	246	6	3,150	16,970
1960	Johnny Beauchamp	2	0	0	0	0	0	0	0	102	0	0	89	60
1961	Fred Lorenzen	14	4	3	1	0	0	1	0	2,369	781	10	2,320	25,830
1962	Speedy Thompson	2	0	0	0	0	0	0	0	185	0	0	463	500
1962	Nelson Stacy	15	0	3	1	0	0	1	2	3,484	371	4	3,171	42,515
1962	Fred Lorenzen	17	3	1	2	4	1	2	1	4,129	452	8	4,230	41,898
1962	Dan Gurney	2	0	0	0	0	1	0	0	174	0	0	435	700
1963	Tiny Lund	5	0	0	0	0	0	0	3	1,299	2	1	1,561	4,375
1963	Dan Gurney	3	0	1	0	0	0	2	0	424	120	1	1,097	18,250
1963	Fireball Roberts	15	0	4	1	0	3	1	2	3,817	662	9	3,895	54,215
1963	Fred Lorenzen	25	9	6	8	3	0	4	1	6,895	2,411	19	5,878	111,335
1963	Jimmy Pardue	1	0	0	0	0	0	0	0	384	0	0	576	1,050
1963	Nelson Stacy	12	0	0	0	1	2	1	5	2,816	76	2	3,179	20,025
1963	Ken Miles	1	0	0	0	0	0	0	0	139	0	0	375	710
1963	Larry Frank	2	0	0	0	0	1	0	0	235	5	1	588	1,800
1963	Dave MacDonald	1	0	0	0	0	0	0	0	176	0	0	475	675
1964	Cale Yarborough	5	0	0	0	0	0	0	3	1,681	0	0	1,382	3,140
1964	Larry Frank	3	0	0	0	0	0	0	2	347	0	0	758	2,475
1964	Bay Darnell	1	0	0	0	0	0	0	0	205	0	0	308	625
1964	Marvin Panch	1	0	0	0	0	1	0	0	44	0	0	125	350
1964	Fred Lorenzen	16	7	8	1	0	1	0	0	4,426	2,375	11	4,181	72,335
1964	Fireball Roberts	10	0	1	2	1	0	1	1	1,702	17	2	2,013	28,345
1964	Don White	1	0	0	0	0	0	0	0	176	0	0	475	825
1964	Skip Hudson	1	0	0	0	0	0	0	1	178	0	0	481	1,075
1964	Dave MacDonald	1	0	0	1	0	0	0	0	138	0	0	414	6,745
1964	Junior Johnson	1	1	0	0	0	0	0	0	8	2	1	3	100
1964	Johnny Rutherford	1	0	0	0	0	0	0	1	156	0	0	390	1,350
1964	Bobby Marshman	2	0	0	0	0	0	0	1	56	0	0	140	925
1964	Bobby Johns	5	0	0	0	0	0	0	1	1,150	0	0	1,193	2,250
1964	Bob Welborn	3	0	0	0	0	0	2	0	506	125	1	286	805
1964	Benny Parsons	1	0	0	0	0	0	0	0	258	0	0	129	250
1965	Dick Hutcherson	50	9	9	9	8	4	2	4	11,427	2,058	22	7,951	49,195
1965	A.J. Foyt	1	0	0	0	0	0	0	1	169	12	1	456	1,035
1965	Bobby Johns	8	0	0	2	2	0	1	0	1,612	35	5	1,914	20,670
1965	Pedro Rodriguez	1	0	0	0	0	0	1	0	391	0	0	587	3,425
1965	Fred Lorenzen	17	6	4	1	0	0	0	1	3,677	981	12	3,998	77,200
1966	Dick Hutcherson	14	2	3	0	2	1	2	1	3,152	400	7	3,042	22,485
1966	Fred Lorenzen	10	2	2	1	0	1	2	0	2,927	758	6	3,216	36,675
1967	Swede Savage	3	0	0	0	0	0	0	2	1,091	0	0	571	1,275
1967	Dick Hutcherson	2	1	0	0	0	1	0	0	632	80	2	316	1,075
1967	Mario Andretti	6	0	1	0	0	0	0	2	867	137	3	1,757	52,165
1967	David Pearson	12	2	0	4	2	1	0	0	3,572	327	7	3,908	53,325
1967	Fred Lorenzen	5	0	1	1	0	0	0	0	895	23	4	1,411	19,125
1967	Jimmy Clark	1	0	0	0	0	0	0	0	144	0	0	144	665
1967	Bobby Allison	2	1	2	0	0	0	0	0	1,000	426	2	750	19,550
1968	A.J. Foyt	1	0	0	0	0	0	0	1	325	0	0	488	1,600
1968	Bobby Allison	2	0	1	1	0	0	0	0	700	317	2	367	3,900
1968	David Pearson	47	12	16	12	4	2	2	2	12,797	3,950	37	9,380	119,987
1968	Donnie Allison	1	0	0	0	0	0	0	0	48	0	0	120	1,000
1968	Frank Gardner	1	0	0	0	0	0	0	0	1	0	0	1	515
1968	Mario Andretti	3	0	0	0	0	0	0	0	297	20	2	751	2,845
1969	Mario Andretti	1	0	0	0	0	0	0	0	132	7	1	356	925
1969	David Pearson	51	13	11	18	9	2	2	2	14,270	3,018	39	11,269	184,885
1969	Parnelli Jones	1	0	0	0	0	0	0	0	22	0	0	59	770
1970	David Pearson	18	2	1	2	2	3	0	2	3,835	580	11	5,618	85,968
1971	Rolf Stommelen	1	0	0	0	0	0	0	0	53	0	0	141	790
1971	A.J. Foyt	1	0	0	0	0	0	0	0	33	0	0	83	655
1971	David Pearson	9	2	2	3	0	2	0	0	2,228	251	9	2,104	24,425
1971	Bobby Allison	23	6	9	5	3	2	0	1	6,991	2,776	21	8,179	209,060
1973	Bobby Unser	1	0	0	0	0	1	0	0	186	0	0	487	4,520
Lifetime		526	85	96	81	44	33	31	51	122,353	24,897	283	119,972	$1,485,003

Year	Driver	Starts	Poles	Finish 1	2	3	4	5	6–10	Laps	Laps Led	Races Led	Miles	$

C.C. Holt

Year	Driver	Starts	Poles	1	2	3	4	5	6–10	Laps	Laps Led	Races Led	Miles	$
1975	Paul Dean Holt	2	0	0	0	0	0	0	0	120	0	0	72	685
Lifetime		2	0	0	0	0	0	0	0	120	0	0	72	$685

Dennis Holt

Year	Driver	Starts	Poles	1	2	3	4	5	6–10	Laps	Laps Led	Races Led	Miles	$
1967	Paul Dean Holt	23	0	0	0	0	0	0	1	2,921	0	0	1,840	4,230
1967	Dr. Don Tarr	1	0	0	0	0	0	0	0	170	0	0	234	680
1967	Bill Ervin	1	0	0	0	0	0	0	0	135	0	0	68	120
1968	Paul Dean Holt	34	0	0	0	0	0	0	0	5,306	0	0	3,184	6,810
1969	Don Biederman	1	0	0	0	0	0	0	0	45	0	0	113	245
1969	J.C. Yarborough	2	0	0	0	0	0	0	0	318	0	0	159	415
1969	Paul Dean Holt	10	0	0	0	0	0	0	0	1,072	0	0	803	3,287
1969	Wendell Scott	1	0	0	0	0	0	0	0	187	0	0	281	1,100
Lifetime		73	0	0	0	0	0	0	1	10,154	0	0	6,680	$16,887

Paul Dean Holt

Year	Driver	Starts	Poles	1	2	3	4	5	6–10	Laps	Laps Led	Races Led	Miles	$
1969	James Sears	1	0	0	0	0	0	0	0	247	0	0	247	725
Lifetime		1	0	0	0	0	0	0	0	247	0	0	247	$725

Gus Holzmueller

Year	Driver	Starts	Poles	1	2	3	4	5	6–10	Laps	Laps Led	Races Led	Miles	$
1955	Ray Chaike	1	0	0	0	0	0	0	0	37	0	0	152	50
1956	Ray Chaike	2	0	0	0	0	0	0	0	430	0	0	215	175
1956	Tiny Lund	19	0	0	0	0	1	0	7	3,357	0	0	2,151	2,415
1957	Tiny Lund	2	0	0	0	0	1	0	0	323	0	0	226	395
1957	Jimmy Thompson	1	0	0	0	0	0	0	0	24	0	0	38	100
Lifetime		25	0	0	0	0	2	0	7	4,171	0	0	2,782	$3,135

Hooker Hood

Year	Driver	Starts	Poles	1	2	3	4	5	6–10	Laps	Laps Led	Races Led	Miles	$
1954	Hooker Hood	2	0	0	0	0	0	0	0	248	0	0	244	75
1955	Hooker Hood	3	0	0	0	0	0	0	0	256	0	0	420	175
1955	Dutch Hoag	1	0	0	0	0	0	0	1	189	0	0	95	150
Lifetime		6	0	0	0	0	0	0	1	693	0	0	759	$400

Lance Hooper

Year	Driver	Starts	Poles	1	2	3	4	5	6–10	Laps	Laps Led	Races Led	Miles	$
1996	Lance Hooper	1	0	0	0	0	0	0	0	302	0	0	302	9,645
Lifetime		1	0	0	0	0	0	0	0	302	0	0	302	$9,645

Randy Hope

Year	Driver	Starts	Poles	1	2	3	4	5	6–10	Laps	Laps Led	Races Led	Miles	$
1988	Patty Moise	2	0	0	0	0	0	0	0	241	0	0	598	4,870
1990	Kenny Wallace	1	0	0	0	0	0	0	0	315	0	0	197	2,550
Lifetime		3	0	0	0	0	0	0	0	556	0	0	795	$7,420

Ronnie Hopkins

Year	Driver	Starts	Poles	1	2	3	4	5	6–10	Laps	Laps Led	Races Led	Miles	$
1971	Tiny Lund	6	0	2	2	0	1	0	1	2,111	250	5	1,009	9,525
Lifetime		6	0	2	2	0	1	0	1	2,111	250	5	1,009	$9,525

Gene Horne

Year	Driver	Starts	Poles	1	2	3	4	5	6–10	Laps	Laps Led	Races Led	Miles	$
1949	Fonty Flock	1	0	0	0	0	0	0	0		0	0		25
1953	Obie Chupp	1	0	0	0	0	0	0	0	36	0	0	148	50
Lifetime		2	0	0	0	0	0	0	0	36	0	0	148	$75

Joe Horner

Year	Driver	Starts	Poles	1	2	3	4	5	6–10	Laps	Laps Led	Races Led	Miles	$
1992	Jimmy Horton	9	0	0	0	0	0	0	0	2,194	0	0	2,930	46,125
1993	Jimmy Horton	13	0	0	0	0	0	0	0	2,198	0	0	3,632	113,305
1995	Jimmy Hensley	2	0	0	0	0	0	0	0	270	0	0	322	17,650
Lifetime		24	0	0	0	0	0	0	0	4,662	0	177,080	6,884	

Roscoe Hough

Year	Driver	Starts	Poles	1	2	3	4	5	6–10	Laps	Laps Led	Races Led	Miles	$
1950	Lee Hough	2	0	0	0	0	0	0	0	60	0	0	30	0

Year	Driver	Starts	Poles	Finish 1	2	3	4	5	6–10	Laps	Laps Led	Races Led	Miles	$

Roscoe Hough *continued*

Year	Driver	Starts	Poles	1	2	3	4	5	6–10	Laps	Laps Led	Races Led	Miles	$
1950	Pappy Hough	4	0	0	0	0	0	0	2	296	0	0	215	275
1951	Pappy Hough	8	0	0	0	0	0	1	3		0	0		925
1952	Pappy Hough	4	1	0	0	0	0	0	1	565	0	0	393	250
1955	Pappy Hough	3	0	0	0	0	0	0	0	422	0	0	256	160
Lifetime		21	1	0	0	0	0	1	6	1,343	0	0	894	$1,610

Jack Housby

Year	Driver	Starts	Poles	1	2	3	4	5	6–10	Laps	Laps Led	Races Led	Miles	$
1972	Ramo Stott	2	0	0	0	0	0	0	1	201	0	0	503	3,740
1972	Pete Hamilton	4	0	0	0	0	0	1	0	889	8	2	1,320	7,095
1973	Pete Hamilton	1	0	0	0	0	0	0	0	33	0	0	83	2,000
1973	Ramo Stott	1	0	0	0	0	0	0	1	240	0	0	480	2,050
1980	Kevin Housby	3	0	0	0	0	0	0	0	524	0	0	1,006	6,165
Lifetime		11	0	0	0	0	0	1	2	1,887	8	2	3,391	$21,050

Bill House

Year	Driver	Starts	Poles	1	2	3	4	5	6–10	Laps	Laps Led	Races Led	Miles	$
1953	Don Oldenberg	4	0	0	0	0	0	1	1	223	0	0	245	375
Lifetime		4	0	0	0	0	0	1	1	223	0	0	245	$375

Don House

Year	Driver	Starts	Poles	1	2	3	4	5	6–10	Laps	Laps Led	Races Led	Miles	$
1961	Joe Kelly	2	0	0	0	0	0	0	0	200	0	0	500	300
1962	Wally Dallenbach	2	0	0	0	0	0	0	1	92	0	0	230	650
1963	Joe Kelly	1	0	0	0	0	0	0	0	120	0	0	60	85
1964	Don Hume	2	0	0	0	0	0	0	0	18	0	0	26	900
1965	Billy DeCoster	1	0	0	0	0	0	0	0	0	0	0	0	100
1965	Don Hume	1	0	0	0	0	0	0	0	146	0	0	219	950
Lifetime		9	0	0	0	0	0	0	1	576	0	0	1,035	$2,985

Stan Hover (Statistics include the Mover Motorsports team owned by both Stan Hover and Stan Hover Jr.)

Year	Driver	Starts	Poles	1	2	3	4	5	6–10	Laps	Laps Led	Races Led	Miles	$
1992	Dave Blaney	1	0	0	0	0	0	0	0	371	0	0	377	4,500
1994	Joe Ruttman	1	0	0	0	0	0	0	0	328	0	0	492	5,690
1994	Jimmy Horton	1	0	0	0	0	0	0	0	199	0	0	498	33,485
1995	Joe Ruttman	1	0	0	0	0	0	0	0	200	0	0	500	39,135
2001	Morgan Shepherd	1	0	0	0	0	0	0	0	159	0	0	398	84,610
Lifetime		5	0	0	0	0	0	0	0	1,257	0	0	2,264	167,420

Hubert Howard

Year	Driver	Starts	Poles	1	2	3	4	5	6–10	Laps	Laps Led	Races Led	Miles	$
1966	Jeff Hawkins	1	0	0	0	0	0	0	0	192	0	0	96	275
1966	Calvin Kelly	2	0	0	0	0	0	0	0	41	0	0	103	1,120
Lifetime		3	0	0	0	0	0	1	0	233	0	0	199	$1,395

Phil Howard

Year	Driver	Starts	Poles	1	2	3	4	5	6–10	Laps	Laps Led	Races Led	Miles	$
1979	Dave Watson	4	0	0	0	0	0	0	1	1,092	7	2	1,161	7,170
1980	John Anderson	1	0	0	0	0	0	0	0	353	0	0	359	750
Lifetime		5	0	0	0	0	0	0	1	1,445	7	2	1,520	$7,920

Richard Howard (Statistics represent teams principly owned by Richard Howard, plus other ventures which included a number of ownership partners.)

Year	Driver	Starts	Poles	1	2	3	4	5	6–10	Laps	Laps Led	Races Led	Miles	$
1970	Fred Lorenzen	2	0	0	0	0	0	0	0	300	47	1	404	2,295
1971	LeeRoy Yarbrough	1	0	0	0	0	0	0	0	120	0	0	180	865
1971	Charlie Glotzbach	14	4	1	2	0	3	1	0	3,897	805	10	3,938	34,055
1972	Jim Paschal	1	0	0	0	0	0	0	0	338	0	0	507	1,825
1972	Lem Blankenship	1	0	0	0	0	0	0	0	50	0	0	76	855
1972	Bobby Allison	31	11	10	12	2	1	0	2	10,063	4,343	30	11,801	305,695
1973	Dick Trickle	1	0	0	0	0	0	1	0	327	2	1	491	3,385
1973	Cale Yarborough	28	5	4	6	4	1	1	3	9,314	3,167	21	9,752	220,135
1973	Billy Scott	1	0	0	0	0	0	0	0	340	0	0	510	1,850
1974	Johnny Rutherford	1	0	0	0	0	0	0	0	202	1	1	303	749
1974	Cale Yarborough	15	2	6	3	1	0	1	1	5,061	1,791	12	5,787	169,810
1974	Billy Scott	1	0	0	0	0	0	0	0	262	0	0	393	1,625
1975	Donnie Allison	2	0	0	0	0	0	0	1	578	1	1	640	3,485
1976	Bobby Isaac	1	0	0	0	0	0	0	1	473	0	0	481	3,280

Year	Driver	Starts	Poles	Finish 1	2	3	4	5	6–10	Laps	Laps Led	Races Led	Miles	$

Richard Howard *continued*

Year	Driver	Starts	Poles	1	2	3	4	5	6–10	Laps	Laps Led	Races Led	Miles	$
1981	Elliott	10	0	0	0	0	0	0	3	1,923	0	0	3,364	26,480
Lifetime		110	22	21	23	7	5	4	11	33,248	10,157	77	38,626	$776,389

Roz Howard

Year	Driver	Starts	Poles	1	2	3	4	5	6–10	Laps	Laps Led	Races Led	Miles	$
1956	Roz Howard	1	0	0	0	0	0	0	0	343	0	0	472	250
1958	Roz Howard	2	0	0	0	0	0	0	1	300	0	0	150	215
1960	Roz Howard	3	0	0	0	0	0	0	2	676	0	0	535	1,490
Lifetime		6	0	0	0	0	0	0	3	1,319	0	0	1,157	$1,955

Ed Huegele

Year	Driver	Starts	Poles	1	2	3	4	5	6–10	Laps	Laps Led	Races Led	Miles	$
1952	Jim Millard	1	0	0	0	0	0	0	1		0	0		100
Lifetime		1	0	0	0	0	0	0	1		0	0		$100

Charlie Hughes

Year	Driver	Starts	Poles	1	2	3	4	5	6–10	Laps	Laps Led	Races Led	Miles	$
1967	Coo Coo Marlin	2	0	0	0	0	0	0	0	38	0	0	95	625
Lifetime		2	0	0	0	0	0	0	0	38	0	0	95	$625

Harry Huhn

Year	Driver	Starts	Poles	1	2	3	4	5	6–10	Laps	Laps Led	Races Led	Miles	$
1960	Arnold Gardner	4	0	0	0	0	0	0	0	614	0	0	904	575
Lifetime		4	0	0	0	0	0	0	0	614	0	0	904	$575

Lloyd Hulette

Year	Driver	Starts	Poles	1	2	3	4	5	6–10	Laps	Laps Led	Races Led	Miles	$
1953	Lloyd Hulette	1	0	0	0	0	0	0	0	328	0	0	451	250
Lifetime		1	0	0	0	0	0	0	0	328	0	0	451	$250

Don Hume

Year	Driver	Starts	Poles	1	2	3	4	5	6–10	Laps	Laps Led	Races Led	Miles	$
1965	Don Hume	3	0	0	0	0	0	0	0	494	0	0	697	1,770
Lifetime		3	0	0	0	0	0	0	0	494	0	0	697	$1,770

Willie Humphries

Year	Driver	Starts	Poles	1	2	3	4	5	6–10	Laps	Laps Led	Races Led	Miles	$
1972	Red Farmer	5	0	0	0	0	1	0	0	474	0	0	1,101	9,575
1973	Red Farmer	3	0	0	0	0	0	0	0	247	0	0	647	4,235
1974	Red Farmer	2	0	0	0	0	0	0	0	329	0	0	875	2,860
Lifetime		10	0	0	0	0	1	0	0	1,050	0	0	2,623	$16,670

T.C. Hunt

Year	Driver	Starts	Poles	1	2	3	4	5	6–10	Laps	Laps Led	Races Led	Miles	$
1969	T.C. Hunt	1	0	0	0	0	0	0	0	53	0	0	141	1,050
1971	Bob Williams	1	0	0	0	0	0	0	0	178	0	0	98	390
Lifetime		2	0	0	0	0	0	0	0	231	0	0	239	$1,440

Lester Hunter

Year	Driver	Starts	Poles	1	2	3	4	5	6–10	Laps	Laps Led	Races Led	Miles	$
1965	Harold Painter	1	0	0	0	0	0	0	0	0	0	0	0	100
1965	Buddy Arrington	1	0	0	0	0	0	0	1	253	0	0	380	800
1965	Cale Yarborough	1	0	0	0	0	0	0	0	193	0	0	290	550
1965	Jeff Hawkins	6	0	0	0	0	0	0	0	322	0	0	261	2,160
1965	Doug Cooper	1	0	0	0	0	0	0	0	198	0	0	272	600
Lifetime		10	0	0	0	0	0	0	1	966	0	0	1,202	$4,210

Tom Hunter

Year	Driver	Starts	Poles	1	2	3	4	5	6–10	Laps	Laps Led	Races Led	Miles	$
1965	Roy Mayne	12	0	0	0	0	1	0	4	2,443	0	0	2,399	7,810
1966	Roy Mayne	15	0	0	0	0	0	1	3	3,762	0	0	3,583	9,555
1967	Roy Mayne	12	0	0	0	0	0	0	1	1,658	0	0	2,028	7,635
1967	Larry Manning	1	0	0	0	0	0	0	0	102	0	0	153	875
1968	Roy Mayne	1	0	0	0	0	0	0	0	77	0	0	116	775
1968	Max Ledbetter	1	0	0	0	0	0	0	0	134	0	0	67	100
1968	Larry Manning	8	0	0	0	0	0	0	0	1,784	0	0	2,088	6,395
1969	Roy Mayne	8	0	0	0	0	0	0	0	2,161	0	0	2,112	6,715
1969	Max Ledbetter	1	0	0	0	0	0	0	0	91	0	0	46	260

Year	Driver	Starts	Poles	Finish 1	2	3	4	5	6–10	Laps	Laps Led	Races Led	Miles	$

Tom Hunter *continued*

Year	Driver	Starts	Poles	1	2	3	4	5	6–10	Laps	Laps Led	Races Led	Miles	$
1970	Roy Mayne	12	0	0	0	0	0	0	3	2,717	0	0	3,736	13,460
1971	Roy Mayne	10	0	0	0	0	0	0	0	1,598	0	0	2,225	8,205
1971	Earl Brooks	1	0	0	0	0	0	0	0	264	0	0	402	585
1972	Roy Mayne	2	0	0	0	0	0	0	0	94	0	0	244	1,620
Lifetime		84	0	0	0	0	1	1	11	16,885	0	0	19,198	$63,990

Walt Hunter

Year	Driver	Starts	Poles	1	2	3	4	5	6–10	Laps	Laps Led	Races Led	Miles	$
1964	J.T. Putney	15	0	0	0	1	0	0	4	3,590	0	0	2,889	6,345
Lifetime		15	0	0	0	1	0	0	4	3,590	0	0	2,889	$6,345

Jim Hurlbert

Year	Driver	Starts	Poles	1	2	3	4	5	6–10	Laps	Laps Led	Races Led	Miles	$
1982	Jim Hurlbert	1	0	0	0	0	0	0	0	1	0	0	3	1,430
Lifetime		1	0	0	0	0	0	0	0	1	0	0	3	$1,430

Mark Hurley

Year	Driver	Starts	Poles	1	2	3	4	5	6–10	Laps	Laps Led	Races Led	Miles	$
1963	Darel Dieringer	1	0	0	0	0	0	0	1	291	0	0	97	240
1963	Mark Hurley	2	0	0	0	0	1	0	0	272	0	0	76	400
1963	Billy Wade	1	0	0	0	0	0	0	0	1	0	0	0	55
Lifetime		4	0	0	0	0	1	0	1	564	0	0	173	$695

George Hutchens

Year	Driver	Starts	Poles	1	2	3	4	5	6–10	Laps	Laps Led	Races Led	Miles	$
1952	Jimmie Lewallen	1	0	0	0	0	1	0	0	78	0	0	98	350
1952	Bill Blair	19	1	1	3	4	2	0	3	2,463	120	4	2,068	7,095
1952	Bobby Myers	1	0	0	0	0	0	0	0	145	0	0	181	0
1952	Dick Rathmann	1	0	0	0	0	0	0	0	85	0	0	85	45
1952	Jim Paschal	3	0	0	0	0	0	0	0	242	0	0	200	50
1953	Jim Paschal	19	1	1	0	1	2	2	3	887	73	1	926	4,575
1953	Cotton Owens	1	0	0	0	0	0	0	0	274	0	0	274	50
1954	Jimmie Lewallen	6	0	0	0	0	0	2	2	856	0	0	558	1,175
1954	Jim Paschal	7	0	0	0	0	1	0	2	776	0	0	577	700
1954	Ray Duhigg	1	0	0	0	0	0	0	0	122	0	0	61	0
1954	Cotton Owens	1	0	0	0	0	0	0	1	183	0	0	92	100
1954	Bob Welborn	3	0	0	0	0	0	0	1	207	0	0	118	325
1955	Jim Paschal	1	0	0	0	0	0	0	0	7	0	0	4	0
Lifetime		64	2	2	3	5	6	4	12	6,325	193	5	5,240	$14,465

James Hylton

Year	Driver	Starts	Poles	1	2	3	4	5	6–10	Laps	Laps Led	Races Led	Miles	$
1968	James Hylton	39	0	0	1	4	8	3	11	9,731	15	3	6,967	26,985
1969	James Hylton	50	0	0	4	9	8	5	12	12,929	162	12	10,482	55,187
1970	James Hylton	45	1	1	4	2	8	7	17	12,492	199	8	10,673	58,215
1971	James Hylton	46	1	0	2	3	5	4	23	12,785	105	5	12,725	54,860
1972	Cale Yarborough	1	0	0	0	0	0	1	0	196	0	0	392	2,150
1972	James Hylton	31	0	1	0	0	5	3	14	9,702	111	4	11,476	89,955
1973	James Hylton	28	0	0	0	0	1	0	10	9,324	1	1	10,058	49,930
1973	Wayne Andrews	1	0	0	0	0	0	0	0	5	0	0	8	1,005
1974	James Hylton	29	0	0	0	0	0	1	7	6,774	29	6	7,970	53,592
1975	James Hylton	30	0	0	0	0	1	1	14	9,650	11	4	11,032	75,880
1976	James Hylton	29	0	0	0	0	1	1	3	7,954	14	4	9,157	67,825
1977	James Hylton	30	0	0	0	0	0	0	11	8,375	3	1	9,592	88,330
1978	James Hylton	18	0	0	0	0	0	0	4	5,773	16	2	5,017	44,365
1978	Al Holbert	12	0	0	0	0	0	0	3	2,479	0	0	3,919	30,885
1978	Walter Ballard	1	0	0	0	0	0	0	0	0	0	0	0	505
1979	James Hylton	30	0	0	0	0	0	0	5	8,658	11	4	9,604	85,375
1980	James Hylton	30	0	0	0	0	0	0	4	8,920	26	1	10,080	92,625
1981	Kirk Shelmerdine	1	0	0	0	0	0	0	0	2	0	0	4	950
1981	Harry Gant	1	0	0	0	0	0	0	1	493	1	1	263	4,270
1981	James Hylton	28	0	0	0	0	0	0	0	7,051	12	2	8,509	81,022
1982	Tommy Gale	1	0	0	0	0	0	0	0	351	0	0	527	5,020
1982	James Hylton	13	0	0	0	0	0	0	0	4,208	0	0	4,332	43,035
1982	Joe Millikan	1	0	0	0	0	0	0	0	343	0	0	469	6,095
1982	Slick Johnson	7	0	0	0	0	0	0	1	1,943	1	1	1,793	23,775
1982	Lennie Pond	3	0	0	0	0	0	0	1	1,065	0	0	1,373	15,540

Year	Driver	Starts	Poles	Finish 1	2	3	4	5	6–10	Laps	Laps Led	Races Led	Miles	$

James Hylton *continued*

Year	Driver	Starts	Poles	1	2	3	4	5	6–10	Laps	Laps Led	Races Led	Miles	$
1982	D.K. Ulrich	3	0	0	0	0	0	0	0	393	0	0	1,007	11,550
1983	Trevor Boys	23	0	0	0	0	0	0	1	5,907	3	2	6,897	87,555
1983	Lennie Pond	4	0	0	0	0	0	0	0	1,189	0	0	1,094	13,900
1983	James Hylton	2	0	0	0	0	0	0	0	556	0	0	662	12,105
1984	Trevor Boys	30	0	0	0	0	0	0	1	8,619	20	3	9,704	139,593
1985	Don Hume	6	0	0	0	0	0	0	0	1,994	0	0	1,749	20,860
1985	Trevor Boys	13	0	0	0	0	0	0	0	3,417	3	1	4,426	53,420
1985	Ron Esau	1	0	0	0	0	0	0	0	10	0	0	26	2,925
1985	Lennie Pond	5	0	0	0	0	0	0	0	1,560	0	0	1,561	32,045
1985	James Hylton	1	0	0	0	0	0	0	0	201	0	0	201	3,945
1985	Greg Sacks	3	0	0	0	0	0	0	0	348	0	0	748	11,350
1986	Eddie Bierschwale	1	0	0	0	0	0	0	0	2	0	0	1	2,515
1986	Jerry Cranmer	5	0	0	0	0	0	0	0	1,727	0	0	1,771	23,510
1986	Trevor Boys	1	0	0	0	0	0	0	0	17	0	0	11	3,035
1986	Morgan Shepherd	1	0	0	0	0	0	0	0	394	0	0	246	3,880
1986	Ron Esau	1	0	0	0	0	0	0	0	92	0	0	241	5,325
1986	Wayne Slark	1	0	0	0	0	0	0	0	96	0	0	98	4,055
1986	Ronnie Thomas	3	0	0	0	0	0	0	0	451	0	0	1,092	20,925
1986	James Hylton	4	0	0	0	0	0	0	0	544	0	0	578	16,825
1986	Johnny Coy Jr.	2	0	0	0	0	0	0	0	591	0	0	593	9,200
1987	Tony Spanos	1	0	0	0	0	0	0	0	386	0	0	203	1,555
1987	Jerry Holden	1	0	0	0	0	0	0	0	133	0	0	354	2,850
1987	James Hylton	2	0	0	0	0	0	0	0	93	0	0	99	2,550
1989	James Hylton	2	0	0	0	0	0	0	0	38	0	0	43	3,775
1989	Bill Flowers	1	0	0	0	0	0	0	0	2	0	0	2	1,800
1989	Trevor Boys	1	0	0	0	0	0	0	0	118	2	1	295	2,575
1990	Freddie Crawford	1	0	0	0	0	0	0	0	6	0	0	6	2,775
1990	James Hylton	1	0	0	0	0	0	0	0	202	0	0	202	2,800
1990	Ben Hess	1	0	0	0	0	0	0	0	169	0	0	338	4,275
1991	James Hylton	4	0	0	0	0	0	0	0	87	0	0	113	14,190
1992	James Hylton	8	0	0	0	0	0	0	0	611	0	0	1,100	35,810
1993	James Hylton	2	0	0	0	0	0	0	0	86	0	0	109	11,945
1993	Trevor Boys	1	0	0	0	0	0	0	0	38	1	1	95	6,540
Lifetime		641	2	2	11	18	37	26	143	171,280	746	67	182,087	$1,629,334

Thomas Hynes

Year	Driver	Starts	Poles	1	2	3	4	5	6–10	Laps	Laps Led	Races Led	Miles	$
1971	Harry Schilling	3	0	0	0	0	0	0	0	222	0	0	561	3,395
Lifetime		3	0	0	0	0	0	0	0	222	0	0	561	$3,395

Tom Hynes

Year	Driver	Starts	Poles	1	2	3	4	5	6–10	Laps	Laps Led	Races Led	Miles	$
1972	Harry Schilling	3	0	0	0	0	0	0	0	587	0	0	923	2,399
Lifetime		3	0	0	0	0	0	0	0	587	0	0	923	$2,399

Jimmy Ingalls

Year	Driver	Starts	Poles	1	2	3	4	5	6–10	Laps	Laps Led	Races Led	Miles	$
1983	Jimmy Ingalls	2	0	0	0	0	0	0	0	901	0	0	901	3,080
Lifetime		2	0	0	0	0	0	0	0	901	0	0	901	$3,080

Paul Ingle

Year	Driver	Starts	Poles	1	2	3	4	5	6–10	Laps	Laps Led	Races Led	Miles	$
1985	Tommy Houston	1	0	0	0	0	0	0	0	47	0	0	64	1,645
1986	Jim Sauter	1	0	0	0	0	0	0	0	26	0	0	69	2,400
1986	Eddie Bierschwale	1	0	0	0	0	0	0	0	374	1	1	561	2,000
Lifetime		3	0	0	0	0	0	0	0	447	1	1	694	$6,045

Jim Ingram

Year	Driver	Starts	Poles	1	2	3	4	5	6–10	Laps	Laps Led	Races Led	Miles	$
1980	Jim Ingram	1	0	0	0	0	0	0	0	437	0	0	437	1,435
Lifetime		1	0	0	0	0	0	0	0	437	0	0	437	$1,435

Tom Ingram

Year	Driver	Starts	Poles	1	2	3	4	5	6–10	Laps	Laps Led	Races Led	Miles	$
1967	Jack Ingram	4	0	0	1	0	0	0	0	506	0	0	218	1,165
1967	Tommy Ingram	2	0	0	0	0	0	0	0	58	0	0	73	1,060
Lifetime		6	0	0	1	0	0	0	0	564	0	0	291	$2,225

Year	Driver	Starts	Poles	Finish 1	2	3	4	5	6–10	Laps	Laps Led	Races Led	Miles	$

Jimmy Insolo

Year	Driver	Starts	Poles	1	2	3	4	5	6–10	Laps	Laps Led	Races Led	Miles	$
1977	Jimmy Insolo	1	0	0	0	0	1	0	0	93	0	0	244	3,900
Lifetime		1	0	0	0	0	1	0	0	93	0	0	244	$3,900

John Irvan

Year	Driver	Starts	Poles	1	2	3	4	5	6–10	Laps	Laps Led	Races Led	Miles	$
1976	J.C. Danielson	1	0	0	0	0	0	0	0	39	0	0	102	890
Lifetime		1	0	0	0	0	0	0	0	39	0	0	102	$890

Bill Irvin

Year	Driver	Starts	Poles	1	2	3	4	5	6–10	Laps	Laps Led	Races Led	Miles	$
1954	Billy Irvin	1	0	0	0	0	0	0	0	127	0	0	64	25
Lifetime		1	0	0	0	0	0	0	0	127	0	0	64	$25

Tommy Irwin

Year	Driver	Starts	Poles	1	2	3	4	5	6–10	Laps	Laps Led	Races Led	Miles	$
1958	Tommy Irwin	5	0	0	0	1	1	0	1	1,255	0	0	689	1,280
1959	Tiny Lund	1	0	0	0	0	0	4	1	147	0	0	49	170
1959	Tommy Irwin	25	1	0	1	2	3	0	6	4,409	174	2	2,847	8,715
1960	Tommy Irwin	13	1	0	0	0	3	1	6	2,104	0	0	1,064	2,370
1961	Tommy Irwin	2	0	0	1	0	0	0	0	296	166	1	148	595
Lifetime		46	2	0	2	3	7	5	14	8,211	340	3	4,797	$13,130

Gene Isenhour

Year	Driver	Starts	Poles	1	2	3	4	5	6–10	Laps	Laps Led	Races Led	Miles	$
1991	Gary Balough	1	0	0	0	0	0	0	0	42	0	0	63	3,110
1992	Rich Bickle	3	0	0	0	0	0	0	0	816	0	0	881	13,370
1993	Rich Bickle	5	0	0	0	0	0	0	0	842	1	1	1,356	33,895
1994	Rich Bickle	1	0	0	0	0	0	0	0	106	0	0	212	8,215
Lifetime		10	0	0	0	0	0	0	0	1,806	1	1	2,512	$58,590

Earl Ivey

Year	Driver	Starts	Poles	1	2	3	4	5	6–10	Laps	Laps Led	Races Led	Miles	$
1967	Joel Davis	5	0	0	0	0	0	0	2	759	0	0	709	1,725
Lifetime		5	0	0	0	0	0	0	2	759	0	0	709	$1,725

Wayne Jacks

Year	Driver	Starts	Poles	1	2	3	4	5	6–10	Laps	Laps Led	Races Led	Miles	$
1993	Wayne Jacks	1	0	0	0	0	0	0	0	48	0	0	48	5,980
Lifetime		1	0	0	0	0	0	0	0	48	0	0	48	$5,980

Beryl Jackson

Year	Driver	Starts	Poles	1	2	3	4	5	6–10	Laps	Laps Led	Races Led	Miles	$
1952	Hershel McGriff	2	0	0	0	0	0	0	1	283	0	0	261	325
1954	Marvin Panch	8	1	0	2	1	0	0	2	1,670	19	1	1,442	4,230
1954	Hershel McGriff	2	1	0	0	0	0	0	0	166	0	0	216	105
1955	John Kieper	1	0	0	1	0	0	0	0	251	89	1	251	1,450
1955	Ed Negre	1	0	0	0	0	0	0	1	239	0	0	239	200
1956	Harold Hardesty	3	0	0	0	0	0	1	0	780	0	0	687	730
1971	Hershel McGriff	2	0	0	0	0	0	0	0	234	3	1	613	2,085
1972	Hershel McGriff	4	0	0	0	0	0	2	1	727	3	1	1,728	12,290
1973	Hershel McGriff	3	0	0	0	0	0	1	1	426	0	0	1,093	8,690
Lifetime		26	2	0	3	1	0	4	6	4,776	114	4	6,528	$30,105

Lacy Jackson

Year	Driver	Starts	Poles	1	2	3	4	5	6–10	Laps	Laps Led	Races Led	Miles	$
1953	Lacy Jackson	1	0	0	0	0	0	0	0	288	0	0	396	130
Lifetime		1	0	0	0	0	0	0	0	288	0	0	396	$130

Larry Jackson

Year	Driver	Starts	Poles	1	2	3	4	5	6–10	Laps	Laps Led	Races Led	Miles	$
1971	Tommy Gale	8	0	0	0	0	0	0	1	1,431	0	0	2,591	7,680
Lifetime		8	0	0	0	0	0	0	1	1,431	0	0	2,591	$7,680

Leo Jackson

Year	Driver	Starts	Poles	1	2	3	4	5	6–10	Laps	Laps Led	Races Led	Miles	$
1990	Harry Gant	28	0	1	0	1	1	0	3	7,441	53	9	9,771	459,950
1990	Phil Parsons	1	0	0	0	0	0	0	0	342	0	0	182	9,080
1991	Harry Gant	29	1	5	2	3	4	0	2	9,428	1,684	17	11,127	782,785
1992	Harry Gant	29	0	2	3	2	0	0	5	9,197	407	15	11,221	775,955

Year	Driver	Starts	Poles	Finish						Laps	Laps Led	Races Led	Miles	$
				1	2	3	4	5	6–10					

Leo Jackson *continued*

Year	Driver	Starts	Poles	1	2	3	4	5	6–10	Laps	Laps Led	Races Led	Miles	$
1993	Harry Gant	30	1	0	0	1	2	0	8	8,843	266	8	10,868	625,440
1994	Robert Pressley	3	0	0	0	0	0	0	0	587	0	0	947	39,485
1994	Harry Gant	30	1	0	0	0	0	0	7	7,347	94	3	9,598	521,820
1995	Robert Pressley	31	0	0	0	0	0	0	1	8,181	37	3	9,996	695,875
1996	Robert Pressley	26	0	0	0	0	1	0	1	6,780	110	7	8,190	605,480
1996	Greg Sacks	1	0	0	0	0	0	0	0	480	0	0	480	23,140
Lifetime		208	3	8	5	7	8	9	27	58,626	2,651	62	72,380	$4,539,010

Leo & Richard Jackson

Year	Driver	Starts	Poles	1	2	3	4	5	6–10	Laps	Laps Led	Races Led	Miles	$
1985	Phil Parsons	14	0	0	0	0	0	0	3	2,187	1	1	4,131	49,995
1985	Benny Parsons	14	0	0	0	0	0	0	5	2,230	8	3	4,279	72,450
1986	Benny Parsons	16	1	0	0	0	0	0	2	2,620	13	7	5,100	100,985
1986	Phil Parsons	15	0	0	0	0	0	0	4	3,159	1	1	5,911	77,160
1987	Phil Parsons	29	0	0	0	0	1	0	6	8,216	18	2	9,674	137,665
1987	Tom Sneva	1	0	0	0	0	0	0	0	182	0	0	455	11,135
1988	Phil Parsons	29	0	1	1	2	1	0	9	8,494	108	10	10,297	409,405
1989	Harry Gant	29	0	1	3	1	2	0	5	8,627	439	11	10,295	487,202
1989	Phil Parsons	28	0	0	0	1	0	0	1	7,341	39	4	9,074	266,767
Lifetime		175	1	2	4	4	4	8	35	43,056	627	39	59,217	$1,612,764

Richard Jackson

Year	Driver	Starts	Poles	1	2	3	4	5	6–10	Laps	Laps Led	Races Led	Miles	$
1990	Irv Hoerr	2	0	0	0	0	0	0	2	164	3	1	407	14,775
1990	Terry Labonte	29	0	0	1	0	3	0	5	8,518	9	3	10,245	390,989
1991	Rick Mast	29	0	0	0	0	1	0	2	8,901	32	3	10,691	329,020
1992	Rick Mast	29	1	0	0	0	0	0	1	8,121	0	0	9,984	344,640
1992	Irv Hoerr	1	0	0	0	0	0	0	0	22	0	0	55	4,725
1993	Rick Mast	30	0	0	0	0	0	1	4	8,488	31	4	9,803	438,145
1994	Rick Mast	31	1	0	1	3	0	0	6	8,756	166	8	10,754	648,385
1995	Rick Mast	31	1	0	0	0	0	0	3	8,559	143	3	10,600	722,200
1996	Rick Mast	31	0	0	0	0	1	0	4	8,972	1	1	10,937	821,432
1997	Morgan Shepherd	18	0	0	0	1	0	0	2	5,333	12	2	7,117	566,235
1997	Lance Hooper	5	0	0	0	0	0	0	0	1,340	0	0	1,408	112,330
1997	Jerry Nadeau	5	0	0	0	0	0	0	0	997	0	0	1,907	108,645
Lifetime		241	3	0	2	4	5	1	29	68,171	397	25	83,909	$4,501,521

Al Jacobs

Year	Driver	Starts	Poles	1	2	3	4	5	6–10	Laps	Laps Led	Races Led	Miles	$
1951	Al Jacobs	1	0	0	0	0	0	0	0		0	0		25
Lifetime		1	0	0	0	0	0	0	0		0	0		$25

Skip Jaehne

Year	Driver	Starts	Poles	1	2	3	4	5	6–10	Laps	Laps Led	Races Led	Miles	$
1987	Hut Stricklin	3	0	0	0	0	0	0	0	912	0	0	1,009	6,085
Lifetime		3	0	0	0	0	0	0	0	912	0	0	1,009	$6,085

Rocco Janette

Year	Driver	Starts	Poles	1	2	3	4	5	6–10	Laps	Laps Led	Races Led	Miles	$
1949	Jack O'Brien	2	0	0	0	0	0	0	0	115	0	0	58	0
Lifetime		2	0	0	0	0	0	0	0	115	0	0	58	$0

Michael Jarema

Year	Driver	Starts	Poles	1	2	3	4	5	6–10	Laps	Laps Led	Races Led	Miles	$
1953	Mike Magill	3	0	0	0	0	0	0	0	244	0	0	336	235
Lifetime		3	0	0	0	0	0	0	0	244	0	0	336	$235

Ned Jarrett

Year	Driver	Starts	Poles	1	2	3	4	5	6–10	Laps	Laps Led	Races Led	Miles	$
1953	Ned Jarrett	1	0	0	0	0	0	0	0	8	0	0	11	100
1955	Ned Jarrett	1	0	0	0	0	0	0	0	70	0	0	44	0
1956	Ned Jarrett	2	0	0	0	0	0	0	0	244	0	0	140	60
1957	Ned Jarrett	1	0	0	0	0	0	0	0	7	0	0	4	50
1959	Ned Jarrett	16	2	2	0	1	0	0	3	2,729	2	2	1,389	3,335
1960	Ned Jarrett	40	5	5	3	4	4	4	6	7,399	382	11	5,479	20,540
1961	Ned Jarrett	2	0	0	0	0	0	0	0	127	0	0	64	110
Lifetime		63	7	7	3	5	4	4	9	10,584	384	13	7,130	$24,195

Year	Driver	Starts	Poles	Finish						Laps	Laps Led	Races Led	Miles	$
				1	2	3	4	5	6–10					

Walt Jarrod

Year	Driver	Starts	Poles	1	2	3	4	5	6–10	Laps	Laps Led	Races Led	Miles	$
1951	Fred Moore	1	0	0	0	0	0	0	0	112	0	0	140	0
Lifetime		1	0	0	0	0	0	0	0	112	0	0	140	$0

George Jefferson

Year	Driver	Starts	Poles	1	2	3	4	5	6–10	Laps	Laps Led	Races Led	Miles	$
1973	Harry Jefferson	1	0	0	0	0	0	0	0	37	0	0	97	1,015
1974	Harry Jefferson	4	0	0	0	0	0	0	1	457	0	0	775	6,083
1975	Harry Jefferson	5	0	0	0	0	0	0	2	1,036	0	0	1,787	11,395
1976	Sonny Easley	1	0	0	0	0	0	0	0	32	0	0	84	685
1976	Harry Jefferson	1	0	0	0	0	0	0	0	14	0	0	37	535
1977	Harry Jefferson	1	0	0	0	0	0	0	0	195	0	0	488	1,600
1978	Hershel McGriff	1	0	0	0	0	0	0	1	118	0	0	309	2,850
1982	Derrike Cope	1	0	0	0	0	0	0	0	42	0	0	110	625
1984	Derrike Cope	3	0	0	0	0	0	0	0	370	0	0	631	9,200
1985	Derrike Cope	2	0	0	0	0	0	0	0	206	0	0	540	7,100
1986	Chad Little	2	0	0	0	0	0	0	0	145	0	0	380	6,065
1987	Chad Little	2	0	0	0	0	0	0	0	211	0	0	553	8,810
1988	Chad Little	1	0	0	0	0	0	0	0	307	0	0	307	4,450
Lifetime		25	0	0	0	0	0	0	4	3,170	0	0	6,096	$60,413

Doreen Jeffrey

Year	Driver	Starts	Poles	1	2	3	4	5	6–10	Laps	Laps Led	Races Led	Miles	$
1988	Rick Jeffrey	2	0	0	0	0	0	0	0	326	0	0	815	14,225
1990	Rick Jeffrey	1	0	0	0	0	0	0	0	467	0	0	475	5,300
Lifetime		3	0	0	0	0	0	0	0	793	0	0	1,290	$19,525

W.S. Jenkins

Year	Driver	Starts	Poles	1	2	3	4	5	6–10	Laps	Laps Led	Races Led	Miles	$
1964	Bobby Keck	1	0	0	0	0	0	0	0	280	0	0	385	850
1966	Hank Thomas	13	0	0	0	1	0	0	3	2,926	0	0	1,435	3,465
Lifetime		14	0	0	0	1	0	2	3	3,206	0	0	1,820	$4,315

Joe Jernigan

Year	Driver	Starts	Poles	1	2	3	4	5	6–10	Laps	Laps Led	Races Led	Miles	$
1950	Joe Jernigan	2	0	0	0	0	0	0	0	166	0	0	296	100
1951	Joe Jernigan	2	0	0	0	0	0	0	0		0	0		25
Lifetime		4	0	0	0	0	0	0	0	166	0	0	296	$125

Shorty Johns

Year	Driver	Starts	Poles	1	2	3	4	5	6–10	Laps	Laps Led	Races Led	Miles	$
1956	Bobby Johns	8	0	0	0	0	0	0	2	1,188	0	0	611	750
1957	Bobby Johns	1	0	0	0	0	0	0	0	335	0	0	461	225
1958	Joe Lee Johnson	1	0	0	0	0	0	0	1	146	0	0	146	375
1958	Bobby Johns	3	0	0	0	0	1	0	0	894	0	0	835	1,625
1959	Bobby Johns	8	1	0	0	1	0	0	1	1,911	129	2	1,440	5,630
1960	Bobby Johns	2	0	0	0	0	0	0	0	665	49	1	333	445
1961	Bobby Johns	13	0	0	0	0	1	1	2	2,217	3	1	2,856	4,570
1962	Bobby Johns	13	0	1	0	1	0	0	1	2,725	614	8	2,946	14,535
1963	Bobby Johns	12	0	0	0	1	0	2	3	2,433	84	3	3,383	15,515
1964	Bobby Johns	6	0	0	0	0	0	0	1	629	0	0	625	2,950
1965	Jim Bray	2	0	0	0	0	0	0	0	6	0	0	15	1,190
1965	Bobby Johns	5	0	0	0	0	0	0	0	1,084	2	1	1,027	2,300
1966	Bub Strickler	1	0	0	0	0	0	0	0	25	0	0	63	0
1966	Bobby Johns	11	0	0	0	0	0	0	1	1,419	0	0	1,236	5,245
1967	Bobby Johns	11	0	0	0	0	0	0	0	1,279	0	0	1,301	6,405
1968	Bobby Johns	7	0	0	0	0	0	0	0	750	0	0	1,108	5,010
1969	Bobby Johns	8	0	0	0	0	0	0	0	1,075	0	0	1,185	5,875
Lifetime		112	1	1	0	3	2	3	12	18,781	881	16	19,570	$72,645

Squirt Johns

Year	Driver	Starts	Poles	1	2	3	4	5	6–10	Laps	Laps Led	Races Led	Miles	$
1958	Squirt Johns	2	0	0	0	0	0	0	0	105	0	0	35	90
Lifetime		2	0	0	0	0	0	0	0	105	0	0	35	$90

Berendt Johnson

Year	Driver	Starts	Poles	1	2	3	4	5	6–10	Laps	Laps Led	Races Led	Miles	$
1994	Billy Standridge	8	0	0	0	0	0	0	0	1,260	0	0	1,706	55,430
1995	Billy Standridge	2	0	0	0	0	0	0	0	594	0	0	859	20,345
Lifetime		10	0	0	0	0	0	0	0	1,854	0	0	2,565	$75,775

Year	Driver	Starts	Poles	Finish 1	2	3	4	5	6–10	Laps	Laps Led	Races Led	Miles	$

Bob Johnson

Year	Driver	Starts	Poles	1	2	3	4	5	6–10	Laps	Laps Led	Races Led	Miles	$
1985	Randy LaJoie	1	0	0	0	0	0	0	0	319	0	0	486	2,925
1986	Randy LaJoie	1	0	0	0	0	0	0	0	144	0	0	360	1,815
1986	Morgan Shepherd	1	0	0	0	0	0	0	0	181	0	0	453	15,465
Lifetime		3	0	0	0	0	0	0	0	644	0	0	1,298	$20,205

Charles Johnson

Year	Driver	Starts	Poles	1	2	3	4	5	6–10	Laps	Laps Led	Races Led	Miles	$
1966	Gene Petro	1	0	0	0	0	0	0	0	35	0	0	88	100
Lifetime		1	0	0	0	0	0	0	0	35	0	0	88	$100

Dick Johnson

Year	Driver	Starts	Poles	1	2	3	4	5	6–10	Laps	Laps Led	Races Led	Miles	$
1967	Dick Johnson	19	0	0	0	0	0	0	0	2,203	0	0	1,433	4,240
1968	Earl Brooks	1	0	0	0	0	0	0	0	189	0	0	284	715
1968	Dick Johnson	9	0	0	0	0	0	0	0	1,786	0	0	1,714	4,515
1969	Dick Johnson	22	0	0	0	0	0	0	4	3,803	0	0	2,910	11,477
1989	Dick Johnson (AUS)	4	0	0	0	0	0	0	0	497	0	0	1,270	11,515
1990	Dick Johnson (AUS)	3	0	0	0	0	0	0	0	166	0	0	304	8,950
1990	Jim Sauter	1	0	0	0	0	0	0	0	199	0	0	498	3,925
Lifetime		59	0	0	0	0	0	0	4	8,843	0	0	8,412	$45,337

Floyd Johnson

Year	Driver	Starts	Poles	1	2	3	4	5	6–10	Laps	Laps Led	Races Led	Miles	$
1956	Len Fraker	1	0	0	0	0	0	0	0	10	0	0	25	30
1956	Jim Cook	4	0	0	0	0	0	1	0	542	0	0	412	475
1957	Jim Cook	1	0	0	0	0	0	0	0	51	0	0	128	85
1959	Danny Letner	1	0	0	0	0	0	0	0	224	0	0	90	100
1959	Jim Cook	2	0	0	0	0	0	0	1	357	0	0	195	325
1960	Jim Cook	2	1	1	0	0	0	0	0	217	1	1	264	1,200
1961	Jim Cook	4	0	0	0	0	1	0	1	314	0	0	421	925
1963	Jim Cook	1	0	0	0	0	0	0	0	143	0	0	386	325
Lifetime		16	1	1	0	0	1	1	2	1,858	1	1	1,920	$3,465

Fred Johnson

Year	Driver	Starts	Poles	1	2	3	4	5	6–10	Laps	Laps Led	Races Led	Miles	$
1949	Fred Johnson	2	0	0	0	0	0	0	0		0	0		0
1950	Fred Johnson	2	0	0	0	0	0	0	1	244	0	0	197	125
Lifetime		4	0	0	0	0	0	0	1	244	0	0	197	$125

J.D. Junior Johnson

Year	Driver	Starts	Poles	1	2	3	4	5	6–10	Laps	Laps Led	Races Led	Miles	$
1979	Slick Johnson	2	0	0	0	0	0	0	1	791	0	0	965	4,300
1980	Slick Johnson	18	0	0	0	0	0	0	5	4,724	7	2	4,731	35,460
1981	Slick Johnson	3	0	0	0	0	0	0	0	501	0	0	602	2,725
Lifetime		23	0	0	0	0	0	0	6	6,016	7	2	6,298	$42,485

Joe Lee Johnson

Year	Driver	Starts	Poles	1	2	3	4	5	6–10	Laps	Laps Led	Races Led	Miles	$
1959	Joe Lee Johnson	10	0	1	0	0	1	1	2	2,538	1	1	1,879	6,487
1960	Joe Lee Johnson	3	0	0	0	1	0	0	0	505	0	0	386	870
1960	Charley Griffin	1	0	0	0	0	0	0	0	132	0	0	198	200
1961	Johnny Allen	5	0	0	0	1	0	0	3	1,464	0	0	1,325	4,120
1961	Bob Welborn	2	0	0	0	0	0	0	0	117	0	0	59	160
1961	Herb Tillman	3	0	0	0	0	0	0	0	518	0	0	450	450
1961	Joe Lee Johnson	9	0	0	0	0	0	0	3	1,276	0	0	1,461	2,615
1962	Charley Griffin	2	0	0	0	0	0	0	0	92	0	0	230	525
1962	Joe Lee Johnson	3	0	0	0	0	0	0	0	379	0	0	190	190
Lifetime		38	0	1	0	2	1	1	8	7,021	1	1	6,176	$15,617

Junior Johnson (Statistics represent teams that were principally owned by Junior Johnson and include a number of partners. The statistics *do not* include mid 1971–mid 1974 when the Johnson managed team was owned by Richard Howard.)

Year	Driver	Starts	Poles	1	2	3	4	5	6–10	Laps	Laps Led	Races Led	Miles	$
1953	Junior Johnson	1	0	0	0	0	0	0	0	222	0	0	305	110
1965	Bobby Isaac	1	1	0	1	0	0	0	0	299	172	1	100	600
1965	Curtis Turner	2	0	0	0	0	0	0	0	101	0	0	47	250
1965	Junior Johnson	36	10	13	2	1	2	0	1	7,144	3,998	30	5,040	59,515
1966	Junior Johnson	7	3	0	0	0	0	1	0	1,813	467	6	1,160	3,610
1966	Gordon Johncock	2	0	0	0	0	1	0	0	709	9	1	876	3,470
1966	Fred Lorenzen	1	0	0	0	0	0	0	0	139	24	1	209	630

Year	Driver	Starts	Poles	Finish 1	2	3	4	5	6–10	Laps	Laps Led	Races Led	Miles	$

Junior Johnson *continued*

Year	Driver	Starts	Poles	1	2	3	4	5	6–10	Laps	Laps Led	Races Led	Miles	$
1966	Darel Dieringer	2	0	0	1	0	0	0	0	798	5	1	965	8,575
1966	Curtis Turner	3	0	0	0	1	0	0	0	662	154	3	607	1,100
1966	Bobby Isaac	8	0	0	1	1	0	0	1	1,094	21	2	1,095	4,915
1966	A.J. Foyt	3	0	0	0	0	0	0	0	129	0	0	332	1,810
1967	Lloyd Ruby	1	0	0	0	0	0	0	0	96	0	0	259	565
1967	LeeRoy Yarbrough	3	0	0	0	1	0	0	0	825	3	1	665	2,705
1967	Darel Dieringer	16	6	1	3	3	0	1	1	3,952	730	10	4,223	30,460
1968	LeeRoy Yarbrough	20	6	2	3	5	1	2	0	5,554	1,300	14	5,475	85,379
1969	LeeRoy Yarbrough	28	0	7	2	0	6	0	5	7,678	1,153	16	8,265	189,640
1970	Donnie Allison	1	0	0	0	1	0	0	0	399	5	1	249	1,975
1970	LeeRoy Yarbrough	17	1	1	1	4	2	0	3	4,126	232	11	5,352	60,960
1970	Fred Lorenzen	1	0	0	0	0	0	0	0	209	0	0	285	1,020
1970	David Pearson	1	0	0	0	0	1	0	0	375	0	0	197	1,525
1971	LeeRoy Yarbrough	4	0	0	0	0	1	0	2	778	26	2	1,224	7,315
1974	Cale Yarborough	15	1	4	1	4	1	1	0	4,337	1,739	14	5,272	135,264
1974	Earl Ross	15	0	1	0	1	1	0	5	4,301	121	5	5,039	43,265
1975	Cale Yarborough	28	3	3	3	3	3	1	0	7,648	2,542	20	8,395	203,125
1976	Cale Yarborough	30	2	9	6	3	2	2	1	9,269	3,771	28	10,548	337,240
1977	Cale Yarborough	30	3	9	6	4	3	3	2	9,747	3,218	28	11,383	440,160
1978	Cale Yarborough	30	8	10	6	1	5	1	1	9,758	3,587	28	11,367	487,963
1979	Cale Yarborough	31	1	4	2	6	4	3	3	9,677	1,323	22	11,193	379,615
1980	Cale Yarborough	31	14	6	4	4	4	1	3	9,440	2,811	28	11,016	432,325
1981	Richard Childress	1	0	0	0	0	0	0	0	5	0	0	13	460
1981	Darrell Waltrip	31	11	12	6	3	0	0	4	9,575	2,504	27	10,975	539,050
1982	Bill Schmitt	1	0	0	0	0	0	0	0	109	0	0	286	1,250
1982	J.D. McDuffie	2	0	0	0	0	0	0	0	574	1	1	538	5,465
1982	Darrell Waltrip	30	7	12	1	3	0	1	3	9,455	3,027	27	10,598	682,085
1983	Darrell Waltrip	30	7	6	8	4	2	2	3	9,403	2,362	22	10,547	650,570
1984	Neil Bonnett	30	1	0	2	0	2	3	7	9,126	641	11	10,460	199,300
1984	Darrell Waltrip	30	4	7	2	3	1	0	7	9,464	2,030	22	10,440	633,923
1985	Darrell Waltrip	28	5	3	6	6	2	1	3	8,931	969	21	10,917	704,448
1985	Neil Bonnett	28	1	2	2	3	1	3	7	8,675	618	15	10,358	438,145
1986	Neil Bonnett	28	0	1	1	1	1	2	6	7,691	323	16	8,992	410,080
1986	Davey Allison	1	0	0	0	0	0	0	1	188	13	1	500	17,820
1986	Darrell Waltrip	29	1	3	2	4	6	6	1	8,327	573	21	9,948	693,945
1987	Terry Labonte	29	4	1	2	2	5	3	9	8,609	592	16	10,159	558,215
1988	Terry Labonte	29	1	1	2	3	4	1	7	9,206	208	17	11,043	520,885
1989	Terry Labonte	29	0	2	2	1	1	3	2	8,306	104	10	9,773	565,702
1990	Geoffrey Bodine	29	2	3	3	2	3	0	8	8,852	976	21	10,748	767,445
1991	Sterling Marlin	29	2	0	2	1	1	3	9	9,205	201	8	11,210	474,235
1991	Geoffrey Bodine	27	2	1	2	1	1	1	6	7,997	152	12	9,591	570,070
1991	Tommy Ellis	2	0	0	0	0	0	0	0	887	0	0	1,085	13,250
1992	Sterling Marlin	29	5	0	3	0	1	2	7	8,462	218	8	10,287	541,065
1992	Bill Elliott	29	2	5	2	3	1	3	3	9,115	1,272	18	11,125	1,197,605
1992	Hut Stricklin	1	0	0	0	0	0	0	0	305	0	0	458	3,800
1993	Bill Elliott	30	2	0	1	2	2	1	9	9,349	15	4	11,351	755,050
1993	Hut Stricklin	30	0	0	0	0	1	0	1	8,356	99	3	10,212	465,550
1994	Jimmy Spencer	29	1	2	0	0	1	0	1	6,904	47	6	8,733	474,335
1994	Jeff Green	1	0	0	0	0	0	0	0	321	0	0	489	8,815
1994	Tom Kendall	1	0	0	0	0	0	0	0	88	0	0	216	9,435
1994	Bill Elliott	31	1	1	1	3	0	1	6	9,173	62	8	11,382	812,260
1995	Elton Sawyer	20	0	0	0	0	0	0	0	4,573	0	0	6,186	416,490
1995	Loy Allen Jr.	5	0	0	0	0	0	0	1	1,459	18	1	2,072	123,505
1995	Jimmy Horton	1	0	0	0	0	0	0	0	192	0	0	480	16,550
1995	Brett Bodine	31	0	0	0	0	0	0	2	9,159	6	1	11,084	830,041
1995	Greg Sacks	1	0	0	0	0	0	0	0	160	0	0	400	22,620
Lifetime		1050	118	132	92	88	73	51	141	303,480	44,442	590	353,797	$17,048,550

Ken Johnson

Year	Driver	Starts	Poles	1	2	3	4	5	6–10	Laps	Laps Led	Races Led	Miles	$
1959	Ken Johnson	4	0	0	0	0	0	0	1	408	0	0	366	370
Lifetime		4	0	0	0	0	0	0	1	408	0	0	366	$370

Lou Johnson

Year	Driver	Starts	Poles	1	2	3	4	5	6–10	Laps	Laps Led	Races Led	Miles	$
1953	Lou Johnson	1	0	0	0	0	0	0	0		0	0		25
Lifetime		1	0	0	0	0	0	0	0		0	0		$25

Year	Driver	Starts	Poles	Finish 1	2	3	4	5	6–10	Laps	Laps Led	Races Led	Miles	$

Norm Johnson

Year	Driver	Starts	Poles	1	2	3	4	5	6–10	Laps	Laps Led	Races Led	Miles	$
1953	Hank Ribet	1	0	0	0	0	0	0	0	68	0	0	34	25
1953	Hank Rivet	1	0	0	0	0	0	0	0	32	0	0	131	25
Lifetime		2	0	0	0	0	0	0	0	100	0	0	165	$50

Raeford Johnson

Year	Driver	Starts	Poles	1	2	3	4	5	6–10	Laps	Laps Led	Races Led	Miles	$
1960	Doug Yates	24	1	0	0	2	1	0	5	4,030	39	1	3,262	5,205
1961	Doug Yates	32	0	0	0	0	0	0	8	5,058	0	0	2,992	5,370
1962	Doug Yates	5	0	0	0	0	0	0	2	777	0	0	351	565
Lifetime		61	1	0	0	2	1	2	15	9,865	39	1	6,604	$11,140

Rush Johnson

Year	Driver	Starts	Poles	1	2	3	4	5	6–10	Laps	Laps Led	Races Led	Miles	$
1974	Jerry Schild	5	0	0	0	0	0	0	1	1,142	0	0	1,750	8,396
Lifetime		5	0	0	0	0	0	0	1	1,142	0	0	1,750	$8,396

Stoney Johnson

Year	Driver	Starts	Poles	1	2	3	4	5	6–10	Laps	Laps Led	Races Led	Miles	$
1962	Herb Thomas	1	0	0	0	0	0	0	0	377	0	0	236	200
Lifetime		1	0	0	0	0	0	0	0	377	0	0	236	$200

Warren Johnson

Year	Driver	Starts	Poles	1	2	3	4	5	6–10	Laps	Laps Led	Races Led	Miles	$
2002	Derrike Cope	1	0	0	0	0	0	0	0	194	0	0	388	41,235
Lifetime		1	0	0	0	0	0	0	0	194	0	0	388	$41,235

Ray Johnstone

Year	Driver	Starts	Poles	1	2	3	4	5	6–10	Laps	Laps Led	Races Led	Miles	$
1970	Ray Johnstone	1	0	0	0	0	0	0	0	26	0	0	68	660
1971	Ray Johnstone	3	0	0	0	0	0	0	0	211	0	0	541	3,405
Lifetime		4	0	0	0	0	0	0	0	237	0	0	609	$4,065

Carl Joiner

Year	Driver	Starts	Poles	1	2	3	4	5	6–10	Laps	Laps Led	Races Led	Miles	$
1963	Carl Joiner	1	0	0	0	0	0	0	0	143	0	0	386	375
1975	Carl Joiner	1	0	0	0	0	0	0	0	87	0	0	228	895
1976	Carl Joiner	2	0	0	0	0	0	0	0	227	0	0	581	2,155
1977	Carl Joiner	1	0	0	0	0	0	0	0	10	0	0	26	740
Lifetime		5	0	0	0	0	0	0	0	467	0	0	1,222	$4,165

Jerry Jolly

Year	Driver	Starts	Poles	1	2	3	4	5	6–10	Laps	Laps Led	Races Led	Miles	$
1984	Jerry Jolly	1	0	0	0	0	0	0	0	10	0	0	26	715
Lifetime		1	0	0	0	0	0	0	0	10	0	0	26	$715

B.J. Jones

Year	Driver	Starts	Poles	1	2	3	4	5	6–10	Laps	Laps Led	Races Led	Miles	$
1956	Wilbur Rakestraw	1	0	0	0	0	0	0	0	29	0	0	15	100
1956	Sonny Black	1	0	0	0	0	0	0	0	79	0	0	79	50
1956	Jack Smith	3	0	0	0	0	0	0	0	153	0	0	77	50
1959	Benny Rakestraw	1	0	0	0	0	0	0	0	182	0	0	91	70
1959	George Alsobrook	4	0	0	0	0	0	0	1	936	0	0	723	1,150
1959	Wilbur Rakestraw	2	0	0	0	0	0	0	1	326	0	0	598	725
1961	Wilbur Rakestraw	5	0	0	0	0	0	0	1	360	0	0	306	635
1961	George Alsobrook	8	0	0	0	0	0	0	1	938	0	0	736	1,825
Lifetime		25	0	0	0	0	0	0	4	3,003	0	0	2,623	$4,605

Billy Jones

Year	Driver	Starts	Poles	1	2	3	4	5	6–10	Laps	Laps Led	Races Led	Miles	$
1997	Buckshot Jones	1	0	0	0	0	0	0	0	38	0	0	58	20,875
1999	Buckshot Jones	9	0	0	0	0	0	0	0	2,342	0	0	3,450	287,810
2000	Buckshot Jones	1	0	0	0	0	0	0	0	277	0	0	427	35,275
Lifetime		11	0	0	0	0	0	0	0	2,657	0	0	3,934	343,960

Hap Jones

Year	Driver	Starts	Poles	1	2	3	4	5	6–10	Laps	Laps Led	Races Led	Miles	$
1954	Hap Jones	1	0	0	0	0	0	0	0	31	0	0	127	0
Lifetime		1	0	0	0	0	0	0	0	31	0	0	127	$0

Year	Driver	Starts	Poles	Finish 1	2	3	4	5	6–10	Laps	Laps Led	Races Led	Miles	$

James Jones

Year	Driver	Starts	Poles	1	2	3	4	5	6–10	Laps	Laps Led	Races Led	Miles	$
1956	James Jones	1	0	0	0	0	0	0	0	169	0	0	85	100
1958	James Jones	1	0	0	0	0	0	0	0	212	0	0	212	100
Lifetime		2	0	0	0	0	0	0	0	381	0	0	297	$200

Joe Jones

Year	Driver	Starts	Poles	1	2	3	4	5	6–10	Laps	Laps Led	Races Led	Miles	$
1958	Wilbur Rakestraw	8	0	0	0	0	1	0	1	1,534	0	0	1,347	1,490
1961	Joe Jones	8	0	0	0	0	0	0	0	893	0	0	637	1,015
1961	George Green	2	0	0	0	0	1	0	0	424	0	0	212	400
1962	Joe Jones	2	0	0	0	0	0	0	0	250	0	0	125	100
Lifetime		20	0	0	0	0	2	0	1	3,101	0	0	2,321	$3,005

Possum Jones

Year	Driver	Starts	Poles	1	2	3	4	5	6–10	Laps	Laps Led	Races Led	Miles	$
1963	Possum Jones	5	0	0	0	0	0	0	1	576	0	0	251	1,080
1963	Joe Weatherly	1	0	0	0	0	0	0	1	191	0	0	96	175
1963	Jim McGuirk	1	0	0	0	0	0	0	0	142	0	0	355	650
Lifetime		7	0	0	0	0	0	0	2	909	0	0	702	$1,905

Preston Jones

Year	Driver	Starts	Poles	1	2	3	4	5	6–10	Laps	Laps Led	Races Led	Miles	$
1951	Oliver Dial	1	0	0	0	0	0	0	0	355	0	0	444	50
Lifetime		1	0	0	0	0	0	0	0	355	0	0	444	$50

Ralph Jones

Year	Driver	Starts	Poles	1	2	3	4	5	6–10	Laps	Laps Led	Races Led	Miles	$
1977	Ralph Jones	4	0	0	0	0	0	0	0	871	0	0	645	3,395
1978	Ralph Jones	7	0	0	0	0	0	0	0	1,871	0	0	1,856	6,305
1979	Ralph Jones	6	0	0	0	0	0	0	0	729	0	0	1,171	12,785
Lifetime		17	0	0	0	0	0	0	0	3,471	0	0	3,673	$22,485

Melvin Joseph

Year	Driver	Starts	Poles	1	2	3	4	5	6–10	Laps	Laps Led	Races Led	Miles	$
1971	Bobby Allison	2	1	1	1	0	0	0	0	748	339	2	289	2,500
Lifetime		2	1	1	1	0	0	0	0	748	339	2	289	$2,500

Dick Joslin

Year	Driver	Starts	Poles	1	2	3	4	5	6–10	Laps	Laps Led	Races Led	Miles	$
1959	Dick Joslin	4	0	0	0	0	0	0	0	338	0	0	793	485
Lifetime		4	0	0	0	0	0	0	0	338	0	0	793	$485

Stuart Joyce

Year	Driver	Starts	Poles	1	2	3	4	5	6–10	Laps	Laps Led	Races Led	Miles	$
1952	Stuart Joyce	1	0	0	0	0	0	0	1	229	0	0	229	200
1952	Leon Meadows	1	0	0	0	0	0	0	0	67	0	0	67	25
Lifetime		2	0	0	0	0	0	0	1	296	0	0	296	$225

C.M. Julian

Year	Driver	Starts	Poles	1	2	3	4	5	6–10	Laps	Laps Led	Races Led	Miles	$
1957	Don Bailey	1	0	0	0	0	0	0	0	62	0	0	62	75
1957	Tiny Lund	1	0	0	0	0	0	0	0	148	0	0	93	100
1957	T.A. Toomes	10	0	0	0	0	0	0	1	1,447	0	0	803	1,250
1957	Johnny Dodson	1	0	0	0	0	0	0	0	19	0	0	12	50
1957	Billy Rafter	2	0	0	0	0	0	0	1	148	0	0	252	340
Lifetime		15	0	0	0	0	0	0	2	1,824	0	0	1,221	$1,815

J.L. Justice

Year	Driver	Starts	Poles	1	2	3	4	5	6–10	Laps	Laps Led	Races Led	Miles	$
1953	J.L. Justice	3	0	0	0	0	0	0	0	226	0	0	307	145
Lifetime		3	0	0	0	0	0	0	0	226	0	0	307	$145

Hoss Kagle

Year	Driver	Starts	Poles	1	2	3	4	5	6–10	Laps	Laps Led	Races Led	Miles	$
1956	Hoss Kagle	1	0	0	0	0	0	0	0	135	0	0	135	100
1956	Reds Kagle	2	0	0	0	0	0	0	0	202	0	0	85	60
1957	Reds Kagle	1	0	0	0	0	0	0	0	23	0	0	12	25
1958	Reds Kagle	3	0	0	0	0	0	1	1	212	0	0	117	365
1959	Reds Kagle	1	0	0	0	0	0	0	0	158	0	0	79	110
Lifetime		8	0	0	0	0	0	1	1	730	0	0	427	$660

Year	Driver	Starts	Poles	Finish 1	2	3	4	5	6–10	Laps	Laps Led	Races Led	Miles	$

Reds Kagle

Year	Driver	Starts	Poles	1	2	3	4	5	6–10	Laps	Laps Led	Races Led	Miles	$
1958	Reds Kagle	10	0	0	0	0	0	1	4	1,337	0	0	687	1,285
1959	Reds Kagle	3	0	0	0	0	1	0	0	469	0	0	261	415
Lifetime		13	0	0	0	0	1	1	4	1,806	0	0	948	$1,700

Iggy Katona

Year	Driver	Starts	Poles	1	2	3	4	5	6–10	Laps	Laps Led	Races Led	Miles	$
1951	Iggy Katona	5	0	0	0	0	0	0	0	559	0	0	643	150
1952	Iggy Katona	2	0	0	0	0	0	0	1	180	0	0	90	125
Lifetime		7	0	0	0	0	0	0	1	739	0	0	733	$275

Bobby Keck

Year	Driver	Starts	Poles	1	2	3	4	5	6–10	Laps	Laps Led	Races Led	Miles	$
1956	Bobby Keck	15	0	0	0	0	0	0	3	2,236	0	0	1,309	1,250
1957	Bobby Keck	16	0	0	0	0	0	0	2	2,144	0	0	1,419	1,525
1957	Speedy Thompson	1	0	0	0	0	0	0	0	99	0	0	50	125
1958	Bobby Keck	30	0	0	0	0	0	0	7	4,345	0	0	2,219	2,885
1959	Bobby Keck	18	0	0	0	0	0	0	0	2,484	0	0	1,152	1,270
Lifetime		80	0	0	0	0	0	0	12	11,308	0	0	6,147	$7,055

Tex Keene

Year	Driver	Starts	Poles	1	2	3	4	5	6–10	Laps	Laps Led	Races Led	Miles	$
1950	Tex Keene	2	0	0	0	0	0	0	0	229	0	0	286	0
Lifetime		2	0	0	0	0	0	0	0	229	0	0	286	$0

Joe Keistler

Year	Driver	Starts	Poles	1	2	3	4	5	6–10	Laps	Laps Led	Races Led	Miles	$
1965	Frank Weathers	5	0	0	0	0	0	0	1	620	0	0	314	640
1965	Don Tilley	2	0	0	0	0	0	0	0	119	0	0	298	1,240
Lifetime		7	0	0	0	0	0	0	1	739	0	0	612	$1,880

N.V. Keith

Year	Driver	Starts	Poles	1	2	3	4	5	6–10	Laps	Laps Led	Races Led	Miles	$
1969	J.D. McDuffie	12	0	0	0	0	0	0	2	2,140	0	0	1,889	7,810
Lifetime		12	0	0	0	0	0	0	2	2,140	0	0	1,889	$7,810

Al Keller

Year	Driver	Starts	Poles	1	2	3	4	5	6–10	Laps	Laps Led	Races Led	Miles	$
1956	Al Keller	4	0	0	1	0	0	0	1	482	0	0	395	1,300
Lifetime		4	0	0	1	0	0	0	1	482	0	0	395	$1,300

Truthful Kelley

Year	Driver	Starts	Poles	1	2	3	4	5	6–10	Laps	Laps Led	Races Led	Miles	$
1951	Bob Reuther	1	0	0	0	0	0	0	0		0	0		0
Lifetime		1	0	0	0	0	0	0	0		0	0		$0

Fran Kelly

Year	Driver	Starts	Poles	1	2	3	4	5	6–10	Laps	Laps Led	Races Led	Miles	$
1970	Dick Trickle	2	0	0	0	0	0	0	0	176	0	0	440	1,415
Lifetime		2	0	0	0	0	0	0	0	176	0	0	440	$1,415

James Kelly

Year	Driver	Starts	Poles	1	2	3	4	5	6–10	Laps	Laps Led	Races Led	Miles	$
1963	Sonny Fogle	8	0	0	0	0	0	0	0	779	0	0	382	600
1963	Billy Oswald	1	0	0	0	0	0	0	0	61	0	0	31	60
Lifetime		9	0	0	0	0	0	0	0	840	0	0	412	$660

Pete Kelly

Year	Driver	Starts	Poles	1	2	3	4	5	6–10	Laps	Laps Led	Races Led	Miles	$
1952	Pete Kelly	2	0	0	0	0	0	0	0	231	0	0	237	35
1959	Pete Kelly	2	0	0	0	0	0	0	0	44	0	0	95	150
Lifetime		4	0	0	0	0	0	0	0	275	0	0	332	$185

Ray Kelly

Year	Driver	Starts	Poles	1	2	3	4	5	6–10	Laps	Laps Led	Races Led	Miles	$
1986	Ray Kelly	1	0	0	0	0	0	0	0	36	0	0	94	850
Lifetime		1	0	0	0	0	0	0	0	36	0	0	94	$850

Year	Driver	Starts	Poles	Finish						Laps	Laps Led	Races Led	Miles	$
				1	2	3	4	5	6–10					

Mike Kempton

Year	Driver	Starts	Poles	1	2	3	4	5	6–10	Laps	Laps Led	Races Led	Miles	$
1977	Mike Kempton	2	0	0	0	0	0	0	0	336	0	0	450	2,555
1977	Terry Bivins	1	0	0	0	0	0	0	0	154	0	0	210	880
1979	Mike Kempton	2	0	0	0	0	0	0	0	499	0	0	487	1,605
1979	Henry Jones	3	0	0	0	0	0	0	0	77	0	0	43	1,160
1980	Henry Jones	3	0	0	0	0	0	0	0	198	0	0	405	3,175
Lifetime		11	0	0	0	0	0	0	0	1,264	0	0	1,595	$9,375

Dave Kennedy

Year	Driver	Starts	Poles	1	2	3	4	5	6–10	Laps	Laps Led	Races Led	Miles	$
1952	Ray Chase	1	0	0	0	0	0	0	0	173	0	0	173	25
1952	Ed Westveer	1	0	0	0	0	0	0	0	45	0	0	45	25
Lifetime		2	0	0	0	0	0	0	0	218	0	0	218	$50

John Kennedy

Year	Driver	Starts	Poles	1	2	3	4	5	6–10	Laps	Laps Led	Races Led	Miles	$
1969	John Kennedy	6	0	0	0	0	0	0	0	996	0	0	1,557	5,187
1977	John Kennedy	1	0	0	0	0	0	0	0	66	0	0	132	880
1977	Jim Hurtubise	1	0	0	0	0	0	0	0	12	0	0	12	460
1978	John Kennedy	5	0	0	0	0	0	0	0	296	0	0	350	2,900
1979	John Kennedy	5	0	0	0	0	0	0	0	600	0	0	942	4,515
1979	Ronnie Thomas	1	0	0	0	0	0	0	0	379	0	0	569	5,490
1979	Dick May	1	0	0	0	0	0	0	0	4	0	0	6	600
Lifetime		20	0	0	0	0	0	0	0	2,353	0	0	3,568	$20,032

Dave Kent

Year	Driver	Starts	Poles	1	2	3	4	5	6–10	Laps	Laps Led	Races Led	Miles	$
1963	Mark Hurley	1	0	0	0	0	0	0	0	296	0	0	148	235
1963	John Hoffman	1	0	0	0	0	0	0	0	51	0	0	13	100
1963	Tiny Lund	8	0	0	0	0	0	0	3	1,360	1	1	684	1,375
1964	Tiny Lund	1	0	0	0	0	0	0	1	215	0	0	108	150
Lifetime		11	0	0	0	0	0	0	4	1,922	1	1	952	$1,860

Joe Kersey

Year	Driver	Starts	Poles	1	2	3	4	5	6–10	Laps	Laps Led	Races Led	Miles	$
1953	Buck Mason	1	0	0	0	0	0	0	0		0	0		50
Lifetime		1	0	0	0	0	0	0	0		0	0		$50

John Keselowski

Year	Driver	Starts	Poles	1	2	3	4	5	6–10	Laps	Laps Led	Races Led	Miles	$
1969	Homer Newland	2	0	0	0	0	0	0	0	179	0	0	393	1,875
1970	Ron Keselowski	17	0	0	0	0	0	0	1	2,339	9	1	2,842	12,015
1970	Dave Marcis	1	0	0	0	0	0	0	0	255	0	0	348	1,145
1971	Ron Keselowski	1	0	0	0	0	0	0	0	0	0	0	0	200
1971	Rene Charland	1	0	0	0	0	0	0	0	33	0	0	12	100
1971	Dick Poling	2	0	0	0	0	0	0	0	228	0	0	345	915
1971	Bill Shirey	1	0	0	0	0	0	0	0	118	0	0	64	325
1971	Bennis Listman	1	0	0	0	0	0	0	0	6	0	0	1	100
1973	Ron Keselowski	2	0	0	0	0	0	1	0	364	0	0	561	2,710
1974	Bob Whitlow	1	0	0	0	0	0	0	0	183	0	0	366	1,055
1975	Jim Vandiver	1	0	0	0	0	0	0	0	3	0	0	8	1,350
Lifetime		30	0	0	0	0	0	1	1	3,708	9	1	4,941	$21,790

Jerry Keyes

Year	Driver	Starts	Poles	1	2	3	4	5	6–10	Laps	Laps Led	Races Led	Miles	$
1954	Jerry Keyes	1	0	0	0	0	0	0	0	338	0	0	169	25
Lifetime		1	0	0	0	0	0	0	0	338	0	0	169	$25

Carl Kiekhaefer

Year	Driver	Starts	Poles	1	2	3	4	5	6–10	Laps	Laps Led	Races Led	Miles	$
1955	Fonty Flock	20	4	2	5	1	0	0	2	2,608	364	6	1,885	10,130
1955	Bob Flock	1	0	0	0	0	0	1	0	195	0	0	293	650
1955	Tim Flock	38	20	18	5	4	1	3	1	6,011	3,495	33	4,457	32,925
1955	Buck Baker	1	0	0	0	0	0	0	1	239	0	0	239	550
1955	Norm Nelson	2	1	1	0	0	0	0	0	273	106	1	354	1,420
1955	Speedy Thompson	2	0	1	0	0	0	0	1	357	64	1	198	1,300
1956	Fonty Flock	4	2	1	0	0	0	0	1	257	150	2	303	1,350
1956	Charlie Scott	1	0	0	0	0	0	0	0		0	0		75
1956	Frank Mundy	9	0	0	1	1	0	1	2	1,589	0	0	1,479	3,585
1956	Herb Thomas	17	1	3	2	2	2	1	3	2,809	222	5	1,675	7,770

Year	Driver	Starts	Poles	Finish 1	2	3	4	5	6–10	Laps	Laps Led	Races Led	Miles	$

Carl Kiekhaefer *continued*

Year	Driver	Starts	Poles	1	2	3	4	5	6–10	Laps	Laps Led	Races Led	Miles	$
1956	Jack Smith	3	0	1	0	0	0	0	0	698	185	1	336	2,475
1956	Speedy Thompson	39	7	8	5	5	4	1	5	6,655	1,956	22	4,476	24,785
1956	Tim Flock	8	3	3	1	2	0	0	1	1,033	314	4	786	8,410
1956	Junior Johnson	1	0	0	1	0	0	0	0	133	0	0	100	700
1956	Buck Baker	44	12	14	7	3	3	2	6	7,779	1,401	23	5,088	29,115
Lifetime		190	50	52	27	18	10	9	23	30,636	8,257	98	21,668	$125,240

John Kieper

Year	Driver	Starts	Poles	1	2	3	4	5	6–10	Laps	Laps Led	Races Led	Miles	$
1955	John Kieper	1	0	0	0	0	0	0	0	72	0	0	72	50
1956	John Kieper	8	2	1	1	1	1	0	3	1,479	67	2	917	3,250
1957	John Kieper	1	0	0	0	0	0	0	0	6	0	0	3	50
1975	John Kieper	2	0	0	0	0	0	0	0	191	0	0	490	2,110
1976	John Kieper	1	0	0	0	0	0	0	0	62	0	0	155	710
1977	Don Noel	1	0	0	0	0	0	0	0	0	0	0	0	500
1977	John Kieper	1	0	0	0	0	0	0	0	50	0	0	125	740
1980	Chuck Bown	1	0	0	0	0	0	0	0	120	0	0	300	1,300
1980	Hershel McGriff	1	0	0	0	0	0	0	0	82	0	0	215	955
1983	Jim Bown	1	0	0	0	0	0	0	0	37	0	0	97	1,025
1984	Jim Bown	2	0	0	0	0	0	0	0	132	4	1	346	2,330
1985	Jim Bown	2	0	0	0	0	0	0	0	185	0	0	485	4,860
1986	Jim Bown	1	0	0	0	0	0	0	0	81	0	0	212	1,175
Lifetime		23	2	1	1	1	1	0	3	2,497	71	3	3,417	$19,055

C.L. Kilpatrick

Year	Driver	Starts	Poles	1	2	3	4	5	6–10	Laps	Laps Led	Races Led	Miles	$
1963	Roy Mayne	19	0	0	0	0	0	1	3	3,854	0	0	1,939	3,065
1963	Jack Deniston	1	0	0	0	0	0	0	0	187	0	0	47	135
1964	Roy Mayne	1	0	0	0	0	0	0	0	13	0	0	12	0
Lifetime		21	0	0	0	0	0	1	3	4,054	0	0	1,998	$3,200

Guy Kimball

Year	Driver	Starts	Poles	1	2	3	4	5	6–10	Laps	Laps Led	Races Led	Miles	$
1961	Danny Letner	1	0	0	0	1	0	0	0	175	0	0	245	750
1961	Danny Weinberg	4	1	0	0	2	0	0	1	446	0	0	453	1,185
Lifetime		5	1	0	0	3	0	0	1	621	0	0	698	$1,935

Bill Kimmel

Year	Driver	Starts	Poles	1	2	3	4	5	6–10	Laps	Laps Led	Races Led	Miles	$
1970	Bill Kimmel	1	0	0	0	0	0	0	0	41	0	0	103	220
Lifetime		1	0	0	0	0	0	0	0	41	0	0	103	$220

A.J. King

Year	Driver	Starts	Poles	1	2	3	4	5	6–10	Laps	Laps Led	Races Led	Miles	$
1967	Bobby Isaac	1	0	0	0	0	0	0	0	76	0	0	38	250
1967	Paul Lewis	8	0	0	0	0	0	1	3	2,013	4	1	2,135	6,710
1967	Paul Moore	5	0	0	0	0	0	2	1	1,318	0	0	1,664	7,100
1968	Paul Moore	9	0	0	0	0	0	0	5	1,907	24	1	1,806	6,965
1968	Pete Hamilton	6	0	0	0	0	0	0	2	1,491	28	2	1,246	4,439
1968	Sam McQuagg	2	0	0	0	0	0	0	0	295	0	0	270	795
1969	Pete Hamilton	2	0	0	0	0	0	0	1	92	14	1	230	2,210
1975	Tiny Lund	1	0	0	0	0	0	0	0	6	0	0	16	620
Lifetime		34	0	0	0	0	0	3	12	7,198	70	5	7,404	$29,089

Bob King

Year	Driver	Starts	Poles	1	2	3	4	5	6–10	Laps	Laps Led	Races Led	Miles	$
1953	Bub King	1	0	0	0	0	0	0	1	182	0	0	91	50
Lifetime		1	0	0	0	0	0	0	1	182	0	0	91	$50

Brownie King

Year	Driver	Starts	Poles	1	2	3	4	5	6–10	Laps	Laps Led	Races Led	Miles	$
1956	Brownie King	15	0	0	0	0	0	0	0	1,994	0	0	1,322	925
Lifetime		15	0	0	0	0	0	0	0	1,994	0	0	1,322	$925

Bub King

Year	Driver	Starts	Poles	1	2	3	4	5	6–10	Laps	Laps Led	Races Led	Miles	$
1951	Bub King	8	0	0	0	0	0	0	2	149	0	0	186	425
1952	Bub King	10	0	0	0	1	1	0	3	1,743	0	0	1,419	2,335

Year	Driver	Starts	Poles	Finish 1	2	3	4	5	6–10	Laps	Laps Led	Races Led	Miles	$

Bub King *continued*

Year	Driver	Starts	Poles	1	2	3	4	5	6–10	Laps	Laps Led	Races Led	Miles	$
1953	Bub King	13	0	0	0	0	0	0	4	847	0	0	922	725
Lifetime		31	0	0	0	1	1	0	9	2,739	0	0	2,527	$3,485

T.L. King

Year	Driver	Starts	Poles	1	2	3	4	5	6–10	Laps	Laps Led	Races Led	Miles	$
1950	Bub King	1	0	0	0	0	0	0	0	329	0	0	411	0
1951	Bub King	1	0	0	0	0	0	0	0	98	0	0	74	25
Lifetime		2	0	0	0	0	0	0	0	427	0	0	485	$25

Pat Kirkwood

Year	Driver	Starts	Poles	1	2	3	4	5	6–10	Laps	Laps Led	Races Led	Miles	$
1949	Pat Kirkwood	1	0	0	0	0	0	0	0		0	0		0
1952	Pat Kirkwood	4	1	0	0	1	0	1	0	764	0	0	972	1,215
Lifetime		5	1	0	0	1	0	1	0	764	0	0	972	$1,215

Ike Kiser

Year	Driver	Starts	Poles	1	2	3	4	5	6–10	Laps	Laps Led	Races Led	Miles	$
1955	Speedy Thompson	1	0	0	0	0	0	0	0	88	0	0	88	50
1955	Dick Beaty	1	0	0	0	0	0	0	0	184	0	0	253	50
1955	Jimmy Thompson	3	0	0	0	0	0	0	1	430	0	0	215	350
1956	Dick Beaty	15	0	0	0	0	0	0	3	1,513	0	0	1,091	910
1957	Dick Beaty	1	0	0	0	0	0	0	0	141	0	0	71	100
Lifetime		21	0	0	0	0	0	0	4	2,356	0	0	1,717	$1,460

Bob Kitchell

Year	Driver	Starts	Poles	1	2	3	4	5	6–10	Laps	Laps Led	Races Led	Miles	$
1963	Lloyd Dane	1	0	0	0	0	0	0	0	131	0	0	354	250
Lifetime		1	0	0	0	0	0	0	0	131	0	0	354	$250

Harold Kite

Year	Driver	Starts	Poles	1	2	3	4	5	6–10	Laps	Laps Led	Races Led	Miles	$
1950	Harold Kite	3	0	1	0	0	0	0	0	382	38	1	618	1,550
1950	Tim Flock	2	1	1	0	0	1	0	0	339	190	2	289	2,000
Lifetime		5	1	2	0	0	1	0	0	721	228	3	907	$3,550

Mike Klapak

Year	Driver	Starts	Poles	1	2	3	4	5	6–10	Laps	Laps Led	Races Led	Miles	$
1950	Mike Klapak	3	0	0	0	0	0	0	0	158	0	0	79	50
1951	Mike Klapak	1	0	0	0	0	0	0	0		0	0		25
Lifetime		4	0	0	0	0	0	0	0	158	0	0	79	$75

Julian Kline

Year	Driver	Starts	Poles	1	2	3	4	5	6–10	Laps	Laps Led	Races Led	Miles	$
1968	Rod Eulenfeld	1	0	0	0	0	0	0	0	174	0	0	435	2,000
Lifetime		1	0	0	0	0	0	0	0	174	0	0	435	$2,000

Frank Klitzer

Year	Driver	Starts	Poles	1	2	3	4	5	6–10	Laps	Laps Led	Races Led	Miles	$
1960	Pat Moore	1	0	0	0	0	0	0	0	72	0	0	36	50
Lifetime		1	0	0	0	0	0	0	0	72	0	0	36	$50

Sam Knox

Year	Driver	Starts	Poles	1	2	3	4	5	6–10	Laps	Laps Led	Races Led	Miles	$
1951	Gober Sosebee	3	1	0	1	0	0	0	0	104	7	1	104	625
1951	Ed Samples	2	0	0	0	0	0	0	0	15	0	0	11	10
1951	Tim Flock	1	1	0	1	0	0	0	0		27	1		1,000
1951	Billy Carden	9	1	0	0	1	1	1	3	519	58	1	613	1,485
1952	Speedy Thompson	1	0	0	0	0	0	0	0	383	0	0	479	280
1952	Gober Sosebee	5	0	1	0	0	0	0	1	549	176	2	458	1,325
1953	Gober Sosebee	2	0	0	0	0	0	0	0	210	0	0	242	100
1954	Stan Kross	5	0	0	0	0	0	0	1	135	0	0	215	150
Lifetime		28	3	1	2	1	1	1	5	1,915	268	5	2,122	$4,975

Robert Koehler

Year	Driver	Starts	Poles	1	2	3	4	5	6–10	Laps	Laps Led	Races Led	Miles	$
1971	Hershel McGriff	1	0	0	0	0	0	0	0	163	1	1	408	1,775
Lifetime		1	0	0	0	0	0	0	0	163	1	1	408	$1,775

Year	Driver	Starts	Poles	Finish 1	2	3	4	5	6–10	Laps	Laps Led	Races Led	Miles	$

Ronnie Kohler

Year	Driver	Starts	Poles	1	2	3	4	5	6–10	Laps	Laps Led	Races Led	Miles	$
1952	Ronnie Kohler	2	0	0	0	0	0	1	0	253	0	0	127	225
1953	Ronnie Kohler	1	0	0	0	0	0	0	0		0	0		75
Lifetime		3	0	0	0	0	0	1	0	253	0	0	127	$300

Phil Kord

Year	Driver	Starts	Poles	1	2	3	4	5	6–10	Laps	Laps Led	Races Led	Miles	$
1975	Ron Esau	1	0	0	0	0	0	0	0	96	0	0	252	1,125
1983	Bob Kennedy (TOCA)	1	0	0	0	0	0	0	0	89	0	0	233	1,990
Lifetime		2	0	0	0	0	0	0	0	185	0	0	485	$3,115

Joe Kosiske

Year	Driver	Starts	Poles	1	2	3	4	5	6–10	Laps	Laps Led	Races Led	Miles	$
1960	Bob Kosiski	2	0	0	0	0	0	0	0	163	0	0	408	250
Lifetime		2	0	0	0	0	0	0	0	163	0	0	408	$250

John Koszein

Year	Driver	Starts	Poles	1	2	3	4	5	6–10	Laps	Laps Led	Races Led	Miles	$
1961	Ernie Gahan	5	0	0	0	0	0	0	1	707	0	0	348	750
Lifetime		5	0	0	0	0	0	0	1	707	0	0	348	$750

Michael Kranefuss

Year	Driver	Starts	Poles	1	2	3	4	5	6–10	Laps	Laps Led	Races Led	Miles	$
1994	Geoff Brabham	1	0	0	0	0	0	0	0	127	0	0	318	27,400
1994	Robby Gordon	1	0	0	0	0	0	0	0	69	0	0	138	7,965
1995	John Andretti	31	1	0	0	0	1	0	4	8,402	69	8	10,174	525,255
1996	John Andretti	22	0	0	0	0	0	1	1	4,832	31	4	7,099	557,481
1996	Jeremy Mayfield	7	0	0	0	0	0	0	0	2,052	0	0	1,665	128,990
1997	Jeremy Mayfield	32	0	0	0	0	1	2	5	9,541	3	2	12,326	921,455
1998	Jeremy Mayfield	33	1	1	1	3	2	5	4	9,745	476	9	12,584	1,892,725
1999	Jeremy Mayfield	34	0	0	1	2	0	2	7	9,870	221	11	12,931	1,879,829
2000	Tom Hubert	1	0	0	0	0	0	0	0	90	0	0	221	33,175
2000	Kyle Petty	1	0	0	0	0	0	0	0	158	0	0	395	97,735
2000	Jeremy Mayfield	32	4	2	3	0	1	0	6	8,268	850	17	10,587	2,044,070
2001	Shawna Robinson	1	0	0	0	0	0	0	0	197	0	0	394	35,190
Lifetime		196	6	3	5	5	5	10	27	53,351	1,650	51	68,830	$8,151,270

Nord Krauskopf

Year	Driver	Starts	Poles	1	2	3	4	5	6–10	Laps	Laps Led	Races Led	Miles	$
1966	Earl Balmer	7	0	0	0	0	0	1	0	1,327	3	1	1,944	5,890
1966	Gordon Johncock	3	0	0	0	0	0	0	1	430	12	1	797	2,015
1967	Bobby Isaac	11	0	0	1	0	0	2	2	2,549	65	3	3,889	22,385
1967	Bobby Allison	2	0	0	0	0	0	0	0	597	0	0	896	2,375
1967	Charlie Glotzbach	9	0	0	0	0	3	0	2	1,783	4	1	2,461	14,870
1967	Sam McQuagg	1	0	0	0	0	0	0	0	57	1	1	143	535
1968	Sam McQuagg	3	0	0	0	0	0	0	2	750	5	1	1,296	4,165
1968	Bobby Isaac	49	3	3	9	7	4	4	9	12,947	1,384	20	9,123	44,730
1969	Bobby Isaac	50	21	17	3	5	3	1	4	12,308	5,072	38	9,230	82,110
1970	Bobby Isaac	47	13	11	9	5	4	3	6	12,726	3,188	35	11,251	124,545
1971	Dave Marcis	1	0	0	0	0	0	0	1	181	38	1	481	6,025
1971	Bobby Isaac	25	5	4	4	2	4	2	1	6,856	1,753	17	7,604	106,025
1972	Bobby Isaac	24	9	1	3	5	0	1	0	5,326	1,314	18	6,458	128,240
1972	Buddy Baker	7	1	1	1	2	1	0	0	2,803	448	6	2,666	48,165
1973	Buddy Baker	27	5	2	4	6	4	0	4	8,369	975	14	8,918	174,345
1974	Buddy Baker	3	0	0	0	2	0	0	0	780	45	1	1,276	14,775
1974	Dave Marcis	2	0	0	0	0	0	0	0	268	0	0	326	2,087
1974	Ray Hendrick	1	0	0	0	0	0	0	0	179	0	0	94	620
1974	Bobby Isaac	1	0	0	0	0	0	0	0	81	0	0	122	1,372
1975	Dave Marcis	30	4	1	1	5	6	3	2	8,324	458	17	9,790	193,460
1976	Dave Marcis	30	7	3	0	1	2	3	7	8,355	893	20	9,733	192,900
1976	Gordon Johncock	1	0	0	0	0	0	0	0	41	0	0	62	870
1977	Neil Bonnett	11	3	0	0	0	1	1	2	2,964	47	4	3,183	53,450
Lifetime		345	71	43	35	40	32	21	43	90,001	15,705	199	91,739	$1,225,954

Art Krebs

Year	Driver	Starts	Poles	1	2	3	4	5	6–10	Laps	Laps Led	Races Led	Miles	$
1956	Jim Cook	2	0	0	0	0	0	0	0	121	0	0	226	65
1959	Jim Blomgren	1	0	0	0	0	0	0	0	49	0	0	49	50
1960	Bruce Worrell	3	0	0	0	0	0	0	2	333	0	0	394	650
Lifetime		6	0	0	0	0	0	0	2	503	0	0	669	$765

Year	Driver	Starts	Poles	Finish 1	2	3	4	5	6–10	Laps	Laps Led	Races Led	Miles	$

Buddy Krebs

Year	Driver	Starts	Poles	1	2	3	4	5	6–10	Laps	Laps Led	Races Led	Miles	$
1955	Buddy Krebs	1	0	0	0	0	0	0	0	50	0	0	50	50
Lifetime		1	0	0	0	0	0	0	0	50	0	0	50	$50

John Krebs

Year	Driver	Starts	Poles	1	2	3	4	5	6–10	Laps	Laps Led	Races Led	Miles	$
1982	John Krebs	1	0	0	0	0	0	0	0	87	0	0	228	1,150
1983	John Krebs	1	0	0	0	0	0	0	0	60	0	0	157	1,100
1984	John Krebs	2	0	0	0	0	0	0	0	54	0	0	141	1,790
1985	John Krebs	1	0	0	0	0	0	0	0	73	0	0	191	2,250
1986	John Krebs	2	0	0	0	0	0	0	0	94	0	0	246	2,075
1987	John Krebs	1	0	0	0	0	0	0	0	80	0	0	210	1,125
1988	John Krebs	1	0	0	0	0	0	0	0	92	0	0	241	1,600
1989	John Krebs	1	0	0	0	0	0	0	0	65	0	0	164	3,000
1990	John Krebs	2	0	0	0	0	0	0	0	366	0	0	477	8,435
1991	John Krebs	1	0	0	0	0	0	0	0	57	1	1	144	3,525
Lifetime		13	0	0	0	0	0	0	0	1,028	1	1	2,199	$26,050

Jeff Krogh

Year	Driver	Starts	Poles	1	2	3	4	5	6–10	Laps	Laps Led	Races Led	Miles	$
1996	Jeff Krogh	2	0	0	0	0	0	0	0	222	0	0	330	19,680
Lifetime		2	0	0	0	0	0	0	0	222	0	0	330	$19,680

Carl Krueger

Year	Driver	Starts	Poles	1	2	3	4	5	6–10	Laps	Laps Led	Races Led	Miles	$
1955	Carl Krueger	7	0	0	0	0	0	1	1	955	0	0	534	585
1955	Lloyd Dane	1	0	0	0	0	0	0	0	0	0	0	0	25
1955	Lee Petty	1	0	0	0	0	0	0	0	116	0	0	116	50
1955	Mario Rossi	1	0	0	0	0	0	0	1	223	0	0	223	200
Lifetime		10	0	0	0	0	0	1	2	1,294	0	0	873	$860

Alan Kulwicki

Year	Driver	Starts	Poles	1	2	3	4	5	6–10	Laps	Laps Led	Races Led	Miles	$
1986	Alan Kulwicki	9	0	0	0	0	0	0	1	3,368	7	2	3,445	31,980
1987	Alan Kulwicki	29	3	0	1	0	1	1	6	7,758	102	8	9,121	284,375
1988	Alan Kulwicki	29	4	1	2	1	1	2	2	8,149	134	8	9,325	364,190
1989	Alan Kulwicki	29	6	0	4	0	0	1	4	8,324	564	14	9,560	425,500
1990	Alan Kulwicki	29	1	1	1	1	1	1	8	8,635	400	10	10,757	403,662
1991	Alan Kulwicki	29	4	1	0	1	1	1	7	8,447	233	9	9,998	518,645
1992	Alan Kulwicki	29	6	2	3	2	2	2	6	8,991	1,235	20	10,853	907,510
1993	Jimmy Hensley	15	0	0	0	0	0	0	2	4,321	1	1	5,408	266,970
1993	Alan Kulwicki	5	0	0	0	1	1	0	1	1,588	4	2	1,995	153,470
1993	Tom Kendall	2	0	0	0	0	0	0	0	158	0	0	392	32,190
Lifetime		205	24	5	11	6	7	8	37	59,739	2,680	74	70,854	$3,388,492

A.J. Kurten

Year	Driver	Starts	Poles	1	2	3	4	5	6–10	Laps	Laps Led	Races Led	Miles	$
1979	Jim Robinson	2	0	0	0	0	0	0	0	176	0	0	449	2,250
1980	Jim Robinson	3	0	0	0	0	0	0	0	288	0	0	742	4,300
Lifetime		5	0	0	0	0	0	0	0	464	0	0	1,191	$6,550

Vic Kurten

Year	Driver	Starts	Poles	1	2	3	4	5	6–10	Laps	Laps Led	Races Led	Miles	$
1974	Sonny Easley	2	0	0	0	0	0	0	1	303	0	0	794	3,300
Lifetime		2	0	0	0	0	0	0	1	303	0	0	794	$3,300

Bobby Labonte

Year	Driver	Starts	Poles	1	2	3	4	5	6–10	Laps	Laps Led	Races Led	Miles	$
1991	Bobby Labonte	2	0	0	0	0	0	0	0	128	0	0	168	8,350
Lifetime		2	0	0	0	0	0	0	0	128	0	0	168	$8,350

Terry Labonte

Year	Driver	Starts	Poles	1	2	3	4	5	6–10	Laps	Laps Led	Races Led	Miles	$
1991	Irv Hoerr	3	0	0	0	0	0	0	0	243	0	0	608	11,125
Lifetime		3	0	0	0	0	0	0	0	243	0	0	608	$11,125

Chip Lain

Year	Driver	Starts	Poles	1	2	3	4	5	6–10	Laps	Laps Led	Races Led	Miles	$
1984	Connie Saylor	4	0	0	0	0	0	0	0	595	1	1	948	5,510
Lifetime		4	0	0	0	0	0	0	0	595	1	1	948	$5,510

Year	Driver	Starts	Poles	Finish						Laps	Laps Led	Races Led	Miles	$
				1	2	3	4	5	6–10	Laps				

Bobby Langdon

| 1960 | Shep Langdon | 2 | 0 | 0 | 0 | 0 | 0 | 0 | 0 | 231 | 0 | 0 | 578 | 400 |
| **Lifetime** | | 2 | 0 | 0 | 0 | 0 | 0 | 0 | 0 | 231 | 0 | 0 | 578 | $400 |

Shep Langdon

1958	Shep Langdon	15	0	0	0	0	0	0	1	2,441	0	0	1,306	1,180
1959	L.D. Austin	1	0	0	0	0	0	0	0	180	0	0	90	70
1959	Shep Langdon	21	0	0	0	0	0	0	6	3,976	0	0	2,259	3,045
1960	Shep Langdon	2	0	0	0	0	0	0	1	357	0	0	179	235
Lifetime		39	0	0	0	0	0	0	8	6,954	0	0	3,834	$4,530

Elmo Langley

1954	Elmo Langley	2	0	0	0	0	0	0	0	340	0	0	466	450
1955	Elmo Langley	3	0	0	0	0	0	0	1	344	0	0	283	300
1956	Elmo Langley	1	0	0	0	0	0	0	0	338	0	0	465	140
1957	Elmo Langley	1	0	0	0	0	0	0	0	189	0	0	95	150
1958	Elmo Langley	7	0	0	0	0	0	1	2	1,116	0	0	759	895
1962	Elmo Langley	3	0	0	0	0	0	0	0	505	0	0	673	820
1963	Elmo Langley	7	0	0	0	0	0	1	1	1,193	0	0	433	920
1965	Buddy Baker	2	0	0	0	0	0	0	0	51	0	0	10	200
1965	Buddy Arrington	1	0	0	0	0	0	0	0	237	0	0	356	700
1965	Bert Robbins	2	0	0	0	0	0	0	1	189	0	0	95	200
1965	Daniel Warlick	1	0	0	0	0	0	0	1	381	0	0	143	250
1965	Darel Dieringer	1	0	0	0	0	0	0	1	282	0	0	94	150
1965	Paul Moore	1	0	0	0	0	0	0	0	23	0	0	12	100
1965	Jack Ingram	1	0	0	0	0	0	0	0	4	0	0	2	100
1965	Elmo Langley	32	0	0	0	2	1	0	6	5,512	19	1	3,729	10,695
1966	Elmo Langley	1	0	0	0	0	0	0	0	14	0	0	7	0
1969	Dub Simpson	3	0	0	0	0	0	0	0	81	0	0	75	940
1969	Clyde Lynn	1	0	0	0	0	0	0	0	40	0	0	41	645
1969	Larry Hess	1	0	0	0	0	0	0	0	122	0	0	183	1,325
1969	J.D. McDuffie	1	0	0	0	0	0	0	0	277	0	0	416	1,175
1969	Elmo Langley	49	1	0	0	1	5	6	15	11,670	40	1	9,131	31,342
1970	John Sears	2	0	0	0	0	0	1	0	242	0	0	138	1,085
1970	Elmo Langley	47	0	0	0	1	0	0	18	10,672	0	0	9,319	33,775
1970	Bill Seifert	1	0	0	0	0	0	1	0	1	0	0	1	430
1971	Clyde Lynn	1	0	0	0	0	0	0	0	15	0	0	9	365
1971	Dick May	4	0	0	0	0	0	0	0	176	0	0	114	900
1971	Elmo Langley	39	0	0	3	0	3	2	10	9,345	48	1	9,404	33,510
1972	Dick May	1	0	0	0	0	0	0	1	141	0	0	369	1,525
1972	Elmo Langley	30	0	0	0	0	0	1	8	8,150	0	0	9,460	44,103
1973	Elmo Langley	27	0	0	0	0	0	0	4	8,016	0	0	8,385	39,150
1974	Dick May	1	0	0	0	0	0	0	0	174	0	0	463	1,485
1974	Dave Marcis	1	0	0	0	0	0	0	0	183	0	0	458	1,525
1974	Elmo Langley	21	0	0	0	0	0	0	3	5,369	0	0	5,327	22,105
1974	Tony Bettenhausen,	1	0	0	0	0	0	0	0	144	0	0	360	1,225
1975	Elmo Langley	27	0	0	0	0	0	1	4	7,898	0	0	9,179	49,260
1975	Tommy Gale	1	0	0	0	0	0	0	0	83	0	0	208	2,625
1975	Bill Champion	1	0	0	0	0	0	0	0	1	0	0	1	530
1976	Ed Negre	1	0	0	0	0	0	0	0	238	0	0	125	880
1976	Tommy Gale	11	0	0	0	0	0	0	0	2,135	0	0	3,027	17,975
1976	Skip Manning	1	0	0	0	0	0	0	0	360	0	0	225	750
1976	Dick Brooks	1	0	0	0	0	0	0	0	45	0	0	27	565
1976	Elmo Langley	7	0	0	0	0	0	0	1	2,451	0	0	1,368	7,515
1977	Elmo Langley	4	0	0	0	0	0	0	0	1,093	0	0	583	4,380
1977	Henley Gray	1	0	0	0	0	0	0	0	376	0	0	235	1,480
1977	Dick Brooks	2	0	0	0	0	0	0	0	358	0	0	394	3,745
1977	Dean Dalton	1	0	0	0	0	0	0	0	113	0	0	60	695
1977	Tommy Gale	18	0	0	0	0	0	0	0	4,493	0	0	6,163	39,190
1978	Dick Brooks	3	0	0	0	0	0	0	0	565	0	0	697	5,240
1978	Elmo Langley	1	0	0	0	0	0	0	0	389	0	0	232	1,165
1978	Tommy Gale	25	0	0	0	0	0	0	0	6,727	0	0	8,482	53,600
1979	Elmo Langley	2	0	0	0	0	0	0	0	461	0	0	248	2,410
1979	Tommy Gale	27	0	0	0	0	0	0	1	7,054	0	0	8,092	64,270
1980	Tommy Gale	28	0	0	0	0	0	0	0	7,411	0	0	8,425	73,250
1981	Tommy Gale	26	0	0	0	0	0	0	0	7,728	2	1	8,974	91,549
1982	Tommy Gale	25	0	0	0	0	0	0	0	7,215	1	1	8,081	95,745
1982	Mark Stahl	1	0	0	0	0	0	0	0	24	0	0	63	1,550

Year	Driver	Starts	Poles	Finish 1	2	3	4	5	6–10	Laps	Laps Led	Races Led	Miles	$

Elmo Langley *continued*

Year	Driver	Starts	Poles	1	2	3	4	5	6–10	Laps	Laps Led	Races Led	Miles	$
1983	Tommy Gale	26	0	0	0	0	0	0	1	6,235	0	0	7,533	84,541
1983	D.K. Ulrich	1	0	0	0	0	0	0	0	101	0	0	265	2,325
1984	Tommy Gale	16	0	0	0	0	0	0	0	4,248	0	0	5,268	69,385
1984	Joe Millikan	1	0	0	0	0	0	0	0	459	0	0	467	4,745
1984	Gary Mayeda	1	0	0	0	0	0	0	0	21	0	0	55	2,215
1984	Ken Schrader	5	0	0	0	0	0	0	0	1,508	0	0	1,632	16,425
1984	Jimmy Hensley	4	0	0	0	0	0	0	0	1,484	0	0	793	12,895
1984	Clark Dwyer	2	0	0	0	0	0	0	0	583	0	0	761	7,525
1985	Clark Dwyer	28	0	0	0	0	0	0	0	7,205	0	0	8,558	128,445
1986	Doug Heveron	1	0	0	0	0	0	0	0	391	0	0	212	4,760
1986	Rick Baldwin	2	0	0	0	0	0	0	0	393	0	0	260	6,905
1986	Pancho Carter	3	0	0	0	0	0	0	0	672	0	0	880	22,550
1986	Tommy Gale	1	0	0	0	0	0	0	0	175	0	0	466	5,845
1986	Morgan Shepherd	1	0	0	0	0	0	0	0	22	0	0	12	2,940
1986	Mike Potter	1	0	0	0	0	0	0	0	375	0	0	381	3,990
1986	Jimmy Hensley	3	0	0	0	0	0	0	0	1,194	0	0	634	11,755
1986	Eddie Bierschwale	5	0	0	0	0	0	0	0	710	0	0	1,584	28,730
1986	Connie Saylor	5	0	0	0	0	0	0	0	1,270	0	0	1,979	28,995
1986	Brian Baker	1	0	0	0	0	0	0	0	252	0	0	252	3,985
1986	Rick McCray	1	0	0	0	0	0	0	0	90	0	0	236	4,060
1987	Rodney Combs	10	0	0	0	0	0	0	0	2,088	0	0	3,561	56,435
1987	Rick McCray	1	0	0	0	0	0	0	0	88	0	0	231	3,200
1987	Jerry Cranmer	5	0	0	0	0	0	0	0	1,914	0	0	1,278	20,660
1987	Curtis Markham	2	0	0	0	0	0	0	0	549	0	0	459	7,070
1987	Connie Saylor	4	0	0	0	0	0	0	0	440	0	0	789	26,390
1987	Trevor Boys	4	0	0	0	0	0	0	0	1,101	1	1	961	17,415
Lifetime		645	1	0	3	4	9	13	79	156,322	111	6	165,664	$1,335,235

Langley-Woodfield

Year	Driver	Starts	Poles	1	2	3	4	5	6–10	Laps	Laps Led	Races Led	Miles	$
1966	Elmo Langley	45	1	2	1	0	4	4	8	9,255	308	5	6,537	19,180
1967	Elmo Langley	43	0	0	1	2	2	4	14	9,161	0	0	6,536	19,245
1968	Bill Seifert	3	0	0	0	0	0	0	0	310	0	0	455	1,525
1968	Elmo Langley	44	0	0	0	1	1	3	20	10,315	0	0	6,993	17,820
1969	Elmo Langley	2	0	0	0	0	1	0	0	557	0	0	279	1,025
Lifetime		137	1	2	2	3	8	11	42	29,598	308	5	20,799	$58,795

Jerry Lankford

Year	Driver	Starts	Poles	1	2	3	4	5	6–10	Laps	Laps Led	Races Led	Miles	$
1973	Sonny Easley	2	0	0	0	0	0	0	0	144	0	0	377	2,015
1974	Sonny Easley	1	0	0	0	0	0	0	0	112	0	0	280	1,500
1975	Sonny Easley	3	0	0	0	0	0	0	0	136	2	1	355	2,405
Lifetime		6	0	0	0	0	0	0	0	392	2	1	1,012	$5,920

John Lansaw

Year	Driver	Starts	Poles	1	2	3	4	5	6–10	Laps	Laps Led	Races Led	Miles	$
1956	John Lansaw	2	0	0	0	0	0	0	0	133	0	0	124	35
Lifetime		2	0	0	0	0	0	0	0	133	0	0	124	$35

Russell Large

Year	Driver	Starts	Poles	1	2	3	4	5	6–10	Laps	Laps Led	Races Led	Miles	$
1974	Jimmy Hensley	1	0	0	0	0	0	0	0	179	9	1	94	610
1974	L.D. Ottinger	4	0	0	0	0	0	0	0	290	0	0	395	4,985
Lifetime		5	0	0	0	0	0	0	0	469	9	1	489	$5,595

Curtis Larimer

Year	Driver	Starts	Poles	1	2	3	4	5	6–10	Laps	Laps Led	Races Led	Miles	$
1965	Bill Morton	5	0	0	0	0	0	0	0	601	0	0	832	2,590
1965	Darel Dieringer	1	0	0	0	0	0	0	0	430	0	0	215	450
1965	Neil Castles	1	0	0	0	0	0	0	0	186	0	0	93	260
1965	Paul Lewis	3	0	0	0	0	0	0	1	997	0	0	753	1,500
1966	Don Tilley	1	0	0	0	0	0	0	0	15	0	0	8	0
Lifetime		11	0	0	0	0	0	0	1	2,229	0	0	1,900	$4,800

Mel Larson

Year	Driver	Starts	Poles	1	2	3	4	5	6–10	Laps	Laps Led	Races Led	Miles	$
1955	Mel Larson	2	0	0	0	0	0	0	1	230	0	0	135	150
1956	Mel Larson	6	0	0	0	0	0	0	1	504	0	0	471	385
1957	Mel Larson	10	1	0	0	0	0	1	4	1,244	0	0	680	1,135

Year	Driver	Starts	Poles	Finish 1	2	3	4	5	6–10	Laps	Laps Led	Races Led	Miles	$

Mel Larson *continued*

Year	Driver	Starts	Poles	1	2	3	4	5	6–10	Laps	Laps Led	Races Led	Miles	$
1958	Mel Larson	4	0	0	0	0	0	0	1	546	0	0	412	280
1959	Mel Larson	2	0	0	0	0	0	0	2	529	0	0	258	350
1960	Mel Larson	4	1	0	1	0	0	0	1	465	19	2	835	1,325
1973	Mel Larson	2	0	0	0	0	0	0	0	109	0	0	110	1,555
1975	Mel Larson	1	0	0	0	0	0	0	0	36	0	0	72	665
Lifetime		31	2	0	1	0	0	1	10	3,663	19	2	2,973	$5,845

Stan Lasky

Year	Driver	Starts	Poles	1	2	3	4	5	6–10	Laps	Laps Led	Races Led	Miles	$
1978	Paul Fess	1	0	0	0	0	0	0	0	75	0	0	188	835
1979	Paul Fess	2	0	0	0	0	0	0	0	232	0	0	532	4,860
Lifetime		3	0	0	0	0	0	0	0	307	0	0	719	$5,695

Fred Lauria

Year	Driver	Starts	Poles	1	2	3	4	5	6–10	Laps	Laps Led	Races Led	Miles	$
1958	Bob Price	2	0	0	0	0	0	0	0	146	0	0	382	110
1959	Bob Price	2	0	0	0	0	0	0	0	427	0	0	176	225
1960	Bob Price	3	0	0	0	0	0	0	0	258	0	0	314	445
1961	Bob Price	2	0	0	0	0	0	0	1	204	0	0	150	180
Lifetime		9	0	0	0	0	0	0	1	1,035	0	0	1,022	$960

Tony Lavati

Year	Driver	Starts	Poles	1	2	3	4	5	6–10	Laps	Laps Led	Races Led	Miles	$
1961	David Pearson	2	0	0	0	0	0	0	0	223	0	0	558	275
Lifetime		2	0	0	0	0	0	0	0	223	0	0	558	$275

Coleman Lawrence

Year	Driver	Starts	Poles	1	2	3	4	5	6–10	Laps	Laps Led	Races Led	Miles	$
1951	Coleman Lawrence	6	0	0	0	0	0	0	2	130	0	0	130	250
1952	Coleman Lawrence	8	0	0	0	0	0	0	3	1,326	0	0	1,045	375
1953	Clyde Minter	3	0	0	0	0	0	0	2		0	0		150
1953	Coleman Lawrence	8	0	0	0	0	0	0	1	263	0	0	263	250
1953	Otis Martin	1	0	0	0	0	0	0	0	281	0	0	281	125
Lifetime		26	0	0	0	0	0	0	8	2,000	0	0	1,719	$1,150

Ed Lawrence

Year	Driver	Starts	Poles	1	2	3	4	5	6–10	Laps	Laps Led	Races Led	Miles	$
1949	Fonty Flock	4	0	0	0	1	1	0	0	304	85	1	153	750
1950	Pee Wee Martin	1	0	0	0	0	0	0	0		12	1		50
1950	Fonty Flock	2	0	0	0	0	0	0	1	76	0	0	214	150
Lifetime		7	0	0	0	1	1	0	1	380	97	2	367	$950

Jack Lawrence

Year	Driver	Starts	Poles	1	2	3	4	5	6–10	Laps	Laps Led	Races Led	Miles	$
1953	Jack Lawrence	2	0	0	0	0	0	0	0	101	0	0	51	50
Lifetime		2	0	0	0	0	0	0	0	101	0	0	51	$50

Mike Laws

Year	Driver	Starts	Poles	1	2	3	4	5	6–10	Laps	Laps Led	Races Led	Miles	$
1986	Mike Laws	2	0	0	0	0	0	0	0	422	0	0	698	3,095
Lifetime		2	0	0	0	0	0	0	0	422	0	0	698	$3,095

Harry Leake

Year	Driver	Starts	Poles	1	2	3	4	5	6–10	Laps	Laps Led	Races Led	Miles	$
1961	Harry Leake	15	0	0	0	0	0	0	7	3,295	0	0	1,935	2,000
1961	E.J. Trivette	1	0	0	0	0	0	0	0	56	0	0	84	100
1962	Harry Leake	1	0	0	0	0	0	0	0	98	0	0	49	50
Lifetime		17	0	0	0	0	0	0	7	3,449	0	0	2,068	$2,150

Dawson Lechlider

Year	Driver	Starts	Poles	1	2	3	4	5	6–10	Laps	Laps Led	Races Led	Miles	$
1951	Dawson Lechlider	4	0	0	0	0	0	0	0	49	0	0	49	75
Lifetime		4	0	0	0	0	0	0	0	49	0	0	49	$75

Bill Ledbetter

Year	Driver	Starts	Poles	1	2	3	4	5	6–10	Laps	Laps Led	Races Led	Miles	$
1951	Bill Ledbetter	3	0	0	0	0	0	0	1		0	0		250
Lifetime		3	0	0	0	0	0	0	1		0	0		$250

Year	Driver	Starts	Poles	Finish 1	2	3	4	5	6–10	Laps	Laps Led	Races Led	Miles	$

Bobby Lee

Year	Driver	Starts	Poles	1	2	3	4	5	6–10	Laps	Laps Led	Races Led	Miles	$
1958	Bobby Lee	5	0	0	0	0	0	0	0	532	0	0	568	285
Lifetime		5	0	0	0	0	0	0	0	532	0	0	568	$285

Jack Lee

Year	Driver	Starts	Poles	1	2	3	4	5	6–10	Laps	Laps Led	Races Led	Miles	$
1983	Ron Esau	2	0	0	0	0	0	0	0	70	0	0	183	1,575
1984	Ron Esau	2	0	0	0	0	0	0	0	170	0	0	445	2,660
Lifetime		4	0	0	0	0	0	0	0	240	0	0	629	$4,235

Jim Lee

Year	Driver	Starts	Poles	1	2	3	4	5	6–10	Laps	Laps Led	Races Led	Miles	$
1974	Jim Lee	1	0	0	0	0	0	0	0	21	0	0	55	650
Lifetime		1	0	0	0	0	0	0	0	21	0	0	55	$650

Jimmie Lee

Year	Driver	Starts	Poles	1	2	3	4	5	6–10	Laps	Laps Led	Races Led	Miles	$
1982	Jim Lee	2	0	0	0	0	0	0	0	125	0	0	328	1,760
Lifetime		2	0	0	0	0	0	0	0	125	0	0	328	$1,760

Ted Lee

Year	Driver	Starts	Poles	1	2	3	4	5	6–10	Laps	Laps Led	Races Led	Miles	$
1953	Ted Lee	4	0	0	0	0	0	0	0	294	0	0	387	125
1954	Ted Lee	2	0	0	0	0	0	0	0	492	0	0	328	65
Lifetime		6	0	0	0	0	0	0	0	786	0	0	715	$190

Warren Lee

Year	Driver	Starts	Poles	1	2	3	4	5	6–10	Laps	Laps Led	Races Led	Miles	$
1956	Possum Jones	1	0	0	0	0	0	0	0	336	0	0	462	110
Lifetime		1	0	0	0	0	0	0	0	336	0	0	462	$110

Bob Lehman

Year	Driver	Starts	Poles	1	2	3	4	5	6–10	Laps	Laps Led	Races Led	Miles	$
1977	Don Graham	1	0	0	0	0	0	0	0	118	0	0	295	1,000
Lifetime		1	0	0	0	0	0	0	0	118	0	0	295	$1,000

Bob Leitzinger

Year	Driver	Starts	Poles	1	2	3	4	5	6–10	Laps	Laps Led	Races Led	Miles	$
1994	Butch Leitzinger	1	0	0	0	0	0	0	0	81	0	0	198	6,330
Lifetime		1	0	0	0	0	0	0	0	81	0	0	198	$6,330

Larry LeMay

Year	Driver	Starts	Poles	1	2	3	4	5	6–10	Laps	Laps Led	Races Led	Miles	$
1977	Larry LeMay	1	0	0	0	0	0	0	0	252	0	0	158	360
Lifetime		1	0	0	0	0	0	0	0	252	0	0	158	$360

Bill Leonard

Year	Driver	Starts	Poles	1	2	3	4	5	6–10	Laps	Laps Led	Races Led	Miles	$
1984	Tommie Crozier	1	0	0	0	0	0	0	0	277	0	0	277	990
1985	Tommie Crozier	3	0	0	0	0	0	0	0	516	0	0	560	4,895
1986	Tommie Crozier	2	0	0	0	0	0	0	0	354	0	0	359	2,475
1989	Tommie Crozier	2	0	0	0	0	0	0	0	112	0	0	136	4,600
Lifetime		8	0	0	0	0	0	0	0	1,259	0	0	1,332	$12,960

Damon Leonard

Year	Driver	Starts	Poles	1	2	3	4	5	6–10	Laps	Laps Led	Races Led	Miles	$
1960	Harold Smith	2	0	0	0	0	0	0	0	105	0	0	263	200
Lifetime		2	0	0	0	0	0	0	0	105	0	0	263	$200

Tracy Leslie

Year	Driver	Starts	Poles	1	2	3	4	5	6–10	Laps	Laps Led	Races Led	Miles	$
1990	Tracy Leslie	1	0	0	0	0	0	0	0	195	0	0	293	4,100
Lifetime		1	0	0	0	0	0	0	0	195	0	0	293	$4,100

Bert Letner

Year	Driver	Starts	Poles	1	2	3	4	5	6–10	Laps	Laps Led	Races Led	Miles	$
1951	Danny Letner	5	0	0	0	0	0	0	2	153	0	0	153	225
1951	Fuzzy Anderson	3	0	0	0	0	0	0	0		0	0		75
1954	Bill West	1	0	0	0	0	0	0	1	476	0	0	238	200
Lifetime		9	0	0	0	0	0	0	3	629	0	0	391	$500

Year	Driver	Starts	Poles	1	2	3	4	5	6–10	Laps	Laps Led	Races Led	Miles	$

Danny Letner

Year	Driver	Starts	Poles	1	2	3	4	5	6–10	Laps	Laps Led	Races Led	Miles	$
1954	Bill West	2	0	0	0	0	0	0	0	412	0	0	319	50
1957	Danny Letner	2	0	0	0	0	0	0	1	209	0	0	137	235
Lifetime		4	0	0	0	0	0	0	1	621	0	0	456	$285

Jimmie Lewallen

Year	Driver	Starts	Poles	1	2	3	4	5	6–10	Laps	Laps Led	Races Led	Miles	$
1949	Jimmie Lewallen	1	0	0	0	0	0	0	0		0	0		25
Lifetime		1	0	0	0	0	0	0	0		0	0		$25

Paul Lewis

Year	Driver	Starts	Poles	1	2	3	4	5	6–10	Laps	Laps Led	Races Led	Miles	$
1962	Tiny Lund	1	0	0	0	0	0	0	0	170	0	0	85	110
1963	Paul Lewis	1	0	0	0	0	0	0	0	2	0	0	3	500
1965	Paul Lewis	21	1	0	0	0	1	0	9	4,957	0	0	4,304	10,300
1966	Paul Lewis	20	0	1	1	6	1	0	5	5,952	67	2	4,434	16,120
1966	Buddy Arrington	1	0	0	0	0	0	0	0	463	0	0	463	805
1967	Paul Lewis	1	0	0	1	0	0	0	0	297	0	0	149	1,170
Lifetime		45	1	1	2	6	2	2	14	11,841	67	2	9,438	$29,005

Raymond Lewis

Year	Driver	Starts	Poles	1	2	3	4	5	6–10	Laps	Laps Led	Races Led	Miles	$
1949	Otis Martin	2	0	0	0	0	0	0	0	66	0	0	33	50
1950	Otis Martin	1	0	0	0	0	0	0	1	47	0	0	196	175
Lifetime		3	0	0	0	0	0	0	1	113	0	0	229	$225

Al Liberty

Year	Driver	Starts	Poles	1	2	3	4	5	6–10	Laps	Laps Led	Races Led	Miles	$
1955	Bill Tanner	5	0	0	0	0	0	0	1	423	0	0	425	475
1956	Bill Tanner	2	0	0	0	0	0	0	0	230	0	0	230	75
Lifetime		7	0	0	0	0	0	0	1	653	0	0	655	$550

Al Liggons

Year	Driver	Starts	Poles	1	2	3	4	5	6–10	Laps	Laps Led	Races Led	Miles	$
1955	Clyde Palmer	1	0	0	0	1	0	0	0	98	0	0	98	450
1955	Mickey McGreevey	1	0	0	0	0	0	0	0	232	0	0	232	150
1956	Clyde Palmer	2	0	0	0	0	0	0	1	293	0	0	219	235
1956	Lyle Matlock	2	1	0	0	0	0	0	0	142	0	0	73	50
Lifetime		6	1	0	0	1	0	0	1	765	0	0	622	$885

Ralph Liguori

Year	Driver	Starts	Poles	1	2	3	4	5	6–10	Laps	Laps Led	Races Led	Miles	$
1952	Ralph Liguori	3	0	0	0	0	1	0	0	680	0	0	646	475
1953	Ralph Liguori	5	0	0	0	0	0	2	1	149	0	0	93	455
1954	Dick Kable	1	0	0	0	0	0	0	0	168	0	0	84	0
1954	Ralph Liguori	21	1	0	0	1	0	0	8	3,072	0	0	2,253	2,820
1955	Ralph Liguori	10	0	0	0	0	0	0	5	865	0	0	660	950
1956	Ralph Liguori	12	0	0	0	0	0	0	3	776	0	0	502	860
Lifetime		52	1	0	0	1	1	2	17	5,710	0	0	4,237	$5,560

Betty Lilly

Year	Driver	Starts	Poles	1	2	3	4	5	6–10	Laps	Laps Led	Races Led	Miles	$
1965	Sam McQuagg	10	0	0	0	1	0	1	2	1,728	31	1	2,132	8,985
1966	Tiny Lund	3	0	0	0	0	0	0	1	442	0	0	785	2,470
1966	Darel Dieringer	1	0	0	0	0	0	0	0	0	0	0	0	100
1966	Curtis Turner	1	0	0	0	0	0	0	0	19	0	0	29	645
1966	Bobby Allison	11	0	0	0	2	1	0	2	2,450	0	0	2,658	9,350
1966	Ned Jarrett	1	0	0	0	0	0	0	0	386	0	0	193	905
1967	Bobby Mausgrover	3	0	0	0	0	0	0	0	337	0	0	312	1,600
1967	Jack Harden	9	0	0	0	0	0	0	0	1,382	0	0	1,948	4,450
Lifetime		39	0	0	0	3	1	1	5	6,744	31	1	8,056	$28,505

Butch Lindley

Year	Driver	Starts	Poles	1	2	3	4	5	6–10	Laps	Laps Led	Races Led	Miles	$
1981	Bobby Allison	1	0	0	0	0	0	0	0	276	0	0	150	5,415
1981	Butch Lindley	3	0	0	0	0	0	0	0	559	28	2	323	2,375
Lifetime		4	0	0	0	0	0	0	0	835	28	2	473	$7,790

Year	Driver	Starts	Poles	Finish 1	2	3	4	5	6–10	Laps	Laps Led	Races Led	Miles	$

John Lindsay

Year	Driver	Starts	Poles	1	2	3	4	5	6–10	Laps	Laps Led	Races Led	Miles	$
1954	John Lindsay	1	0	0	0	0	0	0	0	197	0	0	197	50
1955	John Lindsay	6	0	0	0	0	0	0	3	853	0	0	630	575
1956	John Lindsay	5	0	0	0	0	0	0	1	715	0	0	585	425
1958	John Lindsay	3	0	0	0	0	0	0	1	476	0	0	262	310
Lifetime		15	0	0	0	0	0	0	5	2,241	0	0	1,673	$1,360

Mike Link

Year	Driver	Starts	Poles	1	2	3	4	5	6–10	Laps	Laps Led	Races Led	Miles	$
1974	Terry Link	2	0	0	0	0	0	0	0	146	0	0	388	2,185
1975	Terry Link	1	0	0	0	0	0	0	0	6	0	0	16	595
Lifetime		3	0	0	0	0	0	0	0	152	0	0	404	$2,780

Robert Link

Year	Driver	Starts	Poles	1	2	3	4	5	6–10	Laps	Laps Led	Races Led	Miles	$
1968	Bob Link	1	0	0	0	0	0	0	0	14	0	0	38	500
1969	Robert Link	1	0	0	0	0	0	0	0	62	0	0	167	775
Lifetime		2	0	0	0	0	0	0	0	76	0	0	205	$1,275

Jim Linke

Year	Driver	Starts	Poles	1	2	3	4	5	6–10	Laps	Laps Led	Races Led	Miles	$
1958	Tiny Lund	1	0	0	0	0	0	0	0	285	0	0	392	230
Lifetime		1	0	0	0	0	0	0	0	285	0	0	392	$230

Bob Lipseia

Year	Driver	Starts	Poles	1	2	3	4	5	6–10	Laps	Laps Led	Races Led	Miles	$
1990	Hershel McGriff	1	0	0	0	0	0	0	0	2	0	0	5	3,225
1991	Hershel McGriff	2	0	0	0	0	0	0	0	361	0	0	454	7,475
Lifetime		3	0	0	0	0	0	0	0	363	0	0	459	$10,700

Charles Little

Year	Driver	Starts	Poles	1	2	3	4	5	6–10	Laps	Laps Led	Races Led	Miles	$
1975	Randy Tissot	7	0	0	0	0	0	0	0	1,121	0	0	1,657	10,030
Lifetime		7	0	0	0	0	0	0	0	1,121	0	0	1,657	$10,030

Chuck Little

Year	Driver	Starts	Poles	1	2	3	4	5	6–10	Laps	Laps Led	Races Led	Miles	$
1975	Chuck Little	1	0	0	0	0	0	0	0	35	0	0	92	875
1990	Chad Little	17	0	0	0	0	0	0	0	4,531	0	0	6,120	70,690
1991	Chad Little	28	0	0	0	0	0	0	1	7,784	21	3	9,530	174,440
Lifetime		46	0	0	0	0	0	0	1	12,350	21	3	15,742	$246,005

Joe Littlejohn

Year	Driver	Starts	Poles	1	2	3	4	5	6–10	Laps	Laps Led	Races Led	Miles	$
1950	Joe Littlejohn	1	1	0	0	0	0	0	0	7	0	0	29	25
Lifetime		1	1	0	0	0	0	0	0	7	0	0	29	$25

Virgil Livengood

Year	Driver	Starts	Poles	1	2	3	4	5	6–10	Laps	Laps Led	Races Led	Miles	$
1950	Virgil Livengood	1	0	0	0	0	0	0	0	338	0	0	423	0
1953	Virgil Livengood	3	0	0	0	0	0	0	1	7	0	0	4	100
1954	Virgil Livengood	1	0	0	0	0	0	0	0	35	0	0	144	25
Lifetime		5	0	0	0	0	0	0	1	380	0	0	570	$125

Dub Livingston

Year	Driver	Starts	Poles	1	2	3	4	5	6–10	Laps	Laps Led	Races Led	Miles	$
1952	Dub Livingston	1	0	0	0	0	0	0	0	152	0	0	76	25
1953	Dub Livingston	6	0	0	0	0	0	0	1	309	0	0	252	225
Lifetime		7	0	0	0	0	0	0	1	461	0	0	328	$250

Ed Livingston

Year	Driver	Starts	Poles	1	2	3	4	5	6–10	Laps	Laps Led	Races Led	Miles	$
1962	Ed Livingston	11	0	0	0	0	0	0	0	1,438	0	0	1,986	2,765
1963	Tiny Lund	1	0	0	0	0	0	0	0	71	0	0	36	85
1963	Ed Livingston	8	0	0	0	0	0	0	1	965	0	0	462	850
1963	Frank Graham	3	0	0	0	0	0	0	0	99	0	0	245	1,050
1963	Thomas Cox	1	0	0	0	0	0	0	0	2	0	0	3	250
1964	Ed Livingston	3	0	0	0	0	1	0	0	211	0	0	113	875
1964	Mitch Walker	1	0	0	0	0	0	0	0	174	0	0	87	130
Lifetime		28	0	0	0	0	1	0	1	2,960	0	0	2,931	$6,005

Year	Driver	Starts	Poles	Finish						Laps	Laps Led	Races Led	Miles	$
				1	2	3	4	5	6–10					

Bill Lloyd

Year	Driver	Starts	Poles	1	2	3	4	5	6–10	Laps	Laps Led	Races Led	Miles	$
1961	Harvey Hege	1	0	0	0	0	0	0	0	166	0	0	42	100
1961	Joe Jones	1	0	0	0	0	0	0	0	2	0	0	1	50
Lifetime		2	0	0	0	0	0	0	0	168	0	0	43	$150

Larry Lockamy

Year	Driver	Starts	Poles	1	2	3	4	5	6–10	Laps	Laps Led	Races Led	Miles	$
1997	Jeff Purvis	3	0	0	0	0	0	0	0	376	1	1	661	80,526
Lifetime		3	0	0	0	0	0	0	0	376	1	1	661	$80,526

Les Loeser

Year	Driver	Starts	Poles	1	2	3	4	5	6–10	Laps	Laps Led	Races Led	Miles	$
1970	Les Loeser	1	0	0	0	0	0	0	0	38	0	0	100	830
Lifetime		1	0	0	0	0	0	0	0	38	0	0	100	$830

Bondy Long

Year	Driver	Starts	Poles	1	2	3	4	5	6–10	Laps	Laps Led	Races Led	Miles	$
1963	Larry Frank	5	0	0	0	1	0	0	0	1,108	0	0	843	2,050
1963	Bobby Isaac	26	0	0	0	1	0	2	4	4,932	30	1	4,214	7,935
1964	Joe Schlesser	2	0	0	0	0	0	0	1	231	0	0	578	1,350
1964	Ned Jarrett	56	8	14	7	5	7	5	4	12,693	3,071	27	8,139	60,055
1964	James Hylton	3	0	0	0	0	0	0	0	47	0	0	72	350
1964	Marvin Panch	1	0	0	0	0	0	0	0	3	0	0	7	0
1965	Ned Jarrett	53	9	13	12	10	4	2	3	13,326	2,178	28	9,021	77,266
1965	Dick Hutcherson	1	1	0	0	0	0	0	1	143	7	1	72	150
1966	Ned Jarrett	9	0	0	0	2	1	1	2	2,102	140	2	2,443	12,875
1966	Mario Andretti	1	0	0	0	0	0	0	0	154	0	0	416	580
1967	Dick Hutcherson	31	8	2	9	7	2	1	3	8,261	1,375	19	6,962	74,890
1968	Swede Savage	2	0	0	0	1	0	0	0	841	0	0	592	2,635
1968	A.J. Foyt	1	0	0	0	0	0	0	0	64	0	0	160	475
1968	Bobby Allison	8	0	0	0	1	1	0	0	1,479	130	5	2,255	17,435
1968	Paul Moore	7	0	0	1	0	1	0	2	1,492	27	1	1,413	5,360
Lifetime		206	26	29	29	28	16	11	20	46,876	6,958	84	37,185	$263,406

Carl Long

Year	Driver	Starts	Poles	1	2	3	4	5	6–10	Laps	Laps Led	Races Led	Miles	$
2000	Carl Long	2	0	0	0	0	0	0	0	353	0	0	359	67,625
2000	Darrell Waltrip	1	0	0	0	0	0	0	0	386	0	0	579	33,340
2001	Carl Long	3	0	0	0	0	0	0	0	513	0	0	688	117,514
2002	Carl Long	1	0	0	0	0	0	0	0	18	0	0	45	34,875
Lifetime		7	0	0	0	0	0	0	0	1,270	0	253,354	1,671	

Newman Long

Year	Driver	Starts	Poles	1	2	3	4	5	6–10	Laps	Laps Led	Races Led	Miles	$
1968	Paul Dean Holt	1	0	0	0	0	0	0	0	52	0	0	26	100
1968	Bill Ervin	4	0	0	0	0	0	0	0	636	0	0	318	600
1968	Leonard Brock	3	0	0	0	0	0	0	0	17	0	0	8	175
1969	Bill Ervin	1	0	0	0	0	0	0	0	161	0	0	81	100
Lifetime		9	0	0	0	0	0	0	0	866	0	0	433	$975

Sterling Long

Year	Driver	Starts	Poles	1	2	3	4	5	6–10	Laps	Laps Led	Races Led	Miles	$
1949	Sterling Long	2	0	0	0	0	0	0	1		0	0		150
1950	Sterling Long	1	0	0	0	0	0	0	0		0	0		0
Lifetime		3	0	0	0	0	0	0	1		0	0		$150

William Long

Year	Driver	Starts	Poles	1	2	3	4	5	6–10	Laps	Laps Led	Races Led	Miles	$
1956	Lucky Long	1	0	0	0	0	0	0	0	180	0	0	90	50
1957	Lucky Long	1	0	0	0	0	0	0	0	24	0	0	12	0
1958	Lucky Long	1	0	0	0	0	0	0	0	85	0	0	85	50
1960	Dick Smith	1	0	0	0	0	0	0	1	170	0	0	238	550
1961	Dick Smith	3	0	0	0	1	0	0	0	191	0	0	218	475
Lifetime		7	0	0	0	1	0	0	1	650	0	0	643	$1,125

Fred Lorenzen

Year	Driver	Starts	Poles	1	2	3	4	5	6–10	Laps	Laps Led	Races Led	Miles	$
1956	Fred Lorenzen	7	0	0	0	0	0	0	0	778	0	0	420	235
1960	Fred Lorenzen	10	0	0	0	2	0	1	2	2,086	93	1	2,521	8,005
Lifetime		17	0	0	0	2	0	1	2	2,864	93	1	2,940	$8,240

Year	Driver	Starts	Poles	Finish 1	2	3	4	5	6–10	Laps	Laps Led	Races Led	Miles	$

S.J. Lorenzo

Year	Driver	Starts	Poles	1	2	3	4	5	6–10	Laps	Laps Led	Races Led	Miles	$
1952	Clyde Pittinger	1	0	0	0	0	0	0	0	375	0	0	469	90
Lifetime		1	0	0	0	0	0	0	0	375	0	0	469	$90

Russ Lou

Year	Driver	Starts	Poles	1	2	3	4	5	6–10	Laps	Laps Led	Races Led	Miles	$
1951	Shorty York	5	0	0	1	0	0	0	0	363	0	0	454	725
Lifetime		5	0	0	1	0	0	0	0	363	0	0	454	$725

Ken Love

Year	Driver	Starts	Poles	1	2	3	4	5	6–10	Laps	Laps Led	Races Led	Miles	$
1956	Ken Love	2	0	0	0	0	0	0	0	144	0	0	144	150
1958	Ken Love	3	0	0	0	0	0	0	0	125	0	0	156	135
Lifetime		5	0	0	0	0	0	0	0	269	0	0	300	$285

Fred Lovette

Year	Driver	Starts	Poles	1	2	3	4	5	6–10	Laps	Laps Led	Races Led	Miles	$
1961	Brian Naylor	1	0	0	0	0	0	0	0	1	0	0	3	0
1962	Johnny Allen	12	1	1	0	0	3	0	1	2,529	284	3	1,849	5,175
Lifetime		13	1	1	0	0	3	0	1	2,530	284	3	1,852	$5,175

Rex Lovette

Year	Driver	Starts	Poles	1	2	3	4	5	6–10	Laps	Laps Led	Races Led	Miles	$
1961	Junior Johnson	40	9	7	2	2	3	1	6	6,949	2,361	22	5,127	25,380
1961	Fireball Roberts	4	0	0	0	0	0	1	0	620	51	1	372	745
1961	Curtis Turner	1	0	0	0	0	0	0	1	233	3	1	93	130
1961	Bobby Isaac	1	0	0	0	0	0	0	0	2	0	0	3	50
1962	Junior Johnson	11	1	0	0	2	1	1	0	1,630	143	5	1,089	3,960
1962	Fireball Roberts	1	0	0	0	0	0	1	0	163	0	0	82	450
1962	Johnny Allen	1	0	0	0	0	0	0	0	380	4	1	570	590
Lifetime		59	10	7	2	4	4	4	7	9,977	2,562	30	7,336	$31,305

Jim Lowe / Carl Beckham

Year	Driver	Starts	Poles	1	2	3	4	5	6–10	Laps	Laps Led	Races Led	Miles	$
1955	Fred Johnson	2	0	0	0	0	0	0	0	258	0	0	345	460
1955	Gwyn Staley	1	0	0	0	0	0	2	0	3	0	0	5	150
1955	Buck Baker	1	0	0	0	0	0	5	1	93	0	0	93	100
1955	Junior Johnson	33	2	5	0	2	1	3	6	4,297	790	7	2,934	9,280
Lifetime		37	2	5	0	2	1	10	7	4,651	790	7	3,377	$9,990

James Lowery

Year	Driver	Starts	Poles	1	2	3	4	5	6–10	Laps	Laps Led	Races Led	Miles	$
1958	Bill Morton	8	0	0	0	0	0	0	0	1,370	0	0	917	1,045
Lifetime		8	0	0	0	0	0	0	0	1,370	0	0	917	$1,045

Roger Lubinski

Year	Driver	Starts	Poles	1	2	3	4	5	6–10	Laps	Laps Led	Races Led	Miles	$
1971	Frank Warren	1	0	0	0	0	0	0	0	25	0	0	13	625
1971	J.D. McDuffie	1	0	0	0	0	0	0	0	441	0	0	448	1,015
1971	Ron Keselowski	19	0	0	0	0	0	0	6	3,046	0	0	4,255	17,455
1972	Ron Keselowski	22	0	0	0	0	0	1	2	3,398	0	0	4,976	22,175
1973	Ron Keselowski	3	0	0	0	0	0	0	0	369	0	0	736	3,350
1974	Jim Hurtubise	1	0	0	0	0	0	0	0	232	0	0	353	1,600
1974	Ron Keselowski	4	0	0	0	0	0	0	0	456	0	0	797	5,160
Lifetime		51	0	0	0	0	0	1	8	7,967	0	0	11,579	$51,380

Harold Lucas

Year	Driver	Starts	Poles	1	2	3	4	5	6–10	Laps	Laps Led	Races Led	Miles	$
1951	Harold Lucas	1	0	0	0	0	0	0	0		0	0		25
1951	Oda Greene	6	0	0	0	1	0	1	1	173	0	0	173	875
Lifetime		7	0	0	0	1	0	1	1	173	0	0	173	$900

Tom Lucas

Year	Driver	Starts	Poles	1	2	3	4	5	6–10	Laps	Laps Led	Races Led	Miles	$
1952	Mooney Williamson	1	0	0	0	0	0	0	0		0	0		0
Lifetime		1	0	0	0	0	0	0	0		0	0		$0

Tiny Lund

Year	Driver	Starts	Poles	1	2	3	4	5	6–10	Laps	Laps Led	Races Led	Miles	$
1959	Bunk Moore	2	0	0	0	0	0	0	0	522	0	0	261	150

Year	Driver	Starts	Poles	Finish 1	2	3	4	5	6–10	Laps	Laps Led	Races Led	Miles	$

Tiny Lund *continued*

Year	Driver	Starts	Poles	1	2	3	4	5	6–10	Laps	Laps Led	Races Led	Miles	$
1959	Tom Pistone	1	0	0	0	0	0	0	1	192	0	0	48	175
1959	Rex White	1	0	0	0	0	0	0	0	27	0	0	11	50
1959	Tiny Lund	18	0	0	2	0	3	0	3	3,373	0	0	1,771	3,620
1960	Tiny Lund	1	0	0	0	0	0	0	0	54	0	0	27	50
1960	Bunk Moore	1	0	0	0	0	0	0	0	66	0	0	33	0
Lifetime		24	0	0	2	0	3	0	4	4,234	0	0	2,150	$4,045

Milt Lunda

Year	Driver	Starts	Poles	1	2	3	4	5	6–10	Laps	Laps Led	Races Led	Miles	$
1969	Dave Marcis	34	0	0	0	1	2	0	7	6,575	22	3	6,571	27,317
Lifetime		34	0	0	0	1	2	0	7	6,575	22	3	6,571	$27,317

Leon Lundy

Year	Driver	Starts	Poles	1	2	3	4	5	6–10	Laps	Laps Led	Races Led	Miles	$
1954	Leon Lundy	1	0	0	0	0	0	0	0	192	0	0	192	50
1955	Leon Lundy	1	0	0	0	0	0	0	0	193	0	0	193	150
Lifetime		2	0	0	0	0	0	0	0	385	0	0	385	$200

Frank Luptow

Year	Driver	Starts	Poles	1	2	3	4	5	6–10	Laps	Laps Led	Races Led	Miles	$
1950	Frank Luptow	1	0	0	0	0	0	0	0	43	0	0	179	50
Lifetime		1	0	0	0	0	0	0	0	43	0	0	179	$50

Norman Lynch

Year	Driver	Starts	Poles	1	2	3	4	5	6–10	Laps	Laps Led	Races Led	Miles	$
1952	Norman Lynch	1	0	0	0	0	0	0	0	130	0	0	130	25
Lifetime		1	0	0	0	0	0	0	0	130	0	0	130	$25

Sandy Lynch

Year	Driver	Starts	Poles	1	2	3	4	5	6–10	Laps	Laps Led	Races Led	Miles	$
1951	Sandy Lynch	2	0	0	0	0	0	0	0	215	0	0	269	25
Lifetime		2	0	0	0	0	0	0	0	215	0	0	269	$25

Clyde Lynn

Year	Driver	Starts	Poles	1	2	3	4	5	6–10	Laps	Laps Led	Races Led	Miles	$
1965	Clyde Lynn	24	0	0	0	0	0	0	9	4,522	0	0	2,067	4,520
1965	J.T. Putney	1	0	0	0	0	0	0	0	7	0	0	16	175
1966	Clyde Lynn	38	0	0	1	0	0	0	13	8,527	0	0	5,396	10,470
1967	Clyde Lynn	44	0	0	0	0	2	3	17	9,556	0	0	6,551	17,699
1968	Earl Brooks	4	0	0	0	0	0	0	0	854	0	0	683	1,550
1968	Clyde Lynn	48	0	0	0	0	1	1	23	11,778	0	0	8,509	19,175
1969	Clyde Lynn	2	0	0	0	0	0	0	1	648	0	0	345	1,270
1970	Clyde Lynn	1	0	0	0	0	0	0	1	386	0	0	241	625
1971	Clyde Lynn	2	0	0	0	0	0	0	0	493	0	0	261	715
1971	Elmo Langley	3	0	0	0	0	0	1	1	840	0	0	431	1,840
1973	Ed Negre	5	0	0	0	0	0	0	0	1,148	0	0	1,126	4,935
1973	Bobby Poole	1	0	0	0	0	0	0	0	2	0	0	1	250
Lifetime		173	0	0	1	0	3	5	65	38,761	0	0	25,629	$63,224

Johnny Mackison

Year	Driver	Starts	Poles	1	2	3	4	5	6–10	Laps	Laps Led	Races Led	Miles	$
1957	Johnny Mackison	5	0	0	0	0	0	1	1	769	0	0	693	1,330
1958	Frank Thompson	1	0	0	0	0	0	0	0	5	0	0	21	0
1958	Johnny Mackison	3	0	0	0	0	0	0	0	526	0	0	489	290
Lifetime		9	0	0	0	0	0	1	1	1,300	0	0	1,202	$1,620

Dave Mader

Year	Driver	Starts	Poles	1	2	3	4	5	6–10	Laps	Laps Led	Races Led	Miles	$
1961	Dave Mader	4	0	0	0	0	0	0	0	524	0	0	734	805
Lifetime		4	0	0	0	0	0	0	0	524	0	0	734	$805

Jocko Maggiacomo

Year	Driver	Starts	Poles	1	2	3	4	5	6–10	Laps	Laps Led	Races Led	Miles	$
1977	Jocko Maggiacomo	3	0	0	0	0	0	0	0	467	0	0	806	2,080
1978	Jocko Maggiacomo	1	0	0	0	0	0	0	0	45	0	0	113	815
1979	Jocko Maggiacomo	1	0	0	0	0	0	0	0	172	0	0	430	1,105
1980	Jocko Maggiacomo	2	0	0	0	0	0	0	0	280	0	0	283	1,615
1981	Jocko Maggiacomo	1	0	0	0	0	0	0	0	189	0	0	189	540

Year	Driver	Starts	Poles	Finish 1	2	3	4	5	6–10	Laps	Laps Led	Races Led	Miles	$

Jocko Maggiacomo *continued*

Year	Driver	Starts	Poles	1	2	3	4	5	6–10	Laps	Laps Led	Races Led	Miles	$
1982	Jocko Maggiacomo	4	0	0	0	0	0	0	0	411	0	0	546	3,525
Lifetime		12	0	0	0	0	0	0	0	1,564	0	0	2,367	$9,680

Jim Makar

Year	Driver	Starts	Poles	1	2	3	4	5	6–10	Laps	Laps Led	Races Led	Miles	$
1977	Kenny Brightbill	2	0	0	0	0	0	0	0	206	0	0	497	1,950
1977	Morgan Shepherd	3	0	0	0	0	0	0	1	1,114	0	0	1,433	6,915
1977	Jody Ridley	1	0	0	0	0	0	0	0	316	0	0	481	2,080
1978	Morgan Shepherd	2	0	0	0	0	0	0	0	397	0	0	604	8,115
Lifetime		8	0	0	0	0	0	0	1	2,033	0	0	3,015	$19,060

George Mallinger

Year	Driver	Starts	Poles	1	2	3	4	5	6–10	Laps	Laps Led	Races Led	Miles	$
1957	Ed Fiola	2	0	0	0	0	0	0	0	127	0	0	127	75
Lifetime		2	0	0	0	0	0	0	0	127	0	0	127	$75

Nelson Malloch

Year	Driver	Starts	Poles	1	2	3	4	5	6–10	Laps	Laps Led	Races Led	Miles	$
1979	Elmo Langley	1	0	0	0	0	0	0	0	5	0	0	5	600
1979	Dick Brooks	27	0	0	0	1	0	0	7	6,307	16	1	7,423	61,660
1980	Dick Brooks	16	0	0	0	0	0	2	1	3,236	6	1	4,066	51,765
1980	Ricky Rudd	7	0	0	0	0	0	0	1	1,089	0	0	1,897	18,745
1980	Lake Speed	7	0	0	0	0	0	0	2	1,993	0	0	2,301	38,560
1981	Bruce Hill	1	0	0	0	0	0	0	0	54	0	0	135	3,450
Lifetime		59	0	0	0	1	0	2	11	12,684	22	2	15,827	$174,780

Joe Mangini

Year	Driver	Starts	Poles	1	2	3	4	5	6–10	Laps	Laps Led	Races Led	Miles	$
1951	Woody Brown	3	0	0	0	1	0	1	0	14	0	0	7	1,225
1952	Bill Davis	1	0	0	0	0	0	0	1		0	0		75
1954	Joe Valente	4	0	0	0	0	0	0	1	1,066	0	0	650	275
1954	Woody Brown	4	0	0	0	0	0	0	0	991	0	0	613	175
Lifetime		12	0	0	0	1	0	1	2	2,071	0	0	1,270	$1,750

Lou Mangini

Year	Driver	Starts	Poles	1	2	3	4	5	6–10	Laps	Laps Led	Races Led	Miles	$
1951	Bob Caswell	3	0	0	1	0	0	0	0	247	0	0	154	1,300
1954	Bob Caswell	3	0	0	0	0	0	0	1	751	0	0	498	225
1955	Danny Letner	1	0	0	0	0	0	0	0	91	0	0	91	25
1955	Ed Normi	1	0	0	0	0	0	0	0	237	0	0	237	250
Lifetime		8	0	0	1	0	0	0	1	1,326	0	0	980	$1,800

Jesse Mann

Year	Driver	Starts	Poles	1	2	3	4	5	6–10	Laps	Laps Led	Races Led	Miles	$
1953	Roy Bentley	1	0	0	0	0	0	0	0	220	0	0	220	25
Lifetime		1	0	0	0	0	0	0	0	220	0	0	220	$25

Larry Mann

Year	Driver	Starts	Poles	1	2	3	4	5	6–10	Laps	Laps Led	Races Led	Miles	$
1952	Larry Mann	6	0	0	0	0	0	0	0	767	0	0	632	135
Lifetime		6	0	0	0	0	0	0	0	767	0	0	632	$135

Pete Mann

Year	Driver	Starts	Poles	1	2	3	4	5	6–10	Laps	Laps Led	Races Led	Miles	$
1953	Jimmie Lewallen	1	0	0	0	0	0	0	0	340	0	0	468	350
Lifetime		1	0	0	0	0	0	0	0	340	0	0	468	$350

Larry Manning

Year	Driver	Starts	Poles	1	2	3	4	5	6–10	Laps	Laps Led	Races Led	Miles	$
1965	Larry Manning	10	0	0	0	0	0	0	1	1,683	0	0	1,062	2,465
1965	Red Foote	3	0	0	0	0	0	0	0	181	0	0	88	420
1967	Larry Manning	1	0	0	0	0	0	0	0	362	0	0	226	300
Lifetime		14	0	0	0	0	0	0	1	2,226	0	0	1,376	$3,185

Year	Driver	Starts	Poles	Finish						Laps	Laps Led	Races Led	Miles	$
				1	2	3	4	5	6–10					

Johnny Mantz

Year	Driver	Starts	Poles	1	2	3	4	5	6–10	Laps	Laps Led	Races Led	Miles	$
1951	Johnny Mantz	6	0	0	1	1	0	0	2	532	28	1	454	1,875
1951	George Seeger	1	0	0	0	0	0	0	0		0	0		50
1951	Freddie Farmer	1	0	0	0	0	0	0	1		0	0		100
Lifetime		8	0	0	1	1	0	0	3	532	28	1	454	$2,025

Oscar Maples

Year	Driver	Starts	Poles	1	2	3	4	5	6–10	Laps	Laps Led	Races Led	Miles	$
1956	Jim Blomgren	1	0	0	0	0	0	0	0	141	0	0	141	75
1956	George Seeger	1	0	0	0	0	0	0	1	78	0	0	195	350
1957	George Seeger	6	0	0	1	3	1	0	0	764	19	1	520	2,740
1957	Marvin Porter	1	0	0	0	0	0	0	0	221	0	0	304	100
1957	Parnelli Jones	10	1	1	0	0	0	0	2	743	1	1	582	1,625
1958	Lloyd Dane	1	0	0	1	0	0	0	0	190	0	0	500	1,850
Lifetime		20	1	1	2	3	1	0	3	2,137	20	2	2,242	$6,740

Dave Marcis

Year	Driver	Starts	Poles	1	2	3	4	5	6–10	Laps	Laps Led	Races Led	Miles	$
1969	Dave Marcis	2	0	0	0	0	0	0	0	344	0	0	172	550
1970	Dave Marcis	35	0	0	0	3	0	3	6	6,435	14	1	6,425	28,804
1971	Dave Marcis	23	2	0	1	1	4	1	4	5,382	293	7	5,074	24,970
1971	Bill Seifert	1	0	0	0	0	0	0	0	177	0	0	471	1,950
1972	Dave Marcis	18	0	0	0	2	1	2	2	4,689	4	2	5,102	31,280
1972	Roger McCluskey	1	0	0	0	0	0	0	0	241	0	0	362	1,586
1972	Bill Seifert	1	0	0	0	0	0	0	0	3	0	0	6	1,180
1972	Ray Hendrick	1	0	0	0	0	0	0	0	311	0	0	164	625
1972	Ken Rush	1	0	0	0	0	0	0	0	149	0	0	224	1,625
1973	Dave Marcis	19	0	0	0	0	1	0	3	3,959	0	0	4,202	22,770
1974	Dick Trickle	2	0	0	0	0	0	0	2	812	0	0	985	7,003
1974	Dave Marcis	26	0	0	0	0	2	4	11	7,880	1	1	8,737	59,920
1975	Dick May	1	0	0	0	0	0	0	0	184	0	0	460	1,505
1975	Ed Negre	3	0	0	0	0	0	0	0	585	0	0	951	5,120
1975	John Martin	1	0	0	0	0	0	0	0	53	0	0	133	850
1977	Dave Marcis	2	0	0	0	0	0	0	0	755	2	1	400	5,640
1979	Dave Marcis	25	0	0	0	0	0	1	5	6,842	20	4	7,635	49,305
1980	Dave Marcis	31	0	0	0	1	2	1	10	9,012	94	14	9,791	128,025
1981	Dave Marcis	30	1	0	0	2	1	1	5	7,712	177	14	9,082	142,580
1982	Dave Marcis	29	0	1	1	0	0	0	12	8,279	56	10	9,404	168,760
1983	Dave Marcis	30	0	0	0	0	0	0	7	7,771	24	6	9,171	284,405
1984	Lennie Pond	7	0	0	0	0	0	0	2	2,609	0	0	2,237	31,610
1984	Mike Alexander	19	0	0	0	0	0	0	1	4,656	0	0	5,694	94,820
1985	Dave Marcis	28	0	0	0	0	0	0	5	7,319	30	4	8,737	151,670
1986	Dave Marcis	29	0	0	0	0	0	1	3	7,316	63	11	8,522	181,450
1987	Dave Marcis	29	0	0	0	2	0	0	5	6,880	84	9	8,751	229,340
1988	Dave Marcis	29	0	0	0	0	0	0	2	8,278	62	7	9,618	177,385
1989	Dave Marcis	27	0	0	0	0	0	0	1	7,866	16	5	9,986	195,161
1990	Dave Marcis	29	0	0	0	0	0	0	0	8,940	8	4	10,732	232,724
1991	Dave Marcis	27	0	0	0	0	0	0	1	7,211	3	3	9,024	212,010
1992	Dave Marcis	22	0	0	0	0	0	0	0	4,662	0	0	6,781	172,235
1992	Jim Sauter	7	0	0	0	0	0	0	0	2,604	0	0	2,082	43,265
1993	Terry Fisher	1	0	0	0	0	0	0	0	132	0	0	132	6,040
1993	Dave Marcis	23	0	0	0	0	0	0	0	6,233	14	3	7,819	200,305
1994	Dave Marcis	23	0	0	0	0	0	0	1	5,914	17	4	7,762	259,850
1995	Dave Marcis	28	0	0	0	0	0	0	0	7,318	3	2	9,225	337,863
1996	Dave Marcis	27	0	0	0	0	0	0	0	7,202	20	8	8,699	422,677
1997	Dave Marcis	19	0	0	0	0	0	0	0	5,246	0	0	6,703	416,875
1998	Dave Marcis	13	0	0	0	0	0	0	0	3,378	13	3	4,688	420,550
1999	Dave Marcis	20	0	0	0	0	0	0	0	5,354	9	4	7,362	704,524
2000	Dave Marcis	11	0	0	0	0	0	0	0	3,172	14	2	4,059	346,395
2000	Kerry Earnhardt	1	0	0	0	0	0	0	0	5	0	0	10	21,830
2001	Dick Trickle	1	0	0	0	0	0	0	0	389	0	0	396	33,850
2001	Dave Marcis	3	0	0	0	0	0	0	0	837	0	0	1,149	118,700
2002	Dick Trickle	3	0	0	0	0	0	0	0	587	0	0	572	136,830
2002	Tim Sauter	2	0	0	0	0	0	0	0	607	0	0	553	85,060
2002	Dave Marcis	1	0	0	0	0	0	0	0	79	0	0	198	112,575
2002	Andy Hillenburg	1	0	0	0	0	0	0	0	12	0	0	16	34,598
2002	Jay Sauter	3	0	0	0	0	0	0	0	368	0	0	597	130,087
Lifetime		715	3	1	2	11	11	15	88	186,749	1,041	129	221,049	$6,478,732

Year	Driver	Starts	Poles	Finish 1	2	3	4	5	6–10	Laps	Laps Led	Races Led	Miles	$

John Marcum

Year	Driver	Starts	Poles	1	2	3	4	5	6–10	Laps	Laps Led	Races Led	Miles	$
1951	Mike Klapak	1	0	0	0	0	0	0	1		0	0		100
1951	Dick Linder	1	0	0	0	0	0	0	0		0	0		50
Lifetime		2	0	0	0	0	0	0	1		0	0		$150

Wally Marks

Year	Driver	Starts	Poles	1	2	3	4	5	6–10	Laps	Laps Led	Races Led	Miles	$
1949	Wally Campbell	1	0	0	0	0	0	0	0	166	0	0	166	25
1950	Wally Campbell	2	1	0	0	0	0	0	0	309	0	0	386	175
1951	Red Byron	1	0	0	0	0	0	0	0		0	0		50
1951	Wally Campbell	5	0	0	0	0	0	0	0	21	0	0	11	75
1951	Jack Smith	1	0	0	0	0	0	0	0	323	0	0	404	50
Lifetime		10	1	0	0	0	0	0	0	819	0	0	967	$375

Coo Coo Marlin

Year	Driver	Starts	Poles	1	2	3	4	5	6–10	Laps	Laps Led	Races Led	Miles	$
1981	Sterling Marlin	1	0	0	0	0	0	0	0	193	0	0	290	1,225
Lifetime		1	0	0	0	0	0	0	0	193	0	0	290	$1,225

Gene Marquardt

Year	Driver	Starts	Poles	1	2	3	4	5	6–10	Laps	Laps Led	Races Led	Miles	$
1975	Dick Bown	1	0	0	0	0	0	0	0	17	0	0	45	775
Lifetime		1	0	0	0	0	0	0	0	17	0	0	45	$775

Terry Marra

Year	Driver	Starts	Poles	1	2	3	4	5	6–10	Laps	Laps Led	Races Led	Miles	$
1983	Bob Senneker	5	0	0	0	0	0	0	0	1,317	0	0	2,186	11,335
Lifetime		5	0	0	0	0	0	0	0	1,317	0	0	2,186	$11,335

Ken Marriott

Year	Driver	Starts	Poles	1	2	3	4	5	6–10	Laps	Laps Led	Races Led	Miles	$
1959	Ken Marriott	1	0	0	0	0	0	0	0	1	0	0	3	100
Lifetime		1	0	0	0	0	0	0	0	1	0	0	3	$100

Sam Marshall

Year	Driver	Starts	Poles	1	2	3	4	5	6–10	Laps	Laps Led	Races Led	Miles	$
1949	Sam Marshall	1	0	0	0	0	0	0	0		0	0		0
Lifetime		1	0	0	0	0	0	0	0		0	0		$0

Joe Marsik

Year	Driver	Starts	Poles	1	2	3	4	5	6–10	Laps	Laps Led	Races Led	Miles	$
1974	Chuck Wahl	2	0	0	0	0	0	0	1	275	0	0	702	2,870
1975	Chuck Wahl	2	0	0	0	0	0	0	1	270	0	0	707	3,420
Lifetime		4	0	0	0	0	0	0	2	545	0	0	1,410	$6,290

Mark Martin

Year	Driver	Starts	Poles	1	2	3	4	5	6–10	Laps	Laps Led	Races Led	Miles	$
1981	Morgan Shepherd	1	0	0	0	0	0	0	0	20	0	0	40	1,120
1981	Mark Martin	5	2	0	0	1	0	0	1	1,478	76	2	829	13,950
1982	Mark Martin	30	0	0	0	0	0	2	6	7,449	4	3	8,321	115,600
2002	Matt Kenseth	5	0	1	0	0	0	0	2	1,675	55	1	1,692	468,770
Lifetime		41	2	1	0	1	0	2	9	10,622	135	6	10,883	$599,440

Otis Martin

Year	Driver	Starts	Poles	1	2	3	4	5	6–10	Laps	Laps Led	Races Led	Miles	$
1952	Otis Martin	4	0	0	0	0	0	0	1	483	0	0	474	225
1953	Otis Martin	7	0	0	0	0	0	0	2	238	0	0	327	485
1953	Clyde Minter	1	0	0	0	0	0	0	0	81	0	0	81	25
1954	Otis Martin	3	0	0	0	0	0	0	0	414	0	0	637	225
Lifetime		15	0	0	0	0	0	0	3	1,216	0	0	1,520	$960

Walter Martinson

Year	Driver	Starts	Poles	1	2	3	4	5	6–10	Laps	Laps Led	Races Led	Miles	$
1952	Bud Koehler	1	0	0	0	0	0	0	0	140	0	0	140	25
Lifetime		1	0	0	0	0	0	0	0	140	0	0	140	$25

Filbert Martocci

Year	Driver	Starts	Poles	1	2	3	4	5	6–10	Laps	Laps Led	Races Led	Miles	$
1993	Jeff Burton	1	0	0	0	0	0	0	0	86	0	0	91	9,550

Year	Driver	Starts	Poles	Finish 1	2	3	4	5	6–10	Laps	Laps Led	Races Led	Miles	$

Filbert Martocci *continued*

1994	Kenny Wallace	1	0	0	0	0	0	0	0	198	0	0	396	9,825
1995	Kenny Wallace	11	0	0	0	0	0	0	0	3,127	0	0	4,071	154,350
1996	Kenny Wallace	30	0	0	0	0	0	0	2	8,415	7	2	9,897	451,565
1997	Kenny Wallace	31	2	0	0	0	0	0	2	8,333	0	0	10,868	915,962
1998	Kenny Wallace	31	0	0	0	0	0	0	7	7,076	59	4	9,349	918,940
Lifetime		105	2	0	0	0	0	0	11	27,235	66	6	34,672	$2,460,192

Hammer Mason

| 1972 | Dave Marcis | 1 | 0 | 0 | 0 | 0 | 0 | 0 | 0 | 90 | 0 | 0 | 180 | 735 |
| **Lifetime** | | 1 | 0 | 0 | 0 | 0 | 0 | 0 | 0 | 90 | 0 | 0 | 180 | $735 |

John Masoni

1960	Junior Johnson	28	1	3	2	4	1	0	4	4,636	320	7	3,568	30,195
1961	Marvin Panch	2	1	0	0	0	0	0	2	546	116	1	792	4,085
1961	Junior Johnson	1	1	0	1	0	0	0	0	67	12	1	101	525
1961	Jim Paschal	2	0	0	1	0	0	0	0	69	6	1	173	800
1961	David Pearson	7	1	3	0	1	0	0	0	1,548	247	5	2,179	47,790
Lifetime		40	4	6	4	5	1	3	6	6,866	701	15	6,811	$83,395

Gary Mathews

1974	Gary Mathews	1	0	0	0	0	0	0	0	37	0	0	97	725
1975	Gary Mathews	2	0	0	0	0	0	0	1	298	0	0	781	3,795
Lifetime		3	0	0	0	0	0	0	1	335	0	0	878	$4,520

Jim Mattei (Statistics represent teams owned solely by Jim Mattei, plus partnership with John Porter.)

1998	Geoffrey Bodine	32	0	0	0	0	0	1	4	8,745	33	4	11,016	1,200,055
1999	Michael Waltrip	34	0	0	0	0	0	1	2	9,022	48	6	11,896	1,679,660
2000	Michael Waltrip	13	0	0	0	1	0	0	0	4,009	3	3	4,925	680,290
Lifetime		79	0	0	0	1	0	2	6	21,776	84	13	27,837	$3,560,005

Banjo Matthews

1957	Banjo Matthews	4	0	0	0	1	0	0	0	713	56	1	404	755
1959	Banjo Matthews	3	0	0	0	0	0	0	0	517	55	1	414	1,990
1960	Speedy Thompson	2	0	0	0	0	0	0	1	67	0	0	168	350
1960	Banjo Matthews	12	0	0	0	0	0	0	4	1,894	9	1	2,815	6,740
1961	Banjo Matthews	13	0	0	0	0	1	0	2	1,817	262	6	2,884	5,510
1962	Banjo Matthews	5	2	0	1	0	0	0	1	532	145	3	1,098	11,375
1962	Fireball Roberts	7	2	1	1	0	2	0	1	2,022	450	6	1,875	18,475
1963	Fireball Roberts	5	2	0	1	0	1	0	1	826	30	3	1,575	12,240
1964	A.J. Foyt	4	0	0	0	0	1	0	0	564	2	1	1,194	2,550
1964	Junior Johnson	17	4	2	1	4	0	0	1	4,006	1,098	12	2,323	16,460
1965	A.J. Foyt	1	0	0	0	0	0	0	1	265	119	1	398	1,930
1965	Cale Yarborough	8	0	0	2	0	0	0	0	1,800	142	5	1,798	12,385
1966	A.J. Foyt	1	0	0	0	0	0	0	0	12	0	0	18	580
1966	Cale Yarborough	6	0	0	2	0	0	0	2	1,348	210	2	1,954	23,025
1967	Bosco Lowe	2	0	0	0	0	0	0	0	333	0	0	143	340
1967	A.J. Foyt	7	0	0	1	0	1	0	0	1,060	57	5	1,534	8,035
1968	Bosco Lowe	1	0	0	0	0	0	0	0	220	0	0	117	225
1968	Donnie Allison	12	1	1	1	3	0	0	3	3,781	284	6	3,987	49,815
1968	A.J. Foyt	2	0	0	0	0	0	0	0	183	0	0	458	2,900
1969	Pete Hamilton	1	0	0	0	0	0	1	0	329	0	0	494	3,225
1969	Swede Savage	1	0	0	0	0	0	0	1	485	0	0	243	875
1969	Donnie Allison	16	2	1	2	4	1	2	1	3,893	400	10	5,106	78,055
1970	Donnie Allison	18	0	3	0	1	3	2	2	4,853	692	9	5,424	94,106
1970	Cale Yarborough	1	0	0	0	0	0	0	0	250	0	0	342	1,200
1970	LeeRoy Yarbrough	1	1	0	0	0	0	0	0	102	70	1	54	700
1971	Donnie Allison	2	0	0	0	0	0	0	1	220	11	2	550	1,750
1971	A.J. Foyt	2	0	0	0	0	0	0	0	323	0	0	417	1,569
1972	Bobby Isaac	2	0	0	0	0	0	0	0	291	12	2	404	1,839
1974	Bobby Isaac	2	0	0	1	0	0	0	1	697	2	1	761	10,855
Lifetime		158	14	8	13	13	10	5	24	33,403	4,106	78	38,950	$369,854

Year	Driver	Starts	Poles	Finish						Laps	Laps Led	Races Led	Miles	$
				1	2	3	4	5	6–10	Laps	Led	Led	Miles	$

Billy Matthews

Year	Driver	Starts	Poles	1	2	3	4	5	6–10	Laps	Laps Led	Races Led	Miles	$
1980	Dick Brooks	3	0	0	0	0	0	0	2	742	0	0	1,040	8,935
1981	Dick Brooks	3	0	0	0	0	0	0	0	695	1	1	1,188	11,670
1982	Sterling Marlin	1	0	0	0	0	0	0	0	256	0	0	384	3,615
1982	Joe Millikan	1	0	0	0	0	0	0	0	277	0	0	282	1,020
1983	Ronnie Thomas	1	0	0	0	0	0	0	0	356	0	0	193	1,015
1983	Lennie Pond	2	0	0	0	0	0	0	1	501	0	0	518	3,985
1984	Dick Trickle	1	0	0	0	0	0	0	0	53	0	0	133	7,500
1985	Dick Trickle	2	0	0	0	0	0	0	0	253	0	0	380	2,800
1986	Dick Trickle	2	0	0	0	0	0	0	0	676	0	0	975	19,175
Lifetime		16	0	0	0	0	0	0	3	3,809	1	1	5,092	$59,715

Van Matthews

Year	Driver	Starts	Poles	1	2	3	4	5	6–10	Laps	Laps Led	Races Led	Miles	$
1955	Boyce Hildreth	1	0	0	0	0	0	0	0	41	0	0	21	50
Lifetime		1	0	0	0	0	0	0	0	41	0	0	21	$50

Nace Mattingly

Year	Driver	Starts	Poles	1	2	3	4	5	6–10	Laps	Laps Led	Races Led	Miles	$
1955	Nace Mattingly	3	0	0	0	0	0	1	0	696	0	0	653	700
1956	Lou Spears	1	0	0	0	0	0	0	0	83	0	0	52	0
1956	Nace Mattingly	3	0	0	0	0	0	1	0	311	0	0	219	410
1957	Nace Mattingly	4	0	0	0	0	0	0	0	658	0	0	614	400
1958	Nace Mattingly	4	0	0	0	0	0	0	1	325	0	0	145	285
1958	Thomas Aiken	1	0	0	0	0	0	0	0	93	0	0	93	110
1960	Nace Mattingly	2	0	0	0	0	0	0	1	361	0	0	181	285
Lifetime		18	0	0	0	0	0	2	2	2,527	0	0	1,957	$2,190

Bobby Mausgrover

Year	Driver	Starts	Poles	1	2	3	4	5	6–10	Laps	Laps Led	Races Led	Miles	$
1972	Bobby Mausgrover	4	0	0	0	0	0	0	0	321	0	0	665	3,555
1973	Bobby Mausgrover	2	0	0	0	0	0	0	0	611	0	0	888	2,035
Lifetime		6	0	0	0	0	0	0	0	932	0	0	1,553	$5,590

Joe May

Year	Driver	Starts	Poles	1	2	3	4	5	6–10	Laps	Laps Led	Races Led	Miles	$
1980	Bob Riley	1	0	0	0	0	0	0	0	55	0	0	55	460
1981	Bob Riley	2	0	0	0	0	0	0	0	133	0	0	259	1,425
Lifetime		3	0	0	0	0	0	0	0	188	0	0	314	$1,885

Carl Mays

Year	Driver	Starts	Poles	1	2	3	4	5	6–10	Laps	Laps Led	Races Led	Miles	$
1952	June Cleveland	4	0	0	0	0	1	0	1	450	0	0	261	510
Lifetime		4	0	0	0	0	1	0	1	450	0	0	261	$510

Harold Mays

Year	Driver	Starts	Poles	1	2	3	4	5	6–10	Laps	Laps Led	Races Led	Miles	$
1950	Weldon Adams	2	0	0	0	1	0	0	0	367	0	0	459	725
1951	Wade Fields	2	0	0	0	0	0	0	0		0	0		50
1951	Weldon Adams	8	0	0	0	0	0	0	2	142	0	0	107	375
1952	Jack Smith	2	0	0	0	0	0	0	1		0	0		100
1952	Lucky Mays	2	0	0	0	0	0	0	0	1	0	0	1	60
1966	Joel Davis	11	0	0	0	0	1	0	2	1,750	0	0	1,109	2,685
1967	Eldon Yarbrough	1	0	0	0	0	0	0	0	46	0	0	69	580
1967	Blackie Watt	1	0	0	0	0	0	0	0	283	0	0	425	845
1967	Johnny Allen	2	0	0	0	0	0	0	0	137	0	0	170	1,565
Lifetime		31	0	0	0	1	1	0	5	2,726	0	0	2,339	$6,985

Lloyd McBee

Year	Driver	Starts	Poles	1	2	3	4	5	6–10	Laps	Laps Led	Races Led	Miles	$
1977	Paul Dean Holt	1	0	0	0	0	0	0	0	49	0	0	29	275
Lifetime		1	0	0	0	0	0	0	0	49	0	0	29	$275

Wesley McBell

Year	Driver	Starts	Poles	1	2	3	4	5	6–10	Laps	Laps Led	Races Led	Miles	$
1951	Ben Dixon	1	0	0	0	0	0	0	0		0	0		0
Lifetime		1	0	0	0	0	0	0	0		0	0		$0

							Finish					Laps	Races		
Year	Driver	Starts	Poles	1	2	3	4	5	6–10	Laps	Led	Led	Miles	$

Hub McBride

1950	Hub McBride	1	0	0	0	0	0	0	0	341	0	0	426	0
Lifetime		1	0	0	0	0	0	0	0	341	0	0	426	$0

Jimmy McCain

1971	Jim Hurtubise	3	0	0	0	0	0	0	1	290	0	0	682	4,100
1971	Pedro Rodriguez	1	0	0	0	0	0	0	0	18	0	0	45	1,175
1971	Bill Ward	2	0	0	0	0	0	0	0	281	0	0	747	2,865
Lifetime		6	0	0	0	0	0	0	1	589	0	0	1,474	$8,140

Buz McCall

1997	David Green	26	0	0	0	0	0	0	0	7,282	1	1	9,404	474,044
1997	Todd Bodine	1	0	0	0	0	0	0	0	5	0	0	7	12,270
1998	David Green	11	0	0	0	0	0	0	0	2,636	0	0	3,575	318,750
1998	Kevin Lepage	1	0	0	0	0	0	0	0	390	0	0	293	20,385
1998	Mike Bliss	2	0	0	0	0	0	0	0	743	0	0	510	32,520
1998	Ron Fellows	2	0	0	0	0	0	0	0	355	0	0	472	46,310
1998	Steve Grissom	3	0	0	0	0	0	0	0	573	0	0	1,186	67,595
1998	Ted Musgrave	1	0	0	0	0	0	0	0	397	0	0	298	20,405
1998	Robby Gordon	1	0	0	0	0	0	0	0	102	1	1	199	24,765
1998	Hut Stricklin	5	0	0	0	0	0	0	0	774	0	0	1,359	114,275
Lifetime		53	0	0	0	0	0	0	0	13,257	2	2	17,302	$1,131,319

Buzz McCann

1961	Buzz McCann	1	0	0	0	0	0	0	0	1	0	0	3	0
Lifetime		1	0	0	0	0	0	0	0	1	0	0	3	$0

John McCarthy

1966	Johnny Wynn	20	0	0	0	0	0	0	5	2,781	0	0	2,259	4,225
1971	Charlie Glotzbach	4	0	0	0	0	0	0	3	796	0	0	728	3,780
Lifetime		24	0	0	0	0	0	0	8	3,577	0	0	2,987	$8,005

Alfred McClure

1960	Don Noel	3	0	0	0	0	0	1	0	240	0	0	309	900
1977	Dick May	4	0	0	0	0	0	0	0	1,329	0	0	1,917	7,790
1978	Dick May	5	0	0	0	0	0	0	1	1,201	0	0	2,174	18,055
1979	Dick May	2	0	0	0	0	0	0	0	425	0	0	741	4,185
1979	Ron Hutcherson	1	0	0	0	0	0	0	0	0	0	0	0	1,165
1980	Janet Guthrie	1	0	0	0	0	0	0	0	134	0	0	335	1,140
Lifetime		16	0	0	0	0	0	1	1	3,329	0	0	5,475	$33,235

Jeff McClure

1992	Jeff McClure	1	0	0	0	0	0	0	0	173	0	0	346	5,990
Lifetime		1	0	0	0	0	0	0	0	173	0	0	346	$5,990

Larry McClure

1983	Connie Saylor	1	0	0	0	0	0	0	0	22	0	0	59	1,985
1983	Mark Martin	6	0	0	0	0	0	0	1	1,313	0	0	2,466	17,040
1984	Lennie Pond	4	0	0	0	0	0	0	0	972	0	0	1,101	21,590
1984	Joe Ruttman	3	0	0	0	0	0	0	1	394	1	1	645	5,525
1984	Tommy Ellis	20	0	0	0	0	0	0	1	5,010	1	1	5,356	44,315
1985	Joe Ruttman	16	0	0	0	0	0	1	3	3,378	5	1	4,599	71,425
1986	Rick Wilson	17	0	0	0	0	0	0	4	3,265	7	1	5,310	87,820
1986	Lake Speed	1	0	0	0	0	0	0	0	397	6	1	596	6,400
1987	Rick Wilson	19	0	0	0	0	0	0	1	3,530	20	1	5,577	64,185
1987	A.J. Foyt	1	0	0	0	0	0	0	0	10	0	0	25	7,870
1988	Rick Wilson	28	1	0	1	0	1	0	3	6,870	145	3	8,713	200,925
1989	Rick Wilson	29	0	0	0	0	1	1	5	8,004	29	5	9,992	265,605
1990	Ernie Irvan	26	3	1	2	1	1	1	7	8,008	280	10	9,313	407,419
1990	Phil Parsons	3	0	0	0	0	0	0	0	881	0	0	862	39,350
1991	Ernie Irvan	29	1	2	3	0	4	2	8	8,770	584	16	10,494	811,950
1992	Ernie Irvan	29	3	3	2	1	2	1	2	8,561	477	17	10,280	849,670
1993	Jimmy Hensley	2	0	0	0	0	0	0	0	550	0	0	711	31,895

Year	Driver	Starts	Poles	Finish 1	2	3	4	5	6–10	Laps	Laps Led	Races Led	Miles	$

Larry McClure *continued*

Year	Driver	Starts	Poles	1	2	3	4	5	6–10	Laps	Laps Led	Races Led	Miles	$
1993	Joe Nemechek	2	0	0	0	0	0	0	0	811	0	0	982	32,280
1993	Jeff Purvis	5	0	0	0	0	0	0	0	2,113	3	2	1,762	81,370
1993	Ernie Irvan	21	2	1	3	2	0	1	1	5,058	226	12	6,911	627,545
1994	Sterling Marlin	31	1	1	1	1	0	2	6	9,184	144	11	10,842	928,110
1995	Sterling Marlin	31	1	3	2	0	3	1	13	9,729	475	12	11,939	1,712,155
1996	Sterling Marlin	31	0	2	0	1	1	1	5	8,877	331	10	10,583	1,210,452
1997	Sterling Marlin	32	0	0	0	1	0	1	4	8,584	71	7	10,836	1,251,482
1998	Bobby Hamilton	33	1	1	1	0	1	0	5	9,840	443	6	12,759	1,767,780
1999	Bobby Hamilton	34	0	0	0	0	1	0	9	9,774	3	2	12,914	1,799,954
2000	Bobby Hamilton	34	0	0	0	0	0	0	2	8,903	64	4	11,304	1,584,711
2001	Kevin Lepage	21	0	0	0	0	0	0	0	5,950	10	1	7,369	939,154
2001	Rich Bickle	1	0	0	0	0	0	0	0	494	0	0	259	30,300
2001	Bobby Hamilton Jr.	7	0	0	0	0	0	0	0	2,044	0	0	2,838	305,705
2001	Robby Gordon	5	0	0	0	0	0	0	0	1,426	0	0	2,098	287,545
2002	Mike Skinner	36	0	0	0	0	0	0	1	10,074	2	2	13,136	2,015,720
Lifetime		558	13	14	15	7	15	12	82	152,796	3,327	126	192,629	$17,509,232

John McConnell

Year	Driver	Starts	Poles	1	2	3	4	5	6–10	Laps	Laps Led	Races Led	Miles	$
1970	Tiny Lund	5	0	0	0	0	2	0	0	819	7	2	1,540	11,365
1971	Tiny Lund	5	0	0	1	0	0	0	2	918	8	2	1,199	6,310
Lifetime		10	0	0	1	0	2	0	2	1,737	15	4	2,738	$17,675

Johnny McCoy

Year	Driver	Starts	Poles	1	2	3	4	5	6–10	Laps	Laps Led	Races Led	Miles	$
1956	Ray Thompson	1	0	0	0	0	0	0	0		0	0		50
Lifetime		1	0	0	0	0	0	0	0		0	0		$50

Rick McCray

Year	Driver	Starts	Poles	1	2	3	4	5	6–10	Laps	Laps Led	Races Led	Miles	$
1978	Rick McCray	3	0	0	0	0	0	0	0	220	0	0	575	4,585
1979	Rick McCray	1	0	0	0	0	0	0	0	31	0	0	81	750
1980	Rick McCray	3	0	0	0	0	0	0	0	238	0	0	601	3,415
1981	Rick McCray	1	0	0	0	0	0	0	0	66	0	0	173	1,655
1982	Rick McCray	2	0	0	0	0	0	0	0	151	0	0	396	3,355
1983	Rick McCray	4	0	0	0	0	0	0	0	760	0	0	629	3,710
1984	Rick McCray	2	0	0	0	0	0	0	0	102	0	0	267	2,170
1985	Rick McCray	2	0	0	0	0	0	0	0	47	0	0	123	1,665
1986	Rick McCray	1	0	0	0	0	0	0	0	33	0	0	86	850
1987	Rick McCray	2	0	0	0	0	0	0	0	189	0	0	357	7,475
1988	Rick McCray	1	0	0	0	0	0	0	0	46	0	0	121	1,140
1989	Rick McCray	1	0	0	0	0	0	0	0	72	0	0	181	3,200
Lifetime		23	0	0	0	0	0	0	0	1,955	0	0	3,590	$33,970

Dave McCready

Year	Driver	Starts	Poles	1	2	3	4	5	6–10	Laps	Laps Led	Races Led	Miles	$
1962	Bill Wimble	2	0	0	0	0	0	0	0	231	0	0	578	675
Lifetime		2	0	0	0	0	0	0	0	231	0	0	578	$675

Sam McCuthen

Year	Driver	Starts	Poles	1	2	3	4	5	6–10	Laps	Laps Led	Races Led	Miles	$
1955	Bill Widenhouse	5	0	0	0	0	0	1	2	799	2	1	780	1,065
1956	Pee Wee Jones	1	0	0	0	0	0	0	0	70	0	0	35	0
1956	Jimmie Lewallen	1	0	0	0	0	0	0	0	93	0	0	58	0
1956	Ray Hendrick	1	0	0	0	0	0	0	0	14	0	0	7	50
1956	Jim Donovan	2	0	0	0	0	0	0	0	247	0	0	152	200
1956	Doug Yates	1	0	0	0	0	0	0	0	32	0	0	16	100
Lifetime		11	0	0	0	0	0	1	2	1,255	2	1	1,049	$1,415

J.L. McDonald

Year	Driver	Starts	Poles	1	2	3	4	5	6–10	Laps	Laps Led	Races Led	Miles	$
1950	Alton Haddock	1	0	0	0	0	0	0	0	41	0	0	171	25
Lifetime		1	0	0	0	0	0	0	0	41	0	0	171	$25

Roy McDonald

Year	Driver	Starts	Poles	1	2	3	4	5	6–10	Laps	Laps Led	Races Led	Miles	$
1960	Burrhead Nantz	3	0	0	0	0	0	0	0	66	0	0	133	300
1960	Roy Tyner	4	0	0	0	0	0	0	0	389	0	0	416	475

Year	Driver	Starts	Poles	Finish 1	2	3	4	5	6–10	Laps	Laps Led	Races Led	Miles	$

Roy McDonald *continued*

Year	Driver	Starts	Poles	1	2	3	4	5	6–10	Laps	Laps Led	Races Led	Miles	$
1960	Bob Roberts	1	0	0	0	0	0	0	0	10	0	0	5	50
Lifetime		8	0	0	0	0	0	0	0	465	0	0	554	$825

J.D. McDuffie

Year	Driver	Starts	Poles	1	2	3	4	5	6–10	Laps	Laps Led	Races Led	Miles	$
1963	Larry Manning	1	0	0	0	0	0	0	0	11	0	0	15	500
1963	J.D. McDuffie	12	0	0	0	0	0	0	3	1,918	0	0	765	1,620
1966	J.D. McDuffie	36	0	0	0	0	0	1	8	7,166	0	0	4,255	8,545
1967	J.D. McDuffie	1	0	0	0	0	0	0	0	137	0	0	69	150
1968	J.D. McDuffie	32	0	0	0	0	0	0	9	5,587	0	0	3,018	8,355
1969	J.D. McDuffie	33	0	0	0	0	0	0	10	7,016	0	0	4,986	16,167
1970	J.D. McDuffie	35	0	0	0	0	0	1	9	8,431	0	0	6,242	19,810
1970	Rodney Bruce	1	0	0	0	0	0	0	0	261	0	0	103	225
1970	Tom Usry	1	0	0	0	0	0	0	0	226	0	0	82	255
1971	J.D. McDuffie	40	0	0	0	1	0	1	6	8,694	5	1	8,317	25,725
1972	J.D. McDuffie	24	0	0	0	0	0	0	1	5,444	0	0	6,410	29,765
1973	J.D. McDuffie	27	0	0	0	0	0	3	7	7,388	11	2	8,137	46,698
1974	J.D. McDuffie	30	0	0	0	0	0	0	7	8,283	1	1	9,519	51,573
1975	Dick May	1	0	0	0	0	0	0	0	66	0	0	36	855
1975	Glenn McDuffie	1	0	0	0	0	0	0	0	431	0	0	438	1,130
1975	J.D. McDuffie	26	0	0	0	0	0	1	5	5,832	0	0	7,055	45,270
1975	Henley Gray	2	0	0	0	0	0	0	0	682	0	0	648	2,990
1976	Larry Esau	1	0	0	0	0	0	0	0	169	0	0	443	1,745
1976	J.D. McDuffie	29	0	0	0	0	0	1	7	7,565	0	0	9,269	70,170
1976	Glenn McDuffie	1	0	0	0	0	0	0	0	205	0	0	208	730
1977	J.D. McDuffie	30	0	0	0	0	0	0	4	8,252	1	1	9,689	74,950
1978	J.D. McDuffie	30	1	0	0	0	0	1	5	7,300	15	4	8,716	73,905
1979	J.D. McDuffie	31	0	0	0	0	0	1	6	8,014	116	3	9,634	89,885
1980	Jeff McDuffie	3	0	0	0	0	0	0	0	1,138	0	0	869	2,725
1980	J.D. McDuffie	29	0	0	0	0	0	0	3	5,749	0	0	6,815	70,995
1981	J.D. McDuffie	28	0	0	0	0	0	0	1	10,110	8	2	13,371	95,750
1982	Jeff McDuffie	1	0	0	0	0	0	0	0	377	0	0	236	1,005
1982	J.D. McDuffie	27	0	0	0	0	0	0	1	5,699	0	0	7,092	98,580
1983	J.D. McDuffie	24	0	0	0	0	0	0	0	5,813	0	0	6,309	72,395
1984	J.D. McDuffie	16	0	0	0	0	0	0	0	4,064	0	0	3,422	50,320
1985	J.D. McDuffie	22	0	0	0	0	0	0	0	4,464	0	0	5,336	79,135
1985	Jeff McDuffie	1	0	0	0	0	0	0	0	445	0	0	453	1,875
1986	J.D. McDuffie	14	0	0	0	0	0	0	0	2,982	1	1	3,547	68,115
1987	Charlie Baker	1	0	0	0	0	0	0	0	147	0	0	224	1,350
1987	J.D. McDuffie	14	0	0	0	0	0	0	0	2,405	0	0	2,892	23,375
1988	J.D. McDuffie	2	0	0	0	0	0	0	0	516	1	1	574	3,750
1989	J.D. McDuffie	7	0	0	0	0	0	0	0	1,381	0	0	1,847	25,845
1990	J.D. McDuffie	8	0	0	0	0	0	0	0	1,301	0	0	1,659	26,170
1991	J.D. McDuffie	5	0	0	0	0	0	0	0	732	0	0	1,143	18,095
Lifetime		627	1	0	0	1	0	10	92	146,401	159	16	153,841	$1,210,498

Paul McDuffie

Year	Driver	Starts	Poles	1	2	3	4	5	6–10	Laps	Laps Led	Races Led	Miles	$
1960	Joe Lee Johnson	7	0	1	0	0	1	0	0	1,404	48	1	1,231	29,708
Lifetime		7	0	1	0	0	1	1	0	1,404	48	1	1,231	$29,708

Robert McEntyre

Year	Driver	Starts	Poles	1	2	3	4	5	6–10	Laps	Laps Led	Races Led	Miles	$
1983	Jody Ridley	10	0	0	0	0	0	0	3	1,963	0	0	3,494	45,710
1984	Jody Ridley	14	0	0	0	0	0	0	3	2,891	4	2	4,810	64,135
Lifetime		24	0	0	0	0	0	0	6	4,854	4	2	8,304	$109,845

John McFadden

Year	Driver	Starts	Poles	1	2	3	4	5	6–10	Laps	Laps Led	Races Led	Miles	$
1983	John McFadden	3	0	0	0	0	0	0	0	289	0	0	181	2,260
1989	John McFadden	2	0	0	0	0	0	0	0	213	0	0	291	5,279
Lifetime		5	0	0	0	0	0	0	0	502	0	0	472	$7,539

Charlie McGee

Year	Driver	Starts	Poles	1	2	3	4	5	6–10	Laps	Laps Led	Races Led	Miles	$
1971	David Sisco	4	0	0	0	0	0	0	0	853	0	0	1,019	3,625
1972	Jabe Thomas	1	0	0	0	0	0	0	0	94	0	0	141	814
1972	David Sisco	12	0	0	0	0	0	0	2	2,067	0	0	3,269	14,490

Year	Driver	Starts	Poles	Finish						Laps	Laps Led	Races Led	Miles	$
				1	2	3	4	5	6–10					

Charlie McGee *continued*

Year	Driver	Starts	Poles	1	2	3	4	5	6–10	Laps	Laps Led	Races Led	Miles	$
1973	David Sisco	23	0	0	0	0	1	1	4	6,552	12	2	7,146	33,273
Lifetime		40	0	0	0	0	1	1	6	9,566	12	2	11,575	$52,202

John McGinley

Year	Driver	Starts	Poles	1	2	3	4	5	6–10	Laps	Laps Led	Races Led	Miles	$
1954	John McGinley	3	0	0	0	0	0	0	1	399	0	0	200	275
1955	John McGinley	1	0	0	0	0	0	0	0	157	0	0	79	60
Lifetime		4	0	0	0	0	0	0	1	556	0	0	278	$335

Robert McGrath

Year	Driver	Starts	Poles	1	2	3	4	5	6–10	Laps	Laps Led	Races Led	Miles	$
1952	Bill Holland	1	0	0	0	0	0	0	0	123	0	0	123	25
Lifetime		1	0	0	0	0	0	0	0	123	0	0	123	$25

Hershel McGriff

Year	Driver	Starts	Poles	1	2	3	4	5	6–10	Laps	Laps Led	Races Led	Miles	$
1950	Hershel McGriff	1	0	0	0	0	0	0	1	374	0	0	468	500
1951	Hershel McGriff	3	0	0	0	0	1	0	0	463	1	1	561	1,235
1953	Hershel McGriff	2	0	0	0	0	0	0	0	274	101	1	274	125
1976	Hershel McGriff	2	0	0	0	0	0	0	0	179	0	0	456	1,655
1977	Hershel McGriff	2	0	0	0	0	0	0	1	120	0	0	314	3,240
1978	Hershel McGriff	1	0	0	0	0	0	0	0	90	0	0	236	1,640
1988	Hershel McGriff	3	0	0	0	0	0	0	0	316	0	0	526	5,960
1989	Hershel McGriff	1	0	0	0	0	0	0	0	74	0	0	186	5,075
Lifetime		15	0	0	0	0	1	0	2	1,890	102	2	3,021	$19,430

R.B. McIntosh

Year	Driver	Starts	Poles	1	2	3	4	5	6–10	Laps	Laps Led	Races Led	Miles	$
1949	Jim Roper	1	0	1	0	0	0	0	0	197	47	1	148	2,000
1949	Bill Harrison	1	0	0	0	0	0	0	0		0	0		25
1949	Bill Blair	3	0	0	0	0	0	1	1	190	145	1	279	425
1950	Bill Harrison	1	0	0	0	0	0	0	0	38	0	0	29	0
Lifetime		6	0	1	0	0	0	1	1	425	192	2	455	$2,450

Stewart McKinney

Year	Driver	Starts	Poles	1	2	3	4	5	6–10	Laps	Laps Led	Races Led	Miles	$
1963	Larry Frank	2	0	0	0	0	0	0	0	573	0	0	610	750
1963	Tommy Irwin	6	0	0	0	1	0	0	3	1,330	0	0	1,046	2,415
1963	Fred Lorenzen	3	0	0	0	0	0	0	1	431	0	0	167	380
1963	Tiny Lund	1	0	0	0	0	0	0	0	384	0	0	576	1,150
Lifetime		12	0	0	0	1	0	0	4	2,718	0	0	2,399	$4,695

Sumner McKnight

Year	Driver	Starts	Poles	1	2	3	4	5	6–10	Laps	Laps Led	Races Led	Miles	$
1983	Sumner McKnight	2	0	0	0	0	0	0	0	204	0	0	534	5,275
1984	Sumner McKnight	2	0	0	0	0	0	0	0	192	0	0	503	5,140
1985	Sumner McKnight	1	0	0	0	0	0	0	0	91	0	0	238	3,985
Lifetime		5	0	0	0	0	0	0	0	487	0	0	1,276	$14,400

Jim McLain

Year	Driver	Starts	Poles	1	2	3	4	5	6–10	Laps	Laps Led	Races Led	Miles	$
1955	Jim McLain	1	0	0	0	0	0	0	0	82	0	0	123	50
Lifetime		1	0	0	0	0	0	0	0	82	0	0	123	$50

Sam McMahon III

Year	Driver	Starts	Poles	1	2	3	4	5	6–10	Laps	Laps Led	Races Led	Miles	$
1991	Mickey Gibbs	15	0	0	0	0	0	0	0	4,078	0	0	5,308	98,260
1991	Kenny Wallace	3	0	0	0	0	0	0	0	668	0	0	748	11,425
1991	Jimmy Hensley	4	0	0	0	0	0	0	1	1,708	0	0	1,491	32,125
1991	Dick Trickle	6	0	0	0	0	0	0	1	1,574	0	0	2,106	41,655
1991	Dorsey Schroeder	1	0	0	0	0	0	0	0	90	3	1	221	6,840
Lifetime		29	0	0	0	0	0	0	2	8,118	3	1	9,873	$190,305

Allen McMillion

Year	Driver	Starts	Poles	1	2	3	4	5	6–10	Laps	Laps Led	Races Led	Miles	$
1965	G.T. Nolan	8	0	0	0	0	0	0	1	1,018	0	0	563	1,165
1965	Worth McMillion	10	0	0	0	0	0	0	2	2,290	0	0	1,289	2,120
1965	Alan McMillion	1	0	0	0	0	0	0	0	236	0	0	79	110

Year	Driver	Starts	Poles	Finish 1	2	3	4	5	6–10	Laps	Laps Led	Races Led	Miles	$

Allen McMillion *continued*

Year	Driver	Starts	Poles	1	2	3	4	5	6–10	Laps	Laps Led	Races Led	Miles	$
1965	Earl Brooks	1	0	0	0	0	0	0	0	0	0	0	0	100
1966	G.T. Nolan	3	0	0	0	0	0	0	0	486	0	0	199	305
1966	Worth McMillion	9	0	0	0	0	0	0	3	2,311	0	0	1,450	2,440
1966	Alan McMillion	1	0	0	0	0	0	0	0	250	0	0	125	150
1967	G.T. Nolan	1	0	0	0	0	0	0	0	144	0	0	130	100
1967	Worth McMillion	2	0	0	0	0	0	0	2	497	0	0	249	775
1968	Worth McMillion	3	0	0	0	0	0	1	0	772	0	0	444	875
1968	G.T. Nolan	1	0	0	0	0	0	0	0	123	0	0	62	110
Lifetime		**40**	**0**	**0**	**0**	**0**	**0**	**1**	**8**	**8,127**	**0**	**0**	**4,588**	**$8,250**

Worth McMillion

Year	Driver	Starts	Poles	1	2	3	4	5	6–10	Laps	Laps Led	Races Led	Miles	$
1962	LeeRoy Yarbrough	1	0	0	0	0	0	0	0	259	0	0	356	400
1962	Bunkie Blackburn	2	0	0	0	0	1	0	0	519	0	0	779	2,775
1962	Worth McMillion	4	0	0	0	0	0	0	0	1,105	0	0	517	675
1963	Worth McMillion	15	0	0	0	0	0	0	4	4,177	0	0	2,412	3,145
1963	Joe Weatherly	1	0	0	0	0	0	0	0	48	0	0	18	380
1964	Worth McMillion	18	0	0	0	0	0	0	6	4,681	0	0	2,756	4,710
Lifetime		**41**	**0**	**0**	**0**	**0**	**1**	**0**	**10**	**10,789**	**0**	**0**	**6,838**	**$12,085**

Ralph McNabb

Year	Driver	Starts	Poles	1	2	3	4	5	6–10	Laps	Laps Led	Races Led	Miles	$
1972	Richard D. Brown	15	0	0	0	0	0	0	0	3,355	0	0	4,118	19,570
1974	Marv Acton	1	0	0	0	0	0	0	0	66	0	0	41	365
Lifetime		**16**	**0**	**0**	**0**	**0**	**0**	**1**	**0**	**3,421**	**0**	**0**	**4,159**	**$19,935**

Jim McNeil

Year	Driver	Starts	Poles	1	2	3	4	5	6–10	Laps	Laps Led	Races Led	Miles	$
1959	Jim Lamport	1	0	0	0	0	0	0	0	414	0	0	166	150
1960	Clyde Mitchell	1	0	0	0	0	0	0	1	88	0	0	88	140
1960	John Potter	2	0	0	0	0	0	0	0	126	0	0	158	150
1961	Al Brand	1	0	0	0	0	0	0	0	11	0	0	15	0
1961	Mike Mitchell	1	0	0	0	0	0	0	0	5	0	0	13	50
Lifetime		**6**	**0**	**0**	**0**	**0**	**0**	**0**	**1**	**644**	**0**	**0**	**440**	**$490**

Chip McPherson

Year	Driver	Starts	Poles	1	2	3	4	5	6–10	Laps	Laps Led	Races Led	Miles	$
2000	Jeff Fuller	1	0	0	0	0	0	0	0	115	0	0	173	22,070
Lifetime		**1**	**0**	**0**	**0**	**0**	**0**	**0**	**0**	**115**	**0**	**0**	**173**	**$22,070**

Sam McQuagg

Year	Driver	Starts	Poles	1	2	3	4	5	6–10	Laps	Laps Led	Races Led	Miles	$
1962	Sam McQuagg	1	0	0	0	0	0	0	0	51	0	0	26	120
Lifetime		**1**	**0**	**0**	**0**	**0**	**0**	**0**	**0**	**51**	**0**	**0**	**26**	**$120**

E.A. McQuaig

Year	Driver	Starts	Poles	1	2	3	4	5	6–10	Laps	Laps Led	Races Led	Miles	$
1963	LeeRoy Yarbrough	5	0	0	0	0	0	0	2	947	0	0	1,457	2,940
1963	Fred Thompson	1	0	0	0	0	0	0	1	186	0	0	93	175
1963	Charley Griffin	1	0	0	0	0	0	0	0	182	0	0	91	60
1963	Bob Welborn	2	0	0	0	0	0	0	0	282	0	0	446	675
1964	LeeRoy Yarbrough	1	0	0	0	0	0	0	0	23	0	0	12	50
Lifetime		**10**	**0**	**0**	**0**	**0**	**0**	**0**	**3**	**1,620**	**0**	**0**	**2,098**	**$3,900**

Robert McReynolds

Year	Driver	Starts	Poles	1	2	3	4	5	6–10	Laps	Laps Led	Races Led	Miles	$
1956	Sherman Utsman	1	0	0	0	0	0	0	0	327	0	0	450	75
Lifetime		**1**	**0**	**0**	**0**	**0**	**0**	**0**	**0**	**327**	**0**	**0**	**450**	**$75**

John McVitty

Year	Driver	Starts	Poles	1	2	3	4	5	6–10	Laps	Laps Led	Races Led	Miles	$
1955	John McVitty	7	0	0	0	0	0	0	2	951	0	0	559	550
1956	John McVitty	4	0	0	0	0	0	0	1	431	0	0	228	250
Lifetime		**11**	**0**	**0**	**0**	**0**	**0**	**0**	**3**	**1,382**	**0**	**0**	**787**	**$800**

Charles Meacham

Year	Driver	Starts	Poles	1	2	3	4	5	6–10	Laps	Laps Led	Races Led	Miles	$
1990	Bill Meacham	1	0	0	0	0	0	0	0	87	0	0	65	2,425

Year	Driver	Starts	Poles	Finish 1	2	3	4	5	6–10	Laps	Laps Led	Races Led	Miles	$

Charles Meacham *continued*

Year	Driver	Starts	Poles	1	2	3	4	5	6–10	Laps	Laps Led	Races Led	Miles	$
1991	Bill Meacham	2	0	0	0	0	0	0	0	146	0	0	159	6,535
Lifetime		3	0	0	0	0	0	0	0	233	0	0	225	$8,960

Jimmy Means

Year	Driver	Starts	Poles	1	2	3	4	5	6–10	Laps	Laps Led	Races Led	Miles	$
1978	Jimmy Means	26	0	0	0	0	0	0	2	6,932	0	0	7,591	53,485
1979	Jimmy Means	26	0	0	0	0	0	0	1	5,130	0	0	6,137	53,955
1980	Jimmy Means	27	0	0	0	0	0	0	0	7,649	0	0	8,873	81,590
1981	Charlie Chamblee	1	0	0	0	0	0	0	0	10	0	0	6	830
1981	Cecil Gordon	1	0	0	0	0	0	0	0	8	0	0	5	550
1981	Jimmy Means	29	0	0	0	0	0	0	2	8,320	0	0	8,904	87,690
1981	Baxter Price	1	0	0	0	0	0	0	0	1	0	0	2	900
1982	Jimmy Means	30	0	0	0	0	0	0	2	8,837	2	1	10,274	140,660
1983	Jimmy Means	28	0	0	0	0	0	0	3	7,968	2	1	8,816	118,090
1983	Lennie Pond	1	0	0	0	0	0	0	0	193	0	0	386	4,155
1984	Jimmy Means	22	0	0	0	0	0	0	0	7,044	0	0	7,482	105,105
1984	Morgan Shepherd	1	0	0	0	0	0	0	0	105	0	0	279	4,655
1984	Roy Smith	1	0	0	0	0	0	0	0	70	0	0	183	2,475
1984	Sterling Marlin	1	0	0	0	0	0	0	0	116	0	0	69	2,800
1984	Dale Jarrett	1	0	0	0	0	0	0	0	155	0	0	388	4,995
1984	Bobby Wawak	1	0	0	0	0	0	0	0	180	0	0	450	4,025
1985	Jimmy Means	28	0	0	0	0	0	0	0	6,774	0	0	7,521	132,140
1986	Jimmy Means	26	0	0	0	0	0	0	0	6,472	5	3	8,104	145,440
1987	Jimmy Means	28	0	0	0	0	0	0	1	6,239	21	1	7,184	152,055
1988	Jimmy Means	26	0	0	0	0	0	0	0	4,778	12	4	6,346	131,890
1989	Mickey Gibbs	1	0	0	0	0	0	0	0	76	0	0	190	9,940
1989	Jimmy Means	22	0	0	0	0	0	0	0	4,868	4	1	6,289	60,705
1990	Jimmy Means	27	0	0	0	0	0	0	0	7,419	0	0	8,749	130,415
1991	Bobby Hillin	2	0	0	0	0	0	0	0	564	0	0	675	8,650
1991	Mike Wallace	2	0	0	0	0	0	0	0	315	0	0	351	7,000
1991	Jimmy Means	20	0	0	0	0	0	0	0	4,425	3	3	6,580	105,710
1992	Graham Taylor	2	0	0	0	0	0	0	0	17	0	0	17	8,595
1992	Jimmy Means	22	0	0	0	0	0	0	0	4,370	0	0	5,165	130,860
1992	Brad Teague	1	0	0	0	0	0	0	0	456	0	0	243	7,080
1992	John McFadden	5	0	0	0	0	0	0	0	37	0	0	53	21,810
1992	Scott Gaylord	1	0	0	0	0	0	0	0	124	0	0	124	4,265
1992	Scott Sharp	1	0	0	0	0	0	0	0	51	0	0	125	7,155
1992	Tom Kendall	1	0	0	0	0	0	0	0	74	0	0	186	6,755
1992	Mike Potter	1	0	0	0	0	0	0	0	7	0	0	7	4,025
1993	Mike Potter	1	0	0	0	0	0	0	0	4	0	0	5	5,440
1993	Clay Young	2	0	0	0	0	0	0	0	60	0	0	143	14,370
1993	Scott Gaylord	1	0	0	0	0	0	0	0	75	0	0	184	5,935
1993	Mike Skinner	1	0	0	0	0	0	0	0	145	0	0	198	5,180
1993	Jimmy Means	18	0	0	0	0	0	0	0	4,765	2	2	5,644	134,205
1993	Graham Taylor	1	0	0	0	0	0	0	0	3	0	0	8	6,210
1993	Mike Wallace	1	0	0	0	0	0	0	0	323	0	0	485	4,725
1993	Jimmy Hensley	3	0	0	0	0	0	0	0	680	0	0	657	35,410
1994	Kirk Shelmerdine	1	0	0	0	0	0	0	0	179	0	0	476	11,265
1994	Gary Bradberry	1	0	0	0	0	0	0	0	276	0	0	420	6,600
1994	Bob Keselowski	1	0	0	0	0	0	0	0	17	0	0	43	7,150
1994	Brad Teague	8	0	0	0	0	0	0	0	1,959	0	0	2,095	59,900
1994	Mike Skinner	1	0	0	0	0	0	0	0	469	0	0	477	9,550
Lifetime		453	0	0	0	0	0	0	11	108,739	51	16	128,587	$2,046,390

Bill Meazell

Year	Driver	Starts	Poles	1	2	3	4	5	6–10	Laps	Laps Led	Races Led	Miles	$
1979	Bill Meazell	1	0	0	0	0	0	0	0	46	0	0	92	1,000
Lifetime		1	0	0	0	0	0	0	0	46	0	0	92	$1,000

Chuck Meekins

Year	Driver	Starts	Poles	1	2	3	4	5	6–10	Laps	Laps Led	Races Led	Miles	$
1951	Chuck Meekins	4	0	0	1	0	0	0	0	200	0	0	100	650
Lifetime		4	0	0	1	0	0	0	0	200	0	0	100	$650

Doug Meeks

Year	Driver	Starts	Poles	1	2	3	4	5	6–10	Laps	Laps Led	Races Led	Miles	$
1952	Donald Thomas	11	0	0	0	0	1	1	5	874	0	0	587	1,285
1953	Donald Thomas	9	0	0	0	0	0	0	0	32	0	0	16	225

Year	Driver	Starts	Poles	Finish						Laps	Laps Led	Races Led	Miles	$
				1	2	3	4	5	6–10	Laps	Led	Led	Miles	$

Doug Meeks *continued*

Year	Driver	Starts	Poles	1	2	3	4	5	6–10	Laps	Laps Led	Races Led	Miles	$
1953	Earl Moss	1	0	0	0	0	0	0	0	190	0	0	190	25
Lifetime		21	0	0	0	0	1	1	5	1,096	0	0	793	$1,535

Jack Meeks

Year	Driver	Starts	Poles	1	2	3	4	5	6–10	Laps	Laps Led	Races Led	Miles	$
1961	Bob Pronger	1	0	0	0	0	0	0	0	37	0	0	93	85
1961	Sal Tovella	1	0	0	0	0	0	0	0	31	0	0	47	250
1961	Tim Flock	1	0	0	0	0	0	0	0	184	0	0	460	200
Lifetime		3	0	0	0	0	0	0	0	252	0	0	599	$535

Ken Meisenhelder

Year	Driver	Starts	Poles	1	2	3	4	5	6–10	Laps	Laps Led	Races Led	Miles	$
1969	Ken Meisenhelder	16	0	0	0	0	0	0	0	1,832	0	0	1,285	5,630
1970	Ken Meisenhelder	19	0	0	0	0	0	0	2	2,717	0	0	1,842	7,020
1971	Ken Meisenhelder	14	0	0	0	0	0	0	1	2,150	0	0	1,522	5,170
Lifetime		49	0	0	0	0	0	0	3	6,699	0	0	4,648	$17,820

Harry Melling

Year	Driver	Starts	Poles	1	2	3	4	5	6–10	Laps	Laps Led	Races Led	Miles	$
1982	Bill Elliott	21	1	0	3	3	1	1	1	5,542	151	9	7,887	201,030
1983	Bill Elliott	30	0	1	4	1	3	3	10	9,536	174	15	11,272	318,470
1984	Bill Elliott	30	4	3	1	4	4	1	11	9,848	570	17	11,385	504,708
1985	Bill Elliott	28	11	11	2	0	2	1	2	8,724	1,920	19	10,736	1,969,453
1986	Bill Elliott	29	4	2	0	2	1	3	8	8,549	511	15	10,593	586,730
1987	Bill Elliott	29	8	6	3	1	5	1	4	8,902	1,339	22	10,423	978,500
1988	Bill Elliott	29	6	6	2	2	4	1	7	9,647	1,559	20	11,531	812,775
1989	Bill Elliott	29	2	3	0	1	3	1	6	9,037	380	11	10,836	694,962
1990	Bill Elliott	29	2	1	4	1	5	1	4	9,349	1,182	13	11,189	818,740
1991	Bill Elliott	29	2	1	2	1	0	2	6	9,020	203	6	10,818	586,370
1992	Dorsey Schroeder	1	0	0	0	0	0	0	0	176	0	0	268	10,385
1992	Chad Little	13	0	0	0	0	0	0	1	3,262	0	0	4,799	79,995
1992	Dave Mader III	5	0	0	0	0	0	0	0	1,387	7	1	1,389	51,635
1992	Phil Parsons	2	0	0	0	0	0	0	1	567	0	0	872	58,475
1993	Chad Little	2	0	0	0	0	0	0	0	461	0	0	890	34,865
1993	P.J. Jones	6	0	0	0	0	0	0	1	710	0	0	1,447	50,070
1993	Greg Sacks	1	0	0	0	0	0	0	0	320	0	0	487	10,305
1994	Joe Ruttman	1	0	0	0	0	0	0	0	199	0	0	498	34,005
1994	Phil Parsons	3	0	0	0	0	0	0	0	757	0	0	922	17,165
1994	Rich Bickle	10	0	0	0	0	0	0	0	1,837	0	0	3,260	98,945
1995	Lake Speed	31	0	0	0	0	0	0	2	9,073	17	1	11,197	506,435
1996	Lake Speed	28	0	0	0	0	0	0	1	7,877	10	3	8,900	683,220
1997	Jeff Davis	1	0	0	0	0	0	0	0	60	0	0	151	30,745
1997	Lake Speed	25	0	0	0	0	0	0	0	7,494	3	1	9,424	691,115
1998	Lake Speed	16	0	0	0	0	0	0	0	4,790	0	0	6,357	521,225
1998	Jerry Nadeau	16	0	0	0	0	0	0	0	4,254	0	0	5,399	427,805
1999	Jerry Nadeau	16	0	0	0	0	0	0	1	4,607	0	0	6,302	633,966
Lifetime		460	40	34	21	16	28	15	66	135,985	8,026	153	169,231	$11,412,094

Mark Melling

Year	Driver	Starts	Poles	1	2	3	4	5	6–10	Laps	Laps Led	Races Led	Miles	$
1999	Steve Grissom	3	0	0	0	0	0	0	0	820	0	0	641	78,625
1999	Jerry Nadeau	6	0	0	0	0	0	0	0	1,058	9	1	2,130	255,891
1999	Stacy Compton	3	0	0	0	0	0	0	0	951	0	0	1,092	92,600
1999	Rich Bickle	5	0	0	0	0	0	0	0	1,446	1	1	1,521	142,485
2000	Bobby Hillin	1	0	0	0	0	0	0	0	314	0	0	167	27,525
2000	Stacy Compton	27	0	0	0	0	0	0	0	6,912	4	3	9,188	1,038,160
2001	Stacy Compton	35	2	0	0	0	0	0	1	9,605	29	5	12,810	1,696,457
2002	Stacy Compton	1	0	0	0	0	0	0	0	200	3	1	400	41,615
2002	Robert Pressley	1	0	0	0	0	0	0	0	190	0	0	475	147,709
Lifetime		82	2	0	0	0	0	1	1	21,496	46	11	28,423	$3,521,067

Johnny Mello

Year	Driver	Starts	Poles	1	2	3	4	5	6–10	Laps	Laps Led	Races Led	Miles	$
1958	Art Watts	1	0	0	0	0	0	0	0	165	0	0	434	140
1960	Johnny Mello	1	0	0	0	0	0	0	0	22	0	0	31	0
1960	Art Watts	1	0	0	0	0	0	0	1	168	0	0	235	525
Lifetime		3	0	0	0	0	0	0	1	355	0	0	700	$665

Year	Driver	Starts	Poles	Finish 1	2	3	4	5	6–10	Laps	Laps Led	Races Led	Miles	$

Harry Melton

Year	Driver	Starts	Poles	1	2	3	4	5	6–10	Laps	Laps Led	Races Led	Miles	$
1969	Henley Gray	44	0	0	0	0	0	0	3	8,001	0	0	6,495	21,512
Lifetime		44	0	0	0	0	0	0	3	8,001	0	0	6,495	$21,512

Major Melton

Year	Driver	Starts	Poles	1	2	3	4	5	6–10	Laps	Laps Led	Races Led	Miles	$
1963	Nace Mattingly	1	0	0	0	0	0	0	1	288	0	0	108	240
1963	Joe Weatherly	1	0	0	0	0	0	0	0	98	0	0	49	330
1963	Major Melton	17	0	0	0	0	0	0	0	2,780	0	0	1,287	1,910
Lifetime		19	0	0	0	0	0	0	1	3,166	0	0	1,444	$2,480

John Menard (Statistics include shared ownerships with Robby Gordon and Mike Head.)

Year	Driver	Starts	Poles	1	2	3	4	5	6–10	Laps	Laps Led	Races Led	Miles	$
2000	P.J. Jones	1	0	0	0	0	0	0	0	389	0	0	584	33,345
2000	Robby Gordon	17	0	0	0	0	1	0	1	3,933	14	3	5,219	616,450
Lifetime		18	0	0	0	0	1	0	1	4,322	14	3	5,802	$649,795

Jack Mercer

Year	Driver	Starts	Poles	1	2	3	4	5	6–10	Laps	Laps Led	Races Led	Miles	$
1969	Ben Arnold	1	0	0	0	0	0	0	0	135	0	0	359	1,375
1972	Les Covey	7	0	0	0	0	0	0	0	1,347	0	0	1,540	4,865
Lifetime		8	0	0	0	0	0	0	0	1,482	0	0	1,899	$6,240

Joe Merola

Year	Driver	Starts	Poles	1	2	3	4	5	6–10	Laps	Laps Led	Races Led	Miles	$
1951	Joe Merola	4	0	0	0	0	0	0	1	472	0	0	522	175
Lifetime		4	0	0	0	0	0	0	1	472	0	0	522	$175

Dick Meyer

Year	Driver	Starts	Poles	1	2	3	4	5	6–10	Laps	Laps Led	Races Led	Miles	$
1953	Dick Meyer	1	0	0	0	0	1	0	0	355	0	0	488	1,000
Lifetime		1	0	0	0	0	1	0	0	355	0	0	488	$1,000

William Meyer

Year	Driver	Starts	Poles	1	2	3	4	5	6–10	Laps	Laps Led	Races Led	Miles	$
1957	Peck Peckham	9	0	0	0	0	0	0	0	880	0	0	626	825
1958	Peck Peckham	11	0	0	0	0	0	0	0	1,263	0	0	834	835
Lifetime		20	0	0	0	0	0	0	0	2,143	0	0	1,460	$1,660

Dick Midgley

Year	Driver	Starts	Poles	1	2	3	4	5	6–10	Laps	Laps Led	Races Led	Miles	$
1974	Hershel McGriff	1	0	0	0	0	0	0	0	1	0	0	3	750
1975	Roy Smith	1	0	0	0	0	0	0	0	62	0	0	155	900
1975	Hershel McGriff	2	0	0	0	0	0	0	1	279	0	0	731	3,170
1976	Roy Smith	3	0	0	0	0	0	0	0	225	0	0	569	4,285
1977	Elliott	2	0	0	0	0	0	0	0	527	0	0	606	1,550
1977	Roy Smith	3	0	0	0	0	0	0	0	205	0	0	532	5,365
1978	Roy Smith	1	0	0	0	0	0	0	1	115	0	0	301	2,300
1980	Hershel McGriff	1	0	0	0	0	0	0	0	67	0	0	176	825
1986	George Follmer	2	0	0	0	0	0	0	0	130	0	0	326	3,885
1987	George Follmer	2	0	0	0	0	0	0	0	122	8	1	320	2,880
1989	Roy Smith	1	0	0	0	0	0	0	0	40	0	0	40	4,445
1989	Terry Fisher	1	0	0	0	0	0	0	0	72	0	0	181	2,825
1990	Terry Fisher	1	0	0	0	0	0	0	0	74	0	0	186	4,575
1991	R.K. Smith	1	0	0	0	0	0	0	0	2	0	0	5	3,457
1992	R.K. Smith	1	0	0	0	0	0	0	0	70	0	0	176	4,880
Lifetime		23	0	0	0	0	0	0	2	1,991	8	1	4,307	$46,092

Joe Milahic

Year	Driver	Starts	Poles	1	2	3	4	5	6–10	Laps	Laps Led	Races Led	Miles	$
1977	Joe Mihalic	8	0	0	0	0	0	0	0	1,550	0	0	2,137	7,650
Lifetime		8	0	0	0	0	0	0	0	1,550	0	0	2,137	$7,650

Vel Miletich

Year	Driver	Starts	Poles	1	2	3	4	5	6–10	Laps	Laps Led	Races Led	Miles	$
1956	Parnelli Jones	3	0	0	1	0	0	0	0	591	0	0	564	1,705
1958	Eddie Gray	3	0	1	0	0	0	0	0	437	43	1	807	3,375
1958	Marvin Porter	2	0	0	0	0	0	0	0	124	0	0	211	200
1958	Parnelli Jones	3	2	1	0	0	0	0	0	587	148	2	954	1,010

Year	Driver	Starts	Poles	Finish						Laps	Laps Led	Races Led	Miles	$
				1	2	3	4	5	6–10					

Vel Miletich *continued*

Year	Driver	Starts	Poles	1	2	3	4	5	6–10	Laps	Laps Led	Races Led	Miles	$
1959	Eddie Gray	2	0	1	0	0	0	0	0	317	1	1	187	875
1959	Parnelli Jones	2	0	1	0	0	0	0	0	560	1	1	268	1,905
1960	Parnelli Jones	3	0	0	0	0	0	0	1	204	25	1	371	465
1960	Joe Weatherly	1	0	0	1	0	0	0	0	179	0	0	251	1,250
1960	Marvin Porter	3	0	1	0	0	0	0	0	223	61	2	295	3,800
1963	Marvin Porter	2	0	0	0	0	0	0	0	202	0	0	545	1,100
Lifetime		24	2	5	2	0	0	0	1	3,424	279	8	4,451	$15,685

Les Milfield

Year	Driver	Starts	Poles	1	2	3	4	5	6–10	Laps	Laps Led	Races Led	Miles	$
1955	Lloyd Dane	1	0	0	0	0	0	0	1	242	0	0	242	250
Lifetime		1	0	0	0	0	0	0	1	242	0	0	242	$250

A.L. Miller

Year	Driver	Starts	Poles	1	2	3	4	5	6–10	Laps	Laps Led	Races Led	Miles	$
1951	Tommy Thompson	1	0	0	0	0	0	0	0	148	0	0	185	0
Lifetime		1	0	0	0	0	0	0	0	148	0	0	185	$0

Carl Miller

Year	Driver	Starts	Poles	1	2	3	4	5	6–10	Laps	Laps Led	Races Led	Miles	$
1969	Billy Taylor	2	0	0	0	0	0	0	0	65	0	0	163	1,140
Lifetime		2	0	0	0	0	0	0	0	65	0	0	163	$1,140

George Miller

Year	Driver	Starts	Poles	1	2	3	4	5	6–10	Laps	Laps Led	Races Led	Miles	$
1953	Steve McGrath	2	0	0	0	0	0	0	0		0	0		50
1953	Al Keller	4	0	0	0	0	0	0	0	73	0	0	37	115
1954	Ralph Liguori	2	0	0	0	0	0	0	2	389	0	0	195	350
1954	Junior Johnson	1	0	0	0	0	0	1	0	194	0	0	97	300
1954	Al Keller	12	1	1	2	0	2	0	3	1,761	350	4	1,272	4,135
1954	Jimmie Lewallen	1	0	0	0	0	0	0	0	153	0	0	230	200
1955	Jack Choquette	4	0	0	1	0	0	0	0	469	0	0	371	825
Lifetime		26	1	1	3	0	2	1	5	3,039	350	4	2,201	$5,975

Harold Miller

Year	Driver	Starts	Poles	1	2	3	4	5	6–10	Laps	Laps Led	Races Led	Miles	$
1975	Harold Miller	2	0	0	0	0	0	0	0	247	0	0	494	1,625
1975	Ed Negre	2	0	0	0	0	0	0	0	187	0	0	265	1,960
1976	Dick May	1	0	0	0	0	0	0	0	60	0	0	91	825
1976	Harold Miller	3	0	0	0	0	0	0	0	499	0	0	1,184	4,885
1976	Bob Burcham	4	0	0	0	0	0	0	0	569	0	0	969	5,485
1977	Terry Bivins	1	0	0	0	0	0	0	0	290	0	0	396	1,700
1977	Harold Miller	6	0	0	0	0	0	0	0	1,267	0	0	2,276	8,480
Lifetime		19	0	0	0	0	0	0	0	3,119	0	0	5,675	$24,960

John Miller

Year	Driver	Starts	Poles	1	2	3	4	5	6–10	Laps	Laps Led	Races Led	Miles	$
1967	Tom Raley	1	0	0	0	0	0	0	0	30	0	0	75	100
Lifetime		1	0	0	0	0	0	0	0	30	0	0	75	$100

Junior Miller

Year	Driver	Starts	Poles	1	2	3	4	5	6–10	Laps	Laps Led	Races Led	Miles	$
1976	Dick Brooks	1	0	0	0	0	0	0	0	18	0	0	47	635
1976	Junior Miller	2	0	0	0	0	0	0	0	744	0	0	465	1,325
1976	Ernie Shaw	1	0	0	0	0	0	0	0	372	0	0	202	700
1976	Jerry Sisco	3	0	0	0	0	0	0	0	781	0	0	797	3,070
1976	Gary Myers	11	0	0	0	0	0	0	0	2,493	0	0	2,453	9,230
1976	Jim Hurtubise	1	0	0	0	0	0	0	0	180	0	0	450	3,975
1977	Elmo Langley	1	0	0	0	0	0	0	0	119	0	0	119	540
1977	Junior Miller	5	0	0	0	0	0	0	0	1,028	0	0	648	2,475
1977	Jim Hurtubise	1	0	0	0	0	0	0	0	69	0	0	173	2,050
1978	Junior Miller	1	0	0	0	0	0	0	0	122	0	0	124	630
1978	Ferrel Harris	1	0	0	0	0	0	0	0	453	0	0	238	650
1979	Ernie Shaw	1	0	0	0	0	0	0	0	368	0	0	230	625
1979	Dave Dion	1	0	0	0	0	0	0	0	148	0	0	78	590
1980	Tommy Houston	4	0	0	0	0	0	0	0	1,170	10	1	949	5,020
1980	Junior Miller	11	0	0	0	0	0	0	0	2,654	0	0	1,945	15,260

Year	Driver	Starts	Poles	Finish						Laps	Laps Led	Races Led	Miles	$
				1	2	3	4	5	6–10					

Junior Miller *continued*

Year	Driver	Starts	Poles	1	2	3	4	5	6–10	Laps	Laps Led	Races Led	Miles	$
1981	Jody Ridley	1	0	0	0	0	0	0	0	443	0	0	451	4,290
1981	Junior Miller	2	0	0	0	0	0	0	0	276	0	0	190	3,130
1981	Tommy Gale	1	0	0	0	0	0	0	0	381	0	0	207	2,035
1981	Dick May	1	0	0	0	0	0	0	0	267	0	0	406	2,805
Lifetime		50	0	0	0	0	0	0	0	12,086	10	1	10,172	$59,035

Larry Miller

Year	Driver	Starts	Poles	1	2	3	4	5	6–10	Laps	Laps Led	Races Led	Miles	$
1967	Larry Miller	15	0	0	0	0	0	0	1	1,558	0	0	704	2,075
Lifetime		15	0	0	0	0	0	0	1	1,558	0	0	704	$2,075

Lew Miller

Year	Driver	Starts	Poles	1	2	3	4	5	6–10	Laps	Laps Led	Races Led	Miles	$
1995	Ernie Cope	1	0	0	0	0	0	0	0	19	0	0	19	8,605
Lifetime		1	0	0	0	0	0	0	0	19	0	0	19	$8,605

Scott Miller

Year	Driver	Starts	Poles	1	2	3	4	5	6–10	Laps	Laps Led	Races Led	Miles	$
1982	Dave Marcis	1	0	0	0	0	0	0	0	91	0	0	238	3,030
1983	Scott Miller	2	0	0	0	0	0	0	0	173	0	0	453	2,400
1984	Scott Miller	2	0	0	0	0	0	0	0	98	0	0	257	1,815
Lifetime		5	0	0	0	0	0	0	0	362	0	0	948	$7,245

J. Marvin Mills

Year	Driver	Starts	Poles	1	2	3	4	5	6–10	Laps	Laps Led	Races Led	Miles	$
1972	John Sears	27	0	0	0	0	0	1	5	7,494	0	0	8,752	40,223
1973	John Sears	17	0	0	0	0	0	0	0	3,568	0	0	3,335	16,890
1973	Jim Vandiver	1	0	0	0	0	0	0	0	88	0	0	234	1,290
1973	Ed Negre	3	0	0	0	0	0	0	0	1,046	0	0	1,316	4,990
Lifetime		48	0	0	0	0	0	1	5	12,196	0	0	13,638	$63,393

Chris Milovich

Year	Driver	Starts	Poles	1	2	3	4	5	6–10	Laps	Laps Led	Races Led	Miles	$
1954	Ben Gregory	1	0	0	0	0	0	0	0	228	0	0	228	50
1955	Ben Gregory	1	0	0	0	0	0	0	1	96	0	0	96	200
Lifetime		2	0	0	0	0	0	0	1	324	0	0	324	$250

Clyde Minter

Year	Driver	Starts	Poles	1	2	3	4	5	6–10	Laps	Laps Led	Races Led	Miles	$
1949	Clyde Minter	1	0	0	0	0	1	0	0	199	0	0	100	300
1950	Clyde Minter	8	0	0	0	1	0	2	0	765	0	0	671	1,150
1951	Clyde Minter	3	0	0	0	0	0	0	0	59	0	0	44	50
1951	Bill Lawrence	1	0	0	0	0	0	0	0		0	0		25
1952	Clyde Minter	1	0	0	0	0	0	0	1	175	0	0	88	125
1953	Clyde Minter	4	0	0	0	0	0	0	1	510	0	0	438	230
1954	Billy Minter	1	0	0	0	0	0	0	0	121	0	0	61	25
Lifetime		19	0	0	0	1	1	2	2	1,829	0	0	1,401	$1,905

Pat Mintey

Year	Driver	Starts	Poles	1	2	3	4	5	6–10	Laps	Laps Led	Races Led	Miles	$
1981	Pat Mintey	1	0	0	0	0	0	0	0	40	0	0	105	850
1983	Pat Mintey	1	0	0	0	0	0	0	0	73	0	0	191	1,175
Lifetime		2	0	0	0	0	0	0	0	113	0	0	296	$2,025

Turkey Minton

Year	Driver	Starts	Poles	1	2	3	4	5	6–10	Laps	Laps Led	Races Led	Miles	$
1967	Curtis Turner	1	0	0	0	0	0	0	0	82	0	0	123	800
1967	Tiny Lund	2	0	0	0	0	0	0	0	163	0	0	151	680
1967	Tom Pistone	8	0	0	0	1	0	0	3	1,177	0	0	614	2,150
1968	Tom Pistone	2	0	0	0	0	1	0	0	350	35	1	180	525
Lifetime		13	0	0	0	1	1	0	3	1,772	35	1	1,068	$4,155

Tom Mitchell

Year	Driver	Starts	Poles	1	2	3	4	5	6–10	Laps	Laps Led	Races Led	Miles	$
1985	Chet Fillip	1	0	0	0	0	0	0	0	308	0	0	469	1,425
1986	Chet Fillip	17	0	0	0	0	0	0	0	3,276	0	0	4,552	36,110
Lifetime		18	0	0	0	0	0	0	0	3,584	0	0	5,020	$37,535

Year	Driver	Starts	Poles	Finish						Laps	Laps Led	Races Led	Miles	$
				1	2	3	4	5	6–10	Laps	Led	Led	Miles	$

Charles Mobley

Year	Driver	Starts	Poles	1	2	3	4	5	6–10	Laps	Laps Led	Races Led	Miles	$
1949	Ethel Mobley	2	0	0	0	0	0	0	0		0	0		50
Lifetime		2	0	0	0	0	0	0	0		0	0		$50

Patty Moise

Year	Driver	Starts	Poles	1	2	3	4	5	6–10	Laps	Laps Led	Races Led	Miles	$
1989	Patty Moise	2	0	0	0	0	0	0	0	33	0	0	88	6,180
Lifetime		2	0	0	0	0	0	0	0	33	0	0	88	$6,180

Larry Mollicone

Year	Driver	Starts	Poles	1	2	3	4	5	6–10	Laps	Laps Led	Races Led	Miles	$
1974	Bill Osborne	1	0	0	0	0	0	0	0	68	0	0	178	975
Lifetime		1	0	0	0	0	0	0	0	68	0	0	178	$975

Bill Monaghan

Year	Driver	Starts	Poles	1	2	3	4	5	6–10	Laps	Laps Led	Races Led	Miles	$
1977	Terry Ryan	7	0	0	0	0	0	0	1	1,142	0	0	2,240	12,405
1977	Dave Marcis	1	0	0	0	0	0	0	0	148	0	0	225	700
1977	Terry Bivins	2	0	0	0	0	0	0	1	519	0	0	599	5,700
Lifetime		10	0	0	0	0	0	0	2	1,809	0	0	3,064	$18,805

William Monoghan

Year	Driver	Starts	Poles	1	2	3	4	5	6–10	Laps	Laps Led	Races Led	Miles	$
1976	Terry Ryan	5	0	0	0	0	0	0	2	603	1	1	1,516	24,640
Lifetime		5	0	0	0	0	0	1	2	603	1	1	1,516	$24,640

Chris Monoleos

Year	Driver	Starts	Poles	1	2	3	4	5	6–10	Laps	Laps Led	Races Led	Miles	$
1979	Chris Monoleos	1	0	0	0	0	0	0	0	2	0	0	5	550
Lifetime		1	0	0	0	0	0	0	0	2	0	0	5	$550

Dean Monroe

Year	Driver	Starts	Poles	1	2	3	4	5	6–10	Laps	Laps Led	Races Led	Miles	$
1996	Stacy Compton	2	0	0	0	0	0	0	0	756	0	0	398	18,115
Lifetime		2	0	0	0	0	0	0	0	756	0	0	398	$18,115

Jack Montrangelo

Year	Driver	Starts	Poles	1	2	3	4	5	6–10	Laps	Laps Led	Races Led	Miles	$
1956	Jack Montgangelo	1	0	0	0	0	0	0	0	206	0	0	206	100
Lifetime		1	0	0	0	0	0	0	0	206	0	0	206	$100

Tommy Moon

Year	Driver	Starts	Poles	1	2	3	4	5	6–10	Laps	Laps Led	Races Led	Miles	$
1951	Tommy Moon	1	0	0	0	0	0	0	1		0	0		200
Lifetime		1	0	0	0	0	0	0	1		0	0		$200

Bill Moore

Year	Driver	Starts	Poles	1	2	3	4	5	6–10	Laps	Laps Led	Races Led	Miles	$
1956	Bill Moore	6	0	0	0	0	0	0	2	633	0	0	574	485
Lifetime		6	0	0	0	0	0	0	2	633	0	0	574	$485

Bob Moore

Year	Driver	Starts	Poles	1	2	3	4	5	6–10	Laps	Laps Led	Races Led	Miles	$
1950	Bob Moore (OH)	1	0	0	0	0	0	0	0	0	0	0	0	0
1951	Bob Moore (OH)	2	0	0	0	0	0	0	0		0	0		25
1952	Bob Moore (FL)	1	0	0	0	0	0	0	1		0	0		50
1952	Bob Moore (OH)	4	0	0	0	1	0	0	1	524	0	0	270	525
Lifetime		8	0	0	0	1	0	0	2	524	0	0	270	$600

Bud Moore (Statistics represent the team primarily owned by Bud Moore, including partnerships during the tenure of his ownership.)

Year	Driver	Starts	Poles	1	2	3	4	5	6–10	Laps	Laps Led	Races Led	Miles	$
1961	Joe Weatherly	23	4	8	3	0	1	1	4	5,401	769	17	5,153	39,095
1961	Cotton Owens	1	0	0	0	0	0	0	0	11	0	0	17	60
1961	Bob Welborn	2	0	0	0	1	0	0	1	747	51	1	641	3,860
1961	Fireball Roberts	1	0	0	1	0	0	1	0	319	0	0	199	1,125
1961	Tommy Irwin	1	0	0	0	0	0	0	0	361	0	0	542	500
1962	David Pearson	1	0	0	0	0	0	0	0	261	0	0	392	750
1962	Joe Weatherly	51	7	9	12	10	2	5	6	12,234	1,014	17	7,935	54,765
1963	Joe Weatherly	34	6	3	4	4	2	2	9	8,321	878	12	7,185	50,725

Year	Driver	Starts	Poles	Finish 1	2	3	4	5	6–10	Laps	Laps Led	Races Led	Miles	$

Bud Moore *continued*

Year	Driver	Starts	Poles	1	2	3	4	5	6–10	Laps	Laps Led	Races Led	Miles	$
1963	Bob Welborn	1	0	0	0	0	0	0	0	253	0	0	380	450
1964	Billy Wade	33	5	4	0	3	3	1	12	7,142	954	14	6,139	25,740
1964	Darel Dieringer	15	1	1	0	1	1	0	5	3,439	211	3	2,583	9,645
1964	Bobby Johns	1	0	0	0	0	0	0	0	27	0	0	41	500
1964	Johnny Rutherford	2	0	0	0	0	0	0	0	124	0	0	310	825
1964	Joe Weatherly	2	0	0	1	0	0	0	0	336	84	1	357	2,000
1964	Rex White	5	0	0	0	1	0	1	1	1,427	27	1	1,632	11,735
1965	Darel Dieringer	13	2	1	4	1	1	0	1	3,014	737	10	3,493	41,035
1965	Earl Balmer	9	0	0	1	0	1	0	2	1,320	32	6	2,174	19,045
1966	Darel Dieringer	14	0	2	2	0	0	0	1	2,858	332	6	2,981	39,190
1967	Cale Yarborough	1	0	0	0	0	0	0	0	196	0	0	98	375
1967	Gordon Johncock	2	0	0	0	0	0	1	0	525	1	1	539	2,595
1967	Bobby Allison	4	0	0	0	0	0	0	1	657	0	0	791	2,420
1967	LeeRoy Yarbrough	6	0	0	0	1	0	0	1	1,306	11	1	1,503	8,145
1967	Sam McQuagg	6	0	0	0	0	0	1	0	1,021	2	1	1,608	6,365
1968	Tiny Lund	13	0	0	0	0	1	2	4	3,574	1	1	3,878	15,795
1968	Cale Yarborough	1	0	0	0	0	0	0	0	164	0	0	88	250
1972	LeeRoy Yarbrough	1	0	0	0	0	0	0	0	145	1	1	198	630
1972	Dick Brooks	1	0	0	0	0	0	0	0	119	1	1	121	580
1972	David Pearson	2	0	0	0	0	1	0	0	439	3	1	791	7,860
1972	Donnie Allison	6	0	0	0	0	0	0	1	702	5	2	1,228	5,886
1973	Darrell Waltrip	5	0	0	0	0	0	0	1	818	0	0	945	14,691
1973	Bobby Isaac	19	0	0	2	1	2	0	1	4,177	62	7	4,545	83,950
1974	Buddy Baker	16	2	0	4	3	1	1	1	3,566	336	12	4,615	114,496
1974	George Follmer	11	0	0	0	0	1	2	2	3,029	26	1	3,604	50,180
1975	Buddy Baker	23	3	4	2	4	1	1	1	6,281	748	18	8,114	230,135
1976	Buddy Baker	30	2	1	3	1	4	7	0	7,335	1,028	15	8,610	220,380
1977	Buddy Baker	30	0	0	0	2	4	3	11	8,084	52	7	9,877	192,501
1978	Bobby Allison	30	1	5	3	4	0	2	8	9,283	1,043	19	10,540	355,245
1979	Bobby Allison	31	3	5	7	2	4	0	4	9,585	1,854	24	10,938	362,825
1980	Bobby Allison	31	2	4	2	4	1	1	6	8,244	948	18	9,028	331,630
1981	Benny Parsons	31	0	3	0	3	0	4	2	6,709	537	10	7,515	273,705
1982	Dale Earnhardt	30	1	1	1	3	2	0	5	7,208	1,062	18	7,787	357,270
1983	Dale Earnhardt	30	0	2	3	0	3	1	5	7,701	1,026	19	8,947	401,991
1984	Ricky Rudd	30	4	1	1	3	1	1	9	9,271	566	8	10,584	417,875
1985	Ricky Rudd	28	0	1	2	1	5	4	6	8,474	329	6	10,288	425,410
1986	Ricky Rudd	29	1	2	4	2	3	0	6	7,950	525	7	9,743	523,025
1987	Ricky Rudd	29	0	2	2	4	1	1	3	8,206	493	11	9,893	532,275
1988	Brett Bodine	29	0	0	0	1	1	0	3	7,789	200	5	9,163	396,540
1989	Brett Bodine	29	0	0	0	0	0	1	5	8,202	2	2	10,356	233,182
1990	Morgan Shepherd	29	0	1	2	2	0	2	9	8,794	201	7	10,638	461,697
1991	Morgan Shepherd	29	0	0	0	2	2	0	10	9,023	86	5	10,485	454,920
1992	Geoffrey Bodine	29	0	2	0	2	2	1	4	8,222	474	5	9,780	618,515
1993	Lake Speed	7	0	0	0	0	0	0	0	2,544	0	0	2,504	109,825
1993	Geoffrey Bodine	23	1	1	0	1	0	0	6	6,522	70	10	8,368	586,750
1994	Lake Speed	31	0	0	0	1	1	2	5	9,111	39	5	11,291	732,405
1995	Dick Trickle	31	0	0	0	0	0	0	1	8,940	5	1	11,094	672,220
1996	Wally Dallenbach	30	0	0	0	1	0	0	2	8,191	0	0	10,417	791,551
1998	Ted Musgrave	2	0	0	0	0	0	1	0	219	0	0	385	39,725
1999	Derrike Cope	1	0	0	0	0	0	0	0	328	0	0	492	27,070
2000	Ted Musgrave	1	0	0	0	0	0	0	0	137	0	0	364	34,305
2000	Derrike Cope	3	0	0	0	0	0	0	0	638	0	0	1,139	161,630
Lifetime		959	45	63	66	69	52	48	165	251,024	16,826	337	285,045	$10,559,865

Doug Moore

Year	Driver	Starts	Poles	1	2	3	4	5	6–10	Laps	Laps Led	Races Led	Miles	$
1964	Doug Moore	1	0	0	0	0	0	0	0	66	0	0	91	500
1965	Doug Moore	4	0	0	0	0	0	0	0	613	0	0	315	635
Lifetime		5	0	0	0	0	0	0	0	679	0	0	405	$1,135

Gilbert Moore

Year	Driver	Starts	Poles	1	2	3	4	5	6–10	Laps	Laps Led	Races Led	Miles	$
1979	Steve Moore	1	0	0	0	0	0	0	0	170	0	0	452	2,415
Lifetime		1	0	0	0	0	0	0	0	170	0	0	452	$2,415

Howard Moore

Year	Driver	Starts	Poles	1	2	3	4	5	6–10	Laps	Laps Led	Races Led	Miles	$
1956	Pat Kirkwood	1	0	0	0	0	0	0	1	347	0	0	477	550
Lifetime		1	0	0	0	0	0	0	1	347	0	0	477	$550

Year	Driver	Starts	Poles	Finish 1	2	3	4	5	6–10	Laps	Laps Led	Races Led	Miles	$

Stanley Moore

Year	Driver	Starts	Poles	1	2	3	4	5	6–10	Laps	Laps Led	Races Led	Miles	$
1951	Bobby Booth	3	0	0	0	0	0	0	0	156	0	0	169	25
Lifetime		3	0	0	0	0	0	0	0	156	0	0	169	$25

Steve Moore

Year	Driver	Starts	Poles	1	2	3	4	5	6–10	Laps	Laps Led	Races Led	Miles	$
1984	Steve Moore	2	0	0	0	0	0	0	0	237	0	0	622	5,095
Lifetime		2	0	0	0	0	0	0	0	237	0	0	622	$5,095

Willard Moore

Year	Driver	Starts	Poles	1	2	3	4	5	6–10	Laps	Laps Led	Races Led	Miles	$
1978	Steve Moore	1	0	0	0	0	0	0	0	150	0	0	399	1,590
1980	Steve Moore	4	0	0	0	0	0	0	0	735	0	0	1,469	9,040
1980	Ferrel Harris	1	0	0	0	0	0	0	0	17	0	0	45	1,350
1982	Steve Moore	4	0	0	0	0	0	0	0	456	4	1	727	6,625
Lifetime		10	0	0	0	0	0	0	0	1,358	4	1	2,640	$18,605

Bill Morehart

Year	Driver	Starts	Poles	1	2	3	4	5	6–10	Laps	Laps Led	Races Led	Miles	$
1983	Jim Bown	1	0	0	0	0	0	0	0	81	0	0	212	1,100
Lifetime		1	0	0	0	0	0	0	0	81	0	0	212	$1,100

Beau Morgan

Year	Driver	Starts	Poles	1	2	3	4	5	6–10	Laps	Laps Led	Races Led	Miles	$
1958	Joe Weatherly	1	0	0	0	0	1	0	0	149	0	0	149	650
1958	Fireball Roberts	1	0	0	0	1	0	0	0	100	0	0	100	400
1958	Tim Flock	1	0	0	0	0	0	0	0	98	0	0	98	100
1959	Speedy Thompson	2	0	0	0	0	0	0	0	334	0	0	185	170
1959	L.D. Austin	1	0	0	0	0	0	0	0	469	0	0	235	180
1959	Johnny Beauchamp	1	0	0	1	0	0	0	0	495	0	0	248	1,625
1959	Rex White	2	0	0	0	0	0	0	0	301	0	0	168	175
1959	Tim Flock	2	0	0	0	0	0	0	1	223	0	0	558	850
1960	Curtis Turner	1	0	0	0	0	0	0	0	185	0	0	278	350
1960	Johnny Suddeth	3	0	0	0	0	0	0	0	351	0	0	676	515
1960	Rex White	1	0	0	0	0	0	0	0	172	0	0	86	85
1960	Roscoe Thompson	2	0	0	0	0	0	0	0	402	0	0	603	710
1960	Tim Flock	1	0	0	0	0	0	0	1	213	0	0	293	700
1961	Tim Flock	6	0	0	0	0	0	0	3	1,043	0	0	938	1,405
1961	Jesse James Taylor	1	0	0	0	0	0	0	0	10	0	0	15	250
1961	Jim Bennett	2	0	0	0	0	0	0	0	170	0	0	351	500
1961	Speedy Thompson	2	0	0	0	0	0	0	0	188	0	0	282	275
1961	Johnny Allen	1	0	0	0	0	0	0	0	249	0	0	374	650
Lifetime		31	0	0	1	1	1	0	5	5,152	0	0	5,633	$9,590

Lee Morgan

Year	Driver	Starts	Poles	1	2	3	4	5	6–10	Laps	Laps Led	Races Led	Miles	$
1950	Lee Morgan	1	0	0	0	0	0	0	0	342	0	0	428	0
Lifetime		1	0	0	0	0	0	0	0	342	0	0	428	$0

Sonny Morgan

Year	Driver	Starts	Poles	1	2	3	4	5	6–10	Laps	Laps Led	Races Led	Miles	$
1957	Sonny Morgan	1	0	0	0	0	0	0	0		0	0		25
Lifetime		1	0	0	0	0	0	0	0		0	0		$25

Wayne Morgan

Year	Driver	Starts	Poles	1	2	3	4	5	6–10	Laps	Laps Led	Races Led	Miles	$
1978	Wayne Morgan	2	0	0	0	0	0	0	0	19	0	0	12	785
Lifetime		2	0	0	0	0	0	0	0	19	0	0	12	$785

Wes Morgan

Year	Driver	Starts	Poles	1	2	3	4	5	6–10	Laps	Laps Led	Races Led	Miles	$
1960	Wes Morgan	2	0	0	0	0	0	0	0	277	0	0	378	350
Lifetime		2	0	0	0	0	0	0	0	277	0	0	378	$350

Beth Ann Morganthau

Year	Driver	Starts	Poles	1	2	3	4	5	6–10	Laps	Laps Led	Races Led	Miles	$
2002	Stuart Kirby	1	0	0	0	0	0	0	0	44	0	0	66	53,100
2002	Kevin Lepage	1	0	0	0	0	0	0	0	356	0	0	356	44,650
2002	Derrike Cope	5	0	0	0	0	0	0	0	1,155	0	0	1,529	224,390
2002	Ron Hornaday Jr.	1	0	0	0	0	0	0	0	350	0	0	525	56,150

Year	Driver	Starts	Poles	Finish 1	2	3	4	5	6–10	Laps	Laps Led	Races Led	Miles	$

Beth Ann Morganthau *continued*

Year	Driver	Starts	Poles	1	2	3	4	5	6–10	Laps	Laps Led	Races Led	Miles	$
2002	Shawna Robinson	3	0	0	0	0	0	0	0	450	0	0	794	158,165
2002	Stacy Compton	2	0	0	0	0	0	0	0	274	0	0	629	90,630
Lifetime		13	0	0	0	0	0	0	0	2,629	0	0	3,899	627,085

Dick Moroso

Year	Driver	Starts	Poles	1	2	3	4	5	6–10	Laps	Laps Led	Races Led	Miles	$
1988	Rob Moroso	1	0	0	0	0	0	0	0	142	0	0	89	1,250
1989	Rob Moroso	2	0	0	0	0	0	0	0	583	0	0	671	4,725
1990	Steve Grissom	1	0	0	0	0	0	0	0	322	0	0	490	4,275
1990	Jimmy Hensley	2	0	0	0	0	0	0	0	692	0	0	820	7,475
1990	Chad Little	1	0	0	0	0	0	0	0	309	0	0	309	4,450
1990	Rob Moroso	25	0	0	0	0	0	0	1	5,666	9	3	6,971	141,642
1991	Bobby Hillin	10	0	0	0	0	0	0	1	3,713	0	0	4,113	111,285
1991	Kim Campbell	1	0	0	0	0	0	0	0	64	0	0	157	3,725
1991	Buddy Baker	5	0	0	0	0	0	0	0	810	0	0	1,870	39,260
1991	Sammy Swindell	1	0	0	0	0	0	0	0	28	0	0	70	16,500
1991	Ricky Craven	1	0	0	0	0	0	0	0	221	0	0	225	3,750
1992	Joe Ruttman	1	0	0	0	0	0	0	0	213	0	0	320	5,250
1992	Mike Wallace	1	0	0	0	0	0	0	0	251	0	0	382	5,180
1992	Jimmy Spencer	1	0	0	0	0	0	0	0	487	0	0	260	6,125
1993	Bobby Hamilton	5	0	0	0	0	0	0	0	1,161	0	0	1,833	36,315
1993	Joe Ruttman	5	0	0	0	0	0	1	0	1,133	0	0	1,597	70,700
1994	Jimmy Hensley	1	0	0	0	0	0	0	0	76	0	0	114	4,455
1994	Randy LaJoie	2	0	0	0	0	0	0	0	692	0	0	906	21,990
1994	Bobby Hillin	2	0	0	0	0	0	0	0	274	0	0	628	16,570
Lifetime		68	0	0	0	0	0	1	2	16,837	9	3	21,822	$504,922

B.B. Morris

Year	Driver	Starts	Poles	1	2	3	4	5	6–10	Laps	Laps Led	Races Led	Miles	$
1956	Larry Flynn	2	0	0	0	0	0	0	0	402	0	0	395	250
Lifetime		2	0	0	0	0	0	0	0	402	0	0	395	$250

Bob Morris

Year	Driver	Starts	Poles	1	2	3	4	5	6–10	Laps	Laps Led	Races Led	Miles	$
1984	Jeff Hooker	4	0	0	0	0	0	0	0	980	0	0	861	4,495
1985	Rick Baldwin	1	0	0	0	0	0	0	0	316	0	0	481	1,485
1986	Ken Ragan	1	0	0	0	0	0	0	0	5	0	0	8	1,500
Lifetime		6	0	0	0	0	0	0	0	1,301	0	0	1,349	$7,480

Buckshot Morris

Year	Driver	Starts	Poles	1	2	3	4	5	6–10	Laps	Laps Led	Races Led	Miles	$
1952	Billy Carden	1	0	0	0	0	0	0	0		0	0		0
1952	Jim Paschal	4	0	0	0	0	1	0	0	620	0	0	384	450
1953	Speedy Thompson	6	0	2	2	1	0	0	1	906	99	4	746	5,400
1954	Speedy Thompson	7	0	0	0	0	1	0	2	949	0	0	942	1,115
1954	Joe Weatherly	1	0	0	0	0	0	0	1	196	0	0	98	200
1954	Jim Paschal	1	0	0	0	0	0	0	0	180	0	0	90	25
Lifetime		20	0	2	2	1	2	0	4	2,851	99	4	2,260	$7,190

Bill Morton

Year	Driver	Starts	Poles	1	2	3	4	5	6–10	Laps	Laps Led	Races Led	Miles	$
1955	Bill Morton	2	0	0	0	0	0	0	0	288	0	0	267	110
1957	Bill Morton	5	0	0	0	0	0	0	4	653	0	0	365	600
1959	Bill Morton	3	0	0	0	0	0	0	0	398	0	0	218	100
1961	Bill Morton	5	0	0	0	0	0	0	3	1,697	0	0	886	6,890
1962	Bill Morton	5	0	0	0	0	0	0	2	1,359	0	0	1,255	1,350
Lifetime		20	0	0	0	0	0	0	9	4,395	0	0	2,990	$9,050

Ray Moss

Year	Driver	Starts	Poles	1	2	3	4	5	6–10	Laps	Laps Led	Races Led	Miles	$
1987	Ronnie Sanders	1	0	0	0	0	0	0	0	195	0	0	488	13,930
Lifetime		1	0	0	0	0	0	0	0	195	0	0	488	$13,930

Arden Mounts

Year	Driver	Starts	Poles	1	2	3	4	5	6–10	Laps	Laps Led	Races Led	Miles	$
1955	Herb Thomas	1	0	0	0	0	0	0	0	105	0	0	66	25
1955	Arden Mounts	9	1	0	0	0	0	0	2	1,149	0	0	722	640

Year	Driver	Starts	Poles	Finish 1	2	3	4	5	6–10	Laps	Laps Led	Races Led	Miles	$

Arden Mounts *continued*

Year	Driver	Starts	Poles	1	2	3	4	5	6–10	Laps	Laps Led	Races Led	Miles	$
1956	Arden Mounts	3	0	0	0	0	0	0	0	545	0	0	381	210
Lifetime		13	1	0	0	0	0	0	2	1,799	0	0	1,168	$875

Billy Moyer

Year	Driver	Starts	Poles	1	2	3	4	5	6–10	Laps	Laps Led	Races Led	Miles	$
1975	Terry Bivins	2	0	0	0	0	0	0	1	562	0	0	758	2,735
1975	Jimmy Hensley	2	0	0	0	0	0	0	1	534	0	0	281	1,860
1975	George Follmer	1	0	0	0	0	0	0	0	67	0	0	168	1,650
1975	Don Hoffman	1	0	0	0	0	0	0	0	178	0	0	445	1,650
1976	Bruce Jacobi	2	0	0	0	0	0	0	0	562	0	0	708	1,715
1976	Jimmy Hensley	2	0	0	0	0	0	0	1	474	0	0	249	2,150
1976	Terry Bivins	6	0	0	0	0	0	1	1	1,556	6	1	1,992	16,160
1977	Jimmy Hensley	1	0	0	0	0	0	0	0	321	0	0	169	630
Lifetime		17	0	0	0	0	0	1	4	4,254	6	1	4,769	$28,550

Dailey Moyer

Year	Driver	Starts	Poles	1	2	3	4	5	6–10	Laps	Laps Led	Races Led	Miles	$
1949	Ken Marriott	1	0	0	0	0	0	0	0	169	0	0	169	50
1949	Jack White	1	0	1	0	0	0	0	0	200	66	1	100	1,500
1949	Ken Wagner	3	1	0	0	0	0	0	0	412	0	0	206	100
1950	Jack White	3	0	0	0	0	0	1	1	544	0	0	585	450
1950	Ken Wagner	3	0	0	0	0	0	0	1	274	0	0	313	250
Lifetime		11	1	1	0	0	0	1	2	1,599	66	1	1,373	$2,350

Mueller Brothers

Year	Driver	Starts	Poles	1	2	3	4	5	6–10	Laps	Laps Led	Races Led	Miles	$
1983	Dean Roper	2	0	0	0	0	0	0	0	364	0	0	937	16,485
1984	Dean Roper	3	0	0	0	0	0	0	0	500	0	0	1,274	19,150
1985	Jim Sauter	3	0	0	0	0	0	0	0	565	0	0	1,107	15,465
1986	Jim Sauter	2	0	0	0	0	0	0	0	335	0	0	739	14,875
1987	Jim Sauter	3	0	0	0	0	0	0	1	781	0	0	1,364	14,855
1988	Jim Sauter	5	0	0	0	0	0	0	0	1,037	0	0	1,553	14,760
1988	Michael Waltrip	1	0	0	0	0	0	0	0	197	0	0	493	14,065
1989	Rodney Combs	5	0	0	0	0	0	0	0	610	0	0	836	20,560
1990	Rodney Combs	5	0	0	0	0	0	0	0	988	0	0	1,407	18,865
1991	Jim Sauter	6	0	0	0	0	0	0	0	1,012	0	0	1,843	44,895
1992	Jim Sauter	2	0	0	0	0	0	0	0	225	0	0	353	10,580
1993	Jim Sauter	2	0	0	0	0	0	0	0	307	0	0	714	36,285
Lifetime		39	0	0	0	0	0	0	1	6,921	0	0	12,619	240,840

A.T. Mulherin

Year	Driver	Starts	Poles	1	2	3	4	5	6–10	Laps	Laps Led	Races Led	Miles	$
1966	Rock Harn	1	0	0	0	0	0	0	0	33	0	0	83	0
Lifetime		1	0	0	0	0	0	0	0	33	0	0	83	$0

Jerry Mullins

Year	Driver	Starts	Poles	1	2	3	4	5	6–10	Laps	Laps Led	Races Led	Miles	$
1965	Jabe Thomas	1	0	0	0	0	0	0	0	242	0	0	363	515
1965	Junior Spencer	20	0	0	0	0	0	0	6	3,822	0	0	2,767	8,430
Lifetime		21	0	0	0	0	0	1	6	4,064	0	0	3,130	$8,945

Penny Mullis

Year	Driver	Starts	Poles	1	2	3	4	5	6–10	Laps	Laps Led	Races Led	Miles	$
1949	Buck Baker	1	0	0	0	0	0	0	0		0	0		50
Lifetime		1	0	0	0	0	0	0	0		0	0		$50

Richard Mummert

Year	Driver	Starts	Poles	1	2	3	4	5	6–10	Laps	Laps Led	Races Led	Miles	$
1973	Carl Adams	2	0	0	0	0	0	0	0	290	0	0	760	2,030
1974	Carl Adams	5	0	0	0	0	0	0	0	732	0	0	1,478	5,705
1974	Elmo Langley	2	0	0	0	0	0	0	0	173	0	0	458	2,265
1975	Carl Adams	20	0	0	0	0	0	0	4	5,332	0	0	5,828	24,865
Lifetime		29	0	0	0	0	0	0	4	6,527	0	0	8,523	$34,865

Ralph Murphy

Year	Driver	Starts	Poles	1	2	3	4	5	6–10	Laps	Laps Led	Races Led	Miles	$
1967	Paul Dean Holt	1	0	0	0	0	0	0	0	244	0	0	122	100

Year	Driver	Starts	Poles	1	2	3	4	5	6–10	Laps	Laps Led	Races Led	Miles	$

Ralph Murphy *continued*

Year	Driver	Starts	Poles	1	2	3	4	5	6–10	Laps	Laps Led	Races Led	Miles	$
1967	Ed Negre	1	0	0	0	0	0	0	0	8	0	0	11	555
1967	Bill Ervin	17	0	0	0	0	0	0	0	1,669	0	0	858	1,885
1968	Bill Ervin	1	0	0	0	0	0	0	0	149	0	0	75	100
Lifetime		20	0	0	0	0	0	0	0	2,070	0	0	1,066	$2,640

Ted Musgrave

Year	Driver	Starts	Poles	1	2	3	4	5	6–10	Laps	Laps Led	Races Led	Miles	$
1990	Ted Musgrave	2	0	0	0	0	0	0	0	158	0	0	225	6,590
Lifetime		2	0	0	0	0	0	0	0	158	0	0	225	$6,590

Billy Myers

Year	Driver	Starts	Poles	1	2	3	4	5	6–10	Laps	Laps Led	Races Led	Miles	$
1957	Billy Myers	10	0	0	0	0	1	0	4	1,668	0	0	1,114	2,380
1958	Billy Myers	2	0	0	0	0	0	0	0	28	0	0	115	50
Lifetime		12	0	0	0	0	1	0	4	1,696	0	0	1,229	$2,430

Dean Myers

Year	Driver	Starts	Poles	1	2	3	4	5	6–10	Laps	Laps Led	Races Led	Miles	$
1994	Dick Trickle	25	0	0	0	0	0	0	1	6,422	1	1	7,107	240,206
1995	Chuck Bown	9	0	0	0	0	0	0	0	2,068	0	0	3,026	99,995
1995	Greg Sacks	6	0	0	0	0	0	0	0	853	0	0	1,369	87,130
1995	Michael Ritch	1	0	0	0	0	0	0	0	226	0	0	226	12,655
1995	Ed Berrier	1	0	0	0	0	0	0	0	358	0	0	489	13,460
Lifetime		42	0	0	0	0	0	0	1	9,927	1	1	12,217	$453,446

Gary Myers

Year	Driver	Starts	Poles	1	2	3	4	5	6–10	Laps	Laps Led	Races Led	Miles	$
1976	Gary Myers	3	0	0	0	0	0	0	0	579	0	0	341	1,595
1977	Gary Myers	10	0	0	0	0	0	0	0	2,648	0	0	2,691	10,975
1977	Randy Myers	1	0	0	0	0	0	0	0	377	0	0	383	1,000
1978	Gary Myers	19	0	0	0	0	0	0	0	5,524	0	0	6,134	21,290
Lifetime		33	0	0	0	0	0	0	0	9,128	0	0	9,550	$34,860

Monty Myers

Year	Driver	Starts	Poles	1	2	3	4	5	6–10	Laps	Laps Led	Races Led	Miles	$
1972	Donnie Allison	2	0	0	0	0	0	1	0	472	11	1	883	4,825
Lifetime		2	0	0	0	0	0	1	0	472	11	1	883	$4,825

Kenny Myler

Year	Driver	Starts	Poles	1	2	3	4	5	6–10	Laps	Laps Led	Races Led	Miles	$
1965	Sam McQuagg	2	0	0	0	0	0	0	1	384	0	0	155	350
1965	Cale Yarborough	18	0	1	1	0	5	3	2	3,545	18	1	1,935	6,305
1966	Cale Yarborough	1	0	0	0	0	0	0	1	291	0	0	146	390
Lifetime		21	0	1	1	0	5	3	4	4,220	18	1	2,236	$7,045

Joe Nagle

Year	Driver	Starts	Poles	1	2	3	4	5	6–10	Laps	Laps Led	Races Led	Miles	$
1950	Joe Nagle	1	0	0	0	0	0	0	1	0	0	0	0	75
1950	John Schelesky	1	0	0	0	0	0	0	0		0	0		25
1971	Maynard Troyer	13	0	0	0	0	1	0	2	1,617	0	0	2,884	13,115
1973	Maynard Troyer	1	0	0	0	0	0	0	0	150	0	0	375	1,825
Lifetime		16	0	0	0	0	1	0	3	1,767	0	0	3,259	$15,040

Nash Motor Co.

Year	Driver	Starts	Poles	1	2	3	4	5	6–10	Laps	Laps Led	Races Led	Miles	$
1950	Frank Mundy	2	0	0	0	0	0	0	0		0	0		0
1950	Slick Smith	2	0	0	0	0	0	0	0	31	0	0	16	0
1950	Bill Snowden	3	0	0	0	0	0	0	1	338	0	0	423	100
1951	Bill Holland	1	0	0	0	0	0	0	0		0	0		0
1951	Curtis Turner	4	0	1	0	0	0	0	1	150	104	1	113	1,300
Lifetime		12	0	1	0	0	0	0	2	519	104	1	551	$1,400

Joe Navarro

Year	Driver	Starts	Poles	1	2	3	4	5	6–10	Laps	Laps Led	Races Led	Miles	$
1956	Bill Bade	1	0	0	0	0	0	0	0	214	0	0	214	40
Lifetime		1	0	0	0	0	0	0	0	214	0	0	214	$40

Year	Driver	Starts	Poles	Finish 1	2	3	4	5	6–10	Laps	Laps Led	Races Led	Miles	$

Harry Neal

Year	Driver	Starts	Poles	1	2	3	4	5	6–10	Laps	Laps Led	Races Led	Miles	$
1966	Bill Seifert	1	0	0	0	0	0	0	0	1	0	0	1	125
1966	Blackie Watt	20	0	0	0	0	0	0	9	4,067	0	0	3,003	7,050
Lifetime		21	0	0	0	0	0	0	9	4,068	0	0	3,004	$7,175

Ron Neal

Year	Driver	Starts	Poles	1	2	3	4	5	6–10	Laps	Laps Led	Races Led	Miles	$
1997	Mike Wallace	6	0	0	0	0	0	0	0	1,534	0	0	1,920	130,754
Lifetime		6	0	0	0	0	0	0	0	1,534	0	0	1,920	$130,754

Hal Needham (Statistics represent teams with primary ownership by Hal Needham, and includes co-ownerships with other partners.)

Year	Driver	Starts	Poles	1	2	3	4	5	6–10	Laps	Laps Led	Races Led	Miles	$
1981	Harry Gant	22	3	0	6	1	3	0	3	6,022	852	16	7,459	168,715
1981	Stan Barrett	10	0	0	0	0	0	0	1	1,559	4	2	3,265	28,540
1982	Harry Gant	30	1	2	2	3	1	1	7	8,454	420	17	9,642	275,335
1983	Harry Gant	30	0	1	1	3	1	4	6	9,024	60	10	10,194	361,495
1984	Harry Gant	30	3	3	6	0	5	1	8	9,901	1,186	19	11,396	505,853
1985	Harry Gant	28	3	3	5	3	1	2	5	8,805	1,271	20	10,185	581,690
1986	Harry Gant	29	2	0	3	1	3	2	4	7,965	656	17	9,565	463,450
1987	Harry Gant	29	1	0	0	0	0	0	4	6,494	71	3	7,921	176,145
1988	Harry Gant	24	0	0	0	0	0	0	3	5,896	343	8	6,877	152,615
1988	Morgan Shepherd	5	0	0	1	0	0	0	1	951	110	1	1,587	57,570
1989	Rick Mast	13	0	0	0	0	0	0	1	4,160	14	2	4,439	115,497
Lifetime		250	13	9	24	11	14	10	43	69,231	4,987	115	82,530	$2,886,905

Ed Negre

Year	Driver	Starts	Poles	1	2	3	4	5	6–10	Laps	Laps Led	Races Led	Miles	$
1956	Ed Negre	5	0	0	0	0	1	1	2	936	200	2	597	1,225
1957	Ed Negre	6	0	0	0	0	0	1	2	519	0	0	307	825
1967	Ed Negre	12	0	0	0	0	0	0	0	985	0	0	643	2,250
1968	Ed Negre	24	0	0	0	0	0	0	1	2,930	0	0	1,467	5,085
1969	Ed Negre	13	0	0	0	0	0	0	1	2,310	0	0	1,786	6,000
1970	Henley Gray	1	0	0	0	0	0	0	0	294	0	0	441	1,654
1970	Joe Frasson	2	0	0	0	0	0	0	0	508	0	0	235	695
1970	Ed Negre	31	0	0	0	0	0	0	1	3,345	0	0	2,702	14,580
1971	Ed Negre	34	0	0	0	0	0	0	1	6,549	0	0	5,970	18,065
1972	Ed Negre	25	0	0	0	0	0	0	0	5,588	0	0	6,598	29,893
1973	Ed Negre	15	0	0	0	0	0	1	1	3,853	0	0	4,476	21,116
1974	D.K. Ulrich	1	0	0	0	0	0	0	0	46	0	0	92	955
1974	Ed Negre	25	0	0	0	0	0	0	0	5,152	0	0	6,044	23,597
1975	Dean Dalton	2	0	0	0	0	0	0	0	23	0	0	59	2,405
1975	Ed Negre	21	0	0	0	0	0	0	4	5,428	2	1	5,555	32,785
1975	Dick May	1	0	0	0	0	0	0	0	43	0	0	43	1,000
1975	Dale Earnhardt	1	0	0	0	0	0	0	0	355	0	0	533	2,425
1976	Walter Ballard	1	0	0	0	0	0	0	0	28	0	0	70	550
1976	Ed Negre	24	0	0	0	0	0	0	2	5,821	0	0	6,853	43,895
1976	Gary Mathews	1	0	0	0	0	0	0	0	138	0	0	362	1,395
1977	Ed Negre	23	0	0	0	0	0	0	0	5,446	0	0	5,923	41,625
1978	Dick May	1	0	0	0	0	0	0	0	379	0	0	205	1,370
1978	Ed Negre	20	0	0	0	0	0	0	1	4,823	0	0	4,950	27,840
1978	Ferrel Harris	1	0	0	0	0	0	0	0	3	0	0	3	490
1979	Ed Negre	3	0	0	0	0	0	0	0	849	0	0	1,387	11,215
1981	Buddy Arrington	1	0	0	0	0	0	0	1	414	0	0	247	3,095
Lifetime		294	0	0	0	0	1	3	17	56,765	202	3	57,548	$296,030

Norman Negre

Year	Driver	Starts	Poles	1	2	3	4	5	6–10	Laps	Laps Led	Races Led	Miles	$
1978	Ronnie Thomas	1	0	0	0	0	0	0	0	483	0	0	483	3,560
1980	Dick May	1	0	0	0	0	0	0	0	178	0	0	473	3,550
1980	Cecil Gordon	1	0	0	0	0	0	0	0	10	0	0	14	1,110
1981	Dick May	1	0	0	0	0	0	0	0	353	0	0	482	2,875
1981	Jimmy Means	1	0	0	0	0	0	0	0	327	0	0	491	3,750
1981	Dave Marcis	1	0	0	0	0	0	0	0	292	1	1	174	745
Lifetime		6	0	0	0	0	0	0	0	1,643	1	1	2,117	$15,590

Harold Nelson

Year	Driver	Starts	Poles	1	2	3	4	5	6–10	Laps	Laps Led	Races Led	Miles	$
1951	Eddie Anderson	1	0	0	0	0	0	0	0		0	0	0	0
Lifetime		1	0	0	0	0	0	0	0		0	0		$0

Year	Driver	Starts	Poles	Finish 1	2	3	4	5	6–10	Laps	Laps Led	Races Led	Miles	$

Jon Nelson

Year	Driver	Starts	Poles	1	2	3	4	5	6–10	Laps	Laps Led	Races Led	Miles	$
1973	Eddie Yarboro	1	0	0	0	0	0	0	0	4	0	0	11	610
Lifetime		1	0	0	0	0	0	0	0	4	0	0	11	$610

Norm Nelson

Year	Driver	Starts	Poles	1	2	3	4	5	6–10	Laps	Laps Led	Races Led	Miles	$
1964	Jim Hurtubise	1	0	0	0	0	0	0	0	77	2	1	116	585
1966	Jim Hurtubise	6	0	1	1	0	0	0	2	1,215	158	4	2,434	25,010
1966	Norm Nelson	1	0	0	0	0	0	0	1	176	0	0	475	1,000
1967	Jim Hurtubise	2	0	0	0	0	0	0	1	196	0	0	490	2,600
1967	Norm Nelson	1	0	0	0	1	0	0	0	183	0	0	494	5,250
1970	Roger McCluskey	1	0	0	1	0	0	0	0	193	2	1	506	9,000
Lifetime		12	0	1	2	1	0	1	4	2,040	162	6	4,514	$43,445

Joe Nemechek

Year	Driver	Starts	Poles	1	2	3	4	5	6–10	Laps	Laps Led	Races Led	Miles	$
1993	Joe Nemechek	3	0	0	0	0	0	0	0	303	0	0	534	24,300
1995	Joe Nemechek	29	0	0	0	0	1	0	3	8,502	1	1	10,221	428,925
1996	Joe Nemechek	29	0	0	0	0	0	0	2	8,110	2	1	9,711	660,847
1999	Ron Fellows	1	0	0	1	0	0	0	0	90	3	1	221	67,270
2000	Ron Fellows	1	0	0	0	0	0	0	0	21	0	0	51	24,725
2001	Ron Fellows	2	0	0	0	0	0	0	0	137	23	2	285	72,055
2002	Ron Fellows	1	0	0	0	0	0	0	0	110	0	0	215	47,930
Lifetime		66	0	0	1	0	1	0	5	17,273	29	5	21,238	$1,326,052

Al Neves

Year	Driver	Starts	Poles	1	2	3	4	5	6–10	Laps	Laps Led	Races Led	Miles	$
1954	Clyde Palmer	2	0	0	0	0	1	0	1	526	0	0	263	450
Lifetime		2	0	0	0	0	1	0	1	526	0	0	263	$450

Paul Newkirk

Year	Driver	Starts	Poles	1	2	3	4	5	6–10	Laps	Laps Led	Races Led	Miles	$
1951	Paul Newkirk	1	0	0	0	0	0	1	0	241	0	0	241	500
1952	Paul Newkirk	1	0	0	0	0	0	0	0	27	0	0	27	0
Lifetime		2	0	0	0	0	0	1	0	268	0	0	268	$500

Rick Newsom

Year	Driver	Starts	Poles	1	2	3	4	5	6–10	Laps	Laps Led	Races Led	Miles	$
1972	Rick Newsom	1	0	0	0	0	0	0	0	231	0	0	462	800
1973	Rick Newsom	12	0	0	0	0	0	0	0	3,209	0	0	2,559	8,440
1974	Rick Newsom	3	0	0	0	0	0	0	0	801	0	0	773	2,370
1974	Bob Burcham	1	0	0	0	0	0	0	0	313	0	0	170	760
1975	Rick Newsom	10	0	0	0	0	0	0	0	1,672	0	0	1,695	9,780
1976	Rick Newsom	7	0	0	0	0	0	0	0	1,604	0	0	1,393	5,520
1977	Rick Newsom	7	0	0	0	0	0	0	0	1,240	0	0	888	3,260
1979	Rick Newsom	4	0	0	0	0	0	0	0	484	0	0	1,236	5,530
1980	Rick Newsom	6	0	0	0	0	0	0	0	1,179	0	0	790	3,830
1981	Cecil Gordon	1	0	0	0	0	0	0	0	296	0	0	296	650
1981	Rick Newsom	9	0	0	0	0	0	0	0	1,676	0	0	1,741	8,625
1982	Rick Newsom	8	0	0	0	0	0	0	0	1,143	0	0	1,931	12,390
1983	Rick Newsom	1	0	0	0	0	0	0	0	199	0	0	202	1,225
1984	Rick Newsom	1	0	0	0	0	0	0	0	242	0	0	246	1,235
1985	Rick Newsom	6	0	0	0	0	0	0	0	834	0	0	1,105	8,690
1986	Rick Newsom	3	0	0	0	0	0	0	0	358	0	0	447	4,185
Lifetime		80	0	0	0	0	0	0	0	15,481	0	0	15,933	$77,290

Ray Nichels (Statistics include teams owned by Nichels, plus shared ownership with Paul Goldsmith and a partnership with Chris Vallo.)

Year	Driver	Starts	Poles	1	2	3	4	5	6–10	Laps	Laps Led	Races Led	Miles	$
1957	Darel Dieringer	1	0	0	0	0	0	0	0		0	0		0
1957	Cotton Owens	16	1	1	1	0	0	1	2	2,139	179	3	1,688	12,225
1957	Banjo Matthews	1	1	0	0	0	0	0	0		0	0		100
1961	Darel Dieringer	2	0	0	0	0	0	1	0	230	0	0	575	600
1961	Paul Goldsmith	2	0	0	0	1	0	0	1	239	0	0	598	6,050
1962	Paul Goldsmith	1	0	0	0	0	0	0	1	218	0	0	327	1,375
1962	LeeRoy Yarbrough	2	0	0	0	0	0	0	0	420	0	0	664	1,600
1962	Junior Johnson	1	0	0	0	0	0	0	0	7	0	0	10	200
1963	Len Sutton	4	0	0	0	0	0	0	0	274	0	0	570	1,175
1963	David Pearson	1	0	0	0	0	0	0	0	255	0	0	383	550
1963	A.J. Foyt	3	0	0	1	1	0	0	0	368	8	2	957	7,520

Year	Driver	Starts	Poles	Finish 1	2	3	4	5	6–10	Laps	Laps Led	Races Led	Miles	$

Ray Nichels *continued*

Year	Driver	Starts	Poles	1	2	3	4	5	6–10	Laps	Laps Led	Races Led	Miles	$
1963	Jim McGuirk	2	0	0	0	0	0	0	0	70	0	0	175	550
1963	Paul Goldsmith	6	1	0	1	0	0	0	0	545	22	3	1,058	4,170
1963	Pedro Rodriguez	1	0	0	0	0	0	0	0	54	0	0	135	400
1964	A.J. Foyt	2	0	1	0	0	0	0	0	287	14	1	591	13,400
1964	Bobby Isaac	13	0	1	2	0	0	0	2	2,125	134	6	2,895	24,120
1964	Paul Goldsmith	14	2	0	0	3	0	0	1	2,281	319	8	2,903	20,785
1964	Troy Ruttman	1	0	0	0	0	0	0	1	177	0	0	478	850
1965	Bobby Isaac	3	0	0	0	0	0	0	0	400	11	1	372	1,260
1966	Larry Frank	2	0	0	0	0	0	0	2	232	0	0	580	1,575
1966	Don White	8	0	0	1	2	0	0	2	1,961	8	1	3,199	19,670
1966	Paul Goldsmith	18	1	3	2	2	1	1	0	4,600	436	9	5,159	49,260
1966	Sam McQuagg	16	0	1	0	1	0	2	3	3,575	175	3	3,906	28,480
1967	Don White	6	0	0	0	0	1	0	2	997	0	0	1,691	8,410
1967	Paul Goldsmith	21	0	0	2	3	1	1	1	4,851	397	7	5,409	35,360
1968	Paul Goldsmith	14	0	0	1	0	0	1	2	2,730	304	8	3,473	24,040
1968	Don White	2	0	0	0	0	0	0	1	585	0	0	738	2,105
1969	Don White	1	0	0	0	0	0	0	0	41	0	0	111	835
1969	Charlie Glotzbach	4	1	0	0	0	1	0	1	1,001	80	1	1,419	8,640
1969	Paul Goldsmith	10	0	0	0	3	1	0	1	1,959	20	4	2,950	22,385
1969	Richard Brickhouse	2	0	1	0	0	0	0	0	241	33	1	606	25,420
1970	Don White	1	0	0	0	0	0	0	0	16	0	0	42	880
1970	Charlie Glotzbach	17	4	2	0	3	2	0	1	3,177	417	16	5,161	50,274
1971	Dave Marcis	2	0	0	0	0	0	1	0	507	0	0	713	4,507
1971	Fred Lorenzen	14	1	0	1	0	2	4	2	3,229	152	6	5,038	44,975
1971	David Pearson	7	0	0	0	0	0	0	1	495	0	0	915	6,085
1972	Bobby Unser	1	0	0	0	0	0	0	0	8	0	0	12	603
1972	Don White	1	0	0	0	0	0	0	0	114	0	0	285	1,745
Lifetime		223	12	10	12	19	9	12	27	40,408	2,709	80	55,783	$432,179

Dick Niles

Year	Driver	Starts	Poles	1	2	3	4	5	6–10	Laps	Laps Led	Races Led	Miles	$
1963	Bill Amick	1	0	0	0	0	0	0	1	142	0	0	383	1,000
Lifetime		1	0	0	0	0	0	0	1	142	0	0	383	$1,000

Louis Nissen

Year	Driver	Starts	Poles	1	2	3	4	5	6–10	Laps	Laps Led	Races Led	Miles	$
1973	J.C. Danielson	1	0	0	0	0	0	0	1	176	0	0	461	1,520
1974	J.C. Danielson	1	0	0	0	0	0	0	0	178	0	0	466	1,425
Lifetime		2	0	0	0	0	0	0	1	354	0	0	927	$2,945

O.L. Nixon

Year	Driver	Starts	Poles	1	2	3	4	5	6–10	Laps	Laps Led	Races Led	Miles	$
1970	Jim Vandiver	5	0	0	0	0	0	0	2	1,076	0	0	1,640	6,680
1971	Stick Elliott	2	0	0	0	0	0	0	0	598	0	0	687	1,818
1971	Jim Vandiver	6	0	0	0	0	0	1	3	1,413	0	0	2,551	12,910
1972	Jim Vandiver	14	0	0	0	2	0	0	1	2,506	6	1	3,128	27,408
1973	Jim Vandiver	9	0	0	0	0	0	0	4	2,343	0	0	3,607	17,296
1974	Jim Vandiver	7	0	0	0	0	0	0	1	1,061	1	1	1,996	15,409
1978	Sam Sommers	2	0	0	0	0	0	0	0	512	0	0	748	3,190
1978	Jim Vandiver	2	0	0	0	0	0	0	0	362	0	0	562	3,530
1979	Jim Vandiver	3	0	0	0	0	0	0	0	476	1	1	741	6,215
1980	Jim Vandiver	4	0	0	0	0	0	0	1	610	0	0	1,136	13,185
Lifetime		54	0	0	0	2	0	1	12	10,957	8	3	16,798	$107,641

Charles Noble

Year	Driver	Starts	Poles	1	2	3	4	5	6–10	Laps	Laps Led	Races Led	Miles	$
1976	Gary Mathews	1	0	0	0	0	0	0	0	71	0	0	186	1,015
Lifetime		1	0	0	0	0	0	0	0	71	0	0	186	$1,015

Stan Noble

Year	Driver	Starts	Poles	1	2	3	4	5	6–10	Laps	Laps Led	Races Led	Miles	$
1951	Lloyd Porter	3	0	0	0	0	0	0	0		0	0		25
1951	Stan Noble	3	0	0	0	0	0	0	0		0	0		75
Lifetime		6	0	0	0	0	0	0	0		0	0		$100

Don Noel

Year	Driver	Starts	Poles	1	2	3	4	5	6–10	Laps	Laps Led	Races Led	Miles	$
1967	Don Noel	1	0	0	0	0	0	0	0	131	0	0	354	625

Year	Driver	Starts	Poles	Finish 1	2	3	4	5	6–10	Laps	Laps Led	Races Led	Miles	$

Don Noel *continued*

Year	Driver	Starts	Poles	1	2	3	4	5	6–10	Laps	Laps Led	Races Led	Miles	$
1970	Don Noel	2	0	0	0	0	0	0	0	38	0	0	100	1,450
1971	Don Noel	2	0	0	0	0	0	0	0	65	0	0	166	2,340
1972	Don Noel	2	0	0	0	0	0	0	0	159	0	0	413	2,585
1973	Don Noel	1	0	0	0	0	0	0	0	119	0	0	312	770
1978	Don Noel	2	0	0	0	0	0	0	0	180	0	0	453	1,765
1979	Don Noel	1	0	0	0	0	0	0	0	15	0	0	39	700
Lifetime		11	0	0	0	0	0	0	0	707	0	0	1,836	$10,235

Whitey Norman

Year	Driver	Starts	Poles	1	2	3	4	5	6–10	Laps	Laps Led	Races Led	Miles	$
1956	Whitey Norman	1	0	0	0	0	0	0	1	150	0	0	94	100
1957	Speedy Thompson	1	0	0	0	0	0	0	0	101	0	0	51	100
1957	Whitey Norman	13	0	0	1	0	0	0	3	2,437	0	0	1,614	3,990
1957	Bobby Myers	1	0	0	0	0	0	0	0	26	0	0	13	75
1957	Bill Massey	1	0	0	0	0	0	0	0	86	0	0	43	100
1958	Whitey Norman	8	0	0	0	0	2	0	1	1,238	0	0	683	1,585
1959	Whitey Norman	6	0	0	0	0	0	0	0	899	0	0	403	445
Lifetime		31	0	0	1	0	2	0	5	4,937	0	0	2,900	$6,395

Jim Norris

Year	Driver	Starts	Poles	1	2	3	4	5	6–10	Laps	Laps Led	Races Led	Miles	$
1978	Joe Mihalic	6	0	0	0	0	0	0	0	1,216	0	0	1,537	6,030
1978	John Rezek	1	0	0	0	0	0	0	0	214	0	0	218	675
1979	Wayne Broome	2	0	0	0	0	0	0	0	125	0	0	318	2,140
1979	Bub Strickler	1	0	0	0	0	0	0	0	67	0	0	68	550
1980	Baxter Price	1	0	0	0	0	0	0	0	125	0	0	250	740
1980	Bub Strickler	4	0	0	0	0	0	0	0	832	0	0	534	2,275
Lifetime		15	0	0	0	0	0	0	0	2,579	0	0	2,925	$12,410

Jack Norton

Year	Driver	Starts	Poles	1	2	3	4	5	6–10	Laps	Laps Led	Races Led	Miles	$
1963	Jack Norton	1	0	0	0	0	0	0	0	140	0	0	378	325
Lifetime		1	0	0	0	0	0	0	0	140	0	0	378	$325

James Norton

Year	Driver	Starts	Poles	1	2	3	4	5	6–10	Laps	Laps Led	Races Led	Miles	$
1960	James Norton	5	0	0	0	0	0	0	1	814	0	0	352	540
Lifetime		5	0	0	0	0	0	0	1	814	0	0	352	$540

Paul Nunn

Year	Driver	Starts	Poles	1	2	3	4	5	6–10	Laps	Laps Led	Races Led	Miles	$
1952	Fred Dove	1	0	0	0	0	0	0	0	53	0	0	53	0
1952	Clyde Minter	3	0	0	0	0	0	0	1	349	0	0	258	175
1953	Fred Dove	1	0	0	0	0	0	0	0	8	0	0	33	0
Lifetime		5	0	0	0	0	0	0	1	410	0	0	344	$175

Sam Nunn

Year	Driver	Starts	Poles	1	2	3	4	5	6–10	Laps	Laps Led	Races Led	Miles	$
1952	Fred Dove	2	0	0	0	0	0	0	1	256	0	0	186	140
Lifetime		2	0	0	0	0	0	0	1	256	0	0	186	$140

Don Nuzum

Year	Driver	Starts	Poles	1	2	3	4	5	6–10	Laps	Laps Led	Races Led	Miles	$
1972	Johnny Anderson	4	0	0	0	0	0	0	0	385	0	0	969	4,600
1973	Johnny Anderson	2	0	0	0	0	0	0	0	186	0	0	487	1,840
1974	Johnny Anderson	2	0	0	0	0	0	0	0	154	0	0	403	2,130
Lifetime		8	0	0	0	0	0	0	0	725	0	0	1,860	$8,570

Phil Oates

Year	Driver	Starts	Poles	1	2	3	4	5	6–10	Laps	Laps Led	Races Led	Miles	$
1951	Joe Eubanks	12	0	0	1	2	0	0	0	490	7	1	513	3,175
1952	Joe Eubanks	18	0	0	0	1	1	2	5	2,552	0	0	1,992	2,935
1953	Joe Eubanks	24	1	0	1	2	4	0	8	718	82	2	588	4,725
1954	Joe Eubanks	33	0	0	1	2	5	3	13	5,167	0	0	3,542	7,160
1955	Joe Eubanks	7	0	0	0	0	0	0	3	952	0	0	971	1,450
Lifetime		94	1	0	3	7	10	5	29	9,879	89	3	7,605	$19,445

Year	Driver	Starts	Poles	Finish 1	2	3	4	5	6–10	Laps	Laps Led	Races Led	Miles	$

Mike Ober

Year	Driver	Starts	Poles	1	2	3	4	5	6–10	Laps	Laps Led	Races Led	Miles	$
1969	Dick Bown	1	0	0	0	0	0	0	0	160	0	0	432	1,230
1970	Dick Bown	6	0	0	0	0	0	0	1	836	0	0	1,187	4,275
1971	Dick Bown	4	0	0	0	0	0	0	0	414	0	0	941	4,500
1972	Dick Bown	3	0	0	0	0	0	0	0	459	0	0	1,181	4,465
1973	Dick Bown	2	0	0	0	0	0	0	0	196	0	0	514	1,860
1974	Dick Bown	1	0	0	0	0	0	0	0	24	0	0	63	935
Lifetime		17	0	0	0	0	0	0	1	2,089	0	0	4,317	$17,265

Dan Obrist

Year	Driver	Starts	Poles	1	2	3	4	5	6–10	Laps	Laps Led	Races Led	Miles	$
1995	Dan Obrist	1	0	0	0	0	0	0	0	7	0	0	18	9,760
Lifetime		1	0	0	0	0	0	0	0	7	0	0	18	$9,760

Tony Oddo

Year	Driver	Starts	Poles	1	2	3	4	5	6–10	Laps	Laps Led	Races Led	Miles	$
1972	Mike James	2	0	0	0	0	0	0	0	180	0	0	450	2,620
1973	Mike James	1	0	0	0	0	0	0	0	129	0	0	338	1,065
Lifetime		3	0	0	0	0	0	0	0	309	0	0	788	$3,685

Homer O'Dell

Year	Driver	Starts	Poles	1	2	3	4	5	6–10	Laps	Laps Led	Races Led	Miles	$
1966	Neil Castles	1	0	0	0	0	0	0	0	20	0	0	8	100
1966	Jack Soper	1	0	0	0	0	0	0	0	25	0	0	5	0
1966	Sonny Lamphear	13	0	0	0	0	0	0	1	622	0	0	379	2,270
1966	Jimmy Helms	1	0	0	0	0	0	0	0	183	0	0	92	225
Lifetime		16	0	0	0	0	0	0	1	850	0	0	484	$2,595

Larry Odo

Year	Driver	Starts	Poles	1	2	3	4	5	6–10	Laps	Laps Led	Races Led	Miles	$
1956	Larry Odo	1	0	0	0	0	0	0	0	361	0	0	181	150
1959	Larry Odo	1	0	0	0	0	0	0	0	3	0	0	8	100
Lifetime		2	0	0	0	0	0	0	0	364	0	0	188	$250

Jack Ogden

Year	Driver	Starts	Poles	1	2	3	4	5	6–10	Laps	Laps Led	Races Led	Miles	$
1979	Randy Ogden	3	0	0	0	0	0	0	0	473	0	0	737	2,465
1980	Donnie Allison	1	0	0	0	0	0	0	0	134	0	0	201	1,645
1980	Randy Ogden	3	0	0	0	0	0	0	0	135	0	0	267	2,385
1981	Randy Ogden	4	0	0	0	0	0	0	0	577	0	0	762	3,905
1982	Donnie Allison	3	0	0	0	0	0	0	0	608	0	0	840	9,330
Lifetime		14	0	0	0	0	0	0	0	1,927	0	0	2,808	$19,730

Don Oldenberg

Year	Driver	Starts	Poles	1	2	3	4	5	6–10	Laps	Laps Led	Races Led	Miles	$
1951	Red Duvall	1	0	0	0	1	0	0	0		0	0		500
1951	Don Oldenberg	3	0	0	0	0	0	0	1		0	0		375
1954	Don Oldenberg	6	0	0	0	0	0	0	3	806	0	0	715	900
1955	Don Oldenberg	2	0	0	0	0	0	0	2	260	0	0	178	350
1956	Don Oldenberg	3	0	0	0	0	0	0	0	495	0	0	341	200
Lifetime		15	0	0	0	1	0	1	6	1,561	0	0	1,234	$2,325

Charles Oldham

Year	Driver	Starts	Poles	1	2	3	4	5	6–10	Laps	Laps Led	Races Led	Miles	$
1956	Charles Oldham	1	0	0	0	0	0	0	0		0	0		25
Lifetime		1	0	0	0	0	0	0	0		0	0		$25

Don Oliver

Year	Driver	Starts	Poles	1	2	3	4	5	6–10	Laps	Laps Led	Races Led	Miles	$
1954	Ben Gregory	1	0	0	0	0	0	0	0	222	0	0	111	25
1954	Dick Rathmann	1	0	0	0	1	0	0	0	249	0	0	249	900
1954	Eli Vukovich	1	0	0	0	0	0	0	0	262	0	0	131	25
1955	Dick Rathmann	1	0	0	0	0	0	0	0	197	0	0	197	40
1955	Speedy Thompson	1	0	0	0	0	0	0	1	96	0	0	96	250
1956	Gordon Campbell	1	0	0	0	0	0	0	0	74	0	0	185	75
Lifetime		6	0	0	0	1	0	0	1	1,100	0	0	969	$1,315

Year	Driver	Starts	Poles	Finish 1	2	3	4	5	6–10	Laps	Laps Led	Races Led	Miles	$

Budd Olsen

Year	Driver	Starts	Poles	1	2	3	4	5	6–10	Laps	Laps Led	Races Led	Miles	$
1961	Budd Olsen	1	0	0	0	0	0	0	0	168	0	0	42	175
Lifetime		1	0	0	0	0	0	0	0	168	0	0	42	$175

Herb Onash

Year	Driver	Starts	Poles	1	2	3	4	5	6–10	Laps	Laps Led	Races Led	Miles	$
1964	Sal Tovella	2	0	0	0	0	0	0	0	167	0	0	418	850
Lifetime		2	0	0	0	0	0	0	0	167	0	0	418	$850

J.R. O'Neal

Year	Driver	Starts	Poles	1	2	3	4	5	6–10	Laps	Laps Led	Races Led	Miles	$
1989	Norm Benning	3	0	0	0	0	0	0	0	653	0	0	880	6,875
Lifetime		3	0	0	0	0	0	0	0	653	0	0	880	$6,875

Jerry O'Neal

Year	Driver	Starts	Poles	1	2	3	4	5	6–10	Laps	Laps Led	Races Led	Miles	$
1993	Norm Benning	1	0	0	0	0	0	0	0	1	0	0	1	5,410
Lifetime		1	0	0	0	0	0	0	0	1	0	0	1	$5,410

Heidi O'Neil

Year	Driver	Starts	Poles	1	2	3	4	5	6–10	Laps	Laps Led	Races Led	Miles	$
1993	Jerry O'Neil	1	0	0	0	0	0	0	0	331	0	0	497	4,450
Lifetime		1	0	0	0	0	0	0	0	331	0	0	497	$4,450

Darwin Oordt

Year	Driver	Starts	Poles	1	2	3	4	5	6–10	Laps	Laps Led	Races Led	Miles	$
2000	Wally Dallenbach	30	0	0	0	0	0	0	1	8,226	2	1	10,783	1,141,630
Lifetime		30	0	0	0	0	0	0	1	8,226	2	1	10,783	$1,141,630

Phil Orr

Year	Driver	Starts	Poles	1	2	3	4	5	6–10	Laps	Laps Led	Races Led	Miles	$
1957	Phil Orr	1	0	0	0	0	0	0	0		0	0		110
1958	Phil Orr	1	0	0	0	0	0	0	0	31	0	0	127	50
Lifetime		2	0	0	0	0	0	0	0	31	0	0	127	$160

Bill Osborne

Year	Driver	Starts	Poles	1	2	3	4	5	6–10	Laps	Laps Led	Races Led	Miles	$
1975	Bill Osborne	1	0	0	0	0	0	0	0	125	0	0	328	1,435
1977	Bill Osborne	1	0	0	0	0	0	0	0	188	0	0	470	1,350
1980	Bill Osborne	1	0	0	0	0	0	0	0	22	0	0	22	575
1985	Bill Osborne	2	0	0	0	0	0	0	0	198	0	0	519	3,605
1986	Bill Osborne	1	0	0	0	0	0	0	0	38	0	0	100	850
Lifetime		6	0	0	0	0	0	0	0	571	0	0	1,438	$7,815

George Osborne

Year	Driver	Starts	Poles	1	2	3	4	5	6–10	Laps	Laps Led	Races Led	Miles	$
1953	George Osborne	2	0	0	0	0	0	0	0	477	0	0	528	300
1954	George Osborne	1	0	0	0	0	0	0	0	16	0	0	66	0
Lifetime		3	0	0	0	0	0	0	0	493	0	0	594	$300

Lewis Osborne

Year	Driver	Starts	Poles	1	2	3	4	5	6–10	Laps	Laps Led	Races Led	Miles	$
1962	T.C. Hunt	1	0	0	0	0	0	0	0	196	0	0	270	400
1962	Bubba Farr	1	0	0	0	0	0	0	0	22	0	0	11	75
1962	George Dunn	1	0	0	0	0	1	0	0	108	0	0	27	305
1962	Harry Leake	2	0	0	0	0	0	0	1	225	0	0	56	225
1962	Paul Lewis	4	0	0	0	0	0	0	0	741	0	0	830	1,225
1962	Tiny Lund	1	0	0	0	0	0	0	0	124	0	0	62	75
1962	Tom Pistone	1	0	0	0	0	0	0	0	2	0	0	5	250
1962	LeeRoy Yarbrough	6	0	0	0	0	0	0	0	529	0	0	496	710
1962	Bruce Brantley	1	0	0	0	0	0	0	0	139	0	0	209	275
1963	Cale Yarborough	1	0	0	0	0	0	0	0	9	0	0	23	250
1963	Possum Jones	2	0	0	0	0	0	0	0	341	0	0	511	800
Lifetime		21	0	0	0	0	1	0	1	2,436	0	0	2,499	$4,590

Ray Osborne

Year	Driver	Starts	Poles	1	2	3	4	5	6–10	Laps	Laps Led	Races Led	Miles	$
1963	LeeRoy Yarbrough	1	0	0	0	0	0	0	0	20	0	0	30	600
1964	Jack Anderson	3	0	0	0	0	0	0	0	491	0	0	348	1,100
1964	Jim Cook	1	0	0	0	0	0	0	0	222	0	0	111	150
1964	Reb Wickersham	1	0	0	0	0	0	0	0	186	0	0	279	400

Year	Driver	Starts	Poles	Finish 1	2	3	4	5	6–10	Laps	Laps Led	Races Led	Miles	$

Ray Osborne *continued*

Year	Driver	Starts	Poles	1	2	3	4	5	6–10	Laps	Laps Led	Races Led	Miles	$
1964	Buddy Baker	1	0	0	0	0	0	0	0	43	0	0	39	100
1964	Rodney Bottinger	1	0	0	0	0	0	0	0	8	0	0	4	100
1964	Rodney Williams	2	0	0	0	0	0	0	0	115	0	0	68	550
1964	Cale Yarborough	1	0	0	0	0	0	0	0	74	0	0	111	540
Lifetime		11	0	0	0	0	0	0	0	1,159	0	0	989	$3,540

Bob Osiecki

Year	Driver	Starts	Poles	1	2	3	4	5	6–10	Laps	Laps Led	Races Led	Miles	$
1951	Jim Delaney	7	0	0	0	0	0	1	1	494	0	0	468	425
1952	Charlie Causey	1	0	0	0	0	0	0	0	7	0	0	7	25
1956	Jack Choquette	1	0	0	0	0	0	0	0		0	0		0
1957	Everett Brashear	1	0	0	0	0	0	0	0		0	0		25
1957	Don Oldenberg	1	0	0	0	0	0	0	0		0	0		100
1962	Gary Sain	5	0	0	0	0	0	0	0	986	0	0	533	1,000
1962	Herb Tillman	1	0	0	0	0	0	0	0	194	0	0	291	500
1962	Jimmy Thompson	2	0	0	0	0	0	0	0	483	0	0	725	1,175
1962	Darel Dieringer	7	0	0	0	0	0	1	1	1,878	17	1	1,861	2,890
1962	Ralph Earnhardt	2	0	0	0	0	0	0	1	517	0	0	776	1,675
1962	Marvin Panch	2	0	0	0	0	0	0	0	23	0	0	58	450
Lifetime		30	0	0	0	0	0	2	3	4,582	17	1	4,717	$8,265

Rod Osterlund (Statistics represent teams principly owned by Osterlund, plus a partnership with Nelson Malloch.)

Year	Driver	Starts	Poles	1	2	3	4	5	6–10	Laps	Laps Led	Races Led	Miles	$
1977	Roland Wlodyka	5	0	0	0	0	0	0	0	501	0	0	1,100	5,520
1977	Jimmy Means	1	0	0	0	0	0	0	0	38	0	0	101	875
1977	Marv Acton	2	0	0	0	0	0	0	0	359	0	0	202	945
1977	Dave Marcis	2	0	0	0	0	0	1	0	324	0	0	620	2,510
1977	Dick May	1	0	0	0	0	0	0	0	247	0	0	376	740
1977	Sam Sommers	1	0	0	0	0	0	0	0	377	0	0	236	650
1978	Dave Marcis	30	0	0	1	3	8	2	10	9,672	115	12	10,993	200,930
1978	Dale Earnhardt	1	0	0	0	0	1	0	0	327	0	0	498	7,500
1978	Neil Bonnett	14	0	0	0	1	1	0	1	2,771	278	2	2,897	65,195
1978	Roland Wlodyka	6	0	0	0	0	0	0	0	1,172	0	0	1,707	9,910
1978	Jimmy Insolo	1	0	0	0	0	0	0	1	198	0	0	495	5,640
1979	David Pearson	4	1	1	1	0	1	0	1	1,250	91	2	1,664	64,865
1979	Dale Earnhardt	27	4	1	1	3	4	2	6	8,340	604	16	9,357	237,575
1980	Janet Guthrie	1	0	0	0	0	0	0	0	193	0	0	483	13,925
1980	Dale Earnhardt	31	0	5	3	4	3	4	5	9,615	1,185	25	11,137	449,600
1980	Dan Gurney	1	0	0	0	0	0	0	0	79	0	0	207	1,105
1981	Dale Earnhardt	16	0	0	2	3	0	2	3	4,282	272	7	5,494	220,085
1989	Hut Stricklin	27	0	0	0	0	1	0	3	7,557	3	1	9,287	137,054
1990	Jim Bown	3	0	0	0	0	0	0	0	837	0	0	874	11,655
1990	Jimmy Spencer	26	0	0	0	0	0	0	2	7,576	10	5	9,029	217,675
1991	Buddy Baker	1	0	0	0	0	0	0	0	35	0	0	88	18,800
Lifetime		201	5	7	8	14	19	11	32	55,750	2,558	70	66,844	$1,672,754

Nelson Oswald

Year	Driver	Starts	Poles	1	2	3	4	5	6–10	Laps	Laps Led	Races Led	Miles	$
1978	Nelson Oswald	6	0	0	0	0	0	0	0	1,103	0	0	781	2,955
1979	Dick May	1	0	0	0	0	0	0	0	113	0	0	226	1,100
1979	Nelson Oswald	6	0	0	0	0	0	0	0	842	0	0	1,000	3,610
1979	Bill Seifert	1	0	0	0	0	0	0	0	32	0	0	64	960
1980	Cecil Gordon	1	0	0	0	0	0	0	0	335	0	0	200	450
1980	Dick May	2	0	0	0	0	0	0	0	508	0	0	524	2,315
1980	Nelson Oswald	2	0	0	0	0	0	0	0	184	0	0	374	2,520
Lifetime		19	0	0	0	0	0	0	0	3,117	0	0	3,168	$13,910

Barry Owen

Year	Driver	Starts	Poles	1	2	3	4	5	6–10	Laps	Laps Led	Races Led	Miles	$
1992	Mike Wallace	2	0	0	0	0	0	0	0	791	0	0	965	12,235
1993	Mike Wallace	3	0	0	0	0	0	0	0	964	0	0	1,334	25,400
1996	Mike Wallace	1	0	0	0	0	0	0	0	199	0	0	398	16,665
Lifetime		6	0	0	0	0	0	0	0	1,954	0	0	2,697	$54,300

Cotton Owens

Year	Driver	Starts	Poles	1	2	3	4	5	6–10	Laps	Laps Led	Races Led	Miles	$
1950	Cotton Owens	2	0	0	0	0	0	0	0	131	0	0	252	50
1958	Cotton Owens	1	0	0	0	0	0	0	0	15	0	0	21	100
1960	Cotton Owens	13	3	1	3	1	0	0	0	1,984	185	7	2,276	14,005

Year	Driver	Starts	Poles	1	2	3	4	5	6–10	Laps	Laps Led	Races Led	Miles	$

Cotton Owens *continued*

Year	Driver	Starts	Poles	1	2	3	4	5	6–10	Laps	Laps Led	Races Led	Miles	$
1960	Bobby Johns	4	0	1	0	0	2	0	0	1,173	366	3	1,269	20,040
1961	Marvin Panch	1	0	0	0	0	0	0	1	262	0	0	393	875
1961	Fireball Roberts	1	0	0	0	0	1	0	0	496	2	1	248	850
1961	Cotton Owens	16	2	4	3	1	2	1	0	2,683	58	5	2,108	11,740
1961	Ralph Earnhardt	7	0	0	1	1	0	0	3	1,602	90	3	2,429	10,195
1962	Junior Johnson	4	0	0	1	0	0	0	1	671	166	1	824	7,345
1962	David Pearson	3	0	0	0	0	1	0	1	1,055	2	1	1,076	4,435
1962	Cotton Owens	16	1	0	2	2	2	1	1	2,000	36	2	1,515	5,905
1963	Billy Wade	29	0	0	1	0	2	1	10	5,997	21	2	4,986	13,705
1963	Cotton Owens	1	0	0	0	0	0	0	1	170	0	0	85	175
1963	David Pearson	40	2	0	3	2	5	3	6	8,442	178	6	6,120	20,540
1963	G.C. Spencer	1	0	0	0	0	0	0	0	210	0	0	289	500
1964	Cotton Owens	2	0	1	1	0	0	0	0	466	54	1	299	3,400
1964	Bobby Isaac	3	0	0	1	0	1	0	0	727	0	0	309	1,200
1964	Billy Wade	3	0	0	0	1	0	0	1	485	0	0	585	3,970
1964	Larry Thomas	2	0	0	0	0	0	0	0	403	0	0	579	1,200
1964	Earl Balmer	10	0	0	0	0	1	1	2	2,771	1	1	2,052	5,795
1964	Jim Paschal	9	0	0	0	0	1	2	4	2,305	0	0	1,941	7,115
1964	David Pearson	61	12	8	8	4	7	2	13	13,225	2,256	31	8,906	38,275
1965	David Pearson	14	1	2	2	2	1	1	3	3,242	744	8	1,803	8,925
1966	Bobby Isaac	1	0	0	0	0	0	0	0	293	0	0	293	615
1966	Mario Andretti	1	0	0	0	0	0	0	0	78	0	0	195	395
1966	David Pearson	42	7	15	5	5	1	0	7	10,781	3,174	25	8,437	62,125
1967	Bobby Allison	9	0	1	2	3	1	0	1	1,971	51	5	1,981	16,130
1967	Buddy Baker	4	0	0	0	1	0	0	0	589	0	0	375	1,350
1967	Darel Dieringer	3	0	0	0	0	0	0	0	585	35	1	683	2,310
1967	David Pearson	10	0	2	0	1	1	0	2	2,066	340	6	2,032	16,995
1967	Sam McQuagg	6	0	0	0	0	2	0	0	1,053	8	1	695	2,845
1967	Ray Hendrick	1	0	0	0	0	0	0	0	107	0	0	54	175
1968	Buddy Baker	1	0	0	0	0	0	0	0	59	0	0	159	575
1968	Charlie Glotzbach	19	3	1	3	1	4	0	2	4,336	291	5	4,336	39,710
1968	Al Unser	1	0	0	0	0	1	0	0	200	1	1	500	6,250
1969	Buddy Baker	12	1	0	2	4	0	1	2	3,266	579	10	4,113	50,085
1969	Charlie Glotzbach	6	1	0	2	0	0	1	0	1,443	82	5	1,924	24,550
1969	James Hylton	2	0	0	0	0	0	1	0	611	0	0	355	1,250
1970	Buddy Baker	17	1	1	2	0	1	2	2	3,604	485	11	5,871	63,553
1970	Sam Posey	1	0	0	0	0	0	0	0	82	0	0	215	900
1971	Pete Hamilton	20	2	1	0	5	4	1	1	4,407	214	13	6,858	60,140
1972	Charlie Glotzbach	3	0	0	1	1	0	0	0	709	0	0	1,150	26,175
1973	Peter Gregg	1	0	0	0	0	0	0	0	34	0	0	51	775
1973	Dick Brooks	1	0	0	0	1	0	0	0	197	0	0	493	6,800
Lifetime		404	36	38	43	36	41	18	64	86,986	9,419	155	81,133	$564,043

Ken Pace

Year	Driver	Starts	Poles	1	2	3	4	5	6–10	Laps	Laps Led	Races Led	Miles	$
1954	Billy Minter	1	0	0	0	0	0	0	0	108	0	0	81	25
1954	Clyde Minter	12	0	0	0	0	0	0	6	1,653	0	0	870	900
1954	Ken Pace	2	0	0	0	0	0	0	0	258	0	0	144	25
1954	Fred Dove	2	0	0	0	0	0	0	0	183	0	0	99	0
1955	Fred Dove	2	0	0	0	0	0	0	0	42	0	0	22	25
1955	Clyde Minter	1	0	0	0	0	0	0	1	178	0	0	89	100
1955	Ken Pace	2	0	0	0	0	0	0	0	160	0	0	80	25
Lifetime		22	0	0	0	0	0	0	7	2,582	0	0	1,384	$1,100

Eddie Pagan

Year	Driver	Starts	Poles	1	2	3	4	5	6–10	Laps	Laps Led	Races Led	Miles	$
1954	Eddie Pagan	2	0	0	0	0	0	0	0	682	0	0	453	140
1954	Marian Pagan	1	0	0	0	0	0	0	0	261	0	0	131	25
1955	Eddie Pagan	2	0	0	0	0	0	0	0	287	0	0	287	120
1956	Eddie Pagan	8	2	1	1	0	0	2	0	1,366	31	2	1,037	3,095
1957	Eddie Pagan	15	2	3	3	3	1	1	0	2,611	3	3	1,802	7,165
1958	Eddie Pagan	23	2	0	2	1	1	7	6	3,701	57	2	2,444	6,370
Lifetime		51	6	4	6	4	2	10	6	8,908	91	7	6,152	$16,915

Norm Palmer

Year	Driver	Starts	Poles	1	2	3	4	5	6–10	Laps	Laps Led	Races Led	Miles	$
1977	Norm Palmer	3	0	0	0	0	0	0	1	239	0	0	620	4,560
1978	Norm Palmer	2	0	0	0	0	0	0	0	119	0	0	312	2,100

Year	Driver	Starts	Poles	Finish 1	2	3	4	5	6–10	Laps	Laps Led	Races Led	Miles	$

Norm Palmer *continued*

Year	Driver	Starts	Poles	1	2	3	4	5	6–10	Laps	Laps Led	Races Led	Miles	$
1979	Norm Palmer	1	0	0	0	0	0	0	1	91	0	0	238	2,500
1985	Norm Palmer	1	0	0	0	0	0	0	0	22	0	0	58	745
Lifetime		7	0	0	0	0	0	0	2	471	0	0	1,227	$9,905

Robert Palmer

Year	Driver	Starts	Poles	1	2	3	4	5	6–10	Laps	Laps Led	Races Led	Miles	$
1983	Randy Becker	1	0	0	0	0	0	0	0	23	0	0	60	1,700
Lifetime		1	0	0	0	0	0	0	0	23	0	0	60	$1,700

Walt Palozi

Year	Driver	Starts	Poles	1	2	3	4	5	6–10	Laps	Laps Led	Races Led	Miles	$
1954	Ernie Young	1	0	0	0	0	0	0	0	337	0	0	169	25
1955	Ernie Young	2	0	0	0	0	0	0	1	186	0	0	186	125
1956	Ernie Young	5	0	0	0	0	0	0	0	419	0	0	443	330
1956	Sam Speers	1	0	0	0	0	0	0	1	119	0	0	74	125
1957	Don Johns	2	0	0	0	0	0	0	1	255	0	0	128	200
1957	Ernie Young	2	0	0	0	0	1	0	0	153	0	0	97	375
1958	Ernie Young	1	0	0	0	0	0	0	0	165	0	0	434	130
1959	Bob Hogle	2	0	0	0	0	0	0	0	429	0	0	184	165
1960	Kuzie Kuzmanich	2	0	0	0	0	0	0	1	115	0	0	124	350
Lifetime		18	0	0	0	0	1	0	4	2,178	0	0	1,837	$1,825

Bettie Panch

Year	Driver	Starts	Poles	1	2	3	4	5	6–10	Laps	Laps Led	Races Led	Miles	$
1975	Richie Panch	14	0	0	0	0	0	0	3	2,276	8	3	3,133	32,535
Lifetime		14	0	0	0	0	0	1	3	2,276	8	3	3,133	$32,535

Marvin Panch

Year	Driver	Starts	Poles	1	2	3	4	5	6–10	Laps	Laps Led	Races Led	Miles	$
1951	Sam Hawks	3	0	0	0	0	1	0	0		0	0		800
1951	Marvin Panch	3	0	0	1	0	0	0	1		0	0		950
1953	Marvin Panch	2	0	0	0	0	0	0	0	275	0	0	378	160
1955	Marvin Panch	2	0	0	1	0	0	0	0	169	15	1	134	675
1957	Marvin Panch	20	0	2	2	3	3	0	4	3,595	91	3	2,306	9,995
Lifetime		30	0	2	4	3	4	0	5	4,039	106	4	2,818	$12,580

Chester Papienski

Year	Driver	Starts	Poles	1	2	3	4	5	6–10	Laps	Laps Led	Races Led	Miles	$
1974	Eddie Bradshaw	1	0	0	0	0	0	0	1	123	0	0	322	1,375
1975	Eddie Bradshaw	1	0	0	0	0	0	0	0	63	0	0	165	820
1976	Eddie Bradshaw	2	0	0	0	0	0	0	0	224	0	0	587	2,685
1977	Eddie Bradshaw	2	0	0	0	0	0	0	1	152	0	0	394	2,920
1978	Jack Simpson	1	0	0	0	0	0	0	0	74	0	0	194	1,105
1978	Eddie Bradshaw	1	0	0	0	0	0	0	0	15	0	0	39	600
Lifetime		8	0	0	0	0	0	0	2	651	0	0	1,701	$9,505

Roger Paquette

Year	Driver	Starts	Poles	1	2	3	4	5	6–10	Laps	Laps Led	Races Led	Miles	$
1972	Jimmy Insolo	1	0	0	0	0	0	0	0	130	0	0	341	835
1973	Jimmy Insolo	2	0	0	0	0	1	1	0	335	0	0	878	6,295
1974	Jimmy Insolo	2	0	0	0	0	0	0	0	267	1	1	681	2,575
1975	Jimmy Insolo	3	0	0	0	0	0	0	1	265	18	1	671	4,815
1976	Jimmy Insolo	3	0	0	0	1	0	0	1	454	0	0	1,169	12,105
Lifetime		11	0	0	0	1	1	1	2	1,451	19	2	3,739	$26,625

Jimmy Pardue

Year	Driver	Starts	Poles	1	2	3	4	5	6–10	Laps	Laps Led	Races Led	Miles	$
1955	Jimmy Pardue	1	0	0	0	0	0	0	0	10	0	0	5	0
1955	Bobby Waddell	6	0	0	0	0	0	0	0	805	0	0	849	325
1956	Jimmy Pardue	1	0	0	0	0	0	0	0	142	0	0	71	100
1956	Bobby Waddell	5	0	0	0	0	0	0	0	337	0	0	189	110
1959	Jimmy Pardue	6	0	0	0	0	0	0	1	526	0	0	264	465
1961	Jimmy Pardue	40	0	0	0	0	1	2	13	7,310	0	0	5,439	8,845
1962	Jimmy Pardue	29	0	1	1	1	1	1	11	7,274	200	3	4,855	11,455
1963	Jimmy Pardue	2	0	0	0	0	2	0	0	395	0	0	158	575
Lifetime		90	0	1	1	1	4	3	25	16,799	200	3	11,831	$21,875

Year	Driver	Starts	Poles	Finish 1	2	3	4	5	6–10	Laps	Laps Led	Races Led	Miles	$

J.C. Parker

Year	Driver	Starts	Poles	1	2	3	4	5	6–10	Laps	Laps Led	Races Led	Miles	$
1962	Bob Welborn	18	0	0	1	0	1	2	4	4,470	0	0	2,902	5,695
1962	Nero Steptoe	1	0	0	0	0	0	0	0	78	0	0	39	150
1962	Ned Jarrett	1	0	0	0	0	0	0	1	196	0	0	49	430
1962	Friday Hassler	2	0	0	0	0	0	0	0	257	0	0	321	300
1962	Charley Griffin	1	0	0	0	0	0	0	0	137	0	0	69	100
1963	Hank Thomas	1	0	0	0	0	0	0	0	44	0	0	11	125
1963	Buddy Baker	2	0	0	0	0	0	0	0	289	0	0	209	395
1963	Jimmy Pardue	1	0	0	0	0	0	0	1	193	0	0	48	160
1963	Joe Jones	1	0	0	0	0	0	0	0	186	0	0	47	130
1963	Larry Thomas	3	0	0	0	0	0	0	0	632	0	0	315	570
Lifetime		31	0	0	1	0	1	2	6	6,482	0	0	4,010	$8,055

Ron Parker

Year	Driver	Starts	Poles	1	2	3	4	5	6–10	Laps	Laps Led	Races Led	Miles	$
1990	Tracy Leslie	2	0	0	0	0	0	0	0	121	0	0	212	7,640
Lifetime		2	0	0	0	0	0	0	0	121	0	0	212	$7,640

J.C. Parkett

Year	Driver	Starts	Poles	1	2	3	4	5	6–10	Laps	Laps Led	Races Led	Miles	$
1962	Bob Welborn	1	0	0	0	0	1	0	0	199	0	0	100	300
1964	Buddy Baker	18	0	0	0	1	1	1	2	2,197	0	0	1,088	3,600
Lifetime		19	0	0	0	1	2	1	2	2,396	0	0	1,188	$3,900

Chuck Parkko

Year	Driver	Starts	Poles	1	2	3	4	5	6–10	Laps	Laps Led	Races Led	Miles	$
1961	Don Noel	4	0	0	2	0	0	1	0	493	0	0	518	1,705
Lifetime		4	0	0	2	0	0	1	0	493	0	0	518	$1,705

Paul Parks

Year	Driver	Starts	Poles	1	2	3	4	5	6–10	Laps	Laps Led	Races Led	Miles	$
1960	Paul Parks	3	0	0	0	0	0	0	0	273	0	0	537	250
Lifetime		3	0	0	0	0	0	0	0	273	0	0	537	$250

Raymond Parks

Year	Driver	Starts	Poles	1	2	3	4	5	6–10	Laps	Laps Led	Races Led	Miles	$
1949	Roy Hall	1	0	0	0	0	0	0	1	196	0	0	98	150
1949	Red Byron	6	1	2	0	2	0	0	0	633	103	2	582	4,800
1949	Bob Flock	1	0	0	0	0	0	0	0		0	0		0
1950	Red Byron	4	1	0	1	1	1	0	0	634	85	3	835	3,325
1954	Fonty Flock	2	0	0	0	0	0	1	0	112	0	0	152	300
1955	Curtis Turner	4	0	0	0	1	2	0	0	554	0	0	437	1,625
Lifetime		18	2	2	1	4	3	1	1	2,129	188	5	2,103	$10,200

Stan Parnell

Year	Driver	Starts	Poles	1	2	3	4	5	6–10	Laps	Laps Led	Races Led	Miles	$
1952	Possum Jones	1	0	0	0	0	0	0	0	193	0	0	241	0
Lifetime		1	0	0	0	0	0	0	0	193	0	0	241	$0

George Parrish

Year	Driver	Starts	Poles	1	2	3	4	5	6–10	Laps	Laps Led	Races Led	Miles	$
1954	George Parrish	3	0	0	0	0	0	0	0	440	0	0	482	185
1955	George Parrish	12	0	0	0	0	0	0	1	1,057	0	0	596	740
Lifetime		15	0	0	0	0	0	0	1	1,497	0	0	1,078	$925

Harry Parry

Year	Driver	Starts	Poles	1	2	3	4	5	6–10	Laps	Laps Led	Races Led	Miles	$
1955	Ray Platte	1	0	0	0	0	0	0	0	339	0	0	466	100
Lifetime		1	0	0	0	0	0	0	0	339	0	0	466	$100

Jim Parsley

Year	Driver	Starts	Poles	1	2	3	4	5	6–10	Laps	Laps Led	Races Led	Miles	$
1958	Jim Parsley	10	0	0	0	0	0	0	4	1,720	0	0	760	1,135
1958	Rex White	1	0	0	0	0	0	0	0	187	0	0	94	125
1959	Jim Parsley	1	0	0	0	0	0	0	1	177	0	0	89	150
Lifetime		12	0	0	0	0	0	0	5	2,084	0	0	942	$1,410

Benny Parsons

Year	Driver	Starts	Poles	1	2	3	4	5	6–10	Laps	Laps Led	Races Led	Miles	$
1970	Benny Parsons	2	0	0	0	0	0	0	1	235	0	0	588	2,070
Lifetime		2	0	0	0	0	0	0	1	235	0	0	588	$2,070

Year	Driver	Starts	Poles	Finish 1	2	3	4	5	6–10	Laps	Laps Led	Races Led	Miles	$

Jim Paschal

Year	Driver	Starts	Poles	1	2	3	4	5	6–10	Laps	Laps Led	Races Led	Miles	$
1949	Jim Paschal	1	0	0	0	0	0	0	0		0	0		0
1953	Jim Paschal	1	0	0	0	0	0	0	0		0	0		25
1957	Shorty York	1	0	0	0	0	0	0	0	79	0	0	109	300
1957	Jim Paschal	11	0	0	1	0	1	1	2	1,320	0	0	696	1,800
1958	Jim Paschal	2	0	0	0	0	0	0	0	321	0	0	441	260
Lifetime		16	0	0	1	0	1	1	2	1,720	0	0	1,246	$2,385

Ed Paskovich

Year	Driver	Starts	Poles	1	2	3	4	5	6–10	Laps	Laps Led	Races Led	Miles	$
1955	Ed Paskovich	5	0	0	0	0	0	0	1	333	0	0	346	300
Lifetime		5	0	0	0	0	0	0	1	333	0	0	346	$300

Dick Passwater

Year	Driver	Starts	Poles	1	2	3	4	5	6–10	Laps	Laps Led	Races Led	Miles	$
1953	Dick Passwater	1	0	0	0	0	0	0	1	350	0	0	481	630
Lifetime		1	0	0	0	0	0	0	1	350	0	0	481	$630

Jim Patrick

Year	Driver	Starts	Poles	1	2	3	4	5	6–10	Laps	Laps Led	Races Led	Miles	$
1979	Darrell Basham	1	0	0	0	0	0	0	0	101	0	0	60	385
Lifetime		1	0	0	0	0	0	0	0	101	0	0	60	$385

Dana Patten

Year	Driver	Starts	Poles	1	2	3	4	5	6–10	Laps	Laps Led	Races Led	Miles	$
1988	Dana Patten	4	0	0	0	0	0	0	0	1,059	0	0	1,446	9,595
Lifetime		4	0	0	0	0	0	0	0	1,059	0	0	1,446	$9,595

Otis Patton

Year	Driver	Starts	Poles	1	2	3	4	5	6–10	Laps	Laps Led	Races Led	Miles	$
1969	Bill Massuch	1	0	0	0	0	0	0	0	157	0	0	314	1,075
Lifetime		1	0	0	0	0	0	0	0	157	0	0	314	$1,075

Don Paul

Year	Driver	Starts	Poles	1	2	3	4	5	6–10	Laps	Laps Led	Races Led	Miles	$
1984	Donny Paul	1	0	0	0	0	0	0	0	1	0	0	2	1,005
1985	Donny Paul	1	0	0	0	0	0	0	0	156	0	0	234	1,120
1987	Donny Paul	1	0	0	0	0	0	0	0	104	0	0	208	1,915
Lifetime		3	0	0	0	0	0	0	0	261	0	0	444	$4,040

Bill Payne

Year	Driver	Starts	Poles	1	2	3	4	5	6–10	Laps	Laps Led	Races Led	Miles	$
1954	Charles Pemberton	2	0	0	0	0	0	0	1	525	0	0	381	200
Lifetime		2	0	0	0	0	0	0	1	525	0	0	381	$200

Curtis Payne

Year	Driver	Starts	Poles	1	2	3	4	5	6–10	Laps	Laps Led	Races Led	Miles	$
1979	John Rezek	4	0	0	0	0	0	0	0	584	0	0	1,012	5,035
Lifetime		4	0	0	0	0	0	0	0	584	0	0	1,012	$5,035

William Peach

Year	Driver	Starts	Poles	1	2	3	4	5	6–10	Laps	Laps Led	Races Led	Miles	$
1961	Jack Norton	4	0	0	0	0	0	0	1	352	0	0	418	590
Lifetime		4	0	0	0	0	0	0	1	352	0	0	418	$590

David Pearson

Year	Driver	Starts	Poles	1	2	3	4	5	6–10	Laps	Laps Led	Races Led	Miles	$
1960	David Pearson	22	1	0	1	0	1	1	4	3,885	0	0	3,768	5,030
1961	David Pearson	10	0	0	0	1	1	1	1	1,316	0	0	713	1,515
1985	David Pearson	4	0	0	0	0	0	0	0	203	0	0	372	7,535
1986	Larry Pearson	2	0	0	0	0	0	0	0	358	0	0	566	14,310
1986	David Pearson	2	0	0	0	0	0	0	1	337	0	0	605	8,405
1987	Larry Pearson	4	0	0	0	0	0	0	1	1,162	1	1	1,435	18,555
1988	Larry Pearson	2	0	0	0	0	0	0	0	281	0	0	427	3,705
1989	Larry Pearson	29	0	0	0	0	0	0	2	7,993	5	2	9,737	148,232
1990	Larry Pearson	4	0	0	0	0	0	0	0	1,193	0	0	1,468	41,920
Lifetime		79	1	0	1	1	2	2	9	16,728	6	3	19,091	$249,207

Del Pearson

Year	Driver	Starts	Poles	1	2	3	4	5	6–10	Laps	Laps Led	Races Led	Miles	$
1951	Ted Chamberlain	1	0	0	0	0	0	0	0	340	0	0	425	50

Year	Driver	Starts	Poles	Finish 1	2	3	4	5	6–10	Laps	Laps Led	Races Led	Miles	$

Del Pearson *continued*

| 1951 | Dell Pearson | 8 | 0 | 0 | 1 | 0 | 0 | 0 | 2 | 310 | 0 | 0 | 310 | 900 |
| **Lifetime** | | 9 | 0 | 0 | 1 | 0 | 0 | 0 | 2 | 650 | 0 | 0 | 735 | $950 |

Hugh Pearson

1973	Hugh Pearson	2	0	0	0	0	0	0	0	94	0	0	246	1,720
1974	Hugh Pearson	2	0	0	0	0	0	0	0	116	0	0	302	1,385
1975	Hugh Pearson	2	0	0	0	0	0	0	0	218	0	0	553	2,550
1976	Hugh Pearson	2	0	0	0	0	0	0	0	115	0	0	301	1,930
1977	Hugh Pearson	1	0	0	0	0	0	0	1	114	0	0	299	2,490
Lifetime		9	0	0	0	0	0	0	1	657	0	0	1,701	$10,075

Peck Peckham

1954	Peck Peckham	2	0	0	0	0	0	0	0	313	0	0	157	35
1956	Peck Peckham	3	0	0	0	0	0	0	0	301	0	0	225	225
1957	Peck Peckham	1	0	0	0	0	0	0	0	180	0	0	90	125
Lifetime		6	0	0	0	0	0	0	0	794	0	0	471	$385

Nestor Peles

| 1980 | Nestor Peles | 1 | 0 | 0 | 0 | 0 | 0 | 0 | 0 | 207 | 0 | 0 | 207 | 600 |
| **Lifetime** | | 1 | 0 | 0 | 0 | 0 | 0 | 0 | 0 | 207 | 0 | 0 | 207 | $600 |

Steve Peles

1977	Nestor Peles	2	0	0	0	0	0	0	0	209	0	0	473	1,330
1978	Nestor Peles	3	0	0	0	0	0	0	0	979	0	0	1,249	2,880
1979	Steve Peles	2	0	0	0	0	0	0	0	641	0	0	922	2,180
1979	Nestor Peles	1	0	0	0	0	0	0	0	465	0	0	465	1,000
Lifetime		8	0	0	0	0	0	0	0	2,294	0	0	3,109	$7,390

Bob Penrod

| 1984 | Bob Penrod | 1 | 0 | 0 | 0 | 0 | 0 | 0 | 0 | 55 | 0 | 0 | 84 | 955 |
| **Lifetime** | | 1 | 0 | 0 | 0 | 0 | 0 | 0 | 0 | 55 | 0 | 0 | 84 | $955 |

Roger Penske (Statistics include teams which were solely owned by Roger Penske, plus shared-ownerships with Michael Kranefuss.)

1972	Dave Marcis	7	0	0	0	0	0	0	3	1,547	0	0	2,001	9,906
1972	Mark Donohue	4	0	0	0	0	0	0	0	390	0	0	669	5,580
1972	Donnie Allison	1	0	0	0	1	0	0	0	150	0	0	393	4,025
1973	Dave Marcis	4	0	0	0	0	0	1	0	946	0	0	1,255	7,483
1973	Mark Donohue	2	0	1	0	0	0	0	0	393	138	1	808	16,120
1974	Bobby Allison	7	0	1	0	0	1	3	0	1,925	188	5	2,866	33,935
1974	Dave Marcis	1	0	0	0	0	0	0	1	327	11	1	447	2,025
1974	Gary Bettenhausen	5	0	0	0	0	1	0	2	986	35	1	2,100	12,750
1974	George Follmer	1	1	0	0	0	0	0	0	7	1	1	18	1,000
1975	Bobby Allison	19	3	3	3	1	2	1	0	4,268	578	14	6,227	126,735
1976	Bobby Allison	30	3	0	2	6	5	2	4	8,735	360	18	10,204	197,904
1977	Dave Marcis	12	0	0	0	0	4	1	2	2,777	90	6	4,015	60,755
1980	Rusty Wallace	2	0	0	1	0	0	0	0	653	0	0	987	22,860
1991	Rusty Wallace	29	2	2	0	3	2	2	5	8,316	524	14	10,150	390,330
1992	Rusty Wallace	29	1	1	2	1	1	0	7	8,761	673	11	10,452	556,475
1993	Rusty Wallace	30	3	10	4	2	1	2	2	9,641	2,861	20	11,232	1,144,630
1994	Rusty Wallace	31	2	8	3	1	4	1	3	9,281	2,143	19	10,731	1,413,620
1995	Rusty Wallace	31	0	2	4	6	2	1	4	9,497	1,093	17	11,564	1,380,878
1996	Rusty Wallace	31	0	5	1	0	1	1	10	8,383	965	13	10,160	1,219,412
1997	Rusty Wallace	32	1	1	3	2	0	2	4	8,747	778	11	10,954	1,428,671
1998	Rusty Wallace	33	4	1	2	5	3	4	6	9,603	946	19	12,308	2,017,735
1999	Rusty Wallace	34	4	1	0	1	3	2	9	9,592	1,009	11	12,158	2,128,429
2000	Ryan Newman	1	0	0	0	0	0	0	0	176	0	0	176	37,825
2000	Rusty Wallace	34	9	4	1	1	3	3	8	9,925	1,731	21	12,902	2,956,390
2001	Rusty Wallace	36	0	1	0	2	2	3	6	10,138	1,105	11	13,219	4,037,989
2001	Mike Wallace	8	0	0	1	0	0	0	1	2,556	60	3	3,106	684,647
2001	Jeremy Mayfield	28	0	0	0	3	1	1	2	7,286	60	3	9,906	2,498,058
2001	Ryan Newman	7	1	0	1	0	0	1	0	1,478	13	2	2,350	451,914
2002	Rusty Wallace	36	1	0	4	1	1	0	10	10,591	202	9	13,824	3,927,489

Year	Driver	Starts	Poles	Finish 1	2	3	4	5	6–10	Laps	Laps Led	Races Led	Miles	$

Roger Penske *continued*

Year	Driver	Starts	Poles	1	2	3	4	5	6–10	Laps	Laps Led	Races Led	Miles	$
2002	Ryan Newman	36	6	1	5	1	3	4	8	9,871	753	22	13,101	3,412,491
Lifetime		561	41	42	37	37	40	36	97	156,946	16,317	253	200,282	$30,188,061

Richard Peralta

Year	Driver	Starts	Poles	1	2	3	4	5	6–10	Laps	Laps Led	Races Led	Miles	$
1974	Buck Peralta	1	0	0	0	0	0	0	0	121	0	0	317	1,250
1979	Ed Hale	1	0	0	0	0	0	0	0	85	0	0	223	2,045
Lifetime		2	0	0	0	0	0	0	0	206	0	0	540	$3,295

Bob Perry

Year	Driver	Starts	Poles	1	2	3	4	5	6–10	Laps	Laps Led	Races Led	Miles	$
1958	Bob Perry	2	0	0	0	0	0	0	0	121	0	0	317	200
1958	Joe Lee Johnson	1	0	0	0	0	0	0	1	193	0	0	97	350
1959	Bob Perry	3	0	0	0	0	0	0	1	509	0	0	317	500
1960	Bob Perry	3	0	0	0	0	0	0	1	256	0	0	314	475
1961	Bob Perry	4	0	0	0	0	0	1	2	424	0	0	452	840
1961	Tom Guffy	1	0	0	0	0	0	0	0	29	0	0	41	0
1963	Bob Perry	1	0	0	0	0	0	0	0	175	0	0	473	575
Lifetime		15	0	0	0	0	0	1	5	1,707	0	0	2,010	$2,940

J.E. Peters

Year	Driver	Starts	Poles	1	2	3	4	5	6–10	Laps	Laps Led	Races Led	Miles	$
1952	Gibb Orr	1	0	0	0	0	0	0	0	43	0	0	43	0
Lifetime		1	0	0	0	0	0	0	0	43	0	0	43	$0

Natz Peters

Year	Driver	Starts	Poles	1	2	3	4	5	6–10	Laps	Laps Led	Races Led	Miles	$
1983	Natz Peters	1	0	0	0	0	0	0	0	103	0	0	103	800
Lifetime		1	0	0	0	0	0	0	0	103	0	0	103	$800

Joan Petre

Year	Driver	Starts	Poles	1	2	3	4	5	6–10	Laps	Laps Led	Races Led	Miles	$
1966	Al DeAngelo	1	0	0	0	0	0	0	0	23	0	0	5	0
1966	Pee Wee Ellwanger	1	0	0	0	0	0	0	0	127	0	0	64	250
1966	Earl Brooks	1	0	0	0	0	0	0	0	92	0	0	138	875
1966	Bub Strickler	1	0	0	0	0	0	0	0	57	0	0	29	0
1966	Ernest Eury	4	0	0	0	0	0	0	1	481	0	0	243	495
1966	Buddy Arrington	4	0	0	0	0	0	0	0	339	0	0	284	955
1966	Jimmy Helms	2	0	0	0	0	0	0	0	7	0	0	3	550
1966	Buzz Gregory	2	0	0	0	0	0	0	0	563	0	0	282	500
1966	Buddy Baker	17	0	0	0	0	0	0	4	2,271	0	0	1,213	2,430
1966	Walter Wallace	1	0	0	0	0	0	0	0	379	0	0	190	300
Lifetime		34	0	0	0	0	0	0	5	4,339	0	0	2,449	$6,355

Andy Petree

Year	Driver	Starts	Poles	1	2	3	4	5	6–10	Laps	Laps Led	Races Led	Miles	$
1996	Todd Bodine	3	0	0	0	0	0	0	0	1,014	0	0	1,183	75,780
1996	Robert Pressley	1	0	0	0	0	0	1	0	314	0	0	471	14,995
1997	Ken Schrader	32	2	0	0	0	2	0	6	9,612	46	7	12,364	1,085,993
1998	Ken Schrader	33	2	0	0	0	3	0	8	9,238	60	4	11,800	1,686,685
1998	Hut Stricklin	1	0	0	0	0	0	0	0	31	0	0	78	24,250
1999	Kenny Wallace	34	0	0	1	0	0	1	2	8,805	56	1	11,514	1,343,111
1999	Ken Schrader	34	1	0	0	0	0	0	6	9,676	8	3	12,695	1,706,487
2000	Joe Nemechek	34	1	0	1	1	0	1	6	9,467	8	3	12,281	1,832,570
2000	Kenny Wallace	34	0	0	1	0	0	0	0	8,900	17	2	11,822	1,666,894
2000	Geoffrey Bodine	1	0	0	0	0	0	0	0	11	0	0	17	34,982
2001	Wally Dallenbach	1	0	0	0	0	0	0	0	198	0	0	495	64,410
2001	Scott Pruett	1	0	0	0	0	0	0	0	112	0	0	218	77,020
2001	Joe Nemechek	31	0	1	0	0	0	0	3	8,706	227	6	11,369	2,407,876
2001	Bobby Hamilton	36	0	1	0	0	1	1	4	10,750	239	4	14,100	2,196,224
2001	Bobby Hamilton Jr.	3	0	0	0	0	0	0	0	533	0	0	863	215,180
2002	Greg Biffle	4	0	0	0	0	0	0	0	1,008	12	1	973	218,700
2002	Bobby Hamilton	31	0	0	0	0	0	0	3	8,824	57	3	11,617	2,088,767
2002	Mike Wallace	4	0	0	0	0	0	0	0	726	0	0	1,414	347,312
2002	Ron Hornaday Jr.	1	0	0	0	0	0	0	0	186	0	0	495	52,860
2002	Kenny Wallace	1	0	0	0	0	0	0	0	185	0	0	492	44,775
Lifetime		320	6	2	3	1	6	4	38	88,296	730	34	116,262	$17,184,871

Year	Driver	Starts	Poles	Finish 1	2	3	4	5	6–10	Laps	Laps Led	Races Led	Miles	$

Terry Petris

Year	Driver	Starts	Poles	1	2	3	4	5	6–10	Laps	Laps Led	Races Led	Miles	$
1986	Terry Petris	2	0	0	0	0	0	0	0	149	0	0	390	3,110
1988	Terry Petris	1	0	0	0	0	0	0	0	52	0	0	136	1,150
Lifetime		3	0	0	0	0	0	0	0	201	0	0	527	$4,260

Paul Pettitt

Year	Driver	Starts	Poles	1	2	3	4	5	6–10	Laps	Laps Led	Races Led	Miles	$
1952	Paul Pettitt	3	0	0	0	0	0	0	0	198	0	0	116	60
1954	Paul Pettitt	2	0	0	0	0	0	0	0	166	0	0	149	325
1955	Paul Pettitt	2	0	0	0	0	0	0	0	50	0	0	25	100
Lifetime		7	0	0	0	0	0	1	0	414	0	0	290	$485

Petty Enterprises (Statistics represent the Petty Enterprises team, which has had a number of partnerships and owners, including Lee, Richard, Kyle and Maurice Petty.)

Year	Driver	Starts	Poles	1	2	3	4	5	6–10	Laps	Laps Led	Races Led	Miles	$
1949	Lee Petty	6	0	1	2	0	0	0	2	890	1	1	565	3,375
1950	Lee Petty	17	0	1	1	2	3	2	4	1,558	43	1	1,407	5,775
1951	Lee Petty	32	0	1	4	2	1	3	8	1,103	99	1	1,059	7,300
1952	Lee Petty	32	0	3	6	5	5	2	6	5,094	193	7	3,439	15,670
1953	Jimmie Lewallen	1	0	0	1	0	0	0	0	198	0	0	99	700
1953	Lee Petty	36	0	5	4	10	4	3	6	3,021	210	7	2,201	17,225
1954	Lee Petty	33	3	7	5	5	3	3	8	5,707	681	12	3,962	18,775
1954	Bob Welborn	2	0	0	0	0	0	0	0	209	0	0	105	50
1955	Lee Petty	41	1	6	4	5	4	1	10	6,212	769	6	4,287	16,725
1956	Lee Petty	46	1	2	1	6	2	6	11	7,167	252	6	4,486	13,380
1957	Ralph Earnhardt	8	0	0	0	0	0	0	3	1,301	0	0	682	1,050
1957	Lee Petty	41	3	4	4	3	3	6	13	7,466	449	11	4,595	15,845
1957	Johnny Dodson	1	0	0	0	0	0	0	0	244	0	0	244	425
1957	Tiny Lund	5	0	0	0	0	0	1	1	335	0	0	259	710
1957	Bill Lutz	1	0	0	0	0	0	0	1		0	0		600
1957	Bobby Myers	1	0	0	0	0	0	0	0	27	1	1	37	260
1958	Lee Petty	50	4	7	5	4	9	3	15	9,173	439	14	5,671	21,550
1958	Richard Petty	9	0	0	0	0	0	0	1	977	0	0	410	760
1958	Bob Welborn	1	0	0	0	0	0	0	1	341	0	0	171	565
1958	Jim Linke	2	0	0	0	0	0	0	0	219	0	0	219	100
1958	Jim Reed	1	0	0	0	0	0	0	0	207	0	0	285	315
1958	Jimmy Thompson	1	0	0	0	0	1	0	0	198	0	0	99	575
1958	Joe Weatherly	1	0	0	0	0	0	0	1	489	0	0	245	575
1959	Richard Petty	21	0	0	1	3	1	1	3	3,654	7	1	2,422	7,630
1959	Lee Petty	42	2	11	5	7	4	0	8	8,278	1,011	16	4,977	44,020
1960	Maurice Petty	2	0	0	0	0	0	0	2	375	0	0	142	290
1960	Lee Petty	39	3	5	7	2	6	1	9	7,518	515	10	5,389	26,650
1960	Richard Petty	40	2	3	6	3	3	1	14	8,189	447	6	6,015	35,180
1960	Jim Paschal	8	0	0	0	2	1	0	4	2,559	11	1	2,427	13,595
1961	Marvin Panch	1	0	0	0	0	0	0	0	94	0	0	129	200
1961	Jim Paschal	1	0	0	0	0	0	0	0	25	0	0	13	100
1961	Lee Petty	3	1	1	0	1	0	0	0	433	126	2	291	1,260
1961	Maurice Petty	9	0	0	0	1	1	0	2	1,207	0	0	611	1,460
1961	Richard Petty	42	2	2	4	4	5	3	5	7,866	703	7	5,392	22,670
1961	Darel Dieringer	1	0	0	0	0	0	0	1	263	0	0	395	1,375
1961	Art Malone	1	0	0	0	0	0	0	1	484	0	0	242	500
1962	Jim Paschal	9	0	3	1	0	0	1	3	3,486	767	5	2,617	15,580
1962	Lee Petty	1	0	0	0	0	0	1	0	499	0	0	250	750
1962	Maurice Petty	5	0	0	0	0	1	1	1	800	0	0	443	965
1962	Bunkie Blackburn	6	0	0	0	0	0	0	2	1,424	0	0	1,713	2,740
1962	Speedy Thompson	1	0	0	0	0	0	0	1	258	0	0	387	900
1962	Richard Petty	52	5	8	9	8	5	2	7	11,550	1,396	19	7,561	52,885
1963	Richard Petty	54	8	14	9	2	4	1	9	12,183	2,416	29	7,873	47,965
1963	Jim Paschal	29	1	5	3	5	2	0	3	6,654	392	11	4,179	18,655
1963	Bob James	4	0	0	0	0	0	0	0	589	0	0	876	1,750
1963	Jim Hurtubise	3	0	0	0	0	0	0	0	441	0	0	813	975
1963	Maurice Petty	4	0	0	0	0	0	1	1	654	0	0	238	575
1963	Bob Welborn	4	0	0	1	1	1	0	0	837	0	0	464	2,330
1963	Lee Petty	3	0	0	0	0	1	0	1	291	0	0	179	600
1963	Joe Weatherly	1	0	0	0	0	1	0	0	296	0	0	99	500
1963	Jimmy Massey	2	0	0	0	0	0	0	0	78	0	0	49	250
1964	Jim Paschal	13	0	1	3	1	1	1	1	3,725	155	4	3,590	47,845
1964	Buck Baker	6	0	0	1	0	1	1	1	1,462	21	1	1,605	5,825
1964	Lee Petty	2	0	0	0	0	0	0	0	28	0	0	30	250

Year	Driver	Starts	Poles	Finish						Laps	Laps Led	Races Led	Miles	$
				1	2	3	4	5	6–10					

Petty Enterprises *continued*

Year	Driver	Starts	Poles	1	2	3	4	5	6–10	Laps	Laps Led	Races Led	Miles	$
1964	Maurice Petty	6	0	0	0	0	1	1	3	1,130	0	0	587	1,540
1964	Richard Petty	60	9	9	14	12	0	2	6	13,924	3,483	32	9,374	98,710
1965	Richard Petty	14	7	4	4	2	0	0	0	3,697	1,169	8	1,693	16,200
1965	Jim Paschal	3	0	0	0	1	1	1	0	892	90	2	683	2,700
1965	LeeRoy Yarbrough	1	0	0	0	0	0	0	0	81	0	0	41	150
1966	Paul Lewis	1	0	0	0	0	0	0	0	308	0	0	308	670
1966	Jim Paschal	1	0	0	0	0	0	0	0	281	0	0	141	325
1966	Marvin Panch	4	0	1	0	0	1	0	1	1,187	113	2	1,736	30,765
1966	Richard Petty	39	16	8	9	3	0	0	2	8,737	2,924	26	6,733	88,130
1966	Darel Dieringer	1	0	0	0	0	0	0	0	52	0	0	52	545
1967	Richard Petty	48	19	27	7	2	1	1	2	12,739	5,537	41	9,387	128,475
1967	Tiny Lund	4	0	0	0	0	1	2	0	879	1	1	1,556	11,525
1967	G.C. Spencer	3	0	0	0	1	0	1	0	743	0	0	1,042	10,105
1968	Richard Petty	49	12	16	6	5	2	2	4	12,254	4,242	35	8,869	89,063
1969	Richard Petty	50	6	10	9	9	0	3	7	12,589	2,778	32	10,502	110,155
1970	Dan Gurney	1	1	0	0	0	0	0	1	180	0	0	472	2,400
1970	Jim Paschal	1	0	0	0	0	0	0	0	325	11	1	488	1,800
1970	Pete Hamilton	15	1	3	1	2	0	3	2	3,770	338	9	6,092	130,806
1970	Richard Petty	38	9	16	5	0	0	4	4	10,136	4,791	30	9,611	136,719
1971	Richard Petty	46	9	21	8	7	2	0	3	13,739	4,932	41	12,878	269,150
1971	Buddy Baker	18	1	1	5	5	0	1	3	4,617	683	14	7,523	112,145
1972	Buddy Baker	10	0	1	0	2	0	0	1	1,838	146	8	3,365	54,975
1972	Richard Petty	31	3	8	9	5	2	1	3	10,282	2,093	30	11,996	246,275
1973	Richard Petty	28	3	6	6	1	2	0	2	8,644	1,815	16	9,292	206,955
1974	Hershel McGriff	4	0	0	0	0	0	0	1	558	0	0	1,196	7,635
1974	Richard Petty	30	7	10	8	4	0	0	1	9,097	3,100	24	10,830	335,725
1975	Richard Petty	30	3	13	5	3	0	0	3	9,082	3,198	26	10,847	366,580
1976	Richard Petty	30	1	3	9	3	4	0	3	8,941	1,269	23	10,346	319,774
1977	Richard Petty	30	5	5	6	6	2	1	3	8,840	1,403	24	10,419	351,574
1978	Richard Petty	30	0	0	3	3	3	2	6	8,904	419	15	10,163	215,410
1979	Kyle Petty	5	0	0	0	0	0	0	1	1,069	0	0	2,111	10,810
1979	Richard Petty	31	1	5	7	2	4	5	4	9,367	1,250	16	10,934	416,470
1980	Kyle Petty	14	0	0	0	0	0	0	6	3,306	0	0	4,526	35,270
1980	Richard Petty	31	0	2	4	3	2	4	4	9,314	713	23	10,148	338,365
1981	Richard Petty	31	0	3	1	4	3	1	4	7,276	546	21	8,602	369,505
1981	Kyle Petty	31	0	0	0	0	0	1	9	7,402	20	3	8,484	100,725
1982	Richard Petty	30	0	0	5	2	1	1	7	7,834	355	18	9,025	390,870
1982	Kyle Petty	23	0	0	1	0	1	0	2	5,440	13	3	5,975	98,270
1983	Richard Petty	30	0	3	1	1	1	3	12	9,439	279	16	10,697	389,060
1983	Kyle Petty	30	0	0	0	0	0	0	2	8,345	13	5	9,437	141,291
1984	Kyle Petty	30	0	0	0	0	0	1	5	8,400	2	1	9,302	302,990
1985	Dick Brooks	3	0	0	0	0	0	0	0	683	0	0	982	20,340
1985	Morgan Shepherd	1	0	0	0	0	0	0	0	345	0	0	471	3,415
1986	Richard Petty	28	0	0	1	2	1	0	7	7,516	153	7	8,766	229,940
1987	Richard Petty	29	0	0	1	3	2	3	5	8,306	38	8	9,987	363,850
1988	Richard Petty	29	0	0	0	1	0	0	4	6,207	12	3	7,628	187,056
1989	Richard Petty	25	0	0	0	0	0	0	0	5,567	9	1	7,929	117,300
1990	Richard Petty	29	0	0	0	0	0	0	1	7,438	5	1	9,165	158,715
1991	Richard Petty	29	0	0	0	0	0	0	1	8,341	1	1	9,646	256,035
1992	Richard Petty	29	0	0	0	0	0	0	0	7,977	5	1	9,624	327,620
1993	Rick Wilson	29	0	0	0	0	0	0	1	8,117	1	1	10,330	293,625
1993	Jimmy Hensley	1	0	0	0	0	0	0	0	292	0	0	154	5,875
1994	Wally Dallenbach	14	0	0	0	0	1	0	2	3,568	1	1	5,323	232,492
1994	John Andretti	11	0	0	0	0	0	0	0	3,722	40	3	3,791	116,400
1995	Bobby Hamilton	31	0	0	1	0	2	1	6	9,409	129	7	11,550	665,621
1996	Bobby Hamilton	31	2	1	0	1	0	1	8	9,153	648	11	10,897	942,095
1997	Kyle Petty	32	0	0	0	1	0	1	7	9,192	210	6	11,957	808,150
1997	Bobby Hamilton	32	2	1	1	3	0	1	9	9,535	416	9	12,266	1,317,746
1998	John Andretti	33	1	0	0	2	0	1	7	9,181	136	4	12,037	1,606,900
1998	Kyle Petty	33	0	0	0	0	0	0	2	8,464	0	0	11,239	1,242,035
1999	John Andretti	34	1	1	0	1	1	0	7	8,526	238	10	11,246	1,832,051
1999	Kyle Petty	32	0	0	0	0	0	0	9	8,708	11	4	11,206	1,257,953
2000	John Andretti	34	0	0	0	0	0	0	2	9,217	11	6	11,656	1,909,466
2000	Steve Grissom	5	0	0	0	0	0	0	0	1,569	0	0	1,916	246,785
2000	Kyle Petty	18	0	0	0	0	0	0	1	4,830	8	2	5,994	782,005
2000	Adam Petty	1	0	0	0	0	0	0	0	215	0	0	323	38,675
2001	Kyle Petty	24	0	0	0	0	0	0	0	5,026	1	1	7,569	957,927

Year	Driver	Starts	Poles	Finish 1	2	3	4	5	6–10	Laps	Laps Led	Races Led	Miles	$

Petty Enterprises *continued*

Year	Driver	Starts	Poles	1	2	3	4	5	6–10	Laps	Laps Led	Races Led	Miles	$
2001	John Andretti	35	0	0	1	0	0	0	1	9,994	53	2	12,997	2,788,370
2001	Buckshot Jones	30	0	0	0	0	0	0	0	7,819	2	2	10,352	1,575,471
2002	Kyle Petty	36	0	0	0	0	0	0	1	10,423	22	4	13,701	1,899,237
2002	Buckshot Jones	7	0	0	0	0	0	0	0	2,218	0	0	2,399	373,314
2002	Christian	1	0	0	0	0	0	0	0	252	0	0	252	39,600
2002	John Andretti	36	0	0	0	0	0	0	1	9,743	22	5	12,881	2,849,894
2002	Greg Biffle	2	0	0	0	0	0	0	0	657	0	0	799	96,014
2002	Steve Grissom	10	0	0	0	0	0	0	1	3,070	0	0	4,122	498,505
2002	Jerry Nadeau	14	0	0	0	0	0	0	0	3,029	20	1	4,391	757,852
2002	Ted Musgrave	1	0	0	0	0	0	0	0	246	0	0	379	58,450
Lifetime		2458	155	268	225	184	114	94	363	592,529	61,022	826	619,315	$33,295,961

J.H. Petty

Year	Driver	Starts	Poles	1	2	3	4	5	6–10	Laps	Laps Led	Races Led	Miles	$
1951	Jimmie Lewallen	1	0	0	0	0	0	0	0	111	0	0	111	50
1951	Pap White	1	0	0	0	0	0	0	1	383	0	0	479	400
1952	Julian Petty	1	0	0	0	0	0	0	1	193	0	0	97	125
1952	Bob Welborn	1	0	0	0	0	0	0	0	137	0	0	69	25
1952	Ray Duhigg	9	0	0	0	1	1	1	3	1,365	0	0	759	1,425
1952	Jimmie Lewallen	2	0	0	0	0	0	0	2	377	0	0	213	275
1953	Bob Welborn	3	0	0	0	0	0	0	2		0	0		275
1953	Ray Duhigg	10	0	0	0	2	2	0	3	489	0	0	411	2,625
1954	Bob Welborn	5	0	0	0	0	0	0	1	479	0	0	393	275
1954	Billy Irvin	3	0	0	0	0	0	0	0	344	0	0	234	50
1955	Ralph Liguori	1	0	0	0	0	0	0	1	189	0	0	284	350
1955	Marvin Panch	2	0	0	0	0	0	0	0	401	0	0	508	300
1955	Junior Johnson	1	0	0	1	0	0	0	0	197	0	0	99	700
1955	Julian Petty	2	0	0	0	0	0	0	0	5	0	0	3	75
1955	Jimmie Lewallen	1	0	0	0	0	0	0	0	60	0	0	60	0
1955	Jim Paschal	3	0	0	0	1	0	0	1	535	0	0	287	650
1955	Bob Welborn	20	0	0	0	2	4	3	7	3,051	0	0	1,851	5,175
1956	Bob Welborn	1	0	0	0	0	0	0	1	191	0	0	96	250
1956	Jimmy Massey	1	0	0	0	0	0	0	0	389	0	0	195	300
1956	Jim Paschal	2	0	0	0	0	0	0	0	219	0	0	95	360
1956	Gwyn Staley	1	0	0	0	0	0	0	1	389	0	0	195	350
1957	Gwyn Staley	12	2	3	1	0	2	1	2	2,206	196	4	1,273	8,680
1958	Banjo Matthews	1	0	0	0	0	0	0	0	19	0	0	10	50
1958	Possum Jones	5	0	0	0	0	0	0	0	879	0	0	660	545
1958	Ken Rush	10	1	0	0	0	0	0	3	1,625	0	0	828	1,640
1958	Joe Weatherly	1	0	0	0	0	0	0	0	1	0	0	1	50
1958	Jim Paschal	3	1	1	0	0	1	0	1	591	150	1	381	1,245
1958	Roy Tyner	1	0	0	0	0	0	1	0	157	0	0	98	225
1958	Gwyn Staley	3	0	0	1	0	2	0	0	298	0	0	99	1,030
1958	Tiny Lund	3	1	0	0	0	0	1	0	399	0	0	199	385
1958	Bob Welborn	17	1	5	3	2	0	0	4	3,429	579	7	2,019	12,705
1958	Rex White	14	6	1	4	4	0	1	2	2,267	348	5	1,071	7,265
1959	Joe Weatherly	1	0	0	0	0	0	0	1	188	4	1	94	140
1959	Bob Welborn	1	1	1	0	0	0	0	0	150	117	1	50	600
1959	Tiny Lund	1	0	0	0	0	0	0	0	30	0	0	15	50
1959	Jim Paschal	4	0	0	2	0	0	1	0	758	0	0	337	1,440
1959	Ken Rush	3	0	0	0	0	0	0	0	336	0	0	175	175
1959	Ermon Rush	1	0	0	0	0	0	0	0	188	0	0	47	140
1961	Jim Paschal	20	1	2	3	1	2	3	4	5,370	203	3	3,480	15,928
1962	David Pearson	1	0	0	0	0	0	0	0	90	0	0	56	0
1962	Bob Welborn	4	0	0	0	0	0	0	3	771	0	0	1,235	1,975
1962	Jim Paschal	1	0	0	0	0	0	0	1	198	55	1	99	150
Lifetime		178	14	13	15	13	14	13	45	29,454	1,652	23	18,658	$68,453

Marvin K. Petty

Year	Driver	Starts	Poles	1	2	3	4	5	6–10	Laps	Laps Led	Races Led	Miles	$
1979	Freddy Smith	2	0	0	0	0	0	0	0	765	0	0	936	2,950
1994	Ritchie Petty	1	0	0	0	0	0	0	0	73	0	0	183	8,705
Lifetime		3	0	0	0	0	0	0	0	838	0	0	1,119	$11,655

Maurice Petty

Year	Driver	Starts	Poles	1	2	3	4	5	6–10	Laps	Laps Led	Races Led	Miles	$
1993	Ritchie Petty	3	0	0	0	0	0	0	0	364	0	0	950	22,990
Lifetime		3	0	0	0	0	0	0	0	364	0	0	950	$22,990

Year	Driver	Starts	Poles	Finish 1	2	3	4	5	6–10	Laps	Laps Led	Races Led	Miles	$

Steve Pfeifer

Year	Driver	Starts	Poles	1	2	3	4	5	6–10	Laps	Laps Led	Races Led	Miles	$
1980	Steve Pfeifer	1	0	0	0	0	0	0	0	75	0	0	197	900
1981	Steve Pfeifer	1	0	0	0	0	0	0	0	83	0	0	217	1,055
Lifetime		2	0	0	0	0	0	0	0	158	0	0	414	$1,955

Phillip Duffie

Year	Driver	Starts	Poles	1	2	3	4	5	6–10	Laps	Laps Led	Races Led	Miles	$
1990	Philip Duffie	2	0	0	0	0	0	0	0	191	0	0	419	8,030
Lifetime		2	0	0	0	0	0	0	0	191	0	0	419	$8,030

Bob Phillippi

Year	Driver	Starts	Poles	1	2	3	4	5	6–10	Laps	Laps Led	Races Led	Miles	$
1951	Marvin Burke	1	0	1	0	0	0	0	0	250	156	1	156	1,875
Lifetime		1	0	1	0	0	0	0	0	250	156	1	156	$1,875

Howard Phillippi

Year	Driver	Starts	Poles	1	2	3	4	5	6–10	Laps	Laps Led	Races Led	Miles	$
1956	Howard Phillippi	4	0	0	0	0	0	0	0	501	0	0	398	125
1957	Howard Phillippi	3	0	0	0	0	0	0	1	334	0	0	167	200
1958	Howard Phillippi	2	0	0	0	0	0	0	1	190	0	0	55	320
1958	Marvin Porter	2	0	0	0	0	0	0	1	109	0	0	117	190
Lifetime		11	0	0	0	0	0	0	3	1,134	0	0	737	$835

Wallace Phinney

Year	Driver	Starts	Poles	1	2	3	4	5	6–10	Laps	Laps Led	Races Led	Miles	$
1972	Phil Finney	1	0	0	0	0	0	0	0	321	0	0	174	450
1973	Phil Finney	1	0	0	0	0	0	0	0	55	0	0	146	910
Lifetime		2	0	0	0	0	0	0	0	376	0	0	320	$1,360

Joe Phipps

Year	Driver	Starts	Poles	1	2	3	4	5	6–10	Laps	Laps Led	Races Led	Miles	$
1970	Lennie Pond	1	0	0	0	0	0	0	0	88	0	0	134	1,020
1970	Joe Phipps	7	0	0	0	0	0	0	0	1,506	0	0	1,583	4,090
1971	Joe Phipps	2	0	0	0	0	0	0	0	73	0	0	53	920
1972	Roy Mayne	1	0	0	0	0	0	0	0	1	0	0	3	720
1972	Walter Ballard	1	0	0	0	0	0	0	0	167	0	0	170	865
1972	Buck Baker	1	0	0	0	0	0	0	0	157	0	0	214	935
Lifetime		13	0	0	0	0	0	0	0	1,992	0	0	2,156	$8,550

Andy Pierce

Year	Driver	Starts	Poles	1	2	3	4	5	6–10	Laps	Laps Led	Races Led	Miles	$
1951	Andy Pierce	2	1	0	0	0	0	0	0	98	0	0	49	25
Lifetime		2	1	0	0	0	0	0	0	98	0	0	49	$25

Steve Pierce

Year	Driver	Starts	Poles	1	2	3	4	5	6–10	Laps	Laps Led	Races Led	Miles	$
1955	Possum Jones	1	0	0	0	0	0	0	0	276	0	0	380	60
1958	Speedy Thompson	1	0	0	0	0	0	0	0	344	0	0	473	310
1959	Richard Riley	1	0	0	0	0	0	0	0	42	0	0	21	50
1959	Speedy Thompson	13	1	0	1	0	1	1	2	2,038	226	2	1,600	2,365
Lifetime		16	1	0	1	0	1	1	2	2,700	226	2	2,474	$2,785

Tom Pistone

Year	Driver	Starts	Poles	1	2	3	4	5	6–10	Laps	Laps Led	Races Led	Miles	$
1955	Tom Pistone	1	0	0	0	0	0	0	0	28	0	0	18	0
1956	Tom Pistone	2	0	0	0	0	0	0	0	305	0	0	133	75
1966	Wendell Scott	1	0	0	0	0	0	0	0	119	0	0	119	540
1966	Tom Pistone	27	4	0	3	1	0	2	0	3,825	385	8	2,357	7,625
1967	Tom Pistone	1	0	0	0	0	0	0	1	278	0	0	139	345
1968	Earl Balmer	1	0	0	0	0	0	0	0	59	0	0	89	1,075
1968	Jim Hurtubise	2	0	0	0	0	0	0	0	364	0	0	318	1,000
1968	Tom Pistone	3	0	0	0	1	0	1	0	827	8	1	414	1,425
1970	Jim Hurtubise	2	0	0	0	0	0	0	1	211	0	0	528	2,575
1970	Bunkie Blackburn	1	0	0	0	0	0	0	0	35	0	0	36	620
1970	Richard Brickhouse	3	0	0	0	0	0	0	0	162	2	1	285	3,300
1971	Vic Elford	1	0	0	0	0	0	0	0	46	0	0	115	220
1982	Tighe Scott	1	0	0	0	0	0	0	0	81	0	0	203	5,050
Lifetime		46	4	0	3	2	0	3	2	6,340	395	10	4,751	$23,850

Year	Driver	Starts	Poles	1	2	3	4	5	6–10	Laps	Laps Led	Races Led	Miles	$

Blackie Pitt

Year	Driver	Starts	Poles	1	2	3	4	5	6–10	Laps	Laps Led	Races Led	Miles	$
1958	Blackie Pitt	1	0	0	0	0	0	0	1	93	0	0	84	130
Lifetime		1	0	0	0	0	0	0	1	93	0	0	84	$130

Brownie Pitt

Year	Driver	Starts	Poles	1	2	3	4	5	6–10	Laps	Laps Led	Races Led	Miles	$
1955	Blackie Pitt	12	0	0	0	0	0	0	4	1,537	0	0	1,207	975
1955	Jimmie Lewallen	1	0	0	0	0	0	0	0	14	0	0	57	0
1956	Blackie Pitt	25	0	0	0	0	0	0	4	2,411	0	0	1,580	1,345
1956	Brownie Pitt	1	0	0	0	0	0	0	0	49	0	0	44	100
1958	Blackie Pitt	6	0	0	0	0	0	0	0	268	0	0	133	185
Lifetime		45	0	0	0	0	0	0	8	4,279	0	0	3,022	$2,605

Hoyt Platt

Year	Driver	Starts	Poles	1	2	3	4	5	6–10	Laps	Laps Led	Races Led	Miles	$
1956	Lou Sherman	2	0	0	0	0	0	0	0	267	0	0	134	100
1957	Dick Hoffman	1	0	0	0	0	0	0	0	50	0	0	125	60
Lifetime		3	0	0	0	0	0	0	0	317	0	0	259	$160

B.A. Pless

Year	Driver	Starts	Poles	1	2	3	4	5	6–10	Laps	Laps Led	Races Led	Miles	$
1952	Buck Baker	10	2	1	0	0	2	0	2	1,113	139	3	751	2,235
1952	Buddy Shuman	6	0	1	1	0	0	0	1	816	65	2	589	3,400
1952	Jimmy Thompson	1	0	0	0	0	0	0	0	383	0	0	479	300
1953	Buddy Shuman	2	0	0	0	0	0	0	0	338	0	0	465	380
Lifetime		19	2	2	1	0	2	0	3	2,650	204	5	2,283	$6,315

Dick Poling

Year	Driver	Starts	Poles	1	2	3	4	5	6–10	Laps	Laps Led	Races Led	Miles	$
1973	Buck Baker	1	0	0	0	0	0	0	0	357	0	0	363	670
Lifetime		1	0	0	0	0	0	0	0	357	0	0	363	$670

Greg Pollex

Year	Driver	Starts	Poles	1	2	3	4	5	6–10	Laps	Laps Led	Races Led	Miles	$
1993	Chad Little	1	0	0	0	0	0	0	0	314	0	0	471	4,475
1994	Chad Little	1	0	0	0	0	0	0	0	196	1	1	490	30,805
1995	Chad Little	2	0	0	0	0	0	0	0	195	0	0	508	20,425
1996	Chad Little	5	0	0	0	0	0	0	0	927	0	0	1,611	80,227
1997	Chad Little	15	0	0	0	0	0	0	1	3,822	0	306,720	4,852	
Lifetime		24	0	0	0	0	0	0	1	5,454	1	1	7,932	$442,652

Lennie Pond

Year	Driver	Starts	Poles	1	2	3	4	5	6–10	Laps	Laps Led	Races Led	Miles	$
1981	Lennie Pond	9	0	0	0	0	0	0	0	2,145	0	0	2,263	13,625
Lifetime		9	0	0	0	0	0	0	0	2,145	0	0	2,263	$13,625

Elmer Pooler

Year	Driver	Starts	Poles	1	2	3	4	5	6–10	Laps	Laps Led	Races Led	Miles	$
1952	George Fleming	1	0	0	0	0	0	0	0		0	0		0
1952	Donald Thomas	5	0	0	0	0	0	0	3	999	0	0	816	460
Lifetime		6	0	0	0	0	0	0	3	999	0	0	816	$460

Bill Poor

Year	Driver	Starts	Poles	1	2	3	4	5	6–10	Laps	Laps Led	Races Led	Miles	$
1956	Bill Poor	1	0	0	0	0	0	0	0	364	0	0	182	200
1957	Bill Poor	2	0	0	0	0	0	0	0	167	0	0	84	160
1958	Richard Spittle	1	0	0	0	0	0	0	0	125	0	0	63	50
1958	Darel Dieringer	1	0	0	0	0	0	0	0	114	0	0	57	85
1958	Bill Poor	24	0	0	0	0	0	0	6	3,880	0	0	1,947	3,115
1959	Bill Poor	4	0	0	0	0	0	0	0	484	0	0	219	190
Lifetime		33	0	0	0	0	0	1	6	5,134	0	0	2,550	$3,800

Claude Porter

Year	Driver	Starts	Poles	1	2	3	4	5	6–10	Laps	Laps Led	Races Led	Miles	$
1955	Dutch Cox	1	0	0	0	0	0	0	0	225	0	0	309	150
Lifetime		1	0	0	0	0	0	0	0	225	0	0	309	$150

H.C. Porter

Year	Driver	Starts	Poles	1	2	3	4	5	6–10	Laps	Laps Led	Races Led	Miles	$
1976	Buck Baker	1	0	0	0	0	0	0	0	301	0	0	452	1,235
Lifetime		1	0	0	0	0	0	0	0	301	0	0	452	$1,235

Year	Driver	Starts	Poles	Finish						Laps	Laps Led	Races Led	Miles	$
				1	2	3	4	5	6–10	Laps	Led	Led	Miles	$

Marvin Porter

Year	Driver	Starts	Poles	1	2	3	4	5	6–10	Laps	Led	Led	Miles	$
1957	Marvin Porter	2	0	1	1	0	0	0	0	216	1	1	158	1,350
1958	Marvin Porter	2	0	0	0	0	0	0	1	309	0	0	106	175
1959	Marvin Porter	7	0	0	0	1	1	0	2	1,696	0	0	706	1,940
1959	Bob Reuther	1	0	0	0	0	0	0	1	284	0	0	142	250
Lifetime		12	0	1	1	1	1	0	4	2,505	1	1	1,112	$3,715

Nick Porter

Year	Driver	Starts	Poles	1	2	3	4	5	6–10	Laps	Led	Led	Miles	$
1957	Don Porter	6	0	0	0	0	0	0	4	722	0	0	456	810
Lifetime		6	0	0	0	0	0	0	4	722	0	0	456	$810

Randy Porter

Year	Driver	Starts	Poles	1	2	3	4	5	6–10	Laps	Led	Led	Miles	$
1992	Randy Porter	2	0	0	0	0	0	0	0	502	0	0	962	12,475
Lifetime		2	0	0	0	0	0	0	0	502	0	0	962	$12,475

Jess Potter

Year	Driver	Starts	Poles	1	2	3	4	5	6–10	Laps	Led	Led	Miles	$
1957	George Green	4	0	0	0	0	1	0	0	582	0	0	404	555
1957	Brownie King	36	0	0	0	0	0	1	15	5,756	0	0	3,464	5,030
1958	Brownie King	24	0	0	0	0	0	0	5	3,926	0	0	2,153	3,205
1958	George Green	12	0	0	0	0	0	0	0	1,304	0	0	563	655
1959	Bob Hundley	1	0	0	0	0	0	0	0	141	0	0	71	100
1959	Brownie King	18	0	0	0	0	0	1	4	3,250	0	0	1,904	1,875
1959	Layman Utsman	2	0	0	0	0	0	0	0	235	0	0	131	50
1959	Richard Riley	1	0	0	0	0	0	0	0	149	0	0	75	0
1959	George Green	18	0	0	0	0	0	0	5	3,337	0	0	1,966	2,385
1960	George Green	3	0	0	0	0	0	0	0	237	0	0	327	360
1960	Brownie King	3	0	0	0	0	0	0	1	410	0	0	647	465
1960	Buddy Baker	7	0	0	0	0	0	0	1	1,101	0	0	738	665
1960	Paul Lewis	22	0	0	0	0	0	0	4	3,690	0	0	2,562	3,535
1960	Richard Riley	3	0	0	0	0	0	0	1	466	0	0	348	400
1961	Paul Lewis	18	0	0	0	0	0	0	5	3,036	0	0	2,476	3,675
1961	George Green	2	0	0	0	0	0	0	0	372	0	0	361	550
1962	George Green	46	0	0	0	0	0	1	14	9,279	0	0	5,896	8,210
1963	George Green	3	0	0	0	0	0	0	2	569	0	0	198	425
1963	E.J. Trivette	7	0	0	0	0	0	0	0	1,150	0	0	950	1,410
1963	Bill Morton	1	0	0	0	0	0	0	0	115	0	0	58	125
1964	E.J. Trivette	15	0	0	0	0	0	0	1	1,444	0	0	894	3,460
1964	Jack Anderson	1	0	0	0	0	0	0	0	118	0	0	177	400
1964	Paul Lewis	1	0	0	0	0	0	0	0	27	0	0	17	150
1965	E.J. Trivette	38	0	0	0	0	0	0	7	7,413	0	0	4,899	11,075
Lifetime		286	0	0	0	0	1	3	65	48,107	0	0	31,277	$48,760

Bob Potter

Year	Driver	Starts	Poles	1	2	3	4	5	6–10	Laps	Led	Led	Miles	$
1959	Bob Potter	2	0	0	0	0	0	0	0	46	0	0	115	150
1960	Bob Potter	3	0	0	0	0	0	0	1	708	0	0	822	640
Lifetime		5	0	0	0	0	0	0	1	754	0	0	937	$790

John Potter

Year	Driver	Starts	Poles	1	2	3	4	5	6–10	Laps	Led	Led	Miles	$
1958	Jim Cook	2	0	0	0	0	1	0	0	258	0	0	519	455
Lifetime		2	0	0	0	0	1	0	0	258	0	0	519	$455

Mike Potter

Year	Driver	Starts	Poles	1	2	3	4	5	6–10	Laps	Led	Led	Miles	$
1979	Mike Potter	1	0	0	0	0	0	0	0	73	0	0	74	560
1980	Mike Potter	3	0	0	0	0	0	0	0	450	0	0	535	2,370
1983	Lowell Cowell	1	0	0	0	0	0	0	0	93	0	0	247	3,335
1983	Mike Potter	5	0	0	0	0	0	0	0	587	0	0	1,268	7,850
1988	Brad Teague	1	0	0	0	0	0	0	0	60	0	0	91	1,525
1988	Mike Potter	1	0	0	0	0	0	0	0	44	0	0	110	1,700
Lifetime		12	0	0	0	0	0	0	0	1,307	0	0	2,325	$17,340

Floyd Powell

Year	Driver	Starts	Poles	1	2	3	4	5	6–10	Laps	Led	Led	Miles	$
1962	Floyd Powell	1	0	0	0	0	0	0	0	142	0	0	71	110
1962	Joe Penland	3	0	0	0	0	0	0	0	379	0	0	190	235
1963	Floyd Powell	1	0	0	0	0	0	0	1	154	0	0	139	275

Year	Driver	Starts	Poles	1	2	3	4	5	6–10	Laps	Laps Led	Races Led	Miles	$

Floyd Powell *continued*

Year	Driver	Starts	Poles	1	2	3	4	5	6–10	Laps	Laps Led	Races Led	Miles	$
1963	Joe Weatherly	2	0	0	0	0	2	0	0	394	0	0	197	1,000
Lifetime		7	0	0	0	0	2	0	1	1,069	0	0	596	$1,620

Tex Powell

Year	Driver	Starts	Poles	1	2	3	4	5	6–10	Laps	Laps Led	Races Led	Miles	$
1990	Chuck Bown	3	0	0	0	0	0	0	0	951	0	0	1,280	10,150
1993	John Andretti	4	0	0	0	0	0	0	0	904	0	0	925	24,915
Lifetime		7	0	0	0	0	0	0	0	1,855	0	0	2,205	$35,065

Baxter Price

Year	Driver	Starts	Poles	1	2	3	4	5	6–10	Laps	Laps Led	Races Led	Miles	$
1973	Baxter Price	1	0	0	0	0	0	0	0	3	0	0	2	325
1975	Baxter Price	3	0	0	0	0	0	0	0	331	0	0	548	1,685
1976	Baxter Price	6	0	0	0	0	0	0	0	1,680	0	0	1,432	3,410
1976	Walter Ballard	3	0	0	0	0	0	0	0	852	0	0	669	2,210
1977	Elmo Langley	1	0	0	0	0	0	0	0	182	0	0	108	325
1977	Baxter Price	12	0	0	0	0	0	0	0	2,566	0	0	2,706	10,865
1977	Larry LeMay	1	0	0	0	0	0	0	0	36	0	0	19	350
1977	Walter Ballard	1	0	0	0	0	0	0	0	225	0	0	122	475
1977	Earl Brooks	1	0	0	0	0	0	0	0	131	0	0	82	400
1977	Tighe Scott	1	0	0	0	0	0	0	0	198	0	0	270	845
1978	Baxter Price	23	0	0	0	0	0	0	0	7,164	0	0	7,342	33,630
1979	Baxter Price	24	0	0	0	0	0	0	0	6,791	0	0	6,666	44,405
1979	Roy Smith	1	0	0	0	0	0	0	0	193	0	0	483	2,690
1980	Roy Smith	1	0	0	0	0	0	0	0	114	0	0	299	1,700
1980	Jimmy Means	1	0	0	0	0	0	0	0	35	0	0	18	850
1980	Charlie Chamblee	1	0	0	0	0	0	0	0	298	0	0	454	2,825
1980	Baxter Price	17	0	0	0	0	0	0	0	4,765	0	0	4,680	25,885
1980	Joel Stowe	2	0	0	0	0	0	0	0	835	0	0	694	4,685
1981	Ronnie Thomas	1	0	0	0	0	0	0	0	75	0	0	200	1,805
1981	D.K. Ulrich	2	0	0	0	0	0	0	0	673	0	0	371	1,370
1981	Baxter Price	1	0	0	0	0	0	0	0	16	0	0	9	500
Lifetime		104	0	0	0	0	0	0	0	27,163	0	0	27,174	$141,235

Carl Price

Year	Driver	Starts	Poles	1	2	3	4	5	6–10	Laps	Laps Led	Races Led	Miles	$
1973	Tiny Lund	5	0	0	0	0	0	0	0	388	0	0	410	4,420
Lifetime		5	0	0	0	0	0	0	0	388	0	0	410	$4,420

Chester Price

Year	Driver	Starts	Poles	1	2	3	4	5	6–10	Laps	Laps Led	Races Led	Miles	$
1954	Bud Diamond	2	0	0	0	0	0	0	0	277	0	0	139	25
Lifetime		2	0	0	0	0	0	0	0	277	0	0	139	$25

Norris Price

Year	Driver	Starts	Poles	1	2	3	4	5	6–10	Laps	Laps Led	Races Led	Miles	$
1977	Steve Moore	1	0	0	0	0	0	0	0	139	0	0	370	2,165
1977	Steve Stolarek	1	0	0	0	0	0	0	0	21	0	0	21	490
Lifetime		2	0	0	0	0	0	0	0	160	0	0	391	$2,655

Walt Price

Year	Driver	Starts	Poles	1	2	3	4	5	6–10	Laps	Laps Led	Races Led	Miles	$
1974	Walt Price	2	0	0	0	0	0	0	0	136	0	0	349	1,800
Lifetime		2	0	0	0	0	0	0	0	136	0	0	349	$1,800

Cotton Priddy

Year	Driver	Starts	Poles	1	2	3	4	5	6–10	Laps	Laps Led	Races Led	Miles	$
1953	Cotton Priddy	2	0	0	0	0	0	0	0	35	0	0	144	75
1956	Cotton Priddy	1	0	0	0	0	0	0	0	38	0	0	57	50
Lifetime		3	0	0	0	0	0	0	0	73	0	0	201	$125

Talmadge Prince

Year	Driver	Starts	Poles	1	2	3	4	5	6–10	Laps	Laps Led	Races Led	Miles	$
1970	Talmadge Prince	1	0	0	0	0	0	0	0	18	0	0	45	0
Lifetime		1	0	0	0	0	0	0	0	18	0	0	45	$0

Year	Driver	Starts	Poles	Finish						Laps	Laps Led	Races Led	Miles	$
				1	2	3	4	5	6–10	Laps	Led	Led	Miles	$

Clem Proctor

Year	Driver	Starts	Poles	1	2	3	4	5	6–10	Laps	Laps Led	Races Led	Miles	$
1963	Clem Proctor	2	0	0	0	0	0	0	0	260	0	0	702	850
1972	Clem Proctor	1	0	0	0	0	0	0	0	37	0	0	97	685
Lifetime		3	0	0	0	0	0	0	0	297	0	0	799	$1,535

Bob Pronger

Year	Driver	Starts	Poles	1	2	3	4	5	6–10	Laps	Laps Led	Races Led	Miles	$
1951	Bob Pronger	1	0	0	0	0	0	0	0	332	0	0	415	50
1952	Bob Pronger	1	0	0	0	0	0	0	0	140	0	0	175	0
1953	Bob Pronger	1	1	0	0	0	0	0	0	5	0	0	21	0
1953	Speedy Thompson	1	0	0	0	0	0	0	1	351	0	0	483	750
1958	Bob Pronger	2	0	0	0	0	0	0	0	16	0	0	66	25
1959	Bob Pronger	2	0	0	0	0	0	0	0	156	0	0	390	125
Lifetime		8	1	0	0	0	0	0	1	1,000	0	0	1,549	$950

Oren Prosser

Year	Driver	Starts	Poles	1	2	3	4	5	6–10	Laps	Laps Led	Races Led	Miles	$
1963	Oren Prosser	1	0	0	0	0	0	0	0	95	0	0	257	200
Lifetime		1	0	0	0	0	0	0	0	95	0	0	257	$200

Warren Prout

Year	Driver	Starts	Poles	1	2	3	4	5	6–10	Laps	Laps Led	Races Led	Miles	$
1971	Randy Hutchison	6	0	0	0	0	0	0	1	1,233	0	0	556	2,010
Lifetime		6	0	0	0	0	0	0	1	1,233	0	0	556	$2,010

Don Pruitt

Year	Driver	Starts	Poles	1	2	3	4	5	6–10	Laps	Laps Led	Races Led	Miles	$
1974	Don Pruitt	1	0	0	0	0	0	0	0	28	0	0	73	670
Lifetime		1	0	0	0	0	0	0	0	28	0	0	73	$670

Ervin Pruitt

Year	Driver	Starts	Poles	1	2	3	4	5	6–10	Laps	Laps Led	Races Led	Miles	$
1968	Neil Castles	1	0	0	0	1	0	0	0	152	0	0	137	700
1968	Paul Dean Holt	1	0	0	0	0	0	0	0	1	0	0	1	275
1968	James Hylton	1	0	0	0	0	0	0	1	193	0	0	97	240
1968	Frank Warren	1	0	0	0	0	0	0	0	144	0	0	198	700
1968	Ervin Pruitt	5	0	0	0	0	0	0	1	1,376	0	0	733	1,930
1968	Charlie Glotzbach	1	0	0	0	0	0	1	0	293	0	0	147	475
1968	Roy Tyner	2	0	0	0	0	0	0	0	383	0	0	505	1,275
1969	Roy Mayne	1	0	0	0	0	0	0	0	9	0	0	23	725
1969	Johnny Halford	8	0	0	0	0	0	0	0	1,881	0	0	1,494	4,200
1969	Ervin Pruitt	4	0	0	0	0	0	0	1	565	0	0	371	850
1969	Bobby Mausgrover	13	0	0	0	0	0	0	0	1,192	0	0	995	5,305
1970	Johnny Halford	25	0	0	0	0	0	0	0	3,619	16	1	4,057	15,654
Lifetime		63	0	0	0	1	0	1	3	9,808	16	1	8,754	$32,329

Delbert Puro

Year	Driver	Starts	Poles	1	2	3	4	5	6–10	Laps	Laps Led	Races Led	Miles	$
1975	Dick Trickle	1	0	0	0	0	0	0	0	3	0	0	8	1,705
1975	Bobby Isaac	1	0	0	0	0	0	0	0	40	0	0	60	855
1976	Richie Panch	1	0	0	0	0	0	0	0	252	0	0	384	1,035
1978	Dick Trickle	1	0	0	0	0	0	0	0	24	0	0	36	910
Lifetime		4	0	0	0	0	0	0	0	319	0	0	487	$4,505

Smokey Purser

Year	Driver	Starts	Poles	1	2	3	4	5	6–10	Laps	Laps Led	Races Led	Miles	$
1952	Smokey Purser	1	0	0	0	0	0	0	0	1	0	0	4	0
Lifetime		1	0	0	0	0	0	0	0	1	0	0	4	$0

Matt Puskarich

Year	Driver	Starts	Poles	1	2	3	4	5	6–10	Laps	Laps Led	Races Led	Miles	$
1975	Don Puskarich	3	0	0	0	0	0	0	0	184	0	0	480	3,060
1976	Don Puskarich	3	0	0	0	0	0	0	0	343	0	0	876	3,770
1977	Don Puskarich	2	0	0	0	0	0	0	0	51	0	0	134	1,520
1978	Don Puskarich	1	0	0	0	0	0	0	0	36	0	0	94	700
1979	Don Puskarich	1	0	0	0	0	0	0	0	47	0	0	123	855
1980	Don Puskarich	3	0	0	0	0	0	0	0	201	0	0	526	3,835
1981	Don Puskarich	3	0	0	0	0	0	0	0	211	0	0	553	4,770
1982	Don Puskarich	1	0	0	0	0	0	0	0	87	0	0	228	1,870

Year	Driver	Starts	Poles	Finish						Laps	Laps Led	Races Led	Miles	$
				1	2	3	4	5	6–10					

Matt Puskarich *continued*

Year	Driver	Starts	Poles	1	2	3	4	5	6–10	Laps	Laps Led	Races Led	Miles	$
1983	Doug Wheeler	2	0	0	0	0	0	0	0	203	0	0	532	4,625
Lifetime		19	0	0	0	0	0	0	0	1,363	0	0	3,546	$25,005

J.T. Putney

Year	Driver	Starts	Poles	1	2	3	4	5	6–10	Laps	Laps Led	Races Led	Miles	$
1966	J.T. Putney	35	0	0	1	2	1	0	5	7,159	32	2	6,040	14,285
1967	J.T. Putney	28	0	0	0	1	0	0	9	5,743	0	0	4,510	13,750
Lifetime		63	0	0	1	3	1	0	14	12,902	32	2	10,550	$28,035

W.R. Quann

Year	Driver	Starts	Poles	1	2	3	4	5	6–10	Laps	Laps Led	Races Led	Miles	$
1953	Buck Mason	1	0	0	0	0	0	0	0		0	0		25
Lifetime		1	0	0	0	0	0	0	0		0	0		$25

Dave Quate

Year	Driver	Starts	Poles	1	2	3	4	5	6–10	Laps	Laps Led	Races Led	Miles	$
1953	Ray Duhigg	1	0	0	0	0	0	0	0		0	0		40
1953	Jimmie Lewallen	4	0	0	0	1	0	0	0		0	0		700
1953	Jim Paschal	4	0	0	0	0	0	0	0	292	0	0	292	360
Lifetime		9	0	0	0	1	0	1	0	292	0	0	292	$1,100

Danny Queen

Year	Driver	Starts	Poles	1	2	3	4	5	6–10	Laps	Laps Led	Races Led	Miles	$
1978	Charlie Blanton	1	0	0	0	0	0	0	0	52	0	0	53	590
1979	Melvin Revis	1	0	0	0	0	0	0	0	76	0	0	41	410
Lifetime		2	0	0	0	0	0	0	0	128	0	0	93	$1,000

Grady Quinn

Year	Driver	Starts	Poles	1	2	3	4	5	6–10	Laps	Laps Led	Races Led	Miles	$
1952	Joie Ray	1	0	0	0	0	0	0	0		0	0		0
Lifetime		1	0	0	0	0	0	0	0		0	0		$0

Billy Rafter

Year	Driver	Starts	Poles	1	2	3	4	5	6–10	Laps	Laps Led	Races Led	Miles	$
1956	Chuck Mahoney	2	0	0	0	0	0	0	0	219	0	0	110	200
1956	Billy Rafter	9	0	0	0	0	0	0	1	1,140	0	0	623	975
1957	Ed Jacken	1	0	0	0	0	0	0	0	72	0	0	72	110
1957	Billy Rafter	2	0	0	0	0	0	0	0	102	0	0	52	100
1958	Billy Rafter	19	0	0	0	0	0	0	7	3,160	0	0	1,529	2,490
Lifetime		33	0	0	0	0	0	1	8	4,693	0	0	2,386	$3,875

Marvin Ragan

Year	Driver	Starts	Poles	1	2	3	4	5	6–10	Laps	Laps Led	Races Led	Miles	$
1983	Ken Ragan	8	0	0	0	0	0	0	0	1,984	0	0	3,526	27,905
1984	Ken Ragan	10	0	0	0	0	0	0	0	1,839	1	1	3,467	37,045
1986	Ken Ragan	5	0	0	0	0	0	0	0	1,095	1	1	2,036	20,520
1986	Ron Esau	1	0	0	0	0	0	0	0	76	0	0	199	3,150
1987	Ken Ragan	6	0	0	0	0	0	0	0	1,259	0	0	2,354	30,575
1987	Eddie Bierschwale	3	0	0	0	0	0	0	0	535	0	0	1,018	7,715
1988	Ken Ragan	5	0	0	0	0	0	0	0	731	0	0	1,426	13,555
1989	Ken Ragan	3	0	0	0	0	0	0	0	550	0	0	922	7,295
1990	Ken Ragan	4	0	0	0	0	0	0	0	398	0	0	840	15,720
Lifetime		45	0	0	0	0	0	0	0	8,467	2	2	15,789	$163,480

RahMoc Enterprises (Principal owners were Bob Rahilly and Butch Mock. Statistics include RahMoc Enterprises when Butch Mock took over sole ownership.)

Year	Driver	Starts	Poles	1	2	3	4	5	6–10	Laps	Laps Led	Races Led	Miles	$
1978	Butch Mock	2	0	0	0	0	0	0	0	564	0	0	853	2,390
1979	Bobby Brack	1	0	0	0	0	0	0	0	70	1	1	105	930
1979	Bill Elswick	3	0	0	0	0	0	0	0	1,112	0	0	842	3,400
1979	Butch Mock	1	0	0	0	0	0	0	0	38	0	0	95	2,165
1980	Joe Millikan	3	0	0	0	0	0	1	1	624	1	1	1,043	5,525
1980	Chuck Bown	1	0	0	0	0	0	0	0	364	0	0	497	3,725
1980	John Anderson	7	0	0	0	0	0	0	1	1,958	0	0	1,562	11,585
1980	Kyle Petty	1	0	0	0	0	0	0	0	416	0	0	416	775
1980	Lennie Pond	3	0	0	0	0	0	0	1	903	0	0	1,104	20,115
1980	Harry Gant	3	0	0	0	0	0	2	2	402	1	1	934	10,680
1980	Bill Elswick	11	0	0	0	0	0	0	0	2,252	0	0	2,115	14,680

Year	Driver	Starts	Poles	Finish 1	2	3	4	5	6–10	Laps	Laps Led	Races Led	Miles	$

RahMoc Enterprises *continued*

Year	Driver	Starts	Poles	1	2	3	4	5	6–10	Laps	Laps Led	Races Led	Miles	$
1980	Jim Sauter	1	0	0	0	0	0	0	0	33	0	0	50	900
1981	Gary Balough	10	0	0	0	0	0	0	1	2,267	1	1	3,232	34,430
1981	Tim Richmond	1	0	0	0	0	0	0	0	413	0	0	246	3,450
1981	Joe Millikan	12	0	0	0	0	0	2	5	3,017	15	4	3,578	63,675
1981	Dick May	1	0	0	0	0	0	0	0	184	0	0	368	3,520
1981	Bill Elswick	3	0	0	0	0	0	0	0	662	0	0	1,345	20,100
1982	Gary Balough	5	0	0	0	0	0	0	1	1,359	0	0	1,608	35,735
1982	Jimmy Insolo	1	0	0	0	0	0	0	0	89	0	0	233	2,470
1982	Joe Ruttman	23	0	0	0	0	2	2	2	6,023	30	4	6,586	105,750
1983	Neil Bonnett	30	4	2	1	2	5	0	7	9,418	659	15	10,452	379,365
1984	Dave Marcis	30	0	0	0	0	3	0	6	9,383	30	5	10,387	316,730
1985	Lake Speed	28	0	0	1	0	1	0	12	8,572	8	4	10,087	268,040
1986	Morgan Shepherd	11	0	0	0	1	0	0	1	2,598	227	7	2,661	64,520
1986	Lake Speed	4	0	0	0	0	0	0	2	1,382	4	1	1,676	51,400
1986	Jody Ridley	12	0	0	0	0	0	0	1	3,183	0	0	4,055	84,380
1986	Jim Sauter	4	0	0	0	0	0	0	0	769	2	1	1,509	28,535
1987	Neil Bonnett	26	0	0	0	4	1	0	10	7,834	120	10	9,073	271,495
1987	Joe Ruttman	3	0	0	0	0	0	0	2	936	0	0	1,308	25,280
1988	Morgan Shepherd	3	1	0	0	0	0	0	1	319	4	1	757	27,685
1988	Neil Bonnett	27	0	2	0	0	1	0	4	8,017	324	7	9,140	396,945
1989	Morgan Shepherd	29	1	0	2	0	1	2	8	7,590	139	6	9,910	471,037
1990	Rick Wilson	29	0	0	0	0	0	1	2	8,036	0	0	9,383	230,067
1991	Joe Ruttman	29	0	0	0	1	0	0	3	8,974	11	1	10,776	335,941
1992	Dick Trickle	1	0	0	0	0	0	1	0	200	0	0	500	78,800
1993	Todd Bodine	10	0	0	0	0	0	0	0	2,393	0	0	2,311	62,245
1993	Phil Parsons	1	0	0	0	0	0	0	1	328	3	1	499	11,725
1993	Dick Trickle	18	0	0	0	0	0	1	0	4,381	0	0	5,557	151,700
1994	Todd Bodine	30	0	0	0	1	0	1	5	8,475	60	5	10,479	458,440
1995	Todd Bodine	28	0	0	0	0	1	0	2	6,683	19	2	9,058	664,620
1996	Morgan Shepherd	31	0	0	0	0	0	1	4	8,976	55	4	10,721	630,397
1997	Rick Mast	29	0	0	0	0	0	0	2	8,415	1	1	10,471	811,000
1998	Rick Mast	30	1	0	0	0	0	0	1	7,667	61	2	9,655	866,581
1999	Ted Musgrave	32	0	0	0	0	0	0	2	9,063	5	2	11,670	1,150,306
Lifetime		568	7	4	4	9	15	14	90	156,342	1,781	87	188,905	$8,183,234

A.C. Rakestraw

Year	Driver	Starts	Poles	1	2	3	4	5	6–10	Laps	Laps Led	Races Led	Miles	$
1967	G.C. Spencer	1	0	0	0	0	0	0	1	311	0	0	467	1,125
1967	E.J. Trivette	1	0	0	0	0	0	0	0	129	0	0	194	550
Lifetime		2	0	0	0	0	0	0	1	440	0	0	660	$1,675

Ansel Rakestraw

Year	Driver	Starts	Poles	1	2	3	4	5	6–10	Laps	Laps Led	Races Led	Miles	$
1956	Benny Rakestraw	1	0	0	0	0	0	0	1	156	0	0	78	100
1956	Bobby Myers	2	0	0	0	0	0	0	1	104	0	0	52	200
1957	Ansel Rakestraw	2	0	0	0	0	0	0	0	276	0	0	138	200
Lifetime		5	0	0	0	0	0	0	2	536	0	0	268	$500

Tyre Rakestraw

Year	Driver	Starts	Poles	1	2	3	4	5	6–10	Laps	Laps Led	Races Led	Miles	$
1953	Tyre Rakestraw	1	0	0	0	0	0	0	0	308	0	0	424	160
Lifetime		1	0	0	0	0	0	0	0	308	0	0	424	$160

Tom Raley

Year	Driver	Starts	Poles	1	2	3	4	5	6–10	Laps	Laps Led	Races Led	Miles	$
1967	Tom Raley	8	0	0	0	0	0	0	0	602	0	0	288	825
1967	Dr. Don Tarr	1	0	0	0	0	0	0	0	47	0	0	71	540
Lifetime		9	0	0	0	0	0	0	0	649	0	0	359	$1,365

Robert Ramey

Year	Driver	Starts	Poles	1	2	3	4	5	6–10	Laps	Laps Led	Races Led	Miles	$
1960	Johnny Miller	1	0	0	0	0	0	0	0	26	0	0	36	200
1960	Jimmy Thompson	1	0	0	0	0	0	0	0	397	0	0	199	125
1960	Buzz McCann	1	0	0	0	0	0	0	0	8	0	0	20	0
1960	Bunk Moore	1	0	0	0	0	0	0	0	203	0	0	305	200
1960	Paul Norris	1	0	0	0	0	0	0	0	1	0	0	2	200
1962	Johnny Nave	2	0	0	0	0	0	0	0	170	0	0	106	200
Lifetime		7	0	0	0	0	0	0	0	805	0	0	666	$925

Year	Driver	Starts	Poles	Finish 1	2	3	4	5	6–10	Laps	Laps Led	Races Led	Miles	$

Nick Rampling

Year	Driver	Starts	Poles	1	2	3	4	5	6–10	Laps	Laps Led	Races Led	Miles	$
1964	Jim Bray	3	0	0	0	0	0	0	0	160	0	0	431	1,350
Lifetime		3	0	0	0	0	0	0	0	160	0	0	431	$1,350

Darvin Randahl

Year	Driver	Starts	Poles	1	2	3	4	5	6–10	Laps	Laps Led	Races Led	Miles	$
1956	Darvin Randahl	7	0	0	0	0	0	0	1	528	0	0	448	710
Lifetime		7	0	0	0	0	0	0	1	528	0	0	448	$710

Maurice Randall

Year	Driver	Starts	Poles	1	2	3	4	5	6–10	Laps	Laps Led	Races Led	Miles	$
1984	Maurice Randall	1	0	0	0	0	0	0	0	50	0	0	30	1,010
1985	Maurice Randall	3	0	0	0	0	0	0	0	104	0	0	107	3,450
Lifetime		4	0	0	0	0	0	0	0	154	0	0	137	$4,460

H.B. Ranier

Year	Driver	Starts	Poles	1	2	3	4	5	6–10	Laps	Laps Led	Races Led	Miles	$
1952	Johnny Patterson	3	0	0	1	0	0	1	0	873	0	0	736	3,250
1953	Johnny Patterson	11	0	0	0	0	0	1	1	534	0	0	410	645
1954	Johnny Patterson	4	0	0	0	0	1	0	0	582	0	0	759	1,240
1956	Johnny Patterson	3	0	0	0	0	0	0	1	563	0	0	582	425
1969	Vic Elford	2	0	0	0	0	0	0	0	236	0	0	590	2,950
1969	Andy Hampton	2	0	0	0	0	0	0	1	197	0	0	493	2,500
Lifetime		25	0	0	1	0	1	2	3	2,985	0	0	3,569	$11,010

Harry Ranier (Statistics include shared ownerships with J.T. Lundy and Tom Walsh, along with teams solely owned by Ranier.)

Year	Driver	Starts	Poles	1	2	3	4	5	6–10	Laps	Laps Led	Races Led	Miles	$
1967	Buddy Baker	1	0	0	0	0	0	0	0	465	0	0	233	525
1967	Gary Bettenhausen	3	0	0	0	0	0	0	1	124	0	0	310	1,680
1968	Andy Hampton	1	0	0	0	0	0	0	1	193	0	0	483	2,525
1970	Bobby Watson	1	0	0	0	0	0	0	0	11	0	0	6	430
1975	Jim Vandiver	12	0	0	0	0	1	0	3	2,926	1	1	3,618	22,200
1976	Jim Vandiver	1	0	0	0	0	0	0	0	176	0	0	468	3,735
1977	Jim Vandiver	1	0	0	0	0	0	0	0	137	0	0	343	3,520
1978	Lennie Pond	28	5	1	2	2	1	5	8	8,443	319	12	9,413	159,160
1979	Buddy Baker	26	7	3	2	3	3	1	3	6,107	1,083	20	7,422	255,455
1980	Buddy Baker	19	6	2	2	4	2	0	2	5,042	671	15	6,953	259,200
1981	Bobby Allison	30	2	5	7	4	3	2	5	9,822	1,142	23	11,460	529,250
1982	Joe Ruttman	1	0	0	0	0	0	0	0	20	0	0	52	8,525
1982	Buddy Baker	15	0	0	1	0	0	2	6	4,130	85	6	4,856	183,500
1982	Benny Parsons	14	3	0	0	4	3	0	1	3,579	250	6	4,188	204,535
1983	Cale Yarborough	16	3	4	0	0	0	0	4	3,783	608	13	5,975	254,535
1984	Cale Yarborough	16	4	3	1	3	1	2	0	4,387	736	12	7,140	385,853
1985	Cale Yarborough	16	0	2	2	2	0	0	1	3,450	664	11	5,675	260,465
1986	Cale Yarborough	16	1	0	0	2	0	0	3	3,467	110	4	5,828	106,010
1987	Davey Allison	22	5	2	3	0	0	4	1	5,511	710	11	8,520	337,160
1988	Davey Allison	29	3	2	2	3	2	3	4	8,333	650	14	9,749	704,160
1996	Elton Sawyer	1	0	0	0	0	0	0	0	327	0	0	498	14,015
1997	Lance Hooper	1	0	0	0	0	0	0	0	40	0	0	101	21,820
1997	Greg Sacks	6	0	0	0	0	0	0	0	1,256	3	1	2,058	140,980
Lifetime		276	39	24	22	27	16	19	43	71,729	7,032	149	95,347	$3,859,238

Jim Rathmann

Year	Driver	Starts	Poles	1	2	3	4	5	6–10	Laps	Laps Led	Races Led	Miles	$
1950	Jim Rathmann	1	0	0	0	0	0	0	0	46	0	0	192	50
1958	Banjo Matthews	1	0	0	0	0	0	0	0	17	0	0	70	25
Lifetime		2	0	0	0	0	0	0	0	63	0	0	262	$75

Johnny Ray

Year	Driver	Starts	Poles	1	2	3	4	5	6–10	Laps	Laps Led	Races Led	Miles	$
1953	John Ray	1	0	0	0	0	0	0	0	202	0	0	202	25
1976	Bob Burcham	1	0	0	0	0	0	0	0	52	0	0	138	980
1976	Dale Earnhardt	1	0	0	0	0	0	0	0	260	0	0	396	1,360
1976	Johnny Rutherford	2	0	0	0	0	0	0	0	347	0	0	660	2,745
1977	Dale Earnhardt	1	0	0	0	0	0	0	0	25	0	0	38	1,375
1977	Johnny Rutherford	2	0	0	0	0	0	0	0	79	0	0	149	2,285
1978	Chuck Bown	4	0	0	0	0	0	0	0	539	0	0	732	3,585
Lifetime		12	0	0	0	0	0	0	0	1,504	0	0	2,314	$12,355

Year	Driver	Starts	Poles	Finish 1	2	3	4	5	6–10	Laps	Laps Led	Races Led	Miles	$

Warren Razore

Year	Driver	Starts	Poles	1	2	3	4	5	6–10	Laps	Laps Led	Races Led	Miles	$
1986	Derrike Cope	5	0	0	0	0	0	0	1	1,101	0	0	1,349	8,025
1987	Roy Smith	2	0	0	0	0	0	0	0	29	0	0	76	2,325
1988	Chad Little	2	0	0	0	0	0	0	0	689	0	0	884	5,900
1988	Roy Smith	2	0	0	0	0	0	0	0	303	1	1	441	4,550
1989	Roy Smith	1	0	0	0	0	0	0	0	46	0	0	116	3,375
Lifetime		12	0	0	0	0	0	0	1	2,168	1	1	2,866	$24,175

John Rebhan

Year	Driver	Starts	Poles	1	2	3	4	5	6–10	Laps	Laps Led	Races Led	Miles	$
1980	John Anderson	3	0	0	0	0	0	0	1	289	0	0	612	5,100
1980	Kenny Hemphill	5	0	0	0	0	0	0	1	884	4	1	1,493	8,970
1981	Donnie Allison	3	0	0	0	0	0	1	0	813	2	1	1,196	13,425
Lifetime		11	0	0	0	0	0	1	2	1,986	6	2	3,302	$27,495

James Reed

Year	Driver	Starts	Poles	1	2	3	4	5	6–10	Laps	Laps Led	Races Led	Miles	$
1990	Mark Reed	1	0	0	0	0	0	0	0	269	0	0	269	3,100
1991	Mark Reed	1	0	0	0	0	0	0	0	177	0	0	177	3,375
Lifetime		2	0	0	0	0	0	0	0	446	0	0	446	$6,475

Jim Reed

Year	Driver	Starts	Poles	1	2	3	4	5	6–10	Laps	Laps Led	Races Led	Miles	$
1951	Jim Reed	3	0	0	1	0	0	0	0	199	58	1	100	650
1952	Jim Reed	7	0	0	0	0	0	1	2	597	0	0	336	475
1953	Jim Reed	1	0	0	0	0	0	0	0		0	0		25
1954	Jim Reed	9	0	0	0	0	0	2	1	1,083	0	0	815	965
1954	Charles McDuffie	2	0	0	0	0	0	2	0	150	0	0	75	0
1955	Jim Reed	14	0	0	1	0	1	1	0	1,691	32	1	1,265	2,710
1956	Jim Reed	11	2	0	1	1	2	0	0	1,542	286	3	1,666	4,830
1957	Jim Reed	5	0	0	0	1	1	0	1	892	11	2	980	3,035
1958	Jim Reed	16	2	4	0	5	1	0	2	3,486	692	4	2,189	8,480
1959	Jim Reed	14	1	3	0	1	1	2	2	2,512	289	5	2,071	22,784
1960	Jim Reed	8	0	0	0	1	0	0	0	1,175	28	1	1,670	2,240
1961	Jim Reed	8	0	0	2	0	0	1	1	1,735	32	1	1,717	3,350
Lifetime		98	5	7	5	9	6	9	9	15,062	1,428	18	12,884	$49,544

Norris Reed

Year	Driver	Starts	Poles	1	2	3	4	5	6–10	Laps	Laps Led	Races Led	Miles	$
1971	Gary Myers (H)	1	0	0	0	0	0	0	1	474	0	0	216	500
1972	Paul Tyler	4	0	0	0	0	0	0	1	1,125	0	0	1,312	4,200
1972	David Ray Boggs	1	0	0	0	0	0	0	0	304	0	0	456	1,194
1973	Paul Tyler	5	0	0	0	0	0	0	0	597	0	0	847	5,335
1973	Toby Tobias	1	0	0	0	0	0	0	0	50	0	0	50	680
1974	Kenny Brightbill	1	0	0	0	0	0	0	1	476	0	0	476	1,825
1974	Ramo Stott	7	0	0	0	1	0	0	3	1,725	0	0	2,906	23,325
1975	Bobby Isaac	1	0	0	0	0	0	0	0	208	0	0	312	1,105
1975	Johnny Rutherford	3	0	0	0	0	0	0	0	138	0	0	209	2,850
1975	Ramo Stott	2	0	0	0	0	0	1	0	259	0	0	657	13,030
1976	Ramo Stott	1	1	0	0	0	0	0	0	113	0	0	283	6,830
1977	Ron Hutcherson	1	0	0	0	0	0	0	0	85	0	0	213	4,525
Lifetime		28	1	0	0	1	0	1	6	5,554	0	0	7,936	$65,399

Bud Reeder

Year	Driver	Starts	Poles	1	2	3	4	5	6–10	Laps	Laps Led	Races Led	Miles	$
1983	Mike Potter	6	0	0	0	0	0	0	0	1,329	0	0	1,054	12,325
1983	D.K. Ulrich	4	0	0	0	0	0	0	0	772	0	0	1,228	11,570
1983	Dick May	1	0	0	0	0	0	0	0	301	0	0	411	1,670
1983	Rick Newsom	5	0	0	0	0	0	0	0	1,898	0	0	1,497	13,220
1983	Tommy Gale	2	0	0	0	0	0	0	0	305	0	0	282	3,775
Lifetime		18	0	0	0	0	0	0	0	4,605	0	0	4,472	$42,560

Tom Reet

Year	Driver	Starts	Poles	1	2	3	4	5	6–10	Laps	Laps Led	Races Led	Miles	$
1988	Bob Schacht	1	0	0	0	0	0	0	0	138	0	0	104	1,650
Lifetime		1	0	0	0	0	0	0	0	138	0	0	104	$1,650

Year	Driver	Starts	Poles	Finish 1	2	3	4	5	6–10	Laps	Laps Led	Races Led	Miles	$

Bobby Reeves

Year	Driver	Starts	Poles	1	2	3	4	5	6–10	Laps	Laps Led	Races Led	Miles	$
1978	Raymond Williams	1	0	0	0	0	0	0	0	74	0	0	185	1,290
Lifetime		1	0	0	0	0	0	0	0	74	0	0	185	$1,290

Curtis Reid

Year	Driver	Starts	Poles	1	2	3	4	5	6–10	Laps	Laps Led	Races Led	Miles	$
1956	Eddie Skinner	1	0	0	0	0	0	0	0		0	0		50
Lifetime		1	0	0	0	0	0	0	0		0	0		$50

E.C. Reid

Year	Driver	Starts	Poles	1	2	3	4	5	6–10	Laps	Laps Led	Races Led	Miles	$
1968	E.J. Trivette	11	0	0	0	0	0	0	0	2,071	0	0	2,424	7,820
1968	Bob Burcham	2	0	0	0	0	0	0	0	366	0	0	183	515
1968	Dr. Don Tarr	1	0	0	0	0	0	0	0	242	0	0	363	1,685
1969	Wayne Gillette	16	0	0	0	0	0	0	0	887	0	0	981	6,127
1969	Dick Watson	1	0	0	0	0	0	0	0	171	0	0	107	370
1969	Henley Gray	1	0	0	0	0	0	0	0	34	0	0	51	1,135
1969	E.J. Trivette	47	0	0	0	0	0	0	14	10,649	0	0	8,720	26,892
1969	Danny Turner	3	0	0	0	0	0	0	0	285	0	0	150	1,040
1969	Frank Warren	5	0	0	0	0	0	0	0	961	0	0	1,272	4,725
1969	J.D. McDuffie	1	0	0	0	0	0	0	0	6	0	0	15	600
1970	E.J. Trivette	2	0	0	0	0	0	0	0	47	0	0	116	1,235
Lifetime		90	0	0	0	0	0	0	14	15,719	0	0	14,381	$52,144

Robbie Reiser

Year	Driver	Starts	Poles	1	2	3	4	5	6–10	Laps	Laps Led	Races Led	Miles	$
1999	Matt Kenseth	5	0	0	0	0	1	0	0	1,358	0	0	1,733	143,561
Lifetime		5	0	0	0	0	1	0	0	1,358	0	0	1,733	$143,561

Lee Reitzel

Year	Driver	Starts	Poles	1	2	3	4	5	6–10	Laps	Laps Led	Races Led	Miles	$
1961	Lee Reitzel	17	0	0	0	0	0	0	3	2,566	0	0	2,039	2,910
1961	Darel Dieringer	1	0	0	0	0	0	0	0	1	0	0	1	50
1962	Lee Reitzel	8	0	0	0	0	0	0	1	1,056	0	0	863	1,205
1963	Bobby Keck	1	0	0	0	0	0	0	0	26	0	0	13	100
1963	Lee Reitzel	4	0	0	0	0	0	0	0	496	0	0	275	875
Lifetime		31	0	0	0	0	0	0	4	4,145	0	0	3,190	$5,140

B.E. Renfrow

Year	Driver	Starts	Poles	1	2	3	4	5	6–10	Laps	Laps Led	Races Led	Miles	$
1949	B.E. Renfro	2	0	0	0	0	0	0	0		0	0		25
Lifetime		2	0	0	0	0	0	0	0		0	0		$25

Marc Reno

Year	Driver	Starts	Poles	1	2	3	4	5	6–10	Laps	Laps Led	Races Led	Miles	$
1987	Patty Moise	1	0	0	0	0	0	0	0	53	0	0	130	1,690
1987	Ernie Irvan	2	0	0	0	0	0	0	1	367	1	1	517	9,875
1990	Tom Kendall	3	0	0	0	0	0	0	1	613	4	1	822	14,120
Lifetime		6	0	0	0	0	0	0	2	1,033	5	2	1,468	$25,685

Melvin Revis

Year	Driver	Starts	Poles	1	2	3	4	5	6–10	Laps	Laps Led	Races Led	Miles	$
1980	Melvin Revis	1	0	0	0	0	0	0	0	23	0	0	31	1,115
Lifetime		1	0	0	0	0	0	0	0	23	0	0	31	$1,115

Mamie Reynolds

Year	Driver	Starts	Poles	1	2	3	4	5	6–10	Laps	Laps Led	Races Led	Miles	$
1962	Darel Dieringer	5	0	0	0	0	0	0	1	1,262	0	0	1,099	1,975
1962	Fred Lorenzen	2	0	1	0	0	0	0	0	306	19	1	142	1,050
1963	Ed Livingston	12	0	0	0	0	0	0	0	2,329	0	0	2,734	3,980
1963	Darel Dieringer	1	0	0	0	0	0	1	0	197	0	0	99	275
Lifetime		20	0	1	0	0	0	1	1	4,094	19	1	4,074	$7,280

Tom Reynolds

Year	Driver	Starts	Poles	1	2	3	4	5	6–10	Laps	Laps Led	Races Led	Miles	$
1974	Don Reynolds	2	0	0	0	0	0	0	1	303	0	0	772	2,600
1975	Don Reynolds	1	0	0	0	0	0	0	0	110	0	0	288	1,230
1976	Don Reynolds	1	0	0	0	0	0	0	0	83	0	0	217	1,140
Lifetime		4	0	0	0	0	0	0	1	496	0	0	1,278	$4,970

Year	Driver	Starts	Poles	Finish						Laps	Laps Led	Races Led	Miles	$
				1	2	3	4	5	6–10					

Frank Rhoads

Year	Driver	Starts	Poles	1	2	3	4	5	6–10	Laps	Laps Led	Races Led	Miles	$
1962	Red Farmer	2	0	0	0	0	0	0	0	72	0	0	180	535
Lifetime		2	0	0	0	0	0	0	0	72	0	0	180	$535

Harold Rhodes

Year	Driver	Starts	Poles	1	2	3	4	5	6–10	Laps	Laps Led	Races Led	Miles	$
1965	Frank Warren	4	0	0	0	0	0	0	1	769	0	0	1,088	2,880
1965	Joe Penland	3	0	0	0	0	0	0	0	112	0	0	60	1,260
1966	Frank Warren	11	0	0	0	0	0	0	1	1,989	0	0	2,803	6,740
1967	Frank Warren	12	0	0	0	0	0	0	1	1,805	0	0	2,668	9,185
1968	Frank Warren	5	0	0	0	0	0	0	1	1,256	0	0	1,632	4,265
Lifetime		35	0	0	0	0	0	0	4	5,931	0	0	8,251	$24,330

Floyd Rice

Year	Driver	Starts	Poles	1	2	3	4	5	6–10	Laps	Laps Led	Races Led	Miles	$
1951	Walt Flanders	1	0	0	0	0	0	0	0	145	0	0	145	10
Lifetime		1	0	0	0	0	0	0	0	145	0	0	145	$10

Sam Rice

Year	Driver	Starts	Poles	1	2	3	4	5	6–10	Laps	Laps Led	Races Led	Miles	$
1949	Bill Blair	3	0	0	0	0	0	2	1	573	180	1	385	575
1949	Jimmie Lewallen	2	0	0	0	0	0	0	0		0	0		0
1949	Sam Rice	2	0	0	0	0	2	0	0	192	0	0	96	600
1949	Frank Mundy	4	0	0	0	1	1	0	0	274	0	0	381	1,000
1950	Bill Blair	15	0	1	2	0	0	1	2	1,550	218	3	1,253	4,005
1950	Fireball Roberts	7	1	1	2	1	0	0	1	1,009	60	3	911	6,350
1950	Jimmie Lewallen	2	0	0	0	0	0	0	0	330	0	0	413	25
1951	Fireball Roberts	6	0	0	0	0	0	0	1	238	0	0	154	175
1951	Jim Paschal	1	0	0	0	0	0	0	1		0	0		100
1957	Tiny Lund	2	0	0	0	1	0	0	0	309	0	0	169	450
1957	Jim Paschal	2	0	0	0	0	0	0	0	534	0	0	331	365
1957	Bill Blair	1	0	0	0	0	0	0	0	63	0	0	87	100
1957	Billy Myers	1	0	0	0	0	1	0	0	196	0	0	98	280
1957	Jimmie Lewallen	7	0	0	0	0	0	0	0	895	0	0	865	1,030
1957	Ken Rush	3	1	0	0	1	0	0	1	388	0	0	194	540
1958	Ken Rush	1	0	0	0	0	0	0	0	0	0	0	0	0
1959	Jim Paschal	1	0	0	0	0	0	0	0	371	0	0	186	80
Lifetime		60	2	2	4	4	4	3	7	6,922	458	7	5,521	$15,675

Harlan Richardson

Year	Driver	Starts	Poles	1	2	3	4	5	6–10	Laps	Laps Led	Races Led	Miles	$
1959	Harlan Richardson	10	0	0	0	0	0	0	2	1,893	0	0	948	1,120
Lifetime		10	0	0	0	0	0	0	2	1,893	0	0	948	$1,120

Larry Richardson

Year	Driver	Starts	Poles	1	2	3	4	5	6–10	Laps	Laps Led	Races Led	Miles	$
1974	Larry Richardson	1	0	0	0	0	0	0	0	36	0	0	90	670
Lifetime		1	0	0	0	0	0	0	0	36	0	0	90	$670

J.B. Richter

Year	Driver	Starts	Poles	1	2	3	4	5	6–10	Laps	Laps Led	Races Led	Miles	$
1953	Russell Armentrout	2	0	0	0	0	0	0	0	60	0	0	60	50
Lifetime		2	0	0	0	0	0	0	0	60	0	0	60	$50

Chuck Rider

Year	Driver	Starts	Poles	1	2	3	4	5	6–10	Laps	Laps Led	Races Led	Miles	$
1986	Michael Waltrip	28	0	0	0	0	0	0	0	7,852	6	4	9,147	83,660
1987	Michael Waltrip	29	0	0	0	0	0	0	1	7,790	1	1	8,850	179,010
1988	Michael Waltrip	28	0	0	1	0	0	0	2	7,537	6	2	9,558	203,490
1989	Michael Waltrip	29	0	0	0	0	0	0	5	8,372	9	4	10,113	215,480
1990	Michael Waltrip	29	0	0	0	1	2	2	5	8,226	17	4	10,223	349,669
1991	Michael Waltrip	29	2	0	0	1	0	3	8	8,394	292	11	9,759	342,605
1992	Michael Waltrip	29	0	0	0	0	1	0	1	8,474	3	1	10,184	340,045
1993	Michael Waltrip	30	0	0	0	0	0	0	5	9,378	39	6	11,146	447,905
1994	Michael Waltrip	31	0	0	0	1	0	1	8	9,508	8	5	11,667	630,731
1995	Michael Waltrip	31	0	0	0	1	0	1	6	9,221	45	11	11,400	809,155
1996	Johnny Benson Jr.	30	1	0	0	0	0	1	5	8,507	105	4	10,484	883,580
1997	Johnny Benson Jr.	32	1	0	0	0	0	0	8	9,648	19	7	12,504	1,080,725
1998	Jeff Green	1	0	0	0	0	0	0	0	499	0	0	262	32,350

Year	Driver	Starts	Poles	Finish 1	2	3	4	5	6–10	Laps	Laps Led	Races Led	Miles	$

Chuck Rider *continued*

Year	Driver	Starts	Poles	1	2	3	4	5	6–10	Laps	Laps Led	Races Led	Miles	$
1998	Derrike Cope	28	1	0	0	0	0	0	0	7,526	16	3	9,641	943,887
1999	Derrike Cope	11	0	0	0	0	0	0	0	2,403	0	0	3,379	444,769
Lifetime		395	5	0	1	4	3	8	54	113,335	566	63	138,317	$6,987,061

W.J. Ridgeway

Year	Driver	Starts	Poles	1	2	3	4	5	6–10	Laps	Laps Led	Races Led	Miles	$
1959	Johnny Allen	1	0	0	0	1	0	0	0	99	0	0	248	1,925
1959	Curtis Turner	1	0	0	0	0	1	0	0	150	0	0	150	950
1959	Bob Welborn	2	1	1	0	0	0	0	0	115	42	2	288	1,125
1959	Speedy Thompson	2	0	0	0	0	0	1	0	830	2	1	706	1,465
1960	Joe Lee Johnson	5	0	0	0	0	0	0	0	289	0	0	248	475
1960	Marvin Panch	8	0	0	0	0	0	0	1	1,265	0	0	1,911	2,875
1960	Curtis Turner	1	0	0	0	0	0	0	0	10	0	0	5	50
1960	Bob Welborn	2	0	0	1	0	0	0	0	199	76	1	100	575
1961	Darel Dieringer	1	0	0	0	0	0	0	0	231	0	0	347	250
1961	J.C. Hendrix	1	0	0	0	0	0	0	0	202	0	0	303	300
Lifetime		24	1	1	1	1	1	1	1	3,390	120	4	4,304	$9,990

Bob Riley

Year	Driver	Starts	Poles	1	2	3	4	5	6–10	Laps	Laps Led	Races Led	Miles	$
1983	Bob Riley	3	0	0	0	0	0	0	0	329	0	0	491	3,530
1985	Bob Riley	1	0	0	0	0	0	0	0	449	0	0	449	2,100
Lifetime		4	0	0	0	0	0	0	0	778	0	0	940	$5,630

Richard Riley

Year	Driver	Starts	Poles	1	2	3	4	5	6–10	Laps	Laps Led	Races Led	Miles	$
1958	Jimmy Thompson	1	0	0	0	0	0	0	0	14	0	0	7	70
1958	Bunk Moore	1	0	0	0	0	0	0	0	141	0	0	88	70
1959	Richard Riley	4	0	0	0	0	0	0	1	664	0	0	332	410
1959	Curtis Crider	2	0	0	0	0	0	0	0	244	0	0	122	135
1959	Bunk Moore	5	0	0	0	0	0	0	0	312	0	0	153	280
Lifetime		13	0	0	0	0	0	0	1	1,375	0	0	702	$965

Laurent Rioux

Year	Driver	Starts	Poles	1	2	3	4	5	6–10	Laps	Laps Led	Races Led	Miles	$
1983	Laurent Rioux	2	0	0	0	0	0	0	0	884	0	0	674	2,555
1984	Laurent Rioux	1	0	0	0	0	0	0	0	424	0	0	431	1,695
Lifetime		3	0	0	0	0	0	0	0	1,308	0	0	1,105	$4,250

Pat Rissi

Year	Driver	Starts	Poles	1	2	3	4	5	6–10	Laps	Laps Led	Races Led	Miles	$
1991	Andy Belmont	1	0	0	0	0	0	0	0	11	0	0	11	3,450
1992	Andy Belmont	8	0	0	0	0	0	0	0	779	0	0	1,535	39,820
Lifetime		9	0	0	0	0	0	0	0	790	0	0	1,546	$43,270

Tom Roady

Year	Driver	Starts	Poles	1	2	3	4	5	6–10	Laps	Laps Led	Races Led	Miles	$
1956	Al Pombo	2	0	0	0	0	0	0	0	334	0	0	273	90
1956	Clyde Palmer	4	0	0	1	1	0	1	0	487	129	1	298	1,450
1956	Art Watts	3	0	0	0	0	0	0	2	458	0	0	244	360
Lifetime		9	0	0	1	1	0	1	2	1,279	129	1	815	$1,900

Marty Robbins

Year	Driver	Starts	Poles	1	2	3	4	5	6–10	Laps	Laps Led	Races Led	Miles	$
1970	Marty Robbins	1	0	0	0	0	0	0	0	105	0	0	158	1,160
1971	Marty Robbins	5	0	0	0	0	0	0	1	1,295	0	0	1,991	7,152
1972	Marty Robbins	5	0	0	0	0	0	0	2	1,096	0	0	1,864	7,950
1973	Marty Robbins	4	0	0	0	0	0	0	1	334	1	1	829	5,395
1974	Marty Robbins	4	0	0	0	0	0	1	1	550	0	0	1,343	5,734
1975	Marty Robbins	2	0	0	0	0	0	0	0	65	2	1	172	3,160
1977	Marty Robbins	2	0	0	0	0	0	0	0	229	0	0	482	2,590
1977	Elmo Langley	1	0	0	0	0	0	0	0	1	0	0	2	610
1978	Marty Robbins	1	0	0	0	0	0	0	0	171	0	0	455	2,240
1979	Marty Robbins	3	0	0	0	0	0	0	0	235	0	0	520	3,120
1980	Marty Robbins	2	0	0	0	0	0	0	0	227	0	0	604	4,235
1982	Marty Robbins	2	0	0	0	0	0	0	0	134	0	0	248	2,055
Lifetime		32	0	0	0	0	0	1	5	4,442	3	2	8,667	$45,401

Year	Driver	Starts	Poles	Finish 1	2	3	4	5	6–10	Laps	Laps Led	Races Led	Miles	$

Charlie Roberts

Year	Driver	Starts	Poles	1	2	3	4	5	6–10	Laps	Laps Led	Races Led	Miles	$
1971	Frank Warren	2	0	0	0	0	0	0	1	490	0	0	283	1,370
1971	Roy Mulligan	1	0	0	0	0	0	0	0	83	0	0	221	1,450
1971	Charlie Roberts	17	0	0	0	0	0	0	1	2,145	0	0	2,763	8,755
1972	Charlie Roberts	24	0	0	0	0	0	0	1	6,211	0	0	7,244	25,960
1972	Robert Wales	2	0	0	0	0	0	0	0	14	0	0	37	1,510
1973	Charlie Roberts	24	0	0	0	0	0	0	0	7,017	0	0	6,861	28,550
1973	Dean Dalton	2	0	0	0	0	0	0	0	809	0	0	462	1,230
1974	Charlie Roberts	3	0	0	0	0	0	0	0	226	0	0	471	3,940
1974	Neil Bonnett	1	0	0	0	0	0	0	0	51	0	0	136	1,450
Lifetime		76	0	0	0	0	0	0	3	17,046	0	0	18,478	$74,215

Fireball Roberts

Year	Driver	Starts	Poles	1	2	3	4	5	6–10	Laps	Laps Led	Races Led	Miles	$
1957	Fireball Roberts	22	1	3	2	1	0	2	4	3,285	363	6	2,080	7,160
1957	Marvin Panch	1	0	0	0	0	0	0	0	473	0	0	237	210
Lifetime		23	1	3	2	1	0	2	4	3,758	363	6	2,317	$7,370

J.E. Roberts

Year	Driver	Starts	Poles	1	2	3	4	5	6–10	Laps	Laps Led	Races Led	Miles	$
1954	Johnny Roberts	2	0	0	0	0	0	0	0	160	0	0	159	25
Lifetime		2	0	0	0	0	0	0	0	160	0	0	159	$25

J.F. Roberts

Year	Driver	Starts	Poles	1	2	3	4	5	6–10	Laps	Laps Led	Races Led	Miles	$
1953	Johnny Roberts	2	0	0	0	0	0	0	0	33	0	0	135	50
Lifetime		2	0	0	0	0	0	0	0	33	0	0	135	$50

Johnny Roberts

Year	Driver	Starts	Poles	1	2	3	4	5	6–10	Laps	Laps Led	Races Led	Miles	$
1955	Johnny Roberts	4	0	0	0	0	0	0	1	600	0	0	406	250
1956	Johnny Roberts	4	0	0	0	0	0	0	0	461	0	0	215	210
Lifetime		8	0	0	0	0	0	0	1	1,061	0	0	621	$460

Neil Roberts

Year	Driver	Starts	Poles	1	2	3	4	5	6–10	Laps	Laps Led	Races Led	Miles	$
1953	Neil Roberts	1	0	0	0	0	0	0	0	335	0	0	461	300
Lifetime		1	0	0	0	0	0	0	0	335	0	0	461	$300

Paul Roberts

Year	Driver	Starts	Poles	1	2	3	4	5	6–10	Laps	Laps Led	Races Led	Miles	$
1950	Curtis Turner	1	0	0	0	0	0	0	0	46	0	0	192	50
Lifetime		1	0	0	0	0	0	0	0	46	0	0	192	$50

H.R. Robertson

Year	Driver	Starts	Poles	1	2	3	4	5	6–10	Laps	Laps Led	Races Led	Miles	$
1952	Buck McCardell	1	0	0	0	0	0	0	0		0	0		25
Lifetime		1	0	0	0	0	0	0	0		0	0		$25

Don Robertson

Year	Driver	Starts	Poles	1	2	3	4	5	6–10	Laps	Laps Led	Races Led	Miles	$
1967	Sam McQuagg	1	0	0	0	0	0	0	0	50	0	0	31	175
1967	Jabe Thomas	19	0	0	0	0	0	0	2	2,139	0	0	1,713	6,855
1968	Jabe Thomas	47	0	0	0	0	0	1	14	11,141	0	0	7,250	16,160
1968	Earl Brooks	1	0	0	0	0	0	0	0	18	0	0	27	500
1968	Harold Fagan	1	0	0	0	0	0	0	0	3	0	0	3	250
1969	Wendell Scott	1	0	0	0	0	0	0	0	10	0	0	25	605
1969	Jabe Thomas	49	0	0	0	0	0	0	12	11,782	0	0	9,260	29,172
1969	James Cox	8	0	0	0	0	0	0	0	606	0	0	299	1,935
1969	Paul Dean Holt	3	0	0	0	0	0	0	0	320	0	0	204	733
1970	Dr. Ed Hessert	1	0	0	0	0	0	0	0	60	0	0	90	240
1970	Charlie Glotzbach	2	0	0	0	0	0	0	0	219	0	0	97	475
1970	Jabe Thomas	46	0	0	0	0	0	0	23	10,928	0	0	9,510	32,090
1970	Bobby Allison	3	0	0	1	0	0	0	1	921	0	0	525	5,060
1970	James Cox	7	0	0	0	0	0	0	0	318	0	0	210	2,755
1970	James Hylton	2	0	0	0	0	0	0	0	220	0	0	550	1,490
1970	Richard Petty	2	0	2	0	0	0	0	0	400	216	2	200	2,500
1970	Earl Brooks	1	0	0	0	0	0	0	0	29	0	0	40	815
1970	Wendell Scott	11	0	0	0	0	0	0	0	1,876	0	0	1,929	6,615

Year	Driver	Starts	Poles	Finish 1	2	3	4	5	6–10	Laps	Laps Led	Races Led	Miles	$

Don Robertson *continued*

Year	Driver	Starts	Poles	1	2	3	4	5	6–10	Laps	Laps Led	Races Led	Miles	$
1971	Pedro Rodriguez	1	0	0	0	0	0	0	0	194	0	0	485	1,975
1971	Neil Castles	1	0	0	0	0	0	0	0	2	0	0	3	315
1971	James Cox	5	0	0	0	0	0	0	0	531	0	0	327	1,650
1971	Jabe Thomas	41	0	0	0	0	1	1	13	10,729	0	0	9,172	28,235
1971	Fritz Schulz	1	0	0	0	0	0	0	0	45	0	0	113	205
1971	Bill Seifert	1	0	0	0	0	0	0	0	9	0	0	5	240
1972	Henley Gray	1	0	0	0	0	0	0	0	81	0	0	51	330
1972	Bill Dennis	5	0	0	0	0	0	0	0	737	0	0	916	3,465
1972	Jabe Thomas	27	0	0	0	0	0	0	4	7,038	0	0	8,066	36,755
1972	James Cox	2	0	0	0	0	0	0	0	527	0	0	323	1,220
1972	Mel Larson	3	0	0	0	0	0	0	0	400	0	0	918	2,870
1972	Roy Mayne	1	0	0	0	0	0	0	0	267	0	0	272	650
1972	Vic Elford	1	0	0	0	0	0	0	1	182	0	0	455	3,445
1972	Dr. Ed Hessert	1	0	0	0	0	0	0	0	50	0	0	75	335
1973	Mel Larson	7	0	0	0	0	0	0	0	1,967	0	0	1,666	5,370
1973	Jabe Thomas	23	0	0	0	0	0	0	1	6,553	0	0	7,307	31,768
1973	Roy Mayne	3	0	0	0	0	0	0	1	658	0	0	1,095	5,470
1974	Richie Panch	1	0	0	0	0	0	0	0	56	0	0	33	535
1974	Jabe Thomas	10	0	0	0	0	0	0	1	1,504	0	0	1,007	7,835
1974	Roy Mayne	11	0	0	0	0	0	0	0	1,681	0	0	2,856	14,895
1975	Jabe Thomas	20	0	0	0	0	0	0	2	5,645	0	0	5,191	19,720
1975	Charlie Griffin	2	0	0	0	0	0	0	0	82	0	0	51	720
1975	Earl Brooks	8	0	0	0	0	0	0	0	1,534	0	0	1,681	5,550
1976	Dick May	13	0	0	0	0	0	0	0	3,504	0	0	3,980	21,725
1976	D.K. Ulrich	1	0	0	0	0	0	0	0	168	0	0	447	2,785
1976	Earl Brooks	1	0	0	0	0	0	0	0	313	0	0	428	1,990
1976	Jabe Thomas	6	0	0	0	0	0	0	0	1,944	0	0	1,291	6,160
1977	Dean Dalton	1	0	0	0	0	0	0	0	179	0	0	358	1,775
1977	Ferrel Harris	11	0	0	0	0	0	0	0	2,979	0	0	2,560	19,365
1977	Dick May	1	0	0	0	0	0	0	0	148	0	0	394	3,165
1977	Terry Bivins	4	0	0	0	0	0	0	0	1,009	0	0	909	6,640
1977	Ronnie Thomas	4	0	0	0	0	0	0	0	821	0	0	715	4,590
1978	Ronnie Thomas	26	0	0	0	0	0	0	2	6,804	0	0	7,287	55,350
1979	Ronnie Thomas	28	0	0	0	0	0	0	3	6,171	1	1	7,047	84,520
1980	Ronnie Thomas	30	0	0	0	0	0	0	4	7,522	0	0	9,082	80,985
Lifetime		507	0	2	1	0	1	2	84	113,074	217	3	108,530	$571,028

Charles Robinson

Year	Driver	Starts	Poles	1	2	3	4	5	6–10	Laps	Laps Led	Races Led	Miles	$
1963	Ned Jarrett	50	5	8	7	5	7	4	7	11,370	1,897	18	7,719	38,065
1964	Jimmy Pardue	47	2	0	2	4	4	4	9	9,163	237	5	6,158	34,520
1964	Larry Thomas	3	0	0	0	1	0	1	0	671	0	0	519	1,325
1964	Ned Jarrett	4	1	1	0	0	0	1	1	632	233	3	646	3,275
Lifetime		104	8	9	9	10	11	10	17	21,836	2,367	26	15,042	$77,185

Robbie Robinson

Year	Driver	Starts	Poles	1	2	3	4	5	6–10	Laps	Laps Led	Races Led	Miles	$
1952	Robbie Robinson	4	0	0	0	0	0	0	0	300	0	0	160	75
Lifetime		4	0	0	0	0	0	0	0	300	0	0	160	$75

Truett Rodgers

Year	Driver	Starts	Poles	1	2	3	4	5	6–10	Laps	Laps Led	Races Led	Miles	$
1966	Roy Tyner	24	0	0	0	0	0	0	4	3,241	0	0	1,860	3,735
1967	Roy Tyner	24	0	0	0	0	0	0	1	2,521	0	0	1,638	5,855
1967	Ken Spikes	2	0	0	0	0	0	0	0	305	0	0	423	1,325
1967	Earl Brooks	1	0	0	0	0	0	0	0	215	0	0	134	225
1968	Bill Vanderhoff	1	0	0	0	0	0	0	0	151	0	0	76	100
Lifetime		52	0	0	0	0	0	0	5	6,433	0	0	4,131	$11,240

Kurt Roehrig

Year	Driver	Starts	Poles	1	2	3	4	5	6–10	Laps	Laps Led	Races Led	Miles	$
1998	Tom Hubert	1	0	0	0	0	0	0	0	78	0	0	152	24,685
1999	Tom Hubert	2	0	0	0	0	0	0	0	372	0	0	608	74,120
Lifetime		3	0	0	0	0	0	0	0	450	0	0	760	$98,805

Don Rogalla

Year	Driver	Starts	Poles	1	2	3	4	5	6–10	Laps	Laps Led	Races Led	Miles	$
1949	Al Bonnell	2	1	0	0	0	0	0	1	183	0	0	183	150

Year	Driver	Starts	Poles	1	2	3	4	5	6–10	Laps	Laps Led	Races Led	Miles	$

Don Rogalla *continued*

1950	Dick Linder	9	4	3	1	1	0	0	1	1,144	460	5	847	5,100
1951	Jimmy Florian	3	0	0	0	0	1	0	1		0	0		525
1951	Dick Linder	9	0	0	0	0	0	0	2	21	0	0	11	325
1951	Dan Daniels	2	0	0	0	0	0	0	0		0	0		50
Lifetime		25	5	3	1	1	1	0	5	1,348	460	5	1,041	$6,150

Bob Rogers

1980	Don Sprouse	4	0	0	0	0	0	0	0	1,312	0	0	745	2,880
1981	Don Sprouse	2	0	0	0	0	0	0	0	570	0	0	663	6,850
1981	Tim Richmond	7	0	0	0	0	0	0	1	2,227	24	2	2,438	15,240
1981	Mike Alexander	19	0	0	0	0	0	0	3	4,340	4	1	4,886	33,305
1982	Donnie Allison	5	0	0	0	0	0	1	3	1,174	1	1	1,646	28,105
1982	Neil Bonnett	3	0	0	0	0	0	0	1	1,214	0	0	710	9,530
1982	Tom Sneva	3	0	0	0	0	0	0	0	520	0	0	840	15,585
Lifetime		43	0	0	0	0	0	1	8	11,357	29	4	11,928	$111,495

Buck Rogers

| 1962 | Buck Roger | 1 | 0 | 0 | 0 | 0 | 0 | 0 | 0 | 35 | 0 | 0 | 88 | 50 |
| **Lifetime** | | 1 | 0 | 0 | 0 | 0 | 0 | 0 | 0 | 35 | 0 | 0 | 88 | $50 |

John Rogers

| 1963 | Buck Roger | 2 | 0 | 0 | 0 | 0 | 0 | 0 | 0 | 109 | 0 | 0 | 273 | 625 |
| **Lifetime** | | 2 | 0 | 0 | 0 | 0 | 0 | 0 | 0 | 109 | 0 | 0 | 273 | $625 |

George Rogge

| 1954 | George Rogge | 1 | 0 | 0 | 0 | 0 | 0 | 0 | 0 | 64 | 0 | 0 | 64 | 40 |
| **Lifetime** | | 1 | 0 | 0 | 0 | 0 | 0 | 0 | 0 | 64 | 0 | 0 | 64 | $40 |

R.C. Rollings

| 1955 | Jimmy Roland | 1 | 0 | 0 | 0 | 0 | 0 | 0 | 0 | 137 | 0 | 0 | 188 | 50 |
| **Lifetime** | | 1 | 0 | 0 | 0 | 0 | 0 | 0 | 0 | 137 | 0 | 0 | 188 | $50 |

Shorty Rollins

1958	Jack Smith	1	0	0	0	0	0	0	0	171	0	0	86	0
1958	Shorty Rollins	26	0	1	1	3	5	1	9	4,853	87	4	2,984	10,870
1959	Fritz Wilson	4	0	0	0	0	0	0	1	263	0	0	156	180
1959	Shorty Rollins	8	0	0	0	0	0	0	4	1,286	0	0	890	1,150
1960	Shorty Rollins	4	0	0	0	0	0	0	1	952	0	0	1,480	2,120
1960	Larry Frank	3	0	0	0	0	0	0	1	991	11	1	994	1,335
Lifetime		46	0	1	1	3	5	1	16	8,516	98	5	6,589	$15,655

Paul Romine

| 1990 | Pancho Carter | 1 | 0 | 0 | 0 | 0 | 0 | 0 | 0 | 298 | 0 | 0 | 454 | 3,040 |
| **Lifetime** | | 1 | 0 | 0 | 0 | 0 | 0 | 0 | 0 | 298 | 0 | 0 | 454 | $3,040 |

Slim Rominger

1953	Slim Rominger	2	0	0	0	0	0	0	0	153	0	0	147	125
1957	Darel Dieringer	1	0	0	0	0	0	0	1	279	0	0	279	450
1958	Paul Goldsmith	1	0	0	0	0	0	0	1	139	0	0	46	140
Lifetime		4	0	0	0	0	0	0	2	571	0	0	473	$715

Joyce Ronacher

1970	Dick May	16	0	0	0	0	0	0	0	1,028	0	0	689	5,195
1971	Dick May	1	0	0	0	0	0	0	0	41	0	0	103	0
Lifetime		17	0	0	0	0	0	0	0	1,069	0	0	792	$5,195

Ron Ronacher

| 1971 | Elmo Langley | 4 | 0 | 0 | 0 | 1 | 0 | 1 | 1 | 1,114 | 0 | 0 | 655 | 2,135 |

Year	Driver	Starts	Poles	Finish 1	2	3	4	5	6–10	Laps	Laps Led	Races Led	Miles	$

Ron Ronacher *continued*

| 1971 | Dick May | 12 | 0 | 0 | 0 | 0 | 0 | 0 | 1 | 1,165 | 0 | 0 | 606 | 4,385 |
| **Lifetime** | | 16 | 0 | 0 | 0 | 1 | 0 | 1 | 2 | 2,279 | 0 | 0 | 1,261 | $6,520 |

Ed Rooney

| 1951 | Ed Rooney | 1 | 0 | 0 | 0 | 0 | 0 | 0 | 0 | | 0 | 0 | | 25 |
| **Lifetime** | | 1 | 0 | 0 | 0 | 0 | 0 | 0 | 0 | | 0 | 0 | | $25 |

Bruce Root

| 1952 | Speedy Thompson | 1 | 0 | 0 | 0 | 0 | 0 | 0 | 0 | 26 | 0 | 0 | 33 | 25 |
| **Lifetime** | | 1 | 0 | 0 | 0 | 0 | 0 | 0 | 0 | 26 | 0 | 0 | 33 | $25 |

Charles Roscoe

| 1951 | Bill Stammer | 3 | 0 | 0 | 0 | 0 | 0 | 0 | 2 | | 0 | 0 | | 175 |
| **Lifetime** | | 3 | 0 | 0 | 0 | 0 | 0 | 0 | 2 | | 0 | 0 | | $175 |

Bob Rose

| 1961 | Sal Tovella | 3 | 0 | 0 | 0 | 0 | 0 | 0 | 0 | 362 | 0 | 0 | 761 | 600 |
| **Lifetime** | | 3 | 0 | 0 | 0 | 0 | 0 | 0 | 0 | 362 | 0 | 0 | 761 | $600 |

Mauri Rose

1956	Bob Flock	3	0	0	0	0	0	1	0	390	0	0	345	435
1956	Dink Widenhouse	1	0	0	0	0	0	0	0	64	0	0	32	0
1956	Speedy Thompson	2	0	0	0	0	0	0	0	109	0	0	74	50
1956	Tim Flock	7	0	0	0	0	1	1	2	964	0	0	768	2,219
Lifetime		13	0	0	0	0	1	2	2	1,527	0	0	1,218	$2,704

Sam Rose

1968	Sam Rose	1	0	0	0	0	0	0	0	92	0	0	248	630
1969	Sam Rose	1	0	0	0	0	0	0	0	65	0	0	176	775
1970	Sam Rose	1	0	0	0	0	0	0	0	157	0	0	411	1,175
Lifetime		3	0	0	0	0	0	0	0	314	0	0	835	$2,580

Jim Rosenblum

1983	Jocko Maggiacomo	3	0	0	0	0	0	0	0	312	0	0	722	3,850
1986	Jocko Maggiacomo	2	0	0	0	0	0	0	0	14	0	0	35	2,695
1987	Jocko Maggiacomo	3	0	0	0	0	0	0	0	233	0	0	583	4,885
1988	Jocko Maggiacomo	3	0	0	0	0	0	0	0	125	0	0	321	4,755
1989	Oma Kimbrough	1	0	0	0	0	0	0	0	64	0	0	157	2,135
1989	Randy LaJoie	1	0	0	0	0	0	0	0	178	0	0	445	2,725
1989	Eddie Bierschwale	1	0	0	0	0	0	0	0	83	0	0	208	2,575
1990	Randy LaJoie	2	0	0	0	0	0	0	0	177	0	0	443	6,675
1990	Oma Kimbrough	1	0	0	0	0	0	0	0	40	0	0	98	2,240
1991	Gary Balough	1	0	0	0	0	0	0	0	2	0	0	5	3,300
1991	Oma Kimbrough	1	0	0	0	0	0	0	0	80	0	0	196	3,620
1992	Gary Balough	1	0	0	0	0	0	0	0	131	0	0	197	5,100
1992	Bob Schacht	2	0	0	0	0	0	0	0	107	0	0	265	8,075
1993	Kerry Teague	2	0	0	0	0	0	0	0	223	0	0	558	14,400
Lifetime		24	0	0	0	0	0	0	0	1,769	0	0	4,230	$67,030

Bob Rosenthal

| 1966 | Bunkie Blackburn | 2 | 0 | 0 | 0 | 0 | 0 | 0 | 0 | 65 | 4 | 1 | 163 | 1,070 |
| **Lifetime** | | 2 | 0 | 0 | 0 | 0 | 0 | 0 | 0 | 65 | 4 | 1 | 163 | $1,070 |

H.G. Rosier

1962	H.G. Rosier	4	0	0	0	0	0	0	1	653	0	0	748	1,440
1963	H.G. Rosier	2	0	0	0	0	1	0	0	162	0	0	81	350
Lifetime		6	0	0	0	0	1	0	1	815	0	0	829	$1,790

Year	Driver	Starts	Poles	Finish						Laps	Laps Led	Races Led	Miles	$
				1	2	3	4	5	6–10	Laps	Led	Led	Miles	$

Bob Ross

Year	Driver	Starts	Poles	1	2	3	4	5	6–10	Laps	Laps Led	Races Led	Miles	$
1956	Bob Ross	2	0	0	0	0	0	0	1	411	0	0	323	375
1957	Bob Ross	3	0	0	0	0	0	0	3	396	0	0	314	720
1958	Bob Ross	2	0	0	1	0	0	0	0	135	0	0	192	600
1960	Bob Ross	2	0	0	0	0	0	0	0	104	0	0	116	200
1961	Bob Ross	1	1	0	0	0	0	0	0	13	0	0	18	0
1963	Bob Ross	1	0	0	0	0	0	0	0	175	0	0	473	575
Lifetime		11	1	0	1	0	0	0	4	1,234	0	0	1,436	$2,470

Brian Ross

Year	Driver	Starts	Poles	1	2	3	4	5	6–10	Laps	Laps Led	Races Led	Miles	$
1991	Brian Ross	1	0	0	0	0	0	0	0	37	0	0	37	3,475
Lifetime		1	0	0	0	0	0	0	0	37	0	0	37	$3,475

Mario Rossi

Year	Driver	Starts	Poles	1	2	3	4	5	6–10	Laps	Laps Led	Races Led	Miles	$
1956	Mario Rossi	1	0	0	0	0	0	0	0	97	0	0	97	60
1958	Mario Rossi	2	0	0	0	0	0	0	0	501	0	0	475	220
1968	Darel Dieringer	18	1	0	1	0	3	1	3	4,409	159	2	4,972	27,905
1969	Bobby Allison	23	1	4	3	1	2	2	1	5,570	1,157	13	6,045	65,115
1969	Darel Dieringer	1	0	0	0	0	0	0	0	119	0	0	60	250
1970	Bobby Allison	21	3	1	6	4	2	0	2	5,264	405	13	7,700	100,470
1971	Dick Brooks	15	0	0	1	5	0	3	3	3,936	16	5	4,408	30,420
Lifetime		81	5	5	11	10	7	6	9	19,896	1,737	33	23,757	$224,440

John Rostek

Year	Driver	Starts	Poles	1	2	3	4	5	6–10	Laps	Laps Led	Races Led	Miles	$
1960	John Rostek	5	1	1	0	1	0	0	1	658	65	2	688	2,060
1963	John Rostek	1	0	0	0	0	0	0	0	172	0	0	464	500
Lifetime		6	1	1	0	1	0	0	1	830	65	2	1,152	$2,560

Dr. Gil Roth

Year	Driver	Starts	Poles	1	2	3	4	5	6–10	Laps	Laps Led	Races Led	Miles	$
1982	Dr. Gil Roth	1	0	0	0	0	0	0	0	91	0	0	91	615
Lifetime		1	0	0	0	0	0	0	0	91	0	0	91	$615

Roulo Brothers

Year	Driver	Starts	Poles	1	2	3	4	5	6–10	Laps	Laps Led	Races Led	Miles	$
1993	Jim Sauter	1	0	0	0	0	0	0	0	197	0	0	394	8,195
1993	Dick Trickle	2	0	0	0	0	0	0	0	474	0	0	454	13,920
1993	Chuck Bown	1	0	0	0	0	0	0	0	306	0	0	306	6,610
1993	Scott Lagasse	1	0	0	0	0	0	0	0	90	0	0	221	7,800
1994	Rich Bickle	1	0	0	0	0	0	0	0	144	0	0	144	6,515
1994	Scott Lagasse	1	0	0	0	0	0	0	0	65	0	0	159	6,055
Lifetime		7	0	0	0	0	0	0	0	1,276	0	0	1,678	$49,095

Larry Rouse

Year	Driver	Starts	Poles	1	2	3	4	5	6–10	Laps	Laps Led	Races Led	Miles	$
1991	Robert Sprague	1	0	0	0	0	0	0	0	54	1	1	136	3,500
Lifetime		1	0	0	0	0	0	0	0	54	1	1	136	$3,500

Jack Roush (Statistics represent teams principly owned by Jack Roush, including partnerships with Mark Martin and others.)

Year	Driver	Starts	Poles	1	2	3	4	5	6–10	Laps	Laps Led	Races Led	Miles	$
1988	Mark Martin	29	1	0	1	0	2	0	7	7,595	120	4	9,182	189,420
1989	Mark Martin	29	6	1	5	6	1	1	4	9,010	480	16	10,718	622,878
1990	Mark Martin	29	4	3	5	4	2	2	7	9,636	451	15	11,589	803,095
1991	Mark Martin	29	5	1	1	5	4	3	3	8,903	663	15	10,777	805,105
1992	Mark Martin	29	1	2	5	2	1	0	7	8,954	533	17	10,671	809,505
1992	Wally Dallenbach	29	0	0	0	0	0	1	0	8,105	0	0	9,682	216,745
1993	Mark Martin	30	5	5	3	1	1	2	7	9,381	1,388	20	11,107	1,158,890
1993	Wally Dallenbach	30	0	0	1	0	0	0	3	8,411	3	2	10,056	439,140
1994	Mark Martin	31	1	2	4	2	4	3	5	9,549	726	18	11,404	1,054,237
1994	Ted Musgrave	31	3	0	0	0	0	1	7	9,237	50	4	10,818	579,653
1995	Mark Martin	31	4	4	1	4	1	3	9	9,393	739	14	11,428	1,534,966
1995	Ted Musgrave	31	1	0	2	2	2	1	6	9,290	43	6	11,381	943,675
1996	Jeff Burton	30	1	0	0	1	3	2	6	8,592	208	7	10,552	699,852
1996	Mark Martin	31	4	0	4	5	3	2	9	9,064	701	16	11,067	1,502,558
1996	Ted Musgrave	31	1	0	0	1	1	0	5	9,351	3	2	11,387	852,505
1997	Ted Musgrave	32	0	0	1	1	3	0	3	9,266	131	6	12,095	1,101,965

Year	Driver	Starts	Poles	Finish 1	2	3	4	5	6–10	Laps	Laps Led	Races Led	Miles	$

Jack Roush *continued*

Year	Driver	Starts	Poles	1	2	3	4	5	6–10	Laps	Laps Led	Races Led	Miles	$
1997	Chad Little	12	0	0	0	0	0	0	0	3,910	7	1	4,301	227,955
1997	Jeff Burton	32	0	3	3	3	2	2	5	9,275	685	17	12,346	1,815,145
1997	Mark Martin	32	3	4	2	4	2	4	8	9,599	796	20	12,354	1,803,550
1998	Mark Martin	33	3	7	6	4	3	2	4	9,830	1,731	23	12,744	2,992,220
1998	Ted Musgrave	20	0	0	1	0	0	1	3	5,337	0	0	7,522	912,580
1998	Jeff Burton	33	0	2	4	2	5	5	5	9,488	974	13	12,141	2,072,347
1998	Johnny Benson Jr.	32	0	0	0	0	1	2	7	8,565	93	10	11,108	1,216,320
1998	Kevin Lepage	13	0	0	0	0	0	0	2	3,623	0	0	4,004	447,745
1998	Chad Little	32	0	0	1	0	0	0	6	9,081	69	8	11,828	1,285,460
1999	Jeff Burton	34	1	6	2	3	4	3	5	9,878	1,063	18	12,784	5,150,786
1999	Chad Little	34	0	0	0	0	0	0	5	9,465	3	3	12,160	1,567,879
1999	Kevin Lepage	34	1	0	0	0	0	1	1	9,646	20	2	12,630	1,541,844
1999	Mark Martin	34	1	2	4	5	5	3	7	9,903	701	25	12,848	2,652,296
1999	Johnny Benson Jr.	34	0	0	0	0	0	0	2	9,362	8	3	11,902	1,548,081
2000	Jeff Burton	34	1	4	5	2	1	3	7	9,656	1,131	22	12,626	3,986,460
2000	Chad Little	27	0	0	0	0	0	0	1	7,178	7	5	10,055	1,388,420
2000	Mark Martin	34	0	1	1	7	1	3	7	9,240	494	18	11,758	2,661,615
2000	Matt Kenseth	34	0	1	1	1	0	0	7	9,466	161	7	12,553	2,110,685
2000	Kurt Busch	7	0	0	0	0	0	1	0	2,411	0	0	2,702	311,915
2000	Kevin Lepage	32	0	0	0	0	0	1	2	8,743	38	9	10,936	1,599,922
2001	Mark Martin	36	2	0	0	0	2	1	12	10,138	190	19	13,681	3,338,966
2001	Matt Kenseth	36	0	0	0	0	4	0	5	10,341	100	14	13,568	2,163,514
2001	Kurt Busch	35	1	0	0	1	1	1	3	8,965	160	5	11,994	2,109,687
2001	Jeff Burton	36	0	2	1	2	1	2	8	10,463	401	10	13,937	3,678,464
2002	Greg Biffle	1	0	0	0	0	0	0	0	249	0	0	498	59,050
2002	Mark Martin	36	0	1	3	2	3	3	10	10,517	363	15	13,838	5,086,472
2002	Matt Kenseth	31	1	4	2	1	2	1	6	8,628	637	15	11,736	3,178,977
2002	Kurt Busch	36	1	4	3	2	3	0	8	10,259	933	20	13,099	3,541,682
2002	Jeff Burton	36	0	0	0	3	2	0	9	9,980	124	13	13,205	3,698,099
Lifetime		1342	52	59	72	76	70	59	233	386,933	17,128	477	490,769	$77,462,325

Marvin Rowley

Year	Driver	Starts	Poles	1	2	3	4	5	6–10	Laps	Laps Led	Races Led	Miles	$
1970	Jimmy Insolo	2	0	0	0	0	0	0	0	137	0	0	359	1,635
1971	Jimmy Insolo	3	0	0	0	0	0	0	0	349	0	0	892	3,790
Lifetime		5	0	0	0	0	0	0	0	486	0	0	1,251	$5,425

Al Rudd

Year	Driver	Starts	Poles	1	2	3	4	5	6–10	Laps	Laps Led	Races Led	Miles	$
1976	Ricky Rudd	4	0	0	0	0	0	0	1	876	0	0	1,527	7,175
1977	Ricky Rudd	25	0	0	0	0	1	0	9	6,233	13	3	7,509	60,420
1978	Ricky Rudd	13	0	0	0	0	0	0	4	2,535	16	5	4,334	50,260
1978	James Hylton	1	0	0	0	0	0	0	0	1	0	0	3	1,130
1979	Darrell Waltrip	1	0	0	0	0	0	0	1	200	62	1	500	2,715
1979	Al Rudd Jr.	1	0	0	0	0	0	0	0	39	0	0	78	740
1979	Lennie Pond	2	0	0	0	0	0	0	0	470	2	1	417	10,975
1980	Ricky Rudd	3	0	0	0	0	1	0	1	839	1	1	1,314	23,515
Lifetime		50	0	0	0	0	2	0	16	11,193	94	11	15,682	$156,930

Ricky Rudd

Year	Driver	Starts	Poles	1	2	3	4	5	6–10	Laps	Laps Led	Races Led	Miles	$
1994	Ricky Rudd	31	1	1	0	0	3	2	9	9,728	192	10	12,047	644,931
1995	Ricky Rudd	31	2	1	0	1	4	4	6	8,813	368	11	10,834	1,142,974
1996	Ricky Rudd	31	0	1	2	1	1	0	11	9,281	150	12	11,401	1,170,373
1997	Ricky Rudd	32	0	2	0	1	1	2	5	9,094	77	4	11,619	1,832,731
1998	Ricky Rudd	33	0	1	0	0	0	0	4	9,127	255	3	11,589	1,545,395
1999	Ricky Rudd	34	1	0	0	2	0	1	2	9,230	21	3	12,031	1,614,101
Lifetime		192	4	6	2	5	9	9	37	55,273	1,063	43	69,521	$7,950,505

Charles Rudolph

Year	Driver	Starts	Poles	1	2	3	4	5	6–10	Laps	Laps Led	Races Led	Miles	$
1987	Charlie Rudolph	2	0	0	0	0	0	0	0	658	0	0	952	4,540
Lifetime		2	0	0	0	0	0	0	0	658	0	0	952	$4,540

Jim Ruggles

Year	Driver	Starts	Poles	1	2	3	4	5	6–10	Laps	Laps Led	Races Led	Miles	$
1972	Pete Hamilton	1	0	0	0	0	0	0	0	155	0	0	310	910
Lifetime		1	0	0	0	0	0	0	0	155	0	0	310	$910

Year	Driver	Starts	Poles	Finish						Laps	Laps Led	Races Led	Miles	$
				1	2	3	4	5	6–10	Laps	Led	Led	Miles	$

James Rupe

Year	Driver	Starts	Poles	1	2	3	4	5	6–10	Laps	Led	Led	Miles	$
1971	Dave Marcis	1	0	0	0	0	0	1	0	244	0	0	61	325
1971	Bob Williams	1	0	0	0	0	0	0	0	297	0	0	186	445
1971	Junior Spencer	1	0	0	0	0	0	0	0	112	0	0	51	310
Lifetime		3	0	0	0	0	0	1	0	653	0	0	298	$1,080

Carl Rupert

Year	Driver	Starts	Poles	1	2	3	4	5	6–10	Laps	Led	Led	Miles	$
1955	Tiny Lund	1	0	0	0	0	0	0	0	65	0	0	98	60
1959	Tom Pistone	21	0	2	2	4	2	2	5	3,710	181	7	2,918	10,710
1959	Curtis Turner	2	0	0	0	0	0	0	0	187	19	1	111	195
1960	Tom Pistone	2	0	0	0	0	0	0	1	268	0	0	134	180
Lifetime		26	0	2	2	4	2	2	6	4,230	200	8	3,261	$11,145

James Rush

Year	Driver	Starts	Poles	1	2	3	4	5	6–10	Laps	Led	Led	Miles	$
1955	Chuck Meekins	1	0	0	0	0	0	0	0	226	0	0	226	100
1956	Lou Sherman	1	0	0	0	1	0	0	0	199	0	0	100	500
1956	Chuck Meekins	3	0	0	0	0	0	0	2	412	0	0	431	465
1957	Danny Letner	2	0	0	0	0	0	0	0	315	0	0	158	200
1957	Marshall Sargent	5	0	0	0	0	0	0	2	541	0	0	334	575
1957	John Smith (SJCA)	1	0	0	0	0	0	0	0	61	0	0	31	50
1957	Bob Osborne	1	0	0	0	0	0	0	0	28	0	0	28	25
1957	Jim Hurtubise	2	0	0	0	0	0	0	1	244	0	0	122	210
1957	Chuck Meekins	5	0	0	0	1	2	0	0	423	0	0	364	1,180
1957	Ben Eyerly	1	0	0	0	0	0	0	0	41	0	0	21	50
1958	Marshall Sargent	1	0	0	0	0	0	0	0	135	0	0	355	110
1958	Bob Osborne	1	0	0	0	0	0	0	0	16	0	0	42	100
1959	Bob Ross	2	0	0	0	0	2	0	0	582	0	0	293	935
Lifetime		26	0	0	0	2	4	0	5	3,223	0	0	2,502	$4,500

Jack Russell

Year	Driver	Starts	Poles	1	2	3	4	5	6–10	Laps	Led	Led	Miles	$
1962	Jim Cushman	4	0	0	0	0	0	0	1	782	0	0	883	850
1963	Jim Cushman	2	0	0	0	0	0	0	0	211	0	0	528	625
Lifetime		6	0	0	0	0	0	0	1	993	0	0	1,411	$1,475

Jim Russell

Year	Driver	Starts	Poles	1	2	3	4	5	6–10	Laps	Led	Led	Miles	$
1957	Jim Russell	1	0	0	0	0	0	0	0		0	0		0
Lifetime		1	0	0	0	0	0	0	0		0	0		$0

S.G. Russell

Year	Driver	Starts	Poles	1	2	3	4	5	6–10	Laps	Led	Led	Miles	$
1956	David Ezell	1	0	0	0	0	0	0	0		0	0		50
Lifetime		1	0	0	0	0	0	0	0		0	0		$50

Felix Sabates

Year	Driver	Starts	Poles	1	2	3	4	5	6–10	Laps	Led	Led	Miles	$
1989	Kyle Petty	18	0	0	0	0	1	0	4	4,815	16	1	6,757	92,977
1990	Kyle Petty	29	2	1	0	0	1	0	12	8,485	852	12	10,250	677,790
1991	Tom Kendall	1	0	0	0	0	0	0	0	74	12	1	186	12,450
1991	Kyle Petty	18	2	1	1	0	0	0	2	6,622	553	7	6,547	383,625
1991	Kenny Wallace	2	0	0	0	0	0	0	0	876	1	1	1,075	28,900
1991	Bobby Hillin	8	0	0	0	0	0	0	0	1,321	0	0	2,729	103,005
1992	Kyle Petty	29	3	2	0	4	3	0	8	9,058	971	8	10,938	767,870
1993	Kyle Petty	30	1	1	1	2	2	3	6	9,259	527	13	11,187	659,495
1993	Kenny Wallace	30	0	0	0	0	0	0	3	8,806	1	1	10,552	303,325
1994	Bobby Hamilton	23	0	0	0	0	0	0	1	5,787	24	4	7,731	386,560
1994	Kyle Petty	31	0	0	0	0	1	1	5	9,076	7	2	11,100	693,350
1995	Kyle Petty	30	0	1	0	0	0	0	4	8,127	311	4	10,077	698,875
1996	Greg Sacks	2	0	0	0	0	0	0	0	657	0	0	993	21,190
1996	Robby Gordon	2	0	0	0	0	0	0	0	138	0	0	138	18,565
1996	Kyle Petty	28	0	0	0	0	0	0	2	8,081	72	5	9,683	670,041
1996	Jim Sauter	2	0	0	0	0	0	0	0	633	0	0	631	47,700
1997	Steve Park	1	0	0	0	0	0	0	0	198	0	0	104	14,075
1997	Robby Gordon	20	1	0	0	0	1	0	0	4,395	42	1	5,848	611,850
1997	Phil Parsons	1	0	0	0	0	0	0	0	289	0	0	395	12,845
1997	Wally Dallenbach	22	0	0	0	0	0	0	1	4,598	21	3	6,793	442,690
1997	Greg Sacks	5	0	0	0	0	0	0	0	1,042	5	1	1,537	114,035

Year	Driver	Starts	Poles	Finish 1	2	3	4	5	6–10	Laps	Laps Led	Races Led	Miles	$

Felix Sabates *continued*

Year	Driver	Starts	Poles	1	2	3	4	5	6–10	Laps	Laps Led	Races Led	Miles	$
1997	Joe Nemechek	30	2	0	0	0	0	0	3	8,861	108	6	11,285	721,505
1998	Jeff Green	18	0	0	0	0	0	0	0	4,646	0	0	5,740	449,611
1998	Morgan Shepherd	2	0	0	0	0	0	0	0	743	0	0	758	52,115
1998	Joe Nemechek	32	0	0	0	0	1	0	3	8,771	41	5	11,909	1,298,995
1998	Tom Kendall	1	0	0	0	0	0	0	0	90	0	0	221	19,405
1998	Sterling Marlin	32	0	0	0	0	0	0	6	9,154	342	6	12,012	1,136,040
1998	Wally Dallenbach	4	0	0	0	0	0	0	0	947	0	0	1,632	151,795
1999	Ron Hornaday Jr.	1	0	0	0	0	0	0	0	396	0	0	297	22,810
1999	Joe Nemechek	34	3	1	0	0	0	0	2	9,410	158	6	11,966	1,591,449
1999	Sterling Marlin	34	1	0	0	0	2	0	3	9,711	56	9	12,635	1,613,371
1999	Steve Grissom	1	0	0	0	0	0	0	0	187	0	0	497	32,845
1999	Jeff Green	1	0	0	0	0	0	0	0	199	0	0	498	31,415
2000	Bobby Hamilton Jr.	1	0	0	0	0	0	0	0	319	0	0	491	46,890
2000	Ted Musgrave	12	0	0	0	0	0	0	0	3,802	6	5	4,581	587,420
2000	Sterling Marlin	34	0	0	1	0	0	0	6	9,459	82	6	12,097	1,735,230
2000	P.J. Jones	1	0	0	0	0	0	0	0	90	0	0	221	37,555
2000	Kenny Irwin Jr.	17	0	0	0	0	1	0	0	4,304	2	2	6,138	875,330
Lifetime		587	15	7	3	6	13	4	71	163,426	4,210	109	208,230	$17,164,994

Arnie Sacks

Year	Driver	Starts	Poles	1	2	3	4	5	6–10	Laps	Laps Led	Races Led	Miles	$
1983	Greg Sacks	5	0	0	0	0	0	0	0	638	0	0	1,202	8,060
1984	Greg Sacks	29	0	0	0	0	0	0	1	6,348	0	0	7,781	61,295
1985	Cecil Gordon	1	0	0	0	0	0	0	0	7	0	0	4	2,640
1985	Greg Sacks	3	0	0	0	0	0	0	2	1,006	2	1	1,482	60,410
Lifetime		38	0	0	0	0	0	0	3	7,999	2	1	10,469	$132,405

Greg Sacks

Year	Driver	Starts	Poles	1	2	3	4	5	6–10	Laps	Laps Led	Races Led	Miles	$
1991	Greg Sacks	1	0	0	0	0	0	0	0	20	0	0	50	17,450
Lifetime		1	0	0	0	0	0	0	0	20	0	0	50	$17,450

Sadler Brothers

Year	Driver	Starts	Poles	1	2	3	4	5	6–10	Laps	Laps Led	Races Led	Miles	$
1984	Sterling Marlin	11	0	0	0	0	0	0	2	2,423	0	0	3,420	35,320
1985	Sterling Marlin	7	0	0	0	0	0	0	0	1,102	1	1	2,019	29,805
1985	Mike Alexander	4	0	0	0	0	0	0	0	1,081	0	0	1,197	9,290
1986	Davey Allison	4	0	0	0	0	0	0	0	1,247	0	0	867	6,370
1988	Trevor Boys	1	0	0	0	0	0	0	0	199	0	0	498	15,085
1991	Eddie Bierschwale	2	0	0	0	0	0	0	0	491	0	0	953	9,740
1991	Kerry Teague	1	0	0	0	0	0	0	0	124	0	0	186	3,125
1992	Bob Schacht	4	0	0	0	0	0	0	0	788	2	1	1,350	36,660
1993	Jeremy Mayfield	1	0	0	0	0	0	0	0	324	0	0	486	4,830
1994	Jeff Green	2	0	0	0	0	0	0	0	396	0	0	253	11,455
1994	Jeremy Mayfield	4	0	0	0	0	0	0	0	1,083	0	0	1,315	49,730
1996	Chuck Bown	3	0	0	0	0	0	0	0	338	0	0	723	23,270
1996	Gary Bradberry	9	0	0	0	0	0	0	0	2,212	0	155,785	2,827	
1997	Ed Berrier	3	0	0	0	0	0	0	0	1,119	0	0	909	87,895
1998	Andy Hillenburg	1	0	0	0	0	0	0	0	198	0	0	495	79,505
Lifetime		57	0	0	0	0	0	0	2	13,125	3	2	17,499	$557,865

Hermie Sadler

Year	Driver	Starts	Poles	1	2	3	4	5	6–10	Laps	Laps Led	Races Led	Miles	$
2001	Hermie Sadler	3	0	0	0	0	0	0	0	1,206	0	0	1,141	121,865
2002	Hermie Sadler	7	0	0	0	0	0	0	0	2,372	0	0	1,807	290,465
Lifetime		10	0	0	0	0	0	0	0	3,578	0	0	2,948	412,330

Lee Sage

Year	Driver	Starts	Poles	1	2	3	4	5	6–10	Laps	Laps Led	Races Led	Miles	$
1982	Darryl Sage	5	0	0	0	0	0	0	0	1,552	0	0	1,137	4,970
1983	Darryl Sage	3	0	0	0	0	0	0	0	638	0	0	675	3,060
Lifetime		8	0	0	0	0	0	0	0	2,190	0	0	1,812	$8,030

Bucky Sager

Year	Driver	Starts	Poles	1	2	3	4	5	6–10	Laps	Laps Led	Races Led	Miles	$
1950	Bucky Sager	2	0	0	1	0	0	0	0		146	1		625
1951	Bucky Sager	1	0	0	0	0	0	0	0		0	0		25

Year	Driver	Starts	Poles	Finish						Laps	Laps Led	Races Led	Miles	$
				1	2	3	4	5	6–10					

Bucky Sager *continued*

1954	Bucky Sager	3	0	0	0	0	0	0	0	190	0	0	221	50
Lifetime		6	0	0	1	0	0	0	0	190	146	1	221	$700

Hank Salat

1952	Don Oldenberg	1	0	0	0	0	0	0	0		0	0		25
1952	Red Duvall	4	0	0	0	0	0	0	2	538	0	0	372	275
1954	Red Duvall	1	0	0	0	0	0	0	0	49	0	0	25	0
1955	Jim Ord	2	0	0	0	0	0	0	1	217	0	0	192	225
Lifetime		8	0	0	0	0	0	0	3	804	0	0	588	$525

Patsy Salmon

1986	Charlie Baker	1	0	0	0	0	0	0	0	457	0	0	465	2,500
1987	Charlie Baker	2	0	0	0	0	0	0	0	754	0	0	914	5,210
1988	Charlie Baker	1	0	0	0	0	0	0	0	136	0	0	138	1,590
1989	Charlie Baker	3	0	0	0	0	0	0	0	255	0	0	611	16,370
1990	Charlie Baker	2	0	0	0	0	0	0	0	84	0	0	85	5,325
Lifetime		9	0	0	0	0	0	0	0	1,686	0	0	2,214	$30,995

Ed Samples

1951	Ed Samples	2	0	0	0	0	0	0	2			0	0	275
Lifetime		2	0	0	0	0	0	0	2			0	0	$275

Tony Sampo

1951	George Seeger	2	0	0	0	0	0	0	0	373	0	0	465	175
1951	Danny Weinberg	3	0	1	0	0	0	1	0	200	1	1	100	1,325
Lifetime		5	0	1	0	0	0	1	0	573	1	1	565	$1,500

Roscoe Sanders

1963	Bob James	6	0	0	0	0	0	0	0	825	0	0	1,192	1,625
1964	Roy Gemberling	1	0	0	0	0	0	0	0	34	0	0	85	100
1964	LeeRoy Yarbrough	1	0	0	0	0	0	0	0	482	0	0	241	450
1964	Bunkie Blackburn	2	0	0	0	0	0	0	0	1	0	0	3	850
Lifetime		10	0	0	0	0	0	0	0	1,342	0	0	1,521	$3,025

Irv Sanderson

1981	Dean Combs	2	0	0	0	0	0	0	0	183	0	0	149	1,155
1982	Dean Combs	5	0	0	0	0	0	0	0	639	0	0	1,100	7,940
1983	Dean Combs	5	0	0	0	3	0	0	1	1,296	0	0	1,995	12,275
1984	Dean Combs	12	0	0	0	0	0	0	0	2,399	0	0	3,152	22,385
Lifetime		24	0	0	0	0	0	0	1	4,517	0	0	6,396	$43,755

Bobby Sands

1980	Bobby Sands	1	0	0	0	0	0	0	0	2	0	0	1	450
Lifetime		1	0	0	0	0	0	0	0	2	0	0	1	$450

Marshall Sargent

1961	Marshall Sargent	3	0	0	0	0	0	0	0	369	0	0	690	450
Lifetime		3	0	0	0	0	0	0	0	369	0	0	690	$450

James Satcher

1956	Buck Baker	3	0	0	0	0	1	1	1	526	0	0	276	875
1956	Joe Eubanks	26	2	0	0	3	0	4	6	3,398	107	2	2,529	5,215
1957	Joe Eubanks	1	0	0	0	0	0	0	1	180	0	0	90	100
1957	Cotton Owens	1	0	0	0	0	0	0	1	161	0	0	81	100
Lifetime		31	2	0	0	3	1	5	9	4,265	107	2	2,976	$6,290

Curtis Satterfield

1966	Johnny Rutherford	2	0	0	0	0	0	0	0	150	0	0	375	1,210

Year	Driver	Starts	Poles	Finish 1	2	3	4	5	6–10	Laps	Laps Led	Races Led	Miles	$

Curtis Satterfield *continued*

Year	Driver	Starts	Poles	1	2	3	4	5	6–10	Laps	Laps Led	Races Led	Miles	$
1966	Eldon Yarbrough	1	0	0	0	0	0	0	0	74	0	0	111	500
1966	Bub Strickler	1	0	0	0	0	0	0	0	148	0	0	148	585
1966	Joel Davis	2	0	0	0	0	0	0	0	5	0	0	12	975
Lifetime		6	0	0	0	0	0	0	0	377	0	0	646	$3,270

Don Satterfield

Year	Driver	Starts	Poles	1	2	3	4	5	6–10	Laps	Laps Led	Races Led	Miles	$
1978	Johnny Halford	1	0	0	0	0	0	0	0	84	0	0	85	610
1979	Dick May	2	0	0	0	0	0	0	0	14	0	0	13	865
1979	Slick Johnson	2	0	0	0	0	0	0	0	248	0	0	170	1,060
1981	Bruce Jacobi	1	0	0	0	0	0	0	0	117	0	0	293	955
1981	Don Satterfield	1	0	0	0	0	0	0	0	1	0	0	1	450
1981	Joel Stowe	1	0	0	0	0	0	0	0	14	0	0	7	540
Lifetime		8	0	0	0	0	0	0	0	478	0	0	568	$4,480

Leon Satterfield

Year	Driver	Starts	Poles	1	2	3	4	5	6–10	Laps	Laps Led	Races Led	Miles	$
1983	Slick Johnson	9	0	0	0	0	0	0	0	1,933	0	0	2,097	12,270
1983	Don Satterfield	3	0	0	0	0	0	0	0	645	0	0	359	2,555
1983	Joe Booher	1	0	0	0	0	0	0	0	2	0	0	3	935
1984	Slick Johnson	1	0	0	0	0	0	0	0	70	0	0	96	1,495
Lifetime		14	0	0	0	0	0	0	0	2,650	0	0	2,554	$17,255

Sandy Satullo

Year	Driver	Starts	Poles	1	2	3	4	5	6–10	Laps	Laps Led	Races Led	Miles	$
1979	Sandy Satullo	2	0	0	0	0	0	0	0	210	0	0	429	2,360
1981	John Anderson	1	0	0	0	0	0	0	0	41	0	0	62	965
1981	Sandy Satullo	1	0	0	0	0	0	0	0	68	0	0	181	1,500
Lifetime		4	0	0	0	0	0	0	0	319	0	0	671	$4,825

Joe Savatier

Year	Driver	Starts	Poles	1	2	3	4	5	6–10	Laps	Laps Led	Races Led	Miles	$
1954	Tony Nelson	3	0	0	0	0	0	0	1	995	0	0	616	325
Lifetime		3	0	0	0	0	0	0	1	995	0	0	616	$325

Ed Saverance

Year	Driver	Starts	Poles	1	2	3	4	5	6–10	Laps	Laps Led	Races Led	Miles	$
1951	Fireball Roberts	2	0	0	1	0	0	0	0	587	0	0	584	1,510
1952	Fireball Roberts	6	1	0	0	0	0	0	1	390	15	1	383	175
1953	Fireball Roberts	1	0	0	0	0	0	0	0	154	0	0	154	25
Lifetime		9	1	0	1	0	0	1	1	1,131	15	1	1,120	$1,710

Joe Savoca

Year	Driver	Starts	Poles	1	2	3	4	5	6–10	Laps	Laps Led	Races Led	Miles	$
1970	Harry Shipe	2	0	0	0	0	0	0	0	45	0	0	65	450
Lifetime		2	0	0	0	0	0	0	0	45	0	0	65	$450

Lucky Sawyer

Year	Driver	Starts	Poles	1	2	3	4	5	6–10	Laps	Laps Led	Races Led	Miles	$
1953	Lucky Sawyer	4	0	0	0	0	0	0	0	27	0	0	96	75
Lifetime		4	0	0	0	0	0	0	0	27	0	0	96	$75

Bob Schacht

Year	Driver	Starts	Poles	1	2	3	4	5	6–10	Laps	Laps Led	Races Led	Miles	$
1981	Bob Schacht	2	0	0	0	0	0	0	0	241	0	0	263	1,290
1982	Bob Schacht	3	0	0	0	0	0	0	0	576	0	0	318	2,880
1989	Bob Schacht	1	0	0	0	0	0	0	0	463	0	0	471	2,700
1993	Bob Schacht	2	0	0	0	0	0	0	0	20	0	0	20	13,350
Lifetime		8	0	0	0	0	0	0	0	1,300	0	0	1,072	$20,220

Norm Schihl

Year	Driver	Starts	Poles	1	2	3	4	5	6–10	Laps	Laps Led	Races Led	Miles	$
1956	Norman Schihl	1	0	0	0	0	0	0	0	349	0	0	175	150
Lifetime		1	0	0	0	0	0	0	0	349	0	0	175	$150

Robert Schildnecht

Year	Driver	Starts	Poles	1	2	3	4	5	6–10	Laps	Laps Led	Races Led	Miles	$
1977	Robin Schildnecht	2	0	0	0	0	0	0	0	581	0	0	344	1,575
Lifetime		2	0	0	0	0	0	0	0	581	0	0	344	$1,575

Year	Driver	Starts	Poles	1	2	3	4	5	6–10	Laps	Laps Led	Races Led	Miles	$

Harry Schilling

Year	Driver	Starts	Poles	1	2	3	4	5	6–10	Laps	Laps Led	Races Led	Miles	$
1951	John Soares	1	0	0	0	0	0	0	1		1	1		125
Lifetime		1	0	0	0	0	0	0	1		1	1		$125

Allan Schlauer

Year	Driver	Starts	Poles	1	2	3	4	5	6–10	Laps	Laps Led	Races Led	Miles	$
1969	Larry Baumel	6	0	0	0	0	0	0	0	964	0	0	682	2,760
1970	Larry Baumel	23	1	0	0	0	0	0	1	2,731	0	0	3,697	16,620
1971	Larry Baumel	16	0	0	0	0	0	0	1	2,245	0	0	2,998	10,910
Lifetime		45	1	0	0	0	0	0	2	5,940	0	0	7,376	$30,290

Al Schmidhamer

Year	Driver	Starts	Poles	1	2	3	4	5	6–10	Laps	Laps Led	Races Led	Miles	$
1957	Art Watts	4	4	1	0	1	0	0	1	502	100	1	283	1,620
Lifetime		4	4	1	0	1	0	0	1	502	100	1	283	$1,620

Lee Schmidt

Year	Driver	Starts	Poles	1	2	3	4	5	6–10	Laps	Laps Led	Races Led	Miles	$
1949	Lee Schmidt	1	0	0	0	0	0	0	0	171	0	0	171	50
Lifetime		1	0	0	0	0	0	0	0	171	0	0	171	$50

LeRoy Schmidt

Year	Driver	Starts	Poles	1	2	3	4	5	6–10	Laps	Laps Led	Races Led	Miles	$
1950	Lee Schmidt	1	0	0	0	0	0	0	0	40	0	0	167	25
Lifetime		1	0	0	0	0	0	0	0	40	0	0	167	$25

Bill Schmitt

Year	Driver	Starts	Poles	1	2	3	4	5	6–10	Laps	Laps Led	Races Led	Miles	$
1975	Bill Schmitt	3	0	0	0	0	0	0	1	293	0	0	764	3,970
1976	Bill Schmitt	2	0	0	0	0	0	0	1	318	0	0	816	3,360
1977	Bill Schmitt	3	0	0	0	0	0	0	0	144	0	0	375	3,285
1978	Bill Schmitt	3	0	0	0	0	0	0	1	304	0	0	773	8,430
1979	Bill Schmitt	3	0	0	0	0	1	0	0	325	0	0	828	11,695
1980	Bill Schmitt	4	0	0	0	0	0	1	0	579	0	0	1,473	21,610
1981	Bill Schmitt	3	0	0	0	0	0	0	0	257	1	1	673	6,610
1982	Bill Schmitt	1	0	0	0	0	0	0	0	77	0	0	202	960
1983	Bill Schmitt	2	0	0	0	0	0	0	1	107	0	0	280	4,520
1984	Bill Schmitt	2	0	0	0	0	0	0	0	125	0	0	328	5,270
1985	Bill Schmitt	2	0	0	0	0	0	0	0	157	0	0	411	5,640
1986	Bill Schmitt	2	0	0	0	0	0	0	0	207	0	0	542	7,840
1987	Bill Schmitt	2	0	0	0	0	0	0	0	99	0	0	259	2,500
1988	Bill Schmitt	2	0	0	0	0	0	0	0	252	0	0	406	6,245
1989	Bill Schmitt	2	0	0	0	0	0	0	0	380	0	0	491	7,920
1990	Bill Schmitt	2	0	0	0	0	0	0	0	384	0	0	496	11,525
1991	Bill Schmitt	2	0	0	0	0	0	0	0	210	0	0	322	10,605
1992	Bill Schmitt	2	0	0	0	0	0	0	0	282	0	0	393	13,095
1993	Bill Schmitt	1	0	0	0	0	0	0	0	71	0	0	179	6,815
Lifetime		43	0	0	0	0	1	1	4	4,571	1	1	10,014	$141,895

Frankie Schneider

Year	Driver	Starts	Poles	1	2	3	4	5	6–10	Laps	Laps Led	Races Led	Miles	$
1949	Frankie Schneider	1	0	0	0	0	0	0	1		0	0		150
1957	Frankie Schneider	4	0	0	0	0	0	0	1	917	0	0	613	765
1958	Frankie Schneider	6	0	1	1	0	3	0	0	1,186	106	1	487	1,920
Lifetime		11	0	1	1	0	3	0	2	2,103	106	1	1,100	$2,835

Brittan Schnell

Year	Driver	Starts	Poles	1	2	3	4	5	6–10	Laps	Laps Led	Races Led	Miles	$
1996	Dick Trickle	1	0	0	0	0	0	0	0	9	0	0	23	36,552
Lifetime		1	0	0	0	0	0	0	0	9	0	0	23	$36,552

Lloyd Schoenheit

Year	Driver	Starts	Poles	1	2	3	4	5	6–10	Laps	Laps Led	Races Led	Miles	$
1952	Jim Mayes	1	0	0	0	0	0	0	0		0	0		25
Lifetime		1	0	0	0	0	0	0	0		0	0		$25

Terry Schoonover

Year	Driver	Starts	Poles	1	2	3	4	5	6–10	Laps	Laps Led	Races Led	Miles	$
1984	Terry Schoonover	2	0	0	0	0	0	0	0	543	0	0	614	2,585
Lifetime		2	0	0	0	0	0	0	0	543	0	0	614	$2,585

| | | | | Finish | | | | | | | Laps | Races | | |
|Year|Driver|Starts|Poles|1|2|3|4|5|6–10|Laps|Led|Led|Miles|$|

Ken Schrader

1990	Brian Ross	1	0	0	0	0	0	0	0	175	0	0	438	3,775
1996	Jack Sprague	2	0	0	0	0	0	0	0	333	2	1	345	22,720
Lifetime		3	0	0	0	0	0	0	0	508	2	1	783	$26,495

Ken Schroeder

| | | | | | | | | | | | | | | |
|1949|Ken Schroeder|1|0|0|0|0|0|0|0|168|0|0|168|50|
|**Lifetime**| |1|0|0|0|0|0|0|0|168|0|0|168|$50|

Volney Schulze

1955	Volney Schulze	6	0	0	0	0	0	0	1	674	0	0	456	300
1957	Volney Schulze	3	0	0	0	0	0	0	1	530	0	0	380	340
1958	Volney Schulze	7	0	0	0	0	0	0	0	725	0	0	370	490
Lifetime		16	0	0	0	0	0	0	2	1,929	0	0	1,205	$1,130

Charlie Schwam

1955	Joe Weatherly	5	0	0	0	0	1	0	3	965	140	1	830	2,515
1955	Billy Carden	1	0	0	0	0	0	0	0	55	0	0	83	60
1955	Curtis Turner	5	0	0	1	0	0	0	0	374	14	1	395	980
1956	Billy Carden	3	0	0	0	0	0	0	0	632	0	0	755	350
1956	Curtis Turner	11	0	1	3	0	0	0	1	1,647	287	3	1,196	14,095
1956	Joe Weatherly	13	1	0	0	1	2	1	4	1,784	0	0	1,534	3,310
Lifetime		38	1	1	4	1	3	1	8	5,457	441	5	4,792	$21,310

Max Schwimer

| | | | | | | | | | | | | | | |
|1955|Jack Farris|1|0|0|0|0|0|0|0|30|0|0|123|25|
|**Lifetime**| |1|0|0|0|0|0|0|0|30|0|0|123|$25|

Andrew Scott

| | | | | | | | | | | | | | | |
|1987|Trevor Boys|1|0|0|0|0|0|0|0|198|0|0|495|2,965|
|**Lifetime**| |1|0|0|0|0|0|0|0|198|0|0|495|$2,965|

Lyle Scott

| | | | | | | | | | | | | | | |
|1956|Lyle Scott|1|0|0|0|0|0|0|0| |0|0| |60|
|**Lifetime**| |1|0|0|0|0|0|0|0| |0|0| |$60|

Wendell Scott

1961	Wendell Scott	23	0	0	0	0	0	0	5	4,364	0	0	2,217	3,240
1962	Wendell Scott	41	1	0	0	2	1	1	15	8,542	0	0	4,211	7,133
1962	Earl Brooks	1	0	0	0	0	0	0	0	3	0	0	1	0
1963	Wendell Scott	47	0	0	0	0	0	1	14	9,459	0	0	6,165	8,985
1963	Earl Brooks	3	0	0	0	0	0	1	0	783	0	0	354	725
1964	Wendell Scott	55	0	1	0	0	6	1	16	10,479	27	1	6,375	14,845
1965	Wendell Scott	50	0	0	0	0	2	2	16	9,260	0	0	5,742	14,375
1966	Wendell Scott	44	0	0	0	1	1	1	14	9,674	0	0	7,062	16,235
1967	Wendell Scott	43	0	0	0	0	0	0	11	8,737	0	0	6,217	15,180
1968	Wendell Scott	45	0	0	0	0	0	0	10	9,428	0	0	6,577	15,095
1969	Wendell Scott	48	0	0	0	0	0	0	11	11,362	0	0	8,325	24,482
1970	Wendell Scott	28	0	0	0	0	0	0	9	6,167	0	0	4,815	15,835
1971	Wendell Scott	34	0	0	0	0	0	0	4	7,323	0	0	6,191	17,145
1972	Wendell Scott	6	0	0	0	0	0	0	0	1,763	0	0	1,926	5,595
1973	Wendell Scott	2	0	0	0	0	0	0	0	327	0	0	457	1,730
Lifetime		470	1	1	0	3	10	7	125	97,671	27	1	66,636	$160,600

Arley Scranton

1954	Jim Cook	1	0	0	0	0	0	0	1	226	0	0	113	100
1954	Arley Scranton	1	0	0	0	0	0	0	0	413	0	0	207	25
1956	Arley Scranton	1	0	0	0	0	0	0	0	9	0	0	23	20
1957	Arley Scranton	1	0	0	0	0	0	0	0	25	0	0	25	25
1958	Arley Scranton	2	0	0	0	0	0	0	0	17	0	0	17	100
1959	Arley Scranton	2	0	0	0	0	0	0	0	361	0	0	158	100

Year	Driver	Starts	Poles	Finish 1	2	3	4	5	6–10	Laps	Laps Led	Races Led	Miles	$

Arley Scranton *continued*

Year	Driver	Starts	Poles	1	2	3	4	5	6–10	Laps	Laps Led	Races Led	Miles	$
1961	Arley Scranton	1	0	0	0	0	0	0	0	3	0	0	8	0
Lifetime		9	0	0	0	0	0	0	1	1,054	0	0	549	$370

Rick Scribner

Year	Driver	Starts	Poles	1	2	3	4	5	6–10	Laps	Laps Led	Races Led	Miles	$
1992	Rick Scribner	2	0	0	0	0	0	0	0	75	0	0	178	9,025
Lifetime		2	0	0	0	0	0	0	0	75	0	0	178	$9,025

John Sears

Year	Driver	Starts	Poles	1	2	3	4	5	6–10	Laps	Laps Led	Races Led	Miles	$
1970	Neil Castles	1	0	0	0	0	0	0	0	345	0	0	216	850
1970	John Sears	33	1	0	0	0	3	1	3	6,872	10	1	6,420	21,551
1971	John Sears	37	0	0	0	0	0	0	3	7,512	0	0	6,818	22,651
Lifetime		71	1	0	0	0	3	1	6	14,729	10	1	13,453	$45,052

Frank Secrist

Year	Driver	Starts	Poles	1	2	3	4	5	6–10	Laps	Laps Led	Races Led	Miles	$
1960	Frank Secrist	2	1	0	0	0	0	0	0	105	8	1	123	175
1961	Frank Secrist	1	0	0	0	0	1	0	0	99	0	0	99	400
Lifetime		3	1	0	0	0	1	0	0	204	8	1	222	$575

George Seeger

Year	Driver	Starts	Poles	1	2	3	4	5	6–10	Laps	Laps Led	Races Led	Miles	$
1951	George Seeger	3	0	0	0	0	0	0	1	133	0	0	133	135
Lifetime		3	0	0	0	0	0	0	1	133	0	0	133	$135

Bill Seifert

Year	Driver	Starts	Poles	1	2	3	4	5	6–10	Laps	Laps Led	Races Led	Miles	$
1966	Clyde Lynn	1	0	0	0	0	0	0	0	417	0	0	417	690
1966	Blaine Kauffman	1	0	0	0	0	0	0	0	33	0	0	83	0
1966	Cale Yarborough	1	0	0	0	0	0	0	0	121	0	0	48	100
1966	Bill Seifert	11	0	0	0	0	0	0	3	2,680	0	0	1,576	3,240
1966	Tex McCullough	1	0	0	0	0	0	0	0	5	0	0	5	535
1966	Bill Latham	2	0	0	0	0	0	0	0	160	0	0	54	200
1966	J.T. Putney	1	0	0	0	0	0	0	0	6	0	0	3	0
1966	Jim Tatum	4	0	0	0	0	0	0	0	351	0	0	174	445
1967	Don Biederman	1	0	0	0	0	0	0	0	247	0	0	340	900
1967	Buster Sexton	1	0	0	0	0	0	0	0	15	0	0	8	100
1967	Bill Seifert	41	0	0	0	0	0	0	12	8,171	0	0	5,133	11,910
1968	Bill Seifert	39	0	0	0	0	0	1	7	7,214	0	0	5,141	14,480
1968	Cecil Gordon	4	0	0	0	0	0	0	0	427	0	0	377	1,625
1968	Niles Gage	1	0	0	0	0	0	0	0	274	0	0	91	155
1968	Elmo Langley	3	0	0	0	0	0	0	1	595	0	0	661	1,830
1968	Earl Brooks	1	0	0	0	0	0	0	0	427	0	0	427	890
1969	Bill Seifert	50	0	0	0	0	0	1	14	9,728	0	0	7,473	27,702
1969	Lee Gordon	1	0	0	0	0	0	0	0	160	0	0	80	100
1969	Cecil Gordon	49	0	0	0	0	0	1	7	10,159	0	0	8,594	27,237
1970	Raymond Williams	20	0	0	0	0	0	0	0	3,627	0	0	3,830	11,725
1970	Bill Seifert	38	0	0	0	0	0	1	3	5,188	0	0	5,196	21,720
1971	Raymond Williams	7	0	0	0	0	0	0	0	458	0	0	601	5,035
1971	LeeRoy Yarbrough	1	0	0	0	0	0	0	0	246	0	0	374	1,080
1971	Bill Seifert	35	0	0	0	0	0	0	4	6,366	0	0	6,682	23,654
1971	Dub Simpson	1	0	0	0	0	0	0	0	11	0	0	29	1,100
1972	Vic Parsons	1	0	0	0	0	0	0	1	380	0	0	238	800
1972	Bill Seifert	4	0	0	0	0	0	0	1	468	0	0	644	5,405
1972	LeeRoy Yarbrough	15	0	0	0	1	2	1	4	3,695	5	2	4,161	34,580
1972	Ramo Stott	1	0	0	0	0	0	0	0	238	0	0	476	1,525
1972	Dick Brooks	2	0	0	0	0	0	0	0	214	2	1	303	2,546
1972	Raymond Williams	1	0	0	0	0	0	0	0	422	0	0	429	1,300
1973	Vic Parsons	16	0	0	0	0	0	0	6	3,205	0	0	3,543	16,795
Lifetime		355	0	0	0	1	2	5	63	65,708	7	3	57,190	$219,404

Al Self

Year	Driver	Starts	Poles	1	2	3	4	5	6–10	Laps	Laps Led	Races Led	Miles	$
1963	Al Self	1	0	0	0	0	0	0	0	1	0	0	3	200
Lifetime		1	0	0	0	0	0	0	0	1	0	0	3	$200

Year	Driver	Starts	Poles	Finish 1	2	3	4	5	6–10	Laps	Laps Led	Races Led	Miles	$

David Lee Sellers

Year	Driver	Starts	Poles	1	2	3	4	5	6–10	Laps	Laps Led	Races Led	Miles	$
1976	Jimmy Lee Capps	4	0	0	0	0	0	0	1	505	0	0	1,229	6,950
1977	Jimmy Lee Capps	3	0	0	0	0	0	0	0	815	0	0	1,097	4,800
1978	Jimmy Lee Capps	3	0	0	0	0	0	0	0	586	0	0	701	3,880
Lifetime		10	0	0	0	0	0	0	1	1,906	0	0	3,027	$15,630

Frank Sessoms

Year	Driver	Starts	Poles	1	2	3	4	5	6–10	Laps	Laps Led	Races Led	Miles	$
1969	Frank Sessoms	1	0	0	0	0	0	0	0	128	0	0	340	1,325
1971	Frank Sessoms	2	0	0	0	0	0	0	2	852	0	0	496	1,180
Lifetime		3	0	0	0	0	0	0	2	980	0	0	837	$2,505

Red Sharp

Year	Driver	Starts	Poles	1	2	3	4	5	6–10	Laps	Laps Led	Races Led	Miles	$
1967	Friday Hassler	21	0	0	0	0	1	2	6	4,309	12	1	3,091	10,270
1968	Friday Hassler	20	0	0	0	0	2	1	5	5,012	0	0	4,245	12,000
1969	Friday Hassler	1	0	0	0	0	0	0	1	462	0	0	231	725
Lifetime		42	0	0	0	0	3	3	12	9,783	12	1	7,566	$22,995

Ernie Shaw

Year	Driver	Starts	Poles	1	2	3	4	5	6–10	Laps	Laps Led	Races Led	Miles	$
1969	Ernie Shaw	1	0	0	0	0	0	0	0	149	0	0	396	1,500
1971	Ernie Shaw	2	0	0	0	0	0	0	1	578	0	0	312	775
Lifetime		3	0	0	0	0	0	0	1	727	0	0	708	$2,275

Graham Shaw

Year	Driver	Starts	Poles	1	2	3	4	5	6–10	Laps	Laps Led	Races Led	Miles	$
1964	Tiny Lund	6	0	0	0	0	0	0	1	932	14	1	965	2,025
1964	Graham Shaw	2	0	0	0	0	0	0	0	127	0	0	379	1,000
Lifetime		8	0	0	0	0	0	0	1	1,059	14	1	1,343	$3,025

Red Shaw

Year	Driver	Starts	Poles	1	2	3	4	5	6–10	Laps	Laps Led	Races Led	Miles	$
1966	Johnny Allen	1	0	0	0	0	0	0	0	132	0	0	330	1,135
Lifetime		1	0	0	0	0	0	0	0	132	0	0	330	$1,135

Reid Shaw

Year	Driver	Starts	Poles	1	2	3	4	5	6–10	Laps	Laps Led	Races Led	Miles	$
1965	Buren Skeen	8	0	0	0	0	0	1	2	1,319	0	0	676	2,875
1966	Cale Yarborough	1	0	0	0	0	0	0	1	195	0	0	49	265
1966	Darel Dieringer	4	0	1	0	0	1	0	0	540	178	1	262	1,900
1966	Johnny Allen	2	0	0	0	0	0	0	0	466	0	0	303	450
1966	Bryant Wallace	1	0	0	0	0	0	0	0	39	0	0	20	100
1971	Wayne Andrews	5	0	0	0	0	0	1	2	1,372	0	0	600	1,780
Lifetime		21	0	1	0	0	1	2	5	3,931	178	1	1,910	$7,370

Fred Sheibert

Year	Driver	Starts	Poles	1	2	3	4	5	6–10	Laps	Laps Led	Races Led	Miles	$
1956	Bill Widenhouse	3	0	0	0	0	0	0	0	138	0	0	86	310
Lifetime		3	0	0	0	0	0	1	0	138	0	0	86	$310

Bill Sheldon

Year	Driver	Starts	Poles	1	2	3	4	5	6–10	Laps	Laps Led	Races Led	Miles	$
1951	Ray Chase	2	0	0	0	0	0	0	0	237	0	0	296	50
Lifetime		2	0	0	0	0	0	0	0	237	0	0	296	$50

R.G. Shelton

Year	Driver	Starts	Poles	1	2	3	4	5	6–10	Laps	Laps Led	Races Led	Miles	$
1951	Billy Myers	5	0	0	0	1	0	0	0	113	23	1	113	625
1952	Leon Sales	2	0	0	0	0	0	0	0		0	0		25
1952	Jimmie Lewallen	6	0	0	0	0	0	0	2	980	0	0	755	430
1952	Perk Brown	18	1	0	0	2	0	0	3	2,160	0	0	1,370	1,610
1953	Perk Brown	2	0	0	0	0	0	0	0	14	0	0	57	25
1953	Jimmie Lewallen	11	0	0	0	1	0	1	4	370	0	0	225	1,250
1954	Perk Brown	2	0	0	0	0	0	0	0	174	0	0	126	50
Lifetime		46	1	0	0	4	0	1	9	3,811	23	1	2,645	$4,015

Ron Shephard

Year	Driver	Starts	Poles	1	2	3	4	5	6–10	Laps	Laps Led	Races Led	Miles	$
1987	Ron Shephard	2	0	0	0	0	0	0	0	198	0	0	462	3,745
Lifetime		2	0	0	0	0	0	0	0	198	0	0	462	$3,745

Year	Driver	Starts	Poles	Finish 1	2	3	4	5	6–10	Laps	Laps Led	Races Led	Miles	$

Morgan Shepherd

Year	Driver	Starts	Poles	1	2	3	4	5	6–10	Laps	Laps Led	Races Led	Miles	$
1985	Morgan Shepherd	1	0	0	0	0	0	0	0	180	0	0	479	5,340
1988	Morgan Shepherd	9	0	0	0	0	0	0	0	1,770	0	0	2,008	20,605
Lifetime		10	0	0	0	0	0	0	0	1,950	0	0	2,487	$25,945

John Sheppard

Year	Driver	Starts	Poles	1	2	3	4	5	6–10	Laps	Laps Led	Races Led	Miles	$
1987	Allan Grice	1	0	0	0	0	0	0	0	161	0	0	242	1,700
Lifetime		1	0	0	0	0	0	0	0	161	0	0	242	$1,700

Bill Shirey

Year	Driver	Starts	Poles	1	2	3	4	5	6–10	Laps	Laps Led	Races Led	Miles	$
1969	Bill Shirey	1	0	0	0	0	0	0	0	82	0	0	164	865
1970	Bill Shirey	29	0	0	0	0	0	0	1	3,691	0	0	2,542	12,390
1971	Bill Shirey	26	0	0	0	0	0	0	2	3,549	0	0	2,510	8,835
1971	Jabe Thomas	1	0	0	0	0	0	0	0	339	0	0	212	455
1972	Bill Shirey	12	0	0	0	0	0	0	0	1,600	0	0	1,527	7,305
Lifetime		69	0	0	0	0	0	0	3	9,261	0	0	6,955	$29,850

Monroe Shook

Year	Driver	Starts	Poles	1	2	3	4	5	6–10	Laps	Laps Led	Races Led	Miles	$
1958	Bob Bolheimer	1	0	0	0	0	0	0	0	15	0	0	21	100
1958	Johnny Allen	1	0	0	0	0	0	0	0	56	0	0	56	0
1958	Jerry Draper	1	0	0	0	0	0	0	0	107	0	0	54	0
1958	Doug Yates	1	0	0	0	0	0	0	0	16	0	0	66	25
1960	Emanuel Zervakis	14	1	0	0	1	1	0	8	3,382	0	0	3,457	9,675
1961	Tommy Irwin	1	0	0	0	0	0	0	0	103	0	0	93	150
1961	Emanuel Zervakis	38	1	2	1	3	5	8	9	9,198	386	2	6,664	20,800
1962	Johnny Allen	5	0	0	0	0	0	0	2	963	0	0	427	715
1962	Tommy Irwin	8	0	0	0	0	0	0	3	991	10	1	595	1,175
Lifetime		70	2	2	1	4	6	8	22	14,831	396	3	11,432	$32,640

Barney Shore

Year	Driver	Starts	Poles	1	2	3	4	5	6–10	Laps	Laps Led	Races Led	Miles	$
1958	Barney Shore	12	0	0	0	0	0	1	2	1,741	0	0	835	1,320
1959	Barney Shore	6	0	0	0	0	0	0	2	628	0	0	212	425
1960	Barney Shore	1	0	0	0	0	0	0	0	93	0	0	47	50
Lifetime		19	0	0	0	0	0	1	4	2,462	0	0	1,094	$1,795

Buddy Shuman

Year	Driver	Starts	Poles	1	2	3	4	5	6–10	Laps	Laps Led	Races Led	Miles	$
1952	Buddy Shuman	8	0	0	0	0	0	1	3	593	0	0	354	710
1952	Bill Widenhouse	1	0	0	0	0	0	0	0	19	0	0	24	25
1953	Buddy Shuman	2	0	0	0	0	0	0	0		0	0		50
Lifetime		11	0	0	0	0	0	1	3	612	0	0	378	$785

Larry Shurter

Year	Driver	Starts	Poles	1	2	3	4	5	6–10	Laps	Laps Led	Races Led	Miles	$
1950	Larry Shurter	1	0	0	0	0	0	0	0	37	0	0	154	25
1952	Al Conroy	1	0	0	0	0	0	0	0	308	0	0	385	150
1952	Larry Shurter	4	0	0	0	0	0	0	0	138	0	0	107	125
Lifetime		6	0	0	0	0	0	0	0	483	0	0	646	$300

Lou Sidoit

Year	Driver	Starts	Poles	1	2	3	4	5	6–10	Laps	Laps Led	Races Led	Miles	$
1963	Johnny Allen	2	0	0	0	0	0	0	1	150	0	0	375	700
1963	LeeRoy Yarbrough	2	0	0	0	0	0	1	0	904	0	0	452	1,150
Lifetime		4	0	0	0	0	0	1	1	1,054	0	0	827	$1,850

Ted Sidwell

Year	Driver	Starts	Poles	1	2	3	4	5	6–10	Laps	Laps Led	Races Led	Miles	$
1967	Dorus Wisecraver	2	0	0	0	0	0	0	0	219	0	0	548	2,325
Lifetime		2	0	0	0	0	0	0	0	219	0	0	548	$2,325

Gary Sigman

Year	Driver	Starts	Poles	1	2	3	4	5	6–10	Laps	Laps Led	Races Led	Miles	$
1969	Joe Frasson	1	0	0	0	0	0	0	0	3	0	0	8	825
1970	Kevin Terris	1	0	0	0	0	0	0	0	4	0	0	10	625
1972	Bill Butts	2	0	0	0	0	0	0	0	313	0	0	798	3,060
Lifetime		4	0	0	0	0	0	0	0	320	0	0	816	$4,510

Year	Driver	Starts	Poles	Finish						Laps	Laps Led	Races Led	Miles	$
				1	2	3	4	5	6–10					

Leo Sigmon

Year	Driver	Starts	Poles	1	2	3	4	5	6–10	Laps	Laps Led	Races Led	Miles	$
1951	John Barker	3	0	0	0	0	0	0	0	431	0	0	496	100
1951	Leo Sigmon	2	0	0	0	0	0	0	0		0	0		50
Lifetime		5	0	0	0	0	0	0	0	431	0	0	496	$150

Elmer Simko

Year	Driver	Starts	Poles	1	2	3	4	5	6–10	Laps	Laps Led	Races Led	Miles	$
1982	David Simko	2	0	0	0	0	0	0	0	100	0	0	203	2,700
1983	David Simko	1	0	0	0	0	0	0	0	154	0	0	234	1,315
1984	David Simko	1	0	0	0	0	0	0	0	189	0	0	378	1,800
1986	David Simko	1	0	0	0	0	0	0	0	170	0	0	340	1,625
1987	David Simko	4	0	0	0	0	0	0	0	1,050	0	0	1,611	7,330
1988	David Simko	1	0	0	0	0	0	0	0	9	0	0	18	2,450
Lifetime		10	0	0	0	0	0	0	0	1,672	0	0	2,784	$17,220

Mark Simo

Year	Driver	Starts	Poles	1	2	3	4	5	6–10	Laps	Laps Led	Races Led	Miles	$
1999	Boris Said III	2	0	0	0	0	0	0	0	310	9	1	513	59,260
1999	Randy LaJoie	2	0	0	0	0	0	0	0	436	0	0	528	71,200
Lifetime		4	0	0	0	0	0	0	0	746	9	1	1,042	$130,460

Banks Simpson

Year	Driver	Starts	Poles	1	2	3	4	5	6–10	Laps	Laps Led	Races Led	Miles	$
1955	Bunk Moore	2	0	0	0	0	0	0	0	199	0	0	100	50
1955	Banks Simpson	6	0	0	0	0	0	0	0	931	0	0	1,119	775
Lifetime		8	0	0	0	0	0	0	0	1,130	0	0	1,218	$825

Gene Simpson

Year	Driver	Starts	Poles	1	2	3	4	5	6–10	Laps	Laps Led	Races Led	Miles	$
1955	Gene Simpson	9	0	0	0	0	0	1	2	1,271	0	0	1,027	925
Lifetime		9	0	0	0	0	0	1	2	1,271	0	0	1,027	$925

Sims Brothers

Year	Driver	Starts	Poles	1	2	3	4	5	6–10	Laps	Laps Led	Races Led	Miles	$
1985	Mike Alexander	7	0	0	0	0	0	0	0	1,255	0	0	2,212	34,475
Lifetime		7	0	0	0	0	0	0	0	1,255	0	0	2,212	$34,475

Harry Sims

Year	Driver	Starts	Poles	1	2	3	4	5	6–10	Laps	Laps Led	Races Led	Miles	$
1960	Eddie Gray	3	0	0	0	0	0	0	1	243	0	0	305	580
Lifetime		3	0	0	0	0	0	0	1	243	0	0	305	$580

David Sisco

Year	Driver	Starts	Poles	1	2	3	4	5	6–10	Laps	Laps Led	Races Led	Miles	$
1974	Jerry Sisco	1	0	0	0	0	0	0	0	142	0	0	85	295
1974	David Sisco	27	0	0	0	1	1	1	7	7,168	43	4	8,540	53,055
1975	David Sisco	28	0	0	0	1	0	0	5	7,572	37	4	8,455	52,940
1976	Billy McGinnis	1	0	0	0	0	0	0	0	15	0	0	23	805
1976	David Sisco	27	0	0	0	0	0	0	7	7,077	6	3	8,050	56,090
1977	Ed Negre	1	0	0	0	0	0	0	0	77	0	0	117	1,040
1977	David Sisco	10	0	0	0	0	0	0	0	2,030	0	0	2,186	13,920
Lifetime		95	0	0	0	2	1	1	19	24,081	86	11	27,455	$178,145

Eddie Skinner

Year	Driver	Starts	Poles	1	2	3	4	5	6–10	Laps	Laps Led	Races Led	Miles	$
1957	Eddie Skinner	4	0	0	0	0	0	0	0	833	0	0	534	605
1958	Eddie Skinner	5	0	0	0	0	0	0	0	750	0	0	440	420
Lifetime		9	0	0	0	0	0	0	0	1,583	0	0	973	$1,025

Frank Skinner

Year	Driver	Starts	Poles	1	2	3	4	5	6–10	Laps	Laps Led	Races Led	Miles	$
1960	Gene Marmor	4	0	0	0	0	0	0	1	732	0	0	836	775
1960	Tiny Lund	1	0	0	0	0	0	0	1	375	0	0	563	1,350
1960	Whitey Gerkin	2	0	0	0	0	0	0	0	233	0	0	583	400
Lifetime		7	0	0	0	0	0	0	2	1,340	0	0	1,981	$2,525

William Slate Jr.

Year	Driver	Starts	Poles	1	2	3	4	5	6–10	Laps	Laps Led	Races Led	Miles	$
1996	Hermie Sadler	1	0	0	0	0	0	0	0	349	0	0	349	13,055
Lifetime		1	0	0	0	0	0	0	0	349	0	0	349	$13,055

Year	Driver	Starts	Poles	Finish 1	2	3	4	5	6–10	Laps	Laps Led	Races Led	Miles	$

Archie Smith

Year	Driver	Starts	Poles	1	2	3	4	5	6–10	Laps	Laps Led	Races Led	Miles	$
1964	Jack Smith	3	1	0	1	1	0	0	0	402	20	1	211	1,525
1965	Wayne Smith	25	0	0	0	0	0	0	2	3,744	0	0	2,475	6,790
1966	Wayne Smith	23	0	0	0	0	0	0	1	4,108	0	0	3,655	9,930
1967	Wayne Smith	27	0	0	0	0	0	0	2	4,364	0	0	3,629	10,025
1968	Wayne Smith	17	0	0	0	0	0	0	1	2,350	0	0	1,943	7,135
1969	Wayne Smith	16	0	0	0	0	0	0	2	2,692	0	0	2,951	10,610
Lifetime		111	1	0	1	1	0	0	8	17,660	20	1	14,864	$46,015

Barney Smith

Year	Driver	Starts	Poles	1	2	3	4	5	6–10	Laps	Laps Led	Races Led	Miles	$
1950	Barney Smith	1	0	0	0	0	0	0	0	366	0	0	458	275
1951	Barney Smith	2	0	0	0	0	0	0	0		0	0		75
1952	Barney Smith	3	0	0	0	0	0	0	2	647	0	0	324	285
Lifetime		6	0	0	0	0	0	0	2	1,013	0	0	781	$635

Bob Smith

Year	Driver	Starts	Poles	1	2	3	4	5	6–10	Laps	Laps Led	Races Led	Miles	$
1957	Jim Blomgren	1	0	0	0	0	0	0	0	120	0	0	60	50
1959	John Potter	2	0	0	0	0	0	0	2	549	0	0	277	550
1960	Jim Blomgren	3	0	0	0	0	0	0	2	288	0	0	332	400
1961	Bruce Worrell	4	0	0	0	0	0	0	2	391	0	0	379	540
1961	Jim Blomgren	4	0	0	0	0	1	0	1	401	0	0	406	590
Lifetime		14	0	0	0	0	1	0	7	1,749	0	0	1,454	$2,130

Don Smith

Year	Driver	Starts	Poles	1	2	3	4	5	6–10	Laps	Laps Led	Races Led	Miles	$
1970	Mel Larson	1	0	0	0	0	0	0	1	133	0	0	348	1,115
Lifetime		1	0	0	0	0	0	0	1	133	0	0	348	$1,115

Douglas Smith

Year	Driver	Starts	Poles	1	2	3	4	5	6–10	Laps	Laps Led	Races Led	Miles	$
1989	Joe Ruttman	3	0	0	0	0	0	0	0	743	0	0	923	7,710
1989	Ron Esau	1	0	0	0	0	0	0	0	194	0	0	194	2,960
Lifetime		4	0	0	0	0	0	0	0	937	0	0	1,117	$10,670

F.W. Smith

Year	Driver	Starts	Poles	1	2	3	4	5	6–10	Laps	Laps Led	Races Led	Miles	$
1954	Bill Smith	2	0	0	0	0	0	0	1	373	0	0	228	240
Lifetime		2	0	0	0	0	0	0	1	373	0	0	228	$240

Frank Smith

Year	Driver	Starts	Poles	1	2	3	4	5	6–10	Laps	Laps Led	Races Led	Miles	$
1949	Archie Smith	2	0	0	0	0	0	0	2	161	0	0	81	225
1949	Frank Smith	2	0	0	0	0	0	0	0		0	0		50
Lifetime		4	0	0	0	0	0	0	2	161	0	0	81	$275

Gary Smith

Year	Driver	Starts	Poles	1	2	3	4	5	6–10	Laps	Laps Led	Races Led	Miles	$
1982	Hershel McGriff	2	0	0	0	0	0	0	0	115	0	0	301	1,545
1983	Hershel McGriff	2	0	0	0	0	0	0	1	191	0	0	500	5,650
1984	Hershel McGriff	2	0	0	0	0	0	0	1	149	1	1	390	3,815
1985	Hershel McGriff	2	0	0	0	0	0	0	0	178	0	0	466	2,835
1986	Hershel McGriff	2	0	0	0	0	0	0	0	170	0	0	445	4,080
1987	Hershel McGriff	4	0	0	0	0	0	0	0	367	0	0	896	12,985
Lifetime		14	0	0	0	0	0	0	2	1,170	1	1	2,999	$30,910

George Smith

Year	Driver	Starts	Poles	1	2	3	4	5	6–10	Laps	Laps Led	Races Led	Miles	$
1987	Jimmy Horton	2	0	0	0	0	0	0	0	256	0	0	640	4,405
1987	Eddie Bierschwale	2	0	0	0	0	0	0	0	540	0	0	548	3,250
1988	Jimmy Horton	8	0	0	0	0	0	0	0	2,007	0	0	2,894	19,075
1989	Jimmy Horton	5	0	0	0	0	0	0	0	955	0	0	1,391	14,932
1989	Mark Gibson	1	0	0	0	0	0	0	0	100	0	0	250	2,880
1990	Jimmy Horton	6	0	0	0	0	0	0	0	1,599	0	0	2,175	35,875
Lifetime		24	0	0	0	0	0	0	0	5,457	0	0	7,898	$80,417

Year	Driver	Starts	Poles	Finish						Laps	Laps Led	Races Led	Miles	$
				1	2	3	4	5	6–10					

Gordon Smith

Year	Driver	Starts	Poles	1	2	3	4	5	6–10	Laps	Laps Led	Races Led	Miles	$
1955	Gordon Smith	15	0	0	0	0	0	0	2	1,584	0	0	910	975
Lifetime		15	0	0	0	0	0	0	2	1,584	0	0	910	$975

Harley Smith

Year	Driver	Starts	Poles	1	2	3	4	5	6–10	Laps	Laps Led	Races Led	Miles	$
1971	Larry Smith	4	0	0	0	0	0	0	1	896	0	0	1,699	5,058
1972	Larry Smith	23	0	0	0	0	0	0	7	4,320	0	0	5,831	24,215
1973	Larry Smith	11	0	0	0	0	0	0	1	2,103	0	0	3,576	14,090
Lifetime		38	0	0	0	0	0	0	9	7,319	0	0	11,105	$43,363

Helen Rae Smith

Year	Driver	Starts	Poles	1	2	3	4	5	6–10	Laps	Laps Led	Races Led	Miles	$
1985	Morgan Shepherd	7	0	0	0	0	0	0	0	1,232	1	1	1,351	11,130
1985	Ed Sanger	1	0	0	0	0	0	0	0	358	0	0	224	910
1985	Sterling Marlin	1	0	0	0	0	0	0	0	219	0	0	329	1,350
1985	Phil Barkdoll	2	0	0	0	0	0	0	0	200	0	0	532	5,525
Lifetime		11	0	0	0	0	0	0	0	2,009	1	1	2,435	$18,915

Jack Smith

Year	Driver	Starts	Poles	1	2	3	4	5	6–10	Laps	Laps Led	Races Led	Miles	$
1951	Jack Smith	3	0	0	1	1	0	0	0	34	0	0	26	1,125
1954	Jack Smith	5	0	0	0	0	0	0	1	216	0	0	341	475
1957	Jack Smith	23	2	3	0	1	2	6	3	3,958	314	8	2,575	7,630
1958	Johnny Allen	2	0	0	0	0	0	0	1	108	0	0	127	180
1958	Jack Smith	35	4	2	5	2	3	2	6	5,030	381	7	3,304	10,460
1959	Jack Smith	20	3	4	1	2	1	0	3	3,398	322	7	2,637	11,575
1960	Buck Baker	1	0	1	0	0	0	0	0	364	175	1	501	19,900
1960	Jack Smith	13	4	3	1	2	0	1	0	2,198	514	10	2,570	23,590
1961	Rex White	1	0	0	0	0	0	0	1	345	0	0	474	925
1961	Bob Welborn	5	0	0	1	1	0	0	2	1,305	52	2	1,542	6,555
1961	Larry Frank	2	0	0	0	0	0	0	0	485	0	0	667	880
1961	Jack Smith	25	0	2	2	4	1	1	4	4,695	278	4	4,098	18,260
1961	Bobby Johns	1	1	0	0	0	0	0	0	457	49	1	229	440
1962	Buck Baker	1	0	0	0	0	0	0	1	263	0	0	395	1,125
1962	Jack Smith	51	7	5	6	5	8	3	8	10,781	894	9	7,110	28,485
1962	Art Malone	1	0	0	0	0	0	0	1	95	0	0	238	600
1963	Jack Smith	28	2	0	0	0	1	3	7	5,290	25	2	3,620	8,835
1963	G.C. Spencer	6	0	0	0	0	0	0	1	1,098	8	1	919	2,530
1963	Stick Elliott	6	0	0	0	0	0	0	0	1,143	0	0	1,352	1,975
1964	Jack Smith	1	0	0	0	0	0	0	0	57	0	0	29	50
Lifetime		230	23	20	17	18	16	16	39	41,320	3,012	52	32,750	$145,595

Jim Smith

Year	Driver	Starts	Poles	1	2	3	4	5	6–10	Laps	Laps Led	Races Led	Miles	$
1994	P.J. Jones	1	0	0	0	0	0	0	0	303	0	0	303	6,980
1995	Butch Gilliland	1	0	0	0	0	0	0	0	19	0	0	48	9,760
2000	Michael Waltrip	21	0	0	0	0	0	0	0	4,695	2	2	6,319	959,400
2001	Ted Musgrave	1	0	0	0	0	0	0	0	198	0	0	495	43,565
2001	Robby Gordon	2	0	0	1	0	0	0	0	364	20	1	596	167,335
2001	Kevin Lepage	8	0	0	0	0	0	0	1	2,607	3	1	3,183	436,876
2001	Mike Wallace	21	0	0	0	0	0	0	4	6,128	1	1	7,795	1,331,705
2002	Jason Leffler	2	0	0	0	0	0	0	0	572	0	0	706	78,500
2002	Casey Atwood	34	0	0	0	0	0	0	0	9,193	0	0	12,008	1,845,013
2002	Ted Musgrave	4	0	0	0	0	0	0	0	1,291	0	0	1,565	180,575
Lifetime		95	0	0	1	0	0	0	5	25,370	26	5	33,018	$5,059,709

Louise Smith

Year	Driver	Starts	Poles	1	2	3	4	5	6–10	Laps	Laps Led	Races Led	Miles	$
1949	Louise Smith	3	0	0	0	0	0	0	0	175	0	0	175	75
1950	Louise Smith	5	0	0	0	0	0	0	0	84	0	0	84	25
1951	Buck Clardy	1	0	0	0	0	0	0	0		0	0		25
1952	J.O. Staton	7	0	0	0	0	0	0	1	331	0	0	185	250
1952	E.C. Ramsey	7	0	0	0	0	0	0	0	826	0	0	693	260
1952	Louise Smith	3	0	0	0	0	0	0	0	118	0	0	101	85
Lifetime		26	0	0	0	0	0	0	1	1,534	0	0	1,237	$720

Mark Smith

Year	Driver	Starts	Poles	1	2	3	4	5	6–10	Laps	Laps Led	Races Led	Miles	$
1996	Dick Trickle	8	0	0	0	0	0	0	1	2,349	0	0	2,889	98,470

Year	Driver	Starts	Poles	Finish 1	2	3	4	5	6–10	Laps	Laps Led	Races Led	Miles	$

Mark Smith *continued*

Year	Driver	Starts	Poles	1	2	3	4	5	6–10	Laps	Laps Led	Races Led	Miles	$
1997	Gary Bradberry	10	0	0	0	0	0	0	0	2,622	0	0	3,111	146,341
1997	Loy Allen Jr.	2	0	0	0	0	0	0	0	266	0	0	564	67,300
Lifetime		20	0	0	0	0	0	0	1	5,237	0	0	6,564	$312,111

Perry Smith

Year	Driver	Starts	Poles	1	2	3	4	5	6–10	Laps	Laps Led	Races Led	Miles	$
1951	Mike Klapak	1	0	0	0	0	0	0	0		0	0		0
1951	Bill Rexford	1	0	0	0	0	0	0	0		0	0		25
1951	Frank Mundy	24	4	2	2	1	2	1	3	674	331	4	479	5,435
1951	Perry Smith	1	0	0	0	0	1	0	0		0	0		300
1952	Jack Smith	2	1	0	0	0	0	0	0	216	186	1	123	100
1952	Al Keller	2	0	0	0	0	0	0	0		0	0		75
Lifetime		31	5	2	2	1	3	1	3	890	517	5	602	$5,935

Ralph Smith

Year	Driver	Starts	Poles	1	2	3	4	5	6–10	Laps	Laps Led	Races Led	Miles	$
1962	T.C. Hunt	5	0	0	0	0	0	0	2	561	0	0	273	690
1962	G.C. Spencer	2	0	0	0	0	0	0	0	567	0	0	851	750
1962	Harold Fryar	1	0	0	0	0	0	0	0	187	0	0	62	110
1962	Bill Smith (K)	1	0	0	0	0	0	0	0	60	0	0	30	200
1962	Bill Champion	1	0	0	0	0	0	0	0	15	0	0	21	400
1962	Harry Leake	2	0	0	0	0	0	0	0	346	0	0	173	250
1962	Ralph Smith	2	0	0	0	0	0	0	0	684	0	0	342	300
1962	LeeRoy Yarbrough	1	0	0	0	0	0	1	0	191	0	0	96	275
1963	T.C. Hunt	1	0	0	0	0	0	0	0	184	0	0	92	65
Lifetime		16	0	0	0	0	0	1	2	2,795	0	0	1,939	$3,040

Robert Smith

Year	Driver	Starts	Poles	1	2	3	4	5	6–10	Laps	Laps Led	Races Led	Miles	$
1962	Ralph Earnhardt	11	0	0	0	1	0	1	3	1,183	0	0	910	2,020
1963	Thomas Cox	1	0	0	0	0	0	0	0	6	0	0	9	450
1963	Bunkie Blackburn	2	0	0	0	0	0	0	0	158	0	0	79	250
1963	G.C. Spencer	1	0	0	0	0	0	0	1	177	0	0	89	200
Lifetime		15	0	0	0	1	0	1	4	1,524	0	0	1,086	$2,920

Rollin Smith

Year	Driver	Starts	Poles	1	2	3	4	5	6–10	Laps	Laps Led	Races Led	Miles	$
1952	Rollin Smith	1	0	0	0	0	0	0	0	385	0	0	481	350
Lifetime		1	0	0	0	0	0	0	0	385	0	0	481	$350

Ron Smith

Year	Driver	Starts	Poles	1	2	3	4	5	6–10	Laps	Laps Led	Races Led	Miles	$
1967	Don Stives	3	0	0	0	0	0	0	1	188	0	0	49	510
Lifetime		3	0	0	0	0	0	0	1	188	0	0	49	$510

Ronald Smith

Year	Driver	Starts	Poles	1	2	3	4	5	6–10	Laps	Laps Led	Races Led	Miles	$
1965	Bud Vaughn	4	0	0	0	0	0	0	1	164	0	0	72	840
1965	Robert Vaughn	2	0	0	0	0	0	0	0	5	0	0	13	1,160
Lifetime		6	0	0	0	0	0	0	1	169	0	0	85	$2,000

Scott Smith

Year	Driver	Starts	Poles	1	2	3	4	5	6–10	Laps	Laps Led	Races Led	Miles	$
1980	Don Whittington	1	0	0	0	0	0	0	0	87	0	0	119	1,275
1981	Don Whittington	3	0	0	0	0	0	0	0	346	0	0	883	13,685
Lifetime		4	0	0	0	0	0	0	0	433	0	0	1,002	$14,960

Slick Smith

Year	Driver	Starts	Poles	1	2	3	4	5	6–10	Laps	Laps Led	Races Led	Miles	$
1949	Slick Smith	1	0	0	0	0	0	0	1		0	0		125
1953	Slick Smith	1	0	0	0	0	0	0	1		0	0		125
1954	Buck Baker	1	0	0	0	0	0	0	0	231	0	0	231	100
Lifetime		3	0	0	0	0	0	0	2	231	0	0	231	$350

W.A. Smith

Year	Driver	Starts	Poles	1	2	3	4	5	6–10	Laps	Laps Led	Races Led	Miles	$
1952	June Cleveland	1	0	0	0	0	0	0	0	205	0	0	256	0
Lifetime		1	0	0	0	0	0	0	0	205	0	0	256	$0

Year	Driver	Starts	Poles	Finish 1	2	3	4	5	6–10	Laps	Laps Led	Races Led	Miles	$

Walt Smith

Year	Driver	Starts	Poles	1	2	3	4	5	6–10	Laps	Laps Led	Races Led	Miles	$
1954	Erick Erickson	1	0	0	0	0	0	0	1	477	0	0	239	250
Lifetime		1	0	0	0	0	0	0	1	477	0	0	239	$250

Wayne Smith

Year	Driver	Starts	Poles	1	2	3	4	5	6–10	Laps	Laps Led	Races Led	Miles	$
1965	J.T. Putney	3	0	0	0	0	0	0	0	34	0	0	17	310
1969	Earl Brooks	1	0	0	0	0	0	0	0	183	0	0	252	900
1970	Dave Marcis	1	0	0	0	0	0	0	0	3	0	0	1	200
1970	Wayne Smith	8	0	0	0	0	0	0	0	593	0	0	813	4,505
1971	Wayne Smith	2	0	0	0	0	0	0	0	67	0	0	39	660
1972	Wayne Smith	3	0	0	0	0	0	0	1	270	0	0	624	3,445
Lifetime		18	0	0	0	0	0	0	1	1,150	0	0	1,746	$10,020

Parker Snead

Year	Driver	Starts	Poles	1	2	3	4	5	6–10	Laps	Laps Led	Races Led	Miles	$
1963	Johnny Allen	1	0	0	0	0	0	0	0	134	0	0	201	350
1963	Ted Hairfield	2	0	0	0	0	0	0	0	50	0	0	125	675
Lifetime		3	0	0	0	0	0	0	0	184	0	0	326	$1,025

Grant Sniffen

Year	Driver	Starts	Poles	1	2	3	4	5	6–10	Laps	Laps Led	Races Led	Miles	$
1951	Dick Meyer	6	0	0	1	0	0	2	1		82	1		1,550
Lifetime		6	0	0	1	0	0	2	1		82	1		$1,550

Les Snow

Year	Driver	Starts	Poles	1	2	3	4	5	6–10	Laps	Laps Led	Races Led	Miles	$
1951	Les Snow	2	0	0	0	0	0	0	1	222	0	0	222	375
Lifetime		2	0	0	0	0	0	0	1	222	0	0	222	$375

Bill Snowden

Year	Driver	Starts	Poles	1	2	3	4	5	6–10	Laps	Laps Led	Races Led	Miles	$
1949	Bill Snowden	3	0	0	0	0	0	0	2	182	0	0	91	300
1950	Bill Snowden	1	0	0	0	0	0	1	0	194	0	0	146	200
1951	Bill Snowden	12	0	0	0	0	2	1	6	383	0	0	479	2,325
1952	Fireball Roberts	1	0	0	0	0	0	0	0	53	0	0	53	24
1952	Banjo Matthews	3	0	0	0	0	0	1	0	667	0	0	628	1,000
1952	Bill Snowden	4	0	0	0	0	0	0	1	384	0	0	237	290
Lifetime		24	0	0	0	0	2	3	9	1,863	0	0	1,634	$4,139

Don Snyder

Year	Driver	Starts	Poles	1	2	3	4	5	6–10	Laps	Laps Led	Races Led	Miles	$
1965	Donald Tucker	9	0	0	0	0	1	0	2	1,597	0	0	1,703	5,830
Lifetime		9	0	0	0	0	1	0	2	1,597	0	0	1,703	$5,830

John Soares

Year	Driver	Starts	Poles	1	2	3	4	5	6–10	Laps	Laps Led	Races Led	Miles	$
1951	John Soares	2	0	0	0	0	0	0	0		0	0		0
Lifetime		2	0	0	0	0	0	0	0		0	0		$0

John Soares Jr.

Year	Driver	Starts	Poles	1	2	3	4	5	6–10	Laps	Laps Led	Races Led	Miles	$
1970	John Soares Jr.	1	0	0	0	0	1	0	0	141	0	0	369	3,415
1971	John Soares Jr.	4	0	0	0	0	0	0	1	764	0	0	1,280	4,855
1972	John Soares Jr.	3	0	0	0	0	0	0	0	337	0	0	861	4,315
1975	John Soares Jr.	1	0	0	0	0	0	0	0	18	0	0	47	670
1985	John Soares Jr.	2	0	0	0	0	0	0	0	192	0	0	503	3,100
Lifetime		11	0	0	0	0	1	0	1	1,452	0	0	3,060	$16,355

Rol Soderin

Year	Driver	Starts	Poles	1	2	3	4	5	6–10	Laps	Laps Led	Races Led	Miles	$
1957	Elgin Holmes	1	0	0	0	0	0	0	0	14	0	0	35	35
Lifetime		1	0	0	0	0	0	0	0	14	0	0	35	$35

Lyle Sokoll

Year	Driver	Starts	Poles	1	2	3	4	5	6–10	Laps	Laps Led	Races Led	Miles	$
1957	George Bumgardner	1	0	0	0	0	0	0	0	111	0	0	111	100
1958	Bill Wimble	2	0	0	0	0	0	0	0	241	0	0	121	100
Lifetime		3	0	0	0	0	0	0	0	352	0	0	232	$200

Year	Driver	Starts	Poles	Finish 1	2	3	4	5	6–10	Laps	Laps Led	Races Led	Miles	$

Gober Sosebee

Year	Driver	Starts	Poles	1	2	3	4	5	6–10	Laps	Laps Led	Races Led	Miles	$
1950	Gober Sosebee	1	0	0	0	0	0	0	0	364	4	1	455	290
1951	Gober Sosebee	7	0	0	2	0	0	1	1	613	0	0	607	1,875
1952	Gober Sosebee	3	0	0	0	0	0	3	0	231	0	0	245	775
1953	Gober Sosebee	15	0	0	1	1	0	0	7	733	73	1	686	2,225
1954	Gober Sosebee	17	1	1	0	1	1	0	2	1,817	170	2	1,147	2,525
1955	Gober Sosebee	6	0	0	0	0	2	0	0	344	0	0	218	775
1958	Gober Sosebee	5	1	0	0	0	0	0	3	692	0	0	476	695
1959	Gober Sosebee	1	0	0	0	0	0	0	0	44	0	0	110	100
1979	David Sosebee	3	0	0	0	0	0	0	0	547	0	0	892	2,910
1986	David Sosebee	2	0	0	0	0	0	0	0	267	0	0	404	2,310
Lifetime		60	2	1	3	2	3	4	13	5,652	247	4	5,240	$14,480

Jim Southard

Year	Driver	Starts	Poles	1	2	3	4	5	6–10	Laps	Laps Led	Races Led	Miles	$
1984	Jim Southard	4	0	0	0	0	0	0	0	1,113	0	0	1,653	6,965
1985	Jim Southard	1	0	0	0	0	0	0	0	431	0	0	438	1,970
Lifetime		5	0	0	0	0	0	0	0	1,544	0	0	2,091	$8,935

George Sparks

Year	Driver	Starts	Poles	1	2	3	4	5	6–10	Laps	Laps Led	Races Led	Miles	$
1960	Gene White	2	0	0	0	0	0	0	0	187	0	0	468	200
Lifetime		2	0	0	0	0	0	0	0	187	0	0	468	$200

Ralph Sparks

Year	Driver	Starts	Poles	1	2	3	4	5	6–10	Laps	Laps Led	Races Led	Miles	$
1963	Gary Sain	7	0	0	0	0	0	0	1	994	0	0	523	700
Lifetime		7	0	0	0	0	0	0	1	994	0	0	523	$700

Huck Spaulding

Year	Driver	Starts	Poles	1	2	3	4	5	6–10	Laps	Laps Led	Races Led	Miles	$
1957	Huck Spaulding	8	0	0	0	0	0	0	3	1,006	0	0	659	1,130
Lifetime		8	0	0	0	0	0	0	3	1,006	0	0	659	$1,130

Paul Spaulding

Year	Driver	Starts	Poles	1	2	3	4	5	6–10	Laps	Laps Led	Races Led	Miles	$
1957	Fireball Roberts	1	0	0	0	1	0	0	0	134	0	0	201	1,375
1958	Junior Johnson	26	0	6	2	3	1	0	3	4,096	317	9	2,760	12,205
1958	Lloyd Ragon	2	0	0	0	0	0	0	1	34	0	0	139	230
1958	Huck Spaulding	1	0	0	0	0	0	0	0		0	0		50
1959	Glen Wood	1	0	0	0	0	0	0	1	195	0	0	49	165
1959	Junior Johnson	26	1	5	1	3	2	2	1	4,109	166	7	2,608	8,440
1959	Ned Jarrett	1	0	0	1	0	0	0	0	200	0	0	100	525
1960	Junior Johnson	2	1	0	0	0	0	0	0	98	0	0	49	50
Lifetime		60	2	11	4	7	3	2	6	8,866	483	16	5,907	$23,040

Wayne Spears

Year	Driver	Starts	Poles	1	2	3	4	5	6–10	Laps	Laps Led	Races Led	Miles	$
1989	Bill Sedgwick	1	0	0	0	0	0	0	0	170	0	0	170	3,525
1990	Bill Sedgwick	3	0	0	0	0	0	0	0	730	0	0	653	11,355
1991	Bill Sedgwick	3	0	0	0	0	0	0	0	848	0	0	740	15,150
1992	Bill Sedgwick	2	0	0	0	0	0	0	0	373	0	0	485	16,365
1993	Bill Sedgwick	1	0	0	0	0	0	0	0	73	0	0	184	8,140
1993	Ron Hornaday Jr.	1	0	0	0	0	0	0	0	307	0	0	307	6,660
1994	Ron Hornaday Jr.	2	0	0	0	0	0	0	0	350	1	1	431	13,710
Lifetime		13	0	0	0	0	0	0	0	2,851	1	1	2,969	$74,905

Lake Speed

Year	Driver	Starts	Poles	1	2	3	4	5	6–10	Laps	Laps Led	Races Led	Miles	$
1980	Lake Speed	11	0	0	0	0	0	0	3	1,947	2	1	3,763	29,795
1981	Elmo Langley	1	0	0	0	0	0	0	0	6	0	0	6	575
1981	Lake Speed	25	0	0	0	0	0	0	6	6,517	14	2	7,182	79,505
1982	Lake Speed	1	0	0	0	0	0	0	0	3	0	0	8	5,450
1987	Lake Speed	13	0	0	0	1	0	0	4	2,591	1	1	4,433	88,810
1988	Lake Speed	29	0	1	1	0	1	1	3	7,005	368	6	8,542	205,310
1989	Rodney Combs	1	0	0	0	0	0	0	0	351	0	0	479	6,895
1989	Joe Ruttman	3	0	0	0	0	0	0	0	379	0	0	757	16,650
1989	Eddie Bierschwale	1	0	0	0	0	0	0	0	6	0	0	15	4,260

Year	Driver	Starts	Poles	1	2	3	4	5	6–10	Laps	Laps Led	Races Led	Miles	$

Lake Speed *continued*

Year	Driver	Starts	Poles	1	2	3	4	5	6–10	Laps	Laps Led	Races Led	Miles	$
1989	Lake Speed	24	0	0	0	0	0	1	4	7,028	11	4	8,245	185,227
1990	Lake Speed	6	0	0	0	0	0	0	0	835	3	1	1,753	55,037
1990	Phil Parsons	1	0	0	0	0	0	0	0	330	0	0	495	4,225
1990	Tommy Ellis	1	0	0	0	0	0	0	0	285	0	0	285	3,050
1992	Lake Speed	9	0	0	0	0	0	0	0	2,248	0	0	3,200	49,545
1993	Lake Speed	11	0	0	0	0	0	0	0	2,536	0	0	3,858	115,355
1996	Lake Speed	3	0	0	0	0	0	0	1	616	0	0	1,128	68,455
Lifetime		140	0	1	1	1	1	2	21	32,683	399	15	44,147	$918,144

Tom Spell

Year	Driver	Starts	Poles	1	2	3	4	5	6–10	Laps	Laps Led	Races Led	Miles	$
1964	Ralph Earnhardt	10	0	0	0	0	1	0	0	1,102	0	0	1,047	2,615
Lifetime		10	0	0	0	0	1	0	0	1,102	0	0	1,047	$2,615

G.C. Spencer

Year	Driver	Starts	Poles	1	2	3	4	5	6–10	Laps	Laps Led	Races Led	Miles	$
1959	G.C. Spencer	28	0	0	0	0	1	0	4	4,552	0	0	2,553	3,220
1960	G.C. Spencer	4	0	0	0	0	0	1	0	533	0	0	711	495
1961	G.C. Spencer	31	0	0	0	0	3	0	15	6,218	0	0	3,823	6,515
1962	G.C. Spencer	37	0	0	0	0	2	4	7	6,638	0	0	3,753	6,860
1963	G.C. Spencer	15	0	0	1	0	1	1	3	1,996	0	0	786	3,520
1964	Doug Moore	16	0	0	0	0	0	0	6	2,809	0	0	1,296	3,275
1964	G.C. Spencer	12	0	0	0	1	0	3	1	2,822	0	0	2,253	7,225
1965	G.C. Spencer	46	1	0	3	4	3	4	11	9,063	90	5	6,480	23,130
1966	G.C. Spencer	19	0	0	3	0	0	3	3	4,518	2	1	4,180	25,400
1967	Curtis Turner	1	1	0	0	0	0	0	0	143	6	1	358	6,425
1967	Wendell Scott	1	0	0	0	0	0	0	0	182	0	0	273	950
1967	Ed Negre	1	0	0	0	0	0	0	0	446	0	0	446	1,000
1967	G.C. Spencer	25	0	0	0	2	0	2	4	3,893	0	0	2,648	8,870
1968	Wendell Scott	1	0	0	0	0	0	0	0	436	0	0	218	425
1968	G.C. Spencer	23	0	0	0	0	1	0	4	3,778	0	0	2,645	8,335
1969	Ed Negre	13	0	0	0	0	0	0	3	2,198	0	0	1,622	6,870
1969	Frank Warren	1	0	0	0	0	0	0	0	73	0	0	146	840
1969	E.J. Trivette	2	0	0	0	0	0	0	1	461	0	0	235	775
1969	G.C. Spencer	26	0	0	0	0	2	2	4	4,823	0	0	3,980	21,675
1969	J.D. McDuffie	1	0	0	0	0	0	0	0	380	0	0	238	525
1969	Wendell Scott	1	0	0	0	0	0	0	0	297	0	0	446	1,355
1970	G.C. Spencer	20	0	0	0	0	2	1	6	4,618	0	0	4,091	17,915
1971	Earl Brooks	1	0	0	0	0	0	0	0	67	0	0	102	1,015
1971	Ed Negre	2	0	0	0	0	0	0	0	103	0	0	52	925
1971	G.C. Spencer	16	0	0	0	0	0	2	4	3,116	12	1	2,758	11,030
1971	Neil Castles	1	0	0	0	0	0	0	0	114	0	0	171	834
1972	G.C. Spencer	9	0	0	0	0	0	0	1	1,397	0	0	1,469	7,255
1973	John A. Utsman	3	0	0	0	0	0	0	1	775	0	0	780	2,965
1973	G.C. Spencer	10	0	0	0	0	0	0	1	1,459	0	0	2,043	12,013
1974	G.C. Spencer	10	0	0	0	0	0	0	1	1,205	3	1	1,721	12,985
1975	G.C. Spencer	9	0	0	0	0	0	0	1	906	11	1	1,663	14,945
1976	Henley Gray	1	0	0	0	0	0	0	0	1	0	0	1	585
1976	John A. Utsman	4	0	0	0	0	0	0	0	1,276	0	0	1,859	8,185
1976	G.C. Spencer	4	0	0	0	0	0	0	0	501	0	0	941	4,965
1976	Dick May	1	0	0	0	0	0	0	0	213	0	0	291	1,395
1977	G.C. Spencer	8	0	0	0	0	0	0	1	1,817	0	0	2,908	15,755
1977	Henley Gray	1	0	0	0	0	0	0	0	15	0	0	40	1,230
1978	Connie Saylor	2	0	0	0	0	0	0	0	504	0	0	756	5,105
1978	Claude Ballot-Lena	5	0	0	0	0	0	0	1	776	0	0	1,667	11,780
1979	Claude Ballot-Lena	2	0	0	0	0	0	0	0	251	0	0	463	2,080
1979	Connie Saylor	2	0	0	0	0	0	0	0	262	0	0	565	4,435
1980	Gary Baker	1	0	0	0	0	0	0	0	145	0	0	386	3,440
1980	Connie Saylor	5	0	0	0	0	0	0	0	1,171	5	2	1,729	9,350
1981	Connie Saylor	7	0	0	0	0	0	0	0	4,177	0	0	6,568	18,780
1982	Connie Saylor	7	0	0	0	0	0	0	0	1,450	3	1	1,704	16,225
Lifetime		435	2	0	7	7	15	19	83	82,578	132	13	73,813	$322,877

Jimmy Spencer

Year	Driver	Starts	Poles	1	2	3	4	5	6–10	Laps	Laps Led	Races Led	Miles	$
2000	Boris Said III	1	0	0	0	0	0	0	0	26	0	0	51	36,940
Lifetime		1	0	0	0	0	0	0	0	26	0	0	51	$36,940

Year	Driver	Starts	Poles	Finish 1	2	3	4	5	6–10	Laps	Laps Led	Races Led	Miles	$

Speedy Spiers

Year	Driver	Starts	Poles	1	2	3	4	5	6–10	Laps	Laps Led	Races Led	Miles	$
1964	Larry Frank	1	0	0	0	0	0	0	0	35	0	0	18	100
Lifetime		1	0	0	0	0	0	0	0	35	0	0	18	$100

Ken Spikes

Year	Driver	Starts	Poles	1	2	3	4	5	6–10	Laps	Laps Led	Races Led	Miles	$
1964	Reb Wickersham	2	0	0	0	0	0	0	0	134	0	0	335	825
1964	Ken Spikes	6	0	0	0	0	0	0	1	1,018	0	0	1,570	3,100
1970	J.D. McDuffie	1	0	0	0	0	0	0	0	30	0	0	46	755
1970	Jimmy Watson	1	0	0	0	0	0	0	0	451	0	0	247	505
1970	Ken Spikes	1	0	0	0	0	0	0	0	116	0	0	309	890
1970	Roy Mayne	2	0	0	0	0	0	0	0	189	0	0	380	2,190
1971	Dub Simpson	1	0	0	0	0	0	0	0	48	0	0	120	255
1971	Jimmy Watson	1	0	0	0	0	0	0	0	29	0	0	16	350
Lifetime		15	0	0	0	0	0	0	1	2,015	0	0	3,022	$8,870

Doug Spohn

Year	Driver	Starts	Poles	1	2	3	4	5	6–10	Laps	Laps Led	Races Led	Miles	$
1985	Slick Johnson	1	0	0	0	0	0	0	0	184	0	0	251	2,005
1985	Doug Heveron	1	0	0	0	0	0	0	0	194	0	0	485	2,555
Lifetime		2	0	0	0	0	0	0	0	378	0	0	736	$4,560

Ron Spohn

Year	Driver	Starts	Poles	1	2	3	4	5	6–10	Laps	Laps Led	Races Led	Miles	$
1979	Dick May	1	0	0	0	0	0	0	0	148	0	0	202	1,450
1980	Bruce Jacobi	1	0	0	0	0	0	0	0	189	0	0	378	985
1980	Ralph Jones	2	0	0	0	0	0	0	0	547	0	0	780	3,495
1983	Glenn Jarrett	1	0	0	0	0	0	0	0	24	0	0	60	1,200
1985	Slick Johnson	4	0	0	0	0	0	0	0	1,249	0	0	1,638	11,780
1986	Connie Saylor	1	0	0	0	0	0	0	0	376	0	0	564	2,200
Lifetime		10	0	0	0	0	0	0	0	2,533	0	0	3,623	$21,110

J.D. Stacy

Year	Driver	Starts	Poles	1	2	3	4	5	6–10	Laps	Laps Led	Races Led	Miles	$
1977	Neil Bonnett	12	3	2	0	1	0	0	2	3,029	446	7	3,260	62,180
1977	Tom Sneva	1	0	0	0	0	0	0	0	194	0	0	291	1,150
1978	Neil Bonnett	16	3	0	1	0	1	3	4	3,507	38	4	3,864	86,115
1978	Ferrel Harris	2	0	0	0	0	0	0	2	380	0	0	980	17,250
1979	Neil Bonnett	3	0	0	0	0	0	0	0	95	12	1	225	6,560
1980	Sterling Marlin	2	0	0	0	0	0	0	0	566	0	0	824	6,725
1980	Joe Ruttman	1	0	0	0	0	0	0	0	29	0	0	73	1,055
1981	Joe Ruttman	17	0	0	1	0	0	1	5	4,194	106	7	5,589	110,125
1981	Bob Senneker	1	0	0	0	0	0	0	0	256	0	0	384	1,975
1981	Dale Earnhardt	4	0	0	0	0	0	0	1	770	10	3	1,142	34,300
1982	Tim Richmond	25	1	2	2	0	1	2	5	6,722	319	12	8,132	175,160
1982	Joe Ruttman	5	0	0	0	1	0	0	0	1,311	148	2	1,396	69,155
1982	Rodney Combs	1	0	0	0	0	0	0	1	325	5	1	495	2,900
1982	Jim Sauter	3	0	0	0	0	0	0	1	511	5	1	961	23,270
1982	Robin McCall	2	0	0	0	0	0	0	0	154	0	0	308	2,395
1983	Rodney Combs	1	0	0	0	0	0	0	0	320	0	0	480	1,725
1983	Morgan Shepherd	23	0	0	1	1	1	0	10	6,251	5	4	7,582	250,535
1983	Mark Martin	7	0	0	0	1	0	0	1	2,123	1	1	2,279	75,240
Lifetime		126	7	4	5	4	3	5	32	30,737	1,095	43	38,266	$927,815

Mark Stahl

Year	Driver	Starts	Poles	1	2	3	4	5	6–10	Laps	Laps Led	Races Led	Miles	$
1981	Mark Stahl	1	0	0	0	0	0	0	0	109	0	0	286	1,080
1982	Mark Stahl	1	0	0	0	0	0	0	0	85	0	0	223	2,690
1983	Mark Stahl	2	0	0	0	0	0	0	0	622	0	0	363	1,970
1984	Mark Stahl	3	0	0	0	0	0	0	0	842	0	0	892	4,035
1985	Mark Stahl	1	0	0	0	0	0	0	0	375	0	0	563	3,800
1986	Mark Stahl	3	0	0	0	0	0	0	0	719	0	0	889	5,890
1987	Mark Stahl	9	0	0	0	0	0	0	0	1,635	0	0	2,643	30,270
1988	Mark Stahl	1	0	0	0	0	0	0	0	233	0	0	237	1,615
1989	Mark Stahl	1	0	0	0	0	0	0	0	176	0	0	468	3,785
1990	Mark Stahl	5	0	0	0	0	0	0	0	1,268	0	0	1,890	18,470
1991	Mark Stahl	2	0	0	0	0	0	0	0	30	0	0	35	7,105
Lifetime		29	0	0	0	0	0	0	0	6,094	0	0	8,489	$80,710

Year	Driver	Starts	Poles	1	2	3	4	5	6–10	Laps	Laps Led	Races Led	Miles	$

Bill Stammer

Year	Driver	Starts	Poles	1	2	3	4	5	6–10	Laps	Laps Led	Races Led	Miles	$
1951	Bill Stammer	1	0	0	0	0	0	0	0		0	0		25
1954	Bill Stammer	2	0	0	0	0	0	0	0	631	0	0	316	75
1955	Bill Stammer	1	0	0	0	0	0	0	1	100	0	0	100	150
1956	Bill Stammer	2	0	0	0	0	0	0	0	131	0	0	241	140
Lifetime		6	0	0	0	0	0	0	1	862	0	0	656	$390

Billy Standridge

Year	Driver	Starts	Poles	1	2	3	4	5	6–10	Laps	Laps Led	Races Led	Miles	$
1997	Billy Standridge	1	0	0	0	0	0	0	0	51	0	0	136	21,500
1998	Billy Standridge	4	0	0	0	0	0	0	0	568	0	0	1,476	147,640
Lifetime		5	0	0	0	0	0	0	0	619	0	0	1,612	$169,140

Stanley Smith

Year	Driver	Starts	Poles	1	2	3	4	5	6–10	Laps	Laps Led	Races Led	Miles	$
1991	Stanley Smith	12	0	0	0	0	0	0	0	1,932	12	1	3,201	54,715
1992	Stanley Smith	14	0	0	0	0	0	0	0	2,685	0	0	4,009	89,650
1993	Stanley Smith	1	0	0	0	0	0	0	0	68	0	0	181	7,690
Lifetime		27	0	0	0	0	0	0	0	4,685	12	1	7,390	$152,055

Dick Stanley

Year	Driver	Starts	Poles	1	2	3	4	5	6–10	Laps	Laps Led	Races Led	Miles	$
1960	Jim Whitman	5	0	0	0	0	0	0	0	567	0	0	1,055	1,450
Lifetime		5	0	0	0	0	0	0	0	567	0	0	1,055	$1,450

George Stark

Year	Driver	Starts	Poles	1	2	3	4	5	6–10	Laps	Laps Led	Races Led	Miles	$
1976	John Dineen	1	0	0	0	0	0	0	0	73	0	0	191	1,040
1977	John Dineen	1	0	0	0	0	0	0	0	89	0	0	233	1,400
Lifetime		2	0	0	0	0	0	0	0	162	0	0	424	$2,440

John Stark

Year	Driver	Starts	Poles	1	2	3	4	5	6–10	Laps	Laps Led	Races Led	Miles	$
1988	Larry Moyer	1	0	0	0	0	0	0	0	148	0	0	370	2,355
Lifetime		1	0	0	0	0	0	0	0	148	0	0	370	$2,355

Ralph Stark

Year	Driver	Starts	Poles	1	2	3	4	5	6–10	Laps	Laps Led	Races Led	Miles	$
1960	Herb Tillman	9	0	0	0	0	0	0	0	1,705	0	0	2,244	2,695
1960	Bobby Johns	1	0	0	0	0	0	0	0	57	0	0	29	50
1961	Bobby Allison	4	0	0	0	0	0	0	0	359	0	0	751	650
Lifetime		14	0	0	0	0	0	0	0	2,121	0	0	3,023	$3,395

Flo Starr

Year	Driver	Starts	Poles	1	2	3	4	5	6–10	Laps	Laps Led	Races Led	Miles	$
1969	Wilbur Pickett	1	0	0	0	0	0	0	0	92	0	0	245	1,250
Lifetime		1	0	0	0	0	0	0	0	92	0	0	245	$1,250

Stan Starr

Year	Driver	Starts	Poles	1	2	3	4	5	6–10	Laps	Laps Led	Races Led	Miles	$
1969	Stan Starr Jr.	1	0	0	0	0	0	0	0	82	0	0	218	1,200
Lifetime		1	0	0	0	0	0	0	0	82	0	0	218	$1,200

Ron Staughton

Year	Driver	Starts	Poles	1	2	3	4	5	6–10	Laps	Laps Led	Races Led	Miles	$
1966	Nick Rampling	1	0	0	0	0	0	0	0	27	0	0	68	0
Lifetime		1	0	0	0	0	0	0	0	27	0	0	68	$0

Stavola Brothers

Year	Driver	Starts	Poles	1	2	3	4	5	6–10	Laps	Laps Led	Races Led	Miles	$
1984	Bobby Hillin	16	0	0	0	0	0	0	0	3,452	0	0	5,655	45,020
1985	Bobby Hillin	28	0	0	0	0	0	0	5	8,636	2	2	10,212	120,515
1986	Bobby Hillin	29	0	1	0	1	2	0	10	8,121	25	4	9,980	333,920
1986	Bobby Allison	29	0	1	2	1	1	1	9	8,391	127	11	9,930	388,100
1987	Bobby Hillin	29	0	0	0	0	0	1	3	6,989	1	1	8,615	311,295
1987	Bobby Allison	29	1	1	1	0	1	1	9	7,662	331	10	9,296	458,825
1988	Mike Alexander	16	0	0	0	1	0	1	4	4,677	51	5	6,015	191,620
1988	Bobby Allison	13	0	1	1	0	0	1	3	4,303	104	4	4,762	373,795
1988	Bobby Hillin	29	0	0	0	1	0	0	6	9,383	70	4	11,188	257,330

Year	Driver	Starts	Poles	Finish 1	2	3	4	5	6–10	Laps	Laps Led	Races Led	Miles	$

Stavola Brothers *continued*

Year	Driver	Starts	Poles	1	2	3	4	5	6–10	Laps	Laps Led	Races Led	Miles	$
1989	Dick Trickle	28	0	0	0	3	1	2	3	8,604	80	8	10,129	273,432
1989	Mike Alexander	1	0	0	0	0	0	0	0	188	0	0	470	16,275
1989	Bobby Hillin	28	0	0	0	0	0	1	6	8,377	26	4	10,298	232,204
1990	Bobby Hillin	29	0	0	0	0	0	1	3	8,299	60	5	10,200	280,719
1991	Rick Wilson	29	0	0	0	0	0	0	0	7,966	10	1	9,697	239,025
1992	Rick Wilson	1	0	0	0	0	0	0	0	195	0	0	488	24,045
1992	Dick Trickle	28	0	0	0	0	0	2	6	8,059	5	2	9,383	301,845
1993	Sterling Marlin	30	0	0	1	0	0	0	7	9,153	345	7	11,222	494,120
1994	Jeff Burton	30	0	0	0	0	2	0	1	7,781	122	4	10,240	508,200
1995	Jeff Burton	29	0	0	0	0	0	1	1	8,050	3	2	10,193	628,270
1996	Hut Stricklin	31	0	0	1	0	0	0	0	8,620	163	3	10,633	562,055
1997	Hut Stricklin	29	0	0	0	0	0	0	1	8,494	6	1	10,241	783,165
1998	Hut Stricklin	6	0	0	0	0	0	0	0	1,494	0	0	1,393	152,965
1998	Buckshot Jones	5	0	0	0	0	0	0	1	1,025	0	0	1,769	162,435
1998	Morgan Shepherd	2	0	0	0	0	0	0	0	263	0	0	435	45,955
Lifetime		524	1	4	6	7	7	12	78	148,182	1,531	78	182,444	$7,185,130

Johnny Steele

Year	Driver	Starts	Poles	1	2	3	4	5	6–10	Laps	Laps Led	Races Led	Miles	$
1969	Johnny Steele	1	0	0	0	0	0	0	0	3	0	0	8	750
Lifetime		1	0	0	0	0	0	0	0	3	0	0	8	$750

Happy Steigel

Year	Driver	Starts	Poles	1	2	3	4	5	6–10	Laps	Laps Led	Races Led	Miles	$
1959	Charlie Cregar	3	0	0	0	0	0	0	0	496	0	0	725	560
1959	Jim McGuirk	4	0	0	0	0	0	0	0	314	0	0	590	275
1960	Steve McGrath	1	0	0	0	0	0	0	0	188	0	0	259	200
1960	Dick Joslin	3	0	0	0	0	0	0	0	302	0	0	755	535
1960	Elmo Langley	1	0	0	0	0	0	0	0	24	0	0	36	200
1961	Elmo Langley	3	0	0	0	0	0	0	0	453	0	0	900	550
1962	Ralph Earnhardt	3	0	0	0	0	0	0	0	228	0	0	427	800
Lifetime		18	0	0	0	0	0	0	0	2,005	0	0	3,691	$3,120

Fred Steinbroner

Year	Driver	Starts	Poles	1	2	3	4	5	6–10	Laps	Laps Led	Races Led	Miles	$
1955	Fred Steinbroner	1	0	0	0	0	0	0	0	84	0	0	84	80
1956	Fred Steinbroner	1	0	0	0	0	0	0	0	72	0	0	180	40
Lifetime		2	0	0	0	0	0	0	0	156	0	0	264	$120

Lyle Stelter

Year	Driver	Starts	Poles	1	2	3	4	5	6–10	Laps	Laps Led	Races Led	Miles	$
1958	Chuck Townsen	1	0	0	0	0	0	0	0	152	0	0	400	110
1960	Lyle Stelter	2	0	0	0	0	0	0	0	130	0	0	164	160
1961	Larry Frank	1	0	0	0	0	0	0	0	10	0	0	15	225
1963	LeeRoy Yarbrough	3	1	0	0	0	0	0	2	430	8	1	232	390
1963	Elmo Langley	1	0	0	0	0	0	0	0	314	0	0	471	400
1963	Lyle Stelter	2	0	0	0	0	0	0	0	304	0	0	85	175
1965	Tiny Lund	27	0	1	1	1	3	1	7	3,871	209	2	2,702	10,100
1966	Paul Connors	1	0	0	0	0	0	0	0	38	0	0	95	100
1966	Tiny Lund	26	1	1	2	1	0	1	4	3,564	654	6	2,504	8,685
1966	Paul Dean Holt	4	0	0	0	0	0	0	0	213	0	0	87	475
1966	Mario Caruso	1	0	0	0	0	0	0	0	167	0	0	56	130
1966	Lyle Stelter	2	0	0	0	0	0	0	0	38	0	0	35	0
1966	Harold Smith	2	0	0	0	0	1	0	0	627	0	0	848	3,270
1967	Tiny Lund	10	0	0	0	0	0	1	1	1,564	35	2	1,008	3,210
1968	Harold Smith	1	0	0	0	0	0	0	0	244	0	0	366	1,850
1968	Jim Hurtubise	4	0	0	0	0	0	0	1	618	0	0	1,202	3,490
1968	LeeRoy Yarbrough	6	0	0	0	1	0	1	1	869	0	0	422	1,125
1968	Serge Adams	1	0	0	0	0	0	0	0	24	0	0	33	535
1968	Tiny Lund	2	0	0	0	1	0	1	0	686	0	0	360	1,550
1968	Tom Pistone	2	0	0	0	0	0	0	1	354	0	0	153	300
1968	Tommy Gale	1	0	0	0	0	0	0	0	172	0	0	172	760
1969	Gerald Chamberlain	2	0	0	0	0	0	0	1	324	0	0	453	2,225
1969	Eldon Yarbrough	1	0	0	0	0	0	1	0	194	0	0	97	325
1969	Dr. Ed Hessert	2	0	0	0	0	0	0	0	100	0	0	50	870
1969	LeeRoy Yarbrough	1	0	0	0	0	0	0	0	316	0	0	158	225
Lifetime		106	2	2	3	4	4	6	18	15,323	906	11	12,169	$40,685

Year	Driver	Starts	Poles	Finish						Laps	Laps Led	Races Led	Miles	$
				1	2	3	4	5	6–10	Laps	Led	Led	Miles	$

I.D. Stenstrom

Year	Driver	Starts	Poles	1	2	3	4	5	6–10	Laps	Laps Led	Races Led	Miles	$
1951	Bob Johnson	1	0	0	0	0	0	0	0	214	0	0	268	0
Lifetime		1	0	0	0	0	0	0	0	214	0	0	268	$0

Jim Stephens

Year	Driver	Starts	Poles	1	2	3	4	5	6–10	Laps	Laps Led	Races Led	Miles	$
1956	Tim Flock	1	0	0	0	0	1	0	0	197	0	0	99	365
1956	Cotton Owens	6	0	0	0	0	0	0	2	838	0	0	550	770
1956	Don Carr	4	0	0	0	0	0	0	0	469	0	0	334	210
1956	Junior Johnson	1	0	0	0	0	0	0	0	64	0	0	64	50
1956	Ed Kretz	1	0	0	0	0	0	0	0	11	0	0	45	0
1956	Pat Kirkwood	2	0	0	0	1	0	0	0	368	0	0	451	1,475
1956	Jimmie Lewallen	1	0	0	0	0	0	1	0	15	0	0	15	0
1958	Joe Eubanks	7	0	1	0	0	1	0	1	956	38	2	737	2,055
1958	Cotton Owens	27	2	1	4	2	1	0	9	3,559	241	5	2,124	6,015
1959	Fireball Roberts	5	3	1	0	0	0	0	2	609	147	3	997	10,180
1960	Bobby Johns	4	0	0	2	0	1	0	0	491	23	2	1,029	11,565
1962	Fireball Roberts	11	7	2	2	0	0	0	2	2,127	517	6	2,111	36,085
1963	Bunkie Blackburn	2	0	0	0	0	0	0	1	57	0	0	143	700
Lifetime		72	12	5	8	3	4	1	17	9,761	966	18	8,697	$69,470

Cliff Stewart

Year	Driver	Starts	Poles	1	2	3	4	5	6–10	Laps	Laps Led	Races Led	Miles	$
1962	Thomas Cox	6	0	0	0	0	0	1	2	1,370	0	0	605	1,970
1962	Tiny Lund	2	0	0	0	0	0	0	0	445	0	0	668	825
1962	Ken Rush	1	0	0	0	0	0	0	0	463	0	0	232	150
1962	Bill Foster	5	0	0	0	0	0	0	1	1,230	0	0	740	800
1962	Bob Welborn	1	0	0	0	0	0	0	0	1	0	0	3	275
1962	Jim Paschal	29	0	1	3	3	3	2	3	4,627	34	3	3,153	8,915
1963	Bill Foster	10	0	0	0	0	0	0	2	1,628	0	0	1,049	1,410
1963	Joe Weatherly	10	0	0	1	1	0	0	3	1,308	0	0	471	3,800
1963	Jim Paschal	1	0	0	0	0	0	0	0	32	0	0	8	100
1963	Fred Harb	4	0	0	0	0	1	0	0	365	0	0	175	580
1963	Larry Thomas	1	0	0	0	0	0	0	0	157	0	0	236	300
1963	Jimmy Pardue	3	0	0	0	0	0	0	1	579	0	0	528	825
1963	Curtis Crider	1	0	0	0	0	0	0	0	93	0	0	31	65
1963	Buddy Baker	3	0	0	0	0	0	0	1	615	0	0	456	1,175
1963	Bob Welborn	1	0	0	0	0	0	0	0	4	0	0	6	500
1964	G.C. Spencer	2	0	0	0	0	0	0	0	63	0	0	158	825
1964	Reb Wickersham	1	0	0	0	0	0	0	0	10	0	0	25	450
1964	Doug Cooper	1	0	0	0	0	0	0	0	57	0	0	29	50
1964	Ken Rush	8	0	0	0	0	1	0	1	768	0	0	398	1,640
1964	Fred Harb	2	0	0	0	0	0	1	0	362	0	0	91	375
1964	Jimmy Pardue	2	0	0	0	0	0	0	1	138	0	0	399	1,850
1965	G.C. Spencer	1	0	0	0	0	0	0	0	29	0	0	26	100
1965	Fred Harb	5	0	0	0	0	0	1	1	766	0	0	291	840
1965	T.C. Hunt	1	0	0	0	0	0	0	0	214	0	0	321	550
1971	Jim Paschal	5	0	0	0	2	0	1	1	1,678	0	0	2,105	11,775
1981	Morgan Shepherd	18	1	1	0	0	2	2	5	4,875	371	3	5,172	123,335
1981	Joe Millikan	11	0	0	0	1	0	0	2	3,718	0	0	3,692	76,795
1982	Joe Millikan	6	0	0	0	0	0	0	2	1,788	5	1	1,702	55,210
1982	Geoffrey Bodine	24	2	0	0	1	2	1	6	6,515	118	6	7,932	244,300
1983	Geoffrey Bodine	28	1	0	1	0	2	2	4	7,042	490	13	7,328	183,840
1983	Donnie Allison	2	0	0	0	0	0	0	0	138	0	0	339	6,375
1984	Rusty Wallace	30	0	0	0	0	1	1	2	8,868	11	7	10,024	201,739
1985	Rusty Wallace	28	0	0	0	0	0	1	6	7,271	28	1	8,384	205,775
1986	Kirk Bryant	4	0	0	0	0	0	0	0	842	0	0	978	26,335
Lifetime		265	4	2	5	8	12	13	45	59,419	1,107	36	58,327	$1,136,890

Pete Stewart

Year	Driver	Starts	Poles	1	2	3	4	5	6–10	Laps	Laps Led	Races Led	Miles	$
1954	Pete Stewart	1	0	0	0	0	0	0	0	77	0	0	39	0
1956	Pete Stewart	3	0	0	0	0	0	0	0	756	0	0	356	235
1963	Joe Weatherly	1	0	0	0	0	0	0	0	23	0	0	9	250
1963	Perk Brown	2	0	0	0	0	0	0	1	233	0	0	69	300
1963	Ralph Earnhardt	1	0	0	0	0	0	0	0	59	0	0	89	450
1963	Pete Stewart	2	0	0	0	0	0	0	0	78	0	0	109	150
1963	Jimmy Pardue	44	1	1	0	1	2	1	10	7,885	74	3	5,914	13,059
1963	Darel Dieringer	3	0	0	0	0	1	0	1	946	0	0	425	840

Year	Driver	Starts	Poles	Finish						Laps	Laps Led	Races Led	Miles	$
				1	2	3	4	5	6–10	Laps	Led	Led	Miles	$

Pete Stewart *continued*

1963	Bobby Keck	7	0	0	0	0	0	0	2	883	0	0	429	1,330
1964	Pete Stewart	3	0	0	0	0	0	0	0	717	0	0	620	1,190
1964	Darel Dieringer	1	0	0	0	0	0	0	0	57	0	0	29	50
Lifetime		68	1	1	0	1	3	1	14	11,714	74	3	8,085	$17,854

Ernie Stierly

1976	Ernie Stierly	1	0	0	0	0	0	0	0	21	0	0	55	765
1977	Ernie Stierly	2	0	0	0	0	0	0	0	137	0	0	352	1,805
1978	Ernie Stierly	2	0	0	0	0	0	0	0	141	0	0	369	2,520
Lifetime		5	0	0	0	0	0	0	0	299	0	0	777	$5,090

Paul Stockwell

1971	Bob Kauf	2	0	0	0	0	0	0	0	64	0	0	168	1,675
1972	Bob Kauf	2	0	0	0	0	0	0	0	178	0	0	445	2,500
1973	Bob Kauf	1	0	0	0	0	0	0	0	9	0	0	24	1,015
Lifetime		5	0	0	0	0	0	0	0	251	0	0	637	$5,190

Fred Stoke

1984	Ruben Garcia	2	0	0	0	0	0	0	0	121	0	0	317	1,885
1985	Ruben Garcia	2	0	0	0	0	0	0	0	196	0	0	514	6,525
1985	Blair Aiken	2	0	0	0	0	0	0	0	135	0	0	354	2,020
1986	Ruben Garcia	2	0	0	0	0	0	0	0	169	0	0	443	4,530
1986	Ted Kennedy	2	0	0	0	0	0	0	0	172	0	0	451	3,255
1987	Ruben Garcia	2	0	0	0	0	0	0	0	116	0	0	304	4,180
1987	Derrike Cope	11	0	0	0	0	0	0	0	1,631	0	0	1,978	30,750
1988	Chad Little	1	0	0	0	0	0	0	0	93	3	1	244	3,875
1988	Ruben Garcia	1	0	0	0	0	0	0	0	27	0	0	71	3,380
1989	Bill Cooper	1	0	0	0	0	0	0	0	61	0	0	154	2,360
Lifetime		26	0	0	0	0	0	0	0	2,721	3	1	4,828	$62,760

Gene Stokes

1962	Frank Sessoms	2	0	0	0	0	0	0	0	319	0	0	160	185
Lifetime		2	0	0	0	0	0	0	0	319	0	0	160	$185

Mike Stolarcyk

1985	Mike Stolarcyk	1	0	0	0	0	0	0	0	116	0	0	290	1,615
Lifetime		1	0	0	0	0	0	0	0	116	0	0	290	$1,615

Charlie Stone

1958	Charlie Stone	1	0	0	0	0	0	0	0	35	0	0	144	100
Lifetime		1	0	0	0	0	0	0	0	35	0	0	144	$100

James Stoner

1985	Elton Dotson	1	0	0	0	0	0	0	0	94	0	0	128	1,130
Lifetime		1	0	0	0	0	0	0	0	94	0	0	128	$1,130

Ramo Stott

1967	Ramo Stott	3	0	0	0	0	0	0	1	588	0	0	1,082	3,335
1970	Ramo Stott	3	0	0	0	0	0	0	3	424	2	1	1,089	4,875
1971	Ramo Stott	3	0	0	0	0	0	0	1	476	0	0	1,075	3,715
Lifetime		9	0	0	0	0	0	0	5	1,488	2	1	3,246	$11,925

Ron Stotten

1966	Don Biederman	14	0	0	0	0	0	0	0	2,169	0	0	1,285	2,215
1967	Don Biederman	20	0	0	0	0	0	0	1	2,413	0	0	1,844	4,935
1967	Wendell Scott	1	0	0	0	0	0	0	0	298	0	0	149	330
1968	Don Biederman	1	0	0	0	0	0	0	0	129	0	0	65	100
Lifetime		36	0	0	0	0	0	0	1	5,009	0	0	3,343	$7,580

Year	Driver	Starts	Poles	Finish 1	2	3	4	5	6–10	Laps	Laps Led	Races Led	Miles	$

Al Straub

Year	Driver	Starts	Poles	1	2	3	4	5	6–10	Laps	Laps Led	Races Led	Miles	$
1969	Doug Easton	1	0	0	0	0	0	0	0	0	0	0	0	875
1969	Al Straub	1	0	0	0	0	0	0	0	9	0	0	24	950
1971	Al Straub	1	0	0	0	0	0	0	0	48	0	0	22	300
Lifetime		3	0	0	0	0	0	0	0	57	0	0	46	$2,125

Bill Strauser

Year	Driver	Starts	Poles	1	2	3	4	5	6–10	Laps	Laps Led	Races Led	Miles	$
1994	Mike Chase	1	0	0	0	0	0	0	0	91	0	0	228	21,825
Lifetime		1	0	0	0	0	0	0	0	91	0	0	228	$21,825

John Strauser

Year	Driver	Starts	Poles	1	2	3	4	5	6–10	Laps	Laps Led	Races Led	Miles	$
1992	Hershel McGriff	1	0	0	0	0	0	0	0	19	0	0	48	4,725
1993	Mike Chase	1	0	0	0	0	0	0	0	87	0	0	87	6,015
1993	Hershel McGriff	1	0	0	0	0	0	0	0	27	0	0	68	6,560
1994	Mike Chase	2	0	0	0	0	0	0	0	372	0	0	478	14,265
1995	Ron Hornaday Jr.	1	0	0	0	0	0	0	0	307	0	0	307	9,660
1995	Wally Dallenbach	1	0	0	0	0	0	0	0	41	0	0	103	9,760
Lifetime		7	0	0	0	0	0	0	0	853	0	0	1,092	$50,985

Frank Strickland

Year	Driver	Starts	Poles	1	2	3	4	5	6–10	Laps	Laps Led	Races Led	Miles	$
1958	Fireball Roberts	8	0	6	1	0	0	0	0	2,354	877	7	1,946	31,105
Lifetime		8	0	6	1	0	0	0	0	2,354	877	7	1,946	$31,105

Bub Strickler

Year	Driver	Starts	Poles	1	2	3	4	5	6–10	Laps	Laps Led	Races Led	Miles	$
1965	Bub Strickler	8	0	0	0	0	0	0	2	1,488	0	0	1,699	4,375
1965	Darel Dieringer	5	0	0	0	1	0	0	1	1,155	0	0	525	1,070
1966	Bob Derrington	1	0	0	0	0	0	0	0	36	0	0	90	100
1966	Bub Strickler	1	0	0	0	0	0	0	0	2	0	0	5	1,010
1980	Bub Strickler	1	0	0	0	0	0	0	0	367	0	0	199	925
Lifetime		16	0	0	0	1	0	0	3	3,048	0	0	2,518	$7,480

Doug Stringer

Year	Driver	Starts	Poles	1	2	3	4	5	6–10	Laps	Laps Led	Races Led	Miles	$
1992	Bob Schacht	2	0	0	0	0	0	0	0	445	0	0	670	8,855
1993	Bob Schacht	2	0	0	0	0	0	0	0	252	0	0	345	12,725
Lifetime		4	0	0	0	0	0	0	0	697	0	0	1,015	$21,580

Bill Strong

Year	Driver	Starts	Poles	1	2	3	4	5	6–10	Laps	Laps Led	Races Led	Miles	$
1969	Dub Simpson	10	0	0	0	0	0	0	0	1,812	0	0	1,740	7,690
1970	Dub Simpson	6	0	0	0	0	0	0	1	1,155	0	0	1,111	4,510
1970	Dave Marcis	1	0	0	0	0	0	0	0	70	0	0	35	235
1971	Dub Simpson	7	0	0	0	0	0	0	0	453	0	0	284	3,640
1972	Dub Simpson	5	0	0	0	0	0	0	0	563	0	0	637	3,525
1972	Jim Vandiver	1	0	0	0	0	0	0	0	66	0	0	35	250
1973	Vic Parsons	1	0	0	0	0	0	0	0	108	0	0	108	540
1973	Richard D. Brown	1	0	0	0	0	0	0	0	349	0	0	189	425
1974	Bobby Fleming	1	0	0	0	0	0	0	0	53	0	0	28	500
1974	Dick Simpson	1	0	0	0	0	0	0	0	157	0	0	94	340
1974	Jack Donohue	2	0	0	0	0	0	0	0	333	0	0	237	1,020
Lifetime		36	0	0	0	0	0	0	1	5,119	0	0	4,497	$22,675

Bill Stroppe

Year	Driver	Starts	Poles	1	2	3	4	5	6–10	Laps	Laps Led	Races Led	Miles	$
1955	Johnny Mantz	1	0	0	0	0	0	0	1	102	0	0	102	185
1956	Jim Paschal	2	0	0	0	0	1	0	1	650	102	2	784	2,800
1956	Fonty Flock	1	0	0	0	0	0	0	0	117	0	0	161	80
1956	Bobby Myers	4	0	0	0	0	0	0	0	263	0	0	355	200
1956	Bob Korf	1	0	0	0	0	0	0	1	36	0	0	148	400
1956	Billy Myers	40	1	2	6	2	1	1	8	5,880	103	4	4,055	13,755
1956	Johnny Mantz	1	0	0	0	1	0	0	0	79	0	0	198	1,130
1956	Tim Flock	1	0	1	0	0	0	0	0	63	17	1	258	2,950
1957	Tim Flock	1	0	0	0	0	0	0	0		0	0		135
1957	Jim Paschal	15	0	0	0	1	1	2	4	2,236	0	0	1,197	2,650
1957	Fonty Flock	1	0	0	0	1	0	0	0		0	0		1,500
1957	Billy Myers	16	0	0	0	0	2	0	1	1,899	201	1	1,149	2,875

Year	Driver	Starts	Poles	Finish 1	2	3	4	5	6–10	Laps	Laps Led	Races Led	Miles	$

Bill Stroppe *continued*

Year	Driver	Starts	Poles	1	2	3	4	5	6–10	Laps	Laps Led	Races Led	Miles	$
1958	Tim Flock	1	0	0	0	0	0	0	0	3	0	0	12	0
1962	Troy Ruttman	1	0	0	0	0	0	1	0	218	0	0	327	1,750
1963	Larry Frank	2	0	0	0	0	0	0	0	476	0	0	695	850
1963	Chuck Daigh	1	0	0	0	0	0	0	0	37	0	0	93	75
1963	Darel Dieringer	14	0	1	0	1	2	1	6	4,011	84	3	4,791	24,095
1963	G.C. Spencer	3	0	0	0	0	0	0	2	803	1	1	1,354	3,100
1963	Junior Johnson	1	0	0	0	0	0	1	0	145	0	0	392	1,300
1963	Parnelli Jones	4	0	0	0	0	0	0	1	444	39	1	993	2,000
1963	Rodger Ward	2	0	0	0	0	0	0	0	251	0	0	386	325
1963	Troy Ruttman	5	0	0	0	1	0	0	2	796	0	0	1,699	6,430
1963	Whitey Gerkin	1	0	0	0	0	0	0	0	23	0	0	58	75
1964	Joe Weatherly	1	0	0	0	0	1	0	0	137	0	0	411	2,650
1964	Johnny Allen	2	0	0	0	0	0	0	0	239	0	0	299	925
1964	Bill Amick	1	0	0	0	0	1	0	0	181	0	0	489	2,470
1964	Darel Dieringer	11	0	0	0	0	1	2	2	2,166	27	2	2,753	9,515
1964	Dave MacDonald	4	0	0	0	0	0	0	2	523	0	0	1,185	2,450
1964	Jim McElreath	3	0	0	0	0	0	0	0	336	0	0	667	1,350
1964	Parnelli Jones	4	0	0	0	0	0	0	1	202	9	1	502	2,110
1964	Rodger Ward	1	0	0	0	0	0	0	0	24	0	0	65	525
1965	Parnelli Jones	1	0	0	0	0	0	0	0	37	36	1	100	980
1967	Parnelli Jones	1	0	1	0	0	0	0	0	185	126	1	500	18,720
1967	Curtis Turner	1	0	0	0	0	0	0	0	15	0	0	41	550
1967	Dan Gurney	1	0	0	0	0	0	0	0	143	36	1	386	990
1968	Parnelli Jones	1	0	0	0	1	0	0	0	186	49	1	502	5,600
1997	Butch Gilliland	1	0	0	0	0	0	0	0	74	0	0	186	21,410
Lifetime		152	1	5	6	8	10	8	32	22,980	830	20	27,287	$138,905

D. Wayne Strout

Year	Driver	Starts	Poles	1	2	3	4	5	6–10	Laps	Laps Led	Races Led	Miles	$
1987	D. Wayne Strout	1	0	0	0	0	0	0	0	381	0	0	381	1,700
Lifetime		1	0	0	0	0	0	0	0	381	0	0	381	$1,700

M.J. Sullivan

Year	Driver	Starts	Poles	1	2	3	4	5	6–10	Laps	Laps Led	Races Led	Miles	$
1987	Ken Bouchard	1	0	0	0	0	0	0	0	158	0	0	316	2,075
Lifetime		1	0	0	0	0	0	0	0	158	0	0	316	$2,075

Lem Svajian

Year	Driver	Starts	Poles	1	2	3	4	5	6–10	Laps	Laps Led	Races Led	Miles	$
1956	Tommy Herbert	1	0	0	0	0	0	0	0		0	0		0
1957	Lem Svajian	1	0	0	0	0	0	0	0		0	0		50
Lifetime		2	0	0	0	0	0	0	0		0	0		$50

Dale Swanson

Year	Driver	Starts	Poles	1	2	3	4	5	6–10	Laps	Laps Led	Races Led	Miles	$
1960	Johnny Beauchamp	9	0	1	1	0	0	1	2	2,567	1	1	2,441	15,431
1961	Johnny Beauchamp	1	0	0	0	0	0	0	0	37	0	0	93	75
Lifetime		10	0	1	1	0	0	1	2	2,604	1	1	2,533	$15,506

Glen Sweet

Year	Driver	Starts	Poles	1	2	3	4	5	6–10	Laps	Laps Led	Races Led	Miles	$
1965	Tom Pistone	19	0	0	1	0	0	2	3	2,595	0	0	1,406	5,800
1966	Tom Pistone	1	0	0	0	0	0	0	0	265	0	0	133	150
Lifetime		20	0	0	1	0	0	2	3	2,860	0	0	1,538	$5,950

Ken Swihart

Year	Driver	Starts	Poles	1	2	3	4	5	6–10	Laps	Laps Led	Races Led	Miles	$
1951	Ed Benedict	3	0	0	0	0	0	0	0	445	0	0	538	150
1952	Ed Benedict	3	0	0	0	0	0	1	0	220	0	0	173	235
1952	Chuck Mahoney	1	0	0	0	0	0	0	0		0	0		25
1952	Johnny Thompson	1	0	0	0	0	0	0	0		0	0		25
1952	Bucky Sager	1	0	0	0	0	0	0	0	151	0	0	76	25
1953	Ed Benedict	1	0	0	0	0	0	0	1	189	0	0	95	125
Lifetime		10	0	0	0	0	0	1	1	1,005	0	0	881	$585

G.T. Tallas

Year	Driver	Starts	Poles	1	2	3	4	5	6–10	Laps	Laps Led	Races Led	Miles	$
1970	G.T. Tallas	2	0	0	0	0	0	0	0	139	0	0	364	1,585

Year	Driver	Starts	Poles	Finish						Laps	Laps Led	Races Led	Miles	$
				1	2	3	4	5	6–10					

G.T. Tallas *continued*

Year	Driver	Starts	Poles	1	2	3	4	5	6–10	Laps	Laps Led	Races Led	Miles	$
1971	G.T. Tallas	2	0	0	0	0	0	0	0	189	0	0	491	2,490
1972	G.T. Tallas	1	0	0	0	0	0	0	0	88	0	0	220	1,620
1975	G.T. Tallas	1	0	0	0	0	0	0	0	28	0	0	73	825
Lifetime		6	0	0	0	0	0	0	0	444	0	0	1,149	$6,520

Lou Tanner

Year	Driver	Starts	Poles	1	2	3	4	5	6–10	Laps	Laps Led	Races Led	Miles	$
1952	Johnny Patterson	1	0	0	0	0	0	0	0	76	0	0	38	50
Lifetime		1	0	0	0	0	0	0	0	76	0	0	38	$50

Dr. Don Tarr

Year	Driver	Starts	Poles	1	2	3	4	5	6–10	Laps	Laps Led	Races Led	Miles	$
1968	Dr. Don Tarr	11	0	0	0	0	0	0	0	1,699	0	0	2,052	5,825
1968	Frank Warren	4	0	0	0	0	0	0	0	243	0	0	70	400
1969	Earl Brooks	3	0	0	0	0	0	0	0	560	0	0	566	2,045
1969	Dr. Don Tarr	6	0	0	0	0	0	0	0	594	0	0	1,001	3,465
1969	Ed Negre	2	0	0	0	0	0	0	0	24	0	0	47	1,870
1969	Frank Warren	9	0	0	0	0	0	0	1	1,166	0	0	725	2,570
1969	J.D. McDuffie	2	0	0	0	0	0	0	0	354	0	0	347	1,405
1969	Dick Poling	4	0	0	0	0	0	0	0	410	0	0	688	1,892
1970	Dr. Don Tarr	16	0	0	0	0	0	0	4	2,350	5	1	3,037	14,542
1970	James Sears	1	0	0	0	0	0	0	1	193	0	0	97	275
1971	Dr. Don Tarr	2	0	0	0	0	0	0	0	297	0	0	245	1,060
1971	G.C. Spencer	1	0	0	0	0	0	0	0	209	0	0	115	415
1972	J.D. McDuffie	1	0	0	0	0	0	1	0	466	0	0	248	1,300
Lifetime		62	0	0	0	0	0	1	6	8,565	5	1	9,237	$37,064

Robert Tartaglia

Year	Driver	Starts	Poles	1	2	3	4	5	6–10	Laps	Laps Led	Races Led	Miles	$
1981	Robert Tartaglia	1	0	0	0	0	0	0	0	4	0	0	10	500
Lifetime		1	0	0	0	0	0	0	0	4	0	0	10	$500

Al Tasnady

Year	Driver	Starts	Poles	1	2	3	4	5	6–10	Laps	Laps Led	Races Led	Miles	$
1960	Al Tasnady	1	0	0	0	0	0	0	0	172	0	0	86	110
Lifetime		1	0	0	0	0	0	0	0	172	0	0	86	$110

Acey Taylor

Year	Driver	Starts	Poles	1	2	3	4	5	6–10	Laps	Laps Led	Races Led	Miles	$
1963	Ralph Earnhardt	3	0	0	0	0	0	0	0	344	0	0	557	975
1963	Curtis Crider	1	0	0	0	0	0	0	0	205	0	0	282	450
Lifetime		4	0	0	0	0	0	0	0	549	0	0	839	$1,425

Bill Taylor

Year	Driver	Starts	Poles	1	2	3	4	5	6–10	Laps	Laps Led	Races Led	Miles	$
1955	Leland Sowell	1	0	0	0	0	0	0	0	176	0	0	264	125
Lifetime		1	0	0	0	0	0	0	0	176	0	0	264	$125

Don Taylor

Year	Driver	Starts	Poles	1	2	3	4	5	6–10	Laps	Laps Led	Races Led	Miles	$
1958	Eddie Pagan	1	0	0	0	0	0	0	0	36	0	0	95	100
1959	Don Taylor	2	0	0	0	0	0	0	0	430	0	0	214	200
Lifetime		3	0	0	0	0	0	0	0	466	0	0	309	$300

Jesse James Taylor

Year	Driver	Starts	Poles	1	2	3	4	5	6–10	Laps	Laps Led	Races Led	Miles	$
1950	Jesse James Taylor	1	0	0	0	0	0	0	0	329	0	0	411	0
1951	Jesse James Taylor	10	0	0	1	0	0	0	2	519	104	3	566	3,225
1956	Jesse James Taylor	3	0	0	0	0	0	0	0	269	0	0	186	250
1958	Jesse James Taylor	1	0	0	0	0	0	0	0	95	0	0	131	100
Lifetime		15	0	0	1	0	0	0	2	1,212	104	3	1,294	$3,575

T.W. Taylor

Year	Driver	Starts	Poles	1	2	3	4	5	6–10	Laps	Laps Led	Races Led	Miles	$
1993	T.W. Taylor	3	0	0	0	0	0	0	0	280	1	1	391	19,205
1994	Derrike Cope	2	0	0	0	0	0	0	0	356	0	0	890	35,110
1994	Jeff Purvis	1	0	0	0	0	0	0	0	139	0	0	278	8,715
1994	Randy LaJoie	1	0	0	0	0	0	0	0	318	0	0	484	8,575

Year	Driver	Starts	Poles	Finish 1	2	3	4	5	6–10	Laps	Laps Led	Races Led	Miles	$

T.W. Taylor *continued*

Year	Driver	Starts	Poles	1	2	3	4	5	6–10	Laps	Laps Led	Races Led	Miles	$
1994	Curtis Markham	1	0	0	0	0	0	0	0	32	0	0	49	8,325
1994	Jeremy Mayfield	4	0	0	0	0	0	0	0	1,046	0	0	1,694	39,145
Lifetime		12	0	0	0	0	0	0	0	2,171	1	1	3,785	$119,075

W.O. Taylor

Year	Driver	Starts	Poles	1	2	3	4	5	6–10	Laps	Laps Led	Races Led	Miles	$
1949	Tommy Coates	1	0	0	0	0	0	0	0	167	0	0	167	50
1949	Al Keller	1	0	0	0	0	0	0	1	185	0	0	185	200
1950	Al Keller	2	0	0	0	0	0	0	0	328	0	0	538	50
Lifetime		4	0	0	0	0	0	0	1	680	0	0	890	$300

Kerry Teague

Year	Driver	Starts	Poles	1	2	3	4	5	6–10	Laps	Laps Led	Races Led	Miles	$
1992	Kerry Teague	1	0	0	0	0	0	0	0	122	0	0	305	22,445
Lifetime		1	0	0	0	0	0	0	0	122	0	0	305	$22,445

Marshall Teague

Year	Driver	Starts	Poles	1	2	3	4	5	6–10	Laps	Laps Led	Races Led	Miles	$
1951	Herb Thomas	2	1	1	0	0	0	0	0	200	1	1	100	1,025
1951	Marshall Teague	15	1	5	0	2	0	0	2	1,611	789	8	1,417	7,410
1952	Marshall Teague	4	1	2	0	0	0	0	0	317	236	2	299	2,550
1952	Herb Thomas	2	0	0	2	0	0	0	0	237	1	1	252	1,700
1952	Mike Klapak	1	0	0	0	0	0	0	0		0	0		0
1952	Pepper Cunningham	1	0	0	0	0	0	0	0		0	0		25
Lifetime		25	3	8	2	2	0	0	2	2,365	1,027	12	2,068	$12,710

Buddy Teasley

Year	Driver	Starts	Poles	1	2	3	4	5	6–10	Laps	Laps Led	Races Led	Miles	$
1951	Jimmie Lewallen	1	0	0	0	0	0	0	0	135	0	0	101	25
Lifetime		1	0	0	0	0	0	0	0	135	0	0	101	$25

Steve Temme

Year	Driver	Starts	Poles	1	2	3	4	5	6–10	Laps	Laps Led	Races Led	Miles	$
1977	Ron McGee	1	0	0	0	0	0	0	0	103	0	0	258	950
Lifetime		1	0	0	0	0	0	0	0	103	0	0	258	$950

Dave Terrell

Year	Driver	Starts	Poles	1	2	3	4	5	6–10	Laps	Laps Led	Races Led	Miles	$
1952	Dave Terrell	5	0	0	0	0	0	1	2	477	0	0	306	475
1954	Dave Terrell	29	0	0	0	0	0	0	8	3,858	0	0	2,581	1,750
1955	Dave Terrell	25	0	0	0	2	0	1	7	3,199	9	1	2,433	3,245
1955	Dick Rathmann	1	0	0	0	0	0	0	0	76	0	0	76	25
1956	Dave Terrell	5	0	0	0	0	0	0	1	363	0	0	235	260
1957	Dave Terrell	2	0	0	0	0	0	0	1	290	0	0	290	750
1958	Dave Terrell	1	0	0	0	0	0	0	0	113	0	0	57	50
Lifetime		68	0	0	0	2	0	2	19	8,376	9	1	5,976	$6,555

Kevin Terris

Year	Driver	Starts	Poles	1	2	3	4	5	6–10	Laps	Laps Led	Races Led	Miles	$
1970	Kevin Terris	1	0	0	0	0	0	0	0	165	0	0	432	1,250
1984	Kevin Terris	1	0	0	0	0	0	0	0	78	0	0	204	1,275
Lifetime		2	0	0	0	0	0	0	0	243	0	0	637	$2,525

Bill Terry

Year	Driver	Starts	Poles	1	2	3	4	5	6–10	Laps	Laps Led	Races Led	Miles	$
1982	Dr. Bob Jarvis	1	0	0	0	0	0	0	0	145	0	0	86	595
1982	Bosco Lowe	1	0	0	0	0	0	0	0	381	0	0	572	3,900
1983	Butch Lindley	1	0	0	0	0	0	0	0	122	0	0	64	1,050
1983	Bosco Lowe	1	0	0	0	0	0	0	0	36	0	0	90	5,350
1983	Tommy Ellis	1	0	0	0	0	0	0	0	386	0	0	579	4,350
1985	Alan Kulwicki	5	0	0	0	0	0	0	0	1,843	0	0	1,998	10,290
1986	Alan Kulwicki	14	0	0	0	0	1	0	2	4,530	7	4	5,222	51,470
Lifetime		24	0	0	0	0	1	0	2	7,443	7	4	8,610	$77,005

Jim Testa

Year	Driver	Starts	Poles	1	2	3	4	5	6–10	Laps	Laps Led	Races Led	Miles	$
1979	Chuck Bown	7	0	0	0	0	0	0	2	1,388	0	0	2,143	31,380
1980	Lennie Pond	13	0	0	0	1	1	0	4	2,790	68	6	3,248	36,365

Year	Driver	Starts	Poles	Finish 1	2	3	4	5	6–10	Laps	Laps Led	Races Led	Miles	$

Jim Testa *continued*

Year	Driver	Starts	Poles	1	2	3	4	5	6–10	Laps	Laps Led	Races Led	Miles	$
1980	Chuck Bown	1	0	0	0	0	0	0	0	50	0	0	125	3,350
1980	John Greenwood	2	0	0	0	0	0	0	0	174	0	0	411	2,730
1981	Lennie Pond	2	0	0	0	0	0	0	0	550	0	0	602	7,320
1984	Lennie Pond	1	0	0	0	0	0	0	0	9	0	0	12	1,000
1988	Derrike Cope	26	0	0	0	0	0	0	0	4,772	0	0	6,539	120,435
1989	Derrike Cope	3	0	0	0	0	0	0	0	451	0	0	632	5,440
Lifetime		55	0	0	0	1	1	0	6	10,184	68	6	13,711	$208,020

Marvin Thaxton

Year	Driver	Starts	Poles	1	2	3	4	5	6–10	Laps	Laps Led	Races Led	Miles	$
1982	Glenn Jarrett	1	0	0	0	0	0	0	0	35	0	0	53	735
Lifetime		1	0	0	0	0	0	0	0	35	0	0	53	$735

Donald Thomas

Year	Driver	Starts	Poles	1	2	3	4	5	6–10	Laps	Laps Led	Races Led	Miles	$
1956	Donald Thomas	2	0	0	0	0	0	0	1	103	0	0	52	175
Lifetime		2	0	0	0	0	0	0	1	103	0	0	52	$175

Herb Thomas

Year	Driver	Starts	Poles	1	2	3	4	5	6–10	Laps	Laps Led	Races Led	Miles	$
1949	Herb Thomas	4	0	0	0	0	0	1	0	197	0	0	99	225
1950	Herb Thomas	12	0	1	0	2	1	0	2	719	176	2	438	2,500
1950	Donald Thomas	2	0	0	0	0	0	0	2	141	0	0	71	250
1951	Donald Thomas	17	0	0	0	1	0	3	4	479	0	0	563	2,150
1951	Herb Thomas	31	3	5	1	3	4	1	2	1,719	774	8	1,456	17,075
1952	Donald Thomas	4	1	1	1	1	0	0	0	605	9	1	453	2,255
1952	Herb Thomas	30	10	8	5	3	0	1	3	4,897	1,507	15	3,223	15,925
1952	Smokey Yunick	1	0	0	0	0	0	0	0	7	0	0	4	25
1953	Jim Reed	2	0	0	0	0	1	0	0	260	0	0	358	610
1953	Donald Thomas	8	0	0	0	0	0	0	4	1,002	0	0	1,103	1,275
1953	Herb Thomas	37	11	12	8	3	3	1	4	4,292	1,419	23	3,107	24,300
1954	Herb Thomas	34	8	12	4	1	2	0	8	5,505	1,366	18	3,898	27,540
1954	Donald Thomas	3	0	0	0	0	0	1	0	403	0	0	220	350
1955	Fonty Flock	2	0	0	0	0	0	0	0	85	0	0	43	0
1955	Speedy Thompson	1	0	0	0	0	0	0	0	145	0	0	73	50
1955	Herb Thomas	21	2	3	3	3	3	2	1	3,121	250	7	2,551	16,295
1955	Donald Thomas	10	0	0	0	0	2	0	2	1,320	0	0	855	1,240
1956	Herb Thomas	27	0	1	0	2	5	3	9	4,676	299	2	3,193	8,285
1957	Paul Goldsmith	1	0	0	0	0	0	0	0	83	0	0	33	50
1957	Fonty Flock	1	0	0	0	0	0	0	0	18	0	0	25	100
1957	Herb Thomas	2	0	0	0	0	0	0	0	146	0	0	123	25
1957	Marvin Panch	3	0	1	0	0	0	0	0	326	9	1	320	3,700
Lifetime		253	35	44	22	19	21	13	41	30,146	5,809	77	22,206	$124,225

J.C. Thomas

Year	Driver	Starts	Poles	1	2	3	4	5	6–10	Laps	Laps Led	Races Led	Miles	$
1964	Sam McQuagg	1	0	0	0	0	0	0	0	111	0	0	56	100
Lifetime		1	0	0	0	0	0	0	0	111	0	0	56	$100

J.L. Thomas

Year	Driver	Starts	Poles	1	2	3	4	5	6–10	Laps	Laps Led	Races Led	Miles	$
1964	Sam McQuagg	4	0	0	0	0	0	0	0	542	0	0	787	1,600
Lifetime		4	0	0	0	0	0	0	0	542	0	0	787	$1,600

Jabe Thomas

Year	Driver	Starts	Poles	1	2	3	4	5	6–10	Laps	Laps Led	Races Led	Miles	$
1965	Ned Jarrett	1	0	0	1	0	0	0	0	199	0	0	100	600
1965	Paul Moore	1	0	0	0	0	0	0	0	9	0	0	12	520
1965	Jabe Thomas	9	0	0	0	0	0	0	1	1,919	0	0	1,401	3,735
1965	Junior Spencer	1	0	0	0	0	0	0	0	240	0	0	360	510
1969	Jabe Thomas	1	0	0	0	0	0	0	0	187	0	0	468	2,495
Lifetime		13	0	0	1	0	0	0	1	2,554	0	0	2,341	$7,860

James Thomas

Year	Driver	Starts	Poles	1	2	3	4	5	6–10	Laps	Laps Led	Races Led	Miles	$
1974	Mike James	1	0	0	0	0	0	0	0	103	0	0	270	995
Lifetime		1	0	0	0	0	0	0	0	103	0	0	270	$995

Year	Driver	Starts	Poles	Finish 1	2	3	4	5	6–10	Laps	Laps Led	Races Led	Miles	$

Larry Thomas

Year	Driver	Starts	Poles	1	2	3	4	5	6–10	Laps	Laps Led	Races Led	Miles	$
1964	Larry Thomas	1	0	0	0	0	0	0	1	478	0	0	209	450
Lifetime		1	0	0	0	0	0	0	1	478	0	0	209	$450

Ronnie Thomas

Year	Driver	Starts	Poles	1	2	3	4	5	6–10	Laps	Laps Led	Races Led	Miles	$
1979	Ronnie Thomas	1	0	0	0	0	0	0	0	378	0	0	225	2,020
1981	Joe Booher	1	0	0	0	0	0	0	0	4	0	0	11	1,700
1981	Ronnie Thomas	21	0	0	0	0	0	0	0	5,544	0	0	5,523	49,975
1981	Dick May	1	0	0	0	0	0	0	1	183	0	0	487	8,745
1982	Ronnie Thomas	16	0	0	0	0	0	0	0	2,899	0	0	2,746	17,880
1983	Ronnie Thomas	25	0	0	0	0	0	0	0	6,785	1	1	7,513	46,165
1984	Buddy Arrington	1	0	0	0	0	0	0	0	67	0	0	42	2,485
1984	Ronnie Thomas	21	0	0	0	0	0	0	0	4,976	2	1	5,761	79,325
1985	Ronnie Thomas	7	0	0	0	0	0	0	0	1,510	0	0	1,157	10,505
1986	Ronnie Thomas	3	0	0	0	0	0	0	0	522	0	0	455	4,290
1987	Ronnie Thomas	4	0	0	0	0	0	0	0	874	0	0	694	5,020
Lifetime		101	0	0	0	0	0	0	1	23,742	3	2	24,614	$228,110

Bruce Thompson

Year	Driver	Starts	Poles	1	2	3	4	5	6–10	Laps	Laps Led	Races Led	Miles	$
1949	Jimmy Thompson	2	0	0	0	0	0	0	2		0	0		175
1950	Speedy Thompson	1	0	0	0	0	0	0	0		0	0		0
1959	Jimmy Thompson	3	0	0	0	0	0	0	0	511	0	0	621	625
1959	Speedy Thompson	7	0	0	0	0	1	0	2	1,153	0	0	577	840
1959	Richard Riley	4	0	0	0	0	0	0	1	578	0	0	340	450
1960	Speedy Thompson	1	0	0	0	0	0	1	0	193	0	0	97	250
1960	Bunk Moore	1	0	0	0	0	0	0	0	147	0	0	74	85
Lifetime		19	0	0	0	0	1	1	5	2,582	0	0	1,707	$2,425

Jimmy Thompson

Year	Driver	Starts	Poles	1	2	3	4	5	6–10	Laps	Laps Led	Races Led	Miles	$
1957	Jimmy Thompson	1	0	0	0	0	0	0	0	328	0	0	451	225
Lifetime		1	0	0	0	0	0	0	0	328	0	0	451	$225

Mark Thompson

Year	Driver	Starts	Poles	1	2	3	4	5	6–10	Laps	Laps Led	Races Led	Miles	$
1999	David Murry	1	0	0	0	0	0	0	0	78	0	0	191	21,965
Lifetime		1	0	0	0	0	0	0	0	78	0	0	191	$21,965

Maurice Thompson

Year	Driver	Starts	Poles	1	2	3	4	5	6–10	Laps	Laps Led	Races Led	Miles	$
1955	Jim McLain	1	0	0	0	0	0	0	0	36	0	0	148	35
Lifetime		1	0	0	0	0	0	0	0	36	0	0	148	$35

Speedy Thompson

Year	Driver	Starts	Poles	1	2	3	4	5	6–10	Laps	Laps Led	Races Led	Miles	$
1957	Speedy Thompson	20	3	2	2	0	4	1	4	3,610	593	6	2,452	19,370
1958	Speedy Thompson	37	7	4	2	7	3	3	5	6,464	230	7	3,964	14,670
1958	Jimmy Thompson	1	0	0	0	0	0	0	1	483	0	0	242	375
Lifetime		58	10	6	4	7	7	4	10	10,557	823	13	6,657	$34,415

Tommy Thompson

Year	Driver	Starts	Poles	1	2	3	4	5	6–10	Laps	Laps Led	Races Led	Miles	$
1950	Tommy Thompson	3	0	0	0	0	0	0	0	272	0	0	439	75
1951	Tommy Thompson	4	0	1	0	0	0	0	1	250	58	1	250	5,300
1952	Tommy Thompson	4	0	0	0	0	0	0	1	333	20	1	419	500
1953	Tommy Thompson	2	0	0	0	1	0	0	0	39	0	0	160	840
1954	Tommy Thompson	1	0	0	0	0	0	0	0	15	0	0	62	0
1959	Earl Balmer	2	0	0	0	0	0	0	0	436	0	0	423	250
1959	Tommy Thompson	3	0	0	0	0	0	0	0	367	0	0	422	510
1959	Chuck Tombs	1	0	0	0	0	0	0	0	134	0	0	67	0
1959	Andy Hampton	1	0	0	0	0	0	0	0	76	0	0	38	50
Lifetime		21	0	1	0	1	0	0	2	1,922	78	2	2,279	$7,525

Gene Thonesen

Year	Driver	Starts	Poles	1	2	3	4	5	6–10	Laps	Laps Led	Races Led	Miles	$
1981	Gene Thonesen	1	0	0	0	0	0	0	0	110	0	0	288	2,125
Lifetime		1	0	0	0	0	0	0	0	110	0	0	288	$2,125

Year	Driver	Starts	Poles	Finish 1	2	3	4	5	6–10	Laps	Laps Led	Races Led	Miles	$

Dean Thorne

Year	Driver	Starts	Poles	1	2	3	4	5	6–10	Laps	Laps Led	Races Led	Miles	$
1970	Carl Joiner	1	0	0	0	0	0	0	0	23	0	0	60	800
1971	Carl Joiner	3	0	0	0	0	0	0	1	385	0	0	987	4,250
1972	Carl Joiner	2	0	0	0	0	0	1	0	283	0	0	741	3,420
1973	Carl Joiner	1	0	0	0	0	0	0	0	46	0	0	121	1,015
Lifetime		7	0	0	0	0	0	1	1	737	0	0	1,909	$9,485

Jon Thorne

Year	Driver	Starts	Poles	1	2	3	4	5	6–10	Laps	Laps Led	Races Led	Miles	$
1966	LeeRoy Yarbrough	9	2	1	0	0	1	0	2	1,545	364	5	2,546	23,980
1967	Donnie Allison	7	0	0	0	0	1	0	2	1,869	1	1	2,585	8,815
1967	LeeRoy Yarbrough	5	0	1	0	0	0	0	0	457	20	2	696	4,540
Lifetime		21	2	2	0	0	2	0	4	3,871	385	8	5,827	$37,335

Roy Thornley

Year	Driver	Starts	Poles	1	2	3	4	5	6–10	Laps	Laps Led	Races Led	Miles	$
1974	Richie Panch	26	0	0	0	1	0	1	5	6,105	1	1	6,788	43,616
Lifetime		26	0	0	0	1	0	1	5	6,105	1	1	6,788	$43,616

LeRoy Throop

Year	Driver	Starts	Poles	1	2	3	4	5	6–10	Laps	Laps Led	Races Led	Miles	$
1986	Butch Miller	3	0	0	0	0	0	0	0	799	0	0	891	5,085
1987	Butch Miller	2	0	0	0	0	0	0	0	215	0	0	307	3,145
1989	Butch Miller	9	0	0	0	0	0	0	0	1,129	0	0	1,194	22,520
Lifetime		14	0	0	0	0	0	0	0	2,143	0	0	2,392	$30,750

Ken Thurlby

Year	Driver	Starts	Poles	1	2	3	4	5	6–10	Laps	Laps Led	Races Led	Miles	$
1975	John Banks	3	0	0	0	0	0	0	0	478	0	0	816	2,760
Lifetime		3	0	0	0	0	0	0	0	478	0	0	816	$2,760

Billy Tibbett

Year	Driver	Starts	Poles	1	2	3	4	5	6–10	Laps	Laps Led	Races Led	Miles	$
1951	Billy Tibbett	2	0	0	0	0	0	0	0	318	0	0	398	75
Lifetime		2	0	0	0	0	0	0	0	318	0	0	398	$75

L.W. Tickle

Year	Driver	Starts	Poles	1	2	3	4	5	6–10	Laps	Laps Led	Races Led	Miles	$
1952	Al Fleming	1	0	0	0	0	0	0	0	336	0	0	420	210
Lifetime		1	0	0	0	0	0	0	0	336	0	0	420	$210

Willie Tierney

Year	Driver	Starts	Poles	1	2	3	4	5	6–10	Laps	Laps Led	Races Led	Miles	$
1991	Jerry Hill	1	0	0	0	0	0	0	0	39	0	0	39	3,500
1992	T.W. Taylor	1	0	0	0	0	0	0	0	138	0	0	367	6,045
1992	Jerry Hill	4	0	0	0	0	0	0	0	520	0	0	554	17,705
1993	Jerry Hill	2	0	0	0	0	0	0	0	353	0	0	359	12,885
Lifetime		8	0	0	0	0	0	0	0	1,050	0	0	1,319	$40,135

Adelmo Tiezzi

Year	Driver	Starts	Poles	1	2	3	4	5	6–10	Laps	Laps Led	Races Led	Miles	$
1956	Benny DeRosier	4	0	0	0	0	0	0	0	236	0	0	236	200
Lifetime		4	0	0	0	0	0	0	0	236	0	0	236	$200

Travis Tiller

Year	Driver	Starts	Poles	1	2	3	4	5	6–10	Laps	Laps Led	Races Led	Miles	$
1974	Travis Tiller	13	0	0	0	0	0	0	0	2,180	0	0	2,299	10,465
1975	Travis Tiller	10	0	0	0	0	0	0	0	1,958	0	0	2,178	7,780
1976	Travis Tiller	9	0	0	0	0	0	0	0	2,012	0	0	1,787	6,310
1977	Travis Tiller	3	0	0	0	0	0	0	0	250	0	0	183	1,615
1979	Travis Tiller	5	0	0	0	0	0	0	0	218	0	0	336	5,065
1980	Travis Tiller	3	0	0	0	0	0	0	0	507	0	0	561	2,280
1981	Travis Tiller	1	0	0	0	0	0	0	0	111	0	0	169	850
1982	Travis Tiller	4	0	0	0	0	0	0	0	557	0	0	1,107	6,395
1983	Travis Tiller	2	0	0	0	0	0	0	0	338	0	0	463	4,360
Lifetime		50	0	0	0	0	0	0	0	8,131	0	0	9,084	$45,120

Herb Tillman

Year	Driver	Starts	Poles	1	2	3	4	5	6–10	Laps	Laps Led	Races Led	Miles	$
1953	Herb Tillman	2	0	0	0	0	0	0	0	122	0	0	126	50
Lifetime		2	0	0	0	0	0	0	0	122	0	0	126	$50

Year	Driver	Starts	Poles	Finish						Laps	Laps Led	Races Led	Miles	$
				1	2	3	4	5	6–10					

Leonard Tippett

Year	Driver	Starts	Poles	1	2	3	4	5	6–10	Laps	Laps Led	Races Led	Miles	$
1951	Herb Thomas	1	0	0	0	0	0	0	0	40	0	0	30	25
1951	Leonard Tippett	8	0	0	1	0	0	0	1	359	19	1	270	850
1952	Leonard Tippett	5	0	0	0	0	0	0	0	221	0	0	134	150
Lifetime		14	0	0	1	0	0	0	1	620	19	1	433	$1,025

Randy Tissot

Year	Driver	Starts	Poles	1	2	3	4	5	6–10	Laps	Laps Led	Races Led	Miles	$
1973	Randy Tissot	3	0	0	0	0	0	0	0	816	0	0	1,390	4,245
1974	Randy Tissot	3	0	0	0	0	0	0	0	473	8	1	839	3,750
Lifetime		6	0	0	0	0	0	0	0	1,289	8	1	2,229	$7,995

T.A. Toomes

Year	Driver	Starts	Poles	1	2	3	4	5	6–10	Laps	Laps Led	Races Led	Miles	$
1957	T.A. Toomes	1	0	0	0	0	0	0	0	473	0	0	237	200
Lifetime		1	0	0	0	0	0	0	0	473	0	0	237	$200

Warren Tope

Year	Driver	Starts	Poles	1	2	3	4	5	6–10	Laps	Laps Led	Races Led	Miles	$
1975	Warren Tope	2	0	0	0	0	0	0	0	305	0	0	467	3,170
Lifetime		2	0	0	0	0	0	0	0	305	0	0	467	$3,170

Ward Towers

Year	Driver	Starts	Poles	1	2	3	4	5	6–10	Laps	Laps Led	Races Led	Miles	$
1958	Ward Towers	1	0	0	0	0	0	0	0	34	0	0	139	90
Lifetime		1	0	0	0	0	0	0	0	34	0	0	139	$90

Frank Townsend

Year	Driver	Starts	Poles	1	2	3	4	5	6–10	Laps	Laps Led	Races Led	Miles	$
1969	Marty Kinerk	1	0	0	0	0	0	0	0	40	0	0	108	755
Lifetime		1	0	0	0	0	0	0	0	40	0	0	108	$755

Roy Trantham

Year	Driver	Starts	Poles	1	2	3	4	5	6–10	Laps	Laps Led	Races Led	Miles	$
1968	David Pearson	1	0	0	0	0	0	0	0	300	0	0	150	0
1968	G.C. Spencer	2	0	0	0	0	0	0	1	516	0	0	502	1,200
Lifetime		3	0	0	0	0	0	0	1	816	0	0	652	$1,200

Tom Travis

Year	Driver	Starts	Poles	1	2	3	4	5	6–10	Laps	Laps Led	Races Led	Miles	$
1953	Slow Poke Travis	1	0	0	0	0	0	0	0	33	0	0	135	25
Lifetime		1	0	0	0	0	0	0	0	33	0	0	135	$25

Herb Trimble

Year	Driver	Starts	Poles	1	2	3	4	5	6–10	Laps	Laps Led	Races Led	Miles	$
1951	Herb Trimble	2	0	0	0	0	0	0	1	198	0	0	248	50
Lifetime		2	0	0	0	0	0	0	1	198	0	0	248	$50

Tri-Star Motorsports (Primary Tri-Star Motorsports owners were George Bradshaw and Mark Smith. Statistics represent all Tri-Star Motorsports owners, including changes in ownership during the tenure of the team.)

Year	Driver	Starts	Poles	1	2	3	4	5	6–10	Laps	Laps Led	Races Led	Miles	$
1989	Ron Esau	1	0	0	0	0	0	0	0	117	0	0	311	3,460
1989	Brad Teague	1	0	0	0	0	0	0	0	245	0	0	368	2,350
1990	Stanley Smith	1	0	0	0	0	0	0	0	54	0	0	144	4,285
1990	Bobby Hamilton	2	0	0	0	0	0	0	0	305	0	0	458	6,125
1990	Hut Stricklin	2	0	0	0	0	0	0	0	274	0	0	603	21,525
1991	Bobby Hamilton	28	0	0	0	0	0	0	4	8,214	7	3	10,141	223,955
1992	Bobby Hamilton	29	0	0	0	0	0	0	2	8,998	0	0	10,737	357,065
1993	Loy Allen Jr.	1	0	0	0	0	0	0	0	305	0	0	305	6,560
1993	Greg Sacks	18	0	0	0	0	0	0	1	4,931	1	1	6,732	154,100
1993	Dorsey Schroeder	2	0	0	0	0	0	0	0	69	0	0	174	13,615
1993	Bobby Hamilton	8	0	0	0	0	0	0	0	2,141	0	0	2,455	84,710
1994	Loy Allen Jr.	19	3	0	0	0	0	0	0	4,446	12	3	6,776	215,751
1995	Loy Allen Jr.	6	0	0	0	0	0	0	0	1,248	0	0	2,109	52,165
1995	Phil Parsons	2	0	0	0	0	0	0	0	36	0	0	81	41,450
1995	Ron Fellows	1	0	0	0	0	0	0	0	40	0	0	98	9,035
1996	Loy Allen Jr.	9	0	0	0	0	0	0	0	1,439	0	0	2,772	130,667
Lifetime		130	3	0	0	0	0	0	7	32,862	20	7	44,264	$1,326,818

Year	Driver	Starts	Poles	Finish						Laps	Laps Led	Races Led	Miles	$
				1	2	3	4	5	6–10					

E.J. Trivette

Year	Driver	Starts	Poles	1	2	3	4	5	6–10	Laps	Laps Led	Races Led	Miles	$
1959	E.J. Trivette	4	0	0	0	0	0	0	0	534	0	0	285	175
Lifetime		4	0	0	0	0	0	0	0	534	0	0	285	$175

Bob Tullius

Year	Driver	Starts	Poles	1	2	3	4	5	6–10	Laps	Laps Led	Races Led	Miles	$
1989	Jim Sauter	8	0	0	0	0	0	0	1	1,893	8	1	2,706	30,237
1990	Jimmy Horton	1	0	0	0	0	0	0	0	323	0	0	485	3,525
Lifetime		9	0	0	0	0	0	0	1	2,216	8	1	3,190	$33,762

Reino Tulonen

Year	Driver	Starts	Poles	1	2	3	4	5	6–10	Laps	Laps Led	Races Led	Miles	$
1951	Reino Tulonen	4	0	0	0	0	0	0	0	353	0	0	441	400
Lifetime		4	0	0	0	0	0	1	0	353	0	0	441	$400

Curtis Turner

Year	Driver	Starts	Poles	1	2	3	4	5	6–10	Laps	Laps Led	Races Led	Miles	$
1949	Curtis Turner	3	0	0	0	0	0	0	1		0	0		125
Lifetime		3	0	0	0	0	0	0	1		0	0		$125

James Turner

Year	Driver	Starts	Poles	1	2	3	4	5	6–10	Laps	Laps Led	Races Led	Miles	$
1961	Roscoe Thompson	6	0	0	0	0	0	0	2	721	0	0	1,341	2,535
1961	Darel Dieringer	1	0	0	0	0	0	0	0	238	0	0	357	575
1962	Billy Wade	3	0	0	0	0	0	0	2	872	0	0	483	925
Lifetime		10	0	0	0	0	0	0	4	1,831	0	0	2,181	$4,035

Carl Tyler

Year	Driver	Starts	Poles	1	2	3	4	5	6–10	Laps	Laps Led	Races Led	Miles	$
1958	Carl Tyler	10	0	0	0	0	0	0	0	1,016	0	0	843	745
1959	Carl Tyler	2	0	0	0	0	0	0	0	63	0	0	158	150
Lifetime		12	0	0	0	0	0	0	0	1,079	0	0	1,001	$895

Paul Tyler

Year	Driver	Starts	Poles	1	2	3	4	5	6–10	Laps	Laps Led	Races Led	Miles	$
1971	Paul Tyler	9	0	0	0	0	0	0	0	1,510	0	0	1,679	6,335
Lifetime		9	0	0	0	0	0	0	0	1,510	0	0	1,679	$6,335

Roy Tyner

Year	Driver	Starts	Poles	1	2	3	4	5	6–10	Laps	Laps Led	Races Led	Miles	$
1957	Roy Tyner	10	0	0	0	0	0	0	2	1,705	0	0	1,099	1,055
1958	Roy Tyner	1	0	0	0	0	0	0	0	126	0	0	42	110
1959	Cotton Owens	1	0	0	0	0	0	0	1	290	0	0	145	450
1959	Johnny Allen	1	0	0	0	0	0	0	0	57	0	0	57	50
1959	Roy Tyner	27	0	0	1	0	3	3	7	5,103	0	0	3,269	5,180
1960	Roy Tyner	15	0	0	0	0	1	0	2	1,156	0	0	747	1,815
1960	Jim Austin	2	0	0	0	0	0	0	0	199	0	0	124	310
1961	Roy Tyner	8	0	0	0	0	0	0	1	1,322	0	0	1,109	960
1963	Roy Tyner	8	0	0	0	0	0	0	0	381	0	0	193	1,345
1964	Roy Tyner	46	0	0	0	0	0	0	17	7,327	0	0	4,641	10,505
1965	Darel Dieringer	4	0	0	0	0	0	0	2	658	0	0	346	710
1965	J.T. Putney	1	0	0	0	0	0	0	1	161	0	0	81	140
1965	Roy Tyner	27	0	0	0	0	1	0	5	3,284	0	0	1,729	6,046
1965	William Gardner	2	0	0	0	0	0	0	0	61	0	0	31	200
1966	Roy Tyner	2	0	0	0	0	0	0	0	270	0	0	186	600
1968	Bill Vanderhoff	10	0	0	0	0	0	0	0	788	0	0	364	1,950
1968	Jack Ingram	1	0	0	0	0	0	0	1	481	0	0	241	700
1968	Stan Meserve	1	0	0	0	0	0	0	0	168	0	0	84	100
1968	Wendell Scott	1	0	0	0	0	0	0	0	252	0	0	347	850
1968	Ben Arnold	1	0	0	0	0	0	0	0	284	0	0	391	825
1968	Glenn Luce	1	0	0	0	0	0	0	0	223	0	0	74	125
1968	Roy Tyner	28	0	0	0	0	2	1	6	5,437	0	0	3,015	9,125
1969	Roy Tyner	21	0	0	0	0	0	0	1	3,285	0	0	3,030	12,317
1969	Worth McMillion	1	0	0	0	0	0	0	0	328	0	0	164	480
1969	Earl Brooks	1	0	0	0	0	0	0	0	313	0	0	318	945
1970	Roy Tyner	12	0	0	0	0	0	0	2	1,676	0	0	1,050	4,660
Lifetime		233	0	0	1	0	7	4	48	35,335	0	0	22,872	$61,553

Year	Driver	Starts	Poles	Finish 1	2	3	4	5	6–10	Laps	Laps Led	Races Led	Miles	$

Lynton Tyson

Year	Driver	Starts	Poles	1	2	3	4	5	6–10	Laps	Laps Led	Races Led	Miles	$
1959	Buddy Baker	5	0	0	0	0	1	0	1	794	0	0	397	875
1959	Jim Paschal	1	0	0	0	0	0	0	1	356	0	0	490	1,460
1959	Banjo Matthews	1	0	0	0	0	0	0	0	137	0	0	69	0
1959	Fireball Roberts	1	0	0	0	0	0	0	0	303	0	0	152	75
1959	Buck Baker	12	1	1	0	2	0	0	3	3,029	1	1	1,870	4,295
1960	Buck Baker	1	1	0	0	1	0	0	0	198	35	1	99	375
1960	Larry Frank	3	0	0	0	0	0	0	0	405	0	0	786	400
1960	Buddy Baker	1	0	0	0	0	0	0	0	34	0	0	17	0
Lifetime		25	2	1	0	3	1	0	5	5,256	36	2	3,879	$7,480

D.K. Ulrich (Statistics include several partnerships and shared ownership during the tenure of Ulrich's team.)

Year	Driver	Starts	Poles	1	2	3	4	5	6–10	Laps	Laps Led	Races Led	Miles	$
1971	Roy Mayne	1	0	0	0	0	0	0	1	320	0	0	437	2,050
1971	Dick May	1	0	0	0	0	0	0	0	436	0	0	436	855
1971	D.K. Ulrich	12	0	0	0	0	0	0	0	1,526	0	0	1,064	3,955
1972	D.K. Ulrich	4	0	0	0	0	0	0	0	1,001	0	0	1,041	2,695
1973	D.K. Ulrich	11	0	0	0	0	0	0	0	2,006	0	0	2,125	8,695
1973	Frank Warren	3	0	0	0	0	0	0	0	828	0	0	467	1,705
1974	Tony Bettenhausen,	1	0	0	0	0	0	0	0	443	0	0	451	1,300
1974	Harry Schilling	1	0	0	0	0	0	0	0	65	0	0	170	1,005
1974	Ed Negre	1	0	0	0	0	0	0	0	150	0	0	300	1,025
1974	D.K. Ulrich	14	0	0	0	0	0	0	0	3,148	0	0	3,514	11,000
1975	Randy Bethea	1	0	0	0	0	0	0	0	251	0	0	377	1,055
1975	D.K. Ulrich	16	0	0	0	0	0	0	1	3,448	0	0	4,093	15,775
1978	D.K. Ulrich	22	0	0	0	0	0	0	3	6,175	1	1	7,425	53,800
1979	Al Elmore	1	0	0	0	0	0	0	0	389	0	0	232	1,265
1979	D.K. Ulrich	30	0	0	0	0	0	0	5	8,612	0	0	9,816	99,030
1980	Dick Skillen	1	0	0	0	0	0	0	0	76	0	0	202	2,785
1980	Lennie Pond	1	0	0	0	0	0	0	0	156	0	0	390	5,385
1980	J.D. McDuffie	1	0	0	0	0	0	0	0	145	0	0	218	2,800
1980	Dick May	2	0	0	0	0	0	0	1	962	0	0	741	6,625
1980	D.K. Ulrich	10	0	0	0	0	0	0	1	1,732	0	0	1,896	22,575
1980	Bill Whittington	2	0	0	0	0	0	0	1	183	0	0	472	7,385
1980	Mike Alexander	1	0	0	0	0	0	0	1	409	0	0	244	3,130
1980	Ricky Rudd	3	0	0	0	0	0	0	0	791	6	1	939	8,025
1980	Joe Booher	1	0	0	0	0	0	0	0	376	0	0	204	2,350
1980	Stan Barrett	3	0	0	0	0	0	0	1	987	0	0	1,454	13,760
1980	Sterling Marlin	1	0	0	0	0	0	0	1	413	0	0	246	4,335
1980	Tim Richmond	4	0	0	0	0	0	0	0	1,249	0	0	1,483	14,195
1980	Tommy Gale	1	0	0	0	0	0	0	0	194	0	0	388	3,405
1980	Harry Dinwiddie	1	0	0	0	0	0	0	0	173	0	0	460	5,250
1981	Tommy Gale	3	0	0	0	0	0	0	0	906	0	0	746	3,045
1981	Rick Baldwin	1	0	0	0	0	0	0	0	149	0	0	298	1,550
1981	Al Loquasto	1	0	0	0	0	0	0	0	184	0	0	460	2,345
1981	Bob McElee	2	0	0	0	0	0	0	1	803	0	0	461	5,450
1981	Cecil Gordon	3	0	0	0	0	0	0	0	622	0	0	362	2,020
1981	Tim Richmond	13	0	0	0	0	0	0	3	3,738	0	0	3,904	50,555
1981	Chuck Bown	1	0	0	0	0	0	0	0	118	0	0	177	1,950
1981	D.K. Ulrich	12	0	0	0	0	1	0	0	3,788	0	0	4,023	34,020
1981	Kevin Housby	1	0	0	0	0	0	0	0	53	0	0	133	2,480
1981	Rick Knoop	1	0	0	0	0	0	0	0	197	0	0	394	3,405
1981	Don Hume	1	0	0	0	0	0	0	0	101	0	0	103	590
1981	Elliott	1	0	0	0	0	0	0	0	246	0	0	131	870
1981	Joe Booher	3	0	0	0	0	0	0	0	577	0	0	1,249	3,295
1981	Dick May	2	0	0	0	0	0	0	0	582	0	0	718	3,375
1981	Ronnie Thomas	1	0	0	0	0	0	0	0	137	0	0	206	1,075
1981	Terry Herman	2	0	0	0	0	0	0	0	188	0	0	500	7,035
1981	Sterling Marlin	1	0	0	0	0	0	0	0	244	0	0	145	730
1981	Slick Johnson	1	0	0	0	0	0	0	0	110	0	0	150	1,425
1982	Al Loquasto	5	0	0	0	0	0	0	0	519	0	0	1,228	14,090
1982	Dick May	4	0	0	0	0	0	0	0	1,073	0	0	1,180	5,255
1982	Dr. Bob Jarvis	1	0	0	0	0	0	0	0	47	0	0	118	2,300
1982	Jimmy Hensley	3	0	0	0	0	0	0	1	791	0	0	418	3,205
1982	Randy Becker	1	0	0	0	0	0	0	0	85	0	0	223	1,065
1982	Ferrel Harris	1	0	0	0	0	0	0	0	146	0	0	388	2,625
1982	D.K. Ulrich	22	0	0	0	0	0	0	1	6,709	0	0	6,581	66,580
1982	Slick Johnson	10	0	0	0	0	0	0	0	1,883	2	1	2,437	15,415
1982	Tommy Houston	1	0	0	0	0	0	0	0	238	0	0	129	875

D.K. Ulrich *continued*

Year	Driver	Starts	Poles	1	2	3	4	5	6–10	Laps	Laps Led	Races Led	Miles	$
1982	Stan Barrett	1	0	0	0	0	0	0	0	65	0	0	163	5,585
1982	Joel Stowe	1	0	0	0	0	0	0	0	57	0	0	36	705
1982	Joe Booher	2	0	0	0	0	0	0	0	371	0	0	832	3,300
1982	Terry Herman	1	0	0	0	0	0	0	0	113	0	0	296	4,220
1983	Al Elmore	4	0	0	0	0	0	0	0	1,151	0	0	1,384	13,155
1983	Connie Saylor	1	0	0	0	0	0	0	0	153	0	0	383	4,875
1983	D.K. Ulrich	17	0	0	0	0	0	0	2	6,110	0	0	6,383	71,340
1983	Jim Sauter	4	0	0	0	0	0	0	0	1,093	0	0	1,349	22,765
1983	Mark Martin	2	0	0	0	0	0	0	0	415	0	0	382	5,745
1984	Morgan Shepherd	2	0	0	0	0	0	0	0	496	0	0	577	5,545
1984	Jim Sauter	3	0	0	0	0	0	0	0	737	0	0	1,152	18,015
1984	Doug Heveron	2	0	0	0	0	0	0	0	593	0	0	544	7,645
1984	D.K. Ulrich	9	0	0	0	0	0	0	0	2,565	0	0	2,513	31,040
1984	Clark Dwyer	4	0	0	0	0	0	0	0	1,156	0	0	938	15,855
1984	Connie Saylor	1	0	0	0	0	0	0	0	150	0	0	375	4,330
1984	Jimmy Ingalls	3	0	0	0	0	0	0	0	491	0	0	597	8,865
1985	Eddie Bierschwale	26	0	0	0	0	0	0	0	6,559	0	0	7,761	107,265
1985	D.K. Ulrich	1	0	0	0	0	0	0	0	286	0	0	291	1,350
1986	Trevor Boys	9	0	0	0	0	0	0	0	2,179	2	1	2,214	54,360
1986	Jim Sauter	2	0	0	0	0	0	0	0	300	0	0	750	12,610
1986	D.K. Ulrich	9	0	0	0	0	0	0	0	2,014	0	0	2,191	41,395
1986	Rick Knoop	1	0	0	0	0	0	0	0	88	0	0	216	6,995
1986	Joe Booher	2	0	0	0	0	0	0	0	556	0	0	556	8,930
1986	Richard Petty	1	0	0	0	0	0	0	0	123	0	0	185	5,465
1987	Trevor Boys	1	0	0	0	0	0	0	0	191	0	0	478	16,795
1987	Ron Esau	1	0	0	0	0	0	0	0	90	0	0	236	4,165
1987	Rick Knoop	3	0	0	0	0	0	0	0	686	0	0	1,027	17,375
1987	Ernie Irvan	3	0	0	0	0	0	0	0	974	0	0	794	13,175
1987	D.K. Ulrich	7	0	0	0	0	0	0	0	1,876	0	0	1,844	30,915
1987	Connie Saylor	6	0	0	0	0	0	0	0	1,335	0	0	1,987	33,065
1987	Bobby Baker	1	0	0	0	0	0	0	0	380	0	0	238	3,500
1988	Ernie Irvan	25	0	0	0	0	0	0	0	7,337	1	1	8,855	93,020
1989	Ernie Irvan	29	0	0	0	0	0	0	4	8,286	69	4	9,963	144,347
1990	Charlie Glotzbach	2	0	0	0	0	0	0	0	257	0	0	353	12,255
1990	Troy Beebe	2	0	0	0	0	0	0	0	251	0	0	562	13,115
1990	Eddie Bierschwale	1	0	0	0	0	0	0	0	191	0	0	478	20,125
1990	Ted Musgrave	2	0	0	0	0	0	0	0	628	0	0	795	10,600
1990	Rick Ware	1	0	0	0	0	0	0	0	42	0	0	103	2,295
1990	Rick Mast	14	0	0	0	0	0	0	0	3,935	0	0	4,175	82,570
1990	Jim Sauter	1	0	0	0	0	0	0	0	203	0	0	203	4,900
1990	Jerry O'Neil	1	0	0	0	0	0	0	0	74	0	0	181	2,975
1990	D.K. Ulrich	1	0	0	0	0	0	0	0	185	0	0	139	4,265
1990	Jim Bown	1	0	0	0	0	0	0	0	73	0	0	184	6,675
1991	Ted Musgrave	29	0	0	0	0	0	0	0	9,074	6	5	10,581	197,310
1994	Greg Sacks	31	1	0	0	0	0	0	3	8,346	38	8	10,092	374,728
1994	P.J. Jones	1	0	0	0	0	0	0	0	67	0	0	164	6,085
1995	Davy Jones	7	0	0	0	0	0	0	0	1,680	0	0	2,359	109,925
1995	Bobby Hillin	18	0	0	0	0	0	0	1	4,411	2	2	6,353	237,095
Lifetime		545	1	0	0	0	1	0	32	139,271	127	24	162,348	$2,446,470

Ray Underwood

Year	Driver	Starts	Poles	1	2	3	4	5	6–10	Laps	Laps Led	Races Led	Miles	$
1965	Reb Wickersham	7	0	0	0	0	0	0	2	906	0	0	1,198	4,410
Lifetime		7	0	0	0	0	0	0	2	906	0	0	1,198	$4,410

Sherman Utsman

Year	Driver	Starts	Poles	1	2	3	4	5	6–10	Laps	Laps Led	Races Led	Miles	$
1962	Sherman Utsman	12	0	0	0	0	0	1	3	3,293	0	0	2,314	3,580
1963	Sherman Utsman	3	0	0	0	0	0	0	3	582	0	0	204	555
Lifetime		15	0	0	0	0	0	1	6	3,875	0	0	2,518	$4,135

Walt Valerio

Year	Driver	Starts	Poles	1	2	3	4	5	6–10	Laps	Laps Led	Races Led	Miles	$
1970	Tommy Gale	5	0	0	0	0	0	0	1	391	0	0	659	3,135
Lifetime		5	0	0	0	0	0	0	1	391	0	0	659	$3,135

Year	Driver	Starts	Poles	Finish 1	2	3	4	5	6–10	Laps	Laps Led	Races Led	Miles	$

Gordon Van Liew

Year	Driver	Starts	Poles	1	2	3	4	5	6–10	Laps	Laps Led	Races Led	Miles	$
1973	Tony Bettenhausen,	4	0	0	0	0	0	0	0	854	0	0	1,305	4,115
1974	Tony Bettenhausen,	25	0	0	0	0	0	0	1	4,961	0	0	5,341	30,665
Lifetime		29	0	0	0	0	0	0	1	5,815	0	0	6,646	$34,780

Van Van Wey

Year	Driver	Starts	Poles	1	2	3	4	5	6–10	Laps	Laps Led	Races Led	Miles	$
1954	Van Van Wey	3	0	0	0	0	0	0	0	629	0	0	801	495
Lifetime		3	0	0	0	0	0	0	0	629	0	0	801	$495

Charles Vance

Year	Driver	Starts	Poles	1	2	3	4	5	6–10	Laps	Laps Led	Races Led	Miles	$
1954	John Soares	9	0	1	0	1	0	0	2	2,196	211	1	1,498	3,045
1955	John Soares	1	0	0	0	0	0	0	0	86	0	0	86	25
1955	Allen Adkins	1	0	0	0	0	0	0	0	233	0	0	233	150
Lifetime		11	0	1	0	1	0	0	2	2,515	211	1	1,817	$3,220

J. R. VanCurren

Year	Driver	Starts	Poles	1	2	3	4	5	6–10	Laps	Laps Led	Races Led	Miles	$
1967	Cliff Garner	1	0	0	0	0	0	0	0	25	0	0	68	500
Lifetime		1	0	0	0	0	0	0	0	25	0	0	68	$500

Jim Vandiver

Year	Driver	Starts	Poles	1	2	3	4	5	6–10	Laps	Laps Led	Races Led	Miles	$
1970	Jim Vandiver	4	0	0	0	0	0	0	2	668	6	1	1,208	6,065
Lifetime		4	0	0	0	0	0	0	2	668	6	1	1,208	$6,065

Jenny VanHouten

Year	Driver	Starts	Poles	1	2	3	4	5	6–10	Laps	Laps Led	Races Led	Miles	$
1991	Keith VanHoughten	1	0	0	0	0	0	0	0	13	0	0	13	3,475
Lifetime		1	0	0	0	0	0	0	0	13	0	0	13	$3,475

J.C. VanLandingham

Year	Driver	Starts	Poles	1	2	3	4	5	6–10	Laps	Laps Led	Races Led	Miles	$
1950	J.C. Van Landingham	1	0	0	0	0	0	1	0	48	0	0	200	450
1955	Dick Joslin	1	0	0	0	0	0	0	1	38	0	0	156	425
Lifetime		2	0	0	0	0	0	1	1	86	0	0	356	$875

Frank Vasko

Year	Driver	Starts	Poles	1	2	3	4	5	6–10	Laps	Laps Led	Races Led	Miles	$
1972	Tommy Gale	6	0	0	0	0	0	0	0	1,144	0	0	1,959	7,477
Lifetime		6	0	0	0	0	0	0	0	1,144	0	0	1,959	$7,477

David Vaughn

Year	Driver	Starts	Poles	1	2	3	4	5	6–10	Laps	Laps Led	Races Led	Miles	$
1957	Keith Olson	1	0	0	0	0	0	0	0	17	0	0	9	100
Lifetime		1	0	0	0	0	0	0	0	17	0	0	9	$100

Jimmy Vaughn

Year	Driver	Starts	Poles	1	2	3	4	5	6–10	Laps	Laps Led	Races Led	Miles	$
1969	Jimmy Vaughn	1	0	0	0	0	0	0	1	159	0	0	423	2,000
1971	Jimmy Vaughn	3	0	0	0	0	0	0	0	575	0	0	294	1,015
Lifetime		4	0	0	0	0	0	0	1	734	0	0	717	$3,015

Charles Venable

Year	Driver	Starts	Poles	1	2	3	4	5	6–10	Laps	Laps Led	Races Led	Miles	$
1950	Roscoe Thompson	2	0	0	0	0	0	0	0	69	0	0	218	50
Lifetime		2	0	0	0	0	0	0	0	69	0	0	218	$50

Jim Venable

Year	Driver	Starts	Poles	1	2	3	4	5	6–10	Laps	Laps Led	Races Led	Miles	$
1994	Gary Collins	1	0	0	0	0	0	0	0	43	0	0	108	7,350
Lifetime		1	0	0	0	0	0	0	0	43	0	0	108	$7,350

Bill Venturini

Year	Driver	Starts	Poles	1	2	3	4	5	6–10	Laps	Laps Led	Races Led	Miles	$
1989	Bill Venturini	1	0	0	0	0	0	0	0	80	0	0	160	2,975
1990	Bill Venturini	4	0	0	0	0	0	0	0	702	0	0	1,647	20,670

Year	Driver	Starts	Poles	Finish 1	2	3	4	5	6–10	Laps	Laps Led	Races Led	Miles	$

Bill Venturini *continued*

Year	Driver	Starts	Poles	1	2	3	4	5	6–10	Laps	Laps Led	Races Led	Miles	$
1991	Bill Venturini	2	0	0	0	0	0	0	0	71	0	0	146	7,925
Lifetime		7	0	0	0	0	0	0	0	853	0	0	1,952	$31,570

Tom Vernon

Year	Driver	Starts	Poles	1	2	3	4	5	6–10	Laps	Laps Led	Races Led	Miles	$
1959	Glen Wood	1	0	0	0	0	0	1	0	288	0	0	144	400
1959	Marvin Panch	3	0	0	0	0	0	0	0	603	0	0	841	1,000
1960	Marvin Panch	3	0	0	0	0	0	0	0	217	22	1	411	350
Lifetime		7	0	0	0	0	0	1	0	1,108	22	1	1,396	$1,750

Lou Viglione

Year	Driver	Starts	Poles	1	2	3	4	5	6–10	Laps	Laps Led	Races Led	Miles	$
1974	Joe Mihalic	5	0	0	0	0	0	0	1	1,725	0	0	1,570	7,595
1975	Joe Mihalic	10	0	0	0	0	0	0	1	1,939	0	0	2,695	13,385
1975	Jackie Rogers	7	0	0	0	0	0	0	1	543	2	1	1,191	8,185
1976	Joe Mihalic	9	0	0	0	0	0	0	0	2,171	0	0	3,129	12,925
1976	Jackie Rogers	11	0	0	0	0	0	0	3	2,439	3	2	3,874	21,215
1976	David Sisco	1	0	0	0	0	0	0	0	34	0	0	52	815
1977	Ramo Stott	5	0	0	0	0	0	0	0	688	0	0	1,438	10,170
Lifetime		48	0	0	0	0	0	0	6	9,539	5	3	13,949	$74,290

Chris Virtue

Year	Driver	Starts	Poles	1	2	3	4	5	6–10	Laps	Laps Led	Races Led	Miles	$
1994	Danny Sullivan	1	0	0	0	0	0	0	0	152	0	0	380	22,750
Lifetime		1	0	0	0	0	0	0	0	152	0	0	380	$22,750

Opal Voight

Year	Driver	Starts	Poles	1	2	3	4	5	6–10	Laps	Laps Led	Races Led	Miles	$
1975	Bruce Jacobi	15	0	0	0	0	0	0	3	3,863	0	0	5,767	29,040
1977	Jim Raptis	3	0	0	0	0	0	0	0	116	0	0	252	2,530
Lifetime		18	0	0	0	0	0	0	3	3,979	0	0	6,019	$31,570

Bobby Waddell

Year	Driver	Starts	Poles	1	2	3	4	5	6–10	Laps	Laps Led	Races Led	Miles	$
1957	Bobby Waddell	1	0	0	0	0	0	0	0	39	0	0	20	50
1959	Bobby Waddell	7	0	0	0	0	0	0	0	512	0	0	262	360
1959	Curtis Crider	2	0	0	0	0	0	0	1	209	0	0	105	240
1960	Bobby Waddell	1	0	0	0	0	0	0	0	168	0	0	84	50
1961	Bobby Waddell	4	0	0	0	0	0	0	2	565	0	0	288	455
1962	Bobby Waddell	6	0	0	0	0	0	0	0	303	0	0	161	470
1962	George Fox	1	0	0	0	0	0	0	0	3	0	0	2	50
Lifetime		22	0	0	0	0	0	0	3	1,799	0	0	921	$1,675

Weldon Wagner

Year	Driver	Starts	Poles	1	2	3	4	5	6–10	Laps	Laps Led	Races Led	Miles	$
1960	Darrell Dake	2	0	0	0	0	0	0	1	235	0	0	588	575
1960	G.C. Spencer	21	0	0	0	0	1	1	4	4,073	0	0	2,698	3,215
1961	Darrell Dake	2	0	0	0	0	0	0	0	54	0	0	135	200
Lifetime		25	0	0	0	0	1	1	5	4,362	0	0	3,420	$3,990

Al Wagoner

Year	Driver	Starts	Poles	1	2	3	4	5	6–10	Laps	Laps Led	Races Led	Miles	$
1949	Al Wagoner	1	0	0	0	0	0	0	1	178	0	0	89	75
1949	Bill Snowden	1	0	0	0	0	0	1	0	0	0	0		200
Lifetime		2	0	0	0	0	0	1	1	178	0	0	89	$275

DuWayne Wahl

Year	Driver	Starts	Poles	1	2	3	4	5	6–10	Laps	Laps Led	Races Led	Miles	$
1973	Chuck Wahl	1	0	0	0	0	0	0	0	7	0	0	18	630
1974	Jack Simpson	1	0	0	0	0	0	0	0	105	0	0	275	875
1975	Chuck Wahl	1	0	0	0	0	0	0	0	29	0	0	73	600
1976	Chuck Wahl	2	0	0	0	0	0	0	0	182	3	1	477	2,705
1977	Chuck Wahl	2	0	0	0	0	0	0	0	155	0	0	406	2,420
1978	Chuck Wahl	2	0	0	0	0	0	0	0	102	0	0	262	1,520
1980	Chuck Wahl	1	0	0	0	0	0	0	0	88	0	0	231	1,005
Lifetime		10	0	0	0	0	0	0	0	668	3	1	1,742	$9,755

Year	Driver	Starts	Poles	Finish						Laps	Laps Led	Races Led	Miles	$
				1	2	3	4	5	6–10	Laps	Led	Led	Miles	$

Russell Wainscott

Year	Driver	Starts	Poles	1	2	3	4	5	6–10	Laps	Led	Led	Miles	$
1956	Joy Fair	1	0	0	0	0	0	0	0		0	0		0
Lifetime		1	0	0	0	0	0	0	0		0	0		$0

Frank Waite

Year	Driver	Starts	Poles	1	2	3	4	5	6–10	Laps	Led	Led	Miles	$
1963	Frank Waite	4	0	0	0	0	0	0	0	617	0	0	309	425
1963	James Norton	1	0	0	0	0	0	0	0	84	0	0	126	275
Lifetime		5	0	0	0	0	0	0	0	701	0	0	435	$700

Bob Walden

Year	Driver	Starts	Poles	1	2	3	4	5	6–10	Laps	Led	Led	Miles	$
1953	Bob Walden	4	0	0	0	0	0	0	2	325	0	0	180	250
1958	Eddie Pagan	1	0	0	0	0	0	0	1	143	0	0	48	185
1958	Shep Langdon	1	0	0	0	0	0	0	0	193	0	0	48	165
1958	Johnny Allen	1	0	0	0	0	0	0	0	235	0	0	94	110
1958	Bob Walden	14	0	0	0	0	1	0	8	2,104	0	0	1,167	1,810
1958	Paul Walton	1	0	0	0	0	0	0	0	144	0	0	36	130
Lifetime		22	0	0	0	0	1	0	11	3,144	0	0	1,573	$2,650

Monte Walden

Year	Driver	Starts	Poles	1	2	3	4	5	6–10	Laps	Led	Led	Miles	$
1960	Pappy Crane	1	0	0	0	0	0	0	0	89	0	0	223	200
Lifetime		1	0	0	0	0	0	0	0	89	0	0	223	$200

W.R. Waldron

Year	Driver	Starts	Poles	1	2	3	4	5	6–10	Laps	Led	Led	Miles	$
1955	Larry Flynn	1	0	0	0	0	0	1	0	359	0	0	494	1,175
1956	Buck Hall	1	0	0	0	0	0	0	0	11	0	0	10	25
1956	Bunk Moore	1	0	0	0	0	0	0	0	20	0	0	15	0
1956	George Mantooth	1	0	0	0	0	0	0	0	43	0	0	22	0
1956	Bill Widenhouse	1	0	0	0	0	0	0	0	49	0	0	25	0
Lifetime		5	0	0	0	0	0	1	0	482	0	0	565	$1,200

David Walker

Year	Driver	Starts	Poles	1	2	3	4	5	6–10	Laps	Led	Led	Miles	$
1964	Buck Baker	3	0	0	0	0	0	0	0	352	0	0	198	460
1964	Buddy Baker	1	0	0	0	0	0	0	0	64	0	0	160	725
1964	LeeRoy Yarbrough	2	0	0	0	0	0	0	0	81	0	0	125	750
1964	Marshall Sargent	1	0	0	0	0	0	0	1	77	0	0	39	150
1964	Tiny Lund	4	0	0	0	1	0	0	0	505	0	0	603	1,625
Lifetime		11	0	0	0	1	0	0	1	1,079	0	0	1,123	$3,710

Jimmy Walker

Year	Driver	Starts	Poles	1	2	3	4	5	6–10	Laps	Led	Led	Miles	$
1982	Jimmy Walker	3	0	0	0	0	0	0	0	131	0	0	130	2,320
1984	Mike Potter	1	0	0	0	0	0	0	0	9	0	0	9	710
1985	Mike Potter	6	0	0	0	0	0	0	0	1,434	0	0	1,729	10,855
1985	Jimmy Walker	1	0	0	0	0	0	0	0	180	0	0	180	1,350
1986	Mike Potter	2	0	0	0	0	0	0	0	95	0	0	95	1,900
Lifetime		13	0	0	0	0	0	0	0	1,849	0	0	2,143	$17,135

Murrace Walker

Year	Driver	Starts	Poles	1	2	3	4	5	6–10	Laps	Led	Led	Miles	$
1950	Murrace Walker	1	0	0	0	0	0	0	0	358	0	0	448	0
1951	Murrace Walker	1	0	0	0	0	0	0	0	104	0	0	130	0
Lifetime		2	0	0	0	0	0	0	0	462	0	0	578	$0

B.R. Waller

Year	Driver	Starts	Poles	1	2	3	4	5	6–10	Laps	Led	Led	Miles	$
1951	Frank Gise	2	0	0	0	0	0	0	1	215	0	0	269	100
Lifetime		2	0	0	0	0	0	0	1	215	0	0	269	$100

Dick Walters

Year	Driver	Starts	Poles	1	2	3	4	5	6–10	Laps	Led	Led	Miles	$
1957	Dick Walters	3	0	0	0	0	0	0	1	499	0	0	327	290
1958	Dick Walters	4	0	0	0	0	0	0	0	305	0	0	129	290
Lifetime		7	0	0	0	0	0	0	1	804	0	0	456	$580

Year	Driver	Starts	Poles	Finish 1	2	3	4	5	6–10	Laps	Laps Led	Races Led	Miles	$

Harvey Walters

Year	Driver	Starts	Poles	1	2	3	4	5	6–10	Laps	Laps Led	Races Led	Miles	$
1955	Jim Wilson	1	0	0	0	0	0	0	0	37	0	0	152	50
1956	Buddy Krebs	1	0	0	0	0	0	0	0	1	0	0	4	0
1956	Jim Wilson	2	0	0	0	0	0	0	0	181	0	0	94	50
Lifetime		4	0	0	0	0	0	0	0	219	0	0	250	$100

Nook Walters

Year	Driver	Starts	Poles	1	2	3	4	5	6–10	Laps	Laps Led	Races Led	Miles	$
1960	Nook Walters	1	0	0	0	0	1	0	0	179	0	0	90	275
Lifetime		1	0	0	0	0	1	0	0	179	0	0	90	$275

Ratus Walters

Year	Driver	Starts	Poles	1	2	3	4	5	6–10	Laps	Laps Led	Races Led	Miles	$
1958	Elmo Langley	2	0	0	0	0	0	0	0	124	0	0	115	195
1959	Pedro Rodriguez	1	0	0	0	0	0	0	1	144	0	0	144	300
1959	Elmo Langley	13	0	0	0	1	0	0	1	1,694	0	0	1,314	2,280
1960	Elmo Langley	4	0	0	0	0	0	0	0	358	0	0	437	500
1960	Bill Morgan	1	0	0	0	0	0	0	1	183	0	0	92	130
1961	Hoss Kagle	1	0	0	0	0	0	0	0	2	0	0	1	125
1961	Bill Morgan	3	0	0	0	0	0	0	1	692	0	0	756	1,225
1961	Jimmy Thompson	1	0	0	0	0	0	0	0	113	0	0	170	200
1961	Reds Kagle	3	0	0	0	0	0	0	1	720	0	0	963	1,495
1962	George Alsobrook	4	0	0	0	0	0	0	1	374	0	0	707	825
1962	Elmo Langley	3	0	0	0	0	0	0	0	269	0	0	413	975
1962	Larry Frank	19	0	1	0	0	0	1	6	3,566	85	1	3,506	31,410
1962	Jim Reed	4	0	0	0	0	0	0	0	919	0	0	781	1,030
1962	Ralph Moody	1	0	0	0	0	0	0	0	1	0	0	1	75
1963	Jim Reed	1	0	0	0	0	0	1	0	29	0	0	15	50
1963	Elmo Langley	1	0	0	0	0	0	0	0	8	0	0	4	100
1963	Johnny Allen	5	0	0	0	0	0	0	0	459	0	0	375	1,275
1964	Elmo Langley	1	0	0	0	0	0	0	0	119	0	0	107	100
Lifetime		68	0	1	0	1	0	2	12	9,774	85	1	9,898	$42,290

George Walther

Year	Driver	Starts	Poles	1	2	3	4	5	6–10	Laps	Laps Led	Races Led	Miles	$
1975	Salt Walther	1	0	0	0	0	0	0	0	188	0	0	376	1,005
1976	Salt Walther	1	0	0	0	0	0	0	0	187	0	0	468	5,880
1977	Salt Walther	1	0	0	0	0	0	0	0	114	0	0	285	2,725
Lifetime		3	0	0	0	0	0	0	0	489	0	0	1,129	$9,610

Paul Walton

Year	Driver	Starts	Poles	1	2	3	4	5	6–10	Laps	Laps Led	Races Led	Miles	$
1959	Ken Rush	1	0	0	0	0	1	0	0	246	0	0	98	250
1959	Paul Walton	1	0	0	0	0	0	0	0	112	0	0	70	60
Lifetime		2	0	0	0	0	1	0	0	358	0	0	168	$310

Darrell Waltrip

Year	Driver	Starts	Poles	1	2	3	4	5	6–10	Laps	Laps Led	Races Led	Miles	$
1972	Darrell Waltrip	5	0	0	0	1	0	0	2	1,211	7	1	1,653	8,615
1973	Darrell Waltrip	14	0	0	1	0	0	0	3	2,965	50	3	4,412	27,775
1974	Darrell Waltrip	16	1	0	1	3	2	1	4	4,649	103	5	6,013	63,690
1975	Darrell Waltrip	17	2	1	2	0	3	2	2	4,480	291	8	5,072	98,350
1991	Darrell Waltrip	29	0	2	2	1	0	0	12	9,229	203	12	10,903	428,330
1992	Darrell Waltrip	29	1	3	2	3	0	2	3	8,706	513	14	10,249	773,920
1993	Darrell Waltrip	30	0	0	0	2	1	1	6	9,194	151	9	10,818	643,285
1994	Darrell Waltrip	31	0	0	0	2	2	0	9	9,905	60	8	12,027	662,740
1995	Darrell Waltrip	31	1	0	0	1	3	0	4	8,222	168	8	9,582	782,995
1996	Darrell Waltrip	31	0	0	0	0	0	0	2	7,766	2	2	8,972	712,185
1997	Rich Bickle	1	0	0	0	0	0	0	0	153	0	0	383	56,410
1997	Darrell Waltrip	31	0	0	0	0	0	1	3	8,427	17	6	10,978	919,390
1998	Darrell Waltrip	5	0	0	0	0	0	1	0	1,007	0	0	1,614	206,665
Lifetime		270	5	6	8	13	11	8	50	75,914	1,565	76	92,676	$5,384,350

Michael Waltrip

Year	Driver	Starts	Poles	1	2	3	4	5	6–10	Laps	Laps Led	Races Led	Miles	$
2002	Jerry Nadeau	1	0	0	0	0	0	0	0	217	0	0	326	53,600
2002	Kenny Wallace	3	0	0	0	0	0	0	0	508	0	0	1,037	163,430
Lifetime		4	0	0	0	0	0	0	0	725	0	0	1,363	$217,030

Year	Driver	Starts	Poles	Finish						Laps	Laps Led	Races Led	Miles	$
				1	2	3	4	5	6–10	Laps	Led	Led	Miles	$

Blackie Wangerin

Year	Driver	Starts	Poles	1	2	3	4	5	6–10	Laps	Led	Led	Miles	$
1971	Blackie Wangerin	1	0	0	0	0	0	0	0	16	0	0	40	0
1977	Blackie Wangerin	1	0	0	0	0	0	0	0	260	0	0	396	885
1978	Blackie Wangerin	10	0	0	0	0	0	0	0	1,342	0	0	2,522	13,515
1979	Blackie Wangerin	7	0	0	0	0	0	0	0	894	0	0	1,750	14,300
1980	Blackie Wangerin	3	0	0	0	0	0	0	0	548	0	0	808	6,920
1981	Blackie Wangerin	1	0	0	0	0	0	0	0	17	0	0	43	2,750
1982	Blackie Wangerin	1	0	0	0	0	0	0	0	73	0	0	183	1,600
1983	Blackie Wangerin	2	0	0	0	0	0	0	0	48	0	0	62	1,860
1984	Blackie Wangerin	1	0	0	0	0	0	0	0	0	0	0	0	960
Lifetime		27	0	0	0	0	0	0	0	3,198	0	0	5,803	$42,790

Bill Ward

Year	Driver	Starts	Poles	1	2	3	4	5	6–10	Laps	Led	Led	Miles	$
1975	Bill Ward	1	0	0	0	0	0	0	0	145	0	0	386	1,320
Lifetime		1	0	0	0	0	0	0	0	145	0	0	386	$1,320

Glen Ward

Year	Driver	Starts	Poles	1	2	3	4	5	6–10	Laps	Led	Led	Miles	$
1980	Glen Ward	1	0	0	0	0	0	0	0	77	0	0	193	875
Lifetime		1	0	0	0	0	0	0	0	77	0	0	193	$875

David Warren

Year	Driver	Starts	Poles	1	2	3	4	5	6–10	Laps	Led	Led	Miles	$
1965	Jimmy Helms	35	0	0	0	0	0	0	4	5,248	0	0	3,478	8,140
1965	J.T. Putney	1	0	0	0	0	0	0	0	118	0	0	74	175
1965	David Warren	1	0	0	0	0	0	0	0	32	0	0	16	100
1965	Curtis Crider	1	0	0	0	0	0	0	0	390	0	0	195	375
1965	Pete Stewart	2	0	0	0	0	0	0	0	2	0	0	5	1,165
1966	Marty Robbins	1	0	0	0	0	0	0	0	48	0	0	24	100
1966	Jimmy Helms	25	0	0	0	0	0	0	0	2,823	0	0	2,604	5,030
Lifetime		66	0	0	0	0	0	0	4	8,661	0	0	6,395	$15,085

Frank Warren

Year	Driver	Starts	Poles	1	2	3	4	5	6–10	Laps	Led	Led	Miles	$
1969	Frank Warren	8	0	0	0	0	0	0	0	1,143	0	0	1,679	7,322
1970	Frank Warren	46	0	0	0	0	0	0	2	7,709	71	1	7,763	29,953
1971	Dick Poling	1	0	0	0	0	0	0	0	21	0	0	53	0
1971	Frank Warren	42	0	0	0	0	0	0	7	7,907	0	0	8,067	28,180
1972	Richard Childress	1	0	0	0	0	0	0	0	179	0	0	358	880
1972	Frank Warren	30	0	0	0	0	0	0	2	7,091	0	0	8,404	39,216
1973	Paul Tyler	1	0	0	0	0	0	0	0	105	0	0	107	1,240
1973	Jabe Thomas	1	0	0	0	0	0	0	0	337	0	0	180	700
1973	Frank Warren	21	0	0	0	0	0	0	0	5,640	0	0	6,522	30,057
1973	David Ray Boggs	1	0	0	0	0	0	0	0	116	0	0	158	1,235
1974	Frank Warren	29	0	0	0	0	0	1	1	7,342	0	0	8,994	47,277
1975	Ed Negre	1	0	0	0	0	0	0	0	184	0	0	460	4,390
1975	Frank Warren	27	0	0	0	0	0	0	0	7,758	0	0	9,124	43,970
1976	Frank Warren	28	0	0	0	0	0	0	3	7,309	0	0	9,289	59,055
1977	Frank Warren	29	0	0	0	0	0	0	1	6,466	1	1	8,108	61,960
1978	Frank Warren	30	0	0	0	0	0	0	0	8,481	0	0	9,827	58,580
1979	Frank Warren	31	0	0	0	0	0	0	3	8,477	0	0	10,047	87,400
1980	Frank Warren	7	0	0	0	0	0	0	0	1,591	0	0	2,561	61,375
1980	Joe Booher	2	0	0	0	0	0	0	0	161	0	0	412	3,430
1980	Jim Hurlbert	1	0	0	0	0	0	0	0	33	0	0	83	2,950
1980	Joey Arrington	1	0	0	0	0	0	0	0	368	0	0	199	2,030
1980	Dick May	2	0	0	0	0	0	0	0	502	0	0	624	3,235
1980	Travis Tiller	1	0	0	0	0	0	0	0	323	0	0	172	770
1980	Junior Miller	5	0	0	0	0	0	0	0	1,194	0	0	1,195	8,160
1980	Marty Robbins	1	0	0	0	0	0	0	0	131	0	0	328	2,285
Lifetime		347	0	0	0	0	0	1	19	80,568	72	2	94,712	$585,650

Gayle Warren

Year	Driver	Starts	Poles	1	2	3	4	5	6–10	Laps	Led	Led	Miles	$
1953	Gayle Warren	2	0	0	0	0	0	0	0	327	0	0	348	150
Lifetime		2	0	0	0	0	0	0	0	327	0	0	348	$150

Jerome Warren

Year	Driver	Starts	Poles	1	2	3	4	5	6–10	Laps	Led	Led	Miles	$
1963	Curtis Crider	1	0	0	0	0	0	0	0	397	0	0	199	150

Year	Driver	Starts	Poles	Finish 1	2	3	4	5	6–10	Laps	Laps Led	Races Led	Miles	$

Jerome Warren *continued*

Year	Driver	Starts	Poles	1	2	3	4	5	6–10	Laps	Laps Led	Races Led	Miles	$
1963	Jerome Warren	4	0	0	0	0	0	0	0	146	0	0	77	335
Lifetime		5	0	0	0	0	0	0	0	543	0	0	275	$485

Don Waterman

Year	Driver	Starts	Poles	1	2	3	4	5	6–10	Laps	Laps Led	Races Led	Miles	$
1980	Don Waterman	2	0	0	0	0	0	0	0	250	0	0	633	3,555
1981	Don Waterman	3	0	0	0	0	0	0	1	301	1	1	789	8,570
1982	Don Waterman	2	0	0	0	0	0	0	0	156	1	1	409	3,805
1983	Don Waterman	2	0	0	0	0	0	0	0	189	0	0	495	3,355
Lifetime		9	0	0	0	0	0	0	1	896	2	2	2,325	$19,285

H.L. Waters

Year	Driver	Starts	Poles	1	2	3	4	5	6–10	Laps	Laps Led	Races Led	Miles	$
1982	Delma Cowart	3	0	0	0	0	0	0	0	467	0	0	949	6,790
1983	Delma Cowart	4	0	0	0	0	0	0	0	643	0	0	1,141	7,750
1984	Delma Cowart	2	0	0	0	0	0	0	0	533	0	0	803	4,170
1985	Delma Cowart	2	0	0	0	0	0	0	0	71	0	0	183	9,930
1986	Delma Cowart	3	0	0	0	0	0	0	0	403	0	0	977	7,595
1986	Doug Heveron	1	0	0	0	0	0	0	0	106	1	1	265	2,045
1987	Delma Cowart	1	0	0	0	0	0	0	0	180	0	0	479	3,130
1992	Delma Cowart	3	0	0	0	0	0	0	0	498	0	0	950	33,470
Lifetime		19	0	0	0	0	0	0	0	2,901	1	1	5,746	$74,880

Richard Waters

Year	Driver	Starts	Poles	1	2	3	4	5	6–10	Laps	Laps Led	Races Led	Miles	$
1978	Richard Waters	1	0	0	0	0	0	0	0	13	0	0	8	265
Lifetime		1	0	0	0	0	0	0	0	13	0	0	8	$265

Al Watkins

Year	Driver	Starts	Poles	1	2	3	4	5	6–10	Laps	Laps Led	Races Led	Miles	$
1955	Al Watkins	3	0	0	0	0	0	0	0	491	0	0	386	300
1956	Al Watkins	2	0	0	0	0	0	0	0	253	0	0	127	150
Lifetime		5	0	0	0	0	0	0	0	744	0	0	512	$450

J.B. Watkins

Year	Driver	Starts	Poles	1	2	3	4	5	6–10	Laps	Laps Led	Races Led	Miles	$
1951	Earl Moss	4	0	0	0	0	0	0	1	479	0	0	515	285
Lifetime		4	0	0	0	0	0	0	1	479	0	0	515	$285

Dave Watson

Year	Driver	Starts	Poles	1	2	3	4	5	6–10	Laps	Laps Led	Races Led	Miles	$
1978	Dave Watson	1	0	0	0	0	0	0	0	316	0	0	481	1,600
Lifetime		1	0	0	0	0	0	0	0	316	0	0	481	$1,600

W.H. Watson

Year	Driver	Starts	Poles	1	2	3	4	5	6–10	Laps	Laps Led	Races Led	Miles	$
1959	Speedy Thompson	1	0	0	0	0	0	0	0	29	0	0	26	50
1959	Joe Eubanks	1	0	0	0	0	0	0	0	26	0	0	36	190
1959	Cotton Owens	31	2	1	4	1	2	4	6	5,403	209	4	3,827	10,560
1960	Elmo Henderson	6	0	0	0	0	0	0	0	870	0	0	1,083	1,375
Lifetime		39	2	1	4	1	2	4	6	6,328	209	4	4,972	$12,175

J.M. Wattenbarger

Year	Driver	Starts	Poles	1	2	3	4	5	6–10	Laps	Laps Led	Races Led	Miles	$
1956	Frank Secrist	1	0	0	0	0	0	0	0	207	0	0	207	40
1957	Frank Secrist	1	0	0	0	0	0	0	0	24	0	0	60	45
Lifetime		2	0	0	0	0	0	0	0	231	0	0	267	$85

Art Watts

Year	Driver	Starts	Poles	1	2	3	4	5	6–10	Laps	Laps Led	Races Led	Miles	$
1961	Art Watts	1	0	0	0	0	0	0	0	85	0	0	119	100
Lifetime		1	0	0	0	0	0	0	0	85	0	0	119	$100

Bobby Wawak

Year	Driver	Starts	Poles	1	2	3	4	5	6–10	Laps	Laps Led	Races Led	Miles	$
1967	Bobby Wawak	14	0	0	0	0	0	0	3	2,225	0	0	2,320	8,070
1971	Bobby Wawak	2	0	0	0	0	0	0	0	615	0	0	891	2,665
1977	Bobby Wawak	4	0	0	0	0	0	0	0	1,112	0	0	1,639	5,195

Year	Driver	Starts	Poles	Finish 1	2	3	4	5	6–10	Laps	Laps Led	Races Led	Miles	$

Bobby Wawak *continued*

Year	Driver	Starts	Poles	1	2	3	4	5	6–10	Laps	Laps Led	Races Led	Miles	$
1978	Dick May	2	0	0	0	0	0	0	0	500	0	0	475	1,495
1978	Bobby Wawak	6	0	0	0	0	0	0	0	1,233	0	0	894	4,335
1978	Tommy Gale	1	0	0	0	0	0	0	0	253	0	0	385	700
1978	Joe Booher	2	0	0	0	0	0	0	0	417	0	0	324	1,430
1979	Bobby Wawak	4	0	0	0	0	0	0	0	740	0	0	855	6,785
1980	Henry Jones	1	0	0	0	0	0	0	0	178	0	0	445	1,550
1980	Bob Riley	1	0	0	0	0	0	0	0	141	0	0	353	1,165
1980	Bobby Wawak	19	0	0	0	0	0	0	1	3,965	0	0	4,170	21,080
1980	Joe Booher	2	0	0	0	0	0	0	0	655	0	0	934	9,270
1980	Stuart Huffman	1	0	0	0	0	0	0	0	340	0	0	181	510
1981	Bobby Wawak	14	0	0	0	0	0	0	1	2,734	0	0	3,485	21,790
1981	Cecil Gordon	1	0	0	0	0	0	0	0	2	0	0	1	455
1981	Bob Riley	1	0	0	0	0	0	0	0	6	0	0	6	550
1981	Henry Jones	1	0	0	0	0	0	0	0	363	0	0	197	765
1982	Bobby Wawak	10	0	0	0	0	0	0	0	2,489	2	1	3,981	23,660
1983	Bobby Wawak	9	0	0	0	0	0	0	0	2,167	0	0	3,262	19,130
1984	Bob Riley	1	0	0	0	0	0	0	0	179	0	0	448	1,735
1984	Bobby Wawak	3	0	0	0	0	0	0	0	694	0	0	983	4,550
1985	Bobby Wawak	13	0	0	0	0	0	0	0	2,982	0	0	3,991	38,955
1985	Rick Wilson	1	0	0	0	0	0	0	0	111	0	0	295	2,515
1986	Jim Fitzgerald	1	0	0	0	0	0	0	0	28	0	0	73	925
1986	Jack Ely	2	0	0	0	0	0	0	0	329	0	0	823	5,145
1986	Bobby Wawak	6	0	0	0	0	0	0	0	1,170	0	0	1,634	10,155
1987	Bobby Wawak	8	0	0	0	0	0	0	0	1,648	0	0	2,343	17,755
1988	Randy LaJoie	1	0	0	0	0	0	0	0	89	0	0	89	1,460
1990	Mike Potter	3	0	0	0	0	0	0	0	463	0	0	747	9,775
Lifetime		134	0	0	0	0	0	0	5	27,828	2	1	36,223	$223,570

Dick Wearing

Year	Driver	Starts	Poles	1	2	3	4	5	6–10	Laps	Laps Led	Races Led	Miles	$
1959	Chuck Webb	1	0	0	0	0	0	0	0	63	0	0	63	100
1961	Chuck Webb	2	0	0	0	0	0	0	1	120	0	0	129	200
Lifetime		3	0	0	0	0	0	0	1	183	0	0	192	$300

Bob Weatherly

Year	Driver	Starts	Poles	1	2	3	4	5	6–10	Laps	Laps Led	Races Led	Miles	$
1953	Bob Weatherly	1	0	0	0	0	0	0	0	289	0	0	397	140
1957	Cale Yarborough	1	0	0	0	0	0	0	0	31	0	0	43	100
1959	Cale Yarborough	1	0	0	0	0	0	0	0	219	0	0	301	150
1960	Cale Yarborough	1	0	0	0	0	0	0	0	114	0	0	57	85
Lifetime		4	0	0	0	0	0	0	0	653	0	0	798	$475

Louie Weathersby

Year	Driver	Starts	Poles	1	2	3	4	5	6–10	Laps	Laps Led	Races Led	Miles	$
1964	Louis Weathersbee	4	0	0	0	0	0	0	0	385	0	0	314	610
1964	LeeRoy Yarbrough	17	0	2	2	2	2	0	3	2,970	192	4	1,422	5,755
1964	Doug Yates	1	0	0	0	0	0	1	0	249	0	0	125	450
1964	Bobby Isaac	3	0	0	0	0	0	0	0	311	0	0	155	430
1964	Paul Moore	2	0	0	0	0	0	0	0	206	0	0	227	600
1965	Paul Moore	11	1	0	1	1	1	0	3	1,279	93	2	639	2,590
Lifetime		38	1	2	3	3	3	1	6	5,400	285	6	2,882	$10,435

Gary Weaver

Year	Driver	Starts	Poles	1	2	3	4	5	6–10	Laps	Laps Led	Races Led	Miles	$
1965	LeeRoy Yarbrough	3	0	0	0	0	1	0	1	547	0	0	274	790
1965	Rene Charland	1	0	0	0	0	0	0	0	8	0	0	12	455
1965	Darel Dieringer	3	0	0	0	0	1	0	0	429	0	0	253	1,205
1965	Cale Yarborough	6	0	0	0	1	0	0	1	569	3	1	612	2,610
1965	Bernard Alvarez	2	0	0	0	0	0	0	0	9	0	0	7	600
1965	Tiny Lund	3	0	0	0	0	1	0	2	1,353	0	0	724	1,650
1966	Tiny Lund	1	0	0	0	0	0	0	0	33	0	0	83	0
1966	Paul Bumhaver	1	0	0	0	0	0	0	0	291	0	0	146	200
1966	Jim Paschal	1	0	0	0	0	1	0	0	297	16	1	149	515
Lifetime		21	0	0	0	1	4	0	4	3,536	19	2	2,258	$8,025

J.C. Weaver

Year	Driver	Starts	Poles	1	2	3	4	5	6–10	Laps	Laps Led	Races Led	Miles	$
1987	Dave Pletcher	2	0	0	0	0	0	0	0	210	0	0	548	4,915

Year	Driver	Starts	Poles	Finish 1	2	3	4	5	6–10	Laps	Laps Led	Races Led	Miles	$

J.C. Weaver *continued*

Year	Driver	Starts	Poles	1	2	3	4	5	6–10	Laps	Laps Led	Races Led	Miles	$
1988	Dave Pletcher	1	0	0	0	0	0	0	0	464	0	0	472	2,015
Lifetime		3	0	0	0	0	0	0	0	674	0	0	1,020	$6,930

William P. Webb

Year	Driver	Starts	Poles	1	2	3	4	5	6–10	Laps	Laps Led	Races Led	Miles	$
1955	Bob Dawson	1	0	0	0	0	0	0	0	37	0	0	152	50
Lifetime		1	0	0	0	0	0	0	0	37	0	0	152	$50

Ewell Weddle

Year	Driver	Starts	Poles	1	2	3	4	5	6–10	Laps	Laps Led	Races Led	Miles	$
1950	Ewell Weddle	3	0	0	0	1	0	0	0	158	0	0	79	500
1951	Claude Joyce	1	0	0	0	0	0	0	0		0	0		25
1951	Ewell Weddle	2	0	0	0	0	0	0	0		0	0		50
1952	Ewell Weddle	3	0	0	0	0	0	0	0	465	0	0	316	125
1953	Ewell Weddle	4	0	0	0	0	0	0	1		0	0		125
Lifetime		13	0	0	0	1	0	0	1	623	0	0	395	$825

Larry Wehrs

Year	Driver	Starts	Poles	1	2	3	4	5	6–10	Laps	Laps Led	Races Led	Miles	$
1968	Dave Marcis	10	0	0	0	0	0	0	2	3,240	0	0	3,179	8,199
1969	Dave Marcis	1	0	0	0	0	0	0	1	180	0	0	90	140
Lifetime		11	0	0	0	0	0	0	3	3,420	0	0	3,269	$8,339

Curly Weida

Year	Driver	Starts	Poles	1	2	3	4	5	6–10	Laps	Laps Led	Races Led	Miles	$
1955	Royce Haggerty	1	0	0	0	0	0	0	0	228	0	0	228	100
Lifetime		1	0	0	0	0	0	0	0	228	0	0	228	$100

Charles Weidler

Year	Driver	Starts	Poles	1	2	3	4	5	6–10	Laps	Laps Led	Races Led	Miles	$
1952	Charles Weidler	1	0	0	0	0	0	0	0	27	0	0	14	25
1953	Charles Weidler	2	0	0	0	0	0	0	0	9	0	0	37	25
Lifetime		3	0	0	0	0	0	0	0	36	0	0	50	$50

Danny Weinberg

Year	Driver	Starts	Poles	1	2	3	4	5	6–10	Laps	Laps Led	Races Led	Miles	$
1951	Danny Weinberg	2	0	0	0	0	0	0	1	97	0	0	49	150
Lifetime		2	0	0	0	0	0	0	1	97	0	0	49	$150

Bob Welborn

Year	Driver	Starts	Poles	1	2	3	4	5	6–10	Laps	Laps Led	Races Led	Miles	$
1955	Bob Welborn	9	1	0	1	2	0	3	4	1,776	31	1	1,542	2,850
1955	Marvin Panch	1	0	0	0	0	1	0	0	245	0	0	245	750
1956	Bob Welborn	5	0	0	0	0	0	0	1	783	0	0	379	400
1956	Jimmy Massey	1	0	0	0	0	0	2	1	96	0	0	86	100
1956	Jim Paschal	2	0	0	0	0	0	2	2	353	0	0	177	200
1956	Jimmie Lewallen	3	0	0	0	0	0	0	0	91	0	0	66	100
1957	Tiny Lund	1	0	0	0	0	0	2	0	192	0	0	96	245
1957	Gwyn Staley	1	0	0	0	0	0	1	0	243	0	0	243	400
1957	Possum Jones	6	0	0	0	0	0	0	4	1,443	0	0	1,395	2,375
1957	Curtis Turner	1	0	0	0	0	0	0	0		0	0		50
1957	Bob Welborn	4	0	1	0	0	0	2	0	1,152	457	2	968	5,000
1958	Darel Dieringer	1	0	0	0	0	0	0	0	11	0	0	45	25
1958	Tiny Lund	1	0	0	0	0	0	1	0	9	0	0	37	0
1958	Possum Jones	2	0	0	0	0	0	1	1	340	28	1	145	445
1959	Bob Welborn	25	3	1	1	3	2	0	3	3,431	17	4	1,927	7,395
1960	Bob Welborn	12	0	0	0	0	2	3	4	2,483	18	1	2,402	4,540
1960	Jim Paschal	2	0	0	0	0	0	0	0	193	0	0	287	370
1961	Bob Welborn	4	0	0	0	0	0	0	1	715	1	1	1,128	1,390
Lifetime		81	4	2	2	5	5	17	21	13,556	552	10	11,166	$26,635

Max Welborn

Year	Driver	Starts	Poles	1	2	3	4	5	6–10	Laps	Laps Led	Races Led	Miles	$
1956	Rex White	24	1	0	0	2	0	1	11	4,240	0	0	2,978	4,720
1957	Rex White	7	1	0	1	0	3	0	1	1,561	193	2	1,132	3,570
1958	Possum Jones	1	1	0	0	0	0	0	0	54	0	0	27	0
1958	Rex White	2	0	1	0	1	0	0	0	298	5	1	105	985
Lifetime		34	3	1	1	3	3	1	12	6,153	198	3	4,242	$9,275

Year	Driver	Starts	Poles	1	2	3	4	5	6–10	Laps	Laps Led	Races Led	Miles	$
O.C. Welch														
1989	Mike Potter	1	0	0	0	0	0	0	0	137	0	0	187	2,455
Lifetime		1	0	0	0	0	0	0	0	137	0	0	187	$2,455
Chuck Wellings														
1989	Joe Ruttman	1	0	0	0	0	0	0	0	199	0	0	498	24,505
1990	Joe Ruttman	1	0	0	0	0	0	0	0	196	0	0	490	22,950
Lifetime		2	0	0	0	0	0	0	0	395	0	0	988	$47,455
Cal Wells														
2000	Scott Pruett	28	0	0	0	0	0	0	1	6,216	23	2	8,744	1,105,570
2000	Andy Houston	5	0	0	0	0	0	0	0	1,209	0	0	1,549	141,850
2001	Ricky Craven	36	1	1	1	0	1	1	3	9,670	170	9	12,787	1,864,964
2001	Andy Houston	17	0	0	0	0	0	0	0	3,612	1	1	4,812	850,501
2002	Ricky Craven	36	2	0	0	1	0	2	6	10,054	382	11	13,110	2,361,797
Lifetime		122	3	1	1	1	1	3	10	30,761	576	23	41,002	$6,324,682
Marvin Welty														
1972	Dick Brooks	5	0	0	0	0	0	0	0	236	0	0	467	3,630
Lifetime		5	0	0	0	0	0	0	0	236	0	0	467	$3,630
R.G. Wenschel														
1961	Robert Roeber	1	0	0	0	0	0	0	0	170	0	0	425	200
Lifetime		1	0	0	0	0	0	0	0	170	0	0	425	$200
Jerry Wentz														
1971	Pee Wee Wentz	1	0	0	0	0	0	0	0	100	0	0	46	300
1974	Pee Wee Wentz	1	0	0	0	0	0	0	0	135	0	0	71	570
Lifetime		2	0	0	0	0	0	0	0	235	0	0	117	$870
Carl Wesson														
1955	Bo Fields	3	0	0	0	0	0	0	0	347	0	0	292	100
Lifetime		3	0	0	0	0	0	0	0	347	0	0	292	$100

Hubert Westmoreland (Statistics represent teams primarily owned by Westmoreland, and include assorted ventures with Bill France Sr., Alvin Hawkins and Johnny Mantz.)

Year	Driver	Starts	Poles	1	2	3	4	5	6–10	Laps	Laps Led	Races Led	Miles	$
1949	Curtis Turner	1	0	1	0	0	0	0	0	200	60	1	200	2,250
1949	Glenn Dunnaway	1	0	0	0	0	0	0	0	200	0	0	150	0
1950	Jim Paschal	1	0	0	0	0	0	0	0		0	0		0
1950	Leon Sales	2	0	1	0	0	0	0	0	227	18	1	139	1,000
1950	Ted Swaim	1	0	0	1	0	0	0	0	200	0	0	100	600
1950	Johnny Mantz	1	0	1	0	0	0	0	0	400	351	1	500	10,510
1950	Tim Flock	1	0	0	0	0	1	0	0		0	0		400
1951	Bill Blair	3	0	0	1	0	0	0	1	199	0	0	100	725
1951	Leon Sales	3	0	0	0	0	0	0	2	384	0	0	480	825
1951	Johnny Yountz	1	0	0	0	0	0	0	0	361	0	0	451	50
1951	Jack Smith	1	0	0	0	0	0	0	0		0	0		25
1951	Herb Thomas	1	0	1	0	0	0	0	0	200	179	1	100	1,000
1951	Bill Holland	4	0	0	0	0	1	0	0	144	0	0	111	350
1951	Billy Myers	2	0	0	0	0	0	0	0	496	0	0	589	200
1955	Tim Flock	1	0	0	0	1	0	0	0	197	0	0	99	450
1955	Pee Wee Jones	2	0	0	0	0	0	0	0	204	0	0	102	50
1955	Jimmy Massey	11	0	0	0	1	1	2	4	1,906	0	0	1,721	3,100
1955	Gwyn Staley	23	1	0	1	2	2	2	7	3,193	33	1	2,225	5,665
1955	Billy Myers	2	0	0	0	0	0	0	1	512	0	0	555	215
1956	Gwyn Staley	20	0	0	0	0	2	3	7	2,925	0	0	2,113	4,430
1956	Jimmy Massey	5	0	0	0	0	1	2	0	655	0	0	436	1,145
1957	Billy Carden	2	0	0	0	0	0	0	2	483	0	0	680	1,575
1957	Bill Massey	1	0	0	0	0	0	0	0	129	0	0	81	100
1957	Frankie Schneider	4	1	0	1	0	1	0	2	670	37	1	537	3,095
1958	Frankie Schneider	1	0	0	0	0	0	0	0	29	0	0	119	50
1963	Jimmy Massey	13	0	0	0	0	1	0	7	3,101	0	0	1,384	2,620
1963	Curtis Crider	1	0	0	0	0	0	0	1	285	0	0	107	175

Year	Driver	Starts	Poles	Finish 1	2	3	4	5	6–10	Laps	Laps Led	Races Led	Miles	$

Hubert Westmoreland *continued*

Year	Driver	Starts	Poles	1	2	3	4	5	6–10	Laps	Laps Led	Races Led	Miles	$
1963	Bobby Keck	1	0	0	0	0	0	0	0	26	0	0	16	100
1964	Jimmy Massey	1	0	0	0	0	0	0	0		0	0		0
Lifetime		111	2	4	4	4	10	9	34	17,326	678	6	13,095	$40,705

LeRoy Weyher

Year	Driver	Starts	Poles	1	2	3	4	5	6–10	Laps	Laps Led	Races Led	Miles	$
1954	Howard Phillippi	2	0	0	0	0	0	0	0	264	0	0	232	40
1954	Jim Cook	3	0	0	0	0	0	0	0	759	0	0	472	65
1955	Jim Cook	1	0	0	0	0	0	0	0	110	0	0	110	40
Lifetime		6	0	0	0	0	0	0	0	1,133	0	0	813	$145

Dick Whalen

Year	Driver	Starts	Poles	1	2	3	4	5	6–10	Laps	Laps Led	Races Led	Miles	$
1979	Dick Whalen	1	0	0	0	0	0	0	0	81	0	0	212	950
Lifetime		1	0	0	0	0	0	0	0	81	0	0	212	$950

Fred Wheat

Year	Driver	Starts	Poles	1	2	3	4	5	6–10	Laps	Laps Led	Races Led	Miles	$
1960	Joe Weatherly	3	0	0	0	0	0	0	2	478	0	0	142	515
1960	T.C. Hunt	3	0	0	0	0	0	0	0	353	0	0	497	600
1961	T.C. Hunt	7	0	0	0	0	0	0	0	940	0	0	1,445	2,750
1962	T.C. Hunt	1	0	0	0	0	0	0	0	6	0	0	9	200
Lifetime		14	0	0	0	0	0	0	2	1,777	0	0	2,093	$4,065

Al Wheatley

Year	Driver	Starts	Poles	1	2	3	4	5	6–10	Laps	Laps Led	Races Led	Miles	$
1950	Jim Paschal	3	0	0	1	0	0	0	0	174	0	0	94	600
1951	Ewell Weddle	3	0	0	0	0	0	0	2	743	0	0	799	375
1951	Jim Paschal	2	0	0	0	0	0	0	0	353	0	0	441	50
1951	Bill Holluck	1	0	0	0	0	0	0	0		0	0		25
1951	Billy Carden	1	0	0	0	0	0	0	0		0	0		25
1952	Buck Baker	1	0	0	0	0	0	0	1	388	0	0	485	500
1953	Ralph Liguori	7	0	0	0	0	0	0	0	258	0	0	284	440
1953	Buck Baker	2	0	0	0	0	0	0	1	37	0	0	152	225
1955	Ralph Liguori	1	0	0	0	0	0	0	0	348	0	0	479	400
1955	Johnny Patterson	1	0	0	0	0	0	1	0	342	0	0	470	225
1956	Ralph Liguori	1	0	0	0	0	0	0	0	189	0	0	76	50
Lifetime		23	0	0	1	0	0	1	4	2,832	0	0	3,278	$2,915

R.G. Whelton

Year	Driver	Starts	Poles	1	2	3	4	5	6–10	Laps	Laps Led	Races Led	Miles	$
1951	Bob Flock	1	0	0	0	0	0	0	1		0	0		50
1953	Jimmie Lewallen	1	0	0	0	0	0	1	0		0	0		200
Lifetime		2	0	0	0	0	0	1	1		0	0		$250

Ed Whitaker

Year	Driver	Starts	Poles	1	2	3	4	5	6–10	Laps	Laps Led	Races Led	Miles	$
1978	John A. Utsman	4	0	0	0	0	0	0	0	612	0	0	1,026	7,040
1979	John A. Utsman	1	0	0	0	0	0	0	0	101	0	0	253	2,850
1980	John A. Utsman	1	0	0	0	0	0	0	0	149	0	0	373	2,695
Lifetime		6	0	0	0	0	0	0	0	862	0	0	1,651	$12,585

Bob Whitcomb

Year	Driver	Starts	Poles	1	2	3	4	5	6–10	Laps	Laps Led	Races Led	Miles	$
1988	Ken Bouchard	24	0	0	0	0	0	0	1	7,281	4	1	8,490	93,410
1989	Derrike Cope	20	0	0	0	0	0	0	4	4,931	5	3	6,231	116,340
1989	Ken Bouchard	4	0	0	0	0	0	0	0	911	0	0	1,373	33,930
1990	Derrike Cope	29	0	2	0	0	0	0	4	7,881	109	6	9,595	513,805
1991	Derrike Cope	28	0	0	0	0	1	0	1	6,784	0	0	8,451	390,880
1992	Derrike Cope	29	0	0	0	0	0	0	3	8,483	0	0	10,175	271,115
Lifetime		134	0	2	0	0	1	0	13	36,271	118	10	44,315	$1,419,480

Al White

Year	Driver	Starts	Poles	1	2	3	4	5	6–10	Laps	Laps Led	Races Led	Miles	$
1956	Al White	2	0	0	0	0	0	0	0	330	0	0	165	200
1957	Al White	3	0	0	0	0	0	0	1	161	0	0	200	200
1958	Al White	9	0	0	0	0	0	0	1	1,483	0	0	1,030	920

Year	Driver	Starts	Poles	Finish						Laps	Laps Led	Races Led	Miles	$
				1	2	3	4	5	6–10	Laps	Led	Led	Miles	$

Al White *continued*

Year	Driver	Starts	Poles	1	2	3	4	5	6–10	Laps	Laps Led	Races Led	Miles	$
1959	Al White	5	0	0	0	0	0	0	0	826	0	0	644	575
1960	Al White	2	0	0	0	0	0	0	1	643	0	0	322	450
1962	Al White	1	0	0	0	0	0	0	0	233	0	0	117	125
1963	Al White	1	0	0	0	0	0	0	0	211	0	0	106	150
Lifetime		23	0	0	0	0	0	0	3	3,887	0	0	2,583	$2,620

Bill White

Year	Driver	Starts	Poles	1	2	3	4	5	6–10	Laps	Laps Led	Races Led	Miles	$
1957	Russ Truelove	1	0	0	0	0	0	0	0		0	0		0
Lifetime		1	0	0	0	0	0	0	0		0	0		$0

Billy White

Year	Driver	Starts	Poles	1	2	3	4	5	6–10	Laps	Laps Led	Races Led	Miles	$
1991	Gary Wright	1	0	0	0	0	0	0	0	63	0	0	158	3,750
Lifetime		1	0	0	0	0	0	0	0	63	0	0	158	$3,750

Bob White

Year	Driver	Starts	Poles	1	2	3	4	5	6–10	Laps	Laps Led	Races Led	Miles	$
1956	Russ Truelove	5	0	0	0	0	0	0	2	545	0	0	574	450
Lifetime		5	0	0	0	0	0	0	2	545	0	0	574	$450

Dr. Bradford White

Year	Driver	Starts	Poles	1	2	3	4	5	6–10	Laps	Laps Led	Races Led	Miles	$
1958	Dick Joslin	1	0	0	0	0	0	0	0	6	0	0	25	0
1959	Curtis Turner	6	1	2	1	0	0	0	0	797	419	4	834	2,625
1959	Joe Weatherly	13	0	0	2	0	0	2	2	2,153	178	4	1,365	7,030
1959	Speedy Thompson	1	0	0	0	0	0	0	0	94	0	0	235	375
1959	Jimmy Thompson	1	0	0	0	0	0	0	1	346	0	0	476	805
1960	Joe Weatherly	1	0	0	0	0	0	0	0	49	0	0	25	50
1960	Joe Caspolich	2	0	0	0	0	0	0	0	227	0	0	568	315
1960	Jimmy Thompson	6	0	0	0	0	0	0	0	1,087	0	0	1,400	1,190
1960	Elmo Langley	5	0	0	0	0	0	0	0	827	0	0	687	720
1960	Possum Jones	1	0	0	0	0	0	0	0	291	0	0	437	275
1961	Joe Weatherly	1	0	1	0	0	0	0	0	200	40	1	100	800
1961	Elmo Langley	9	0	0	0	0	0	1	4	1,683	0	0	1,120	1,820
Lifetime		47	1	3	3	0	0	3	7	7,760	637	9	7,270	$16,005

Dave White

Year	Driver	Starts	Poles	1	2	3	4	5	6–10	Laps	Laps Led	Races Led	Miles	$
1958	Dave White	2	0	0	0	0	0	0	1	205	0	0	266	150
1959	Dave White	5	0	0	0	0	0	0	1	1,253	0	0	533	660
Lifetime		7	0	0	0	0	0	0	2	1,458	0	0	799	$810

Don White

Year	Driver	Starts	Poles	1	2	3	4	5	6–10	Laps	Laps Led	Races Led	Miles	$
1954	Don White	1	0	0	0	0	0	0	0	38	0	0	156	90
1955	Don White	3	0	0	2	1	0	0	0	296	0	0	198	1,750
Lifetime		4	0	0	2	1	0	0	0	334	0	0	354	$1,840

Gene White

Year	Driver	Starts	Poles	1	2	3	4	5	6–10	Laps	Laps Led	Races Led	Miles	$
1958	Billy Carden	1	0	0	0	0	0	0	0	141	0	0	71	0
1958	Gene White	9	0	0	0	0	0	0	2	1,641	0	0	1,295	1,400
1958	Jack Smith	1	0	0	0	0	0	0	0	338	0	0	169	305
1959	Gene White	7	0	0	0	0	0	0	2	1,210	0	0	1,012	1,360
Lifetime		18	0	0	0	0	0	0	4	3,330	0	0	2,546	$3,065

Herschel White

Year	Driver	Starts	Poles	1	2	3	4	5	6–10	Laps	Laps Led	Races Led	Miles	$
1957	Pat Kirkwood	1	0	0	0	0	0	0	0		0	0		50
Lifetime		1	0	0	0	0	0	0	0		0	0		$50

Jack White

Year	Driver	Starts	Poles	1	2	3	4	5	6–10	Laps	Laps Led	Races Led	Miles	$
1974	Bob Burcham	12	0	0	0	0	1	0	3	2,776	0	0	3,604	18,510
Lifetime		12	0	0	0	0	1	0	3	2,776	0	0	3,604	$18,510

Year	Driver	Starts	Poles	Finish 1	2	3	4	5	6–10	Laps	Laps Led	Races Led	Miles	$

Jim White

Year	Driver	Starts	Poles	1	2	3	4	5	6–10	Laps	Laps Led	Races Led	Miles	$
1951	Bill Majot	3	0	0	0	0	0	0	0	233	0	0	233	75
1961	Harlan Richardson	4	0	0	0	0	0	0	0	284	0	0	640	525
Lifetime		7	0	0	0	0	0	0	0	517	0	0	873	$600

Mike White

Year	Driver	Starts	Poles	1	2	3	4	5	6–10	Laps	Laps Led	Races Led	Miles	$
1975	Richard White	1	0	0	0	0	0	0	0	117	0	0	307	1,285
1977	Richard White	2	0	0	0	0	0	0	0	251	0	0	637	2,375
1978	Richard White	3	0	0	0	0	0	0	0	346	2	1	884	4,550
1979	Richard White	3	0	0	0	0	0	0	0	234	0	0	599	4,070
Lifetime		9	0	0	0	0	0	0	0	948	2	1	2,426	$12,280

Rex White (Statistics represent teams primarily owned by Rex White plus a partnership with Crawford Clements.)

Year	Driver	Starts	Poles	1	2	3	4	5	6–10	Laps	Laps Led	Races Led	Miles	$
1958	Rex White	5	1	0	0	1	0	0	2	1,096	118	1	853	2,700
1959	Rex White	20	5	5	2	2	1	1	2	4,416	826	9	2,860	11,290
1960	Rex White	37	3	6	6	7	4	2	8	8,405	342	11	6,557	44,555
1961	Rex White	46	7	7	8	8	2	4	8	9,962	1,224	15	7,067	47,905
1962	Tommy Irwin	1	0	0	0	0	0	0	0	124	0	0	186	300
1962	Rex White	37	9	8	3	3	1	3	5	7,683	1,129	15	5,760	30,643
1963	Rex White	25	3	0	3	2	0	0	9	5,595	171	6	5,490	23,670
Lifetime		171	28	26	22	23	8	10	34	37,281	3,810	57	28,773	$161,063

Paul Whiteman

Year	Driver	Starts	Poles	1	2	3	4	5	6–10	Laps	Laps Led	Races Led	Miles	$
1954	Gwyn Staley	2	0	0	0	0	0	0	1	357	0	0	480	670
1954	Junior Johnson	3	1	0	0	0	0	0	0	341	0	0	292	250
1954	Al Keller	1	0	1	0	0	0	0	0	50	28	1	100	1,000
1955	Junior Johnson	1	0	0	0	0	0	0	0	51	0	0	26	25
Lifetime		7	1	1	0	0	0	0	1	799	28	1	897	$1,945

John Whitford

Year	Driver	Starts	Poles	1	2	3	4	5	6–10	Laps	Laps Led	Races Led	Miles	$
1956	Bill Champion	13	0	0	0	0	0	0	3	2,110	0	0	1,532	1,470
1956	Joe Weatherly	1	0	0	0	0	1	0	0	197	0	0	99	350
1956	Buck Baker	1	0	0	0	0	0	0	1	190	0	0	95	100
1957	Pee Wee Jones	1	0	0	0	0	0	0	0	262	0	0	262	225
1957	Bill Champion	5	0	0	0	0	0	0	1	804	0	0	748	590
1957	Darel Dieringer	7	0	0	0	0	0	0	2	983	0	0	570	760
1958	Jimmy Massey	1	0	0	0	0	0	0	1	458	0	0	458	500
1958	Curtis Turner	2	0	0	0	0	0	0	0	414	0	0	305	275
1958	Marvin Panch	11	2	0	1	1	1	2	0	1,833	157	3	1,576	3,805
Lifetime		42	2	0	1	1	2	2	8	7,251	157	3	5,645	$8,075

Bob Whitmire

Year	Driver	Starts	Poles	1	2	3	4	5	6–10	Laps	Laps Led	Races Led	Miles	$
1957	Bob Whitmire	1	0	0	0	0	0	0	0	153	0	0	77	100
Lifetime		1	0	0	0	0	0	0	0	153	0	0	77	$100

Robert Whitmire

Year	Driver	Starts	Poles	1	2	3	4	5	6–10	Laps	Laps Led	Races Led	Miles	$
1957	Rod Perry	1	0	0	0	0	0	0	0		0	0		100
Lifetime		1	0	0	0	0	0	0	0		0	0		$100

Ken Whitney

Year	Driver	Starts	Poles	1	2	3	4	5	6–10	Laps	Laps Led	Races Led	Miles	$
1949	Jack Russell	3	0	0	0	0	0	0	2	178	0	0	89	175
1952	Jim Fiebelkorn	1	0	0	0	0	0	0	0	35	0	0	35	0
1955	Bill Blair	1	0	0	0	0	0	0	0	6	0	0	25	0
Lifetime		5	0	0	0	0	0	0	2	219	0	0	149	$175

Basil Whittaker

Year	Driver	Starts	Poles	1	2	3	4	5	6–10	Laps	Laps Led	Races Led	Miles	$
1965	Bud Harless	4	0	0	0	0	0	0	0	627	0	0	316	1,460
Lifetime		4	0	0	0	0	0	0	0	627	0	0	316	$1,460

Don Whittington

Year	Driver	Starts	Poles	1	2	3	4	5	6–10	Laps	Laps Led	Races Led	Miles	$
1980	Don Whittington	2	0	0	0	0	0	0	0	196	0	0	497	3,970
Lifetime		2	0	0	0	0	0	0	0	196	0	0	497	$3,970

Year	Driver	Starts	Poles	Finish						Laps	Laps Led	Races Led	Miles	$
				1	2	3	4	5	6–10	Laps	Led	Led	Miles	$

Reb Wickersham

Year	Driver	Starts	Poles	1	2	3	4	5	6–10	Laps	Laps Led	Races Led	Miles	$
1960	Reb Wickersham	7	0	0	0	0	0	0	0	1,119	0	0	1,948	2,575
1961	Bryant Wallace	2	0	0	0	0	0	0	0	81	0	0	40	100
1961	Reb Wickersham	8	0	0	0	0	0	0	1	1,343	0	0	1,199	1,345
1962	Reb Wickersham	1	0	0	0	0	0	0	0	133	0	0	67	0
1962	Jerry Burnett	1	0	0	0	0	0	0	0	143	0	0	57	75
1963	Reb Wickersham	14	0	0	0	0	0	0	1	3,501	0	0	2,577	3,800
1963	Jimmy Pardue	1	0	0	0	0	0	0	1	283	0	0	71	175
Lifetime		34	0	0	0	0	0	0	3	6,603	0	0	5,958	$8,070

Bill Widenhouse

Year	Driver	Starts	Poles	1	2	3	4	5	6–10	Laps	Laps Led	Races Led	Miles	$
1950	Bill Widenhouse	1	0	0	0	0	0	0	0	350	0	0	438	0
1951	Bill Widenhouse	4	0	0	0	0	0	0	0	371	0	0	464	225
Lifetime		5	0	0	0	0	0	0	0	721	0	0	901	$225

Bob Widenhouse

Year	Driver	Starts	Poles	1	2	3	4	5	6–10	Laps	Laps Led	Races Led	Miles	$
1954	Bill Widenhouse	6	0	0	0	0	0	0	0	987	0	0	999	425
1956	Bill Widenhouse	2	0	0	0	0	0	0	0	324	0	0	301	150
Lifetime		8	0	0	0	0	0	0	0	1,311	0	0	1,300	$575

Dink Widenhouse

Year	Driver	Starts	Poles	1	2	3	4	5	6–10	Laps	Laps Led	Races Led	Miles	$
1954	Dink Widenhouse	6	0	0	0	0	1	0	1	620	0	0	401	625
1955	Dink Widenhouse	15	1	0	0	0	0	0	6	1,743	0	0	1,166	1,660
1956	Dink Widenhouse	6	0	0	0	0	1	0	2	670	0	0	503	940
Lifetime		27	1	0	0	0	2	0	9	3,033	0	0	2,070	$3,225

Felix Wilkes

Year	Driver	Starts	Poles	1	2	3	4	5	6–10	Laps	Laps Led	Races Led	Miles	$
1949	Felix Wilkes	3	0	0	0	0	0	0	0	38	0	0	38	0
1950	Felix Wilkes	1	0	0	0	0	0	0	0		0	0		0
1951	Felix Wilkes	2	0	0	0	0	0	0	0	18	0	0	14	10
1952	Felix Wilkes	1	0	0	0	0	0	0	0	141	0	0	141	35
Lifetime		7	0	0	0	0	0	0	0	197	0	0	193	$45

Thurman Wilkes

Year	Driver	Starts	Poles	1	2	3	4	5	6–10	Laps	Laps Led	Races Led	Miles	$
1962	Jim Bennett	5	0	0	0	0	0	1	1	402	0	0	341	950
Lifetime		5	0	0	0	0	0	1	1	402	0	0	341	$950

Chet Williams

Year	Driver	Starts	Poles	1	2	3	4	5	6–10	Laps	Laps Led	Races Led	Miles	$
1953	Chet Williams	2	0	0	0	0	0	0	0	374	0	0	429	135
Lifetime		2	0	0	0	0	0	0	0	374	0	0	429	$135

Ewell Williams

Year	Driver	Starts	Poles	1	2	3	4	5	6–10	Laps	Laps Led	Races Led	Miles	$
1962	Art Brady	1	0	0	0	0	0	0	0	176	0	0	440	400
Lifetime		1	0	0	0	0	0	0	0	176	0	0	440	$400

Jack Williams

Year	Driver	Starts	Poles	1	2	3	4	5	6–10	Laps	Laps Led	Races Led	Miles	$
1981	Jim Robinson	3	0	0	0	0	0	0	2	264	0	0	692	9,505
Lifetime		3	0	0	0	0	0	0	2	264	0	0	692	$9,505

Lois Williams

Year	Driver	Starts	Poles	1	2	3	4	5	6–10	Laps	Laps Led	Races Led	Miles	$
1982	Jim Robinson	2	0	0	0	0	0	0	0	150	0	0	393	2,220
1983	Jim Robinson	2	0	0	0	0	0	0	0	204	0	0	534	6,075
1984	Jim Robinson	2	0	0	0	0	0	0	0	189	0	0	495	7,560
1985	Jim Robinson	2	0	0	0	0	0	0	0	209	0	0	548	10,820
1986	Jim Robinson	2	0	0	0	0	0	0	0	192	0	0	503	9,300
1987	Jim Robinson	2	0	0	0	0	0	0	0	157	0	0	411	5,685
Lifetime		12	0	0	0	0	0	0	0	1,101	0	0	2,885	$41,660

Raymond Williams

Year	Driver	Starts	Poles	1	2	3	4	5	6–10	Laps	Laps Led	Races Led	Miles	$
1971	J.D. McDuffie	1	0	0	0	0	0	0	0	222	0	0	333	1,117
1971	Raymond Williams	13	0	0	0	0	0	0	0	2,364	0	0	3,471	9,550

Year	Driver	Starts	Poles	Finish 1	2	3	4	5	6–10	Laps	Laps Led	Races Led	Miles	$

Raymond Williams *continued*

Year	Driver	Starts	Poles	1	2	3	4	5	6–10	Laps	Laps Led	Races Led	Miles	$
1972	Raymond Williams	27	0	0	0	0	0	0	5	6,337	0	0	7,650	30,965
1973	Raymond Williams	22	0	0	0	0	0	0	3	4,684	0	0	5,233	22,728
Lifetime		63	0	0	0	0	0	0	8	13,607	0	0	16,687	$64,360

Tom Williams

Year	Driver	Starts	Poles	1	2	3	4	5	6–10	Laps	Laps Led	Races Led	Miles	$
1975	Grant Adcox	1	0	0	0	0	0	0	0	133	0	0	354	1,615
1975	Tom Reynolds	2	0	0	0	0	0	0	0	203	0	0	524	2,195
1975	Walter Ballard	1	0	0	0	0	0	0	0	94	0	0	235	885
1976	Tom Williams	1	0	0	0	0	0	0	0	41	0	0	103	1,615
Lifetime		5	0	0	0	0	0	0	0	471	0	0	1,215	$6,310

Wildcat Williams

Year	Driver	Starts	Poles	1	2	3	4	5	6–10	Laps	Laps Led	Races Led	Miles	$
1961	Bunkie Blackburn	5	0	0	0	0	0	0	0	478	0	0	485	1,175
1962	Art Brady	1	0	0	0	0	0	0	0	3	0	0	8	50
1962	T.C. Hunt	2	0	0	0	0	0	0	0	157	0	0	63	50
1962	Cale Yarborough	1	0	0	0	0	0	0	0	212	0	0	318	375
1962	Jimmy Thompson	1	0	0	0	0	0	0	0	364	0	0	546	475
1962	Bunkie Blackburn	1	0	0	0	0	0	0	0	23	0	0	35	200
1963	Cotton Hodges	1	0	0	0	0	0	0	0	9	0	0	5	50
Lifetime		12	0	0	0	0	0	0	0	1,246	0	0	1,458	$2,375

Tim Williamson

Year	Driver	Starts	Poles	1	2	3	4	5	6–10	Laps	Laps Led	Races Led	Miles	$
1979	Tim Williamson	3	0	0	0	0	0	0	1	340	0	0	868	5,580
Lifetime		3	0	0	0	0	0	0	1	340	0	0	868	$5,580

Buzz Wilson

Year	Driver	Starts	Poles	1	2	3	4	5	6–10	Laps	Laps Led	Races Led	Miles	$
1958	Buzz Wilson	2	0	0	0	0	0	0	0	270	0	0	135	175
Lifetime		2	0	0	0	0	0	0	0	270	0	0	135	$175

C.D. Wilson

Year	Driver	Starts	Poles	1	2	3	4	5	6–10	Laps	Laps Led	Races Led	Miles	$
1952	Tommy Moon	6	1	0	1	0	0	0	1	487	0	0	428	1,145
1953	Tommy Moon	1	0	0	0	0	0	0	0	5	0	0	21	0
Lifetime		7	1	0	1	0	0	1	1	492	0	0	449	$1,145

E.C. Wilson

Year	Driver	Starts	Poles	1	2	3	4	5	6–10	Laps	Laps Led	Races Led	Miles	$
1959	Fireball Roberts	1	0	0	0	0	0	0	0	385	0	0	193	85
1959	Joe Weatherly	2	0	0	0	0	1	1	0	239	7	2	598	2,125
1960	Charley Griffin	2	0	0	0	0	0	0	0	445	0	0	668	1,000
1960	Roy Tyner	4	0	0	0	0	0	0	2	531	0	0	645	640
1960	Joe Lee Johnson	7	0	0	1	0	0	1	2	1,255	0	0	787	2,235
1960	Friday Hassler	2	0	0	0	0	0	0	0	251	0	0	377	425
1960	Tommy Irwin	1	0	0	0	0	0	0	0	59	0	0	30	0
Lifetime		19	0	0	1	0	1	2	4	3,165	7	2	3,296	$6,510

Elmer Wilson

Year	Driver	Starts	Poles	1	2	3	4	5	6–10	Laps	Laps Led	Races Led	Miles	$
1950	Elmer Wilson	2	0	0	0	0	0	0	0	360	0	0	450	150
1951	Elmer Wilson	3	0	0	0	0	0	0	0	80	0	0	80	25
Lifetime		5	0	0	0	0	0	0	0	440	0	0	530	$175

Fritz Wilson

Year	Driver	Starts	Poles	1	2	3	4	5	6–10	Laps	Laps Led	Races Led	Miles	$
1959	Fritz Wilson	3	0	0	1	0	0	0	0	388	4	1	304	700
1960	Fritz Wilson	4	0	0	0	0	2	0	0	284	0	0	367	1,100
Lifetime		7	0	0	1	0	2	0	0	672	4	1	671	$1,800

Gus Wilson

Year	Driver	Starts	Poles	1	2	3	4	5	6–10	Laps	Laps Led	Races Led	Miles	$
1957	Gus Wilson	1	0	0	0	0	0	0	0	98	0	0	49	50
1958	Gus Wilson	3	0	0	0	0	0	0	0	359	0	0	163	175
1959	Gus Wilson	1	0	0	0	0	0	0	0	100	0	0	50	50
Lifetime		5	0	0	0	0	0	0	0	557	0	0	262	$275

Year	Driver	Starts	Poles	Finish 1	2	3	4	5	6–10	Laps	Laps Led	Races Led	Miles	$

Jim Wilson

Year	Driver	Starts	Poles	1	2	3	4	5	6–10	Laps	Laps Led	Races Led	Miles	$
1993	Jay Hedgecock	1	0	0	0	0	0	0	0	372	0	0	233	4,780
1994	Jay Hedgecock	2	0	0	0	0	0	0	0	537	0	0	288	9,475
1994	Pancho Carter	1	0	0	0	0	0	0	0	322	0	0	490	9,130
1996	Randy MacDonald	3	0	0	0	0	0	0	0	680	0	0	1,285	31,610
1996	Billy Standridge	3	0	0	0	0	0	0	0	789	0	0	1,123	27,780
1997	Billy Standridge	5	0	0	0	0	0	0	0	1,148	0	0	1,864	118,085
1997	Gary Bradberry	6	0	0	0	0	0	0	0	1,585	0	0	1,893	95,650
1997	Tom Hubert	1	0	0	0	0	0	0	0	73	0	0	184	21,350
1998	Gary Bradberry	12	0	0	0	0	0	0	0	3,280	0	0	4,400	277,731
Lifetime		34	0	0	0	0	0	0	0	8,786	0	0	11,760	$595,591

Rick Wilson

Year	Driver	Starts	Poles	1	2	3	4	5	6–10	Laps	Laps Led	Races Led	Miles	$
1980	Rick Wilson	3	0	0	0	0	0	0	0	262	0	0	595	5,510
1981	Rick Wilson	8	0	0	0	0	0	0	0	989	7	2	1,713	15,625
1982	Rick Wilson	8	0	0	0	0	0	0	2	1,404	0	0	2,612	33,230
1983	Rick Wilson	1	0	0	0	0	0	0	0	55	0	0	146	2,135
Lifetime		20	0	0	0	0	0	0	2	2,710	7	2	5,066	$56,500

Woodrow Wilson

Year	Driver	Starts	Poles	1	2	3	4	5	6–10	Laps	Laps Led	Races Led	Miles	$
1949	Woodie Wilson	1	0	0	0	0	0	0	0		0	0		25
Lifetime		1	0	0	0	0	0	0	0		0	0		$25

Jerry Wimbish

Year	Driver	Starts	Poles	1	2	3	4	5	6–10	Laps	Laps Led	Races Led	Miles	$
1951	Jerry Wimbish	2	0	0	0	0	0	0	1	51	0	0	51	75
1952	Jerry Wimbish	4	0	0	0	0	0	1	0	222	0	0	113	395
1953	Jerry Wimbish	1	0	0	0	0	0	1	0		0	0		200
1954	Jerry Wimbish	1	0	0	0	0	0	0	0	92	0	0	92	25
Lifetime		8	0	0	0	0	0	2	1	365	0	0	256	$695

Andy Winfree

Year	Driver	Starts	Poles	1	2	3	4	5	6–10	Laps	Laps Led	Races Led	Miles	$
1953	Andy Winfree	7	0	0	0	0	0	0	3	277	0	0	277	440
1954	Andy Winfree	3	0	0	0	0	0	0	1	301	0	0	216	175
Lifetime		10	0	0	0	0	0	0	4	578	0	0	493	$615

Tom Winkle

Year	Driver	Starts	Poles	1	2	3	4	5	6–10	Laps	Laps Led	Races Led	Miles	$
1986	J.D. McDuffie	6	0	0	0	0	0	0	0	1,768	0	0	1,537	26,500
1987	J.D. McDuffie	3	0	0	0	0	0	0	0	1,054	0	0	1,170	17,430
1987	Steve Christman	20	0	0	0	0	0	0	0	4,404	0	0	5,101	46,115
1988	Joe Ruttman	1	0	0	0	0	0	0	0	71	0	0	72	1,550
1988	Morgan Shepherd	3	1	0	0	0	0	0	1	900	7	2	743	27,145
1988	Rodney Combs	17	0	0	0	0	0	0	0	3,469	0	0	4,570	44,390
1988	Tommy Ellis	2	0	0	0	0	0	0	0	178	0	0	267	3,125
1989	Greg Sacks	9	0	0	0	0	0	0	0	1,742	2	1	2,061	23,550
1989	Mickey Gibbs	3	0	0	0	0	0	0	0	745	0	0	712	8,630
Lifetime		64	1	0	0	0	0	0	1	14,331	9	3	16,233	$198,435

Hans Winter

Year	Driver	Starts	Poles	1	2	3	4	5	6–10	Laps	Laps Led	Races Led	Miles	$
1950	Al Gross	1	0	0	0	0	1	0	0	48	0	0	200	550
1952	Johnny Thompson	2	0	0	0	0	0	0	0		0	0		25
Lifetime		3	0	0	0	0	1	0	0	48	0	0	200	$575

Joe Winter

Year	Driver	Starts	Poles	1	2	3	4	5	6–10	Laps	Laps Led	Races Led	Miles	$
1951	Frank Luptow	4	0	0	0	0	0	1	0	161	0	0	125	250
Lifetime		4	0	0	0	0	0	1	0	161	0	0	125	$250

Wood Brothers

Year	Driver	Starts	Poles	1	2	3	4	5	6–10	Laps	Laps Led	Races Led	Miles	$
1953	Glen Wood	2	0	0	0	0	0	0	0	274	0	0	274	125
1955	Glen Wood	1	0	0	0	0	0	0	0	55	0	0	28	0
1956	Glen Wood	1	0	0	0	0	0	0	0	110	0	0	55	0
1957	Glen Wood	6	0	0	0	0	0	0	1	1,062	0	0	847	1,670
1957	Jimmy Massey	2	0	0	1	0	0	0	1	652	7	1	345	2,115

Wood Brothers *continued*

Year	Driver	Starts	Poles	1	2	3	4	5	6–10	Laps	Laps Led	Races Led	Miles	$
1958	Glen Wood	10	3	0	1	0	0	0	6	2,348	360	4	1,331	3,120
1958	Jimmy Massey	1	0	0	0	0	0	1	0	148	0	0	49	255
1958	Curtis Turner	1	0	0	0	0	0	0	0	26	0	0	7	125
1959	Joe Weatherly	1	0	0	0	0	0	0	1	196	0	0	49	200
1959	Glen Wood	18	3	0	5	1	1	1	3	3,703	98	2	2,100	6,310
1959	Junior Johnson	2	0	0	0	0	1	0	0	324	0	0	137	275
1959	Johnny Beauchamp	1	0	0	0	0	0	0	0	132	0	0	132	190
1960	Curtis Turner	1	0	0	0	0	0	0	0	78	0	0	70	50
1960	Junior Johnson	2	1	0	0	0	1	0	0	247	0	0	124	345
1960	Joe Weatherly	2	0	0	0	0	1	0	0	394	0	0	237	585
1960	Jimmy Massey	3	0	0	1	1	0	0	0	835	26	1	368	2,085
1960	Glen Wood	9	4	3	0	2	0	1	1	2,206	766	5	973	5,260
1960	Fred Harb	1	0	0	0	0	0	0	0	370	0	0	185	275
1960	Speedy Thompson	3	0	2	0	0	1	0	0	797	208	2	996	15,985
1960	Bob Welborn	1	0	0	0	0	0	0	0	127	0	0	32	125
1961	Glen Wood	6	1	0	2	1	0	0	0	1,101	138	1	445	2,000
1961	Curtis Turner	7	0	0	1	0	0	0	0	949	159	5	1,164	5,960
1961	Speedy Thompson	1	0	0	0	0	0	0	0	252	0	0	378	825
1961	Banjo Matthews	1	0	0	0	0	0	0	0	202	0	0	126	100
1962	Marvin Panch	14	0	0	2	3	0	0	3	3,552	156	3	3,667	23,470
1963	Marvin Panch	12	3	1	2	5	1	0	3	3,510	291	6	3,742	37,396
1963	Glen Wood	3	2	1	0	1	0	0	0	571	268	2	143	1,070
1963	Tommy Irwin	1	0	0	0	0	0	1	0	198	0	0	59	240
1963	Tiny Lund	7	0	1	1	1	1	1	1	1,979	124	3	2,024	32,620
1963	Dave MacDonald	1	0	0	1	0	0	0	0	147	92	1	397	4,655
1963	Fred Lorenzen	1	0	0	0	0	0	0	0	158	8	1	427	530
1964	Nelson Stacy	1	0	0	0	0	0	0	0	5	0	0	7	500
1964	Marvin Panch	29	4	3	7	3	3	1	3	6,452	648	10	4,899	31,785
1964	Glen Wood	2	1	0	0	1	0	0	0	305	5	1	76	530
1964	Dan Gurney	4	0	1	0	0	0	0	1	433	142	1	1,103	14,770
1965	A.J. Foyt	2	0	1	0	0	0	0	0	251	30	1	537	9,075
1965	Curtis Turner	4	0	1	0	1	0	1	0	1,208	256	2	1,171	17,380
1965	Dan Gurney	1	0	1	0	0	0	0	0	185	126	1	500	13,625
1965	Marvin Panch	20	5	4	1	4	1	2	2	4,743	856	12	4,716	54,205
1966	Dan Gurney	1	0	1	0	0	0	0	0	185	148	1	500	18,445
1966	Cale Yarborough	5	0	0	0	0	1	0	0	1,876	42	2	1,748	4,350
1966	Marvin Panch	6	0	0	0	0	1	0	0	1,231	70	3	1,531	4,400
1966	Curtis Turner	6	0	0	1	0	1	0	0	1,275	80	4	1,830	6,790
1967	Earl Balmer	1	0	0	0	0	0	0	0	102	0	0	140	625
1967	Cale Yarborough	15	4	2	3	1	1	0	1	3,532	908	9	3,570	56,210
1968	Cale Yarborough	20	4	6	2	1	0	3	0	5,497	1,065	16	5,622	133,886
1968	Dan Gurney	1	1	1	0	0	0	0	0	186	124	1	502	21,250
1969	Dan Gurney	1	0	0	0	0	0	0	0	66	0	0	178	980
1969	Swede Savage	2	0	0	0	0	0	1	0	173	0	0	433	2,970
1969	Cale Yarborough	19	6	2	2	1	2	0	1	4,341	946	16	5,482	75,065
1970	Parnelli Jones	1	0	0	0	0	0	0	0	168	88	1	440	1,275
1970	Cale Yarborough	18	5	3	4	3	0	1	2	4,784	906	14	5,896	116,400
1971	Donnie Allison	11	5	1	1	1	2	2	1	2,797	795	6	3,784	67,985
1971	A.J. Foyt	4	4	2	1	1	0	0	0	778	392	4	1,624	86,350
1972	A.J. Foyt	6	3	2	2	0	1	0	0	1,417	344	6	2,778	101,340
1972	David Pearson	14	4	6	1	3	1	0	1	4,377	1,567	14	5,756	133,165
1973	David Pearson	18	8	11	2	1	0	0	0	5,338	2,658	16	7,197	224,566
1974	David Pearson	19	11	7	5	2	1	0	0	4,630	1,167	18	7,746	215,475
1975	David Pearson	21	7	3	6	2	2	0	1	5,653	1,323	18	8,580	187,665
1976	David Pearson	22	8	10	3	2	1	0	2	6,194	1,233	19	9,049	328,490
1977	David Pearson	22	5	2	7	2	2	3	0	5,694	868	17	8,181	211,095
1978	David Pearson	22	7	4	2	1	1	3	0	5,375	757	13	7,603	186,605
1979	Neil Bonnett	17	4	3	0	0	1	0	2	3,766	556	13	5,427	131,875
1979	David Pearson	5	1	0	1	0	0	0	0	1,021	173	4	1,564	22,815
1980	Neil Bonnett	22	0	2	4	1	1	2	3	5,173	331	14	7,504	207,240
1981	Neil Bonnett	22	1	3	1	0	3	0	1	4,917	1,549	16	6,366	180,920
1982	Neil Bonnett	22	0	1	0	2	1	2	2	5,516	412	12	7,194	123,760
1983	Buddy Baker	21	1	1	1	2	0	1	7	5,111	174	7	6,816	201,355
1984	Buddy Baker	21	1	0	1	2	0	1	8	6,216	84	2	7,451	133,635
1984	Bobby Rahal	1	0	0	0	0	0	0	0	44	0	0	115	875
1985	Kyle Petty	28	0	0	1	1	1	4	5	8,796	75	6	10,384	248,590
1986	Kyle Petty	29	0	1	0	1	0	2	10	8,446	17	6	10,204	352,375
1987	Kyle Petty	29	0	1	1	4	0	0	8	8,523	103	7	10,401	431,010

Year	Driver	Starts	Poles	Finish 1	2	3	4	5	6–10	Laps	Laps Led	Races Led	Miles	$

Wood Brothers *continued*

Year	Driver	Starts	Poles	1	2	3	4	5	6–10	Laps	Laps Led	Races Led	Miles	$
1988	Kyle Petty	29	0	0	0	0	0	2	6	8,883	66	3	10,524	327,295
1989	Tommy Ellis	3	0	0	0	0	0	0	0	996	0	0	885	15,385
1989	Neil Bonnett	26	0	0	0	0	0	0	11	7,795	23	6	9,488	227,052
1990	Neil Bonnett	5	0	0	0	0	0	0	0	1,179	0	0	1,635	62,600
1990	Dale Jarrett	24	0	0	0	0	1	0	6	6,801	74	5	7,800	208,265
1991	Dale Jarrett	29	0	1	0	0	0	2	5	7,767	47	7	9,440	399,070
1992	Morgan Shepherd	29	0	0	2	0	0	1	8	9,093	60	3	10,840	567,090
1993	Morgan Shepherd	30	0	1	1	0	1	0	12	9,442	92	9	11,407	602,635
1994	Morgan Shepherd	31	0	0	2	2	1	4	7	9,788	81	10	11,951	864,715
1995	Morgan Shepherd	31	0	0	1	1	1	1	6	9,274	32	8	11,547	862,041
1996	Michael Waltrip	31	0	0	0	0	0	1	10	9,279	18	5	11,166	856,825
1997	Michael Waltrip	32	0	0	0	0	0	0	6	9,277	11	5	12,041	984,295
1998	Michael Waltrip	32	0	0	0	0	0	0	5	9,519	14	7	12,493	1,330,685
1999	Elliott Sadler	34	0	0	0	0	0	0	1	9,851	5	3	12,855	1,534,954
2000	Elliott Sadler	33	0	0	0	0	0	0	1	8,644	6	5	11,045	1,548,815
2001	Elliott Sadler	36	0	1	0	1	0	0	0	10,392	125	8	13,541	2,419,917
2002	Elliott Sadler	36	0	0	2	0	0	0	5	9,789	29	8	13,183	3,265,134
Lifetime		1128	117	97	85	62	39	45	170	301,252	24,402	442	369,346	$20,586,436

Gifford Wood

Year	Driver	Starts	Poles	1	2	3	4	5	6–10	Laps	Laps Led	Races Led	Miles	$
1953	Gifford Wood	2	0	0	0	0	0	0	0	136	0	0	68	50
1954	Gifford Wood	1	0	0	0	0	0	0	0	152	0	0	76	25
Lifetime		3	0	0	0	0	0	0	0	288	0	0	144	$75

Richard Woodland

Year	Driver	Starts	Poles	1	2	3	4	5	6–10	Laps	Laps Led	Races Led	Miles	$
1993	Rich Woodland	1	0	0	0	0	0	0	0	114	0	0	114	6,030
1996	Rich Woodland	1	0	0	0	0	0	0	0	68	0	0	171	10,095
Lifetime		2	0	0	0	0	0	0	0	182	0	0	285	$16,125

Ernest Woods

Year	Driver	Starts	Poles	1	2	3	4	5	6–10	Laps	Laps Led	Races Led	Miles	$
1953	Emory Lewis	2	0	0	0	0	0	0	1	387	0	0	364	255
1953	Tommy Thompson	1	0	0	0	0	0	0	0		0	0		25
1954	Bob Flock	2	0	0	0	0	0	0	0	167	0	0	84	25
1954	Buck Baker	14	6	2	1	3	1	2	3	2,410	432	8	1,445	5,600
1954	Elbert Allen	1	0	0	0	0	0	0	0	179	0	0	90	25
1954	Emory Lewis	5	0	0	0	0	0	0	2	422	0	0	378	475
1954	Jim Paschal	14	1	0	0	0	0	1	4	1,886	0	0	1,419	2,060
1954	Joel Million	9	0	0	0	0	0	0	1	1,298	0	0	1,324	875
1954	Tim Flock	1	0	0	0	0	0	0	0	39	0	0	160	0
1954	Ray Duhigg	1	0	0	0	0	0	0	0	2	0	0	1	0
1955	Joel Million	8	0	0	1	0	1	0	4	973	0	0	605	1,685
1955	Jimmie Lewallen	22	1	0	2	0	4	0	5	2,913	0	0	2,249	4,365
1955	Jim Paschal	31	2	3	3	2	2	1	7	4,126	306	7	2,829	9,000
1955	Fred Harb	1	0	0	0	0	0	0	0	93	0	0	93	60
1955	Dick Rathmann	1	0	0	0	0	0	0	0	38	0	0	156	100
1956	Banjo Matthews	1	0	0	0	0	0	0	0	149	0	0	224	200
1956	Joel Million	2	0	0	0	0	0	0	0	175	0	0	88	50
1956	Blackie Pitt	2	0	0	0	0	0	0	1	291	0	0	173	200
1956	Jimmie Lewallen	4	0	0	0	0	1	0	0	407	0	0	350	1,000
1956	Ralph Liguori	2	0	0	0	0	0	0	0	390	0	0	503	300
1957	Jim Linke	2	0	0	0	0	0	0	1	213	0	0	179	300
Lifetime		126	10	5	7	5	9	4	29	16,558	738	15	12,710	$26,600

Buzz Woodward

Year	Driver	Starts	Poles	1	2	3	4	5	6–10	Laps	Laps Led	Races Led	Miles	$
1957	Buzz Woodward	1	0	0	0	0	0	0	1	87	0	0	87	165
1958	Buzz Woodward	8	0	0	0	0	0	0	2	1,436	0	0	992	1,135
1959	Buzz Woodward	1	0	0	0	0	0	1	0	191	0	0	96	225
1961	Buzz Woodward	1	0	0	0	0	0	0	1	459	0	0	115	400
Lifetime		11	0	0	0	0	0	1	4	2,173	0	0	1,290	$1,925

Wayne Woodward

Year	Driver	Starts	Poles	1	2	3	4	5	6–10	Laps	Laps Led	Races Led	Miles	$
1966	Wayne Woodward	6	0	0	0	0	0	0	0	936	0	0	489	1,290
Lifetime		6	0	0	0	0	0	0	0	936	0	0	489	$1,290

Year	Driver	Starts	Poles	Finish 1	2	3	4	5	6–10	Laps	Laps Led	Races Led	Miles	$

Dick Wright

Year	Driver	Starts	Poles	1	2	3	4	5	6–10	Laps	Laps Led	Races Led	Miles	$
1960	Larry Frank	2	0	0	0	0	0	0	0	93	0	0	60	125
1960	Jimmy Thompson	1	0	0	0	0	0	0	0	157	9	1	236	325
1961	Larry Frank	5	0	0	0	0	0	0	1	483	0	0	904	1,275
Lifetime		8	0	0	0	0	0	0	1	733	9	1	1,199	$1,725

Earl Wright

Year	Driver	Starts	Poles	1	2	3	4	5	6–10	Laps	Laps Led	Races Led	Miles	$
1955	Dick Allwine	1	0	0	0	0	0	0	0	202	0	0	278	50
1955	Russ Graham	5	0	0	0	0	0	0	0	735	0	0	702	375
1956	Russ Graham	1	0	0	0	0	0	0	0	26	0	0	36	50
1956	Dick Allwine	2	0	0	0	0	0	0	0	294	0	0	294	200
Lifetime		9	0	0	0	0	0	0	0	1,257	0	0	1,309	$675

Millard Wright

Year	Driver	Starts	Poles	1	2	3	4	5	6–10	Laps	Laps Led	Races Led	Miles	$
1954	Tommie Elliott	3	0	0	0	0	0	0	3	546	0	0	273	400
1954	Ronnie Kohler	2	0	0	0	0	0	0	1	368	0	0	276	150
1955	Millard Wright	1	0	0	0	0	0	0	0	182	0	0	91	60
1956	Millard Wright	1	0	0	0	0	0	0	0	178	0	0	89	50
Lifetime		7	0	0	0	0	0	0	4	1,274	0	0	729	$660

R.H. Yandell

Year	Driver	Starts	Poles	1	2	3	4	5	6–10	Laps	Laps Led	Races Led	Miles	$
1951	Buddy Shuman	7	0	0	0	1	0	0	6	391	0	0	489	2,200
Lifetime		7	0	0	0	1	0	0	6	391	0	0	489	$2,200

Eddie Yarboro

Year	Driver	Starts	Poles	1	2	3	4	5	6–10	Laps	Laps Led	Races Led	Miles	$
1968	Eddie Yarboro	2	0	0	0	0	0	0	0	784	0	0	433	580
1970	Eddie Yarboro	1	0	0	0	0	0	0	1	338	0	0	201	800
1971	Eddie Yarboro	7	0	0	0	0	0	0	0	1,624	0	0	1,310	3,685
1971	Wendell Scott	1	0	0	0	0	0	0	0	251	0	0	132	425
1972	Eddie Yarboro	6	0	0	0	0	0	0	0	1,728	0	0	1,336	3,435
Lifetime		17	0	0	0	0	0	0	1	4,725	0	0	3,412	$8,925

Cale Yarborough

Year	Driver	Starts	Poles	1	2	3	4	5	6–10	Laps	Laps Led	Races Led	Miles	$
1987	Cale Yarborough	16	0	0	0	0	1	1	2	2,671	11	2	4,519	88,525
1988	Dale Jarrett	19	0	0	0	0	0	0	1	5,361	4	1	5,514	59,610
1988	Cale Yarborough	10	0	0	0	0	0	0	3	1,653	6	2	3,169	56,065
1989	Dale Jarrett	29	0	0	0	0	0	2	3	7,798	99	3	9,180	215,317
1990	Dick Trickle	29	1	0	0	1	0	1	2	8,291	82	4	9,908	293,490
1991	Dick Trickle	4	0	0	0	0	0	0	0	1,362	0	0	1,736	61,235
1991	Dorsey Schroeder	1	0	0	0	0	0	0	0	2	0	0	3	5,105
1991	Lake Speed	20	0	0	0	0	0	0	0	4,513	0	0	5,053	147,400
1991	Chuck Bown	1	0	0	0	0	0	0	0	391	0	0	244	5,225
1991	Randy LaJoie	3	0	0	0	0	0	0	0	926	0	0	1,062	19,625
1992	Jimmy Hensley	22	0	0	0	0	0	0	4	6,804	22	3	8,492	213,930
1992	Bobby Hillin	1	0	0	0	0	0	0	0	393	0	0	246	5,260
1992	Chad Little	6	0	0	0	0	0	0	0	1,852	0	0	1,909	55,810
1993	Derrike Cope	30	0	0	0	0	0	0	1	8,406	38	3	9,966	396,015
1994	Jeremy Mayfield	12	0	0	0	0	0	0	0	3,452	0	0	4,304	137,785
1994	Derrike Cope	16	0	0	0	0	0	0	0	4,261	7	1	5,029	183,186
1995	Jeremy Mayfield	27	0	0	0	0	0	0	1	7,943	79	3	10,441	436,805
1996	John Andretti	8	0	0	0	0	0	0	0	3,018	1	1	2,813	117,030
1996	Jeremy Mayfield	23	1	0	0	0	1	1	0	5,862	20	4	7,845	462,263
1997	John Andretti	32	1	1	0	1	1	1	0	9,333	135	5	11,965	1,100,056
1998	Rich Bickle	21	0	0	0	0	1	0	0	5,691	0	0	6,938	662,755
1998	Greg Sacks	7	0	0	0	0	0	0	0	1,821	0	0	2,312	280,130
1999	Rick Mast	34	0	0	0	0	0	0	2	9,487	25	3	12,542	1,255,546
Lifetime		371	3	1	0	2	4	6	19	101,291	529	35	125,189	$6,258,168

Doug Yates

Year	Driver	Starts	Poles	1	2	3	4	5	6–10	Laps	Laps Led	Races Led	Miles	$
1952	Doug Yates	1	0	0	0	0	0	0	0		0	0		25
1964	Doug Yates	14	1	0	1	0	0	1	4	2,262	9	1	991	2,790
1965	Doug Yates	4	0	0	0	0	0	0	1	271	13	1	150	550
Lifetime		19	1	0	1	0	0	1	5	2,533	22	2	1,142	$3,365

Year	Driver	Starts	Poles	Finish 1	2	3	4	5	6–10	Laps	Laps Led	Races Led	Miles	$

Robert Yates

Year	Driver	Starts	Poles	1	2	3	4	5	6–10	Laps	Laps Led	Races Led	Miles	$
1989	Davey Allison	29	1	2	1	0	2	2	6	8,287	253	13	10,113	560,904
1990	Davey Allison	29	0	2	0	1	0	2	5	9,154	222	8	10,918	536,505
1991	Davey Allison	29	3	5	4	2	1	0	4	8,770	1,528	23	10,613	1,031,295
1992	Davey Allison	29	2	5	1	1	5	3	2	8,976	1,377	18	10,999	1,192,230
1993	Robby Gordon	1	0	0	0	0	0	0	0	55	0	0	146	7,665
1993	Lake Speed	3	0	0	0	0	0	0	1	772	2	1	856	60,620
1993	Davey Allison	16	0	1	1	2	1	1	2	5,061	275	9	6,215	476,085
1993	Ernie Irvan	9	2	2	1	1	0	1	1	3,176	894	7	3,249	415,995
1994	Kenny Wallace	10	0	0	0	0	1	0	1	4,040	4	3	3,790	211,810
1994	Ernie Irvan	20	5	3	6	2	0	2	2	5,357	1,783	17	7,644	1,033,955
1995	Ernie Irvan	3	0	0	0	0	0	0	2	924	142	2	945	54,875
1995	Dale Jarrett	31	1	1	1	2	1	4	5	8,671	324	8	10,418	1,259,224
1996	Ernie Irvan	31	1	2	2	0	6	2	4	8,617	383	15	10,218	1,457,177
1996	Dale Jarrett	31	2	4	7	4	2	0	4	9,307	743	20	11,181	2,218,880
1997	Dale Jarrett	32	3	7	4	4	2	3	3	9,769	2,086	22	12,646	2,374,243
1997	Ernie Irvan	32	2	1	2	0	1	1	8	8,757	439	15	11,592	1,429,150
1998	Kenny Irwin Jr.	32	1	0	0	0	0	1	3	8,182	129	4	10,548	1,414,867
1998	Dale Jarrett	33	2	3	5	6	2	3	3	9,475	831	22	12,360	3,286,035
1999	Kenny Irwin Jr.	34	2	0	0	1	0	1	4	9,445	35	3	12,234	1,955,024
1999	Dale Jarrett	34	0	4	6	4	5	5	5	9,900	1,100	22	12,987	3,565,319
2000	Dale Jarrett	34	3	2	3	1	5	4	9	9,750	333	15	12,714	4,887,305
2000	Ricky Rudd	34	2	0	1	5	3	3	7	10,048	362	14	13,013	2,304,365
2001	Dale Jarrett	36	5	4	2	1	4	1	7	10,744	512	17	14,047	4,330,537
2001	Ricky Rudd	36	1	2	2	5	4	1	8	10,536	568	16	13,843	3,740,227
2002	Dale Jarrett	36	1	2	1	3	2	2	8	9,881	441	15	13,041	3,736,796
2002	Ricky Rudd	36	1	1	0	4	2	1	4	10,195	357	11	13,559	3,849,197
Lifetime		680	40	53	50	49	49	43	108	197,849	15,123	320	249,889	$47,390,285

Clay Young

Year	Driver	Starts	Poles	1	2	3	4	5	6–10	Laps	Laps Led	Races Led	Miles	$
1986	Clay Young	1	0	0	0	0	0	0	0	90	0	0	236	1,400
1992	Clay Young	1	0	0	0	0	0	0	0	40	0	0	106	5,690
Lifetime		2	0	0	0	0	0	0	0	130	0	0	342	$7,090

Kaylan Young

Year	Driver	Starts	Poles	1	2	3	4	5	6–10	Laps	Laps Led	Races Led	Miles	$
1992	Mike Chase	1	0	0	0	0	0	0	0	69	0	0	174	6,330
Lifetime		1	0	0	0	0	0	0	0	69	0	0	174	$6,330

Wade Younts

Year	Driver	Starts	Poles	1	2	3	4	5	6–10	Laps	Laps Led	Races Led	Miles	$
1961	Larry Thomas	12	0	0	0	0	0	0	4	2,547	0	0	1,185	1,900
1962	Larry Thomas	37	0	0	0	0	2	1	9	7,268	0	0	4,889	8,580
1963	Larry Thomas	27	0	0	0	2	1	3	7	5,829	0	0	3,099	6,955
1963	Joe Weatherly	2	0	0	0	0	0	0	2	664	0	0	284	1,150
1964	Larry Thomas	21	0	0	0	1	0	1	11	3,819	0	0	2,062	5,920
1964	Major Melton	3	0	0	0	0	0	0	1	737	0	0	648	1,100
1964	Darrell Bryant	1	0	0	0	0	0	0	0	1	0	0	1	275
Lifetime		103	0	0	0	3	3	5	34	20,865	0	0	12,168	$25,880

Pete Yow

Year	Driver	Starts	Poles	1	2	3	4	5	6–10	Laps	Laps Led	Races Led	Miles	$
1956	Pete Yow	11	0	0	0	0	0	0	2	1,221	0	0	680	700
Lifetime		11	0	0	0	0	0	0	2	1,221	0	0	680	$700

Smokey Yunick

Year	Driver	Starts	Poles	1	2	3	4	5	6–10	Laps	Laps Led	Races Led	Miles	$
1956	Paul Goldsmith	9	0	1	0	0	2	1	2	2,292	182	1	2,090	8,200
1956	Herb Thomas	2	1	1	0	0	0	0	1	142	1	1	201	1,350
1956	Tim Flock	1	0	0	0	1	0	0	0	149	41	1	149	725
1957	Paul Goldsmith	19	4	3	3	1	1	0	4	3,003	547	9	2,105	10,350
1957	Curtis Turner	1	0	0	0	0	0	0	0	346	51	1	476	1,060
1957	Ralph Moody	1	0	0	0	0	0	0	0	25	0	0	13	75
1958	Paul Goldsmith	1	1	1	0	0	0	0	0	39	39	1	160	4,550
1958	Cotton Owens	1	0	0	0	0	0	0	0	126	0	0	63	0
1961	Fireball Roberts	14	6	1	3	2	1	0	1	3,318	771	10	3,893	38,030
1961	Marvin Panch	5	0	1	1	0	1	0	0	615	13	1	1,262	24,005
1963	Bobby Isaac	1	0	0	0	0	0	2	0	57	0	0	86	425

Year	Driver	Starts	Poles	Finish						Laps	Laps Led	Races Led	Miles	$
				1	2	3	4	5	6–10					

Smokey Yunick *continued*

Year	Driver	Starts	Poles	1	2	3	4	5	6–10	Laps	Laps Led	Races Led	Miles	$
1963	Banjo Matthews	1	0	0	0	0	0	0	0	358	0	0	537	700
1963	Buck Baker	1	0	0	0	0	0	0	1	356	0	0	490	1,025
1963	A.J. Foyt	2	0	0	0	0	0	0	0	271	56	1	552	1,330
1963	Johnny Rutherford	2	0	1	0	0	0	0	1	236	6	1	590	2,350
1966	Mario Andretti	2	0	0	0	0	0	0	0	68	1	1	170	1,165
1966	Bobby Allison	1	0	0	0	0	0	0	0	3	0	0	5	630
1966	Curtis Turner	6	1	0	0	0	1	0	0	685	71	3	1,078	6,115
1967	Curtis Turner	1	1	0	0	0	0	0	0	1	0	0	3	100
1969	Bobby Unser	2	0	0	0	0	1	0	0	106	2	2	265	1,900
1969	Charlie Glotzbach	1	0	0	0	0	1	0	0	333	5	1	500	3,585
1969	Swede Savage	1	0	0	0	0	0	0	0	266	0	0	399	1,275
1969	Joe Leonard	1	0	0	0	0	0	0	0	47	0	0	118	720
Lifetime		76	14	9	7	4	8	3	10	12,842	1,786	34	15,200	$109,665

Zanworth Racing Team (Owned by Dick Ozan and Jim Wigglesworth.)

Year	Driver	Starts	Poles	1	2	3	4	5	6–10	Laps	Laps Led	Races Led	Miles	$
1986	Mike Skinner	3	0	0	0	0	0	0	0	807	0	0	635	4,255
Lifetime			3	0	0	0	0	0	0	807	0	0	635	$4,255

Johnny Zeke

Year	Driver	Starts	Poles	1	2	3	4	5	6–10	Laps	Laps Led	Races Led	Miles	$
1953	Johnny Zeke	1	0	0	0	0	0	0	0	84	0	0	84	25
Lifetime		1	0	0	0	0	0	0	0	84	0	0	84	$25

Emanuel Zervakis

Year	Driver	Starts	Poles	1	2	3	4	5	6–10	Laps	Laps Led	Races Led	Miles	$
1956	Emanuel Zervakis	6	0	0	0	0	0	0	0	773	0	0	831	475
1957	Emanuel Zervakis	2	0	0	0	0	0	0	0	140	0	0	70	150
1962	Emanuel Zervakis	11	0	0	0	0	0	0	2	2,151	5	1	2,357	4,545
1963	Jack Anderson	3	0	0	0	0	0	0	0	532	0	0	231	475
1963	Emanuel Zervakis	3	0	0	0	0	0	0	0	436	0	0	586	1,400
1974	Sonny Hutchins	1	0	0	0	0	0	0	0	150	79	1	79	590
1981	Geoffrey Bodine	3	0	0	0	0	0	0	1	678	14	2	821	8,610
1982	Butch Lindley	4	0	0	1	0	0	0	0	1,020	165	2	548	16,695
1983	Mark Martin	1	0	0	0	0	0	0	0	279	0	0	419	1,640
1983	Butch Lindley	1	0	0	0	0	0	0	0	396	7	1	215	2,485
1983	Morgan Shepherd	1	0	0	0	0	0	0	0	8	0	0	4	1,000
1984	Dale Jarrett	2	0	0	0	0	0	0	0	641	0	0	410	2,350
1984	Sam Ard	1	0	0	0	0	0	0	0	1	0	0	1	1,100
Lifetime		39	0	0	1	0	0	0	3	7,205	270	7	6,572	$41,515

John Zink

Year	Driver	Starts	Poles	1	2	3	4	5	6–10	Laps	Laps Led	Races Led	Miles	$
1956	Jack Zink	1	0	0	0	0	0	0	0	10	0	0	5	100
Lifetime		1	0	0	0	0	0	0	0	10	0	0	5	$100

PART 5
THE TRACKS

Alabama

Birmingham Int'l Raceway
Birmingham, AL
Half-mile Dirt Track

(aka Birmingham Int'l Speedway; Birmingham Super Speedway; Birmingham Super Raceway, Fairgrounds Raceway) Originally built as 1-mile horse track circa 1906. The half-mile dirt track was built circa 1933. First NASCAR Winston Cup (then Grand National) race 9/7/58 (Fireball Roberts won). Final Grand National event took place on 6/8/68 (won by Richard Petty). Track is still in operation and is now measured at .625-miles.

Winston Cup Starts
Buck Baker 5
Ned Jarrett 5
Richard Petty 5
Wendell Scott 5

Winston Cup Victories
Ned Jarrett 3

Winston Cup Poles
Jim Paschal 2
David Pearson 2

Winston Cup Money
Richard Petty $3,800

Most Cars Started
21—November 4, 1962

Fewest Cars Started
13—June 4, 1961

Narrowest Margin of Victory
1 car length—June 10, 1967

Slowest Race
56.364 MPH—June 6, 1965
Birmingham 200

Race Record
89.153 MPH—June 8, 1968

Most Cautions
N/A

Most Race Leaders
N/A

Most Cars Running at Finish
16—November 4, 1962

1958 Grand National Race No. 43
September 7, 1958 Average Speed: 60.678

Driver	Owner	Car #	Make	Laps	Winnings
1. Fireball Roberts	Frank Strickland	22	57 Chev	200	800
2. Buck Baker	Buck Baker	87	57 Chev	200	525
3. Lee Petty	Petty Enterprises	42	57 Olds	199	450
4. Joe Eubanks	Jim Stephens	6	57 Pont	194	325
5. Tiny Lund	J. H. Petty	48	57 Chev	194	225

1961 Grand National Race No. 26
June 4, 1961 Average Speed: 61.068

Driver	Owner	Car #	Make	Laps	Winnings
1. Ned Jarrett	Bee Gee Holloway	11	61 Chev	200	800
2. Jim Paschal	J. H. Petty	14	61 Pont	198	525
3. Jack Smith	Jack Smith	46	61 Pont	198	375
4. Rex White	Rex White	4	60 Chev	197	375
5. Tommy Wells		39	60 Chev	192	250

1963 Grand National Race No. 1
November 4, 1962 Average Speed: 68.350

Driver	Owner	Car #	Make	Laps	Winnings
1. Jim Paschal	Petty Enterprises	41	62 Plym	200	1,000
2. Richard Petty	Petty Enterprises	43	62 Plym	199	600
3. Buck Baker	Buck Baker	87	62 Chrys	196	400
4. Jimmy Pardue	Jimmy Pardue	54	62 Pont	196	300
5. Darel Dieringer	Mamie Reynolds	26	62 Ford	197	275

1963 Grand National Race No. 27
June 9, 1963 Average Speed: 68.195

Driver	Owner	Car #	Make	Laps	Winnings
1. Richard Petty	Petty Enterprises	41	63 Plym	200	1,000
2. Junior Johnson	Ray Fox	3	63 Chev	200	600
3. Buck Baker	Buck Baker	87	63 Pont	198	400
4. Ned Jarrett	Charles Robinson	11	63 Ford	196	300
5. Jack Smith	Jack Smith	47	63 Plym	195	275

1964 Grand National Race No. 32
June 21, 1964 Average Speed: 67.643

Driver	Owner	Car #	Make	Laps	Winnings
1. Ned Jarrett	Bondy Long	11	64 Ford	200	1,150
2. Richard Petty	Petty Enterprises	43	64 Plym	199	600
3. Billy Wade	Bud Moore	1	64 Merc	198	450
4. David Pearson	Cotton Owens	6	64 Dodg	198	300
5. Buck Baker	Ray Fox	3	64 Dodg	194	275

1965 Grand National Race No. 24 Birmingham 200
June 6, 1965 Average Speed: 56.364

Driver	Owner	Car #	Make	Laps	Winnings
1. Ned Jarrett	Bondy Long	11	65 Ford	108	1,000
2. Dick Hutcherson	Holman-Moody	29	65 Ford	108	600
3. G. C. Spencer	G. C. Spencer	49	64 Ford	108	400
4. Tom Pistone	Emory Gilliam	00	64 Ford	108	300
5. Junior Spencer	Jerry Mullins	17	64 Ford	107	275

1967 Grand National Race No. 24
June 10, 1967 Average Speed: 88.999

Driver	Owner	Car #	Make	Laps	Winnings
1. Bobby Allison	Cotton Owens	6	67 Dodg	160	1,000
2. Jim Paschal	Tom Friedkin	14	67 Plym	160	600
3. Richard Petty	Petty Enterprises	43	67 Plym	160	400
4. James Hylton	Bud Hartje	48	65 Dodg	158	300
5. Friday Hassler	Red Sharp	39	66 Chev	157	275

1968 Grand National Race No. 22
June 8, 1968 Average Speed: 89.153

Driver	Owner	Car #	Make	Laps	Winnings
1. Richard Petty	Petty Enterprises	43	68 Plym	160	1,200
2. Bobby Isaac	Nord Krauskopf	71	67 Dodg	160	600
3. James Hylton	James Hylton	48	67 Dodg	158	400
4. Friday Hassler	Red Sharp	39	66 Chev	157	300
5. Bobby Allison	Bobby Allison	2	66 Chev	157	275

Chisholm Speedway
Montgomery, AL
Half-mile Dirt Track

Half-mile dirt oval built circa 1951. Only NASCAR Winston Cup (then Grand National) race staged on 9/9/56 (won by Buck Baker) before a sparse crowd of 2,000. Promoters lost money on the event and the track closed shortly thereafter.

Winston Cup Victories
Buck Baker   1

Winston Cup Poles
Tim Flock   1

Winston Cup Money
Buck Baker $950

Most Cars Started
21—September 9, 1956

Narrowest Margin of Victory
N/A

Race Record
60.893 MPH—September 9, 1956

Most Race Leaders
4—September 9, 1956

Most Cars Running at Finish
15—September 9, 1956

1956 Grand National Race No. 45
September 9, 1956 Average Speed: 60.893

Driver	Owner	Car #	Make	Laps	Winnings
1. Buck Baker	Carl Kiekhaefer	87	56 Chrys	200	950
2. Ralph Moody	Pete DePaolo	12	56 Ford	200	675
3. Marvin Panch	Tom Harbison	98	56 Ford	199	475
4. Fireball Roberts	Pete DePaolo	22	56 Ford	195	365
5. Johnny Allen	Spook Crawford	264	56 Plym	194	320

Dixie Speedway
Birmingham, AL
Quarter-mile Paved Track

(aka Midfield Speedway) Quarter-mile paved oval built in 1958. Located in Birmingham suburb of Midfield. Only NASCAR Winston Cup (then Grand National) race staged on 8/3/60 (won by Ned Jarrett). The 50-mile event saw three Petty racers (Lee, Richard, and Maurice) all finish in the top 10; Richard was second, Lee third, and Maurice eighth. Track continued weekly operation until 1974.

Winston Cup Victories
Ned Jarrett   1

Winston Cup Poles
Ned Jarrett   1

Winston Cup Money
Ned Jarrett $770

Most Cars Started
16—August 3, 1960

Narrowest Margin of Victory
2 laps-plus—August 3, 1960

Race Record
54.463 MPH—August 3, 1960

Most Race Leaders
1—August 3, 1960

Most Cars Running at Finish
11—August 3, 1960

1960 Grand National Race No. 28
August 3, 1960 Average Speed: 54.463

Driver	Owner	Car #	Make	Laps	Winnings
1. Ned Jarrett	Ned Jarrett	11	60 Ford	200	770
2. Richard Petty	Petty Enterprises	43	60 Plym	198	535
3. Lee Petty	Petty Enterprises	42	60 Plym	196	485
4. Joe Lee Johnson	Paul McDuffie	89	60 Chev	195	365
5. Johnny Beauchamp	Dale Swanson	73	60 Chev	192	245

Huntsville Speedway
Huntsville, AL
Quarter-mile Paved Track

(aka Huntsville Motor Speedway; Huntsville Int'l Speedway; Huntsville Int'l Raceway) Quarter-mile paved track built circa 1961. Only NASCAR Winston Cup (then Grand National) race held on 8/8/62 (won by Richard Petty). Track still active today.

Winston Cup Victories
Richard Petty   1

Winston Cup Poles
Richard Petty   1

Winston Cup Money
Richard Petty $580

Most Cars Started
16—August 8, 1962

Narrowest Margin of Victory
1 lap-plus—August 8, 1962

Race Record
54.644 MPH—August 8, 1962

Most Race Leaders
1—August 8, 1962

Most Cars Running at Finish
13—August 8, 1962

1962 Grand National Race No. 39
August 8, 1962 Average Speed: 54.644

Driver	Owner	Car #	Make	Laps	Winnings
1. Richard Petty	Petty Enterprises	43	62 Plym	200	580
2. Bob Welborn	J. C. Parker	49	62 Pont	199	475
3. Jim Paschal	Cliff Stewart	2	62 Pont	198	400
4. Buck Baker	Buck Baker	87	62 Chrys	198	325
5. Ned Jarrett	Bee Gee Holloway	11	62 Chev	198	450

Lakeview Speedway
Mobile, AL
.75-mile Dirt Track

(aka Lake View Estates) 0.75-mile dirt oval built in 1948. First NASCAR Winston Cup (then Grand National) race run on 4/8/51 (Tim Flock won) and was promoted by Fonty Flock. Track also held '51 season finale on 11/25/51 (won by Frank Mundy in a Studebaker). Track closed circa 1953.

Winston Cup Starts
Sonny Black	2
Bud Erb	2
Bob Flock	2
Tim Flock	2
Fonty Flock	2
Lee Petty	2
Gene Tapia	2
Herb Thomas	2

Winston Cup Victories
Tim Flock   1
Frank Mundy   1

Winston Cup Poles
Frank Mundy   1

Winston Cup Money
Tim Flock $1,600

Most Cars Started
24—April 8, 1951

Fewest Cars Started
23—November 25, 1951

Narrowest Margin of Victory
Half-lap—April 8, 1951

Slowest Race
50.260 MPH—April 8, 1951

Race Record
50.260 MPH—April 8, 1951

Most Race Leaders
2—April 8, 1951

Most Cars Running at Finish
15—April 8, 1951

1951 Grand National Race No. 3
April 8, 1951 Average Speed: 50.260

Driver	Owner	Car #	Make	Laps	Winnings
1. Tim Flock	Ted Chester	91	51 Olds	150	1,000
2. Fonty Flock	Frank Christian	14	50 Olds	150	600
3. Herb Thomas	Herb Thomas	92	50 Plym	149	400
4. Bill Osborne		9	50 Olds	148	300
5. Donald Thomas	Herb Thomas	93	50 Plym	—	250

1951 Grand National Race No. 41
November 25, 1951

Driver	Owner	Car #	Make	Laps	Winnings
1. Frank Mundy	Perry Smith	23	51 Stud	150	1,000
2. Tim Flock	Ted Chester	91	51 Huds	149	600
3. Red Duvall	Hank Salat	87	51 Pack	—	500
4. Fonty Flock	Frank Christian	14	51 Olds	—	400
5. Don Oldenberg	Don Oldenberg	142	51 Pack	—	300

Montgomery Motor Speedway
Montgomery, AL
Half-mile Dirt Track

(aka Montgomery Int'l Raceway) Half-mile paved oval built in 1955. First NASCAR Winston Cup (then Grand National) race staged on 4/17/55 (Tim Flock won). Last race run on 12/8/68 (Bobby Allison won). Bobby Allison was promoter in late '60s. Track still in operation.

Winston Cup Starts
Buck Baker   5

Winston Cup Victories
Tim Flock   2

Winston Cup Poles
Richard Petty   3

Winston Cup Money
Richard Petty $2,400

Most Cars Started
30—November 26, 1967

Fewest Cars Started
14—July 29, 1956

Narrowest Margin of Victory
4 feet—December 8, 1968

Slowest Race
60.872 MPH—April 17, 1955

Race Record
73.200 MPH—December 8, 1968
Alabama 200

Most Cautions
4—November 26, 1967

Most Race Leaders
3—April 17, 1955
3—December 8, 1968 Alabama 200

Most Cars Running at Finish
18—September 11, 1955

1955 Grand National Race No. 9
April 17, 1955 Average Speed: 60.872

Driver	Owner	Car #	Make	Laps	Winnings
1. Tim Flock	Carl Kiekhaefer	300	55 Chrys	200	1,000
2. Joel Million	Ernest Woods	88	55 Olds	196	650
3. Fonty Flock	Frank Christian	14	55 Chev	196	450
4. Curtis Turner	Raymond Parks	99	55 Olds	192	350
5. Herb Thomas	Herb Thomas	92	55 Chev	190	300

1955 Grand National Race No. 36
September 11, 1955 Average Speed: 63.773

Driver	Owner	Car #	Make	Laps	Winnings
1. Tim Flock	Carl Kiekhaefer	300	55 Chrys	200	1,100
2. Herb Thomas	Herb Thomas	92	55 Chev	199	700
3. Bob Welborn	Bob Welborn	49	55 Chev	197	475
4. Lee Petty	Petty Enterprises	42	55 Dodg	196	365
5. Buck Baker	Buck Baker	89	55 Buick	195	310

1956 Grand National Race No. 35
July 29, 1956 Average Speed: 67.252

Driver	Owner	Car #	Make	Laps	Winnings
1. Marvin Panch	Tom Harbison	98	56 Ford	200	950
2. Buck Baker	Carl Kiekhaefer	300	56 Chrys	199	675
3. Bill Amick	Pete DePaolo	97	56 Ford	197	475
4. Speedy Thompson	Carl Kiekhaefer	500	56 Dodg	197	365
5. Lee Petty	Petty Enterprises	42	56 Dodg	195	320

1967 Grand National Race No. 27
June 27, 1967 Average Speed: 72.435

Driver	Owner	Car #	Make	Laps	Winnings
1. Jim Paschal	Tom Friedkin	14	67 Plym	200	1,000
2. Richard Petty	Petty Enterprises	43	67 Plym	200	600
3. Bobby Allison	Cotton Owens	6	67 Dodg	198	400
4. James Hylton	Bud Hartje	48	65 Dodg	196	300
5. Elmo Langley	Henry Woodfield	64	66 Ford	193	275

1968 Grand National Race No. 2
November 26, 1967 Average Speed: 70.644

Driver	Owner	Car #	Make	Laps	Winnings
1. Richard Petty	Petty Enterprises	43	67 Plym	200	1,200
2. Bobby Allison	Holman-Moody	11	67 Ford	200	600
3. Bobby Isaac	Nord Krauskopf	37	67 Dodg	196	400
4. Tom Pistone	Turkey Minton	74	67 Chev	196	300
5. Paul Lewis	Bobby Allison	2	65 Chev	195	275

1969 Grand National Race No. 2 Alabama 200
December 8, 1968 Average Speed: 73.200

Driver	Owner	Car #	Make	Laps	Winnings
1. Bobby Allison	Tom Friedkin	14	68 Plym	200	1,000
2. Richard Petty	Petty Enterprises	43	68 Plym	200	600
3. James Hylton	James Hylton	48	68 Dodg	195	400
4. Bobby Isaac	Nord Krauskopf	71	68 Dodg	193	300
5. Neil Castles	Neil Castles	06	67 Plym	188	275

Talladega Superspeedway
Talladega, AL
2.66-mile Superspeedway

(aka Alabama Int'l Motor Speedway) 2.66-mile tri-oval opened in September, 1969 with inaugural Talladega 500 on 9/14/69 (Richard Brickhouse won). Turns are banked 33 degrees. Patterned after the Daytona Int'l Speedway. Inaugural event hit by driver's boycott, citing dangerous conditions and tires that would tear apart after only a few laps. Regarded as fastest closed circuit in the country. Track was the site of the all-time Winston Cup qualifying record (212.809 MPH, Bill Elliott, 4/30/87) and the fastest 500-mile stock car race (186.288 MPH), won by Bill Elliott on May 5, 1985.

Winston Cup Starts
Dave Marcis   61

Winston Cup Victories
Dale Earnhardt   10

Winston Cup Poles
Bill Elliott   8

Winston Cup Money
Dale Earnhardt $2,698,931

Most Cars Started
60—May 6, 1973 Winston 500

Fewest Cars Started
36—September 14, 1969 Talladega 500

Narrowest Margin of Victory
0.005 seconds—July 25, 1993
DieHard 500

Slowest Race
130.220 MPH—May 5, 1974
Winston 500

Race Record
188.354 MPH—May 10, 1997

Most Cautions
9—May 7, 1972 Winston 500
9—May 4, 1986 Winston 500
9—July 27, 1986 Talladega 500
9—May 3, 1987 Winston 500

Most Race Leaders
26—July 27, 1986 Talladega 500

Most Cars Running at Finish
40—April 22, 2001

1969 Grand National Race No. 44 Talladega 500
September 14, 1969 Average Speed: 153.778

Driver	Owner	Car #	Make	Laps	Winnings
1. Richard Brickhouse	Ray Nichels	99	69 Dodg	188	24,550
2. Jim Vandiver	Ray Fox	3	69 Dodg	188	12,400
3. Ramo Stott	Bill Ellis	14	69 Dodg	188	7,050
4. Bobby Isaac	Nord Krauskopf	71	69 Dodg	187	4,725
5. Dick Brooks	Dick Brooks	32	69 Plym	180	3,300

1970 Grand National Race No. 10 Alabama 500
April 12, 1970 Average Speed: 152.321

Driver	Owner	Car #	Make	Laps	Winnings
1. Pete Hamilton	Petty Enterprises	40	70 Plym	188	26,650
2. Bobby Isaac	Nord Krauskopf	71	69 Dodg	188	12,500
3. David Pearson	Holman-Moody	17	69 Ford	187	8,675
4. Benny Parsons	L. G. DeWitt	72	69 Ford	187	5,825
5. Cale Yarborough	Wood Brothers	21	69 Merc	183	4,425

1970 Grand National Race No. 35 Talladega 500
August 23, 1970 Average Speed: 158.517

Driver	Owner	Car #	Make	Laps	Winnings
1. Pete Hamilton	Petty Enterprises	40	70 Plym	188	23,165
2. Bobby Isaac	Nord Krauskopf	71	69 Dodg	188	11,490
3. Charlie Glotzbach	Ray Nichels	99	69 Dodg	187	7,380
4. David Pearson	Holman-Moody	17	69 Ford	184	5,540
5. Buddy Baker	Cotton Owens	6	69 Dodg	184	3,915

1971 Winston Cup GN Race No. 18 Winston 500
May 16, 1971 Average Speed: 147.419

Driver	Owner	Car #	Make	Laps	Winnings
1. Donnie Allison	Wood Brothers	21	69 Merc	188	31,140
2. Bobby Allison	Holman-Moody	12	69 Merc	188	19,225
3. Buddy Baker	Petty Enterprises	11	71 Dodg	188	9,825
4. Pete Hamilton	Cotton Owens	6	71 Plym	187	5,825
5. Fred Lorenzen	Ray Nichels	99	71 Plym	187	3,950

1971 Winston Cup GN Race No. 37 Talladega 500
August 22, 1971 Average Speed: 145.945

Driver	Owner	Car #	Make	Laps	Winnings
1. Bobby Allison	Holman-Moody	12	69 Merc	188	19,565
2. Richard Petty	Petty Enterprises	43	71 Plym	188	10,040
3. Pete Hamilton	Cotton Owens	6	71 Plym	187	6,265
4. Fred Lorenzen	Ray Nichels	99	71 Plym	184	4,290
5. James Hylton	James Hylton	48	69 Merc	183	4,340

1972 Winston Cup GN Race No. 11 Winston 500
May 7, 1972 Average Speed: 134.400

Driver	Owner	Car #	Make	Laps	Winnings
1. David Pearson	Wood Brothers	21	71 Merc	188	23,745
2. Bobby Isaac	Nord Krauskopf	71	72 Dodg	188	15,895
3. Buddy Baker	Petty Enterprises	11	72 Dodg	188	9,995
4. Fred Lorenzen	Hoss Ellington	28	72 Ford	188	6,095
5. Richard Petty	Petty Enterprises	43	72 Dodg	187	6,970

1972 Winston Cup GN Race No. 21 Talladega 500
August 6, 1972 Average Speed: 148.728

Driver	Owner	Car #	Make	Laps	Winnings
1. James Hylton	James Hylton	48	71 Merc	188	24,865
2. Ramo Stott	Junie Donlavey	90	72 Ford	188	9,440
3. Bobby Allison	Richard Howard	12	72 Chev	183	9,465
4. Red Farmer	Willie Humphries	97	72 Ford	180	4,540
5. Buddy Arrington	Buddy Arrington	67	70 Dodg	179	3,615

1973 Winston Cup GN Race No. 10 Winston 500
May 6, 1973 Average Speed: 131.956

Driver	Owner	Car #	Make	Laps	Winnings
1. David Pearson	Wood Brothers	21	71 Merc	188	26,345
2. Donnie Allison	DiGard	08	72 Chev	187	11,445
3. Benny Parsons	L. G. DeWitt	72	72 Chev	187	8,935
4. Clarence Lovell	Don Bierschwale	61	73 Chev	185	5,870
5. Cecil Gordon	Cecil Gordon	24	73 Chev	184	4,495

1973 Winston Cup GN Race No. 20 Talladega 500
August 12, 1973 Average Speed: 145.454

Driver	Owner	Car #	Make	Laps	Winnings
1. Dick Brooks	Crawford Brothers	22	72 Plym	188	20,815
2. Buddy Baker	Nord Krauskopf	71	73 Dodg	188	14,590
3. David Pearson	Wood Brothers	21	71 Merc	188	9,540
4. James Hylton	James Hylton	48	71 Merc	186	5,590
5. David Sisco	Charlie McGee	05	72 Chev	186	4,665

1974 Winston Cup GN Race No. 10 Winston 500
May 5, 1974 Average Speed: 130.220

Driver	Owner	Car #	Make	Laps	Winnings
1. David Pearson	Wood Brothers	21	73 Merc	188	20,785
2. Benny Parsons	L. G. DeWitt	72	74 Chev	188	15,015
3. Richard Petty	Petty Enterprises	43	74 Dodg	188	11,245
4. Charlie Glotzbach	Junie Donlavey	90	72 Ford	188	6,490
5. Lennie Pond	Ronnie Elder	54	74 Chev	187	4,640

Talladega Superspeedway *continued*

1974 Winston Cup GN Race No. 21 Talladega 500
August 11, 1974 Average Speed: 148.637

Driver	Owner	Car #	Make	Laps	Winnings
1. Richard Petty	Petty Enterprises	43	74 Dodg	188	24,465
2. David Pearson	Wood Brothers	21	73 Merc	188	12,890
3. Bobby Allison	Bobby Allison	12	74 Chev	187	7,140
4. Cale Yarborough	Junior Johnson	11	74 Chev	186	8,285
5. Benny Parsons	L. G. DeWitt	72	74 Chev	186	7,465

1975 Winston Cup GN Race No. 19 Talladega 500
August 17, 1975 Average Speed: 130.892

Driver	Owner	Car #	Make	Laps	Winnings
1. Buddy Baker	Bud Moore	15	75 Ford	188	26,390
2. Richard Petty	Petty Enterprises	43	74 Dodg	188	17,295
3. Donnie Allison	Hoss Ellington	28	75 Chev	187	9,295
4. Dave Marcis	Nord Krauskopf	71	74 Dodg	186	9,620
5. Coo Coo Marlin	H. B. Cunningham	14	75 Chev	186	5,220

1976 Winston Cup GN Race No. 19 Talladega 500
August 8, 1976 Average Speed: 157.547

Driver	Owner	Car #	Make	Laps	Winnings
1. Dave Marcis	Nord Krauskopf	71	Dodg	188	26,110
2. Buddy Baker	Bud Moore	15	Ford	188	20,865
3. Dick Brooks	Junie Donlavey	90	Ford	187	11,945
4. James Hylton	James Hylton	48	Chev	186	8,260
5. Lennie Pond	Ronnie Elder	54	Chev	182	6,750

1977 Winston Cup GN Race No. 19 Talladega 500
August 7, 1977 Average Speed: 162.524

Driver	Owner	Car #	Make	Laps	Winnings
1. Donnie Allison	Hoss Ellington	1	Chev	188	26,375
2. Cale Yarborough	Junior Johnson	11	Chev	188	18,300
3. Skip Manning	Billy Hagan	92	Chev	188	14,700
4. Ricky Rudd	Al Rudd	22	Chev	186	8,000
5. Lennie Pond	Ronnie Elder	54	Chev	186	8,050

1978 Winston Cup GN Race No. 19 Talladega 500
August 6, 1978 Average Speed: 174.700

Driver	Owner	Car #	Make	Laps	Winnings
1. Lennie Pond	Harry Ranier	54	Olds	188	26,025
2. Donnie Allison	Hoss Ellington	1	Olds	188	16,250
3. Benny Parsons	L. G. DeWitt	72	Olds	188	15,350
4. Cale Yarborough	Junior Johnson	11	Olds	188	17,850
5. David Pearson	Wood Brothers	21	Merc	187	6,400

1979 Winston Cup GN Race No. 20 Talladega 500
August 5, 1979 Average Speed: 161.229

Driver	Owner	Car #	Make	Laps	Winnings
1. Darrell Waltrip	DiGard	88	Olds	188	32,325
2. David Pearson	Rod Osterlund	2	Olds	188	20,925
3. Ricky Rudd	Junie Donlavey	90	Merc	186	13,920
4. Richard Petty	Petty Enterprises	43	Olds	186	11,475
5. Jody Ridley	Junie Donlavey	77	Merc	186	6,025

1980 Winston Cup GN Race No. 20 Talladega 500
August 3, 1980 Average Speed: 166.894

Driver	Owner	Car #	Make	Laps	Winnings
1. Neil Bonnett	Wood Brothers	21	Merc	188	35,675
2. Cale Yarborough	Junior Johnson	11	Olds	188	20,625
3. Dale Earnhardt	Rod Osterlund	2	Olds	188	16,975
4. Benny Parsons	M. C. Anderson	27	Olds	188	12,125
5. Harry Gant	Jack Beebe	47	Olds	188	9,550

1975 Winston Cup GN Race No. 10 Winston 500
May 4, 1975 Average Speed: 144.948

Driver	Owner	Car #	Make	Laps	Winnings
1. Buddy Baker	Bud Moore	15	75 Ford	188	28,725
2. David Pearson	Wood Brothers	21	73 Merc	188	14,600
3. Dick Brooks	Junie Donlavey	90	73 Ford	188	9,750
4. Darrell Waltrip	Darrell Waltrip	17	75 Chev	182	9,825
5. Coo Coo Marlin	H. B. Cunningham	14	75 Chev	182	6,800

1976 Winston Cup GN Race No. 10 Winston 500
May 2, 1976 Average Speed: 169.887

Driver	Owner	Car #	Make	Laps	Winnings
1. Buddy Baker	Bud Moore	15	Ford	188	32,735
2. Cale Yarborough	Junior Johnson	11	Chev	188	19,670
3. Bobby Allison	Roger Penske	2	Merc	187	14,960
4. Richard Petty	Petty Enterprises	43	Dodg	186	13,805
5. Terry Ryan	Bill Monaghan	81	Chev	184	6,335

1977 Winston Cup GN Race No. 10 Winston 500
May 1, 1977 Average Speed: 164.877

Driver	Owner	Car #	Make	Laps	Winnings
1. Darrell Waltrip	DiGard	88	Chev	188	26,875
2. Cale Yarborough	Junior Johnson	11	Chev	188	23,310
3. Benny Parsons	L. G. DeWitt	72	Chev	188	16,500
4. Donnie Allison	Hoss Ellington	1	Chev	188	12,100
5. Dave Marcis	Roger Penske	2	Merc	188	10,250

1978 Winston Cup GN Race No. 10 Winston 500
May 14, 1978 Average Speed: 155.699

Driver	Owner	Car #	Make	Laps	Winnings
1. Cale Yarborough	Junior Johnson	11	Olds	188	34,300
2. Buddy Baker	M. C. Anderson	27	Olds	188	21,900
3. A. J. Foyt	A. J. Foyt	51	Buick	187	12,200
4. Skip Manning	Billy Hagan	92	Buick	187	11,350
5. Grant Adcox	Herb Adcox	41	Chev	186	7,650

1979 Winston Cup GN Race No. 10 Winston 500
May 6, 1979 Average Speed: 154.770

Driver	Owner	Car #	Make	Laps	Winnings
1. Bobby Allison	Bud Moore	15	Ford	188	33,750
2. Darrell Waltrip	DiGard	88	Olds	187	25,025
3. Buddy Arrington	Buddy Arrington	67	Dodg	186	18,120
4. Richard Petty	Petty Enterprises	43	Olds	185	13,100
5. Joe Millikan	L. G. DeWitt	72	Olds	185	11,900

1980 Winston Cup GN Race No. 10 Winston 500
May 4, 1980 Average Speed: 170.481

Driver	Owner	Car #	Make	Laps	Winnings
1. Buddy Baker	Harry Ranier	28	Olds	188	32,150
2. Dale Earnhardt	Rod Osterlund	2	Olds	188	28,700
3. David Pearson	Hoss Ellington	1	Olds	188	23,150
4. Lennie Pond	Jim Testa	68	Olds	187	10,500
5. Tighe Scott	Walter Ballard	30	Olds	186	9,200

1981 Winston Cup GN Race No. 10 Winston 500
May 3, 1981 Average Speed: 149.376

Driver	Owner	Car #	Make	Laps	Winnings
1. Bobby Allison	Harry Ranier	28	Buick	188	41,500
2. Buddy Baker	Hoss Ellington	1	Buick	188	34,450
3. Darrell Waltrip	Junior Johnson	11	Buick	188	20,325
4. Ricky Rudd	DiGard	88	Olds	188	18,750
5. Donnie Allison	John Rebhan	77	Olds	187	10,050

Talladega Superspeedway *continued*

1981 Winston Cup GN Race No. 20 Talladega 500
August 2, 1981 Average Speed: 156.737

Driver	Owner	Car #	Make	Laps	Winnings
1. Ron Bouchard	Jack Beebe	47	Buick	188	38,905
2. Darrell Waltrip	Junior Johnson	11	Buick	188	23,000
3. Terry Labonte	Billy Hagan	44	Buick	188	18,500
4. Harry Gant	Hal Needham	33	Buick	188	10,000
5. Bobby Allison	Harry Ranier	28	Buick	188	17,825

1982 Winston Cup GN Race No. 19 Talladega 500
August 1, 1982 Average Speed: 168.157

Driver	Owner	Car #	Make	Laps	Winnings
1. Darrell Waltrip	Junior Johnson	11	Buick	188	58,770
2. Buddy Baker	Harry Ranier	28	Pont	188	34,350
3. Richard Petty	Petty Enterprises	43	Pont	188	26,975
4. Cale Yarborough	M. C. Anderson	27	Buick	188	11,625
5. Terry Labonte	Billy Hagan	44	Buick	188	13,095

1983 Winston Cup GN Race No. 19 Talladega 500
July 31, 1983 Average Speed: 170.611

Driver	Owner	Car #	Make	Laps	Winnings
1. Dale Earnhardt	Bud Moore	15	Ford	188	46,950
2. Darrell Waltrip	Junior Johnson	11	Chev	188	32,965
3. Tim Richmond	Raymond Beadle	27	Pont	188	20,680
4. Richard Petty	Petty Enterprises	43	Pont	188	17,475
5. Harry Gant	Hal Needham	33	Buick	188	17,650

1984 Winston Cup GN Race No. 19 Talladega 500
July 29, 1984 Average Speed: 155.485

Driver	Owner	Car #	Make	Laps	Winnings
1. Dale Earnhardt	Richard Childress	3	Chev	188	47,100
2. Buddy Baker	Wood Brothers	21	Ford	188	28,225
3. Terry Labonte	Billy Hagan	44	Chev	188	22,455
4. Bobby Allison	DiGard	22	Buick	188	24,350
5. Cale Yarborough	Harry Ranier	28	Chev	188	15,350

1985 Winston Cup GN Race No. 17 Talladega 500
July 28, 1985 Average Speed: 148.772

Driver	Owner	Car #	Make	Laps	Winnings
1. Cale Yarborough	Harry Ranier	28	Ford	188	48,655
2. Neil Bonnett	Junior Johnson	12	Chev	188	34,250
3. Ron Bouchard	Jack Beebe	47	Buick	188	23,205
4. Bill Elliott	Harry Melling	9	Ford	188	29,475
5. A. J. Foyt	A. J. Foyt	14	Olds	187	11,625

1986 Winston Cup Race No. 17 Talladega 500
July 27, 1986 Average Speed: 151.522

Driver	Owner	Car #	Make	Laps	Winnings
1. Bobby Hillin Jr.	Stavola Brothers	8	Buick	188	60,055
2. Tim Richmond	Rick Hendrick	25	Chev	188	34,345
3. Ricky Rudd	Bud Moore	15	Ford	188	29,255
4. Sterling Marlin	Hoss Ellington	1	Chev	188	15,750
5. Benny Parsons	Richard Jackson	55	Olds	188	12,815

1987 Winston Cup Race No. 17 Talladega 500
July 26, 1987 Average Speed: 171.293

Driver	Owner	Car #	Make	Laps	Winnings
1. Bill Elliott	Harry Melling	9	Ford	188	70,920
2. Davey Allison	Harry Ranier	28	Ford	188	39,115
3. Dale Earnhardt	Richard Childress	3	Chev	188	35,050
4. Darrell Waltrip	Rick Hendrick	17	Chev	188	19,120
5. Cale Yarborough	Cale Yarborough	29	Olds	188	13,465

1982 Winston Cup GN Race No. 9 Winston 500
May 2, 1982 Average Speed: 156.697

Driver	Owner	Car #	Make	Laps	Winnings
1. Darrell Waltrip	Junior Johnson	11	Buick	188	44,250
2. Terry Labonte	Billy Hagan	44	Buick	188	29,230
3. Benny Parsons	Harry Ranier	28	Pont	188	33,565
4. Kyle Petty	Petty Enterprises	42	Pont	188	17,095
5. Morgan Shepherd	Ron Benfield	98	Buick	188	11,100

1983 Winston Cup GN Race No. 8 Winston 500
May 1, 1983 Average Speed: 153.936

Driver	Owner	Car #	Make	Laps	Winnings
1. Richard Petty	Petty Enterprises	43	Pont	188	46,650
2. Benny Parsons	Johnny Hayes	55	Buick	188	24,575
3. Lake Speed	Hoss Ellington	1	Chev	188	18,975
4. Harry Gant	Hal Needham	33	Buick	188	22,425
5. Bill Elliott	Harry Melling	9	Ford	188	15,905

1984 Winston Cup GN Race No. 9 Winston 500
May 6, 1984 Average Speed: 172.988

Driver	Owner	Car #	Make	Laps	Winnings
1. Cale Yarborough	Harry Ranier	28	Chev	188	42,300
2. Harry Gant	Hal Needham	33	Chev	188	31,780
3. Buddy Baker	Wood Brothers	21	Ford	188	22,250
4. Bobby Allison	DiGard	22	Buick	188	31,250
5. Benny Parsons	Johnny Hayes	55	Chev	188	19,650

1985 Winston Cup GN Race No. 9 Winston 500
May 5, 1985 Average Speed: 186.288

Driver	Owner	Car #	Make	Laps	Winnings
1. Bill Elliott	Harry Melling	9	Ford	188	60,500
2. Kyle Petty	Wood Brothers	7	Ford	188	34,905
3. Cale Yarborough	Harry Ranier	28	Ford	188	37,750
4. Bobby Allison	DiGard	22	Buick	187	23,075
5. Ricky Rudd	Bud Moore	15	Ford	187	21,025

1986 Winston Cup Race No. 9 Winston 500
May 4, 1986 Average Speed: 157.698

Driver	Owner	Car #	Make	Laps	Winnings
1. Bobby Allison	Stavola Brothers	22	Buick	188	77,905
2. Dale Earnhardt	Richard Childress	3	Chev	188	53,900
3. Buddy Baker	Buddy Baker & Danny Schiff	88	Olds	188	27,600
4. Bobby Hillin Jr.	Stavola Brothers	8	Buick	188	21,470
5. Phil Parsons	Richard Jackson	66	Olds	188	15,525

1987 Winston Cup Race No. 9 Winston 500
May 3, 1987 Average Speed: 154.228

Driver	Owner	Car #	Make	Laps	Winnings
1. Davey Allison	Harry Ranier	28	Ford	178	71,250
2. Terry Labonte	Junior Johnson	11	Chev	178	47,060
3. Kyle Petty	Wood Brothers	21	Ford	178	30,915
4. Dale Earnhardt	Richard Childress	3	Chev	178	31,350
5. Bobby Hillin Jr.	Stavola Brothers	8	Buick	178	25,055

1988 Winston Cup Race No. 9 Winston 500
May 1, 1988 Average Speed: 156.547

Driver	Owner	Car #	Make	Laps	Winnings
1. Phil Parsons	Richard Jackson	55	Olds	188	86,850
2. Bobby Allison	Stavola Brothers	12	Buick	188	50,060
3. Geoff Bodine	Rick Hendrick	5	Chev	188	37,560
4. Terry Labonte	Junior Johnson	11	Chev	188	28,425
5. Ken Schrader	Rick Hendrick	25	Chev	188	27,165

Talladega Superspeedway *continued*

1988 Winston Cup Race No. 17 Talladega DieHard 500
July 31, 1988 Average Speed: 154.505

Driver	Owner	Car #	Make	Laps	Winnings
1. Ken Schrader	Rick Hendrick	25	Chev	188	67,920
2. Geoff Bodine	Rick Hendrick	5	Chev	188	39,915
3. Dale Earnhardt	Richard Childress	3	Chev	188	37,775
4. Rick Wilson	Larry McClure	4	Olds	188	20,075
5. Rusty Wallace	Raymond Beadle	27	Pont	188	23,215

1989 Winston Cup Race No. 17 Talladega DieHard 500
July 30, 1989 Average Speed: 157.354

Driver	Owner	Car #	Make	Laps	Winnings
1. Terry Labonte	Junior Johnson	11	Ford	188	73,920
2. Darrell Waltrip	Rick Hendrick	17	Chev	188	47,965
3. Mark Martin	Jack Roush	6	Ford	188	37,950
4. Ken Schrader	Rick Hendrick	25	Chev	188	28,400
5. Rick Wilson	Larry McClure	4	Olds	188	20,200

1990 Winston Cup Series Race No. 17 DieHard 500
July 29, 1990 Average Speed: 174.430

Driver	Owner	Car #	Make	Laps	Winnings
1. Dale Earnhardt	Richard Childress	3	Chev	188	152,975
2. Bill Elliott	Harry Melling	9	Ford	188	48,390
3. Sterling Marlin	Billy Hagan	94	Olds	188	34,050
4. Alan Kulwicki	Alan Kulwicki	7	Ford	188	24,750
5. Ricky Rudd	Rick Hendrick	5	Chev	188	22,050

1991 Winston Cup Series Race No. 17 DieHard 500
July 28, 1991 Average Speed: 147.383

Driver	Owner	Car #	Make	Laps	Winnings
1. Dale Earnhardt	Richard Childress	3	Chev	188	88,670
2. Bill Elliott	Harry Melling	9	Ford	188	51,185
3. Mark Martin	Jack Roush	6	Ford	188	46,390
4. Ricky Rudd	Rick Hendrick	5	Chev	188	29,400
5. Sterling Marlin	Junior Johnson	22	Ford	188	27,075

1992 Winston Cup Race No. 17 DieHard 500
July 26, 1992 Average Speed: 176.309

Driver	Owner	Car #	Make	Laps	Winnings
1. Ernie Irvan	Larry McClure	4	Chev	188	81,815
2. Sterling Marlin	Junior Johnson	22	Ford	188	54,760
3. Davey Allison	Robert Yates	28	Ford	188	42,845
4. Ricky Rudd	Rick Hendrick	5	Chev	187	32,195
5. Bill Elliott	Junior Johnson	11	Ford	187	27,965

1993 Winston Cup Series Race No. 18 DieHard 500
July 25, 1993 Average Speed: 153.858

Driver	Owner	Car #	Make	Laps	Winnings
1. Dale Earnhardt	Richard Childress	3	Chev	188	87,315
2. Ernie Irvan	Larry McClure	4	Chev	188	53,210
3. Mark Martin	Jack Roush	6	Ford	188	40,495
4. Kyle Petty	Felix Sabates	42	Pont	188	31,395
5. Dale Jarrett	Joe Gibbs	18	Chev	188	30,390

1994 Winston Cup Series Race No. 18 DieHard 500
July 24, 1994 Average Speed: 163.217

Driver	Owner	Car #	Make	Laps	Winnings
1. Jimmy Spencer	Junior Johnson	27	Ford	188	81,450
2. Bill Elliott	Junior Johnson	11	Ford	188	52,445
3. Ernie Irvan	Robert Yates	28	Ford	188	47,130
4. Ken Schrader	Rick Hendrick	25	Chev	188	33,530
5. Sterling Marlin	Larry McClure	4	Chev	188	32,675

1989 Winston Cup Race No. 9 Winston 500
May 7, 1989 Average Speed: 155.869

Driver	Owner	Car #	Make	Laps	Winnings
1. Davey Allison	Robert Yates	28	Ford	188	98,675
2. Terry Labonte	Junior Johnson	11	Ford	188	51,275
3. Mark Martin	Jack Roush	6	Ford	188	39,850
4. Morgan Shepherd	Bob Rahilly & Butch Mock	75	Pont	188	34,250
5. Darrell Waltrip	Rick Hendrick	17	Chev	188	28,900

1990 Winston Cup Series Race No. 9 Winston 500
May 6, 1990 Average Speed: 159.571

Driver	Owner	Car #	Make	Laps	Winnings
1. Dale Earnhardt	Richard Childress	3	Chev	188	98,975
2. Greg Sacks	Rick Hendrick	18	Chev	188	46,900
3. Mark Martin	Jack Roush	6	Ford	188	39,050
4. Ernie Irvan	Larry McClure	4	Olds	188	30,150
5. Michael Waltrip	Chuck Rider	30	Pont	188	26,425

1991 Winston Cup Series Race No. 9 Winston 500
May 6, 1991 Average Speed: 165.620

Driver	Owner	Car #	Make	Laps	Winnings
1. Harry Gant	Leo Jackson	33	Olds	188	81,950
2. Darrell Waltrip	Darrell Waltrip	17	Chev	188	47,400
3. Dale Earnhardt	Richard Childress	3	Chev	188	56,100
4. Sterling Marlin	Junior Johnson	22	Ford	188	25,450
5. Michael Waltrip	Chuck Rider	30	Pont	188	25,800

1992 Winston Cup Race No. 9 Winston 500
May 3, 1992 Average Speed: 167.609

Driver	Owner	Car #	Make	Laps	Winnings
1. Davey Allison	Robert Yates	28	Ford	188	189,325
2. Bill Elliott	Junior Johnson	11	Ford	188	56,225
3. Dale Earnhardt	Richard Childress	3	Chev	188	46,970
4. Sterling Marlin	Junior Johnson	22	Ford	188	45,470
5. Ernie Irvan	Larry McClure	4	Chev	188	35,840

1993 Winston Cup Series Race No. 9 Winston 500
May 2, 1993 Average Speed: 155.412

Driver	Owner	Car #	Make	Laps	Winnings
1. Ernie Irvan	Larry McClure	4	Chev	188	85,875
2. Jimmy Spencer	Bobby Allison	12	Ford	188	56,850
3. Dale Jarrett	Joe Gibbs	18	Chev	188	44,870
4. Dale Earnhardt	Richard Childress	3	Chev	188	39,870
5. Joe Ruttman	Dick Moroso	20	Ford	188	25,765

1994 Winston Cup Series Race No. 9 Winston Select 500
May 1, 1994 Average Speed: 157.478

Driver	Owner	Car #	Make	Laps	Winnings
1. Dale Earnhardt	Richard Childress	3	Chev	188	94,865
2. Ernie Irvan	Robert Yates	28	Ford	188	67,990
3. Michael Waltrip	Chuck Rider	30	Pont	188	50,995
4. Jimmy Spencer	Junior Johnson	27	Ford	188	32,570
5. Ken Schrader	Rick Hendrick	25	Chev	188	33,540

1995 Winston Cup Series Race No. 9 Winston Select 500
April 30, 1995 Average Speed: 178.902

Driver	Owner	Car #	Make	Laps	Winnings
1. Mark Martin	Jack Roush	6	Ford	188	98,565
2. Jeff Gordon	Rick Hendrick	24	Chev	188	165,315
3. Morgan Shepherd	Wood Brothers	21	Ford	188	62,145
4. Darrell Waltrip	Darrell Waltrip	17	Chev	188	43,095
5. Bobby Labonte	Joe Gibbs	18	Chev	188	40,115

Talladega Superspeedway *continued*

1995 Winston Cup Series Race No. 18 DieHard 500
July 23, 1995 Average Speed: 173.188

Driver	Owner	Car #	Make	Laps	Winnings
1. Sterling Marlin	Larry McClure	4	Chev	188	219,425
2. Dale Jarrett	Robert Yates	28	Ford	188	65,895
3. Dale Earnhardt	Richard Childress	3	Chev	188	57,105
4. Morgan Shepherd	Wood Brothers	21	Ford	188	40,805
5. Bill Elliott	Bill Elliott	94	Ford	188	32,325

1996 Winston Cup Series Race No. 18 DieHard 500
July 28, 1996 Average Speed: 133.387

Driver	Owner	Car #	Make	Laps	Winnings
1. Jeff Gordon	Rick Hendrick	24	Chev	129	272,550
2. Dale Jarrett	Robert Yates	88	Ford	129	55,070
3. Mark Martin	Jack Roush	6	Ford	129	53,980
4. Ernie Irvan	Robert Yates	28	Ford	129	44,455
5. Jimmy Spencer	Travis Carter	23	Ford	129	50,025

1997 Winston Cup Series Race No. 29
October 12, 1997 Average Speed: 156.601

Driver	Owner	Car #	Make	Laps	Winnings
1. Terry Labonte	Rick Hendrick	5	Chev	188	116,725
2. Bobby Labonte	Joe Gibbs	18	Pont	188	76,670
3. John Andretti	Cale Yarborough	98	Ford	188	58,530
4. Ken Schrader	Andy Petree	33	Chev	188	53,715
5. Ernie Irvan	Robert Yates	28	Ford	188	57,275

1998 Winston Cup Series Race No. 29
October 11, 1998 Average Speed: 159.318

Driver	Owner	Car #	Make	Laps	Winnings
1. Dale Jarrett	Robert Yates	88	Ford	188	1,110,125
2. Jeff Gordon	Rick Hendrick	24	Chev	188	86,245
3. Terry Labonte	Rick Hendrick	5	Chev	188	68,860
4. Jimmy Spencer	Travis Carter	23	Ford	188	69,550
5. Jeremy Mayfield	Michael Kranefuss	12	Ford	188	51,000

1999 Winston Cup Series Race No. 30
October 17, 1999 Average Speed: 166.632

Driver	Owner	Car #	Make	Laps	Winnings
1. Dale Earnhardt	Richard Childress	3	Chev	188	120,290
2. Dale Jarrett	Robert Yates	88	Ford	188	85,345
3. Ricky Rudd	Ricky Rudd	10	Ford	188	82,325
4. Ward Burton	Bill Davis	22	Pont	188	72,200
5. Kenny Wallace	Andy Petree	55	Chev	188	58,065

2000 Winston Cup Series Race No. 30
October 15, 2000 Average Speed: 165.681

Driver	Owner	Car #	Make	Laps	Winnings
1. Dale Earnhardt	Richard Childress	3	Chev	188	135,900
2. Kenny Wallace	Andy Petree	55	Chev	188	98,170
3. Joe Nemechek	Andy Petree	33	Chev	188	85,685
4. Jeff Gordon	Rick Hendrick	24	Chev	188	82,100
5. Terry Labonte	Rick Hendrick	5	Chev	188	73,700

2001 Winston Cup Series Race No. 31
October 21, 2001 Average Speed: 164.185

Driver	Owner	Car #	Make	Laps	Winnings
1. Dale Earnhardt, Jr.	Dale Earnhardt, Inc.	8	Chev	188	1,165,773
2. Tony Stewart	Joe Gibbs	20	Pont	188	104,700
3. Jeff Burton	Jack Roush	99	Ford	188	120,271
4. Matt Kenseth	Jack Roush	17	Ford	188	77,550
5. Bobby Hamilton	Andy Petree	55	Chev	188	81,450

1996 Winston Cup Series Race No. 9 Winston Select 500
April 28, 1996 Average Speed: 149.999

Driver	Owner	Car #	Make	Laps	Winnings
1. Sterling Marlin	Larry McClure	4	Chev	188	109,845
2. Dale Jarrett	Robert Yates	88	Ford	188	64,145
3. Dale Earnhardt	Richard Childress	3	Chev	188	64,620
4. Terry Labonte	Rick Hendrick	5	Chev	188	60,570
5. Michael Waltrip	Wood Brothers	21	Ford	188	44,490

1997 Winston Cup Series Race No. 10
May 10, 1997 Average Speed: 188.354

Driver	Owner	Car #	Make	Laps	Winnings
1. Mark Martin	Jack Roush	6	Ford	188	92,220
2. Dale Earnhardt	Richard Childress	3	Chev	188	85,445
3. Bobby Labonte	Joe Gibbs	18	Pont	188	61,845
4. John Andretti	Cale Yarborough	98	Ford	188	57,920
5. Jeff Gordon	Rick Hendrick	24	Chev	188	54,440

1998 Winston Cup Series Race No. 9
April 26, 1998 Average Speed: 163.439

Driver	Owner	Car #	Make	Laps	Winnings
1. Bobby Labonte	Joe Gibbs	18	Pont	188	141,870
2. Jimmy Spencer	Travis Carter	23	Ford	188	97,920
3. Dale Jarrett	Robert Yates	88	Ford	188	82,370
4. Terry Labonte	Rick Hendrick	5	Chev	188	85,520
5. Jeff Gordon	Rick Hendrick	24	Chev	188	74,490

1999 Winston Cup Series Race No. 9
April 25, 1999 Average Speed: 163.395

Driver	Owner	Car #	Make	Laps	Winnings
1. Dale Earnhardt	Richard Childress	3	Chev	188	147,795
2. Dale Jarrett	Robert Yates	88	Ford	188	104,955
3. Mark Martin	Jack Roush	6	Ford	188	91,230
4. Bobby Labonte	Joe Gibbs	18	Pont	188	84,380
5. Tony Stewart	Joe Gibbs	20	Pont	188	59,855

2000 Winston Cup Series Race No. 9
April 16, 2000 Average Speed: 161.157

Driver	Owner	Car #	Make	Laps	Winnings
1. Jeff Gordon	Rick Hendrick	24	Chev	188	159,755
2. Mike Skinner	Richard Childress	31	Chev	188	115,680
3. Dale Earnhardt	Richard Childress	3	Chev	188	92,630
4. Kenny Irwin, Jr.	Felix Sabates	42	Chev	188	86,280
5. Jimmy Spencer	Travis Carter	26	Ford	188	76,665

2001 Winston Cup Series Race No. 9
April 22, 2001 Average Speed: 184.003

Driver	Owner	Car #	Make	Laps	Winnings
1. Bobby Hamilton	Andy Petree	55	Chev	188	173,855
2. Tony Stewart	Joe Gibbs	20	Pont	188	137,630
3. Kurt Busch	Jack Roush	97	Ford	188	107,780
4. Mark Martin	Jack Roush	6	Ford	188	126,126
5. Bobby Labonte	Joe Gibbs	18	Pont	188	128,842

2002 Winston Cup Series Race No. 9
April 21, 2002 Average Speed: 159.022

Driver	Owner	Car #	Make	Laps	Winnings
1. Dale Earnhardt, Jr.	Dale Earnhardt, Inc.	8	Chev	188	184,830
2. Michael Waltrip	Dale Earnhardt, Inc.	15	Chev	188	131,855
3. Kurt Busch	Jack Roush	97	Ford	188	120,255
4. Jeff Gordon	Rick Hendrick	24	Chev	188	143,003
5. Sterling Marlin	Chip Ganassi	40	Dodg	188	127,182

Talladega Superspeedway *continued*

2002 Winston Cup Series Race No. 30
October 6, 2002 Average Speed: 183.665

Driver	Owner	Car #	Make	Laps	Winnings
1. Dale Earnhardt, Jr.	Dale Earnhardt, Inc.	8	Chev	188	1,166,040
2. Tony Stewart	Joe Gibbs	20	Pont	188	152,258
3. Ricky Rudd	Robert Yates	28	Ford	188	134,972
4. Kurt Busch	Jack Roush	97	Ford	188	86,665
5. Jeff Green	Richard Childress	30	Chev	188	68,265

Arizona

Arizona State Fairgrounds
Phoenix, AZ
1-mile Dirt Track

(aka Phoenix Fairgrounds) Originally built as 1-mile dirt oval in 1910. First NASCAR Winston Cup (then Grand National) race staged on 4/29/51 (won by Marshall Teague). Final Grand National race run on 4/3/60 (John Rostek won). Track closed in 1963. Re-opened as 1/8-mile dirt oval in 1985.

Winston Cup Starts
Lloyd Dane   4

Winston Cup Victories
Buck Baker   1
Tim Flock   1
John Rostek   1
Marshall Teague   1

Winston Cup Poles
Bill Amick   1
Fonty Flock   1
Mel Larson   1
Joe Weatherly   1

Winston Cup Money
Tim Flock $2,160

Most Cars Started
30—April 22, 1951
30—January 22, 1956

Fewest Cars Started
19—April 3, 1960
Copper Cup Championship

Narrowest Margin of Victory
1/4-mile—April 22, 1951

Slowest Race
60.153 MPH—April 22, 1951

Race Record
71.899 MPH—April 3, 1960
Copper Cup Championship

Most Race Leaders
4—April 3, 1960
Copper Cup Championship

Most Cars Running at Finish
21—May 8, 1955

1951 Grand National Race No. 6
April 22, 1951 Average Speed: 60.153

Driver	Owner	Car #	Make	Laps	Winnings
1. Marshall Teague	Marshall Teague	6	51 Huds	150	1,100
2. Erick Erickson		1	48 Pont	150	750
3. Tim Flock	Ted Chester	91	51 Olds	—	450
4. Fonty Flock	Frank Christian	14	50 Olds	—	300
5. Dick Meyer	Grant Sniffen	9	50 Merc	—	200

1955 Grand National Race No. 13
May 8, 1955 Average Speed: 71.485

Driver	Owner	Car #	Make	Laps	Winnings
1. Tim Flock	Carl Kiekhaefer	301	55 Chrys	100	1,000
2. Marvin Panch	John Hernandez	98	55 Merc	99	650
3. Clyde Palmer		47	55 Merc	98	450
4. Bill Amick		3	55 Dodg	97	350
5. Allen Adkins		7	54 Dodg	97	300

1956 Grand National Race No. 5
January 22, 1956 Average Speed: 64.408

Driver	Owner	Car #	Make	Laps	Winnings
1. Buck Baker	Carl Kiekhaefer	301	55 Chrys	150	1,500
2. Frank Mundy	Carl Kiekhaefer	30	55 Chrys	150	970
3. Tim Flock	Carl Kiekhaefer	300	55 Chrys	150	710
4. Marvin Panch	Tom Harbison	98	56 Ford	149	560
5. Lee Petty	Petty Enterprises	42	56 Dodg	149	415

1960 Grand National Race No. 8 Copper Cup Championship
April 3, 1960 Average Speed: 71.899

Driver	Owner	Car #	Make	Laps	Winnings
1. John Rostek	John Rostek	19	58 Ford	100	800
2. Mel Larson	Mel Larson	35	60 Pont	100	525
3. Scotty Cain	Scotty Cain	4	59 Ford	97	375
4. Fritz Wilson	Fritz Wilson	48	58 Ford	95	275
5. Lloyd Dane	Lloyd Dane	44	59 Ford	95	250

Phoenix Int'l Raceway
Phoenix, AZ
1-mile Superspeedway

1-mile paved oval opened in 1964 with USAC IndyCar race. A. J. Foyt won first event. First NASCAR Winston Cup race 11/6/88 (Alan Kulwicki won). Track hosts a variety of NASCAR, USAC, and Indy Racing League events.

Winston Cup Starts
15 drivers tied with 9

Winston Cup Victories
Davey Allison 2

Winston Cup Poles
Rusty Wallace 3

Winston Cup Money
Mark Martin $819,854

Most Cars Started
44—October 29, 1995 Dura-Lube 500
44—October 27, 1996 Dura-Lube 500

Fewest Cars Started
42—November 1, 1992 Pyroil 500

Narrowest Margin of Victory
0.170 seconds October 31, 1993
Slick 50 500

Slowest Race
90.457 MPH—November 6, 1988
Checker 500

Race Record
118.132 MPH—November 7, 1999

Most Cautions
10—November 3, 1991 Pyroil 500

Most Race Leaders
13—November 3, 1991 Pyroil 500

Most Cars Running at Finish
41—November 7, 1999

1988 Winston Cup Race No. 28 Checker 500
November 6, 1988 Average Speed: 90.457

Driver	Owner	Car #	Make	Laps	Winnings
1. Alan Kulwicki	Alan Kulwicki	7	Ford	312	54,100
2. Terry Labonte	Junior Johnson	11	Chev	312	31,075
3. Davey Allison	Harry Ranier	28	Ford	312	24,275
4. Bill Elliott	Harry Melling	9	Ford	312	19,475
5. Rusty Wallace	Raymond Beadle	27	Pont	312	20,400

1989 Winston Cup Race No. 28 Autoworks 500
November 5, 1989 Average Speed: 105.683

Driver	Owner	Car #	Make	Laps	Winnings
1. Bill Elliott	Harry Melling	9	Ford	312	57,900
2. Terry Labonte	Junior Johnson	11	Ford	312	34,275
3. Mark Martin	Jack Roush	6	Ford	312	23,725
4. Darrell Waltrip	Rick Hendrick	17	Chev	312	20,290
5. Dale Jarrett	Cale Yarborough	29	Pont	312	22,112

1990 Winston Cup Series Race No. 28 Checker 500
November 4, 1990 Average Speed: 96.786

Driver	Owner	Car #	Make	Laps	Winnings
1. Dale Earnhardt	Richard Childress	3	Chev	312	72,100
2. Ken Schrader	Rick Hendrick	25	Chev	312	32,900
3. Morgan Shepherd	Bud Moore	15	Ford	312	23,357
4. Darrell Waltrip	Rick Hendrick	17	Chev	312	21,500
5. Bill Elliott	Harry Melling	9	Ford	312	19,775

1991 Winston Cup Series Race No. 28 Pyroil 500
November 3, 1991 Average Speed: 95.746

Driver	Owner	Car #	Make	Laps	Winnings
1. Davey Allison	Robert Yates	28	Ford	312	78,500
2. Darrell Waltrip	Darrell Waltrip	17	Chev	312	37,225
3. Sterling Marlin	Junior Johnson	22	Ford	312	25,000
4. Alan Kulwicki	Alan Kulwicki	7	Ford	312	22,600
5. Rusty Wallace	Roger Penske	2	Pont	312	16,475

1992 Winston Cup Race No. 28 Pyroil 500
November 1, 1992 Average Speed: 103.885

Driver	Owner	Car #	Make	Laps	Winnings
1. Davey Allison	Robert Yates	28	Ford	312	65,285
2. Mark Martin	Jack Roush	6	Ford	312	40,555
3. Darrell Waltrip	Darrell Waltrip	17	Chev	312	32,130
4. Alan Kulwicki	Alan Kulwicki	7	Ford	312	25,730
5. Jimmy Spencer	Bobby Allison	12	Ford	312	22,105

1993 Winston Cup Series Race No. 29 Slick 50 500
October 31, 1993 Average Speed: 100.375

Driver	Owner	Car #	Make	Laps	Winnings
1. Mark Martin	Jack Roush	6	Ford	312	67,035
2. Ernie Irvan	Robert Yates	28	Ford	312	44,155
3. Kyle Petty	Felix Sabates	42	Pont	312	28,430
4. Dale Earnhardt	Richard Childress	3	Chev	312	29,980
5. Bill Elliott	Junior Johnson	11	Ford	312	31,655

1994 Winston Cup Series Race No. 30 Slick 50 500
October 30, 1994 Average Speed: 107.463

Driver	Owner	Car #	Make	Laps	Winnings
1. Terry Labonte	Rick Hendrick	5	Chev	312	67,885
2. Mark Martin	Jack Roush	6	Ford	312	46,155
3. Sterling Marlin	Larry McClure	4	Chev	312	40,330
4. Jeff Gordon	Rick Hendrick	24	Chev	311	26,780
5. Ted Musgrave	Jack Roush	16	Ford	311	25,405

1995 Winston Cup Series Race No. 30 Dura-Lube 500
October 29, 1995 Average Speed: 102.128

Driver	Owner	Car #	Make	Laps	Winnings
1. Ricky Rudd	Ricky Rudd	10	Ford	312	78,260
2. Derrike Cope	Bobby Allison	12	Ford	312	52,205
3. Dale Earnhardt	Richard Childress	3	Chev	312	49,105
4. Rusty Wallace	Roger Penske	2	Ford	312	36,118
5. Jeff Gordon	Rick Hendrick	24	Chev	312	33,580

1996 Winston Cup Series Race No. 30 Dura-Lube 500
October 27, 1996 Average Speed: 109.709

Driver	Owner	Car #	Make	Laps	Winnings
1. Bobby Hamilton	Petty Enterprises	43	Pont	312	95,550
2. Mark Martin	Jack Roush	6	Ford	312	59,795
3. Terry Labonte	Rick Hendrick	5	Chev	312	61,590
4. Ted Musgrave	Jack Roush	16	Ford	312	35,153
5. Jeff Gordon	Rick Hendrick	24	Chev	312	45,065

1997 Winston Cup Series Race No. 31
November 2, 1997 Average Speed: 110.824

Driver	Owner	Car #	Make	Laps	Winnings
1. Dale Jarrett	Robert Yates	88	Ford	312	98,830
2. Rusty Wallace	Roger Penske	2	Ford	312	63,355
3. Bobby Hamilton	Petty Enterprises	43	Pont	312	47,225
4. Ken Schrader	Andy Petree	33	Chev	312	38,588
5. Dale Earnhardt	Richard Childress	3	Chev	312	39,300

Phoenix Int'l Raceway *continued*

1998 Winston Cup Series Race No. 31
October 25, 1998 Average Speed: 108.211

Driver	Owner	Car #	Make	Laps	Winnings
1. Rusty Wallace	Roger Penske	2	Ford	257	78,005
2. Mark Martin	Jack Roush	6	Ford	257	68,430
3. Dale Earnhardt	Richard Childress	3	Chev	257	57,175
4. Jeff Burton	Jack Roush	99	Ford	257	50,512
5. Ted Musgrave	Bill Elliott	13	Ford	257	33,950

1999 Winston Cup Series Race No. 32
November 7, 1999 Average Speed: 118.132

Driver	Owner	Car #	Make	Laps	Winnings
1. Tony Stewart	Joe Gibbs	20	Pont	312	168,485
2. Mark Martin	Jack Roush	6	Ford	312	125,200
3. Bobby Labonte	Joe Gibbs	18	Pont	312	105,450
4. Jeff Burton	Jack Roush	99	Ford	312	90,535
5. Ricky Rudd	Ricky Rudd	10	Ford	312	86,240

2000 Winston Cup Series Race No. 32
November 5, 2000 Average Speed: 105.041

Driver	Owner	Car #	Make	Laps	Winnings
1. Jeff Burton	Jack Roush	99	Ford	312	197,345
2. Jeremy Mayfield	Michael Kranefuss	12	Ford	312	124,925
3. Steve Park	Dale Earnhardt, Inc.	1	Chev	312	112,250
4. Rusty Wallace	Roger Penske	2	Ford	312	98,860
5. Bobby Labonte	Joe Gibbs	18	Pont	312	100,250

2001 Winston Cup Series Race No. 32
October 28, 2001 Average Speed: 102.613

Driver	Owner	Car #	Make	Laps	Winnings
1. Jeff Burton	Jack Roush	99	Ford	312	213,491
2. Mike Wallace	Roger Penske	12	Ford	312	160,759
3. Ricky Rudd	Robert Yates	28	Ford	312	135,497
4. Matt Kenseth	Jack Roush	17	Ford	312	97,960
5. Tony Stewart	Joe Gibbs	20	Pont	312	96,675

2002 Winston Cup Series Race No. 35
November 10, 2002 Average Speed: 113.857

Driver	Owner	Car #	Make	Laps	Winnings
1. Matt Kenseth	Mark Martin	17	Ford	312	211,895
2. Rusty Wallace	Roger Penske	2	Ford	312	163,825
3. Jeff Gordon	Rick Hendrick	24	Chev	312	152,328
4. Mark Martin	Jack Roush	6	Ford	312	129,218
5. Dale Earnhardt, Jr.	Dale Earnhardt, Inc.	8	Chev	312	97,850

Tucson Rodeo Grounds
Tucson, AZ
Half-mile Dirt Track

Half-mile dirt track opened in November, 1939. Only NASCAR Winston Cup (then Grand National) race run on 5/15/55 (won by Danny Letner). Automobile racing was discontinued shortly after the conclusion of the NASCAR event.

Winston Cup Victories		**Winston Cup Money**		**Narrowest Margin of Victory**	**Most Race Leaders**
Danny Letner	1	Danny Letner	$1,000	1 lap plus—May 15, 1955	5—May 15, 1955
Winston Cup Poles		**Most Cars Started**		**Race Record**	**Most Cars Running at Finish**
Bill Amick	1	19—May 15, 1955		51.428 MPH—May 15, 1955	12—May 15, 1955

1955 Grand National Race No. 14
May 15, 1955 Average Speed: 51.428

Driver	Owner	Car #	Make	Laps	Winnings
1. Danny Letner	Coz Concilla	6	54 Olds	200	1,000
2. Allen Adkins		7	54 Dodg	199	650
3. Lloyd Dane	Lloyd Dane	33	53 Huds	198	450
4. Chuck Meekins	Larry Dorsey	65	52 Olds	196	350
5. Bill Amick		3	55 Dodg	194	300

Arkansas

Memphis-Arkansas Speedway
LeHi, Arkansas
1.5-mile Dirt Track

1.5-mile high-banked dirt track opened with NASCAR Winston Cup (then Grand National) race on 10/10/54 (won by Buck Baker; Junior Johnson won the pole in a Cadillac). Final NASCAR race was held on 7/14/57 (won by Marvin Panch). Track was extremely dangerous and was the site of two NASCAR fatalities in 1956 (Clint McHugh and Thomas "Cotton" Priddy). Track was closed when major highways were built in the area, blocking all access to the track. It never re-opened following the completion of the highway project.

Winston Cup Starts
Buck Baker	5
Lee Petty	5

Winston Cup Victories
Buck Baker	1
Fonty Flock	1
Ralph Moody	1
Marvin Panch	1
Speedy Thompson	1

Winston Cup Poles
Fonty Flock	2

Winston Cup Money
Marvin Panch	$5,350

Most Cars Started
52—October 10, 1954 Mid-South 250

Fewest Cars Started
28—July 14, 1957

Narrowest Margin of Victory
4.000 seconds June 10, 1956

Slowest Race
67.167 MPH—July 14, 1957

Race Record
89.892 MPH—August 14, 1955 Mid-South 250

Most Cautions
5—June 10, 1956

Most Race Leaders
4—June 10, 1956
4—July 14, 1957

Most Cars Running at Finish
28—October 10, 1954 Mid-South 250

1954 Grand National Race No. 35 Mid-South 250
October 10, 1954 Average Speed: 89.013

Driver	Owner	Car #	Make	Laps	Winnings
1. Buck Baker	Griffin Motors	87	54 Olds	167	2,750
2. Dick Rathmann	John Ditz	3	54 Huds	162	1,150
3. Lee Petty	Petty Enterprises	42	54 Chrys	161	850
4. Herb Thomas	Herb Thomas	92	54 Huds	161	700
5. Herschel Buchanan	Herschel Buchanan	4	54 Huds	160	500

1955 Grand National Race No. 33 Mid-South 250
August 14, 1955 Average Speed: 89.892

Driver	Owner	Car #	Make	Laps	Winnings
1. Fonty Flock	Carl Kiekhaefer	301	55 Chrys	167	2,950
2. Speedy Thompson	Griffin Motors	87	54 Olds	167	1,675
3. Tim Flock	Carl Kiekhaefer	300	55 Chrys	165	1,175
4. Jim Paschal	Ernest Woods	78	55 Olds	163	815
5. Buck Baker	Buck Baker	89	55 Buick	161	685

1955 Grand National Race No. 40
October 9, 1955 Average Speed: 83.948

Driver	Owner	Car #	Make	Laps	Winnings
1. Speedy Thompson	Pete DePaolo	297	55 Ford	200	2,900
2. Marvin Panch	Pete DePaolo	98	55 Ford	200	1,450
3. Jimmy Massey	Hubert Westmoreland	04	55 Chev	196	1,000
4. Tim Flock	Carl Kiekhaefer	300	55 Chrys	195	850
5. Bob Flock	Carl Kiekhaefer	308	55 Chrys	195	650

1956 Grand National Race No. 25
June 10, 1956 Average Speed: 74.313

Driver	Owner	Car #	Make	Laps	Winnings
1. Ralph Moody	Pete DePaolo	12	56 Ford	167	4,100
2. Jim Paschal	Frank Hayworth	75	56 Merc	167	2,100
3. Pat Kirkwood	Jim Stephens	286	56 Pont	165	1,325
4. Tim Flock	Mauri Rose	11	56 Chev	164	950
5. Joe Eubanks	James Satcher	82	56 Ford	163	650

1957 Grand National Race No. 30
July 14, 1957 Average Speed: 67.167

Driver	Owner	Car #	Make	Laps	Winnings
1. Marvin Panch	Herb Thomas	92	57 Pont	134	3,500
2. Bill Amick	Bill Amick	97	57 Ford	134	2,075
3. Fireball Roberts	Paul Spaulding	11	57 Ford	134	1,375
4. Buck Baker	Buck Baker	87	57 Chev	132	950
5. Bob Welborn	Bob Welborn	49	57 Chev	131	750

California

Ascot Stadium
Los Angeles, CA
.4-mile Dirt Track

(aka Bill McKay's Los Angeles Speedway; Ascot Park; Ascot Speedway) Half-mile dirt oval built in May 1957. Final race run in 1990. First Winston Cup race staged on 6/8/57 (won by Eddie Pagan). Final Winston Cup race run on 5/27/61 (won by Eddie Cray). Track closed in 1990. Now the site of an industrial park.

Winston Cup Starts

Scotty Cain	3
Jim Cook	3
Lloyd Dane	3
Dick Getty	3
Eddie Gray	3
Eddie Pagan	3

Winston Cup Victories

Eddie Gray	1
Parnelli Jones	1
Eddie Pagan	1

Winston Cup Poles

Eddie Pagan	1
Jim Reed	1
Danny Weinberg	1

Winston Cup Money
Parnelli Jones $1,855

Most Cars Started
33—May 30, 1959

Fewest Cars Started
22—May 27, 1961

Narrowest Margin of Victory
N/A

Slowest Race
50.982 MPH—May 30, 1959

Race Record
68.833 MPH—May 27, 1961

Most Race Leaders
N/A

Most Cars Running at Finish
17—May 30, 1959

1957 Grand National Race No. 22
June 8, 1957

Driver	Owner	Car #	Make	Laps	Winnings
1. Eddie Pagan	Eddie Pagan	45	57 Ford	150	800
2. Lloyd Dane	Lloyd Dane	44	57 Ford	149	550
3. Chuck Meekins	Jim Rush	1	57 Chev	148	400
4. George Seeger	Oscar Maples	12	57 Ford	148	305
5. Eddie Gray	Chuck Green	18	56 Chev	147	270

1959 Grand National Race No. 17
May 30, 1959 Average Speed: 50.982

Driver	Owner	Car #	Make	Laps	Winnings
1. Parnelli Jones	Vel Miletich	97	59 Ford	487	1,805
2. Lloyd Dane	Lloyd Dane	44	57 Ford	487	900
3. Marvin Porter	Marvin Porter	12	57 Ford	485	700
4. Bob Ross	Bob Ross	34	57 Chev	482	600
5. Bob Keefe	Jack Chatenay	11	58 Plym	459	500

1961 Grand National Race No. 23
May 27, 1961 Average Speed: 68.833

Driver	Owner	Car #	Make	Laps	Winnings
1. Eddie Gray	Eddie Gray	98	61 Ford	200	850
2. Don Noel	Chuck Parkko	7	61 Ford	199	500
3. Danny Weinberg	Guy Kimball	76	61 Ford	196	370
4. Jim Blomgren	Bob Smith	10	60 Ford	196	305
5. Ron Hornaday	Frank Galpin	2	60 Ford	196	250

Bay Meadows Race Track
San Mateo, CA
1-mile Dirt Track

(aka Bay Meadows Race Course) 1-mile dirt track opened in November of 1950. First Winston Cup race staged on 8/22/54 (Hershel McGriff won). Last Winston Cup race run on 8/19/56 (Eddie Pagan won). Still a famous horse track.

Winston Cup Starts

Buck Baker	3
Jim Cook	3
Lloyd Dane	3
Chuck Meekins	3
Eddie Pagan	3
Bill West	3

Winston Cup Victories

Tim Flock	1
Hershel McGriff	1
Eddie Pagan	1

Winston Cup Poles

Hershel McGriff	1
Eddie Pagan	1

Winston Cup Money
Hershel McGriff $2,425

Most Cars Started
41—August 22, 1954

Fewest Cars Started
34—July 31, 1955

Narrowest Margin of Victory
N/A

Slowest Race
64.710 MPH—August 22, 1954

Race Record
68.571 MPH—July 31, 1955

Most Race Leaders
3—July 31, 1955

Most Cars Running at Finish
32—August 22, 1954

1954 Grand National Race No. 29
August 22, 1954 Average Speed: 64.710

Driver	Owner	Car #	Make	Laps	Winnings
1. Hershel McGriff	Frank Christian	14	54 Olds	250	2,425
2. Bill Amick	Frank Dodge	28	53 Olds	250	1,500
3. Dick Rathmann	Don Oliver	12	53 Olds	249	900
4. Allen Adkins	Gus Davis	68	54 Dodg	249	700
5. Lee Petty	Petty Enterprises	42	54 Chrys	247	500

1955 Grand National Race No. 30
July 31, 1955 Average Speed: 68.571

Driver	Owner	Car #	Make	Laps	Winnings
1. Tim Flock	Carl Kiekhaefer	300	55 Chrys	252	2,050
2. John Kieper	John Kieper	11	55 Olds	251	1,450
3. Danny Letner	Coz Concilla	6	54 Olds	249	700
4. Marvin Panch	John Hernandez	98	55 Merc	247	650
5. Buck Baker	Buck Baker	89	55 Buick	247	550

1956 Grand National Race No. 39
August 19, 1956 Average Speed: 68.161

Driver	Owner	Car #	Make	Laps	Winnings
1. Eddie Pagan	Eddie Pagan	45	56 Ford	241	1,475
2. Parnelli Jones	Vel Miletich	11	56 Ford	241	1,575
3. Chuck Meekins		56	56 Chev	239	1,100
4. Lloyd Dane	Lloyd Dane	225	56 Merc	239	750
5. Scotty Cain		21	56 Ford	239	550

California Speedway
Fontana, CA
2-mile Superspeedway

A 2-mile D-shaped oval. First oval superspeedway in Southern California since the demise of the Ontario Motor Speedway in 1980. Construction began in November, 1995. Track opened in June, 1997. Jeff Gordon won the inaugural NASCAR Winston Cup race. Track holds the distinction of having the all-time official closed course qualifying record of 241.428 mph set by Gil de Ferran for an open wheel Indy Car event on October 28, 2000. Track contains nearly 100,000 grandstand seats. Variety of motorsports events comprise the annual calendar, including NASCAR stocks, Indy Cars, Sports Cars, Motorcycles and vintage racing cars.

Winston Cup Starts
21 drivers tied at

Winston Cup Victories
Jeff Gordon   2

Winston Cup Poles
6 drivers tied at

Winston Cup Money
Jeff Gordon $737,745

Most Cars Started
43—5 times

Fewest Cars Started
42—June 22, 1997

Narrowest Margin of Victory
.270 seconds—April 29, 2001

Slowest Race
140.220 MPH—May 3, 1998

Race Record
155.025 MPH—June 22, 1997

Most Cautions
6—2 times

Most Race Leaders
15—April 30, 2000

Most Cars Running at Finish
40—April 29, 2001

1997 Winston Cup Series Race No. 15
June 22, 1997 Average Speed: 155.025

Driver	Owner	Car #	Make	Laps	Winnings
1. Jeff Gordon	Rick Hendrick	24	Chev	250	144,600
2. Terry Labonte	Rick Hendrick	5	Chev	250	100,825
3. Ricky Rudd	Ricky Rudd	10	Ford	250	78,525
4. Ted Musgrave	Jack Roush	16	Ford	250	64,975
5. Jimmy Spencer	Travis Carter	23	Ford	250	54,775

1998 Winston Cup Series Race No. 10
May 3, 1998 Average Speed: 140.22

Driver	Owner	Car #	Make	Laps	Winnings
1. Mark Martin	Jack Roush	6	Ford	250	141,375
2. Jeremy Mayfield	Michael Kranefuss	12	Ford	250	88,800
3. Terry Labonte	Rick Hendrick	5	Chev	250	96,200
4. Jeff Gordon	Rick Hendrick	24	Chev	250	98,800
5. Darrell Waltrip	Dale Earnhardt, Inc.	1	Chev	250	47,950

1999 Winston Cup Series Race No. 10
May 2, 1999 Average Speed: 150.28

Driver	Owner	Car #	Make	Laps	Winnings
1. Jeff Gordon	Rick Hendrick	24	Chev	250	155,890
2. Jeff Burton	Jack Roush	99	Ford	250	125,375
3. Bobby Labonte	Joe Gibbs	18	Pont	250	99,850
4. Tony Stewart	Joe Gibbs	20	Pont	250	68,175
5. Dale Jarrett	Robert Yates	88	Ford	250	71,140

2000 Winston Cup Series Race No. 10
April 30, 2000 Average Speed: 149.378

Driver	Owner	Car #	Make	Laps	Winnings
1. Jeremy Mayfield	Michael Kranefuss	12	Ford	250	125,925
2. Bobby Labonte	Joe Gibbs	18	Pont	250	135,300
3. Matt Kenseth	Jack Roush	17	Ford	250	114,325
4. Ricky Rudd	Robert Yates	28	Ford	250	86,525
5. Jeff Burton	Jack Roush	99	Ford	250	77,575

2001 Winston Cup Series Race No. 10
April 29, 2001 Average Speed: 143.118

Driver	Owner	Car #	Make	Laps	Winnings
1. Rusty Wallace	Roger Penske	2	Ford	250	195,090
2. Jeff Gordon	Rick Hendrick	24	Chev	250	163,902
3. Dale Earnhardt, Jr.	Dale Earnhardt, Inc.	8	Chev	250	136,873
4. Tony Stewart	Joe Gibbs	20	Pont	250	107,072
5. Jeremy Mayfield	Roger Penske	12	Ford	250	105,884

2002 Winston Cup Series Race No. 10
April 28, 2002 Average Speed: 150.088

Driver	Owner	Car #	Make	Laps	Winnings
1. Jimmie Johnson	Rick Hendrick	48	Chev	250	176,750
2. Kurt Busch	Jack Roush	97	Ford	250	140,075
3. Ricky Rudd	Robert Yates	28	Ford	250	148,117
4. Bill Elliott	Ray Evernham	9	Dodg	250	125,856
5. Mark Martin	Jack Roush	6	Ford	250	110,458

California State Fairgrounds
Sacramento, CA
1-mile Dirt Track

(aka Sacramento Fairgrounds) Originally built as horse track in 1906. 1-mile dirt track (September 1946–October 1970). First NASCAR Winston Cup (then Grand National) race staged on 7/8/56 (Lloyd Dane won). Last Grand National race run on 9/10/61 (won by Eddie Gray). Track closed after October 1970 event. Now a shopping center.

Winston Cup Starts
Jim Blomgren	6
Jim Cook	6

Winston Cup Victories
Eddie Gray	2

Winston Cup Poles
Bill Amick	1
Jim Cook	1
Danny Graves	1
Parnelli Jones	1
Eddie Pagan	1

Winston Cup Money
Eddie Gray	$2,325

Most Cars Started
32—September 10, 1961

Fewest Cars Started
21—July 8, 1956

Narrowest Margin of Victory
N/A

Slowest Race
54.753 MPH—September 13, 1959

Race Record
74.074 MPH—July 8, 1956

Most Race Leaders
4—July 8, 1956

Most Cars Running at Finish
20—September 10, 1961

1956 Grand National Race No. 32
July 8, 1956 Average Speed: 74.074

Driver	Owner	Car #	Make	Laps	Winnings
1. Lloyd Dane	Lloyd Dane	225	56 Merc	100	1,100
2. Chuck Meekins		56	56 Chev	100	700
3. John Kieper	John Kieper	88	56 Olds	100	475
4. Gordon Haines		77	56 Dodg	100	365
5. Clyde Palmer		1	56 Dodg	99	310

1957 Grand National Race No. 43
September 8, 1957 Average Speed: 68.663

Driver	Owner	Car #	Make	Laps	Winnings
1. Danny Graves	Danny Graves	81	57 Chev	100	800
2. Marvin Porter	Marvin Porter	12	57 Ford	100	550
3. Eddie Pagan	Eddie Pagan	45	57 Ford	100	450
4. Chuck Meekins		1	57 Chev	100	325
5. Dick Getty	Dick Getty	00	56 Chev	100	325

1958 Grand National Race No. 44
September 7, 1958 Average Speed: 65.550

Driver	Owner	Car #	Make	Laps	Winnings
1. Parnelli Jones	Vel Miletich	97	56 Ford	100	700
2. Bob Ross		43	56 Merc	100	500
3. Danny Weinberg		8	57 Ford	99	425
4. Jim Cook		5	57 Ford	98	335
5. Harold Hardesty		22N	56 Ford	98	300

1959 Grand National Race No. 39
September 13, 1959 Average Speed: 54.753

Driver	Owner	Car #	Make	Laps	Winnings
1. Eddie Gray	Vel Miletich	1	59 Ford	100	700
2. Scotty Cain	Scotty Cain	3	59 Ford	100	500
3. Danny Weinberg	Carl Dane	16	58 Merc	100	425
4. Bob Ross	Jim Rush	34	57 Chev	100	335
5. Lucky Long		10	57 Chev	97	300

1960 Grand National Race No. 37
September 11, 1960 Average Speed: 70.629

Driver	Owner	Car #	Make	Laps	Winnings
1. Jim Cook	Floyd Johnson	0	60 Dodg	100	1,100
2. Scotty Cain	Scotty Cain	4	59 Ford	100	700
3. Lloyd Dane	Lloyd Dane	44	59 Ford	99	500
4. Ron Hornaday	Frank Galpin	2	60 Ford	96	400
5. Danny Weinberg	Carl Dane	16	60 Ford	95	300

1961 Grand National Race No. 45
September 10, 1961

Driver	Owner	Car #	Make	Laps	Winnings
1. Eddie Gray	Eddie Gray	98	61 Ford	100	1,300
2. Bob Ross		6	61 Olds	99	800
3. Danny Weinberg	Guy Kimball	76	61 Ford	99	500
4. Frank Secrist		36	60 Ford	99	400
5. Don Noel	Chuck Parkko	7	61 Ford	98	300

Capital Speedway
Sacramento, CA
Half-mile Dirt Track

(aka West Capital Speedway; West Capital Raceway) Quarter-mile dirt track built in 1947. Half-mile dirt track oval 1954–72. Only NASCAR Winston Cup (then Grand National) race held on 6/22/57 (Bill Amick won). Track closed in 1980.

Winston Cup Victories
Bill Amick 1

Winston Cup Poles
Art Watts 1

Winston Cup Money
Bill Amick $900

Most Cars Started
31—June 22, 1957

Narrowest Margin of Victory
1lap plus—June 22, 1957

Race Record
59.580 MPH—June 22, 1957

Most Race Leaders
1—June 22, 1957

Most Cars Running at Finish
17—June 22, 1957

1957 Grand National Race No. 25
June 22, 1957 Average Speed: 59.580

Driver	Owner	Car #	Make	Laps	Winnings
1. Bill Amick	Bill Amick	97	57 Ford	199	900
2. Lloyd Dane	Lloyd Dane	44	57 Ford	198	600
3. George Seeger	Oscar Maples	12	57 Ford	197	475
4. Scotty Cain	Scotty Cain	14	56 Merc	196	365
5. Danny Graves	Danny Graves	81	57 Chev	196	320

Carrell Speedway
Gardena, CA
Half-mile Dirt Track

(aka Gardena Bowl) Half-mile dirt oval built in 1940. Half-mile dirt oval opened in 1948. Closed circa 1954. First NASCAR Winston Cup (then Grand National) race run on 4/8/51 (Marshall Teague won). Final race staged on 5/30/54 (won by John Soares). Track closed in early '50s to make room for Artesia Boulevard.

Winston Cup Starts
Fred Bince 4
Lloyd Dane 4
Erick Erickson 4
Chuck Meekins 4
George Seeger 4

Winston Cup Victories
Lou Figaro 1
Bill Norton 1
John Soares 1
Marshall Teague 1

Winston Cup Poles
Lou Figaro 1
Fonty Flock 1
Danny Letner 1
Andy Pierce 1

Winston Cup Money
John Soares $1,525

Most Cars Started
32—May 30, 1954

Fewest Cars Started
20—April 8, 1951

Narrowest Margin of Victory
100 yards—June 30,1951

Slowest Race
53.438 MPH—May 30, 1954

Race Record
61.047 MPH—April 8, 1951

Most Cautions
1—April 8, 1951
1—June 30, 1951

Most Race Leaders
4—November 11, 1951

Most Cars Running at Finish
21—May 30, 1954

1951 Grand National Race No. 4
April 8, 1951 Average Speed: 61.047

Driver	Owner	Car #	Make	Laps	Winnings
1. Marshall Teague	Marshall Teague	6	51 Huds	200	1,000
2. Johnny Mantz	Johnny Mantz	98	51 Nash	200	700
3. George Seeger	Bill Cramer	2	49 Plym	199	400
4. Fred Steinbroner	Bob Carpenter	16	48 Ford	198	300
5. Erick Erickson		1	48 Pont	195	250

1951 Grand National Race No. 13
June 30, 1951

Driver	Owner	Car #	Make	Laps	Winnings
1. Lou Figaro	Jack Gaynor	33	51 Huds	200	1,000
2. Chuck Meekins	Chuck Meekins	7	49 Plym	200	600
3. Lloyd Dane	Lloyd Dane	22	51 Ford	—	400
4. Fred Bince		11	48 Pont	—	300
5. Fred Steinbroner	Bob Carpenter	16	50 Ford	—	250

1951 Grand National Race No. 40
November 11, 1951

Driver	Owner	Car #	Make	Laps	Winnings
1. Bill Norton	Larry Bettinger	48	51 Merc	200	1,000
2. Dick Meyer	Grant Sniffen	9	50 Merc	—	600
3. Erick Erickson	Erick Erickson	25	51 KAI	—	500
4. Lou Figaro	Jack Gaynor	33	51 Huds	—	400
5. Danny Weinberg	Tony Sampo	2	51 Stud	—	300

1954 Grand National Race No. 16
May 30, 1954 Average Speed: 53.438

Driver	Owner	Car #	Make	Laps	Winnings
1. John Soares	Charles Vance	4	54 Dodg	496	1,500
2. Lloyd Dane	Lloyd Dane	33	53 Huds	495	800
3. Danny Letner	Joe Berreschick	39	52 Huds	490	600
4. Ben Gregory	Don Oliver	12	53 Olds	486	400
5. George Seeger	Carl Dane	73	54 Ford	486	350

Marchbanks Speedway
Hanford, CA
1.4-mile Paved Track

(aka Hanford Motor Speedway) California's first high-banked paved superspeedway to be run under NASCAR sanction. 1.4-mile track opened in June 1960. Half-mile oval originally built in 1951. First Grand National event was staged on 10/28/51 (won by Danny Weinberg). Fireball Roberts won the first race on the the high-banked superspeedway and led every lap (3/12/61). He remains the only driver to lead from start to finish on a long-distance superspeedway event. Track also had a road course that was closed circa 1965. Additionally, .333-mile and .75-mile tracks held motor racing events. Complex torn down in 1984.

Winston Cup Starts
Lloyd Dane	3
Danny Weinberg	3

Winston Cup Victories
Marvin Porter	1
Fireball Roberts	1
Danny Weinberg	1

Winston Cup Poles
Bob Ross	1
Frank Secrist	1

Winston Cup Money
Marvin Porter	$2,100

Most Cars Started
36—March 12, 1961

Fewest Cars Started
33—June 12, 1960 California 250

Narrowest Margin of Victory
46 seconds June 12, 1960 California 250

Slowest Race
88.032 MPH—June 12, 1960 California 250

Race Record
95.621 MPH—March 12, 1961

Most Race Leaders
5—June 12, 1960 California 250

Most Cars Running at Finish
18—March 12, 1961

1951 Grand National Race No. 37
October 28, 1951

	Driver	Owner	Car #	Make	Laps	Winnings
1.	Danny Weinberg	Tony Sampo	2	51 Stud	200	1,000
2.	Marvin Panch	Marvin Panch	56	50 Merc	—	600
3.	Bill Norton	Larry Bettinger	48	50 Merc	—	500
4.	Lloyd Dane	Lloyd Dane	22	51 Ford	—	400
5.	Woody Brown	Joe Mangini	88	50 Olds	—	300

1960 Grand National Race No. 20 California 250
June 12, 1960 Average Speed: 88.032

	Driver	Owner	Car #	Make	Laps	Winnings
1.	Marvin Porter	Vel Miletich	98	59 Ford	179	2,000
2.	Joe Weatherly	Vel Miletich	97	60 Ford	179	1,250
3.	John Rostek	John Rostek	19	60 Ford	175	750
4.	Fritz Wilson	Fritz Wilson	48	58 Ford	173	600
5.	Don Noel	A. L. McClure	7	59 Ford	172	575

1961 Grand National Race No. 8
March 12, 1961 Average Speed: 95.621

	Driver	Owner	Car #	Make	Laps	Winnings
1.	Fireball Roberts	J. D. Braswell	75	61 Pont	178	2,000
2.	Eddie Gray	Eddie Gray	98	61 Ford	176	1,250
3.	Danny Letner	Guy Kimball	76	61 Ford	175	750
4.	Tubby Gonzales	Tubby Gonzales	80	61 Ford	168	600
5.	Eddie Pagan	Bill Clinton	45	61 Ford	168	575

Merced Fairgrounds Speedway
Merced, CA
Half-mile Dirt Track

.2-mile dirt oval built circa 1946. Half-mile dirt track built for NASCAR Winston Cup (then Grand National) race run on 6/3/56 (won by Herb Thomas). Current configuration is a quarter-mile dirt oval.

Winston Cup Victories
Herb Thomas	1

Winston Cup Poles
Herb Thomas	1

Winston Cup Money
Herb Thomas	$910

Most Cars Started
28—June 3, 1956

Narrowest Margin of Victory
N/A

Race Record
47.325 MPH—June 3, 1956

Most Race Leaders
N/A

Most Cars Running at Finish
17—June 3, 1956

1956 Grand National Race No. 24
June 3, 1956 Average Speed: 47.325

	Driver	Owner	Car #	Make	Laps	Winnings
1.	Herb Thomas	Carl Kiekhaefer	300B	56 Chrys	200	910
2.	Harold Hardesty		52	56 Chev	200	650
3.	Jim Graham		30	56 Plym	200	495
4.	Lloyd Dane	Lloyd Dane	225	56 Merc	198	375
5.	Eddie Pagan	Eddie Pagan	45	56 Ford	197	310

Oakland Stadium
Oakland, CA
Half-mile Paved and Dirt Track

(aka Oakland Speedway) 1-mile high-banked dirt oval built in 1931. Scene of 500-mile races in 1930s. Half-mile flat oval built inside big track. A .625-mile track that utilized high-banked turns, sloping upwards to 45 degrees, was built in 1946. First NASCAR Winston Cup (then Grand National) race held on 10/14/51 (won by Marvin Burke). Final NASCAR race run on 8/1/54 (Danny Letner won). The 1954 events used dirt turns and paved straightaways.

Winston Cup Starts
Woody Brown	3
Robert Caswell	3
Lloyd Dane	3
Sam Hawks	3
Marvin Panch	3
John Soares	3

Winston Cup Victories
Marvin Burke	1
Danny Letner	1
Dick Rathmann	1

Winston Cup Poles
Fonty Flock	1
Hershel McGriff	1
Marvin Panch	1

Winston Cup Money
Marvin Burke	$1,875

Most Cars Started
32—August 1, 1954

Fewest Cars Started
26—March 28, 1954

Narrowest Margin of Victory
2 car lengths—August 1, 1954

Slowest Race
50.692 MPH—March 28, 1954

Race Record
78.748 MPH—October 14, 1951

Most Race Leaders
N/A

Most Cars Running at Finish
18—March 28, 1954
18—August 1, 1954

1951 Grand National Race No. 35
October 14, 1951 Average Speed: 78.748

Driver	Owner	Car #	Make	Laps	Winnings
1. Marvin Burke	Bob Phillippi	18	50 Merc	250	1,875
2. Robert Caswell	Lou Mangini	84	50 Plym	247	1,250
3. Woody Brown	Joe Mangini	88	50 Olds	—	900
4. Sam Hawks	Marvin Panch	55	50 Plym	—	750
5. Dick Meyer	Grant Sniffen	9	50 Merc	—	500

1954 Grand National Race No. 6
March 28, 1954 Average Speed: 50.692

Driver	Owner	Car #	Make	Laps	Winnings
1. Dick Rathmann	Ray Erickson	3	52 Huds	250	1,000
2. Marvin Panch	Beryl Jackson	98	54 Dodg	249	650
3. John Soares	Charles Vance	4	54 Dodg	247	450
4. Clyde Palmer	Al Neves	1	51 Merc	238	350
5. Lloyd Dane	Lloyd Dane	18	50 Olds	234	300

1954 Grand National Race No. 27
August 1, 1954 Average Speed: 53.045

Driver	Owner	Car #	Make	Laps	Winnings
1. Danny Letner	Joe Berreschick	3	52 Huds	297	1,000
2. Marvin Panch	Beryl Jackson	98	54 Dodg	297	650
3. Allen Adkins	Gus Davis	68	54 Dodg	296	450
4. Ben Gregory	Chris Milovich	6	54 Olds	296	350
5. Lloyd Dane	Lloyd Dane	33	53 Huds	295	300

Ontario Motor Speedway
Ontario, CA
2.5-mile Paved Track

2.5-mile rectangular shaped track opened in 1970 with USAC IndyCar race. First NASCAR Winston Cup Grand National race staged on 2/28/71 (the 1,000th NASCAR Winston Cup race to be run); won by A. J. Foyt. Final NASCAR event staged on 11/15/80 (Benny Parsons won). The track, then regarded as the premier motorsports facility in America, was purchased by Chevron Oil Co. and leveled in 1981.

Winston Cup Starts
Bobby Allison 9
Cecil Gordon 9
James Hylton 9
J. D. McDuffie 9
Benny Parsons 9
Richard Petty 9

Winston Cup Victories
Bobby Allison 2
A. J. Foyt 2
Benny Parsons 2

Winston Cup Poles
Cale Yarborough 3

Winston Cup Money
Bobby Allison $99,655

Most Cars Started
51—February 28, 1971
Miller High Life 500
51—March 5, 1972 Miller High Life 500

Fewest Cars Started
37—November 18, 1979
Los Angeles Times 500

Narrowest Margin of Victory
2 car lengths—November 20, 1977
Los Angeles Times 500

Slowest Race
127.082 MPH—March 5, 1972
Miller High Life 500

Race Record
140.712 MPH—November 23, 1975
Los Angeles Times 500

Most Cautions
6—November 18, 1979
Los Angeles Times 500
6—November 15, 1980
Los Angeles Times 500

Most Race Leaders
11—November 20, 1977
Los Angeles Times 500

Most Cars Running at Finish
33—March 5, 1972
Miller High Life 500

1971 Winston Cup GN Race No. 5 Miller High Life 500
February 28, 1971 Average Speed: 134.168

Driver	Owner	Car #	Make	Laps	Winnings
1. A. J. Foyt	Wood Brothers	21	69 Merc	200	51,850
2. Buddy Baker	Petty Enterprises	11	71 Dodg	200	15,325
3. Richard Petty	Petty Enterprises	43	71 Plym	200	12,825
4. Bobby Isaac	Nord Krauskopf	71	71 Dodg	199	9,325
5. Dick Brooks	Mario Rossi	22	70 Dodg	198	5,025

1972 Winston Cup GN Race No. 4 Miller High Life 500
March 5, 1972 Average Speed: 127.082

Driver	Owner	Car #	Make	Laps	Winnings
1. A. J. Foyt	Wood Brothers	21	71 Merc	200	31,695
2. Bobby Allison	R. Howard & J. Johnson	12	72 Chev	200	16,945
3. Buddy Baker	Petty Enterprises	11	72 Dodg	200	11,670
4. Richard Petty	Petty Enterprises	43	72 Plym	199	9,970
5. Ray Elder	Fred Elder	96	72 Dodg	194	5,845

1974 Winston Cup GN Race No. 30 Los Angeles Times 500
November 24, 1974 Average Speed: 134.963

Driver	Owner	Car #	Make	Laps	Winnings
1. Bobby Allison	Roger Penske	12	74 Mata	200	15,125
2. David Pearson	Wood Brothers	21	73 Merc	200	9,925
3. Cale Yarborough	Junior Johnson	11	74 Chev	200	10,125
4. A. J. Foyt	Hoss Ellington	28	74 Chev	199	5,725
5. Buddy Baker	Bud Moore	15	73 Ford	197	6,825

1975 Winston Cup GN Race No. 30 Los Angeles Times 500
November 23, 1975 Average Speed: 140.712

Driver	Owner	Car #	Make	Laps	Winnings
1. Buddy Baker	Bud Moore	15	75 Ford	200	35,300
2. David Pearson	Wood Brothers	21	73 Merc	200	14,300
3. Dave Marcis	Nord Krauskopf	71	74 Dodg	200	12,000
4. Cale Yarborough	Junior Johnson	11	75 Chev	199	8,825
5. Bobby Allison	Roger Penske	16	75 Mata	199	4,925

1976 Winston Cup GN Race No. 30 Los Angeles Times 500
November 21, 1976 Average Speed: 137.101

Driver	Owner	Car #	Make	Laps	Winnings
1. David Pearson	Wood Brothers	21	Merc	200	27,715
2. Lennie Pond	Ronnie Elder	54	Chev	199	14,690
3. Benny Parsons	L. G. DeWitt	72	Chev	198	11,670
4. Dick Brooks	Junie Donlavey	90	Ford	198	7,810
5. James Hylton	James Hylton	48	Chev	196	6,250

1977 Winston Cup GN Race No. 30 Los Angeles Times 500
November 20, 1977 Average Speed: 128.296

Driver	Owner	Car #	Make	Laps	Winnings
1. Neil Bonnett	Jim Stacy	5	Dodg	200	22,510
2. Richard Petty	Petty Enterprises	43	Dodg	200	17,535
3. Cale Yarborough	Junior Johnson	11	Chev	200	14,285
4. Buddy Baker	Bud Moore	15	Ford	200	9,385
5. David Pearson	Wood Brothers	21	Merc	199	5,285

1978 Winston Cup GN Race No. 30 Los Angeles Times 500
November 19, 1978 Average Speed: 137.783

Driver	Owner	Car #	Make	Laps	Winnings
1. Bobby Allison	Bud Moore	15	Ford	200	24,025
2. Cale Yarborough	Junior Johnson	11	Olds	200	19,700
3. Donnie Allison	Hoss Ellington	1	Chev	200	12,925
4. Buddy Baker	M. C. Anderson	27	Chev	199	8,600
5. Darrell Waltrip	DiGard	88	Chev	199	9,200

1979 Winston Cup GN Race No. 31 Los Angeles Times 500
November 18, 1979 Average Speed: 132.822

Driver	Owner	Car #	Make	Laps	Winnings
1. Benny Parsons	M. C. Anderson	27	Chev	200	27,050
2. Bobby Allison	Bud Moore	15	Ford	200	17,350
3. Cale Yarborough	Junior Johnson	11	Olds	200	18,000
4. Buddy Baker	Harry Ranier	28	Chev	200	7,000
5. Richard Petty	Petty Enterprises	43	Chev	200	9,025

1980 Winston Cup GN Race No. 31 Los Angeles Times 500
November 15, 1980 Average Speed: 129.441

Driver	Owner	Car #	Make	Laps	Winnings
1. Benny Parsons	M. C. Anderson	27	Chev	200	24,835
2. Neil Bonnett	Wood Brothers	21	Merc	200	13,335
3. Cale Yarborough	Junior Johnson	11	Chev	200	17,035
4. Bobby Allison	Bud Moore	15	Ford	200	10,985
5. Dale Earnhardt	Rod Osterlund	2	Chev	200	10,835

Redwood Speedway
Eureka, CA
.625-mile Dirt Track

(aka Redwood Acres Speedway; Redwood Acres Raceway; Redwood Acres Fairgrounds; Eureka Speedway) Alternate configurations: .375-mile dirt track (1947–1987); .375-mile paved track (1988–present); .625-mile dirt oval (1956–1957). First NASCAR Winston Cup (then Grand National) race staged on 5/30/56 (Herb Thomas won). Final Grand National race staged on 5/30/57 (Lloyd Dane won). Track is still in operation.

Winston Cup Starts

Lloyd Dane	2
Harold Hardesty	2
Bob Havenmann	2
Ed Negre	2
Don Porter	2

Winston Cup Victories

Lloyd Dane	1
Herb Thomas	1

Winston Cup Poles

Parnelli Jones	1
John Kieper	1

Winston Cup Money

Lloyd Dane	$1,375

Most Cars Started

25—May 30, 1956

Fewest Cars Started

15—May 30, 1957

Narrowest Margin of Victory

1 lap plus—May 30, 1956

Slowest Race

38.814 MPH—May 30, 1956

Race Record

55.957 MPH—May 30, 1957

Most Race Leaders

N/A

Most Cars Running at Finish

16—May 30, 1956

1956 Grand National Race No. 22
May 30, 1956 Average Speed: 38.814

Driver	Owner	Car #	Make	Laps	Winnings
1. Herb Thomas	Carl Kiekhaefer	300B	56 Chrys	125	1,000
2. Gordon Haines		77	56 Dodg	124	700
3. Lloyd Dane	Lloyd Dane	225	56 Merc	124	475
4. Bob Keefe		14	56 Ford	124	365
5. Jim Cook		9	56 Pont	123	310

1957 Grand National Race No. 19
May 30, 1957 Average Speed: 55.957

Driver	Owner	Car #	Make	Laps	Winnings
1. Lloyd Dane	Lloyd Dane	44	57 Ford	153	900
2. George Seeger	Oscar Maples	12	57 Ford	147	650
3. Eddie Pagan	Eddie Pagan	45	57 Ford	146	475
4. Cliff Yiskis		25	56 Ford	140	365
5. Ed Negre	Ed Negre	98	55 Olds	139	310

Riverside Int'l Raceway
Riverside, CA
2.631-mile Paved Road Course

Road course with four different length built in 1957. Closed in 1988. First NASCAR Winston Cup (then Grand National) race staged on 6/1/58 (won by Eddie Gray). Final NASCAR event staged on 6/12/88 (won by Rusty Wallace). Track sold and turned into shopping complex.

Winston Cup Starts
Richard Petty   45

Winston Cup Victories
Bobby Allison   6

Winston Cup Poles
Darrell Waltrip   9

Winston Cup Money
Bobby Allison $390,350

Most Cars Started
46—June 1, 1958 Crown America 500

Fewest Cars Started
27—May 21, 1961

Narrowest Margin of Victory
0.240 seconds November 22, 1981
    Winston Western 500

Slowest Race
79.481 MPH—June 1, 1958
    Crown America 500

Race Record
107.820 MPH—January 14, 1979 Winston
    Western 500

Most Cautions
7—November 22, 1981
    Winston Western 500
7—November 16, 1986
    Winston Western 500
7—June 12, 1988 Budweiser 400

Most Race Leaders
9—January 18, 1976
    Winston Western 500
9—January 11, 1981
    Winston Western 500
9—November 22, 1981
    Winston Western 500
9—June 12, 1988 Budweiser 400

Most Cars Running at Finish
31—June 12, 1988 Budweiser 400

1958 Grand National Race No. 21 Crown America 500
June 1, 1958 Average Speed: 79.481

Driver	Owner	Car #	Make	Laps	Winnings
1. Eddie Gray	Eddie Gray	98	57 Ford	190	3,225
2. Lloyd Dane	Lloyd Dane	44	58 Ford	190	1,850
3. Jack Smith	Jack Smith	47	58 Pont	186	1,375
4. Lee Petty	Petty Enterprises	42	57 Olds	184	1,100
5. Bob Keefe		15	56 Ford	181	725

1961 Grand National Race No. 22
May 21, 1961 Average Speed: 82.512

Driver	Owner	Car #	Make	Laps	Winnings
1. Lloyd Dane	Lloyd Dane	44	61 Chev	39	825
2. Don Noel	Chuck Parkko	7	61 Ford	39	505
3. Dick Smith		18	60 Ford	38	350
4. Jim Cook	Floyd Johnson	0	60 Dodg	38	290
5. Bob Perry	Bob Perry	84	59 Ford	38	250

1963 Grand National Race No. 4 Riverside 500
January 20, 1963 Average Speed: 84.965

Driver	Owner	Car #	Make	Laps	Winnings
1. Dan Gurney	Holman-Moody	28	63 Ford	185	14,400
2. A. J. Foyt	Ray Nichels	02	63 Pont	185	6,570
3. Troy Ruttman	Bill Stroppe	14	63 Merc	184	3,980
4. Fireball Roberts	Banjo Matthews	22	63 Pont	184	2,630
5. Bobby Johns	Shorty Johns	7	63 Pont	182	1,750

1963 Grand National Race No. 55 Golden State 400
November 3, 1963 Average Speed: 91.465

Driver	Owner	Car #	Make	Laps	Winnings
1. Darel Dieringer	Bill Stroppe	16	63 Merc	148	7,875
2. Dave MacDonald	Wood Brothers	21	63 Ford	147	4,655
3. Marvin Panch	Wood Brothers	121	63 Ford	147	2,860
4. Fireball Roberts	Holman-Moody	22	63 Ford	147	1,775
5. Junior Johnson	Bill Stroppe	26	63 Merc	145	1,300

1964 Grand National Race No. 5 Motor Trend 500
January 19, 1964 Average Speed: 91.245

Driver	Owner	Car #	Make	Laps	Winnings
1. Dan Gurney	Wood Brothers	121	64 Ford	185	12,870
2. Marvin Panch	Wood Brothers	21	64 Ford	184	6,650
3. Fireball Roberts	Holman-Moody	22	64 Ford	183	3,900
4. Bill Amick	Dick Niles	9W	63 Merc	181	2,470
5. Ned Jarrett	Bondy Long	11	64 Ford	180	1,750

1965 Grand National Race No. 1 Motor Trend 500
January 17, 1965 Average Speed: 87.708

Driver	Owner	Car #	Make	Laps	Winnings
1. Dan Gurney	Wood Brothers	121	65 Ford	185	13,625
2. Junior Johnson	Rex Lovette	27	65 Ford	185	7,310
3. Marvin Panch	Wood Brothers	21	65 Ford	184	4,075
4. Darel Dieringer		06	65 Ford	181	2,625
5. Gene Davis	Bill Groves	5	64 Merc	177	1,850

1966 Grand National Race No. 2 Motor Trend 500
January 23, 1966 Average Speed: 97.952

Driver	Owner	Car #	Make	Laps	Winnings
1. Dan Gurney	Wood Brothers	121	66 Ford	185	18,445
2. David Pearson	Cotton Owens	6	65 Dodg	185	8,395
3. Paul Goldsmith	Ray Nichels	99	65 Plym	183	5,055
4. Curtis Turner	Wood Brothers	41	66 Ford	183	3,445
5. Dick Hutcherson	Holman-Moody	29	66 Ford	182	2,120

1967 Grand National Race No. 2 Motor Trend 500
January 22 & 29, 1967 Average Speed: 91.080

Driver	Owner	Car #	Make	Laps	Winnings
1. Parnelli Jones	Wood Brothers	115	67 Ford	185	18,720
2. Paul Goldsmith	Ray Nichels	99	66 Plym	183	8,600
3. Norm Nelson	Norm Nelson	11	67 Plym	183	5,250
4. Don White	Ray Nichels	31	66 Dodg	183	3,325
5. James Hylton	Bud Hartje	48	65 Dodg	178	2,175

1968 Grand National Race No. 3 Motor Trend 500
January 21, 1968 Average Speed: 100.598

Driver	Owner	Car #	Make	Laps	Winnings
1. Dan Gurney	Wood Brothers	121	68 Ford	186	21,250
2. David Pearson	Holman-Moody	17	68 Ford	186	9,600
3. Parnelli Jones	Bill Stroppe	115	68 Ford	186	5,600
4. Bobby Allison	Bondy Long	29	68 Ford	185	3,250
5. Cale Yarborough	Wood Brothers	21	68 Ford	184	2,225

1969 Grand National Race No. 3 Motor Trend 500
February 1, 1969 Average Speed: 105.498

Driver	Owner	Car #	Make	Laps	Winnings
1. Richard Petty	Petty Enterprises	43	69 Ford	186	19,650
2. A. J. Foyt	Jack Bowsher	1	69 Ford	186	10,200
3. David Pearson	Holman-Moody	17	69 Ford	184	6,775
4. Al Unser		41	69 Dodg	183	3,825
5. James Hylton	James Hylton	48	67 Dodg	177	2,450

Riverside Int'l Raceway *continued*

1970 Grand National Race No. 1 Motor Trend 500
January 18, 1970 Average Speed: 97.450

Driver	Owner	Car #	Make	Laps	Winnings
1. A. J. Foyt	Jack Bowsher	11	70 Ford	193	19,700
2. Roger McCluskey	Norm Nelson	1	70 Plym	193	9,000
3. LeeRoy Yarbrough	Junior Johnson	98	70 Ford	193	6,275
4. Donnie Allison	Banjo Matthews	27	70 Ford	190	4,475
5. Richard Petty	Petty Enterprises	43	70 Plym	186	3,000

1970 Grand National Race No. 20 Falstaff 400
June 14, 1970 Average Speed: 101.120

Driver	Owner	Car #	Make	Laps	Winnings
1. Richard Petty	Petty Enterprises	43	70 Plym	153	18,840
2. Bobby Allison	Mario Rossi	22	69 Dodg	152	9,365
3. James Hylton	James Hylton	48	69 Ford	144	5,340
4. John Soares Jr.	John Soares	08	70 Plym	141	3,415
5. Dick Gulstrand	James Good	44	68 Chev	139	2,540

1971 Winston Cup GN Race No. 1 Motor Trend 500
January 10, 1971 Average Speed: 100.783

Driver	Owner	Car #	Make	Laps	Winnings
1. Ray Elder	Fred Elder	96	70 Dodg	191	18,715
2. Bobby Allison	Bobby Allison	12	70 Dodg	191	9,215
3. Benny Parsons	L. G. DeWitt	72	69 Ford	189	6,390
4. Bobby Isaac	Nord Krauskopf	71	71 Dodg	189	4,540
5. James Hylton	James Hylton	48	70 Ford	185	2,915

1971 Winston Cup GN Race No. 24 Winston Golden State 400
June 20, 1971 Average Speed: 93.427

Driver	Owner	Car #	Make	Laps	Winnings
1. Bobby Allison	Bobby Allison	12	70 Dodg	153	14,395
2. Ray Elder	Fred Elder	96	71 Dodg	153	7,695
3. Cecil Gordon	Cecil Gordon	24	69 Merc	147	4,595
4. James Hylton	James Hylton	48	70 Ford	146	2,870
5. Jerry Oliver	Coz Cancilla	6	70 Dodg	145	1,945

1972 Winston Cup GN Race No. 1 Winston Western 500
January 23, 1972 Average Speed: 104.016

Driver	Owner	Car #	Make	Laps	Winnings
1. Richard Petty	Petty Enterprises	43	72 Plym	149	18,170
2. Bobby Allison	R. Howard & J. Johnson	12	72 Chev	149	10,720
3. Bobby Isaac	Nord Krauskopf	71	71 Dodg	146	7,845
4. Ray Elder	Fred Elder	96	72 Dodg	146	4,945
5. Hershel McGriff	Beryl Jackson	04	70 Plym	145	3,120

1972 Winston Cup GN Race No. 15 Golden State 400
June 18, 1972 Average Speed: 98.761

Driver	Owner	Car #	Make	Laps	Winnings
1. Ray Elder	Fred Elder	96	71 Dodg	153	12,375
2. Benny Parsons	L. G. DeWitt	72	71 Merc	152	6,850
3. Donnie Allison	Roger Penske	16	72 Mata	150	4,025
4. James Hylton	James Hylton	48	70 Ford	149	3,300
5. Carl Joiner	Dean Thorne	26	72 Chev	148	2,150

1973 Winston Cup GN Race No. 1 Winston Western 500
January 21, 1973 Average Speed: 104.055

Driver	Owner	Car #	Make	Laps	Winnings
1. Mark Donohue	Roger Penske	16	73 Mata	191	15,170
2. Bobby Allison	Bobby Allison	12	73 Chev	190	10,770
3. Ray Elder	Fred Elder	96	72 Dodg	189	6,120
4. Bobby Unser	Holman-Moody	41	72 Ford	186	4,520
5. Jimmy Insolo	Roger Paquette	38	72 Chev	184	3,070

1973 Winston Cup GN Race No. 15 Tuborg 400
June 17, 1973 Average Speed: 100.215

Driver	Owner	Car #	Make	Laps	Winnings
1. Bobby Allison	Bobby Allison	12	73 Chev	153	12,750
2. Richard Petty	Petty Enterprises	43	73 Dodg	153	10,275
3. Benny Parsons	L. G. DeWitt	72	72 Chev	152	5,325
4. Jimmy Insolo	Roger Paquette	38	72 Chev	151	3,225
5. Cecil Gordon	Cecil Gordon	24	72 Chev	149	2,650

1974 Winston Cup GN Race No. 1 Winston Western 500
January 20 & 26, 1974 Average Speed: 101.140

Driver	Owner	Car #	Make	Laps	Winnings
1. Cale Yarborough	R. Howard & J. Johnson	11	74 Chev	191	19,325
2. Richard Petty	Petty Enterprises	43	74 Dodg	191	12,825
3. David Pearson	Wood Brothers	21	71 Merc	191	8,525
4. Benny Parsons	L. G. DeWitt	72	74 Chev	188	8,825
5. Bobby Allison	Bobby Allison	12	74 Chev	188	6,975

1974 Winston Cup GN Race No. 14 Tuborg 400
June 9, 1974 Average Speed: 102.489

Driver	Owner	Car #	Make	Laps	Winnings
1. Cale Yarborough	R. Howard & J. Johnson	11	74 Chev	138	17,925
2. Bobby Allison	Bobby Allison	12	74 Chev	138	11,400
3. Benny Parsons	L. G. DeWitt	72	72 Chev	136	8,800
4. Cecil Gordon	Cecil Gordon	24	72 Chev	134	3,550
5. Frank Warren	Frank Warren	79	74 Dodg	130	2,850

1975 Winston Cup GN Race No. 1 Winston Western 500
January 19, 1975 Average Speed: 98.627

Driver	Owner	Car #	Make	Laps	Winnings
1. Bobby Allison	Roger Penske	16	75 Mata	191	14,735
2. David Pearson	Wood Brothers	21	73 Merc	191	11,135
3. Cecil Gordon	Cecil Gordon	24	75 Chev	184	8,535
4. Dave Marcis	Nord Krauskopf	71	74 Dodg	183	8,235
5. Elmo Langley	Elmo Langley	64	72 Ford	178	4,535

1975 Winston Cup GN Race No. 14 Tuborg 400
June 8, 1975 Average Speed: 101.028

Driver	Owner	Car #	Make	Laps	Winnings
1. Richard Petty	Petty Enterprises	43	74 Dodg	153	18,135
2. Bobby Allison	Roger Penske	16	75 Mata	153	10,410
3. Benny Parsons	L. G. DeWitt	72	75 Chev	152	8,510
4. Ray Elder	Fred Elder	96	74 Dodg	152	4,185
5. Dave Marcis	Nord Krauskopf	71	74 Dodg	148	6,135

1976 Winston Cup GN Race No. 1 Winston Western 500
January 18, 1976 Average Speed: 99.180

Driver	Owner	Car #	Make	Laps	Winnings
1. David Pearson	Wood Brothers	21	Merc	191	17,295
2. Cale Yarborough	Junior Johnson	11	Chev	191	14,920
3. Jimmy Insolo	Roger Paquette	38	Chev	191	8,620
4. Ray Elder	Fred Elder	96	Dodg	160	6,745
5. Benny Parsons	L. G. DeWitt	72	Chev	189	4,445

1976 Winston Cup GN Race No. 14 Riverside 400
June 13, 1976 Average Speed: 106.279

Driver	Owner	Car #	Make	Laps	Winnings
1. David Pearson	Wood Brothers	21	Merc	95	15,150
2. Bobby Allison	Roger Penske	2	Merc	95	10,695
3. Benny Parsons	L. G. DeWitt	72	Chev	94	7,550
4. Ray Elder	Fred Elder	96	Dodg	94	4,970
5. Buddy Baker	Bud Moore	15	Ford	94	5,540

Riverside Int'l Raceway *continued*

1977 Winston Cup GN Race No. 1 Winston Western 500
January 16, 1977 Average Speed: 107.038

Driver	Owner	Car #	Make	Laps	Winnings
1. David Pearson	Wood Brothers	21	Merc	119	15,400
2. Cale Yarborough	Junior Johnson	11	Chev	119	16,220
3. Richard Petty	Petty Enterprises	43	Dodg	118	11,095
4. Dave Marcis	Roger Penske	2	Chev	116	8,645
5. Sonny Easley	Jerry Lankford	67	Ford	115	6,290

1977 Winston Cup GN Race No. 14 NAPA 400
June 12, 1977 Average Speed: 105.021

Driver	Owner	Car #	Make	Laps	Winnings
1. Richard Petty	Petty Enterprises	43	Dodg	95	18,255
2. David Pearson	Wood Brothers	21	Merc	95	10,400
3. Cale Yarborough	Junior Johnson	11	Chev	95	10,475
4. Jimmy Insolo	Jimmy Insolo	51	Ford	93	3,900
5. Buddy Baker	Bud Moore	15	Ford	93	6,400

1978 Winston Cup GN Race No. 1 Winston Western 500
January 22, 1978 Average Speed: 102.269

Driver	Owner	Car #	Make	Laps	Winnings
1. Cale Yarborough	Junior Johnson	11	Olds	119	20,850
2. Benny Parsons	L. G. DeWitt	72	Chev	119	14,800
3. David Pearson	Wood Brothers	21	Merc	119	9,850
4. Neil Bonnett	Jim Stacy	5	Dodg	119	8,800
5. Dave Marcis	Rod Osterlund	2	Chev	118	4,050

1978 Winston Cup GN Race No. 14 NAPA 400
June 11, 1978 Average Speed: 104.311

Driver	Owner	Car #	Make	Laps	Winnings
1. Benny Parsons	L. G. DeWitt	72	Chev	95	22,750
2. Richard Petty	Petty Enterprises	43	Dodg	95	14,200
3. Bobby Allison	Bud Moore	15	Ford	95	10,050
4. Dave Marcis	Rod Osterlund	2	Chev	95	5,850
5. Cale Yarborough	Junior Johnson	11	Olds	94	8,400

1979 Winston Cup GN Race No. 1 Winston Western 500
January 14, 1979 Average Speed: 107.820

Driver	Owner	Car #	Make	Laps	Winnings
1. Darrell Waltrip	DiGard	88	Chev	119	21,150
2. David Pearson	Wood Brothers	21	Merc	119	14,200
3. Cale Yarborough	Junior Johnson	11	Olds	119	12,675
4. Bill Schmitt	Bill Schmitt	73	Olds	118	8,000
5. Donnie Allison	Hoss Ellington	1	Chev	118	7,550

1979 Winston Cup GN Race No. 15 NAPA Riverside 400
June 10, 1979 Average Speed: 103.732

Driver	Owner	Car #	Make	Laps	Winnings
1. Bobby Allison	Bud Moore	15	Ford	95	22,700
2. Darrell Waltrip	DiGard	88	Chev	95	14,875
3. Richard Petty	Petty Enterprises	43	Chev	95	10,350
4. Cale Yarborough	Junior Johnson	11	Chev	95	11,800
5. Benny Parsons	M. C. Anderson	27	Chev	94	6,800

1980 Winston Cup GN Race No. 1 Winston Western 500
January 13 & 19, 1980 Average Speed: 94.974

Driver	Owner	Car #	Make	Laps	Winnings
1. Darrell Waltrip	DiGard	88	Chev	119	24,700
2. Dale Earnhardt	Rod Osterlund	2	Chev	119	19,400
3. Richard Petty	Petty Enterprises	43	Chev	119	15,100
4. Joe Millikan	L. G. DeWitt	72	Chev	119	10,200
5. Bill Schmitt	Bill Schmitt	73	Olds	119	7,455

1980 Winston Cup GN Race No. 15 Warner W. Hodgdon 400
June 8, 1980 Average Speed: 101.846

Driver	Owner	Car #	Make	Laps	Winnings
1. Darrell Waltrip	DiGard	88	Chev	95	22,100
2. Neil Bonnett	Wood Brothers	21	Merc	95	10,950
3. Benny Parsons	M. C. Anderson	27	Chev	95	10,950
4. Cale Yarborough	Junior Johnson	11	Chev	95	9,650
5. Dale Earnhardt	Rod Osterlund	2	Chev	95	9,100

1981 Winston Cup GN Race No. 1 Winston Western 500
January 11, 1981 Average Speed: 95.263

Driver	Owner	Car #	Make	Laps	Winnings
1. Bobby Allison	Harry Ranier	28	Chev	119	24,600
2. Terry Labonte	Billy Hagan	44	Chev	119	19,600
3. Dale Earnhardt	Rod Osterlund	2	Pont	119	16,325
4. Richard Childress	Richard Childress	3	Chev	119	8,510
5. Richard Petty	Petty Enterprises	42	Chev	119	4,250

1981 Winston Cup GN Race No. 15 Warner W. Hodgdon 400
June 14, 1981 Average Speed: 93.597

Driver	Owner	Car #	Make	Laps	Winnings
1. Darrell Waltrip	Junior Johnson	11	Buick	95	23,650
2. Dale Earnhardt	Rod Osterlund	2	Pont	95	18,725
3. Richard Petty	Petty Enterprises	43	Buick	95	12,200
4. Neil Bonnett	Wood Brothers	21	Ford	95	4,650
5. Ricky Rudd	DiGard	88	Buick	95	8,900

1981 Winston Cup GN Race No. 31 Winston Western 500
November 22, 1981 Average Speed: 95.288

Driver	Owner	Car #	Make	Laps	Winnings
1. Bobby Allison	Harry Ranier	28	Buick	119	24,300
2. Joe Ruttman	Jim Stacy	2	Buick	119	17,675
3. Terry Labonte	Billy Hagan	44	Buick	119	16,450
4. Dale Earnhardt	Richard Childress	3	Pont	119	10,560
5. Joe Millikan	Cliff Stewart	5	Pont	119	9,125

1982 Winston Cup GN Race No. 14 Budweiser 400
June 13, 1982 Average Speed: 103.000

Driver	Owner	Car #	Make	Laps	Winnings
1. Tim Richmond	Jim Stacy	2	Buick	95	21,530
2. Terry Labonte	Billy Hagan	44	Buick	95	17,930
3. Geoff Bodine	Cliff Stewart	50	Pont	95	14,670
4. Dale Earnhardt	Bud Moore	15	Ford	95	11,935
5. Neil Bonnett	Wood Brothers	21	Ford	95	3,485

1982 Winston Cup GN Race No. 30 Winston Western 500
November 21, 1982 Average Speed: 99.823

Driver	Owner	Car #	Make	Laps	Winnings
1. Tim Richmond	Jim Stacy	2	Buick	119	24,730
2. Ricky Rudd	Richard Childress	3	Pont	119	16,980
3. Darrell Waltrip	Junior Johnson	11	Buick	119	21,150
4. Neil Bonnett	Wood Brothers	21	Ford	119	6,100
5. Mark Martin	Bo Reeder	02	Buick	118	7,760

1983 Winston Cup GN Race No. 13 Budweiser 400
June 5, 1983 Average Speed: 88.063

Driver	Owner	Car #	Make	Laps	Winnings
1. Ricky Rudd	Richard Childress	3	Chev	95	24,530
2. Bill Elliott	Harry Melling	9	Ford	95	14,655
3. Harry Gant	Hal Needham	33	Buick	95	14,775
4. Dale Earnhardt	Bud Moore	15	Ford	95	11,475
5. Dick Brooks	Junie Donlavey	90	Ford	95	6,760

Riverside Int'l Raceway *continued*

1983 Winston Cup GN Race No. 30 Winston Western 500
November 20, 1983 Average Speed: 95.859

Driver	Owner	Car #	Make	Laps	Winnings
1. Bill Elliott	Harry Melling	9	Ford	119	26,380
2. Benny Parsons	Johnny Hayes	55	Chev	119	13,225
3. Neil Bonnett	Bob Rahilly & Butch Mock	75	Chev	119	18,375
4. Dale Earnhardt	Bud Moore	15	Ford	119	13,725
5. Tim Richmond	Raymond Beadle	27	Pont	119	8,930

1984 Winston Cup GN Race No. 30 Winston Western 500
November 18, 1984 Average Speed: 98.448

Driver	Owner	Car #	Make	Laps	Winnings
1. Geoff Bodine	Rick Hendrick	5	Chev	119	31,900
2. Tim Richmond	Raymond Beadle	27	Pont	119	21,325
3. Terry Labonte	Billy Hagan	44	Chev	119	17,255
4. Bill Elliott	Harry Melling	9	Ford	119	13,500
5. Benny Parsons	Johnny Hayes	55	Chev	119	8,450

1985 Winston Cup GN Race No. 28 Winston Western 500
November 17, 1985 Average Speed: 105.065

Driver	Owner	Car #	Make	Laps	Winnings
1. Ricky Rudd	Bud Moore	15	Ford	119	37,875
2. Terry Labonte	Billy Hagan	44	Chev	119	38,375
3. Neil Bonnett	Junior Johnson	12	Chev	119	18,550
4. Harry Gant	Hal Needham	33	Chev	119	16,225
5. Dale Earnhardt	Richard Childress	3	Chev	119	13,175

1986 Winston Cup Race No. 29 Winston Western 500
November 16, 1986 Average Speed: 101.246

Driver	Owner	Car #	Make	Laps	Winnings
1. Tim Richmond	Rick Hendrick	25	Chev	119	50,955
2. Dale Earnhardt	Richard Childress	3	Chev	119	26,750
3. Geoff Bodine	Rick Hendrick	5	Chev	119	20,175
4. Darrell Waltrip	Junior Johnson	11	Chev	119	22,350
5. Joe Ruttman	Kenny Bernstein	26	Buick	119	11,945

1987 Winston Cup Race No. 28 Winston Western 500
November 8, 1987 Average Speed: 98.035

Driver	Owner	Car #	Make	Laps	Winnings
1. Rusty Wallace	Raymond Beadle	27	Pont	119	47,725
2. Benny Parsons	Rick Hendrick	35	Chev	119	28,700
3. Kyle Petty	Wood Brothers	21	Ford	119	21,125
4. Richard Petty	Petty Enterprises	43	Pont	119	13,780
5. Bobby Allison	Stavola Brothers	22	Buick	119	14,575

1984 Winston Cup GN Race No. 13 Budweiser 400
June 3, 1984 Average Speed: 102.910

Driver	Owner	Car #	Make	Laps	Winnings
1. Terry Labonte	Billy Hagan	44	Chev	95	31,955
2. Neil Bonnett	Junior Johnson	12	Chev	95	15,670
3. Bobby Allison	DiGard	22	Buick	95	18,850
4. Geoff Bodine	Rick Hendrick	5	Chev	95	11,600
5. Dale Earnhardt	Richard Childress	3	Chev	95	10,950

1985 Winston Cup GN Race No. 12 Budweiser 400
June 2, 1985 Average Speed: 104.276

Driver	Owner	Car #	Make	Laps	Winnings
1. Terry Labonte	Billy Hagan	44	Chev	95	39,200
2. Harry Gant	Hal Needham	33	Chev	95	23,450
3. Bobby Allison	DiGard	22	Buick	95	15,900
4. Ricky Rudd	Bud Moore	15	Ford	95	11,825
5. Kyle Petty	Wood Brothers	7	Ford	95	9,330

1986 Winston Cup Race No. 12 Budweiser 400
June 1, 1986 Average Speed: 105.083

Driver	Owner	Car #	Make	Laps	Winnings
1. Darrell Waltrip	Junior Johnson	11	Chev	95	49,000
2. Tim Richmond	Rick Hendrick	25	Chev	95	22,155
3. Ricky Rudd	Bud Moore	15	Ford	95	18,650
4. Rusty Wallace	Raymond Beadle	27	Pont	95	12,775
5. Dale Earnhardt	Richard Childress	3	Chev	95	14,125

1987 Winston Cup Race No. 13 Budweiser 400
June 21, 1987 Average Speed: 102.183

Driver	Owner	Car #	Make	Laps	Winnings
1. Tim Richmond	Rick Hendrick	25	Chev	95	36,450
2. Ricky Rudd	Bud Moore	15	Ford	95	28,450
3. Neil Bonnett	Bob Rahilly & Butch Mock	75	Pont	95	17,005
4. Terry Labonte	Junior Johnson	11	Chev	95	19,125
5. Bill Elliott	Harry Melling	9	Ford	95	13,850

1988 Winston Cup Race No. 12 Budweiser 400
June 12, 1988 Average Speed: 88.341

Driver	Owner	Car #	Make	Laps	Winnings
1. Rusty Wallace	Raymond Beadle	27	Pont	95	49,100
2. Terry Labonte	Junior Johnson	11	Chev	95	26,175
3. Ricky Rudd	Kenny Bernstein	26	Buick	95	20,950
4. Dale Earnhardt	Richard Childress	3	Chev	95	18,600
5. Phil Parsons	Richard Jackson	55	Olds	95	10,725

Santa Clara Fairgrounds
San Jose, CA
Half-mile Dirt Track

(aka San Jose Fairgrounds) Half-mile dirt oval built in 1948. Only NASCAR Winston Cup (then Grand National) race staged on 9/15/57 (won by Marvin Porter). Half-mile track closed in 1990. A .333-mile track opened in 1991.

Winston Cup Victories
Marvin Porter   1

Winston Cup Poles
Lloyd Dane   1

Winston Cup Money
Marvin Porter $800

Most Cars Started
22—September 15, 1957

Narrowest Margin of Victory
None, red flag—September 15, 1957

Most Race Leaders
N/A

Most Cars Running at Finish
5—September 15, 1957

1957 Grand National Race No. 44
September 15, 1957

Driver	Owner	Car #	Make	Laps	Winnings
1. Marvin Porter	Marvin Porter	12	57 Ford	116	800
2. Eddie Pagan	Eddie Pagan	45	57 Ford	116	550
3. Lloyd Dane	Lloyd Dane	44	57 Ford	115	450
4. Ernie Young	Walt Palozi	8	57 Pont	113	350
5. Jim Blomgren	Bob Smith	5	57 Ford	112	310

Sears Point Int'l Raceway
Sonoma, CA
2.52-mile Paved Road Course

1.7- and 2.52-mile road course built in 1968. First NASCAR Winston Cup race staged on 6/11/89 (Ricky Rudd won).

Winston Cup Starts
9 drivers tied with 14

Winston Cup Victories
Jeff Gordon   3

Winston Cup Poles
Ricky Rudd   4

Winston Cup Money
Jeff Gordon $847,110

Most Cars Started
44—3 times

Fewest Cars Started
42—June 11, 1989
Banquet Frozen Foods 300

Narrowest Margin of Victory
0.197 seconds June 27, 1999

Slowest Race
69.245 MPH—June 10, 1990
Banquet Frozen Foods 300

Race Record
81.412 MPH—June 7, 1992
Save Mart Supermarkets 300K

Most Cautions
9—June 10, 1990 Banquet Frozen
Foods 300

Most Race Leaders
9—June 28, 1998

Most Cars Running at Finish
44—May 5, 1996
Save Mart Supermarkets 300K

1989 Winston Cup Race No. 12 Banquet Frozen Foods 300
June 11, 1989 Average Speed: 76.088

Driver	Owner	Car #	Make	Laps	Winnings
1. Ricky Rudd	Kenny Bernstein	26	Buick	74	62,350
2. Rusty Wallace	Raymond Beadle	27	Pont	74	39,225
3. Bill Elliott	Harry Melling	9	Ford	74	28,375
4. Dale Earnhardt	Richard Childress	3	Chev	74	20,350
5. Lake Speed	Lake Speed	83	Olds	74	18,507

1990 Winston Cup Series Race No. 12 Banquet Frozen Foods 300
June 10, 1990 Average Speed: 69.245

Driver	Owner	Car #	Make	Laps	Winnings
1. Rusty Wallace	Raymond Beadle	27	Pont	74	69,100
2. Mark Martin	Jack Roush	6	Ford	74	34,000
3. Ricky Rudd	Rick Hendrick	5	Chev	74	28,675
4. Geoff Bodine	Junior Johnson	11	Ford	74	20,650
5. Bobby Hillin Jr.	Stavola Brothers	8	Buick	74	17,007

1991 Winston Cup Series Race No. 12 Banquet Frozen Foods 300
June 9, 1991 Average Speed: 72.970

Driver	Owner	Car #	Make	Laps	Winnings
1. Davey Allison	Robert Yates	28	Ford	74	61,950
2. Ricky Rudd	Rick Hendrick	5	Chev	74	41,975
3. Rusty Wallace	Roger Penske	2	Pont	74	34,975
4. Ernie Irvan	Larry McClure	4	Chev	74	20,350
5. Ken Schrader	Rick Hendrick	25	Chev	74	17,225

1992 Winston Cup Race No. 12 Save Mart Supermarkets 300K
June 7, 1992 Average Speed: 81.413

Driver	Owner	Car #	Make	Laps	Winnings
1. Ernie Irvan	Larry McClure	4	Chev	74	61,810
2. Terry Labonte	Billy Hagan	94	Olds	74	36,685
3. Mark Martin	Jack Roush	6	Ford	74	28,185
4. Ricky Rudd	Rick Hendrick	5	Chev	74	25,710
5. Bill Elliott	Junior Johnson	11	Ford	74	32,585

1993 Winston Cup Series Race No. 10 Save Mart Supermarkets 300K
May 16, 1993 Average Speed: 77.013

Driver	Owner	Car #	Make	Laps	Winnings
1. Geoff Bodine	Bud Moore	15	Ford	74	66,510
2. Ernie Irvan	Larry McClure	4	Chev	74	41,190
3. Ricky Rudd	Rick Hendrick	5	Chev	74	29,590
4. Ken Schrader	Rick Hendrick	25	Chev	74	22,415
5. Kyle Petty	Felix Sabates	42	Pont	74	22,715

1994 Winston Cup Series Race No. 10 Save Mart Supermarkets 300K
May 15, 1994 Average Speed: 77.458

Driver	Owner	Car #	Make	Laps	Winnings
1. Ernie Irvan	Robert Yates	28	Ford	74	78,810
2. Geoff Bodine	Geoff Bodine	7	Ford	74	45,640
3. Dale Earnhardt	Richard Childress	3	Chev	74	37,825
4. Wally Dallenbach Jr.	Petty Enterprises	43	Pont	74	24,920
5. Rusty Wallace	Roger Penske	2	Ford	74	25,970

1995 Winston Cup Series Race No. 10 Save Mart Supermarkets 300K
May 7, 1993 Average Speed: 70.681

Driver	Owner	Car #	Make	Laps	Winnings
1. Dale Earnhardt	Richard Childress	3	Chev	74	74,860
2. Mark Martin	Jack Roush	6	Ford	74	68,915
3. Jeff Gordon	Rick Hendrick	24	Chev	74	41,625
4. Ricky Rudd	Ricky Rudd	10	Ford	74	39,870
5. Terry Labonte	Rick Hendrick	5	Chev	74	35,020

1996 Winston Cup Series Race No. 10 Save Mart Supermarkets 300K
May 5, 1996 Average Speed: 77.673

Driver	Owner	Car #	Make	Laps	Winnings
1. Rusty Wallace	Roger Penske	2	Ford	74	58,395
2. Mark Martin	Jack Roush	6	Ford	74	58,640
3. Wally Dallenbach Jr.	Bud Moore	15	Ford	74	50,850
4. Dale Earnhardt	Richard Childress	3	Chev	74	39,160
5. Terry Labonte	Rick Hendrick	5	Chev	74	41,995

1997 Winston Cup Series Race No. 9
May 4, 1997 Average Speed: 75.788

Driver	Owner	Car #	Make	Laps	Winnings
1. Mark Martin	Jack Roush	6	Ford	74	113,995
2. Jeff Gordon	Rick Hendrick	24	Chev	74	66,065
3. Terry Labonte	Rick Hendrick	5	Chev	74	63,700
4. Dale Jarrett	Robert Yates	88	Ford	74	50,135
5. Darrell Waltrip	Darrell Waltrip	17	Chev	74	35,920

1998 Winston Cup Series Race No. 16
June 28, 1998 Average Speed: 72.387

Driver	Owner	Car #	Make	Laps	Winnings
1. Jeff Gordon	Rick Hendrick	24	Chev	112	160,675
2. Bobby Hamilton	Larry McClure	4	Chev	112	81,575
3. John Andretti	Petty Enterprises	43	Pont	112	61,150
4. Bobby Labonte	Joe Gibbs	18	Pont	112	59,340
5. Rusty Wallace	Roger Penske	2	Ford	112	49,715

Sears Point Int'l Raceway *continued*

1999 Winston Cup Series Race No. 16
June 27, 1999 Average Speed: 70.378

Driver	Owner	Car #	Make	Laps	Winnings
1. Jeff Gordon	Rick Hendrick	24	Chev	112	125,040
2. Mark Martin	Jack Roush	6	Ford	112	86,775
3. John Andretti	Petty Enterprises	43	Pont	112	72,675
4. Rusty Wallace	Roger Penske	2	Ford	112	56,340
5. Jimmy Spencer	Travis Carter	23	Ford	112	61,055

2000 Winston Cup Series Race No. 16
June 25, 2000 Average Speed: 78.789

Driver	Owner	Car #	Make	Laps	Winnings
1. Jeff Gordon	Rick Hendrick	24	Chev	112	143,025
2. Sterling Marlin	Felix Sabates	40	Chev	112	90,725
3. Mark Martin	Jack Roush	6	Ford	112	75,950
4. Bobby Labonte	Joe Gibbs	18	Pont	112	81,290
5. Ricky Rudd	Robert Yates	28	Ford	112	67,915

2001 Winston Cup Series Race No. 16
June 24, 2001 Average Speed: 75.889

Driver	Owner	Car #	Make	Laps	Winnings
1. Tony Stewart	Joe Gibbs	20	Pont	112	139,875
2. Robby Gordon	Jim Smith	7	Chev	112	114,035
3. Jeff Gordon	Rick Hendrick	24	Chev	112	129,277
4. Ricky Rudd	Robert Yates	28	Ford	112	98,847
5. Rusty Wallace	Roger Penske	2	Ford	112	94,780

2002 Winston Cup Series Race No. 16
June 23, 2002 Average Speed: 81.007

Driver	Owner	Car #	Make	Laps	Winnings
1. Ricky Rudd	Robert Yates	28	Ford	110	184,992
2. Tony Stewart	Joe Gibbs	20	Pont	110	143,203
3. Terry Labonte	Rick Hendrick	5	Chev	110	113,933
4. Kurt Busch	Jack Roush	97	Ford	110	81,765
5. Jeff Green	Richard Childress	30	Chev	110	63,990

Willow Springs Int'l Raceway
Lancaster, CA
2.5-mile Oiled Dirt Road Course

(aka Willow Springs Speedway; Kern County Speedway) 2-mile oiled dirt road course built in 1953. First NASCAR Winston Cup (then Grand National) race run on 11/20/55 (won by Chuck Stevenson), and was a part of 1956 season schedule. Final NASCAR race run on 11/11/56 (Marvin Panch won), and the race was counted as 1957 season opener. Track is still in operation.

Winston Cup Starts
15 drivers tied with 2

Winston Cup Victories
Marvin Panch   1
Chuck Stevenson   1

Winston Cup Poles
Marvin Panch   1
Jim Reed   1

Winston Cup Money
Marvin Panch $2,680

Most Cars Started
37—November 20, 1955

Fewest Cars Started
34—November 11, 1956

Narrowest Margin of Victory
500 feet—November 20, 1955

Slowest Race
66.512 MPH—November 20, 1955

Race Record
78.648 MPH—November 11, 1956

Most Cautions
Both races ran caution-free

Most Race Leaders
2—November 20, 1955
2—November 11, 1956

Most Cars Running at Finish
32—November 20, 1955

1956 Grand National Race No. 3
November 20, 1955 Average Speed: 66.512

Driver	Owner	Car #	Make	Laps	Winnings
1. Chuck Stevenson	Carl Dane	22	56 Ford	80	1,570
2. Marvin Panch	Tom Harbison	98	56 Ford	80	1,130
3. Johnny Mantz	Bill Stroppe	15	56 Merc	79	1,130
4. Jim Reed	Jim Reed	7	56 Chev	79	580
5. Allen Adkins	Gus Davis	2	55 Dodg	78	445

1957 Grand National Race No. 1
November 11, 1956 Average Speed: 78.648

Driver	Owner	Car #	Make	Laps	Winnings
1. Marvin Panch	Pete DePaolo	98	56 Ford	60	1,550
2. Fireball Roberts	Pete DePaolo	22	56 Ford	60	1,000
3. George Seeger	Oscar Maples	12	56 Ford	60	755
4. Jim Paschal	Frank Hayworth	75	56 Merc	59	570
5. Eddie Pagan	Eddie Pagan	45	56 Ford	50	430

Connecticut

Thompson Int'l Speedway
Thompson, CT
Half-mile Paved Track

(aka Thompson Speedway; New Thompson Speedway) .625-mile paved track built in 1940. Originally listed as half-mile track, currently measured as .542-mile oval. Also included a road course (1952–1970s), a quarter-mile Midget oval, and a drag strip. First NASCAR Winston Cup (then Grand National) race staged on 10/12/51 (won by Neil Cole). Final big NASCAR race run on 7/12/70 (Bobby Isaac won). Track is still in operation.

Winston Cup Starts
16 drivers tied with 2

Winston Cup Victories
Neil Cole	1
Bobby Isaac	1
David Pearson	1

Winston Cup Poles
Neil Cole	1
Bobby Isaac	1
David Pearson	1

Winston Cup Money
Bobby Isaac $2,500

Most Cars Started
38—October 12, 1951

Fewest Cars Started
30—July 9, 1970
Thompson Speedway 200

Narrowest Margin of Victory
N/A

Slowest Race
80.296 MPH—July 9, 1970
Thompson Speedway 200

Race Record
89.498 MPH—July 10, 1969
Thompson Speedway 200

Most Cautions
2—July 10, 1969
Thompson Speedway 200

Most Race Leaders
4—October 12, 1951

Most Cars Running at Finish
19—July 9, 1970
Thompson Speedway 200

1951 Grand National Race No. 32
October 12, 1951

Driver	Owner	Car #	Make	Laps	Winnings
1. Neil Cole	John Golabek	52	50 Olds	200	1,000
2. Jim Reed	Jim Reed	67	51 Ford	199	600
3. Dick Eagan	Dick Eagan		50 Plym	—	500
4. Billy Carden	Sam Knox	8	50 Olds	—	400
5. Reino Tulonen	Reino Tulonen	32	51 HEN	—	300

1969 Grand National Race No. 30 Thompson Speedway 200
July 10, 1969 Average Speed: 89.498

Driver	Owner	Car #	Make	Laps	Winnings
1. David Pearson	Holman-Moody	17	69 Ford	200	2,200
2. James Hylton	James Hylton	48	69 Dodg	199	1,500
3. John Sears	L. G. DeWitt	4	68 Ford	199	1,000
4. G. C. Spencer	G. C. Spencer	49	68 Plym	197	900
5. Richard Brickhouse	Dub Clewis	03	67 Plym	193	800

1970 Grand National Race No. 26 Thompson Speedway 200
July 9, 1970 Average Speed: 80.296

Driver	Owner	Car #	Make	Laps	Winnings
1. Bobby Isaac	Nord Krauskopf	71	69 Dodg	200	2,500
2. Richard Petty	Petty Enterprises	43	70 Plym	200	1,800
3. Benny Parsons	L. G. DeWitt	72	69 Ford	198	1,100
4. Dick Brooks	Dick Brooks	32	69 Plym	198	900
5. Neil Castles	Neil Castles	06	69 Dodg	198	800

Delaware

Dover Downs Int'l Speedway
Dover, DE
1-mile Paved Track

1-mile paved track built in 1969. First NASCAR Winston Cup (then Grand National) race staged on 7/6/69 (won by Richard Petty). Elevated horse track sits inside NASCAR oval. First superspeedway to offer air-conditioned general seating.

Winston Cup Starts
Dave Marcis   54

Winston Cup Victories
Richard Petty   7

Winston Cup Poles
David Pearson   6

Winston Cup Money
Mark Martin $1,611,763

Most Cars Started
43—11 times

Fewest Cars Started
31—May 20, 1979 Mason-Dixon 500

Narrowest Margin of Victory
0.091 seconds—June 1, 1997

Slowest Race
100.334 MPH—September 19, 1993
    SplitFire Spark Plug 500

Race Record
132.719 MPH—September 21, 1997

Most Cautions
16—September 19, 1993
    SplitFire Spark Plug 500

Most Race Leaders
13—June 1, 1997

Most Cars Running at Finish
42—June 4, 2000

1969 Grand National Race No. 29 Mason-Dixon 300
July 6, 1969 Average Speed: 115.772

Driver	Owner	Car #	Make	Laps	Winnings
1. Richard Petty	Petty Enterprises	43	69 Ford	300	4,725
2. Sonny Hutchins	Junie Donlavey	90	67 Ford	294	2,050
3. James Hylton	James Hylton	48	69 Dodg	294	1,275
4. John Sears	L. G. DeWitt	4	69 Ford	293	825
5. Elmo Langley	Elmo Langley	84	68 Ford	287	725

1970 Grand National Race No. 41 Mason-Dixon 300
September 20, 1970 Average Speed: 112.103

Driver	Owner	Car #	Make	Laps	Winnings
1. Richard Petty	Petty Enterprises	43	70 Plym	300	6,195
2. Bobby Allison	Mario Rossi	22	69 Dodg	300	3,095
3. Charlie Glotzbach	Ray Nichels	99	69 Dodg	299	2,170
4. David Pearson	Holman-Moody	17	70 Ford	296	1,885
5. Benny Parsons	L. G. DeWitt	72	69 Ford	296	1,280

1971 Winston Cup GN Race No. 22 Mason-Dixon 500
June 6, 1971 Average Speed: 123.119

Driver	Owner	Car #	Make	Laps	Winnings
1. Bobby Allison	Holman-Moody	12	71 Ford	500	15,720
2. Fred Lorenzen	Ray Nichels	99	71 Plym	499	9,045
3. Richard Petty	Petty Enterprises	43	71 Plym	498	5,020
4. Bobby Isaac	Nord Krauskopf	71	71 Dodg	496	3,495
5. G. C. Spencer	G. C. Spencer	49	69 Plym	486	2,020

1971 Winston Cup GN Race No. 43 Delaware 500
October 17, 1971 Average Speed: 123.254

Driver	Owner	Car #	Make	Laps	Winnings
1. Richard Petty	Petty Enterprises	43	71 Plym	500	14,570
2. Charlie Glotzbach	R. Howard & J. Johnson	98	71 Chev	499	7,945
3. Bobby Isaac	Nord Krauskopf	71	71 Dodg	499	4,970
4. Bobby Allison	Holman-Moody	12	69 Merc	498	2,695
5. Bill Dennis	Junie Donlavey	90	69 Merc	483	1,595

1972 Winston Cup GN Race No. 13 Mason-Dixon 500
June 4, 1972 Average Speed: 118.019

Driver	Owner	Car #	Make	Laps	Winnings
1. Bobby Allison	R. Howard & J. Johnson	12	72 Chev	500	14,625
2. Richard Petty	Petty Enterprises	43	72 Dodg	499	10,375
3. LeeRoy Yarbrough	Bill Seifert	45	72 Merc	486	4,850
4. Jackie Oliver	Junie Donlavey	90	71 Ford	486	3,550
5. John Sears	J Marvin Mills	4	70 Plym	484	2,750

1972 Winston Cup GN Race No. 26 Delaware 500
September 17, 1972 Average Speed: 120.506

Driver	Owner	Car #	Make	Laps	Winnings
1. David Pearson	Wood Brothers	21	71 Merc	500	13,250
2. Richard Petty	Petty Enterprises	43	72 Plym	497	10,600
3. Ramo Stott	Junie Donlavey	90	71 Ford	486	4,950
4. James Hylton	James Hylton	48	71 Ford	478	3,550
5. Cecil Gordon	Cecil Gordon	24	71 Merc	477	2,885

1973 Winston Cup GN Race No. 13 Mason-Dixon 500
June 3, 1973 Average Speed: 119.745

Driver	Owner	Car #	Make	Laps	Winnings
1. David Pearson	Wood Brothers	21	71 Merc	500	14,025
2. Cale Yarborough	R. Howard & J. Johnson	11	73 Chev	500	10,700
3. Bobby Allison	Bobby Allison	12	73 Chev	497	6,775
4. Richard Petty	Petty Enterprises	43	73 Dodg	492	5,475
5. Cecil Gordon	Cecil Gordon	24	72 Chev	490	2,750

1973 Winston Cup GN Race No. 24 Delaware 500
September 16, 1973 Average Speed: 112.852

Driver	Owner	Car #	Make	Laps	Winnings
1. David Pearson	Wood Brothers	21	71 Merc	500	16,325
2. Bobby Allison	Bobby Allison	12	73 Chev	500	10,125
3. Buddy Baker	Nord Krauskopf	71	73 Dodg	500	7,050
4. Benny Parsons	L. G. DeWitt	72	73 Chev	493	4,175
5. J. D. McDuffie	J. D. McDuffie	70	72 Chev	484	3,275

Dover Downs Int'l Speedway *continued*

1974 Winston Cup GN Race No. 12 Mason-Dixon 500
May 19, 1974 Average Speed: 115.057

Driver	Owner	Car #	Make	Laps	Winnings
1. Cale Yarborough	R. Howard & J. Johnson	11	74 Chev	500	18,300
2. David Pearson	Wood Brothers	21	73 Merc	500	8,900
3. Richard Petty	Petty Enterprises	43	74 Dodg	498	8,250
4. Benny Parsons	L. G. DeWitt	72	74 Chev	492	7,150
5. George Follmer	Bud Moore	15	73 Ford	492	5,850

1974 Winston Cup GN Race No. 25 Delaware 500
September 15, 1974 Average Speed: 113.640

Driver	Owner	Car #	Make	Laps	Winnings
1. Richard Petty	Petty Enterprises	43	74 Dodg	500	18,175
2. Buddy Baker	Bud Moore	15	73 Ford	497	11,425
3. Earl Ross	Junior Johnson	52	74 Chev	491	5,750
4. Benny Parsons	L. G. DeWitt	72	74 Chev	488	7,250
5. Dave Marcis	Dave Marcis	2	73 Dodg	486	3,275

1975 Winston Cup GN Race No. 12 Mason-Dixon 500
May 18 & 19, 1975 Average Speed: 100.820

Driver	Owner	Car #	Make	Laps	Winnings
1. David Pearson	Wood Brothers	21	73 Merc	500	15,425
2. Cecil Gordon	Cecil Gordon	24	75 Chev	493	10,400
3. Richard Petty	Petty Enterprises	43	74 Dodg	490	10,050
4. James Hylton	James Hylton	48	74 Chev	487	6,950
5. David Sisco	David Sisco	05	75 Chev	486	3,725

1975 Winston Cup GN Race No. 22 Delaware 500
September 14, 1975 Average Speed: 111.372

Driver	Owner	Car #	Make	Laps	Winnings
1. Richard Petty	Petty Enterprises	43	74 Dodg	500	18,250
2. Dick Brooks	Junie Donlavey	90	73 Ford	500	10,425
3. Benny Parsons	L. G. DeWitt	72	75 Chev	170	8,975
4. Cale Yarborough	Junior Johnson	11	75 Chev	497	7,050
5. Bruce Hill	Bruce Hill	47	75 Chev	496	3,725

1976 Winston Cup GN Race No. 12 Mason-Dixon 500
May 16, 1976 Average Speed: 115.436

Driver	Owner	Car #	Make	Laps	Winnings
1. Benny Parsons	L. G. DeWitt	72	Chev	500	18,890
2. David Pearson	Wood Brothers	21	Merc	500	11,190
3. Dave Marcis	Nord Krauskopf	71	Dodg	499	9,620
4. Bobby Allison	Roger Penske	2	Merc	497	7,360
5. Buddy Baker	Bud Moore	15	Ford	495	6,525

1976 Winston Cup GN Race No. 24 Delaware 500
September 19, 1976 Average Speed: 115.740

Driver	Owner	Car #	Make	Laps	Winnings
1. Cale Yarborough	Junior Johnson	11	Chev	500	18,075
2. Richard Petty	Petty Enterprises	43	Dodg	500	14,990
3. David Pearson	Wood Brothers	21	Merc	498	7,620
4. Bobby Allison	Roger Penske	2	Merc	496	7,285
5. Buddy Baker	Bud Moore	15	Ford	493	6,525

1977 Winston Cup GN Race No. 12 Mason-Dixon 500
May 15, 1977 Average Speed: 123.327

Driver	Owner	Car #	Make	Laps	Winnings
1. Cale Yarborough	Junior Johnson	11	Chev	500	17,175
2. David Pearson	Wood Brothers	21	Merc	500	9,600
3. Richard Petty	Petty Enterprises	43	Dodg	499	9,830
4. Darrell Waltrip	DiGard	88	Chev	496	7,870
5. Dick Brooks	Junie Donlavey	90	Ford	496	5,250

1977 Winston Cup GN Race No. 24 Delaware 500
September 18, 1977 Average Speed: 114.708

Driver	Owner	Car #	Make	Laps	Winnings
1. Benny Parsons	L. G. DeWitt	72	Chev	500	15,675
2. David Pearson	Wood Brothers	21	Merc	500	9,600
3. Cale Yarborough	Junior Johnson	11	Chev	499	10,925
4. Donnie Allison	Hoss Ellington	1	Chev	498	3,900
5. Darrell Waltrip	DiGard	88	Chev	497	6,400

1978 Winston Cup GN Race No. 11 Mason-Dixon 500
May 21, 1978 Average Speed: 114.664

Driver	Owner	Car #	Make	Laps	Winnings
1. David Pearson	Wood Brothers	21	Merc	500	16,600
2. Cale Yarborough	Junior Johnson	11	Olds	500	15,100
3. Lennie Pond	Harry Ranier	54	Chev	499	8,200
4. Benny Parsons	L. G. DeWitt	72	Chev	498	8,000
5. Neil Bonnett	Jim Stacy	5	Dodg	497	6,500

1978 Winston Cup GN Race No. 24 Delaware 500
September 17, 1978 Average Speed: 119.323

Driver	Owner	Car #	Make	Laps	Winnings
1. Bobby Allison	Bud Moore	15	Ford	500	19,500
2. Cale Yarborough	Junior Johnson	11	Olds	500	15,100
3. Buddy Baker	M. C. Anderson	27	Chev	499	8,700
4. David Pearson	Wood Brothers	21	Merc	498	4,600
5. Darrell Waltrip	DiGard	88	Chev	497	7,000

1979 Winston Cup GN Race No. 12 Mason-Dixon 500
May 20, 1979 Average Speed: 111.269

Driver	Owner	Car #	Make	Laps	Winnings
1. Neil Bonnett	Wood Brothers	21	Merc	500	17,750
2. Cale Yarborough	Junior Johnson	11	Chev	500	14,800
3. Buddy Baker	Harry Ranier	28	Chev	498	10,650
4. Bobby Allison	Bud Moore	15	Ford	498	8,100
5. Dale Earnhardt	Rod Osterlund	2	Chev	497	7,750

1979 Winston Cup GN Race No. 25 CRC Chemicals 500
September 16, 1979 Average Speed: 114.366

Driver	Owner	Car #	Make	Laps	Winnings
1. Richard Petty	Petty Enterprises	43	Chev	500	21,650
2. Donnie Allison	Hoss Ellington	1	Chev	500	11,350
3. Cale Yarborough	Junior Johnson	11	Chev	500	11,250
4. Buddy Baker	Harry Ranier	28	Chev	499	4,700
5. Joe Millikan	L. G. DeWitt	72	Chev	499	7,500

1980 Winston Cup GN Race No. 12 Mason-Dixon 500
May 18, 1980 Average Speed: 113.866

Driver	Owner	Car #	Make	Laps	Winnings
1. Bobby Allison	Bud Moore	15	Ford	500	21,900
2. Richard Petty	Petty Enterprises	43	Chev	500	16,775
3. Buddy Baker	Harry Ranier	28	Chev	497	7,800
4. Harry Gant	Jack Beebe	47	Chev	495	7,530
5. Terry Labonte	Billy Hagan	44	Chev	494	6,255

1980 Winston Cup GN Race No. 25 CRC Chemicals 500
September 14, 1980 Average Speed: 116.024

Driver	Owner	Car #	Make	Laps	Winnings
1. Darrell Waltrip	DiGard	88	Chev	500	22,900
2. Harry Gant	Jack Beebe	47	Chev	500	12,930
3. Buddy Baker	Harry Ranier	28	Chev	500	8,150
4. Cale Yarborough	Junior Johnson	11	Chev	499	10,700
5. Benny Parsons	M. C. Anderson	27	Chev	499	8,425

Dover Downs Int'l Speedway *continued*

1981 Winston Cup GN Race No. 12 Mason-Dixon 500
May 17, 1981 Average Speed: 116.595

Driver	Owner	Car #	Make	Laps	Winnings
1. Jody Ridley	Junie Donlavey	90	Ford	500	22,560
2. Bobby Allison	Harry Ranier	28	Buick	500	16,725
3. Dale Earnhardt	Rod Osterlund	2	Pont	499	15,125
4. D. K. Ulrich	D. K. Ulrich	99	Buick	491	7,160
5. Ricky Rudd	DiGard	88	Buick	490	9,450

1982 Winston Cup GN Race No. 11 Mason-Dixon 500
May 16, 1982 Average Speed: 120.136

Driver	Owner	Car #	Make	Laps	Winnings
1. Bobby Allison	DiGard	88	Chev	500	25,350
2. Dave Marcis	Dave Marcis	71	Chev	497	14,605
3. Dale Earnhardt	Bud Moore	15	Ford	497	15,700
4. Terry Labonte	Billy Hagan	44	Chev	496	8,305
5. Mark Martin	Bo Reeder	02	Buick	496	7,710

1983 Winston Cup GN Race No. 10 Mason-Dixon 500
May 15, 1983 Average Speed: 114.847

Driver	Owner	Car #	Make	Laps	Winnings
1. Bobby Allison	DiGard	22	Buick	500	28,500
2. Darrell Waltrip	Junior Johnson	11	Chev	500	20,425
3. Joe Ruttman	Ron Benfield	98	Buick	499	13,565
4. Bill Elliott	Harry Melling	9	Ford	498	8,655
5. Buddy Baker	Wood Brothers	21	Ford	497	4,550

1984 Winston Cup GN Race No. 11 Budweiser 500
May 20, 1984 Average Speed: 118.717

Driver	Owner	Car #	Make	Laps	Winnings
1. Richard Petty	Mike Curb	43	Pont	500	28,105
2. Tim Richmond	Raymond Beadle	27	Pont	500	19,220
3. Terry Labonte	Billy Hagan	44	Chev	500	13,075
4. Bill Elliott	Harry Melling	9	Ford	500	13,250
5. Dale Earnhardt	Richard Childress	3	Chev	499	11,600

1985 Winston Cup GN Race No. 10 Budweiser 500
May 19, 1985 Average Speed: 123.094

Driver	Owner	Car #	Make	Laps	Winnings
1. Bill Elliott	Harry Melling	9	Ford	500	44,500
2. Harry Gant	Hal Needham	33	Chev	499	29,950
3. Kyle Petty	Wood Brothers	7	Ford	499	19,055
4. Ricky Rudd	Bud Moore	15	Ford	498	15,375
5. Darrell Waltrip	Junior Johnson	11	Chev	497	15,975

1986 Winston Cup Race No. 10 Budweiser 500
May 18, 1986 Average Speed: 115.009

Driver	Owner	Car #	Make	Laps	Winnings
1. Geoff Bodine	Rick Hendrick	5	Chev	500	51,700
2. Bobby Allison	Stavola Brothers	22	Buick	500	29,150
3. Dale Earnhardt	Richard Childress	3	Chev	499	24,900
4. Ricky Rudd	Bud Moore	15	Ford	498	18,875
5. Darrell Waltrip	Junior Johnson	11	Chev	498	18,975

1987 Winston Cup Race No. 11 Budweiser 500
May 31, 1987 Average Speed: 112.958

Driver	Owner	Car #	Make	Laps	Winnings
1. Davey Allison	Harry Ranier	28	Ford	500	46,600
2. Bill Elliott	Harry Melling	9	Ford	500	35,575
3. Terry Labonte	Junior Johnson	11	Chev	499	25,575
4. Dale Earnhardt	Richard Childress	3	Chev	498	20,775
5. Benny Parsons	Rick Hendrick	35	Chev	498	18,025

1981 Winston Cup GN Race No. 25 CRC Chemicals 500
September 20, 1981 Average Speed: 119.561

Driver	Owner	Car #	Make	Laps	Winnings
1. Neil Bonnett	Wood Brothers	21	Ford	500	19,000
2. Darrell Waltrip	Junior Johnson	11	Buick	499	16,025
3. Bobby Allison	Harry Ranier	28	Buick	499	13,000
4. Ron Bouchard	Jack Beebe	47	Buick	495	9,060
5. Ricky Rudd	DiGard	88	Chev	495	11,375

1982 Winston Cup GN Race No. 24 CRC Chemicals 500
September 19, 1982 Average Speed: 107.642

Driver	Owner	Car #	Make	Laps	Winnings
1. Darrell Waltrip	Junior Johnson	11	Buick	500	29,600
2. Kyle Petty	Petty Enterprises	42	Pont	500	11,500
3. Bill Elliott	Harry Melling	9	Ford	500	8,400
4. Geoff Bodine	Cliff Stewart	50	Pont	500	12,650
5. Benny Parsons	Johnny Hayes	55	Buick	496	4,150

1983 Winston Cup GN Race No. 24 Budweiser 500
September 18, 1983 Average Speed: 116.077

Driver	Owner	Car #	Make	Laps	Winnings
1. Bobby Allison	DiGard	22	Buick	500	30,985
2. Geoff Bodine	Cliff Stewart	88	Pont	500	16,190
3. Tim Richmond	Raymond Beadle	27	Pont	500	11,565
4. Terry Labonte	Billy Hagan	44	Chev	499	10,470
5. Darrell Waltrip	Junior Johnson	11	Chev	499	14,335

1984 Winston Cup GN Race No. 24 Delaware 500
September 16, 1984 Average Speed: 111.856

Driver	Owner	Car #	Make	Laps	Winnings
1. Harry Gant	Hal Needham	33	Chev	500	40,005
2. Terry Labonte	Billy Hagan	44	Chev	500	17,870
3. Ricky Rudd	Bud Moore	15	Ford	498	17,200
4. Dave Marcis	Bob Rahilly & Butch Mock	75	Pont	497	15,020
5. Dale Earnhardt	Richard Childress	3	Chev	497	11,710

1985 Winston Cup GN Race No. 22 Delaware 500
September 15, 1985 Average Speed: 120.538

Driver	Owner	Car #	Make	Laps	Winnings
1. Harry Gant	Hal Needham	33	Chev	501	44,950
2. Darrell Waltrip	Junior Johnson	11	Chev	500	29,750
3. Ricky Rudd	Bud Moore	15	Ford	499	31,450
4. Bobby Allison	Bobby Allison	22	Ford	496	9,975
5. Neil Bonnett	Junior Johnson	12	Chev	496	14,275

1986 Winston Cup Race No. 23 Delaware 500
September 14, 1986 Average Speed: 114.329

Driver	Owner	Car #	Make	Laps	Winnings
1. Ricky Rudd	Bud Moore	15	Ford	500	51,500
2. Neil Bonnett	Junior Johnson	12	Chev	500	30,800
3. Kyle Petty	Wood Brothers	7	Ford	500	22,850
4. Buddy Baker	Buddy Baker & Danny Schiff	88	Olds	499	8,975
5. Dave Marcis	Dave Marcis	71	Chev	498	12,830

1987 Winston Cup Race No. 23 Delaware 500
September 20, 1987 Average Speed: 124.706

Driver	Owner	Car #	Make	Laps	Winnings
1. Ricky Rudd	Bud Moore	15	Ford	500	54,550
2. Davey Allison	Harry Ranier	28	Ford	500	25,875
3. Neil Bonnett	Bob Rahilly & Butch Mock	75	Pont	500	21,335
4. Bill Elliott	Harry Melling	9	Ford	500	19,375
5. Sterling Marlin	Billy Hagan	44	Olds	500	17,620

Dover Downs Int'l Speedway *continued*

1988 Winston Cup Race No. 11 Budweiser 500
June 5, 1988 Average Speed: 118.726

Driver	Owner	Car #	Make	Laps	Winnings
1. Bill Elliott	Harry Melling	9	Ford	500	53,000
2. Morgan Shepherd	Hal Needham	33	Chev	500	29,300
3. Rusty Wallace	Raymond Beadle	27	Pont	500	26,350
4. Lake Speed	Lake Speed	83	Olds	499	13,550
5. Davey Allison	Harry Ranier	28	Ford	499	20,150

1988 Winston Cup Race No. 23 Delaware 500
September 18, 1988 Average Speed: 109.349

Driver	Owner	Car #	Make	Laps	Winnings
1. Bill Elliott	Harry Melling	9	Ford	500	56,400
2. Dale Earnhardt	Richard Childress	3	Chev	500	37,450
3. Rusty Wallace	Raymond Beadle	27	Pont	500	26,200
4. Davey Allison	Harry Ranier	28	Ford	500	21,600
5. Geoff Bodine	Rick Hendrick	5	Chev	500	16,250

1989 Winston Cup Race No. 11 Budweiser 500
June 4, 1989 Average Speed: 121.670

Driver	Owner	Car #	Make	Laps	Winnings
1. Dale Earnhardt	Richard Childress	3	Chev	500	59,350
2. Mark Martin	Jack Roush	6	Ford	500	38,950
3. Ken Schrader	Rick Hendrick	25	Chev	500	36,525
4. Terry Labonte	Junior Johnson	11	Ford	500	18,425
5. Rusty Wallace	Raymond Beadle	27	Pont	500	20,975

1989 Winston Cup Race No. 23 Peak Performance 500
September 17, 1989 Average Speed: 122.909

Driver	Owner	Car #	Make	Laps	Winnings
1. Dale Earnhardt	Richard Childress	3	Chev	500	59,950
2. Mark Martin	Jack Roush	6	Ford	500	35,540
3. Ken Schrader	Rick Hendrick	25	Chev	500	25,875
4. Bill Elliott	Harry Melling	9	Ford	499	23,125
5. Ricky Rudd	Kenny Bernstein	26	Buick	498	18,375

1990 Winston Cup Series Race No. 11
June 3, 1990 Average Speed: 123.960

Driver	Owner	Car #	Make	Laps	Winnings
1. Derrike Cope	Bob Whitcomb	10	Chev	500	55,050
2. Ken Schrader	Rick Hendrick	25	Chev	500	34,575
3. Dick Trickle	Cale Yarborough	66	Pont	500	29,125
4. Mark Martin	Jack Roush	6	Ford	500	23,575
5. Sterling Marlin	Billy Hagan	94	Olds	500	16,325

1990 Winston Cup Series Race No. 23 Peak AntiFreeze 500
September 16, 1990 Average Speed: 125.945

Driver	Owner	Car #	Make	Laps	Winnings
1. Bill Elliott	Harry Melling	9	Ford	500	83,100
2. Mark Martin	Jack Roush	6	Ford	500	35,325
3. Dale Earnhardt	Richard Childress	3	Chev	500	29,375
4. Harry Gant	Leo Jackson	33	Olds	499	19,425
5. Michael Waltrip	Chuck Rider	30	Pont	499	16,825

1991 Winston Cup Series Race No. 11 Budweiser 500
June 2, 1991 Average Speed: 120.152

Driver	Owner	Car #	Make	Laps	Winnings
1. Ken Schrader	Rick Hendrick	25	Chev	500	64,800
2. Dale Earnhardt	Richard Childress	3	Chev	500	44,275
3. Harry Gant	Leo Jackson	33	Olds	500	28,800
4. Ernie Irvan	Larry McClure	4	Chev	500	21,750
5. Mark Martin	Jack Roush	6	Ford	500	23,325

1991 Winston Cup Series Race No. 23 Peak AntiFreeze 500
September 15, 1991 Average Speed: 110.179

Driver	Owner	Car #	Make	Laps	Winnings
1. Harry Gant	Leo Jackson	33	Olds	500	67,100
2. Geoff Bodine	Junior Johnson	11	Ford	499	42,225
3. Morgan Shepherd	Bud Moore	15	Ford	499	31,250
4. Hut Stricklin	Bobby Allison	12	Buick	499	20,350
5. Michael Waltrip	Chuck Rider	30	Pont	498	17,625

1992 Winston Cup Race No. 11 Budweiser 500
May 31, 1992 Average Speed: 109.456

Driver	Owner	Car #	Make	Laps	Winnings
1. Harry Gant	Leo Jackson	33	Olds	500	65,145
2. Dale Earnhardt	Richard Childress	3	Chev	500	43,720
3. Rusty Wallace	Roger Penske	2	Pont	499	25,795
4. Ernie Irvan	Larry McClure	4	Chev	499	29,445
5. Darrell Waltrip	Darrell Waltrip	17	Chev	499	25,140

1992 Winston Cup Race No. 23 Peak AntiFreeze 500
September 20, 1992 Average Speed: 115.289

Driver	Owner	Car #	Make	Laps	Winnings
1. Ricky Rudd	Rick Hendrick	5	Chev	500	64,965
2. Bill Elliott	Junior Johnson	11	Ford	500	51,260
3. Kyle Petty	Felix Sabates	42	Pont	500	27,310
4. Davey Allison	Robert Yates	28	Ford	499	29,410
5. Morgan Shepherd	Wood Brothers	21	Ford	498	21,980

1993 Winston Cup Series Race No. 12 Budweiser 500
June 6, 1993 Average Speed: 105.600

Driver	Owner	Car #	Make	Laps	Winnings
1. Dale Earnhardt	Richard Childress	3	Chev	500	68,030
2. Dale Jarrett	Joe Gibbs	18	Chev	500	42,435
3. Davey Allison	Robert Yates	28	Ford	500	38,240
4. Mark Martin	Jack Roush	6	Ford	500	28,100
5. Ken Schrader	Rick Hendrick	25	Chev	500	25,330

1993 Winston Cup Series Race No. 24 SplitFire Spark Plug 500
September 19, 1993 Average Speed: 100.334

Driver	Owner	Car #	Make	Laps	Winnings
1. Rusty Wallace	Roger Penske	2	Pont	500	77,645
2. Ken Schrader	Rick Hendrick	25	Chev	500	53,115
3. Darrell Waltrip	Darrell Waltrip	17	Chev	500	38,410
4. Dale Jarrett	Joe Gibbs	18	Chev	500	31,035
5. Harry Gant	Leo Jackson	33	Chev	500	27,830

1994 Winston Cup Series Race No. 12 Budweiser 500
June 6, 1994 Average Speed: 102.529

Driver	Owner	Car #	Make	Laps	Winnings
1. Rusty Wallace	Roger Penske	2	Ford	500	70,605
2. Ernie Irvan	Robert Yates	28	Ford	500	54,830
3. Ken Schrader	Rick Hendrick	25	Chev	500	35,605
4. Mark Martin	Jack Roush	6	Ford	500	29,765
5. Jeff Gordon	Rick Hendrick	24	Chev	500	33,570

1994 Winston Cup Series Race No. 25 SplitFire Spark Plug 500
September 18, 1994 Average Speed: 112.556

Driver	Owner	Car #	Make	Laps	Winnings
1. Rusty Wallace	Roger Penske	2	Ford	500	55,055
2. Dale Earnhardt	Richard Childress	3	Chev	500	47,980
3. Darrell Waltrip	Darrell Waltrip	17	Chev	500	36,705
4. Ken Schrader	Rick Hendrick	25	Chev	500	32,965
5. Geoff Bodine	Geoff Bodine	7	Ford	500	31,520

Dover Downs Int'l Speedway *continued*

1995 Winston Cup Series Race No. 12 Miller Genuine Draft 500
June 4, 1995 Average Speed: 119.880

Driver	Owner	Car #	Make	Laps	Winnings
1. Kyle Petty	Felix Sabates	42	Pont	500	77,655
2. Bobby Labonte	Joe Gibbs	18	Chev	500	61,555
3. Ted Musgrave	Jack Roush	16	Ford	500	43,305
4. Hut Stricklin	Kenny Bernstein	26	Ford	500	35,615
5. Dale Earnhardt	Richard Childress	3	Chev	500	45,545

1995 Winston Cup Series Race No. 25 MBNA 500
September 17, 1995 Average Speed: 124.740

Driver	Owner	Car #	Make	Laps	Winnings
1. Jeff Gordon	Rick Hendrick	24	Chev	500	74,655
2. Bobby Hamilton	Petty Enterprises	43	Pont	500	62,505
3. Rusty Wallace	Roger Penske	2	Ford	500	46,905
4. Joe Nemechek	Joe Nemechek	87	Chev	500	34,465
5. Dale Earnhardt	Richard Childress	3	Chev	500	40,970

1996 Winston Cup Series Race No. 12 Miller 500
June 2, 1996 Average Speed: 122.741

Driver	Owner	Car #	Make	Laps	Winnings
1. Jeff Gordon	Rick Hendrick	24	Chev	500	138,730
2. Terry Labonte	Rick Hendrick	5	Chev	500	57,480
3. Dale Earnhardt	Richard Childress	3	Chev	500	60,080
4. Ernie Irvan	Robert Yates	28	Ford	500	42,440
5. Bobby Labonte	Joe Gibbs	18	Chev	499	42,295

1996 Winston Cup Series Race No. 25 MBNA 500
September 15, 1996 Average Speed: 105.646

Driver	Owner	Car #	Make	Laps	Winnings
1. Jeff Gordon	Rick Hendrick	24	Chev	500	153,630
2. Rusty Wallace	Roger Penske	2	Ford	500	54,580
3. Dale Jarrett	Robert Yates	88	Ford	500	40,880
4. Bobby Labonte	Joe Gibbs	18	Chev	500	50,390
5. Mark Martin	Jack Roush	6	Ford	500	48,820

1997 Winston Cup Series Race No. 12
June 1, 1997 Average Speed: 114.635

Driver	Owner	Car #	Make	Laps	Winnings
1. Ricky Rudd	Ricky Rudd	10	Ford	500	95,255
2. Mark Martin	Jack Roush	6	Ford	500	52,405
3. Jeff Burton	Jack Roush	99	Ford	500	53,155
4. Jeremy Mayfield	Michael Kranefuss	37	Ford	500	37,090
5. Kyle Petty	Petty Enterprises	44	Pont	500	31,820

1997 Winston Cup Series Race No. 26
September 21, 1997 Average Speed: 132.719

Driver	Owner	Car #	Make	Laps	Winnings
1. Mark Martin	Jack Roush	6	Ford	400	195,305
2. Dale Earnhardt	Richard Childress	3	Chev	400	63,105
3. Kyle Petty	Petty Enterprises	44	Pont	400	40,205
4. Bobby Labonte	Joe Gibbs	18	Pont	400	41,465
5. Dale Jarrett	Robert Yates	88	Ford	399	39,845

1998 Winston Cup Series Race No. 12
May 31, 1998 Average Speed: 119.522

Driver	Owner	Car #	Make	Laps	Winnings
1. Dale Jarrett	Robert Yates	88	Ford	400	89,950
2. Jeff Burton	Jack Roush	99	Ford	400	62,250
3. Jeff Gordon	Rick Hendrick	24	Chev	400	79,350
4. Bobby Labonte	Joe Gibbs	18	Pont	400	55,500
5. Jeremy Mayfield	Michael Kranefuss	12	Ford	399	42,325

1998 Winston Cup Series Race No. 26
September 20, 1998 Average Speed: 113.834

Driver	Owner	Car #	Make	Laps	Winnings
1. Mark Martin	Jack Roush	6	Ford	400	126,130
2. Jeff Gordon	Rick Hendrick	24	Chev	400	77,005
3. Jeremy Mayfield	Michael Kranefuss	12	Ford	400	49,305
4. Bobby Labonte	Joe Gibbs	18	Pont	400	57,410
5. Rusty Wallace	Roger Penske	2	Ford	400	40,370

1999 Winston Cup Series Race No. 13
June 6, 1999 Average Speed: 120.603

Driver	Owner	Car #	Make	Laps	Winnings
1. Bobby Labonte	Joe Gibbs	18	Pont	400	144,820
2. Jeff Gordon	Rick Hendrick	24	Chev	400	96,805
3. Mark Martin	Jack Roush	6	Ford	399	77,480
4. Tony Stewart	Joe Gibbs	20	Pont	399	63,205
5. Dale Jarrett	Robert Yates	88	Ford	399	67,745

1999 Winston Cup Series Race No. 27
September 26, 1999 Average Speed: 127.434

Driver	Owner	Car #	Make	Laps	Winnings
1. Mark Martin	Jack Roush	6	Ford	400	115,710
2. Tony Stewart	Joe Gibbs	20	Pont	400	88,875
3. Dale Jarrett	Robert Yates	88	Ford	400	74,935
4. Matt Kenseth	Robbie Reiser	17	Ford	400	51,160
5. Bobby Labonte	Joe Gibbs	18	Pont	400	56,285

2000 Winston Cup Series Race No. 13
June 4, 2000 Average Speed: 109.514

Driver	Owner	Car #	Make	Laps	Winnings
1. Tony Stewart	Joe Gibbs	20	Pont	400	152,830
2. Matt Kenseth	Jack Roush	17	Ford	400	119,755
3. Bobby Labonte	Joe Gibbs	18	Pont	400	96,105
4. Dale Jarrett	Robert Yates	88	Ford	400	95,755
5. Ricky Rudd	Robert Yates	28	Ford	400	78,280

2000 Winston Cup Series Race No. 27
September 24, 2000 Average Speed: 115.191

Driver	Owner	Car #	Make	Laps	Winnings
1. Tony Stewart	Joe Gibbs	20	Pont	400	158,535
2. Johnny Benson, Jr.	Tim Beverley	10	Pont	400	99,710
3. Ricky Rudd	Robert Yates	28	Ford	400	93,160
4. Steve Park	Dale Earnhardt, Inc.	1	Chev	400	81,010
5. Bobby Labonte	Joe Gibbs	18	Pont	400	82,670

2001 Winston Cup Series Race No. 13
June 3, 2001 Average Speed: 120.361

Driver	Owner	Car #	Make	Laps	Winnings
1. Jeff Gordon	Rick Hendrick	24	Chev	400	183,907
2. Steve Park	Dale Earnhardt, Inc.	1	Chev	400	128,148
3. Dale Earnhardt, Jr.	Dale Earnhardt, Inc.	8	Chev	400	113,648
4. Ricky Craven	Cal Wells	32	Ford	400	79,900
5. Dale Jarrett	Robert Yates	88	Ford	400	115,007

2001 Winston Cup Series Race No. 27
September 23, 2001 Average Speed: 101.559

Driver	Owner	Car #	Make	Laps	Winnings
1. Dale Earnhardt, Jr.	Dale Earnhardt, Inc.	8	Chev	400	168,858
2. Jerry Nadeau	Rick Hendrick	25	Chev	400	106,960
3. Ricky Rudd	Robert Yates	28	Ford	400	117,507
4. Jeff Gordon	Rick Hendrick	24	Chev	400	117,832
5. Tony Stewart	Joe Gibbs	20	Pont	400	89,270

Dover Downs Int'l Speedway *continued*

2002 Winston Cup Series Race No. 13
June 2, 2002 Average Speed: 117.551

Driver	Owner	Car #	Make	Laps	Winnings
1. Jimmie Johnson	Rick Hendrick	48	Chev	400	152,400
2. Bill Elliott	Ray Evernham	9	Dodg	400	139,106
3. Jeff Burton	Jack Roush	99	Ford	400	134,267
4. Ryan Newman	Roger Penske	12	Ford	400	103,425
5. Dale Jarrett	Robert Yates	88	Ford	400	125,453

2002 Winston Cup Series Race No. 28
September 22, 2002 Average Speed: 120.805

Driver	Owner	Car #	Make	Laps	Winnings
1. Jimmie Johnson	Rick Hendrick	48	Chev	400	152,735
2. Mark Martin	Jack Roush	6	Ford	400	148,593
3. Dale Jarrett	Robert Yates	88	Ford	400	120,480
4. Matt Kenseth	Jack Roush	17	Ford	400	91,680
5. Tony Stewart	Joe Gibbs	20	Pont	400	115,073

Florida

Beach & Road Course
Daytona Beach, FL
4.17-mile Beach & Road Course

4.1-mile sand and paved course, utilizing highway A-1-A and the beachfront at south tip of Daytona Beach in Ponce Inlet. First Beach-Road course built in 1936 (near Daytona Beach Shores), and later moved south due to beachfront development. First NASCAR Winston Cup (then Strictly Stock) race staged on 7/10/49 (won by Red Byron). Final auto racing event staged on 2/23/58 (won by Paul Goldsmith). Track continued to present annual motorcycle races through 1960. Concrete blocks that held the South Turn grandstand are still in the ground today. The South Turn is still recognizable today, and Brewster's Restaurant is currently located at the old North Turn.

Winston Cup Starts
Buck Baker	10
Tim Flock	10
Curtis Turner	10

Winston Cup Victories
Tim Flock	2
Marshall Teague	2

Winston Cup Poles
Tim Flock	3

Winston Cup Money
Tim Flock	$9,360

Most Cars Started
76—February 26, 1956

Fewest Cars Started
28—July 10, 1949

Narrowest Margin of Victory
5 car lengths—February 23, 1958

Slowest Race
80.883 MPH—July 10, 1949

Race Record
101.541 MPH—February 17, 1957

Most Cautions
2—February 26, 1956

Most Race Leaders
2—July 10, 1949
2—February 5, 1950
2—February 11, 1951
2—February 10, 1952
2—February 15, 1953
2—February 21, 1954
2—February 26, 1956
2—February 17, 1957

Most Cars Running at Finish
47—February 21, 1954

1949 Strictly Stock Race No. 2
July 10, 1949 Average Speed: 80.883

Driver	Owner	Car #	Make	Laps	Winnings
1. Red Byron	Raymond Parks	22	49 Olds	40	2,000
2. Tim Flock	Buddy Elliott	90	49 Olds	40	1,000
3. Frank Mundy	Sam Rice	5	49 Olds	40	500
4. Joe Littlejohn	Frank Christian	7	49 Olds	40	300
5. Bill Blair	R. B. McIntosh	44	49 Linc	40	200

1950 Grand National Race No. 1
February 5, 1950 Average Speed: 89.894

Driver	Owner	Car #	Make	Laps	Winnings
1. Harold Kite	Harold Kite	21	49 Linc	48	1,500
2. Red Byron	Raymond Parks	22	50 Olds	48	1,000
3. Lloyd Moore	Julian Buesink	59	49 Linc	48	600
4. Al Gross	Hans Winter	88	50 Olds	48	550
5. J. C. Van Landingham	J. C. Van Landingham	35	50 Buick	48	450

1951 Grand National Race No. 1
February 11, 1951 Average Speed: 82.328

Driver	Owner	Car #	Make	Laps	Winnings
1. Marshall Teague	Marshall Teague	6	51 Huds	39	1,500
2. Tim Flock	Sam Knox	91	50 Linc	—	1,000
3. Fonty Flock	Frank Christian	14	50 Olds	—	600
4. Bill Blair	Bill Blair	41.5	49 Olds	—	550
5. Buck Baker	Griffin Motors	87	50 Olds	—	450

1952 Grand National Race No. 2
February 10, 1952 Average Speed: 85.612

Driver	Owner	Car #	Make	Laps	Winnings
1. Marshall Teague	Marshall Teague	6	52 Huds	37	1,500
2. Herb Thomas	Marshall Teague	92	52 Huds	37	1,000
3. Pat Kirkwood	Pat Kirkwood	99	51 Chrys	37	600
4. Fonty Flock	Frank Christian	14	51 Olds	—	550
5. Gober Sosebee	Gober Sosebee	51	51 Olds	—	450

1953 Grand National Race No. 2
February 15, 1953 Average Speed: 89.789

Driver	Owner	Car #	Make	Laps	Winnings
1. Bill Blair	Bill Blair	2	53 Olds	39	1,500
2. Fonty Flock	Frank Christian	14	53 Olds	39	1,000
3. Tommy Thompson	Tommy Thompson	40	53 Linc	39	800
4. Herb Thomas	Herb Thomas	92	53 Huds	39	600
5. Tim Flock	Ted Chester	91	52 Huds	39	500

1954 Grand National Race No. 2
February 21, 1954 Average Speed: 89.108

Driver	Owner	Car #	Make	Laps	Winnings
1. Lee Petty	Petty Enterprises	42	54 Chrys	39	1,700
2. Buck Baker	Griffin Motors	87	53 Olds	39	1,325
3. Curtis Turner	Frank Christian	14	54 Olds	39	900
4. Dick Rathmann	John Ditz	3	54 Huds	38	625
5. Bill Blair	Bill Blair	2	54 Olds	38	475

1955 Grand National Race No. 4
February 27, 1955 Average Speed: 91.999

Driver	Owner	Car #	Make	Laps	Winnings
1. Tim Flock	Carl Kiekhaefer	300	55 Chrys	39	2,350
2. Lee Petty	Petty Enterprises	42	55 Chrys	39	1,600
3. Ray Duhigg	J. O. Goode	24	55 Buick	39	1,000
4. Curtis Turner	Raymond Parks	99	55 Olds	39	800
5. Fonty Flock	Frank Christian	14	55 Olds	39	625

1956 Grand National Race No. 6
February 26, 1956 Average Speed: 90.657

Driver	Owner	Car #	Make	Laps	Winnings
1. Tim Flock	Carl Kiekhaefer	300A	56 Chrys	37	4,025
2. Billy Myers	Bill Stroppe	14W	56 Merc	37	2,375
3. Ralph Moody	Pete DePaolo	12	56 Ford	37	1,450
4. Jimmie Lewallen	Ernest Woods	88	56 Olds	—	900
5. Jim Reed	Jim Reed	7	56 Chev	—	700

Beach & Road Course *continued*

1957 Grand National Race No. 4
February 17, 1957 Average Speed: 101.541

Driver	Owner	Car #	Make	Laps	Winnings
1. Cotton Owens	Ray Nichels	6	57 Pont	39	4,250
2. Johnny Beauchamp	Hugh Babb	50	57 Chev	39	2,450
3. Fonty Flock	Bill Stroppe	18	57 Merc	—	1,500
4. Buck Baker	Hugh Babb	87	57 Chev	—	900
5. Marvin Panch	Pete DePaolo	98	57 Ford	—	700

1958 Grand National Race No. 2
February 23, 1958 Average Speed: 101.113

Driver	Owner	Car #	Make	Laps	Winnings
1. Paul Goldsmith	Smokey Yunick	3	58 Pont	39	4,550
2. Curtis Turner	Holman-Moody	26	58 Ford	39	2,600
3. Jack Smith	Jack Smith	47	57 Pont	39	1,575
4. Joe Weatherly	Holman-Moody	12	58 Ford	39	900
5. Gwyn Staley	Buck Baker	187	57 Chev	38	700

Daytona Int'l Speedway
Daytona Beach, FL
2.5-mile Superspeedway

2.5-mile high-banked speedway opened in February 1959, and was the first ultra-fast speedway in NASCAR circuit. First race staged on 2/20/59 (Convertible race won by Shorty Rollins). The first Daytona 500 (originally named the International Sweepstakes 500) was won by Lee Petty on 2/22/59. The road course is set in the infield, site of the 24 Hours of Daytona. Track is banked 31 degrees. When asked why the degree of banking was set at 31, founder Bill France said, "Because they couldn't lay asphalt any steeper." Just prior to opening, driver Jimmy Thompson offered his assessment of the new facility, "There have been other tracks that separated the men from the boys. This is the track that will separate the brave from the weak after the boys are gone."

Winston Cup Starts
Richard Petty   74

Winston Cup Victories
Richard Petty   10

Winston Cup Poles
Cale Yarborough   13

Winston Cup Money
Dale Jarrett $4,599,002

Most Cars Started
68—February 14, 1960 Daytona 500

Fewest Cars Started
21—February 12, 1965
(40-lap race)

Narrowest Margin of Victory
0.029 seconds—July 5, 1997

Slowest Race
111.076 MPH—February 12, 1965
(40-lap race)

Race Record
183.295 MPH—February 19, 1970

Most Cautions
12—July 1, 1989 Pepsi 400

Most Race Leaders
15—3 times

Most Cars Running at Finish
39—3 times

1959 Grand National Race No. 2
February 20, 1959 Average Speed: 143.198

Driver	Owner	Car #	Make	Laps	Winnings
1. Bob Welborn	W. J. Ridgeway	49	59 Chev	40	800
2. Fritz Wilson	Fritz Wilson	64	59 Ford	40	525
3. Tom Pistone	Carl Rupert	59	59 Ford	40	350
4. Joe Weatherly	E. C. Wilson	48	59 Chev	40	250
5. Eduardo Dibos	Eduardo Dibos	37	59 Ford	39	225

1959 Grand National Race No. 3 Daytona 500
February 22, 1959 Average Speed: 135.521

Driver	Owner	Car #	Make	Laps	Winnings
1. Lee Petty	Petty Enterprises	42	59 Olds	200	19,050
2. Johnny Beauchamp	Roy Burdick Gar	73	59 Ford	200	7,650
3. Charley Griffith	Charley Griffith	18	57 Pont	199	4,600
4. Cotton Owens	W. H. Watson	6	58 Pont	199	2,525
5. Joe Weatherly	E. C. Wilson	48	59 Chev	199	1,875

1959 Grand National Race No. 26 Firecracker 250
July 4, 1959 Average Speed: 140.581

Driver	Owner	Car #	Make	Laps	Winnings
1. Fireball Roberts	Jim Stephens	3	59 Pont	100	7,050
2. Joe Weatherly	Doc White	12	59 Ford	100	4,625
3. Johnny Allen	W. J. Ridgeway	22	59 Chev	99	1,925
4. Jack Smith	Jack Smith	47	59 Chev	99	1,175
5. Eduardo Dibos	Eduardo Dibos	37	59 Ford	98	725

1960 Grand National Race No. 3
February 12, 1960 Average Speed: 137.614

Driver	Owner	Car #	Make	Laps	Winnings
1. Fireball Roberts	John Hines	22	60 Pont	40	1,000
2. Cotton Owens	Cotton Owens	6	60 Pont	40	600
3. Fred Lorenzen	Fred Lorenzen	28	60 Ford	40	400
4. Joe Weatherly	Holman-Moody	12	60 Ford	40	300
5. Junior Johnson	John Masoni	27	59 Chev	40	275

1960 Grand National Race No. 4
February 12, 1960 Average Speed: 146.520

Driver	Owner	Car #	Make	Laps	Winnings
1. Jack Smith	Jack Smith	47	60 Pont	40	1,000
2. Bobby Johns	Jim Stephens	3	59 Pont	40	600
3. Jim Reed	Jim Reed	7	60 Chev	40	400
4. Rex White	Rex White	4	60 Chev	40	300
5. Bob Welborn	Bob Welborn	49	60 Chev	40	275

1960 Grand National Race No. 5 Daytona 500
February 14, 1960

Driver	Owner	Car #	Make	Laps	Winnings
1. Junior Johnson	John Masoni	27	59 Chev	200	19,600
2. Bobby Johns	Jim Stephens	3	59 Pont	200	8,600
3. Richard Petty	Petty Enterprises	43	60 Plym	200	6,450
4. Lee Petty	Petty Enterprises	42	60 Plym	200	3,650
5. Johnny Allen	Hanley Dawson	69	60 Chev	199	3,300

1960 Grand National Race No. 23 Firecracker 250
July 4, 1960 Average Speed: 146.842

Driver	Owner	Car #	Make	Laps	Winnings
1. Jack Smith	Jack Smith	47	60 Pont	100	11,500
2. Cotton Owens	Cotton Owens	6	60 Pont	100	5,100
3. Fred Lorenzen	Fred Lorenzen	28	60 Ford	99	2,600
4. Lee Petty	Petty Enterprises	42	60 Plym	99	1,525
5. Bunkie Blackburn	Spook Crawford	64	60 Ford	98	1,150

1961 Grand National Race No. 3
February 24, 1961 Average Speed: 129.711

Driver	Owner	Car #	Make	Laps	Winnings
1. Fireball Roberts	Jim Stephens	22	61 Pont	39	1,000
2. Jim Paschal	John Masoni	3	61 Pont	39	600
3. Jack Smith	Jack Smith	47	61 Pont	39	400
4. Buck Baker	Buck Baker	87	61 Chrys	39	300
5. Ned Jarrett	Bee Gee Holloway	11	61 Chev	39	275

1961 Grand National Race No. 4
February 24, 1961 Average Speed: 152.671

Driver	Owner	Car #	Make	Laps	Winnings
1. Joe Weatherly	Bud Moore	8	61 Pont	40	1,000
2. Marvin Panch	Smokey Yunick	20	60 Pont	40	600
3. Cotton Owens	Cotton Owens	6	61 Pont	40	400
4. Banjo Matthews	Banjo Matthews	94	61 Ford	39	300
5. Darel Dieringer	Ray Nichels	32	61 Pont	39	275

1961 Grand National Race No. 5 Daytona 500
February 26, 1961 Average Speed: 149.601

Driver	Owner	Car #	Make	Laps	Winnings
1. Marvin Panch	Smokey Yunick	20	60 Pont	200	21,050
2. Joe Weatherly	Bud Moore	8	61 Pont	200	9,150
3. Paul Goldsmith	Ray Nichels	31	61 Pont	200	5,900
4. Fred Lorenzen	Tubby Gonzales	80	61 Ford	198	3,825
5. Cotton Owens	Cotton Owens	6	61 Pont	198	2,975

Daytona Int'l Speedway *continued*

1961 Grand National Race No. 32 Firecracker 250
July 4, 1961 Average Speed: 154.294

Driver	Owner	Car #	Make	Laps	Winnings
1. David Pearson	John Masoni	3	Pont	100	8,450
2. Fred Lorenzen	Holman-Moody	28	61 Ford	100	4,275
3. Jack Smith	Jack Smith	46	61 Pont	99	2,700
4. Marvin Panch	Smokey Yunick	20	60 Pont	99	1,525
5. Fireball Roberts	Jim Stephens	22	61 Pont	98	1,525

1962 Grand National Race No. 3
February 16, 1962 Average Speed: 156.999

Driver	Owner	Car #	Make	Laps	Winnings
1. Fireball Roberts	Jim Stephens	22	62 Pont	40	1,000
2. Jack Smith	Jack Smith	47	62 Pont	40	600
3. Cotton Owens	Cotton Owens	6	62 Pont	40	400
4. Dan Gurney	Holman-Moody	0	62 Ford	40	300
5. Junior Johnson	Rex Lovette	27	62 Pont	40	300

1962 Grand National Race No. 4
February 16, 1962 Average Speed: 145.395

Driver	Owner	Car #	Make	Laps	Winnings
1. Joe Weatherly	Bud Moore	8	62 Pont	40	1,000
2. Nelson Stacy	Holman-Moody	29	62 Ford	40	600
3. Rex White	Rex White	4	62 Chev	40	400
4. Richard Petty	Petty Enterprises	43	62 Plym	39	300
5. Johnny Allen	Bee Gee Holloway	7	62 Chev	39	300

1962 Grand National Race No. 5 Daytona 500
February 18, 1962 Average Speed: 152.529

Driver	Owner	Car #	Make	Laps	Winnings
1. Fireball Roberts	Jim Stephens	22	62 Pont	200	24,190
2. Richard Petty	Petty Enterprises	43	62 Plym	200	10,250
3. Joe Weatherly	Bud Moore	8	62 Pont	199	7,100
4. Jack Smith	Jack Smith	47	62 Pont	199	4,025
5. Fred Lorenzen	Holman-Moody	28	62 Ford	199	2,975

1962 Grand National Race No. 29 Firecracker 250
July 4, 1962 Average Speed: 153.688

Driver	Owner	Car #	Make	Laps	Winnings
1. Fireball Roberts	Banjo Matthews	22	62 Pont	100	9,850
2. Junior Johnson	Cotton Owens	6	62 Pont	100	5,450
3. Marvin Panch	Wood Brothers	21	62 Ford	98	3,400
4. Jack Smith	Jack Smith	47	62 Pont	98	1,675
5. Jimmy Pardue	Jimmy Pardue	54	62 Pont	97	1,225

1963 Grand National Race No. 5
February 22, 1963 Average Speed: 164.083

Driver	Owner	Car #	Make	Laps	Winnings
1. Junior Johnson	Ray Fox	3	63 Chev	40	1,100
2. Paul Goldsmith	Ray Nichels	01	63 Pont	40	600
3. A. J. Foyt	Ray Nichels	02	63 Pont	40	400
4. Larry Frank	Holman-Moody	06	63 Ford	40	300
5. Dan Gurney	Dan Gurney	0	63 Ford	40	300

1963 Grand National Race No. 6
February 22, 1963 Average Speed: 162.969

Driver	Owner	Car #	Make	Laps	Winnings
1. Johnny Rutherford	Smokey Yunick	13	63 Chev	40	1,100
2. Rex White	Rex White	4	63 Chev	40	600
3. Fred Lorenzen	Holman-Moody	28	63 Ford	40	400
4. Ned Jarrett	Charles Robinson	11	63 Ford	40	300
5. Nelson Stacy	Holman-Moody	29	63 Ford	40	300

1963 Grand National Race No. 7 Daytona 500
February 24, 1963 Average Speed: 151.566

Driver	Owner	Car #	Make	Laps	Winnings
1. Tiny Lund	Wood Brothers	21	63 Ford	200	24,550
2. Fred Lorenzen	Holman-Moody	28	63 Ford	200	15,450
3. Ned Jarrett	Charles Robinson	11	63 Ford	200	8,700
4. Nelson Stacy	Holman-Moody	29	63 Ford	199	8,275
5. Dan Gurney	Holman-Moody	0	63 Ford	199	3,550

1963 Grand National Race No. 29 Firecracker 400
July 4, 1963 Average Speed: 150.927

Driver	Owner	Car #	Make	Laps	Winnings
1. Fireball Roberts	Holman-Moody	22	63 Ford	160	12,100
2. Fred Lorenzen	Holman-Moody	28	63 Ford	160	8,015
3. Marvin Panch	Wood Brothers	21	63 Ford	160	5,310
4. Darel Dieringer	Bill Stroppe	16	63 Merc	158	3,175
5. Ned Jarrett	Charles Robinson	11	63 Ford	156	1,900

1964 Grand National Race No. 6
February 21, 1964 Average Speed: 170.777

Driver	Owner	Car #	Make	Laps	Winnings
1. Junior Johnson	Ray Fox	3	64 Dodg	40	1,100
2. Buck Baker	Petty Enterprises	41	64 Plym	40	600
3. David Pearson	Cotton Owens	6	64 Dodg	40	400
4. Marvin Panch	Wood Brothers	21	64 Ford	40	300
5. Darel Dieringer	Bill Stroppe	16	64 Merc	40	300

1964 Grand National Race No. 7
February 21, 1964 Average Speed: 169.811

Driver	Owner	Car #	Make	Laps	Winnings
1. Bobby Isaac	Ray Nichels	26	64 Dodg	40	1,100
2. Jimmy Pardue	Charles Robinson	54	64 Plym	40	600
3. Richard Petty	Petty Enterprises	43	64 Plym	40	400
4. A. J. Foyt	Banjo Matthews	00	64 Ford	40	300
5. Jim Paschal	Cotton Owens	5	64 Dodg	40	300

1964 Grand National Race No. 8 Daytona 500
February 23, 1964 Average Speed: 154.334

Driver	Owner	Car #	Make	Laps	Winnings
1. Richard Petty	Petty Enterprises	43	64 Plym	200	33,300
2. Jimmy Pardue	Charles Robinson	54	64 Plym	199	11,600
3. Paul Goldsmith	Ray Nichels	25	64 Plym	198	8,600
4. Marvin Panch	Wood Brothers	21	64 Ford	198	4,350
5. Jim Paschal	Cotton Owens	5	64 Dodg	197	3,700

1964 Grand National Race No. 35 Firecracker 400
July 4, 1964 Average Speed: 151.451

Driver	Owner	Car #	Make	Laps	Winnings
1. A. J. Foyt	Ray Nichels	47	64 Dodg	160	13,000
2. Bobby Isaac	Ray Nichels	26	64 Dodg	160	8,895
3. Jimmy Pardue	Charles Robinson	54	64 Plym	160	5,430
4. Buck Baker	Ray Fox	3	64 Dodg	158	3,475
5. Jim Paschal	Petty Enterprises	41	64 Plym	158	2,200

1965 Grand National Race No. 2
February 12, 1965 Average Speed: 165.669

Driver	Owner	Car #	Make	Laps	Winnings
1. Darel Dieringer	Bud Moore	16	64 Merc	40	1,100
2. Ned Jarrett	Bondy Long	11	65 Ford	40	600
3. Bobby Johns	Holman-Moody	7	65 Ford	40	400
4. Larry Frank	Larry Frank	76	64 Ford	39	300
5. H. B. Bailey	H. B. Bailey	04	64 Pont	39	300

Daytona Int'l Speedway *continued*

1965 Grand National Race No. 3
February 12, 1965 Average Speed: 111.076

Driver	Owner	Car #	Make	Laps	Winnings
1. Junior Johnson	Rex Lovette	27	65 Ford	40	1,100
2. Fred Lorenzen	Holman-Moody	28	65 Ford	40	600
3. Marvin Panch	Wood Brothers	21	65 Ford	40	400
4. Donald Tucker	Don Snyder	74	63 Ford	38	300
5. Sam McQuagg	Betty Lilly	24	65 Ford	38	300

1965 Grand National Race No. 4 Daytona 500
February 14, 1965 Average Speed: 141.539

Driver	Owner	Car #	Make	Laps	Winnings
1. Fred Lorenzen	Holman-Moody	28	65 Ford	133	27,100
2. Darel Dieringer	Bud Moore	16	64 Merc	132	12,900
3. Bobby Johns	Holman-Moody	7	65 Ford	132	7,850
4. Earl Balmer	Bud Moore	15	64 Merc	132	4,350
5. Ned Jarrett	Bondy Long	11	65 Ford	132	3,750

1965 Grand National Race No. 29 Firecracker 400
July 4, 1965 Average Speed: 150.046

Driver	Owner	Car #	Make	Laps	Winnings
1. A. J. Foyt	Wood Brothers	41	65 Ford	160	8,500
2. Buddy Baker	Buck Baker	86	65 Plym	160	5,400
3. G. C. Spencer	G. C. Spencer	49	64 Ford	158	4,200
4. J. T. Putney	Herman Beam	19	65 Chev	153	2,525
5. Neil Castles	Buck Baker	88	64 Dodg	152	1,725

1966 Grand National Race No. 3
February 25, 1966 Average Speed: 160.427

Driver	Owner	Car #	Make	Laps	Winnings
1. Paul Goldsmith	Ray Nichels	99	65 Plym	40	1,100
2. Richard Petty	Petty Enterprises	43	66 Plym	40	600
3. Don White	Ray Nichels	07	65 Dodg	40	400
4. Marvin Panch	Wood Brothers	21	66 Ford	40	300
5. Fred Lorenzen	Holman-Moody	28	66 Ford	40	300

1966 Grand National Race No. 4
February 25, 1966 Average Speed: 153.191

Driver	Owner	Car #	Make	Laps	Winnings
1. Earl Balmer	Ray Fox	3	65 Dodg	40	1,000
2. Jim Hurtubise	Norm Nelson	56	65 Plym	40	600
3. Dick Hutcherson	Holman-Moody	29	66 Ford	40	400
4. LeeRoy Yarbrough	Jon Thorne	12	66 Dodg	40	300
5. Ned Jarrett	Bondy Long	11	66 Ford	40	500

1966 Grand National Race No. 5 Daytona 500
February 27, 1966 Average Speed: 160.627

Driver	Owner	Car #	Make	Laps	Winnings
1. Richard Petty	Petty Enterprises	43	66 Plym	198	28,150
2. Cale Yarborough	Banjo Matthews	27	66 Ford	197	12,800
3. David Pearson	Cotton Owens	6	66 Dodg	196	7,950
4. Fred Lorenzen	Holman-Moody	28	66 Ford	196	4,250
5. Sam McQuagg	Ray Nichels	98	66 Dodg	195	3,600

1966 Grand National Race No. 28 Firecracker 400
July 4, 1966 Average Speed: 153.613

Driver	Owner	Car #	Make	Laps	Winnings
1. Sam McQuagg	Ray Nichels	98	66 Dodg	160	13,600
2. Darel Dieringer	Bud Moore	16	66 Merc	160	8,870
3. Jim Paschal	Tom Friedkin	14	66 Plym	159	5,985
4. Curtis Turner	Smokey Yunick	13	66 Chev	159	3,100
5. Jim Hurtubise	Norm Nelson	56	66 Plym	158	1,550

1967 Grand National Race No. 3
February 24, 1967 Average Speed: 163.934

Driver	Owner	Car #	Make	Laps	Winnings
1. LeeRoy Yarbrough	Jon Thorne	12	67 Dodg	40	1,350
2. A. J. Foyt	Banjo Matthews	27	67 Ford	40	650
3. Paul Goldsmith	Ray Nichels	99	67 Plym	40	400
4. Buddy Baker	Ray Fox	3	67 Dodg	40	400
5. Tiny Lund	Petty Enterprises	42	66 Plym	39	300

1967 Grand National Race No. 4
February 24, 1967 Average Speed: 174.587

Driver	Owner	Car #	Make	Laps	Winnings
1. Fred Lorenzen	Holman-Moody	28	67 Ford	40	1,350
2. Darel Dieringer	Junior Johnson	26	67 Ford	40	650
3. Cale Yarborough	Wood Brothers	21	67 Ford	40	400
4. Dick Hutcherson	Bondy Long	29	67 Ford	40	300
5. Richard Petty	Petty Enterprises	43	67 Plym	40	300

1967 Grand National Race No. 5 Daytona 500
February 26, 1967 Average Speed: 146.926

Driver	Owner	Car #	Make	Laps	Winnings
1. Mario Andretti	Holman-Moody	11	67 Ford	200	48,900
2. Fred Lorenzen	Holman-Moody	28	67 Ford	200	15,950
3. James Hylton	Bud Hartje	48	65 Dodg	199	10,925
4. Tiny Lund	Petty Enterprises	42	66 Plym	198	6,675
5. Jerry Grant	Tom Friedkin	40	67 Plym	197	4,725

1967 Grand National Race No. 28 Firecracker 400
July 4, 1967 Average Speed: 143.583

Driver	Owner	Car #	Make	Laps	Winnings
1. Cale Yarborough	Wood Brothers	21	67 Ford	160	15,725
2. Dick Hutcherson	Bondy Long	29	67 Ford	160	8,395
3. Darel Dieringer	Junior Johnson	26	67 Ford	160	5,905
4. David Pearson	Holman-Moody	17	67 Ford	160	3,525
5. Bobby Isaac	Nord Krauskopf	71	67 Dodg	159	1,950

1968 Grand National Race No. 4 Daytona 500
February 25, 1968 Average Speed: 143.251

Driver	Owner	Car #	Make	Laps	Winnings
1. Cale Yarborough	Wood Brothers	21	68 Merc	200	47,250
2. LeeRoy Yarbrough	Junior Johnson	26	68 Merc	200	17,525
3. Bobby Allison	Bondy Long	29	68 Ford	200	10,150
4. Al Unser	Cotton Owens	6	68 Dodg	200	6,250
5. David Pearson	Holman-Moody	17	68 Ford	199	4,750

1968 Grand National Race No. 25 Firecracker 400
July 4, 1968 Average Speed: 167.247

Driver	Owner	Car #	Make	Laps	Winnings
1. Cale Yarborough	Wood Brothers	21	68 Merc	160	15,400
2. LeeRoy Yarbrough	Junior Johnson	98	68 Merc	158	8,545
3. David Pearson	Holman-Moody	17	68 Ford	157	5,730
4. Darel Dieringer	Mario Rossi	22	68 Plym	157	2,975
5. Tiny Lund	Bud Moore	16	68 Merc	157	1,875

1969 Grand National Race No. 4
February 20, 1969 Average Speed: 152.181

Driver	Owner	Car #	Make	Laps	Winnings
1. David Pearson	Holman-Moody	17	69 Ford	50	1,200
2. Cale Yarborough	Wood Brothers	21	69 Merc	50	800
3. Donnie Allison	Banjo Matthews	27	69 Ford	50	550
4. A. J. Foyt	Jack Bowsher	11	69 Ford	49	500
5. Benny Parsons	Russ Dawson	88	69 Ford	49	450

Daytona Int'l Speedway *continued*

1969 Grand National Race No. 5
February 20, 1969 Average Speed: 151.668

Driver	Owner	Car #	Make	Laps	Winnings
1. Bobby Isaac	Nord Krauskopf	71	69 Dodg	50	1,200
2. Charlie Glotzbach	Cotton Owens	6	69 Dodg	50	800
3. Paul Goldsmith	Ray Nichels	99	69 Dodg	50	550
4. Bobby Unser	Smokey Yunick	13	69 Ford	50	500
5. Swede Savage	Wood Brothers	41	68 Merc	50	450

1969 Grand National Race No. 6 Daytona 500
February 23, 1969 Average Speed: 157.950

Driver	Owner	Car #	Make	Laps	Winnings
1. LeeRoy Yarbrough	Junior Johnson	98	69 Ford	200	38,950
2. Charlie Glotzbach	Cotton Owens	6	69 Dodg	200	18,425
3. Donnie Allison	Banjo Matthews	27	69 Ford	199	13,275
4. A. J. Foyt	Jack Bowsher	11	69 Ford	199	5,800
5. Buddy Baker	Ray Fox	3	69 Dodg	198	10,050

1969 Grand National Race No. 28 Firecracker 400
July 4, 1969 Average Speed: 160.875

Driver	Owner	Car #	Make	Laps	Winnings
1. LeeRoy Yarbrough	Junior Johnson	98	69 Ford	160	22,175
2. Buddy Baker	Cotton Owens	6	69 Dodg	160	11,195
3. Donnie Allison	Banjo Matthews	27	69 Ford	159	6,905
4. David Pearson	Holman-Moody	17	69 Ford	156	4,050
5. Richard Petty	Petty Enterprises	43	69 Ford	156	1,950

1970 Grand National Race No. 2
February 19, 1970 Average Speed: 183.295

Driver	Owner	Car #	Make	Laps	Winnings
1. Cale Yarborough	Wood Brothers	21	69 Merc	50	1,300
2. Bobby Isaac	Nord Krauskopf	71	69 Dodg	50	800
3. LeeRoy Yarbrough	Junior Johnson	98	69 Ford	50	550
4. Donnie Allison	Banjo Matthews	27	69 Ford	50	500
5. Pete Hamilton	Petty Enterprises	40	70 Plym	50	450

1970 Grand National Race No. 3
February 19, 1970 Average Speed: 147.734

Driver	Owner	Car #	Make	Laps	Winnings
1. Charlie Glotzbach	Ray Nichels	99	69 Dodg	50	1,300
2. Buddy Baker	Cotton Owens	6	69 Dodg	50	800
3. Bobby Allison	Mario Rossi	22	69 Dodg	50	550
4. Tiny Lund	John McConnell	55	69 Dodg	49	500
5. Richard Brickhouse	Bill Ellis	14	70 Plym	49	450

1970 Grand National Race No. 4 Daytona 500
February 22, 1970 Average Speed: 149.601

Driver	Owner	Car #	Make	Laps	Winnings
1. Pete Hamilton	Petty Enterprises	40	70 Plym	200	44,850
2. David Pearson	Holman-Moody	17	69 Ford	200	17,650
3. Bobby Allison	Mario Rossi	22	69 Dodg	199	9,950
4. Charlie Glotzbach	Ray Nichels	99	69 Dodg	199	5,850
5. Bobby Isaac	Nord Krauskopf	71	69 Dodg	198	4,450

1970 Grand National Race No. 24 Firecracker 400
July 4, 1970 Average Speed: 162.235

Driver	Owner	Car #	Make	Laps	Winnings
1. Donnie Allison	Banjo Matthews	27	69 Ford	160	21,025
2. Buddy Baker	Cotton Owens	6	69 Dodg	160	10,795
3. Bobby Allison	Mario Rossi	22	69 Dodg	160	7,005
4. Charlie Glotzbach	Ray Nichels	99	69 Dodg	159	3,825
5. Dick Brooks	Dick Brooks	32	70 Plym	158	2,500

1971 Winston Cup GN Race No. 2
February 11, 1971 Average Speed: 175.029

Driver	Owner	Car #	Make	Laps	Winnings
1. Pete Hamilton	Cotton Owens	6	71 Plym	50	1,300
2. A. J. Foyt	Wood Brothers	21	69 Merc	50	800
3. Richard Petty	Petty Enterprises	43	71 Plym	50	550
4. LeeRoy Yarbrough	Junior Johnson	98	69 Merc	50	500
5. Fred Lorenzen	Ray Nichels	99	71 Plym	50	450

1971 Winston Cup GN Race No. 3
February 11, 1971 Average Speed: 168.728

Driver	Owner	Car #	Make	Laps	Winnings
1. David Pearson	Holman-Moody	17	69 Merc	50	1,200
2. Buddy Baker	Petty Enterprises	11	71 Dodg	50	800
3. Dick Brooks	Mario Rossi	22	69 Dodg	50	550
4. Bill Dennis	Junie Donlavey	90	69 Merc	50	500
5. Benny Parsons	L. G. DeWitt	72	69 Ford	50	450

1971 Winston Cup GN Race No. 4 Daytona 500
February 14, 1971 Average Speed: 144.462

Driver	Owner	Car #	Make	Laps	Winnings
1. Richard Petty	Petty Enterprises	43	71 Plym	200	45,450
2. Buddy Baker	Petty Enterprises	11	71 Dodg	200	16,100
3. A. J. Foyt	Wood Brothers	21	69 Merc	200	14,500
4. David Pearson	Holman-Moody	17	69 Merc	199	4,225
5. Fred Lorenzen	Ray Nichels	99	71 Plym	199	3,825

1971 Winston Cup GN Race No. 27 Firecracker 400
July 4, 1971 Average Speed: 161.947

Driver	Owner	Car #	Make	Laps	Winnings
1. Bobby Isaac	Nord Krauskopf	71	71 Dodg	160	16,450
2. Richard Petty	Petty Enterprises	43	71 Plym	160	8,825
3. Buddy Baker	Petty Enterprises	11	71 Dodg	160	6,325
4. Pete Hamilton	Cotton Owens	6	71 Plym	160	3,275
5. Donnie Allison	Wood Brothers	21	69 Merc	160	2,200

1972 Winston Cup GN Race No. 2 Daytona 500
February 20, 1972 Average Speed: 161.550

Driver	Owner	Car #	Make	Laps	Winnings
1. A. J. Foyt	Wood Brothers	21	71 Merc	200	45,400
2. Charlie Glotzbach	Cotton Owens	6	71 Dodg	199	16,250
3. Jim Vandiver	O. L. Nixon	31	70 Dodg	194	10,475
4. Benny Parsons	L. G. DeWitt	72	70 Merc	194	7,150
5. James Hylton	James Hylton	48	71 Ford	191	5,925

1972 Winston Cup GN Race No. 17 Firecracker 400
July 4, 1972 Average Speed: 160.821

Driver	Owner	Car #	Make	Laps	Winnings
1. David Pearson	Wood Brothers	21	71 Merc	160	15,650
2. Richard Petty	Petty Enterprises	43	72 Dodg	160	11,725
3. Bobby Allison	R. Howard & J. Johnson	12	72 Chev	160	8,925
4. Coo Coo Marlin	H. B. Cunningham	14	72 Chev	157	4,275
5. James Hylton	James Hylton	48	70 Ford	157	3,600

1973 Winston Cup GN Race No. 2 Daytona 500
February 18, 1973 Average Speed: 157.205

Driver	Owner	Car #	Make	Laps	Winnings
1. Richard Petty	Petty Enterprises	43	73 Dodg	200	36,100
2. Bobby Isaac	Bud Moore	15	73 Ford	198	17,300
3. Dick Brooks	Cotton Owens	6	73 Dodg	197	9,800
4. A. J. Foyt	Banjo Matthews	50	73 Chev	196	7,020
5. Hershel McGriff	Beryl Jackson	04	72 Plym	195	6,025

Daytona Int'l Speedway *continued*

1973 Winston Cup GN Race No. 17 Firecracker 400
July 4, 1973 Average Speed: 158.468

Driver	Owner	Car #	Make	Laps	Winnings
1. David Pearson	Wood Brothers	21	71 Merc	160	16,100
2. Richard Petty	Petty Enterprises	43	73 Dodg	160	11,875
3. Buddy Baker	Nord Krauskopf	71	73 Dodg	156	9,375
4. Gordon Johncock	Hoss Ellington	28	73 Chev	156	4,350
5. Benny Parsons	L. G. DeWitt	72	73 Chev	156	4,200

1974 Winston Cup GN Race No. 16 Firecracker 400
July 4, 1974 Average Speed: 138.310

Driver	Owner	Car #	Make	Laps	Winnings
1. David Pearson	Wood Brothers	21	73 Merc	160	17,350
2. Richard Petty	Petty Enterprises	43	74 Dodg	160	12,825
3. Cale Yarborough	Junior Johnson	11	74 Chev	160	12,187
3. Buddy Baker	Bud Moore	15	73 Ford	160	12,237
5. Bobby Allison	Roger Penske	16	74 Mata	159	4,100

1975 Winston Cup GN Race No. 16 Firecracker 400
July 4, 1975 Average Speed: 158.381

Driver	Owner	Car #	Make	Laps	Winnings
1. Richard Petty	Petty Enterprises	43	74 Dodg	160	19,935
2. Buddy Baker	Bud Moore	15	75 Ford	160	15,635
3. Dave Marcis	Nord Krauskopf	71	74 Dodg	159	11,635
4. Darrell Waltrip	Darrell Waltrip	17	75 Chev	159	8,810
5. Donnie Allison	DiGard	88	75 Chev	158	5,810

1976 Winston Cup GN Race No. 16 Firecracker 400
July 4, 1976 Average Speed: 160.966

Driver	Owner	Car #	Make	Laps	Winnings
1. Cale Yarborough	Junior Johnson	11	Chev	160	22,215
2. David Pearson	Wood Brothers	21	Merc	160	13,615
3. Bobby Allison	Roger Penske	2	Merc	160	13,245
4. A. J. Foyt	Hoss Ellington	28	Chev	159	7,440
5. Dave Marcis	Nord Krauskopf	71	Dodg	157	7,810

1977 Winston Cup GN Race No. 16 Firecracker 400
July 4, 1977 Average Speed: 142.716

Driver	Owner	Car #	Make	Laps	Winnings
1. Richard Petty	Petty Enterprises	43	Dodg	160	23,075
2. Darrell Waltrip	DiGard	88	Chev	160	16,350
3. Benny Parsons	L. G. DeWitt	72	Chev	160	12,300
4. David Pearson	Wood Brothers	21	Merc	160	6,900
5. A. J. Foyt	A. J. Foyt	51	Chev	160	4,700

1978 Winston Cup GN Race No. 16 Firecracker 400
July 4, 1978 Average Speed: 154.340

Driver	Owner	Car #	Make	Laps	Winnings
1. David Pearson	Wood Brothers	21	Merc	160	18,450
2. Cale Yarborough	Junior Johnson	11	Olds	160	18,350
3. Darrell Waltrip	DiGard	88	Chev	159	13,550
4. Richard Petty	Petty Enterprises	43	Dodg	159	10,800
5. Lennie Pond	Harry Ranier	54	Chev	158	7,350

1979 Winston Cup GN Race No. 17 Firecracker 400
July 4, 1979 Average Speed: 172.890

Driver	Owner	Car #	Make	Laps	Winnings
1. Neil Bonnett	Wood Brothers	21	Merc	160	21,705
2. Benny Parsons	M. C. Anderson	27	Olds	160	16,875
3. Dale Earnhardt	Rod Osterlund	2	Olds	160	14,980
4. Darrell Waltrip	DiGard	88	Olds	159	12,280
5. Richard Petty	Petty Enterprises	43	Olds	158	9,480

1974 Winston Cup GN Race No. 2 Daytona 500
February 17, 1974 Average Speed: 140.894

Driver	Owner	Car #	Make	Laps	Winnings
1. Richard Petty	Petty Enterprises	43	74 Dodg	200	39,650
2. Cale Yarborough	R. Howard & J. Johnson	11	74 Chev	200	21,250
3. Ramo Stott	Norris Reed	83	74 Chev	200	11,390
4. Coo Coo Marlin	H. B. Cunningham	14	73 Chev	200	8,350
5. A. J. Foyt	Banjo Matthews	50	74 Chev	199	8,465

1975 Winston Cup GN Race No. 2 Daytona 500
February 16, 1975 Average Speed: 153.649

Driver	Owner	Car #	Make	Laps	Winnings
1. Benny Parsons	L. G. DeWitt	72	75 Chev	200	43,905
2. Bobby Allison	Roger Penske	16	75 Mata	199	26,700
3. Cale Yarborough	Junior Johnson	11	75 Chev	198	21,850
4. David Pearson	Wood Brothers	21	73 Merc	198	18,150
5. Ramo Stott	Norris Reed	83	75 Chev	197	11,650

1976 Winston Cup GN Race No. 2 Daytona 500
February 15, 1976 Average Speed: 152.181

Driver	Owner	Car #	Make	Laps	Winnings
1. David Pearson	Wood Brothers	21	Merc	200	46,800
2. Richard Petty	Petty Enterprises	43	Dodg	199	35,750
3. Benny Parsons	L. G. DeWitt	72	Chev	199	23,680
4. Lennie Pond	Ronnie Elder	54	Chev	198	16,890
5. Neil Bonnett	Neil Bonnett	12	Chev	197	14,000

1977 Winston Cup GN Race No. 2 Daytona 500
February 20, 1977 Average Speed: 153.218

Driver	Owner	Car #	Make	Laps	Winnings
1. Cale Yarborough	Junior Johnson	11	Chev	200	63,700
2. Buddy Baker	Bud Moore	15	Ford	199	28,075
2. Benny Parsons	L. G. DeWitt	72	Chev	200	38,825
4. Coo Coo Marlin	H. B. Cunningham	14	Chev	198	17,825
5. Dick Brooks	Junie Donlavey	90	Ford	198	18,100

1978 Winston Cup GN Race No. 2 Daytona 500
February 19, 1978 Average Speed: 159.730

Driver	Owner	Car #	Make	Laps	Winnings
1. Bobby Allison	Bud Moore	15	Ford	200	56,300
2. Cale Yarborough	Junior Johnson	11	Olds	200	41,900
3. Benny Parsons	L. G. DeWitt	72	Olds	199	31,865
4. Ron Hutcherson	A. J. Foyt	53	Buick	199	22,250
5. Dick Brooks	Junie Donlavey	90	Merc	198	19,925

1979 Winston Cup GN Race No. 2 Daytona 500
February 18, 1979 Average Speed: 143.977

Driver	Owner	Car #	Make	Laps	Winnings
1. Richard Petty	Petty Enterprises	43	Olds	200	73,900
2. Darrell Waltrip	DiGard	88	Olds	200	59,350
3. A. J. Foyt	A. J. Foyt	51	Olds	200	38,550
4. Donnie Allison	Hoss Ellington	1	Olds	199	39,600
5. Cale Yarborough	Junior Johnson	11	Olds	199	34,525

1980 Winston Cup GN Race No. 2 Daytona 500
February 17,1980 Average Speed: 177.602

Driver	Owner	Car #	Make	Laps	Winnings
1. Buddy Baker	Harry Ranier	28	Olds	200	102,175
2. Bobby Allison	Bud Moore	15	Ford	200	54,450
3. Neil Bonnett	Wood Brothers	21	Merc	199	51,100
4. Dale Earnhardt	Rod Osterlund	2	Olds	199	36,350
5. Benny Parsons	M. C. Anderson	27	Olds	197	32,375

Daytona Int'l Speedway *continued*

1980 Winston Cup GN Race No. 17 Firecracker 400
July 4, 1980 Average Speed: 173.473

Driver	Owner	Car #	Make	Laps	Winnings
1. Bobby Allison	Bud Moore	15	Ford	160	24,805
2. David Pearson	Hoss Ellington	1	Olds	160	14,230
3. Dale Earnhardt	Rod Osterlund	2	Chev	160	16,580
4. Buddy Baker	Harry Ranier	28	Olds	160	8,880
5. Richard Petty	Petty Enterprises	43	Olds	160	12,130

1981 Winston Cup GN Race No. 17 Firecracker 400
July 4, 1981 Average Speed: 142.588

Driver	Owner	Car #	Make	Laps	Winnings
1. Cale Yarborough	M. C. Anderson	27	Buick	160	24,625
2. Harry Gant	Hal Needham	33	Buick	160	15,350
3. Richard Petty	Petty Enterprises	43	Buick	160	17,200
4. Buddy Baker	Hoss Ellington	1	Olds	160	8,765
5. Johnny Rutherford	Ron Benfield	98	Pont	160	7,075

1982 Winston Cup GN Race No. 16 Firecracker 400
July 4, 1982 Average Speed: 163.099

Driver	Owner	Car #	Make	Laps	Winnings
1. Bobby Allison	DiGard	88	Buick	160	42,100
2. Bill Elliott	Harry Melling	9	Ford	160	21,800
3. Ron Bouchard	Jack Beebe	47	Buick	160	22,500
4. Morgan Shepherd	Ron Benfield	98	Buick	160	13,030
5. David Pearson	Bobby Hawkins	03	Buick	160	8,190

1983 Winston Cup GN Race No. 16 Firecracker 400
July 4, 1983 Average Speed: 167.442

Driver	Owner	Car #	Make	Laps	Winnings
1. Buddy Baker	Wood Brothers	21	Ford	160	32,950
2. Morgan Shepherd	Jim Stacy	2	Buick	160	27,175
3. David Pearson	Bobby Hawkins	16	Chev	160	13,275
4. Ron Bouchard	Jack Beebe	47	Buick	160	13,380
5. Terry Labonte	Billy Hagan	44	Chev	160	13,545

1984 Winston Cup GN Race No. 16 Pepsi Firecracker 400
July 4, 1984 Average Speed: 171.204

Driver	Owner	Car #	Make	Laps	Winnings
1. Richard Petty	Mike Curb	43	Pont	160	43,755
2. Harry Gant	Hal Needham	33	Chev	160	25,570
3. Cale Yarborough	Harry Ranier	28	Chev	160	23,640
4. Bobby Allison	DiGard	22	Buick	160	21,850
5. Benny Parsons	Johnny Hayes	55	Chev	160	10,450

1985 Winston Cup GN Race No. 15 Pepsi Firecracker 400
July 4, 1985 Average Speed: 158.730

Driver	Owner	Car #	Make	Laps	Winnings
1. Greg Sacks	DiGard	10	Chev	160	45,350
2. Bill Elliott	Harry Melling	9	Ford	160	41,900
3. Darrell Waltrip	Junior Johnson	11	Chev	160	26,100
4. Ron Bouchard	Jack Beebe	47	Buick	160	16,730
5. Kyle Petty	Wood Brothers	7	Ford	160	15,570

1986 Winston Cup Race No. 15 Pepsi Firecracker 400
July 4, 1986 Average Speed: 131.916

Driver	Owner	Car #	Make	Laps	Winnings
1. Tim Richmond	Rick Hendrick	25	Chev	160	58,655
2. Sterling Marlin	Hoss Ellington	1	Chev	160	37,700
3. Bobby Hillin Jr.	Stavola Brothers	8	Buick	160	24,545
4. Darrell Waltrip	Junior Johnson	11	Chev	160	24,750
5. Kyle Petty	Wood Brothers	7	Ford	160	19,725

1981 Winston Cup GN Race No. 2 Daytona 500
February 15, 1981 Average Speed: 169.651

Driver	Owner	Car #	Make	Laps	Winnings
1. Richard Petty	Petty Enterprises	43	Buick	200	90,575
2. Bobby Allison	Harry Ranier	28	Pont	200	84,050
3. Ricky Rudd	DiGard	88	Olds	200	53,115
4. Buddy Baker	Hoss Ellington	1	Olds	200	35,740
5. Dale Earnhardt	Rod Osterlund	2	Pont	200	37,365

1982 Winston Cup GN Race No. 1 Daytona 500
February 14, 1982 Average Speed: 153.991

Driver	Owner	Car #	Make	Laps	Winnings
1. Bobby Allison	DiGard	88	Buick	200	120,630
2. Cale Yarborough	M. C. Anderson	27	Buick	200	70,725
3. Joe Ruttman	Jim Stacy	2	Buick	200	54,820
4. Terry Labonte	Billy Hagan	44	Buick	199	51,975
5. Bill Elliott	Harry Melling	9	Ford	198	36,125

1983 Winston Cup GN Race No. 1 Daytona 500
February 20, 1983 Average Speed: 155.979

Driver	Owner	Car #	Make	Laps	Winnings
1. Cale Yarborough	Harry Ranier	28	Pont	200	119,600
2. Bill Elliott	Harry Melling	9	Ford	200	66,425
3. Buddy Baker	Wood Brothers	21	Ford	200	59,650
4. Joe Ruttman	Ron Benfield	98	Chev	200	55,980
5. Dick Brooks	Junie Donlavey	90	Ford	199	44,545

1984 Winston Cup GN Race No. 1 Daytona 500
February 19, 1984 Average Speed: 150.994

Driver	Owner	Car #	Make	Laps	Winnings
1. Cale Yarborough	Harry Ranier	28	Chev	200	160,300
2. Dale Earnhardt	Richard Childress	3	Chev	200	81,825
3. Darrell Waltrip	Junior Johnson	11	Chev	200	68,650
4. Neil Bonnett	Junior Johnson	12	Chev	200	50,000
5. Bill Elliott	Harry Melling	9	Ford	200	58,700

1985 Winston Cup GN Race No. 1 Daytona 500
February 17, 1985 Average Speed: 172.265

Driver	Owner	Car #	Make	Laps	Winnings
1. Bill Elliott	Harry Melling	9	Ford	200	185,500
2. Lake Speed	Bob Rahilly & Butch Mock	75	Pont	200	85,705
3. Darrell Waltrip	Junior Johnson	11	Chev	199	79,350
4. Buddy Baker	Buddy Baker & Danny Schiff	88	Olds	199	53,075
5. Ricky Rudd	Bud Moore	15	Ford	199	52,900

1986 Winston Cup Race No. 1 Daytona 500
February 16, 1986 Average Speed: 148.124

Driver	Owner	Car #	Make	Laps	Winnings
1. Geoff Bodine	Rick Hendrick	5	Chev	200	192,715
2. Terry Labonte	Billy Hagan	44	Olds	200	103,240
3. Darrell Waltrip	Junior Johnson	11	Chev	200	80,515
4. Bobby Hillin Jr.	Stavola Brothers	8	Chev	200	58,975
5. Benny Parsons	Richard Jackson	55	Olds	199	47,415

1987 Winston Cup Race No. 1 Daytona 500
February 15, 1987 Average Speed: 176.263

Driver	Owner	Car #	Make	Laps	Winnings
1. Bill Elliott	Harry Melling	9	Ford	200	204,150
2. Benny Parsons	Rick Hendrick	35	Chev	200	122,420
3. Richard Petty	Petty Enterprises	43	Pont	200	76,040
4. Buddy Baker	Buddy Baker & Danny Schiff	88	Olds	200	74,450
5. Dale Earnhardt	Richard Childress	3	Chev	200	64,925

Daytona Int'l Speedway *continued*

1987 Winston Cup Race No. 15 Pepsi Firecracker 400
July 4, 1987 Average Speed: 161.074

Driver	Owner	Car #	Make	Laps	Winnings
1. Bobby Allison	Stavola Brothers	22	Buick	160	57,375
2. Buddy Baker	Buddy Baker & Danny Schiff	88	Olds	160	30,800
3. Dave Marcis	Dave Marcis	71	Chev	160	27,805
4. Darrell Waltrip	Rick Hendrick	17	Chev	160	17,470
5. Morgan Shepherd	Kenny Bernstein	26	Buick	160	17,130

1988 Winston Cup Race No. 15 Pepsi Firecracker 400
July 2, 1988 Average Speed: 163.302

Driver	Owner	Car #	Make	Laps	Winnings
1. Bill Elliott	Harry Melling	9	Ford	160	63,500
2. Rick Wilson	Larry McClure	4	Olds	160	45,825
3. Phil Parsons	Richard Jackson	55	Olds	160	22,250
4. Dale Earnhardt	Richard Childress	3	Chev	160	22,825
5. Darrell Waltrip	Rick Hendrick	17	Chev	160	25,430

1989 Winston Cup Race No. 15 Pepsi 400
July 1, 1989 Average Speed: 132.207

Driver	Owner	Car #	Make	Laps	Winnings
1. Davey Allison	Robert Yates	28	Ford	160	65,000
2. Morgan Shepherd	Bob Rahilly & Butch Mock	75	Pont	160	39,975
3. Phil Parsons	Richard Jackson	55	Olds	160	27,700
4. Bill Elliott	Harry Melling	9	Ford	160	27,750
5. Alan Kulwicki	Alan Kulwicki	7	Ford	160	19,855

1990 Winston Cup Series Race No. 15 Pepsi 400
July 7, 1990 Average Speed: 160.000

Driver	Owner	Car #	Make	Laps	Winnings
1. Dale Earnhardt	Richard Childress	3	Chev	160	72,850
2. Alan Kulwicki	Alan Kulwicki	7	Ford	160	38,700
3. Ken Schrader	Rick Hendrick	25	Chev	160	31,400
4. Terry Labonte	Richard Jackson	1	Olds	160	23,450
5. Sterling Marlin	Billy Hagan	94	Olds	160	21,250

1991 Winston Cup Series Race No. 15 Pepsi 400
July 6, 1991 Average Speed: 159.116

Driver	Owner	Car #	Make	Laps	Winnings
1. Bill Elliott	Harry Melling	9	Ford	160	75,000
2. Geoff Bodine	Junior Johnson	11	Ford	160	48,325
3. Davey Allison	Robert Yates	28	Ford	160	36,950
4. Ken Schrader	Rick Hendrick	25	Chev	160	27,450
5. Ernie Irvan	Larry McClure	4	Chev	160	36,525

1992 Winston Cup Race No. 15 Pepsi 400
July 4, 1992 Average Speed: 170.457

Driver	Owner	Car #	Make	Laps	Winnings
1. Ernie Irvan	Larry McClure	4	Chev	160	86,300
2. Sterling Marlin	Junior Johnson	22	Ford	160	50,025
3. Dale Jarrett	Joe Gibbs	18	Chev	160	37,200
4. Geoff Bodine	Bud Moore	15	Ford	160	26,075
5. Bill Elliott	Junior Johnson	11	Ford	160	26,500

1993 Winston Cup Series Race No. 15 Pepsi 400
July 3, 1993 Average Speed: 151.755

Driver	Owner	Car #	Make	Laps	Winnings
1. Dale Earnhardt	Richard Childress	3	Chev	160	75,940
2. Sterling Marlin	Stavola Brothers	8	Ford	160	46,000
3. Ken Schrader	Rick Hendrick	25	Chev	160	37,125
4. Ricky Rudd	Rick Hendrick	5	Chev	160	28,250
5. Jeff Gordon	Rick Hendrick	24	Chev	160	24,625

1988 Winston Cup Race No. 1 Daytona 500
February 14, 1988 Average Speed: 137.531

Driver	Owner	Car #	Make	Laps	Winnings
1. Bobby Allison	Stavola Brothers	12	Buick	200	202,940
2. Davey Allison	Harry Ranier	28	Ford	200	113,760
3. Phil Parsons	Richard Jackson	55	Olds	200	81,625
4. Neil Bonnett	Bob Rahilly & Butch Mock	75	Pont	200	67,290
5. Terry Labonte	Junior Johnson	11	Chev	200	62,415

1989 Winston Cup Race No. 1 Daytona 500
February 19, 1989 Average Speed: 148.466

Driver	Owner	Car #	Make	Laps	Winnings
1. Darrell Waltrip	Rick Hendrick	17	Chev	200	184,900
2. Ken Schrader	Rick Hendrick	25	Chev	200	182,700
3. Dale Earnhardt	Richard Childress	3	Chev	200	95,550
4. Geoff Bodine	Rick Hendrick	5	Chev	200	79,250
5. Phil Parsons	Richard Jackson	55	Olds	200	70,325

1990 Winston Cup Series Race No. 1 Daytona 500
February 18, 1990 Average Speed: 165.761

Driver	Owner	Car #	Make	Laps	Winnings
1. Derrike Cope	Bob Whitcomb	10	Chev	200	188,150
2. Terry Labonte	Richard Jackson	1	Olds	200	117,800
3. Bill Elliott	Harry Melling	9	Ford	200	114,100
4. Ricky Rudd	Rick Hendrick	5	Chev	200	77,050
5. Dale Earnhardt	Richard Childress	3	Chev	200	109,325

1991 Winston Cup Series Race No. 1 Daytona 500
February 19, 1991 Average Speed: 148.148

Driver	Owner	Car #	Make	Laps	Winnings
1. Ernie Irvan	Larry McClure	4	Chev	200	233,000
2. Sterling Marlin	Junior Johnson	22	Ford	200	133,925
3. Joe Ruttman	Bob Rahilly & Butch Mock	75	Olds	200	111,450
4. Rick Mast	Richard Jackson	1	Olds	200	100,900
5. Dale Earnhardt	Richard Childress	3	Chev	200	113,850

1992 Winston Cup Race No. 1 Daytona 500
February 16, 1992 Average Speed: 160.256

Driver	Owner	Car #	Make	Laps	Winnings
1. Davey Allison	Robert Yates	28	Ford	200	244,050
2. Morgan Shepherd	Wood Brothers	21	Ford	200	161,300
3. Geoff Bodine	Bud Moore	15	Ford	200	116,250
4. Alan Kulwicki	Alan Kulwicki	7	Ford	200	87,500
5. Dick Trickle	Butch Mock	75	Olds	200	78,800

1993 Winston Cup Series Race No. 1 Daytona 500
February 14, 1993 Average Speed: 154.972

Driver	Owner	Car #	Make	Laps	Winnings
1. Dale Jarrett	Joe Gibbs	18	Chev	200	238,200
2. Dale Earnhardt	Richard Childress	3	Chev	200	181,825
3. Geoff Bodine	Bud Moore	15	Ford	200	141,450
4. Hut Stricklin	Junior Johnson	27	Ford	200	95,950
5. Jeff Gordon	Rick Hendrick	24	Chev	200	111,150

1994 Winston Cup Series Race No. 1 Daytona 500
February 20, 1994 Average Speed: 156.931

Driver	Owner	Car #	Make	Laps	Winnings
1. Sterling Marlin	Larry McClure	4	Chev	200	253,275
2. Ernie Irvan	Robert Yates	28	Ford	200	190,750
3. Terry Labonte	Rick Hendrick	5	Chev	200	138,475
4. Jeff Gordon	Rick Hendrick	24	Chev	200	112,525
5. Morgan Shepherd	Wood Brothers	21	Ford	200	92,805

Daytona Int'l Speedway *continued*

1994 Winston Cup Series Race No. 15 Pepsi 400
July 2, 1994 Average Speed: 155.558

Driver	Owner	Car #	Make	Laps	Winnings
1. Jimmy Spencer	Junior Johnson	27	Ford	160	75,880
2. Ernie Irvan	Robert Yates	28	Ford	160	50,275
3. Dale Earnhardt	Richard Childress	3	Chev	160	50,050
4. Mark Martin	Jack Roush	6	Ford	160	36,575
5. Ken Schrader	Rick Hendrick	25	Chev	160	30,150

1995 Winston Cup Series Race No. 1 Daytona 500
February 19, 1995 Average Speed: 141.710

Driver	Owner	Car #	Make	Laps	Winnings
1. Sterling Marlin	Larry McClure	4	Chev	200	300,460
2. Dale Earnhardt	Richard Childress	3	Chev	200	212,250
3. Mark Martin	Jack Roush	6	Ford	200	153,700
4. Ted Musgrave	Jack Roush	16	Ford	200	111,200
5. Dale Jarrett	Robert Yates	28	Ford	200	119,855

1995 Winston Cup Series Race No. 15 Pepsi 400
July 1, 1995 Average Speed: 166.976

Driver	Owner	Car #	Make	Laps	Winnings
1. Jeff Gordon	Rick Hendrick	24	Chev	160	96,580
2. Sterling Marlin	Larry McClure	4	Chev	160	63,450
3. Dale Earnhardt	Richard Childress	3	Chev	160	66,200
4. Mark Martin	Jack Roush	6	Ford	160	43,225
5. Ted Musgrave	Jack Roush	16	Ford	160	39,075

1996 Winston Cup Series Race No. 1 Daytona 500
February 18, 1996 Average Speed: 154.308

Driver	Owner	Car #	Make	Laps	Winnings
1. Dale Jarrett	Robert Yates	88	Ford	200	360,775
2. Dale Earnhardt	Richard Childress	3	Chev	200	215,065
3. Ken Schrader	Rick Hendrick	25	Chev	200	169,547
4. Mark Martin	Jack Roush	6	Ford	200	118,840
5. Jeff Burton	Jack Roush	99	Ford	200	91,702

1996 Winston Cup Series Race No. 15 Pepsi 400
July 6, 1996 Average Speed: 161.602

Driver	Owner	Car #	Make	Laps	Winnings
1. Sterling Marlin	Larry McClure	4	Chev	117	106,565
2. Terry Labonte	Rick Hendrick	5	Chev	117	63,335
3. Jeff Gordon	Rick Hendrick	24	Chev	117	63,735
4. Dale Earnhardt	Richard Childress	3	Chev	117	97,960
5. Ernie Irvan	Robert Yates	28	Ford	117	44,210

1997 Winston Cup Series Race No. 1
February 16, 1997 Average Speed: 148.295

Driver	Owner	Car #	Make	Laps	Winnings
1. Jeff Gordon	Rick Hendrick	24	Chev	200	377,410
2. Terry Labonte	Rick Hendrick	5	Chev	200	194,925
3. Ricky Craven	Rick Hendrick	25	Chev	200	155,625
4. Bill Elliott	Bill Elliott	94	Ford	200	133,200
5. Sterling Marlin	Larry McClure	4	Chev	200	121,080

1997 Winston Cup Series Race No. 16
July 5, 1997 Average Speed: 157.791

Driver	Owner	Car #	Make	Laps	Winnings
1. John Andretti	Cale Yarborough	98	Ford	160	109,525
2. Terry Labonte	Rick Hendrick	5	Chev	160	74,975
3. Sterling Marlin	Larry McClure	4	Chev	160	53,775
4. Dale Earnhardt	Richard Childress	3	Chev	160	52,475
5. Dale Jarrett	Robert Yates	88	Ford	160	45,975

1998 Winston Cup Series Race No. 1
February 15, 1998 Average Speed: 172.712

Driver	Owner	Car #	Make	Laps	Winnings
1. Dale Earnhardt	Richard Childress	3	Chev	200	1,079,533
2. Bobby Labonte	Joe Gibbs	18	Pont	200	548,555
3. Jeremy Mayfield	Michael Kranefuss	12	Ford	200	375,005
4. Ken Schrader	Andy Petree	33	Chev	200	312,780
5. Rusty Wallace	Roger Penske	2	Ford	200	232,005

1998 Winston Cup Series Race No. 30
October 17, 1998 Average Speed: 144.549

Driver	Owner	Car #	Make	Laps	Winnings
1. Jeff Gordon	Rick Hendrick	24	Chev	160	184,325
2. Bobby Labonte	Joe Gibbs	18	Pont	160	98,825
3. Mike Skinner	Richard Childress	31	Chev	160	71,475
4. Jeremy Mayfield	Michael Kranefuss	12	Ford	160	62,325
5. Rusty Wallace	Roger Penske	2	Ford	160	59,175

1999 Winston Cup Series Race No. 1
February 14, 1999 Average Speed: 161.551

Driver	Owner	Car #	Make	Laps	Winnings
1. Jeff Gordon	Rick Hendrick	24	Chev	200	1,172,246
2. Dale Earnhardt	Richard Childress	3	Chev	200	613,659
3. Kenny Irwin, Jr.	Robert Yates	28	Ford	200	440,584
4. Mike Skinner	Richard Childress	31	Chev	200	350,634
5. Michael Waltrip	Jim Mattei	7	Chev	200	290,596

1999 Winston Cup Series Race No. 17
July 3, 1999 Average Speed: 169.213

Driver	Owner	Car #	Make	Laps	Winnings
1. Dale Jarrett	Robert Yates	88	Ford	160	164,955
2. Dale Earnhardt	Richard Childress	3	Chev	160	92,175
3. Jeff Burton	Jack Roush	99	Ford	160	93,775
4. Mike Skinner	Richard Childress	31	Chev	160	79,825
5. Bobby Labonte	Joe Gibbs	18	Pont	160	71,890

2000 Winston Cup Series Race No. 1
February 20, 2000 Average Speed: 155.669

Driver	Owner	Car #	Make	Laps	Winnings
1. Dale Jarrett	Robert Yates	88	Ford	200	2,277,975
2. Jeff Burton	Jack Roush	99	Ford	200	840,825
3. Bill Elliott	Bill Elliott	94	Ford	200	528,475
4. Rusty Wallace	Roger Penske	2	Ford	200	420,775
5. Mark Martin	Jack Roush	6	Ford	200	326,175

2000 Winston Cup Series Race No. 17
July 1, 2000 Average Speed: 148.576

Driver	Owner	Car #	Make	Laps	Winnings
1. Jeff Burton	Jack Roush	99	Ford	160	152,450
2. Dale Jarrett	Robert Yates	88	Ford	160	126,350
3. Rusty Wallace	Roger Penske	2	Ford	160	88,750
4. Mark Martin	Jack Roush	6	Ford	160	83,650
5. Ricky Rudd	Robert Yates	28	Ford	160	79,900

2001 Winston Cup Series Race No. 1
February 18, 2001 Average Speed: 161.783

Driver	Owner	Car #	Make	Laps	Winnings
1. Michael Waltrip	Dale Earnhardt, Inc.	15	Chev	200	1,331,185
2. Dale Earnhardt, Jr.	Dale Earnhardt, Inc.	8	Chev	200	975,907
3. Rusty Wallace	Roger Penske	2	Ford	200	676,224
4. Ricky Rudd	Robert Yates	28	Ford	200	517,831
5. Bill Elliott	Ray Evernham	9	Dodg	200	392,582

Daytona Int'l Speedway *continued*

2001 Winston Cup Series Race No. 17
July 7, 2001 Average Speed: 157.601

Driver	Owner	Car #	Make	Laps	Winnings
1. Dale Earnhardt, Jr.	Dale Earnhardt, Inc.	8	Chev	160	185,873
2. Michael Waltrip	Dale Earnhardt, Inc.	15	Chev	160	108,850
3. Elliott Sadler	Wood Brothers	21	Ford	160	112,610
4. Ward Burton	Bill Davis	22	Dodg	160	123,285
5. Bobby Labonte	Joe Gibbs	18	Pont	160	127,777

2002 Winston Cup Series Race No. 1
February 17, 2002 Average Speed: 130.81

Driver	Owner	Car #	Make	Laps	Winnings
1. Ward Burton	Bill Davis	22	Dodg	200	1,383,017
2. Elliott Sadler	Wood Brothers	21	Ford	200	957,037
3. Geoffrey Bodine	James Finch	09	Ford	200	644,187
4. Kurt Busch	Jack Roush	97	Ford	200	499,462
5. Michael Waltrip	Dale Earnhardt, Inc.	15	Chev	200	409,159

2002 Winston Cup Series Race No. 17
July 7, 2002 Average Speed: 135.952

Driver	Owner	Car #	Make	Laps	Winnings
1. Michael Waltrip	Dale Earnhardt, Inc.	15	Chev	160	172,975
2. Rusty Wallace	Roger Penske	2	Ford	160	151,350
3. Sterling Marlin	Chip Ganassi	40	Dodg	160	158,292
4. Jimmy Spencer	Chip Ganassi	41	Dodg	160	109,575
5. Mark Martin	Jack Roush	6	Ford	160	117,883

Five Flags Speedway
Pensacola, FL
Half-mile Dirt Track

Half-mile dirt oval opened in May 1953. Only NASCAR Winston Cup (then Grand National) event run on 6/14/53 (won by Herb Thomas). Track is currently the site of the Snowball Derby.

Winston Cup Victories
Herb Thomas   1

Winston Cup Money
Herb Thomas $1,000

Most Cars Started
18—June 14, 1953

Narrowest Margin of Victory
N/A

Race Record
63.316 MPH—June 14, 1953

Most Race Leaders
N/A

Most Cars Running at Finish
N/A

1953 Grand National Race No. 15
June 14, 1953 Average Speed: 63.316

Driver	Owner	Car #	Make	Laps	Winnings
1. Herb Thomas	Herb Thomas	92	53 Huds	140	1,000
2. Dick Rathmann	Walt Chapman	120	53 Huds	—	900
3. Lee Petty	Petty Enterprises	42	53 Dodg	—	450
4. Buck Baker	Griffin Motors	87	53 Olds	—	350
5. Tim Flock	Ted Chester	91	53 Huds	—	200

Golden Gate Speedway
Tampa, FL
.333-mile Dirt Track

Located on the Northeast side of town. The .333 mile track opened in May of 1962. Only NASCAR Winston Cup (then Grand National) race staged on 11/11/62 (won by Richard Petty). Track closed in 1978 and re-opened in 1981. Closed for good in 1984.

Winston Cup Victories
Richard Petty   1

Winston Cup Poles
Rex White   1

Winston Cup Money
Richard Petty $780

Most Cars Started
24—November 11, 1962

Narrowest Margin of Victory
1 car length—November 11, 1962

Race Record
57.167 MPH—November 11, 1962

Most Cautions
2—November 11, 1962

Most Race Leaders
3—November 11, 1962

Most Cars Running at Finish
18—November 11, 1962

1963 Grand National Race No. 2
November 11, 1962 Average Speed: 57.167

Driver	Owner	Car #	Make	Laps	Winnings
1. Richard Petty	Petty Enterprises	43	62 Plym	200	780
2. Jim Paschal	Petty Enterprises	41	62 Plym	200	490
3. Joe Weatherly	Bud Moore	8	62 Pont	200	580
4. Jimmy Pardue	Jimmy Pardue	54	62 Pont	199	275
5. Tommy Irwin	Wood Brothers	21	62 Ford	198	240

Homestead-Miami Speedway
Homestead, FL
1.5-mile Superspeedway

Mile-and-a-half speedway originally opened in November, 1995. Built by Ralph Sanchez and originally named Metro Dade Homestead Motorsports Complex. First race was a NASCAR Busch Series event on November 5, 1995, won by Dale Jarrett. Original track configuration was a rounded rectangle, similar to Indianapolis Motor Speedway. Track was sold to International Speedway Corp., which opened the doors for a Winston Cup event. Turns were re-shaped in 1998 to a more conventional oval, with further adjustments in banking scheduled for 2003. First Winston Cup race run on November 14, 1999, won by rookie Tony Stewart. Track hosts a variety of motorsports events, including open wheel Indy Cars and Sports Cars on the infield road course.

Winston Cup Starts		**Winston Cup Money**		**Narrowest Margin of Victory**		**Most Cautions**	
21 drivers tied at	4	Tony Stewart	$717,493	1.420 seconds—November 11, 2001		6—2 times	

Winston Cup Victories		**Most Cars Started**		**Slowest Race**		**Most Race Leaders**	
Tony Stewart	2	43—4 times		116.462 MPH—November 17, 200		10—November 14, 1999	

Winston Cup Poles		**Fewest Cars Started**		**Race Record**		**Most Cars Running at Finish**	
Bill Elliott	1	43—4 times		140.335 MPH—November 14, 1999		42—November 11, 2001	

1999 Winston Cup Series Race No. 33
November 14, 1999 Average Speed: 140.335

Driver	Owner	Car #	Make	Laps	Winnings
1. Tony Stewart	Joe Gibbs	20	Pont	267	278,265
2. Bobby Labonte	Joe Gibbs	18	Pont	267	214,675
3. Jeff Burton	Jack Roush	99	Ford	267	164,100
4. Mark Martin	Jack Roush	6	Ford	267	116,200
5. Dale Jarrett	Robert Yates	88	Ford	267	100,865

2000 Winston Cup Series Race No. 33
November 12, 2000 Average Speed: 127.48

Driver	Owner	Car #	Make	Laps	Winnings
1. Tony Stewart	Joe Gibbs	20	Pont	267	291,325
2. Jeremy Mayfield	Michael Kranefuss	12	Ford	267	206,825
3. Mark Martin	Jack Roush	6	Ford	267	161,625
4. Bobby Labonte	Joe Gibbs	18	Pont	267	129,575
5. Jimmy Spencer	Travis Carter	26	Ford	267	105,575

2001 Winston Cup Series Race No. 34
November 11, 2001 Average Speed: 117.449

Driver	Owner	Car #	Make	Laps	Winnings
1. Bill Elliott	Ray Evernham	9	Dodg	267	319,273
2. Michael Waltrip	Dale Earnhardt, Inc.	15	Chev	267	201,925
3. Casey Atwood	Ray Evernham	19	Dodg	267	155,825
4. Jeff Burton	Jack Roush	99	Ford	267	149,371
5. Sterling Marlin	Chip Ganassi	40	Dodg	267	115,585

2002 Winston Cup Series Race No. 36
November 17, 2002 Average Speed: 116.462

Driver	Owner	Car #	Make	Laps	Winnings
1. Kurt Busch	Jack Roush	97	Ford	267	297,100
2. Joe Nemechek	Rick Hendrick	25	Chev	267	221,875
3. Jeff Burton	Jack Roush	99	Ford	267	195,342
4. Mark Martin	Jack Roush	6	Ford	267	148,083
5. Jeff Gordon	Rick Hendrick	24	Chev	267	152,278

Jacksonville Speedway Park
Jacksonville, FL
Half-mile Dirt Track

(aka Speedway Park) Half-mile dirt track opened in March 1947. First NASCAR Winston Cup (then Grand National) race held on 11/4/51 (won by Herb Thomas). Final big NASCAR race was staged on 12/1/63 (won by Wendell Scott, the only win by an African-American driver in the history of big-league NASCAR racing), and was included on 1964 championship season schedule. Track closed in 1973.

Winston Cup Starts
Buck Baker 5
Lee Petty 5

Winston Cup Victories
Lee Petty 2
Herb Thomas 2

Winston Cup Poles
Junior Johnson 1
Dick Rathmann 1
Jack Smith 1
Marshall Teague 1
Herb Thomas 1
Curtis Turner 1

Winston Cup Money
Herb Thomas $3,150

Most Cars Started
29—March 6, 1952

Fewest Cars Started
19—February 13, 1955

Narrowest Margin of Victory
N/A

Slowest Race
53.412 MPH—November 4, 1951

Race Record
69.031 MPH—February 13, 1955

Most Cautions
5—December 1, 1963

Most Race Leaders
4—November 20, 1960
4—December 1, 1963

Most Cars Running at Finish
N/A

1951 Grand National Race No. 38
November 4, 1951 Average Speed: 53.412

Driver	Owner	Car #	Make	Laps	Winnings
1. Herb Thomas	Marshall Teague	6	51 Huds	200	1,000
2. Jack Smith	Jack Smith	44	51 Huds	—	600
3. Fonty Flock	Frank Christian	14	51 Olds	—	500
4. Bill Snowden	Bill Snowden	16	51 Ford	—	400
5. Frank Mundy	Perry Smith	23	51 Stud	—	300

1952 Grand National Race No. 3
March 6, 1952 Average Speed: 55.197

Driver	Owner	Car #	Make	Laps	Winnings
1. Marshall Teague	Marshall Teague	6	52 Huds	200	1,000
2. Herb Thomas	Marshall Teague	4	52 Huds	200	700
3. Frankie Schneider		88	51 Olds	200	450
4. Tim Flock	Ted Chester	91	51 Huds	—	350
5. Tommy Moon	C. D. Wilson	157	51 Huds	—	200

1954 Grand National Race No. 3
March 7, 1954 Average Speed: 56.461

Driver	Owner	Car #	Make	Laps	Winnings
1. Herb Thomas	Herb Thomas	92	53 Huds	200	1,000
2. Fonty Flock	Frank Christian	14	53 Huds	198	650
3. Lee Petty	Petty Enterprises	42	54 Dodg	197	450
4. Joe Eubanks	Phil Oates	82	51 Huds	197	350
5. Buck Baker	Griffin Motors	87	53 Olds	194	300

1955 Grand National Race No. 3
February 13, 1955 Average Speed: 69.031

Driver	Owner	Car #	Make	Laps	Winnings
1. Lee Petty	Petty Enterprises	42	54 Chrys	200	1,000
2. Dick Rathmann	John Ditz	3	54 Huds	200	650
3. Herb Thomas	Herb Thomas	92	54 Huds	200	450
4. Buck Baker	Griffin Motors	87	54 Olds	194	350
5. Junior Johnson	B & L Motors	55	55 Olds	191	300

1961 Grand National Race No. 2
November 20, 1960 Average Speed: 64.400

Driver	Owner	Car #	Make	Laps	Winnings
1. Lee Petty	Petty Enterprises	42	60 Plym	200	800
2. Tommy Irwin	Tom Daniels	2	60 Chev	199	525
3. Rex White	Rex White	4	59 Chev	198	475
4. Richard Petty	Petty Enterprises	43	60 Plym	197	275
5. Doug Yates	Raeford Johnson	23	59 Plym	194	250

1964 Grand National Race No. 3
December 1, 1963 Average Speed: 58.252

Driver	Owner	Car #	Make	Laps	Winnings
1. Wendell Scott	Wendell Scott	34	62 Chev	202	1,000
2. Buck Baker	Buck Baker	87	63 Pont	200	600
3. Jack Smith	Jack Smith	47	63 Plym	199	400
4. Ed Livingston	Ed Livingston	68	62 Ford	195	300
5. Richard Petty	Petty Enterprises	42	63 Plym	193	275

Palm Beach Speedway
West Palm Beach, FL
Half-mile Dirt Track

(aka West Palm Beach Speedway; West Palm Beach Fairgrounds; South Florida Fairgrounds Speedway; Palm Beach County Fairgrounds; Southland Speedway) Half-mile dirt oval built in 1949. First NASCAR Winston Cup (then Grand National) race staged on 1/20/52 (won by Tim Flock). Final race staged on 3/4/56 (won by Billy Myers). Track paved in 1955, and torn down in 1984.

Winston Cup Starts		**Winston Cup Money**		**Narrowest Margin of Victory**		**Most Cautions**	
Lee Petty	7	Herb Thomas	$5,150	3 car lengths—February 6, 1955		2—January 20, 1952	

Winston Cup Victories — Herb Thomas 4
Most Cars Started — 30—March 4, 1956
Slowest Race — 56.013 MPH—February 6, 1955
Most Race Leaders — 4—February 7, 1954

Winston Cup Poles — Dick Rathmann 3
Fewest Cars Started — 16—February 6, 1955
Race Record — 68.990 MPH—March 4, 1956
Most Cars Running at Finish — 19—March 4, 1956

1952 Grand National Race No. 1
January 20, 1952

Driver	Owner	Car #	Make	Laps	Winnings
1. Tim Flock	Ted Chester	91	51 Huds	200	1,025
2. Lee Petty	Petty Enterprises	42	51 Plym	—	700
3. Fonty Flock	Frank Christian	14	51 Olds	—	450
4. Frankie Schneider		88	51 Olds	—	360
5. Buddy Shuman	Buddy Shuman	17	51 Ford	—	210

1952 Grand National Race No. 34
November 30, 1952 Average Speed: 58.008

Driver	Owner	Car #	Make	Laps	Winnings
1. Herb Thomas	Herb Thomas	92	52 Huds	200	1,000
2. Fonty Flock	Frank Christian	14	52 Olds	198	700
3. Perk Brown	R. G. Shelton	22	52 Huds	196	450
4. Lee Petty	Petty Enterprises	42	51 Plym	194	350
5. Marion Edwards			50 Dodg	183	200

1953 Grand National Race No. 1
February 1, 1953 Average Speed: 60.220

Driver	Owner	Car #	Make	Laps	Winnings
1. Lee Petty	Petty Enterprises	42	53 Dodg	200	1,000
2. Jimmie Lewallen	Petty Enterprises	41	52 Plym	198	700
3. Tim Flock	Ted Chester	91	52 Huds	197	450
4. Herschel Buchanan	Herschel Buchanan	1	52 Nash	192	350
5. Don Oldenberg	Bill House	86	53 Linc	186	200

1954 Grand National Race No. 1
February 7, 1954 Average Speed: 58.938

Driver	Owner	Car #	Make	Laps	Winnings
1. Herb Thomas	Herb Thomas	92	53 Huds	200	1,600
2. Buck Baker	Griffin Motors	87	53 Olds	198	1,050
3. Lee Petty	Petty Enterprises	42	54 Dodg	198	750
4. Jim Paschal	George Hutchens	80	54 Dodg	196	350
5. Ray Duhigg	J. O. Goode	24	50 Plym	190	300

1955 Grand National Race No. 2
February 6, 1955 Average Speed: 56.013

Driver	Owner	Car #	Make	Laps	Winnings
1. Herb Thomas	Herb Thomas	92	54 Huds	200	1,000
2. Jack Choquette	George Miller	23	54 Huds	200	650
3. Buck Baker	Griffin Motors	87	54 Olds	200	450
4. Dick Rathmann	John Ditz	3	54 Huds	200	350
5. Lee Petty	Petty Enterprises	42	54 Chrys	196	300

1956 Grand National Race No. 4
December 11, 1955 Average Speed: 65.009

Driver	Owner	Car #	Make	Laps	Winnings
1. Herb Thomas	Herb Thomas	92	56 Chev	199	1,100
2. Al Keller	Al Keller	64	56 Chev	198	700
3. Billy Myers	Hugh Babb	46	55 Chev	197	475
4. Buck Baker	James Satcher	87	56 Ford	195	365
5. Lee Petty	Petty Enterprises	42	56 Dodg	193	310

1956 Grand National Race No. 7
March 4, 1956 Average Speed: 68.990

Driver	Owner	Car #	Make	Laps	Winnings
1. Billy Myers	Bill Stroppe	14W	56 Merc	199	900
2. Buck Baker	Carl Kiekhaefer	500B	56 Dodg	199	600
3. Herb Thomas	Smokey Yunick	92	56 Chev	195	425
4. Joe Weatherly	Charlie Schwam	9	56 Ford	191	335
5. Fireball Roberts	Pete DePaolo	22	56 Ford	191	290

Titusville-Cocoa Speedway
Titusville, FL
1.6-mile Paved Road Course

1.6-mile road course utilizing runways at airport. Only Winston Cup (then Grand National) race staged on 12/30/56 (counted toward 1957 season and won by Fireball Roberts). Last race run in July 1958.

Winston Cup Victories
Fireball Roberts   1

Winston Cup Poles
Paul Goldsmith   1

Winston Cup Money
Fireball Roberts $850

Most Cars Started
15—December 30, 1956

Narrowest Margin of Victory
N/A

Race Record
69.106 MPH—December 30, 1956

Most Race Leaders
2—December 30, 1956

Most Cars Running at Finish
12—December 30, 1956

1957 Grand National Race No. 3
December 30, 1956 Average Speed: 69.106

Driver	Owner	Car #	Make	Laps	Winnings
1. Fireball Roberts	Pete DePaolo	22	56 Ford	56	850
2. Curtis Turner	Pete DePaolo	C22	56 Ford	56	625
3. Marvin Panch	Pete DePaolo	98	56 Ford	56	450
4. Ralph Moody	Pete DePaolo	12	56 Ford	56	350
5. Doug Cox	John Foster	86	56 Ford	55	310

Georgia

Atlanta Motor Speedway
Hampton, GA
1.522-mile Superspeedway

(aka Atlanta Int'l Raceway) 1.522-mile banked oval opened in 1960. Originally measured as 1.5-mile oval. First NASCAR Winston Cup (then Grand National) race staged on 7/31/60 (won by Fireball Roberts). Track scheduled to open in 1959, but construction delays and bad weather forced postponement until summer of 1960.

Winston Cup Starts
Richard Petty   65

Winston Cup Victories
Dale Earnhardt   9

Winston Cup Poles
Buddy Baker   7

Winston Cup Money
Dale Earnhardt $1,796,825

Most Cars Started
46—March 26, 1961   Atlanta 500
46—June 10, 1962   Atlanta 500
46—March 17, 1963   Atlanta 500

Fewest Cars Started
35—June 7, 1964   Dixie 400

Narrowest Margin of Victory
.006 seconds—March 11, 2001

Slowest Race
101.983 MPH—June 10, 1962
Atlanta 500

Race Record
163.633 MPH—November 12, 1995
NAPA 500

Most Cautions
11—March 31, 1968   Atlanta 500
11—August 4, 1968   Dixie 500
11—November 14, 1993   Hooters 500

Most Race Leaders
17—March 12, 2000

Most Cars Running at Finish
39—October 27, 2002

1960 Grand National Race No. 27 Dixie 300
July 31, 1960 Average Speed: 112.652

Driver	Owner	Car #	Make	Laps	Winnings
1. Fireball Roberts	John Hines	22	60 Pont	200	10,130
2. Cotton Owens	Cotton Owens	6	60 Pont	200	5,215
3. Jack Smith	Jack Smith	47	60 Pont	200	3,090
4. Bobby Johns	Jim Stephens	3	60 Pont	199	1,865
5. Fred Lorenzen	Fred Lorenzen	28	60 Ford	199	1,565

1960 Grand National Race No. 44 Atlanta 500
October 30, 1960 Average Speed: 108.408

Driver	Owner	Car #	Make	Laps	Winnings
1. Bobby Johns	Cotton Owens	5	60 Pont	334	15,975
2. Johnny Allen	Hanley Dawson	69	60 Chev	333	7,475
3. Jim Paschal	Petty Enterprises	44	60 Plym	333	4,425
4. Speedy Thompson	Wood Brothers	21	60 Ford	330	2,475
5. Rex White	Rex White	4	60 Chev	330	1,850

1961 Grand National Race No. 9 Atlanta 500
March 26, 1961 Average Speed: 124.172

Driver	Owner	Car #	Make	Laps	Winnings
1. Bob Burdick	Roy Burdick Gar	53	61 Pont	334	15,775
2. Rex White	Rex White	4	61 Chev	334	8,850
3. Ralph Earnhardt	Cotton Owens	6	61 Pont	334	4,850
4. Nelson Stacy	Dudley Farrell	29	61 Ford	333	2,475
5. Ned Jarrett	Bee Gee Holloway	11	61 Chev	332	1,775

1961 Grand National Race No. 33 Festival 250
July 9, 1961 Average Speed: 118.067

Driver	Owner	Car #	Make	Laps	Winnings
1. Fred Lorenzen	Holman-Moody	28	61 Ford	167	7,085
2. Bob Welborn	Jack Smith	47	61 Pont	166	3,580
3. Richard Petty	Petty Enterprises	43	61 Plym	164	2,275
4. Emanuel Zervakis	Monroe Shook	85	61 Chev	163	1,475
5. Jack Smith	Jack Smith	46	61 Pont	161	1,310

1961 Grand National Race No. 46 Dixie 400
September 17, 1961 Average Speed: 125.384

Driver	Owner	Car #	Make	Laps	Winnings
1. David Pearson	John Masoni	3	61 Pont	267	9,330
2. Junior Johnson	Rex Lovette	27	61 Pont	267	4,795
3. Fireball Roberts	Jim Stephens	22	61 Pont	267	3,165
4. Jack Smith	Jack Smith	47	61 Pont	264	2,250
5. Richard Petty	Petty Enterprises	43	61 Plym	264	1,625

1962 Grand National Race No. 24 Atlanta 500
June 10, 1962 Average Speed: 101.983

Driver	Owner	Car #	Make	Laps	Winnings
1. Fred Lorenzen	Holman-Moody	28	62 Ford	219	15,555
2. Banjo Matthews	Banjo Matthews	02	62 Pont	219	9,490
3. Bobby Johns	Shorty Johns	72	62 Pont	218	5,220
4. Fireball Roberts	Banjo Matthews	22	62 Pont	218	2,525
5. Troy Ruttman	Bill Stroppe	98	62 Merc	218	1,750

1962 Grand National Race No. 53 Dixie 400
October 28, 1962 Average Speed: 124.740

Driver	Owner	Car #	Make	Laps	Winnings
1. Rex White	Rex White	4	62 Chev	267	10,315
2. Joe Weatherly	Bud Moore	8	62 Pont	267	5,270
3. Marvin Panch	Wood Brothers	21	62 Ford	267	3,535
4. Richard Petty	Petty Enterprises	43	62 Plym	266	2,415
5. Fred Lorenzen	Holman-Moody	28	62 Ford	266	2,000

1963 Grand National Race No. 11 Atlanta 500
March 17, 1963 Average Speed: 130.582

Driver	Owner	Car #	Make	Laps	Winnings
1. Fred Lorenzen	Holman-Moody	28	63 Ford	334	16,855
2. Fireball Roberts	Banjo Matthews	22	63 Pont	333	8,655
3. Bobby Johns	Shorty Johns	7	63 Pont	333	5,700
4. Joe Weatherly	Bud Moore	8	63 Pont	333	3,790
5. Tiny Lund	Wood Brothers	21	63 Ford	331	1,875

Atlanta Motor Speedway *continued*

1963 Grand National Race No. 28 Dixie 400
June 30, 1963 Average Speed: 121.139

Driver	Owner	Car #	Make	Laps	Winnings
1. Junior Johnson	Ray Fox	3	63 Chev	267	12,445
2. Fred Lorenzen	Holman-Moody	28	63 Ford	267	6,190
3. Marvin Panch	Wood Brothers	21	63 Ford	267	3,370
4. Darel Dieringer	Bill Stroppe	26	63 Merc	266	2,245
5. Joe Weatherly	Bud Moore	8	63 Pont	266	2,050

1964 Grand National Race No. 28 Dixie 400
June 7, 1964 Average Speed: 112.535

Driver	Owner	Car #	Make	Laps	Winnings
1. Ned Jarrett	Bondy Long	11	64 Ford	267	11,500
2. Richard Petty	Petty Enterprises	43	64 Plym	267	5,790
3. Paul Goldsmith	Ray Nichels	25	64 Plym	266	3,530
4. Darel Dieringer	Bill Stroppe	16	64 Merc	266	2,425
5. Rex White	Bud Moore	4	64 Merc	266	2,025

1965 Grand National Race No. 25 Dixie 400
June 13, 1965 Average Speed: 110.120

Driver	Owner	Car #	Make	Laps	Winnings
1. Marvin Panch	Wood Brothers	21	65 Ford	267	12,300
2. Darel Dieringer	Bud Moore	16	64 Merc	267	6,770
3. Ned Jarrett	Bondy Long	11	65 Ford	267	3,730
4. Junior Johnson	Rex Lovette	26	65 Ford	265	2,975
5. Buddy Baker	Buck Baker	88	64 Dodg	263	1,675

1966 Grand National Race No. 37 Dixie 400
August 7, 1966 Average Speed: 130.244

Driver	Owner	Car #	Make	Laps	Winnings
1. Richard Petty	Petty Enterprises	43	66 Plym	267	13,525
2. Buddy Baker	Ray Fox	3	66 Dodg	267	8,345
3. Sam McQuagg	Ray Nichels	98	66 Dodg	260	3,505
4. James Hylton	Bud Hartje	48	65 Dodg	259	3,000
5. Jerry Grant	Tom Friedkin	04	65 Plym	255	1,925

1967 Grand National Race No. 36 Dixie 500
August 6, 1967 Average Speed: 132.286

Driver	Owner	Car #	Make	Laps	Winnings
1. Dick Hutcherson	Bondy Long	29	67 Ford	334	16,500
2. Paul Goldsmith	Ray Nichels	99	67 Plym	334	7,900
3. LeeRoy Yarbrough	Bud Moore	16	67 Merc	331	4,725
4. Donnie Allison	Jon Thorne	12	67 Ford	323	2,550
5. Bud Moore	A. J. King	53	67 Dodg	323	1,925

1968 Grand National Race No. 33 Dixie 500
August 4, 1968 Average Speed: 127.068

Driver	Owner	Car #	Make	Laps	Winnings
1. LeeRoy Yarbrough	Junior Johnson	98	68 Merc	334	17,260
2. Bobby Isaac	Nord Krauskopf	71	68 Dodg	334	8,440
3. Donnie Allison	Banjo Matthews	27	68 Ford	334	5,925
4. David Pearson	Holman-Moody	17	68 Ford	334	3,005
5. Richard Petty	Petty Enterprises	43	68 Plym	333	2,535

1969 Grand National Race No. 36 Dixie 500
August 10, 1969 Average Speed: 133.001

Driver	Owner	Car #	Make	Laps	Winnings
1. LeeRoy Yarbrough	Junior Johnson	98	69 Ford	334	18,620
2. David Pearson	Holman-Moody	17	69 Ford	334	9,750
3. Richard Petty	Petty Enterprises	43	69 Ford	334	6,100
4. Charlie Glotzbach	Smokey Yunick	13	69 Ford	333	3,585
5. Donnie Allison	Banjo Matthews	27	69 Ford	333	2,775

1964 Grand National Race No. 13 Atlanta 500
April 5, 1964 Average Speed: 134.137

Driver	Owner	Car #	Make	Laps	Winnings
1. Fred Lorenzen	Holman-Moody	28	64 Ford	334	18,000
2. Bobby Isaac	Ray Nichels	26	64 Dodg	332	8,065
3. Ned Jarrett	Bondy Long	11	64 Ford	331	4,500
4. Junior Johnson	Ray Fox	3	64 Dodg	330	2,925
5. Buck Baker	Petty Enterprises	41	64 Plym	327	1,850

1965 Grand National Race No. 9 Atlanta 500
April 11, 1965 Average Speed: 129.410

Driver	Owner	Car #	Make	Laps	Winnings
1. Marvin Panch	Wood Brothers	21	65 Ford	334	18,420
2. Bobby Johns	Holman-Moody	7	65 Ford	334	7,995
3. Ned Jarrett	Bondy Long	11	65 Ford	330	4,700
4. Dick Hutcherson	Holman-Moody	29	65 Ford	327	2,775
5. Buddy Baker	Buck Baker	88	64 Dodg	325	1,850

1966 Grand National Race No. 8 Atlanta 500
March 27, 1966 Average Speed: 131.247

Driver	Owner	Car #	Make	Laps	Winnings
1. Jim Hurtubise	Norm Nelson	56	66 Plym	334	17,920
2. Fred Lorenzen	Holman-Moody	28	66 Ford	333	8,290
3. Dick Hutcherson	Holman-Moody	29	66 Ford	333	4,825
4. Paul Goldsmith	Ray Nichels	99	66 Plym	331	2,750
5. Jim Paschal	Tom Friedkin	14	66 Plym	330	1,925

1967 Grand National Race No. 10 Atlanta 500
April 2, 1967 Average Speed: 131.238

Driver	Owner	Car #	Make	Laps	Winnings
1. Cale Yarborough	Wood Brothers	21	67 Ford	334	21,035
2. Dick Hutcherson	Bondy Long	29	67 Ford	333	8,600
3. Buddy Baker	Ray Fox	3	67 Dodg	332	4,900
4. Charlie Glotzbach	Nord Krauskopf	37	65 Dodg	327	2,750
5. Bobby Isaac	Nord Krauskopf	71	67 Dodg	326	1,875

1968 Grand National Race No. 7 Atlanta 500
March 31, 1968 Average Speed: 125.564

Driver	Owner	Car #	Make	Laps	Winnings
1. Cale Yarborough	Wood Brothers	21	68 Merc	334	20,680
2. LeeRoy Yarbrough	Junior Johnson	26	68 Merc	334	9,360
3. Donnie Allison	Banjo Matthews	27	68 Ford	333	5,415
4. Charlie Glotzbach	Cotton Owens	6	68 Dodg	332	3,225
5. Darel Dieringer	Mario Rossi	2	68 Plym	332	2,300

1969 Grand National Race No. 10 Atlanta 500
March 30, 1969 Average Speed: 132.191

Driver	Owner	Car #	Make	Laps	Winnings
1. Cale Yarborough	Wood Brothers	21	69 Merc	334	21,590
2. David Pearson	Holman-Moody	17	69 Ford	334	10,630
3. Paul Goldsmith	Ray Nichels	99	69 Dodg	332	6,225
4. Bobby Allison	Mario Rossi	22	69 Dodg	331	4,100
5. Pete Hamilton	Banjo Matthews	27	69 Ford	329	3,225

1970 Grand National Race No. 8 Atlanta 500
March 29, 1970 Average Speed: 139.554

Driver	Owner	Car #	Make	Laps	Winnings
1. Bobby Allison	Mario Rossi	22	69 Dodg	328	21,825
2. Cale Yarborough	Wood Brothers	21	69 Merc	328	11,375
3. Pete Hamilton	Petty Enterprises	40	70 Plym	326	6,550
4. LeeRoy Yarbrough	Junior Johnson	98	69 Ford	325	4,300
5. Richard Petty	Petty Enterprises	43	70 Plym	321	3,375

Atlanta Motor Speedway *continued*

1970 Grand National Race No. 31 Dixie 500
August 2, 1970 Average Speed: 142.712

Driver	Owner	Car #	Make	Laps	Winnings
1. Richard Petty	Petty Enterprises	43	70 Plym	328	19,600
2. Cale Yarborough	Wood Brothers	21	69 Merc	327	11,525
3. LeeRoy Yarbrough	Junior Johnson	98	69 Merc	326	7,200
4. Buddy Baker	Cotton Owens	6	69 Dodg	326	3,775
5. Donnie Allison	Banjo Matthews	27	69 Ford	325	2,800

1971 Winston Cup GN Race No. 10 Atlanta 500
April 4, 1971 Average Speed: 131.375

Driver	Owner	Car #	Make	Laps	Winnings
1. A. J. Foyt	Wood Brothers	21	69 Merc	328	19,200
2. Richard Petty	Petty Enterprises	43	71 Plym	328	10,700
3. Pete Hamilton	Cotton Owens	6	71 Plym	327	6,975
4. David Pearson	Holman-Moody	17	70 Ford	327	4,490
5. Bobby Isaac	Nord Krauskopf	71	71 Dodg	327	3,500

1971 Winston Cup GN Race No. 33 Dixie 500
August 1, 1971 Average Speed: 129.061

Driver	Owner	Car #	Make	Laps	Winnings
1. Richard Petty	Petty Enterprises	43	71 Plym	328	20,220
2. Bobby Allison	Holman-Moody	12	69 Merc	328	9,530
3. Benny Parsons	L. G. DeWitt	72	69 Merc	319	6,225
4. Charlie Glotzbach	R. Howard & J. Johnson	3	71 Chev	318	4,525
5. Friday Hassler	Friday Hassler	39	70 Chev	317	3,375

1972 Winston Cup GN Race No. 6 Atlanta 500
March 26, 1972 Average Speed: 128.214

Driver	Owner	Car #	Make	Laps	Winnings
1. Bobby Allison	R. Howard & J. Johnson	12	72 Chev	328	21,605
2. A. J. Foyt	Wood Brothers	21	71 Merc	328	10,600
3. Bobby Isaac	Nord Krauskopf	71	72 Dodg	328	10,380
4. David Pearson	Bud Moore	15	72 Ford	327	4,800
5. Donnie Allison	Monty Myers	27	72 Chev	327	3,530

1972 Winston Cup GN Race No. 20 Dixie 500
July 23, 1972 Average Speed: 131.295

Driver	Owner	Car #	Make	Laps	Winnings
1. Bobby Allison	R. Howard & J. Johnson	12	72 Chev	328	17,955
2. Richard Petty	Petty Enterprises	43	72 Dodg	328	11,005
3. David Pearson	Wood Brothers	21	71 Merc	325	6,380
4. Benny Parsons	L. G. DeWitt	72	71 Merc	323	5,230
5. LeeRoy Yarbrough	Junie Donlavey	90	71 Ford	322	4,230

1973 Winston Cup GN Race No. 6 Atlanta 500
April 1, 1973 Average Speed: 139.351

Driver	Owner	Car #	Make	Laps	Winnings
1. David Pearson	Wood Brothers	21	71 Merc	328	16,625
2. Bobby Isaac	Bud Moore	15	72 Ford	326	11,325
3. Benny Parsons	L. G. DeWitt	72	72 Chev	323	6,700
4. Buddy Baker	Nord Krauskopf	71	73 Dodg	322	6,525
5. Cale Yarborough	R. Howard & J. Johnson	11	73 Chev	321	6,575

1973 Winston Cup GN Race No. 19 Dixie 500
July 22, 1973 Average Speed: 130.211

Driver	Owner	Car #	Make	Laps	Winnings
1. David Pearson	Wood Brothers	21	71 Merc	328	16,650
2. Cale Yarborough	R. Howard & J. Johnson	11	73 Chev	327	10,625
3. Donnie Allison	DiGard	88	73 Chev	323	6,075
4. Joe Frasson	Joe Frasson	18	73 Dodg	321	4,800
5. Jody Ridley	Junie Donlavey	90	71 Merc	319	4,535

1974 Winston Cup GN Race No. 6 Atlanta 500
March 24, 1974 Average Speed: 136.910

Driver	Owner	Car #	Make	Laps	Winnings
1. Cale Yarborough	R. Howard & J. Johnson	11	74 Chev	328	18,650
2. David Pearson	Wood Brothers	21	73 Merc	328	9,950
3. Buddy Baker	Nord Krauskopf	71	74 Dodg	327	6,650
4. George Follmer	Bud Moore	15	72 Ford	327	7,300
5. Donnie Allison	DiGard	88	74 Chev	326	4,150

1974 Winston Cup GN Race No. 19 Dixie 500
July 28, 1974 Average Speed: 131.651

Driver	Owner	Car #	Make	Laps	Winnings
1. Richard Petty	Petty Enterprises	43	74 Dodg	328	19,350
2. David Pearson	Wood Brothers	21	73 Merc	328	9,225
3. Buddy Baker	Bud Moore	15	73 Ford	327	9,425
4. Darrell Waltrip	Darrell Waltrip	95	74 Chev	324	5,800
5. Lennie Pond	Ronnie Elder	54	74 Chev	319	4,425

1975 Winston Cup GN Race No. 6 Atlanta 500
March 23, 1975 Average Speed: 133.496

Driver	Owner	Car #	Make	Laps	Winnings
1. Richard Petty	Petty Enterprises	43	74 Dodg	328	19,500
2. Buddy Baker	Bud Moore	15	75 Ford	328	13,025
3. David Pearson	Wood Brothers	21	73 Merc	327	8,025
4. Dick Brooks	Junie Donlavey	90	73 Ford	324	5,525
5. Darrell Waltrip	Darrell Waltrip	17	75 Chev	323	6,525

1975 Winston Cup GN Race No. 29 Dixie 500
November 9, 1975 Average Speed: 130.990

Driver	Owner	Car #	Make	Laps	Winnings
1. Buddy Baker	Bud Moore	15	75 Ford	328	18,550
2. Dave Marcis	Nord Krauskopf	71	74 Dodg	328	13,375
3. Richard Petty	Petty Enterprises	43	74 Dodg	328	10,725
4. David Pearson	Wood Brothers	21	73 Merc	327	6,150
5. Cale Yarborough	Junior Johnson	11	75 Chev	327	7,600

1976 Winston Cup GN Race No. 6 Atlanta 500
March 21, 1976 Average Speed: 128.904

Driver	Owner	Car #	Make	Laps	Winnings
1. David Pearson	Wood Brothers	21	Merc	328	16,750
2. Benny Parsons	L. G. DeWitt	72	Chev	328	13,375
3. Cale Yarborough	Junior Johnson	11	Chev	327	17,855
4. Lennie Pond	Ronnie Elder	54	Chev	326	5,870
5. Darrell Waltrip	DiGard	88	Chev	325	7,360

1976 Winston Cup GN Race No. 29 Dixie 500
November 7, 1976 Average Speed: 127.396

Driver	Owner	Car #	Make	Laps	Winnings
1. Dave Marcis	Nord Krauskopf	71	Dodg	328	20,165
2. David Pearson	Wood Brothers	21	Merc	328	11,765
3. Donnie Allison	Hoss Ellington	1	Chev	328	7,790
4. Cale Yarborough	Junior Johnson	11	Chev	328	8,670
5. Buddy Baker	Bud Moore	15	Ford	327	8,985

1977 Winston Cup GN Race No. 5 Atlanta 500
March 20, 1977 Average Speed: 144.093

Driver	Owner	Car #	Make	Laps	Winnings
1. Richard Petty	Petty Enterprises	43	Dodg	328	22,550
2. David Pearson	Wood Brothers	21	Merc	328	12,850
3. Cale Yarborough	Junior Johnson	11	Chev	327	13,025
4. Donnie Allison	Hoss Ellington	1	Chev	327	6,000
5. Buddy Baker	Bud Moore	15	Ford	326	7,650

Atlanta Motor Speedway *continued*

1977 Winston Cup GN Race No. 29 Dixie 500
November 6, 1977 Average Speed: 110.052

Driver	Owner	Car #	Make	Laps	Winnings
1. Darrell Waltrip	DiGard	88	Chev	268	20,425
2. David Pearson	Wood Brothers	21	Merc	268	11,500
3. Benny Parsons	L. G. DeWitt	72	Chev	268	11,250
4. Donnie Allison	Hoss Ellington	1	Chev	268	18,250
5. Cale Yarborough	Junior Johnson	11	Chev	268	9,450

1978 Winston Cup GN Race No. 29 Dixie 500
November 5, 1978 Average Speed: 124.312

Driver	Owner	Car #	Make	Laps	Winnings
1. Donnie Allison	Hoss Ellington	1	Chev	328	19,850
2. Richard Petty	Petty Enterprises	43	Chev	328	14,750
3. Dave Marcis	Rod Osterlund	2	Chev	328	9,750
4. Dale Earnhardt	Rod Osterlund	98	Chev	327	7,500
5. Benny Parsons	L. G. DeWitt	72	Olds	327	9,000

1979 Winston Cup GN Race No. 30 Dixie 500
November 4, 1979 Average Speed: 140.120

Driver	Owner	Car #	Make	Laps	Winnings
1. Neil Bonnett	Wood Brothers	21	Merc	328	20,050
2. Dale Earnhardt	Rod Osterlund	2	Chev	328	16,700
3. Cale Yarborough	Junior Johnson	11	Olds	328	23,150
4. Bobby Allison	Bud Moore	15	Ford	328	10,200
5. Darrell Waltrip	DiGard	88	Chev	327	9,100

1980 Winston Cup GN Race No. 30 Atlanta Journal 500
November 2, 1980 Average Speed: 131.190

Driver	Owner	Car #	Make	Laps	Winnings
1. Cale Yarborough	Junior Johnson	11	Chev	328	31,600
2. Neil Bonnett	Wood Brothers	21	Merc	328	12,600
3. Dale Earnhardt	Rod Osterlund	2	Chev	327	14,700
4. Buddy Baker	Harry Ranier	28	Buick	327	7,050
5. Terry Labonte	Billy Hagan	44	Chev	327	9,850

1981 Winston Cup GN Race No. 30 Atlanta Journal 500
November 8, 1981 Average Speed: 130.391

Driver	Owner	Car #	Make	Laps	Winnings
1. Neil Bonnett	Wood Brothers	21	Ford	328	31,500
2. Darrell Waltrip	Junior Johnson	11	Buick	328	17,350
3. Cale Yarborough	M. C. Anderson	27	Buick	328	8,800
4. Bobby Allison	Harry Ranier	28	Buick	328	12,090
5. Jody Ridley	Junie Donlavey	90	Ford	328	11,700

1982 Winston Cup GN Race No. 29 Atlanta Journal 500
November 7, 1982 Average Speed: 130.884

Driver	Owner	Car #	Make	Laps	Winnings
1. Bobby Allison	DiGard	88	Buick	328	45,500
2. Harry Gant	Hal Needham	33	Buick	328	19,230
3. Darrell Waltrip	Junior Johnson	11	Buick	328	19,700
4. Tim Richmond	Jim Stacy	2	Buick	328	9,895
5. Joe Ruttman	Bob Rahilly & Butch Mock	75	Buick	327	8,775

1983 Winston Cup GN Race No. 29 Atlanta Journal 500
November 6, 1983 Average Speed: 137.643

Driver	Owner	Car #	Make	Laps	Winnings
1. Neil Bonnett	Bob Rahilly & Butch Mock	75	Chev	328	36,975
2. Buddy Baker	Wood Brothers	21	Ford	328	15,800
3. Bobby Allison	DiGard	22	Buick	328	31,025
4. Terry Labonte	Billy Hagan	44	Chev	327	12,955
5. Richard Petty	Petty Enterprises	43	Pont	326	12,100

1978 Winston Cup GN Race No. 5 Atlanta 500
March 19, 1978 Average Speed: 142.520

Driver	Owner	Car #	Make	Laps	Winnings
1. Bobby Allison	Bud Moore	15	Ford	328	33,050
2. Dave Marcis	Rod Osterlund	2	Chev	327	16,925
3. Donnie Allison	Hoss Ellington	1	Chev	327	11,000
4. Cale Yarborough	Junior Johnson	11	Olds	327	23,600
5. Lennie Pond	Harry Ranier	54	Chev	327	5,950

1979 Winston Cup GN Race No. 5 Atlanta 500
March 18, 1979 Average Speed: 135.136

Driver	Owner	Car #	Make	Laps	Winnings
1. Buddy Baker	Harry Ranier	28	Olds	328	35,975
2. Bobby Allison	Bud Moore	15	Ford	328	32,875
3. Darrell Waltrip	DiGard	88	Chev	328	15,400
4. Cale Yarborough	Junior Johnson	11	Olds	327	11,725
5. Benny Parsons	M. C. Anderson	27	Chev	327	5,775

1980 Winston Cup GN Race No. 5 Atlanta 500
March 16, 1980 Average Speed: 134.808

Driver	Owner	Car #	Make	Laps	Winnings
1. Dale Earnhardt	Rod Osterlund	2	Chev	328	36,200
2. Rusty Wallace	Roger Penske	16	Chev	328	14,250
3. Bobby Allison	Bud Moore	15	Ford	328	16,250
4. Dave Marcis	Dave Marcis	71	Olds	327	13,600
5. Dick Brooks	Nelson Malloch	7	Chev	325	9,490

1981 Winston Cup GN Race No. 5 Coca-Cola 500
March 15, 1981 Average Speed: 133.619

Driver	Owner	Car #	Make	Laps	Winnings
1. Cale Yarborough	M. C. Anderson	27	Buick	328	28,950
2. Harry Gant	Jack Beebe	47	Buick	328	32,705
3. Dale Earnhardt	Rod Osterlund	2	Pont	327	19,400
4. Bobby Allison	Harry Ranier	28	Pont	327	14,415
5. Benny Parsons	Bud Moore	15	Ford	326	11,975

1982 Winston Cup GN Race No. 4 Coca-Cola 500
March 21, 1982 Average Speed: 124.824

Driver	Owner	Car #	Make	Laps	Winnings
1. Darrell Waltrip	Junior Johnson	11	Buick	287	49,615
2. Richard Petty	Petty Enterprises	43	Pont	287	37,725
3. Cale Yarborough	M. C. Anderson	27	Buick	287	16,250
4. Benny Parsons	Harry Ranier	28	Pont	287	19,345
5. Harry Gant	Hal Needham	33	Buick	286	12,890

1983 Winston Cup GN Race No. 4 Coca-Cola 500
March 27, 1983 Average Speed: 124.055

Driver	Owner	Car #	Make	Laps	Winnings
1. Cale Yarborough	Harry Ranier	28	Chev	328	33,300
2. Neil Bonnett	Bob Rahilly & Butch Mock	75	Chev	328	34,530
3. Buddy Baker	Wood Brothers	21	Ford	328	12,125
4. Joe Ruttman	Ron Benfield	98	Buick	328	13,620
5. Richard Petty	Petty Enterprises	43	Pont	328	12,650

1984 Winston Cup GN Race No. 4 Coca-Cola 500
March 18, 1984 Average Speed: 144.945

Driver	Owner	Car #	Make	Laps	Winnings
1. Benny Parsons	Johnny Hayes	55	Chev	328	51,110
2. Dale Earnhardt	Richard Childress	3	Chev	328	26,935
3. Cale Yarborough	Harry Ranier	28	Chev	328	12,550
4. Richard Petty	Mike Curb	43	Pont	327	8,650
5. Bobby Allison	DiGard	22	Buick	326	18,050

Atlanta Motor Speedway *continued*

1984 Winston Cup GN Race No. 29 Atlanta Journal 500
November 11, 1984 Average Speed: 134.610

Driver	Owner	Car #	Make	Laps	Winnings
1. Dale Earnhardt	Richard Childress	3	Chev	328	40,610
2. Bill Elliott	Harry Melling	9	Ford	328	28,085
3. Ricky Rudd	Bud Moore	15	Ford	328	19,350
4. Benny Parsons	Johnny Hayes	55	Chev	328	7,000
5. Bobby Allison	DiGard	22	Buick	327	16,850

1985 Winston Cup GN Race No. 27 Atlanta Journal 500
November 3, 1985 Average Speed: 139.597

Driver	Owner	Car #	Make	Laps	Winnings
1. Bill Elliott	Harry Melling	9	Ford	328	57,650
2. Cale Yarborough	Harry Ranier	28	Ford	328	29,600
3. Darrell Waltrip	Junior Johnson	11	Chev	328	21,125
4. Dale Earnhardt	Richard Childress	3	Chev	328	15,300
5. Morgan Shepherd	Bobby Hawkins	16	Chev	327	7,150

1986 Winston Cup Race No. 28 Atlanta Journal 500
November 2, 1986 Average Speed: 152.523

Driver	Owner	Car #	Make	Laps	Winnings
1. Dale Earnhardt	Richard Childress	3	Chev	328	67,950
2. Richard Petty	Petty Enterprises	43	Pont	327	26,130
3. Bill Elliott	Harry Melling	9	Ford	327	26,450
4. Tim Richmond	Rick Hendrick	25	Chev	327	12,845
5. Buddy Baker	Buddy Baker & Danny Schiff	88	Olds	327	7,725

1987 Winston Cup Race No. 29 Atlanta Journal 500
November 22, 1987 Average Speed: 139.047

Driver	Owner	Car #	Make	Laps	Winnings
1. Bill Elliott	Harry Melling	9	Ford	328	74,200
2. Dale Earnhardt	Richard Childress	3	Chev	328	35,350
3. Ricky Rudd	Bud Moore	15	Ford	328	22,585
4. Bobby Allison	Stavola Brothers	22	Buick	328	16,725
5. Davey Allison	Harry Ranier	28	Ford	327	9,985

1988 Winston Cup Race No. 29 Atlanta Journal 500
November 20, 1988 Average Speed: 129.024

Driver	Owner	Car #	Make	Laps	Winnings
1. Rusty Wallace	Raymond Beadle	27	Pont	328	87,575
2. Davey Allison	Harry Ranier	28	Ford	328	35,625
3. Mike Alexander	Stavola Brothers	12	Buick	328	23,610
4. Ricky Rudd	Kenny Bernstein	26	Buick	328	14,725
5. Darrell Waltrip	Rick Hendrick	17	Chev	328	16,525

1989 Winston Cup Race No. 29 Atlanta Journal 500
November 19, 1989 Average Speed: 140.229

Driver	Owner	Car #	Make	Laps	Winnings
1. Dale Earnhardt	Richard Childress	3	Chev	328	81,700
2. Geoff Bodine	Rick Hendrick	5	Chev	328	33,625
3. Sterling Marlin	Billy Hagan	94	Olds	328	25,275
4. Ken Schrader	Rick Hendrick	25	Chev	328	18,875
5. Darrell Waltrip	Rick Hendrick	17	Chev	327	18,800

1990 Winston Cup Series Race No. 29 Atlanta Journal 500
November 18, 1990 Average Speed: 140.911

Driver	Owner	Car #	Make	Laps	Winnings
1. Morgan Shepherd	Bud Moore	15	Ford	328	62,250
2. Geoff Bodine	Junior Johnson	11	Ford	328	40,850
3. Dale Earnhardt	Richard Childress	3	Chev	328	26,700
4. Dale Jarrett	Wood Brothers	21	Ford	328	17,225
5. Darrell Waltrip	Rick Hendrick	17	Chev	327	22,300

1985 Winston Cup GN Race No. 4 Coca-Cola 500
March 17, 1985 Average Speed: 140.273

Driver	Owner	Car #	Make	Laps	Winnings
1. Bill Elliott	Harry Melling	9	Ford	328	59,800
2. Geoff Bodine	Rick Hendrick	5	Chev	328	29,800
3. Neil Bonnett	Junior Johnson	12	Chev	328	23,700
4. Ricky Rudd	Bud Moore	15	Ford	327	15,825
5. Bobby Allison	DiGard	22	Buick	327	15,000

1986 Winston Cup Race No. 4 Motorcraft 500
March 16, 1986 Average Speed: 132.126

Driver	Owner	Car #	Make	Laps	Winnings
1. Morgan Shepherd	Jack Beebe	47	Buick	328	62,350
2. Dale Earnhardt	Richard Childress	3	Chev	328	51,300
3. Terry Labonte	Billy Hagan	44	Olds	328	22,150
4. Darrell Waltrip	Junior Johnson	11	Chev	328	24,075
5. Bill Elliott	Harry Melling	9	Ford	328	18,250

1987 Winston Cup Race No. 4 Motorcraft Quality Parts 500
March 15, 1987 Average Speed: 133.689

Driver	Owner	Car #	Make	Laps	Winnings
1. Ricky Rudd	Bud Moore	15	Ford	328	62,400
2. Benny Parsons	Rick Hendrick	35	Chev	328	36,125
3. Rusty Wallace	Raymond Beadle	27	Pont	328	25,950
4. Terry Labonte	Junior Johnson	11	Chev	328	20,825
5. Davey Allison	Harry Ranier	28	Ford	327	18,550

1988 Winston Cup Race No. 4 Motorcraft Quality Parts 500
March 20, 1988 Average Speed: 137.588

Driver	Owner	Car #	Make	Laps	Winnings
1. Dale Earnhardt	Richard Childress	3	Chev	328	67,950
2. Rusty Wallace	Raymond Beadle	27	Pont	328	37,875
3. Darrell Waltrip	Rick Hendrick	17	Chev	327	26,150
4. Terry Labonte	Junior Johnson	11	Chev	327	19,575
5. Kyle Petty	Wood Brothers	21	Ford	327	18,750

1989 Winston Cup Race No. 3 Motorcraft Quality Parts 500
March 19, 1989 Average Speed: 139.684

Driver	Owner	Car #	Make	Laps	Winnings
1. Darrell Waltrip	Rick Hendrick	17	Chev	328	63,500
2. Dale Earnhardt	Richard Childress	3	Chev	328	39,675
3. Dick Trickle	Stavola Brothers	84	Buick	328	30,250
4. Kyle Petty	Felix Sabates	42	Pont	327	13,250
5. Sterling Marlin	Billy Hagan	94	Olds	326	22,500

1990 Winston Cup Series Race No. 4 Motorcraft Quality Parts 500
March 18, 1990 Average Speed: 156.849

Driver	Owner	Car #	Make	Laps	Winnings
1. Dale Earnhardt	Richard Childress	3	Chev	328	85,000
2. Morgan Shepherd	Bud Moore	15	Ford	328	36,000
3. Ernie Irvan	Larry McClure	4	Olds	328	31,957
4. Ken Schrader	Rick Hendrick	25	Chev	328	22,900
5. Mark Martin	Jack Roush	6	Ford	328	20,850

1991 Winston Cup Series Race No. 4 Motorcraft Quality Parts 500
March 18, 1991 Average Speed: 140.470

Driver	Owner	Car #	Make	Laps	Winnings
1. Ken Schrader	Rick Hendrick	25	Chev	328	69,250
2. Bill Elliott	Harry Melling	9	Ford	328	47,675
3. Dale Earnhardt	Richard Childress	3	Chev	328	37,000
4. Morgan Shepherd	Bud Moore	15	Ford	328	23,600
5. Michael Waltrip	Chuck Rider	30	Pont	328	21,400

Atlanta Motor Speedway *continued*

1991 Winston Cup Series Race No. 29 Hardee's 500
November 17, 1991 Average Speed: 137.968

Driver	Owner	Car #	Make	Laps	Winnings
1. Mark Martin	Jack Roush	6	Ford	328	88,950
2. Ernie Irvan	Larry McClure	4	Chev	328	39,025
3. Bill Elliott	Harry Melling	9	Ford	328	36,950
4. Harry Gant	Leo Jackson	33	Olds	328	21,250
5. Dale Earnhardt	Richard Childress	3	Chev	328	27,825

1992 Winston Cup Race No. 29 Hooters 500
November 15, 1992 Average Speed: 133.322

Driver	Owner	Car #	Make	Laps	Winnings
1. Bill Elliott	Junior Johnson	11	Ford	328	93,600
2. Alan Kulwicki	Alan Kulwicki	7	Ford	328	56,000
3. Geoff Bodine	Bud Moore	15	Ford	328	32,400
4. Jimmy Spencer	Bobby Allison	12	Ford	328	27,000
5. Terry Labonte	Billy Hagan	94	Chev	328	22,235

1993 Winston Cup Series Race No. 30 Hooters 500
November 14, 1993 Average Speed: 125.221

Driver	Owner	Car #	Make	Laps	Winnings
1. Rusty Wallace	Roger Penske	2	Pont	328	93,100
2. Ricky Rudd	Rick Hendrick	5	Chev	328	57,225
3. Darrell Waltrip	Darrell Waltrip	17	Chev	328	40,175
4. Bill Elliott	Junior Johnson	11	Ford	328	34,250
5. Dick Trickle	Larry Hedrick	41	Chev	328	24,300

1994 Winston Cup Series Race No. 31 Hooters 500
November 13, 1994 Average Speed: 148.982

Driver	Owner	Car #	Make	Laps	Winnings
1. Mark Martin	Jack Roush	6	Ford	328	104,200
2. Dale Earnhardt	Richard Childress	3	Chev	328	55,950
3. Todd Bodine	Butch Mock	75	Ford	328	44,000
4. Lake Speed	Bud Moore	15	Ford	328	32,000
5. Mike Wallace	Junie Donlavey	90	Ford	328	23,800

1995 Winston Cup Series Race No. 31 NAPA 500
November 12, 1995 Average Speed: 163.633

Driver	Owner	Car #	Make	Laps	Winnings
1. Dale Earnhardt	Richard Childress	3	Chev	328	141,850
2. Sterling Marlin	Larry McClure	4	Chev	328	58,250
3. Rusty Wallace	Roger Penske	2	Ford	328	40,300
4. Bill Elliott	Bill Elliott	94	Ford	328	29,700
5. Ward Burton	Bill Davis	22	Pont	328	30,000

1996 Winston Cup Series Race No. 31 NAPA 500
November 10, 1996 Average Speed: 134.661

Driver	Owner	Car #	Make	Laps	Winnings
1. Bobby Labonte	Joe Gibbs	18	Chev	328	274,900
2. Dale Jarrett	Robert Yates	88	Ford	328	59,500
3. Jeff Gordon	Rick Hendrick	24	Chev	328	71,600
4. Dale Earnhardt	Richard Childress	3	Chev	328	47,400
5. Terry Labonte	Rick Hendrick	5	Chev	328	48,800

1997 Winston Cup Series Race No. 32
November 16, 1997 Average Speed: 159.904

Driver	Owner	Car #	Make	Laps	Winnings
1. Bobby Labonte	Joe Gibbs	18	Pont	325	158,600
2. Dale Jarrett	Robert Yates	88	Ford	325	79,600
3. Mark Martin	Jack Roush	6	Ford	325	60,300
4. Jeff Green	Gary Bechtel	29	Chev	324	43,475
5. Derrike Cope	Nelson Bowers	36	Pont	324	38,100

1992 Winston Cup Race No. 4 Motorcraft Quality Parts 500
March 15, 1992 Average Speed: 147.746

Driver	Owner	Car #	Make	Laps	Winnings
1. Bill Elliott	Junior Johnson	11	Ford	328	71,000
2. Harry Gant	Leo Jackson	33	Olds	328	45,875
3. Dale Earnhardt	Richard Childress	3	Chev	328	36,850
4. Davey Allison	Robert Yates	28	Ford	328	32,550
5. Dick Trickle	Stavola Brothers	8	Ford	328	28,125

1993 Winston Cup Series Race No. 4 Motorcraft Quality Parts 500
March 20, 1993 Average Speed: 150.442

Driver	Owner	Car #	Make	Laps	Winnings
1. Morgan Shepherd	Wood Brothers	21	Ford	328	70,350
2. Ernie Irvan	Larry McClure	4	Chev	328	45,950
3. Rusty Wallace	Roger Penske	2	Pont	328	41,550
4. Jeff Gordon	Rick Hendrick	24	Chev	327	32,000
5. Ricky Rudd	Rick Hendrick	5	Chev	327	26,550

1994 Winston Cup Series Race No. 4 Motorcraft Quality Parts 500
March 13, 1994 Average Speed: 146.136

Driver	Owner	Car #	Make	Laps	Winnings
1. Ernie Irvan	Robert Yates	28	Ford	328	86,100
2. Morgan Shepherd	Wood Brothers	21	Ford	328	48,300
3. Darrell Waltrip	Darrell Waltrip	17	Chev	328	39,450
4. Jeff Burton	Stavola Brothers	8	Ford	328	32,600
5. Mark Martin	Jack Roush	6	Ford	327	30,300

1995 Winston Cup Series Race No. 4 Purolator 500
March 12, 1995 Average Speed: 150.115

Driver	Owner	Car #	Make	Laps	Winnings
1. Jeff Gordon	Rick Hendrick	24	Chev	328	104,950
2. Bobby Labonte	Joe Gibbs	18	Chev	328	50,000
3. Terry Labonte	Rick Hendrick	5	Chev	328	44,150
4. Dale Earnhardt	Richard Childress	3	Chev	328	52,950
5. Dale Jarrett	Robert Yates	28	Ford	327	33,725

1996 Winston Cup Series Race No. 4 Purolator 500
March 10, 1996 Average Speed: 161.298

Driver	Owner	Car #	Make	Laps	Winnings
1. Dale Earnhardt	Richard Childress	3	Chev	328	91,050
2. Terry Labonte	Rick Hendrick	5	Chev	328	60,500
3. Jeff Gordon	Rick Hendrick	24	Chev	328	61,600
4. Ernie Irvan	Robert Yates	28	Ford	328	40,400
5. Jeremy Mayfield	Cale Yarborough	98	Ford	328	32,100

1997 Winston Cup Series Race No. 4
March 9, 1997 Average Speed: 132.731

Driver	Owner	Car #	Make	Laps	Winnings
1. Dale Jarrett	Robert Yates	88	Ford	328	137,650
2. Ernie Irvan	Robert Yates	28	Ford	328	73,000
3. Morgan Shepherd	Richard Jackson	1	Pont	328	59,400
4. Bobby Labonte	Joe Gibbs	18	Pont	328	46,000
5. Jeff Burton	Jack Roush	99	Ford	328	41,000

1998 Winston Cup Series Race No. 4
March 9, 1998 Average Speed: 139.501

Driver	Owner	Car #	Make	Laps	Winnings
1. Bobby Labonte	Joe Gibbs	18	Pont	325	106,800
2. Dale Jarrett	Robert Yates	88	Ford	325	72,600
3. Jeremy Mayfield	Michael Kranefuss	12	Ford	325	54,400
4. Rusty Wallace	Roger Penske	2	Ford	325	50,250
5. Kenny Irwin, Jr.	Robert Yates	28	Ford	325	58,150

Atlanta Motor Speedway *continued*

1998 Winston Cup Series Race No. 33
November 8, 1998 Average Speed: 114.915

Driver	Owner	Car #	Make	Laps	Winnings
1. Jeff Gordon	Rick Hendrick	24	Chev	221	164,450
2. Dale Jarrett	Robert Yates	88	Ford	221	100,400
3. Mark Martin	Jack Roush	6	Ford	221	67,350
4. Jeff Burton	Jack Roush	99	Ford	221	64,600
5. Todd Bodine	Joe Falk	91	Chev	221	55,000

1999 Winston Cup Series Race No. 34
November 21, 1999 Average Speed: 137.942

Driver	Owner	Car #	Make	Laps	Winnings
1. Bobby Labonte	Joe Gibbs	18	Pont	325	174,300
2. Dale Jarrett	Robert Yates	88	Ford	325	94,400
3. Jeremy Mayfield	Michael Kranefuss	12	Ford	325	75,875
4. Mark Martin	Jack Roush	6	Ford	325	75,850
5. Jeff Burton	Jack Roush	99	Ford	325	70,000

2000 Winston Cup Series Race No. 34
November 19, 2000 Average Speed: 141.296

Driver	Owner	Car #	Make	Laps	Winnings
1. Jerry Nadeau	Rick Hendrick	25	Chev	325	180,550
2. Dale Earnhardt	Richard Childress	3	Chev	325	99,750
3. Ward Burton	Bill Davis	22	Pont	325	98,150
4. Jeff Gordon	Rick Hendrick	24	Chev	325	88,800
5. Bobby Labonte	Joe Gibbs	18	Pont	325	76,200

2001 Winston Cup Series Race No. 35
November 18, 2001 Average Speed: 151.756

Driver	Owner	Car #	Make	Laps	Winnings
1. Bobby Labonte	Joe Gibbs	18	Pont	325	233,227
2. Sterling Marlin	Chip Ganassi	40	Dodg	325	142,460
3. Kevin Harvick	Richard Childress	29	Chev	325	135,477
4. Jerry Nadeau	Rick Hendrick	25	Chev	325	110,100
5. Ward Burton	Bill Davis	22	Dodg	325	113,435

1999 Winston Cup Series Race No. 4
March 14, 1999 Average Speed: 143.296

Driver	Owner	Car #	Make	Laps	Winnings
1. Jeff Gordon	Rick Hendrick	24	Chev	325	117,650
2. Bobby Labonte	Joe Gibbs	18	Pont	325	98,850
3. Mark Martin	Jack Roush	6	Ford	325	62,775
4. Jeff Burton	Jack Roush	99	Ford	325	64,900
5. Dale Jarrett	Robert Yates	88	Ford	325	53,675

2000 Winston Cup Series Race No. 4
March 12, 2000 Average Speed: 131.759

Driver	Owner	Car #	Make	Laps	Winnings
1. Dale Earnhardt	Richard Childress	3	Chev	325	123,100
2. Bobby Labonte	Joe Gibbs	18	Pont	325	88,200
3. Mark Martin	Jack Roush	6	Ford	325	67,900
4. Steve Park	Dale Earnhardt, Inc.	1	Chev	325	60,250
5. Joe Nemechek	Andy Petree	33	Chev	325	60,050

2001 Winston Cup Series Race No. 4
March 11, 2001 Average Speed: 143.416

Driver	Owner	Car #	Make	Laps	Winnings
1. Kevin Harvick	Richard Childress	29	Chev	325	158,427
2. Jeff Gordon	Rick Hendrick	24	Chev	325	143,077
3. Jerry Nadeau	Rick Hendrick	25	Chev	325	80,650
4. Dale Jarrett	Robert Yates	88	Ford	325	114,927
5. Terry Labonte	Rick Hendrick	5	Chev	325	92,630

2002 Winston Cup Series Race No. 4
March 10, 2002 Average Speed: 148.443

Driver	Owner	Car #	Make	Laps	Winnings
1. Tony Stewart	Joe Gibbs	20	Pont	325	174,978
2. Dale Earnhardt, Jr.	Dale Earnhardt, Inc.	8	Chev	325	104,600
3. Jimmie Johnson	Rick Hendrick	48	Chev	325	72,350
4. Matt Kenseth	Jack Roush	17	Ford	325	91,700
5. Ricky Craven	Cal Wells	32	Ford	325	69,950

2002 Winston Cup Series Race No. 33
October 27, 2002 Average Speed: 127.519

Driver	Owner	Car #	Make	Laps	Winnings
1. Kurt Busch	Jack Roush	97	Ford	248	212,100
2. Joe Nemechek	Rick Hendrick	25	Chev	248	153,400
3. Dale Jarrett	Robert Yates	88	Ford	248	137,178
4. Tony Stewart	Joe Gibbs	20	Pont	248	137,178
5. Dale Earnhardt, Jr.	Dale Earnhardt, Inc.	8	Chev	248	97,950

Augusta Int'l Raceway
Augusta, GA
3-mile Paved Road Course

3-mile road course opened in 1963. Only NASCAR Winston Cup (then Grand National) race staged on 11/10/63 (won by Fireball Roberts—his 33rd and final Winston Cup victory; race counted in the 1964 championship season). Track was abandoned and left to decay after first and only event.

Winston Cup Victories
Fireball Roberts   1

Winston Cup Money
Fireball Roberts $13,190

Narrowest Margin of Victory
1 lap and 28 seconds—November 17, 1963

Most Race Leaders
5—November 17, 1963

Winston Cup Poles
Fred Lorenzen   1

Most Cars Started
36—November 17, 1963

Race Record
86.320 MPH—November 17, 1963

Most Cars Running at Finish
16—November 17, 1963

1964 Grand National Race No. 2
November 17, 1963 Average Speed: 86.320

Driver	Owner	Car #	Make	Laps	Winnings
1. Fireball Roberts	Holman-Moody	22	63 Ford	139	13,190
2. Dave MacDonald	Holman-Moody	29	63 Ford	138	6,745
3. Billy Wade	Cotton Owens	5	63 Dodg	137	3,730
4. Joe Weatherly	Bill Stroppe	26	63 Merc	137	2,650
5. Ned Jarrett	Charles Robinson	11	63 Ford	132	1,675

Augusta Int'l Speedway
Augusta, GA
Half-mile Dirt Track

(aka Augusta Speedway; New Augusta Speedway) Half-mile dirt oval built in 1961. First NASCAR Winston Cup (then Grand National) race staged on 6/19/62 (won by Joe Weatherly). Track paved in 1964. Final NASCAR race staged on 10/19/69 (won by Bobby Isaac). Track closed in 1970.

Winston Cup Starts
Richard Petty   11
Wendell Scott   11

Winston Cup Victories
Bobby Isaac   2
David Pearson   2
Richard Petty   2
Joe Weatherly   2

Winston Cup Poles
Bobby Isaac   3

Winston Cup Money
Richard Petty $7,785

Most Cars Started
30—November 1, 1964 Jaycee 300
30—November 14, 1965
    Georgia Cracker 300

Fewest Cars Started
15—April 4, 1963

Narrowest Margin of Victory
2.750 seconds August 15, 1965

Slowest Race
55.104 MPH—July 17, 1962

Race Record
78.740 MPH—October 19, 1969

Most Cautions
6—November 1, 1964 Jaycee 300

Most Race Leaders
4—November 1, 1964 Jaycee 300
4—November 14, 1965
    Georgia Cracker 300

Most Cars Running at Finish
21—November 14, 1965
    Georgia Cracker 300

1962 Grand National Race No. 26
June 19, 1962 Average Speed: 59.850

Driver	Owner	Car #	Make	Laps	Winnings
1. Joe Weatherly	Bud Moore	8	61 Pont	200	1,000
2. Ned Jarrett	Bee Gee Holloway	11	62 Chev	199	800
3. Richard Petty	Petty Enterprises	43	62 Plym	198	400
4. Jim Paschal	Cliff Stewart	2	62 Pont	193	300
5. G. C. Spencer	G. C. Spencer	48	60 Chev	193	275

1962 Grand National Race No. 33
July 17, 1962 Average Speed: 55.104

Driver	Owner	Car #	Make	Laps	Winnings
1. Joe Weatherly	Bud Moore	8	61 Pont	200	1,000
2. Richard Petty	Petty Enterprises	43	62 Plym	200	600
3. Buck Baker	Buck Baker	87	62 Chrys	198	400
4. Buddy Baker	Buck Baker	86	61 Chrys	196	300
5. Bob Welborn	J. C. Parker	49	62 Pont	195	275

1962 Grand National Race No. 49
September 13, 1962 Average Speed: 60.759

Driver	Owner	Car #	Make	Laps	Winnings
1. Fred Lorenzen	Mamie Reynolds	26	62 Ford	200	1,000
2. Richard Petty	Petty Enterprises	41	62 Plym	200	600
3. Joe Weatherly	Bud Moore	8	62 Pont	197	400
4. Ned Jarrett	Bee Gee Holloway	11	62 Chev	190	500
5. Wendell Scott	Wendell Scott	34	61 Chev	190	275

1963 Grand National Race No. 14
April 4, 1963 Average Speed: 60.089

Driver	Owner	Car #	Make	Laps	Winnings
1. Ned Jarrett	Charles Robinson	11	63 Ford	112	1,000
2. Richard Petty	Petty Enterprises	43	62 Plym	112	600
3. Curtis Crider	Curtis Crider	62	62 Merc	110	400
4. H. G. Rosier	H. G. Rosier	5	61 Pont	108	300
5. Buck Baker	Buck Baker	87	62 Chrys	106	275

1964 Grand National Race No. 61 Jaycee 300
November 1, 1964 Average Speed: 68.641

Driver	Owner	Car #	Make	Laps	Winnings
1. Darel Dieringer	Bud Moore	16	64 Merc	300	1,750
2. Bobby Isaac	Cotton Owens	5	64 Dodg	300	800
3. Larry Thomas	Charles Robinson	36	64 Plym	298	600
4. Doug Cooper	Bob Cooper	60	64 Ford	283	500
4. Billy Wade	Bud Moore	1	64 Merc	293	525

1965 Grand National Race No. 40
August 15, 1965 Average Speed: 71.499

Driver	Owner	Car #	Make	Laps	Winnings
1. Dick Hutcherson	Holman-Moody	29	65 Ford	200	1,000
2. David Pearson	Cotton Owens	6	65 Dodg	200	600
3. Ned Jarrett	Bondy Long	11	65 Ford	200	400
4. LeeRoy Yarbrough	Gary Weaver	10	64 Ford	199	300
5. G. C. Spencer	G. C. Spencer	49	64 Ford	196	375

1966 Grand National Race No. 1 Georgia Cracker 300
November 14, 1965 Average Speed: 73.569

Driver	Owner	Car #	Make	Laps	Winnings
1. Richard Petty	Petty Enterprises	42	65 Plym	300	1,700
2. Bobby Isaac	Rex Lovette	26	65 Ford	300	850
3. Ned Jarrett	Bondy Long	11	65 Ford	300	820
4. Jim Paschal	Gary Weaver	10	64 Ford	297	515
5. Roy Mayne	Tom Hunter	46	65 Chev	296	490

1967 Grand National Race No. 1 Augusta 300
November 13, 1966 Average Speed: 71.809

Driver	Owner	Car #	Make	Laps	Winnings
1. Richard Petty	Petty Enterprises	43	66 Plym	300	1,735
2. Paul Lewis	Paul Lewis	1	65 Plym	297	1,170
3. David Pearson	Cotton Owens	6	66 Dodg	297	1,050
4. James Hylton	Bud Hartje	48	65 Dodg	296	645
5. Tiny Lund	Lyle Stelter	55	64 Ford	289	605

1968 Grand National Race No. 13 Dixie 250
May 3, 1968 Average Speed: 73.099

Driver	Owner	Car #	Make	Laps	Winnings
1. Bobby Isaac	Nord Krauskopf	71	67 Dodg	250	1,100
2. Buddy Baker	Ray Fox	3	67 Dodg	249	700
3. Tom Pistone	Jon Thorne	12	68 Merc	249	600
4. James Hylton	James Hylton	48	67 Dodg	244	500
5. Buck Baker	Buck Baker	87	67 Olds	239	425

1968 Grand National Race No. 46 Augusta 200
October 5, 1968 Average Speed: 75.821

Driver	Owner	Car #	Make	Laps	Winnings
1. David Pearson	Holman-Moody	17	68 Ford	200	1,000
2. Bobby Allison	Tom Friedkin	14	68 Plym	200	600
3. Richard Petty	Petty Enterprises	43	68 Plym	200	600
4. Bobby Isaac	Nord Krauskopf	71	68 Dodg	199	300
5. John Sears	L. G. DeWitt	4	67 Ford	194	275

Augusta Int'l Speedway *continued*

1969 Grand National Race No. 8 Cracker 200
March 16, 1969 Average Speed: 77.586

Driver	Owner	Car #	Make	Laps	Winnings
1. David Pearson	Holman-Moody	17	69 Ford	200	1,200
2. Richard Petty	Petty Enterprises	43	69 Ford	200	600
3. Bobby Isaac	Nord Krauskopf	71	69 Dodg	200	400
4. James Hylton	James Hylton	48	67 Dodg	196	350
5. John Sears	L. G. DeWitt	4	67 Ford	195	325

1969 Grand National Race No. 50
October 19, 1969 Average Speed: 78.740

Driver	Owner	Car #	Make	Laps	Winnings
1. Bobby Isaac	Nord Krauskopf	71	69 Dodg	200	1,000
2. Richard Petty	Petty Enterprises	43	69 Ford	200	600
3. David Pearson	Holman-Moody	17	69 Ford	199	600
4. LeeRoy Yarbrough	Junior Johnson	98	69 Ford	198	350
5. Elmo Langley	Elmo Langley	64	68 Ford	195	325

Central City Speedway
Macon, GA
Half-mile Dirt Track

(aka Central City Park Speedway; Macon Speedway; Macon Fairgrounds Speedway; Georgia State Fairgrounds) Originally built in 1920s as 1-mile dirt track. Half-mile dirt track built in 1947. First NASCAR Winston Cup (then Grand National) race staged on 9/9/51 (won by Herb Thomas). Final Grand National race run on 9/12/54 (won by Hershel McGriff). Track operated until May 1956.

Winston Cup Starts

Joe Eubanks	7
Jim Paschal	7
Lee Petty	7
Herb Thomas	7

Winston Cup Victories

Herb Thomas	2

Winston Cup Poles

Joe Eubanks	1
Bob Flock	1
Tim Flock	1
Fonty Flock	1
Dick Rathmann	1
Jack Smith	1

Winston Cup Money

Herb Thomas	$3,980

Most Cars Started
28—April 27, 1952

Fewest Cars Started
20—September 13, 1953

Narrowest Margin of Victory
N/A

Slowest Race
48.404 MPH—September 7, 1952

Race Record
56.417 MPH—April 26, 1953

Most Race Leaders
5—September 13, 1953

Most Cars Running at Finish
20—April 27, 1952

1951 Grand National Race No. 26
September 8, 1951 Average Speed: 53.222

Driver	Owner	Car #	Make	Laps	Winnings
1. Herb Thomas	Herb Thomas	92	51 Plym	200	1,000
2. Gober Sosebee	Gober Sosebee	51	51 Olds	198	600
3. Jim Paschal	Julian Buesink	60	50 Ford	—	500
4. Fonty Flock	Frank Christian	14	51 Olds	—	400
5. Donald Thomas	Herb Thomas	93	51 Plym	—	300

1952 Grand National Race No. 26
September 7, 1952 Average Speed: 48.404

Driver	Owner	Car #	Make	Laps	Winnings
1. Lee Petty	Petty Enterprises	42	51 Plym	300	1,260
2. Herb Thomas	Herb Thomas	92	52 Huds	300	810
3. Tim Flock	Ted Chester	91	52 Huds	298	630
4. Joe Eubanks	Phil Oates	82	52 Huds	295	500
5. Herschel Buchanan	Herschel Buchanan	1	52 Nash	289	300

1953 Grand National Race No. 31
September 13, 1953 Average Speed: 55.172

Driver	Owner	Car #	Make	Laps	Winnings
1. Speedy Thompson	Buckshot Morris	12	53 Olds	200	1,000
2. Lee Petty	Petty Enterprises	42	53 Dodg	—	700
3. Gober Sosebee	Gober Sosebee	51	53 Olds	—	450
4. Joe Eubanks	Phil Oates	82	53 Huds	—	350
5. Tim Flock	Ted Chester	91	53 Huds	—	200

1952 Grand National Race No. 8
April 27, 1952 Average Speed: 53.853

Driver	Owner	Car #	Make	Laps	Winnings
1. Herb Thomas	Herb Thomas	92	52 Huds	198	1,270
2. Fonty Flock	Frank Christian	14	51 Olds	198	800
3. Ed Samples	Claude Alexander	9	51 Olds	198	600
4. Buck Baker	B. A. Pless	89	52 Huds	197	500
5. Gober Sosebee	Gober Sosebee	51	50 Olds	195	300

1953 Grand National Race No. 7
April 26, 1953 Average Speed: 56.417

Driver	Owner	Car #	Make	Laps	Winnings
1. Dick Rathmann	Walt Chapman	120	52 Huds	200	1,000
2. Herb Thomas	Herb Thomas	92	53 Huds	—	700
3. Jimmie Lewallen	Dave Quate	43	53 Olds	—	450
4. Fonty Flock	Frank Christian	14	53 Olds	—	350
5. Dick Passwater	Frank Arford	78	53 Olds	—	200

1954 Grand National Race No. 9
April 25, 1954 Average Speed: 55.410

Driver	Owner	Car #	Make	Laps	Winnings
1. Gober Sosebee	Gober Sosebee	51	54 Olds	200	1,000
2. Dick Rathmann	John Ditz	3	54 Huds	200	650
3. Jim Paschal	Griffin Motors	87	53 Olds	199	450
4. Al Keller	George Miller	23	54 Huds	199	350
5. Curtis Turner	Frank Christian	14	53 Olds	199	300

1954 Grand National Race No. 32
September 12, 1954 Average Speed: 50.536

Driver	Owner	Car #	Make	Laps	Winnings
1. Hershel McGriff	Frank Christian	14	51 Olds	200	1,000
2. Tim Flock	Buck Baker	89	53 Olds	200	650
3. Lee Petty	Petty Enterprises	42	54 Chrys	200	450
4. Joe Eubanks	Phil Oates	82	51 Huds	199	350
5. Ralph Liguori	Ralph Liguori	6	54 Dodg	197	300

Columbus Speedway
Columbus, GA
Half-mile Dirt Track

Half-mile dirt track built circa 1949. Only NASCAR Winston Cup (then Grand National) event staged on 6/10/51 (won by Tim Flock). Track closed in late '50s.

Winston Cup Victories
Tim Flock   1

Winston Cup Poles
Gober Sosebee   1

Winston Cup Money
Tim Flock $1,000

Most Cars Started
31—June 10, 1951

Narrowest Margin of Victory
N/A

Most Cautions
4—June 10, 1951

Most Race Leaders
1—June 10, 1951

Most Cars Running at Finish
N/A

1951 Grand National Race No. 10
June 10, 1951

Driver	Owner	Car #	Make	Laps	Winnings
1. Tim Flock	Ted Chester	91	51 Olds	200	1,000
2. Gober Sosebee	Sam Knox	51	50 Cad	—	600
3. Herb Thomas	Herb Thomas	92	50 Plym	—	400
4. Jim Paschal	Julian Buesink	60	50 Ford	—	300
5. Lee Petty	Petty Enterprises	42	49 Plym	—	250

Hayloft Speedway
Augusta, GA
Half-mile Dirt Track

(aka Augusta Speedway; Gordon Park Speedway) Opened in March 1948. Only NASCAR Winston Cup (then Grand National) race staged on 6/1/52 (won by Gober Sosebee). Track closed in 1955. Dirt track was built on grounds in 1980s.

Winston Cup Victories
Gober Sosebee   1

Winston Cup Poles
Tommy Moon   1

Winston Cup Money
Gober Sosebee $1,000

Most Cars Started
14—June 1, 1952

Narrowest Margin of Victory
22 seconds June 1, 1952

Most Race Leaders
N/A

Most Cars Running at Finish
10—June 1, 1952

1952 Grand National Race No. 13
June 1, 1952

Driver	Owner	Car #	Make	Laps	Winnings
1. Gober Sosebee	Sam Knox	51	52 Chrys	154	1,000
2. Tommy Moon	C. D. Wilson	57	52 Huds	154	700
3. David Ezell			52 Huds	153	450
4. June Cleveland	Carl Mays	17	51 Chrys	150	350
5. Jerry Wimbish	Jerry Wimbish		50 Olds	150	300

Jeffco Speedway
Jefferson, GA
Half-mile Paved Track

(aka Peach State Speedway; Georgia Int'l Speedway) Half-mile paved oval opened in July 1967. First NASCAR Winston Cup (then Grand National) race staged on 11/3/68 (won by Cale Yarborough). Only other NASCAR event staged on 11/2/69 (won by Bobby Isaac). Track is still in operation.

Winston Cup Starts
18 drivers tied with 2

Winston Cup Victories
Bobby Isaac   1
Cale Yarborough   1

Winston Cup Poles
David Pearson   2

Winston Cup Money
Bobby Isaac $1,500

Most Cars Started
29—November 3, 1968 Peach State 200

Fewest Cars Started
27—November 2, 1969 Jeffco 200

Narrowest Margin of Victory
Half lap—November 3, 1968

Slowest Race
77.737 MPH—November 3, 1968
Peach State 200

Race Record
85.106 MPH—November 2, 1969
Jeffco 200

Most Cautions
N/A

Most Race Leaders
3—November 3, 1968 Peach State 200

Most Cars Running at Finish
21—November 3, 1968 Peach State 200
21—November 2, 1969 Jeffco 200

1968 Grand National Race No. 49 Peach State 200
November 3, 1968 Average Speed: 77.737

Driver	Owner	Car #	Make	Laps	Winnings
1. Cale Yarborough	Wood Brothers	21	68 Merc	200	1,000
2. Richard Petty	Petty Enterprises	43	68 Plym	200	800
3. David Pearson	Holman-Moody	17	68 Ford	199	400
4. James Hylton	James Hylton	48	68 Dodg	199	300
5. LeeRoy Yarbrough	Lyle Stelter	56	67 Merc	197	275

1969 Grand National Race No. 52 Jeffco 200
November 2, 1969 Average Speed: 85.106

Driver	Owner	Car #	Make	Laps	Winnings
1. Bobby Isaac	Nord Krauskopf	71	69 Dodg	200	1,350
2. David Pearson	Holman-Moody	17	69 Ford	200	950
3. Richard Petty	Petty Enterprises	43	69 Ford	198	500
4. LeeRoy Yarbrough	Junior Johnson	98	69 Ford	196	350
5. Neil Castles	Neil Castles	06	69 Dodg	191	325

Lakewood Speedway
Atlanta, GA
1-mile Dirt Track

(aka Lakewood Park; Lakewood Fairgrounds) Originally built in 1915. First auto race was run in 1917. Held AM Indy Car races in '40s and '50s. Sam Nunis ran two Strictly Stock races (not sanctioned by NASCAR) in 1949. Tim Flock and June Cleveland won, and both were mistakenly given credit for Winston Cup victories. First NASCAR Winston Cup (then Grand National) race staged on 11/11/51 (won by Tim Flock). Final Grand National race run on 6/14/59 (won by Lee Petty after successfully protesting Richard Petty's apparent first Winston Cup victory). Track closed following completion of Atlanta Int'l Raceway. Re-opened for selected shows (NASCAR Grand American, Sprint Cars, Dirt Late Models). Final event held on Labor Day 1979.

Winston Cup Starts
Lee Petty   11

Winston Cup Victories
Buck Baker   2
Herb Thomas   2

Winston Cup Poles
Tim Flock   3

Winston Cup Money
Lee Petty $5,860

Most Cars Started
40—October 26, 1958
40—June 14, 1959

Fewest Cars Started
17—July 12, 1953

Narrowest Margin of Victory
1 car length—March 21, 1954

Slowest Race
58.499 MPH—June 14, 1959

Race Record
79.016 MPH—April 13, 1958

Most Cautions
N/A

Most Race Leaders
4—April 20, 1952
4—November 16, 1952
4—November 1, 1953

Most Cars Running at Finish
21—October 26, 1958
21—June 14, 1959

1951 Grand National Race No. 39
November 11, 1951 Average Speed: 59.960

Driver	Owner	Car #	Make	Laps	Winnings
1. Tim Flock	Ted Chester	91	51 Huds	100	1,000
2. Bob Flock	Ted Chester	7	51 Olds	—	600
3. Jack Smith	Jack Smith	44X	51 Huds	—	500
4. Frank Mundy	Perry Smith	23	51 Stud	—	400
5. Gober Sosebee	Gober Sosebee	51	51 Olds	—	300

1952 Grand National Race No. 7
April 20, 1952 Average Speed: 66.877

Driver	Owner	Car #	Make	Laps	Winnings
1. Bill Blair	George Hutchens	2	52 Olds	100	1,000
2. Ed Samples	Claude Alexander	9	51 Olds	100	700
3. Lee Petty	Petty Enterprises	42	51 Plym	100	450
4. Buck Baker	B. A. Pless	89	52 Huds	99	350
5. Ed Benedict	Ken Swihart	118	52 Huds	98	200

1952 Grand National Race No. 33
November 16, 1952 Average Speed: 64.853

Driver	Owner	Car #	Make	Laps	Winnings
1. Donald Thomas	Herb Thomas	9	52 Huds	100	1,080
2. Lee Petty	Petty Enterprises	42	51 Plym	100	700
3. Joe Eubanks	Phil Oates	82	52 Huds	100	450
4. Tim Flock	Ted Chester	91	52 Huds	99	385
5. Gober Sosebee	Gober Sosebee	51	52 Chrys	98	200

1953 Grand National Race No. 22
July 12, 1953 Average Speed: 70.685

Driver	Owner	Car #	Make	Laps	Winnings
1. Herb Thomas	Herb Thomas	92	53 Huds	100	1,000
2. Dick Rathmann	Walt Chapman	120	53 Huds	—	700
3. Lee Petty	Petty Enterprises	42	53 Dodg	—	450
4. Joe Eubanks	Phil Oates	82	52 Huds	—	350
5. Jerry Wimbish	Jerry Wimbish		52 Huds	—	200

1953 Grand National Race No. 37
November 1, 1953 Average Speed: 63.180

Driver	Owner	Car #	Make	Laps	Winnings
1. Buck Baker	Griffin Motors	87	53 Olds	100	1,000
2. Fonty Flock	Frank Christian	14	53 Huds	—	700
3. Lee Petty	Petty Enterprises	42	53 Dodg	—	450
4. Jim Paschal	George Hutchens	80	53 Dodg	—	350
5. Jimmie Lewallen	R. G. Shelton	22	53 Olds	—	200

1954 Grand National Race No. 4
March 21, 1954 Average Speed: 60.494

Driver	Owner	Car #	Make	Laps	Winnings
1. Herb Thomas	Herb Thomas	92	53 Huds	100	1,000
2. Buck Baker	Griffin Motors	87	53 Olds	100	650
3. Dick Rathmann	John Ditz	3	54 Huds	100	450
4. Gober Sosebee	Gober Sosebee	51	54 Olds	99	350
5. Fonty Flock		99	53 Huds	99	300

1956 Grand National Race No. 9
March 25, 1956 Average Speed: 70.643

Driver	Owner	Car #	Make	Laps	Winnings
1. Buck Baker	Carl Kiekhaefer	300c	56 Chrys	100	1,400
2. Speedy Thompson	Carl Kiekhaefer	500	56 Dodg	100	800
3. Herb Thomas	Herb Thomas	92	56 Chev	99	550
4. Jimmy Massey	Hubert Westmoreland	2	56 Chev	99	365
5. Lee Petty	Petty Enterprises	42	56 Dodg	99	310

1958 Grand National Race No. 10
April 13, 1958 Average Speed: 79.016

Driver	Owner	Car #	Make	Laps	Winnings
1. Curtis Turner	Holman-Moody	26	58 Ford	100	1,540
2. Joe Weatherly	Holman-Moody	12	58 Ford	100	545
3. Fireball Roberts	Beau Morgan	494	57 Ford	100	400
4. Marvin Panch	John Whitford	98	57 Ford	100	250
5. Joe Lee Johnson	S. T. Campbell	310	57 Chev	99	225

1958 Grand National Race No. 51
October 26, 1958 Average Speed: 69.570

Driver	Owner	Car #	Make	Laps	Winnings
1. Junior Johnson	Paul Spaulding	11	57 Ford	150	1,925
2. Fireball Roberts	Frank Strickland	22	57 Chev	150	1,200
3. Lee Petty	Petty Enterprises	2	57 Olds	150	950
4. Joe Weatherly	Beau Morgan	45	58 Ford	149	650
5. Charlie Micney		29	57 Chev	148	550

1959 Grand National Race No. 6
March 22, 1959 Average Speed: 75.172

Driver	Owner	Car #	Make	Laps	Winnings
1. Johnny Beauchamp	Roy Burdick Gar	73	59 Ford	100	800
2. Buck Baker	Buck Baker	87	59 Chev	99	525
3. Tom Pistone	Carl Rupert	59	59 Ford	97	350
4. Speedy Thompson	Steve Pierce	1	57 Chev	96	250
5. Joe Eubanks	Don Every	82	58 Ford	95	225

Lakewood Speedway *continued*

1959 Grand National Race No. 20
June 14, 1959 Average Speed: 58.499

Driver	Owner	Car #	Make	Laps	Winnings
1. Lee Petty	Petty Enterprises	42	59 Plym	150	2,200
2. Richard Petty	Petty Enterprises	43	57 Olds	150	1,400
3. Buck Baker	Buck Baker	87	59 Chev	150	1,025
4. Curtis Turner	W. J. Ridgeway	22	59 Chev	150	950
5. Tom Pistone	Carl Rupert	59	59 Ford	148	625

Middle Georgia Raceway
Macon, GA
Half-mile Paved Track

(aka Macon Raceway; Peach State Fairgrounds) Half-mile track built in 1966 on site of former Central City Speedway. Re-measured as .5479-mile paved oval. First NASCAR Winston Cup (then Grand National) race staged on 5/10/66 (won by Richard Petty). Final race staged on 11/7/71 (won by Bobby Allison). A fully operative moonshine still was found beneath the track shortly before 1968 season opener. The entrance to the still was through a ticket booth. A 35-foot ladder led to a trap door. Authorities found a 125-foot tunnel leading to the still. "This is one of the most cleverly run moonshine operations I have ever seen," said one federal agent. Promoter was arrested, but later acquitted. The race went on as scheduled.

Winston Cup Starts
Wendell Scott   9

Winston Cup Victories
Richard Petty   4

Winston Cup Poles
David Pearson   3
Richard Petty   3

Winston Cup Money
Richard Petty $13,765

Most Cars Started
32—November 7, 1971 Georgia 500

Fewest Cars Started
15—May 10, 1966
Speedy Morelock 200

Narrowest Margin of Victory
5 car lengths—November 9, 1969
Georgia 500

Slowest Race
73.717 MPH—June 1, 1969 Macon 300

Race Record
85.121 MPH—November 17, 1968

Most Cautions
10—November 9, 1969 Georgia 500

Most Race Leaders
4—November 17, 1968
4—November 12, 1967
   Middle Georgia 500
4—November 9, 1969 Georgia 500
4—November 8, 1970 Georgia 500
4—November 7, 1971 Georgia 500

Most Cars Running at Finish
17—November 8, 1970 Georgia 500

1966 Grand National Race No. 17 Speedy Morelock 200
May 10, 1966 Average Speed: 82.023

Driver	Owner	Car #	Make	Laps	Winnings
1. Richard Petty	Petty Enterprises	43	66 Plym	200	1,000
2. Tom Pistone	Tom Pistone	59	64 Ford	200	600
3. Bobby Allison	Betty Lilly	24	66 Ford	197	400
4. James Hylton	Bud Hartje	48	65 Dodg	193	300
5. Neil Castles	Buck Baker	86	66 Plym	184	275

1967 Grand National Race No. 22 Macon 300
June 6, 1967 Average Speed: 80.321

Driver	Owner	Car #	Make	Laps	Winnings
1. Richard Petty	Petty Enterprises	43	67 Plym	300	1,400
2. James Hylton	Bud Hartje	48	65 Dodg	295	1,000
3. Elmo Langley	L. G. DeWitt	4	66 Ford	292	700
4. Bobby Allison	George Davis	07	67 Chev	290	575
5. Doug Cooper	Bob Cooper	02	66 Chev	286	425

1968 Grand National Race No. 1 Middle Georgia 500
November 12, 1967 Average Speed: 81.001

Driver	Owner	Car #	Make	Laps	Winnings
1. Bobby Allison	Holman-Moody	11	67 Ford	500	3,300
2. Richard Petty	Petty Enterprises	43	67 Plym	499	2,040
3. Tiny Lund	Lyle Stelter	55	66 Ford	491	1,275
4. Red Farmer	Roy Buckner	97	67 Ford	476	900
5. Dub Simpson	Buck Baker	88	67 Olds	470	800

1968 Grand National Race No. 20 Macon 300
June 2, 1968 Average Speed: 79.342

Driver	Owner	Car #	Make	Laps	Winnings
1. David Pearson	Holman-Moody	17	68 Ford	300	1,400
2. Bobby Isaac	Nord Krauskopf	71	67 Dodg	300	1,000
3. Richard Petty	Petty Enterprises	43	68 Plym	300	900
4. James Hylton	James Hylton	48	67 Dodg	297	575
5. Tiny Lund	Bud Moore	16	68 Merc	292	425

1969 Grand National Race No. 1
November 17, 1968 Average Speed: 85.121

Driver	Owner	Car #	Make	Laps	Winnings
1. Richard Petty	Petty Enterprises	43	68 Plym	500	3,500
2. David Pearson	Holman-Moody	17	68 Ford	500	2,345
3. James Hylton	James Hylton	48	68 Dodg	490	1,375
4. Elmo Langley	Elmo Langley	64	66 Ford	476	925
5. John Sears	L. G. DeWitt	4	66 Ford	466	825

1969 Grand National Race No. 22 Macon 300
June 1, 1969 Average Speed: 73.717

Driver	Owner	Car #	Make	Laps	Winnings
1. Bobby Isaac	Nord Krauskopf	71	69 Dodg	300	2,500
2. David Pearson	Holman-Moody	17	69 Ford	300	1,700
3. Richard Petty	Petty Enterprises	43	69 Ford	299	1,000
4. John Sears	L. G. DeWitt	4	67 Ford	295	750
5. Neil Castles	Neil Castles	06	67 Plym	295	600

1969 Grand National Race No. 53 Georgia 500
November 9, 1969 Average Speed: 81.079

Driver	Owner	Car #	Make	Laps	Winnings
1. Bobby Allison	Mario Rossi	22	69 Dodg	500	3,050
2. David Pearson	Holman-Moody	17	69 Ford	500	2,025
3. Bobby Isaac	Nord Krauskopf	71	69 Dodg	500	1,300
4. John Sears	L. G. DeWitt	4	67 Ford	482	775
5. Bill Champion	Bill Champion	10	68 Ford	471	675

1970 Grand National Race No. 46 Georgia 500
November 8, 1970 Average Speed: 83.284

Driver	Owner	Car #	Make	Laps	Winnings
1. Richard Petty	Petty Enterprises	43	70 Plym	500	3,275
2. Bobby Isaac	Nord Krauskopf	71	70 Dodg	500	1,800
3. Dick Brooks	Dick Brooks	32	69 Plym	498	1,150
4. Bobby Allison	Bobby Allison	22	69 Dodg	497	925
5. John Sears	John Sears	4	69 Dodg	487	700

1971 Winston Cup GN Race No. 45 Georgia 500
November 7, 1971 Average Speed: 80.859

Driver	Owner	Car #	Make	Laps	Winnings
1. Bobby Allison	Holman-Moody	12	71 Ford	500	3,275
2. Tiny Lund	Ronnie Hopkins	55	70 Chev	499	2,000
3. Friday Hassler	Friday Hassler	39	70 Chev	490	1,200
4. Neil Castles	Neil Castles	06	70 Dodg	486	800
5. Bill Champion	Bill Champion	10	71 Ford	483	700

Oglethorpe Speedway
Savannah, GA
Half-mile Dirt Track

Half-mile dirt track opened in May 1951. First NASCAR Winston Cup (then Grand National) race staged on 3/28/54 (won by Al Keller). Final race staged on 3/6/55 (won by Lee Petty). The track still conducts weekly NASCAR racing.

Winston Cup Starts

Buck Baker	2
Jimmie Lewallen	2
Jim Paschal	2
Eddie Skinner	2
Gober Sosebee	2
Dave Terrell	2
Herb Thomas	2

Winston Cup Victories

Al Keller	1
Lee Petty	1

Winston Cup Poles

Dick Rathmann	1
Herb Thomas	1

Winston Cup Money

Al Keller	$1,000
Lee Petty	$1,000

Most Cars Started
21—March 28, 1954

Fewest Cars Started
18—March 6, 1955

Narrowest Margin of Victory
2 laps plus—March 28, 1954

Slowest Race
59.820 MPH—March 28, 1954

Race Record
60.150 MPH—March 6, 1955

Most Race Leaders
2—March 28, 1954
2—March 6, 1955

Most Cars Running at Finish
12—March 6, 1955

1954 Grand National Race No. 5
March 28, 1954 Average Speed: 59.820

Driver	Owner	Car #	Make	Laps	Winnings
1. Al Keller	George Miller	23	54 Huds	200	1,000
2. Buck Baker	Griffin Motors	87	53 Olds	198	650
3. Gober Sosebee	Gober Sosebee	51	54 Olds	194	450
4. Donald Thomas	John Ditz	3	54 Huds	189	350
5. Joe Eubanks	Phil Oates	82	51 Huds	188	300

1955 Grand National Race No. 5
March 6, 1955 Average Speed: 60.150

Driver	Owner	Car #	Make	Laps	Winnings
1. Lee Petty	Petty Enterprises	42	54 Chrys	200	1,000
2. Don White	Don White	1	55 Olds	196	650
3. Dick Rathmann	John Ditz	3	54 Huds	194	450
4. Herb Thomas	Herb Thomas	92	54 Huds	192	350
5. Eddie Skinner	Frank Dodge	28	53 Olds	185	300

Savannah Speedway
Savannah, GA
Half-mile Paved Track

(aka New Savannah Speedway) Half-mile dirt track built in 1962. First NASCAR Winston Cup (then Grand National) race staged on 3/17/62 (won by Jack Smith). LeeRoy Yarbrough won his first Grand National race here on 5/1/64. Track paved in 1969. Final Grand National race run on 3/15/70 (won by Richard Petty). Track closed in 1981.

Winston Cup Starts
Richard Petty   10

Winston Cup Victories
Richard Petty   3

Winston Cup Poles
Richard Petty   3

Winston Cup Money
Richard Petty $5,785

Most Cars Started
29—October 17, 1969

Fewest Cars Started
12—May 1, 1964 Savannah 200
12—October 9, 1964

Narrowest Margin of Victory
N/A

Slowest Race
58.775 MPH—March 17, 1962
St. Patrick's Day 200

Race Record
82.418 MPH—March 15, 1970
Savannah 200

Most Cautions
3—March 17, 1962 St. Patrick's Day 200
3—December 29, 1963 Sunshine 200

Most Race Leaders
4—March 17, 1962 St. Patrick's Day 200
4—April 28, 1967

Most Cars Running at Finish
23—October 17, 1969

1962 Grand National Race No. 8 St. Patrick's Day 200
March 17, 1962 Average Speed: 58.775

Driver	Owner	Car #	Make	Laps	Winnings
1. Jack Smith	Jack Smith	47	61 Pont	200	1,000
2. Cotton Owens	Cotton Owens	6	60 Pont	200	600
3. Joe Weatherly	Bud Moore	8	61 Pont	198	400
4. Curtis Crider	Curtis Crider	62	61 Merc	190	300
5. Rex White	Rex White	4	61 Chev	183	275

1962 Grand National Race No. 34
July 20, 1962 Average Speed: 67.239

Driver	Owner	Car #	Make	Laps	Winnings
1. Joe Weatherly	Bud Moore	8	61 Pont	200	1,000
2. Tommy Irwin	Melvin Bradley	27	62 Chev	200	600
3. Richard Petty	Petty Enterprises	43	62 Plym	200	400
4. Bob Welborn	J. C. Parker	49	62 Pont	199	300
5. Jim Paschal	Cliff Stewart	2	62 Pont	198	275

1963 Grand National Race No. 31
July 10, 1963 Average Speed: 59.622

Driver	Owner	Car #	Make	Laps	Winnings
1. Ned Jarrett	Charles Robinson	11	63 Ford	200	1,000
2. David Pearson	Cotton Owens	6	63 Dodg	200	600
3. Jimmy Pardue	Pete Stewart	57	62 Pont	199	400
4. Jack Smith	Jack Smith	48	63 Plym	199	300
5. Cale Yarborough	Herman Beam	19	62 Ford	198	275

1964 Grand National Race No. 4 Sunshine 200
December 29, 1963 Average Speed: 68.143

Driver	Owner	Car #	Make	Laps	Winnings
1. Richard Petty	Petty Enterprises	43	63 Plym	200	1,000
2. Jack Smith	Jack Smith	47	63 Plym	199	600
3. Tiny Lund	Dave Kent	32	63 Ford	196	400
4. Maurice Petty	Petty Enterprises	42	63 Plym	195	300
5. Curtis Crider	Curtis Crider	62	63 Ford	194	275

1964 Grand National Race No. 20 Savannah 200
May 1, 1964 Average Speed: 70.326

Driver	Owner	Car #	Make	Laps	Winnings
1. LeeRoy Yarbrough	Louie Weathersby	45	63 Plym	200	1,000
2. Marvin Panch	Wood Brothers	21	64 Ford	199	600
3. Richard Petty	Petty Enterprises	43	64 Plym	197	400
4. Buddy Baker	J. C. Parker	87	63 Dodg	197	300
5. Cale Yarborough	Herman Beam	19	64 Ford	185	275

1964 Grand National Race No. 57
October 9, 1964 Average Speed: 68.663

Driver	Owner	Car #	Make	Laps	Winnings
1. Ned Jarrett	Bondy Long	11	64 Ford	200	1,000
2. Richard Petty	Petty Enterprises	43	64 Plym	199	600
3. David Pearson	Cotton Owens	6	64 Dodg	198	400
4. Jack Anderson	Dave Kent	32	64 Ford	193	300
5. Wendell Scott	Wendell Scott	34	63 Ford	192	275

1967 Grand National Race No. 15
April 28, 1967 Average Speed: 66.802

Driver	Owner	Car #	Make	Laps	Winnings
1. Bobby Allison	Bobby Allison	2	65 Chev	200	1,000
2. Richard Petty	Petty Enterprises	43	67 Plym	200	600
3. Jim Paschal	Tom Friedkin	14	67 Plym	198	400
4. Elmo Langley	Henry Woodfield	64	66 Ford	194	300
5. Clyde Lynn	Clyde Lynn	20	66 Ford	194	275

1967 Grand National Race No. 39
August 25, 1967 Average Speed: 65.041

Driver	Owner	Car #	Make	Laps	Winnings
1. Richard Petty	Petty Enterprises	43	67 Plym	200	1,000
2. Elmo Langley	Henry Woodfield	64	66 Ford	195	600
3. Tom Pistone	Turkey Minton	74	67 Chev	194	400
4. Neil Castles	Neil Castles	91	65 Plym	190	300
5. George Davis	George Davis	07	66 Chev	186	275

1969 Grand National Race No. 49
October 17, 1969 Average Speed: 78.482

Driver	Owner	Car #	Make	Laps	Winnings
1. Bobby Isaac	Nord Krauskopf	71	69 Dodg	200	1,000
2. Richard Petty	Petty Enterprises	43	69 Ford	200	600
3. David Pearson	Holman-Moody	17	69 Ford	200	600
4. LeeRoy Yarbrough	Junior Johnson	98	69 Ford	198	350
5. Elmo Langley	Elmo Langley	64	68 Ford	194	325

1970 Grand National Race No. 7 Savannah 200
March 15, 1970 Average Speed: 82.418

Driver	Owner	Car #	Make	Laps	Winnings
1. Richard Petty	Petty Enterprises	43	70 Plym	200	1,000
2. Bobby Isaac	Nord Krauskopf	71	69 Dodg	199	600
3. James Hylton	James Hylton	48	69 Ford	196	400
4. Benny Parsons	L. G. DeWitt	72	69 Ford	195	350
5. Dave Marcis	Dave Marcis	30	69 Dodg	195	325

Valdosta 75 Speedway
Valdosta, GA
Half-mile Dirt Track

(aka I-75 Speedway; Valdosta Speedway) Half-mile dirt track built in April 1962. First NASCAR Winston Cup (then Grand National) race staged on 8/25/62 (won by Ned Jarrett). Final race staged on 6/25/65 (won by Cale Yarborough, his first Grand National victory). Track closed in 1966.

Winston Cup Starts

Ned Jarrett	3
Wendell Scott	3

Winston Cup Victories

Buck Baker	1
Ned Jarrett	1
Cale Yarborough	1

Winston Cup Poles

Dick Hutcherson	1
Ned Jarrett	1
Richard Petty	1

Winston Cup Money

Ned Jarrett	$1,410

Most Cars Started

23—June 23, 1964

Fewest Cars Started

13—August 25, 1962

Narrowest Margin of Victory

15.000 seconds June 23, 1964

Slowest Race

58.862 MPH—June 27, 1965

Race Record

61.454 MPH—August 25, 1962

Most Race Leaders

3—June 23, 1964
3—June 27, 1965

Most Cars Running at Finish

13—June 23, 1964

1962 Grand National Race No. 44
August 25, 1962 Average Speed: 61.454

Driver	Owner	Car #	Make	Laps	Winnings
1. Ned Jarrett	Bee Gee Holloway	11	62 Chev	200	1,200
2. Richard Petty	Petty Enterprises	43	62 Plym	199	600
3. Joe Weatherly	Bud Moore	8	61 Pont	197	400
4. G. C. Spencer	G. C. Spencer	48	62 Chev	191	300
5. LeeRoy Yarbrough	Ralph Smith	179	62 Chev	191	275

1964 Grand National Race No. 33
June 23, 1964 Average Speed: 61.328

Driver	Owner	Car #	Make	Laps	Winnings
1. Buck Baker	Ray Fox	3	64 Dodg	200	1,000
2. LeeRoy Yarbrough	Louie Weathersby	45	63 Plym	200	600
3. Tiny Lund	David Walker	89	64 Plym	196	400
4. Wendell Scott	Wendell Scott	34	63 Ford	195	300
5. Curtis Crider	Curtis Crider	02	63 Merc	193	275

1965 Grand National Race No. 28
June 27, 1965 Average Speed: 58.862

Driver	Owner	Car #	Make	Laps	Winnings
1. Cale Yarborough	Kenny Myler	06	64 Ford	200	1,000
2. J. T. Putney	Herman Beam	19	64 Ford	197	600
3. G. C. Spencer	G. C. Spencer	49	64 Ford	196	400
4. Stick Elliott	Toy Bolton	18	65 Chev	196	300
5. Harvey Jones	Sam Fogle	31	63 Ford	195	275

Illinois

Chicagoland Speedway
Joliet, IL
1.5-mile Superspeedway

Modern 1.5-mile D-shaped speedway is a product of Motorsports Alliance, a consortium of big-time racing interests that include Indianapolis Motor Speedway and International Speedway Corp. Ceremonial ground breaking occurred on September 28, 1999. Inaugural racing weekend hosted NASCAR Busch Series and Winston Cup. Rookie Kevin Harvick took top honors on inaugural Winston Cup event on July 15, 2001. Track is built on 930 acres and is adjacent to a short track and a drag strip. All purpose facility with corporate skyboxes and spacious grandstands.

Winston Cup Starts
36 drivers tied at

Winston Cup Victories
Kevin Harvick 2

Winston Cup Poles
Todd Bodine 1
Ryan Newman 1

Winston Cup Money
Kevin Harvick $362,528

Most Cars Started
43—2 times

Fewest Cars Started
43—2 times

Narrowest Margin of Victory
0.649 seconds—July 15, 2001

Slowest Race
121.200 MPH—July 15, 2001

Race Record
136.832 MPH—July 14, 2002

Most Cautions
10—July 15, 2001

Most Race Leaders
11—July 14, 2002

Most Cars Running at Finish
34—July 15, 2001

2001 Winston Cup Series Race No. 18
July 15, 2001 Average Speed: 121.2

Driver	Owner	Car #	Make	Laps	Winnings
1. Kevin Harvick	Richard Childress	29	Chev	267	162,500
2. Robert Pressley	Doug Bawel	77	Ford	267	126,600
3. Ricky Rudd	Robert Yates	28	Ford	267	112,600
4. Dale Jarrett	Robert Yates	88	Ford	267	101,300
5. Jimmy Spencer	Travis Carter	26	Ford	267	94,200

2002 Winston Cup Series Race No. 18
July 14, 2002 Average Speed: 136.832

Driver	Owner	Car #	Make	Laps	Winnings
1. Kevin Harvick	Richard Childress	29	Chev	267	200,028
2. Jeff Gordon	Rick Hendrick	24	Chev	267	180,268
3. Tony Stewart	Joe Gibbs	20	Pont	267	153,928
4. Jimmie Johnson	Rick Hendrick	48	Chev	267	88,175
5. Ryan Newman	Roger Penske	12	Ford	267	115,725

Santa Fe Speedway
Willow Springs, IL
Half-mile Dirt Track

Half-mile dirt track opened in May 1953. Only NASCAR Winston Cup (then Grand National) race run on 7/10/54 (won by Dick Rathmann). Track still active in 1990s.

Winston Cup Victories
Dick Rathmann 1

Winston Cup Poles
Buck Baker 1

Winston Cup Money
Dick Rathmann $1,000

Most Cars Started
23—July 10, 1954

Narrowest Margin of Victory
3/4 lap—July 10, 1954

Race Record
72.216 MPH—July 10, 1954

Most Race Leaders
2—July 10, 1954

Most Cars Running at Finish
16—July 10, 1954

1954 Grand National Race No. 24
July 10, 1954 Average Speed: 72.216

Driver	Owner	Car #	Make	Laps	Winnings
1. Dick Rathmann	John Ditz	3	54 Huds	200	1,000
2. Herb Thomas	Herb Thomas	92	54 Huds	200	650
3. Hershel McGriff	Frank Christian	14	51 Olds	200	450
4. Lee Petty	Petty Enterprises	42	54 Chrys	199	350
5. Buck Baker	Ernest Woods	88	54 Olds	197	300

Soldier Field
Chicago, IL
Half-mile Paved Track

Famous football stadium built in 1926. Quarter-mile cinder oval built inside stadium in 1935. Half-mile paved track ran from 1956-67. A .375-mile track followed in 1968. Track torn out in 1970 following protests by hippies who objected to city financing of auto racing. Only NASCAR Winston Cup (then Grand National) race staged on 7/21/56 (won by Fireball Roberts).

Winston Cup Victories
Fireball Roberts   1

Winston Cup Poles
Billy Myers   1

Winston Cup Money
Fireball Roberts $850

Most Cars Started
25—July 21, 1956

Narrowest Margin of Victory
N/A

Race Record
61.037 MPH—July 21, 1956

Most Race Leaders
N/A

Most Cars Running at Finish
15—July 21, 1956

1956 Grand National Race No. 33
July 21, 1956 Average Speed: 61.037

Driver	Owner	Car #	Make	Laps	Winnings
1. Fireball Roberts	Pete DePaolo	22	56 Ford	200	850
2. Jim Paschal	Frank Hayworth	75	56 Merc	200	625
3. Ralph Moody	Pete DePaolo	12	56 Ford	200	450
4. Speedy Thompson	Carl Kiekhaefer	500	56 Dodg	200	350
5. Frank Mundy	Carl Kiekhaefer	500B	56 Dodg	200	310

Indiana

Indianapolis Motor Speedway
Speedway, IN
2.5-mile Superspeedway

Since 1911, the scene of the Greatest Spectacle in Racing, the Indianapolis 500. 2.5-mile rectangular shaped track was built in 1909 with 3.2-million bricks, hence the nickname "Brickyard". Track was built by the Carl Fisher group. Eddie Rickenbacker was president during Depression years. Following the Second World War, Anton Hulman purchased track. First NASCAR Winston Cup race staged on 8/6/94 (won by Jeff Gordon).

Winston Cup Starts
31 drivers tied with 3

Winston Cup Victories
Dale Earnhardt   1
Jeff Gordon   1
Dale Jarrett   1

Winston Cup Poles
Jeff Gordon   2

Winston Cup Money
Jeff Gordon $1,049,791

Most Cars Started
43—August 6, 1994 Brickyard 400

Fewest Cars Started
40—August 3, 1996 Brickyard 400

Narrowest Margin of Victory
0.370 seconds August 5, 1995
  Brickyard 400

Slowest Race
131.977 MPH—August 6, 1994
  Brickyard 400

Race Record
155.206 MPH—August 5, 1995
  Brickyard 400

Most Cautions
6—August 6, 1994 Brickyard 400

Most Race Leaders
13—August 6, 1994 Brickyard 400
13—August 3, 1996 Brickyard 400

Most Cars Running at Finish
36—August 6, 1994 Brickyard 400
36—August 5, 1995 Brickyard 400

1994 Winston Cup Series Race No. 19 Brickyard 400
August 6, 1994 Average Speed: 131.977

Driver	Owner	Car #	Make	Laps	Winnings
1. Jeff Gordon	Rick Hendrick	24	Chev	160	613,000
2. Brett Bodine	Kenny Bernstein	26	Ford	160	203,575
3. Bill Elliott	Junior Johnson	11	Ford	160	164,850
4. Rusty Wallace	Roger Penske	2	Ford	160	140,600
5. Dale Earnhardt	Richard Childress	3	Chev	160	121,625

1995 Winston Cup Series Race No. 19 Brickyard 400
August 5, 1995 Average Speed: 155.206

Driver	Owner	Car #	Make	Laps	Winnings
1. Dale Earnhardt	Richard Childress	3	Chev	160	565,600
2. Rusty Wallace	Roger Penske	2	Ford	160	250,500
3. Dale Jarrett	Robert Yates	28	Ford	160	203,200
4. Bill Elliott	Bill Elliott	94	Ford	160	233,450
5. Mark Martin	Jack Roush	6	Ford	160	144,850

1996 Winston Cup Series Race No. 19 Brickyard 400
August 3, 1996 Average Speed: 139.508

Driver	Owner	Car #	Make	Laps	Winnings
1. Dale Jarrett	Robert Yates	88	Ford	160	564,035
2. Ernie Irvan	Robert Yates	28	Ford	160	267,285
3. Terry Labonte	Rick Hendrick	5	Chev	160	209,535
4. Mark Martin	Jack Roush	6	Ford	160	195,235
5. Morgan Shepherd	Butch Mock	75	Ford	160	140,135

Playland Park Speedway
South Bend, IN
Half-mile Dirt Track

Half-mile dirt track built in 1919. Only NASCAR Winston Cup (then Grand National) race staged on 7/20/52 (won by Tim Flock). Track closed circa 1956.

Winston Cup Victories
Tim Flock   1

Winston Cup Poles
Herb Thomas   1

Winston Cup Money
Tim Flock $1,000

Most Cars Started
19—July 20, 1952

Narrowest Margin of Victory
N/A

Race Record
41.889 MPH—July 20, 1952

Most Race Leaders
2—July 20, 1952

Most Cars Running at Finish
8—July 20, 1952

1952 Grand National Race No. 22
July 20, 1952 Average Speed: 41.889

Driver	Owner	Car #	Make	Laps	Winnings
1. Tim Flock	Ted Chester	91	51 Huds	200	1,000
2. Lee Petty	Petty Enterprises	42	52 Chrys	200	700
3. Bub King	Bub King	55	52 Huds	189	450
4. Herschel Buchanan	Frank Christian	4	51 Olds	186	350
5. Dick Passwater	Frank Arford	77	52 DES	184	200

Winchester Speedway
Winchester, IN
Half-mile Oiled Dirt Track

(aka Funk's Speedway; Funk's Lake; Funk's Motor Speedway) Half-mile dirt track built by Frank Funk in a cornfield in 1914. High-banks were added in 1929. Only Winston Cup (then Grand National) race run on 10/15/50 (won by Lloyd Moore). Track paved in 1951. Still active today, hosting a variety of open wheel and stock car events.

Winston Cup Victories
Lloyd Moore   1

Winston Cup Poles
Dick Linder   1

Winston Cup Money
Lloyd Moore $1,000

Most Cars Started
13—October 15, 1950

Narrowest Margin of Victory
N/A

Race Record
63.875 MPH—October 15, 1950

Most Race Leaders
3—October 15, 1950

Most Cars Running at Finish
N/A

1950 Grand National Race No. 18
October 15, 1950 Average Speed: 63.875

Driver	Owner	Car #	Make	Laps	Winnings
1. Lloyd Moore	Julian Buesink	59	50 Merc	200	1,000
2. Bucky Sager		101	49 Plym	—	625
3. Bill Rexford	Julian Buesink	60	49 Ford	—	400
4. Chuck James			46 Ford	—	300
5. Ray Duhigg		10	50 Plym	—	225

Iowa

Davenport Speedway
Davenport, IA
Half-mile Dirt Track

Half-mile dirt oval opened in August 1920. Only NASCAR Winston Cup (then Grand National) race run on 8/2/53 (won by Herb Thomas). Track still active today.

Winston Cup Victories	**Winston Cup Money**	**Narrowest Margin of Victory**	**Most Race Leaders**
Herb Thomas 1	Herb Thomas $1,000	N/A	N/A

Winston Cup Poles	**Most Cars Started**	**Race Record**	**Most Cars Running at Finish**
Buck Baker 1	14—August 2, 1953	62.500 MPH—August 2, 1953	N/A

1953 Grand National Race No. 25
August 2, 1953 Average Speed: 62.500

Driver	Owner	Car #	Make	Laps	Winnings
1. Herb Thomas	Herb Thomas	92	53 Huds	200	1,000
2. Buck Baker	Griffin Motors	87	53 Olds	—	700
3. Lee Petty	Petty Enterprises	42	53 Dodg	—	450
4. Dick Rathmann	Walt Chapman	120	53 Huds	—	350
5. Fonty Flock	Frank Christian	14	53 Huds	—	200

Kansas

Kansas Speedway
Kansas City, KS
1.5-mile Superspeedway

Construction on the $250 million multi purpose motorsports facility began in May, 1999. Mile-and-a-half D-shaped track opened in July, 2001. Eddie Cheever won the first major open wheel Indy Racing League event on July 8, 2001. First NASCAR Winston Cup race staged on September 30, 2001, won by Jeff Gordon. One of the many new motorsports facilities under the corporate umbrella operated by International Speedway Corp.

Winston Cup Starts	**Winston Cup Money**	**Narrowest Margin of Victory**	**Most Cautions**
33 drivers tied at 2	Jeff Gordon $472,305	0.413 seconds—September 30, 2001	13—September 30, 2001
Winston Cup Victories	**Most Cars Started**	**Slowest Race**	**Most Race Leaders**
Jeff Gordon 2	43—2 times	110.576 MPH—September 30, 2001	12—September 30, 2001
Winston Cup Poles	**Fewest Cars Started**	**Race Record**	**Most Cars Running at Finish**
Dale Earnhardt, Jr. 1	43—2 times	119.394 MPH—September 29, 2002	30—September 30, 2001

2001 Winston Cup Series Race No. 28
September 30, 2001 Average Speed: 110.576

Driver	Owner	Car #	Make	Laps	Winnings
1. Jeff Gordon	Rick Hendrick	24	Chev	267	254,377
2. Ryan Newman	Roger Penske	02	Ford	267	100,100
3. Ricky Rudd	Robert Yates	28	Ford	267	138,947
4. Rusty Wallace	Roger Penske	2	Ford	267	130,140
5. Sterling Marlin	Chip Ganassi	40	Dodg	267	98,760

2002 Winston Cup Series Race No. 29
September 29, 2002 Average Speed: 119.394

Driver	Owner	Car #	Make	Laps	Winnings
1. Jeff Gordon	Rick Hendrick	24	Chev	267	217,928
2. Ryan Newman	Roger Penske	12	Ford	267	150,140
3. Rusty Wallace	Roger Penske	2	Ford	267	140,800
4. Joe Nemechek	Rick Hendrick	25	Chev	267	105,025
5. Bill Elliott	Ray Evernham	9	Dodg	267	106,231

Kentucky

Corbin Speedway
Corbin, KY
Half-mile Dirt Track

Half-mile dirt track opened circa 1953. Only NASCAR Winston Cup (then Grand National) race staged on 8/29/54 (won by Lee Petty). Track closed in early 1960s.

Winston Cup Victories
Lee Petty   1

Winston Cup Poles
Jim Paschal   1

Winston Cup Money
Lee Petty $1,000

Most Cars Started
21—August 29, 1954

Narrowest Margin of Victory
N/A

Race Record
63.080 MPH—August 29, 1954

Most Race Leaders
N/A

Most Cars Running at Finish
13—August 29, 1954

1954 Grand National Race No. 30
August 29, 1954 Average Speed: 63.080

Driver	Owner	Car #	Make	Laps	Winnings
1. Lee Petty	Petty Enterprises	42	54 Chrys	200	1,000
2. Hershel McGriff	Frank Christian	14	52 Olds	200	650
3. Buck Baker	Griffin Motors	87	53 Olds	198	450
4. Herb Thomas	Herb Thomas	92	54 Huds	195	350
5. Donald Thomas	Herb Thomas	9	53 Huds	191	300

Louisiana

Louisiana Fairgrounds
Shreveport, LA
Half-mile Dirt Track

(aka Louisiana Speedway; Louisiana State Fair Speedway) Originally built as 1-mile horse track in 1905. Autos first raced at facility in 1910. The legendary Barney Oldfield won first race. Half-mile dirt oval built circa 1931. Only NASCAR Winston Cup (then Grand National) race staged on 6/7/53 (won by Lee Petty). Track closed in 1980.

Winston Cup Victories		**Winston Cup Money**		**Narrowest Margin of Victory**	**Most Race Leaders**
Lee Petty	1	Lee Petty	$1,000	N/A	N/A

Winston Cup Poles		**Most Cars Started**	**Race Record**	**Most Cars Running at Finish**
Herb Thomas	1	19—June 7, 1953	53.199 MPH—June 7, 1953	N/A

1953 Grand National Race No. 14
June 7, 1953 Average Speed: 53.199

Driver	Owner	Car #	Make	Laps	Winnings
1. Lee Petty	Petty Enterprises	42	53 Dodg	200	1,000
2. Dick Rathmann	Walt Chapman	120	53 Huds	—	700
3. Herb Thomas	Herb Thomas	92	53 Huds	—	650
4. Tim Flock	Ted Chester	91	52 Huds	—	350
5. Buck Baker	Griffin Motors	87	53 Olds	—	200

Maine

Oxford Plains Speedway
Oxford, ME
.333-mile Paved Track

Half-mile dirt oval opened in May 1950. Track reconfigured to .333-mile paved oval in June 1960. First NASCAR Winston Cup (then Grand National) race staged on 7/12/66 (won by Bobby Allison, his first of 85 career victories). Final Grand National race held on 7/9/68 (won by Richard Petty). Track still active today.

Winston Cup Starts
Many drivers tied with 3

Winston Cup Victories
Bobby Allison   2

Winston Cup Poles
Bobby Allison   1
Buddy Baker   1
James Hylton   1

Winston Cup Money
Bobby Allison $2,575

Most Cars Started
30—July 11, 1967 Maine 300

Fewest Cars Started
27—July 12, 1966
27—July 9, 1968 Maine 300

Narrowest Margin of Victory
12 seconds July 9, 1968 Maine 300

Slowest Race
56.782 MPH—July 12, 1966

Race Record
63.717 MPH—July 9, 1968 Maine 300

Most Cautions
4—July 12, 1966

Most Race Leaders
4—July 11, 1967 Maine 300

Most Cars Running at Finish
15—July 9, 1968 Maine 300

1966 Grand National Race No. 31
July 12, 1966 Average Speed: 56.782

	Driver	Owner	Car #	Make	Laps	Winnings
1.	Bobby Allison	Bobby Allison	2	65 Chev	300	1,100
2.	Tiny Lund	Lyle Stelter	55	64 Ford	299	675
3.	Richard Petty	Petty Enterprises	43	66 Plym	299	450
4.	Neil Castles	Buck Baker	87	66 Olds	297	325
5.	James Hylton	Bud Hartje	48	65 Dodg	297	315

1967 Grand National Race No. 30 Maine 300
July 11, 1967 Average Speed: 61.697

	Driver	Owner	Car #	Make	Laps	Winnings
1.	Bobby Allison	Bobby Allison	2	65 Chev	300	1,150
2.	Richard Petty	Petty Enterprises	43	67 Plym	299	700
3.	Jim Paschal	Tom Friedkin	14	67 Plym	297	450
4.	James Hylton	Bud Hartje	48	65 Dodg	297	325
5.	Neil Castles	Neil Castles	06	65 Dodg	294	315

1968 Grand National Race No. 27 Maine 300
July 9, 1968 Average Speed: 63.717

	Driver	Owner	Car #	Make	Laps	Winnings
1.	Richard Petty	Petty Enterprises	43	68 Plym	300	1,350
2.	David Pearson	Holman-Moody	17	68 Ford	300	700
3.	Buddy Baker	Ray Fox	3	67 Dodg	297	450
4.	Bobby Allison	Bobby Allison	2	66 Chev	297	325
5.	Bobby Isaac	Nord Krauskopf	71	67 Dodg	292	315

Maryland

Beltsville Speedway
Beltsville, MD
Half-mile Paved Track

(aka Baltimore-Washington Speedway) Half-mile paved oval opened in July 1965. First NASCAR Winston Cup (then Grand National) race staged on 8/25/65 (won by Ned Jarrett). Final race held on 5/15/70 (won by Bobby Isaac). Nearby residents, who built homes in the area long after the track was built, complained about noise, prompting track officials to apply mufflers to all race cars in the early '70s. Track closed in 1979.

Winston Cup Starts
Elmo Langley 10
Wendell Scott 10

Winston Cup Victories
Bobby Isaac 3

Winston Cup Poles
Richard Petty 5

Winston Cup Money
Bobby Isaac $7,120

Most Cars Started
31—June 15, 1966 Beltsville 200

Fewest Cars Started
16—May 19, 1967 Beltsville 200

Narrowest Margin of Victory
2 feet—June 15, 1966
Beltsville 200

Slowest Race
68.899 MPH—August 24, 1966
Maryland 200

Race Record
77.253 MPH—July 15, 1969
Maryland 300

Most Cautions
3—May 19, 1967 Beltsville 200
3—May 16, 1969 Beltsville 300

Most Race Leaders
4—July 15, 1969 Maryland 300
4—May 15, 1970 Beltsville 300

Most Cars Running at Finish
15—June 15, 1966 Beltsville 200

1965 Grand National Race No. 43
August 25, 1965 Average Speed: 74.165

Driver	Owner	Car #	Make	Laps	Winnings
1. Ned Jarrett	Bondy Long	11	65 Ford	200	1,000
2. Tiny Lund	Lyle Stelter	55	64 Ford	198	600
3. Darel Dieringer	Lanty McClung	37	64 Ford	198	400
4. Dick Dixon	Dan Colone	8	63 Ford	197	300
5. Wendell Scott	Wendell Scott	34	63 Ford	191	275

1966 Grand National Race No. 26 Beltsville 200
June 15, 1966 Average Speed: 73.409

Driver	Owner	Car #	Make	Laps	Winnings
1. Tiny Lund	Lyle Stelter	55	64 Ford	200	1,000
2. James Hylton	Bud Hartje	48	65 Dodg	200	600
3. Hank Thomas	W. S. Jenkins	92	64 Ford	195	400
4. John Sears	L. G. DeWitt	4	64 Ford	195	300
5. G. C. Spencer	Henley Gray	97	66 Ford	193	275

1966 Grand National Race No. 40 Maryland 200
August 24, 1966 Average Speed: 68.899

Driver	Owner	Car #	Make	Laps	Winnings
1. Bobby Allison	Bobby Allison	2	65 Chev	200	1,000
2. Elmo Langley	Henry Woodfield	64	64 Ford	199	600
3. James Hylton	Bud Hartje	48	65 Dodg	196	400
4. Buck Baker	Buck Baker	87	66 Olds	195	300
5. Tiny Lund	Lyle Stelter	55	64 Ford	194	275

1967 Grand National Race No. 18 Beltsville 200
May 19, 1967 Average Speed: 71.036

Driver	Owner	Car #	Make	Laps	Winnings
1. Jim Paschal	Tom Friedkin	14	67 Plym	200	1,000
2. Richard Petty	Petty Enterprises	43	67 Plym	200	600
3. Bobby Allison	Cotton Owens	6	67 Dodg	200	400
4. Donnie Allison	Bobby Allison	2	65 Chev	198	300
5. Paul Lewis	Emory Gilliam	00	65 Dodg	195	275

1967 Grand National Race No. 43 Maryland 300
September 15, 1967 Average Speed: 76.563

Driver	Owner	Car #	Make	Laps	Winnings
1. Richard Petty	Petty Enterprises	43	67 Plym	300	1,400
2. Bobby Allison	Bobby Allison	2	65 Chev	298	1,000
3. Jim Paschal	Tom Friedkin	14	67 Plym	298	700
4. James Hylton	Bud Hartje	48	65 Dodg	292	575
5. John Sears	L. G. DeWitt	4	66 Ford	286	425

1968 Grand National Race No. 16 Beltsville 300
May 17, 1968 Average Speed: 74.844

Driver	Owner	Car #	Make	Laps	Winnings
1. David Pearson	Holman-Moody	17	68 Ford	300	1,400
2. Bobby Isaac	Nord Krauskopf	71	67 Dodg	299	1,000
3. Buddy Baker	Ray Fox	3	67 Dodg	297	700
4. James Hylton	James Hylton	48	67 Dodg	297	575
5. John Sears	L. G. DeWitt	4	67 Ford	285	425

1968 Grand National Race No. 42 Maryland 300
September 13, 1968 Average Speed: 71.033

Driver	Owner	Car #	Make	Laps	Winnings
1. Bobby Isaac	Nord Krauskopf	71	67 Dodg	300	1,400
2. Bobby Allison	Bobby Allison	2	66 Chev	298	1,000
3. Richard Petty	Petty Enterprises	43	68 Plym	294	700
4. G. C. Spencer	G. C. Spencer	49	67 Plym	294	750
5. Roy Tyner	Roy Tyner	9	67 Pont	285	425

1969 Grand National Race No. 19 Beltsville 300
May 16, 1969 Average Speed: 73.059

Driver	Owner	Car #	Make	Laps	Winnings
1. Bobby Isaac	Nord Krauskopf	71	69 Dodg	300	2,500
2. Neil Castles	Neil Castles	06	67 Plym	298	1,500
3. John Sears	L. G. DeWitt	4	67 Ford	295	1,000
4. Elmo Langley	Elmo Langley	64	68 Ford	295	750
5. James Hylton	James Hylton	48	69 Dodg	292	600

Beltsville Speedway *continued*

1969 Grand National Race No. 32 Maryland 300
July 15, 1969 Average Speed: 77.253

Driver	Owner	Car #	Make	Laps	Winnings
1. Richard Petty	Petty Enterprises	43	69 Ford	300	2,500
2. David Pearson	Holman-Moody	17	69 Ford	300	1,700
3. James Hylton	James Hylton	48	69 Dodg	299	1,000
4. Neil Castles	Neil Castles	06	67 Plym	296	750
5. John Sears	L. G. DeWitt	4	68 Ford	294	600

1970 Grand National Race No. 14 Beltsville 300
May 15, 1970 Average Speed: 76.370

Driver	Owner	Car #	Make	Laps	Winnings
1. Bobby Isaac	Nord Krauskopf	71	70 Dodg	300	1,900
2. James Hylton	James Hylton	48	69 Ford	299	1,300
3. Bobby Allison	Bobby Allison	22	69 Dodg	298	900
4. Neil Castles	Neil Castles	06	69 Dodg	297	600
5. Dave Marcis	Dave Marcis	30	69 Dodg	294	475

Massachusetts

Norwood Arena
Norwood, MA
Quarter-mile Asphalt

Quarter-mile paved oval opened in June 1948. Only NASCAR Winston Cup (then Grand National) event run on 6/17/61 (won by Emanuel Zervakis). Track closed in 1972 and is now the site of an industrial park.

Winston Cup Victories
Emanuel Zervakis   1

Winston Cup Poles
Rex White   1

Winston Cup Money
Emanuel Zervakis $2,250

Most Cars Started
18—June 17, 1961 Yankee 500

Narrowest Margin of Victory
1/4 lap—June 17, 1961

Race Record
53.827 MPH—June 17, 1961 Yankee 500

Most Cautions
1—June 17, 1961 Yankee 500

Most Race Leaders
3—June 17, 1961 Yankee 500

Most Cars Running at Finish
11—June 17, 1961 Yankee 500

1961 Grand National Race No. 29 Yankee 500
June 17, 1961 Average Speed: 53.827

Driver	Owner	Car #	Make	Laps	Winnings
1. Emanuel Zervakis	Monroe Shook	85	60 Chev	500	2,250
2. Rex White	Rex White	4	60 Chev	500	1,000
3. Ned Jarrett	Bee Gee Holloway	11	61 Chev	491	800
4. Buck Baker	Buck Baker	86	61 Chrys	476	700
5. Jim Reed	Jim Reed	7	61 Chev	473	600

Michigan

Grand River Speedrome
Grand Rapids, MI
Half-mile Dirt Track

(aka Comstock Park; West Michigan State Fair; Kent County Fairgrounds; Comstock Park Fairgrounds; Grand River Speedway) Original track built in 1903, a 1.125-mile dirt oval. Quarter mile and half-mile dirt track built in 1950. First NASCAR Winston Cup (then Grand National) race staged on 7/1/51 (won by Marshall Teague). The only other big NASCAR race was run on 7/11/54 (won by Lee Petty). Track closed in 1966 to make way for US 131 Expressway.

Winston Cup Starts

Ray Duhigg	2
Lee Petty	2
Dick Rathmann	2
Donald Thomas	2
Herb Thomas	2

Winston Cup Victories

| Lee Petty | 1 |
| Marshall Teague | 1 |

Winston Cup Poles

| Tim Flock | 1 |
| Herb Thomas | 1 |

Winston Cup Money

| Lee Petty | $1,200 |

Most Cars Started

25—July 11, 1954

Fewest Cars Started

22—July 1, 1951

Narrowest Margin of Victory

N/A

Slowest Race

52.090 MPH—July 11, 1954

Race Record

52.090 MPH—July 11, 1954

Most Race Leaders

3—July 11, 1954

Most Cars Running at Finish

15—July 11, 1954

1951 Grand National Race No. 14
July 1, 1951

Driver	Owner	Car #	Make	Laps	Winnings
1. Marshall Teague	Marshall Teague	6	51 Huds	200	1,000
2. Dick Rathmann	Walt Chapman	120	51 Huds	—	600
3. Fonty Flock	Frank Christian	14	50 Olds	—	400
4. Tim Flock	Ted Chester	91	51 Olds	—	300
5. Lloyd Moore	Julian Buesink	59	51 Ford	—	250

1954 Grand National Race No. 25
July 11, 1954 Average Speed: 52.090

Driver	Owner	Car #	Make	Laps	Winnings
1. Lee Petty	Petty Enterprises	42	54 Chrys	200	1,000
2. Buck Baker	Ernest Woods	88	54 Olds	196	650
3. Dick Rathmann	John Ditz	3	54 Huds	196	450
4. Ray Duhigg	J. O. Goode	24	51 Plym	193	350
5. Jim Reed	Jim Reed	7	54 Huds	192	300

Michigan Int'l Speedway
Brooklyn, MI
2.04-mile Paved Track

2-mile oval opened in October 1968 with USAC IndyCar race. First NASCAR Winston Cup (then Grand National) event staged on 6/15/69 (won by Cale Yarborough). Built by Larry LoPatin (rhymes with Go Skatin'), who operated the track under American Raceways corporate umbrella. Roger Penske bought track in 1973.

Winston Cup Starts
Dave Marcis   56

Winston Cup Victories
David Pearson   9

Winston Cup Poles
David Pearson   10

Winston Cup Money
Dale Jarrett $1,515,066

Most Cars Started
44—August 17, 1969 Yankee 600

Fewest Cars Started
36—June 16, 1974 Motor State 400
36—August 25, 1974 Yankee 400
36—June 15, 1975 Motor State 400
36—August 24, 1975
    Champion Spark Plug 400
36—June 20, 1976 Cam 2 Motor Oil 400
36—August 22, 1976
    Champion Spark Plug 400
36—June 19, 1977 Cam 2 Motor Oil 400
36—August 22, 1977
    Champion Spark Plug 400
36—June 18, 1978 Gabriel 400
36—August 20, 1978
    Champion Spark Plug 400
36—June 17, 1979 Gabriel 400
36—August 19, 1979
    Champion Spark Plug 400
36—August 16, 1981
    Champion Spark Plug 400

Narrowest Margin of Victory
085 seconds—June 10, 2001

Slowest Race
107.583 MPH—August 24, 1975
    Champion Spark Plug 400

Race Record
173.997 MPH—June 13, 1999

Most Cautions
9—August 16, 1981
    Champion Spark Plug 400

Most Race Leaders
15—June 20, 1982 Gabriel 400

Most Cars Running at Finish
42—June 13, 1999

1969 Grand National Race No. 24 Motor State 500
June 15, 1969 Average Speed: 139.254

Driver	Owner	Car #	Make	Laps	Winnings
1. Cale Yarborough	Wood Brothers	21	69 Merc	250	17,625
2. David Pearson	Holman-Moody	17	69 Ford	250	10,100
3. Richard Petty	Petty Enterprises	43	69 Ford	250	5,875
4. LeeRoy Yarbrough	Junior Johnson	98	69 Merc	249	4,100
5. Charlie Glotzbach	Cotton Owens	6	69 Dodg	249	3,150

1969 Grand National Race No. 37 Yankee 600
August 17, 1969 Average Speed: 115.508

Driver	Owner	Car #	Make	Laps	Winnings
1. David Pearson	Holman-Moody	17	69 Ford	165	21,950
2. Buddy Baker	Cotton Owens	6	69 Dodg	165	10,880
3. Richard Petty	Petty Enterprises	43	69 Ford	165	7,020
4. Cale Yarborough	Wood Brothers	21	69 Merc	165	3,675
5. Bobby Allison	Mario Rossi	22	69 Dodg	165	2,775

1970 Grand National Race No. 19 Motor State 400
June 7, 1970 Average Speed: 138.302

Driver	Owner	Car #	Make	Laps	Winnings
1. Cale Yarborough	Wood Brothers	21	69 Merc	200	14,675
2. Pete Hamilton	Petty Enterprises	40	70 Plym	200	7,120
3. David Pearson	Holman-Moody	17	69 Ford	200	4,980
4. LeeRoy Yarbrough	Junior Johnson	98	69 Ford	200	2,800
5. Bobby Isaac	Nord Krauskopf	71	69 Dodg	199	2,025

1970 Grand National Race No. 34 Yankee 400
August 16, 1970 Average Speed: 147.571

Driver	Owner	Car #	Make	Laps	Winnings
1. Charlie Glotzbach	Ray Nichels	99	69 Dodg	197	14,275
2. Bobby Allison	Mario Rossi	22	69 Dodg	197	6,845
3. Dick Brooks	Dick Brooks	32	70 Plym	196	4,430
4. Bobby Isaac	Nord Krauskopf	71	69 Dodg	196	2,800
5. Pete Hamilton	Petty Enterprises	40	70 Plym	196	1,975

1971 Winston Cup GN Race No. 23 Motor State 400
June 13, 1971 Average Speed: 149.567

Driver	Owner	Car #	Make	Laps	Winnings
1. Bobby Allison	Holman-Moody	12	69 Merc	197	14,945
2. Bobby Isaac	Nord Krauskopf	71	71 Dodg	197	7,620
3. Pete Hamilton	Cotton Owens	6	71 Plym	197	4,920
4. Donnie Allison	Wood Brothers	21	69 Merc	197	2,945
5. Buddy Baker	Petty Enterprises	11	71 Dodg	195	1,945

1971 Winston Cup GN Race No. 36 Yankee 400
August 15, 1971 Average Speed: 149.862

Driver	Owner	Car #	Make	Laps	Winnings
1. Bobby Allison	Holman-Moody	12	69 Merc	197	15,395
2. Richard Petty	Petty Enterprises	43	71 Plym	197	7,870
3. Buddy Baker	Petty Enterprises	11	71 Dodg	196	4,700
4. Maynard Troyer	David Nagle	60	69 Merc	193	2,870
5. Joe Frasson	Joe Frasson	18	70 Dodg	192	2,020

1972 Winston Cup GN Race No. 14 Motor State 400
June 11, 1972 Average Speed: 146.639

Driver	Owner	Car #	Make	Laps	Winnings
1. David Pearson	Wood Brothers	21	71 Merc	200	12,935
2. Bobby Allison	R. Howard & J. Johnson	12	72 Chev	200	8,980
3. Richard Petty	Petty Enterprises	43	72 Dodg	200	6,925
4. James Hylton	James Hylton	48	70 Ford	195	3,350
5. Ron Keselowski	Roger Lubinski	88	70 Dodg	194	2,150

1972 Winston Cup GN Race No. 22 Yankee 400
August 20, 1972 Average Speed: 134.416

Driver	Owner	Car #	Make	Laps	Winnings
1. David Pearson	Wood Brothers	21	71 Merc	200	13,385
2. Bobby Allison	R. Howard & J. Johnson	12	72 Chev	200	9,230
3. Bobby Isaac	Nord Krauskopf	71	72 Dodg	199	6,525
4. Richard Petty	Petty Enterprises	43	72 Dodg	199	5,475
5. Cale Yarborough	James Hylton	98	71 Merc	196	2,150

Michigan Int'l Speedway *continued*

1973 Winston Cup GN Race No. 16 Motor State 400
June 24, 1973 Average Speed: 153.485

Driver	Owner	Car #	Make	Laps	Winnings
1. David Pearson	Wood Brothers	21	71 Merc	200	12,710
2. Buddy Baker	Nord Krauskopf	71	73 Dodg	200	9,055
3. Richard Petty	Petty Enterprises	43	73 Dodg	199	6,800
4. Bobby Allison	Bobby Allison	12	73 Chev	199	4,575
5. Ron Keselowski	Roger Lubinski	99	71 Dodg	197	2,000

1974 Winston Cup GN Race No. 22 Yankee 400
August 25, 1974 Average Speed: 133.045

Driver	Owner	Car #	Make	Laps	Winnings
1. David Pearson	Wood Brothers	21	73 Merc	200	15,765
2. Richard Petty	Petty Enterprises	43	74 Dodg	200	11,155
3. Cale Yarborough	Junior Johnson	11	74 Chev	200	7,700
4. Buddy Baker	Bud Moore	15	73 Ford	199	6,000
5. Bobby Allison	Roger Penske	12	74 Mata	198	2,050

1975 Winston Cup GN Race No. 20 Champion Spark Plug 400
August 24, 1975 Average Speed: 107.583

Driver	Owner	Car #	Make	Laps	Winnings
1. Richard Petty	Petty Enterprises	43	74 Dodg	200	18,140
2. David Pearson	Wood Brothers	21	73 Merc	200	10,735
3. Cale Yarborough	Junior Johnson	11	75 Chev	200	9,385
4. Bobby Allison	Roger Penske	16	75 Mata	200	4,060
5. Dave Marcis	Nord Krauskopf	71	74 Dodg	199	6,310

1976 Winston Cup GN Race No. 20 Champion Spark Plug 400
August 22, 1976 Average Speed: 140.078

Driver	Owner	Car #	Make	Laps	Winnings
1. David Pearson	Wood Brothers	21	Merc	200	16,700
2. Cale Yarborough	Junior Johnson	11	Chev	200	13,705
3. Richard Petty	Petty Enterprises	43	Dodg	200	10,985
4. Bobby Allison	Roger Penske	2	Merc	200	7,375
5. Dave Marcis	Nord Krauskopf	71	Dodg	199	6,565

1977 Winston Cup GN Race No. 20 Champion Spark Plug 400
August 22, 1977 Average Speed: 137.944

Driver	Owner	Car #	Make	Laps	Winnings
1. Darrell Waltrip	DiGard	88	Chev	200	16,820
2. David Pearson	Wood Brothers	21	Merc	200	10,300
3. Benny Parsons	L. G. DeWitt	72	Chev	200	9,350
4. Sam Sommers	M. C. Anderson	27	Chev	200	4,900
5. Cale Yarborough	Junior Johnson	11	Chev	200	8,100

1978 Winston Cup GN Race No. 20 Champion Spark Plug 400
August 20, 1978 Average Speed: 129.566

Driver	Owner	Car #	Make	Laps	Winnings
1. David Pearson	Wood Brothers	21	Merc	200	16,025
2. Cale Yarborough	Junior Johnson	11	Olds	200	14,275
3. Darrell Waltrip	DiGard	88	Chev	200	10,950
4. Dave Marcis	Rod Osterlund	2	Chev	200	6,500
5. Bobby Allison	Bud Moore	15	Ford	198	7,550

1979 Winston Cup GN Race No. 21 Champion Spark Plug 400
August 19, 1979 Average Speed: 130.376

Driver	Owner	Car #	Make	Laps	Winnings
1. Richard Petty	Petty Enterprises	43	Chev	200	21,100
2. Buddy Baker	Harry Ranier	28	Chev	200	12,425
3. Benny Parsons	M. C. Anderson	27	Chev	200	12,820
4. David Pearson	Rod Osterlund	2	Chev	199	10,215
5. John Anderson	Russ Draime	08	Chev	199	4,355

1974 Winston Cup GN Race No. 15 Motor State 400
June 16, 1974 Average Speed: 127.098

Driver	Owner	Car #	Make	Laps	Winnings
1. Richard Petty	Petty Enterprises	43	74 Dodg	180	17,190
2. Earl Ross	Allan J. Clarke	52	74 Chev	180	7,930
3. David Pearson	Wood Brothers	21	74 Merc	180	3,475
4. Gary Bettenhausen	Roger Penske	16	74 Mata	178	2,400
5. Marty Robbins	Marty Robbins	42	74 Dodg	178	2,050

1975 Winston Cup GN Race No. 15 Motor State 400
June 15, 1975 Average Speed: 131.398

Driver	Owner	Car #	Make	Laps	Winnings
1. David Pearson	Wood Brothers	21	73 Merc	200	14,405
2. Richard Petty	Petty Enterprises	43	74 Dodg	200	13,130
3. Dave Marcis	Nord Krauskopf	71	74 Dodg	199	9,205
4. Cale Yarborough	Junior Johnson	11	75 Chev	199	7,180
5. Darrell Waltrip	Darrell Waltrip	17	75 Chev	199	5,530

1976 Winston Cup GN Race No. 15 Cam 2 Motor Oil 400
June 20, 1976 Average Speed: 141.148

Driver	Owner	Car #	Make	Laps	Winnings
1. David Pearson	Wood Brothers	21	Merc	200	15,845
2. Cale Yarborough	Junior Johnson	11	Chev	200	11,845
3. Bobby Allison	Roger Penske	2	Merc	200	9,275
4. Richard Petty	Petty Enterprises	43	Dodg	200	9,065
5. Buddy Baker	Bud Moore	15	Ford	199	6,630

1977 Winston Cup GN Race No. 15 Cam 2 Motor Oil 400
June 19, 1977 Average Speed: 135.033

Driver	Owner	Car #	Make	Laps	Winnings
1. Cale Yarborough	Junior Johnson	11	Chev	200	20,625
2. Richard Petty	Petty Enterprises	43	Dodg	200	14,425
3. Benny Parsons	L. G. DeWitt	72	Chev	200	10,700
4. Dave Marcis	Roger Penske	2	Chev	199	4,750
5. David Pearson	Wood Brothers	21	Merc	199	4,550

1978 Winston Cup GN Race No. 15 Gabriel 400
June 18, 1978 Average Speed: 149.563

Driver	Owner	Car #	Make	Laps	Winnings
1. Cale Yarborough	Junior Johnson	11	Olds	200	21,555
2. David Pearson	Wood Brothers	21	Merc	200	12,580
3. Benny Parsons	L. G. DeWitt	72	Olds	200	10,880
4. Dave Marcis	Rod Osterlund	2	Chev	200	6,830
5. Donnie Allison	Hoss Ellington	1	Chev	199	4,080

1979 Winston Cup GN Race No. 16 Gabriel 400
June 17, 1979 Average Speed: 135.798

Driver	Owner	Car #	Make	Laps	Winnings
1. Buddy Baker	Harry Ranier	28	Chev	200	16,870
2. Donnie Allison	Hoss Ellington	1	Chev	200	12,970
3. Cale Yarborough	Junior Johnson	11	Olds	200	12,620
4. Neil Bonnett	Wood Brothers	21	Merc	200	7,410
5. Richard Petty	Petty Enterprises	43	Chev	200	8,325

1980 Winston Cup GN Race No. 16 Gabriel 400
June 15, 1980 Average Speed: 131.808

Driver	Owner	Car #	Make	Laps	Winnings
1. Benny Parsons	M. C. Anderson	27	Chev	200	24,800
2. Cale Yarborough	Junior Johnson	11	Chev	200	16,300
3. Buddy Baker	Harry Ranier	28	Chev	200	9,300
4. Neil Bonnett	Wood Brothers	21	Merc	200	6,325
5. Richard Petty	Petty Enterprises	43	Chev	199	13,075

Michigan Int'l Speedway *continued*

1980 Winston Cup GN Race No. 21 Champion Spark Plug 400
August 17, 1980 Average Speed: 145.352

Driver	Owner	Car #	Make	Laps	Winnings
1. Cale Yarborough	Junior Johnson	11	Chev	200	19,700
2. Neil Bonnett	Wood Brothers	21	Merc	200	12,875
3. Donnie Allison	Kennie Childers	12	Chev	200	9,050
4. Darrell Waltrip	Joel Halpern	02	Chev	200	6,050
5. Richard Petty	Petty Enterprises	43	Chev	200	11,075

1981 Winston Cup GN Race No. 16 Gabriel 400
June 21, 1981 Average Speed: 130.589

Driver	Owner	Car #	Make	Laps	Winnings
1. Bobby Allison	Harry Ranier	28	Buick	200	24,075
2. Harry Gant	Hal Needham	33	Pont	200	10,825
3. Benny Parsons	Bud Moore	15	Ford	200	14,325
4. Jody Ridley	Junie Donlavey	90	Ford	200	10,005
5. Dale Earnhardt	Rod Osterlund	2	Pont	200	11,925

1981 Winston Cup GN Race No. 21 Champion Spark Plug 400
August 16, 1981 Average Speed: 123.457

Driver	Owner	Car #	Make	Laps	Winnings
1. Richard Petty	Petty Enterprises	43	Buick	200	23,750
2. Darrell Waltrip	Junior Johnson	11	Buick	200	17,525
3. Ricky Rudd	DiGard	88	Chev	200	15,150
4. Harry Gant	Hal Needham	33	Pont	200	6,000
5. Buddy Baker	Hoss Ellington	1	Buick	200	5,175

1982 Winston Cup GN Race No. 15 Gabriel 400
June 20, 1982 Average Speed: 118.101

Driver	Owner	Car #	Make	Laps	Winnings
1. Cale Yarborough	M. C. Anderson	27	Buick	200	24,700
2. Darrell Waltrip	Junior Johnson	11	Buick	200	25,650
3. Bill Elliott	Harry Melling	9	Ford	200	12,500
4. Bobby Allison	DiGard	88	Buick	200	16,100
5. Ricky Rudd	Richard Childress	3	Pont	200	11,530

1982 Winston Cup GN Race No. 20 Champion Spark Plug 400
August 22, 1982 Average Speed: 136.454

Driver	Owner	Car #	Make	Laps	Winnings
1. Bobby Allison	DiGard	88	Buick	200	26,900
2. Richard Petty	Petty Enterprises	43	Pont	200	20,505
3. Harry Gant	Hal Needham	33	Buick	200	13,255
4. Geoff Bodine	Cliff Stewart	50	Pont	200	15,200
5. Benny Parsons	Johnny Hayes	55	Buick	200	6,725

1983 Winston Cup GN Race No. 15 Gabriel 400
June 19, 1983 Average Speed: 138.728

Driver	Owner	Car #	Make	Laps	Winnings
1. Cale Yarborough	Harry Ranier	28	Chev	200	24,170
2. Bobby Allison	DiGard	22	Buick	200	23,800
3. Tim Richmond	Raymond Beadle	27	Pont	200	16,310
4. Darrell Waltrip	Junior Johnson	11	Chev	200	19,825
5. Terry Labonte	Billy Hagan	44	Chev	200	16,595

1983 Winston Cup GN Race No. 20 Champion Spark Plug 400
August 21, 1983 Average Speed: 147.511

Driver	Owner	Car #	Make	Laps	Winnings
1. Cale Yarborough	Harry Ranier	28	Chev	200	26,100
2. Darrell Waltrip	Junior Johnson	11	Chev	200	23,775
3. Bill Elliott	Harry Melling	9	Ford	200	17,205
4. Terry Labonte	Billy Hagan	44	Chev	200	13,245
5. Tim Richmond	Raymond Beadle	27	Pont	200	10,205

1984 Winston Cup GN Race No. 15 Miller High Life 400
June 17, 1984 Average Speed: 134.705

Driver	Owner	Car #	Make	Laps	Winnings
1. Bill Elliott	Harry Melling	9	Ford	200	41,600
2. Dale Earnhardt	Richard Childress	3	Chev	200	28,175
3. Darrell Waltrip	Junior Johnson	11	Chev	200	24,350
4. Harry Gant	Hal Needham	33	Chev	200	15,605
5. Lake Speed	Hoss Ellington	1	Chev	200	9,850

1984 Winston Cup GN Race No. 20 Champion Spark Plug 400
August 12, 1984 Average Speed: 153.863

Driver	Owner	Car #	Make	Laps	Winnings
1. Darrell Waltrip	Junior Johnson	11	Chev	200	40,800
2. Terry Labonte	Billy Hagan	44	Chev	200	26,030
3. Bill Elliott	Harry Melling	9	Ford	200	22,150
4. Harry Gant	Hal Needham	33	Chev	200	12,920
5. Cale Yarborough	Harry Ranier	28	Chev	200	8,100

1985 Winston Cup GN Race No. 14 Miller 400
June 16, 1985 Average Speed: 144.724

Driver	Owner	Car #	Make	Laps	Winnings
1. Bill Elliott	Harry Melling	9	Ford	200	48,600
2. Darrell Waltrip	Junior Johnson	11	Chev	200	32,100
3. Cale Yarborough	Harry Ranier	28	Ford	200	16,900
4. Tim Richmond	Raymond Beadle	27	Pont	200	15,630
5. Dale Earnhardt	Richard Childress	3	Chev	200	17,925

1985 Winston Cup GN Race No. 18 Champion Spark Plug 400
August 11, 1985 Average Speed: 137.430

Driver	Owner	Car #	Make	Laps	Winnings
1. Bill Elliott	Harry Melling	9	Ford	200	57,600
2. Darrell Waltrip	Junior Johnson	11	Chev	200	29,050
3. Harry Gant	Hal Needham	33	Chev	200	23,100
4. Kyle Petty	Wood Brothers	7	Ford	200	13,780
5. Benny Parsons	Richard Jackson	55	Chev	199	8,575

1986 Winston Cup Race No. 14 Miller American 400
June 15, 1986 Average Speed: 138.851

Driver	Owner	Car #	Make	Laps	Winnings
1. Bill Elliott	Harry Melling	9	Ford	200	56,900
2. Harry Gant	Hal Needham	33	Chev	200	37,400
3. Geoff Bodine	Rick Hendrick	5	Chev	200	25,600
4. Buddy Baker	Buddy Baker & Danny Schiff	88	Olds	200	11,825
5. Darrell Waltrip	Junior Johnson	11	Chev	200	21,625

1986 Winston Cup Race No. 19 Champion Spark Plug 400
August 17, 1986 Average Speed: 135.376

Driver	Owner	Car #	Make	Laps	Winnings
1. Bill Elliott	Harry Melling	9	Ford	200	55,950
2. Tim Richmond	Rick Hendrick	25	Chev	200	27,980
3. Darrell Waltrip	Junior Johnson	11	Chev	200	27,275
4. Geoff Bodine	Rick Hendrick	5	Chev	200	17,225
5. Dale Earnhardt	Richard Childress	3	Chev	199	18,750

1987 Winston Cup Race No. 14 Miller American 400
June 28, 1987 Average Speed: 148.454

Driver	Owner	Car #	Make	Laps	Winnings
1. Dale Earnhardt	Richard Childress	3	Chev	200	60,250
2. Davey Allison	Harry Ranier	28	Ford	200	27,575
3. Kyle Petty	Wood Brothers	21	Ford	200	26,025
4. Tim Richmond	Rick Hendrick	25	Chev	200	13,175
5. Rusty Wallace	Raymond Beadle	27	Pont	200	25,150

Michigan Int'l Speedway *continued*

1987 Winston Cup Race No. 19 Champion Spark Plug 400
August 16, 1987 Average Speed: 138.648

Driver	Owner	Car #	Make	Laps	Winnings
1. Bill Elliott	Harry Melling	9	Ford	200	52,875
2. Dale Earnhardt	Richard Childress	3	Chev	200	34,325
3. Morgan Shepherd	Kenny Bernstein	26	Buick	200	20,505
4. Rusty Wallace	Raymond Beadle	27	Pont	200	20,650
5. Davey Allison	Harry Ranier	28	Ford	200	13,500

1988 Winston Cup Race No. 19 Champion Spark Plug 400
August 21, 1988 Average Speed: 156.863

Driver	Owner	Car #	Make	Laps	Winnings
1. Davey Allison	Harry Ranier	28	Ford	200	60,475
2. Rusty Wallace	Raymond Beadle	27	Pont	200	37,250
3. Bill Elliott	Harry Melling	9	Ford	200	31,775
4. Morgan Shepherd	Buddy Baker & Danny Schiff	88	Olds	200	19,600
5. Lake Speed	Lake Speed	83	Olds	200	14,650

1989 Winston Cup Race No. 19 Champion Spark Plug 400
August 20, 1989 Average Speed: 157.704

Driver	Owner	Car #	Make	Laps	Winnings
1. Rusty Wallace	Raymond Beadle	27	Pont	200	67,900
2. Morgan Shepherd	Bob Rahilly & Butch Mock	75	Pont	200	38,975
3. Harry Gant	Leo Jackson	33	Olds	200	28,425
4. Hut Stricklin	Rod Osterlund	57	Pont	200	20,232
5. Geoff Bodine	Rick Hendrick	5	Chev	200	23,750

1990 Winston Cup Series Race No. 19 Champion Spark Plug 400
August 19, 1990 Average Speed: 138.822

Driver	Owner	Car #	Make	Laps	Winnings
1. Mark Martin	Jack Roush	6	Ford	200	71,200
2. Greg Sacks	Rick Hendrick	17	Chev	200	41,600
3. Rusty Wallace	Raymond Beadle	27	Pont	200	33,900
4. Bill Elliott	Harry Melling	9	Ford	200	27,000
5. Ricky Rudd	Rick Hendrick	5	Chev	200	20,607

1991 Winston Cup Series Race No. 19 Champion Spark Plug 400
August 18, 1991 Average Speed: 142.972

Driver	Owner	Car #	Make	Laps	Winnings
1. Dale Jarrett	Wood Brothers	21	Ford	200	74,150
2. Davey Allison	Robert Yates	28	Ford	200	47,700
3. Rusty Wallace	Roger Penske	2	Pont	200	23,600
4. Mark Martin	Jack Roush	6	Ford	200	30,050
5. Bill Elliott	Harry Melling	9	Ford	200	26,600

1992 Winston Cup Race No. 19 Champion Spark Plug 400
August 16, 1992 Average Speed: 146.056

Driver	Owner	Car #	Make	Laps	Winnings
1. Harry Gant	Leo Jackson	33	Olds	200	71,545
2. Darrell Waltrip	Darrell Waltrip	17	Chev	200	45,670
3. Bill Elliott	Junior Johnson	11	Ford	200	45,820
4. Ernie Irvan	Larry McClure	4	Chev	200	28,920
5. Davey Allison	Robert Yates	28	Ford	200	29,265

1993 Winston Cup Series Race No. 20 Champion Spark Plug 400
August 15, 1993 Average Speed: 144.564

Driver	Owner	Car #	Make	Laps	Winnings
1. Mark Martin	Jack Roush	6	Ford	200	76,645
2. Morgan Shepherd	Wood Brothers	21	Ford	200	47,320
3. Jeff Gordon	Rick Hendrick	24	Chev	200	34,745
4. Dale Jarrett	Joe Gibbs	18	Chev	200	29,045
5. Ted Musgrave	Ray DeWitt	55	Ford	200	27,990

1988 Winston Cup Race No. 14 Miller High Life 400
June 26, 1988 Average Speed: 153.551

Driver	Owner	Car #	Make	Laps	Winnings
1. Rusty Wallace	Raymond Beadle	27	Pont	200	64,100
2. Bill Elliott	Harry Melling	9	Ford	200	42,875
3. Terry Labonte	Junior Johnson	11	Chev	200	28,075
4. Dale Earnhardt	Richard Childress	3	Chev	200	26,175
5. Geoff Bodine	Rick Hendrick	5	Chev	200	20,325

1989 Winston Cup Race No. 14 Miller High Life 400
June 25, 1989 Average Speed: 139.023

Driver	Owner	Car #	Make	Laps	Winnings
1. Bill Elliott	Harry Melling	9	Ford	200	71,450
2. Rusty Wallace	Raymond Beadle	27	Pont	200	53,025
3. Darrell Waltrip	Rick Hendrick	17	Chev	200	31,600
4. Ricky Rudd	Kenny Bernstein	26	Buick	200	24,575
5. Brett Bodine	Bud Moore	15	Ford	200	22,025

1990 Winston Cup Series Race No. 14 Miller Genuine Draft 400
June 24, 1990 Average Speed: 150.219

Driver	Owner	Car #	Make	Laps	Winnings
1. Dale Earnhardt	Richard Childress	3	Chev	200	72,950
2. Ernie Irvan	Larry McClure	4	Chev	200	41,000
3. Geoff Bodine	Junior Johnson	11	Ford	200	33,375
4. Mark Martin	Jack Roush	6	Ford	200	25,400
5. Harry Gant	Leo Jackson	33	Olds	200	23,425

1991 Winston Cup Series Race No. 14 Miller Genuine Draft 400
June 23, 1991 Average Speed: 160.912

Driver	Owner	Car #	Make	Laps	Winnings
1. Davey Allison	Robert Yates	28	Ford	200	90,650
2. Hut Stricklin	Bobby Allison	12	Buick	200	41,925
3. Mark Martin	Jack Roush	6	Ford	200	37,650
4. Dale Earnhardt	Richard Childress	3	Chev	200	30,950
5. Ernie Irvan	Larry McClure	4	Chev	200	24,725

1992 Winston Cup Race No. 14 Miller Genuine Draft 400
June 21, 1992 Average Speed: 152.672

Driver	Owner	Car #	Make	Laps	Winnings
1. Davey Allison	Robert Yates	28	Ford	200	150,665
2. Darrell Waltrip	Darrell Waltrip	17	Chev	200	47,840
3. Alan Kulwicki	Alan Kulwicki	7	Ford	200	38,215
4. Kyle Petty	Felix Sabates	42	Pont	200	25,265
5. Ricky Rudd	Rick Hendrick	5	Chev	200	25,760

1993 Winston Cup Series Race No. 14 Miller Genuine Draft 400
June 20, 1993 Average Speed: 148.484

Driver	Owner	Car #	Make	Laps	Winnings
1. Ricky Rudd	Rick Hendrick	5	Chev	200	77,890
2. Jeff Gordon	Rick Hendrick	24	Chev	200	44,915
3. Ernie Irvan	Larry McClure	4	Chev	200	41,240
4. Dale Jarrett	Joe Gibbs	18	Chev	200	29,590
5. Rusty Wallace	Roger Penske	2	Pont	200	26,160

1994 Winston Cup Series Race No. 14 Miller Genuine Draft 400
June 19, 1994 Average Speed: 125.022

Driver	Owner	Car #	Make	Laps	Winnings
1. Rusty Wallace	Roger Penske	2	Ford	200	66,980
2. Dale Earnhardt	Richard Childress	3	Chev	200	55,905
3. Mark Martin	Jack Roush	6	Ford	200	42,330
4. Ricky Rudd	Ricky Rudd	10	Ford	200	31,430
5. Morgan Shepherd	Wood Brothers	21	Ford	200	31,025

Michigan Int'l Speedway *continued*

1994 Winston Cup Series Race No. 21 GM Goodwrench Dealers 400
August 21, 1994 Average Speed: 139.914

Driver	Owner	Car #	Make	Laps	Winnings
1. Geoff Bodine	Geoff Bodine	7	Ford	200	89,595
2. Mark Martin	Jack Roush	6	Ford	200	50,320
3. Rick Mast	Richard Jackson	1	Ford	200	38,320
4. Rusty Wallace	Roger Penske	2	Ford	200	34,070
5. Bobby Labonte	Bill Davis	22	Pont	200	28,415

1995 Winston Cup Series Race No. 21 GM Goodwrench Dealers 400
August 20, 1995 Average Speed: 157.739

Driver	Owner	Car #	Make	Laps	Winnings
1. Bobby Labonte	Joe Gibbs	18	Chev	200	97,445
2. Terry Labonte	Rick Hendrick	5	Chev	200	52,695
3. Jeff Gordon	Rick Hendrick	24	Chev	200	46,420
4. Sterling Marlin	Larry McClure	4	Chev	200	38,170
5. Rusty Wallace	Roger Penske	2	Ford	200	37,690

1996 Winston Cup Series Race No. 21 GM Goodwrench Dealers 400
August 18, 1996 Average Speed: 139.792

Driver	Owner	Car #	Make	Laps	Winnings
1. Dale Jarrett	Robert Yates	88	Ford	200	83,195
2. Mark Martin	Jack Roush	6	Ford	200	79,170
3. Terry Labonte	Rick Hendrick	5	Chev	200	57,120
4. Ernie Irvan	Robert Yates	28	Ford	200	43,770
5. Jeff Gordon	Rick Hendrick	24	Chev	200	44,040

1997 Winston Cup Series Race No. 21
August 17, 1997 Average Speed: 126.88

Driver	Owner	Car #	Make	Laps	Winnings
1. Mark Martin	Jack Roush	6	Ford	200	93,045
2. Jeff Gordon	Rick Hendrick	24	Chev	200	85,728
3. Ted Musgrave	Jack Roush	16	Ford	200	59,945
4. Ernie Irvan	Robert Yates	28	Ford	200	46,295
5. Dale Jarrett	Robert Yates	88	Ford	200	46,848

1998 Winston Cup Series Race No. 21
August 16, 1998 Average Speed: 151.995

Driver	Owner	Car #	Make	Laps	Winnings
1. Jeff Gordon	Rick Hendrick	24	Chev	200	120,302
2. Bobby Labonte	Joe Gibbs	18	Pont	200	73,555
3. Dale Jarrett	Robert Yates	88	Ford	200	61,805
4. Mark Martin	Jack Roush	6	Ford	200	53,525
5. Jeff Burton	Jack Roush	99	Ford	200	48,390

1999 Winston Cup Series Race No. 22
August 22, 1999 Average Speed: 144.332

Driver	Owner	Car #	Make	Laps	Winnings
1. Bobby Labonte	Joe Gibbs	18	Pont	200	121,230
2. Jeff Gordon	Rick Hendrick	24	Chev	200	83,030
3. Tony Stewart	Joe Gibbs	20	Pont	200	60,505
4. Dale Jarrett	Robert Yates	88	Ford	200	57,650
5. Dale Earnhardt	Richard Childress	3	Chev	200	51,005

2000 Winston Cup Series Race No. 22
August 20, 2000 Average Speed: 132.597

Driver	Owner	Car #	Make	Laps	Winnings
1. Rusty Wallace	Roger Penske	2	Ford	200	110,460
2. Ricky Rudd	Robert Yates	28	Ford	200	94,530
3. Bobby Labonte	Joe Gibbs	18	Pont	200	73,430
4. Dale Jarrett	Robert Yates	88	Ford	200	70,275
5. Johnny Benson, Jr.	Tim Beverley	10	Pont	200	44,740

1995 Winston Cup Series Race No. 14 Miller Genuine Draft 400
June 18, 1995 Average Speed: 134.141

Driver	Owner	Car #	Make	Laps	Winnings
1. Bobby Labonte	Joe Gibbs	18	Chev	200	84,080
2. Jeff Gordon	Rick Hendrick	24	Chev	200	72,530
3. Rusty Wallace	Roger Penske	2	Ford	200	44,780
4. John Andretti	Michael Kranefuss & Carl Haas	37	Ford	200	31,375
5. Morgan Shepherd	Wood Brothers	21	Ford	200	36,075

1996 Winston Cup Series Race No. 14 Miller Genuine Draft 400
June 23, 1996 Average Speed: 166.033

Driver	Owner	Car #	Make	Laps	Winnings
1. Rusty Wallace	Roger Penske	2	Ford	200	71,380
2. Terry Labonte	Rick Hendrick	5	Chev	200	59,730
3. Sterling Marlin	Larry McClure	4	Chev	200	55,930
4. Jimmy Spencer	Travis Carter	23	Ford	200	43,775
5. Ernie Irvan	Robert Yates	28	Ford	200	40,525

1997 Winston Cup Series Race No. 14
June 15, 1997 Average Speed: 153.321

Driver	Owner	Car #	Make	Laps	Winnings
1. Ernie Irvan	Robert Yates	28	Ford	200	93,830
2. Bill Elliott	Bill Elliott	94	Ford	200	73,830
3. Mark Martin	Jack Roush	6	Ford	200	48,805
4. Ted Musgrave	Jack Roush	16	Ford	200	47,200
5. Jeff Gordon	Rick Hendrick	24	Chev	200	47,425

1998 Winston Cup Series Race No. 14
June 14, 1998 Average Speed: 158.695

Driver	Owner	Car #	Make	Laps	Winnings
1. Mark Martin	Jack Roush	6	Ford	200	92,375
2. Dale Jarrett	Robert Yates	88	Ford	200	76,125
3. Jeff Gordon	Rick Hendrick	24	Chev	200	84,375
4. Jeff Burton	Jack Roush	99	Ford	200	54,235
5. Jeremy Mayfield	Michael Kranefuss	12	Ford	200	44,500

1999 Winston Cup Series Race No. 14
June 13, 1999 Average Speed: 173.997

Driver	Owner	Car #	Make	Laps	Winnings
1. Dale Jarrett	Robert Yates	88	Ford	200	151,240
2. Jeff Gordon	Rick Hendrick	24	Chev	200	90,050
3. Jeff Burton	Jack Roush	99	Ford	200	56,985
4. Ward Burton	Bill Davis	22	Pont	200	56,985
5. Bobby Labonte	Joe Gibbs	18	Pont	200	55,565

2000 Winston Cup Series Race No. 14
June 11, 2000 Average Speed: 143.926

Driver	Owner	Car #	Make	Laps	Winnings
1. Tony Stewart	Joe Gibbs	20	Pont	194	123,800
2. Dale Earnhardt	Richard Childress	3	Chev	194	80,575
3. Bobby Labonte	Joe Gibbs	18	Pont	194	79,175
4. Dale Jarrett	Robert Yates	88	Ford	194	71,285
5. Robert Pressley	Doug Bawel	77	Ford	194	51,000

2001 Winston Cup Series Race No. 14
June 10, 2001 Average Speed: 134.203

Driver	Owner	Car #	Make	Laps	Winnings
1. Jeff Gordon	Rick Hendrick	24	Chev	200	240,137
2. Ricky Rudd	Robert Yates	28	Ford	200	123,257
3. Sterling Marlin	Chip Ganassi	40	Dodg	200	95,280
4. Jeremy Mayfield	Roger Penske	12	Ford	200	98,814
5. Ryan Newman	Roger Penske	02	Ford	200	47,315

Michigan Int'l Speedway *continued*

2001 Winston Cup Series Race No. 23
August 19, 2001 Average Speed: 140.513

Driver	Owner	Car #	Make	Laps	Winnings
1. Sterling Marlin	Chip Ganassi	40	Dodg	162	157,830
2. Ricky Craven	Cal Wells	32	Ford	162	92,545
3. Bill Elliott	Ray Evernham	9	Dodg	162	106,128
4. Matt Kenseth	Jack Roush	17	Ford	162	70,050
5. Johnny Benson, Jr.	Nelson Bowers	10	Pont	162	68,015

2002 Winston Cup Series Race No. 15
June 16, 2002 Average Speed: 154.822

Driver	Owner	Car #	Make	Laps	Winnings
1. Matt Kenseth	Jack Roush	17	Ford	200	154,100
2. Dale Jarrett	Robert Yates	88	Ford	200	142,028
3. Ryan Newman	Roger Penske	12	Ford	200	100,575
4. Michael Waltrip	Dale Earnhardt, Inc.	15	Chev	200	80,500
5. Jeff Gordon	Rick Hendrick	24	Chev	200	112,025

2002 Winston Cup Series Race No. 23
August 18, 2002 Average Speed: 140.555

Driver	Owner	Car #	Make	Laps	Winnings
1. Dale Jarrett	Robert Yates	88	Ford	200	179,530
2. Tony Stewart	Joe Gibbs	20	Pont	200	136,183
3. Kevin Harvick	Richard Childress	29	Chev	200	116,938
4. Jeff Burton	Jack Roush	99	Ford	200	112,812
5. Mark Martin	Jack Roush	6	Ford	200	107,138

Michigan State Fairgrounds
Detroit, MI
1-mile Dirt Track

1-mile dirt oval built in 1899. Automobiles ran there in early 1900s. First NASCAR Winston Cup (then Grand National) race held on 8/12/51 (won by Tommy Thompson). The event was titled Motor City 250 in honor of Detroit's 250th anniversary. The only other Grand National event was staged on 6/29/52 (won by Tim Flock). The track is now the site of parking lots for the fairgrounds.

Winston Cup Starts
17 drivers tied with 2

Winston Cup Victories
Tim Flock   1
Tommy Thompson   1

Winston Cup Poles
Dick Rathmann   1
Marshall Teague   1

Winston Cup Money
Tim Flock $5,175

Most Cars Started
59—August 12, 1951 Motor City 250

Fewest Cars Started
47—June 29, 1952 Motor City 250

Narrowest Margin of Victory
N/A

Slowest Race
57.588 MPH—August 12, 1951
Motor City 250

Race Record
59.908 MPH—June 29, 1952
Motor City 250

Most Cautions
N/A

Most Race Leaders
6—August 12, 1951 Motor City 250

Most Cars Running at Finish
N/A

1951 Grand National Race No. 20 Motor City 250
August 12, 1951 Average Speed: 57.588

Driver	Owner	Car #	Make	Laps	Winnings
1. Tommy Thompson	Tommy Thompson	40	51 Chrys	250	5,000
2. Joe Eubanks	Phil Oates	82	50 Olds	250	2,000
3. Johnny Mantz	Johnny Mantz	98	51 Nash	244	1,000
4. Red Byron	B. J. Dantone	83	50 Ford	241	600
5. Paul Newkirk		43	51 Nash	241	500

1952 Grand National Race No. 17 Motor City 250
June 29, 1952 Average Speed: 59.908

Driver	Owner	Car #	Make	Laps	Winnings
1. Tim Flock	Ted Chester	91	51 Huds	250	5,050
2. Buddy Shuman	B. A. Pless	89	52 Huds	250	2,225
3. Herb Thomas	Herb Thomas	92	51 Huds	249	1,000
4. Bill Blair	George Hutchens	2	52 Olds	249	600
5. Pat Kirkwood	Pat Kirkwood	99	51 Chrys	246	500

Monroe Speedway
Monroe, MI
Half-mile Dirt Track

(aka Fairgrounds Speedway) Half-mile dirt track opened in July 1949. Only NASCAR Winston Cup (then Grand National) race held on 7/6/52 (won by Tim Flock). The track was later shortened to a quarter-mile and then closed circa 1954.

Winston Cup Victories
Tim Flock   1

Winston Cup Poles
Tim Flock   1

Winston Cup Money
Tim Flock $1,000

Most Cars Started
15—July 6, 1952

Narrowest Margin of Victory
N/A

Race Record
44.499 MPH—July 6, 1952

Most Race Leaders
N/A

Most Cars Running at Finish
9—July 6, 1952

1952 Grand National Race No. 20
July 6, 1952 Average Speed: 44.499

Driver	Owner	Car #	Make	Laps	Winnings
1. Tim Flock	Ted Chester	91	51 Huds	200	1,000
2. Herb Thomas	Herb Thomas	92	52 Huds	200	700
3. Lee Petty	Petty Enterprises	42	52 Plym	199	450
4. Fonty Flock	Frank Christian	14	52 Olds	194	350
5. Ray Duhigg	J. H. Petty	44	51 Plym	193	200

Nebraska

Lincoln City Fairgrounds
North Platte, NE
Half-mile Dirt Track

(aka Lincoln County Raceway; North Platte Speedway) Half-mile dirt track built circa 1951. Only NASCAR Winston Cup (then Grand National) race staged on 7/26/53 (won by Dick Rathmann). Track still active today.

Winston Cup Victories
Dick Rathmann   1

Winston Cup Poles
Herb Thomas   1

Winston Cup Money
Dick Rathmann $1,000

Most Cars Started
18—July 26, 1953

Narrowest Margin of Victory
6 feet—July 26, 1953

Race Record
54.380 MPH—July 26, 1953

Most Race Leaders
2—July 26, 1953

Most Cars Running at Finish
N/A

1953 Grand National Race No. 24
July 26, 1953 Average Speed: 54.380

Driver	Owner	Car #	Make	Laps	Winnings
1. Dick Rathmann	Walt Chapman	120	53 Huds	200	1,000
2. Herb Thomas	Herb Thomas	92	53 Huds	200	700
3. Lee Petty	Petty Enterprises	42	53 Dodg	—	450
4. Buck Baker	Griffin Motors	87	53 Olds	—	350
5. Marvin Copple			49 Olds	—	200

Nevada

Las Vegas Motor Speedway
Las Vegas, NV
1.5-mile Superspeedway

Construction began in 1995 on state-of-the-art 1.5-mile facility. Built on 1,600 acres just north of Las Vegas, the speedway is coined the "Diamond in the Desert". Track opened on September 15, 1996 with an Indy Racing League open wheel event, won by Richie Hearn. First NASCAR Winston Cup event staged on March 1, 1998, won by Mark Martin. Spacious grounds also contain a 0.375-mile short dirt track oval for Sprint and stock car racing, and a drag strip. A custom-designed lighting system features 2,600 lighting fixtures on 200 light poles.

Winston Cup Starts
21 drivers tied at   5

Winston Cup Victories
Jeff Burton   2

Winston Cup Poles
Dale Jarrett   2

Winston Cup Money
Jeff Burton $1,086,182

Most Cars Started
43—5 times

Narrowest Margin of Victory
1.074 seconds—March 7, 1999

Slowest Race
119.985 MPH—March 5, 2000

Race Record
146.530 MPH—March 1, 1998

Most Cautions
6—2 times

Most Race Leaders
13—March 4, 2001

Most Cars Running at Finish
42—March 5, 2000

1998 Winston Cup Series Race No. 3
March 1, 1998 Average Speed: 146.53

Driver	Owner	Car #	Make	Laps	Winnings
1. Mark Martin	Jack Roush	6	Ford	267	313,900
2. Jeff Burton	Jack Roush	99	Ford	267	202,850
3. Rusty Wallace	Roger Penske	2	Ford	267	156,500
4. Johnny Benson, Jr.	Jack Roush	26	Ford	267	121,200
5. Jeremy Mayfield	Michael Kranefuss	12	Ford	267	101,500

1999 Winston Cup Series Race No. 3
March 7, 1999 Average Speed: 137.535

Driver	Owner	Car #	Make	Laps	Winnings
1. Jeff Burton	Jack Roush	99	Ford	267	336,590
2. Ward Burton	Bill Davis	22	Pont	267	217,275
3. Jeff Gordon	Rick Hendrick	24	Chev	267	179,400
4. Mike Skinner	Richard Childress	31	Chev	267	133,175
5. Bobby Labonte	Joe Gibbs	18	Pont	267	118,540

2000 Winston Cup Series Race No. 3
March 5, 2000 Average Speed: 119.982

Driver	Owner	Car #	Make	Laps	Winnings
1. Jeff Burton	Jack Roush	99	Ford	148	358,925
2. Tony Stewart	Joe Gibbs	20	Pont	148	221,250
3. Mark Martin	Jack Roush	6	Ford	148	169,900
4. Bill Elliott	Bill Elliott	94	Ford	148	142,950
5. Bobby Labonte	Joe Gibbs	18	Pont	148	119,600

2001 Winston Cup Series Race No. 3
March 4, 2001 Average Speed

Driver	Owner	Car #	Make	Laps	Winnings
1. Jeff Gordon	Rick Hendrick	24	Chev	267	369,602
2. Dale Jarrett	Robert Yates	88	Ford	267	257,977
3. Sterling Marlin	Chip Ganassi	40	Dodg	267	183,760
4. Johnny Benson, Jr.	Nelson Bowers	10	Pont	267	129,600
5. Todd Bodine	Travis Carter	66	Ford	267	108,350

2002 Winston Cup Series Race No. 3
March 3, 2002 Average Speed: 136.754

Driver	Owner	Car #	Make	Laps	Winnings
1. Sterling Marlin	Chip Ganassi	40	Dodg	267	412,842
2. Jeremy Mayfield	Ray Evernham	19	Dodg	267	222,550
3. Mark Martin	Jack Roush	6	Ford	267	199,233
4. Ryan Newman	Roger Penske	12	Ford	267	162,125
5. Tony Stewart	Joe Gibbs	20	Pont	267	153,953

Las Vegas Park Speedway
Las Vegas, NV
1-mile Dirt Track

Originally the 1-mile Las Vegas Jockey Club horse track. The track only hosted three races, one of which was a NASCAR Winston Cup (then Grand National) event on 10/16/55 (won by Norm Nelson). Other events were an AM IndyCar Championship event (1954) and a USAC Late Model race (1959). Now the site of the Las Vegas Hilton.

Winston Cup Victories
Norm Nelson   1

Winston Cup Poles
Norm Nelson   1

Winston Cup Money
Norm Nelson $1,325

Most Cars Started
27—October 16, 1955

Narrowest Margin of Victory
2 laps plus—October 16, 1955

Race Record
44.449 MPH—October 16, 1955

Most Race Leaders
2—October 16, 1955

Most Cars Running at Finish
13—October 16, 1955

1955 Grand National Race No. 43
October 16, 1955 Average Speed: 44.449

Driver	Owner	Car #	Make	Laps	Winnings
1. Norm Nelson	Carl Kiekhaefer	299	55 Chrys	111	1,325
2. Bill Hyde		96	53 Olds	109	820
3. Bill West	Jim Dane	33	53 Huds	107	560
4. Sherman Clark	Sherman Clark	34	55 Chev	104	340
5. Jim Murray		46	55 Buick	102	270

New Hampshire

New Hampshire Int'l Speedway
Loudon, NH
1.058-mile Superspeedway

1.063-mile paved oval opened in July 1990. First NASCAR Winston Cup event was staged on 7/11/93 (won by Rusty Wallace); the event was also Davey Allison's final race—he was mortally injured in a helicopter crash the following day). Track is located on the site of the former Bryar Motorsports Park, which opened in early 1960s.

Winston Cup Starts
27 drivers tied with 4

Winston Cup Victories
Jeff Gordon	1
Ernie Irvan	1
Ricky Rudd	1
Rusty Wallace	1

Winston Cup Poles
Mark Martin   2

Winston Cup Money
Jeff Gordon $237,425

Most Cars Started
42—July 10, 1994 Slick 50 300

Fewest Cars Started
40—July 11, 1993 Slick 50 300
40—July 14, 1996 Slick 50 300

Narrowest Margin of Victory
0.690 seconds July 10, 1994
Slick 50 300

Slowest Race
87.599 MPH—July 10, 1994 Slick 50 300

Race Record
107.029 MPH—July 9, 1995 Slick 50 300

Most Cautions
17—July 10, 1994 Slick 50 300

Most Race Leaders
15—July 14, 1996 Slick 50 300

Most Cars Running at Finish
33—July 9, 1995 Slick 50 300
33—July 14, 1996 Slick 50 300

1993 Winston Cup Series Race No. 16 Slick 50 300
July 11, 1993 Average Speed: 105.947

Driver	Owner	Car #	Make	Laps	Winnings
1. Rusty Wallace	Roger Penske	2	Pont	300	77,500
2. Mark Martin	Jack Roush	6	Ford	300	74,800
3. Davey Allison	Robert Yates	28	Ford	300	44,725
4. Dale Jarrett	Joe Gibbs	18	Chev	300	33,850
5. Ricky Rudd	Rick Hendrick	5	Chev	300	25,375

1994 Winston Cup Series Race No. 16 Slick 50 300
July 10, 1994 Average Speed: 87.599

Driver	Owner	Car #	Make	Laps	Winnings
1. Ricky Rudd	Ricky Rudd	10	Ford	300	91,875
2. Dale Earnhardt	Richard Childress	3	Chev	300	68,000
3. Rusty Wallace	Roger Penske	2	Ford	300	38,975
4. Mark Martin	Jack Roush	6	Ford	300	33,625
5. Todd Bodine	Butch Mock	75	Ford	300	21,850

1995 Winston Cup Series Race No. 16 Slick 50 300
July 9, 1995 Average Speed: 107.029

Driver	Owner	Car #	Make	Laps	Winnings
1. Jeff Gordon	Rick Hendrick	24	Chev	300	160,300
2. Morgan Shepherd	Wood Brothers	21	Ford	300	61,500
3. Mark Martin	Jack Roush	6	Ford	300	54,650
4. Terry Labonte	Rick Hendrick	5	Chev	300	37,925
5. Ricky Rudd	Ricky Rudd	10	Ford	300	35,125

1996 Winston Cup Series Race No. 16 Slick 50 300
July 14, 1996 Average Speed: 98.930

Driver	Owner	Car #	Make	Laps	Winnings
1. Ernie Irvan	Robert Yates	28	Ford	300	112,625
2. Dale Jarrett	Robert Yates	88	Ford	300	59,725
3. Ricky Rudd	Ricky Rudd	10	Ford	300	49,825
4. Jeff Burton	Jack Roush	99	Ford	300	31,600
5. Robert Pressley	Leo Jackson & Andy Petree	33	Chev	300	34,825

New Jersey

Linden Airport
Linden, NJ
2-mile Paved Road Course

2-mile road course utilizing runways at airport. Site of first NASCAR Winston Cup (then Grand National) road race on 6/13/54 (won by Al Keller in a Jaguar). For this special NASCAR event, foreign cars were permitted to compete. Track was originally a 2.2-mile course opened in August of 1949. Track was never again used for auto racing sometime after 1955.

Winston Cup Victories
Al Keller   1

Winston Cup Poles
Buck Baker   1

Winston Cup Money
Al Keller $1,000

Most Cars Started
43—June 13, 1954

Narrowest Margin of Victory
N/A

Race Record
77.569 MPH—June 13, 1954

Most Cautions
4—June 13, 1954

Most Race Leaders
3—June 13, 1954

Most Cars Running at Finish
N/A

1954 Grand National Race No. 18
June 13, 1954 Average Speed: 77.569

Driver	Owner	Car #	Make	Laps	Winnings
1. Al Keller	Paul Whiteman	4	JAG	50	1,000
2. Joe Eubanks	Phil Oates	82	51 Huds	50	650
3. Buck Baker	Ernest Woods	88	54 Olds	49	500
4. Bob Grossman		32	JAG	49	400
5. Harry LaVois		7-A	JAG	49	275

Morristown Speedway
Morristown, NJ
Half-mile Dirt Track

(aka Soranno Park; Morristown Raceway) Half-mile dirt track opened in June 1950. First NASCAR Winston Cup (then Grand National) race staged on 8/24/51 (won by Tim Flock). Final NASCAR race run on 7/15/55 (also won by Tim Flock). Track closed in October 1955.

Winston Cup Starts	**Winston Cup Money**	**Narrowest Margin of Victory**	**Most Cautions**
Lee Petty 5	Lee Petty $3,000	N/A	N/A
Winston Cup Victories	**Most Cars Started**	**Slowest Race**	**Most Race Leaders**
Tim Flock 2	44—August 24, 1951	58.092 MPH—July 15, 1955	3—July 11, 1952
Winston Cup Poles	**Fewest Cars Started**	**Race Record**	**Most Cars Running at Finish**
Tim Flock 2	23—July 10, 1953	69.417 MPH—July 10, 1953	20—July 30, 1954
Herb Thomas 2			20—July 15, 1955

1951 Grand National Race No. 22
August 24, 1951

Driver	Owner	Car #	Make	Laps	Winnings
1. Tim Flock	Ted Chester	91	51 Olds	200	1,000
2. Lee Petty	Petty Enterprises	42	51 Plym	—	700
3. Ronnie Kohler			51 Plym	—	450
4. John DuBoise			50 Plym	—	350
5. Jim Delaney	Bob Osiecki	21	50 Ford	—	200

1952 Grand National Race No. 21
July 11, 1952 Average Speed: 59.661

Driver	Owner	Car #	Make	Laps	Winnings
1. Lee Petty	Petty Enterprises	42	51 Plym	200	1,000
2. Tim Flock	Ted Chester	91	51 Huds	200	700
3. Neil Cole	John Golabek	52	50 Plym	196	450
4. Ralph Liguori	Ralph Liguori	00	51 Huds	196	350
5. Ronnie Kohler			50 Plym	192	200

1953 Grand National Race No. 21
July 10, 1953 Average Speed: 69.417

Driver	Owner	Car #	Make	Laps	Winnings
1. Dick Rathmann	Walt Chapman	120	53 Huds	200	1,000
2. Herb Thomas	Herb Thomas	92	53 Huds	199	700
3. Lee Petty	Petty Enterprises	42	53 Dodg	198	450
4. Jim Paschal	George Hutchens	80	53 Dodg	—	350
5. Ronnie Kohler	John Golabek	53	50 Plym	—	200

1954 Grand National Race No. 26
July 30, 1954 Average Speed: 58.968

Driver	Owner	Car #	Make	Laps	Winnings
1. Buck Baker	Ernest Woods	88	54 Olds	200	1,000
2. Herb Thomas	Herb Thomas	92	54 Huds	199	650
3. Hershel McGriff	Frank Christian	14	53 Olds	199	450
4. Dick Rathmann	John Ditz	3	54 Huds	196	350
5. Jimmie Lewallen	Joe Blair	5	54 Merc	195	300

1955 Grand National Race No. 27
July 15, 1955 Average Speed: 58.092

Driver	Owner	Car #	Make	Laps	Winnings
1. Tim Flock	Carl Kiekhaefer	300	55 Chrys	200	900
2. Lee Petty	Petty Enterprises	42	55 Chrys	198	600
3. Dave Terrell	Dave Terrell	98	54 Olds	197	425
4. Junior Johnson	B & L Motors	55	54 Olds	196	335
5. Jim Reed	Jim Reed	7	55 Chev	195	290

Old Bridge Stadium
Old Bridge, NJ
Half-mile Paved Track

Half-mile paved oval opened in August 1953. First NASCAR Winston Cup (then Grand National) event staged on 8/17/56 (won by Ralph Moody). Final NASCAR Grand National event run on 7/9/65 (won by Junior Johnson). Track closed in 1968.

Winston Cup Starts
Lee Petty   5

Winston Cup Victories
Junior Johnson   1
Ralph Moody   1
Lee Petty   1
Jim Reed   1
Fireball Roberts   1
Billy Wade   1

Winston Cup Poles
Jim Reed   2

Winston Cup Money
Jim Reed $1,775

Most Cars Started
27—April 27, 1958

Fewest Cars Started
20—July 19, 1963
20—July 9, 1965 Old Bridge 200

Narrowest Margin of Victory
6 car lengths—July 19, 1963

Slowest Race
65.170 MPH—August 17, 1956

Race Record
73.891 MPH—July 10, 1964
Fireball Roberts 200

Most Cautions
4—July 19, 1963

Most Race Leaders
3—August 16, 1957
3—July 10, 1964 Fireball Roberts 200
3—July 9, 1965 Old Bridge 200

Most Cars Running at Finish
16—August 16, 1957

1956 Grand National Race No. 38
August 17, 1956 Average Speed: 65.170

Driver	Owner	Car #	Make	Laps	Winnings
1. Ralph Moody	Pete DePaolo	12	56 Ford	200	650
2. Jim Reed	Jim Reed	7	56 Chev	200	525
3. Billy Myers	Bill Stroppe	4	56 Merc	199	400
4. Fireball Roberts	Pete DePaolo	22	56 Ford	199	320
5. Jim Paschal	Frank Hayworth	75	56 Merc	197	290

1957 Grand National Race No. 38
August 16, 1957 Average Speed: 65.813

Driver	Owner	Car #	Make	Laps	Winnings
1. Lee Petty	Petty Enterprises	42	57 Olds	200	1,000
2. Rex White	Bob Welborn	44	57 Chev	200	625
3. Jim Reed	Jim Reed	7	57 Ford	200	400
4. Marvin Panch	Marvin Panch	98	57 Ford	200	295
5. Jack Smith	Jack Smith	47	57 Chev	199	255

1958 Grand National Race No. 14
April 27, 1958 Average Speed: 68.438

Driver	Owner	Car #	Make	Laps	Winnings
1. Jim Reed	Jim Reed	7	57 Ford	187	800
2. Eddie Pagan	Eddie Pagan	45	57 Ford	186	525
3. Rex White	J. H. Petty	44	57 Chev	185	350
4. Frankie Schneider	Frankie Schneider	62	57 Chev	184	250
5. Elmo Langley	Elmo Langley	8	56 Chev	184	225

1963 Grand National Race No. 35
July 19, 1963 Average Speed: 73.022

Driver	Owner	Car #	Make	Laps	Winnings
1. Fireball Roberts	Holman-Moody	22	63 Ford	200	1,000
2. Rex White	Rex White	4	63 Merc	200	600
3. Fred Lorenzen	Holman-Moody	28	63 Ford	199	400
4. Ned Jarrett	Charles Robinson	11	63 Ford	199	300
5. Bobby Isaac	Bondy Long	99	63 Ford	196	275

1964 Grand National Race No. 37 Fireball Roberts 200
July 10, 1964 Average Speed: 73.891

Driver	Owner	Car #	Make	Laps	Winnings
1. Billy Wade	Bud Moore	1	63 Merc	200	1,000
2. Ned Jarrett	Bondy Long	11	64 Ford	199	600
3. Richard Petty	Petty Enterprises	43	64 Plym	198	400
4. Jimmy Pardue	Charles Robinson	54	64 Plym	195	300
5. David Pearson	Cotton Owens	6	64 Dodg	193	275

1965 Grand National Race No. 31 Old Bridge 200
July 9, 1965 Average Speed: 72.087

Driver	Owner	Car #	Make	Laps	Winnings
1. Junior Johnson	Rex Lovette	26	65 Ford	200	1,000
2. Dick Hutcherson	Holman-Moody	29	65 Ford	199	600
3. Marvin Panch	Wood Brothers	21	65 Ford	199	400
4. Darel Dieringer	Bud Moore	16	64 Merc	198	300
5. Ned Jarrett	Bondy Long	11	65 Ford	198	275

Trenton Speedway
Trenton, NJ
1-Mile Paved Track

(aka New Jersey State Fairgrounds; Trenton Int'l Speedway) Half-mile dirt track originally built in 1900. 1-mile dirt track opened in May 1946. Track paved in 1957. A 500-mile NASCAR Winston Cup (then Grand National) race was staged on 5/30/58 (won by Fireball Roberts). Track was lengthened to 1.5 miles in the shape of a peanut in 1969. Final Winston Cup race run on 7/16/72 (won by Bobby Allison). Another Winston Cup event was scheduled in 1973 but was rained out after qualifying trials had determined the field. The event was never rescheduled.

Winston Cup Starts
Elmo Langley   8

Winston Cup Victories
Richard Petty   3

Winston Cup Poles
Bobby Isaac   3

Winston Cup Money
Richard Petty $22,755

Most Cars Started
40—July 18, 1971 Northern 300

Fewest Cars Started
18—May 17, 1959

Narrowest Margin of Victory
1.400 seconds July 16, 1972
    Northern 300

Slowest Race
84.522 MPH—May 30, 1958
    Northern 500

Race Record
121.008 MPH—July 13, 1969
    Northern 300

Most Cautions
5—July 14, 1968 Northern 300
5—July 16, 1972 Northern 300

Most Race Leaders
6—July 12, 1970 Schaefer 300

Most Cars Running at Finish
22—July 12, 1970 Schaefer 300
22—July 18, 1971 Northern 300
22—July 16, 1972 Northern 300

1958 Grand National Race No. 20 Northern 500
May 30, 1958 Average Speed: 84.522

Driver	Owner	Car #	Make	Laps	Winnings
1. Fireball Roberts	Frank Strickland	22	57 Chev	500	6,500
2. Junior Johnson	Paul Spaulding	11	57 Ford	498	3,160
3. Lee Petty	Petty Enterprises	42	57 Olds	492	2,125
4. Jim Reed	Jim Reed	7	57 Ford	489	1,510
5. Eddie Pagan	Eddie Pagan	45	57 Ford	488	1,225

1959 Grand National Race No. 14
May 17, 1959

Driver	Owner	Car #	Make	Laps	Winnings
1. Tom Pistone	Carl Rupert	59	59 Ford	150	1,450
2. Cotton Owens	W. H. Watson	6	58 Pont	150	750
3. Lee Petty	Petty Enterprises	42	59 Plym	149	575
4. Jim Reed	Jim Reed	7	59 Chev	148	375
5. Tommy Irwin	Tommy Irwin	36	59 Ford	147	350

1967 Grand National Race No. 29 Northern 300
July 9, 1967 Average Speed: 95.208

Driver	Owner	Car #	Make	Laps	Winnings
1. Richard Petty	Petty Enterprises	43	67 Plym	300	4,350
2. Darel Dieringer	Junior Johnson	26	67 Ford	300	1,965
3. Jim Paschal	Tom Friedkin	14	67 Plym	297	1,310
4. Paul Goldsmith	Ray Nichels	99	67 Plym	293	700
5. Elmo Langley	Henry Woodfield	64	66 Ford	288	625

1968 Grand National Race No. 29 Northern 300
July 14, 1968 Average Speed: 89.079

Driver	Owner	Car #	Make	Laps	Winnings
1. LeeRoy Yarbrough	Junior Johnson	98	68 Ford	300	2,900
2. David Pearson	Holman-Moody	17	68 Ford	299	1,475
3. Bobby Allison	Bobby Allison	2	66 Chev	299	1,025
4. Charlie Glotzbach	Cotton Owens	6	68 Dodg	297	675
5. Pete Hamilton	Rocky Hinton	5	68 Ford	294	625

1969 Grand National Race No. 31 Northern 300
July 13, 1969 Average Speed: 121.008

Driver	Owner	Car #	Make	Laps	Winnings
1. David Pearson	Holman-Moody	17	69 Ford	200	5,300
2. Bobby Allison	Mario Rossi	22	69 Dodg	199	2,050
3. Bobby Isaac	Nord Krauskopf	71	69 Dodg	199	1,350
4. James Hylton	James Hylton	48	69 Dodg	198	725
5. LeeRoy Yarbrough	L. G. DeWitt	14	69 Ford	196	675

1970 Grand National Race No. 27 Schaefer 300
July 12, 1970 Average Speed: 120.724

Driver	Owner	Car #	Make	Laps	Winnings
1. Richard Petty	Petty Enterprises	43	70 Plym	200	6,730
2. Bobby Allison	Mario Rossi	22	69 Dodg	200	2,470
3. Charlie Glotzbach	Ray Nichels	99	69 Dodg	200	1,720
4. Dick Brooks	Dick Brooks	32	70 Plym	198	1,320
5. James Hylton	James Hylton	48	69 Ford	196	1,045

1971 Winston Cup GN Race No. 31 Northern 300
July 18, 1971 Average Speed: 120.347

Driver	Owner	Car #	Make	Laps	Winnings
1. Richard Petty	Petty Enterprises	43	71 Plym	200	6,760
2. Buddy Baker	Neil Castles	06	70 Dodg	200	2,980
3. Bobby Allison	Holman-Moody	12	71 Ford	199	2,055
4. Dave Marcis	Dave Marcis	2	69 Dodg	198	1,370
5. Pete Hamilton	Cotton Owens	6	71 Plym	198	1,075

1972 Winston Cup GN Race No. 19 Northern 300
July 16, 1972 Average Speed: 114.030

Driver	Owner	Car #	Make	Laps	Winnings
1. Bobby Allison	Richard Howard	12	72 Chev	200	7,900
2. Bobby Isaac	Nord Krauskopf	71	72 Dodg	200	4,825
3. Richard Petty	Petty Enterprises	43	72 Plym	199	3,800
4. Fred Lorenzen	Junie Donlavey	90	71 Ford	197	1,475
5. Cecil Gordon	Cecil Gordon	24	71 Merc	194	1,325

Wall Stadium
Belmar, NJ
.333-Mile Paved Track

.333-mile paved track opened in May 1950. Only NASCAR Winston Cup (the Grand National) event staged on 7/26/58 (won by Jim Reed).
Track is still in operation.

Winston Cup Victories
Jim Reed   1

Winston Cup Poles
Rex White   1

Winston Cup Money
Jim Reed $800

Most Cars Started
19—July 26, 1958

Narrowest Margin of Victory
1 car length—July 26, 1958

Race Record
65.395 MPH—July 26, 1958

Most Cautions
1—July 26, 1958

Most Race Leaders
1—July 26, 1958

Most Cars Running at Finish
14—July 26, 1958

1958 Grand National Race No. 34
July 26, 1958 Average Speed: 65.395

Driver	Owner	Car #	Make	Laps	Winnings
1. Jim Reed	Jim Reed	7	57 Ford	300	800
2. Rex White	J. H. Petty	44	57 Chev	300	525
3. Buck Baker	Buck Baker	87	57 Chev	300	350
4. Lee Petty	Petty Enterprises	42	57 Olds	300	250
5. Jack Smith	Jack Smith	47	57 Chev	291	225

New York

Airborne Speedway
Plattsburg, NY
Half-mile Dirt Track

(aka Plattsburg Speedway) Half-mile dirt track built in 1954. Only NASCAR Winston Cup (then Grand National) event staged on 6/19/55 (won by Lee Petty). Track was paved in 1961 and is still in operation.

Winston Cup Victories
Lee Petty   1

Winston Cup Poles
Lee Petty   1

Winston Cup Money
Lee Petty $1,000

Most Cars Started
16—June 19, 1955

Narrowest Margin of Victory
1 lap plus—June 19, 1955

Race Record
59.074 MPH—June 19, 1955

Most Race Leaders
2—June 19, 1955

Most Cars Running at Finish
10—June 19, 1955

1955 Grand National Race No. 22
June 19, 1955 Average Speed: 59.074

Driver	Owner	Car #	Make	Laps	Winnings
1. Lee Petty	Petty Enterprises	42	55 Chrys	200	1,000
2. Buck Baker	Griffin Motors	87	54 Olds	199	650
3. Tim Flock	Hubert Westmoreland	2	55 Chev	197	450
4. Bob Welborn	J. H. Petty	44	55 Chev	194	350
5. Carl Krueger	Carl Krueger	302	55 Chrys	190	300

Albany-Saratoga Speedway
Malta, NY
.362-mile Paved Track

(aka Malta Speedway) .362-mile paved oval opened in May 1965, built by Joe Lesik. First NASCAR Winston Cup (then Grand National) race staged on 7/7/70 (won by Richard Petty). Only other Winston Cup Grand National event run on 7/14/71 (also won by Richard Petty). Track closed in 1975, but one final event was conducted in 1991.

Winston Cup Starts
20 drivers tied with 2

Winston Cup Victories
Richard Petty   2

Winston Cup Poles
Bobby Isaac   1
Richard Petty   1

Winston Cup Money
Richard Petty $3,000

Most Cars Started
34—July 14, 1971 Albany-Saratoga 250

Fewest Cars Started
28—July 7, 1970 Albany-Saratoga 250

Narrowest Margin of Victory
1 lap plus—July 7, 1970

Slowest Race
66.748 MPH—July 14, 1971
Albany-Saratoga 250

Race Record
68.589 MPH—July 7, 1970
Albany-Saratoga 250

Most Cautions
2—July 14, 1971 Albany-Saratoga 250

Most Race Leaders
4—July 14, 1971 Albany-Saratoga 250

Most Cars Running at Finish
18—July 7, 1970 Albany-Saratoga 250

1970 Grand National Race No. 25 Albany-Saratoga 250
July 7, 1970 Average Speed: 68.589

Driver	Owner	Car #	Make	Laps	Winnings
1. Richard Petty	Petty Enterprises	43	70 Plym	250	1,500
2. Bobby Allison	Bobby Allison	22	69 Dodg	249	900
3. Dave Marcis	Dave Marcis	30	69 Dodg	246	500
4. Neil Castles	Neil Castles	06	69 Dodg	243	350
5. G. C. Spencer	G. C. Spencer	49	69 Plym	240	325

1971 Winston Cup GN Race No. 29 Albany-Saratoga 250
July 14, 1971 Average Speed: 66.748

Driver	Owner	Car #	Make	Laps	Winnings
1. Richard Petty	Petty Enterprises	43	71 Plym	250	1,500
2. Dave Marcis	Dave Marcis	2	69 Dodg	248	900
3. J. D. McDuffie	J. D. McDuffie	70	69 Merc	244	500
4. James Hylton	James Hylton	48	71 Ford	243	350
5. Elmo Langley	Ron Ronacher	67	69 Ford	242	325

Altamont-Schenectady Fairgrounds
Altamont, NY
Half-mile Dirt Track

(aka Altamont Speedway; Tri-County Fairgrounds; Albany-Schenectady Fairgrounds) Half-mile dirt oval opened in July 1932. First NASCAR Winston Cup (then Grand National) race staged on 8/1/51 (won by Fonty Flock). Last NASCAR race held on 7/29/55 (won by Junior Johnson). Track closed shortly after the final Grand National event.

Winston Cup Starts		Winston Cup Victories		Winston Cup Money		Narrowest Margin of Victory
Pappy Hough	2	Fonty Flock	1	Fonty Flock $1,000		N/A
Lee Petty	2	Junior Johnson	1	**Most Cars Started**		**Most Race Leaders**
Jim Reed	2	**Winston Cup Poles**		25—July 29, 1955		3—July 29, 1955
		Tim Flock	1	**Fewest Cars Started**		**Most Cars Running at Finish**
		Fonty Flock	1	21—August 1, 1951		16—July 29, 1955

1951 Grand National Race No. 19
August 1, 1951

Driver	Owner	Car #	Make	Laps	Winnings
1. Fonty Flock	Frank Christian	14	51 Olds	200	1,000
2. Herb Thomas	Herb Thomas	92	51 Plym	—	600
3. Lee Petty	Petty Enterprises	42	51 Plym	—	400
4. Perry Smith	Perry Smith	23	51 Stud	—	300
5. Jerry Morese		227	51 Ford	—	250

1955 Grand National Race No. 28
July 29, 1955

Driver	Owner	Car #	Make	Laps	Winnings
1. Junior Johnson	B & L Motors	55	55 Olds	177	900
2. Jim Paschal	Ernest Woods	78	55 Olds	176	600
3. Lee Petty	Petty Enterprises	42	55 Chrys	172	525
4. Jimmie Lewallen	Ernest Woods	88	55 Olds	170	335
5. Gene Simpson	Gene Simpson	40	55 Buick	170	200

Bridgehampton Race Circuit
Bridgehampton, NY
2.85-mile Paved Road Course

(aka Bridgehampton Raceway) 2.85-mile road course located on eastern reaches of Long Island, opened in September 1957. First NASCAR Winston Cup (then Grand National) race held on 8/2/58 (won by Jack Smith). Richard Petty's first career win on a road course came here on 7/21/63. Final Grand National run on 7/10/66 (won by David Pearson). Track is still in operation.

Winston Cup Starts		Winston Cup Poles		Fewest Cars Started	Race Record
Buck Baker	4	Richard Petty	2	17—August 2, 1958	87.707 MPH—July 12, 1964
Winston Cup Victories		**Winston Cup Money**		17—July 21, 1963	**Most Race Leaders**
David Pearson	1	David Pearson $2,075		**Narrowest Margin of Victory**	4—July 12, 1964
Richard Petty	1	**Most Cars Started**		12.000 seconds August 2, 1958	**Most Cars Running at Finish**
Jack Smith	1	28—July 10, 1966		**Slowest Race**	20—July 10, 1966
Billy Wade	1			80.696 MPH—August 2, 1958	

1958 Grand National Race No. 35
August 2, 1958 Average Speed: 80.696

Driver	Owner	Car #	Make	Laps	Winnings
1. Jack Smith	Jack Smith	47	57 Chev	35	800
2. Cotton Owens	Jim Stephens	3	58 Pont	35	525
3. Jim Reed	Jim Reed	7	57 Ford	35	350
4. Junior Johnson	Paul Spaulding	11	57 Ford	35	250
5. Buck Baker	Buck Baker	87	57 Chev	35	225

1963 Grand National Race No. 36
July 21, 1963 Average Speed: 86.047

Driver	Owner	Car #	Make	Laps	Winnings
1. Richard Petty	Petty Enterprises	43	63 Plym	35	1,000
2. Fred Lorenzen	Holman-Moody	28	63 Ford	35	600
3. Marvin Panch	Wood Brothers	21	63 Ford	35	400
4. David Pearson	Cotton Owens	6	63 Dodg	35	300
5. Fireball Roberts	Holman-Moody	22	63 Ford	35	275

1964 Grand National Race No. 38
July 12, 1964 Average Speed: 87.707

Driver	Owner	Car #	Make	Laps	Winnings
1. Billy Wade	Bud Moore	1	64 Merc	50	1,225
2. Buck Baker	Ray Fox	3	64 Dodg	50	675
3. Walt Hansgen	Walt Hansgen	46	64 Ford	48	500
4. Marvin Panch	Holman-Moody	06	64 Ford	44	350
5. Curtis Crider	Curtis Crider	02	63 Merc	42	350

1966 Grand National Race No. 30
July 10, 1966 Average Speed: 86.949

Driver	Owner	Car #	Make	Laps	Winnings
1. David Pearson	Cotton Owens	6	65 Dodg	52	1,375
2. James Hylton	Bud Hartje	48	65 Dodg	52	775
3. Marvin Panch		22	64 Ford	51	570
4. Roy Hallquist	Roy Hallquist	144	64 Ford	51	350
5. Elmo Langley	Henry Woodfield	64	64 Ford	51	350

Buffalo Civic Stadium
Buffalo, NY
Quarter-mile Paved Track

(aka Jopp Stadium; War Memorial Stadium) Quarter-mile cinder track opened for auto racing in May 1940. Track paved in August 1940. Only NASCAR Winston Cup (then Grand National) event staged on 7/19/58 (won by Jim Reed). The stadium is where Buffalo Bills played football in their early AFL days.

Winston Cup Victories		Winston Cup Money		Narrowest Margin of Victory	Most Race Leaders
Jim Reed	1	Jim Reed	$605	N/A	2—July 19, 1958
Winston Cup Poles		**Most Cars Started**		**Race Record**	**Most Cars Running at Finish**
Rex White	1	19—July 19, 1958		46.972 MPH—July 19, 1958	17—July 19, 1958

1958 Grand National Race No. 32
July 19, 1958 Average Speed: 46.972

	Driver	Owner	Car #	Make	Laps	Winnings
1.	Jim Reed	Jim Reed	7	57 Ford	100	605
2.	Cotton Owens	Jim Stephens	6	57 Pont	100	450
3.	Johnny Mackison	Ken Corman	23	57 Merc	100	320
4.	Shorty Rollins	Shorty Rollins	99	58 Ford	99	275
5.	Rex White	J. H. Petty	44	57 Chev	99	250

Fonda Speedway
Fonda, NY
Half-mile Paved Track

(aka Montgomery County Fairgrounds; Fonda-Fultonville Speedway) A half-mile dirt oval that opened circa 1926 and closed in 1939. Re-opened in 1948 and closed again later that same year. Refurbished and opened a third time in May 1953. First NASCAR Winston Cup (then Grand National) race staged on 6/18/55 (won by Junior Johnson). Final Grand National event run on 7/11/68 (won by Richard Petty). Track is still in operation.

Winston Cup Starts		Winston Cup Money		Narrowest Margin of Victory	Most Cautions
Buck Baker	4	Richard Petty	$3,025	N/A	5—July 13, 1967
Winston Cup Victories		**Most Cars Started**		**Slowest Race**	**Most Race Leaders**
Richard Petty	2	31—July 14, 1966		58.413 MPH—June 18, 1955	4—July 14, 1966
Winston Cup Poles		**Fewest Cars Started**		**Race Record**	**Most Cars Running at Finish**
Richard Petty	2	19—June 18, 1955		65.826 MPH—July 13, 1967	15—July 14, 1966
					15—July 13, 1967

1955 Grand National Race No. 21
June 18, 1955 Average Speed: 58.413

Driver	Owner	Car #	Make	Laps	Winnings
1. Junior Johnson	B & L Motors	55	55 Olds	200	1,000
2. Tim Flock	Carl Kiekhaefer	300	55 Chrys	199	650
3. Lee Petty	Petty Enterprises	42	55 Chrys	191	450
4. Buck Baker	Griffin Motors	87	54 Olds	188	350
5. Bob Welborn	J. H. Petty	44	55 Chev	188	300

1966 Grand National Race No. 32
July 14, 1966 Average Speed: 61.010

Driver	Owner	Car #	Make	Laps	Winnings
1. David Pearson	Cotton Owens	6	65 Dodg	200	1,100
2. Richard Petty	Petty Enterprises	43	66 Plym	200	675
3. Rene Charland	Ed Ackerman	03	64 Ford	199	450
4. Roy Hallquist	Roy Hallquist	144	64 Ford	196	300
5. Buck Baker	Buck Baker	87	66 Olds	193	275

1967 Grand National Race No. 31
July 13, 1967 Average Speed: 65.826

Driver	Owner	Car #	Make	Laps	Winnings
1. Richard Petty	Petty Enterprises	43	67 Plym	200	1,150
2. Bobby Allison	Bobby Allison	2	65 Chev	199	700
3. G. C. Spencer	G. C. Spencer	49	66 Plym	197	450
4. John Sears	L. G. DeWitt	4	66 Ford	196	300
5. James Hylton	Bud Hartje	48	65 Dodg	196	275

1968 Grand National Race No. 28 Fonda 200
July 11, 1968 Average Speed: 64.935

Driver	Owner	Car #	Make	Laps	Winnings
1. Richard Petty	Petty Enterprises	43	68 Plym	200	1,200
2. Buddy Baker	Ray Fox	3	68 Dodg	200	600
3. Bobby Allison	Bobby Allison	2	66 Chev	200	400
4. Bobby Isaac	Nord Krauskopf	71	67 Dodg	197	300
5. David Pearson	Holman-Moody	17	68 Ford	196	275

Hamburg Speedway
Hamburg, NY
Half-mile Dirt Track

(aka Erie County Fairgrounds) A half-mile dirt oval that opened circa 1929 for automobile racing. The original horse track was built in the 1840s. First NASCAR Winston Cup (then Strictly Stock) race held on 9/18/49 (won by Jack White; the fifth Winston Cup race ever run). Only other big NASCAR event held on 8/27/50 (won by Dick Linder). Track is still in operation.

Winston Cup Starts
Ted Chamberlain	2
Chuck Mahoney	2
Bill Rexford	2
Frankie Schneider	2
Jack White	2

Winston Cup Victories
Dick Linder	1
Jack White	1

Winston Cup Poles
Dick Linder	1

Winston Cup Money
Jack White	$1,800

Most Cars Started
33—August 27, 1950

Fewest Cars Started
16—September 18, 1949

Narrowest Margin of Victory
20 yards—August 27, 1950

Slowest Race
50.747 MPH—August 27, 1950

Race Record
50.747 MPH—August 27, 1950

Most Cautions
N/A

Most Race Leaders
3—August 27, 1950

Most Cars Running at Finish
N/A

1949 Strictly Stock Race No. 5
September 18, 1949

Driver	Owner	Car #	Make	Laps	Winnings
1. Jack White	Dailey Moyer	25	49 Linc	200	1,500
2. Ray Erickson	Ed Hastings	5	49 Merc	200	750
3. Billy Rafter			49 Ford	—	400
4. Mike Eagan			49 Merc	—	300
5. Bill Rexford	Julian Buesink	59	49 Ford	—	175

1950 Grand National Race No. 12
August 27, 1950 Average Speed: 50.747

Driver	Owner	Car #	Make	Laps	Winnings
1. Dick Linder	Don Rogalla	25	50 Olds	200	1,500
2. Fireball Roberts	Sam Rice	11	49 Olds	200	750
3. Curtis Turner	John Eanes	41	50 Olds	199	500
4. Lloyd Moore	Julian Buesink	59	50 Linc	—	400
5. Jack White	Dailey Moyer		50 Merc	—	300

Islip Speedway
Islip, NY
.2-mile Paved Track

.2-mile paved oval opened in August 1947. First NASCAR Winston Cup (then Grand National) race was held on 7/15/64 (won by Billy Wade). Final big NASCAR event staged on 7/15/71 (won by Richard Petty). The track was the scene of the World Figure 8 Championships that frequently aired on ABC's Wide World of Sports. Final event run on 9/8/84. The property is now the site of a cookie factory.

Winston Cup Starts
Neil Castles	6
Wendell Scott	6

Winston Cup Victories
Bobby Allison	2
Richard Petty	2

Winston Cup Poles
Richard Petty	2

Winston Cup Money
Richard Petty	$3,650

Most Cars Started
33—July 15, 1971 Islip 250

Fewest Cars Started
22—July 15, 1964
22—July 14, 1965

Narrowest Margin of Victory
6 car lengths—July 7, 1968

Slowest Race
42.428 MPH—July 15, 1967 Islip 300

Race Record
49.925 MPH—July 15, 1971 Islip 250

Most Cautions
5—July 15, 1967 Islip 300

Most Race Leaders
4—July 15, 1967 Islip 300
4—July 7, 1968 Islip 300

Most Cars Running at Finish
14—July 7, 1968 Islip 300

1964 Grand National Race No. 39
July 15, 1964 Average Speed: 46.252

Driver	Owner	Car #	Make	Laps	Winnings
1. Billy Wade	Bud Moore	1	64 Merc	300	1,000
2. Ned Jarrett	Bondy Long	11	64 Ford	299	600
3. Richard Petty	Petty Enterprises	41	64 Plym	295	400
4. Jimmy Pardue	Charles Robinson	54	64 Plym	283	300
5. Bob Welborn	Holman-Moody	06	64 Ford	273	275

1965 Grand National Race No. 32
July 14, 1965 Average Speed: 43.838

Driver	Owner	Car #	Make	Laps	Winnings
1. Marvin Panch	Wood Brothers	21	65 Ford	250	1,000
2. Dick Hutcherson	Holman-Moody	29	65 Ford	249	600
3. Ned Jarrett	Bondy Long	11	65 Ford	246	400
4. Cale Yarborough	Kenny Myler	06	64 Ford	245	300
5. Dick Dixon	Dan Colone	8	64 Ford	242	275

1966 Grand National Race No. 33
July 16, 1966 Average Speed: 47.285

Driver	Owner	Car #	Make	Laps	Winnings
1. Bobby Allison	Bobby Allison	2	65 Chev	300	1,100
2. James Hylton	Bud Hartje	48	65 Dodg	298	675
3. Ned Jarrett	Bernard Alvarez	11	64 Ford	297	650
4. David Pearson	Cotton Owens	6	65 Dodg	295	300
5. Elmo Langley	Henry Woodfield	64	64 Ford	290	275

1967 Grand National Race No. 32 Islip 300
July 15, 1967 Average Speed: 42.428

Driver	Owner	Car #	Make	Laps	Winnings
1. Richard Petty	Petty Enterprises	43	67 Plym	300	1,150
2. James Hylton	Bud Hartje	48	65 Dodg	297	800
3. G. C. Spencer	G. C. Spencer	49	66 Plym	297	500
4. John Sears	L. G. DeWitt	4	66 Ford	295	300
5. Jim Paschal	Tom Friedkin	14	67 Plym	294	275

1968 Grand National Race No. 26 Islip 300
July 7, 1968 Average Speed: 48.561

Driver	Owner	Car #	Make	Laps	Winnings
1. Bobby Allison	Bobby Allison	2	66 Chev	300	1,000
2. David Pearson	Holman-Moody	17	68 Ford	300	600
3. Buddy Baker	Ray Fox	3	68 Dodg	299	400
4. Richard Petty	Petty Enterprises	43	68 Plym	298	500
5. James Hylton	James Hylton	48	67 Dodg	294	275

1971 Winston Cup GN Race No. 30 Islip 250
July 15, 1971 Average Speed: 49.925

Driver	Owner	Car #	Make	Laps	Winnings
1. Richard Petty	Petty Enterprises	43	71 Plym	230	1,500
2. Friday Hassler	Friday Hassler	39	70 Chev	228	900
3. Elmo Langley	Elmo Langley	67	69 Merc	224	500
4. Bobby Allison	Holman-Moody	12	69 Merc	223	350
5. G. C. Spencer	G. C. Spencer	49	69 Plym	222	325

Monroe County Fairgrounds
Rochester, NY
Half-mile Dirt Track

Half-mile dirt track built circa 1948. First NASCAR Winston Cup (then Grand National) event staged on 7/2/50 (won by Curtis Turner). Final NASCAR event held on 7/25/58 (won by Cotton Owens). Track closed circa 1962 and was briefly re-opened in 1981.

Winston Cup Starts

Lee Petty	8

Winston Cup Victories

Tim Flock	2
Lee Petty	2

Winston Cup Poles

Buck Baker	1
Fonty Flock	1
Jim Paschal	1
Herb Thomas	1
Curtis Turner	1
Rex White	1

Winston Cup Money

Lee Petty	$3,500

Most Cars Started
32—June 25, 1954

Fewest Cars Started
18—July 3, 1953

Narrowest Margin of Victory
10 car lengths—July 3, 1953

Slowest Race
50.614 MPH—July 2, 1950

Race Record
59.990 MPH—July 25, 1958

Most Cautions
N/A

Most Race Leaders
3—August 15, 1952
3—July 25, 1958

Most Cars Running at Finish
24—June 25, 1954

1950 Grand National Race No. 8
July 2, 1950 Average Speed: 50.614

Driver	Owner	Car #	Make	Laps	Winnings
1. Curtis Turner	John Eanes	41	50 Olds	200	1,500
2. Bill Blair	Sam Rice	2	50 Merc	197	600
3. Lee Petty	Petty Enterprises	42	50 Plym	197	400
4. Jimmy Florian	Jimmy Florian	27	50 Ford	192	300
5. Bill Rexford	Julian Buesink	80	50 Olds	192	225

1951 Grand National Race No. 18
July 31, 1951

Driver	Owner	Car #	Make	Laps	Winnings
1. Lee Petty	Petty Enterprises	42	51 Plym	200	1,000
2. Charles Gattalia			51 Ford	—	600
3. Ronnie Kohler			51 Plym	—	400
4. Don Bailey		54	51 Stud	—	300
5. Pappy Hough	Pappy Hough	81	51 Ford	—	250

1952 Grand National Race No. 23
August 15, 1952

Driver	Owner	Car #	Make	Laps	Winnings
1. Tim Flock	Ted Chester	91	52 Huds	176	1,000
2. Herb Thomas	Herb Thomas	92	52 Huds	176	700
3. Dick Rathmann	Walt Chapman	120	52 Huds	174	450
4. Lee Petty	Petty Enterprises	42	52 Plym	174	350
5. Jim Reed	Jim Reed	47	51 Ford	173	200

1953 Grand National Race No. 19
July 3, 1953 Average Speed: 56.939

Driver	Owner	Car #	Make	Laps	Winnings
1. Herb Thomas	Herb Thomas	92	53 Huds	200	1,000
2. Dick Rathmann	Walt Chapman	120	53 Huds	200	700
3. Lee Petty	Petty Enterprises	42	53 Dodg	200	450
4. Tim Flock	Ted Chester	91	53 Huds	199	350
5. Bill Rexford	Julian Buesink	60	53 Chev	—	200

1954 Grand National Race No. 20
June 25, 1954 Average Speed: 52.455

Driver	Owner	Car #	Make	Laps	Winnings
1. Lee Petty	Petty Enterprises	42	54 Chrys	200	1,000
2. Herb Thomas	Herb Thomas	92	54 Huds	200	650
3. Dick Rathmann	John Ditz	3	54 Huds	199	450
4. Buck Baker	Griffin Motors	87	53 Olds	198	350
5. Hershel McGriff	Frank Christian	14	54 Olds	198	300

1955 Grand National Race No. 20
June 17, 1955 Average Speed: 57.170

Driver	Owner	Car #	Make	Laps	Winnings
1. Tim Flock	Carl Kiekhaefer	300	55 Chrys	200	1,000
2. Fonty Flock	Carl Kiekhaefer	301	55 Chrys	199	650
3. Bob Welborn	J. H. Petty	44	55 Chev	196	450
4. Jimmie Lewallen	Ernest Woods	88	55 Olds	194	350
5. Harvey Henderson	Harvey Henderson	121	53 Huds	191	300

1956 Grand National Race No. 27
June 22, 1956 Average Speed: 57.288

Driver	Owner	Car #	Make	Laps	Winnings
1. Speedy Thompson	Carl Kiekhaefer	300c	56 Chrys	200	850
2. Jim Paschal	Frank Hayworth	75	56 Merc	199	625
3. Herb Thomas	Carl Kiekhaefer	500B	56 Dodg	199	450
4. Buck Baker	Carl Kiekhaefer	300	56 Chrys	197	350
5. Bob Duell	Julian Buesink	95	56 Ford	192	310

1958 Grand National Race No. 33
July 25, 1958 Average Speed: 59.990

Driver	Owner	Car #	Make	Laps	Winnings
1. Cotton Owens	Jim Stephens	6	57 Pont	200	800
2. Buck Baker	Buck Baker	87	57 Chev	198	525
3. Speedy Thompson	Speedy Thompson	46	57 Chev	198	350
4. Lee Petty	Petty Enterprises	42	57 Olds	197	250
5. Bob Duell	Julian Buesink	95	57 Ford	195	225

Montgomery Air Base
Montgomery, NY
2-mile Paved Track

(aka Stewart Air Force Base) 1.85-mile concrete road course opened for first race in August 1956. Track was laid out on runways in a triangular fashion with "kinks" or chicanes in each of the three corners to incorporate quick left- and right-hand turns. Only NASCAR Winston Cup (then Grand National) race run on 7/17/60 (won by Rex White). NASCAR course did not include chicanes, and drivers frequently ran into the dirt beyond the course boundaries in order to set up a more favorable angle into each flat corner. The NASCAR course measured 2 miles. Final motor racing event held on track in August 1960.

Winston Cup Victories
Rex White   1

Winston Cup Poles
John Rostek   1

Winston Cup Money
Rex White $2,970

Most Cars Started
19—July 17, 1960 Empire State 200

Narrowest Margin of Victory
1 lap plus—July 17, 1960
Empire State 200

Race Record
88.626 MPH—July 17, 1960
Empire State 200

Most Cautions
1—July 17, 1960 Empire State 200

Most Race Leaders
4—July 17, 1960 Empire State 200

Most Cars Running at Finish
14—July 17, 1960 Empire State 200

1960 Grand National Race No. 25 Empire State 200
July 17, 1960 Average Speed: 88.626

Driver	Owner	Car #	Make	Laps	Winnings
1. Rex White	Rex White	4	60 Chev	100	2,970
2. Richard Petty	Petty Enterprises	43	60 Plym	99	1,600
3. Lee Petty	Petty Enterprises	42	60 Plym	97	1,200
4. Ned Jarrett	Ned Jarrett	11	60 Ford	96	725
5. Buck Baker	Buck Baker	87	60 Chev	96	625

New York State Fairgrounds
Syracuse, NY
1.0-mile Dirt Track

1-mile dirt track originally built as a horse track in 1880. Its premier auto racing event was staged in September 1909. First NASCAR Winston Cup (then Grand National) race held on 7/30/55 (won by Tim Flock). Final big NASCAR event held on 9/5/57 (won by Gwyn Staley). Track is now home of the Syracuse Nationals. In 1911, Lee Oldfield crashed through a fence and plunged into the crowd. Eleven spectators were killed in one of America's worst racing accidents. Early AAA champion and Indianapolis 500 winner Jimmy Murphy was also killed here in 1924.

Winston Cup Starts
Lee Petty   3
Jim Reed   3

Winston Cup Victories
Buck Baker   1
Tim Flock   1
Gwyn Staley   1

Winston Cup Poles
Buck Baker   1
Tim Flock   1
Gwyn Staley   1

Winston Cup Money
Buck Baker $2,000

Most Cars Started
24—May 30, 1956
24—September 5, 1957

Fewest Cars Started
22—July 30, 1955

Narrowest Margin of Victory
N/A

Slowest Race
76.522 MPH—July 30, 1955

Race Record
86.179 MPH—May 30, 1956

Most Cautions
N/A

Most Race Leaders
2—May 30, 1956
2—September 5, 1957

Most Cars Running at Finish
18—July 30, 1955

1955 Grand National Race No. 29
July 30, 1955 Average Speed: 76.522

Driver	Owner	Car #	Make	Laps	Winnings
1. Tim Flock	Carl Kiekhaefer	300	55 Chrys	100	950
2. Jimmie Lewallen	Ernest Woods	88	55 Olds	100	650
3. Lee Petty	Petty Enterprises	42	55 Chrys	99	525
4. Bob Welborn	J. H. Petty	44	55 Chev	98	385
5. Jim Paschal	Ernest Woods	78	55 Olds	98	290

1956 Grand National Race No. 23
May 30, 1956 Average Speed: 86.179

Driver	Owner	Car #	Make	Laps	Winnings
1. Buck Baker	Carl Kiekhaefer	300	56 Chrys	150	1,900
2. Jim Paschal	Frank Hayworth	75	56 Merc	147	1,300
3. Jim Reed	Jim Reed	7	56 Chev	146	950
4. Lee Petty	Petty Enterprises	42	56 Dodg	145	700
5. Gwyn Staley	Hubert Westmoreland	2	56 Chev	145	535

1957 Grand National Race No. 41
September 5, 1957 Average Speed: 80.591

Driver	Owner	Car #	Make	Laps	Winnings
1. Gwyn Staley	J. H. Petty	38	57 Chev	100	1,000
2. Lee Petty	Petty Enterprises	42	57 Olds	99	625
3. Bill Walker		150	57 Ford	99	400
4. Dean Layfield	William Dickenson	916	56 Ford	97	295
5. Fireball Roberts	Fireball Roberts	22	57 Ford	95	255

Shangri-La Speedway
Oswego, NY
Half-mile Paved Track

(aka Tioga Speedway) Half-mile paved oval opened in July 1946. Only NASCAR Winston Cup (then Grand National) race staged on 7/4/52 (won by Tim Flock). Track is still in operation.

Winston Cup Victories
Tim Flock   1

Winston Cup Poles
Tim Flock   1

Winston Cup Money
Tim Flock $1,000

Most Cars Started
26—July 4, 1952

Narrowest Margin of Victory
N/A

Race Record
56.603 MPH—July 4, 1952

Most Race Leaders
N/A

Most Cars Running at Finish
16—July 4, 1952

1952 Grand National Race No. 19
July 4, 1952 Average Speed: 56.603

Driver	Owner	Car #	Make	Laps	Winnings
1. Tim Flock	Ted Chester	91	51 Huds	200	1,000
2. Herb Thomas	Herb Thomas	92	52 Huds	200	700
3. Dick Rathmann	Walt Chapman	120	51 Huds	199	450
4. Bucky Sager	Ken Swihart	118	51 Huds	199	350
5. Lee Petty	Petty Enterprises	42	50 Plym	198	200

State Line Speedway
Busti, NY
.333-Mile Dirt Track

.333-mile paved oval opened in July 1956. Only NASCAR Winston Cup (then Grand National) race staged on 7/16/58 (won by rookie Shorty Rollins). Track is still in operation and should not be confused with the other track in Busti, named Satan's Bowl-O-Death.

Winston Cup Victories		**Winston Cup Money**		**Narrowest Margin of Victory**	**Most Race Leaders**
Shorty Rollins	1	Shorty Rollins	$600	N/A	N/A

Winston Cup Poles		**Most Cars Started**	**Race Record**	**Most Cars Running at Finish**
Lee Petty	1	23—July 16, 1958	47.110 MPH—July 16, 1958	14—July 16, 1958

1958 Grand National Race No. 30
July 16, 1958 Average Speed: 47.110

Driver	Owner	Car #	Make	Laps	Winnings
1. Shorty Rollins	Shorty Rollins	99	58 Ford	150	600
2. Bob Duell	Julian Buesink	95	57 Ford	150	470
3. Ken Johnson		36	56 Ford	149	375
4. Emory Mahon		8	57 Chev	149	270
5. John Seeley		16	57 Ford	143	245

Vernon Fairgrounds
Vernon, NY
Half-mile Dirt Track

Half-mile dirt oval opened in 1949. First Winston Cup (then Grand National) race held on 6/18/50 (won by Bill Blair). Only other Grand National ran on 10/1/50 (won by Dick Linder). Track closed circa 1951. It is currently a training track for the Vernon Downs horse track.

Winston Cup Starts		**Winston Cup Victories**		**Winston Cup Money**		**Narrowest Margin of Victory**
Dick Linder	2	Bill Blair	1	Bill Blair	$1,255	5 car lengths—October 1, 1950
Chuck Mahoney	2	Dick Linder	1			
Lloyd Moore	2			**Most Cars Started**		**Most Race Leaders**
Lee Petty	2	**Winston Cup Poles**		29—October 1, 1950		3—June 18, 1950
Bill Rexford	2	Dick Linder	1			
Herb Thomas	2	Chuck Mahoney	1	**Fewest Cars Started**		**Most Cars Running at Finish**
				23—June 18, 1950		N/A

1950 Grand National Race No. 6
June 18, 1950

Driver	Owner	Car #	Make	Laps	Winnings
1. Bill Blair	Sam Rice	2	50 Merc	200	1,255
2. Lloyd Moore	Julian Buesink	59	50 Ford	—	680
3. Chuck Mahoney	Brooks Motors	77	50 Merc	—	490
4. Dick Burns		18	50 Merc	—	300
5. Lee Petty	Petty Enterprises	42	49 Plym	—	225

1950 Grand National Race No. 16
October 1, 1950

Driver	Owner	Car #	Make	Laps	Winnings
1. Dick Linder	Don Rogalla	25	50 Olds	200	1,025
2. Ted Swaim	Hubert Westmoreland	38	50 Plym	200	600
3. Lloyd Moore	Julian Buesink	59	50 Merc	198	400
4. Tim Flock	Buddy Elliott	9	50 Olds	198	300
5. Jack Reynolds			50 Plym	—	225

Watkins Glen International
Watkins Glen, NY
2.428-mile Road Course

2.3-mile road course opened on 9/15/56. Track was built following the destruction of the 6.6-mile street and road course through the Watkins Glen village in 1952. First NASCAR Winston Cup (then Grand National) race held on 8/4/57 (won by Buck Baker). Site of United States Formula One Grand Prix from 1960–81. 2.428-mile course played host to return of the Winston Cup Series on 8/10/86 (won by Tim Richmond).

Winston Cup Starts

Ricky Rudd	17
KenSchrader	17
Rusty Wallace	17
Michael Waltrip	17

Winston Cup Victories

Jeff Gordon	4

Winston Cup Poles

Dale Earnhardt	3
Mark Martin	3

Winston Cup Money

Mark Martin	$900,309

Most Cars Started

43—5 times

Fewest Cars Started

19—July 18, 1965

Narrowest Margin of Victory

0.172 seconds August 12, 2001

Slowest Race

74.096 MPH—August 14, 1988
The Budweiser at the Glen

Race Record

103.030 MPH—August 13, 1995
The Budweiser at the Glen

Most Cautions

8—August 14, 1988
The Budweiser at the Glen

Most Race Leaders

11—August 12, 2001

Most Cars Running at Finish

41—August 9, 1998

1957 Grand National Race No. 35
August 4, 1957 Average Speed: 83.064

Driver	Owner	Car #	Make	Laps	Winnings
1. Buck Baker	Buck Baker	87	57 Chev	44	1,000
2. Fireball Roberts	Fireball Roberts	22	57 Ford	44	625
3. Tiny Lund	A. L. Bumgarner	55	57 Pont	44	400
4. Frankie Schneider	Hubert Westmoreland	2	57 Chev	43	295
5. Johnny Allen	Spook Crawford	64	57 Plym	43	255

1964 Grand National Race No. 40
July 19, 1964 Average Speed: 97.988

Driver	Owner	Car #	Make	Laps	Winnings
1. Billy Wade	Bud Moore	1	64 Merc	66	1,400
2. LeeRoy Yarbrough	Ray Fox	03	64 Dodg	66	800
3. Walt Hansgen	Walt Hansgen	46	64 Chev	65	600
4. Buck Baker	Ray Fox	3	64 Dodg	65	500
5. Bob Welborn	Holman-Moody	06	64 Ford	64	400

1965 Grand National Race No. 33
July 18, 1965 Average Speed: 98.182

Driver	Owner	Car #	Make	Laps	Winnings
1. Marvin Panch	Wood Brothers	21	65 Ford	66	1,425
2. Ned Jarrett	Bondy Long	11	65 Ford	66	650
3. Buddy Baker	Buck Baker	88	64 Dodg	64	490
4. Cale Yarborough	Kenny Myler	06	64 Ford	63	415
5. Tiny Lund	Lyle Stelter	55	64 Ford	58	385

1986 Winston Cup Race No. 18 The Budweiser at the Glen
August 10, 1986 Average Speed: 90.463

Driver	Owner	Car #	Make	Laps	Winnings
1. Tim Richmond	Rick Hendrick	25	Chev	90	50,955
2. Darrell Waltrip	Junior Johnson	11	Chev	90	32,450
3. Dale Earnhardt	Richard Childress	3	Chev	90	25,250
4. Bill Elliott	Harry Melling	9	Ford	90	20,350
5. Neil Bonnett	Junior Johnson	12	Chev	90	18,575

1987 Winston Cup Race No. 18 The Budweiser at the Glen
August 10, 1987 Average Speed: 90.682

Driver	Owner	Car #	Make	Laps	Winnings
1. Rusty Wallace	Raymond Beadle	27	Pont	90	52,925
2. Terry Labonte	Junior Johnson	11	Chev	90	35,850
3. Dave Marcis	Dave Marcis	71	Chev	90	23,880
4. Ricky Rudd	Bud Moore	15	Ford	90	20,135
5. Benny Parsons	Rick Hendrick	35	Chev	90	19,655

1988 Winston Cup Race No. 18 The Budweiser at the Glen
August 14, 1988 Average Speed: 74.096

Driver	Owner	Car #	Make	Laps	Winnings
1. Ricky Rudd	Kenny Bernstein	26	Buick	90	49,625
2. Rusty Wallace	Raymond Beadle	27	Pont	90	33,900
3. Bill Elliott	Harry Melling	9	Ford	90	26,640
4. Phil Parsons	Richard Jackson	55	Olds	90	16,540
5. Mike Alexander	Stavola Brothers	12	Buick	90	19,295

1989 Winston Cup Race No. 18 The Budweiser at the Glen
August 13, 1989 Average Speed: 87.242

Driver	Owner	Car #	Make	Laps	Winnings
1. Rusty Wallace	Raymond Beadle	27	Pont	90	56,400
2. Mark Martin	Jack Roush	6	Ford	90	32,550
3. Dale Earnhardt	Richard Childress	3	Chev	90	38,140
4. Davey Allison	Robert Yates	28	Ford	90	21,005
5. Bobby Hillin Jr.	Stavola Brothers	8	Buick	90	16,690

1990 Winston Cup Series Race No. 18 Budweiser at the Glen
August 12, 1990 Average Speed: 92.452

Driver	Owner	Car #	Make	Laps	Winnings
1. Ricky Rudd	Rick Hendrick	5	Chev	90	55,000
2. Geoff Bodine	Junior Johnson	11	Ford	90	33,900
3. Brett Bodine	Kenny Bernstein	26	Buick	90	22,490
4. Michael Waltrip	Chuck Rider	30	Pont	90	16,980
5. Mark Martin	Jack Roush	6	Ford	90	20,790

1991 Winston Cup Series Race No. 18 The Budweiser at the Glen
August 11, 1991 Average Speed: 98.977

Driver	Owner	Car #	Make	Laps	Winnings
1. Ernie Irvan	Larry McClure	4	Chev	90	64,850
2. Ricky Rudd	Rick Hendrick	5	Chev	90	37,325
3. Mark Martin	Jack Roush	6	Ford	90	31,440
4. Rusty Wallace	Roger Penske	2	Pont	90	16,680
5. Dale Jarrett	Wood Brothers	21	Ford	90	18,565

1992 Winston Cup Race No. 18 The Budweiser at the Glen
August 9, 1992 Average Speed: 88.980

Driver	Owner	Car #	Make	Laps	Winnings
1. Kyle Petty	Felix Sabates	42	Pont	51	50,895
2. Morgan Shepherd	Wood Brothers	21	Ford	51	48,545
3. Ernie Irvan	Larry McClure	4	Chev	51	35,060
4. Mark Martin	Jack Roush	6	Ford	51	28,325
5. Wally Dallenbach Jr.	Jack Roush	16	Ford	51	13,480

Watkins Glen International *continued*

1993 Winston Cup Series Race No. 19 The Budweiser at the Glen
August 8, 1993 Average Speed: 84.771

Driver	Owner	Car #	Make	Laps	Winnings
1. Mark Martin	Jack Roush	6	Ford	90	166,110
2. Wally Dallenbach Jr.	Jack Roush	16	Ford	90	37,045
3. Jimmy Spencer	Bobby Allison	12	Ford	90	31,135
4. Bill Elliott	Junior Johnson	11	Ford	90	28,075
5. Ken Schrader	Rick Hendrick	25	Chev	90	24,655

1994 Winston Cup Series Race No. 20 The Budweiser at the Glen
August 14, 1994 Average Speed: 93.752

Driver	Owner	Car #	Make	Laps	Winnings
1. Mark Martin	Jack Roush	6	Ford	90	85,100
2. Ernie Irvan	Robert Yates	28	Ford	90	42,015
3. Dale Earnhardt	Richard Childress	3	Chev	90	39,605
4. Ken Schrader	Rick Hendrick	25	Chev	90	26,245
5. Ricky Rudd	Ricky Rudd	10	Ford	90	20,875

1995 Winston Cup Series Race No. 20 The Budweiser at the Glen
August 13, 1995 Average Speed: 103.030

Driver	Owner	Car #	Make	Laps	Winnings
1. Mark Martin	Jack Roush	6	Ford	90	95,290
2. Wally Dallenbach Jr.	Bill Davis	22	Pont	90	54,140
3. Jeff Gordon	Rick Hendrick	24	Chev	90	42,205
4. Ricky Rudd	Ricky Rudd	10	Ford	90	34,320
5. Terry Labonte	Rick Hendrick	5	Chev	90	36,325

1996 Winston Cup Series Race No. 20 The Budweiser at the Glen
August 11, 1996 Average Speed: 92.334

Driver	Owner	Car #	Make	Laps	Winnings
1. Geoff Bodine	Geoff Bodine	7	Ford	90	88,740
2. Terry Labonte	Rick Hendrick	5	Chev	90	51,390
3. Mark Martin	Jack Roush	6	Ford	90	44,755
4. Jeff Gordon	Rick Hendrick	24	Chev	90	44,370
5. Bobby Labonte	Joe Gibbs	18	Chev	90	35,325

1997 Winston Cup Series Race No. 20
August 10, 1997 Average Speed: 91.294

Driver	Owner	Car #	Make	Laps	Winnings
1. Jeff Gordon	Rick Hendrick	24	Chev	90	139,120
2. Geoffrey Bodine	Geoffrey Bodine	7	Ford	90	71,895
3. Rusty Wallace	Roger Penske	2	Ford	90	43,810
4. Robby Gordon	Felix Sabates	40	Chev	90	39,200
5. Mark Martin	Jack Roush	6	Ford	90	36,700

1998 Winston Cup Series Race No. 20
August 9, 1998 Average Speed: 94.446

Driver	Owner	Car #	Make	Laps	Winnings
1. Jeff Gordon	Rick Hendrick	24	Chev	90	152,970
2. Mark Martin	Jack Roush	6	Ford	90	65,820
3. Mike Skinner	Richard Childress	31	Chev	90	53,085
4. Rusty Wallace	Roger Penske	2	Ford	90	47,050
5. Dale Jarrett	Robert Yates	88	Ford	90	52,980

1999 Winston Cup Series Race No. 21
August 15, 1999 Average Speed: 87.722

Driver	Owner	Car #	Make	Laps	Winnings
1. Jeff Gordon	Rick Hendrick	24	Chev	90	119,860
2. Ron Fellows	Joe Nemechek	87	Chev	90	67,270
3. Rusty Wallace	Roger Penske	2	Ford	90	64,460
4. Dale Jarrett	Robert Yates	88	Ford	90	59,900
5. Jerry Nadeau	Mark Melling	9	Ford	90	53,120

2000 Winston Cup Series Race No. 21
August 13, 2000 Average Speed: 91.336

Driver	Owner	Car #	Make	Laps	Winnings
1. Steve Park	Dale Earnhardt, Inc.	1	Chev	90	124,870
2. Mark Martin	Jack Roush	6	Ford	90	73,870
3. Jeff Burton	Jack Roush	99	Ford	90	75,685
4. Robby Gordon	John Menard	13	Ford	90	52,600
5. Bobby Labonte	Joe Gibbs	18	Pont	90	60,605

2001 Winston Cup Series Race No. 22
August 12, 2001 Average Speed: 89.081

Driver	Owner	Car #	Make	Laps	Winnings
1. Jeff Gordon	Rick Hendrick	24	Chev	90	173,402
2. Jeff Burton	Jack Roush	99	Ford	90	125,371
3. Jeremy Mayfield	Roger Penske	12	Ford	90	97,834
4. Ricky Rudd	Robert Yates	28	Ford	90	96,322
5. Todd Bodine	Travis Carter	66	Ford	90	57,350

2002 Winston Cup Series Race No. 22
August 11, 2002 Average Speed: 82.208

Driver	Owner	Car #	Make	Laps	Winnings
1. Tony Stewart	Joe Gibbs	20	Pont	90	165,303
2. Ryan Newman	Roger Penske	12	Ford	90	107,725
3. Robby Gordon	Richard Childress	31	Chev	90	108,706
4. P.J. Jones	A.J. Foyt	14	Pont	90	65,950
5. Ricky Rudd	Robert Yates	28	Ford	90	109,867

North Carolina

Asheville-Weaverville Speedway
Weaverville, NC
Half-mile Dirt Track

(aka Skyline Speedway) Half-mile dirt oval opened in May 1950. First NASCAR Winston Cup (then Grand National) race staged on 7/29/51 (won by Fonty Flock). Track was paved in 1958. This was often referred to as the fastest half-mile track in the nation. Final Grand National event held on 8/24/69 (won by Bobby Isaac). The track was the scene of a riot during a Grand National event held on 8/13/61 when the race was shortened from 500 to 258 laps. Spectators held drivers and crewmen hostage, and teams were held captive inside the speedway for nearly four hours. Law enforcement officials could not disperse crowd, and the riot fizzled out near dark with no serious injuries reported. Track closed in 1970. Last activity on track was slow-pitch soft-ball.

Winston Cup Starts
Buck Baker   23

Winston Cup Victories
Rex White   5

Winston Cup Poles
Junior Johnson   4
Rex White   4

Winston Cup Money
Richard Petty $16,135

Most Cars Started
41—August 16, 1959
Western North Carolina 500

Fewest Cars Started
15—March 5, 1961

Narrowest Margin of Victory
70 feet—September 8, 1957

Slowest Race
56.435 MPH—July 1, 1956

Race Record
83.360 MPH—March 5, 1967
Fireball 300

Most Cautions
10—November 5, 1967
Western North Carolina 500

Most Race Leaders
6—August 14, 1960
Western North Carolina 500

Most Cars Running at Finish
28—August 13, 1961
Western North Carolina 500

1951 Grand National Race No. 17
July 29, 1951

Driver	Owner	Car #	Make	Laps	Winnings
1. Fonty Flock	Frank Christian	14	51 Olds	200	1,000
2. Gober Sosebee	Gober Sosebee	51	50 Olds	—	600
3. Herb Thomas	Herb Thomas	92	50 Plym	—	400
4. Frank Mundy	Perry Smith	23	51 Stud	—	300
5. Speedy Thompson			51 Stud	—	250

1952 Grand National Race No. 24
August 17, 1952 Average Speed: 57.288

Driver	Owner	Car #	Make	Laps	Winnings
1. Bob Flock	Ted Chester	7	51 Huds	200	1,000
2. Tim Flock	Ted Chester	91	52 Huds	198	700
3. Herb Thomas	Herb Thomas	92	52 Huds	195	450
4. Gene Comstock	Gene Comstock	8	52 Huds	192	350
5. Herschel Buchanan	Herschel Buchanan	1	52 Nash	189	200

1953 Grand National Race No. 27
August 16, 1953 Average Speed: 62.434

Driver	Owner	Car #	Make	Laps	Winnings
1. Fonty Flock	Frank Christian	14	53 Huds	200	1,000
2. Herb Thomas	Herb Thomas	92	53 Huds	—	700
3. Bill Blair	Bill Blair	2	53 Olds	—	450
4. Buck Baker	Griffin Motors	87	53 Olds	—	350
5. Jimmie Lewallen	R. G. Shelton	22	52 Olds	—	200

1954 Grand National Race No. 23
July 4, 1954 Average Speed: 61.318

Driver	Owner	Car #	Make	Laps	Winnings
1. Herb Thomas	Herb Thomas	92	54 Huds	200	1,000
2. Jimmie Lewallen	Joe Blair	5	54 Merc	199	650
3. Dick Rathmann	John Ditz	3	54 Huds	199	450
4. Lee Petty	Gary Drake	100	54 Olds	196	350
5. Gober Sosebee	Gober Sosebee	51	54 Olds	193	300

1955 Grand National Race No. 26
July 10, 1955 Average Speed: 62.739

Driver	Owner	Car #	Make	Laps	Winnings
1. Tim Flock	Carl Kiekhaefer	300	55 Chrys	200	1,000
2. Fonty Flock	Carl Kiekhaefer	301	55 Chrys	199	700
3. Jim Paschal	Ernest Woods	78	55 Olds	198	475
4. Donald Thomas	Herb Thomas	9	54 Huds	189	365
5. Eddie Skinner	Frank Dodge	28	53 Olds	180	310

1956 Grand National Race No. 29
July 1, 1956 Average Speed: 56.435

Driver	Owner	Car #	Make	Laps	Winnings
1. Lee Petty	Petty Enterprises	42	56 Dodg	200	850
2. Jim Paschal	Frank Hayworth	75	56 Merc	200	625
3. Joe Eubanks	James Satcher	82	56 Ford	197	450
4. Gwyn Staley	Hubert Westmoreland	2	56 Chev	194	350
5. Herb Thomas	Carl Kiekhaefer	300B	56 Chrys	193	310

1957 Grand National Race No. 8
March 31, 1957 Average Speed: 65.693

Driver	Owner	Car #	Make	Laps	Winnings
1. Buck Baker	Hugh Babb	87	57 Chev	200	850
2. Speedy Thompson	Hugh Babb	46	57 Chev	199	625
3. Jim Paschal	Bill Stroppe	17	57 Merc	198	350
4. Jack Smith	Hugh Babb	47	57 Chev	189	300
5. Dick Beaty	Dick Beaty	34	56 Ford	188	310

1957 Grand National Race No. 42
September 8, 1957 Average Speed: 67.950

Driver	Owner	Car #	Make	Laps	Winnings
1. Lee Petty	Petty Enterprises	42	57 Olds	200	1,000
2. Buck Baker	Buck Baker	87	57 Chev	200	625
3. Bill Amick	Bill Amick	97	57 Ford	200	400
4. Rex White	Bob Welborn	44	57 Chev	200	295
5. Jack Smith	Jack Smith	47	57 Chev	199	255

Asheville-Weaverville Speedway *continued*

1958 Grand National Race No. 27
June 29, 1958 Average Speed: 73.892

Driver	Owner	Car #	Make	Laps	Winnings
1. Rex White	J. H. Petty	44	57 Chev	200	800
2. Buck Baker	Buck Baker	87	57 Chev	199	525
3. Speedy Thompson	Speedy Thompson	46	57 Chev	196	350
4. Jim Paschal	J. H. Petty	4	57 Chev	196	250
5. Eddie Pagan	Eddie Pagan	45	57 Ford	196	225

1958 Grand National Race No. 38 Western North Carolina 500
August 17, 1958 Average Speed: 66.780

Driver	Owner	Car #	Make	Laps	Winnings
1. Fireball Roberts	Frank Strickland	22	57 Chev	500	2,650
2. Bob Welborn	J. H. Petty	49	57 Chev	499	1,800
3. Lee Petty	Petty Enterprises	42	57 Olds	497	1,250
4. Speedy Thompson	Speedy Thompson	46	57 Chev	494	925
5. Buck Baker	Buck Baker	87	57 Chev	493	775

1959 Grand National Race No. 25
June 28, 1959 Average Speed: 72.934

Driver	Owner	Car #	Make	Laps	Winnings
1. Rex White	Rex White	4	59 Chev	200	900
2. Lee Petty	Petty Enterprises	42	59 Plym	200	525
3. Junior Johnson	Paul Spaulding	11	57 Ford	196	350
4. Roy Tyner	Roy Tyner	9	57 Chev	194	250
5. Herman Beam	Herman Beam	19	57 Chev	190	225

1959 Grand National Race No. 32 Western North Carolina 500
August 16, 1959 Average Speed: 71.833

Driver	Owner	Car #	Make	Laps	Winnings
1. Bob Welborn	Bob Welborn	49	59 Chev	500	3,200
2. Lee Petty	Petty Enterprises	42	59 Plym	497	2,025
3. Jack Smith	Jack Smith	47	59 Chev	493	1,325
4. Joe Lee Johnson	Joe Lee Johnson	77	57 Chev	489	975
5. Rex White	Rex White	4	59 Chev	489	800

1959 Grand National Race No. 42
October 11, 1959 Average Speed: 76.433

Driver	Owner	Car #	Make	Laps	Winnings
1. Lee Petty	Petty Enterprises	42	59 Plym	200	900
2. Glen Wood	Wood Brothers	16	58 Ford	200	525
3. Jack Smith	Jack Smith	47	59 Chev	199	375
4. Rex White	Rex White	4	59 Chev	199	275
5. Richard Petty	Petty Enterprises	43	59 Plym	198	250

1960 Grand National Race No. 15
April 24, 1960 Average Speed: 63.368

Driver	Owner	Car #	Make	Laps	Winnings
1. Lee Petty	Petty Enterprises	42	60 Plym	167	900
2. Joe Lee Johnson	E. C. Wilson	78	60 Chev	166	625
3. Ned Jarrett	Ned Jarrett	11	60 Ford	164	375
4. Bob Welborn	Bob Welborn	49	60 Chev	158	275
5. G. C. Spencer	Weldon Wagner	48	58 Chev	157	250

1960 Grand National Race No. 30 Western North Carolina 500
August 14, 1960 Average Speed: 65.024

Driver	Owner	Car #	Make	Laps	Winnings
1. Rex White	Rex White	4	60 Chev	500	3,650
2. Possum Jones	Tom Daniels	2	60 Chev	496	2,225
3. Emanuel Zervakis	Monroe Shook	85	60 Chev	492	1,525
4. Bobby Johns	Cotton Owens	5	60 Pont	479	975
5. Jack Smith	Jack Smith	47	60 Pont	479	800

1961 Grand National Race No. 7
March 5, 1961 Average Speed: 72.492

Driver	Owner	Car #	Make	Laps	Winnings
1. Rex White	Rex White	4	61 Chev	200	900
2. Cotton Owens	Cotton Owens	5	60 Pont	200	525
3. Ned Jarrett	Bee Gee Holloway	11	60 Ford	200	375
4. Richard Petty	Petty Enterprises	43	60 Plym	196	275
5. Emanuel Zervakis	Monroe Shook	85	61 Chev	194	250

1961 Grand National Race No. 39 Western North Carolina 500
August 13, 1961 Average Speed: 65.704

Driver	Owner	Car #	Make	Laps	Winnings
1. Junior Johnson	Rex Lovette	27	60 Pont	258	2,000
2. Joe Weatherly	Bud Moore	8	61 Pont	255	1,400
3. Rex White	Rex White	4	61 Chev	254	1,100
4. Ned Jarrett	Bee Gee Holloway	11	61 Chev	254	850
5. Emanuel Zervakis	Monroe Shook	85	61 Chev	254	750

1962 Grand National Race No. 2
November 12, 1961 Average Speed: 68.467

Driver	Owner	Car #	Make	Laps	Winnings
1. Rex White	Rex White	4	61 Chev	200	800
2. Buck Baker	Buck Baker	86	61 Chrys	200	525
3. Joe Weatherly	Bud Moore	8	61 Pont	200	375
4. Jack Smith	Jack Smith	46	61 Pont	200	275
5. Ned Jarrett	Bee Gee Holloway	11	61 Chev	200	350

1962 Grand National Race No. 7
March 4, 1962 Average Speed: 75.471

Driver	Owner	Car #	Make	Laps	Winnings
1. Joe Weatherly	Bud Moore	8	61 Pont	200	1,000
2. Jim Paschal	Cliff Stewart	2	62 Pont	197	600
3. Buddy Baker	Buck Baker	87	61 Chrys	197	400
4. Maurice Petty	Petty Enterprises	41	62 Plym	192	300
5. Jack Smith	Jack Smith	47	61 Pont	191	275

1962 Grand National Race No. 40 Western North Carolina 500
August 12, 1962 Average Speed: 77.492

Driver	Owner	Car #	Make	Laps	Winnings
1. Jim Paschal	Petty Enterprises	42	62 Plym	500	2,350
2. Joe Weatherly	Bud Moore	8	62 Pont	497	1,625
3. Rex White	Rex White	4	62 Chev	495	1,150
4. Ned Jarrett	Bee Gee Holloway	11	62 Chev	494	1,150
5. Jack Smith	Jack Smith	47	62 Pont	488	800

1963 Grand National Race No. 9
March 3, 1963 Average Speed: 76.664

Driver	Owner	Car #	Make	Laps	Winnings
1. Richard Petty	Petty Enterprises	43	63 Plym	200	1,000
2. Buck Baker	Buck Baker	87	62 Chrys	200	600
3. Junior Johnson	Ray Fox	3	63 Chev	200	400
4. Joe Weatherly	Fred Harb	17	62 Pont	200	500
5. Ned Jarrett	Herman Beam	19	62 Ford	195	275

1963 Grand National Race No. 41 Western North Carolina 500
August 11, 1963 Average Speed: 77.673

Driver	Owner	Car #	Make	Laps	Winnings
1. Fred Lorenzen	Holman-Moody	28	63 Ford	500	2,550
2. Richard Petty	Petty Enterprises	43	63 Plym	499	1,425
3. Jim Paschal	Petty Enterprises	42	63 Plym	498	1,150
4. David Pearson	Cotton Owens	6	63 Dodg	494	950
5. Billy Wade	Cotton Owens	5	63 Dodg	493	800

Asheville-Weaverville Speedway *continued*

1964 Grand National Race No. 14
April 11, 1964 Average Speed: 81.669

Driver	Owner	Car #	Make	Laps	Winnings
1. Marvin Panch	Wood Brothers	21	64 Ford	200	1,150
2. Junior Johnson	Ray Fox	3	64 Dodg	199	700
3. Billy Wade	Bud Moore	1	64 Merc	199	450
4. David Pearson	Cotton Owens	6	64 Dodg	198	300
5. Jimmy Pardue	Charles Robinson	54	64 Plym	198	275

1964 Grand National Race No. 45 Western North Carolina 500
August 9, 1964 Average Speed: 77.600

Driver	Owner	Car #	Make	Laps	Winnings
1. Ned Jarrett	Bondy Long	11	64 Ford	500	2,550
2. David Pearson	Cotton Owens	6	64 Dodg	500	1,400
3. Junior Johnson	Banjo Matthews	27	64 Ford	496	1,100
4. Darel Dieringer	Bud Moore	16	64 Merc	494	875
5. Buck Baker	Ray Fox	3	64 Dodg	485	750

1965 Grand National Race No. 6
February 28, 1965 Average Speed: 75.678

Driver	Owner	Car #	Make	Laps	Winnings
1. Ned Jarrett	Bondy Long	11	65 Ford	200	1,150
2. Dick Hutcherson	Holman-Moody	29	65 Ford	200	700
3. Cale Yarborough	Gary Weaver	10	64 Ford	197	450
4. G. C. Spencer	G. C. Spencer	49	64 Ford	196	300
5. Danny Byrd	Glenn Sweet	08	64 Ford	195	275

1965 Grand National Race No. 37 Western North Carolina 500
August 8, 1965 Average Speed: 74.343

Driver	Owner	Car #	Make	Laps	Winnings
1. Richard Petty	Petty Enterprises	43	65 Plym	500	3,200
2. Ned Jarrett	Bondy Long	11	65 Ford	498	1,650
3. Dick Hutcherson	Holman-Moody	29	65 Ford	495	1,200
4. Buddy Baker	Buck Baker	88	64 Dodg	488	900
5. Cale Yarborough	Kenny Myler	06	64 Ford	487	800

1966 Grand National Race No. 25 Fireball 300
June 12, 1966 Average Speed: 81.423

Driver	Owner	Car #	Make	Laps	Winnings
1. Richard Petty	Petty Enterprises	43	66 Plym	300	1,400
2. David Pearson	Cotton Owens	6	66 Dodg	300	1,000
3. Paul Lewis	Paul Lewis	1	65 Plym	298	700
4. Buck Baker	Buck Baker	87	66 Olds	290	575
5. John Sears	L. G. DeWitt	4	64 Ford	289	425

1966 Grand National Race No. 39 Western North Carolina 500
August 21, 1966 Average Speed: 76.700

Driver	Owner	Car #	Make	Laps	Winnings
1. Darel Dieringer	Bud Moore	16	66 Merc	500	3,150
2. G. C. Spencer	G. C. Spencer	49	65 Plym	492	1,750
3. James Hylton	Bud Hartje	48	65 Dodg	486	1,250
4. John Sears	L. G. DeWitt	4	64 Ford	478	900
5. Friday Hassler	Red Sharp	09	66 Chev	470	800

1967 Grand National Race No. 6 Fireball 300
March 5, 1967 Average Speed: 83.360

Driver	Owner	Car #	Make	Laps	Winnings
1. Richard Petty	Petty Enterprises	43	67 Plym	300	1,800
2. Darel Dieringer	Junior Johnson	26	67 Ford	298	1,050
3. Bobby Allison	Bobby Allison	2	66 Chev	297	700
4. David Pearson	Cotton Owens	6	66 Dodg	295	775
5. John Sears	L. G. DeWitt	4	66 Ford	289	425

1967 Grand National Race No. 49 Western North Carolina 500
November 5, 1967 Average Speed: 76.291

Driver	Owner	Car #	Make	Laps	Winnings
1. Bobby Allison	Holman-Moody	11	67 Ford	500	3,250
2. Richard Petty	Petty Enterprises	43	67 Plym	500	2,300
3. David Pearson	Holman-Moody	17	67 Ford	500	1,500
4. Dick Hutcherson	Holman-Moody	66	67 Ford	490	900
5. Friday Hassler	Red Sharp	39	66 Chev	471	800

1968 Grand National Race No. 14 Fireball 300
May 5, 1968 Average Speed: 75.167

Driver	Owner	Car #	Make	Laps	Winnings
1. David Pearson	Holman-Moody	17	68 Ford	300	1,400
2. Bobby Isaac	Nord Krauskopf	71	67 Dodg	298	1,000
3. Richard Petty	Petty Enterprises	43	68 Plym	297	900
4. James Hylton	James Hylton	48	67 Dodg	295	575
5. Elmo Langley	Elmo Langley	64	66 Ford	291	425

1968 Grand National Race No. 36 Western North Carolina 500
August 18, 1968 Average Speed: 73.686

Driver	Owner	Car #	Make	Laps	Winnings
1. David Pearson	Holman-Moody	17	68 Ford	500	2,150
2. Bobby Isaac	Nord Krauskopf	71	67 Dodg	497	1,270
3. Neil Castles	Neil Castles	06	67 Plym	472	1,050
4. Roy Tyner	Roy Tyner	9	67 Pont	467	850
5. Bill Seifert	Bill Seifert	45	68 Ford	457	750

1969 Grand National Race No. 17 Fireball 300
May 4, 1969 Average Speed: 72.581

Driver	Owner	Car #	Make	Laps	Winnings
1. Bobby Isaac	Nord Krauskopf	71	68 Dodg	300	2,050
2. James Hylton	James Hylton	48	68 Dodg	299	1,275
3. John Sears	L. G. DeWitt	4	67 Ford	298	1,000
4. Neil Castles	Neil Castles	06	67 Plym	297	625
5. Earl Brooks	Earl Brooks	26	67 Ford	284	475

1969 Grand National Race No. 40 Western North Carolina 500
August 24, 1969 Average Speed: 80.450

Driver	Owner	Car #	Make	Laps	Winnings
1. Bobby Isaac	Nord Krauskopf	71	69 Dodg	500	2,800
2. David Pearson	Holman-Moody	17	69 Ford	496	1,725
3. Dick Brooks	Dick Brooks	32	69 Plym	487	1,050
4. Elmo Langley	Elmo Langley	64	68 Ford	481	850
5. James Hylton	James Hylton	48	68 Dodg	467	750

Bowman-Gray Stadium
Winston-Salem, NC
Quarter-mile Paved Track

Quarter-mile paved oval opened in June 1947. First NASCAR Winston Cup (then Grand National) race staged on 5/24/58 (won by Bob Welborn). Final Winston Cup Grand National race staged on 8/6/71 (won by Bobby Allison in a Mustang). Richard Petty's 100th career Winston Cup victory came on this track on 8/22/69 while driving a Ford. The track still hosts weekly racing.

Winston Cup Starts
Richard Petty 26

Winston Cup Victories
Rex White 6

Winston Cup Poles
Richard Petty 8

Winston Cup Money
Richard Petty $10,855

Most Cars Started
29—August 6, 1971 Myers Brothers Memorial

Fewest Cars Started
15—April 18, 1960

Narrowest Margin of Victory
6 inches—June 16, 1962 Myers Brothers Memorial

Slowest Race
39.258 MPH—August 22, 1958

Race Record
51.527 MPH—August 28, 1970 Myers Brothers Memorial

Most Cautions
6—August 6, 1971 Myers Brothers Memorial

Most Race Leaders
3—August 22, 1958
3—July 13, 1963
3—August 27, 1966 Myers Brothers Memorial
3—March 27, 1967

Most Cars Running at Finish
20—August 22, 1958
20—August 21, 1959

1958 Grand National Race No. 19
May 24, 1958 Average Speed: 40.407

Driver	Owner	Car #	Make	Laps	Winnings
1. Bob Welborn	J. H. Petty	49	57 Chev	150	600
2. Rex White	J. H. Petty	44	57 Chev	150	475
3. Jim Reed	Jim Reed	7	57 Ford	150	355
4. Fred Harb	Fred Harb	17	57 Merc	149	275
5. Barney Shore	Barney Shore	97	57 Chev	148	230

1958 Grand National Race No. 39
August 22, 1958 Average Speed: 39.258

Driver	Owner	Car #	Make	Laps	Winnings
1. Lee Petty	Petty Enterprises	42	57 Olds	200	765
2. Shorty Rollins	Shorty Rollins	99	58 Ford	200	550
3. Jim Reed	Jim Reed	7	57 Ford	200	495
4. Fred Harb	Fred Harb	17	57 Merc	199	295
5. Buck Baker	Buck Baker	87	57 Chev	199	250

1959 Grand National Race No. 8
March 30, 1959 Average Speed: 43.562

Driver	Owner	Car #	Make	Laps	Winnings
1. Jim Reed	Jim Reed	7	57 Ford	200	550
2. Lee Petty	Petty Enterprises	43	57 Olds	200	480
3. Rex White	Rex White	4	59 Chev	200	350
4. Bob Welborn	Bob Welborn	49	59 Chev	198	270
5. Buck Baker	Buck Baker	89	59 Chev	197	230

1959 Grand National Race No. 24
June 27, 1959 Average Speed: 41.228

Driver	Owner	Car #	Make	Laps	Winnings
1. Rex White	Rex White	4	59 Chev	200	675
2. Ken Rush	Manley Britt	14	57 Ford	200	480
3. Bob Welborn	Bob Welborn	49	57 Chev	199	375
4. Junior Johnson	Paul Spaulding	11	57 Ford	198	270
5. Jim Reed	Jim Reed	7	59 Chev	196	235

1959 Grand National Race No. 33
August 21, 1959 Average Speed: 44.085

Driver	Owner	Car #	Make	Laps	Winnings
1. Rex White	Rex White	4	59 Chev	200	1,125
2. Glen Wood	Wood Brothers	16	58 Ford	200	690
3. Lee Petty	Petty Enterprises	42	59 Plym	198	595
4. Bob Welborn	Bob Welborn	49	59 Chev	197	425
5. Jim Reed	Jim Reed	7	57 Ford	196	290

1960 Grand National Race No. 13
April 18, 1960 Average Speed: 43.082

Driver	Owner	Car #	Make	Laps	Winnings
1. Glen Wood	Wood Brothers	16	58 Ford	200	600
2. Rex White	Rex White	4	60 Chev	200	475
3. Jimmy Massey	Wood Brothers	21	59 Ford	199	400
4. Richard Petty	Petty Enterprises	43	60 Plym	199	305
5. Ned Jarrett	Ned Jarrett	11	60 Ford	196	245

1960 Grand National Race No. 22
June 26, 1960 Average Speed: 45.872

Driver	Owner	Car #	Make	Laps	Winnings
1. Glen Wood	Wood Brothers	16	58 Ford	200	1,125
2. Lee Petty	Petty Enterprises	42	60 Plym	200	595
3. Rex White	Rex White	4	59 Chev	198	415
4. Richard Petty	Petty Enterprises	43	60 Plym	197	250
5. Ned Jarrett	Ned Jarrett	11	60 Ford	195	255

1960 Grand National Race No. 34
August 23, 1960 Average Speed: 44.389

Driver	Owner	Car #	Make	Laps	Winnings
1. Glen Wood	Wood Brothers	16	58 Ford	200	770
2. Lee Petty	Petty Enterprises	42	60 Plym	199	635
3. Junior Johnson	John Masoni	27	59 Chev	199	365
4. Rex White	Rex White	4	59 Chev	199	260
5. Buck Baker	Buck Baker	87	60 Chev	198	245

1961 Grand National Race No. 12
April 3, 1961 Average Speed: 45.500

Driver	Owner	Car #	Make	Laps	Winnings
1. Rex White	Rex White	4	60 Chev	150	700
2. Glen Wood	Wood Brothers	21	61 Ford	150	500
3. Richard Petty	Petty Enterprises	43	60 Plym	147	375
4. Fred Harb	Fred Harb	17	59 Ford	147	305
5. Ned Jarrett	Bee Gee Holloway	11	61 Chev	147	245

1961 Grand National Race No. 28 Myers Brothers Memorial
June 10, 1961 Average Speed: 42.714

Driver	Owner	Car #	Make	Laps	Winnings
1. Rex White	Rex White	4	60 Chev	200	900
2. Jim Reed	Jim Reed	7	61 Chev	200	525
3. Junior Johnson	Rex Lovette	27	60 Pont	199	375
4. Emanuel Zervakis	Monroe Shook	85	60 Chev	198	275
5. Richard Petty	Petty Enterprises	43	60 Plym	198	250

Bowman-Gray Stadium *continued*

1961 Grand National Race No. 38
August 9, 1961 Average Speed: 42.452

Driver	Owner	Car #	Make	Laps	Winnings
1. Rex White	Rex White	4	60 Chev	150	665
2. Glen Wood	Wood Brothers	21	61 Ford	150	500
3. Ned Jarrett	Bee Gee Holloway	11	61 Chev	150	370
4. Emanuel Zervakis	Monroe Shook	85	60 Chev	149	305
5. Richard Petty	Petty Enterprises	43	61 Plym	149	225

1962 Grand National Race No. 16
April 23, 1962 Average Speed: 43.392

Driver	Owner	Car #	Make	Laps	Winnings
1. Rex White	Rex White	4	62 Chev	108	565
2. Jack Smith	Jack Smith	47	61 Pont	108	475
3. Joe Weatherly	Bud Moore	8	62 Pont	108	370
4. George Dunn	Lewis Osborne	97	62 Chev	108	305
5. Richard Petty	Petty Enterprises	43	61 Plym	107	225

1962 Grand National Race No. 25 Myers Brothers Memorial
June 16, 1962 Average Speed: 45.466

Driver	Owner	Car #	Make	Laps	Winnings
1. Johnny Allen	Fred Lovette	58	61 Pont	200	580
2. Rex White	Rex White	4	62 Chev	200	500
3. Richard Petty	Petty Enterprises	43	62 Plym	196	375
4. Larry Thomas	Wade Younts	36	62 Dodg	195	305
5. Joe Weatherly	Bud Moore	8	61 Pont	194	275

1962 Grand National Race No. 42 International 200
August 18, 1962 Average Speed: 46.875

Driver	Owner	Car #	Make	Laps	Winnings
1. Richard Petty	Petty Enterprises	43	62 Plym	200	600
2. Jack Smith	Jack Smith	47	61 Pont	199	450
3. Joe Weatherly	Bud Moore	8	61 Pont	199	400
4. Jimmy Pardue	Jimmy Pardue	54	62 Pont	199	290
5. G. C. Spencer	G. C. Spencer	48	62 Chev	196	250

1963 Grand National Race No. 18
April 15, 1963 Average Speed: 46.814

Driver	Owner	Car #	Make	Laps	Winnings
1. Jim Paschal	Petty Enterprises	43	62 Plym	200	575
2. Fred Harb	Fred Harb	12	62 Pont	198	465
3. Larry Thomas	Wade Younts	36	62 Dodg	195	370
4. Buck Baker	Buck Baker	87	62 Chrys	195	290
5. Ned Jarrett	Charles Robinson	11	63 Ford	194	275

1963 Grand National Race No. 33
July 13, 1963 Average Speed: 44.390

Driver	Owner	Car #	Make	Laps	Winnings
1. Glen Wood	Wood Brothers	21	63 Ford	200	575
2. Ned Jarrett	Charles Robinson	11	63 Ford	200	480
3. Buck Baker	Buck Baker	87	63 Pont	198	350
4. Lee Petty	Petty Enterprises	41	63 Plym	197	300
5. Jack Smith	Jack Smith	48	63 Plym	195	240

1963 Grand National Race No. 43 International 200
August 16, 1963 Average Speed: 46.320

Driver	Owner	Car #	Make	Laps	Winnings
1. Junior Johnson	Ray Fox	3	63 Plym	200	580
2. Richard Petty	Petty Enterprises	43	63 Plym	199	500
3. Glen Wood	Wood Brothers	21	63 Ford	198	370
4. David Pearson	Cotton Owens	6	63 Dodg	196	275
5. Ned Jarrett	Charles Robinson	11	63 Ford	196	225

1964 Grand National Race No. 12
March 30, 1964 Average Speed: 47.796

Driver	Owner	Car #	Make	Laps	Winnings
1. Marvin Panch	Wood Brothers	21	64 Ford	200	820
2. Ned Jarrett	Bondy Long	11	64 Ford	200	530
3. Richard Petty	Petty Enterprises	43	64 Plym	199	425
4. Jim Paschal	Cotton Owens	5	64 Dodg	198	325
5. David Pearson	Cotton Owens	6	64 Dodg	197	290

1964 Grand National Race No. 49 Myers Brothers Memorial
August 22, 1964 Average Speed: 46.192

Driver	Owner	Car #	Make	Laps	Winnings
1. Junior Johnson	Banjo Matthews	27	64 Ford	250	1,000
2. Richard Petty	Petty Enterprises	43	64 Plym	249	600
3. Ned Jarrett	Bondy Long	11	64 Ford	249	400
4. David Pearson	Cotton Owens	6	64 Dodg	245	300
5. Fred Harb	Cliff Stewart	2	63 Pont	240	275

1965 Grand National Race No. 17
May 15, 1965 Average Speed: 47.911

Driver	Owner	Car #	Make	Laps	Winnings
1. Junior Johnson	Rex Lovette	26	65 Ford	200	850
2. Ned Jarrett	Bondy Long	11	65 Ford	198	550
3. Dick Hutcherson	Holman-Moody	29	65 Ford	196	430
4. G. C. Spencer	G. C. Spencer	49	64 Ford	193	330
5. Buren Skeen	Reid Shaw	23	64 Ford	193	285

1965 Grand National Race No. 44 Myers Brothers Memorial
August 28, 1965 Average Speed: 46.632

Driver	Owner	Car #	Make	Laps	Winnings
1. Junior Johnson	Rex Lovette	26	65 Ford	250	1,000
2. Richard Petty	Petty Enterprises	43	65 Plym	246	800
3. Dick Hutcherson	Holman-Moody	29	65 Ford	245	400
4. Ned Jarrett	Bondy Long	11	65 Ford	243	300
5. Cale Yarborough	Kenny Myler	06	64 Ford	240	275

1966 Grand National Race No. 12
April, 11, 1966 Average Speed: 51.341

Driver	Owner	Car #	Make	Laps	Winnings
1. David Pearson	Cotton Owens	6	64 Dodg	200	850
2. Tom Pistone	Tom Pistone	59	64 Ford	200	550
3. Richard Petty	Petty Enterprises	43	65 Plym	198	425
4. Bobby Allison	Betty Lilly	24	66 Ford	198	330
5. Elmo Langley	Henry Woodfield	64	64 Ford	197	305

1966 Grand National Race No. 41 Myers Brothers Memorial
August 27, 1966 Average Speed: 45.928

Driver	Owner	Car #	Make	Laps	Winnings
1. David Pearson	Cotton Owens	6	65 Dodg	250	1,000
2. Richard Petty	Petty Enterprises	42	66 Plym	250	600
3. James Hylton	Bud Hartje	48	65 Dodg	246	400
4. John Sears	L. G. DeWitt	4	64 Ford	246	300
5. Tom Pistone	Tom Pistone	59	64 Ford	240	275

1967 Grand National Race No. 9
March 27, 1967 Average Speed: 49.248

Driver	Owner	Car #	Make	Laps	Winnings
1. Bobby Allison	Bobby Allison	2	65 Chev	200	820
2. Richard Petty	Petty Enterprises	43	67 Plym	198	550
3. John Sears	L. G. DeWitt	4	66 Ford	196	430
4. Clyde Lynn	Clyde Lynn	20	66 Ford	195	320
5. James Hylton	Bud Hartje	48	65 Dodg	192	300

Bowman-Gray Stadium *continued*

1967 Grand National Race No. 37 Myers Brothers Memorial
August 12, 1967 Average Speed: 50.893

Driver	Owner	Car #	Make	Laps	Winnings
1. Richard Petty	Petty Enterprises	43	67 Plym	250	100
2. Jim Paschal	Tom Friedkin	14	67 Plym	247	600
3. Bobby Allison	Bobby Allison	2	65 Chev	247	400
4. John Sears	L. G. DeWitt	4	66 Ford	245	300
5. James Hylton	Bud Hartje	48	65 Dodg	243	275

1968 Grand National Race No. 35 Myers Brothers Memorial
August 10, 1968 Average Speed: 42.940

Driver	Owner	Car #	Make	Laps	Winnings
1. David Pearson	Holman-Moody	17	68 Ford	250	1,000
2. Richard Petty	Petty Enterprises	43	68 Plym	250	850
3. Bobby Isaac	Nord Krauskopf	71	67 Dodg	246	400
4. James Hylton	James Hylton	48	68 Dodg	244	300
5. Elmo Langley	Elmo Langley	64	66 Ford	244	275

1969 Grand National Race No. 39 Myers Brothers Stock Car Spectacle
August 22, 1969 Average Speed: 47.458

Driver	Owner	Car #	Make	Laps	Winnings
1. Richard Petty	Petty Enterprises	43	69 Ford	250	1,000
2. Bobby Isaac	Nord Krauskopf	71	69 Dodg	250	600
3. David Pearson	Holman-Moody	17	69 Ford	250	600
4. Elmo Langley	Elmo Langley	64	68 Ford	248	350
5. James Hylton	James Hylton	48	68 Dodg	246	325

1970 Grand National Race No. 36 Myers Brothers Memorial
August 28, 1970 Average Speed: 51.527

Driver	Owner	Car #	Make	Laps	Winnings
1. Richard Petty	Petty Enterprises	43	70 Plym	250	1,000
2. Bobby Allison	Bobby Allison	22	69 Dodg	250	600
3. Bobby Isaac	Nord Krauskopf	71	70 Dodg	247	400
4. James Hylton	James Hylton	48	69 Ford	246	350
5. Benny Parsons	L. G. DeWitt	72	69 Ford	243	325

1971 Winston Cup GN Race No. 34 Myers Brothers Memorial
August 6, 1971 Average Speed: 44.792

Driver	Owner	Car #	Make	Laps	Winnings
1. Bobby Allison	Melvin Joseph	49	70 Ford	250	1,000
2. Richard Petty	Petty Enterprises	43	70 Plym	250	600
3. Jim Paschal	Cliff Stewart	14	70 Mata	249	400
4. Buck Baker	Buck Baker	87	71 Pont	247	350
5. Dave Marcis	James Rush	11	69 Chev	244	325

Champion Speedway
Fayetteville, NC
.333-mile Paved Track

.333-mile paved oval built by Harold Brasington and opened in May 1953. First NASCAR Winston Cup (then Grand National) race staged on 11/3/57 (won by Rex White; race was included in the 1958 championship season). Final Grand National race run on 11/9/58 (won by Bob Welborn; race was included in the 1959 championship season). Track closed in 1959.

Winston Cup Starts

L. D. Austin	4
Buck Baker	4
Clarence DeZalia	4
Fred Harb	4
Brownie King	4
Lee Petty	4
Rex White	4

Winston Cup Victories

Bob Welborn   2

Winston Cup Poles

Lee Petty   2

Winston Cup Money

Bob Welborn $1,365

Most Cars Started

29—April 5, 1958

Fewest Cars Started

22—November 3, 1957

Narrowest Margin of Victory

1 car length—March 15, 1958

Slowest Race

50.229 MPH—April 5, 1958

Race Record

59.170 MPH—November 3, 1957

Most Cautions

2—April 5, 1958

Most Race Leaders

3—November 3, 1957
3—March 15, 1958
3—April 5, 1958

Most Cars Running at Finish

20—November 9, 1958

1958 Grand National Race No. 1
November 3, 1957 Average Speed: 59.170

Driver	Owner	Car #	Make	Laps	Winnings
1. Rex White	J. H. Petty	44	57 Chev	150	630
2. Lee Petty	Petty Enterprises	42	57 Olds	150	500
3. Tiny Lund	Lonnie Fish	76	57 Chev	149	380
4. Gwyn Staley	J. H. Petty	38	57 Chev	148	310
5. Jimmy Massey	Wood Brothers	21	56 Ford	148	255

1958 Grand National Race No. 4
March 15, 1958 Average Speed: 56.141

Driver	Owner	Car #	Make	Laps	Winnings
1. Curtis Turner	Holman-Moody	21	57 Ford	150	600
2. Gwyn Staley	J. H. Petty	38	57 Chev	150	470
3. Buck Baker	Buck Baker	87	57 Chev	150	350
4. Frankie Schneider	Frankie Schneider	62	57 Chev	150	275
5. Fred Harb	Fred Harb	17	57 Merc	—	225

1958 Grand National Race No. 7
April 5, 1958 Average Speed: 50.229

Driver	Owner	Car #	Make	Laps	Winnings
1. Bob Welborn	J. H. Petty	38	57 Chev	150	600
2. Frankie Schneider	Frankie Schneider	62	57 Chev	150	470
3. Speedy Thompson	Speedy Thompson	46	57 Chev	150	350
4. Curtis Turner	Holman-Moody	126	58 Ford	150	275
5. Eddie Pagan	Eddie Pagan	45	57 Ford	149	225

1959 Grand National Race No. 1
November 9, 1958 Average Speed: 56.001

Driver	Owner	Car #	Make	Laps	Winnings
1. Bob Welborn	J. H. Petty	46	57 Chev	150	600
2. Glen Wood	Wood Brothers	21	58 Ford	150	475
3. Buck Baker	Buck Baker	86	58 Chev	150	350
4. Roy Tyner	Roy Tyner	49	57 Chev	149	250
5. Junior Johnson	Paul Spaulding	11	57 Ford	148	215

Charlotte Speedway
Charlotte, NC
.75-mile Dirt Track

.75-mile dirt track built by Harvey and Pat Charles and opened in June 1948. The track was the site of the inaugural NASCAR Winston Cup (then Strictly Stock) championship race on 6/19/49 (won by Jim Roper). Final Grand National race staged on 10/17/56 (won by Buck Baker), and the track was closed soon thereafter.

Winston Cup Starts
Lee Petty   11
Herb Thomas   11

Winston Cup Victories
Buck Baker   3

Winston Cup Poles
Fonty Flock   3

Winston Cup Money
Tim Flock $4,235

Most Cars Started
40—April 1, 1951

Fewest Cars Started
24—June 15, 1952

Narrowest Margin of Victory
1/2 car length—November 20, 1955

Slowest Race
N/A

Race Record
72.268 MPH—October 17, 1956

Most Cautions
N/A

Most Race Leaders
6—April 5, 1953

Most Cars Running at Finish
N/A

1949 Strictly Stock Race No. 1
June 19, 1949

	Driver	Owner	Car #	Make	Laps	Winnings
1.	Jim Roper	R. B. McIntosh	34	49 Linc	197	2,000
2.	Fonty Flock		47	49 Huds	—	1,000
3.	Red Byron	Raymond Parks	22	49 Olds	—	500
4.	Sam Rice	Sam Rice	2	49 Olds	—	300
5.	Tim Flock	Buddy Elliott	90	49 Olds	—	200

1950 Grand National Race No. 2
April 2, 1950

	Driver	Owner	Car #	Make	Laps	Winnings
1.	Tim Flock	Harold Kite	21	49 Linc	200	1,500
2.	Bob Flock	Frank Christian	7	49 Olds	200	750
3.	Clyde Minter	Clyde Minter	19	50 Merc	197	500
4.	Red Byron	Raymond Parks	22	50 Olds	196	300
5.	Bill Snowden	Bill Snowden		49 Buick	194	200

1950 Grand National Race No. 9
July 23, 1950

	Driver	Owner	Car #	Make	Laps	Winnings
1.	Curtis Turner	John Eanes	41	50 Olds	200	1,500
2.	Chuck Mahoney	Brooks Motors	77	50 Merc	—	600
3.	Herb Thomas	Herb Thomas	92	50 Plym	—	400
4.	Jimmie Lewallen			50 Merc	—	300
5.	Dick Burns		18	50 Olds	—	225

1951 Grand National Race No. 2
April 1, 1951 Average Speed: 70.545

	Driver	Owner	Car #	Make	Laps	Winnings
1.	Curtis Turner	Nash Motor Co.	41	51 Nash	150	1,000
2.	Lee Petty	Petty Enterprises	42	49 Plym	150	700
3.	Marshall Teague	Marshall Teague	6	51 Huds	148	450
4.	Herb Thomas	Herb Thomas	92	50 Plym	145	350
5.	Frank Luptow	Frank Luptow	88	50 Olds	143	200

1951 Grand National Race No. 28
September 23, 1951

	Driver	Owner	Car #	Make	Laps	Winnings
1.	Herb Thomas	Herb Thomas	92	51 Huds	200	1,000
2.	Shorty York	Russ Lou	90	50 Plym	—	600
3.	Donald Thomas	Herb Thomas	93	50 Plym	—	500
4.	Bill Blair	Bill Blair	2	51 Ford	—	400
5.	Jimmie Lewallen	Hubert Hamilton	0	51 Plym	—	300

1952 Grand National Race No. 16
June 15, 1952 Average Speed: 64.820

	Driver	Owner	Car #	Make	Laps	Winnings
1.	Herb Thomas	Herb Thomas	92	52 Huds	150	1,000
2.	Tim Flock	Ted Chester	91	51 Huds	150	700
3.	Bill Blair	George Hutchens	2	52 Olds	149	450
4.	Lee Petty	Petty Enterprises	42	51 Plym	146	350
5.	Dick Rathmann	Walt Chapman	120	51 Huds	145	200

1953 Grand National Race No. 5
April 5, 1953

	Driver	Owner	Car #	Make	Laps	Winnings
1.	Dick Passwater	Frank Arford	78	53 Olds	150	1,000
2.	Gober Sosebee	Gober Sosebee	51	53 Olds	150	700
3.	Herschel Buchanan	Herschel Buchanan	1	52 Nash	150	450
4.	Tim Flock	Ted Chester	91	53 Huds	150	350
5.	Pop McGinnis	Irving Frye	13	52 Huds	149	200

1954 Grand National Race No. 15
May 30, 1954 Average Speed: 49.805

	Driver	Owner	Car #	Make	Laps	Winnings
1.	Buck Baker	Griffin Motors	87	53 Olds	133	1,000
2.	Lee Petty	Petty Enterprises	42	54 Chrys	133	650
3.	Joe Eubanks	Phil Oates	82	51 Huds	132	450
4.	Russ Hepler	Walt Chapman	120	53 Huds	128	350
5.	Bill Blair	Bill Blair	2	53 Huds	126	300

1955 Grand National Race No. 11
May 1, 1955 Average Speed: 52.630

	Driver	Owner	Car #	Make	Laps	Winnings
1.	Buck Baker	Buck Baker	89	55 Buick	133	1,000
2.	Tim Flock	Carl Kiekhaefer	300	55 Chrys	133	650
3.	Dave Terrell	Dave Terrell	98	55 Olds	131	450
4.	Gober Sosebee	Gober Sosebee	51	55 Olds	127	350
5.	Bob Welborn	J. H. Petty	44	55 Chev	127	300

1956 Grand National Race No. 2
November 20, 1955 Average Speed: 61.825

	Driver	Owner	Car #	Make	Laps	Winnings
1.	Fonty Flock	Carl Kiekhaefer	301	55 Chrys	134	1,100
2.	Tim Flock	Carl Kiekhaefer	300	55 Chrys	134	700
3.	Lee Petty	Petty Enterprises	42	56 Dodg	134	475
4.	Joe Weatherly	Charlie Schwam	9	56 Ford	133	365
5.	Buck Baker	James Satcher	87	56 Ford	133	310

Charlotte Speedway *continued*

1956 Grand National Race No. 20
May 27, 1956 Average Speed: 64.866

Driver	Owner	Car #	Make	Laps	Winnings
1. Speedy Thompson	Carl Kiekhaefer	300c	56 Chrys	133	1,100
2. Junior Johnson	Carl Kiekhaefer	502	56 Dodg	133	700
3. Buck Baker	Carl Kiekhaefer	300	56 Chrys	132	475
4. Jim Paschal	Frank Hayworth	75	56 Merc	131	465
5. Lee Petty	Petty Enterprises	42	56 Dodg	131	310

1956 Grand National Race No. 52
October 17, 1956 Average Speed: 72.268

Driver	Owner	Car #	Make	Laps	Winnings
1. Buck Baker	Carl Kiekhaefer	300B	56 Chrys	133	950
2. Ralph Moody	Pete DePaolo	12	56 Ford	133	675
3. Marvin Panch	Tom Harbison	98	56 Ford	132	475
4. Jim Paschal	Frank Hayworth	75	56 Merc	132	365
5. Bill Amick	Pete DePaolo	97	56 Ford	130	320

Charlotte Motor Speedway
Charlotte, NC
1.5-mile Superspeedway

1.5-mile paved tri-oval opened in June 1960. First World 600 staged on 6/19/60 (won by Joe Lee Johnson). Curtis Turner and Bruton Smith, the original builders, were ousted in 1961 following bankruptcy as the project greatly exceeded the original cost estimates. Promoter Richard Howard subsequently elevated the facility to one of America's hottest properties before Smith regained control in 1975. Permanent lights were erected in 1992, and the track is currently the site of the annual All-Star race.

Winston Cup Starts
Richard Petty   64

Winston Cup Victories
Bobby Allison   6
Darrell Waltrip   6

Winston Cup Poles
David Pearson   14

Winston Cup Money
Mark Martin $3,126,563

Most Cars Started
60—June 19, 1960 World 600

Fewest Cars Started
19—May 21, 1961

Narrowest Margin of Victory
0.17 seconds—May 27, 1990

Slowest Race
104.207 MPH—May 26, 1968 World 600

Race Record
160.306 MPH—October 10, 1999

Most Cautions
14—May 25, 1980 World 600

Most Race Leaders
18—May 29, 1988 Coca-Cola 600

Most Cars Running at Finish
38—May 25, 1997
38—May 24, 1998

1960 Grand National Race No. 21 World 600
June 19, 1960 Average Speed: 107.735

Driver	Owner	Car #	Make	Laps	Winnings
1. Joe Lee Johnson	Paul McDuffie	89	60 Chev	400	27,150
2. Johnny Beauchamp	Dale Swanson	73	60 Chev	396	9,110
3. Bobby Johns	Petty Enterprises	46	60 Plym	394	6,975
4. Gerald Duke	Gerald Duke & Robert Davis	92	59 Ford	388	3,675
5. Buck Baker	Buck Baker	87	60 Chev	386	3,075

1960 Grand National Race No. 42 National 400
October 16, 1960 Average Speed: 112.905

Driver	Owner	Car #	Make	Laps	Winnings
1. Speedy Thompson	Wood Brothers	21	60 Ford	267	12,710
2. Richard Petty	Petty Enterprises	43	60 Plym	266	5,550
3. Ned Jarrett	Ned Jarrett	11	60 Ford	266	3,275
4. Bobby Johns	Cotton Owens	5	60 Pont	265	2,880
5. Junior Johnson	John Masoni	27	60 Pont	265	1,855

1961 Grand National Race No. 20
May 21, 1961 Average Speed: 133.554

Driver	Owner	Car #	Make	Laps	Winnings
1. Richard Petty	Petty Enterprises	43	61 Plym	67	800
2. Ralph Earnhardt	Cotton Owens	6	61 Pont	67	525
3. Bob Welborn	Jack Smith	47	61 Pont	67	375
4. Bobby Johns	Shorty Johns	72	61 Ford	67	275
5. Fred Lorenzen	Holman-Moody	28	61 Ford	67	250

1961 Grand National Race No. 21
May 21, 1961 Average Speed: 115.591

Driver	Owner	Car #	Make	Laps	Winnings
1. Joe Weatherly	Bud Moore	8	61 Pont	67	800
2. Junior Johnson	John Masoni	3	61 Pont	67	525
3. Jack Smith	Jack Smith	46	61 Pont	66	375
4. Nelson Stacy	Dudley Farrell	29	61 Ford	66	275
5. Marvin Porter		44	60 Plym	66	250

1961 Grand National Race No. 24 World 600
May 28, 1961 Average Speed: 111.633

Driver	Owner	Car #	Make	Laps	Winnings
1. David Pearson	John Masoni	3	61 Pont	400	24,280
2. Fireball Roberts	Jim Stephens	22	61 Pont	398	9,320
3. Rex White	Rex White	4	61 Chev	397	7,070
4. Ned Jarrett	Bee Gee Holloway	11	61 Chev	397	4,475
5. Jim Paschal	J. H. Petty	14	61 Pont	394	3,150

1961 Grand National Race No. 49 National 400
October 15, 1961 Average Speed: 119.950

Driver	Owner	Car #	Make	Laps	Winnings
1. Joe Weatherly	Bud Moore	8	61 Pont	267	9,510
2. Richard Petty	Petty Enterprises	43	61 Plym	267	4,870
3. Bob Welborn	Bud Moore	18	61 Pont	267	3,275
4. Cotton Owens	Cotton Owens	6	61 Pont	266	2,275
5. Rex White	Rex White	4	61 Chev	264	1,800

1962 Grand National Race No. 23 World 600
May 27, 1962 Average Speed: 125.552

Driver	Owner	Car #	Make	Laps	Winnings
1. Nelson Stacy	Holman-Moody	29	62 Ford	400	25,505
2. Joe Weatherly	Bud Moore	8	62 Pont	400	11,105
3. Fred Lorenzen	Holman-Moody	0	62 Ford	399	6,870
4. Richard Petty	Petty Enterprises	43	62 Plym	397	5,400
5. Larry Frank	Ratus Walters	66	62 Ford	395	3,475

1962 Grand National Race No. 52 National 400
October 14, 1962 Average Speed: 132.085

Driver	Owner	Car #	Make	Laps	Winnings
1. Junior Johnson	Ray Fox	3	62 Pont	267	11,355
2. Fireball Roberts	Jim Stephens	22	62 Pont	265	5,420
3. Fred Lorenzen	Holman-Moody	28	62 Ford	264	3,230
5. Joe Weatherly	Bud Moore	8	62 Pont	261	1,725

1963 Grand National Race No. 26 World 600
June 2, 1963 Average Speed: 132.417

Driver	Owner	Car #	Make	Laps	Winnings
1. Fred Lorenzen	Holman-Moody	28	63 Ford	400	27,780
2. Junior Johnson	Ray Fox	3	63 Chev	400	17,460
3. Rex White	Rex White	4	63 Chev	398	8,310
4. Joe Weatherly	Bud Moore	8	63 Pont	397	6,275
5. David Pearson	Cotton Owens	6	63 Dodg	396	4,425

1963 Grand National Race No. 52 National 400
October 13, 1963 Average Speed: 132.105

Driver	Owner	Car #	Make	Laps	Winnings
1. Junior Johnson	Ray Fox	3	63 Chev	267	11,720
2. Fred Lorenzen	Holman-Moody	28	63 Ford	267	6,215
3. Marvin Panch	Wood Brothers	21	63 Ford	267	3,596
4. Fireball Roberts	Holman-Moody	22	63 Ford	263	2,225
5. Joe Weatherly	Bud Moore	8	63 Merc	261	2,075

Charlotte Motor Speedway *continued*

1964 Grand National Race No. 25 World 600
May 24, 1964 Average Speed: 125.772

Driver	Owner	Car #	Make	Laps	Winnings
1. Jim Paschal	Petty Enterprises	41	64 Plym	400	24,785
2. Richard Petty	Petty Enterprises	43	64 Plym	396	10,455
3. Rex White	Bud Moore	4	64 Merc	393	8,095
4. Fred Lorenzen	Holman-Moody	28	64 Ford	393	6,425
5. Billy Wade	Bud Moore	1	64 Merc	390	4,050

1964 Grand National Race No. 59 National 400
October 18, 1964 Average Speed: 134.475

Driver	Owner	Car #	Make	Laps	Winnings
1. Fred Lorenzen	Holman-Moody	28	64 Ford	267	11,185
2. Jim Paschal	Petty Enterprises	41	64 Plym	266	5,725
3. Richard Petty	Petty Enterprises	43	64 Plym	265	4,245
4. Ned Jarrett	Bondy Long	11	64 Ford	265	2,375
5. LeeRoy Yarbrough	Ray Fox	03	64 Dodg	264	1,650

1965 Grand National Race No. 19 World 600
May 23, 1965 Average Speed: 121.722

Driver	Owner	Car #	Make	Laps	Winnings
1. Fred Lorenzen	Holman-Moody	28	65 Ford	400	27,270
2. Earl Balmer	Bud Moore	15	64 Merc	400	10,900
3. Dick Hutcherson	Holman-Moody	29	65 Ford	397	6,895
4. Buddy Baker	Buck Baker	88	64 Dodg	392	4,250
5. Pedro Rodriguez	Holman-Moody	51	65 Ford	391	3,425

1965 Grand National Race No. 52 National 400
October 17, 1965 Average Speed: 119.117

Driver	Owner	Car #	Make	Laps	Winnings
1. Fred Lorenzen	Holman-Moody	28	65 Ford	267	9,920
2. Dick Hutcherson	Holman-Moody	29	65 Ford	267	5,225
3. Curtis Turner	Wood Brothers	47	65 Ford	267	3,340
4. Ned Jarrett	Bondy Long	11	65 Ford	266	2,390
5. LeeRoy Yarbrough	Ray Fox	3	65 Chev	265	1,630

1966 Grand National Race No. 20 World 600
May 22, 1966 Average Speed: 135.042

Driver	Owner	Car #	Make	Laps	Winnings
1. Marvin Panch	Petty Enterprises	42	65 Plym	400	26,060
2. G. C. Spencer	G. C. Spencer	49	65 Plym	398	10,980
3. Don White	Ray Nichels	31	66 Dodg	394	7,045
4. James Hylton	Bud Hartje	48	65 Dodg	391	4,325
5. Neil Castles	Buck Baker	87	66 Olds	371	3,440

1966 Grand National Race No. 48 National 500
October 16, 1966 Average Speed: 130.576

Driver	Owner	Car #	Make	Laps	Winnings
1. LeeRoy Yarbrough	Jon Thorne	12	66 Dodg	334	17,455
2. Darel Dieringer	Junior Johnson	15	66 Ford	334	7,670
3. Paul Goldsmith	Ray Nichels	99	66 Plym	334	4,205
4. Gordon Johncock	Junior Johnson	26	66 Ford	334	2,865
5. Earl Balmer	Nord Krauskopf	71	66 Dodg	332	1,975

1967 Grand National Race No. 20 World 600
May 28, 1967 Average Speed: 135.832

Driver	Owner	Car #	Make	Laps	Winnings
1. Jim Paschal	Tom Friedkin	14	67 Plym	400	28,450
2. David Pearson	Holman-Moody	17	67 Ford	400	12,530
3. Bobby Allison	Cotton Owens	6	67 Dodg	400	7,670
4. Richard Petty	Petty Enterprises	43	67 Plym	397	4,875
5. Tiny Lund	Petty Enterprises	42	67 Plym	396	4,000

1967 Grand National Race No. 47 National 500
October 15, 1967 Average Speed: 130.317

Driver	Owner	Car #	Make	Laps	Winnings
1. Buddy Baker	Ray Fox	3	67 Dodg	334	18,950
2. Bobby Isaac	Nord Krauskopf	71	67 Dodg	333	9,480
3. Dick Hutcherson	Bondy Long	29	67 Ford	332	5,860
4. Charlie Glotzbach	Nord Krauskopf	72	65 Dodg	329	4,250
5. G. C. Spencer	Petty Enterprises	42	67 Plym	328	3,375

1968 Grand National Race No. 18 World 600
May 26, 1968 Average Speed: 104.207

Driver	Owner	Car #	Make	Laps	Winnings
1. Buddy Baker	Ray Fox	3	68 Dodg	255	27,780
2. Donnie Allison	Banjo Matthews	27	68 Ford	255	12,975
3. LeeRoy Yarbrough	Junior Johnson	98	68 Merc	254	9,290
4. David Pearson	Holman-Moody	17	68 Ford	254	6,300
5. Bobby Isaac	Nord Krauskopf	71	68 Dodg	253	5,475

1968 Grand National Race No. 47 National 500
October 20, 1968 Average Speed: 156.324

Driver	Owner	Car #	Make	Laps	Winnings
1. Charlie Glotzbach	Cotton Owens	6	68 Dodg	334	19,280
2. Paul Goldsmith	Ray Nichels	99	68 Dodg	334	9,505
3. David Pearson	Holman-Moody	17	68 Ford	334	6,800
4. Bobby Allison	Tom Friedkin	14	68 Plym	332	4,195
5. Cale Yarborough	Wood Brothers	21	68 Merc	332	3,335

1969 Grand National Race No. 21 World 600
May 25, 1969 Average Speed: 134.361

Driver	Owner	Car #	Make	Laps	Winnings
1. LeeRoy Yarbrough	Junior Johnson	98	69 Merc	400	29,325
2. Donnie Allison	Banjo Matthews	27	69 Ford	398	14,755
3. James Hylton	James Hylton	48	69 Dodg	382	9,670
4. G. C. Spencer	G. C. Spencer	49	67 Plym	381	6,300
5. Bobby Isaac	Nord Krauskopf	71	69 Dodg	374	5,375

1969 Grand National Race No. 48 National 500
October 12, 1969 Average Speed: 131.271

Driver	Owner	Car #	Make	Laps	Winnings
1. Donnie Allison	Banjo Matthews	27	69 Ford	334	20,280
2. Bobby Allison	Mario Rossi	22	69 Dodg	334	10,465
3. Buddy Baker	Cotton Owens	6	69 Dodg	334	6,550
4. Charlie Glotzbach	Ray Nichels	99	69 Dodg	334	4,025
5. David Pearson	Holman-Moody	17	69 Ford	332	3,800

1970 Grand National Race No. 16 World 600
May 24, 1970 Average Speed: 129.680

Driver	Owner	Car #	Make	Laps	Winnings
1. Donnie Allison	Banjo Matthews	27	69 Ford	400	39,750
2. Cale Yarborough	Wood Brothers	21	69 Merc	398	17,080
3. Benny Parsons	L. G. DeWitt	72	69 Ford	396	11,445
4. Tiny Lund	John McConnell	55	69 Dodg	395	7,575
5. James Hylton	James Hylton	48	69 Ford	395	6,200

1970 Grand National Race No. 44 National 500
October 11, 1970 Average Speed: 123.246

Driver	Owner	Car #	Make	Laps	Winnings
1. LeeRoy Yarbrough	Junior Johnson	98	69 Merc	334	23,700
2. Bobby Allison	Mario Rossi	22	69 Dodg	334	10,950
3. Fred Lorenzen	Ray Fox	3	69 Dodg	333	6,400
4. Benny Parsons	L. G. DeWitt	72	69 Ford	329	3,955
5. Bobby Isaac	Nord Krauskopf	71	69 Dodg	323	3,330

Charlotte Motor Speedway *continued*

1971 Winston Cup GN Race No. 21 World 600
May 30, 1971 Average Speed: 140.422

Driver	Owner	Car #	Make	Laps	Winnings
1. Bobby Allison	Holman-Moody	12	69 Merc	400	28,400
2. Donnie Allison	Wood Brothers	21	69 Merc	400	14,900
3. Pete Hamilton	Cotton Owens	6	71 Plym	399	10,425
4. Richard Petty	Petty Enterprises	43	71 Plym	398	7,175
5. Fred Lorenzen	Ray Nichels	99	71 Plym	395	5,600

1971 Winston Cup GN Race No. 42 National 500
October 10, 1971 Average Speed: 126.140

Driver	Owner	Car #	Make	Laps	Winnings
1. Bobby Allison	Holman-Moody	12	69 Merc	238	18,450
2. Bobby Isaac	Nord Krauskopf	71	71 Dodg	238	10,525
3. Donnie Allison	Wood Brothers	21	69 Merc	238	6,050
4. Richard Petty	Petty Enterprises	43	71 Plym	238	4,025
5. Charlie Glotzbach	R. Howard & J. Johnson	3	71 Chev	238	2,975

1972 Winston Cup GN Race No. 12 World 600
May 28, 1972 Average Speed: 142.255

Driver	Owner	Car #	Make	Laps	Winnings
1. Buddy Baker	Petty Enterprises	11	72 Dodg	400	22,075
2. Bobby Allison	R. Howard & J. Johnson	12	72 Chev	400	18,950
3. Charlie Glotzbach	Cotton Owens	6	72 Dodg	395	9,625
4. Benny Parsons	L. G. DeWitt	72	71 Merc	391	7,350
5. LeeRoy Yarbrough	Bill Seifert	45	71 Merc	382	6,325

1972 Winston Cup GN Race No. 29 National 500
October 8, 1972 Average Speed: 133.234

Driver	Owner	Car #	Make	Laps	Winnings
1. Bobby Allison	R. Howard & J. Johnson	12	72 Chev	334	21,450
2. Buddy Baker	Nord Krauskopf	71	72 Dodg	334	12,400
3. David Pearson	Wood Brothers	21	71 Merc	332	6,815
4. A. J. Foyt	Wood Brothers	41	71 Merc	332	4,090
5. Butch Hartman	Junie Donlavey	90	72 Ford	326	3,570

1973 Winston Cup GN Race No. 12 World 600
May 27, 1973 Average Speed: 134.890

Driver	Owner	Car #	Make	Laps	Winnings
1. Buddy Baker	Nord Krauskopf	71	73 Dodg	400	27,200
2. David Pearson	Wood Brothers	21	71 Merc	400	14,850
3. Cale Yarborough	R. Howard & J. Johnson	11	73 Chev	399	11,700
4. Bobby Isaac	Bud Moore	15	73 Ford	397	10,200
5. Benny Parsons	L. G. DeWitt	72	73 Chev	393	6,715

1973 Winston Cup GN Race No. 27 National 500
October 7, 1973 Average Speed: 145.240

Driver	Owner	Car #	Make	Laps	Winnings
1. Cale Yarborough	R. Howard & J. Johnson	11	73 Chev	334	45,425
2. Richard Petty	Petty Enterprises	43	73 Dodg	334	17,275
3. Bobby Allison	Bobby Allison	12	73 Chev	331	8,815
4. Benny Parsons	L. G. DeWitt	72	73 Chev	330	4,630
5. Dick Trickle	Richard Howard	1	73 Chev	327	3,385

1974 Winston Cup GN Race No. 13 World 600
May 26, 1974 Average Speed: 135.720

Driver	Owner	Car #	Make	Laps	Winnings
1. David Pearson	Wood Brothers	21	73 Merc	400	26,400
2. Richard Petty	Petty Enterprises	43	74 Dodg	400	21,200
3. Bobby Allison	Bobby Allison	12	74 Chev	395	12,975
4. Darrell Waltrip	Darrell Waltrip	95	74 Chev	395	7,875
5. Earl Ross	Allan J. Clarke	52	74 Chev	392	5,930

1974 Winston Cup GN Race No. 28 National 500
October 6, 1974 Average Speed: 119.912

Driver	Owner	Car #	Make	Laps	Winnings
1. David Pearson	Wood Brothers	21	73 Merc	334	22,575
2. Richard Petty	Petty Enterprises	43	74 Dodg	334	13,475
3. Darrell Waltrip	Darrell Waltrip	95	72 Chev	334	8,765
4. Donnie Allison	DiGard	88	74 Chev	334	6,055
5. Bobby Allison	Roger Penske	12	74 Mata	333	5,935

1975 Winston Cup GN Race No. 13 World 600
May 25, 1975 Average Speed: 145.327

Driver	Owner	Car #	Make	Laps	Winnings
1. Richard Petty	Petty Enterprises	43	74 Dodg	400	30,290
2. Cale Yarborough	Junior Johnson	1	75 Chev	399	16,915
3. David Pearson	Wood Brothers	21	73 Merc	396	10,790
4. Darrell Waltrip	Darrell Waltrip	17	75 Chev	395	10,265
5. Buddy Baker	Bud Moore	15	75 Ford	395	9,640

1975 Winston Cup GN Race No. 25 National 500
October 5, 1975 Average Speed: 132.209

Driver	Owner	Car #	Make	Laps	Winnings
1. Richard Petty	Petty Enterprises	43	74 Dodg	334	30,970
2. David Pearson	Wood Brothers	21	73 Merc	334	23,445
3. Buddy Baker	Bud Moore	15	75 Ford	334	12,450
4. Benny Parsons	L. G. DeWitt	72	75 Chev	330	9,370
5. Cecil Gordon	Cecil Gordon	24	75 Chev	324	5,955

1976 Winston Cup GN Race No. 13 World 600
May 30, 1976 Average Speed: 137.352

Driver	Owner	Car #	Make	Laps	Winnings
1. David Pearson	Wood Brothers	21	Merc	400	49,990
2. Richard Petty	Petty Enterprises	43	Dodg	400	22,465
3. Cale Yarborough	Junior Johnson	11	Chev	399	19,220
4. Bobby Allison	Roger Penske	2	Merc	397	12,555
5. Benny Parsons	L. G. DeWitt	72	Chev	396	10,750

1976 Winston Cup GN Race No. 27 National 500
October 10, 1976 Average Speed: 141.226

Driver	Owner	Car #	Make	Laps	Winnings
1. Donnie Allison	Hoss Ellington	1	Chev	334	22,435
2. Cale Yarborough	Junior Johnson	11	Chev	334	22,955
3. Bobby Allison	Roger Penske	2	Merc	334	17,069
4. Buddy Baker	Bud Moore	15	Ford	334	17,710
5. Benny Parsons	L. G. DeWitt	72	Chev	333	9,279

1977 Winston Cup GN Race No. 13 World 600
May 29, 1977 Average Speed: 137.676

Driver	Owner	Car #	Make	Laps	Winnings
1. Richard Petty	Petty Enterprises	43	Dodg	400	69,550
2. David Pearson	Wood Brothers	21	Merc	400	38,535
3. Benny Parsons	L. G. DeWitt	72	Chev	398	16,735
4. Lennie Pond	Ronnie Elder	54	Chev	397	12,850
5. Buddy Baker	Bud Moore	15	Ford	397	12,240

1977 Winston Cup GN Race No. 27 NAPA National 500
October 9, 1977 Average Speed: 142.780

Driver	Owner	Car #	Make	Laps	Winnings
1. Benny Parsons	L. G. DeWitt	72	Chev	334	41,075
2. Cale Yarborough	Junior Johnson	11	Chev	333	25,900
3. David Pearson	Wood Brothers	21	Merc	333	22,500
4. Buddy Baker	Bud Moore	15	Ford	333	12,100
5. Darrell Waltrip	DiGard	88	Chev	333	10,250

Charlotte Motor Speedway *continued*

1978 Winston Cup GN Race No. 12 World 600
May 28, 1978 Average Speed: 138.355

Driver	Owner	Car #	Make	Laps	Winnings
1. Darrell Waltrip	DiGard	88	Chev	400	48,608
2. Donnie Allison	Hoss Ellington	1	Chev	400	27,000
3. Bobby Allison	Bud Moore	15	Ford	400	19,695
4. Cale Yarborough	Junior Johnson	11	Olds	400	31,133
5. David Pearson	Wood Brothers	21	Merc	400	28,135

1978 Winston Cup GN Race No. 27 NAPA National 500
October 8, 1978 Average Speed: 141.826

Driver	Owner	Car #	Make	Laps	Winnings
1. Bobby Allison	Bud Moore	15	Ford	334	40,000
2. Darrell Waltrip	DiGard	88	Chev	334	23,575
3. Dave Marcis	Rod Osterlund	2	Chev	334	20,050
4. Donnie Allison	Hoss Ellington	1	Chev	334	16,775
5. David Pearson	Wood Brothers	21	Merc	333	23,750

1979 Winston Cup GN Race No. 13 World 600
May 27, 1979 Average Speed: 136.674

Driver	Owner	Car #	Make	Laps	Winnings
1. Darrell Waltrip	DiGard	88	Chev	400	55,400
2. Richard Petty	Petty Enterprises	43	Chev	400	35,650
3. Dale Earnhardt	Rod Osterlund	2	Chev	400	27,100
4. Cale Yarborough	Junior Johnson	11	Olds	398	18,225
5. Benny Parsons	M. C. Anderson	27	Chev	398	13,570

1979 Winston Cup GN Race No. 27 NAPA National 500
October 7, 1979 Average Speed: 134.266

Driver	Owner	Car #	Make	Laps	Winnings
1. Cale Yarborough	Junior Johnson	11	Chev	334	39,000
2. Bobby Allison	Bud Moore	15	Ford	333	27,475
3. Darrell Waltrip	DiGard	88	Chev	332	23,100
4. Richard Petty	Petty Enterprises	43	Chev	332	15,375
5. Donnie Allison	Hoss Ellington	1	Chev	331	7,700

1980 Winston Cup GN Race No. 13 World 600
May 25, 1980 Average Speed: 119.265

Driver	Owner	Car #	Make	Laps	Winnings
1. Benny Parsons	M. C. Anderson	27	Chev	400	44,850
2. Darrell Waltrip	DiGard	88	Chev	400	38,700
3. Terry Labonte	Billy Hagan	44	Chev	398	22,660
4. Richard Petty	Petty Enterprises	43	Chev	397	19,550
5. Neil Bonnett	Wood Brothers	21	Merc	397	11,250

1980 Winston Cup GN Race No. 28 National 500
October 5, 1980 Average Speed: 135.243

Driver	Owner	Car #	Make	Laps	Winnings
1. Dale Earnhardt	Rod Osterlund	2	Chev	334	49,050
2. Cale Yarborough	Junior Johnson	11	Chev	334	30,200
3. Buddy Baker	Harry Ranier	28	Buick	334	21,850
4. Ricky Rudd	Al Rudd	22	Chev	334	15,350
5. Donnie Allison	Kennie Childers	12	Chev	333	8,400

1981 Winston Cup GN Race No. 13 World 600
May 24, 1981 Average Speed: 129.326

Driver	Owner	Car #	Make	Laps	Winnings
1. Bobby Allison	Harry Ranier	28	Buick	400	60,200
2. Harry Gant	Hal Needham	33	Chev	400	28,600
3. Cale Yarborough	M. C. Anderson	27	Buick	398	22,425
4. Ricky Rudd	DiGard	88	Buick	397	18,975
5. Kyle Petty	Petty Enterprises	42	Buick	396	13,080

1981 Winston Cup GN Race No. 28 National 500
October 11, 1981 Average Speed: 117.483

Driver	Owner	Car #	Make	Laps	Winnings
1. Darrell Waltrip	Junior Johnson	11	Buick	334	51,600
2. Bobby Allison	Harry Ranier	28	Chev	334	27,400
3. Ricky Rudd	DiGard	88	Chev	334	29,925
4. Tommy Ellis	Tommy Ellis	55	Chev	333	11,400
5. Ron Bouchard	Jack Beebe	47	Buick	332	12,180

1982 Winston Cup GN Race No. 12 World 600
May 30, 1982 Average Speed: 130.058

Driver	Owner	Car #	Make	Laps	Winnings
1. Neil Bonnett	Wood Brothers	21	Ford	400	50,650
2. Bill Elliott	Harry Melling	9	Ford	400	35,625
3. Bobby Allison	DiGard	88	Buick	399	29,525
4. Cale Yarborough	M. C. Anderson	27	Buick	398	15,850
5. Buddy Baker	Hoss Ellington	1	Buick	398	17,440

1982 Winston Cup GN Race No. 26 National 500
October 10, 1982 Average Speed: 137.208

Driver	Owner	Car #	Make	Laps	Winnings
1. Harry Gant	Hal Needham	33	Buick	334	47,740
2. Bill Elliott	Harry Melling	9	Ford	334	33,040
3. David Pearson	Bobby Hawkins	03	Buick	333	13,915
4. Joe Ruttman	Bob Rahilly & Butch Mock	75	Buick	331	14,010
5. Benny Parsons	Johnny Hayes	55	Buick	331	8,765

1983 Winston Cup GN Race No. 12 World 600
May 29, 1983 Average Speed: 140.707

Driver	Owner	Car #	Make	Laps	Winnings
1. Neil Bonnett	Bob Rahilly & Butch Mock	75	Chev	400	50,405
2. Richard Petty	Petty Enterprises	43	Pont	400	31,450
3. Bobby Allison	DiGard	22	Buick	400	61,925
4. Darrell Waltrip	Junior Johnson	11	Chev	399	23,425
5. Dale Earnhardt	Bud Moore	15	Ford	399	28,700

1983 Winston Cup GN Race No. 27 Miller High Life 500
October 9, 1983 Average Speed: 139.998

Driver	Owner	Car #	Make	Laps	Winnings
1. Richard Petty	Petty Enterprises	43	Pont	334	40,400
2. Darrell Waltrip	Junior Johnson	11	Chev	334	34,850
3. Benny Parsons	Johnny Hayes	55	Chev	334	43,775
4. Terry Labonte	Billy Hagan	44	Chev	334	16,230
5. Tim Richmond	Raymond Beadle	27	Pont	334	35,195

1984 Winston Cup GN Race No. 12 World 600
May 27, 1984 Average Speed: 129.233

Driver	Owner	Car #	Make	Laps	Winnings
1. Bobby Allison	DiGard	22	Buick	400	88,500
2. Dale Earnhardt	Richard Childress	3	Chev	400	49,625
3. Ron Bouchard	Jack Beebe	47	Buick	399	24,430
4. Harry Gant	Hal Needham	33	Chev	399	42,005
5. Geoff Bodine	Rick Hendrick	5	Chev	399	20,500

1984 Winston Cup GN Race No. 26 Miller High Life 500
October 7, 1984 Average Speed: 148.861

Driver	Owner	Car #	Make	Laps	Winnings
1. Bill Elliott	Harry Melling	9	Ford	334	52,633
2. Benny Parsons	Johnny Hayes	55	Chev	334	68,475
3. Cale Yarborough	Harry Ranier	28	Chev	334	23,258
4. Harry Gant	Hal Needham	33	Chev	334	34,938
5. Terry Labonte	Billy Hagan	44	Chev	333	19,228

Charlotte Motor Speedway *continued*

1985 Winston Cup GN Race No. 11 Coca-Cola World 600
May 26, 1985 Average Speed: 141.807

Driver	Owner	Car #	Make	Laps	Winnings
1. Darrell Waltrip	Junior Johnson	11	Chev	400	90,733
2. Harry Gant	Hal Needham	33	Chev	400	49,300
3. Bobby Allison	DiGard	22	Buick	400	30,900
4. Dale Earnhardt	Richard Childress	3	Chev	399	49,238
5. Terry Labonte	Billy Hagan	44	Chev	398	24,000

1985 Winston Cup GN Race No. 25 Miller High Life 500
October 6, 1985 Average Speed: 136.761

Driver	Owner	Car #	Make	Laps	Winnings
1. Cale Yarborough	Harry Ranier	28	Ford	334	51,600
2. Bill Elliott	Harry Melling	9	Ford	334	65,400
3. Geoff Bodine	Rick Hendrick	5	Chev	334	33,625
4. Darrell Waltrip	Junior Johnson	11	Chev	333	23,450
5. Joe Ruttman	Larry McClure	4	Chev	333	12,400

1986 Winston Cup Race No. 11 Coca-Cola 600
May 25, 1986 Average Speed: 140.406

Driver	Owner	Car #	Make	Laps	Winnings
1. Dale Earnhardt	Richard Childress	3	Chev	400	98,150
2. Tim Richmond	Rick Hendrick	25	Chev	400	64,355
3. Cale Yarborough	Harry Ranier	28	Ford	400	34,375
4. Harry Gant	Hal Needham	33	Chev	400	35,630
5. Darrell Waltrip	Junior Johnson	11	Chev	400	27,250

1986 Winston Cup Race No. 26 Oakwood Homes 500
October 5, 1986 Average Speed: 132.403

Driver	Owner	Car #	Make	Laps	Winnings
1. Dale Earnhardt	Richard Childress	3	Chev	334	82,050
2. Harry Gant	Hal Needham	33	Chev	334	54,100
3. Neil Bonnett	Junior Johnson	12	Chev	333	33,125
4. Ricky Rudd	Bud Moore	15	Ford	333	25,700
5. Buddy Baker	Buddy Baker & Danny Schiff	88	Olds	333	15,200

1987 Winston Cup Race No. 10 Coca-Cola 600
May 24, 1987 Average Speed: 131.483

Driver	Owner	Car #	Make	Laps	Winnings
1. Kyle Petty	Wood Brothers	21	Ford	400	89,405
2. Morgan Shepherd	Kenny Bernstein	26	Buick	399	49,070
3. Lake Speed	Lake Speed	83	Olds	399	27,625
4. Richard Petty	Petty Enterprises	43	Pont	398	24,925
5. Darrell Waltrip	Rick Hendrick	17	Chev	398	16,900

1987 Winston Cup Race No. 26 Oakwood Homes 500
October 11, 1987 Average Speed: 128.443

Driver	Owner	Car #	Make	Laps	Winnings
1. Bill Elliott	Harry Melling	9	Ford	334	74,040
2. Bobby Allison	Stavola Brothers	22	Buick	334	67,765
3. Sterling Marlin	Billy Hagan	44	Olds	334	34,770
4. Terry Labonte	Junior Johnson	11	Chev	333	30,240
5. Richard Petty	Petty Enterprises	43	Pont	333	31,860

1988 Winston Cup Race No. 10 Coca-Cola 600
May 29, 1988 Average Speed: 124.460

Driver	Owner	Car #	Make	Laps	Winnings
1. Darrell Waltrip	Rick Hendrick	17	Chev	400	104,250
2. Rusty Wallace	Raymond Beadle	27	Pont	400	56,425
3. Alan Kulwicki	Alan Kulwicki	7	Ford	400	38,100
4. Brett Bodine	Bud Moore	15	Ford	400	49,305
5. Davey Allison	Harry Ranier	28	Ford	400	62,050

1988 Winston Cup Race No. 25 Oakwood Homes 500
October 9, 1988 Average Speed: 130.677

Driver	Owner	Car #	Make	Laps	Winnings
1. Rusty Wallace	Raymond Beadle	27	Pont	334	84,300
2. Darrell Waltrip	Rick Hendrick	17	Chev	334	54,525
3. Brett Bodine	Bud Moore	15	Ford	334	43,350
4. Bill Elliott	Harry Melling	9	Ford	334	35,900
5. Sterling Marlin	Billy Hagan	44	Olds	334	28,200

1989 Winston Cup Race No. 10 Coca-Cola 600
May 28, 1989 Average Speed: 144.077

Driver	Owner	Car #	Make	Laps	Winnings
1. Darrell Waltrip	Rick Hendrick	17	Chev	400	126,400
2. Sterling Marlin	Billy Hagan	94	Olds	400	61,675
3. Ken Schrader	Rick Hendrick	25	Chev	400	44,275
4. Geoff Bodine	Rick Hendrick	5	Chev	399	30,950
5. Bill Elliott	Harry Melling	9	Ford	399	32,305

1989 Winston Cup Race No. 25 All Pro Auto Parts 500
October 8, 1989 Average Speed: 149.863

Driver	Owner	Car #	Make	Laps	Winnings
1. Ken Schrader	Rick Hendrick	25	Chev	334	91,700
2. Harry Gant	Leo Jackson	33	Olds	334	50,375
3. Mark Martin	Jack Roush	6	Ford	334	55,075
4. Bill Elliott	Harry Melling	9	Ford	334	75,650
5. Davey Allison	Robert Yates	28	Ford	334	27,990

1990 Winston Cup Series Race No. 10 Coca-Cola 600
May 27, 1990 Average Speed: 137.650

Driver	Owner	Car #	Make	Laps	Winnings
1. Rusty Wallace	Raymond Beadle	27	Pont	400	151,000
2. Bill Elliott	Harry Melling	9	Ford	400	67,450
3. Mark Martin	Jack Roush	6	Ford	400	51,700
4. Michael Waltrip	Chuck Rider	30	Pont	400	32,600
5. Ernie Irvan	Larry McClure	4	Olds	400	28,350

1990 Winston Cup Series Race No. 26 Mello Yello 500
October 7, 1990 Average Speed: 137.428

Driver	Owner	Car #	Make	Laps	Winnings
1. Davey Allison	Robert Yates	28	Ford	334	90,650
2. Morgan Shepherd	Bud Moore	15	Ford	334	51,800
3. Michael Waltrip	Chuck Rider	30	Pont	334	38,100
4. Kyle Petty	Felix Sabates	42	Pont	334	30,450
5. Alan Kulwicki	Alan Kulwicki	7	Ford	334	24,757

1991 Winston Cup Series Race No. 10 Coca-Cola 600
May 26, 1991 Average Speed: 138.951

Driver	Owner	Car #	Make	Laps	Winnings
1. Davey Allison	Robert Yates	28	Ford	400	137,100
2. Ken Schrader	Rick Hendrick	25	Chev	400	84,850
3. Dale Earnhardt	Richard Childress	3	Chev	400	53,650
4. Harry Gant	Leo Jackson	33	Olds	400	37,700
5. Dale Jarrett	Wood Brothers	21	Ford	400	27,400

1991 Winston Cup Series Race No. 26 Mello Yello 500
October 6, 1991 Average Speed: 138.984

Driver	Owner	Car #	Make	Laps	Winnings
1. Geoff Bodine	Junior Johnson	11	Ford	334	92,200
2. Davey Allison	Robert Yates	28	Ford	334	69,350
3. Alan Kulwicki	Alan Kulwicki	7	Ford	333	47,250
4. Harry Gant	Leo Jackson	33	Olds	333	31,350
5. Sterling Marlin	Junior Johnson	22	Ford	331	25,100

Charlotte Motor Speedway *continued*

1992 Winston Cup Race No. 10 Coca-Cola 600
May 24, 1992 Average Speed: 132.980

Driver	Owner	Car #	Make	Laps	Winnings
1. Dale Earnhardt	Richard Childress	3	Chev	400	125,100
2. Ernie Irvan	Larry McClure	4	Chev	400	67,275
3. Kyle Petty	Felix Sabates	42	Pont	400	60,900
4. Davey Allison	Robert Yates	28	Ford	400	45,750
5. Harry Gant	Leo Jackson	33	Olds	400	35,800

1993 Winston Cup Series Race No. 11 Coca-Cola 600
May 30, 1993 Average Speed: 145.504

Driver	Owner	Car #	Make	Laps	Winnings
1. Dale Earnhardt	Richard Childress	3	Chev	400	156,650
2. Jeff Gordon	Rick Hendrick	24	Chev	400	79,050
3. Dale Jarrett	Joe Gibbs	18	Chev	400	73,100
4. Ken Schrader	Rick Hendrick	25	Chev	400	91,550
5. Ernie Irvan	Larry McClure	4	Chev	400	46,600

1994 Winston Cup Series Race No. 11 Coca-Cola 600
May 29, 1994 Average Speed: 139.445

Driver	Owner	Car #	Make	Laps	Winnings
1. Jeff Gordon	Rick Hendrick	24	Chev	400	196,500
2. Rusty Wallace	Roger Penske	2	Ford	400	88,075
3. Geoff Bodine	Geoff Bodine	7	Ford	400	75,500
4. Dale Jarrett	Joe Gibbs	18	Chev	400	54,600
5. Ernie Irvan	Robert Yates	28	Ford	400	47,800

1995 Winston Cup Series Race No. 11 Coca-Cola 600
May 28, 1995 Average Speed: 151.952

Driver	Owner	Car #	Make	Laps	Winnings
1. Bobby Labonte	Joe Gibbs	18	Chev	400	163,850
2. Terry Labonte	Rick Hendrick	5	Chev	400	93,050
3. Michael Waltrip	Chuck Rider	30	Pont	400	70,650
4. Sterling Marlin	Larry McClure	4	Chev	399	62,700
5. Ricky Rudd	Ricky Rudd	10	Ford	399	49,000

1996 Winston Cup Series Race No. 11 Coca-Cola 600
May 26, 1996 Average Speed: 147.581

Driver	Owner	Car #	Make	Laps	Winnings
1. Dale Jarrett	Robert Yates	88	Ford	400	165,250
2. Dale Earnhardt	Richard Childress	3	Chev	400	97,000
3. Terry Labonte	Rick Hendrick	5	Chev	400	75,300
4. Jeff Gordon	Rick Hendrick	24	Chev	400	118,200
5. Ken Schrader	Rick Hendrick	25	Chev	399	46,350

1997 Winston Cup Series Race No. 11
May 25, 1997 Average Speed: 136.745

Driver	Owner	Car #	Make	Laps	Winnings
1. Jeff Gordon	Rick Hendrick	24	Chev	333	224,900
2. Rusty Wallace	Roger Penske	2	Ford	333	108,025
3. Mark Martin	Jack Roush	6	Ford	333	77,500
4. Bill Elliott	Bill Elliott	94	Ford	333	73,300
5. Jeff Burton	Jack Roush	99	Ford	333	61,750

1998 Winston Cup Series Race No. 11
May 24, 1998 Average Speed: 136.424

Driver	Owner	Car #	Make	Laps	Winnings
1. Jeff Gordon	Rick Hendrick	24	Chev	400	346,500
2. Rusty Wallace	Roger Penske	2	Ford	400	109,500
3. Bobby Labonte	Joe Gibbs	18	Pont	400	102,550
4. Mark Martin	Jack Roush	6	Ford	400	95,500
5. Dale Jarrett	Robert Yates	88	Ford	400	78,700

1992 Winston Cup Race No. 26 Mello Yello 500
October 11, 1992 Average Speed: 153.537

Driver	Owner	Car #	Make	Laps	Winnings
1. Mark Martin	Jack Roush	6	Ford	334	101,500
2. Alan Kulwicki	Alan Kulwicki	7	Ford	334	89,000
3. Kyle Petty	Felix Sabates	42	Pont	334	68,600
4. Jimmy Spencer	Bobby Allison	12	Ford	334	41,200
5. Ricky Rudd	Rick Hendrick	5	Chev	334	35,550

1993 Winston Cup Series Race No. 27 Mello Yello 500
October 10, 1993 Average Speed: 154.537

Driver	Owner	Car #	Make	Laps	Winnings
1. Ernie Irvan	Robert Yates	28	Ford	334	147,450
2. Mark Martin	Jack Roush	6	Ford	334	67,900
3. Dale Earnhardt	Richard Childress	3	Chev	334	56,900
4. Rusty Wallace	Roger Penske	2	Pont	334	42,950
5. Jeff Gordon	Rick Hendrick	24	Chev	334	56,875

1994 Winston Cup Series Race No. 28 Mello Yello 500
October 10, 1994 Average Speed: 145.922

Driver	Owner	Car #	Make	Laps	Winnings
1. Dale Jarrett	Joe Gibbs	18	Chev	334	106,800
2. Morgan Shepherd	Wood Brothers	21	Ford	334	71,900
3. Dale Earnhardt	Richard Childress	3	Chev	334	66,000
4. Ken Schrader	Rick Hendrick	25	Chev	334	47,800
5. Lake Speed	Bud Moore	15	Ford	334	42,925

1995 Winston Cup Series Race No. 28 UAW - GM Quality 500
October 8, 1995 Average Speed: 145.358

Driver	Owner	Car #	Make	Laps	Winnings
1. Mark Martin	Jack Roush	6	Ford	334	105,650
2. Dale Earnhardt	Richard Childress	3	Chev	334	86,800
3. Terry Labonte	Rick Hendrick	5	Chev	334	73,750
4. Ricky Rudd	Ricky Rudd	10	Ford	334	90,200
5. Dale Jarrett	Robert Yates	28	Ford	334	51,400

1996 Winston Cup Series Race No. 28 UAW - GM Quality 500
October 6, 1996 Average Speed: 143.143

Driver	Owner	Car #	Make	Laps	Winnings
1. Terry Labonte	Rick Hendrick	5	Chev	334	133,950
2. Mark Martin	Jack Roush	6	Ford	334	85,100
3. Dale Jarrett	Robert Yates	88	Ford	334	58,300
4. Sterling Marlin	Larry McClure	4	Chev	334	60,100
5. Ricky Craven	Larry Hedrick	41	Chev	334	63,400

1997 Winston Cup Series Race No. 28
October 5, 1997 Average Speed: 144.323

Driver	Owner	Car #	Make	Laps	Winnings
1. Dale Jarrett	Robert Yates	88	Ford	334	130,000
2. Bobby Labonte	Joe Gibbs	18	Pont	334	110,900
3. Dale Earnhardt	Richard Childress	3	Chev	334	85,650
4. Mark Martin	Jack Roush	6	Ford	334	66,050
5. Jeff Gordon	Rick Hendrick	24	Chev	334	62,200

1998 Winston Cup Series Race No. 28
October 4, 1998 Average Speed: 123.188

Driver	Owner	Car #	Make	Laps	Winnings
1. Mark Martin	Jack Roush	6	Ford	334	151,950
2. Ward Burton	Bill Davis	22	Pont	334	96,700
3. Jeff Burton	Jack Roush	99	Ford	334	76,250
4. Bobby Hamilton	Larry McClure	4	Chev	334	83,300
5. Jeff Gordon	Rick Hendrick	24	Chev	334	79,450

Charlotte Motor Speedway *continued*

1999 Winston Cup Series Race No. 12
May 30, 1999 Average Speed: 151.367

Driver	Owner	Car #	Make	Laps	Winnings
1. Jeff Burton	Jack Roush	99	Ford	400	1,212,500
2. Bobby Labonte	Joe Gibbs	18	Pont	400	170,400
3. Mark Martin	Jack Roush	6	Ford	400	97,875
4. Tony Stewart	Joe Gibbs	20	Pont	400	76,275
5. Dale Jarrett	Robert Yates	88	Ford	400	81,125

1999 Winston Cup Series Race No. 29
October 10, 1999 Average Speed: 160.306

Driver	Owner	Car #	Make	Laps	Winnings
1. Jeff Gordon	Rick Hendrick	24	Chev	334	140,350
2. Bobby Labonte	Joe Gibbs	18	Pont	334	157,250
3. Mike Skinner	Richard Childress	31	Chev	334	87,800
4. Mark Martin	Jack Roush	6	Ford	334	85,750
5. Ward Burton	Bill Davis	22	Pont	334	73,075

2000 Winston Cup Series Race No. 12
May 28, 2000 Average Speed: 142.64

Driver	Owner	Car #	Make	Laps	Winnings
1. Matt Kenseth	Jack Roush	17	Ford	400	200,950
2. Bobby Labonte	Joe Gibbs	18	Pont	400	138,600
3. Dale Earnhardt	Richard Childress	3	Chev	400	103,250
4. Dale Earnhardt, Jr.	Dale Earnhardt, Inc.	8	Chev	400	110,900
5. Dale Jarrett	Robert Yates	88	Ford	400	95,000

2000 Winston Cup Series Race No. 29
October 8, 2000 Average Speed: 133.63

Driver	Owner	Car #	Make	Laps	Winnings
1. Bobby Labonte	Joe Gibbs	18	Pont	334	220,700
2. Jeremy Mayfield	Michael Kranefuss	12	Ford	334	89,550
3. Ricky Rudd	Robert Yates	28	Ford	334	104,950
4. Tony Stewart	Joe Gibbs	20	Pont	334	84,650
5. Mark Martin	Jack Roush	6	Ford	334	70,250

2001 Winston Cup Series Race No. 12
May 27, 2001 Average Speed: 130.107

Driver	Owner	Car #	Make	Laps	Winnings
1. Jeff Burton	Jack Roush	99	Ford	400	258,846
2. Kevin Harvick	Richard Childress	29	Chev	400	189,827
3. Tony Stewart	Joe Gibbs	20	Pont	400	132,300
4. Mark Martin	Jack Roush	6	Ford	400	139,651
5. Bobby Labonte	Joe Gibbs	18	Pont	400	139,077

2001 Winston Cup Series Race No. 29
October 7, 2001 Average Speed: 139.006

Driver	Owner	Car #	Make	Laps	Winnings
1. Sterling Marlin	Chip Ganassi	40	Dodg	334	196,360
2. Tony Stewart	Joe Gibbs	20	Pont	334	131,100
3. Ward Burton	Bill Davis	22	Dodg	334	119,185
4. Dale Earnhardt, Jr.	Dale Earnhardt, Inc.	8	Chev	334	104,923
5. Jeff Burton	Jack Roush	99	Ford	334	110,746

2002 Winston Cup Series Race No. 12
May 26, 2002 Average Speed: 137.729

Driver	Owner	Car #	Make	Laps	Winnings
1. Mark Martin	Jack Roush	6	Ford	400	1,280,033
2. Matt Kenseth	Jack Roush	17	Ford	400	170,600
3. Ricky Craven	Cal Wells	32	Ford	400	139,250
4. Ricky Rudd	Robert Yates	28	Ford	400	158,617
5. Jeff Gordon	Rick Hendrick	24	Chev	400	144,928

2002 Winston Cup Series Race No. 31
October 13, 2002 Average Speed: 141.586

Driver	Owner	Car #	Make	Laps	Winnings
1. Jamie McMurray	Chip Ganassi	40	Dodg	334	215,717
2. Bobby Labonte	Joe Gibbs	18	Pont	334	152,678
3. Tony Stewart	Joe Gibbs	20	Pont	334	136,628
4. Jeff Gordon	Rick Hendrick	24	Chev	334	125,778
5. Rusty Wallace	Roger Penske	2	Ford	334	111,100

Cleveland County Fairgrounds
Shelby, NC
Half-mile Dirt Track

(aka Shelby Fairgrounds; Shelby Motor Speedway) Half-mile dirt oval built in 1924. First Winston Cup (then Grand National) race held on 7/17/56 (won by Speedy Thompson). Final Grand National race run on 8/5/65 (won by Ned Jarrett). Track was leased by team owner Carl Kiekhaefer in 1956 and inserted late in the championship season in order to give his drivers (Baker and Thompson) an additional chance to cut into point leader Herb Thomas's (who had quit Kiekhaefer's team in mid-season) lead. In the race run on 10/23/56, Thompson hooked Thomas on the straightaway, sending him into the retaining wall. Thomas was critically injured. Essentially, Thomas's career ended, and he lost the 1956 championship to Baker (who ended up winning the race). The track has been the scene of recent demolition derbies during the fair in October.

Winston Cup Starts
Buck Baker 5

Winston Cup Victories
Buck Baker 2
Ned Jarrett 2

Winston Cup Poles
Buck Baker 1
Doug Cox 1
Dick Hutcherson 1
Tiny Lund 1
Ralph Moody 1
David Pearson 1

Winston Cup Money
Buck Baker $2,395

Most Cars Started
26—October 23, 1956

Fewest Cars Started
14—August 5, 1965

Narrowest Margin of Victory
2 car lengths—October 23, 1956

Slowest Race
53.699 MPH—July 27, 1956
53.699 MPH—September 21, 1957

Race Record
64.748 MPH—August 5, 1965

Most Cautions
4—September 21, 1957

Most Race Leaders
4—May 4, 1957
4—September 21, 1957

Most Cars Running at Finish
15—October 23, 1956

1956 Grand National Race No. 34
July 27, 1956 Average Speed: 53.699

Driver	Owner	Car #	Make	Laps	Winnings
1. Speedy Thompson	Carl Kiekhaefer	500	56 Dodg	201	950
2. Ralph Moody	Pete DePaolo	12	58 Ford	201	675
3. Billy Myers	Bill Stroppe	14	56 Merc	200	475
4. Fireball Roberts	Pete DePaolo	22	56 Ford	200	365
5. Buck Baker	Carl Kiekhaefer	500B	56 Dodg	197	320

1956 Grand National Race No. 53
October 23, 1956 Average Speed: 54.054

Driver	Owner	Car #	Make	Laps	Winnings
1. Buck Baker	Carl Kiekhaefer	300B	56 Chrys	200	850
2. Bill Amick	Pete DePaolo	97	56 Ford	200	625
3. Marvin Panch	Tom Harbison	98	56 Ford	200	450
4. Speedy Thompson	Carl Kiekhaefer	500B	56 Dodg	197	350
5. Joe Eubanks	James Satcher	82	56 Ford	191	310

1957 Grand National Race No. 15
May 4, 1957 Average Speed: 54.861

Driver	Owner	Car #	Make	Laps	Winnings
1. Fireball Roberts	Pete DePaolo	22	57 Ford	200	700
2. Paul Goldsmith	Smokey Yunick	3	57 Ford	200	525
3. Marvin Panch	Pete DePaolo	98	57 Ford	200	400
4. Jim Paschal	Bill Stroppe	17	57 Merc	197	330
5. Jack Smith	Hugh Babb	47	57 Chev	196	270

1957 Grand National Race No. 47
September 21, 1957 Average Speed: 53.699

Driver	Owner	Car #	Make	Laps	Winnings
1. Buck Baker	Buck Baker	87	57 Chev	200	900
2. Marvin Panch	Marvin Panch	98	57 Ford	200	575
3. Bill Amick	Bill Amick	97	57 Ford	198	375
4. Gwyn Staley	J. H. Petty	38	57 Chev	198	280
5. Lee Petty	Petty Enterprises	42	57 Olds	195	245

1965 Grand National Race No. 20
May 27, 1965 Average Speed: 63.909

Driver	Owner	Car #	Make	Laps	Winnings
1. Ned Jarrett	Bondy Long	11	65 Ford	200	1,000
2. Bud Moore	Louie Weathersby	45	65 Plym	178	600
3. Dick Hutcherson	Holman-Moody	29	65 Ford	175	400
4. Doug Cooper	Bob Cooper	60	64 Ford	175	300
5. Bob Derrington	Bob Derrington	68	63 Ford	172	275

1965 Grand National Race No. 36
August 5, 1965 Average Speed: 64.748

Driver	Owner	Car #	Make	Laps	Winnings
1. Ned Jarrett	Bondy Long	11	65 Ford	200	1,000
2. Richard Petty	Petty Enterprises	43	64 Plym	196	600
3. Dick Hutcherson	Holman-Moody	29	65 Ford	189	400
4. Neil Castles	Buck Baker	89	65 Olds	185	300
5. David Pearson	Cotton Owens	6	65 Dodg	184	275

Concord Speedway
Concord, NC
Half-mile Dirt Track

(aka Concord Int'l Speedway; New Concord Speedway) Half-mile dirt track opened in 1955. First NASCAR Winston Cup (then Grand National) race held on 5/6/56 (won by Speedy Thompson). Final Grand National race run on 6/11/64 (won by Richard Petty). Track closed in 1978, and later re-opened for NDRA Dirt Late Model race in 1979.

Winston Cup Starts
Cotton Owens 9
Jack Smith 9

Winston Cup Victories
Jack Smith 3

Winston Cup Poles
Speedy Thompson 2
Joe Weatherly 2

Winston Cup Money
Jack Smith $3,945

Most Cars Started
34—October 25, 1959
Lee Kirby Memorial

Fewest Cars Started
19—March 8, 1959
19—June 11, 1964

Narrowest Margin of Victory
3 car lengths—March 2, 1958

Slowest Race
53.161 MPH—February 25, 1962

Race Record
66.352 MPH—June 11, 1964

Most Cautions
5—October 13, 1957

Most Race Leaders
4—October 13, 1957
4—November 10, 1963 Textile 250

Most Cars Running at Finish
21—October 13, 1957

1956 Grand National Race No. 14
May 6, 1956 Average Speed: 61.633

Driver	Owner	Car #	Make	Laps	Winnings
1. Speedy Thompson	Carl Kiekhaefer	300c	56 Chrys	200	1,100
2. Buck Baker	Carl Kiekhaefer	300	56 Chrys	200	700
3. Herb Thomas	Carl Kiekhaefer	300B	56 Chrys	198	475
4. Tim Flock	Jim Stephens	285	56 Pont	197	365
5. Rex White	Bob Welborn	X	56 Chev	195	310

1957 Grand National Race No. 5
March 3, 1957 Average Speed: 59.860

Driver	Owner	Car #	Make	Laps	Winnings
1. Jack Smith	Hugh Babb	47	57 Chev	200	650
2. Buck Baker	Hugh Babb	87	57 Chev	200	525
3. Speedy Thompson	Hugh Babb	46	57 Chev	200	400
4. Fireball Roberts	Pete DePaolo	22	57 Ford	200	320
5. Mel Larson	Mel Larson	55	56 Ford	189	290

1958 Grand National Race No. 3
March 2, 1958 Average Speed: 58.555

Driver	Owner	Car #	Make	Laps	Winnings
1. Lee Petty	Petty Enterprises	42	57 Olds	200	800
2. Curtis Turner	Holman-Moody	21	58 Ford	200	525
3. Speedy Thompson	Speedy Thompson	46	57 Chev	200	350
4. Gwyn Staley	J. H. Petty	38	57 Chev	—	250
5. Eddie Pagan	Eddie Pagan	45	57 Ford	—	225

1959 Grand National Race No. 44 Lee Kirby Memorial
October 25, 1959 Average Speed: 54.005

Driver	Owner	Car #	Make	Laps	Winnings
1. Jack Smith	Jack Smith	47	59 Chev	300	1,500
2. Lee Petty	Petty Enterprises	42	59 Plym	299	1,000
3. Buck Baker	Lynton Tyson	87	59 Chev	293	700
4. Buddy Baker	Lynton Tyson	88	59 Chev	291	500
5. Glen Wood	Tom Vernon	98	59 Ford	288	400

1962 Grand National Race No. 6
February 25, 1962 Average Speed: 53.161

Driver	Owner	Car #	Make	Laps	Winnings
1. Joe Weatherly	Bud Moore	8	61 Pont	78	500
2. Richard Petty	Petty Enterprises	43	62 Plym	78	300
3. Ralph Earnhardt	Robert Smith	75	61 Pont	77	200
4. Jack Smith	Jack Smith	47	61 Pont	77	150
5. Buddy Baker	Buck Baker	87	61 Chrys	77	138

1957 Grand National Race No. 2
December 2, 1956 Average Speed: 55.883

Driver	Owner	Car #	Make	Laps	Winnings
1. Marvin Panch	Pete DePaolo	98	56 Ford	200	650
2. Paul Goldsmith	Smokey Yunick	3	56 Chev	200	525
3. Bill Amick	Pete DePaolo	97	56 Ford	199	400
4. Tiny Lund	Gus Holzmueller	16	56 Chev	194	320
5. Lee Petty	Petty Enterprises	42	56 Dodg	193	290

1957 Grand National Race No. 51
October 13, 1957 Average Speed: 59.553

Driver	Owner	Car #	Make	Laps	Winnings
1. Fireball Roberts	Fireball Roberts	22	57 Ford	200	900
2. Lee Petty	Petty Enterprises	42	57 Olds	200	575
3. Ken Rush	Sam Rice	26	57 Ford	197	375
4. Marvin Panch	Marvin Panch	98	57 Ford	193	280
5. Jack Smith	Jack Smith	47	57 Chev	192	245

1959 Grand National Race No. 5
March 8, 1959 Average Speed: 59.239

Driver	Owner	Car #	Make	Laps	Winnings
1. Curtis Turner	Doc White	41	59 Ford	200	800
2. Cotton Owens	W. H. Watson	6	58 Pont	199	525
3. Lee Petty	Petty Enterprises	42	57 Olds	198	350
4. Junior Johnson	Paul Spaulding	11	57 Ford	196	250
5. Speedy Thompson	Steve Pierce	1	57 Chev	196	225

1962 Grand National Race No. 1
November 5, 1961 Average Speed: 59.405

Driver	Owner	Car #	Make	Laps	Winnings
1. Jack Smith	Jack Smith	46	61 Pont	200	800
2. Joe Weatherly	Bud Moore	8	61 Pont	200	525
3. Cotton Owens	Cotton Owens	6	61 Pont	198	375
4. Rex White	Rex White	4	61 Chev	198	275
5. Ned Jarrett	Bee Gee Holloway	11	61 Chev	196	350

1962 Grand National Race No. 20
May 6, 1962 Average Speed: 57.052

Driver	Owner	Car #	Make	Laps	Winnings
1. Joe Weatherly	Bud Moore	8	61 Pont	200	1,000
2. Cotton Owens	Cotton Owens	6	60 Pont	200	600
3. Wendell Scott	Wendell Scott	34	61 Chev	192	400
4. Jack Smith	Jack Smith	47	61 Pont	191	300
5. Maurice Petty	Petty Enterprises	41	62 Plym	188	275

Concord Speedway *continued*

1964 Grand National Race No. 1 Textile 250
November 10, 1963 Average Speed: 56.897

Driver	Owner	Car #	Make	Laps	Winnings
1. Ned Jarrett	Charles Robinson	11	63 Ford	250	1,350
2. Joe Weatherly	Bud Moore	8	63 Pont	250	1,000
3. Richard Petty	Petty Enterprises	42	63 Plym	248	650
4. David Pearson	Cotton Owens	5	63 Dodg	241	500
5. Maurice Petty	Petty Enterprises	41	63 Plym	241	400

1964 Grand National Race No. 29
June 11, 1964 Average Speed: 66.352

Driver	Owner	Car #	Make	Laps	Winnings
1. Richard Petty	Petty Enterprises	43	64 Plym	200	1,000
2. David Pearson	Cotton Owens	6	64 Dodg	200	600
3. Ned Jarrett	Bondy Long	11	64 Ford	198	400
4. Wendell Scott	Wendell Scott	34	63 Ford	191	300
5. Curtis Crider	Curtis Crider	02	63 Merc	185	275

Dog Track Speedway
Moyock, NC
Quarter-mile Dirt Track

(aka Dogtrack Raceway; Moyock Speedway) Quarter-mile dirt oval opened in August 1960. First NASCAR Winston Cup (then Grand National) race staged on 9/11/62 (won by Ned Jarrett). Track paved in 1964 and enlarged to .333-mile oval. Final Grand National event held on 5/29/66 (won by David Pearson).

Winston Cup Starts
Wendell Scott   7

Winston Cup Victories
Ned Jarrett   4

Winston Cup Poles
Ned Jarrett   2
Richard Petty   2

Winston Cup Money
Ned Jarrett $4,631

Most Cars Started
25—November 7, 1965 Tidewater 300
25—May 29, 1966

Fewest Cars Started
14—July 11, 1963

Narrowest Margin of Victory
N/A

Slowest Race
43.000 MPH—September 24, 1963

Race Record
63.965 MPH—August 13, 1964
Moyock 300

Most Cautions
N/A

Most Race Leaders
3—November 7, 1965 Tidewater 300

Most Cars Running at Finish
15—November 7, 1965 Tidewater 300

1962 Grand National Race No. 48
September 11, 1962 Average Speed: 43.078

Driver	Owner	Car #	Make	Laps	Winnings
1. Ned Jarrett	Bee Gee Holloway	11	62 Chev	250	775
2. Joe Weatherly	Bud Moore	8	61 Pont	249	500
3. Curtis Crider	Curtis Crider	62	62 Merc	240	380
4. Melvin Bradley	Melvin Bradley	27	62 Chev	235	290
5. George Green	Jess Potter	1	60 Chev	228	245

1963 Grand National Race No. 49
September 24, 1963 Average Speed: 43.000

Driver	Owner	Car #	Make	Laps	Winnings
1. Ned Jarrett	Charles Robinson	11	63 Ford	300	645
2. Joe Weatherly	Bud Moore	8	63 Merc	300	680
3. David Pearson	Cotton Owens	5	63 Dodg	291	375
4. Richard Petty	Petty Enterprises	42	63 Plym	290	300
5. Fred Lorenzen	Holman-Moody	28	63 Ford	289	250

1965 Grand National Race No. 42 Moyock 300
August 24, 1965 Average Speed: 63.047

Driver	Owner	Car #	Make	Laps	Winnings
1. Dick Hutcherson	Holman-Moody	29	65 Ford	300	1,000
2. Ned Jarrett	Bondy Long	11	65 Ford	300	600
3. Richard Petty	Petty Enterprises	43	65 Plym	300	600
4. Tiny Lund	Lyle Stelter	55	64 Ford	298	300
5. Sonny Hutchins	Junie Donlavey	90	64 Ford	297	275

1963 Grand National Race No. 32
July 11, 1963 Average Speed: 45.464

Driver	Owner	Car #	Make	Laps	Winnings
1. Jimmy Pardue	Pete Stewart	54	63 Ford	250	550
2. Ned Jarrett	Charles Robinson	11	63 Ford	250	500
3. Buck Baker	Buck Baker	87	63 Pont	246	365
4. Mark Hurley	Mark Hurley	61	63 Ford	241	300
5. Neil Castles	Buck Baker	86	62 Chrys	236	255

1964 Grand National Race No. 46 Moyock 300
August 13, 1964 Average Speed: 63.965

Driver	Owner	Car #	Make	Laps	Winnings
1. Ned Jarrett	Bondy Long	11	64 Ford	300	1,000
2. David Pearson	Cotton Owens	6	64 Dodg	299	600
3. Richard Petty	Petty Enterprises	43	64 Plym	296	400
4. Bunkie Blackburn	Casper Hensley	82	64 Pont	294	300
5. Bill McMahan	Casper Hensley	42	63 Pont	286	275

1965 Grand National Race No. 55 Tidewater 300
November 7, 1965 Average Speed: 63.773

Driver	Owner	Car #	Make	Laps	Winnings
1. Ned Jarrett	Bondy Long	11	65 Ford	300	1,111
2. Bobby Isaac	Rex Lovette	26	65 Ford	299	600
3. Buddy Baker	Buck Baker	87	65 Chev	297	400
4. Jim Paschal	Petty Enterprises	42	65 Plym	297	300
5. Tom Pistone	Glenn Sweet	59	64 Ford	295	275

1966 Grand National Race No. 21
May 29, 1966 Average Speed: 61.913

Driver	Owner	Car #	Make	Laps	Winnings
1. David Pearson	Cotton Owens	6	64 Dodg	301	1,000
2. Tiny Lund	Lyle Stelter	55	64 Ford	300	600
3. James Hylton	Bud Hartje	48	65 Dodg	298	400
4. John Sears	L. G. DeWitt	4	64 Ford	294	300
5. Wendell Scott	Wendell Scott	34	65 Ford	291	275

Forsyth County Fairgrounds
Winston-Salem, NC
Half-mile Dirt Track

(aka Winston-Salem Fairgrounds; Dixie Classic Fairgrounds) Half-mile dirt oval built circa 1929. First NASCAR Winston Cup (then Grand National) race staged on 5/29/55 (won by Lee Petty). Only other NASCAR race was run on 8/7/55 (won by Lee Petty). Final auto racing event was held in October 1963.

Winston Cup Starts
13 drivers tied with 2

Winston Cup Victories
Lee Petty   2

Winston Cup Poles
Tim Flock   1
Fonty Flock   1

Winston Cup Money
Lee Petty $2,100

Most Cars Started
23—May 29, 1955

Fewest Cars Started
22—August 7, 1955

Narrowest Margin of Victory
6 car lengths—August 2, 1955

Slowest Race
50.111 MPH—August 7, 1955

Race Record
50.583 MPH—May 29, 1955

Most Cautions
8—May 29, 1955

Most Race Leaders
3—May 29, 1955

Most Cars Running at Finish
12—May 29, 1955
12—August 7, 1955

1955 Grand National Race No. 18
May 29, 1955 Average Speed: 50.583

Driver	Owner	Car #	Make	Laps	Winnings
1. Lee Petty	Petty Enterprises	42	54 Chrys	200	1,000
2. Jim Paschal	Ernest Woods	78	55 Olds	200	650
3. Fred Dove	Fred Dove	71	55 Olds	197	450
4. Dick Rathmann	John Ditz	3	55 Chrys	193	350
5. John Dodd Jr.	John Dodd, Sr.	171	55 Dodg	190	300

1955 Grand National Race No. 32
August 7, 1955 Average Speed: 50.111

Driver	Owner	Car #	Make	Laps	Winnings
1. Lee Petty	Petty Enterprises	42	55 Dodg	200	1,100
2. Jim Paschal	Ernest Woods	78	55 Olds	200	700
3. Buck Baker	Buck Baker	89	55 Buick	199	475
4. Billy Carden	Bishop Brothers	8	55 Buick	198	365
5. Eddie Skinner	Frank Dodge	28	53 Olds	189	310

Gastonia Fairgrounds
Gastonia, NC
.333-Mile Dirt Track

(aka Spindle City Fairgrounds; Gaston Speedway; Lowell Fairgrounds) .333-mile dirt oval built circa 1953. Only NASCAR Winston Cup (then Grand National) race staged on 9/12/58 (won by Buck Baker). Track closed in late 1980s.

Winston Cup Victories
Buck Baker   1

Winston Cup Poles
Tiny Lund   1

Winston Cup Money
Buck Baker $800

Most Cars Started
19—September 12, 1958

Narrowest Margin of Victory
N/A

Race Record
47.856 MPH—September 12, 1958

Most Race Leaders
N/A

Most Cars Running at Finish
14—September 12, 1958

1958 Grand National Race No. 45
September 12, 1958 Average Speed: 47.856

Driver	Owner	Car #	Make	Laps	Winnings
1. Buck Baker	Buck Baker	87	57 Chev	200	800
2. Lee Petty	Petty Enterprises	42	57 Olds	200	525
3. Bob Welborn	J. H. Petty	49	57 Chev	200	350
4. Whitey Norman	Whitey Norman	41	57 Chev	196	250
5. Speedy Thompson	Speedy Thompson	46	57 Chev	193	225

Greensboro Agricultural Fairgrounds
Greensboro, NC
.333-mile Dirt Track

(aka Central Carolina Fairgrounds; Greensboro Fairgrounds) Track originally built circa 1926. A .333-mile track opened in June 1953. Grandstands burned down on 5/1/55, and bleachers were rebuilt later that year. First NASCAR Winston Cup (then Grand National) race staged on 4/28/57 (won by Paul Goldsmith). Final race staged on 5/11/58 (won by Bob Welborn). Track closed in 1957.

Winston Cup Starts
L. D. Austin	3
Buck Baker	3
Brownie King	3
Lee Petty	3
Jack Smith	3
Speedy Thompson	3

Winston Cup Victories
Buck Baker	1
Paul Goldsmith	1
Bob Welborn	1

Winston Cup Poles
Buck Baker	1
Ken Rush	1
Bob Welborn	1

Winston Cup Money
Buck Baker	$1,520

Most Cars Started
31—October 27, 1957

Fewest Cars Started
19—April 28, 1957

Narrowest Margin of Victory
5 seconds April 28, 1957

Slowest Race
38.927 MPH—October 27, 1957

Race Record
49.905 MPH—April 28, 1957

Most Cautions
4—April 28, 1957

Most Race Leaders
2—April 28, 1957
2—October 27, 1957
2—May 11, 1958

Most Cars Running at Finish
N/A

1957 Grand National Race No. 13
April 28, 1957 Average Speed: 49.905

	Driver	Owner	Car #	Make	Laps	Winnings
1.	Paul Goldsmith	Smokey Yunick	3	57 Ford	250	700
2.	Jack Smith	Hugh Babb	47	57 Chev	250	525
3.	Buck Baker	Hugh Babb	87	57 Chev	249	400
4.	Ralph Moody	Pete DePaolo	12	57 Ford	248	430
5.	Fireball Roberts	Pete DePaolo	22	57 Ford	247	270

1957 Grand National Race No. 53
October 27, 1957 Average Speed: 38.927

	Driver	Owner	Car #	Make	Laps	Winnings
1.	Buck Baker	Buck Baker	87	57 Chev	250	900
2.	Speedy Thompson	Speedy Thompson	46	57 Chev	—	575
3.	Joe Weatherly	Holman-Moody	12	57 Ford	—	375
4.	Jack Smith	Jack Smith	47	57 Chev	—	280
5.	Lee Petty	Petty Enterprises	42	57 Olds	—	245

1958 Grand National Race No. 16
May 11, 1958 Average Speed: 45.628

	Driver	Owner	Car #	Make	Laps	Winnings
1.	Bob Welborn	J. H. Petty	44	57 Chev	150	600
2.	Lee Petty	Petty Enterprises	42	57 Olds	149	500
3.	Junior Johnson	Paul Spaulding	11	57 Ford	148	355
4.	Speedy Thompson	Speedy Thompson	46	57 Chev	147	260
5.	Doug Cox	Doug Cox	30	57 Ford	147	240

Harnett Speedway
Spring Lake, NC
Half-mile Dirt Track

Half-mile dirt track built in 1952. One Winston Cup (then Grand National) race run on 3/8/53 (won by Herb Thomas). Track closed circa 1970.

Winston Cup Victories
Herb Thomas	1

Winston Cup Poles
Herb Thomas	1

Winston Cup Money
Herb Thomas	$1,000

Most Cars Started
32—March 8, 1953

Narrowest Margin of Victory
3 laps plus—March 8, 1953

Race Record
48.826 MPH—March 8, 1953

Most Race Leaders
1—March 8, 1953

Most Cars Running at Finish
N/A

1953 Grand National Race No. 3
March 8, 1953 Average Speed: 48.826

	Driver	Owner	Car #	Make	Laps	Winnings
1.	Herb Thomas	Herb Thomas	92	53 Huds	200	1,000
2.	Dick Rathmann	Walt Chapman	120	53 Huds	197	700
3.	Lee Petty	Petty Enterprises	42	53 Dodg	—	450
4.	Dick Passwater	Frank Arford	78	53 Olds	—	350
5.	Herschel Buchanan	Herschel Buchanan	1	53 Nash	—	200

Harris Speedway
Harris, NC
.333-mile Paved Track

(aka Tri-City Motor Speedway; Harris Motor Speedway) .3-mile paved track built in 1964. First NASCAR Winston Cup (then Grand National) race staged on 5/5/56 (won by Speedy Thompson). Final NASCAR event held on 5/30/65 (won by Ned Jarrett). Track is still in operation.

Winston Cup Starts

Buddy Arrington	2
Neil Castles	2
Doug Cooper	2
Ned Jarrett	2
Larry Manning	2
J. T. Putney	2
Wendell Scott	2
Roy Tyner	2

Winston Cup Victories

Ned Jarrett	1
Richard Petty	1

Winston Cup Poles

Paul Lewis	1
Billy Wade	1

Winston Cup Money

Ned Jarrett	$1,600

Most Cars Started
22—May 30, 1965

Fewest Cars Started
21—October 25, 1964

Narrowest Margin of Victory
1 lap plus—October 25, 1964

Slowest Race
56.851 MPH—May 30, 1965

Race Record
59.009 MPH—October 25, 1964

Most Cautions
3—October 25, 1964

Most Race Leaders
3—October 25, 1964

Most Cars Running at Finish
12—October 25, 1964

1964 Grand National Race No. 60
October 25, 1964 Average Speed: 59.009

Driver	Owner	Car #	Make	Laps	Winnings
1. Richard Petty	Petty Enterprises	41	64 Plym	334	1,000
2. Ned Jarrett	Bondy Long	11	64 Ford	333	600
3. Curtis Crider	Curtis Crider	02	63 Merc	325	400
4. Bobby Isaac	Cotton Owens	5	64 Dodg	324	300
5. Larry Thomas	Wade Younts	36	63 Dodg	321	275

1965 Grand National Race No. 22
May 30, 1965 Average Speed: 56.851

Driver	Owner	Car #	Make	Laps	Winnings
1. Ned Jarrett	Bondy Long	11	65 Ford	334	1,000
2. G. C. Spencer	G. C. Spencer	49	64 Ford	330	600
3. Dick Dixon	Dan Colone	8	63 Ford	326	400
4. Dick Hutcherson	Holman-Moody	29	65 Ford	325	300
5. J. T. Putney	Herman Beam	19	65 Chev	317	275

Hickory Speedway
Hickory, NC
Half-mile Dirt Track

(aka Hickory Motor Speedway) Dirt track built in 1951. Originally measured at half-mile. Later re-measured at .4-mile and today listed as .362-mile. First NASCAR Winston Cup (then Grand National) race staged on 5/16/53 (won by Tim Flock). Track paved in 1967. First Grand National race run on pavement was 9/8/67 (won by Richard Petty, his 5th of his record-setting 10 straight wins). Final Winston Cup Grand National race run on 8/28/71 (won by Tiny Lund in a Camaro). The track still hosts a variety of NASCAR weekly and special events.

Winston Cup Starts
Buck Baker   24

Winston Cup Victories
Junior Johnson   7

Winston Cup Poles
Junior Johnson   6

Winston Cup Money
Richard Petty $14,975

Most Cars Started
33—September 8, 1967
Buddy Shuman Memorial

Fewest Cars Started
12—August 29, 1953

Narrowest Margin of Victory
1 car length—June 28, 1958

Slowest Race
56.962 MPH—November 13, 1955

Race Record
82.872 MPH—June 19, 1954

Most Cautions
6—May 7, 1955
6—May 12, 1956
6—April 3, 1966 Hickory 250
6—September 8, 1967
Buddy Shuman Memorial

Most Race Leaders
6—July 20, 1957
6—April 9, 1967 Hickory 250

Most Cars Running at Finish
23—June 28, 1958

1953 Grand National Race No. 10
May 16, 1953

Driver	Owner	Car #	Make	Laps	Winnings
1. Tim Flock	Ted Chester	91	53 Huds	200	1,000
2. Joe Eubanks	Phil Oates	82	52 Huds	—	700
3. Ray Duhigg	J. H. Petty	44	52 Plym	—	450
4. Dick Passwater	Frank Arford	78	53 Olds	—	350
5. Dick Rathmann	Walt Chapman	120	53 Huds	—	200

1953 Grand National Race No. 29
August 29, 1953

Driver	Owner	Car #	Make	Laps	Winnings
1. Fonty Flock	Frank Christian	14	53 Huds	200	1,000
2. Herb Thomas	Herb Thomas	92	53 Huds	—	700
3. Joe Eubanks	Phil Oates	82	52 Huds	—	450
4. Lee Petty	Petty Enterprises	42	53 Dodg	—	350
5. Jimmie Lewallen		22	52 Plym	—	200

1954 Grand National Race No. 19
June 19, 1954 Average Speed: 82.872

Driver	Owner	Car #	Make	Laps	Winnings
1. Herb Thomas	Herb Thomas	92	54 Huds	200	1,000
2. Lee Petty	Petty Enterprises	42	54 Chrys	200	650
3. Buck Baker	Ernest Woods	88	54 Olds	198	450
4. Dick Rathmann	John Ditz	3	54 Huds	198	350
5. Junior Johnson	George Miller	23	54 Huds	194	300

1955 Grand National Race No. 12
May 7, 1955 Average Speed: 58.823

Driver	Owner	Car #	Make	Laps	Winnings
1. Junior Johnson	B & L Motors	55	55 Olds	200	1,000
2. Tim Flock	Carl Kiekhaefer	300	55 Chrys	200	650
3. Jim Paschal	Ernest Woods	78	55 Olds	200	450
4. Lee Petty	Petty Enterprises	42	55 Chrys	198	350
5. Jimmie Lewallen	Joe Blair	5	54 Merc	196	300

1956 Grand National Race No. 1
November 13, 1955 Average Speed: 56.962

Driver	Owner	Car #	Make	Laps	Winnings
1. Tim Flock	Carl Kiekhaefer	301	55 Chrys	200	1,150
2. Curtis Turner	Charlie Schwam	99	56 Ford	200	720
3. Lee Petty	Petty Enterprises	42	56 Dodg	200	505
4. Dink Widenhouse	Dink Widenhouse	B-29	56 Ford	199	365
5. Jim Paschal	Bob Welborn	44	55 Chev	199	360

1956 Grand National Race No. 16
May 12, 1956 Average Speed: 59.442

Driver	Owner	Car #	Make	Laps	Winnings
1. Speedy Thompson	Carl Kiekhaefer	300c	56 Chrys	200	1,100
2. Billy Myers	Bill Stroppe	14	56 Merc	200	700
3. Buck Baker	Carl Kiekhaefer	500B	56 Dodg	200	475
4. Herb Thomas	Carl Kiekhaefer	502	56 Dodg	200	365
5. Gwyn Staley	Hubert Westmoreland	2	56 Chev	200	310

1956 Grand National Race No. 55 Buddy Shuman Memorial
November 11, 1956 Average Speed: 66.420

Driver	Owner	Car #	Make	Laps	Winnings
1. Speedy Thompson	Carl Kiekhaefer	300	56 Chrys	250	850
2. Ralph Earnhardt	Pete DePaolo	22	56 Ford	250	625
3. Buck Baker	Carl Kiekhaefer	300B	56 Chrys	249	450
4. Ralph Moody	Pete DePaolo	12	56 Ford	249	350
5. Doug Cox	John Foster	86	56 Ford	247	310

1957 Grand National Race No. 32
July 20, 1957 Average Speed: 58.737

Driver	Owner	Car #	Make	Laps	Winnings
1. Jack Smith	Jack Smith	47	57 Chev	250	1,000
2. Lee Petty	Petty Enterprises	42	57 Olds	250	625
3. Joe Weatherly	Holman-Moody	12	57 Ford	250	400
4. Gwyn Staley	J. H. Petty	38	57 Chev	250	280
5. Fireball Roberts	Fireball Roberts	22	57 Ford	250	245

1958 Grand National Race No. 26
June 28, 1958 Average Speed: 62.413

Driver	Owner	Car #	Make	Laps	Winnings
1. Lee Petty	Petty Enterprises	42	57 Olds	250	800
2. Junior Johnson	Paul Spaulding	11	57 Ford	250	525
3. Speedy Thompson	Speedy Thompson	46	57 Chev	250	350
4. Jack Smith	Jack Smith	47	57 Chev	248	250
5. Shorty Rollins	Shorty Rollins	99	58 Ford	247	225

1959 Grand National Race No. 12
May 2, 1959 Average Speed: 62.165

Driver	Owner	Car #	Make	Laps	Winnings
1. Junior Johnson	Paul Spaulding	11	57 Ford	250	800
2. Joe Weatherly	Doc White	41	59 Ford	248	525
3. Lee Petty	Petty Enterprises	42	57 Olds	247	350
4. Ken Rush	Paul Walton	40	57 Chev	246	250
5. Cotton Owens	W. H. Watson	6	58 Pont	246	225

Hickory Speedway *continued*

1959 Grand National Race No. 37
September 11, 1959 Average Speed: 63.380

Driver	Owner	Car #	Make	Laps	Winnings
1. Lee Petty	Petty Enterprises	42	59 Plym	250	900
2. Buck Baker	Lynton Tyson	88	59 Chev	249	525
3. Rex White	Rex White	4	59 Chev	248	375
4. Junior Johnson	Wood Brothers	21	58 Ford	248	275
5. Brownie King	Jess Potter	31	57 Chev	243	250

1960 Grand National Race No. 11
April 15, 1960 Average Speed: 66.347

Driver	Owner	Car #	Make	Laps	Winnings
1. Joe Weatherly	Holman-Moody	12	60 Ford	250	800
2. Ned Jarrett	Ned Jarrett	11	60 Ford	250	525
3. Richard Petty	Petty Enterprises	43	60 Plym	249	375
4. Bob Welborn	Bob Welborn	49	60 Chev	247	275
5. Tom Pistone	W. T. Coppedge	59	60 Chev	246	250

1960 Grand National Race No. 36 Buddy Shuman Memorial
September 9, 1960 Average Speed: 69.998

Driver	Owner	Car #	Make	Laps	Winnings
1. Junior Johnson	John Masoni	27	60 Chev	250	800
2. Possum Jones	Tom Daniels	2	60 Chev	249	525
3. Rex White	Rex White	4	59 Chev	246	375
4. David Pearson	David Pearson	67	59 Chev	246	275
5. Ned Jarrett	Ned Jarrett	11	60 Ford	241	250

1961 Grand National Race No. 16
April 22, 1961 Average Speed: 66.654

Driver	Owner	Car #	Make	Laps	Winnings
1. Junior Johnson	Rex Lovette	27	61 Pont	250	950
2. Buck Baker	Buck Baker	86	62 Chrys	250	625
3. Rex White	Rex White	4	60 Chev	245	525
4. G. C. Spencer	G. C. Spencer	48	60 Chev	245	275
5. Jimmy Pardue	Jimmy Pardue	54	59 Chev	242	250

1961 Grand National Race No. 43 Buddy Shuman Memorial
September 8, 1961 Average Speed: 67.529

Driver	Owner	Car #	Make	Laps	Winnings
1. Rex White	Rex White	4	61 Chev	250	900
2. Jack Smith	Jack Smith	47	61 Pont	249	525
3. Buck Baker	Buck Baker	86	61 Chrys	249	375
4. Cotton Owens	Cotton Owens	6	60 Pont	248	275
5. Emanuel Zervakis	Monroe Shook	85	60 Chev	246	250

1962 Grand National Race No. 19 Hickory 250
May 5, 1962 Average Speed: 71.216

Driver	Owner	Car #	Make	Laps	Winnings
1. Jack Smith	Jack Smith	47	61 Pont	250	1,000
2. Rex White	Rex White	4	62 Chev	248	600
3. Joe Weatherly	Bud Moore	8	61 Pont	246	400
4. Jim Paschal	Cliff Stewart	2	62 Pont	240	300
5. Ralph Earnhardt	Robert Smith	75	61 Pont	237	275

1962 Grand National Race No. 46 Buddy Shuman Memorial
September 7, 1962 Average Speed: 70.574

Driver	Owner	Car #	Make	Laps	Winnings
1. Rex White	Rex White	4	62 Chev	250	1,000
2. Jimmy Pardue	Jimmy Pardue	54	62 Pont	241	600
3. Buck Baker	Buck Baker	87	62 Chrys	240	400
4. Larry Thomas	Wade Younts	36	62 Dodg	240	300
5. Joe Weatherly	Bud Moore	8	61 Pont	239	275

1963 Grand National Race No. 12 Hickory 250
March 24, 1963 Average Speed: 67.950

Driver	Owner	Car #	Make	Laps	Winnings
1. Junior Johnson	Ray Fox	3	63 Chev	250	1,150
2. Richard Petty	Petty Enterprises	43	63 Plym	249	700
3. Ned Jarrett	Charles Robinson	11	63 Ford	248	450
4. Jim Paschal	Petty Enterprises	41	62 Plym	246	300
5. Roy Mayne	C. L. Kilpatrick	33	62 Chev	237	275

1963 Grand National Race No. 46 Buddy Shuman Memorial
September 6, 1963 Average Speed: 62.926

Driver	Owner	Car #	Make	Laps	Winnings
1. Junior Johnson	Ray Fox	3	63 Chev	250	1,775
2. G. C. Spencer	G. C. Spencer	03	62 Chev	246	700
3. Bob Welborn	Fred Harb	17	62 Pont	237	450
4. Jimmy Massey	Hubert Westmoreland	96	61 Chev	232	300
5. Larry Thomas	Wade Younts	36	62 Dodg	232	275

1964 Grand National Race No. 23 Hickory 250
May 16, 1964 Average Speed: 69.364

Driver	Owner	Car #	Make	Laps	Winnings
1. Ned Jarrett	Bondy Long	11	64 Ford	250	1,150
2. David Pearson	Cotton Owens	6	64 Dodg	249	600
3. Richard Petty	Petty Enterprises	43	64 Plym	249	400
4. LeeRoy Yarbrough	Louie Weathersby	45	63 Plym	248	300
5. Buddy Baker	J. C. Parker	87	63 Dodg	244	275

1964 Grand National Race No. 52 Buddy Shuman Memorial
September 11, 1964 Average Speed: 67.797

Driver	Owner	Car #	Make	Laps	Winnings
1. David Pearson	Cotton Owens	6	64 Dodg	250	2,035
2. Larry Thomas	Herman Beam	19	64 Ford	247	600
3. Buck Baker	Ray Fox	3	64 Dodg	246	400
4. Jimmy Pardue	Charles Robinson	54	64 Plym	246	300
5. Richard Petty	Petty Enterprises	43	64 Plym	238	275

1965 Grand National Race No. 18 Hickory 250
May 16, 1965 Average Speed: 72.130

Driver	Owner	Car #	Make	Laps	Winnings
1. Junior Johnson	Rex Lovette	26	65 Ford	250	1,000
2. Ned Jarrett	Bondy Long	11	65 Ford	250	600
3. G. C. Spencer	G. C. Spencer	49	64 Ford	245	400
4. Paul Lewis	Paul Lewis	27	64 Ford	241	300
5. Buddy Baker	Buck Baker	87	65 Olds	240	275

1965 Grand National Race No. 46 Buddy Shuman Memorial
September 10, 1965 Average Speed: 74.365

Driver	Owner	Car #	Make	Laps	Winnings
1. Richard Petty	Petty Enterprises	43	65 Plym	250	1,200
2. David Pearson	Cotton Owens	6	65 Dodg	250	600
3. Ned Jarrett	Bondy Long	11	65 Ford	248	400
4. Junior Johnson	Rex Lovette	26	65 Ford	248	300
5. J. T. Putney	Herman Beam	19	65 Chev	246	275

1966 Grand National Race No. 9 Hickory 250
April 3, 1966 Average Speed: 68.428

Driver	Owner	Car #	Make	Laps	Winnings
1. David Pearson	Cotton Owens	6	64 Dodg	250	1,000
2. Curtis Turner	Wood Brothers	41	66 Ford	250	600
3. Bobby Isaac	Junior Johnson	26	66 Ford	248	400
4. Ned Jarrett	Bondy Long	11	66 Ford	248	500
5. Paul Goldsmith	Bob Cooper	02	65 Plym	247	275

Hickory Speedway *continued*

1966 Grand National Race No. 43 Buddy Shuman Memorial
September 9, 1966 Average Speed: 76.923

Driver	Owner	Car #	Make	Laps	Winnings
1. David Pearson	Cotton Owens	6	65 Dodg	250	1,000
2. Richard Petty	Petty Enterprises	42	66 Plym	249	600
3. Paul Lewis	Paul Lewis	1	65 Plym	248	400
4. James Hylton	Bud Hartje	48	65 Dodg	242	300
5. Hank Thomas	W. S. Jenkins	92	64 Ford	240	275

1967 Grand National Race No. 12 Hickory 250
April 9, 1967 Average Speed: 69.699

Driver	Owner	Car #	Make	Laps	Winnings
1. Richard Petty	Petty Enterprises	43	67 Plym	250	1,000
2. Dick Hutcherson	Bondy Long	29	67 Ford	248	600
3. James Hylton	Bud Hartje	48	65 Dodg	247	400
4. Jim Paschal	Tom Friedkin	14	65 Plym	246	300
5. Bobby Allison	Bobby Allison	2	65 Chev	245	275

1967 Grand National Race No. 41 Buddy Shuman Memorial
September 8, 1967 Average Speed: 71.414

Driver	Owner	Car #	Make	Laps	Winnings
1. Richard Petty	Petty Enterprises	43	67 Plym	250	1,500
2. Jack Ingram	Tommy Ingram	81	66 Chev	249	600
3. Jim Paschal	Tom Friedkin	14	67 Plym	248	400
4. James Hylton	Bud Hartje	48	65 Dodg	245	300
5. Elmo Langley	Henry Woodfield	64	66 Ford	244	275

1968 Grand National Race No. 8
April 7, 1968 Average Speed: 79.435

Driver	Owner	Car #	Make	Laps	Winnings
1. Richard Petty	Petty Enterprises	43	67 Plym	250	1,200
2. David Pearson	Holman-Moody	17	68 Ford	250	600
3. Bobby Isaac	Nord Krauskopf	71	67 Dodg	250	400
4. Friday Hassler	Red Sharp	39	66 Chev	246	300
5. James Hylton	James Hylton	48	67 Dodg	244	275

1968 Grand National Race No. 40 Buddy Shuman Memorial
September 6, 1968 Average Speed: 80.357

Driver	Owner	Car #	Make	Laps	Winnings
1. David Pearson	Holman-Moody	17	68 Ford	250	1,000
2. Bobby Isaac	Nord Krauskopf	71	67 Dodg	250	600
3. Buddy Baker	Ray Fox	3	68 Dodg	249	400
4. Richard Petty	Petty Enterprises	43	68 Plym	244	500
5. Elmo Langley	Elmo Langley	64	66 Ford	244	275

1969 Grand National Race No. 12 Hickory 250
April 6, 1969 Average Speed: 79.086

Driver	Owner	Car #	Make	Laps	Winnings
1. Bobby Isaac	Nord Krauskopf	71	69 Dodg	250	1,700
2. Richard Petty	Petty Enterprises	43	69 Ford	248	1,300
3. David Pearson	Holman-Moody	17	69 Ford	245	1,100
4. Dave Marcis	Milt Lunda	30	69 Dodg	244	700
5. G. C. Spencer	G. C. Spencer	49	67 Plym	243	600

1969 Grand National Race No. 42 Buddy Shuman Memorial
September 5, 1969 Average Speed: 80.519

Driver	Owner	Car #	Make	Laps	Winnings
1. Bobby Isaac	Nord Krauskopf	71	69 Dodg	250	1,700
2. Neil Castles	Neil Castles	06	69 Dodg	249	1,200
3. Richard Petty	Petty Enterprises	43	69 Ford	247	900
4. John Sears	L. G. DeWitt	4	69 Ford	246	700
5. Buddy Young	Fred Bear	31	67 Chev	245	600

1970 Grand National Race No. 21 Hickory 276
June 20, 1970 Average Speed: 68.011

Driver	Owner	Car #	Make	Laps	Winnings
1. Bobby Isaac	Nord Krauskopf	71	69 Dodg	276	2,200
2. Dick Brooks	Dick Brooks	32	69 Plym	274	1,500
3. Dave Marcis	Dave Marcis	30	69 Dodg	272	1,000
4. G. C. Spencer	G. C. Spencer	49	69 Plym	269	700
5. Bill Seifert	Bill Seifert	45	69 Ford	268	600

1970 Grand National Race No. 39 Buddy Shuman Memorial
September 11, 1970 Average Speed: 73.365

Driver	Owner	Car #	Make	Laps	Winnings
1. Bobby Isaac	Nord Krauskopf	71	70 Dodg	276	2,200
2. Richard Petty	Petty Enterprises	43	70 Plym	276	1,500
3. Bobby Allison	Bobby Allison	22	69 Dodg	276	1,000
4. Dick Brooks	Dick Brooks	32	69 Plym	273	700
5. James Hylton	James Hylton	48	69 Ford	273	600

1971 Winston Cup GN Race No. 8 Hickory 276
March 21, 1971 Average Speed: 67.700

Driver	Owner	Car #	Make	Laps	Winnings
1. Richard Petty	Petty Enterprises	43	71 Plym	276	2,200
2. David Pearson	Richard Giachetti	44	71 Ford	275	1,500
3. Benny Parsons	L. G. DeWitt	72	70 Ford	273	1,000
4. James Hylton	James Hylton	48	70 Ford	273	700
5. Elmo Langley	Elmo Langley	64	69 Merc	273	600

1971 Winston Cup GN Race No. 39 Buddy Shuman Memorial
August 28, 1971 Average Speed: 72.937

Driver	Owner	Car #	Make	Laps	Winnings
1. Tiny Lund	Ronnie Hopkins	55	69 Chev	276	1,500
2. Elmo Langley	Elmo Langley	64	71 Ford	276	900
3. Richard Petty	Petty Enterprises	43	71 Plym	276	500
4. Bobby Allison	Bobby Allison	12	70 Dodg	276	350
5. Wayne Andrews	Reid Shaw	15	71 Ford	274	325

Jacksonville Speedway
Jacksonville, NC
Half-mile Dirt Track

(aka Onslow Speedway) Half-mile dirt track built in 1952. First NASCAR Winston Cup (then Grand National) race run on 6/30/57 (won by Buck Baker). Final NASCAR Winston Cup (then Grand National) race staged on 11/8/64 (won by Ned Jarrett, the season finale in 1964). Track closed shortly thereafter.

Winston Cup Starts
Buck Baker 2
Tiny Lund 2

Winston Cup Victories
Buck Baker 1
Ned Jarrett 1

Winston Cup Poles
Lee Petty 1
Doug Yates 1

Winston Cup Money
Buck Baker $1,050

Most Cars Started
25—November 8, 1964

Fewest Cars Started
19—June 30, 1957

Narrowest Margin of Victory
1 lap plus—November 8, 1964

Slowest Race
55.342 MPH—June 30, 1957

Race Record
57.535 MPH—November 8, 1964

Most Cautions
4—November 8, 1964

Most Race Leaders
4—November 8, 1964

Most Cars Running at Finish
12—November 8, 1964

1957 Grand National Race No. 27
June 30, 1957 Average Speed: 55.342

Driver	Owner	Car #	Make	Laps	Winnings
1. Buck Baker	Buck Baker	87	57 Chev	200	1,000
2. Jim Paschal	Jim Paschal	17	57 Merc	197	575
3. Tiny Lund	Sam Rice	80	57 Pont	191	400
4. George Green	Jess Potter	33	56 Chev	187	295
5. Jack Smith	Jack Smith	47	57 Chev	179	255

1964 Grand National Race No. 62
November 8, 1964 Average Speed: 57.535

Driver	Owner	Car #	Make	Laps	Winnings
1. Ned Jarrett	Bondy Long	11	64 Ford	200	1,000
2. Richard Petty	Petty Enterprises	43	64 Plym	199	600
3. G. C. Spencer	G. C. Spencer	49	64 Ford	196	400
4. Doug Cooper	Bob Cooper	60	64 Ford	195	300
5. Larry Thomas	Charles Robinson	36	64 Plym	190	275

McCormick Field
Asheville, NC
Quarter-mile Paved Track

Quarter-mile paved oval built circa 1949. Track was laid around a baseball diamond where the minor league baseball team the Asheville Tourists played. Only NASCAR Winston Cup (then Grand National) race staged on 7/12/58 (won by Jim Paschal). Lee Petty crashed into the dugout in preliminary event to Grand National. Races were discontinued in 1959.

Winston Cup Victories
Jim Paschal 1

Winston Cup Poles
Jim Paschal 1

Winston Cup Money
Jim Paschal $570

Most Cars Started
15—July 12, 1958

Narrowest Margin of Victory
1 car length—July 12, 1958

Race Record
46.440 MPH—July 12, 1958

Most Race Leaders
1—July 12, 1958

Most Cars Running at Finish
12—July 12, 1958

1958 Grand National Race No. 29
July 12, 1958 Average Speed: 46.440

Driver	Owner	Car #	Make	Laps	Winnings
1. Jim Paschal	J. H. Petty	49	57 Chev	150	570
2. Cotton Owens	Jim Stephens	6	57 Pont	150	465
3. Rex White	J. H. Petty	44	57 Chev	150	340
4. Lee Petty	Petty Enterprises	42	57 Olds	149	265
5. Jack Smith	Jack Smith	47	57 Chev	148	235

New Asheville Speedway
Asheville, NC
.4-mile Paved Track

(aka Asheville Speedway; New Asheville Motor Speedway; Asheville Motor Speedway) .333-mile paved oval built in 1961 and originally measured at .4-mile oval. First NASCAR Winston Cup (then Grand National) race run on 7/13/62 (won by Jack Smith). Final Winston Cup Grand National race held on 5/12/71 (won by Richard Petty). Track is still in operation.

Winston Cup Starts
Richard Petty 7
Wendell Scott 7

Winston Cup Victories
Ned Jarrett 2
Richard Petty 2

Winston Cup Poles
Richard Petty 5

Winston Cup Money
Richard Petty $4,800

Most Cars Started
23—May 31, 1968 Asheville 300

Fewest Cars Started
17—May 21, 1971 Asheville 300

Narrowest Margin of Victory
N/A

Slowest Race
63.080 MPH—June 2, 1967 Asheville 300

Race Record
78.294 MPH—July 13, 1962

Most Race Leaders
4—July 14, 1963
4—June 2, 1967 Asheville 300

Most Cars Running at Finish
14—July 13, 1962
14—May 31, 1968 Asheville 300

1962 Grand National Race No. 31
July 13, 1962 Average Speed: 78.294

Driver	Owner	Car #	Make	Laps	Winnings
1. Jack Smith	Jack Smith	47	61 Pont	250	1,000
2. Joe Weatherly	Bud Moore	8	61 Pont	249	600
3. Richard Petty	Petty Enterprises	43	62 Plym	248	400
4. Buck Baker	Buck Baker	87	62 Chrys	244	300
5. Ned Jarrett	Bee Gee Holloway	11	62 Chev	241	475

1963 Grand National Race No. 34
July 14, 1963 Average Speed: 63.384

Driver	Owner	Car #	Make	Laps	Winnings
1. Ned Jarrett	Charles Robinson	11	63 Ford	300	1,000
2. Richard Petty	Petty Enterprises	43	63 Plym	300	600
3. David Pearson	Cotton Owens	6	63 Dodg	297	400
4. Joe Weatherly	Petty Enterprises	41	63 Plym	296	500
5. Buck Baker	Buck Baker	87	63 Pont	291	275

1964 Grand National Race No. 27
May 31, 1964 Average Speed: 66.538

Driver	Owner	Car #	Make	Laps	Winnings
1. Ned Jarrett	Bondy Long	11	64 Ford	300	1,000
2. Richard Petty	Petty Enterprises	43	674 Plym	298	600
3. Marvin Panch	Wood Brothers	21	64 Ford	297	400
4. David Pearson	Cotton Owens	6	64 Dodg	293	300
5. Cale Yarborough	Herman Beam	19	64 Ford	293	275

1965 Grand National Race No. 21
May 29, 1965 Average Speed: 66.293

Driver	Owner	Car #	Make	Laps	Winnings
1. Junior Johnson	Rex Lovette	26	65 Ford	300	1,000
2. Ned Jarrett	Bondy Long	11	65 Ford	296	600
3. Dick Dixon	Dan Colone	8	63 Ford	284	400
4. J. T. Putney	Herman Beam	19	65 Chev	283	300
5. Neil Castles	Buck Baker	39	65 Olds	278	275

1966 Grand National Race No. 22 Asheville 300
June 2, 1966 Average Speed: 64.917

Driver	Owner	Car #	Make	Laps	Winnings
1. David Pearson	Cotton Owens	6	64 Dodg	300	1,000
2. J. T. Putney	J. T. Putney	19	66 Chev	299	600
3. John Sears	L. G. DeWitt	4	64 Ford	286	400
4. James Hylton	Bud Hartje	48	65 Dodg	285	300
5. Hank Thomas	W. S. Jenkins	92	64 Ford	284	275

1967 Grand National Race No. 21 Asheville 300
June 2, 1967 Average Speed: 63.080

Driver	Owner	Car #	Make	Laps	Winnings
1. Jim Paschal	Tom Friedkin	14	67 Plym	300	1,000
2. Donnie Allison	Bobby Allison	2	66 Chev	300	600
3. Richard Petty	Petty Enterprises	43	67 Plym	298	400
4. James Hylton	Bud Hartje	48	65 Dodg	297	300
5. Buddy Arrington	Buddy Arrington	67	65 Dodg	281	275

1968 Grand National Race No. 19 Asheville 300
May 31, 1968 Average Speed: 65.741

Driver	Owner	Car #	Make	Laps	Winnings
1. Richard Petty	Petty Enterprises	43	68 Plym	300	1,200
2. Buddy Baker	Ray Fox	3	67 Dodg	299	600
3. Bobby Isaac	Nord Krauskopf	71	67 Dodg	296	400
4. James Hylton	James Hylton	48	67 Dodg	292	300
5. Elmo Langley	Elmo Langley	64	66 Ford	288	275

1971 Winston Cup GN Race No. 19 Asheville 300
May 21, 1971 Average Speed: 71.231

Driver	Owner	Car #	Make	Laps	Winnings
1. Richard Petty	Petty Enterprises	43	71 Plym	300	1,500
2. Elmo Langley	Elmo Langley	64	69 Merc	296	900
3. Cecil Gordon	Cecil Gordon	24	69 Merc	284	500
4. Jabe Thomas	Don Robertson	25	69 Plym	281	350
5. Bill Champion	Bill Champion	10	69 Ford	259	325

North Carolina Motor Speedway
Rockingham, NC
1.017-mile Superspeedway

1-mile track built in 1965. Harold Brasington was consultant in track layout. First NASCAR Winston Cup (then Grand National) race run on 10/31/65 (won by Curtis Turner). Victory was the first and final win for Turner after being re-instated by NASCAR following his "lifetime" suspension for Teamster Union involvement in 1961. David Pearson also scored his 100th career victory here on 3/5/78.

Winston Cup Starts
Dave Marcis   61

Winston Cup Victories
Richard Petty   11

Winston Cup Poles
Mark Martin   5
David Pearson   5
Kyle Petty   5

Winston Cup Money
Rusty Wallace $1,344,830

Most Cars Started
44—March 13, 1966 Peach Blossom 500
44—October 30, 1966 American 500
44—June 18, 1967 Carolina 500
44—October 29, 1967 American 500
44—June 16, 1968 Carolina 500
44—October 27, 1968 American 500

Fewest Cars Started
31—March 2, 1975 Carolina 500

Narrowest Margin of Victory
0.06 seconds—October 23, 1994

Slowest Race
97.860 MPH—March 13, 1977
Carolina 500

Race Record
131.103 MPH—October 24, 1999

Most Cautions
14—March 1, 1981 Carolina 500
14—October 22, 1989 AC Delco 500

Most Race Leaders
13—October 22, 1978 American 500

Most Cars Running at Finish
42—February 27, 2000

1965 Grand National Race No. 54 American 500
October 31, 1965 Average Speed: 101.942

Driver	Owner	Car #	Make	Laps	Winnings
1. Curtis Turner	Wood Brothers	41	65 Ford	500	13,090
2. Cale Yarborough	Banjo Matthews	27	65 Ford	500	6,450
3. Marvin Panch	Wood Brothers	21	65 Ford	498	4,010
4. G. C. Spencer	G. C. Spencer	49	64 Ford	490	2,450
5. Jim Paschal	Petty Enterprises	42	65 Plym	486	2,000

1966 Grand National Race No. 6 Peach Blossom 500
March 13, 1966 Average Speed: 100.027

Driver	Owner	Car #	Make	Laps	Winnings
1. Paul Goldsmith	Ray Nichels	99	66 Plym	500	14,340
2. Cale Yarborough	Banjo Matthews	27	66 Ford	500	7,875
3. Bobby Allison	Betty Lilly	24	65 Ford	488	4,250
4. Harold Smith	Lyle Stelter	55	64 Ford	480	2,675
5. John Sears	L. G. DeWitt	04	64 Ford	478	1,750

1966 Grand National Race No. 49 American 500
October 30, 1966 Average Speed: 104.348

Driver	Owner	Car #	Make	Laps	Winnings
1. Fred Lorenzen	Holman-Moody	28	66 Ford	500	14,550
2. Don White	Ray Nichels	31	66 Dodg	496	7,350
3. Ned Jarrett	Banjo Matthews	11	66 Ford	496	4,700
4. Cale Yarborough	Wood Brothers	21	66 Ford	494	2,250
5. Junior Johnson	Junior Johnson	47	66 Ford	494	1,475

1967 Grand National Race No. 25 Carolina 500
June 18, 1967 Average Speed: 104.682

Driver	Owner	Car #	Make	Laps	Winnings
1. Richard Petty	Petty Enterprises	43	67 Plym	500	16,175
2. Buddy Baker	Ray Fox	3	67 Dodg	499	9,700
3. Dick Hutcherson	Bondy Long	29	67 Ford	498	5,200
4. Cale Yarborough	Wood Brothers	21	67 Ford	496	2,650
5. Darel Dieringer	Junior Johnson	26	67 Ford	494	1,875

1967 Grand National Race No. 48 American 500
October 29, 1967 Average Speed: 98.420

Driver	Owner	Car #	Make	Laps	Winnings
1. Bobby Allison	Holman-Moody	11	67 Ford	500	16,300
2. David Pearson	Holman-Moody	17	67 Ford	499	10,150
3. Paul Goldsmith	Ray Nichels	99	67 Plym	499	5,250
4. A. J. Foyt	Banjo Matthews	27	67 Ford	498	2,800
5. Gordon Johncock	Bud Moore	16	67 Merc	497	1,875

1968 Grand National Race No. 23 Carolina 500
June 16, 1968 Average Speed: 99.338

Driver	Owner	Car #	Make	Laps	Winnings
1. Donnie Allison	Banjo Matthews	27	68 Ford	500	16,675
2. Bobby Allison	Bobby Allison	2	66 Chev	498	9,650
3. James Hylton	James Hylton	48	67 Dodg	494	5,150
4. Richard Brickhouse	Dub Clewis	03	67 Plym	470	2,650
5. Roy Tyner	Don Culpepper	76	66 Ford	469	1,850

1968 Grand National Race No. 48 American 500
October 27, 1968 Average Speed: 105.060

Driver	Owner	Car #	Make	Laps	Winnings
1. Richard Petty	Petty Enterprises	43	68 Plym	500	17,075
2. David Pearson	Holman-Moody	17	68 Ford	500	9,775
3. LeeRoy Yarbrough	Junior Johnson	98	68 Ford	498	5,225
4. Tiny Lund	Bud Moore	16	68 Merc	497	2,800
5. Bobby Allison	Tom Friedkin	14	68 Plym	496	1,850

1969 Grand National Race No. 7 Carolina 500
March 9, 1969 Average Speed: 102.569

Driver	Owner	Car #	Make	Laps	Winnings
1. David Pearson	Holman-Moody	17	69 Ford	500	16,150
2. Bobby Allison	Mario Rossi	22	69 Dodg	500	9,500
3. Cale Yarborough	Wood Brothers	21	69 Merc	498	4,975
4. Paul Goldsmith	Ray Nichels	99	69 Dodg	497	2,700
5. Richard Petty	Petty Enterprises	43	69 Ford	492	1,850

1969 Grand National Race No. 51 American 500
October 26, 1969 Average Speed: 111.938

Driver	Owner	Car #	Make	Laps	Winnings
1. LeeRoy Yarbrough	Junior Johnson	98	69 Ford	492	17,600
2. David Pearson	Holman-Moody	17	69 Ford	491	10,725
3. Buddy Baker	Cotton Owens	6	69 Dodg	485	5,350
4. Dave Marcis	Milt Lunda	30	69 Dodg	472	2,850
5. John Sears	L. G. DeWitt	4	69 Ford	465	2,070

1970 Grand National Race No. 6 Carolina 500
March 8, 1970 Average Speed: 116.117

Driver	Owner	Car #	Make	Laps	Winnings
1. Richard Petty	Petty Enterprises	43	70 Plym	492	16,715
2. Cale Yarborough	Wood Brothers	21	70 Merc	489	9,890
3. Dick Brooks	Dick Brooks	32	70 Plym	484	5,265
4. Bobby Allison	Mario Rossi	22	69 Dodg	483	3,315
5. Pete Hamilton	Petty Enterprises	40	70 Plym	475	2,090

North Carolina Motor Speedway *continued*

1970 Grand National Race No. 47 American 500
November 15, 1970 Average Speed: 117.811

Driver	Owner	Car #	Make	Laps	Winnings
1. Cale Yarborough	Wood Brothers	21	69 Merc	492	20,445
2. David Pearson	Holman-Moody	17	69 Ford	492	11,170
3. Bobby Allison	Mario Rossi	22	69 Dodg	489	6,195
4. Donnie Allison	Banjo Matthews	27	69 Ford	486	3,045
5. Buddy Baker	Cotton Owens	6	69 Dodg	485	2,190

1971 Winston Cup GN Race No. 7 Carolina 500
March 14, 1971 Average Speed: 118.696

Driver	Owner	Car #	Make	Laps	Winnings
1. Richard Petty	Petty Enterprises	43	71 Plym	492	17,315
2. Bobby Isaac	Nord Krauskopf	71	71 Dodg	492	11,240
3. Buddy Baker	Petty Enterprises	11	71 Dodg	492	5,065
4. Fred Lorenzen	Ray Nichels	99	71 Plym	488	3,815
5. Dick Brooks	Mario Rossi	22	69 Dodg	488	1,875

1971 Winston Cup GN Race No. 44 American 500
October 24, 1971 Average Speed: 113.405

Driver	Owner	Car #	Make	Laps	Winnings
1. Richard Petty	Petty Enterprises	43	71 Plym	492	17,120
2. Buddy Baker	Petty Enterprises	11	71 Dodg	492	9,745
3. Bobby Allison	Holman-Moody	12	71 Merc	488	6,320
4. Pete Hamilton	Cotton Owens	6	71 Plym	487	4,195
5. Bobby Isaac	Nord Krauskopf	71	71 Dodg	483	3,920

1972 Winston Cup GN Race No. 5 Carolina 500
March 12, 1972 Average Speed: 113.895

Driver	Owner	Car #	Make	Laps	Winnings
1. Bobby Isaac	Nord Krauskopf	71	72 Dodg	492	17,250
2. Richard Petty	Petty Enterprises	43	72 Plym	491	11,825
3. Jim Vandiver	O. L. Nixon	31	70 Dodg	491	5,550
4. LeeRoy Yarbrough	Bill Seifert	45	71 Ford	477	6,250
5. Dave Marcis	Dave Marcis	2	70 Dodg	477	3,300

1972 Winston Cup GN Race No. 30 American 500
October 22, 1972 Average Speed: 118.275

Driver	Owner	Car #	Make	Laps	Winnings
1. Bobby Allison	R. Howard & J. Johnson	12	72 Chev	492	19,400
2. Richard Petty	Petty Enterprises	43	72 Plym	490	12,050
3. Buddy Baker	Nord Krauskopf	71	72 Dodg	489	8,425
4. David Pearson	Wood Brothers	21	71 Merc	488	5,400
5. Pete Hamilton	Jack Housby	9	72 Plym	486	3,850

1973 Winston Cup GN Race No. 4 Carolina 500
March 18, 1973 Average Speed: 118.649

Driver	Owner	Car #	Make	Laps	Winnings
1. David Pearson	Wood Brothers	21	71 Merc	492	15,475
2. Cale Yarborough	R. Howard & J. Johnson	11	73 Chev	492	10,125
3. Buddy Baker	Nord Krauskopf	71	73 Dodg	491	7,325
4. Bobby Allison	Bobby Allison	12	73 Chev	490	6,000
5. Dick Brooks	Junie Donlavey	90	72 Ford	486	3,600

1973 Winston Cup GN Race No. 28 American 500
October 21, 1973 Average Speed: 117.749

Driver	Owner	Car #	Make	Laps	Winnings
1. David Pearson	Wood Brothers	21	71 Merc	492	16,795
2. Buddy Baker	Nord Krauskopf	71	73 Dodg	491	11,050
3. Cale Yarborough	R. Howard & J. Johnson	11	73 Chev	491	7,925
4. Bobby Allison	Bobby Allison	12	73 Chev	488	6,525
5. Dave Marcis	Roger Penske	2	73 Mata	484	4,175

1974 Winston Cup GN Race No. 4 Carolina 500
March 3, 1974 Average Speed: 121.622

Driver	Owner	Car #	Make	Laps	Winnings
1. Richard Petty	Petty Enterprises	43	74 Dodg	492	18,025
2. Cale Yarborough	R. Howard & J. Johnson	11	74 Chev	491	11,600
3. Bobby Allison	Bobby Allison	12	74 Chev	486	8,400
4. Charlie Glotzbach	Hoss Ellington	28	74 Chev	483	4,125
5. George Follmer	Bud Moore	15	73 Ford	483	6,475

1974 Winston Cup GN Race No. 29 American 500
October 20, 1974 Average Speed: 118.493

Driver	Owner	Car #	Make	Laps	Winnings
1. David Pearson	Wood Brothers	21	73 Merc	492	16,350
2. Cale Yarborough	Junior Johnson	11	74 Chev	492	11,925
3. Richard Petty	Petty Enterprises	43	74 Dodg	490	9,725
4. Bobby Allison	Roger Penske	12	74 Mata	487	4,600
5. Darrell Waltrip	Darrell Waltrip	95	72 Chev	487	4,200

1975 Winston Cup GN Race No. 4 Carolina 500
March 2, 1975 Average Speed: 117.588

Driver	Owner	Car #	Make	Laps	Winnings
1. Cale Yarborough	Junior Johnson	11	75 Chev	492	17,200
2. David Pearson	Wood Brothers	21	73 Merc	492	10,815
3. Richard Petty	Petty Enterprises	43	74 Dodg	483	10,925
4. Dick Brooks	Junie Donlavey	90	73 Ford	478	5,200
5. Bruce Hill	Bruce Hill	47	75 Chev	465	3,950

1975 Winston Cup GN Race No. 27 American 500
October 19, 1975 Average Speed: 120.129

Driver	Owner	Car #	Make	Laps	Winnings
1. Cale Yarborough	Junior Johnson	11	75 Chev	492	19,930
2. Bobby Allison	Roger Penske	16	75 Mata	492	10,355
3. Dave Marcis	Nord Krauskopf	71	74 Dodg	491	11,505
4. Lennie Pond	Ronnie Elder	54	75 Chev	488	5,580
5. A. J. Foyt	Hoss Ellington	28	75 Chev	487	4,530

1976 Winston Cup GN Race No. 3 Carolina 500
February 29, 1976 Average Speed: 113.665

Driver	Owner	Car #	Make	Laps	Winnings
1. Richard Petty	Petty Enterprises	43	Dodg	492	19,915
2. Darrell Waltrip	DiGard	88	Chev	490	14,055
3. Cale Yarborough	Junior Johnson	11	Chev	490	10,665
4. Buddy Baker	Bud Moore	15	Ford	487	8,250
5. Benny Parsons	L. G. DeWitt	72	Chev	477	7,190

1976 Winston Cup GN Race No. 28 American 500
October 24, 1976 Average Speed: 117.718

Driver	Owner	Car #	Make	Laps	Winnings
1. Richard Petty	Petty Enterprises	43	Dodg	492	20,395
2. Lennie Pond	Ronnie Elder	54	Chev	491	12,870
3. Darrell Waltrip	DiGard	88	Chev	489	10,075
4. Bobby Allison	Roger Penske	2	Merc	489	7,965
5. Cale Yarborough	Junior Johnson	11	Chev	488	7,255

1977 Winston Cup GN Race No. 4 Carolina 500
March 13, 1977 Average Speed: 97.860

Driver	Owner	Car #	Make	Laps	Winnings
1. Richard Petty	Petty Enterprises	43	Dodg	492	18,594
2. Darrell Waltrip	DiGard	88	Chev	492	14,170
3. Donnie Allison	Hoss Ellington	1	Chev	491	8,520
4. Buddy Baker	Bud Moore	15	Ford	491	7,770
5. Neil Bonnett	Nord Krauskopf	71	Dodg	488	7,070

North Carolina Motor Speedway *continued*

1977 Winston Cup GN Race No. 28 American 500
October 23, 1977 Average Speed: 113.584

Driver	Owner	Car #	Make	Laps	Winnings
1. Donnie Allison	Hoss Ellington	1	Chev	492	17,135
2. Richard Petty	Petty Enterprises	43	Dodg	492	14,350
3. Darrell Waltrip	DiGard	88	Chev	492	10,800
4. Cale Yarborough	Junior Johnson	11	Chev	490	9,550
5. Dick Brooks	Junie Donlavey	90	Ford	489	6,250

1978 Winston Cup GN Race No. 28 American 500
October 22, 1978 Average Speed: 117.288

Driver	Owner	Car #	Make	Laps	Winnings
1. Cale Yarborough	Junior Johnson	11	Olds	492	23,360
2. Bobby Allison	Bud Moore	15	Ford	490	14,650
3. Darrell Waltrip	DiGard	88	Chev	488	11,400
4. Benny Parsons	L. G. DeWitt	72	Chev	486	8,500
5. Dick Brooks	Junie Donlavey	90	Ford	486	6,330

1979 Winston Cup GN Race No. 29 American 500
October 21, 1979 Average Speed: 108.356

Driver	Owner	Car #	Make	Laps	Winnings
1. Richard Petty	Petty Enterprises	43	Chev	492	20,960
2. Benny Parsons	M. C. Anderson	27	Chev	492	15,950
3. Cale Yarborough	Junior Johnson	11	Chev	492	11,800
4. Donnie Allison	Hoss Ellington	1	Chev	490	5,000
5. Dale Earnhardt	Rod Osterlund	2	Chev	488	8,300

1980 Winston Cup GN Race No. 29 American 500
October 19, 1980 Average Speed: 114.159

Driver	Owner	Car #	Make	Laps	Winnings
1. Cale Yarborough	Junior Johnson	11	Chev	492	20,160
2. Harry Gant	Jack Beebe	47	Chev	492	14,030
3. Darrell Waltrip	DiGard	88	Chev	490	12,700
4. Terry Labonte	Billy Hagan	44	Chev	487	9,400
5. Jody Ridley	Junie Donlavey	90	Ford	486	7,030

1981 Winston Cup GN Race No. 29 American 500
November 1, 1981 Average Speed: 107.399

Driver	Owner	Car #	Make	Laps	Winnings
1. Darrell Waltrip	Junior Johnson	11	Buick	492	23,410
2. Bobby Allison	Harry Ranier	28	Buick	492	17,100
3. Harry Gant	Hal Needham	33	Pont	492	10,150
4. Richard Petty	Petty Enterprises	43	Buick	492	10,400
5. Joe Ruttman	Jim Stacy	2	Pont	492	9,700

1982 Winston Cup GN Race No. 28 Warner W. Hodgdon American 500
October 31, 1982 Average Speed: 115.122

Driver	Owner	Car #	Make	Laps	Winnings
1. Darrell Waltrip	Junior Johnson	11	Buick	492	26,610
2. Bobby Allison	DiGard	88	Chev	492	20,100
3. Neil Bonnett	Wood Brothers	21	Ford	492	8,100
4. Terry Labonte	Billy Hagan	44	Buick	491	8,480
5. Morgan Shepherd	Ron Benfield	98	Buick	491	7,455

1983 Winston Cup GN Race No. 28 Warner W. Hodgdon American 500
October 30, 1983 Average Speed: 119.324

Driver	Owner	Car #	Make	Laps	Winnings
1. Terry Labonte	Billy Hagan	44	Chev	492	25,505
2. Tim Richmond	Raymond Beadle	27	Pont	492	18,490
3. Ricky Rudd	Richard Childress	3	Chev	491	11,370
4. Neil Bonnett	Bob Rahilly & Butch Mock	75	Chev	490	13,410
5. Darrell Waltrip	Junior Johnson	11	Chev	489	14,335

1978 Winston Cup GN Race No. 4 Carolina 500
March 5, 1978 Average Speed: 116.681

Driver	Owner	Car #	Make	Laps	Winnings
1. David Pearson	Wood Brothers	21	Merc	492	16,665
2. Bobby Allison	Bud Moore	15	Ford	492	14,570
3. Benny Parsons	L. G. DeWitt	72	Chev	492	11,220
4. Richard Petty	Petty Enterprises	43	Dodg	490	8,470
5. Lennie Pond	Harry Ranier	54	Chev	489	3,920

1979 Winston Cup GN Race No. 3 Carolina 500
March 4, 1979 Average Speed: 122.727

Driver	Owner	Car #	Make	Laps	Winnings
1. Bobby Allison	Bud Moore	15	Ford	492	21,555
2. Joe Millikan	L. G. DeWitt	72	Chev	491	15,670
3. Dick Brooks	Nelson Malloch	05	Olds	487	8,220
4. Tighe Scott	Walter Ballard	30	Buick	485	7,520
5. Richard Childress	Richard Childress	3	Chev	484	6,320

1980 Winston Cup GN Race No. 4 Carolina 500
March 9, 1980 Average Speed: 108.735

Driver	Owner	Car #	Make	Laps	Winnings
1. Cale Yarborough	Junior Johnson	11	Olds	492	19,280
2. Richard Petty	Petty Enterprises	43	Chev	492	18,720
3. Dale Earnhardt	Rod Osterlund	2	Chev	491	14,420
4. Darrell Waltrip	DiGard	88	Chev	491	11,270
5. Donnie Allison	Hoss Ellington	1	Chev	491	6,750

1981 Winston Cup GN Race No. 4 Carolina 500
March 1, 1981 Average Speed: 114.594

Driver	Owner	Car #	Make	Laps	Winnings
1. Darrell Waltrip	Junior Johnson	11	Buick	492	21,655
2. Cale Yarborough	M. C. Anderson	27	Buick	492	12,370
3. Richard Petty	Petty Enterprises	43	Buick	492	14,370
4. Neil Bonnett	Wood Brothers	21	Ford	492	6,920
5. Buddy Baker	Hoss Ellington	1	Olds	491	3,895

1982 Winston Cup GN Race No. 5 Warner W. Hodgdon Carolina 500
March 28, 1982 Average Speed: 108.992

Driver	Owner	Car #	Make	Laps	Winnings
1. Cale Yarborough	M. C. Anderson	27	Buick	492	17,360
2. Terry Labonte	Billy Hagan	44	Chev	491	13,705
3. Benny Parsons	Harry Ranier	28	Pont	491	17,300
4. Bobby Allison	DiGard	88	Chev	491	10,825
5. Morgan Shepherd	Ron Benfield	98	Buick	489	4,825

1983 Winston Cup GN Race No. 3 Warner W. Hodgdon Carolina 500
March 13, 1983 Average Speed: 113.055

Driver	Owner	Car #	Make	Laps	Winnings
1. Richard Petty	Petty Enterprises	43	Pont	492	24,150
2. Bill Elliott	Harry Melling	9	Ford	492	14,990
3. Darrell Waltrip	Junior Johnson	11	Chev	492	17,760
4. Lake Speed	Hoss Ellington	1	Chev	489	5,110
5. Harry Gant	Hal Needham	33	Buick	489	12,335

1984 Winston Cup GN Race No. 3 Warner W. Hodgdon Carolina 500
March 4, 1984 Average Speed: 122.931

Driver	Owner	Car #	Make	Laps	Winnings
1. Bobby Allison	DiGard	22	Buick	492	33,150
2. Terry Labonte	Billy Hagan	44	Chev	492	17,830
3. Lake Speed	Hoss Ellington	1	Chev	492	13,015
4. Richard Petty	Mike Curb	43	Pont	491	5,545
5. Buddy Baker	Wood Brothers	21	Ford	488	6,875

North Carolina Motor Speedway *continued*

1984 Winston Cup GN Race No. 28 Warner W. Hodgdon American 500
October 21, 1984 Average Speed: 112.617

Driver	Owner	Car #	Make	Laps	Winnings
1. Bill Elliott	Harry Melling	9	Ford	492	30,400
2. Harry Gant	Hal Needham	33	Chev	492	20,230
3. Terry Labonte	Billy Hagan	44	Chev	492	13,115
4. Darrell Waltrip	Junior Johnson	11	Chev	492	13,845
5. Bobby Allison	DiGard	22	Buick	491	15,625

1985 Winston Cup GN Race No. 3 Carolina 500
March 3, 1985 Average Speed: 114.953

Driver	Owner	Car #	Make	Laps	Winnings
1. Neil Bonnett	Junior Johnson	12	Chev	492	35,505
2. Harry Gant	Hal Needham	33	Chev	492	26,330
3. Terry Labonte	Billy Hagan	44	Chev	492	23,310
4. Lake Speed	Bob Rahilly & Butch Mock	75	Pont	492	11,360
5. Kyle Petty	Wood Brothers	7	Ford	491	10,520

1985 Winston Cup GN Race No. 26 Nationwise 500
October 20, 1985 Average Speed: 118.344

Driver	Owner	Car #	Make	Laps	Winnings
1. Darrell Waltrip	Junior Johnson	11	Chev	492	40,900
2. Ron Bouchard	Jack Beebe	47	Buick	492	21,055
3. Harry Gant	Hal Needham	33	Chev	492	20,900
4. Bill Elliott	Harry Melling	9	Ford	492	15,675
5. Geoff Bodine	Rick Hendrick	5	Chev	492	14,400

1986 Winston Cup Race No. 3 Goodwrench 500
March 2, 1986 Average Speed: 120.488

Driver	Owner	Car #	Make	Laps	Winnings
1. Terry Labonte	Billy Hagan	44	Olds	492	44,550
2. Harry Gant	Hal Needham	33	Chev	492	28,110
3. Richard Petty	Petty Enterprises	43	Pont	492	15,970
4. Morgan Shepherd	Jack Beebe	47	Buick	491	9,255
5. Darrell Waltrip	Junior Johnson	11	Chev	491	18,615

1986 Winston Cup Race No. 27 Nationwise 500
October 19, 1986 Average Speed: 126.381

Driver	Owner	Car #	Make	Laps	Winnings
1. Neil Bonnett	Junior Johnson	12	Chev	492	47,000
2. Ricky Rudd	Bud Moore	15	Ford	492	26,550
3. Darrell Waltrip	Junior Johnson	11	Chev	492	23,650
4. Harry Gant	Hal Needham	33	Chev	492	16,525
5. Buddy Baker	Buddy Baker & Danny Schiff	88	Olds	492	8,575

1987 Winston Cup Race No. 2 Goodwrench 500
March 1, 1987 Average Speed: 117.556

Driver	Owner	Car #	Make	Laps	Winnings
1. Dale Earnhardt	Richard Childress	3	Chev	492	53,900
2. Ricky Rudd	Bud Moore	15	Ford	492	28,135
3. Neil Bonnett	Bob Rahilly & Butch Mock	75	Pont	492	17,875
4. Bill Elliott	Harry Melling	9	Ford	492	17,405
5. Morgan Shepherd	Kenny Bernstein	26	Buick	491	12,010

1987 Winston Cup Race No. 27 AC Delco 500
October 25, 1987 Average Speed: 118.258

Driver	Owner	Car #	Make	Laps	Winnings
1. Bill Elliott	Harry Melling	9	Ford	492	50,025
2. Dale Earnhardt	Richard Childress	3	Chev	492	38,915
3. Darrell Waltrip	Rick Hendrick	17	Chev	492	16,690
4. Terry Labonte	Junior Johnson	11	Chev	492	19,315
5. Morgan Shepherd	Kenny Bernstein	26	Buick	492	16,160

1988 Winston Cup Race No. 3 Goodwrench 500
March 6, 1988 Average Speed: 120.159

Driver	Owner	Car #	Make	Laps	Winnings
1. Neil Bonnett	Bob Rahilly & Butch Mock	75	Pont	492	45,800
2. Lake Speed	Lake Speed	83	Olds	492	22,310
3. Sterling Marlin	Billy Hagan	44	Olds	492	19,195
4. Alan Kulwicki	Alan Kulwicki	7	Ford	492	14,330
5. Dale Earnhardt	Richard Childress	3	Chev	492	19,865

1988 Winston Cup Race No. 27 AC Delco 500
October 23, 1988 Average Speed: 111.557

Driver	Owner	Car #	Make	Laps	Winnings
1. Rusty Wallace	Raymond Beadle	27	Pont	492	52,150
2. Ricky Rudd	Kenny Bernstein	26	Buick	492	26,985
3. Terry Labonte	Junior Johnson	11	Chev	492	25,095
4. Bill Elliott	Harry Melling	9	Ford	491	23,480
5. Dale Earnhardt	Richard Childress	3	Chev	491	27,965

1989 Winston Cup Race No. 2 Goodwrench 500
March 5, 1989 Average Speed: 115.122

Driver	Owner	Car #	Make	Laps	Winnings
1. Rusty Wallace	Raymond Beadle	27	Pont	492	72,100
2. Alan Kulwicki	Alan Kulwicki	7	Ford	492	29,600
3. Dale Earnhardt	Richard Childress	3	Chev	492	24,200
4. Geoff Bodine	Rick Hendrick	5	Chev	492	17,975
5. Mark Martin	Jack Roush	6	Ford	492	15,963

1989 Winston Cup Race No. 27 AC Delco 500
October 22, 1989 Average Speed: 114.079

Driver	Owner	Car #	Make	Laps	Winnings
1. Mark Martin	Jack Roush	6	Ford	492	52,800
2. Rusty Wallace	Raymond Beadle	27	Pont	492	33,675
3. Darrell Waltrip	Rick Hendrick	17	Chev	492	32,225
4. Ken Schrader	Rick Hendrick	25	Chev	491	16,725
5. Dick Trickle	Stavola Brothers	84	Buick	491	15,250

1990 Winston Cup Series Race No. 3 GM Goodwrench 500
March 4, 1990 Average Speed: 122.864

Driver	Owner	Car #	Make	Laps	Winnings
1. Kyle Petty	Felix Sabates	42	Pont	492	284,450
2. Geoff Bodine	Junior Johnson	11	Ford	492	31,825
3. Ken Schrader	Rick Hendrick	25	Chev	491	24,575
4. Sterling Marlin	Billy Hagan	94	Olds	490	17,725
5. Rusty Wallace	Raymond Beadle	27	Pont	490	21,625

1990 Winston Cup Series Race No. 27 AC Delco 500
October 21, 1990 Average Speed: 126.452

Driver	Owner	Car #	Make	Laps	Winnings
1. Alan Kulwicki	Alan Kulwicki	7	Ford	492	53,300
2. Bill Elliott	Harry Melling	9	Ford	492	40,775
3. Harry Gant	Leo Jackson	33	Olds	492	23,575
4. Geoff Bodine	Junior Johnson	11	Ford	492	23,625
5. Ken Schrader	Rick Hendrick	25	Chev	492	26,025

1991 Winston Cup Series Race No. 3 GM Goodwrench 500
March 3, 1991 Average Speed: 124.083

Driver	Owner	Car #	Make	Laps	Winnings
1. Kyle Petty	Felix Sabates	42	Pont	492	131,450
2. Ken Schrader	Rick Hendrick	25	Chev	492	34,575
3. Harry Gant	Leo Jackson	33	Olds	491	23,950
4. Ricky Rudd	Rick Hendrick	5	Chev	491	20,250
5. Bill Elliott	Harry Melling	9	Ford	491	21,275

North Carolina Motor Speedway *continued*

1991 Winston Cup Series Race No. 27 AC Delco 500
October 20, 1991 Average Speed: 127.292

Driver	Owner	Car #	Make	Laps	Winnings
1. Davey Allison	Robert Yates	28	Ford	492	66,050
2. Harry Gant	Leo Jackson	33	Olds	492	34,675
3. Mark Martin	Jack Roush	6	Ford	492	29,350
4. Geoff Bodine	Junior Johnson	11	Ford	492	26,450
5. Ken Schrader	Rick Hendrick	25	Chev	491	17,325

1992 Winston Cup Race No. 27 AC Delco 500
October 25, 1992 Average Speed: 130.748

Driver	Owner	Car #	Make	Laps	Winnings
1. Kyle Petty	Felix Sabates	42	Pont	492	153,100
2. Ernie Irvan	Larry McClure	4	Chev	492	31,225
3. Ricky Rudd	Rick Hendrick	5	Chev	491	31,225
4. Bill Elliott	Junior Johnson	11	Ford	491	26,200
5. Sterling Marlin	Junior Johnson	22	Ford	491	20,075

1993 Winston Cup Series Race No. 28 AC Delco 500
October 24, 1993 Average Speed: 114.036

Driver	Owner	Car #	Make	Laps	Winnings
1. Rusty Wallace	Roger Penske	2	Pont	492	52,850
2. Dale Earnhardt	Richard Childress	3	Chev	492	49,550
3. Bill Elliott	Junior Johnson	11	Ford	492	35,675
4. Harry Gant	Leo Jackson	33	Chev	492	29,225
5. Mark Martin	Jack Roush	6	Ford	491	33,150

1994 Winston Cup Series Race No. 29 AC Delco 500
October 23, 1994 Average Speed: 126.408

Driver	Owner	Car #	Make	Laps	Winnings
1. Dale Earnhardt	Richard Childress	3	Chev	492	60,600
2. Rick Mast	Richard Jackson	1	Ford	492	45,425
3. Morgan Shepherd	Wood Brothers	21	Ford	492	32,100
4. Ricky Rudd	Ricky Rudd	10	Ford	492	28,076
5. Terry Labonte	Rick Hendrick	5	Chev	492	28,750

1995 Winston Cup Series Race No. 29 AC Delco 500
October 22, 1995 Average Speed: 114.778

Driver	Owner	Car #	Make	Laps	Winnings
1. Ward Burton	Bill Davis	22	Pont	393	70,250
2. Rusty Wallace	Roger Penske	2	Ford	393	50,050
3. Mark Martin	Jack Roush	6	Ford	393	44,850
4. Terry Labonte	Rick Hendrick	5	Chev	393	34,925
5. Jeff Burton	Stavola Brothers	8	Ford	393	40,325

1996 Winston Cup Series Race No. 29 AC Delco 400
October 20, 1996 Average Speed: 122.320

Driver	Owner	Car #	Make	Laps	Winnings
1. Ricky Rudd	Ricky Rudd	10	Ford	393	90,025
2. Dale Jarrett	Robert Yates	88	Ford	393	62,125
3. Terry Labonte	Rick Hendrick	5	Chev	393	46,725
4. Ernie Irvan	Robert Yates	28	Ford	393	35,950
5. Jeff Burton	Jack Roush	99	Ford	393	25,675

1997 Winston Cup Series Race No. 30
October 26, 1997 Average Speed: 121.73

Driver	Owner	Car #	Make	Laps	Winnings
1. Bobby Hamilton	Petty Enterprises	43	Pont	393	89,150
2. Dale Jarrett	Robert Yates	88	Ford	393	65,175
3. Ricky Craven	Rick Hendrick	25	Chev	393	45,625
4. Jeff Gordon	Rick Hendrick	24	Chev	393	41,150
5. Dick Trickle	Junie Donlavey	90	Ford	393	30,800

1992 Winston Cup Race No. 2 GM Goodwrench 500
March 1, 1992 Average Speed: 126.125

Driver	Owner	Car #	Make	Laps	Winnings
1. Bill Elliott	Junior Johnson	11	Ford	492	57,800
2. Davey Allison	Robert Yates	28	Ford	492	48,875
3. Harry Gant	Leo Jackson	33	Olds	492	31,600
4. Michael Waltrip	Chuck Rider	30	Pont	491	18,650
5. Ken Schrader	Rick Hendrick	25	Chev	491	21,650

1993 Winston Cup Series Race No. 2 GM Goodwrench 500
February 28, 1993 Average Speed: 124.486

Driver	Owner	Car #	Make	Laps	Winnings
1. Rusty Wallace	Roger Penske	2	Pont	492	42,735
2. Dale Earnhardt	Richard Childress	3	Chev	492	47,585
3. Ernie Irvan	Larry McClure	4	Chev	492	33,785
4. Alan Kulwicki	Alan Kulwicki	7	Ford	492	28,085
5. Mark Martin	Jack Roush	6	Ford	492	29,160

1994 Winston Cup Series Race No. 2 GM Goodwrench 500
February 27, 1994 Average Speed: 125.239

Driver	Owner	Car #	Make	Laps	Winnings
1. Rusty Wallace	Roger Penske	2	Ford	492	52,885
2. Sterling Marlin	Larry McClure	4	Chev	492	48,935
3. Rick Mast	Richard Jackson	1	Ford	492	31,085
4. Mark Martin	Jack Roush	6	Ford	491	28,986
5. Ernie Irvan	Robert Yates	28	Ford	491	26,410

1995 Winston Cup Series Race No. 2 GM Goodwrench 500
February 26, 1995 Average Speed: 125.305

Driver	Owner	Car #	Make	Laps	Winnings
1. Jeff Gordon	Rick Hendrick	24	Chev	492	167,600
2. Bobby Labonte	Joe Gibbs	18	Chev	492	61,350
3. Dale Earnhardt	Richard Childress	3	Chev	492	40,740
4. Ricky Rudd	Ricky Rudd	10	Ford	492	33,480
5. Dale Jarrett	Robert Yates	28	Ford	491	34,075

1996 Winston Cup Series Race No. 2 Goodwrench Service 400
February 25,1996 Average Speed: 113.959

Driver	Owner	Car #	Make	Laps	Winnings
1. Dale Earnhardt	Richard Childress	3	Chev	393	83,840
2. Dale Jarrett	Robert Yates	88	Ford	393	48,960
3. Ricky Craven	Larry Hedrick	41	Chev	393	47,760
4. Ricky Rudd	Ricky Rudd	10	Ford	393	35,810
5. Steve Grissom	Gary Bechtel	29	Chev	393	31,475

1997 Winston Cup Series Race No. 2
February 23, 1997 Average Speed: 125.927

Driver	Owner	Car #	Make	Laps	Winnings
1. Jeff Gordon	Rick Hendrick	24	Chev	393	93,115
2. Dale Jarrett	Robert Yates	88	Ford	393	68,760
3. Jeff Burton	Jack Roush	99	Ford	393	42,260
4. Ricky Rudd	Ricky Rudd	10	Ford	393	39,210
5. Ricky Craven	Rick Hendrick	25	Chev	393	35,050

1998 Winston Cup Series Race No. 2
February 22, 1998 Average Speed: 117.065

Driver	Owner	Car #	Make	Laps	Winnings
1. Jeff Gordon	Rick Hendrick	24	Chev	393	90,090
2. Rusty Wallace	Roger Penske	2	Ford	393	49,240
3. Mark Martin	Jack Roush	6	Ford	393	51,940
4. Jimmy Spencer	Travis Carter	23	Ford	393	43,120
5. Geoffrey Bodine	Jim Mattei	7	Ford	393	39,225

North Carolina Motor Speedway *continued*

1998 Winston Cup Series Race No. 32
November 1, 1998 Average Speed: 128.423

Driver	Owner	Car #	Make	Laps	Winnings
1. Jeff Gordon	Rick Hendrick	24	Chev	393	111,575
2. Dale Jarrett	Robert Yates	88	Ford	393	75,625
3. Rusty Wallace	Roger Penske	2	Ford	393	54,275
4. Mark Martin	Jack Roush	6	Ford	393	53,750
5. Jeff Burton	Jack Roush	99	Ford	393	41,325

1999 Winston Cup Series Race No. 2
February 21, 1999 Average Speed: 120.75

Driver	Owner	Car #	Make	Laps	Winnings
1. Mark Martin	Jack Roush	6	Ford	393	104,635
2. Dale Jarrett	Robert Yates	88	Ford	393	83,675
3. Bobby Labonte	Joe Gibbs	18	Pont	393	71,335
4. Jeff Burton	Jack Roush	99	Ford	393	65,195
5. Jeremy Mayfield	Michael Kranefuss	12	Ford	393	45,610

1999 Winston Cup Series Race No. 31
October 24, 1999 Average Speed: 131.103

Driver	Owner	Car #	Make	Laps	Winnings
1. Jeff Burton	Jack Roush	99	Ford	393	104,715
2. Ward Burton	Bill Davis	22	Pont	393	78,625
3. Bobby Labonte	Joe Gibbs	18	Pont	393	67,075
4. Dale Jarrett	Robert Yates	88	Ford	393	61,175
5. Rusty Wallace	Roger Penske	2	Ford	393	60,875

2000 Winston Cup Series Race No. 2
February 27, 2000 Average Speed: 127.875

Driver	Owner	Car #	Make	Laps	Winnings
1. Bobby Labonte	Joe Gibbs	18	Pont	393	131,385
2. Dale Earnhardt	Richard Childress	3	Chev	393	78,610
3. Ward Burton	Bill Davis	22	Pont	393	70,410
4. Tony Stewart	Joe Gibbs	20	Pont	393	65,120
5. Dale Jarrett	Robert Yates	88	Ford	392	64,060

2000 Winston Cup Series Race No. 31
October 22, 2000 Average Speed: 110.418

Driver	Owner	Car #	Make	Laps	Winnings
1. Dale Jarrett	Robert Yates	88	Ford	393	125,850
2. Jeff Gordon	Rick Hendrick	24	Chev	393	81,300
3. Ricky Rudd	Robert Yates	28	Ford	393	65,300
4. Jeff Burton	Jack Roush	99	Ford	393	62,925
5. Rusty Wallace	Roger Penske	2	Ford	393	50,875

2001 Winston Cup Series Race No. 2
February 25, 2001 Average Speed: 111.966

Driver	Owner	Car #	Make	Laps	Winnings
1. Steve Park	Dale Earnhardt, Inc.	1	Chev	393	144,593
2. Bobby Labonte	Joe Gibbs	18	Pont	393	125,727
3. Jeff Gordon	Rick Hendrick	24	Chev	393	125,987
4. Tony Stewart	Joe Gibbs	20	Pont	393	75,245
5. Ricky Craven	Cal Wells	32	Ford	393	50,160

2001 Winston Cup Series Race No. 33
November 4, 2001 Average Speed: 128.933

Driver	Owner	Car #	Make	Laps	Winnings
1. Joe Nemechek	Andy Petree	33	Chev	393	157,535
2. Kenny Wallace	Dale Earnhardt, Inc.	1	Chev	393	113,233
3. Johnny Benson, Jr.	Nelson Bowers	10	Pont	393	75,350
4. Dale Jarrett	Robert Yates	88	Ford	393	103,252
5. Jerry Nadeau	Rick Hendrick	25	Chev	393	65,350

2002 Winston Cup Series Race No. 2
February 24, 2002 Average Speed: 115.478

Driver	Owner	Car #	Make	Laps	Winnings
1. Matt Kenseth	Jack Roush	17	Ford	393	157,400
2. Sterling Marlin	Chip Ganassi	40	Dodg	393	125,142
3. Bobby Labonte	Joe Gibbs	18	Pont	393	114,178
4. Tony Stewart	Joe Gibbs	20	Pont	393	109,378
5. Ricky Craven	Cal Wells	32	Ford	393	70,900

2002 Winston Cup Series Race No. 34
November 3, 2002 Average Speed: 128.526

Driver	Owner	Car #	Make	Laps	Winnings
1. Johnny Benson, Jr.	Nelson Bowers	10	Pont	393	162,965
2. Mark Martin	Jack Roush	6	Ford	393	130,923
3. Kurt Busch	Jack Roush	97	Ford	393	80,400
4. Jeff Burton	Jack Roush	99	Ford	393	106,267
5. Jeff Gordon	Rick Hendrick	24	Chev	393	106,713

North Carolina State Fairgrounds
Raleigh, NC
Half-mile Dirt Track

(aka Raleigh Speedway; State Fair Speedway) Originally a 1-mile dirt track built circa 1926. Half-mile dirt track built in 1940 and re-opened in October 1946. First NASCAR Winston Cup (then Grand National) race staged on 5/28/55 (won by Junior Johnson). Final Grand National race run on 9/30/70 (won by Richard Petty). Track hosted the final Winston Cup (then Grand National) race on a dirt track. Petty won in a Plymouth owned by Don Robertson. Track closed after 1970 Grand National event.

Winston Cup Starts
14 drivers tied with 2

Winston Cup Victories

Junior Johnson	1
David Pearson	1
Richard Petty	1

Winston Cup Poles

Tim Flock	1
Bobby Isaac	1
John Sears	1

Winston Cup Money
Richard Petty $1,600

Most Cars Started
27—May 28, 1955

Fewest Cars Started
23—Sept. 30, 1970 Home State 200

Narrowest Margin of Victory
1 lap plus—May 28, 1955

Slowest Race
50.522 MPH—May 28, 1955

Race Record
68.376 MPH—Sept. 30, 1970
Home State 200

Most Cautions
6—May 28, 1955

Most Race Leaders
3—Sept. 30, 1970 Home State 200

Most Cars Running at Finish
18—May 28, 1955

1955 Grand National Race No. 17
May 28, 1955 Average Speed: 50.522

Driver	Owner	Car #	Make	Laps	Winnings
1. Junior Johnson	B & L Motors	55	55 Olds	172	1,350
2. Fonty Flock	Carl Kiekhaefer	301	55 Chrys	171	875
3. Buck Baker	Griffin Motors	87	54 Olds	171	550
4. Lee Petty	Petty Enterprises	42	55 Chrys	170	400
5. Gwyn Staley	Hubert Westmoreland	2	55 Chev	167	315

1969 Grand National Race No. 27 North State 200
June 26, 1969 Average Speed: 65.418

Driver	Owner	Car #	Make	Laps	Winnings
1. David Pearson	Holman-Moody	17	69 Ford	200	1,200
2. Richard Petty	Petty Enterprises	43	69 Ford	197	600
3. James Hylton	James Hylton	48	67 Dodg	189	400
4. John Sears	L. G. DeWitt	4	67 Ford	184	350
5. Elmo Langley	Elmo Langley	64	68 Ford	183	325

1970 Grand National Race No. 42 Home State 200 Sept. 30, 1970
Average Speed: 68.376

Driver	Owner	Car #	Make	Laps	Winnings
1. Richard Petty	Don Robertson	43	69 Plym	200	1,000
2. Neil Castles	Neil Castles	06	69 Dodg	198	600
3. Bobby Isaac	Nord Krauskopf	71	69 Dodg	195	400
4. James Hylton	James Hylton	48	70 Ford	193	350
5. Cecil Gordon	Cecil Gordon	97	68 Ford	186	325

North Wilkesboro Speedway
North Wilkesboro, NC
.625-mile Short Track

.625-mile dirt track opened in May 1947. First NASCAR Winston Cup (then Strictly Stock) race held on 10/16/49 (won by Bob Flock). Event was the finale for the 1949 season. Track paved in 1957, and the Winston Cup race staged here on 9/29/96 was likely the last race ever run here. The track was purchased by Bruton Smith and Bob Bahre, and annual events have been shifted to the new Texas Motor Speedway and New Hampshire Int'l Speedway for the 1997 season. It is uncertain what the future holds for this track.

Winston Cup Starts
Richard Petty   66

Winston Cup Victories
Richard Petty   15

Winston Cup Poles
Darrell Waltrip   9

Winston Cup Money
Dale Earnhardt $853,685

Most Cars Started
38—April 29, 1951

Fewest Cars Started
20—April 7, 1957

Narrowest Margin of Victory
3 feet—April 3, 1955

Slowest Race
53.364 MPH—October 16, 1949

Race Record
107.360 MPH—October 5, 1992
Tyson/Holly Farms 400

Most Cautions
17—April 21, 1991 First Union 400

Most Race Leaders
13—October 1, 1995
Tyson/Holly Farms 400

Most Cars Running at Finish
37—September 29, 1996
Tyson/Holly Farms 400

1949 Strictly Stock Race No. 8
October 16, 1949 Average Speed: 53.364

Driver	Owner	Car #	Make	Laps	Winnings
1. Bob Flock	Frank Christian	7	49 Olds	200	1,500
2. Lee Petty	Petty Enterprises	42	49 Plym	200	750
3. Fonty Flock	Ed Lawrence	47	47 Buick	199	400
4. Clyde Minter	Clyde Minter	19	47 Ford	199	300
5. Herb Thomas	Herb Thomas	92	49 Ford	197	175

1950 Grand National Race No. 15
September 24, 1950

Driver	Owner	Car #	Make	Laps	Winnings
1. Leon Sales	Hubert Westmoreland	98	50 Plym	200	1,000
2. Jack Smith	Bishop Brothers		50 Plym	—	600
3. Ewell Weddle	Ewell Weddle	78	49 Linc	—	400
4. Herb Thomas	Herb Thomas	92	50 Plym	—	300
5. Gayle Warren		44	50 Plym	—	225

1951 Grand National Race No. 7
April 29, 1951

Driver	Owner	Car #	Make	Laps	Winnings
1. Fonty Flock	Frank Christian	14	50 Olds	150	1,000
2. Tim Flock	Ted Chester	91	51 Olds	—	600
3. Lee Petty	Petty Enterprises	42	49 Plym	—	400
4. Bill Holland	Hubert Westmoreland	98	50 Plym	—	300
5. Donald Thomas	Herb Thomas	93	50 Plym	—	250

1951 Grand National Race No. 36
October 21, 1951 Average Speed: 67.791

Driver	Owner	Car #	Make	Laps	Winnings
1. Fonty Flock	Ted Chester	7	51 Olds	200	1,000
2. Lee Petty	Petty Enterprises	42	51 Plym	—	600
3. Joe Eubanks	Phil Oates	82	50 Olds	—	500
4. Tim Flock	Ted Chester	91	51 Olds	—	400
5. Cotton Owens	Cotton Owens	71	51 Stud	—	300

1952 Grand National Race No. 4
March 30, 1952 Average Speed: 58.597

Driver	Owner	Car #	Make	Laps	Winnings
1. Herb Thomas	Herb Thomas	92	52 Huds	200	1,000
2. Fonty Flock	Frank Christian	14	51 Olds	199	700
3. Bill Blair	George Hutchens	2	52 Olds	—	450
4. Donald Thomas	Doug Meeks	72	51 Ford	—	350
5. Dave Terrell	Dave Terrell	126	51 Plym	—	200

1952 Grand National Race No. 32
October 26, 1952 Average Speed: 67.044

Driver	Owner	Car #	Make	Laps	Winnings
1. Herb Thomas	Herb Thomas	9	52 Huds	200	1,000
2. Fonty Flock	Frank Christian	14	52 Olds	200	700
3. Donald Thomas	Herb Thomas	92	52 Huds	200	450
4. Tim Flock	Ted Chester	91	51 Huds	199	350
5. Dick Rathmann	Walt Chapman	120	52 Huds	194	200

1953 Grand National Race No. 4
March 29, 1953 Average Speed: 71.907

Driver	Owner	Car #	Make	Laps	Winnings
1. Herb Thomas	Herb Thomas	92	53 Huds	200	1,000
2. Dick Rathmann	Walt Chapman	120	53 Huds	200	700
3. Fonty Flock	Frank Christian	14	53 Olds	—	450
4. Lee Petty	Petty Enterprises	42	53 Dodg	—	350
5. Jimmie Lewallen	Dave Quate	43	53 Dodg	—	200

1953 Grand National Race No. 35
October 11, 1953 Average Speed: 71.202

Driver	Owner	Car #	Make	Laps	Winnings
1. Speedy Thompson	Buckshot Morris	12	53 Olds	160	1,000
2. Fonty Flock	Frank Christian	14	53 Huds	158	700
3. Ray Duhigg	J. H. Petty	44	52 Plym	156	450
4. Bob Welborn	J. O. Goode	24	51 Plym	156	350
5. Lee Petty	Petty Enterprises	42	53 Dodg	155	200

1954 Grand National Race No. 7
April 4, 1954 Average Speed: 68.545

Driver	Owner	Car #	Make	Laps	Winnings
1. Dick Rathmann	John Ditz	3	54 Huds	160	1,000
2. Herb Thomas	Herb Thomas	92	54 Huds	160	650
3. Joe Eubanks	Phil Oates	82	51 Huds	160	450
4. Curtis Turner	Frank Christian	14	52 Olds	158	350
5. Lee Petty	Petty Enterprises	42	54 Dodg	156	300

1954 Grand National Race No. 37
October 24, 1954 Average Speed: 65.175

Driver	Owner	Car #	Make	Laps	Winnings
1. Hershel McGriff	Frank Christian	14	54 Olds	157	1,000
2. Buck Baker	Griffin Motors	87	54 Olds	157	650
3. Herb Thomas	Herb Thomas	92	54 Huds	157	450
4. Slick Smith	Frank Christian	143	51 Olds	156	350
5. Dick Rathmann	John Ditz	3	54 Huds	156	300

North Wilkesboro Speedway *continued*

1955 Grand National Race No. 8
April 3, 1955 Average Speed: 73.126

Driver	Owner	Car #	Make	Laps	Winnings
1. Buck Baker	Griffin Motors	87	54 Olds	160	1,000
2. Dick Rathmann	John Ditz	3	54 Huds	160	650
3. Curtis Turner	Raymond Parks	99	55 Olds	156	450
4. Lee Petty	Petty Enterprises	42	55 Chrys	155	350
5. Eddie Skinner	Frank Dodge	28	53 Olds	154	300

1955 Grand National Race No. 44
October 23, 1955 Average Speed: 72.347

Driver	Owner	Car #	Make	Laps	Winnings
1. Buck Baker	Pete DePaolo	87	56 Ford	160	1,100
2. Lee Petty	Petty Enterprises	42	55 Dodg	160	700
3. Gwyn Staley	Hubert Westmoreland	2	55 Chev	159	475
4. Joe Weatherly	Charlie Schwam	9	56 Ford	159	365
5. Tim Flock	Carl Kiekhaefer	300	55 Chrys	159	310

1956 Grand National Race No. 10
April 8, 1956 Average Speed: 71.034

Driver	Owner	Car #	Make	Laps	Winnings
1. Tim Flock	Carl Kiekhaefer	300A	56 Chrys	160	1,100
2. Billy Myers	Bill Stroppe	14	56 Merc	160	700
3. Jim Paschal	Frank Hayworth	75	56 Merc	160	475
4. Herb Thomas	Herb Thomas	92	56 Chev	160	365
5. Ralph Moody	Pete DePaolo	12	56 Ford	159	310

1957 Grand National Race No. 9
April 7, 1957 Average Speed: 75.015

Driver	Owner	Car #	Make	Laps	Winnings
1. Fireball Roberts	Pete DePaolo	22	57 Ford	160	850
2. Paul Goldsmith	Pete DePaolo	97	57 Ford	160	625
3. Ralph Moody	Pete DePaolo	12	57 Ford	160	450
4. Marvin Panch	Pete DePaolo	98	57 Ford	159	350
5. Buck Baker	Hugh Babb	87	57 Chev	149	310

1957 Grand National Race No. 52
October 20, 1957 Average Speed: 69.902

Driver	Owner	Car #	Make	Laps	Winnings
1. Jack Smith	Jack Smith	47	57 Chev	160	900
2. Lee Petty	Petty Enterprises	42	57 Olds	160	575
3. Banjo Matthews	Banjo Matthews	84	57 Ford	160	375
4. Speedy Thompson	Speedy Thompson	46	57 Chev	160	280
5. Cotton Owens	Ray Nichels	6	57 Pont	160	245

1958 Grand National Race No. 18
May 18 , 1958 Average Speed: 78.636

Driver	Owner	Car #	Make	Laps	Winnings
1. Junior Johnson	Paul Spaulding	11	57 Ford	160	800
2. Jack Smith	Jack Smith	47	57 Chev	160	525
3. Rex White	J. H. Petty	44	57 Chev	160	350
4. Buck Baker	Buck Baker	87	57 Chev	159	250
5. Eddie Pagan	Eddie Pagan	45	57 Ford	157	225

1958 Grand National Race No. 50
October 19, 1958 Average Speed: 84.906

Driver	Owner	Car #	Make	Laps	Winnings
1. Junior Johnson	Paul Spaulding	11	57 Ford	160	800
2. Glen Wood	Wood Brothers	21	58 Ford	159	525
3. Speedy Thompson	Speedy Thompson	46	57 Chev	158	350
4. Cotton Owens	Jim Stephens	3	58 Pont	158	250
5. Jack Smith	Buck Baker	86	57 Chev	155	225

1959 Grand National Race No. 10
April 5, 1959 Average Speed: 71.985

Driver	Owner	Car #	Make	Laps	Winnings
1. Lee Petty	Petty Enterprises	43	57 Olds	160	800
2. Jack Smith	Jack Smith	47	59 Chev	160	525
3. Cotton Owens	W. H. Watson	6	58 Pont	159	350
4. Tiny Lund	Tiny Lund	5	57 Chev	159	250
5. Fred Harb	Fred Harb	17	57 Merc	154	225

1959 Grand National Race No. 43
October 18, 1959 Average Speed: 74.829

Driver	Owner	Car #	Make	Laps	Winnings
1. Lee Petty	Petty Enterprises	42	59 Plym	160	900
2. Rex White	Rex White	4	59 Chev	160	525
3. Richard Petty	Petty Enterprises	43	59 Plym	160	375
4. Tom Pistone	Carl Rupert	49	59 Ford	159	275
5. Junior Johnson	Paul Spaulding	11	59 Dodg	159	250

1960 Grand National Race No. 7
March 27, 1960 Average Speed: 66.347

Driver	Owner	Car #	Make	Laps	Winnings
1. Lee Petty	Petty Enterprises	42	60 Plym	160	900
2. Rex White	Rex White	4	59 Chev	160	525
3. Glen Wood	Wood Brothers	21	59 Ford	160	375
4. Ned Jarrett	Ned Jarrett	11	60 Ford	160	275
5. Junior Johnson	John Masoni	27	59 Chev	160	250

1960 Grand National Race No. 41 Wilkes 200
October 2, 1960 Average Speed: 77.444

Driver	Owner	Car #	Make	Laps	Winnings
1. Rex White	Rex White	4	60 Chev	320	2,200
2. Junior Johnson	John Masoni	27	60 Chev	320	1,225
3. Possum Jones	Tom Daniels	2	60 Chev	320	800
4. Joe Weatherly	Wood Brothers	16	58 Ford	318	525
5. Buck Baker	Buck Baker	87	60 Chev	314	375

1961 Grand National Race No. 14
April 16, 1961 Average Speed: 83.248

Driver	Owner	Car #	Make	Laps	Winnings
1. Rex White	Rex White	4	61 Chev	400	2,455
2. Tommy Irwin	Tom Daniels	2	60 Chev	398	1,175
3. Richard Petty	Petty Enterprises	43	61 Plym	396	900
4. Fireball Roberts	Jim Stephens	22	60 Pont	390	575
5. Johnny Allen	Bee Gee Holloway	69	61 Chev	387	575

1961 Grand National Race No. 48 Wilkes 200
October 1, 1961 Average Speed: 84.675

Driver	Owner	Car #	Make	Laps	Winnings
1. Rex White	Rex White	4	61 Chev	320	3,105
2. Fireball Roberts	Bud Moore	18	61 Pont	319	1,125
3. Richard Petty	Petty Enterprises	42	61 Plym	316	850
4. Junior Johnson	Rex Lovette	27	61 Pont	315	1,265
5. Ned Jarrett	Bee Gee Holloway	11	61 Chev	315	575

1962 Grand National Race No. 12 Gwyn Staley 400
April 15, 1962 Average Speed: 84.737

Driver	Owner	Car #	Make	Laps	Winnings
1. Richard Petty	Petty Enterprises	43	62 Plym	400	2,725
2. Fred Lorenzen	Holman-Moody	28	62 Ford	400	1,450
3. Junior Johnson	Rex Lovette	27	62 Pont	399	1,110
4. Fireball Roberts	Banjo Matthews	22	62 Pont	398	850
5. Darel Dieringer	Bob Osiecki	90	62 Dodg	396	675

North Wilkesboro Speedway *continued*

1962 Grand National Race No. 51 Wilkes 320
September 30, 1962 Average Speed: 86.186

Driver	Owner	Car #	Make	Laps	Winnings
1. Richard Petty	Petty Enterprises	43	62 Plym	320	2,560
2. Marvin Panch	Wood Brothers	21	62 Ford	320	1,400
3. Joe Weatherly	Bud Moore	8	62 Pont	320	875
4. Junior Johnson	Rex Lovette	27	62 Pont	319	765
5. Jim Paschal	Petty Enterprises	41	62 Plym	319	650

1963 Grand National Race No. 50 Wilkes 250
September 29, 1963 Average Speed: 89.428

Driver	Owner	Car #	Make	Laps	Winnings
1. Marvin Panch	Wood Brothers	21	63 Ford	400	3,225
2. Fred Lorenzen	Holman-Moody	28	62 Ford	400	2,050
3. Nelson Stacy	Holman-Moody	29	63 Ford	398	1,450
4. Fireball Roberts	Holman-Moody	22	63 Ford	397	1,225
5. Ned Jarrett	Charles Robinson	11	63 Ford	397	625

1964 Grand National Race No. 58 Wilkes 400
October 11, 1964 Average Speed: 91.398

Driver	Owner	Car #	Make	Laps	Winnings
1. Marvin Panch	Wood Brothers	21	64 Ford	400	3,225
2. Fred Lorenzen	Holman-Moody	28	64 Ford	400	2,150
3. Darel Dieringer	Bud Moore	16	64 Merc	397	1,225
4. Billy Wade	Bud Moore	1	64 Merc	394	850
5. Buck Baker	Ray Fox	3	64 Dodg	390	625

1965 Grand National Race No. 51 Wilkes 400
October 3, 1965 Average Speed: 88.801

Driver	Owner	Car #	Make	Laps	Winnings
1. Junior Johnson	Rex Lovette	26	65 Ford	400	4,475
2. Cale Yarborough	Banjo Matthews	27	65 Ford	398	2,125
3. Ned Jarrett	Bondy Long	11	65 Ford	398	1,275
4. David Pearson	Cotton Owens	6	65 Dodg	397	825
5. Curtis Turner	Wood Brothers	47	65 Ford	396	675

1966 Grand National Race No. 47 Wilkes 400
October 2, 1966 Average Speed: 89.012

Driver	Owner	Car #	Make	Laps	Winnings
1. Dick Hutcherson	Bondy Long	29	66 Ford	400	4,325
2. David Pearson	Cotton Owens	6	66 Dodg	400	2,225
3. Paul Lewis	Paul Lewis	1	65 Plym	400	1,325
4. Jim Paschal	Tom Friedkin	14	66 Plym	397	800
5. James Hylton	Bud Hartje	48	65 Dodg	395	625

1967 Grand National Race No. 46 Wilkes 400
October 1, 1967 Average Speed: 94.837

Driver	Owner	Car #	Make	Laps	Winnings
1. Richard Petty	Petty Enterprises	43	67 Plym	400	4,725
2. Dick Hutcherson	Bondy Long	29	67 Ford	398	2,400
3. LeeRoy Yarbrough	Junior Johnson	26	67 Ford	398	1,300
4. Bobby Allison	Bobby Allison	2	65 Chev	398	1,125
5. Jim Paschal	Tom Friedkin	14	67 Plym	398	650

1968 Grand National Race No. 45 Wilkes 400
September 29, 1968 Average Speed: 94.103

Driver	Owner	Car #	Make	Laps	Winnings
1. Richard Petty	Petty Enterprises	43	68 Plym	400	5,975
2. David Pearson	Holman-Moody	17	68 Ford	399	2,500
3. LeeRoy Yarbrough	Junior Johnson	98	68 Merc	399	1,450
4. Bobby Allison	Tom Friedkin	14	68 Plym	397	1,150
5. Cale Yarborough	Wood Brothers	21	68 Merc	395	625

1963 Grand National Race No. 20 Gwyn Staley 400
April 28, 1963 Average Speed: 83.301

Driver	Owner	Car #	Make	Laps	Winnings
1. Richard Petty	Petty Enterprises	43	63 Plym	257	3,575
2. Fred Lorenzen	Holman-Moody	28	63 Ford	256	2,575
3. Tiny Lund	Wood Brothers	21	63 Ford	256	1,300
4. Jim Paschal	Petty Enterprises	41	63 Plym	254	825
5. Buck Baker	Buck Baker	87	63 Pont	254	700

1964 Grand National Race No. 18 Gwyn Staley 400
April 19, 1964 Average Speed: 81.930

Driver	Owner	Car #	Make	Laps	Winnings
1. Fred Lorenzen	Holman-Moody	28	64 Ford	400	3,950
2. Ned Jarrett	Bondy Long	11	64 Ford	400	1,900
3. Marvin Panch	Wood Brothers	21	64 Ford	399	1,250
4. Junior Johnson	Ray Fox	3	64 Dodg	395	850
5. Darel Dieringer	Bill Stroppe	16	64 Merc	395	625

1965 Grand National Race No. 11 Gwyn Staley 400
April 18, 1965 Average Speed: 95.047

Driver	Owner	Car #	Make	Laps	Winnings
1. Junior Johnson	Rex Lovette	26	65 Ford	400	4,900
2. Bobby Johns	Holman-Moody	7	65 Ford	400	2,125
3. Ned Jarrett	Bondy Long	11	65 Ford	399	1,300
4. Dick Hutcherson	Holman-Moody	29	65 Ford	393	850
5. Marvin Panch	Wood Brothers	21	65 Ford	389	675

1966 Grand National Race No. 13 Gwyn Staley 400
April 17, 1966 Average Speed: 89.045

Driver	Owner	Car #	Make	Laps	Winnings
1. Jim Paschal	Tom Friedkin	14	66 Plym	400	4,950
2. G. C. Spencer	G. C. Spencer	49	65 Plym	394	2,225
3. David Pearson	Cotton Owens	6	66 Dodg	382	1,350
4. Wendell Scott	Wendell Scott	34	65 Ford	378	825
5. Henley Gray	Henley Gray	97	66 Ford	375	625

1967 Grand National Race No. 13 Gwyn Staley 400
April 16, 1967 Average Speed: 93.594

Driver	Owner	Car #	Make	Laps	Winnings
1. Darel Dieringer	Junior Johnson	26	67 Ford	400	5,150
2. Cale Yarborough	Wood Brothers	21	67 Ford	399	2,275
3. Dick Hutcherson	Bondy Long	29	67 Ford	396	1,325
4. Jim Paschal	Tom Friedkin	14	67 Plym	396	825
5. Paul Lewis	A. J. King	1	67 Dodg	392	625

1968 Grand National Race No. 11 Gwyn Staley 400
April 21, 1968 Average Speed: 90.425

Driver	Owner	Car #	Make	Laps	Winnings
1. David Pearson	Holman-Moody	17	68 Ford	400	5,100
2. Buddy Baker	Ray Fox	3	68 Dodg	399	2,275
3. Bobby Isaac	Nord Krauskopf	71	67 Dodg	399	1,325
4. Darel Dieringer	Mario Rossi	22	68 Plym	396	825
5. LeeRoy Yarbrough	Junior Johnson	98	68 Ford	391	750

1969 Grand National Race No. 15 Gwyn Staley 400
April 20, 1969 Average Speed: 95.268

Driver	Owner	Car #	Make	Laps	Winnings
1. Bobby Allison	Mario Rossi	22	69 Dodg	400	5,125
2. LeeRoy Yarbrough	Junior Johnson	98	69 Merc	400	3,750
3. David Pearson	Holman-Moody	17	69 Ford	400	2,100
4. Buddy Baker	Ray Fox	3	69 Dodg	400	1,150
5. James Hylton	Cotton Owens	6	69 Dodg	398	775

North Wilkesboro Speedway *continued*

1969 Grand National Race No. 47 Wilkes 400
October 5, 1969 Average Speed: 93.429

Driver	Owner	Car #	Make	Laps	Winnings
1. David Pearson	Holman-Moody	17	69 Ford	400	5,750
2. Richard Petty	Petty Enterprises	43	69 Ford	400	3,000
3. Bobby Isaac	Nord Krauskopf	71	69 Dodg	399	2,075
4. LeeRoy Yarbrough	Junior Johnson	98	69 Ford	397	1,125
5. Buddy Baker	Cotton Owens	6	69 Dodg	396	875

1970 Grand National Race No. 43 Wilkes 400
October 4, 1970 Average Speed: 90.162

Driver	Owner	Car #	Make	Laps	Winnings
1. Bobby Isaac	Nord Krauskopf	71	70 Dodg	400	5,825
2. Richard Petty	Petty Enterprises	43	70 Plym	400	2,850
3. Donnie Allison	Junior Johnson	98	70 Ford	399	1,975
4. Bobby Allison	Mario Rossi	22	70 Dodg	395	1,250
5. James Hylton	James Hylton	48	70 Ford	393	900

1971 Winston Cup GN Race No. 47 Wilkes 400
November 21, 1971 Average Speed: 96.174

Driver	Owner	Car #	Make	Laps	Winnings
1. Tiny Lund	Ronnie Hopkins	55	70 Chev	400	3,875
2. Charlie Glotzbach	R. Howard & J. Johnson	3	71 Chev	400	3,525
3. Richard Petty	Petty Enterprises	43	70 Plym	400	1,650
4. Dave Marcis	Dave Marcis	2	69 Dodg	398	1,175
5. Benny Parsons	L. G. DeWitt	72	71 Ford	394	1,000

1972 Winston Cup GN Race No. 28 Wilkes 400
October 1, 1972 Average Speed: 95.816

Driver	Owner	Car #	Make	Laps	Winnings
1. Richard Petty	Petty Enterprises	43	72 Plym	400	7,200
2. Bobby Allison	R. Howard & J. Johnson	12	72 Chev	400	4,550
3. Buddy Baker	Nord Krauskopf	71	72 Dodg	396	3,950
4. Benny Parsons	L. G. DeWitt	72	71 Merc	392	1,475
5. John Sears	Hoss Ellington	28	72 Chev	388	950

1973 Winston Cup GN Race No. 25 Wilkes 400
September 23, 1973 Average Speed: 95.198

Driver	Owner	Car #	Make	Laps	Winnings
1. Bobby Allison	Bobby Allison	12	73 Chev	400	7,425
2. Richard Petty	Petty Enterprises	43	73 Dodg	400	4,800
3. Cale Yarborough	R. Howard & J. Johnson	11	73 Chev	400	3,475
4. Buddy Baker	Nord Krauskopf	71	73 Dodg	399	2,930
5. Benny Parsons	L. G. DeWitt	72	73 Chev	395	1,200

1974 Winston Cup GN Race No. 26 Wilkes 400
September 22, 1974 Average Speed: 80.782

Driver	Owner	Car #	Make	Laps	Winnings
1. Cale Yarborough	Junior Johnson	11	74 Chev	400	9,275
2. Richard Petty	Petty Enterprises	43	74 Dodg	400	6,300
3. Buddy Baker	Bud Moore	15	73 Ford	399	4,625
4. Earl Ross	Junior Johnson	52	74 Chev	394	1,700
5. Dave Marcis	Dave Marcis	2	73 Dodg	393	1,600

1975 Winston Cup GN Race No. 23 Wilkes 400
September 21, 1975 Average Speed: 88.986

Driver	Owner	Car #	Make	Laps	Winnings
1. Richard Petty	Petty Enterprises	43	74 Dodg	400	9,960
2. Cale Yarborough	Junior Johnson	11	75 Chev	400	5,960
3. Darrell Waltrip	DiGard	88	75 Chev	396	4,535
4. Buddy Baker	Bud Moore	15	75 Ford	394	4,060
5. Lennie Pond	Ronnie Elder	54	75 Chev	394	1,810

1970 Grand National Race No. 11 Gwyn Staley 400
April 18, 1970 Average Speed: 94.246

Driver	Owner	Car #	Make	Laps	Winnings
1. Richard Petty	Petty Enterprises	43	70 Plym	400	6,025
2. Bobby Isaac	Nord Krauskopf	71	69 Dodg	399	3,725
3. LeeRoy Yarbrough	Junior Johnson	98	70 Ford	399	2,350
4. James Hylton	James Hylton	48	69 Ford	396	1,500
5. Dick Brooks	Dick Brooks	32	69 Plym	394	1,250

1971 Winston Cup GN Race No. 14 Gwyn Staley 400
April 18, 1971 Average Speed: 98.479

Driver	Owner	Car #	Make	Laps	Winnings
1. Richard Petty	Petty Enterprises	43	71 Plym	400	4,545
2. David Pearson	Holman-Moody	17	70 Ford	399	2,570
3. Dick Brooks	Mario Rossi	22	70 Dodg	396	1,745
4. Benny Parsons	L. G. DeWitt	72	71 Ford	394	1,145
5. Bobby Allison	Bobby Allison	12	71 Dodg	394	895

1972 Winston Cup GN Race No. 9 Gwyn Staley 400
April 23, 1972 Average Speed: 86.381

Driver	Owner	Car #	Make	Laps	Winnings
1. Richard Petty	Petty Enterprises	43	72 Plym	400	6,600
2. Bobby Allison	R. Howard & J. Johnson	12	72 Chev	400	4,375
3. Bobby Isaac	Nord Krauskopf	71	72 Dodg	400	3,950
4. James Hylton	James Hylton	48	70 Ford	392	1,550
5. Benny Parsons	L. G. DeWitt	72	70 Merc	392	1,200

1973 Winston Cup GN Race No. 7 Gwyn Staley 400
April 8, 1973 Average Speed: 97.224

Driver	Owner	Car #	Make	Laps	Winnings
1. Richard Petty	Petty Enterprises	43	73 Dodg	400	6,230
2. Benny Parsons	L. G. DeWitt	72	72 Chev	396	2,805
3. Buddy Baker	Nord Krauskopf	71	72 Dodg	394	3,380
4. Bobby Allison	Bobby Allison	12	73 Chev	394	3,205
5. Cecil Gordon	Cecil Gordon	24	72 Chev	394	1,205

1974 Winston Cup GN Race No. 8 Gwyn Staley 400
April 21, 1974 Average Speed: 96.200

Driver	Owner	Car #	Make	Laps	Winnings
1. Richard Petty	Petty Enterprises	43	74 Dodg	400	8,250
2. Cale Yarborough	R. Howard & J. Johnson	11	74 Chev	398	5,550
3. Bobby Allison	Bobby Allison	12	74 Chev	396	4,725
4. Benny Parsons	L. G. DeWitt	72	74 Chev	392	3,400
5. Lennie Pond	Ronnie Elder	54	74 Chev	392	1,150

1975 Winston Cup GN Race No. 7 Gwyn Staley 400
April 6, 1975 Average Speed: 90.009

Driver	Owner	Car #	Make	Laps	Winnings
1. Richard Petty	Petty Enterprises	43	74 Dodg	400	8,675
2. Cale Yarborough	Junior Johnson	11	75 Chev	397	5,825
3. Buddy Baker	Bud Moore	15	75 Ford	394	4,975
4. Dave Marcis	Nord Krauskopf	71	74 Dodg	394	4,025
5. Lennie Pond	Ronnie Elder	54	75 Chev	393	1,850

1976 Winston Cup GN Race No. 7 Gwyn Staley 400
April 4, 1976 Average Speed: 96.858

Driver	Owner	Car #	Make	Laps	Winnings
1. Cale Yarborough	Junior Johnson	11	Chev	400	11,125
2. Richard Petty	Petty Enterprises	43	Dodg	399	8,125
3. Bobby Allison	Roger Penske	2	Merc	397	5,575
4. Benny Parsons	L. G. DeWitt	72	Chev	397	4,370
5. J. D. McDuffie	J. D. McDuffie	70	Chev	393	2,100

North Wilkesboro Speedway *continued*

1976 Winston Cup GN Race No. 26 Wilkes 400
October 3, 1976 Average Speed: 96.380

Driver	Owner	Car #	Make	Laps	Winnings
1. Cale Yarborough	Junior Johnson	11	Chev	400	11,885
2. Benny Parsons	L. G. DeWitt	72	Chev	399	6,975
3. Richard Petty	Petty Enterprises	43	Dodg	399	6,705
4. Buddy Baker	Bud Moore	15	Ford	399	4,370
5. Lennie Pond	Ronnie Elder	54	Chev	395	2,925

1977 Winston Cup GN Race No. 26 Wilkes 400
October 2, 1977 Average Speed: 86.713

Driver	Owner	Car #	Make	Laps	Winnings
1. Darrell Waltrip	DiGard	88	Chev	400	12,500
2. Cale Yarborough	Junior Johnson	11	Chev	400	8,775
3. Neil Bonnett	Jim Stacy	5	Dodg	399	5,700
4. Bobby Allison	Bobby Allison	12	Mata	397	3,225
5. Benny Parsons	L. G. DeWitt	72	Chev	396	3,875

1978 Winston Cup GN Race No. 26 Wilkes 400
October 1, 1978 Average Speed: 97.847

Driver	Owner	Car #	Make	Laps	Winnings
1. Cale Yarborough	Junior Johnson	11	Olds	400	14,000
2. Darrell Waltrip	DiGard	88	Chev	400	13,450
3. Bobby Allison	Bud Moore	15	Ford	399	6,075
4. Richard Petty	Petty Enterprises	43	Chev	397	4,875
5. Neil Bonnett	Jim Stacy	5	Chev	397	4,400

1979 Winston Cup GN Race No. 28 Holly Farms 400
October 14, 1979 Average Speed: 91.454

Driver	Owner	Car #	Make	Laps	Winnings
1. Benny Parsons	M. C. Anderson	27	Chev	400	12,225
2. Bobby Allison	Bud Moore	15	Ford	400	8,200
3. Richard Petty	Petty Enterprises	43	Chev	399	6,500
4. Dale Earnhardt	Rod Osterlund	2	Chev	398	10,425
5. Ricky Rudd	Junie Donlavey	90	Ford	398	3,325

1980 Winston Cup GN Race No. 26 Holly Farms 400
September 21, 1980 Average Speed: 75.510

Driver	Owner	Car #	Make	Laps	Winnings
1. Bobby Allison	Bud Moore	15	Ford	400	17,725
2. Darrell Waltrip	DiGard	88	Chev	400	11,175
3. Dave Marcis	Dave Marcis	71	Chev	400	6,685
4. Harry Gant	Jack Beebe	47	Chev	399	5,235
5. Dale Earnhardt	Rod Osterlund	2	Chev	399	6,925

1981 Winston Cup GN Race No. 27 Holly Farms 400
October 4, 1981 Average Speed: 93.091

Driver	Owner	Car #	Make	Laps	Winnings
1. Darrell Waltrip	Junior Johnson	11	Buick	400	23,725
2. Bobby Allison	Harry Ranier	28	Buick	399	12,725
3. Joe Millikan	Cliff Stewart	5	Pont	399	9,600
4. Dale Earnhardt	Richard Childress	3	Pont	399	7,270
5. Ron Bouchard	Jack Beebe	47	Buick	398	5,145

1982 Winston Cup GN Race No. 25 Holly Farms 400
October 3, 1982 Average Speed: 98.071

Driver	Owner	Car #	Make	Laps	Winnings
1. Darrell Waltrip	Junior Johnson	11	Buick	400	32,775
2. Harry Gant	Hal Needham	33	Buick	400	11,985
3. Terry Labonte	Billy Hagan	44	Chev	399	8,395
4. Richard Petty	Petty Enterprises	43	Pont	399	11,125
5. Geoff Bodine	Cliff Stewart	50	Pont	399	9,775

1977 Winston Cup GN Race No. 6 Gwyn Staley 400
March 27, 1977 Average Speed: 88.950

Driver	Owner	Car #	Make	Laps	Winnings
1. Cale Yarborough	Junior Johnson	11	Chev	400	14,600
2. Richard Petty	Petty Enterprises	43	Dodg	400	8,025
3. Benny Parsons	L. G. DeWitt	72	Chev	400	6,175
4. Buddy Baker	Bud Moore	15	Ford	399	4,400
5. Bobby Allison	Bobby Allison	12	Mata	398	2,125

1978 Winston Cup GN Race No. 8 Gwyn Staley 400
April 16, 1978 Average Speed: 92.345

Driver	Owner	Car #	Make	Laps	Winnings
1. Darrell Waltrip	DiGard	88	Chev	400	13,075
2. Richard Petty	Petty Enterprises	43	Dodg	400	7,950
3. Benny Parsons	L. G. DeWitt	72	Chev	399	9,300
4. Lennie Pond	Harry Ranier	54	Chev	399	3,175
5. Dave Marcis	Rod Osterlund	2	Chev	398	1,675

1979 Winston Cup GN Race No. 6 Northwestern Bank 400
March 25, 1979 Average Speed: 88.400

Driver	Owner	Car #	Make	Laps	Winnings
1. Bobby Allison	Bud Moore	15	Ford	400	13,750
2. Richard Petty	Petty Enterprises	43	Chev	400	8,300
3. Benny Parsons	M. C. Anderson	27	Chev	400	8,600
4. Dale Earnhardt	Rod Osterlund	2	Chev	400	4,275
5. Darrell Waltrip	DiGard	88	Chev	399	4,575

1980 Winston Cup GN Race No. 8 Northwestern Bank 400
April 20, 1980 Average Speed: 95.501

Driver	Owner	Car #	Make	Laps	Winnings
1. Richard Petty	Petty Enterprises	43	Chev	400	18,925
2. Harry Gant	Jack Beebe	47	Chev	399	9,160
3. Bobby Allison	Bud Moore	15	Ford	399	13,675
4. Cale Yarborough	Junior Johnson	11	Chev	397	8,475
5. Benny Parsons	M. C. Anderson	27	Chev	397	5,925

1981 Winston Cup GN Race No. 7 Northwestern Bank 400
April 5, 1981 Average Speed: 85.381

Driver	Owner	Car #	Make	Laps	Winnings
1. Richard Petty	Petty Enterprises	43	Buick	400	18,850
2. Bobby Allison	Harry Ranier	28	Pont	400	12,350
3. Darrell Waltrip	Junior Johnson	11	Buick	400	9,875
4. Dave Marcis	Dave Marcis	71	Chev	400	10,470
5. Harry Gant	Kennie Childers	12	Olds	400	2,550

1982 Winston Cup GN Race No. 7 Northwestern Bank 400
April 18, 1982 Average Speed: 97.646

Driver	Owner	Car #	Make	Laps	Winnings
1. Darrell Waltrip	Junior Johnson	11	Buick	400	32,300
2. Terry Labonte	Billy Hagan	44	Chev	400	13,835
3. Dale Earnhardt	Bud Moore	15	Ford	400	12,425
4. Benny Parsons	Harry Ranier	28	Pont	400	11,525
5. Richard Petty	Petty Enterprises	43	Pont	399	10,000

1983 Winston Cup GN Race No. 6 Northwestern Bank 400
April 17, 1983 Average Speed: 91.436

Driver	Owner	Car #	Make	Laps	Winnings
1. Darrell Waltrip	Junior Johnson	11	Chev	400	28,075
2. Bobby Allison	DiGard	22	Buick	400	16,975
3. Harry Gant	Hal Needham	33	Buick	400	12,885
4. Neil Bonnett	Bob Rahilly & Butch Mock	75	Chev	400	10,995
5. Geoff Bodine	Cliff Stewart	88	Pont	400	7,070

North Wilkesboro Speedway *continued*

1983 Winston Cup GN Race No. 26 Holly Farms 400
October 2, 1983 Average Speed: 100.716

Driver	Owner	Car #	Make	Laps	Winnings
1. Darrell Waltrip	Junior Johnson	11	Chev	400	34,800
2. Dale Earnhardt	Bud Moore	15	Ford	400	15,500
3. Bobby Allison	DiGard	22	Buick	400	12,855
4. Bill Elliott	Harry Melling	9	Ford	400	6,345
5. Terry Labonte	Billy Hagan	44	Chev	399	5,820

1984 Winston Cup GN Race No. 27 Holly Farms 400
October 14, 1984 Average Speed: 90.525

Driver	Owner	Car #	Make	Laps	Winnings
1. Darrell Waltrip	Junior Johnson	11	Chev	400	38,900
2. Harry Gant	Hal Needham	33	Chev	400	15,230
3. Bobby Allison	DiGard	22	Buick	400	17,000
4. Neil Bonnett	Junior Johnson	12	Chev	400	6,630
5. Rusty Wallace	Cliff Stewart	88	Pont	400	7,510

1985 Winston Cup GN Race No. 24 Holly Farms 400
September 29, 1985 Average Speed: 95.077

Driver	Owner	Car #	Make	Laps	Winnings
1. Harry Gant	Hal Needham	33	Chev	400	32,025
2. Geoff Bodine	Rick Hendrick	5	Chev	400	25,000
3. Terry Labonte	Billy Hagan	44	Chev	400	15,860
4. Dale Earnhardt	Richard Childress	3	Chev	400	10,960
5. Ricky Rudd	Bud Moore	15	Ford	399	9,500

1986 Winston Cup Race No. 25 Holly Farms 400
September 28, 1986 Average Speed: 95.612

Driver	Owner	Car #	Make	Laps	Winnings
1. Darrell Waltrip	Junior Johnson	11	Chev	400	38,100
2. Geoff Bodine	Rick Hendrick	5	Chev	400	20,700
3. Richard Petty	Petty Enterprises	43	Pont	400	12,105
4. Rusty Wallace	Raymond Beadle	27	Pont	400	10,500
5. Harry Gant	Hal Needham	33	Chev	400	11,800

1987 Winston Cup Race No. 25 Holly Farms 400
October 4, 1987 Average Speed: 96.051

Driver	Owner	Car #	Make	Laps	Winnings
1. Terry Labonte	Junior Johnson	11	Chev	400	45,575
2. Dale Earnhardt	Richard Childress	3	Chev	400	26,950
3. Bill Elliott	Harry Melling	9	Ford	399	25,450
4. Morgan Shepherd	Kenny Bernstein	26	Buick	398	11,205
5. Geoff Bodine	Rick Hendrick	5	Chev	398	11,975

1988 Winston Cup Race No. 26 Holly Farms 400
October 16, 1988 Average Speed: 94.192

Driver	Owner	Car #	Make	Laps	Winnings
1. Rusty Wallace	Raymond Beadle	27	Pont	400	47,000
2. Phil Parsons	Richard Jackson	55	Olds	400	22,900
3. Geoff Bodine	Rick Hendrick	5	Chev	400	16,750
4. Terry Labonte	Junior Johnson	11	Chev	400	12,825
5. Bill Elliott	Harry Melling	9	Ford	400	21,625

1989 Winston Cup Race No. 26 Holly Farms 400
October 15, 1989 Average Speed: 90.289

Driver	Owner	Car #	Make	Laps	Winnings
1. Geoff Bodine	Rick Hendrick	5	Chev	400	47,800
2. Mark Martin	Jack Roush	6	Ford	400	28,075
3. Terry Labonte	Junior Johnson	11	Ford	400	18,300
4. Harry Gant	Leo Jackson	33	Olds	400	12,775
5. Morgan Shepherd	Bob Rahilly & Butch Mock	75	Pont	400	15,200

1984 Winston Cup GN Race No. 6 Northwestern Bank 400
April 8, 1984 Average Speed: 97.830

Driver	Owner	Car #	Make	Laps	Winnings
1. Tim Richmond	Raymond Beadle	27	Pont	400	24,780
2. Harry Gant	Hal Needham	33	Chev	400	16,455
3. Ricky Rudd	Bud Moore	15	Ford	400	22,190
4. Terry Labonte	Billy Hagan	44	Chev	400	7,355
5. Kyle Petty	Petty Enterprises	7	Ford	400	11,220

1985 Winston Cup GN Race No. 7 Northwestern Bank 400
April 21, 1985 Average Speed: 93.818

Driver	Owner	Car #	Make	Laps	Winnings
1. Neil Bonnett	Junior Johnson	12	Chev	400	30,025
2. Darrell Waltrip	Junior Johnson	11	Chev	400	27,500
3. Bobby Allison	DiGard	22	Buick	400	12,965
4. Ricky Rudd	Bud Moore	15	Ford	400	9,870
5. Geoff Bodine	Rick Hendrick	5	Chev	400	11,955

1986 Winston Cup Race No. 7 First Union 400
April 20, 1986 Average Speed: 88.408

Driver	Owner	Car #	Make	Laps	Winnings
1. Dale Earnhardt	Richard Childress	3	Chev	400	38,550
2. Ricky Rudd	Bud Moore	15	Ford	400	20,075
3. Geoff Bodine	Rick Hendrick	5	Chev	400	17,415
4. Darrell Waltrip	Junior Johnson	11	Chev	400	13,750
5. Joe Ruttman	Kenny Bernstein	26	Buick	400	4,415

1987 Winston Cup Race No. 6 First Union 400
April 5, 1987 Average Speed: 94.103

Driver	Owner	Car #	Make	Laps	Winnings
1. Dale Earnhardt	Richard Childress	3	Chev	400	44,675
2. Kyle Petty	Wood Brothers	21	Ford	400	20,055
3. Neil Bonnett	Bob Rahilly & Butch Mock	75	Pont	400	14,470
4. Alan Kulwicki	Alan Kulwicki	7	Ford	400	12,935
5. Ricky Rudd	Bud Moore	15	Ford	399	14,890

1988 Winston Cup Race No. 7 First Union 400
April 17, 1988 Average Speed: 99.075

Driver	Owner	Car #	Make	Laps	Winnings
1. Terry Labonte	Junior Johnson	11	Chev	400	48,050
2. Ricky Rudd	Kenny Bernstein	26	Buick	400	21,025
3. Dale Earnhardt	Richard Childress	3	Chev	400	22,115
4. Rusty Wallace	Raymond Beadle	27	Pont	400	14,650
5. Kyle Petty	Wood Brothers	21	Ford	400	12,965

1989 Winston Cup Race No. 7 First Union 400
April 16, 1989 Average Speed: 89.937

Driver	Owner	Car #	Make	Laps	Winnings
1. Dale Earnhardt	Richard Childress	3	Chev	400	51,225
2. Alan Kulwicki	Alan Kulwicki	7	Ford	400	25,575
3. Mark Martin	Jack Roush	6	Ford	400	19,425
4. Dick Trickle	Stavola Brothers	84	Buick	400	13,800
5. Terry Labonte	Junior Johnson	11	Ford	400	14,025

1990 Winston Cup Series Race No. 7 First Union 400
April 22, 1990 Average Speed: 83.908

Driver	Owner	Car #	Make	Laps	Winnings
1. Brett Bodine	Kenny Bernstein	26	Buick	400	50,682
2. Darrell Waltrip	Rick Hendrick	17	Chev	400	31,625
3. Dale Earnhardt	Richard Childress	3	Chev	400	21,775
4. Ricky Rudd	Rick Hendrick	5	Chev	400	12,775
5. Morgan Shepherd	Bud Moore	15	Ford	400	12,100

North Wilkesboro Speedway *continued*

1990 Winston Cup Series Race No. 25 Tyson/Holly Farms 400
September 30, 1990 Average Speed: 93.818

Driver	Owner	Car #	Make	Laps	Winnings
1. Mark Martin	Jack Roush	6	Ford	400	52,875
2. Dale Earnhardt	Richard Childress	3	Chev	400	32,075
3. Brett Bodine	Kenny Bernstein	26	Buick	400	18,750
4. Bill Elliott	Harry Melling	9	Ford	400	16,775
5. Ken Schrader	Rick Hendrick	25	Chev	400	15,325

1991 Winston Cup Series Race No. 25 Tyson/Holly Farms 400
September 29, 1991 Average Speed: 94.113

Driver	Owner	Car #	Make	Laps	Winnings
1. Dale Earnhardt	Richard Childress	3	Chev	400	69,350
2. Harry Gant	Leo Jackson	33	Olds	400	40,575
3. Morgan Shepherd	Bud Moore	15	Ford	400	25,375
4. Davey Allison	Robert Yates	28	Ford	400	19,600
5. Mark Martin	Jack Roush	6	Ford	400	18,875

1992 Winston Cup Race No. 25 Tyson/Holly Farms 400
October 5, 1992 Average Speed: 107.360

Driver	Owner	Car #	Make	Laps	Winnings
1. Geoff Bodine	Bud Moore	15	Ford	400	71,625
2. Mark Martin	Jack Roush	6	Ford	400	36,475
3. Kyle Petty	Felix Sabates	42	Pont	399	20,325
4. Rusty Wallace	Roger Penske	2	Pont	399	18,600
5. Sterling Marlin	Junior Johnson	22	Ford	399	20,000

1993 Winston Cup Series Race No. 26 Tyson/Holly Farms 400
October 3, 1993 Average Speed: 96.920

Driver	Owner	Car #	Make	Laps	Winnings
1. Rusty Wallace	Roger Penske	2	Pont	400	46,260
2. Dale Earnhardt	Richard Childress	3	Chev	400	46,285
3. Ernie Irvan	Robert Yates	28	Ford	400	39,435
4. Kyle Petty	Felix Sabates	42	Pont	400	20,085
5. Ricky Rudd	Rick Hendrick	5	Chev	399	21,235

1994 Winston Cup Series Race No. 27 Tyson/Holly Farms 400
October 2, 1994 Average Speed: 98.522

Driver	Owner	Car #	Make	Laps	Winnings
1. Geoff Bodine	Geoff Bodine	7	Ford	400	61,440
2. Terry Labonte	Rick Hendrick	5	Chev	399	39,365
3. Rick Mast	Richard Jackson	1	Ford	399	32,590
4. Rusty Wallace	Roger Penske	2	Ford	399	23,590
5. Mark Martin	Jack Roush	6	Ford	398	24,090

1995 Winston Cup Series Race No. 27 Tyson/Holly Farms 400
October 1, 1995 Average Speed: 102.998

Driver	Owner	Car #	Make	Laps	Winnings
1. Mark Martin	Jack Roush	6	Ford	400	71,590
2. Rusty Wallace	Roger Penske	2	Ford	400	38,915
3. Jeff Gordon	Rick Hendrick	24	Chev	400	33,065
4. Terry Labonte	Rick Hendrick	5	Chev	400	28,595
5. Ricky Rudd	Ricky Rudd	10	Ford	400	31,640

1991 Winston Cup Series Race No. 7 First Union 400
April 21, 1991 Average Speed: 79.604

Driver	Owner	Car #	Make	Laps	Winnings
1. Darrell Waltrip	Darrell Waltrip	17	Chev	400	53,800
2. Dale Earnhardt	Richard Childress	3	Chev	400	35,225
3. Jimmy Spencer	Travis Carter	98	Chev	400	20,350
4. Morgan Shepherd	Bud Moore	15	Ford	400	16,450
5. Ken Schrader	Rick Hendrick	25	Chev	400	14,725

1992 Winston Cup Race No. 7 First Union 400
April 12, 1992 Average Speed: 90.653

Driver	Owner	Car #	Make	Laps	Winnings
1. Davey Allison	Robert Yates	28	Ford	400	51,740
2. Rusty Wallace	Roger Penske	2	Pont	400	29,140
3. Ricky Rudd	Rick Hendrick	5	Chev	400	23,465
4. Geoff Bodine	Bud Moore	15	Ford	400	22,665
5. Harry Gant	Leo Jackson	33	Olds	400	19,590

1993 Winston Cup Series Race No. 7 First Union 400
April 18, 1993 Average Speed: 92.602

Driver	Owner	Car #	Make	Laps	Winnings
1. Rusty Wallace	Roger Penske	2	Pont	400	43,535
2. Kyle Petty	Felix Sabates	42	Pont	400	29,210
3. Ken Schrader	Rick Hendrick	25	Chev	400	40,235
4. Davey Allison	Robert Yates	28	Ford	400	28,285
5. Darrell Waltrip	Darrell Waltrip	17	Chev	400	25,935

1994 Winston Cup Series Race No. 7 First Union 400
April 17, 1994 Average Speed: 95.816

Driver	Owner	Car #	Make	Laps	Winnings
1. Terry Labonte	Rick Hendrick	5	Chev	400	61,640
2. Rusty Wallace	Roger Penske	2	Ford	400	42,215
3. Ernie Irvan	Robert Yates	28	Ford	400	41,565
4. Kyle Petty	Felix Sabates	42	Pont	400	32,165
5. Dale Earnhardt	Richard Childress	3	Chev	400	26,740

1995 Winston Cup Series Race No. 7 First Union 400
April 9, 1995 Average Speed: 102.424

Driver	Owner	Car #	Make	Laps	Winnings
1. Dale Earnhardt	Richard Childress	3	Chev	400	77,400
2. Jeff Gordon	Rick Hendrick	24	Chev	400	61,625
3. Mark Martin	Jack Roush	6	Ford	400	40,250
4. Rusty Wallace	Roger Penske	2	Ford	400	29,630
5. Steve Grissom	Gary Bechtel	29	Chev	400	20,655

1996 Winston Cup Series Race No. 7 First Union 400
April 14, 1996 Average Speed: 96.370

Driver	Owner	Car #	Make	Laps	Winnings
1. Terry Labonte	Rick Hendrick	5	Chev	400	229,025
2. Jeff Gordon	Rick Hendrick	24	Chev	400	52,750
3. Dale Earnhardt	Richard Childress	3	Chev	400	38,525
4. Robert Pressley	Leo Jackson & Andy Petree	33	Chev	400	35,305
5. Sterling Marlin	Larry McClure	4	Chev	400	31,855

1996 Winston Cup Series Race No. 27 Tyson/Holly Farms 400
September 29, 1996 Average Speed: 96.837

Driver	Owner	Car #	Make	Laps	Winnings
1. Jeff Gordon	Rick Hendrick	24	Chev	400	91,350
2. Dale Earnhardt	Richard Childress	3	Chev	400	51,940
3. Dale Jarrett	Robert Yates	88	Ford	400	35,790
4. Jeff Burton	Jack Roush	99	Ford	400	27,570
5. Terry Labonte	Rick Hendrick	5	Chev	400	31,115

Occoneechee Speedway
Hillsboro, NC
1-mile Dirt Track

(aka Orange Speedway in Hillsborough, NC) Track opened in June of 1948. First NASCAR Winston Cup (then Strictly Stock) race held on 8/7/49 (won by Bob Flock, the third big league NASCAR race ever staged). Originally measured at 1-mile, the track was re-measured at 0.9-mile in 1956. Final Grand National race held on 9/15/68 (won by Richard Petty). The superspeedway at Talladega assumed its race date in 1969.

Winston Cup Starts
Buck Baker   22

Winston Cup Victories
Buck Baker   3
Lee Petty   3
Richard Petty   3

Winston Cup Poles
Richard Petty   4
Joe Weatherly   4

Winston Cup Money
Buck Baker $8,660

Most Cars Started
33—April 15, 1951
33—September 28, 1958

Fewest Cars Started
18—March 23, 1958
18—September 18, 1960

Narrowest Margin of Victory
1 car length—April 18, 1954

Slowest Race
70.465 MPH—October 30, 1955

Race Record
90.663 MPH—March 14, 1965

Most Cautions
4—September 30, 1956
4—September 28, 1958

Most Race Leaders
4—September 28, 1958

Most Cars Running at Finish
21—April 18, 1954
21—May 13, 1956

1949 Strictly Stock Race No. 3
August 7, 1949 Average Speed: 76.800

Driver	Owner	Car #	Make	Laps	Winnings
1. Bob Flock	Frank Christian	7	48 Olds	200	2,000
2. Gober Sosebee	Leon Chester	50	49 Olds	—	1,000
3. Glenn Dunnaway	Glenn Dunnaway	55	49 Olds	—	500
4. Fonty Flock	Ed Lawrence	47	47 Buick	—	300
5. Bill Snowden	Al Wagoner	3	49 Chev	—	200

1950 Grand National Race No. 10
August 13, 1950

Driver	Owner	Car #	Make	Laps	Winnings
1. Fireball Roberts	Sam Rice	71	49 Olds	100	1,125
2. Curtis Turner	John Eanes	41	50 Olds	100	775
3. Dick Linder	Don Rogalla	25	50 Olds	—	400
4. Bill Rexford	Julian Buesink	80	50 Olds	—	300
5. Clyde Minter	Clyde Minter	19	50 Merc	—	225

1950 Grand National Race No. 19
October 29, 1950

Driver	Owner	Car #	Make	Laps	Winnings
1. Lee Petty	Petty Enterprises	42	49 Plym	175	1,500
2. Buck Baker	Griffin Motors	87	50 Olds	—	1,000
3. Weldon Adams	Harold Mays	72	50 Plym	—	500
4. Tim Flock	Hubert Westmoreland	98	50 Plym	—	400
5. Bill Blair	Bill Blair	41.5	50 Olds	—	300

1951 Grand National Race No. 5
April 15, 1951 Average Speed: 80.889

Driver	Owner	Car #	Make	Laps	Winnings
1. Fonty Flock	Frank Christian	14	50 Olds	95	1,300
2. Frank Mundy	Perry Smith	23	51 Stud	95	800
3. Bill Blair	Bill Blair	41.5	50 Olds	—	600
4. Tim Flock	Ted Chester	91	51 Olds	—	500
5. Neil Cole	John Golabek	52	50 Olds	—	300

1951 Grand National Race No. 31
October 7, 1951 Average Speed: 72.454

Driver	Owner	Car #	Make	Laps	Winnings
1. Herb Thomas	Herb Thomas	92	51 Huds	150	1,000
2. Leonard Tippett	Leonard Tippett	99	51 Huds	149	600
3. Joe Eubanks	Phil Oates	82	50 Olds	148	500
4. Jim Paschal	Julian Buesink	60	50 Ford	147	400
5. Lee Petty	Petty Enterprises	42	51 Plym	147	300

1952 Grand National Race No. 15
June 8, 1952 Average Speed: 81.008

Driver	Owner	Car #	Make	Laps	Winnings
1. Tim Flock	Ted Chester	91	51 Huds	100	1,000
2. Fonty Flock	Frank Christian	14	52 Olds	100	700
3. Dick Rathmann	Walt Chapman	120	51 Huds	100	450
4. Bill Blair	George Hutchens	2	52 Olds	98	350
5. Jimmie Lewallen			52 Ford	97	200

1952 Grand National Race No. 30
October 12, 1952 Average Speed: 73.489

Driver	Owner	Car #	Make	Laps	Winnings
1. Fonty Flock	Frank Christian	14	52 Olds	150	1,200
2. Donald Thomas	Herb Thomas	9	52 Huds	150	700
3. Bill Blair	George Hutchens	2	52 Olds	150	500
4. Tim Flock	Ted Chester	91	52 Huds	149	450
5. Lee Petty	Petty Enterprises	42	51 Plym	147	400

1953 Grand National Race No. 26
August 9, 1953 Average Speed: 75.125

Driver	Owner	Car #	Make	Laps	Winnings
1. Curtis Turner	Frank Christian	41	53 Olds	100	1,000
2. Herb Thomas	Herb Thomas	92	53 Huds	100	700
3. Lee Petty	Petty Enterprises	42	53 Dodg	99	450
4. Joe Eubanks	Phil Oates	82	52 Huds	—	350
5. Bill Blair	Bill Blair	2	53 Olds	—	200

1954 Grand National Race No. 8
April 18, 1954 Average Speed: 77.386

Driver	Owner	Car #	Make	Laps	Winnings
1. Herb Thomas	Herb Thomas	92	54 Huds	100	1,000
2. Donald Thomas	John Ditz	31	53 Huds	100	650
3. Buck Baker	Ernest Woods	88	54 Olds	100	450
4. Dick Rathmann	John Ditz	3	54 Huds	100	350
5. Curtis Turner	Frank Christian	14	54 Olds	99	300

1955 Grand National Race No. 7
March 27, 1955 Average Speed: 82.304

Driver	Owner	Car #	Make	Laps	Winnings
1. Jim Paschal	Ernest Woods	78	55 Olds	100	1,000
2. Buck Baker	Griffin Motors	87	54 Olds	100	650
3. Don White	Don White	1	55 Olds	100	450
4. Joel Million	Ernest Woods	88	55 Olds	99	350
5. Fonty Flock	Frank Christian	14	55 Chev	99	300

Occoneechee Speedway *continued*

1955 Grand National Race No. 45
October 30, 1955 Average Speed: 70.465

Driver	Owner	Car #	Make	Laps	Winnings
1. Tim Flock	Carl Kiekhaefer	301	55 Chrys	100	1,100
2. Curtis Turner	Charlie Schwam	99	56 Ford	100	700
3. Buck Baker	Pete DePaolo	87	56 Ford	100	475
4. Herb Thomas	Herb Thomas	92	55 Chev	100	365
5. Dave Terrell	Dave Terrell	198	55 Olds	100	310

1956 Grand National Race No. 17
May 13, 1956 Average Speed: 83.720

Driver	Owner	Car #	Make	Laps	Winnings
1. Buck Baker	Carl Kiekhaefer	300	56 Chrys	100	1,100
2. Speedy Thompson	Carl Kiekhaefer	300c	56 Chrys	100	700
3. Lee Petty	Petty Enterprises	42	56 Dodg	100	475
4. Fireball Roberts	Pete DePaolo	22	56 Ford	100	365
5. Cotton Owens	Jim Stephens	286	56 Pont	99	310

1956 Grand National Race No. 50
September 30, 1956 Average Speed: 72.734

Driver	Owner	Car #	Make	Laps	Winnings
1. Fireball Roberts	Pete DePaolo	22	56 Ford	110	950
2. Buck Baker	Carl Kiekhaefer	300B	56 Chrys	110	675
3. Speedy Thompson	Carl Kiekhaefer	300	56 Chrys	108	475
4. Herb Thomas	Herb Thomas	92	56 Chev	108	365
5. Bunk Moore		35	56 Ford	107	320

1957 Grand National Race No. 7
March 24, 1957 Average Speed: 82.233

Driver	Owner	Car #	Make	Laps	Winnings
1. Buck Baker	Hugh Babb	87	57 Chev	110	650
2. Speedy Thompson	Hugh Babb	46	57 Chev	110	525
3. Jack Smith	Hugh Babb	47	57 Chev	109	400
4. Paul Goldsmith	Pete DePaolo	99	57 Ford	109	320
5. Lee Petty	Petty Enterprises	42	57 Olds	107	290

1958 Grand National Race No. 6
March 23, 1958 Average Speed: 78.502

Driver	Owner	Car #	Make	Laps	Winnings
1. Buck Baker	Buck Baker	87	57 Chev	110	800
2. Marvin Panch	John Whitford	98	57 Ford	110	525
3. Speedy Thompson	Speedy Thompson	46	57 Chev	110	350
4. Lee Petty	Petty Enterprises	42	57 Olds	110	250
5. Curtis Turner	Holman-Moody	21	57 Ford	108	225

1958 Grand National Race No. 47
September 28, 1958 Average Speed: 72.439

Driver	Owner	Car #	Make	Laps	Winnings
1. Joe Eubanks	Jim Stephens	6	57 Pont	110	800
2. Doug Cox	Doug Cox	30	57 Ford	110	525
3. Buck Baker	Buck Baker	87	57 Chev	109	350
4. Tommy Irwin	Tommy Irwin	16	57 Ford	109	250
5. Lee Petty	Petty Enterprises	42	57 Olds	108	225

1959 Grand National Race No. 4
March 1, 1959 Average Speed: 81.612

Driver	Owner	Car #	Make	Laps	Winnings
1. Curtis Turner	Doc White	41	59 Ford	110	800
2. Tom Pistone	Carl Rupert	59	59 Ford	110	525
3. Bob Welborn	Bob Welborn	49	59 Chev	109	350
4. Lee Petty	Petty Enterprises	42	57 Olds	109	250
5. Buck Baker	Buck Baker	88	59 Chev	109	225

1959 Grand National Race No. 40
September 20, 1959 Average Speed: 77.868

Driver	Owner	Car #	Make	Laps	Winnings
1. Lee Petty	Petty Enterprises	42	59 Plym	110	900
2. Cotton Owens	Cotton Owens	6	59 Ford	109	525
3. Richard Petty	Petty Enterprises	43	59 Plym	100	375
4. Larry Frank	Larry Frank	76	57 Chev	100	250
5. Roy Tyner	Roy Tyner	9	57 Chev	100	250

1960 Grand National Race No. 18
May 29, 1960 Average Speed: 83.583

Driver	Owner	Car #	Make	Laps	Winnings
1. Lee Petty	Petty Enterprises	42	60 Plym	110	900
2. Ned Jarrett	Ned Jarrett	11	60 Ford	108	525
3. Jack Smith	Jack Smith	47	60 Pont	108	375
4. Tommy Irwin	Tommy Irwin	36	59 Ford	107	275
5. Buck Baker	Buck Baker	87	60 Chev	107	250

1960 Grand National Race No. 39
September 18, 1960 Average Speed: 80.161

Driver	Owner	Car #	Make	Laps	Winnings
1. Richard Petty	Petty Enterprises	43	60 Plym	110	800
2. Ned Jarrett	Ned Jarrett	11	60 Ford	109	525
3. Rex White	Rex White	4	59 Chev	106	375
4. Herman Beam	Herman Beam	19	60 Ford	103	275
5. Jimmy Pardue	Ebart Clifton	54	59 Dodg	103	250

1961 Grand National Race No. 11
April 2, 1961 Average Speed: 84.695

Driver	Owner	Car #	Make	Laps	Winnings
1. Cotton Owens	Cotton Owens	6	60 Pont	110	800
2. Richard Petty	Petty Enterprises	42	60 Plym	110	525
3. Buck Baker	Buck Baker	86	61 Chrys	110	375
4. Junior Johnson	Rex Lovette	27	60 Pont	109	275
5. Rex White	Rex White	4	60 Chev	109	350

1961 Grand National Race No. 52
October 29, 1961 Average Speed: 85.249

Driver	Owner	Car #	Make	Laps	Winnings
1. Joe Weatherly	Bud Moore	8	61 Pont	165	1,150
2. Rex White	Rex White	4	61 Chev	164	850
3. Ned Jarrett	Bee Gee Holloway	11	61 Chev	163	475
4. Maurice Petty	Petty Enterprises	42	61 Plym	155	375
5. Fireball Roberts	Rex Lovette	22	61 Pont	154	325

1962 Grand National Race No. 9
March 18, 1962 Average Speed: 86.948

Driver	Owner	Car #	Make	Laps	Winnings
1. Rex White	Rex White	4	61 Chev	110	1,000
2. Richard Petty	Petty Enterprises	43	62 Plym	110	600
3. Jim Paschal	Cliff Stewart	2	62 Pont	110	400
4. Jack Smith	Jack Smith	47	61 Pont	110	300
5. Buddy Baker	Buck Baker	87	61 Chrys	109	275

1963 Grand National Race No. 10
March 10, 1963 Average Speed: 83.129

Driver	Owner	Car #	Make	Laps	Winnings
1. Junior Johnson	Ray Fox	3	63 Chev	165	1,550
2. Jim Paschal	Petty Enterprises	41	62 Plym	165	1,100
3. Richard Petty	Petty Enterprises	43	63 Plym	165	750
4. Ned Jarrett	Charles Robinson	11	63 Ford	161	575
5. Jimmy Pardue	Pete Stewart	54	62 Pont	157	425

Occoneechee Speedway *continued*

1963 Grand National Race No. 54
October 27, 1963 Average Speed: 85.559

Driver	Owner	Car #	Make	Laps	Winnings
1. Joe Weatherly	Bud Moore	8	63 Pont	167	1,600
2. Bob Welborn	Petty Enterprises	41	63 Plym	166	1,000
3. Doug Cooper	Bob Cooper	02	62 Pont	154	700
4. Buck Baker	Buck Baker	87	63 Pont	152	550
5. Curtis Crider	Curtis Crider	62	63 Merc	149	425

1964 Grand National Race No. 55
September 20, 1964 Average Speed: 86.725

Driver	Owner	Car #	Make	Laps	Winnings
1. Ned Jarrett	Bondy Long	11	64 Ford	167	1,550
2. Cotton Owens	Cotton Owens	5	64 Dodg	166	1,000
3. Larry Thomas	Herman Beam	19	64 Ford	162	750
4. Wendell Scott	Wendell Scott	34	63 Ford	156	575
5. Buddy Arrington	Buddy Arrington	78	63 Dodg	153	425

1965 Grand National Race No. 53
October 24, 1965 Average Speed: 87.462

Driver	Owner	Car #	Make	Laps	Winnings
1. Dick Hutcherson	Holman-Moody	47	65 Ford	112	1,000
2. Tom Pistone	Glenn Sweet	59	64 Ford	109	600
3. Jim Paschal	Petty Enterprises	43	64 Plym	109	400
4. Cale Yarborough	Kenny Myler	06	64 Ford	106	300
5. Paul Lewis	Curtis Larimer	56	64 Ford	105	275

1967 Grand National Race No. 44 Hillsborough 150
September 17, 1967 Average Speed: 81.574

Driver	Owner	Car #	Make	Laps	Winnings
1. Richard Petty	Petty Enterprises	43	67 Plym	167	1,500
2. Dick Hutcherson	Bondy Long	29	67 Ford	167	1,050
3. Buddy Baker	Cotton Owens	6	67 Dodg	165	700
4. James Hylton	Bud Hartje	48	65 Dodg	164	575
5. G. C. Spencer	G. C. Spencer	49	67 Plym	164	425

1964 Grand National Race No. 15 Joe Weatherly Memorial 150
April 12, 1964 Average Speed: 83.319

Driver	Owner	Car #	Make	Laps	Winnings
1. David Pearson	Cotton Owens	6	64 Dodg	167	1,400
2. Dick Hutcherson	Dick Hutcherson	1	64 Ford	164	1,100
3. Larry Thomas	Wade Younts	36	62 Dodg	160	700
4. Ralph Earnhardt	Tom Spell	31	63 Ford	160	575
5. Bobby Keck	E. B. Rich	23	63 Ford	155	425

1965 Grand National Race No. 8
March 14, 1965 Average Speed: 90.663

Driver	Owner	Car #	Make	Laps	Winnings
1. Ned Jarrett	Bondy Long	11	65 Ford	167	1,400
2. Junior Johnson	Rex Lovette	26	65 Ford	166	1,000
3. Bud Moore	Louie Weathersby	45	64 Plym	162	700
4. Elmo Langley	Elmo Langley	64	64 Ford	161	575
5. Buddy Arrington	Buddy Arrington	67	64 Dodg	160	425

1966 Grand National Race No. 45 Joe Weatherly Memorial 150
September 18, 1966 Average Speed: 90.603

Driver	Owner	Car #	Make	Laps	Winnings
1. Dick Hutcherson	Bondy Long	29	66 Ford	167	1,400
2. David Pearson	Cotton Owens	6	65 Dodg	167	1,000
3. Paul Lewis	Paul Lewis	1	65 Plym	165	700
4. James Hylton	Bud Hartje	48	65 Dodg	163	575
5. John Sears	L. G. DeWitt	4	64 Ford	163	425

1968 Grand National Race No. 43 Hillsborough 150
September 15, 1968 Average Speed: 87.681

Driver	Owner	Car #	Make	Laps	Winnings
1. Richard Petty	Petty Enterprises	43	68 Plym	167	1,600
2. James Hylton	James Hylton	48	67 Ford	160	1,000
3. Neil Castles	Sherral Pruitt	57	67 Dodg	152	700
4. John Sears	L. G. DeWitt	4	66 Ford	150	575
5. Worth McMillion	Allen McMillion	83	67 Pont	145	425

Raleigh Speedway
Raleigh, NC
1-mile Paved Track

(aka Southland Speedway; Dixie Speedway) Modern 1-mile high-banked paved oval was North Carolina's first superspeedway. Opened to AAA IndyCar championship event in 1952. First NASCAR Winston Cup (then Grand National) race staged on 5/30/53 (won by Fonty Flock). During the inaugural NASCAR 300-mile event, Tim Flock gave up second place in order to remove a monkey (Jocko Flocko) from his car when the animal broke loose from his seat. Flock had the monkey riding with him as promotional gimmick in 1953. Lights erected in 1955, the first superspeedway race held at night was held on 8/20/55 (won by Herb Thomas). Final Grand National race held on 7/4/58 (won by Fireball Roberts). Track lost its July 4 date when Daytona Int'l Speedway opened in 1959 and never re-opened.

Winston Cup Starts

Buck Baker	7
Jim Paschal	7
Lee Petty	7
Speedy Thompson	7

Winston Cup Victories

Fonty Flock	2
Fireball Roberts	2
Herb Thomas	2

Winston Cup Poles

Tim Flock	1
Fonty Flock	1
Cotton Owens	1
Lee Petty	1
Frankie Schneider	1
Slick Smith	1
Herb Thomas	1

Winston Cup Money

Fireball Roberts	$7,275

Most Cars Started
55—July 4, 1958 Raleigh 250

Fewest Cars Started
29—August 20, 1955

Narrowest Margin of Victory
6 car lengths—September 30, 1955

Slowest Race
70.629 MPH—May 30, 1953 Raleigh 300

Race Record
79.822 MPH—July 4, 1956 Raleigh 250

Most Cautions
8—July 4, 1958 Raleigh 250

Most Race Leaders
7—July 4, 1958 Raleigh 250

Most Cars Running at Finish
41—July 4, 1957 Raleigh 250

1953 Grand National Race No. 13 Raleigh 300
May 30, 1953 Average Speed: 70.629

Driver	Owner	Car #	Make	Laps	Winnings
1. Fonty Flock	Frank Christian	14	53 Huds	300	3,500
2. Speedy Thompson	Buckshot Morris	12	53 Olds	298	1,800
3. Tim Flock	Ted Chester	91	53 Huds	297	1,200
4. Herb Thomas	Herb Thomas	92	53 Huds	296	1,000
5. Dick Passwater	Frank Arford	78	53 Olds	296	800

1954 Grand National Race No. 14 Raleigh 250
May 29, 1954 Average Speed: 73.909

Driver	Owner	Car #	Make	Laps	Winnings
1. Herb Thomas	Herb Thomas	92	54 Huds	250	2,250
2. Dick Rathmann	John Ditz	3	54 Huds	248	1,175
3. Hershel McGriff	Frank Christian	14	54 Olds	246	800
4. Lee Petty	Petty Enterprises	42	54 Dodg	244	700
5. Jimmie Lewallen	George Hutchens	80	54 Merc	241	600

1955 Grand National Race No. 34
August 20, 1955 Average Speed: 76.400

Driver	Owner	Car #	Make	Laps	Winnings
1. Herb Thomas	Herb Thomas	92	55 Buick	100	1,500
2. Tim Flock	Carl Kiekhaefer	300	55 Chrys	100	1,000
3. Bob Welborn	J. H. Petty	44	55 Chev	100	600
4. Jimmie Lewallen	Ernest Woods	88	55 Olds	100	500
5. Gwyn Staley	Hubert Westmoreland	2	55 Chev	99	400

1955 Grand National Race No. 38
September 30, 1955 Average Speed: 73.289

Driver	Owner	Car #	Make	Laps	Winnings
1. Fonty Flock	Carl Kiekhaefer	301	55 Chrys	100	1,100
2. Herb Thomas	Herb Thomas	92	55 Chev	100	700
3. Tim Flock	Carl Kiekhaefer	300	55 Chrys	100	475
4. Donald Thomas	Herb Thomas	91	55 Buick	100	365
5. Bill Widenhouse	Sam McCuthen	25	55 Chev	100	310

1956 Grand National Race No. 30 Raleigh 250
July 4, 1956 Average Speed: 79.822

Driver	Owner	Car #	Make	Laps	Winnings
1. Fireball Roberts	Pete DePaolo	22	56 Ford	250	3,000
2. Speedy Thompson	Carl Kiekhaefer	500	56 Dodg	248	2,000
3. Frank Mundy	Carl Kiekhaefer	502	56 Dodg	247	1,275
4. Herb Thomas	Herb Thomas	92	56 Chev	246	925
5. Tim Flock	Mauri Rose	11	56 Chev	243	750

1957 Grand National Race No. 28 Raleigh 250
July 4, 1957 Average Speed: 75.693

Driver	Owner	Car #	Make	Laps	Winnings
1. Paul Goldsmith	Smokey Yunick	3	57 Ford	250	4,000
2. Frankie Schneider	Hubert Westmoreland	44	57 Chev	250	2,475
3. Joe Weatherly	Holman-Moody	12	57 Ford	249	1,575
4. Speedy Thompson	Speedy Thompson	46	57 Chev	249	1,050
5. Bob Welborn	Bob Welborn	49	57 Chev	248	850

1958 Grand National Race No. 28 Raleigh 250
July 4, 1958 Average Speed: 73.691

Driver	Owner	Car #	Make	Laps	Winnings
1. Fireball Roberts	Frank Strickland	22	57 Chev	250	3,800
2. Buck Baker	Buck Baker	87	57 Chev	249	2,325
3. Rex White	J. H. Petty	44	57 Chev	248	1,575
4. Shorty Rollins	Shorty Rollins	99	58 Ford	248	1,075
5. Speedy Thompson	Speedy Thompson	46	57 Chev	248	850

Salisbury Superspeedway
Salisbury, NC
.625-Mile Dirt Track

A superspeedway in name only. Track, built in 1958, was measured at .625-paved oval. Track opened with Winston Cup (then Grand National) race on 10/5/58 (won by Lee Petty). Track closed in 1961.

Winston Cup Victories
Lee Petty   1

Winston Cup Poles
Gober Sosebee   1

Winston Cup Money
Lee Petty $800

Most Cars Started
30—October 5, 1958

Narrowest Margin of Victory
N/A

Race Record
58.271 MPH—October 5, 1958

Most Race Leaders
N/A

Most Cars Running at Finish
25—October 5, 1958

1958 Grand National Race No. 48
October 5, 1958 Average Speed: 58.271

Driver	Owner	Car #	Make	Laps	Winnings
1. Lee Petty	Petty Enterprises	42	57 Olds	160	800
2. Buck Baker	Buck Baker	87	57 Chev	160	525
3. Cotton Owens	Jim Stephens	3	58 Pont	157	350
4. George Dunn	Manley Britt	14	57 Merc	157	250
5. Roy Tyner	J. H. Petty	49	57 Chev	157	225

Southern States Fairgrounds
Charlotte, NC
Half-mile Dirt Track

(aka Charlotte Fairgrounds) Half-mile dirt track built circa 1926. First NASCAR Winston Cup (then Grand National) race staged on 8/13/54 (won by Lee Petty). Final Grand National race was held on 11/6/60 (won by Richard Petty, who won his first career race here on 2/28/60). Track closed to auto racing with the construction of Charlotte Motor Speedway in 1960.

Winston Cup Starts
Buck Baker   17
Lee Petty   17

Winston Cup Victories
Lee Petty   3

Winston Cup Poles
Lee Petty   4

Winston Cup Money
Lee Petty $6,110

Most Cars Started
35—July 26, 1959

Fewest Cars Started
15—August 5, 1955

Narrowest Margin of Victory
20 yards—May 22, 1959

Slowest Race
48.806 MPH—August 5, 1955

Race Record
59.435 MPH—November 6, 1960

Most Cautions
9—July 26, 1959

Most Race Leaders
4—July 12, 1957
4—September 5, 1958
4—May 22, 1959
4—November 8, 1959

Most Cars Running at Finish
17—July 26, 1959

1954 Grand National Race No. 28
August 13, 1954 Average Speed: 51.362

Driver	Owner	Car #	Make	Laps	Winnings
1. Lee Petty	Petty Enterprises	42	54 Chrys	200	1,000
2. Dick Rathmann	John Ditz	3	54 Huds	198	650
3. Bob Welborn	Griffin Motors	87	53 Olds	196	450
4. Dink Widenhouse	Dink Widenhouse	B-29	53 Olds	196	350
5. Buck Baker	Ernest Woods	88	54 Olds	192	300

1954 Grand National Race No. 33
September 24, 1954 Average Speed: 53.167

Driver	Owner	Car #	Make	Laps	Winnings
1. Hershel McGriff	Frank Christian	14	54 Olds	200	1,000
2. Lee Petty	Petty Enterprises	42	54 Chrys	199	650
3. Buck Baker	Griffin Motors	87	54 Olds	199	450
4. Dick Rathmann	John Ditz	3	54 Huds	196	350
5. Joe Eubanks	Phil Oates	82	51 Huds	195	300

1955 Grand National Race No. 23
June 24, 1955 Average Speed: 51.289

Driver	Owner	Car #	Make	Laps	Winnings
1. Tim Flock	Carl Kiekhaefer	301	55 Chrys	200	1,000
2. Buck Baker	Griffin Motors	87	54 Olds	198	650
3. Gwyn Staley	Hubert Westmoreland	2	55 Chev	198	450
4. Bob Welborn	J. H. Petty	44	55 Chev	198	350
5. Junior Johnson	B & L Motors	55	55 Olds	194	300

1955 Grand National Race No. 31
August 5, 1955 Average Speed: 48.806

Driver	Owner	Car #	Make	Laps	Winnings
1. Jim Paschal	Ernest Woods	78	55 Olds	200	1,100
2. Gwyn Staley	Hubert Westmoreland	2	55 Chev	198	700
3. Buck Baker	Henry Ford	303	55 Chrys	198	475
4. Bob Welborn	J. H. Petty	44	55 Chev	195	365
5. Tim Flock	Carl Kiekhaefer	300	55 Chrys	192	310

1956 Grand National Race No. 26
June 15, 1956 Average Speed: 56.022

Driver	Owner	Car #	Make	Laps	Winnings
1. Speedy Thompson	Carl Kiekhaefer	300c	56 Chrys	200	650
2. Curtis Turner	Charlie Schwam	99	56 Ford	195	525
3. Lee Petty	Petty Enterprises	42	56 Dodg	195	400
4. Fireball Roberts	Pete DePaolo	22	56 Ford	193	320
5. Buck Baker	Carl Kiekhaefer	300	56 Chrys	189	290

1956 Grand National Race No. 46
September 12, 1956 Average Speed: 52.847

Driver	Owner	Car #	Make	Laps	Winnings
1. Ralph Moody	Pete DePaolo	12	56 Ford	200	850
2. Billy Myers	Bill Stroppe	4	56 Merc	200	625
3. Joe Eubanks	James Satcher	82	56 Ford	200	450
4. Marvin Panch	Tom Harbison	98	56 Ford	199	350
5. Herb Thomas	Herb Thomas	92	56 Chev	196	310

1957 Grand National Race No. 11
April 19, 1957 Average Speed: 52.083

Driver	Owner	Car #	Make	Laps	Winnings
1. Fireball Roberts	Pete DePaolo	22	57 Ford	200	700
2. Marvin Panch	Pete DePaolo	98	57 Ford	200	595
3. Buck Baker	Hugh Babb	87	57 Chev	200	400
4. Lee Petty	Petty Enterprises	42	57 Olds	191	300
5. Jim Paschal	Bill Stroppe	17	57 Merc	190	270

1957 Grand National Race No. 29
July 12, 1957 Average Speed: 56.302

Driver	Owner	Car #	Make	Laps	Winnings
1. Marvin Panch	Marvin Panch	98	57 Ford	200	700
2. Buck Baker	Buck Baker	87	57 Chev	200	525
3. Lee Petty	Petty Enterprises	42	57 Olds	200	400
4. Speedy Thompson	Speedy Thompson	46	57 Chev	199	330
5. Fireball Roberts	Dick Beaty	34	56 Ford	195	270

1957 Grand National Race No. 48
October 5, 1957 Average Speed: 51.583

Driver	Owner	Car #	Make	Laps	Winnings
1. Lee Petty	Petty Enterprises	42	57 Olds	200	900
2. Fireball Roberts	Fireball Roberts	22	57 Ford	200	575
3. Eddie Pagan	Eddie Pagan	45	57 Ford	199	375
4. Buck Baker	Buck Baker	87	57 Chev	195	280
5. Tiny Lund	Bob Welborn	48	57 Chev	192	245

1958 Grand National Race No. 11
April 18, 1958 Average Speed: 53.254

Driver	Owner	Car #	Make	Laps	Winnings
1. Curtis Turner	Holman-Moody	26	58 Ford	200	800
2. Jack Smith	Jack Smith	47	57 Chev	199	525
3. Johnny Allen	Spook Crawford	64	57 Plym	196	350
4. Lee Petty	Petty Enterprises	42	57 Olds	196	250
5. Joe Weatherly	Holman-Moody	12	58 Ford	195	225

Southern States Fairgrounds *continued*

1958 Grand National Race No. 42
September 5, 1958 Average Speed: 52.280

Driver	Owner	Car #	Make	Laps	Winnings
1. Buck Baker	Buck Baker	87	57 Chev	200	800
2. Speedy Thompson	Speedy Thompson	46	57 Chev	199	525
3. Shorty Rollins	Shorty Rollins	99	58 Ford	191	350
4. Bob Walden	Bob Walden	52	57 Ford	183	250
5. Bill Poor	Bill Poor	711	56 Chev	179	225

1959 Grand National Race No. 28
July 26, 1959 Average Speed: 49.553

Driver	Owner	Car #	Make	Laps	Winnings
1. Jack Smith	Jack Smith	47	59 Chev	200	900
2. Bob Welborn	Bob Welborn	49	57 Chev	200	525
3. Buck Baker	Lynton Tyson	87	59 Chev	200	350
4. Cotton Owens	W. H. Watson	6	58 Pont	200	250
5. Larry Frank	Larry Frank	76	57 Chev	200	225

1960 Grand National Race No. 1
November 8, 1959 Average Speed: 52.409

Driver	Owner	Car #	Make	Laps	Winnings
1. Jack Smith	Jack Smith	47	59 Chev	200	800
2. Bob Welborn	W. J. Ridgeway	22	59 Chev	199	525
3. Buck Baker	Buck Baker	87	59 Chev	198	375
4. Roy Tyner	Roy Tyner	9	57 Chev	196	275
5. Speedy Thompson	Bruce Thompson	2	57 Chev	193	250

1959 Grand National Race No. 15
May 22, 1959 Average Speed: 55.300

Driver	Owner	Car #	Make	Laps	Winnings
1. Lee Petty	Petty Enterprises	42	57 Olds	200	800
2. Tiny Lund	Tiny Lund	5	57 Chev	200	525
3. Cotton Owens	Don Every	82	58 Ford	200	350
4. Speedy Thompson	Bruce Thompson	2	57 Chev	200	250
5. Buck Baker	Buck Baker	87	59 Chev	199	225

1959 Grand National Race No. 30
August 2, 1959 Average Speed: 52.794

Driver	Owner	Car #	Make	Laps	Winnings
1. Ned Jarrett	Ned Jarrett	11	57 Ford	200	800
2. Jim Paschal	J. H. Petty	48	57 Chev	199	525
3. Bob Welborn	Bob Welborn	49	59 Chev	199	350
4. Tommy Irwin	Tommy Irwin	36	57 Ford	193	250
5. Larry Frank	Larry Frank	76	57 Chev	190	225

1960 Grand National Race No. 6
February 28, 1960 Average Speed: 53.404

Driver	Owner	Car #	Make	Laps	Winnings
1. Richard Petty	Petty Enterprises	43	59 Plym	200	800
2. Rex White	Rex White	4	59 Chev	200	525
3. Doug Yates	Raeford Johnson	23	59 Plym	199	375
4. Junior Johnson	Wood Brothers	21	59 Ford	198	275
5. Joe Eubanks	Don Every	82	59 Chev	193	250

1961 Grand National Race No. 1
November 6, 1960 Average Speed: 59.435

Driver	Owner	Car #	Make	Laps	Winnings
1. Joe Weatherly	Doc White	16	58 Ford	200	800
2. Rex White	Rex White	4	59 Chev	200	525
3. Lee Petty	Petty Enterprises	42	60 Plym	196	375
4. Buck Baker	Buck Baker	87	60 Chev	194	275
5. David Pearson	David Pearson	67	59 Chev	190	250

Starlite Speedway
Monroe, NC
Half-mile Dirt Track

Half-mile dirt track built circa 1962. Only NASCAR Winston Cup (then Grand National) race staged on 5/13/66 (won by Darel Dieringer). No factory backed teams were permitted to compete in race. James Sears was killed here in August 1973 after striking an opening in the guard rail, an event which ultimately led to the track's closure.

Winston Cup Victories
Darel Dieringer   1

Winston Cup Poles
James Hylton   1

Winston Cup Money
Darel Dieringer $1,000

Most Cars Started
25—May 13, 1966

Narrowest Margin of Victory
8 laps plus—May 13, 1966

Race Record
60.140 MPH—May 13, 1966

Most Cautions
3—May 13, 1966

Most Race Leaders
4—May 13, 1966

Most Cars Running at Finish
7—May 13, 1966

1966 Grand National Race No. 18
May 13, 1966 Average Speed: 60.140

Driver	Owner	Car #	Make	Laps	Winnings
1. Darel Dieringer	Reid Shaw	0	64 Ford	250	1,000
2. Clyde Lynn	Clyde Lynn	20	64 Ford	242	600
3. Wendell Scott	Wendell Scott	34	65 Ford	238	400
4. Neil Castles	Buck Baker	86	65 Plym	237	300
5. Henley Gray	Henley Gray	97	66 Ford	230	275

Tar Heel Speedway
Randleman, NC
Quarter-mile Dirt Track

(aka Kings Kountry Motor Speedway) Quarter-mile paved track opened in May 1957; built by Harold Brasington. First NASCAR Winston Cup (then Grand National) race staged on 11/22/62 (won by Jim Paschal; race was included in 1963 championship season). Final Grand National race run on 10/5/63 (won by Richard Petty). Track closed circa 1967, but may have run a special event in 1975.

Winston Cup Starts

Curtis Crider	3
Ned Jarrett	3
Jimmy Pardue	3
Jim Paschal	3
Richard Petty	3
Wendell Scott	3
Larry Thomas	3
Joe Weatherly	3

Winston Cup Victories
Jim Paschal   2

Winston Cup Poles
Ned Jarrett   1
Fred Lorenzen   1
Glen Wood   1

Winston Cup Money
Joe Weatherly $1,995

Most Cars Started
24—November 22, 1962 Turkey Day 200

Fewest Cars Started
15—May 5, 1963

Narrowest Margin of Victory
4 car lengths—October 5, 1963

Slowest Race
46.001 MPH—October 5, 1963

Race Record
48.605 MPH—May 5, 1963

Most Race Leaders
2—November 22, 1962 Turkey Day 200
2—May 5, 1963
2—October 5, 1963

Most Cars Running at Finish
16—November 22, 1962 Turkey Day 200

1963 Grand National Race No. 3 Turkey Day 200
November 22, 1962 Average Speed: 47.544

Driver	Owner	Car #	Make	Laps	Winnings
1. Jim Paschal	Petty Enterprises	41	62 Plym	200	575
2. Joe Weatherly	Bud Moore	8	62 Pont	198	650
3. Tommy Irwin	Stewart McKinney	44	62 Ford	197	350
4. David Pearson	Cotton Owens	6	62 Dodg	197	290
5. Maurice Petty	Petty Enterprises	42	62 Plym	196	225

1963 Grand National Race No. 22
May 5, 1963 Average Speed: 48.605

Driver	Owner	Car #	Make	Laps	Winnings
1. Jim Paschal	Petty Enterprises	43	62 Plym	200	570
2. Joe Weatherly	Cliff Stewart	2	62 Pont	196	675
3. Ned Jarrett	Charles Robinson	11	63 Ford	196	400
4. Jimmy Pardue	Pete Stewart	57	62 Pont	195	290
5. Larry Thomas	Wade Younts	36	62 Dodg	195	240

1963 Grand National Race No. 51
October 5, 1963 Average Speed: 46.001

Driver	Owner	Car #	Make	Laps	Winnings
1. Richard Petty	Petty Enterprises	43	63 Plym	200	580
2. Joe Weatherly	Bud Moore	8	63 Merc	200	670
3. Bob Welborn	Petty Enterprises	42	63 Plym	199	380
4. Darel Dieringer		14	63 Ford	196	290
5. Fred Lorenzen	Holman-Moody	28	63 Ford	194	275

Tri-City Speedway
High Point, NC
Half-mile Dirt Track

(aka High Point Motor Speedway) Originally a 1-mile track built in 1940. Half-mile track built sometime in the early '50s. First NASCAR Winston Cup (then Grand National) race staged on 6/26/53 (won by Herb Thomas). Only other Grand National race staged on 11/7/54 (won by Lee Petty; race was the 1955 season opener). Track closed in late '50s or early '60s.

Winston Cup Starts
12 drivers tied with 2

Winston Cup Victories
Lee Petty   1
Herb Thomas   1

Winston Cup Poles
Herb Thomas   2

Winston Cup Money
Herb Thomas $1,450

Most Cars Started
23—June 26, 1953

Fewest Cars Started
21—November 7, 1954

Narrowest Margin of Victory
1/2 lap—November 7, 1954

Slowest Race
58.186 MPH—June 26, 1953

Race Record
62.882 MPH—November 7, 1954

Most Race Leaders
N/A

Most Cars Running at Finish
N/A

1953 Grand National Race No. 17
June 26, 1953 Average Speed: 58.186

Driver	Owner	Car #	Make	Laps	Winnings
1. Herb Thomas	Herb Thomas	92	53 Huds	200	1,000
2. Dick Rathmann	Walt Chapman	120	53 Huds	—	700
3. Joe Eubanks	Phil Oates	82	52 Huds	—	450
4. Buck Baker	Griffin Motors	87	53 Olds	—	350
5. Lee Petty	Petty Enterprises	42	53 Dodg	—	200

1955 Grand National Race No. 1
November 7, 1954 Average Speed: 62.882

Driver	Owner	Car #	Make	Laps	Winnings
1. Lee Petty	Petty Enterprises	42	54 Chrys	200	1,000
2. Buck Baker	Frank Christian	14	54 Olds	200	650
3. Herb Thomas	Herb Thomas	92	54 Huds	199	450
4. Gober Sosebee	Gober Sosebee	51	54 Olds	196	350
5. Jimmie Lewallen	Joe Blair	5	54 Merc	196	300

Wilson Speedway
Wilson, NC
Half-mile Dirt Track

(aka Wilson Fairgrounds; Wilson County Speedway; Legion Speedway) Half-mile dirt track built in 1934. First NASCAR Winston Cup (then Grand National) race staged on 9/30/51 (won by Fonty Flock). Final Grand National race held on 4/17/60 (won by Joe Weatherly). Track operated weekly and special events until it closed sometime in 1989.

Winston Cup Starts		Winston Cup Money		Narrowest Margin of Victory		Most Race Leaders	
Buck Baker	12	Buck Baker	$4,895	1 foot—November 18, 1956		4—March 29, 1959	

Winston Cup Victories
Herb Thomas 3

Most Cars Started
32—March 18, 1956

Slowest Race
35.398 MPH—September 28, 1952

Most Cars Running at Finish
18—March 18, 1956

Winston Cup Poles
Herb Thomas 3

Fewest Cars Started
16—May 9, 1954

Race Record
58.065 MPH—June 20, 1959

1951 Grand National Race No. 30
September 30, 1951

Driver	Owner	Car #	Make	Laps	Winnings
1. Fonty Flock	Frank Christian	14	51 Olds	200	1,000
2. Bob Flock	Ted Chester	7	51 Olds	—	600
3. Jimmie Lewallen	Hubert Hamilton	0	51 Plym	—	500
4. Jim Paschal	Julian Buesink	60	50 Ford	—	400
5. Bill Snowden	Bill Snowden	16	51 Ford	—	300

1952 Grand National Race No. 29
September 28, 1952 Average Speed: 35.398

Driver	Owner	Car #	Make	Laps	Winnings
1. Herb Thomas	Herb Thomas	92	52 Huds	200	1,000
2. Lee Petty	Petty Enterprises	42	51 Plym	199	700
3. Bill Blair	George Hutchens	2	52 Olds	199	450
4. Jim Paschal	Buckshot Morris	12	52 Olds	199	350
5. Dick Rathmann	Walt Chapman	120	52 Huds	198	200

1953 Grand National Race No. 18
June 28, 1953 Average Speed: 53.803

Driver	Owner	Car #	Make	Laps	Winnings
1. Fonty Flock	Frank Christian	14	53 Huds	200	1,000
2. Dick Rathmann	Walt Chapman	120	53 Huds	—	700
3. Herb Thomas	Herb Thomas	92	53 Huds	—	450
4. Joe Eubanks	Phil Oates	82	52 Huds	—	350
5. Buck Baker	Griffin Motors	87	53 Olds	—	200

1953 Grand National Race No. 34
October 4, 1953 Average Speed: 56.022

Driver	Owner	Car #	Make	Laps	Winnings
1. Herb Thomas	Herb Thomas	92	53 Huds	200	1,000
2. Speedy Thompson	Buckshot Morris	12	53 Olds	—	700
3. Fonty Flock	Frank Christian	14	53 Huds	—	450
4. Lee Petty	Petty Enterprises	42	53 Dodg	—	350
5. Ralph Liguori		45	51 Plym	—	200

1954 Grand National Race No. 11
May 9, 1954 Average Speed: 52.279

Driver	Owner	Car #	Make	Laps	Winnings
1. Buck Baker	Ernest Woods	88	54 Olds	200	1,000
2. Al Keller	George Miller	23	54 Huds	199	650
3. Ralph Liguori	Ralph Liguori	6	53 Dodg	199	450
4. Lee Petty	Petty Enterprises	42	54 Dodg	197	350
5. Jim Paschal	Griffin Motors	87	53 Olds	196	300

1956 Grand National Race No. 8
March 18, 1956 Average Speed: 46.287

Driver	Owner	Car #	Make	Laps	Winnings
1. Herb Thomas	Smokey Yunick	92	56 Chev	106	1,100
2. Buck Baker	Carl Kiekhaefer	500B	56 Dodg	106	700
3. Tim Flock	Carl Kiekhaefer	300B	56 Chrys	106	475
4. Jim Paschal	Frank Hayworth	75	56 Merc	105	365
5. Bill Widenhouse		68	56 Ford	105	310

1956 Grand National Race No. 56
November 18, 1956 Average Speed: 50.597

Driver	Owner	Car #	Make	Laps	Winnings
1. Buck Baker	Carl Kiekhaefer	300B	56 Chrys	200	950
2. Joe Weatherly	Pete DePaolo	112	56 Ford	200	675
3. Speedy Thompson	Carl Kiekhaefer	300	56 Chrys	200	475
4. Fireball Roberts	Pete DePaolo	22	56 Ford	200	365
5. Bill Amick	Pete DePaolo	97	56 Ford	199	320

1957 Grand National Race No. 6
March 17, 1957 Average Speed: 55.079

Driver	Owner	Car #	Make	Laps	Winnings
1. Ralph Moody	Pete DePaolo	12	57 Ford	200	850
2. Buck Baker	Hugh Babb	87	57 Chev	198	625
3. Speedy Thompson	Hugh Babb	46	57 Chev	196	450
4. Lee Petty	Petty Enterprises	42	57 Olds	195	350
5. Tiny Lund	Petty Enterprises	188	57 Olds	195	310

1958 Grand National Race No. 5
March 16, 1958 Average Speed: 48.459

Driver	Owner	Car #	Make	Laps	Winnings
1. Lee Petty	Petty Enterprises	42	57 Olds	200	800
2. Buck Baker	Buck Baker	87	57 Chev	196	525
3. Marvin Panch	John Whitford	98	57 Ford	193	350
4. Jack Smith	Jack Smith	47	57 Chev	192	250
5. Reds Kagle	Hoss Kagle	88	57 Chev	191	225

1959 Grand National Race No. 7
March 29, 1959 Average Speed: 50.300

Driver	Owner	Car #	Make	Laps	Winnings
1. Junior Johnson	Paul Spaulding	11	57 Ford	200	800
2. Curtis Turner	Doc White	41	59 Ford	200	525
3. Richard Petty	Petty Enterprises	43	57 Olds	198	350
4. Lee Petty	Petty Enterprises	42	57 Olds	196	250
5. Tom Pistone	Carl Rupert	59	59 Ford	196	225

Wilson Speedway *continued*

1959 Grand National Race No. 22
June 20, 1959 Average Speed: 58.065

Driver	Owner	Car #	Make	Laps	Winnings
1. Junior Johnson	Paul Spaulding	11	57 Ford	200	800
2. Tom Pistone	Carl Rupert	59	59 Ford	200	525
3. Glen Wood	Wood Brothers	21	58 Ford	196	350
4. Lee Petty	Petty Enterprises	42	57 Olds	194	250
5. Buck Baker	Buck Baker	87	59 Chev	194	225

1960 Grand National Race No. 12
April 17, 1960 Average Speed: 55.113

Driver	Owner	Car #	Make	Laps	Winnings
1. Joe Weatherly	Holman-Moody	12	60 Ford	200	1,275
2. Lee Petty	Petty Enterprises	42	60 Plym	199	750
3. Tom Pistone	W. T. Coppedge	59	60 Chev	199	525
4. Rex White	Rex White	4	50 Chev	198	275
5. Buck Baker	Buck Baker	87	60 Chev	198	250

Ohio

Bainbridge Fairgrounds
Bainbridge, OH
1-mile Dirt Track

1-mile dirt track opened in June 1946. Half-mile dirt track utilized for only one NASCAR Winston Cup (then Grand National) race on 7/8/51 (won by Fonty Flock). Auto races were discontinued after 1951, and the track became the Grandview Race Track for horse racing in 1950s.

Winston Cup Victories
Fonty Flock   1

Winston Cup Poles
Fonty Flock   1

Winston Cup Money
Fonty Flock $1,000

Most Cars Started
34—July 8, 1951

Narrowest Margin of Victory
N/A

Race Record
65.753 MPH—July 8, 1951

Most Race Leaders
1—July 8, 1951

Most Cars Running at Finish
N/A

1951 Grand National Race No. 15
July 8, 1951 Average Speed: 65.753

Driver	Owner	Car #	Make	Laps	Winnings
1. Fonty Flock	Frank Christian	14	50 Olds	100	1,000
2. Dick Rathmann	Walt Chapman	120	51 Huds	—	600
3. Frank Mundy	Perry Smith	23	51 Stud	—	400
4. Jimmy Florian	Jimmy Florian	27	51 Ford	—	300
5. Oda Greene	Harold Lucas	22	51 Huds	—	250

Canfield Fairgrounds
Canfield, OH
Half-mile Dirt Track

(aka Canfield Motor Speedway; Mahoning County Fairgrounds) Half-mile dirt oval built circa 1929. First NASCAR Winston Cup (then Grand National) race staged on 5/30/50 (won by Bill Rexford, his only Grand National win came in his championship season). Event was named "Poor Man's 500"—and was run on the same day as the Indianapolis 500. Final NASCAR race held on 5/30/52 (won by Herb Thomas). Track closed in 1973.

Winston Cup Starts
Tim Flock	3
Lloyd Moore	3
Lee Petty	3
Bill Rexford	3

Winston Cup Victories
Bill Rexford	1
Marshall Teague	1
Herb Thomas	1

Winston Cup Poles
Jimmy Florian	1
Dick Rathmann	1
Bill Rexford	1

Winston Cup Money
Bill Rexford	$1,525

Most Cars Started
38—May 30, 1951 Poor Man's 500

Fewest Cars Started
29—May 30, 1950 Poor Man's 500

Narrowest Margin of Victory
4 feet—May 30, 1952
Poor Man's 500

Slowest Race
48.057 MPH—May 30, 1952
Poor Man's 500

Race Record
49.308 MPH—May 30, 1951
Poor Man's 500

Most Cautions
4—May 30, 1952 Poor Man's 500

Most Race Leaders
2—May 30, 1950 Poor Man's 500
2—May 30, 1952 Poor Man's 500

Most Cars Running at Finish
N/A

1950 Grand National Race No. 5 Poor Man's 500
May 30, 1950

Driver	Owner	Car #	Make	Laps	Winnings
1. Bill Rexford	Julian Buesink	60	50 Olds	200	1,400
2. Glenn Dunnaway	Glenn Dunnaway	49	49 Plym	198	750
3. Lloyd Moore	Julian Buesink	59	50 Ford	198	500
4. Lee Petty	Petty Enterprises	42	49 Plym	195	400
5. Bill Blair	Sam Rice	22	50 Merc	195	300

1951 Grand National Race No. 9 Poor Man's 500
May 30, 1951 Average Speed: 49.308

Driver	Owner	Car #	Make	Laps	Winnings
1. Marshall Teague	Marshall Teague	6	51 Huds	200	1,000
2. Tim Flock	Ted Chester	91	51 Olds	197	600
3. Fonty Flock	Frank Christian	14	50 Olds	—	400
4. Herb Thomas	Herb Thomas	92	50 Plym	—	300
5. Lee Petty	Petty Enterprises	42	49 Plym	—	250

1952 Grand National Race No. 12 Poor Man's 500
May 30, 1952 Average Speed: 48.057

Driver	Owner	Car #	Make	Laps	Winnings
1. Herb Thomas	Herb Thomas	92	52 Huds	200	1,000
2. Bill Blair	George Hutchens	2	52 Olds	200	700
3. Bob Moore	Bob Moore	78	51 Olds	199	450
4. Tim Flock	Ted Chester	91	51 Huds	196	350
5. Curtis Turner	John Eanes	41	51 Huds	189	200

Dayton Speedway
Dayton, OH
Half-mile Paved Track

(aka Greater Dayton Speedway) Half-mile high-banked dirt oval opened in 1939. First NASCAR Winston Cup (then Grand National) race staged on 6/25/50 (won by Jimmy Florian, the first driver to win a Grand National event in a Ford). Final Grand National race run on 5/18/52 (won by Dick Rathmann). Track closed in 1982 and is now a landfill.

Winston Cup Starts
Lloyd Moore   6
Lee Petty   6

Winston Cup Victories
Dick Rathmann   2

Winston Cup Poles
Fonty Flock   3

Winston Cup Money
Dick Rathmann $3,125

Most Cars Started
31—September 23, 1951

Fewest Cars Started
15—May 18, 1952

Narrowest Margin of Victory
5.000 seconds September 21, 1952

Slowest Race
61.643 MPH—September 21, 1952

Race Record
65.526 MPH—May 18, 1952

Most Cautions
N/A

Most Race Leaders
4—June 25, 1950

Most Cars Running at Finish
21—September 21, 1952

1950 Grand National Race No. 7
June 25, 1950 Average Speed: 63.351

Driver	Owner	Car #	Make	Laps	Winnings
1. Jimmy Florian	Jimmy Florian	27	50 Ford	200	1,160
2. Dick Linder	Don Rogalla	25	50 Olds	—	625
3. Buck Barr			50 Ford	—	400
4. Curtis Turner	John Eanes	41	50 Olds	—	620
5. Art Lamey		9	49 Plym	—	225

1950 Grand National Race No. 11
August 20, 1950

Driver	Owner	Car #	Make	Laps	Winnings
1. Dick Linder	Don Rogalla	25	50 Olds	195	1,125
2. Red Harvey			49 Olds	—	600
3. Herb Thomas	Herb Thomas	92	50 Plym	—	400
4. Lee Petty	Petty Enterprises	42	49 Plym	—	300
5. Art Lamey			49 Plym	—	225

1951 Grand National Race No. 12
June 24, 1951

Driver	Owner	Car #	Make	Laps	Winnings
1. Curtis Turner	John Eanes	41	51 Olds	200	1,000
2. Dick Rathmann	Walt Chapman	120	51 Huds	200	600
3. Tim Flock	Ted Chester	91	51 Olds	—	400
4. Fonty Flock	Frank Christian	14	51 Olds	—	300
5. Lloyd Moore	Julian Buesink	59	51 Ford	—	250

1951 Grand National Race No. 29
September 23, 1951

Driver	Owner	Car #	Make	Laps	Winnings
1. Fonty Flock	Frank Christian	14	51 Olds	200	1,000
2. Neil Cole	John Golabek	52	50 Olds	199	600
3. Lloyd Moore	Julian Buesink	59	51 Ford	—	500
4. Lee Petty	Petty Enterprises	42	51 Plym	—	400
5. Harvey Riley	Joe Beccue	66	51 Huds	—	300

1952 Grand National Race No. 11
May 18, 1952 Average Speed: 65.526

Driver	Owner	Car #	Make	Laps	Winnings
1. Dick Rathmann	Walt Chapman	120	51 Huds	200	1,000
2. Lloyd Moore	Julian Buesink	59	51 Ford	199	700
3. Tim Flock	Ted Chester	91	51 Huds	195	450
4. Lee Petty	Petty Enterprises	42	51 Plym	195	350
5. Donald Thomas	Doug Meeks	72	51 Ford	192	200

1952 Grand National Race No. 28
September 21, 1952 Average Speed: 61.643

Driver	Owner	Car #	Make	Laps	Winnings
1. Dick Rathmann	Walt Chapman	120	51 Huds	300	1,500
2. Lee Petty	Petty Enterprises	42	51 Plym	300	1,000
3. Ray Duhigg	J. O. Goode	24	50 Plym	297	700
4. Lloyd Moore	Julian Buesink	59	51 Ford	295	600
5. Herb Thomas	Herb Thomas	92	52 Huds	293	350

Ft. Miami Speedway
Toledo, OH
Half-mile Dirt Track

1-mile dirt track built in October 1902. Half-mile dirt track opened in September 1941. Closed during war, re-opened in July of 1947. First NASCAR Winston Cup (then Grand National) race staged on 8/19/51 (won by Tim Flock). Final Grand National race run 6/1/52 (also won by Tim Flock). Half-mile track closed in 1956. A .375-mile track operated in 1957 and 1958.

Winston Cup Starts

Ray Duhigg	2
Joe Eubanks	2
Tim Flock	2
Fonty Flock	2
Bob Moore	2
Lee Petty	2
Dick Rathmann	2
Herb Thomas	2

Winston Cup Victories

Tim Flock	2

Winston Cup Poles

Fonty Flock	2

Winston Cup Money

Tim Flock	$2,000

Most Cars Started

33—August 19, 1951

Fewest Cars Started

24—June 1, 1952

Narrowest Margin of Victory

N/A

Slowest Race

47.175 MPH—June 1, 1952

Race Record

50.847 MPH—August 19, 1951

Most Cautions

N/A

Most Race Leaders

3—August 19, 1951

Most Cars Running at Finish

N/A

1951 Grand National Race No. 21
August 19, 1951 Average Speed: 50.847

Driver	Owner	Car #	Make	Laps	Winnings
1. Tim Flock	Ted Chester	91	51 Olds	200	1,000
2. Dell Pearson	Del Pearson	88	51 Plym	—	600
3. Oda Greene	Harold Lucas	22	51 Huds	—	400
4. Lou Figaro	Jack Gaynor	33	51 Huds	—	300
5. Herb Thomas	Herb Thomas	92	51 Plym	—	250

1952 Grand National Race No. 14
June 1, 1952 Average Speed: 47.175

Driver	Owner	Car #	Make	Laps	Winnings
1. Tim Flock	Ted Chester	91	51 Huds	200	1,000
2. Dick Rathmann	Walt Chapman	120	51 Huds	200	700
3. Lee Petty	Petty Enterprises	42	51 Plym	194	450
4. Ray Duhigg	J. H. Petty	44	51 Plym	193	350
5. Fonty Flock	Frank Christian	14	50 Olds	175	200

Powell Motor Speedway
Columbus, OH
Half-mile Dirt Track

(aka Powell Speedway) Half-mile dirt track originally built in 1939. Re-opened after the war in June 1946. Only NASCAR Winston Cup (then Grand National) race staged on 5/24/53 (won by Herb Thomas). Half-mile track closed in 1959. Smaller tracks were built on site and ran until 1965.

Winston Cup Victories

Herb Thomas	1

Winston Cup Poles

Fonty Flock	1

Winston Cup Money

Herb Thomas	$1,000

Most Cars Started

27—May 24, 1953

Narrowest Margin of Victory

3 car lengths—May 24, 1953

Race Record

56.127 MPH—May 24, 1953

Most Race Leaders

N/A

Most Cars Running at Finish

15—May 24, 1953

1953 Grand National Race No. 12
May 24, 1953 Average Speed: 56.127

Driver	Owner	Car #	Make	Laps	Winnings
1. Herb Thomas	Herb Thomas	92	53 Huds	200	1,000
2. Dick Rathmann	Walt Chapman	120	53 Huds	200	700
3. Buck Baker	Griffin Motors	87	53 Olds	198	450
4. Curtis Turner	John Eanes	41	53 Olds	198	350
5. Pop McGinnis	Irving Frye	13	53 Huds	193	200

Oklahoma

Oklahoma State Fairgrounds
Oklahoma City, OK
Half-mile Dirt Track

(aka State Fair Speedway) Half-mile dirt track opened in 1954. Only Winston Cup (then Grand National) race held on 8/3/56 (won by Jim Paschal). Track still in operation.

Winston Cup Victories
Jim Paschal   1

Winston Cup Poles
Speedy Thompson   1

Winston Cup Money
Jim Paschal $850

Most Cars Started
12—August, 1956

Narrowest Margin of Victory
1/4 lap—August 3, 1956

Race Record
60.100 MPH—August 3, 1956

Most Race Leaders
3—August 3, 1956

Most Cars Running at Finish
7—August 3, 1956

1956 Grand National Race No. 36
August 3, 1956 Average Speed: 60.100

Driver	Owner	Car #	Make	Laps	Winnings
1. Jim Paschal	Frank Hayworth	75	56 Merc	200	850
2. Ralph Moody	Pete DePaolo	12	56 Ford	200	625
3. Fireball Roberts	Pete DePaolo	22	56 Ford	198	450
4. Herb Thomas	Herb Thomas	92	56 Chev	196	350
5. Lee Petty	Petty Enterprises	42	56 Dodg	193	310

Oregon

Portland Speedway
Portland, OR
Half-mile Paved Track

(aka Union Avenue Speedway; Rankin Speedway; City of Roses Speedway; Portland Drive-In Speedway; Rose City Speedway) .625-mile dirt track built in 1924 and paved in 1951. Shortened to half-mile in 1952. First NASCAR Winston Cup (then Grand National) race staged on 5/27/56 (won by Herb Thomas). Final Grand National race run on 7/14/57 (won by Eddie Pagan). The infield was the parking lot for a drive-in theater; with the screen just off the backstretch. Track is still in operation and currently hosts a variety of NASCAR events.

Winston Cup Starts		Winston Cup Poles		Fewest Cars Started	Race Record
Harold Beal	7	Art Watts	3	16—April 28, 1957	64.754 MPH—April 28, 1957
Lloyd Dane	7	**Winston Cup Money**		**Narrowest Margin of Victory**	**Most Race Leaders**
Art Watts	7	Eddie Pagan	$3,665	N/A	4—May 27, 1956
Winston Cup Victories		**Most Cars Started**		**Slowest Race**	**Most Cars Running at Finish**
Eddie Pagan	2	23—May 26, 1957		62.586 MPH—June 24, 1956	17—May 27, 1956
					17—August 26, 1956

1956 Grand National Race No. 21
May 27, 1956 Average Speed: 63.815

Driver	Owner	Car #	Make	Laps	Winnings
1. Herb Thomas	Carl Kiekhaefer	300B	56 Chrys	150	1,000
2. John Kieper	John Kieper	98	55 Olds	150	700
3. Clyde Palmer		1C	56 Dodg	150	475
4. Ed Negre		88	56 Olds	149	365
5. Curley Barker		11	56 Chev	148	310

1956 Grand National Race No. 28
June 24, 1956 Average Speed: 62.586

Driver	Owner	Car #	Make	Laps	Winnings
1. John Kieper	John Kieper	98	55 Olds	200	950
2. Clyde Palmer		1C	56 Dodg	200	665
3. Lou Sherman	Jim Rush	56	56 Merc	199	500
4. Harold Beal		50	56 Ford	199	395
5. Ed Negre		6	54 Olds	199	310

1956 Grand National Race No. 43
August 26, 1956 Average Speed: 63.429

Driver	Owner	Car #	Make	Laps	Winnings
1. Royce Haggerty	Curly Weida	15N	56 Dodg	246	1,200
2. Clyde Palmer		1	56 Ford	246	730
3. Curley Barker		11	56 Chev	246	500
4. Chuck Meekins		56	56 Chev	245	400
5. Eddie Pagan	Eddie Pagan	45	56 Ford	244	350

1956 Grand National Race No. 48
September 23, 1956

Driver	Owner	Car #	Make	Laps	Winnings
1. Lloyd Dane	Lloyd Dane	1	56 Ford	250	1,020
2. Eddie Pagan	Eddie Pagan	45	56 Ford	249	650
3. Curley Barker		11N	56 Chev	249	450
4. John Kieper	John Kieper	57	56 Chev	248	370
5. Harold Hardesty	Beryl Jackson	80N	56 Olds	247	330

1957 Grand National Race No. 14
April 28, 1957 Average Speed: 64.754

Driver	Owner	Car #	Make	Laps	Winnings
1. Art Watts	Al Schmidhamer	22N	56 Ford	100	940
2. Eddie Pagan	Eddie Pagan	45	57 Ford	100	635
3. George Seeger	Oscar Maples	12	57 Ford	100	480
4. Chuck Meekins	Jim Rush	1	57 Chev	99	340
5. Jack McCoy		22	56 Ford	99	270

1957 Grand National Race No. 18
May 26, 1957 Average Speed: 64.732

Driver	Owner	Car #	Make	Laps	Winnings
1. Eddie Pagan	Eddie Pagan	45	57 Ford	150	930
2. Lloyd Dane	Lloyd Dane	44	57 Ford	150	600
3. Clyde Palmer	Hugh Babb	82	57 Chev	149	470
4. Scotty Cain	Scotty Cain	44	56 Merc	147	345
5. Dick Getty	Dick Getty	00	56 Chev	146	270

1957 Grand National Race No. 31
July 14, 1957 Average Speed: 64.539

Driver	Owner	Car #	Make	Laps	Winnings
1. Eddie Pagan	Eddie Pagan	45	57 Ford	200	1,000
2. Lloyd Dane	Lloyd Dane	44	57 Ford	198	625
3. Danny Graves	Danny Graves	81	57 Chev	198	400
4. Scotty Cain	Scotty Cain	14	56 Merc	197	295
5. Dick Getty	Dick Getty	00	56 Chev	194	255

Pennsylvania

Bloomsburg Fairgrounds
Bloomsburg, PA
Half-mile Dirt Track

Built on Columbia County Fairgrounds circa 1927. Only NASCAR Winston Cup (then Grand National) race staged on 10/3/53 (won by Herb Thomas). Track closed in mid-1980s.

Winston Cup Victories
Herb Thomas   1

Winston Cup Poles
Jim Paschal   1

Winston Cup Money
Herb Thomas $1,000

Most Cars Started
21—October 3, 1953

Narrowest Margin of Victory
N/A

Most Race Leaders
N/A

Most Cars Running at Finish
N/A

1953 Grand National Race No. 33
October 3, 1953

Driver	Owner	Car #	Make	Laps	Winnings
1. Herb Thomas	Herb Thomas	92	53 Huds	200	1,000
2. Dick Rathmann	Walt Chapman	120	53 Huds	—	700
3. Buck Baker	Griffin Motors	87	53 Olds	—	450
4. Elton Hildreth	Elton Hildreth	167	53 Nash	—	350
5. Bob Welborn	J. O. Goode	24	51 Plym	—	200

Heidelberg Raceway
Pittsburgh, PA
Quarter-mile Dirt Track

(aka Heidelberg Speedway; Heidelberg Stadium) Half-mile and quarter-mile tracks opened in May 1948. First NASCAR Winston Cup (then Grand National) race staged on 10/2/49 (won by Lee Petty, his first of 54 Grand National victories). Last Grand National race run 7/10/60 (won by Lee Petty). Track paved in 1966. Final event run 10/7/73.

Winston Cup Starts
Lee Petty   4

Winston Cup Victories
Lee Petty   2

Winston Cup Poles
Dick Bailey   1
Al Bonnell   1
Fonty Flock   1
Lee Petty   1

Winston Cup Money
Lee Petty $2,775

Most Cars Started
42—July 15, 1951

Fewest Cars Started
17—July 10, 1960

Narrowest Margin of Victory
N/A

Slowest Race
45.000 MPH—July 21, 1959

Race Record
67.450 MPH—July 10, 1960

Most Cautions
N/A

Most Race Leaders
4—July 21, 1959

Most Cars Running at Finish
14—July 10, 1960

1949 Strictly Stock Race No. 7
October 2, 1949 Average Speed: 57.458

Driver	Owner	Car #	Make	Laps	Winnings
1. Lee Petty	Petty Enterprises	42	49 Plym	200	1,500
2. Dick Linder	La Belle Motors	8	KAI	195	750
3. Bill Rexford	Julian Buesink	4	49 Ford	193	400
4. Sam Rice	Sam Rice	2	49 Chev	192	300
5. Sara Christian	Frank Christian	1	49 Ford	190	175

1959 Grand National Race No. 27
July 21, 1959 Average Speed: 45.000

Driver	Owner	Car #	Make	Laps	Winnings
1. Jim Reed	Jim Reed	7	59 Chev	200	900
2. Rex White	Rex White	4	59 Chev	200	525
3. Lee Petty	Petty Enterprises	42	59 Plym	197	350
4. Marvin Porter	Marvin Porter	12	57 Ford	195	250
5. Cotton Owens	W. H. Watson	6	59 Pont	193	225

1951 Grand National Race No. 16
July 15, 1951

Driver	Owner	Car #	Make	Laps	Winnings
1. Herb Thomas	Hubert Westmoreland	2	51 Olds	200	1,000
2. Jim Fiebelkorn	Jim Fiebelkorn	10	51 Merc	199	600
3. Augie Walackas			51 Merc	—	400
4. Bud Farrell			51 Plym	—	300
5. Tom Jerris	William Gundaker		51 Buick	—	250

1960 Grand National Race No. 24
July 10, 1960 Average Speed: 67.450

Driver	Owner	Car #	Make	Laps	Winnings
1. Lee Petty	Petty Enterprises	42	60 Plym	188	900
2. Richard Petty	Petty Enterprises	43	60 Plym	185	525
3. Rex White	Rex White	4	59 Chev	184	375
4. Nook Walters	Nook Walters	1	59 Chev	179	275
5. L. D. Austin	L. D. Austin	74	58 Chev	174	250

Langhorne Speedway
Langhorne, PA
1-mile Dirt Track

1-mile circular track opened in May 1926. First named Philadelphia Speedway. Closed on 5/10/92. Re-opened after the war in June 1946. First NASCAR Winston Cup (then Grand National) race staged on 9/11/49 (won by Curtis Turner). Sara Christian, the first woman to compete at top level NASCAR racing, finished 6th in the field of 45 and was invited to share Victory Lane ceremonies with Turner. Final Grand National race run on 9/15/57 (won by Gwyn Staley). The track was commonly referred to as the "Track that ate the heroes" due to its danger. Track paved in 1965 and hosted USAC IndyCar races. Final event was 10/17/71. Now a shopping center.

Winston Cup Starts
Lee Petty   17

Winston Cup Victories
Dick Rathmann   3
Herb Thomas   3

Winston Cup Poles
Herb Thomas   4

Winston Cup Money
Lee Petty $11,515

Most Cars Started
63—September 26, 1954

Fewest Cars Started
24—May 2, 1954

Narrowest Margin of Victory
N/A

Slowest Race
64.434 MPH—June 21, 1953

Race Record
85.850 MPH—April 14, 1957

Most Cautions
9—September 23, 1956

Most Race Leaders
5—April 16, 1950
5—September 14, 1952
5—September 23, 1956

Most Cars Running at Finish
35—September 26, 1954

1949 Strictly Stock Race No. 4
September 11, 1949 Average Speed: 69.403

Driver	Owner	Car #	Make	Laps	Winnings
1. Curtis Turner	Hubert Westmoreland	41	49 Olds	200	2,250
2. Bob Flock	Frank Christian	7	49 Olds	200	1,000
3. Red Byron	Raymond Parks	22	49 Olds	199	800
4. Frank Mundy	Sam Rice	44	49 Cad	196	500
5. Bill Blair	Sam Rice	46	49 Cad	196	350

1950 Grand National Race No. 3
April 16, 1950 Average Speed: 69.399

Driver	Owner	Car #	Make	Laps	Winnings
1. Curtis Turner	John Eanes	41	50 Olds	150	1,500
2. Lloyd Moore	Julian Buesink	59	49 Linc	149	1,000
3. Jimmy Florian	Jimmy Florian	27	50 Ford	144	700
4. Tim Flock	Harold Kite	21	49 Linc	139	500
5. Lee Petty	Petty Enterprises	42	49 Plym	139	300

1950 Grand National Race No. 14
September 17, 1950 Average Speed: 72.801

Driver	Owner	Car #	Make	Laps	Winnings
1. Fonty Flock	Frank Christian	47	50 Olds	200	1,500
2. Bill Blair	Sam Rice	2	49 Olds	200	1,000
3. Fireball Roberts	Sam Rice	82	50 Olds	—	700
4. Lee Petty	Petty Enterprises	42	49 Plym	—	400
5. Neil Cole			49 Ford	—	300

1951 Grand National Race No. 27
September 15, 1951 Average Speed: 71.043

Driver	Owner	Car #	Make	Laps	Winnings
1. Herb Thomas	Herb Thomas	92	51 Huds	150	1,275
2. Fonty Flock	Frank Christian	14	51 Olds	150	800
3. Dick Rathmann	Walt Chapman	21	51 Huds	—	600
4. John McGinley	Walt Chapman	120	51 Huds	—	500
5. Tim Flock	Ted Chester	91	51 Olds	—	300

1952 Grand National Race No. 9
May 4, 1952 Average Speed: 67.669

Driver	Owner	Car #	Make	Laps	Winnings
1. Dick Rathmann	Walt Chapman	120	52 Huds	150	1,275
2. Tim Flock	Ted Chester	91	51 Huds	145	810
3. Lee Petty	Petty Enterprises	42	51 Plym	140	600
4. Jack Reynolds		421	50 Plym	140	500
5. Fonty Flock	Frank Christian	14	51 Olds	139	310

1952 Grand National Race No. 27
September 14, 1952 Average Speed: 72.463

Driver	Owner	Car #	Make	Laps	Winnings
1. Lee Petty	Petty Enterprises	42	51 Plym	250	2,500
2. Bill Blair	George Hutchens	2	52 Olds	250	1,250
3. Herschel Buchanan	Herschel Buchanan	1	52 Nash	248	750
4. Tim Flock	Ted Chester	91	52 Huds	247	500
5. Dick Rathmann	Walt Chapman	120	52 Huds	246	450

1953 Grand National Race No. 8
May 3, 1953 Average Speed: 72.743

Driver	Owner	Car #	Make	Laps	Winnings
1. Buck Baker	Griffin Motors	87	53 Olds	150	1,525
2. Lee Petty	Petty Enterprises	42	53 Dodg	150	1,000
3. Fonty Flock	Frank Christian	14	53 Olds	—	800
4. Herschel Buchanan	Herschel Buchanan	1	52 Nash	—	600
5. Tim Flock	Ted Chester	91	53 Huds	—	500

1953 Grand National Race No. 16
June 21, 1953 Average Speed: 64.434

Driver	Owner	Car #	Make	Laps	Winnings
1. Dick Rathmann	Walt Chapman	120	53 Huds	200	2,500
2. Lee Petty	Petty Enterprises	42	53 Dodg	196	1,500
3. Jim Paschal	George Hutchens	80	53 Dodg	191	900
4. Herb Thomas	Herb Thomas	92	53 Huds	188	700
5. Bill Blair	Bill Blair	2	53 Olds	187	500

1953 Grand National Race No. 32
September 20, 1953 Average Speed: 67.046

Driver	Owner	Car #	Make	Laps	Winnings
1. Dick Rathmann	Walt Chapman	120	53 Huds	250	2,500
2. Herb Thomas	Herb Thomas	92	53 Huds	249	1,250
3. Speedy Thompson	Buckshot Morris	46	53 Olds	248	750
4. Jim Reed	Herb Thomas	9	52 Huds	—	500
5. Jim Paschal	George Hutchens	80	53 Dodg	—	450

1954 Grand National Race No. 10
May 2, 1954 Average Speed: 74.883

Driver	Owner	Car #	Make	Laps	Winnings
1. Herb Thomas	Herb Thomas	92	54 Huds	150	1,685
2. Al Keller	George Miller	23	54 Huds	149	810
3. Dick Rathmann	John Ditz	3	54 Huds	149	610
4. Joe Eubanks	Phil Oates	82	51 Huds	133	510
5. Paul Pettitt	Paul Pettitt	45	53 Huds	132	325

Langhorne Speedway *continued*

1954 Grand National Race No. 34
September 26, 1954 Average Speed: 71.186

Driver	Owner	Car #	Make	Laps	Winnings
1. Herb Thomas	Herb Thomas	92	54 Huds	250	2,450
2. Lee Petty	Petty Enterprises	42	54 Chrys	250	1,150
3. Hershel McGriff	Frank Christian	14	54 Olds	250	850
4. Buck Baker	Griffin Motors	87	54 Olds	245	625
5. Erick Erickson	Erick Erickson	23	54 Buick	245	600

1955 Grand National Race No. 10
April 24, 1955 Average Speed: 72.893

Driver	Owner	Car #	Make	Laps	Winnings
1. Tim Flock	Carl Kiekhaefer	300	55 Chrys	124	1,430
2. Buck Baker	Griffin Motors	87	54 Olds	124	860
3. Junior Johnson	B & L Motors	55	55 Olds	124	600
4. Dick Rathmann	John Ditz	3	54 Huds	124	515
5. Herb Thomas	Herb Thomas	92	55 Buick	122	350

1955 Grand National Race No. 37
September 18, 1955 Average Speed: 77.888

Driver	Owner	Car #	Make	Laps	Winnings
1. Tim Flock	Carl Kiekhaefer	300	55 Chrys	250	2,250
2. Herb Thomas	Herb Thomas	92	55 Chev	249	1,525
3. Fonty Flock	Carl Kiekhaefer	301	55 Chrys	246	950
4. Marvin Panch	J. H. Petty	44	5 Chev	245	750
5. Jimmy Massey	Hubert Westmoreland	04	55 Chev	244	600

1956 Grand National Race No. 11
April 22, 1956 Average Speed: 75.928

Driver	Owner	Car #	Make	Laps	Winnings
1. Buck Baker	Carl Kiekhaefer	87	56 Chrys	150	1,750
2. Herb Thomas	Carl Kiekhaefer	92	56 Chrys	149	1,000
3. Tim Flock	Smokey Yunick	3	56 Chev	149	725
4. Lee Petty	Petty Enterprises	42	56 Dodg	149	530
5. Jimmy Massey	Hubert Westmoreland	2	56 Chev	146	345

1956 Grand National Race No. 47
September 23, 1956 Average Speed: 70.615

Driver	Owner	Car #	Make	Laps	Winnings
1. Paul Goldsmith	Smokey Yunick	3	56 Chev	300	4,150
2. Lee Petty	Petty Enterprises	42	56 Dodg	293	1,800
3. Speedy Thompson	Carl Kiekhaefer	67	56 Dodg	292	1,175
4. Jim Paschal	Bill Stroppe	26	56 Merc	292	950
5. Herb Thomas	Herb Thomas	92	56 Chev	290	700

1957 Grand National Race No. 10
April 14, 1957 Average Speed: 85.850

Driver	Owner	Car #	Make	Laps	Winnings
1. Fireball Roberts	Pete DePaolo	22	57 Ford	150	1,890
2. Paul Goldsmith	Smokey Yunick	3	57 Ford	150	1,125
3. Speedy Thompson	Hugh Babb	46	57 Chev	147	750
4. Billy Myers	Bill Stroppe	14	57 Merc	146	540
5. Buck Baker	Hugh Babb	87	57 Chev	145	345

1957 Grand National Race No. 45
September 15, 1957 Average Speed: 72.759

Driver	Owner	Car #	Make	Laps	Winnings
1. Gwyn Staley	J. H. Petty	38	57 Chev	300	4,500
2. Whitey Norman	Whitey Norman	0	57 Ford	298	2,350
3. Johnny Allen	Spook Crawford	64	57 Plym	295	1,700
4. Rex White	Bob Welborn	44	57 Chev	295	1,135
5. Buck Baker	Buck Baker	87	57 Chev	295	960

Lincoln Speedway
Abbottstown, PA (New Oxford, PA)
Half-mile Dirt Track

Half-mile dirt track built in 1951. First Winston Cup (then Grand National) race run on 6/10/55 (won by Junior Johnson). Final Grand National race run on 9/14/65 (won by Dick Hutcherson). Track still in operation.

Winston Cup Starts
Buck Baker   6

Winston Cup Victories
Buck Baker   2

Winston Cup Poles
Junior Johnson   1
Tiny Lund   1
Marvin Panch   1
David Pearson   1
Richard Petty   1
Ken Rush   1
Speedy Thompson   1

Winston Cup Money
Buck Baker $2,900

Most Cars Started
32—August 10, 1957

Fewest Cars Started
17—May 25, 1956

Narrowest Margin of Victory
1 car length—May 25, 1956

Slowest Race
65.371 MPH—June 10, 1955

Race Record
82.607 MPH—September 14, 1965
Pennsylvania 200 Classic

Most Cautions
N/A

Most Race Leaders
3—June 10, 1955
3—May 25, 1956

Most Cars Running at Finish
20—May 30, 1957

1955 Grand National Race No. 19
June 10, 1955 Average Speed: 65.371

Driver	Owner	Car #	Make	Laps	Winnings
1. Junior Johnson	B & L Motors	55	55 Olds	200	1,000
2. Tim Flock	Carl Kiekhaefer	300	55 Chrys	198	650
3. Buck Baker	Griffin Motors	87	54 Olds	197	450
4. Jim Reed	Jim Reed	7	55 Chev	195	350
5. Nace Mattingly	Nace Mattingly	54	55 Ford	190	300

1956 Grand National Race No. 19
May 25, 1956 Average Speed: 69.619

Driver	Owner	Car #	Make	Laps	Winnings
1. Buck Baker	Carl Kiekhaefer	500B	56 Dodg	200	1,100
2. Jim Paschal	Frank Hayworth	75	56 Merc	200	700
3. Lee Petty	Petty Enterprises	42	56 Dodg	200	475
4. Herb Thomas	Carl Kiekhaefer	502	56 Dodg	195	365
5. Nace Mattingly	Nace Mattingly	54	56 Ford	185	310

1957 Grand National Race No. 20
May 30, 1957 Average Speed: 76.126

Driver	Owner	Car #	Make	Laps	Winnings
1. Buck Baker	Hugh Babb	87	57 Chev	200	700
2. Fireball Roberts	Pete DePaolo	22	57 Ford	200	525
3. Paul Goldsmith	Smokey Yunick	3	57 Ford	200	400
4. Marvin Panch	Pete DePaolo	98	57 Ford	200	330
5. Speedy Thompson	Hugh Babb	46	57 Chev	200	270

1957 Grand National Race No. 37
August 10, 1957 Average Speed: 77.569

Driver	Owner	Car #	Make	Laps	Winnings
1. Marvin Panch	Marvin Panch	98	57 Ford	200	1,000
2. Speedy Thompson	Speedy Thompson	46	57 Chev	200	625
3. Tiny Lund	A. L. Bumgarner	55	57 Pont	198	400
4. Johnny Allen	Spook Crawford	64	57 Plym	191	295
5. Johnny Mackison	Johnny Mackison	104	57 Ford	188	255

1958 Grand National Race No. 25
June 25, 1958 Average Speed: 69.726

Driver	Owner	Car #	Make	Laps	Winnings
1. Lee Petty	Petty Enterprises	42	57 Olds	200	800
2. Buck Baker	Buck Baker	87	57 Chev	200	525
3. Bob Welborn	J. H. Petty	49	57 Chev	199	350
4. Shorty Rollins	Shorty Rollins	99	58 Ford	196	250
5. Reds Kagle	Hoss Kagle	88	57 Chev	194	225

1964 Grand National Race No. 41 Pennsylvania 200 Classic
July 21, 1964 Average Speed: 82.568

Driver	Owner	Car #	Make	Laps	Winnings
1. David Pearson	Cotton Owens	6	64 Dodg	200	1,000
2. Richard Petty	Petty Enterprises	41	64 Plym	200	600
3. Jimmy Pardue	Charles Robinson	54	64 Plym	194	400
4. Wendell Scott	Wendell Scott	34	63 Ford	193	300
5. Doug Yates	Doug Yates	72	64 Plym	192	275

1965 Grand National Race No. 47 Pennsylvania 200 Classic
September 14, 1965 Average Speed: 82.607

Driver	Owner	Car #	Make	Laps	Winnings
1. Dick Hutcherson	Holman-Moody	29	65 Ford	200	1,000
2. G. C. Spencer	G. C. Spencer	49	64 Ford	192	600
3. David Pearson	Cotton Owens	6	65 Dodg	190	400
4. Ned Jarrett	Bondy Long	11	65 Ford	190	300
5. Buddy Baker	Buck Baker	86	64 Dodg	189	275

New Bradford Speedway
Bradford, PA
.333-mile Dirt Track

.333-mile dirt oval built in 1958. Staged first Winston Cup (then Grand National) race on 6/12/58 (won by Junior Johnson). Track now measured at a quarter-mile.

Winston Cup Victories
Junior Johnson   1

Winston Cup Poles
Bob Duell   1

Winston Cup Money
Junior Johnson $550

Most Cars Started
21—June 12, 1958

Narrowest Margin of Victory
N/A

Race Record
59.840 MPH—June 12, 1958

Most Race Leaders
N/A

Most Cars Running at Finish
14—June 12, 1958

1958 Grand National Race No. 23
June 12, 1958 Average Speed: 59.840

Driver	Owner	Car #	Make	Laps	Winnings
1. Junior Johnson	Paul Spaulding	11	57 Ford	150	550
2. Lee Petty	Petty Enterprises	42	57 Olds	150	450
3. Bob Duell	Julian Buesink	95	57 Ford	148	325
4. Jack Smith	Jack Smith	47	57 Chev	148	250
5. Billy Rafter	Billy Rafter	57	57 Ford	147	215

Pine Grove Speedway
Shippenville, PA
Half-mile Dirt Track

Half-mile dirt track built in 1950. Only NASCAR Winston Cup (then Grand National) race staged on 10/14/51 (won by Tim Flock). Track conducted races in sporadic manner until it closed in 1960s.

Winston Cup Victories
Tim Flock   1

Winston Cup Money
Tim Flock $1,000

Most Cars Started
20—October 14, 1951

Narrowest Margin of Victory
N/A

Most Race Leaders
N/A

Most Cars Running at Finish
N/A

1951 Grand National Race No. 33
October 14, 1951

Driver	Owner	Car #	Make	Laps	Winnings
1. Tim Flock	Ted Chester	91	51 Olds	200	1,000
2. John McGinley	Walt Chapman	120	51 Huds	—	600
3. Billy Carden	Sam Knox	8	50 Olds	—	500
4. Jimmy Florian	Jimmy Florian		50 Olds	—	400
5. Lloyd Moore	Julian Buesink	59	51 Ford	—	300

Pocono Int'l Raceway
Long Pond, PA
2.5-mile Paved Track

Proposed in 1960, but not constructed until 1969. First track was .75-mile oval. Road courses were also built. 2.5-mile triangular speedway opened with USAC IndyCar race on 7/3/71. First Winston Cup Grand National race staged on 8/4/74 (won by Richard Petty). Track has three straightaways of different lengths and three corners, each with a different radius and banking.

Winston Cup Starts
Ricky Rudd   47

Winston Cup Victories
Bill Elliott   5

Winston Cup Poles
Ken Schrader   5

Winston Cup Money
Dale Jarrett $1,535,667

Most Cars Started
43—10 times

Fewest Cars Started
35—August 4, 1974 Purolator 500
35—August 3, 1975 Purolator 500
35—July 31, 1977 Coca-Cola 500
35—July 26, 1981 Mountain Dew 500

Narrowest Margin of Victory
0.050 seconds July 20, 1986
Summer 500

Slowest Race
111.179 MPH—August 3, 1975
Purolator 500

Race Record
144.892 MPH—July 21, 1996
Miller Genuine Draft 500

Most Cautions
13—June 17, 1990
Miller Genuine Draft 500

Most Race Leaders
16—June 17, 1990
Miller Genuine Draft 500

Most Cars Running at Finish
40—July 29, 2001

1974 Winston Cup GN Race No. 20 Purolator 500
August 4, 1974 Average Speed: 115.593

Driver	Owner	Car #	Make	Laps	Winnings
1. Richard Petty	Petty Enterprises	43	74 Dodg	192	17,000
2. Buddy Baker	Bud Moore	15	73 Ford	192	10,650
3. Cale Yarborough	Junior Johnson	11	74 Chev	192	7,350
4. David Pearson	Wood Brothers	21	73 Merc	192	3,750
5. Benny Parsons	L. G. DeWitt	72	74 Chev	190	6,100

1975 Winston Cup GN Race No. 18 Purolator 500
August 3, 1975 Average Speed: 111.179

Driver	Owner	Car #	Make	Laps	Winnings
1. David Pearson	Wood Brothers	21	73 Merc	200	15,725
2. Richard Petty	Petty Enterprises	43	74 Dodg	200	13,000
3. Buddy Baker	Bud Moore	15	73 Ford	200	9,200
4. Benny Parsons	L. G. DeWitt	72	75 Chev	200	6,725
5. Richard Childress	Tom Garn	96	75 Chev	196	3,525

1976 Winston Cup GN Race No. 18 Purolator 500
August 1, 1976 Average Speed: 115.875

Driver	Owner	Car #	Make	Laps	Winnings
1. Richard Petty	Petty Enterprises	43	Dodg	200	20,640
2. Buddy Baker	Bud Moore	15	Ford	200	13,465
3. Benny Parsons	L. G. DeWitt	72	Chev	200	9,790
4. David Pearson	Wood Brothers	21	Merc	200	5,060
5. Lennie Pond	Ronnie Elder	54	Chev	198	5,400

1977 Winston Cup GN Race No. 18 Coca-Cola 500
July 31, 1977 Average Speed: 128.379

Driver	Owner	Car #	Make	Laps	Winnings
1. Benny Parsons	L. G. DeWitt	72	Chev	200	15,475
2. Richard Petty	Petty Enterprises	43	Dodg	200	12,200
3. Darrell Waltrip	DiGard	88	Chev	200	9,825
4. Bobby Allison	Bobby Allison	12	Mata	200	6,150
5. Dick Brooks	Junie Donlavey	90	Ford	198	5,200

1978 Winston Cup GN Race No. 18 Coca-Cola 500
July 30, 1978 Average Speed: 142.540

Driver	Owner	Car #	Make	Laps	Winnings
1. Darrell Waltrip	DiGard	88	Chev	200	20,890
2. David Pearson	Wood Brothers	21	Merc	200	11,165
3. Bobby Allison	Bud Moore	15	Ford	199	10,965
4. Dave Marcis	Rod Osterlund	2	Chev	197	6,665
5. Buddy Baker	M. C. Anderson	27	Chev	197	5,615

1979 Winston Cup GN Race No. 19 Coca-Cola 500
July 30, 1979 Average Speed: 115.207

Driver	Owner	Car #	Make	Laps	Winnings
1. Cale Yarborough	Junior Johnson	11	Chev	200	21,465
2. Richard Petty	Petty Enterprises	43	Chev	200	15,465
3. Buddy Baker	Harry Ranier	28	Chev	200	8,490
4. Benny Parsons	M. C. Anderson	27	Chev	200	7,765
5. Ricky Rudd	Junie Donlavey	90	Merc	200	6,215

1980 Winston Cup GN Race No. 19 Coca-Cola 500
July 27, 1980 Average Speed: 124.395

Driver	Owner	Car #	Make	Laps	Winnings
1. Neil Bonnett	Wood Brothers	21	Merc	200	19,915
2. Buddy Baker	Harry Ranier	28	Buick	200	12,590
3. Cale Yarborough	Junior Johnson	11	Chev	200	13,640
4. Dale Earnhardt	Rod Osterlund	2	Chev	200	11,415
5. Harry Gant	Jack Beebe	47	Chev	200	7,545

1981 Winston Cup GN Race No. 19 Mountain Dew 500
July 26, 1981 Average Speed: 119.111

Driver	Owner	Car #	Make	Laps	Winnings
1. Darrell Waltrip	Junior Johnson	11	Buick	200	23,640
2. Richard Petty	Petty Enterprises	43	Buick	200	18,915
3. Benny Parsons	Bud Moore	15	Ford	200	13,515
4. Harry Gant	Hal Needham	33	Pont	200	4,990
5. Cale Yarborough	M. C. Anderson	27	Buick	200	4,290

1982 Winston Cup GN Race No. 13 Van Scoy Diamond Mine 500
June 6, 1982 Average Speed: 113.579

Driver	Owner	Car #	Make	Laps	Winnings
1. Bobby Allison	DiGard	88	Buick	200	25,500
2. Tim Richmond	Jim Stacy	2	Buick	200	15,430
3. Benny Parsons	Harry Ranier	28	Pont	199	17,375
4. Harry Gant	Hal Needham	33	Buick	199	10,180
5. Terry Labonte	Billy Hagan	44	Chev	199	8,735

1982 Winston Cup GN Race No. 18 Mountain Dew 500
July 25, 1982 Average Speed: 115.496

Driver	Owner	Car #	Make	Laps	Winnings
1. Bobby Allison	DiGard	88	Buick	200	24,200
2. Richard Petty	Petty Enterprises	43	Pont	200	21,500
3. Terry Labonte	Billy Hagan	44	Buick	200	12,755
4. Ron Bouchard	Jack Beebe	47	Buick	200	14,100
5. Buddy Baker	Harry Ranier	28	Pont	200	13,850

Pocono Int'l Raceway *continued*

1983 Winston Cup GN Race No. 14 Van Scoy Diamond Mine 500
June 12, 1983 Average Speed: 128.636

Driver	Owner	Car #	Make	Laps	Winnings
1. Bobby Allison	DiGard	22	Buick	200	31,100
2. Darrell Waltrip	Junior Johnson	11	Chev	200	25,950
3. Richard Petty	Petty Enterprises	43	Pont	200	17,225
4. Tim Richmond	Raymond Beadle	27	Pont	199	10,580
5. Benny Parsons	Johnny Hayes	55	Buick	199	7,100

1983 Winston Cup GN Race No. 18 Like Cola 500
July 24, 1983 Average Speed: 114.818

Driver	Owner	Car #	Make	Laps	Winnings
1. Tim Richmond	Raymond Beadle	27	Pont	200	27,430
2. Darrell Waltrip	Junior Johnson	11	Chev	200	23,375
3. Bobby Allison	DiGard	22	Buick	200	21,950
4. Neil Bonnett	Bob Rahilly & Butch Mock	75	Chev	200	16,525
5. Harry Gant	Hal Needham	33	Buick	200	14,700

1984 Winston Cup GN Race No. 14 Van Scoy Diamond Mine 500
June 10, 1984 Average Speed: 138.164

Driver	Owner	Car #	Make	Laps	Winnings
1. Cale Yarborough	Harry Ranier	28	Chev	200	30,850
2. Harry Gant	Hal Needham	33	Chev	200	21,980
3. Terry Labonte	Billy Hagan	44	Chev	200	17,295
4. Bill Elliott	Harry Melling	9	Ford	200	16,150
5. Tim Richmond	Raymond Beadle	27	Pont	200	14,900

1984 Winston Cup GN Race No. 18 Like Cola 500
July 22, 1984 Average Speed: 121.351

Driver	Owner	Car #	Make	Laps	Winnings
1. Harry Gant	Hal Needham	33	Chev	200	34,605
2. Cale Yarborough	Harry Ranier	28	Chev	200	17,275
3. Bill Elliott	Harry Melling	9	Ford	200	24,250
4. Terry Labonte	Billy Hagan	44	Chev	200	13,695
5. Benny Parsons	Johnny Hayes	55	Chev	200	8,450

1985 Winston Cup GN Race No. 13 Van Scoy Diamond Mine 500
June 9, 1985 Average Speed: 138.974

Driver	Owner	Car #	Make	Laps	Winnings
1. Bill Elliott	Harry Melling	9	Ford	200	44,525
2. Harry Gant	Hal Needham	33	Chev	200	27,675
3. Darrell Waltrip	Junior Johnson	11	Chev	200	23,100
4. Geoff Bodine	Rick Hendrick	5	Chev	200	28,325
5. Neil Bonnett	Junior Johnson	12	Chev	199	15,525

1985 Winston Cup GN Race No. 16 Summer 500
July 21, 1985 Average Speed: 134.008

Driver	Owner	Car #	Make	Laps	Winnings
1. Bill Elliott	Harry Melling	9	Ford	200	41,750
2. Neil Bonnett	Junior Johnson	12	Chev	200	38,450
3. Darrell Waltrip	Junior Johnson	11	Chev	200	25,375
4. Geoff Bodine	Rick Hendrick	5	Chev	200	18,325
5. Harry Gant	Hal Needham	33	Chev	200	17,425

1986 Winston Cup Race No. 13 Miller High Life 500
June 8, 1986 Average Speed: 113.279

Driver	Owner	Car #	Make	Laps	Winnings
1. Tim Richmond	Rick Hendrick	25	Chev	200	46,705
2. Dale Earnhardt	Richard Childress	3	Chev	200	29,750
3. Cale Yarborough	Harry Ranier	28	Ford	200	15,450
4. Ricky Rudd	Bud Moore	15	Ford	200	18,375
5. Bill Elliott	Harry Melling	9	Ford	200	19,725

1986 Winston Cup Race No. 16 Summer 500
July 20, 1986 Average Speed: 124.218

Driver	Owner	Car #	Make	Laps	Winnings
1. Tim Richmond	Rick Hendrick	25	Chev	150	46,805
2. Ricky Rudd	Bud Moore	15	Ford	150	29,500
3. Geoff Bodine	Rick Hendrick	5	Chev	150	22,350
4. Darrell Waltrip	Junior Johnson	11	Chev	150	23,825
5. Bobby Allison	Stavola Brothers	22	Buick	150	17,525

1987 Winston Cup Race No. 12 Miller High Life 500
June 14, 1987 Average Speed: 122.166

Driver	Owner	Car #	Make	Laps	Winnings
1. Tim Richmond	Rick Hendrick	25	Chev	200	40,325
2. Bill Elliott	Harry Melling	9	Ford	200	30,600
3. Kyle Petty	Wood Brothers	21	Ford	200	24,575
4. Cale Yarborough	Cale Yarborough	29	Olds	200	11,505
5. Dale Earnhardt	Richard Childress	3	Chev	200	22,400

1987 Winston Cup Race No. 16 Summer 500
July 19, 1987 Average Speed: 121.745

Driver	Owner	Car #	Make	Laps	Winnings
1. Dale Earnhardt	Richard Childress	3	Chev	200	55,875
2. Alan Kulwicki	Alan Kulwicki	7	Ford	200	32,880
3. Buddy Baker	Buddy Baker & Danny Schiff	88	Olds	200	18,100
4. Benny Parsons	Rick Hendrick	35	Chev	200	21,445
5. Davey Allison	Harry Ranier	28	Ford	200	11,650

1988 Winston Cup Race No. 13 Miller High Life 500
June 19, 1988 Average Speed: 126.147

Driver	Owner	Car #	Make	Laps	Winnings
1. Geoff Bodine	Rick Hendrick	5	Chev	200	51,200
2. Michael Waltrip	Chuck Rider	30	Pont	200	31,100
3. Rusty Wallace	Raymond Beadle	27	Pont	200	26,500
4. Mark Martin	Jack Roush	6	Ford	200	15,080
5. Davey Allison	Harry Ranier	28	Ford	200	20,925

1988 Winston Cup Race No. 16 AC Spark Plug 500
July 24, 1988 Average Speed: 122.866

Driver	Owner	Car #	Make	Laps	Winnings
1. Bill Elliott	Harry Melling	9	Ford	200	53,200
2. Ken Schrader	Rick Hendrick	25	Chev	200	30,725
3. Davey Allison	Harry Ranier	28	Ford	200	26,275
4. Geoff Bodine	Rick Hendrick	5	Chev	200	17,775
5. Darrell Waltrip	Rick Hendrick	17	Chev	200	17,925

1989 Winston Cup Race No. 13 Miller High Life 500
June 18, 1989 Average Speed: 131.320

Driver	Owner	Car #	Make	Laps	Winnings
1. Terry Labonte	Junior Johnson	11	Ford	200	54,807
2. Harry Gant	Leo Jackson	33	Olds	200	33,875
3. Dale Earnhardt	Richard Childress	3	Chev	200	29,250
4. Ken Schrader	Rick Hendrick	25	Chev	200	20,600
5. Morgan Shepherd	Bob Rahilly & Butch Mock	75	Pont	200	21,850

1989 Winston Cup Race No. 16 AC Spark Plug 500
July 23, 1989 Average Speed: 117.847

Driver	Owner	Car #	Make	Laps	Winnings
1. Bill Elliott	Harry Melling	9	Ford	200	58,400
2. Rusty Wallace	Raymond Beadle	27	Pont	200	46,875
3. Mark Martin	Jack Roush	6	Ford	200	26,300
4. Darrell Waltrip	Rick Hendrick	17	Chev	200	23,850
5. Harry Gant	Leo Jackson	33	Olds	200	20,350

Pocono Int'l Raceway *continued*

1990 Winston Cup Series Race No. 13 Miller Genuine Draft 500
June 17, 1990 Average Speed: 120.600

Driver	Owner	Car #	Make	Laps	Winnings
1. Harry Gant	Leo Jackson	33	Olds	200	54,350
2. Rusty Wallace	Raymond Beadle	27	Pont	200	37,307
3. Geoff Bodine	Junior Johnson	11	Ford	200	30,750
4. Brett Bodine	Kenny Bernstein	26	Buick	200	19,850
5. Davey Allison	Robert Yates	28	Ford	200	20,700

1990 Winston Cup Series Race No. 16 AC Spark Plug 500
July 22, 1990 Average Speed: 124.070

Driver	Owner	Car #	Make	Laps	Winnings
1. Geoff Bodine	Junior Johnson	11	Ford	200	58,500
2. Bill Elliott	Harry Melling	9	Ford	200	33,650
3. Rusty Wallace	Raymond Beadle	27	Pont	200	30,000
4. Dale Earnhardt	Richard Childress	3	Chev	200	22,800
5. Davey Allison	Robert Yates	28	Ford	200	25,950

1991 Winston Cup Series Race No. 13 Champion Spark Plug 500
June 16, 1991 Average Speed: 122.666

Driver	Owner	Car #	Make	Laps	Winnings
1. Darrell Waltrip	Darrell Waltrip	17	Chev	200	60,650
2. Dale Earnhardt	Richard Childress	3	Chev	200	43,775
3. Mark Martin	Jack Roush	6	Ford	200	38,875
4. Harry Gant	Leo Jackson	33	Olds	200	22,600
5. Geoff Bodine	Junior Johnson	97	Ford	200	15,125

1991 Winston Cup Series Race No. 16 Miller Genuine Draft 500
July 21, 1991 Average Speed: 115.459

Driver	Owner	Car #	Make	Laps	Winnings
1. Rusty Wallace	Roger Penske	2	Pont	179	34,100
2. Mark Martin	Jack Roush	6	Ford	179	41,475
3. Geoff Bodine	Junior Johnson	11	Ford	179	32,350
4. Hut Stricklin	Bobby Allison	12	Buick	179	21,750
5. Sterling Marlin	Junior Johnson	22	Ford	179	14,100

1992 Winston Cup Race No. 13 Champion Spark Plug 500
June 14, 1992 Average Speed: 144.023

Driver	Owner	Car #	Make	Laps	Winnings
1. Alan Kulwicki	Alan Kulwicki	7	Ford	200	74,255
2. Mark Martin	Jack Roush	6	Ford	200	39,480
3. Bill Elliott	Junior Johnson	11	Ford	200	32,355
4. Ken Schrader	Rick Hendrick	25	Chev	200	32,980
5. Davey Allison	Robert Yates	28	Ford	200	27,175

1992 Winston Cup Race No. 16 Miller Genuine Draft 500
July 19, 1992 Average Speed: 134.058

Driver	Owner	Car #	Make	Laps	Winnings
1. Darrell Waltrip	Darrell Waltrip	17	Chev	200	63,445
2. Harry Gant	Leo Jackson	33	Olds	200	40,520
3. Alan Kulwicki	Alan Kulwicki	7	Ford	200	42,095
4. Ricky Rudd	Rick Hendrick	5	Chev	200	24,695
5. Ted Musgrave	D. K. Ulrich & Ray DeWitt	55	Ford	200	22,365

1993 Winston Cup Series Race No. 13 Champion Spark Plug 500
June 13, 1993 Average Speed: 138.005

Driver	Owner	Car #	Make	Laps	Winnings
1. Kyle Petty	Felix Sabates	42	Pont	200	44,960
2. Ken Schrader	Rick Hendrick	25	Chev	200	58,435
3. Harry Gant	Leo Jackson	33	Chev	200	38,335
4. Jimmy Spencer	Bobby Allison	12	Ford	200	31,410
5. Ted Musgrave	Ray DeWitt	55	Ford	200	24,040

1993 Winston Cup Series Race No. 17 Miller Genuine Draft 500
July 18, 1993 Average Speed: 133.343

Driver	Owner	Car #	Make	Laps	Winnings
1. Dale Earnhardt	Richard Childress	3	Chev	200	66,795
2. Rusty Wallace	Roger Penske	2	Pont	200	35,145
3. Bill Elliott	Junior Johnson	11	Ford	200	39,720
4. Morgan Shepherd	Wood Brothers	21	Ford	200	26,345
5. Brett Bodine	Kenny Bernstein	26	Ford	200	25,940

1994 Winston Cup Series Race No. 13 UAW-GM Teamwork 500
June 12, 1994 Average Speed: 128.801

Driver	Owner	Car #	Make	Laps	Winnings
1. Rusty Wallace	Roger Penske	2	Ford	200	84,525
2. Dale Earnhardt	Richard Childress	3	Chev	200	46,425
3. Ken Schrader	Rick Hendrick	25	Chev	200	33,400
4. Morgan Shepherd	Wood Brothers	21	Ford	200	24,900
5. Mark Martin	Jack Roush	6	Ford	200	30,400

1994 Winston Cup Series Race No. 17 Miller Genuine Draft 500
July 17, 1994 Average Speed: 136.075

Driver	Owner	Car #	Make	Laps	Winnings
1. Geoff Bodine	Geoff Bodine	7	Ford	200	103,270
2. Ward Burton	A. G. Dillard	31	Chev	200	39,720
3. Joe Nemechek	Larry Hedrick	41	Chev	200	29,790
4. Jeff Burton	Stavola Brothers	8	Ford	200	29,640
5. Morgan Shepherd	Wood Brothers	21	Ford	200	30,635

1995 Winston Cup Series Race No. 13 UAW-GM Teamwork 500
June 11, 1995 Average Speed: 137.720

Driver	Owner	Car #	Make	Laps	Winnings
1. Terry Labonte	Rick Hendrick	5	Chev	200	71,175
2. Ted Musgrave	Jack Roush	16	Ford	200	50,525
3. Ken Schrader	Rick Hendrick	25	Chev	200	45,550
4. Sterling Marlin	Larry McClure	4	Chev	200	35,250
5. Hut Stricklin	Kenny Bernstein	26	Ford	200	30,900

1995 Winston Cup Series Race No. 17 Miller Genuine Draft 500
July 16, 1995 Average Speed: 134.038

Driver	Owner	Car #	Make	Laps	Winnings
1. Dale Jarrett	Robert Yates	28	Ford	200	72,970
2. Jeff Gordon	Rick Hendrick	24	Chev	200	48,520
3. Ricky Rudd	Ricky Rudd	10	Ford	200	41,010
4. Ted Musgrave	Jack Roush	16	Ford	200	32,135
5. Bill Elliott	Bill Elliott	94	Ford	200	32,780

1996 Winston Cup Series Race No. 13 UAW-GM Teamwork 500
June 16, 1996 Average Speed: 139.104

Driver	Owner	Car #	Make	Laps	Winnings
1. Jeff Gordon	Rick Hendrick	24	Chev	200	96,980
2. Ricky Rudd	Ricky Rudd	10	Ford	200	52,900
3. Geoff Bodine	Geoff Bodine	7	Ford	200	54,700
4. Mark Martin	Jack Roush	6	Ford	200	38,975
5. Bobby Hamilton	Petty Enterprises	43	Pont	200	31,875

1996 Winston Cup Series Race No. 17 Miller Genuine Draft 500
July 21, 1996 Average Speed: 144.892

Driver	Owner	Car #	Make	Laps	Winnings
1. Rusty Wallace	Roger Penske	2	Ford	200	59,165
2. Ricky Rudd	Ricky Rudd	10	Ford	200	56,615
3. Dale Jarrett	Robert Yates	88	Ford	200	35,705
4. Ernie Irvan	Robert Yates	28	Ford	200	44,590
5. Johnny Benson Jr.	Chuck Rider	30	Pont	200	36,400

Pocono Int'l Raceway *continued*

1997 Winston Cup Series Race No. 13
June 8, 1997 Average Speed: 139.828

Driver	Owner	Car #	Make	Laps	Winnings
1. Jeff Gordon	Rick Hendrick	24	Chev	200	166,080
2. Jeff Burton	Jack Roush	99	Ford	200	52,550
3. Dale Jarrett	Robert Yates	88	Ford	200	53,245
4. Mark Martin	Jack Roush	6	Ford	200	39,620
5. Jeremy Mayfield	Michael Kranefuss	37	Ford	200	33,070

1997 Winston Cup Series Race No. 18
July 20, 1997 Average Speed: 142.068

Driver	Owner	Car #	Make	Laps	Winnings
1. Dale Jarrett	Robert Yates	88	Ford	200	104,570
2. Jeff Gordon	Rick Hendrick	24	Chev	200	56,745
3. Jeff Burton	Jack Roush	99	Ford	200	44,195
4. Ted Musgrave	Jack Roush	16	Ford	200	39,070
5. Mark Martin	Jack Roush	6	Ford	200	36,040

1998 Winston Cup Series Race No. 15
June 21, 1998 Average Speed: 117.801

Driver	Owner	Car #	Make	Laps	Winnings
1. Jeremy Mayfield	Michael Kranefuss	12	Ford	200	111,580
2. Jeff Gordon	Rick Hendrick	24	Chev	200	79,500
3. Dale Jarrett	Robert Yates	88	Ford	200	62,220
4. Jeff Burton	Jack Roush	99	Ford	200	49,080
5. Mark Martin	Jack Roush	6	Ford	200	40,645

1998 Winston Cup Series Race No. 18
July 26, 1998 Average Speed: 134.66

Driver	Owner	Car #	Make	Laps	Winnings
1. Jeff Gordon	Rick Hendrick	24	Chev	200	165,495
2. Mark Martin	Jack Roush	6	Ford	200	89,220
3. Jeff Burton	Jack Roush	99	Ford	200	73,170
4. Bobby Labonte	Joe Gibbs	18	Pont	200	75,545
5. Dale Jarrett	Robert Yates	88	Ford	200	63,815

1999 Winston Cup Series Race No. 15
June 20, 1999 Average Speed: 118.898

Driver	Owner	Car #	Make	Laps	Winnings
1. Bobby Labonte	Joe Gibbs	18	Pont	200	151,110
2. Jeff Gordon	Rick Hendrick	24	Chev	200	86,670
3. Dale Jarrett	Robert Yates	88	Ford	200	86,670
4. Sterling Marlin	Felix Sabates	40	Chev	200	85,245
5. Mark Martin	Jack Roush	6	Ford	200	78,290

1999 Winston Cup Series Race No. 19
July 25, 1999 Average Speed: 116.982

Driver	Owner	Car #	Make	Laps	Winnings
1. Bobby Labonte	Joe Gibbs	18	Pont	200	139,385
2. Dale Jarrett	Robert Yates	88	Ford	200	95,695
3. Mark Martin	Jack Roush	6	Ford	200	82,320
4. Tony Stewart	Joe Gibbs	20	Pont	200	70,970
5. Wally Dallenbach	Rick Hendrick	25	Chev	200	59,855

2000 Winston Cup Series Race No. 15
June 18, 2000 Average Speed: 139.741

Driver	Owner	Car #	Make	Laps	Winnings
1. Jeremy Mayfield	Michael Kranefuss	12	Ford	200	121,020
2. Dale Jarrett	Robert Yates	88	Ford	200	131,520
3. Ricky Rudd	Robert Yates	28	Ford	200	95,870
4. Dale Earnhardt	Richard Childress	3	Chev	200	87,495
5. Mark Martin	Jack Roush	6	Ford	200	71,565

2000 Winston Cup Series Race No. 19
July 23, 2000 Average Speed: 130.662

Driver	Owner	Car #	Make	Laps	Winnings
1. Rusty Wallace	Roger Penske	2	Ford	200	125,745
2. Jeff Burton	Jack Roush	99	Ford	200	121,245
3. Jeff Gordon	Rick Hendrick	24	Chev	200	92,045
4. Dale Jarrett	Robert Yates	88	Ford	200	97,470
5. Matt Kenseth	Jack Roush	17	Ford	200	71,590

2001 Winston Cup Series Race No. 15
June 17, 2001 Average Speed: 134.389

Driver	Owner	Car #	Make	Laps	Winnings
1. Ricky Rudd	Robert Yates	28	Ford	200	189,542
2. Jeff Gordon	Rick Hendrick	24	Chev	200	148,897
3. Dale Jarrett	Robert Yates	88	Ford	200	119,947
4. Sterling Marlin	Chip Ganassi	40	Dodg	200	92,350
5. Mark Martin	Jack Roush	6	Ford	200	102,016

2001 Winston Cup Series Race No. 20
July 29, 2001 Average Speed: 134.59

Driver	Owner	Car #	Make	Laps	Winnings
1. Bobby Labonte	Joe Gibbs	18	Pont	200	189,427
2. Dale Earnhardt, Jr.	Dale Earnhardt, Inc.	8	Chev	200	119,923
3. Tony Stewart	Joe Gibbs	20	Pont	200	91,800
4. Bill Elliott	Ray Evernham	9	Dodg	200	90,948
5. Johnny Benson, Jr.	Nelson Bowers	10	Pont	200	68,895

2002 Winston Cup Series Race No. 14
June 9, 2002 Average Speed: 143.426

Driver	Owner	Car #	Make	Laps	Winnings
1. Dale Jarrett	Robert Yates	88	Ford	200	206,298
2. Mark Martin	Jack Roush	6	Ford	200	141,003
3. Jimmie Johnson	Rick Hendrick	48	Chev	200	83,570
4. Sterling Marlin	Chip Ganassi	40	Dodg	200	113,772
5. Jeff Gordon	Rick Hendrick	24	Chev	200	125,003

2002 Winston Cup Series Race No. 20
July 28, 2002 Average Speed: 125.809

Driver	Owner	Car #	Make	Laps	Winnings
1. Bill Elliott	Ray Evernham	9	Dodg	175	193,401
2. Kurt Busch	Jack Roush	97	Ford	175	113,570
3. Sterling Marlin	Chip Ganassi	40	Dodg	175	136,487
4. Dale Jarrett	Robert Yates	88	Ford	175	109,355
5. Ryan Newman	Roger Penske	12	Ford	175	85,975

Reading Fairgrounds
Reading, PA
Half-mile Dirt Track

One of the most famous tracks in the East. Built in 1924, the first race was run on 9/20/24. Ralph Hankinson was the first promoter. Sam Nunis operated track from 1946–1954. First NASCAR Winston Cup (then Grand National) race staged on 6/15/58 (won by Junior Johnson). Only other Grand National race run 4/26/59 (also won by Johnson). Final event run in June of 1979. Now the site of an art mall.

Winston Cup Starts
9 drivers tied with   2

Winston Cup Victories
Junior Johnson   2

Winston Cup Poles
Speedy Thompson   1

Winston Cup Money
Junior Johnson $1,600

Most Cars Started
30—June 15, 1958

Fewest Cars Started
25—April 26, 1959

Narrowest Margin of Victory
10 car lengths—June 15, 1954

Slowest Race
53.011 MPH—April 26, 1959

Race Record
53.763 MPH—June 15, 1958

Most Cautions
N/A

Most Race Leaders
4—June 15, 1958

Most Cars Running at Finish
19—June 15, 1958

1958 Grand National Race No. 24
June 15, 1958 Average Speed: 53.763

Driver	Owner	Car #	Make	Laps	Winnings
1. Junior Johnson	Paul Spaulding	11	57 Ford	200	800
2. Eddie Pagan	Eddie Pagan	45	57 Ford	200	525
3. Buck Baker	Buck Baker	87	57 Chev	199	350
4. Lee Petty	Petty Enterprises	42	57 Olds	199	250
5. Speedy Thompson	Speedy Thompson	46	57 Chev	198	225

1959 Grand National Race No. 11
April 26, 1959 Average Speed: 53.011

Driver	Owner	Car #	Make	Laps	Winnings
1. Junior Johnson	Paul Spaulding	11	57 Ford	200	800
2. Speedy Thompson	Steve Pierce	1	57 Chev	196	525
3. Tom Pistone	Carl Rupert	59	59 Ford	196	350
4. Tommy Irwin	Tommy Irwin	36	59 Ford	192	250
5. Buzz Woodward	Buzz Woodward	90	57 Ford	191	225

Sharon Speedway
Sharon, PA
Half-mile Dirt Track

(actually located in Hartford, OH; named for nearest big city) Half-mile dirt track opened in 1929. Only NASCAR Winston Cup (then Grand National) race staged on 5/24/54 (won by Lee Petty). Track paved in 1971 and subsequently went back to dirt in 1981. Still in operation.

Winston Cup Victories
Lee Petty   1

Winston Cup Poles
Dick Rathmann   1

Winston Cup Money
Lee Petty $1,000

Most Cars Started
22—May 23, 1954

Narrowest Margin of Victory
1 lap plus—May 23, 1954

Most Race Leaders
3—May 23, 1954

Most Cars Running at Finish
13—May 23, 1954

1954 Grand National Race No. 13
May 23, 1954

Driver	Owner	Car #	Make	Laps	Winnings
1. Lee Petty	Petty Enterprises	42	54 Chrys	160	1,000
2. Buck Baker	Griffin Motors	87	53 Olds	159	650
3. Dick Rathmann	John Ditz	3	54 Huds	157	450
4. Joe Eubanks	Phil Oates	82	51 Huds	154	350
5. Laird Bruner	Carmen Amica	21	53 Olds	153	300

Williams Grove Speedway
Mechanicsburg, PA
Half-mile Dirt Track

Half-mile dirt track opened in May 1939; built by Roy Richwine. Only NASCAR Winston Cup (then Grand National) race staged on 6/17/54 (won by Herb Thomas). Track still in operation.

Winston Cup Victories
Herb Thomas   1

Winston Cup Poles
Dick Rathmann   1

Winston Cup Money
Herb Thomas $1,000

Most Cars Started
41—June 27, 1954

Narrowest Margin of Victory
4 car lengths—June 27, 1954

Race Record
51.085 MPH—June 27, 1954

Most Race Leaders
2—June 27, 1954

Most Cars Running at Finish
27—June 27, 1954

1954 Grand National Race No. 21
June 27, 1954 Average Speed: 51.085

Driver	Owner	Car #	Make	Laps	Winnings
1. Herb Thomas	Herb Thomas	92	54 Huds	200	1,000
2. Dick Rathmann	John Ditz	3	54 Huds	200	650
3. Hershel McGriff	Frank Christian	14	54 Olds	199	450
4. Joe Eubanks	Phil Oates	82	51 Huds	199	350
5. Jimmie Lewallen	George Hutchens	80	54 Merc	197	300

South Carolina

Coastal Speedway
Myrtle Beach, SC
Half-mile Dirt Track

Half-mile dirt track originally built as horse track circa 1940s. Opened to auto racing in 1950s. First NASCAR Winston Cup (then Grand National) race staged on 8/25/56 (won by Fireball Roberts). Only other Grand National race run 8/26/57 (won by Gwyn Staley). Now the site of a bank across the street from the Convention Center.

Winston Cup Starts

Johnny Allen	2
Buck Baker	2
Lee Petty	2
Fireball Roberts	2
Speedy Thompson	2

Winston Cup Victories

Fireball Roberts	1
Gwyn Staley	1

Winston Cup Poles

Johnny Allen	1
Ralph Moody	1

Winston Cup Money

Fireball Roberts	$1,350

Most Cars Started
20—August 25, 1956

Fewest Cars Started
15—August 26, 1957

Narrowest Margin of Victory
N/A

Slowest Race
50.576 MPH—August 25, 1956

Race Record
50.782 MPH—August 26, 1957

Most Race Leaders
N/A

Most Cars Running at Finish
10—August 25, 1956
10—August 26, 1957

1956 Grand National Race No. 42
August 25, 1956 Average Speed: 50.576

Driver	Owner	Car #	Make	Laps	Winnings
1. Fireball Roberts	Pete DePaolo	22	56 Ford	200	950
2. Billy Myers	Bill Stroppe	4	56 Merc	200	675
3. Jim Paschal	Frank Hayworth	75	56 Merc	199	475
4. Buck Baker	Carl Kiekhaefer	300	56 Chrys	196	365
5. Speedy Thompson	Carl Kiekhaefer	501	56 Dodg	196	320

1957 Grand National Race No. 39
August 26, 1957 Average Speed: 50.782

Driver	Owner	Car #	Make	Laps	Winnings
1. Gwyn Staley	J. H. Petty	38	57 Chev	200	1,000
2. Eddie Pagan	Eddie Pagan	45	57 Ford	199	625
3. Fireball Roberts	Fireball Roberts	22	57 Ford	198	400
4. Buck Baker	Buck Baker	87	57 Chev	183	295
5. L. D. Austin	L. D. Austin	74	56 Chev	180	255

Columbia Speedway
Columbia, SC
Half-mile Paved Track

Half-mile dirt track originally built in 1932. First NASCAR Winston Cup (then Grand National) race staged on 6/16/51 (won by Frank Mundy in a Studebaker). Track paved in 1971. Final Grand National race run on 8/27/71 (won by Richard Petty). Track closed in 1977.

Winston Cup Starts
Buck Baker 28

Winston Cup Victories
Richard Petty 7

Winston Cup Poles
Richard Petty 7

Winston Cup Money
Richard Petty $15,025

Most Cars Started
34—June 16, 1951

Fewest Cars Started
13—August 29, 1959

Narrowest Margin of Victory
1/2 car length—August 8, 1968 Sandlapper 200

Slowest Race
48.264 MPH—August 29, 1959

Race Record
76.514 MPH—April 8, 1971 Sandlapper 200

Most Cautions
13—May 2, 1963

Most Race Leaders
5—April 16, 1964 Columbia 200
5—August 21, 1964 Sandlapper 200
5—April 3, 1969 Columbia 200

Most Cars Running at Finish
20—August 18, 1966

1951 Grand National Race No. 11
June 16, 1951 Average Speed: 50.683

Driver	Owner	Car #	Make	Laps	Winnings
1. Frank Mundy	Perry Smith	23	51 Stud	200	1,000
2. Bill Blair	Hubert Westmoreland	98	50 Plym	199	600
3. Marshall Teague	Marshall Teague	6	51 Huds	—	400
4. Herb Thomas	Herb Thomas	92	50 Plym	—	300
5. Buck Baker	Buck Baker	87	50 Plym	—	250

1951 Grand National Race No. 25
September 7, 1951

Driver	Owner	Car #	Make	Laps	Winnings
1. Tim Flock	Ted Chester	91	51 Olds	200	1,000
2. Fireball Roberts	Ed Saverance	11	51 Ford	200	600
3. Jimmie Lewallen	Hubert Hamilton	0	51 Plym	—	500
4. Bob Flock	Ted Chester	7	51 Olds	—	400
5. Buck Baker	Griffin Motors	87	51 Olds	—	300

1952 Grand National Race No. 6
April 12, 1952 Average Speed: 53.460

Driver	Owner	Car #	Make	Laps	Winnings
1. Buck Baker	B. A. Pless	89	52 Huds	200	1,000
2. Lee Petty	Petty Enterprises	42	51 Plym	200	700
3. Dick Rathmann	Walt Chapman	120	51 Huds	—	450
4. Frankie Schneider		88	51 Olds	—	350
5. Joe Eubanks	Phil Oates	82	50 Olds	—	200

1953 Grand National Race No. 9
May 9, 1953 Average Speed: 53.707

Driver	Owner	Car #	Make	Laps	Winnings
1. Buck Baker	Griffin Motors	87	53 Olds	200	1,000
2. Tim Flock	Ted Chester	91	53 Huds	—	700
3. Jimmie Lewallen	R. G. Shelton	32	51 Huds	—	450
4. Ray Duhigg	J. H. Petty	44	52 Plym	—	350
5. Lee Petty	Petty Enterprises	42	53 Dodg	—	200

1954 Grand National Race No. 17
June 6, 1954 Average Speed: 56.719

Driver	Owner	Car #	Make	Laps	Winnings
1. Curtis Turner	Elmer Brooks	44	52 Olds	200	1,000
2. Hershel McGriff	Frank Christian	14	54 Olds	198	650
3. Dick Rathmann	John Ditz	3	54 Huds	197	450
4. Speedy Thompson	Buckshot Morris	12	53 Olds	197	350
5. Lee Petty	Petty Enterprises	42	54 Chrys	195	300

1955 Grand National Race No. 6
March 26, 1955

Driver	Owner	Car #	Make	Laps	Winnings
1. Fonty Flock	Frank Christian	14	55 Chev	200	1,000
2. Don White	Don White	1	55 Olds	—	650
3. Dick Rathmann	John Ditz	3	54 Huds	—	450
4. Buck Baker	Griffin Motors	87	54 Olds	—	350
5. Tim Flock	Carl Kiekhaefer	300	55 Chrys	—	300

1955 Grand National Race No. 25
July 9, 1955 Average Speed: 55.469

Driver	Owner	Car #	Make	Laps	Winnings
1. Jim Paschal	Ernest Woods	78	54 Olds	200	1,000
2. Jimmie Lewallen	Ernest Woods	88	55 Olds	200	700
3. Tim Flock	Carl Kiekhaefer	300	55 Chrys	200	475
4. Billy Carden	Bishop Brothers	8	55 Buick	197	365
5. Buck Baker	Henry Ford	303	55 Chrys	195	310

1955 Grand National Race No. 41
October 15, 1955 Average Speed: 55.393

Driver	Owner	Car #	Make	Laps	Winnings
1. Tim Flock	Carl Kiekhaefer	300	55 Chrys	200	1,100
2. Buck Baker	Pete DePaolo	87	56 Ford	200	700
3. Herb Thomas	Herb Thomas	92	55 Chev	197	475
4. Gwyn Staley	Hubert Westmoreland	2	55 Chev	194	365
5. Jimmy Massey	Hubert Westmoreland	04	55 Chev	194	310

1956 Grand National Race No. 13
May 5, 1956 Average Speed: 54.545

Driver	Owner	Car #	Make	Laps	Winnings
1. Speedy Thompson	Carl Kiekhaefer	500	56 Dodg	200	1,100
2. Buck Baker	Carl Kiekhaefer	500b	56 Dodg	198	700
3. Joe Weatherly	Charlie Schwam	9	56 Ford	196	475
4. Tiny Lund	Gus Holzmueller	37	56 Pont	192	365
5. Bob Flock	Mauri Rose	49	56 Chev	191	310

1956 Grand National Race No. 49
September 29, 1956 Average Speed: 61.193

Driver	Owner	Car #	Make	Laps	Winnings
1. Buck Baker	Carl Kiekhaefer	500B	56 Dodg	200	950
2. Ralph Moody	Pete DePaolo	12	56 Ford	200	675
3. Speedy Thompson	Carl Kiekhaefer	500	56 Dodg	200	475
4. Fireball Roberts	Pete DePaolo	22	56 Ford	200	360
5. Billy Myers	Bill Stroppe	4	56 Merc	198	320

Columbia Speedway *continued*

1957 Grand National Race No. 24
June 20, 1957 Average Speed: 58.045

Driver	Owner	Car #	Make	Laps	Winnings
1. Jack Smith	Jack Smith	47	57 Chev	200	1,000
2. Buck Baker	Buck Baker	87	57 Chev	200	625
3. Marvin Panch	Marvin Panch	98	57 Ford	200	400
4. Jim Paschal	Jim Paschal	17	57 Merc	199	295
5. Speedy Thompson	Speedy Thompson	46	57 Chev	199	255

1957 Grand National Race No. 46
September 19, 1957 Average Speed: 60.514

Driver	Owner	Car #	Make	Laps	Winnings
1. Buck Baker	Buck Baker	87	57 Chev	200	900
2. Gwyn Staley	J. H. Petty	38	57 Chev	199	575
3. Bill Amick	Bill Amick	97	57 Ford	198	375
4. Billy Myers	Sam Rice	26	57 Ford	196	280
5. Brownie King	Jess Potter	32	57 Chev	194	245

1958 Grand National Race No. 8
April 10, 1958

Driver	Owner	Car #	Make	Laps	Winnings
1. Speedy Thompson	Speedy Thompson	46	57 Chev	200	800
2. Jack Smith	Jack Smith	47	57 Chev	200	525
3. Tiny Lund	Don Angel	37	56 Ford	199	350
4. Lee Petty	Petty Enterprises	42	57 Olds	199	250
5. Eddie Pagan	Eddie Pagan	45	57 Ford	198	225

1958 Grand National Race No. 22
June 5, 1958 Average Speed: 54.752

Driver	Owner	Car #	Make	Laps	Winnings
1. Junior Johnson	Paul Spaulding	11	57 Ford	200	800
2. George Dunn	Manley Britt	14	57 Merc	192	525
3. Fred Harb	Fred Harb	17	57 Merc	192	350
4. Wilbur Rakestraw	Joe Jones	999	57 Ford	190	250
5. Shorty Rollins	Spook Crawford	67	57 Plym	189	225

1958 Grand National Race No. 36
August 7, 1958 Average Speed: 54.820

Driver	Owner	Car #	Make	Laps	Winnings
1. Speedy Thompson	Speedy Thompson	46	57 Chev	200	800
2. Bob Welborn	J. H. Petty	49	57 Chev	200	525
3. Cotton Owens	Jim Stephens	6	57 Pont	195	350
4. Shorty Rollins	Shorty Rollins	99	58 Ford	193	250
5. George Dunn	Manley Britt	14	57 Merc	183	225

1959 Grand National Race No. 9
April 4, 1959 Average Speed: 57.343

Driver	Owner	Car #	Make	Laps	Winnings
1. Jack Smith	Jack Smith	47	59 Chev	200	900
2. Ned Jarrett	Paul Spaulding	11	57 Ford	200	525
3. Lee Petty	Petty Enterprises	42	57 Olds	191	350
4. Tiny Lund	Tiny Lund	5	57 Chev	190	250
5. Cotton Owens	W. H. Watson	6	58 Pont	186	225

1959 Grand National Race No. 21
June 18, 1959 Average Speed: 58.726

Driver	Owner	Car #	Make	Laps	Winnings
1. Lee Petty	Petty Enterprises	42	59 Plym	200	900
2. Tommy Irwin	Tommy Irwin	36	59 Ford	200	525
3. Buck Baker	Buck Baker	87	59 Chev	200	350
4. Benny Rakestraw	Talmadge Cochrane	20	57 Merc	196	250
5. Joe Weatherly	Doc White	41	59 Ford	196	225

1959 Grand National Race No. 35
August 29, 1959 Average Speed: 48.264

Driver	Owner	Car #	Make	Laps	Winnings
1. Lee Petty	Petty Enterprises	42	59 Plym	200	900
2. Tiny Lund	Tiny Lund	5	57 Chev	199	525
3. Fred Harb	Fred Harb	17	57 Ford	197	375
4. Roy Tyner	Roy Tyner	49	57 Chev	194	275
5. Glen Wood	Wood Brothers	21	58 Ford	193	250

1960 Grand National Race No. 2
November 26, 1959 Average Speed: 55.071

Driver	Owner	Car #	Make	Laps	Winnings
1. Ned Jarrett	Ned Jarrett	38	57 Ford	200	800
2. Jack Smith	Jack Smith	47	59 Chev	200	525
3. Joe Lee Johnson	Joe Lee Johnson	77	59 Chev	200	375
4. Lee Petty	Petty Enterprises	42	59 Plym	200	275
5. Bobby Johns	Shorty Johns	72	57 Chev	195	250

1960 Grand National Race No. 9
April 5, 1960 Average Speed: 50.697

Driver	Owner	Car #	Make	Laps	Winnings
1. Rex White	Rex White	4	60 Chev	200	800
2. Buck Baker	Buck Baker	87	60 Chev	199	525
3. Doug Yates	Raeford Johnson	23	59 Plym	199	375
4. Lee Petty	Petty Enterprises	42	60 Plym	199	375
5. Joe Lee Johnson	E. C. Wilson	78	59 Chev	197	350

1960 Grand National Race No. 32
August 18, 1960 Average Speed: 54.265

Driver	Owner	Car #	Make	Laps	Winnings
1. Rex White	Rex White	4	60 Chev	300	1,000
2. Richard Petty	Petty Enterprises	43	60 Plym	300	600
3. Buck Baker	Buck Baker	87	60 Chev	293	450
4. Ned Jarrett	Ned Jarrett	11	60 Ford	293	350
5. Tommy Irwin	Tommy Irwin	36	59 Ford	293	325

1961 Grand National Race No. 15
April 20, 1961 Average Speed: 51.940

Driver	Owner	Car #	Make	Laps	Winnings
1. Cotton Owens	Cotton Owens	6	60 Pont	200	950
2. Ned Jarrett	Bee Gee Holloway	11	61 Chev	199	625
3. Emanuel Zervakis	Monroe Shook	85	60 Chev	199	425
4. G. C. Spencer	G. C. Spencer	48	60 Chev	197	275
5. Rex White	Rex White	4	60 Chev	197	350

1961 Grand National Race No. 34
July 20, 1961 Average Speed: 62.198

Driver	Owner	Car #	Make	Laps	Winnings
1. Cotton Owens	Cotton Owens	6	60 Pont	200	950
2. Jim Paschal	J. H. Petty	14	61 Chev	200	625
3. Ned Jarrett	Bee Gee Holloway	11	61 Chev	200	425
4. Junior Johnson	Rex Lovette	27	60 Pont	198	275
5. Joe Weatherly	Bud Moore	8	61 Pont	198	250

1962 Grand National Race No. 11 Arclite 200
April 13, 1962 Average Speed: 56.710

Driver	Owner	Car #	Make	Laps	Winnings
1. Ned Jarrett	Bee Gee Holloway	11	62 Chev	200	1,200
2. Joe Weatherly	Bud Moore	8	61 Pont	200	600
3. Jack Smith	Jack Smith	47	61 Pont	198	400
4. Jim Paschal	Cliff Stewart	2	62 Pont	198	300
5. G. C. Spencer	G. C. Spencer	48	60 Chev	197	275

Columbia Speedway *continued*

1962 Grand National Race No. 30
July 7, 1962 Average Speed: 62.370

Driver	Owner	Car #	Make	Laps	Winnings
1. Rex White	Rex White	4	62 Chev	200	1,000
2. Joe Weatherly	Bud Moore	8	61 Pont	200	600
3. Jack Smith	Jack Smith	47	61 Pont	199	400
4. Cotton Owens	Cotton Owens	6	62 Pont	199	300
5. Ned Jarrett	Bee Gee Holloway	11	62 Chev	199	475

1963 Grand National Race No. 21
May 2, 1963 Average Speed: 51.650

Driver	Owner	Car #	Make	Laps	Winnings
1. Richard Petty	Petty Enterprises	41	63 Plym	200	1,000
2. Buck Baker	Buck Baker	87	63 Pont	200	600
3. Ned Jarrett	Charles Robinson	11	63 Ford	200	400
4. Buddy Baker	Buck Baker	7	62 Chrys	200	300
5. Jack Smith	Jack Smith	47	63 Plym	200	275

1963 Grand National Race No. 40 Sandlapper 200
August 8, 1963 Average Speed: 55.598

Driver	Owner	Car #	Make	Laps	Winnings
1. Richard Petty	Petty Enterprises	43	63 Plym	200	1,140
2. David Pearson	Cotton Owens	6	63 Dodg	200	600
3. Bobby Isaac	Bondy Long	99	63 Ford	200	400
4. Ned Jarrett	Charles Robinson	11	63 Ford	200	350
5. G. C. Spencer	G. C. Spencer	03	62 Chev	198	275

1964 Grand National Race No. 17 Columbia 200
April 16, 1964 Average Speed: 64.412

Driver	Owner	Car #	Make	Laps	Winnings
1. Ned Jarrett	Bondy Long	11	64 Ford	200	1,150
2. Marvin Panch	Wood Brothers	21	64 Ford	199	700
3. LeeRoy Yarbrough	Louie Weathersby	45	63 Plym	198	400
4. Billy Wade	Bud Moore	1	64 Merc	198	300
5. Dick Hutcherson	Dick Hutcherson	7	64 Ford	198	275

1964 Grand National Race No. 48 Sandlapper 200
August 21, 1964 Average Speed: 61.697

Driver	Owner	Car #	Make	Laps	Winnings
1. David Pearson	Cotton Owens	6	64 Dodg	200	1,000
2. Doug Yates	Doug Yates	72	63 Plym	198	600
3. Jimmy Pardue	Charles Robinson	54	64 Plym	196	400
4. Ned Jarrett	Bondy Long	11	64 Ford	193	300
5. Doug Cooper	Bob Cooper	60	63 Ford	186	275

1965 Grand National Race No. 13 Columbia 200
April 28, 1965 Average Speed: 55.591

Driver	Owner	Car #	Make	Laps	Winnings
1. Tiny Lund	Lyle Stelter	55	64 Ford	124	1,000
2. Ned Jarrett	Bondy Long	11	65 Ford	124	600
3. Neil Castles	Buck Baker	86	65 Plym	122	400
4. Darel Dieringer	Gary Weaver	10	65 Ford	121	300
5. Dick Hutcherson	Holman-Moody	29	65 Ford	120	275

1965 Grand National Race No. 41 Sandlapper 200
August 19, 1965 Average Speed: 57.361

Driver	Owner	Car #	Make	Laps	Winnings
1. David Pearson	Cotton Owens	6	65 Dodg	200	1,000
2. Richard Petty	Petty Enterprises	43	65 Plym	200	800
3. Dick Hutcherson	Holman-Moody	29	65 Ford	200	400
4. Tiny Lund	Lyle Stelter	55	64 Ford	198	300
5. Cale Yarborough	Kenny Myler	06	64 Ford	197	275

1966 Grand National Race No. 10
April 7, 1966 Average Speed: 65.574

Driver	Owner	Car #	Make	Laps	Winnings
1. David Pearson	Cotton Owens	6	64 Dodg	200	1,000
2. Paul Goldsmith	Bob Cooper	02	65 Plym	200	600
3. Tom Pistone	Tom Pistone	59	64 Ford	198	400
4. J. T. Putney	J. T. Putney	19	66 Chev	198	300
5. John Sears	L. G. DeWitt	04	64 Ford	195	275

1966 Grand National Race No. 38
August 18, 1966 Average Speed: 66.128

Driver	Owner	Car #	Make	Laps	Winnings
1. David Pearson	Cotton Owens	6	65 Dodg	200	1,000
2. Richard Petty	Petty Enterprises	42	66 Plym	200	600
3. Curtis Turner	Junior Johnson	26	66 Ford	200	400
4. James Hylton	Bud Hartje	48	65 Dodg	198	300
5. Dick Hutcherson	Holman-Moody	29	66 Ford	198	275

1967 Grand National Race No. 11 Sandlapper 200
April 6, 1967 Average Speed: 65.455

Driver	Owner	Car #	Make	Laps	Winnings
1. Richard Petty	Petty Enterprises	43	67 Plym	200	1,000
2. Jim Paschal	Tom Friedkin	14	67 Plym	199	600
3. Dick Hutcherson	Bondy Long	29	67 Ford	198	400
4. James Hylton	Bud Hartje	48	65 Dodg	197	300
5. Neil Castles	Buck Baker	88	66 Olds	193	275

1967 Grand National Race No. 38
August 17, 1967 Average Speed: 64.274

Driver	Owner	Car #	Make	Laps	Winnings
1. Richard Petty	Petty Enterprises	43	67 Plym	200	1,000
2. John Sears	L. G. DeWitt	4	66 Ford	199	600
3. Elmo Langley	Henry Woodfield	64	66 Ford	197	400
4. Bobby Allison	Bobby Allison	2	66 Chev	197	300
5. James Hylton	Bud Hartje	48	65 Dodg	196	275

1968 Grand National Race No. 10
April 18, 1968 Average Speed: 71.358

Driver	Owner	Car #	Make	Laps	Winnings
1. Bobby Isaac	Nord Krauskopf	37	67 Dodg	200	1,000
2. Charlie Glotzbach	Cotton Owens	6	67 Dodg	200	600
3. James Hylton	James Hylton	48	67 Dodg	200	400
4. Buddy Baker	Ray Fox	3	67 Dodg	199	300
5. Richard Petty	Petty Enterprises	43	68 Plym	198	475

1968 Grand National Race No. 34 Sandlapper 200
August 8, 1968 Average Speed: 67.039

Driver	Owner	Car #	Make	Laps	Winnings
1. David Pearson	Holman-Moody	17	68 Ford	200	1,000
2. Charlie Glotzbach	Cotton Owens	6	68 Dodg	200	600
3. LeeRoy Yarbrough	Lyle Stelter	56	67 Ford	199	400
4. Elmo Langley	Elmo Langley	64	66 Ford	198	300
5. Neil Castles	Neil Castles	06	67 Plym	197	275

1969 Grand National Race No. 11 Columbia 200
April 3, 1969 Average Speed: 68.558

Driver	Owner	Car #	Make	Laps	Winnings
1. Bobby Isaac	Nord Krauskopf	71	69 Dodg	200	1,000
2. David Pearson	Holman-Moody	17	69 Ford	200	800
3. Richard Petty	Petty Enterprises	43	69 Ford	199	400
4. James Hylton	James Hylton	48	67 Dodg	197	350
5. John Sears	L. G. DeWitt	4	67 Ford	197	325

Columbia Speedway *continued*

1969 Grand National Race No. 45 Sandlapper 200
September 18, 1969 Average Speed: 70.230

Driver	Owner	Car #	Make	Laps	Winnings
1. Bobby Isaac	Nord Krauskopf	71	69 Dodg	200	1,000
2. Richard Petty	Petty Enterprises	43	69 Ford	200	600
3. James Hylton	James Hylton	48	69 Dodg	196	400
4. John Sears	L. G. DeWitt	4	69 Ford	195	350
5. Eldon Yarbrough	Lyle Stelter	56	67 Ford	194	325

1970 Grand National Race No. 12 Columbia 200
April 30, 1970 Average Speed: 62.685

Driver	Owner	Car #	Make	Laps	Winnings
1. Richard Petty	Don Robertson	43	70 Plym	200	1,500
2. Bobby Allison	Bobby Allison	22	69 Dodg	199	900
3. Bobby Isaac	Nord Krauskopf	71	69 Dodg	197	500
4. Neil Castles	Neil Castles	06	69 Dodg	197	350
5. James Hylton	James Hylton	48	69 Ford	195	325

1970 Grand National Race No. 32 Sandlapper 200
August 6, 1970 Average Speed: 67.101

Driver	Owner	Car #	Make	Laps	Winnings
1. Bobby Isaac	Nord Krauskopf	71	70 Dodg	200	1,500
2. Richard Petty	Petty Enterprises	43	70 Plym	200	900
3. Bobby Allison	Bobby Allison	22	69 Dodg	199	500
4. John Sears	John Sears	4	69 Dodg	197	350
5. Neil Castles	Neil Castles	06	69 Dodg	196	325

1971 Winston Cup GN Race No. 11 Sandlapper 200
April 8, 1971 Average Speed: 76.514

Driver	Owner	Car #	Make	Laps	Winnings
1. Richard Petty	Petty Enterprises	43	71 Plym	200	1,700
2. Benny Parsons	L. G. DeWitt	72	69 Ford	200	1,200
3. Dick Brooks	Mario Rossi	22	70 Dodg	200	800
4. James Hylton	James Hylton	48	60 Ford	198	550
5. Elmo Langley	Clyde Lynn	20	70 Ford	198	425

1971 Winston Cup GN Race No. 38 Sandlapper 200
August 27, 1971 Average Speed: 64.831

Driver	Owner	Car #	Make	Laps	Winnings
1. Richard Petty	Petty Enterprises	43	70 Plym	200	1,500
2. Tiny Lund	Ronnie Hopkins	55	69 Chev	200	900
3. Jim Paschal	Cliff Stewart	14	70 Mata	200	500
4. James Hylton	James Hylton	48	70 Ford	197	350
5. Jabe Thomas	Don Robertson	25	70 Plym	196	325

Darlington Raceway
Darlington, SC
1.366-mile Superspeedway

Built in 1948–50 by Harold Brasington. First race was inaugural Southern 500 (9/4/50), won by Johnny Mantz. Original measurement was 1.25-mile egg-shaped oval. Configuration determined by location of minnow pond. Track upgraded and lengthened to 1.375-mile oval in 1953. Currently measured at 1.366-miles. AM and USAC IndyCars have also run on track on occasion from 1950–56.

Winston Cup Starts
Richard Petty 65

Winston Cup Victories
David Pearson 10

Winston Cup Poles
David Pearson 12

Winston Cup Money
Jeff Gordon $2,359,142

Most Cars Started
82—September 3, 1951 Southern 500

Fewest Cars Started
24—May 10, 1952 (100-mile race)

Narrowest Margin of Victory
0.144 seconds—August 31, 1997

Slowest Race
74.512 MPH—September 1, 1952 Southern 500

Race Record
141.410 MPH—March 23, 1997

Most Cautions
15—March 26, 1995 TranSouth 400

Most Race Leaders
17—September 6, 1982 Southern 500

Most Cars Running at Finish
50—September 4, 1950 Southern 500

1950 Grand National Race No. 13 Southern 500
September 4, 1950 Average Speed: 75.250

Driver	Owner	Car #	Make	Laps	Winnings
1. Johnny Mantz	Johnny Mantz & Bill France	98	50 Plym	400	10,510
2. Fireball Roberts	Sam Rice	82	50 Olds	391	3,500
3. Red Byron	Raymond Parks	22	50 Cad	390	2,000
4. Bill Rexford	Julian Buesink	59	50 Olds	385	1,500
5. Chuck Mahoney	Brooks Motors	77	50 Merc	381	1,000

1951 Grand National Race No. 24 Southern 500
September 3, 1951 Average Speed: 76.906

Driver	Owner	Car #	Make	Laps	Winnings
1. Herb Thomas	Herb Thomas	92	51 Huds	400	8,800
2. Jesse James Taylor	Jesse James Taylor	31	51 Huds	399	2,800
3. Buddy Shuman	R. H. Yandell	17	51 Ford	391	1,500
4. Hershel McGriff		77	51 Olds	390	1,210
5. Fireball Roberts	Ed Saverance	11	51 Ford	387	910

1952 Grand National Race No. 10
May 10, 1952 Average Speed: 83.818

Driver	Owner	Car #	Make	Laps	Winnings
1. Dick Rathmann	Walt Chapman	120	51 Huds	80	1,000
2. Tim Flock	Ted Chester	91	51 Huds	80	700
3. Fonty Flock	Frank Christian	14	51 Olds	78	450
4. Jimmie Lewallen	George Hutchens	2	52 Olds	78	350
5. Joe Eubanks	Phil Oates	82	52 Huds	78	200

1952 Grand National Race No. 25 Southern 500
September 1, 1952 Average Speed: 74.512

Driver	Owner	Car #	Make	Laps	Winnings
1. Fonty Flock	Frank Christian	14	52 Olds	400	9,430
2. Johnny Patterson	H. B. Ranier	58	52 Huds	399	3,000
3. Herb Thomas	Herb Thomas	92	52 Huds	399	1,590
4. Bub King	Bub King	55	52 Huds	398	1,230
5. Banjo Matthews	Bill Snowden	16	52 Huds	393	950

1953 Grand National Race No. 30 Southern 500
September 7, 1953 Average Speed: 92.881

Driver	Owner	Car #	Make	Laps	Winnings
1. Buck Baker	Griffin Motors	87	53 Olds	364	6,285
2. Fonty Flock	Frank Christian	14	53 Huds	361	3,040
3. Curtis Turner	Frank Christian	44	53 Olds	359	1,500
4. Dick Meyer	Dick Meyer	49	53 Dodg	355	1,000
5. Herb Thomas	Herb Thomas	92	53 Huds	354	1,550

1954 Grand National Race No. 31
September 6, 1954 Average Speed: 95.026

Driver	Owner	Car #	Make	Laps	Winnings
1. Herb Thomas	Herb Thomas	92	54 Huds	364	6,830
2. Curtis Turner	Elmer Brooks	44	52 Olds	364	6,245
3. Marvin Panch	Beryl Jackson	98	54 Dodg	362	2,155
4. Johnny Patterson	H. B. Ranier	58	54 Merc	360	1,165
5. Jim Paschal	Ernest Woods	88	54 Olds	357	975

1955 Grand National Race No. 35 Southern 500
September 5, 1955 Average Speed: 92.281

Driver	Owner	Car #	Make	Laps	Winnings
1. Herb Thomas	Herb Thomas	92	55 Chev	366	7,480
2. Jim Reed	Jim Reed	7	55 Chev	365	1,550
3. Tim Flock	Carl Kiekhaefer	16	55 Chrys	363	2,500
4. Gwyn Staley	Hubert Westmoreland	2	55 Chev	359	1,300
5. Larry Flynn	W. O. Taylor	96	55 Ford	359	1,175

1956 Grand National Race No. 44 Southern 500
September 3, 1956 Average Speed: 95.167

Driver	Owner	Car #	Make	Laps	Winnings
1. Curtis Turner	Charlie Schwam	99	56 Ford	364	11,750
2. Speedy Thompson	Carl Kiekhaefer	57	56 Chrys	362	5,000
3. Marvin Panch	Pete DePaolo	8	56 Ford	359	3,370
4. Jim Reed	Jim Reed	7	56 Chev	350	1,850
5. Paul Goldsmith	Smokey Yunick	3	56 Chev	358	1,300

1957 Grand National Race No. 40 Southern 500
September 2, 1957 Average Speed: 100.094

Driver	Owner	Car #	Make	Laps	Winnings
1. Speedy Thompson	Speedy Thompson	46	57 Chev	364	13,590
2. Cotton Owens	Ray Nichels	6	57 Pont	361	6,100
3. Marvin Panch	Marvin Panch	98	57 Ford	360	3,745
4. Jim Reed	Jim Reed	7	57 Ford	356	2,155
5. Buck Baker	Buck Baker	87	57 Chev	356	1,650

1958 Grand National Race No. 41 Southern 500
September 1, 1958 Average Speed: 102.585

Driver	Owner	Car #	Make	Laps	Winnings
1. Fireball Roberts	Frank Strickland	22	57 Chev	364	13,220
2. Buck Baker	Buck Baker	87	57 Chev	359	5,750
3. Shorty Rollins	Shorty Rollins	99	58 Ford	359	3,815
4. Jimmy Thompson	Speedy Thompson	46	57 Chev	358	1,995
5. Marvin Panch	John Whitford	98	58 Ford	357	1,525

Darlington Raceway *continued*

1959 Grand National Race No. 36 Southern 500
September 7, 1959 Average Speed: 111.836

Driver	Owner	Car #	Make	Laps	Winnings
1. Jim Reed	Jim Reed	7	57 Chev	364	17,250
2. Bob Burdick	Roy Burdick Gar	73	59 Ford	362	7,760
3. Bobby Johns	Shorty Johns	72	57 Chev	362	4,760
4. Richard Petty	Petty Enterprises	43	59 Plym	361	2,830
5. Tommy Irwin	Tommy Irwin	36	59 Ford	358	2,010

1960 Grand National Race No. 35 Southern 500
September 5, 1960 Average Speed: 105.901

Driver	Owner	Car #	Make	Laps	Winnings
1. Buck Baker	Jack Smith	47	60 Pont	364	19,900
2. Rex White	Rex White	4	60 Chev	364	9,780
3. Jim Paschal	Petty Enterprises	44	60 Plym	362	5,595
4. Emanuel Zervakis	Monroe Shook	85	60 Chev	362	3,125
5. Ned Jarrett	Ned Jarrett	11	60 Ford	362	2,000

1961 Grand National Race No. 42 Southern 500
September 4, 1961 Average Speed: 117.787

Driver	Owner	Car #	Make	Laps	Winnings
1. Nelson Stacy	Dudley Farrell	29	61 Ford	364	18,430
2. Fireball Roberts	Jim Stephens	22	61 Pont	364	10,670
3. David Pearson	John Masoni	3	Pont	363	5,060
4. Jim Paschal	J. H. Petty	44	61 Pont	359	2,625
5. Emanuel Zervakis	Monroe Shook	85	61 Chev	359	2,450

1962 Grand National Race No. 45 Southern 500
September 3, 1962 Average Speed: 117.965

Driver	Owner	Car #	Make	Laps	Winnings
1. Larry Frank	Ratus Walters	66	62 Ford	364	21,730
2. Junior Johnson	Ray Fox	3	62 Pont	364	10,155
3. Marvin Panch	Wood Brothers	21	62 Ford	364	5,150
4. David Pearson	Cotton Owens	6	62 Pont	364	3,325
5. Richard Petty	Petty Enterprises	43	62 Plym	363	5,450

1963 Grand National Race No. 45 Southern 500
September 2, 1963 Average Speed: 129.784

Driver	Owner	Car #	Make	Laps	Winnings
1. Fireball Roberts	Holman-Moody	22	63 Ford	364	22,150
2. Marvin Panch	Wood Brothers	21	63 Ford	364	12,650
3. Fred Lorenzen	Holman-Moody	28	73 Ford	364	6,550
4. Nelson Stacy	Holman-Moody	29	63 Ford	363	3,500
5. Darel Dieringer	Bill Stroppe	26	63 Merc	360	2,625

1964 Grand National Race No. 51 Southern 500
September 7, 1964 Average Speed: 117.757

Driver	Owner	Car #	Make	Laps	Winnings
1. Buck Baker	Ray Fox	3	64 Dodg	364	21,230
2. Jim Paschal	Petty Enterprises	41	64 Plym	362	8,960
3. Richard Petty	Petty Enterprises	43	64 Plym	360	8,170
4. Ned Jarrett	Bondy Long	11	64 Ford	359	3,575
5. Jimmy Pardue	Charles Robinson	54	64 Plym	358	2,955

1965 Grand National Race No. 45 Southern 500
September 6, 1965 Average Speed: 115.878

Driver	Owner	Car #	Make	Laps	Winnings
1. Ned Jarrett	Bondy Long	11	65 Ford	364	21,060
2. Buck Baker	Buck Baker	86	65 Plym	350	9,170
3. Darel Dieringer	Bud Moore	16	64 Merc	345	7,200
4. Roy Mayne	Tom Hunter	46	65 Chev	345	3,225
5. Buddy Arrington	Buddy Arrington	67	64 Dodg	344	2,400

1960 Grand National Race No. 16 Rebel 300
May 7 & 14, 1960 Average Speed: 102.640

Driver	Owner	Car #	Make	Laps	Winnings
1. Joe Weatherly	Holman-Moody	12	60 Ford	219	9,250
2. Richard Petty	Petty Enterprises	43	60 Plym	219	4,875
3. Rex White	Rex White	4	60 Chev	218	2,900
4. Lee Petty	Petty Enterprises	42	60 Plym	218	1,940
5. Buck Baker	Buck Baker	87	60 Chev	216	1,500

1961 Grand National Race No. 19 Rebel 300
May 6, 1961 Average Speed: 119.520

Driver	Owner	Car #	Make	Laps	Winnings
1. Fred Lorenzen	Holman-Moody	28	61 Ford	219	8,420
2. Curtis Turner	Wood Brothers	21	61 Ford	219	4,600
3. Johnny Allen	Bee Gee Holloway	69	61 Chev	218	3,200
4. Bob Burdick	Roy Burdick Gar	53	61 Pont	218	2,400
5. Fireball Roberts	Bud Moore	22	61 Pont	218	1,665

1962 Grand National Race No. 21 Rebel 300
May 12, 1962 Average Speed: 117.429

Driver	Owner	Car #	Make	Laps	Winnings
1. Nelson Stacy	Holman-Moody	29	62 Ford	219	7,900
2. Marvin Panch	Wood Brothers	21	62 Ford	219	4,890
3. Fred Lorenzen	Holman-Moody	28	62 Ford	218	3,400
4. Jack Smith	Jack Smith	47	62 Pont	217	2,270
5. Cotton Owens	Cotton Owens	6	62 Pont	216	1,765

1963 Grand National Race No. 23 Rebel 300
May 11, 1963

Driver	Owner	Car #	Make	Laps	Winnings
1. Joe Weatherly	Bud Moore	8	63 Pont	220	11,100
2. Fireball Roberts	Holman-Moody	22	63 Ford	219	6,200
3. Richard Petty	Petty Enterprises	42	63 Plym	219	4,980
4. Tiny Lund	Wood Brothers	21	63 Ford	219	2,665
5. Bobby Johns	Shorty Johns	7	63 UNK	218	1,965

1964 Grand National Race No. 21 Rebel 300
May 9, 1964 Average Speed: 130.013

Driver	Owner	Car #	Make	Laps	Winnings
1. Fred Lorenzen	Holman-Moody	28	64 Ford	219	10,265
2. Fireball Roberts	Holman-Moody	22	64 Ford	219	5,990
3. Junior Johnson	Banjo Matthews	27	64 Ford	218	4,510
4. Ned Jarrett	Bondy Long	11	64 Ford	216	2,995
5. Jimmy Pardue	Charles Robinson	54	64 Plym	215	2,170

1965 Grand National Race No. 15 Rebel 300
May 8, 1965 Average Speed: 111.849

Driver	Owner	Car #	Make	Laps	Winnings
1. Junior Johnson	Rex Lovette	26	65 Ford	219	10,490
2. Darel Dieringer	Bud Moore	16	64 Merc	219	6,155
3. Ned Jarrett	Bondy Long	11	65 Ford	218	4,460
4. Dick Hutcherson	Holman-Moody	29	65 Ford	217	2,925
5. Bobby Johns	Holman-Moody	7	65 Ford	217	1,100

1966 Grand National Race No. 15 Rebel 400
April 30, 1966 Average Speed: 131.993

Driver	Owner	Car #	Make	Laps	Winnings
1. Richard Petty	Petty Enterprises	43	66 Plym	291	12,115
2. Paul Goldsmith	Ray Nichels	99	65 Plym	288	6,570
3. David Pearson	Cotton Owens	6	65 Dodg	288	4,145
4. Bunkie Blackburn	Ray Fox	3	65 Dodg	283	2,225
5. G. C. Spencer	G. C. Spencer	49	65 Plym	283	1,670

Darlington Raceway *continued*

1966 Grand National Race No. 42 Southern 500
September 5, 1966 Average Speed: 114.830

Driver	Owner	Car #	Make	Laps	Winnings
1. Darel Dieringer	Bud Moore	16	66 Merc	364	20,900
2. Richard Petty	Petty Enterprises	43	66 Plym	364	8,975
3. David Pearson	Cotton Owens	6	66 Dodg	361	4,700
4. Marvin Panch	Petty Enterprises	42	66 Plym	360	2,725
5. Fred Lorenzen	Holman-Moody	28	66 Ford	360	2,300

1967 Grand National Race No. 40 Southern 500
September 4, 1967 Average Speed: 130.423

Driver	Owner	Car #	Make	Laps	Winnings
1. Richard Petty	Petty Enterprises	43	67 Plym	364	26,900
2. David Pearson	Holman-Moody	17	67 Ford	359	10,825
3. G. C. Spencer	Petty Enterprises	42	67 Plym	359	6,175
4. Charlie Glotzbach	Nord Krauskopf	72	67 Dodg	356	3,325
5. Bud Moore	A. J. King	53	67 Dodg	355	2,725

1968 Grand National Race No. 39 Southern 500
September 2, 1968 Average Speed: 126.132

Driver	Owner	Car #	Make	Laps	Winnings
1. Cale Yarborough	Wood Brothers	21	68 Merc	364	25,415
2. David Pearson	Holman-Moody	17	68 Ford	364	10,850
3. Buddy Baker	Ray Fox	3	68 Dodg	362	6,200
4. Charlie Glotzbach	Cotton Owens	6	68 Dodg	360	3,800
5. Paul Goldsmith	Ray Nichels	99	68 Dodg	357	3,075

1969 Grand National Race No. 41 Southern 500
September 1, 1969 Average Speed: 105.612

Driver	Owner	Car #	Make	Laps	Winnings
1. LeeRoy Yarbrough	Junior Johnson	98	69 Ford	230	21,800
2. David Pearson	Holman-Moody	17	69 Ford	230	12,250
3. Buddy Baker	Cotton Owens	6	69 Dodg	230	6,700
4. Donnie Allison	Banjo Matthews	27	69 Ford	227	3,325
5. Bobby Allison	Mario Rossi	22	69 Dodg	225	2,750

1970 Grand National Race No. 38 Southern 500
September 7, 1970 Average Speed: 128.817

Driver	Owner	Car #	Make	Laps	Winnings
1. Buddy Baker	Cotton Owens	6	69 Dodg	367	27,450
2. Bobby Isaac	Nord Krauskopf	71	69 Dodg	366	11,825
3. Pete Hamilton	Petty Enterprises	40	70 Plym	364	7,000
4. David Pearson	Holman-Moody	17	69 Ford	363	6,175
5. Richard Petty	Petty Enterprises	43	70 Plym	362	3,100

1971 Winston Cup GN Race No. 40 Southern 500
September 6, 1971 Average Speed: 131.398

Driver	Owner	Car #	Make	Laps	Winnings
1. Bobby Allison	Holman-Moody	12	69 Merc	367	22,450
2. Richard Petty	Petty Enterprises	43	71 Plym	366	10,050
3. Buddy Baker	Petty Enterprises	11	71 Dodg	363	6,575
4. Bobby Isaac	Nord Krauskopf	71	71 Dodg	361	4,625
5. Dave Marcis	Ray Nichels	99	71 Plym	355	3,600

1972 Winston Cup GN Race No. 24 Southern 500
September 4, 1972 Average Speed: 128.124

Driver	Owner	Car #	Make	Laps	Winnings
1. Bobby Allison	R. Howard & J. Johnson	12	72 Chev	367	23,990
2. David Pearson	Wood Brothers	21	71 Merc	367	11,065
3. Richard Petty	Petty Enterprises	43	72 Dodg	360	8,990
4. Fred Lorenzen	Hoss Ellington	28	72 Chev	354	4,940
5. H. B. Bailey	Vernon Blank	66	71 Pont	351	4,630

1967 Grand National Race No. 17 Rebel 300
May 13, 1967 Average Speed: 125.738

Driver	Owner	Car #	Make	Laps	Winnings
1. Richard Petty	Petty Enterprises	43	67 Plym	291	14,090
2. David Pearson	Holman-Moody	17	67 Ford	290	8,285
3. Dick Hutcherson	Bondy Long	29	67 Ford	285	5,005
4. Bobby Allison	Cotton Owens	6	67 Dodg	285	2,775
5. Sam McQuagg	Bud Moore	16	67 Merc	283	2,175

1968 Grand National Race No. 15 Rebel 400
May 11, 1968 Average Speed: 132.699

Driver	Owner	Car #	Make	Laps	Winnings
1. David Pearson	Holman-Moody	17	68 Ford	291	13,700
2. Darel Dieringer	Mario Rossi	22	68 Plym	291	7,620
3. Richard Petty	Petty Enterprises	43	68 Plym	291	5,330
4. Buddy Baker	Ray Fox	3	67 Dodg	290	2,675
5. LeeRoy Yarbrough	Junior Johnson	26	68 Ford	287	2,225

1969 Grand National Race No. 18 Rebel 400
May 10, 1969 Average Speed: 131.572

Driver	Owner	Car #	Make	Laps	Winnings
1. LeeRoy Yarbrough	Junior Johnson	98	69 Merc	291	14,700
2. Cale Yarborough	Wood Brothers	21	69 Merc	290	8,020
3. Paul Goldsmith	Ray Nichels	99	69 Dodg	288	5,005
4. Bobby Allison	Mario Rossi	22	69 Dodg	287	2,650
5. David Pearson	Holman-Moody	17	69 Ford	285	2,550

1970 Grand National Race No. 13 Rebel 400
May 9, 1970 Average Speed: 129.668

Driver	Owner	Car #	Make	Laps	Winnings
1. David Pearson	Holman-Moody	17	69 Ford	291	15,650
2. Dick Brooks	Dick Brooks	32	70 Plym	288	8,170
3. Bobby Isaac	Nord Krauskopf	71	69 Dodg	284	5,580
4. James Hylton	James Hylton	48	69 Ford	282	3,350
5. Benny Parsons	L. G. DeWitt	72	69 Ford	279	2,600

1971 Winston Cup GN Race No. 16 Rebel 400
May 2, 1971 Average Speed: 130.678

Driver	Owner	Car #	Make	Laps	Winnings
1. Buddy Baker	Petty Enterprises	11	71 Dodg	293	16,065
2. Dick Brooks	Mario Rossi	22	70 Dodg	286	8,165
3. Dave Marcis	Dave Marcis	2	69 Dodg	286	5,540
4. Donnie Allison	Wood Brothers	21	71 Merc	283	4,090
5. Jim Vandiver	O. L. Nixon	31	70 Dodg	276	2,215

1972 Winston Cup GN Race No. 8 Rebel 400
April 16, 1972 Average Speed: 124.406

Driver	Owner	Car #	Make	Laps	Winnings
1. David Pearson	Wood Brothers	21	71 Merc	293	16,850
2. Richard Petty	Petty Enterprises	43	72 Plym	292	10,375
3. Joe Frasson	Joe Frasson	18	71 Dodg	285	5,475
4. Benny Parsons	L. G. DeWitt	72	71 Merc	284	4,675
5. James Hylton	James Hylton	48	71 Ford	281	2,875

1973 Winston Cup GN Race No. 8 Rebel 500
April 15, 1973 Average Speed: 122.655

Driver	Owner	Car #	Make	Laps	Winnings
1. David Pearson	Wood Brothers	21	71 Merc	367	16,335
2. Benny Parsons	L. G. DeWitt	72	72 Chev	354	8,885
3. Bobby Allison	Bobby Allison	12	73 Chev	349	7,585
4. Richard Childress	Tom Garn	96	73 Chev	346	4,035
5. J. D. McDuffie	J. D. McDuffie	70	72 Chev	344	3,685

Darlington Raceway *continued*

1973 Winston Cup GN Race No. 22 Southern 500
September 3, 1973 Average Speed: 134.033

Driver	Owner	Car #	Make	Laps	Winnings
1. Cale Yarborough	R. Howard & J. Johnson	11	73 Chev	367	23,140
2. David Pearson	Wood Brothers	21	71 Merc	367	12,130
3. Buddy Baker	Nord Krauskopf	71	73 Dodg	366	8,585
4. Richard Petty	Petty Enterprises	43	73 Dodg	361	7,510
5. Benny Parsons	L. G. DeWitt	72	73 Chev	360	4,685

1974 Winston Cup GN Race No. 23 Southern 500
September 2, 1974 Average Speed: 111.075

Driver	Owner	Car #	Make	Laps	Winnings
1. Cale Yarborough	Junior Johnson	11	74 Chev	367	28,000
2. Darrell Waltrip	Darrell Waltrip	95	74 Chev	366	11,000
3. David Sisco	David Sisco	05	74 Chev	365	7,575
4. Dave Marcis	Dave Marcis	2	73 Dodg	362	5,850
5. James Hylton	James Hylton	48	74 Chev	360	4,650

1975 Winston Cup GN Race No. 21 Southern 500
September 1, 1975 Average Speed: 116.825

Driver	Owner	Car #	Make	Laps	Winnings
1. Bobby Allison	Roger Penske	16	75 Mata	367	20,870
2. Richard Petty	Petty Enterprises	43	75 Dodg	367	16,395
3. David Sisco	David Sisco	05	75 Chev	358	9,120
4. Jim Vandiver	Jim Vandiver	31	74 Dodg	353	6,495
5. Bruce Hill	Bruce Hill	47	75 Chev	352	5,600

1976 Winston Cup GN Race No. 22 Southern 500
September 6, 1976 Average Speed: 120.534

Driver	Owner	Car #	Make	Laps	Winnings
1. David Pearson	Wood Brothers	21	Merc	367	16,155
2. Richard Petty	Petty Enterprises	43	Dodg	367	18,055
3. Darrell Waltrip	DiGard	88	Chev	367	13,135
4. Dave Marcis	Nord Krauskopf	71	Dodg	367	10,800
5. Lennie Pond	Ronnie Elder	54	Chev	365	8,315

1977 Winston Cup GN Race No. 22 Southern 500
September 5, 1977 Average Speed: 106.797

Driver	Owner	Car #	Make	Laps	Winnings
1. David Pearson	Wood Brothers	21	Merc	367	24,550
2. Donnie Allison	Hoss Ellington	1	Chev	367	14,285
3. Buddy Baker	Bud Moore	15	Ford	367	12,710
4. Richard Petty	Petty Enterprises	43	Dodg	365	10,360
5. Cale Yarborough	Junior Johnson	11	Chev	362	12,435

1978 Winston Cup GN Race No. 22 Southern 500
September 4, 1978 Average Speed: 116.828

Driver	Owner	Car #	Make	Laps	Winnings
1. Cale Yarborough	Junior Johnson	11	Olds	367	30,175
2. Darrell Waltrip	DiGard	88	Chev	367	18,450
3. Richard Petty	Petty Enterprises	43	Chev	366	13,175
4. Terry Labonte	Billy Hagan	92	Chev	356	9,850
5. Bobby Allison	Bud Moore	15	Ford	355	10,875

1979 Winston Cup GN Race No. 23 Southern 500
September 3, 1979 Average Speed: 126.259

Driver	Owner	Car #	Make	Laps	Winnings
1. David Pearson	Rod Osterlund	2	Chev	367	29,925
2. Bill Elliott	George Elliott	17	Merc	365	19,235
3. Terry Labonte	Billy Hagan	44	Chev	365	13,460
4. Buddy Baker	Harry Ranier	28	Chev	365	7,975
5. Benny Parsons	M. C. Anderson	27	Chev	364	8,915

1974 Winston Cup GN Race No. 7 Rebel 450
April 7, 1974 Average Speed: 117.543

Driver	Owner	Car #	Make	Laps	Winnings
1. David Pearson	Wood Brothers	21	73 Merc	330	16,575
2. Bobby Allison	Bobby Allison	12	74 Chev	330	11,725
3. Buddy Baker	Nord Krauskopf	71	74 Dodg	330	6,275
4. Donnie Allison	DiGard	88	74 Chev	329	4,825
5. Cale Yarborough	R. Howard & J. Johnson	11	74 Chev	328	6,025

1975 Winston Cup GN Race No. 8 Rebel 500
April 13, 1975 Average Speed: 117.597

Driver	Owner	Car #	Make	Laps	Winnings
1. Bobby Allison	Roger Penske	16	75 Mata	367	15,080
2. Darrell Waltrip	Darrell Waltrip	17	75 Chev	367	13,180
3. Donnie Allison	DiGard	88	75 Chev	367	8,080
4. Dave Marcis	Nord Krauskopf	71	74 Dodg	364	7,880
5. Coo Coo Marlin	H. B. Cunningham	14	75 Chev	357	4,580

1976 Winston Cup GN Race No. 8 Rebel 500
April 11, 1976 Average Speed: 122.973

Driver	Owner	Car #	Make	Laps	Winnings
1. David Pearson	Wood Brothers	21	Merc	367	17,570
2. Buddy Baker	Bud Moore	15	Ford	367	14,875
3. Benny Parsons	L. G. DeWitt	72	Chev	365	12,055
4. Lennie Pond	Ronnie Elder	54	Chev	363	6,015
5. Dave Marcis	Nord Krauskopf	71	Dodg	362	7,580

1977 Winston Cup GN Race No. 7 Rebel 500
April 3, 1977 Average Speed: 128.817

Driver	Owner	Car #	Make	Laps	Winnings
1. Darrell Waltrip	DiGard	88	Chev	367	19,270
2. Donnie Allison	Hoss Ellington	1	Chev	367	11,875
3. Richard Petty	Petty Enterprises	43	Dodg	367	11,600
4. David Pearson	Wood Brothers	21	Merc	367	6,600
5. Benny Parsons	L. G. DeWitt	72	Chev	365	7,720

1978 Winston Cup GN Race No. 7 Rebel 500
April 9, 1978 Average Speed: 127.544

Driver	Owner	Car #	Make	Laps	Winnings
1. Benny Parsons	L. G. DeWitt	72	Chev	367	21,700
2. Darrell Waltrip	DiGard	88	Chev	367	16,550
3. Lennie Pond	Harry Ranier	54	Olds	366	8,755
4. Dave Marcis	Rod Osterlund	2	Chev	365	5,700
5. Richard Petty	Petty Enterprises	43	Dodg	364	8,500

1979 Winston Cup GN Race No. 8 CRC Chemicals Rebel 500
April 8, 1979 Average Speed: 121.721

Driver	Owner	Car #	Make	Laps	Winnings
1. Darrell Waltrip	DiGard	88	Chev	367	23,400
2. Richard Petty	Petty Enterprises	43	Chev	367	16,100
3. Donnie Allison	Hoss Ellington	1	Chev	367	13,650
4. Benny Parsons	M. C. Anderson	27	Chev	365	5,700
5. Buddy Baker	Harry Ranier	28	Chev	365	8,500

1980 Winston Cup GN Race No. 7 CRC Chemicals Rebel 500
April 13, 1980 Average Speed: 112.397

Driver	Owner	Car #	Make	Laps	Winnings
1. David Pearson	Hoss Ellington	1	Chev	189	21,430
2. Benny Parsons	M. C. Anderson	27	Chev	189	19,475
3. Harry Gant	Jack Beebe	47	Chev	189	10,180
4. Darrell Waltrip	DiGard	88	Chev	188	10,500
5. Dick Brooks	Nelson Malloch	7	Chev	187	7,310

Darlington Raceway *continued*

1980 Winston Cup GN Race No. 23 Southern 500
September 1, 1980 Average Speed: 115.210

Driver	Owner	Car #	Make	Laps	Winnings
1. Terry Labonte	Billy Hagan	44	Chev	367	27,325
2. David Pearson	Hoss Ellington	1	Chev	367	15,540
3. Harry Gant	Jack Beebe	47	Chev	367	15,190
4. Benny Parsons	M. C. Anderson	27	Chev	367	14,625
5. Neil Bonnett	Wood Brothers	21	Merc	367	7,575

1981 Winston Cup GN Race No. 23 Southern 500
September 7, 1981 Average Speed: 126.410

Driver	Owner	Car #	Make	Laps	Winnings
1. Neil Bonnett	Wood Brothers	21	Ford	367	33,375
2. Darrell Waltrip	Junior Johnson	11	Buick	367	19,365
3. Dave Marcis	Dave Marcis	71	Buick	367	14,330
4. Terry Labonte	Billy Hagan	44	Buick	367	13,225
5. Buddy Baker	Hoss Ellington	1	Buick	367	6,500

1982 Winston Cup GN Race No. 22 Southern 500
September 6, 1982 Average Speed: 115.224

Driver	Owner	Car #	Make	Laps	Winnings
1. Cale Yarborough	M. C. Anderson	27	Buick	367	34,300
2. Richard Petty	Petty Enterprises	43	Pont	367	26,165
3. Dale Earnhardt	Bud Moore	15	Ford	367	21,225
4. Bill Elliott	Harry Melling	9	Ford	367	13,925
5. Buddy Baker	Harry Ranier	28	Pont	365	16,140

1983 Winston Cup GN Race No. 22 Southern 500
September 5, 1983 Average Speed: 123.343

Driver	Owner	Car #	Make	Laps	Winnings
1. Bobby Allison	DiGard	22	Buick	367	42,050
2. Bill Elliott	Harry Melling	9	Ford	367	19,045
3. Darrell Waltrip	Junior Johnson	11	Chev	367	23,475
4. Neil Bonnett	Bob Rahilly & Butch Mock	75	Chev	367	19,320
5. Terry Labonte	Billy Hagan	44	Chev	367	11,045

1984 Winston Cup GN Race No. 22 Southern 500
September 2, 1984 Average Speed: 128.270

Driver	Owner	Car #	Make	Laps	Winnings
1. Harry Gant	Hal Needham	33	Chev	367	46,180
2. Tim Richmond	Raymond Beadle	27	Pont	367	29,420
3. Buddy Baker	Wood Brothers	21	Ford	367	12,200
4. Rusty Wallace	Cliff Stewart	88	Pont	365	14,405
5. Ricky Rudd	Bud Moore	15	Ford	364	17,050

1985 Winston Cup GN Race No. 20 Southern 500
September 1, 1985 Average Speed: 121.254

Driver	Owner	Car #	Make	Laps	Winnings
1. Bill Elliott	Harry Melling	9	Ford	367	1,053,725
2. Cale Yarborough	Harry Ranier	28	Ford	367	22,050
3. Geoff Bodine	Rick Hendrick	5	Chev	367	21,975
4. Neil Bonnett	Junior Johnson	12	Chev	366	17,425
5. Ron Bouchard	Jack Beebe	47	Buick	366	13,330

1986 Winston Cup Race No. 21 Southern 500
August 31, 1986 Average Speed: 121.068

Driver	Owner	Car #	Make	Laps	Winnings
1. Tim Richmond	Rick Hendrick	25	Chev	367	60,005
2. Bobby Allison	Stavola Brothers	22	Buick	367	31,500
3. Bill Elliott	Harry Melling	9	Ford	367	25,625
4. Morgan Shepherd	Jack Beebe	47	Buick	367	11,125
5. Darrell Waltrip	Junior Johnson	11	Chev	367	21,055

1981 Winston Cup GN Race No. 8 CRC Chemicals Rebel 500
April 12, 1981 Average Speed: 126.703

Driver	Owner	Car #	Make	Laps	Winnings
1. Darrell Waltrip	Junior Johnson	11	Buick	367	23,225
2. Harry Gant	Hal Needham	33	Pont	367	11,000
3. Dave Marcis	Dave Marcis	71	Chev	366	12,860
4. Bill Elliott	George Elliott	9	Ford	366	7,625
5. Benny Parsons	Bud Moore	15	Ford	366	10,750

1982 Winston Cup GN Race No. 6 CRC Chemicals Rebel 500
April 4, 1982 Average Speed: 123.554

Driver	Owner	Car #	Make	Laps	Winnings
1. Dale Earnhardt	Bud Moore	15	Ford	367	31,450
2. Cale Yarborough	M. C. Anderson	27	Buick	367	12,550
3. Bill Elliott	Harry Melling	9	Ford	367	9,900
4. Benny Parsons	Harry Ranier	28	Pont	367	14,275
5. Tim Richmond	Jim Stacy	2	Buick	366	9,180

1983 Winston Cup GN Race No. 5 TranSouth 500
April 10, 1983 Average Speed: 130.406

Driver	Owner	Car #	Make	Laps	Winnings
1. Harry Gant	Hal Needham	33	Buick	367	30,050
2. Darrell Waltrip	Junior Johnson	11	Chev	367	24,525
3. Mark Martin	Jim Stacy	2	Buick	367	17,530
4. Ricky Rudd	Richard Childress	3	Chev	366	9,905
5. Bill Elliott	Harry Melling	9	Ford	365	9,225

1984 Winston Cup GN Race No. 7 TranSouth 500
April 15, 1984 Average Speed: 119.925

Driver	Owner	Car #	Make	Laps	Winnings
1. Darrell Waltrip	Junior Johnson	11	Chev	367	39,450
2. Terry Labonte	Billy Hagan	44	Chev	367	22,180
3. Bill Elliott	Harry Melling	9	Ford	366	17,775
4. Cale Yarborough	Harry Ranier	28	Chev	366	6,850
5. Dale Earnhardt	Richard Childress	3	Chev	366	12,825

1985 Winston Cup GN Race No. 6 TranSouth 500
April 14, 1985 Average Speed: 126.295

Driver	Owner	Car #	Make	Laps	Winnings
1. Bill Elliott	Harry Melling	9	Ford	367	42,900
2. Darrell Waltrip	Junior Johnson	11	Chev	367	26,550
3. Tim Richmond	Raymond Beadle	27	Pont	367	15,860
4. Terry Labonte	Billy Hagan	44	Chev	366	17,105
5. Rusty Wallace	Cliff Stewart	2	Pont	365	11,800

1986 Winston Cup Race No. 6 TranSouth 500
April 13, 1986 Average Speed: 128.994

Driver	Owner	Car #	Make	Laps	Winnings
1. Dale Earnhardt	Richard Childress	3	Chev	367	52,250
2. Darrell Waltrip	Junior Johnson	11	Chev	367	31,600
3. Bobby Allison	Stavola Brothers	22	Buick	366	13,355
4. Neil Bonnett	Junior Johnson	12	Chev	366	16,480
5. Tim Richmond	Rick Hendrick	25	Chev	364	7,305

1987 Winston Cup Race No. 5 TranSouth 500
March 29, 1987 Average Speed: 122.540

Driver	Owner	Car #	Make	Laps	Winnings
1. Dale Earnhardt	Richard Childress	3	Chev	367	52,985
2. Bill Elliott	Harry Melling	9	Ford	367	31,485
3. Richard Petty	Petty Enterprises	43	Pont	367	20,450
4. Sterling Marlin	Billy Hagan	44	Olds	367	17,105
5. Ken Schrader	Junie Donlavey	90	Ford	367	16,650

Darlington Raceway *continued*

1987 Winston Cup Race No. 21 Southern 500
September 6, 1987 Average Speed: 115.520

Driver	Owner	Car #	Make	Laps	Winnings
1. Dale Earnhardt	Richard Childress	3	Chev	202	64,650
2. Rusty Wallace	Raymond Beadle	27	Pont	202	33,695
3. Richard Petty	Petty Enterprises	43	Pont	202	22,530
4. Sterling Marlin	Billy Hagan	44	Olds	202	18,665
5. Terry Labonte	Junior Johnson	11	Chev	202	19,945

1988 Winston Cup Race No. 21 Southern 500
September 4, 1988 Average Speed: 128.297

Driver	Owner	Car #	Make	Laps	Winnings
1. Bill Elliott	Harry Melling	9	Ford	367	75,800
2. Rusty Wallace	Raymond Beadle	27	Pont	367	38,850
3. Dale Earnhardt	Richard Childress	3	Chev	367	31,375
4. Darrell Waltrip	Rick Hendrick	17	Chev	367	19,850
5. Sterling Marlin	Billy Hagan	44	Olds	367	21,130

1989 Winston Cup Race No. 21 Heinz Southern 500
September 3, 1989 Average Speed: 135.462

Driver	Owner	Car #	Make	Laps	Winnings
1. Dale Earnhardt	Richard Childress	3	Chev	367	71,150
2. Mark Martin	Jack Roush	6	Ford	367	37,550
3. Ricky Rudd	Kenny Bernstein	26	Buick	367	26,865
4. Rusty Wallace	Raymond Beadle	27	Pont	367	24,330
5. Ken Schrader	Rick Hendrick	25	Chev	367	20,390

1990 Winston Cup Series Race No. 21 Heinz Southern 500
September 2, 1990 Average Speed: 123.141

Driver	Owner	Car #	Make	Laps	Winnings
1. Dale Earnhardt	Richard Childress	3	Chev	367	210,350
2. Ernie Irvan	Larry McClure	4	Chev	367	35,900
3. Alan Kulwicki	Alan Kulwicki	7	Ford	367	23,340
4. Bill Elliott	Harry Melling	9	Ford	367	24,380
5. Harry Gant	Leo Jackson	33	Olds	367	21,340

1991 Winston Cup Series Race No. 21 Heinz Southern 500
September 1, 1991 Average Speed: 133.508

Driver	Owner	Car #	Make	Laps	Winnings
1. Harry Gant	Leo Jackson	33	Olds	367	179,450
2. Ernie Irvan	Larry McClure	4	Chev	367	40,525
3. Ken Schrader	Rick Hendrick	25	Chev	367	26,940
4. Derrike Cope	Bob Whitcomb	10	Chev	366	24,330
5. Terry Labonte	Billy Hagan	94	Olds	366	19,515

1992 Winston Cup Race No. 21 Mountain Dew Southern 500
September 6, 1992 Average Speed: 129.114

Driver	Owner	Car #	Make	Laps	Winnings
1. Darrell Waltrip	Darrell Waltrip	17	Chev	298	66,030
2. Mark Martin	Jack Roush	6	Ford	298	41,355
3. Bill Elliott	Junior Johnson	11	Ford	298	32,620
4. Brett Bodine	Kenny Bernstein	26	Ford	298	23,260
5. Davey Allison	Robert Yates	28	Ford	298	38,845

1993 Winston Cup Series Race No. 22 Mountain Dew Southern 500
September 5, 1993 Average Speed: 137.932

Driver	Owner	Car #	Make	Laps	Winnings
1. Mark Martin	Jack Roush	6	Ford	351	67,765
2. Brett Bodine	Kenny Bernstein	26	Ford	351	40,690
3. Rusty Wallace	Roger Penske	2	Pont	351	27,495
4. Dale Earnhardt	Richard Childress	3	Chev	351	31,090
5. Ernie Irvan	Robert Yates	28	Ford	350	28,395

1988 Winston Cup Race No. 5 TranSouth 500
March 27, 1988 Average Speed: 131.284

Driver	Owner	Car #	Make	Laps	Winnings
1. Lake Speed	Lake Speed	83	Olds	367	49,435
2. Alan Kulwicki	Alan Kulwicki	7	Ford	367	30,905
3. Davey Allison	Harry Ranier	28	Ford	367	26,095
4. Bill Elliott	Harry Melling	9	Ford	366	19,260
5. Sterling Marlin	Billy Hagan	44	Olds	366	14,800

1989 Winston Cup Race No. 5 TranSouth 500
April 2, 1989 Average Speed: 115.475

Driver	Owner	Car #	Make	Laps	Winnings
1. Harry Gant	Leo Jackson	33	Olds	367	59,935
2. Davey Allison	Robert Yates	28	Ford	367	35,435
3. Geoff Bodine	Rick Hendrick	5	Chev	367	25,345
4. Mark Martin	Jack Roush	6	Ford	367	18,810
5. Sterling Marlin	Billy Hagan	94	Olds	367	18,270

1990 Winston Cup Series Race No. 5 TranSouth 500
April 1, 1990 Average Speed: 124.073

Driver	Owner	Car #	Make	Laps	Winnings
1. Dale Earnhardt	Richard Childress	3	Chev	367	61,985
2. Mark Martin	Jack Roush	6	Ford	367	34,460
3. Davey Allison	Robert Yates	28	Ford	367	25,795
4. Geoff Bodine	Junior Johnson	11	Ford	367	28,110
5. Morgan Shepherd	Bud Moore	15	Ford	367	17,610

1991 Winston Cup Series Race No. 5 TranSouth 500
April 7, 1991 Average Speed: 135.594

Driver	Owner	Car #	Make	Laps	Winnings
1. Ricky Rudd	Rick Hendrick	5	Chev	367	62,185
2. Davey Allison	Robert Yates	28	Ford	367	38,860
3. Michael Waltrip	Chuck Rider	30	Pont	367	20,320
4. Mark Martin	Jack Roush	6	Ford	366	22,710
5. Rusty Wallace	Roger Penske	2	Pont	365	10,260

1992 Winston Cup Race No. 5 TranSouth 500
March 29, 1992 Average Speed: 139.364

Driver	Owner	Car #	Make	Laps	Winnings
1. Bill Elliott	Junior Johnson	11	Ford	367	64,290
2. Harry Gant	Leo Jackson	33	Olds	367	40,715
3. Mark Martin	Jack Roush	6	Ford	367	29,375
4. Davey Allison	Robert Yates	28	Ford	366	35,315
5. Ricky Rudd	Rick Hendrick	5	Chev	366	21,020

1993 Winston Cup Series Race No. 5 TranSouth 500
March 28, 1993 Average Speed: 139.958

Driver	Owner	Car #	Make	Laps	Winnings
1. Dale Earnhardt	Richard Childress	3	Chev	367	64,815
2. Mark Martin	Jack Roush	6	Ford	367	38,875
3. Dale Jarrett	Joe Gibbs	18	Chev	367	30,685
4. Ken Schrader	Rick Hendrick	25	Chev	367	23,125
5. Rusty Wallace	Roger Penske	2	Pont	366	20,400

1994 Winston Cup Series Race No. 5 TranSouth 500
March 27, 1994 Average Speed: 132.432

Driver	Owner	Car #	Make	Laps	Winnings
1. Dale Earnhardt	Richard Childress	3	Chev	293	70,190
2. Mark Martin	Jack Roush	6	Ford	293	42,835
3. Bill Elliott	Junior Johnson	11	Ford	293	35,285
4. Dale Jarrett	Joe Gibbs	18	Chev	293	27,550
5. Lake Speed	Bud Moore	15	Ford	293	26,300

Darlington Raceway *continued*

1994 Winston Cup Series Race No. 23 Mountain Dew Southern 500
September 4, 1994 Average Speed: 127.952

Driver	Owner	Car #	Make	Laps	Winnings
1. Bill Elliott	Junior Johnson	11	Ford	367	68,330
2. Dale Earnhardt	Richard Childress	3	Chev	367	45,030
3. Morgan Shepherd	Wood Brothers	21	Ford	367	32,730
4. Ricky Rudd	Ricky Rudd	10	Ford	367	24,715
5. Sterling Marlin	Larry McClure	4	Chev	367	26,870

1995 Winston Cup Series Race No. 23 Mountain Dew Southern 500
September 3, 1995 Average Speed: 121.231

Driver	Owner	Car #	Make	Laps	Winnings
1. Jeff Gordon	Rick Hendrick	24	Chev	367	70,630
2. Dale Earnhardt	Richard Childress	3	Chev	367	62,155
3. Rusty Wallace	Roger Penske	2	Ford	367	40,580
4. Ward Burton	Bill Davis	22	Pont	367	39,090
5. Michael Waltrip	Chuck Rider	30	Pont	367	28,870

1996 Winston Cup Series Race No. 23 Mountain Dew Southern 500
September 1, 1996 Average Speed: 135.757

Driver	Owner	Car #	Make	Laps	Winnings
1. Jeff Gordon	Rick Hendrick	24	Chev	367	99,630
2. Hut Stricklin	Stavola Brothers	8	Ford	367	52,405
3. Mark Martin	Jack Roush	6	Ford	367	45,430
4. Ken Schrader	Rick Hendrick	25	Chev	366	40,590
5. John Andretti	Michael Kranefuss & Carl Haas	37	Ford	366	32,120

1997 Winston Cup Series Race No. 23
August 31, 1997 Average Speed: 121.149

Driver	Owner	Car #	Make	Laps	Winnings
1. Jeff Gordon	Rick Hendrick	24	Chev	367	131,330
2. Jeff Burton	Jack Roush	99	Ford	367	57,280
3. Dale Jarrett	Robert Yates	88	Ford	367	49,505
4. Bill Elliott	Bill Elliott	94	Ford	367	49,965
5. Ricky Rudd	Ricky Rudd	10	Ford	367	39,345

1998 Winston Cup Series Race No. 24
September 6, 1998 Average Speed: 139.031

Driver	Owner	Car #	Make	Laps	Winnings
1. Jeff Gordon	Rick Hendrick	24	Chev	367	1,134,655
2. Jeff Burton	Jack Roush	99	Ford	367	98,180
3. Dale Jarrett	Robert Yates	88	Ford	367	79,220
4. Dale Earnhardt	Richard Childress	3	Chev	367	64,465
5. Jeremy Mayfield	Michael Kranefuss	12	Ford	366	52,245

1999 Winston Cup Series Race No. 24
September 5, 1999 Average Speed: 107.811

Driver	Owner	Car #	Make	Laps	Winnings
1. Jeff Burton	Jack Roush	99	Ford	270	1,148,170
2. Ward Burton	Bill Davis	22	Pont	270	96,155
3. Jeremy Mayfield	Michael Kranefuss	12	Ford	270	70,320
4. Mark Martin	Jack Roush	6	Ford	270	74,065
5. Kevin Lepage	Jack Roush	16	Ford	270	63,510

2000 Winston Cup Series Race No. 24
September 3, 2000 Average Speed: 108.275

Driver	Owner	Car #	Make	Laps	Winnings
1. Bobby Labonte	Joe Gibbs	18	Pont	328	198,180
2. Jeff Burton	Jack Roush	99	Ford	328	106,705
3. Dale Earnhardt	Richard Childress	3	Chev	328	82,745
4. Jeff Gordon	Rick Hendrick	24	Chev	328	82,540
5. Dale Jarrett	Robert Yates	88	Ford	328	80,570

1995 Winston Cup Series Race No. 5 TranSouth 400
March 26, 1995 Average Speed: 111.392

Driver	Owner	Car #	Make	Laps	Winnings
1. Sterling Marlin	Larry McClure	4	Chev	293	86,185
2. Dale Earnhardt	Richard Childress	3	Chev	293	54,355
3. Ted Musgrave	Jack Roush	16	Ford	293	43,565
4. Todd Bodine	Butch Mock	75	Ford	293	36,570
5. Derrike Cope	Bobby Allison	12	Ford	293	22,950

1996 Winston Cup Series Race No. 5 TranSouth 400
March 24, 1996 Average Speed: 124.792

Driver	Owner	Car #	Make	Laps	Winnings
1. Jeff Gordon	Rick Hendrick	24	Chev	293	97,310
2. Bobby Labonte	Joe Gibbs	18	Chev	293	57,550
3. Ricky Craven	Larry Hedrick	41	Chev	293	46,690
4. Rusty Wallace	Roger Penske	2	Ford	293	29,480
5. Terry Labonte	Rick Hendrick	5	Chev	293	34,325

1997 Winston Cup Series Race No. 5
March 23, 1997 Average Speed: 141.41

Driver	Owner	Car #	Make	Laps	Winnings
1. Dale Jarrett	Robert Yates	88	Ford	293	142,860
2. Ted Musgrave	Jack Roush	16	Ford	293	54,330
3. Jeff Gordon	Rick Hendrick	24	Chev	293	56,240
4. Jeff Burton	Jack Roush	99	Ford	293	34,420
5. Bobby Labonte	Joe Gibbs	18	Pont	293	38,275

1998 Winston Cup Series Race No. 5
March 22, 1998 Average Speed: 127.962

Driver	Owner	Car #	Make	Laps	Winnings
1. Dale Jarrett	Robert Yates	88	Ford	293	110,035
2. Jeff Gordon	Rick Hendrick	24	Chev	293	75,705
3. Rusty Wallace	Roger Penske	2	Ford	293	52,240
4. Jeremy Mayfield	Michael Kranefuss	12	Ford	293	45,930
5. Jeff Burton	Jack Roush	99	Ford	293	40,075

1999 Winston Cup Series Race No. 5
March 21, 1999 Average Speed: 121.294

Driver	Owner	Car #	Make	Laps	Winnings
1. Jeff Burton	Jack Roush	99	Ford	164	161,900
2. Jeremy Mayfield	Michael Kranefuss	12	Ford	164	62,455
3. Jeff Gordon	Rick Hendrick	24	Chev	164	83,940
4. Dale Jarrett	Robert Yates	88	Ford	164	60,305
5. Mark Martin	Jack Roush	6	Ford	164	50,500

2000 Winston Cup Series Race No. 5
March 19, 2000 Average Speed: 128.076

Driver	Owner	Car #	Make	Laps	Winnings
1. Ward Burton	Bill Davis	22	Pont	293	132,725
2. Dale Jarrett	Robert Yates	88	Ford	293	90,905
3. Dale Earnhardt	Richard Childress	3	Chev	293	68,590
4. Tony Stewart	Joe Gibbs	20	Pont	293	68,230
5. Jeff Burton	Jack Roush	99	Ford	293	65,925

2001 Winston Cup Series Race No. 5
March 18, 2001 Average Speed: 126.558

Driver	Owner	Car #	Make	Laps	Winnings
1. Dale Jarrett	Robert Yates	88	Ford	293	214,612
2. Steve Park	Dale Earnhardt, Inc.	1	Chev	293	105,173
3. Jeremy Mayfield	Roger Penske	12	Ford	293	98,049
4. Jimmy Spencer	Travis Carter	26	Ford	293	83,640
5. Sterling Marlin	Chip Ganassi	40	Dodg	293	68,998

Darlington Raceway *continued*

2001 Winston Cup Series Race No. 25
September 2, 2001 Average Speed: 122.773

Driver	Owner	Car #	Make	Laps	Winnings
1. Ward Burton	Bill Davis	22	Dodg	367	181,435
2. Jeff Gordon	Rick Hendrick	24	Chev	367	153,127
3. Bobby Labonte	Joe Gibbs	18	Pont	367	133,327
4. Tony Stewart	Joe Gibbs	20	Pont	367	93,900
5. Bill Elliott	Ray Evernham	9	Dodg	367	92,583

2002 Winston Cup Series Race No. 5
March 17, 2002 Average Speed: 126.07

Driver	Owner	Car #	Make	Laps	Winnings
1. Sterling Marlin	Chip Ganassi	40	Dodg	293	190,442
2. Elliott Sadler	Wood Brothers	21	Ford	293	98,395
3. Kevin Harvick	Richard Childress	29	Chev	293	108,443
4. Dale Earnhardt, Jr.	Dale Earnhardt, Inc.	8	Chev	293	96,542
5. Ryan Newman	Roger Penske	12	Ford	293	77,175

2002 Winston Cup Series Race No. 25
September 1, 2002 Average Speed: 118.62

Driver	Owner	Car #	Make	Laps	Winnings
1. Jeff Gordon	Rick Hendrick	24	Chev	367	0
2. Ryan Newman	Roger Penske	12	Ford	367	0
3. Bill Elliott	Ray Evernham	9	Dodg	367	1
4. Sterling Marlin	Chip Ganassi	40	Dodg	367	0
5. Dale Jarrett	Robert Yates	88	Ford	367	0

Gamecock Speedway
Sumter, SC
Quarter-mile Dirt Track

(aka Sumter Rebel Speedway; Sumter Speedway; Rebel Speedway) Quarter-mile dirt track built circa 1955. Cale Yarborough began career here. Only NASCAR Winston Cup (then Grand National) race staged on 9/15/60 (won by Ned Jarrett). Track closed in 1984, re-opened in 1987, and closed again in 1993.

Winston Cup Victories
Ned Jarrett   1

Winston Cup Poles
David Pearson   1

Winston Cup Money
Ned Jarrett $770

Most Cars Started
13—September 15, 1960

Narrowest Margin of Victory
N/A

Race Record
41.208 MPH—September 15, 1960

Most Race Leaders
N/A

Most Cars Running at Finish
10—September 15, 1960

1960 Grand National Race No. 38
September 15, 1960 Average Speed: 41.208

Driver	Owner	Car #	Make	Laps	Winnings
1. Ned Jarrett	Ned Jarrett	11	60 Ford	200	770
2. David Pearson	David Pearson	67	59 Chev	200	535
3. Junior Johnson	John Masoni	27	60 Chev	199	385
4. G. C. Spencer	Weldon Wagner	48	58 Chev	195	270
5. Lee Petty	Petty Enterprises	42	60 Plym	195	325

Greenville-Pickens Speedway
Greenville, SC
Half-mile Paved Track

Half-mile dirt track built in 1940. First NASCAR Winston Cup (then Grand National) race staged on 8/25/51 (won by Bob Flock). Track paved in April 1970. The April 10, 1971, race was the first official Winston Cup point race to be televised live in its entirety on network television. Final Winston Cup Grand National race conducted on 6/26/71 (won by Richard Petty). Still an active track, hosting a variety of NASCAR events.

Winston Cup Starts
Richard Petty   20

Winston Cup Victories
Richard Petty   6

Winston Cup Poles
David Pearson   5

Winston Cup Money
Richard Petty $11,710

Most Cars Started
29—June 27, 1970 Greenville 200
29—June 26, 1971 Pickens 200

Fewest Cars Started
15—August 25, 1951

Narrowest Margin of Victory
1 car length—April 17, 1965

Slowest Race
51.480 MPH—June 13, 1959

Race Record
78.159 MPH—April 10, 1971
Greenville 200

Most Cautions
7—April 13, 1963

Most Race Leaders
5—April 13, 1963
5—April 8, 1969 Greenville 200

Most Cars Running at Finish
20—October 6, 1955

1951 Grand National Race No. 23
August 25, 1951

Driver	Owner	Car #	Make	Laps	Winnings
1. Bob Flock	Ted Chester	7	51 Olds	200	1,000
2. Tim Flock	Ted Chester	91	51 Olds	—	600
3. Buck Baker	Buck Baker	87	51 Plym	—	400
4. Fonty Flock	Frank Christian	14	51 Olds	—	300
5. Erick Erickson		1-X	51 Pont	—	250

1955 Grand National Race No. 39
October 6, 1955 Average Speed: 57.942

Driver	Owner	Car #	Make	Laps	Winnings
1. Tim Flock	Carl Kiekhaefer	300	55 Chrys	199	1,100
2. Junior Johnson	J. H. Petty	44	55 Chev	197	700
3. Bob Welborn	Bob Welborn	49	55 Chev	197	475
4. Jimmy Massey	Hubert Westmoreland	04	55 Chev	197	365
5. Buck Baker	Pete DePaolo	87	55 Ford	197	310

1956 Grand National Race No. 15
May 10, 1956 Average Speed: 60.362

Driver	Owner	Car #	Make	Laps	Winnings
1. Buck Baker	Carl Kiekhaefer	500B	56 Dodg	200	1,100
2. Curtis Turner	Charlie Schwam	99	56 Ford	199	700
3. Joe Eubanks	James Satcher	82	56 Ford	197	475
4. Gwyn Staley	Hubert Westmoreland	2	56 Chev	195	365
5. Joe Weatherly	Charlie Schwam	9	56 Ford	192	310

1958 Grand National Race No. 15
May 3, 1958 Average Speed: 62.295

Driver	Owner	Car #	Make	Laps	Winnings
1. Jack Smith	Jack Smith	47	57 Chev	200	800
2. Buck Baker	Buck Baker	87	57 Chev	199	525
3. Junior Johnson	Paul Spaulding	11	57 Ford	197	350
4. Doug Cox	Doug Cox	30	57 Ford	196	250
5. Eddie Pagan	Eddie Pagan	45	57 Ford	192	225

1959 Grand National Race No. 19
June 13, 1959 Average Speed: 51.480

Driver	Owner	Car #	Make	Laps	Winnings
1. Junior Johnson	Paul Spaulding	11	57 Ford	200	800
2. Roy Tyner	Roy Tyner	9	57 Chev	198	525
3. Lee Petty	Petty Enterprises	42	57 Olds	198	350
4. Tiny Lund	Tiny Lund	5	57 Chev	196	250
5. Tommy Irwin	Tommy Irwin	36	59 Ford	193	225

1959 Grand National Race No. 34
August 22, 1959 Average Speed: 58.055

Driver	Owner	Car #	Make	Laps	Winnings
1. Buck Baker	Lynton Tyson	88	59 Chev	200	800
2. Cotton Owens	W. H. Watson	6	58 Pont	200	525
3. Ned Jarrett	Ned Jarrett	11	57 Ford	200	375
4. Jack Smith	Gerald Duke & Robert Davis	92	59 Ford	196	275
5. Jim Paschal	J. H. Petty	48	57 Chev	190	250

1960 Grand National Race No. 14
April 23, 1960 Average Speed: 62.337

Driver	Owner	Car #	Make	Laps	Winnings
1. Ned Jarrett	Ned Jarrett	11	60 Ford	200	800
2. Lee Petty	Petty Enterprises	42	60 Plym	200	625
3. Richard Petty	Petty Enterprises	43	60 Plym	199	375
4. Tommy Irwin	Tommy Irwin	36	59 Ford	194	275
5. Bob Welborn	Bob Welborn	49	60 Chev	192	250

1961 Grand National Race No. 10
April 1, 1961 Average Speed: 52.189

Driver	Owner	Car #	Make	Laps	Winnings
1. Emanuel Zervakis	Monroe Shook	85	60 Chev	200	800
2. Richard Petty	Petty Enterprises	43	60 Plym	200	525
3. Rex White	Rex White	4	60 Chev	199	475
4. G. C. Spencer	G. C. Spencer	48	60 Chev	199	275
5. Buck Baker	Buck Baker	86	61 Chrys	196	250

1961 Grand National Race No. 27
June 8, 1961 Average Speed: 58.441

Driver	Owner	Car #	Make	Laps	Winnings
1. Jack Smith	Jack Smith	47	61 Pont	200	800
2. Ned Jarrett	Bee Gee Holloway	11	61 Chev	199	525
3. Emanuel Zervakis	Monroe Shook	85	61 Chev	198	375
4. Joe Weatherly	Bud Moore	8	61 Pont	198	275
5. Jim Paschal	J. H. Petty	14	61 Pont	196	250

1961 Grand National Race No. 51
October 28, 1961 Average Speed: 63.346

Driver	Owner	Car #	Make	Laps	Winnings
1. Junior Johnson	Rex Lovette	27	61 Pont	200	950
2. Joe Weatherly	Bud Moore	8	61 Pont	199	625
3. Rex White	Rex White	4	61 Chev	198	425
4. Richard Petty	Petty Enterprises	42	61 Plym	195	275
5. Curtis Crider	Curtis Crider	62	61 Merc	192	250

Greenville-Pickens Speedway *continued*

1962 Grand National Race No. 13
April 19, 1962 Average Speed: 57.480

Driver	Owner	Car #	Make	Laps	Winnings
1. Ned Jarrett	Bee Gee Holloway	11	62 Chev	200	1,200
2. Jim Paschal	Cliff Stewart	2	62 Pont	200	600
3. Joe Weatherly	Bud Moore	8	61 Pont	200	400
4. Wendell Scott	Wendell Scott	34	61 Chev	194	300
5. Jim Bennett	Thurman Wilkes	25	61 Ford	191	275

1962 Grand National Race No. 32
July 14, 1962 Average Speed: 62.219

Driver	Owner	Car #	Make	Laps	Winnings
1. Richard Petty	Petty Enterprises	43	62 Plym	200	1,000
2. Jack Smith	Jack Smith	47	61 Pont	197	600
3. Wendell Scott	Wendell Scott	34	61 Chev	194	400
4. Tommy Irwin	Melvin Bradley	27	62 Chev	194	300
5. Rex White	Rex White	4	62 Chev	192	275

1963 Grand National Race No. 16
April 13, 1963 Average Speed: 54.853

Driver	Owner	Car #	Make	Laps	Winnings
1. Buck Baker	Buck Baker	87	63 Pont	200	1,000
2. Ned Jarrett	Charles Robinson	11	63 Ford	200	600
3. G. C. Spencer	G. C. Spencer	03	62 Chev	200	400
4. Richard Petty	Petty Enterprises	41	62 Plym	199	300
5. David Pearson	Cotton Owens	6	63 Dodg	199	275

1963 Grand National Race No. 38
July 30, 1963 Average Speed: 62.456

Driver	Owner	Car #	Make	Laps	Winnings
1. Richard Petty	Petty Enterprises	41	63 Plym	200	1,000
2. Ned Jarrett	Charles Robinson	11	63 Ford	200	600
3. Buck Baker	Buck Baker	87	63 Pont	199	400
4. Fred Harb	Cliff Stewart	2	62 Pont	195	300
5. Bobby Isaac	Bondy Long	99	63 Ford	195	275

1964 Grand National Race No. 11
March 28, 1964 Average Speed: 57.554

Driver	Owner	Car #	Make	Laps	Winnings
1. David Pearson	Cotton Owens	6	64 Dodg	200	1,100
2. Ned Jarrett	Bondy Long	11	64 Ford	200	700
3. Marvin Panch	Wood Brothers	21	64 Ford	200	450
4. LeeRoy Yarbrough	Louie Weathersby	45	63 Plym	197	300
5. Tiny Lund	Herman Beam	19	63 Ford	196	275

1964 Grand National Race No. 26
May 30, 1964 Average Speed: 56.559

Driver	Owner	Car #	Make	Laps	Winnings
1. LeeRoy Yarbrough	Louie Weathersby	45	63 Plym	199	1,000
2. Richard Petty	Petty Enterprises	43	63 Plym	199	600
3. J. T. Putney	Walt Hunter	46	62 Chev	197	400
4. Bobby Keck	E. B. Rich	23	63 Ford	197	300
5. G. C. Spencer	Paul Clayton	75	62 Pont	193	275

1965 Grand National Race No. 10
April 17, 1965 Average Speed: 56.899

Driver	Owner	Car #	Make	Laps	Winnings
1. Dick Hutcherson	Holman-Moody	29	65 Ford	200	1,000
2. Ned Jarrett	Bondy Long	11	65 Ford	200	600
3. Buddy Baker	Buck Baker	86	64 Dodg	197	400
4. Bud Moore	Louie Weathersby	45	65 Plym	197	300
5. Fred Harb	Cliff Stewart	2	64 Pont	193	275

1965 Grand National Race No. 26
June 19, 1965 Average Speed: 55.274

Driver	Owner	Car #	Make	Laps	Winnings
1. Dick Hutcherson	Holman-Moody	29	65 Ford	200	1,000
2. Stick Elliott	Toy Bolton	18	65 Chev	197	600
3. J. T. Putney	Herman Beam	19	65 Chev	196	400
4. Roy Tyner	Roy Tyner	9	64 Chev	190	300
5. Buddy Arrington	Buddy Arrington	62	64 Dodg	188	275

1966 Grand National Race No. 11
April 9, 1966 Average Speed: 68.850

Driver	Owner	Car #	Make	Laps	Winnings
1. David Pearson	Cotton Owens	6	64 Dodg	200	1,000
2. Richard Petty	Petty Enterprises	43	65 Plym	199	600
3. Tiny Lund	Lyle Stelter	55	64 Ford	194	400
4. Neil Castles	Buck Baker	86	65 Plym	192	300
5. Jeff Hawkins	Hubert Howard	23	64 Ford	192	275

1966 Grand National Race No. 27
June 25, 1966 Average Speed: 66.286

Driver	Owner	Car #	Make	Laps	Winnings
1. David Pearson	Cotton Owens	6	64 Dodg	200	1,000
2. Tom Pistone	Tom Pistone	59	64 Ford	196	600
3. Elmo Langley	Gene Black	74	64 Ford	192	400
4. Stick Elliott	Toy Bolton	61	66 Chev	189	300
5. Henley Gray	Henley Gray	97	66 Ford	188	275

1967 Grand National Race No. 8
March 25, 1967 Average Speed: 61.824

Driver	Owner	Car #	Make	Laps	Winnings
1. David Pearson	Cotton Owens	6	66 Dodg	200	1,200
2. Jim Paschal	Tom Friedkin	14	65 Plym	197	600
3. John Sears	L. G. DeWitt	4	66 Ford	197	400
4. Buddy Baker	Toy Bolton	47	66 Chev	191	300
5. James Hylton	Bud Hartje	48	65 Dodg	190	275

1967 Grand National Race No. 26
June 24, 1967 Average Speed: 61.781

Driver	Owner	Car #	Make	Laps	Winnings
1. Richard Petty	Petty Enterprises	43	67 Plym	200	1,000
2. Dick Hutcherson	Bondy Long	29	67 Ford	200	600
3. Elmo Langley	Henry Woodfield	64	64 Ford	195	400
4. Clyde Lynn	Clyde Lynn	20	66 Ford	192	300
5. Doug Cooper	Bob Cooper	02	67 Chev	191	275

1968 Grand National Race No. 9
April 13, 1968 Average Speed: 63.347

Driver	Owner	Car #	Make	Laps	Winnings
1. Richard Petty	Petty Enterprises	43	68 Plym	200	1,200
2. Bobby Isaac	Nord Krauskopf	37	67 Dodg	197	600
3. Charlie Glotzbach	Cotton Owens	6	67 Dodg	197	400
4. Roy Tyner	Roy Tyner	9	67 Pont	195	300
5. Tiny Lund	Lyle Stelter	56	66 Ford	195	275

1968 Grand National Race No. 24
June 22, 1968 Average Speed: 64.609

Driver	Owner	Car #	Make	Laps	Winnings
1. Richard Petty	Petty Enterprises	43	68 Plym	200	1,200
2. David Pearson	Holman-Moody	17	68 Ford	200	600
3. John Sears	L. G. DeWitt	4	66 Ford	195	400
4. Clyde Lynn	Clyde Lynn	20	66 Ford	194	300
5. Jabe Thomas	Don Robertson	25	67 Ford	193	275

Greenville-Pickens Speedway *continued*

1969 Grand National Race No. 13 Greenville 200
April 8, 1969 Average Speed: 64.389

Driver	Owner	Car #	Make	Laps	Winnings
1. Bobby Isaac	Nord Krauskopf	71	69 Dodg	200	1,000
2. James Hylton	James Hylton	48	69 Dodg	199	600
3. David Pearson	Holman-Moody	17	69 Ford	198	600
4. Elmo Langley	Elmo Langley	64	68 Ford	197	350
5. Richard Petty	Petty Enterprises	43	69 Ford	197	325

1969 Grand National Race No. 26 Greenville 200
June 21, 1969 Average Speed: 61.813

Driver	Owner	Car #	Make	Laps	Winnings
1. Bobby Isaac	Nord Krauskopf	71	69 Dodg	200	1,000
2. David Pearson	Holman-Moody	17	69 Ford	200	800
3. Richard Petty	Petty Enterprises	43	69 Ford	200	400
4. James Hylton	James Hylton	48	68 Dodg	196	350
5. Neil Castles	Neil Castles	06	67 Plym	195	325

1970 Grand National Race No. 23 Greenville 200
June 27, 1970 Average Speed: 75.345

Driver	Owner	Car #	Make	Laps	Winnings
1. Bobby Isaac	Nord Krauskopf	71	70 Dodg	200	1,500
2. Bobby Allison	Bobby Allison	22	69 Dodg	200	900
3. Dick Brooks	Dick Brooks	32	69 Plym	198	400
4. James Hylton	James Hylton	48	69 Ford	197	350
5. Benny Parsons	L. G. DeWitt	72	69 Ford	196	325

1971 Winston Cup GN Race No. 12 Greenville 200
April 10, 1971 Average Speed: 78.159

Driver	Owner	Car #	Make	Laps	Winnings
1. Bobby Isaac	Nord Krauskopf	71	71 Dodg	200	1,430
2. David Pearson	Holman-Moody	17	70 Ford	198	1,030
3. Dick Brooks	Mario Rossi	22	70 Dodg	198	830
4. Dave Marcis	Dave Marcis	2	69 Dodg	198	780
5. Benny Parsons	L. G. DeWitt	72	70 Ford	198	755

1971 Winston Cup GN Race No. 26 Pickens 200
June 26, 1971 Average Speed: 74.297

Driver	Owner	Car #	Make	Laps	Winnings
1. Richard Petty	Petty Enterprises	43	71 Plym	200	1,500
2. Tiny Lund	John McConnell	55	70 Dodg	199	900
3. Bill Dennis	Junie Donlavey	90	69 Merc	199	500
4. Elmo Langley	Elmo Langley	64	71 Ford	197	350
5. Walter Ballard	Walter Ballard	30	71 Ford	197	325

Hartsville Speedway
Hartsville, SC
.333-mile Dirt Track

.333-mile dirt oval opened circa 1956. Only NASCAR Winston Cup (then Grand National) race staged on 6/23/61 (won by Buck Baker). Track closed circa 1962.

Winston Cup Victories
Buck Baker   1

Winston Cup Poles
Emanuel Zervakis   1

Winston Cup Money
Buck Baker $760

Most Cars Started
18—June 23, 1961

Narrowest Margin of Victory
1/2 lap—June 23, 1961

Race Record
46.234 MPH—June 23, 1961

Most Race Leaders
N/A

Most Cars Running at Finish
14—June 23, 1961

1961 Grand National Race No. 30
June 23, 1961 Average Speed: 46.234

Driver	Owner	Car #	Make	Laps	Winnings
1. Buck Baker	Buck Baker	86	61 Chrys	150	760
2. Jack Smith	Jack Smith	47	61 Pont	150	520
3. Rex White	Rex White	4	60 Chev	149	460
4. David Pearson	David Pearson	67	60 Chev	148	265
5. Junior Johnson	Rex Lovette	27	60 Pont	148	260

Lancaster Speedway
Lancaster, SC
Half-mile Dirt Track

Half-mile dirt track opened in 1954. First NASCAR Winston Cup (then Grand National) race staged on 6/1/57 (won by Paul Goldsmith). Only other Grand National race held on 7/30/57 (won by Speedy Thompson). This event has disappeared from all official NASCAR records and Thompson is listed as having 19 career Grand National wins instead of 20. Track still in operation.

Winston Cup Starts
13 drivers tied with   2

Winston Cup Victories
Paul Goldsmith   1
Speedy Thompson   1

Winston Cup Poles
Buck Baker   1
Speedy Thompson   1

Winston Cup Money
Speedy Thompson $1,270

Most Cars Started
19—July 30, 1957

Fewest Cars Started
17—June 1, 1957

Slowest Race
61.622 MPH—June 1, 1957

Narrowest Margin of Victory
N/A

Race Record
66.543 MPH—July 30, 1957

Most Race Leaders
N/A

Most Cars Running at Finish
15—June 1, 1957

1957 Grand National Race No. 21
June 1, 1957 Average Speed: 61.622

Driver	Owner	Car #	Make	Laps	Winnings
1. Paul Goldsmith	Smokey Yunick	3	57 Ford	200	700
2. Buck Baker	Hugh Babb	87	57 Chev	200	525
3. Lee Petty	Petty Enterprises	42	57 Olds	199	400
4. Marvin Panch	Pete DePaolo	98	57 Ford	198	330
5. Speedy Thompson	Hugh Babb	46	57 Chev	198	270

1957 Grand National Race No. 34
July 30, 1957 Average Speed: 66.543

Driver	Owner	Car #	Make	Laps	Winnings
1. Speedy Thompson	Speedy Thompson	46	57 Chev	200	1,000
2. Bill Amick	Bill Amick	97	57 Ford	200	625
3. Marvin Panch	Marvin Panch	98	57 Ford	197	400
4. Buck Baker	Buck Baker	87	57 Chev	194	295
5. Lee Petty	Petty Enterprises	42	57 Olds	192	255

Newberry Speedway
Newberry, SC
Half-mile Dirt Track

Half-mile dirt track opened in August 1952. Only NASCAR Winston Cup (then Grand National) race staged on 10/12/57 (Fireball Roberts won). Has the distinction of having the smallest crowd ever recorded at a top level NASCAR event (900 in attendance). Track shortened to quarter-mile circa 1961. Closed circa 1979.

Winston Cup Victories
Fireball Roberts   1

Winston Cup Poles
Jack Smith   1

Winston Cup Money
Fireball Roberts $900

Most Cars Started
23—October 12, 1957

Narrowest Margin of Victory
1 lap plus—October 12, 1957

Race Record
50.398 MPH—October 12, 1957

Most Race Leaders
4—October 12, 1957

Most Cars Running at Finish
17—October 12, 1957

1957 Grand National Race No. 50
October 12, 1957 Average Speed: 50.398

Driver	Owner	Car #	Make	Laps	Winnings
1. Fireball Roberts	Fireball Roberts	22	57 Ford	200	900
2. Buck Baker	Buck Baker	87	57 Chev	199	575
3. Jack Smith	Jack Smith	47	57 Chev	198	375
4. Marvin Panch	Marvin Panch	98	57 Ford	197	280
5. Gwyn Staley	J. H. Petty	38	57 Chev	194	245

Piedmont Interstate Fairgrounds
Spartanburg, SC
Half-mile Dirt Track

(aka Hub City Speedway) Half-mile dirt track opened in October 1937. First NASCAR Winston Cup (then Grand National) race staged on 7/4/53 (won by Lee Petty). Final Grand National race run on 6/4/66 (won by Elmo Langley, his first of two career victories). Closed circa 1986.

Winston Cup Starts
Buck Baker   14

Winston Cup Victories
Ned Jarrett   6

Winston Cup Poles
Dick Hutcherson   3
Cotton Owens   3

Winston Cup Money
Ned Jarrett $7,990

Most Cars Started
27—July 6, 1955
27—April 12, 1958

Fewest Cars Started
15—May 19, 1962

Narrowest Margin of Victory
60 feet (20 yards)—August 16, 1960

Slowest Race
46.287 MPH—June 29, 1957

Race Record
66.367 MPH—February 27, 1965

Most Cautions
6—July 6, 1955

Most Race Leaders
4—August 14, 1963
4—June 26, 1964

Most Cars Running at Finish
17—April 12, 1958

1953 Grand National Race No. 20
July 4, 1953 Average Speed: 56.934

Driver	Owner	Car #	Make	Laps	Winnings
1. Lee Petty	Petty Enterprises	42	53 Dodg	200	1,000
2. Buck Baker	Griffin Motors	87	53 Olds	—	700
3. Herb Thomas	Herb Thomas	92	53 Huds	—	450
4. Fonty Flock	Frank Christian	14	53 Huds	—	350
5. Johnny Patterson	H. B. Ranier	58	52 Huds	—	200

1954 Grand National Race No. 22
July 3, 1954 Average Speed: 59.181

Driver	Owner	Car #	Make	Laps	Winnings
1. Herb Thomas	Herb Thomas	92	54 Huds	200	1,000
2. Jimmie Lewallen	Joe Blair	5	54 Merc	199	650
3. Lee Petty	Petty Enterprises	42	54 Chrys	199	450
4. Buck Baker	Ernest Woods	88	54 Olds	196	350
5. Joe Eubanks	Phil Oates	82	52 Huds	194	300

1955 Grand National Race No. 24
July 6, 1955 Average Speed: 49.106

Driver	Owner	Car #	Make	Laps	Winnings
1. Tim Flock	Carl Kiekhaefer	300	55 Chrys	200	1,100
2. Fonty Flock	Carl Kiekhaefer	301	55 Chrys	200	650
3. Lee Petty	Petty Enterprises	42	55 Chrys	200	450
4. Buck Baker	Henry Ford	303	55 Chrys	198	350
5. Cotton Owens	Lancaster Brothers	70	55 Chev	195	300

1956 Grand National Race No. 31
July 7, 1956 Average Speed: 50.483

Driver	Owner	Car #	Make	Laps	Winnings
1. Lee Petty	Petty Enterprises	42	56 Dodg	200	850
2. Fireball Roberts	Pete DePaolo	22	56 Ford	200	625
3. Marvin Panch	Tom Harbison	99	56 Ford	198	450
4. Bill Amick	Pete DePaolo	66	56 Ford	189	350
5. Joe Eubanks	James Satcher	82	56 Ford	186	310

1956 Grand National Race No. 41
August 23, 1956 Average Speed: 54.372

Driver	Owner	Car #	Make	Laps	Winnings
1. Ralph Moody	Pete DePaolo	12	56 Ford	200	850
2. Jim Paschal	Frank Hayworth	75	56 Merc	198	625
3. Rex White	Bob Welborn	X	56 Chev	198	450
4. Herb Thomas	Herb Thomas	92	56 Chev	196	350
5. Speedy Thompson	Pete DePaolo	296	56 Ford	193	310

1957 Grand National Race No. 12
April 27, 1957 Average Speed: 55.130

Driver	Owner	Car #	Make	Laps	Winnings
1. Marvin Panch	Pete DePaolo	98	57 Ford	200	700
2. Fireball Roberts	Pete DePaolo	22	57 Ford	200	525
3. Ralph Moody	Pete DePaolo	12	57 Ford	200	500
4. Lee Petty	Petty Enterprises	42	57 Olds	199	330
5. Johnny Allen	Spook Crawford	64	57 Plym	191	320

1957 Grand National Race No. 26
June 29, 1957 Average Speed: 46.287

Driver	Owner	Car #	Make	Laps	Winnings
1. Lee Petty	Petty Enterprises	42	57 Olds	187	1,000
2. Bill Amick	Bill Amick	97	57 Ford	187	575
3. Buck Baker	Buck Baker	87	57 Chev	187	400
4. Speedy Thompson	Speedy Thompson	46	57 Chev	187	295
5. Jack Smith	Jack Smith	47	57 Chev	186	255

1958 Grand National Race No. 9
April 12, 1958 Average Speed: 56.613

Driver	Owner	Car #	Make	Laps	Winnings
1. Speedy Thompson	Speedy Thompson	46	57 Chev	200	800
2. Jack Smith	Jack Smith	47	57 Chev	200	525
3. Junior Johnson	Paul Spaulding	11	57 Ford	196	350
4. Eddie Pagan	Eddie Pagan	45	57 Ford	196	250
5. Possum Jones	Bob Welborn	2B	57 Chev	193	225

1959 Grand National Race No. 18
June 5, 1959 Average Speed: 55.547

Driver	Owner	Car #	Make	Laps	Winnings
1. Jack Smith	Jack Smith	47	59 Chev	200	1,000
2. Joe Eubanks	Don Every	82	58 Ford	199	525
3. Junior Johnson	Paul Spaulding	11	57 Ford	198	350
4. G. C. Spencer	G. C. Spencer	34	57 Chev	197	250
5. Roy Tyner	Roy Tyner	9	57 Chev	195	225

1960 Grand National Race No. 17
May 28, 1960 Average Speed: 51.843

Driver	Owner	Car #	Make	Laps	Winnings
1. Ned Jarrett	Ned Jarrett	11	60 Ford	200	800
2. Lee Petty	Petty Enterprises	42	60 Plym	200	625
3. Cotton Owens	Cotton Owens	5	60 Pont	199	375
4. Tommy Irwin	Tommy Irwin	36	59 Ford	198	275
5. David Pearson	David Pearson	67	59 Chev	198	250

Piedmont Interstate Fairgrounds *continued*

1960 Grand National Race No. 31
August 16, 1960 Average Speed: 59.681

Driver	Owner	Car #	Make	Laps	Winnings
1. Cotton Owens	Cotton Owens	5	60 Pont	200	800
2. Lee Petty	Petty Enterprises	42	60 Plym	200	625
3. Junior Johnson	John Masoni	27	60 Chev	198	375
4. Ned Jarrett	Ned Jarrett	11	60 Ford	198	275
5. Rex White	Rex White	4	60 Chev	198	250

1961 Grand National Race No. 6
March 4, 1961 Average Speed: 59.152

Driver	Owner	Car #	Make	Laps	Winnings
1. Cotton Owens	Cotton Owens	5	60 Pont	200	800
2. Richard Petty	Petty Enterprises	43	60 Plym	199	525
3. David Pearson	David Pearson	67	60 Chev	197	375
4. Jimmy Pardue	Jimmy Pardue	54	59 Chev	195	275
5. Doug Yates	Raeford Johnson	23	59 Plym	193	250

1961 Grand National Race No. 25
June 2, 1961 Average Speed: 55.495

Driver	Owner	Car #	Make	Laps	Winnings
1. Jim Paschal	J. H. Petty	14	61 Pont	200	800
2. Cotton Owens	Cotton Owens	6	60 Pont	198	525
3. Maurice Petty	Petty Enterprises	42	60 Plym	197	375
4. Herman Beam	Herman Beam	19	60 Ford	188	275
5. Ned Jarrett	Bee Gee Holloway	11	61 Chev	187	250

1962 Grand National Race No. 22
May 19, 1962 Average Speed: 60.080

Driver	Owner	Car #	Make	Laps	Winnings
1. Ned Jarrett	Bee Gee Holloway	11	62 Chev	200	1,200
2. Jim Paschal	Cliff Stewart	2	62 Pont	200	600
3. Richard Petty	Petty Enterprises	43	60 Plym	200	400
4. G. C. Spencer	G. C. Spencer	48	60 Chev	198	300
5. Joe Weatherly	Bud Moore	8	61 Pont	197	275

1962 Grand National Race No. 43
August 21, 1962 Average Speed: 59.870

Driver	Owner	Car #	Make	Laps	Winnings
1. Richard Petty	Petty Enterprises	43	62 Plym	200	1,000
2. Joe Weatherly	Bud Moore	8	61 Pont	200	600
3. Jack Smith	Jack Smith	47	61 Pont	197	400
4. Cotton Owens	Cotton Owens	6	60 Pont	197	300
5. G. C. Spencer	G. C. Spencer	48	62 Chev	195	275

1963 Grand National Race No. 8
March 2, 1963 Average Speed: 55.598

Driver	Owner	Car #	Make	Laps	Winnings
1. Richard Petty	Petty Enterprises	43	63 Plym	200	1,000
2. Ned Jarrett	Charles Robinson	11	63 Ford	199	600
3. Jim Paschal	Petty Enterprises	42	63 Plym	199	400
4. Joe Weatherly	Fred Harb	17	62 Pont	194	500
5. Wendell Scott	Wendell Scott	34	61 Chev	190	275

1963 Grand National Race No. 42
August 14, 1963 Average Speed: 52.424

Driver	Owner	Car #	Make	Laps	Winnings
1. Ned Jarrett	Charles Robinson	11	63 Ford	200	1,000
2. Richard Petty	Petty Enterprises	43	63 Plym	200	600
3. Buck Baker	Buck Baker	87	63 Pont	200	400
4. Billy Wade	Cotton Owens	5	63 Dodg	199	300
5. Cale Yarborough	Herman Beam	19	62 Ford	195	275

1964 Grand National Race No. 16
April 14, 1964 Average Speed: 58.852

Driver	Owner	Car #	Make	Laps	Winnings
1. Ned Jarrett	Bondy Long	11	64 Ford	200	1,150
2. Marvin Panch	Wood Brothers	21	64 Ford	200	700
3. David Pearson	Cotton Owens	6	64 Dodg	197	400
4. Ken Rush	Cliff Stewart	2	63 Pont	195	300
5. Elmo Henderson	Paul Clayton	75	62 Pont	191	275

1964 Grand National Race No. 34
June 26, 1964 Average Speed: 58.233

Driver	Owner	Car #	Make	Laps	Winnings
1. Richard Petty	Petty Enterprises	43	64 Plym	200	1,000
2. LeeRoy Yarbrough	Louie Weathersby	45	63 Plym	199	600
3. Doug Cooper	Bob Cooper	60	63 Ford	193	400
4. Wendell Scott	Wendell Scott	34	63 Ford	190	300
5. Ned Jarrett	Bondy Long	11	64 Ford	185	275

1965 Grand National Race No. 5
February 27, 1965 Average Speed: 66.367

Driver	Owner	Car #	Make	Laps	Winnings
1. Ned Jarrett	Bondy Long	11	65 Ford	200	1,150
2. G. C. Spencer	G. C. Spencer	49	64 Ford	178	700
3. Bob Derrington	Bob Derrington	68	64 Ford	177	450
4. Gene Hobby	Gene Hobby	99	64 Dodg	179	300
5. Dick Hutcherson	Holman-Moody	29	64 Ford	160	275

1965 Grand National Race No. 39
August 14, 1965 Average Speed: 56.926

Driver	Owner	Car #	Make	Laps	Winnings
1. Ned Jarrett	Bondy Long	11	65 Ford	200	1,000
2. Cale Yarborough	Kenny Myler	06	64 Ford	198	600
3. Elmo Langley	Elmo Langley	64	64 Ford	191	400
4. Wendell Scott	Wendell Scott	34	63 Ford	187	300
5. G. C. Spencer	G. C. Spencer	49	64 Ford	185	275

1966 Grand National Race No. 23
June 4, 1966 Average Speed: 60.050

Driver	Owner	Car #	Make	Laps	Winnings
1. Elmo Langley	Henry Woodfield	64	64 Ford	200	1,000
2. Neil Castles	Buck Baker	86	65 Dodg	196	600
3. Doug Cooper	Bob Cooper	02	65 Plym	195	400
4. Joel Davis	Harold Mays	77	64 Plym	190	300
5. J. D. McDuffie	J. D. McDuffie	70	64 Ford	189	275

Rambi Race Track
Myrtle Beach, SC
Half-mile Dirt Track

(aka Myrtle Beach Speedway; Rambi Raceway) Track built in 1958. Rambi stood for Racing Association of Myrtle Beach, Inc. Half-mile dirt track played to host first Winston Cup (then Grand National) race on 8/23/58 (won by Bob Welborn). Final Grand National race run on 6/24/65 (won by Dick Hutcherson). Track remains the only speedway in the world to host all three generations of Pettys (Lee, Richard, and Kyle) and never yielded a victory to any of them. Kyle drove in two weekly-dirt-track events in 1979. Track was paved in 1971. Promoters laid dirt over pavement in 1976, only to go back to pavement in 1977. Pavement torn up again in 1978, paved again in 1987. Track still in operation.

Winston Cup Starts
Ned Jarrett   8
Richard Petty   8

Winston Cup Victories
Ned Jarrett   3

Winston Cup Poles
Ned Jarrett   3

Winston Cup Money
Ned Jarrett $5,140

Most Cars Started
27—August 1, 1959

Fewest Cars Started
12—August 7, 1964

Narrowest Margin of Victory
N/A

Slowest Race
52.941 MPH—August 1, 1959

Race Record
64.171 MPH—July 21, 1962

Most Race Leaders
3—July 7, 1963 Speedorama 200
3—June 24, 1965

Most Cars Running at Finish
16—August 1, 1959

1958 Grand National Race No. 40
August 23, 1958 Average Speed: 60.443

Driver	Owner	Car #	Make	Laps	Winnings
1. Bob Welborn	J. H. Petty	49	57 Chev	200	800
2. Buck Baker	Buck Baker	87	57 Chev	200	525
3. Shorty Rollins	Shorty Rollins	99	58 Ford	200	350
4. Tiny Lund	Don Angel	37	56 Ford	198	250
5. Lee Petty	Petty Enterprises	42	57 Olds	197	225

1959 Grand National Race No. 29
August 1, 1959 Average Speed: 52.941

Driver	Owner	Car #	Make	Laps	Winnings
1. Ned Jarrett	Ned Jarrett	11	57 Ford	200	800
2. Jim Paschal	J. H. Petty	48	57 Chev	199	525
3. Tommy Irwin	Tommy Irwin	36	57 Ford	199	350
4. Glen Wood	Wood Brothers	21	58 Ford	198	250
5. Joe Weatherly	Doc White	41	59 Ford	197	225

1960 Grand National Race No. 26
July 23, 1960 Average Speed: 60.985

Driver	Owner	Car #	Make	Laps	Winnings
1. Buck Baker	Buck Baker	87	60 Chev	200	800
2. Lee Petty	Petty Enterprises	42	60 Plym	200	625
3. Rex White	Rex White	4	60 Chev	198	375
4. Junior Johnson	John Masoni	27	60 Chev	197	275
5. Richard Petty	Petty Enterprises	43	60 Plym	197	250

1961 Grand National Race No. 35
July 22, 1961 Average Speed: 57.655

Driver	Owner	Car #	Make	Laps	Winnings
1. Joe Weatherly	Bud Moore	8	61 Pont	200	950
2. Jim Paschal	J. H. Petty	14	61 Pont	200	625
3. Ned Jarrett	Bee Gee Holloway	11	61 Chev	199	425
4. George Green	Joe Jones	77	60 Ford	188	275
5. Emanuel Zervakis	Monroe Shook	85	61 Chev	185	250

1962 Grand National Race No. 14
April 21, 1962 Average Speed: 63.036

Driver	Owner	Car #	Make	Laps	Winnings
1. Jack Smith	Jack Smith	47	61 Pont	200	1,000
2. Richard Petty	Petty Enterprises	43	60 Plym	198	600
3. Ned Jarrett	Bee Gee Holloway	11	62 Chev	195	600
4. Thomas Cox	Ray Herlocker	60	60 Plym	188	300
5. Curtis Crider	Curtis Crider	62	61 Merc	183	275

1962 Grand National Race No. 35
July 21, 1962 Average Speed: 64.171

Driver	Owner	Car #	Make	Laps	Winnings
1. Ned Jarrett	Bee Gee Holloway	11	62 Chev	200	1,200
2. Joe Weatherly	Bud Moore	8	60 Pont	199	600
3. Jack Smith	Jack Smith	47	62 Pont	196	400
4. Buddy Baker	Buck Baker	86	61 Chrys	195	300
5. Bob Welborn	J. C. Parker	49	62 Pont	190	275

1963 Grand National Race No. 30 Speedorama 200
July 7, 1963 Average Speed: 60.996

Driver	Owner	Car #	Make	Laps	Winnings
1. Ned Jarrett	Charles Robinson	11	63 Ford	200	1,000
2. Buck Baker	Buck Baker	87	63 Pont	193	600
3. Joe Weatherly	Cliff Stewart	2	62 Pont	191	600
4. Neil Castles	Buck Baker	86	62 Chrys	190	300
5. Cale Yarborough	Herman Beam	19	62 Ford	185	275

1964 Grand National Race No. 44
August 7, 1964 Average Speed: 61.750

Driver	Owner	Car #	Make	Laps	Winnings
1. David Pearson	Cotton Owens	6	64 Dodg	200	1,000
2. Richard Petty	Petty Enterprises	43	64 Plym	199	600
3. LeeRoy Yarbrough	Louie Weathersby	45	63 Plym	195	400
4. Ned Jarrett	Bondy Long	11	64 Ford	192	300
5. Neil Castles	Buck Baker	88	62 Chrys	187	275

1965 Grand National Race No. 27
June 24, 1965 Average Speed: 59.701

Driver	Owner	Car #	Make	Laps	Winnings
1. Dick Hutcherson	Holman-Moody	29	65 Ford	200	1,000
2. Ned Jarrett	Bondy Long	11	65 Ford	200	600
3. Tiny Lund	Lyle Stelter	55	64 Ford	195	400
4. Cale Yarborough	Kenny Myler	06	64 Ford	193	300
5. G. C. Spencer	G. C. Spencer	49	64 Ford	183	275

South Dakota

Rapid Valley Speedway
Rapid City, SD
Half-mile Dirt Track

(aka Rapid Valley Race Track; Black Hills Speedway) Half-mile dirt track opened circa 1949. Only NASCAR Winston Cup (then Grand National) race staged on 7/22/53 (Herb Thomas won). Track still in operation.

Winston Cup Victories
Herb Thomas   1

Winston Cup Money
Herb Thomas $1,000

Narrowest Margin of Victory
N/A

Most Race Leaders
N/A

Winston Cup Poles
Herb Thomas   1

Most Cars Started
15—July 22, 1953

Race Record
57.270 MPH—July 22, 1953

Most Cars Running at Finish
N/A

1953 Grand National Race No. 23
July 22, 1953 Average Speed: 57.270

Driver	Owner	Car #	Make	Laps	Winnings
1. Herb Thomas	Herb Thomas	92	53 Huds	200	1,000
2. Dick Rathmann	Walt Chapman	120	53 Huds	—	700
3. Fonty Flock	Frank Christian	14	53 Huds	—	450
4. Lee Petty	Petty Enterprises	42	53 Dodg	—	350
5. Buck Baker	Griffin Motors	87	53 Olds	—	200

Tennessee

Boyd Speedway
Chattanooga, TN
.333-mile Paved Track

(aka Chattanooga Int'l Raceway; Chattanooga Raceway Park) Actually located just south of Georgia-Tennessee state line. A .333-mile dirt track that opened in 1952, and was paved in 1962. First NASCAR Winston Cup (then Grand National) race staged on 8/3/62 (won by Joe Weatherly). Final Grand National race run on 6/19/64 (won by David Pearson). Track still in operation.

Winston Cup Starts

Buddy Baker	2
Buck Baker	2
Curtis Crider	2
Ned Jarrett	2
Richard Petty	2
Wendell Scott	2
G. C. Spencer	2

Winston Cup Victories

David Pearson	1
Joe Weatherly	1

Winston Cup Poles

Richard Petty	2

Winston Cup Money

David Pearson	$1,000
Joe Weatherly	$1,000

Most Cars Started
21—August 3, 1962 Confederate 200

Fewest Cars Started
18—June 19, 1964 Confederate 300

Narrowest Margin of Victory
N/A

Slowest Race
70.051 MPH—June 19, 1964 Confederate 300

Race Record
71.145 MPH—August 3, 1962 Confederate 200

Most Race Leaders
3—August 3, 1962 Confederate 200

Most Cars Running at Finish
16—August 3, 1962 Confederate 200

1962 Grand National Race No. 37 Confederate 200
August 3, 1962 Average Speed: 71.145

Driver	Owner	Car #	Make	Laps	Winnings
1. Joe Weatherly	Bud Moore	8	61 Pont	200	1,000
2. Fireball Roberts	Jim Stephens	22	62 Pont	200	600
3. Jim Paschal	Cliff Stewart	2	62 Pont	197	400
4. Richard Petty	Petty Enterprises	42	62 Plym	197	300
5. Sherman Utsman	Sherman Utsman	61	62 Ford	196	275

1964 Grand National Race No. 31 Confederate 300
June 19, 1964 Average Speed: 70.051

Driver	Owner	Car #	Make	Laps	Winnings
1. David Pearson	Cotton Owens	6	64 Dodg	300	1,000
2. Richard Petty	Petty Enterprises	43	64 Plym	298	600
3. Buck Baker	Ray Fox	3	64 Dodg	293	400
4. Ned Jarrett	Bondy Long	11	64 Ford	290	300
5. G. C. Spencer	G. C. Spencer	49	64 Chev	289	275

Bristol Motor Speedway
Bristol, TN
.533-mile Paved Track

(aka Bristol Int'l Raceway; Bristol Int'l Speedway) Half-mile paved oval built in 1961. First NASCAR Winston Cup (then Grand National) race staged on 7/29/61 (won by Jack Smith with relief help from Johnny Allen). Track originally had a football field in the infield to attract NFL pre-season games. Track was re-designed in 1969, banking turns to 36 degrees, which are the steepest banks on the current Winston Cup schedule.

Winston Cup Starts
Richard Petty   60

Winston Cup Victories
Darrell Waltrip   12

Winston Cup Poles
Cale Yarborough   9

Winston Cup Money
Rusty Wallace $1,713,965

Most Cars Started
44—July 29, 1962 Southeastern 500

Fewest Cars Started
23—March 16, 1975 Southeastern 500

Narrowest Margin of Victory
1 foot—April 14, 1991

Slowest Race
61.826 MPH—July 25, 1965
Volunteer 500

Race Record
101.074 MPH—July 11, 1971
Volunteer 500

Most Cautions
20—2 times

Most Race Leaders
16—April 9, 1989 Valleydale Meats 500

Most Cars Running at Finish
40—April 11, 1999

1961 Grand National Race No. 36 Volunteer 500
July 30, 1961 Average Speed: 68.373

Driver	Owner	Car #	Make	Laps	Winnings
1. Jack Smith	Jack Smith	46	61 Pont	500	3,025
2. Fireball Roberts	Jim Stephens	22	61 Pont	498	1,325
3. Ned Jarrett	Bee Gee Holloway	11	61 Chev	495	1,125
4. Richard Petty	Petty Enterprises	43	61 Plym	493	800
5. Buddy Baker	Buck Baker	87	61 Chrys	492	750

1961 Grand National Race No. 50 Southeastern 500
October 22, 1961 Average Speed: 72.452

Driver	Owner	Car #	Make	Laps	Winnings
1. Joe Weatherly	Bud Moore	8	61 Pont	500	3,680
2. Rex White	Rex White	4	61 Chev	500	2,365
3. Nelson Stacy	Dudley Farrell	29	61 Ford	500	1,525
4. Jim Paschal	J. H. Petty	44	61 Pont	498	1,125
5. Emanuel Zervakis	Monroe Shook	85	61 Chev	495	950

1962 Grand National Race No. 17 Volunteer 500
April 29, 1962 Average Speed: 73.397

Driver	Owner	Car #	Make	Laps	Winnings
1. Bobby Johns	Shorty Johns	72	62 Pont	500	4,405
2. Fireball Roberts	Banjo Matthews	22	62 Pont	494	2,500
3. Jack Smith	Jack Smith	47	62 Pont	492	1,635
4. Ned Jarrett	Bee Gee Holloway	11	62 Chev	475	1,400
5. Thomas Cox	Ray Herlocker	60	60 Plym	470	850

1962 Grand National Race No. 36 Southeastern 500
July 29, 1962 Average Speed: 75.276

Driver	Owner	Car #	Make	Laps	Winnings
1. Jim Paschal	Petty Enterprises	42	62 Plym	500	3,930
2. Fred Lorenzen	Holman-Moody	20	62 Ford	500	2,370
3. Richard Petty	Petty Enterprises	43	62 Plym	500	1,540
4. Johnny Allen	Fred Lovette	46	62 Pont	498	1,270
5. Nelson Stacy	Holman-Moody	29	62 Ford	498	875

1963 Grand National Race No. 13 Southeastern 500
March 31, 1963 Average Speed: 76.910

Driver	Owner	Car #	Make	Laps	Winnings
1. Fireball Roberts	Holman-Moody	22	63 Ford	500	4,060
2. Fred Lorenzen	Holman-Moody	28	63 Ford	500	2,395
3. Junior Johnson	Ray Fox	3	63 Chev	497	1,725
4. Richard Petty	Petty Enterprises	43	63 Plym	495	1,225
5. LeeRoy Yarbrough	Lou Sidoit	69	62 Merc	490	975

1963 Grand National Race No. 37 Volunteer 500
July 28, 1963 Average Speed: 74.844

Driver	Owner	Car #	Make	Laps	Winnings
1. Fred Lorenzen	Holman-Moody	28	63 Ford	500	4,540
2. Richard Petty	Petty Enterprises	43	63 Plym	500	2,365
3. Jim Paschal	Petty Enterprises	42	63 Plym	499	1,825
4. Marvin Panch	Wood Brothers	21	63 Ford	492	1,225
5. David Pearson	Cotton Owens	6	63 Dodg	491	1,075

1964 Grand National Race No. 10 Southeastern 500
March 22, 1964 Average Speed: 72.196

Driver	Owner	Car #	Make	Laps	Winnings
1. Fred Lorenzen	Holman-Moody	28	64 Ford	500	4,300
2. Fireball Roberts	Holman-Moody	22	64 Ford	500	2,150
3. Paul Goldsmith	Ray Nichels	25	64 Plym	497	1,685
4. Buck Baker	Petty Enterprises	41	64 Plym	496	1,075
5. Marvin Panch	Wood Brothers	21	64 Ford	494	1,075

1964 Grand National Race No. 42 Volunteer 500
July 26, 1964 Average Speed: 78.044

Driver	Owner	Car #	Make	Laps	Winnings
1. Fred Lorenzen	Holman-Moody	28	64 Ford	500	4,185
2. Richard Petty	Petty Enterprises	43	64 Plym	499	2,730
3. Jim Paschal	Petty Enterprises	41	64 Plym	499	1,500
4. LeeRoy Yarbrough	Ray Fox	03	64 Dodg	489	1,260
5. Larry Thomas	Herman Beam	19	64 Ford	482	975

1965 Grand National Race No. 14 Southeastern 500
May 2, 1965 Average Speed: 74.937

Driver	Owner	Car #	Make	Laps	Winnings
1. Junior Johnson	Rex Lovette	26	65 Ford	500	4,550
2. Dick Hutcherson	Holman-Moody	29	65 Ford	500	2,460
3. Ned Jarrett	Bondy Long	11	65 Ford	500	1,730
4. Marvin Panch	Wood Brothers	21	65 Ford	487	1,375
5. Wendell Scott	Wendell Scott	34	63 Ford	468	1,035

1965 Grand National Race No. 34 Volunteer 500
July 25, 1965 Average Speed: 61.826

Driver	Owner	Car #	Make	Laps	Winnings
1. Ned Jarrett	Bondy Long	11	65 Ford	500	4,315
2. Dick Hutcherson	Holman-Moody	29	65 Ford	500	2,275
3. Sam McQuagg	Betty Lilly	24	65 Ford	494	1,650
4. Jim Paschal	Tom Friedkin	41	65 Chev	494	1,125
5. Buck Baker	Buck Baker	87	65 Chev	484	1,025

Bristol Motor Speedway *continued*

1966 Grand National Race No. 7 Southeastern 500
March 20, 1966 Average Speed: 69.952

Driver	Owner	Car #	Make	Laps	Winnings
1. Dick Hutcherson	Holman-Moody	29	66 Ford	500	4,150
2. Paul Lewis	Paul Lewis	1	65 Plym	496	1,825
3. James Hylton	Bud Hartje	48	65 Dodg	494	1,550
4. Elmo Langley	Henry Woodfield	64	64 Ford	492	1,125
5. Sam McQuagg	Ray Nichels	98	66 Dodg	489	1,000

1966 Grand National Race No. 34 Volunteer 500
July 24, 1966 Average Speed: 77.963

Driver	Owner	Car #	Make	Laps	Winnings
1. Paul Goldsmith	Ray Nichels	99	66 Plym	500	5,400
2. Richard Petty	Petty Enterprises	43	66 Plym	500	2,950
3. David Pearson	Cotton Owens	6	66 Dodg	496	2,150
4. Paul Lewis	Paul Lewis	1	65 Plym	492	1,200
5. Bobby Allison	Bobby Allison	2	65 Chev	490	1,060

1967 Grand National Race No. 7 Southeastern 500
March 19, 1967 Average Speed: 75.937

Driver	Owner	Car #	Make	Laps	Winnings
1. David Pearson	Cotton Owens	6	67 Dodg	500	5,290
2. Cale Yarborough	Wood Brothers	21	67 Ford	500	3,050
3. Darel Dieringer	Junior Johnson	26	67 Ford	497	2,700
4. Neil Castles	Emory Gilliam	00	65 Plym	485	1,400
5. Dick Hutcherson	Bondy Long	29	67 Ford	482	1,125

1967 Grand National Race No. 33 Volunteer 500
July 23, 1967 Average Speed: 78.705

Driver	Owner	Car #	Make	Laps	Winnings
1. Richard Petty	Petty Enterprises	43	67 Plym	500	6,050
2. Dick Hutcherson	Bondy Long	29	67 Ford	500	3,250
3. Darel Dieringer	Junior Johnson	26	67 Ford	498	2,300
4. Jim Paschal	Tom Friedkin	14	67 Plym	492	1,325
5. James Hylton	Bud Hartje	48	65 Dodg	486	1,100

1968 Grand National Race No. 5 Southeastern 500
March 17, 1968 Average Speed: 77.247

Driver	Owner	Car #	Make	Laps	Winnings
1. David Pearson	Holman-Moody	17	68 Ford	500	5,725
2. Richard Petty	Petty Enterprises	43	68 Plym	500	4,125
3. LeeRoy Yarbrough	Junior Johnson	26	68 Ford	499	2,100
4. Darel Dieringer	Mario Rossi	22	68 Plym	492	1,325
5. Bobby Isaac	Nord Krauskopf	71	67 Dodg	491	900

1968 Grand National Race No. 30 Volunteer 500
July 21, 1968 Average Speed: 76.310

Driver	Owner	Car #	Make	Laps	Winnings
1. David Pearson	Holman-Moody	17	68 Ford	500	5,175
2. Cale Yarborough	Wood Brothers	21	68 Merc	499	2,650
3. Swede Savage	Bondy Long	29	68 Ford	498	1,700
4. Bobby Isaac	Nord Krauskopf	71	67 Dodg	497	900
5. Friday Hassler	Red Sharp	39	66 Chev	488	800

1969 Grand National Race No. 9 Southeastern 500
March 23, 1969 Average Speed: 81.455

Driver	Owner	Car #	Make	Laps	Winnings
1. Bobby Allison	Mario Rossi	22	69 Dodg	500	5,025
2. LeeRoy Yarbrough	Junior Johnson	98	69 Ford	496	3,000
3. David Pearson	Holman-Moody	17	69 Ford	495	2,400
4. Cale Yarborough	Wood Brothers	21	69 Merc	494	1,275
5. Donnie Allison	Banjo Matthews	27	69 Ford	491	800

1969 Grand National Race No. 33 Volunteer 500
July 20, 1969 Average Speed: 79.737

Driver	Owner	Car #	Make	Laps	Winnings
1. David Pearson	Holman-Moody	17	69 Ford	500	5,525
2. Bobby Isaac	Nord Krauskopf	71	69 Dodg	497	3,150
3. Donnie Allison	Banjo Matthews	27	69 Ford	487	2,300
4. James Hylton	James Hylton	48	69 Dodg	477	1,500
5. Cecil Gordon	Bill Seifert	47	68 Ford	431	1,000

1970 Grand National Race No. 9 Southeastern 500
April 5, 1970 Average Speed: 87.543

Driver	Owner	Car #	Make	Laps	Winnings
1. Donnie Allison	Banjo Matthews	27	70 Ford	500	6,670
2. Bobby Allison	Don Robertson	22	69 Plym	497	3,820
3. Cale Yarborough	Wood Brothers	21	70 Merc	456	2,345
4. James Hylton	James Hylton	48	69 Ford	453	1,295
5. Dick Brooks	Dick Brooks	32	70 Plym	447	1,020

1970 Grand National Race No. 28 Volunteer 500
July 19, 1970 Average Speed: 84.880

Driver	Owner	Car #	Make	Laps	Winnings
1. Bobby Allison	Bobby Allison	22	69 Dodg	500	4,850
2. LeeRoy Yarbrough	Junior Johnson	98	69 Ford	498	2,850
3. Bobby Isaac	Nord Krauskopf	71	70 Dodg	491	2,075
4. G. C. Spencer	G. C. Spencer	49	69 Plym	479	1,385
5. Richard Petty	Petty Enterprises	43	70 Plym	464	1,050

1971 Winston Cup GN Race No. 9 Southeastern 500
March 28, 1971 Average Speed: 91.704

Driver	Owner	Car #	Make	Laps	Winnings
1. David Pearson	Holman-Moody	17	71 Ford	500	6,120
2. Richard Petty	Petty Enterprises	43	71 Plym	500	3,570
3. Dick Brooks	Mario Rossi	22	70 Dodg	489	2,245
4. Bobby Allison	Bobby Allison	12	71 Dodg	487	1,320
5. Benny Parsons	L. G. DeWitt	72	70 Ford	485	1,045

1971 Winston Cup GN Race No. 28 Volunteer 500
July 11, 1971 Average Speed: 101.074

Driver	Owner	Car #	Make	Laps	Winnings
1. Charlie Glotzbach	R. Howard & J. Johnson	3	71 Chev	500	5,675
2. Bobby Allison	Holman-Moody	12	70 Ford	497	3,450
3. Richard Petty	Petty Enterprises	43	71 Plym	494	2,575
4. Cecil Gordon	Cecil Gordon	24	69 Merc	477	1,200
5. James Hylton	James Hylton	48	70 Ford	473	1,025

1972 Winston Cup GN Race No. 7 Southeastern 500
April 9, 1972 Average Speed: 92.826

Driver	Owner	Car #	Make	Laps	Winnings
1. Bobby Allison	R. Howard & J. Johnson	12	72 Chev	500	8,325
2. Bobby Isaac	Nord Krauskopf	71	72 Dodg	496	5,350
3. Richard Petty	Petty Enterprises	43	72 Plym	491	4,225
4. LeeRoy Yarbrough	Bill Seifert	45	71 Ford	483	1,720
5. Cecil Gordon	Cecil Gordon	24	71 Merc	474	1,325

1972 Winston Cup GN Race No. 18 Volunteer 500
July 9, 1972 Average Speed: 92.735

Driver	Owner	Car #	Make	Laps	Winnings
1. Bobby Allison	R. Howard & J. Johnson	12	72 Chev	500	8,400
2. Richard Petty	Petty Enterprises	43	72 Plym	497	5,700
3. Dave Marcis	Dave Marcis	2	70 Dodg	489	2,775
4. Benny Parsons	L. G. DeWitt	72	71 Merc	477	1,750
5. J. D. McDuffie	Dr. Don Tarr	70	70 Dodg	466	1,300

Bristol Motor Speedway *continued*

1973 Winston Cup GN Race No. 5 Southeastern 500
March 25, 1973 Average Speed: 88.952

Driver	Owner	Car #	Make	Laps	Winnings
1. Cale Yarborough	R. Howard & J. Johnson	11	73 Chev	500	8,030
2. Richard Petty	Petty Enterprises	43	73 Dodg	498	5,305
3. Bobby Allison	Bobby Allison	12	73 Chev	495	3,855
4. Dave Marcis	Dave Marcis	2	73 Dodg	484	1,440
5. Benny Parsons	L. G. DeWitt	72	71 Merc	484	1,330

1973 Winston Cup GN Race No. 18 Volunteer 500
July 8, 1973 Average Speed: 91.342

Driver	Owner	Car #	Make	Laps	Winnings
1. Benny Parsons	L. G. DeWitt	72	73 Chev	500	6,800
2. L. D. Ottinger	James Bryant	45	73 Chev	493	4,060
3. Cecil Gordon	Cecil Gordon	24	73 Chev	492	2,875
4. Lennie Pond	Ronnie Elder	54	73 Chev	485	1,475
5. J. D. McDuffie	J. D. McDuffie	70	72 Chev	473	1,435

1974 Winston Cup GN Race No. 5 Southeastern 500
March 17, 1974 Average Speed: 64.533

Driver	Owner	Car #	Make	Laps	Winnings
1. Cale Yarborough	R. Howard & J. Johnson	11	74 Chev	500	8,655
2. Bobby Isaac	Banjo Matthews	27	74 Chev	499	4,030
3. Benny Parsons	L. G. DeWitt	72	74 Chev	498	4,905
4. Bobby Allison	Bobby Allison	12	74 Chev	497	3,355
5. Donnie Allison	DiGard	88	74 Chev	491	1,980

1974 Winston Cup GN Race No. 17 Volunteer 500
July 14, 1974 Average Speed: 75.430

Driver	Owner	Car #	Make	Laps	Winnings
1. Cale Yarborough	Junior Johnson	11	74 Chev	500	7,725
2. Buddy Baker	Bud Moore	15	73 Ford	500	5,525
3. Richard Petty	Petty Enterprises	43	74 Dodg	498	4,900
4. Charlie Glotzbach	Junie Donlavey	90	72 Ford	494	1,700
5. Bobby Allison	Bobby Allison	12	74 Chev	494	1,025

1975 Winston Cup GN Race No. 5 Southeastern 500
March 16, 1975 Average Speed: 97.053

Driver	Owner	Car #	Make	Laps	Winnings
1. Richard Petty	Petty Enterprises	43	74 Dodg	500	7,350
2. Benny Parsons	L. G. DeWitt	72	75 Chev	494	5,325
3. Buddy Baker	Bud Moore	15	75 Ford	493	5,500
4. Cecil Gordon	Cecil Gordon	24	75 Chev	486	2,300
5. James Hylton	James Hylton	48	74 Chev	482	1,900

1975 Winston Cup GN Race No. 28 Volunteer 500
November 2, 1975 Average Speed: 97.016

Driver	Owner	Car #	Make	Laps	Winnings
1. Richard Petty	Petty Enterprises	43	74 Dodg	500	7,560
2. Lennie Pond	Ronnie Elder	54	75 Chev	499	4,110
3. Darrell Waltrip	DiGard	88	75 Chev	498	4,355
4. Dave Marcis	Nord Krauskopf	71	74 Dodg	494	4,060
5. Benny Parsons	L. G. DeWitt	72	75 Chev	488	3,035

1976 Winston Cup GN Race No. 5 Southeastern 400
March 14, 1976 Average Speed: 87.377

Driver	Owner	Car #	Make	Laps	Winnings
1. Cale Yarborough	Junior Johnson	11	Chev	400	18,070
2. Darrell Waltrip	DiGard	88	Chev	399	7,910
3. Benny Parsons	L. G. DeWitt	72	Chev	398	5,330
4. Dave Marcis	Nord Krauskopf	71	Dodg	398	4,280
5. Bobby Allison	Roger Penske	2	Merc	395	3,950

1976 Winston Cup GN Race No. 21 Volunteer 400
August 29, 1976 Average Speed: 99.175

Driver	Owner	Car #	Make	Laps	Winnings
1. Cale Yarborough	Junior Johnson	11	Chev	400	10,025
2. Richard Petty	Petty Enterprises	43	Dodg	398	7,800
3. Darrell Waltrip	DiGard	88	Chev	398	5,700
4. Benny Parsons	L. G. DeWitt	72	Chev	395	4,320
5. Buddy Baker	Bud Moore	15	Ford	394	3,950

1977 Winston Cup GN Race No. 8 Southeastern 500
April 17, 1977 Average Speed: 100.989

Driver	Owner	Car #	Make	Laps	Winnings
1. Cale Yarborough	Junior Johnson	11	Chev	500	23,300
2. Dick Brooks	Junie Donlavey	90	Ford	493	7,750
3. Richard Petty	Petty Enterprises	43	Dodg	491	6,100
4. Neil Bonnett	Nord Krauskopf	71	Dodg	490	4,200
5. Benny Parsons	L. G. DeWitt	72	Chev	488	3,950

1977 Winston Cup GN Race No. 21 Volunteer 400
August 28, 1977 Average Speed: 79.726

Driver	Owner	Car #	Make	Laps	Winnings
1. Cale Yarborough	Junior Johnson	11	Chev	400	12,100
2. Darrell Waltrip	DiGard	88	Chev	400	7,200
3. Benny Parsons	L. G. DeWitt	72	Chev	399	5,670
4. Dick Brooks	Junie Donlavey	90	Ford	396	3,400
5. Tighe Scott	Walter Ballard	30	Chev	389	2,900

1978 Winston Cup GN Race No. 6 Southeastern 500
April 2, 1978 Average Speed: 92.401

Driver	Owner	Car #	Make	Laps	Winnings
1. Darrell Waltrip	DiGard	88	Chev	500	19,200
2. Benny Parsons	L. G. DeWitt	72	Chev	499	15,300
3. Dave Marcis	Rod Osterlund	2	Chev	497	45,100
4. Cale Yarborough	Junior Johnson	11	Olds	494	6,850
5. Lennie Pond	Harry Ranier	54	Chev	494	2,000

1978 Winston Cup GN Race No. 21 Volunteer 500
August 26, 1978 Average Speed: 88.628

Driver	Owner	Car #	Make	Laps	Winnings
1. Cale Yarborough	Junior Johnson	11	Olds	500	15,910
2. Benny Parsons	L. G. DeWitt	72	Olds	500	8,350
3. Darrell Waltrip	DiGard	88	Chev	499	7,100
4. Dick Brooks	Junie Donlavey	90	Ford	497	1,950
5. Richard Petty	Petty Enterprises	43	Chev	495	4,350

1979 Winston Cup GN Race No. 7 Southeastern 500
April 1, 1979 Average Speed: 91.033

Driver	Owner	Car #	Make	Laps	Winnings
1. Dale Earnhardt	Rod Osterlund	2	Chev	500	19,800
2. Bobby Allison	Bud Moore	15	Ford	500	11,150
3. Darrell Waltrip	DiGard	88	Chev	500	8,300
4. Richard Petty	Petty Enterprises	43	Olds	498	5,850
5. Benny Tracons	M. C. Anderson	27	Olds	497	3,150

1979 Winston Cup GN Race No. 22 Volunteer 500
August 25, 1979 Average Speed: 91.493

Driver	Owner	Car #	Make	Laps	Winnings
1. Darrell Waltrip	DiGard	88	Chev	500	13,510
2. Richard Petty	Petty Enterprises	43	Chev	500	10,100
3. Bobby Allison	Bud Moore	15	Ford	500	6,950
4. Benny Parsons	M. C. Anderson	27	Chev	499	4,900
5. Cale Yarborough	Junior Johnson	11	Chev	497	5,600

Bristol Motor Speedway *continued*

1980 Winston Cup GN Race No. 6 Valleydale Southeastern 500
March 30, 1980 Average Speed: 96.977

Driver	Owner	Car #	Make	Laps	Winnings
1. Dale Earnhardt	Rod Osterlund	2	Chev	500	20,625
2. Darrell Waltrip	DiGard	88	Chev	500	13,100
3. Bobby Allison	Bud Moore	15	Ford	500	9,400
4. Benny Parsons	M. C. Anderson	27	Chev	499	6,835
5. Cale Yarborough	Junior Johnson	11	Chev	498	7,100

1980 Winston Cup GN Race No. 22 Busch Volunteer 500
August 23, 1980 Average Speed: 86.973

Driver	Owner	Car #	Make	Laps	Winnings
1. Cale Yarborough	Junior Johnson	11	Chev	500	16,550
2. Dale Earnhardt	Rod Osterlund	2	Chev	500	11,450
3. Darrell Waltrip	DiGard	88	Chev	500	7,500
4. Richard Petty	Petty Enterprises	43	Chev	499	7,700
5. Benny Parsons	M. C. Anderson	27	Chev	499	5,450

1981 Winston Cup GN Race No. 6 Valleydale 500
March 29, 1981 Average Speed: 89.530

Driver	Owner	Car #	Make	Laps	Winnings
1. Darrell Waltrip	Junior Johnson	11	Buick	500	22,450
2. Ricky Rudd	DiGard	88	Olds	500	14,375
3. Bobby Allison	Harry Ranier	28	Pont	500	10,450
4. Morgan Shepherd	Cliff Stewart	5	Pont	500	4,600
5. Benny Parsons	Bud Moore	15	Ford	499	7,375

1981 Winston Cup GN Race No. 22 Busch 500
August 22, 1981 Average Speed: 84.723

Driver	Owner	Car #	Make	Laps	Winnings
1. Darrell Waltrip	Junior Johnson	11	Buick	500	18,800
2. Ricky Rudd	DiGard	88	Chev	499	12,375
3. Terry Labonte	Billy Hagan	44	Buick	498	8,800
4. Bobby Allison	Harry Ranier	28	Buick	497	7,075
5. Ron Bouchard	Jack Beebe	47	Buick	497	5,650

1982 Winston Cup GN Race No. 3 Valleydale 500
March 14, 1982 Average Speed: 94.025

Driver	Owner	Car #	Make	Laps	Winnings
1. Darrell Waltrip	Junior Johnson	11	Buick	500	26,520
2. Dale Earnhardt	Bud Moore	15	Ford	500	18,480
3. Morgan Shepherd	Ron Benfield	98	Buick	500	6,705
4. Terry Labonte	Billy Hagan	44	Chev	499	6,575
5. Bobby Allison	DiGard	88	Chev	498	7,680

1982 Winston Cup GN Race No. 21 Busch 500
August 28, 1982 Average Speed: 94.318

Driver	Owner	Car #	Make	Laps	Winnings
1. Darrell Waltrip	Junior Johnson	11	Buick	500	22,925
2. Bobby Allison	DiGard	88	Chev	500	16,325
3. Harry Gant	Hal Needham	33	Buick	500	7,395
4. Terry Labonte	Billy Hagan	44	Buick	499	6,495
5. Morgan Shepherd	Ron Benfield	98	Buick	499	5,150

1983 Winston Cup GN Race No. 11 Valleydale 500
May 21, 1983 Average Speed: 93.445

Driver	Owner	Car #	Make	Laps	Winnings
1. Darrell Waltrip	Junior Johnson	11	Chev	500	29,965
2. Bobby Allison	DiGard	22	Buick	500	16,955
3. Morgan Shepherd	Jim Stacy	2	Buick	499	13,260
4. Neil Bonnett	Bob Rahilly & Butch Mock	75	Chev	499	7,700
5. Richard Petty	Petty Enterprises	43	Pont	498	7,930

1983 Winston Cup GN Race No. 21 Busch 500
August 27, 1983 Average Speed: 89.430

Driver	Owner	Car #	Make	Laps	Winnings
1. Darrell Waltrip	Junior Johnson	11	Chev	419	30,400
2. Dale Earnhardt	Bud Moore	15	Ford	419	15,725
3. Bobby Allison	DiGard	22	Buick	419	13,360
4. Geoff Bodine	Cliff Stewart	88	Pont	418	7,370
5. Terry Labonte	Billy Hagan	44	Chev	418	5,770

1984 Winston Cup GN Race No. 5 Valleydale 500
April 1, 1984 Average Speed: 93.967

Driver	Owner	Car #	Make	Laps	Winnings
1. Darrell Waltrip	Junior Johnson	11	Chev	500	31,670
2. Terry Labonte	Billy Hagan	44	Chev	500	15,885
3. Ron Bouchard	Jack Beebe	47	Buick	500	11,010
4. Dave Marcis	Bob Rahilly & Butch Mock	75	Pont	499	10,630
5. Tim Richmond	Raymond Beadle	27	Pont	499	6,490

1984 Winston Cup GN Race No. 21 Busch 500
August 25, 1984 Average Speed: 85.365

Driver	Owner	Car #	Make	Laps	Winnings
1. Terry Labonte	Billy Hagan	44	Chev	500	28,480
2. Bobby Allison	DiGard	22	Buick	500	22,475
3. Dick Brooks	Junie Donlavey	90	Ford	498	11,930
4. Dave Marcis	Bob Rahilly & Butch Mock	75	Pont	494	11,300
5. Harry Gant	Hal Needham	33	Chev	494	6,910

1985 Winston Cup GN Race No. 5 Valleydale 500
April 6, 1985 Average Speed: 81.790

Driver	Owner	Car #	Make	Laps	Winnings
1. Dale Earnhardt	Richard Childress	3	Chev	500	31,525
2. Ricky Rudd	Bud Moore	15	Ford	500	18,050
3. Terry Labonte	Billy Hagan	44	Chev	498	16,625
4. Buddy Baker	Buddy Baker & Danny Schiff	88	Olds	498	4,470
5. Rusty Wallace	Cliff Stewart	2	Pont	497	8,230

1985 Winston Cup GN Race No. 19 Busch 500
August 24, 1985 Average Speed: 81.388

Driver	Owner	Car #	Make	Laps	Winnings
1. Dale Earnhardt	Richard Childress	3	Chev	500	34,675
2. Tim Richmond	Raymond Beadle	27	Pont	500	19,230
3. Neil Bonnett	Junior Johnson	12	Chev	500	13,900
4. Darrell Waltrip	Junior Johnson	11	Chev	500	12,500
5. Bill Elliott	Harry Melling	9	Ford	499	11,350

1986 Winston Cup Race No. 5 Valleydale 500
April 6, 1986 Average Speed: 89.747

Driver	Owner	Car #	Make	Laps	Winnings
1. Rusty Wallace	Raymond Beadle	27	Pont	500	34,780
2. Ricky Rudd	Bud Moore	15	Ford	500	20,125
3. Darrell Waltrip	Junior Johnson	11	Chev	500	17,825
4. Harry Gant	Hal Needham	33	Chev	499	11,770
5. Bill Elliott	Harry Melling	9	Ford	499	12,050

1986 Winston Cup Race No. 20 Busch 500
August 23, 1986 Average Speed: 86.934

Driver	Owner	Car #	Make	Laps	Winnings
1. Darrell Waltrip	Junior Johnson	11	Chev	500	41,725
2. Terry Labonte	Billy Hagan	44	Chev	500	21,350
3. Geoff Bodine	Rick Hendrick	5	Chev	499	17,025
4. Dale Earnhardt	Richard Childress	3	Chev	499	12,800
5. Harry Gant	Hal Needham	33	Chev	499	12,950

Bristol Motor Speedway *continued*

1987 Winston Cup Race No. 7 Valleydale Meats 500
April 12, 1987 Average Speed: 75.621

Driver	Owner	Car #	Make	Laps	Winnings
1. Dale Earnhardt	Richard Childress	3	Chev	500	43,850
2. Richard Petty	Petty Enterprises	43	Pont	500	21,030
3. Ricky Rudd	Bud Moore	15	Ford	500	17,175
4. Bill Elliott	Harry Melling	9	Ford	500	12,570
5. Alan Kulwicki	Alan Kulwicki	7	Ford	500	11,605

1987 Winston Cup Race No. 20 Busch 500
August 22, 1987 Average Speed: 90.373

Driver	Owner	Car #	Make	Laps	Winnings
1. Dale Earnhardt	Richard Childress	3	Chev	500	47,175
2. Rusty Wallace	Raymond Beadle	27	Pont	500	26,300
3. Ricky Rudd	Bud Moore	15	Ford	500	20,275
4. Terry Labonte	Junior Johnson	11	Chev	500	17,500
5. Richard Petty	Petty Enterprises	43	Pont	500	10,030

1988 Winston Cup Race No. 6 Valleydale Meats 500
April 10, 1988 Average Speed: 83.115

Driver	Owner	Car #	Make	Laps	Winnings
1. Bill Elliott	Harry Melling	9	Ford	500	45,750
2. Mark Martin	Jack Roush	6	Ford	500	21,250
3. Geoff Bodine	Rick Hendrick	5	Chev	500	17,425
4. Rusty Wallace	Raymond Beadle	27	Pont	499	14,370
5. Bobby Allison	Stavola Brothers	12	Buick	498	12,625

1988 Winston Cup Race No. 20 Busch 500
August 27, 1988 Average Speed: 78.775

Driver	Owner	Car #	Make	Laps	Winnings
1. Dale Earnhardt	Richard Childress	3	Chev	500	48,500
2. Bill Elliott	Harry Melling	9	Ford	500	29,150
3. Geoff Bodine	Rick Hendrick	5	Chev	499	17,475
4. Davey Allison	Harry Ranier	28	Ford	499	16,775
5. Alan Kulwicki	Alan Kulwicki	7	Ford	499	16,410

1989 Winston Cup Race No. 6 Valleydale Meats 500
April 9, 1989 Average Speed: 76.034

Driver	Owner	Car #	Make	Laps	Winnings
1. Rusty Wallace	Raymond Beadle	27	Pont	500	48,750
2. Darrell Waltrip	Rick Hendrick	17	Chev	500	28,900
3. Geoff Bodine	Rick Hendrick	5	Chev	500	21,950
4. Davey Allison	Robert Yates	28	Ford	500	17,802
5. Dick Trickle	Stavola Brothers	84	Buick	400	12,950

1989 Winston Cup Race No. 20 Busch 500
August 26, 1989 Average Speed: 85.554

Driver	Owner	Car #	Make	Laps	Winnings
1. Darrell Waltrip	Rick Hendrick	17	Chev	500	52,450
2. Alan Kulwicki	Alan Kulwicki	7	Ford	500	30,875
3. Ricky Rudd	Kenny Bernstein	26	Buick	500	19,200
4. Harry Gant	Leo Jackson	33	Olds	500	13,300
5. Terry Labonte	Junior Johnson	11	Ford	499	13,400

1990 Winston Cup Series Race No. 6 Valleydale Meats 500
April 8, 1990 Average Speed: 87.258

Driver	Owner	Car #	Make	Laps	Winnings
1. Davey Allison	Robert Yates	28	Ford	500	50,100
2. Mark Martin	Jack Roush	6	Ford	500	31,300
3. Ricky Rudd	Rick Hendrick	5	Chev	500	19,775
4. Terry Labonte	Richard Jackson	1	Olds	500	13,500
5. Rick Wilson	Bob Rahilly & Butch Mock	75	Pont	500	13,857

1990 Winston Cup Series Race No. 20 Busch 500
August 25, 1990 Average Speed: 91.782

Driver	Owner	Car #	Make	Laps	Winnings
1. Ernie Irvan	Larry McClure	4	Chev	500	49,600
2. Rusty Wallace	Raymond Beadle	27	Pont	500	32,850
3. Mark Martin	Jack Roush	6	Ford	500	22,830
4. Terry Labonte	Richard Jackson	1	Olds	500	14,150
5. Sterling Marlin	Billy Hagan	94	Olds	500	12,900

1991 Winston Cup Series Race No. 6 Valleydale Meats 500
April 14, 1991 Average Speed: 72.809

Driver	Owner	Car #	Make	Laps	Winnings
1. Rusty Wallace	Roger Penske	2	Pont	500	51,300
2. Ernie Irvan	Larry McClure	4	Chev	500	26,000
3. Davey Allison	Robert Yates	28	Ford	500	18,950
4. Mark Martin	Jack Roush	6	Ford	500	18,950
5. Ricky Rudd	Rick Hendrick	5	Chev	500	37,950

1991 Winston Cup Series Race No. 20 Bud 500
August 24, 1991 Average Speed: 82.028

Driver	Owner	Car #	Make	Laps	Winnings
1. Alan Kulwicki	Alan Kulwicki	7	Ford	500	61,400
2. Sterling Marlin	Junior Johnson	22	Ford	500	30,275
3. Ken Schrader	Rick Hendrick	25	Chev	500	22,950
4. Mark Martin	Jack Roush	6	Ford	499	19,700
5. Ricky Rudd	Rick Hendrick	5	Chev	499	16,450

1992 Winston Cup Race No. 6 Food City 500
April 5, 1992 Average Speed: 86.316

Driver	Owner	Car #	Make	Laps	Winnings
1. Alan Kulwicki	Alan Kulwicki	7	Ford	500	83,360
2. Dale Jarrett	Joe Gibbs	18	Chev	500	29,835
3. Ken Schrader	Rick Hendrick	25	Chev	500	29,410
4. Terry Labonte	Billy Hagan	94	Olds	499	20,010
5. Dick Trickle	Stavola Brothers	8	Ford	499	18,410

1992 Winston Cup Race No. 20 Bud 500
August 29, 1992 Average Speed: 91.198

Driver	Owner	Car #	Make	Laps	Winnings
1. Darrell Waltrip	Darrell Waltrip	17	Chev	500	73,050
2. Dale Earnhardt	Richard Childress	3	Chev	500	39,325
3. Ken Schrader	Rick Hendrick	25	Chev	500	28,350
4. Kyle Petty	Felix Sabates	42	Pont	500	18,000
5. Alan Kulwicki	Alan Kulwicki	7	Ford	499	19,800

1993 Winston Cup Series Race No. 6 Food City 500
April 4, 1993 Average Speed: 84.730

Driver	Owner	Car #	Make	Laps	Winnings
1. Rusty Wallace	Roger Penske	2	Pont	500	107,610
2. Dale Earnhardt	Richard Childress	3	Chev	500	47,760
3. Kyle Petty	Felix Sabates	42	Pont	500	31,485
4. Jimmy Spencer	Bobby Allison	12	Ford	500	26,050
5. Davey Allison	Robert Yates	28	Ford	500	25,180

1993 Winston Cup Series Race No. 21 Bud 500
August 28, 1993 Average Speed: 88.172

Driver	Owner	Car #	Make	Laps	Winnings
1. Mark Martin	Jack Roush	6	Ford	500	80,125
2. Rusty Wallace	Roger Penske	2	Pont	500	31,875
3. Dale Earnhardt	Richard Childress	3	Chev	500	32,325
4. Harry Gant	Leo Jackson	33	Chev	500	28,150
5. Rick Mast	Richard Jackson	1	Ford	500	22,000

Bristol Motor Speedway *continued*

1994 Winston Cup Series Race No. 6 Food City 500
April 10, 1994 Average Speed: 89.647

Driver	Owner	Car #	Make	Laps	Winnings
1. Dale Earnhardt	Richard Childress	3	Chev	500	72,570
2. Ken Schrader	Rick Hendrick	25	Chev	500	43,445
3. Lake Speed	Bud Moore	15	Ford	500	35,020
4. Geoff Bodine	Geoff Bodine	7	Ford	499	24,356
5. Michael Waltrip	Chuck Rider	30	Pont	497	20,135

1994 Winston Cup Series Race No. 22 Goody's 500
August 27, 1994 Average Speed: 91.363

Driver	Owner	Car #	Make	Laps	Winnings
1. Rusty Wallace	Roger Penske	2	Ford	500	53,015
2. Mark Martin	Jack Roush	6	Ford	500	35,915
3. Dale Earnhardt	Richard Childress	3	Chev	500	33,265
4. Darrell Waltrip	Darrell Waltrip	17	Chev	500	28,730
5. Bill Elliott	Junior Johnson	11	Ford	500	22,275

1995 Winston Cup Series Race No. 6 Food City 500
April 2, 1995 Average Speed: 92.011

Driver	Owner	Car #	Make	Laps	Winnings
1. Jeff Gordon	Rick Hendrick	24	Chev	500	67,645
2. Rusty Wallace	Roger Penske	2	Ford	500	42,045
3. Darrell Waltrip	Darrell Waltrip	17	Chev	500	35,845
4. Bobby Hamilton	Petty Enterprises	43	Pont	500	28,631
5. Ricky Rudd	Ricky Rudd	10	Ford	500	32,260

1995 Winston Cup Series Race No. 22 Goody's 500
August 26, 1995 Average Speed: 81.979

Driver	Owner	Car #	Make	Laps	Winnings
1. Terry Labonte	Rick Hendrick	5	Chev	500	66,940
2. Dale Earnhardt	Richard Childress	3	Chev	500	66,890
3. Dale Jarrett	Robert Yates	28	Ford	500	39,390
4. Darrell Waltrip	Darrell Waltrip	17	Chev	500	32,780
5. Mark Martin	Jack Roush	6	Ford	500	41,775

1996 Winston Cup Series Race No. 6 Food City 500
March 31, 1996 Average Speed: 91.308

Driver	Owner	Car #	Make	Laps	Winnings
1. Jeff Gordon	Rick Hendrick	24	Chev	342	93,765
2. Terry Labonte	Rick Hendrick	5	Chev	342	54,215
3. Mark Martin	Jack Roush	6	Ford	342	44,815
4. Dale Earnhardt	Richard Childress	3	Chev	342	35,351
5. Rusty Wallace	Roger Penske	2	Ford	342	29,895

1996 Winston Cup Series Race No. 22 Goody's 500
August 24, 1996 Average Speed: 91.267

Driver	Owner	Car #	Make	Laps	Winnings
1. Rusty Wallace	Roger Penske	2	Ford	500	77,090
2. Jeff Gordon	Rick Hendrick	24	Chev	500	54,590
3. Mark Martin	Jack Roush	6	Ford	500	46,490
4. Dale Jarrett	Robert Yates	88	Ford	500	32,980
5. Terry Labonte	Rick Hendrick	5	Chev	500	37,875

1997 Winston Cup Series Race No. 7
April 13, 1997 Average Speed: 75.035

Driver	Owner	Car #	Make	Laps	Winnings
1. Jeff Gordon	Rick Hendrick	24	Chev	500	83,640
2. Rusty Wallace	Roger Penske	2	Ford	500	64,090
3. Terry Labonte	Rick Hendrick	5	Chev	500	51,490
4. Dale Jarrett	Robert Yates	88	Ford	500	39,265
5. Mark Martin	Jack Roush	6	Ford	500	37,520

1997 Winston Cup Series Race No. 22
August 23, 1997 Average Speed: 80.01

Driver	Owner	Car #	Make	Laps	Winnings
1. Dale Jarrett	Robert Yates	88	Ford	500	101,500
2. Mark Martin	Jack Roush	6	Ford	500	46,775
3. Dick Trickle	Junie Donlavey	90	Ford	500	42,625
4. Jeff Burton	Jack Roush	99	Ford	500	40,875
5. Steve Grissom	Larry Hedrick	41	Chev	500	37,125

1998 Winston Cup Series Race No. 6
March 29, 1998 Average Speed: 82.85

Driver	Owner	Car #	Make	Laps	Winnings
1. Jeff Gordon	Rick Hendrick	24	Chev	500	90,860
2. Terry Labonte	Rick Hendrick	5	Chev	500	57,960
3. Dale Jarrett	Robert Yates	88	Ford	500	57,660
4. Jeff Burton	Jack Roush	99	Ford	500	47,670
5. Johnny Benson, Jr.	Jack Roush	26	Ford	500	31,770

1998 Winston Cup Series Race No. 22
August 22, 1998 Average Speed: 86.918

Driver	Owner	Car #	Make	Laps	Winnings
1. Mark Martin	Jack Roush	6	Ford	500	80,315
2. Jeff Burton	Jack Roush	99	Ford	500	58,615
3. Rusty Wallace	Roger Penske	2	Ford	500	58,165
4. Dale Jarrett	Robert Yates	88	Ford	500	58,855
5. Jeff Gordon	Rick Hendrick	24	Chev	500	58,650

1999 Winston Cup Series Race No. 7
April 11, 1999 Average Speed: 93.366

Driver	Owner	Car #	Make	Laps	Winnings
1. Rusty Wallace	Roger Penske	2	Ford	500	92,435
2. Mark Martin	Jack Roush	6	Ford	500	73,585
3. Dale Jarrett	Robert Yates	88	Ford	500	68,650
4. John Andretti	Petty Enterprises	43	Pont	500	64,295
5. Jeff Burton	Jack Roush	99	Ford	500	57,335

1999 Winston Cup Series Race No. 23
August 28, 1999 Average Speed: 91.276

Driver	Owner	Car #	Make	Laps	Winnings
1. Dale Earnhardt	Richard Childress	3	Chev	500	89,880
2. Jimmy Spencer	Travis Carter	23	Ford	500	76,265
3. Ricky Rudd	Ricky Rudd	10	Ford	500	64,190
4. Jeff Gordon	Rick Hendrick	24	Chev	500	71,505
5. Tony Stewart	Joe Gibbs	20	Pont	500	64,915

2000 Winston Cup Series Race No. 6
March 26, 2000 Average Speed: 88.018

Driver	Owner	Car #	Make	Laps	Winnings
1. Rusty Wallace	Roger Penske	2	Ford	500	87,585
2. Johnny Benson, Jr.	Tim Beverley	10	Pont	500	87,535
3. Ward Burton	Bill Davis	22	Pont	500	81,135
4. Jeremy Mayfield	Michael Kranefuss	12	Ford	500	49,795
5. Terry Labonte	Rick Hendrick	5	Chev	500	60,745

2000 Winston Cup Series Race No. 23
August 26, 2000 Average Speed: 85.394

Driver	Owner	Car #	Make	Laps	Winnings
1. Rusty Wallace	Roger Penske	2	Ford	500	107,540
2. Tony Stewart	Joe Gibbs	20	Pont	500	92,540
3. Mark Martin	Jack Roush	6	Ford	500	61,890
4. Dale Earnhardt	Richard Childress	3	Chev	500	62,980
5. Steve Park	Dale Earnhardt, Inc.	1	Chev	500	53,525

Bristol Motor Speedway *continued*

2001 Winston Cup Series Race No. 6
March 25, 2001 Average Speed: 86.949

Driver	Owner	Car #	Make	Laps	Winnings
1. Elliott Sadler	Wood Brothers	21	Ford	500	124,700
2. John Andretti	Petty Enterprises	43	Dodg	500	136,842
3. Jeremy Mayfield	Roger Penske	12	Ford	500	105,709
4. Jeff Gordon	Rick Hendrick	24	Chev	500	126,352
5. Ward Burton	Bill Davis	22	Dodg	500	100,580

2001 Winston Cup Series Race No. 24
August 25, 2001 Average Speed: 85.106

Driver	Owner	Car #	Make	Laps	Winnings
1. Tony Stewart	Joe Gibbs	20	Pont	500	189,415
2. Kevin Harvick	Richard Childress	29	Chev	500	167,267
3. Jeff Gordon	Rick Hendrick	24	Chev	500	155,692
4. Ricky Rudd	Robert Yates	28	Ford	500	124,527
5. Rusty Wallace	Roger Penske	2	Ford	500	107,640

2002 Winston Cup Series Race No. 6
March 24, 2002 Average Speed: 82.281

Driver	Owner	Car #	Make	Laps	Winnings
1. Kurt Busch	Jack Roush	97	Ford	500	143,840
2. Jimmy Spencer	Chip Ganassi	41	Dodg	500	110,665
3. Ricky Rudd	Robert Yates	28	Ford	500	123,242
4. Dale Earnhardt, Jr.	Dale Earnhardt, Inc.	8	Chev	500	87,850
5. Bobby Labonte	Joe Gibbs	18	Pont	500	113,423

2002 Winston Cup Series Race No. 24
August 24, 2002 Average Speed: 77.097

Driver	Owner	Car #	Make	Laps	Winnings
1. Jeff Gordon	Rick Hendrick	24	Chev	500	245,543
2. Rusty Wallace	Roger Penske	2	Ford	500	173,240
3. Dale Earnhardt, Jr.	Dale Earnhardt, Inc.	8	Chev	500	131,090
4. Kevin Harvick	Richard Childress	29	Chev	500	137,033
5. Matt Kenseth	Jack Roush	17	Ford	500	98,375

Kingsport Speedway
Kingsport, TN
.4-mile Paved Track

(aka MARCA Motorsports Community; Raceland Kingsport; Kingsport Motor Speedway; New Kingsport Speedway; Kingsport Int'l Speedway; Tri-Cities Speedway) .4-mile paved oval opened circa 1967. First NASCAR Winston Cup (then Grand National) race staged on 6/19/69 (won by Richard Petty). Re-measured in 1970 at .337-mile oval. Final Winston Cup Grand National race run 5/23/71 (won by Bobby Isaac). Pavement torn up in 1984. Still active today.

Winston Cup Starts
12 drivers tied with 3

Winston Cup Victories
Richard Petty   2

Winston Cup Poles
Bobby Isaac   2

Winston Cup Money
Richard Petty $2,790

Most Cars Started
25—May 23, 1971 Kingsport 300

Fewest Cars Started
22—June 26, 1970 Kingsport 100

Narrowest Margin of Victory
1 lap plus—June 19, 1969 Kingsport 250

Slowest Race
63.242 MPH—May 23, 1971
Kingsport 300

Race Record
73.619 MPH—June 19, 1969
Kingsport 250

Most Cautions
6—May 23, 1971 Kingsport 300

Most Race Leaders
3—June 19, 1969 Kingsport 250

Most Cars Running at Finish
13—June 19, 1969 Kingsport 250

1969 Grand National Race No. 25 Kingsport 250
June 19, 1969 Average Speed: 73.619

Driver	Owner	Car #	Make	Laps	Winnings
1. Richard Petty	Petty Enterprises	43	69 Ford	250	1,000
2. John Sears	L. G. DeWitt	4	68 Ford	249	600
3. David Pearson	Holman-Moody	17	69 Ford	248	600
4. Neil Castles	Neil Castles	06	67 Plym	247	350
5. G. C. Spencer	G. C. Spencer	49	67 Plym	246	325

1970 Grand National Race No. 22 Kingsport 100
June 26, 1970 Average Speed: 68.583

Driver	Owner	Car #	Make	Laps	Winnings
1. Richard Petty	Petty Enterprises	43	70 Plym	297	1,500
2. James Hylton	James Hylton	48	69 Ford	295	900
3. Dave Marcis	Dave Marcis	30	69 Dodg	293	500
4. Bobby Allison	Bobby Allison	22	69 Dodg	292	350
5. Neil Castles	Neil Castles	06	69 Dodg	292	325

1971 Winston Cup GN Race No. 20 Kingsport 300
May 23, 1971 Average Speed: 63.242

Driver	Owner	Car #	Make	Laps	Winnings
1. Bobby Isaac	Nord Krauskopf	71	71 Dodg	300	1,800
2. Elmo Langley	Elmo Langley	64	71 Ford	295	1,100
3. James Hylton	James Hylton	48	71 Ford	293	800
4. Cecil Gordon	Cecil Gordon	24	69 Merc	283	600
5. Bill Champion	Bill Champion	10	69 Ford	282	500

Nashville Speedway
Nashville, TN
Half-mile Paved Track

(aka Nashville Speedway USA; Nashville Motor Speedway; Nashville Int'l Speedway; Cumberland Park; Fairgrounds Speedway) Originally built in 1907 as a 1-mile horse track. Track paved and shortened to half-mile in 1958. First NASCAR Winston Cup (then Grand National) race staged on 8/10/58 (won by Joe Weatherly, his first of 25 career wins). Track renovated to .675-mile high-banked (35 degree turns) in 1970. Following several fatalities, turns were shaved down to 24 degrees. Final Winston Cup race run on 7/14/84 (Geoff Bodine won). The track is still active today, hosting a variety of NASCAR events and weekly Late Model Stock racing.

Winston Cup Starts
Richard Petty   39

Winston Cup Victories
Richard Petty   9

Winston Cup Poles
Richard Petty   7
Darrell Waltrip   7

Winston Cup Money
Darrell Waltrip $238,120

Most Cars Started
36—July 25, 1970 Nashville 420

Fewest Cars Started
12—May 24, 1959

Narrowest Margin of Victory
1/2 car length—July 26, 1969
Nashville 400

Slowest Race
56.455 MPH—August 6, 1961
Nashville 500

Race Record
98.419 MPH—May 12, 1973
Music City 420

Most Cautions
10—July 16, 1977 Nashville 420

Most Race Leaders
7—May 8, 1976 Music City USA 420
7—July 14, 1984 Pepsi 420

Most Cars Running at Finish
25—May 10, 1980 Music City USA 420

1958 Grand National Race No. 37
August 10, 1958 Average Speed: 59.269

Driver	Owner	Car #	Make	Laps	Winnings
1. Joe Weatherly	Holman-Moody	72	58 Ford	200	1,850
2. Bob Welborn	J. H. Petty	49	57 Chev	200	1,050
3. Larry Frank	Larry Frank	76	57 Chev	200	800
4. Jimmy Thompson	Petty Enterprises	2	57 Olds	198	575
5. Lee Petty	Petty Enterprises	42	57 Olds	197	475

1959 Grand National Race No. 16
May 24, 1959 Average Speed: 71.006

Driver	Owner	Car #	Make	Laps	Winnings
1. Rex White	Rex White	4	59 Chev	200	900
2. Junior Johnson	Paul Spaulding	11	57 Ford	200	525
3. Tommy Irwin	Tommy Irwin	36	59 Ford	199	350
4. Buck Baker	Buck Baker	87	59 Chev	198	250
5. Joe Lee Johnson	Joe Lee Johnson	77	57 Chev	198	225

1959 Grand National Race No. 31
August 9, 1959 Average Speed: 63.343

Driver	Owner	Car #	Make	Laps	Winnings
1. Joe Lee Johnson	Joe Lee Johnson	77	57 Chev	300	2,912
2. Larry Frank	Larry Frank	76	57 Chev	297	1,453
3. Elmo Langley	Ratus Walters	10	59 Buick	297	1,125
4. Lee Petty	Petty Enterprises	42	59 Plym	297	900
5. Tommy Irwin	Tommy Irwin	36	59 Ford	295	750

1960 Grand National Race No. 29
August 7, 1960 Average Speed: 56.966

Driver	Owner	Car #	Make	Laps	Winnings
1. Johnny Beauchamp	Dale Swanson	73	60 Chev	333	3,666
2. Rex White	Rex White	4	60 Chev	333	2,390
3. Buck Baker	Buck Baker	87	60 Chev	331	1,225
4. Lee Petty	Petty Enterprises	42	60 Plym	330	825
5. Joe Lee Johnson	Paul McDuffie	89	60 Chev	330	718

1961 Grand National Race No. 37 Nashville 500
August 6, 1961 Average Speed: 56.455

Driver	Owner	Car #	Make	Laps	Winnings
1. Jim Paschal	J. H. Petty	44	61 Pont	403	2,523
2. Ned Jarrett	Bee Gee Holloway	11	61 Chev	403	1,275
3. Johnny Allen	Joe Lee Johnson	14	61 Chev	401	975
4. Buck Baker	Buck Baker	86	61 Chrys	401	675
5. Emanuel Zervakis	Monroe Shook	85	61 Chev	397	575

1962 Grand National Race No. 38 Nashville 500
August 5, 1962 Average Speed: 64.469

Driver	Owner	Car #	Make	Laps	Winnings
1. Jim Paschal	Petty Enterprises	42	62 Plym	500	3,250
2. Richard Petty	Petty Enterprises	43	62 Pont	489	1,875
3. Buck Baker	Buck Baker	87	62 Chrys	493	1,350
4. Joe Weatherly	Bud Moore	8	62 Pont	489	800
5. Thomas Cox	Cliff Stewart	2	62 Pont	471	700

1963 Grand National Race No. 39 Nashville 400
August 4, 1963 Average Speed: 60.126

Driver	Owner	Car #	Make	Laps	Winnings
1. Jim Paschal	Petty Enterprises	42	63 Plym	350	2,500
2. Billy Wade	Cotton Owens	5	63 Dodg	349	1,350
3. Joe Weatherly	Bud Moore	8	63 Pont	349	1,025
4. Richard Petty	Petty Enterprises	43	63 Plym	348	675
5. Buck Baker	Buck Baker	87	63 Pont	348	475

1964 Grand National Race No. 30
June 14, 1964 Average Speed: 76.498

Driver	Owner	Car #	Make	Laps	Winnings
1. Richard Petty	Petty Enterprises	43	64 Plym	200	1,000
2. David Pearson	Cotton Owens	6	64 Dodg	199	600
3. Buck Baker	Ray Fox	3	64 Dodg	199	400
4. Jimmy Pardue	Charles Robinson	54	64 Plym	195	300
5. G. C. Spencer	G. C. Spencer	49	64 Chev	191	275

1964 Grand National Race No. 43
August 2, 1964 Average Speed: 73.208

Driver	Owner	Car #	Make	Laps	Winnings
1. Richard Petty	Petty Enterprises	43	64 Plym	400	2,150
2. Jim Paschal	Petty Enterprises	41	64 Plym	400	1,000
3. David Pearson	Cotton Owens	6	64 Dodg	399	800
4. Earl Balmer	Cotton Owens	5	64 Dodg	392	500
5. Ned Jarrett	Bondy Long	11	64 Ford	392	575

1965 Grand National Race No. 23
June 3, 1965 Average Speed: 71.386

Driver	Owner	Car #	Make	Laps	Winnings
1. Dick Hutcherson	Holman-Moody	29	65 Ford	200	1,000
2. Ned Jarrett	Jabe Thomas	25	64 Ford	199	600
3. J. T. Putney	Herman Beam	19	65 Chev	199	400
4. Wendell Scott	Wendell Scott	34	63 Ford	196	300
5. Henley Gray	Gene Cline	97	64 Ford	177	275

Nashville Speedway *continued*

1965 Grand National Race No. 35 Nashville 400
July 31, 1965 Average Speed: 72.383

Driver	Owner	Car #	Make	Laps	Winnings
1. Richard Petty	Petty Enterprises	43	65 Plym	400	2,350
2. Ned Jarrett	Bondy Long	11	65 Ford	394	1,100
3. Buddy Arrington	Buddy Arrington	67	64 Dodg	382	750
4. J. T. Putney	Herman Beam	19	65 Chev	381	500
5. G. C. Spencer	G. C. Spencer	49	64 Ford	374	475

1966 Grand National Race No. 36
July 30, 1966 Average Speed: 71.770

Driver	Owner	Car #	Make	Laps	Winnings
1. Richard Petty	Petty Enterprises	43	66 Plym	400	2,750
2. Buck Baker	Buck Baker	87	66 Olds	395	1,400
3. Bobby Allison	Bobby Allison	2	65 Chev	394	850
4. Henley Gray	Gene Black	74	66 Ford	383	500
5. John Sears	L. G. DeWitt	4	64 Ford	383	475

1967 Grand National Race No. 35 Nashville 400
July 29, 1967 Average Speed: 70.866

Driver	Owner	Car #	Make	Laps	Winnings
1. Richard Petty	Petty Enterprises	43	67 Plym	400	2,050
2. James Hylton	Bud Hartje	48	65 Dodg	395	1,500
3. John Sears	L. G. DeWitt	4	66 Ford	390	900
4. Sam McQuagg	Cotton Owens	6	67 Dodg	390	500
5. Clyde Lynn	Clyde Lynn	20	66 Ford	375	475

1968 Grand National Race No. 32 Nashville 400
July 27, 1968 Average Speed: 72.980

Driver	Owner	Car #	Make	Laps	Winnings
1. David Pearson	Holman-Moody	17	68 Ford	301	2,950
2. Richard Petty	Petty Enterprises	43	68 Plym	298	1,700
3. Bobby Allison	Bobby Allison	2	66 Chev	295	900
4. Bobby Isaac	Nord Krauskopf	71	67 Dodg	294	500
5. Charlie Glotzbach	Sherral Pruitt	57	67 Dodg	293	475

1969 Grand National Race No. 34 Nashville 400
July 26, 1969 Average Speed: 78.740

Driver	Owner	Car #	Make	Laps	Winnings
1. Richard Petty	Petty Enterprises	43	69 Ford	400	3,000
2. Bobby Isaac	Nord Krauskopf	71	69 Dodg	400	1,700
3. James Hylton	James Hylton	48	68 Dodg	387	950
4. John Sears	L. G. DeWitt	4	68 Ford	384	550
5. Neil Castles	Neil Castles	06	67 Plym	379	500

1970 Grand National Race No. 30 Nashville 420
July 25, 1970 Average Speed: 87.943

Driver	Owner	Car #	Make	Laps	Winnings
1. Bobby Isaac	Nord Krauskopf	71	69 Dodg	420	3,310
2. Bobby Allison	Bobby Allison	22	69 Dodg	418	1,910
3. Neil Castles	Neil Castles	06	69 Dodg	394	1,310
4. Cecil Gordon	Cecil Gordon	24	68 Ford	391	1,010
5. J. D. McDuffie	J. D. McDuffie	70	69 Merc	385	910

1971 Winston Cup GN Race No. 32 Nashville 420
July 24, 1971 Average Speed: 89.667

Driver	Owner	Car #	Make	Laps	Winnings
1. Richard Petty	Petty Enterprises	43	71 Plym	420	4,325
2. James Hylton	James Hylton	48	70 Ford	416	2,415
3. Benny Parsons	L. G. DeWitt	72	70 Merc	416	1,600
4. Earl Brooks	Earl Brooks	26	69 Ford	411	1,160
5. J. D. McDuffie	J. D. McDuffie	70	69 Merc	403	1,025

1972 Winston Cup GN Race No. 23 Nashville 420
August 27, 1972 Average Speed: 92.578

Driver	Owner	Car #	Make	Laps	Winnings
1. Bobby Allison	R. Howard & J. Johnson	12	72 Chev	420	6,925
2. Richard Petty	Petty Enterprises	43	72 Plym	420	5,010
3. Darrell Waltrip	Darrell Waltrip	95	71 Merc	404	2,040
4. Benny Parsons	L. G. DeWitt	72	71 Merc	400	1,630
5. Elmo Langley	Elmo Langley	64	71 Ford	387	1,400

1973 Winston Cup GN Race No. 11 Music City 420
May 12, 1973 Average Speed: 98.419

Driver	Owner	Car #	Make	Laps	Winnings
1. Cale Yarborough	R. Howard & J. Johnson	11	73 Chev	420	6,755
2. Benny Parsons	L. G. DeWitt	72	72 Chev	418	3,365
3. Buddy Baker	Nord Krauskopf	71	73 Dodg	415	3,680
4. Cecil Gordon	Cecil Gordon	24	72 Chev	413	1,710
5. Bobby Allison	Bobby Allison	12	73 Chev	411	2,755

1973 Winston Cup GN Race No. 21 Nashville 420
August 25, 1973 Average Speed: 89.310

Driver	Owner	Car #	Make	Laps	Winnings
1. Buddy Baker	Nord Krauskopf	71	73 Dodg	420	6,750
2. Richard Petty	Petty Enterprises	43	73 Dodg	416	4,960
3. Coo Coo Marlin	H. B. Cunningham	14	72 Chev	409	2,125
4. David Sisco	Charlie McGee	05	72 Chev	402	1,750
5. Ed Negre	Ed Negre	8	73 Dodg	399	1,570

1974 Winston Cup GN Race No. 11 Music City USA 420
May 11 & 12, 1974 Average Speed: 82.240

Driver	Owner	Car #	Make	Laps	Winnings
1. Richard Petty	Petty Enterprises	43	74 Dodg	420	7,900
2. Donnie Allison	DiGard	88	74 Chev	420	3,850
3. Darrell Waltrip	Darrell Waltrip	95	74 Chev	416	2,390
4. Bob Burcham	Jack White	57	74 Chev	415	1,370
5. Dave Marcis	Dave Marcis	2	73 Dodg	414	1,520

1974 Winston Cup GN Race No. 18 Nashville 420
July 20, 1974 Average Speed: 76.368

Driver	Owner	Car #	Make	Laps	Winnings
1. Cale Yarborough	Junior Johnson	11	74 Chev	420	8,025
2. Bobby Allison	Bobby Allison	12	74 Chev	420	3,675
3. Darrell Waltrip	Darrell Waltrip	95	74 Chev	416	2,855
4. David Sisco	David Sisco	05	74 Chev	416	1,675
5. Alton Jones	Butch Hawkersmith	68	72 Chev	415	1,230

1975 Winston Cup GN Race No. 11 Music City USA 420
May 10, 1975 Average Speed: 94.107

Driver	Owner	Car #	Make	Laps	Winnings
1. Darrell Waltrip	Darrell Waltrip	17	75 Chev	420	8,000
2. Benny Parsons	L. G. DeWitt	72	75 Chev	418	5,450
3. Coo Coo Marlin	H. B. Cunningham	14	75 Chev	409	2,700
4. Dave Marcis	Nord Krauskopf	71	74 Dodg	407	3,400
5. Cecil Gordon	Cecil Gordon	24	75 Chev	407	1,550

1975 Winston Cup GN Race No. 17 Nashville 420
July 20, 1975 Average Speed: 89.792

Driver	Owner	Car #	Make	Laps	Winnings
1. Cale Yarborough	Junior Johnson	11	75 Chev	420	7,735
2. Richard Petty	Petty Enterprises	43	74 Dodg	419	6,205
3. Dave Marcis	Nord Krauskopf	71	74 Dodg	418	4,560
4. Benny Parsons	L. G. DeWitt	72	75 Chev	412	3,185
5. Cecil Gordon	Cecil Gordon	24	75 Chev	407	1,585

Nashville Speedway *continued*

1976 Winston Cup GN Race No. 11 Music City USA 420
May 8, 1976 Average Speed: 84.512

Driver	Owner	Car #	Make	Laps	Winnings
1. Cale Yarborough	Junior Johnson	11	Chev	420	8,565
2. Richard Petty	Petty Enterprises	43	Dodg	420	6,965
3. Benny Parsons	L. G. DeWitt	72	Chev	420	4,645
4. Buddy Baker	Bud Moore	15	Ford	419	3,585
5. Bobby Allison	Roger Penske	2	Merc	417	3,465

1976 Winston Cup GN Race No. 17 Nashville 420
July 17, 1976 Average Speed: 86.908

Driver	Owner	Car #	Make	Laps	Winnings
1. Benny Parsons	L. G. DeWitt	72	Chev	420	8,315
2. Richard Petty	Petty Enterprises	43	Dodg	420	7,140
3. Darrell Waltrip	DiGard	88	Chev	420	4,395
4. Lennie Pond	Ronnie Elder	54	Chev	419	2,685
5. Cale Yarborough	Junior Johnson	11	Chev	418	3,615

1977 Winston Cup GN Race No. 11 Music City USA 420
May 7, 1977 Average Speed: 87.490

Driver	Owner	Car #	Make	Laps	Winnings
1. Benny Parsons	L. G. DeWitt	72	Chev	420	9,565
2. Cale Yarborough	Junior Johnson	11	Chev	420	7,965
3. Darrell Waltrip	DiGard	88	Chev	418	5,215
4. Dave Marcis	Roger Penske	2	Chev	417	3,565
5. Richard Petty	Petty Enterprises	43	Dodg	416	3,465

1977 Winston Cup GN Race No. 17 Nashville 420
July 16, 1977 Average Speed: 78.999

Driver	Owner	Car #	Make	Laps	Winnings
1. Darrell Waltrip	DiGard	88	Chev	420	9,415
2. Bobby Allison	Bobby Allison	12	Mata	419	5,540
3. Richard Petty	Petty Enterprises	43	Dodg	418	4,965
4. Cale Yarborough	Junior Johnson	11	Chev	417	4,965
5. Dick Brooks	Junie Donlavey	90	Ford	416	2,515

1978 Winston Cup GN Race No. 13 Music City USA 420
June 3, 1978 Average Speed: 87.541

Driver	Owner	Car #	Make	Laps	Winnings
1. Cale Yarborough	Junior Johnson	11	Olds	420	11,215
2. Lennie Pond	Harry Ranier	54	Chev	418	5,315
3. Richard Petty	Petty Enterprises	43	Dodg	416	5,265
4. Dave Marcis	Rod Osterlund	2	Chev	415	2,465
5. Neil Bonnett	Jim Stacy	5	Dodg	413	3,715

1978 Winston Cup GN Race No. 17 Nashville 420
July 15, 1978 Average Speed: 88.924

Driver	Owner	Car #	Make	Laps	Winnings
1. Cale Yarborough	Junior Johnson	11	Olds	420	11,240
2. Darrell Waltrip	DiGard	88	Chev	418	6,715
3. Richard Childress	Richard Childress	3	Olds	415	3,860
4. Dave Marcis	Rod Osterlund	2	Chev	414	2,690
5. J. D. McDuffie	J. D. McDuffie	70	Chev	413	2,445

1979 Winston Cup GN Race No. 11 Sun-Drop Music City USA 420
May 12, 1979 Average Speed: 88.652

Driver	Owner	Car #	Make	Laps	Winnings
1. Cale Yarborough	Junior Johnson	11	Olds	420	12,275
2. Richard Petty	Petty Enterprises	43	Chev	420	8,150
3. Bobby Allison	Bud Moore	15	Ford	419	6,450
4. Dale Earnhardt	Rod Osterlund	2	Chev	419	5,350
5. J. D. McDuffie	J. D. McDuffie	70	Chev	418	3,080

1979 Winston Cup GN Race No. 18 Busch Nashville 420
July 14, 1979 Average Speed: 92.227

Driver	Owner	Car #	Make	Laps	Winnings
1. Darrell Waltrip	DiGard	88	Chev	420	14,000
2. Cale Yarborough	Junior Johnson	11	Chev	419	8,700
3. Dale Earnhardt	Rod Osterlund	2	Chev	417	7,200
4. Benny Parsons	M. C. Anderson	27	Chev	417	3,650
5. Richard Petty	Petty Enterprises	43	Chev	406	4,280

1980 Winston Cup GN Race No. 11 Music City USA 420
May 10, 1980 Average Speed: 89.471

Driver	Owner	Car #	Make	Laps	Winnings
1. Richard Petty	Petty Enterprises	43	Chev	420	15,350
2. Benny Parsons	M. C. Anderson	27	Chev	420	10,310
3. Cale Yarborough	Junior Johnson	11	Chev	420	8,660
4. Darrell Waltrip	DiGard	88	Chev	419	5,750
5. Bobby Allison	Bud Moore	15	Ford	418	5,130

1980 Winston Cup GN Race No. 18 Busch Nashville 420
July 12, 1980 Average Speed: 93.821

Driver	Owner	Car #	Make	Laps	Winnings
1. Dale Earnhardt	Rod Osterlund	2	Chev	420	14,600
2. Cale Yarborough	Junior Johnson	11	Chev	420	10,160
3. Benny Parsons	M. C. Anderson	27	Chev	420	7,910
4. Darrell Waltrip	DiGard	88	Chev	419	5,750
5. Richard Petty	Petty Enterprises	43	Chev	416	6,630

1981 Winston Cup GN Race No. 11 Melling Tool 420
May 9, 1981 Average Speed: 89.756

Driver	Owner	Car #	Make	Laps	Winnings
1. Benny Parsons	Bud Moore	15	Ford	420	15,950
2. Darrell Waltrip	Junior Johnson	11	Buick	420	10,950
3. Bobby Allison	Harry Ranier	28	Pont	420	8,500
4. Richard Petty	Petty Enterprises	43	Buick	419	6,950
5. Ricky Rudd	DiGard	88	Buick	419	7,375

1981 Winston Cup GN Race No. 18 Busch Nashville 420
July 11, 1981 Average Speed: 90.052

Driver	Owner	Car #	Make	Laps	Winnings
1. Darrell Waltrip	Junior Johnson	11	Buick	420	15,700
2. Bobby Allison	Harry Ranier	28	Buick	420	10,975
3. Benny Parsons	Bud Moore	15	Ford	420	8,750
4. Ricky Rudd	DiGard	88	Chev	419	7,450
5. Terry Labonte	Billy Hagan	44	Buick	418	6,300

1982 Winston Cup GN Race No. 10 Cracker Barrel Country Store 420
May 8, 1982 Average Speed: 83.502

Driver	Owner	Car #	Make	Laps	Winnings
1. Darrell Waltrip	Junior Johnson	11	Buick	420	24,025
2. Terry Labonte	Billy Hagan	44	Chev	419	9,095
3. Ron Bouchard	Jack Beebe	47	Buick	418	10,110
4. Joe Ruttman	Bob Rahilly & Butch Mock	75	Buick	417	4,730
5. Neil Bonnett	Bob Rogers	37	Buick	417	4,235

1982 Winston Cup GN Race No. 17 Busch Nashville 420
July 10, 1982 Average Speed: 86.524

Driver	Owner	Car #	Make	Laps	Winnings
1. Darrell Waltrip	Junior Johnson	11	Buick	420	22,025
2. Terry Labonte	Billy Hagan	44	Chev	419	8,595
3. Harry Gant	Hal Needham	33	Buick	419	6,805
4. Ricky Rudd	Richard Childress	3	Pont	419	5,360
5. Tim Richmond	Jim Stacy	2	Buick	419	4,175

Nashville Speedway *continued*

1983 Winston Cup GN Race No. 9 Marty Robbins 420
May 7, 1983 Average Speed: 70.717

Driver	Owner	Car #	Make	Laps	Winnings
1. Darrell Waltrip	Junior Johnson	11	Chev	420	25,650
2. Bobby Allison	DiGard	22	Buick	419	13,650
3. Harry Gant	Hal Needham	33	Buick	419	11,285
4. Morgan Shepherd	Jim Stacy	2	Buick	418	9,000
5. Bill Elliott	Harry Melling	9	Ford	416	4,520

1983 Winston Cup GN Race No. 17 Busch Nashville 420
July 16, 1983 Average Speed: 85.726

Driver	Owner	Car #	Make	Laps	Winnings
1. Dale Earnhardt	Bud Moore	15	Ford	420	23,125
2. Darrell Waltrip	Junior Johnson	11	Chev	420	16,425
3. Tim Richmond	Raymond Beadle	27	Pont	419	8,030
4. Bobby Allison	DiGard	22	Buick	419	9,400
5. Ricky Rudd	Richard Childress	3	Chev	417	4,770

1984 Winston Cup GN Race No. 10 Coors 420
May 12, 1984 Average Speed: 85.702

Driver	Owner	Car #	Make	Laps	Winnings
1. Darrell Waltrip	Junior Johnson	11	Chev	420	29,300
2. Neil Bonnett	Junior Johnson	12	Chev	420	13,500
3. Geoff Bodine	Rick Hendrick	5	Chev	420	12,025
4. Ricky Rudd	Bud Moore	15	Ford	420	10,450
5. Ron Bouchard	Jack Beebe	47	Buick	420	6,785

1984 Winston Cup GN Race No. 17 Pepsi 420
July 14, 1984 Average Speed: 80.908

Driver	Owner	Car #	Make	Laps	Winnings
1. Geoff Bodine	Rick Hendrick	5	Chev	420	25,800
2. Darrell Waltrip	Junior Johnson	11	Chev	420	16,125
3. Dale Earnhardt	Richard Childress	3	Chev	419	10,775
4. Ron Bouchard	Jack Beebe	47	Buick	419	6,330
5. Bobby Allison	DiGard	22	Buick	419	13,450

Smoky Mountain Raceway
Maryville, TN
Half-mile Paved Track

(aka Smoky Mountain Race Park; Smoky Mountain Speedway) Half-mile dirt track opened circa 1965. First NASCAR Winston Cup (then Grand National) race staged on 8/13/65 (won by Dick Hutcherson). Track paved in 1968. Final Winston Cup Grand National race was 4/15/71 (won by Richard Petty). Track still active.

Winston Cup Starts
Henley Gray 12
Elmo Langley 12
Wendell Scott 12

Winston Cup Victories
Richard Petty 6

Winston Cup Poles
David Pearson 3

Winston Cup Money
Richard Petty $8,170

Most Cars Started
33—July 27, 1967 Smoky 200

Fewest Cars Started
20—June 8, 1967 East Tennessee 200

Narrowest Margin of Victory
1 car length—July 25, 1968
1 car length—July 27, 1969
1 car length—July 24, 1970

Slowest Race
65.455 MPH—August 13, 1965

Race Record
88.697 MPH—April 15, 1971 Maryville 200

Most Cautions
N/A

Most Race Leaders
3—July 28, 1966 Smoky 200
3—June 6, 1968
3—July 27, 1969 Smoky 200
3—July 24, 1970 East Tennessee 200
3—April 15, 1971 Maryville 200

Most Cars Running at Finish
21—July 28, 1966 Smoky 200
21—July 27, 1967 Smoky 200

1965 Grand National Race No. 38
August 13, 1965 Average Speed: 65.455

Driver	Owner	Car #	Make	Laps	Winnings
1. Dick Hutcherson	Holman-Moody	29	65 Ford	200	1,000
2. Buddy Baker	Buck Baker	88	64 Dodg	196	600
3. Richard Petty	Petty Enterprises	43	64 Plym	195	400
4. Jim Hunter	Casper Hensley	82	64 Pont	191	300
5. Paul Lewis	Paul Lewis	1	64 Ford	186	275

1966 Grand National Race No. 35 Smoky 200
July 28, 1966 Average Speed: 69.822

Driver	Owner	Car #	Make	Laps	Winnings
1. Paul Lewis	Paul Lewis	1	65 Plym	200	1,000
2. David Pearson	Cotton Owens	6	65 Dodg	200	600
3. J. T. Putney	J. T. Putney	19	66 Chev	199	400
4. Doug Cooper	Bob Cooper	02	65 Plym	195	300
5. Bobby Allison	Bobby Allison	2	65 Chev	194	275

1967 Grand National Race No. 34 Smoky 200
July 27, 1967 Average Speed: 65.765

Driver	Owner	Car #	Make	Laps	Winnings
1. Dick Hutcherson	Bondy Long	29	67 Ford	200	1,050
2. Richard Petty	Petty Enterprises	43	67 Plym	200	600
3. Jim Hunter	Casper Hensley	85	65 Chev	199	400
4. James Hylton	Bud Hartje	48	65 Dodg	199	300
5. Bobby Allison	Bobby Allison	2	65 Chev	197	275

1968 Grand National Race No. 31 Smoky 200
July 25, 1968 Average Speed: 71.513

Driver	Owner	Car #	Make	Laps	Winnings
1. Richard Petty	Petty Enterprises	43	68 Plym	200	1,200
2. Bud Moore	Bondy Long	29	68 Ford	200	600
3. David Pearson	Holman-Moody	17	68 Ford	199	400
4. Buddy Baker	Ray Fox	3	68 Dodg	199	300
5. James Hylton	James Hylton	48	67 Dodg	197	275

1969 Grand National Race No. 35 Smoky 200
July 27, 1969 Average Speed: 82.417

Driver	Owner	Car #	Make	Laps	Winnings
1. Richard Petty	Petty Enterprises	43	69 Ford	200	1,000
2. David Pearson	Holman-Moody	17	69 Ford	200	800
3. Neil Castles	Neil Castles	06	67 Plym	195	400
4. Elmo Langley	Elmo Langley	64	68 Ford	189	350
5. James Hylton	James Hylton	48	68 Dodg	189	325

1966 Grand National Race No. 24 East Tennessee 200
June 9, 1966 Average Speed: 71.986

Driver	Owner	Car #	Make	Laps	Winnings
1. David Pearson	Cotton Owens	6	64 Dodg	200	1,000
2. Buck Baker	Buck Baker	87	66 Olds	198	600
3. Paul Lewis	Paul Lewis	1	65 Plym	198	400
4. Elmo Langley	Henry Woodfield	64	64 Ford	197	300
5. Doug Cooper	Bob Cooper	02	65 Plym	196	275

1967 Grand National Race No. 23 East Tennessee 200
June 8, 1967 Average Speed: 72.919

Driver	Owner	Car #	Make	Laps	Winnings
1. Richard Petty	Petty Enterprises	43	67 Plym	200	1,000
2. Jim Paschal	Tom Friedkin	14	67 Plym	200	600
3. Dick Hutcherson	Bondy Long	29	67 Ford	200	400
4. Friday Hassler	Red Sharp	39	66 Chev	199	300
5. Elmo Langley	L. G. DeWitt	4	66 Ford	199	275

1968 Grand National Race No. 21
June 6, 1968 Average Speed: 76.743

Driver	Owner	Car #	Make	Laps	Winnings
1. Richard Petty	Petty Enterprises	43	68 Plym	200	1,200
2. Pete Hamilton	Rocky Hinton	5	68 Ford	199	600
3. James Hylton	James Hylton	48	67 Dodg	199	400
4. Curtis Turner	Tom Friedkin	14	68 Plym	195	300
5. John Sears	L. G. DeWitt	4	66 Ford	192	275

1969 Grand National Race No. 23 Maryville 300
June 5, 1969 Average Speed: 81.706

Driver	Owner	Car #	Make	Laps	Winnings
1. Bobby Isaac	Nord Krauskopf	71	69 Dodg	300	1,400
2. David Pearson	Holman-Moody	17	69 Ford	294	1,250
3. James Hylton	James Hylton	48	69 Dodg	293	825
4. Neil Castles	Neil Castles	06	67 Plym	292	650
5. Elmo Langley	Elmo Langley	64	68 Ford	287	500

1970 Grand National Race No. 17 Maryville 200
May 28, 1970 Average Speed: 82.558

Driver	Owner	Car #	Make	Laps	Winnings
1. Bobby Isaac	Nord Krauskopf	71	70 Dodg	200	1,500
2. James Hylton	James Hylton	48	69 Ford	199	900
3. Neil Castles	Neil Castles	06	69 Dodg	199	500
4. Dick Brooks	Dick Brooks	32	69 Plym	197	350
5. Dave Marcis	Dave Marcis	30	69 Dodg	195	325

Smoky Mountain Raceway *continued*

1970 Grand National Race No. 29 East Tennessee 200
July 24, 1970 Average Speed: 84.956

Driver	Owner	Car #	Make	Laps	Winnings
1. Richard Petty	Petty Enterprises	43	70 Plym	200	1,500
2. Bobby Isaac	Nord Krauskopf	71	69 Dodg	200	900
3. Dick Brooks	Dick Brooks	32	69 Plym	198	500
4. James Hylton	James Hylton	48	69 Ford	196	350
5. Friday Hassler	Friday Hassler	39	69 Chev	196	325

1971 Winston Cup GN Race No. 13 Maryville 200
April 15, 1971 Average Speed: 88.697

Driver	Owner	Car #	Make	Laps	Winnings
1. Richard Petty	Petty Enterprises	43	71 Plym	200	1,000
2. Benny Parsons	L. G. DeWitt	72	70 Ford	200	600
3. Friday Hassler	Friday Hassler	39	69 Chev	199	400
4. Elmo Langley	Elmo Langley	64	70 Ford	196	350
5. Dick Brooks	Mario Rossi	22	70 Dodg	196	325

Tennessee-Carolina Speedway
Newport, TN
Half-mile Dirt Track

(aka Newport Fairgrounds; Cocke County Fairgrounds) Half-mile dirt track opened in 1956. First NASCAR Winston Cup (then Grand National) race staged on 10/7/56 (won by Fireball Roberts). Only other Grand National race run 6/15/57 (also won by Roberts). Track closed in 1967.

Winston Cup Starts
11 drivers tied with 2

Winston Cup Victories
Fireball Roberts   2

Winston Cup Poles
Joe Eubanks   1
Speedy Thompson   1

Winston Cup Money
Fireball Roberts $1,850

Most Cars Started
22—October 7, 1956

Fewest Cars Started
17—June 15, 1957

Narrowest Margin of Victory
N/A

Slowest Race
60.687 MPH—June 15, 1957

Race Record
61.475 MPH—October 7, 1956

Most Race Leaders
N/A

Most Cars Running at Finish
14—October 7, 1956

1956 Grand National Race No. 51
October 7, 1956 Average Speed: 61.475

Driver	Owner	Car #	Make	Laps	Winnings
1. Fireball Roberts	Pete DePaolo	22	56 Ford	200	850
2. Buck Baker	Carl Kiekhaefer	300B	56 Chrys	200	625
3. Bill Amick	Pete DePaolo	97	56 Ford	199	450
4. Joe Weatherly	John Whitford	31	56 Ford	197	350
5. Herb Thomas	Herb Thomas	92	56 Chev	196	310

1957 Grand National Race No. 23
June 15, 1957 Average Speed: 60.687

Driver	Owner	Car #	Make	Laps	Winnings
1. Fireball Roberts	Fireball Roberts	22	57 Ford	200	1,000
2. Marvin Panch	Marvin Panch	98	57 Ford	200	625
3. Buck Baker	Buck Baker	87	57 Chev	200	400
4. Jack Smith	Jack Smith	47	57 Chev	199	295
5. Jim Paschal	Jim Paschal	17	57 Merc	190	255

Texas

Meyer Speedway
Houston, TX
Half-mile Paved Track

(aka Joseph F. Meyer Speedway) Half-mile paved oval opened in October 1959. Only NASCAR Winston Cup (then Grand National) race staged on 6/23/71 (won by Bobby Allison). Track closed in 1979.

Winston Cup Victories
Bobby Allison   1

Winston Cup Poles
Bobby Allison   1

Winston Cup Money
Bobby Allison $2,200

Most Cars Started
14—June 23, 1971 Space City 300

Narrowest Margin of Victory
2 laps plus—June 23, 1971
Space City 300

Race Record
73.489 MPH—June 23, 1971
Space City 300

Most Race Leaders
3—June 23, 1971 Space City 300

Most Cars Running at Finish
11—June 23, 1971 Space City 300

1971 Winston Cup GN Race No. 25 Space City 300
June 23, 1971 Average Speed: 73.489

Driver	Owner	Car #	Make	Laps	Winnings
1. Bobby Allison	Bobby Allison	12	70 Dodg	300	2,200
2. James Hylton	James Hylton	48	70 Ford	298	1,500
3. Walter Ballard	Walter Ballard	30	71 Ford	292	1,000
4. Elmo Langley	Elmo Langley	64	69 Merc	290	700
5. Frank Warren	H. B. Bailey	36	70 Pont	289	650

Texas Motor Speedway
Fort Worth, TX
1.5-mile Superspeedway

Modern 1.5-mile quad-oval speedway located in the Dallas /Ft. Worth metroplex in Texas. Groundbreaking began on August 18, 1995. First event was the NASCAR Busch Series and Winston Cup races on April 5 and 6, 1997. Inaugural NASCAR Winston Cup event won by Jeff Burton, his first triumph in NASCAR Winston Cup competition. Facility seats nearly 180,000 in its spacious grandstands. Speedway also hosts Indy Racing League open wheel events. Fully lighted facility is one of the most fan friendly speedways in motorsports.

Winston Cup Starts
19 drivers tied at 6

Winston Cup Victories
6 drivers tied at 6

Winston Cup Poles
6 drivers tied at 1

Winston Cup Money
Dale Jarrett $1,206,355

Most Cars Started
43—6 times

Fewest Cars Started
43—6 times

Narrowest Margin of Victory
0.573 seconds—April 5, 1998

Slowest Race
125.105 MPH—April 6, 1997

Race Record
144.276 MPH—March 28, 1999

Most Cautions
12—April 2, 2000

Most Race Leaders
17—April 2,2000

Most Cars Running at Finish
38—April 7, 2002

1997 Winston Cup Series Race No. 6
April 6, 1997 Average Speed: 125.105

Driver	Owner	Car #	Make	Laps	Winnings
1. Jeff Burton	Jack Roush	99	Ford	334	354,350
2. Dale Jarrett	Robert Yates	88	Ford	334	232,800
3. Bobby Labonte	Joe Gibbs	18	Pont	334	174,500
4. Terry Labonte	Rick Hendrick	5	Chev	334	170,600
5. Ricky Rudd	Ricky Rudd	10	Ford	334	118,775

1998 Winston Cup Series Race No. 7
April 5, 1998 Average Speed: 136.771

Driver	Owner	Car #	Make	Laps	Winnings
1. Mark Martin	Jack Roush	6	Ford	334	356,850
2. Chad Little	Jack Roush	97	Ford	334	238,550
3. Robert Pressley	Doug Bawel	77	Ford	334	161,750
4. Joe Nemechek	Felix Sabates	42	Chev	334	155,100
5. Johnny Benson, Jr.	Jack Roush	26	Ford	334	113,650

1999 Winston Cup Series Race No. 6
March 28, 1999 Average Speed: 144.276

Driver	Owner	Car #	Make	Laps	Winnings
1. Terry Labonte	Rick Hendrick	5	Chev	334	376,840
2. Dale Jarrett	Robert Yates	88	Ford	334	250,100
3. Bobby Labonte	Joe Gibbs	18	Pont	334	181,650
4. Rusty Wallace	Roger Penske	2	Ford	334	151,675
5. Jeremy Mayfield	Michael Kranefuss	12	Ford	334	119,925

2000 Winston Cup Series Race No. 7
April 2, 2000 Average Speed: 131.152

Driver	Owner	Car #	Make	Laps	Winnings
1. Dale Earnhardt, Jr.	Dale Earnhardt, Inc.	8	Chev	334	374,675
2. Jeff Burton	Jack Roush	99	Ford	334	259,550
3. Bobby Labonte	Joe Gibbs	18	Pont	334	186,500
4. Rusty Wallace	Roger Penske	2	Ford	334	155,450
5. Kevin Lepage	Jack Roush	16	Ford	334	128,800

2001 Winston Cup Series Race No. 7
April 1, 2001 Average Speed: 141.804

Driver	Owner	Car #	Make	Laps	Winnings
1. Dale Jarrett	Robert Yates	88	Ford	334	444,527
2. Steve Park	Dale Earnhardt, Inc.	1	Chev	334	270,443
3. Johnny Benson, Jr.	Nelson Bowers	10	Pont	334	193,050
4. Kurt Busch	Jack Roush	97	Ford	334	162,150
5. Jeff Gordon	Rick Hendrick	24	Chev	334	165,502

2002 Winston Cup Series Race No. 7
April 7, 2002 Average Speed: 142.435

Driver	Owner	Car #	Make	Laps	Winnings
1. Matt Kenseth	Jack Roush	17	Ford	334	418,275
2. Jeff Gordon	Rick Hendrick	24	Chev	334	296,478
3. Mark Martin	Jack Roush	6	Ford	334	219,358
4. Ricky Rudd	Robert Yates	28	Ford	334	201,717
5. Tony Stewart	Joe Gibbs	20	Pont	334	168,053

Texts World Speedway
College Station, TX
2-mile Paved Track

(aka Texas Int'l Speedway) Built in 1969 by Larry LoPatin. Part of the American Raceways complex. First NASCAR Winston Cup (then Grand National) race staged on 12/12/69 (won by Bobby Isaac, his first superspeedway victory). Final Winston Cup Grand National race staged on 6/7/81 (won by Benny Parsons, before a sparse crowd of 18,000). Track closed in 1989, and was purchased by Japanese businessmen in 1991. The grandstands were later declared unsafe and only a few minor sportscar events were staged thereafter.

Winston Cup Starts

Bobby Allison	8
Cecil Gordon	8
James Hylton	8
Benny Parsons	8
Richard Petty	8

Winston Cup Victories

| Richard Petty | 3 |

Winston Cup Poles

| Buddy Baker | 3 |

Winston Cup Money

| Richard Petty | $94,755 |

Most Cars Started

49—December 12, 1971 Texas 500

Fewest Cars Started

31—June 1, 1980 NASCAR 400

Narrowest Margin of Victory

1/2 car length—November 12, 1972 Texas 500

Slowest Race

132.475 MPH—June 7, 1981 Budweiser NASCAR 400

Race Record

159.046 MPH—June 1, 1980 NASCAR 400

Most Cautions

5—November 12, 1972 Texas 500
5—June 10, 1973 Alamo 500
5—June 7, 1981 Budweiser NASCAR 400

Most Race Leaders

9—June 7, 1981 Budweiser NASCAR 400

Most Cars Running at Finish

29—November 12, 1972 Texas 500

1969 Grand National Race No. 54 Texas 500
December 7, 1969 Average Speed: 144.277

Driver	Owner	Car #	Make	Laps	Winnings
1. Bobby Isaac	Nord Krauskopf	71	69 Dodg	250	15,640
2. Donnie Allison	Banjo Matthews	27	69 Ford	248	8,200
3. Benny Parsons	Russ Dawson	18	69 Ford	247	4,000
4. James Hylton	James Hylton	48	69 Dodg	239	3,700
5. Dick Brooks	Dick Brooks	32	69 Plym	237	3,350

1972 Winston Cup GN Race No. 16 Lone Star 500
June 25, 1972 Average Speed: 144.185

Driver	Owner	Car #	Make	Laps	Winnings
1. Richard Petty	Petty Enterprises	43	72 Plym	250	16,245
2. Bobby Allison	R. Howard & J. Johnson	12	72 Chev	249	8,670
3. Coo Coo Marlin	H. B. Cunningham	14	72 Chev	244	5,045
4. Benny Parsons	L. G. DeWitt	72	71 Merc	244	4,355
5. Bobby Isaac	Nord Krauskopf	71	72 Dodg	244	5,400

1973 Winston Cup GN Race No. 14 Alamo 500
June 10, 1973 Average Speed: 142.114

Driver	Owner	Car #	Make	Laps	Winnings
1. Richard Petty	Petty Enterprises	43	73 Dodg	250	17,820
2. Darrell Waltrip	Darrell Waltrip	95	71 Merc	248	7,720
3. Joe Frasson	Joe Frasson	18	73 Dodg	247	5,795
4. Cale Yarborough	R. Howard & J. Johnson	11	73 Chev	247	6,445
5. Cecil Gordon	Cecil Gordon	24	72 Chev	245	4,200

1980 Winston Cup GN Race No. 14 NASCAR 400
June 1, 1980 Average Speed: 159.046

Driver	Owner	Car #	Make	Laps	Winnings
1. Cale Yarborough	Junior Johnson	11	Chev	200	21,000
2. Richard Petty	Petty Enterprises	43	Chev	199	16,800
3. Bobby Allison	Bud Moore	15	Ford	199	13,500
4. Darrell Waltrip	DiGard	88	Chev	197	11,550
5. Terry Labonte	Billy Hagan	44	Chev	196	8,680

1971 Winston Cup GN Race No. 48 Texas 500
December 12, 1971 Average Speed: 144.000

Driver	Owner	Car #	Make	Laps	Winnings
1. Richard Petty	Petty Enterprises	43	71 Plym	250	13,395
2. Buddy Baker	Petty Enterprises	11	71 Dodg	250	6,805
3. Bobby Allison	Holman-Moody	12	71 Merc	248	5,125
4. Pete Hamilton	Cotton Owens	6	71 Plym	245	3,865
5. Bill Dennis	Junie Donlavey	90	69 Merc	239	3,100

1972 Winston Cup GN Race No. 31 Texas 500
November 12, 1972 Average Speed: 147.059

Driver	Owner	Car #	Make	Laps	Winnings
1. Buddy Baker	Nord Krauskopf	71	71 Dodg	250	14,920
2. A. J. Foyt	Wood Brothers	2	71 Merc	250	7,545
3. Richard Petty	Petty Enterprises	43	72 Dodg	250	8,220
4. Bobby Allison	R. Howard & J. Johnson	12	72 Chev	249	7,345
5. Hershel McGriff	Beryl Jackson	04	72 Plym	248	3,725

1979 Winston Cup GN Race No. 14 Texas 400
June 3, 1979 Average Speed: 156.216

Driver	Owner	Car #	Make	Laps	Winnings
1. Darrell Waltrip	DiGard	88	Chev	200	21,750
2. Bobby Allison	Bud Moore	15	Ford	199	14,600
3. Buddy Baker	Harry Ranier	28	Chev	199	13,950
4. Cale Yarborough	Junior Johnson	11	Chev	199	12,150
5. Terry Labonte	Billy Hagan	44	Chev	196	12,150

1981 Winston Cup GN Race No. 14 Budweiser NASCAR 400
June 7, 1981 Average Speed: 132.475

Driver	Owner	Car #	Make	Laps	Winnings
1. Benny Parsons	Bud Moore	15	Ford	200	22,750
2. Dale Earnhardt	Rod Osterlund	2	Pont	200	18,650
3. Bobby Allison	Harry Ranier	28	Buick	200	14,650
4. Richard Petty	Petty Enterprises	43	Buick	199	12,550
5. Dave Marcis	Dave Marcis	71	Buick	198	8,935

Virginia

Langley Field Speedway
Hampton, VA
.4-mile Paved Track

(aka Dude Ranch Speedway; Langley Field; Langley Speedway) .333-mile dirt oval opened circa 1949. Closed in 1953. .4-mile dirt oval re-opened in 1963. First NASCAR Winston Cup (then Grand National) race staged on 5/15/64 (won by Ned Jarrett). Track paved and re-measured at .395-mile in 1968. Final Winston Cup Grand National race was run 11/22/70 (won by Bobby Allison). Track active today.

Winston Cup Starts
Elmo Langley   9
Wendell Scott   9

Winston Cup Victories
David Pearson   3

Winston Cup Poles
David Pearson   3
Richard Petty   3

Winston Cup Money
David Pearson $4,920

Most Cars Started
30—November 22, 1970 Tidewater 300

Fewest Cars Started
16—May 20, 1967 Tidewater 250

Narrowest Margin of Victory
100 yards—May 18, 1970 Tidewater 250

Slowest Race
57.815 MPH—May 14, 1965
Tidewater 250

Race Record
75.789 MPH—May 17, 1969
Tidewater 375

Most Cautions
2—May 18, 1970 Tidewater 300
2—November 22, 1970 Tidewater 300

Most Race Leaders
3—May 20, 1967 Tidewater 250
3—May 18, 1968 Tidewater 250
3—May 18, 1970 Tidewater 300

Most Cars Running at Finish
20—November 22, 1970 Tidewater 300

1964 Grand National Race No. 22 Tidewater 250
May 15, 1964 Average Speed: 65.300

Driver	Owner	Car #	Make	Laps	Winnings
1. Ned Jarrett	Bondy Long	11	64 Ford	250	1,000
2. Marvin Panch	Wood Brothers	21	64 Ford	247	600
3. Buddy Baker	J. C. Parker	87	63 Dodg	242	400
4. Wendell Scott	Wendell Scott	34	63 Ford	240	300
5. Curtis Crider	Curtis Crider	02	63 Merc	234	275

1965 Grand National Race No. 16 Tidewater 250
May 14, 1965 Average Speed: 57.815

Driver	Owner	Car #	Make	Laps	Winnings
1. Ned Jarrett	Bondy Long	11	65 Ford	250	1,000
2. Dick Hutcherson	Holman-Moody	29	65 Ford	249	600
3. Elmo Langley	Elmo Langley	64	64 Ford	240	400
4. Buddy Arrington	Buddy Arrington	6	64 Dodg	237	300
5. Neil Castles	Buck Baker	86	65 Plym	233	275

1966 Grand National Race No. 16 Tidewater 250
May 7, 1966 Average Speed: 60.616

Driver	Owner	Car #	Make	Laps	Winnings
1. Richard Petty	Petty Enterprises	43	66 Plym	250	1,000
2. James Hylton	Bud Hartje	48	65 Dodg	250	600
3. Neil Castles	Buck Baker	86	66 Plym	246	400
4. Elmo Langley	Henry Woodfield	64	64 Ford	244	300
5. Tom Pistone	Tom Pistone	59	64 Ford	244	275

1967 Grand National Race No. 19 Tidewater 250
May 20, 1967 Average Speed: 66.704

Driver	Owner	Car #	Make	Laps	Winnings
1. Richard Petty	Petty Enterprises	43	67 Plym	250	1,000
2. Bobby Allison	Cotton Owens	6	67 Dodg	250	600
3. James Hylton	Bud Hartje	48	65 Dodg	246	400
4. Elmo Langley	Henry Woodfield	64	66 Ford	233	300
5. Donnie Allison	Bobby Allison	2	65 Chev	230	275

1968 Grand National Race No. 17 Tidewater 250
May 18, 1968 Average Speed: 71.457

Driver	Owner	Car #	Make	Laps	Winnings
1. David Pearson	Holman-Moody	17	68 Ford	250	1,000
2. Bobby Isaac	Nord Krauskopf	71	67 Dodg	250	600
3. Buddy Baker	Ray Fox	3	67 Dodg	249	400
4. James Hylton	James Hylton	48	67 Dodg	246	300
5. Pete Hamilton	Rocky Hinton	5	68 Ford	243	275

1968 Grand National Race No. 38 Crabber 250
August 24, 1968 Average Speed: 75.582

Driver	Owner	Car #	Make	Laps	Winnings
1. David Pearson	Holman-Moody	17	68 Ford	250	1,000
2. Richard Petty	Petty Enterprises	43	68 Plym	250	800
3. Bobby Isaac	Nord Krauskopf	71	67 Dodg	249	400
4. Bobby Allison	Bobby Allison	2	66 Chev	247	300
5. Ray Hendrick	Tom Friedkin	15	68 Plym	245	255

1969 Grand National Race No. 20 Tidewater 375
May 17, 1969 Average Speed: 75.789

Driver	Owner	Car #	Make	Laps	Winnings
1. David Pearson	Holman-Moody	17	69 Ford	375	2,700
2. James Hylton	James Hylton	48	69 Dodg	370	1,500
3. Dave Marcis	Milt Lunda	30	69 Dodg	369	1,000
4. Bobby Isaac	Nord Krauskopf	71	69 Dodg	368	750
5. Neil Castles	Neil Castles	06	Plym	366	600

1970 Grand National Race No. 15 Tidewater 300
May 18, 1970 Average Speed: 73.245

Driver	Owner	Car #	Make	Laps	Winnings
1. Bobby Isaac	Nord Krauskopf	71	70 Dodg	300	1,700
2. Bobby Allison	Bobby Allison	22	69 Dodg	298	1,035
3. Neil Castles	Neil Castles	06	69 Dodg	298	630
4. James Hylton	James Hylton	48	69 Ford	296	440
5. Benny Parsons	L. G. DeWitt	72	69 Ford	296	350

Langley Field Speedway *continued*

1970 Grand National Race No. 48 Tidewater 300
November 22, 1970 Average Speed: 69.584

Driver	Owner	Car #	Make	Laps	Winnings
1. Bobby Allison	Bobby Allison	22	70 Dodg	300	1,635
2. Benny Parsons	L. G. DeWitt	72	69 Ford	300	1,100
3. Pete Hamilton	Dick Brooks	32	69 Plym	299	600
4. John Sears	John Sears	4	69 Dodg	298	425
5. James Hylton	James Hylton	48	70 Ford	297	355

Martinsville Speedway
Martinsville, VA
.526-mile Paved Track

Half-mile dirt track opened in July 1947. First NASCAR Winston Cup (then Grand National) race staged on 9/25/49 (won by Red Byron). Track paved in mid-1955, between the spring and fall races. Track re-measured as .525-mile in 1970. Re-measured at .526-mile in late '80s.

Winston Cup Starts
Richard Petty 67

Winston Cup Victories
Richard Petty 15

Winston Cup Poles
Darrell Waltrip 8

Winston Cup Money
Rusty Wallace $1,506,025

Most Cars Started
47—April 20, 1958 Virginia 500
47—September 27, 1959
Virginia Sweepstakes 500

Fewest Cars Started
15—September 25, 1949

Narrowest Margin of Victory
0.141 seconds—October 15, 2001

Slowest Race
42.862 MPH—April 6, 1952

Race Record
82.223 MPH—September 22, 1996
Goody's 500

Most Cautions
17—September 28, 1980
Old Dominion 500

Most Race Leaders
14—October 15, 2001

Most Cars Running at Finish
42—April 18, 1999

1949 Strictly Stock Race No. 6
September 25, 1949

Driver	Owner	Car #	Make	Laps	Winnings
1. Red Byron	Raymond Parks	22	49 Olds	200	1,500
2. Lee Petty	Petty Enterprises	42	49 Plym	197	750
3. Ray Erickson	Ed Hastings	5	49 Merc	197	400
4. Clyde Minter	Mitchell Motors	19	46 Ford	187	300
5. Bill Blair	Sam Rice	2	49 Chev	186	175

1950 Grand National Race No. 4
May 21, 1950

Driver	Owner	Car #	Make	Laps	Winnings
1. Curtis Turner	John Eanes	41	50 Olds	150	1,250
2. Jim Paschal	Al Wheatley	79	47 Ford	148	600
3. Lee Petty	Petty Enterprises	42	49 Plym	144	400
4. Glenn Dunnaway	Glenn Dunnaway	49	49 Plym	144	300
5. Clyde Minter	Clyde Minter	19	50 Merc	143	225

1950 Grand National Race No. 17
October 15, 1950

Driver	Owner	Car #	Make	Laps	Winnings
1. Herb Thomas	Herb Thomas	92	50 Plym	200	1,000
2. Lee Petty	Petty Enterprises	42	49 Plym	199	600
3. Buck Baker	Griffin Motors	87	40 Olds	198	400
4. Fonty Flock	Frank Christian	7	50 Olds	197	325
5. Weldon Adams	Harold Mays	52	50 Plym	193	225

1951 Grand National Race No. 8
May 6, 1951

Driver	Owner	Car #	Make	Laps	Winnings
1. Curtis Turner	John Eanes	41	50 Olds	200	1,000
2. Frank Mundy	Perry Smith	23	51 Stud	—	600
3. Tim Flock	Ted Chester	91	51 Olds	—	400
4. Herb Thomas	Herb Thomas	92	50 Plym	—	300
5. Fonty Flock	Frank Christian	14	50 Olds	—	250

1951 Grand National Race No. 34
October 14, 1951

Driver	Owner	Car #	Make	Laps	Winnings
1. Frank Mundy	Ted Chester	7	51 Olds	200	1,000
2. Lee Petty	Petty Enterprises	42	51 Plym	—	600
3. Billy Myers	R. G. Shelton	22	51 Huds	—	500
4. Bill Snowden	Bill Snowden	16	51 Ford	—	400
5. Jimmie Lewallen	Hubert Hamilton	0	51 Plym	—	300

1952 Grand National Race No. 5
April 6, 1952 Average Speed: 42.862

Driver	Owner	Car #	Make	Laps	Winnings
1. Dick Rathmann	Walt Chapman	120	51 Huds	200	1,000
2. Bill Blair	George Hutchens	2	52 Olds	200	700
3. Perk Brown	R. G. Shelton	22	51 Huds	199	450
4. Lee Petty	Petty Enterprises	42	51 Plym	199	350
5. Bobby Courtwright	Bobby Courtwright		50 Olds	197	200

1952 Grand National Race No. 31
October 19, 1952 Average Speed: 47.556

Driver	Owner	Car #	Make	Laps	Winnings
1. Herb Thomas	Herb Thomas	92	52 Huds	200	1,000
2. Fonty Flock	Frank Christian	14	52 Olds	200	700
3. Lee Petty	Petty Enterprises	42	52 Plym	199	450
4. Tim Flock	Ted Chester	91	52 Huds	195	350
5. Johnny Patterson	H. B. Ranier	58	52 Huds	194	200

1953 Grand National Race No. 11
May 17, 1953

Driver	Owner	Car #	Make	Laps	Winnings
1. Lee Petty	Petty Enterprises	42	53 Dodg	200	1,000
2. Herb Thomas	Herb Thomas	92	53 Huds	200	700
3. Dick Rathmann	Walt Chapman	120	53 Huds	—	450
4. Ray Duhigg	J. H. Petty	44	52 Plym	—	350
5. Ralph Liguori		46	53 Linc	—	200

1953 Grand National Race No. 36
October 18, 1953 Average Speed: 56.013

Driver	Owner	Car #	Make	Laps	Winnings
1. Jim Paschal	George Hutchens	80	53 Dodg	200	1,000
2. Lee Petty	Petty Enterprises	42	53 Dodg	200	700
3. Bill Blair	Bill Blair	2	53 Olds	199	450
4. Fonty Flock	Frank Christian	14	53 Huds	199	350
5. Carl Burris			51 Plym	194	200

1954 Grand National Race No. 12
May 16, 1954 Average Speed: 46.153

Driver	Owner	Car #	Make	Laps	Winnings
1. Jim Paschal	Griffin Motors	87	53 Olds	200	1,000
2. Lee Petty	Petty Enterprises	42	54 Chrys	199	650
3. Curtis Turner	Carmen Amica	21	53 Olds	198	450
4. Al Keller	George Miller	23	54 Huds	195	350
5. Laird Bruner	Frank Dodge	28	53 Olds	187	300

Martinsville Speedway *continued*

1954 Grand National Race No. 36
October 17, 1954 Average Speed: 44.547

Driver	Owner	Car #	Make	Laps	Winnings
1. Lee Petty	Petty Enterprises	42	Chrys	165	1,000
2. Hershel McGriff	Frank Christian	14	54 Olds	165	650
3. Buck Baker	Griffin Motors	87	54 Olds	163	450
4. Dick Rathmann	John Ditz	3	54 Huds	163	350
5. Jim Reed	Jim Reed	7	52 Huds	162	300

1955 Grand National Race No. 42
October 16, 1955

Driver	Owner	Car #	Make	Laps	Winnings
1. Speedy Thompson	Carl Kiekhaefer	30	55 Chrys	200	1,100
2. Bob Welborn	Bob Welborn	49	55 Chev	200	700
3. Jim Paschal	J. H. Petty	44	55 Chev	200	475
4. Herb Thomas	Herb Thomas	92	55 Chev	199	365
5. Jim Reed	Jim Reed	7	55 Chev	198	310

1956 Grand National Race No. 54 Mixed 400
October 28, 1956 Average Speed: 61.136

Driver	Owner	Car #	Make	Laps	Winnings
1. Jack Smith	Carl Kiekhaefer	5	56 Dodg	400	2,275
2. Marvin Panch	Tom Harbison	98	56 Ford	400	1,400
3. Bill Amick	Pete DePaolo	97	56 Ford	400	950
4. Speedy Thompson	Carl Kiekhaefer	300	56 Chrys	396	700
5. Fireball Roberts	Pete DePaolo	22	56 Ford	394	600

1957 Grand National Race No. 49 Sweepstakes 500
October 6, 1957 Average Speed: 63.025

Driver	Owner	Car #	Make	Laps	Winnings
1. Bob Welborn	Bob Welborn	49	57 Chev	500	3,100
2. Jimmy Massey	Wood Brothers	11	56 Ford	500	1,975
3. Lee Petty	Petty Enterprises	42	57 Olds	498	1,425
4. Rex White	Bob Welborn	44	57 Chev	497	1,150
5. Joe Weatherly	Holman-Moody	12	57 Ford	493	850

1958 Grand National Race No. 49 Old Dominion 500
October 12, 1958 Average Speed: 64.344

Driver	Owner	Car #	Make	Laps	Winnings
1. Fireball Roberts	Frank Strickland	22	57 Chev	350	2,875
2. Speedy Thompson	Speedy Thompson	46	57 Chev	349	1,925
3. Rex White	Rex White	40	58 Chev	348	1,405
4. Bobby Johns	Shorty Johns	77	57 Chev	347	1,075
5. Buck Baker	Buck Baker	87	58 Chev	347	850

1959 Grand National Race No. 41 Virginia Sweepstakes 500
September 27, 1959 Average Speed: 60.500

Driver	Owner	Car #	Make	Laps	Winnings
1. Rex White	Rex White	4	59 Chev	500	3,250
2. Glen Wood	Wood Brothers	16	58 Ford	500	1,975
3. Jim Reed	Jim Reed	7	59 Chev	497	1,425
4. Tommy Irwin	Tommy Irwin	36	59 Ford	497	1,175
5. Speedy Thompson	W. J. Ridgeway	22	59 Chev	497	900

1960 Grand National Race No. 40 Old Dominion 500
September 25, 1960 Average Speed: 60.439

Driver	Owner	Car #	Make	Laps	Winnings
1. Rex White	Rex White	4	60 Chev	500	3,110
2. Joe Weatherly	Holman-Moody	12	60 Ford	500	1,790
3. Junior Johnson	John Masoni	27	59 Chev	499	975
4. Jim Paschal	Petty Enterprises	44	60 Plym	497	625
5. Buck Baker	Buck Baker	87	60 Chev	494	575

1955 Grand National Race No. 15
May 15, 1955 Average Speed: 52.554

Driver	Owner	Car #	Make	Laps	Winnings
1. Tim Flock	Carl Kiekhaefer	300	55 Chrys	200	1,000
2. Lee Petty	Petty Enterprises	42	55 Chrys	200	650
3. Junior Johnson	B & L Motors	55	55 Olds	198	450
4. Jimmie Lewallen	Ernest Woods	88	55 Olds	198	350
5. Bob Welborn	J. H. Petty	44	55 Chev	194	300

1956 Grand National Race No. 18 Virginia 500
May 20, 1956 Average Speed: 60.824

Driver	Owner	Car #	Make	Laps	Winnings
1. Buck Baker	Carl Kiekhaefer	502	56 Dodg	500	3,100
2. Speedy Thompson	Carl Kiekhaefer	500	56 Dodg	500	1,500
3. Lee Petty	Petty Enterprises	42	56 Dodg	497	1,025
4. Paul Goldsmith	Smokey Yunick	3	56 Chev	596	750
5. Gwyn Staley	Hubert Westmoreland	2	56 Chev	491	600

1957 Grand National Race No. 17 Virginia 500
May 19, 1957 Average Speed: 57.318

Driver	Owner	Car #	Make	Laps	Winnings
1. Buck Baker	Hugh Babb	87	57 Chev	441	3,170
2. Curtis Turner	Pete DePaolo	99	57 Ford	441	1,770
3. Tom Pistone	Hugh Babb	50	57 Chev	441	1,125
4. Billy Myers	Bill Stroppe	14	57 Merc	441	980
5. Lee Petty	Petty Enterprises	42	57 Olds	440	675

1958 Grand National Race No. 12 Virginia 500
April 20, 1958 Average Speed: 66.007

Driver	Owner	Car #	Make	Laps	Winnings
1. Bob Welborn	J. H. Petty	4	57 Chev	500	3,640
2. Rex White	J. H. Petty	44	57 Chev	500	1,675
3. Jim Reed	Jim Reed	7	57 Ford	500	1,125
4. Whitey Norman	Whitey Norman	41	57 Chev	495	800
5. Marvin Panch	John Whitford	98	57 Ford	494	675

1959 Grand National Race No. 13 Virginia 500
May 3, 1959 Average Speed: 59.512

Driver	Owner	Car #	Make	Laps	Winnings
1. Lee Petty	Petty Enterprises	42	57 Olds	500	3,630
2. Johnny Beauchamp	Beau Morgan	76	57 Chev	495	1,625
3. Junior Johnson	Paul Spaulding	11	57 Ford	495	1,205
4. Tom Pistone	Carl Rupert	59	59 Ford	491	775
5. Roy Tyner	Roy Tyner	9	57 Chev	491	600

1960 Grand National Race No. 10 Virginia 500
April 10, 1960 Average Speed: 63.943

Driver	Owner	Car #	Make	Laps	Winnings
1. Richard Petty	Petty Enterprises	43	60 Plym	500	3,340
2. Jimmy Massey	Wood Brothers	21	58 Ford	500	1,535
3. Glen Wood	Wood Brothers	24	58 Ford	499	1,155
4. Rex White	Rex White	4	60 Chev	499	835
5. Bob Welborn	Bob Welborn	49	60 Chev	495	650

1961 Grand National Race No. 13 Virginia 500
April 9, 1961 Average Speed: 68.366

Driver	Owner	Car #	Make	Laps	Winnings
1. Fred Lorenzen	Holman-Moody	28	61 Ford	149	1,150
2. Rex White	Rex White	4	61 Ford	149	1,275
3. Glen Wood	Wood Brothers	21	61 Ford	147	500
4. Emanuel Zervakis	Monroe Shook	85	61 Chev	147	325
5. Ned Jarrett	Bee Gee Holloway	11	61 Chev	147	450

Martinsville Speedway *continued*

1961 Grand National Race No. 18 Virginia 500 Sweepstakes
April 30, 1961 Average Speed: 66.278

Driver	Owner	Car #	Make	Laps	Winnings
1. Junior Johnson	Rex Lovette	27	61 Pont	500	2,315
2. Emanuel Zervakis	Monroe Shook	85	61 Chev	496	1,200
3. Fireball Roberts	Jim Stephens	75	61 Pont	496	825
4. Tommy Irwin	Tom Daniels	2	60 Chev	491	625
5. Buck Baker	Buck Baker	86	61 Chrys	491	550

1962 Grand National Race No. 15 Virginia 500
April 22, 1962 Average Speed: 66.425

Driver	Owner	Car #	Make	Laps	Winnings
1. Richard Petty	Petty Enterprises	43	62 Plym	500	3,400
2. Joe Weatherly	Bud Moore	8	62 Pont	500	1,625
3. Rex White	Rex White	4	62 Chev	499	1,210
4. Fred Lorenzen	Holman-Moody	28	61 Ford	499	860
5. Lee Petty	Petty Enterprises	41	62 Plym	499	750

1963 Grand National Race No. 19 Virginia 500
April 21, 1963 Average Speed: 64.823

Driver	Owner	Car #	Make	Laps	Winnings
1. Richard Petty	Petty Enterprises	43	63 Plym	500	3,375
2. Tiny Lund	Wood Brothers	21	63 Ford	499	1,675
3. Darel Dieringer	Bill Stroppe	26	63 Merc	496	1,225
4. Ned Jarrett	Charles Robinson	11	63 Ford	495	875
5. Fred Lorenzen	Holman-Moody	28	63 Ford	494	1,150

1964 Grand National Race No. 19 Virginia 500
April 26, 1964 Average Speed: 70.098

Driver	Owner	Car #	Make	Laps	Winnings
1. Fred Lorenzen	Holman-Moody	28	64 Ford	500	4,175
2. Marvin Panch	Wood Brothers	21	64 Ford	499	1,925
3. Junior Johnson	Banjo Matthews	00	64 Ford	497	1,250
4. Ned Jarrett	Bondy Long	11	64 Ford	495	850
5. Fireball Roberts	Holman-Moody	22	64 Ford	494	800

1965 Grand National Race No. 12 Virginia 500
April 25, 1965 Average Speed: 66.765

Driver	Owner	Car #	Make	Laps	Winnings
1. Fred Lorenzen	Holman-Moody	28	65 Ford	500	4,350
2. Marvin Panch	Wood Brothers	21	65 Ford	500	2,075
3. Dick Hutcherson	Holman-Moody	29	65 Ford	494	1,250
4. Tiny Lund	Gary Weaver	10	64 Ford	487	775
5. Buddy Arrington	Buddy Arrington	67	64 Dodg	472	725

1966 Grand National Race No. 14 Virginia 500
April 24, 1966 Average Speed: 69.156

Driver	Owner	Car #	Make	Laps	Winnings
1. Jim Paschal	Tom Friedkin	14	66 Plym	500	4,550
2. Paul Goldsmith	Ray Nichels	99	65 Plym	500	2,150
3. Richard Petty	Petty Enterprises	43	66 Plym	495	1,250
4. Elmo Langley	Henry Woodfield	64	64 Ford	488	775
5. G. C. Spencer	G. C. Spencer	49	65 Plym	486	725

1967 Grand National Race No. 14 Virginia 500
April 23, 1967 Average Speed: 67.446

Driver	Owner	Car #	Make	Laps	Winnings
1. Richard Petty	Petty Enterprises	43	67 Plym	500	4,450
2. Cale Yarborough	Wood Brothers	21	67 Ford	500	2,300
3. J. T. Putney	J. T. Putney	11	66 Chev	491	1,300
4. Dick Hutcherson	Bondy Long	99	67 Ford	488	925
5. Paul Goldsmith	Ray Nichels	99	67 Plym	488	725

1961 Grand National Race No. 47 Old Dominion 500
September 24, 1961 Average Speed: 62.586

Driver	Owner	Car #	Make	Laps	Winnings
1. Joe Weatherly	Bud Moore	8	61 Pont	500	3,595
2. Rex White	Rex White	4	61 Pont	500	2,000
3. Junior Johnson	Rex Lovette	27	61 Pont	499	1,570
4. Fireball Roberts	Cotton Owens	6	61 Pont	496	850
5. Ken Rush	Lynn Holloway	59	61 Pont	494	750

1962 Grand National Race No. 50 Old Dominion 500
September 23, 1962 Average Speed: 66.874

Driver	Owner	Car #	Make	Laps	Winnings
1. Nelson Stacy	Holman-Moody	29	62 Ford	500	3,655
2. Richard Petty	Petty Enterprises	43	672 Plym	497	1,650
3. Ned Jarrett	Bee Gee Holloway	11	62 Chev	496	1,500
4. Jack Smith	Jack Smith	47	62 Pont	495	850
5. Joe Weatherly	Bud Moore	8	62 Pont	495	920

1963 Grand National Race No. 48 Old Dominion 500
September 22, 1963 Average Speed: 67.486

Driver	Owner	Car #	Make	Laps	Winnings
1. Fred Lorenzen	Holman-Moody	28	63 Ford	500	3,800
2. Marvin Panch	Wood Brothers	21	63 Ford	499	1,675
3. Joe Weatherly	Bud Moore	8	63 Merc	497	1,475
4. David Pearson	Cotton Owens	6	63 Dodg	496	875
5. Richard Petty	Petty Enterprises	41	63 Plym	496	775

1964 Grand National Race No. 56 Old Dominion 500
September 27, 1964 Average Speed: 67.320

Driver	Owner	Car #	Make	Laps	Winnings
1. Fred Lorenzen	Holman-Moody	28	64 Ford	500	4,175
2. Richard Petty	Petty Enterprises	43	64 Plym	500	1,725
3. Junior Johnson	Banjo Matthews	27	64 Ford	500	1,250
4. Marvin Panch	Wood Brothers	21	64 Ford	499	850
5. Ned Jarrett	Bondy Long	11	64 Ford	497	775

1965 Grand National Race No. 50 Old Dominion 500
September 26, 1965 Average Speed: 67.056

Driver	Owner	Car #	Make	Laps	Winnings
1. Junior Johnson	Rex Lovette	26	65 Ford	500	4,625
2. Richard Petty	Petty Enterprises	43	65 Plym	499	2,400
3. David Pearson	Cotton Owens	6	65 Dodg	497	1,250
4. Ned Jarrett	Bondy Long	11	65 Ford	495	775
5. Marvin Panch	Wood Brothers	21	65 Ford	495	725

1966 Grand National Race No. 46 Old Dominion 500
September 25, 1966 Average Speed: 69.177

Driver	Owner	Car #	Make	Laps	Winnings
1. Fred Lorenzen	Holman-Moody	28	66 Ford	500	4,350
2. Darel Dieringer	Bud Moore	16	66 Merc	495	2,100
3. Bobby Allison	Bobby Allison	2	65 Chev	494	1,425
4. Dick Hutcherson	Bondy Long	29	66 Ford	492	775
5. James Hylton	Bud Hartje	48	65 Dodg	490	725

1967 Grand National Race No. 45 Old Dominion 500
September 24, 1967 Average Speed: 69.605

Driver	Owner	Car #	Make	Laps	Winnings
1. Richard Petty	Petty Enterprises	43	67 Plym	500	4,400
2. Dick Hutcherson	Bondy Long	29	67 Ford	496	2,075
3. David Pearson	Holman-Moody	17	67 Ford	495	1,475
4. James Hylton	Bud Hartje	48	65 Ford	493	775
5. Jim Paschal	Tom Friedkin	14	67 Plym	493	800

Martinsville Speedway *continued*

1968 Grand National Race No. 12 Virginia 500
April 28, 1968 Average Speed: 66.686

Driver	Owner	Car #	Make	Laps	Winnings
1. Cale Yarborough	Wood Brothers	21	68 Merc	500	5,476
2. David Pearson	Holman-Moody	17	68 Ford	500	2,797
3. Donnie Allison	Banjo Matthews	27	68 Ford	498	1,245
4. LeeRoy Yarbrough	Junior Johnson	26	68 Ford	498	800
5. Tom Pistone	Jon Thorne	12	68 Ford	497	725

1968 Grand National Race No. 44 Old Dominion 500
September 22, 1968 Average Speed: 65.808

Driver	Owner	Car #	Make	Laps	Winnings
1. Richard Petty	Petty Enterprises	43	68 Plym	500	5,999
2. Cale Yarborough	Wood Brothers	21	68 Merc	497	2,700
3. LeeRoy Yarbrough	Junior Johnson	98	68 Ford	497	1,244
4. Bud Moore	Bondy Long	29	68 Ford	494	775
5. Bobby Isaac	Nord Krauskopf	71	67 Dodg	494	725

1969 Grand National Race No. 16 Virginia 500
April 27, 1969 Average Speed: 64.405

Driver	Owner	Car #	Make	Laps	Winnings
1. Richard Petty	Petty Enterprises	43	69 Ford	500	10,275
2. David Pearson	Holman-Moody	17	69 Ford	500	5,050
3. Bobby Allison	Mario Rossi	22	69 Dodg	500	2,840
4. LeeRoy Yarbrough	Junior Johnson	98	69 Merc	496	1,550
5. Buddy Arrington	Buddy Arrington	67	69 Dodg	496	1,075

1969 Grand National Race No. 46 Old Dominion 500
September 28, 1969 Average Speed: 63.127

Driver	Owner	Car #	Make	Laps	Winnings
1. Richard Petty	Petty Enterprises	43	69 Ford	500	10,085
2. David Pearson	Holman-Moody	17	69 Ford	500	5,190
3. Buddy Baker	Cotton Owens	6	69 Dodg	496	2,675
4. James Hylton	James Hylton	48	69 Dodg	496	2,525
5. Buddy Arrington	Buddy Arrington	67	69 Dodg	489	1,075

1970 Grand National Race No. 18 Virginia 500
May 31, 1970 Average Speed: 68.584

Driver	Owner	Car #	Make	Laps	Winnings
1. Bobby Isaac	Nord Krauskopf	71	69 Dodg	377	10,795
2. Bobby Allison	Bobby Allison	22	69 Dodg	377	5,140
3. Cale Yarborough	Wood Brothers	21	70 Merc	376	3,100
4. David Pearson	Junior Johnson	98	70 Ford	375	1,525
5. Dick Brooks	Dick Brooks	32	69 Plym	373	1,025

1970 Grand National Race No. 45 Old Dominion 500
October 18, 1970 Average Speed: 72.235

Driver	Owner	Car #	Make	Laps	Winnings
1. Richard Petty	Petty Enterprises	43	70 Plym	500	8,775
2. Bobby Allison	Mario Rossi	22	69 Dodg	499	6,175
3. Cale Yarborough	Wood Brothers	21	70 Merc	498	4,100
4. Bobby Isaac	Nord Krauskopf	71	70 Dodg	498	3,525
5. Donnie Allison	Banjo Matthews	27	69 Ford	497	2,125

1971 Winston Cup GN Race No. 15 Virginia 500
April 25, 1971 Average Speed: 77.707

Driver	Owner	Car #	Make	Laps	Winnings
1. Richard Petty	Petty Enterprises	43	71 Plym	500	5,075
2. David Pearson	Holman-Moody	17	71 Ford	500	2,550
3. Bobby Isaac	Nord Krauskopf	71	71 Dodg	492	2,350
4. Dave Marcis	Dave Marcis	2	69 Dodg	486	1,525
5. James Hylton	James Hylton	48	70 Ford	483	1,225

1971 Winston Cup GN Race No. 41 Old Dominion 500
September 26, 1971 Average Speed: 73.681

Driver	Owner	Car #	Make	Laps	Winnings
1. Bobby Isaac	Nord Krauskopf	71	71 Dodg	500	6,250
2. Bobby Allison	Holman-Moody	12	71 Ford	499	2,600
3. Richard Petty	Petty Enterprises	43	71 Plym	499	2,200
4. Charlie Glotzbach	R. Howard & J. Johnson	3	71 Chev	496	1,575
5. Donnie Allison	Wood Brothers	21	71 Merc	495	1,250

1972 Winston Cup GN Race No. 10 Virginia 500
April 30, 1972 Average Speed: 72.657

Driver	Owner	Car #	Make	Laps	Winnings
1. Richard Petty	Petty Enterprises	43	72 Plym	500	8,250
2. Bobby Allison	R. Howard & J. Johnson	12	72 Chev	493	5,800
3. Dave Marcis	Dave Marcis	2	72 Dodg	487	2,675
4. Cecil Gordon	Cecil Gordon	24	71 Merc	485	1,825
5. Richard Brown	Ralph McNabb	91	72 Chev	479	1,250

1972 Winston Cup GN Race No. 27 Old Dominion 500
September 24, 1972 Average Speed: 69.989

Driver	Owner	Car #	Make	Laps	Winnings
1. Richard Petty	Petty Enterprises	43	72 Plym	500	7,350
2. Bobby Allison	R. Howard & J. Johnson	12	72 Chev	500	10,600
3. David Pearson	Wood Brothers	21	71 Merc	498	2,775
4. Buddy Baker	Nord Krauskopf	71	70 Dodg	496	3,225
5. Jimmy Hensley	Junie Donlavey	90	71 Ford	493	1,400

1973 Winston Cup GN Race No. 9 Virginia 500
April 29, 1973 Average Speed: 70.251

Driver	Owner	Car #	Make	Laps	Winnings
1. David Pearson	Wood Brothers	21	71 Merc	500	11,250
2. Cale Yarborough	R. Howard & J. Johnson	11	73 Chev	500	11,500
3. Bobby Isaac	Bud Moore	15	73 Ford	495	4,500
4. Buddy Baker	Nord Krauskopf	71	72 Dodg	494	3,500
5. Cecil Gordon	Cecil Gordon	24	72 Chev	490	1,750

1973 Winston Cup GN Race No. 26 Old Dominion 500
September 30, 1973 Average Speed: 68.831

Driver	Owner	Car #	Make	Laps	Winnings
1. Richard Petty	Petty Enterprises	43	73 Dodg	480	11,750
2. Cale Yarborough	R. Howard & J. Johnson	11	73 Chev	479	12,500
3. Bobby Allison	Bobby Allison	12	73 Chev	476	4,500
4. Buddy Baker	Nord Krauskopf	71	73 Dodg	475	3,500
5. Jack McCoy	Ernie Conn	07	73 Dodg	469	1,750

1974 Winston Cup GN Race No. 9 Virginia 500
April 28, 1974 Average Speed: 70.427

Driver	Owner	Car #	Make	Laps	Winnings
1. Cale Yarborough	R. Howard & J. Johnson	11	74 Chev	500	20,000
2. Richard Petty	Petty Enterprises	43	74 Dodg	500	8,000
3. Bobby Allison	Bobby Allison	12	74 Chev	496	5,000
4. Benny Parsons	L. G. DeWitt	72	74 Chev	494	4,250
5. Lennie Pond	Ronnie Elder	54	74 Chev	491	1,750

1974 Winston Cup GN Race No. 27 Old Dominion 500
September 29, 1974 Average Speed: 66.232

Driver	Owner	Car #	Make	Laps	Winnings
1. Earl Ross	Junior Johnson	52	72 Chev	500	14,550
2. Buddy Baker	Bud Moore	15	74 Ford	499	10,000
3. Donnie Allison	DiGard	88	74 Chev	497	4,250
4. Dave Marcis	Dave Marcis	2	73 Dodg	497	3,375
5. Richie Panch	Roy Thornley	98	72 Chev	488	2,000

Martinsville Speedway *continued*

1975 Winston Cup GN Race No. 9 Virginia 500
April 27, 1975 Average Speed: 69.282

Driver	Owner	Car #	Make	Laps	Winnings
1. Richard Petty	Petty Enterprises	43	74 Dodg	500	20,000
2. Darrell Waltrip	Darrell Waltrip	17	75 Chev	500	8,700
3. Cale Yarborough	Junior Johnson	11	75 Chev	499	6,550
4. Bobby Allison	Roger Penske	16	75 Mata	496	4,000
5. Dave Marcis	Nord Krauskopf	71	74 Dodg	493	4,500

1975 Winston Cup GN Race No. 24 Old Dominion 500
September 28, 1975 Average Speed: 75.819

Driver	Owner	Car #	Make	Laps	Winnings
1. Dave Marcis	Nord Krauskopf	71	74 Dodg	500	14,500
2. Benny Parsons	L. G. DeWitt	72	75 Chev	500	8,550
3. Bobby Allison	Roger Penske	16	75 Mata	496	4,850
4. Richard Childress	Tom Garn	96	75 Chev	487	3,785
5. Richie Panch	Bettie Panch	98	75 Chev	487	2,885

1976 Winston Cup GN Race No. 9 Virginia 500
April 25, 1976 Average Speed: 71.759

Driver	Owner	Car #	Make	Laps	Winnings
1. Darrell Waltrip	DiGard	88	Chev	500	22,500
2. Cale Yarborough	Junior Johnson	11	Chev	499	10,450
3. David Pearson	Wood Brothers	21	Merc	498	6,080
4. Richard Petty	Petty Enterprises	43	Dodg	498	7,070
5. Dick Brooks	Junie Donlavey	90	Ford	493	2,950

1976 Winston Cup GN Race No. 25 Old Dominion 500
September 26, 1976 Average Speed: 75.370

Driver	Owner	Car #	Make	Laps	Winnings
1. Cale Yarborough	Junior Johnson	11	Chev	340	22,700
2. Darrell Waltrip	DiGard	88	Chev	340	11,700
3. Buddy Baker	Bud Moore	15	Ford	338	7,130
4. Richard Petty	Petty Enterprises	43	Dodg	338	7,070
5. Benny Parsons	L. G. DeWitt	72	Chev	336	4,700

1977 Winston Cup GN Race No. 9 Virginia 500
April 24, 1977 Average Speed: 77.405

Driver	Owner	Car #	Make	Laps	Winnings
1. Cale Yarborough	Junior Johnson	11	Chev	384	21,600
2. Benny Parsons	L. G. DeWitt	72	Chev	384	12,200
3. Richard Petty	Petty Enterprises	43	Dodg	381	7,750
4. Lennie Pond	Ronnie Elder	54	Chev	381	5,700
5. David Pearson	Wood Brothers	21	Merc	380	2,900

1977 Winston Cup GN Race No. 25 Old Dominion 500
September 25, 1977 Average Speed: 73.447

Driver	Owner	Car #	Make	Laps	Winnings
1. Cale Yarborough	Junior Johnson	11	Chev	500	23,700
2. Benny Parsons	L. G. DeWitt	72	Chev	500	11,850
3. David Pearson	Wood Brothers	21	Merc	500	5,700
4. Richard Petty	Petty Enterprises	43	Dodg	499	5,850
5. Sam Sommers	M. C. Anderson	27	Chev	491	3,550

1978 Winston Cup GN Race No. 9 Virginia 500
April 23, 1978 Average Speed: 77.971

Driver	Owner	Car #	Make	Laps	Winnings
1. Darrell Waltrip	DiGard	88	Chev	500	22,700
2. Neil Bonnett	Jim Stacy	5	Dodg	497	11,450
3. Richard Petty	Petty Enterprises	43	Dodg	497	8,700
4. Dave Marcis	Rod Osterlund	2	Chev	489	4,000
5. Buddy Arrington	Buddy Arrington	67	Dodg	485	4,950

1978 Winston Cup GN Race No. 25 Old Dominion 500
September 24, 1978 Average Speed: 79.185

Driver	Owner	Car #	Make	Laps	Winnings
1. Cale Yarborough	Junior Johnson	11	Olds	500	24,950
2. Darrell Waltrip	DiGard	88	Chev	500	11,700
3. Benny Parsons	L. G. DeWitt	72	Chev	498	8,700
4. Neil Bonnett	Jim Stacy	5	Chev	498	6,700
5. Lennie Pond	Harry Ranier	54	Chev	497	6,950

1979 Winston Cup GN Race No. 9 Virginia 500
April 22, 1979 Average Speed: 76.562

Driver	Owner	Car #	Make	Laps	Winnings
1. Richard Petty	Petty Enterprises	43	Chev	500	23,400
2. Buddy Baker	Harry Ranier	28	Chev	500	14,700
3. Darrell Waltrip	DiGard	88	Chev	499	10,200
4. Bobby Allison	Bud Moore	15	Ford	498	7,100
5. Joe Millikan	L. G. DeWitt	72	Chev	497	6,550

1979 Winston Cup GN Race No. 26 Old Dominion 500
September 23, 1979 Average Speed: 75.119

Driver	Owner	Car #	Make	Laps	Winnings
1. Buddy Baker	Harry Ranier	28	Chev	500	19,900
2. Richard Petty	Petty Enterprises	43	Chev	500	12,550
3. Joe Millikan	L. G. DeWitt	72	Chev	499	9,650
4. Bobby Allison	Bud Moore	15	Ford	495	6,950
5. Dave Marcis	Dave Marcis	71	Chev	494	3,150

1980 Winston Cup GN Race No. 9 Virginia 500
April 27, 1980 Average Speed: 69.049

Driver	Owner	Car #	Make	Laps	Winnings
1. Darrell Waltrip	DiGard	88	Chev	500	26,850
2. Benny Parsons	M. C. Anderson	27	Chev	500	15,400
3. Richard Petty	Petty Enterprises	43	Chev	500	13,475
4. Cale Yarborough	Junior Johnson	11	Chev	500	8,750
5. Joe Millikan	L. G. DeWitt	72	Chev	496	6,800

1980 Winston Cup GN Race No. 27 Old Dominion 500
September 28, 1980 Average Speed: 69.654

Driver	Owner	Car #	Make	Laps	Winnings
1. Dale Earnhardt	Rod Osterlund	2	Chev	500	25,375
2. Buddy Baker	Harry Ranier	28	Chev	500	16,400
3. Cale Yarborough	Junior Johnson	11	Olds	500	11,975
4. Benny Parsons	M. C. Anderson	27	Chev	499	7,700
5. Dave Marcis	Dave Marcis	71	Chev	499	5,860

1981 Winston Cup GN Race No. 9 Virginia 500
April 26, 1981 Average Speed: 75.019

Driver	Owner	Car #	Make	Laps	Winnings
1. Morgan Shepherd	Cliff Stewart	5	Pont	500	24,525
2. Neil Bonnett	Wood Brothers	21	Ford	500	12,650
3. Ricky Rudd	DiGard	88	Buick	499	15,250
4. Harry Gant	Kennie Childers	12	Olds	497	7,700
5. Terry Labonte	Billy Hagan	44	Buick	497	7,725

1981 Winston Cup GN Race No. 26 Old Dominion 500
September 27, 1981 Average Speed: 70.089

Driver	Owner	Car #	Make	Laps	Winnings
1. Darrell Waltrip	Junior Johnson	11	Buick	500	29,275
2. Harry Gant	Hal Needham	33	Pont	500	18,570
3. Mark Martin	Ray Dillon	02	Pont	497	7,525
4. Neil Bonnett	Wood Brothers	21	Ford	497	4,500
5. Joe Millikan	Cliff Stewart	5	Pont	497	7,425

Martinsville Speedway *continued*

1982 Winston Cup GN Race No. 8 Virginia National Bank 500
April 25, 1982 Average Speed: 75.073

Driver	Owner	Car #	Make	Laps	Winnings
1. Harry Gant	Hal Needham	33	Buick	500	26,795
2. Butch Lindley	Emanuel Zervakis	01	Buick	499	14,250
3. Neil Bonnett	Wood Brothers	21	Ford	497	8,275
4. Ricky Rudd	Richard Childress	3	Pont	496	8,520
5. Darrell Waltrip	Junior Johnson	11	Buick	496	12,600

1982 Winston Cup GN Race No. 27 Old Dominion 500
October 17, 1982 Average Speed: 71.315

Driver	Owner	Car #	Make	Laps	Winnings
1. Darrell Waltrip	Junior Johnson	11	Buick	500	33,225
2. Ricky Rudd	Richard Childress	3	Pont	500	22,770
3. Richard Petty	Petty Enterprises	43	Pont	500	14,925
4. Terry Labonte	Billy Hagan	44	Chev	498	8,270
5. Joe Ruttman	Bob Rahilly & Butch Mock	75	Buick	498	6,500

1983 Winston Cup GN Race No. 7 Virginia National Bank 500
April 24, 1983 Average Speed: 66.460

Driver	Owner	Car #	Make	Laps	Winnings
1. Darrell Waltrip	Junior Johnson	11	Chev	500	35,225
2. Harry Gant	Hal Needham	33	Buick	500	20,200
3. Bobby Allison	DiGard	22	Buick	500	15,780
4. Joe Ruttman	Ron Benfield	98	Buick	500	8,870
5. Ricky Rudd	Richard Childress	3	Chev	500	9,670

1983 Winston Cup GN Race No. 25 Goody's 500
September 25, 1983 Average Speed: 76.134

Driver	Owner	Car #	Make	Laps	Winnings
1. Ricky Rudd	Richard Childress	3	Chev	500	31,395
2. Bobby Allison	DiGard	22	Buick	500	19,600
3. Darrell Waltrip	Junior Johnson	11	Chev	500	20,150
4. Dale Earnhardt	Bud Moore	15	Ford	499	11,200
5. Geoff Bodine	Cliff Stewart	88	Pont	499	7,670

1984 Winston Cup GN Race No. 8 Sovran Bank 500
April 29, 1984 Average Speed: 73.264

Driver	Owner	Car #	Make	Laps	Winnings
1. Geoff Bodine	Rick Hendrick	5	Chev	500	29,880
2. Ron Bouchard	Jack Beebe	47	Buick	500	18,905
3. Darrell Waltrip	Junior Johnson	11	Chev	500	17,450
4. Bobby Allison	DiGard	22	Buick	500	18,000
5. Neil Bonnett	Junior Johnson	12	Chev	499	4,900

1984 Winston Cup GN Race No. 25 Goody's 500
September 23, 1984 Average Speed: 75.532

Driver	Owner	Car #	Make	Laps	Winnings
1. Darrell Waltrip	Junior Johnson	11	Chev	500	38,300
2. Terry Labonte	Billy Hagan	44	Chev	499	19,905
3. Bill Elliott	Harry Melling	9	Ford	499	15,550
4. Harry Gant	Hal Needham	33	Chev	498	9,530
5. Neil Bonnett	Junior Johnson	12	Chev	498	8,960

1985 Winston Cup GN Race No. 8 Sovran Bank 500
April 28, 1985 Average Speed: 73.022

Driver	Owner	Car #	Make	Laps	Winnings
1. Harry Gant	Hal Needham	33	Chev	500	38,525
2. Ricky Rudd	Bud Moore	15	Ford	500	22,450
3. Geoff Bodine	Rick Hendrick	5	Chev	500	19,825
4. Bobby Allison	DiGard	22	Buick	500	12,050
5. Neil Bonnett	Junior Johnson	12	Chev	500	10,550

1985 Winston Cup GN Race No. 23 Goody's 500
September 22, 1985 Average Speed: 70.694

Driver	Owner	Car #	Make	Laps	Winnings
1. Dale Earnhardt	Richard Childress	3	Chev	500	37,725
2. Darrell Waltrip	Junior Johnson	11	Chev	500	24,650
3. Harry Gant	Hal Needham	33	Chev	499	18,225
4. Ricky Rudd	Bud Moore	15	Ford	499	12,350
5. Kyle Petty	Wood Brothers	7	Ford	498	8,430

1986 Winston Cup Race No. 8 Sovran Bank 500
April 27, 1986 Average Speed: 76.882

Driver	Owner	Car #	Make	Laps	Winnings
1. Ricky Rudd	Bud Moore	15	Ford	500	40,850
2. Joe Ruttman	Kenny Bernstein	26	Buick	499	17,325
3. Terry Labonte	Billy Hagan	44	Olds	496	17,125
4. Alan Kulwicki	Bill Terry	35	Ford	496	8,350
5. Kyle Petty	Wood Brothers	7	Ford	496	11,050

1986 Winston Cup Race No. 24 Goody's 500
September 21, 1986 Average Speed: 73.191

Driver	Owner	Car #	Make	Laps	Winnings
1. Rusty Wallace	Raymond Beadle	27	Pont	500	40,175
2. Geoff Bodine	Rick Hendrick	5	Chev	500	28,250
3. Harry Gant	Hal Needham	33	Chev	500	19,625
4. Darrell Waltrip	Junior Johnson	11	Chev	499	16,350
5. Joe Ruttman	Kenny Bernstein	26	Buick	499	9,730

1987 Winston Cup Race No. 8 Sovran Bank 500
April 26, 1987 Average Speed: 72.808

Driver	Owner	Car #	Make	Laps	Winnings
1. Dale Earnhardt	Richard Childress	3	Chev	500	50,850
2. Rusty Wallace	Raymond Beadle	27	Pont	500	27,325
3. Geoff Bodine	Rick Hendrick	5	Chev	500	20,750
4. Phil Parsons	Richard Jackson	55	Olds	500	10,275
5. Terry Labonte	Junior Johnson	11	Chev	498	16,425

1987 Winston Cup Race No. 24 Goody's 500
September 27, 1987 Average Speed: 76.410

Driver	Owner	Car #	Make	Laps	Winnings
1. Darrell Waltrip	Rick Hendrick	17	Chev	500	43,830
2. Dale Earnhardt	Richard Childress	3	Chev	500	29,875
3. Terry Labonte	Junior Johnson	11	Chev	500	23,950
4. Neil Bonnett	Bob Rahilly & Butch Mock	75	Pont	498	13,005
5. Morgan Shepherd	Kenny Bernstein	26	Buick	497	12,335

1988 Winston Cup Race No. 8 Pannill Sweatshirts 500
April 24, 1988 Average Speed: 74.740

Driver	Owner	Car #	Make	Laps	Winnings
1. Dale Earnhardt	Richard Childress	3	Chev	500	53,550
2. Sterling Marlin	Billy Hagan	44	Olds	500	29,975
3. Bobby Hillin Jr.	Stavola Brothers	8	Buick	499	20,775
4. Terry Labonte	Junior Johnson	11	Chev	498	14,550
5. Darrell Waltrip	Rick Hendrick	17	Chev	498	14,250

1988 Winston Cup Race No. 24 Goody's 500
September 25, 1988 Average Speed: 74.988

Driver	Owner	Car #	Make	Laps	Winnings
1. Darrell Waltrip	Rick Hendrick	17	Chev	500	48,750
2. Alan Kulwicki	Alan Kulwicki	7	Ford	500	28,225
3. Rusty Wallace	Raymond Beadle	27	Pont	500	26,825
4. Ken Schrader	Rick Hendrick	25	Chev	499	13,500
5. Geoff Bodine	Rick Hendrick	5	Chev	499	13,050

Martinsville Speedway *continued*

1989 Winston Cup Race No. 8 Pannill Sweatshirts 500
April 23, 1989 Average Speed: 79.025

Driver	Owner	Car #	Make	Laps	Winnings
1. Darrell Waltrip	Rick Hendrick	17	Chev	500	53,600
2. Dale Earnhardt	Richard Childress	3	Chev	500	34,525
3. Dick Trickle	Stavola Brothers	84	Buick	500	21,050
4. Rick Wilson	Larry McClure	4	Olds	499	15,975
5. Terry Labonte	Junior Johnson	11	Ford	499	15,575

1989 Winston Cup Race No. 24 Goody's 500
September 24, 1989 Average Speed: 76.571

Driver	Owner	Car #	Make	Laps	Winnings
1. Darrell Waltrip	Rick Hendrick	17	Chev	500	55,650
2. Harry Gant	Leo Jackson	33	Olds	500	33,802
3. Dick Trickle	Stavola Brothers	84	Buick	500	22,250
4. Rusty Wallace	Raymond Beadle	27	Pont	500	18,875
5. Dale Jarrett	Cale Yarborough	29	Pont	500	15,125

1990 Winston Cup Series Race No. 8 Hanes Activewear 500
April 29, 1990 Average Speed: 77.423

Driver	Owner	Car #	Make	Laps	Winnings
1. Geoff Bodine	Junior Johnson	11	Ford	500	95,950
2. Rusty Wallace	Raymond Beadle	27	Pont	500	36,800
3. Morgan Shepherd	Bud Moore	15	Ford	500	19,750
4. Darrell Waltrip	Rick Hendrick	17	Chev	500	19,600
5. Dale Earnhardt	Richard Childress	3	Chev	499	20,800

1990 Winston Cup Series Race No. 24 Goody's 500
September 23, 1990 Average Speed: 76.386

Driver	Owner	Car #	Make	Laps	Winnings
1. Geoff Bodine	Junior Johnson	11	Ford	500	53,850
2. Dale Earnhardt	Richard Childress	3	Chev	500	30,550
3. Mark Martin	Jack Roush	6	Ford	500	24,450
4. Brett Bodine	Kenny Bernstein	26	Buick	500	16,807
5. Harry Gant	Leo Jackson	33	Olds	500	18,100

1991 Winston Cup Series Race No. 8 Hanes 500
April 28, 1991 Average Speed: 75.139

Driver	Owner	Car #	Make	Laps	Winnings
1. Dale Earnhardt	Richard Childress	3	Chev	500	63,600
2. Kyle Petty	Felix Sabates	42	Pont	500	29,625
3. Darrell Waltrip	Darrell Waltrip	17	Chev	500	16,150
4. Brett Bodine	Kenny Bernstein	26	Buick	500	15,550
5. Harry Gant	Leo Jackson	33	Olds	499	17,625

1991 Winston Cup Series Race No. 24 Goody's 500
September 22, 1991 Average Speed: 74.535

Driver	Owner	Car #	Make	Laps	Winnings
1. Harry Gant	Leo Jackson	33	Olds	500	64,000
2. Brett Bodine	Kenny Bernstein	26	Buick	500	36,625
3. Dale Earnhardt	Richard Childress	3	Chev	500	30,350
4. Ernie Irvan	Larry McClure	4	Chev	500	19,300
5. Mark Martin	Jack Roush	6	Ford	500	24,575

1992 Winston Cup Race No. 8 Hanes 500
April 26, 1992 Average Speed: 78.086

Driver	Owner	Car #	Make	Laps	Winnings
1. Mark Martin	Jack Roush	6	Ford	500	59,300
2. Sterling Marlin	Junior Johnson	22	Ford	500	32,775
3. Darrell Waltrip	Darrell Waltrip	17	Chev	499	30,700
4. Terry Labonte	Billy Hagan	94	Olds	499	19,700
5. Harry Gant	Leo Jackson	33	Olds	498	22,875

1992 Winston Cup Race No. 24 Goody's 500
September 28, 1992 Average Speed: 75.424

Driver	Owner	Car #	Make	Laps	Winnings
1. Geoff Bodine	Bud Moore	15	Ford	500	60,550
2. Rusty Wallace	Roger Penske	2	Pont	500	39,400
3. Brett Bodine	Kenny Bernstein	26	Ford	500	29,125
4. Kyle Petty	Felix Sabates	42	Pont	500	22,000
5. Alan Kulwicki	Alan Kulwicki	7	Ford	500	23,330

1993 Winston Cup Series Race No. 8 Hanes 500
April 25, 1993 Average Speed: 79.078

Driver	Owner	Car #	Make	Laps	Winnings
1. Rusty Wallace	Roger Penske	2	Pont	500	45,175
2. Davey Allison	Robert Yates	28	Ford	500	49,725
3. Dale Jarrett	Joe Gibbs	18	Chev	500	30,350
4. Darrell Waltrip	Darrell Waltrip	17	Chev	500	28,800
5. Kyle Petty	Felix Sabates	42	Pont	499	21,050

1993 Winston Cup Series Race No. 25 Goody's 500
September 26, 1993 Average Speed: 74.102

Driver	Owner	Car #	Make	Laps	Winnings
1. Ernie Irvan	Robert Yates	28	Ford	500	75,300
2. Rusty Wallace	Roger Penske	2	Pont	500	31,875
3. Jimmy Spencer	Bobby Allison	12	Ford	500	31,000
4. Ricky Rudd	Rick Hendrick	5	Chev	500	25,250
5. Dale Jarrett	Joe Gibbs	18	Chev	499	22,675

1994 Winston Cup Series Race No. 8 Hanes 500
April 24, 1994 Average Speed: 76.700

Driver	Owner	Car #	Make	Laps	Winnings
1. Rusty Wallace	Roger Penske	2	Ford	500	173,675
2. Ernie Irvan	Robert Yates	28	Ford	500	41,750
3. Mark Martin	Jack Roush	6	Ford	500	33,425
4. Darrell Waltrip	Darrell Waltrip	17	Chev	500	23,050
5. Morgan Shepherd	Wood Brothers	21	Ford	500	23,875

1994 Winston Cup Series Race No. 26 Goody's 500
September 25, 1994 Average Speed: 77.139

Driver	Owner	Car #	Make	Laps	Winnings
1. Rusty Wallace	Roger Penske	2	Ford	500	69,125
2. Dale Earnhardt	Richard Childress	3	Chev	500	42,400
3. Bill Elliott	Junior Johnson	11	Ford	500	29,525
4. Kenny Wallace	Robert Yates	28	Ford	500	30,650
5. Dale Jarrett	Joe Gibbs	18	Chev	500	26,775

1995 Winston Cup Series Race No. 8 Hanes 500
April 23, 1995 Average Speed: 72.145

Driver	Owner	Car #	Make	Laps	Winnings
1. Rusty Wallace	Roger Penske	2	Ford	356	61,945
2. Ted Musgrave	Jack Roush	16	Ford	356	42,965
3. Jeff Gordon	Rick Hendrick	24	Chev	356	37,895
4. Darrell Waltrip	Darrell Waltrip	17	Chev	356	42,695
5. Mark Martin	Jack Roush	6	Ford	356	33,195

1995 Winston Cup Series Race No. 26 Goody's 500
September 24, 1995 Average Speed: 73.946

Driver	Owner	Car #	Make	Laps	Winnings
1. Dale Earnhardt	Richard Childress	3	Chev	500	78,150
2. Terry Labonte	Rick Hendrick	5	Chev	500	45,600
3. Rusty Wallace	Roger Penske	2	Ford	500	42,400
4. Bobby Hamilton	Petty Enterprises	43	Pont	500	24,450
5. Geoff Bodine	Geoff Bodine	7	Ford	500	32,100

Martinsville Speedway *continued*

1996 Winston Cup Series Race No. 8 Goody's 500
April 21, 1996 Average Speed: 81.410

Driver	Owner	Car #	Make	Laps	Winnings
1. Rusty Wallace	Roger Penske	2	Ford	500	59,245
2. Ernie Irvan	Robert Yates	28	Ford	500	57,395
3. Jeff Gordon	Rick Hendrick	24	Chev	500	57,495
4. Jeremy Mayfield	Cale Yarborough	98	Ford	500	32,545
5. Dale Earnhardt	Richard Childress	3	Chev	500	35,195

1997 Winston Cup Series Race No. 8
April 20, 1997 Average Speed: 70.29

Driver	Owner	Car #	Make	Laps	Winnings
1. Jeff Gordon	Rick Hendrick	24	Chev	500	99,225
2. Bobby Hamilton	Petty Enterprises	43	Pont	500	50,575
3. Mark Martin	Jack Roush	6	Ford	500	42,375
4. Terry Labonte	Rick Hendrick	5	Chev	500	42,925
5. Rusty Wallace	Roger Penske	2	Ford	500	33,875

1998 Winston Cup Series Race No. 8
April 20, 1998 Average Speed: 70.709

Driver	Owner	Car #	Make	Laps	Winnings
1. Bobby Hamilton	Larry McClure	4	Chev	500	227,025
2. Ted Musgrave	Jack Roush	16	Ford	500	65,675
3. Dale Jarrett	Robert Yates	88	Ford	500	58,525
4. Dale Earnhardt	Richard Childress	3	Chev	500	49,475
5. Randy LaJoie	Rick Hendrick	50	Chev	500	44,325

1999 Winston Cup Series Race No. 8
April 18, 1999 Average Speed: 75.653

Driver	Owner	Car #	Make	Laps	Winnings
1. John Andretti	Petty Enterprises	43	Pont	500	105,275
2. Jeff Burton	Jack Roush	99	Ford	500	89,865
3. Jeff Gordon	Rick Hendrick	24	Chev	500	71,800
4. Mike Skinner	Richard Childress	31	Chev	500	57,355
5. Mark Martin	Jack Roush	6	Ford	500	52,925

2000 Winston Cup Series Race No. 8
April 9, 2000 Average Speed: 71.161

Driver	Owner	Car #	Make	Laps	Winnings
1. Mark Martin	Jack Roush	6	Ford	500	104,650
2. Jeff Burton	Jack Roush	99	Ford	500	91,150
3. Michael Waltrip	Jim Mattei	7	Chev	500	79,850
4. Jeff Gordon	Rick Hendrick	24	Chev	500	65,530
5. Dale Jarrett	Robert Yates	88	Ford	500	65,125

2001 Winston Cup Series Race No. 8
April 8, 2001 Average Speed: 70.799

Driver	Owner	Car #	Make	Laps	Winnings
1. Dale Jarrett	Robert Yates	88	Ford	500	170,027
2. Ricky Rudd	Robert Yates	28	Ford	500	106,047
3. Jeff Burton	Jack Roush	99	Ford	500	108,596
4. Bobby Hamilton	Andy Petree	55	Chev	500	77,675
5. Sterling Marlin	Chip Ganassi	40	Dodg	500	67,110

2002 Winston Cup Series Race No. 8
April 14, 2002 Average Speed: 73.951

Driver	Owner	Car #	Make	Laps	Winnings
1. Bobby Labonte	Joe Gibbs	18	Pont	500	168,078
2. Matt Kenseth	Jack Roush	17	Ford	500	97,165
3. Tony Stewart	Joe Gibbs	20	Pont	500	111,953
4. Dale Jarrett	Robert Yates	88	Ford	500	112,553
5. Dale Earnhardt, Jr.	Dale Earnhardt, Inc.	8	Chev	500	88,862

1996 Winston Cup Series Race No. 26 Hanes 500
September 22, 1996 Average Speed: 82.223

Driver	Owner	Car #	Make	Laps	Winnings
1. Jeff Gordon	Rick Hendrick	24	Chev	500	93,825
2. Terry Labonte	Rick Hendrick	5	Chev	500	56,175
3. Bobby Hamilton	Petty Enterprises	43	Pont	500	50,425
4. Rick Mast	Richard Jackson	1	Pont	500	36,125
5. John Andretti	Cale Yarborough	98	Ford	500	26,235

1997 Winston Cup Series Race No. 27
September 29, 1997 Average Speed: 73.072

Driver	Owner	Car #	Make	Laps	Winnings
1. Jeff Burton	Jack Roush	99	Ford	500	78,675
2. Dale Earnhardt	Richard Childress	3	Chev	500	65,800
3. Bobby Hamilton	Petty Enterprises	43	Pont	500	40,075
4. Jeff Gordon	Rick Hendrick	24	Chev	500	40,225
5. Bill Elliott	Bill Elliott	94	Ford	500	34,775

1998 Winston Cup Series Race No. 27
September 27, 1998 Average Speed: 73.35

Driver	Owner	Car #	Make	Laps	Winnings
1. Ricky Rudd	Ricky Rudd	10	Ford	500	102,575
2. Jeff Gordon	Rick Hendrick	24	Chev	500	73,525
3. Mark Martin	Jack Roush	6	Ford	500	56,875
4. Rich Bickle	Cale Yarborough	98	Ford	500	54,525
5. Jeff Burton	Jack Roush	99	Ford	500	46,925

1999 Winston Cup Series Race No. 28
October 3, 1999 Average Speed: 72.624

Driver	Owner	Car #	Make	Laps	Winnings
1. Jeff Gordon	Rick Hendrick	24	Chev	500	110,090
2. Dale Earnhardt	Richard Childress	3	Chev	500	70,225
3. Geoffrey Bodine	Joe Bessey	60	Chev	500	50,475
4. Rusty Wallace	Roger Penske	2	Ford	500	53,325
5. Kenny Wallace	Andy Petree	55	Chev	500	51,715

2000 Winston Cup Series Race No. 28
October 1, 2000 Average Speed: 73.859

Driver	Owner	Car #	Make	Laps	Winnings
1. Tony Stewart	Joe Gibbs	20	Pont	500	125,875
2. Dale Earnhardt	Richard Childress	3	Chev	500	77,925
3. Jeff Burton	Jack Roush	99	Ford	500	83,225
4. Ricky Rudd	Robert Yates	28	Ford	500	59,275
5. Jeff Gordon	Rick Hendrick	24	Chev	500	59,075

2001 Winston Cup Series Race No. 30
October 15, 2001 Average Speed: 75.75

Driver	Owner	Car #	Make	Laps	Winnings
1. Ricky Craven	Cal Wells	32	Ford	500	130,475
2. Dale Jarrett	Robert Yates	88	Ford	500	114,252
3. Ward Burton	Bill Davis	22	Dodg	500	94,460
4. Bobby Labonte	Joe Gibbs	18	Pont	500	104,537
5. Jeff Burton	Jack Roush	99	Ford	500	96,846

2002 Winston Cup Series Race No. 32
October 20, 2002 Average Speed: 74.651

Driver	Owner	Car #	Make	Laps	Winnings
1. Kurt Busch	Jack Roush	97	Ford	500	142,175
2. Johnny Benson, Jr.	Nelson Bowers	10	Pont	500	105,450
3. Ricky Rudd	Robert Yates	28	Ford	500	110,417
4. Dale Earnhardt, Jr.	Dale Earnhardt, Inc.	8	Chev	500	75,870
5. Ward Burton	Bill Davis	22	Dodg	500	106,675

Norfolk Speedway
Norfolk, VA
.4-mile Dirt Track

Half-mile dirt track opened briefly in 1949. Re-opened in 1956. First NASCAR Winston Cup (then Grand National) race staged on 8/22/56 (won by Billy Myers). Final Grand National race run on 7/24/57 (won by Buck Baker). Track closed shortly after last NASCAR race.

Winston Cup Starts

Johnny Allen	2
Buck Baker	2
Bill Champion	2
Billy Myers	2
Jim Paschal	2
Lee Petty	2
Fireball Roberts	2
Joe Weatherly	2

Winston Cup Victories

Buck Baker	1
Billy Myers	1

Winston Cup Poles

Bill Amick	1
Ralph Moody	1

Winston Cup Money

Buck Baker	$1,250

Most Cars Started
23—July 24, 1957

Fewest Cars Started
14—August 22, 1956

Narrowest Margin of Victory
N/A

Slowest Race
47.987 MPH—July 24, 1957

Race Record
56.408 MPH—August 22, 1956

Most Race Leaders
N/A

Most Cars Running at Finish
14—July 24, 1957

1956 Grand National Race No. 40
August 22, 1956 Average Speed: 56.408

Driver	Owner	Car #	Make	Laps	Winnings
1. Billy Myers	Bill Stroppe	4	56 Merc	250	850
2. Jim Paschal	Frank Hayworth	75	56 Merc	249	625
3. Rex White	Bob Welborn	X	56 Chev	246	450
4. Buck Baker	Carl Kiekhaefer	501	56 Dodg	245	350
5. Johnny Allen	Spook Crawford	264	56 Plym	241	310

1957 Grand National Race No. 33
July 24, 1957 Average Speed: 47.987

Driver	Owner	Car #	Make	Laps	Winnings
1. Buck Baker	Buck Baker	87	57 Chev	250	900
2. Joe Weatherly	Holman-Moody	12	57 Ford	249	575
3. Jim Paschal	Frank Hayworth	75	56 Merc	249	375
4. Billy Myers	Billy Myers	14	57 Merc	248	280
5. Jack Smith	Jack Smith	47	57 Chev	245	245

Old Dominion Speedway
Manassas, VA
.375-Mile Paved Track

(aka Longview Speedway) .375-mile dirt track opened in September 1948. Track paved in 1952. Re-measured at .333-mile oval. First NASCAR Winston Cup (then Grand National) race staged on 4/25/58 (won by Frankie Schneider). Final Grand National race run on 7/7/66 (won by Elmo Langley). Track still in operation.

Winston Cup Starts
Elmo Langley   7

Winston Cup Victories
Ned Jarrett   2
Richard Petty   2

Winston Cup Poles
Ned Jarrett   3

Winston Cup Money
Ned Jarrett $4,275

Most Cars Started
30—September 17, 1965

Fewest Cars Started
16—May 18, 1963

Narrowest Margin of Victory
N/A

Slowest Race
67.590 MPH—April 25, 1958

Race Record
70.275 MPH—May 18, 1963

Most Cautions
2—July 7, 1966

Most Race Leaders
3—September 18, 1964
3—September 17, 1965
3—July 7, 1966

Most Cars Running at Finish
22—September 17, 1965

1958 Grand National Race No. 13
April 25, 1958 Average Speed: 67.590

Driver	Owner	Car #	Make	Laps	Winnings
1. Frankie Schneider	Frankie Schneider	62	57 Chev	150	600
2. Jack Smith	Jack Smith	47	57 Chev	150	475
3. Rex White	J. H. Petty	44	57 Chev	148	355
4. Lee Petty	Petty Enterprises	42	57 Olds	148	280
5. Johnny Allen	Spook Crawford	64	57 Plym	147	240

1964 Grand National Race No. 36 Old Dominion 400
July 8, 1964 Average Speed: 67.652

Driver	Owner	Car #	Make	Laps	Winnings
1. Ned Jarrett	Bondy Long	11	64 Ford	400	1,100
2. David Pearson	Cotton Owens	6	64 Dodg	399	625
3. Jimmy Pardue	Charles Robinson	54	64 Plym	388	450
4. Curtis Crider	Curtis Crider	02	63 Merc	371	350
5. Buddy Arrington	Buddy Arrington	78	63 Dodg	370	325

1965 Grand National Race No. 30
July 8, 1965 Average Speed: 68.165

Driver	Owner	Car #	Make	Laps	Winnings
1. Junior Johnson	Rex Lovette	26	65 Ford	400	1,100
2. Dick Hutcherson	Holman-Moody	29	65 Ford	400	625
3. Ned Jarrett	Bondy Long	11	65 Ford	398	450
4. Cale Yarborough	Kenny Myler	06	64 Ford	393	350
5. Dick Dixon	Dan Colone	8	63 Ford	388	325

1963 Grand National Race No. 24
May 18, 1963 Average Speed: 70.275

Driver	Owner	Car #	Make	Laps	Winnings
1. Richard Petty	Petty Enterprises	41	63 Pont	300	1,000
2. Ned Jarrett	Charles Robinson	11	63 Ford	299	600
3. Jim Paschal	Petty Enterprises	43	63 Plym	298	400
4. Larry Thomas	Wade Younts	36	62 Dodg	292	300
5. Elmo Langley	Henry Woodfield	64	62 Ford	289	275

1964 Grand National Race No. 54
September 18, 1964 Average Speed: 68.842

Driver	Owner	Car #	Make	Laps	Winnings
1. Ned Jarrett	Bondy Long	11	64 Ford	500	1,500
2. David Pearson	Cotton Owens	6	64 Dodg	499	1,000
3. Richard Petty	Petty Enterprises	41	64 Plym	496	725
4. Larry Thomas	Herman Beam	19	64 Ford	480	600
5. Bert Robbins	Henry Woodfield	84	63 Ford	467	400

1965 Grand National Race No. 48
September 17, 1965 Average Speed: 67.890

Driver	Owner	Car #	Make	Laps	Winnings
1. Richard Petty	Petty Enterprises	43	65 Plym	400	1,300
2. Ned Jarrett	Bondy Long	11	65 Ford	399	625
3. Buddy Baker	Buck Baker	86	64 Dodg	396	450
4. Tiny Lund	Lyle Stelter	55	64 Ford	396	350
5. Tom Pistone	Glenn Sweet	59	64 Ford	393	325

1966 Grand National Race No. 29
July 7, 1966 Average Speed: 68.079

Driver	Owner	Car #	Make	Laps	Winnings
1. Elmo Langley	Henry Woodfield	64	64 Ford	400	1,100
2. John Sears	L. G. DeWitt	4	64 Ford	393	625
3. James Hylton	Bud Hartje	48	65 Dodg	393	450
4. Larry Manning	Bob Adams	63	65 Plym	393	350
5. Buck Baker	Buck Baker	87	66 Olds	392	325

Princess Anne Speedway
Norfolk, VA
Half-mile Dirt Track

First opened as 1-mile dirt track in 1930s. Half-mile dirt track built in 1950. Only NASCAR Winston Cup (then Grand National) race staged on 8/23/53 (won by Herb Thomas). Closed in 1954. Sold for housing development in 1955. Now the site of a shopping center.

Winston Cup Victories
Herb Thomas   1

Winston Cup Poles
Curtis Turner   1

Winston Cup Money
Herb Thomas $1,000

Most Cars Started
19—August 23, 1953

Narrowest Margin of Victory
N/A

Race Record
51.040 MPH—August 23, 1953

Most Race Leaders
N/A

Most Cars Running at Finish
N/A

1953 Grand National Race No. 28
August 23, 1953 Average Speed: 51.040

Driver	Owner	Car #	Make	Laps	Winnings
1. Herb Thomas	Herb Thomas	92	53 Huds	200	1,000
2. Fonty Flock	Frank Christian	14	53 Huds	—	700
3. Lee Petty	Petty Enterprises	42	53 Dodg	—	450
4. Dick Rathmann	Walt Chapman	120	53 Huds	—	350
5. Jim Paschal	George Hutchens	80	53 Dodg	—	200

Richmond Int'l Raceway
Richmond, VA
.75-mile Paved Track

(aka Fairgrounds Speedway; Strawberry Hill; Atlantic Rural Exposition Fairgrounds; Virginia State Fairgrounds; Strawberry Hill Speedway; Richmond Fairgrounds) Half-mile dirt oval opened in October 1946. First NASCAR Winston Cup (then Grand National) race staged on 4/19/53 (Lee Petty won). Track paved in 1968. Re-measured as .563-mile oval in 1970. Re-measured in 1971 as .542-mile oval. Track re-designed in 1988 as .75-mile D-shaped oval. Davey Allison won first race on big track (9/11/88).

Winston Cup Starts
Richard Petty   63

Winston Cup Victories
Richard Petty   13

Winston Cup Poles
Bobby Allison   8
Richard Petty   8

Winston Cup Money
Rusty Wallace $1,350,660

Most Cars Started
43—11 times

Fewest Cars Started
12—April 23, 1961

Narrowest Margin of Victory
0.051 seconds—September 12, 1998

Slowest Race
45.535 MPH—April 19, 1953

Race Record
108.707 MPH—September 6, 1997

Most Cautions
14—3 times

Most Race Leaders
12—September 7, 1986
Wrangler Jeans Indigo 400

Most Cars Running at Finish
42—September 8, 2001

1953 Grand National Race No. 6
April 19, 1953 Average Speed: 45.535

Driver	Owner	Car #	Make	Laps	Winnings
1. Lee Petty	Petty Enterprises	42	53 Dodg	200	1,000
2. Dick Rathmann	Walt Chapman	120	52 Huds	—	700
3. Buck Baker	Griffin Motors	87	53 Olds	—	450
4. Dick Passwater	Frank Arford	78	53 Olds	—	350
5. Bill Blair	Bill Blair	2	53 Olds	—	200

1956 Grand National Race No. 12
April 29, 1956 Average Speed: 56.232

Driver	Owner	Car #	Make	Laps	Winnings
1. Buck Baker	Carl Kiekhaefer	87	56 Dodg	200	1,100
2. Herb Thomas	Carl Kiekhaefer	92	56 Dodg	199	700
3. Speedy Thompson	Carl Kiekhaefer	300	56 Chrys	199	475
4. Billy Myers	Bill Stroppe	14	56 Merc	198	365
5. Jimmy Massey	Hubert Westmoreland	2	56 Chev	197	310

1958 Grand National Race No. 46
September 14, 1958 Average Speed: 57.878

Driver	Owner	Car #	Make	Laps	Winnings
1. Speedy Thompson	Speedy Thompson	46	57 Chev	200	800
2. Lee Petty	Petty Enterprises	42	57 Olds	200	525
3. Tommy Irwin	Tommy Irwin	16	57 Ford	197	350
4. Buck Baker	Buck Baker	87	57 Chev	195	250
5. John Findlay	John Findlay	100	57 Chev	189	225

1959 Grand National Race No. 38
September 13, 1959 Average Speed: 60.382

Driver	Owner	Car #	Make	Laps	Winnings
1. Cotton Owens	Cotton Owens	6	59 Ford	200	800
2. Lee Petty	Petty Enterprises	42	59 Plym	200	625
3. Tom Pistone	Carl Rupert	59	59 Ford	198	375
4. Reds Kagle	Hoss Kagle	88	57 Chev	194	275
5. Runt Harris	Junie Donlavey	90	57 Chev	193	250

1960 Grand National Race No. 43
October 23, 1960 Average Speed: 63.739

Driver	Owner	Car #	Make	Laps	Winnings
1. Speedy Thompson	Wood Brothers	21	60 Ford	200	800
2. Junior Johnson	John Masoni	27	59 Chev	200	525
3. Ned Jarrett	Ned Jarrett	11	60 Ford	200	375
4. Richard Petty	Petty Enterprises	43	60 Plym	197	275
5. Fred Harb	Fred Harb	17	59 Ford	197	250

1955 Grand National Race No. 16
May 22, 1955 Average Speed: 54.298

Driver	Owner	Car #	Make	Laps	Winnings
1. Tim Flock	Carl Kiekhaefer	300	55 Chrys	200	1,000
2. Fonty Flock	Carl Kiekhaefer	301	55 Chrys	200	650
3. Lee Petty	Petty Enterprises	42	55 Chrys	200	450
4. Jim Paschal	Ernest Woods	78	55 Olds	199	350
5. Junior Johnson	B & L Motors	55	55 Olds	197	300

1957 Grand National Race No. 16
May 5, 1957 Average Speed: 62.445

Driver	Owner	Car #	Make	Laps	Winnings
1. Paul Goldsmith	Pete DePaolo	12	57 Ford	200	700
2. Fireball Roberts	Pete DePaolo	22	57 Ford	199	525
3. Marvin Panch	Pete DePaolo	98	57 Ford	199	400
4. Frankie Schneider	Hugh Babb	45	57 Chev	194	330
5. Jim Paschal	Bill Stroppe	17	57 Merc	188	270

1959 Grand National Race No. 23
June 21, 1959 Average Speed: 56.881

Driver	Owner	Car #	Make	Laps	Winnings
1. Tom Pistone	Carl Rupert	59	59 Ford	200	900
2. Glen Wood	Wood Brothers	21	58 Ford	200	525
3. Buck Baker	Buck Baker	87	59 Chev	200	350
4. Bob Welborn	Jerry Draper	79	57 Chev	199	250
5. Cotton Owens	W. H. Watson	6	58 Pont	191	225

1960 Grand National Race No. 19
June 5, 1960 Average Speed: 62.251

Driver	Owner	Car #	Make	Laps	Winnings
1. Lee Petty	Petty Enterprises	42	60 Plym	200	900
2. Rex White	Rex White	4	59 Chev	200	525
3. Ned Jarrett	Ned Jarrett	11	60 Ford	199	375
4. Doug Yates	Raeford Johnson	23	59 Plym	198	275
5. Glen Wood	Wood Brothers	21	59 Ford	197	250

1961 Grand National Race No. 17
April 23, 1961 Average Speed: 62.456

Driver	Owner	Car #	Make	Laps	Winnings
1. Richard Petty	Petty Enterprises	43	60 Plym	200	950
2. Cotton Owens	Cotton Owens	6	60 Pont	199	625
3. Buck Baker	Buck Baker	86	61 Chrys	193	425
4. Ned Jarrett	Bee Gee Holloway	11	61 Chev	186	275
5. Elmo Langley	Doc White	61	59 Ford	186	250

Richmond Int'l Raceway *continued*

1961 Grand National Race No. 44
September 10, 1961 Average Speed: 61.677

Driver	Owner	Car #	Make	Laps	Winnings
1. Joe Weatherly	Bud Moore	8	61 Pont	250	1,350
2. Junior Johnson	Rex Lovette	27	60 Pont	250	850
3. Rex White	Rex White	4	61 Chev	249	750
4. Ned Jarrett	Bee Gee Holloway	11	61 Chev	249	450
5. Jim Paschal	J. H. Petty	44	61 Pont	248	300

1962 Grand National Race No. 47 Capital City 300
September 9, 1962 Average Speed: 64.981

Driver	Owner	Car #	Make	Laps	Winnings
1. Joe Weatherly	Bud Moore	8	62 Pont	300	2,000
2. Jim Paschal	Petty Enterprises	41	62 Plym	299	1,350
3. Fred Lorenzen	Holman-Moody	26	62 Ford	296	950
4. Richard Petty	Petty Enterprises	42	62 Plym	296	675
5. Rex White	Rex White	4	62 Chev	294	510

1963 Grand National Race No. 47 Capital City 300
September 8, 1963 Average Speed: 66.339

Driver	Owner	Car #	Make	Laps	Winnings
1. Ned Jarrett	Charles Robinson	11	63 Ford	300	2,200
2. Rex White	Rex White	4	63 Merc	298	1,475
3. Larry Frank	Bondy Long	99	63 Ford	293	1,050
4. G. C. Spencer	G. C. Spencer	03	62 Chev	291	775
5. Fred Lorenzen	Holman-Moody	28	63 Ford	289	560

1964 Grand National Race No. 53 Capital City 300
September 14, 1964 Average Speed: 61.955

Driver	Owner	Car #	Make	Laps	Winnings
1. Cotton Owens	Cotton Owens	5	64 Dodg	300	2,400
2. David Pearson	Cotton Owens	6	64 Dodg	299	1,600
3. Richard Petty	Petty Enterprises	41	64 Plym	292	1,200
4. Larry Thomas	Herman Beam	19	64 Ford	289	900
5. Ned Jarrett	Bondy Long	11	64 Ford	280	710

1965 Grand National Race No. 49 Capital City 300
September 18, 1965 Average Speed: 60.983

Driver	Owner	Car #	Make	Laps	Winnings
1. David Pearson	Cotton Owens	6	65 Dodg	300	2,300
2. Darel Dieringer	Bud Moore	15	64 Merc	299	1,525
3. Junior Johnson	Rex Lovette	26	65 Ford	298	1,200
4. J. T. Putney	Herman Beam	19	65 Chev	298	875
5. Neil Castles	Buck Baker	89	65 Olds	278	710

1966 Grand National Race No. 44 Capital City 300
September 11, 1966 Average Speed: 62.886

Driver	Owner	Car #	Make	Laps	Winnings
1. David Pearson	Cotton Owens	6	66 Dodg	300	2,350
2. Buck Baker	Buck Baker	87	66 Olds	295	1,600
3. Paul Lewis	Paul Lewis	1	65 Plym	295	1,250
4. Curtis Turner	Toy Bolton	47	66 Chev	292	875
5. Elmo Langley	Henry Woodfield	64	64 Ford	286	710

1967 Grand National Race No. 42 Capital City 300
September 10, 1967 Average Speed: 57.631

Driver	Owner	Car #	Make	Laps	Winnings
1. Richard Petty	Petty Enterprises	43	67 Plym	300	2,450
2. Dick Hutcherson	Bondy Long	29	67 Ford	300	1,540
3. Paul Goldsmith	Ray Nichels	99	67 Plym	299	1,210
4. Sam McQuagg	Cotton Owens	6	67 Dodg	289	875
5. James Hylton	Bud Hartje	48	65 Dodg	285	710

1962 Grand National Race No. 10 Richmond 250
April 1, 1962 Average Speed: 51.363

Driver	Owner	Car #	Make	Laps	Winnings
1. Rex White	Rex White	4	61 Chev	180	1,850
2. Ned Jarrett	Bee Gee Holloway	11	62 Chev	179	1,300
3. Junior Johnson	Rex Lovette	27	61 Pont	178	800
4. Joe Weatherly	Bud Moore	8	61 Pont	168	600
5. Fireball Roberts	Rex Lovette	22	61 Pont	163	450

1963 Grand National Race No. 15 Richmond 250
April 7, 1963 Average Speed: 58.624

Driver	Owner	Car #	Make	Laps	Winnings
1. Joe Weatherly	Bud Moore	8	63 Pont	250	2,400
2. Ned Jarrett	Charles Robinson	11	63 Ford	249	1,300
3. Rex White	Rex White	4	62 Chev	247	900
4. Billy Wade	Cotton Owens	5	63 Dodg	245	625
5. Junior Johnson	Ray Fox	3	63 Chev	242	450

1964 Grand National Race No. 9 Richmond 250
March 8 & 10, 1964 Average Speed: 60.233

Driver	Owner	Car #	Make	Laps	Winnings
1. David Pearson	Cotton Owens	6	64 Dodg	250	1,500
2. Richard Petty	Petty Enterprises	43	64 Plym	250	1,000
3. Billy Wade	Bud Moore	1	64 Merc	250	750
4. Junior Johnson	Ray Fox	3	64 Dodg	249	600
5. Doug Yates	Louie Weathersby	45	63 Plym	249	450

1965 Grand National Race No. 7 Richmond 250
March 7, 1965 Average Speed: 61.416

Driver	Owner	Car #	Make	Laps	Winnings
1. Junior Johnson	Rex Lovette	26	65 Ford	250	2,200
2. Buck Baker	Buck Baker	88	64 Dodg	250	1,275
3. J. T. Putney	Herman Beam	19	65 Chev	242	900
4. Curtis Crider	Curtis Crider	02	64 Merc	238	600
5. Bob Derrington	Bob Derrington	68	63 Ford	237	450

1966 Grand National Race No. 19 Richmond 250
May 15, 1966 Average Speed: 66.539

Driver	Owner	Car #	Make	Laps	Winnings
1. David Pearson	Cotton Owens	6	64 Dodg	250	2,050
2. Richard Petty	Petty Enterprises	43	66 Plym	248	1,250
3. J. T. Putney	J. T. Putney	19	66 Chev	244	950
4. Darel Dieringer	Reid Shaw	0	64 Ford	242	700
5. Paul Goldsmith	Ray Nichels	99	65 Plym	241	550

1967 Grand National Race No. 16 Richmond 250
April 30, 1967 Average Speed: 65.982

Driver	Owner	Car #	Make	Laps	Winnings
1. Richard Petty	Petty Enterprises	43	67 Plym	250	2,150
2. Bobby Allison	Cotton Owens	6	67 Dodg	250	1,300
3. Dick Hutcherson	Bondy Long	29	67 Ford	247	950
4. James Hylton	Bud Hartje	48	65 Dodg	241	700
5. Clyde Lynn	Clyde Lynn	20	66 Ford	231	550

1968 Grand National Race No. 6 Richmond 250
March 24, 1968 Average Speed: 65.217

Driver	Owner	Car #	Make	Laps	Winnings
1. David Pearson	Holman-Moody	17	68 Ford	250	2,300
2. Charlie Glotzbach	Cotton Owens	6	67 Dodg	249	1,275
3. Elmo Langley	Elmo Langley	64	66 Ford	237	950
4. Neil Castles	Neil Castles	88	67 Olds	237	700
5. Clyde Lynn	Clyde Lynn	20	66 Ford	232	550

Richmond Int'l Raceway *continued*

1968 Grand National Race No. 41 Capital City 300
September 8, 1968 Average Speed: 85.659

Driver	Owner	Car #	Make	Laps	Winnings
1. Richard Petty	Petty Enterprises	43	68 Plym	300	2,400
2. David Pearson	Holman-Moody	17	68 Ford	300	1,490
3. Cale Yarborough	Wood Brothers	21	68 Merc	299	1,210
4. Bobby Allison	Bobby Allison	2	66 Chev	299	875
5. Buddy Baker	Ray Fox	3	68 Dodg	298	710

1969 Grand National Race No. 43 Capital City 250
September 7, 1969 Average Speed: 76.388

Driver	Owner	Car #	Make	Laps	Winnings
1. Bobby Allison	Mario Rossi	22	69 Dodg	462	5,000
2. Sonny Hutchins	Junie Donlavey	90	67 Ford	459	2,575
3. Bobby Isaac	Nord Krauskopf	71	69 Dodg	456	1,775
4. David Pearson	Holman-Moody	17	69 Ford	455	1,250
5. John Sears	L. G. DeWitt	4	69 Ford	454	925

1970 Grand National Race No. 40 Capital City 500
September 13, 1970 Average Speed: 81.476

Driver	Owner	Car #	Make	Laps	Winnings
1. Richard Petty	Petty Enterprises	43	70 Plym	500	4,675
2. Bobby Allison	Bobby Allison	22	69 Dodg	498	2,550
3. Donnie Allison	Banjo Matthews	27	70 Ford	497	1,800
4. Bobby Isaac	Nord Krauskopf	71	69 Dodg	496	1,175
5. Sonny Hutchins	Junie Donlavey	90	69 Ford	492	950

1971 Winston Cup GN Race No. 46 Capital City 500
November 14, 1971 Average Speed: 80.025

Driver	Owner	Car #	Make	Laps	Winnings
1. Richard Petty	Petty Enterprises	43	71 Plym	500	4,450
2. Bobby Allison	Holman-Moody	12	71 Ford	499	2,585
3. Pete Hamilton	Cotton Owens	6	71 Plym	490	1,750
4. Charlie Glotzbach	R. Howard & J. Johnson	98	71 Chev	487	1,175
5. Elmo Langley	Elmo Langley	64	71 Ford	480	965

1972 Winston Cup GN Race No. 25 Capital City 500
September 10, 1972 Average Speed: 75.899

Driver	Owner	Car #	Make	Laps	Winnings
1. Richard Petty	Petty Enterprises	43	72 Plym	500	6,775
2. Bobby Allison	R. Howard & J. Johnson	12	72 Chev	500	4,825
3. Bill Dennis	H. J. Brooking	17	72 Chev	492	2,100
4. James Hylton	James Hylton	48	71 Ford	482	1,650
5. Dave Marcis	Dave Marcis	2	72 Dodg	479	1,400

1973 Winston Cup GN Race No. 23 Capital City 500
September 9, 1973 Average Speed: 63.215

Driver	Owner	Car #	Make	Laps	Winnings
1. Richard Petty	Petty Enterprises	43	73 Dodg	500	6,775
2. Cale Yarborough	R. Howard & J. Johnson	11	73 Chev	498	4,425
3. Bobby Allison	Bobby Allison	12	73 Chev	497	4,150
4. Benny Parsons	L. G. DeWitt	72	73 Chev	492	1,750
5. Buddy Arrington	Buddy Arrington	67	72 Dodg	482	1,580

1974 Winston Cup GN Race No. 24 Capital City 500
September 8, 1974 Average Speed: 64.430

Driver	Owner	Car #	Make	Laps	Winnings
1. Richard Petty	Petty Enterprises	43	74 Dodg	500	8,740
2. Benny Parsons	L. G. DeWitt	72	74 Chev	500	6,010
3. Richie Panch	Roy Thornley	98	72 Chev	493	3,295
4. Charlie Glotzbach	Junie Donlavey	90	72 Ford	491	1,985
5. Walter Ballard	Walter Ballard	30	74 Chev	487	1,510

1969 Grand National Race No. 14 Richmond 500
April 13, 1969 Average Speed: 73.752

Driver	Owner	Car #	Make	Laps	Winnings
1. David Pearson	Holman-Moody	17	69 Ford	500	3,650
2. Richard Petty	Petty Enterprises	43	69 Ford	499	1,800
3. Elmo Langley	Elmo Langley	64	68 Ford	483	1,075
4. Bill Seifert	Bill Seifert	45	68 Ford	465	675

1970 Grand National Race No. 5 Richmond 500
March 1, 1970 Average Speed: 82.044

Driver	Owner	Car #	Make	Laps	Winnings
1. James Hylton	James Hylton	48	69 Ford	500	5,195
2. Richard Petty	Petty Enterprises	43	70 Plym	500	2,970
3. Elmo Langley	Elmo Langley	64	69 Ford	491	1,845
4. Bobby Isaac	Nord Krauskopf	71	69 Dodg	485	1,220
5. Neil Castles	Neil Castles	06	69 Dodg	482	945

1971 Winston Cup GN Race No. 6 Richmond 500
March 7, 1971 Average Speed: 79.836

Driver	Owner	Car #	Make	Laps	Winnings
1. Richard Petty	Petty Enterprises	43	70 Plym	500	4,425
2. Bobby Isaac	Nord Krauskopf	71	70 Dodg	498	2,850
3. Benny Parsons	L. G. DeWitt	72	69 Ford	492	1,525
4. Bobby Allison	Bobby Allison	12	69 Dodg	491	1,125
5. Dave Marcis	Dave Marcis	2	69 Dodg	490	1,075

1972 Winston Cup GN Race No. 3 Richmond 500
February 27, 1972 Average Speed: 76.258

Driver	Owner	Car #	Make	Laps	Winnings
1. Richard Petty	Petty Enterprises	43	72 Plym	500	5,300
2. Bobby Allison	R. Howard & J. Johnson	12	72 Chev	499	4,025
3. Bobby Isaac	Nord Krauskopf	71	72 Dodg	493	3,175
4. Dave Marcis	Dave Marcis	2	70 Dodg	488	1,575
5. Bill Dennis	Junie Donlavey	90	71 Ford	485	1,400

1973 Winston Cup GN Race No. 3 Richmond 500
February 25, 1973 Average Speed: 74.764

Driver	Owner	Car #	Make	Laps	Winnings
1. Richard Petty	Petty Enterprises	43	73 Dodg	500	6,350
2. Buddy Baker	Nord Krauskopf	71	71 Dodg	500	4,050
3. Cale Yarborough	R. Howard & J. Johnson	11	73 Chev	497	3,450
4. Bobby Isaac	Bud Moore	15	72 Ford	495	2,900
5. Dave Marcis	Dave Marcis	2	71 Dodg	491	1,150

1974 Winston Cup GN Race No. 3 Richmond 500
February 24, 1974 Average Speed: 80.095

Driver	Owner	Car #	Make	Laps	Winnings
1. Bobby Allison	Bobby Allison	12	74 Chev	500	8,330
2. Richard Petty	Petty Enterprises	43	74 Dodg	500	5,455
3. Cale Yarborough	R. Howard & J. Johnson	11	74 Chev	494	5,505
4. Lennie Pond	Ronnie Elder	54	74 Chev	492	1,730
5. Dave Marcis	Dave Marcis	2	73 Dodg	487	1,705

1975 Winston Cup GN Race No. 3 Richmond 500
February 23, 1975 Average Speed: 74.913

Driver	Owner	Car #	Make	Laps	Winnings
1. Richard Petty	Petty Enterprises	43	74 Dodg	500	8,265
2. Lennie Pond	Ronnie Elder	54	75 Chev	494	4,410
3. Benny Parsons	L. G. DeWitt	72	75 Chev	491	4,435
4. Dick Brooks	Junie Donlavey	90	73 Ford	489	2,010
5. Elmo Langley	Elmo Langley	64	73 Ford	476	1,435

Richmond Int'l Raceway *continued*

1975 Winston Cup GN Race No. 26 Capital City 500
October 12, 1975 Average Speed: 81.886

Driver	Owner	Car #	Make	Laps	Winnings
1. Darrell Waltrip	DiGard	88	75 Chev	500	7,835
2. Lennie Pond	Ronnie Elder	54	75 Chev	499	4,210
3. Dick Brooks	Junie Donlavey	90	73 Ford	494	3,295
4. Cecil Gordon	Cecil Gordon	24	75 Chev	484	2,285
5. J. D. McDuffie	J. D. McDuffie	70	75 Chev	483	1,785

1976 Winston Cup GN Race No. 23 Capital City 400
September 12, 1976 Average Speed: 77.993

Driver	Owner	Car #	Make	Laps	Winnings
1. Cale Yarborough	Junior Johnson	11	Chev	400	10,300
2. Bobby Allison	Roger Penske	2	Merc	400	7,250
3. Richard Petty	Petty Enterprises	43	Dodg	399	7,180
4. Darrell Waltrip	DiGard	88	Chev	399	4,770
5. Buddy Baker	Bud Moore	15	Ford	398	4,225

1977 Winston Cup GN Race No. 23 Capital City 400
September 11, 1977 Average Speed: 80.644

Driver	Owner	Car #	Make	Laps	Winnings
1. Neil Bonnett	Jim Stacy	5	Dodg	400	8,700
2. Richard Petty	Petty Enterprises	43	Dodg	400	7,775
3. Benny Parsons	L. G. DeWitt	72	Chev	400	6,800
4. Cale Yarborough	Junior Johnson	11	Chev	400	5,950
5. Lennie Pond	Ronnie Elder	54	Chev	400	3,340

1978 Winston Cup GN Race No. 23 Capital City 400
September 10, 1978 Average Speed: 79.568

Driver	Owner	Car #	Make	Laps	Winnings
1. Darrell Waltrip	DiGard	88	Chev	400	13,800
2. Bobby Allison	Bud Moore	15	Ford	400	8,800
3. Neil Bonnett	Jim Stacy	5	Chev	400	6,575
4. Cale Yarborough	Junior Johnson	11	Olds	399	6,450
5. Dick Brooks	Junie Donlavey	90	Ford	397	3,300

1979 Winston Cup GN Race No. 24 Capital City 400
September 9, 1979 Average Speed: 80.604

Driver	Owner	Car #	Make	Laps	Winnings
1. Bobby Allison	Bud Moore	15	Ford	400	15,400
2. Darrell Waltrip	DiGard	88	Chev	400	9,525
3. Ricky Rudd	Junie Donlavey	90	Ford	399	5,650
4. Dale Earnhardt	Rod Osterlund	2	Chev	399	7,250
5. Cale Yarborough	Junior Johnson	11	Olds	398	5,975

1980 Winston Cup GN Race No. 24 Capital City 400
September 7, 1980 Average Speed: 79.722

Driver	Owner	Car #	Make	Laps	Winnings
1. Bobby Allison	Bud Moore	15	Ford	400	17,175
2. Richard Petty	Petty Enterprises	43	Chev	400	13,350
3. Lennie Pond	Jim Testa	68	Chev	400	5,150
4. Dale Earnhardt	Rod Osterlund	2	Chev	399	7,575
5. Jody Ridley	Junie Donlavey	90	Ford	398	4,710

1981 Winston Cup GN Race No. 24 Wrangler Sanfor-Set 400
September 13, 1981 Average Speed: 69.998

Driver	Owner	Car #	Make	Laps	Winnings
1. Benny Parsons	Bud Moore	15	Ford	400	18,525
2. Harry Gant	Hal Needham	33	Pont	400	10,195
3. Darrell Waltrip	Junior Johnson	11	Buick	400	12,500
4. Terry Labonte	Billy Hagan	44	Buick	400	7,550
5. Bobby Allison	Harry Ranier	28	Buick	400	7,275

1976 Winston Cup GN Race No. 4 Richmond 400
March 7, 1976 Average Speed: 72.792

Driver	Owner	Car #	Make	Laps	Winnings
1. Dave Marcis	Nord Krauskopf	71	Dodg	400	9,300
2. Richard Petty	Petty Enterprises	43	Dodg	400	8,025
3. Bobby Allison	Roger Penske	2	Merc	399	6,230
4. Cale Yarborough	Junior Johnson	11	Chev	388	4,745
5. Terry Bivins	Billy Moyer	63	Chev	386	2,050

1977 Winston Cup GN Race No. 3 Richmond 400
February 27, 1977 Average Speed: 73.084

Driver	Owner	Car #	Make	Laps	Winnings
1. Cale Yarborough	Junior Johnson	11	Chev	245	12,100
2. Darrell Waltrip	DiGard	88	Chev	245	7,775
3. Benny Parsons	L. G. DeWitt	72	Chev	245	6,325
4. Dave Marcis	Roger Penske	2	Chev	244	4,700
5. Bobby Allison	Bobby Allison	12	Mata	244	2,000

1978 Winston Cup GN Race No. 3 Richmond 400
February 26, 1978 Average Speed: 80.304

Driver	Owner	Car #	Make	Laps	Winnings
1. Benny Parsons	L. G. DeWitt	72	Chev	400	13,200
2. Lennie Pond	Harry Ranier	54	Chev	400	6,050
3. Cale Yarborough	Junior Johnson	11	Olds	399	8,050
4. Darrell Waltrip	DiGard	88	Chev	399	5,250
5. Dick Brooks	Junie Donlavey	90	Ford	397	3,325

1979 Winston Cup GN Race No. 4 Richmond 400
March 11, 1979 Average Speed: 83.608

Driver	Owner	Car #	Make	Laps	Winnings
1. Cale Yarborough	Junior Johnson	11	Olds	400	16,275
2. Bobby Allison	Bud Moore	15	Ford	400	10,750
3. Darrell Waltrip	DiGard	88	Chev	399	6,925
4. Benny Parsons	M. C. Anderson	27	Chev	399	2,550
5. Richard Petty	Petty Enterprises	43	Chev	399	4,800

1980 Winston Cup GN Race No. 3 Richmond 400
February 24, 1980 Average Speed: 67.703

Driver	Owner	Car #	Make	Laps	Winnings
1. Darrell Waltrip	DiGard	88	Chev	400	17,800
2. Bobby Allison	Bud Moore	15	Ford	400	10,975
3. Richard Petty	Petty Enterprises	43	Chev	400	9,375
4. Dave Marcis	Dave Marcis	71	Chev	400	4,310
5. Dale Earnhardt	Rod Osterlund	2	Chev	398	6,550

1981 Winston Cup GN Race No. 3 Richmond 400
February 22, 1981 Average Speed: 76.570

Driver	Owner	Car #	Make	Laps	Winnings
1. Darrell Waltrip	Junior Johnson	11	Buick	400	18,800
2. Ricky Rudd	DiGard	88	Olds	400	13,400
3. Richard Petty	Petty Enterprises	43	Buick	399	9,775
4. Morgan Shepherd	Cliff Stewart	5	Pont	399	5,100
5. Benny Parsons	Bud Moore	15	Ford	399	7,050

1982 Winston Cup GN Race No. 2 Richmond 400
February 21, 1982 Average Speed: 72.914

Driver	Owner	Car #	Make	Laps	Winnings
1. Dave Marcis	Dave Marcis	71	Chev	250	19,145
2. Richard Petty	Petty Enterprises	43	Pont	250	16,325
3. Benny Parsons	Harry Ranier	28	Pont	250	15,475
4. Dale Earnhardt	Bud Moore	15	Ford	250	10,960
5. Terry Labonte	Billy Hagan	44	Chev	249	6,330

Richmond Int'l Raceway *continued*

1982 Winston Cup GN Race No. 23 Wrangler Sanfor-Set 400
September 12, 1982 Average Speed: 82.800

Driver	Owner	Car #	Make	Laps	Winnings
1. Bobby Allison	DiGard	88	Chev	400	25,750
2. Tim Richmond	Jim Stacy	2	Buick	400	13,795
3. Darrell Waltrip	Junior Johnson	11	Buick	399	15,525
4. Ricky Rudd	Richard Childress	3	Pont	399	7,930
5. Neil Bonnett	Wood Brothers	21	Ford	398	3,710

1983 Winston Cup GN Race No. 2 Richmond 400
February 27, 1983 Average Speed: 79.584

Driver	Owner	Car #	Make	Laps	Winnings
1. Bobby Allison	DiGard	22	Chev	400	23,725
2. Dale Earnhardt	Bud Moore	15	Ford	400	16,575
3. Neil Bonnett	Bob Rahilly & Butch Mock	75	Chev	400	9,975
4. Geoff Bodine	Cliff Stewart	88	Pont	399	8,445
5. Harry Gant	Hal Needham	33	Buick	399	11,260

1983 Winston Cup GN Race No. 23 Wrangler Sanfor-Set 400
September 11, 1983 Average Speed: 79.381

Driver	Owner	Car #	Make	Laps	Winnings
1. Bobby Allison	DiGard	22	Buick	400	39,925
2. Ricky Rudd	Richard Childress	3	Chev	400	19,025
3. Darrell Waltrip	Junior Johnson	11	Chev	399	24,010
4. Bill Elliott	Harry Melling	9	Ford	399	8,270
5. Terry Labonte	Billy Hagan	44	Chev	398	8,005

1984 Winston Cup GN Race No. 2 Miller High Life 400
February 26, 1984 Average Speed: 76.736

Driver	Owner	Car #	Make	Laps	Winnings
1. Ricky Rudd	Bud Moore	15	Ford	400	31,775
2. Darrell Waltrip	Junior Johnson	11	Chev	400	27,865
3. Terry Labonte	Billy Hagan	44	Chev	400	12,465
4. Bill Elliott	Harry Melling	9	Ford	399	11,000
5. Neil Bonnett	Junior Johnson	12	Chev	399	4,820

1984 Winston Cup GN Race No. 23 Wrangler Sanfor-Set 400
September 9, 1984 Average Speed: 74.780

Driver	Owner	Car #	Make	Laps	Winnings
1. Darrell Waltrip	Junior Johnson	11	Chev	400	46,550
2. Ricky Rudd	Bud Moore	15	Ford	400	22,325
3. Dale Earnhardt	Richard Childress	3	Chev	400	13,450
4. Geoff Bodine	Rick Hendrick	5	Chev	399	10,400
5. Richard Petty	Mike Curb	43	Pont	399	7,730

1985 Winston Cup GN Race No. 2 Miller High Life 400
February 24, 1985 Average Speed: 67.945

Driver	Owner	Car #	Make	Laps	Winnings
1. Dale Earnhardt	Richard Childress	3	Chev	400	33,625
2. Geoff Bodine	Rick Hendrick	5	Chev	400	22,165
3. Darrell Waltrip	Junior Johnson	11	Chev	400	21,110
4. Ron Bouchard	Jack Beebe	47	Buick	400	9,530
5. Harry Gant	Hal Needham	33	Chev	399	12,120

1985 Winston Cup GN Race No. 21 Wrangler Sanfor-Set 400
September 8, 1985 Average Speed: 72.508

Driver	Owner	Car #	Make	Laps	Winnings
1. Darrell Waltrip	Junior Johnson	11	Chev	400	35,300
2. Terry Labonte	Billy Hagan	44	Chev	400	23,850
3. Richard Petty	Mike Curb	43	Pont	400	14,625
4. Dale Earnhardt	Richard Childress	3	Chev	400	12,050
5. Ricky Rudd	Bud Moore	15	Ford	400	9,900

1986 Winston Cup Race No. 2 Miller High Life 400
February 23, 1986 Average Speed: 71.078

Driver	Owner	Car #	Make	Laps	Winnings
1. Kyle Petty	Wood Brothers	7	Ford	400	37,880
2. Joe Ruttman	Kenny Bernstein	26	Buick	400	16,215
3. Dale Earnhardt	Richard Childress	3	Chev	400	19,310
4. Bobby Allison	Stavola Brothers	22	Buick	399	6,275
5. Darrell Waltrip	Junior Johnson	11	Chev	398	14,295

1986 Winston Cup Race No. 22 Wrangler Jeans Indigo 400
September 7, 1986 Average Speed: 70.161

Driver	Owner	Car #	Make	Laps	Winnings
1. Tim Richmond	Rick Hendrick	25	Chev	400	35,005
2. Dale Earnhardt	Richard Childress	3	Chev	400	24,525
3. Morgan Shepherd	Bob Rahilly & Butch Mock	75	Pont	400	13,655
4. Richard Petty	Petty Enterprises	43	Pont	400	10,260
5. Neil Bonnett	Junior Johnson	12	Chev	400	12,075

1987 Winston Cup Race No. 3 Miller High Life 400
March 8, 1987 Average Speed: 81.520

Driver	Owner	Car #	Make	Laps	Winnings
1. Dale Earnhardt	Richard Childress	3	Chev	400	49,150
2. Geoff Bodine	Rick Hendrick	5	Chev	400	24,010
3. Rusty Wallace	Raymond Beadle	27	Pont	400	18,225
4. Bill Elliott	Harry Melling	9	Ford	400	14,285
5. Terry Labonte	Junior Johnson	11	Chev	400	13,590

1987 Winston Cup Race No. 22 Wrangler Jeans Indigo 400
September 13, 1987 Average Speed: 67.074

Driver	Owner	Car #	Make	Laps	Winnings
1. Dale Earnhardt	Richard Childress	3	Chev	400	44,950
2. Darrell Waltrip	Rick Hendrick	17	Chev	400	22,680
3. Ricky Rudd	Bud Moore	15	Ford	400	20,050
4. Bill Elliott	Harry Melling	9	Ford	400	14,675
5. Richard Petty	Petty Enterprises	43	Pont	399	10,180

1988 Winston Cup Race No. 2 Pontiac Excitement 400
February 21, 1988 Average Speed: 66.401

Driver	Owner	Car #	Make	Laps	Winnings
1. Neil Bonnett	Bob Rahilly & Butch Mock	75	Pont	400	45,900
2. Ricky Rudd	Kenny Bernstein	26	Buick	400	25,660
3. Richard Petty	Petty Enterprises	43	Pont	400	16,975
4. Darrell Waltrip	Rick Hendrick	17	Chev	400	14,185
5. Sterling Marlin	Billy Hagan	44	Olds	400	12,315

1988 Winston Cup Race No. 22 Miller High Life 400
September 11, 1988 Average Speed: 95.770

Driver	Owner	Car #	Make	Laps	Winnings
1. Davey Allison	Harry Ranier	28	Ford	400	57,800
2. Dale Earnhardt	Richard Childress	3	Chev	400	29,625
3. Terry Labonte	Junior Johnson	11	Chev	400	20,525
4. Mark Martin	Jack Roush	6	Ford	400	10,925
5. Alan Kulwicki	Alan Kulwicki	7	Ford	400	15,825

1989 Winston Cup Race No. 4 Pontiac Excitement 400
March 26, 1989 Average Speed: 89.619

Driver	Owner	Car #	Make	Laps	Winnings
1. Rusty Wallace	Raymond Beadle	27	Pont	400	63,025
2. Alan Kulwicki	Alan Kulwicki	7	Ford	400	28,625
3. Dale Earnhardt	Richard Childress	3	Chev	400	30,900
4. Ricky Rudd	Kenny Bernstein	26	Buick	400	13,600
5. Davey Allison	Robert Yates	28	Ford	399	17,607

Richmond Int'l Raceway *continued*

1989 Winston Cup Race No. 22 Miller High Life 400
September 10, 1989 Average Speed: 88.380

Driver	Owner	Car #	Make	Laps	Winnings
1. Rusty Wallace	Raymond Beadle	27	Pont	400	55,650
2. Dale Earnhardt	Richard Childress	3	Chev	400	31,475
3. Geoff Bodine	Rick Hendrick	5	Chev	400	21,750
4. Ricky Rudd	Kenny Bernstein	26	Buick	399	16,450
5. Harry Gant	Leo Jackson	33	Olds	399	15,175

1990 Winston Cup Series Race No. 22 Miller Genuine Draft 400
September 9, 1990 Average Speed: 95.567

Driver	Owner	Car #	Make	Laps	Winnings
1. Dale Earnhardt	Richard Childress	3	Chev	400	59,225
2. Mark Martin	Jack Roush	6	Ford	400	30,550
3. Darrell Waltrip	Rick Hendrick	17	Chev	400	25,107
4. Bill Elliott	Harry Melling	9	Ford	400	16,950
5. Rusty Wallace	Raymond Beadle	27	Pont	400	19,525

1991 Winston Cup Series Race No. 22 Miller Genuine Draft 400
September 7, 1991 Average Speed: 101.361

Driver	Owner	Car #	Make	Laps	Winnings
1. Harry Gant	Leo Jackson	33	Olds	400	63,650
2. Davey Allison	Robert Yates	28	Ford	400	39,425
3. Rusty Wallace	Roger Penske	2	Pont	400	21,700
4. Ernie Irvan	Larry McClure	4	Chev	400	20,800
5. Ricky Rudd	Rick Hendrick	5	Chev	400	18,125

1992 Winston Cup Race No. 22 Miller Genuine Draft 400
September 12, 1992 Average Speed: 104.661

Driver	Owner	Car #	Make	Laps	Winnings
1. Rusty Wallace	Roger Penske	2	Pont	400	47,115
2. Mark Martin	Jack Roush	6	Ford	400	48,365
3. Darrell Waltrip	Darrell Waltrip	17	Chev	400	44,360
4. Dale Earnhardt	Richard Childress	3	Chev	400	29,655
5. Geoff Bodine	Bud Moore	15	Ford	400	19,980

1993 Winston Cup Series Race No. 23 Miller Genuine Draft 400
September 11, 1993 Average Speed: 99.917

Driver	Owner	Car #	Make	Laps	Winnings
1. Rusty Wallace	Roger Penske	2	Pont	400	49,415
2. Bill Elliott	Junior Johnson	11	Ford	400	54,665
3. Dale Earnhardt	Richard Childress	3	Chev	400	35,780
4. Ricky Rudd	Rick Hendrick	5	Chev	400	26,505
5. Brett Bodine	Kenny Bernstein	26	Ford	400	21,580

1994 Winston Cup Series Race No. 24 Miller Genuine Draft 400
September 10, 1994 Average Speed: 104.156

Driver	Owner	Car #	Make	Laps	Winnings
1. Terry Labonte	Rick Hendrick	5	Chev	400	67,765
2. Jeff Gordon	Rick Hendrick	24	Chev	400	40,365
3. Dale Earnhardt	Richard Childress	3	Chev	400	38,830
4. Rusty Wallace	Roger Penske	2	Ford	400	30,780
5. Ricky Rudd	Ricky Rudd	10	Ford	400	26,705

1995 Winston Cup Series Race No. 24 Miller Genuine Draft 400
September 9, 1995 Average Speed: 104.459

Driver	Owner	Car #	Make	Laps	Winnings
1. Rusty Wallace	Roger Penske	2	Ford	400	64,515
2. Terry Labonte	Rick Hendrick	5	Chev	400	49,065
3. Dale Earnhardt	Richard Childress	3	Chev	400	54,005
4. Dale Jarrett	Robert Yates	28	Ford	400	40,605
5. Bobby Hamilton	Petty Enterprises	43	Pont	400	26,805

1990 Winston Cup Series Race No. 2 Pontiac Excitement 400
February 25, 1990 Average Speed: 92.158

Driver	Owner	Car #	Make	Laps	Winnings
1. Mark Martin	Jack Roush	6	Ford	400	59,150
2. Dale Earnhardt	Richard Childress	3	Chev	400	42,600
3. Ricky Rudd	Rick Hendrick	5	Chev	400	25,050
4. Bill Elliott	Harry Melling	9	Ford	400	16,650
5. Dick Trickle	Cale Yarborough	66	Pont	400	14,325

1991 Winston Cup Series Race No. 2 Pontiac Excitement 400
February 24, 1991 Average Speed: 105.937

Driver	Owner	Car #	Make	Laps	Winnings
1. Dale Earnhardt	Richard Childress	3	Chev	400	67,950
2. Ricky Rudd	Rick Hendrick	5	Chev	400	45,675
3. Harry Gant	Leo Jackson	33	Olds	400	25,500
4. Rusty Wallace	Roger Penske	2	Pont	400	13,050
5. Alan Kulwicki	Alan Kulwicki	7	Ford	400	19,025

1992 Winston Cup Race No. 3 Pontiac Excitement 400
March 8, 1992 Average Speed: 104.378

Driver	Owner	Car #	Make	Laps	Winnings
1. Bill Elliott	Junior Johnson	11	Ford	400	272,700
2. Alan Kulwicki	Alan Kulwicki	7	Ford	400	36,525
3. Harry Gant	Leo Jackson	33	Olds	400	31,950
4. Davey Allison	Robert Yates	28	Ford	400	25,100
5. Darrell Waltrip	Darrell Waltrip	17	Chev	400	21,775

1993 Winston Cup Series Race No. 3 Pontiac Excitement 400
March 7, 1993 Average Speed: 107.000

Driver	Owner	Car #	Make	Laps	Winnings
1. Davey Allison	Robert Yates	28	Ford	400	70,125
2. Rusty Wallace	Roger Penske	2	Pont	400	31,550
3. Alan Kulwicki	Alan Kulwicki	7	Ford	400	39,225
4. Dale Jarrett	Joe Gibbs	18	Chev	400	29,050
5. Kyle Petty	Felix Sabates	42	Pont	400	21,600

1994 Winston Cup Series Race No. 3 Pontiac Excitement 400
March 4, 1994 Average Speed: 98.334

Driver	Owner	Car #	Make	Laps	Winnings
1. Ernie Irvan	Robert Yates	28	Ford	400	66,175
2. Rusty Wallace	Roger Penske	2	Ford	400	39,575
3. Jeff Gordon	Rick Hendrick	24	Chev	400	34,000
4. Dale Earnhardt	Richard Childress	3	Chev	400	29,550
5. Kyle Petty	Felix Sabates	42	Pont	400	26,500

1995 Winston Cup Series Race No. 3 Pontiac Excitement 400
March 5, 1995 Average Speed: 106.425

Driver	Owner	Car #	Make	Laps	Winnings
1. Terry Labonte	Rick Hendrick	5	Chev	400	82,950
2. Dale Earnhardt	Richard Childress	3	Chev	400	57,200
3. Rusty Wallace	Roger Penske	2	Ford	400	29,600
4. Ken Schrader	Rick Hendrick	25	Chev	400	31,100
5. Sterling Marlin	Larry McClure	4	Chev	400	34,400

1996 Winston Cup Series Race No. 3 Pontiac Excitement 400
March 3, 1996 Average Speed: 102.750

Driver	Owner	Car #	Make	Laps	Winnings
1. Jeff Gordon	Rick Hendrick	24	Chev	400	92,400
2. Dale Jarrett	Robert Yates	88	Ford	400	44,225
3. Ted Musgrave	Jack Roush	16	Ford	400	42,200
4. Jeff Burton	Jack Roush	99	Ford	400	22,350
5. Mark Martin	Jack Roush	6	Ford	400	37,850

Richmond Int'l Raceway *continued*

1996 Winston Cup Series Race No. 24 Miller Genuine Draft 400
September 7, 1996 Average Speed: 105.469

Driver	Owner	Car #	Make	Laps	Winnings
1. Ernie Irvan	Robert Yates	28	Ford	400	86,665
2. Jeff Gordon	Rick Hendrick	24	Chev	400	59,640
3. Jeff Burton	Jack Roush	99	Ford	400	50,755
4. Dale Jarrett	Robert Yates	88	Ford	400	30,505
5. Terry Labonte	Rick Hendrick	5	Chev	400	37,155

1997 Winston Cup Series Race No. 3
March 2, 1997 Average Speed: 108.499

Driver	Owner	Car #	Make	Laps	Winnings
1. Rusty Wallace	Roger Penske	2	Ford	400	86,775
2. Geoffrey Bodine	Geoffrey Bodine	7	Ford	400	56,875
3. Dale Jarrett	Robert Yates	88	Ford	400	50,750
4. Jeff Gordon	Rick Hendrick	24	Chev	399	46,200
5. Bobby Hamilton	Petty Enterprises	43	Pont	399	28,945

1997 Winston Cup Series Race No. 24
September 6, 1997 Average Speed: 108.707

Driver	Owner	Car #	Make	Laps	Winnings
1. Dale Jarrett	Robert Yates	88	Ford	400	91,490
2. Jeff Burton	Jack Roush	99	Ford	400	70,240
3. Jeff Gordon	Rick Hendrick	24	Chev	400	52,355
4. Geoffrey Bodine	Geoffrey Bodine	7	Ford	400	40,005
5. Rusty Wallace	Roger Penske	2	Ford	400	39,050

1998 Winston Cup Series Race No. 13
June 6, 1998 Average Speed: 97.044

Driver	Owner	Car #	Make	Laps	Winnings
1. Terry Labonte	Rick Hendrick	5	Chev	400	99,975
2. Dale Jarrett	Robert Yates	88	Ford	400	75,625
3. Rusty Wallace	Roger Penske	2	Ford	400	56,875
4. Ken Schrader	Andy Petree	33	Chev	400	62,075
5. Mark Martin	Jack Roush	6	Ford	400	65,025

1998 Winston Cup Series Race No. 25
September 12, 1998 Average Speed: 91.985

Driver	Owner	Car #	Make	Laps	Winnings
1. Jeff Burton	Jack Roush	99	Ford	400	108,495
2. Jeff Gordon	Rick Hendrick	24	Chev	400	85,190
3. Mark Martin	Jack Roush	6	Ford	400	60,580
4. Ken Schrader	Andy Petree	33	Chev	400	65,230
5. John Andretti	Petty Enterprises	43	Pont	400	52,280

1999 Winston Cup Series Race No. 11
May 15, 1999 Average Speed: 100.102

Driver	Owner	Car #	Make	Laps	Winnings
1. Dale Jarrett	Robert Yates	88	Ford	400	169,715
2. Mark Martin	Jack Roush	6	Ford	400	89,700
3. Bobby Labonte	Joe Gibbs	18	Pont	400	69,775
4. Bobby Hamilton	Larry McClure	4	Chev	400	64,875
5. Rusty Wallace	Roger Penske	2	Ford	400	49,450

1999 Winston Cup Series Race No. 25
September 11, 1999 Average Speed: 104.006

Driver	Owner	Car #	Make	Laps	Winnings
1. Tony Stewart	Joe Gibbs	20	Pont	400	136,160
2. Bobby Labonte	Joe Gibbs	18	Pont	400	77,990
3. Dale Jarrett	Robert Yates	88	Ford	400	64,605
4. Sterling Marlin	Felix Sabates	40	Chev	400	60,105
5. Kenny Irwin, Jr.	Robert Yates	28	Ford	400	49,570

2000 Winston Cup Series Race No. 11
May 6, 2000 Average Speed: 99.374

Driver	Owner	Car #	Make	Laps	Winnings
1. Dale Earnhardt, Jr.	Dale Earnhardt, Inc.	8	Chev	400	118,850
2. Terry Labonte	Rick Hendrick	5	Chev	400	85,925
3. Dale Jarrett	Robert Yates	88	Ford	400	78,525
4. Ricky Rudd	Robert Yates	28	Ford	400	63,025
5. Rusty Wallace	Roger Penske	2	Ford	400	68,625

2000 Winston Cup Series Race No. 25
September 9, 2000 Average Speed: 99.871

Driver	Owner	Car #	Make	Laps	Winnings
1. Jeff Gordon	Rick Hendrick	24	Chev	400	130,220
2. Dale Earnhardt	Richard Childress	3	Chev	400	81,190
3. Mark Martin	Jack Roush	6	Ford	400	69,130
4. Steve Park	Dale Earnhardt, Inc.	1	Chev	400	60,610
5. Jeff Burton	Jack Roush	99	Ford	400	79,780

2001 Winston Cup Series Race No. 11
May 5, 2001 Average Speed: 95.872

Driver	Owner	Car #	Make	Laps	Winnings
1. Tony Stewart	Joe Gibbs	20	Pont	400	150,175
2. Jeff Gordon	Rick Hendrick	24	Chev	400	133,827
3. Rusty Wallace	Roger Penske	2	Ford	400	117,740
4. Steve Park	Dale Earnhardt, Inc.	1	Chev	400	95,493
5. Ricky Rudd	Robert Yates	28	Ford	400	93,297

2001 Winston Cup Series Race No. 26
September 8, 2001 Average Speed: 95.146

Driver	Owner	Car #	Make	Laps	Winnings
1. Ricky Rudd	Robert Yates	28	Ford	400	0
2. Kevin Harvick	Richard Childress	29	Chev	400	0
3. Dale Earnhardt, Jr.	Dale Earnhardt, Inc.	8	Chev	400	0
4. Dale Jarrett	Robert Yates	88	Ford	400	0
5. Rusty Wallace	Roger Penske	2	Ford	400	0

2002 Winston Cup Series Race No. 11
May 5, 2002 Average Speed: 86.824

Driver	Owner	Car #	Make	Laps	Winnings
1. Tony Stewart	Joe Gibbs	20	Pont	400	185,653
2. Ryan Newman	Roger Penske	12	Ford	400	121,950
3. Jeff Burton	Jack Roush	99	Ford	400	126,067
4. Mark Martin	Jack Roush	6	Ford	400	106,708
5. Jeremy Mayfield	Ray Evernham	19	Dodg	400	67,950

2002 Winston Cup Series Race No. 26
September 7, 2002 Average Speed: 94.787

Driver	Owner	Car #	Make	Laps	Winnings
1. Matt Kenseth	Jack Roush	17	Ford	400	163,595
2. Ryan Newman	Roger Penske	12	Ford	400	127,340
3. Jeff Green	Richard Childress	30	Chev	400	80,930
4. Dale Earnhardt, Jr.	Dale Earnhardt, Inc.	8	Chev	400	87,205
5. Todd Bodine	Travis Carter	26	Ford	400	92,142

South Boston Speedway
South Boston, VA
Quarter-mile Paved Track

Quarter-mile dirt oval opened in August 1957. First NASCAR Winston Cup (then Grand National) race staged on 8/20/60 (won by Junior Johnson). Re-measured as .375-mile oval in 1962 and again as .357-mile oval in 1970. Final Winston Cup Grand National race run on 5/9/71 (won by Benny Parsons, his first Winston Cup victory). Track still in operation, operating as .4-mile oval.

Winston Cup Starts
Richard Petty 10

Winston Cup Victories
Richard Petty 5

Winston Cup Poles
Bobby Isaac 2
Ned Jarrett 2
Richard Petty 2
Jack Smith 2

Winston Cup Money
Richard Petty $8,735

Most Cars Started
28—May 9, 1971 Halifax County 100

Fewest Cars Started
15—August 20, 1960

Narrowest Margin of Victory
5 car lengths—August 23, 1968

Narrowest Margin of Victory
8.000 seconds May 17, 1964

Slowest Race
48.348 MPH—August 27, 1961

Race Record
76.906 MPH—August 21, 1969
South Boston 100

Most Cautions
3—May 17, 1964

Most Race Leaders
4—October 20, 1963 South Boston 400
4—May 17, 1964

Most Cars Running at Finish
17—June 23, 1962

1960 Grand National Race No. 33
August 20, 1960 Average Speed: 50.732

Driver	Owner	Car #	Make	Laps	Winnings
1. Junior Johnson	John Masoni	27	59 Chev	150	810
2. Possum Jones	Tom Daniels	2	60 Chev	149	545
3. Rex White	Rex White	4	59 Chev	148	410
4. Buck Baker	Buck Baker	87	60 Chev	147	290
5. Fred Harb	Fred Harb	17	58 Ford	146	260

1961 Grand National Race No. 41
August 27, 1961 Average Speed: 48.348

Driver	Owner	Car #	Make	Laps	Winnings
1. Junior Johnson	Rex Lovette	27	60 Pont	200	800
2. Jim Reed	Jim Reed	7	61 Chev	199	525
3. Ned Jarrett	Bee Gee Holloway	11	61 Chev	197	375
4. Emanuel Zervakis	Monroe Shook	85	60 Chev	196	275
5. Rex White	Rex White	4	60 Chev	195	350

1962 Grand National Race No. 28
June 23, 1962 Average Speed: 72.540

Driver	Owner	Car #	Make	Laps	Winnings
1. Rex White	Rex White	4	62 Chev	267	1,000
2. Jack Smith	Jack Smith	47	61 Pont	267	600
3. Richard Petty	Petty Enterprises	43	62 Plym	267	400
4. Johnny Allen	Fred Lovette	58	61 Pont	265	300
5. Larry Thomas	Wade Younts	36	62 Dodg	262	275

1963 Grand National Race No. 17 South Boston 400
April 14, 1963 Average Speed: 75.229

Driver	Owner	Car #	Make	Laps	Winnings
1. Richard Petty	Petty Enterprises	43	63 Plym	400	1,500
2. Jim Paschal	Petty Enterprises	41	62 Plym	398	900
3. Ned Jarrett	Charles Robinson	11	63 Ford	394	700
4. Larry Manning	Bob Adams	09	62 Chev	374	550
5. Earl Brooks	Wendell Scott	134	61 Chev	369	450

1963 Grand National Race No. 53 South Boston 400
October 20, 1963 Average Speed: 76.325

Driver	Owner	Car #	Make	Laps	Winnings
1. Richard Petty	Petty Enterprises	41	63 Plym	400	1,550
2. David Pearson	Cotton Owens	6	63 Dodg	397	900
3. Joe Weatherly	Bud Moore	8	63 Pont	396	925
4. Bob Welborn	Petty Enterprises	42	63 Plym	394	550
5. Larry Thomas	Wade Younts	36	62 Dodg	388	450

1964 Grand National Race No. 24
May 17, 1964 Average Speed: 71.957

Driver	Owner	Car #	Make	Laps	Winnings
1. Richard Petty	Petty Enterprises	43	63 Plym	267	1,000
2. Marvin Panch	Wood Brothers	21	64 Ford	267	600
3. Ned Jarrett	Bondy Long	11	64 Ford	265	400
4. David Pearson	Cotton Owens	6	64 Dodg	260	300
5. Roy Mayne	Bob Adams	09	62 Chev	256	275

1968 Grand National Race No. 37
August 23, 1968 Average Speed: 75.916

Driver	Owner	Car #	Make	Laps	Winnings
1. Richard Petty	Petty Enterprises	43	68 Plym	267	1,200
2. David Pearson	Holman-Moody	17	68 Ford	267	600
3. Bobby Isaac	Nord Krauskopf	71	67 Dodg	267	400
4. Charlie Glotzbach	Cotton Owens	6	68 Dodg	265	300
5. Buddy Baker	Ray Fox	3	68 Dodg	264	255

1969 Grand National Race No. 38 South Boston 100
August 21, 1969 Average Speed: 76.906

Driver	Owner	Car #	Make	Laps	Winnings
1. Bobby Isaac	Nord Krauskopf	71	68 Dodg	267	1,000
2. David Pearson	Holman-Moody	17	69 Ford	267	800
3. Richard Petty	Petty Enterprises	43	69 Ford	266	400
4. James Hylton	James Hylton	48	68 Dodg	261	350
5. Elmo Langley	Elmo Langley	64	68 Ford	259	325

1970 Grand National Race No. 37 Halifax County 100
August 29, 1970 Average Speed: 73.060

Driver	Owner	Car #	Make	Laps	Winnings
1. Richard Petty	Petty Enterprises	43	70 Plym	281	1,500
2. Bobby Isaac	Nord Krauskopf	71	70 Dodg	281	900
3. Bobby Allison	Bobby Allison	22	69 Dodg	280	500
4. Benny Parsons	L. G. DeWitt	72	69 Ford	279	350
5. James Hylton	James Hylton	48	70 Ford	277	325

1971 Winston Cup GN Race No. 17 Halifax County 100
May 9, 1971 Average Speed: 72.271

Driver	Owner	Car #	Make	Laps	Winnings
1. Benny Parsons	L. G. DeWitt	72	70 Ford	281	1,500
2. Richard Petty	Petty Enterprises	43	71 Plym	280	900
3. James Hylton	James Hylton	48	71 Ford	277	500
4. Walter Ballard	Walter Ballard	30	71 Ford	273	350
5. Cecil Gordon	Cecil Gordon	24	69 Merc	273	325

Southside Speedway
Richmond, VA
Quarter-mile Paved Track

(aka Royall Speedway) .2-mile paved oval built in 1947. Lengthened to quarter-mile track in April 1950. First NASCAR Winston Cup (then Grand National) race staged on 8/18/61 (won by Junior Johnson). Re-measured at .333-mile in 1962. Final Grand National race run on 5/19/63 (won by Ned Jarett). Track still in operation.

Winston Cup Starts

Curtis Crider	4
Ned Jarrett	4
Jimmy Pardue	4
Richard Petty	4
Wendell Scott	4
Larry Thomas	4

Winston Cup Victories

Ned Jarrett	1
Junior Johnson	1
Jimmy Pardue	1
Jim Paschal	1

Winston Cup Poles

Rex White	2

Winston Cup Money

Ned Jarrett	$2,265

Most Cars Started
25—June 22, 1962

Fewest Cars Started
16—May 4, 1962

Narrowest Margin of Victory
N/A

Slowest Race
51.605 MPH—August 18, 1961

Race Record
67.747 MPH—May 4, 1962

Most Cautions
N/A

Most Race Leaders
3—June 22, 1962

Most Cars Running at Finish
19—June 22, 1962

1961 Grand National Race No. 40
August 18, 1961 Average Speed: 51.605

Driver	Owner	Car #	Make	Laps	Winnings
1. Junior Johnson	Rex Lovette	27	60 Pont	150	600
2. Ned Jarrett	Bee Gee Holloway	11	61 Chev	149	475
3. Emanuel Zervakis	Monroe Shook	85	61 Chev	149	380
4. Rex White	Rex White	4	60 Chev	148	425
5. Jimmy Pardue	Jimmy Pardue	54	60 Chev	148	225

1962 Grand National Race No. 18
May 4, 1962 Average Speed: 67.747

Driver	Owner	Car #	Make	Laps	Winnings
1. Jimmy Pardue	Jimmy Pardue	54	62 Pont	200	550
2. Jack Smith	Jack Smith	47	61 Pont	200	480
3. Richard Petty	Petty Enterprises	43	60 Plym	199	375
4. Joe Weatherly	Fred Harb	17	61 Ford	197	290
5. Jim Paschal	Cliff Stewart	2	62 Pont	196	275

1962 Grand National Race No. 27
June 22, 1962 Average Speed: 66.293

Driver	Owner	Car #	Make	Laps	Winnings
1. Jim Paschal	Cliff Stewart	2	62 Pont	300	1,010
2. Rex White	Rex White	4	62 Chev	299	650
3. Jimmy Pardue	Jimmy Pardue	54	62 Pont	298	400
4. Johnny Allen	Fred Lovette	58	61 Pont	297	300
5. Jim Reed	Ratus Walters	77	62 Pont	296	290

1963 Grand National Race No. 25
May 19, 1963 Average Speed: 65.052

Driver	Owner	Car #	Make	Laps	Winnings
1. Ned Jarrett	Charles Robinson	11	63 Ford	300	1,000
2. Richard Petty	Petty Enterprises	41	63 Plym	298	600
3. Larry Thomas	Wade Younts	36	62 Dodg	294	400
4. Jimmy Pardue	Pete Stewart	57	62 Pont	291	300
5. Ray Hendrick	Rebel Racing	35	61 Pont	288	275

Starkey Speedway
Roanoke, VA
Quarter-mile Paved Track

Quarter-mile paved oval opened in October 1950. First NASCAR Winston Cup (then Grand National) race staged on 5/15/58 (Jim Reed won).
Last Grand National race staged on 8/23/64 (won by Junior Johnson). Track closed in 1966.

Winston Cup Starts

Curtis Crider	3
Fred Harb	3
Ned Jarrett	3
Jimmy Pardue	3
Richard Petty	3
Wendell Scott	3
Larry Thomas	3

Winston Cup Victories

Junior Johnson	2

Winston Cup Poles

Jim Reed	1
Jack Smith	1
Rex White	1
Glen Wood	1

Winston Cup Money

Junior Johnson	$1,750

Most Cars Started

22—May 15, 1958
22—August 23, 1964

Fewest Cars Started

18—August 15, 1962

Narrowest Margin of Victory

N/A

Slowest Race

49.504 MPH—May 15, 1958

Race Record

51.165 MPH—August 15, 1962

Most Race Leaders

N/A

Most Cars Running at Finish

19—May 15, 1958

1958 Grand National Race No. 17
May 15, 1958 Average Speed: 49.504

Driver	Owner	Car #	Make	Laps	Winnings
1. Jim Reed	Jim Reed	7	57 Ford	150	550
2. Rex White	J. H. Petty	44	57 Chev	150	450
3. Eddie Pagan	Eddie Pagan	45	57 Ford	149	325
4. Frankie Schneider	Frankie Schneider	62	57 Chev	148	250
5. Curtis Turner	Holman-Moody	26	58 Ford	148	215

1961 Grand National Race No. 31
June 24, 1961 Average Speed: 49.907

Driver	Owner	Car #	Make	Laps	Winnings
1. Junior Johnson	Rex Lovette	27	60 Pont	150	900
2. Rex White	Rex White	4	60 Chev	149	725
3. Jim Paschal	J. H. Petty	14	61 Pont	149	475
4. Richard Petty	Petty Enterprises	43	61 Plym	147	295
5. Emanuel Zervakis	Monroe Shook	85	60 Chev	146	250

1962 Grand National Race No. 41
August 15, 1962 Average Speed: 51.165

Driver	Owner	Car #	Make	Laps	Winnings
1. Richard Petty	Petty Enterprises	42	62 Plym	200	550
2. Joe Weatherly	Bud Moore	8	62 Pont	200	480
3. Ned Jarrett	Bee Gee Holloway	11	62 Chev	200	575
4. Bob Welborn	J. C. Parker	49	62 Pont	200	325
5. Jack Smith	Jack Smith	47	62 Pont	200	245

1964 Grand National Race No. 50
August 23, 1964 Average Speed: 49.847

Driver	Owner	Car #	Make	Laps	Winnings
1. Junior Johnson	Banjo Matthews	27	64 Ford	200	850
2. Ned Jarrett	Bondy Long	11	64 Ford	199	530
3. Glen Wood	Wood Brothers	21	64 Ford	199	430
4. David Pearson	Cotton Owens	6	64 Dodg	199	350
5. Jimmy Pardue	Charles Robinson	54	64 Plym	199	300

Washington

Bremerton Raceway
Bremerton, WA
.9-mile Paved Road Course

(aka Kitsap County Airport; Sea Fair Races; Thunderbird Stadium) Originated as 1.25-mile dirt oval. Started using airport runways for races in 1950. Three different size road courses (.9-mile, 2-mile, and 4-mile) were used from 1955–57. Only NASCAR Winston Cup (then Grand National) race staged on 8/4/57 (won by Parnelli Jones on .9-mile track). Course discontinued in 1958.

Winston Cup Victories
Parnelli Jones   1

Winston Cup Poles
Art Watts   1

Winston Cup Money
Parnelli Jones $900

Most Cars Started
14—August 4, 1957

Narrowest Margin of Victory
N/A

Race Record
38.959 MPH—August 4, 1957

Most Race Leaders
1—August 4, 1957

Most Cars Running at Finish
12—August 4, 1957

1957 Grand National Race No. 36
August 4, 1957 Average Speed: 38.959

Driver	Owner	Car #	Make	Laps	Winnings
1. Parnelli Jones	Oscar Maples	11	57 Ford	80	900
2. Lloyd Dane	Lloyd Dane	44	57 Ford	80	610
3. Art Watts	Al Schmidhamer	22N	56 Ford	80	465
4. Eddie Pagan	Eddie Pagan	45	57 Ford	79	315
5. Bob Rauscher		21N	57 Ford	77	270

West Virginia

West Virginia Int'l Speedway
Huntington, WV
.4375-mile Paved Track

(aka Huntington Int'l Speedway; Int'l Raceway Park; Dick Clark's Int'l Raceway Park) Once owned by TV personality Dick Clark, the .375-mile paved track opened with NASCAR Winston Cup (then Grand National) race on 8/18/63 (Fred Lorenzen won). Re-measured as .4375-mile oval in 1964. Final Winston Cup Grand National race run on 8/8/71 (won by Richard Petty). Track closed in 1972.

Winston Cup Starts
Neil Castles	4
Richard Petty	4
Wendell Scott	4

Winston Cup Victories
Richard Petty	3

Winston Cup Poles
Bobby Allison	2

Winston Cup Money
Richard Petty $6,800

Most Cars Started
35—August 8, 1971 West Virginia 500

Fewest Cars Started
20—August 18, 1963 Mountaineer 300

Narrowest Margin of Victory
1 lap plus—August 18, 1963 Mountaineer 300

Slowest Race
59.340 MPH—August 18, 1963 Mountaineer 300

Race Record
83.805 MPH—August 8, 1971 West Virginia 500

Most Cautions
7—August 18, 1963 Mountaineer 300

Most Race Leaders
4—August 18, 1963 Mountaineer 300
4—August 16, 1964 Mountaineer 500

Most Cars Running at Finish
16—August 18, 1963 Mountaineer 300

1963 Grand National Race No. 44 Mountaineer 300
August 18, 1963 Average Speed: 59.340

Driver	Owner	Car #	Make	Laps	Winnings
1. Fred Lorenzen	Holman-Moody	28	63 Ford	300	1,600
2. Joe Weatherly	Bud Moore	8	63 Pont	299	1,225
3. Jim Paschal	Petty Enterprises	42	63 Plym	299	750
4. Ned Jarrett	Charles Robinson	11	63 Ford	297	600
5. Buck Baker	Buck Baker	87	63 Pont	296	450

1964 Grand National Race No. 47 Mountaineer 500
August 16, 1964 Average Speed: 70.488

Driver	Owner	Car #	Make	Laps	Winnings
1. Richard Petty	Petty Enterprises	43	64 Plym	500	2,550
2. Junior Johnson	Banjo Matthews	27	64 Ford	497	1,600
3. Ned Jarrett	Bondy Long	11	64 Ford	494	1,225
4. Jim Paschal	Petty Enterprises	41	64 Plym	494	1,000
5. Earl Balmer	Cotton Owens	5	64 Dodg	489	800

1970 Grand National Race No. 33 West Virginia 300
August 11, 1970 Average Speed: 78.358

Driver	Owner	Car #	Make	Laps	Winnings
1. Richard Petty	Petty Enterprises	43	70 Plym	300	1,700
2. James Hylton	James Hylton	48	70 Ford	292	1,100
3. Neil Castles	Neil Castles	06	69 Dodg	290	600
4. John Sears	John Sears	4	69 Dodg	290	480
5. Dave Marcis	Cecil Gordon	97	68 Ford	283	425

1971 Winston Cup GN Race No. 35 West Virginia 500
August 8, 1971 Average Speed: 83.805

Driver	Owner	Car #	Make	Laps	Winnings
1. Richard Petty	Petty Enterprises	43	71 Plym	500	2,300
2. Bobby Allison	Melvin Joseph	49	70 Ford	498	1,500
3. James Hylton	James Hylton	48	71 Ford	495	950
4. Tiny Lund	Ronnie Hopkins	55	70 Chev	493	750
5. Cecil Gordon	Cecil Gordon	24	69 Merc	482	650

Wisconsin

Road America
Elkhart Lake, WI
4.1-mile Road Course

4.0-mile road course opened in September 1955. Track was built after races through the street and village were discontinued. Only NASCAR Winston Cup (then Grand National) race staged on 8/12/56 (won by Tim Flock, his final Grand National victory). The NASCAR race was run in the rain. Old store-bought-type tires, then utilized in big-league NASCAR racing, had treaded grooves, so the race went on as scheduled. A second event was scheduled in 1957, but was canceled due to conflicting race dates with other NASCAR events. Today the site of IndyCar races and sportscar events.

Winston Cup Victories
Tim Flock   1

Winston Cup Poles
Frank Mundy   1

Winston Cup Money
Tim Flock $2,950

Most Cars Started
26—August 12, 1956

Narrowest Margin of Victory
17 seconds August 12, 1956

Race Record
73.858 MPH—August 12, 1956

Most Race Leaders
4—August 12, 1956

Most Cars Running at Finish
14—August 12, 1956

1956 Grand National Race No. 37
August 12, 1956 Average Speed: 73.858

Driver	Owner	Car #	Make	Laps	Winnings
1. Tim Flock	Bill Stroppe	15	56 Merc	63	2,950
2. Billy Myers	Bill Stroppe	14	56 Merc	63	1,900
3. Fireball Roberts	Pete DePaolo	22	56 Ford	63	1,275
4. Paul Goldsmith	Smokey Yunick	3	56 Chev	63	900
5. Joe Eubanks	James Satcher	56	56 Ford	63	675

Canada

Canadian National Exposition Speedway
Toronto, Canada
.333-Mile Paved Track

(aka CNE Stadium) Originally built as horse track in 1904, and converted to a .333-mile track circa 1952. Paved in mid-'50s. First NASCAR Winston Cup (then Grand National) race staged on 7/18/58 (won by Lee Petty). Site of Richard Petty's first Winston Cup (then Grand National) start. Lorne Greene, of Bonanza *fame. served as public address announcer in 1950s. Track closed in 1966, but special events have been run into the '90s. Both the Toronto Blue Jays baseball team and Canadian football team, the Toronto Argonauts played in the stadium in later years until a new downtown sports facility was built.*

Winston Cup Victories
Lee Petty   1

Winston Cup Poles
Rex White   1

Winston Cup Money
Lee Petty $575

Most Cars Started
19—July 18, 1958

Narrowest Margin of Victory
N/A

Race Record
43.184 MPH—July 18, 1958

Most Race Leaders
2—July 18, 1958

Most Cars Running at Finish
16—July 18, 1958

1958 Grand National Race No. 31
July 18, 1958 Average Speed: 43.184

Driver	Owner	Car #	Make	Laps	Winnings
1. Lee Petty	Petty Enterprises	42	57 Olds	100	575
2. Cotton Owens	Jim Stephens	6	57 Pont	100	480
3. Jim Reed	Jim Reed	7	57 Ford	100	305
4. Shorty Rollins	Shorty Rollins	99	58 Ford	100	275
5. Johnny Mackison	Ken Corman	23	57 Merc	99	220

Stamford Park
Niagara Falls, ONT
Half-mile Dirt Track

Originally a horse track built in 1950. Half-mile dirt track was the site of first NASCAR Winston Cup (then Grand National) race run outside the boundaries of the United States. Buddy Shuman won the 7/1/52 event. Closed after final auto race in July of 1953.

Winston Cup Victories
Buddy Shuman   1

Winston Cup Poles
Herb Thomas   1

Winston Cup Money
Buddy Shuman $1,000

Most Cars Started
17—July 1, 1952

Narrowest Margin of Victory
2 laps plus—July 1, 1952

Race Record
45.610 MPH—July 1, 1952

Most Cautions
3—July 1, 1952

Most Race Leaders
2—July 1, 1952

Most Cars Running at Finish
6—July 1, 1952

1952 Grand National Race No. 18
July 1, 1952 Average Speed: 45.610

Driver	Owner	Car #	Make	Laps	Winnings
1. Buddy Shuman	B. A. Pless	89	52 Huds	200	1,000
2. Herb Thomas	Herb Thomas	92	52 Huds	198	700
3. Ray Duhigg	J. H. Petty	44	51 Plym	193	450
4. Jack Reynolds	Wiss Brothers	421	51 Plym	183	350
5. Perk Brown			50 Ford	176	200

PART 6
THE RACES

Cum. No.	Yr. No.	Date	Site	Track Length	Surface	Miles	Race Winner	Make	Speed	Pole Winner	Make	Pole Speed
1951												
28	1	2/11/51	Daytona Beach, FL	4.1	B-R	159.9	Marshall Teague	Hudson	82.328	Tim Flock	Lincoln	102.200
29	2	4/1/51	Charlotte, NC	0.75	D	112.5	Curtis Turner	Nash	70.545	Fonty Flock	Olds	68.337
30	3	4/8/51	Mobile, AL	0.75	D	112.5	Tim Flock	Olds	50.260	No Time Trials	NTT	NTT
31	4	4/8/51	Gardena, CA	0.5	D	100	Marshall Teague	Hudson	61.047	Andy Pierce	Buick	62.959
32	5	4/15/51	Hillsboro, NC	1.0	D	95	Fonty Flock	Olds	80.889	Fonty Flock	Olds	88.278
33	6	4/29/51	Phoenix, AZ	1.0	D	150	Marshall Teague	Hudson	60.153	Fonty Flock	Olds	N/A
34	7	4/29/51	N. Wilkesboro, NC	0.625	D	93.75	Fonty Flock	Olds	None	Fonty Flock	Olds	72.184
35	8	5/6/51	Martinsville, VA	0.5	D	100	Curtis Turner	Olds	N/A	Tim Flock	Olds	55.062
36	9	5/30/51	Canfield, OH	0.5	D	100	Marshall Teague	Hudson	49.308	Bill Rexford	Olds	54.233
37	10	6/10/51	Columbus, GA	0.5	D	100	Tim Flock	Olds	N/A	Gober Sosebee	Cadillac	57.766
38	11	6/16/51	Columbia, SC	0.5	D	100	Frank Mundy	Studebaker	50.683	Frank Mundy	Studebaker	57.563
39	12	6/24/51	Dayton, OH	0.5	P	100	Curtis Turner	Olds	N/A	Tim Flock	Olds	70.838

Key

CUM. NO. The cumulative number of all Winston Cup races ever run. For example, the number 28 besides the first race in 1951 indicates that race was the 28th Winston Cup race ever run. Counting through the end of the 1996 season, there have been a grand total of 1789 Winston Cup races

YR. NO. The number of races run that year. For example, the 6 next to the April 29 race indicates that race was the 6th of the season

TRACK LENGTH Track configuration when that race was run

SURFACE The type of track surface

  B-R Beach and Road course

  D Dirt track

  P Paved track

MILES Number of miles driven that race

MAKE Car manufacturer

SPEED Average speed

POLE SPEED Pole winner's qualifying speed

Cum. No.	Yr. No.	Date	Site	Track Length	Surface	Miles	Race Winner	Make	Speed	Pole Winner	Make	Pole Speed

CHRONOLOGICAL LISTING OF RACES

1949

Cum. No.	Yr. No.	Date	Site	Track Length	Surface	Miles	Race Winner	Make	Speed	Pole Winner	Make	Pole Speed
1	1	6/19/49	Charlotte, NC	0.75	D	150	Jim Roper	Lincoln	N/A	Bob Flock	Hudson	67.958
2	2	7/10/49	Daytona Beach, FL	4.15	B-R	166	Red Byron	Olds	80.883	Gober Sosebee	Olds	N/A
3	3	8/7/49	Hillsboro, NC	1	D	200	Bob Flock	Olds	76.8	N/A	N/A	N/A
4	4	9/11/49	Langhorne, PA	1	D	200	Curtis Turner	Olds	69.403	Red Byron	Olds	77.482
5	5	9/18/49	Hamburg, NY	0.5	D	100	Jack White	Lincoln	N/A	N/A	N/A	N/A
6	6	9/25/49	Martinsville, VA	0.5	D	100	Red Byron	Olds	N/A	Curtis Turner	Olds	N/A
7	7	10/2/49	Pittsburg, PA	0.5	D	100	Lee Petty	Plymouth	57.458	Al Bonnell	Olds	61.475
8	8	10/16/49	N. Wilkesboro, NC	0.5	D	100	Bob Flock	Olds	53.364	Ken Wagner	Lincoln	57.563

1950

Cum. No.	Yr. No.	Date	Site	Track Length	Surface	Miles	Race Winner	Make	Speed	Pole Winner	Make	Pole Speed
9	1	2/5/50	Daytona Beach, FL	4.17	B-R	200.16	Harold Kite	Lincoln	89.894	Joe Littlejohn	Olds	98.84
10	2	4/2/50	Charlotte, NC	0.75	D	150	Tim Flock	Lincoln	N/A	Red Byron	Olds	67.839
11	3	4/16/50	Langhorne, PA	1	D	150	Curtis Turner	Olds	69.399	Tim Flock	Lincoln	N/A
12	4	5/21/50	Martinsville, VA	0.5	D	75	Curtis Turner	Olds	N/A	Buck Baker	Ford	54.216
13	5	5/30/50	Canfield, OH	0.5	D	100	Bill Rexford	Olds	N/A	Jimmy Florian	Ford	N/A
14	6	6/18/50	Vernon, NY	0.5	D	100	Bill Blair	Mercury	N/A	Chuck Mahoney	Mercury	N/A
15	7	6/25/50	Dayton, OH	0.5	D	100	Jimmy Florian	Ford	63.351	Dick Linder	Olds	66.543
16	8	7/2/50	Rochester, NY	0.5	D	100	Curtis Turner	Olds	50.614	Curtis Turner	Olds	54.794
17	9	7/23/50	Charlotte, NC	0.75	D	150	Curtis Turner	Olds	N/A	Curtis Turner	Olds	N/A
18	10	8/13/50	Hillsboro, NC	1	D	100	Fireball Roberts	Olds	N/A	Dick Linder	Olds	N/A
19	11	8/20/50	Dayton, OH	0.5	D	100	Dick Linder	Olds	None	Curtis Turner	Olds	N/A
20	12	8/27/50	Hamburg, NY	0.5	D	100	Dick Linder	Olds	50.747	Dick Linder	Olds	53.113
21	13	9/4/50	Darlington, SC	1.25	P	500	Johnny Mantz	Plymouth	75.25	Curtis Turner	Olds	82.034
22	14	9/17/50	Langhorne, PA	1	D	200	Fonty Flock	Olds	72.801	Wally Campbell	Olds	77.104
23	15	9/24/50	N. Wilkesboro, NC	0.625	D	125	Leon Sales	Plymouth	N/A	Fireball Roberts	Olds	73.266
24	16	10/1/50	Vernon, NY	0.5	D	100	Dick Linder	Olds	N/A	Dick Linder	Olds	N/A
25	17	10/15/50	Martinsville, VA	0.5	D	100	Herb Thomas	Plymouth	N/A	Fonty Flock	Olds	54.761
26	18	10/15/50	Winchester, IN	0.5	P	100	Lloyd Moore	Mercury	63.875	Dick Linder	Olds	68.834
27	19	10/29/50	Hillsboro, NC	1	D	175	Lee Petty	Plymouth	N/A	Fonty Flock	Olds	85.898

1951

Cum. No.	Yr. No.	Date	Site	Track Length	Surface	Miles	Race Winner	Make	Speed	Pole Winner	Make	Pole Speed
28	1	2/11/51	Daytona Beach, FL	4.1	B-R	159.9	Marshall Teague	Hudson	82.328	Tim Flock	Lincoln	102.2
29	2	4/1/51	Charlotte, NC	0.75	D	112.5	Curtis Turner	Nash	70.545	Fonty Flock	Olds	68.337
30	3	4/8/51	Mobile, AL	0.75	D	112.5	Tim Flock	Olds	50.26	Red Harrelson	Ford	NTT
31	4	4/8/51	Gardena, CA	0.5	D	100	Marshall Teague	Hudson	61.047	Andy Pierce	Buick	62.959
32	5	4/15/51	Hillsboro, NC	1	D	150	Fonty Flock	Olds	80.889	Fonty Flock	Olds	88.287
33	6	4/22/51	Phoenix, AZ	1	D	150	Marshall Teague	Hudson	60.153	Fonty Flock	Olds	70.936
34	7	4/29/51	N. Wilkesboro, NC	0.625	D	93.75	Fonty Flock	Olds	None	Fonty Flock	Olds	72.184
35	8	5/6/51	Martinsville, VA	0.5	D	100	Curtis Turner	Olds	N/A	Tim Flock	Olds	55.062
36	9	5/30/51	Canfield, OH	0.5	D	100	Marshall Teague	Hudson	49.308	Bill Rexford	Olds	54.233
37	10	6/10/51	Columbus, GA	0.5	D	100	Tim Flock	Olds	N/A	Gober Sosebee	Cadillac	57.766
38	11	6/16/51	Columbia, SC	0.5	D	100	Frank Mundy	Studebaker	50.683	Frank Mundy	Studebaker	57.563
39	12	6/24/51	Dayton, OH	0.5	P	100	Curtis Turner	Olds	N/A	Tim Flock	Olds	70.838
40	13	6/30/51	Gardena, CA	0.5	D	100	Lou Figaro	Hudson	N/A	Lou Figaro	Hudson	76.988
41	14	7/1/51	Grand Rapids, MI	0.5	D	100	Marshall Teague	Hudson	N/A	Tim Flock	Olds	84.3
42	15	7/8/51	Bainbridge, OH	1	D	100	Fonty Flock	Olds	65.753	Fonty Flock	Olds	N/A
43	16	7/15/51	Heidelberg, PA	0.5	D	100	Herb Thomas	Olds	None	Fonty Flock	Olds	61.983
44	17	7/29/51	Weaverville, NC	0.5	D	100	Fonty Flock	Olds	N/A	Fonty Flock	Olds	64.608
45	18	7/31/51	Rochester, NY	0.5	D	100	Lee Petty	Plymouth	N/A	Fonty Flock	Olds	N/A
46	19	8/1/51	Altamont, NY	0.5	D	100	Fonty Flock	Olds	N/A	N/A	N/A	N/A
47	20	8/12/51	Detroit, MI	1	D	250	Tommy Thompson	Chrysler	57.588	Marshall Teague	Hudson	69.131
48	21	8/19/51	Toledo, OH	0.5	D	100	Tim Flock	Olds	50.847	Fonty Flock	Olds	55.521
49	22	8/24/51	Morristown, NJ	0.5	D	100	Tim Flock	Olds	N/A	Tim Flock	Olds	58.67
50	23	8/25/51	Greenville, SC	0.5	D	100	Bob Flock	Olds	N/A	N/A	N/A	N/A
51	24	9/3/51	Darlington, SC	1.25	P	500	Herb Thomas	Hudson	76.906	Frank Mundy	Studebaker	84.173
52	25	9/7/51	Columbia, SC	0.5	D	100	Tim Flock	Olds	N/A	Tim Flock	Olds	58.843
53	26	9/9/51	Macon, GA	0.5	D	100	Herb Thomas	Plymouth	53.222	Bob Flock	Olds	54.266
54	27	9/15/51	Langhorne, PA	1	D	150	Herb Thomas	Hudson	71.043	Fonty Flock	Olds	81.733
55	28	9/23/51	Charlotte, NC	0.75	D	150	Herb Thomas	Hudson	N/A	Billy Carden	Olds	66.914
56	29	9/23/51	Dayton, OH	0.5	P	100	Fonty Flock	Olds	N/A	Fonty Flock	Olds	N/A

Cum. No.	Yr. No.	Date	Site	Track Length	Surface	Miles	Race Winner	Make	Speed	Pole Winner	Make	Pole Speed
57	30	9/30/51	Wilson, NC	0.5	D	100	Fonty Flock	Olds	N/A	Fonty Flock	Olds	N/A
58	31	10/7/51	Hillsboro, NC	1	D	150	Herb Thomas	Hudson	72.454	Herb Thomas	Hudson	79.628
59	32	10/12/51	Thompson, CT	0.5	P	100	Neil Cole	Olds	N/A	Neil Cole	Olds	59.269
60	33	10/14/51	Shippenville, PA	0.5	D	100	Tim Flock	Olds	N/A	N/A	N/A	N/A
61	34	10/14/51	Martinsville, VA	0.5	D	100	Frank Mundy	Olds	N/A	Herb Thomas	Hudson	56.109
62	35	10/14/51	Oakland, CA	0.625	D	156.25	Marvin Burke	Mercury	78.748	N/A	N/A	N/A
63	36	10/21/51	N. Wilkesboro, NC	0.625	D	125	Fonty Flock	Olds	67.791	Herb Thomas	Hudson	68.828
64	37	10/28/51	Hanford, CA	0.5	D	100	Danny Weinberg	Studebaker	N/A	N/A	N/A	N/A
65	38	11/4/51	Jacksonville, FL	0.5	D	100	Herb Thomas	Hudson	53.412	Herb Thomas	Hudson	64.818
66	39	11/11/51	Atlanta, GA	1	D	100	Tim Flock	Hudson	59.96	Frank Mundy	Studebaker	74.013
67	40	11/11/51	Gardena, CA	0.5	D	100	Bill Norton	Mercury	N/A	Fonty Flock	Olds	N/A
68	41	11/25/51	Mobile, AL	0.75	D	112.5	Frank Mundy	Studebaker	N/A	Frank Mundy	Studebaker	61.113

1952

Cum. No.	Yr. No.	Date	Site	Track Length	Surface	Miles	Race Winner	Make	Speed	Pole Winner	Make	Pole Speed
69	1	1/20/52	West Palm Beach, FL	0.5	D	100	Tim Flock	Hudson	None	Tim Flock	Hudson	67.794
70	2	2/10/52	Daytona Beach, FL	4.1	B-R	200.9	Marshall Teague	Hudson	85.612	Pat Kirkwood	Chrysler	110.97
71	3	3/6/52	Jacksonville, FL	0.5	D	100	Marshall Teague	Hudson	55.197	Marshall Teague	Hudson	60.1
72	4	3/30/52	N. Wilkesboro, NC	0.625	D	125	Herb Thomas	Hudson	58.597	Herb Thomas	Hudson	75.075
73	5	4/6/52	Martinsville, VA	0.5	D	100	Dick Rathmann	Hudson	42.862	Buck Baker	Hudson	54.945
74	6	4/12/52	Columbia, SC	0.5	D	100	Buck Baker	Hudson	53.46	Buck Baker	Hudson	N/A
75	7	4/20/52	Atlanta, GA	1	D	100	Bill Blair	Olds	66.877	Tim Flock	Hudson	71.613
76	8	4/27/52	Macon, GA	0.5	D	150	Herb Thomas	Hudson	53.853	Jack Smith	Studebaker	54.429
77	9	5/4/52	Langhorne, PA	1	D	150	Dick Rathmann	Hudson	67.669	Herb Thomas	Hudson	76.045
78	10	5/10/52	Darlington, SC	1.25	P	100	Dick Rathmann	Hudson	83.818	Fireball Roberts	Ford	N/A
79	11	5/18/52	Dayton, OH	0.5	P	100	Dick Rathmann	Hudson	65.526	Fonty Flock	Olds	71.884
80	12	5/30/52	Canfield, OH	0.5	D	100	Herb Thomas	Hudson	48.057	Dick Rathmann	Ford	58.102
81	13	6/1/52	Augusta, GA	0.5	D	77	Gober Sosebee	Chrysler	None	Tommy Moon	Hudson	51.561
82	14	6/1/52	Toledo, OH	0.5	D	100	Tim Flock	Hudson	47.175	Fonty Flock	Olds	57.034
83	15	6/8/52	Hillsboro, NC	1	D	100	Tim Flock	Hudson	81.008	Fonty Flock	Olds	91.977
84	16	6/15/52	Charlotte, NC	0.75	D	112.5	Herb Thomas	Hudson	64.82	Fonty Flock	Olds	70.038
85	17	6/29/52	Detroit, MI	1	D	250	Tim Flock	Hudson	59.908	Dick Rathmann	Hudson	70.23
86	18	7/1/52	Niagara Falls, ONT	0.5	D	100	Buddy Shuman	Hudson	45.61	Herb Thomas	Hudson	52.401
87	19	7/4/52	Owego, NY	0.5	D	100	Tim Flock	Hudson	56.603	Tim Flock	Hudson	67.669
88	20	7/6/52	Monroe, MI	0.5	D	100	Tim Flock	Hudson	44.499	Tim Flock	Hudson	57.6
89	21	7/11/52	Morristown, NJ	0.5	D	100	Lee Petty	Plymouth	59.661	Herb Thomas	Hudson	60.996
90	22	7/20/52	South Bend, IN	0.5	D	100	Tim Flock	Hudson	41.889	Herb Thomas	Hudson	58.12
91	23	8/15/52	Rochester, NY	0.5	D	100	Tim Flock	Hudson	None	NTT	NTT	NTT
92	24	8/17/52	Weaverville, NC	0.5	D	100	Bob Flock	Hudson	57.288	Herb Thomas	Hudson	64.888
93	25	9/1/52	Darlington, SC	1.25	P	500	Fonty Flock	Olds	74.512	Fonty Flock	Olds	88.55
94	26	9/7/52	Macon, GA	0.5	D	150	Lee Petty	Plymouth	48.404	Fonty Flock	Olds	59.113
95	27	9/14/52	Langhorne, PA	1	D	250	Lee Petty	Plymouth	72.463	Herb Thomas	Hudson	85.287
96	28	9/21/52	Dayton, OH	0.5	P	150	Dick Rathmann	Hudson	61.643	Fonty Flock	Olds	71.741
97	29	9/28/52	Wilson, NC	0.5	D	100	Herb Thomas	Hudson	35.398	Herb Thomas	Hudson	55.883
98	30	10/12/52	Hillsboro, NC	1	D	150	Fonty Flock	Olds	73.489	Bill Blair	Olds	75.901
99	31	10/19/52	Martinsville, VA	0.5	D	100	Herb Thomas	Hudson	47.556	Perk Brown	Hudson	55.333
100	32	10/26/52	N. Wilkesboro, NC	0.625	D	125	Herb Thomas	Hudson	67.044	Herb Thomas	Hudson	76.013
101	33	11/16/52	Atlanta, GA	1	D	100	Donald Thomas	Hudson	64.853	Donald Thomas	Hudson	72.874
102	34	11/30/52	West Palm Beach, FL	0.5	D	100	Herb Thomas	Hudson	58.008	Herb Thomas	Hudson	63.716

1953

Cum. No.	Yr. No.	Date	Site	Track Length	Surface	Miles	Race Winner	Make	Speed	Pole Winner	Make	Pole Speed
103	1	2/1/53	West Palm Beach, FL	0.5	D	100	Lee Petty	Dodge	60.22	Dick Rathmann	Hudson	65.028
104	2	2/15/53	Daytona Beach, FL	4.1	B-R	159.9	Bill Blair	Olds	89.789	Bob Pronger	Olds	115.77
105	3	3/8/53	Spring Lake, NC	0.5	D	100	Herb Thomas	Hudson	48.826	Herb Thomas	Hudson	51.918
106	4	3/29/53	N. Wilkesboro, NC	0.625	D	125	Herb Thomas	Hudson	71.907	Herb Thomas	Hudson	78.424
107	5	4/5/53	Charlotte, NC	0.75	D	112.5	Dick Passwater	Olds	N/A	Tim Flock	Hudson	71.108
108	6	4/19/53	Richmond, VA	0.5	D	100	Lee Petty	Dodge	45.535	Buck Baker	Olds	48.465
109	7	4/26/53	Macon, GA	0.5	D	100	Dick Rathmann	Hudson	56.417	N/A	N/A	N/A
110	8	5/3/53	Langhorne, PA	1	D	150	Buck Baker	Olds	72.743	NTT	NTT	NTT
111	9	5/9/53	Columbia, SC	0.5	D	100	Buck Baker	Olds	53.707	Herb Thomas	Hudson	58.67
112	10	5/16/53	Hickory, NC	0.5	D	100	Tim Flock	Hudson	N/A	N/A	N/A	N/A
113	11	5/17/53	Martinsville, VA	0.5	D	100	Lee Petty	Dodge	N/A	N/A	N/A	N/A
114	12	5/24/53	Columbus, OH	0.5	D	100	Herb Thomas	Hudson	56.127	Fonty Flock	Olds	59.288
115	13	5/30/53	Raleigh, NC	1	P	300	Fonty Flock	Hudson	70.629	Slick Smith	Olds	76.23

Cum. No.	Yr. No.	Date	Site	Track Length	Surface	Miles	Race Winner	Make	Speed	Pole Winner	Make	Pole Speed
116	14	6/7/53	Shreveport, LA	0.5	D	100	Lee Petty	Dodge	53.199	Herb Thomas	Hudson	58.727
117	15	6/14/53	Pensacola, FL	0.5	D	100	Herb Thomas	Hudson	63.316	Dick Rathmann	Hudson	67.039
118	16	6/21/53	Langhorne, PA	1	D	200	Dick Rathmann	Hudson	64.434	Lloyd Shaw	Jaguar	82.2
119	17	6/26/53	High Point, NC	0.5	D	100	Herb Thomas	Hudson	58.186	Herb Thomas	Hudson	66.152
120	18	6/28/53	Wilson, NC	0.5	D	100	Fonty Flock	Hudson	53.803	N/A	N/A	N/A
121	19	7/3/53	Rochester, NY	0.5	D	100	Herb Thomas	Hudson	56.939	NTT	NTT	NTT
122	20	7/4/53	Spartanburg, SC	0.5	D	100	Lee Petty	Dodge	56.934	Buck Baker	Olds	58.027
123	21	7/10/53	Morristown, NJ	0.5	D	100	Dick Rathmann	Hudson	69.417	Herb Thomas	Hudson	61.016
124	22	7/12/53	Atlanta, GA	1	D	100	Herb Thomas	Hudson	70.685	Herb Thomas	Hudson	72.756
125	23	7/22/53	Rapid City, SD	0.5	D	100	Herb Thomas	Hudson	57.27	Herb Thomas	Hudson	55.727
126	24	7/26/53	North Platte, NE	0.5	D	100	Dick Rathmann	Hudson	54.38	Herb Thomas	Hudson	54.397
127	25	8/2/53	Davenport, IA	0.5	D	100	Herb Thomas	Hudson	62.5	Buck Baker	Olds	54.397
128	26	8/9/53	Hillsboro, NC	1	D	100	Curtis Turner	Olds	75.125	Curtis Turner	Olds	89.078
129	27	8/16/53	Weaverville, NC	0.5	D	100	Fonty Flock	Hudson	62.434	Curtis Turner	Olds	N/A
130	28	8/23/53	Norfolk, VA	0.5	D	100	Herb Thomas	Hudson	51.04	Curtis Turner	Olds	54.2
131	29	8/29/53	Hickory, NC	0.5	D	100	Fonty Flock	Hudson	N/A	Tim Flock	Hudson	79.362
132	30	9/7/53	Darlington, SC	1.375	P	500.5	Buck Baker	Olds	92.881	Fonty Flock	Hudson	107.983
133	31	9/13/53	Macon, GA	0.5	D	100	Speedy Thompson	Olds	55.172	Joe Eubanks	Hudson	60.81
134	32	9/20/53	Langhorne, PA	1	D	250	Dick Rathmann	Hudson	67.046	Herb Thomas	Hudson	N/A
135	33	10/3/53	Bloomsburg, PA	0.5	D	100	Herb Thomas	Hudson	N/A	Jim Paschal	Dodge	55.935
136	34	10/4/53	Wilson, NC	0.5	D	100	Herb Thomas	Hudson	56.022	Herb Thomas	Hudson	56.962
137	35	10/11/53	N. Wilkesboro, NC	0.625	D	100	Speedy Thompson	Olds	71.202	Buck Baker	Olds	78.288
138	36	10/18/53	Martinsville, VA	0.5	D	100	Jim Paschal	Dodge	56.013	Fonty Flock	Hudson	58.958
139	37	11/1/53	Atlanta, GA	1	D	100	Buck Baker	Olds	63.18	Tim Flock	Hudson	73.58

1954

Cum. No.	Yr. No.	Date	Site	Track Length	Surface	Miles	Race Winner	Make	Speed	Pole Winner	Make	Pole Speed
140	1	2/7/54	West Palm Beach, FL	0.5	D	100	Herb Thomas	Hudson	58.938	Dick Rathmann	Hudson	66.371
141	2	2/21/54	Daytona Beach, FL	4.1	B-R	159.9	Lee Petty	Chrysler	89.108	Lee Petty	Chrysler	123.41
142	3	3/7/54	Jacksonville, FL	0.5	D	100	Herb Thomas	Hudson	56.461	Curtis Turner	Olds	63.581
143	4	3/21/54	Atlanta, GA	1	D	100	Herb Thomas	Hudson	60.494	Herb Thomas	Hudson	75.514
144	5	3/28/54	Savannah, GA	0.5	D	100	Al Keller	Hudson	59.82	Herb Thomas	Hudson	63.202
145	6	3/28/54	Oakland, CA	0.5	D	125	Dick Rathmann	Hudson	50.692	Hershel McGriff	Olds	55.624
146	7	4/4/54	N. Wilkesboro, NC	0.625	D	100	Dick Rathmann	Hudson	68.545	Gober Sosebee	Olds	78.698
147	8	4/18/54	Hillsboro, NC	1	D	100	Herb Thomas	Hudson	77.386	Buck Baker	Olds	86.767
148	9	4/25/54	Macon, GA	0.5	D	100	Gober Sosebee	Olds	55.41	Dick Rathmann	Hudson	57.859
149	10	5/2/54	Langhorne, PA	1	D	150	Herb Thomas	Hudson	74.883	Lee Petty	Chrysler	87.217
150	11	5/9/54	Wilson, NC	0.5	D	100	Buck Baker	Olds	52.279	Jim Paschal	Olds	55.469
151	12	5/16/54	Martinsville, VA	0.5	D	100	Jim Paschal	Olds	46.153	NTT	NTT	NTT
152	13	5/23/54	Sharon, PA	0.5	D	100	Lee Petty	Chrysler	None	Dick Rathmann	Hudson	62.09
153	14	5/29/54	Raleigh, NC	1	P	200	Herb Thomas	Hudson	73.909	Herb Thomas	Hudson	76.66
154	15	5/30/54	Charlotte, NC	0.75	D	99.75	Buck Baker	Olds	49.805	Al Keller	Hudson	68.947
155	16	5/30/54	Gardena, CA	0.5	D	250	John Soares	Dodge	53.438	Danny Letner	Hudson	62.849
156	17	6/6/54	Columbia, SC	0.5	D	100	Curtis Turner	Olds	56.719	Buck Baker	Olds	62.24
157	18	6/13/54	Linden, NJ	2	P	100	Al Keller	Jaguar	77.569	Buck Baker	Olds	80.536
158	19	6/19/54	Hickory, NC	0.5	D	100	Herb Thomas	Hudson	82.872	Herb Thomas	Hudson	81.669
159	20	6/25/54	Rochester, NY	0.5	D	100	Lee Petty	Chrysler	52.455	Herb Thomas	Hudson	60.422
160	21	6/17/54	Mechanicsburg, PA	0.5	D	100	Herb Thomas	Hudson	51.085	Dick Rathmann	Hudson	54.945
161	22	7/3/54	Spartanburg, SC	0.5	D	100	Herb Thomas	Hudson	59.181	Hershel McGriff	Olds	58.12
162	23	7/4/54	Weaverville, NC	0.5	D	100	Herb Thomas	Hudson	61.318	Herb Thomas	Hudson	67.771
163	24	7/10/54	Willow Springs, IL	0.5	D	100	Dick Rathmann	Hudson	72.216	Buck Baker	Olds	75.662
164	25	7/11/54	Grand Rapids, MI	0.5	D	100	Lee Petty	Chrysler	52.09	Herb Thomas	Hudson	59.055
165	26	7/30/54	Morristown, NJ	0.5	D	100	Buck Baker	Olds	58.968	Buck Baker	Olds	66.666
166	27	8/1/54	Oakland, CA	0.5	D	150	Danny Letner	Hudson	53.045	Marvin Panch	Dodge	55.248
167	28	8/13/54	Charlotte, NC	0.5	D	100	Lee Petty	Chrysler	51.362	Buck Baker	Olds	57.27
168	29	8/22/54	San Mateo, CA	1	D	250	Hershel McGriff	Olds	64.71	Hershel McGriff	Olds	75.566
169	30	8/29/54	Corbin, KY	0.5	D	100	Lee Petty	Chrysler	63.08	Jim Paschal	Olds	65.789
170	31	9/6/54	Darlington, SC	1.375	P	500.5	Herb Thomas	Hudson	95.026	Buck Baker	Olds	108.261
171	32	9/12/54	Macon, GA	0.5	D	100	Hershel McGriff	Olds	50.536	Tim Flock	Olds	56.907
172	33	9/24/54	Charlotte, NC	0.5	D	100	Hershel McGriff	Olds	53.167	Hershel McGriff	Olds	54.054
173	34	9/26/54	Langhorne, PA	1	D	250	Herb Thomas	Hudson	71.186	Herb Thomas	Hudson	89.418
174	35	10/10/54	LeHi, Arkansas	1.5	D	250.5	Buck Baker	Olds	89.013	Junior Johnson	Cadillac	N/A
175	36	10/17/54	Martinsville, VA	0.5	D	100	Lee Petty	Chrysler	44.547	Lee Petty	Chrysler	53.191
176	37	10/24/54	N. Wilkesboro, NC	0.625	D	100	Hershel McGriff	Olds	65.175	Hershel McGriff	Olds	77.612

1955

Cum. No.	Yr. No.	Date	Site	Track Length	Surface	Miles	Race Winner	Make	Speed	Pole Winner	Make	Pole Speed
177	1	11/7/54	High Point, NC	0.5	D	100	Lee Petty	Chrysler	62.882	Herb Thomas	Hudson	71.942
178	2	2/6/55	West Palm Beach, FL	0.5	D	100	Herb Thomas	Hudson	56.013	Dick Rathmann	Hudson	65.454
179	3	2/13/55	Jacksonville, FL	0.5	D	100	Lee Petty	Chrysler	69.031	Dick Rathmann	Hudson	63.514
180	4	2/27/55	Daytona Beach, FL	4.1	B-R	159.9	Tim Flock	Chrysler	91.999	Tim Flock	Chrysler	130.293
181	5	3/6/55	Savannah, GA	0.5	D	100	Lee Petty	Chrysler	60.15	Dick Rathmann	Hudson	62.805
182	6	3/26/55	Columbia, SC	0.5	D	100	Fonty Flock	Chevrolet	None	Tim Flock	Chrysler	N/A
183	7	3/27/55	Hillsboro, NC	1	D	100	Jim Paschal	Olds	82.304	Tim Flock	Chrysler	91.696
184	8	4/3/55	N. Wilkesboro, NC	0.625	D	100	Buck Baker	Olds	73.126	Dink Widenhouse	Olds	77.72
185	9	4/17/55	Montgomery, AL	0.5	D	100	Tim Flock	Chrysler	60.872	Jim Paschal	Olds	64.29
186	10	4/24/55	Langhorne, PA	1	D	150	Tim Flock	Chrysler	72.893	Tim Flock	Chrysler	86.699
187	11	5/1/55	Charlotte, NC	0.75	D	99.75	Buck Baker	Buick	52.63	Herb Thomas	Buick	70.184
188	12	5/7/55	Hickory, NC	0.4	D	80	Junior Johnson	Olds	58.823	Tim Flock	Chrysler	67.478
189	13	5/8/55	Phoenix, AZ	1	D	100	Tim Flock	Chrysler	71.485	Bill Amick	Dodge	75.519
190	14	5/15/55	Tucson, AZ	0.5	D	100	Danny Letner	Olds	51.428	Bill Amick	Dodge	56.179
191	15	5/15/55	Martinsville, VA	0.5	D	100	Tim Flock	Chrysler	52.554	Jim Paschal	Olds	58.823
192	16	5/22/55	Richmond, VA	0.5	D	100	Tim Flock	Chrysler	54.298	No Time Trials	NTT	NTT
193	17	5/28/55	Raleigh, NC	0.5	D	100	Junior Johnson	Olds	50.522	Tim Flock	Chrysler	58.612
194	18	5/29/55	Winston-Salem, NC	0.5	D	100	Lee Petty	Chrysler	50.583	Fonty Flock	Chrysler	56.71
195	19	6/10/55	New Oxford, PA	0.5	D	100	Junior Johnson	Olds	65.371	Junior Johnson	Olds	75.853
196	20	6/17/55	Rochester, NY	0.5	D	100	Tim Flock	Chrysler	57.17	Buck Baker	Olds	61.141
197	21	6/18/55	Fonda, NY	0.5	D	100	Junior Johnson	Olds	58.413	Tim Flock	Chrysler	61.77
198	22	6/19/55	Plattsburg, NY	0.5	D	100	Lee Petty	Chrysler	59.074	Lee Petty	Chrysler	55.744
199	23	6/24/55	Charlotte, NC	0.5	D	100	Tim Flock	Chrysler	51.289	Tim Flock	Chrysler	57.915
200	24	7/6/55	Spartanburg, SC	0.5	D	100	Tim Flock	Chrysler	49.106	Tim Flock	Chrysler	58.517
201	25	7/9/55	Columbia, SC	0.5	D	100	Jim Paschal	Olds	55.469	Jimmie Lewallen	Olds	59.741
202	26	7/10/55	Weaverville, NC	0.5	D	100	Tim Flock	Chrysler	62.739	Tim Flock	Chrysler	69.31
203	27	7/15/55	Morristown, NJ	0.5	D	100	Tim Flock	Chrysler	58.092	Tim Flock	Chrysler	63.649
204	28	7/29/55	Altamont, NY	0.5	D	100	Junior Johnson	Olds	None	Tim Flock	Chrysler	56.603
205	29	7/30/55	Syracuse, NY	1	D	200	Tim Flock	Chrysler	76.522	Tim Flock	Chrysler	78.311
206	30	7/31/55	San Mateo, CA	1	D	250	Tim Flock	Chrysler	68.571	Tim Flock	Chrysler	79.33
207	31	8/5/55	Charlotte, NC	0.5	D	100	Jim Paschal	Olds	48.806	Tim Flock	Chrysler	57.859
208	32	8/7/55	Winston-Salem, NC	0.5	D	100	Lee Petty	Dodge	50.111	Tim Flock	Chrysler	59.016
209	33	8/14/55	LeHi, Arkansas	1.5	D	250.5	Fonty Flock	Chrysler	89.892	Fonty Flock	Chrysler	99.944
210	34	8/20/55	Raleigh, NC	1	P	100	Herb Thomas	Buick	76.4	Tim Flock	Chrysler	78.722
211	35	9/5/55	Darlington, SC	1.375	P	503.25	Herb Thomas	Chevrolet	None	Fireball Roberts	Buick	110.682
212	36	9/11/55	Montgomery, AL	0.5	D	100	Tim Flock	Chrysler	63.773	Tim Flock	Chrysler	68.728
213	37	9/18/55	Langhorne, PA	1	D	250	Tim Flock	Chrysler	77.888	Tim Flock	Chrysler	92.095
214	38	9/30/55	Raleigh, NC	1	P	100	Fonty Flock	Chrysler	73.289	Fonty Flock	Chrysler	82.098
215	39	10/6/55	Greenville, SC	0.5	D	100	Tim Flock	Chrysler	57.942	Bob Welborn	Chevrolet	58.037
216	40	10/9/55	LeHi, Arkansas	1.5	D	300	Speedy Thompson	Ford	83.948	Fonty Flock	Chrysler	100.39
217	41	10/15/55	Columbia, SC	0.5	D	100	Tim Flock	Chrysler	55.393	Junior Johnson	Olds	61.728
218	42	10/16/55	Martinsville, VA	0.5	P	100	Speedy Thompson	Chrysler	None	No Time Trials	NTT	NTT
219	43	10/16/55	Las Vegas, NV	1	D	200	Norm Nelson	Chrysler	44.449	Norm Nelson	Chrysler	74.518
220	44	10/23/55	N. Wilkesboro, NC	0.625	D	100	Buck Baker	Ford	72.347	Buck Baker	Ford	79.815
221	45	10/30/55	Hillsboro, NC	1	D	100	Tim Flock	Chrysler	70.465	Tim Flock	Chrysler	81.673

1956

Cum. No.	Yr. No.	Date	Site	Track Length	Surface	Miles	Race Winner	Make	Speed	Pole Winner	Make	Pole Speed
222	1	11/13/55	Hickory, NC	0.4	D	80	Tim Flock	Chrysler	56.962	Tim Flock	Chrysler	N/A
223	2	11/20/55	Charlotte, NC	0.75	D	100.5	Fonty Flock	Chrysler	61.825	Fonty Flock	Chrysler	70.496
224	3	11/20/55	Lancaster, CA	2.5	D	200	Chuck Stevenson	Ford	66.512	Jim Reed	Chevrolet	76.556
225	4	12/11/55	West Palm Beach, FL	0.5	P	100	Herb Thomas	Chevrolet	65.009	Fonty Flock	Chrysler	78.912
226	5	1/22/56	Phoenix, AZ	1	D	150	Buck Baker	Chrysler	64.408	Joe Weatherly	Ford	71.315
227	6	2/26/56	Daytona Beach, FL	4.1	B-R	159.9	Tim Flock	Chrysler	90.657	Tim Flock	Chrysler	135.747
228	7	3/4/56	West Palm Beach, FL	0.5	P	100	Billy Myers	Mercury	68.99	Buck Baker	Dodge	81.081
229	8	3/18/56	Wilson, NC	0.5	D	100	Herb Thomas	Chevrolet	46.287	Herb Thomas	Chevrolet	57.197
230	9	3/25/56	Atlanta, GA	1	D	100	Buck Baker	Chrysler	70.643	Tim Flock	Chrysler	82.154
231	10	4/8/56	N. Wilkesboro, NC	0.625	D	100	Tim Flock	Chrysler	71.034	Junior Johnson	Pontiac	78.37
232	11	4/22/56	Langhorne, PA	1	D	150	Buck Baker	Chrysler	75.928	Buck Baker	Chrysler	104.59
233	12	4/29/56	Richmond, VA	0.5	D	100	Buck Baker	Dodge	56.232	Buck Baker	Dodge	67.091
234	13	5/5/56	Columbia, SC	0.5	D	100	Speedy Thompson	Dodge	54.545	Buck Baker	Dodge	63.274
235	14	5/6/56	Concord, NC	0.5	D	100	Speedy Thompson	Chrysler	61.633	Speedy Thompson	Chrysler	65.241
236	15	5/10/56	Greenville, SC	0.5	D	100	Buck Baker	Dodge	60.362	Rex White	Chevrolet	61.1

Cum. No.	Yr. No.	Date	Site	Track Length	Surface	Miles	Race Winner	Make	Speed	Pole Winner	Make	Pole Speed
237	16	5/12/56	Hickory, NC	0.4	D	80	Speedy Thompson	Chrysler	59.442	Speedy Thompson	Chrysler	67.447
238	17	5/13/56	Hillsboro, NC	0.9	D	90	Buck Baker	Chrysler	83.72	Buck Baker	Chrysler	89.305
239	18	5/20/56	Martinsville, VA	0.5	P	250	Buck Baker	Dodge	60.824	Buck Baker	Dodge	66.103
240	19	5/25/56	Abbottstown, PA	0.5	D	100	Buck Baker	Dodge	69.619	Speedy Thompson	Dodge	76.628
241	20	5/27/56	Charlotte, NC	0.75	D	99.75	Speedy Thompson	Chrysler	64.866	Speedy Thompson	Chrysler	76.966
242	21	5/27/56	Portland, OR	0.5	P	75	Herb Thomas	Chrysler	63.815	Lyle Matlock	Mercury	67.239
243	22	5/30/56	Eureka, CA	0.625	D	100	Herb Thomas	Chrysler	38.814	John Kieper	Oldsmobile	66.04
244	23	5/30/56	Syracuse, NY	1	D	150	Buck Baker	Chrysler	86.179	Buck Baker	Chrysler	83.975
245	24	6/3/56	Merced, CA	0.5	D	100	Herb Thomas	Chrysler	47.325	Herb Thomas	Chrysler	58.234
246	25	6/10/56	LeHi, Arkansas	1.5	D	250.5	Ralph Moody	Ford	74.313	Buck Baker	Chrysler	98.504
247	26	6/15/56	Charlotte, NC	0.5	D	100	Speedy Thompson	Chrysler	56.022	Fireball Roberts	Ford	59.661
248	27	6/22/56	Rochester, NY	0.5	D	100	Speedy Thompson	Chrysler	57.288	Jim Paschal	Mercury	57.434
249	28	6/24/56	Portland, OR	0.5	P	100	John Kieper	Olds	62.586	Herb Thomas	Chrysler	65.934
250	29	7/1/56	Weaverville, NC	0.5	D	100	Lee Petty	Dodge	56.435	Fireball Roberts	Ford	72.26
251	30	7/4/56	Raleigh, NC	1	P	250	Fireball Roberts	Ford	79.822	Lee Petty	Dodge	82.587
252	31	7/7/56	Spartanburg, SC	0.5	D	100	Lee Petty	Dodge	50.483	Fireball Roberts	Ford	58.9
253	32	7/8/56	Sacramento, CA	1	D	100	Lloyd Dane	Mercury	74.074	Eddie Pagan	Ford	76.612
254	33	7/21/56	Chicago, IL	0.5	P	100	Fireball Roberts	Ford	61.037	Billy Myers	Mercury	N/A
255	34	7/27/56	Shelby, NC	0.5	D	100	Speedy Thompson	Dodge	53.699	Ralph Moody	Ford	55.658
256	35	7/29/56	Montgomery, AL	0.5	D	100	Marvin Panch	Ford	67.252	Marvin Panch	Ford	69.444
257	36	8/3/56	Oklahoma City, OK	0.5	D	100	Jim Paschal	Mercury	60.1	Speedy Thompson	Dodge	64.655
258	37	8/12/56	Elkhart Lake, WI	4.1	P	258.3	Tim Flock	Mercury	73.858	Frank Mundy	Dodge	N/A
259	38	8/17/56	Old Bridge, NJ	0.5	P	100	Ralph Moody	Ford	65.17	Jim Reed	Chevrolet	72.028
260	39	8/19/56	San Mateo, CA	1	D	250	Eddie Pagan	Ford	68.161	Eddie Pagan	Ford	81.614
261	40	8/22/56	Norfolk, VA	0.4	D	100	Billy Myers	Mercury	56.408	Ralph Moody	Ford	58.631
262	41	8/23/56	Spartanburg, SC	0.5	D	100	Ralph Moody	Ford	54.372	Ralph Moody	Ford	61.433
263	42	8/25/56	Myrtle Beach, SC	0.5	D	100	Fireball Roberts	Ford	50.576	Ralph Moody	Ford	58.346
264	43	8/26/56	Portland, OR	0.5	P	125	Royce Haggerty	Dodge	None	John Kieper	Olds	65.861
265	44	9/3/56	Darlington, SC	1.375	P	500.5	Curtis Turner	Ford	95.167	Speedy Thompson	Chrysler	119.659
266	45	9/9/56	Montgomery, AL	0.5	D	100	Buck Baker	Chrysler	60.893	Tim Flock	Ford	64.864
267	46	9/12/56	Charlotte, NC	0.5	D	100	Ralph Moody	Ford	52.847	Joe Eubanks	Ford	59.464
268	47	9/23/56	Langhorne, PA	1	D	300	Paul Goldsmith	Chevrolet	70.615	Buck Baker	Chrysler	93.628
269	48	9/23/56	Portland, OR	0.5	P	125	Lloyd Dane	Ford	None	Royce Haggerty	Dodge	N/A
270	49	9/29/56	Columbia, SC	0.5	D	100	Buck Baker	Dodge	61.193	Tim Flock	Ford	61.94
271	50	9/30/56	Hillsboro, NC	0.9	D	99	Fireball Roberts	Ford	72.734	Speedy Thompson	Chrysler	88.067
272	51	10/7/56	Newport, TN	0.5	D	100	Fireball Roberts	Ford	61.475	Joe Eubanks	Ford	65.597
273	52	10/17/56	Charlotte, NC	0.75	D	99.75	Buck Baker	Chrysler	72.268	Ralph Moody	Ford	75.041
274	53	10/23/56	Shelby, NC	0.5	D	100	Buck Baker	Chrysler	54.054	Doug Cox	Ford	58.479
275	54	10/28/56	Martinsville, VA	0.5	P	200	Jack Smith	Dodge	61.136	Buck Baker	Chrysler	67.643
276	55	11/11/56	Hickory, NC	0.4	D	100	Speedy Thompson	Chrysler	66.42	Ralph Earnhardt	Ford	68.278
277	56	11/18/56	Wilson, NC	0.5	D	100	Buck Baker	Chrysler	50.597	Buck Baker	Chrysler	60.16

1957

Cum. No.	Yr. No.	Date	Site	Track Length	Surface	Miles	Race Winner	Make	Speed	Pole Winner	Make	Pole Speed
278	1	11/11/56	Lancaster, CA	2.5	D	150	Marvin Panch	Ford	78.648	Marvin Panch	Ford	78.596
279	2	12/2/56	Concord, NC	0.5	D	100	Marvin Panch	Ford	55.883	Curtis Turner	Ford	62.586
280	3	12/30/56	Titusville, FL	1.6	P	89.6	Fireball Roberts	Ford	69.106	Paul Goldsmith	Chevrolet	69.106
281	4	2/17/57	Daytona Beach, FL	4.1	B-R	159.9	Cotton Owens	Pontiac	101.541	Banjo Matthews	Pontiac	134.382
282	5	3/3/57	Concord, NC	0.5	D	100	Jack Smith	Chevrolet	59.86	Mel Larson	Ford	62.225
283	6	3/17/57	Wilson, NC	0.5	D	100	Ralph Moody	Ford	55.079	Fireball Roberts	Ford	59.269
284	7	3/24/57	Hillsboro, NC	0.9	D	99	Buck Baker	Chevrolet	82.233	Fireball Roberts	Ford	87.828
285	8	3/31/57	Weaverville, NC	0.5	D	100	Buck Baker	Chevrolet	65.693	Marvin Panch	Ford	73.649
286	9	4/7/57	N. Wilkesboro, NC	0.625	D	100	Fireball Roberts	Ford	75.015	Fireball Roberts	Ford	81.5
287	10	4/14/57	Langhorne, PA	1	D	150	Fireball Roberts	Ford	85.85	Paul Goldsmith	Ford	93.701
288	11	4/19/57	Charlotte, NC	0.5	D	100	Fireball Roberts	Ford	52.083	Marvin Panch	Ford	60.06
289	12	4/27/57	Spartanburg, SC	0.5	D	100	Marvin Panch	Ford	55.13	Speedy Thompson	Chevrolet	61.538
290	13	4/28/57	Greensboro, NC	0.333	D	83.25	Paul Goldsmith	Ford	49.905	Buck Baker	Chevrolet	50.12
291	14	4/28/57	Portland, OR	0.5	P	50	Art Watts	Ford	64.754	Art Watts	Ford	65.813
292	15	5/4/57	Shelby, NC	0.5	D	100	Fireball Roberts	Ford	54.861	Tiny Lund	Pontiac	57.544
293	16	5/5/57	Richmond, VA	0.5	D	100	Paul Goldsmith	Ford	62.445	Russ Hepler	Pontiac	64.239
294	17	5/19/57	Martinsville, VA	0.5	P	250	Buck Baker	Chevrolet	57.318	Paul Goldsmith	Ford	65.693
295	18	5/26/57	Portland, OR	0.5	P	75	Eddie Pagan	Ford	64.732	Art Watts	Ford	66.732
296	19	5/30/57	Eureka, CA	0.625	D	100	Lloyd Dane	Ford	55.957	Parnelli Jones	Ford	63.92
297	20	5/30/57	New Oxford, PA	0.5	D	100	Buck Baker	Chevrolet	76.126	Marvin Panch	Ford	78.238

Cum. No.	Yr. No.	Date	Site	Track Length	Surface	Miles	Race Winner	Make	Speed	Pole Winner	Make	Pole Speed
298	21	6/1/57	Lancaster, SC	0.5	D	100	Paul Goldsmith	Ford	61.622	Buck Baker	Chevrolet	67.365
299	22	6/8/57	Los Angeles, CA	0.5	D	100	Eddie Pagan	Ford	None	Eddie Pagan	Ford	67.29
300	23	6/15/57	Newport, TN	0.5	D	100	Fireball Roberts	Ford	60.687	Speedy Thompson	Chevrolet	61.813
301	24	6/20/57	Columbia, SC	0.5	D	100	Jack Smith	Chevrolet	58.045	Buck Baker	Chevrolet	64.585
302	25	6/22/57	Sacramento, CA	0.5	D	100	Bill Amick	Ford	59.58	Art Watts	Ford	69.337
303	26	6/29/57	Spartanburg, SC	0.5	D	100	Lee Petty	Olds	46.287	Lee Petty	Olds	59.642
304	27	6/30/57	Jacksonville, NC	0.5	D	100	Buck Baker	Chevrolet	55.342	Lee Petty	Olds	61.328
305	28	7/4/57	Raleigh, NC	1	P	250	Paul Goldsmith	Ford	75.693	Frankie Schneider	Chevrolet	83.371
306	29	7/12/57	Charlotte, NC	0.5	D	100	Marvin Panch	Ford	56.302	Tiny Lund	Pontiac	60.913
307	30	7/14/57	LeHi, Arkansas	1.5	D	201	Marvin Panch	Pontiac	67.167	Speedy Thompson	Chevrolet	98.991
308	31	7/14/57	Portland, OR	0.5	P	100	Eddie Pagan	Ford	64.539	Art Watts	Ford	66.396
309	32	7/20/57	Hickory, NC	0.4	D	100	Jack Smith	Chevrolet	58.737	Gwyn Staley	Chevrolet	66.085
310	33	7/24/57	Norfolk, VA	0.4	D	100	Buck Baker	Chevrolet	47.987	Bill Amick	Ford	56.338
311	34	7/30/57	Lancaster, SC	0.5	D	100	Speedy Thompson	Chevrolet	66.543	Speedy Thompson	Chevrolet	67.694
312	35	8/4/57	Watkins Glen, NY	2.3	P	101.2	Buck Baker	Chevrolet	83.064	Buck Baker	Chevrolet	87.071
313	36	8/4/57	Bremerton, WA	0.9	P	72	Parnelli Jones	Ford	38.959	Art Watts	Ford	62.657
314	37	8/10/57	New Oxford, PA	0.5	D	100	Marvin Panch	Ford	77.569	Tiny Lund	Pontiac	80.971
315	38	8/16/57	Old Bridge, NJ	0.5	P	100	Lee Petty	Olds	65.813	Rex White	Ford	71.599
316	39	8/26/57	Myrtle Beach, SC	0.5	D	100	Gwyn Staley	Chevrolet	50.782	Johnny Allen	Plymouth	58.139
317	40	9/2/57	Darlington, SC	1.375	P	500.5	Speedy Thompson	Chevrolet	100.094	Cotton Owens	Pontiac	117.416
318	41	9/5/57	Syracuse, NY	1	D	100	Gwyn Staley	Chevrolet	80.591	Gwyn Staley	Chevrolet	83.045
319	42	9/8/57	Weaverville, NC	0.5	P	100	Lee Petty	Olds	67.95	Bill Amick	Ford	77.687
320	43	9/8/57	Sacramento, CA	1	D	100	Danny Graves	Chevrolet	68.663	Danny Graves	Chevrolet	78.007
321	44	9/15/57	San Jose, CA	0.5	D	100	Marvin Porter	Ford	None	No Time Trials	NTT	NTT
322	45	9/15/57	Langhorne, PA	1	D	300	Gwyn Staley	Chevrolet	72.759	Paul Goldsmith	Ford	92.072
323	46	9/19/57	Columbia, SC	0.5	D	100	Buck Baker	Chevrolet	60.514	Buck Baker	Chevrolet	63.649
324	47	9/21/57	Shelby, NC	0.5	D	100	Buck Baker	Chevrolet	53.699	Buck Baker	Chevrolet	58.177
325	48	10/5/57	Charlotte, NC	0.5	D	100	Lee Petty	Olds	51.583	Lee Petty	Olds	60.585
326	49	10/6/57	Martinsville, VA	0.5	P	250	Bob Welborn	Chevrolet	63.025	Eddie Pagan	Ford	65.837
327	50	10/12/57	Newberry, SC	0.5	D	100	Fireball Roberts	Ford	50.398	Jack Smith	Chevrolet	56.514
328	51	10/13/57	Concord, NC	0.5	D	100	Fireball Roberts	Ford	59.553	Jack Smith	Chevrolet	65.052
329	52	10/20/57	N. Wilkesboro, NC	0.625	D	100	Jack Smith	Chevrolet	69.902	Fireball Roberts	Ford	81.64
330	53	10/27/57	Greensboro, NC	0.333	D	83.25	Buck Baker	Chevrolet	38.927	Ken Rush	Ford	48.358

1958

Cum. No.	Yr. No.	Date	Site	Track Length	Surface	Miles	Race Winner	Make	Speed	Pole Winner	Make	Pole Speed
331	1	11/3/57	Fayetteville, NC	0.333	P	49.95	Rex White	Chevrolet	59.17	Jack Smith	Chevrolet	62.665
332	2	2/23/58	Daytona Beach, FL	4.1	B-R	159.9	Paul Goldsmith	Pontiac	101.113	Paul Goldsmith	Pontiac	140.57
333	3	3/2/58	Concord, NC	0.5	D	100	Lee Petty	Olds	58.555	Speedy Thompson	Chevrolet	N/A
334	4	3/15/58	Fayetteville, NC	0.333	P	49.95	Curtis Turner	Ford	56.141	Lee Petty	Olds	62.6
335	5	3/16/58	Wilson, NC	0.5	D	100	Lee Petty	Olds	48.459	Marvin Panch	Ford	58.901
336	6	3/23/58	Hillsboro, NC	0.9	D	99	Buck Baker	Chevrolet	78.502	Buck Baker	Chevrolet	83.076
337	7	4/5/58	Fayetteville, NC	0.333	P	49.95	Bob Welborn	Chevrolet	50.229	Lee Petty	Olds	60.576
338	8	4/10/58	Columbia, SC	0.5	D	100	Speedy Thompson	Chevrolet	None	Possum Jones	Chevrolet	66.201
339	9	4/12/58	Spartanburg, SC	0.5	D	100	Speedy Thompson	Chevrolet	56.613	Speedy Thompson	Chevrolet	61.412
340	10	4/13/58	Atlanta, GA	1	D	100	Curtis Turner	Ford	79.016	Joe Weatherly	Ford	81.577
341	11	4/18/58	Charlotte, NC	0.5	D	100	Curtis Turner	Ford	53.254	Curtis Turner	Ford	57.471
342	12	4/20/58	Martinsville, VA	0.5	P	250	Bob Welborn	Chevrolet	66.007	Buck Baker	Chevrolet	61.166
343	13	4/25/58	Manassas, VA	0.375	D	56.25	Frankie Schneider	Chevrolet	67.59	Eddie Pagan	Ford	69.018
344	14	4/27/58	Old Bridge, NJ	0.5	P	100	Jim Reed	Ford	68.438	Jim Reed	Ford	71.371
345	15	5/3/58	Greenville, SC	0.5	D	100	Jack Smith	Chevrolet	62.295	Jack Smith	Chevrolet	60.484
346	16	5/11/58	Greensboro, NC	0.333	D	49.95	Bob Welborn	Chevrolet	45.628	Bob Welborn	Chevrolet	46.25
347	17	5/15/58	Roanoke, VA	0.25	P	37.5	Jim Reed	Ford	49.504	Jim Reed	Ford	51.963
348	18	5/18/58	N. Wilkesboro, NC	0.625	P	100	Junior Johnson	Ford	78.636	Jack Smith	Chevrolet	82.056
349	19	5/24/58	Winston-Salem, NC	0.25	P	37.5	Bob Welborn	Chevrolet	40.407	Rex White	Chevrolet	46.851
350	20	5/30/58	Trenton, NJ	1	P	500	Fireball Roberts	Chevrolet	84.522	Marvin Panch	Ford	89.02
351	21	6/1/58	Riverside, CA	2.631	P	499.89	Eddie Gray	Ford	79.481	Danny Graves	Chevrolet	N/A
352	22	6/5/58	Columbia, SC	0.5	D	100	Junior Johnson	Ford	54.752	Buck Baker	Chevrolet	64.308
353	23	6/12/58	Bradford, PA	0.333	D	49.95	Junior Johnson	Ford	59.84	Bob Duell	Ford	65.831
354	24	6/15/58	Reading, PA	0.5	D	100	Junior Johnson	Ford	53.763	Speedy Thompson	Chevrolet	60.687
355	25	6/25/58	New Oxford, PA	0.5	D	100	Lee Petty	Olds	69.726	Ken Rush	Ford	82.796
356	26	6/28/58	Hickory, NC	0.4	D	100	Lee Petty	Olds	62.413	Speedy Thompson	Chevrolet	68.768
357	27	6/29/58	Weaverville, NC	0.5	P	100	Rex White	Chevrolet	73.892	Rex White	Chevrolet	76.857
358	28	7/4/58	Raleigh, NC	1	P	250	Fireball Roberts	Chevrolet	73.691	Cotton Owens	Pontiac	83.896

Cum. No.	Yr. No.	Date	Site	Track Length	Surface	Miles	Race Winner	Make	Speed	Pole Winner	Make	Pole Speed
359	29	7/12/58	Asheville, NC	0.25	P	37.5	Jim Paschal	Chevrolet	46.44	Jim Paschal	Chevrolet	50.336
360	30	7/16/58	Busti, NY	0.333	D	49.95	Shorty Rollins	Ford	47.11	Lee Petty	Olds	N/A
361	31	7/18/58	Toronto, Canada	0.333	P	33.3	Lee Petty	Olds	43.184	Rex White	Chevrolet	51.406
362	32	7/19/58	Buffalo, NY	0.25	P	25	Jim Reed	Ford	46.972	Rex White	Chevrolet	38.593
363	33	7/25/58	Rochester, NY	0.5	D	100	Cotton Owens	Pontiac	59.99	Rex White	Chevrolet	62.871
364	34	7/26/58	Belmar, NJ	0.333	P	99.9	Jim Reed	Chevrolet	65.395	Rex White	Chevrolet	68.936
365	35	8/2/58	Bridgehampton, NY	2.85	P	99.75	Jack Smith	Chevrolet	80.696	Jack Smith	Chevrolet	82.001
366	36	8/7/58	Columbia, SC	0.5	D	100	Speedy Thompson	Chevrolet	54.82	Speedy Thompson	Chevrolet	64.24
367	37	8/10/58	Nashville, TN	0.5	P	100	Joe Weatherly	Ford	59.269	Rex White	Chevrolet	71.315
368	38	8/17/58	Weaverville, NC	0.5	P	250	Fireball Roberts	Chevrolet	66.78	Jimmy Massey	Pontiac	76.596
369	39	8/22/58	Winston-Salem, NC	0.25	P	50	Lee Petty	Olds	39.258	George Dunn	Mercury	46.68
370	40	8/23/58	Myrtle Beach, SC	0.5	D	100	Bob Welborn	Chevrolet	60.443	Speedy Thompson	Chevrolet	66.667
371	41	9/1/58	Darlington, SC	1.375	P	500.5	Fireball Roberts	Chevrolet	102.585	Eddie Pagan	Ford	116.952
372	42	9/5/58	Charlotte, NC	0.5	D	100	Buck Baker	Chevrolet	52.28	Lee Petty	Olds	576.897
373	43	9/7/58	Birmingham, AL	0.5	D	100	Fireball Roberts	Chevrolet	60.678	Cotton Owens	Pontiac	64.034
374	44	9/7/58	Sacramento, CA	1	D	100	Parnelli Jones	Ford	65.55	Parnelli Jones	Ford	77.922
375	45	9/12/58	Gastonia, NC	0.333	D	66.6	Buck Baker	Chevrolet	47.856	Tiny Lund	Chevrolet	51.65
376	46	9/14/58	Richmond, VA	0.5	D	100	Speedy Thompson	Chevrolet	57.878	Speedy Thompson	Chevrolet	62.915
377	47	9/28/58	Hillsboro, NC	0.9	D	99	Joe Eubanks	Pontiac	72.439	Tiny Lund	Chevrolet	87.308
378	48	10/5/58	Salisbury, NC	0.625	D	100	Lee Petty	Olds	58.271	Gober Sosebee	Chevrolet	72.162
379	49	10/12/58	Martinsville, VA	0.5	P	250	Fireball Roberts	Chevrolet	64.344	Glen Wood	Ford	67.95
380	50	10/19/58	N. Wilkesboro, NC	0.625	P	100	Junior Johnson	Ford	84.906	Glen Wood	Ford	86.805
381	51	10/26/58	Atlanta, GA	1	D	150	Junior Johnson	Ford	69.57	Glen Wood	Ford	81.522

1959

Cum. No.	Yr. No.	Date	Site	Track Length	Surface	Miles	Race Winner	Make	Speed	Pole Winner	Make	Pole Speed
382	1	11/9/58	Fayetteville, NC	0.333	P	49.95	Bob Welborn	Chevrolet	56.001	Bob Welborn	Chevrolet	61.985
383	2	2/20/59	Daytona Beach, FL	2.5	P	100	Bob Welborn	Chevrolet	143.198	Fireball Roberts	Pontiac	140.581
384	3	2/22/59	Daytona Beach, FL	2.5	P	500	Lee Petty	Oldsmobile	135.521	Bob Welborn	Chevrolet	140.121
385	4	3/1/59	Hillsboro, NC	0.9	D	99	Curtis Turner	T-Bird	81.612	Curtis Turner	T-Bird	87.544
386	5	3/8/59	Concord, NC	0.5	D	100	Curtis Turner	T-Bird	59.239	Buck Baker	Chevrolet	66.42
387	6	3/22/59	Atlanta, GA	1	D	100	Johnny Beauchamp	T-Bird	75.172	Buck Baker	Chevrolet	77.888
388	7	3/29/59	Wilson, NC	0.5	D	100	Junior Johnson	Ford	50.3	No Time Trials	NTT	NTT
389	8	3/30/59	Winston-Salem, NC	0.25	P	50	Jim Reed	Ford	43.562	Rex White	Chevrolet	46.296
390	9	4/4/59	Columbia, SC	0.5	P	100	Jack Smith	Chevrolet	57.343	Jack Smith	Chevrolet	60.73
391	10	4/5/59	N. Wilkesboro, NC	0.625	P	100	Lee Petty	Olds	71.985	Speedy Thompson	Chevrolet	85.746
392	11	4/26/59	Reading, PA	0.5	D	100	Junior Johnson	Ford	53.011	Junior Johnson	Ford	68.9
393	12	5/2/59	Hickory, NC	0.4	D	100	Junior Johnson	Ford	62.165	Bobby Johns	Chevrolet	66.03
394	13	5/3/59	Martinsville, VA	0.5	P	250	Lee Petty	Olds	59.512	Bob Burdick	T-Bird	88.95
395	14	5/17/59	Trenton, NJ	1	P	150	Tom Pistone	T-Bird	87.35	Bob Welborn	Chevrolet	57.95
396	15	5/22/59	Charlotte, NC	0.5	D	100	Lee Petty	Olds	55.3	Rex White	Chevrolet	70.89
397	16	5/24/59	Nashville, TN	0.5	P	100	Rex White	Chevrolet	71.006	Jim Reed	Chevrolet	53.59
398	17	5/30/59	Los Angeles, CA	0.4	D	194.8	Parnelli Jones	Ford	50.982	Cotton Owens	Pontiac	63.18
399	18	6/5/59	Spartanburg, SC	0.5	D	100	Jack Smith	Chevrolet	55.547	Jack Smith	Chevrolet	65.838
400	19	6/13/59	Greenville, SC	0.5	D	100	Junior Johnson	Ford	51.48	No Time Trials	NTT	NTT
401	20	6/14/59	Atlanta, GA	1	D	150	Lee Petty	Plymouth	58.499	Bob Burdick	T-Bird	64.865
402	21	6/18/59	Columbia, SC	0.5	D	100	Lee Petty	Plymouth	58.726	No Time Trials	NTT	NTT
403	22	6/20/59	Wilson, NC	0.5	D	100	Junior Johnson	Ford	58.065	Buck Baker	Chevrolet	66.42
404	23	6/21/59	Richmond, VA	0.5	D	100	Tom Pistone	T-Bird	56.881	Lee Petty	Plymouth	47.071
405	24	6/27/59	Winston-Salem, NC	0.25	P	50	Rex White	Chevrolet	41.228	Glen Wood	Ford	76.82
406	25	6/28/59	Weaverville, NC	0.5	P	100	Rex White	Chevrolet	72.934	Fireball Roberts	Pontiac	144.997
407	26	7/4/59	Daytona Beach, FL	2.5	P	250	Fireball Roberts	Pontiac	140.581	Dick Bailey	Plymouth	47.97
408	27	7/21/59	Pittsburg, PA	0.25	D	50	Jim Reed	Chevrolet	45	Buck Baker	Chevrolet	63.07
409	28	7/26/59	Charlotte, NC	0.5	D	100	Jack Smith	Chevrolet	49.553	Bob Welborn	Chevrolet	66.47
410	29	8/1/59	Myrtle Beach, SC	0.5	D	100	Ned Jarrett	Ford	52.941	Bob Welborn	Chevrolet	62.54
411	30	8/2/59	Charlotte, NC	0.5	D	100	Ned Jarrett	Ford	52.794	Rex White	Chevrolet	74.044
412	31	8/9/59	Nashville, TN	0.5	P	150	Joe Lee Johnson	Chevrolet	63.343	Rex White	Chevrolet	77.687
413	32	8/16/59	Weaverville, NC	0.5	P	250	Bob Welborn	Chevrolet	71.833	Rex White	Chevrolet	47.443
414	33	8/21/59	Winston-Salem, NC	0.25	P	50	Rex White	Chevrolet	44.085	Lee Petty	Plymouth	63.313
415	34	8/22/59	Greenville, SC	0.5	D	100	Buck Baker	Chevrolet	58.055	No Time Trials	NTT	NTT
416	35	8/29/59	Columbia, SC	0.5	D	100	Lee Petty	Plymouth	48.264	Fireball Roberts	Pontiac	123.734
417	36	9/7/59	Darlington, SC	1.375	P	500.5	Jim Reed	Chevrolet	111.836	No Time Trials	NTT	NTT
418	37	9/11/59	Hickory, NC	0.4	D	100	Lee Petty	Plymouth	63.38	Cotton Owens	T-Bird	62.674
419	38	9/13/59	Richmond, VA	0.5	D	100	Cotton Owens	T-Bird	60.382	No Time Trials	NTT	NTT

Cum. No.	Yr. No.	Date	Site	Track Length	Surface	Miles	Race Winner	Make	Speed	Pole Winner	Make	Pole Speed
420	39	9/13/59	Sacramento, CA	1	D	100	Eddie Gray	Ford	54.753	Jack Smith	Chevrolet	85.533
421	40	9/20/59	Hillsboro, NC	0.9	D	99	Lee Petty	Plymouth	77.868	Glen Wood	Ford	69.471
422	41	9/27/59	Martinsville, VA	0.5	P	250	Rex White	Chevrolet	60.5	Tommy Irwin	T-Bird	78.568
423	42	10/11/59	Weaverville, NC	0.5	P	100	Lee Petty	Plymouth	76.433	Glen Wood	Ford	86.806
424	43	10/18/59	N. Wilkesboro, NC	0.625	P	100	Lee Petty	Plymouth	74.829	No Time Trials	NTT	NTT
425	44	10/25/59	Concord, NC	0.5	D	150	Jack Smith	Chevrolet	54.005	Buck Baker	Chevrolet	64.103

1960

Cum. No.	Yr. No.	Date	Site	Track Length	Surface	Miles	Race Winner	Make	Speed	Pole Winner	Make	Pole Speed
426	1	11/8/59	Charlotte, NC	0.5	D	100	Jack Smith	Chevrolet	52.409	Junior Johnson	Dodge	65.217
427	2	11/26/59	Columbia, SC	0.5	D	100	Ned Jarrett	Ford	55.071	Cotton Owens	Pontiac	149.892
428	3	2/12/60	Daytona Beach, FL	2.5	P	100	Fireball Roberts	Pontiac	137.614	Jack Smith	Pontiac	148.157
429	4	2/12/60	Daytona Beach, FL	2.5	P	100	Jack Smith	Pontiac	146.52	Cotton Owens	Pontiac	149.892
430	5	2/14/60	Daytona Beach, FL	2.5	P	500	Junior Johnson	Chevrolet	124.74	Lee Petty	Plymouth	62.11
431	6	2/28/60	Charlotte, NC	0.5	D	100	Richard Petty	Plymouth	53.404	Junior Johnson	Chevrolet	83.86
432	7	3/27/60	N. Wilkesboro, NC	0.625	P	100	Lee Petty	Plymouth	66.347	Mel Larson	Pontiac	78.93
433	8	4/3/60	Phoenix, AZ	1	D	100	John Rostek	Ford	71.899	Doug Yates	Plymouth	66.03
434	9	4/5/60	Columbia, SC	0.5	D	100	Rex White	Chevrolet	50.697	Glen Wood	Ford	69.15
435	10	4/10/60	Martinsville, VA	0.5	P	250	Richard Petty	Plymouth	63.943	Rex White	Chevrolet	71.08
436	11	4/16/60	Hickory, NC	0.4	D	100	Joe Weatherly	Ford	66.347	Emanuel Zervakis	Chevrolet	60.5
437	12	4/17/60	Wilson, NC	0.5	D	100	Joe Weatherly	Ford	55.113	Glen Wood	Ford	47.24
438	13	4/18/60	Winston-Salem, NC	0.25	P	50	Glen Wood	Ford	43.082	Curtis Turner	Ford	64.72
439	14	4/23/60	Greenville, SC	0.5	D	100	Ned Jarrett	Ford	62.337	Junior Johnson	Ford	78.09
440	15	4/24/60	Weaverville, NC	0.5	P	83.5	Lee Petty	Plymouth	63.368	Fireball Roberts	Pontiac	127.75
441	16	5/14/60	Darlington, SC	1.375	P	301.125	Joe Weatherly	Ford	102.64	Jack Smith	Pontiac	64.22
442	17	5/28/60	Spartanburg, SC	0.5	D	100	Ned Jarrett	Ford	51.843	Richard Petty	Plymouth	88.19
443	18	5/29/60	Hillsboro, NC	0.9	D	99	Lee Petty	Plymouth	83.583	Ned Jarrett	Ford	64.56
444	19	6/5/60	Richmond, VA	0.5	D	100	Lee Petty	Plymouth	62.251	Frank Secrist	Ford	93.04
445	20	6/12/60	Hanford, CA	1.4	P	250.6	Marvin Porter	Ford	88.032	Fireball Roberts	Pontiac	133.904
446	21	6/19/60	Charlotte, NC	1.5	P	600	Joe Lee Johnson	Chevrolet	107.735	Lee Petty	Plymouth	47.85
447	22	6/26/60	Winston-Salem, NC	0.25	P	50	Glen Wood	Ford	45.872	Jack Smith	Pontiac	152.129
448	23	7/4/60	Daytona Beach, FL	2.5	P	250	Jack Smith	Pontiac	146.842	Lee Petty	Plymouth	71.97
449	24	7/10/60	Pittsburg, PA	0.5	D	94	Lee Petty	Plymouth	67.45	John Rostek	Ford	91.65
450	25	7/17/60	Montgomery, NY	2	P	200	Rex White	Chevrolet	88.626	Ned Jarrett	Ford	64.61
451	26	7/23/60	Myrtle Beach, SC	0.5	D	100	Buck Baker	Chevrolet	60.985	Fireball Roberts	Pontiac	133.87
452	27	7/31/60	Hampton, GA	1.5	P	300	Fireball Roberts	Pontiac	112.652	Ned Jarrett	Ford	55.866
453	28	8/3/60	Birmingham, AL	0.25	P	50	Ned Jarrett	Ford	54.463	Rex White	Chevrolet	74.81
454	29	8/7/60	Nashville, TN	0.5	P	166.5	Johnny Beauchamp	Chevrolet	56.966	Jack Smith	Pontiac	77.85
455	30	8/14/60	Weaverville, NC	0.5	P	250	Rex White	Chevrolet	65.024	Cotton Owens	Pontiac	63.25
456	31	8/16/60	Spartanburg, SC	0.5	D	100	Cotton Owens	Pontiac	59.681	Tommy Irwin	T-Bird	60.36
457	32	8/18/60	Columbia, SC	0.5	D	150	Rex White	Chevrolet	54.265	Ned Jarrett	Ford	51.903
458	33	8/20/60	South Boston, VA	0.25	D	37.5	Junior Johnson	Chevrolet	50.732	Glen Wood	Ford	46.97
459	34	8/23/60	Winston-Salem, NC	0.25	P	50	Glen Wood	Ford	44.389	Fireball Roberts	Pontiac	125.459
460	35	9/5/60	Darlington, SC	1.375	P	500.5	Buck Baker	Pontiac	105.901	Buck Baker	Chevrolet	71.18
461	36	9/9/60	Hickory, NC	0.4	D	100	Junior Johnson	Chevrolet	69.998	Jim Cook	Dodge	78.45
462	37	9/11/60	Sacramento, CA	1	D	100	Jim Cook	Dodge	70.629	David Pearson	Chevrolet	45.07
463	38	9/15/60	Sumter, SC	0.25	D	50	Ned Jarrett	Ford	41.208	Richard Petty	Plymouth	85.285
464	39	9/18/60	Hillsboro, NC	0.9	D	99	Richard Petty	Plymouth	80.161	Glen Wood	Ford	68.44
465	40	9/25/60	Martinsville, VA	0.5	P	250	Rex White	Chevrolet	60.439	Rex White	Chevrolet	93.399
466	41	10/2/60	N. Wilkesboro, NC	0.625	P	200	Rex White	Chevrolet	77.444	Fireball Roberts	Pontiac	133.465
467	42	10/16/60	Charlotte, NC	1.5	P	400.5	Speedy Thompson	Ford	112.905	Ned Jarrett	Ford	64.41
468	43	10/23/60	Richmond, VA	0.5	D	100	Speedy Thompson	Ford	63.739	Fireball Roberts	Pontiac	134.596
469	44	10/30/60	Hampton, GA	1.5	P	501	Bobby Johns	Pontiac	108.408	Lee Petty	Plymouth	63.581

1961

Cum. No.	Yr. No.	Date	Site	Track Length	Surface	Miles	Race Winner	Make	Speed	Pole Winner	Make	Pole Speed
470	1	11/6/60	Charlotte, NC	0.5	D	100	Joe Weatherly	Ford	59.435	Junior Johnson	Pontiac	68.623
471	2	11/20/60	Jacksonville, FL	0.5	D	100	Lee Petty	Plymouth	64.4	Fireball Roberts	Pontiac	133.037
472	3	2/24/61	Daytona Beach, FL	2.5	P	97.5	Fireball Roberts	Pontiac	129.711	Joe Weatherly	Pontiac	154.122
473	4	2/24/61	Daytona Beach, FL	2.5	P	100	Joe Weatherly	Pontiac	152.671	Fireball Roberts	Pontiac	155.709
474	5	2/26/61	Daytona Beach, FL	2.5	P	500	Marvin Panch	Pontiac	149.601	Ned Jarrett	Ford	63.92
475	6	3/4/61	Spartanburg, SC	0.5	D	100	Cotton Owens	Pontiac	59.152	Rex White	Chevrolet	79.295
476	7	3/5/61	Weaverville, NC	0.5	P	100	Rex White	Chevrolet	72.492	Bob Ross	Ford	98.37
477	8	3/12/61	Hanford, CA	1.4	P	249.2	Fireball Roberts	Pontiac	95.621	Marvin Panch	Pontiac	135.755
478	9	3/26/61	Hampton, GA	1.5	P	501	Bob Burdick	Pontiac	124.172	Junior Johnson	Pontiac	62.09

Cum. No.	Yr. No.	Date	Site	Track Length	Surface	Miles	Race Winner	Make	Speed	Pole Winner	Make	Pole Speed
479	10	4/1/61	Greenville, SC	0.5	D	100	Emanuel Zervakis	Chevrolet	52.189	Ned Jarrett	Chevrolet	91.836
480	11	4/2/61	Hillsboro, NC	0.9	D	99	Cotton Owens	Pontiac	84.695	Glen Wood	Ford	48.7
481	12	4/3/61	Winston-Salem, NC	0.25	P	37.5	Rex White	Chevrolet	45.5	Rex White	Chevrolet	70.28
482	13	4/9/61	Martinsville, VA	0.5	P	74.5	Fred Lorenzen	Ford	68.366	Junior Johnson	Pontiac	95.66
483	14	4/16/61	N. Wilkesboro, NC	0.625	P	250	Rex White	Chevrolet	83.248	Ned Jarrett	Chevrolet	64.38
484	15	4/20/61	Columbia, SC	0.5	D	100	Cotton Owens	Pontiac	51.94	Junior Johnson	Pontiac	74.074
485	16	4/22/61	Hickory, NC	0.4	D	100	Junior Johnson	Pontiac	66.654	Richard Petty	Plymouth	66.667
486	17	4/23/61	Richmond, VA	0.5	D	100	Richard Petty	Plymouth	62.456	Rex White	Chevrolet	71.32
487	18	4/30/61	Martinsville, VA	0.5	P	250	Junior Johnson	Pontiac	66.278	Fred Lorenzen	Ford	128.965
488	19	5/6/61	Darlington, SC	1.375	P	301.125	Fred Lorenzen	Ford	119.52	Fred Lorenzen	Ford	137.48
489	20	5/21/61	Charlotte, NC	1.5	P	100.5	Richard Petty	Plymouth	133.554	Junior Johnson	Pontiac	136.951
490	21	5/21/61	Charlotte, NC	1.5	P	100.5	Joe Weatherly	Pontiac	115.591	Eddie Gray	Ford	85.21
491	22	5/21/61	Riverside, CA	2.58	P	100.62	Lloyd Dane	Chevrolet	82.512	Danny Weinberg	Ford	71.94
492	23	5/27/61	Los Angeles, CA	0.5	D	100	Eddie Gray	Ford	68.833	Richard Petty	Plymouth	131.611
493	24	5/28/61	Charlotte, NC	1.5	P	600	David Pearson	Pontiac	111.633	Joe Weatherly	Pontiac	61.25
494	25	6/2/61	Spartanburg, SC	0.5	D	100	Jim Paschal	Pontiac	55.495	Johnny Allen	Chevrolet	65.91
495	26	6/4/61	Birmingham, AL	0.5	D	100	Ned Jarrett	Chevrolet	61.068	Ned Jarrett	Chevrolet	65.48
496	27	6/8/61	Greenville, SC	0.5	D	100	Jack Smith	Pontiac	58.441	Junior Johnson	Pontiac	47.72
497	28	6/10/61	Winston-Salem, NC	0.25	P	50	Rex White	Chevrolet	42.714	Rex White	Chevrolet	55.87
498	29	6/17/61	Norwood, MA	0.25	P	125	Emanuel Zervakis	Chevrolet	53.827	Emanuel Zervakis	Chevrolet	54.97
499	30	6/23/61	Hartsville, SC	0.333	D	49.95	Buck Baker	Chrysler	46.234	Rex White	Chevrolet	53.7
500	31	6/24/61	Roanoke, VA	0.25	P	37.5	Junior Johnson	Pontiac	49.907	Fireball Roberts	Pontiac	157.15
501	32	7/4/61	Daytona Beach, FL	2.5	P	250	David Pearson	Pontiac	154.294	Fireball Roberts	Pontiac	136.088
502	33	7/9/61	Hampton, GA	1.5	P	250.5	Fred Lorenzen	Ford	118.067	Cotton Owens	Pontiac	67.65
503	34	7/20/61	Columbia, SC	0.5	D	100	Cotton Owens	Pontiac	62.198	Joe Weatherly	Pontiac	66.69
504	35	7/22/61	Myrtle Beach, SC	0.5	D	100	Joe Weatherly	Pontiac	57.655	Fred Lorenzen	Ford	79.225
505	36	7/29/61	Bristol, TN	0.5	P	250	Jack Smith	Pontiac	68.373	Rex White	Chevrolet	76.69
506	37	8/6/61	Nashville, TN	0.5	P	201.5	Jim Paschal	Pontiac	56.455	Junior Johnson	Pontiac	48.05
507	38	8/9/61	Winston-Salem, NC	0.25	P	37.5	Rex White	Chevrolet	42.452	Jim Paschal	Pontiac	80.43
508	39	8/13/61	Weaverville, NC	0.5	P	129	Junior Johnson	Pontiac	65.704	Junior Johnson	Pontiac	58.86
509	40	8/18/61	Richmond, VA	0.25	P	37.5	Junior Johnson	Pontiac	51.605	Cotton Owens	Pontiac	52.63
510	41	8/27/61	South Boston, VA	0.25	D	50	Junior Johnson	Pontiac	48.348	Fireball Roberts	Pontiac	128.68
511	42	9/4/61	Darlington, SC	1.375	P	500.5	Nelson Stacy	Ford	117.787	Rex White	Chevrolet	72.29
512	43	9/8/61	Hickory, NC	0.4	D	100	Rex White	Chevrolet	67.529	Junior Johnson	Pontiac	65.01
513	44	9/10/61	Richmond, VA	0.5	D	125	Joe Weatherly	Pontiac	61.677	Bill Amick	Pontiac	79.26
514	45	9/10/61	Sacramento, CA	1	D	100	Eddie Gray	Ford	None	Fireball Roberts	Pontiac	136.778
515	46	9/17/61	Hampton, GA	1.5	P	400.5	David Pearson	Pontiac	125.384	Fred Lorenzen	Ford	70.73
516	47	9/24/61	Martinsville, VA	0.5	P	250	Joe Weatherly	Pontiac	62.586	Junior Johnson	Pontiac	94.54
517	48	10/1/61	N. Wilkesboro, NC	0.625	P	200	Rex White	Chevrolet	84.675	David Pearson	Pontiac	138.577
518	49	10/15/61	Charlotte, NC	1.5	P	400.5	Joe Weatherly	Pontiac	119.95	Bobby Johns	Pontiac	80.645
519	50	10/22/61	Bristol, TN	0.5	P	250	Joe Weatherly	Pontiac	72.452	Buck Baker	Chrysler	66.667
520	51	10/28/61	Greenville, SC	0.5	D	100	Junior Johnson	Pontiac	63.346	Joe Weatherly	Pontiac	95.154
521	52	10/29/61	Hillsboro, NC	0.9	D	148.5	Joe Weatherly	Pontiac	85.249	Joe Weatherly	Pontiac	68.543

1962

Cum. No.	Yr. No.	Date	Site	Track Length	Surface	Miles	Race Winner	Make	Speed	Pole Winner	Make	Pole Speed
522	1	11/5/61	Concord, NC	0.5	D	100	Jack Smith	Pontiac	59.405	Joe Weatherly	Pontiac	81.743
523	2	11/12/61	Weaverville, NC	0.5	P	100	Rex White	Chevrolet	68.467	Fireball Roberts	Pontiac	158.744
524	3	2/16/62	Daytona Beach, FL	2.5	P	100	Fireball Roberts	Pontiac	156.999	Darel Dieringer	Pontiac	155.086
525	4	2/16/62	Daytona Beach, FL	2.5	P	100	Joe Weatherly	Pontiac	145.395	Fireball Roberts	Pontiac	156.999
526	5	2/18/62	Daytona Beach, FL	2.5	P	500	Fireball Roberts	Pontiac	152.529	Joe Weatherly	Pontiac	N/A
527	6	2/25/62	Concord, NC	0.5	D	39	Joe Weatherly	Pontiac	53.161	Rex White	Chevrolet	80.46
528	7	3/4/62	Weaverville, NC	0.5	P	100	Joe Weatherly	Pontiac	75.471	Rex White	Chevrolet	70.588
529	8	3/17/62	Savannah, GA	0.5	D	100	Jack Smith	Pontiac	58.775	Joe Weatherly	Pontiac	96.285
530	9	3/18/62	Hillsboro, NC	0.9	D	99	Rex White	Chevrolet	86.948	No Time Trials	NTT	NTT
531	10	4/1/62	Richmond, VA	0.5	D	90	Rex White	Chevrolet	51.363	Joe Weatherly	Pontiac	64.423
532	11	4/13/62	Columbia, SC	0.5	D	100	Ned Jarrett	Chevrolet	56.71	Junior Johnson	Pontiac	94.142
533	12	4/15/62	N. Wilkesboro, NC	0.625	P	250	Richard Petty	Plymouth	84.737	Ned Jarrett	Chevrolet	66.568
534	13	4/19/62	Greenville, SC	0.5	D	100	Ned Jarrett	Chevrolet	57.48	Ned Jarrett	Chevrolet	68.939
535	14	4/21/62	Myrtle Beach, SC	0.5	D	100	Jack Smith	Pontiac	63.036	Fred Lorenzen	Ford	71.287
536	15	4/22/62	Martinsville, VA	0.5	P	250	Richard Petty	Plymouth	66.425	Rex White	Chevrolet	48.417
537	16	4/23/62	Winston-Salem, NC	0.25	P	27	Rex White	Chevrolet	43.392	Fireball Roberts	Pontiac	81.374
538	17	4/29/62	Bristol, TN	0.5	P	250	Bobby Johns	Pontiac	73.397	Rex White	Chevrolet	71.145
539	18	5/4/62	Richmond, VA	0.333	P	66.6	Jimmy Pardue	Pontiac	67.747	Jack Smith	Pontiac	74.074

Cum. No.	Yr. No.	Date	Site	Track Length	Surface	Miles	Race Winner	Make	Speed	Pole Winner	Make	Pole Speed
540	19	5/5/62	Hickory, NC	0.4	D	100	Jack Smith	Pontiac	71.216	No Time Trials	NTT	NTT
541	20	5/6/62	Concord, NC	0.5	D	100	Joe Weatherly	Pontiac	57.052	Fred Lorenzen	Ford	129.81
542	21	5/12/62	Darlington, SC	1.375	P	301.125	Nelson Stacy	Ford	117.429	Cotton Owens	Pontiac	64.423
543	22	5/19/62	Spartanburg, SC	0.5	D	100	Ned Jarrett	Chevrolet	60.08	Fireball Roberts	Pontiac	140.15
544	23	5/27/62	Charlotte, NC	1.5	P	600	Nelson Stacy	Ford	125.552	Banjo Matthews	Pontiac	137.64
545	24	6/10/62	Hampton, GA	1.5	P	328.5	Fred Lorenzen	Ford	101.983	Rex White	Chevrolet	48.179
546	25	6/16/62	Winston-Salem, NC	0.25	P	50	Johnny Allen	Pontiac	45.466	Joe Weatherly	Pontiac	63.069
547	26	6/19/62	Augusta, GA	0.5	D	100	Joe Weatherly	Pontiac	59.85	Rex White	Chevrolet	70.435
548	27	6/22/62	Richmond, VA	0.333	P	99.9	Jim Paschal	Pontiac	66.293	Jack Smith	Pontiac	79.458
549	28	6/23/62	South Boston, VA	0.375	P	100.125	Rex White	Chevrolet	72.54	Banjo Matthews	Pontiac	160.499
550	29	7/4/62	Daytona Beach, FL	2.5	P	250	Fireball Roberts	Pontiac	53.688	Jack Smith	Pontiac	66.667
551	30	7/7/62	Columbia, SC	0.5	D	100	Rex White	Chevrolet	62.37	Rex White	Chevrolet	82.285
552	31	7/13/62	Asheville, NC	0.4	P	100	Jack Smith	Pontiac	78.294	Rex White	Chevrolet	66.055
553	32	7/14/62	Greenville, SC	0.5	D	100	Richard Petty	Plymouth	62.219	Jack Smith	Pontiac	65.885
554	33	7/17/62	Augusta, GA	0.5	D	100	Joe Weatherly	Pontiac	55.104	Wendell Scott	Chevrolet	71.627
555	34	7/20/62	Savannah, GA	0.5	D	100	Joe Weatherly	Pontiac	67.239	Ned Jarrett	Chevrolet	68.467
556	35	7/21/62	Myrtle Beach, SC	0.5	D	100	Ned Jarrett	Chevrolet	64.171	Fireball Roberts	Pontiac	80.321
557	36	7/29/62	Bristol, TN	0.5	P	250	Jim Paschal	Plymouth	75.276	Richard Petty	Plymouth	73.365
558	37	8/3/62	Chattanooga, TN	0.333	P	66.6	Joe Weatherly	Pontiac	71.145	Johnny Allen	Pontiac	77.854
559	38	8/5/62	Nashville, TN	0.5	P	250	Jim Paschal	Plymouth	77.854	Richard Petty	Plymouth	54.086
560	39	8/8/62	Huntsville, AL	0.25	P	50	Richard Petty	Plymouth	54.644	Jack Smith	Pontiac	82.72
561	40	8/12/62	Weaverville, NC	0.5	P	250	Jim Paschal	Plymouth	77.492	Jack Smith	Pontiac	54.086
562	41	8/15/62	Roanoke, VA	0.25	P	50	Richard Petty	Plymouth	51.165	Jack Smith	Pontiac	48.102
563	42	8/18/62	Winston-Salem, NC	0.25	P	50	Richard Petty	Plymouth	46.875	Richard Petty	Plymouth	61.59
564	43	8/21/62	Spartanburg, SC	0.5	D	100	Richard Petty	Plymouth	59.87	Richard Petty	Plymouth	59.386
565	44	8/25/62	Valdosta, GA	0.5	D	100	Ned Jarrett	Chevrolet	61.454	Fireball Roberts	Pontiac	130.246
566	45	9/3/62	Darlington, SC	1.375	P	500.5	Larry Frank	Ford	117.965	Junior Johnson	Pontiac	71.357
567	46	9/7/62	Hickory, NC	0.4	P	100	Rex White	Chevrolet	70.574	Rex White	Chevrolet	66.127
568	47	9/9/62	Richmond, VA	0.5	D	150	Joe Weatherly	Pontiac	64.981	Ned Jarrett	Chevrolet	45.569
569	48	9/11/62	Moyock, NC	0.25	D	62.5	Ned Jarrett	Chevrolet	43.078	Joe Weatherly	Pontiac	65.241
570	49	9/13/62	Augusta, GA	0.5	D	100	Fred Lorenzen	Ford	60.759	Fireball Roberts	Pontiac	71.513
571	50	9/23/62	Martinsville, VA	0.5	P	250	Nelson Stacy	Ford	66.874	Fred Lorenzen	Ford	94.657
572	51	9/30/62	N. Wilkesboro, NC	0.625	P	200	Richard Petty	Plymouth	86.186	Fireball Roberts	Pontiac	140.287
573	52	10/14/62	Charlotte, NC	1.5	P	400.5	Junior Johnson	Pontiac	132.085	Fireball Roberts	Pontiac	138.978
574	53	10/28/62	Hampton, GA	1.5	P	400.5	Rex White	Chevrolet	124.74	Jim Paschal	Plymouth	73.952

1963

Cum. No.	Yr. No.	Date	Site	Track Length	Surface	Miles	Race Winner	Make	Speed	Pole Winner	Make	Pole Speed
575	1	11/4/62	Birmingham, AL	0.5	D	100	Jim Paschal	Plymouth	68.35	Rex White	Chevrolet	60.09
576	2	11/11/62	Tampa, FL	0.3	D	60	Richard Petty	Plymouth	57.167	Glen Wood	Ford	51.933
577	3	11/22/62	Randleman, NC	0.25	D	50	Jim Paschal	Plymouth	47.544	Paul Goldsmith	Pontiac	99.59
578	4	1/20/63	Riverside, CA	2.7	P	499.5	Dan Gurney	Ford	84.965	Fireball Roberts	Pontiac	163.681
579	5	2/22/63	Daytona Beach, FL	2.5	P	100	Junior Johnson	Chevrolet	164.083	Fred Lorenzen	Ford	165.183
580	6	2/22/63	Daytona Beach, FL	2.5	P	100	Johnny Rutherford	Chevrolet	162.969	Fireball Roberts	Pontiac	165.183
581	7	2/24/63	Daytona Beach, FL	2.5	P	500	Tiny Lund	Ford	151.566	Junior Johnson	Chevrolet	64.47
582	8	3/2/63	Spartanburg, SC	0.5	D	100	Richard Petty	Plymouth	55.598	Junior Johnson	Chevrolet	82.75
583	9	3/3/63	Weaverville, NC	0.5	P	100	Richard Petty	Plymouth	76.664	Joe Weatherly	Pontiac	95.716
584	10	3/10/63	Hillsboro, NC	0.9	D	99	Junior Johnson	Chevrolet	83.129	Junior Johnson	Chevrolet	141.038
585	11	3/17/63	Hampton, GA	1.5	P	501	Fred Lorenzen	Ford	130.582	Junior Johnson	Chevrolet	75.235
586	12	3/24/63	Hickory, NC	0.4	D	100	Junior Johnson	Chevrolet	67.95	Fred Lorenzen	Ford	80.681
587	13	3/31/63	Bristol, TN	0.5	P	250	Fireball Roberts	Ford	76.91	LeeRoy Yarbrough	Mercury	64.61
588	14	4/4/63	Augusta, GA	0.5	D	56	Ned Jarrett	Ford	60.089	Rex White	Chevrolet	69.151
589	15	4/7/63	Richmond, VA	0.5	D	125	Joe Weatherly	Pontiac	58.624	Jimmy Pardue	Ford	66.27
590	16	4/13/63	Greenville, SC	0.5	D	100	Buck Baker	Pontiac	54.853	Ned Jarrett	Ford	78.72
591	17	4/14/63	South Boston, VA	0.375	P	150	Richard Petty	Plymouth	75.229	Richard Petty	Plymouth	48.28
592	18	4/15/63	Winston-Salem, NC	0.25	P	50	Jim Paschal	Plymouth	46.814	Rex White	Chevrolet	72
593	19	4/21/63	Martinsville, VA	0.5	P	250	Richard Petty	Plymouth	64.823	Fred Lorenzen	Ford	96.15
594	20	4/28/63	N. Wilkesboro, NC	0.625	P	160.625	Richard Petty	Plymouth	83.301	Richard Petty	Plymouth	68.08
595	21	5/2/63	Columbia, SC	0.5	D	100	Richard Petty	Plymouth	51.65	Ned Jarrett	Ford	50.856
596	22	5/5/63	Randleman, NC	0.25	D	50	Jim Paschal	Plymouth	48.605	Fred Lorenzen	Ford	131.718
597	23	5/11/63	Darlington, SC	1.375	P	302.5	Joe Weatherly	Pontiac	122.745	Richard Petty	Plymouth	71.58
598	24	5/18/63	Manassas, VA	0.375	D	112.5	Richard Petty	Plymouth	70.275	Ned Jarrett	Ford	70.642
599	25	5/19/63	Richmond, VA	0.333	P	99.9	Ned Jarrett	Ford	65.052	Junior Johnson	Chevrolet	141.148
600	26	6/2/63	Charlotte, NC	1.5	P	600	Fred Lorenzen	Ford	132.417	Jack Smith	Plymouth	71.146

Cum. No.	Yr. No.	Date	Site	Track Length	Surface	Miles	Race Winner	Make	Speed	Pole Winner	Make	Pole Speed
601	27	6/9/63	Birmingham, AL	0.5	D	100	Richard Petty	Plymouth	68.195	Marvin Panch	Ford	140.753
602	28	6/30/63	Hampton, GA	1.5	P	400.5	Junior Johnson	Chevrolet	121.139	Junior Johnson	Chevrolet	166.005
603	29	7/4/63	Daytona Beach, FL	2.5	P	400	Fireball Roberts	Ford	150.927	Richard Petty	Plymouth	68.7
604	30	7/7/63	Myrtle Beach, SC	0.5	D	100	Ned Jarrett	Ford	60.996	Richard Petty	Plymouth	71.34
605	31	7/10/63	Savannah, GA	0.5	D	100	Ned Jarrett	Ford	59.622	Junior Johnson	Chevrolet	47.12
606	32	7/11/63	Moyock, NC	0.25	D	62.5	Jimmy Pardue	Ford	45.464	Glen Wood	Ford	48.387
607	33	7/13/63	Winston-Salem, NC	0.25	P	50	Glen Wood	Ford	44.39	David Pearson	Dodge	67.235
608	34	7/14/63	Asheville, NC	0.333	P	99.9	Ned Jarrett	Ford	63.384	Joe Weatherly	Pontiac	75.85
609	35	7/19/63	Old Bridge, NJ	0.5	P	100	Fireball Roberts	Ford	73.022	Richard Petty	Plymouth	86.301
610	36	7/21/63	Bridgehampton, NY	2.85	P	99.75	Richard Petty	Plymouth	86.047	Fred Lorenzen	Ford	82.229
611	37	7/28/63	Bristol, TN	0.5	P	250	Fred Lorenzen	Ford	74.844	Ned Jarrett	Ford	65.526
612	38	7/30/63	Greenville, SC	0.5	D	100	Richard Petty	Plymouth	62.456	Richard Petty	Plymouth	78.878
613	39	8/4/63	Nashville, TN	0.5	P	175	Jim Paschal	Plymouth	60.126	Richard Petty	Plymouth	69.014
614	40	8/8/63	Columbia, SC	0.5	D	100	Richard Petty	Plymouth	55.598	No Time Trials	NTT	NTT
615	41	8/11/63	Weaverville, NC	0.5	P	250	Fred Lorenzen	Ford	77.673	Joe Weatherly	Pontiac	64.958
616	42	8/14/63	Spartanburg, SC	0.5	D	100	Ned Jarrett	Ford	52.424	Junior Johnson	Chevrolet	49.806
617	43	8/16/63	Winston-Salem, NC	0.25	P	50	Junior Johnson	Chevrolet	46.32	Fred Lorenzen	Ford	66.568
618	44	8/18/63	Huntington, WV	0.375	P	112.5	Fred Lorenzen	Ford	59.34	Fred Lorenzen	Ford	133.648
619	45	9/2/63	Darlington, SC	1.375	P	500.5	Fireball Roberts	Ford	129.784	David Pearson	Dodge	72.471
620	46	9/6/63	Hickory, NC	0.4	D	100	Junior Johnson	Chevrolet	62.926	Joe Weatherly	Mercury	68.104
621	47	9/8/63	Richmond, VA	0.5	D	150	Ned Jarrett	Ford	66.339	Junior Johnson	Chevrolet	73.379
622	48	9/22/63	Martinsville, VA	0.5	P	250	Fred Lorenzen	Ford	67.486	Joe Weatherly	Mercury	45.988
623	49	9/24/63	Moyock, NC	0.25	D	75	Ned Jarrett	Ford	43	Fred Lorenzen	Ford	96.566
624	50	9/29/63	N. Wilkesboro, NC	0.625	P	250	Marvin Panch	Ford	89.428	Fred Lorenzen	Ford	51.724
625	51	10/5/63	Randleman, NC	0.25	P	50	Richard Petty	Plymouth	46.001	Marvin Panch	Ford	143.017
626	52	10/13/63	Charlotte, NC	1.5	P	400.5	Junior Johnson	Chevrolet	132.105	Jack Smith	Plymouth	81.081
627	53	10/20/63	South Boston, VA	0.375	P	150	Richard Petty	Plymouth	76.325	Joe Weatherly	Pontiac	93.156
628	54	10/27/63	Hillsboro, NC	0.9	D	150.3	Joe Weatherly	Pontiac	85.559	Marvin Panch	Ford	101.05
629	55	11/3/63	Riverside, CA	2.7	P	399.6	Darel Dieringer	Mercury	91.465	David Pearson	Dodge	69.257

1964

Cum. No.	Yr. No.	Date	Site	Track Length	Surface	Miles	Race Winner	Make	Speed	Pole Winner	Make	Pole Speed
630	1	11/10/63	Concord, NC	0.5	D	125	Ned Jarrett	Ford	56.897	Fred Lorenzen	Ford	89.545
631	2	11/17/63	Augusta, GA	3	P	417	Fireball Roberts	Ford	86.32	Jack Smith	Plymouth	70.921
632	3	12/1/63	Jacksonville, FL	0.5	D	100	Wendell Scott	Chevrolet	58.252	Fred Lorenzen	Ford	102.433
633	4	1/19/64	Riverside, CA	2.7	P	499.5	Dan Gurney	Ford	91.245	Ned Jarrett	Ford	73.529
634	5	12/29/63	Savannah, GA	0.5	D	100	Richard Petty	Plymouth	68.143	Paul Goldsmith	Plymouth	174.91
635	6	2/21/64	Daytona Beach, FL	2.5	P	100	Junior Johnson	Dodge	170.777	Paul Goldsmith	Plymouth	174.91
636	7	2/23/64	Daytona Beach, FL	2.5	P	500	Richard Petty	Plymouth	154.334	Richard Petty	Plymouth	174.418
637	8	2/21/64	Daytona Beach, FL	2.5	P	100	Bobby Isaac	Dodge	169.811	Ned Jarrett	Ford	69.07
638	9	3/8/64	Richmond, VA	0.5	D	125	David Pearson	Dodge	60.233	Marvin Panch	Ford	80.64
639	10	3/22/64	Bristol, TN	0.5	P	250	Fred Lorenzen	Ford	72.196	Dick Hutcherson	Ford	66.74
640	11	3/28/64	Greenville, SC	0.5	D	100	David Pearson	Dodge	57.554	Fred Lorenzen	Ford	146.47
641	12	4/5/64	Hampton, GA	1.5	P	501	Fred Lorenzen	Ford	134.137	Marvin Panch	Ford	49.83
642	13	3/30/64	Winston-Salem, NC	0.25	P	50	Marvin Panch	Ford	47.796	Dick Hutcherson	Ford	69.044
643	14	4/11/64	Weaverville, NC	0.5	P	100	Marvin Panch	Ford	81.669	David Pearson	Dodge	99.784
644	15	4/14/64	Spartanburg, SC	0.5	D	100	Ned Jarrett	Ford	58.852	David Pearson	Dodge	71.485
645	16	4/12/64	Hillsboro, NC	0.9	D	150.3	David Pearson	Dodge	83.319	Fred Lorenzen	Ford	94.024
646	17	4/16/64	Columbia, SC	0.5	D	100	Ned Jarrett	Ford	64.412	Fred Lorenzen	Ford	74.472
647	18	4/19/64	N. Wilkesboro, NC	0.625	P	250	Fred Lorenzen	Ford	81.93	Jimmy Pardue	Plymouth	73.111
648	19	4/26/64	Martinsville, VA	0.5	P	250	Fred Lorenzen	Ford	70.098	Fred Lorenzen	Ford	135.727
649	20	5/1/64	Savannah, GA	0.5	D	100	LeeRoy Yarbrough	Plymouth	70.326	David Pearson	Dodge	67.542
650	21	5/9/64	Darlington, SC	1.375	P	301.125	Fred Lorenzen	Ford	130.013	Junior Johnson	Ford	76.882
651	22	5/15/64	Hampton, VA	0.4	D	100	Ned Jarrett	Ford	65.3	Marvin Panch	Ford	80.023
652	23	5/16/64	Hickory, NC	0.4	D	100	Ned Jarrett	Ford	69.364	Jimmy Pardue	Plymouth	144.346
653	24	5/17/64	South Boston, VA	0.375	P	100.125	Richard Petty	Plymouth	71.957	Marvin Panch	Ford	68.05
654	25	5/24/64	Charlotte, NC	1.5	P	600	Jim Paschal	Plymouth	125.772	Richard Petty	Plymouth	69.889
655	26	5/30/64	Greenville, SC	0.5	D	100	LeeRoy Yarbrough	Plymouth	56.559	Junior Johnson	Ford	145.906
656	27	5/31/64	Asheville, NC	0.333	P	99.9	Ned Jarrett	Ford	66.538	Richard Petty	Plymouth	68.233
657	28	6/7/64	Hampton, GA	1.5	P	400.5	Ned Jarrett	Ford	112.535	David Pearson	Dodge	80.142
658	29	6/11/64	Concord, NC	0.5	D	100	Richard Petty	Plymouth	66.352	David Pearson	Dodge	72.115
659	30	6/14/64	Nashville, TN	0.5	P	100	Richard Petty	Plymouth	76.498	Richard Petty	Plymouth	75.235
660	31	6/21/64	Birmingham, AL	0.5	P	100	Ned Jarrett	Ford	67.643	Ned Jarrett	Ford	65.146
661	32	6/19/64	Chattanooga, TN	0.333	P	99.9	David Pearson	Dodge	70.051	David Pearson	Dodge	66.939

Cum. No.	Yr. No.	Date	Site	Track Length	Surface	Miles	Race Winner	Make	Speed	Pole Winner	Make	Pole Speed
662	33	6/23/64	Valdosta, GA	0.5	D	100	Buck Baker	Dodge	61.328	Darel Dieringer	Mercury	172.678
663	34	6/26/64	Spartanburg, SC	0.5	D	100	Richard Petty	Plymouth	58.233	Ned Jarrett	Ford	73.609
664	35	7/4/64	Daytona Beach, FL	2.5	P	400	A.J. Foyt	Dodge	151.451	Billy Wade	Mercury	76.66
665	36	7/8/64	Manassas, VA	0.375	P	150	Ned Jarrett	Ford	67.652	Billy Wade	Mercury	51.1
666	37	7/10/64	Old Bridge, NJ	0.5	P	100	Billy Wade	Mercury	73.891	Richard Petty	Plymouth	90.6
667	38	7/15/64	Islip, NY	0.2	P	60	Billy Wade	Mercury	46.252	Billy Wade	Mercury	102.222
668	39	7/12/64	Bridgehampton, NY	2.85	P	142.5	Billy Wade	Mercury	87.707	David Pearson	Dodge	86.289
669	40	7/19/64	Watkins Glen, NY	2.3	P	151.8	Billy Wade	Mercury	97.988	Richard Petty	Plymouth	82.91
670	41	7/21/64	New Oxford, PA	0.5	D	100	David Pearson	Dodge	82.568	Richard Petty	Plymouth	80.826
671	42	7/26/64	Bristol, TN	0.5	P	250	Fred Lorenzen	Ford	78.044	David Pearson	Dodge	69.659
672	43	8/2/64	Nashville, TN	0.5	P	200	Richard Petty	Plymouth	73.208	Junior Johnson	Ford	84.626
673	44	8/7/64	Myrtle Beach, SC	0.5	D	100	David Pearson	Dodge	61.75	Ned Jarrett	Ford	67.643
674	45	8/9/64	Weaverville, NC	0.5	P	250	Ned Jarrett	Ford	77.6	Billy Wade	Mercury	79.505
675	46	8/13/64	Moyock, NC	0.333	P	99.9	Ned Jarrett	Ford	63.965	Ned Jarrett	Ford	69.15
676	47	8/16/64	Huntington, WV	0.4375	P	218.75	Richard Petty	Plymouth	70.488	Glen Wood	Ford	55.97
677	48	8/21/64	Columbia, SC	0.5	D	100	David Pearson	Dodge	61.697	Junior Johnson	Ford	49.846
678	49	8/23/64	Roanoke, VA	0.25	P	50	Junior Johnson	Ford	49.847	Richard Petty	Plymouth	136.815
679	50	8/22/64	Winston-Salem, NC	0.25	P	62.5	Junior Johnson	Ford	46.192	David Pearson	Dodge	74.418
680	51	9/7/64	Darlington, SC	1.375	P	500.5	Buck Baker	Dodge	117.757	Ned Jarrett	Ford	66.89
681	52	9/11/64	Hickory, NC	0.4	D	100	David Pearson	Dodge	67.797	David Pearson	Dodge	74.626
682	53	9/14/64	Richmond, VA	0.5	D	150	Cotton Owens	Dodge	61.955	David Pearson	Dodge	89.28
683	54	9/18/64	Manassas, VA	0.375	P	187.5	Ned Jarrett	Ford	68.842	Fred Lorenzen	Ford	74.196
684	55	9/20/64	Hillsboro, NC	0.9	D	150.3	Ned Jarrett	Ford	86.725	Ned Jarrett	Ford	68.886
685	56	9/27/64	Martinsville, VA	0.5	P	250	Fred Lorenzen	Ford	67.32	Junior Johnson	Ford	100.761
686	57	10/9/64	Savannah, GA	0.5	D	100	Ned Jarrett	Ford	68.663	Richard Petty	Plymouth	150.711
687	58	10/11/64	N. Wilkesboro, NC	0.625	P	250	Marvin Panch	Ford	91.398	Billy Wade	Mercury	64.787
688	59	10/18/64	Charlotte, NC	1.5	P	400.5	Fred Lorenzen	Ford	134.475	Ned Jarrett	Ford	82.455
689	60	10/25/64	Harris, NC	0.333	P	111.222	Richard Petty	Plymouth	59.009	Doug Yates	Plymouth	64.285
690	61	11/1/64	Augusta, GA	0.5	P	150	Darel Dieringer	Mercury	68.641	Junior Johnson	Ford	102.846
691	62	11/8/64	Jacksonville, NC	0.5	D	100	Ned Jarrett	Ford	57.535	Darel Dieringer	Mercury	171.151

1965

Cum. No.	Yr. No.	Date	Site	Track Length	Surface	Miles	Race Winner	Make	Speed	Pole Winner	Make	Pole Speed
692	1	1/17/65	Riverside, CA	2.7	P	499.5	Dan Gurney	Ford	87.708	Junior Johnson	Ford	170.551
693	2	2/12/65	Daytona Beach, FL	2.5	P	100	Darel Dieringer	Mercury	165.669	Darel Dieringer	Mercury	171.151
694	3	2/12/65	Daytona Beach, FL	2.5	P	100	Junior Johnson	Ford	111.076	Dick Hutcherson	Ford	70.644
695	4	2/14/65	Daytona Beach, FL	2.5	P	332.5	Fred Lorenzen	Ford	141.539	Ned Jarrett	Ford	84.23
696	5	2/27/65	Spartanburg, SC	0.5	D	100	Ned Jarrett	Ford	66.367	Junior Johnson	Ford	67.847
697	6	2/28/65	Weaverville, NC	0.5	P	100	Ned Jarrett	Ford	75.678	Junior Johnson	Ford	98.57
698	7	3/7/65	Richmond, VA	0.5	D	125	Junior Johnson	Ford	61.416	Marvin Panch	Ford	145.581
699	8	3/14/65	Hillsboro, NC	0.9	D	150.3	Ned Jarrett	Ford	90.663	Paul Moore	Plymouth	67.695
700	9	4/11/65	Hampton, GA	1.5	P	501	Marvin Panch	Ford	129.41	Junior Johnson	Ford	101.033
701	10	4/17/65	Greenville, SC	0.5	D	100	Dick Hutcherson	Ford	56.899	Junior Johnson	Ford	74.503
702	11	4/18/65	N. Wilkesboro, NC	0.625	P	250	Junior Johnson	Ford	95.047	Ned Jarrett	Ford	71.061
703	12	4/25/65	Martinsville, VA	0.5	P	250	Fred Lorenzen	Ford	66.765	Marvin Panch	Ford	84.626
704	13	4/28/65	Columbia, SC	0.5	D	100	Tiny Lund	Ford	55.591	Fred Lorenzen	Ford	138.133
705	14	5/2/65	Bristol, TN	0.5	P	250	Junior Johnson	Ford	74.937	Dick Hutcherson	Ford	66.79
706	15	5/8/65	Darlington, SC	1.375	P	301.125	Junior Johnson	Ford	111.849	Junior Johnson	Ford	49.261
707	16	5/14/65	Hampton, VA	0.4	D	100	Ned Jarrett	Ford	57.815	G.C. Spencer	Ford	76.312
708	17	5/15/65	Winston-Salem, NC	0.25	P	50	Junior Johnson	Ford	47.911	Fred Lorenzen	Ford	145.268
709	18	5/16/65	Hickory, NC	0.4	D	100	Junior Johnson	Ford	72.13	Dick Hutcherson	Ford	65.862
710	19	5/23/65	Charlotte, NC	1.5	P	600	Fred Lorenzen	Ford	121.722	Junior Johnson	Ford	70.601
711	20	5/27/65	Shelby, NC	0.5	D	100	Ned Jarrett	Ford	63.909	Paul Lewis	Ford	61.644
712	21	5/29/65	Asheville, NC	0.333	P	99.9	Junior Johnson	Ford	66.293	Tom Pistone	Ford	79.155
713	22	5/30/65	Harris, NC	0.3	P	100.2	Ned Jarrett	Ford	56.851	Ned Jarrett	Ford	71.575
714	23	6/3/65	Nashville, TN	0.5	P	100	Dick Hutcherson	Ford	71.386	Fred Lorenzen	Ford	143.407
715	24	6/6/65	Birmingham, AL	0.5	P	100	Ned Jarrett	Ford	56.364	Ned Jarrett	Ford	65.574
716	25	6/13/65	Hampton, GA	1.5	P	400.5	Marvin Panch	Ford	110.12	Dick Hutcherson	Ford	66.421
717	26	6/19/65	Greenville, SC	0.5	D	100	Dick Hutcherson	Ford	55.274	Dick Hutcherson	Ford	64.54
718	27	6/24/65	Myrtle Beach, SC	0.5	D	100	Dick Hutcherson	Ford	59.701	Marvin Panch	Ford	171.51
719	28	6/27/65	Valdosta, GA	0.5	D	100	Cale Yarborough	Ford	58.862	Ned Jarrett	Ford	73.569
720	29	7/4/65	Daytona Beach, FL	2.5	P	400	A.J. Foyt	Ford	150.046	Marvin Panch	Ford	77.286
721	30	7/8/65	Manassas, VA	0.375	P	150	Junior Johnson	Ford	68.165	Marvin Panch	Ford	51.246
722	31	7/9/65	Old Bridge, NJ	0.5	P	100	Junior Johnson	Ford	72.087	No Time Trials	NTT	NTT

Cum. No.	Yr. No.	Date	Site	Track Length	Surface	Miles	Race Winner	Make	Speed	Pole Winner	Make	Pole Speed
723	32	7/14/65	Islip, NY	0.2	P	50	Marvin Panch	Ford	43.838	Fred Lorenzen	Ford	84.348
724	33	7/18/65	Watkins Glen, NY	2.3	P	151.8	Marvin Panch	Ford	98.182	Richard Petty	Plymouth	82.117
725	34	7/25/65	Bristol, TN	0.5	P	250	Ned Jarrett	Ford	61.826	David Pearson	Dodge	67.797
726	35	7/31/65	Nashville, TN	0.5	P	200	Richard Petty	Plymouth	72.383	Richard Petty	Plymouth	86.455
727	36	8/5/65	Shelby, NC	0.5	D	100	Ned Jarrett	Ford	64.748	Ned Jarrett	Ford	77.62
728	37	8/8/65	Weaverville, NC	0.5	P	250	Richard Petty	Plymouth	74.343	Dick Hutcherson	Ford	66.89
729	38	8/13/65	Maryville, TN	0.5	D	100	Dick Hutcherson	Ford	65.455	Ned Jarrett	Ford	81.118
730	39	8/14/65	Spartanburg, SC	0.5	D	100	Ned Jarrett	Ford	56.926	Dick Hutcherson	Ford	71.343
731	40	8/15/65	Augusta, GA	0.5	P	100	Dick Hutcherson	Ford	71.499	Richard Petty	Plymouth	68.493
732	41	8/19/65	Columbia, SC	0.5	D	100	David Pearson	Dodge	57.361	Ned Jarrett	Ford	79.26
733	42	8/24/65	Moyock, NC	0.333	P	99.9	Dick Hutcherson	Ford	63.047	Richard Petty	Plymouth	50.195
734	43	8/25/65	Beltsville, MD	0.5	P	100	Ned Jarrett	Ford	74.165	Junior Johnson	Ford	137.571
735	44	8/28/65	Winston-Salem, NC	0.25	P	62.5	Junior Johnson	Ford	46.632	Junior Johnson	Ford	74.766
736	45	9/6/65	Darlington, SC	1.375	P	500.5	Ned Jarrett	Ford	115.878	Richard Petty	Plymouth	86.705
737	46	9/10/65	Hickory, NC	0.4	D	100	Richard Petty	Plymouth	74.365	Ned Jarrett	Ford	73.851
738	47	9/14/65	New Oxford, PA	0.5	D	100	Dick Hutcherson	Ford	82.607	Dick Hutcherson	Ford	67.34
739	48	9/17/65	Manassas, VA	0.375	P	150	Richard Petty	Plymouth	67.89	Richard Petty	Plymouth	74.503
740	49	9/18/65	Richmond, VA	0.5	D	150	David Pearson	Dodge	60.983	Fred Lorenzen	Ford	101.58
741	50	9/26/65	Martinsville, VA	0.5	P	250	Junior Johnson	Ford	67.056	Fred Lorenzen	Ford	147.773
742	51	10/3/65	N. Wilkesboro, NC	0.625	P	250	Junior Johnson	Ford	88.801	Dick Hutcherson	Ford	98.81
743	52	10/17/65	Charlotte, NC	1.5	P	400.5	Fred Lorenzen	Ford	119.117	Richard Petty	Plymouth	116.26
744	53	10/24/65	Hillsboro, NC	0.9	D	100.8	Dick Hutcherson	Ford	87.462	Bobby Isaac	Ford	68.143
745	54	10/31/65	Rockingham, NC	1	P	500	Curtis Turner	Ford	101.942	Richard Petty	Plymouth	82.987
746	55	11/7/65	Moyock, NC	0.333	P	99.9	Ned Jarrett	Ford	63.773	David Pearson	Dodge	106.078

1966

Cum. No.	Yr. No.	Date	Site	Track Length	Surface	Miles	Race Winner	Make	Speed	Pole Winner	Make	Pole Speed
747	1	11/14/65	Augusta, GA	0.5	P	150	Richard Petty	Plymouth	73.569	Richard Petty	Plymouth	175.165
748	2	1/23/66	Riverside, CA	2.7	P	499.5	Dan Gurney	Ford	97.952	Dick Hutcherson	Ford	174.317
749	3	2/25/66	Daytona Beach, FL	2.5	P	100	Paul Goldsmith	Plymouth	160.427	Richard Petty	Plymouth	175.163
750	4	2/25/66	Daytona Beach, FL	2.5	P	100	Earl Balmer	Dodge	153.191	Paul Goldsmith	Plymouth	116.684
751	5	2/27/66	Daytona Beach, FL	2.5	P	500	Richard Petty	Plymouth	160.627	David Pearson	Dodge	86.248
752	6	3/13/66	Rockingham, NC	1	P	500	Paul Goldsmith	Plymouth	100.027	Richard Petty	Plymouth	147.742
753	7	3/20/66	Bristol, TN	0.5	P	250	Dick Hutcherson	Ford	69.952	Elmo Langley	Ford	75.117
754	8	3/27/66	Hampton, GA	1.5	P	501	Jim Hurtubise	Plymouth	131.247	Tom Pistone	Ford	72.202
755	9	4/3/66	Hickory, NC	0.4	D	100	David Pearson	Dodge	68.428	Tiny Lund	Ford	68.208
756	10	4/7/66	Columbia, SC	0.5	D	100	David Pearson	Dodge	65.574	David Pearson	Dodge	54.479
757	11	4/9/66	Greenville, SC	0.5	D	100	David Pearson	Dodge	68.85	Jim Paschal	Plymouth	102.693
758	12	4/11/66	Winston-Salem, NC	0.25	P	50	David Pearson	Dodge	51.341	Jim Paschal	Plymouth	76.345
759	13	4/17/66	N. Wilkesboro, NC	0.625	P	250	Jim Paschal	Plymouth	89.045	Richard Petty	Plymouth	140.815
760	14	4/24/66	Martinsville, VA	0.5	P	250	Jim Paschal	Plymouth	69.156	Richard Petty	Plymouth	66.821
761	15	4/30/66	Darlington, SC	1.375	P	400.125	Richard Petty	Plymouth	131.993	Richard Petty	Plymouth	85.026
762	16	5/7/66	Hampton, VA	1.5	P	375	Richard Petty	Plymouth	60.616	James Hylton	Dodge	65.099
763	17	5/10/66	Macon, GA	0.5	P	100	Richard Petty	Plymouth	82.023	Tom Pistone	Ford	70.978
764	18	5/13/66	Monroe, NC	0.5	D	125	Darel Dieringer	Ford	60.14	Richard Petty	Plymouth	148.637
765	19	5/15/66	Richmond, VA	0.5	D	125	David Pearson	Dodge	66.539	Richard Petty	Plymouth	69.164
766	20	5/22/66	Charlotte, NC	1.5	P	600	Marvin Panch	Plymouth	135.042	Richard Petty	Plymouth	72.964
767	21	5/29/66	Moyock, NC	0.333	P	99.9	David Pearson	Dodge	61.913	David Pearson	Dodge	68.027
768	22	6/2/66	Asheville, NC	0.333	P	99.9	David Pearson	Dodge	64.917	Tom Pistone	Ford	78.947
769	23	6/4/66	Spartanburg, SC	0.5	D	100	Elmo Langley	Ford	60.05	Richard Petty	Plymouth	86.455
770	24	6/9/66	Maryville, TN	0.5	D	100	David Pearson	Dodge	71.986	Richard Petty	Plymouth	80.25
771	25	6/12/66	Weaverville, NC	0.5	P	150	Richard Petty	Plymouth	81.423	David Pearson	Dodge	69.365
772	26	6/15/66	Beltsville, MD	0.5	P	100	Tiny Lund	Ford	73.409	LeeRoy Yarbrough	Dodge	176.66
773	27	6/25/66	Greenville, SC	0.5	D	100	David Pearson	Dodge	66.286	Bobby Allison	Chevrolet	73.973
774	28	7/4/66	Daytona Beach, FL	2.5	P	400	Sam McQuagg	Dodge	153.613	David Pearson	Dodge	Qual. Race
775	29	7/7/66	Manassas, VA	0.375	P	150	Elmo Langley	Ford	68.079	Bobby Allison	Chevrolet	65.681
776	30	7/10/66	Bridgehampton, NY	2.85	P	148.2	David Pearson	Dodge	86.949	Richard Petty	Plymouth	71.514
777	31	7/12/66	Oxford, ME	0.333	P	99.9	Bobby Allison	Chevrolet	56.782	Tom Pistone	Ford	55.919
778	32	7/14/66	Fonda, NY	0.5	D	100	David Pearson	Dodge	61.01	Curtis Turner	Chevrolet	84.309
779	33	7/16/66	Islip, NY	0.2	P	60	Bobby Allison	Chevrolet	47.285	Buddy Baker	Dodge	77.821
780	34	7/24/66	Bristol, TN	0.5	P	250	Paul Goldsmith	Plymouth	77.963	Richard Petty	Plymouth	82.493
781	35	7/28/66	Maryville, TN	0.5	D	100	Paul Lewis	Plymouth	69.822	Curtis Turner	Chevrolet	148.331
782	36	7/30/66	Nashville, TN	0.5	P	200	Richard Petty	Plymouth	71.77	Bobby Allison	Chevrolet	73.469
783	37	8/7/66	Hampton, GA	1.5	P	400.5	Richard Petty	Plymouth	130.244	Junior Johnson	Ford	86.831

Cum. No.	Yr. No.	Date	Site	Track Length	Surface	Miles	Race Winner	Make	Speed	Pole Winner	Make	Pole Speed
784	38	8/18/66	Columbia, SC	0.5	D	100	David Pearson	Dodge	66.128	Bobby Allison	Chevrolet	79.33
785	39	8/21/66	Weaverville, NC	0.5	P	250	Darel Dieringer	Mercury	76.7	Richard Petty	Plymouth	54.348
786	40	8/24/66	Beltsville, MD	0.5	P	100	Bobby Allison	Chevrolet	68.899	LeeRoy Yarbrough	Dodge	140.058
787	41	8/27/66	Winston-Salem, NC	0.25	P	62.5	David Pearson	Dodge	45.928	Richard Petty	Plymouth	76.923
788	42	9/5/66	Darlington, SC	1.375	P	500.5	Darel Dieringer	Mercury	114.83	David Pearson	Dodge	70.644
789	43	9/9/66	Hickory, NC	0.4	D	100	David Pearson	Dodge	76.923	Dick Hutcherson	Ford	95.716
790	44	9/11/66	Richmond, VA	0.5	D	150	David Pearson	Dodge	62.886	Junior Johnson	Ford	75.598
791	45	9/18/66	Hillsboro, NC	0.9	D	150.3	Dick Hutcherson	Ford	90.603	Junior Johnson	Ford	103.069
792	46	9/25/66	Martinsville, VA	0.5	P	250	Fred Lorenzen	Ford	69.177	Fred Lorenzen	Ford	150.533
793	47	10/2/66	N. Wilkesboro, NC	0.625	P	250	Dick Hutcherson	Ford	89.012	Fred Lorenzen	Ford	115.988
794	48	10/16/66	Charlotte, NC	1.5	P	501	LeeRoy Yarbrough	Dodge	130.576	Dick Hutcherson	Ford	84.112
795	49	10/30/66	Rockingham, NC	1	P	500	Fred Lorenzen	Ford	104.348	Dick Hutcherson	Ford	106.951

1967

Cum. No.	Yr. No.	Date	Site	Track Length	Surface	Miles	Race Winner	Make	Speed	Pole Winner	Make	Pole Speed
796	1	11/13/66	Augusta, GA	0.5	P	150	Richard Petty	Plymouth	71.809	Curtis Turner	Chevrolet	180.831
797	2	1/29/67	Riverside, CA	2.7	P	499.5	Parnelli Jones	Ford	91.08	Richard Petty	Plymouth	179.068
798	3	2/24/67	Daytona Beach, FL	2.5	P	100	LeeRoy Yarbrough	Dodge	163.934	Curtis Turner	Chevrolet	180.831
799	4	2/24/67	Daytona Beach, FL	2.5	P	100	Fred Lorenzen	Ford	174.587	Darel Dieringer	Ford	88.626
800	5	2/26/67	Daytona Beach, FL	2.5	P	500	Mario Andretti	Ford	146.926	Darel Dieringer	Ford	87.124
801	6	3/5/67	Weaverville, NC	0.5	P	150	Richard Petty	Plymouth	83.36	Dick Hutcherson	Ford	70.313
802	7	3/19/67	Bristol, TN	0.5	P	250	David Pearson	Dodge	75.937	Bobby Allison	Chevrolet	53.476
803	8	3/25/67	Greenville, SC	0.5	D	100	David Pearson	Dodge	61.824	Cale Yarborough	Ford	148.996
804	9	3/27/67	Winston-Salem, NC	0.25	P	50	Bobby Allison	Chevrolet	49.248	Dick Hutcherson	Ford	74.166
805	10	4/2/67	Hampton, GA	1.5	P	501	Cale Yarborough	Ford	131.238	Richard Petty	Plymouth	79.12
806	11	4/6/67	Columbia, SC	0.5	D	100	Richard Petty	Plymouth	65.455	Darel Dieringer	Ford	104.603
807	12	4/9/67	Hickory, NC	0.4	D	100	Richard Petty	Plymouth	69.699	Darel Dieringer	Ford	77.319
808	13	4/16/67	N. Wilkesboro, NC	0.625	P	250	Darel Dieringer	Ford	93.594	John Sears	Ford	72.173
809	14	4/23/67	Martinsville, VA	0.5	P	250	Richard Petty	Plymouth	67.446	Richard Petty	Plymouth	70.038
810	15	4/28/67	Savannah, GA	0.5	P	100	Bobby Allison	Chevrolet	66.802	David Pearson	Ford	144.536
811	16	4/30/67	Richmond, VA	0.5	D	125	Richard Petty	Plymouth	65.982	Richard Petty	Plymouth	80.286
812	17	5/13/67	Darlington, SC	1.375	P	400.125	Richard Petty	Plymouth	125.738	Richard Petty	Plymouth	68.214
813	18	5/19/67	Beltsville, MD	0.5	P	100	Jim Paschal	Plymouth	71.036	Cale Yarborough	Ford	154.385
814	19	5/20/67	Hampton, VA	0.4	D	100	Richard Petty	Plymouth	66.704	Richard Petty	Plymouth	73.71
815	20	5/28/67	Charlotte, NC	1.5	P	600	Jim Paschal	Plymouth	135.832	Richard Petty	Plymouth	86.538
816	21	6/2/67	Asheville, NC	0.333	P	99.9	Jim Paschal	Plymouth	63.08	Jim Hunter	Chevrolet	79.051
817	22	6/6/67	Macon, GA	0.5	P	150	Richard Petty	Plymouth	80.321	Jim Paschal	Plymouth	94.142
818	23	6/8/67	Maryville, TN	0.5	D	100	Richard Petty	Plymouth	72.919	Dick Hutcherson	Ford	116.486
819	24	6/10/67	Birmingham, AL	0.625	P	100	Bobby Allison	Dodge	88.999	Richard Petty	Plymouth	69.498
820	25	6/18/67	Rockingham, NC	1	P	500	Richard Petty	Plymouth	104.682	Richard Petty	Plymouth	77.088
821	26	6/24/67	Greenville, SC	0.5	D	100	Richard Petty	Plymouth	61.781	Darel Dieringer	Ford	179.802
822	27	6/27/67	Montgomery, AL	0.5	P	100	Jim Paschal	Plymouth	72.435	Richard Petty	Plymouth	101.208
823	28	7/4/67	Daytona Beach, FL	2.5	P	400	Cale Yarborough	Ford	143.583	James Hylton	Dodge	66.043
824	29	7/9/67	Trenton, NJ	1	P	300	Richard Petty	Plymouth	95.208	Richard Petty	Plymouth	72.173
825	30	7/11/67	Oxford, ME	0.333	P	99.9	Bobby Allison	Chevrolet	61.697	Richard Petty	Plymouth	51.136
826	31	7/13/67	Fonda, NY	0.5	D	100	Richard Petty	Plymouth	65.826	Richard Petty	Plymouth	86.621
827	32	7/15/67	Islip, NY	0.2	P	60	Richard Petty	Plymouth	42.428	Dick Hutcherson	Ford	79.54
828	33	7/23/67	Bristol, TN	0.5	P	250	Richard Petty	Plymouth	78.705	Dick Hutcherson	Ford	84.26
829	34	7/27/67	Maryville, TN	0.5	D	100	Dick Hutcherson	Ford	65.765	Darel Dieringer	Ford	150.669
830	35	7/29/67	Nashville, TN	0.5	P	200	Richard Petty	Plymouth	70.866	Richard Petty	Plymouth	53.16
831	36	8/6/67	Hampton, GA	1.5	P	501	Dick Hutcherson	Ford	132.286	Richard Petty	Plymouth	74.968
832	37	8/12/67	Winston-Salem, NC	0.25	P	62.5	Richard Petty	Plymouth	50.893	Richard Petty	Plymouth	71.942
833	38	8/17/67	Columbia, SC	0.5	D	100	Richard Petty	Plymouth	64.274	Richard Petty	Plymouth	143.436
834	39	8/25/67	Savannah, GA	0.5	P	100	Richard Petty	Plymouth	65.041	Dick Hutcherson	Ford	86.538
835	40	9/4/67	Darlington, SC	1.375	P	500.5	Richard Petty	Plymouth	130.423	No Time Trials	NTT	NTT
836	41	9/8/67	Hickory, NC	0.4	P	100	Richard Petty	Plymouth	71.414	Richard Petty	Plymouth	81.044
837	42	9/10/67	Richmond, VA	0.5	D	150	Richard Petty	Plymouth	57.631	Richard Petty	Plymouth	94.159
838	43	9/15/67	Beltsville, MD	0.5	P	150	Richard Petty	Plymouth	76.563	Cale Yarborough	Ford	77.386
839	44	9/17/67	Hillsboro, NC	0.9	D	150.3	Richard Petty	Plymouth	81.574	Dick Hutcherson	Ford	104.312
840	45	9/24/67	Martinsville, VA	0.5	P	250	Richard Petty	Plymouth	69.605	Cale Yarborough	Ford	154.872
841	46	10/1/67	N. Wilkesboro, NC	0.625	P	250	Richard Petty	Plymouth	94.837	David Pearson	Ford	117.12
842	47	10/15/67	Charlotte, NC	1.5	P	501	Buddy Baker	Dodge	130.317	Bobby Allison	Ford	90.407
843	48	10/29/67	Rockingham, NC	1	P	500	Bobby Allison	Ford	98.42	LeeRoy Yarbrough	Ford	94.323
844	49	11/5/67	Weaverville, NC	0.5	P	250	Bobby Allison	Ford	76.291	Richard Petty	Plymouth	79.964

Cum. No.	Yr. No.	Date	Site	Track Length	Surface	Miles	Race Winner	Make	Speed	Pole Winner	Make	Pole Speed
1968												
845	1	11/12/67	Macon, GA	0.534	P	267	Bobby Allison	Ford	81.001	Dan Gurney	Ford	110.971
846	2	11/26/67	Montgomery, AL	0.5	P	100	Richard Petty	Plymouth	70.644	Cale Yarborough	Mercury	189.222
847	3	1/21/68	Riverside, CA	2.7	P	502.2	Dan Gurney	Ford	100.598	Richard Petty	Plymouth	88.582
848	4	2/25/68	Daytona Beach, FL	2.5	P	500	Cale Yarborough	Mercury	143.251	Bobby Isaac	Dodge	67.822
849	5	3/17/68	Bristol, TN	0.5	P	250	David Pearson	Ford	77.247	LeeRoy Yarbrough	Mercury	155.646
850	6	3/24/68	Richmond, VA	0.5	D	125	David Pearson	Ford	65.217	David Pearson	Ford	86.975
851	7	3/31/68	Hampton, GA	1.5	P	501	Cale Yarborough	Mercury	125.564	David Pearson	Ford	67.848
852	8	4/7/68	Hickory, NC	0.4	P	100	Richard Petty	Plymouth	79.435	Richard Petty	Plymouth	75.282
853	9	4/13/68	Greenville, SC	0.5	D	100	Richard Petty	Plymouth	63.347	David Pearson	Ford	104.993
854	10	4/18/68	Columbia, SC	0.5	D	100	Bobby Isaac	Dodge	71.358	David Pearson	Ford	78.23
855	11	4/21/68	N. Wilkesboro, NC	0.625	P	250	David Pearson	Ford	90.425	Bobby Isaac	Dodge	83.877
856	12	4/28/68	Martinsville, VA	0.5	P	250	Cale Yarborough	Mercury	66.686	David Pearson	Ford	89.708
857	13	5/3/68	Augusta, GA	0.5	P	125	Bobby Isaac	Dodge	73.099	LeeRoy Yarbrough	Ford	148.85
858	14	5/5/68	Weaverville, NC	0.5	P	150	David Pearson	Ford	75.167	Richard Petty	Plymouth	83.604
859	15	5/11/68	Darlington, SC	1.375	P	400.125	David Pearson	Ford	132.699	Richard Petty	Plymouth	80.801
860	16	5/17/68	Beltsville, MD	0.5	P	150	David Pearson	Ford	74.844	Donnie Allison	Ford	159.223
861	17	5/18/68	Hampton, VA	0.4	P	100	David Pearson	Ford	71.457	Richard Petty	Plymouth	74.349
862	18	5/26/68	Charlotte, NC	1.5	P	382.5	Buddy Baker	Dodge	104.207	David Pearson	Ford	86.873
863	19	5/31/68	Asheville, NC	0.333	P	99.9	Richard Petty	Plymouth	65.741	David Pearson	Ford	88.583
864	20	6/2/68	Macon, GA	0.5	P	150	David Pearson	Ford	79.342	David Pearson	Ford	97.784
865	21	6/6/68	Maryville, TN	0.5	P	100	Richard Petty	Plymouth	76.743	LeeRoy Yarbrough	Ford	118.644
866	22	6/8/68	Birmingham, AL	0.625	P	100	Richard Petty	Plymouth	89.153	David Pearson	Ford	68.834
867	23	6/16/68	Rockingham, NC	1	P	500	Donnie Allison	Ford	99.338	Charlie Glotzbach	Dodge	185.156
868	24	6/22/68	Greenville, SC	0.5	D	100	Richard Petty	Plymouth	64.609	Buddy Baker	Dodge	51.873
869	25	7/4/68	Daytona Beach, FL	2.5	P	400	Cale Yarborough	Mercury	167.247	Buddy Baker	Dodge	67.835
870	26	7/7/68	Islip, NY	0.2	P	60	Bobby Allison	Chevrolet	48.561	David Pearson	Ford	73.8
871	27	7/9/68	Oxford, ME	0.333	P	99.9	Richard Petty	Plymouth	63.717	LeeRoy Yarbrough	Ford	103.717
872	28	7/11/68	Fonda, NY	0.5	P	100	Richard Petty	Plymouth	64.935	LeeRoy Yarbrough	Ford	87.421
873	29	7/14/68	Trenton, NJ	1	P	300	LeeRoy Yarbrough	Ford	89.079	Bobby Isaac	Dodge	86.538
874	30	7/21/68	Bristol, TN	0.5	P	250	David Pearson	Ford	76.31	Richard Petty	Plymouth	85.066
875	31	7/25/68	Maryville, TN	0.5	P	100	Richard Petty	Plymouth	71.513	Buddy Baker	Dodge	153.361
876	32	7/27/68	Nashville, TN	0.5	P	150.5	David Pearson	Ford	72.98	Buddy Baker	Dodge	74.196
877	33	8/4/68	Hampton, GA	1.5	P	501	LeeRoy Yarbrough	Ford	127.068	Richard Petty	Plymouth	53.828
878	34	8/8/68	Columbia, SC	0.5	D	100	David Pearson	Ford	67.039	Darel Dieringer	Plymouth	88.409
879	35	8/10/68	Winston-Salem, NC	0.25	P	62.5	David Pearson	Ford	42.94	Richard Petty	Plymouth	84.428
880	36	8/18/68	Weaverville, NC	0.5	P	250	David Pearson	Ford	73.686	David Pearson	Ford	78.007
881	37	8/23/68	South Boston, VA	0.375	P	100.125	Richard Petty	Plymouth	75.916	Charlie Glotzbach	Dodge	144.83
882	38	8/24/68	Hampton, VA	0.4	P	100	David Pearson	Ford	75.582	Richard Petty	Plymouth	85.868
883	39	9/2/68	Darlington, SC	1.375	P	500.5	Cale Yarborough	Mercury	126.132	Cale Yarborough	Mercury	103.178
884	40	9/6/68	Hickory, NC	0.4	P	100	David Pearson	Ford	80.357	Cale Yarborough	Mercury	81.311
885	41	9/8/68	Richmond, VA	0.5	P	150	Richard Petty	Plymouth	85.659	Richard Petty	Plymouth	93.245
886	42	9/13/68	Beltsville, MD	0.5	P	150	Bobby Isaac	Dodge	71.033	Cale Yarborough	Mercury	77.279
887	43	9/15/68	Hillsboro, NC	0.9	D	150.3	Richard Petty	Plymouth	87.681	Bobby Allison	Plymouth	104.525
888	44	9/22/68	Martinsville, VA	0.5	P	250	Richard Petty	Plymouth	65.808	Bobby Allison	Plymouth	84.822
889	45	9/29/68	N. Wilkesboro, NC	0.625	P	250	Richard Petty	Plymouth	94.103	Charlie Glotzbach	Dodge	156.06
890	46	10/5/68	Augusta, GA	0.5	P	100	David Pearson	Ford	75.821	Cale Yarborough	Mercury	118.717
891	47	10/20/68	Charlotte, NC	1.5	P	501	Charlie Glotzbach	Dodge	156.324	David Pearson	Ford	90.694
892	48	10/27/68	Rockingham, NC	1	P	500	Richard Petty	Plymouth	105.06	David Pearson	Ford	95.472
893	49	11/3/68	Jefferson, GA	0.5	P	100	Cale Yarborough	Mercury	77.737	Richard Petty	Plymouth	80.899
1969												
894	1	11/17/68	Macon, GA	0.5	P	250	Richard Petty	Plymouth	85.121	A.J. Foyt	Ford	110.323
895	2	12/8/68	Montgomery, AL	0.5	P	100	Bobby Allison	Plymouth	73.2	Buddy Baker	Dodge	188.901
896	3	2/1/69	Riverside, CA	2.7	P	502.2	Richard Petty	Ford	105.498	Bobby Isaac	Dodge	188.726
897	4	2/20/69	Daytona Beach, FL	2.5	P	125	David Pearson	Ford	152.181	Buddy Baker	Dodge	188.901
898	5	2/20/69	Daytona Beach, FL	2.5	P	125	Bobby Isaac	Dodge	151.668	David Pearson	Ford	119.619
899	6	2/23/69	Daytona Beach, FL	2.5	P	500	LeeRoy Yarbrough	Ford	157.95	Bobby Isaac	Dodge	86.901
900	7	3/9/69	Rockingham, NC	1	P	500	David Pearson	Ford	102.569	Bobby Isaac	Dodge	88.669
901	8	3/16/69	Augusta, GA	0.5	P	100	David Pearson	Ford	77.586	Charlie Glotzbach	Dodge	156.794
902	9	3/23/69	Bristol, TN	0.5	P	250	Bobby Allison	Dodge	81.455	Bobby Isaac	Dodge	73.806
903	10	3/30/69	Hampton, GA	1.5	P	501	Cale Yarborough	Mercury	132.191	Bobby Isaac	Dodge	85.612
904	11	4/3/69	Columbia, SC	0.5	D	100	Bobby Isaac	Dodge	68.558	David Pearson	Ford	70.359

Cum. No.	Yr. No.	Date	Site	Track Length	Surface	Miles	Race Winner	Make	Speed	Pole Winner	Make	Pole Speed
905	12	4/6/69	Hickory, NC	0.4	P	100	Bobby Isaac	Dodge	79.086	David Pearson	Ford	82.538
906	13	4/8/69	Greenville, SC	0.5	D	100	Bobby Isaac	Dodge	64.389	Bobby Isaac	Dodge	82.538
907	14	4/13/69	Richmond, VA	0.5	P	250	David Pearson	Ford	73.752	Bobby Isaac	Dodge	106.731
908	15	4/20/69	N. Wilkesboro, NC	0.625	P	250	Bobby Allison	Dodge	95.268	Bobby Allison	Dodge	78.26
909	16	4/27/69	Martinsville, VA	0.5	P	250	Richard Petty	Ford	64.405	Bobby Isaac	Dodge	90.361
910	17	5/4/69	Weaverville, NC	0.5	P	150	Bobby Isaac	Dodge	72.581	Cale Yarborough	Mercury	152.293
911	18	5/10/69	Darlington, SC	1.375	P	400.125	LeeRoy Yarbrough	Mercury	131.572	Bobby Isaac	Dodge	83.329
912	19	5/16/69	Beltsville, MD	0.5	P	150	Bobby Isaac	Dodge	73.059	David Pearson	Ford	80.236
913	20	5/17/69	Hampton, VA	0.4	P	150	David Pearson	Ford	75.789	Donnie Allison	Ford	159.296
914	21	5/25/69	Charlotte, NC	1.5	P	600	LeeRoy Yarbrough	Mercury	134.361	David Pearson	Ford	87.946
915	22	6/1/69	Macon, GA	0.5	P	150	Bobby Isaac	Dodge	73.717	David Pearson	Ford	87.976
916	23	6/5/69	Maryville, TN	0.5	P	150	Bobby Isaac	Dodge	81.706	Donnie Allison	Ford	160.135
917	24	6/15/69	Brooklyn, MI	2	P	500	Cale Yarborough	Mercury	139.254	Bobby Isaac	Dodge	90.112
918	25	6/19/69	Kingsport, TN	0.4	P	100	Richard Petty	Ford	73.619	Bobby Isaac	Dodge	66.03
919	26	6/21/69	Greenville, SC	0.5	D	100	Bobby Isaac	Dodge	61.813	Bobby Isaac	Dodge	72.942
920	27	6/26/69	Raleigh, NC	0.5	D	100	David Pearson	Ford	65.418	Cale Yarborough	Mercury	190.706
921	28	7/4/69	Daytona Beach, FL	2.5	P	400	LeeRoy Yarbrough	Ford	160.875	David Pearson	Ford	130.43
922	29	7/6/69	Dover, DE	1	P	300	Richard Petty	Ford	115.772	David Pearson	Ford	99.8
923	30	7/10/69	Thompson, CT	0.625	P	125	David Pearson	Ford	89.498	Bobby Isaac	Dodge	132.668
924	31	7/13/69	Trenton, NJ	1	P	200	David Pearson	Ford	121.008	Richard Petty	Ford	82.094
925	32	7/15/69	Beltsville, MD	0.5	P	150	Richard Petty	Ford	77.253	Cale Yarborough	Mercury	103.432
926	33	7/20/69	Bristol, TN	0.5	P	250	David Pearson	Ford	79.737	Richard Petty	Ford	84.918
927	34	7/26/69	Nashville, TN	0.5	P	200	Richard Petty	Ford	78.74	David Pearson	Ford	87.434
928	35	7/27/69	Maryville, TN	0.5	P	100	Richard Petty	Ford	82.417	Cale Yarborough	Mercury	155.413
929	36	8/10/69	Hampton, GA	1.5	P	501	LeeRoy Yarbrough	Ford	133.001	David Pearson	Ford	161.714
930	37	8/17/69	Brooklyn, MI	2	P	330	David Pearson	Ford	115.508	Bobby Isaac	Dodge	84.959
931	38	8/21/69	South Boston, VA	0.375	P	100.125	Bobby Isaac	Dodge	76.906	Richard Petty	Ford	54.253
932	39	8/22/69	Winston-Salem, NC	0.25	P	62.5	Richard Petty	Ford	47.458	Bobby Isaac	Dodge	89
933	40	8/24/69	Weaverville, NC	0.5	P	250	Bobby Isaac	Dodge	80.45	Cale Yarborough	Mercury	151.985
934	41	9/1/69	Darlington, SC	1.375	P	316.25	LeeRoy Yarbrough	Ford	105.612	Bobby Isaac	Dodge	86.212
935	42	9/5/69	Hickory, NC	0.4	P	100	Bobby Isaac	Dodge	80.519	Richard Petty	Ford	91.257
936	43	9/7/69	Richmond, VA	0.542	P	250.404	Bobby Allison	Dodge	76.388	Bobby Isaac	Dodge	196.386
937	44	9/14/69	Talladega, AL	2.66	P	500.08	Richard Brickhouse	Dodge	153.778	Richard Petty	Ford	73.108
938	45	9/18/69	Columbia, SC	0.5	D	100	Bobby Isaac	Dodge	70.23	David Pearson	Ford	83.197
939	46	9/28/69	Martinsville, VA	0.5	P	250	Richard Petty	Ford	63.127	Bobby Isaac	Dodge	106.032
940	47	10/5/69	N. Wilkesboro, NC	0.625	P	250	David Pearson	Ford	93.429	Cale Yarborough	Mercury	162.162
941	48	10/12/69	Charlotte, NC	1.5	P	501	Donnie Allison	Ford	131.271	Bobby Isaac	Dodge	86.095
942	49	10/17/69	Savannah, GA	0.5	P	100	Bobby Isaac	Dodge	78.482	Bobby Isaac	Dodge	85.689
943	50	10/19/69	Augusta, GA	0.5	P	100	Bobby Isaac	Dodge	78.74	Charlie Glotzbach	Dodge	136.972
944	51	10/26/69	Rockingham, NC	1.017	P	500.364	LeeRoy Yarbrough	Ford	111.938	David Pearson	Ford	89.565
945	52	11/2/69	Jefferson, GA	0.5	P	100	Bobby Isaac	Dodge	85.106	Bobby Isaac	Dodge	98.148
946	53	11/9/69	Macon, GA	0.548	P	274	Bobby Allison	Dodge	81.079	Elmo Langley	Ford	98.148
947	54	12/7/69	College Station, TX	2	P	500	Bobby Isaac	Dodge	144.277	Buddy Baker	Dodge	176.284

1970

Cum. No.	Yr. No.	Date	Site	Track Length	Surface	Miles	Race Winner	Make	Speed	Pole Winner	Make	Pole Speed
948	1	1/18/70	Riverside, CA	2.62	P	505.66	A.J. Foyt	Ford	97.45	Dan Gurney	Plymouth	112.06
949	2	2/19/70	Daytona Beach, FL	2.5	P	125	Cale Yarborough	Mercury	183.295	Cale Yarborough	Mercury	194.015
950	3	2/19/70	Daytona Beach, FL	2.5	P	125	Charlie Glotzbach	Dodge	147.734	Buddy Baker	Dodge	192.624
951	4	2/22/70	Daytona Beach, FL	2.5	P	500	Pete Hamilton	Plymouth	149.601	Cale Yarborough	Mercury	194.015
952	5	3/1/70	Richmond, VA	0.542	P	271	James Hylton	Ford	82.044	Richard Petty	Plymouth	89.137
953	6	3/8/70	Rockingham, NC	1.017	P	500.364	Richard Petty	Plymouth	116.117	Bobby Allison	Dodge	139.048
954	7	3/15/70	Savannah, GA	0.5	P	100	Richard Petty	Plymouth	82.418	Richard Petty	Plymouth	85.874
955	8	3/29/70	Hampton, GA	1.522	P	499.216	Bobby Allison	Dodge	139.554	Cale Yarborough	Mercury	159.929
956	9	4/5/70	Bristol, TN	0.533	P	266.5	Donnie Allison	Ford	87.543	David Pearson	Ford	107.079
957	10	4/12/70	Talladega, AL	2.66	P	500.08	Pete Hamilton	Plymouth	152.321	Bobby Isaac	Dodge	199.658
958	11	4/18/70	N. Wilkesboro, NC	0.625	P	250	Richard Petty	Plymouth	94.246	Bobby Isaac	Dodge	107.041
959	12	4/30/70	Columbia, SC	0.5	D	100	Richard Petty	Plymouth	62.685	Larry Baumel	Ford	72.329
960	13	5/9/70	Darlington, SC	1.366	P	397.506	David Pearson	Ford	129.668	Charlie Glotzbach	Dodge	153.822
961	14	5/15/70	Beltsville, MD	0.5	P	150	Bobby Isaac	Dodge	76.37	James Hylton	Ford	83.128
962	15	5/18/70	Hampton, VA	0.4	P	120	Bobby Isaac	Dodge	73.245	Bobby Isaac	Dodge	79.659
963	16	5/24/70	Charlotte, NC	1.5	P	600	Donnie Allison	Ford	129.68	Bobby Isaac	Dodge	159.277

Cum. No.	Yr. No.	Date	Site	Track Length	Surface	Miles	Race Winner	Make	Speed	Pole Winner	Make	Pole Speed
964	17	5/28/70	Maryville, TN	0.52	P	104	Bobby Isaac	Dodge	82.558	Bobby Allison	Dodge	92.094
965	18	5/31/70	Martinsville, VA	0.525	P	197.925	Bobby Isaac	Dodge	68.584	Donnie Allison	Ford	82.609
966	19	6/7/70	Brooklyn, MI	2	P	400	Cale Yarborough	Mercury	138.302	Pete Hamilton	Plymouth	162.737
967	20	6/14/70	Riverside, CA	2.62	P	400.86	Richard Petty	Plymouth	101.12	Bobby Allison	Dodge	111.621
968	21	6/20/70	Hickory, NC	0.363	P	100.188	Bobby Isaac	Dodge	68.011	Bobby Isaac	Dodge	79.596
969	22	6/26/70	Kingsport, TN	0.337	P	100.089	Richard Petty	Plymouth	68.583	Richard Petty	Plymouth	75.056
970	23	6/27/70	Greenville, SC	0.5	P	100	Bobby Isaac	Dodge	75.345	Bobby Isaac	Dodge	82.327
971	24	7/4/70	Daytona Beach, FL	2.5	P	400	Donnie Allison	Ford	162.235	Cale Yarborough	Mercury	191.64
972	25	7/7/70	Malta, NY	0.362	P	90.5	Richard Petty	Plymouth	68.589	Bobby Isaac	Dodge	73.213
973	26	7/9/70	Thompson, CT	0.542	P	108.4	Bobby Isaac	Dodge	80.296	Bobby Isaac	Dodge	87.029
974	27	7/12/70	Trenton, NJ	1.5	P	300	Richard Petty	Plymouth	120.724	Bobby Isaac	Dodge	131.749
975	28	7/19/70	Bristol, TN	0.533	P	266.5	Bobby Allison	Dodge	84.88	Cale Yarborough	Mercury	107.375
976	29	7/24/70	Maryville, TN	0.52	P	104	Richard Petty	Plymouth	84.956	Richard Petty	Plymouth	91.264
977	30	7/25/70	Nashville, TN	0.596	P	250.32	Bobby Isaac	Dodge	87.943	LeeRoy Yarbrough	Ford	114.115
978	31	8/2/70	Hampton, GA	1.522	P	499.216	Richard Petty	Plymouth	142.712	Fred Lorenzen	Dodge	157.625
979	32	8/6/70	Columbia, SC	0.5	D	100	Bobby Isaac	Dodge	67.101	Richard Petty	Plymouth	72.695
980	33	8/11/70	Ona, WV	0.437	P	131.1	Richard Petty	Plymouth	78.358	Bobby Allison	Dodge	150.555
981	34	8/16/70	Brooklyn, MI	2.04	P	401.88	Charlie Glotzbach	Dodge	147.571	Charlie Glotzbach	Dodge	157.363
982	35	8/23/70	Talladega, AL	2.66	P	500.08	Pete Hamilton	Plymouth	158.517	Bobby Isaac	Dodge	186.834
983	36	8/28/70	Winston-Salem, NC	0.25	P	62.5	Richard Petty	Plymouth	51.527	Richard Petty	Plymouth	54.553
984	37	8/29/70	South Boston, VA	0.357	P	100.317	Richard Petty	Plymouth	73.06	Richard Petty	Plymouth	81.187
985	38	9/7/70	Darlington, SC	1.366	P	501.322	Buddy Baker	Dodge	128.817	David Pearson	Ford	150.555
986	39	9/11/70	Hickory, NC	0.363	P	100.188	Bobby Isaac	Dodge	73.365	Bobby Isaac	Dodge	78.411
987	40	9/13/70	Richmond, VA	0.542	P	271	Richard Petty	Plymouth	81.476	Richard Petty	Plymouth	87.014
988	41	9/20/70	Dover, DE	1	P	300	Richard Petty	Plymouth	112.103	Bobby Isaac	Dodge	129.538
989	42	9/30/70	Raleigh, NC	0.5	D	100	Richard Petty	Plymouth	68.376	John Sears	Dodge	71.38
990	43	10/4/70	N. Wilkesboro, NC	0.625	P	250	Bobby Isaac	Dodge	90.162	Bobby Isaac	Dodge	105.406
991	44	10/11/70	Charlotte, NC	1.5	P	501	LeeRoy Yarbrough	Mercury	123.246	Charlie Glotzbach	Dodge	147.273
992	45	10/18/70	Martinsville, VA	0.525	P	262.5	Richard Petty	Plymouth	72.235	Bobby Allison	Dodge	82.167
993	46	11/8/70	Macon, GA	0.548	P	274	Richard Petty	Plymouth	83.284	Richard Petty	Plymouth	94.064
994	47	11/15/70	Rockingham, NC	1.017	P	500.364	Cale Yarborough	Mercury	117.811	Charlie Glotzbach	Dodge	136.498
995	48	11/22/70	Hampton, VA	0.395	P	118.5	Bobby Allison	Dodge	69.584	Benny Parsons	Ford	78.239

1971

Cum. No.	Yr. No.	Date	Site	Track Length	Surface	Miles	Race Winner	Make	Speed	Pole Winner	Make	Pole Speed
996	1	1/10/71	Riverside, CA	2.62	P	500.42	Ray Elder	Dodge	100.783	Richard Petty	Plymouth	107.084
997	2	2/11/71	Daytona Beach, FL	2.5	P	125	Pete Hamilton	Plymouth	175.029	A.J. Foyt	Mercury	182.744
998	3	2/11/71	Daytona Beach, FL	2.5	P	125	David Pearson	Mercury	168.728	Bobby Isaac	Dodge	180.05
999	4	2/14/71	Daytona Beach, FL	2.5	P	500	Richard Petty	Plymouth	144.462	A.J. Foyt	Mercury	182.744
1000	5	2/28/71	Ontario, CA	2.5	P	500	A.J. Foyt	Mercury	134.168	A.J. Foyt	Mercury	151.711
1001	6	3/7/71	Richmond, VA	0.542	P	271	Richard Petty	Plymouth	79.836	Dave Marcis	Dodge	87.178
1002	7	3/14/71	Rockingham, NC	1.017	P	500.364	Richard Petty	Plymouth	118.696	Fred Lorenzen	Plymouth	133.892
1003	8	3/21/71	Hickory, NC	0.363	P	100.188	Richard Petty	Plymouth	67.7	Bobby Allison	Dodge	79.001
1004	9	3/28/71	Bristol, TN	0.533	P	266.5	David Pearson	Ford	91.704	David Pearson	Ford	105.525
1005	10	4/4/71	Hampton, GA	1.522	P	499.216	A.J. Foyt	Mercury	131.375	A.J. Foyt	Mercury	155.152
1006	11	4/8/71	Columbia, SC	0.5	P	100	Richard Petty	Plymouth	76.514	James Hylton	Ford	84.229
1007	12	4/10/71	Greenville, SC	0.5	P	100	Bobby Isaac	Dodge	78.159	David Pearson	Ford	82.257
1008	13	4/15/71	Maryville, TN	0.52	P	104	Richard Petty	Plymouth	88.697	Friday Hassler	Chevrolet	91.464
1009	14	4/18/71	N. Wilkesboro, NC	0.625	P	250	Richard Petty	Plymouth	98.479	Bobby Isaac	Dodge	106.217
1010	15	4/25/71	Martinsville, VA	0.525	P	262.5	Richard Petty	Plymouth	77.707	Donnie Allison	Mercury	82.529
1011	16	5/2/71	Darlington, SC	1.366	P	400.238	Buddy Baker	Dodge	130.678	Donnie Allison	Mercury	149.826
1012	17	5/9/71	South Boston, VA	0.357	P	100.317	Benny Parsons	Ford	72.271	Bobby Isaac	Dodge	81.548
1013	18	5/16/71	Talladega, AL	2.66	P	500.08	Donnie Allison	Mercury	147.419	Donnie Allison	Mercury	185.869
1014	19	5/21/71	Asheville, NC	0.333	P	99.9	Richard Petty	Plymouth	71.231	Richard Petty	Plymouth	79.598
1015	20	5/23/71	Kingsport, TN	0.337	P	101.1	Bobby Isaac	Dodge	63.242	Bobby Isaac	Dodge	75.167
1016	21	5/30/71	Charlotte, NC	1.5	P	600	Bobby Allison	Mercury	140.422	Charlie Glotzbach	Chevrolet	157.788
1017	22	6/6/71	Dover, DE	1	P	500	Bobby Allison	Mercury	123.119	Richard Petty	Plymouth	129.486
1018	23	6/13/71	Brooklyn, MI	2.04	P	401.88	Bobby Allison	Mercury	149.567	Bobby Allison	Mercury	161.19
1019	24	6/20/71	Riverside, CA	2.62	P	400.86	Bobby Allison	Mercury	93.427	Bobby Allison	Mercury	107.315
1020	25	6/23/71	Houston, TX	0.5	P	150	Bobby Allison	Dodge	73.489	Bobby Allison	Dodge	78.226
1021	26	6/26/71	Greenville, SC	0.5	P	100	Richard Petty	Plymouth	74.297	Bobby Allison	Ford	81.555
1022	27	7/4/71	Daytona Beach, FL	2.5	P	400	Bobby Isaac	Dodge	161.947	Donnie Allison	Mercury	183.228

Cum. No.	Yr. No.	Date	Site	Track Length	Surface	Miles	Race Winner	Make	Speed	Pole Winner	Make	Pole Speed
1023	28	7/11/71	Bristol, TN	0.533	P	266.5	Charlie Glotzbach	Chevrolet	101.074	Richard Petty	Plymouth	104.589
1024	29	7/14/71	Malta, NY	0.362	P	90.5	Richard Petty	Plymouth	66.748	Richard Petty	Plymouth	74.896
1025	30	7/15/71	Islip, NY	0.2	P	46	Richard Petty	Plymouth	49.925	Richard Petty	Plymouth	46.133
1026	31	7/18/71	Trenton, NJ	1.5	P	300	Richard Petty	Plymouth	120.347	Friday Hassler	Chevrolet	129.134
1027	32	7/24/71	Nashville, TN	0.596	P	250.32	Richard Petty	Plymouth	89.667	Richard Petty	Plymouth	114.628
1028	33	8/1/71	Hampton, GA	1.522	P	499.216	Richard Petty	Plymouth	129.061	Buddy Baker	Dodge	155.796
1029	34	8/6/71	Winston-Salem, NC	0.25	P	62.5	Bobby Allison	Mustang	44.792	Richard Petty	Plymouth	55.283
1030	35	8/8/71	Ona, WV	0.455	P	227.5	Richard Petty	Plymouth	83.805	Bobby Allison	Mustang	84.053
1031	36	8/15/71	Brooklyn, MI	2.04	P	401.88	Bobby Allison	Mercury	149.862	Pete Hamilton	Plymouth	161.901
1032	37	8/22/71	Talladega, AL	2.66	P	500.08	Bobby Allison	Mercury	145.945	Donnie Allison	Mercury	187.323
1033	38	8/27/71	Columbia, SC	0.5	P	100	Richard Petty	Plymouth	64.831	Richard Petty	Plymouth	85.137
1034	39	9/28/71	Hickory, NC	0.363	P	100.188	Tiny Lund	Camaro	72.937	Dave Marcis	Dodge	80.147
1035	40	9/6/71	Darlington, SC	1.366	P	501.322	Bobby Allison	Mercury	131.398	Bobby Allison	Mercury	147.915
1036	41	9/26/71	Martinsville, VA	0.525	P	262.5	Bobby Isaac	Dodge	73.681	Bobby Isaac	Dodge	83.635
1037	42	10/10/71	Charlotte, NC	1.5	P	357	Bobby Allison	Mercury	126.14	Charlie Glotzbach	Chevrolet	157.085
1038	43	10/17/71	Dover, DE	1	P	500	Richard Petty	Plymouth	123.254	Bobby Allison	Mercury	132.811
1039	44	10/24/71	Rockingham, NC	1.017	P	500.364	Richard Petty	Plymouth	113.405	Charlie Glotzbach	Chevrolet	135.167
1040	45	11/7/71	Macon, GA	0.548	P	274	Bobby Allison	Ford	80.859	Bobby Allison	Ford	95.334
1041	46	11/14/71	Richmond, VA	0.542	P	271	Richard Petty	Plymouth	80.025	Bill Dennis	Mercury	N/A
1042	47	11/21/71	N. Wilkesboro, NC	0.625	P	250	Tiny Lund	Camaro	96.174	Charlie Glotzbach	Chevrolet	107.558
1043	48	12/12/71	College Station, TX	2	P	500	Richard Petty	Plymouth	144	Pete Hamilton	Plymouth	170.83

1972

Cum. No.	Yr. No.	Date	Site	Track Length	Surface	Miles	Race Winner	Make	Speed	Pole Winner	Make	Pole Speed
1044	1	1/23/72	Riverside, CA	2.62	P	390.38	Richard Petty	Plymouth	104.016	A.J. Foyt	Mercury	110.033
1045	2	2/20/72	Daytona Beach, FL	2.5	P	500	A.J. Foyt	Mercury	161.55	Bobby Isaac	Dodge	186.632
1046	3	2/27/72	Richmond, VA	0.542	P	271	Richard Petty	Plymouth	76.258	Bobby Allison	Chevrolet	76.258
1047	4	3/5/72	Ontario, CA	2.5	P	500	A.J. Foyt	Mercury	127.082	A.J. Foyt	Mercury	153.217
1048	5	3/12/72	Rockingham, NC	1.017	P	500.364	Bobby Isaac	Dodge	113.895	Bobby Isaac	Dodge	137.539
1049	6	3/26/72	Hampton, GA	1.522	P	499.216	Bobby Allison	Chevrolet	128.214	Bobby Allison	Chevrolet	156.245
1050	7	4/9/72	Bristol, TN	0.533	P	266.5	Bobby Allison	Chevrolet	92.826	Bobby Allison	Chevrolet	106.875
1051	8	4/16/72	Darlington, SC	1.366	P	400.238	David Pearson	Mercury	124.406	David Pearson	Mercury	148.209
1052	9	4/23/72	N. Wilkesboro, NC	0.625	P	250	Richard Petty	Plymouth	86.381	Bobby Isaac	Dodge	107.506
1053	10	4/30/72	Martinsville, VA	0.526	P	263	Richard Petty	Plymouth	72.657	Bobby Allison	Chevrolet	84.163
1054	11	5/7/72	Talladega, AL	2.66	P	500.08	David Pearson	Mercury	134.4	Bobby Isaac	Dodge	192.428
1055	12	5/28/72	Charlotte, NC	1.5	P	600	Buddy Baker	Dodge	142.255	Bobby Allison	Chevrolet	158.162
1056	13	6/4/72	Dover, DE	1	P	500	Bobby Allison	Chevrolet	118.019	Bobby Isaac	Dodge	130.809
1057	14	6/11/72	Brooklyn, MI	2	P	400	David Pearson	Mercury	146.639	Bobby Isaac	Dodge	160.764
1058	15	6/18/72	Riverside, CA	2.62	P	400.86	Ray Elder	Dodge	98.761	Richard Petty	Plymouth	108.688
1059	16	6/25/72	College Station, TX	2	P	500	Richard Petty	Plymouth	144.185	Richard Petty	Plymouth	169.412
1060	17	7/4/72	Daytona Beach, FL	2.5	P	400	David Pearson	Mercury	160.821	Bobby Isaac	Dodge	186.277
1061	18	7/9/72	Bristol, TN	0.533	P	266.5	Bobby Allison	Chevrolet	92.735	Bobby Allison	Chevrolet	107.279
1062	19	7/16/72	Trenton, NJ	1.5	P	300	Bobby Allison	Chevrolet	114.03	Bobby Isaac	Dodge	133.126
1063	20	7/23/72	Hampton, GA	1.522	P	499.216	Bobby Allison	Chevrolet	131.295	David Pearson	Mercury	158.353
1064	21	8/6/72	Talladega, AL	2.66	P	500.08	James Hylton	Mercury	148.728	Bobby Isaac	Dodge	190.677
1065	22	8/20/72	Brooklyn, MI	2	P	400	David Pearson	Mercury	134.16	Richard Petty	Dodge	157.607
1066	23	8/27/72	Nashville, TN	0.596	P	250.32	Bobby Allison	Chevrolet	92.578	Bobby Allison	Chevrolet	116.932
1067	24	9/4/72	Darlington, SC	1.366	P	501.322	Bobby Allison	Chevrolet	128.124	Bobby Allison	Chevrolet	152.342
1068	25	9/10/72	Richmond, VA	0.542	P	271	Richard Petty	Plymouth	75.899	Bobby Allison	Chevrolet	89.669
1069	26	9/17/72	Dover, DE	1	P	500	David Pearson	Mercury	120.506	Bobby Allison	Chevrolet	133.323
1070	27	9/24/72	Martinsville, VA	0.526	P	263	Richard Petty	Plymouth	69.989	Bobby Allison	Chevrolet	85.89
1071	28	10/1/72	N. Wilkesboro, NC	0.625	P	250	Richard Petty	Plymouth	95.816	Buddy Baker	Dodge	105.922
1072	29	10/8/72	Charlotte, NC	1.5	P	501	Bobby Allison	Chevrolet	133.234	David Pearson	Mercury	158.539
1073	30	10/22/72	Rockingham, NC	1.017	P	500.364	Bobby Allison	Chevrolet	118.275	David Pearson	Mercury	137.528
1074	31	11/12/72	College Station, TX	2	P	500	Buddy Baker	Dodge	147.059	A.J. Foyt	Mercury	170.273

1973

Cum. No.	Yr. No.	Date	Site	Track Length	Surface	Miles	Race Winner	Make	Speed	Pole Winner	Make	Pole Speed
1075	1	1/21/73	Riverside, CA	2.62	P	500.42	Mark Donohue	Matador	104.055	David Pearson	Mercury	110.856
1076	2	2/18/73	Daytona Beach, FL	2.5	P	500	Richard Petty	Dodge	157.205	Buddy Baker	Dodge	185.662
1077	3	2/25/73	Richmond, VA	0.542	P	271	Richard Petty	Dodge	74.764	Bobby Allison	Chevrolet	90.952
1078	4	3/18/73	Rockingham, NC	1.017	P	500.364	David Pearson	Mercury	118.649	David Pearson	Mercury	134.021
1079	5	3/25/73	Bristol, TN	0.533	P	266.5	Cale Yarborough	Chevrolet	88.952	Cale Yarborough	Chevrolet	107.608
1080	6	4/1/73	Hampton, GA	1.522	P	499.216	David Pearson	Mercury	139.351	No Time Trials	NTT	NTT

Cum. No.	Yr. No.	Date	Site	Track Length	Surface	Miles	Race Winner	Make	Speed	Pole Winner	Make	Pole Speed
1081	7	4/8/73	N. Wilkesboro, NC	0.625	P	250	Richard Petty	Dodge	97.224	Bobby Allison	Chevrolet	106.75
1082	8	4/15/73	Darlington, SC	1.366	P	501.322	David Pearson	Mercury	122.655	David Pearson	Mercury	153.463
1083	9	4/29/73	Martinsville, VA	0.526	P	263	David Pearson	Mercury	70.251	David Pearson	Mercury	86.369
1084	10	5/6/73	Talladega, AL	2.66	P	500.08	David Pearson	Mercury	131.956	Buddy Baker	Dodge	193.435
1085	11	5/12/73	Nashville, TN	0.596	P	250.32	Cale Yarborough	Chevrolet	98.419	Cale Yarborough	Chevrolet	105.741
1086	12	5/27/73	Charlotte, NC	1.5	P	600	Buddy Baker	Dodge	134.89	Buddy Baker	Dodge	158.051
1087	13	6/3/73	Dover, DE	1	P	500	David Pearson	Mercury	119.745	David Pearson	Mercury	133.111
1088	14	6/10/73	College Station, TX	2	P	500	Richard Petty	Dodge	142.114	Buddy Baker	Dodge	169.248
1089	15	6/17/73	Riverside, CA	2.62	P	400.86	Bobby Allison	Chevrolet	100.215	Richard Petty	Dodge	110.027
1090	16	6/24/73	Brooklyn, MI	2	P	400	David Pearson	Mercury	153.485	Buddy Baker	Dodge	158.273
1091	17	7/4/73	Daytona Beach, FL	2.5	P	400	David Pearson	Mercury	158.468	Bobby Allison	Chevrolet	179.619
1092	18	7/8/73	Bristol, TN	0.533	P	266.5	Benny Parsons	Chevrolet	91.342	Cale Yarborough	Chevrolet	106.472
1093	19	7/22/73	Hampton, GA	1.522	P	499.216	David Pearson	Mercury	130.211	Richard Petty	Dodge	157.163
1094	20	8/12/73	Talladega, AL	2.66	P	500.08	Dick Brooks	Plymouth	145.454	Bobby Allison	Chevrolet	187.064
1095	21	8/25/73	Nashville, TN	0.596	P	250.32	Buddy Baker	Dodge	89.31	Cale Yarborough	Chevrolet	103.024
1096	22	9/3/73	Darlington, SC	1.366	P	501.322	Cale Yarborough	Chevrolet	134.033	David Pearson	Mercury	150.366
1097	23	9/9/73	Richmond, VA	0.542	P	271	Richard Petty	Dodge	63.215	Bobby Allison	Chevrolet	90.245
1098	24	9/16/73	Dover, DE	1	P	500	David Pearson	Mercury	112.852	David Pearson	Mercury	124.649
1099	25	9/23/73	N. Wilkesboro, NC	0.625	P	250	Bobby Allison	Chevrolet	95.198	Bobby Allison	Chevrolet	105.619
1100	26	9/30/73	Martinsville, VA	0.526	P	252.48	Richard Petty	Dodge	68.831	Cale Yarborough	Chevrolet	85.922
1101	27	10/7/73	Charlotte, NC	1.5	P	501	Cale Yarborough	Chevrolet	145.24	David Pearson	Mercury	158.315
1102	28	10/21/73	Rockingham, NC	1.017	P	500.364	David Pearson	Mercury	117.749	Richard Petty	Dodge	135.748

1974

Cum. No.	Yr. No.	Date	Site	Track Length	Surface	Miles	Race Winner	Make	Speed	Pole Winner	Make	Pole Speed
1103	1	1/26/74	Riverside, CA	2.62	P	500.42	Cale Yarborough	Chevrolet	101.14	David Pearson	Mercury	110.098
1104	2	2/17/74	Daytona Beach, FL	2.5	P	500	Richard Petty	Dodge	140.894	David Pearson	Mercury	185.817
1105	3	2/24/74	Richmond, VA	0.542	P	271	Bobby Allison	Chevrolet	80.095	Bobby Allison	Chevrolet	90.353
1106	4	3/3/74	Rockingham, NC	1.017	P	500.364	Richard Petty	Dodge	121.622	Cale Yarborough	Chevrolet	134.868
1107	5	3/17/74	Bristol, TN	0.533	P	266.5	Cale Yarborough	Chevrolet	64.533	Donnie Allison	Chevrolet	107.785
1108	6	3/24/74	Hampton, GA	1.522	P	499.216	Cale Yarborough	Chevrolet	136.91	David Pearson	Mercury	159.242
1109	7	4/7/74	Darlington, SC	1.366	P	450.78	David Pearson	Mercury	117.543	Donnie Allison	Chevrolet	150.689
1110	8	4/21/74	N. Wilkesboro, NC	0.625	P	250	Richard Petty	Dodge	96.2	Bobby Allison	Chevrolet	105.669
1111	9	4/28/74	Martinsville, VA	0.526	P	263	Cale Yarborough	Chevrolet	70.427	Cale Yarborough	Chevrolet	84.362
1112	10	5/5/74	Talladega, AL	2.66	P	500.08	David Pearson	Mercury	130.22	David Pearson	Mercury	186.086
1113	11	5/12/74	Nashville, TN	0.596	P	250.32	Richard Petty	Dodge	82.24	Bobby Allison	Chevrolet	100.088
1114	12	5/19/74	Dover, DE	1	P	500	Cale Yarborough	Chevrolet	115.057	David Pearson	Mercury	134.403
1115	13	5/26/74	Charlotte, NC	1.5	P	600	David Pearson	Mercury	135.72	David Pearson	Mercury	157.498
1116	14	6/9/74	Riverside, CA	2.62	P	361.56	Cale Yarborough	Chevrolet	102.489	George Follmer	Matador	109.093
1117	15	6/16/74	Brooklyn, MI	2	P	360	Richard Petty	Dodge	127.098	David Pearson	Mercury	156.426
1118	16	7/4/74	Daytona Beach, FL	2.5	P	400	David Pearson	Mercury	138.31	David Pearson	Mercury	180.759
1119	17	7/14/74	Bristol, TN	0.533	P	266.5	Cale Yarborough	Chevrolet	75.43	Richard Petty	Dodge	107.351
1120	18	7/20/74	Nashville, TN	0.596	P	250.32	Cale Yarborough	Chevrolet	76.368	Darrell Waltrip	Chevrolet	101.274
1121	19	7/28/74	Hampton, GA	1.522	P	499.216	Richard Petty	Dodge	131.651	Cale Yarborough	Chevrolet	156.75
1122	20	8/4/74	Pocono, PA	2.5	P	480	Richard Petty	Dodge	115.593	Buddy Baker	Ford	144.122
1123	21	8/11/74	Talladega, AL	2.66	P	500.08	Richard Petty	Dodge	148.637	David Pearson	Mercury	184.926
1124	22	8/25/74	Brooklyn, MI	2	P	400	David Pearson	Mercury	133.045	David Pearson	Mercury	157.946
1125	23	9/2/74	Darlington, SC	1.366	P	501.322	Cale Yarborough	Chevrolet	111.075	Richard Petty	Dodge	150.132
1126	24	9/8/74	Richmond, VA	0.542	P	271	Richard Petty	Dodge	64.43	Richard Petty	Dodge	88.852
1127	25	9/15/74	Dover, DE	1	P	500	Richard Petty	Dodge	113.64	Buddy Baker	Ford	133.64
1128	26	9/22/74	N. Wilkesboro, NC	0.625	P	250	Cale Yarborough	Chevrolet	80.782	Richard Petty	Dodge	105.087
1129	27	9/29/74	Martinsville, VA	0.526	P	263	Earl Ross	Chevrolet	66.232	Richard Petty	Dodge	84.119
1130	28	10/6/74	Charlotte, NC	1.5	P	501	David Pearson	Mercury	119.912	David Pearson	Mercury	158.749
1131	29	10/20/74	Rockingham, NC	1.017	P	500.364	David Pearson	Mercury	118.493	Richard Petty	Dodge	135.297
1132	30	11/24/74	Ontario, CA	2.5	P	500	Bobby Allison	Matador	134.963	Richard Petty	Dodge	149.94

1975

Cum. No.	Yr. No.	Date	Site	Track Length	Surface	Miles	Race Winner	Make	Speed	Pole Winner	Make	Pole Speed
1133	1	1/19/75	Riverside, CA	2.62	P	500.42	Bobby Allison	Matador	98.627	Bobby Allison	Matador	110.382
1134	2	2/16/75	Daytona Beach, FL	2.5	P	500	Benny Parsons	Chevrolet	153.649	Donnie Allison	Chevrolet	185.827
1135	3	2/23/75	Richmond, VA	0.542	P	271	Richard Petty	Dodge	74.913	Richard Petty	Dodge	93.34
1136	4	3/2/75	Rockingham, NC	1.017	P	500.364	Cale Yarborough	Chevrolet	117.588	Buddy Baker	Ford	137.611
1137	5	3/16/75	Bristol, TN	0.533	P	266.5	Richard Petty	Dodge	97.053	Buddy Baker	Ford	110.951
1138	6	3/23/75	Hampton, GA	1.522	P	499.216	Richard Petty	Dodge	133.496	Richard Petty	Dodge	159.029

Cum. No.	Yr. No.	Date	Site	Track Length	Surface	Miles	Race Winner	Make	Speed	Pole Winner	Make	Pole Speed
1139	7	4/6/75	N. Wilkesboro, NC	0.625	P	250	Richard Petty	Dodge	90.009	Darrell Waltrip	Chevrolet	105.52
1140	8	4/13/75	Darlington, SC	1.366	P	501.322	Bobby Allison	Matador	117.597	David Pearson	Mercury	155.433
1141	9	4/27/75	Martinsville, VA	0.526	P	263	Richard Petty	Dodge	69.282	Benny Parsons	Chevrolet	85.789
1142	10	5/4/75	Talladega, AL	2.66	P	500.08	Buddy Baker	Ford	144.948	Buddy Baker	Ford	189.947
1143	11	5/10/75	Nashville, TN	0.596	P	250.32	Darrell Waltrip	Chevrolet	94.107	Darrell Waltrip	Chevrolet	103.793
1144	12	5/18/75	Dover, DE	1	P	500	David Pearson	Mercury	100.82	David Pearson	Mercury	136.612
1145	13	5/25/75	Charlotte, NC	1.5	P	600	Richard Petty	Dodge	145.327	David Pearson	Mercury	159.353
1146	14	6/8/75	Riverside, CA	2.62	P	400.86	Richard Petty	Dodge	101.028	Bobby Allison	Matador	110.353
1147	15	6/15/75	Brooklyn, MI	2	P	400	David Pearson	Mercury	131.398	Cale Yarborough	Chevrolet	158.541
1148	16	7/4/75	Daytona Beach, FL	2.5	P	400	Richard Petty	Dodge	158.381	Donnie Allison	Chevrolet	186.737
1149	17	7/20/75	Nashville, TN	0.596	P	250.32	Cale Yarborough	Chevrolet	89.792	Benny Parsons	Chevrolet	103.247
1150	18	8/3/75	Pocono, PA	2.5	P	500	David Pearson	Mercury	111.179	Bobby Allison	Matador	146.491
1151	19	8/17/75	Talladega, AL	2.66	P	500.08	Buddy Baker	Ford	130.892	Dave Marcis	Dodge	191.34
1152	20	8/24/75	Brooklyn, MI	2	P	400	Richard Petty	Dodge	107.583	David Pearson	Mercury	159.798
1153	21	9/1/75	Darlington, SC	1.366	P	501.322	Bobby Allison	Matador	116.825	David Pearson	Mercury	153.401
1154	22	9/14/75	Dover, DE	1	P	500	Richard Petty	Dodge	111.372	Dave Marcis	Dodge	133.953
1155	23	9/21/75	N. Wilkesboro, NC	0.625	P	250	Richard Petty	Dodge	88.986	Richard Petty	Dodge	105.5
1156	24	9/28/75	Martinsville, VA	0.526	P	263	Dave Marcis	Dodge	75.819	Cale Yarborough	Chevrolet	86.199
1157	25	10/5/75	Charlotte, NC	1.5	P	501	Richard Petty	Dodge	132.209	David Pearson	Mercury	161.701
1158	26	10/12/75	Richmond, VA	0.542	P	271	Darrell Waltrip	Chevrolet	81.886	Benny Parsons	Chevrolet	91.071
1159	27	10/19/75	Rockingham, NC	1.017	P	500.364	Cale Yarborough	Chevrolet	120.129	Dave Marcis	Dodge	132.021
1160	28	11/2/75	Bristol, TN	0.533	P	266.5	Richard Petty	Dodge	97.016	Cale Yarborough	Chevrolet	110.162
1161	29	11/9/75	Hampton, GA	1.522	P	499.216	Buddy Baker	Ford	130.99	Dave Marcis	Dodge	160.662
1162	30	11/23/75	Ontario, CA	2.5	P	500	Buddy Baker	Ford	140.712	David Pearson	Mercury	153.525

1976

Cum. No.	Yr. No.	Date	Site	Track Length	Surface	Miles	Race Winner	Make	Speed	Pole Winner	Make	Pole Speed
1163	1	1/18/76	Riverside, CA	2.62	P	500.42	David Pearson	Mercury	99.18	Bobby Allison	Matador	112.416
1164	2	2/15/76	Daytona Beach, FL	2.5	P	500	David Pearson	Mercury	152.181	Ramo Stott	Chevrolet	183.456
1165	3	2/29/76	Rockingham, NC	1.017	P	500.364	Richard Petty	Dodge	113.665	Dave Marcis	Dodge	138.287
1166	4	3/7/76	Richmond, VA	0.542	P	216.8	Dave Marcis	Dodge	72.792	Bobby Allison	Mercury	92.715
1167	5	3/14/76	Bristol, TN	0.533	P	213.2	Cale Yarborough	Chevrolet	87.377	Buddy Baker	Ford	110.72
1168	6	3/21/76	Hampton, GA	1.522	P	499.216	David Pearson	Mercury	128.904	Dave Marcis	Dodge	160.709
1169	7	4/4/76	N. Wilkesboro, NC	0.625	P	250	Cale Yarborough	Chevrolet	96.858	Dave Marcis	Dodge	108.585
1170	8	4/11/76	Darlington, SC	1.366	P	501.322	David Pearson	Mercury	122.973	David Pearson	Mercury	154.171
1171	9	4/25/76	Martinsville, VA	0.526	P	263	Darrell Waltrip	Chevrolet	71.759	Dave Marcis	Dodge	86.286
1172	10	5/2/76	Talladega, AL	2.66	P	500.08	Buddy Baker	Ford	169.887	Dave Marcis	Dodge	189.197
1173	11	5/8/76	Nashville, TN	0.596	P	250.32	Cale Yarborough	Chevrolet	84.512	Benny Parsons	Chevrolet	104.328
1174	12	5/16/76	Dover, DE	1	P	500	Benny Parsons	Chevrolet	115.436	Dave Marcis	Dodge	136.013
1175	13	5/30/76	Charlotte, NC	1.5	P	600	David Pearson	Mercury	137.352	David Pearson	Mercury	159.132
1176	14	6/13/76	Riverside, CA	2.62	P	248.9	David Pearson	Mercury	106.279	David Pearson	Mercury	111.437
1177	15	6/20/76	Brooklyn, MI	2	P	400	David Pearson	Mercury	141.148	Richard Petty	Dodge	158.569
1178	16	7/4/76	Daytona Beach, FL	2.5	P	400	Cale Yarborough	Chevrolet	160.966	A. J. Foyt	Chevrolet	183.09
1179	17	7/17/76	Nashville, TN	0.596	P	250.32	Benny Parsons	Chevrolet	86.908	Bobby Allison	Mercury	103.049
1180	18	8/1/76	Pocono, PA	2.5	P	500	Richard Petty	Dodge	115.875	Cale Yarborough	Chevrolet	147.865
1181	19	8/8/76	Talladega, AL	2.66	P	500.08	Dave Marcis	Dodge	157.547	Dave Marcis	Dodge	190.651
1182	20	8/22/76	Brooklyn, MI	2	P	400	David Pearson	Mercury	140.078	David Pearson	Mercury	160.875
1183	21	8/29/76	Bristol, TN	0.533	P	213.2	Cale Yarborough	Chevrolet	99.175	Darrell Waltrip	Chevrolet	110.3
1184	22	9/6/76	Darlington, SC	1.366	P	501.322	David Pearson	Mercury	120.534	David Pearson	Mercury	154.699
1185	23	9/12/76	Richmond, VA	0.542	P	216.8	Cale Yarborough	Chevrolet	77.993	Benny Parsons	Chevrolet	92.46
1186	24	9/19/76	Dover, DE	1	P	500	Cale Yarborough	Chevrolet	115.74	Cale Yarborough	Chevrolet	115.74
1187	25	9/26/76	Martinsville, VA	0.526	P	178.84	Cale Yarborough	Chevrolet	75.37	Darrell Waltrip	Chevrolet	88.484
1188	26	10/3/76	N. Wilkesboro, NC	0.625	P	250	Cale Yarborough	Chevrolet	96.38	Darrell Waltrip	Chevrolet	107.449
1189	27	10/10/76	Charlotte, NC	1.5	P	501	Donnie Allison	Chevrolet	141.226	David Pearson	Mercury	161.223
1190	28	10/24/76	Rockingham, NC	1.017	P	500.364	Richard Petty	Dodge	117.718	David Pearson	Mercury	139.117
1191	29	11/7/76	Hampton, GA	1.522	P	499.216	Dave Marcis	Dodge	127.396	Buddy Baker	Ford	161.652
1192	30	11/21/76	Ontario, CA	2.5	P	500	David Pearson	Mercury	137.101	David Pearson	Mercury	153.964

1977

Cum. No.	Yr. No.	Date	Site	Track Length	Surface	Miles	Race Winner	Make	Speed	Pole Winner	Make	Pole Speed
1193	1	1/16/77	Riverside, CA	2.62	P	311.78	David Pearson	Mercury	107.038	Cale Yarborough	Chevrolet	112.686
1194	2	2/20/77	Daytona Beach, FL	2.5	P	500	Cale Yarborough	Chevrolet	153.218	Donnie Allison	Chevrolet	188.048
1195	3	2/27/77	Richmond, VA	0.542	P	132.79	Cale Yarborough	Chevrolet	73.084	Neil Bonnett	Dodge	93.632
1196	4	3/13/77	Rockingham, NC	1.017	P	500.364	Richard Petty	Dodge	97.86	Donnie Allison	Chevrolet	135.387

Cum. No.	Yr. No.	Date	Site	Track Length	Surface	Miles	Race Winner	Make	Speed	Pole Winner	Make	Pole Speed
1197	5	3/20/77	Hampton, GA	1.522	P	499.216	Richard Petty	Dodge	144.093	Richard Petty	Dodge	162.501
1198	6	3/27/77	N. Wilkesboro, NC	0.625	P	250	Cale Yarborough	Chevrolet	88.95	Neil Bonnett	Dodge	107.537
1199	7	4/3/77	Darlington, SC	1.366	P	501.322	Darrell Waltrip	Chevrolet	128.817	David Pearson	Mercury	151.269
1200	8	4/17/77	Bristol, TN	0.533	P	266.5	Cale Yarborough	Chevrolet	100.989	Cale Yarborough	Chevrolet	110.168
1201	9	4/24/77	Martinsville, VA	0.526	P	201.984	Cale Yarborough	Chevrolet	77.405	Neil Bonnett	Dodge	88.923
1202	10	5/1/77	Talladega, AL	2.66	P	500.08	Darrell Waltrip	Chevrolet	164.877	A.J. Foyt	Chevrolet	192.424
1203	11	5/7/77	Nashville, TN	0.596	P	250.32	Benny Parsons	Chevrolet	87.49	Darrell Waltrip	Chevrolet	103.643
1204	12	5/15/77	Dover, DE	1	P	500	Cale Yarborough	Chevrolet	123.327	Richard Petty	Dodge	136.033
1205	13	5/29/77	Charlotte, NC	1.5	P	600	Richard Petty	Dodge	137.676	David Pearson	Mercury	161.435
1206	14	6/12/77	Riverside, CA	2.62	P	248.9	Richard Petty	Dodge	105.021	Richard Petty	Dodge	112.432
1207	15	6/19/77	Brooklyn, MI	2	P	400	Cale Yarborough	Chevrolet	135.033	David Pearson	Mercury	159.175
1208	16	7/4/77	Daytona Beach, FL	2.5	P	400	Richard Petty	Dodge	142.716	Neil Bonnett	Dodge	187.191
1209	17	7/17/77	Nashville, TN	0.596	P	250.32	Darrell Waltrip	Chevrolet	78.999	Benny Parsons	Chevrolet	104.21
1210	18	7/31/77	Pocono, PA	2.5	P	500	Benny Parsons	Chevrolet	128.379	Darrell Waltrip	Chevrolet	147.591
1211	19	8/7/77	Talladega, AL	2.66	P	500.08	Donnie Allison	Chevrolet	162.524	Benny Parsons	Chevrolet	192.684
1212	20	8/22/77	Brooklyn, MI	2	P	400	Darrell Waltrip	Chevrolet	137.944	David Pearson	Mercury	160.346
1213	21	8/28/77	Bristol, TN	0.533	P	213.2	Cale Yarborough	Chevrolet	79.726	Cale Yarborough	Chevrolet	109.746
1214	22	9/5/77	Darlington, SC	1.366	P	501.322	David Pearson	Mercury	106.797	Darrell Waltrip	Chevrolet	153.493
1215	23	9/11/77	Richmond, VA	0.542	P	216.8	Neil Bonnett	Dodge	80.644	Benny Parsons	Chevrolet	92.281
1216	24	9/18/77	Dover, DE	1	P	500	Benny Parsons	Chevrolet	114.708	Neil Bonnett	Dodge	134.233
1217	25	9/25/77	Martinsville, VA	0.526	P	263	Cale Yarborough	Chevrolet	73.447	Neil Bonnett	Dodge	87.637
1218	26	10/2/77	N. Wilkesboro, NC	0.625	P	250	Darrell Waltrip	Chevrolet	86.713	Richard Petty	Dodge	108.35
1219	27	10/9/77	Charlotte, NC	1.5	P	501	Benny Parsons	Chevrolet	142.78	David Pearson	Mercury	160.892
1220	28	10/23/77	Rockingham, NC	1.017	P	500.364	Donnie Allison	Chevrolet	113.584	Donnie Allison	Chevrolet	138.685
1221	29	11/6/77	Hampton, GA	1.522	P	407.896	Darrell Waltrip	Chevrolet	110.052	Sam Sommers	Chevrolet	160.229
1222	30	11/20/77	Ontario, CA	2.5	P	500	Neil Bonnett	Dodge	128.296	Richard Petty	Dodge	154.905

1978

Cum. No.	Yr. No.	Date	Site	Track Length	Surface	Miles	Race Winner	Make	Speed	Pole Winner	Make	Pole Speed
1223	1	1/22/78	Riverside, CA	2.62	P	311.78	Cale Yarborough	Oldsmobile	102.269	David Pearson	Mercury	113.204
1224	2	2/19/78	Daytona Beach, FL	2.5	P	500	Bobby Allison	Ford	159.73	Cale Yarborough	Oldsmobile	187.536
1225	3	2/26/78	Richmond, VA	0.542	P	216.8	Benny Parsons	Oldsmobile	80.304	Neil Bonnett	Dodge	93.382
1226	4	3/5/78	Rockingham, NC	1.017	P	500.364	David Pearson	Mercury	116.681	Neil Bonnett	Dodge	141.94
1227	5	3/19/78	Hampton, GA	1.522	P	499.216	Bobby Allison	Ford	142.52	Cale Yarborough	Oldsmobile	162.006
1228	6	4/2/78	Bristol, TN	0.533	P	266.5	Darrell Waltrip	Chevrolet	92.401	Neil Bonnett	Dodge	110.409
1229	7	4/9/78	Darlington, SC	1.366	P	501.322	Benny Parsons	Chevrolet	127.544	Bobby Allison	Ford	151.862
1230	8	4/16/78	N. Wilkesboro, NC	0.625	P	250	Darrell Waltrip	Chevrolet	92.345	Benny Parsons	Chevrolet	108.51
1231	9	4/23/78	Martinsville, VA	0.526	P	263	Darrell Waltrip	Chevrolet	77.971	Lennie Pond	Chevrolet	88.637
1232	10	5/14/78	Talladega, AL	2.66	P	500.08	Cale Yarborough	Oldsmobile	155.699	Cale Yarborough	Oldsmobile	191.904
1233	11	5/21/78	Dover, DE	1	P	500	David Pearson	Mercury	114.664	Buddy Baker	Chevrolet	135.452
1234	12	5/28/78	Charlotte, NC	1.5	P	600	Darrell Waltrip	Chevrolet	138.355	David Pearson	Mercury	160.551
1235	13	6/3/78	Nashville, TN	0.596	P	250.32	Cale Yarborough	Oldsmobile	87.541	Lennie Pond	Chevrolet	105.094
1236	14	6/11/78	Riverside, CA	2.62	P	248.9	Benny Parsons	Chevrolet	104.311	David Pearson	Mercury	112.882
1237	15	6/18/78	Brooklyn, MI	2	P	400	Cale Yarborough	Oldsmobile	149.563	David Pearson	Mercury	163.936
1238	16	7/4/78	Daytona Beach, FL	2.5	P	400	David Pearson	Mercury	154.34	Cale Yarborough	Oldsmobile	186.803
1239	17	7/15/78	Nashville, TN	0.596	P	250.32	Cale Yarborough	Oldsmobile	88.924	Lennie Pond	Chevrolet	104.257
1240	18	7/30/78	Pocono, PA	2.5	P	500	Darrell Waltrip	Chevrolet	142.54	Benny Parsons	Chevrolet	149.236
1241	19	8/6/78	Talladega, AL	2.66	P	500.08	Lennie Pond	Oldsmobile	174.7	Cale Yarborough	Oldsmobile	192.917
1242	20	8/20/78	Brooklyn, MI	2	P	400	David Pearson	Mercury	129.566	David Pearson	Mercury	164.073
1243	21	8/26/78	Bristol, TN	0.533	P	266.5	Cale Yarborough	Oldsmobile	88.628	Lennie Pond	Oldsmobile	110.958
1244	22	9/4/78	Darlington, SC	1.366	P	501.322	Cale Yarborough	Oldsmobile	116.828	David Pearson	Mercury	153.685
1245	23	9/10/78	Richmond, VA	0.542	P	216.8	Darrell Waltrip	Chevrolet	79.568	Darrell Waltrip	Chevrolet	91.964
1246	24	9/17/78	Dover, DE	1	P	500	Bobby Allison	Ford	119.323	J.D. McDuffie	Chevrolet	135.48
1247	25	9/24/78	Martinsville, VA	0.526	P	263	Cale Yarborough	Oldsmobile	79.185	Lennie Pond	Chevrolet	86.558
1248	26	10/1/78	N. Wilkesboro, NC	0.625	P	250	Cale Yarborough	Oldsmobile	97.847	Darrell Waltrip	Chevrolet	109.397
1249	27	10/8/78	Charlotte, NC	1.5	P	501	Bobby Allison	Ford	141.826	David Pearson	Mercury	161.355
1250	28	10/22/78	Rockingham, NC	1.017	P	500.364	Cale Yarborough	Oldsmobile	117.288	Cale Yarborough	Oldsmobile	142.067
1251	29	11/5/78	Hampton, GA	1.522	P	499.216	Donnie Allison	Chevrolet	124.312	Cale Yarborough	Oldsmobile	168.425
1252	30	11/19/78	Ontario, CA	2.5	P	500	Bobby Allison	Ford	137.783	Cale Yarborough	Oldsmobile	156.19

1979

Cum. No.	Yr. No.	Date	Site	Track Length	Surface	Miles	Race Winner	Make	Speed	Pole Winner	Make	Pole Speed
1253	1	1/14/79	Riverside, CA	2.62	P	311.78	Darrell Waltrip	Chevrolet	107.82	David Pearson	Mercury	113.659
1254	2	2/18/79	Daytona Beach, FL	2.5	P	500	Richard Petty	Oldsmobile	143.977	Buddy Baker	Oldsmobile	196.049

Cum. No.	Yr. No.	Date	Site	Track Length	Surface	Miles	Race Winner	Make	Speed	Pole Winner	Make	Pole Speed
1255	3	3/4/79	Rockingham, NC	1.017	P	500.364	Bobby Allison	Ford	122.727	Bobby Allison	Ford	136.79
1256	4	3/11/79	Richmond, VA	0.542	P	216.8	Cale Yarborough	Oldsmobile	83.608	Bobby Allison	Ford	92.957
1257	5	3/18/79	Hampton, GA	1.522	P	499.216	Buddy Baker	Oldsmobile	135.136	Buddy Baker	Oldsmobile	165.951
1258	6	3/25/79	N. Wilkesboro, NC	0.625	P	250	Bobby Allison	Ford	88.4	Benny Parsons	Chevrolet	108.136
1259	7	4/1/79	Bristol, TN	0.533	P	266.5	Dale Earnhardt	Chevrolet	91.033	Buddy Baker	Chevrolet	111.668
1260	8	4/8/79	Darlington, SC	1.366	P	501.322	Darrell Waltrip	Chevrolet	121.721	Donnie Allison	Chevrolet	154.797
1261	9	4/22/79	Martinsville, VA	0.526	P	263	Richard Petty	Chevrolet	76.562	Darrell Waltrip	Chevrolet	87.383
1262	10	5/6/79	Talladega, AL	2.66	P	500.08	Bobby Allison	Ford	154.77	Darrell Waltrip	Chevrolet	195.644
1263	11	5/12/79	Nashville, TN	0.596	P	250.32	Cale Yarborough	Oldsmobile	88.652	Joe Millikan	Chevrolet	104.155
1264	12	5/20/79	Dover, DE	1	P	500	Neil Bonnett	Mercury	111.269	Darrell Waltrip	Chevrolet	136.103
1265	13	5/27/79	Charlotte, NC	1.5	P	600	Darrell Waltrip	Chevrolet	136.674	Neil Bonnett	Mercury	160.125
1266	14	6/3/79	College Station, TX	2	P	400	Darrell Waltrip	Chevrolet	156.216	Buddy Baker	Chevrolet	167.903
1267	15	6/10/79	Riverside, CA	2.62	P	248.9	Bobby Allison	Ford	103.732	Dale Earnhardt	Chevrolet	113.089
1268	16	6/17/79	Brooklyn, MI	2	P	400	Buddy Baker	Chevrolet	135.798	Neil Bonnett	Mercury	162.371
1269	17	7/4/79	Daytona Beach, FL	2.5	P	400	Neil Bonnett	Mercury	172.89	Buddy Baker	Oldsmobile	193.196
1270	18	7/14/79	Nashville, TN	0.596	P	250.32	Darrell Waltrip	Chevrolet	92.227	Darrell Waltrip	Chevrolet	105.43
1271	19	7/30/79	Pocono, PA	2.5	P	500	Cale Yarborough	Chevrolet	115.207	Harry Gant	Chevrolet	148.711
1272	20	8/5/79	Talladega, AL	2.66	P	500.08	Darrell Waltrip	Chevrolet	161.229	Neil Bonnett	Mercury	193.6
1273	21	8/19/79	Brooklyn, MI	2	P	400	Richard Petty	Chevrolet	130.376	David Pearson	Chevrolet	162.992
1274	22	8/25/79	Bristol, TN	0.533	P	266.5	Darrell Waltrip	Chevrolet	91.493	Richard Petty	Chevrolet	120.524
1275	23	9/3/79	Darlington, SC	1.366	P	501.322	David Pearson	Chevrolet	126.259	Bobby Allison	Ford	154.88
1276	24	9/9/79	Richmond, VA	0.542	P	216.8	Bobby Allison	Ford	80.604	Dale Earnhardt	Chevrolet	92.605
1277	25	9/16/79	Dover, DE	1	P	500	Richard Petty	Chevrolet	114.366	Dale Earnhardt	Chevrolet	135.726
1278	26	9/23/79	Martinsville, VA	0.526	P	263	Buddy Baker	Chevrolet	75.119	Darrell Waltrip	Chevrolet	88.265
1279	27	10/7/79	Charlotte, NC	1.5	P	501	Cale Yarborough	Chevrolet	134.266	Neil Bonnett	Mercury	164.304
1280	28	10/14/79	N. Wilkesboro, NC	0.625	P	250	Benny Parsons	Chevrolet	91.454	Dale Earnhardt	Chevrolet	112.783
1281	29	10/21/79	Rockingham, NC	1.017	P	500.364	Richard Petty	Chevrolet	108.356	Buddy Baker	Chevrolet	141.315
1282	30	11/4/79	Hampton, GA	1.522	P	499.216	Neil Bonnett	Mercury	140.12	Buddy Baker	Chevrolet	164.813
1283	31	11/18/79	Ontario, CA	2.5	P	500	Benny Parsons	Chevrolet	132.822	Cale Yarborough	Oldsmobile	154.902

1980

Cum. No.	Yr. No.	Date	Site	Track Length	Surface	Miles	Race Winner	Make	Speed	Pole Winner	Make	Pole Speed
1284	1	1/19/80	Riverside, CA	2.62	P	311.78	Darrell Waltrip	Chevrolet	94.974	Darrell Waltrip	Chevrolet	113.404
1285	2	2/17/80	Daytona Beach, FL	2.5	P	500	Buddy Baker	Oldsmobile	177.602	Buddy Baker	Oldsmobile	194.009
1286	3	2/24/80	Richmond, VA	0.542	P	216.8	Darrell Waltrip	Chevrolet	67.703	Darrell Waltrip	Chevrolet	93.695
1287	4	3/9/80	Rockingham, NC	1.017	P	500.364	Cale Yarborough	Oldsmobile	108.735	Darrell Waltrip	Chevrolet	139.905
1288	5	3/16/80	Hampton, GA	1.522	P	499.216	Dale Earnhardt	Chevrolet	134.808	Buddy Baker	Oldsmobile	166.212
1289	6	3/30/80	Bristol, TN	0.533	P	266.5	Dale Earnhardt	Chevrolet	96.977	Cale Yarborough	Chevrolet	111.688
1290	7	4/13/80	Darlington, SC	1.366	P	258.174	David Pearson	Chevrolet	112.397	Benny Parsons	Chevrolet	155.866
1291	8	4/20/80	N. Wilkesboro, NC	0.625	P	250	Richard Petty	Chevrolet	95.501	Bobby Allison	Ford	113.797
1292	9	4/27/80	Martinsville, VA	0.526	P	263	Darrell Waltrip	Chevrolet	69.049	Darrell Waltrip	Chevrolet	88.566
1293	10	5/4/80	Talladega, AL	2.66	P	500.08	Buddy Baker	Oldsmobile	170.481	David Pearson	Oldsmobile	197.704
1294	11	5/10/80	Nashville, TN	0.596	P	250.32	Richard Petty	Chevrolet	89.471	Cale Yarborough	Chevrolet	106.591
1295	12	5/18/80	Dover, DE	1	P	500	Bobby Allison	Ford	113.866	Cale Yarborough	Chevrolet	138.814
1296	13	5/25/80	Charlotte, NC	1.5	P	600	Benny Parsons	Chevrolet	119.265	Cale Yarborough	Chevrolet	165.194
1297	14	6/1/80	College Station, TX	2	P	400	Cale Yarborough	Chevrolet	159.046	Cale Yarborough	Chevrolet	170.709
1298	15	6/8/80	Riverside, CA	2.62	P	248.9	Darrell Waltrip	Chevrolet	101.846	Cale Yarborough	Chevrolet	113.792
1299	16	6/15/80	Brooklyn, MI	2	P	400	Benny Parsons	Chevrolet	131.808	Benny Parsons	Chevrolet	163.662
1300	17	7/4/80	Daytona Beach, FL	2.5	P	400	Bobby Allison	Mercury	173.473	Cale Yarborough	Oldsmobile	194.67
1301	18	7/12/80	Nashville, TN	0.596	P	250.32	Dale Earnhardt	Chevrolet	93.821	Cale Yarborough	Chevrolet	104.817
1302	19	7/27/80	Pocono, PA	2.5	P	500	Neil Bonnett	Mercury	124.395	Cale Yarborough	Chevrolet	151.469
1303	20	8/3/80	Talladega, AL	2.66	P	500.08	Neil Bonnett	Mercury	166.894	Buddy Baker	Oldsmobile	198.545
1304	21	8/17/80	Brooklyn, MI	2	P	400	Cale Yarborough	Chevrolet	145.352	Buddy Baker	Chevrolet	162.693
1305	22	8/23/80	Bristol, TN	0.533	P	266.5	Cale Yarborough	Chevrolet	86.973	Cale Yarborough	Chevrolet	110.99
1306	23	9/1/80	Darlington, SC	1.366	P	501.322	Terry Labonte	Chevrolet	115.21	Darrell Waltrip	Oldsmobile	153.838
1307	24	9/7/80	Richmond, VA	0.542	P	216.8	Bobby Allison	Ford	79.722	Cale Yarborough	Chevrolet	93.466
1308	25	9/14/80	Dover, DE	1	P	500	Darrell Waltrip	Oldsmobile	116.024	Cale Yarborough	Chevrolet	137.583
1309	26	9/21/80	N. Wilkesboro, NC	0.625	P	250	Bobby Allison	Ford	75.51	Cale Yarborough	Chevrolet	111.996
1310	27	9/28/80	Martinsville, VA	0.526	P	263	Dale Earnhardt	Chevrolet	69.654	Buddy Baker	Chevrolet	88.5
1311	28	10/5/80	Charlotte, NC	1.5	P	501	Dale Earnhardt	Chevrolet	135.243	Buddy Baker	Buick	165.634
1312	29	10/19/80	Rockingham, NC	1.017	P	500.364	Cale Yarborough	Chevrolet	114.159	Donnie Allison	Chevrolet	142.648
1313	30	11/2/80	Hampton, GA	1.522	P	499.216	Cale Yarborough	Chevrolet	131.19	Bobby Allison	Mercury	165.62
1314	31	11/15/80	Ontario, CA	2.5	P	500	Benny Parsons	Chevrolet	129.441	Cale Yarborough	Chevrolet	155.499

Cum. No.	Yr. No.	Date	Site	Track Length	Surface	Miles	Race Winner	Make	Speed	Pole Winner	Make	Pole Speed
1981												
1315	1	1/11/81	Riverside, CA	2.62	P	311.78	Bobby Allison	Chevrolet	95.263	Darrell Waltrip	Buick	114.711
1316	2	2/15/81	Daytona Beach, FL	2.5	P	500	Richard Petty	Buick	169.651	Bobby Allison	Pontiac	194.624
1317	3	2/22/81	Richmond, VA	0.542	P	216.8	Darrell Waltrip	Buick	76.57	Morgan Shepherd	Pontiac	92.821
1318	4	3/1/81	Rockingham, NC	1.017	P	500.364	Darrell Waltrip	Buick	114.594	Cale Yarborough	Buick	140.448
1319	5	3/15/81	Hampton, GA	1.522	P	499.216	Cale Yarborough	Buick	133.619	Terry Labonte	Buick	162.94
1320	6	3/29/81	Bristol, TN	0.533	P	266.5	Darrell Waltrip	Buick	89.53	Darrell Waltrip	Buick	112.125
1321	7	4/5/81	N. Wilkesboro, NC	0.625	P	250	Richard Petty	Buick	85.381	Dave Marcis	Chevrolet	114.647
1322	8	4/12/81	Darlington, SC	1.366	P	501.322	Darrell Waltrip	Buick	126.703	Bill Elliott	Ford	153.896
1323	9	4/26/81	Martinsville, VA	0.526	P	263	Morgan Shepherd	Pontiac	75.019	Ricky Rudd	Buick	89.056
1324	10	5/3/81	Talladega, AL	2.66	P	500.08	Bobby Allison	Buick	149.376	Bobby Allison	Buick	195.864
1325	11	5/9/81	Nashville, TN	0.596	P	250.32	Benny Parsons	Ford	89.756	Ricky Rudd	Buick	104.409
1326	12	5/17/81	Dover, DE	1	P	500	Jody Ridley	Ford	116.595	David Pearson	Oldsmobile	138.425
1327	13	5/24/81	Charlotte, NC	1.5	P	600	Bobby Allison	Buick	129.326	Neil Bonnett	Ford	158.115
1328	14	6/7/81	College Station, TX	2	P	400	Benny Parsons	Ford	132.475	Terry Labonte	Buick	167.543
1329	15	6/14/81	Riverside, CA	2.62	P	248.9	Darrell Waltrip	Buick	93.597	Darrell Waltrip	Buick	114.378
1330	16	6/21/81	Brooklyn, MI	2	P	400	Bobby Allison	Buick	130.589	Darrell Waltrip	Buick	160.471
1331	17	7/4/81	Daytona Beach, FL	2.5	P	400	Cale Yarborough	Buick	142.588	Cale Yarborough	Buick	192.852
1332	18	7/11/81	Nashville, TN	0.596	P	250.32	Darrell Waltrip	Buick	90.052	Mark Martin	Pontiac	104.353
1333	19	7/26/81	Pocono, PA	2.5	P	500	Darrell Waltrip	Buick	119.111	Darrell Waltrip	Buick	150.148
1334	20	8/2/81	Talladega, AL	2.66	P	500.08	Ron Bouchard	Buick	156.737	Harry Gant	Buick	195.897
1335	21	8/16/81	Brooklyn, MI	2	P	400	Richard Petty	Buick	123.457	Ron Bouchard	Buick	161.501
1336	22	8/22/81	Bristol, TN	0.533	P	266.5	Darrell Waltrip	Buick	84.723	Darrell Waltrip	Buick	110.818
1337	23	9/7/81	Darlington, SC	1.366	P	501.322	Neil Bonnett	Ford	126.41	Harry Gant	Pontiac	152.693
1338	24	9/13/81	Richmond, VA	0.542	P	216.8	Benny Parsons	Ford	69.998	Mark Martin	Pontiac	93.435
1339	25	9/20/81	Dover, DE	1	P	500	Neil Bonnett	Ford	119.561	Ricky Rudd	Chevrolet	136.757
1340	26	9/27/81	Martinsville, VA	0.526	P	263	Darrell Waltrip	Buick	70.089	Darrell Waltrip	Buick	89.014
1341	27	10/4/81	N. Wilkesboro, NC	0.625	P	250	Darrell Waltrip	Buick	93.091	Darrell Waltrip	Buick	114.065
1342	28	10/11/81	Charlotte, NC	1.5	P	501	Darrell Waltrip	Buick	117.483	Darrell Waltrip	Buick	162.744
1343	29	11/1/81	Rockingham, NC	1.017	P	500.364	Darrell Waltrip	Buick	107.399	Darrell Waltrip	Buick	138.164
1344	30	11/8/81	Hampton, GA	1.522	P	499.216	Neil Bonnett	Ford	130.391	Harry Gant	Pontiac	163.266
1345	31	11/22/81	Riverside, CA	2.62	P	311.78	Bobby Allison	Buick	95.288	Darrell Waltrip	Buick	114.981
1982												
1346	1	2/14/82	Daytona Beach, FL	2.5	P	500	Bobby Allison	Buick	153.991	Benny Parsons	Pontiac	196.317
1347	2	2/21/82	Richmond, VA	0.542	P	135.5	Dave Marcis	Chevrolet	72.914	Darrell Waltrip	Buick	93.256
1348	3	3/14/82	Bristol, TN	0.533	P	266.5	Darrell Waltrip	Buick	94.025	Darrell Waltrip	Buick	111.068
1349	4	3/21/82	Hampton, GA	1.522	P	436.814	Darrell Waltrip	Buick	124.824	Dale Earnhardt	Ford	163.774
1350	5	3/28/82	Rockingham, NC	1.017	P	500.364	Cale Yarborough	Buick	108.992	Benny Parsons	Pontiac	141.577
1351	6	4/4/82	Darlington, SC	1.366	P	501.322	Dale Earnhardt	Ford	123.554	Buddy Baker	Buick	153.979
1352	7	4/18/82	N. Wilkesboro, NC	0.625	P	250	Darrell Waltrip	Buick	97.646	Darrell Waltrip	Buick	114.801
1353	8	4/25/82	Martinsville, VA	0.526	P	263	Harry Gant	Buick	75.073	Terry Labonte	Chevrolet	89.988
1354	9	5/2/82	Talladega, AL	2.66	P	500.08	Darrell Waltrip	Buick	156.697	Benny Parsons	Pontiac	200.176
1355	10	5/8/82	Nashville, TN	0.596	P	250.32	Darrell Waltrip	Buick	83.502	Darrell Waltrip	Buick	102.773
1356	11	5/16/82	Dover, DE	1	P	500	Bobby Allison	Chevrolet	120.136	Darrell Waltrip	Buick	139.308
1357	12	5/30/82	Charlotte, NC	1.5	P	600	Neil Bonnett	Ford	130.058	David Pearson	Buick	162.511
1358	13	6/6/82	Pocono, PA	2.5	P	500	Bobby Allison	Buick	113.579	No Time Trials	NTT	NTT
1359	14	6/13/82	Riverside, CA	2.62	P	248.9	Tim Richmond	Buick	103	Terry Labonte	Buick	114.352
1360	15	6/20/82	Brooklyn, MI	2	P	400	Cale Yarborough	Buick	118.101	Ron Bouchard	Buick	162.404
1361	16	7/4/82	Daytona Beach, FL	2.5	P	400	Bobby Allison	Buick	163.099	Geoffrey Bodine	Pontiac	194.721
1362	17	7/10/82	Nashville, TN	0.596	P	250.32	Darrell Waltrip	Buick	86.524	Morgan Shepherd	Buick	103.959
1363	18	7/25/82	Pocono, PA	2.5	P	500	Bobby Allison	Buick	115.496	Cale Yarborough	Buick	150.764
1364	19	8/1/82	Talladega, AL	2.66	P	500.08	Darrell Waltrip	Buick	168.157	Geoffrey Bodine	Pontiac	199.4
1365	20	8/22/82	Brooklyn, MI	2	P	400	Bobby Allison	Buick	136.454	Bill Elliott	Ford	162.995
1366	21	8/28/82	Bristol, TN	0.533	P	266.5	Darrell Waltrip	Buick	94.318	Tim Richmond	Buick	112.507
1367	22	9/6/82	Darlington, SC	1.366	P	501.322	Cale Yarborough	Buick	115.224	David Pearson	Buick	155.739
1368	23	9/12/82	Richmond, VA	0.542	P	216.8	Bobby Allison	Chevrolet	82.8	Bobby Allison	Chevrolet	93.435
1369	24	9/19/82	Dover, DE	1	P	500	Darrell Waltrip	Buick	107.642	Ricky Rudd	Pontiac	139.384
1370	25	10/3/82	N. Wilkesboro, NC	0.625	P	250	Darrell Waltrip	Buick	98.071	Darrell Waltrip	Buick	113.86
1371	26	10/10/82	Charlotte, NC	1.5	P	501	Harry Gant	Buick	137.208	Harry Gant	Buick	164.694
1372	27	10/17/82	Martinsville, VA	0.526	P	263	Darrell Waltrip	Buick	71.315	Ricky Rudd	Pontiac	89.132
1373	28	10/31/82	Rockingham, NC	1.017	P	500.364	Darrell Waltrip	Buick	115.122	Cale Yarborough	Buick	143.22

Cum. No.	Yr. No.	Date	Site	Track Length	Surface	Miles	Race Winner	Make	Speed	Pole Winner	Make	Pole Speed
1374	29	11/7/82	Hampton, GA	1.522	P	499.216	Bobby Allison	Buick	130.884	Morgan Shepherd	Buick	166.779
1375	30	11/21/82	Riverside, CA	2.62	P	311.78	Tim Richmond	Buick	99.823	Darrell Waltrip	Buick	114.995

1983

1376	1	2/20/83	Daytona Beach, FL	2.5	P	500	Cale Yarborough	Pontiac	155.979	Ricky Rudd	Chevrolet	198.864
1377	2	2/27/83	Richmond, VA	0.542	P	216.8	Bobby Allison	Chevrolet	79.584	Ricky Rudd	Chevrolet	93.439
1378	3	3/13/83	Rockingham, NC	1.017	P	500.364	Richard Petty	Pontiac	113.055	Ricky Rudd	Chevrolet	143.413
1379	4	3/27/83	Hampton, GA	1.522	P	499.216	Cale Yarborough	Chevrolet	124.055	Geoffrey Bodine	Pontiac	167.703
1380	5	4/10/83	Darlington, SC	1.366	P	501.322	Harry Gant	Buick	130.406	Tim Richmond	Pontiac	157.818
1381	6	4/17/83	N. Wilkesboro, NC	0.625	P	250	Darrell Waltrip	Chevrolet	91.436	Neil Bonnett	Chevrolet	112.332
1382	7	4/24/83	Martinsville, VA	0.526	P	263	Darrell Waltrip	Chevrolet	66.46	Ricky Rudd	Chevrolet	89.91
1383	8	5/1/83	Talladega, AL	2.66	P	500.08	Richard Petty	Pontiac	153.936	Cale Yarborough	Chevrolet	202.65
1384	9	5/7/83	Nashville, TN	0.596	P	250.32	Darrell Waltrip	Chevrolet	70.717	Darrell Waltrip	Chevrolet	103.119
1385	10	5/15/83	Dover, DE	1	P	500	Bobby Allison	Buick	114.847	Joe Ruttman	Buick	139.616
1386	11	5/21/83	Bristol, TN	0.533	P	266.5	Darrell Waltrip	Chevrolet	93.445	Neil Bonnett	Chevrolet	110.409
1387	12	5/29/83	Charlotte, NC	1.5	P	600	Neil Bonnett	Chevrolet	140.707	Buddy Baker	Ford	162.841
1388	13	6/5/83	Riverside, CA	2.62	P	248.9	Ricky Rudd	Chevrolet	88.063	Darrell Waltrip	Chevrolet	116.421
1389	14	6/12/83	Pocono, PA	2.5	P	500	Bobby Allison	Buick	128.636	Darrell Waltrip	Chevrolet	152.315
1390	15	6/19/83	Brooklyn, MI	2	P	400	Cale Yarborough	Chevrolet	138.728	Terry Labonte	Chevrolet	161.965
1391	16	7/4/83	Daytona Beach, FL	2.5	P	400	Buddy Baker	Ford	167.442	Cale Yarborough	Chevrolet	196.635
1392	17	7/16/83	Nashville, TN	0.596	P	250.32	Dale Earnhardt	Ford	85.726	Ron Bouchard	Buick	103.02
1393	18	7/24/83	Pocono, PA	2.5	P	500	Tim Richmond	Pontiac	114.818	Tim Richmond	Pontiac	151.981
1394	19	7/31/83	Talladega, AL	2.66	P	500.08	Dale Earnhardt	Ford	170.611	Cale Yarborough	Chevrolet	201.744
1395	20	8/21/83	Brooklyn, MI	2	P	400	Cale Yarborough	Chevrolet	147.511	Terry Labonte	Chevrolet	162.437
1396	21	8/27/83	Bristol, TN	0.533	P	223.327	Darrell Waltrip	Chevrolet	89.43	Joe Ruttman	Pontiac	111.923
1397	22	9/5/83	Darlington, SC	1.366	P	501.322	Bobby Allison	Buick	123.343	Neil Bonnett	Chevrolet	157.187
1398	23	9/11/83	Richmond, VA	0.542	P	216.8	Bobby Allison	Buick	79.381	Darrell Waltrip	Chevrolet	96.069
1399	24	9/18/83	Dover, DE	1	P	500	Bobby Allison	Buick	116.077	Terry Labonte	Chevrolet	139.573
1400	25	9/25/83	Martinsville, VA	0.526	P	263	Ricky Rudd	Chevrolet	76.134	Darrell Waltrip	Chevrolet	89.342
1401	26	10/2/83	N. Wilkesboro, NC	0.625	P	250	Darrell Waltrip	Chevrolet	100.716	Darrell Waltrip	Chevrolet	114.539
1402	27	10/9/83	Charlotte, NC	1.5	P	501	Richard Petty	Pontiac	139.998	Tim Richmond	Pontiac	163.073
1403	28	10/30/83	Rockingham, NC	1.017	P	500.364	Terry Labonte	Chevrolet	119.324	Neil Bonnett	Chevrolet	143.876
1404	29	11/6/83	Hampton, GA	1.522	P	499.216	Neil Bonnett	Chevrolet	137.643	Tim Richmond	Pontiac	168.151
1405	30	11/20/83	Riverside, CA	2.62	P	311.78	Bill Elliott	Ford	95.859	Darrell Waltrip	Chevrolet	116.782

1984

1406	1	2/19/84	Daytona Beach, FL	2.5	P	500	Cale Yarborough	Chevrolet	150.994	Cale Yarborough	Chevrolet	201.848
1407	2	2/26/84	Richmond, VA	0.542	P	216.8	Ricky Rudd	Ford	76.736	Darrell Waltrip	Chevrolet	93.817
1408	3	3/4/84	Rockingham, NC	1.017	P	500.364	Bobby Allison	Buick	122.931	Harry Gant	Chevrolet	145.084
1409	4	3/18/84	Hampton, GA	1.522	P	499.216	Benny Parsons	Chevrolet	144.945	Buddy Baker	Ford	166.642
1410	5	4/1/84	Bristol, TN	0.533	P	266.5	Darrell Waltrip	Chevrolet	93.967	Ricky Rudd	Ford	111.39
1411	6	4/8/84	N. Wilkesboro, NC	0.625	P	250	Tim Richmond	Pontiac	97.83	Ricky Rudd	Ford	113.487
1412	7	4/15/84	Darlington, SC	1.366	P	501.322	Darrell Waltrip	Chevrolet	119.925	Benny Parsons	Chevrolet	156.328
1413	8	4/29/84	Martinsville, VA	0.526	P	263	Geoffrey Bodine	Chevrolet	73.264	Joe Ruttman	Chevrolet	89.426
1414	9	5/6/84	Talladega, AL	2.66	P	500.08	Cale Yarborough	Chevrolet	172.988	Cale Yarborough	Chevrolet	202.692
1415	10	5/12/84	Nashville, TN	0.596	P	250.32	Darrell Waltrip	Chevrolet	85.702	Darrell Waltrip	Chevrolet	104.439
1416	11	5/20/84	Dover, DE	1	P	500	Richard Petty	Pontiac	118.717	Ricky Rudd	Ford	140.807
1417	12	5/27/84	Charlotte, NC	1.5	P	600	Bobby Allison	Buick	129.233	Harry Gant	Chevrolet	162.496
1418	13	6/3/84	Riverside, CA	2.62	P	248.9	Terry Labonte	Chevrolet	102.91	Terry Labonte	Chevrolet	115.921
1419	14	6/10/84	Pocono, PA	2.5	P	500	Cale Yarborough	Chevrolet	138.164	Neil Bonnett	Chevrolet	150.921
1420	15	6/17/84	Brooklyn, MI	2	P	400	Bill Elliott	Ford	134.705	Bill Elliott	Ford	164.339
1421	16	7/4/84	Daytona Beach, FL	2.5	P	400	Richard Petty	Pontiac	171.204	Cale Yarborough	Chevrolet	199.743
1422	17	7/14/84	Nashville, TN	0.596	P	250.32	Geoffrey Bodine	Chevrolet	80.908	Ricky Rudd	Ford	104.12
1423	18	7/22/84	Pocono, PA	2.5	P	500	Harry Gant	Chevrolet	121.351	Bill Elliott	Ford	152.184
1424	19	7/29/84	Talladega, AL	2.66	P	500.08	Dale Earnhardt	Chevrolet	155.485	Cale Yarborough	Chevrolet	202.474
1425	20	8/12/84	Brooklyn, MI	2	P	400	Darrell Waltrip	Chevrolet	153.863	Bill Elliott	Ford	165.217
1426	21	8/25/84	Bristol, TN	0.533	P	266.5	Terry Labonte	Chevrolet	85.365	Geoffrey Bodine	Chevrolet	111.734
1427	22	9/2/84	Darlington, SC	1.366	P	501.322	Harry Gant	Chevrolet	128.27	Harry Gant	Chevrolet	155.502
1428	23	9/9/84	Richmond, VA	0.542	P	216.8	Darrell Waltrip	Chevrolet	74.78	Darrell Waltrip	Chevrolet	92.518
1429	24	9/16/84	Dover, DE	1	P	500	Harry Gant	Chevrolet	111.856	No Time Trials	NTT	NTT
1430	25	9/23/84	Martinsville, VA	0.526	P	263	Darrell Waltrip	Chevrolet	75.532	Geoffrey Bodine	Chevrolet	89.523
1431	26	10/7/84	Charlotte, NC	1.5	P	501	Bill Elliott	Ford	146.861	Benny Parsons	Chevrolet	165.579

Cum. No.	Yr. No.	Date	Site	Track Length	Surface	Miles	Race Winner	Make	Speed	Pole Winner	Make	Pole Speed
1432	27	10/14/84	N. Wilkesboro, NC	0.625	P	250	Darrell Waltrip	Chevrolet	90.525	Darrell Waltrip	Chevrolet	113.304
1433	28	10/21/84	Rockingham, NC	1.017	P	500.364	Bill Elliott	Ford	112.617	Geoffrey Bodine	Chevrolet	144.415
1434	29	11/11/84	Hampton, GA	1.522	P	499.216	Dale Earnhardt	Chevrolet	134.61	Bill Elliott	Ford	170.193
1435	30	11/18/84	Riverside, CA	2.62	P	311.78	Geoffrey Bodine	Chevrolet	98.448	Terry Labonte	Chevrolet	116.714

1985

Cum. No.	Yr. No.	Date	Site	Track Length	Surface	Miles	Race Winner	Make	Speed	Pole Winner	Make	Pole Speed
1436	1	2/17/85	Daytona Beach, FL	2.5	P	500	Bill Elliott	Ford	172.265	Bill Elliott	Ford	205.114
1437	2	2/24/85	Richmond, VA	0.542	P	216.8	Dale Earnhardt	Chevrolet	67.945	Darrell Waltrip	Chevrolet	95.218
1438	3	3/3/85	Rockingham, NC	1.017	P	500.364	Neil Bonnett	Chevrolet	114.953	Terry Labonte	Chevrolet	145.067
1439	4	3/17/85	Hampton, GA	1.522	P	499.216	Bill Elliott	Ford	140.273	Neil Bonnett	Chevrolet	170.278
1440	5	4/6/85	Bristol, TN	0.533	P	266.5	Dale Earnhardt	Chevrolet	81.79	Harry Gant	Chevrolet	112.778
1441	6	4/14/85	Darlington, SC	1.366	P	501.322	Bill Elliott	Ford	126.295	Bill Elliott	Ford	157.454
1442	7	4/21/85	N. Wilkesboro, NC	0.625	P	250	Neil Bonnett	Chevrolet	93.818	Darrell Waltrip	Chevrolet	111.899
1443	8	4/28/85	Martinsville, VA	0.526	P	263	Harry Gant	Chevrolet	73.022	Darrell Waltrip	Chevrolet	90.279
1444	9	5/5/85	Talladega, AL	2.66	P	500.08	Bill Elliott	Ford	186.288	Bill Elliott	Ford	209.398
1445	10	5/19/85	Dover, DE	1	P	500	Bill Elliott	Ford	123.094	Terry Labonte	Chevrolet	138.106
1446	11	5/26/85	Charlotte, NC	1.5	P	600	Darrell Waltrip	Chevrolet	141.807	Bill Elliott	Ford	164.703
1447	12	6/2/85	Riverside, CA	2.62	P	248.9	Terry Labonte	Chevrolet	104.276	Darrell Waltrip	Chevrolet	115.533
1448	13	6/9/85	Pocono, PA	2.5	P	500	Bill Elliott	Ford	138.974	Bill Elliott	Ford	152.563
1449	14	6/16/85	Brooklyn, MI	2	P	400	Bill Elliott	Ford	144.724	No Time Trials	NTT	NTT
1450	15	7/4/85	Daytona Beach, FL	2.5	P	400	Greg Sacks	Chevrolet	158.73	Bill Elliott	Ford	201.523
1451	16	7/21/85	Pocono, PA	2.5	P	500	Bill Elliott	Ford	134.008	Darrell Waltrip	Chevrolet	151.973
1452	17	7/28/85	Talladega, AL	2.66	P	500.08	Cale Yarborough	Ford	148.772	Bill Elliott	Ford	207.578
1453	18	8/11/85	Brooklyn, MI	2	P	400	Bill Elliott	Ford	137.43	Bill Elliott	Ford	165.479
1454	19	8/24/85	Bristol, TN	0.533	P	266.5	Dale Earnhardt	Chevrolet	81.388	Dale Earnhardt	Chevrolet	113.586
1455	20	9/1/85	Darlington, SC	1.366	P	501.322	Bill Elliott	Ford	121.254	Bill Elliott	Ford	156.641
1456	21	9/8/85	Richmond, VA	0.542	P	216.8	Darrell Waltrip	Chevrolet	72.508	Geoffrey Bodine	Chevrolet	94.535
1457	22	9/15/85	Dover, DE	1	P	500	Harry Gant	Chevrolet	120.538	Bill Elliott	Ford	141.543
1458	23	9/22/85	Martinsville, VA	0.526	P	263	Dale Earnhardt	Chevrolet	70.694	Geoffrey Bodine	Chevrolet	90.521
1459	24	9/29/85	N. Wilkesboro, NC	0.625	P	250	Harry Gant	Chevrolet	95.077	Geoffrey Bodine	Chevrolet	113.967
1460	25	10/6/85	Charlotte, NC	1.5	P	501	Cale Yarborough	Ford	136.761	Harry Gant	Chevrolet	166.139
1461	26	10/25/85	Rockingham, NC	1.017	P	500.364	Darrell Waltrip	Chevrolet	118.344	Terry Labonte	Chevrolet	141.841
1462	27	11/3/85	Hampton, GA	1.522	P	499.216	Bill Elliott	Ford	139.597	Harry Gant	Chevrolet	167.94
1463	28	11/17/85	Riverside, CA	2.62	P	311.78	Ricky Rudd	Ford	105.065	Terry Labonte	Chevrolet	116.938

1986

Cum. No.	Yr. No.	Date	Site	Track Length	Surface	Miles	Race Winner	Make	Speed	Pole Winner	Make	Pole Speed
1464	1	2/16/86	Daytona Beach, FL	2.5	P	500	Geoffrey Bodine	Chevrolet	148.124	Bill Elliott	Ford	205.039
1465	2	2/23/86	Richmond, VA	0.542	P	216.8	Kyle Petty	Ford	71.078	No Time Trials	NTT	NTT
1466	3	3/2/86	Rockingham, NC	1.017	P	500.364	Terry Labonte	Oldsmobile	120.488	Terry Labonte	Oldsmobile	146.348
1467	4	3/16/86	Hampton, GA	1.522	P	499.216	Morgan Shepherd	Buick	132.126	Dale Earnhardt	Chevrolet	170.713
1468	5	4/6/86	Bristol, TN	0.533	P	266.5	Rusty Wallace	Pontiac	89.747	Geoffrey Bodine	Chevrolet	114.85
1469	6	4/13/86	Darlington, SC	1.366	P	501.322	Dale Earnhardt	Chevrolet	128.994	Geoffrey Bodine	Chevrolet	159.197
1470	7	4/20/86	N. Wilkesboro, NC	0.625	P	250	Dale Earnhardt	Chevrolet	88.408	Geoffrey Bodine	Chevrolet	112.419
1471	8	4/27/86	Martinsville, VA	0.526	P	263	Ricky Rudd	Ford	76.882	Tim Richmond	Chevrolet	90.716
1472	9	5/4/86	Talladega, AL	2.66	P	500.08	Bobby Allison	Buick	157.698	Bill Elliott	Ford	212.229
1473	10	5/18/86	Dover, DE	1	P	500	Geoffrey Bodine	Chevrolet	115.009	Ricky Rudd	Ford	138.217
1474	11	5/25/86	Charlotte, NC	1.5	P	600	Dale Earnhardt	Chevrolet	140.406	Geoffrey Bodine	Chevrolet	164.511
1475	12	6/1/86	Riverside, CA	2.62	P	248.9	Darrell Waltrip	Chevrolet	105.083	Darrell Waltrip	Chevrolet	117.006
1476	13	6/8/86	Pocono, PA	2.5	P	500	Tim Richmond	Chevrolet	113.279	Geoffrey Bodine	Chevrolet	153.625
1477	14	6/15/86	Brooklyn, MI	2	P	400	Bill Elliott	Ford	138.851	Tim Richmond	Chevrolet	172.031
1478	15	7/4/86	Daytona Beach, FL	2.5	P	400	Tim Richmond	Chevrolet	131.916	Cale Yarborough	Ford	203.519
1479	16	7/20/86	Pocono, PA	2.5	P	375	Tim Richmond	Chevrolet	124.218	Harry Gant	Chevrolet	154.392
1480	17	7/27/86	Talladega, AL	2.66	P	500.08	Bobby Hillin	Chevrolet	151.522	Bill Elliott	Ford	209.005
1481	18	8/10/86	Watkins Glen, NY	2.45	P	220.5	Tim Richmond	Chevrolet	90.463	Tim Richmond	Chevrolet	117.563
1482	19	8/17/86	Brooklyn, MI	2	P	400	Bill Elliott	Ford	135.376	Benny Parsons	Oldsmobile	171.924
1483	20	8/23/86	Bristol, TN	0.533	P	266.5	Darrell Waltrip	Chevrolet	86.934	Geoffrey Bodine	Chevrolet	114.665
1484	21	8/31/86	Darlington, SC	1.366	P	501.322	Tim Richmond	Chevrolet	121.068	Tim Richmond	Chevrolet	158.489
1485	22	9/7/86	Richmond, VA	0.542	P	216.8	Tim Richmond	Chevrolet	70.161	Harry Gant	Chevrolet	93.966
1486	23	9/14/86	Dover, DE	1	P	500	Ricky Rudd	Ford	114.329	Geoffrey Bodine	Chevrolet	146.205
1487	24	9/21/86	Martinsville, VA	0.526	P	263	Rusty Wallace	Pontiac	73.191	Geoffrey Bodine	Chevrolet	90.599
1488	25	9/28/86	N. Wilkesboro, NC	0.625	P	250	Darrell Waltrip	Chevrolet	95.612	Tim Richmond	Chevrolet	113.447
1489	26	10/5/86	Charlotte, NC	1.5	P	501	Dale Earnhardt	Chevrolet	132.403	Tim Richmond	Chevrolet	167.078

Cum. No.	Yr. No.	Date	Site	Track Length	Surface	Miles	Race Winner	Make	Speed	Pole Winner	Make	Pole Speed
1490	27	10/19/86	Rockingham, NC	1.017	P	500.364	Neil Bonnett	Chevrolet	126.381	Tim Richmond	Chevrolet	146.948
1491	28	11/2/86	Hampton, GA	1.522	P	499.216	Dale Earnhardt	Chevrolet	152.523	Bill Elliott	Ford	172.905
1492	29	11/16/86	Riverside, CA	2.62	P	311.78	Tim Richmond	Chevrolet	101.246	Tim Richmond	Chevrolet	118.247

1987

Cum. No.	Yr. No.	Date	Site	Track Length	Surface	Miles	Race Winner	Make	Speed	Pole Winner	Make	Pole Speed
1493	1	2/15/87	Daytona Beach, FL	2.5	P	500	Bill Elliott	Ford	176.263	Bill Elliott	Ford	210.364
1494	2	3/1/87	Rockingham, NC	1.017	P	500.364	Dale Earnhardt	Chevrolet	117.556	Davey Allison	Ford	146.989
1495	3	3/8/87	Richmond, VA	0.542	P	216.8	Dale Earnhardt	Chevrolet	81.52	Alan Kulwicki	Ford	95.153
1496	4	3/15/87	Hampton, GA	1.522	P	499.216	Ricky Rudd	Ford	133.689	Dale Earnhardt	Chevrolet	175.497
1497	5	3/29/87	Darlington, SC	1.366	P	501.322	Dale Earnhardt	Chevrolet	122.54	Ken Schrader	Ford	158.387
1498	6	4/5/87	N. Wilkesboro, NC	0.625	P	250	Dale Earnhardt	Chevrolet	94.103	Bill Elliott	Ford	116.003
1499	7	4/12/87	Bristol, TN	0.533	P	266.5	Dale Earnhardt	Chevrolet	75.621	Harry Gant	Oldsmobile	115.674
1500	8	4/26/87	Martinsville, VA	0.526	P	263	Dale Earnhardt	Chevrolet	72.808	Morgan Shepherd	Buick	92.355
1501	9	5/3/87	Talladega, AL	2.66	P	473.48	Davey Allison	Ford	154.228	Bill Elliott	Ford	212.809
1502	10	5/24/87	Charlotte, NC	1.5	P	600	Kyle Petty	Ford	131.483	Bill Elliott	Ford	170.901
1503	11	5/31/87	Dover, DE	1	P	500	Davey Allison	Ford	112.958	Bill Elliott	Ford	145.056
1504	12	6/14/87	Pocono, PA	2.5	P	500	Tim Richmond	Chevrolet	122.166	Terry Labonte	Chevrolet	155.502
1505	13	6/21/87	Riverside, CA	2.62	P	248.9	Tim Richmond	Chevrolet	102.183	Terry Labonte	Chevrolet	117.541
1506	14	6/28/87	Brooklyn, MI	2	P	400	Dale Earnhardt	Chevrolet	148.454	Rusty Wallace	Pontiac	170.746
1507	15	7/4/87	Daytona Beach, FL	2.5	P	400	Bobby Allison	Buick	161.074	Davey Allison	Ford	198.085
1508	16	7/19/87	Pocono, PA	2.5	P	500	Dale Earnhardt	Chevrolet	121.745	Tim Richmond	Chevrolet	155.979
1509	17	7/26/87	Talladega, AL	2.66	P	500.08	Bill Elliott	Ford	171.293	Bill Elliott	Ford	203.827
1510	18	8/10/87	Watkins Glen, NY	2.45	P	220.5	Rusty Wallace	Pontiac	90.682	Terry Labonte	Chevrolet	117.956
1511	19	8/16/87	Brooklyn, MI	2	P	400	Bill Elliott	Ford	138.648	Davey Allison	Ford	170.705
1512	20	8/22/87	Bristol, TN	0.533	P	266.5	Dale Earnhardt	Chevrolet	90.373	Terry Labonte	Chevrolet	115.758
1513	21	9/6/87	Darlington, SC	1.366	P	275.932	Dale Earnhardt	Chevrolet	115.52	Davey Allison	Ford	157.232
1514	22	9/13/87	Richmond, VA	0.542	P	216.8	Dale Earnhardt	Chevrolet	67.074	Alan Kulwicki	Ford	94.052
1515	23	9/20/87	Dover, DE	1	P	500	Ricky Rudd	Ford	124.706	Alan Kulwicki	Ford	145.826
1516	24	9/27/87	Martinsville, VA	0.526	P	263	Darrell Waltrip	Chevrolet	76.41	Geoffrey Bodine	Chevrolet	91.218
1517	25	10/4/87	N. Wilkesboro, NC	0.625	P	250	Terry Labonte	Chevrolet	96.051	Bill Elliott	Ford	115.196
1518	26	10/11/87	Charlotte, NC	1.5	P	501	Bill Elliott	Ford	128.443	Bobby Allison	Buick	171.636
1519	27	10/25/87	Rockingham, NC	1.017	P	500.364	Bill Elliott	Ford	118.258	Davey Allison	Ford	145.609
1520	28	11/8/87	Riverside, CA	2.62	P	311.78	Rusty Wallace	Pontiac	98.035	Geoffrey Bodine	Chevrolet	117.934
1521	29	11/22/87	Hampton, GA	1.522	P	499.216	Bill Elliott	Ford	139.047	Bill Elliott	Ford	174.341

1988

Cum. No.	Yr. No.	Date	Site	Track Length	Surface	Miles	Race Winner	Make	Speed	Pole Winner	Make	Pole Speed
1522	1	2/14/88	Daytona Beach, FL	2.5	P	500	Bobby Allison	Buick	137.531	Ken Schrader	Chevrolet	193.823
1523	2	2/21/88	Richmond, VA	0.542	P	216.8	Neil Bonnett	Pontiac	66.401	Morgan Shepherd	Buick	94.645
1524	3	3/6/88	Rockingham, NC	1.017	P	500.364	Neil Bonnett	Pontiac	120.159	Bill Elliott	Ford	146.612
1525	4	3/20/88	Hampton, GA	1.522	P	499.216	Dale Earnhardt	Chevrolet	137.588	Geoffrey Bodine	Chevrolet	176.623
1526	5	3/27/88	Darlington, SC	1.366	P	501.322	Lake Speed	Oldsmobile	131.284	Ken Schrader	Chevrolet	162.657
1527	6	4/10/88	Bristol, TN	0.533	P	266.5	Bill Elliott	Ford	83.115	Rick Wilson	Oldsmobile	117.552
1528	7	4/17/88	N. Wilkesboro, NC	0.625	P	250	Terry Labonte	Chevrolet	99.075	Terry Labonte	Chevrolet	117.322
1529	8	4/24/88	Martinsville, VA	0.526	P	263	Dale Earnhardt	Chevrolet	74.74	Ricky Rudd	Buick	91.328
1530	9	5/1/88	Talladega, AL	2.66	P	500.08	Phil Parsons	Oldsmobile	156.547	Davey Allison	Ford	198.969
1531	10	5/29/88	Charlotte, NC	1.5	P	600	Darrell Waltrip	Chevrolet	124.46	Davey Allison	Ford	173.594
1532	11	6/5/88	Dover, DE	1	P	500	Bill Elliott	Ford	118.726	Alan Kulwicki	Ford	146.681
1533	12	6/12/88	Riverside, CA	2.62	P	248.9	Rusty Wallace	Pontiac	88.341	Ricky Rudd	Buick	118.484
1534	13	6/19/88	Pocono, PA	2.5	P	500	Geoffrey Bodine	Chevrolet	126.147	Alan Kulwicki	Ford	158.806
1535	14	6/26/88	Brooklyn, MI	2	P	400	Rusty Wallace	Pontiac	153.551	Bill Elliott	Ford	172.687
1536	15	7/2/88	Daytona Beach, FL	2.5	P	400	Bill Elliott	Ford	163.302	Darrell Waltrip	Chevrolet	193.819
1537	16	7/24/88	Pocono, PA	2.5	P	500	Bill Elliott	Ford	122.866	Morgan Shepherd	Pontiac	157.153
1538	17	7/31/88	Talladega, AL	2.66	P	500.08	Ken Schrader	Chevrolet	154.505	Darrell Waltrip	Chevrolet	196.274
1539	18	8/14/88	Watkins Glen, NY	2.45	P	220.5	Ricky Rudd	Buick	74.096	Geoffrey Bodine	Chevrolet	120.541
1540	19	8/21/88	Brooklyn, MI	2	P	400	Davey Allison	Ford	156.863	Bill Elliott	Ford	174.94
1541	20	8/27/88	Bristol, TN	0.533	P	266.5	Dale Earnhardt	Chevrolet	78.775	Alan Kulwicki	Ford	116.893
1542	21	9/4/88	Darlington, SC	1.366	P	501.322	Bill Elliott	Ford	128.297	Bill Elliott	Ford	160.827
1543	22	9/11/88	Richmond, VA	0.75	P	300	Davey Allison	Ford	95.77	Davey Allison	Ford	122.85
1544	23	9/18/88	Dover, DE	1	P	500	Bill Elliott	Ford	109.349	Mark Martin	Ford	148.075
1545	24	9/25/88	Martinsville, VA	0.526	P	263	Darrell Waltrip	Chevrolet	74.988	Rusty Wallace	Pontiac	91.372
1546	25	10/9/88	Charlotte, NC	1.5	P	501	Rusty Wallace	Pontiac	130.677	Alan Kulwicki	Ford	175.896
1547	26	10/16/88	N. Wilkesboro, NC	0.625	P	250	Rusty Wallace	Pontiac	94.192	Bill Elliott	Ford	116.901

Cum. No.	Yr. No.	Date	Site	Track Length	Surface	Miles	Race Winner	Make	Speed	Pole Winner	Make	Pole Speed
1548	27	10/23/88	Rockingham, NC	1.017	P	500.364	Rusty Wallace	Pontiac	111.557	Bill Elliott	Ford	148.359
1549	28	11/6/88	Phoenix, AZ	1	P	312	Alan Kulwicki	Ford	90.457	Geoffrey Bodine	Chevrolet	123.203
1550	29	11/20/88	Hampton, GA	1.522	P	499.216	Rusty Wallace	Pontiac	129.024	Rusty Wallace	Pontiac	179.499

1989

Cum. No.	Yr. No.	Date	Site	Track Length	Surface	Miles	Race Winner	Make	Speed	Pole Winner	Make	Pole Speed
1551	1	2/19/89	Daytona Beach, FL	2.5	P	500	Darrell Waltrip	Chevrolet	148.466	Ken Schrader	Chevrolet	196.996
1552	2	3/5/89	Rockingham, NC	1.017	P	500.364	Rusty Wallace	Pontiac	115.122	Rusty Wallace	Pontiac	148.793
1553	3	3/19/89	Hampton, GA	1.522	P	499.216	Darrell Waltrip	Chevrolet	139.684	Alan Kulwicki	Ford	176.925
1554	4	3/26/89	Richmond, VA	0.75	P	300	Rusty Wallace	Pontiac	89.619	Geoffrey Bodine	Chevrolet	120.573
1555	5	4/2/89	Darlington, SC	1.366	P	501.322	Harry Gant	Oldsmobile	115.475	Mark Martin	Ford	161.111
1556	6	4/9/89	Bristol, TN	0.533	P	266.5	Rusty Wallace	Pontiac	76.034	Mark Martin	Ford	120.278
1557	7	4/16/89	N. Wilkesboro, NC	0.625	P	250	Dale Earnhardt	Chevrolet	89.937	Rusty Wallace	Pontiac	117.524
1558	8	4/23/89	Martinsville, VA	0.526	P	263	Darrell Waltrip	Chevrolet	79.025	Geoffrey Bodine	Chevrolet	93.097
1559	9	5/7/89	Talladega, AL	2.66	P	500.08	Davey Allison	Ford	155.869	Mark Martin	Ford	193.061
1560	10	5/28/89	Charlotte, NC	1.5	P	600	Darrell Waltrip	Chevrolet	144.077	Alan Kulwicki	Ford	173.021
1561	11	6/4/89	Dover, DE	1	P	500	Dale Earnhardt	Chevrolet	121.67	Mark Martin	Ford	144.387
1562	12	6/11/89	Sonoma, CA	2.52	P	186.48	Ricky Rudd	Buick	76.088	Rusty Wallace	Pontiac	90.041
1563	13	6/18/89	Pocono, PA	2.5	P	500	Terry Labonte	Ford	131.32	Rusty Wallace	Pontiac	157.489
1564	14	6/25/89	Brooklyn, MI	2	P	400	Bill Elliott	Ford	139.023	Ken Schrader	Chevrolet	174.728
1565	15	7/1/89	Daytona Beach, FL	2.5	P	400	Davey Allison	Ford	132.207	Mark Martin	Ford	191.861
1566	16	7/23/89	Pocono, PA	2.5	P	500	Bill Elliott	Ford	117.847	Ken Schrader	Chevrolet	157.809
1567	17	7/30/89	Talladega, AL	2.66	P	500.08	Terry Labonte	Ford	157.354	Mark Martin	Ford	194.8
1568	18	8/13/89	Watkins Glen, NY	2.45	P	220.5	Rusty Wallace	Pontiac	87.242	Morgan Shepherd	Pontiac	120.456
1569	19	8/20/89	Brooklyn, MI	2	P	400	Rusty Wallace	Pontiac	157.704	Geoffrey Bodine	Chevrolet	175.962
1570	20	8/26/89	Bristol, TN	0.533	P	266.5	Darrell Waltrip	Chevrolet	85.554	Alan Kulwicki	Ford	117.043
1571	21	9/3/89	Darlington, SC	1.366	P	501.322	Dale Earnhardt	Chevrolet	135.462	Alan Kulwicki	Ford	160.156
1572	22	9/10/89	Richmond, VA	0.75	P	300	Rusty Wallace	Pontiac	88.38	Bill Elliott	Ford	121.136
1573	23	9/17/89	Dover, DE	1	P	500	Dale Earnhardt	Chevrolet	122.909	Davey Allison	Ford	146.169
1574	24	9/24/89	Martinsville, VA	0.526	P	263	Darrell Waltrip	Chevrolet	76.571	Dale Earnhardt	Chevrolet	91.913
1575	25	10/8/89	Charlotte, NC	1.5	P	501	Ken Schrader	Chevrolet	149.863	Bill Elliott	Ford	174.081
1576	26	10/15/89	N. Wilkesboro, NC	0.625	P	250	Geoffrey Bodine	Chevrolet	90.289	No Time Trials	NTT	NTT
1577	27	10/22/89	Rockingham, NC	1.017	P	500.364	Mark Martin	Ford	114.079	Alan Kulwicki	Ford	114.079
1578	28	11/5/89	Phoenix, AZ	1	P	312	Bill Elliott	Ford	105.683	Ken Schrader	Chevrolet	124.645
1579	29	11/19/89	Hampton, GA	1.522	P	499.216	Dale Earnhardt	Chevrolet	140.229	Alan Kulwicki	Ford	179.112

1990

Cum. No.	Yr. No.	Date	Site	Track Length	Surface	Miles	Race Winner	Make	Speed	Pole Winner	Make	Pole Speed
1580	1	2/18/90	Daytona Beach, FL	2.5	P	500	Derrike Cope	Chevrolet	165.761	Ken Schrader	Chevrolet	196.515
1581	2	2/25/90	Richmond, VA	0.75	P	300	Mark Martin	Ford	92.158	Ricky Rudd	Chevrolet	119.617
1582	3	3/4/90	Rockingham, NC	1.017	P	500.364	Kyle Petty	Pontiac	122.864	Kyle Petty	Pontiac	148.751
1583	4	3/18/90	Hampton, GA	1.522	P	499.216	Dale Earnhardt	Chevrolet	156.849	No Time Trials	NTT	NTT
1584	5	4/1/90	Darlington, SC	1.366	P	501.322	Dale Earnhardt	Chevrolet	124.073	Geoffrey Bodine	Ford	162.996
1585	6	4/8/90	Bristol, TN	0.533	P	266.5	Davey Allison	Ford	87.258	Ernie Irvan	Oldsmobile	116.157
1586	7	4/22/90	N. Wilkesboro, NC	0.625	P	250	Brett Bodine	Buick	83.908	Mark Martin	Ford	117.475
1587	8	4/29/90	Martinsville, VA	0.526	P	263	Geoffrey Bodine	Ford	77.423	Geoffrey Bodine	Ford	91.726
1588	9	5/6/90	Talladega, AL	2.66	P	500.08	Dale Earnhardt	Chevrolet	159.571	Bill Elliott	Ford	199.388
1589	10	5/27/90	Charlotte, NC	1.5	P	600	Rusty Wallace	Pontiac	137.65	Ken Schrader	Chevrolet	173.963
1590	11	6/3/90	Dover, DE	1	P	500	Derrike Cope	Chevrolet	123.96	Dick Trickle	Pontiac	145.814
1591	12	6/10/90	Sonoma, CA	2.52	P	186.48	Rusty Wallace	Pontiac	69.245	Ricky Rudd	Chevrolet	99.743
1592	13	6/17/90	Pocono, PA	2.5	P	500	Harry Gant	Oldsmobile	120.6	Ernie Irvan	Oldsmobile	158.75
1593	14	6/24/90	Brooklyn, MI	2	P	400	Dale Earnhardt	Chevrolet	150.219	No Time Trials	NTT	NTT
1594	15	7/7/90	Daytona Beach, FL	2.5	P	400	Dale Earnhardt	Chevrolet	160.894	Greg Sacks	Chevrolet	195.533
1595	16	7/22/90	Pocono, PA	2.5	P	500	Geoffrey Bodine	Ford	124.07	Mark Martin	Ford	158.264
1596	17	7/29/90	Talladega, AL	2.66	P	500.08	Dale Earnhardt	Chevrolet	174.43	Dale Earnhardt	Chevrolet	192.513
1597	18	8/12/90	Watkins Glen, NY	2.45	P	220.5	Ricky Rudd	Chevrolet	92.452	Dale Earnhardt	Chevrolet	121.19
1598	19	8/19/90	Brooklyn, MI	2	P	400	Mark Martin	Ford	138.822	Alan Kulwicki	Ford	174.982
1599	20	8/25/90	Bristol, TN	0.533	P	266.5	Ernie Irvan	Chevrolet	91.782	Dale Earnhardt	Chevrolet	115.604
1600	21	9/2/90	Darlington, SC	1.366	P	501.322	Dale Earnhardt	Chevrolet	123.141	Dale Earnhardt	Chevrolet	158.448
1601	22	9/9/90	Richmond, VA	0.75	P	300	Dale Earnhardt	Chevrolet	95.567	Ernie Irvan	Chevrolet	119.872
1602	23	9/16/90	Dover, DE	1	P	500	Bill Elliott	Ford	125.945	Bill Elliott	Ford	144.928
1603	24	9/23/90	Martinsville, VA	0.526	P	263	Geoffrey Bodine	Ford	76.386	Mark Martin	Ford	91.571
1604	25	9/30/90	N. Wilkesboro, NC	0.625	P	250	Mark Martin	Ford	93.818	Kyle Petty	Pontiac	116.387
1605	26	10/7/90	Charlotte, NC	1.5	P	501	Davey Allison	Ford	137.428	Brett Bodine	Buick	174.385

Cum. No.	Yr. No.	Date	Site	Track Length	Surface	Miles	Race Winner	Make	Speed	Pole Winner	Make	Pole Speed
1606	27	10/21/90	Rockingham, NC	1.017	P	500.364	Alan Kulwicki	Ford	126.452	Ken Schrader	Chevrolet	147.814
1607	28	11/4/90	Phoenix, AZ	1	P	312	Dale Earnhardt	Chevrolet	96.786	Rusty Wallace	Pontiac	124.443
1608	29	11/18/90	Hampton, GA	1.522	P	499.216	Morgan Shepherd	Ford	140.911	Rusty Wallace	Pontiac	175.222

1991

Cum. No.	Yr. No.	Date	Site	Track Length	Surface	Miles	Race Winner	Make	Speed	Pole Winner	Make	Pole Speed
1609	1	2/19/91	Daytona Beach, FL	2.5	P	500	Ernie Irvan	Chevrolet	148.148	Davey Allison	Ford	195.955
1610	2	2/24/91	Richmond, VA	0.75	P	300	Dale Earnhardt	Chevrolet	105.937	Davey Allison	Ford	120.428
1611	3	3/3/91	Rockingham, NC	1.017	P	500.364	Kyle Petty	Pontiac	124.083	Kyle Petty	Pontiac	149.205
1612	4	3/18/91	Hampton, GA	1.522	P	499.216	Ken Schrader	Chevrolet	140.47	Alan Kulwicki	Ford	174.413
1613	5	4/7/91	Darlington, SC	1.366	P	501.322	Ricky Rudd	Chevrolet	135.594	Geoffrey Bodine	Ford	161.939
1614	6	4/14/91	Bristol, TN	0.533	P	266.5	Rusty Wallace	Pontiac	72.809	Rusty Wallace	Pontiac	118.051
1615	7	4/21/91	N. Wilkesboro, NC	0.625	P	250	Darrell Waltrip	Chevrolet	79.604	Brett Bodine	Buick	116.237
1616	8	4/28/91	Martinsville, VA	0.526	P	263	Dale Earnhardt	Chevrolet	75.139	Mark Martin	Ford	91.949
1617	9	5/6/91	Talladega, AL	2.66	P	500.08	Harry Gant	Oldsmobile	165.62	Ernie Irvan	Chevrolet	195.186
1618	10	5/26/91	Charlotte, NC	1.5	P	600	Davey Allison	Ford	138.951	Mark Martin	Ford	174.82
1619	11	6/2/91	Dover, DE	1	P	500	Ken Schrader	Chevrolet	120.152	Michael Waltrip	Pontiac	143.392
1620	12	6/9/91	Sonoma, CA	2.52	P	186.48	Davey Allison	Ford	72.97	Ricky Rudd	Chevrolet	90.634
1621	13	6/16/91	Pocono, PA	2.5	P	500	Darrell Waltrip	Chevrolet	122.666	Mark Martin	Ford	161.996
1622	14	6/23/91	Brooklyn, MI	2	P	400	Davey Allison	Ford	160.912	Michael Waltrip	Pontiac	174.351
1623	15	7/6/91	Daytona Beach, FL	2.5	P	400	Bill Elliott	Ford	159.116	Sterling Marlin	Ford	190.331
1624	16	7/21/91	Pocono, PA	2.5	P	447.5	Rusty Wallace	Pontiac	115.459	Alan Kulwicki	Ford	161.473
1625	17	7/28/91	Talladega, AL	2.66	P	500.08	Dale Earnhardt	Chevrolet	147.383	Sterling Marlin	Ford	192.085
1626	18	8/11/91	Watkins Glen, NY	2.45	P	220.5	Ernie Irvan	Chevrolet	98.977	Terry Labonte	Oldsmobile	121.652
1627	19	8/18/91	Brooklyn, MI	2	P	400	Dale Jarrett	Ford	142.972	Alan Kulwicki	Ford	173.431
1628	20	8/24/91	Bristol, TN	0.533	P	266.5	Alan Kulwicki	Ford	82.028	Bill Elliott	Ford	116.957
1629	21	9/1/91	Darlington, SC	1.366	P	501.322	Harry Gant	Oldsmobile	133.508	Davey Allison	Ford	162.506
1630	22	9/7/91	Richmond, VA	0.75	P	300	Harry Gant	Oldsmobile	101.361	Rusty Wallace	Pontiac	120.59
1631	23	9/15/91	Dover, DE	1	P	500	Harry Gant	Oldsmobile	110.179	Alan Kulwicki	Ford	146.825
1632	24	9/22/91	Martinsville, VA	0.526	P	263	Harry Gant	Oldsmobile	74.535	Mark Martin	Ford	93.171
1633	25	9/29/91	N. Wilkesboro, NC	0.625	P	250	Dale Earnhardt	Chevrolet	94.113	Harry Gant	Oldsmobile	116.871
1634	26	10/6/91	Charlotte, NC	1.5	P	501	Geoffrey Bodine	Ford	138.984	Mark Martin	Ford	176.499
1635	27	10/20/91	Rockingham, NC	1.017	P	500.364	Davey Allison	Ford	127.292	Kyle Petty	Pontiac	149.461
1636	28	11/3/91	Phoenix, AZ	1	P	312	Davey Allison	Ford	95.746	Geoffrey Bodine	Ford	127.589
1637	29	11/17/91	Hampton, GA	1.522	P	499.216	Mark Martin	Ford	137.968	Bill Elliott	Ford	177.937

1992

Cum. No.	Yr. No.	Date	Site	Track Length	Surface	Miles	Race Winner	Make	Speed	Pole Winner	Make	Pole Speed
1638	1	2/16/92	Daytona Beach, FL	2.5	P	500	Davey Allison	Ford	160.256	Sterling Marlin	Ford	192.213
1639	2	3/1/92	Rockingham, NC	1.017	P	500.364	Bill Elliott	Ford	126.125	Kyle Petty	Pontiac	149.926
1640	3	3/8/92	Richmond, VA	0.75	P	300	Bill Elliott	Ford	104.378	Bill Elliott	Ford	121.337
1641	4	3/15/92	Hampton, GA	1.522	P	499.216	Bill Elliott	Ford	147.746	Mark Martin	Ford	179.923
1642	5	3/29/92	Darlington, SC	1.366	P	501.322	Bill Elliott	Ford	139.364	Sterling Marlin	Ford	163.067
1643	6	4/5/92	Bristol, TN	0.533	P	266.5	Alan Kulwicki	Ford	86.316	Alan Kulwicki	Ford	122.474
1644	7	4/12/92	N. Wilkesboro, NC	0.625	P	250	Davey Allison	Ford	90.653	Alan Kulwicki	Ford	117.242
1645	8	4/26/92	Martinsville, VA	0.526	P	263	Mark Martin	Ford	78.086	Darrell Waltrip	Chevrolet	92.956
1646	9	5/3/92	Talladega, AL	2.66	P	500.08	Davey Allison	Ford	167.609	Ernie Irvan	Chevrolet	192.831
1647	10	5/24/92	Charlotte, NC	1.5	P	600	Dale Earnhardt	Chevrolet	132.98	Bill Elliott	Ford	175.479
1648	11	5/31/92	Dover, DE	1	P	500	Harry Gant	Oldsmobile	109.456	Brett Bodine	Ford	147.408
1649	12	6/7/92	Sonoma, CA	2.52	P	186.48	Ernie Irvan	Chevrolet	81.412	Ricky Rudd	Chevrolet	90.985
1650	13	6/14/92	Pocono, PA	2.5	P	500	Alan Kulwicki	Ford	144.023	Ken Schrader	Chevrolet	162.499
1651	14	6/21/92	Brooklyn, MI	2	P	400	Davey Allison	Ford	152.672	Davey Allison	Ford	176.258
1652	15	7/4/92	Daytona Beach, FL	2.5	P	400	Ernie Irvan	Chevrolet	170.457	Sterling Marlin	Ford	189.366
1653	16	7/19/92	Pocono, PA	2.5	P	500	Darrell Waltrip	Chevrolet	134.058	Davey Allison	Ford	162.022
1654	17	7/26/92	Talladega, AL	2.66	P	500.08	Ernie Irvan	Chevrolet	176.309	Sterling Marlin	Ford	190.586
1655	18	8/9/92	Watkins Glen, NY	2.45	P	124.95	Kyle Petty	Pontiac	88.98	Dale Earnhardt	Chevrolet	116.882
1656	19	8/16/92	Brooklyn, MI	2	P	400	Harry Gant	Oldsmobile	146.056	Alan Kulwicki	Ford	178.196
1657	20	8/29/92	Bristol, TN	0.533	P	266.5	Darrell Waltrip	Chevrolet	91.198	Ernie Irvan	Chevrolet	120.535
1658	21	9/6/92	Darlington, SC	1.366	P	407.068	Darrell Waltrip	Chevrolet	129.114	Sterling Marlin	Ford	162.249
1659	22	9/12/92	Richmond, VA	0.75	P	300	Rusty Wallace	Pontiac	104.661	Ernie Irvan	Chevrolet	120.784
1660	23	9/20/92	Dover, DE	1	P	500	Ricky Rudd	Chevrolet	115.289	Alan Kulwicki	Ford	145.267
1661	24	9/28/92	Martinsville, VA	0.526	P	263	Geoffrey Bodine	Ford	75.424	Kyle Petty	Pontiac	92.497
1662	25	10/5/92	N. Wilkesboro, NC	0.625	P	250	Geoffrey Bodine	Ford	107.36	Alan Kulwicki	Ford	117.133
1663	26	10/11/92	Charlotte, NC	1.5	P	501	Mark Martin	Ford	153.537	Alan Kulwicki	Ford	179.027

Cum. No.	Yr. No.	Date	Site	Track Length	Surface	Miles	Race Winner	Make	Speed	Pole Winner	Make	Pole Speed
1664	27	10/25/92	Rockingham, NC	1.017	P	500.364	Kyle Petty	Pontiac	130.748	Kyle Petty	Pontiac	149.675
1665	28	11/1/92	Phoenix, AZ	1	P	312	Davey Allison	Ford	103.885	Rusty Wallace	Pontiac	128.141
1666	29	11/15/92	Hampton, GA	1.522	P	499.216	Bill Elliott	Ford	133.322	Rick Mast	Oldsmobile	180.183

1993

Cum. No.	Yr. No.	Date	Site	Track Length	Surface	Miles	Race Winner	Make	Speed	Pole Winner	Make	Pole Speed
1667	1	2/14/93	Daytona Beach, FL	2.5	P	500	Dale Jarrett	Chevrolet	154.972	Kyle Petty	Pontiac	189.426
1668	2	2/28/93	Rockingham, NC	1.017	P	500.364	Rusty Wallace	Pontiac	124.486	Mark Martin	Ford	149.547
1669	3	3/7/93	Richmond, VA	0.75	P	300	Davey Allison	Ford	107.709	Ken Schrader	Chevrolet	123.164
1670	4	3/20/93	Hampton, GA	1.522	P	499.216	Morgan Shepherd	Ford	150.442	Rusty Wallace	Pontiac	178.749
1671	5	3/28/93	Darlington, SC	1.366	P	501.322	Dale Earnhardt	Chevrolet	139.958	No Time Trials	NTT	NTT
1672	6	4/4/93	Bristol, TN	0.533	P	266.5	Rusty Wallace	Pontiac	84.73	Rusty Wallace	Pontiac	120.938
1673	7	4/18/93	N. Wilkesboro, NC	0.625	P	250	Rusty Wallace	Pontiac	92.602	Brett Bodine	Ford	117.017
1674	8	4/25/93	Martinsville, VA	0.526	P	263	Rusty Wallace	Pontiac	79.078	Geoffrey Bodine	Ford	93.887
1675	9	5/2/93	Talladega, AL	2.66	P	500.08	Ernie Irvan	Chevrolet	155.415	Dale Earnhardt	Chevrolet	192.355
1676	10	5/16/93	Sonoma, CA	2.52	P	186.48	Geoffrey Bodine	Ford	77.013	Dale Earnhardt	Chevrolet	91.838
1677	11	5/30/93	Charlotte, NC	1.5	P	600	Dale Earnhardt	Chevrolet	145.504	Ken Schrader	Chevrolet	177.352
1678	12	6/6/93	Dover, DE	1	P	500	Dale Earnhardt	Chevrolet	105.6	Ernie Irvan	Chevrolet	151.541
1679	13	6/13/93	Pocono, PA	2.5	P	500	Kyle Petty	Pontiac	138.005	Ken Schrader	Chevrolet	162.816
1680	14	6/20/93	Brooklyn, MI	2	P	400	Ricky Rudd	Chevrolet	148.484	Brett Bodine	Ford	175.456
1681	15	7/3/93	Daytona Beach, FL	2.5	P	400	Dale Earnhardt	Chevrolet	151.755	Ernie Irvan	Chevrolet	190.327
1682	16	7/11/93	Loudon, NH	1.058	P	317.4	Rusty Wallace	Pontiac	105.947	Mark Martin	Ford	126.871
1683	17	7/18/93	Pocono, PA	2.5	P	500	Dale Earnhardt	Chevrolet	133.343	Ken Schrader	Chevrolet	162.934
1684	18	7/25/93	Talladega, AL	2.66	P	500.08	Dale Earnhardt	Chevrolet	153.858	Bill Elliott	Ford	192.397
1685	19	8/8/93	Watkins Glen, NY	2.45	P	220.5	Mark Martin	Ford	84.771	Mark Martin	Ford	119.118
1686	20	8/15/93	Brooklyn, MI	2	P	400	Mark Martin	Ford	144.564	Ken Schrader	Chevrolet	180.75
1687	21	8/28/93	Bristol, TN	0.533	P	266.5	Mark Martin	Ford	88.172	Mark Martin	Ford	121.405
1688	22	9/5/93	Darlington, SC	1.366	P	479.466	Mark Martin	Ford	137.932	Ken Schrader	Chevrolet	161.259
1689	23	9/11/93	Richmond, VA	0.75	P	300	Rusty Wallace	Pontiac	99.917	Bobby Labonte	Ford	122.006
1690	24	9/19/93	Dover, DE	1	P	500	Rusty Wallace	Pontiac	100.334	Rusty Wallace	Pontiac	151.464
1691	25	9/26/93	Martinsville, VA	0.526	P	263	Ernie Irvan	Ford	74.101	Ernie Irvan	Ford	92.583
1692	26	10/3/93	N. Wilkesboro, NC	0.625	P	250	Rusty Wallace	Pontiac	96.92	Ernie Irvan	Ford	116.786
1693	27	10/10/93	Charlotte, NC	1.5	P	501	Ernie Irvan	Ford	154.537	Jeff Gordon	Chevrolet	177.684
1694	28	10/24/93	Rockingham, NC	1.017	P	500.364	Rusty Wallace	Pontiac	114.036	Mark Martin	Ford	148.353
1695	29	10/31/93	Phoenix, AZ	1	P	312	Mark Martin	Ford	100.375	Bill Elliott	Ford	129.482
1696	30	11/14/93	Hampton, GA	1.522	P	499.216	Rusty Wallace	Pontiac	125.221	Harry Gant	Chevrolet	176.902

1994

Cum. No.	Yr. No.	Date	Site	Track Length	Surface	Miles	Race Winner	Make	Speed	Pole Winner	Make	Pole Speed
1697	1	2/20/94	Daytona Beach, FL	2.5	P	500	Sterling Marlin	Chevrolet	156.931	Loy Allen, Jr.	Ford	190.158
1698	2	2/27/94	Rockingham, NC	1.017	P	500.364	Rusty Wallace	Ford	125.239	Geoffrey Bodine	Ford	151.716
1699	3	3/6/94	Richmond, VA	0.75	P	300	Ernie Irvan	Ford	98.334	Ted Musgrave	Ford	123.474
1700	4	3/13/94	Hampton, GA	1.522	P	499.216	Ernie Irvan	Ford	146.136	Loy Allen, Jr.	Ford	180.207
1701	5	3/27/94	Darlington, SC	1.366	P	400.238	Dale Earnhardt	Chevrolet	132.432	Bill Elliott	Ford	165.553
1702	6	4/10/94	Bristol, TN	0.533	P	266.5	Dale Earnhardt	Chevrolet	89.647	Chuck Bown	Ford	124.946
1703	7	4/17/94	N. Wilkesboro, NC	0.625	P	250	Terry Labonte	Chevrolet	95.816	Ernie Irvan	Ford	119.016
1704	8	4/24/94	Martinsville, VA	0.526	P	263	Rusty Wallace	Ford	76.7	Rusty Wallace	Ford	92.942
1705	9	5/1/94	Talladega, AL	2.66	P	500.08	Dale Earnhardt	Chevrolet	157.478	Ernie Irvan	Ford	193.298
1706	10	5/15/94	Sonoma, CA	2.52	P	186.48	Ernie Irvan	Ford	77.458	Ernie Irvan	Ford	91.514
1707	11	5/29/94	Charlotte, NC	1.5	P	600	Jeff Gordon	Chevrolet	139.445	Jeff Gordon	Chevrolet	181.439
1708	12	6/5/94	Dover, DE	1	P	500	Rusty Wallace	Ford	102.529	Ernie Irvan	Ford	151.956
1709	13	6/12/94	Pocono, PA	2.5	P	500	Rusty Wallace	Ford	128.801	Rusty Wallace	Ford	164.558
1710	14	6/19/94	Brooklyn, MI	2	P	400	Rusty Wallace	Ford	125.022	Loy Allen, Jr.	Ford	180.641
1711	15	7/2/94	Daytona Beach, FL	2.5	P	400	Jimmy Spencer	Ford	155.558	Dale Earnhardt	Chevrolet	191.339
1712	16	7/10/94	Loudon, NH	1.058	P	317.4	Ricky Rudd	Ford	87.599	Ernie Irvan	Ford	127.197
1713	17	7/17/94	Pocono, PA	2.5	P	500	Geoffrey Bodine	Ford	136.075	Geoffrey Bodine	Ford	163.869
1714	18	7/24/94	Talladega, AL	2.66	P	500.08	Jimmy Spencer	Ford	163.217	Dale Earnhardt	Chevrolet	193.47
1715	19	8/6/94	Indianapolis, IN	2.5	P	400	Jeff Gordon	Chevrolet	131.977	Rick Mast	Ford	172.414
1716	20	8/14/94	Watkins Glen, NY	2.45	P	220.5	Mark Martin	Ford	93.752	Mark Martin	Ford	118.326
1717	21	8/21/94	Brooklyn, MI	2	P	400	Geoffrey Bodine	Ford	139.914	Geoffrey Bodine	Ford	181.082
1718	22	8/27/94	Bristol, TN	0.533	P	266.5	Rusty Wallace	Ford	91.363	Harry Gant	Chevrolet	124.186
1719	23	9/4/94	Darlington, SC	1.366	P	501.322	Bill Elliott	Ford	127.952	Geoffrey Bodine	Ford	166.998
1720	24	9/10/94	Richmond, VA	0.75	P	300	Terry Labonte	Chevrolet	104.156	Ted Musgrave	Ford	124.052
1721	25	9/18/94	Dover, DE	1	P	500	Rusty Wallace	Ford	112.556	Geoffrey Bodine	Ford	152.84

Cum. No.	Yr. No.	Date	Site	Track Length	Surface	Miles	Race Winner	Make	Speed	Pole Winner	Make	Pole Speed
1722	26	9/25/94	Martinsville, VA	0.526	P	263	Rusty Wallace	Ford	77.139	Ted Musgrave	Ford	94.129
1723	27	10/2/94	N. Wilkesboro, NC	0.625	P	250	Geoffrey Bodine	Ford	98.522	Jimmy Spencer	Ford	118.558
1724	28	10/9/94	Charlotte, NC	1.5	P	501	Dale Jarrett	Chevrolet	145.922	Ward Burton	Chevrolet	185.759
1725	29	10/23/94	Rockingham, NC	1.017	P	500.364	Dale Earnhardt	Chevrolet	126.408	Ricky Rudd	Ford	157.099
1726	30	10/30/94	Phoenix, AZ	1	P	312	Terry Labonte	Chevrolet	107.463	Sterling Marlin	Chevrolet	129.833
1727	31	11/13/94	Hampton, GA	1.522	P	499.216	Mark Martin	Ford	148.982	Greg Sacks	Ford	185.83

1995

Cum. No.	Yr. No.	Date	Site	Track Length	Surface	Miles	Race Winner	Make	Speed	Pole Winner	Make	Pole Speed
1728	1	2/19/95	Daytona Beach, FL	2.5	P	500	Sterling Marlin	Chevrolet	141.71	Dale Jarrett	Ford	193.498
1729	2	2/26/95	Rockingham, NC	1.017	P	500.364	Jeff Gordon	Chevrolet	125.305	Jeff Gordon	Chevrolet	157.62
1730	3	3/5/95	Richmond, VA	0.75	P	300	Terry Labonte	Chevrolet	106.425	Jeff Gordon	Chevrolet	124.757
1731	4	3/12/95	Hampton, GA	1.522	P	499.216	Jeff Gordon	Chevrolet	150.115	Dale Earnhardt	Chevrolet	185.077
1732	5	3/26/95	Darlington, SC	1.366	P	400.238	Sterling Marlin	Chevrolet	111.392	Jeff Gordon	Chevrolet	170.833
1733	6	4/2/95	Bristol, TN	0.533	P	266.5	Jeff Gordon	Chevrolet	92.011	Mark Martin	Ford	124.605
1734	7	4/9/95	N. Wilkesboro, NC	0.625	P	250	Dale Earnhardt	Chevrolet	102.424	Jeff Gordon	Chevrolet	118.765
1735	8	4/23/95	Martinsville, VA	0.526	P	187.256	Rusty Wallace	Ford	72.145	Bobby Labonte	Chevrolet	93.308
1736	9	4/30/95	Talladega, AL	2.66	P	500.08	Mark Martin	Ford	178.902	Terry Labonte	Chevrolet	196.532
1737	10	5/7/95	Sonoma, CA	2.52	P	186.48	Dale Earnhardt	Chevrolet	70.681	Ricky Rudd	Ford	92.132
1738	11	5/28/95	Charlotte, NC	1.5	P	600	Bobby Labonte	Chevrolet	151.952	Jeff Gordon	Chevrolet	183.861
1739	12	6/4/95	Dover, DE	1	P	500	Kyle Petty	Pontiac	119.88	Jeff Gordon	Chevrolet	153.669
1740	13	6/11/95	Pocono, PA	2.5	P	500	Terry Labonte	Chevrolet	137.72	Ken Schrader	Chevrolet	163.375
1741	14	6/18/95	Brooklyn, MI	2	P	400	Bobby Labonte	Chevrolet	134.141	Jeff Gordon	Chevrolet	186.611
1742	15	7/1/95	Daytona Beach, FL	2.5	P	400	Jeff Gordon	Chevrolet	166.976	Dale Earnhardt	Chevrolet	191.355
1743	16	7/9/95	Loudon, NH	1.058	P	317.4	Jeff Gordon	Chevrolet	107.029	Mark Martin	Ford	128.815
1744	17	7/16/95	Pocono, PA	2.5	P	500	Dale Jarrett	Ford	134.038	Bill Elliott	Ford	162.496
1745	18	7/23/95	Talladega, AL	2.66	P	500.08	Sterling Marlin	Chevrolet	173.188	Sterling Marlin	Chevrolet	194.212
1746	19	8/5/95	Indianapolis, IN	2.5	P	400	Dale Earnhardt	Chevrolet	155.206	Jeff Gordon	Chevrolet	172.536
1747	20	8/13/95	Watkins Glen, NY	2.45	P	220.5	Mark Martin	Ford	103.03	Mark Martin	Ford	120.411
1748	21	8/20/95	Brooklyn, MI	2	P	400	Bobby Labonte	Chevrolet	157.739	Bobby Labonte	Chevrolet	184.403
1749	22	8/26/95	Bristol, TN	0.533	P	266.5	Terry Labonte	Chevrolet	81.979	Mark Martin	Ford	125.093
1750	23	9/3/95	Darlington, SC	1.366	P	501.322	Jeff Gordon	Chevrolet	121.231	John Andretti	Ford	167.379
1751	24	9/9/95	Richmond, VA	0.75	P	300	Rusty Wallace	Ford	104.459	Dale Earnhardt	Chevrolet	122.543
1752	25	9/17/95	Dover, DE	1	P	500	Jeff Gordon	Chevrolet	124.74	Rick Mast	Ford	153.446
1753	26	9/24/95	Martinsville, VA	0.526	P	263	Dale Earnhardt	Chevrolet	73.946	No Time Trials	NTT	NTT
1754	27	10/1/95	N. Wilkesboro, NC	0.625	P	250	Mark Martin	Ford	102.998	Ted Musgrave	Ford	118.396
1755	28	10/8/95	Charlotte, NC	1.5	P	501	Mark Martin	Ford	145.358	Ricky Rudd	Ford	180.758
1756	29	10/22/95	Rockingham, NC	1.017	P	399.681	Ward Burton	Pontiac	114.778	Hut Stricklin	Ford	155.379
1757	30	10/29/95	Phoenix, AZ	1	P	312	Ricky Rudd	Ford	102.128	Bill Elliott	Ford	130.02
1758	31	11/12/95	Hampton, GA	1.522	P	499.216	Dale Earnhardt	Chevrolet	163.633	Darrell Waltrip	Chevrolet	185.046

1996

Cum. No.	Yr. No.	Date	Site	Track Length	Surface	Miles	Race Winner	Make	Speed	Pole Winner	Make	Pole Speed
1759	1	2/18/96	Daytona Beach, FL	2.5	P	500	Dale Jarrett	Ford	154.308	Dale Earnhardt	Chevrolet	189.51
1760	2	2/25/96	Rockingham, NC	1.017	P	399.681	Dale Earnhardt	Chevrolet	113.959	Terry Labonte	Chevrolet	156.87
1761	3	3/3/96	Richmond, VA	0.75	P	300	Jeff Gordon	Chevrolet	102.75	Terry Labonte	Chevrolet	123.728
1762	4	3/10/96	Hampton, GA	1.522	P	499.216	Dale Earnhardt	Chevrolet	161.298	Johnny Benson, Jr.	Pontiac	185.434
1763	5	3/24/96	Darlington, SC	1.366	P	400.238	Jeff Gordon	Chevrolet	124.792	Ward Burton	Pontiac	173.797
1764	6	3/31/96	Bristol, TN	0.533	P	182.286	Jeff Gordon	Chevrolet	91.308	Mark Martin	Ford	123.578
1765	7	4/14/96	N. Wilkesboro, NC	0.625	P	250	Terry Labonte	Chevrolet	96.37	Terry Labonte	Chevrolet	116.659
1766	8	4/21/96	Martinsville, VA	0.526	P	263	Rusty Wallace	Ford	81.41	Ricky Craven	Chevrolet	93.079
1767	9	4/28/96	Talladega, AL	2.66	P	500.08	Sterling Marlin	Chevrolet	149.999	Ernie Irvan	Ford	192.855
1768	10	5/5/96	Sonoma, CA	2.52	P	186.48	Rusty Wallace	Ford	77.673	Terry Labonte	Chevrolet	92.524
1769	11	5/26/96	Charlotte, NC	1.5	P	600	Dale Jarrett	Ford	147.581	Jeff Gordon	Chevrolet	183.773
1770	12	6/2/96	Dover, DE	1	P	500	Jeff Gordon	Chevrolet	122.741	Jeff Gordon	Chevrolet	154.785
1771	13	6/16/96	Pocono, PA	2.5	P	500	Jeff Gordon	Chevrolet	139.104	Jeff Gordon	Chevrolet	169.725
1772	14	6/23/96	Brooklyn, MI	2	P	400	Rusty Wallace	Ford	166.033	Bobby Hamilton	Pontiac	185.166
1773	15	7/6/96	Daytona Beach, FL	2.5	P	292.5	Sterling Marlin	Chevrolet	161.602	Jeff Gordon	Chevrolet	188.869
1774	16	7/14/96	Loudon, NH	1.058	P	317.4	Ernie Irvan	Ford	98.93	Ricky Craven	Chevrolet	129.379
1775	17	7/21/96	Pocono, PA	2.5	P	500	Rusty Wallace	Ford	144.892	Mark Martin	Ford	168.41
1776	18	7/28/96	Talladega, AL	2.66	P	343.14	Jeff Gordon	Chevrolet	133.387	Jeremy Mayfield	Ford	192.37
1777	19	8/3/96	Indianapolis, IN	2.5	P	400	Dale Jarrett	Ford	139.508	Jeff Gordon	Chevrolet	176.419
1778	20	8/11/96	Watkins Glen, NY	2.45	P	220.5	Geoffrey Bodine	Ford	92.334	Dale Earnhardt	Chevrolet	73.054
1779	21	8/18/96	Brooklyn, MI	2	P	400	Dale Jarrett	Ford	139.792	Jeff Burton	Ford	185.395

Cum. No.	Yr. No.	Date	Site	Track Length	Surface	Miles	Race Winner	Make	Speed	Pole Winner	Make	Pole Speed
1780	22	8/24/96	Bristol, TN	0.533	P	266.5	Rusty Wallace	Ford	91.267	Mark Martin	Ford	124.857
1781	23	9/1/96	Darlington, SC	1.366	P	501.322	Jeff Gordon	Chevrolet	135.757	Dale Jarrett	Ford	170.934
1782	24	9/7/96	Richmond, VA	0.75	P	300	Ernie Irvan	Ford	105.469	Mark Martin	Ford	122.744
1783	25	9/15/96	Dover, DE	1	P	500	Jeff Gordon	Chevrolet	105.646	Bobby Labonte	Chevrolet	155.086
1784	26	9/22/96	Martinsville, VA	0.526	P	263	Jeff Gordon	Chevrolet	82.223	Bobby Hamilton	Pontiac	94.12
1785	27	9/29/96	N. Wilkesboro, NC	0.625	P	250	Jeff Gordon	Chevrolet	96.837	Ted Musgrave	Ford	118.054
1786	28	10/6/96	Charlotte, NC	1.5	P	501	Terry Labonte	Chevrolet	143.143	Bobby Labonte	Chevrolet	184.068
1787	29	10/20/96	Rockingham, NC	1.017	P	399.681	Ricky Rudd	Ford	122.32	Dale Jarrett	Ford	157.194
1788	30	10/27/96	Phoenix, AZ	1	P	312	Bobby Hamilton	Pontiac	109.709	Bobby Labonte	Chevrolet	131.076
1789	31	11/10/96	Hampton, GA	1.522	P	499.216	Bobby Labonte	Chevrolet	134.661	Bobby Labonte	Chevrolet	185.887

1997

Cum. No.	Yr. No.	Date	Site	Track Length	Surface	Miles	Race Winner	Make	Speed	Pole Winner	Make	Pole Speed
1790	1	2/16/97	Daytona Beach, FL	2.5	P	500	Jeff Gordon	Chevrolet	148.295	Mike Skinner	Chevrolet	189.813
1791	2	2/23/97	Rockingham, NC	1.017	P	399.681	Jeff Gordon	Chevrolet	125.927	Mark Martin	Ford	157.885
1792	3	3/2/97	Richmond, VA	0.75	P	300	Rusty Wallace	Ford	108.499	No Time Trials	NTT	NTT
1793	4	3/9/97	Hampton, GA	1.522	P	499.216	Dale Jarrett	Ford	132.731	Robby Gordon	Chevrolet	186.987
1794	5	3/23/97	Darlington, SC	1.366	P	400.238	Dale Jarrett	Ford	141.41	Dale Jarrett	Ford	171.095
1795	6	4/6/97	Fort Worth, TX	1.5	P	501	Jeff Burton	Ford	125.105	No Time Trials	NTT	NTT
1796	7	4/13/97	Bristol, TN	0.533	P	266.5	Jeff Gordon	Chevrolet	75.035	Rusty Wallace	Ford	123.586
1797	8	4/20/97	Martinsville, VA	0.526	P	263	Jeff Gordon	Chevrolet	70.29	Kenny Wallace	Ford	93.961
1798	9	5/4/97	Sonoma, CA	2.52	P	186.48	Mark Martin	Ford	75.788	Mark Martin	Ford	92.807
1799	10	5/10/97	Talladega, AL	2.66	P	500.08	Mark Martin	Ford	188.354	John Andretti	Ford	193.627
1800	11	5/25/97	Charlotte, NC	1.5	P	499.5	Jeff Gordon	Chevrolet	136.745	Jeff Gordon	Chevrolet	184.3
1801	12	6/1/97	Dover, DE	1	P	500	Ricky Rudd	Ford	114.635	Bobby Labonte	Pontiac	152.788
1802	13	6/8/97	Pocono, PA	2.5	P	500	Jeff Gordon	Chevrolet	139.828	Bobby Hamilton	Pontiac	168.089
1803	14	6/15/97	Brooklyn, MI	2	P	400	Ernie Irvan	Ford	153.321	Dale Jarrett	Ford	183.669
1804	15	6/22/97	Fontana, CA	2	P	500	Jeff Gordon	Chevrolet	155.025	Joe Nemechek	Chevrolet	183.015
1805	16	7/5/97	Daytona Beach, FL	2.5	P	400	John Andretti	Ford	157.791	Mike Skinner	Chevrolet	189.777
1806	17	7/13/97	Loudon, NH	1.058	P	317.4	Jeff Burton	Ford	117.194	Ken Schrader	Chevrolet	129.423
1807	18	7/20/97	Pocono, PA	2.5	P	500	Dale Jarrett	Ford	142.068	Joe Nemechek	Chevrolet	168.831
1808	19	8/2/97	Indianapolis, IN	2.5	P	400	Ricky Rudd	Ford	130.828	Ernie Irvan	Ford	177.736
1809	20	8/10/97	Watkins Glen, NY	2.45	P	220.5	Jeff Gordon	Chevrolet	91.294	Todd Bodine	Chevrolet	120.505
1810	21	8/17/97	Brooklyn, MI	2	P	400	Mark Martin	Ford	126.88	Johnny Benson, Jr.	Pontiac	183.332
1811	22	8/23/97	Bristol, TN	0.533	P	266.5	Dale Jarrett	Ford	80.01	Kenny Wallace	Ford	123.039
1812	23	8/31/97	Darlington, SC	1.366	P	501.322	Jeff Gordon	Chevrolet	121.149	Bobby Labonte	Pontiac	170.661
1813	24	9/6/97	Richmond, VA	0.75	P	300	Dale Jarrett	Ford	108.707	Bill Elliott	Ford	124.723
1814	25	9/14/97	Loudon, NH	1.058	P	317.4	Jeff Gordon	Chevrolet	100.376	Ken Schrader	Chevrolet	129.182
1815	26	9/21/97	Dover, DE	1	P	500	Mark Martin	Ford	132.719	Mark Martin	Ford	152.033
1816	27	9/29/97	Martinsville, VA	0.526	P	263	Jeff Burton	Ford	73.072	Ward Burton	Pontiac	93.41
1817	28	10/5/97	Charlotte, NC	1.5	P	600	Dale Jarrett	Ford	144.323	Geoffrey Bodine	Ford	184.256
1818	29	10/12/97	Talladega, AL	2.66	P	500.08	Terry Labonte	Chevrolet	156.601	Ernie Irvan	Ford	193.271
1819	30	10/26/97	Rockingham, NC	1.017	P	400.698	Bobby Hamilton	Pontiac	121.73	Bobby Labonte	Pontiac	156.696
1820	31	11/2/97	Phoenix, AZ	1	P	312	Dale Jarrett	Ford	110.824	Bobby Hamilton	Pontiac	131.579
1821	32	11/16/97	Hampton, GA	1.522	P	499.216	Bobby Labonte	Pontiac	159.904	Geoffrey Bodine	Ford	197.478

1998

Cum. No.	Yr. No.	Date	Site	Track Length	Surface	Miles	Race Winner	Make	Speed	Pole Winner	Make	Pole Speed
1822	1	2/15/98	Daytona Beach, FL	2.5	P	500	Dale Earnhardt	Chevrolet	172.712	Bobby Labonte	Pontiac	192.415
1823	2	2/22/98	Rockingham, NC	1.017	P	399.681	Jeff Gordon	Chevrolet	117.065	Rick Mast	Ford	156.361
1824	3	3/1/98	Las Vegas, NV	1.5	P	400.5	Mark Martin	Ford	146.53	Dale Jarrett	Ford	168.224
1825	4	3/9/98	Hampton, GA	1.54	P	500.5	Bobby Labonte	Pontiac	139.501	John Andretti	Pontiac	192.956
1826	5	3/22/98	Darlington, SC	1.366	P	400.238	Dale Jarrett	Ford	127.962	Mark Martin	Ford	168.665
1827	6	3/29/98	Bristol, TN	0.533	P	266.5	Jeff Gordon	Chevrolet	82.85	Rusty Wallace	Ford	124.275
1828	7	4/5/98	Fort Worth, TX	1.5	P	501	Mark Martin	Ford	136.771	Jeremy Mayfield	Ford	185.906
1829	8	4/20/98	Martinsville, VA	0.525	P	262.5	Bobby Hamilton	Chevrolet	70.709	Bobby Hamilton	Chevrolet	93.175
1830	9	4/26/98	Talladega, AL	2.66	P	500.08	Bobby Labonte	Pontiac	163.439	Bobby Labonte	Pontiac	195.728
1831	10	5/3/98	Fontana, CA	2	P	500	Mark Martin	Ford	140.22	Jeff Gordon	Chevrolet	181.772
1832	11	5/24/98	Charlotte, NC	1.5	P	600	Jeff Gordon	Chevrolet	136.424	Jeff Gordon	Chevrolet	182.976
1833	12	5/31/98	Dover, DE	1	P	400	Dale Jarrett	Ford	119.522	Rusty Wallace	Ford	155.898
1834	13	6/6/98	Richmond, VA	0.75	P	300	Terry Labonte	Chevrolet	97.044	Jeff Gordon	Chevrolet	125.558
1835	14	6/14/98	Brooklyn, MI	2	P	400	Mark Martin	Ford	158.695	Ward Burton	Pontiac	181.561
1836	15	6/21/98	Pocono, PA	2.5	P	500	Jeremy Mayfield	Ford	117.801	Jeff Gordon	Chevrolet	168.042
1837	16	6/28/98	Sonoma, CA	1.95	P	218.4	Jeff Gordon	Chevrolet	72.387	Jeff Gordon	Chevrolet	98.711

Cum. No.	Yr. No.	Date	Site	Track Length	Surface	Miles	Race Winner	Make	Speed	Pole Winner	Make	Pole Speed
1838	17	7/12/98	Loudon, NH	1.058	P	317.4	Jeff Burton	Ford	102.996	Ricky Craven	Chevrolet	128.394
1839	18	7/26/98	Pocono, PA	2.5	P	500	Jeff Gordon	Chevrolet	134.66	Ward Burton	Pontiac	168.805
1840	19	8/1/98	Indianapolis, IN	2.5	P	400	Jeff Gordon	Chevrolet	126.77	Ernie Irvan	Pontiac	179.394
1841	20	8/9/98	Watkins Glen, NY	2.45	P	220.5	Jeff Gordon	Chevrolet	94.446	Jeff Gordon	Chevrolet	120.331
1842	21	8/16/98	Brooklyn, MI	2	P	400	Jeff Gordon	Chevrolet	151.995	Ernie Irvan	Pontiac	183.416
1843	22	8/22/98	Bristol, TN	0.533	P	266.5	Mark Martin	Ford	86.918	Rusty Wallace	Ford	123.554
1844	23	8/30/98	Loudon, NH	1.058	P	317.4	Jeff Gordon	Chevrolet	112.078	Jeff Gordon	Chevrolet	129.033
1845	24	9/6/98	Darlington, SC	1.366	P	501.322	Jeff Gordon	Chevrolet	139.031	Dale Jarrett	Ford	168.879
1846	25	9/12/98	Richmond, VA	0.75	P	300	Jeff Burton	Ford	91.985	Rusty Wallace	Ford	125.377
1847	26	9/20/98	Dover, DE	1	P	400	Mark Martin	Ford	113.834	Mark Martin	Ford	155.966
1848	27	9/27/98	Martinsville, VA	0.525	P	262.5	Ricky Rudd	Ford	73.35	Ernie Irvan	Pontiac	93.608
1849	28	10/4/98	Charlotte, NC	1.5	P	501	Mark Martin	Ford	123.188	Derrike Cope	Pontiac	181.69
1850	29	10/11/98	Talladega, AL	2.66	P	500.08	Dale Jarrett	Ford	159.318	Ken Schrader	Chevrolet	196.153
1851	30	10/17/98	Daytona Beach, FL	2.5	P	400	Jeff Gordon	Chevrolet	144.549	Bobby Labonte	Pontiac	193.611
1852	31	10/25/98	Phoenix, AZ	1	P	257	Rusty Wallace	Ford	108.211	Ken Schrader	Chevrolet	131.234
1853	32	11/1/98	Rockingham, NC	1.017	P	399.681	Jeff Gordon	Chevrolet	128.423	Mark Martin	Ford	156.502
1854	33	11/8/98	Hampton, GA	1.54	P	340.34	Jeff Gordon	Chevrolet	114.915	Kenny Irwin, Jr.	Ford	193.461

1999

Cum. No.	Yr. No.	Date	Site	Track Length	Surface	Miles	Race Winner	Make	Speed	Pole Winner	Make	Pole Speed
1855	1	2/14/99	Daytona Beach, FL	2.5	P	500	Jeff Gordon	Chevrolet	161.551	Jeff Gordon	Chevrolet	195.067
1856	2	2/21/99	Rockingham, NC	1.017	P	399.681	Mark Martin	Ford	120.75	Ricky Rudd	Ford	157.241
1857	3	3/7/99	Las Vegas, NV	1.5	P	400.5	Jeff Burton	Ford	137.535	Bobby Labonte	Pontiac	170.643
1858	4	3/14/99	Hampton, GA	1.54	P	500.5	Jeff Gordon	Chevrolet	143.296	Bobby Labonte	Pontiac	194.957
1859	5	3/21/99	Darlington, SC	1.366	P	224.024	Jeff Burton	Ford	121.294	Jeff Gordon	Chevrolet	173.167
1860	6	3/28/99	Fort Worth, TX	1.5	P	501	Terry Labonte	Chevrolet	144.276	Kenny Irwin, Jr.	Ford	190.154
1861	7	4/11/99	Bristol, TN	0.533	P	266.5	Rusty Wallace	Ford	93.366	Rusty Wallace	Ford	125.142
1862	8	4/18/99	Martinsville, VA	0.525	P	262.5	John Andretti	Pontiac	75.653	Tony Stewart	Pontiac	95.275
1863	9	4/25/99	Talladega, AL	2.66	P	500.08	Dale Earnhardt	Chevrolet	163.395	Ken Schrader	Chevrolet	197.765
1864	10	5/2/99	Fontana, CA	2	P	500	Jeff Gordon	Chevrolet	150.28	No Time Trials	NTT	NTT
1865	11	5/15/99	Richmond, VA	0.75	P	300	Dale Jarrett	Ford	100.102	Jeff Gordon	Chevrolet	126.499
1866	12	5/30/99	Charlotte, NC	1.5	P	600	Jeff Burton	Ford	151.367	Bobby Labonte	Pontiac	185.23
1867	13	6/6/99	Dover, DE	1	P	400	Bobby Labonte	Pontiac	120.603	Bobby Labonte	Pontiac	159.32
1868	14	6/13/99	Brooklyn, MI	2	P	400	Dale Jarrett	Ford	173.997	Jeff Gordon	Chevrolet	186.945
1869	15	6/20/99	Pocono, PA	2.5	P	500	Bobby Labonte	Pontiac	118.898	Sterling Marlin	Chevrolet	170.506
1870	16	6/27/99	Sonoma, CA	1.95	P	218.4	Jeff Gordon	Chevrolet	70.378	Jeff Gordon	Chevrolet	98.519
1871	17	7/3/99	Daytona Beach, FL	2.5	P	400	Dale Jarrett	Ford	169.213	Joe Nemechek	Chevrolet	194.86
1872	18	7/11/99	Loudon, NH	1.058	P	317.4	Jeff Burton	Ford	101.876	Jeff Gordon	Chevrolet	131.171
1873	19	7/25/99	Pocono, PA	2.5	P	500	Bobby Labonte	Pontiac	116.982	Mike Skinner	Chevrolet	170.451
1874	20	8/7/99	Indianapolis, IN	2.5	P	400	Dale Jarrett	Ford	148.228	Jeff Gordon	Chevrolet	179.612
1875	21	8/15/99	Watkins Glen, NY	2.45	P	220.5	Jeff Gordon	Chevrolet	87.722	Rusty Wallace	Ford	121.234
1876	22	8/22/99	Brooklyn, MI	2	P	400	Bobby Labonte	Pontiac	144.332	Ward Burton	Pontiac	188.843
1877	23	8/28/99	Bristol, TN	0.533	P	266.5	Dale Earnhardt	Chevrolet	91.276	Tony Stewart	Pontiac	124.589
1878	24	9/5/99	Darlington, SC	1.366	P	368.82	Jeff Burton	Ford	107.811	Kenny Irwin, Jr.	Ford	170.97
1879	25	9/11/99	Richmond, VA	0.75	P	300	Tony Stewart	Pontiac	104.006	Mike Skinner	Chevrolet	125.465
1880	26	9/19/99	Loudon, NH	1.058	P	317.4	Joe Nemechek	Chevrolet	100.673	Rusty Wallace	Ford	129.82
1881	27	9/26/99	Dover, DE	1	P	400	Mark Martin	Ford	127.434	Rusty Wallace	Ford	159.964
1882	28	10/3/99	Martinsville, VA	0.525	P	262.5	Jeff Gordon	Chevrolet	72.624	Joe Nemechek	Chevrolet	95.223
1883	29	10/10/99	Charlotte, NC	1.5	P	501	Jeff Gordon	Chevrolet	160.306	Bobby Labonte	Pontiac	185.682
1884	30	10/17/99	Talladega, AL	2.66	P	500.08	Dale Earnhardt	Chevrolet	166.632	Joe Nemechek	Chevrolet	198.331
1885	31	10/24/99	Rockingham, NC	1.017	P	399.681	Jeff Burton	Ford	131.103	Mark Martin	Ford	157.383
1886	32	11/7/99	Phoenix, AZ	1	P	257	Tony Stewart	Pontiac	118.132	John Andretti	Pontiac	132.67
1887	33	11/14/99	Homestead, FL	1.51	P	403.17	Tony Stewart	Pontiac	140.335	David Green	Pontiac	155.759
1888	34	11/21/99	Hampton, GA	1.54	P	500.5	Bobby Labonte	Pontiac	137.942	Kevin Lepage	Ford	193.731

2000

Cum. No.	Yr. No.	Date	Site	Track Length	Surface	Miles	Race Winner	Make	Speed	Pole Winner	Make	Pole Speed
1889	1	2/20/00	Daytona Beach, FL	2.5	P	500	Dale Jarrett	Ford	155.669	Dale Jarrett	Ford	191.091
1890	2	2/27/00	Rockingham, NC	1.017	P	399.681	Bobby Labonte	Pontiac	127.875	Rusty Wallace	Ford	158.035
1891	3	3/5/00	Las Vegas, NV	1.5	P	222	Jeff Burton	Ford	119.982	Ricky Rudd	Ford	172.563
1892	4	3/12/00	Hampton, GA	1.54	P	500.5	Dale Earnhardt	Chevrolet	131.759	Dale Jarrett	Ford	192.574
1893	5	3/19/00	Darlington, SC	1.366	P	400.238	Ward Burton	Pontiac	128.076	Jeff Gordon	Chevrolet	172.662
1894	6	3/26/00	Bristol, TN	0.533	P	266.5	Rusty Wallace	Ford	88.018	Steve Park	Chevrolet	126.37
1895	7	4/2/00	Fort Worth, TX	1.5	P	501	Dale Earnhardt, Jr.	Chevrolet	131.152	Terry Labonte	Chevrolet	192.137

Cum. No.	Yr. No.	Date	Site	Track Length	Surface	Miles	Race Winner	Make	Speed	Pole Winner	Make	Pole Speed
1896	8	4/9/00	Martinsville, VA	0.525	P	262.5	Mark Martin	Ford	71.161	Rusty Wallace	Ford	94.827
1897	9	4/16/00	Talladega, AL	2.66	P	500.08	Jeff Gordon	Chevrolet	161.157	Jeremy Mayfield	Ford	186.969
1898	10	4/30/00	Fontana, CA	2	P	500	Jeremy Mayfield	Ford	149.378	Mike Skinner	Chevrolet	186.061
1899	11	5/6/00	Richmond, VA	0.75	P	300	Dale Earnhardt, Jr.	Chevrolet	99.374	Rusty Wallace	Ford	124.74
1900	12	5/28/00	Charlotte, NC	1.5	P	600	Matt Kenseth	Ford	142.64	Dale Earnhardt, Jr.	Chevrolet	186.034
1901	13	6/4/00	Dover, DE	1	P	400	Tony Stewart	Pontiac	109.514	Rusty Wallace	Ford	157.411
1902	14	6/11/00	Brooklyn, MI	2	P	388	Tony Stewart	Pontiac	143.926	Bobby Labonte	Pontiac	189.883
1903	15	6/18/00	Pocono, PA	2.5	P	500	Jeremy Mayfield	Ford	139.741	Rusty Wallace	Ford	171.625
1904	16	6/25/00	Sonoma, CA	1.95	P	218.4	Jeff Gordon	Chevrolet	78.789	Rusty Wallace	Ford	99.309
1905	17	7/1/00	Daytona Beach, FL	2.5	P	400	Jeff Burton	Ford	148.576	Dale Jarrett	Ford	187.547
1906	18	7/9/00	Loudon, NH	1.058	P	288.834	Tony Stewart	Pontiac	103.145	Rusty Wallace	Ford	132.089
1907	19	7/23/00	Pocono, PA	2.5	P	500	Rusty Wallace	Ford	130.662	Tony Stewart	Pontiac	172.391
1908	20	8/5/00	Indianapolis, IN	2.5	P	400	Bobby Labonte	Pontiac	155.912	Ricky Rudd	Ford	181.068
1909	21	8/13/00	Watkins Glen, NY	2.45	P	220.5	Steve Park	Chevrolet	91.336	No Time Trials	NTT	NTT
1910	22	8/20/00	Brooklyn, MI	2	P	400	Rusty Wallace	Ford	132.597	Dale Earnhardt, Jr.	Chevrolet	191.149
1911	23	8/26/00	Bristol, TN	0.533	P	266.5	Rusty Wallace	Ford	85.394	Rusty Wallace	Ford	125.477
1912	24	9/3/00	Darlington, SC	1.366	P	448.048	Bobby Labonte	Pontiac	108.275	Jeremy Mayfield	Ford	169.444
1913	25	9/9/00	Richmond, VA	0.75	P	300	Jeff Gordon	Chevrolet	99.871	Jeff Burton	Ford	125.78
1914	26	9/17/00	Loudon, NH	1.058	P	317.4	Jeff Burton	Ford	102.003	Bobby Labonte	Pontiac	127.632
1915	27	9/24/00	Dover, DE	1	P	400	Tony Stewart	Pontiac	115.191	Jeremy Mayfield	Ford	159.872
1916	28	10/1/00	Martinsville, VA	0.525	P	262.5	Tony Stewart	Pontiac	73.859	Tony Stewart	Pontiac	95.371
1917	29	10/8/00	Charlotte, NC	1.5	P	501	Bobby Labonte	Pontiac	133.63	Jeff Gordon	Chevrolet	185.561
1918	30	10/15/00	Talladega, AL	2.66	P	500.08	Dale Earnhardt	Chevrolet	165.681	Joe Nemechek	Chevrolet	190.279
1919	31	10/22/00	Rockingham, NC	1.017	P	399.681	Dale Jarrett	Ford	110.418	Jeremy Mayfield	Ford	157.342
1920	32	11/5/00	Phoenix, AZ	1	P	312	Jeff Burton	Ford	105.041	Rusty Wallace	Ford	134.178
1921	33	11/12/00	Homestead, FL	1.51	P	403.17	Tony Stewart	Pontiac	127.48	Steve Park	Chevrolet	156.44
1922	34	11/19/00	Hampton, GA	1.54	P	500.5	Jerry Nadeau	Chevrolet	141.296	Jeff Gordon	Chevrolet	194.274

2001

Cum. No.	Yr. No.	Date	Site	Track Length	Surface	Miles	Race Winner	Make	Speed	Pole Winner	Make	Pole Speed
1923	1	2/18/01	Daytona Beach, FL	2.5	P	500	Michael Waltrip	Chevrolet	161.783	Bill Elliott	Dodge	183.565
1924	2	2/25/01	Rockingham, NC	1.017	P	399.681	Steve Park	Chevrolet	111.966	Jeff Gordon	Chevrolet	156.455
1925	3	3/4/01	Las Vegas, NV	1.5	P	400.5	Jeff Gordon	Chevrolet	135.546	Dale Jarrett	Ford	172.106
1926	4	3/11/01	Hampton, GA	1.54	P	500.5	Kevin Harvick	Chevrolet	143.416	Dale Jarrett	Ford	192.748
1927	5	3/18/01	Darlington, SC	1.366	P	400.238	Dale Jarrett	Ford	126.558	No Time Trials	NTT	NTT
1928	6	3/25/01	Bristol, TN	0.533	P	266.5	Elliott Sadler	Ford	86.949	Mark Martin	Ford	126.303
1929	7	4/1/01	Fort Worth, TX	1.5	P	501	Dale Jarrett	Ford	141.804	Dale Earnhardt, Jr.	Chevrolet	190.678
1930	8	4/8/01	Martinsville, VA	0.525	P	262.5	Dale Jarrett	Ford	70.799	Jeff Gordon	Chevrolet	94.087
1931	9	4/22/01	Talladega, AL	2.66	P	500.08	Bobby Hamilton	Chevrolet	184.003	Stacy Compton	Dodge	184.861
1932	10	4/29/01	Fontana, CA	2	P	500	Rusty Wallace	Ford	143.118	Bobby Labonte	Pontiac	182.635
1933	11	5/5/01	Richmond, VA	0.75	P	300	Tony Stewart	Pontiac	95.872	Mark Martin	Ford	124.613
1934	12	5/27/01	Charlotte, NC	1.5	P	600	Jeff Burton	Ford	130.107	Ryan Newman	Ford	185.217
1935	13	6/3/01	Dover, DE	1	P	400	Jeff Gordon	Chevrolet	120.361	No Time Trials	NTT	NTT
1936	14	6/10/01	Brooklyn, MI	2	P	400	Jeff Gordon	Chevrolet	134.203	Jeff Gordon	Chevrolet	188.25
1937	15	6/17/01	Pocono, PA	2.5	P	500	Ricky Rudd	Ford	134.389	Ricky Rudd	Ford	170.503
1938	16	6/24/01	Sonoma, CA	1.95	P	218.4	Tony Stewart	Pontiac	75.889	Jeff Gordon	Chevrolet	93.699
1939	17	7/7/01	Daytona Beach, FL	2.5	P	400	Dale Earnhardt, Jr.	Chevrolet	157.601	Sterling Marlin	Dodge	183.778
1940	18	7/15/01	Joliet, IL	1.5	P	400.5	Kevin Harvick	Chevrolet	121.2	Todd Bodine	Ford	183.717
1941	19	7/22/01	Loudon, NH	1.058	P	317.4	Dale Jarrett	Ford	102.131	Jeff Gordon	Chevrolet	131.77
1942	20	7/29/01	Pocono, PA	2.5	P	500	Bobby Labonte	Pontiac	134.59	Todd Bodine	Ford	170.326
1943	21	8/5/01	Indianapolis, IN	2.5	P	400	Jeff Gordon	Chevrolet	130.79	Jimmy Spencer	Ford	179.666
1944	22	8/12/01	Watkins Glen, NY	2.45	P	220.5	Jeff Gordon	Chevrolet	89.081	Dale Jarrett	Ford	122.698
1945	23	8/19/01	Brooklyn, MI	2	P	400	Sterling Marlin	Dodge	140.513	Ricky Craven	Ford	188.127
1946	24	8/25/01	Bristol, TN	0.533	P	266.5	Tony Stewart	Pontiac	85.106	Jeff Green	Chevrolet	123.674
1947	25	9/2/01	Darlington, SC	1.366	P	501.322	Ward Burton	Dodge	122.773	Kurt Busch	Ford	168.048
1948	26	9/8/01	Richmond, VA	0.75	P	300	Ricky Rudd	Ford	95.146	Jeff Gordon	Chevrolet	124.902
1949	27	9/23/01	Dover, DE	1	P	400	Dale Earnhardt, Jr.	Chevrolet	101.559	Dale Jarrett	Ford	154.919
1950	28	9/30/01	Kansas City, KS	1.5	P	400.5	Jeff Gordon	Chevrolet	110.576	Jason Leffler	Dodge	176.499
1951	29	10/7/01	Charlotte, NC	1.5	P	501	Sterling Marlin	Dodge	139.006	Jimmy Spencer	Ford	185.147
1952	30	10/15/01	Martinsville, VA	0.525	P	262.5	Ricky Craven	Ford	75.75	Todd Bodine	Ford	93.724
1953	31	10/21/01	Talladega, AL	2.66	P	500.08	Dale Earnhardt, Jr.	Chevrolet	164.185	Stacy Compton	Dodge	185.24
1954	32	10/28/01	Phoenix, AZ	1	P	312	Jeff Burton	Ford	102.613	Casey Atwood	Dodge	131.296
1955	33	11/4/01	Rockingham, NC	1.017	P	399.681	Joe Nemechek	Chevrolet	128.933	Kenny Wallace	Chevrolet	154.69

Cum. No.	Yr. No.	Date	Site	Track Length	Surface	Miles	Race Winner	Make	Speed	Pole Winner	Make	Pole Speed
1956	34	11/11/01	Homestead, FL	1.51	P	403.17	Bill Elliott	Dodge	117.449	Bill Elliott	Dodge	155.226
1957	35	11/18/01	Hampton, GA	1.54	P	500.5	Bobby Labonte	Pontiac	151.756	Dale Earnhardt, Jr.	Chevrolet	192.047
1958	36	11/23/01	Loudon, NH	1.058	P	317.4	Robby Gordon	Chevrolet	103.594	No Time Trials	NTT	NTT

2002

Cum. No.	Yr. No.	Date	Site	Track Length	Surface	Miles	Race Winner	Make	Speed	Pole Winner	Make	Pole Speed
1959	1	2/17/02	Daytona Beach, FL	2.5	P	500	Ward Burton	Dodge	130.81	Jimmie Johnson	Chevrolet	185.831
1960	2	2/24/02	Rockingham, NC	1.017	P	399.681	Matt Kenseth	Ford	115.478	Ricky Craven	Ford	156.008
1961	3	3/3/02	Las Vegas, NV	1.5	P	400.5	Sterling Marlin	Dodge	136.754	Todd Bodine	Ford	172.85
1962	4	3/10/02	Hampton, GA	1.54	P	500.5	Tony Stewart	Pontiac	148.443	Bill Elliott	Dodge	191.542
1963	5	3/17/02	Darlington, SC	1.366	P	400.238	Sterling Marlin	Dodge	126.07	Ricky Craven	Ford	170.089
1964	6	3/24/02	Bristol, TN	0.533	P	266.5	Kurt Busch	Ford	82.281	Jeff Gordon	Chevrolet	127.316
1965	7	4/7/02	Fort Worth, TX	1.5	P	501	Matt Kenseth	Ford	142.435	Bill Elliott	Dodge	194.224
1966	8	4/14/02	Martinsville, VA	0.525	P	262.5	Bobby Labonte	Pontiac	73.951	Jeff Gordon	Chevrolet	94.161
1967	9	4/21/02	Talladega, AL	2.66	P	500.08	Dale Earnhardt, Jr.	Chevrolet	159.022	Jimmie Johnson	Chevrolet	186.532
1968	10	4/28/02	Fontana, CA	2	P	500	Jimmie Johnson	Chevrolet	150.088	Ryan Newman	Ford	187.432
1969	11	5/5/02	Richmond, VA	0.75	P	300	Tony Stewart	Pontiac	86.824	Ward Burton	Dodge	127.388
1970	12	5/26/02	Charlotte, NC	1.5	P	600	Mark Martin	Ford	137.729	Jimmie Johnson	Chevrolet	186.464
1971	13	6/2/02	Dover, DE	1	P	400	Jimmie Johnson	Chevrolet	117.551	Matt Kenseth	Ford	154.938
1972	14	6/9/02	Pocono, PA	2.5	P	500	Dale Jarrett	Ford	143.426	No Time Trials	NTT	NTT
1973	15	6/16/02	Brooklyn, MI	2	P	400	Matt Kenseth	Ford	154.822	Dale Jarrett	Ford	189.071
1974	16	6/23/02	Sonoma, CA	1.95	P	214.5	Ricky Rudd	Ford	81.007	Tony Stewart	Pontiac	93.476
1975	17	7/7/02	Daytona Beach, FL	2.5	P	400	Michael Waltrip	Chevrolet	135.952	Kevin Harvick	Chevrolet	185.04
1976	18	7/14/02	Joliet, IL	1.5	P	400.5	Kevin Harvick	Chevrolet	136.832	Ryan Newman	Ford	183.051
1977	19	7/21/02	Loudon, NH	1.058	P	317.4	Ward Burton	Dodge	92.342	Bill Elliott	Dodge	131.469
1978	20	7/28/02	Pocono, PA	2.5	P	437.5	Bill Elliott	Dodge	125.809	Bill Elliott	Dodge	170.568
1979	21	8/4/02	Indianapolis, IN	2.5	P	400	Bill Elliott	Dodge	125.033	Tony Stewart	Pontiac	182.96
1980	22	8/11/02	Watkins Glen, NY	2.45	P	220.5	Tony Stewart	Pontiac	82.208	Ricky Rudd	Ford	122.696
1981	23	8/18/02	Brooklyn, MI	2	P	400	Dale Jarrett	Ford	140.555	Dale Earnhardt, Jr.	Chevrolet	189.668
1982	24	8/24/02	Bristol, TN	0.533	P	266.5	Jeff Gordon	Chevrolet	77.097	Jeff Gordon	Chevrolet	124.034
1983	25	9/1/02	Darlington, SC	1.366	P	501.322	Jeff Gordon	Chevrolet	118.62	No Time Trials	NTT	NTT
1984	26	9/7/02	Richmond, VA	0.75	P	300	Matt Kenseth	Ford	94.787	Jimmie Johnson	Chevrolet	126.145
1985	27	9/15/02	Loudon, NH	1.058	P	219.006	Ryan Newman	Ford	105.081	Ryan Newman	Ford	132.241
1986	28	9/22/02	Dover, DE	1	P	400	Jimmie Johnson	Chevrolet	120.805	Rusty Wallace	Ford	156.822
1987	29	9/29/02	Kansas City, KS	1.5	P	400.5	Jeff Gordon	Chevrolet	119.394	Dale Earnhardt, Jr.	Chevrolet	177.924
1988	30	10/6/02	Talladega, AL	2.66	P	500.08	Dale Earnhardt, Jr.	Chevrolet	183.665	No Time Trials	NTT	NTT
1989	31	10/13/02	Charlotte, NC	1.5	P	501	Jamie McMurray	Dodge	141.586	No Time Trials	NTT	NTT
1990	32	10/20/02	Martinsville, VA	0.525	P	262.5	Kurt Busch	Ford	74.651	Ryan Newman	Ford	92.837
1991	33	10/27/02	Atlanta, GA	1.54	P	381.92	Kurt Busch	Ford	127.519	No Time Trials	NTT	NTT
1992	34	11/3/02	Rockingham, NC	1.017	P	399.681	Johnny Benson	Pontiac	128.526	Ryan Newman	Ford	155.836
1993	35	11/10/02	Phoenix, AZ	1	P	312	Matt Kenseth	Ford	113.857	Ryan Newman	Ford	132.655
1994	36	11/17/02	Homestead, FL	1.51	P	403.17	Kurt Busch	Ford	116.462	Kurt Busch	Ford	154.365

Cum. No.	Yr. No.	Date	Site	Track Length	Surface	Miles	Race Winner	Make	Speed	Pole Winner	Make	Pole Speed

Selected Race Histories

Atlanta Motor Speedway
Spring 500-Miler
Fall 500-Miler
Festival 250

Bristol Int'l Speedway
Spring Race
Summer Race

California Speedway

Chicagoland Speedway

Darlington Raceway
Southern 500
Spring Race

Daytona Int'l Speedway
Daytona 500
Firecracker/Pepsi 250/400

Dover Downs Int'l Speedway
Spring Race
Fall Race

Homestead-Miami Speedway

Indianapolis Speedway

Infineon Speedway

Kansas Speedway

Las Vegas Motor Speedway

Lowes Motor Speedway

Martinsville Speedway
Spring 500-Lapper
Fall 500-Lapper

Michigan Int'l Speedway
June 500/400-Miler
August 600/400-Miler

New Hampshire Int'l Motor Speedway

North Carolina Motor Speedway
Spring 500/400-Miler
Fall 500/400-Miler

Phoenix Int'l Speedway

Pocono Int'l Raceway
June 500-Miler
July 500-Miler

Richmond Int'l Raceway

Talladega Superspeedway
Alabama/Winston 500
Talladega/DieHard 500

Texas Motor Speedway

Watkins Glen International

Race	Date	Winner	Start Pos.	Make	Speed	Lead Ch.	No. Lds.	No. Caut.	Caut. Laps	Owner	Pole Winner	Pole Speed

ATLANTA MOTOR SPEEDWAY
Spring 500-Miler

Race	Date	Winner	Start Pos.	Make	Speed	Lead Ch.	No. Lds.	No. Caut.	Caut. Laps	Owner	Pole Winner	Pole Speed
Atlanta 500	10/30/60	Bobby Johns	5	60 Pontiac	108.408	7	4			Cotton Owens	Fireball Roberts	134.596
Atlanta 500	3/26/61	Bob Burdick	7	61 Pontiac	124.172			2		Roy Burdick	Marvin Panch	135.755
Atlanta 500	6/10/62	Fred Lorenzen	7	62 Ford	101.983	23	7	3	61	Holman-Moody	Banjo Matthews	137.640
Atlanta 500	3/17/63	Fred Lorenzen	2	63 Ford	130.582	13	8			Holman-Moody	Junior Johnson	141.038
Atlanta 500	4/5/64	Fred Lorenzen	1	1964 Ford	134.137	0	1	4	19	Holman-Moody	Fred Lorenzen	146.470
Atlanta 500	4/11/65	Marvin Panch	1	1965 Ford	129.410	8	5	5	26	Wood Brothers	Marvin Panch	145.581
Atlanta 500	3/27/66	Jim Hurtubise	5	1966 Plymouth	131.247	23	9	5	31	Norm Nelson	Richard Petty	147.742
Atlanta 500	4/2/67	Cale Yarborough	1	1967 Ford	131.238	9	5	6	39	Wood Brothers	Cale Yarborough	148.996

Key

START POS.	Position where winner started
MAKE	Car manufacturer
SPEED	Average speed
LEAD CH.	Number of lead changes in race
NO LDS.	Number of race leaders
NO CAUT.	Number of cautions issued during race
CAUT. LAPS	Number of laps run under caution
NTT	No time trial

Please note that blank fields indicate that the information is unavailable.

Race	Date	Winner	Start Pos.	Make	Speed	Lead Ch.	No. Lds.	No. Caut.	Caut. Laps	Owner	Pole Winner	Pole Speed

SELECTED RACE HISTORIES

ATLANTA MOTOR SPEEDWAY
Spring 500-Miler

Race	Date	Winner	Start Pos.	Make	Speed	Lead Ch.	No. Lds.	No. Caut.	Caut. Laps	Owner	Pole Winner	Pole Speed
Atlanta 500	10/30/60	Bobby Johns	5	60 Pontiac	108.408	7	4			Cotton Owens	Fireball Roberts	134.596
Atlanta 500	3/26/61	Bob Burdick	7	61 Pontiac	124.172			2		Roy Burdick	Marvin Panch	135.755
Atlanta 500	6/10/62	Fred Lorenzen	7	62 Ford	101.983	23	7	3	61	Holman-Moody	Banjo Matthews	137.640
Atlanta 500	3/17/63	Fred Lorenzen	2	63 Ford	130.582	13	8			Holman-Moody	Junior Johnson	141.038
Atlanta 500	4/5/64	Fred Lorenzen	1	1964 Ford	134.137	0	1	4	19	Holman-Moody	Fred Lorenzen	146.470
Atlanta 500	4/11/65	Marvin Panch	1	1965 Ford	129.410	8	5	5	26	Wood Brothers	Marvin Panch	145.581
Atlanta 500	3/27/66	Jim Hurtubise	5	1966 Plymouth	131.247	23	9	5	31	Norm Nelson	Richard Petty	147.742
Atlanta 500	4/2/67	Cale Yarborough	1	1967 Ford	131.238	9	5	6	39	Wood Brothers	Cale Yarborough	148.996
Atlanta 500	3/31/68	Cale Yarborough	4	1968 Mercury	125.564	15	6	11	73	Wood Brothers	LeeRoy Yarbrough	155.646
Atlanta 500	3/30/69	Cale Yarborough	5	1969 Mercury	132.191	11	4	5	53	Wood Brothers	Charlie Glotzbach	156.794
Atlanta 500	3/29/70	Bobby Allison	9	Dodge	139.554	20	8	4	23	Mario Rossi	Cale Yarborough	159.929
Atlanta 500	4/4/71	A.J. Foyt	1	Mercury	131.375	23	6	4	31	Wood Brothers	A.J. Foyt	155.152
Atlanta 500	3/26/72	Bobby Allison	1	Chevrolet	128.214	18	6	6	47	Richard Howard	Bobby Allison	156.245
Atlanta 500	4/1/73	David Pearson	9	Mercury	139.351	23	4	4	31	Wood Brothers	Gordon Johncock	
Atlanta 500	3/24/74	Cale Yarborough	9	Chevrolet	136.910	12	7	3	24	Richard Howard	David Pearson	159.242
Atlanta 500	3/23/75	Richard Petty	1	Dodge	133.496	22	7	5	43	Petty Enterprises	Richard Petty	159.029
Atlanta 500	3/21/76	David Pearson	2	Mercury	128.904	33	10	8	47	Wood Brothers	Dave Marcis	160.709
Atlanta 500	3/20/77	Richard Petty	1	Dodge	144.093	15	3	2	11	Petty Enterprises	Richard Petty	162.501
Atlanta 500	3/19/78	Bobby Allison	4	Ford	142.520	9	6	4	16	Bud Moore	Cale Yarborough	162.006
Atlanta 500	3/18/79	Buddy Baker	1	Oldsmobile	135.136	29	6	5	42	Harry Ranier	Buddy Baker	165.951
Atlanta 500	3/16/80	Dale Earnhardt	31	Chevrolet	134.808	27	11	7	45	Rod Osterlund	Buddy Baker	166.212
Coca-Cola 500	3/15/81	Cale Yarborough	17	Buick	133.619	23	9	5	39	M.C. Anderson	Terry Labonte	162.940
Coca-Cola 500	3/21/82	Darrell Waltrip	14	Buick	124.824	31	8	7	47	Junior Johnson	Dale Earnhardt	163.774
Coca-Cola 500	3/27/83	Cale Yarborough	22	Chevrolet	124.055	20	10	7	62	Harry Ranier	Geoffrey Bodine	167.703
Coca-Cola 500	3/18/84	Benny Parsons	8	Chevrolet	144.945	20	4	3	17	Johnny Hayes	Buddy Baker	166.642
Coca-Cola 500	3/17/85	Bill Elliott	3	Ford	140.273	17	10	6	31	Harry Melling	Neil Bonnett	170.278
Motorcraft 500	3/16/86	Morgan Shepherd	3	Buick	132.126	18	7	9	56	Jack Beebe	Dale Earnhardt	170.713
Motorcraft Qualit Parts 500	3/15/87	Ricky Rudd	6	Ford	133.689	32	10	9	51	Bud Moore	Dale Earnhardt	175.497
Motorcraft Quality Parts 500	3/20/88	Dale Earnhardt	2	Chevrolet	137.588	19	10	7	40	Richard Childress	Geoffrey Bodine	176.623
Motorcraft Quality Parts 500	3/19/89	Darrell Waltrip	4	Chevrolet	139.684	29	11	6	41	Rick Hendrick	Alan Kulwicki	176.925
Motorcraft Quality Parts 500	3/18/90	Dale Earnhardt	1	Chevrolet	156.849	21	9	3	10	Richard Childress	Dale Earnhardt	
Motorcraft Quality Parts 500	3/18/91	Ken Schrader	5	Chevrolet	140.470	16	9	4	33	Rick Hendrick	Alan Kulwicki	174.413
Motorcraft Quality Parts 500	3/15/92	Bill Elliott	4	Ford	147.746	10	6	7	26	Junior Johnson	Mark Martin	179.923
Motorcraft Quality Parts 500	3/20/93	Morgan Shepherd	7	Ford	150.442	19	9	4	19	Wood Brothers	Rusty Wallace	178.749
Purolator 500	3/13/94	Ernie Irvan	7	Ford	146.136	19	7	5	27	Robert Yates	Loy Allen, Jr.	180.207
Purolator 500	3/12/95	Jeff Gordon	3	Chevrolet	150.115	9	7	5	27	Rick Hendrick	Dale Earnhardt	185.077
Purolator 500	3/10/96	Dale Earnhardt	18	Chevrolet	161.298	30	12	3	13	Richard Childress	Johnny Benson, Jr.	185.434
Primestar 500	3/9/97	Dale Jarrett	9	Ford	132.731	16	7	7	45	Robert Yates	Robby Gordon	186.987
Primestar 500	3/9/98	Bobby Labonte	14	Pontiac	139.501	29	14	7	52	Joe Gibbs	John Andretti	192.956
Cracker Barrel 500	3/14/99	Jeff Gordon	8	Chevrolet	143.296	25	10	6	44	Rick Hendrick	Bobby Labonte	194.957
Cracker Barrel Old Country Store 500	3/12/00	Dale Earnhardt	35	Chevrolet	131.759	30	17	10	62	Richard Childress	Dale Jarrett	192.574
Cracker Barrel 500	3/11/01	Kevin Harvick	5	Chevrolet	143.416	25	11	8	42	Richard Childress	Dale Jarrett	192.748
MBNA America 500	3/10/02	Tony Stewart	9	Pontiac	148.443	34	8	7	37	Joe Gibbs	Bill Elliott	191.542

Fall 500–Miler

Race	Date	Winner	Start Pos.	Make	Speed	Lead Ch.	No. Lds.	No. Caut.	Caut. Laps	Owner	Pole Winner	Pole Speed
Dixie 300	7/31/60	Fireball Roberts	1	60 Pontiac	112.652	12	6			John Hines	Fireball Roberts	133.870
Dixie 400	9/17/61	David Pearson	5	61 Pontiac	125.384	7	4			John Masoni	Fireball Roberts	136.778
Dixie 400	10/28/62	Rex White	5	62 Chevrolet	124.740	16	6	3		Rex White	Fireball Roberts	138.978
Dixie 400	6/30/63	Junior Johnson	2	63 Chevrolet	121.139	18	6	2	32	Ray Fox	Marvin Panch	140.753
Dixie 400	6/7/64	Ned Jarrett	17	1964 Ford	112.535	35	13	3	63	Bondy Long	Junior Johnson	145.906

Race	Date	Winner	Start Pos.	Make	Speed	Lead Ch.	No. Lds.	No. Caut.	Caut. Laps	Owner	Pole Winner	Pole Speed
Dixie 400	6/13/65	Marvin Panch	2	1965 Ford	110.120	17	7	8	98	Wood Brothers	Fred Lorenzen	143.407
Dixie 400	8/7/66	Richard Petty	5	1966 Plymouth	130.244	18	7	6	37	Petty Enterprises	Curtis Turner	148.331
Dixie 500	8/6/67	Dick Hutcherson	8	1967 Ford	132.286	13	1	6	38	Bondy Long	Darel Dieringer	150.669
Dixie 500	8/4/68	LeeRoy Yarbrough	5	1968 Ford	127.068	29	9	11	67	Junior Johnson	Buddy Baker	153.361
Dixie 500	8/10/69	LeeRoy Yarbrough	2	1969 Ford	133.001	19	7	3	31	Junior Johnson	Cale Yarborough	155.413
Dixie 500	8/2/70	Richard Petty	6	Plymouth	142.712	10	4	1	10	Petty Enterprises	Fred Lorenzen	157.625
Dixie 500	8/1/71	Richard Petty	3	Plymouth	129.061	27	4	5	48	Petty Enterprises	Buddy Baker	155.796
Dixie 500	7/23/72	Bobby Allison	3	Chevrolet	131.295	24	9	5	40	Richard Howard	David Pearson	158.353
Dixie 500	7/22/73	David Pearson	5	Mercury	130.211	14	5	6	47	Wood Brothers	Richard Petty	157.163
Dixie 500	7/28/74	Richard Petty	2	Dodge	131.651	23	7	5	38	Petty Enterprises	Cale Yarborough	156.750
Dixie 500	11/9/75	Buddy Baker	3	Ford	130.990	18	8	2	40	Bud Moore	Dave Marcis	160.662
Dixie 500	11/7/76	Dave Marcis	2	Dodge	127.396	17	5	4	41	Nord Krauskopf	Buddy Baker	161.652
Dixie 500	11/6/77	Darrell Waltrip	8	Chevrolet	110.052	12	6	5	99	DiGard	Sam Sommers	160.229
Dixie 500	11/5/78	Donnie Allison	13	Chevrolet	124.312	25	8	7	63	Hoss Ellington	Cale Yarborough	168.425
Dixie 500	11/4/79	Neil Bonnett	4	Mercury	140.120	25	7	5	29	Wood Brothers	Buddy Baker	164.813
Atlanta Journal 500	11/2/80	Cale Yarborough	12	Chevrolet	131.190	28	13	6	49	Junior Johnson	Bobby Allison	165.620
Atlanta Journal 500	11/8/81	Neil Bonnett	5	Ford	130.391	36	11	7	50	Wood Brothers	Harry Gant	163.266
Atlanta Journal 500	11/7/82	Bobby Allison	9	Buick	130.884	45	14	10	56	DiGard	Morgan Shepherd	166.779
Atlanta Journal 500	11/6/83	Neil Bonnett	15	Chevrolet	137.643	28	8	6	39	RahMoc Enterprises	Tim Richmond	168.151
Atlanta Journal 500	11/11/84	Dale Earnhardt	10	Chevrolet	134.610	25	11	7	44	Richard Childress	Bill Elliott	170.193
Atlanta Journal 500	11/3/85	Bill Elliott	3	Ford	139.597	12	4	6	39	Harry Melling	Harry Gant	167.940
Atlanta Journal 500	11/2/86	Dale Earnhardt	4	Chevrolet	152.523	19	8	2	7	Richard Childress	Bill Elliott	172.905
Atlanta Journal 500	11/22/87	Bill Elliott	1	Ford	139.047	12	8	5	33	Harry Melling	Bill Elliott	174.341
Atlanta Journal 500	11/20/88	Rusty Wallace	1	Pontiac	129.024	33	15	9	55	Raymond Beadle	Rusty Wallace	179.499
Atlanta Journal 500	11/19/89	Dale Earnhardt	3	Chevrolet	140.229	21	8	6	35	Richard Childress	Alan Kulwicki	179.112
Atlanta Journal 500	11/18/90	Morgan Shepherd	20	Ford	140.911	19	9	3	34	Bud Moore	Rusty Wallace	175.222
Hardee's 500	11/17/91	Mark Martin	4	Ford	137.968	21	12	6	37	Jack Roush	Bill Elliott	177.937
Hooters 500	11/15/92	Bill Elliott	11	Ford	133.322	20	9	7	45	Junior Johnson	Rick Mast	180.183
Hooters 500	11/14/93	Rusty Wallace	20	Pontiac	125.221	26	12	11	58	Roger Penske	Harry Gant	176.902
Hooters 500	11/13/94	Mark Martin	5	Ford	148.982	30	13	4	27	Jack Roush	Greg Sacks	185.830
NAPA 500	11/12/95	Dale Earnhardt	11	Chevrolet	163.633	22	8	2	11	Richard Childress	Darrell Waltrip	185.046
NAPA 500	11/10/96	Bobby Labonte	1	Chevrolet	134.661	27	12	8	47	Joe Gibbs	Bobby Labonte	185.887
NAPA 500	11/16/97	Bobby Labonte	21	Pontiac	159.904	24	11	4	25	Joe Gibbs	Geoffrey Bodine	197.478
NAPA 500	11/8/98	Jeff Gordon	21	Chevrolet	114.915	12	8	5	68	Rick Hendrick	Kenny Irwin, Jr.	193.461
NAPA 500	11/21/99	Bobby Labonte	37	Pontiac	137.942	38	15	8	53	Joe Gibbs	Kevin Lepage	193.731
NAPA 500	11/19/00	Jerry Nadeau	2	Chevrolet	141.296	24	13	8	44	Rick Hendrick	Jeff Gordon	194.274
NAPA 500	11/18/01	Bobby Labonte	39	Pontiac	151.756	23	13	5	28	Joe Gibbs	Dale Earnhardt, Jr.	192.047
NAPA 500	10/27/02	Kurt Busch	8	Ford	127.519	19	9	5	50	Jack Roush	Tony Stewart	

Festival 250

Race	Date	Winner	Start Pos.	Make	Speed	Lead Ch.	No. Lds.	No. Caut.	Caut. Laps	Owner	Pole Winner	Pole Speed
Festival 250	7/9/61	Fred Lorenzen	5	61 Ford	118.067		7	1	12	Holman-Moody	Fireball Roberts	136.088

BRISTOL INT'L RACEWAY
Spring Race

Race	Date	Winner	Start Pos.	Make	Speed	Lead Ch.	No. Lds.	No. Caut.	Caut. Laps	Owner	Pole Winner	Pole Speed
Southeastern 500	10/22/61	Joe Weatherly	2	61 Pontiac	72.452	6	5	3		Bud Moore	Bobby Johns	80.645
Southeastern 500	7/29/62	Jim Paschal	12	62 Plymouth	75.276	12	6	4	21	Petty Enterprises	Fireball Roberts	80.321
Southeastern 500	3/31/63	Fireball Roberts	3	63 Ford	76.910	8	5	1	9	Holman-Moody	Fred Lorenzen	80.681
Southeastern 500	3/22/64	Fred Lorenzen	2	1964 Ford	72.196	1	2	4	54	Holman-Moody	Marvin Panch	80.640
Southeastern 500	5/2/65	Junior Johnson	3	1965 Ford	74.937	8	4	7	39	Junior Johnson	Marvin Panch	84.626
Southeastern 500	3/20/66	Dick Hutcherson	6	1966 Ford	69.952	7	4	7	92	Holman-Moody	David Pearson	86.248
Southeastern 500	3/19/67	David Pearson	14	1967 Dodge	75.937	13	6	6	59	Cotton Owens	Darel Dieringer	87.124
Southeastern 500	3/17/68	David Pearson	2	1968 Ford	77.247	18	4	11	81	Holman-Moody	Richard Petty	88.582
Southeastern 500	3/23/69	Bobby Allison	4	1969 Dodge	81.455	9	3	4	32	Mario Rossi	Bobby Isaac	88.669
Southeastern 500	4/5/70	Donnie Allison	2	Ford	87.543	10	6	6	58	Banjo Matthews	David Pearson	107.079
Southeastern 500	3/28/71	David Pearson	1	Ford	91.704	9	5	5	45	Holman-Moody	David Pearson	105.525
Southeastern 500	4/9/72	Bobby Allison	1	Chevrolet	92.826	6	4	2	25	Richard Howard	Bobby Allison	106.875
Southeastern 500	3/25/73	Cale Yarborough	1	Chevrolet	88.952	0	1	7	56	Richard Howard	Cale Yarborough	107.608
Southeastern 500	3/17/74	Cale Yarborough	3	Chevrolet	64.533	5	5	3	28	Richard Howard	Donnie Allison	107.785
Southeastern 500	3/16/75	Richard Petty	2	Dodge	97.053	6	4	2	27	Petty Enterprises	Buddy Baker	110.951
Southeastern 400	3/14/76	Cale Yarborough	3	Chevrolet	87.377	16	7	6	79	Junior Johnson	Buddy Baker	110.720
Southeastern 500	4/17/77	Cale Yarborough	1	Chevrolet	100.989	5	4	2	9	Junior Johnson	Cale Yarborough	110.168
Southeastern 500	4/2/78	Darrell Waltrip	7	Chevrolet	92.401	13	3	4	40	DiGard	Neil Bonnett	110.409
Southeastern 500	4/1/79	Dale Earnhardt	9	Chevrolet	91.033	8	6	6	44	Rod Osterlund	Buddy Baker	111.668

Race	Date	Winner	Start Pos.	Make	Speed	Lead Ch.	No. Lds.	No. Caut.	Caut. Laps	Owner	Pole Winner	Pole Speed
Valleydale												
Southeastern 500	3/30/80	Dale Earnhardt	4	Chevrolet	96.977	15	6	3	14	Rod Osterlund	Cale Yarborough	111.688
Valleydale 500	3/29/81	Darrell Waltrip	1	Buick	89.530	21	11	8	44	Junior Johnson	Darrell Waltrip	112.125
Valleydale 500	3/14/82	Darrell Waltrip	1	Buick	94.025	10	6	3	25	Junior Johnson	Darrell Waltrip	111.068
Valleydale 500	5/21/83	Darrell Waltrip	13	Chevrolet	93.445	12	5	4	22	Junior Johnson	Neil Bonnett	110.409
Valleydale 500	4/1/84	Darrell Waltrip	3	Chevrolet	93.967	17	7	4	19	Junior Johnson	Ricky Rudd	111.390
Valleydale 500	4/6/85	Dale Earnhardt	12	Chevrolet	81.790	18	10	14	90	Richard Childress	Harry Gant	112.778
Valleydale 500	4/6/86	Rusty Wallace	14	Pontiac	89.747	14	8	7	56	Raymond Beadle	Geoffrey Bodine	114.850
Valleydale Meats 500	4/12/87	Dale Earnhardt	3	Chevrolet	75.621	19	11	13	125	Richard Childress	Harry Gant	115.674
Valleydale Meats 500	4/10/88	Bill Elliott	13	Ford	83.115	11	8	12	70	Harry Melling	Rick Wilson	117.552
Valleydale Meats 500	4/9/89	Rusty Wallace	8	Pontiac	76.034	33	16	20	98	Raymond Beadle	Mark Martin	120.278
Valleydale Meats 500	4/8/90	Davey Allison	19	Ford	87.258	11	9	13	65	Robert Yates	Ernie Irvan	116.157
Valleydale Meats 500	4/14/91	Rusty Wallace	1	Pontiac	72.809	40	8	19	133	Roger Penske	Rusty Wallace	118.051
Food City 500	4/5/92	Alan Kulwicki	1	Ford	86.316	11	7	10	74	Alan Kulwicki	Alan Kulwicki	122.474
Food City 500	4/4/93	Rusty Wallace	1	Pontiac	84.730	19	10	17	87	Roger Penske	Rusty Wallace	120.938
Food City 500	4/10/94	Dale Earnhardt	24	Chevrolet	89.647	11	5	10	75	Richard Childress	Chuck Bown	124.946
Food City 500	4/2/95	Jeff Gordon	2	Chevrolet	92.011	12	5	7	65	Rick Hendrick	Mark Martin	124.605
Food City 500	3/31/96	Jeff Gordon	8	Chevrolet	91.308	7	7	5	37	Rick Hendrick	Mark Martin	123.578
Food City 500	4/13/97	Jeff Gordon	5	Chevrolet	75.035	13	6	20	132	Rick Hendrick	Rusty Wallace	123.586
Food City 500	3/29/98	Jeff Gordon	2	Chevrolet	82.850	19	10	14	88	Rick Hendrick	Rusty Wallace	124.275
Food City 500	4/11/99	Rusty Wallace	1	Ford	93.366	7	5	7	57	Roger Penske	Rusty Wallace	125.142
Food City 500	3/26/00	Rusty Wallace	6	Ford	88.018	18	9	11	76	Roger Penske	Steve Park	126.370
Food City 500	3/25/01	Elliott Sadler	38	Ford	86.949	18	10	13	87	Wood Brothers	Mark Martin	126.303
Food City 500	3/24/02	Kurt Busch	27	Ford	82.281	14	6	14	101	Jack Roush	Jeff Gordon	127.316
Summer Race												
Volunteer 500	7/29/61	Jack Smith	12	61 Pontiac	68.373	7	5	8		Jack Smith	Fred Lorenzen	79.225
Volunteer 500	4/29/62	Bobby Johns	6	62 Pontiac	73.397	5	3	4	37	Shorty Johns	Fireball Roberts	81.374
Volunteer 500	7/28/63	Fred Lorenzen	1	63 Ford	74.844	6	4	7	36	Holman-Moody	Fred Lorenzen	82.229
Volunteer 500	7/26/64	Fred Lorenzen	8	1964 Ford	78.044	5	4	1	14	Holman-Moody	Richard Petty	82.910
Volunteer 500	7/25/65	Ned Jarrett	6	1965 Ford	61.826	9	4	8	167	Bondy Long	Fred Lorenzen	84.348
Volunteer 500	7/24/66	Paul Goldsmith	4	1966 Plymouth	77.963	3	3	2	24	Ray Nichels	Curtis Turner	84.309
Volunteer 500	7/23/67	Richard Petty	1	1967 Plymouth	78.705	11	2	6	42	Petty Enterprises	Richard Petty	86.621
Volunteer 500	7/21/68	David Pearson	6	1968 Ford	76.310	8	2	13	92	Holman-Moody	LeeRoy Yarbrough	87.421
Volunteer 500	7/20/69	David Pearson	3	1969 Ford	79.737	9	7	8	58	Holman-Moody	Cale Yarborough	103.432
Volunteer 500	7/19/70	Bobby Allison	10	Dodge	84.880	9	2	8	54	Bobby Allison	Cale Yarborough	107.375
Volunteer 500	7/11/71	Charlie Glotzbach	2	Chevrolet	101.074	7	3	0	0	Richard Howard	Richard Petty	104.589
Volunteer 500	7/9/72	Bobby Allison	1	Chevrolet	92.735	4	3	5	30	Richard Howard	Bobby Allison	107.279
Volunteer 500	7/8/73	Benny Parsons	2	Chevrolet	91.342	5	3	5	33	L.G. DeWitt	Cale Yarborough	106.472
Volunteer 500	7/14/74	Cale Yarborough	3	Chevrolet	75.430	22	5	9	105	Junior Johnson	Richard Petty	107.351
Volunteer 500	11/2/75	Richard Petty	4	Dodge	97.016	12	5	5	28	Petty Enterprises	Cale Yarborough	110.162
Volunteer 400	8/29/76	Cale Yarborough	2	Chevrolet	99.175	1	2	2	13	Junior Johnson	Darrell Waltrip	110.300
Volunteer 500	8/28/77	Cale Yarborough	1	Chevrolet	79.726	14	6	6	92	Junior Johnson	Cale Yarborough	109.746
Volunteer 500	8/26/78	Cale Yarborough	4	Oldsmobile	88.628	16	7	10	59	Junior Johnson	Lennie Pond	110.958
Volunteer 500	8/25/79	Darrell Waltrip	5	Chevrolet	91.493	18	6	6	60	DiGard	Richard Petty	120.524
Busch Volunteer 500	8/23/80	Cale Yarborough	1	Chevrolet	86.973	19	8	10	57	Junior Johnson	Cale Yarborough	110.990
Busch 500	8/22/81	Darrell Waltrip	1	Buick	84.723	11	5	7	52	Junior Johnson	Darrell Waltrip	110.818
Busch 500	8/28/82	Darrell Waltrip	8	Buick	94.318	15	8	3	15	Junior Johnson	Tim Richmond	112.507
Busch 500	8/27/83	Darrell Waltrip	2	Chevrolet	89.430	12	6	5	31	Junior Johnson	Joe Ruttman	111.923
Busch 500	8/25/84	Terry Labonte	6	Chevrolet	85.365	12	6	12	66	Billy Hagan	Geoffrey Bodine	
Busch 500	8/24/85	Dale Earnhardt	1	Chevrolet	81.388	18	8	11	82	Richard Childress	Dale Earnhardt	113.586
Busch 500	8/23/86	Darrell Waltrip	10	Chevrolet	86.934	15	9	6	56	Junior Johnson	Geoffrey Bodine	114.665
Busch 500	8/22/87	Dale Earnhardt	6	Chevrolet	90.373	12	7	8	49	Richard Childress	Terry Labonte	115.758
Busch 500	8/27/88	Dale Earnhardt	5	Chevrolet	78.775	22	13	14	83	Richard Childress	Alan Kulwicki	116.893
Busch 500	8/26/89	Darrell Waltrip	9	Chevrolet	85.554	11	5	11	69	Rick Hendrick	Alan Kulwicki	117.043
Busch 500	8/25/90	Ernie Irvan	6	Chevrolet	91.782	9	4	10	47	Larry McClure	Dale Earnhardt	115.604
Bud 500	8/24/91	Alan Kulwicki	5	Ford	82.028	14	8	11	81	Alan Kulwicki	Bill Elliott	116.957
Bud 500	8/29/92	Darrell Waltrip	9	Chevrolet	91.198	14	8	10	55	Darrell Waltrip	Ernie Irvan	120.535
Bud 500	8/28/93	Mark Martin	1	Ford	88.172	8	4	11	71	Jack Roush	Mark Martin	121.405
Goody's 500	8/27/94	Rusty Wallace	4	Ford	91.363	16	10	12	73	Roger Penske	Harry Gant	124.186
Goody's 500	8/26/95	Terry Labonte	2	Chevrolet	81.979	16	10	15	106	Rick Hendrick	Mark Martin	125.093
Goody's 500	8/24/96	Rusty Wallace	5	Ford	91.267	8	5	8	67	Roger Penske	Mark Martin	124.857
Goody's Headache 500	8/23/97	Dale Jarrett	3	Ford	80.010	12	5	12	97	Robert Yates	Kenny Wallace	123.039

Race	Date	Winner	Start Pos.	Make	Speed	Lead Ch.	No. Lds.	No. Caut.	Caut. Laps	Owner	Pole Winner	Pole Speed
Goody's Headache Powder 500	8/22/98	Mark Martin	4	Ford	86.918	12	7	13	86	Jack Roush	Rusty Wallace	123.554
Goody's Headache Powder 500	8/28/99	Dale Earnhardt	26	Chevrolet	91.276	11	5	10	61	Richard Childress	Tony Stewart	124.589
goracing.com 500	8/26/00	Rusty Wallace	1	Ford	85.394	19	12	13	85	Roger Penske	Rusty Wallace	125.477
Sharpie 500	8/25/01	Tony Stewart	18	Pontiac	85.106	11	8	16	92	Joe Gibbs	Jeff Green	123.674
Sharpie 500	8/24/02	Jeff Gordon	1	Chevrolet	77.097	10	7	15	118	Rick Hendrick	Jeff Gordon	124.034

CALIFORNIA SPEEDWAY

Race	Date	Winner	Start Pos.	Make	Speed	Lead Ch.	No. Lds.	No. Caut.	Caut. Laps	Owner	Pole Winner	Pole Speed
California 500	6/22/97	Jeff Gordon	3	Chevrolet	155.025	21	12	4	22	Rick Hendrick	Joe Nemechek	183.015
California 500	5/3/98	Mark Martin	3	Ford	140.220	18	8	6	35	Jack Roush	Jeff Gordon	181.772
California 500	5/2/99	Jeff Gordon	5	Chevrolet	150.280	28	13	5	23	Rick Hendrick	Jeff Burton	
NAPA Auto Parts 500	4/30/00	Jeremy Mayfield	24	Ford	149.378	22	15	5	22	Michael Kranefuss	Mike Skinner	186.061
NAPA Auto Parts 500	4/29/01	Rusty Wallace	19	Ford	143.118	29	14	6	29	Roger Penske	Bobby Labonte	182.635
NAPA Auto Parts 500	4/28/02	Jimmie Johnson	4	Chevrolet	150.088	20	8	5	24	Rick Hendrick	Ryan Newman	187.432

CHICAGOLAND SPEEDWAY

Race	Date	Winner	Start Pos.	Make	Speed	Lead Ch.	No. Lds.	No. Caut.	Caut. Laps	Owner	Pole Winner	Pole Speed
Tropicana 400	7/15/01	Kevin Harvick	6	Chevrolet	121.200	14	10	10	56	Richard Childress	Todd Bodine	183.717
Tropicana 400	7/14/02	Kevin Harvick	32	Chevrolet	136.832	19	11	7	35	Richard Childress	Ryan Newman	183.051

DARLINGTON RACEWAY
Southern 500

Race	Date	Winner	Start Pos.	Make	Speed	Lead Ch.	No. Lds.	No. Caut.	Caut. Laps	Owner	Pole Winner	Pole Speed
Southern 500	9/4/50	Johnny Mantz	43	50 Plymouth	75.250	4	4	2	13	Hubert Westmoreland	Curtis Turner	82.034
Southern 500	9/3/51	Herb Thomas	2	51 Hudson	76.906	6	5	4	26	Herb Thomas	Frank Mundy	84.173
Southern 500	9/1/52	Fonty Flock	1	52 Olds	74.512	6	4	7	40	Frank Christian	Fonty Flock	88.550
Southern 500	9/7/53	Buck Baker	7	53 Olds	92.881	35	4	4	17	Bobby Griffin	Fonty Flock	107.983
Southern 500	9/6/54	Herb Thomas	23	54 Hudson	95.026	12	6	2	4	Herb Thomas	Buck Baker	108.261
Southern 500	9/5/55	Herb Thomas	8	55 Chevrolet		10	7	8	51	Herb Thomas	Fireball Roberts	110.682
Southern 500	9/3/56	Curtis Turner	11	56 Ford	95.167	14	6	7	68	Charlie Schwam	Speedy Thompson	119.659
Southern 500	9/2/57	Speedy Thompson	7	57 Chevrolet	100.094	13	8	6	23	Speedy Thompson	Cotton Owens	117.416
Southern 500	9/1/58	Fireball Roberts	2	57 Chevrolet	102.585	8	6	6	28	Frank Strickland	Eddie Pagan	116.952
Southern 500	9/7/59	Jim Reed	14	57 Chevrolet	111.836	11	8	2	12	Jim Reed	Fireball Roberts	123.734
Southern 500	9/5/60	Buck Baker	2	60 Pontiac	105.901	14	7	5	61	Jack Smith	Fireball Roberts	125.459
Southern 500	9/4/61	Nelson Stacy	3	61 Ford	117.787	19	6	6	21	Dudley Farrell	Fireball Roberts	128.680
Southern 500	9/3/62	Larry Frank	10	62 Ford	117.965	9	7	4	27	Ratus Walters	Fireball Roberts	130.246
Southern 500	9/2/63	Fireball Roberts	10	63 Ford	129.784	9	4	0	0	Holman-Moody	Fred Lorenzen	133.648
Southern 500	9/7/64	Buck Baker	6	1964 Dodge	117.757	12	7	7	50	Ray Fox	Richard Petty	136.815
Southern 500	9/6/65	Ned Jarrett	10	1965 Ford	115.878	23	8	7	44	Bondy Long	Junior Johnson	137.571
Southern 500	9/5/66	Darel Dieringer	3	1966 Mercury	114.830	28	10	8	80	Bud Moore	LeeRoy Yarbrough	140.058
Southern 500	9/4/67	Richard Petty	1	1967 Plymouth	130.423	6	4	3	25	Petty Enterprises	Richard Petty	143.436
Southern 500	9/2/68	Cale Yarborough	2	1968 Mercury	126.132	13	6	7	65	Wood Brothers	Charlie Glotzbach	144.830
Southern 500	9/1/69	LeeRoy Yarbrough	4	1969 Ford	105.612	20	8	7	85	Junior Johnson	Cale Yarborough	151.985
Southern 500	9/7/70	Buddy Baker	2	Dodge	128.817	19	8	9	50	Cotton Owens	David Pearson	150.555
Southern 500	9/6/71	Bobby Allison	1	Mercury	131.398	14	3	5	32	Holman-Moody	Bobby Allison	147.915
Southern 500	9/4/72	Bobby Allison	1	Chevrolet	128.124	31	7	5	43	Richard Howard	Bobby Allison	152.342
Southern 500	9/3/73	Cale Yarborough	8	Chevrolet	134.033	25	5	7	38	Richard Howard	David Pearson	150.366
Southern 500	9/2/74	Cale Yarborough	4	Chevrolet	111.075	26	13	11	101	Junior Johnson	Richard Petty	150.132
Southern 500	9/1/75	Bobby Allison	3	Matador	116.825	20	8	10	72	Roger Penske	David Pearson	153.401
Southern 500	9/6/76	David Pearson	1	Mercury	120.534	31	10	8	65	Wood Brothers	David Pearson	154.699
Southern 500	9/5/77	David Pearson	5	Mercury	106.797	32	7	6	93	Wood Brothers	Darrell Waltrip	153.493
Southern 500	9/4/78	Cale Yarborough	6	Oldsmobile	116.828	21	10	9	72	Junior Johnson	David Pearson	153.685
Southern 500	9/3/79	David Pearson	5	Chevrolet	126.259	18	7	9	52	Rod Osterlund	Bobby Allison	154.880
Southern 500	9/1/80	Terry Labonte	10	Chevrolet	115.210	27	12	14	79	Billy Hagan	Darrell Waltrip	153.838
Southern 500	9/7/81	Neil Bonnett	3	Ford	126.410	23	9	8	45	Wood Brothers	Harry Gant	152.693
Southern 500	9/6/82	Cale Yarborough	9	Buick	115.224	41	17	14	87	M.C. Anderson	David Pearson	155.739
Southern 500	9/5/83	Bobby Allison	14	Buick	123.343	17	9	9	60	DiGard	Neil Bonnett	157.187
Southern 500	9/2/84	Harry Gant	1	Chevrolet	128.270	17	9	8	51	Hal Needham	Harry Gant	155.502
Southern 500	9/1/85	Bill Elliott	1	Ford	121.254	20	9	14	70	Harry Melling	Bill Elliott	156.641
Southern 500	8/31/86	Tim Richmond	1	Chevrolet	121.068	16	9	12	79	Rick Hendrick	Tim Richmond	158.489
Southern 500	9/6/87	Dale Earnhardt	5	Chevrolet	115.520	13	6	5	50	Richard Childress	Davey Allison	157.232
Southern 500	9/4/88	Bill Elliott	1	Ford	128.297	24	12	10	39	Harry Melling	Bill Elliott	160.827
Heinz Southern 500	9/3/89	Dale Earnhardt	10	Chevrolet	135.462	26	10	4	24	Richard Childress	Alan Kulwicki	160.156
Heinz Southern 500	9/2/90	Dale Earnhardt	1	Chevrolet	123.141	20	8	10	51	Richard Childress	Dale Earnhardt	158.448

Race	Date	Winner	Start Pos.	Make	Speed	Lead Ch.	No. Lds.	No. Caut.	Caut. Laps	Owner	Pole Winner	Pole Speed
Heinz Southern 500	9/1/91	Harry Gant	5	Oldsmobile	133.508	20	10	8	33	Leo Jackson	Davey Allison	162.506
Mt. Dew Southern 500	9/6/92	Darrell Waltrip	5	Chevrolet	129.114	23	11	5	28	Darrell Waltrip	Sterling Marlin	162.249
Mt. Dew Southern 500	9/5/93	Mark Martin	4	Ford	137.932	21	10	3	16	Jack Roush	Ken Schrader	161.259
Mt. Dew Southern 500	9/4/94	Bill Elliott	9	Ford	127.952	28	10	6	42	Junior Johnson	Geoffrey Bodine	166.998
Mt. Dew Southern 500	9/3/95	Jeff Gordon	5	Chevrolet	121.231	21	11	12	94	Rick Hendrick	John Andretti	167.379
Mt. Dew Southern 500	9/1/96	Jeff Gordon	2	Chevrolet	135.757	29	14	6	37	Rick Hendrick	Dale Jarrett	170.934
Mt. Dew Southern 500	8/31/97	Jeff Gordon	7	Chevrolet	121.149	7	9	11	67	Rick Hendrick	Bobby Labonte	170.661
Southern 500	9/6/98	Jeff Gordon	5	Chevrolet	139.031	12	6	2	16	Rick Hendrick	Dale Jarrett	168.879
Pepsi Southern 500	9/5/99	Jeff Burton	15	Ford	107.811	20	10	6	62	Jack Roush	Kenny Irwin, Jr.	170.970
Pepsi Southern 500	9/3/00	Bobby Labonte	37	Pontiac	108.275	22	15	9	69	Joe Gibbs	Jeremy Mayfield	169.444
Southern 500	9/2/01	Ward Burton	37	Dodge	122.773	19	9	11	51	Bill Davis	Kurt Busch	168.048
Southern 500	9/1/02	Jeff Gordon	3	Chevrolet	118.620	14	9	9	63	Rick Hendrick	Sterling Marlin	

Spring Race

Race	Date	Winner	Start Pos.	Make	Speed	Lead Ch.	No. Lds.	No. Caut.	Caut. Laps	Owner	Pole Winner	Pole Speed
Darlington 100	5/10/52	Dick Rathmann	4	51 Hudson	83.818	7	5			Walt Chapman	Fireball Roberts	
Rebel 300	5/14/60	Joe Weatherly	2	60 Ford	102.640	7	4	4		Holman-Moody	Fireball Roberts	127.750
Rebel 300	5/6/61	Fred Lorenzen	1	61 Ford	119.520	16	8	1		Holman-Moody	Fred Lorenzen	128.965
Rebel 300	5/12/62	Nelson Stacy	3	62 Ford	117.429	9	7	6		Holman-Moody	Fred Lorenzen	129.810
Rebel 300	5/11/63	Joe Weatherly	6	63 Pontiac	122.745	9	6	3	14	Bud Moore	Fred Lorenzen	131.718
Rebel 300	5/9/64	Fred Lorenzen	1	1964 Ford	130.013	10	2	1	5	Holman-Moody	Fred Lorenzen	135.727
Rebel 300	5/8/65	Junior Johnson	3	1965 Ford	111.849	11	7	6	50	Junior Johnson	Fred Lorenzen	138.133
Rebel 400	4/30/66	Richard Petty	1	1966 Plymouth	131.993	6	5	1	5	Petty Enterprises	Richard Petty	140.815
Rebel 300	5/13/67	Richard Petty	2	1967 Plymouth	125.738	12	6	5	31	Petty Enterprises	David Pearson	144.536
Rebel 400	5/11/68	David Pearson	2	1968 Ford	132.699	13	7	4	23	Holman-Moody	LeeRoy Yarbrough	148.850
Rebel 400	5/10/69	LeeRoy Yarbrough	4	1969 Mercury	131.572	11	6	4	24	Junior Johnson	Cale Yarborough	152.293
Rebel 400	5/9/70	David Pearson	3	Ford	129.668	20	7	4	37	Holman-Moody	Charlie Glotzbach	153.822
Rebel 400	5/2/71	Buddy Baker	5	Dodge	130.678	13	6	5	30	Petty Enterprises	Donnie Allison	149.826
Rebel 400	4/16/72	David Pearson	1	Mercury	124.406	14	7	5	37	Wood Brothers	David Pearson	148.209
Rebel 500	4/15/73	David Pearson	1	Mercury	122.655	21	5	11	71	Wood Brothers	David Pearson	153.463
Rebel 450	4/7/74	David Pearson	2	Mercury	117.543	29	8	7	66	Wood Brothers	Donnie Allison	150.689
Rebel 500	4/13/75	Bobby Allison	5	Matador	117.597	22	10	11	79	Roger Penske	David Pearson	155.433
Rebel 500	4/11/76	David Pearson	1	Mercury	122.973	32	10	8	54	Wood Brothers	David Pearson	154.171
Rebel 500	4/3/77	Darrell Waltrip	4	Chevrolet	128.817	28	7	6	39	DiGard	David Pearson	151.269
Rebel 500	4/9/78	Benny Parsons	8	Chevrolet	127.544	24	9	7	44	L.G. DeWitt	Bobby Allison	151.862
CRC Chemicals Rebel 500	4/8/79	Darrell Waltrip	2	Chevrolet	121.721	25	8	6	53	DiGard	Donnie Allison	154.797
CRC Chemicals Rebel 500	4/13/80	David Pearson	2	Chevrolet	112.397	12	7	7	47	Hoss Ellington	Benny Parsons	155.866
CRC Chemicals Rebel 500	4/12/81	Darrell Waltrip	3	Buick	126.703	20	5	6	40	Junior Johnson	Bill Elliott	153.896
CRC Chemicals Rebel 500	4/4/82	Dale Earnhardt	5	Ford	123.554	30	11	8	53	Bud Moore	Buddy Baker	153.979
TranSouth 500	4/10/83	Harry Gant	5	Buick	130.406	20	8	5	37	Hal Needham	Tim Richmond	157.818
TranSouth 500	4/15/84	Darrell Waltrip	9	Chevrolet	119.925	19	11	9	65	Junior Johnson	Benny Parsons	156.328
TranSouth 500	4/14/85	Bill Elliott	1	Ford	126.295	22	9	7	51	Harry Melling	Bill Elliott	157.454
TranSouth 500	4/13/86	Dale Earnhardt	4	Chevrolet	128.994	17	8	11	54	Richard Childress	Geoffrey Bodine	159.197
TranSouth 500	3/29/87	Dale Earnhardt	2	Chevrolet	122.540	27	11	10	71	Richard Childress	Ken Schrader	158.387
TranSouth 500	3/27/88	Lake Speed	8	Oldsmobile	131.284	18	11	8	42	Lake Speed	Ken Schrader	162.657
TranSouth 500	4/2/89	Harry Gant	10	Oldsmobile	115.475	14	9	7	68	Leo & Richard Jackson	Mark Martin	161.111
TranSouth 500	4/1/90	Dale Earnhardt	15	Chevrolet	124.073	20	10	10	51	Richard Childress	Geoffrey Bodine	162.996
TranSouth 500	4/7/91	Ricky Rudd	13	Chevrolet	135.594	15	7	3	19	Rick Hendrick	Geoffrey Bodine	161.939
TranSouth 500	3/29/92	Bill Elliott	2	Ford	139.364	21	7	4	21	Junior Johnson	Sterling Marlin	163.067
TranSouth 500	3/28/93	Dale Earnhardt	1	Chevrolet	139.958	18	11	3	14	Richard Childress	Dale Earnhardt	
TranSouth 400	3/27/94	Dale Earnhardt	9	Chevrolet	132.432	28	10	5	26	Richard Childress	Bill Elliott	165.553
TranSouth 400	3/26/95	Sterling Marlin	5	Chevrolet	111.392	16	11	15	87	Larry McClure	Jeff Gordon	170.833
TranSouth 400	3/24/96	Jeff Gordon	2	Chevrolet	124.792	15	9	11	56	Rick Hendrick	Ward Burton	173.797
TranSouth Financial 400	3/23/97	Dale Jarrett	1	Ford	141.410	15	7	10	60	Robert Yates	Dale Jarrett	171.095
TranSouth 400	3/22/98	Dale Jarrett	2	Ford	127.962	18	6	5	31	Robert Yates	Mark Martin	168.665
TranSouth 400	3/21/99	Jeff Burton	9	Ford	121.294	13	8	3	18	Jack Roush	Jeff Gordon	173.167
Mall.com 400	3/19/00	Ward Burton	3	Pontiac	128.076	13	7	5	30	Bill Davis	Jeff Gordon	172.662
Carolina Dodge Dealers 400	3/18/01	Dale Jarrett	2	Ford	126.558	12	7	7	38	Robert Yates	Jeff Gordon	0.000

Race	Date	Winner	Start Pos.	Make	Speed	Lead Ch.	No. Lds.	No. Caut.	Caut. Laps	Owner	Pole Winner	Pole Speed
Carolina												
Dodge Dealers 400	3/17/02	Sterling Marlin	11	Dodge	126.070	11	8	5	40	Chip Ganassi	Ricky Craven	170.089

DAYTONA INT'L SPEEDWAY
Daytona 500

Race	Date	Winner	Start Pos.	Make	Speed	Lead Ch.	No. Lds.	No. Caut.	Caut. Laps	Owner	Pole Winner	Pole Speed
Daytona 500	2/22/59	Lee Petty	15	59 Olds	135.521	34	7	0	0	Petty Enterprises	Bob Welborn	140.121
Daytona 500	2/14/60	Junior Johnson	9	59 Chevrolet	124.740	13	8		32	John Masoni	Cotton Owens	149.892
Daytona 500	2/26/61	Marvin Panch	4	60 Pontiac	149.601	9	5	0	0	Smokey Yunick	Fireball Roberts	155.709
Daytona 500	2/18/62	Fireball Roberts	1	62 Pontiac	152.529	22	5	0	0	Jim Stephens	Fireball Roberts	156.999
Daytona 500	2/24/63	Tiny Lund	12	63 Ford	151.566	30	11	2	10	Wood Brothers	Fireball Roberts	165.183
Daytona 500	2/23/64	Richard Petty	2	1964 Plymouth	154.334	1	2	3	19	Petty Enterprises	Paul Goldsmith	174.910
Daytona 500	2/14/65	Fred Lorenzen	4	1965 Ford	141.539	7	4	3	43	Holman-Moody	Darel Dieringer	171.151
Daytona 500	2/27/66	Richard Petty	1	1966 Plymouth	160.627	14	6	4	22	Petty Enterprises	Richard Petty	175.163
Daytona 500	2/26/67	Mario Andretti	12	1967 Ford	146.926	36	9	6	54	Holman-Moody	Curtis Turner	180.831
Daytona 500	2/25/68	Cale Yarborough	1	1968 Mercury	143.251	21	9	11	60	Wood Brothers	Cale Yarborough	189.222
Daytona 500	2/23/69	LeeRoy Yarbrough	19	1969 Ford	157.950	17	8	5	38	Junior Johnson	Buddy Baker	188.901
Daytona 500	2/22/70	Pete Hamilton	9	Plymouth	149.601	24	10	6	45	Petty Enterprises	Cale Yarborough	194.015
Daytona 500	2/14/71	Richard Petty	5	Plymouth	144.462	48	11	7	44	Petty Enterprises	A.J. Foyt	182.744
Daytona 500	2/20/72	A.J. Foyt	2	Mercury	161.550	13	3	3	17	Wood Brothers	Bobby Isaac	186.632
Daytona 500	2/18/73	Richard Petty	7	Dodge	157.205	20	5	4	28	Petty Enterprises	Buddy Baker	185.662
Daytona 500	2/17/74	Richard Petty	2	Dodge	140.894	59	15	10	53	Petty Enterprises	David Pearson	185.817
Daytona 500	2/16/75	Benny Parsons	32	Chevrolet	153.649	19	7	3	21	L.G. DeWitt	Donnie Allison	185.827
Daytona 500	2/15/76	David Pearson	7	Mercury	152.181	36	11	7	35	Wood Brothers	Ramo Stott	183.456
Daytona 500	2/20/77	Cale Yarborough	4	Chevrolet	153.218	30	10	6	37	Junior Johnson	Donnie Allison	188.048
Daytona 500	2/19/78	Bobby Allison	33	Ford	159.730	37	6	5	24	Bud Moore	Cale Yarborough	187.536
Daytona 500	2/18/79	Richard Petty	13	Oldsmobile	143.977	36	13	7	57	Petty Enterprises	Buddy Baker	196.049
Daytona 500	2/17/80	Buddy Baker	1	Oldsmobile	177.602	29	7	5	15	Harry Ranier	Buddy Baker	194.009
Daytona 500	2/15/81	Richard Petty	8	Buick	169.651	49	9	4	18	Petty Enterprises	Bobby Allison	194.624
Daytona 500	2/14/82	Bobby Allison	7	Buick	153.991	31	10	5	34	DiGard	Benny Parsons	196.317
Daytona 500	2/20/83	Cale Yarborough	8	Pontiac	155.979	58	11	6	36	Harry Ranier	Ricky Rudd	198.864
Daytona 500	2/19/84	Cale Yarborough	1	Chevrolet	150.994	34	9	7	39	Harry Ranier	Cale Yarborough	201.848
Daytona 500	2/17/85	Bill Elliott	1	Ford	172.265	22	9	5	18	Harry Melling	Bill Elliott	205.114
Daytona 500	2/16/86	Geoffrey Bodine	2	Chevrolet	148.124	27	12	8	46	Rick Hendrick	Bill Elliott	205.039
Daytona 500	2/15/87	Bill Elliott	1	Ford	176.263	28	10	4	15	Harry Melling	Bill Elliott	210.364
Daytona 500	2/14/88	Bobby Allison	3	Buick	137.531	26	12	7	42	Stavola Brothers	Ken Schrader	193.823
Daytona 500	2/19/89	Darrell Waltrip	2	Chevrolet	148.466	30	15	7	30	Rick Hendrick	Ken Schrader	196.996
Daytona 500	2/18/90	Derrike Cope	12	Chevrolet	165.761	27	13	3	15	Bob Whitcomb	Ken Schrader	196.515
Daytona 500	2/19/91	Ernie Irvan	2	Chevrolet	148.148	21	9	9	36	Larry McClure	Davey Allison	195.955
Daytona 500	2/16/92	Davey Allison	6	Ford	160.256	15	7	4	22	Robert Yates	Sterling Marlin	192.213
Daytona 500 by STP	2/14/93	Dale Jarrett	2	Chevrolet	154.972	38	13	7	30	Joe Gibbs	Kyle Petty	189.426
Daytona 500 by STP	2/20/94	Sterling Marlin	4	Chevrolet	156.931	33	13	4	23	Larry McClure	Loy Allen, Jr.	190.158
Daytona 500	2/19/95	Sterling Marlin	3	Chevrolet	141.710	12	7	10	41	Larry McClure	Dale Jarrett	193.498
Daytona 500	2/18/96	Dale Jarrett	7	Ford	154.308	32	15	6	26	Robert Yates	Dale Earnhardt	189.510
Daytona 500	2/16/97	Jeff Gordon	6	Chevrolet	148.295	12	9	8	29	Rick Hendrick	Mike Skinner	189.813
Daytona 500	2/15/98	Dale Earnhardt	4	Chevrolet	172.712	13	8	3	9	Richard Childress	Bobby Labonte	192.415
Daytona 500	2/14/99	Jeff Gordon	1	Chevrolet	161.551	14	7	4	20	Rick Hendrick	Jeff Gordon	195.067
Daytona 500	2/20/00	Dale Jarrett	1	Ford	155.669	9	7	6	24	Robert Yates	Dale Jarrett	191.091
Daytona 500	2/18/01	Michael Waltrip	19	Chevrolet	161.783	49	14	3	14	Dale Earnhardt, Inc.	Bill Elliott	183.565
Daytona 500	2/17/02	Ward Burton	19	Dodge	130.810	20	12	9	38	Bill Davis	Jimmie Johnson	185.831

Firecracker/Pepsi 250/400

Race	Date	Winner	Start Pos.	Make	Speed	Lead Ch.	No. Lds.	No. Caut.	Caut. Laps	Owner	Pole Winner	Pole Speed
Firecracker 250	7/4/59	Fireball Roberts	1	59 Pontiac	140.581	7	4	0	0	Jim Stephens	Fireball Roberts	144.997
Firecracker 250	7/4/60	Jack Smith	1	60 Pontiac	146.842	10	3	0	0	Jack Smith	Jack Smith	152.129
Firecracker 250	7/4/61	David Pearson	2	61 Pontiac	154.294	12	6	0	0	John Masoni	Fireball Roberts	157.150
Firecracker 250	7/4/62	Fireball Roberts	4	62 Pontiac	53.688	14	3	2	7	Banjo Matthews	Banjo Matthews	160.499
Firecracker 400	7/4/63	Fireball Roberts	3	63 Ford	150.927	39	6	3	19	Holman-Moody	Junior Johnson	166.005
Firecracker 400	7/4/64	A.J. Foyt	19	1964 Dodge	151.451	19	4	5	25	Ray Nichels	Darel Dieringer	172.678
Firecracker 400	7/4/65	A.J. Foyt	11	1965 Ford	150.046	19	7	3	20	Wood Brothers	Marvin Panch	171.510
Firecracker 400	7/4/66	Sam McQuagg	4	1966 Dodge	153.613	17	6	4	23	Ray Nichels	LeeRoy Yarbrough	176.660
Firecracker 400	7/4/67	Cale Yarborough	2	1967 Ford	143.583	41	8	4	43	Wood Brothers	Darel Dieringer	179.802
Firecracker 400	7/4/68	Cale Yarborough	4	1968 Mercury	167.247	8	4	2	14	Wood Brothers	Charlie Glotzbach	185.156
Firecracker 400	7/4/69	LeeRoy Yarbrough	9	1969 Ford	160.875	16	7	2	27	Junior Johnson	Cale Yarborough	190.706
Firecracker 400	7/4/70	Donnie Allison	15	Ford	162.235	32	10	3	17	Banjo Matthews	Cale Yarborough	191.640
Firecracker 400	7/4/71	Bobby Isaac	21	Dodge	161.947	33	8	2	11	Nord Krauskopf	Donnie Allison	183.228

Race	Date	Winner	Start Pos.	Make	Speed	Lead Ch.	No. Lds.	No. Caut.	Caut. Laps	Owner	Pole Winner	Pole Speed
Firecracker 400	7/4/72	David Pearson	2	Mercury	160.821	23	6	2	14	Wood Brothers	Bobby Isaac	186.277
Firecracker 400	7/4/73	David Pearson	6	Mercury	158.468	25	5	2	17	Wood Brothers	Bobby Allison	179.619
Firecracker 400	7/4/74	David Pearson	1	Mercury	138.310	48	9	6	41	Wood Brothers	David Pearson	180.759
Firecracker 400	7/4/75	Richard Petty	13	Dodge	158.381	16	6	3	17	Petty Enterprises	Donnie Allison	186.737
Firecracker 400	7/4/76	Cale Yarborough	2	Chevrolet	160.966	41	8	2	14	Junior Johnson	A.J. Foyt	183.090
Firecracker 400	7/4/77	Richard Petty	5	Dodge	142.716	34	8	2	26	Petty Enterprises	Neil Bonnett	187.191
Firecracker 400	7/4/78	David Pearson	3	Mercury	154.340	29	10	4	21	Wood Brothers	Cale Yarborough	186.803
Firecracker 400	7/4/79	Neil Bonnett	2	Mercury	172.890	28	8	2	11	Wood Brothers	Buddy Baker	193.196
Firecracker 400	7/4/80	Bobby Allison	14	Mercury	173.473	40	8	3	11	Bud Moore	Cale Yarborough	194.670
Firecracker 400	7/4/81	Cale Yarborough	1	Buick	142.588	35	10	6	37	M.C. Anderson	Cale Yarborough	192.852
Firecracker 400	7/4/82	Bobby Allison	9	Buick	163.099	28	8	5	25	DiGard	Geoffrey Bodine	194.721
Firecracker 400	7/4/83	Buddy Baker	8	Ford	167.442	39	11	3	16	Wood Brothers	Cale Yarborough	196.635
Firecracker 400	7/4/84	Richard Petty	6	Pontiac	171.204	28	8	3	15	Mike Curb	Cale Yarborough	199.743
Firecracker 400	7/4/85	Greg Sacks	9	Chevrolet	158.730	19	10	6	26	DiGard	Bill Elliott	201.523
Firecracker 400	7/4/86	Tim Richmond	9	Chevrolet	131.916	31	14	8	58	Rick Hendrick	Cale Yarborough	203.519
Pepsi Firecracker 400	7/4/87	Bobby Allison	11	Buick	161.074	24	12	4	20	Stavola Brothers	Davey Allison	198.085
Pepsi Firecracker 400	7/2/88	Bill Elliott	38	Ford	163.302	21	9	3	15	Harry Melling	Darrell Waltrip	193.819
Pepsi 400	7/1/89	Davey Allison	8	Ford	132.207	28	11	12	42	Robert Yates	Mark Martin	191.861
Pepsi 400	7/7/90	Dale Earnhardt	3	Chevrolet	160.894	15	8	4	14	Richard Childress	Greg Sacks	195.533
Pepsi 400	7/6/91	Bill Elliott	10	Ford	159.116	18	11	4	18	Harry Melling	Sterling Marlin	190.331
Pepsi 400	7/4/92	Ernie Irvan	6	Chevrolet	170.457	17	8	2	8	Larry McClure	Sterling Marlin	189.366
Pepsi 400	7/3/93	Dale Earnhardt	5	Chevrolet	151.755	28	13	6	22	Richard Childress	Ernie Irvan	190.327
Pepsi 400	7/2/94	Jimmy Spencer	3	Ford	155.558	18	10	4	19	Junior Johnson	Dale Earnhardt	191.339
Pepsi 400	7/1/95	Jeff Gordon	3	Chevrolet	166.976	8	4	3	11	Rick Hendrick	Dale Earnhardt	191.355
Pepsi 400	7/6/96	Sterling Marlin	2	Chevrolet	161.602	9	6	3	11	Larry McClure	Jeff Gordon	188.869
Pepsi 400	7/5/97	John Andretti	3	Ford	157.791	16	11	4	16	Cale Yarborough	Mike Skinner	189.777
Pepsi 400	10/17/98	Jeff Gordon	8	Chevrolet	144.549	16	9	6	26	Rick Hendrick	Bobby Labonte	193.611
Pepsi 400	7/3/99	Dale Jarrett	12	Ford	169.213	17	9	3	9	Robert Yates	Joe Nemechek	194.860
Pepsi 400	7/1/00	Jeff Burton	9	Ford	148.576	10	8	5	23	Jack Roush	Dale Jarrett	187.547
Pepsi 400	7/7/01	Dale Earnhardt, Jr.	13	Chevrolet	157.601	14	9	3	15	Dale Earnhardt, Inc.	Sterling Marlin	183.778
Pepsi 400	7/7/02	Michael Waltrip	7	Chevrolet	135.952	6	6	9	39	Dale Earnhardt, Inc.	Kevin Harvick	185.040
Daytona 100	2/20/59	Bob Welborn	7	59 Chevrolet	143.198	10	4	0	0	W.J. Ridgeway	Fireball Roberts	140.581
Daytona 100	2/12/60	Fireball Roberts	2	60 Pontiac	137.614	1	1	2	5	John Hines	Jack Smith	149.892
Daytona 100	2/12/60	Jack Smith	1	60 Pontiac	146.520	0	1	2	2	Jack Smith	Jack Smith	148.157
Daytona 100	2/24/61	Fireball Roberts	1	61 Pontiac	129.711			5	10	Smokey Yunick	Fireball Roberts	133.037
Daytona 100	2/24/61	Joe Weatherly	1	61 Pontiac	152.671	8	3			Bud Moore	Fireball Roberts	154.122
Daytona 100	2/16/62	Fireball Roberts	1	62 Pontiac	156.999			0	0	Jim Stephens	Fireball Roberts	158.744
Daytona 100	2/16/62	Joe Weatherly	3	62 Pontiac	145.395	2	2			Bud Moore	Darel Dieringer	155.086
Daytona 100	2/22/63	Johnny Rutherford	9	63 Chevrolet	164.083					Smokey Yunick	Fireball Roberts	163.681
Daytona 100	2/22/63	Junior Johnson	2	63 Chevrolet	162.969	4	3			Ray Fox	Fireball Roberts	165.183
Daytona 100	2/21/64	Junior Johnson	2	1964 Dodge	170.777	4	3			Ray Fox	Richard Petty	174.910
Daytona 100	2/21/64	Bobby Isaac	4	1964 Dodge	169.811	6	4	0	0	Ray Nichels	Paul Goldsmith	174.418
100 Mile Qualifier	2/12/65	Junior Johnson	1	1965 Ford	165.669	3	3	0	0	Junior Johnson	Junior Johnson	171.151
100 Mile Qualifier	2/12/65	Darel Dieringer	1	1964 Mercury	111.076	10	3	1	13	Bud Moore	Darel Dieringer	170.551
100 Mile Qualifier	2/25/66	Earl Balmer	6	1965 Dodge	160.427	5	3	1	3	Ray Fox	Dick Hutcherson	175.165
100 Mile Qualifier	2/25/66	Paul Goldsmith	8	1965 Plymouth	153.191	5	5	1	7	Ray Nichels	Richard Petty	174.317
100 Mile Qualifier	2/24/67	Fred Lorenzen	6	1967 Ford	163.934	13	4	1		Holman-Moody	Curtis Turner	180.831
100 Mile Qualifier	2/24/67	LeeRoy Yarbrough	3	1967 Dodge	174.587	15	6	0	0	Jon Thorne	Curtis Turner	179.068
Twin 125 Qualifier	2/20/69	Bobby Isaac	1	1969 Dodge	152.181	6	5	2	15	Nord Krauskopf	Bobby Isaac	188.901
Twin 125 Qualifier	2/20/69	David Pearson	15	1969 Ford	151.668		5	2	16	Holman-Moody	Bobby Isaac	188.726
Twin 125 Qualifier #1	2/19/70	Cale Yarborough	1	Mercury	147.734	4	3	1	13	Wood Brothers	Buddy Baker	192.624
Twin 125 Qualifier #1	2/11/71	Pete Hamilton	2	Plymouth	168.728	20	4	1	3	Cotton Owens	A.J. Foyt	180.050
Twin 125 Qualifier #2	2/19/70	Charlie Glotzbach	2	Dodge	147.734	4	3	1	13	Ray Nichels	Cale Yarborough	192.624
Twin 125 Qualifier #2	2/11/71	David Pearson	4	Mercury	168.728	20	4	1	3	Holman-Moody	Bobby Isaac	180.050

DOVER DOWNS INT'L SPEEDWAY
Spring Race

Race	Date	Winner	Start Pos.	Make	Speed	Lead Ch.	No. Lds.	No. Caut.	Caut. Laps	Owner	Pole Winner	Pole Speed
Mason-Dixon 300	7/6/69	Richard Petty	3	1969 Ford	115.772	7	3	4	27	Petty Enterprises	David Pearson	130.430
Mason-Dixon 300	9/20/70	Richard Petty	2	Plymouth	112.103	10	3	4	27	Petty Enterprises	Bobby Isaac	129.538
Mason-Dixon 500	6/6/71	Bobby Allison	2	Mercury	123.119	21	6	0	0	Holman-Moody	Richard Petty	129.486
Mason-Dixon 500	6/4/72	Bobby Allison	2	Chevrolet	118.019	13	4	3	25	Richard Howard	Bobby Isaac	130.809
Mason-Dixon 500	6/3/73	David Pearson	1	Mercury	119.745	13	4	3	22	Wood Brothers	David Pearson	133.111

Race	Date	Winner	Start Pos.	Make	Speed	Lead Ch.	No. Lds.	No. Caut.	Caut. Laps	Owner	Pole Winner	Pole Speed
Mason-Dixon 500	5/19/74	Cale Yarborough	3	Chevrolet	115.057	9	3	3	25	Richard Howard	David Pearson	134.403
Mason-Dixon 500	5/18/75	David Pearson	1	Mercury	100.820	19	5	8	101	Wood Brothers	David Pearson	136.612
Mason-Dixon 500	5/16/76	Benny Parsons	7	Chevrolet	115.436	17	5	6	38	L.G. DeWitt	Dave Marcis	136.013
Mason-Dixon 500	5/15/77	Cale Yarborough	6	Chevrolet	123.327	11	5	2	10	Junior Johnson	Richard Petty	136.033
Mason-Dixon 500	5/21/78	David Pearson	3	Mercury	114.664	16	9	6	37	Wood Brothers	Buddy Baker	135.452
Mason-Dixon 500	5/20/79	Neil Bonnett	5	Mercury	111.269	26	8	6	48	Wood Brothers	Darrell Waltrip	136.103
Mason-Dixon 500	5/18/80	Bobby Allison	8	Ford	113.866	17	6	9	67	Bud Moore	Cale Yarborough	138.814
Mason-Dixon 500	5/17/81	Jody Ridley	11	Ford	116.595	12	5	2	24	Junie Donlavey	David Pearson	138.425
Mason-Dixon 500	5/16/82	Bobby Allison	3	Chevrolet	120.136	9	3	6	32	DiGard	Darrell Waltrip	139.308
Mason-Dixon 500	5/15/83	Bobby Allison	10	Buick	114.847	28	9	9	53	DiGard	Joe Ruttman	139.616
Budweiser 500	5/20/84	Richard Petty	5	Pontiac	118.717	26	7	6	40	Mike Curb	Ricky Rudd	140.807
Budweiser 500	5/19/85	Bill Elliott	4	Ford	123.094	7	4	5	37	Harry Melling	Terry Labonte	138.106
Budweiser 500	5/18/86	Geoffrey Bodine	3	Chevrolet	115.009	29	10	8	67	Rick Hendrick	Ricky Rudd	138.217
Budweiser 500	5/31/87	Davey Allison	2	Ford	112.958	18	8	9	59	Harry Ranier	Bill Elliott	145.056
Budweiser 500	6/5/88	Bill Elliott	17	Ford	118.726	25	11	7	45	Harry Melling	Alan Kulwicki	146.681
Budweiser 500	6/4/89	Dale Earnhardt	2	Chevrolet	121.670	19	7	6	36	Richard Childress	Mark Martin	144.387
Dover 500	6/3/90	Derrike Cope	15	Chevrolet	123.960	22	9	5	32	Bob Whitcomb	Dick Trickle	145.814
Budweiser 500	6/2/91	Ken Schrader	19	Chevrolet	120.152	22	9	6	42	Rick Hendrick	Michael Waltrip	143.392
Budweiser 500	5/31/92	Harry Gant	15	Oldsmobile	109.456	20	11	7	98	Leo Jackson	Brett Bodine	147.408
Budweiser 500	6/6/93	Dale Earnhardt	8	Chevrolet	105.600	25	12	14	78	Richard Childress	Ernie Irvan	151.541
Budweiser 500	6/5/94	Rusty Wallace	6	Ford	102.529	22	8	12	99	Roger Penske	Ernie Irvan	151.956
Miller Genuine Draft 500	6/4/95	Kyle Petty	37	Pontiac	119.880	20	8	5	38	Felix Sabates	Jeff Gordon	153.669
Miller 500	6/2/96	Jeff Gordon	1	Chevrolet	122.741	19	6	5	38	Rick Hendrick	Jeff Gordon	154.785
Miller 500	6/1/97	Ricky Rudd	13	Ford	114.635	23	13	8	54	Ricky Rudd	Bobby Labonte	152.788
MBNA Platinum 400	5/31/98	Dale Jarrett	4	Ford	119.522	13	7	5	35	Robert Yates	Rusty Wallace	155.898
MBNA Platinum 400	6/6/99	Bobby Labonte	1	Pontiac	120.603	15	7	4	31	Joe Gibbs	Bobby Labonte	159.320
MBNA Platinum 400	6/4/00	Tony Stewart	16	Pontiac	109.514	14	10	10	58	Joe Gibbs	Rusty Wallace	157.411
MBNA Platinum 400	6/3/01	Jeff Gordon	2	Chevrolet	120.361	16	8	5	31	Rick Hendrick	Dale Jarrett	
MBNA Platinum 400	6/2/02	Jimmie Johnson	10	Chevrolet	117.551	14	8	7	40	Rick Hendrick	Matt Kenseth	154.938

Fall Race

Race	Date	Winner	Start Pos.	Make	Speed	Lead Ch.	No. Lds.	No. Caut.	Caut. Laps	Owner	Pole Winner	Pole Speed
Delaware 500	10/17/71	Richard Petty	4	Plymouth	123.254	3	3	2	9	Petty Enterprises	Bobby Allison	132.811
Delaware 500	9/17/72	David Pearson	2	Mercury	120.506	14	4	2	22	Wood Brothers	Bobby Allison	133.323
Delaware 500	9/16/73	David Pearson	1	Mercury	112.852	22	5	7	56	Wood Brothers	David Pearson	124.649
Delaware 500	9/15/74	Richard Petty	2	Dodge	113.640	6	6	7	55	Petty Enterprises	Buddy Baker	133.640
Delaware 500	9/14/75	Richard Petty	3	Dodge	111.372	18	7	5	41	Petty Enterprises	Dave Marcis	133.953
Delaware 500	9/19/76	Cale Yarborough	1	Chevrolet	115.740	21	6	2	27	Junior Johnson	Cale Yarborough	115.740
Delaware 500	9/18/77	Benny Parsons	7	Chevrolet	114.708	9	4	3	25	L.G. DeWitt	Neil Bonnett	134.233
Delaware 500	9/17/78	Bobby Allison	2	Ford	119.323	7	5	3	18	Bud Moore	J.D. McDuffie	135.480
CRC Chemicals 500	9/16/79	Richard Petty	4	Chevrolet	114.366	27	7	11	49	Petty Enterprises	Dale Earnhardt	135.726
CRC Chemicals 500	9/14/80	Darrell Waltrip	2	Oldsmobile	116.024	29	11	8	39	DiGard	Cale Yarborough	137.583
CRC Chemicals 500	9/20/81	Neil Bonnett	3	Ford	119.561	17	9	4	22	Wood Brothers	Ricky Rudd	136.757
CRC Chemicals 500	9/19/82	Darrell Waltrip	3	Buick	107.642	26	11	9	67	Junior Johnson	Ricky Rudd	139.384
Budweiser Delaware 500	9/18/83	Bobby Allison	7	Buick	116.077	21	8	7	51	DiGard	Terry Labonte	139.573
Delaware 500	9/16/84	Harry Gant	3	Chevrolet	111.856	19	9	10	73	Hal Needham	Terry Labonte	
Delaware 500	9/15/85	Harry Gant	4	Chevrolet	120.538	17	6	6	45	Hal Needham	Bill Elliott	141.543
Delaware 500	9/14/86	Ricky Rudd	11	Ford	114.329	27	11	13	88	Bud Moore	Geoffrey Bodine	146.205
Delaware 500	9/20/87	Ricky Rudd	13	Ford	124.706	19	7	6	31	Bud Moore	Alan Kulwicki	145.826
Delaware 500	9/18/88	Bill Elliott	3	Ford	109.349	22	8	14	84	Harry Melling	Mark Martin	148.075
Peak Performance 500	9/17/89	Dale Earnhardt	15	Chevrolet	122.909	18	7	5	31	Richard Childress	Davey Allison	146.169
Peak AntiFreeze 500	9/16/90	Bill Elliott	1	Ford	125.945	11	5	6	29	Harry Melling	Bill Elliott	144.928
Peak AntiFreeze 500	9/15/91	Harry Gant	10	Oldsmobile	110.179	10	7	9	70	Leo Jackson	Alan Kulwicki	146.825
Peak AntiFreeze 500	9/20/92	Ricky Rudd	6	Chevrolet	115.289	13	7	9	48	Rick Hendrick	Alan Kulwicki	145.267
SplitFire Spark Plug 500	9/19/93	Rusty Wallace	1	Pontiac	100.334	18	8	16	103	Roger Penske	Rusty Wallace	151.464
SplitFire Spark Plug 500	9/18/94	Rusty Wallace	10	Ford	112.556	26	12	13	72	Roger Penske	Geoffrey Bodine	152.840
MBNA 500	9/17/95	Jeff Gordon	2	Chevrolet	124.740	10	7	5	34	Rick Hendrick	Rick Mast	153.446
MBNA 500	9/15/96	Jeff Gordon	3	Chevrolet	105.646	28	12	14	91	Rick Hendrick	Bobby Labonte	155.086
MBNA 500	9/21/97	Mark Martin	1	Ford	132.719	10	4	1	11	Jack Roush	Mark Martin	152.033
MBNA Gold 400	9/20/98	Mark Martin	1	Ford	113.834	9	4	7	47	Jack Roush	Mark Martin	155.966
MBNA Gold 400	9/26/99	Mark Martin	8	Ford	127.434	25	10	4	22	Jack Roush	Rusty Wallace	159.964
MBNA.com 400	9/24/00	Tony Stewart	27	Pontiac	115.191	25	13	8	45	Joe Gibbs	Jeremy Mayfield	159.872
MBNA Cal Ripken, Jr. 400	9/23/01	Dale Earnhardt, Jr.	3	Chevrolet	101.559	13	7	11	71	Dale Earnhardt, Inc.	Dale Jarrett	154.919

Race	Date	Winner	Start Pos.	Make	Speed	Lead Ch.	No. Lds.	No. Caut.	Caut. Laps	Owner	Pole Winner	Pole Speed
MBNA All-American Heroes 400	9/22/02	Jimmie Johnson	19	Chevrolet	120.805	15	7	6	37	Rick Hendrick	Rusty Wallace	156.822
HOMESTEAD-MIAMI SPEEDWAY												
Pennzoil 400	11/14/99	Tony Stewart	7	Pontiac	140.335	19	10	1	5	Joe Gibbs	David Green	155.759
Pennzoil 400	11/12/00	Tony Stewart	13	Pontiac	127.480	15	7	4	25	Joe Gibbs	Steve Park	156.440
Pennzoil Freedom 400	11/11/01	Bill Elliott	1	Dodge	117.449	19	7	6	41	Ray Evernham	Bill Elliott	155.226
Ford 400	11/17/02	Kurt Busch	1	Ford	116.462	12	6	6	41	Jack Roush	Kurt Busch	154.365
INDIANAPOLIS MOTOR SPEEDWAY												
Brickyard 400	8/6/94	Jeff Gordon	3	Chevrolet	131.977	21	13	6	25	Rick Hendrick	Rick Mast	172.414
Brickyard 400	8/5/95	Dale Earnhardt	13	Chevrolet	155.206	17	10	1	4	Richard Childress	Jeff Gordon	172.536
Brickyard 400	8/3/96	Dale Jarrett	24	Ford	139.508	18	13	5	21	Robert Yates	Jeff Gordon	176.419
Brickyard 400	8/2/97	Ricky Rudd	7	Ford	130.828	20	11	6	25	Ricky Rudd	Ernie Irvan	177.736
Brickyard 400	8/1/98	Jeff Gordon	3	Chevrolet	126.770	10	7	9	34	Rick Hendrick	Ernie Irvan	179.394
Brickyard 400	8/7/99	Dale Jarrett	4	Ford	148.228	13	6	3	12	Robert Yates	Jeff Gordon	179.612
Brickyard 400	8/5/00	Bobby Labonte	3	Pontiac	155.912	9	5	2	7	Joe Gibbs	Ricky Rudd	181.068
Brickyard 400	8/5/01	Jeff Gordon	27	Chevrolet	130.790	18	12	7	28	Rick Hendrick	Jimmy Spencer	179.666
Brickyard 400	8/4/02	Bill Elliott	2	Dodge	125.033	16	10	8	36	Ray Evernham	Tony Stewart	182.960
INFINEON RACEWAY												
Banquet Frozen Foods 300	6/11/89	Ricky Rudd	4	Buick	76.088	3	3	3	16	Kenny Bernstein	Rusty Wallace	90.041
Banquet Frozen Foods 300	6/10/90	Rusty Wallace	11	Pontiac	69.245	8	6	9	24	Raymond Beadle	Ricky Rudd	99.743
Banquet Frozen Foods 300	6/9/91	Davey Allison	13	Ford	72.970	9	7	5	14	Robert Yates	Ricky Rudd	90.634
Save Mart 300k	6/7/92	Ernie Irvan	2	Chevrolet	81.412	7	8	3	7	Larry McClure	Ricky Rudd	90.985
Save Mart 300k	5/16/93	Geoffrey Bodine	3	Ford	77.013	9	6	5	11	Bud Moore	Dale Earnhardt	91.838
Save Mart Supermarkets 300k	5/15/94	Ernie Irvan	1	Ford	77.458	7	5	4	10	Robert Yates	Ernie Irvan	91.514
Save Mart Supermarkets 300k	5/7/95	Dale Earnhardt	4	Chevrolet	70.681	4	4	5	14	Richard Childress	Ricky Rudd	92.132
Save Mart 300k	5/5/96	Rusty Wallace	7	Ford	77.673	9	7	5	10	Roger Penske	Terry Labonte	92.524
Save Mart Supermarkets 300	5/4/97	Mark Martin	1	Ford	75.788	6	4	3	9	Jack Roush	Mark Martin	92.807
SaveMart Supermarkets 300	6/28/98	Jeff Gordon	1	Chevrolet	72.387	9	9	5	23	Rick Hendrick	Jeff Gordon	98.711
SaveMart / Kragen 350	6/27/99	Jeff Gordon	1	Chevrolet	70.378	7	4	7	26	Rick Hendrick	Jeff Gordon	98.519
SaveMart / Kragen 350	6/25/00	Jeff Gordon	5	Chevrolet	78.789	10	7	4	13	Rick Hendrick	Rusty Wallace	99.309
Dodge / SaveMart 350	6/24/01	Tony Stewart	3	Pontiac	75.889	10	8	5	17	Joe Gibbs	Jeff Gordon	93.699
Dodge / SaveMart 350	6/23/02	Ricky Rudd	7	Ford	81.007	10	9	3	9	Robert Yates	Tony Stewart	93.476
KANSAS SPEEDWAY												
Protection One 400	9/30/01	Jeff Gordon	2	Chevrolet	110.576	19	12	13	70	Rick Hendrick	Jason Leffler	176.499
Protection One 400	9/29/02	Jeff Gordon	10	Chevrolet	119.394	13	10	11	52	Rick Hendrick	Dale Earnhardt, Jr.	177.924
LAS VEGAS MOTOR SPEEDWAY												
Las Vegas 400	3/1/98	Mark Martin	7	Ford	146.530	24	12	2	9	Jack Roush	Dale Jarrett	168.224
Las Vegas 400	3/7/99	Jeff Burton	19	Ford	137.535	25	10	5	22	Jack Roush	Bobby Labonte	170.643
CarsDirect.com 400	3/5/00	Jeff Burton	11	Ford	119.982	13	7	2	28	Jack Roush	Ricky Rudd	172.563
UAW-Daimler Chrysler 400	3/4/01	Jeff Gordon	24	Chevrolet		20	13	6	25	Rick Hendrick	Dale Jarrett	172.106
UAW-Daimler Chrysler 400	3/3/02	Sterling Marlin	24	Dodge	136.754	21	13	6	25	Chip Ganassi	Todd Bodine	172.850
LOWES MOTOR SPEEDWAY												
World 600	6/19/60	Joe Lee Johnson	20	60 Chevrolet	107.735	11	6	8	45	Paul McDuffie	Fireball Roberts	133.904
World 600	5/28/61	David Pearson	3	61 Pontiac	111.633	17	7	7	57	John Masoni	Richard Petty	131.611
World 600	5/27/62	Nelson Stacy	18	62 Ford	125.552	18	7	2	14	Holman-Moody	Fireball Roberts	140.150
World 600	6/2/63	Fred Lorenzen	2	63 Ford	132.417	15	6	2	14	Holman-Moody	Junior Johnson	141.148
World 600	5/24/64	Jim Paschal	12	1964 Plymouth	125.772	14	8	7	48	Petty Enterprises	Jimmy Pardue	144.346
World 600	5/23/65	Fred Lorenzen	1	1965 Ford	121.722	22	6	11	80	Holman-Moody	Fred Lorenzen	145.268
World 600	5/22/66	Marvin Panch	7	1965 Plymouth	135.042	14	8	5	18	Petty Enterprises	Richard Petty	148.637
World 600	5/28/67	Jim Paschal	10	1967 Plymouth	135.832	11	7	5	32	Friedkin Ent	Cale Yarborough	154.385

Race	Date	Winner	Start Pos.	Make	Speed	Lead Ch.	No. Lds.	No. Caut.	Caut. Laps	Owner	Pole Winner	Pole Speed
World 600	5/26/68	Buddy Baker	12	1968 Dodge	104.207	16	8	6	110	Ray Fox	Donnie Allison	159.223
World 600	5/25/69	LeeRoy Yarbrough	2	1969 Mercury	134.361	13	7	5	45	Junior Johnson	Donnie Allison	159.296
World 600	5/24/70	Donnie Allison	9	Ford	129.680	28	11	10	66	Banjo Matthews	Bobby Isaac	159.277
World 600	5/30/71	Bobby Allison	2	Mercury	140.422	13	5	3	24	Holman-Moody	Charlie Glotzbach	157.788
World 600	5/28/72	Buddy Baker	6	Dodge	142.255	22	4	3	24	Petty Enterprises	Bobby Allison	158.162
World 600	5/27/73	Buddy Baker	1	Dodge	134.890	23	6	6	48	Nord Krauskopf	Buddy Baker	158.051
World 600	5/26/74	David Pearson	1	Mercury	135.720	37	5	8	48	Wood Brothers	David Pearson	157.498
World 600	5/25/75	Richard Petty	3	Dodge	145.327	17	5	3	12	Petty Enterprises	David Pearson	159.353
World 600	5/30/76	David Pearson	1	Mercury	137.352	37	5	7	38	Wood Brothers	David Pearson	159.132
World 600	5/29/77	Richard Petty	2	Dodge	137.676	25	8	6	31	Petty Enterprises	David Pearson	161.435
World 600	5/28/78	Darrell Waltrip	17	Chevrolet	138.355	43	6	6	32	DiGard	David Pearson	160.551
World 600	5/27/79	Darrell Waltrip	3	Chevrolet	136.674	59	10	9	48	DiGard	Neil Bonnett	160.125
World 600	5/25/80	Benny Parsons	6	Chevrolet	119.265	47	12	14	113	M.C. Anderson	Cale Yarborough	165.194
World 600	5/24/81	Bobby Allison	7	Buick	129.326	32	7	7	50	Harry Ranier	Neil Bonnett	158.115
World 600	5/30/82	Neil Bonnett	13	Ford	130.058	47	12	10	62	Wood Brothers	David Pearson	162.511
World 600	5/29/83	Neil Bonnett	5	Chevrolet	140.707	23	9	5	28	RahMoc Enterprises	Buddy Baker	162.841
World 600	5/27/84	Bobby Allison	16	Buick	129.233	22	6	5	48	DiGard	Harry Gant	162.496
Coca-Cola World 600	5/26/85	Darrell Waltrip	4	Chevrolet	141.807	29	8	7	34	Junior Johnson	Bill Elliott	164.703
Coca-Cola 600	5/25/86	Dale Earnhardt	3	Chevrolet	140.406	38	15	6	32	Richard Childress	Geoffrey Bodine	164.511
Coca-Cola 600	5/24/87	Kyle Petty	7	Ford	131.483	23	10	12	68	Wood Brothers	Bill Elliott	170.901
Coca-Cola 600	5/29/88	Darrell Waltrip	5	Chevrolet	124.460	43	18	13	89	Rick Hendrick	Davey Allison	173.594
Coca-Cola 600	5/28/89	Darrell Waltrip	4	Chevrolet	144.077	21	12	7	36	Rick Hendrick	Alan Kulwicki	173.021
Coca-Cola 600	5/27/90	Rusty Wallace	9	Pontiac	137.650	15	10	11	48	Raymond Beadle	Ken Schrader	173.963
Coca-Cola 600	5/26/91	Davey Allison	10	Ford	138.951	22	10	9	54	Robert Yates	Mark Martin	174.820
Coca-Cola 600	5/24/92	Dale Earnhardt	13	Chevrolet	132.980	27	14	12	62	Richard Childress	Bill Elliott	175.479
Coca-Cola 600	5/30/93	Dale Earnhardt	14	Chevrolet	145.504	29	10	7	33	Richard Childress	Ken Schrader	177.352
Coca-Cola 600	5/29/94	Jeff Gordon	1	Chevrolet	139.445	24	8	9	47	Rick Hendrick	Jeff Gordon	181.439
Coca-Cola 600	5/28/95	Bobby Labonte	2	Chevrolet	151.952	32	12	7	33	Joe Gibbs	Jeff Gordon	183.861
Coca-Cola 600	5/26/96	Dale Jarrett	15	Ford	147.581	20	8	6	35	Robert Yates	Jeff Gordon	183.773
Coca-Cola 600	5/25/97	Jeff Gordon	1	Chevrolet	136.745	27	12	7	50	Rick Hendrick	Jeff Gordon	184.300
Coca-Cola 600	5/24/98	Jeff Gordon	1	Chevrolet	136.424	33	12	8	52	Rick Hendrick	Jeff Gordon	182.976
Coca-Cola 600	5/30/99	Jeff Burton	2	Ford	151.367	23	9	5	23	Jack Roush	Bobby Labonte	185.230
Coca-Cola 600	5/28/00	Matt Kenseth	21	Ford	142.640	25	11	7	38	Jack Roush	Dale Earnhardt, Jr.	186.034
Coca-Cola 600	5/27/01	Jeff Burton	18	Ford	130.107	28	14	6	45	Jack Roush	Ryan Newman	185.217
Coca-Cola Racing Family 600	5/26/02	Mark Martin	25	Ford	137.729	21	11	9	48	Jack Roush	Jimmie Johnson	186.464
National 400	10/16/60	Speedy Thompson	3	60 Ford	112.905	8	5	7	34	Wood Brothers	Fireball Roberts	133.465
National 400	10/15/61	Joe Weatherly	6	61 Pontiac	119.950	13	5	3	18	Bud Moore	David Pearson	138.577
National 400	10/14/62	Junior Johnson	3	62 Pontiac	132.085	10	4	1	6	Ray Fox	Fireball Roberts	140.287
National 400	10/13/63	Junior Johnson	2	63 Chevrolet	132.105	13	5	3	17	Ray Fox	Marvin Panch	143.017
National 400	10/18/64	Fred Lorenzen	3	1964 Ford	134.475	10	4	4	21	Holman-Moody	Richard Petty	150.711
National 400	10/17/65	Fred Lorenzen	1	1965 Ford	119.117	28	9	6	47	Holman-Moody	Fred Lorenzen	147.773
National 500	10/16/66	LeeRoy Yarbrough	17	1966 Dodge	130.576	14	6	6	46	Jon Thorne	Fred Lorenzen	150.533
National 500	10/15/67	Buddy Baker	4	1967 Dodge	130.317	22	11	9	64	Ray Fox	Cale Yarborough	154.872
National 500	10/20/68	Charlie Glotzbach	1	1968 Dodge	156.324	27	9	6	49	Cotton Owens	Charlie Glotzbach	156.060
National 500	10/12/69	Donnie Allison	3	1969 Ford	131.271	28	6	9	50	Banjo Matthews	Cale Yarborough	162.162
National 500	10/11/70	LeeRoy Yarbrough	5	Mercury	123.246	23	8	8	63	Junior Johnson	Charlie Glotzbach	147.273
National 500	10/10/71	Bobby Allison	3	Mercury	126.140	12	5	6	37	Holman-Moody	Charlie Glotzbach	157.085
National 500	10/8/72	Bobby Allison	4	Chevrolet	133.234	21	6	6	40	Richard Howard	David Pearson	158.539
National 500	10/7/73	Cale Yarborough	2	Chevrolet	145.240	12	7	2	16	Richard Howard	David Pearson	158.315
National 500	10/6/74	David Pearson	1	Mercury	119.912	47	11	9	79	Wood Brothers	David Pearson	158.749
National 500	10/5/75	Richard Petty	9	Dodge	132.209	29	13	7	53	Petty Enterprises	David Pearson	161.701
National 500	10/10/76	Donnie Allison	15	Chevrolet	141.226	26	7	3	18	Hoss Ellington	David Pearson	161.223
NAPA National 500	10/9/77	Benny Parsons	8	Chevrolet	142.780	18	7	4	18	L.G. DeWitt	David Pearson	160.892
NAPA National 500	10/8/78	Bobby Allison	8	Ford	141.826	40	9	4	21	Bud Moore	David Pearson	161.355
NAPA National 500	10/7/79	Cale Yarborough	4	Chevrolet	134.266	28	14	8	40	Junior Johnson	Neil Bonnett	164.304
National 500	10/5/80	Dale Earnhardt	4	Chevrolet	135.243	43	11	8	44	Rod Osterlund	Buddy Baker	165.634
National 500	10/11/81	Darrell Waltrip	1	Buick	117.483	27	13	12	78	Junior Johnson	Darrell Waltrip	162.744
National 500	10/10/82	Harry Gant	1	Buick	137.208	12	6	6	34	Hal Needham	Harry Gant	164.694
Miller High Life 500	10/9/83	Richard Petty	20	Pontiac	139.998	30	13	8	35	Petty Enterprises	Tim Richmond	163.073
Miller High Life 500	10/7/84	Bill Elliott	2	Ford	146.861	22	7	3	15	Harry Melling	Benny Parsons	165.579

Race	Date	Winner	Start Pos.	Make	Speed	Lead Ch.	No. Lds.	No. Caut.	Caut. Laps	Owner	Pole Winner	Pole Speed
Miller High Life 500	10/6/85	Cale Yarborough	7	Ford	136.761	15	6	6	41	Harry Ranier	Harry Gant	166.139
Oakwood Homes 500	10/5/86	Dale Earnhardt	3	Chevrolet	132.403	26	9	6	44	Richard Childress	Tim Richmond	167.078
Oakwood Homes 500	10/11/87	Bill Elliott	7	Ford	128.443	29	17	7	59	Harry Melling	Bobby Allison	171.636
Oakwood Homes 500	10/9/88	Rusty Wallace	3	Pontiac	130.677	36	15	10	63	Raymond Beadle	Alan Kulwicki	175.896
All Pro Auto Parts 500	10/8/89	Ken Schrader	2	Chevrolet	149.863	19	9	4	21	Rick Hendrick	Bill Elliott	174.081
Mello Yello 500	10/7/90	Davey Allison	5	Ford	137.428	14	10	6	37	Robert Yates	Brett Bodine	174.385
Mello Yello 500	10/6/91	Geoffrey Bodine	6	Ford	138.984	10	4	6	38	Junior Johnson	Mark Martin	176.499
Mello Yello 500	10/11/92	Mark Martin	4	Ford	153.537	21	8	3	12	Jack Roush	Alan Kulwicki	179.027
Mello Yello 500	10/10/93	Ernie Irvan	2	Ford	154.537	9	4	2	11	Robert Yates	Jeff Gordon	
Mello Yello 500	10/9/94	Dale Jarrett	22	Chevrolet	145.922	30	16	7	34	Joe Gibbs	Ward Burton	185.759
UAW-GM Quality 500	10/8/95	Mark Martin	5	Ford	145.358	19	11	7	35	Jack Roush	Ricky Rudd	180.758
UAW-GM 500	10/6/96	Terry Labonte	16	Chevrolet	143.143	21	9	5	37	Rick Hendrick	Bobby Labonte	184.068
UAW-GM Quality 500	10/5/97	Dale Jarrett	5	Ford	144.323	20	9	4	33	Robert Yates	Geoffrey Bodine	184.256
UAW-GM Quality 500	10/4/98	Mark Martin	2	Ford	123.188	17	8	11	65	Jack Roush	Derrike Cope	181.690
UAW-GM Quality 500	10/10/99	Jeff Gordon	22	Chevrolet	160.306	21	10	2	9	Rick Hendrick	Bobby Labonte	185.682
UAW-GM Quality 500	10/8/00	Bobby Labonte	2	Pontiac	133.630	46	13	9	51	Joe Gibbs	Jeff Gordon	185.561
UAW-GM 500	10/7/01	Sterling Marlin	13	Dodge	139.006	19	9	8	40	Chip Ganassi	Jimmy Spencer	185.147
UAW-GM Quality 500	10/13/02	Jamie McMurray	5	Dodge	141.586	23	11	5	33	Chip Ganassi	Tony Stewart	
Charlotte 100	5/21/61	Joe Weatherly	3	61 Pontiac	115.591	3	3	2	14	Bud Moore	Fred Lorenzen	136.951
Charlotte 100	5/21/61	Richard Petty	7	61 Plymouth	133.554	2	3	0	0	Petty Enterprises	Eddie Gray	137.480

MARTINSVILLE SPEEDWAY
Spring 500–Lapper

Race	Date	Winner	Start Pos.	Make	Speed	Lead Ch.	No. Lds.	No. Caut.	Caut. Laps	Owner	Pole Winner	Pole Speed
Martinsville 75	5/21/50	Curtis Turner		50 Olds		1	2			John Eanes	Buck Baker	54.216
Martinsville 200	5/6/51	Curtis Turner	7	50 Olds		7	4			John Eanes	Tim Flock	55.062
Martinsville 200	4/6/52	Dick Rathmann	9	51 Hudson	42.862	7	5	4		Walt Chapman	Buck Baker	54.945
Martinsville 200	5/17/53	Lee Petty		53 Dodge		2	3			Petty Enterprises		
Martinsville 200	5/16/54	Jim Paschal		53 Olds	46.153	2	2	3		Bobby Griffin	Ralph Liguori	
Martinsville 200	5/15/55	Tim Flock	4	55 Chrysler	52.554	2	2	2		Carl Kiekhaefer	Bill Amick	58.823
Virginia 500	5/20/56	Buck Baker	1	56 Dodge	60.824	5	3	7	20	Carl Kiekhaefer	Buck Baker	66.103
Virginia 500	5/19/57	Buck Baker	14	57 Chevrolet	57.318	5	4	3	51	Hugh Babb	Paul Goldsmith	65.693
Virginia 500	4/20/58	Bob Welborn	20	57 Chevrolet	66.007	5	4	4		J.H. Petty	Buck Baker	61.166
Virginia 500	5/3/59	Lee Petty	24	57 Olds	59.512	4	4	3		Petty Enterprises	Bobby Johns	66.030
Virginia 500	4/10/60	Richard Petty	4	60 Plymouth	63.943	8	6	8		Petty Enterprises	Glen Wood	69.150
Virginia 500	4/9/61	Fred Lorenzen	2	61 Ford	68.366	1	2	2		Holman-Moody	Rex White	70.280
Virginia 500 Sweepstakes	4/30/61	Junior Johnson	17	61 Pontiac	66.278	2	3	1	6	Rex Lovette	Rex White	71.320
Virginia 500	4/22/62	Richard Petty	7	62 Plymouth	66.425	6	6	2		Petty Enterprises	Fred Lorenzen	71.287
Virginia 500	4/21/63	Richard Petty	8	63 Plymouth	64.823	3	3	5		Petty Enterprises	Rex White	72.000
Virginia 500	4/26/64	Fred Lorenzen	1	1964 Ford	70.098	5	3	2	14	Holman-Moody	Fred Lorenzen	74.472
Virginia 500	4/25/65	Fred Lorenzen	2	1965 Ford	66.765	6	3	5	49	Holman-Moody	Junior Johnson	74.503
Virginia 500	4/24/66	Jim Paschal	1	1966 Plymouth	69.156	6	4	1	6	Friedkin Ent	Jim Paschal	76.345
Virginia 500	4/23/67	Richard Petty	2	1967 Plymouth	67.446	11	4	8	57	Petty Enterprises	Darel Dieringer	77.319
Virginia 500	4/28/68	Cale Yarborough	3	1968 Mercury	66.686	9	5	10	72	Wood Brothers	David Pearson	78.230
Virginia 500	4/27/69	Richard Petty	6	1969 Ford	64.405	11	5	8	61	Petty Enterprises	Bobby Allison	78.260
Virginia 500	5/31/70	Bobby Isaac	2	Dodge	68.584	4	3	7	46	Nord Krauskopf	LeeRoy Yarbrough	82.609
Virginia 500	4/25/71	Richard Petty	3	Plymouth	77.707	10	4	1	3	Petty Enterprises	Donnie Allison	82.529
Virginia 500	4/30/72	Richard Petty	3	Plymouth	72.657	15	5	4	24	Petty Enterprises	Bobby Allison	84.163
Virginia 500	4/29/73	David Pearson	1	Mercury	70.251	11	3	7	49	Wood Brothers	David Pearson	86.369
Virginia 500	4/28/74	Cale Yarborough	1	Chevrolet	70.427	5	3	12	70	Richard Howard	Cale Yarborough	84.362
Virginia 500	4/27/75	Richard Petty	6	Dodge	69.282	18	7	4	58	Petty Enterprises	Benny Parsons	85.789
Virginia 500	4/25/76	Darrell Waltrip	4	Chevrolet	71.759	11	4	6	47	DiGard	Dave Marcis	86.286
Virginia 500	4/24/77	Cale Yarborough	5	Chevrolet	77.405	8	5	3	22	Junior Johnson	Neil Bonnett	88.923
Virginia 500	4/23/78	Darrell Waltrip	3	Chevrolet	77.971	6	3	4	27	DiGard	Lennie Pond	88.637
Virginia 500	4/22/79	Richard Petty	2	Chevrolet	76.562	11	5	5	32	Petty Enterprises	Darrell Waltrip	87.383
Virginia 500	4/27/80	Darrell Waltrip	1	Chevrolet	69.049	5	5	8	91	DiGard	Darrell Waltrip	88.566
Virginia 500	4/26/81	Morgan Shepherd	12	Pontiac	75.019	13	6	5	38	Cliff Stewart	Ricky Rudd	89.056
Virginia National Bank 500	4/25/82	Harry Gant	3	Buick	75.073	14	7	9	46	Hal Needham	Terry Labonte	89.988
Virginia National Bank 500	4/24/83	Darrell Waltrip	3	Chevrolet	66.460	13	7	9	105	Junior Johnson	Ricky Rudd	89.910
Sovran Bank 500	4/29/84	Geoffrey Bodine	6	Chevrolet	73.264	13	6	11	54	Rick Hendrick	Joe Ruttman	89.426

Race	Date	Winner	Start Pos.	Make	Speed	Lead Ch.	No. Lds.	No. Caut.	Caut. Laps	Owner	Pole Winner	Pole Speed
Sovran Bank 500	4/28/85	Harry Gant	13	Chevrolet	73.022	12	7	10	57	Hal Needham	Darrell Waltrip	90.279
Sovran Bank 500	4/27/86	Ricky Rudd	4	Ford	76.882	15	8	7	33	Bud Moore	Tim Richmond	90.716
Sovran Bank 500	4/26/87	Dale Earnhardt	4	Chevrolet	72.808	14	7	11	65	Richard Childress	Morgan Shepherd	92.355
Pannill Sweatshirts 500	4/24/88	Dale Earnhardt	14	Chevrolet	74.740	10	7	7	46	Richard Childress	Ricky Rudd	91.328
Pannill Sweatshirts 500	4/23/89	Darrell Waltrip	10	Chevrolet	79.025	12	6	5	31	Rick Hendrick	Geoffrey Bodine	93.097
Hanes Activewear 500	4/29/90	Geoffrey Bodine	1	Ford	77.423	12	5	10	44	Junior Johnson	Geoffrey Bodine	91.726
Hanes Activewear 500	4/28/91	Dale Earnhardt	10	Chevrolet	75.139	13	4	11	53	Richard Childress	Mark Martin	91.949
Hanes 500	4/26/92	Mark Martin	14	Ford	78.086	11	6	11	59	Jack Roush	Darrell Waltrip	92.956
Hanes 500	4/25/93	Rusty Wallace	5	Pontiac	79.078	10	4	8	49	Roger Penske	Geoffrey Bodine	93.887
Hanes 500	4/24/94	Rusty Wallace	1	Ford	76.700	11	5	11	65	Roger Penske	Rusty Wallace	92.942
Hanes 500	4/23/95	Rusty Wallace	15	Ford	72.145	8	5	7	84	Roger Penske	Bobby Labonte	93.308
Goody's Headache Powders 500	4/21/96	Rusty Wallace	5	Ford	81.410	18	7	6	36	Roger Penske	Ricky Craven	93.079
Goody's 500	4/20/97	Jeff Gordon	4	Chevrolet	70.290	4	3	11	103	Rick Hendrick	Kenny Wallace	93.961
Goody's 500	4/20/98	Bobby Hamilton	1	Chevrolet	70.709	15	6	14	96	Larry McClure	Bobby Hamilton	93.175
Goody's Body Pain 500	4/18/99	John Andretti	21	Pontiac	75.653	20	10	10	70	Petty Enterprises	Tony Stewart	95.275
Goody's Body Pain 500	4/9/00	Mark Martin	21	Ford	71.161	14	8	17	112	Jack Roush	Rusty Wallace	94.827
Virginia 500	4/8/01	Dale Jarrett	13	Ford	70.799	15	11	12	98	Robert Yates	Jeff Gordon	94.087
Virginia 500	4/14/02	Bobby Labonte	15	Pontiac	73.951	19	13	14	104	Joe Gibbs	Jeff Gordon	94.161

Fall 500-Lapper

Race	Date	Winner	Start Pos.	Make	Speed	Lead Ch.	No. Lds.	No. Caut.	Caut. Laps	Owner	Pole Winner	Pole Speed
Martinsville 100	9/25/49	Red Byron	3	49 Olds		2	3			Raymond Parks	Curtis Turner	0.000
Martinsville 100	10/15/50	Herb Thomas	19	50 Plymouth		2	0			Herb Thomas	Fonty Flock	54.761
Martinsville 200	10/14/51	Frank Mundy	3	51 Olds		4	5			Ted Chester	Herb Thomas	56.109
Martinsville 200	10/19/52	Herb Thomas	2	52 Hudson	47.556	7	3			Herb Thomas	Perk Brown	55.333
Martinsville 200	10/18/53	Jim Paschal		53 Dodge	56.013	2	2			George Hutchens	Fonty Flock	58.958
Martinsville 200	10/17/54	Lee Petty	1	Chrysler	44.547	4	2	3		Petty Enterprises	Lee Petty	53.191
Martinsville 200	10/16/55	Speedy Thompson	17	55 Chrysler		7	5	3		Carl Kiekhaefer	Gwyn Staley	
Mixed 400	10/28/56	Jack Smith	23	56 Dodge	61.136	7	6	4		Carl Kiekhaefer	Buck Baker	67.643
Sweepstakes 500	10/6/57	Bob Welborn	2	57 Chevrolet	63.025	6	4	4	14	Bob Welborn	Eddie Pagan	65.837
Old Dominion 500	10/12/58	Fireball Roberts	4	57 Chevrolet	64.344	1	2			Frank Strickland	Glen Wood	67.950
Virginia Sweepstakes 500	9/27/59	Rex White	14	59 Chevrolet	60.500	6	5	7		Rex White	Glen Wood	69.471
Old Dominion 500	9/25/60	Rex White	2	60 Chevrolet	60.439					Rex White	Glen Wood	68.440
Old Dominion 500	9/24/61	Joe Weatherly	4	61 Pontiac	62.586			7		Bud Moore	Fred Lorenzen	70.730
Old Dominion 500	9/23/62	Nelson Stacy	3	62 Ford	66.874	4	4	2		Holman-Moody	Fireball Roberts	71.513
Old Dominion 500	9/22/63	Fred Lorenzen	2	63 Ford	67.486	3	2	5	18	Holman-Moody	Junior Johnson	73.379
Old Dominion 500	9/27/64	Fred Lorenzen	1	1964 Ford	67.320	6	4	6	28	Holman-Moody	Fred Lorenzen	74.196
Old Dominion 500	9/26/65	Junior Johnson	3	1965 Ford	67.056	5	2	3	19	Junior Johnson	Richard Petty	74.503
Old Dominion 500	9/25/66	Fred Lorenzen	2	1966 Ford	69.177	6	4	4	26	Holman-Moody	Junior Johnson	75.598
Old Dominion 500	9/24/67	Richard Petty	5	1967 Plymouth	69.605	3	5	7	43	Petty Enterprises	Cale Yarborough	77.386
Old Dominion 500	9/22/68	Richard Petty	6	1968 Plymouth	65.808	11	5	7	60	Petty Enterprises	Cale Yarborough	77.279
Old Dominion 500	9/28/69	Richard Petty	6	1969 Ford	63.127	13	6	11	61	Petty Enterprises	David Pearson	83.197
Old Dominion 500	10/18/70	Richard Petty	4	Plymouth	72.235	5	4	5	32	Petty Enterprises	Bobby Allison	82.167
Old Dominion 500	9/26/71	Bobby Isaac	1	Dodge	73.681	12	3	3	33	Nord Krauskopf	Bobby Isaac	83.635
Old Dominion 500	9/24/72	Richard Petty	4	Plymouth	69.989	13	3	8	58	Petty Enterprises	Bobby Allison	85.890
Old Dominion 500	9/30/73	Richard Petty	6	Dodge	68.831	6	3	6	69	Petty Enterprises	Cale Yarborough	85.922
Old Dominion 500	9/29/74	Earl Ross	11	Chevrolet	66.232	11	7	10	78	Junior Johnson	Richard Petty	84.119
Old Dominion 500	9/28/75	Dave Marcis	7	Dodge	75.819	19	7	7	40	Nord Krauskopf	Cale Yarborough	86.199
Old Dominion 500	9/26/76	Cale Yarborough	4	Chevrolet	75.370	7	2	3	27	Junior Johnson	Darrell Waltrip	88.484
Old Dominion 500	9/25/77	Cale Yarborough	3	Chevrolet	73.447	13	5	9	57	Junior Johnson	Neil Bonnett	87.637
Old Dominion 500	9/24/78	Cale Yarborough	6	Oldsmobile	79.185	6	4	4	19	Junior Johnson	Lennie Pond	86.558
Old Dominion 500	9/23/79	Buddy Baker	7	Chevrolet	75.119	12	5	10	54	Harry Ranier	Darrell Waltrip	88.265
Old Dominion 500	9/28/80	Dale Earnhardt	7	Chevrolet	69.654	25	9	17	79	Rod Osterlund	Buddy Baker	88.500
Old Dominion 500	9/27/81	Darrell Waltrip	1	Buick	70.089	14	9	11	72	Junior Johnson	Darrell Waltrip	89.014
Old Dominion 500	10/17/82	Darrell Waltrip	3	Buick	71.315	23	11	10	70	Junior Johnson	Ricky Rudd	89.132
Goody's 500	9/25/83	Ricky Rudd	2	Chevrolet	76.134	6	5	6	37	Richard Childress	Darrell Waltrip	89.342
Goody's 500	9/23/84	Darrell Waltrip	3	Chevrolet	75.532	11	8	8	39	Junior Johnson	Geoffrey Bodine	89.523
Goody's 500	9/22/85	Dale Earnhardt	11	Chevrolet	70.694	11	7	12	65	Richard Childress	Geoffrey Bodine	90.521
Goody's 500	9/21/86	Rusty Wallace	8	Pontiac	73.191	15	9	12	54	Raymond Beadle	Geoffrey Bodine	90.599
Goody's 500	9/27/87	Darrell Waltrip	14	Chevrolet	76.410	13	6	8	35	Rick Hendrick	Geoffrey Bodine	91.218
Goody's 500	9/25/88	Darrell Waltrip	20	Chevrolet	74.988	11	6	11	53	Rick Hendrick	Rusty Wallace	91.372
Goody's 500	9/24/89	Darrell Waltrip	2	Chevrolet	76.571	18	7	8	46	Rick Hendrick	Dale Earnhardt	91.913

Race	Date	Winner	Start Pos.	Make	Speed	Lead Ch.	No. Lds.	No. Caut.	Caut. Laps	Owner	Pole Winner	Pole Speed
Goody's 500	9/23/90	Geoffrey Bodine	14	Ford	76.386	16	10	11	57	Junior Johnson	Mark Martin	91.571
Goody's 500	9/22/91	Harry Gant	12	Oldsmobile	74.535	20	12	15	81	Leo Jackson	Mark Martin	93.171
Goody's 500	9/28/92	Geoffrey Bodine	7	Ford	75.424	12	8	12	67	Bud Moore	Kyle Petty	92.497
Goody's 500	9/26/93	Ernie Irvan	1	Ford	74.101	9	4	11	74	Robert Yates	Ernie Irvan	92.583
Goody's 500	9/25/94	Rusty Wallace	7	Ford	77.139	18	9	11	62	Roger Penske	Ted Musgrave	94.129
Goody's 500	9/24/95	Dale Earnhardt	2	Chevrolet	73.946	16	8	10	85	Richard Childress	Jeff Gordon	
Hanes 500	9/22/96	Jeff Gordon	10	Chevrolet	82.223	11	4	7	35	Rick Hendrick	Bobby Hamilton	94.120
Hanes 500	9/29/97	Jeff Burton	10	Ford	73.072	15	7	11	83	Jack Roush	Ward Burton	93.410
NAPA Auto Care 500	9/27/98	Ricky Rudd	2	Ford	73.350	11	5	11	82	Ricky Rudd	Ernie Irvan	93.608
NAPA Auto Care 500	10/3/99	Jeff Gordon	5	Chevrolet	72.624	17	11	8	75	Rick Hendrick	Joe Nemechek	95.223
NAPA AutoCare 500	10/1/00	Tony Stewart	1	Pontiac	73.859	12	7	13	88	Joe Gibbs	Tony Stewart	95.371
Old Dominion 500	10/15/01	Ricky Craven	6	Ford	75.750	19	14	13	81	Cal Wells	Todd Bodine	93.724
Old Dominion 500	10/20/02	Kurt Busch	36	Ford	74.651	12	9	12	65	Jack Roush	Ryan Newman	92.837

MICHIGAN INT'L SPEEDWAY
June 500/400-Miler

Race	Date	Winner	Start Pos.	Make	Speed	Lead Ch.	No. Lds.	No. Caut.	Caut. Laps	Owner	Pole Winner	Pole Speed
Motor State 500	6/15/69	Cale Yarborough	4	1969 Mercury	139.254	35	9	7	35	Wood Brothers	Donnie Allison	160.135
Motor State 400	6/7/70	Cale Yarborough	4	Mercury	138.302	15	6	3	28	Wood Brothers	Pete Hamilton	162.737
Motor State 400	6/13/71	Bobby Allison	1	Mercury	149.567	32	5	2	13	Holman-Moody	Bobby Allison	161.190
Motor State 400	6/11/72	David Pearson	3	Mercury	146.639	20	6	2	12	Wood Brothers	Bobby Isaac	160.764
Motor State 400	6/24/73	David Pearson	2	Mercury	153.485	25	5	0	0	Wood Brothers	Buddy Baker	158.273
Motor State 360	6/16/74	Richard Petty	4	Dodge	127.098	50	9	6	40	Petty Enterprises	David Pearson	156.426
Motor State 400	6/15/75	David Pearson	3	Mercury	131.398	44	9	5	36	Wood Brothers	Cale Yarborough	158.541
Cam 2 Motor Oil 400	6/20/76	David Pearson	8	Mercury	141.148	17	7	3	20	Wood Brothers	Richard Petty	158.569
Cam 2 Motor Oil 400	6/19/77	Cale Yarborough	4	Chevrolet	135.033	19	8	4	25	Junior Johnson	David Pearson	159.175
Gabriel 400	6/18/78	Cale Yarborough	3	Oldsmobile	149.563	25	7	1	8	Junior Johnson	David Pearson	163.936
Gabriel 400	6/17/79	Buddy Baker	3	Chevrolet	135.798	46	12	6	33	Harry Ranier	Neil Bonnett	162.371
Gabriel 400	6/15/80	Benny Parsons	1	Chevrolet	131.808	25	5	7	43	M.C. Anderson	Benny Parsons	163.662
Gabriel 400	6/21/81	Bobby Allison	4	Buick	130.589	47	11	7	36	Harry Ranier	Darrell Waltrip	160.471
Gabriel 400	6/20/82	Cale Yarborough	4	Buick	118.101	24	15	3	42	M.C. Anderson	Ron Bouchard	162.404
Gabriel 400	6/19/83	Cale Yarborough	9	Chevrolet	138.728	15	6	5	22	Harry Ranier	Terry Labonte	161.965
Miller 400	6/17/84	Bill Elliott	1	Ford	134.705	20	10	6	28	Harry Melling	Bill Elliott	164.339
Miller 400	6/16/85	Bill Elliott	1	Ford	144.724	19	9	2	15	Harry Melling	Bill Elliott	
Miller American 400	6/15/86	Bill Elliott	8	Ford	138.851	34	12	8	39	Harry Melling	Tim Richmond	172.031
Miller American 400	6/28/87	Dale Earnhardt	5	Chevrolet	148.454	13	7	5	18	Richard Childress	Rusty Wallace	170.746
Miller High Life 400	6/26/88	Rusty Wallace	5	Pontiac	153.551	13	9	4	15	Raymond Beadle	Bill Elliott	172.687
Miller High Life 400	6/25/89	Bill Elliott	2	Ford	139.023	12	6	5	23	Harry Melling	Ken Schrader	174.728
Miller Genuine Draft 400	6/24/90	Dale Earnhardt	5	Chevrolet	150.219	16	7	4	16	Richard Childress	Mark Martin	
Miller Genuine Draft 400	6/23/91	Davey Allison	4	Ford	160.912	31	11	1	4	Robert Yates	Michael Waltrip	174.351
Miller Genuine Draft 400	6/21/92	Davey Allison	1	Ford	152.672	14	6	4	13	Robert Yates	Davey Allison	176.258
Miller Genuine Draft 400	6/20/93	Ricky Rudd	2	Chevrolet	148.484	16	8	5	20	Rick Hendrick	Brett Bodine	175.456
Miller Genuine Draft 400	6/19/94	Rusty Wallace	5	Ford	125.022	13	7	7	52	Roger Penske	Loy Allen, Jr.	180.641
Miller Genuine Draft 400	6/18/95	Bobby Labonte	19	Chevrolet	134.141	20	10	8	44	Joe Gibbs	Jeff Gordon	186.611
Miller Genuine Draft 400	6/23/96	Rusty Wallace	18	Ford	166.033	17	9	2	8	Roger Penske	Bobby Hamilton	185.166
Miller 400	6/15/97	Ernie Irvan	20	Ford	153.321	26	11	3	18	Robert Yates	Dale Jarrett	183.669
Miller Lite 400	6/14/98	Mark Martin	7	Ford	158.695	15	9	2	11	Jack Roush	Ward Burton	181.561
Kmart 400	6/13/99	Dale Jarrett	6	Ford	173.997	12	7	0	0	Robert Yates	Jeff Gordon	186.945
Kmart 400	6/11/00	Tony Stewart	28	Pontiac	143.926	19	11	4	20	Joe Gibbs	Bobby Labonte	189.883
Kmart 400	6/10/01	Jeff Gordon	1	Chevrolet	134.203	17	7	8	34	Rick Hendrick	Jeff Gordon	188.250
Sirius Satellite Radio 400	6/16/02	Matt Kenseth	20	Ford	154.822	15	10	4	16	Jack Roush	Dale Jarrett	189.071

August 600/400-Miler

Race	Date	Winner	Start Pos.	Make	Speed	Lead Ch.	No. Lds.	No. Caut.	Caut. Laps	Owner	Pole Winner	Pole Speed
Yankee 600	8/17/69	David Pearson	1	1969 Ford	115.508	26	12	7	78	Holman-Moody	David Pearson	161.714
Yankee 400	8/16/70	Charlie Glotzbach	1	Dodge	147.571	18	8	1	9	Ray Nichels	Charlie Glotzbach	157.363
Yankee 400	8/15/71	Bobby Allison	2	Mercury	149.862	29	5	2	12	Holman-Moody	Pete Hamilton	161.901
Yankee 400	8/20/72	David Pearson	4	Mercury	134.160	19	7	3	26	Wood Brothers	Richard Petty	157.607

Race	Date	Winner	Start Pos.	Make	Speed	Lead Ch.	No. Lds.	No. Caut.	Caut. Laps	Owner	Pole Winner	Pole Speed
Yankee 400	8/25/74	David Pearson	1	Mercury	133.045	45	8	5	30	Wood Brothers	David Pearson	157.946
Champion Spark Plug 400	8/24/75	Richard Petty	4	Dodge	107.583	25	13	6	63	Petty Enterprises	David Pearson	159.798
Champion Spark Plug 400	8/22/76	David Pearson	1	Mercury	140.078	34	10	4	20	Wood Brothers	David Pearson	160.875
Champion Spark Plug 400	8/22/77	Darrell Waltrip	3	Chevrolet	137.944	31	6	5	24	DiGard	David Pearson	160.346
Champion Spark Plug 400	8/20/78	David Pearson	1	Mercury	129.566	34	10	7	35	Wood Brothers	David Pearson	164.073
Champion Spark Plug 400	8/19/79	Richard Petty	5	Chevrolet	130.376	21	8	5	35	Petty Enterprises	David Pearson	162.992
Champion Spark Plug 400	8/17/80	Cale Yarborough	2	Chevrolet	145.352	31	9	4	17	Junior Johnson	Buddy Baker	162.693
Champion Spark Plug 400	8/16/81	Richard Petty	7	Buick	123.457	65	14	9	51	Petty Enterprises	Ron Bouchard	161.501
Champion Spark Plug 400	8/22/82	Bobby Allison	10	Buick	136.454	31	12	5	29	DiGard	Bill Elliott	162.995
Champion Spark Plug 400	8/21/83	Cale Yarborough	7	Chevrolet	147.511	27	11	2	7	Harry Ranier	Terry Labonte	162.437
Champion Spark Plug 400	8/12/84	Darrell Waltrip	7	Chevrolet	153.863	7	5	0	0	Junior Johnson	Bill Elliott	165.217
Champion Spark Plug 400	8/11/85	Bill Elliott	1	Ford	137.430	14	7	5	28	Harry Melling	Bill Elliott	165.479
Champion Spark Plug 400	8/17/86	Bill Elliott	3	Ford	135.376	23	10	5	38	Harry Melling	Benny Parsons	171.924
Champion Spark Plug 400	8/16/87	Bill Elliott	3	Ford	138.648	16	9	5	25	Harry Melling	Davey Allison	170.705
Champion Spark Plug 400	8/21/88	Davey Allison	4	Ford	156.863	21	9	2	9	Harry Ranier	Bill Elliott	174.940
Champion Spark Plug 400	8/20/89	Rusty Wallace	2	Pontiac	157.704	20	11	2	8	Raymond Beadle	Geoffrey Bodine	175.962
Champion Spark Plug 400	8/19/90	Mark Martin	5	Ford	138.822	23	11	6	26	Jack Roush	Alan Kulwicki	174.982
Champion Spark Plug 400	8/18/91	Dale Jarrett	11	Ford	142.972	24	12	4	22	Wood Brothers	Alan Kulwicki	173.431
Champion Spark Plug 400	8/16/92	Harry Gant	24	Oldsmobile	146.056	16	8	5	25	Leo Jackson	Alan Kulwicki	178.196
Champion Spark Plug 400	8/15/93	Mark Martin	12	Ford	144.564	15	8	8	27	Jack Roush	Ken Schrader	180.750
GM Goodwrench Dealer 400	8/21/94	Geoffrey Bodine	1	Ford	139.914	14	8	5	30	Geoffrey Bodine	Geoffrey Bodine	181.082
GM Goodwrench Dealer 400	8/20/95	Bobby Labonte	1	Chevrolet	157.739	17	8	3	16	Joe Gibbs	Bobby Labonte	184.403
GM Goodwrench 400	8/18/96	Dale Jarrett	11	Ford	139.792	13	8	8	36	Robert Yates	Jeff Burton	185.395
ITW DevilBliss 400	8/17/97	Mark Martin	2	Ford	126.880	19	8	3	46	Jack Roush	Johnny Benson, Jr.	183.332
Pepsi 400	8/16/98	Jeff Gordon	3	Chevrolet	151.995	25	9	3	18	Rick Hendrick	Ernie Irvan	183.416
Pepsi 400	8/22/99	Bobby Labonte	19	Pontiac	144.332	23	11	6	26	Joe Gibbs	Ward Burton	188.843
Pepsi 400	8/20/00	Rusty Wallace	10	Ford	132.597	21	8	8	38	Roger Penske	Dale Earnhardt, Jr.	191.149
Pepsi 400 presented by Meijer	8/19/01	Sterling Marlin	15	Dodge	140.513	16	8	3	18	Chip Ganassi	Ricky Craven	188.127
Pepsi 400	8/18/02	Dale Jarrett	8	Ford	140.555	23	12	7	30	Robert Yates	Dale Earnhardt, Jr.	189.668

NEW HAMPSHIRE INT'L SPEEDWAY

Race	Date	Winner	Start Pos.	Make	Speed	Lead Ch.	No. Lds.	No. Caut.	Caut. Laps	Owner	Pole Winner	Pole Speed
Slick 50 500k	7/11/93	Rusty Wallace	33	Pontiac	105.947	13	6	6	27	Roger Penske	Mark Martin	126.871
Slick 50 500k	7/10/94	Ricky Rudd	3	Ford	87.599	19	11	17	78	Ricky Rudd	Ernie Irvan	127.197
Slick 50 300	7/9/95	Jeff Gordon	21	Chevrolet	107.029	16	8	6	29	Rick Hendrick	Mark Martin	128.815
Jiffy Lube 300	7/14/96	Ernie Irvan	6	Ford	98.930	23	15	8	49	Robert Yates	Ricky Craven	129.379
Jiffy Lube 300	7/13/97	Jeff Burton	15	Ford	117.194	14	8	2	10	Jack Roush	Ken Schrader	129.423
Jiffy Lube 300	7/12/98	Jeff Burton	5	Ford	102.996	17	9	6	40	Jack Roush	Ricky Craven	128.394
Jiffy Lube 300	7/11/99	Jeff Burton	38	Ford	101.876	9	6	7	51	Jack Roush	Jeff Gordon	131.171
thatlook.com 300	7/9/00	Tony Stewart	6	Pontiac	103.145	12	12	5	38	Joe Gibbs	Rusty Wallace	132.089
New England 300	7/22/01	Dale Jarrett	9	Ford	102.131	10	8	10	53	Robert Yates	Jeff Gordon	131.770
New England 300	7/21/02	Ward Burton	31	Dodge	92.342	23	12	14	77	Bill Davis	Bill Elliott	131.469

Race	Date	Winner	Start Pos.	Make	Speed	Lead Ch.	No. Lds.	No. Caut.	Caut. Laps	Owner	Pole Winner	Pole Speed
CMT 300	9/14/97	Jeff Gordon	13	Chevrolet	100.376	8	15	8	49	Rick Hendrick	Ken Schrader	129.182
Farm Aid on CMT 300	8/30/98	Jeff Gordon	1	Chevrolet	112.078	11	9	4	25	Rick Hendrick	Jeff Gordon	129.033
Dura Lube 300	9/19/99	Joe Nemechek	11	Chevrolet	100.673	12	9	11	59	Felix Sabates	Rusty Wallace	129.820
Dura Lube / Kmart 300	9/17/00	Jeff Burton	2	Ford	102.003	0	1	7	42	Jack Roush	Bobby Labonte	127.632
New Hampshire 300	11/23/01	Robby Gordon	31	Chevrolet	103.594	10	5	7	50	Richard Childress	Jeff Gordon	
New Hampshire 300	9/15/02	Ryan Newman	1	Ford	105.081	7	6	3	24	Roger Penske	Ryan Newman	132.241

NORTH CAROLINA MOTOR SPEEDWAY
Spring 500/400-Miler

Race	Date	Winner	Start Pos.	Make	Speed	Lead Ch.	No. Lds.	No. Caut.	Caut. Laps	Owner	Pole Winner	Pole Speed
Peach Blossom 500	3/13/66	Paul Goldsmith	1	1966 Plymouth	100.027	25	10	10	70	Ray Nichels	Paul Goldsmith	116.684
Carolina 500	6/18/67	Richard Petty	2	1967 Plymouth	104.682	20	5	9	45	Petty Enterprises	Dick Hutcherson	116.486
Carolina 500	6/16/68	Donnie Allison	7	1968 Ford	99.338	20	3	8	74	Banjo Matthews	LeeRoy Yarbrough	118.644
Carolina 500	3/9/69	David Pearson	1	1969 Ford	102.569	23	7	10	82	Holman-Moody	David Pearson	119.619
Carolina 500	3/8/70	Richard Petty	8	Plymouth	116.117	24	7	9	67	Petty Enterprises	Bobby Allison	139.048
Carolina 500	3/14/71	Richard Petty	2	Plymouth	118.696	19	7	7	36	Petty Enterprises	Fred Lorenzen	133.892
Carolina 500	3/12/72	Bobby Isaac	1	Dodge	113.895	13	4	8	57	Nord Krauskopf	Bobby Isaac	137.539
Carolina 500	3/18/73	David Pearson	1	Mercury	118.649	0	2	7	47	Wood Brothers	David Pearson	134.021
Carolina 500	3/3/74	Richard Petty	2	Dodge	121.622	9	3	2	15	Petty Enterprises	Cale Yarborough	134.868
Carolina 500	3/2/75	Cale Yarborough	7	Chevrolet	117.588	15	5	4	34	Junior Johnson	Buddy Baker	137.611
Carolina 500	2/29/76	Richard Petty	3	Dodge	113.665	13	5	5	45	Petty Enterprises	Dave Marcis	138.287
Carolina 500	3/13/77	Richard Petty	2	Dodge	97.860	30	10	11	118	Petty Enterprises	Donnie Allison	135.387
Carolina 500	3/5/78	David Pearson	9	Mercury	116.681	24	9	8	62	Wood Brothers	Neil Bonnett	141.940
Carolina 500	3/4/79	Bobby Allison	1	Ford	122.727	13	5	7	39	Bud Moore	Bobby Allison	136.790
Carolina 500	3/9/80	Cale Yarborough	21	Oldsmobile	108.735	19	6	12	93	Junior Johnson	Darrell Waltrip	139.905
Carolina 500	3/1/81	Darrell Waltrip	4	Buick	114.594	36	10	14	75	Junior Johnson	Cale Yarborough	140.448
Carolina 500	3/28/82	Cale Yarborough	11	Buick	108.992	31	12	9	86	M.C. Anderson	Benny Parsons	141.577
Carolina 500	3/13/83	Richard Petty	12	Pontiac	113.055	30	11	10	94	Petty Enterprises	Ricky Rudd	143.413
Carolina 500	3/4/84	Bobby Allison	15	Buick	122.931	23	6	6	42	DiGard	Harry Gant	145.084
Carolina 500	3/3/85	Neil Bonnett	4	Chevrolet	114.953	29	6	10	76	Junior Johnson	Terry Labonte	145.067
Goodwrench 500	3/2/86	Terry Labonte	1	Oldsmobile	120.488	22	10	9	50	Billy Hagan	Terry Labonte	146.348
Goodwrench 500	3/1/87	Dale Earnhardt	14	Chevrolet	117.556	26	10	10	55	Richard Childress	Davey Allison	146.989
Goodwrench 500	3/6/88	Neil Bonnett	30	Pontiac	120.159	23	9	7	40	RahMoc Enterprises	Bill Elliott	146.612
Goodwrench 500	3/5/89	Rusty Wallace	1	Pontiac	115.122	29	11	10	64	Raymond Beadle	Rusty Wallace	148.793
GM Goodwrench 500	3/4/90	Kyle Petty	1	Pontiac	122.864	18	9	8	36	Felix Sabates	Kyle Petty	148.751
GM Goodwrench 500	3/3/91	Kyle Petty	1	Pontiac	124.083	13	5	7	29	Felix Sabates	Kyle Petty	149.205
GM Goodwrench 500	3/1/92	Bill Elliott	2	Ford	126.125	11	5	7	28	Junior Johnson	Kyle Petty	149.926
GM Goodwrench 500	2/28/93	Rusty Wallace	10	Pontiac	124.486	20	9	7	40	Roger Penske	Mark Martin	149.547
Goodwrench 500	2/27/94	Rusty Wallace	14	Ford	125.239	19	8	5	38	Roger Penske	Geoffrey Bodine	151.716
Goodwrench 500	2/26/95	Jeff Gordon	1	Chevrolet	125.305	19	7	11	58	Rick Hendrick	Jeff Gordon	157.620
Goodwrench 400	2/25/96	Dale Earnhardt	18	Chevrolet	113.959	22	6	10	66	Richard Childress	Terry Labonte	156.870
Goodwrench 400	2/23/97	Jeff Gordon	4	Chevrolet	125.927	9	6	7	47	Rick Hendrick	Mark Martin	157.885
Goodwrench 400	2/22/98	Jeff Gordon	4	Chevrolet	117.065	27	12	6	50	Rick Hendrick	Rick Mast	156.361
Dura-Lube/Big K 400	2/21/99	Mark Martin	5	Ford	120.750	25	6	6	40	Jack Roush	Ricky Rudd	157.241
Dura-Lube/Kmart 400	2/27/00	Bobby Labonte	3	Pontiac	127.875	22	10	4	21	Joe Gibbs	Rusty Wallace	158.035
Dura-Lube 400	2/25/01	Steve Park	2	Chevrolet	111.966	20	10	4	52	Dale Earnhardt, Inc.	Jeff Gordon	156.455
Subway 400	2/24/02	Matt Kenseth	25	Ford	115.478	17	7	10	57	Jack Roush	Ricky Craven	156.008

Fall 500/400-Miler

Race	Date	Winner	Start Pos.	Make	Speed	Lead Ch.	No. Lds.	No. Caut.	Caut. Laps	Owner	Pole Winner	Pole Speed
American 500	10/31/65	Curtis Turner	4	1965 Ford	101.942	16	6	8	55	Wood Brothers	Richard Petty	116.260
American 500	10/30/66	Fred Lorenzen	1	1966 Ford	104.348	20	2	4	35	Holman-Moody	Fred Lorenzen	115.988
American 500	10/29/67	Bobby Allison	3	1967 Ford	98.420	26	4	9	81	Holman-Moody	David Pearson	117.120
American 500	10/27/68	Richard Petty	4	1968 Plymouth	105.060	18	7	6	46	Petty Enterprises	Cale Yarborough	118.717
American 500	10/26/69	LeeRoy Yarbrough	9	1969 Ford	111.938	25	7	7	66	Junior Johnson	Charlie Glotzbach	136.972
American 500	11/15/70	Cale Yarborough	2	Mercury	117.811	13	5	7	46	Wood Brothers	Charlie Glotzbach	136.498
American 500	10/24/71	Richard Petty	5	Plymouth	113.405	14	5	9	58	Petty Enterprises	Charlie Glotzbach	135.167
American 500	10/22/72	Bobby Allison	5	Chevrolet	118.275	20	8	4	35	Richard Howard	David Pearson	137.528
American 500	10/21/73	David Pearson	2	Mercury	117.749	20	6	5	36	Wood Brothers	Richard Petty	135.748
American 500	10/20/74	David Pearson	3	Mercury	118.493	23	5	4	37	Wood Brothers	Richard Petty	135.297
American 500	10/19/75	Cale Yarborough	4	Chevrolet	120.129	15	4	4	23	Junior Johnson	Dave Marcis	132.021
American 500	10/24/76	Richard Petty	4	Dodge	117.718	15	5	6	35	Petty Enterprises	David Pearson	139.117
American 500	10/23/77	Donnie Allison	1	Chevrolet	113.584	24	5	9	75	Hoss Ellington	Donnie Allison	138.685
American 500	10/22/78	Cale Yarborough	1	Oldsmobile	117.288	19	13	5	52	Junior Johnson	Cale Yarborough	142.067

Race	Date	Winner	Start Pos.	Make	Speed	Lead Ch.	No. Lds.	No. Caut.	Caut. Laps	Owner	Pole Winner	Pole Speed
American 500	10/21/79	Richard Petty	7	Chevrolet	108.356	23	8	12	82	Petty Enterprises	Buddy Baker	141.315
American 500	10/19/80	Cale Yarborough	2	Chevrolet	114.159	35	12	9	61	Junior Johnson	Donnie Allison	142.648
American 500	11/1/81	Darrell Waltrip	1	Buick	107.399	33	11	12	97	Junior Johnson	Darrell Waltrip	138.164
American 500	10/31/82	Darrell Waltrip	4	Buick	115.122	33	10	8	55	Junior Johnson	Cale Yarborough	143.220
American 500	10/30/83	Terry Labonte	3	Chevrolet	119.324	36	10	10	63	Billy Hagan	Neil Bonnett	143.876
American 500	10/21/84	Bill Elliott	2	Ford	112.617	28	12	10	91	Harry Melling	Geoffrey Bodine	144.415
Nationwise 500	10/25/85	Darrell Waltrip	20	Chevrolet	118.344	27	9	10	64	Junior Johnson	Terry Labonte	141.841
Nationwise 500	10/19/86	Neil Bonnett	6	Chevrolet	126.381	22	8	6	29	Junior Johnson	Tim Richmond	146.948
AC-Delco 500	10/25/87	Bill Elliott	3	Ford	118.258	31	11	8	46	Harry Melling	Davey Allison	145.609
AC-Delco 500	10/23/88	Rusty Wallace	3	Pontiac	111.557	18	10	11	76	Raymond Beadle	Bill Elliott	148.359
AC-Delco 500	10/22/89	Mark Martin	7	Ford	114.079	35	10	14	69	Jack Roush	Alan Kulwicki	114.079
AC Delco 500	10/21/90	Alan Kulwicki	3	Ford	126.452	21	8	7	28	Alan Kulwicki	Ken Schrader	147.814
AC Delco 500	10/20/91	Davey Allison	10	Ford	127.292	26	6	5	24	Robert Yates	Kyle Petty	149.461
AC Delco 500	10/25/92	Kyle Petty	1	Pontiac	130.748	9	4	2	12	Felix Sabates	Kyle Petty	149.675
AC Delco 500	10/24/93	Rusty Wallace	18	Pontiac	114.036	23	11	8	54	Roger Penske	Mark Martin	148.353
AC Delco 500	10/23/94	Dale Earnhardt	20	Chevrolet	126.408	26	12	10	52	Richard Childress	Ricky Rudd	157.099
AC Delco 400	10/22/95	Ward Burton	3	Pontiac	114.778	14	10	7	64	Bill Davis	Hut Stricklin	155.379
AC Delco 400	10/20/96	Ricky Rudd	2	Ford	122.320	21	10	7	46	Ricky Rudd	Dale Jarrett	157.194
AC Delco 400	10/26/97	Bobby Hamilton	28	Pontiac	121.730	20	9	5	40	Petty Enterprises	Bobby Labonte	156.696
AC-Delco 400	11/1/98	Jeff Gordon	9	Chevrolet	128.423	20	10	4	25	Rick Hendrick	Mark Martin	156.502
Pop Secret Microwave Popcorn 400	10/24/99	Jeff Burton	6	Ford	131.103	18	8	3	18	Jack Roush	Mark Martin	157.383
Pop Secret Popcorn 400	10/22/00	Dale Jarrett	21	Ford	110.418	23	10	9	60	Robert Yates	Jeremy Mayfield	157.342
Pop Secret Popcorn 400	11/4/01	Joe Nemechek	13	Chevrolet	128.933	15	6	2	16	Andy Petree	Kenny Wallace	154.690
Pop Secret Popcorn 400	11/3/02	Johnny Benson, Jr.	26	Pontiac	128.526	22	9	4	22	Nelson Bowers	Ryan Newman	155.836

PHOENIX INT'L RACEWAY

Race	Date	Winner	Start Pos.	Make	Speed	Lead Ch.	No. Lds.	No. Caut.	Caut. Laps	Owner	Pole Winner	Pole Speed
Checker 500	11/6/88	Alan Kulwicki	21	Ford	90.457	14	7	6	53	Alan Kulwicki	Geoffrey Bodine	123.203
Autoworks 500	11/5/89	Bill Elliott	13	Ford	105.683	17	9	5	24	Harry Melling	Ken Schrader	124.645
Checker 500	11/4/90	Dale Earnhardt	3	Chevrolet	96.786	1	2	9	48	Richard Childress	Rusty Wallace	124.443
Pyroil 500k	11/3/91	Davey Allison	13	Ford	95.746	18	13	10	5	Robert Yates	Geoffrey Bodine	127.589
Pyroil 500k	11/1/92	Davey Allison	12	Ford	103.885	8	7	7	34	Robert Yates	Rusty Wallace	128.141
Slick 50 500k	10/31/93	Mark Martin	3	Ford	100.375	20	11	9	45	Jack Roush	Bill Elliott	129.482
Slick 50 500k	10/30/94	Terry Labonte	19	Chevrolet	107.463	13	9	4	27	Rick Hendrick	Sterling Marlin	129.833
Dura-Lube 500k	10/29/95	Ricky Rudd	29	Ford	102.128	11	8	8	39	Ricky Rudd	Bill Elliott	130.020
Dura-Lube 500	10/27/96	Bobby Hamilton	17	Pontiac	109.709	19	9	5	25	Petty Enterprises	Bobby Labonte	131.076
Dura-Lube 500	11/2/97	Dale Jarrett	9	Ford	110.824	13	9	4	23	Robert Yates	Bobby Hamilton	131.579
Dura Lube 500	10/25/98	Rusty Wallace	6	Ford	108.211	8	7	4	25	Roger Penske	Ken Schrader	131.234
Dura Lube 500	11/7/99	Tony Stewart	11	Pontiac	118.132	12	7	2	10	Joe Gibbs	John Andretti	132.670
Checker/Dura Lube 500	11/5/00	Jeff Burton	2	Ford	105.041	23	13	6	38	Jack Roush	Rusty Wallace	134.178
Checker 500	10/28/01	Jeff Burton	3	Ford	102.613	15	6	7	45	Jack Roush	Casey Atwood	131.296
Checker Auto Parts 500	11/10/02	Matt Kenseth	28	Ford	113.857	14	9	4	18	Mark Martin	Ryan Newman	132.655

POCONO INT'L RACEWAY
June 500-Miler

Race	Date	Winner	Start Pos.	Make	Speed	Lead Ch.	No. Lds.	No. Caut.	Caut. Laps	Owner	Pole Winner	Pole Speed
Van Scoy Diamond Mine 500	6/6/82	Bobby Allison	3	Buick	113.579	44	11	7	51	DiGard	Terry Labonte	
Van Scoy Diamond Mine 500	6/12/83	Bobby Allison	7	Buick	128.636	22	11	6	25	DiGard	Darrell Waltrip	152.315
Van Scoy Diamond Mine 500	6/10/84	Cale Yarborough	12	Chevrolet	138.164	32	12	3	12	Harry Ranier	Neil Bonnett	150.921
Van Scoy Diamond Mine 500	6/9/85	Bill Elliott	1	Ford	138.974	13	4	3	10	Harry Melling	Bill Elliott	152.563
Miller High Life 500	6/8/86	Tim Richmond	3	Chevrolet	113.279	18	11	9	53	Rick Hendrick	Geoffrey Bodine	153.625
Miller High Life 500	6/14/87	Tim Richmond	3	Chevrolet	122.166	17	9	9	45	Rick Hendrick	Terry Labonte	155.502
Miller High Life 500	6/19/88	Geoffrey Bodine	3	Chevrolet	126.147	16	7	6	31	Rick Hendrick	Alan Kulwicki	158.806
Miller High Life 500	6/18/89	Terry Labonte	23	Ford	131.320	23	12	6	23	Junior Johnson	Rusty Wallace	157.489
Miller Genuine Draft 500	6/17/90	Harry Gant	16	Oldsmobile	120.600	26	16	13	44	Leo Jackson	Ernie Irvan	158.750
Champion Spark Plug 500	6/16/91	Darrell Waltrip	13	Chevrolet	122.666	23	14	7	37	Darrell Waltrip	Mark Martin	161.996
Champion Spark Plug 500	6/14/92	Alan Kulwicki	6	Ford	144.023	26	11	3	13	Alan Kulwicki	Ken Schrader	162.499

Race	Date	Winner	Start Pos.	Make	Speed	Lead Ch.	No. Lds.	No. Caut.	Caut. Laps	Owner	Pole Winner	Pole Speed
Champion												
Spark Plug 500	6/13/93	Kyle Petty	8	Pontiac	138.005	22	13	6	24	Felix Sabates	Ken Schrader	162.816
UAW-GM Teamwork 500	6/12/94	Rusty Wallace	1	Ford	128.801	22	12	5	35	Roger Penske	Rusty Wallace	164.558
UAW-GM Teamwork 500	6/11/95	Terry Labonte	27	Chevrolet	137.720	24	11	6	20	Rick Hendrick	Ken Schrader	163.375
UAW-GM Teamwork 500	6/16/96	Jeff Gordon	1	Chevrolet	139.104	26	12	4	23	Rick Hendrick	Jeff Gordon	169.725
Pocono 500	6/8/97	Jeff Gordon	11	Chevrolet	139.828	25	15	4	22	Rick Hendrick	Bobby Hamilton	168.089
Pocono 500	6/21/98	Jeremy Mayfield	3	Ford	117.801	18	12	9	47	Michael Kranefuss	Jeff Gordon	168.042
Pocono 500	6/20/99	Bobby Labonte	3	Pontiac	118.898	22	13	11	46	Joe Gibbs	Sterling Marlin	170.506
Pocono 500	6/18/00	Jeremy Mayfield	22	Ford	139.741	24	11	5	17	Michael Kranefuss	Rusty Wallace	171.625
Pocono 500	6/17/01	Ricky Rudd	1	Ford	134.389	13	5	7	26	Robert Yates	Ricky Rudd	170.503
Pocono 500	6/9/02	Dale Jarrett	13	Ford	143.426	17	12	5	17	Robert Yates	Sterling Marlin	

July 500-Miler

Race	Date	Winner	Start Pos.	Make	Speed	Lead Ch.	No. Lds.	No. Caut.	Caut. Laps	Owner	Pole Winner	Pole Speed
Purolator 500	8/4/74	Richard Petty	3	Dodge	115.593	20	5	4	42	Petty Enterprises	Buddy Baker	144.122
Purolator 500	8/3/75	David Pearson	2	Mercury	111.179	44	6	5	47	Wood Brothers	Bobby Allison	146.491
Purolator 500	8/1/76	Richard Petty	5	Dodge	115.875	48	8	7	38	Petty Enterprises	Cale Yarborough	147.865
Coca-Cola 500	7/31/77	Benny Parsons	4	Chevrolet	128.379	47	6	4	22	L.G. DeWitt	Darrell Waltrip	147.591
Coca-Cola 500	7/30/78	Darrell Waltrip	4	Chevrolet	142.540	37	4	1	3	DiGard	Benny Parsons	149.236
Coca-Cola 500	7/30/79	Cale Yarborough	2	Chevrolet	115.207	56	8	7	46	Junior Johnson	Harry Gant	148.711
Coca-Cola 500	7/27/80	Neil Bonnett	2	Mercury	124.395	49	11	5	26	Wood Brothers	Cale Yarborough	151.469
Mountain Dew 500	7/26/81	Darrell Waltrip	1	Buick	119.111	27	10	6	39	Junior Johnson	Darrell Waltrip	150.148
Mountain Dew 500	7/25/82	Bobby Allison	4	Buick	115.496	46	11	6	43	DiGard	Cale Yarborough	150.764
Like Cola 500	7/24/83	Tim Richmond	1	Pontiac	114.818	41	11	5	52	Raymond Beadle	Tim Richmond	151.981
Like Cola 500	7/22/84	Harry Gant	3	Chevrolet	121.351	26	11	9	41	Hal Needham	Bill Elliott	152.184
Summer 500	7/21/85	Bill Elliott	2	Ford	134.008	37	12	6	24	Harry Melling	Darrell Waltrip	151.973
Summer 500	7/20/86	Tim Richmond	5	Chevrolet	124.218	20	6	8	33	Rick Hendrick	Harry Gant	154.392
Summer 500	7/19/87	Dale Earnhardt	16	Chevrolet	121.745	35	15	9	46	Richard Childress	Tim Richmond	155.979
AC Spark Plug 500	7/24/88	Bill Elliott	2	Ford	122.866	22	9	5	42	Harry Melling	Morgan Shepherd	157.153
AC Spark Plug 500	7/23/89	Bill Elliott	14	Ford	117.847	29	14	9	42	Harry Melling	Ken Schrader	157.809
AC Spark Plug 500	7/22/90	Geoffrey Bodine	4	Ford	124.070	22	9	10	35	Junior Johnson	Mark Martin	158.264
Miller Genuine Draft 500	7/21/91	Rusty Wallace	10	Pontiac	115.459	21	11	11	48	Roger Penske	Alan Kulwicki	161.473
Miller Genuine Draft 500	7/19/92	Darrell Waltrip	8	Chevrolet	134.058	13	7	3	23	Darrell Waltrip	Davey Allison	162.022
Miller Genuine Draft 500	7/18/93	Dale Earnhardt	11	Chevrolet	133.343	22	12	8	27	Richard Childress	Ken Schrader	162.934
Miller Genuine Draft 500	7/17/94	Geoffrey Bodine	1	Ford	136.075	18	9	5	23	Geoffrey Bodine	Geoffrey Bodine	163.869
Miller Genuine Draft 500	7/16/95	Dale Jarrett	15	Ford	134.038	37	13	5	25	Robert Yates	Bill Elliott	162.496
Miller Genuine Draft 500	7/21/96	Rusty Wallace	13	Ford	144.892	23	12	4	17	Roger Penske	Mark Martin	168.410
Pennsylvania 500	7/20/97	Dale Jarrett	4	Ford	142.068	23	14	4	18	Robert Yates	Joe Nemechek	168.831
Pennsylvania 500	7/26/98	Jeff Gordon	2	Chevrolet	134.660	10	7	5	25	Rick Hendrick	Ward Burton	168.805
Pennsylvania 500	7/25/99	Bobby Labonte	4	Pontiac	116.982	27	15	9	49	Joe Gibbs	Mike Skinner	170.451
Pennsylvania 500	7/23/00	Rusty Wallace	2	Ford	130.662	25	10	7	32	Roger Penske	Tony Stewart	172.391
Pennsylvania 500	7/29/01	Bobby Labonte	11	Pontiac	134.590	20	12	6	24	Joe Gibbs	Todd Bodine	170.326
Pennsylvania 500	7/28/02	Bill Elliott	1	Dodge	125.809	17	11	5	29	Ray Evernham	Bill Elliott	170.568

RICHMOND INT'L RACEWAY

Race	Date	Winner	Start Pos.	Make	Speed	Lead Ch.	No. Lds.	No. Caut.	Caut. Laps	Owner	Pole Winner	Pole Speed
Richmond 200	4/19/53	Lee Petty		53 Dodge	45.535					Petty Enterprises	Buck Baker	48.465
Richmond 200	5/22/55	Tim Flock	22	55 Chrysler	54.298	4	3			Carl Kiekhaefer	Arden Mounts	
Richmond 200	4/29/56	Buck Baker	1	56 Dodge	56.232	2	2			Carl Kiekhaefer	Buck Baker	67.091
Richmond 200	5/5/57	Paul Goldsmith	7	57 Ford	62.445	2	2			Peter DePaolo	Russ Hepler	64.239
Richmond 100	6/21/59	Tom Pistone	12	59 T-Bird	56.881					Carl Rupert	Buck Baker	66.420
Richmond 200	6/5/60	Lee Petty	10	60 Plymouth	62.251	7	6	1	6	Petty Enterprises	Ned Jarrett	64.560
Richmond 200	4/23/61	Richard Petty	1	60 Plymouth	62.456	2	2			Petty Enterprises	Richard Petty	66.667
Richmond 250	4/1/62	Rex White	20	61 Chevrolet	51.363	7	6	5	32	Rex White	Herman Beam	62.090
Richmond 250	4/7/63	Joe Weatherly	3	63 Pontiac	58.624	11	4	6	37	Bud Moore	Rex White	69.151
Richmond 250	3/8/64	David Pearson	10	1964 Dodge	60.233	5	4	2		Cotton Owens	Ned Jarrett	69.070
Richmond 250	3/7/65	Junior Johnson	1	1965 Ford	61.416	5	4	8	45	Junior Johnson	Junior Johnson	67.847
Richmond 250	5/15/66	David Pearson	4	1964 Dodge	66.539	5	4	2	14	Cotton Owens	Tom Pistone	70.978
Richmond 250	4/30/67	Richard Petty	1	1967 Plymouth	65.982	6	3	6	32	Petty Enterprises	Richard Petty	70.038
Richmond 250	3/24/68	David Pearson	16	1968 Ford	65.217	7	4			Holman-Moody	Bobby Isaac	67.822
Richmond 250	4/13/69	David Pearson	1	1969 Ford	73.752	6	4	6	40	Holman-Moody	David Pearson	82.538
Richmond 500	3/1/70	James Hylton	3	Ford	82.044	2	3	1	7	James Hylton	Richard Petty	89.137
Richmond 500	3/7/71	Richard Petty	30	Plymouth	79.836	6	4	3	18	Petty Enterprises	Dave Marcis	87.178
Richmond 500	2/27/72	Richard Petty	3	Plymouth	76.258	13	3	3	46	Petty Enterprises	Bobby Allison	76.258
Richmond 500	2/25/73	Richard Petty	8	Dodge	74.764	19	7	8	78	Petty Enterprises	Bobby Allison	90.952

Race	Date	Winner	Start Pos.	Make	Speed	Lead Ch.	No. Lds.	No. Caut.	Caut. Laps	Owner	Pole Winner	Pole Speed
Richmond 400	2/24/74	Bobby Allison	1	Chevrolet	80.095	11	4	3	16	Bobby Allison	Bobby Allison	90.353
Richmond 400	2/23/75	Richard Petty	1	Dodge	74.913	2	2	7	89	Petty Enterprises	Richard Petty	93.340
Richmond 400	3/7/76	Dave Marcis	2	Dodge	72.792	19	5	7		Nord Krauskopf	Bobby Allison	92.715
Richmond 400	2/27/77	Cale Yarborough	7	Chevrolet	73.084	9	7	4	35	Junior Johnson	Neil Bonnett	93.632
Richmond 400	2/26/78	Benny Parsons	3	Oldsmobile	80.304	10	6	5	33	L.G. DeWitt	Neil Bonnett	93.382
Richmond 400	3/11/79	Cale Yarborough	9	Oldsmobile	83.608	3	2	2	8	Junior Johnson	Bobby Allison	92.957
Richmond 400	2/24/80	Darrell Waltrip	1	Chevrolet	67.703	19	7	9	72	DiGard	Darrell Waltrip	93.695
Richmond 400	2/22/81	Darrell Waltrip	7	Buick	76.570	4	4	7	50	Junior Johnson	Morgan Shepherd	92.821
Richmond 400	2/21/82	Dave Marcis	6	Chevrolet	72.914	11	7	6	33	Dave Marcis	Darrell Waltrip	93.256
Richmond 400	2/27/83	Bobby Allison	6	Chevrolet	79.584	15	8	5	25	DiGard	Ricky Rudd	93.439
Miller High Life 400	2/26/84	Ricky Rudd	4	Ford	76.736	11	4	9	40	Bud Moore	Darrell Waltrip	93.817
Miller High Life 400	2/24/85	Dale Earnhardt	4	Chevrolet	67.945	9	6	10	74	Richard Childress	Darrell Waltrip	95.218
Miller High Life 400	2/23/86	Kyle Petty	12	Ford	71.078	11	8	8	63	Wood Brothers	Geoffrey Bodine	
Miller High Life 400	3/8/87	Dale Earnhardt	3	Chevrolet	81.520	12	8	6	35	Richard Childress	Alan Kulwicki	95.153
Pontiac Excitement 400	2/21/88	Neil Bonnett	3	Pontiac	66.401	11	6	14	83	RahMoc Enterprises	Morgan Shepherd	94.645
Pontiac Excitement 400	3/26/89	Rusty Wallace	2	Pontiac	89.619	19	7	12	67	Raymond Beadle	Geoffrey Bodine	120.573
Pontiac Excitement 400	2/25/90	Mark Martin	6	Ford	92.158	18	8	12	75	Jack Roush	Ricky Rudd	119.617
Pontiac Excitement 400	2/24/91	Dale Earnhardt	19	Chevrolet	105.937	25	7	6	23	Richard Childress	Davey Allison	120.428
Pontiac Excitement 400	3/8/92	Bill Elliott	1	Ford	104.378	5	4	4	23	Junior Johnson	Bill Elliott	121.337
Pontiac Excitement 400	3/7/93	Davey Allison	14	Ford	107.709	12	6	3	19	Robert Yates	Ken Schrader	123.164
Pontiac Excitement 400	3/6/94	Ernie Irvan	7	Ford	98.334	15	8	8	51	Robert Yates	Ted Musgrave	123.474
Pontiac Excitement 400	3/5/95	Terry Labonte	24	Chevrolet	106.425	17	6	5	28	Rick Hendrick	Jeff Gordon	124.757
Pontiac 400	3/3/96	Jeff Gordon	2	Chevrolet	102.750	25	11	8	36	Rick Hendrick	Terry Labonte	123.728
Pontiac Excitement 400	3/2/97	Rusty Wallace	7	Ford	108.499	15	7	3	12	Roger Penske	Terry Labonte	
Pontiac Excitement 400	6/6/98	Terry Labonte	16	Chevrolet	97.044	17	8	7	47	Rick Hendrick	Jeff Gordon	125.558
Pontiac Excitement 400	5/15/99	Dale Jarrett	21	Ford	100.102	19	9	8	58	Robert Yates	Jeff Gordon	126.499
Pontiac Excitement 400	5/6/00	Dale Earnhardt, Jr.	5	Chevrolet	99.374	21	10	9	59	Dale Earnhardt, Inc.	Rusty Wallace	124.740
Pontiac Excitement 400	5/5/01	Tony Stewart	7	Pontiac	95.872	12	5	8	58	Joe Gibbs	Mark Martin	124.613
Pontiac Excitement 400	5/5/02	Tony Stewart	3	Pontiac	86.824	13	10	14	103	Joe Gibbs	Ward Burton	127.388
Southside 200	5/4/62	Jimmy Pardue	12	62 Pontiac	67.747	1	2			Jimmy Pardue	Rex White	71.145
Southside 300	6/22/62	Jim Paschal	3	62 Pontiac	66.293	2	3	1		Cliff Stewart	Rex White	70.435
Southside 300	5/19/63	Ned Jarrett	1	63 Ford	65.052	4	2	1	6	Charles Robinson	Ned Jarrett	70.642
Richmond 200	9/14/58	Speedy Thompson	1	57 Chevrolet	57.878	4	3			Speedy Thompson	Speedy Thompson	62.915
Richmond 200	9/13/59	Cotton Owens	1	59 T-Bird	60.382					W.H. Watson	Bill Jarick	62.674
Richmond 100	10/23/60	Speedy Thompson	3	60 Ford	63.739	3	3			Wood Brothers	Ned Jarrett	64.410
Richmond 150	8/18/61	Junior Johnson	1	60 Pontiac	51.605	0	1	1	8	Rex Lovette	Junior Johnson	58.860
Richmond 250	9/10/61	Joe Weatherly	7	61 Pontiac	61.677					Bud Moore	Bill Amick	65.010
Capital City 300	9/9/62	Joe Weatherly	2	62 Pontiac	64.981			1	9	Bud Moore	Rex White	66.127
Capital City 300	9/8/63	Ned Jarrett	7	63 Ford	66.339	4	3			Charles Robinson	Joe Weatherly	68.104
Capital City 300	9/14/64	Cotton Owens	3	1964 Dodge	61.955	7	3	5	23	Cotton Owens	Ned Jarrett	66.890
Capitol City 300	9/18/65	David Pearson	2	1965 Dodge	60.983	10	5			Cotton Owens	Dick Hutcherson	67.340
Capitol City 300	9/11/66	David Pearson	1	1966 Dodge	62.886	4	3	5	29	Cotton Owens	David Pearson	70.644
Capitol City 300	9/10/67	Richard Petty	2	1967 Plymouth	57.631	8	2	10	71	Petty Enterprises	Earl Brooks	
Capitol City 300	9/8/68	Richard Petty	1	1968 Plymouth	85.659	13	5	10	52	Petty Enterprises	Richard Petty	103.178
Capitol City 250	9/7/69	Bobby Allison	25	1969 Dodge	76.388	3	2	6	39	Mario Rossi	Richard Petty	91.257
Capital City 500	9/13/70	Richard Petty	1	Plymouth	81.476	2	2	2	9	Petty Enterprises	Richard Petty	87.014
Capital City 500	11/14/71	Richard Petty	11	Plymouth	80.025	9	4	4	24	Petty Enterprises	Bill Dennis	
Capital City 500	9/10/72	Richard Petty	3	Plymouth	75.899	18	4	8	57	Petty Enterprises	Bobby Allison	89.669
Capital City 500	9/9/73	Richard Petty	5	Dodge	63.215	6	3	5	123	Petty Enterprises	Bobby Allison	90.245
Capital City 500	9/8/74	Richard Petty	1	Dodge	64.430	6	4	13	123	Petty Enterprises	Richard Petty	88.852
Capital City 400	10/12/75	Darrell Waltrip	2	Chevrolet	81.886	10	5	4	23	DiGard	Benny Parsons	91.071
Capital City 400	9/12/76	Cale Yarborough	6	Chevrolet	77.993	12	5	2	37	Junior Johnson	Benny Parsons	92.460
Capital City 400	9/11/77	Neil Bonnett	2	Dodge	80.644	12	6	5	30	J.D. Stacy	Benny Parsons	92.281
Capital City 400	9/10/78	Darrell Waltrip	1	Chevrolet	79.568	15	6	5	27	DiGard	Darrell Waltrip	91.964
Capital City 400	9/9/79	Bobby Allison	2	Ford	80.604	6	4	2	20	Bud Moore	Dale Earnhardt	92.605
Capital City 400 Wrangler	9/7/80	Bobby Allison	2	Ford	79.722	18	8	7	31	Bud Moore	Cale Yarborough	93.466
Sanfor-Set 400 Wrangler	9/13/81	Benny Parsons	4	Ford	69.998	18	8	9	63	Bud Moore	Mark Martin	93.435

Race	Date	Winner	Start Pos.	Make	Speed	Lead Ch.	No. Lds.	No. Caut.	Caut. Laps	Owner	Pole Winner	Pole Speed
Sanfor-Set 400 Wrangler	9/12/82	Bobby Allison	1	Chevrolet	82.800	6	4	2	12	DiGard	Bobby Allison	93.435
Sanfor-Set 400 Wrangler	9/11/83	Bobby Allison	6	Buick	79.381	6	4	4	22	DiGard	Darrell Waltrip	96.069
Sanfor-Set 400 Wrangler	9/9/84	Darrell Waltrip	1	Chevrolet	74.780	9	5	9	42	Junior Johnson	Darrell Waltrip	92.518
Sanfor-Set 400 Wrangler Jeans	9/8/85	Darrell Waltrip	22	Chevrolet	72.508	14	7	7	65	Junior Johnson	Geoffrey Bodine	94.535
Indigo 400 Wrangler Jeans	9/7/86	Tim Richmond	4	Chevrolet	70.161	15	12	12	75	Rick Hendrick	Harry Gant	93.966
Indigo 400	9/13/87	Dale Earnhardt	8	Chevrolet	67.074	13	7	12	82	Richard Childress	Alan Kulwicki	94.052
Miller 400	9/11/88	Davey Allison	1	Ford	95.770	14	7	5	42	Harry Ranier	Davey Allison	122.850
Miller 400	9/10/89	Rusty Wallace	6	Pontiac	88.380	9	7	14	76	Raymond Beadle	Bill Elliott	121.136
Miller Genuine Draft 400	9/9/90	Dale Earnhardt	6	Chevrolet	95.567	17	6	9	55	Richard Childress	Ernie Irvan	119.872
Miller Genuine Draft 400	9/7/91	Harry Gant	13	Oldsmobile	101.361	15	9	9	43	Leo Jackson	Rusty Wallace	120.590
Miller Genuine Draft 400	9/12/92	Rusty Wallace	3	Pontiac	104.661	12	6	3	20	Roger Penske	Ernie Irvan	120.784
Miller Genuine Draft 400	9/11/93	Rusty Wallace	3	Pontiac	99.917	12	6	8	47	Roger Penske	Bobby Labonte	122.006
Miller Genuine Draft 400	9/10/94	Terry Labonte	3	Chevrolet	104.156	17	8	5	35	Rick Hendrick	Ted Musgrave	124.052
Miller Genuine Draft 400	9/9/95	Rusty Wallace	7	Ford	104.459	15	7	4	30	Roger Penske	Dale Earnhardt	122.543
Miller 400	9/7/96	Ernie Irvan	16	Ford	105.469	16	9	4	24	Robert Yates	Mark Martin	122.744
Exide Select Batteries 400	9/6/97	Dale Jarrett	23	Ford	108.707	9	10	3	16	Robert Yates	Bill Elliott	124.723
Exide NASCAR Select 400	9/12/98	Jeff Burton	3	Ford	91.985	24	11	8	66	Jack Roush	Rusty Wallace	125.377
Exide NASCAR Select 400	9/11/99	Tony Stewart	2	Pontiac	104.006	13	5	6	45	Joe Gibbs	Mike Skinner	125.465
Chevrolet Monte Carlo 400	9/9/00	Jeff Gordon	13	Chevrolet	99.871	16	9	8	57	Rick Hendrick	Jeff Burton	125.780
Chevrolet Monte Carlo 400	9/8/01	Ricky Rudd	9	Ford	95.146	8	6	12	80	Robert Yates	Jeff Gordon	124.902
Chevrolet Monte Carlo 400	9/7/02	Matt Kenseth	25	Ford	94.787	14	11	10	65	Jack Roush	Jimmie Johnson	126.145

Talladega Superspeedway
Alabama/Winston 500

Race	Date	Winner	Start Pos.	Make	Speed	Lead Ch.	No. Lds.	No. Caut.	Caut. Laps	Owner	Pole Winner	Pole Speed
Alabama 500	4/12/70	Pete Hamilton	6	Plymouth	152.321	32	8	6	42	Petty Enterprises	Bobby Isaac	199.658
Winston 500	5/16/71	Donnie Allison	1	Mercury	147.419	45	4	7	45	Wood Brothers	Donnie Allison	185.869
Winston 500	5/7/72	David Pearson	2	Mercury	134.400	53	7	9	62	Wood Brothers	Bobby Isaac	192.428
Winston 500	5/6/73	David Pearson	2	Mercury	131.956	13	10	4	54	Wood Brothers	Buddy Baker	
Winston 500	5/5/74	David Pearson	1	Mercury	130.220	53	13	6	60	Wood Brothers	David Pearson	186.086
Winston 500	5/4/75	Buddy Baker	1	Ford	144.948	51	12	5	45	Bud Moore	Buddy Baker	189.947
Winston 500	5/2/76	Buddy Baker	12	Ford	169.887	24	8	3	14	Bud Moore	Dave Marcis	189.197
Winston 500	5/1/77	Darrell Waltrip	11	Chevrolet	164.877	63	11	6	27	DiGard	A.J. Foyt	192.424
Winston 500	5/14/78	Cale Yarborough	1	Oldsmobile	155.699	44	8	5	30	Junior Johnson	Cale Yarborough	191.904
Winston 500	5/6/79	Bobby Allison	12	Ford	154.770	21	8	4	30	Bud Moore	Darrell Waltrip	195.644
Winston 500	5/4/80	Buddy Baker	2	Oldsmobile	170.481	40	12	6	28	Harry Ranier	David Pearson	197.704
Winston 500	5/3/81	Bobby Allison	1	Buick	149.376	43	10	7	44	Harry Ranier	Bobby Allison	195.864
Winston 500	5/2/82	Darrell Waltrip	2	Buick	156.697	51	13	8	39	Junior Johnson	Benny Parsons	200.176
Winston 500	5/1/83	Richard Petty	15	Pontiac	153.936	27	13	7	42	Petty Enterprises	Cale Yarborough	202.650
Winston 500	5/6/84	Cale Yarborough	1	Chevrolet	172.988	75	13	4	17	Harry Ranier	Cale Yarborough	202.692
Winston 500	5/5/85	Bill Elliott	1	Ford	186.288	28	10	2	8	Harry Melling	Bill Elliott	209.398
Winston 500	5/4/86	Bobby Allison	2	Buick	157.698	24	9	9	41	Stavola Brothers	Bill Elliott	212.229
Winston 500	5/3/87	Davey Allison	3	Ford	154.228	18	10	9	39	Harry Ranier	Bill Elliott	212.809
Winston 500	5/1/88	Phil Parsons	3	Oldsmobile	156.547	23	9	7	29	Leo & Richard Jackson	Davey Allison 198.969	
Winston 500	5/7/89	Davey Allison	2	Ford	155.869	28	9	7	26	Robert Yates	Mark Martin	193.061

Race	Date	Winner	Start Pos.	Make	Speed	Lead Ch.	No. Lds.	No. Caut.	Caut. Laps	Owner	Pole Winner	Pole Speed
Winston 500	5/6/90	Dale Earnhardt	5	Chevrolet	159.571	25	12	7	28	Richard Childress	Bill Elliott	199.388
Winston 500	5/6/91	Harry Gant	2	Oldsmobile	165.620	24	11	3	18	Leo Jackson	Ernie Irvan	195.186
Winston 500	5/3/92	Davey Allison	2	Ford	167.609	16	6	5	21	Robert Yates	Ernie Irvan	192.831
Winston 500	5/2/93	Ernie Irvan	16	Chevrolet	155.415	22	7	4	25	Larry McClure	Dale Earnhardt	192.355
Winston Select 500	5/1/94	Dale Earnhardt	4	Chevrolet	157.478	30	11	4	23	Richard Childress	Ernie Irvan	193.298
Winston Select 500	4/30/95	Mark Martin	3	Ford	178.902	24	10	2	8	Jack Roush	Terry Labonte	196.532
Winston Select 500	4/28/96	Sterling Marlin	4	Chevrolet	149.999	24	14	6	31	Larry McClure	Ernie Irvan	192.855
Winston 500	5/10/97	Mark Martin	18	Ford	188.354	26	13	0	0	Jack Roush	John Andretti	193.627
Die Hard 500	4/26/98	Bobby Labonte	1	Pontiac	163.439	19	9	3	16	Joe Gibbs	Bobby Labonte	195.728
Die Hard 500	4/25/99	Dale Earnhardt	17	Chevrolet	163.395	28	14	3	18	Richard Childress	Ken Schrader	197.765
Die Hard 500	4/16/00	Jeff Gordon	36	Chevrolet	161.157	27	10	4	17	Rick Hendrick	Jeremy Mayfield	186.969
Talladega 500	4/22/01	Bobby Hamilton	14	Chevrolet	184.003	37	26	0	0	Andy Petree	Stacy Compton	184.861
Talladega 500	4/21/02	Dale Earnhardt, Jr.	4	Chevrolet	159.022	26	10	3	19	Dale Earnhardt, Inc.	Jimmie Johnson	186.532

Talladega/DieHard 500

Race	Date	Winner	Start Pos.	Make	Speed	Lead Ch.	No. Lds.	No. Caut.	Caut. Laps	Owner	Pole Winner	Pole Speed
Talladega 500	9/14/69	Richard Brickhouse	9	1969 Dodge	153.778	35	7	7	38	Ray Nichels	Bobby Isaac	196.386
Talladega 500	8/23/70	Pete Hamilton	4	Plymouth	158.517	23	9	4	30	Petty Enterprises	Bobby Isaac	186.834
Talladega 500	8/22/71	Bobby Allison	2	Mercury	145.945	54	6	5	43	Holman-Moody	Donnie Allison	187.323
Talladega 500	8/6/72	James Hylton	22	Mercury	148.728	30	9	5	37	James Hylton	Bobby Isaac	190.677
Talladega 500	8/12/73	Dick Brooks	24	Plymouth	145.454	64	15	7	52	Crawford Enterprises	Bobby Allison	187.064
Talladega 500	8/11/74	Richard Petty	3	Dodge	148.637	34	11	6	40	Petty Enterprises	David Pearson	184.926
Talladega 500	8/17/75	Buddy Baker	2	Ford	130.892	60	17	8	61	Bud Moore	Dave Marcis	191.340
Talladega 500	8/8/76	Dave Marcis	1	Dodge	157.547	58	8	3	25	Nord Krauskopf	Dave Marcis	190.651
Talladega 500	8/7/77	Donnie Allison	2	Chevrolet	162.524	49	9	5	27	Hoss Ellington	Benny Parsons	192.684
Talladega 500	8/6/78	Lennie Pond	5	Oldsmobile	174.700	67	9	4	17	Harry Ranier	Cale Yarborough	192.917
Talladega 500	8/5/79	Darrell Waltrip	8	Chevrolet	161.229	34	8	5	28	DiGard	Neil Bonnett	193.600
Talladega 500	8/3/80	Neil Bonnett	2	Mercury	166.894	36	11	5	25	Wood Brothers	Buddy Baker	198.545
Talladega 500	8/2/81	Ron Bouchard	10	Buick	156.737	39	10	8	36	Jack Beebe	Harry Gant	195.897
Talladega 500	8/1/82	Darrell Waltrip	2	Buick	168.157	38	11	5	25	Junior Johnson	Geoffrey Bodine	199.400
Talladega 500	7/31/83	Dale Earnhardt	4	Ford	170.611	46	10	2	16	Bud Moore	Cale Yarborough	201.744
Talladega 500	7/29/84	Dale Earnhardt	3	Chevrolet	155.485	67	16	7	37	Richard Childress	Cale Yarborough	202.474
Talladega 500	7/28/85	Cale Yarborough	2	Ford	148.772	30	12	7	44	Harry Ranier	Bill Elliott	207.578
Talladega 500	7/27/86	Bobby Hillin	13	Chevrolet	151.522	49	26	9	44	Stavola Brothers	Bill Elliott	209.005
Talladega 500	7/26/87	Bill Elliott	1	Ford	171.293	23	9	4	18	Harry Melling	Bill Elliott	203.827
Talladega DieHard 500	7/31/88	Ken Schrader	7	Chevrolet	154.505	30	14	8	31	Rick Hendrick	Darrell Waltrip	196.274
DieHard 500	7/30/89	Terry Labonte	5	Ford	157.354	48	9	6	25	Junior Johnson	Mark Martin	194.800
DieHard 500	7/29/90	Dale Earnhardt	1	Chevrolet	174.430	23	13	2	12	Richard Childress	Dale Earnhardt	192.513
DieHard 500	7/28/91	Dale Earnhardt	4	Chevrolet	147.383	32	13	7	43	Richard Childress	Sterling Marlin	192.085
DieHard 500	7/26/92	Ernie Irvan	7	Chevrolet	176.309	17	8	2	11	Larry McClure	Sterling Marlin	190.586
DieHard 500	7/25/93	Dale Earnhardt	11	Chevrolet	153.858	26	10	5	27	Richard Childress	Bill Elliott	192.397
DieHard 500	7/24/94	Jimmy Spencer	2	Ford	163.217	24	10	5	20	Junior Johnson	Dale Earnhardt	193.470
DieHard 500	7/23/95	Sterling Marlin	1	Chevrolet	173.188	21	9	2	11	Larry McClure	Sterling Marlin	194.212
DieHard 500	7/28/96	Jeff Gordon	2	Chevrolet	133.387	24	10	5	35	Rick Hendrick	Jeremy Mayfield	192.370
DieHard 500	10/12/97	Terry Labonte	6	Chevrolet	156.601	32	16	4	22	Rick Hendrick	Ernie Irvan	193.271
Winston 500	10/11/98	Dale Jarrett	3	Ford	159.318	20	12	4	20	Robert Yates	Ken Schrader	196.153
Winston 500	10/17/99	Dale Earnhardt	27	Chevrolet	166.632	32	16	3	17	Richard Childress	Joe Nemechek	198.331
Winston 500	10/15/00	Dale Earnhardt	20	Chevrolet	165.681	49	21	3	13	Richard Childress	Joe Nemechek	190.279
EA Sports 500	10/21/01	Dale Earnhardt, Jr.	6	Chevrolet	164.185	32	13	3	16	Dale Earnhardt, Inc.	Stacy Compton	185.240
EA Sports 500	10/6/02	Dale Earnhardt, Jr.	13	Chevrolet	183.665	35	12	0	0	Dale Earnhardt, Inc.	Jimmie Johnson	

TEXAS MOTOR SPEEDWAY

Race	Date	Winner	Start Pos.	Make	Speed	Lead Ch.	No. Lds.	No. Caut.	Caut. Laps	Owner	Pole Winner	Pole Speed
Interstate Batteries 500	4/6/97	Jeff Burton	5	Ford	125.105	19	10	10	73	Jack Roush	Dale Jarrett	
Texas 500	4/5/98	Mark Martin	7	Ford	136.771	24	9	8	43	Jack Roush	Jeremy Mayfield	185.906
Primestar 500	3/28/99	Terry Labonte	4	Chevrolet	144.276	24	11	8	39	Rick Hendrick	Kenny Irwin, Jr.	190.154
DirecTV 500	4/2/00	Dale Earnhardt, Jr.	4	Chevrolet	131.152	29	17	12	62	Dale Earnhardt, Inc.	Terry Labonte	192.137
Harrah's 500	4/1/01	Dale Jarrett	3	Ford	141.804	18	7	10	44	Robert Yates	Dale Earnhardt, Jr.	190.678
Samsung / Radio Shack 500	4/7/02	Matt Kenseth	31	Ford	142.435	24	15	7	41	Jack Roush	Bill Elliott	194.224

WATKINS GLEN INTERNATIONAL

Race	Date	Winner	Start Pos.	Make	Speed	Lead Ch.	No. Lds.	No. Caut.	Caut. Laps	Owner	Pole Winner	Pole Speed
Watkins Glen, NY	8/4/57	Buck Baker	1	57 Chevrolet	83.064	0	1	0	0	Buck Baker	Art Watts	87.071
Watkins Glen 150	7/19/64	Billy Wade	1	1964 Mercury	97.988	5	3			Bud Moore	Billy Wade	102.222
Watkins Glen 150	7/18/65	Marvin Panch	3	1965 Ford	98.182	3	3	0	0	Wood Brothers	Dick Hutcherson	

Race	Date	Winner	Start Pos.	Make	Speed	Lead Ch.	No. Lds.	No. Caut.	Caut. Laps	Owner	Pole Winner	Pole Speed
The Budweiser at the Glen	8/10/86	Tim Richmond	1	Chevrolet	90.463	11	5	4	16	Rick Hendrick	Tim Richmond	117.563
The Budweiser at the Glen	8/10/87	Rusty Wallace	2	Pontiac	90.682	7	5	5	15	Raymond Beadle	Terry Labonte	117.956
The Budweiser at the Glen	8/14/88	Ricky Rudd	6	Buick	74.096	13	10	8	36	Kenny Bernstein	Geoffrey Bodine	120.541
The Budweiser at the Glen	8/13/89	Rusty Wallace	13	Pontiac	87.242	12	9	6	19	Raymond Beadle	Morgan Shepherd	120.456
Budweiser at the Glen	8/12/90	Ricky Rudd	12	Chevrolet	92.452	11	8	5	15	Rick Hendrick	Dale Earnhardt	121.190
Budweiser at the Glen	8/11/91	Ernie Irvan	3	Chevrolet	98.977	14	9	5	11	Larry McClure	Terry Labonte	121.652
Budweiser at the Glen	8/9/92	Kyle Petty	2	Pontiac	88.980	6	4	3	13	Felix Sabates	Dale Earnhardt	116.882
Budweiser at the Glen	8/8/93	Mark Martin	1	Ford	84.771	8	4	7	20	Jack Roush	Mark Martin	
Budweiser at the Glen	8/14/94	Mark Martin	1	Ford	93.752	7	5	4	11	Jack Roush	Mark Martin	118.326
The Bud at the Glen	8/13/95	Mark Martin	1	Ford	103.030	9	6	3	7	Jack Roush	Mark Martin	120.411
The Bud at the Glen	8/11/96	Geoffrey Bodine	13	Ford	92.334	8	6	4	11	Geoffrey Bodine	Dale Earnhardt	73.054
Budweiser at the Glen	8/10/97	Jeff Gordon	11	Chevrolet	91.294	10	9	5	11	Rick Hendrick	Todd Bodine	120.505
Bud at the Glen	8/9/98	Jeff Gordon	1	Chevrolet	94.446	8	6	4	9	Rick Hendrick	Jeff Gordon	120.331
Frontier at the Glen	8/15/99	Jeff Gordon	3	Chevrolet	87.722	11	8	7	15	Rick Hendrick	Rusty Wallace	121.234
Global Crossing @ the Glen	8/13/00	Steve Park	18	Chevrolet	91.336	8	7	5	13	Dale Earnhardt, Inc.	Bobby Labonte	0.000
Global Crossing @ the Glen	8/12/01	Jeff Gordon	13	Chevrolet	89.081	13	11	5	13	Rick Hendrick	Dale Jarrett	122.698
Sirius Satellite at the Glen	8/11/02	Tony Stewart	3	Pontiac	82.208	12	9	7	18	Joe Gibbs	Ricky Rudd	122.696